Arithmetic Operations:

$$ab + ac = a(b + c)$$

$$\frac{a}{b} + \frac{c}{d} = \frac{ad + bc}{bd}$$

$$\frac{a + b}{c} = \frac{a}{c} + \frac{b}{c}$$

$$\frac{\left(\dfrac{a}{b}\right)}{\left(\dfrac{c}{d}\right)} = \frac{ad}{bc}$$

$$a\left(\frac{b}{c}\right) = \frac{ab}{c}$$

$$\frac{a - b}{c - d} = \frac{b - a}{d - c}$$

$$\frac{ab + ac}{a} = b + c, \; a \neq 0$$

$$\frac{\left(\dfrac{a}{b}\right)}{c} = \frac{a}{bc}$$

$$\frac{a}{\left(\dfrac{b}{c}\right)} = \frac{ac}{b}$$

Exponents and Radicals:

$$a^0 = 1, \; a \neq 0$$

$$\frac{a^x}{a^y} = a^{x-y}$$

$$\left(\frac{a}{b}\right)^x = \frac{a^x}{b^x}$$

$$\sqrt[n]{a^m} = a^{m/n} = \left(\sqrt[n]{a}\right)^m$$

$$a^{-x} = \frac{1}{a^x}$$

$$(a^x)^y = a^{xy}$$

$$\sqrt{a} = a^{1/2}$$

$$\sqrt[n]{ab} = \sqrt[n]{a}\,\sqrt[n]{b}$$

$$a^x a^y = a^{x+y}$$

$$(ab)^x = a^x b^x$$

$$\sqrt[n]{a} = a^{1/n}$$

$$\sqrt[n]{\left(\frac{a}{b}\right)} = \frac{\sqrt[n]{a}}{\sqrt[n]{b}}$$

Algebraic Errors to Avoid:

$$\frac{a}{x + b} \neq \frac{a}{x} + \frac{a}{b}$$ (To see this error, let $a = b = x = 1$.)

$$\sqrt{x^2 + a^2} \neq x + a$$ (To see this error, let $x = 3$ and $a = 4$.)

$$a - b(x - 1) \neq a - bx - b$$ [Remember to distribute negative signs. The equation should be $a - b(x - 1) = a - bx + b$.]

$$\frac{\left(\dfrac{x}{a}\right)}{b} \neq \frac{bx}{a}$$ [To divide fractions, invert and multiply. The equation should be
$$\frac{\left(\dfrac{x}{a}\right)}{b} = \frac{\left(\dfrac{x}{a}\right)}{\left(\dfrac{b}{1}\right)} = \left(\frac{x}{a}\right)\left(\frac{1}{b}\right) = \frac{x}{ab}.]$$

$$\sqrt{-x^2 + a^2} \neq -\sqrt{x^2 - a^2}$$ (The negative sign cannot be factored out of the square root.)

$$\frac{a + bx}{a} \neq 1 + bx$$ (This is one of many examples of incorrect cancellation. The equation should be
$$\frac{a + bx}{a} = \frac{a}{a} + \frac{bx}{a} = 1 + \frac{bx}{a}.)$$

$$\frac{1}{x^{1/2} - x^{1/3}} \neq x^{-1/2} - x^{-1/3}$$ (This error is a more complex version of the first error.)

$$(x^2)^3 \neq x^5$$ [This equation should be $(x^2)^3 = x^2 x^2 x^2 = x^6$.]

Conversion Table:

1 centimeter ≈ 0.394 inch	1 joule ≈ 0.738 foot-pound	1 mile ≈ 1.609 kilometers
1 meter ≈ 39.370 inches	1 gram ≈ 0.035 ounce	1 gallon ≈ 3.785 liters
≈ 3.281 feet	1 kilogram ≈ 2.205 pounds	1 pound ≈ 4.448 newtons
1 kilometer ≈ 0.621 mile	1 inch ≈ 2.540 centimeters	1 foot-lb ≈ 1.356 joules
1 liter ≈ 0.264 gallon	1 foot ≈ 30.480 centimeters	1 ounce ≈ 28.350 grams
1 newton ≈ 0.225 pound	≈ 0.305 meter	1 pound ≈ 0.454 kilogram

Instructor's Annotated Edition

Precalculus

Sixth Edition

► **Ron Larson**
► **Robert P. Hostetler**

The Pennsylvania State University
The Behrend College

► **With the assistance of David C. Falvo**

The Pennsylvania State University
The Behrend College

Houghton Mifflin Company   **Boston   New York**

Publisher : Jack Shira
Managing Editor: Cathy Cantin
Development Manager: Maureen Ross
Development Editor: Laura Wheel
Assistant Editor: Jennifer King
Assistant Editor: James Cohen
Supervising Editor: Karen Carter
Senior Project Editor: Patty Bergin
Production Technology Supervisor: Gary Crespo
Senior Marketing Manager: Danielle Potvin
Marketing Associate: Nicole Mollica
Senior Manufacturing Coordinator: Jane Spelman
Composition and Art: Meridian Creative Group
Cover Design Manager: Diana Coe

Cover Image: © Ralph Mercer

Printed in the U.S.A.

Library of Congress Catalog Card Number: 2002109501

ISBN: 0-618-31436-9

56789–DOW–07 06 05

Contents

A Word from the Authors

Welcome to *Precalculus*, Sixth Edition. In this revision we continue to focus on promoting student success, while providing an accessible text that offers flexible teaching and learning options.

In keeping with our philosophy that students learn best when they know what they are expected to learn, we have retained the thematic study thread from the Fifth Edition. We first introduce this study thread in the Chapter Opener. Each chapter begins with a study guide that contains a comprehensive overview of the chapter concepts (*What you should learn*), a list of *Important Vocabulary* integral to learning the chapter concepts, a list of additional chapter-specific *Study Tools*, and additional text-specific resources. The study guide allows students to get organized and prepare for the chapter. Then, each section opens with a a set of learning objectives outlining the concepts and skills students are expected to learn (*What you should learn*), followed by an interesting real-life application used to illustrate why it is important to learn the concepts in that section (*Why you should learn it*). *Study Tips* at point-of-use provide support as students read through the section. And finally, to provide study support and a comprehensive review of the chapter, each chapter concludes with a chapter summary (*What did you learn?*), which reinforces the section objectives, and chapter *Review Exercises*, which are correlated to the chapter summary.

In addition to providing in-text study support, we have taken care to write a text for the student. We paid careful attention to the presentation, using precise mathematical language and clear writing, to create an effective learning tool. We are committed to providing a text that makes the mathematics within it accessible to all students. In the Sixth Edition, we have revised and improved upon many text features designed for this purpose. The *Technology*, *Exploration* features have been expanded. *Chapter Tests*, which gave students an opportunity for self-assessment, are included in every chapter. We have retained the *Synthesis* exercises, which check students' conceptual understanding, and the *Review* exercises, which reinforce skills learned in previous sections within each section exercise set. Also, students have access to several media resources that offer additional text-specific resources to enhance the learning process.

From the time we first began writing in the early 1970s, we have always viewed part of our authoring role as that of providing instructors with flexible teaching programs. The optional features within the text allow instructors with different pedagogical approaches to design their course to meet both their instructional needs and the needs of their students. Instructors who stress applications and problem solving, or exploration and technology, and more traditional methods will be able to use this text successfully. We hope you enjoy the Sixth Edition.

Ron Larson

Ron Larson

Robert P. Hostetler

Robert P. Hostetler

Acknowledgments

We would like to thank the many people who helped us at various stages of this project. Their encouragement, criticisms, and suggestions have been invaluable to us.

Sixth Edition Reviewers

Ahmad Abusaid, Southern Polytechnic University; Catherine Banks, Texas Woman's College; Jared Burch, College of the Sequoias; Dr. Michelle R. DeDeo, University of North Florida; Brian Hickey, East Central College; Gangadhar R. Hiremath, Miles College; Erick Hofacker, University of Wisconsin-River Falls; Dr. Kevin W. Hopkins, Southwest Baptist University; Charles W. Johnson, South Georgia College; Gary S. Kersting, North Central Michigan College; Namyong Lee, Minnesota State University; Mary Leeseberg, Manatee Community College; Tristan Londré, Blue River Community College; Bruce N. Lundberg, University of Southern Colorado; Dr. Carl V. Lutzer, Rochester Institute of Technology; Rudy Maglio, Oakton Community College; James Miller, West Virginia University; Steve O'Donnell, Rogue Community College; Armando I. Perez, Laredo Community College; Rita Randolfi, Brevard Community College; David Ray, The University of Tennessee at Martin; Miguel San Miguel Gonzalez, Texas A&M International University; Scott Satake, North Idaho College; Jed Soifer, Atlantic Cape Community College; Dr. Roy N. Tucker, Palo Alto College and The University of Texas at San Antonio; Karen Villarreal, Xavier University of Louisiana; Carol Walker, Hinds Community College; J. Lewis Walston, Methodist College; Jun Wang, Alabama State University; Ibrahim Wazir, American International School; Robert Wylie, Carl Albert State College.

Previous Edition Reviewers

James Alsobrook, Southern Union State Community College; Sherry Biggers, Clemson University; Charles Biles, Humboldt State University; Randall Boan, Aims Community College; Jeremy Carr, Pensacola Junior College; D. J. Clark, Portland Community College; Donald Clayton, Madisonville Community College; Linda Crabtree, Metropolitan Community College; David DeLatte, University of North Texas; Gregory Dlabach, Northeastern Oklahoma A & M College; Joseph Lloyd Harris, Gulf Coast Community College; Jeff Heiking, St. Petersburg Junior College; Celeste Hernandez, Richland College; Heidi Howard, Florida Community College at Jacksonville; Wanda Long, St. Charles County Community College; Wayne F. Mackey, University of Arkansas; Rhonda MacLeod, Florida State University; M. Maheswaran, University of Wisconsin–Marathon County; Valerie Miller, Georgia State University; Katharine Muller, Cisco Junior College; Bonnie Oppenheimer, Mississippi University for Women; James Pohl, Florida Atlantic University; Hari Pulapaka, Valdosta State University; Michael Russo, Suffolk County Community College; Cynthia Floyd Sikes, Georgia Southern University; Susan Schindler, Baruch College–CUNY; Stanley Smith, Black Hills State University

We would like to extend a special thanks to all of the instructors who took time to participate in our phone interviews.

We would like to thank the staff of Larson Texts, Inc. and the staff of Meridian Creative Group, who assisted in proofreading the manuscript, preparing and proofreading the art package, and typesetting the supplements.

We are grateful to our wives, Deanna Gilbert Larson and Eloise Hostetler, for their love, patience, and support. Also, a special thanks goes to R. Scott O'Neil.

If you have suggestions for improving this text, please feel free to write to us. Over the years we have received many useful comments from both instructors and students, and we value these comments very much.

Ron Larson
Robert P. Hostetler

How can this book help you

Support for Student Success

- Larson provides clear, easy-to-read examples that include all the steps needed to understand a new concept.
- Numerous examples are provided throughout the book that correspond to the exercise sets, giving students support with the key concepts in their homework assignments.
- Additional resources are also available, such as SMARTHINKING's live, one-on-one online tutoring service. This enables students to receive tutorial help from the comfort and privacy of their own home.
- Key course material is also presented on a DVD by a qualified instructor, making it easy to review content or material missed due to an absence.

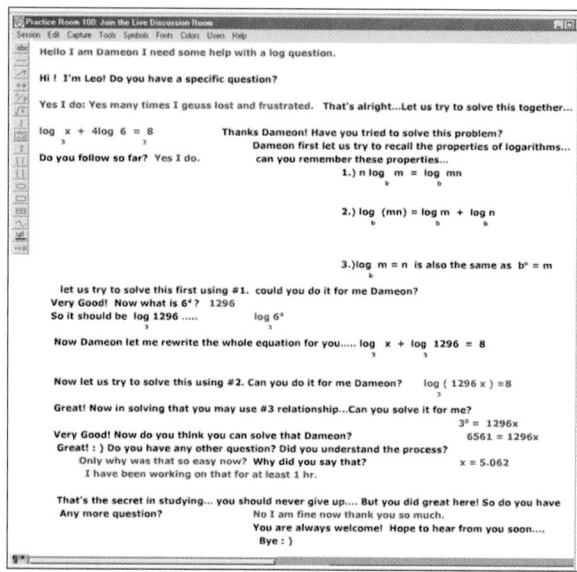

Options for Students and Instructors

- Concepts are presented through examples, applications, technology, or explorations to adapt the course to the curriculum needs or student learning styles.
- A variety of exercises that increase in difficulty allows professors the flexibility to assign homework to students with various learning styles. Exercise options include skills, technology, critical thinking, writing, applications, modeling data, true/false, proofs, and theoretical questions.
- The P.S. Problem Solving section at the end of every chapter offers more challenging exercises for advanced students.
- This text provides a solid mathematical foundation by foreshadowing concepts that will be used in future courses. Topics that will be especially helpful to students in Calculus are labeled with an "Algebra of Calculus" ∫ icon.

◀ **E x p l o r a t i o n** ▶

Graph each of the functions with a graphing utility. Determine whether the function is *even*, *odd*, or *neither*.

Technology

You can use a graphing utility to determine the domain of a composition of functions. For the composition in Example 5, enter the function

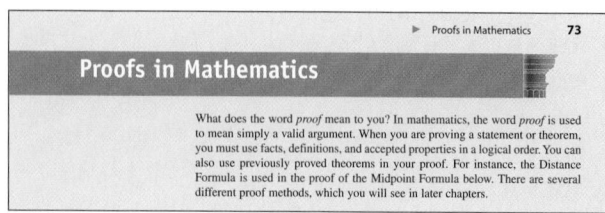

▶ Proofs in Mathematics **73**

Proofs in Mathematics

What does the word *proof* mean to you? In mathematics, the word *proof* is used to mean simply a valid argument. When you are proving a statement or theorem, you must use facts, definitions, and accepted properties in a logical order. You can also use previously proved theorems in your proof. For instance, the Distance Formula is used in the proof of the Midpoint Formula below. There are several different proof methods, which you will see in later chapters.

succeed in your math course?

For more information, see pages xii–xxv.

Applications That Motivate Students

- Applications in the exposition, examples, and exercises use real life data for students to see the relevance of what they are learning.
- Interesting topics are included throughout the book to help students see the practical, as well as theoretical, side of mathematics.
- Sourced data sets are included throughout the text, allowing students the opportunity to generate mathematical models that represent real data.

Readable and Understandable Text for Students

- Examples, explanations, and proofs begin and end on the same page to allow students to see concepts as a whole, without page-turning distractions. This unique design is one more example of the carefully developed texts created by the Larson Team.
- Examples include detailed solutions that show all steps to make it easy for students to understand the material being presented.
- Many examples include numerical, algebraic, and/or graphical presentations to provide students an opportunity to see the solution represented in a way that is most clear to them.

Section 2.1 ▶ Quadratic Functions **119**

83. Height of a Ball The height y (in feet) of a ball thrown by a child is

$$y = -\frac{1}{12}x^2 + 2x + 4$$

where x is the horizontal distance (in feet) from the point at which the ball is thrown (see figure).

(a) How high is the ball when it leaves the child's hand? (*Hint:* Find y when $x = 0$.)
(b) What is the maximum height of the ball?
(c) How far from the child does the ball strike the ground?

84. Path of a Diver The path of a diver is

$$y = -\frac{4}{9}x^2 + \frac{24}{9}x + 12$$

where y is the height (in feet) and x is the horizontal distance from the end of the diving board (in feet). What is the maximum height of the diver?

85. Graphical Analysis From 1960 to 2000, the per capita consumption C of cigarettes by Americans (age 18 and older) can be modeled by

$$C = 4258 + 6.5t - 1.62t^2, \quad 0 \le t \le 40$$

where t is the year, with $t = 0$ corresponding to 1960. (Source: *Tobacco Situation and Outlook Yearbook*)

(a) Use a graphing utility to graph the model.

▶ **Model It**

86. Data Analysis The numbers y (in thousands) of hairdressers and cosmetologists in the United States for the years 1995 through 2000 are shown in the table. (Source: U.S. Bureau of Labor Statistics)

Year	Number of hairdressers and cosmetologists, y
1995	750
1996	737
1997	748
1998	763
1999	784
2000	820

(a) Use a graphing utility to create a scatter plot of the data. Let x represent the year, with $x = 5$ corresponding to 1995.
(b) Use the *regression* feature of a graphing utility to find a quadratic model for the data.
(c) Use a graphing utility to graph the model in the same viewing window as the scatter plot. How well does the model fit the data?
(d) Use the *trace* feature of the graphing utility to approximate the year in which the number of hairdressers and cosmetologists was the least.
(e) Use the model to predict the number of hairdressers and cosmetologists in 2005.

87. Wind Drag The number of horsepower y required to overcome wind drag on an automobile is approximated by

---

72 Chapter 1 ▶ Functions and Their Graphs

Technology

You can use a graphing utility to determine the domain of a composition of functions. For the composition in Example 5, enter the function composition as

$$y = \left(\sqrt{9 - x^2}\right)^2 - 9.$$

You should obtain the graph shown below. Use the *trace* feature to determine that the x-coordinates of points on the graph extend from -3 to 3. So, the domain of $(f \circ g)(x)$ is $-3 \le x \le 3$.

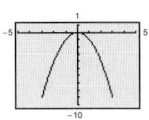

Example 5 Finding the Domain of a Composite Function

Find the composition $(f \circ g)(x)$ for the functions

$$f(x) = x^2 - 9 \quad \text{and} \quad g(x) = \sqrt{9 - x^2}.$$

Then find the domain of $(f \circ g)$.

Solution

$$\begin{aligned}
(f \circ g)(x) &= f(g(x)) \\
&= f\left(\sqrt{9 - x^2}\right) \\
&= \left(\sqrt{9 - x^2}\right)^2 - 9 \\
&= 9 - x^2 - 9 \\
&= -x^2
\end{aligned}$$

From this, it might appear that the domain of the composition is the set of all real numbers. Because the domain of f is the set of all real numbers and the domain of g is $-3 \le x \le 3$, the domain of $(f \circ g)$ is $-3 \le x \le 3$.

In Examples 4 and 5, you formed the composition of two given functions. In calculus, it is also important to be able to identify two functions that make up a given composite function. For instance, the function h given by

$$h(x) = (3x - 5)^3$$

is the composition of f with g, where $f(x) = x^3$ and $g(x) = 3x - 5$. That is,

$$h(x) = (3x - 5)^3 = [g(x)]^3 = f(g(x)).$$

Basically, to "decompose" a composite function, look for an "inner" function and an "outer" function. In the function h above, $g(x) = 3x - 5$ is the inner function and $f(x) = x^3$ is the outer function.

Example 6 Finding Components of Composite Functions

Express the function $h(x) = \dfrac{1}{(x - 2)^2}$ as a composition of two functions.

Solution

One way to write h as a composition of two functions is to take the inner function to be $g(x) = x - 2$ and the outer function to be

$$f(x) = \frac{1}{x^2} = x^{-2}.$$

Then you can write

$$h(x) = \frac{1}{(x - 2)^2} = (x - 2)^{-2} = f(x - 2) = f(g(x)).$$

Student Success Tools

How to study Chapter 1

▶ **What you should learn**

In this chapter you will learn the following skills and concepts:

- How to sketch the graphs of equations
- How to find and use the slopes of lines to write and graph linear equations in two variables
- How to evaluate functions and find their domains
- How to analyze graphs of functions
- How to identify and graph rigid and nonrigid transformations of functions
- How to find arithmetic combinations and compositions of functions
- How to find inverse functions graphically and algebraically
- How to write algebraic models for direct, inverse, and joint variation

▶ **Important Vocabulary**

As you encounter each new vocabulary term in this chapter, add the term and its definition to your notebook glossary.

Graph of an equation (p. 2)	Implied domain (p. 31)
Intercepts (p. 4)	Vertical Line Test (p. 42)
Symmetry (p. 5)	Zeros of a function (p. 43)
Linear equation in two variables (p. 12)	Relative minimum (p. 45)
Slope (p. 12)	Relative maximum (p. 45)
Slope-intercept form (p. 12)	Even function (p. 46)
Point-slope form (p. 17)	Odd function (p. 46)
General form (p. 18)	Rigid transformation (p. 63)
Parallel (p. 19)	Nonrigid transformation (p. 63)
Perpendicular (p. 19)	Inverse function (p. 77)
Function (p. 27)	Horizontal Line Test (p. 80)
Domain (p. 27)	One-to-one function (p. 80)
Range (p. 27)	Directly proportional (p. 88)
Independent variable (p. 29)	Inversely proportional (p. 90)
Dependent variable (p. 29)	Jointly proportional (p. 91)
Function notation (p. 29)	

Study Tools

Learning objectives in each section
Chapter Summary (p. 99)
Review Exercises (pp. 100–103)
Chapter Test (p. 104)

Additional Resources

Study and Solutions Guide
Interactive Precalculus
Videotapes/DVD for Chapter 1
Precalculus Website
Student Success Organizer

Functions and Their Graphs

"How to Study This Chapter"

The chapter-opening study guide includes: *What you should learn*, an objective-based overview of the main concepts of the chapter, *Important Vocabulary*, key mathematical terms integral to learning the concepts outlined in *What you should learn*, a list of *Study Tools*, additional study resources within the text chapter, and *Additional Resources*, text-specific supplemental resources available for each chapter.

Section Openers include: "What you should learn"

A list of section objectives outlining the main concepts to help students focus while reading through the section.

"Why you should learn it"

A real-life application or a reference to other branches of mathematics illustrates the relevance of the section's content. The real-life application is showcased in *Model It* found in the section exercise set.

1.2   Linear Equations in Two Variables

▶ **What you should learn**

- How to use slope to graph linear equations in two variables
- How to find slopes of lines
- How to write linear equations in two variables
- How to use slope to identify parallel and perpendicular lines
- How to use linear equations in two variables to model and solve real-life problems

▶ **Why you should learn it**

Linear equations in two variables can be used to model and solve real-life problems. For instance, in Exercise 119 on page 25, a linear equation is used to model the average monthly cellular phone bills for subscribers in the United States.

Using Slope

The simplest mathematical model for relating two variables is the **linear equation in two variables** $y = mx + b$. The equation is called *linear* because its graph is a line. (In mathematics, the term *line* means *straight line*.) By letting $x = 0$, you can see that the line crosses the y-axis at $y = b$, as shown in Figure 1.15. In other words, the y-intercept is $(0, b)$. The steepness or slope of the line is m.

$$y = mx + b$$

Slope   y-Intercept

The **slope** of a nonvertical line is the number of units the line rises (or falls) vertically for each unit of horizontal change from left to right, as shown in Figure 1.15 and Figure 1.16.

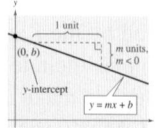

Positive slope, line rises.
FIGURE 1.15

Negative slope, line falls.
FIGURE 1.16

A linear equation that is written in the form $y = mx + b$ is said to be written in **slope-intercept form.**

The Slope-Intercept Form of the Equation of a Line

The graph of the equation

$$y = mx + b$$

is a line whose slope is m and whose y-intercept is $(0, b)$.

Exploration

Use a graphing utility to compare the slopes of the lines $y = mx$ where $m = 0.5, 1, 2,$ and 4. Which line rises most quickly? Now, let $m = -0.5, -1, -2,$ and -4. Which line falls most quickly? Use a square setting to obtain a true geometric perspective. What can you conclude about the slope and the "rate" at which the line rises or falls?

The icon identifies examples and concepts related to features of the Learning Tools CD-ROM and the *Interactive* and *Internet* versions of this text. For more details see the chart on pages xxi–xxv.

114. *Rental Demand* A real estate office handles an apartment complex with 50 units. When the rent per unit is $580 per month, all 50 units are occupied. However, when the rent is $625 per month, the average number of occupied units drops to 47. Assume that the relationship between the monthly rent p and the demand x is linear.

(a) Write the equation of the line giving the demand x in terms of the rent p.

(b) Use this equation to predict the number of units occupied when the rent is $655.

(c) Predict the number of units occupied when the rent is $595.

115. *Geometry* The length and width of a rectangular garden are 15 meters and 10 meters, respectively. A walkway of width x surrounds the garden.

(a) Draw a diagram that gives a visual representation of the problem.

(b) Write the equation for the perimeter y of the walkway in terms of x.

(c) Use a graphing utility to graph the equation for the perimeter.

(d) Determine the slope of the graph in part (c). For each additional one-meter increase in the width of the walkway, determine the increase in its perimeter.

116. *Monthly Salary* A pharmaceutical salesperson receives a monthly salary of $2500 plus a commission of 7% of sales. Write a linear equation for the salesperson's monthly wage W in terms of monthly sales S.

117. *Business Costs* A sales representative of a company using a personal car receives $120 per day for lodging and meals plus $0.35 per mile driven. Write a linear equation giving the daily cost C to the company in terms of x, the number of miles driven.

118. *Sports* The average annual salaries of major league baseball players (in thousands of dollars) from 1995 to 2002 are shown in the scatter plot. Find the equation of the line that you think best fits this data. (Let y represent the average salary and let t represent the year, with $t = 5$ corresponding to 1995.) (Source: The Associated Press)

FIGURE FOR 118

▶ **Model It**

119. *Data Analysis* The average monthly cellular phone bills y (in dollars) for subscribers in the United States from 1990 through 1999, where x is the year, are shown as data points (x, y). (Source: Cellular Telecommunications Industry Association)

(1990, 80.90)   (1995, 51.00)
(1991, 72.74)   (1996, 47.70)
(1992, 68.68)   (1997, 42.78)
(1993, 61.48)   (1998, 39.43)
(1994, 56.21)   (1999, 41.24)

(a) Sketch a scatter plot of the data. Let $x = 0$ correspond to 1990.

(b) Sketch the best-fitting line through the points.

(c) Find the equation of the line from part (b). Explain the procedure you used.

(d) Write a short paragraph explaining the meaning of the slope and y-intercept of the line in terms of the data.

(e) Compare the values obtained using your model with the actual values.

(f) Use your model to estimate the average monthly cellular phone bill in 2005.

Chapter Summary

▶ **What did you learn?**

Section 1.1	Review Exercises
☐ How to sketch and find x- and y-intercepts of graphs of equations	1–8
☐ How to use symmetry to sketch graphs of equations	9–12
☐ How to find equations and sketch graphs of circles	13–18
☐ How to use graphs of equations in solving real-life problems	19, 20

Section 1.2	
☐ How to find and use slopes of lines to graph linear equations	21–28
☐ How to write linear equations and identify parallel and perpendicular lines	29–40
☐ How to use linear equations to model and solve real-life problems	41, 42

Section 1.3	
☐ How to determine whether relations between two variables are functions	43–46
☐ How to use function notation, evaluate functions, and find the domains of functions	47–52
☐ How to use functions to model and solve real-life problems	53, 54

Section 1.4	
☐ How to use the Vertical Line Test and find the zeros of functions	55–62
☐ How to determine intervals on which functions are increasing or decreasing	63, 64
☐ How to identify even and odd functions	65–68

Section 1.5	
☐ How to identify and graph linear, squaring, cubic, square root, reciprocal, step, and other piecewise-defined functions	69–80
☐ How to recognize graphs of common functions	81, 82

Section 1.6	
☐ How to use transformations to sketch graphs of functions	83–90

Section 1.7	
☐ How to find combinations and compositions of functions	91–96
☐ How to use combinations of functions to model and solve real-life problems	97, 98

Section 1.8	
☐ How to find inverse functions and verify that two functions are inverse functions	99, 100
☐ How to use graphs to determine whether functions have inverse functions	101, 102
☐ How to use the Horizontal Line Test to determine if functions are one-to-one	103–106
☐ How to find inverse functions algebraically	107–112

Section 1.9	
☐ How to use mathematical models to approximate sets of data points	113
☐ How to write mathematical models for direct, inverse, and joint variation	114–117
☐ How to use a graphing utility to find the equation of a least squares regression line	118

Review Exercises

1.1 In Exercises 1–4, complete a table of values. Use the solution points to sketch the graph of the equation.

1. $y = 3x - 5$
2. $y = -\frac{1}{3}x + 2$
3. $y = x^2 - 3x$
4. $y = 2x^2 - x - 9$

In Exercises 5–8, find the x- and y-intercepts of the graph of the equation.

5. $y = 2x - 9$
6. $y = |x - 4| - 4$
7. $y = (x + 1)^2$
8. $y = x\sqrt{9 - x^2}$

In Exercises 9–12, use symmetry to sketch the graph of the equation.

9. $y = 5 - x^2$
10. $y = x^3 + 3$
11. $y = \sqrt{x + 5}$
12. $y = 1 - |x|$

In Exercises 13–16, find the center and radius of the circle and sketch its graph.

13. $x^2 + y^2 = 9$
14. $x^2 + y^2 = 4$
15. $(x + 2)^2 + y^2 = 16$
16. $x^2 + (y - 8)^2 = 81$

17. Find the standard form of the equation of the circle for which the endpoints of a diameter are $(0, 0)$ and $(4, -6)$.

18. Find the standard form of the equation of the circle for which the endpoints of a diameter are $(-2, -3)$ and $(4, -10)$.

19. *Number of Stores* The number N of Home Depot stores from 1993 to 2000 can be approximated by the model $y = 9.53t^2 + 162$, where t is the time (in years), with $t = 3$ corresponding to 1995. Sketch a graph of the model, and then use the graph to estimate the year in which the number of stores will be 2000. (Source: Home Depot, Inc.)

20. *Geometry* You have 100 feet of fencing to use for three sides of a rectangular fence, with your house enclosing the fourth side. The area of the enclosure is given by $A = -2x^2 + 100x$. Graph the equation to find the maximum area possible, and how long each side needs to be to obtain that area.

1.2 In Exercises 21–24, find the slope and y-intercept (if possible) of the equation of the line. Sketch the line.

21. $y = 6$
22. $x = -3$
23. $y = 3x + 13$
24. $y = -10x + 9$

In Exercises 25–28, plot the points and find the slope of the line passing through the pair of points.

25. $(3, -4), (-7, 1)$
26. $(-1, 8), (6, 5)$
27. $(-4.5, 6), (2.1, 3)$
28. $(-3, 2), (8, 2)$

In Exercises 29–32, find an equation of the line that passes through the points.

29. $(0, 0), (0, 10)$
30. $(2, 5), (-2, -1)$
31. $(-1, 4), (2, 0)$
32. $(11, -2), (6, -1)$

In Exercises 33–36, find an equation of the line that passes through the given point and has the specified slope. Sketch the line.

Point	Slope	Point	Slope
33. $(0, -5)$	$m = \frac{3}{2}$	**34.** $(-2, 6)$	$m = 0$
35. $(10, -3)$	$m = -\frac{1}{2}$	**36.** $(-8, 5)$	Undefined

In Exercises 37–40, write an equation of the line through the point (a) parallel to the given line and (b) perpendicular to the given line.

	Point	Line
37.	$(3, -2)$	$5x - 4y = 8$
38.	$(-8, 3)$	$2x + 3y = 5$
39.	$(4, -1)$	$x = 3$
40.	$(-2, 5)$	$y = -4$

Rate of Change In Exercises 41 and 42, you are given the dollar value of a product in the year 2004 *and* the rate at which the value of the item is expected to change during the next 5 years. Write a linear equation that gives the dollar value V of the product in terms of the year t. (Let $t = 4$ represent 2004.)

	2004 Value	Rate
41.	$12,500	$850 increase per year
42.	$72.95	$5.15 increase per year

1.3 In Exercises 43–46, determine whether the equation represents y as a function of x.

43. $16x - y^4 = 0$
44. $y = \sqrt{1 - x}$
45. $2x - y - 3 = 0$
46. $|y| = x + 2$

NEW! Model It

Often involving real-life data, these multi-part applications, referenced in *Why you should learn it*, offer students the opportunity to generate and analyze mathematical models.

"What did you learn?" Chapter Summary

The chapter summary provides a concise, section-by-section review of the section objectives. These objectives are correlated to the chapter Review Exercises allowing students to identify sections and concepts needing further review and study.

Review Exercises

Following the chapter summary, the Review Exercises provide additional practice and review of chapter concepts. The Review Exercises are organized by section and keyed directly to the section objectives listed in the chapter summary.

Additional Student Success Tools include point-of-use *Study Tips* and *Chapter* and *Cumulative Tests*.

FEATURES

Exploration

Before introducing selected topics, *Explorations* engage students in active discovery of mathematical concepts and relationships, often through the power of technology, while strengthening their critical thinking skills and developing an intuitive understanding of theoretical concepts.

Examples

Each example was carefully chosen to illustrate a particular mathematical concept or problem solving skill. Every example contains step-by-step solutions, most with side-by-side explanations that lead students through the solution process.

Technology

Point-of-use instructions for graphing utilities appear in the margin. Emphasis is placed on using technology as a tool for visualizing mathematical concepts, for verifying solutions, and for facilitating mathematical computation. The use of technology is optional and this feature and related exercises, identified by the icon ⚗, can be omitted without loss of continuity in coverage of topics.

Algebra of Calculus

Special emphasis is given to the algebraic techniques used in calculus. Algebra of Calculus examples and exercises are integrated throughout the text and are identified by the symbol ∫.

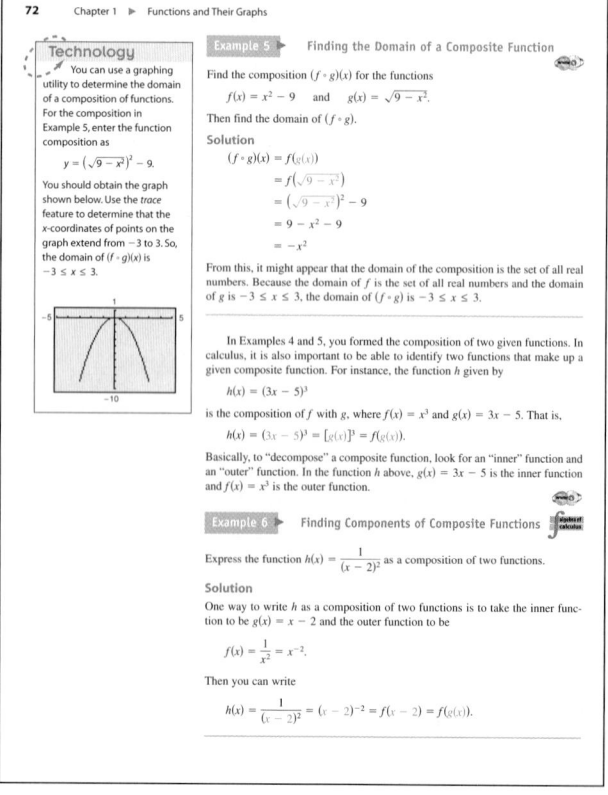

P.S. **Problem Solving**

1. As a salesperson, you receive a monthly salary of $2000, plus a commission of 7% of sales. You are offered a new job at $2300 per month, plus a commission of 5% of sales.
   (a) Write a linear equation for your current monthly wage W_1 in terms of your monthly sales S.
   (b) Write a linear equation for the monthly wage W_2 of your new job offer in terms of the monthly sales S.
   (c) Use a graphing utility to graph both equations in the same viewing window. Find the point of intersection. What does it signify?
   (d) You think you can sell $20,000 per month. Should you change jobs? Explain.

2. For the numbers 2 through 9 on a telephone keypad (see figure), create two relations: one mapping numbers onto letters, and the other mapping letters onto numbers. Are both relations functions? Explain.

3. What can be said about the sum and difference of each of the following?
   (a) Two even functions
   (b) Two odd functions
   (c) An odd function and an even function

4. The two functions
   $$f(x) = x \text{ and } g(x) = -x$$
   are their own inverse functions. Graph each function and explain why this is true. Graph other linear functions that are their own inverse functions. Find a general formula for a family of linear functions that are their own inverse functions.

5. Prove that a function of the following form is even.
   $$y = a_{2n}x^{2n} + a_{2n-2}x^{2n-2} + \cdots + a_2x^2 + a_0$$

6. A miniature golf professional is trying to make a hole-in-one on the miniature golf green shown. A coordinate plane is placed over the golf green. The golf ball is at the point $(2.5, 2)$ and the hole is at the point $(9.5, 2)$. The professional wants to bank the ball off the side wall of the green at the point (x, y). Find the coordinates of the point (x, y). Then write an equation for the path of the ball.

7. At 2:00 P.M. on April 11, 1912, the *Titanic* left Cobh, Ireland, on her voyage to New York City. At 11:40 P.M. on April 14, the *Titanic* struck an iceberg and sank, having covered only about 2100 miles of the approximately 3400-mile trip.
   (a) What was the total length of the *Titanic's* voyage in hours?
   (b) What was the *Titanic's* average speed in miles per hour?
   (c) Write a function relating the *Titanic's* distance from New York City and the number of hours traveled. Find the domain and range of the function.
   (d) Graph the function from part (c).

8. Consider the functions $f(x) = 4x$ and $g(x) = x + 6$.
   (a) Find $(f \circ g)(x)$.
   (b) Find $(f \circ g)^{-1}(x)$.
   (c) Find $f^{-1}(x)$ and $g^{-1}(x)$.
   (d) Find $(g^{-1} \circ f^{-1})(x)$ and compare the result with that of part (b).
   (e) Repeat parts (a) through (d) for $f(x) = x^3 + 1$ and $g(x) = 2x$.
   (f) Write two one-to-one functions f and g, and repeat parts (a) through (d) for these functions.
   (g) Make a conjecture about $(f \circ g)^{-1}(x)$ and $(g^{-1} \circ f^{-1})(x)$.

9. You are in a boat 2 miles from the nearest point on the coast. You are to travel to a point Q, 3 miles down the coast and 1 mile inland (see figure). You can row at 2 miles per hour and walk at 4 miles per hour.

   (a) Write the total time T of the trip as a function of x.
   (b) Determine the domain of the function.
   (c) Use a graphing utility to graph the function. Be sure to choose an appropriate viewing window.
   (d) Use the *zoom* and *trace* features to find the value of x that minimizes T.
   (e) Write a brief paragraph interpreting these values.

10. The Heaviside function $H(x)$ is widely used in engineering applications. (See figure.) To print an enlarged copy of the graph, go to the website *www.mathgraphs.com*.
    $$H(x) = \begin{cases} 1, & x \geq 0 \\ 0, & x < 0 \end{cases}$$
    Sketch the graph of each function by hand.
    (a) $H(x) - 2$ (b) $H(x - 2)$ (c) $-H(x)$
    (d) $H(-x)$ (e) $\frac{1}{2}H(x)$ (f) $-H(x - 2) + 2$

11. Let $f(x) = \dfrac{1}{1-x}$.
    (a) What are the domain and range of f?
    (b) Find $f(f(x))$. What is the domain of this function?
    (c) Find $f(f(f(x)))$. Is the graph a line? Why or why not?

12. Show that the Associative Property holds for compositions of functions—that is,
    $$(f \circ (g \circ h))(x) = ((f \circ g) \circ h)(x).$$

13. Consider the graph of the function f shown in the figure. Use this graph to sketch the graph of each function. To print an enlarged copy of the graph, go to the website *www.mathgraphs.com*.
    (a) $f(x + 1)$ (b) $f(x) + 1$ (c) $2f(x)$ (d) $f(-x)$
    (e) $-f(x)$ (f) $|f(x)|$ (g) $f(|x|)$

14. Use the graphs of f and f^{-1} to complete each table of function values.

(a)

x	$f(f^{-1}(x))$
-4	
-2	
0	
4	

(b)

x	$(f + f^{-1})(x)$
-3	
-2	
0	
1	

(c)

x	$(f \cdot f^{-1})(x)$
-3	
-2	
0	
1	

(d)

x	$|f^{-1}(x)|$
-4	
-3	
0	
4	

106

107

NEW! P.S. Problem Solving

Each chapter concludes with a collection of thought-provoking and challenging exercises that further explore and expand upon the chapter concepts. These exercises have unusual characteristics that set them apart from traditional text exercises.

NEW! Proofs in Mathematics

At the end of every chapter, Proofs in Mathematics emphasizes the importance of proofs in mathematics. Proofs of important mathematical properties and theorems are presented as well as discussions of various proof techniques.

---

192 Chapter 2 ▶ Polynomial and Rational Functions

Proofs in Mathematics

These two pages contain proofs of four important theorems and polynomial functions. The first two theorems are from Section 2.3, and the second two theorems are from Section 2.5.

> **The Remainder Theorem** *(p. 138)*
> If a polynomial $f(x)$ is divided by $x - k$, the remainder is
> $$r = f(k).$$

Proof

From the Division Algorithm, you have
$$f(x) = (x - k)q(x) + r(x)$$
and because either $r(x) = 0$ or the degree of $r(x)$ is less than the degree of $x - k$, you know that $r(x)$ must be a constant. That is, $r(x) = r$. Now, by evaluating $f(x)$ at $x = k$, you have
$$f(k) = (k - k)q(k) + r$$
$$= (0)q(k) + r = r.$$

To be successful in algebra, it is important that you understand the connection among *factors* of a polynomial, *zeros* of a polynomial function, and *solutions* or *roots* of a polynomial equation. The Factor Theorem is the basis for this connection.

> **The Factor Theorem** *(p. 138)*
> A polynomial $f(x)$ has a factor $(x - k)$ if and only if $f(k) = 0$.

Proof

Using the Division Algorithm with the factor $(x - k)$, you have
$$f(x) = (x - k)q(x) + r(x).$$
By the Remainder Theorem, $r(x) = r = f(k)$, and you have
$$f(x) = (x - k)q(x) + f(k)$$
where $q(x)$ is a polynomial of lesser degree than $f(x)$. If $f(k) = 0$, then
$$f(x) = (x - k)q(x)$$
and you see that $(x - k)$ is a factor of $f(x)$. Conversely, if $(x - k)$ is a factor of $f(x)$, division of $f(x)$ by $(x - k)$ yields a remainder of 0. So, by the Remainder Theorem, you have $f(k) = 0$.

FEATURES

---

130   Chapter 2 ▶ Polynomial and Rational Functions

2.2 Exercises

In Exercises 1–8, match the polynomial function with its graph. [The graphs are labeled (a), (b), (c), (d), (e), (f), (g), and (h).]

(a)

(b)

(c)

(d)

(e)

(f)

(g)

(h)

1. $f(x) = -2x + 3$
2. $f(x) = x^2 - 4x$
3. $f(x) = -2x^2 - 5x$
4. $f(x) = 2x^3 - 3x + 1$
5. $f(x) = -\frac{1}{4}x^4 + 3x^2$
6. $f(x) = -\frac{1}{3}x^3 + x^2 - \frac{4}{3}$
7. $f(x) = x^4 + 2x^3$
8. $f(x) = \frac{1}{5}x^5 - 2x^3 + \frac{9}{5}x$

In Exercises 9–12, sketch the graph of $y = x^n$ and each transformation.

9. $y = x^3$
   (a) $f(x) = (x - 2)^3$ (b) $f(x) = x^3 - 2$
   (c) $f(x) = -\frac{1}{2}x^3$ (d) $f(x) = (x - 2)^3 - 2$
10. $y = x^5$
    (a) $f(x) = (x + 1)^5$ (b) $f(x) = x^5 + 1$
    (c) $f(x) = 1 - \frac{1}{2}x^5$ (d) $f(x) = -\frac{1}{2}(x + 1)^5$
11. $y = x^4$
    (a) $f(x) = (x + 3)^4$ (b) $f(x) = x^4 - 3$
    (c) $f(x) = 4 - x^4$ (d) $f(x) = \frac{1}{2}(x - 1)^4$
    (e) $f(x) = (2x)^4 + 1$ (f) $f(x) = \left(\frac{1}{2}x\right)^4 - 2$
12. $y = x^6$
    (a) $f(x) = -\frac{1}{8}x^6$ (b) $f(x) = (x + 2)^6 - 4$
    (c) $f(x) = x^6 - 4$ (d) $f(x) = -\frac{1}{4}x^6 + 1$
    (e) $f(x) = \left(\frac{1}{4}x\right)^6 - 2$ (f) $f(x) = (2x)^6 - 1$

In Exercises 13–22, determine the right-hand and left-hand behavior of the graph of the polynomial function.

13. $f(x) = \frac{1}{3}x^3 + 5x$
14. $f(x) = 2x^2 - 3x + 1$
15. $g(x) = 5 - \frac{7}{2}x - 3x^2$
16. $h(x) = 1 - x^6$
17. $f(x) = -2.1x^5 + 4x^3 - 2$
18. $f(x) = 2x^5 - 5x + 7.5$
19. $f(x) = 6 - 2x + 4x^2 - 5x^3$
20. $f(x) = \dfrac{3x^4 - 2x + 5}{4}$
21. $h(x) = -\frac{2}{3}(t^2 - 5t + 3)$
22. $f(s) = -\frac{7}{8}(s^3 + 5s^2 - 7s + 1)$

Graphical Analysis In Exercises 23–26, use a graphing utility to graph the functions f and g in the same viewing window. Zoom out sufficiently far to show that the right-hand and left-hand behaviors of f and g appear identical.

23. $f(x) = 3x^3 - 9x + 1$, $g(x) = 3x^3$
24. $f(x) = -\frac{1}{3}(x^3 - 3x + 2)$, $g(x) = -\frac{1}{3}x^3$
25. $f(x) = -(x^4 - 4x^3 + 16x)$, $g(x) = -x^4$
26. $f(x) = 3x^4 - 6x^2$, $g(x) = 3x^4$

Section 2.2 ▶ Polynomial Functions of Higher Degree   **133**

Synthesis

True or False? In Exercises 93–95, determine whether the statement is true or false. Justify your answer.

93. A fifth-degree polynomial can have five turning points in its graph.
94. It is possible for a sixth-degree polynomial to have only one solution.
95. The graph of the function
$$f(x) = 2 + x - x^2 + x^3 - x^4 + x^5 + x^6 - x^7$$
rises to the left and falls to the right.

96. *Graphical Analysis* Describe a polynomial function that could represent the graph. (Indicate the degree of the function and the sign of its leading coefficient.)

(a)   (b)

(c)   (d)

97. *Graphical Reasoning* Sketch a graph of the function $f(x) = x^4$. Explain how the graph of g differs (if it does) from the graph of f. Determine whether g is odd, even, or neither.
(a) $g(x) = f(x) + 2$ (b) $g(x) = f(x + 2)$
(c) $g(x) = f(-x)$ (d) $g(x) = -f(x)$
(e) $g(x) = f\left(\frac{1}{2}x\right)$ (f) $g(x) = \frac{1}{2}f(x)$
(g) $g(x) = f(x^{3/4})$ (h) $g(x) = (f \circ f)(x)$

98. *Exploration* Explore the transformations of the form $g(x) = a(x - h)^5 + k$.
(a) Use a graphing utility to graph the functions
$$y_1 = -\frac{1}{3}(x - 2)^5 + 1$$
and
$$y_2 = \frac{3}{5}(x + 2)^5 - 3.$$
Determine whether the graphs are increasing or decreasing. Explain.
(b) Will the graph of g always be increasing or decreasing? If so, is this behavior determined by a, h, or k? Explain.
(c) Use a graphing utility to graph the function
$$H(x) = x^5 - 3x^3 + 2x + 1.$$
Use the graph and the result of part (b) to determine whether H can be written in the form $H(x) = a(x - h)^5 + k$. Explain.

Review

In Exercises 99–102, solve the equation by factoring.
99. $2x^2 - x - 28 = 0$ 100. $3x^2 - 22x - 16 = 0$
101. $12x^2 + 11x - 5 = 0$ 102. $x^2 + 24x + 144 = 0$

In Exercises 103–106, solve the equation by completing the square.
103. $x^2 - 2x - 21 = 0$ 104. $x^2 - 8x + 2 = 0$
105. $2x^2 + 5x - 20 = 0$ 106. $3x^2 + 4x - 9 = 0$

In Exercises 107–110, factor the expression completely.
107. $5x^2 + 7x - 24$ 108. $6x^3 - 61x^2 + 10x$
109. $4x^4 - 7x^3 - 15x^2$ 110. $y^3 + 216$

In Exercises 111–116, describe the transformation from a common function that occurs in the function. Then sketch its graph.
111. $f(x) = (x + 4)^2$ 112. $f(x) = 3 - x^2$
113. $f(x) = \sqrt{x + 1} - 5$ 114. $f(x) = 7 - \sqrt{x - 6}$
115. $f(x) = 2[\![x]\!] + 9$ 116. $f(x) = 10 - \frac{1}{3}[\![x + 3]\!]$

Exercise

A hallmark feature of the text, the exercise sets contain a variety of computational, conceptual, and applied problems. Each section exercise set contains *Synthesis* exercises, which promote further exploration of mathematical concepts, critical thinking skills, and writing about mathematics and *Review* exercises, which provide continuous review of previously learned skills and concepts.

Applications

Demonstrating the relevance of mathematics to the real world, a wide variety of practical, real-life applications, many with sourced data, are found in examples and exercises throughout the text.

Additional Features

Additional carefully crafted learning tools designed to create a rich learning environment for all students can be found throughout the text. These learning tools include Historical Notes, Writing About Mathematics, and an extensive art program.

Section 2.1 ▶ Quadratic Functions   **119**

83. *Height of a Ball* The height y (in feet) of a ball thrown by a child is
$$y = -\frac{1}{12}x^2 + 2x + 4$$
where x is the horizontal distance (in feet) from the point at which the ball is thrown (see figure).
(a) How high is the ball when it leaves the child's hand? (*Hint:* Find y when $x = 0$.)
(b) What is the maximum height of the ball?
(c) How far from the child does the ball strike the ground?

84. *Path of a Diver* The path of a diver is
$$y = -\frac{4}{9}x^2 + \frac{24}{9}x + 12$$
where y is the height (in feet) and x is the horizontal distance from the end of the diving board (in feet). What is the maximum height of the diver?

85. *Graphical Analysis* From 1960 to 2000, the per capita consumption C of cigarettes by Americans (age 18 and older) can be modeled by
$$C = 4258 + 6.5t - 1.62t^2, \quad 0 \le t \le 40$$
where t is the year, with $t = 0$ corresponding to 1960. (Source: *Tobacco Situation and Outlook Yearbook*)
(a) Use a graphing utility to graph the model.
(b) Use the graph of the model to approximate the maximum average annual consumption. Beginning in 1966, all cigarette packages were required by law to carry a health warning. Do you think the warning had any effect? Explain.
(c) In 1990, the U.S. population (age 18 and over) was 185,105,441. Of those, about 63,423,167 were smokers. What was the average annual cigarette consumption *per smoker* in 1990? What was the average daily cigarette consumption *per smoker*?

▶ **Model It**

86. *Data Analysis* The numbers y (in thousands) of hairdressers and cosmetologists in the United States for the years 1995 through 2000 are shown in the table. (Source: U.S. Bureau of Labor Statistics)

Year	Number of hairdressers and cosmetologists, y
1995	750
1996	737
1997	748
1998	763
1999	784
2000	820

(a) Use a graphing utility to create a scatter plot of the data. Let x represent the year, with $x = 5$ corresponding to 1995.
(b) Use the *regression* feature of a graphing utility to find a quadratic model for the data.
(c) Use a graphing utility to graph the model in the same viewing window as the scatter plot. How well does the model fit the data?
(d) Use the *trace* feature of the graphing utility to approximate the year in which the number of hairdressers and cosmetologists was the least.
(e) Use the model to predict the number of hairdressers and cosmetologists in 2005.

87. *Wind Drag* The number of horsepower y required to overcome wind drag on an automobile is approximated by
$$y = 0.002s^2 + 0.005s - 0.029, \quad 0 \le s \le 100$$
where s is the speed of the car (in miles per hour).
(a) Use a graphing utility to graph the function.
(b) Graphically estimate the maximum speed of the car if the power required to overcome wind drag is not to exceed 10 horsepower. Verify your estimate analytically.

Program Components

Precalculus, Student Edition
Precalculus, Instructor's Annotated Edition

Interactive Precalculus 3.0 CD-ROM (can be used alone or with the printed textbook)
Internet Precalculus 3.0 (can be used alone or with the printed textbook)

Additional Resources

Student Resources

Student Success Organizer

Study and Solutions Guide
by Dianna L. Zook, (Indiana University/Purdue University–Fort Wayne)

Student Technology Resources

Instructional Videotapes for Graphing Calculators
by Dana Mosely

Learning Tools Student CD-ROM

Smarthinking™.com live online tutoring

Instructional DVDs by Dana Mosely

Instructional Videotapes for Graphing Calculators
by Dana Mosely

Interactive Precalculus 3.0 CD-ROM

Internet Precalculus 3.0

HM eduSpace website

BlackBoard Course Cartridge

WebCT e-pack

Textbook website (math.college.hmco.com)

For more information on these and other resources available, visit our website at **math.college.hmco.com.**

Instructor Resources

Instructor Success Organizer

Complete Solutions Guide
by Dianna L. Zook, (Indiana University/Purdue University–Fort Wayne)

Instructor's Annotated Edition

Test Item File

Instructor Technology Resources

HMClassPrep™ Instructor's CD-ROM

HM Testing 6.03

PowerPoint Presentations

Instructional Videotapes by Dana Mosely
(ideal for libraries and resource centers)

Interactive Precalculus 3.0 CD-ROM

Internet Precalculus 3.0

HM eduSpace website

BlackBoard Course Cartridge

WebCT e-pack

Textbook website (math.college.hmco.com)

Interactive Precalculus 3.0 CD-ROM and Internet Precalculus 3.0

To accommodate a wide variety of teaching and learning styles, *Precalculus* is also available as *Interactive Precalculus* 3.0 on an interactive CD-ROM and *Internet Precalculus* 3.0. Students using the interactive CD-ROM or those with internet access will benefit from a wide range of compelling, interactive pedagogy, plus solutions to all odd exercises in the text. For instructors who conduct part of their course online, the internet version is an ideal solution, offering the additional advantages of online interaction with instructors and course management tools.

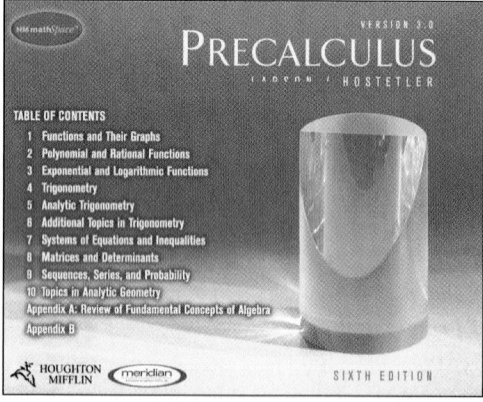

Classroom and Syllabus Management Systems

All of the content of the Sixth Edition—a wealth of applications, exercises, worked-out examples, and detailed explanations—is included in *Interactive Precalculus* 3.0 on CD-ROM and *Internet Precalculus* 3.0. Instructors have the flexibility of customizing content and interactive features for students as desired. Instructors may simply add dates to a default syllabus or may modify the order of topics. Either way, a customized syllabus is easy to distribute electronically and update instantly. This tool is particularly useful for managing distance learning courses.

Hands-on Interaction

- The graphing calculator emulator provides students with an onscreen graphing utility that can be used for computation and exploration.
- The animations, simulations, and editable graph explorations make mathematical concepts come alive.
- Guided and synthesis examples are designed to have students work through a solution one step at a time.
- Section quizzes require students to enter free-response answers, click and drag answers into place, or click on correct answers.

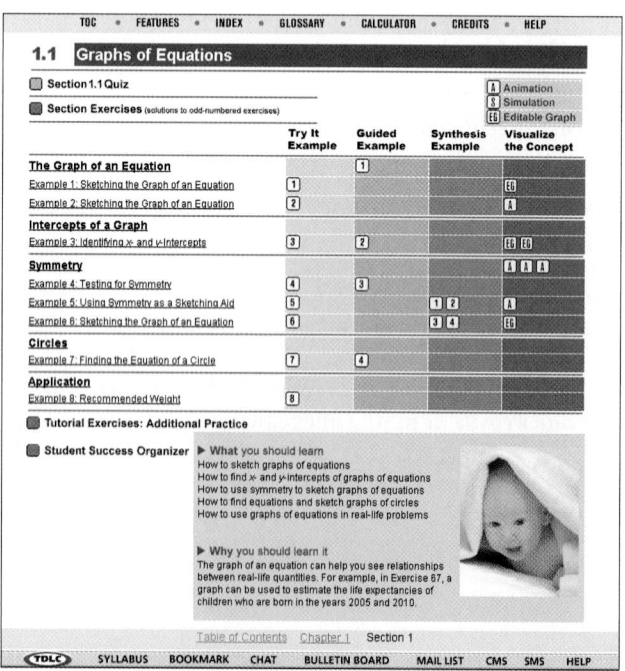

Features

Interactive Precalculus **3.0 CD-ROM and**
Internet Precalculus **3.0**

Exercises with full worked-out solutions to all of the odd exercises in the text provide immediate feedback for students.

Try Its allow students to try problems similar to the examples and to check their work using the worked-out solutions provided.

Guided Examples provide a full range of support by walking students step-by-step through problems that relate to a specific concept in the text.

Synthesis Examples require the use of more than one concept from a section and encourage students to work through a solution of a problem one step at a time.

Animations, which use motion and sound to explain concepts, can be played, paused, stopped, and replayed as many times as the student desires.

Simulations are interactive activities that encourage exploration and hands-on use of mathematical concepts.

Editable Graphs encourage students to explore concepts by graphing "editable" graphs. Students can also change the viewing window and use *zoom* and *trace* features.

MathGraphs are enlarged, printable versions of graphs from exercises in the book in which students are asked to draw on the graphs.

Tutorial Exercises are *additional* exercises that furnish students with much needed guided practice and refer back to a **Guided Example** for help if necessary.

Graphing Calculator Emulator is a powerful tool built into the program for convenient computation and exploration, and is also useful for working exercises that require the use of a graphing calculator.

Section Quizzes with responses and **Chapter Tests** with answers help students assess their mastery of the material.

Chapter Pre-Tests and **Post-Tests** offer added practice and assessment opportunities.

Glossary of Terms provides a comprehensive list of important mathematical terms, which students can quickly and easily access at any time.

Index and **Features Index** facilitate cross-referencing by providing complete searchable text-specific content.

Syllabus Builder enables instructors to save administrative time and to convey important information online.

Precalculus, Sixth Edition
Learning Tools Student CD-ROM

The Learning Tools Student CD-ROM that accompanies the text provides students with an unprecedented quantity of support materials and resources that help bring mathematics to life with motion and sound. These electronic learning tools are separated into three components described below. The CD-ROM also provides access to MathGraphs, ACE Practice Tests, and SMARTHINKING, the online tutoring center.

Study the Lesson

The Glossary of Terms provides a comprehensive list of important mathematical terms for each chapter with a short definition of each term.

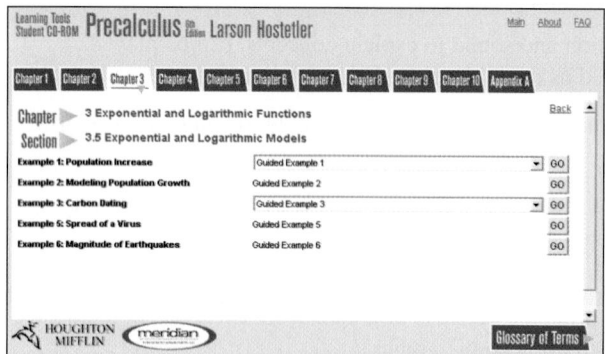

Review and Practice

- **Guided Examples** provide a full range of support by walking students step-by-step through problems that relate to a specific concept in the text.

- **Synthesis Examples** require the use of more than one concept from a section and encourage students to work through a solution of a problem one step at a time.

Visualize and Extend the Concepts

- **Animations** use motion and sound to explain concepts and can be played, paused, stopped, and replayed as many times as the student desires.

- **Simulations** encourage students to explore mathematical concepts experimentally.

- **Editable Graph Explorations** engage students in active discovery of mathematical concepts and relationships through the use of technology.

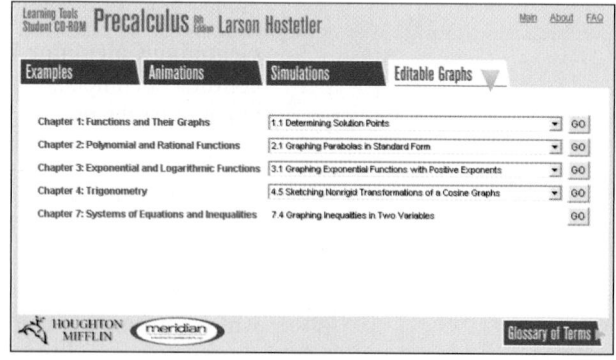

Precalculus, Sixth Edition
Learning Tools Student CD-ROM

Selected examples and concepts throughout the text are identified by the Learning Tools Student CD-ROM icon ⟨www ⊙⟩. The chart on this and the following pages indicates the feature(s) of the CD—Guided Example, Synthesis Example, Animation, Simulation, and Editable Graph Exploration—that corresponds to the example or concept.

Chapter	Section	Example/Concept	Guided Example	Synthesis Example	Animation	Simulation	Editable Graph
1	1	The Graph of an Equation	✓				
1	1	Example 1					✓
1	1	Example 2			✓		
1	1	Example 3	✓				✓
1	1	Symmetry			✓		
1	1	Examples 4, 7	✓				
1	1	Example 5		✓	✓		
1	1	Example 6		✓			✓
1	2	Using Slope	✓			✓	
1	2	Example 1		✓			
1	2	Examples 4, 5	✓	✓			
1	2	Examples 6, 7	✓				
1	2	Parallel and Perpendicular Lines	✓				
1	3	Examples 2, 6, 7, 9	✓				
1	3	Examples 3, 5	✓	✓			
1	4	Examples 1, 2	✓				
1	4	Examples 4, 6	✓	✓			
1	4	Even and Odd Functions				✓	
1	5	Example 2	✓				
1	5	Example 3		✓			
1	6	Shifting Graphs	✓		✓		
1	6	Example 1	✓				
1	6	Reflecting Graphs			✓		
1	6	Examples 2, 4		✓			
1	6	Nonrigid Transformations			✓		
1	7	Combinations of Functions	✓		✓		
1	7	Examples 2, 4, 5	✓				
1	7	Composition of Functions			✓		
1	7	Example 6		✓			
1	8	Examples 1, 2, 7	✓				
1	8	Graph of an Inverse Function			✓		
1	8	Examples 5, 6	✓	✓			
1	8	Finding Inverse Functions	✓				
1	9	Examples 2, 4, 5	✓	✓			
1	9	Example 3	✓				
1	9	Example 6				✓	
2	1	Example 2					✓
2	1	Example 3		✓			✓
2	1	Example 4	✓				
2	1	Example 5	✓			✓	
2	2	Examples 3, 4, 7	✓				
2	2	Example 5		✓			
2	2	Example 6	✓	✓			
2	3	Example 1	✓	✓			

Chapter	Section	Example/Concept	Guided Example	Synthesis Example	Animation	Simulation	Editable Graph
2	3	Example 2		✓	✓		
2	3	Example 4	✓		✓		
2	3	Example 6	✓				
2	4	The Imaginary Unit i	✓				
2	4	Examples 1, 3, 4, 6	✓				
2	4	Examples 2, 5	✓	✓			
2	5	Examples 1, 5, 6, 8, 9	✓				
2	5	Examples 3, 7		✓			
2	5	Tests for Zeros of Polynomials	✓				
2	5	Example 10	✓	✓	✓		
2	6	Examples 2, 3, 5	✓				
2	6	Example 6	✓		✓		
2	6	Example 7	✓	✓			
2	6	Example 8		✓			
2	7	Example 1	✓	✓			
2	7	Examples 2, 3	✓				
2	7	Example 4		✓			
3	1	Example 2		✓			✓
3	1	Example 3	✓				✓
3	1	Example 4	✓	✓	✓		
3	1	Examples 5, 7, 8	✓				
3	1	Applications				✓	
3	2	Example 1	✓	✓			
3	2	Examples 2, 7, 8, 10	✓				
3	2	Example 4			✓		
3	2	Example 6	✓	✓	✓		
3	3	Examples 1, 2, 6	✓				
3	3	Example 4	✓	✓			
3	3	Example 5		✓			
3	4	Examples 1, 2, 4–8, 10	✓				
3	4	Example 3	✓	✓			
3	5	Example 1	✓	✓			
3	5	Examples 2, 3, 5, 6	✓				
4	1	Examples 1, 3, 4, 7	✓				
4	1	Example 2	✓		✓		
4	1	Degree Measure	✓	✓			
4	1	Example 5	✓			✓	
4	2	The Unit Circle		✓	✓		
4	2	The Trigonometric Functions			✓		
4	2	Examples 1, 2, 3, 4	✓				
4	2	Domain and Period of Sine and Cosine	✓				
4	3	Trigonometric Functions			✓		
4	3	Examples 1, 4, 7	✓	✓			
4	3	Example 3	✓		✓		
4	3	Example 6	✓				
4	4	Examples 1, 2, 5	✓				
4	4	Reference Angles				✓	
4	4	Examples 4, 7	✓	✓			
4	5	Amplitude and Period	✓				
4	5	Example 2		✓			✓
4	5	Example 4					✓
4	5	Example 5	✓		✓		

Chapter	Section	Example/Concept	Guided Example	Synthesis Example	Animation	Simulation	Editable Graph
4	5	Example 6	✓				✓
4	5	Mathematical Modeling	✓				
4	6	Examples 1, 3–6	✓				
4	6	Example 2			✓		
4	6	Reciprocal Functions					✓
4	7	Example 2			✓		
4	7	Inverse Trigonometric Functions		✓	✓		
4	7	Examples 3, 5, 6	✓				
4	7	Examples 4, 7	✓	✓			
4	8	Examples 1, 3, 5, 6	✓				
4	8	Example 4	✓	✓			
5	1	Examples 1–3, 5, 8	✓				
5	1	Example 4	✓	✓			
5	1	Example 6		✓			
5	2	Introduction			✓		
5	2	Examples 1, 3, 5	✓				
5	3	Examples 3, 4, 6, 8	✓				
5	3	Equations of Quadratic Type	✓				
5	3	Example 5		✓			
5	3	Functions Involving Multiple Angles		✓			
5	4	Sum and Difference Formulas		✓			
5	4	Examples 1, 3, 4, 8	✓				
5	4	Example 2		✓			
5	5	Multiple-Angle Formulas			✓		
5	5	Examples 1, 9	✓				
5	5	Example 3		✓			
5	5	Power-Reducing Formulas			✓		
5	5	Example 5	✓	✓			
5	5	Half-Angle Formulas			✓		
5	5	Example 6	✓	✓			
5	5	Product-to-Sum Formulas	✓				
6	1	Examples 1, 3, 5–7	✓				
6	1	The Ambiguous Case (SSA)				✓	
6	2	Example 1	✓	✓			
6	2	Examples 2, 4, 5	✓				
6	2	Example 3		✓			
6	3	Examples 2, 9	✓				
6	3	Vector Operations			✓		
6	3	Example 3	✓	✓	✓		
6	3	Unit Vectors	✓				
6	3	Examples 6, 7		✓			
6	3	Direction Angles		✓			
6	4	Examples 1, 2, 6, 8	✓				
6	4	Example 4	✓	✓			
6	4	Finding Vector Components				✓	
6	5	Examples 1–3, 6, 8	✓				
6	5	Examples 4, 5	✓	✓			
6	5	Roots of Complex Numbers		✓			
7	1	Examples 1, 5–7	✓				
7	1	Example 3	✓	✓	✓		
7	1	Example 4			✓		
7	2	Examples 1, 5, 6, 9	✓				
7	2	Example 3	✓	✓			

Chapter	Section	Example/Concept	Guided Example	Synthesis Example	Animation	Simulation	Editable Graph
7	2	Example 4			✓		
7	2	Applications	✓				
7	3	Examples 3–5, 7–10	✓				
7	3	Nonsquare Systems	✓				
7	3	Applications	✓				
7	4	The Graph of an Inequality	✓				
7	4	Example 1					✓
7	4	Example 4	✓	✓	✓		
7	4	Examples 5, 9	✓				
7	5	Example 1			✓		
7	5	Examples 3–6	✓				
8	1	Examples 1, 2, 5, 7–9	✓				
8	1	Example 6	✓	✓	✓		
8	2	Examples 1, 8	✓				
8	2	Example 3	✓	✓			
8	2	Examples 7, 11	✓		✓		
8	3	Examples 1, 4, 5	✓				
8	3	Example 3	✓		✓		
8	4	Determinant of a 2 x 2 Matrix		✓			
8	4	Example 1	✓				
8	4	Example 3	✓	✓			
8	4	Example 4		✓			
8	5	Examples 1, 3–5, 7, 8	✓				
8	5	Example 2	✓	✓	✓		
9	1	Example 3		✓			
9	1	Factorial Notation		✓			
9	1	Examples 5–7	✓				
9	1	Summation Notation		✓			
9	2	Examples 1, 6–8	✓				
9	2	Examples 2, 3		✓			
9	3	Examples 1–4, 6, 8	✓				
9	3	Geometric Series			✓		
9	3	Example 7		✓			
9	4	Introduction		✓			
9	4	Examples 1, 4	✓				
9	5	Examples 2, 4, 7	✓				
9	5	Example 5		✓	✓		
9	6	Examples 4–9	✓				
9	7	Examples 1, 2, 5, 8, 9, 11	✓				
9	7	Example 3	✓			✓	
10	1	Inclination of a Line				✓	
10	1	Example 1	✓	✓			
10	1	Angle Between Two Lines				✓	
10	1	Examples 2, 3, 4	✓				
10	2	Conics			✓		
10	2	Examples 1, 2, 4	✓				
10	2	Example 3	✓	✓			
10	3	Introduction			✓		
10	3	Example 1	✓	✓			
10	3	Example 2		✓			
10	3	Application		✓			
10	3	Eccentricity	✓				
10	4	Example 1	✓	✓			
10	4	Examples 2, 4, 6	✓				

Chapter	Section	Example/Concept	Guided Example	Synthesis Example	Animation	Simulation	Editable Graph
10	5	Examples 1, 3, 4	✓				
10	6	Plane Curves			✓		
10	6	Example 1			✓		
10	6	Example 2	✓				
10	6	Example 3	✓	✓			
10	6	Finding Parametric Equations		✓			
10	6	Example 4		✓			
10	6	Example 5	✓		✓		
10	7	Introduction			✓		
10	7	Examples 3, 4, 5	✓				
10	7	Equation Conversion	✓				
10	8	Introduction		✓			
10	8	Symmetry	✓				
10	8	Example 2		✓			
10	8	Examples 3, 5, 6	✓				
10	8	Example 4			✓		
10	8	Special Polar Graphs		✓			
10	9	Polar Equations of Conics				✓	
10	9	Examples 1, 2, 4	✓				
10	9	Example 3	✓	✓			
A	1	Real Numbers	✓				
A	1	Ordering Real Numbers	✓				
A	1	Example 1	✓		✓		
A	1	Example 2	✓				
A	1	Absolute Value and Distance		✓			
A	1	Examples 4, 5	✓	✓			
A	1	Algebraic Expressions	✓		✓		
A	1	Basic Rules of Algebra	✓				
A	2	Examples 1, 2	✓	✓			
A	2	Scientific Notation	✓				
A	2	Examples 3–6, 9–15	✓				
A	2	Example 8		✓			
A	3	Polynomials	✓				
A	3	Examples 2, 5, 7, 8, 11, 13, 14	✓				
A	3	Example 3	✓	✓		✓	
A	3	Example 4	✓	✓			
A	3	Example 10		✓			
A	3	Example 12	✓	✓	✓		
A	4	Examples 1–6, 8	✓				
A	4	Example 7	✓	✓			
A	5	Solutions of Equations	✓	✓			
A	5	Examples 1, 4, 5	✓	✓			
A	5	Quadratic Equations	✓				
A	5	Examples 6, 8, 9, 11, 12	✓				
A	5	Example 7			✓		
A	5	Example 10	✓	✓			
A	6	Examples 1, 2, 3	✓				
A	6	Examples 4–6	✓	✓			
A	6	Example 7		✓			
A	7	Algebraic Errors to Avoid	✓				
A	7	Examples 3–6	✓				
A	8	Examples 1, 3, 4, 7	✓				
A	8	Examples 2, 8			✓		
A	8	Example 6		✓			

How to study Chapter 1

► **What you should learn**

In this chapter you will learn the following skills and concepts:

- How to sketch the graphs of equations
- How to find and use the slopes of lines to write and graph linear equations in two variables
- How to evaluate functions and find their domains
- How to analyze graphs of functions
- How to identify and graph rigid and nonrigid transformations of functions
- How to find arithmetic combinations and compositions of functions
- How to find inverse functions graphically and algebraically
- How to write algebraic models for direct, inverse, and joint variation

► **Important Vocabulary**

As you encounter each new vocabulary term in this chapter, add the term and its definition to your notebook glossary.

Graph of an equation (p. 2)
Intercepts (p. 4)
Symmetry (p. 5)
Linear equation in two variables (p. 12)
Slope (p. 12)
Slope-intercept form (p. 12)
Point-slope form (p. 17)
General form (p. 18)
Parallel (p. 19)
Perpendicular (p. 19)
Function (p. 27)
Domain (p. 27)
Range (p. 27)
Independent variable (p. 29)
Dependent variable (p. 29)
Function notation (p. 29)

Implied domain (p. 31)
Vertical Line Test (p. 42)
Zeros of a function (p. 43)
Relative minimum (p. 45)
Relative maximum (p. 45)
Even function (p. 46)
Odd function (p. 46)
Rigid transformation (p. 63)
Nonrigid transformation (p. 63)
Inverse function (p. 77)
Horizontal Line Test (p. 80)
One-to-one function (p. 80)
Directly proportional (p. 88)
Inversely proportional (p. 90)
Jointly proportional (p. 91)

Study Tools

Learning objectives in each section
Chapter Summary (p. 99)
Review Exercises (pp. 100–103)
Chapter Test (p. 104)

Additional Resources

Study and Solutions Guide
Interactive Precalculus
Videotapes/DVD for Chapter 1
Precalculus Website
Student Success Organizer

Andreas Stirnberg/Getty Images

Functions and Their Graphs

1

1.1 Graphs of Equations

▶ **What you should learn**

- How to sketch graphs of equations
- How to find *x*- and *y*-intercepts of graphs of equations
- How to use symmetry to sketch graphs of equations
- How to find equations and sketch graphs of circles
- How to use graphs of equations in solving real-life problems

▶ **Why you should learn it**

The graph of an equation can help you see relationships between real-life quantities. For example, in Exercise 75 on page 11, a graph can be used to estimate the life expectancies of children who are born in the years 2005 and 2010.

Bruce Forster/Tony Stone Images

The Graph of an Equation

A coordinate system is used to represent graphically the relationship between two quantities. The graphical picture consists of a collection of points in a coordinate plane.

Frequently, a relationship between two quantities is expressed as an **equation in two variables.** For instance, $y = 7 - 3x$ is an equation in x and y. An ordered pair (a, b) is a **solution** or **solution point** of an equation in x and y if the equation is true when a is substituted for x and b is substituted for y. For instance, $(1, 4)$ is a solution of $y = 7 - 3x$ because $4 = 7 - 3(1)$ is a true statement.

In this section you will review some basic procedures for sketching the graph of an equation in two variables. The **graph of an equation** is the set of all points that are solutions of the equation.

Example 1 ▶ Sketching the Graph of an Equation

Sketch the graph of $y = 7 - 3x$.

Solution

The simplest way to sketch the graph of an equation is the *point-plotting method.* With this method, you construct a table of values that consists of several solution points of the equation. For instance, when $x = 0$,

$$y = 7 - 3(0)$$
$$= 7$$

which implies that $(0, 7)$ is a solution point of the graph.

x	$y = 7 - 3x$	(x, y)
0	7	$(0, 7)$
1	4	$(1, 4)$
2	1	$(2, 1)$
3	-2	$(3, -2)$
4	-5	$(4, -5)$

From the table, it follows that

$$(0, 7), (1, 4), (2, 1), (3, -2), \text{ and } (4, -5)$$

are solution points of the equation. After plotting these points, you can see that they appear to lie on a line, as shown in Figure 1.1. The graph of the equation is the line that passes through the five plotted points.

FIGURE **1.1**

See Appendix A for a review of the rectangular coordinate system and other basic algebraic concepts.

The icon identifies examples and concepts related to features of the Learning Tools CD-ROM and the *Interactive* and *Internet* versions of this text. For more details see the chart on pages *xxi-xxv*.

The *Interactive* CD-ROM and *Internet* versions of this text offer a Try It for each example in the text.

Example 2 ▶ **Sketching the Graph of an Equation**

Sketch the graph of

$$y = x^2 - 2.$$

Solution

Begin by constructing a table of values.

x	-2	-1	0	1	2	3
$y = x^2 - 2$	2	-1	-2	-1	2	7
(x, y)	$(-2, 2)$	$(-1, -1)$	$(0, -2)$	$(1, -1)$	$(2, 2)$	$(3, 7)$

Next, plot the points given in the table, as shown in Figure 1.2. Finally, connect the points with a smooth curve, as shown in Figure 1.3.

STUDY TIP

One of your goals in this course is to learn to classify the basic shape of a graph from its equation. For instance, you will learn that the *linear equation* in Example 1 has the form

$$y = mx + b$$

and its graph is a line, whereas the *quadratic equation* in Example 2 has the form

$$y = ax^2 + bx + c$$

and its graph is a parabola.

FIGURE 1.2

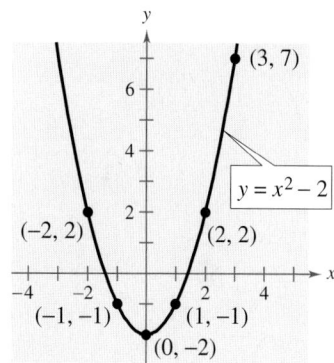

FIGURE 1.3

The point-plotting technique demonstrated in Examples 1 and 2 is easy to use, but it has some shortcomings. With too few solution points, you can misrepresent the graph of an equation. For instance, if only the four points

$$(-2, 2), (-1, -1), (1, -1), \text{ and } (2, 2)$$

in Figure 1.2 were plotted, any one of the three graphs in Figure 1.4 would be reasonable.

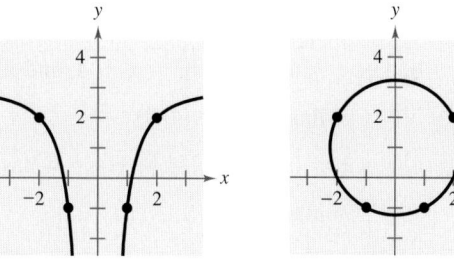

FIGURE 1.4

Intercepts of a Graph

It is often easy to determine the solution points that have zero as either the *x*-coordinate or the *y*-coordinate. These points are called **intercepts** because they are the points at which the graph intersects the *x*- or *y*-axis. It is possible for a graph to have no intercepts or several intercepts, as shown in Figure 1.5.

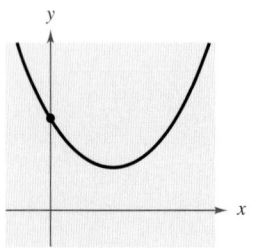

No x-intercept
One y-intercept
FIGURE 1.5

Three x-intercepts
One y-intercept

One x-intercept
Two y-intercepts

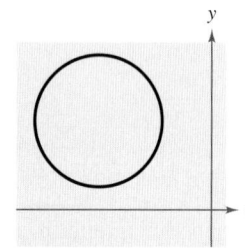

No intercepts

Note that an *x*-intercept is written as the ordered pair $(x, 0)$ and a *y*-intercept is written as the ordered pair $(0, y)$.

Finding Intercepts

1. To find *x*-intercepts, let *y* be zero and solve the equation for *x*.

2. To find *y*-intercepts, let *x* be zero and solve the equation for *y*.

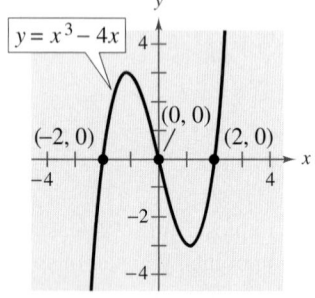

FIGURE 1.6

Example 3 ▶   Finding *x*- and *y*-Intercepts

Find the *x*- and *y*-intercepts of the graph of each equation.

a. $y = x^3 - 4x$

b. $y^2 = x + 4$

Solution

a. Let $y = 0$. Then $0 = x^3 - 4x = x(x^2 - 4)$ has solutions $x = 0$ and $x = \pm 2$.

   x-intercepts: $(0, 0), (2, 0), (-2, 0)$

   Let $x = 0$. Then $y = (0)^3 - 4(0) = 0$.

   y-intercept: $(0, 0)$ (See Figure 1.6)

b. Let $y = 0$. Then $(0)^2 = x + 4$, and $x = -4$.

   x-intercept: $(-4, 0)$

   Let $x = 0$. Then $y^2 = 0 + 4 = 4$ has solutions $y = \pm 2$.

   y-intercepts: $(0, 2), (0, -2)$ (See Figure 1.7)

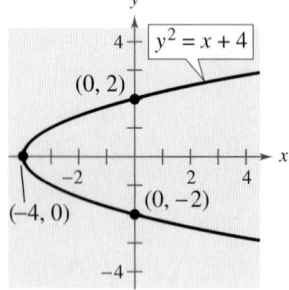

FIGURE 1.7

Symmetry

Graphs of equations can have **symmetry** with respect to one of the coordinate axes or with respect to the origin. Symmetry with respect to the x-axis means that if the Cartesian plane were folded along the x-axis, the portion of the graph above the x-axis would coincide with the portion below the x-axis. Symmetry with respect to the y-axis or the origin can be described in a similar manner, as shown in Figure 1.8.

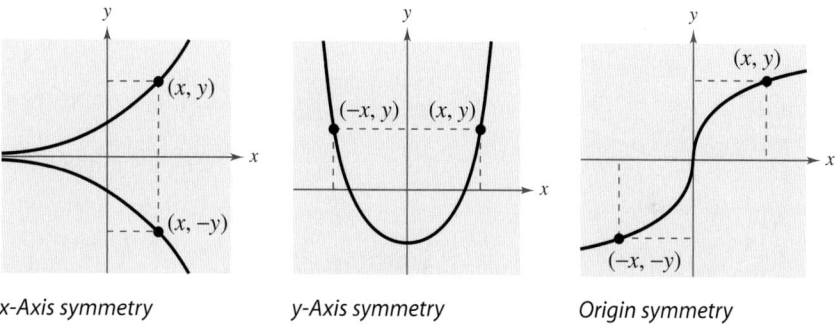

x-Axis symmetry   y-Axis symmetry   Origin symmetry

FIGURE **1.8**

Knowing the symmetry of a graph *before* attempting to sketch it is helpful, because then you need only half as many solution points to sketch the graph. There are three basic types of symmetry, described as follows.

Graphical Tests for Symmetry

1. A graph is **symmetric with respect to the x-axis** if, whenever (x, y) is on the graph, $(x, -y)$ is also on the graph.

2. A graph is **symmetric with respect to the y-axis** if, whenever (x, y) is on the graph, $(-x, y)$ is also on the graph.

3. A graph is **symmetric with respect to the origin** if, whenever (x, y) is on the graph, $(-x, -y)$ is also on the graph.

Example 4 ▶ **Testing for Symmetry**

The graph of

$$y = x^2 - 2$$

is symmetric with respect to the y-axis because the point $(-x, y)$ is also on the graph of $y = x^2 - 2$. (See Figure 1.9.) The table below confirms that the graph is symmetric with respect to the y-axis.

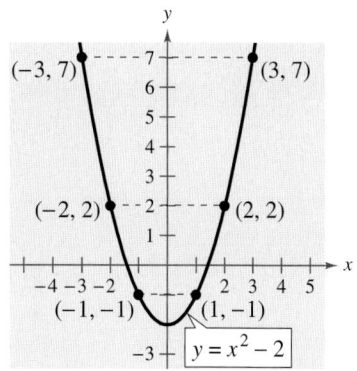

FIGURE **1.9** *y-Axis symmetry*

x	-3	-2	-1	1	2	3
y	7	2	-1	-1	2	7
(x, y)	$(-3, 7)$	$(-2, 2)$	$(-1, -1)$	$(1, -1)$	$(2, 2)$	$(3, 7)$

> ## Algebraic Tests for Symmetry
>
> 1. The graph of an equation is symmetric with respect to the x-axis if replacing y with $-y$ yields an equivalent equation.
>
> 2. The graph of an equation is symmetric with respect to the y-axis if replacing x with $-x$ yields an equivalent equation.
>
> 3. The graph of an equation is symmetric with respect to the origin if replacing x with $-x$ and y with $-y$ yields an equivalent equation.

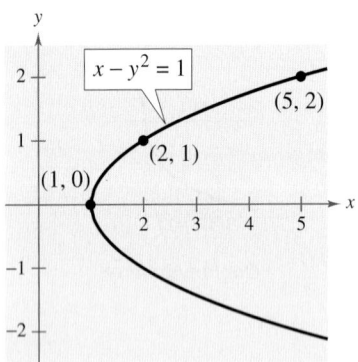

FIGURE 1.10

Example 5 ▶ Using Symmetry as a Sketching Aid

Use symmetry to sketch the graph of

$$x - y^2 = 1.$$

Solution

Of the three tests for symmetry, the only one that is satisfied is the test for x-axis symmetry because $x - (-y)^2 = 1$ is equivalent to $x - y^2 = 1$. So, the graph is symmetric with respect to the x-axis. Using symmetry, you need only to find the solution points above the x-axis and then reflect them to obtain the graph, as shown in Figure 1.10.

y	$x = y^2 + 1$	(x, y)
0	1	$(1, 0)$
1	2	$(2, 1)$
2	5	$(5, 2)$

STUDY TIP

Notice that when creating the table in Example 5, it is easier to choose y-values and then find the corresponding x-values of the ordered pairs.

Example 6 ▶ Sketching the Graph of an Equation

Sketch the graph of

$$y = |x - 1|.$$

Solution

This equation fails all three tests for symmetry and consequently its graph is not symmetric with respect to either axis or to the origin. The absolute value sign indicates that y is always nonnegative. Create a table of values and plot the points as shown in Figure 1.11. From the table, you can see that $x = 0$ when $y = 1$. So, the y-intercept is $(0, 1)$. Similarly, $y = 0$ when $x = 1$. So, the x-intercept is $(1, 0)$.

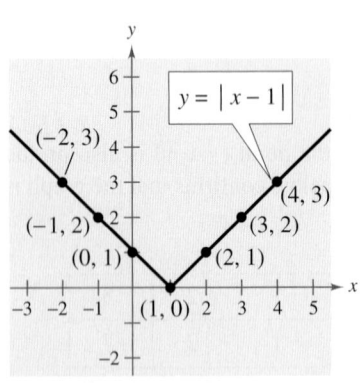

FIGURE 1.11

x	-2	-1	0	1	2	3	4
$y = |x - 1|$	3	2	1	0	1	2	3
(x, y)	$(-2, 3)$	$(-1, 2)$	$(0, 1)$	$(1, 0)$	$(2, 1)$	$(3, 2)$	$(4, 3)$

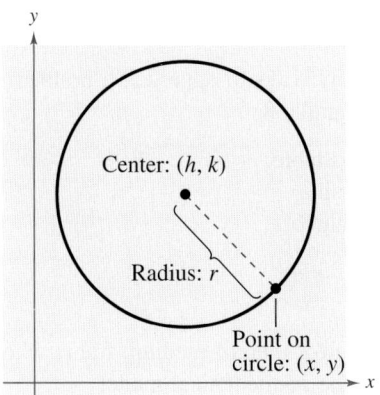

FIGURE 1.12

Throughout this course, you will learn to recognize several types of graphs from their equations. For instance, you will learn to recognize that the graph of a second-degree equation of the form

$$y = ax^2 + bx + c$$

is a parabola (see Example 2). Another easily recognized graph is that of a **circle.**

Circles

Consider the circle shown in Figure 1.12. A point (x, y) is on the circle if and only if its distance from the center (h, k) is r. By the Distance Formula,

$$\sqrt{(x - h)^2 + (y - k)^2} = r.$$

By squaring each side of this equation, you obtain the **standard form of the equation of a circle.**

> **Standard Form of the Equation of a Circle**
>
> The point (x, y) lies on the circle of radius r and center (h, k) if and only if
>
> $$(x - h)^2 + (y - k)^2 = r^2.$$

STUDY TIP

To find the correct h and k, it may be helpful to rewrite the quantities $(x + 1)^2$ and $(y - 2)^2$, using subtraction.

$$(x + 1)^2 = [x - (-1)]^2,$$

$$h = -1$$

$$(y - 2)^2 = [y - (2)]^2,$$

$$k = 2$$

From this result, you can see that the standard form of the equation of a circle *with its center at the origin*, $(h, k) = (0, 0)$, is simply

$$x^2 + y^2 = r^2.$$ Circle with center at origin

Example 7 ▶ **Finding the Equation of a Circle**

The point $(3, 4)$ lies on a circle whose center is at $(-1, 2)$, as shown in Figure 1.13. Write the standard form of the equation of this circle.

Solution

The radius of the circle is the distance between $(-1, 2)$ and $(3, 4)$.

$$r = \sqrt{(x - h)^2 + (y - k)^2}$$ Distance Formula

$$r = \sqrt{[3 - (-1)]^2 + (4 - 2)^2}$$ Substitute for x, y, h, and k.

$$= \sqrt{4^2 + 2^2}$$ Simplify.

$$= \sqrt{16 + 4}$$ Simplify.

$$= \sqrt{20}$$ Radius

Using $(h, k) = (-1, 2)$ and $r = \sqrt{20}$, the equation of the circle is

$$(x - h)^2 + (y - k)^2 = r^2$$ Equation of circle

$$[x - (-1)]^2 + (y - 2)^2 = \left(\sqrt{20}\right)^2$$ Substitute for h, k, and r.

$$(x + 1)^2 + (y - 2)^2 = 20.$$ Standard form

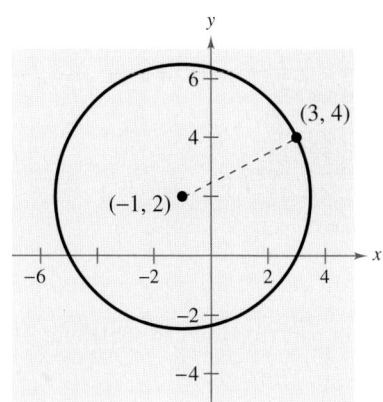

FIGURE 1.13

Additional Examples

a. Write the standard form of the equation of a circle whose endpoints of a diameter are $(-4, 1)$ and $(2, -7)$.

Answer: $(x + 1)^2 + (y + 3)^2 = 25$

b. Identify any symmetry: $y = \sqrt{4 - x^2}$.

Answer: y-axis symmetry

Application

In this course, you will learn that there are many ways to approach a problem. Three common approaches are illustrated in Example 8.

A *Numerical Approach:* Construct and use a table.
A *Graphical Approach:* Draw and use a graph.
An *Analytical Approach:* Use the rules of algebra.

Example 8 ▶   **Recommended Weight**

The median recommended weight y (in pounds) for men of medium frame who are 25 to 59 years old can be approximated by the mathematical model

$$y = 0.073x^2 - 6.99x + 289.0, \quad 62 \le x \le 76$$

where x is the man's height in inches.   (Source: Metropolitan Life Insurance Company)

a. Construct a table of values that shows the median recommended weights for men with heights of 62, 64, 66, 68, 70, 72, 74, and 76 inches.

b. Use the table of values to sketch a graph of the model. Then use the graph to estimate *graphically* the median recommended weight for a man whose height is 71 inches.

c. Use the model to confirm *analytically* the estimate you found in part (b).

Solution

a. You can use a calculator to complete the table, as shown at the left.

b. The table of values can be used to sketch the graph of the function, as shown in Figure 1.14. From the graph, you can estimate that a height of 71 inches corresponds to a weight of about 161 pounds.

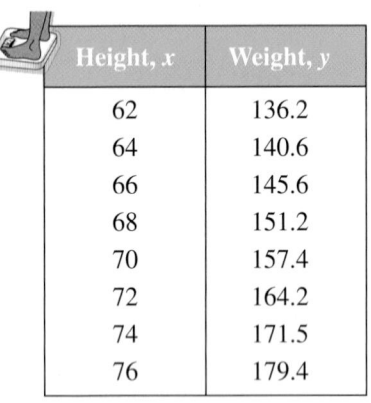

Height, x	Weight, y
62	136.2
64	140.6
66	145.6
68	151.2
70	157.4
72	164.2
74	171.5
76	179.4

Recommended Weight

FIGURE 1.14

c. To confirm algebraically the estimate found in part (b), you can substitute 71 for x in the model.

$$y = 0.073(71)^2 - 6.99(71) + 289.0 \approx 160.70$$

So, the graphical estimate of 161 pounds is fairly good.

1.1 Exercises

The *Interactive* CD-ROM and *Internet* versions of this text contain step-by-step solutions to all odd-numbered exercises. They also provide Tutorial Exercises for additional help.

In Exercises 1–4, determine whether each point lies on the graph of the equation.

Equation	Points
1. $y = \sqrt{x + 4}$	(a) $(0, 2)$ (b) $(5, 3)$
2. $y = x^2 - 3x + 2$	(a) $(2, 0)$ (b) $(-2, 8)$
3. $y = 4 - |x - 2|$	(a) $(1, 5)$ (b) $(6, 0)$
4. $y = \frac{1}{3}x^3 - 2x^2$	(a) $\left(2, -\frac{16}{3}\right)$ (b) $(-3, 9)$

In Exercises 5–8, complete the table. Use the resulting solution points to sketch the graph of the equation.

5. $y = -2x + 5$

x	-1	0	1	2	$\frac{5}{2}$
y					
(x, y)					

6. $y = \frac{3}{4}x - 1$

x	-2	0	1	$\frac{4}{3}$	2
y					
(x, y)					

7. $y = x^2 - 3x$

x	-1	0	1	2	3
y					
(x, y)					

8. $y = 5 - x^2$

x	-2	-1	0	1	2
y					
(x, y)					

In Exercises 9–20, find the *x*- and *y*-intercepts of the graph of the equation.

9. $y = 16 - 4x^2$

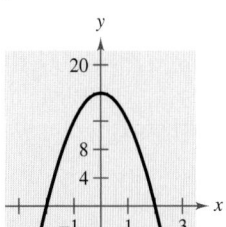

10. $y = (x + 3)^2$

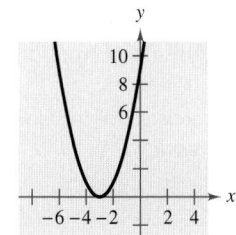

11. $y = 5x - 6$

12. $y = 8 - 3x$

13. $y = \sqrt{x + 4}$

14. $y = \sqrt{2x - 1}$

15. $y = |3x - 7|$

16. $y = -|x + 10|$

17. $y = 2x^3 - 4x^2$

18. $y = x^4 - 25$

19. $y^2 = 6 - x$

20. $y^2 = x + 1$

In Exercises 21–28, use the algebraic tests to check for symmetry with respect to both axes and the origin.

21. $x^2 - y = 0$

22. $x - y^2 = 0$

23. $y = x^3$

24. $y = x^4 - x^2 + 3$

25. $y = \dfrac{x}{x^2 + 1}$

26. $y = \dfrac{1}{x^2 + 1}$

27. $xy^2 + 10 = 0$

28. $xy = 4$

In Exercises 29–32, assume that the graph has the indicated type of symmetry. Sketch the complete graph of the equation. To print an enlarged copy of the graph, go to the website *www.mathgraphs.com*.

29.

y-Axis symmetry

30.

x-Axis symmetry

31.

Origin symmetry

32.

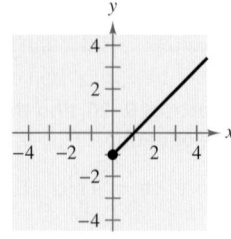

y-Axis symmetry

In Exercises 33–44, use symmetry to sketch the graph of the equation.

33. $y = -3x + 1$

34. $y = 2x - 3$

35. $y = x^2 - 2x$

36. $y = -x^2 - 2x$

37. $y = x^3 + 3$

38. $y = x^3 - 1$

39. $y = \sqrt{x - 3}$

40. $y = \sqrt{1 - x}$

41. $y = |x - 6|$

42. $y = 1 - |x|$

43. $x = y^2 - 1$

44. $x = y^2 - 5$

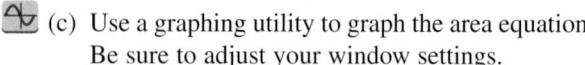 **In Exercises 45–56, use a graphing utility to graph the equation. Use a standard setting. Approximate any intercepts.**

45. $y = 3 - \frac{1}{2}x$

46. $y = \frac{2}{3}x - 1$

47. $y = x^2 - 4x + 3$

48. $y = x^2 + x - 2$

49. $y = \dfrac{2x}{x - 1}$

50. $y = \dfrac{4}{x^2 + 1}$

51. $y = \sqrt[3]{x}$

52. $y = \sqrt[3]{x + 1}$

53. $y = x\sqrt{x + 6}$

54. $y = (6 - x)\sqrt{x}$

55. $y = |x + 3|$

56. $y = 2 - |x|$

In Exercises 57–64, write the standard form of the equation of the specified circle.

57. Center: $(0, 0)$; Radius: 4

58. Center: $(0, 0)$; Radius: 5

59. Center: $(2, -1)$; Radius: 4

60. Center: $(-7, -4)$; Radius: 7

61. Center: $(-1, 2)$; Solution point: $(0, 0)$

62. Center: $(3, -2)$; Solution point: $(-1, 1)$

63. Endpoints of a diameter: $(0, 0)$, $(6, 8)$

64. Endpoints of a diameter: $(-4, -1)$, $(4, 1)$

In Exercises 65–70, find the center and radius of the circle, and sketch its graph.

65. $x^2 + y^2 = 25$

66. $x^2 + y^2 = 16$

67. $(x - 1)^2 + (y + 3)^2 = 9$

68. $x^2 + (y - 1)^2 = 1$

69. $\left(x - \frac{1}{2}\right)^2 + \left(y - \frac{1}{2}\right)^2 = \frac{9}{4}$

70. $(x - 2)^2 + (y + 1)^2 = 3$

71. *Depreciation* A manufacturing plant purchases a new molding machine for $225,000. The depreciated value y after t years is

$$y = 225,000 - 20,000t, \qquad 0 \le t \le 8.$$

Sketch the graph of the equation.

72. *Consumerism* You purchase a jet ski for $8100. The depreciated value y after t years is

$$y = 8100 - 929t, \qquad 0 \le t \le 6.$$

Sketch the graph of the equation.

73. *Geometry* A rectangle of length x and width w has a perimeter of 12 meters.

(a) Draw a rectangle that gives a visual representation of the problem. Use the specified variables to label the sides of the rectangle.

(b) Show that the width of the rectangle is $w = 6 - x$ and its area is $A = x(6 - x)$.

(c) Use a graphing utility to graph the area equation.

(d) From the graph in part (c), estimate the dimensions of the rectangle that yield a maximum area.

74. *Geometry* A rectangle of length x and width w has a perimeter of 22 yards.

(a) Draw a rectangle that gives a visual representation of the problem. Use the specified variables to label the sides of the rectangle.

(b) Show that the width of the rectangle is $w = 11 - x$ and its area is $A = x(11 - x)$.

(c) Use a graphing utility to graph the area equation. Be sure to adjust your window settings.

(d) From the graph in part (c), estimate the dimensions of the rectangle that yield a maximum area.

The symbol ⚏ indicates an exercise or parts of an exercise in which you are instructed to use a graphing utility.

▶ Model It

75. Population Statistics The table shows the life expectancy of a child (at birth) in the United States for selected years from 1920 to 2000. (Source: U.S. National Center for Health Statistics, U.S. Census Bureau)

Year, t	Life expectancy, y
1920	54.1
1930	59.7
1940	62.9
1950	68.2
1960	69.7
1970	70.8
1980	73.7
1990	75.4
2000	76.4

A model for the life expectancy during this period is

$$y = -0.0025t^2 + 0.572t + 44.31$$

where y represents the life expectancy and t is the time in years, with $t = 20$ corresponding to 1920.

(a) Sketch a scatter plot of the data.

(b) Graph the model for the data and compare the scatter plot and the graph.

(c) Use the graph of the model to estimate the life expectancy of a child for the years 2005 and 2010.

(d) Do you think this model can be used to predict the life expectancy of a child 50 years from now? Explain.

 76. Federal Debt The per capita federal debt y (in dollars) of the United States from 1950 through 2000 can be approximated by the model

$$y = 0.047t^3 + 9.23t^2 - 206.3t + 1984$$

where t is the time in years, with $t = 0$ corresponding to 1950. Use a graphing utility to graph the model and estimate the per capita federal debt for the year 2005. (Sources: U.S. Census Bureau and U.S. Department of the Treasury)

 77. Electronics The resistance y (in ohms) of 1000 feet of solid copper wire at 68 degrees Fahrenheit can be approximated by the model

$$y = \frac{10{,}770}{x^2} - 0.37, \qquad 5 \le x \le 100$$

where x is the diameter of the wire in mils (0.001 in.). Use a graphing utility to graph the model and estimate the resistance when $x = 50$. (Source: American Wire Gage)

Synthesis

True or False? In Exercises 78 and 79, determine whether the statement is true or false. Justify your answer.

78. In order to find the y-intercepts of the graph of an equation, let $y = 0$ and solve the equation for x.

79. The graph of a linear equation of the form $y = mx + b$ has one y-intercept.

80. Think About It Suppose you correctly enter an expression for the variable y on a graphing utility. However, no graph appears on the display when you graph the equation. Give a possible explanation and the steps you could take to remedy the problem. Illustrate your explanation with an example.

81. Think About It Find a and b if the graph of $y = ax^2 + bx^3$ is symmetric with respect to (a) the y-axis and (b) the origin. (There are many correct answers.)

82. In your own words, explain how the display of a graphing utility changes if the maximum setting for x is changed from 10 to 20.

Review

83. Identify the terms: $9x^5 + 4x^3 - 7$.

84. Rewrite the expression using exponential notation.

$$-(7 \times 7 \times 7 \times 7)$$

In Exercises 85–90, simplify the expression.

85. $\sqrt{18x} - \sqrt{2x}$

86. $\sqrt[4]{x^5}$

87. $\dfrac{70}{\sqrt{7x}}$

88. $\dfrac{55}{\sqrt{20} - 3}$

89. $\sqrt[6]{t^2}$

90. $\sqrt[3]{\sqrt{y}}$

1.2   Linear Equations in Two Variables

▶ **What you should learn**

- How to use slope to graph linear equations in two variables
- How to find slopes of lines
- How to write linear equations in two variables
- How to use slope to identify parallel and perpendicular lines
- How to use linear equations in two variables to model and solve real-life problems

▶ **Why you should learn it**

Linear equations in two variables can be used to model and solve real-life problems. For instance, in Exercise 119 on page 25, a linear equation is used to model the average monthly cellular phone bills for subscribers in the United States.

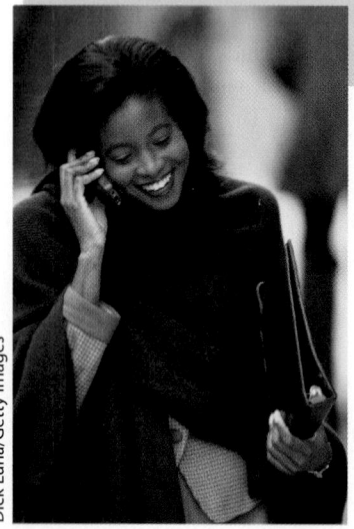

Dick Luria/Getty Images

Using Slope

The simplest mathematical model for relating two variables is the **linear equation in two variables** $y = mx + b$. The equation is called *linear* because its graph is a line. (In mathematics, the term *line* means *straight line*.) By letting $x = 0$, you can see that the line crosses the y-axis at $y = b$, as shown in Figure 1.15. In other words, the y-intercept is $(0, b)$. The steepness or slope of the line is m.

$$y = mx + b$$

Slope ⎯⎯⎯┘   └⎯⎯⎯ y-Intercept

The **slope** of a nonvertical line is the number of units the line rises (or falls) vertically for each unit of horizontal change from left to right, as shown in Figure 1.15 and Figure 1.16.

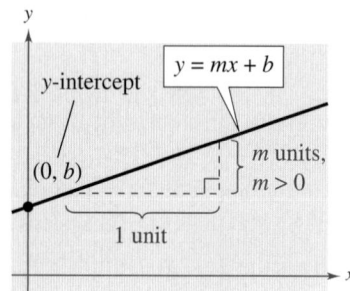

Positive slope, line rises.
FIGURE 1.15

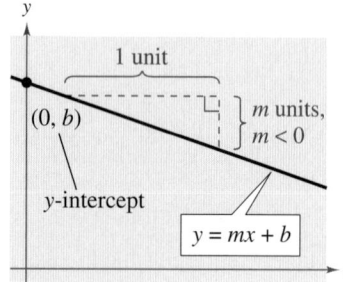

Negative slope, line falls.
FIGURE 1.16

A linear equation that is written in the form $y = mx + b$ is said to be written in **slope-intercept form.**

The Slope-Intercept Form of the Equation of a Line

The graph of the equation

$$y = mx + b$$

is a line whose slope is m and whose y-intercept is $(0, b)$.

◀ **E x p l o r a t i o n** ▶

Use a graphing utility to compare the slopes of the lines $y = mx$ where $m = 0.5, 1, 2,$ and 4. Which line rises most quickly? Now, let $m = -0.5, -1, -2,$ and -4. Which line falls most quickly? Use a square setting to obtain a true geometric perspective. What can you conclude about the slope and the "rate" at which the line rises or falls?

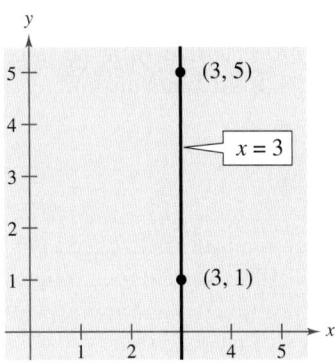

FIGURE 1.17 *Slope is undefined.*

Common Error

Many students confuse the line $x = a$ with the point $x = a$ on the real number line, or the line $y = b$ with the point $y = b$. Point out to students that they need to be aware of the context in which $x = a$ or $y = b$ is presented to know whether it refers to the line in the plane or the point on the number line.

Once you have determined the slope and the y-intercept of a line, it is a relatively simple matter to sketch its graph. In the next example, note that none of the lines is vertical. A vertical line has an equation of the form

$$x = a. \qquad \text{Vertical line}$$

The equation of a vertical line cannot be written in the form $y = mx + b$ because the slope of a vertical line is undefined, as indicated in Figure 1.17.

Example 1 ▶ **Graphing a Linear Equation**

Sketch the graph of each linear equation.

a. $y = 2x + 1$

b. $y = 2$

c. $x + y = 2$

Solution

a. Because $b = 1$, the y-intercept is $(0, 1)$. Moreover, because the slope is $m = 2$, the line *rises* two units for each unit the line moves to the right, as shown in Figure 1.18.

b. By writing this equation in the form $y = (0)x + 2$, you can see that the y-intercept is $(0, 2)$ and the slope is zero. A zero slope implies that the line is horizontal—that is, it doesn't rise *or* fall, as shown in Figure 1.19.

c. By writing this equation in slope-intercept form

$$x + y = 2 \qquad \text{Write original equation.}$$

$$y = -x + 2 \qquad \text{Subtract } x \text{ from each side.}$$

$$y = (-1)x + 2 \qquad \text{Write in slope-intercept form.}$$

you can see that the y-intercept is $(0, 2)$. Moreover, because the slope is $m = -1$, the line *falls* one unit for each unit the line moves to the right, as shown in Figure 1.20.

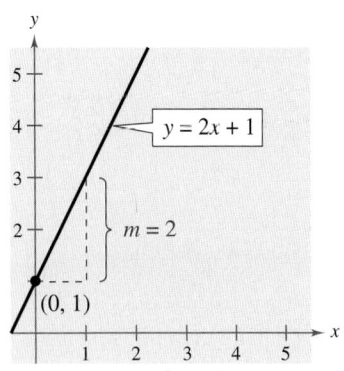

When m is positive, the line rises.
FIGURE 1.18

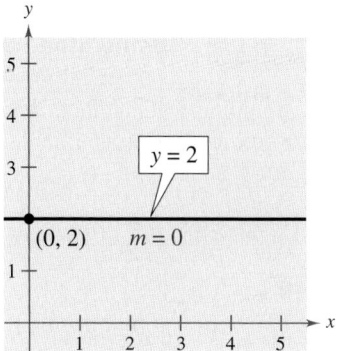

When m is 0, the line is horizontal.
FIGURE 1.19

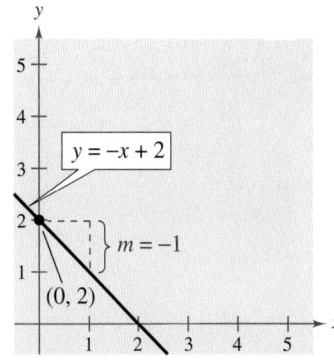

When m is negative, the line falls.
FIGURE 1.20

In real-life problems, the slope of a line can be interpreted as either a *ratio* or a *rate*. If the *x*-axis and *y*-axis have the same unit of measure, then the slope has no units and is a **ratio.** If the *x*-axis and *y*-axis have different units of measure, then the slope is a **rate** or **rate of change.**

Example 2 ▶   **Using Slope as a Ratio**

The maximum recommended slope of a wheelchair ramp is $\frac{1}{12}$. A business is installing a wheelchair ramp that rises 22 inches over a horizontal length of 24 feet. Is the ramp steeper than recommended? (Source: Americans with Disabilities Act Handbook)

Solution

The horizontal length of the ramp is 24 feet or $12(24) = 288$ inches, as shown in Figure 1.21. So, the slope of the ramp is

$$\text{Slope} = \frac{\text{vertical change}}{\text{horizontal change}}$$

$$= \frac{22 \text{ in.}}{288 \text{ in.}}$$

$$\approx 0.076.$$

Because $\frac{1}{12} \approx 0.083$, the slope of the ramp is not steeper than recommended.

FIGURE 1.21

Example 3 ▶   **Using Slope as a Rate of Change**

A kitchen appliance manufacturing company determines that the total cost in dollars of producing *x* units of a blender is

$$C = 25x + 3500. \qquad \text{Cost equation}$$

Describe the practical significance of the *y*-intercept and slope of this line.

Solution

The *y*-intercept (0, 3500) tells you that the cost of producing zero units is $3500. This is the *fixed cost* of production—it includes costs that must be paid regardless of the number of units produced. The slope of $m = 25$ tells you that the cost of producing each unit is $25, as shown in Figure 1.22. Economists call the cost per unit the *marginal cost*. If the production increases by one unit, then the "margin," or extra amount of cost, is $25. So, the cost increases at a rate of $25 per unit.

FIGURE 1.22 *Production cost*

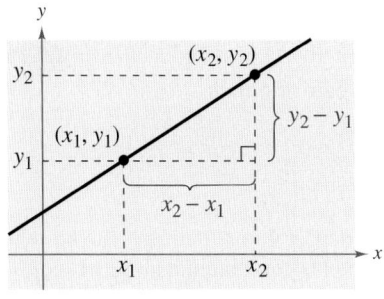

FIGURE 1.23

Finding the Slope of a Line

Given an equation of a line, you can find its slope by writing the equation in slope-intercept form. If you are not given an equation, you can still find the slope of a line. For instance, suppose you want to find the slope of the line passing through the points (x_1, y_1) and (x_2, y_2), as shown in Figure 1.23. As you move from left to right along this line, a change of $(y_2 - y_1)$ units in the vertical direction corresponds to a change of $(x_2 - x_1)$ units in the horizontal direction.

$$y_2 - y_1 = \text{the change in } y = \text{rise}$$

and

$$x_2 - x_1 = \text{the change in } x = \text{run}$$

The ratio of $(y_2 - y_1)$ to $(x_2 - x_1)$ represents the slope of the line that passes through the points (x_1, y_1) and (x_2, y_2).

$$\text{Slope} = \frac{\text{change in } y}{\text{change in } x}$$

$$= \frac{\text{rise}}{\text{run}}$$

$$= \frac{y_2 - y_1}{x_2 - x_1}$$

> ## The Slope of a Line Passing Through Two Points
>
> The **slope** m of the nonvertical line through (x_1, y_1) and (x_2, y_2) is
>
> $$m = \frac{y_2 - y_1}{x_2 - x_1}$$
>
> where $x_1 \neq x_2$.

When this formula is used for slope, the *order of subtraction* is important. Given two points on a line, you are free to label either one of them as (x_1, y_1) and the other as (x_2, y_2). However, once you have done this, you must form the numerator and denominator using the same order of subtraction.

$$m = \frac{y_2 - y_1}{x_2 - x_1} \qquad m = \frac{y_1 - y_2}{x_1 - x_2} \qquad m = \frac{y_2 - y_1}{x_1 - x_2}$$

Correct   Correct   Incorrect

For instance, the slope of the line passing through the points $(3, 4)$ and $(5, 7)$ can be calculated as

$$m = \frac{7 - 4}{5 - 3} = \frac{3}{2}$$

or, reversing the subtraction order in both the numerator and denominator, as

$$m = \frac{4 - 7}{3 - 5} = \frac{-3}{-2} = \frac{3}{2}.$$

Example 4 ▶	Finding the Slope of a Line Through Two Points

Find the slope of the line passing through each pair of points.

a. $(-2,\ 0)$ and $(3, 1)$ **b.** $(-1,\ 2)$ and $(2, 2)$

c. $(0, 4)$ and $(1, -1)$ **d.** $(3, 4)$ and $(3, 1)$

Solution

a. Letting $(x_1,\ y_1) = (-2,\ 0)$ and $(x_2, y_2) = (3, 1)$, you obtain a slope of

$$m = \frac{y_2 - y_1}{x_2 - x_1} = \frac{1 - 0}{3 - (-2)} = \frac{1}{5}. \qquad \text{See Figure 1.24.}$$

b. The slope of the line passing through $(-1, 2)$ and $(2, 2)$ is

$$m = \frac{2 - 2}{2 - (-1)} = \frac{0}{3} = 0. \qquad \text{See Figure 1.25.}$$

c. The slope of the line passing through $(0, 4)$ and $(1, -1)$ is

$$m = \frac{-1 - 4}{1 - 0} = \frac{-5}{1} = -5. \qquad \text{See Figure 1.26.}$$

d. The slope of the line passing through $(3, 4)$ and $(3, 1)$ is

$$m = \frac{1 - 4}{3 - 3} = \frac{-3}{0}. \qquad \text{See Figure 1.27.}$$

Because division by 0 is undefined, the slope is undefined and the line is vertical.

Common Error

A common error when finding the slope of a line is combining x- and y-coordinates in either the numerator or denominator, or both, as in

$$m = \frac{y_2 - x_1}{x_2 - y_1}.$$

STUDY TIP

In Figures 1.24 to 1.27, note the relationships between slope and the orientation of the line.

a. Positive slope; line rises from left to right

b. Zero slope; line is horizontal

c. Negative slope; line falls from left to right

d. Undefined slope; line is vertical

FIGURE 1.24

FIGURE 1.25

FIGURE 1.26

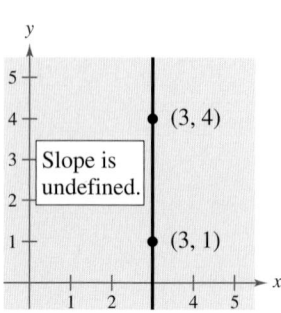

FIGURE 1.27

Writing Linear Equations in Two Variables

If (x_1, y_1) is a point on a line of slope m and (x, y) is *any other* point on the line, then

$$\frac{y - y_1}{x - x_1} = m.$$

This equation, involving the variables x and y, can be rewritten in the form

$$y - y_1 = m(x - x_1)$$

which is the **point-slope form** of the equation of a line.

Point-Slope Form of the Equation of a Line

The equation of the line with slope m passing through the point (x_1, y_1) is

$$y - y_1 = m(x - x_1).$$

The point-slope form is most useful for *finding* the equation of a line. You should remember this form.

Example 5 ▶ **Using the Point-Slope Form**

Find the slope-intercept form of the equation of the line that has a slope of 3 and passes through the point $(1, -2)$.

Solution

Use the point-slope form with $m = 3$ and $(x_1, y_1) = (1, -2)$.

$$y - y_1 = m(x - x_1) \qquad \text{Point-slope form}$$

$$y - (-2) = 3(x - 1) \qquad \text{Substitute for } m, x_1, \text{ and } y_1.$$

$$y + 2 = 3x - 3 \qquad \text{Simplify.}$$

$$y = 3x - 5 \qquad \text{Write in slope-intercept form.}$$

The slope-intercept form of the equation of the line is $y = 3x - 5$. The graph of this line is shown in Figure 1.28.

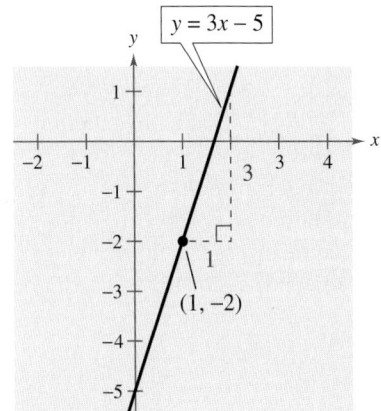

FIGURE **1.28**

The point-slope form can be used to find an equation of the line passing through two points (x_1, y_1) and (x_2, y_2). To do this, first find the slope of the line

$$m = \frac{y_2 - y_1}{x_2 - x_1}, \qquad x_1 \neq x_2$$

and then use the point-slope form to obtain the equation

$$y - y_1 = \frac{y_2 - y_1}{x_2 - x_1}(x - x_1). \qquad \text{Two-point form}$$

This is sometimes called the **two-point form** of the equation of a line.

eBay Inc.

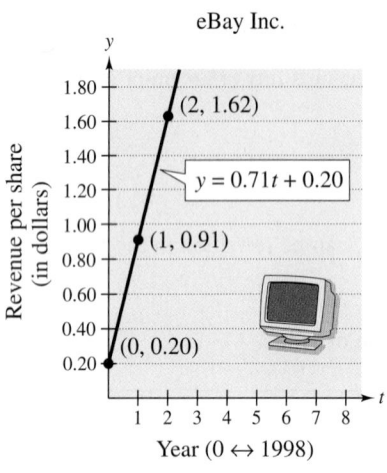

FIGURE **1.29**

Example 6 ▶ **Predicting Revenue per Share**

The revenue per share for eBay Inc. was \$0.20 in 1998 and \$0.91 in 1999. Using only this information, write a linear equation that gives the revenue per share in terms of the year. Then predict the revenue per share for 2000. (Source: eBay Inc.)

Solution

Let $t = 0$ represent 1998. Then the two given values are represented by the data points $(0, 0.20)$ and $(1, 0.91)$. The slope of the line through these points is

$$m = \frac{0.91 - 0.20}{1 - 0}$$

$$= 0.71.$$

Using the point-slope form, you can find the equation that relates the revenue per share y and the year t to be

$$y - 0.20 = 0.71(t - 0) \qquad \text{Write in point-slope form.}$$

$$y = 0.71t + 0.20. \qquad \text{Write in slope-intercept form.}$$

According to this equation, the revenue per share in 2000 was \$1.62, as shown in Figure 1.29. (In this case, the prediction is quite good—the actual revenue per share in 2000 was \$1.60.)

Linear extrapolation
FIGURE **1.30**

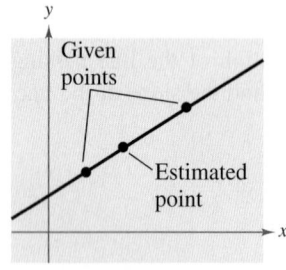

Linear interpolation
FIGURE **1.31**

The prediction method illustrated in Example 6 is called **linear extrapolation.** Note in Figure 1.30 that an extrapolated point does not lie between the given points. When the estimated point lies between two given points, as shown in Figure 1.31, the procedure is called **linear interpolation.**

Because the slope of a vertical line is not defined, its equation cannot be written in slope-intercept form. However, every line has an equation that can be written in the **general form**

$$Ax + By + C = 0 \qquad \text{General form}$$

where A and B are not both zero. For instance, the vertical line given by $x = a$ can be represented by the general form $x - a = 0$.

Equations of Lines

1. General form:	$Ax + By + C = 0$
2. Vertical line:	$x = a$
3. Horizontal line:	$y = b$
4. Slope-intercept form:	$y = mx + b$
5. Point-slope form:	$y - y_1 = m(x - x_1)$
6. Two-point form:	$y - y_1 = \dfrac{y_2 - y_1}{x_2 - x_1}(x - x_1)$

Find d_1 and d_2 in terms of m_1 and m_2, respectively (see figure). Then use the Pythagorean Theorem to find a relationship between m_1 and m_2.

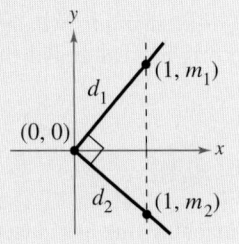

Parallel and Perpendicular Lines

Slope can be used to decide whether two nonvertical lines in a plane are parallel, perpendicular, or neither.

Parallel and Perpendicular Lines

1. Two distinct nonvertical lines are **parallel** if and only if their slopes are equal. That is, $m_1 = m_2$.

2. Two nonvertical lines are **perpendicular** if and only if their slopes are negative reciprocals of each other. That is, $m_1 = -1/m_2$.

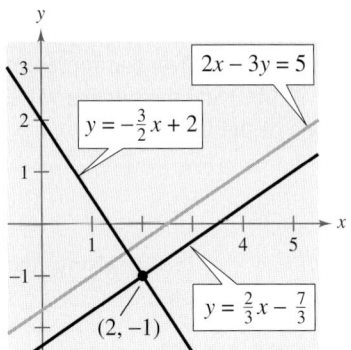

FIGURE 1.32

Example 7 ▶ Finding Parallel and Perpendicular Lines

Find the slope-intercept forms of the equations of the lines that pass through the point $(2, -1)$ and are (a) parallel to and (b) perpendicular to the line $2x - 3y = 5$.

Solution

By writing the equation of the given line in slope-intercept form

$$2x - 3y = 5 \qquad \text{Write original equation.}$$
$$-3y = -2x + 5 \qquad \text{Subtract } 2x \text{ from each side.}$$
$$y = \tfrac{2}{3}x - \tfrac{5}{3} \qquad \text{Write in slope-intercept form.}$$

you can see that it has a slope of $m = \tfrac{2}{3}$, as shown in Figure 1.32.

a. Any line parallel to the given line must also have a slope of $\tfrac{2}{3}$. So, the line through $(2, -1)$ that is parallel to the given line has the following equation.

$$y - (-1) = \tfrac{2}{3}(x - 2) \qquad \text{Write in point-slope form.}$$
$$3(y + 1) = 2(x - 2) \qquad \text{Multiply each side by 3.}$$
$$3y + 3 = 2x - 4 \qquad \text{Distributive Property}$$
$$2x - 3y - 7 = 0 \qquad \text{Write in general form.}$$
$$y = \tfrac{2}{3}x - \tfrac{7}{3} \qquad \text{Write in slope-intercept form.}$$

b. Any line perpendicular to the given line must have a slope of $-1/(2/3)$ or $-3/2$. So, the line through $(2, -1)$ that is perpendicular to the given line has the following equation.

$$y - (-1) = -\tfrac{3}{2}(x - 2) \qquad \text{Write in point-slope form.}$$
$$2(y + 1) = -3(x - 2) \qquad \text{Multiply each side by 2.}$$
$$2y + 2 = -3x + 6 \qquad \text{Distributive Property}$$
$$3x + 2y - 4 = 0 \qquad \text{Write in general form.}$$
$$y = -\tfrac{3}{2}x + 2 \qquad \text{Write in slope-intercept form.}$$

Technology

On a graphing utility, lines will not appear to have the correct slope unless you use a viewing window that has a square setting. For instance, try graphing the lines in Example 7 using the standard setting $-10 \leq x \leq 10$ and $-10 \leq y \leq 10$. Then reset the viewing window with the square setting $-9 \leq x \leq 9$ and $-6 \leq y \leq 6$. On which setting do the lines $y = \tfrac{2}{3}x - \tfrac{5}{3}$ and $y = -\tfrac{3}{2}x + 2$ appear perpendicular?

Notice in Example 7 how the slope-intercept form is used to obtain information about the graph of a line, whereas the point-slope form is used to write the equation of a line.

Application

Most business expenses can be deducted in the same year they occur. One exception is the cost of property that has a useful life of more than 1 year. Such costs must be *depreciated* over the useful life of the property. If the *same amount* is depreciated each year, the procedure is called *linear* or *straight-line depreciation*. The *book value* is the difference between the original value and the total amount of depreciation accumulated to date.

Example 8 ▶ **Straight-Line Depreciation**

Your publishing company has purchased a $12,000 machine that has a useful life of 8 years. The salvage value at the end of 8 years is $2000. Write a linear equation that describes the book value of the machine each year.

Solution

Let V represent the value of the machine at the end of year t. You can represent the initial value of the machine by the data point $(0, 12,000)$ and the salvage value of the machine by the data point $(8, 2000)$. The slope of the line is

$$m = \frac{2000 - 12,000}{8 - 0} = -\$1250$$

which represents the annual depreciation in *dollars per year*. Using the point-slope form, you can write the equation of the line as follows.

$$V - 12,000 = -1250(t - 0) \qquad \text{Write in point-slope form.}$$

$$V = -1250t + 12,000 \qquad \text{Write in slope-intercept form.}$$

The table shows the book value at the end of each year, and the graph of the equation is shown in Figure 1.33.

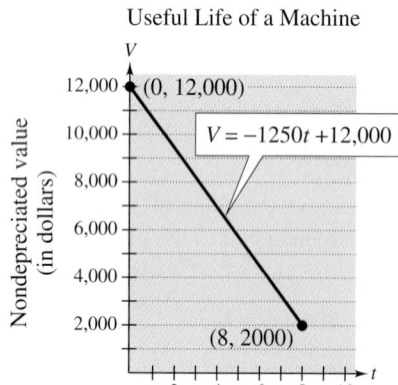

Useful Life of a Machine

FIGURE 1.33   *Straight-line depreciation*

Year, t	Value, V
0	12,000
1	10,750
2	9,500
3	8,250
4	7,000
5	5,750
6	4,500
7	3,250
8	2,000

1.2 Exercises

In Exercises 1 and 2, identify the line that has each slope.

1. (a) $m = \frac{2}{3}$

(b) m is undefined.

(c) $m = -2$

2. (a) $m = 0$

(b) $m = -\frac{3}{4}$

(c) $m = 1$

 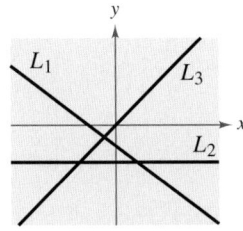

In Exercises 3 and 4, sketch the lines through the point with the indicated slopes on the same set of coordinate axes.

Point   *Slopes*

3. $(2, 3)$ (a) 0   (b) 1   (c) 2   (d) -3

4. $(-4, 1)$ (a) 3   (b) -3 (c) $\frac{1}{2}$ (d) Undefined

In Exercises 5–8, estimate the slope of the line.

5.

6.

7.

8.

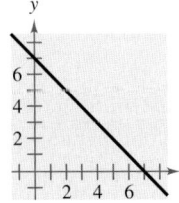

In Exercises 9–20, find the slope and y-intercept (if possible) of the equation of the line. Sketch the line.

9. $y = 5x + 3$

10. $y = x - 10$

11. $y = -\frac{1}{2}x + 4$

12. $y = -\frac{3}{2}x + 6$

13. $5x - 2 = 0$

14. $3y + 5 = 0$

15. $7x + 6y = 30$

16. $2x + 3y = 9$

17. $y - 3 = 0$

18. $y + 4 = 0$

19. $x + 5 = 0$

20. $x - 2 = 0$

In Exercises 21–28, plot the points and find the slope of the line passing through the pair of points.

21. $(-3, -2), (1, 6)$

22. $(2, 4), (4, -4)$

23. $(-6, -1), (-6, 4)$

24. $(0, -10), (-4, 0)$

25. $\left(\frac{11}{2}, -\frac{4}{3}\right), \left(-\frac{3}{2}, -\frac{1}{3}\right)$

26. $\left(\frac{7}{8}, \frac{3}{4}\right), \left(\frac{5}{4}, -\frac{1}{4}\right)$

27. $(4.8, 3.1), (-5.2, 1.6)$

28. $(-1.75, -8.3), (2.25, -2.6)$

In Exercises 29–38, use the point on the line and the slope of the line to find three additional points through which the line passes. (There are many correct answers.)

Point	*Slope*
29. $(2, 1)$	$m = 0$
30. $(-4, 1)$	m is undefined.
31. $(5, -6)$	$m = 1$
32. $(10, -6)$	$m = -1$
33. $(-8, 1)$	m is undefined.
34. $(-3, -1)$	$m = 0$
35. $(-5, 4)$	$m = 2$
36. $(0, -9)$	$m = -2$
37. $(7, -2)$	$m = \frac{1}{2}$
38. $(-1, -6)$	$m = -\frac{1}{2}$

In Exercises 39–42, determine whether the lines L_1 and L_2 passing through the pairs of points are parallel, perpendicular, or neither.

39. L_1: $(0, -1), (5, 9)$

L_2: $(0, 3), (4, 1)$

40. L_1: $(-2, -1), (1, 5)$

L_2: $(1, 3), (5, -5)$

41. L_1: $(3, 6), (-6, 0)$

L_2: $(0, -1), \left(5, \frac{7}{3}\right)$

42. L_1: $(4, 8), (-4, 2)$

L_2: $(3, -5), \left(-1, \frac{1}{3}\right)$

43. *Sales*   The following are the slopes of lines representing annual sales y in terms of time x in years. Use the slopes to interpret any change in annual sales for a one-year increase in time.

(a) The line has a slope of $m = 135$.

(b) The line has a slope of $m = 0$.

(c) The line has a slope of $m = -40$.

44. *Revenue* The following are the slopes of lines representing daily revenues y in terms of time x in days. Use the slopes to interpret any change in daily revenues for a one-day increase in time.

(a) The line has a slope of $m = 400$.

(b) The line has a slope of $m = 100$.

(c) The line has a slope of $m = 0$.

45. *Earnings per Share* The graph shows the earnings per share of stock for Auto Zone, Inc. for the years 1991 through 2001. (Source: Auto Zone, Inc.)

Year (1 ↔ 1991)

(a) Use the slopes to determine the years in which the earnings per share showed the greatest increase and the smallest increase.

(b) Find the slope of the line segment connecting the years 1991 and 2001.

(c) Interpret the meaning of the slope in part (b) in the context of the problem.

46. *Net Profit* The graph shows the net profit (in millions of dollars) for Outback Steakhouse for the years 1991 through 2001. (Source: Outback Steakhouse, Inc.)

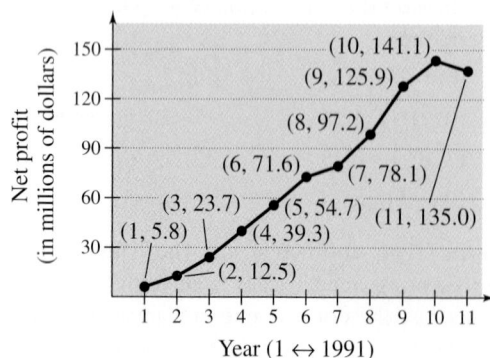

Year (1 ↔ 1991)

(a) Use the slopes to determine the years in which the net profit showed the greatest increase and the smallest increase.

(b) Find the slope of the line segment connecting the years 1991 and 2001.

(c) Interpret the meaning of the slope in part (b) in the context of the problem.

47. *Road Grade* From the top of a mountain road, a surveyor takes several horizontal measurements x and several vertical measurements y, as shown in the table (x and y are measured in feet).

x	y
300	-25
600	-50
900	-75
1200	-100
1500	-125
1800	-150
2100	-175

(a) Sketch a scatter plot of the data.

(b) Use a straightedge to sketch the best-fitting line through the points.

(c) Find an equation for the line you sketched in part (b).

(d) Interpret the meaning of the slope of the line in part (c) in the context of the problem.

(e) The surveyor needs to put up a road sign that indicates the steepness of the road. For instance, a surveyor would put up a sign that states "8% grade" on a road with a downhill grade that has a slope of $-\frac{8}{100}$. What should the sign state for the road in this problem?

48. *Road Grade* You are driving on a road that has a 6% uphill grade. This means that the slope of the road is $\frac{6}{100}$. Approximate the amount of vertical change in your position if you drive 200 feet.

Rate of Change   In Exercises 49 and 50, you are given the dollar value of a product in 2003 and the rate at which the value of the product is expected to change during the next 5 years. Use this information to write a linear equation that gives the dollar value *V* of the product in terms of the year *t*. (Let $t = 3$ represent 2003.)

	2003 Value	*Rate*
49.	$2540	$125 increase per year
50.	$156	$4.50 increase per year

Graphical Interpretation   In Exercises 51–54, match the description of the situation with its graph. Also determine the slope of each graph and interpret the slope in the context of the situation. [The graphs are labeled (a), (b), (c), and (d).]

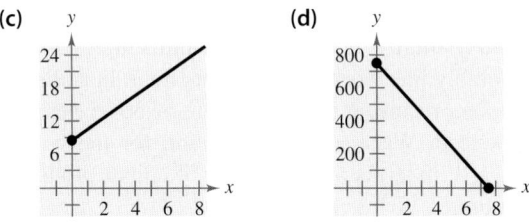

51. A person is paying $20 per week to a friend to repay a $200 loan.

52. An employee is paid $8.50 per hour plus $2 for each unit produced per hour.

53. A sales representative receives $30 per day for food plus $0.32 for each mile traveled.

54. A word processor that was purchased for $750 depreciates $100 per year.

In Exercises 55–66, find the slope-intercept form of the equation of the line that passes through the given point and has the indicated slope. Sketch the line.

	Point	*Slope*
55.	$(0, -2)$	$m = 3$
56.	$(0, 10)$	$m = -1$
57.	$(-3, 6)$	$m = -2$
58.	$(0, 0)$	$m = 4$

59.	$(4, 0)$	$m = -\frac{1}{3}$
60.	$(-2, -5)$	$m = \frac{3}{4}$
61.	$(6, -1)$	m is undefined.
62.	$(-10, 4)$	m is undefined.
63.	$\left(4, \frac{5}{2}\right)$	$m = 0$
64.	$\left(-\frac{1}{2}, \frac{3}{2}\right)$	$m = 0$
65.	$(-5.1, 1.8)$	$m = 5$
66.	$(2.3, -8.5)$	$m = -\frac{5}{2}$

In Exercises 67–80, find the slope-intercept form of the equation of the line passing through the points. Sketch the line.

67. $(5, -1), (-5, 5)$ **68.** $(4, 3), (-4, -4)$

69. $(-8, 1), (-8, 7)$ **70.** $(-1, 4), (6, 4)$

71. $\left(2, \frac{1}{2}\right), \left(\frac{1}{2}, \frac{5}{4}\right)$ **72.** $(1, 1), \left(6, -\frac{2}{3}\right)$

73. $\left(-\frac{1}{10}, -\frac{3}{5}\right), \left(\frac{9}{10}, -\frac{9}{5}\right)$

74. $\left(\frac{3}{4}, \frac{3}{2}\right), \left(-\frac{4}{3}, \frac{7}{4}\right)$

75. $(1, 0.6), (-2, -0.6)$

76. $(-8, 0.6), (2, -2.4)$

77. $(2, -1), \left(\frac{1}{3}, -1\right)$

78. $\left(\frac{1}{5}, -2\right), (-6, -2)$

79. $\left(\frac{7}{3}, -8\right), \left(\frac{7}{3}, 1\right)$

80. $(1.5, -2), (1.5, 0.2)$

In Exercises 81–86, use the *intercept form* to find the equation of the line with the given intercepts. The intercept form of the equation of a line with intercepts $(a, 0)$ and $(0, b)$ is

$$\frac{x}{a} + \frac{y}{b} = 1, \quad a \neq 0, \ b \neq 0.$$

81. x-intercept: $(2, 0)$ **82.** x-intercept: $(-3, 0)$
 y-intercept: $(0, 3)$ y-intercept: $(0, 4)$

83. x-intercept: $\left(-\frac{1}{6}, 0\right)$ **84.** x-intercept: $\left(\frac{2}{3}, 0\right)$
 y-intercept: $\left(0, -\frac{2}{3}\right)$ y-intercept: $(0, -2)$

85. Point on line: $(1, 2)$
 x-intercept: $(c, 0)$
 y-intercept: $(0, c), \quad c \neq 0$

86. Point on line: $(-3, 4)$
 x-intercept: $(d, 0)$
 y-intercept: $(0, d), \quad d \neq 0$

In Exercises 87–96, write the slope-intercept forms of the equations of the lines through the given point (a) parallel to the given line and (b) perpendicular to the given line.

	Point	Line
87.	$(2, 1)$	$4x - 2y = 3$
88.	$(-3, 2)$	$x + y = 7$
89.	$\left(-\frac{2}{3}, \frac{7}{8}\right)$	$3x + 4y = 7$
90.	$\left(\frac{7}{8}, \frac{3}{4}\right)$	$5x + 3y = 0$
91.	$(-1, 0)$	$y = -3$
92.	$(4, -2)$	$y = 1$
93.	$(2, 5)$	$x = 4$
94.	$(-5, 1)$	$x = -2$
95.	$(2.5, 6.8)$	$x - y = 4$
96.	$(-3.9, -1.4)$	$6x + 2y = 9$

Graphical Interpretation   In Exercises 97–100, identify any relationships that exist among the lines, and then use a graphing utility to graph the three equations in the same viewing window. Adjust the viewing window so that the slope appears visually correct—that is, so that parallel lines appear parallel and perpendicular lines appear to intersect at a right angle.

97. (a) $y = 2x$ (b) $y = -2x$ (c) $y = \frac{1}{2}x$

98. (a) $y = \frac{2}{3}x$ (b) $y = -\frac{3}{2}x$ (c) $y = \frac{2}{3}x + 2$

99. (a) $y = -\frac{1}{2}x$ (b) $y = -\frac{1}{2}x + 3$ (c) $y = 2x - 4$

100. (a) $y = x - 8$ (b) $y = x + 1$ (c) $y = -x + 3$

In Exercises 101–104, find a relationship between x and y such that (x, y) is equidistant from the two points.

101. $(4, -1), (-2, 3)$

102. $(6, 5), (1, -8)$

103. $\left(3, \frac{5}{2}\right), (-7, 1)$

104. $\left(-\frac{1}{2}, -4\right), \left(\frac{7}{2}, \frac{5}{4}\right)$

105. *Cash Flow per Share*   The cash flow per share for Timberland Co. was $0.18 in 1995 and $3.65 in 2000. Write a linear equation that gives the cash flow per share in terms of the year. Let $t = 0$ represent 1995. Then predict the cash flows for the years 2005 and 2010.   (Source: Timberland Co.)

106. *Number of Stores*   In 1996 there were 3927 J.C. Penney stores and in 2000 there were 3800 stores. Write a linear equation that gives the number of stores in terms of the year. Let $t = 0$ represent 1996. Then predict the numbers of stores for the years 2005 and 2010.   (Source: J.C. Penney Co.)

107. *Annual Salary*   A jeweler's salary was $28,500 in 1998 and $32,900 in 2000. The jeweler's salary follows a linear growth pattern. What will the jeweler's salary be in 2005?

108. *College Enrollment*   Ohio University had 27,913 students in 1999 and 28,197 students in 2001. The enrollment appears to follow a linear growth pattern. How many students will Ohio University have in 2005?   (Source: Ohio University)

109. *Depreciation*   A sub shop purchases a used pizza oven for $875. After 5 years, the oven will have to be replaced. Write a linear equation giving the value V of the equipment during the 5 years it will be in use.

110. *Depreciation*   A school district purchases a high-volume printer, copier, and scanner for $25,000. After 10 years, the equipment will have to be replaced. Its value at that time is expected to be $2000. Write a linear equation giving the value V of the equipment during the 10 years it will be in use.

111. *Sales*   A discount outlet is offering a 15% discount on all items. Write a linear equation giving the sale price S for an item with a list price L.

112. *Hourly Wage*   A microchip manufacturer pays its assembly line workers $11.50 per hour. In addition, workers receive a piecework rate of $0.75 per unit produced. Write a linear equation for the hourly wage W in terms of the number of units x produced per hour.

113. *Cost, Revenue, and Profit*   A roofing contractor purchases a shingle delivery truck with a shingle elevator for $36,500. The vehicle requires an average expenditure of $5.25 per hour for fuel and maintenance, and the operator is paid $11.50 per hour.

(a) Write a linear equation giving the total cost C of operating this equipment for t hours. (Include the purchase cost of the equipment.)

(b) Assuming that customers are charged $27 per hour of machine use, write an equation for the revenue R derived from t hours of use.

(c) Use the formula for profit $(P = R - C)$ to write an equation for the profit derived from t hours of use.

(d) Use the result of part (c) to find the break-even point—that is, the number of hours this equipment must be used to yield a profit of 0 dollars.

114. *Rental Demand* A real estate office handles an apartment complex with 50 units. When the rent per unit is $580 per month, all 50 units are occupied. However, when the rent is $625 per month, the average number of occupied units drops to 47. Assume that the relationship between the monthly rent p and the demand x is linear.

(a) Write the equation of the line giving the demand x in terms of the rent p.

(b) Use this equation to predict the number of units occupied when the rent is $655.

(c) Predict the number of units occupied when the rent is $595.

115. *Geometry* The length and width of a rectangular garden are 15 meters and 10 meters, respectively. A walkway of width x surrounds the garden.

(a) Draw a diagram that gives a visual representation of the problem.

(b) Write the equation for the perimeter y of the walkway in terms of x.

 (c) Use a graphing utility to graph the equation for the perimeter.

 (d) Determine the slope of the graph in part (c). For each additional one-meter increase in the width of the walkway, determine the increase in its perimeter.

116. *Monthly Salary* A pharmaceutical salesperson receives a monthly salary of $2500 plus a commission of 7% of sales. Write a linear equation for the salesperson's monthly wage W in terms of monthly sales S.

117. *Business Costs* A sales representative of a company using a personal car receives $120 per day for lodging and meals plus $0.35 per mile driven. Write a linear equation giving the daily cost C to the company in terms of x, the number of miles driven.

118. *Sports* The average annual salaries of major league baseball players (in thousands of dollars) from 1995 to 2002 are shown in the scatter plot. Find the equation of the line that you think best fits this data. (Let y represent the average salary and let t represent the year, with $t = 5$ corresponding to 1995.) (Source: The Associated Press)

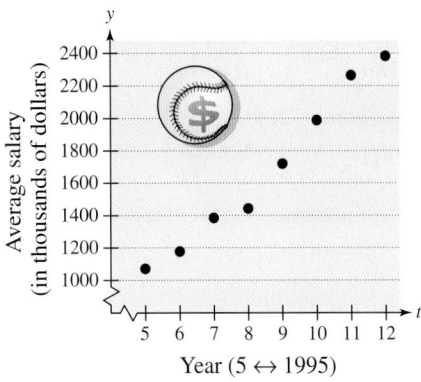

FIGURE FOR 118

▶ **Model It**

119. *Data Analysis* The average monthly cellular phone bills y (in dollars) for subscribers in the United States from 1990 through 1999, where x is the year, are shown as data points (x, y). (Source: Cellular Telecommunications Industry Association)

(1990, 80.90) (1995, 51.00)
(1991, 72.74) (1996, 47.70)
(1992, 68.68) (1997, 42.78)
(1993, 61.48) (1998, 39.43)
(1994, 56.21) (1999, 41.24)

(a) Sketch a scatter plot of the data. Let $x = 0$ correspond to 1990.

(b) Sketch the best-fitting line through the points.

(c) Find the equation of the line from part (b). Explain the procedure you used.

(d) Write a short paragraph explaining the meaning of the slope and y-intercept of the line in terms of the data.

(e) Compare the values obtained using your model with the actual values.

(f) Use your model to estimate the average monthly cellular phone bill in 2005.

120. *Data Analysis* An instructor gives regular 20-point quizzes and 100-point exams in an algebra course. Average scores for six students, given as data points (x, y) where x is the average quiz score and y is the average test score, are $(18, 87), (10, 55),$ $(19, 96)$, $(16, 79)$, $(13, 76)$, and $(15, 82)$. [*Note:* There are many correct answers for parts (b)–(d).]

(a) Sketch a scatter plot of the data.

(b) Use a straightedge to sketch the best-fitting line through the points.

(c) Find an equation for the line sketched in part (b).

(d) Use the equation in part (c) to estimate the average test score for a person with an average quiz score of 17.

(e) The instructor adds 4 points to the average test score of everyone in the class. Describe the changes in the positions of the plotted points and the change in the equation of the line.

Synthesis

True or False? **In Exercises 121 and 122, determine whether the statement is true or false. Justify your answer.**

121. A line with a slope of $-\frac{5}{7}$ is steeper than a line with a slope of $-\frac{6}{7}$.

122. The line through $(-8, 2)$ and $(-1, 4)$ and the line through $(0, -4)$ and $(-7, 7)$ are parallel.

123. Explain how you could show that the points $A\ (2, 3)$, $B\ (2, 9)$, and $C\ (4, 3)$ are the vertices of a right triangle.

124. Explain why the slope of a vertical line is said to be undefined.

125. With the information given in the graphs, is it possible to determine the slope of each line? Is it possible that the lines could have the same slope? Explain.

(a)   (b)

 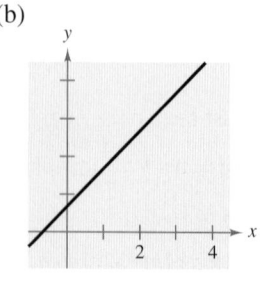

126. The slopes of two lines are -4 and $\frac{5}{2}$. Which is steeper? Explain.

127. The value V of a molding machine t years after it is purchased is

$$V = -4000t + 58{,}500, \quad 0 \le t \le 5.$$

Explain what the V-intercept and slope measure.

128. *Think About It* Is it possible for two lines with positive slopes to be perpendicular? Explain.

Review

In Exercises 129–132, match the equation with its graph. [The graphs are labeled (a), (b), (c), and (d).]

(a)   (b)

(c)   (d)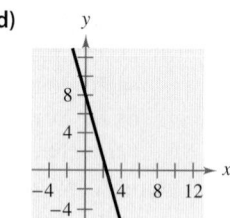

129. $y = 8 - 3x$

130. $y = 8 - \sqrt{x}$

131. $y = \frac{1}{2}x^2 + 2x + 1$

132. $y = |x + 2| - 1$

In Exercises 133–138, find all the solutions of the equation. Check your solution(s) in the original equation.

133. $-7(3 - x) = 14(x - 1)$

134. $\dfrac{8}{2x - 7} = \dfrac{4}{9 - 4x}$

135. $2x^2 - 21x + 49 = 0$

136. $x^2 - 8x + 3 = 0$

137. $\sqrt{x - 9} + 15 = 0$

138. $3x - 16\sqrt{x} + 5 = 0$

1.3 Functions

▶ What you should learn

- How to determine whether relations between two variables are functions
- How to use function notation and evaluate functions
- How to find the domains of functions
- How to use functions to model and solve real-life problems

▶ Why you should learn it

Functions can be used to model and solve real-life problems. For instance, in Exercise 99 on page 40, you will use a function to find the number of threatened and endangered fish in the world.

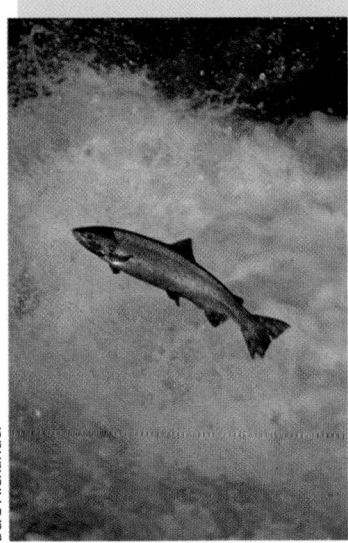

B&C Alexander

Introduction to Functions

Many everyday phenomena involve two quantities that are related to each other by some rule of correspondence. The mathematical term for such a rule of correspondence is a **relation.** In mathematics, relations are often represented by mathematical equations and formulas. For instance, the simple interest I earned on $1000 for 1 year is related to the annual interest rate r by the formula $I = 1000r$.

The formula $I = 1000r$ represents a special kind of relation that matches each item from one set with exactly one item from a different set. Such a relation is called a **function.**

Definition of a Function

A **function** f from a set A to a set B is a relation that assigns to each element x in the set A exactly one element y in the set B. The set A is the **domain** (or set of inputs) of the function f, and the set B contains the **range** (or set of outputs).

To help understand this definition, look at the function that relates the time of day to the temperature in Figure 1.34.

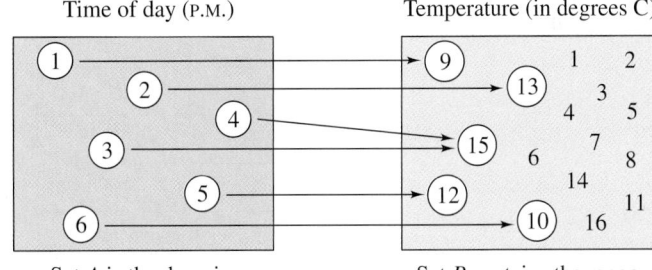

Set A is the domain.
Inputs: 1, 2, 3, 4, 5, 6

Set B contains the range.
Outputs: 9, 10, 12, 13, 15

FIGURE **1.34**

This function can be represented by the following ordered pairs, in which the first coordinate is the input and the second coordinate is the output.

$$\{(1, 9°), (2, 13°), (3, 15°), (4, 15°), (5, 12°), (6, 10°)\}$$

Characteristics of a Function from Set A to Set B

1. Each element in A must be matched with an element in B.

2. Some elements in B may not be matched with any element in A.

3. Two or more elements in A may be matched with the same element in B.

4. An element in A (the domain) cannot be matched with two different elements in B.

Have your students pay special attention to the concepts of function, domain, and range because they will be used throughout this text and in calculus.

Functions are commonly represented in four ways.

> ## Four Ways to Represent a Function
>
> 1. *Verbally* by a sentence that describes how the input variable is related to the output variable
>
> 2. *Numerically* by a table or a list of ordered pairs that matches input values with output values
>
> 3. *Graphically* by points on a graph in a coordinate plane in which the input values are represented by the horizontal axis and the output values are represented by the vertical axis
>
> 4. *Algebraically* by an equation in two variables

To determine whether or not a relation is a function, you must decide whether each input value is matched with exactly one output value. If any input value is matched with two or more output values, the relation is not a function.

Example 1 ▶   Testing for Functions

Determine whether the relation represents y as a function of x.

a. The input value x is the number of representatives from a state, and the output value y is the number of senators.

b.

Input x	Output y
2	11
2	10
3	8
4	5
5	1

c.

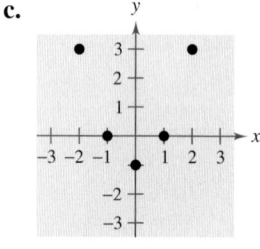

FIGURE 1.35

Solution

a. This verbal description *does* describe y as a function of x. Regardless of the value of x, the value of y is always 2. Such functions are called *constant functions*.

b. This table *does not* describe y as a function of x. The input value 2 is matched with two different y-values.

c. The graph in Figure 1.35 *does* describe y as a function of x. Each input value is matched with exactly one output value.

Representing functions by sets of ordered pairs is common in *discrete mathematics*. In algebra, however, it is more common to represent functions by equations or formulas involving two variables. For instance, the equation

$$y = x^2 \qquad \text{\small y is a function of x.}$$

represents the variable y as a function of the variable x. In this equation, x is

Historical Note
Leonhard Euler (1707–1783), a Swiss mathematician, is considered to have been the most prolific and productive mathematician in history. One of his greatest influences on mathematics was his use of symbols, or notation. The function notation $y = f(x)$ was introduced by Euler.

the **independent variable** and y is the **dependent variable.** The domain of the function is the set of all values taken on by the independent variable x, and the range of the function is the set of all values taken on by the dependent variable y.

Example 2 ▶ Testing for Functions Represented Algebraically

Which of the equations represent(s) y as a function of x?

a. $x^2 + y = 1$ **b.** $-x + y^2 = 1$

Solution

To determine whether y is a function of x, try to solve for y in terms of x.

a. Solving for y yields

$x^2 + y = 1$	Write original equation.
$y = 1 - x^2.$	Solve for y.

To each value of x there corresponds exactly one value of y. So, y is a function of x.

b. Solving for y yields

$-x + y^2 = 1$	Write original equation.
$y^2 = 1 + x$	Add x to each side.
$y = \pm\sqrt{1 + x}.$	Solve for y.

The $\pm$ indicates that to a given value of x there correspond two values of y. So, y is not a function of x.

Function Notation

When an equation is used to represent a function, it is convenient to name the function so that it can be referenced easily. For example, you know that the equation $y = 1 - x^2$ describes y as a function of x. Suppose you give this function the name "f." Then you can use the following **function notation.**

Input	Output	Equation
x	$f(x)$	$f(x) = 1 - x^2$

The symbol $f(x)$ is read as *the value of f at x* or simply *f of x.* The symbol $f(x)$ corresponds to the y-value for a given x. So, you can write $y = f(x)$. Keep in mind that f is the *name* of the function, whereas $f(x)$ is the *value* of the function at x. For instance, the function

$$f(x) = 3 - 2x$$

has *function values* denoted by $f(-1), f(0), f(2)$, and so on. To find these values, substitute the specified input values into the given equation.

For $x = -1$, $f(-1) = 3 - 2(-1) = 3 + 2 = 5.$

For $x = 0$, $f(0) = 3 - 2(0) = 3 - 0 = 3.$

For $x = 2$, $f(2) = 3 - 2(2) = 3 - 4 = -1.$

Although f is often used as a convenient function name and x is often used as the independent variable, you can use other letters. For instance,

$$f(x) = x^2 - 4x + 7, \quad f(t) = t^2 - 4t + 7, \quad \text{and} \quad g(s) = s^2 - 4s + 7$$

all define the same function. In fact, the role of the independent variable is that of a "placeholder." Consequently, the function could be described by

$$f() = ()^2 - 4() + 7.$$

Example 3 ▶ **Evaluating a Function** www

Let $g(x) = -x^2 + 4x + 1$. Find

a. $g(2)$ **b.** $g(t)$ **c.** $g(x + 2)$.

Solution

a. Replacing x with 2 in $g(x) = -x^2 + 4x + 1$ yields the following.

$$g(2) = -(2)^2 + 4(2) + 1 = -4 + 8 + 1 = 5$$

b. Replacing x with t yields the following.

$$g(t) = -(t)^2 + 4(t) + 1 = -t^2 + 4t + 1$$

c. Replacing x with $x + 2$ yields the following.

$$g(x + 2) = -(x + 2)^2 + 4(x + 2) + 1$$
$$= -(x^2 + 4x + 4) + 4x + 8 + 1$$
$$= -x^2 - 4x - 4 + 4x + 8 + 1$$
$$= -x^2 + 5$$

Students often have difficulty understanding how to evaluate piecewise-defined functions. You may want to use the following additional examples to demonstrate evaluation of piecewise-defined functions.

a. Evaluate at $x = 0, 1, 3$.

$$f(x) = \begin{cases} \dfrac{x}{2} + 1, & x \leq 1 \\ 3x + 2, & x > 1 \end{cases}$$

Solution

Because $x = 0$ is less than or equal to 1, use $f(x) = (x/2) + 1$ to obtain

$$f(0) = \frac{0}{2} + 1 = 1.$$

For $x = 1$, use $f(x) = (x/2) + 1$ to obtain

$$f(1) = \frac{1}{2} + 1 = 1\frac{1}{2}.$$

For $x = 3$, use $f(x) = 3x + 2$ to obtain
$f(3) = 3(3) + 2 = 11.$

b. Evaluate at $x = 0, 3, 5$.

$$f(x) = \begin{cases} x^2 + 3, & x < 2 \\ 7, & 2 \leq x \leq 4 \\ 2x - 1, & x > 4 \end{cases}$$

Solution

Because $x = 0$ is less than 2, use $f(x) = x^2 + 3$ to obtain
$f(0) = 0^2 + 3 = 3.$
For $x = 3$, use $f(x) = 7$ to obtain
$f(3) = 7.$
For $x = 5$, use $f(x) = 2x - 1$ to obtain
$f(5) = 2(5) - 1 = 9.$

A function defined by two or more equations over a specified domain is called a **piecewise-defined function.**

Example 4 ▶ **A Piecewise-Defined Function**

Evaluate the function when $x = -1, 0,$ and 1.

$$f(x) = \begin{cases} x^2 + 1, & x < 0 \\ x - 1, & x \geq 0 \end{cases}$$

Solution

Because $x = -1$ is less than 0, use $f(x) = x^2 + 1$ to obtain

$$f(-1) = (-1)^2 + 1 = 2.$$

For $x = 0$, use $f(x) = x - 1$ to obtain

$$f(0) = (0) - 1 = -1.$$

For $x = 1$, use $f(x) = x - 1$ to obtain

$$f(1) = (1) - 1 = 0.$$

Technology

Use a graphing utility to graph $y = \sqrt{4 - x^2}$. What is the domain of this function? Then graph $y = \sqrt{x^2 - 4}$. What is the domain of this function? Do the domains of these two functions overlap? If so, for what values?

The Domain of a Function

The domain of a function can be described explicitly or it can be *implied* by the expression used to define the function. The **implied domain** is the set of all real numbers for which the expression is defined. For instance, the function

$$f(x) = \frac{1}{x^2 - 4}$$
Domain excludes x-values that result in division by zero.

has an implied domain that consists of all real x other than $x = \pm 2$. These two values are excluded from the domain because division by zero is undefined. Another common type of implied domain is that used to avoid even roots of negative numbers. For example, the function

$$f(x) = \sqrt{x}$$
Domain excludes x-values that result in even roots of negative numbers.

is defined only for $x \geq 0$. So, its implied domain is the interval $[0, \infty)$. In general, the domain of a function *excludes* values that would cause division by zero *or* that would result in the even root of a negative number.

Example 5 ▶ Finding the Domain of a Function

Find the domain of each function.

a. f: $\{(-3, 0), (-1, 4), (0, 2), (2, 2), (4, -1)\}$ **b.** $g(x) = \dfrac{1}{x + 5}$

c. Volume of a sphere: $V = \frac{4}{3}\pi r^3$ **d.** $h(x) = \sqrt{4 - x^2}$

Solution

a. The domain of f consists of all first coordinates in the set of ordered pairs.

Domain $= \{-3, -1, 0, 2, 4\}$

b. Excluding x-values that yield zero in the denominator, the domain of g is the set of all real numbers $x \neq -5$.

c. Because this function represents the volume of a sphere, the values of the radius r must be positive. So, the domain is the set of all real numbers r such that $r > 0$.

d. This function is defined only for x-values for which

$$4 - x^2 \geq 0.$$

Using the methods described in Section A.6, you can conclude that $-2 \leq x \leq 2$. So, the domain is the interval $[-2, 2]$.

In Example 5(c), note that the domain of a function may be implied by the physical context. For instance, from the equation

$$V = \frac{4}{3}\pi r^3$$

you would have no reason to restrict r to positive values, but the physical context implies that a sphere cannot have a negative radius.

$$\boxed{\dfrac{h}{r} = 4}$$

|←— r —→|

h

FIGURE **1.36**

Applications

▶ **The Dimensions of a Container**

You work in the marketing department of a soft-drink company and are experimenting with a new can for iced tea that is slightly narrower and taller than a standard can. For your experimental can, the ratio of the height to the radius is 4, as shown in Figure 1.36.

a. Write the volume of the can as a function of the radius r.

b. Write the volume of the can as a function of the height h.

Solution

a. $V(r) = \pi r^2 h = \pi r^2(4r) = 4\pi r^3$ Write V as a function of r.

b. $V(h) = \pi \left(\dfrac{h}{4}\right)^2 h = \dfrac{\pi h^3}{16}$ Write V as a function of h.

▶ **The Path of a Baseball**

A baseball is hit at a point 3 feet above ground at a velocity of 100 feet per second and an angle of 45°. The path of the baseball is given by the function

$$f(x) = -0.0032x^2 + x + 3$$

where y and x are measured in feet, as shown in Figure 1.37. Will the baseball clear a 10-foot fence located 300 feet from home plate?

Solution

When $x = 300$, the height of the baseball is

$$f(300) = -0.0032(300)^2 + 300 + 3$$

$$= 15 \text{ feet.}$$

So, the ball will clear the fence.

FIGURE **1.37**

In the equation in Example 7, the height of the baseball is a function of the distance from home plate.

Pieces of Mail Handled
by U.S. Postal Service

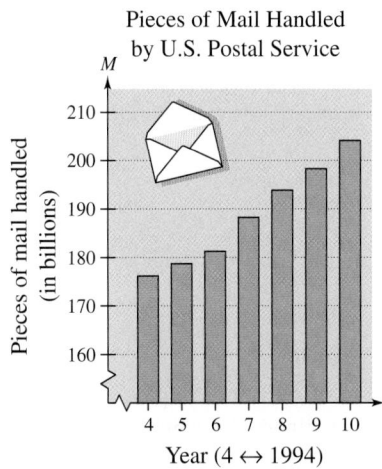

FIGURE **1.38**

Example 8 ▶ **Pieces of Mail Handled**

The number M (in billions) of pieces of mail handled by the U.S. Postal Service increased in a linear pattern from 1994 to 1996, as shown in Figure 1.38. Then, in 1997, the number handled took a jump and, until 2000, increased in a *different* linear pattern. These two patterns can be approximated by the function

$$M(t) = \begin{cases} 167.2 + 2.70t, & 4 \leq t \leq 6 \\ 152.0 + 5.57t, & 7 \leq t \leq 10 \end{cases}$$

where $t = 4$ represents 1994. Use this function to approximate the total number of pieces of mail handled from 1994 to 2000. (Source: U.S. Postal Service)

Solution

From 1994 to 1996, use $M(t) = 167.2 + 2.70t$.

$$\underbrace{178.0,}_{1994} \quad \underbrace{180.7,}_{1995} \quad \underbrace{183.4}_{1996}$$

From 1997 to 2000, use $M(t) = 152.0 + 5.57t$.

$$\underbrace{191.0,}_{1997} \quad \underbrace{196.6,}_{1998} \quad \underbrace{202.1,}_{1999} \quad \underbrace{207.7}_{2000}$$

The total of these seven amounts is 1339.5, which implies that the total number of pieces of mail handled was approximately 1.3 trillion.

One of the basic definitions in calculus employs the ratio

$$\frac{f(x + h) - f(x)}{h}, \qquad h \neq 0.$$

This ratio is called a **difference quotient,** as illustrated in Example 9.

Example 9 ▶ **Evaluating a Difference Quotient**

For $f(x) = x^2 - 4x + 7$, find $\dfrac{f(x + h) - f(x)}{h}$.

Solution

$$\frac{f(x + h) - f(x)}{h} = \frac{[(x + h)^2 - 4(x + h) + 7] - (x^2 - 4x + 7)}{h}$$

$$= \frac{x^2 + 2xh + h^2 - 4x - 4h + 7 - x^2 + 4x - 7}{h}$$

$$= \frac{2xh + h^2 - 4h}{h} = \frac{h(2x + h - 4)}{h} = 2x + h - 4, \ h \neq 0$$

The symbol ∫ indicates an example or exercise that highlights algebraic techniques specifically used in calculus.

Activities

1. Evaluate $f(x) = 2 + 3x - x^2$ for
   a. $f(-3)$
   b. $f(x + 1)$
   c. $f(x + \Delta x) - f(x)$.
   Answers: a. -16
   b. $-x^2 + x + 4$
   c. $3\,\Delta x - 2x\,\Delta x - (\Delta x)^2$

2. Determine whether y is a function of x.
   $2x^3 + 3x^2y^2 + 1 = 0$
   Answer: No

3. Find the domain: $f(x) = \dfrac{3}{x + 1}$.
   Answer: All real numbers $x \neq -1$

Summary of Function Terminology

Function: A **function** is a relationship between two variables such that to each value of the independent variable there corresponds exactly one value of the dependent variable.

Function Notation: $y = f(x)$

f is the *name* of the function.

y is the **dependent variable.**

x is the **independent variable.**

$f(x)$ is the *value of the function at x.*

Domain: The **domain** of a function is the set of all values (inputs) of the independent variable for which the function is defined. If x is in the domain of f, f is said to be *defined* at x. If x is not in the domain of f, f is said to be *undefined* at x.

Range: The range of a function is the set of all values (outputs) assumed by the dependent variable (that is, the set of all function values).

Implied Domain: If f is defined by an algebraic expression and the domain is not specified, the **implied domain** consists of all real numbers for which the expression is defined.

Writing ABOUT MATHEMATICS

Everyday Functions In groups of two or three, identify common real-life functions. Consider everyday activities, events, and expenses, such as long distance telephone calls and car insurance. Here are two examples.

a. The statement, "Your happiness is a function of the grade you receive in this course" *is not* a correct mathematical use of the word "function." The word "happiness" is ambiguous.

b. The statement, "Your federal income tax is a function of your adjusted gross income" *is* a correct mathematical use of the word "function." Once you have determined your adjusted gross income, your income tax can be determined.

Describe your functions in words. Avoid using ambiguous words. Can you find an example of a piecewise-defined function?

1.3 Exercises

In Exercises 1–4, is the relationship a function?

1. *Domain   Range*

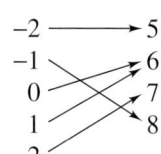

2. *Domain   Range*

-2 ⟶ 3
-1 ⟶ 4
0 ⟶ 5
1 ⟶
2 ⟶

3. *Domain   Range*

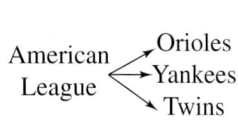

National League ⟶ Cubs / Pirates / Dodgers

American League ⟶ Orioles / Yankees / Twins

4. *Domain   Range*

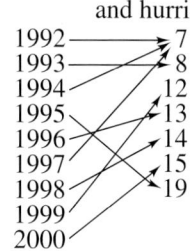

(Year)   (Number of North Atlantic tropical storms and hurricanes)

1992 ⟶ 7
1993 ⟶ 8
1994 ⟶ 12
1995 ⟶ 13
1996 ⟶ 14
1997 ⟶ 15
1998 ⟶ 19
1999 ⟶
2000 ⟶

In Exercises 5–8, does the table describe a function? Explain your reasoning.

5.

Input value	−2	−1	0	1	2
Output value	−8	−1	0	1	8

6.

Input value	0	1	2	1	0
Output value	−4	−2	0	2	4

7.

Input value	10	7	4	7	10
Output value	3	6	9	12	15

8.

Input value	0	3	9	12	15
Output value	3	3	3	3	3

In Exercises 9 and 10, which sets of ordered pairs represent functions from *A* to *B*? Explain.

9. $A = \{0, 1, 2, 3\}$ and $B = \{-2, -1, 0, 1, 2\}$

(a) $\{(0, 1), (1, -2), (2, 0), (3, 2)\}$

(b) $\{(0, -1), (2, 2), (1, -2), (3, 0), (1, 1)\}$

(c) $\{(0, 0), (1, 0), (2, 0), (3, 0)\}$

(d) $\{(0, 2), (3, 0), (1, 1)\}$

10. $A = \{a, b, c\}$ and $B = \{0, 1, 2, 3\}$

(a) $\{(a, 1), (c, 2), (c, 3), (b, 3)\}$

(b) $\{(a, 1), (b, 2), (c, 3)\}$

(c) $\{(1, a), (0, a), (2, c), (3, b)\}$

(d) $\{(c, 0), (b, 0), (a, 3)\}$

Circulation of Newspapers **In Exercises 11 and 12, use the graph, which shows the circulation (in millions) of daily newspapers in the United States.** (Source: Editor & Publisher Company)

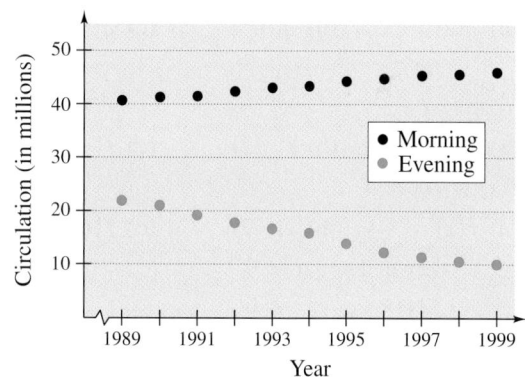

11. Is the circulation of morning newspapers a function of the year? Is the circulation of evening newspapers a function of the year? Explain.

12. Let $f(x)$ represent the circulation of evening newspapers in year x. Find $f(1998)$.

In Exercises 13–22, determine whether the equation represents *y* as a function of *x*.

13. $x^2 + y^2 = 4$

14. $x = y^2$

15. $x^2 + y = 4$

16. $x + y^2 = 4$

17. $2x + 3y = 4$

18. $(x - 2)^2 + y^2 = 4$

19. $y^2 = x^2 - 1$

20. $y = \sqrt{x + 5}$

21. $y = |4 - x|$

22. $|y| = 4 - x$

In Exercises 23–36, evaluate the function at each specified value of the independent variable and simplify.

23. $f(x) = 2x - 3$
   (a) $f(1)$ (b) $f(-3)$ (c) $f(x - 1)$

24. $g(y) = 7 - 3y$
   (a) $g(0)$ (b) $g(\frac{7}{3})$ (c) $g(s + 2)$

25. $V(r) = \frac{4}{3}\pi r^3$
   (a) $V(3)$ (b) $V(\frac{3}{2})$ (c) $V(2r)$

26. $h(t) = t^2 - 2t$
   (a) $h(2)$ (b) $h(1.5)$ (c) $h(x + 2)$

27. $f(y) = 3 - \sqrt{y}$
   (a) $f(4)$ (b) $f(0.25)$ (c) $f(4x^2)$

28. $f(x) = \sqrt{x + 8} + 2$
   (a) $f(-8)$ (b) $f(1)$ (c) $f(x - 8)$

29. $q(x) = \dfrac{1}{x^2 - 9}$
   (a) $q(0)$ (b) $q(3)$ (c) $q(y + 3)$

30. $q(t) = \dfrac{2t^2 + 3}{t^2}$
   (a) $q(2)$ (b) $q(0)$ (c) $q(-x)$

31. $f(x) = \dfrac{|x|}{x}$
   (a) $f(2)$ (b) $f(-2)$ (c) $f(x - 1)$

32. $f(x) = |x| + 4$
   (a) $f(2)$ (b) $f(-2)$ (c) $f(x^2)$

33. $f(x) = \begin{cases} 2x + 1, & x < 0 \\ 2x + 2, & x \geq 0 \end{cases}$
   (a) $f(-1)$ (b) $f(0)$ (c) $f(2)$

34. $f(x) = \begin{cases} x^2 + 2, & x \leq 1 \\ 2x^2 + 2, & x > 1 \end{cases}$
   (a) $f(-2)$ (b) $f(1)$ (c) $f(2)$

35. $f(x) = \begin{cases} 3x - 1, & x < -1 \\ 4, & -1 \leq x \leq 1 \\ x^2, & x > 1 \end{cases}$
   (a) $f(-2)$ (b) $f(-\frac{1}{2})$ (c) $f(3)$

36. $f(x) = \begin{cases} 4 - 5x, & x \leq -2 \\ 0, & -2 < x \leq 2 \\ x^2 + 1, & x > 2 \end{cases}$
   (a) $f(-3)$ (b) $f(4)$ (c) $f(-1)$

In Exercises 37–42, complete the table.

37. $f(x) = x^2 - 3$

x	$f(x)$
-2	
-1	
0	
1	
2	

38. $g(x) = \sqrt{x - 3}$

x	$g(x)$
3	
4	
5	
6	
7	

39. $h(t) = \frac{1}{2}|t + 3|$

t	$h(t)$
-5	
-4	
-3	
-2	
-1	

40. $f(s) = \dfrac{|s - 2|}{s - 2}$

s	$f(s)$
0	
1	
$\frac{3}{2}$	
$\frac{5}{2}$	
4	

41. $f(x) = \begin{cases} -\frac{1}{2}x + 4, & x \leq 0 \\ (x - 2)^2, & x > 0 \end{cases}$

x	$f(x)$
-2	
-1	
0	
1	
2	

42. $h(x) = \begin{cases} 9 - x^2, & x < 3 \\ x - 3, & x \geq 3 \end{cases}$

x	$h(x)$
1	
2	
3	
4	
5	

In Exercises 43–50, find all real values of x such that $f(x) = 0$.

43. $f(x) = 15 - 3x$

44. $f(x) = 5x + 1$

45. $f(x) = \dfrac{3x - 4}{5}$

46. $f(x) = \dfrac{12 - x^2}{5}$

47. $f(x) = x^2 - 9$

48. $f(x) = x^2 - 8x + 15$

49. $f(x) = x^3 - x$

50. $f(x) = x^3 - x^2 - 4x + 4$

In Exercises 51–54, find the value(s) of x for which $f(x) = g(x)$.

51. $f(x) = x^2 + 2x + 1, \quad g(x) = 3x + 3$

52. $f(x) = x^4 - 2x^2, \quad g(x) = 2x^2$

53. $f(x) = \sqrt{3x} + 1, \quad g(x) = x + 1$

54. $f(x) = \sqrt{x} - 4, \quad g(x) = 2 - x$

In Exercises 55–68, find the domain of the function.

55. $f(x) = 5x^2 + 2x - 1$

56. $g(x) = 1 - 2x^2$

57. $h(t) = \dfrac{4}{t}$

58. $s(y) = \dfrac{3y}{y + 5}$

59. $g(y) = \sqrt{y - 10}$

60. $f(t) = \sqrt[3]{t + 4}$

61. $f(x) = \sqrt[4]{1 - x^2}$

62. $f(x) = \sqrt[4]{x^2 + 3x}$

63. $g(x) = \dfrac{1}{x} - \dfrac{3}{x + 2}$

64. $h(x) = \dfrac{10}{x^2 - 2x}$

65. $f(s) = \dfrac{\sqrt{s - 1}}{s - 4}$

66. $f(x) = \dfrac{\sqrt{x + 6}}{6 + x}$

67. $f(x) = \dfrac{x - 4}{\sqrt{x}}$

68. $f(x) = \dfrac{x - 5}{\sqrt{x^2 - 9}}$

In Exercises 69–72, assume that the domain of f is the set $A = \{-2, -1, 0, 1, 2\}$. Determine the set of ordered pairs that represents the function f.

69. $f(x) = x^2$

70. $f(x) = x^2 - 3$

71. $f(x) = |x| + 2$

72. $f(x) = |x + 1|$

Exploration In Exercises 73–76, match the data with one of the following functions

$$f(x) = cx, \quad g(x) = cx^2, \quad h(x) = c\sqrt{|x|}, \quad \text{and} \quad r(x) = \dfrac{c}{x}$$

and determine the value of the constant c that will make the function fit the data in the table.

73.

x	y
-4	-32
-1	-2
0	0
1	-2
4	-32

74.

x	y
-4	-1
-1	$-\frac{1}{4}$
0	0
1	$\frac{1}{4}$
4	1

75.

x	y
-4	-8
-1	-32
0	Undef.
1	32
4	8

76.

x	y
-4	6
-1	3
0	0
1	3
4	6

∫ In Exercises 77–84, find the difference quotient and simplify your answer.

77. $f(x) = x^2 - x + 1, \quad \dfrac{f(2 + h) - f(2)}{h}, h \neq 0$

78. $f(x) = 5x - x^2, \quad \dfrac{f(5 + h) - f(5)}{h}, h \neq 0$

79. $f(x) = x^3 + 3x, \quad \dfrac{f(x + h) - f(x)}{h}, h \neq 0$

80. $f(x) = 4x^2 - 2x, \quad \dfrac{f(x + h) - f(x)}{h}, h \neq 0$

81. $g(x) = \dfrac{1}{x^2}, \quad \dfrac{g(x) - g(3)}{x - 3}, x \neq 3$

82. $f(t) = \dfrac{1}{t - 2}, \quad \dfrac{f(t) - f(1)}{t - 1}, t \neq 1$

83. $f(x) = \sqrt{5x}, \quad \dfrac{f(x) - f(5)}{x - 5}, x \neq 5$

84. $f(x) = x^{2/3} + 1, \quad \dfrac{f(x) - f(8)}{x - 8}, x \neq 8$

The symbol ∫ indicates an example or exercise that highlights algebraic techniques specifically used in calculus.

85. *Geometry* Write the area A of a square as a function of its perimeter P.

86. *Geometry* Write the area A of a circle as a function of its circumference C.

87. *Maximum Volume* An open box of maximum volume is to be made from a square piece of material 24 centimeters on a side by cutting equal squares from the corners and turning up the sides (see figure).

(a) The table shows the volume V (in cubic centimeters) of the box for various heights x (in centimeters). Use the table to estimate the maximum volume.

Height, x	Volume, V
1	484
2	800
3	972
4	1024
5	980
6	864

(b) Plot the points (x, V). Does the relation defined by the ordered pairs represent V as a function of x?

(c) If V is a function of x, write the function and determine its domain.

 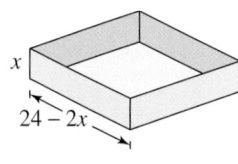

$x \hspace{0.3em} \vdash\!\!-\! 24 - 2x \!-\!\dashv \hspace{0.3em} x$

88. *Maximum Profit* The cost per unit in the production of a radio model is $60. The manufacturer charges $90 per unit for orders of 100 or less. To encourage large orders, the manufacturer reduces the charge by $0.15 per radio for each unit ordered in excess of 100 (for example, there would be a charge of $87 per radio for an order size of 120).

(a) The table shows the profit P (in dollars) for various numbers of units ordered, x. Use the table to estimate the maximum profit.

Units, x	Profit, P
110	3135
120	3240
130	3315
140	3360
150	3375
160	3360
170	3315

(b) Plot the points (x, P). Does the relation defined by the ordered pairs represent P as a function of x?

(c) If P is a function of x, write the function and determine its domain.

89. *Geometry* A right triangle is formed in the first quadrant by the x- and y-axes and a line through the point $(2, 1)$ (see figure). Write the area A of the triangle as a function of x, and determine the domain of the function.

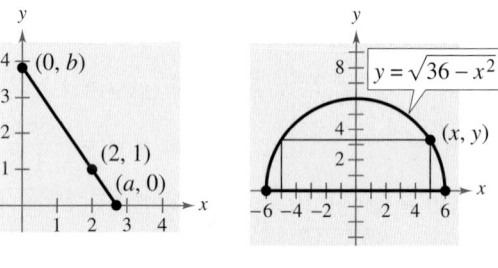

FIGURE FOR 89   FIGURE FOR 90

90. *Geometry* A rectangle is bounded by the x-axis and the semicircle $y = \sqrt{36 - x^2}$ (see figure). Write the area A of the rectangle as a function of x, and determine the domain of the function.

91. *Average Price* The average price p (in thousands of dollars) of a new mobile home in the United States from 1990 to 1999 (see figure) can be approximated by the model

$$p(t) = \begin{cases} 0.543t^2 - 0.75t + 27.8, & 0 \le t \le 4 \\ 1.89t + 27.1, & 5 \le t \le 9 \end{cases}$$

where $t = 0$ represents 1990. Use this model to find the average prices of a mobile home in 1990, 1994, 1996, and 1999. (Source: U.S. Census Bureau)

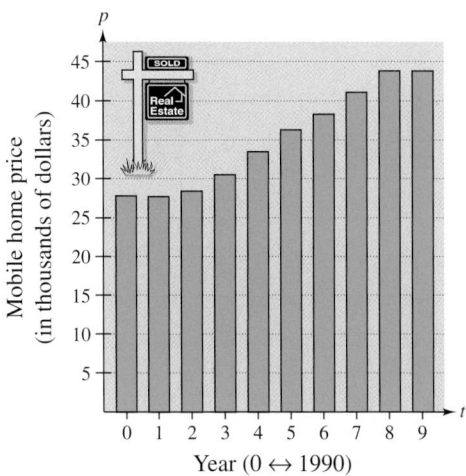

92. Postal Regulations A rectangular package to be sent by the U.S. Postal Service can have a maximum combined length and girth (perimeter of a cross section) of 108 inches (see figure).

(a) Write the volume V of the package as a function of x. What is the domain of the function?

(b) Use a graphing utility to graph your function. Be sure to use the appropriate window setting.

(c) What dimensions will maximize the volume of the package? Explain your answer.

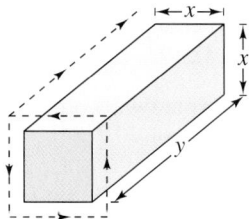

93. Cost, Revenue, and Profit A company produces a product for which the variable cost is $12.30 per unit and the fixed costs are $98,000. The product sells for $17.98. Let x be the number of units produced and sold.

(a) The total cost for a business is the sum of the variable cost and the fixed costs. Write the total cost C as a function of the number of units produced.

(b) Write the revenue R as a function of the number of units sold.

(c) Write the profit P as a function of the number of units sold. (*Note:* $P = R - C$.)

94. Average Cost The inventor of a new game believes that the variable cost for producing the game is $0.95 per unit and the fixed costs are $6000. The inventor sells each game for $1.69. Let x be the number of games sold.

(a) The total cost for a business is the sum of the variable cost and the fixed costs. Write the total cost C as a function of the number of games sold.

(b) Write the average cost per unit $\overline{C} = C/x$ as a function of x.

95. Transportation For groups of 80 or more people, a charter bus company determines the rate per person according to the formula

$$\text{Rate} = 8 - 0.05(n - 80), \qquad n \geq 80$$

where the rate is given in dollars and n is the number of people.

(a) Write the revenue R for the bus company as a function of n.

(b) Use the function in part (a) to complete the table. What can you conclude?

n	90	100	110	120	130	140	150
$R(n)$							

96. Physics The force F (in tons) of water against the face of a dam is estimated by the function $F(y) = 149.76\sqrt{10}\,y^{5/2}$, where y is the depth of the water in feet.

(a) Complete the table. What can you conclude from the table?

y	5	10	20	30	40
$F(y)$					

(b) Use the table to approximate the depth at which the force against the dam is 1,000,000 tons.

(c) Find the depth at which the force against the dam is 1,000,000 tons algebraically.

97. Height of a Balloon A balloon carrying a transmitter ascends vertically from a point 3000 feet from the receiving station.

(a) Draw a diagram that gives a visual representation of the problem. Let h represent the height of the balloon and let d represent the distance between the balloon and the receiving station.

(b) Write the height of the balloon as a function of d. What is the domain of the function?

98. *Path of a Ball* The height y (in feet) of a baseball thrown by a child is

$$y = -\frac{1}{10}x^2 + 3x + 6$$

where x is the horizontal distance (in feet) from where the ball was thrown. Will the ball fly over the head of another child 30 feet away trying to catch the ball? (Assume that the child who is trying to catch the ball holds a baseball glove at a height of 5 feet.)

▶ **Model It**

99. *Wildlife* The graph shows the number of threatened and endangered fish species in the world from 1996 through 2001. Let $f(t)$ represent the number of threatened and endangered fish species in the year t. (Source: U.S. Fish and Wildlife Service)

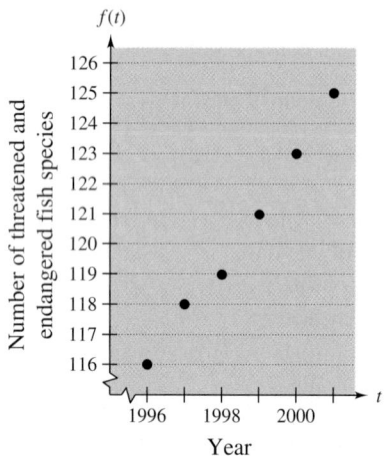

(a) Find

$$\frac{f(2001) - f(1996)}{2001 - 1996}$$

and interpret the result in the context of the problem.

(b) Find a linear model for the data algebraically. Let N represent the number of threatened and endangered fish species and let $x = 6$ correspond to 1996.

(c) Use the model found in part (b) to complete the table.

▶ **Model It** *(continued)*

x	N
6	
7	
8	
9	
10	
11	

(d) Compare your results from part (c) with the actual data.

 (e) Use a graphing utility to find a linear model for the data. Let $x = 6$ correspond to 1996. How does the model you found in part (b) compare with the model given by the graphing utility?

Synthesis

True or False? In Exercises 100 and 101, determine whether the statement is true or false. Justify your answer.

100. The domain of the function $f(x) = x^4 - 1$ is $(-\infty, \infty)$, and the range of $f(x)$ is $(0, \infty)$.

101. The set of ordered pairs $\{(-8, -2), (-6, 0), (-4, 0), (-2, 2), (0, 4), (2, -2)\}$ represents a function.

102. *Writing* In your own words, explain the meanings of *domain* and *range*.

Review

In Exercises 103–106, solve the equation.

103. $\dfrac{t}{3} + \dfrac{t}{5} = 1$

104. $\dfrac{3}{t} + \dfrac{5}{t} = 1$

105. $\dfrac{3}{x(x+1)} - \dfrac{4}{x} = \dfrac{1}{x+1}$

106. $\dfrac{12}{x} - 3 = \dfrac{4}{x} + 9$

In Exercises 107–110, find the equation of the line passing through the pair of points.

107. $(-2, -5), (4, -1)$

108. $(10, 0), (1, 9)$

109. $(-6, 5), (3, -5)$

110. $\left(-\frac{1}{2}, 3\right), \left(\frac{11}{2}, -\frac{1}{3}\right)$

1.4 Analyzing Graphs of Functions

▶ **Why you should learn it**

Graphs of functions can help you visualize relationships between variables in real life. For instance, in Exercise 76 on page 49, you will use the graph of a function to represent visually the merchandise trade balance for the United States.

The Graph of a Function

In Section 1.3, you studied functions from an algebraic point of view. In this section, you will study functions from a graphical perspective.

The **graph of a function** f is the collection of ordered pairs $(x, f(x))$ such that x is in the domain of f. As you study this section, remember that

$x =$ the directed distance from the y-axis

$f(x) =$ the directed distance from the x-axis

as shown in Figure 1.39.

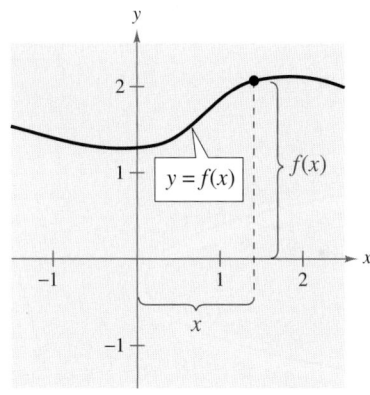

FIGURE 1.39

Example 1 ▶ Finding the Domain and Range of a Function

Use the graph of the function f, shown in Figure 1.40, to find (a) the domain of f, (b) the function values $f(-1)$ and $f(2)$, and (c) the range of f.

Solution

a. The closed dot at $(-1, 1)$ indicates that $x = -1$ is in the domain of f, whereas the open dot at $(5, 2)$ indicates $x = 5$ is not in the domain. So, the domain of f is all x in the interval $[-1, 5)$.

b. Because $(-1, 1)$ is a point on the graph of f, it follows that $f(-1) = 1$. Similarly, because $(2, -3)$ is a point on the graph of f, it follows that $f(2) = -3$.

c. Because the graph does not extend below $f(2) = -3$ or above $f(0) = 3$, the range of f is the interval $[-3, 3]$.

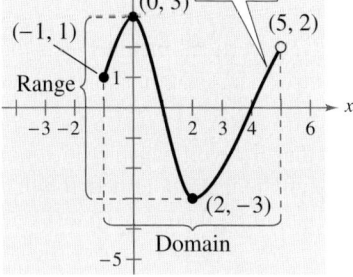

FIGURE 1.40

The use of dots (open or closed) at the extreme left and right points of a graph indicates that the graph does not extend beyond these points. If no such dots are shown, assume that the graph extends beyond these points.

By the definition of a function, at most one y-value corresponds to a given x-value. This means that the graph of a function cannot have two or more different points with the same x-coordinate, and no two points on the graph of a function can be vertically above and below each other. It follows, then, that a vertical line can intersect the graph of a function at most once. This observation provides a convenient visual test called the **Vertical Line Test** for functions.

Vertical Line Test for Functions

A set of points in a coordinate plane is the graph of y as a function of x if and only if no *vertical* line intersects the graph at more than one point.

Example 2 ▶   **Vertical Line Test for Functions**

Use the Vertical Line Test to decide whether the graphs in Figure 1.41 represent y as a function of x.

(a)

(b)

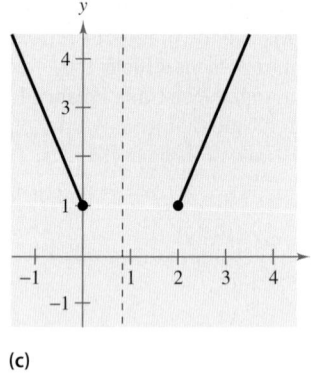

(c)

FIGURE 1.41

Solution

a. This *is not* a graph of y as a function of x, because you can find a vertical line that intersects the graph twice. That is, for a particular input x, there is more than one output y.

b. This *is* a graph of y as a function of x, because every vertical line intersects the graph at most once. That is, for a particular input x, there is at most one output y.

c. This *is* a graph of y as a function of x. (Note that if a vertical line does not intersect the graph, it simply means that the function is undefined for that particular value of x.) That is, for a particular input x, there is at most one output y.

Zeros of a Function

If the graph of a function of x has an x-intercept at $(a, 0)$, then a is a **zero** of the function.

Zeros of a Function

The **zeros of a function** f of x are the x-values for which $f(x) = 0$.

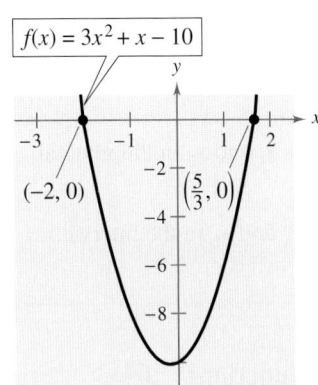

$f(x) = 3x^2 + x - 10$

$(-2, 0)$ $\left(\frac{5}{3}, 0\right)$

Zeros of f: $x = -2, x = \frac{5}{3}$

FIGURE **1.42**

Example 3 ▶ **Finding the Zeros of a Function**

Find the zeros of each function.

a. $f(x) = 3x^2 + x - 10$ **b.** $g(x) = \sqrt{10 - x^2}$ **c.** $h(t) = \dfrac{2t - 3}{t + 5}$

Solution

To find the zeros of a function, set the function equal to zero and solve for the independent variable.

a. $3x^2 + x - 10 = 0$ Set $f(x)$ equal to 0.

   $(3x - 5)(x + 2) = 0$ Factor.

      $3x - 5 = 0$ ⟹ $x = \frac{5}{3}$ Set 1st factor equal to 0.

      $x + 2 = 0$ ⟹ $x = -2$ Set 2nd factor equal to 0.

The zeros of f are $x = \frac{5}{3}$ and $x = -2$. In Figure 1.42, note that the graph of f has $\left(\frac{5}{3}, 0\right)$ and $(-2, 0)$ as its x-intercepts.

b. $\sqrt{10 - x^2} = 0$ Set $g(x)$ equal to 0.

   $10 - x^2 = 0$ Square each side.

      $10 = x^2$ Add x^2 to each side.

   $\pm\sqrt{10} = x$ Extract square root.

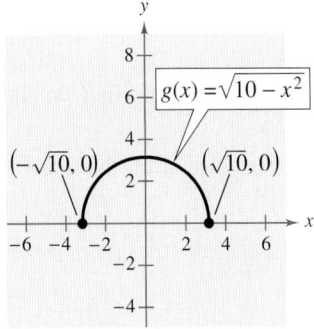

$g(x) = \sqrt{10 - x^2}$

$\left(-\sqrt{10}, 0\right)$ $\left(\sqrt{10}, 0\right)$

Zeros of g: $x = \pm\sqrt{10}$

FIGURE **1.43**

The zeros of g are $x = -\sqrt{10}$ and $x = \sqrt{10}$. In Figure 1.43, note that the graph of g has $\left(-\sqrt{10}, 0\right)$ and $\left(\sqrt{10}, 0\right)$ as its x-intercepts.

c. $\dfrac{2t - 3}{t + 5} = 0$ Set $h(t)$ equal to 0.

   $2t - 3 = 0$ Multiply each side by $t + 5$.

      $2t = 3$ Add 3 to each side.

      $t = \dfrac{3}{2}$ Divide each side by 2.

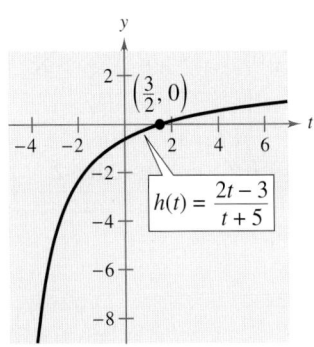

$\left(\frac{3}{2}, 0\right)$

$h(t) = \dfrac{2t - 3}{t + 5}$

Zero of h: $t = \frac{3}{2}$

FIGURE **1.44**

The zero of h is $t = \frac{3}{2}$. In Figure 1.44, note that the graph of h has $\left(\frac{3}{2}, 0\right)$ as its t-intercept.

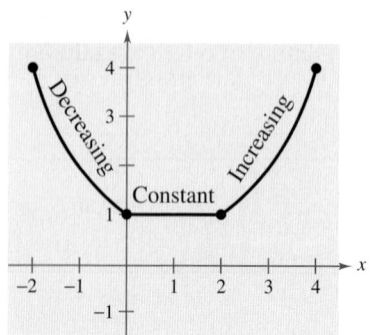

FIGURE **1.45**

Increasing and Decreasing Functions

The more you know about the graph of a function, the more you know about the function itself. Consider the graph shown in Figure 1.45. As you move from *left to right*, this graph decreases, then is constant, and then increases.

> ### Increasing, Decreasing, and Constant Functions
>
> A function f is **increasing** on an interval if, for any x_1 and x_2 in the interval, $x_1 < x_2$ implies $f(x_1) < f(x_2)$.
>
> A function f is **decreasing** on an interval if, for any x_1 and x_2 in the interval, $x_1 < x_2$ implies $f(x_1) > f(x_2)$.
>
> A function f is **constant** on an interval if, for any x_1 and x_2 in the interval, $f(x_1) = f(x_2)$.

Example 4 ▶ Increasing and Decreasing Functions

In Figure 1.46, use the graphs to describe the increasing or decreasing behavior of each function.

Solution

a. This function is increasing over the entire real line.

b. This function is increasing on the interval $(-\infty, -1)$, decreasing on the interval $(-1, 1)$, and increasing on the interval $(1, \infty)$.

c. This function is increasing on the interval $(-\infty, 0)$, constant on the interval $(0, 2)$, and decreasing on the interval $(2, \infty)$.

(a)

(b)

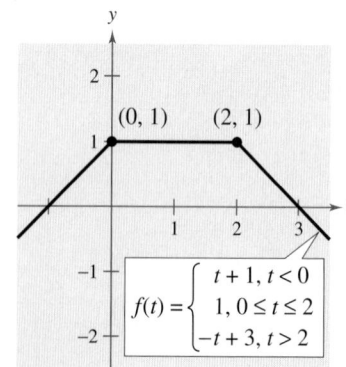

(c)

FIGURE **1.46**

To help you decide whether a function is increasing, decreasing, or constant on an interval, you can evaluate the function for several values of x. However, calculus is needed to determine, for certain, all intervals on which a function is increasing, decreasing, or constant.

The points at which a function changes its increasing, decreasing, or constant behavior are helpful in determining the **relative minimum** or **relative maximum** values of the function.

Definition of Relative Minimum and Relative Maximum

A function value $f(a)$ is called a **relative minimum** of f if there exists an interval (x_1, x_2) that contains a such that

$$x_1 < x < x_2 \quad \text{implies} \quad f(a) \le f(x).$$

A function value $f(a)$ is called a **relative maximum** of f if there exists an interval (x_1, x_2) that contains a such that

$$x_1 < x < x_2 \quad \text{implies} \quad f(a) \ge f(x).$$

Figure 1.47 shows several different examples of relative minima and relative maxima. In Section 2.1, you will study a technique for finding the *exact point* at which a second-degree polynomial function has a relative minimum or relative maximum. For the time being, however, you can use a graphing utility to find reasonable approximations of these points.

Use a graphing utility to approximate the relative minimum of the function $f(x) = 3x^2 - 4x - 2$.

Solution

The graph of f is shown in Figure 1.48. By using the *zoom* and *trace* features of a graphing utility, you can estimate that the function has a relative minimum at the point

$$(0.67, -3.33). \qquad \text{Relative minimum}$$

Later, in Section 2.1, you will be able to determine that the exact point at which the relative minimum occurs is $\left(\frac{2}{3}, -\frac{10}{3}\right)$.

You can also use the *table* feature of a graphing utility to approximate numerically the relative minimum of the function in Example 5. Using a table that begins at 0.6 and increments the value of x by 0.01, you can approximate that the minimum of $f(x) = 3x^2 - 4x - 2$ occurs at the point $(0.67, -3.33)$.

STUDY TIP

A relative minimum or relative maximum is also referred to as a *local* minimum or *local* maximum.

FIGURE **1.47**

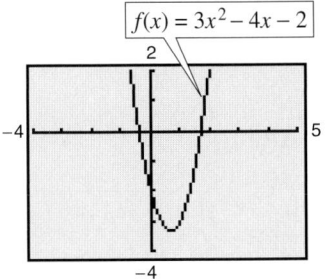

FIGURE **1.48**

Technology

If you use a graphing utility to estimate the x- and y-values of a relative minimum or relative maximum, the *automatic zoom* feature will often produce graphs that are nearly flat. To overcome this problem, you can manually change the vertical setting of the viewing window. The graph will stretch vertically if the values of Ymin and Ymax are closer together.

Even and Odd Functions

In Section 1.1, you studied different types of symmetry of a graph. In the terminology of functions, a function is said to be **even** if its graph is symmetric with respect to the y-axis and to be **odd** if its graph is symmetric with respect to the origin. The symmetry tests in Section 1.1 yield the following tests for even and odd functions.

Tests for Even and Odd Functions

A function $y = f(x)$ is **even** if, for each x in the domain of f,

$$f(-x) = f(x).$$

A function $y = f(x)$ is **odd** if, for each x in the domain of f,

$$f(-x) = -f(x).$$

Example 6 ▶   Even and Odd Functions

a. The function $g(x) = x^3 - x$ is odd because $g(-x) = -g(x)$, as follows.

$$g(-x) = (-x)^3 - (-x) \qquad \text{Substitute } -x \text{ for } x.$$
$$= -x^3 + x \qquad \text{Simplify.}$$
$$= -(x^3 - x) \qquad \text{Distributive Property}$$
$$= -g(x) \qquad \text{Test for odd function}$$

b. The function $h(x) = x^2 + 1$ is even because $h(-x) = h(x)$, as follows.

$$h(-x) = (-x)^2 + 1 \qquad \text{Substitute } -x \text{ for } x.$$
$$= x^2 + 1 \qquad \text{Simplify.}$$
$$= h(x) \qquad \text{Test for even function}$$

The graphs of these two functions are shown in Figure 1.49.

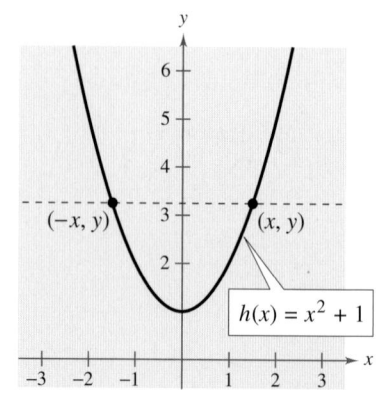

(a) Symmetric to origin: Odd Function
FIGURE 1.49

(b) Symmetric to y-axis: Even Function

1.4 Exercises

In Exercises 1–4, use the graph of the function to find the domain and range of *f*.

1.

2.

3.

4.

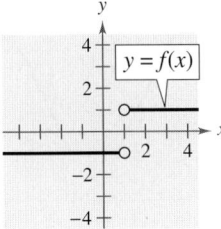

In Exercises 5–8, use the graph of the function to find the indicated function values.

5. (a) $f(-2)$ (b) $f(-1)$
    (c) $f\left(\frac{1}{2}\right)$ (d) $f(1)$

6. (a) $f(-1)$ (b) $f(2)$
    (c) $f(0)$ (d) $f(1)$

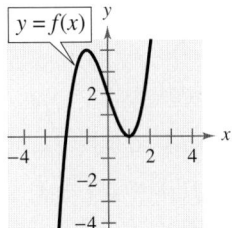

7. (a) $f(-2)$ (b) $f(1)$
    (c) $f(0)$ (d) $f(2)$

8. (a) $f(2)$ (b) $f(1)$
    (c) $f(3)$ (d) $f(-1)$

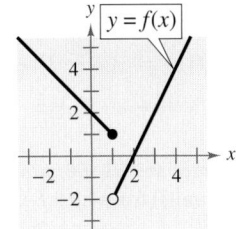

In Exercises 9–14, use the Vertical Line Test to determine whether *y* is a function of *x*. To print an enlarged copy of the graph, go to the website *www.mathgraphs.com*.

9. $y = \frac{1}{2}x^2$

10. $y = \frac{1}{4}x^3$

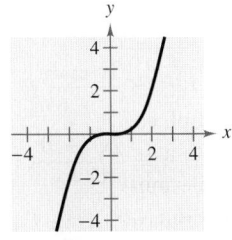

11. $x - y^2 = 1$

12. $x^2 + y^2 = 25$

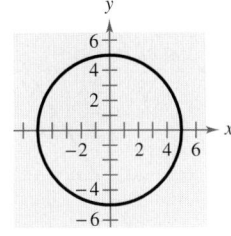

13. $x^2 = 2xy - 1$

14. $x = |y + 2|$

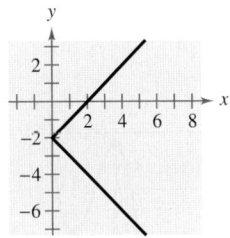

In Exercises 15–24, find the zeros of the function algebraically.

15. $f(x) = 2x^2 - 7x - 30$

16. $f(x) = 3x^2 + 22x - 16$

17. $f(x) = \dfrac{x}{9x^2 - 4}$ **18.** $f(x) = \dfrac{x^2 - 9x + 14}{4x}$

19. $f(x) = \frac{1}{2}x^3 - x$

20. $f(x) = x^3 - 4x^2 - 9x + 36$

21. $f(x) = 4x^3 - 24x^2 - x + 6$

22. $f(x) = 9x^4 - 25x^2$

23. $f(x) = \sqrt{2x} - 1$

24. $f(x) = \sqrt{3x + 2}$

In Exercises 25–30, use a graphing utility to graph the function and find the zeros of the function. Verify your results algebraically.

25. $f(x) = 3 + \dfrac{5}{x}$

26. $f(x) = x(x - 7)$

27. $f(x) = \sqrt{2x + 11}$

28. $f(x) = \sqrt{3x - 14} - 8$

29. $f(x) = \dfrac{3x - 1}{x - 6}$

30. $f(x) = \dfrac{2x^2 - 9}{3 - x}$

In Exercises 31–38, determine the intervals over which the function is increasing, decreasing, or constant.

31. $f(x) = \frac{3}{2}x$

32. $f(x) = x^2 - 4x$

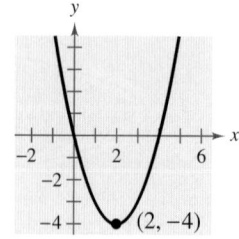

33. $f(x) = x^3 - 3x^2 + 2$

34. $f(x) = \sqrt{x^2 - 1}$

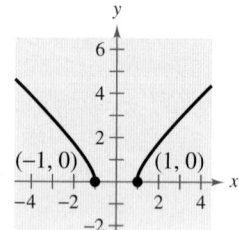

35. $f(x) = \begin{cases} x + 3, & x \le 0 \\ 3, & 0 < x \le 2 \\ 2x + 1, & x > 2 \end{cases}$

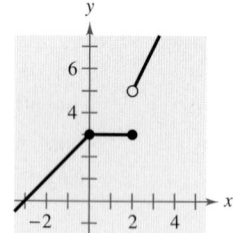

36. $f(x) = \begin{cases} 2x + 1, & x \le -1 \\ x^2 - 2, & x > -1 \end{cases}$

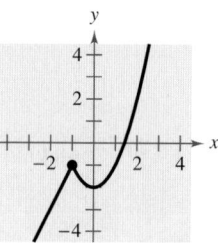

37. $f(x) = |x + 1| + |x - 1|$ **38.** $f(x) = \dfrac{x^2 + x + 1}{x + 1}$

 In Exercises 39–48, (a) use a graphing utility to graph the function and visually determine the intervals over which the function is increasing, decreasing, or constant, and (b) make a table of values to verify whether the function is increasing, decreasing, or constant over the intervals you identified in part (a).

39. $f(x) = 3$

40. $g(x) = x$

41. $g(s) = \dfrac{s^2}{4}$

42. $h(x) = x^2 - 4$

43. $f(t) = -t^4$

44. $f(x) = 3x^4 - 6x^2$

45. $f(x) = \sqrt{1 - x}$

46. $f(x) = x\sqrt{x + 3}$

47. $f(x) = x^{3/2}$

48. $f(x) = x^{2/3}$

 In Exercises 49–52, use a graphing utility to approximate the relative minimum/relative maximum of each function.

49. $f(x) = (x - 4)(x + 2)$ **50.** $f(x) = 3x^2 - 2x - 5$

51. $f(x) = x(x - 2)(x + 3)$

52. $f(x) = x^3 - 3x^2 - x + 1$

In Exercises 53–60, graph the function and determine the interval(s) for which $f(x) \ge 0$.

53. $f(x) = 4 - x$

54. $f(x) = 4x + 2$

55. $f(x) = x^2 + x$

56. $f(x) = x^2 - 4x$

57. $f(x) = \sqrt{x - 1}$

58. $f(x) = \sqrt{x + 2}$

59. $f(x) = -\left(1 + |x|\right)$

60. $f(x) = \frac{1}{2}\left(2 + |x|\right)$

In Exercises 61–66, determine whether the function is even, odd, or neither.

61. $f(x) = x^6 - 2x^2 + 3$ **62.** $h(x) = x^3 - 5$

63. $g(x) = x^3 - 5x$ **64.** $f(x) = x\sqrt{1 - x^2}$

65. $f(t) = t^2 + 2t - 3$ **66.** $g(s) = 4s^{2/3}$

 In Exercises 67–70, write the height h of the rectangle as a function of x.

67.

68.

69.

70.

 In Exercises 71–74, write the length L of the rectangle as a function of y.

71.

72.

73.

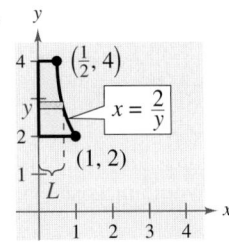

74.

75. *Electronics* The number of lumens (time rate of flow of light) L from a fluorescent lamp can be approximated by the model

$$L = -0.294x^2 + 97.744x - 664.875, \quad 20 \le x \le 90$$

where x is the wattage of the lamp.

(a) Use a graphing utility to graph the function.

(b) Use the graph from part (a) to estimate the wattage necessary to obtain 2000 lumens.

▶ **Model It**

76. *Data Analysis* The table shows the amount y (in billions of dollars) of the merchandise trade balance of the United States for the years 1991 through 1999. The merchandise trade balance is the difference between the values of exports and imports. A negative merchandise trade balance indicates that imports exceeded exports. (Source: U.S. International Trade Administration and U.S. Foreign Trade Highlights)

Year, x	Trade balance, y
1991	−66.8
1992	−84.5
1993	−115.6
1994	−150.7
1995	−158.7
1996	−170.2
1997	−181.5
1998	−229.8
1999	−330.0

(a) Use a graphing utility to create a scatter plot of the data.

(b) Use the graph in part (a) to determine whether the data represents y as a function of x.

(c) Use the *regression* feature of a graphing utility to find a cubic model (a model of the form $y = ax^3 + bx^2 + cx + d$) for the data. Let x be the time (in years), with $x = 1$ corresponding to 1991.

(d) What is the domain of the model?

(e) Use a graphing utility to graph the model in the same viewing window you used in part (a).

(f) For which year does the model most accurately estimate the actual data? During which year is it least accurate?

77. *Coordinate Axis Scale* Each function models the specified data for the years 1995 through 2002, with $t = 5$ corresponding to 1995. Estimate a reasonable scale for the vertical axis (e.g., hundreds, thousands, millions, etc.) of the graph and justify your answer. (There are many correct answers.)

(a) $f(t)$ represents the average salary of college professors.

(b) $f(t)$ represents the U.S. population.

(c) $f(t)$ represents the percent of the civilian work force that is unemployed.

78. *Geometry* Corners of equal size are cut from a square with sides of length 8 meters (see figure).

(a) Write the area A of the resulting figure as a function of x. Determine the domain of the function.

(b) Use a graphing utility to graph the area function over its domain. Use the graph to find the range of the function.

(c) Identify the figure that would result if x were chosen to be the maximum value in the domain of the function. What would be the length of each side of the figure?

Synthesis

True or False? In Exercises 79 and 80, determine whether the statement is true or false. Justify your answer.

79. A function with a square root cannot have a domain that is the set of real numbers.

80. It is possible for an odd function to have the interval $[0, \infty)$ as its domain.

81. If f is an even function, determine whether g is even, odd, or neither. Explain.

(a) $g(x) = -f(x)$ (b) $g(x) = f(-x)$

(c) $g(x) = f(x) - 2$ (d) $g(x) = f(x - 2)$

82. *Think About It* Does the graph in Exercise 11 represent x as a function of y? Explain.

Think About It In Exercises 83–86, find the coordinates of a second point on the graph of a function f if the given point is on the graph and the function is (a) even and (b) odd.

83. $\left(-\frac{3}{2}, 4\right)$ **84.** $\left(-\frac{5}{3}, -7\right)$

85. $(4, 9)$ **86.** $(5, -1)$

87. *Writing* Use a graphing utility to graph each function. Write a paragraph describing any similarities and differences you observe among the graphs.

(a) $y = x$ (b) $y = x^2$

(c) $y = x^3$ (d) $y = x^4$

(e) $y = x^5$ (f) $y = x^6$

88. *Conjecture* Use the results of Exercise 87 to make a conjecture about the graphs of $y = x^7$ and $y = x^8$. Use a graphing utility to graph the functions and compare the results with your conjecture.

Review

In Exercises 89–92, solve the equation.

89. $x^2 - 10x = 0$ **90.** $100 - (x - 5)^2 = 0$

91. $x^3 - x = 0$ **92.** $16x^2 - 40x + 25 = 0$

In Exercises 93–96, evaluate the function at each specified value of the independent variable and simplify.

93. $f(x) = 5x - 8$

(a) $f(9)$ (b) $f(-4)$ (c) $f(x - 7)$

94. $f(x) = x^2 - 10x$

(a) $f(4)$ (b) $f(-8)$ (c) $f(x - 4)$

95. $f(x) = \sqrt{x - 12} - 9$

(a) $f(12)$ (b) $f(40)$ (c) $f\left(-\sqrt{36}\right)$

96. $f(x) = x^4 - x - 5$

(a) $f(-1)$ (b) $f\left(\frac{1}{2}\right)$ (c) $f\left(2\sqrt{3}\right)$

In Exercises 97 and 98, find the difference quotient and simplify your answer.

97. $f(x) = x^2 - 2x + 9$, $\dfrac{f(3 + h) - f(3)}{h}$, $h \neq 0$

98. $f(x) = 5 + 6x - x^2$, $\dfrac{f(6 + h) - f(6)}{h}$, $h \neq 0$

1.5 A Library of Functions

▶ **What you should learn**

- How to identify and graph linear and squaring functions
- How to identify and graph cubic, square root, and reciprocal functions
- How to identify and graph step and other piecewise-defined functions
- How to recognize graphs of common functions

▶ **Why you should learn it**

Piecewise-defined functions can be used to model real-life situations. For instance, in Exercise 68 on page 58, you will use a piecewise-defined function to model the monthly revenue of a landscaping business.

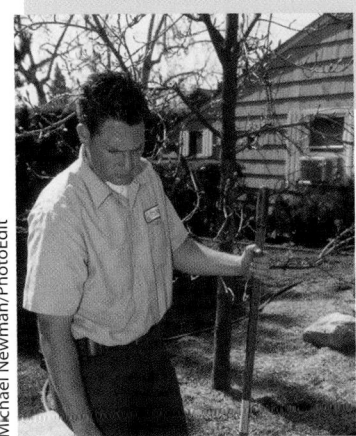

Michael Newman/PhotoEdit

Additional Example

Write the linear function f for which $f(0) = -1$ and $f(5) = 8$.

Solution

$$m = \frac{y_2 - y_1}{x_2 - x_1} = \frac{8 - (-1)}{5 - 0} = \frac{9}{5}$$

$$y - y_1 = m(x - x_1)$$

$$y - (-1) = \frac{9}{5}(x - 0)$$

$$y + 1 = \frac{9}{5}x$$

$$y = \frac{9}{5}x - 1$$

Linear and Squaring Functions

One of the goals of this text is to enable you to recognize the basic shapes of the graphs of different types of functions. For instance, you know that the graph of the **linear function** $f(x) = ax + b$ is a line with slope $m = a$ and y-intercept at $(0, b)$. The graph of the linear function has the following features.

- The domain of the function is the set of all real numbers.
- The range of the function is the set of all real numbers.
- The graph has one intercept, $(0, b)$.
- The graph is increasing if $m > 0$, decreasing if $m < 0$, and constant if $m = 0$.

Example 1 ▶ **Writing a Linear Function**

Write the linear function f for which $f(1) = 3$ and $f(4) = 0$.

Solution

To find the equation of the line that passes through $(x_1, y_1) = (1, 3)$ and $(x_2, y_2) = (4, 0)$, first find the slope of the line.

$$m = \frac{y_2 - y_1}{x_2 - x_1} = \frac{0 - 3}{4 - 1} = \frac{-3}{3} = -1$$

Next, use the point-slope form of the equation of a line.

$$y - y_1 = m(x - x_1) \qquad \text{Point-slope form}$$

$$y - 3 = -1(x - 1) \qquad \text{Substitute for } x_1, y_1, \text{ and } m.$$

$$y = -x + 4 \qquad \text{Simplify.}$$

$$f(x) = -x + 4 \qquad \text{Function notation}$$

The graph of this function is shown in Figure 1.50.

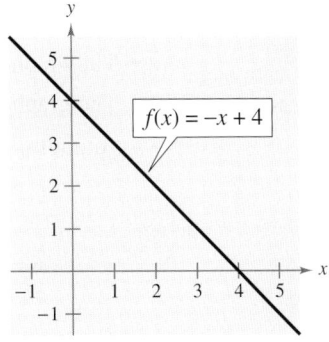

FIGURE **1.50**

There are two special types of linear functions, the **constant function** and the **identity function.** A constant function has the form

$$f(x) = c$$

and has the domain of all real numbers with a range consisting of a single real number c. The graph of a constant function is a horizontal line, as shown in Figure 1.51. The identity function has the form

$$f(x) = x.$$

Its domain and range are the set of all real numbers. The identity function has a slope of $m = 1$ and a y-intercept $(0, 0)$. The graph of the identity function is a line for which each x-coordinate equals the corresponding y-coordinate. The graph is always increasing, as shown in Figure 1.52.

FIGURE 1.51

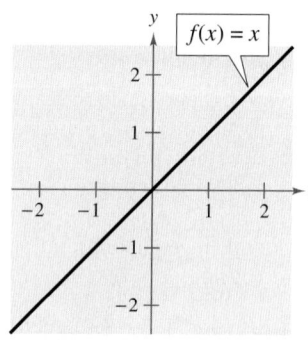

FIGURE 1.52

The graph of the **squaring function**

$$f(x) = x^2$$

is a U-shaped curve with the following features.

- The domain of the function is the set of all real numbers.
- The range of the function is the set of all nonnegative real numbers.
- The function is even.
- The graph has an intercept at $(0, 0)$.
- The graph is decreasing on the interval $(-\infty, 0)$ and increasing on the interval $(0, \infty)$.
- The graph is symmetric with respect to the y-axis.
- The graph has a relative minimum at $(0, 0)$.

The graph of the squaring function is shown in Figure 1.53.

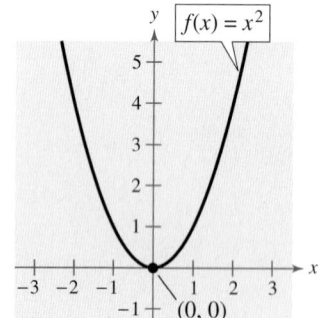

FIGURE 1.53

Cubic, Square Root, and Reciprocal Functions

Special features of the graphs of the **cubic, square root,** and **reciprocal func-tions** are summarized below.

1. The graph of the *cubic* function

$$f(x) = x^3$$

has the following features.

- The domain of the function is the set of all real numbers.
- The range of the function is the set of all real numbers.
- The function is odd.
- The graph has an intercept at $(0, 0)$.
- The graph is increasing on the interval $(-\infty, \infty)$.
- The graph is symmetric with respect to the origin.

The graph of the cubic function is shown in Figure 1.54.

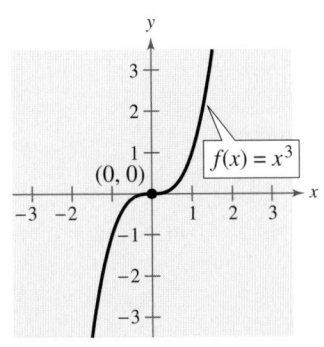

Cubic function
FIGURE **1.54**

2. The graph of the *square root* function

$$f(x) = \sqrt{x}$$

has the following features.

- The domain of the function is the set of all nonnegative real numbers.
- The range of the function is the set of all nonnegative real numbers.
- The graph has an intercept at $(0, 0)$.
- The graph is increasing on the interval $(0, \infty)$.

The graph of the square root function is shown in Figure 1.55.

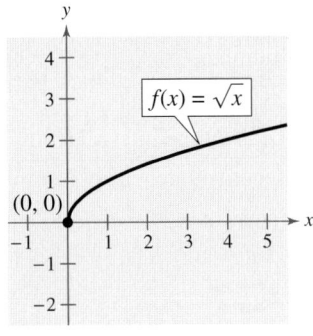

Square root function
FIGURE **1.55**

3. The graph of the *reciprocal* function

$$f(x) = \frac{1}{x}$$

has the following features.

- The domain of the function is $(-\infty, 0) \cup (0, \infty)$.
- The range of the function is $(-\infty, 0) \cup (0, \infty)$.
- The function is odd.
- The graph does not have any intercepts.
- The graph is decreasing on the intervals $(-\infty, 0)$ and $(0, \infty)$.
- The graph is symmetric with respect to the origin.

The graph of the reciprocal function is shown in Figure 1.56.

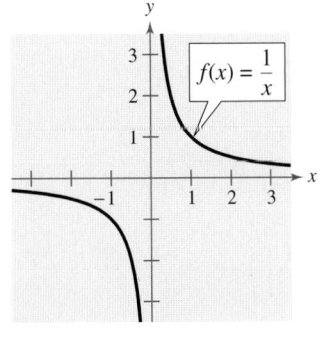

Reciprocal function
FIGURE **1.56**

Step and Piecewise-Defined Functions

Functions whose graphs resemble sets of stairsteps are known as **step functions.** The most famous of the step functions is the **greatest integer function,** which is denoted by $[\![x]\!]$ and defined as

$$f(x) = [\![x]\!] = \text{the greatest integer less than or equal to } x.$$

Some values of the greatest integer function are as follows.

$$[\![-1]\!] = (\text{greatest integer} \leq -1) = -1$$

$$\left[\!\left[-\tfrac{1}{2}\right]\!\right] = \left(\text{greatest integer} \leq -\tfrac{1}{2}\right) = -1$$

$$\left[\!\left[\tfrac{1}{10}\right]\!\right] = \left(\text{greatest integer} \leq \tfrac{1}{10}\right) = 0$$

$$[\![1.5]\!] = (\text{greatest integer} \leq 1.5) = 1$$

The graph of the greatest integer function

$$f(x) = [\![x]\!]$$

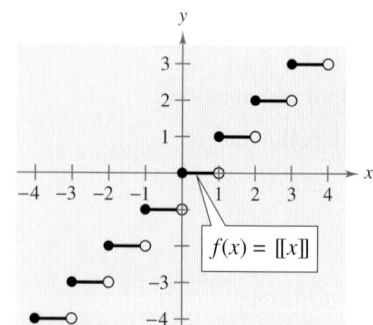

FIGURE **1.57**

has the following features, as shown in Figure 1.57.

- The domain of the function is the set of all real numbers.
- The range of the function is the set of all integers.
- The graph has a y-intercept at $(0, 0)$ and x-intercepts in the interval $[0, 1)$.
- The graph is constant between each pair of consecutive integers.
- The graph jumps vertically one unit at each integer value.

Example 2 ▶ **Evaluating a Step Function**

Evaluate the function when $x = -1, 2$, and $\tfrac{3}{2}$.

$$f(x) = [\![x]\!] + 1$$

Solution

For $x = -1$, the greatest integer ≤ -1 is -1, so

$$f(-1) = [\![-1]\!] + 1 = -1 + 1 = 0.$$

For $x = 2$, the greatest integer ≤ 2 is 2, so

$$f(2) = [\![2]\!] + 1 = 2 + 1 = 3.$$

For $x = \tfrac{3}{2}$, the greatest integer $\leq \tfrac{3}{2}$ is 1, so

$$f\!\left(\tfrac{3}{2}\right) = \left[\!\left[\tfrac{3}{2}\right]\!\right] + 1 = 1 + 1 = 2.$$

The graph of $f(x) = [\![x]\!] + 1$ is shown in Figure 1.58.

FIGURE **1.58**

Recall from Section 1.3 that a piecewise-defined function is defined by two or more equations over a specified domain. To graph a piecewise-defined function, graph each equation separately over the specified domain, as shown in Example 3.

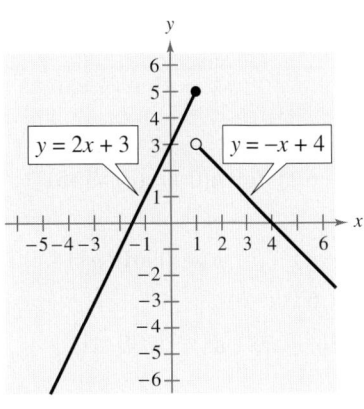

FIGURE **1.59**

Example 3 ▶ Graphing a Piecewise-Defined Function

Sketch the graph of

$$f(x) = \begin{cases} 2x + 3, & x \le 1 \\ -x + 4, & x > 1 \end{cases}.$$

Solution

This piecewise-defined function is composed of two linear functions. At $x = 1$ and to the left of $x = 1$ the graph is the line $y = 2x + 3$, and to the right of $x = 1$ the graph is the line $y = -x + 4$, as shown in Figure 1.59.

Common Functions

The eight graphs shown in Figure 1.60 represent the most commonly used functions in algebra. Familiarity with the basic characteristics of these simple graphs will help you analyze the shapes of more complicated graphs—in particular, graphs obtained from these graphs by the rigid and nonrigid transformations studied in the next section.

(a) **Constant Function**

(b) **Identity Function**

(c) **Absolute Value Function**

(d) **Square Root Function**

(e) **Quadratic Function**

(f) **Cubic Function**

(g) **Reciprocal Function**

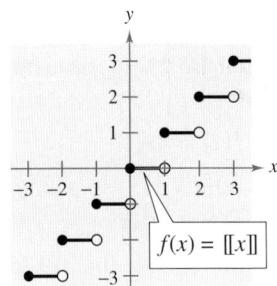

(h) **Greatest Integer Function**

FIGURE **1.60**

1.5 Exercises

In Exercises 1–8, write the linear function that has the indicated function values. Then sketch the graph of the function.

1. $f(1) = 4, f(0) = 6$

2. $f(-3) = -8, f(1) = 2$

3. $f(5) = -4, f(-2) = 17$

4. $f(3) = 9, f(-1) = -11$

5. $f(-5) = -1, f(5) = -1$

6. $f(-10) = 12, f(16) = -1$

7. $f\left(\frac{1}{2}\right) = -6, f(4) = -3$

8. $f\left(\frac{2}{3}\right) = -\frac{15}{2}, f(-4) = -11$

 In Exercises 9–28, use a graphing utility to graph the function. Be sure to choose an appropriate viewing window.

9. $f(x) = -x - \frac{3}{4}$

10. $f(x) = 3x - \frac{5}{2}$

11. $f(x) = -\frac{1}{6}x - \frac{5}{2}$

12. $f(x) = \frac{5}{6} - \frac{2}{3}x$

13. $f(x) = x^2 - 2x$

14. $f(x) = -x^2 + 8x$

15. $h(x) = -x^2 + 4x + 12$

16. $g(x) = x^2 - 6x - 16$

17. $f(x) = x^3 - 1$

18. $f(x) = 8 - x^3$

19. $f(x) = (x - 1)^3 + 2$

20. $g(x) = 2(x + 3)^3 + 1$

21. $f(x) = 4\sqrt{x}$

22. $f(x) = 4 - 2\sqrt{x}$

23. $g(x) = 2 - \sqrt{x + 4}$

24. $h(x) = \sqrt{x + 2} + 3$

25. $f(x) = -\dfrac{1}{x}$

26. $f(x) = 4 + \dfrac{1}{x}$

27. $h(x) = \dfrac{1}{x + 2}$

28. $k(x) = \dfrac{1}{x - 3}$

In Exercise 29–36, evaluate the function for the indicated values.

29. $f(x) = [\![x]\!]$
(a) $f(2.1)$ (b) $f(2.9)$ (c) $f(-3.1)$ (d) $f\left(\frac{7}{2}\right)$

30. $g(x) = 2[\![x]\!]$
(a) $g(-3)$ (b) $g(0.25)$ (c) $g(9.5)$ (d) $g\left(\frac{11}{3}\right)$

31. $h(x) = [\![x + 3]\!]$
(a) $h(-2)$ (b) $h\left(\frac{1}{2}\right)$ (c) $h(4.2)$ (d) $h(-21.6)$

32. $f(x) = 4[\![x]\!] + 7$
(a) $f(0)$ (b) $f(-1.5)$ (c) $f(6)$ (d) $f\left(\frac{5}{3}\right)$

33. $h(x) = [\![3x - 1]\!]$
(a) $h(2.5)$ (b) $h(-3.2)$ (c) $h\left(\frac{7}{3}\right)$ (d) $h\left(-\frac{21}{3}\right)$

34. $k(x) = \left[\!\left[\frac{1}{2}x + 6\right]\!\right]$
(a) $k(5)$ (b) $k(-6.1)$ (c) $k(0.1)$ (d) $k(15)$

35. $g(x) = 3[\![x - 2]\!] + 5$
(a) $g(-2.7)$ (b) $g(-1)$ (c) $g(0.8)$ (d) $g(14.5)$

36. $g(x) = -7[\![x + 4]\!] + 6$
(a) $g\left(\frac{1}{8}\right)$ (b) $g(9)$ (c) $g(-4)$ (d) $g\left(\frac{3}{2}\right)$

In Exercises 37–42, sketch the graph of the function.

37. $g(x) = -[\![x]\!]$

38. $g(x) = 4[\![x]\!]$

39. $g(x) = [\![x]\!] - 2$

40. $g(x) = [\![x]\!] - 1$

41. $g(x) = [\![x + 1]\!]$

42. $g(x) = [\![x - 3]\!]$

In Exercises 43–50, graph the function.

43. $f(x) = \begin{cases} 2x + 3, & x < 0 \\ 3 - x, & x \geq 0 \end{cases}$

44. $g(x) = \begin{cases} x + 6, & x \leq -4 \\ \frac{1}{2}x - 4, & x > -4 \end{cases}$

45. $f(x) = \begin{cases} \sqrt{4 + x}, & x < 0 \\ \sqrt{4 - x}, & x \geq 0 \end{cases}$

46. $f(x) = \begin{cases} 1 - (x - 1)^2, & x \leq 2 \\ \sqrt{x - 2}, & x > 2 \end{cases}$

47. $f(x) = \begin{cases} x^2 + 5, & x \leq 1 \\ -x^2 + 4x + 3, & x > 1 \end{cases}$

48. $h(x) = \begin{cases} 3 - x^2, & x < 0 \\ x^2 + 2, & x \geq 0 \end{cases}$

49. $h(x) = \begin{cases} 4 - x^2, & x < -2 \\ 3 + x, & -2 \leq x < 0 \\ x^2 + 1, & x \geq 0 \end{cases}$

50. $k(x) = \begin{cases} 2x + 1, & x \leq -1 \\ 2x^2 - 1, & -1 < x \leq 1 \\ 1 - x^2, & x > 1 \end{cases}$

In Exercises 51 and 52, use a graphing utility to graph the function. State the domain and range of the function. Describe the pattern of the graph.

51. $s(x) = 2\left(\frac{1}{4}x - \left[\!\left[\frac{1}{4}x\right]\!\right]\right)$

52. $g(x) = 2\left(\frac{1}{4}x - \left[\!\left[\frac{1}{4}x\right]\!\right]\right)^2$

In Exercises 53–62, identify the common function and the transformed common function shown in the graph. Write an equation for the function shown in the graph. Then use a graphing utility to verify your answer.

53.

54.

55.

56.

57.

58.

59.

60.

61.

62.

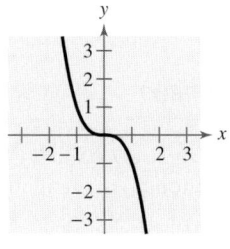

63. *Communications*   The cost of a telephone call between Denver and Boise is $0.60 for the first minute and $0.42 for each additional minute or portion of a minute. A model for the total cost C (in dollars) of the phone call is

$$C = 0.60 - 0.42[\![1 - t]\!], \quad t > 0$$

where t is the length of the phone call in minutes.

(a) Sketch the graph of the model.

(b) Determine the cost of a call lasting 12 minutes and 30 seconds.

64. *Communications*   The cost of using a telephone calling card is $1.05 for the first minute and $0.38 for each additional minute or portion of a minute.

(a) A customer needs a model for the cost C of using a calling card for a call lasting t minutes. Which of the following is the appropriate model? Explain.

$$C_1(t) = 1.05 + 0.38[\![t - 1]\!]$$

$$C_2(t) = 1.05 - 0.38[\![-(t - 1)]\!]$$

(b) Graph the appropriate model. Determine the cost of a call lasting 18 minutes and 45 seconds.

65. *Delivery Charges*   The cost of sending an overnight package from Los Angeles to Miami is $10.75 for a package weighing up to but not including 1 pound and $3.95 for each additional pound or portion of a pound. A model for the total cost C (in dollars) of sending the package is

$$C = 10.75 + 3.95[\![x]\!], \quad x > 0$$

where x is the weight in pounds.

(a) Sketch a graph of the model.

(b) Determine the cost of sending a package that weighs 10.33 pounds.

66. *Delivery Charges*   The cost of sending an overnight package from New York to Atlanta is $9.80 for a package weighing up to but not including 1 pound and $2.50 for each additional pound or portion of a pound.

(a) Use the greatest integer function to create a model for the cost C of overnight delivery of a package weighing x pounds, $x > 0$.

(b) Sketch the graph of the function.

67. *Wages*   A mechanic is paid $12.00 per hour for regular time and time-and-a-half for overtime. The weekly wage function is

$$W(h) = \begin{cases} 12h, & 0 < h \le 40 \\ 18(h - 40) + 480, & h > 40 \end{cases}$$

where h is the number of hours worked in a week.

(a) Evaluate $W(30)$, $W(40)$, $W(45)$, and $W(50)$.

(b) The company increased the regular work week to 45 hours. What is the new weekly wage function?

▶ Model It

68. Revenue The table shows the monthly revenue *y* (in thousands of dollars) of a landscaping business for the year 2002, with *x* = 1 representing January.

Month, x	Revenue, y
1	5.2
2	5.6
3	6.6
4	8.3
5	11.5
6	15.8
7	12.8
8	10.1
9	8.6
10	6.9
11	4.5
12	2.7

A mathematical model that represents this data is

$$f(x) = \begin{cases} -1.97x + 26.3 \\ 0.505x^2 - 1.47x + 6.3 \end{cases}.$$

(a) What is the domain of each part of the piecewise-defined function? How can you tell? Explain your reasoning.

(b) Sketch a graph of the model.

(c) Find $f(5)$ and $f(11)$, and interpret your results in the context of the problem.

(d) How do the values obtained from the model in part (b) compare with the actual data values?

69. Fluid Flow The intake pipe of a 100-gallon tank has a flow rate of 10 gallons per minute, and two drainpipes have flow rates of 5 gallons per minute each. The figure shows the volume *V* of fluid in the tank as a function of time *t*. Determine the combination of the input pipe and drain pipes in which the fluid is flowing in specific subintervals of the 1 hour of time shown on the graph. (There are many correct answers.)

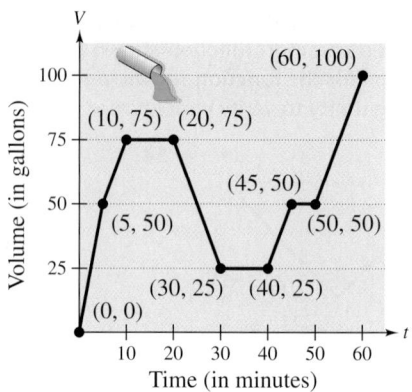

FIGURE FOR 69

Synthesis

True or False? In Exercises 70 and 71, determine whether the statement is true or false. Justify your answer.

70. A piecewise-defined function will always have at least one *x*-intercept or at least one *y*-intercept.

71. $f(x) = \begin{cases} 2, & 1 \le x < 2 \\ 4, & 2 \le x < 3 \\ 6, & 3 \le x < 4 \end{cases}$

can be rewritten as $f(x) = 2[\![x]\!], \quad 1 \le x < 4.$

72. Exploration Write equations for the piecewise-defined function shown in the graph.

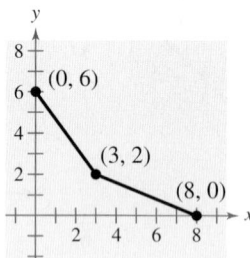

Review

In Exercise 73 and 74, solve the inequality and sketch the solution on the real number line.

73. $3x + 4 \le 12 - 5x$ **74.** $2x + 1 > 6x - 9$

In Exercises 75 and 76, determine whether the lines L_1 and L_2 passing through the pairs of points are parallel, perpendicular, or neither.

75. L_1: $(-2, -2), (2, 10)$ **76.** L_1: $(-1, -7), (4, 3)$
    L_2: $(-1, 3), (3, 9)$ L_2: $(1, 5), (-2, -7)$

1.6 Shifting, Reflecting, and Stretching Graphs

Shifting, Reflecting, and Stretching Graphs

▶ **What you should learn**

- How to use vertical and horizontal shifts to sketch graphs of functions
- How to use reflections to sketch graphs of functions
- How to use nonrigid transformations to sketch graphs of functions

▶ **Why you should learn it**

Knowing the graphs of common functions and knowing how to shift, reflect, and stretch graphs of functions can help you sketch a wide variety of simple functions by hand. This skill is useful in sketching graphs of functions that model real-life data, such as in Exercise 63 on page 67, where you are asked to sketch the graph of a function that models the amount of fuel used by trucks from 1980 through 1999.

Chuck Keeler/The Stock Market

Shifting Graphs

Many functions have graphs that are simple transformations of the common graphs summarized in Section 1.5. For example, you can obtain the graph of

$$h(x) = x^2 + 2$$

by shifting the graph of $f(x) = x^2$ *up* two units, as shown in Figure 1.61. In function notation, h and f are related as follows.

$$h(x) = x^2 + 2 = f(x) + 2 \qquad \text{Upward shift of two units}$$

Similarly, you can obtain the graph of

$$g(x) = (x - 2)^2$$

by shifting the graph of $f(x) = x^2$ to the *right* two units, as shown in Figure 1.62. In this case, the functions g and f have the following relationship.

$$g(x) = (x - 2)^2 = f(x - 2) \qquad \text{Right shift of two units}$$

FIGURE **1.61**

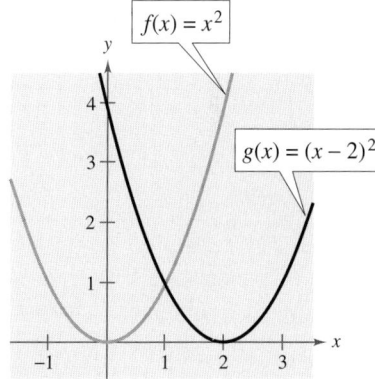

FIGURE **1.62**

The following list summarizes this discussion about horizontal and vertical shifts.

STUDY TIP

In items 3 and 4, be sure you see that $h(x) = f(x - c)$ corresponds to a *right* shift and $h(x) = f(x + c)$ corresponds to a *left* shift for $c > 0$.

Vertical and Horizontal Shifts

Let c be a positive real number. **Vertical and horizontal shifts** in the graph of $y = f(x)$ are represented as follows.

1. Vertical shift c units *upward:* $h(x) = f(x) + c$

2. Vertical shift c units *downward:* $h(x) = f(x) - c$

3. Horizontal shift c units to the *right:* $h(x) = f(x - c)$

4. Horizontal shift c units to the *left:* $h(x) = f(x + c)$

You might also wish to illustrate simple transformations of functions numerically using tables to emphasize what happens to individual ordered pairs. For instance, if you have $f(x) = x^2$, $h(x) = x^2 + 2 = f(x) + 2$, and $g(x) = (x - 2)^2 = f(x - 2)$, you can illustrate these transformations with the following tables.

x	$f(x)$	$h(x) = f(x) + 2$
-2	4	$4 + 2 = 6$
-1	1	$1 + 2 = 3$
0	0	$0 + 2 = 2$
1	1	$1 + 2 = 3$
2	4	$4 + 2 = 6$

x	$x - 2$	$g(x) = f(x - 2)$
0	$0 - 2 = -2$	4
1	$1 - 2 = -1$	1
2	$2 - 2 = 0$	0
3	$3 - 2 = 1$	1
4	$4 - 2 = 2$	4

Some graphs can be obtained from combinations of vertical and horizontal shifts, as demonstrated in Example 1(b). Vertical and horizontal shifts generate a *family of functions*, each with the same shape but at different locations in the plane.

Example 1 ▶ Shifts in the Graphs of a Function

Use the graph of $f(x) = x^3$ to sketch the graph of each function.

a. $g(x) = x^3 - 1$

b. $h(x) = (x + 2)^3 + 1$

Solution

a. Relative to the graph of $f(x) = x^3$, the graph of $g(x) = x^3 - 1$ is a downward shift of one unit, as shown in Figure 1.63.

b. Relative to the graph of $f(x) = x^3$, the graph of $h(x) = (x + 2)^3 + 1$ involves a left shift of two units and an upward shift of one unit, as shown in Figure 1.64.

FIGURE 1.63

FIGURE 1.64

In Figure 1.64, notice that the same result is obtained if the vertical shift precedes the horizontal shift *or* if the horizontal shift precedes the vertical shift.

◀ Exploration ▶

Graphing utilities are ideal tools for exploring translations of functions. Graph f, g, and h in same viewing window. Before looking at the graphs, try to predict how the graphs of g and h relate to the graph of f.

a. $f(x) = x^2$, $g(x) = (x - 4)^2$, $h(x) = (x - 4)^2 + 3$

b. $f(x) = x^2$, $g(x) = (x + 1)^2$, $h(x) = (x + 1)^2 - 2$

c. $f(x) = x^2$, $g(x) = (x + 4)^2$, $h(x) = (x + 4)^2 + 2$

FIGURE **1.65**

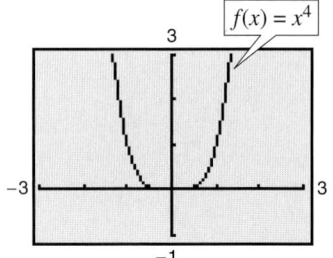

FIGURE **1.66**

Reflecting Graphs

The second common type of transformation is a **reflection.** For instance, if you consider the x-axis to be a mirror, the graph of

$$h(x) = -x^2$$

is the mirror image (or reflection) of the graph of $f(x) = x^2$, as shown in Figure 1.65.

Reflections in the Coordinate Axes

Reflections in the coordinate axes of the graph of $y = f(x)$ are represented as follows.

1. Reflection in the x-axis: $h(x) = -f(x)$

2. Reflection in the y-axis: $h(x) = f(-x)$

Example 2 ▶ **Finding Equations from Graphs**

The graph of the function

$$f(x) = x^4$$

is shown in Figure 1.66. Each of the graphs in Figure 1.67 is a transformation of the graph of f. Find an equation for each of these functions.

(a)

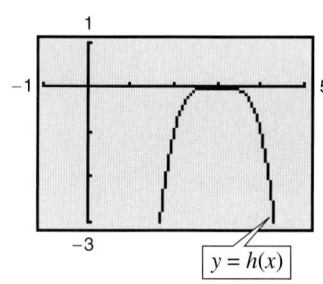

(b)

FIGURE **1.67**

Solution

a. The graph of g is a reflection in the x-axis *followed by* an upward shift of two units of the graph of $f(x) = x^4$. So, the equation for g is

$$g(x) = -x^4 + 2.$$

b. The graph of h is a horizontal shift of three units to the right *followed by* a reflection in the x-axis of the graph of $f(x) = x^4$. So, the equation for h is

$$h(x) = -(x - 3)^4.$$

◀ **E x p l o r a t i o n** ▶

Reverse the order of transformations in Example 2(a). Do you obtain the same graph? Do the same for Example 2(b). Do you obtain the same graph? Explain.

Example 3 ▶   **Reflections and Shifts**

Compare the graph of each function with the graph of $f(x) = \sqrt{x}$.

a. $g(x) = -\sqrt{x}$ **b.** $h(x) = \sqrt{-x}$ **c.** $k(x) = -\sqrt{x + 2}$

Solution

a. The graph of g is a reflection of the graph of f in the x-axis because

$$g(x) = -\sqrt{x}$$
$$= -f(x).$$

The graph of g compared with f is shown in Figure 1.68.

b. The graph of h is a reflection of the graph of f in the y-axis because

$$h(x) = \sqrt{-x}$$
$$= f(-x).$$

The graph of h compared with f is shown in Figure 1.69.

c. The graph of k is a left shift of two units, followed by a reflection in the x-axis because

$$k(x) = -\sqrt{x + 2}$$
$$= -f(x + 2).$$

The graph of k compared with f is shown in Figure 1.70.

FIGURE **1.68**

FIGURE **1.69**

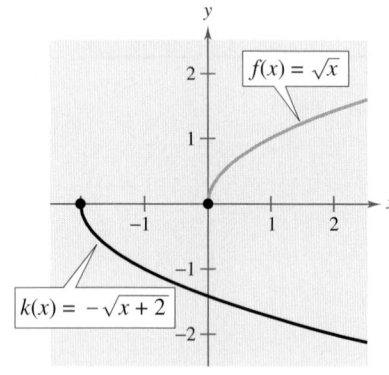

FIGURE **1.70**

When sketching the graphs of functions involving square roots, remember that the domain must be restricted to exclude negative numbers inside the radical. For instance, here are the domains of the functions in Example 3.

Domain of $g(x) = -\sqrt{x}$: $x \geq 0$

Domain of $h(x) = \sqrt{-x}$: $x \leq 0$

Domain of $k(x) = -\sqrt{x + 2}$: $x \geq -2$

Nonrigid Transformations

Horizontal shifts, vertical shifts, and reflections are **rigid transformations** because the basic shape of the graph is unchanged. These transformations change only the *position* of the graph in the *xy*-plane. **Nonrigid transformations** are those that cause a *distortion*—a change in the shape of the original graph. For instance, a nonrigid transformation of the graph of $y = f(x)$ is represented by $g(x) = cf(x)$, where the transformation is a **vertical stretch** if $c > 1$ and a **vertical shrink** if $0 < c < 1$. Another nonrigid transformation of the graph of $y = f(x)$ is represented by $h(x) = f(cx)$, where the transformation is a **horizontal shrink** if $c > 1$ and a **horizontal stretch** if $0 < c < 1$.

Example 4 ▶ Nonrigid Transformations

Compare the graph of each function with the graph of $f(x) = |x|$.

a. $h(x) = 3|x|$ **b.** $g(x) = \frac{1}{3}|x|$

Solution

a. Relative to the graph of $f(x) = |x|$, the graph of

$$h(x) = 3|x| = 3f(x)$$

is a vertical stretch (each *y*-value is multiplied by 3) of the graph of *f*. (See Figure 1.71.)

b. Similarly, the graph of

$$g(x) = \tfrac{1}{3}|x| = \tfrac{1}{3}f(x)$$

is a vertical shrink $\left(\text{each } y\text{-value is multiplied by } \tfrac{1}{3}\right)$ of the graph of *f*. (See Figure 1.72.)

Example 5 ▶ Nonrigid Transformations

Compare the graph of each function with the graph of $f(x) = 2 - x^3$.

a. $g(x) = f(2x)$ **b.** $h(x) = f\left(\tfrac{1}{2}x\right)$

Solution

a. Relative to the graph of $f(x) = 2 - x^3$, the graph of

$$g(x) = f(2x) = 2 - (2x)^3 = 2 - 8x^3$$

is a horizontal shrink $\left(\text{each } x\text{-value is multiplied by } \tfrac{1}{2}\right)$ of the graph of *f*. (See Figure 1.73.)

b. Similarly, the graph of

$$h(x) = f\left(\tfrac{1}{2}x\right) = 2 - \left(\tfrac{1}{2}x\right)^3 = 2 - \tfrac{1}{8}x^3$$

is a horizontal stretch (each *x*-value is multiplied by 2) of the graph of *f*. (See Figure 1.74.)

FIGURE **1.71**

FIGURE **1.72**

FIGURE **1.73**

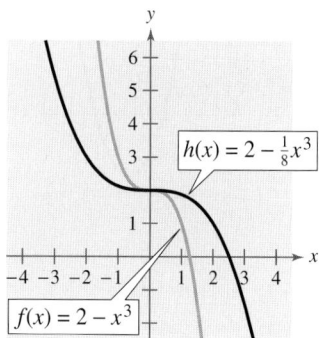

FIGURE **1.74**

1.6 **Exercises**

1. For each function, sketch (on the same set of coordinate axes) a graph of each function for $c = -1, 1,$ and 3.

   (a) $f(x) = |x| + c$ (b) $f(x) = |x - c|$

   (c) $f(x) = |x + 4| + c$

2. For each function, sketch (on the same set of coordinate axes) a graph of each function for $c = -3, -1, 1,$ and 3.

   (a) $f(x) = \sqrt{x} + c$ (b) $f(x) = \sqrt{x - c}$

   (c) $f(x) = \sqrt{x - 3} + c$

3. For each function, sketch (on the same set of coordinate axes) a graph of each function for $c = -2, 0,$ and 2.

   (a) $f(x) = [\![x]\!] + c$ (b) $f(x) = [\![x + c]\!]$

   (c) $f(x) = [\![x - 1]\!] + c$

4. For each function, sketch (on the same set of coordinate axes) a graph of each function for $c = -3, -1, 1,$ and 3.

   (a) $f(x) = \begin{cases} x^2 + c, & x < 0 \\ -x^2 + c, & x \geq 0 \end{cases}$

   (b) $f(x) = \begin{cases} (x + c)^2, & x < 0 \\ -(x + c)^2, & x \geq 0 \end{cases}$

5. Use the graph of f to sketch each graph. To print an enlarged copy of the graph, go to the website *www.mathgraphs.com*.

   (a) $y = f(x) + 2$

   (b) $y = f(x - 2)$

   (c) $y = 2f(x)$

   (d) $y = -f(x)$

   (e) $y = f(x + 3)$

   (f) $y = f(-x)$

   (g) $y = f\left(\frac{1}{2}x\right)$

6. Use the graph of f to sketch each graph. To print an enlarged copy of the graph, go to the website *www.mathgraphs.com*.

   (a) $y = f(-x)$

   (b) $y = f(x) + 4$

   (c) $y = 2f(x)$

   (d) $y = -f(x - 4)$

   (e) $y = f(x) - 3$

   (f) $y = -f(x) - 1$

   (g) $y = f(2x)$

7. Use the graph of f to sketch each graph. To print an enlarged copy of the graph, go to the website *www.mathgraphs.com*.

   (a) $y = f(x) - 1$

   (b) $y = f(x - 1)$

   (c) $y = f(-x)$

   (d) $y = f(x + 1)$

   (e) $y = -f(x - 2)$

   (f) $y = \frac{1}{2}f(x)$

   (g) $y = f(2x)$

8. Use the graph of f to sketch each graph. To print an enlarged copy of the graph, go to the website *www.mathgraphs.com*.

   (a) $y = f(x - 5)$

   (b) $y = -f(x) + 3$

   (c) $y = \frac{1}{3}f(x)$

   (d) $y = -f(x + 1)$

   (e) $y = f(-x)$

   (f) $y = f(x) - 10$

   (g) $y = f\left(\frac{1}{3}x\right)$

9. Use the graph of $f(x) = x^2$ to write an equation for each function whose graph is shown.

   (a)

   (b)

   (c)

   (d)
   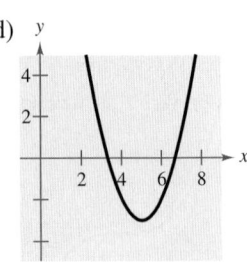

10. Use the graph of $f(x) = x^3$ to write an equation for each function whose graph is shown.

(a)

(b)

(c)

(d)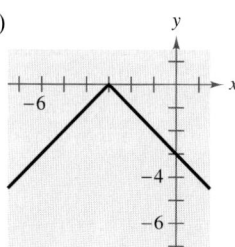

11. Use the graph of $f(x) = |x|$ to write an equation for each function whose graph is shown.

(a)

(b)

(c)

(d)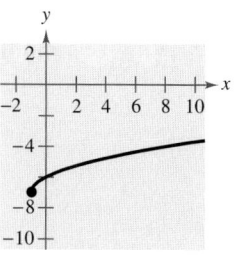

12. Use the graph of $f(x) = \sqrt{x}$ to write an equation for each function whose graph is shown.

(a)

(b)

(c)

(d)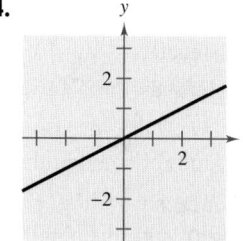

In Exercises 13–18, identify the common function and the transformation shown in the graph. Write an equation for the function shown in the graph.

13.

14.

15.

16.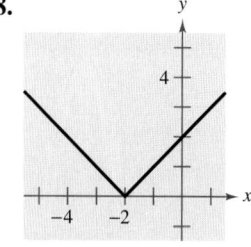

17.

18.

In Exercises 19–38, describe the transformation from a common function that occurs in the function. Then sketch its graph.

19. $f(x) = 12 - x^2$

20. $f(x) = (x - 8)^2$

21. $f(x) = x^3 + 7$

22. $f(x) = -x^3 - 1$

23. $f(x) = 2 - (x + 5)^2$

24. $f(x) = -(x + 10)^2 + 5$

25. $f(x) = (x - 1)^3 + 2$

26. $f(x) = (x + 3)^3 - 10$

27. $f(x) = -|x| - 2$

28. $f(x) = 6 - |x + 5|$

29. $f(x) = -|x + 4| + 8$

30. $f(x) = |-x + 3| + 9$

31. $f(x) = 3 - [\![x]\!]$

32. $f(x) = 2[\![x + 5]\!]$

33. $f(x) = \sqrt{x - 9}$ **34.** $f(x) = \sqrt{x + 4} + 8$

35. $f(x) = \sqrt{7 - x} - 2$ **36.** $f(x) = -\sqrt{x + 1} - 6$

37. $f(x) = \sqrt{\frac{1}{2}x} - 4$ **38.** $f(x) = \sqrt{3x} + 1$

In Exercises 39–46, write an equation for the function that is described by the given characteristics.

39. The shape of $f(x) = x^2$, but moved two units to the right and eight units downward

40. The shape of $f(x) = x^2$, but moved three units to the left, seven units upward, and reflected in the x-axis

41. The shape of $f(x) = x^3$, but moved 13 units to the right

42. The shape of $f(x) = x^3$, but moved six units to the left, six units downward, and reflected in the y-axis

43. The shape of $f(x) = |x|$, but moved 10 units upward and reflected in the x-axis

44. The shape of $f(x) = |x|$, but moved one unit to the left and seven units downward

45. The shape of $f(x) = \sqrt{x}$, but moved six units to the left and reflected in both the x-axis and the y-axis

46. The shape of $f(x) = \sqrt{x}$, but moved nine units downward and reflected in both the x-axis and the y-axis

47. Use the graph of $f(x) = x^2$ to write an equation for each function whose graph is shown.

(a)   (b)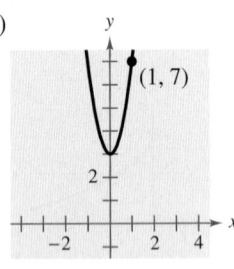

48. Use the graph of $f(x) = x^3$ to write an equation for each function whose graph is shown.

(a) (b)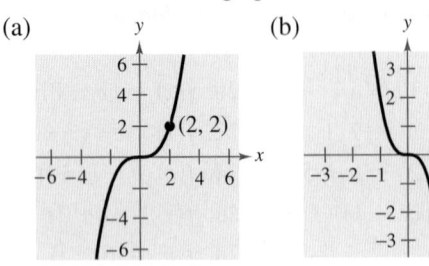

49. Use the graph of $f(x) = |x|$ to write an equation for each function whose graph is shown.

(a)   (b)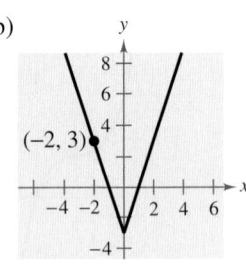

50. Use the graph of $f(x) = \sqrt{x}$ to write an equation for each function whose graph is shown.

(a)   (b)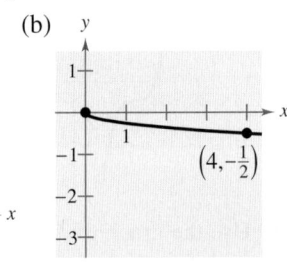

In Exercises 51–56, identify the common function and the transformation shown in the graph. Write an equation for the function shown in the graph. Then use a graphing utility to verify your answer.

51.   **52.**

53.   **54.**

55.   **56.**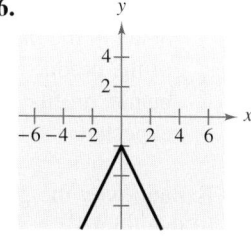

Graphical Analysis In Exercises 57–60, use the viewing window shown to write a possible equation for the transformation of the common function.

57.

58.

59.

60.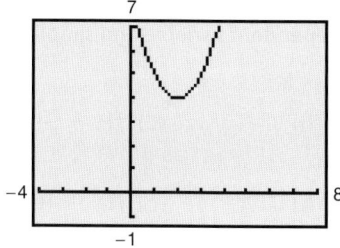

Graphical Reasoning In Exercises 61 and 62, use the graph of *f* to sketch the graph of *g*. To print an enlarged copy of the graph, go to the website *www.mathgraphs.com*.

61.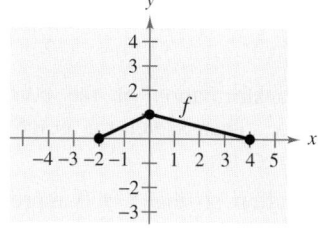

(a) $g(x) = f(x) + 2$ (b) $g(x) = f(x) - 1$
(c) $g(x) = f(-x)$ (d) $g(x) = -2f(x)$
(e) $g(x) = f(4x)$ (f) $g(x) = f\left(\frac{1}{2}x\right)$

62.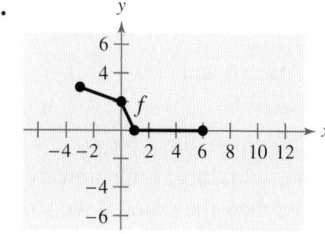

(a) $g(x) = f(x) - 5$ (b) $g(x) = f(x) + \frac{1}{2}$
(c) $g(x) = f(-x)$ (d) $g(x) = -4f(x)$
(e) $g(x) = f(2x) + 1$ (f) $g(x) = f\left(\frac{1}{4}x\right) - 2$

▶ **Model It**

63. *Fuel Use* The amount of fuel *F* (in billions of gallons) used by trucks from 1980 through 1999 can be approximated by the function

$$F = f(t) = 20.5 + 0.035t^2$$

where *t* = 0 represents 1980. (Source: U.S. Federal Highway Administration)

(a) Describe the transformation of the common function $f(x) = x^2$. Then sketch the graph over the interval $0 \le t \le 19$.

(b) Find and interpret $\dfrac{f(19) - f(0)}{19 - 0}$.

(c) Rewrite the function so that $t = 0$ represents 1990. Explain how you got your answer.

(d) Use the model from part (c) to predict the amount of fuel used by trucks in 2005. Does your answer seem reasonable? Explain.

64. *Finance* The amount M (in trillions of dollars) of mortgage debt outstanding in the United States from 1980 through 1999 can be approximated by the function $M = f(t) = 0.0037(t + 14.979)^2$, where $t = 0$ represents 1980. (Source: Board of Governors of the Federal Reserve System)

(a) Describe the transformation of the common function $f(x) = x^2$. Then sketch the graph over the interval $0 \le t \le 19$.

(b) Rewrite the function so that $t = 0$ represents 1990. Explain how you got your answer.

Synthesis

True or False? In Exercises 65 and 66, determine whether the statement is true or false. Justify your answer.

65. The graphs of $f(x) = |x| + 6$ and $f(x) = |-x| + 6$ are identical.

66. If the graph of the common function $f(x) = x^2$ is moved six units to the right, three units upward, and reflected in the x-axis, then the point $(-2, 19)$ will lie on the graph of the transformation.

67. *Describing Profits* Management originally predicted that the profits from the sales of a new product would be approximated by the graph of the function f shown. The actual profits are shown by the function g along with a verbal description. Use the concepts of transformations of graphs to write g in terms of f.

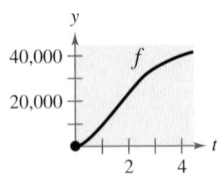

(a) The profits were only three-fourths as large as expected.

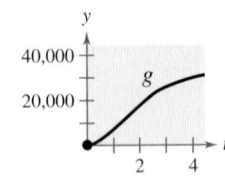

(b) The profits were consistently $10,000 greater than predicted.

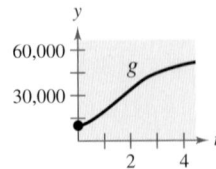

(c) There was a two-year delay in the introduction of the product. After sales began, profits grew as expected.

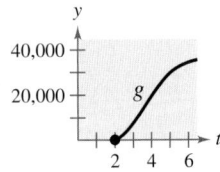

68. Explain why the graph of $y = -f(x)$ is a reflection of the graph of $y = f(x)$ about the x-axis.

69. The graph of $y = f(x)$ passes through the points $(0, 1)$, $(1, 2)$, and $(2, 3)$. Find the corresponding points on the graph of $y = f(x + 2) - 1$.

70. *Think About It* You can use either of two methods to graph a function: plotting points or translating a common function as shown in this section. Which method of graphing do you prefer to use for each function? Explain.

(a) $f(x) = 3x^2 - 4x + 1$

(b) $f(x) = 2(x - 1)^2 - 6$

Review

In Exercises 71–78, perform the operation and simplify.

71. $\dfrac{4}{x} + \dfrac{4}{1 - x}$

72. $\dfrac{2}{x + 5} - \dfrac{2}{x - 5}$

73. $\dfrac{3}{x - 1} - \dfrac{2}{x(x - 1)}$

74. $\dfrac{x}{x - 5} + \dfrac{1}{2}$

75. $(x - 4)\left(\dfrac{1}{\sqrt{x^2 - 4}}\right)$

76. $\left(\dfrac{x}{x^2 - 4}\right)\left(\dfrac{x^2 - x - 2}{x^2}\right)$

77. $(x^2 - 9) \div \left(\dfrac{x + 3}{5}\right)$

78. $\left(\dfrac{x}{x^2 - 3x - 28}\right) \div \left(\dfrac{x^2 + 3x}{x^2 + 5x + 4}\right)$

In Exercises 79 and 80, evaluate the function at the specified values of the independent variable and simplify.

79. $f(x) = x^2 - 6x + 11$

(a) $f(-3)$ (b) $f\left(-\tfrac{1}{2}\right)$ (c) $f(x - 3)$

80. $f(x) = \sqrt{x + 10} - 3$

(a) $f(-10)$ (b) $f(26)$ (c) $f(x - 10)$

In Exercises 81–84, find the domain of the function.

81. $f(x) = \dfrac{2}{11 - x}$

82. $f(x) = \dfrac{\sqrt{x - 3}}{x - 8}$

83. $f(x) = \sqrt{81 - x^2}$

84. $f(x) = \sqrt[3]{4 - x^2}$

1.7 Combinations of Functions

▶ What you should learn

- How to add, subtract, multiply, and divide functions
- How to find the composition of one function with another function
- How to use combinations of functions to model and solve real-life problems

▶ Why you should learn it

Combinations of functions can be used to model and solve real-life problems. For instance, in Exercise 33 on page 75, combinations of functions are used to analyze U.S. health expenditures.

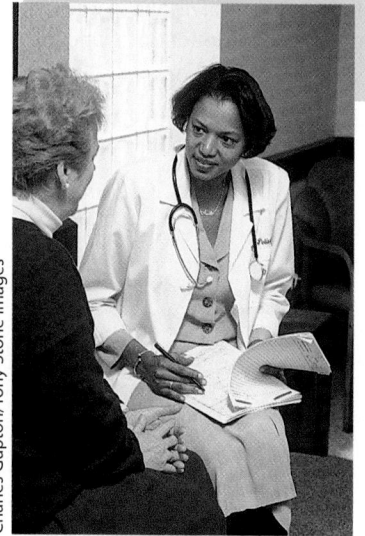

Charles Gupton/Tony Stone Images

Arithmetic Combinations of Functions

Just as two real numbers can be combined by the operations of addition, subtraction, multiplication, and division to form other real numbers, two *functions* can be combined to create new functions. For example, the functions $f(x) = 2x - 3$ and $g(x) = x^2 - 1$ can be combined to form the sum, difference, product, and quotient of f and g.

$$f(x) + g(x) = (2x - 3) + (x^2 - 1)$$
$$= x^2 + 2x - 4 \qquad \text{Sum}$$
$$f(x) - g(x) = (2x - 3) - (x^2 - 1)$$
$$= -x^2 + 2x - 2 \qquad \text{Difference}$$
$$f(x)g(x) = (2x - 3)(x^2 - 1)$$
$$= 2x^3 - 3x^2 - 2x + 3 \qquad \text{Product}$$
$$\frac{f(x)}{g(x)} = \frac{2x - 3}{x^2 - 1}, \quad x \neq \pm 1 \qquad \text{Quotient}$$

The domain of an **arithmetic combination** of functions f and g consists of all real numbers that are common to the domains of f and g. In the case of the quotient $f(x)/g(x)$, there is the further restriction that $g(x) \neq 0$.

Sum, Difference, Product, and Quotient of Functions

Let f and g be two functions with overlapping domains. Then, for all x common to both domains, the *sum*, *difference*, *product*, and *quotient* of f and g are defined as follows.

1. *Sum:* $(f + g)(x) = f(x) + g(x)$
2. *Difference:* $(f - g)(x) = f(x) - g(x)$
3. *Product:* $(fg)(x) = f(x) \cdot g(x)$
4. *Quotient:* $\left(\dfrac{f}{g}\right)(x) = \dfrac{f(x)}{g(x)}, \qquad g(x) \neq 0$

Example 1 ▶ **Finding the Sum of Two Functions**

Given $f(x) = 2x + 1$ and $g(x) = x^2 + 2x - 1$, find $(f + g)(x)$.

Solution
$$(f + g)(x) = f(x) + g(x) = (2x + 1) + (x^2 + 2x - 1) = x^2 + 4x$$

Example 2 ▶   **Finding the Difference of Two Functions**

Given $f(x) = 2x + 1$ and $g(x) = x^2 + 2x - 1$, find $(f - g)(x)$. Then evaluate the difference when $x = 2$.

Solution

The difference of f and g is

$$(f - g)(x) = f(x) - g(x)$$

$$= (2x + 1) - (x^2 + 2x - 1)$$

$$= -x^2 + 2.$$

When $x = 2$, the value of this difference is

$$(f - g)(2) = -(2)^2 + 2$$

$$= -2.$$

In Examples 1 and 2, both f and g have domains that consist of all real numbers. So, the domains of $(f + g)$ and $(f - g)$ are also the set of all real numbers. Remember that any restrictions on the domains of f and g must be considered when forming the sum, difference, product, or quotient of f and g.

Example 3 ▶   **Finding the Domains of Quotients of Functions**

Find the domains of $\left(\dfrac{f}{g}\right)(x)$ and $\left(\dfrac{g}{f}\right)(x)$ for the functions

$$f(x) = \sqrt{x} \qquad \text{and} \qquad g(x) = \sqrt{4 - x^2}.$$

Solution

The quotient of f and g is

$$\left(\dfrac{f}{g}\right)(x) = \dfrac{f(x)}{g(x)} = \dfrac{\sqrt{x}}{\sqrt{4 - x^2}}$$

and the quotient of g and f is

$$\left(\dfrac{g}{f}\right)(x) = \dfrac{g(x)}{f(x)} = \dfrac{\sqrt{4 - x^2}}{\sqrt{x}}.$$

The domain of f is $[0, \infty)$ and the domain of g is $[-2, 2]$. The intersection of these domains is $[0, 2]$. So, the domains of $\left(\dfrac{f}{g}\right)$ and $\left(\dfrac{g}{f}\right)$ are as follows.

$$\text{Domain of } \left(\dfrac{f}{g}\right): [0, 2) \qquad \text{Domain of } \left(\dfrac{g}{f}\right): (0, 2]$$

Can you see why these two domains differ slightly?

Composition of Functions

Another way of combining two functions is to form the **composition** of one with the other. For instance, if $f(x) = x^2$ and $g(x) = x + 1$, the composition of f with g is

$$f(g(x)) = f(x + 1)$$
$$= (x + 1)^2.$$

This composition is denoted as $(f \circ g)$.

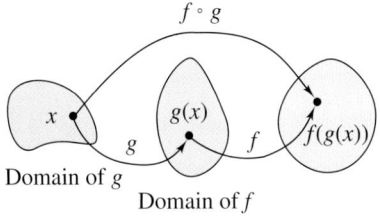

$f \circ g$

Domain of g

Domain of f

FIGURE 1.75

Definition of Composition of Two Functions

The **composition** of the function f with the function g is

$$(f \circ g)(x) = f(g(x)).$$

The domain of $(f \circ g)$ is the set of all x in the domain of g such that $g(x)$ is in the domain of f. (See Figure 1.75.)

STUDY TIP

The following tables of values help illustrate the composition $(f \circ g)(x)$ given in Example 4.

x	0	1	2	3
$g(x)$	4	3	0	-5

$g(x)$	4	3	0	-5
$f(g(x))$	6	5	2	-3

x	0	1	2	3
$f(g(x))$	6	5	2	-3

Note that the first two tables can be combined (or "composed") to produce the values given in the third table.

Example 4 ▶ **Composition of Functions**

Given $f(x) = x + 2$ and $g(x) = 4 - x^2$, find the following.

a. $(f \circ g)(x)$ **b.** $(g \circ f)(x)$ **c.** $(g \circ f)(-2)$

Solution

a. The composition of f with g is as follows.

$$(f \circ g)(x) = f(g(x)) \qquad \text{Definition of } f \circ g$$
$$= f(4 - x^2) \qquad \text{Definition of } g(x)$$
$$= (4 - x^2) + 2 \qquad \text{Definition of } f(x)$$
$$= -x^2 + 6 \qquad \text{Simplify.}$$

b. The composition of g with f is as follows.

$$(g \circ f)(x) = g(f(x)) \qquad \text{Definition of } g \circ f$$
$$= g(x + 2) \qquad \text{Definition of } f(x)$$
$$= 4 - (x + 2)^2 \qquad \text{Definition of } g(x)$$
$$= 4 - (x^2 + 4x + 4) \qquad \text{Expand.}$$
$$= -x^2 - 4x \qquad \text{Simplify.}$$

Note that, in this case, $(f \circ g)(x) \neq (g \circ f)(x)$.

c. Using the result of part (b), you can write the following.

$$(g \circ f)(-2) = -(-2)^2 - 4(-2) \qquad \text{Substitute.}$$
$$= -4 + 8 \qquad \text{Simplify.}$$
$$= 4 \qquad \text{Simplify.}$$

Technology

You can use a graphing utility to determine the domain of a composition of functions. For the composition in Example 5, enter the function composition as

$$y = \left(\sqrt{9 - x^2}\right)^2 - 9.$$

You should obtain the graph shown below. Use the *trace* feature to determine that the x-coordinates of points on the graph extend from -3 to 3. So, the domain of $(f \circ g)(x)$ is $-3 \le x \le 3$.

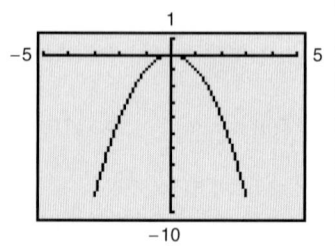

Activities

1. Given $f(x) = 3x^2 + 2$ and $g(x) = 2x$, find $f \circ g$.

   Answer: $(f \circ g)(x) = 12x^2 + 2$

2. Given the functions

   $$f(x) = \frac{1}{x - 2} \text{ and } g(x) = \sqrt{x},$$

   find the composition of f with g. Then find the domain of the composition.

   Answer: $(f \circ g)(x) = \dfrac{1}{\sqrt{x} - 2}$. The domain of $(f \circ g)$ is the set of all non-negative real numbers except $x = 4$.

3. Find two functions f and g such that $(f \circ g)(x) = h(x)$. (There are many correct answers.)

   a. $h(x) = \dfrac{1}{\sqrt{3x + 1}}$

      Answer: $f(x) = \dfrac{1}{\sqrt{x}}$ and $g(x) = 3x + 1$

   b. $h(x) = (2x + 3)^4$

      Answer: $f(x) = x^4$ and $g(x) = 2x + 3$

Example 5 ▶ Finding the Domain of a Composite Function

Find the composition $(f \circ g)(x)$ for the functions

$$f(x) = x^2 - 9 \quad \text{and} \quad g(x) = \sqrt{9 - x^2}.$$

Then find the domain of $(f \circ g)$.

Solution

$$
\begin{aligned}
(f \circ g)(x) &= f(g(x)) \\
&= f\left(\sqrt{9 - x^2}\right) \\
&= \left(\sqrt{9 - x^2}\right)^2 - 9 \\
&= 9 - x^2 - 9 \\
&= -x^2
\end{aligned}
$$

From this, it might appear that the domain of the composition is the set of all real numbers. Because the domain of f is the set of all real numbers and the domain of g is $-3 \le x \le 3$, the domain of $(f \circ g)$ is $-3 \le x \le 3$.

In Examples 4 and 5, you formed the composition of two given functions. In calculus, it is also important to be able to identify two functions that make up a given composite function. For instance, the function h given by

$$h(x) = (3x - 5)^3$$

is the composition of f with g, where $f(x) = x^3$ and $g(x) = 3x - 5$. That is,

$$h(x) = (3x - 5)^3 = [g(x)]^3 = f(g(x)).$$

Basically, to "decompose" a composite function, look for an "inner" function and an "outer" function. In the function h above, $g(x) = 3x - 5$ is the inner function and $f(x) = x^3$ is the outer function.

Example 6 ▶ Finding Components of Composite Functions

Express the function $h(x) = \dfrac{1}{(x - 2)^2}$ as a composition of two functions.

Solution

One way to write h as a composition of two functions is to take the inner function to be $g(x) = x - 2$ and the outer function to be

$$f(x) = \frac{1}{x^2} = x^{-2}.$$

Then you can write

$$h(x) = \frac{1}{(x - 2)^2} = (x - 2)^{-2} = f(x - 2) = f(g(x)).$$

◀ E x p l o r a t i o n ▶

You are buying an automobile whose price is $18,500. Which of the following options would you choose? Explain.

a. You are given a factory rebate of $2000, followed by a dealer discount of 10%.

b. You are given a dealer discount of 10%, followed by a factory rebate of $2000.

Let $f(x) = x - 2000$ and let $g(x) = 0.9x$. Which option is represented by the composite $f(g(x))$? Which is represented by the composite $g(f(x))$?

Writing About Mathematics

To expand on this activity, you might consider asking your students to use the tables they created in parts (a) and (b), along with a table of values for x and $f(x)$, to demonstrate and explain how the tables can be manipulated to yield tables of values for $h(x)$ and $g(x)$.

Application

Example 7 ▶ Bacteria Count

The number N of bacteria in a refrigerated food is

$$N(T) = 20T^2 - 80T + 500, \qquad 2 \le T \le 14$$

where T is the temperature of the food in degrees Celsius. When the food is removed from refrigeration, the temperature is

$$T(t) = 4t + 2, \qquad 0 \le t \le 3$$

where t is the time in hours. (a) Find the composite $N(T(t))$ and interpret its meaning in context. (b) Find the time when the bacterial count reaches 2000.

Solution

a. $N(T(t)) = 20(4t + 2)^2 - 80(4t + 2) + 500$

$\qquad\qquad = 20(16t^2 + 16t + 4) - 320t - 160 + 500$

$\qquad\qquad = 320t^2 + 320t + 80 - 320t - 160 + 500$

$\qquad\qquad = 320t^2 + 420$

The composite function $N(T(t))$ represents the number of bacteria in the food as a function of time.

b. The bacterial count will reach 2000 when $320t^2 + 420 = 2000$. Solve this equation to find that the count will reach 2000 when $t \approx 2.2$ hours. When you solve this equation, note that the negative value is rejected because it is not in the domain of the composite function.

Writing ABOUT MATHEMATICS

Analyzing Arithmetic Combinations of Functions

a. Use the graphs of f and $(f + g)$ in Figure 1.76 to make a table showing the values of $g(x)$ when $x = 1, 2, 3, 4, 5,$ and 6. Explain your reasoning.

b. Use the graphs of f and $(f - h)$ in Figure 1.76 to make a table showing the values of $h(x)$ when $x = 1, 2, 3, 4, 5,$ and 6. Explain your reasoning.

  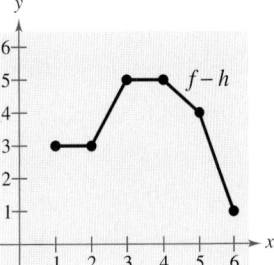

FIGURE 1.76

1.7 Exercises

In Exercises 1–4, use the graphs of f and g to graph $h(x) = (f + g)(x)$. To print an enlarged copy of the graph, go to the website *www.mathgraphs.com*.

1.

2.

3.

4.
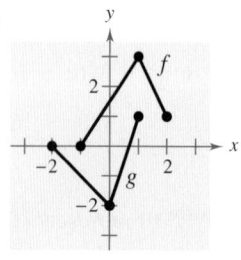

In Exercises 5–12, find (a) $(f + g)(x)$, (b) $(f - g)(x)$, (c) $(fg)(x)$, and (d) $(f/g)(x)$. What is the domain of f/g?

5. $f(x) = x + 2$, $\quad g(x) = x - 2$

6. $f(x) = 2x - 5$, $\quad g(x) = 2 - x$

7. $f(x) = x^2$, $\quad g(x) = 4x - 5$

8. $f(x) = 2x - 5$, $\quad g(x) = 4$

9. $f(x) = x^2 + 6$, $\quad g(x) = \sqrt{1 - x}$

10. $f(x) = \sqrt{x^2 - 4}$, $\quad g(x) = \dfrac{x^2}{x^2 + 1}$

11. $f(x) = \dfrac{1}{x}$, $\quad g(x) = \dfrac{1}{x^2}$

12. $f(x) = \dfrac{x}{x + 1}$, $\quad g(x) = x^3$

In Exercises 13–24, evaluate the indicated function for $f(x) = x^2 + 1$ and $g(x) = x - 4$.

13. $(f + g)(2)$

14. $(f - g)(-1)$

15. $(f - g)(0)$

16. $(f + g)(1)$

17. $(f - g)(3t)$

18. $(f + g)(t - 2)$

19. $(fg)(6)$

20. $(fg)(-6)$

21. $\left(\dfrac{f}{g}\right)(5)$

22. $\left(\dfrac{f}{g}\right)(0)$

23. $\left(\dfrac{f}{g}\right)(-1) - g(3)$

24. $(fg)(5) + f(4)$

In Exercises 25–28, graph the functions f, g, and f + g on the same set of coordinate axes.

25. $f(x) = \frac{1}{2}x$, $\quad g(x) = x - 1$

26. $f(x) = \frac{1}{3}x$, $\quad g(x) = -x + 4$

27. $f(x) = x^2$, $\quad g(x) = -2x$

28. $f(x) = 4 - x^2$, $\quad g(x) = x$

 Graphical Reasoning In Exercises 29 and 30, use a graphing utility to graph f, g, and f + g in the same viewing window. Which function contributes most to the magnitude of the sum when $0 \le x \le 2$? Which function contributes most to the magnitude of the sum when $x > 6$?

29. $f(x) = 3x$, $\quad g(x) = -\dfrac{x^3}{10}$

30. $f(x) = \dfrac{x}{2}$, $\quad g(x) = \sqrt{x}$

31. *Stopping Distance* The research and development department of an automobile manufacturer has determined that when required to stop quickly to avoid an accident, the distance (in feet) a car travels during the driver's reaction time is given by $R(x) = \frac{3}{4}x$, where x is the speed of the car in miles per hour. The distance (in feet) traveled while the driver is braking is $B(x) = \frac{1}{15}x^2$. Find the function that represents the total stopping distance T. Graph the functions R, B, and T on the same set of coordinate axes for $0 \le x \le 60$.

 32. *Sales* From 1997 to 2002, the sales R_1 (in thousands of dollars) for one of two restaurants owned by the same parent company can be modeled by

$$R_1 = 480 - 8t - 0.8t^2, \qquad t = 0, 1, 2, 3, 4, 5$$

where $t = 0$ represents 1997. During the same six-year period, the sales R_2 (in thousands of dollars) for the second restaurant can be modeled by

$$R_2 = 254 + 0.78t, \qquad t = 0, 1, 2, 3, 4, 5.$$

Write a function that represents the total sales of the two restaurants owned by the same parent company. Use a graphing utility to graph the total sales function.

▶ Model It

33. *Health Care Costs* The table shows the total amount (in billions of dollars) spent on health services and supplies in the United States (including Puerto Rico) for the years 1993 through 1999. The variables y_1, y_2, and y_3 represent out-of-pocket payments, insurance premiums, and other types of payments, respectively. (Source: Centers for Medicare and Medicaid Services)

Year	y_1	y_2	y_3
1993	148.9	295.7	39.1
1994	146.2	308.9	40.8
1995	149.2	322.3	44.8
1996	155.0	337.4	47.9
1997	165.5	355.6	52.0
1998	176.1	376.8	54.8
1999	186.5	401.2	58.9

(a) Use the *regression* feature of a graphing utility to find a quadratic model for y_1 and linear models for y_2 and y_3. Let $t = 3$ represent 1993.

(b) Find $y_1 + y_2 + y_3$. What does this sum represent?

(c) Use a graphing utility to graph y_1, y_2, y_3, and $y_1 + y_2 + y_3$ in the same viewing window.

(d) Use the model from part (b) to estimate the total amount spent on health services and supplies in the years 2003 and 2005.

34. *Graphical Reasoning* An electronically controlled thermostat in a home is programmed to lower the temperature automatically during the night. The temperature in the house T (in degrees Fahrenheit) is given in terms of t, the time in hours on a 24-hour clock (see figure).

(a) Explain why T is a function of t.

(b) Approximate $T(4)$ and $T(15)$.

(c) The thermostat is reprogrammed to produce a temperature H for which $H(t) = T(t - 1)$. How does this change the temperature?

(d) The thermostat is reprogrammed to produce a temperature H for which $H(t) = T(t) - 1$. How does this change the temperature?

(e) Write a piecewise-defined function that represents the graph.

FIGURE FOR **34**

In Exercises 35–38, find (a) $f \circ g$, (b) $g \circ f$, and (c) $f \circ f$.

35. $f(x) = x^2$, $\qquad\qquad$ $g(x) = x - 1$

36. $f(x) = 3x + 5$, $\qquad\quad$ $g(x) = 5 - x$

37. $f(x) = \sqrt[3]{x - 1}$, $\qquad$ $g(x) = x^3 + 1$

38. $f(x) = x^3$, $\qquad\qquad$ $g(x) = \dfrac{1}{x}$

In Exercises 39–46, find (a) $f \circ g$ and (b) $g \circ f$. Find the domain of each function and each composite function.

39. $f(x) = \sqrt{x + 4}$, $\qquad$ $g(x) = x^2$

40. $f(x) = \sqrt[3]{x - 5}$, $\qquad$ $g(x) = x^3 + 1$

41. $f(x) = x^2 + 1$, $\qquad\;$ $g(x) = \sqrt{x}$

42. $f(x) = x^{2/3}$, $\qquad\qquad$ $g(x) = x^6$

43. $f(x) = |x|$, $\qquad\qquad$ $g(x) = x + 6$

44. $f(x) = |x - 4|$, $\qquad\;$ $g(x) = 3 - x$

45. $f(x) = \dfrac{1}{x}$, $\qquad\qquad$ $g(x) = x + 3$

46. $f(x) = \dfrac{3}{x^2 - 1}$, $\qquad$ $g(x) = x + 1$

In Exercises 47–50, use the graphs of f and g to evaluate the functions.

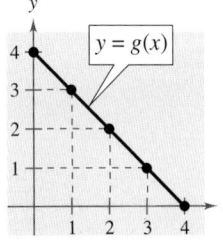

47. (a) $(f + g)(3)$ $\qquad$ (b) $(f/g)(2)$

48. (a) $(f - g)(1)$ $\qquad$ (b) $(fg)(4)$

49. (a) $(f \circ g)(2)$ (b) $(g \circ f)(2)$

50. (a) $(f \circ g)(1)$ (b) $(g \circ f)(3)$

In Exercises 51–58, find two functions f and g such that $(f \circ g)(x) = h(x)$. (There is more than one correct answer.)

51. $h(x) = (2x + 1)^2$

52. $h(x) = (1 - x)^3$

53. $h(x) = \sqrt[3]{x^2 - 4}$

54. $h(x) = \sqrt{9 - x}$

55. $h(x) = \dfrac{1}{x + 2}$

56. $h(x) = \dfrac{4}{(5x + 2)^2}$

57. $h(x) = \dfrac{-x^2 + 3}{4 - x^2}$

58. $h(x) = \dfrac{27x^3 + 6x}{10 - 27x^3}$

59. Geometry A square concrete foundation is prepared as a base for a cylindrical tank (see figure).

(a) Write the radius r of the tank as a function of the length x of the sides of the square.

(b) Write the area A of the circular base of the tank as a function of the radius r.

(c) Find and interpret $(A \circ r)(x)$.

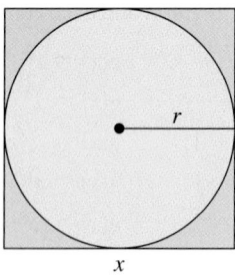

x

60. Physics A pebble is dropped into a calm pond, causing ripples in the form of concentric circles (see figure). The radius (in feet) of the outer ripple is $r(t) = 0.6t$, where t is the time in seconds after the pebble strikes the water. The area of the circle is given by the function $A(r) = \pi r^2$. Find and interpret $(A \circ r)(t)$.

Synthesis

True or False? **In Exercises 61 and 62, determine whether the statement is true or false. Justify your answer.**

61. If $f(x) = x + 1$ and $g(x) = 6x$, then $(f \circ g)(x) = (g \circ f)(x)$.

62. If you are given two functions $f(x)$ and $g(x)$, you can calculate $(f \circ g)(x)$ if and only if the range of g is a subset of the domain of f.

63. Think About It You are a sales representative for an automobile manufacturer. You are paid an annual salary, plus a bonus of 3% of your sales over \$500,000. Consider the two functions

$$f(x) = x - 500,000 \quad \text{and} \quad g(x) = 0.03x.$$

If x is greater than \$500,000, which of the following represents your bonus? Explain your reasoning.

(a) $f(g(x))$ (b) $g(f(x))$

64. Proof Prove that the product of two odd functions is an even function, and that the product of two even functions is an even function.

65. Conjecture Use examples to hypothesize whether the product of an odd function and an even function is even or odd. Then prove your hypothesis.

Review

66. Find the domain of the function.

$$f(x) = \frac{x}{5x + 7}$$

Average Rate of Change **In Exercises 67–70, find the difference quotient**

$$\frac{f(x + h) - f(x)}{h}$$

and simplify your answer.

67. $f(x) = 3x - 4$

68. $f(x) = 1 - x^2$

69. $f(x) = \dfrac{4}{x}$

70. $f(x) = \sqrt{2x + 1}$

In Exercises 71–74, find an equation of the line that passes through the given point and has the indicated slope. Sketch the line.

71. $(2, -4), m = 3$

72. $(-6, 3), m = -1$

73. $(8, -1), m = -\frac{3}{2}$

74. $(7, 0), m = \frac{5}{7}$

1.8 Inverse Functions

▶ What you should learn

- How to find inverse functions informally and verify that two functions are inverse functions of each other
- How to use graphs of functions to determine whether functions have inverse functions
- How to use the Horizontal Line Test to determine if functions are one-to-one
- How to find inverse functions algebraically

▶ Why you should learn it

Inverse functions can be used to model and solve real-life problems. For instance, in Exercise 79 on page 85, an inverse function can be used to determine the year in which there were a given number of households in the United States.

Michelle Bridwell/PhotoEdit

Inverse Functions

Recall from Section 1.3 that a function can be represented by a set of ordered pairs. For instance, the function $f(x) = x + 4$ from the set $A = \{1, 2, 3, 4\}$ to the set $B = \{5, 6, 7, 8\}$ can be written as follows.

$$f(x) = x + 4: \ \{(1, 5), (2, 6), (3, 7), (4, 8)\}$$

In this case, by interchanging the first and second coordinates of each of these ordered pairs, you can form the **inverse function** of f, which is denoted by f^{-1}. It is a function from the set B to the set A, and can be written as follows.

$$f^{-1}(x) = x - 4: \ \{(5, 1), (6, 2), (7, 3), (8, 4)\}$$

Note that the domain of f is equal to the range of f^{-1}, and vice versa, as shown in Figure 1.77. Also note that the functions f and f^{-1} have the effect of "undoing" each other. In other words, when you form the composition of f with f^{-1} or the composition of f^{-1} with f, you obtain the identity function.

$$f(f^{-1}(x)) = f(x - 4) = (x - 4) + 4 = x$$
$$f^{-1}(f(x)) = f^{-1}(x + 4) = (x + 4) - 4 = x$$

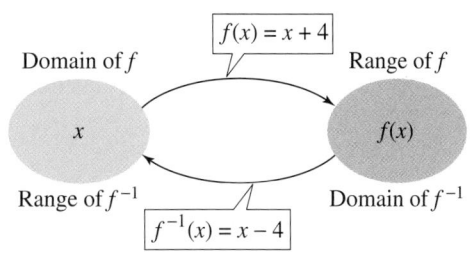

FIGURE 1.77

Example 1 ▶ **Finding Inverse Functions Informally**

Find the inverse function of $f(x) = 4x$. Then verify that both $f(f^{-1}(x))$ and $f^{-1}(f(x))$ are equal to the identity function.

Solution

The function f *multiplies* each input by 4. To "undo" this function, you need to *divide* each input by 4. So, the inverse function of $f(x) = 4x$ is

$$f^{-1}(x) = \frac{x}{4}.$$

You can verify that both $f(f^{-1}(x))$ and $f^{-1}(f(x))$ are equal to the identity function as follows.

$$f(f^{-1}(x)) = f\left(\frac{x}{4}\right) = 4\left(\frac{x}{4}\right) = x \qquad f^{-1}(f(x)) = f^{-1}(4x) = \frac{4x}{4} = x$$

◀ E x p l o r a t i o n ▶

Consider the functions

$$f(x) = x + 2$$

and

$$f^{-1}(x) = x - 2.$$

Evaluate $f(f^{-1}(x))$ and $f^{-1}(f(x))$ for the indicated values of x. What can you conclude about the functions?

x	-10	0	7	45
$f(f^{-1}(x))$				
$f^{-1}(f(x))$				

Definition of Inverse Function

Let f and g be two functions such that

$$f(g(x)) = x \qquad \text{for every } x \text{ in the domain of } g$$

and

$$g(f(x)) = x \qquad \text{for every } x \text{ in the domain of } f.$$

Under these conditions, the function g is the **inverse function** of the function f. The function g is denoted by f^{-1} (read "f-inverse"). So,

$$f(f^{-1}(x)) = x \qquad \text{and} \qquad f^{-1}(f(x)) = x.$$

The domain of f must be equal to the range of f^{-1}, and the range of f must be equal to the domain of f^{-1}.

Don't be confused by the use of -1 to denote the inverse function f^{-1}. In this text, whenever f^{-1} is written, it *always* refers to the inverse function of the function f and *not* to the reciprocal of $f(x)$.

If the function g is the inverse function of the function f, it must also be true that the function f is the inverse function of the function g. For this reason, you can say that the functions f and g are *inverse functions of each other.*

Additional Examples

Determine whether the two functions are inverse functions of each other.

a. $f(x) = 3x - 2,\ g(x) = \dfrac{1}{3}x + 2$

b. $f(x) = \dfrac{1}{4}x - 3,\ g(x) = 12 + 4x$

c. $f(x) = 2x + 4,\ g(x) = \dfrac{1}{2}x - 2$

Solution

The functions in parts (b) and (c) are inverse functions of each other because $f(g(x)) = g(f(x)) = x$.

The functions in part (a) are not inverse functions of each other.

Example 2 ▶ Verifying Inverse Functions

Which of the functions is the inverse function of $f(x) = \dfrac{5}{x - 2}$?

$$g(x) = \frac{x - 2}{5} \qquad\qquad h(x) = \frac{5}{x} + 2$$

Solution

By forming the composition of f with g, you have

$$f(g(x)) = f\left(\frac{x - 2}{5}\right)$$

$$= \frac{5}{\left(\dfrac{x - 2}{5}\right) - 2} \qquad \text{Substitute } \frac{x-2}{5} \text{ for } x.$$

$$= \frac{25}{x - 12} \neq x.$$

Because this composition is not equal to the identity function x, it follows that g *is not* the inverse function of f. By forming the composition of f with h, you have

$$f(h(x)) = f\left(\frac{5}{x} + 2\right) = \frac{5}{\left(\dfrac{5}{x} + 2\right) - 2} = \frac{5}{\left(\dfrac{5}{x}\right)} = x.$$

So, it appears that h *is* the inverse function of f. You can confirm this by showing that the composition of h with f is also equal to the identity function.

The Graph of an Inverse Function

The graphs of a function f and its inverse function f^{-1} are related to each other in the following way. If the point (a, b) lies on the graph of f, then the point (b, a) must lie on the graph of f^{-1}, and vice versa. This means that the graph of f^{-1} is a *reflection* of the graph of f in the line $y = x$, as shown in Figure 1.78.

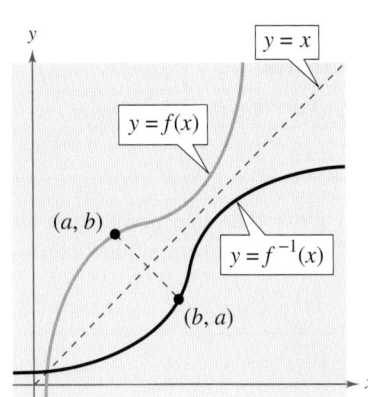

FIGURE **1.78**

Example 3 ▶ The Graphs of f and f^{-1}

Sketch the graphs of the inverse functions $f(x) = 2x - 3$ and $f^{-1}(x) = \frac{1}{2}(x + 3)$ on the same rectangular coordinate system and show that the graphs are reflections of each other in the line $y = x$.

Solution

The graphs of f and f^{-1} are shown in Figure 1.79. It appears that the graphs are reflections of each other in the line $y = x$. You can further verify this reflective property by testing a few points on each graph. Note in the following list that if the point (a, b) is on the graph of f, the point (b, a) is on the graph of f^{-1}.

Graph of $f(x) = 2x - 3$	Graph of $f^{-1}(x) = \frac{1}{2}(x + 3)$
$(-1, -5)$	$(-5, -1)$
$(0, -3)$	$(-3, 0)$
$(1, -1)$	$(-1, 1)$
$(2, 1)$	$(1, 2)$
$(3, 3)$	$(3, 3)$

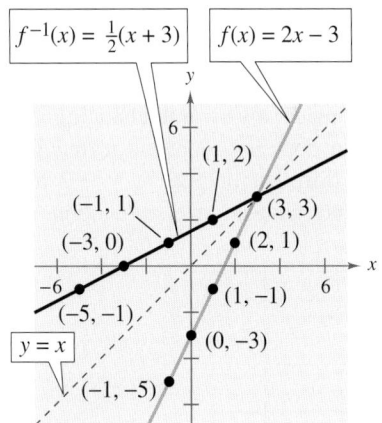

FIGURE **1.79**

Example 4 ▶ Finding Inverse Functions Graphically

Sketch the graphs of the inverse functions $f(x) = x^2 (x \geq 0)$ and $f^{-1}(x) = \sqrt{x}$ on the same rectangular coordinate system and show that the graphs are reflections of each other in the line $y = x$.

Solution

The graphs of f and f^{-1} are shown in Figure 1.80. It appears that the graphs are reflections of each other in the line $y = x$. You can further verify this reflective property by testing a few points on each graph. Note in the following list that if the point (a, b) is on the graph of f, the point (b, a) is on the graph of f^{-1}.

Graph of $f(x) = x^2$, $x \geq 0$	Graph of $f^{-1}(x) = \sqrt{x}$
$(0, 0)$	$(0, 0)$
$(1, 1)$	$(1, 1)$
$(2, 4)$	$(4, 2)$
$(3, 9)$	$(9, 3)$

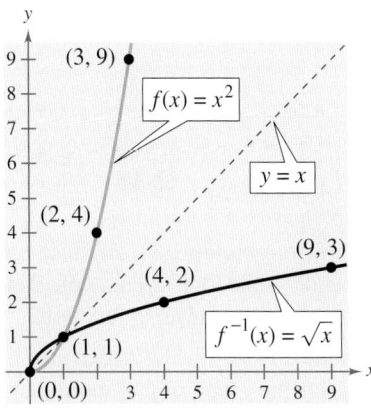

FIGURE **1.80**

Try showing that $f(f^{-1}(x)) = x$ and $f^{-1}(f(x)) = x$.

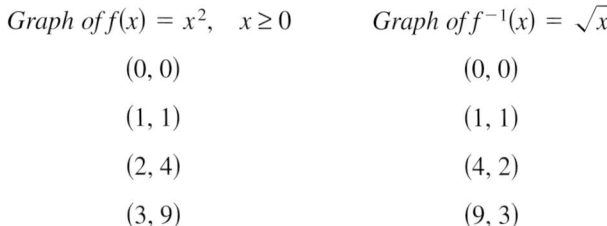

One-to-One Functions

The reflective property of the graphs of inverse functions gives you a nice *geometric* test for determining whether a function has an inverse function. This test is called the **Horizontal Line Test** for inverse functions.

> ### Horizontal Line Test for Inverse Functions
>
> A function f has an inverse function if and only if no *horizontal* line intersects the graph of f at more than one point.

If no horizontal line intersects the graph of f at more than one point, then no y-value is matched with more than one x-value. This is the essential characteristic of what are called **one-to-one** functions.

> ### One-to-One Functions
>
> A function f is **one-to-one** if each value of the dependent variable corresponds to exactly one value of the independent variable. A function f has an inverse function if and only if f is one-to-one.

Consider the function $f(x) = x^2$. The table on the left is a table of values for $f(x) = x^2$. The table of values on the right is made up by interchanging the columns of the first table. The table on the right does not represent a function because the input $x = 4$ is matched with two different outputs: $y = -2$ and $y = 2$. So, $f(x) = x^2$ is not one-to-one and does not have an inverse function.

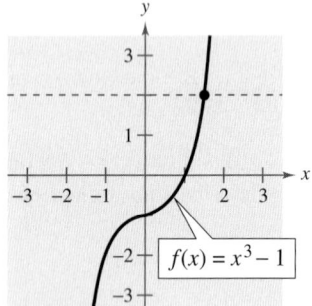

FIGURE **1.81**

x	$f(x)$
-2	4
-1	1
0	0
1	1
2	4
3	9

x	y
4	-2
1	-1
0	0
1	1
4	2
9	3

Example 5 ▶ Applying the Horizontal Line Test

a. The graph of the function $f(x) = x^3 - 1$ is shown in Figure 1.81. Because no horizontal line intersects the graph of f at more than one point, you can conclude that f *is* a one-to-one function and *does* have an inverse function.

b. The graph of the function $f(x) = x^2 - 1$ is shown in Figure 1.82. Because it is possible to find a horizontal line that intersects the graph of f at more than one point, you can conclude that f *is not* a one-to-one function and *does not* have an inverse function.

FIGURE **1.82**

Finding Inverse Functions Algebraically

For simple functions (such as the one in Example 1), you can find inverse functions by inspection. For more complicated functions, however, it is best to use the following guidelines. The key step in these guidelines is Step 3—interchanging the roles of x and y. This step corresponds to the fact that inverse functions have ordered pairs with the coordinates reversed.

Finding an Inverse Function

1. Use the Horizontal Line Test to decide whether f has an inverse function.

2. In the equation for $f(x)$, replace $f(x)$ by y.

3. Interchange the roles of x and y, and solve for y.

4. Replace y by $f^{-1}(x)$ in the new equation.

5. Verify that f and f^{-1} are inverse functions of each other by showing that the domain of f is equal to the range of f^{-1}, the range of f is equal to the domain of f^{-1}, and $f(f^{-1}(x)) = x = f^{-1}(f(x))$.

Example 6 ▶ Finding an Inverse Function Algebraically

Find the inverse function of

$$f(x) = \frac{5 - 3x}{2}.$$

Solution

The graph of f is a line, as shown in Figure 1.83. This graph passes the Horizontal Line Test. So, you know that f is one-to-one and has an inverse function.

$$f(x) = \frac{5 - 3x}{2} \qquad \text{Write original function.}$$

$$y = \frac{5 - 3x}{2} \qquad \text{Replace } f(x) \text{ by } y.$$

$$x = \frac{5 - 3y}{2} \qquad \text{Interchange } x \text{ and } y.$$

$$2x = 5 - 3y \qquad \text{Multiply each side by 2.}$$

$$3y = 5 - 2x \qquad \text{Isolate the } y\text{-term.}$$

$$y = \frac{5 - 2x}{3} \qquad \text{Solve for } y.$$

$$f^{-1}(x) = \frac{5 - 2x}{3} \qquad \text{Replace } y \text{ by } f^{-1}(x).$$

Note that both f and f^{-1} have domains and ranges that consist of the entire set of real numbers. Check that $f(f^{-1}(x)) = x$ and $f^{-1}(f(x)) = x$.

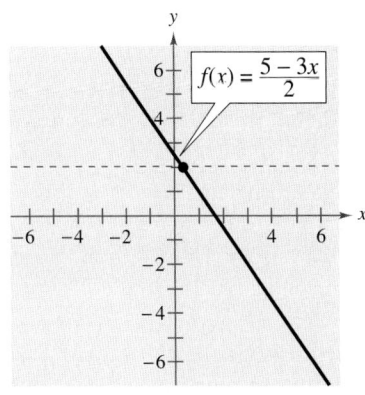

FIGURE 1.83

Example 7 ▶ **Finding an Inverse Function**

Find the inverse function of

$$f(x) = \sqrt[3]{x + 1}.$$

Solution

The graph of f is a curve, as shown in Figure 1.84. Because this graph passes the Horizontal Line Test, you know that f is one-to-one and has an inverse function.

$$f(x) = \sqrt[3]{x + 1} \qquad \text{Write original function.}$$
$$y = \sqrt[3]{x + 1} \qquad \text{Replace } f(x) \text{ by } y.$$
$$x = \sqrt[3]{y + 1} \qquad \text{Interchange } x \text{ and } y.$$
$$x^3 = y + 1 \qquad \text{Cube each side.}$$
$$x^3 - 1 = y \qquad \text{Solve for } y.$$
$$x^3 - 1 = f^{-1}(x) \qquad \text{Replace } y \text{ by } f^{-1}(x).$$

Both f and f^{-1} have domains and ranges that consist of the entire set of real numbers. You can verify this result numerically as shown in the tables below.

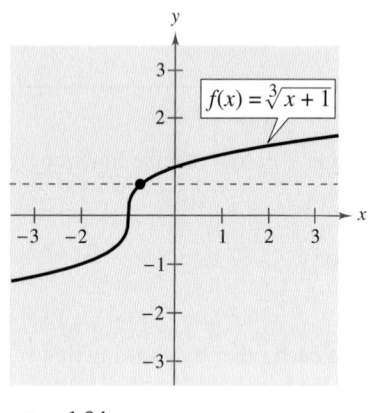

$f(x) = \sqrt[3]{x + 1}$

FIGURE 1.84

x	$f(x)$
-28	-3
-9	-2
-2	-1
-1	0
0	1
7	2
26	3

x	$f^{-1}(x)$
-3	-28
-2	-9
-1	-2
0	-1
1	0
2	7
3	26

Activities

1. Given $f(x) = 5x - 7$, find $f^{-1}(x)$.

   Answer: $f^{-1}(x) = \dfrac{x + 7}{5}$

2. Show that f and g are inverse functions by showing that $f(g(x)) = x$ and $g(f(x)) = x$.
   $f(x) = 3x^3 + 1$
   $g(x) = \sqrt[3]{\dfrac{x - 1}{3}}$

3. Describe the graphs of functions that have inverse functions and show how the graphs of a function and its inverse function are related.

Writing ABOUT MATHEMATICS

The Existence of an Inverse Function Write a short paragraph describing why the following functions do or do not have inverse functions.

a. Let x represent the retail price of an item (in dollars), and let $f(x)$ represent the sales tax on the item. Assume that the sales tax is 6% of the retail price *and* that the sales tax is rounded to the nearest cent. Does this function have an inverse function? (*Hint:* Can you undo this function?

For instance, if you know that the sales tax is $0.12, can you determine exactly what the retail price is?)

b. Let x represent the temperature in degrees Celsius, and let $f(x)$ represent the temperature in degrees Fahrenheit. Does this function have an inverse function? (*Hint:* The formula for converting from degrees Celsius to degrees Fahrenheit is $F = \frac{9}{5}C + 32$.)

1.8 Exercises

In Exercises 1–4, match the graph of the function with the graph of its inverse function. [The graphs of the inverse functions are labeled (a), (b), (c), and (d).]

(a)

(b)

(c)

(d)

1.

2.

3.

4.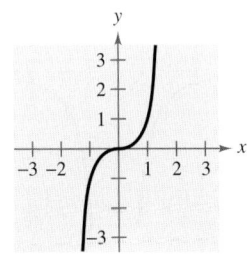

In Exercises 5–12, find the inverse function of f informally. Verify that $f(f^{-1}(x)) = x$ and $f^{-1}(f(x)) = x$.

5. $f(x) = 6x$

6. $f(x) = \frac{1}{3}x$

7. $f(x) = x + 9$

8. $f(x) = x - 4$

9. $f(x) = 3x + 1$

10. $f(x) = \dfrac{x - 1}{5}$

11. $f(x) = \sqrt[3]{x}$

12. $f(x) = x^5$

In Exercises 13–24, show that f and g are inverse functions (a) algebraically and (b) graphically.

13. $f(x) = 2x,$ $g(x) = \dfrac{x}{2}$

14. $f(x) = x - 5,$ $g(x) = x + 5$

15. $f(x) = 7x + 1,$ $g(x) = \dfrac{x - 1}{7}$

16. $f(x) = 3 - 4x,$ $g(x) = \dfrac{3 - x}{4}$

17. $f(x) = \dfrac{x^3}{8},$ $g(x) = \sqrt[3]{8x}$

18. $f(x) = \dfrac{1}{x},$ $g(x) = \dfrac{1}{x}$

19. $f(x) = \sqrt{x - 4},$ $g(x) = x^2 + 4, \quad x \geq 0$

20. $f(x) = 1 - x^3,$ $g(x) = \sqrt[3]{1 - x}$

21. $f(x) = 9 - x^2, \quad x \geq 0, \quad g(x) = \sqrt{9 - x}, \quad x \leq 9$

22. $f(x) = \dfrac{1}{1 + x}, \quad x \geq 0$

$g(x) = \dfrac{1 - x}{x}, \quad 0 < x \leq 1$

23. $f(x) = \dfrac{x - 1}{x + 5},$ $g(x) = -\dfrac{5x + 1}{x - 1}$

24. $f(x) = \dfrac{x + 3}{x - 2},$ $g(x) = \dfrac{2x + 3}{x - 1}$

In Exercises 25 and 26, does the function have an inverse function?

25.

x	$f(x)$
-1	-2
0	1
1	2
2	1
3	-2
4	-6

26.

x	$f(x)$
-3	10
-2	6
-1	4
0	1
2	-3
3	-10

In Exercises 27 and 28, use the table of values for $y = f(x)$ to complete a table for $y = f^{-1}(x)$.

27.

x	-2	-1	0	1	2	3
$f(x)$	-2	0	2	4	6	8

28.

x	-3	-2	-1	0	1	2
$f(x)$	-10	-7	-4	-1	2	5

In Exercises 29–32, does the function have an inverse function?

29.

30.

31.

32.

 In Exercises 33–38, use a graphing utility to graph the function, and use the Horizontal Line Test to determine whether the function is one-to-one and so has an inverse function.

33. $g(x) = \dfrac{4 - x}{6}$

34. $f(x) = 10$

35. $h(x) = |x + 4| - |x - 4|$

36. $g(x) = (x + 5)^3$

37. $f(x) = -2x\sqrt{16 - x^2}$

38. $f(x) = \frac{1}{8}(x + 2)^2 - 1$

In Exercises 39–54, find the inverse function of f. Then graph both f and f^{-1} on the same set of coordinate axes.

39. $f(x) = 2x - 3$

40. $f(x) = 3x + 1$

41. $f(x) = x^5 - 2$

42. $f(x) = x^3 + 1$

43. $f(x) = \sqrt{x}$

44. $f(x) = x^2, \quad x \geq 0$

45. $f(x) = \sqrt{4 - x^2}, \quad 0 \leq x \leq 2$

46. $f(x) = x^2 - 2, \quad x \leq 0$

47. $f(x) = \dfrac{4}{x}$

48. $f(x) = -\dfrac{2}{x}$

49. $f(x) = \dfrac{x + 1}{x - 2}$

50. $f(x) = \dfrac{x - 3}{x + 2}$

51. $f(x) = \sqrt[3]{x - 1}$

52. $f(x) = x^{3/5}$

53. $f(x) = \dfrac{6x + 4}{4x + 5}$

54. $f(x) = \dfrac{8x - 4}{2x + 6}$

In Exercises 55–68, determine whether the function has an inverse function. If it does, find the inverse function.

55. $f(x) = x^4$

56. $f(x) = \dfrac{1}{x^2}$

57. $g(x) = \dfrac{x}{8}$

58. $f(x) = 3x + 5$

59. $p(x) = -4$

60. $f(x) = \dfrac{3x + 4}{5}$

61. $f(x) = (x + 3)^2, \quad x \geq -3$

62. $q(x) = (x - 5)^2$

63. $f(x) = \begin{cases} x + 3, & x < 0 \\ 6 - x, & x \geq 0 \end{cases}$

64. $f(x) = \begin{cases} -x, & x \leq 0 \\ x^2 - 3x, & x > 0 \end{cases}$

65. $h(x) = -\dfrac{4}{x^2}$

66. $f(x) = |x - 2|, \quad x \leq 2$

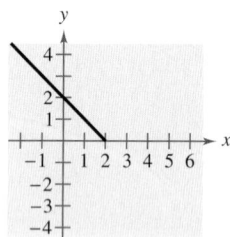

67. $f(x) = \sqrt{2x + 3}$

68. $f(x) = \sqrt{x - 2}$

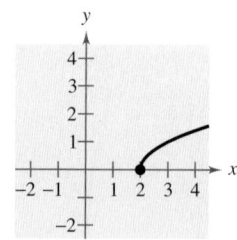

In Exercises 69–74, use the functions $f(x) = \frac{1}{8}x - 3$ and $g(x) = x^3$ to find the indicated value or function.

69. $(f^{-1} \circ g^{-1})(1)$

70. $(g^{-1} \circ f^{-1})(-3)$

71. $(f^{-1} \circ f^{-1})(6)$

72. $(g^{-1} \circ g^{-1})(-4)$

73. $(f \circ g)^{-1}$

74. $g^{-1} \circ f^{-1}$

In Exercises 75–78, use the functions $f(x) = x + 4$ and $g(x) = 2x - 5$ to find the specified function.

75. $g^{-1} \circ f^{-1}$

76. $f^{-1} \circ g^{-1}$

77. $(f \circ g)^{-1}$

78. $(g \circ f)^{-1}$

▶ **Model It**

79. *U.S. Households* The number of households f (in thousands) in the United States from 1994 to 2000 are shown in the table. The time (in years) is given by t, with $t = 4$ corresponding to 1994. (Source: U.S. Census Bureau)

Year, t	Households, $f(t)$
4	97,107
5	98,990
6	99,627
7	101,018
8	102,528
9	103,874
10	104,705

(a) Find $f^{-1}(103,874)$.

(b) What does f^{-1} mean in the context of the problem?

(c) Use the *regression* feature of a graphing utility to find a linear model for the data, $y = mx + b$. (Round m and b to two decimal places.)

(d) Algebraically find the inverse function of the linear model in part (c).

(e) Use the inverse function of the linear model you found in part (d) to approximate $f^{-1}(111, 254)$.

80. *Bottled Water Consumption* The per capita consumption f (in gallons) of bottled water in the United States from 1994 through 1999 is shown in the table. The time (in years) is given by t, with $t = 4$ corresponding to 1994. (Source: U.S. Department of Agriculture)

t	$f(t)$
4	10.7
5	11.6
6	12.5
7	13.1
8	16.0
9	18.1

(a) Does f^{-1} exist?

(b) If f^{-1} exists, what does it represent in the context of the problem?

(c) If f^{-1} exists, find $f^{-1}(16.0)$.

81. *Miles Traveled* The total number f (in billions) of miles traveled by motor vehicles in the United States from 1992 through 1999 is shown in the table below. The time (in years) is given by t, with $t = 2$ corresponding to 1992. (Source: U.S. Federal Highway Administration)

Year, t	Miles traveled, $f(t)$
2	2247
3	2296
4	2358
5	2423
6	2486
7	2562
8	2632
9	2691

(a) Does f^{-1} exist?

(b) If f^{-1} exists, what does it mean in the context of the problem?

(c) If f^{-1} exists, find $f^{-1}(2632)$.

(d) If the table was extended to 2000 and if the total number of miles traveled by motor vehicles for that year was 2423 billion, would f^{-1} exist? Explain.

82. *Hourly Wage* Your wage is $8.00 per hour plus $0.75 for each unit produced per hour. So, your hourly wage y in terms of the number of units produced is $y = 8 + 0.75x$.

(a) Find the inverse function.

(b) What does each variable represent in the inverse function?

(c) Determine the number of units produced when your hourly wage is $22.25.

83. *Diesel Mechanics* The function

$$y = 0.03x^2 + 245.50, \qquad 0 < x < 100$$

approximates the exhaust temperature y in degrees Fahrenheit, where x is the percent load for a diesel engine.

(a) Find the inverse function. What does each variable represent in the inverse function?

(b) Use a graphing utility to graph the inverse function.

(c) The exhaust temperature of the engine must not exceed 500 degrees Fahrenheit. What is the percent load interval?

84. *Cost* You need a total of 50 pounds of two types of ground beef costing $1.25 and $1.60 per pound, respectively. A model for the total cost y of the two types of beef is

$$y = 1.25x + 1.60(50 - x)$$

where x is the number of pounds of the less expensive ground beef.

(a) Find the inverse function of the cost function. What does each variable represent in the inverse function?

(b) Use the context of the problem to determine the domain of the inverse function.

(c) Determine the number of pounds of the less expensive ground beef purchased when the total cost is $73.

Synthesis

True or False? **In Exercises 85 and 86, determine whether the statement is true or false. Justify your answer.**

85. If f is an even function, f^{-1} exists.

86. If the inverse function of f exists and the graph of f has a y-intercept, the y-intercept of f is an x-intercept of f^{-1}.

In Exercises 87–90, use the graph of the function f to create a table of values for the given points. Then create a second table that can be used to find f^{-1}, and sketch the graph of f^{-1} if possible.

87.

88.

89.

90.
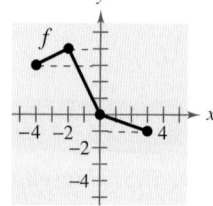

91. *Think About It* The function

$$f(x) = k(2 - x - x^3)$$

has an inverse function, and $f^{-1}(3) = -2$. Find k.

92. *Think About It* The function

$$f(x) = k(x^3 + 3x - 4)$$

has an inverse function, and $f^{-1}(-5) = 2$. Find k.

Review

In Exercises 93–100, solve the equation by any convenient method.

93. $x^2 = 64$

94. $(x - 5)^2 = 8$

95. $4x^2 - 12x + 9 = 0$

96. $9x^2 + 12x + 3 = 0$

97. $x^2 - 6x + 4 = 0$

98. $2x^2 - 4x - 6 = 0$

99. $50 + 5x = 3x^2$

100. $2x^2 + 4x - 9 = 2(x - 1)^2$

101. Find two consecutive positive even integers whose product is 288.

102. *Geometry* A triangular sign has a height that is twice its base. The area of the sign is 10 square feet. Find the base and height of the sign.

1.9 Mathematical Modeling

▶ **Why you should learn it**

You can use functions as models to represent a wide variety of real-life data sets. For instance, in Exercise 63 on page 96, a variation model can be used to model the water temperature of the ocean at various depths.

Introduction

You have already studied some techniques for fitting models to data. For instance, in Section 1.2, you learned how to find the equation of a line that passes through two points. In this section, you will study other techniques for fitting models to data: *direct and inverse variation* and *least squares regression*. The resulting models are either polynomial functions or rational functions. (Rational functions will be studied in Chapter 2.)

Example 1 ▶ A Mathematical Model

The numbers of insured commercial banks *y* (in thousands) in the United States for the years 1995 to 1999 are shown in the table. (Source: Federal Deposit Insurance Corporation)

Year	Insured commercial banks, y
1995	9.94
1996	9.53
1997	9.14
1998	8.77
1999	8.58

A linear model that approximates this data is $y = -0.348t + 11.63$ for $5 \le t \le 9$, where *t* is the year, with $t = 5$ corresponding to 1995. Plot the actual data *and* the model on the same graph. How closely does the model represent the data?

Solution

The actual data is plotted in Figure 1.85, along with the graph of the linear model. From the graph, it appears that the model is a "good fit" for the actual data. You can see how well the model fits by comparing the actual values of *y* with the values of *y* given by the model. The values given by the model are labeled *y*∗ in the table below.

t	5	6	7	8	9
y	9.94	9.53	9.14	8.77	8.58
$y*$	9.89	9.54	9.19	8.85	8.50

U. S. Banks

Insured commercial banks (in thousands)

Year (5 ↔ 1995)

FIGURE 1.85

Note in Example 1 that you could have chosen any two points to find a line that fits the data. However, the given linear model was found using the *regression* feature of a graphing utility and is the line that *best* fits the data. This concept of a "best-fitting" line is discussed later in this section.

Direct Variation

There are two basic types of linear models. The more general model has a y-intercept that is nonzero.

$$y = mx + b, \quad b \neq 0$$

The simpler model

$$y = kx$$

has a y-intercept that is zero. In the simpler model, y is said to **vary directly** as x, or to be **directly proportional** to x.

Direct Variation

The following statements are equivalent.

1. y **varies directly** as x.

2. y is **directly proportional** to x.

3. $y = kx$ for some nonzero constant k.

k is the **constant of variation** or the **constant of proportionality**.

Example 2 ▶ Direct Variation

In Pennsylvania, the state income tax is directly proportional to *gross income*. You are working in Pennsylvania and your state income tax deduction is $42 for a gross monthly income of $1500. Find a mathematical model that gives the Pennsylvania state income tax in terms of gross income.

Solution

Verbal Model: State income tax $= k \cdot$ Gross income

Labels:
State income tax $= y$ (dollars)
Gross income $= x$ (dollars)
Income tax rate $= k$ (percent in decimal form)

Equation: $y = kx$

To solve for k, substitute the given information into the equation $y = kx$, and then solve for k.

$$y = kx \qquad \text{Write direct variation model.}$$

$$42 = k(1500) \qquad \text{Substitute } y = 42 \text{ and } x = 1500.$$

$$0.028 = k \qquad \text{Simplify.}$$

So, the equation (or model) for state income tax in Pennsylvania is

$$y = 0.028x.$$

In other words, Pennsylvania has a state income tax rate of 2.8% of gross income. The graph of this equation is shown in Figure 1.86.

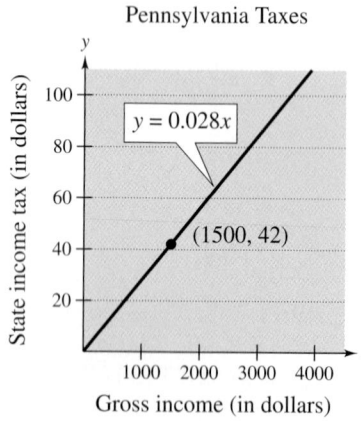

Pennsylvania Taxes

FIGURE 1.86

Direct Variation as an *n*th Power

Another type of direct variation relates one variable to a *power* of another variable. For example, in the formula for the area of a circle

$$A = \pi r^2$$

the area A is directly proportional to the square of the radius r. Note that for this formula, π is the constant of proportionality.

Direct Variation as an *n*th Power

The following statements are equivalent.

1. y **varies directly as the *n*th power** of x.

2. y is **directly proportional to the *n*th power** of x.

3. $y = kx^n$ for some constant k.

Example 3 ▶ Direct Variation as *n*th Power

The distance a ball rolls down an inclined plane is directly proportional to the square of the time it rolls. During the first second, the ball rolls 8 feet. (See Figure 1.87.)

a. Write an equation relating the distance traveled to the time.

b. How far will the ball roll during the first 3 seconds?

Solution

a. Letting d be the distance (in feet) the ball rolls and letting t be the time (in seconds), you have

$$d = kt^2.$$

Now, because $d = 8$ when $t = 1$, you can see that $k = 8$, as follows.

$$d = kt^2$$
$$8 = k(1)^2$$
$$8 = k$$

So, the equation relating distance to time is

$$d = 8t^2.$$

b. When $t = 3$, the distance traveled is $d = 8(3)^2 = 8(9) = 72$ feet.

$t = 0$ sec
$t = 1$ sec
10
20
30
40
50
60
70
$t = 3$ sec

FIGURE **1.87**

In Examples 2 and 3, the direct variations are such that an *increase* in one variable corresponds to an *increase* in the other variable. This is also true in the model $d = \frac{1}{5}F$, $F > 0$, where an increase in F results in an increase in d. You should not, however, assume that this always occurs with direct variation. For example, in the model $y = -3x$, an increase in x results in a *decrease* in y, and yet y is said to vary directly as x.

Inverse Variation

> ### Inverse Variation
>
> The following statements are equivalent.
>
> **1.** y **varies inversely** as x. **2.** y is **inversely proportional** to x.
>
> **3.** $y = \dfrac{k}{x}$ for some constant k.

If x and y are related by an equation of the form $y = k/x^n$, then y varies inversely as the nth power of x (or y is inversely proportional to the nth power of x).

Example 4 ▶ Inverse Variation

A gas law states that the volume of an enclosed gas varies directly as the temperature *and* inversely as the pressure, as shown in Figure 1.88. The pressure of a gas is 0.75 kilogram per square centimeter when the temperature is 294 K and the volume is 8000 cubic centimeters.

a. Write an equation relating pressure, temperature, and volume.

b. Find the pressure when the temperature is 300 K and the volume is 7000 cubic centimeters.

Solution

a. Let V be volume (in cubic centimeters), let P be pressure (in kilograms per square centimeter), and let T be temperature (in Kelvin). Because V varies directly as T and inversely as P,

$$V = \frac{kT}{P}.$$

Now, because $P = 0.75$ when $T = 294$ and $V = 8000$,

$$8000 = \frac{k(294)}{0.75}$$

$$\frac{8000(0.75)}{294} = k$$

$$k = \frac{6000}{294} = \frac{1000}{49}.$$

So, the equation relating pressure, temperature, and volume is

$$V = \frac{1000}{49}\left(\frac{T}{P}\right).$$

b. When $T = 300$ and $V = 7000$, the pressure is

$$P = \frac{1000}{49}\left(\frac{300}{7000}\right) = \frac{300}{343} \approx 0.87 \text{ kilogram per square centimeter.}$$

FIGURE 1.88 *If the temperature is held constant and pressure increases, volume decreases.*

Joint Variation

In Example 4, note that when a direct variation and an inverse variation occur in the same statement, they are coupled with the word "and." To describe two different *direct* variations in the same statement, the word **jointly** is used.

Joint Variation

The following statements are equivalent.

1. z **varies jointly** as x and y.

2. z is **jointly proportional** to x and y.

3. $z = kxy$ for some constant k.

If x, y, and z are related by an equation of the form

$$z = kx^n y^m$$

then z varies jointly as the nth power of x and the mth power of y.

Example 5 ▶ **Joint Variation**

The *simple* interest for a certain savings account is jointly proportional to the time and the principal. After one quarter (3 months), the interest on a principal of $5000 is $43.75.

a. Write an equation relating the interest, principal, and time.

b. Find the interest after three quarters.

Solution

a. Let I = interest (in dollars), P = principal (in dollars), and t = time (in years). Because I is jointly proportional to P and t,

$$I = kPt.$$

For $I = 43.75$, $P = 5000$, and $t = \frac{1}{4}$,

$$43.75 = k(5000)\left(\frac{1}{4}\right)$$

which implies that $k = 4(43.75)/5000 = 0.035$. So, the equation relating interest, principal, and time is

$$I = 0.035Pt$$

which is the familiar equation for simple interest where the constant of proportionality, 0.035, represents an annual interest rate of 3.5%.

b. When $P = \$5000$ and $t = \frac{3}{4}$, the interest is

$$I = (0.035)(5000)\left(\frac{3}{4}\right)$$

$$= \$131.25.$$

Activities

1. Find a mathematical model for "a is jointly proportional to y and z."

   Answer: $a = kyz$

2. Determine the constant of proportionality if x is inversely proportional to the square of y, when $y = 7$ and $x = 3$.

   Answer: 147

3. Write a sentence using variation terminology to describe the formula

   $F = k\dfrac{m_1 m_2}{t^2}.$

   Answer: F is jointly proportional to m_1 and m_2 and inversely proportional to the square of t.

Least Squares Regression and Graphing Utilities

This subsection along with Exercises 71–74 can be omitted if technology is not used in your course.

So far in this text, you have worked with many different types of mathematical models that approximate real-life data. In some instances the model was given, whereas in other instances you were asked to find the model using simple algebraic techniques or a graphing utility.

To find a model that approximates the data most accurately, statisticians use a measure called the **sum of square differences,** which is the sum of the squares of the differences between actual data values and model values. The "best-fitting" linear model is the one with the least sum of square differences. This best-fitting linear model is called the **least squares regression line.** Recall that you can approximate this line visually by plotting the data points and drawing the line that appears to fit best—or you can enter the data points into a calculator or computer and use the calculator's or computer's linear regression program. When you run a linear regression program, the "*r*-value" or **correlation coefficient** gives a measure of how well the model fits the data. The closer the value of $|r|$ is to 1, the better the fit.

Example 6 ▶ Finding a Least Squares Regression Line

The amounts p (in millions of dollars) of total annual prize money awarded at the Indianapolis 500 race from 1993 to 2001 are shown in the table. Construct a scatter plot that represents the data and find a linear model that approximates the data.   (Source: Indy Racing League)

Indianapolis 500

FIGURE **1.89**

Year	Prize money, p
1993	7.68
1994	7.86
1995	8.06
1996	8.11
1997	8.61
1998	8.72
1999	9.05
2000	9.48
2001	9.62

Solution

Let $t = 3$ represent 1993. The scatter plot for the points is shown in Figure 1.89. Using the *regression* feature of a graphing utility, you can determine that the equation of the least squares regression line is

$$p = 0.254t + 6.80.$$

To check this model, compare the actual p-values with the p-values given by the model, which are labeled $p*$ in the table at the left. The correlation coefficient for this model is $r \approx 0.988$, which implies that the model is a good fit.

t	p	$p*$
3	7.68	7.56
4	7.86	7.82
5	8.06	8.07
6	8.11	8.32
7	8.61	8.58
8	8.72	8.83
9	9.05	9.09
10	9.48	9.34
11	9.62	9.59

1.9 Exercises

1. **Employment** The total numbers of employees (in thousands) in the United States from 1992 to 1999 are given by the following ordered pairs.

(1992, 128,105)	(1996, 133,943)
(1993, 129,200)	(1997, 136,297)
(1994, 131,056)	(1998, 137,673)
(1995, 132,304)	(1999, 139,368)

A linear model that approximates this data is $y = 124{,}420 + 1649.6t$, where y represents the number of employees (in thousands) and $t = 2$ represents 1992. Plot the actual data and the model on the same set of coordinate axes. How closely does the model represent the data? (Source: U.S. Bureau of Labor Statistics)

2. **Sports** The winning times (in minutes) in the women's 400-meter freestyle swimming event in the Olympics from 1948 to 2000 are given by the following ordered pairs.

(1948, 5.30)	(1976, 4.16)
(1952, 5.20)	(1980, 4.15)
(1956, 4.91)	(1984, 4.12)
(1960, 4.84)	(1988, 4.06)
(1964, 4.72)	(1992, 4.12)
(1968, 4.53)	(1996, 4.12)
(1972, 4.32)	(2000, 4.10)

A linear model that approximates this data is $y = 5.06 - 0.024t$, where y represents the winning time in minutes and $t = 0$ represents 1950. Plot the actual data and the model on the same set of coordinate axes. How closely does the model represent the data? (Source: *The World Almanac and Book of Facts*)

Think About It In Exercises 3 and 4, use the graph to determine whether y varies directly as some power of x or inversely as some power of x. Explain.

3.

4.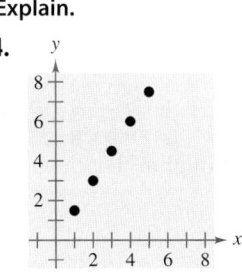

In Exercises 5–8, use the given value of k to complete the table for the direct variation model $y = kx^2$. Plot the points on a rectangular coordinate system.

x	2	4	6	8	10
$y = kx^2$					

5. $k = 1$

6. $k = 2$

7. $k = \frac{1}{2}$

8. $k = \frac{1}{4}$

In Exercises 9–12, use the given value of k to complete the table for the inverse variation model

$$y = \frac{k}{x^2}.$$

Plot the points on a rectangular coordinate system.

x	2	4	6	8	10
$y = \dfrac{k}{x^2}$					

9. $k = 2$

10. $k = 5$

11. $k = 10$

12. $k = 20$

In Exercises 13–16, determine whether the variation model is of the form $y = kx$ or $y = k/x$, and find k.

13.

x	y
5	1
10	$\frac{1}{2}$
15	$\frac{1}{3}$
20	$\frac{1}{4}$
25	$\frac{1}{5}$

14.

x	y
5	2
10	4
15	6
20	8
25	10

15.

x	y
5	-3.5
10	-7
15	-10.5
20	-14
25	-17.5

16.

x	y
5	24
10	12
15	8
20	6
25	$\frac{24}{5}$

Direct Variation In Exercises 17–20, assume that *y* is directly proportional to *x*. Use the given *x*-value and *y*-value to find a linear model that relates *y* and *x*.

x-Value	*y-Value*		*x-Value*	*y-Value*
17. $x = 5$	$y = 12$		**18.** $x = 2$	$y = 14$
19. $x = 10$	$y = 2050$		**20.** $x = 6$	$y = 580$

21. *Simple Interest* The simple interest on an investment is directly proportional to the amount of the investment. By investing $2500 in a certain bond issue, you obtained an interest payment of $87.50 after 1 year. Find a mathematical model that gives the interest *I* for this bond issue after 1 year in terms of the amount invested *P*.

22. *Simple Interest* The simple interest on an investment is directly proportional to the amount of the investment. By investing $5000 in a municipal bond, you obtained an interest payment of $187.50 after 1 year. Find a mathematical model that gives the interest *I* for this municipal bond after 1 year in terms of the amount invested *P*.

23. *Measurement* On a yardstick with scales in inches and centimeters, you notice that 13 inches is approximately the same length as 33 centimeters. Use this information to find a mathematical model that relates centimeters to inches. Then use the model to find the number of centimeters in 10 inches and 20 inches.

24. *Measurement* When buying gasoline, you notice that 14 gallons of gasoline is approximately the same amount of gasoline as 53 liters. Use this information to find a linear model that relates gallons to liters. Use the model to find the number of liters in 5 gallons and 25 gallons.

25. *Taxes* Property tax is based on the assessed value of the property. A house that has an assessed value of $150,000 has a property tax of $5520. Find a mathematical model that gives the amount of property tax *y* in terms of the assessed value *x* of the property. Use the model to find the property tax on a house that has an assessed value of $200,000.

26. *Taxes* State sales tax is based on retail price. An item that sells for $145.99 has a sales tax of $10.22. Find a mathematical model that gives the amount of sales tax *y* in terms of the retail price *x*. Use the model to find the sales tax on a $540.50 purchase.

Hooke's Law In Exercises 27–30, use Hooke's Law for springs, which states that the distance a spring is stretched (or compressed) varies directly as the force on the spring.

27. A force of 265 newtons stretches a spring 0.15 meter (see figure).

(a) How far will a force of 90 newtons stretch the spring?

(b) What force is required to stretch the spring 0.1 meter?

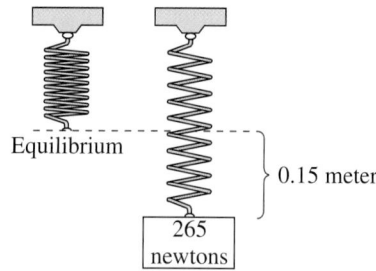

Equilibrium

0.15 meter

265 newtons

28. A force of 220 newtons stretches a spring 0.12 meter. What force is required to stretch the spring 0.16 meter?

29. The coiled spring of a toy supports the weight of a child. The spring is compressed a distance of 1.9 inches by the weight of a 25-pound child. The toy will not work properly if its spring is compressed more than 3 inches. What is the weight of the heaviest child who should be allowed to use the toy?

30. An overhead garage door has two springs, one on each side of the door (see figure). A force of 15 pounds is required to stretch each spring 1 foot. Because of a pulley system, the springs stretch only one-half the distance the door travels. The door moves a total of 8 feet, and the springs are at their natural length when the door is open. Find the combined lifting force applied to the door by the springs when the door is closed.

8 ft

In Exercises 31–40, find a mathematical model for the verbal statement.

31. A varies directly as the square of r.

32. V varies directly as the cube of e.

33. y varies inversely as the square of x.

34. h varies inversely as the square root of s.

35. F varies directly as g and inversely as r^2.

36. z is jointly proportional to the square of x and y^3.

37. Boyle's Law: For a constant temperature, the pressure P of a gas is inversely proportional to the volume V of the gas.

38. Newton's Law of Cooling: The rate of change R of the temperature of an object is proportional to the difference between the temperature T of the object and the temperature T_e of the environment in which the object is placed.

39. Newton's Law of Universal Gravitation: The gravitational attraction F between two objects of masses m_1 and m_2 is proportional to the product of the masses and inversely proportional to the square of the distance r between the objects.

40. Logistic growth: The rate of growth R of a population is jointly proportional to the size S of the population and the difference between S and the maximum population size L that the environment can support.

In Exercises 41–46, write a sentence using the variation terminology of this section to describe the formula.

41. Area of a triangle: $A = \frac{1}{2}bh$

42. Surface area of a sphere: $S = 4\pi r^2$

43. Volume of a sphere: $V = \frac{4}{3}\pi r^3$

44. Volume of a right circular cylinder: $V = \pi r^2 h$

45. Average speed: $r = \dfrac{d}{t}$

46. Free vibrations: $\omega = \sqrt{\dfrac{kg}{W}}$

In Exercises 47–54, find a mathematical model representing the statement. (In each case, determine the constant of proportionality.)

47. A varies directly as r^2. ($A = 9\pi$ when $r = 3$.)

48. y varies inversely as x. ($y = 3$ when $x = 25$.)

49. y is inversely proportional to x. ($y = 7$ when $x = 4$.)

50. z varies jointly as x and y. ($z = 64$ when $x = 4$ and $y = 8$.)

51. F is jointly proportional to r and the third power of s. ($F = 4158$ when $r = 11$ and $s = 3$.)

52. P varies directly as x and inversely as the square of y. $\left(P = \frac{28}{3}\text{ when } x = 42 \text{ and } y = 9.\right)$

53. z varies directly as the square of x and inversely as y. ($z = 6$ when $x = 6$ and $y = 4$.)

54. v varies jointly as p and q and inversely as the square of s. ($v = 1.5$ when $p = 4.1$, $q = 6.3$, and $s = 1.2$.)

Ecology **In Exercises 55 and 56, use the fact that the diameter of the largest particle that can be moved by a stream varies approximately directly as the square of the velocity of the stream.**

55. A stream with a velocity of $\frac{1}{4}$ mile per hour can move coarse sand particles about 0.02 inch in diameter. Approximate the velocity required to carry particles 0.12 inch in diameter.

56. A stream of velocity v can move particles of diameter d or less. By what factor does d increase when the velocity is doubled?

Resistance **In Exercises 57 and 58, use the fact that the resistance of a wire carrying an electrical current is directly proportional to its length and inversely proportional to its cross-sectional area.**

57. If #28 copper wire (which has a diameter of 0.0126 inch) has a resistance of 66.17 ohms per thousand feet, what length of #28 copper wire will produce a resistance of 33.5 ohms?

58. A 14-foot piece of copper wire produces a resistance of 0.05 ohm. Use the constant of proportionality from Exercise 57 to find the diameter of the wire.

59. *Free Fall* Neglecting air resistance, the distance s an object falls varies directly as the square of the duration t of the fall. An object falls a distance of 144 feet in 3 seconds. How far will it fall in 5 seconds?

60. *Spending* The prices of three sizes of pizza at a pizza shop are as follows.

9-inch: $8.78, 12-inch: $11.78, 15-inch: $14.18

You would expect that the price of a certain size of pizza would be directly proportional to its surface area. Is that the case for this pizza shop? If not, which size of pizza is the best buy?

61. *Fluid Flow* The velocity v of a fluid flowing in a conduit is inversely proportional to the cross-sectional area of the conduit. (Assume that the volume of the flow per unit of time is held constant.) Determine the change in the velocity of water flowing from a hose when a person places a finger over the end of the hose to decrease its cross-sectional area by 25%.

62. *Beam Load* The maximum load that can be safely supported by a horizontal beam varies jointly as the width of the beam and the square of its depth, and inversely as the length of the beam. Determine the change in the maximum safe load under the following conditions.

(a) The width and length of the beam are doubled.

(b) The width and depth of the beam are doubled.

(c) All three of the dimensions are doubled.

(d) The depth of the beam is halved.

▶ **Model It**

63. *Data Analysis* An oceanographer took readings of the water temperature C (in degrees Celsius) at depth d (in meters). The data collected is shown in the table.

Depth, d	Temperature, C
1000	4.2°
2000	1.9°
3000	1.4°
4000	1.2°
5000	0.9°

(a) Sketch a scatter plot of the data.

(b) Does it appear that the data can be modeled by the inverse variation model $C = k/d$? If so, find k for each pair of coordinates.

(c) Determine the mean value of k from part (b) to find the inverse variation model $C = k/d$.

(d) Use a graphing utility to plot the data points and the inverse model in part (c).

(e) Use the model to approximate the depth at which the water temperature is 3°C.

---

64. *Data Analysis* An experiment in a physics lab requires a student to measure the compressed length y (in centimeters) of a spring when a force of F pounds is applied. The data is shown in the table.

Force, F	Length, y
0	0
2	1.15
4	2.3
6	3.45
8	4.6
10	5.75
12	6.9

(a) Sketch a scatter plot of the data.

(b) Does it appear that the data can be modeled by Hooke's Law? If so, estimate k. (See Exercises 27–30.)

(c) Use the model in part (b) to approximate the force required to compress the spring 9 centimeters.

65. *Data Analysis* A light probe is located x centimeters from a light source, and the intensity y (in microwatts per square centimeter) of the light is measured. The results are shown in the table.

x	y
30	0.1881
34	0.1543
38	0.1172
42	0.0998
46	0.0775
50	0.0645

A model for the data is $y = 262.76/x^{2.12}$.

(a) Use a graphing utility to plot the data points and the model in the same viewing window.

(b) Use the model to approximate the light intensity 25 centimeters from the light source.

66. *Illumination* The illumination from a light source varies inversely as the square of the distance from the light source. When the distance from a light source is doubled, how does the illumination change? Discuss this model in terms of the data given in Exercise 65. Give a possible explanation of the difference.

In Exercises 67–70, sketch the line that you think best approximates the data in the scatter plot. Then find an equation of the line. To print an enlarged copy of the graph, go to the website *www.mathgraphs.com*.

67.

68.

69.

70.
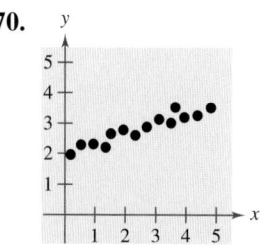

71. Sports The lengths (in feet) of the winning men's discus throws in the Olympics from 1908 to 2000 are listed below. (Source: *The World Almanac and Book of Facts*)

1908	134.2	1948	173.2	1976	221.4
1912	145.0	1952	180.5	1980	218.7
1920	146.6	1956	184.9	1984	218.5
1924	151.4	1960	194.2	1988	225.8
1928	155.2	1964	200.1	1992	213.7
1932	162.4	1968	212.5	1996	227.7
1936	165.6	1972	211.3	2000	227.3

(a) Sketch a scatter plot of the data. Let y represent the length of the winning discus throw (in feet) and let $t = 8$ represent 1908.

(b) Use a straightedge to sketch the best-fitting line through the points and find an equation of the line.

(c) Use the *regression* feature of a graphing utility to find the least squares regression line that fits this data.

(d) Compare the linear model you found in part (b) with the linear model given by the graphing utility in part (c).

(e) Use the models from parts (b) and (c) to estimate the winning men's discus throw in the year 2004.

(f) Use your school's library, the Internet, or some other reference source to analyze the accuracy of the estimate in part (e).

72. Sales The total sales (in millions of dollars) for Barnes & Noble from 1992 to 2000 are listed below. (Source: Barnes & Noble, Inc.)

1992	1086.7	1995	1976.9	1998	3005.6
1993	1337.4	1996	2448.1	1999	3486.0
1994	1622.7	1997	2796.8	2000	4375.8

(a) Sketch a scatter plot of the data. Let y represent the total sales (in millions of dollars) and let $t = 2$ represent 1992.

(b) Use a straightedge to sketch the best-fitting line through the points and find an equation of the line.

(c) Use the *regression* feature of a graphing utility to find the least squares regression line that fits this data.

(d) Compare the linear model you found in part (b) with the linear model given by the graphing utility in part (c).

(e) Use the models from parts (b) and (c) to estimate the sales of Barnes & Noble in 2002.

(f) Use your school's library, the Internet, or some other reference source to analyze the accuracy of the estimate in part (c).

73. Movie Theaters The table shows the annual receipts R (in millions of dollars) for motion picture movie theaters in the United States from 1993 through 2001. (Source: Motion Picture Association of America)

Year	Receipts, R
1993	5154
1994	5396
1995	5494
1996	5912
1997	6366
1998	6949
1999	7448
2000	7661
2001	8413

(a) Use a graphing utility to create a scatter plot of the data. Let $t = 3$ represent 1993.

(b) Use the *regression* feature of a graphing utility to find the equation of the least squares regression line that fits this data.

(c) Use the graphing utility to graph the scatter plot you found in part (a) and the model you found in part (b) in the same viewing window.

(d) Use the model to estimate the annual receipts in 2000 and 2002.

(e) Interpret the meaning of the slope of the linear model in the context of the problem.

74. *Data Analysis*   The table shows the number x (in millions) of households with cable television and the number y (in millions) of daily newspapers in circulation in the United States from 1993 through 1999. (Source: Nielsen Media Research and Editor & Publisher Co.)

Households with cable, x	Daily newspapers, y
58.8	59.8
60.5	59.3
63.0	58.2
64.6	57.0
65.9	56.7
67.4	56.2
68.0	56.0

(a) Use the *regression* feature of a graphing utility to find the equation of the least squares regression line that fits this data.

(b) Use the graphing utility to create a scatter plot of the data. Then graph the model you found in part (a) and the scatter plot in the same viewing window.

(c) Use the model to estimate the number of daily newspapers in circulation if the number of households with cable television is 70 million.

(d) Interpret the meaning of the slope of the linear model in the context of the problem.

Synthesis

True or False?   In Exercises 75 and 76, decide whether the statement is true or false. Justify your answer.

75. If y varies directly as x, then if x increases, y will increase as well.

76. In the equation for kinetic energy, $E = \frac{1}{2}mv^2$, the amount of kinetic energy E is directly proportional to the mass m of an object and the square of its velocity v.

77. *Writing*   A linear mathematical model for predicting prize winnings at a race is based on data for 3 years. Write a paragraph discussing the potential accuracy or inaccuracy of such a model.

78. Discuss how well the data shown in each scatter plot can be approximated by a linear model.

(a)   (b)

(c)   (d)

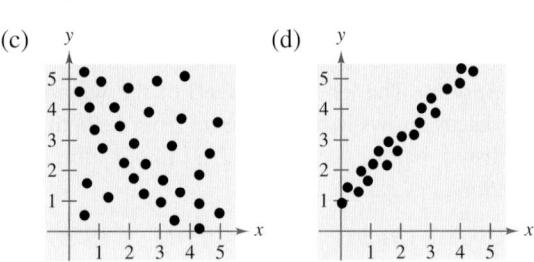

Review

In Exercises 79–82, solve the inequality and graph the solution on the real number line.

79. $(x - 5)^2 \geq 1$

80. $3(x + 1)(x - 3) < 0$

81. $6x^3 - 30x^2 > 0$

82. $x^4(x - 8) \geq 0$

In Exercises 83 and 84, evaluate the function at each value of the independent variable and simplify.

83. $f(x) = \dfrac{x^2 + 5}{x - 3}$

(a) $f(0)$ (b) $f(-3)$ (c) $f(4)$

84. $f(x) = \begin{cases} -x^2 + 10, & x \geq -2 \\ 6x^2 - 1, & x < -2 \end{cases}$

(a) $f(-2)$ (b) $f(1)$ (c) $f(-8)$

Chapter Summary

▶ *What* did you learn?

Review Exercises

1.1 In Exercises 1–4, complete a table of values. Use the solution points to sketch the graph of the equation.

1. $y = 3x - 5$

2. $y = -\frac{1}{2}x + 2$

3. $y = x^2 - 3x$

4. $y = 2x^2 - x - 9$

In Exercises 5–8, find the x- and y-intercepts of the graph of the equation.

5. $y = 2x - 9$

6. $y = |x - 4| - 4$

7. $y = (x + 1)^2$

8. $y = x\sqrt{9 - x^2}$

In Exercises 9–12, use symmetry to sketch the graph of the equation.

9. $y = 5 - x^2$

10. $y = x^3 + 3$

11. $y = \sqrt{x + 5}$

12. $y = 1 - |x|$

In Exercises 13–16, find the center and radius of the circle and sketch its graph.

13. $x^2 + y^2 = 9$

14. $x^2 + y^2 = 4$

15. $(x + 2)^2 + y^2 = 16$

16. $x^2 + (y - 8)^2 = 81$

17. Find the standard form of the equation of the circle for which the endpoints of a diameter are $(0, 0)$ and $(4, -6)$.

18. Find the standard form of the equation of the circle for which the endpoints of a diameter are $(-2, -3)$ and $(4, -10)$.

19. *Number of Stores* The number N of Home Depot stores from 1993 to 2000 can be approximated by the model $y = 9.53t^2 + 162$, where t is the time (in years), with $t = 3$ corresponding to 1995. Sketch a graph of the model, and then use the graph to estimate the year in which the number of stores will be 2000. (Source: Home Depot, Inc.)

20. *Geometry* You have 100 feet of fencing to use for three sides of a rectangular fence, with your house enclosing the fourth side. The area of the enclosure is given by $A = -2x^2 + 100x$. Graph the equation to find the maximum area possible, and how long each side needs to be to obtain that area.

1.2 In Exercises 21–24, find the slope and y-intercept (if possible) of the equation of the line. Sketch the line.

21. $y = 6$

22. $x = -3$

23. $y = 3x + 13$

24. $y = -10x + 9$

In Exercises 25–28, plot the points and find the slope of the line passing through the pair of points.

25. $(3, -4), (-7, 1)$

26. $(-1, 8), (6, 5)$

27. $(-4.5, 6), (2.1, 3)$

28. $(-3, 2), (8, 2)$

In Exercises 29–32, find an equation of the line that passes through the points.

29. $(0, 0), (0, 10)$

30. $(2, 5), (-2, -1)$

31. $(-1, 4), (2, 0)$

32. $(11, -2), (6, -1)$

In Exercises 33–36, find an equation of the line that passes through the given point and has the specified slope. Sketch the line.

Point	Slope	Point	Slope
33. $(0, -5)$	$m = \frac{3}{2}$	**34.** $(-2, 6)$	$m = 0$
35. $(10, -3)$	$m = -\frac{1}{2}$	**36.** $(-8, 5)$	Undefined

In Exercises 37–40, write an equation of the line through the point (a) parallel to the given line and (b) perpendicular to the given line.

Point	Line
37. $(3, -2)$	$5x - 4y = 8$
38. $(-8, 3)$	$2x + 3y = 5$
39. $(4, -1)$	$x = 3$
40. $(-2, 5)$	$y = -4$

Rate of Change In Exercises 41 and 42, you are given the dollar value of a product in the year 2004 *and* the rate at which the value of the item is expected to change during the next 5 years. Write a linear equation that gives the dollar value V of the product in terms of the year t. (Let $t = 4$ represent 2004.)

2004 Value	Rate
41. $12,500	$850 increase per year
42. $72.95	$5.15 increase per year

1.3 In Exercises 43–46, determine whether the equation represents y as a function of x.

43. $16x - y^4 = 0$

44. $y = \sqrt{1 - x}$

45. $2x - y - 3 = 0$

46. $|y| = x + 2$

In Exercises 47 and 48, evaluate the function as indicated. Simplify your answers.

47. $f(x) = x^2 + 1$

(a) $f(2)$ (b) $f(-4)$ (c) $f(t^2)$ (d) $-f(x+1)$

48. $g(x) = \begin{cases} 2x + 1, & x \le -1 \\ x^2 + 2, & x > -1 \end{cases}$

(a) $g(-2)$ (b) $g(-1)$ (c) $g(0)$ (d) $g(2)$

In Exercises 49–52, determine the domain of the function. Verify your result with a graph.

49. $f(x) = \sqrt{25 - x^2}$

50. $f(x) = 3x + 4$

51. $h(x) = \dfrac{x}{x^2 - x - 6}$

52. $h(t) = |t + 1|$

53. *Velocity* The velocity of a ball thrown vertically upward from ground level is $v(t) = -32t + 48$, where t is the time in seconds and v is the velocity in feet per second.

(a) Find the velocity when $t = 1$.

(b) Find the time when the ball reaches its maximum height. [*Hint:* Find the time when $v(t) = 0$.]

(c) Find the velocity when $t = 2$.

54. *Mixture Problem* From a full 50-liter container of a 40% concentration of acid, x liters is removed and replaced with 100% acid.

(a) Write the amount of acid in the final mixture as a function of x.

(b) Determine the domain and range of the function.

(c) Determine x if the final mixture is 50% acid.

1.4 In Exercises 55–58, use the Vertical Line Test to determine whether y is a function of x. To print an enlarged copy of the graph, go to the website *www.mathgraphs.com*.

55. $y = (x - 3)^2$

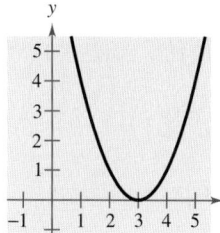

56. $y = -\frac{3}{5}x^3 - 2x + 1$

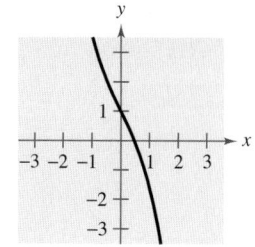

57. $x - 4 = y^2$

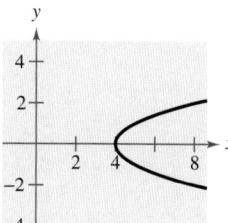

58. $x = -|4 - y|$

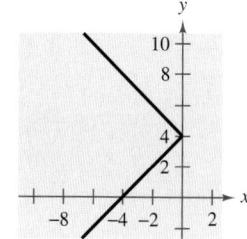

In Exercises 59–62, find the zeros of the function.

59. $f(x) = 3x^2 - 16x + 21$

60. $f(x) = 5x^2 + 4x - 1$

61. $f(x) = \dfrac{8x + 3}{11 - x}$

62. $f(x) = x^3 - x^2 - 25x + 25$

In Exercises 63 and 64, determine the intervals over which the function is increasing, decreasing, or constant.

63. $f(x) = |x| + |x + 1|$ **64.** $f(x) = (x^2 - 4)^2$

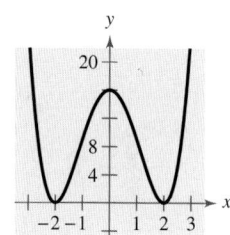

In Exercises 65–68, determine whether the function is even, odd, or neither.

65. $f(x) = x^5 + 4x - 7$

66. $f(x) = x^4 - 20x^2$

67. $f(x) = 2x\sqrt{x^2 + 3}$

68. $f(x) = \sqrt[5]{6x^2}$

1.5 In Exercises 69 and 70, write the linear function f so that it has the indicated function values. Sketch a graph of the function.

69. $f(2) = -6$, $f(-1) = 3$

70. $f(0) = -5$, $f(4) = -8$

In Exercises 71–80, graph the function.

71. $f(x) = 3 - x^2$ **72.** $h(x) = x^3 - 2$

73. $f(x) = -\sqrt{x}$ **74.** $f(x) = \sqrt{x + 1}$

75. $g(x) = \dfrac{3}{x}$

76. $g(x) = \dfrac{1}{x + 5}$

77. $f(x) = [\![x]\!] - 2$

78. $g(x) = [\![x + 4]\!]$

79. $f(x) = \begin{cases} 5x - 3, & x \geq -1 \\ -4x + 5, & x < -1 \end{cases}$

80. $f(x) = \begin{cases} x^2 - 2, & x < -2 \\ 5, & -2 \leq x \leq 0 \\ 8x - 5, & x > 0 \end{cases}$

In Exercises 81 and 82, identify the transformed common function shown in the graph.

81.

82.

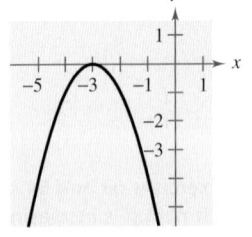

1.6 In Exercises 83–90, identify the transformation of the graph of f and sketch the graph of h.

83. $f(x) = x^2,$ $h(x) = x^2 - 9$

84. $f(x) = \sqrt{x},$ $h(x) = \sqrt{x - 7}$

85. $f(x) = |x|,$ $h(x) = |x + 3| - 5$

86. $f(x) = x^2,$ $h(x) = -(x + 3)^2 + 1$

87. $f(x) = \sqrt{x},$ $h(x) = -\sqrt{x + 1} + 9$

88. $f(x) = x^3,$ $h(x) = -\frac{1}{3}x^3$

89. $f(x) = [\![x]\!],$ $h(x) = -[\![x]\!] + 6$

90. $f(x) = [\![x]\!],$ $h(x) = 5[\![x - 9]\!]$

1.7 In Exercises 91 and 92, find (a) $(f + g)(x)$, (b) $(f - g)(x)$, (c) $(fg)(x)$, and (d) $(f/g)(x)$. What is the domain of f/g?

91. $f(x) = x^2 + 3,\ g(x) = 2x - 1$

92. $f(x) = x^2 - 4,\ g(x) = \sqrt{3 - x}$

In Exercises 93 and 94, find (a) $f \circ g$ and (b) $g \circ f$. Find the domain of each function and each composite function.

93. $f(x) = \frac{1}{3}x - 3,\ g(x) = 3x + 1$

94. $f(x) = x^3 - 4,\ g(x) = \sqrt[3]{x + 7}$

In Exercises 95 and 96, find two functions f and g such that $(f \circ g)(x) = h(x)$. (There is more than one correct answer.)

95. $h(x) = (6x - 5)^3$ **96.** $h(x) = \sqrt[3]{x + 2}$

Data Analysis In Exercises 97 and 98, use the table, which shows the total values (in billions of dollars) of U.S. imports from Mexico and Canada for the years 1995 through 1999. The variables y_1 and y_2 represent the total values of imports from Mexico and Canada, respectively. (Source: U.S. Census Bureau)

Year	y_1	y_2
1995	62.1	144.4
1996	74.3	155.9
1997	85.9	168.2
1998	94.6	173.3
1999	109.7	198.3

97. Use a graphing utility to find quadratic models for y_1 and y_2. Let $t = 5$ represent 1995.

98. Use a graphing utility to graph y_1, y_2, and $y_1 + y_2$ in the same viewing window. Use the model to estimate the total value of U.S. imports from Canada and Mexico in 2005.

1.8 In Exercises 99 and 100, find the inverse of f informally. Verify that $f(f^{-1}(x)) = x = f^{-1}(f(x))$.

99. $f(x) = x - 7$ **100.** $f(x) = x + 5$

In Exercises 101 and 102, determine whether the function has an inverse function.

101.

102.

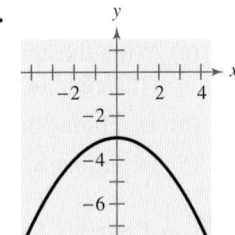

In Exercises 103–106, use a graphing utility to graph the function. Use the Horizontal Line Test to determine if the function is one-to-one and so has an inverse function.

103. $f(x) = 4 - \dfrac{1}{3}x$ **104.** $f(x) = (x - 1)^2$

105. $h(t) = \dfrac{2}{t - 3}$ **106.** $g(x) = \sqrt{x + 6}$

In Exercises 107–110, (a) find f^{-1}, (b) sketch the graphs of f and f^{-1} on the same coordinate system, and (c) verify that $f^{-1}(f(x)) = x = f(f^{-1}(x))$.

107. $f(x) = \frac{1}{2}x - 3$ **108.** $f(x) = 5x - 7$

109. $f(x) = \sqrt{x+1}$ **110.** $f(x) = x^3 + 2$

In Exercises 111 and 112, restrict the domain of the function f to an interval over which the function is increasing and determine f^{-1} over that interval.

111. $f(x) = 2(x-4)^2$ **112.** $f(x) = |x-2|$

1.9 **113.** *Data Analysis*   The federal minimum wage rates R (in dollars) in the United States for selected years from 1955 through 2000 are shown in the table. A linear model that approximates this data is

$$R = 0.099t - 0.08$$

where t represents the year, with $t = 5$ corresponding to 1955. (Source: U.S. Department of Labor)

Year	R	Year	R
1955	0.75	1980	3.10
1960	1.00	1985	3.35
1965	1.25	1990	3.80
1970	1.60	1995	4.25
1975	2.10	2000	5.15

(a) Plot the actual data and the model on the same set of coordinate axes.

(b) How closely does the model represent the data?

114. *Measurement*   You notice a billboard indicating that it is 2.5 miles or 4 kilometers to the next restaurant of a national fast-food chain. Use this information to find a linear model that relates miles to kilometers. Use the model to find the numbers of kilometers in 2 miles and 10 miles.

115. *Demand*   A company has found that the daily demand x for its product is inversely proportional to the price p. When the price is $5, the demand is 800 units. The price increases to $6. Approximate the demand.

116. *Predator-Prey*   The number N of prey t months after a natural predator is introduced into a test area is inversely proportional to $t + 1$. If $N = 500$ when $t = 0$, find N when $t = 4$.

117. *Frictional Force*   The frictional force F between the tires and the road required to keep a car on a curved section of a highway is directly proportional to the square of the speed s of the car. If the speed of the car is doubled, the force will change by what factor?

118. *Recording Media*   The table shows the numbers y (in millions) of CDs shipped in the United States during the years 1990 through 1999. (Source: Recording Industry Association of America)

Year	CDs shipped, y
1990	286.5
1991	333.3
1992	407.5
1993	495.4
1994	662.1
1995	722.9
1996	778.9
1997	753.1
1998	847.0
1999	938.9

(a) Use the *regression* feature of a graphing utility to find the equation of the least squares regression line that fits the data.

(b) Use the model to estimate the number of CDs shipped during the year 2005.

(c) Interpret the meaning of the slope of the linear model in the context of the problem.

Synthesis

True or False?   In Exercises 119 and 120, determine whether the statement is true or false. Justify your answer.

119. Relative to the graph of $f(x) = \sqrt{x}$, the function $h(x) = -\sqrt{x+9} - 13$ is shifted nine units to the left and 13 units downward, then reflected in the x-axis.

120. If f and g are two inverse functions, then the domain of g is equal to the range of f.

121. *Writing*   Explain the difference between the Vertical Line Test and the Horizontal Line Test.

122. If y is directly proportional to x for a particular linear model, what is the y-intercept of the graph of the model?

Chapter Test

Take this test as you would take a test in class. When you are finished, check your work against the answers given in the back of the book.

In Exercises 1–3, use intercepts and symmetry to sketch the graph of the equation.

1. $y = 3 - 5x$ **2.** $y = 4 - |x|$ **3.** $y = x^2 - 1$

4. Write the standard form of the equation of the circle shown at the left.

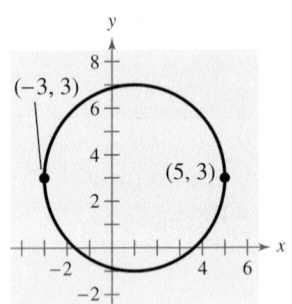

FIGURE FOR **4**

In Exercises 5 and 6, find an equation of the line passing through the given points.

5. $(2, -3), (-4, 9)$ **6.** $(3, 0.8), (7, -6)$

7. Find an equation of the line that passes through the point $(3, 8)$ and is (a) parallel to and (b) perpendicular to the line $-4x + 7y = -5$.

8. Evaluate $f(x) = \dfrac{\sqrt{x + 9}}{x^2 - 81}$ at each value: (a) $f(7)$ (b) $f(-5)$ (c) $f(x - 9)$.

9. Determine the domain of $f(x) = \sqrt{100 - x^2}$.

In Exercises 10–12, (a) find the zeros of the function, (b) use a graphing utility to graph the function, (c) approximate the intervals over which the function is increasing, decreasing, or constant, and (d) determine whether the function is even, odd, or neither.

10. $f(x) = 2x^6 + 5x^4 - x^2$ **11.** $f(x) = 4x\sqrt{3 - x}$ **12.** $f(x) = |x + 5|$

13. Sketch the graph of $f(x) = \begin{cases} 3x + 7, & x \le -3 \\ 4x^2 - 1, & x > -3 \end{cases}$.

In Exercises 14 and 15, identify the common function in the transformation. Then sketch a graph of the function.

14. $h(x) = -[\![x]\!]$ **15.** $h(x) = -\sqrt{x + 5} + 8$

In Exercises 16 and 17, find (a) $(f + g)(x)$, (b) $(f - g)(x)$, (c) $(fg)(x)$, (d) $(f/g)(x)$, (e) $(f \circ g)(x)$, and (f) $(g \circ f)(x)$.

16. $f(x) = 3x^2 - 7, \quad g(x) = -x^2 - 4x + 5$ **17.** $f(x) = \dfrac{1}{x}, \quad g(x) = 2\sqrt{x}$

In Exercises 18–20, determine whether or not the function has an inverse function, and if so, find the inverse function.

18. $f(x) = x^3 + 8$ **19.** $f(x) = |x^2 - 3| + 6$ **20.** $f(x) = 3x\sqrt{x}$

In Exercises 21–23, find a mathematical model representing the statement. (In each case, determine the constant of proportionality.)

21. v varies directly as the square root of s. ($v = 24$ when $s = 16$.)

22. A varies jointly as x and y. ($A = 500$ when $x = 15$ and $y = 8$.)

23. b varies inversely as a. ($b = 32$ when $a = 1.5$.)

The *Interactive* CD-ROM and *Internet* versions of this text offer Chapter Pre-Tests and Chapter Post-Tests, both of which have randomly generated exercises with diagnostic capabilities.

Proofs in Mathematics

Conditional Statements

Many theorems are written in the **if-then form** "if p, then q," which is denoted by

$$p \rightarrow q \qquad \text{Conditional statement}$$

where p is the **hypothesis** and q is the **conclusion.** Here are some other ways to express the conditional statement $p \rightarrow q$.

p implies q. p, only if q. p is sufficient for q.

Conditional statements can be either true or false. The conditional statement $p \rightarrow q$ is false only when p is true and q is false. To show that a conditional statement is true, you must prove that the conclusion follows for all cases that fulfill the hypothesis. To show that a conditional statement is false, you need only to describe a single **counterexample** that shows that the statement is not always true.

For instance, $x = -4$ is a counterexample that shows that the following statement is false.

If $x^2 = 16$, then $x = 4$.

The hypothesis "$x^2 = 16$" is true because $(-4)^2 = 16$. However, the conclusion "$x = 4$" is false. This implies that the given conditional statement is false.

For the conditional statement $p \rightarrow q$, there are three important associated conditional statements.

1. The **converse** of $p \rightarrow q$: $q \rightarrow p$
2. The **inverse** of $p \rightarrow q$: $\sim p \rightarrow \sim q$
3. The **contrapositive** of $p \rightarrow q$: $\sim q \rightarrow \sim p$

The symbol $\sim$ means the **negation** of a statement. For instance, the negation of "The engine is running" is "The engine is not running."

> **Example** ▶ **Writing the Converse, Inverse, and Contrapositive**

Write the converse, inverse, and contrapositive of the conditional statement "If I get a B on my test, then I will pass the course."

Solution

a. *Converse:* If I pass the course, then I got a B on my test.

b. *Inverse:* If I do not get a B on my test, then I will not pass the course.

c. *Contrapositive:* If I do not pass the course, then I did not get a B on my test.

In the example above, notice that neither the converse nor the inverse is logically equivalent to the original conditional statement. On the other hand, the contrapositive *is* logically equivalent to the original conditional statement.

1. As a salesperson, you receive a monthly salary of $2000, plus a commission of 7% of sales. You are offered a new job at $2300 per month, plus a commission of 5% of sales.

   (a) Write a linear equation for your current monthly wage W_1 in terms of your monthly sales S.

   (b) Write a linear equation for the monthly wage W_2 of your new job offer in terms of the monthly sales S.

   (c) Use a graphing utility to graph both equations in the same viewing window. Find the point of intersection. What does it signify?

   (d) You think you can sell $20,000 per month. Should you change jobs? Explain.

2. For the numbers 2 through 9 on a telephone keypad (see figure), create two relations: one mapping numbers onto letters, and the other mapping letters onto numbers. Are both relations functions? Explain.

3. What can be said about the sum and difference of each of the following?

   (a) Two even functions

   (b) Two odd functions

   (c) An odd function and an even function

4. The two functions

   $f(x) = x$ and $g(x) = -x$

   are their own inverse functions. Graph each function and explain why this is true. Graph other linear functions that are their own inverse functions. Find a general formula for a family of linear functions that are their own inverse functions.

5. Prove that a function of the following form is even.

   $$y = a_{2n}x^{2n} + a_{2n-2}x^{2n-2} + \cdots + a_2x^2 + a_0$$

6. A miniature golf professional is trying to make a hole-in-one on the miniature golf green shown. A coordinate plane is placed over the golf green. The golf ball is at the point $(2.5, 2)$ and the hole is at the point $(9.5, 2)$. The professional wants to bank the ball off the side wall of the green at the point (x, y). Find the coordinates of the point (x, y). Then write an equation for the path of the ball.

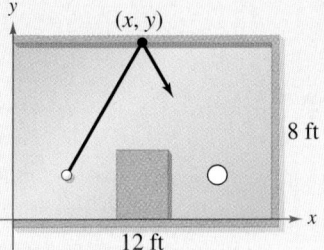

7. At 2:00 P.M. on April 11, 1912, the *Titanic* left Cobh, Ireland, on her voyage to New York City. At 11:40 P.M. on April 14, the *Titanic* struck an iceberg and sank, having covered only about 2100 miles of the approximately 3400-mile trip.

   (a) What was the total length of the *Titanic's* voyage in hours?

   (b) What was the *Titanic's* average speed in miles per hour?

   (c) Write a function relating the *Titanic's* distance from New York City and the number of hours traveled. Find the domain and range of the function.

   (d) Graph the function from part (c).

8. Consider the functions $f(x) = 4x$ and $g(x) = x + 6$.

   (a) Find $(f \circ g)(x)$.

   (b) Find $(f \circ g)^{-1}(x)$.

   (c) Find $f^{-1}(x)$ and $g^{-1}(x)$.

   (d) Find $(g^{-1} \circ f^{-1})(x)$ and compare the result with that of part (b).

   (e) Repeat parts (a) through (d) for $f(x) = x^3 + 1$ and $g(x) = 2x$.

   (f) Write two one-to-one functions f and g, and repeat parts (a) through (d) for these functions.

   (g) Make a conjecture about $(f \circ g)^{-1}(x)$ and $(g^{-1} \circ f^{-1})(x)$.

9. You are in a boat 2 miles from the nearest point on the coast. You are to travel to a point Q, 3 miles down the coast and 1 mile inland (see figure). You can row at 2 miles per hour and walk at 4 miles per hour.

(a) Write the total time T of the trip as a function of x.

(b) Determine the domain of the function.

(c) Use a graphing utility to graph the function. Be sure to choose an appropriate viewing window.

(d) Use the *zoom* and *trace* features to find the value of x that minimizes T.

(e) Write a brief paragraph interpreting these values.

10. The Heaviside function $H(x)$ is widely used in engineering applications. (See figure.) To print an enlarged copy of the graph, go to the website *www.mathgraphs.com*.

$$H(x) = \begin{cases} 1, & x \geq 0 \\ 0, & x < 0 \end{cases}$$

Sketch the graph of each function by hand.

(a) $H(x) - 2$ (b) $H(x - 2)$ (c) $-H(x)$

(d) $H(-x)$ (e) $\frac{1}{2}H(x)$ (f) $-H(x - 2) + 2$

11. Let $f(x) = \dfrac{1}{1 - x}$.

(a) What are the domain and range of f?

(b) Find $f(f(x))$. What is the domain of this function?

(c) Find $f(f(f(x)))$. Is the graph a line? Why or why not?

12. Show that the Associative Property holds for compositions of functions—that is,

$$(f \circ (g \circ h))(x) = ((f \circ g) \circ h)(x).$$

13. Consider the graph of the function f shown in the figure. Use this graph to sketch the graph of each function. To print an enlarged copy of the graph, go to the website *www.mathgraphs.com*.

(a) $f(x + 1)$ (b) $f(x) + 1$ (c) $2f(x)$ (d) $f(-x)$

(e) $-f(x)$ (f) $|f(x)|$ (g) $f(|x|)$

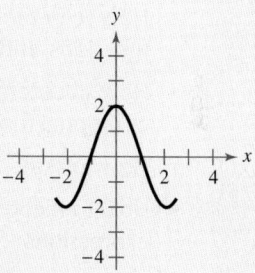

14. Use the graphs of f and f^{-1} to complete each table of function values.

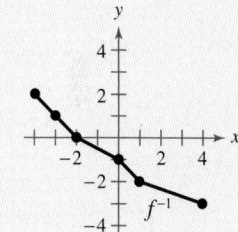

(a)

x	$f(f^{-1}(x))$
-4	
-2	
0	
4	

(b)

x	$(f + f^{-1})(x)$
-3	
-2	
0	
1	

(c)

x	$(f \cdot f^{-1})(x)$
-3	
-2	
0	
1	

(d)

x	$|f^{-1}(x)|$
-4	
-3	
0	
4	

How to study Chapter 2

▶ **What you should learn**

In this chapter you will learn the following skills and concepts:

- How to sketch and analyze graphs of polynomial functions
- How to use long division and synthetic division to divide polynomials by other polynomials
- How to perform operations with complex numbers
- How to determine the numbers of rational and real zeros of polynomial functions, and find the zeros
- How to determine the domains of rational functions and find asymptotes of rational functions
- How to sketch the graphs of rational functions
- How to recognize and find partial fraction decompositions of rational expressions

▶ **Important Vocabulary**

As you encounter each new vocabulary term in this chapter, add the term and its definition to your notebook glossary.

Polynomial function (p. 110)
Parabola (p. 110)
Vertex (of a parabola) (p. 111)
Standard form of a quadratic function (p. 113)
Continuous (p. 121)
Leading Coefficient Test (p. 123)
Repeated zero (p. 125)
Test intervals (p. 126)
Intermediate Value Theorem (p. 128)
Improper (rational expression) (p. 135)
Proper (rational expression) (p. 135)
Remainder Theorem (p. 138)
Factor Theorem (p. 138)
Complex number (p. 143)

Imaginary number (p. 143)
Complex conjugates (p. 146)
Fundamental Theorem of Algebra (p. 150)
Linear Factorization Theorem (p. 150)
Rational Zero Test (p. 151)
Descartes's Rule of Signs (p. 157)
Upper bound (p. 158)
Lower bound (p. 158)
Rational function (p. 165)
Vertical asymptote (p. 166)
Horizontal asymptote (p. 166)
Slant (or oblique) asymptote (p. 171)
Partial fraction (p. 178)
Basic equation (p. 179)

Study Tools

Learning objectives in each section
Chapter Summary (p. 186)
Review Exercises (pp. 187–190)
Chapter Test (p. 191)

Additional Resources

Study and Solutions Guide
Interactive Precalculus
Videotapes/DVD for Chapter 2
Precalculus Website
Student Success Organizer

David Pu'u/Corbis

2

Polynomial and Rational Functions

2.1   Quadratic Functions

▶ **What you should learn**

- How to analyze graphs of quadratic functions
- How to write quadratic functions in standard form and use the results to sketch graphs of functions
- How to use quadratic functions to model and solve real-life problems

▶ **Why you should learn it**

Quadratic functions can be used to model data to analyze consumer behavior. For instance, in Exercise 86 on page 119, you will use a quadratic function to model the number of hairdressers and cosmetologists in the United States.

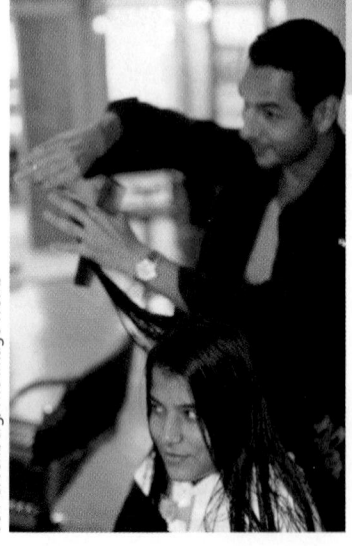

Jeff Greenberg/The Image Works

The Graph of a Quadratic Function

In this and the next section you will study the graphs of polynomial functions. In Section 1.5, you were introduced to the following basic functions.

$$f(x) = ax + b \qquad \text{Linear function}$$

$$f(x) = c \qquad \text{Constant function}$$

$$f(x) = x^2 \qquad \text{Squaring function}$$

These functions are examples of **polynomial functions.**

Definition of Polynomial Function

Let n be a nonnegative integer and let $a_n, a_{n-1}, \ldots, a_2, a_1, a_0$ be real numbers with $a_n \neq 0$. The function

$$f(x) = a_n x^n + a_{n-1} x^{n-1} + \cdots + a_2 x^2 + a_1 x + a_0$$

is called a **polynomial function of x with degree n.**

Polynomial functions are classified by degree. For instance, a constant function has degree 0 and a linear function has degree 1. In this section you will study second-degree polynomial functions, which are called **quadratic functions.**

For instance, each of the following functions is a quadratic function.

$$f(x) = x^2 + 6x + 2$$

$$g(x) = 2(x + 1)^2 - 3$$

$$h(x) = 9 + \tfrac{1}{4}x^2$$

$$k(x) = -3x^2 + 4$$

$$m(x) = (x - 2)(x + 1)$$

Note that the squaring function is a simple quadratic function that has degree 2.

Definition of Quadratic Function

Let a, b, and c be real numbers with $a \neq 0$. The function

$$f(x) = ax^2 + bx + c \qquad \text{Quadratic function}$$

is called a **quadratic function.**

The graph of a quadratic function is a special type of "U"-shaped curve called a **parabola.** Parabolas occur in many real-life applications—especially those involving reflective properties of satellite dishes and flashlight reflectors. You will study these properties in Section 10.2.

All parabolas are symmetric with respect to a line called the **axis of symmetry,** or simply the **axis** of the parabola. The point where the axis intersects the parabola is the **vertex** of the parabola, as shown in Figure 2.1. If the leading coefficient is positive, the graph of $f(x) = ax^2 + bx + c$ is a parabola that opens upward. If the leading coefficient is negative, the graph of $f(x) = ax^2 + bx + c$ is a parabola that opens downward.

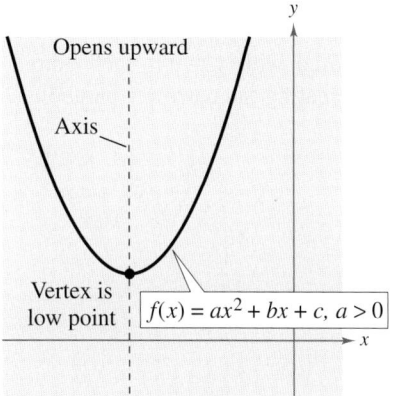

Leading coefficient is positive.   *Leading coefficient is negative.*

FIGURE 2.1

The simplest type of quadratic function is

$$f(x) = ax^2.$$

Its graph is a parabola whose vertex is $(0, 0)$. If $a > 0$, the vertex is the point with the *minimum* y-value on the graph, and if $a < 0$, the vertex is the point with the *maximum* y-value on the graph, as shown in Figure 2.2.

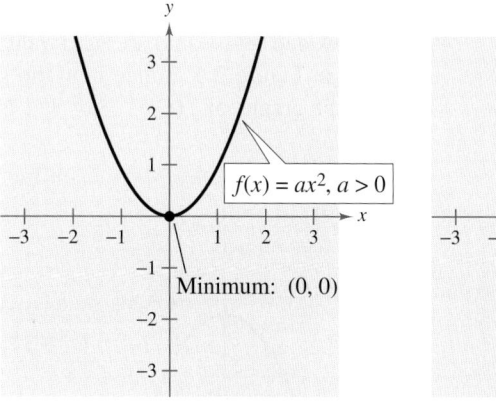

Leading coefficient is positive.   *Leading coefficient is negative.*

FIGURE 2.2

When sketching the graph of $f(x) = ax^2$, it is helpful to use the graph of $y = x^2$ as a reference, as discussed in Section 1.6.

◀ **Exploration** ▶

Graph $y = ax^2$ for $a = -2, -1,$ $-0.5, 0.5, 1,$ and 2. How does changing the value of a affect the graph?

Graph $y = (x - h)^2$ for $h = -4,$ $-2, 2,$ and 4. How does changing the value of h affect the graph?

Graph $y = x^2 + k$ for $k = -4,$ $-2, 2,$ and 4. How does changing the value of k affect the graph?

Example 1 ▶   **Sketching Graphs of Quadratic Functions**

a. Compare the graphs of $y = x^2$ and $f(x) = \frac{1}{3}x^2$.

b. Compare the graphs of $y = x^2$ and $g(x) = 2x^2$.

Solution

a. Compared with $y = x^2$, each output of $f(x) = \frac{1}{3}x^2$ "shrinks" by a factor of $\frac{1}{3}$, creating the broader parabola shown in Figure 2.3.

b. Compared with $y = x^2$, each output of $g(x) = 2x^2$ "stretches" by a factor of 2, creating the narrower parabola shown in Figure 2.4.

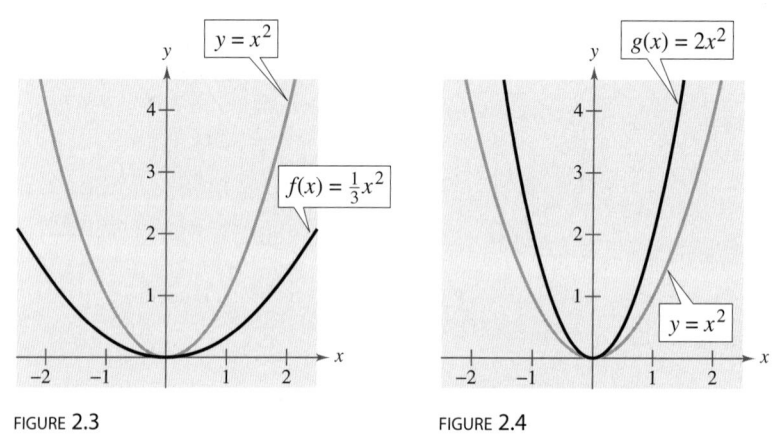

FIGURE **2.3**   FIGURE **2.4**

In Example 1, note that the coefficient a determines how widely the parabola given by $f(x) = ax^2$ opens. If $|a|$ is small, the parabola opens more widely than if $|a|$ is large.

Recall from Section 1.6 that the graphs of $y = f(x \pm c)$, $y = f(x) \pm c$, $y = f(-x)$, and $y = -f(x)$ are rigid transformations of the graph of $y = f(x)$. For instance, in Figure 2.5, notice how the graph of $y = x^2$ can be transformed to produce the graphs of $f(x) = -x^2 + 1$ and $g(x) = (x + 2)^2 - 3$.

 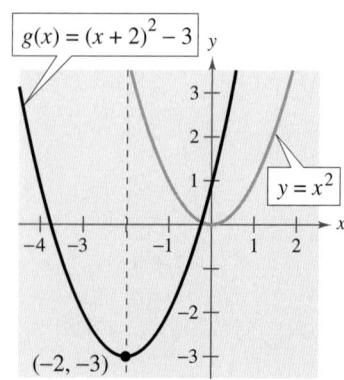

FIGURE **2.5**

The Standard Form of a Quadratic Function

The **standard form** of a quadratic function is

$$f(x) = a(x - h)^2 + k.$$

This form is especially convenient for sketching a parabola because it identifies the vertex of the parabola.

STUDY TIP

The standard form of a quadratic function identifies four basic transformations of the graph of $y = x^2$.

a. The factor $|a|$ produces a vertical stretch or shrink.

b. If $a < 0$, the graph is reflected in the x-axis.

c. The factor $(x - h)^2$ represents a horizontal shift of h units.

d. The term k represents a vertical shift of k units.

Standard Form of a Quadratic Function

The quadratic function

$$f(x) = a(x - h)^2 + k, \qquad a \neq 0$$

is in **standard form.** The graph of f is a parabola whose axis is the vertical line $x = h$ and whose vertex is the point (h, k). If $a > 0$, the parabola opens upward, and if $a < 0$, the parabola opens downward.

To graph a parabola, it is helpful to begin by writing the quadratic function in standard form using the process of completing the square, as illustrated in Example 2.

To prepare for rewriting a function $f(x)$ in standard form, review the process of completing the square for an algebraic expression, paying special attention to problems in which $a \neq 1$.

Example 2 ▶ Graphing a Parabola in Standard Form

Sketch the graph of

$$f(x) = 2x^2 + 8x + 7$$

and identify the vertex and the axis of the parabola.

Solution

Begin by writing the quadratic function in standard form. Notice that the first step in completing the square is to factor out any coefficient of x^2 that is not 1.

$f(x) = 2x^2 + 8x + 7$	Write original function.
$= 2(x^2 + 4x) + 7$	Factor 2 out of x-terms.
$= 2(x^2 + 4x + 4 - 4) + 7$	Add and subtract 4 within parentheses.

$$\underbrace{\qquad}_{(4/2)^2}$$

$= 2(x^2 + 4x + 4) - 2(4) + 7$	Regroup terms.
$= 2(x^2 + 4x + 4) - 8 + 7$	Simplify.
$= 2(x + 2)^2 - 1$	Write in standard form.

From this form, you can see that the graph of f is a parabola that opens upward and has its vertex at $(-2, -1)$. This corresponds to a left shift of two units and a downward shift of one unit relative to the graph of $y = 2x^2$, as shown in Figure 2.6. In the figure, you can see that the axis of the parabola is the vertical line through the vertex, $x = -2$.

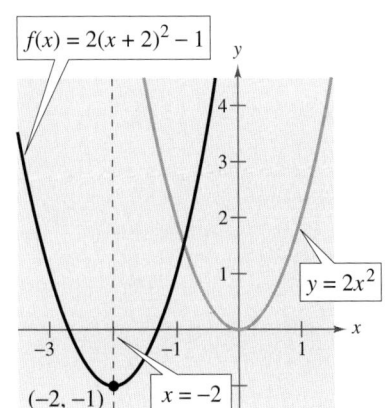

$f(x) = 2(x + 2)^2 - 1$

$y = 2x^2$

$x = -2$

$(-2, -1)$

FIGURE **2.6**

The icon identifies examples and concepts related to features of the Learning Tools CD-ROM and the *Interactive* and *Internet* versions of this text. For more details see the chart on pages *xxi-xxv*.

To find the x-intercepts of the graph of $f(x) = ax^2 + bx + c$, you must solve the equation $ax^2 + bx + c = 0$. If $ax^2 + bx + c$ does not factor, you can use the Quadratic Formula to find the x-intercepts. Remember, however, that a parabola may have no x-intercepts.

The *Interactive* CD-ROM and *Internet* versions of this text offer a Try It for each example in the text.

Example 3 ▶ Finding the Vertex and x-Intercepts of a Parabola

Sketch the graph of $f(x) = -x^2 + 6x - 8$ and identify the vertex and x-intercepts.

Solution

As in Example 2, begin by writing the quadratic function in standard form.

$$f(x) = -x^2 + 6x - 8 \qquad \text{Write original function.}$$
$$= -(x^2 - 6x) - 8 \qquad \text{Factor } -1 \text{ out of } x\text{-terms.}$$
$$= -(x^2 - 6x + 9 - 9) - 8 \qquad \text{Add and subtract 9 within parentheses.}$$

$$\underbrace{\qquad}_{(-6/2)^2}$$

$$= -(x^2 - 6x + 9) - (-9) - 8 \qquad \text{Regroup terms.}$$
$$= -(x - 3)^2 + 1 \qquad \text{Write in standard form.}$$

From this form, you can see that the vertex is $(3, 1)$. To find the x-intercepts of the graph, solve the equation $-x^2 + 6x - 8 = 0$.

$$-(x^2 - 6x + 8) = 0 \qquad \text{Factor out } -1.$$
$$-(x - 2)(x - 4) = 0 \qquad \text{Factor.}$$
$$x - 2 = 0 \quad \Longrightarrow \quad x = 2 \qquad \text{Set 1st factor equal to 0.}$$
$$x - 4 = 0 \quad \Longrightarrow \quad x = 4 \qquad \text{Set 2nd factor equal to 0.}$$

The x-intercepts are $(2, 0)$ and $(4, 0)$. So, the graph of f is a parabola that opens downward, as shown in Figure 2.7.

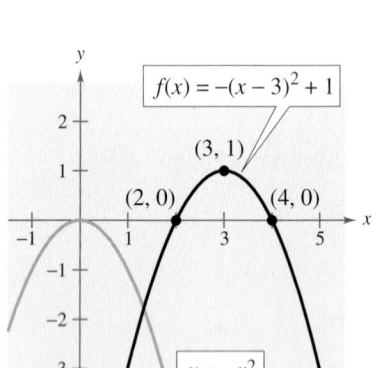

FIGURE 2.7

Example 4 ▶ Writing the Equation of a Parabola

Write the standard form of the equation of the parabola whose vertex is $(1, 2)$ and that passes through the point $(0, 0)$, as shown in Figure 2.8.

Solution

Because the vertex of the parabola is at $(h, k) = (1, 2)$, the equation has the form

$$f(x) = a(x - 1)^2 + 2. \qquad \text{Substitute for } h \text{ and } k \text{ in standard form.}$$

Because the parabola passes through the point $(0, 0)$, it follows that $f(0) = 0$. So,

$$0 = a(0 - 1)^2 + 2 \quad \Longrightarrow \quad a = -2 \qquad \text{Substitute 0 for } x; \text{ solve for } a.$$

which implies that the equation is

$$f(x) = -2(x - 1)^2 + 2. \qquad \text{Substitute for } a \text{ in standard form.}$$

So, the equation of this parabola is $y = -2(x - 1)^2 + 2$.

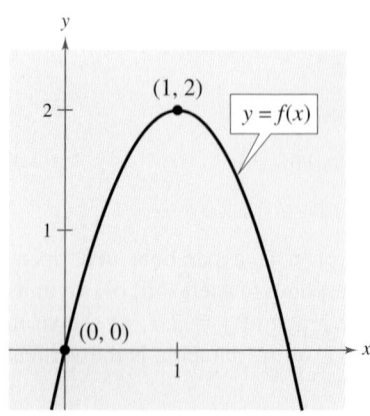

FIGURE 2.8

Application

Many applications involve finding the maximum or minimum value of a quadratic function. Some quadratic functions are not easily written in standard form. For such functions, it is useful to have an alternative method for finding the vertex. For a quadratic function in the form $f(x) = ax^2 + bx + c$, the vertex occurs when $x = -b/2a$. (You are asked to verify this in Exercise 91.)

Vertex of a Parabola

The vertex of the graph of $f(x) = ax^2 + bx + c$ is $\left(-\dfrac{b}{2a},\ f\left(-\dfrac{b}{2a}\right)\right)$.

Example 5 ▶ **The Maximum Height of a Baseball**

A baseball is hit at a point 3 feet above the ground at a velocity of 100 feet per second and at an angle of 45° with respect to the ground. The path of the baseball is given by the function

$$f(x) = -0.0032x^2 + x + 3$$

where $f(x)$ is the height of the baseball (in feet) and x is the horizontal distance from home plate (in feet). What is the maximum height reached by the baseball?

Solution

For this quadratic function, you have

$$f(x) = ax^2 + bx + c$$
$$= -0.0032x^2 + x + 3.$$

So, $a = -0.0032$ and $b = 1$. Because the function has a maximum at $x = -b/2a$, you can conclude that the baseball reaches its maximum height when it is x feet from home plate, where x is

$$x = -\frac{b}{2a}$$
$$= -\frac{1}{2(-0.0032)} \qquad \text{Substitute for } a \text{ and } b.$$
$$= 156.25 \text{ feet.}$$

To find the maximum height, you must determine the value of the function when $x = 156.25$.

$$f(156.25) = -0.0032(156.25)^2 + 156.25 + 3$$
$$= 81.125 \text{ feet.}$$

The path of the baseball is shown in Figure 2.9. You can estimate from the graph in Figure 2.9 that the ball hits the ground at a distance of about 320 feet from home plate. The actual distance is the x-intercept of the graph of f, which you can find by solving the equation $-0.0032x^2 + x + 3 = 0$ and taking the positive solution, $x \approx 315.5$.

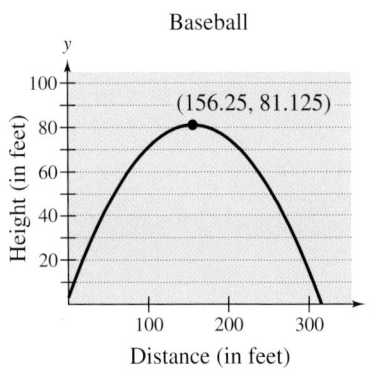

FIGURE **2.9**

2.1 Exercises

The *Interactive* CD-ROM and *Internet* versions of this text contain step-by-step solutions to all odd-numbered exercises. They also provide Tutorial Exercises for additional help.

In Exercises 1–8, match the quadratic function with its graph. [The graphs are labeled (a), (b), (c), (d), (e), (f), (g), and (h).]

(a)

(b)

(c)

(d)

(e)

(f)

(g)

(h)
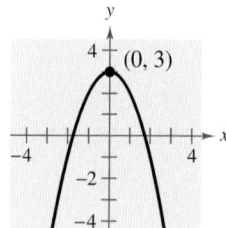

1. $f(x) = (x - 2)^2$

2. $f(x) = (x + 4)^2$

3. $f(x) = x^2 - 2$

4. $f(x) = 3 - x^2$

5. $f(x) = 4 - (x - 2)^2$

6. $f(x) = (x + 1)^2 - 2$

7. $f(x) = -(x - 3)^2 - 2$

8. $f(x) = -(x - 4)^2$

In Exercises 9–12, graph each function. Compare the graph of each function with the graph of $y = x^2$.

9. (a) $f(x) = \frac{1}{2}x^2$ (b) $g(x) = -\frac{1}{8}x^2$
   (c) $h(x) = \frac{3}{2}x^2$ (d) $k(x) = -3x^2$

10. (a) $f(x) = x^2 + 1$ (b) $g(x) = x^2 - 1$
   (c) $h(x) = x^2 + 3$ (d) $k(x) = x^2 - 3$

11. (a) $f(x) = (x - 1)^2$ (b) $g(x) = (3x)^2 + 1$
   (c) $h(x) = \left(\frac{1}{3}x\right)^2 - 3$ (d) $k(x) = (x + 3)^2$

12. (a) $f(x) = -\frac{1}{2}(x - 2)^2 + 1$
   (b) $g(x) = \left[\frac{1}{2}(x - 1)\right]^2 - 3$
   (c) $h(x) = -\frac{1}{2}(x + 2)^2 - 1$
   (d) $k(x) = [2(x + 1)]^2 + 4$

In Exercises 13–28, sketch the graph of the quadratic function without using a graphing utility. Identify the vertex and x-intercept(s).

13. $f(x) = x^2 - 5$ **14.** $h(x) = 25 - x^2$

15. $f(x) = \frac{1}{2}x^2 - 4$ **16.** $f(x) = 16 - \frac{1}{4}x^2$

17. $f(x) = (x + 5)^2 - 6$ **18.** $f(x) = (x - 6)^2 + 3$

19. $h(x) = x^2 - 8x + 16$ **20.** $g(x) = x^2 + 2x + 1$

21. $f(x) = x^2 - x + \frac{5}{4}$ **22.** $f(x) = x^2 + 3x + \frac{1}{4}$

23. $f(x) = -x^2 + 2x + 5$ **24.** $f(x) = -x^2 - 4x + 1$

25. $h(x) = 4x^2 - 4x + 21$

26. $f(x) = 2x^2 - x + 1$

27. $f(x) = \frac{1}{4}x^2 - 2x - 12$

28. $f(x) = -\frac{1}{3}x^2 + 3x - 6$

In Exercises 29–36, use a graphing utility to graph the quadratic function. Identify the vertex and x-intercepts. Then check your results algebraically by writing the quadratic function in standard form.

29. $f(x) = -(x^2 + 2x - 3)$

30. $f(x) = -(x^2 + x - 30)$

31. $g(x) = x^2 + 8x + 11$

32. $f(x) = x^2 + 10x + 14$

33. $f(x) = 2x^2 - 16x + 31$

34. $f(x) = -4x^2 + 24x - 41$

35. $g(x) = \frac{1}{2}(x^2 + 4x - 2)$

36. $f(x) = \frac{3}{5}(x^2 + 6x - 5)$

In Exercises 37–42, find the standard form of the quadratic function.

37.

38.

39.

40.

41.

42.

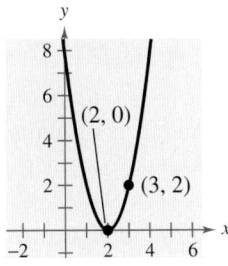

In Exercises 43–52, find the quadratic function that has the indicated vertex and whose graph passes through the given point.

43. Vertex: $(-2, 5)$; Point: $(0, 9)$

44. Vertex: $(4, -1)$; Point: $(2, 3)$

45. Vertex: $(3, 4)$; Point: $(1, 2)$

46. Vertex: $(2, 3)$; Point: $(0, 2)$

47. Vertex: $(5, 12)$; Point: $(7, 15)$

48. Vertex: $(-2, -2)$; Point: $(-1, 0)$

49. Vertex: $\left(-\frac{1}{4}, \frac{3}{2}\right)$; Point: $(-2, 0)$

50. Vertex: $\left(\frac{5}{2}, -\frac{3}{4}\right)$; Point: $(-2, 4)$

51. Vertex: $\left(-\frac{5}{2}, 0\right)$; Point: $\left(-\frac{7}{2}, -\frac{16}{3}\right)$

52. Vertex: $(6, 6)$; Point: $\left(\frac{61}{10}, \frac{3}{2}\right)$

Graphical Reasoning In Exercises 53–56, determine the x-intercept(s) of the graph visually. Then find the x-intercepts algebraically to confirm your results.

53. $y = x^2 - 16$

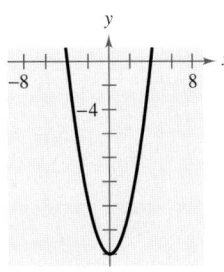

54. $y = x^2 - 6x + 9$

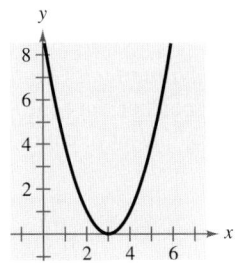

55. $y = x^2 - 4x - 5$

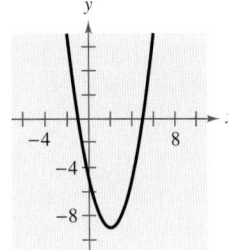

56. $y = 2x^2 + 5x - 3$

 In Exercises 57–64, use a graphing utility to graph the quadratic function. Find the x-intercepts of the graph and compare them with the solutions of the corresponding quadratic equation when $y = 0$.

57. $f(x) = x^2 - 4x$

58. $f(x) = -2x^2 + 10x$

59. $f(x) = x^2 - 9x + 18$

60. $f(x) = x^2 - 8x - 20$

61. $f(x) = 2x^2 - 7x - 30$

62. $f(x) = 4x^2 + 25x - 21$

63. $f(x) = -\frac{1}{2}(x^2 - 6x - 7)$

64. $f(x) = \frac{7}{10}(x^2 + 12x - 45)$

In Exercises 65–70, find two quadratic functions, one that opens upward and one that opens downward, whose graphs have the given x-intercepts. (There are many correct answers.)

65. $(-1, 0), (3, 0)$

66. $(-5, 0), (5, 0)$

67. $(0, 0), (10, 0)$

68. $(4, 0), (8, 0)$

69. $(-3, 0), \left(-\frac{1}{2}, 0\right)$

70. $\left(-\frac{5}{2}, 0\right), (2, 0)$

In Exercises 71–74, find two positive real numbers whose product is a maximum.

71. The sum is 110.   **72.** The sum is S.

73. The sum of the first and twice the second is 24.

74. The sum of the first and three times the second is 42.

75. *Numerical, Graphical, and Analytical Analysis*   A rancher has 200 feet of fencing to enclose two adjacent rectangular corrals (see figure).

(a) Write the area A of the corral as a function of x.

(b) Create a table showing possible values of x and the corresponding area of the corral. Use the table to estimate the dimensions that will enclose the maximum area.

(c) Use a graphing utility to graph the area function. Use the graph to approximate the dimensions that will produce the maximum enclosed area.

(d) Write the area function in standard form to find analytically the dimensions that will produce the maximum area.

76. *Geometry*   An indoor physical fitness room consists of a rectangular region with a semicircle on each end (see figure). The perimeter of the room is to be a 200-meter single-lane running track.

(a) Determine the radius of the semicircular ends of the room. Determine the distance, in terms of y, around the inside edge of the two semicircular parts of the track.

(b) Use the result of part (a) to write an equation, in terms of x and y, for the distance traveled in one lap around the track. Solve for y.

(c) Use the result of part (b) to write the area A of the rectangular region as a function of x. What dimensions will produce a maximum area of the rectangle?

77. *Maximum Revenue*   Find the number of units sold that yields a maximum annual revenue for a company that produces health food supplements. The total revenue R (in dollars) is given by $R = 900x - 0.1x^2$, where x is the number of units sold.

78. *Maximum Revenue*   Find the number of units sold that yields a maximum annual revenue for a sporting goods manufacturer. The total revenue R (in dollars) is given by $R = 100x - 0.0002x^2$, where x is the number of units sold.

79. *Minimum Cost*   A manufacturer of lighting fixtures has daily production costs of

$$C = 800 - 10x + 0.25x^2$$

where C is the total cost (in dollars) and x is the number of units produced. How many fixtures should be produced each day to yield a minimum cost?

80. *Minimum Cost*   A textile manufacturer has daily production costs of $C = 100{,}000 - 110x + 0.045x^2$, where C is the total cost (in dollars) and x is the number of units produced. How many units should be produced each day to yield a minimum cost?

81. *Maximum Profit*   The profit P (in dollars) for a company that produces antivirus and system utilities software is

$$P = -0.0002x^2 + 140x - 250{,}000$$

where x is the number of units sold. What sales level will yield a maximum profit?

82. *Maximum Profit*   The profit P (in hundreds of dollars) that a company makes depends on the amount x (in hundreds of dollars) the company spends on advertising according to the model

$$P = 230 + 20x - 0.5x^2.$$

What expenditure for advertising will yield a maximum profit?

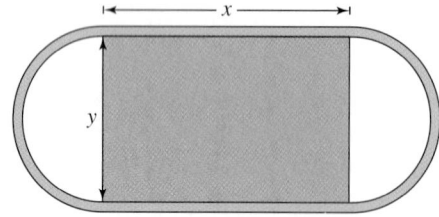

83. *Height of a Ball* The height y (in feet) of a ball thrown by a child is

$$y = -\frac{1}{12}x^2 + 2x + 4$$

where x is the horizontal distance (in feet) from the point at which the ball is thrown (see figure).

(a) How high is the ball when it leaves the child's hand? (*Hint:* Find y when $x = 0$.)

(b) What is the maximum height of the ball?

(c) How far from the child does the ball strike the ground?

84. *Path of a Diver* The path of a diver is

$$y = -\frac{4}{9}x^2 + \frac{24}{9}x + 12$$

where y is the height (in feet) and x is the horizontal distance from the end of the diving board (in feet). What is the maximum height of the diver?

85. *Graphical Analysis* From 1960 to 2000, the per capita consumption C of cigarettes by Americans (age 18 and older) can be modeled by

$$C = 4258 + 6.5t - 1.62t^2, \qquad 0 \le t \le 40$$

where t is the year, with $t = 0$ corresponding to 1960. (Source: *Tobacco Situation and Outlook Yearbook*)

(a) Use a graphing utility to graph the model.

(b) Use the graph of the model to approximate the maximum average annual consumption. Beginning in 1966, all cigarette packages were required by law to carry a health warning. Do you think the warning had any effect? Explain.

(c) In 1990, the U.S. population (age 18 and over) was 185,105,441. Of those, about 63,423,167 were smokers. What was the average annual cigarette consumption *per smoker* in 1990? What was the average daily cigarette consumption *per smoker*?

▶ **Model It**

86. *Data Analysis* The numbers y (in thousands) of hairdressers and cosmetologists in the United States for the years 1995 through 2000 are shown in the table. (Source: U.S. Bureau of Labor Statistics)

Year	Number of hairdressers and cosmetologists, y
1995	750
1996	737
1997	748
1998	763
1999	784
2000	820

(a) Use a graphing utility to create a scatter plot of the data. Let x represent the year, with $x = 5$ corresponding to 1995.

(b) Use the *regression* feature of a graphing utility to find a quadratic model for the data.

(c) Use a graphing utility to graph the model in the same viewing window as the scatter plot. How well does the model fit the data?

(d) Use the *trace* feature of the graphing utility to approximate the year in which the number of hairdressers and cosmetologists was the least.

(e) Use the model to predict the number of hairdressers and cosmetologists in 2005.

87. *Wind Drag* The number of horsepower y required to overcome wind drag on an automobile is approximated by

$$y = 0.002s^2 + 0.005s - 0.029, \qquad 0 \le s \le 100$$

where s is the speed of the car (in miles per hour).

(a) Use a graphing utility to graph the function.

(b) Graphically estimate the maximum speed of the car if the power required to overcome wind drag is not to exceed 10 horsepower. Verify your estimate analytically.

88. Maximum Fuel Economy A study was done to compare the speed x (in miles per hour) with the mileage y (in miles per gallon) of an automobile. The results are shown in the table. (Source: Federal Highway Administration)

Speed, x	Mileage, y
15	22.3
20	25.5
25	27.5
30	29.0
35	28.8
40	30.0
45	29.9
50	30.2
55	30.4
60	28.8
65	27.4
70	25.3
75	23.3

(a) Use a graphing utility to create a scatter plot of the data.

(b) Use the *regression* feature of a graphing utility to find a quadratic model for the data.

(c) Use a graphing utility to graph the model in the same viewing window as the scatter plot.

(d) Estimate the speed for which the miles per gallon is greatest.

Synthesis

True or False? In Exercises 89 and 90, determine whether the statement is true or false. Justify your answer.

89. The function $f(x) = -12x^2 - 1$ has no x-intercepts.

90. The graphs of

$$f(x) = -4x^2 - 10x + 7$$

and

$$g(x) = 12x^2 + 30x + 1$$

have the same axis of symmetry.

91. Write the quadratic equation

$$f(x) = ax^2 + bx + c$$

in standard form to verify that the vertex occurs at

$$\left(-\frac{b}{2a}, \; f\left(-\frac{b}{2a}\right)\right).$$

92. Profit The profit P (in millions of dollars) for a recreational vehicle retailer is modeled by a quadratic function of the form

$$P = at^2 + bt + c$$

where t represents the year. If you were president of the company, which of the models below would you prefer? Explain your reasoning.

(a) a is positive and $-b/(2a) \le t$.

(b) a is positive and $t \le -b/(2a)$.

(c) a is negative and $-b/(2a) \le t$.

(d) a is negative and $t \le -b/(2a)$.

93. Is it possible for a quadratic equation to have only one x-intercept? Explain.

94. Assume that the function

$$f(x) = ax^2 + bx + c, \qquad a \ne 0$$

has two real zeros. Show that the x-coordinate of the vertex of the graph is the average of the zeros of f. (*Hint:* Use the Quadratic Formula.)

Review

In Exercises 95–98, find the equation of the line in slope-intercept form that has the given characteristics.

95. Contains the points $(-4, 3)$ and $(2, 1)$

96. Contains the point $\left(\frac{7}{2}, 2\right)$ and has a slope of $\frac{3}{2}$

97. Contains the point $(0, 3)$ and is perpendicular to the line $4x + 5y = 10$

98. Contains the point $(-8, 4)$ and is parallel to the line $y = -3x + 2$

In Exercises 99–104, let $f(x) = 14x - 3$ and let $g(x) = 8x^2$. Find the indicated value.

99. $(f + g)(-3)$

100. $(g - f)(2)$

101. $(fg)\left(-\frac{4}{7}\right)$

102. $\left(\frac{f}{g}\right)(-1.5)$

103. $(f \circ g)(-1)$

104. $(g \circ f)(0)$

2.2 Polynomial Functions of Higher Degree

▶ **What you should learn**

- How to use transformations to sketch graphs of polynomial functions
- How to use the Leading Coefficient Test to determine the end behavior of graphs of polynomial functions
- How to use zeros of polynomial functions as sketching aids
- How to use the Intermediate Value Theorem to help locate zeros of polynomial functions

▶ **Why you should learn it**

You can use polynomial functions to model real-life processes, such as the growth of a red oak tree, as discussed in Exercise 91 on page 132.

Graphs of Polynomial Functions

In this section you will study basic features of the graphs of polynomial functions. The first feature is that the graph of a polynomial function is **continuous.** Essentially, this means that the graph of a polynomial function has no breaks, holes, or gaps, as shown in Figure 2.10(a).

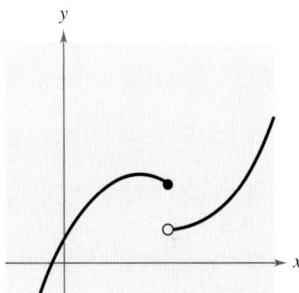

(a) **Polynomial functions have continuous graphs.**

(b) **Functions with graphs that are not continuous are not polynomial functions.**

FIGURE 2.10

The second feature is that the graph of a polynomial function has only smooth, rounded turns, as shown in Figure 2.11. A polynomial function cannot have a sharp turn. For instance, the function $f(x) = |x|$, which has a sharp turn at the point $(0, 0)$, as shown in Figure 2.12, is not a polynomial function.

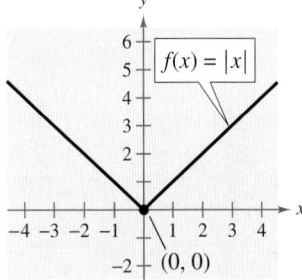

Polynomial functions have graphs with rounded turns.

FIGURE 2.11

Functions whose graphs have sharp turns are not polynomial functions.

FIGURE 2.12

Point out to students that although all polynomial functions are continuous and have rounded turns, not all graphs that are continuous and have rounded turns are polynomials.

The graphs of polynomial functions of degree greater than 2 are more difficult to analyze than the graphs of polynomials of degree 0, 1, or 2. However, using the features presented in this section, together with point plotting, intercepts, and symmetry, you should be able to make reasonably accurate sketches *by hand.*

Leonard Lee Rue/Earth Scenes

The polynomial functions that have the simplest graphs are monomials of the form $f(x) = x^n$, where n is an integer greater than zero. From Figure 2.13, you can see that when n is *even*, the graph is similar to the graph of $f(x) = x^2$, and when n is *odd*, the graph is similar to the graph of $f(x) = x^3$. Moreover, the greater the value of n, the flatter the graph near the origin. Polynomial functions of the form $f(x) = x^n$ are often referred to as **power functions.**

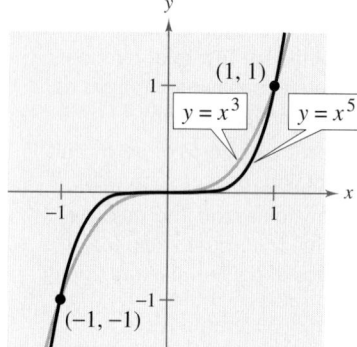

(a) If n is even, the graph of $y = x^n$ touches the axis at the x-intercept.

(b) If n is odd, the graph of $y = x^n$ crosses the axis at the x-intercept.

FIGURE 2.13

Example 1 ▶ **Sketching Transformations of Monomial Functions**

Sketch the graph of each function.

a. $f(x) = -x^5$

b. $h(x) = (x + 1)^4$

Solution

a. Because the degree of $f(x) = -x^5$ is odd, its graph is similar to the graph of $y = x^3$. In Figure 2.14, note that the negative coefficient has the effect of reflecting the graph in the x-axis.

b. The graph of $h(x) = (x + 1)^4$, as shown in Figure 2.15, is a left shift by one unit of the graph of $y = x^4$.

FIGURE 2.14

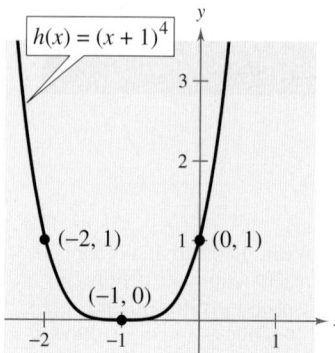

FIGURE 2.15

Exploration

For each function, identify the degree of the function and whether the degree of the function is even or odd. Identify the leading coefficient and whether the leading coefficient is greater than 0 or less than 0. Use a graphing utility to graph each function. Describe the relationship between the degree and the sign of the leading coefficient of the function and the right- and left-hand behavior of the graph of the function.

a. $f(x) = x^3 - 2x^2 - x + 1$

b. $f(x) = 2x^5 + 2x^2 - 5x + 1$

c. $f(x) = -2x^5 - x^2 + 5x + 3$

d. $f(x) = -x^3 + 5x - 2$

e. $f(x) = 2x^2 + 3x - 4$

f. $f(x) = x^4 - 3x^2 + 2x - 1$

g. $f(x) = x^2 + 3x + 2$

STUDY TIP

The notation "$f(x) \to -\infty$ as $x \to -\infty$" indicates that the graph falls to the left. The notation "$f(x) \to \infty$ as $x \to \infty$" indicates that the graph rises to the right.

A review of the shapes of the graphs of polynomial functions of degrees 0, 1, and 2 may be used to illustrate the Leading Coefficient Test.

The Leading Coefficient Test

In Example 1, note that both graphs eventually rise or fall without bound as x moves to the right. Whether the graph of a polynomial function eventually rises or falls can be determined by the function's degree (even or odd) and by its leading coefficient, as indicated in the **Leading Coefficient Test.**

Leading Coefficient Test

As x moves without bound to the left or to the right, the graph of the polynomial function $f(x) = a_n x^n + \cdots + a_1 x + a_0$ eventually rises or falls in the following manner.

1. When n is *odd:*

 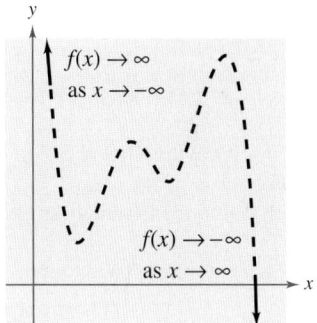

If the leading coefficient is positive $(a_n > 0)$, the graph falls to the left and rises to the right.

If the leading coefficient is negative $(a_n < 0)$, the graph rises to the left and falls to the right.

2. When n is *even:*

 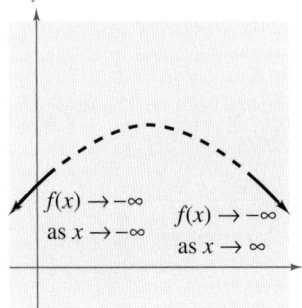

If the leading coefficient is positive $(a_n > 0)$, the graph rises to the left and right.

If the leading coefficient is negative $(a_n < 0)$, the graph falls to the left and right.

The dashed portions of the graphs indicate that the test determines *only* the right-hand and left-hand behavior of the graph.

Zeros of Polynomial Functions

It can be shown that for a polynomial function f of degree n, the following statements are true.

1. The graph of f has, at most, $n - 1$ turning points. (Turning points are points at which the graph changes from increasing to decreasing or vice versa.)

2. The function f has, at most, n real zeros. (You will study this result in detail in the discussion of the Fundamental Theorem of Algebra in Section 2.5.)

Finding the zeros of polynomial functions is one of the most important problems in algebra. There is a strong interplay between graphical and algebraic approaches to this problem. Sometimes you can use information about the graph of a function to help find its zeros, and in other cases you can use information about the zeros of a function to help sketch its graph.

Real Zeros of Polynomial Functions

If f is a polynomial function and a is a real number, the following statements are equivalent.

1. $x = a$ is a *zero* of the function f.

2. $x = a$ is a *solution* of the polynomial equation $f(x) = 0$.

3. $(x - a)$ is a *factor* of the polynomial $f(x)$.

4. $(a, 0)$ is an *x-intercept* of the graph of f.

Example 4 ▶ Finding the Zeros of a Polynomial Function

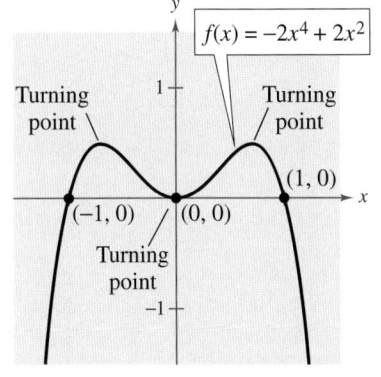

FIGURE **2.19**

Find all real zeros of $f(x) = -2x^4 + 2x^2$. Use the graph in Figure 2.19 to determine the number of turning points of the graph of the function.

Solution

In this case, the polynomial factors as follows.

$$f(x) = -2x^2(x^2 - 1) \qquad \text{Remove common monomial factor.}$$

$$= -2x^2(x - 1)(x + 1) \qquad \text{Factor completely.}$$

So, the real zeros are $x = 0$, $x = 1$, and $x = -1$, and the corresponding x-intercepts are $(0, 0)$, $(1, 0)$, and $(-1, 0)$, as shown in Figure 2.19. Note in the figure that the graph has three turning points. This is consistent with the fact that a fourth-degree polynomial can have *at most* three turning points.

Repeated Zeros

A factor $(x - a)^k$, $k > 1$, yields a **repeated zero** $x = a$ of **multiplicity** k.

1. If k is odd, the graph *crosses* the x-axis at $x = a$.

2. If k is even, the graph *touches* the x-axis (but does not cross the x-axis) at $x = a$.

a.

b.

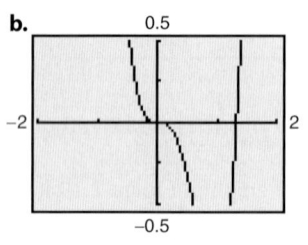

To graph polynomial functions, you can use the fact that a polynomial function can change signs only at its zeros. Between two consecutive zeros, a polynomial must be entirely positive or entirely negative. This means that when the real zeros of a polynomial function are put in order, they divide the real number line into intervals in which the function has no sign changes. These resulting intervals are **test intervals** in which a representative x-value in the interval is chosen to determine if the value of the polynomial function is positive (the graph lies above the x-axis) or negative (the graph lies below the x-axis).

Example 5 ▶   **Sketching the Graph of a Polynomial Function**

Sketch the graph of $f(x) = 3x^4 - 4x^3$.

Solution

1. *Apply the Leading Coefficient Test.*   Because the leading coefficient is positive and the degree is even, you know that the graph eventually rises to the left and to the right (see Figure 2.20).

2. *Find the Zeros of the Polynomial.*   By factoring $f(x) = 3x^4 - 4x^3 = x^3(3x - 4)$ you can see that the zeros of f are $x = 0$ and $x = \frac{4}{3}$ (both of odd multiplicity). So, the x-intercepts occur at $(0, 0)$ and $\left(\frac{4}{3}, 0\right)$. Add these points to your graph, as shown in Figure 2.20.

3. *Plot a Few Additional Points.*   Use the zeros of the polynomial to find the test intervals. In each test interval, choose a representative x-value and evaluate the polynomial function, as shown in the table.

Test interval	Representative x-value	Value of f	Sign	Point on Graph
$(-\infty, 0)$	-1	$f(-1) = 7$	Positive	$(-1, 7)$
$\left(0, \frac{4}{3}\right)$	1	$f(1) = -1$	Negative	$(1, -1)$
$\left(\frac{4}{3}, \infty\right)$	1.5	$f(1.5) = 1.6875$	Positive	$(1.5, 1.6875)$

4. *Draw the Graph.*   Draw a continuous curve through the points, as shown in Figure 2.21. Because both zeros are of odd multiplicity, you know that the graph should cross the x-axis at $x = 0$ and $x = \frac{4}{3}$.

STUDY TIP

If you are unsure of the shape of a portion of the graph of a polynomial function, plot some additional points, such as the point $(0.5, -0.3125)$ as shown in Figure 2.21.

FIGURE 2.20

FIGURE 2.21

STUDY TIP

A polynomial function is written in **standard form** if its terms are written in descending order of exponents from left to right. Before applying the Leading Coefficient Test to a polynomial function, it is a good idea to check that the polynomial function is written in standard form.

STUDY TIP

Observe in Example 6 that the sign of $f(x)$ is positive to the left of and negative to the right of the zero $x = 0$. Similarly, the sign of $f(x)$ is negative to the left and to the right of the zero $x = \frac{3}{2}$. This suggests that if the zero of a polynomial function is of *odd* multiplicity, then the sign of $f(x)$ changes from one side of the zero to the other side. If the zero is of *even* multiplicity, then the sign of $f(x)$ does not change from one side of the zero to the other side.

Example 6 ▶ Sketching the Graph of a Polynomial Function

Sketch the graph of $f(x) = -2x^3 + 6x^2 - \frac{9}{2}x$.

Solution

1. *Apply the Leading Coefficient Test.* Because the leading coefficient is negative and the degree is odd, you know that the graph eventually rises to the left and falls to the right (see Figure 2.22).

2. *Find the Zeros of the Polynomial.* By factoring

$$f(x) = -2x^3 + 6x^2 - \frac{9}{2}x$$

$$= -\frac{1}{2}x(4x^2 - 12x + 9) = -\frac{1}{2}x(2x - 3)^2$$

you can see that the zeros of f are $x = 0$ (odd multiplicity) and $x = \frac{3}{2}$ (even multiplicity). So, the x-intercepts occur at $(0, 0)$ and $\left(\frac{3}{2}, 0\right)$. Add these points to your graph, as shown in Figure 2.22.

3. *Plot a Few Additional Points.* Use the zeros of the polynomial to find the test intervals. In each test interval, choose a representative x-value and evaluate the polynomial function, as shown in the table.

Test interval	Representative x-value	Value of f	Sign	Point on Graph
$(-\infty, 0)$	-0.5	$f(-0.5) = 4$	Positive	$(-0.5, 4)$
$\left(0, \frac{3}{2}\right)$	0.5	$f(0.5) = -1$	Negative	$(0.5, -1)$
$\left(\frac{3}{2}, \infty\right)$	2	$f(2) = -1$	Negative	$(2, -1)$

4. *Draw the Graph.* Draw a continuous curve through the points, as shown in Figure 2.23. As indicated by the multiplicities of the zeros, the graph crosses the x-axis at $(0, 0)$ but does not cross the x-axis at $\left(\frac{3}{2}, 0\right)$.

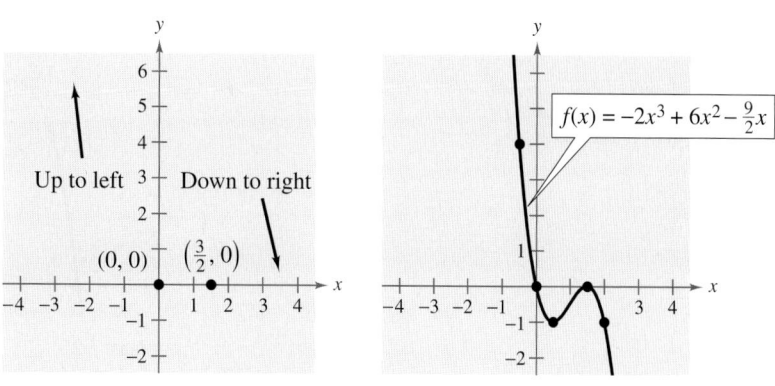

FIGURE 2.22

FIGURE 2.23

The Intermediate Value Theorem

The next theorem, called the **Intermediate Value Theorem,** tells you of the existence of real zeros of polynomial functions. This theorem implies that if $(a, f(a))$ and $(b, f(b))$ are two points on the graph of a polynomial function such that $f(a) \neq f(b)$, then for any number d between $f(a)$ and $f(b)$ there must be a number c between a and b such that $f(c) = d$. (See Figure 2.24.)

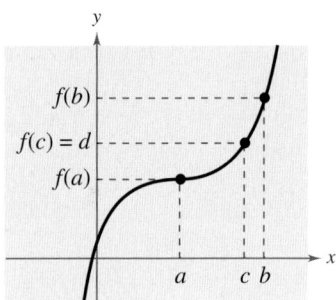

FIGURE 2.24

Intermediate Value Theorem

Let a and b be real numbers such that $a < b$. If f is a polynomial function such that $f(a) \neq f(b)$, then, in the interval $[a, b]$, f takes on every value between $f(a)$ and $f(b)$.

The Intermediate Value Theorem helps you locate the real zeros of a polynomial function in the following way. If you can find a value $x = a$ at which a polynomial function is positive, and another value $x = b$ at which it is negative, you can conclude that the function has at least one real zero between these two values. For example, the function $f(x) = x^3 + x^2 + 1$ is negative when $x = -2$ and positive when $x = -1$. Therefore, it follows from the Intermediate Value Theorem that f must have a real zero somewhere between -2 and -1, as shown in Figure 2.25.

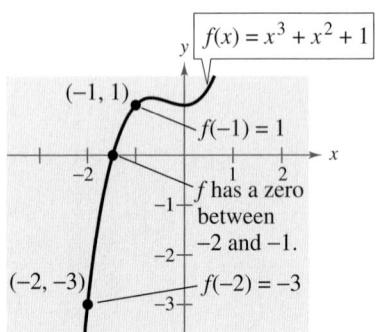

FIGURE 2.25

By continuing this line of reasoning, you can approximate any real zeros of a polynomial function to any desired accuracy. This concept is further demonstrated in Example 7.

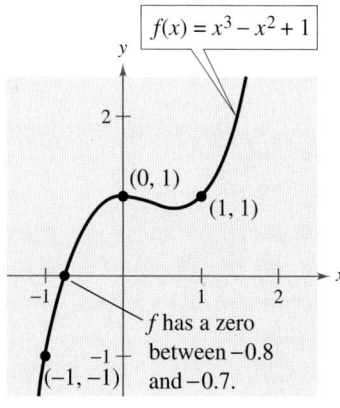

$f(x) = x^3 - x^2 + 1$

(0, 1)

(1, 1)

f has a zero
between -0.8
and -0.7.

$(-1, -1)$

FIGURE **2.26**

The approximation process in Example 7 adapts very well to a graphing utility. Have students repeatedly use the *zoom* and *trace* features to find that the real zero of $f(x) = x^3 - x^2 + 1$ occurs between -0.755 and -0.754.

Example 7 ▶ Approximating a Zero of a Polynomial Function

Use the Intermediate Value Theorem to approximate the real zero of

$$f(x) = x^3 - x^2 + 1.$$

Solution

Begin by computing a few function values, as follows.

x	$f(x)$
-2	-11
-1	-1
0	1
1	1

Because $f(-1)$ is negative and $f(0)$ is positive, you can apply the Intermediate Value Theorem to conclude that the function has a zero between -1 and 0. To pinpoint this zero more closely, divide the interval $[-1, 0]$ into tenths and evaluate the function at each point. When you do this, you will find that

$$f(-0.8) = -0.152 \quad \text{and} \quad f(-0.7) = 0.167.$$

So, f must have a zero between -0.8 and -0.7, as shown in Figure 2.26. For a more accurate approximation, compute function values between $f(-0.8)$ and $f(-0.7)$ and apply the Intermediate Value Theorem again. By continuing this process, you can approximate this zero to any desired accuracy.

Technology

You can use the *table* feature of a graphing utility to approximate the zeros of a polynomial function. For instance, for the function

$$f(x) = -2x^3 - 3x^2 + 3$$

create a table that shows the function values for $-20 \leq x \leq 20$, as shown in the table on the left. Scroll through the table looking for consecutive function values that differ in sign. From the table on the left, you can see that $f(0)$ and $f(1)$ differ in sign. So, you can

conclude from the Intermediate Value Theorem that the function has a zero between 0 and 1. You can adjust your table to show function values for $0 \leq x \leq 1$ using increments of 0.1, as shown in the table on the right. By scrolling through the table on the right, you can see that $f(0.8)$ and $f(0.9)$ differ in sign. So, the function has a zero between 0.8 and 0.9. If you repeat this process several times, you should obtain $x \approx 0.806$ as the zero of the function. Use the *zero* or *root* feature of a graphing utility to confirm this result.

X	Y₁	
-2	7	
-1	2	
0	3	
1	-2	
2	-25	
3	-78	
4	-173	
X=1		

X	Y₁	
.4	2.392	
.5	2	
.6	1.488	
.7	.844	
.8	.056	
.9	-.888	
1	-2	
X=.9		

2.2 Exercises

In Exercises 1–8, match the polynomial function with its graph. [The graphs are labeled (a), (b), (c), (d), (e), (f), (g), and (h).]

(a)

(b)

(c)

(d)

(e)

(f)

(g)

(h)
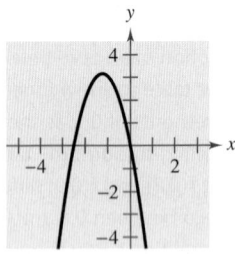

1. $f(x) = -2x + 3$

2. $f(x) = x^2 - 4x$

3. $f(x) = -2x^2 - 5x$

4. $f(x) = 2x^3 - 3x + 1$

5. $f(x) = -\frac{1}{4}x^4 + 3x^2$

6. $f(x) = -\frac{1}{3}x^3 + x^2 - \frac{4}{3}$

7. $f(x) = x^4 + 2x^3$

8. $f(x) = \frac{1}{5}x^5 - 2x^3 + \frac{9}{5}x$

In Exercises 9–12, sketch the graph of $y = x^n$ and each transformation.

9. $y = x^3$

   (a) $f(x) = (x - 2)^3$ (b) $f(x) = x^3 - 2$

   (c) $f(x) = -\frac{1}{2}x^3$ (d) $f(x) = (x - 2)^3 - 2$

10. $y = x^5$

   (a) $f(x) = (x + 1)^5$ (b) $f(x) = x^5 + 1$

   (c) $f(x) = 1 - \frac{1}{2}x^5$ (d) $f(x) = -\frac{1}{2}(x + 1)^5$

11. $y = x^4$

   (a) $f(x) = (x + 3)^4$ (b) $f(x) = x^4 - 3$

   (c) $f(x) = 4 - x^4$ (d) $f(x) = \frac{1}{2}(x - 1)^4$

   (e) $f(x) = (2x)^4 + 1$ (f) $f(x) = \left(\frac{1}{2}x\right)^4 - 2$

12. $y = x^6$

   (a) $f(x) = -\frac{1}{8}x^6$ (b) $f(x) = (x + 2)^6 - 4$

   (c) $f(x) = x^6 - 4$ (d) $f(x) = -\frac{1}{4}x^6 + 1$

   (e) $f(x) = \left(\frac{1}{4}x\right)^6 - 2$ (f) $f(x) = (2x)^6 - 1$

In Exercises 13–22, determine the right-hand and left-hand behavior of the graph of the polynomial function.

13. $f(x) = \frac{1}{3}x^3 + 5x$

14. $f(x) = 2x^2 - 3x + 1$

15. $g(x) = 5 - \frac{7}{2}x - 3x^2$

16. $h(x) = 1 - x^6$

17. $f(x) = -2.1x^5 + 4x^3 - 2$

18. $f(x) = 2x^5 - 5x + 7.5$

19. $f(x) = 6 - 2x + 4x^2 - 5x^3$

20. $f(x) = \dfrac{3x^4 - 2x + 5}{4}$

21. $h(t) = -\frac{2}{3}(t^2 - 5t + 3)$

22. $f(s) = -\frac{7}{8}(s^3 + 5s^2 - 7s + 1)$

Graphical Analysis **In Exercises 23–26, use a graphing utility to graph the functions f and g in the same viewing window. Zoom out sufficiently far to show that the right-hand and left-hand behaviors of f and g appear identical.**

23. $f(x) = 3x^3 - 9x + 1$, $g(x) = 3x^3$

24. $f(x) = -\frac{1}{3}(x^3 - 3x + 2)$, $g(x) = -\frac{1}{3}x^3$

25. $f(x) = -(x^4 - 4x^3 + 16x)$, $g(x) = -x^4$

26. $f(x) = 3x^4 - 6x^2$, $g(x) = 3x^4$

In Exercises 27–42, find all the real zeros of the polynomial function. Determine the multiplicity of each zero.

27. $f(x) = x^2 - 25$

28. $f(x) = 49 - x^2$

29. $h(t) = t^2 - 6t + 9$

30. $f(x) = x^2 + 10x + 25$

31. $f(x) = \frac{1}{3}x^2 + \frac{1}{3}x - \frac{2}{3}$

32. $f(x) = \frac{1}{2}x^2 + \frac{5}{2}x - \frac{3}{2}$

33. $f(x) = 3x^3 - 12x^2 + 3x$

34. $g(x) = 5x(x^2 - 2x - 1)$

35. $f(t) = t^3 - 4t^2 + 4t$

36. $f(x) = x^4 - x^3 - 20x^2$

37. $g(t) = t^5 - 6t^3 + 9t$

38. $f(x) = x^5 + x^3 - 6x$

39. $f(x) = 5x^4 + 15x^2 + 10$

40. $f(x) = 2x^4 - 2x^2 - 40$

41. $g(x) = x^3 + 3x^2 - 4x - 12$

42. $f(x) = x^3 - 4x^2 - 25x + 100$

 Graphical Analysis In Exercises 43–46, use a graphing utility to graph the function. Use the graph to approximate any *x*-intercepts of the graph. Set *y* = 0 and solve the resulting equation. Compare the result with any *x*-intercepts of the graph.

43. $y = 4x^3 - 20x^2 + 25x$

44. $y = 4x^3 + 4x^2 - 7x + 2$

45. $y = x^5 - 5x^3 + 4x$

46. $y = \frac{1}{4}x^3(x^2 - 9)$

In Exercises 47–56, find a polynomial function that has the given zeros. (There are many correct answers.)

47. $0, 10$

48. $0, -3$

49. $2, -6$

50. $-4, 5$

51. $0, -2, -3$

52. $0, 2, 5$

53. $4, -3, 3, 0$

54. $-2, -1, 0, 1, 2$

55. $1 + \sqrt{3}, 1 - \sqrt{3}$

56. $2, 4 + \sqrt{5}, 4 - \sqrt{5}$

In Exercises 57–66, find a polynomial of degree *n* that has the given zero(s). (There are many correct answers.)

57. Zero: $x = -2$ Degree: $n = 2$

58. Zeros: $x = -8, -4$ Degree: $n = 2$

59. Zeros: $x = -3, 0, 1$ Degree: $n = 3$

60. Zeros: $x = -2, 4, 7$ Degree: $n = 3$

61. Zeros: $x = 0, \sqrt{3}, -\sqrt{3}$ Degree: $n = 3$

62. Zero: $x = 9$ Degree: $n = 3$

63. Zeros: $x = -5, 1, 2$ Degree: $n = 4$

64. Zeros: $x = -4, -1, 3, 6$ Degree: $n = 4$

65. Zeros: $x = 0, -4$ Degree: $n = 5$

66. Zeros: $x = -3, 1, 5, 6$ Degree: $n = 5$

In Exercises 67–80, sketch the graph of the function by (a) applying the Leading Coefficient Test, (b) finding the zeros of the polynomial, (c) plotting sufficient solution points, and (d) drawing a continuous curve through the points.

67. $f(x) = x^3 - 9x$

68. $g(x) = x^4 - 4x^2$

69. $f(t) = \frac{1}{4}(t^2 - 2t + 15)$

70. $g(x) = -x^2 + 10x - 16$

71. $f(x) = x^3 - 3x^2$

72. $f(x) = 1 - x^3$

73. $f(x) = 3x^3 - 15x^2 + 18x$

74. $f(x) = -4x^3 + 4x^2 + 15x$

75. $f(x) = -5x^2 - x^3$

76. $f(x) = -48x^2 + 3x^4$

77. $f(x) = x^2(x - 4)$

78. $h(x) = \frac{1}{3}x^3(x - 4)^2$

79. $g(t) = -\frac{1}{4}(t - 2)^2(t + 2)^2$

80. $g(x) = \frac{1}{10}(x + 1)^2(x - 3)^3$

 In Exercises 81–84, use a graphing utility to graph the function. Use the *zero* or *root* feature to approximate zeros of the function. Determine the multiplicity of each zero.

81. $f(x) = x^3 - 4x$

82. $f(x) = \frac{1}{4}x^4 - 2x^2$

83. $g(x) = \frac{1}{5}(x + 1)^2(x - 3)(2x - 9)$

84. $h(x) = \frac{1}{5}(x + 2)^2(3x - 5)^2$

In Exercises 85–88, use the Intermediate Value Theorem and the *table* feature of a graphing utility to find intervals one unit in length in which the polynomial function is guaranteed to have a zero. Adjust the table to approximate the zeros of the function. Use the *zero* or *root* feature of a graphing utility to verify your results.

85. $f(x) = x^3 - 3x^2 + 3$

86. $f(x) = 0.11x^3 - 2.07x^2 + 9.81x - 6.88$

87. $g(x) = 3x^4 + 4x^3 - 3$

88. $h(x) = x^4 - 10x^2 + 3$

89. *Numerical and Graphical Analysis* An open box is to be made from a square piece of material, 36 inches on a side, by cutting equal squares with sides of length x from the corners and turning up the sides (see figure).

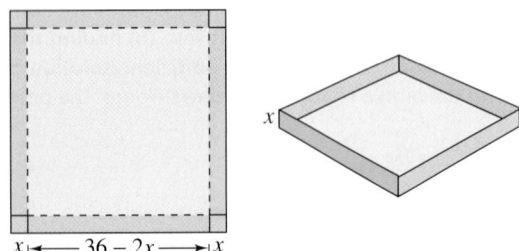

(a) Verify that the volume of the box is given by the function $V(x) = x(36 - 2x)^2$.

(b) Determine the domain of the function.

(c) Use a graphing utility to create a table that shows the box height x and the corresponding volumes V. Use the table to estimate the dimensions that will produce a maximum volume.

(d) Use a graphing utility to graph V and use the graph to estimate the value of x for which $V(x)$ is maximum. Compare your result with that of part (c).

90. *Maximum Volume* An open box with locking tabs is to be made from a square piece of material 24 inches on a side. This is to be done by cutting equal squares from the corners and folding along the dashed lines shown in the figure.

(a) Verify that the volume of the box is given by the function

$$V(x) = 8x(6 - x)(12 - x).$$

(b) Determine the domain of the function V.

(c) Sketch a graph of the function and estimate the value of x for which $V(x)$ is maximum.

▶ **Model It**

91. *Tree Growth* The growth of a red oak tree is approximated by the function

$$G = -0.003t^3 + 0.137t^2 + 0.458t - 0.839$$

where G is the height of the tree (in feet) and t ($2 \le t \le 34$) is its age (in years).

(a) Use a graphing utility to graph the function. (*Hint:* Use a viewing window in which $-10 \le x \le 45$ and $-5 \le y \le 60$.)

(b) Estimate the age of the tree when it is growing most rapidly. This point is called the *point of diminishing returns* because the increase in size will be less with each additional year.

(c) Using calculus, the point of diminishing returns can also be found by finding the vertex of the parabola given by

$$y = -0.009t^2 + 0.274t + 0.458.$$

Find the vertex of this parabola.

(d) Compare your results from parts (b) and (c).

---

92. *Revenue* The total revenue R (in millions of dollars) for a company is related to its advertising expense by the function

$$R = \frac{1}{100,000}(-x^3 + 600x^2), \qquad 0 \le x \le 400$$

where x is the amount spent on advertising (in tens of thousands of dollars). Use the graph of this function, shown in the figure, to estimate the point on the graph at which the function is increasing most rapidly. This point is called the *point of diminishing returns* because any expense above this amount will yield less return per dollar invested in advertising.

Advertising expense
(in tens of thousands of dollars)

Synthesis

True or False? **In Exercises 93–95, determine whether the statement is true or false. Justify your answer.**

93. A fifth-degree polynomial can have five turning points in its graph.

94. It is possible for a sixth-degree polynomial to have only one solution.

95. The graph of the function

$$f(x) = 2 + x - x^2 + x^3 - x^4 + x^5 + x^6 - x^7$$

rises to the left and falls to the right.

96. *Graphical Analysis* Describe a polynomial function that could represent the graph. (Indicate the degree of the function and the sign of its leading coefficient.)

(a)

(b)

(c)

(d)

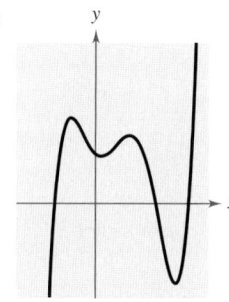

97. *Graphical Reasoning* Sketch a graph of the function $f(x) = x^4$. Explain how the graph of g differs (if it does) from the graph of f. Determine whether g is odd, even, or neither.

(a) $g(x) = f(x) + 2$ (b) $g(x) = f(x + 2)$

(c) $g(x) = f(-x)$ (d) $g(x) = -f(x)$

(e) $g(x) = f\left(\frac{1}{2}x\right)$ (f) $g(x) = \frac{1}{2}f(x)$

(g) $g(x) = f\left(x^{3/4}\right)$ (h) $g(x) = (f \circ f)(x)$

98. *Exploration* Explore the transformations of the form $g(x) = a(x - h)^5 + k$.

(a) Use a graphing utility to graph the functions

$$y_1 = -\frac{1}{3}(x - 2)^5 + 1$$

and

$$y_2 = \frac{3}{5}(x + 2)^5 - 3.$$

Determine whether the graphs are increasing or decreasing. Explain.

(b) Will the graph of g always be increasing or decreasing? If so, is this behavior determined by a, h, or k? Explain.

(c) Use a graphing utility to graph the function

$$H(x) = x^5 - 3x^3 + 2x + 1.$$

Use the graph and the result of part (b) to determine whether H can be written in the form $H(x) = a(x - h)^5 + k$. Explain.

Review

In Exercises 99–102, solve the equation by factoring.

99. $2x^2 - x - 28 = 0$ **100.** $3x^2 - 22x - 16 = 0$

101. $12x^2 + 11x - 5 = 0$ **102.** $x^2 + 24x + 144 = 0$

In Exercises 103–106, solve the equation by completing the square.

103. $x^2 - 2x - 21 = 0$ **104.** $x^2 - 8x + 2 = 0$

105. $2x^2 + 5x - 20 = 0$ **106.** $3x^2 + 4x - 9 = 0$

In Exercises 107–110, factor the expression completely.

107. $5x^2 + 7x - 24$ **108.** $6x^3 - 61x^2 + 10x$

109. $4x^4 - 7x^3 - 15x^2$ **110.** $y^3 + 216$

In Exercises 111–116, describe the transformation from a common function that occurs in the function. Then sketch its graph.

111. $f(x) = (x + 4)^2$ **112.** $f(x) = 3 - x^2$

113. $f(x) = \sqrt{x + 1} - 5$ **114.** $f(x) = 7 - \sqrt{x - 6}$

115. $f(x) = 2[\![x]\!] + 9$ **116.** $f(x) = 10 - \frac{1}{3}[\![x + 3]\!]$

2.3 Polynomial and Synthetic Division

▶ **What you should learn**

- How to use long division to divide polynomials by other polynomials
- How to use synthetic division to divide polynomials by binomials of the form $(x - k)$
- How to use the Remainder Theorem and the Factor Theorem

▶ **Why you should learn it**

Synthetic division can help you evaluate polynomial functions. For instance, in Exercise 75 on page 141, you will use synthetic division to determine the number of U.S. military personnel in 2005.

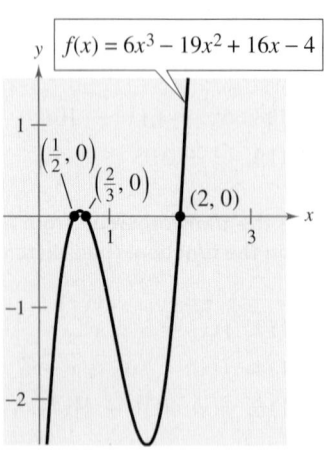

Long Division of Polynomials

In this section you will study two procedures for *dividing* polynomials. These procedures are especially valuable in factoring and finding the zeros of polynomial functions. To begin, suppose you are given the graph of

$$f(x) = 6x^3 - 19x^2 + 16x - 4.$$

Notice that a zero of f occurs at $x = 2$, as shown in Figure 2.27. Because $x = 2$ is a zero of f, you know that $(x - 2)$ is a factor of $f(x)$. This means that there exists a second-degree polynomial $q(x)$ such that

$$f(x) = (x - 2) \cdot q(x).$$

To find $q(x)$, you can use **long division,** as illustrated in Example 1.

Example 1 ▶ Long Division of Polynomials

Divide $6x^3 - 19x^2 + 16x - 4$ by $x - 2$, and use the result to factor the polynomial completely.

Solution

Think $\dfrac{6x^3}{x} = 6x^2$.

Think $\dfrac{-7x^2}{x} = -7x$.

Think $\dfrac{2x}{x} = 2$.

$$
\begin{array}{r}
6x^2 - 7x + 2 \\
x - 2 \overline{) 6x^3 - 19x^2 + 16x - 4} \\
\underline{6x^3 - 12x^2} \quad\quad\quad\quad\quad\quad\;\; \\
-7x^2 + 16x \quad\quad\quad \\
\underline{-7x^2 + 14x} \quad\quad\quad \\
2x - 4 \\
\underline{2x - 4} \\
0
\end{array}
$$

Multiply: $6x^2(x - 2)$.
Subtract.
Multiply: $-7x(x - 2)$.
Subtract.
Multiply: $2(x - 2)$.
Subtract.

From this division, you can conclude that

$$6x^3 - 19x^2 + 16x - 4 = (x - 2)(6x^2 - 7x + 2)$$

and by factoring the quadratic $6x^2 - 7x + 2$, you have

$$6x^3 - 19x^2 + 16x - 4 = (x - 2)(2x - 1)(3x - 2).$$

Note that this factorization agrees with the graph shown in Figure 2.27 in that the three x-intercepts occur at $x = 2$, $x = \frac{1}{2}$, and $x = \frac{2}{3}$.

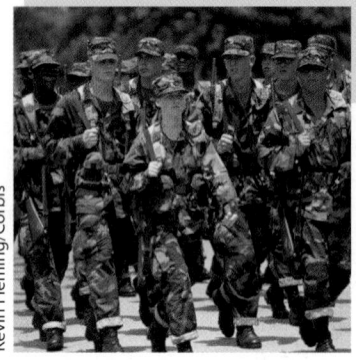

FIGURE 2.27

Note that one of the many uses of polynomial division is to write a function as a sum of terms to find slant asymptotes (see Section 2.6). This is a skill that is also used frequently in calculus.

In Example 1, $x - 2$ is a factor of the polynomial $6x^3 - 19x^2 + 16x - 4$, and the long division process produces a remainder of zero. Often, long division will produce a nonzero remainder. For instance, if you divide $x^2 + 3x + 5$ by $x + 1$, you obtain the following.

$$
\begin{array}{r}
x + 2 \quad \longleftarrow \text{Quotient} \\
\text{Divisor} \longrightarrow \quad x + 1 \,\overline{)\, x^2 + 3x + 5} \quad \longleftarrow \text{Dividend} \\
\underline{x^2 + x} \\
2x + 5 \\
\underline{2x + 2} \\
3 \quad \longleftarrow \text{Remainder}
\end{array}
$$

In fractional form, you can write this result as follows.

$$
\underbrace{\frac{x^2 + 3x + 5}{x + 1}}_{\substack{\text{Dividend} \\ \text{Divisor}}} = \underbrace{x + 2}_{\text{Quotient}} + \underbrace{\frac{3}{x + 1}}_{\substack{\text{Remainder} \\ \text{Divisor}}}
$$

This implies that

$$x^2 + 3x + 5 = (x + 1)(x + 2) + 3 \qquad \text{Multiply each side by } (x + 1).$$

which illustrates the following theorem, called the **Division Algorithm.**

The Division Algorithm

If $f(x)$ and $d(x)$ are polynomials such that $d(x) \neq 0$, and the degree of $d(x)$ is less than or equal to the degree of $f(x)$, there exist unique polynomials $q(x)$ and $r(x)$ such that

$$
\underset{\substack{\uparrow \\ \text{Dividend}}}{f(x)} = \underset{\substack{\uparrow \\ \text{Divisor}}}{d(x)} \underset{\substack{\uparrow \\ \text{Quotient}}}{q(x)} + \underset{\substack{\uparrow \\ \text{Remainder}}}{r(x)}
$$

where $r(x) = 0$ *or* the degree of $r(x)$ is less than the degree of $d(x)$. If the remainder $r(x)$ is zero, $d(x)$ *divides evenly* into $f(x)$.

The Division Algorithm can also be written as

$$\frac{f(x)}{d(x)} = q(x) + \frac{r(x)}{d(x)}.$$

In the Division Algorithm, the rational expression $f(x)/d(x)$ is **improper** because the degree of $f(x)$ is greater than or equal to the degree of $d(x)$. On the other hand, the rational expression $r(x)/d(x)$ is **proper** because the degree of $r(x)$ is less than the degree of $d(x)$.

Before you apply the Division Algorithm, follow these steps.

1. Write the dividend and divisor in descending powers of the variable.

2. Insert placeholders with zero coefficients for missing powers of the variable.

Example 2 ▶ **Long Division of Polynomials**

Divide $x^3 - 1$ by $x - 1$.

Solution

Because there is no x^2-term or x-term in the dividend, you need to line up the subtraction by using zero coefficients (or leaving spaces) for the missing terms.

$$
\begin{array}{r}
x^2 + x + 1 \\
x - 1 \overline{)\, x^3 + 0x^2 + 0x - 1} \\
\underline{x^3 - x^2} \\
x^2 + 0x \\
\underline{x^2 - x} \\
x - 1 \\
\underline{x - 1} \\
0
\end{array}
$$

So, $x - 1$ divides evenly into $x^3 - 1$, and you can write

$$\frac{x^3 - 1}{x - 1} = x^2 + x + 1, \quad x \neq 1.$$

You can check the result of Example 2 by multiplying.

$$(x - 1)(x^2 + x + 1) = x^3 + x^2 + x - x^2 - x - 1 = x^3 - 1$$

Example 3 ▶ **Long Division of Polynomials**

Divide $2x^4 + 4x^3 - 5x^2 + 3x - 2$ by $x^2 + 2x - 3$.

Solution

$$
\begin{array}{r}
2x^2 + 1 \\
x^2 + 2x - 3 \overline{)\, 2x^4 + 4x^3 - 5x^2 + 3x - 2} \\
\underline{2x^4 + 4x^3 - 6x^2} \\
x^2 + 3x - 2 \\
\underline{x^2 + 2x - 3} \\
x + 1
\end{array}
$$

Note that the first subtraction eliminated two terms from the dividend. When this happens, the quotient skips a term. You can write the result as

$$\frac{2x^4 + 4x^3 - 5x^2 + 3x - 2}{x^2 + 2x - 3} = 2x^2 + 1 + \frac{x + 1}{x^2 + 2x - 3}.$$

Remind students that when division yields a remainder, it is important that they write the remainder term correctly.

Synthetic Division

There is a nice shortcut for long division of polynomials when dividing by divisors of the form $x - k$. This shortcut is called **synthetic division.** The pattern for synthetic division of a cubic polynomial is summarized as follows. (The pattern for higher-degree polynomials is similar.)

Synthetic Division (for a Cubic Polynomial)

To divide $ax^3 + bx^2 + cx + d$ by $x - k$, use the following pattern.

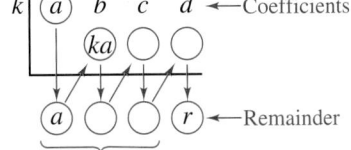

Vertical pattern: Add terms.
Diagonal pattern: Multiply by k.

Point out to students that a graphing utility can be used to check the answer to a polynomial division problem. When students graph both the original polynomial division problem and the answer in the same viewing window, the graphs should coincide.

Synthetic division works only for divisors of the form $x - k$. [Remember that $x + k = x - (-k)$.] You cannot use synthetic division to divide a polynomial by a quadratic such as $x^2 - 3$.

Example 4 ▶ Using Synthetic Division

Use synthetic division to divide $x^4 - 10x^2 - 2x + 4$ by $x + 3$.

Solution

You should set up the array as follows. Note that a zero is included for the missing x^3-term in the dividend.

$$-3 \quad | \quad 1 \quad 0 \quad -10 \quad -2 \quad 4$$

Then, use the synthetic division pattern by adding terms in columns and multiplying the results by -3.

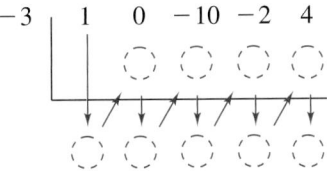

Divisor: $x + 3$ Dividend: $x^4 - 10x^2 - 2x + 4$

$$
\begin{array}{r|rrrrr}
-3 & 1 & 0 & -10 & -2 & 4 \\
   &   & -3 & 9 & 3 & -3 \\
\hline
   & 1 & -3 & -1 & 1 & \boxed{1}
\end{array}
$$

← Remainder: 1

Quotient: $x^3 - 3x^2 - x + 1$

So, you have

$$\frac{x^4 - 10x^2 - 2x + 4}{x + 3} = x^3 - 3x^2 - x + 1 + \frac{1}{x + 3}.$$

The Remainder and Factor Theorems

The remainder obtained in the synthetic division process has an important interpretation, as described in the **Remainder Theorem.**

The Remainder Theorem

If a polynomial $f(x)$ is divided by $x - k$, the remainder is

$$r = f(k).$$

For a proof of the Remainder Theorem, see Proofs in Mathematics on page 192.

The Remainder Theorem tells you that synthetic division can be used to evaluate a polynomial function. That is, to evaluate a polynomial function $f(x)$ when $x = k$, divide $f(x)$ by $x - k$. The remainder will be $f(k)$, as illustrated in Example 5.

Example 5 ▶ Using the Remainder Theorem

Use the Remainder Theorem to evaluate the following function at $x = -2$.

$$f(x) = 3x^3 + 8x^2 + 5x - 7$$

Solution

Using synthetic division, you obtain the following.

$$
\begin{array}{r|rrrr}
-2 & 3 & 8 & 5 & -7 \\
   &   & -6 & -4 & -2 \\
\hline
   & 3 & 2 & 1 & -9
\end{array}
$$

Because the remainder is $r = -9$, you can conclude that

$$f(-2) = -9. \qquad {\scriptstyle r = f(x)}$$

This means that $(-2, -9)$ is a point on the graph of f. You can check this by substituting $x = -2$ in the original function.

Check

$$f(-2) = 3(-2)^3 + 8(-2)^2 + 5(-2) - 7$$
$$= 3(-8) + 8(4) - 10 - 7 = -9$$

Additional Example

Use the Remainder Theorem to evaluate $f(x) = 4x^2 - 10x - 21$ when $x = 5$.

Solution

Using synthetic division, you obtain the following.

$$
\begin{array}{r|rrr}
5 & 4 & -10 & -21 \\
  &   & 20 & 50 \\
\hline
  & 4 & 10 & 29
\end{array}
$$

Because the remainder is 29, you can conclude that $f(5) = 29$.

Another important theorem is the **Factor Theorem,** stated below. This theorem states that you can test to see whether a polynomial has $(x - k)$ as a factor by evaluating the polynomial at $x = k$. If the result is 0, $(x - k)$ is a factor.

The Factor Theorem

A polynomial $f(x)$ has a factor $(x - k)$ if and only if $f(k) = 0$.

For a proof of the Factor Theorem, see Proofs in Mathematics on page 192.

Example 6 ► **Factoring a Polynomial: Repeated Division**

Show that $(x - 2)$ and $(x + 3)$ are factors of

$$f(x) = 2x^4 + 7x^3 - 4x^2 - 27x - 18.$$

Then find the remaining factors of $f(x)$.

Solution

Using synthetic division with the factor $(x - 2)$, you obtain the following.

$$
\begin{array}{r|rrrrr}
2 & 2 & 7 & -4 & -27 & -18 \\
  &   & 4 & 22 & 36 & 18 \\
\hline
  & 2 & 11 & 18 & 9 & 0
\end{array}
$$
→ 0 remainder, so $f(2) = 0$ and $(x - 2)$ is a factor.

Take the result of this division and perform synthetic division again using the factor $(x + 3)$.

$$
\begin{array}{r|rrrr}
-3 & 2 & 11 & 18 & 9 \\
   &   & -6 & -15 & -9 \\
\hline
   & 2 & 5 & 3 & 0
\end{array}
$$
→ 0 remainder, so $f(-3) = 0$ and $(x + 3)$ is a factor.

Because the resulting quadratic expression factors as

$$2x^2 + 5x + 3 = (2x + 3)(x + 1)$$

the complete factorization of $f(x)$ is

$$f(x) = (x - 2)(x + 3)(2x + 3)(x + 1).$$

Note that this factorization implies that f has four real zeros:

$$x = 2, \; x = -3, \; x = -\tfrac{3}{2}, \text{ and } x = -1.$$

This is confirmed by the graph of f, which is shown in Figure 2.28.

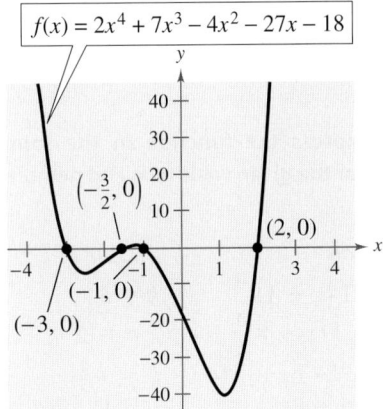

$f(x) = 2x^4 + 7x^3 - 4x^2 - 27x - 18$

FIGURE 2.28

Uses of the Remainder in Synthetic Division

The remainder r, obtained in the synthetic division of $f(x)$ by $x - k$, provides the following information.

1. The remainder r gives the value of f at $x = k$. That is, $r = f(k)$.

2. If $r = 0$, $(x - k)$ is a factor of $f(x)$.

3. If $r = 0$, $(k, 0)$ is an x-intercept of the graph of f.

Throughout this text, the importance of developing several problem-solving strategies is emphasized. In the exercises for this section, try using more than one strategy to solve several of the exercises. For instance, if you find that $x - k$ divides evenly into $f(x)$ (with no remainder), try sketching the graph of f. You should find that $(k, 0)$ is an x-intercept of the graph.

Activities

1. Use synthetic division to determine if $(x + 3)$ is a factor of $f(x) = 3x^3 + 4x^2 - 18x - 3$.

   Answer: No, it is not.

2. Divide using long division.

   $$\frac{4x^5 - x^3 + 2x^2 - x}{2x + 1}$$

   Answer: $2x^4 - x^3 + x - 1 + \dfrac{1}{2x + 1}$

3. Use the Remainder Theorem to evaluate $f(-3)$ for $f(x) = 2x^3 - 4x^2 + 1$.

   Answer: -89

2.3 Exercises

Analytical Analysis In Exercises 1 and 2, use long division to verify that $y_1 = y_2$.

1. $y_1 = \dfrac{x^2}{x + 2}$, $y_2 = x - 2 + \dfrac{4}{x + 2}$

2. $y_1 = \dfrac{x^4 - 3x^2 - 1}{x^2 + 5}$, $y_2 = x^2 - 8 + \dfrac{39}{x^2 + 5}$

Graphical Analysis In Exercises 3 and 4, use a graphing utility to graph the two equations in the same viewing window. Use the graphs to verify that the expressions are equivalent. Use long division to verify the results algebraically.

3. $y_1 = \dfrac{x^5 - 3x^3}{x^2 + 1}$, $y_2 = x^3 - 4x + \dfrac{4x}{x^2 + 1}$

4. $y_1 = \dfrac{x^3 - 2x^2 + 5}{x^2 + x + 1}$, $y_2 = x - 3 + \dfrac{2(x + 4)}{x^2 + x + 1}$

In Exercises 5–18, use long division to divide.

5. $(2x^2 + 10x + 12) \div (x + 3)$

6. $(5x^2 - 17x - 12) \div (x - 4)$

7. $(4x^3 - 7x^2 - 11x + 5) \div (4x + 5)$

8. $(6x^3 - 16x^2 + 17x - 6) \div (3x - 2)$

9. $(x^4 + 5x^3 + 6x^2 - x - 2) \div (x + 2)$

10. $(x^3 + 4x^2 - 3x - 12) \div (x - 3)$

11. $(7x + 3) \div (x + 2)$

12. $(8x - 5) \div (2x + 1)$

13. $(6x^3 + 10x^2 + x + 8) \div (2x^2 + 1)$

14. $(x^3 - 9) \div (x^2 + 1)$

15. $\dfrac{x^4 + 3x^2 + 1}{x^2 - 2x + 3}$

16. $\dfrac{x^5 + 7}{x^3 - 1}$

17. $\dfrac{x^4}{(x - 1)^3}$

18. $\dfrac{2x^3 - 4x^2 - 15x + 5}{(x - 1)^2}$

In Exercises 19–36, use synthetic division to divide.

19. $(3x^3 - 17x^2 + 15x - 25) \div (x - 5)$

20. $(5x^3 + 18x^2 + 7x - 6) \div (x + 3)$

21. $(4x^3 - 9x + 8x^2 - 18) \div (x + 2)$

22. $(9x^3 - 16x - 18x^2 + 32) \div (x - 2)$

23. $(-x^3 + 75x - 250) \div (x + 10)$

24. $(3x^3 - 16x^2 - 72) \div (x - 6)$

25. $(5x^3 - 6x^2 + 8) \div (x - 4)$

26. $(5x^3 + 6x + 8) \div (x + 2)$

27. $\dfrac{10x^4 - 50x^3 - 800}{x - 6}$

28. $\dfrac{x^5 - 13x^4 - 120x + 80}{x + 3}$

29. $\dfrac{x^3 + 512}{x + 8}$

30. $\dfrac{x^3 - 729}{x - 9}$

31. $\dfrac{-3x^4}{x - 2}$

32. $\dfrac{-3x^4}{x + 2}$

33. $\dfrac{180x - x^4}{x - 6}$

34. $\dfrac{5 - 3x + 2x^2 - x^3}{x + 1}$

35. $\dfrac{4x^3 + 16x^2 - 23x - 15}{x + \frac{1}{2}}$

36. $\dfrac{3x^3 - 4x^2 + 5}{x - \frac{3}{2}}$

In Exercises 37–44, express the function in the form $f(x) = (x - k)q(x) + r$ for the given value of k, and demonstrate that $f(k) = r$.

	Function	*Value of k*
37.	$f(x) = x^3 - x^2 - 14x + 11$	$k = 4$
38.	$f(x) = x^3 - 5x^2 - 11x + 8$	$k = -2$
39.	$f(x) = 15x^4 + 10x^3 - 6x^2 + 14$	$k = -\frac{2}{3}$
40.	$f(x) = 10x^3 - 22x^2 - 3x + 4$	$k = \frac{1}{5}$
41.	$f(x) = x^3 + 3x^2 - 2x - 14$	$k = \sqrt{2}$
42.	$f(x) = x^3 + 2x^2 - 5x - 4$	$k = -\sqrt{5}$
43.	$f(x) = -4x^3 + 6x^2 + 12x + 4$	$k = 1 - \sqrt{3}$
44.	$f(x) = -3x^3 + 8x^2 + 10x - 8$	$k = 2 + \sqrt{2}$

In Exercises 45–48, use synthetic division to find each function value. Verify your answer using another method.

45. $f(x) = 4x^3 - 13x + 10$

(a) $f(1)$ (b) $f(-2)$ (c) $f\left(\frac{1}{2}\right)$ (d) $f(8)$

46. $g(x) = x^6 - 4x^4 + 3x^2 + 2$

(a) $g(2)$ (b) $g(-4)$ (c) $g(3)$ (d) $g(-1)$

47. $h(x) = 3x^3 + 5x^2 - 10x + 1$

(a) $h(3)$ (b) $h\left(\frac{1}{3}\right)$ (c) $h(-2)$ (d) $h(-5)$

48. $f(x) = 0.4x^4 - 1.6x^3 + 0.7x^2 - 2$

(a) $f(1)$ (b) $f(-2)$ (c) $f(5)$ (d) $f(-10)$

In Exercises 49–56, use synthetic division to show that *x* is a zero of the third-degree polynomial equation, and use the result to factor the polynomial completely. List all real zeros of the function.

Polynomial Equation	*Value of x*
49. $x^3 - 7x + 6 = 0$	$x = 2$
50. $x^3 - 28x - 48 = 0$	$x = -4$
51. $2x^3 - 15x^2 + 27x - 10 = 0$	$x = \frac{1}{2}$
52. $48x^3 - 80x^2 + 41x - 6 = 0$	$x = \frac{2}{3}$
53. $x^3 + 2x^2 - 3x - 6 = 0$	$x = \sqrt{3}$
54. $x^3 + 2x^2 - 2x - 4 = 0$	$x = \sqrt{2}$
55. $x^3 - 3x^2 + 2 = 0$	$x = 1 + \sqrt{3}$
56. $x^3 - x^2 - 13x - 3 = 0$	$x = 2 - \sqrt{5}$

In Exercises 57–64, (a) verify the given factors of the function *f*, (b) find the remaining factors of *f*, (c) use your results to write the complete factorization of *f*, (d) list all real zeros of *f*, and (e) confirm your results by using a graphing utility to graph the function.

Function	*Factors*
57. $f(x) = 2x^3 + x^2 - 5x + 2$	$(x + 2), (x - 1)$
58. $f(x) = 3x^3 + 2x^2 - 19x + 6$	$(x + 3), (x - 2)$
59. $f(x) = x^4 - 4x^3 - 15x^2 + 58x - 40$	$(x - 5), (x + 4)$
60. $f(x) = 8x^4 - 14x^3 - 71x^2 - 10x + 24$	$(x + 2), (x - 4)$
61. $f(x) = 6x^3 + 41x^2 - 9x - 14$	$(2x + 1), (3x - 2)$
62. $f(x) = 10x^3 - 11x^2 - 72x + 45$	$(2x + 5), (5x - 3)$
63. $f(x) = 2x^3 - x^2 - 10x + 5$	$(2x - 1), (x + \sqrt{5})$
64. $f(x) = x^3 + 3x^2 - 48x - 144$	$(x + 4\sqrt{3}), (x + 3)$

 Graphical Analysis In Exercises 65–68, (a) use the *zero* or *root* feature of a graphing utility to approximate the zeros of the function accurate to three decimal places and (b) determine one of the exact zeros, use synthetic division to verify your result, and then factor the polynomial completely.

65. $f(x) = x^3 - 2x^2 - 5x + 10$

66. $g(x) = x^3 - 4x^2 - 2x + 8$

67. $h(t) = t^3 - 2t^2 - 7t + 2$

68. $f(s) = s^3 - 12s^2 + 40s - 24$

In Exercises 69–74, simplify the rational expression.

69. $\dfrac{4x^3 - 8x^2 + x + 3}{2x - 3}$

70. $\dfrac{x^3 + x^2 - 64x - 64}{x + 8}$

71. $\dfrac{x^3 + 3x^2 - x - 3}{x + 1}$

72. $\dfrac{2x^3 + 3x^2 - 3x - 2}{x - 1}$

73. $\dfrac{x^4 + 6x^3 + 11x^2 + 6x}{x^2 + 3x + 2}$

74. $\dfrac{x^4 + 9x^3 - 5x^2 - 36x + 4}{x^2 - 4}$

▶ Model It

75. *Data Analysis* The numbers *M* (in thousands) of United States military personnel on active duty for the years 1990 through 2000 are shown in the table, where *t* represents the time (in years), with $t = 0$ corresponding to 1990. (Source: U.S. Department of Defense)

Year, *t*	Military personnel, *M*
0	2044
1	1986
2	1807
3	1705
4	1610
5	1518
6	1472
7	1439
8	1407
9	1386
10	1384

(a) Use a graphing utility to create a scatter plot of the data.

(b) Use the *regression* feature of the graphing utility to find a cubic model for the data. Then graph the model in the same viewing window as the scatter plot.

(c) Use the model to create a table of estimated values of *M*. Compare the model with the data.

(d) Use synthetic division to evaluate the model for the year 2005. Even though the model is relatively accurate for estimating the given data, would you use this model to predict the number of military personnel in the future? Explain.

76. *Data Analysis*   The average monthly basic rates R (in dollars) for cable television in the United States for the years 1990 through 1999 are shown in the table, where t represents the time (in years), with $t = 0$ corresponding to 1990.   (Source: Paul Kagan Associates, Inc.)

Year, t	Basic rate, R
0	16.78
1	18.10
2	19.08
3	19.39
4	21.62
5	23.07
6	24.41
7	26.48
8	27.81
9	28.92

(a) Use a graphing utility to create a scatter plot of the data.

(b) Use the *regression* feature of the graphing utility to find a cubic model for the data. Then graph the model in the same viewing window as the scatter plot. Compare the model with the data.

(c) Use synthetic division to evaluate the model for the year 2005.

Synthesis

True or False?   In Exercises 77–79, determine whether the statement is true or false. Justify your answer.

77. If $(7x + 4)$ is a factor of some polynomial function f, then $\frac{4}{7}$ is a zero of f.

78. $(2x - 1)$ is a factor of the polynomial $6x^6 + x^5 - 92x^4 + 45x^3 + 184x^2 + 4x - 48$.

79. The rational expression

$$\frac{x^3 + 2x^2 - 13x + 10}{x^2 - 4x - 12}$$

is improper.

80. *Exploration*   Use the form

$$f(x) = (x - k)q(x) + r$$

to create a cubic function that (a) passes through the point $(2, 5)$ and rises to the right, and (b) passes through the point $(-3, 1)$ and falls to the right. (There are many correct answers.)

Think About It   In Exercises 81 and 82, perform the division by assuming that n is a positive integer.

81. $\dfrac{x^{3n} + 9x^{2n} + 27x^n + 27}{x^n + 3}$

82. $\dfrac{x^{3n} - 3x^{2n} + 5x^n - 6}{x^n - 2}$

83. *Writing*   Briefly explain what it means for a divisor to divide evenly into a dividend.

84. *Writing*   Briefly explain how to check polynomial division, and justify your reasoning. Give an example.

Exploration   In Exercises 85 and 86, find the constant c such that the denominator will divide evenly into the numerator.

85. $\dfrac{x^3 + 4x^2 - 3x + c}{x - 5}$ **86.** $\dfrac{x^5 - 2x^2 + x + c}{x + 2}$

Think About It   In Exercises 87 and 88, answer the questions about the division

$$\frac{f(x)}{x - k}$$

where $f(x) = (x + 3)^2(x - 3)(x + 1)^3$.

87. What is the remainder when $k = -3$? Explain.

88. If it is necessary to find $f(2)$, is it easier to evaluate the function directly or to use synthetic division? Explain.

Review

In Exercises 89–94, use any method to solve the quadratic equation.

89. $9x^2 - 25 = 0$ **90.** $16x^2 - 21 = 0$

91. $5x^2 - 3x - 14 = 0$ **92.** $8x^2 - 22x + 15 = 0$

93. $2x^2 + 6x + 3 = 0$ **94.** $x^2 + 3x - 3 = 0$

In Exercises 95–98, find a polynomial function that has the given zeros. There are many correct answers.

95. $0, 3, 4$ **96.** $-6, 1$

97. $-3, 1 + \sqrt{2}, 1 - \sqrt{2}$

98. $1, -2, 2 + \sqrt{3}, 2 - \sqrt{3}$

2.4 Complex Numbers

▶ What you should learn

- How to use the imaginary unit i to write complex numbers
- How to add, subtract, and multiply complex numbers
- How to use complex conjugates to write the quotient of two complex numbers in standard form
- How to find complex solutions of quadratic equations

▶ Why you should learn it

You can use complex numbers to model and solve real-life problems in electronics. For instance, in Exercise 84 on page 149, you will learn how to use complex numbers to find the impedance of an electrical circuit.

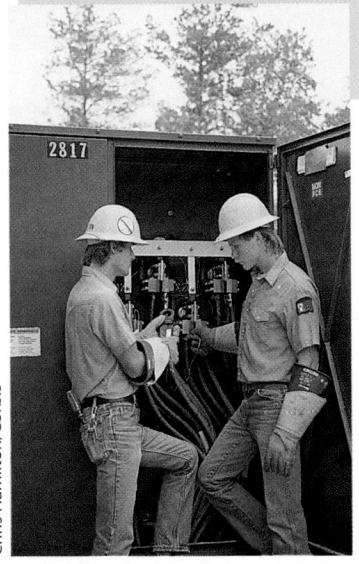

Chris Hamilton/Corbis

The Imaginary Unit i

You have learned that some quadratic equations have no real solutions. For instance, the quadratic equation

$$x^2 + 1 = 0 \qquad \text{Equation with no real solution}$$

has no real solution because there is no real number x that can be squared to produce -1. To overcome this deficiency, mathematicians created an expanded system of numbers using the **imaginary unit i,** defined as

$$i = \sqrt{-1} \qquad \text{Imaginary unit}$$

where $i^2 = -1$. By adding real numbers to real multiples of this imaginary unit, the set of **complex numbers** is obtained. Each complex number can be written in the **standard form $a + bi$.** The real number a is called the **real part** of the **complex number $a + bi$,** and the number bi (where b is a real number) is called the **imaginary part** of the complex number.

Definition of a Complex Number

If a and b are real numbers, the number $a + bi$ is a **complex number,** and it is said to be written in **standard form.** If $b = 0$, the number $a + bi = a$ is a real number. If $b \neq 0$, the number $a + bi$ is called an **imaginary number.** A number of the form bi, where $b \neq 0$, is called a **pure imaginary number.**

The set of real numbers is a subset of the set of complex numbers, as shown in Figure 2.29. This is true because every real number a can be written as a complex number using $b = 0$. That is, for every real number a, you can write $a = a + 0i$.

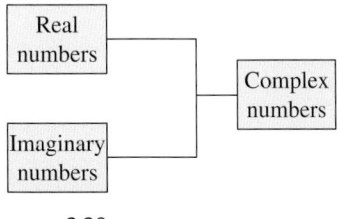

FIGURE 2.29

Equality of Complex Numbers

Two complex numbers $a + bi$ and $c + di$, written in standard form, are equal to each other

$$a + bi = c + di \qquad \text{Equality of two complex numbers}$$

if and only if $a = c$ and $b = d$.

Operations with Complex Numbers

To add (or subtract) two complex numbers, you add (or subtract) the real and imaginary parts of the numbers separately.

For each operation on complex numbers, you can show the parallel operation on polynomials.

> ### Addition and Subtraction of Complex Numbers
>
> If $a + bi$ and $c + di$ are two complex numbers written in standard form, their sum and difference are defined as follows.
>
> *Sum:* $(a + bi) + (c + di) = (a + c) + (b + d)i$
>
> *Difference:* $(a + bi) - (c + di) = (a - c) + (b - d)i$

The **additive identity** in the complex number system is zero (the same as in the real number system). Furthermore, the **additive inverse** of the complex number $a + bi$ is

$$-(a + bi) = -a - bi.$$ Additive inverse

So, you have

$$(a + bi) + (-a - bi) = 0 + 0i = 0.$$

Example 1 ▶ **Adding and Subtracting Complex Numbers**

a. $(4 + 7i) + (1 - 6i) = 4 + 7i + 1 - 6i$ Remove parentheses.

$\qquad\qquad\qquad\quad = (4 + 1) + (7i - 6i)$ Group like terms.

$\qquad\qquad\qquad\quad = 5 + i$ Write in standard form.

b. $(1 + 2i) - (4 + 2i) = 1 + 2i - 4 - 2i$ Remove parentheses.

$\qquad\qquad\qquad\quad = (1 - 4) + (2i - 2i)$ Group like terms.

$\qquad\qquad\qquad\quad = -3 + 0$ Simplify.

$\qquad\qquad\qquad\quad = -3$ Write in standard form.

c. $3i - (-2 + 3i) - (2 + 5i) = 3i + 2 - 3i - 2 - 5i$

$\qquad\qquad\qquad\qquad\quad = (2 - 2) + (3i - 3i - 5i)$

$\qquad\qquad\qquad\qquad\quad = 0 - 5i$

$\qquad\qquad\qquad\qquad\quad = -5i$

d. $(3 + 2i) + (4 - i) - (7 + i) = 3 + 2i + 4 - i - 7 - i$

$\qquad\qquad\qquad\qquad\qquad = (3 + 4 - 7) + (2i - i - i)$

$\qquad\qquad\qquad\qquad\qquad = 0 + 0i$

$\qquad\qquad\qquad\qquad\qquad = 0$

Note in Examples 1(b) and 1(d) that the sum of two complex numbers can be a real number.

Exploration

Complete the following.

$i^1 = i$ $i^7 = \boxed{}$

$i^2 = -1$ $i^8 = \boxed{}$

$i^3 = -i$ $i^9 = \boxed{}$

$i^4 = 1$ $i^{10} = \boxed{}$

$i^5 = \boxed{}$ $i^{11} = \boxed{}$

$i^6 = \boxed{}$ $i^{12} = \boxed{}$

What pattern do you see? Write a brief description of how you would find i raised to any positive integer power.

Many of the properties of real numbers are valid for complex numbers as well. Here are some examples.

Associative Properties of Addition and Multiplication

Commutative Properties of Addition and Multiplication

Distributive Property of Multiplication Over Addition

Notice below how these properties are used when two complex numbers are multiplied.

$$(a + bi)(c + di) = a(c + di) + bi(c + di) \qquad \text{Distributive Property}$$
$$= ac + (ad)i + (bc)i + (bd)i^2 \qquad \text{Distributive Property}$$
$$= ac + (ad)i + (bc)i + (bd)(-1) \qquad i^2 = -1$$
$$= ac - bd + (ad)i + (bc)i \qquad \text{Commutative Property}$$
$$= (ac - bd) + (ad + bc)i \qquad \text{Associative Property}$$

Rather than trying to memorize this multiplication rule, you should simply remember how the Distributive Property is used to multiply two complex numbers.

Example 2 ▶ Multiplying Complex Numbers

a. $4(-2 + 3i) = 4(-2) + 4(3i)$ Distributive Property

$\qquad\qquad\quad = -8 + 12i$ Simplify.

b. $(2 - i)(4 + 3i) = 2(4 + 3i) - i(4 + 3i)$ Distributive Property

$\qquad\qquad\qquad = 8 + 6i - 4i - 3i^2$ Distributive Property

$\qquad\qquad\qquad = 8 + 6i - 4i - 3(-1)$ $i^2 = -1$

$\qquad\qquad\qquad = (8 + 3) + (6i - 4i)$ Group like terms.

$\qquad\qquad\qquad = 11 + 2i$ Write in standard form.

c. $(3 + 2i)(3 - 2i) = 3(3 - 2i) + 2i(3 - 2i)$ Distributive Property

$\qquad\qquad\qquad = 9 - 6i + 6i - 4i^2$ Distributive Property

$\qquad\qquad\qquad = 9 - 6i + 6i - 4(-1)$ $i^2 = -1$

$\qquad\qquad\qquad = 9 + 4$ Simplify.

$\qquad\qquad\qquad = 13$ Write in standard form.

d. $(3 + 2i)^2 = (3 + 2i)(3 + 2i)$ Square of a binomial

$\qquad\qquad\quad = 3(3 + 2i) + 2i(3 + 2i)$ Distributive Property

$\qquad\qquad\quad = 9 + 6i + 6i + 4i^2$ Distributive Property

$\qquad\qquad\quad = 9 + 6i + 6i + 4(-1)$ $i^2 = -1$

$\qquad\qquad\quad = 9 + 12i - 4$ Simplify.

$\qquad\qquad\quad = 5 + 12i$ Write in standard form.

Complex Conjugates

Notice in Example 2(c) that the product of two complex numbers can be a real number. This occurs with pairs of complex numbers of the form $a + bi$ and $a - bi$, called **complex conjugates.**

A comparison with the method of rationalizing denominators (Section A.2) may be helpful.

$$(a + bi)(a - bi) = a^2 - abi + abi - b^2i^2$$
$$= a^2 - b^2(-1)$$
$$= a^2 + b^2$$

Example 3 ▶ **Multiplying Conjugates**

Multiply each complex number by its complex conjugate.

a. $1 + i$ **b.** $4 - 3i$

Solution

a. The complex conjugate of $1 + i$ is $1 - i$.

$$(1 + i)(1 - i) = 1^2 - i^2 = 1 - (-1) = 2$$

b. The complex conjugate of $4 - 3i$ is $4 + 3i$.

$$(4 - 3i)(4 + 3i) = 4^2 - (3i)^2 = 16 - 9i^2 = 16 - 9(-1) = 25$$

To write the quotient of $a + bi$ and $c + di$ in standard form, where c and d are not both zero, multiply the numerator and denominator by the complex conjugate of the *denominator* to obtain

$$\frac{a + bi}{c + di} = \frac{a + bi}{c + di}\left(\frac{c - di}{c - di}\right)$$

$$= \frac{(ac + bd) + (bc - ad)i}{c^2 + d^2}. \qquad \text{Standard form}$$

Example 4 ▶ **Writing a Quotient of Complex Numbers**
in Standard Form

$$\frac{2 + 3i}{4 - 2i} = \frac{2 + 3i}{4 - 2i}\left(\frac{4 + 2i}{4 + 2i}\right) \qquad \text{Multiply numerator and denominator by complex conjugate of denominator.}$$

$$= \frac{8 + 4i + 12i + 6i^2}{16 - 4i^2} \qquad \text{Expand.}$$

$$= \frac{8 - 6 + 16i}{16 + 4} \qquad i^2 = -1$$

$$= \frac{2 + 16i}{20} \qquad \text{Simplify.}$$

$$= \frac{1}{10} + \frac{4}{5}i \qquad \text{Write in standard form.}$$

Complex Solutions of Quadratic Equations

When using the Quadratic Formula to solve a quadratic equation, you often obtain a result such as $\sqrt{-3}$, which you know is not a real number. By factoring out $i = \sqrt{-1}$, you can write this number in standard form.

$$\sqrt{-3} = \sqrt{3(-1)} = \sqrt{3}\sqrt{-1} = \sqrt{3}\,i$$

The number $\sqrt{3}\,i$ is called the *principal square root* of -3.

> ### Principal Square Root of a Negative Number
>
> If a is a positive number, the **principal square root** of the negative number $-a$ is defined as
>
> $$\sqrt{-a} = \sqrt{a}\,i.$$

STUDY TIP

The definition of principal square root uses the rule

$$\sqrt{ab} = \sqrt{a}\sqrt{b}$$

for $a > 0$ and $b < 0$. This rule is not valid if *both* a and b are negative. For example,

$$\sqrt{-5}\sqrt{-5} = \sqrt{5(-1)}\sqrt{5(-1)}$$
$$= \sqrt{5}\,i\sqrt{5}\,i$$
$$= \sqrt{25}\,i^2$$
$$= 5i^2 = -5$$

whereas

$$\sqrt{(-5)(-5)} = \sqrt{25} = 5.$$

To avoid problems with square roots of negative numbers, be sure to convert to standard form *before* multiplying.

Example 5 ▶ Writing Complex Numbers in Standard Form

a. $\sqrt{-3}\sqrt{-12} = \sqrt{3}\,i\sqrt{12}\,i = \sqrt{36}\,i^2 = 6(-1) = -6$

b. $\sqrt{-48} - \sqrt{-27} = \sqrt{48}\,i - \sqrt{27}\,i = 4\sqrt{3}\,i - 3\sqrt{3}\,i = \sqrt{3}\,i$

c. $\left(-1 + \sqrt{-3}\right)^2 = \left(-1 + \sqrt{3}\,i\right)^2$
$$= (-1)^2 - 2\sqrt{3}\,i + \left(\sqrt{3}\right)^2(i^2)$$
$$= 1 - 2\sqrt{3}\,i + 3(-1)$$
$$= -2 - 2\sqrt{3}\,i$$

Example 6 ▶ Complex Solutions of a Quadratic Equation

Solve (a) $x^2 + 4 = 0$ and (b) $3x^2 - 2x + 5 = 0$.

Solution

a. $x^2 + 4 = 0$ Write original equation.

     $x^2 = -4$ Subtract 4 from each side.

     $x = \pm 2i$ Extract square roots.

b. $3x^2 - 2x + 5 = 0$ Write original equation.

$$x = \frac{-(-2) \pm \sqrt{(-2)^2 - 4(3)(5)}}{2(3)}$$ Quadratic Formula

$$= \frac{2 \pm \sqrt{-56}}{6}$$ Simplify.

$$= \frac{2 \pm 2\sqrt{14}\,i}{6}$$ Write $\sqrt{-56}$ in standard form.

$$= \frac{1}{3} \pm \frac{\sqrt{14}}{3}\,i$$ Write in standard form.

Activities

1. Perform the indicated operations and write the result in standard form.
$$\left(4 - \sqrt{-9}\right)\left(2 + \sqrt{-9}\right)$$
Answer: $17 + 6i$

2. Write $\dfrac{3 + i}{i}$ in standard form.

Answer: $1 - 3i$

3. Use the Quadratic Formula to solve $2x^2 - 5x + 7 = 0$.

Answer: $x = \dfrac{5}{4} \pm \dfrac{\sqrt{31}}{4}\,i$

2.4 Exercises

In Exercises 1–4, find real numbers a and b such that the equation is true.

1. $a + bi = -10 + 6i$

2. $a + bi = 13 + 4i$

3. $(a - 1) + (b + 3)i = 5 + 8i$

4. $(a + 6) + 2bi = 6 - 5i$

In Exercises 5–16, write the complex number in standard form.

5. $4 + \sqrt{-9}$ **6.** $3 + \sqrt{-16}$

7. $2 - \sqrt{-27}$ **8.** $1 + \sqrt{-8}$

9. $\sqrt{-75}$ **10.** $\sqrt{-4}$

11. 8 **12.** 45

13. $-6i + i^2$ **14.** $-4i^2 + 2i$

15. $\sqrt{-0.09}$ **16.** $\sqrt{-0.0004}$

In Exercises 17–26, perform the addition or subtraction and write the result in standard form.

17. $(5 + i) + (6 - 2i)$

18. $(13 - 2i) + (-5 + 6i)$

19. $(8 - i) - (4 - i)$

20. $(3 + 2i) - (6 + 13i)$

21. $\left(-2 + \sqrt{-8}\right) + \left(5 - \sqrt{-50}\right)$

22. $\left(8 + \sqrt{-18}\right) - \left(4 + 3\sqrt{2}i\right)$

23. $13i - (14 - 7i)$

24. $22 + (-5 + 8i) + 10i$

25. $-\left(\frac{3}{2} + \frac{5}{2}i\right) + \left(\frac{5}{3} + \frac{11}{3}i\right)$

26. $(1.6 + 3.2i) + (-5.8 + 4.3i)$

In Exercises 27–40, perform the operation and write the result in standard form.

27. $\sqrt{-6} \cdot \sqrt{-2}$ **28.** $\sqrt{-5} \cdot \sqrt{-10}$

29. $\left(\sqrt{-10}\right)^2$ **30.** $\left(\sqrt{-75}\right)^2$

31. $(1 + i)(3 - 2i)$

32. $(6 - 2i)(2 - 3i)$

33. $6i(5 - 2i)$

34. $-8i(9 + 4i)$

35. $\left(\sqrt{14} + \sqrt{10}i\right)\left(\sqrt{14} - \sqrt{10}i\right)$

36. $\left(3 + \sqrt{-5}\right)\left(7 - \sqrt{-10}\right)$

37. $(4 + 5i)^2$

38. $(2 - 3i)^2$

39. $(2 + 3i)^2 + (2 - 3i)^2$

40. $(1 - 2i)^2 - (1 + 2i)^2$

In Exercises 41–48, write the complex conjugate of the complex number. Then multiply the number by its complex conjugate.

41. $6 + 3i$ **42.** $7 - 12i$

43. $-1 - \sqrt{5}i$ **44.** $-3 + \sqrt{2}i$

45. $\sqrt{-20}$ **46.** $\sqrt{-15}$

47. $\sqrt{8}$ **48.** $1 + \sqrt{8}$

In Exercises 49–58, write the quotient in standard form.

49. $\dfrac{5}{i}$ **50.** $-\dfrac{14}{2i}$

51. $\dfrac{2}{4 - 5i}$ **52.** $\dfrac{5}{1 - i}$

53. $\dfrac{3 + i}{3 - i}$ **54.** $\dfrac{6 - 7i}{1 - 2i}$

55. $\dfrac{6 - 5i}{i}$ **56.** $\dfrac{8 + 16i}{2i}$

57. $\dfrac{3i}{(4 - 5i)^2}$ **58.** $\dfrac{5i}{(2 + 3i)^2}$

In Exercises 59–62, perform the operation and write the result in standard form.

59. $\dfrac{2}{1 + i} - \dfrac{3}{1 - i}$ **60.** $\dfrac{2i}{2 + i} + \dfrac{5}{2 - i}$

61. $\dfrac{i}{3 - 2i} + \dfrac{2i}{3 + 8i}$ **62.** $\dfrac{1 + i}{i} - \dfrac{3}{4 - i}$

In Exercises 63–72, use the Quadratic Formula to solve the quadratic equation.

63. $x^2 - 2x + 2 = 0$ **64.** $x^2 + 6x + 10 = 0$

65. $4x^2 + 16x + 17 = 0$ **66.** $9x^2 - 6x + 37 = 0$

67. $4x^2 + 16x + 15 = 0$ **68.** $16t^2 - 4t + 3 = 0$

69. $\frac{3}{2}x^2 - 6x + 9 = 0$ **70.** $\frac{7}{8}x^2 - \frac{3}{4}x + \frac{5}{16} = 0$

71. $1.4x^2 - 2x - 10 = 0$

72. $4.5x^2 - 3x + 12 = 0$

In Exercises 73–80, simplify the complex number and write it in standard form.

73. $-6i^3 + i^2$

74. $4i^2 - 2i^3$

75. $-5i^5$

76. $(-i)^3$

77. $\left(\sqrt{-75}\right)^3$

78. $\left(\sqrt{-2}\right)^6$

79. $\dfrac{1}{i^3}$

80. $\dfrac{1}{(2i)^3}$

81. Cube each complex number.

(a) 2 (b) $-1 + \sqrt{3}i$ (c) $-1 - \sqrt{3}i$

82. Raise each complex number to the fourth power.

(a) 2 (b) -2 (c) $2i$ (d) $-2i$

83. Express each of the powers of i as i, $-i$, 1, or -1.

(a) i^{40} (b) i^{25} (c) i^{50} (d) i^{67}

▶ **Model It**

84. *Impedance* The opposition to current in an electrical circuit is called its impedance. The impedance z in a parallel circuit with two pathways satisfies the equation

$$\frac{1}{z} = \frac{1}{z_1} + \frac{1}{z_2}$$

where z_1 is the impedance (in ohms) of pathway 1 and z_2 is the impedance of pathway 2.

(a) The impedance of each pathway in a parallel circuit is found by adding the impedances of all components in the pathway. Use the table to find z_1 and z_2.

(b) Find the impedance z.

	Resistor	Inductor	Capacitor
Symbol	─W─ $a\Omega$	─000─ $b\Omega$	─┤├─ $c\Omega$
Impedance	a	bi	$-ci$

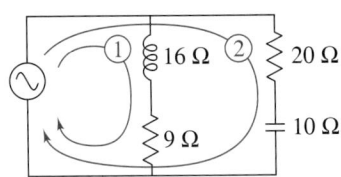

Synthesis

True or False? In Exercises 85–87, determine whether the statement is true or false. Justify your answer.

85. There is no complex number that is equal to its complex conjugate.

86. $-i\sqrt{6}$ is a solution of $x^4 - x^2 + 14 = 56$.

87. $i^{44} + i^{150} - i^{74} - i^{109} + i^{61} = -1$

88. *Error Analysis* Describe the error.

$$\sqrt{-6}\sqrt{-6} = \sqrt{(-6)(-6)} = \sqrt{36} = 6$$

89. *Proof* Prove that the complex conjugate of the product of two complex numbers $a_1 + b_1i$ and $a_2 + b_2i$ is the product of their complex conjugates.

90. *Proof* Prove that the complex conjugate of the sum of two complex numbers $a_1 + b_1i$ and $a_2 + b_2i$ is the sum of their complex conjugates.

Review

In Exercises 91–94, perform the operation and write the result in standard form.

91. $(4 + 3x) + (8 - 6x - x^2)$

92. $(x^3 - 3x^2) - (6 - 2x - 4x^2)$

93. $\left(3x - \frac{1}{2}\right)(x + 4)$

94. $(2x - 5)^2$

In Exercises 95–98, solve the equation and check your solution.

95. $-x - 12 = 19$

96. $8 - 3x = -34$

97. $4(5x - 6) - 3(6x + 1) = 0$

98. $5[x - (3x + 11)] = 20x - 15$

99. *Volume of an Oblate Spheroid*

Solve for a: $V = \frac{4}{3}\pi a^2 b$

100. *Newton's Law of Universal Gravitation*

Solve for r: $F = \alpha \dfrac{m_1 m_2}{r^2}$

101. *Mixture Problem* A five-liter container contains a mixture with a concentration of 50%. How much of this mixture must be withdrawn and replaced by 100% concentrate to bring the mixture up to 60% concentration?

2.5   Zeros of Polynomial Functions

▶ **What you should learn**

- How to use the Fundamental Theorem of Algebra to determine the number of zeros of polynomial functions
- How to find rational zeros of polynomial functions
- How to find conjugate pairs of complex zeros
- How to find zeros of polynomials by factoring
- How to use Descartes's Rule of Signs and the Upper and Lower Bound Rules to find zeros of polynomials

▶ **Why you should learn it**

Finding zeros of polynomial functions is an important part of solving real-life problems. For instance, in Exercise 107 on page 163, the zeros of a polynomial function can help you analyze the attendance at women's college basketball games.

The Fundamental Theorem of Algebra

You know that an nth-degree polynomial can have at most n real zeros. In the complex number system, this statement can be improved. That is, in the complex number system, every nth-degree polynomial function has *precisely* n zeros. This important result is derived from the **Fundamental Theorem of Algebra,** first proved by the German mathematician Carl Friedrich Gauss (1777–1855).

> **The Fundamental Theorem of Algebra**
>
> If $f(x)$ is a polynomial of degree n, where $n > 0$, then f has at least one zero in the complex number system.

Using the Fundamental Theorem of Algebra and the equivalence of zeros and factors, you obtain the **Linear Factorization Theorem.**

> **Linear Factorization Theorem**
>
> If $f(x)$ is a polynomial of degree n, where $n > 0$, then f has precisely n linear factors
>
> $$f(x) = a_n(x - c_1)(x - c_2) \cdots (x - c_n)$$
>
> where $c_1, c_2, \ldots, c_n$ are complex numbers.

For a proof of the Linear Factorization Theorem, see Proofs in Mathematics on page 193.

Note that the Fundamental Theorem of Algebra and the Linear Factorization Theorem tell you only that the zeros or factors of a polynomial exist, not how to find them. Such theorems are called *existence theorems.*

Example 1 ▶   Zeros of Polynomial Functions

a. The first-degree polynomial $f(x) = x - 2$ has exactly *one* zero: $x = 2$.

b. Counting multiplicity, the second-degree polynomial function

$$f(x) = x^2 - 6x + 9 = (x - 3)(x - 3)$$

has exactly *two* zeros: $x = 3$ and $x = 3$. (This is called a *repeated zero.*)

c. The third-degree polynomial function

$$f(x) = x^3 + 4x = x(x^2 + 4) = x(x - 2i)(x + 2i)$$

has exactly *three* zeros: $x = 0$, $x = 2i$, and $x = -2i$.

d. The fourth-degree polynomial function

$$f(x) = x^4 - 1 = (x - 1)(x + 1)(x - i)(x + i)$$

has exactly *four* zeros: $x = 1$, $x = -1$, $x = i$, and $x = -i$.

Jonathan Daniel/Getty Images

Finding zeros of polynomial functions is a very important concept in algebra. This is a good place to discuss the fact that polynomials do not necessarily have rational zeros but may have zeros that are irrational or complex.

Fogg Art Museum

Historical Note

Although they were not contemporaries, Jean Le Rond d'Alembert (1717–1783) worked independently of Carl Gauss in trying to prove the Fundamental Theorem of Algebra. His efforts were such that, in France, the Fundamental Theorem of Algebra is frequently known as the Theorem of d'Alembert.

The Rational Zero Test

The **Rational Zero Test** relates the possible rational zeros of a polynomial (having integer coefficients) to the leading coefficient and to the constant term of the polynomial.

The Rational Zero Test

If the polynomial $f(x) = a_n x^n + a_{n-1} x^{n-1} + \cdots + a_2 x^2 + a_1 x + a_0$ has *integer* coefficients, every rational zero of f has the form

$$\text{Rational zero} = \frac{p}{q}$$

where p and q have no common factors other than 1, and

$$p = \text{a factor of the constant term } a_0$$

$$q = \text{a factor of the leading coefficient } a_n.$$

To use the Rational Zero Test, you should first list all rational numbers whose numerators are factors of the constant term and whose denominators are factors of the leading coefficient.

$$\text{Possible rational zeros} = \frac{\text{factors of constant term}}{\text{factors of leading coefficient}}$$

Having formed this list of *possible rational zeros*, use a trial-and-error method to determine which, if any, are actual zeros of the polynomial. Note that when the leading coefficient is 1, the possible rational zeros are simply the factors of the constant term.

Example 2 ▶ **Rational Zero Test with Leading Coefficient of 1**

Find the rational zeros of

$$f(x) = x^3 + x + 1.$$

Solution

Because the leading coefficient is 1, the possible rational zeros are ± 1, the factors of the constant term. By testing these possible zeros, you can see that neither works.

$$f(1) = (1)^3 + 1 + 1$$
$$= 3$$
$$f(-1) = (-1)^3 + (-1) + 1$$
$$= -1$$

So, you can conclude that the given polynomial has *no* rational zeros. Note from the graph of f in Figure 2.30 that f does have one real zero between -1 and 0. However, by the Rational Zero Test, you know that this real zero is *not* a rational number.

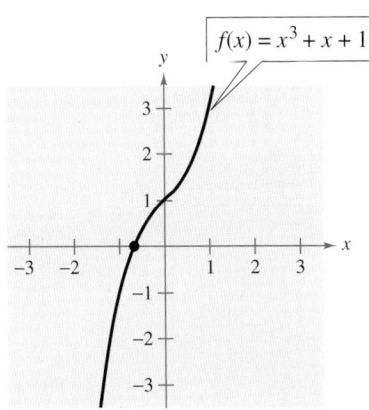

$f(x) = x^3 + x + 1$

FIGURE 2.30

Example 3 ▶ **Rational Zero Test with Leading Coefficient of 1**

Find the rational zeros of $f(x) = x^4 - x^3 + x^2 - 3x - 6$.

Solution

Because the leading coefficient is 1, the possible rational zeros are the factors of the constant term.

Possible rational zeros: $\pm 1, \pm 2, \pm 3, \pm 6$

A test of these possible zeros shows that $x = -1$ and $x = 2$ are the only two rational zeros. Check the others to be sure.

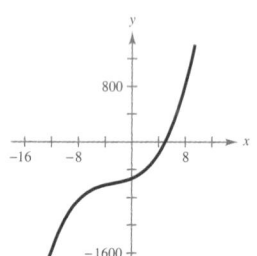
If the leading coefficient of a polynomial is not 1, the list of possible rational zeros can increase dramatically. In such cases, the search can be shortened in several ways: (1) a programmable calculator can be used to speed up the calculations; (2) a graph, drawn either by hand or with a graphing utility, can give a good estimate of the locations of the zeros; (3) the Intermediate Value Theorem along with a table generated by a graphing utility can give approximations of zeros; and (4) synthetic division can be used to test the possible rational zeros.

To see how to use synthetic division to test the possible rational zeros, take another look at the function $f(x) = x^4 - x^3 + x^2 - 3x - 6$ from Example 3. To test that $x = -1$ and $x = 2$ are zeros of f, you can apply synthetic division successively, as follows.

$$
\begin{array}{r|rrrrr}
-1 & 1 & -1 & 1 & -3 & -6 \\
   &   & -1 & 2 & -3 & 6 \\
\hline
   & 1 & -2 & 3 & -6 & 0
\end{array}
$$

$$
\begin{array}{r|rrrr}
2 & 1 & -2 & 3 & -6 \\
  &   & 2 & 0 & 6 \\
\hline
  & 1 & 0 & 3 & 0
\end{array}
$$

So, you have

$$f(x) = (x + 1)(x - 2)(x^2 + 3).$$

Because the factor $(x^2 + 3)$ produces no real zeros, you can conclude that $x = -1$ and $x = 2$ are the only *real* zeros of f, which is verified in Figure 2.31.

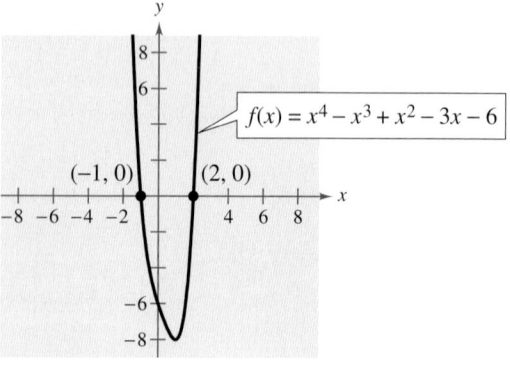

FIGURE **2.31**

Finding the first zero is often the hardest part. After that, the search is simplified by using the lower-degree polynomial obtained in synthetic division.

Example 4 ▶ **Using the Rational Zero Test**

Find the rational zeros of $f(x) = 2x^3 + 3x^2 - 8x + 3$.

Solution

The leading coefficient is 2 and the constant term is 3.

$$Possible\ rational\ zeros: \frac{Factors\ of\ 3}{Factors\ of\ 2} = \frac{\pm 1, \pm 3}{\pm 1, \pm 2} = \pm 1, \pm 3, \pm\frac{1}{2}, \pm\frac{3}{2}$$

By synthetic division, you can determine that $x = 1$ is a rational zero.

$$
\begin{array}{r|rrrr}
1 & 2 & 3 & -8 & 3 \\
  &   & 2 & 5 & -3 \\
\hline
  & 2 & 5 & -3 & 0 \\
\end{array}
$$

So, $f(x)$ factors as

$$f(x) = (x - 1)(2x^2 + 5x - 3)$$
$$= (x - 1)(2x - 1)(x + 3)$$

and you can conclude that the rational zeros of f are $x = 1$, $x = \frac{1}{2}$, and $x = -3$.

Example 5 ▶ **Using the Rational Zero Test** www

Find all the real zeros of $f(x) = -10x^3 + 15x^2 + 16x - 12$.

Solution

The leading coefficient is -10 and the constant term is -12.

$$Possible\ rational\ zeros: \frac{Factors\ of\ -12}{Factors\ of\ -10} = \frac{\pm 1, \pm 2, \pm 3, \pm 4, \pm 6, \pm 12}{\pm 1, \pm 2, \pm 5, \pm 10}$$

With so many possibilities (32, in fact), it is worth your time to stop and sketch a graph. From Figure 2.32, it looks like three reasonable choices would be $x = -\frac{6}{5}$, $x = \frac{1}{2}$, and $x = 2$. Testing these by synthetic division shows that only $x = 2$ is a zero. So, you have

$$f(x) = (x - 2)(-10x^2 - 5x + 6).$$

Using the Quadratic Formula for the second factor, you find that the two additional zeros are irrational numbers.

$$x = \frac{-(-5) + \sqrt{265}}{-20} \approx -1.0639$$

and

$$x = \frac{-(-5) - \sqrt{265}}{-20} \approx 0.5639$$

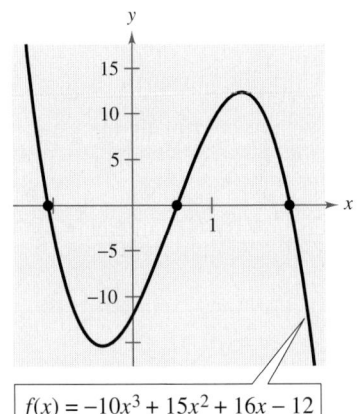

$f(x) = -10x^3 + 15x^2 + 16x - 12$

FIGURE **2.32**

Conjugate Pairs

In Example 1(c) and (d), note that the pairs of complex zeros are **conjugates.** That is, they are of the form $a + bi$ and $a - bi$.

Complex Zeros Occur in Conjugate Pairs

Let $f(x)$ be a polynomial function that has *real coefficients*. If $a + bi$, where $b \neq 0$, is a zero of the function, the conjugate $a - bi$ is also a zero of the function.

Be sure you see that this result is true only if the polynomial function has *real coefficients*. For instance, the result applies to the function $f(x) = x^2 + 1$ but not to the function $g(x) = x - i$.

Example 6 ▶ **Finding a Polynomial with Given Zeros**

Find a fourth-degree polynomial function with real coefficients that has $-1, -1,$ and $3i$ as zeros.

Solution

Because $3i$ is a zero *and* the polynomial is stated to have real coefficients, you know that the conjugate $-3i$ must also be a zero. So, from the Linear Factorization Theorem, $f(x)$ can be written as

$$f(x) = a(x + 1)(x + 1)(x - 3i)(x + 3i).$$

For simplicity, let $a = 1$ to obtain

$$f(x) = (x^2 + 2x + 1)(x^2 + 9)$$
$$= x^4 + 2x^3 + 10x^2 + 18x + 9.$$

Factoring a Polynomial

The Linear Factorization Theorem shows that you can write any nth-degree polynomial as the product of n linear factors.

$$f(x) = a_n(x - c_1)(x - c_2)(x - c_3) \cdots (x - c_n)$$

However, this result includes the possibility that some of the values of c_i are complex. The following theorem says that even if you do not want to get involved with "complex factors," you can still write $f(x)$ as the product of linear and/or quadratic factors. For a proof of this theorem, see Proofs in Mathematics on page 193.

Factors of a Polynomial

Every polynomial of degree $n > 0$ with real coefficients can be written as the product of linear and quadratic factors with real coefficients, where the quadratic factors have no real zeros.

You may want to remind students that a graphing calculator is helpful in determining real zeros, which in turn are useful in finding the complex zeros.

A quadratic factor with no real zeros is said to be *prime* or **irreducible over the reals.** Be sure you see that this is not the same as being *irreducible over the rationals.* For example, the quadratic

$$x^2 + 1 = (x - i)(x + i)$$

is irreducible over the reals (and therefore over the rationals). On the other hand, the quadratic

$$x^2 - 2 = \left(x - \sqrt{2}\right)\left(x + \sqrt{2}\right)$$

is irreducible over the rationals but *reducible* over the reals.

Example 7 ▶ **Finding the Zeros of a Polynomial Function**

Find all the zeros of

$$f(x) = x^4 - 3x^3 + 6x^2 + 2x - 60$$

given that $1 + 3i$ is a zero of f.

Solution

Because complex zeros occur in conjugate pairs, you know that $1 - 3i$ is also a zero of f. This means that both

$$[x - (1 + 3i)] \quad \text{and} \quad [x - (1 - 3i)]$$

are factors of f. Multiplying these two factors produces

$$
\begin{aligned}
[x - (1 + 3i)][x - (1 - 3i)] &= [(x - 1) - 3i][(x - 1) + 3i] \\
&= (x - 1)^2 - 9i^2 \\
&= x^2 - 2x + 1 - 9(-1) \\
&= x^2 - 2x + 10.
\end{aligned}
$$

Using long division, you can divide $x^2 - 2x + 10$ into f to obtain the following.

$$
\begin{array}{r}
x^2 - x - 6 \\
x^2 - 2x + 10 \overline{)\, x^4 - 3x^3 + 6x^2 + 2x - 60} \\
\underline{x^4 - 2x^3 + 10x^2} \\
-x^3 - 4x^2 + 2x \\
\underline{-x^3 + 2x^2 - 10x} \\
-6x^2 + 12x - 60 \\
\underline{-6x^2 + 12x - 60} \\
0
\end{array}
$$

So, you have

$$
\begin{aligned}
f(x) &= (x^2 - 2x + 10)(x^2 - x - 6) \\
&= (x^2 - 2x + 10)(x - 3)(x + 2)
\end{aligned}
$$

and you can conclude that the zeros of f are $x = 1 + 3i$, $x = 1 - 3i$, $x = 3$, and $x = -2$.

STUDY TIP

In Example 7, if you were not told that $1 + 3i$ is a zero of f, you could still find all zeros of the function by using synthetic division to find the real zeros -2 and 3. Then you could factor the polynomial as $(x + 2)(x - 3)(x^2 - 2x + 10)$. Finally, by using the Quadratic Formula, you could determine that the zeros are $x = -2$, $x = 3$, $x = 1 + 3i$, and $x = 1 - 3i$.

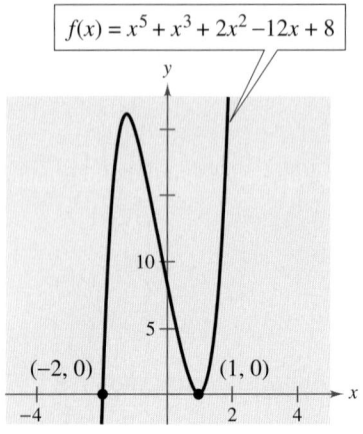

$f(x) = x^5 + x^3 + 2x^2 - 12x + 8$

(−2, 0) (1, 0)

FIGURE **2.33**

Example 8 shows how to find all the zeros of a polynomial function, including complex zeros.

Example 8 ▶ **Finding the Zeros of a Polynomial Function**

Write $f(x) = x^5 + x^3 + 2x^2 - 12x + 8$ as the product of linear factors, and list all of its zeros.

Solution

The possible rational zeros are $\pm 1, \pm 2, \pm 4,$ and ± 8. Synthetic division produces the following.

$$
\begin{array}{r|rrrrrr}
1 & 1 & 0 & 1 & 2 & -12 & 8 \\
  &   & 1 & 1 & 2 & 4 & -8 \\
\hline
  & 1 & 1 & 2 & 4 & -8 & 0
\end{array}
\longrightarrow \text{1 is a zero.}
$$

$$
\begin{array}{r|rrrrr}
-2 & 1 & 1 & 2 & 4 & -8 \\
   &   & -2 & 2 & -8 & 8 \\
\hline
   & 1 & -1 & 4 & -4 & 0
\end{array}
\longrightarrow \text{-2 is a zero.}
$$

So, you have

$$f(x) = x^5 + x^3 + 2x^2 - 12x + 8$$
$$= (x - 1)(x + 2)(x^3 - x^2 + 4x - 4).$$

You can factor $x^3 - x^2 + 4x - 4$ as $(x - 1)(x^2 + 4)$, and by factoring $x^2 + 4$ as

$$x^2 - (-4) = \left(x - \sqrt{-4}\right)\left(x + \sqrt{-4}\right)$$
$$= (x - 2i)(x + 2i)$$

you obtain

$$f(x) = (x - 1)(x - 1)(x + 2)(x - 2i)(x + 2i)$$

which gives the following five zeros of f.

$$x = 1, x = 1, x = -2, x = 2i, \quad \text{and} \quad x = -2i$$

From the graph of f shown in Figure 2.33, you can see that the *real* zeros are the only ones that appear as *x*-intercepts. Note that $x = 1$ is a repeated zero.

STUDY TIP

In Example 8, the fifth-degree polynomial function has three real zeros. In such cases, you can use the *zoom* and *trace* features or the *zero* or *root* feature of a graphing utility to approximate the real zeros. You can then use these real zeros to determine the complex zeros algebraically.

Technology

You can use the *table* feature of a graphing utility to help you determine which of the possible rational zeros are zeros of the polynomial in Example 8. The table should be set to *ask* mode. Then enter each of the possible rational zeros in the table. When you do this, you will see that there are two rational zeros, −2 and 1, as shown at the right.

X	Y1
-8	-33048
-4	-1000
-2	0
-1	20
1	0
2	32
4	1080

X=4

Other Tests for Zeros of Polynomials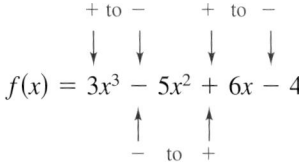

You know that an nth-degree polynomial function can have *at most n* real zeros. Of course, many nth-degree polynomials do not have that many real zeros. For instance, $f(x) = x^2 + 1$ has no real zeros, and $f(x) = x^3 + 1$ has only one real zero. The following theorem, called **Descartes's Rule of Signs,** sheds more light on the number of real zeros of a polynomial.

Descartes's Rule of Signs

Let $f(x) = a_n x^n + a_{n-1} x^{n-1} + \cdots + a_2 x^2 + a_1 x + a_0$ be a polynomial with real coefficients and $a_0 \neq 0$.

1. The number of *positive real zeros* of f is either equal to the number of variations in sign of $f(x)$ or less than that number by an even integer.

2. The number of *negative real zeros* of f is either equal to the number of variations in sign of $f(-x)$ or less than that number by an even integer.

A **variation in sign** means that two consecutive coefficients have opposite signs.

When using Descartes's Rule of Signs, a zero of multiplicity k should be counted as k zeros. For instance, the polynomial $x^3 - 3x + 2$ has two variations in sign, and so has either two positive or no positive real zeros. Because

$$x^3 - 3x + 2 = (x - 1)(x - 1)(x + 2)$$

you can see that the two positive real zeros are $x = 1$ of multiplicity 2.

Example 9 ▶ **Using Descartes's Rule of Signs**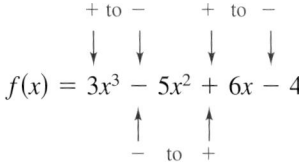

Describe the possible real zeros of

$$f(x) = 3x^3 - 5x^2 + 6x - 4.$$

Solution

The original polynomial has *three* variations in sign.

$$
\begin{array}{ccc}
+ \text{ to } - & & + \text{ to } - \\
\downarrow \quad \downarrow & & \downarrow \quad \downarrow
\end{array}
$$

$$f(x) = 3x^3 - 5x^2 + 6x - 4$$

$$
\begin{array}{cc}
\uparrow & \uparrow \\
- \text{ to } & +
\end{array}
$$

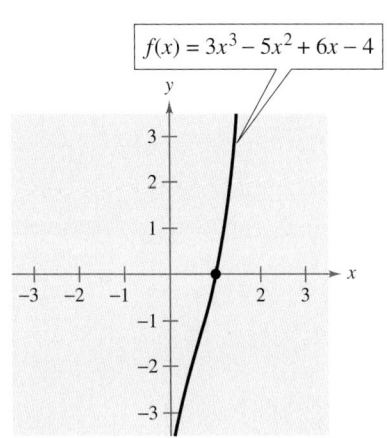

FIGURE **2.34**

$f(x) = 3x^3 - 5x^2 + 6x - 4$

The polynomial

$$f(-x) = 3(-x)^3 - 5(-x)^2 + 6(-x) - 4$$
$$= -3x^3 - 5x^2 - 6x - 4$$

has no variations in sign. So, from Descartes's Rule of Signs, the polynomial $f(x) = 3x^3 - 5x^2 + 6x - 4$ has either three positive real zeros or one positive real zero, and has no negative real zeros. From the graph in Figure 2.34, you can see that the function has only one real zero (it is a positive number, near $x = 1$).

Another test for zeros of a polynomial function is related to the sign pattern in the last row of the synthetic division array. This test can give you an upper or lower bound of the real zeros of f. A real number b is an **upper bound** for the real zeros of f if no zeros are greater than b. Similarly, b is a **lower bound** if no real zeros of f are less than b.

Upper and Lower Bound Rules

Let $f(x)$ be a polynomial with real coefficients and a positive leading coefficient. Suppose $f(x)$ is divided by $x - c$, using synthetic division.

1. If $c > 0$ and each number in the last row is either positive or zero, c is an *upper bound* for the real zeros of f.

2. If $c < 0$ and the numbers in the last row are alternately positive and negative (zero entries count as positive or negative), c is a *lower bound* for the real zeros of f.

Example 10 ▶ Finding the Zeros of a Polynomial Function

Find the real zeros of

$$f(x) = 6x^3 - 4x^2 + 3x - 2.$$

Solution

The possible real zeros are as follows.

$$\frac{\text{Factors of } 2}{\text{Factors of } 6} = \frac{\pm 1, \pm 2}{\pm 1, \pm 2, \pm 3, \pm 6}$$

$$= \pm 1, \pm\frac{1}{2}, \pm\frac{1}{3}, \pm\frac{1}{6}, \pm\frac{2}{3}, \pm 2$$

Because $f(x)$ has three variations in sign and $f(-x)$ has none, you can apply Descartes's Rule of Signs to conclude that there are three positive real zeros or one positive real zero, and no negative zeros. Trying $x = 1$ produces the following.

$$
\begin{array}{r|rrrr}
1 & 6 & -4 & 3 & -2 \\
  &   & 6 & 2 & 5 \\
\hline
  & 6 & 2 & 5 & 3
\end{array}
$$

In Example 10, notice how the Rational Zero Test, Descartes's Rule of Signs, and the Upper and Lower Bound Rules may be used together in a search for all real zeros of a polynomial function.

So, $x = 1$ is not a zero, but because the last row has all positive entries, you know that $x = 1$ is an upper bound for the real zeros. So, you can restrict the search to zeros between 0 and 1. By trial and error, you can determine that $x = \frac{2}{3}$ is a zero. So,

$$f(x) = \left(x - \frac{2}{3}\right)(6x^2 + 3).$$

Because $6x^2 + 3$ has no real zeros, it follows that $x = \frac{2}{3}$ is the only real zero.

Before concluding this section, here are two additional hints that can help you find the real zeros of a polynomial.

1. If the terms of $f(x)$ have a common monomial factor, it should be factored out before applying the tests in this section. For instance, by writing

$$f(x) = x^4 - 5x^3 + 3x^2 + x = x(x^3 - 5x^2 + 3x + 1)$$

you can see that $x = 0$ is a zero of f and that the remaining zeros can be obtained by analyzing the cubic factor.

2. If you are able to find all but two zeros of $f(x)$, you can always use the Quadratic Formula on the remaining quadratic factor. For instance, if you succeeded in writing

$$f(x) = x^4 - 5x^3 + 3x^2 + x = x(x - 1)(x^2 - 4x - 1)$$

you can apply the Quadratic Formula to $x^2 - 4x - 1$ to conclude that the two remaining zeros are $x = 2 + \sqrt{5}$ and $x = 2 - \sqrt{5}$.

Example 11 ▶   Using a Polynomial Model

You are designing candle-making kits. Each kit contains 25 cubic inches of candle wax and a mold for making a pyramid-shaped candle. You want the height of the candle to be 2 inches less than the length of each side of the candle's square base. What should the dimensions of your candle mold be?

Solution

The volume of a pyramid is $V = \frac{1}{3}Bh$, where B is the area of the base and h is the height. The area of the base is x^2 and the height is $(x - 2)$. So, the volume of the pyramid is $V = \frac{1}{3}x^2(x - 2)$. Substituting 25 for the volume yields the following.

$$25 = \frac{1}{3}x^2(x - 2) \qquad \text{Substitute 25 for } V.$$

$$75 = x^3 - 2x^2 \qquad \text{Multiply each side by 3.}$$

$$0 = x^3 - 2x^2 - 75 \qquad \text{Write in general form.}$$

The possible rational zeros are $x = \pm 1, \pm 3, \pm 5, \pm 15, \pm 25, \pm 75$. Using synthetic division, you can determine that $x = 5$ is a solution. The other two solutions, which satisfy $x^2 + 3x + 15 = 0$, are imaginary and can be discarded. You can conclude that the base of the candle mold should be 5 inches by 5 inches and the height of the mold should be $5 - 2 = 3$ inches.

Activities

1. Write as a product of linear factors:
   $f(x) = x^4 - 16$.
   Answer: $(x - 2)(x + 2)(x - 2i)(x + 2i)$

2. Find a third-degree polynomial with integer coefficients that has $2, 3 + i$, and $3 - i$ as zeros.
   Answer: $x^3 - 8x^2 + 22x - 20$

3. Use the zero $x = 2i$ to find the zeros of $f(x) = x^4 - x^3 - 2x^2 - 4x - 24$.
   Answer: $-2, 3, 2i, -2i$

Writing ABOUT MATHEMATICS

Factoring Polynomials Compile a list of all the various techniques for factoring a polynomial that have been covered so far in the text. Give an example illustrating each technique, and write a paragraph discussing when the use of each technique is appropriate.

2.5 **Exercises**

In Exercises 1–6, find all the zeros of the function.

1. $f(x) = x(x - 6)^2$ **2.** $f(x) = x^2(x + 3)(x^2 - 1)$

3. $g(x) = (x - 2)(x + 4)^3$

4. $f(x) = (x + 5)(x - 8)^2$

5. $f(x) = (x + 6)(x + i)(x - i)$

6. $h(t) = (t - 3)(t - 2)(t - 3i)(t + 3i)$

In Exercises 7–10, use the Rational Zero Test to list all possible rational zeros of f. Verify that the zeros of f shown on the graph are contained in the list.

7. $f(x) = x^3 + 3x^2 - x - 3$

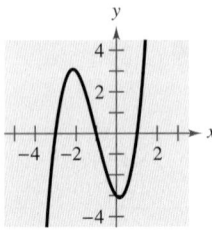

8. $f(x) = x^3 - 4x^2 - 4x + 16$

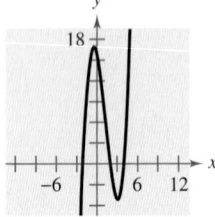

9. $f(x) = 2x^4 - 17x^3 + 35x^2 + 9x - 45$

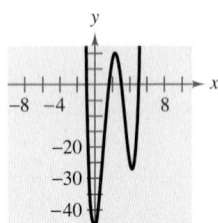

10. $f(x) = 4x^5 - 8x^4 - 5x^3 + 10x^2 + x - 2$

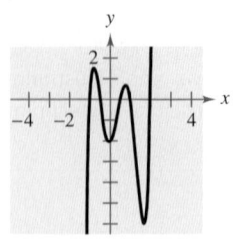

In Exercises 11–20, find all the real zeros of the function.

11. $f(x) = x^3 - 6x^2 + 11x - 6$

12. $f(x) = x^3 - 7x - 6$

13. $g(x) = x^3 - 4x^2 - x + 4$

14. $h(x) = x^3 - 9x^2 + 20x - 12$

15. $h(t) = t^3 + 12t^2 + 21t + 10$

16. $p(x) = x^3 - 9x^2 + 27x - 27$

17. $C(x) = 2x^3 + 3x^2 - 1$

18. $f(x) = 3x^3 - 19x^2 + 33x - 9$

19. $f(x) = 9x^4 - 9x^3 - 58x^2 + 4x + 24$

20. $f(x) = 2x^4 - 15x^3 + 23x^2 + 15x - 25$

In Exercises 21–24, find all real solutions of the polynomial equation.

21. $z^4 - z^3 - 2z - 4 = 0$

22. $x^4 - 13x^2 - 12x = 0$

23. $2y^4 + 7y^3 - 26y^2 + 23y - 6 = 0$

24. $x^5 - x^4 - 3x^3 + 5x^2 - 2x = 0$

In Exercises 25–28, (a) list the possible rational zeros of f, (b) sketch the graph of f so that some of the possible zeros in part (a) can be disregarded, and then (c) determine all real zeros of f.

25. $f(x) = x^3 + x^2 - 4x - 4$

26. $f(x) = -3x^3 + 20x^2 - 36x + 16$

27. $f(x) = -4x^3 + 15x^2 - 8x - 3$

28. $f(x) = 4x^3 - 12x^2 - x + 15$

In Exercises 29–32, (a) list the possible rational zeros of f, (b) use a graphing utility to graph f so that some of the possible zeros in part (a) can be disregarded, and then (c) determine all real zeros of f.

29. $f(x) = -2x^4 + 13x^3 - 21x^2 + 2x + 8$

30. $f(x) = 4x^4 - 17x^2 + 4$

31. $f(x) = 32x^3 - 52x^2 + 17x + 3$

32. $f(x) = 4x^3 + 7x^2 - 11x - 18$

Graphical Analysis In Exercises 33–36, (a) use the *zero* or *root* feature of a graphing utility to approximate the zeros of the function accurate to three decimal places and (b) determine one of the exact zeros, use synthetic division to verify your result, and then factor the polynomial completely.

33. $f(x) = x^4 - 3x^2 + 2$

34. $P(t) = t^4 - 7t^2 + 12$

35. $h(x) = x^5 - 7x^4 + 10x^3 + 14x^2 - 24x$

36. $g(x) = 6x^4 - 11x^3 - 51x^2 + 99x - 27$

In Exercises 37–42, find a polynomial function with integer coefficients that has the given zeros. (There are many correct answers.)

37. $1, 5i, -5i$

38. $4, 3i, -3i$

39. $6, -5 + 2i, -5 - 2i$

40. $2, 4 + i, 4 - i$

41. $\frac{2}{3}, -1, 3 + \sqrt{2}i$

42. $-5, -5, 1 + \sqrt{3}i$

In Exercises 43–46, write the polynomial (a) as the product of factors that are irreducible over the *rationals*, (b) as the product of linear and quadratic factors that are irreducible over the *reals*, and (c) in completely factored form.

43. $f(x) = x^4 + 6x^2 - 27$

44. $f(x) = x^4 - 2x^3 - 3x^2 + 12x - 18$
    (*Hint:* One factor is $x^2 - 6$.)

45. $f(x) = x^4 - 4x^3 + 5x^2 - 2x - 6$
    (*Hint:* One factor is $x^2 - 2x - 2$.)

46. $f(x) = x^4 - 3x^3 - x^2 - 12x - 20$
    (*Hint:* One factor is $x^2 + 4$.)

In Exercises 47–54, use the given zero to find all the zeros of the function.

Function	Zero
47. $f(x) = 2x^3 + 3x^2 + 50x + 75$	$5i$
48. $f(x) = x^3 + x^2 + 9x + 9$	$3i$
49. $f(x) = 2x^4 - x^3 + 7x^2 - 4x - 4$	$2i$
50. $g(x) = x^3 - 7x^2 - x + 87$	$5 + 2i$
51. $g(x) = 4x^3 + 23x^2 + 34x - 10$	$-3 + i$
52. $h(x) = 3x^3 - 4x^2 + 8x + 8$	$1 - \sqrt{3}i$
53. $f(x) = x^4 + 3x^3 - 5x^2 - 21x + 22$	$-3 + \sqrt{2}i$
54. $f(x) = x^3 + 4x^2 + 14x + 20$	$-1 - 3i$

In Exercises 55–72, find all the zeros of the function and write the polynomial as a product of linear factors.

55. $f(x) = x^2 + 25$

56. $f(x) = x^2 - x + 56$

57. $h(x) = x^2 - 4x + 1$

58. $g(x) = x^2 + 10x + 23$

59. $f(x) = x^4 - 81$

60. $f(y) = y^4 - 625$

61. $f(z) = z^2 - 2z + 2$

62. $h(x) = x^3 - 3x^2 + 4x - 2$

63. $g(x) = x^3 - 6x^2 + 13x - 10$

64. $f(x) = x^3 - 2x^2 - 11x + 52$

65. $h(x) = x^3 - x + 6$

66. $h(x) = x^3 + 9x^2 + 27x + 35$

67. $f(x) = 5x^3 - 9x^2 + 28x + 6$

68. $g(x) = 3x^3 - 4x^2 + 8x + 8$

69. $g(x) = x^4 - 4x^3 + 8x^2 - 16x + 16$

70. $h(x) = x^4 + 6x^3 + 10x^2 + 6x + 9$

71. $f(x) = x^4 + 10x^2 + 9$

72. $f(x) = x^4 + 29x^2 + 100$

 In Exercises 73–78, find all the zeros of the function. When there is an extended list of possible rational zeros, use a graphing utility to graph the function in order to discard any rational zeros that are obviously not zeros of the function.

73. $f(x) = x^3 + 24x^2 + 214x + 740$

74. $f(s) = 2s^3 - 5s^2 + 12s - 5$

75. $f(x) = 16x^3 - 20x^2 - 4x + 15$

76. $f(x) = 9x^3 - 15x^2 + 11x - 5$

77. $f(x) = 2x^4 + 5x^3 + 4x^2 + 5x + 2$

78. $g(x) = x^5 - 8x^4 + 28x^3 - 56x^2 + 64x - 32$

In Exercises 79–86, use Descartes's Rule of Signs to determine the possible number of positive and negative zeros of the function.

79. $g(x) = 5x^5 + 10x$

80. $h(x) = 4x^2 - 8x + 3$

81. $h(x) = 3x^4 + 2x^2 + 1$

82. $h(x) = 2x^4 - 3x + 2$

83. $g(x) = 2x^3 - 3x^2 - 3$

84. $f(x) = 4x^3 - 3x^2 + 2x - 1$

85. $f(x) = -5x^3 + x^2 - x + 5$

86. $f(x) = 3x^3 + 2x^2 + x + 3$

In Exercises 87–90, use synthetic division to verify the upper and lower bounds of the real zeros of *f*.

87. $f(x) = x^4 - 4x^3 + 15$

   (a) Upper: $x = 4$ (b) Lower: $x = -1$

88. $f(x) = 2x^3 - 3x^2 - 12x + 8$

   (a) Upper: $x = 4$ (b) Lower: $x = -3$

89. $f(x) = x^4 - 4x^3 + 16x - 16$

   (a) Upper: $x = 5$ (b) Lower: $x = -3$

90. $f(x) = 2x^4 - 8x + 3$

   (a) Upper: $x = 3$ (b) Lower: $x = -4$

In Exercises 91–94, find all the real zeros of the function.

91. $f(x) = 4x^3 - 3x - 1$

92. $f(z) = 12z^3 - 4z^2 - 27z + 9$

93. $f(y) = 4y^3 + 3y^2 + 8y + 6$

94. $g(x) = 3x^3 - 2x^2 + 15x - 10$

In Exercises 95–98, find all the rational zeros of the polynomial function.

95. $P(x) = x^4 - \frac{25}{4}x^2 + 9 = \frac{1}{4}(4x^4 - 25x^2 + 36)$

96. $f(x) = x^3 - \frac{3}{2}x^2 - \frac{23}{2}x + 6 = \frac{1}{2}(2x^3 - 3x^2 - 23x + 12)$

97. $f(x) = x^3 - \frac{1}{4}x^2 - x + \frac{1}{4} = \frac{1}{4}(4x^3 - x^2 - 4x + 1)$

98. $f(z) = z^3 + \frac{11}{6}z^2 - \frac{1}{2}z - \frac{1}{3} = \frac{1}{6}(6z^3 + 11z^2 - 3z - 2)$

In Exercises 99–102, match the cubic function with the numbers of rational and irrational zeros.

(a) Rational zeros: 0;   Irrational zeros: 1

(b) Rational zeros: 3;   Irrational zeros: 0

(c) Rational zeros: 1;   Irrational zeros: 2

(d) Rational zeros: 1;   Irrational zeros: 0

99. $f(x) = x^3 - 1$

100. $f(x) = x^3 - 2$

101. $f(x) = x^3 - x$

102. $f(x) = x^3 - 2x$

103. ***Geometry*** An open box is to be made from a rectangular piece of material, 15 centimeters by 9 centimeters, by cutting equal squares from the corners and turning up the sides.

   (a) Let *x* represent the length of the sides of the squares removed. Draw a diagram showing the squares removed from the original piece of material and the resulting dimensions of the open box.

   (b) Use the diagram to write the volume *V* of the box as a function of *x*. Determine the domain of the function.

   (c) Sketch the graph of the function and approximate the dimensions of the box that will yield a maximum volume.

   (d) Find values of *x* such that $V = 56$. Which of these values is a physical impossibility in the construction of the box? Explain.

104. ***Geometry*** A rectangular package to be sent by a delivery service (see figure) can have a maximum combined length and girth (perimeter of a cross section) of 120 inches.

   (a) Show that the volume of the package is

$$V(x) = 4x^2(30 - x).$$

  (b) Use a graphing utility to graph the function and approximate the dimensions of the package that will yield a maximum volume.

   (c) Find values of *x* such that $V = 13,500$. Which of these values is a physical impossibility in the construction of the package? Explain.

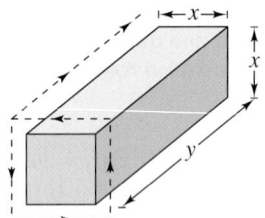

105. ***Advertising Cost*** A company that produces portable cassette players estimates that the profit *P* (in dollars) for selling a particular model is

$$P = -76x^3 + 4830x^2 - 320{,}000, \quad 0 \le x \le 60$$

where *x* is the advertising expense (in tens of thousands of dollars). Using this model, find the smaller of two advertising amounts that will yield a profit of $2,500,000.

106. ***Advertising Cost*** A company that manufactures bicycles estimates that the profit *P* (in dollars) for selling a particular model is

$$P = -45x^3 + 2500x^2 - 275{,}000, \quad 0 \le x \le 50$$

where *x* is the advertising expense (in tens of thousands of dollars). Using this model, find the smaller of two advertising amounts that will yield a profit of $800,000.

▶ Model It

107. *Athletics* The attendance A (in millions) at NCAA women's college basketball games for the years 1994 through 2000 is shown in the table, where t represents the year, with $t = 4$ corresponding to 1994. (Source: National Collegiate Athletic Association)

Year, t	Attendance, A
4	4.557
5	4.962
6	5.234
7	6.734
8	7.387
9	8.698
10	8.825

(a) Use the *regression* feature of a graphing utility to find a cubic model for the data.

(b) Use the graphing utility to create a scatter plot of the data. Then graph the model and the scatter plot in the same viewing window. How do they compare?

(c) According to the model found in part (a), in what year did attendance reach 5.5 million?

(d) According to the model found in part (a), in what year did attendance reach 8 million?

(e) According to the right-hand behavior of the model, will the attendance continue to increase? Explain.

108. *Cost* The ordering and transportation cost C (in thousands of dollars) for the components used in manufacturing a product is

$$C = 100\left(\frac{200}{x^2} + \frac{x}{x + 30}\right), \quad x \ge 1$$

where x is the order size (in hundreds). In calculus, it can be shown that the cost is a minimum when

$$3x^3 - 40x^2 - 2400x - 36{,}000 = 0.$$

Use a calculator to approximate the optimal order size to the nearest hundred units.

109. *Height of a Baseball* A baseball is thrown upward from ground level with an initial velocity of 48 feet per second, and its height h (in feet) is

$$h(t) = -16t^2 + 48t, \quad 0 \le t \le 3$$

where t is the time (in seconds). You are told the ball reaches a height of 64 feet. Is this possible?

110. *Profit* The demand equation for a certain product is $p = 140 - 0.0001x$, where p is the unit price (in dollars) of the product and x is the number of units produced and sold. The cost equation for the product is $C = 80x + 150{,}000$, where C is the total cost (in dollars) and x is the number of units produced. The total profit obtained by producing and selling x units is

$$P = R - C = xp - C.$$

You are working in the marketing department of the company that produces this product, and you are asked to determine a price p that will yield a profit of 9 million dollars. Is this possible? Explain.

Synthesis

True or False? In Exercises 111 and 112, decide whether the statement is true or false. Justify your answer.

111. It is possible for a third-degree polynomial function with integer coefficients to have no real zeros.

112. If $x = -i$ is a zero of the function $f(x) = x^3 + ix^2 + ix - 1$, then $x = i$ must also be a zero of f.

Think About It In Exercises 113–118, determine (if possible) the zeros of the function g if the function f has zeros at $x = r_1$, $x = r_2$, and $x = r_3$.

113. $g(x) = -f(x)$ **114.** $g(x) = 3f(x)$

115. $g(x) = f(x - 5)$ **116.** $g(x) = f(2x)$

117. $g(x) = 3 + f(x)$ **118.** $g(x) = f(-x)$

119. *Exploration* Use a graphing utility to graph the function $f(x) = x^4 - 4x^2 + k$ for different values of k. Find values of k such that the zeros of f satisfy the specified characteristics. (Some parts do not have unique answers.)

(a) Four real zeros

(b) Two real zeros, each of multiplicity 2

(c) Two real zeros and two complex roots

(d) Four complex zeros

120. *Think About It* Will the answers to Exercise 119 change for the function g?

(a) $g(x) = f(x - 2)$　　(b) $g(x) = f(2x)$

121. *Think About It* A third-degree polynomial function f has real zeros -2, $\frac{1}{2}$, and 3, and its leading coefficient is negative. Write an equation for f. Sketch the graph of f. How many different polynomial functions are possible for f?

122. *Think About It* Sketch the graph of a fifth-degree polynomial function whose leading coefficient is positive and that has one root at $x = 3$ of multiplicity 2.

123. Use the information in the table.

Interval	Value of $f(x)$
$(-\infty, -2)$	Positive
$(-2, 1)$	Negative
$(1, 4)$	Negative
$(4, \infty)$	Positive

(a) What are the three real zeros of the polynomial function f?

(b) What can be said about the behavior of the graph of f at $x = 1$?

(c) What is the least possible degree of f? Explain. Can the degree of f ever be odd? Explain.

(d) Is the leading coefficient of f positive or negative? Explain.

(e) Write an equation for f. There are many correct answers.

(f) Sketch a graph of the equation you wrote in part (e).

124. Use the information in the table.

Interval	Value of $f(x)$
$(-\infty, -2)$	Negative
$(-2, 0)$	Positive
$(0, 2)$	Positive
$(2, \infty)$	Negative

(a) What are the three real zeros of the polynomial function f?

(b) What can be said about the behavior of the graph of f at $x = 0$?

(c) What is the least possible degree of f? Explain. Can the degree of f ever be odd? Explain.

(d) Is the leading coefficient of f positive or negative? Explain.

(e) Write an equation for f. There are many correct answers.

(f) Sketch a graph of the equation you wrote in part (e).

125. (a) Find a quadratic function f (with integer coefficients) that has $\pm \sqrt{b}i$ as zeros. Assume that b is a positive integer.

(b) Find a quadratic function f (with integer coefficients) that has $a \pm bi$ as zeros. Assume that b is a positive integer.

126. *Graphical Reasoning* The graph of one of the following functions is shown below. Identify the function shown in the graph. Explain why each of the others is not the correct function. Use a graphing utility to verify your result.

(a) $f(x) = x^2(x + 2)(x - 3.5)$

(b) $g(x) = (x + 2)(x - 3.5)$

(c) $h(x) = (x + 2)(x - 3.5)(x^2 + 1)$

(d) $k(x) = (x + 1)(x + 2)(x - 3.5)$

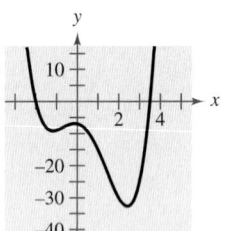

Review

In Exercises 127–130, perform the operation and simplify.

127. $(-3 + 6i) - (8 - 3i)$　　**128.** $(12 - 5i) + 16i$

129. $(6 - 2i)(1 + 7i)$　　**130.** $(9 - 5i)(9 + 5i)$

In Exercises 131–136, use the graph of f to sketch the graph of g. To print an enlarged copy of the graph, go to the website *www.mathgraphs.com*.

131. $g(x) = f(x - 2)$

132. $g(x) = f(x) - 2$

133. $g(x) = 2f(x)$

134. $g(x) = f(-x)$

135. $g(x) = f(2x)$

136. $g(x) = f\left(\frac{1}{2}x\right)$

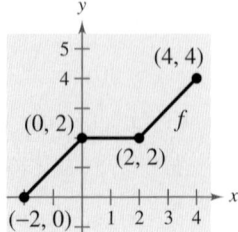

2.6 Rational Functions

▶ **Why you should learn it**

You can use rational functions to model average speed over a distance. For example, see Exercise 74 on page 177.

Baron Wolman/Tony Stone Images

Introduction

A **rational function** can be written in the form

$$f(x) = \frac{N(x)}{D(x)}$$

where $N(x)$ and $D(x)$ are polynomials and $D(x)$ is not the zero polynomial. In this section it is assumed that $N(x)$ and $D(x)$ have no common factors.

In general, the *domain* of a rational function of x includes all real numbers except x-values that make the denominator zero. Much of the discussion of rational functions will focus on their graphical behavior near the x-values excluded from the domain.

Example 1 ▶ **Finding the Domain of a Rational Function**

Find the domain of $f(x) = 1/x$ and discuss the behavior of f near any excluded x-values.

Solution

Because the denominator is zero when $x = 0$, the domain of f is all real numbers except $x = 0$. To determine the behavior of f near this excluded value, evaluate $f(x)$ to the left and right of $x = 0$, as indicated in the following tables.

x	-1	-0.5	-0.1	-0.01	-0.001	$\longrightarrow 0$
$f(x)$	-1	-2	-10	-100	-1000	$\longrightarrow -\infty$

x	0	$\longleftarrow$	0.001	0.01	0.1	0.5	1
$f(x)$	∞	$\longleftarrow$	1000	100	10	2	1

Note that as x approaches 0 *from the left*, $f(x)$ decreases without bound. In contrast, as x approaches 0 *from the right*, $f(x)$ increases without bound. The graph of f is shown in Figure 2.35.

STUDY TIP

Note that the rational function

$$f(x) = \frac{1}{x}$$

is also referred to as the reciprocal function, as discussed in Section 1.5.

FIGURE 2.35

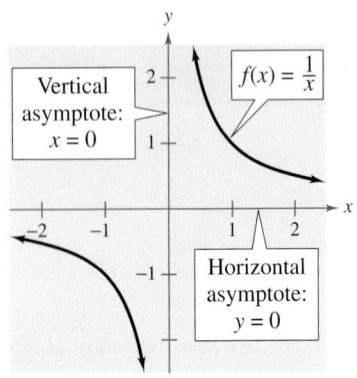

FIGURE **2.36**

Horizontal and Vertical Asymptotes

In Example 1, the behavior of f near $x = 0$ is denoted as follows.

$$f(x) \longrightarrow -\infty \text{ as } x \longrightarrow 0^- \qquad f(x) \longrightarrow \infty \text{ as } x \longrightarrow 0^+$$

$f(x)$ decreases without bound as x approaches 0 from the left. $f(x)$ increases without bound as x approaches 0 from the right.

The line $x = 0$ is a **vertical asymptote** of the graph of f, as shown in Figure 2.36. From this figure, you can see that the graph of f also has a **horizontal asymptote**—the line $y = 0$. This means that the values of $f(x) = 1/x$ approach zero as x increases or decreases without bound.

$$f(x) \longrightarrow 0 \text{ as } x \longrightarrow -\infty \qquad f(x) \longrightarrow 0 \text{ as } x \longrightarrow \infty$$

$f(x)$ approaches 0 as x decreases without bound. $f(x)$ approaches 0 as x increases without bound.

Definition of Vertical and Horizontal Asymptotes

1. The line $x = a$ is a **vertical asymptote** of the graph of f if

$$f(x) \longrightarrow \infty \quad \text{or} \quad f(x) \longrightarrow -\infty$$

as $x \longrightarrow a$, either from the right or from the left.

2. The line $y = b$ is a **horizontal asymptote** of the graph of f if

$$f(x) \longrightarrow b$$

as $x \longrightarrow \infty$ or $x \longrightarrow -\infty$.

Eventually (as $x \longrightarrow \infty$ or $x \longrightarrow -\infty$), the distance between the horizontal asymptote and the points on the graph must approach zero. Figure 2.37 shows the horizontal and vertical asymptotes of the graphs of three rational functions.

(a)

(b)

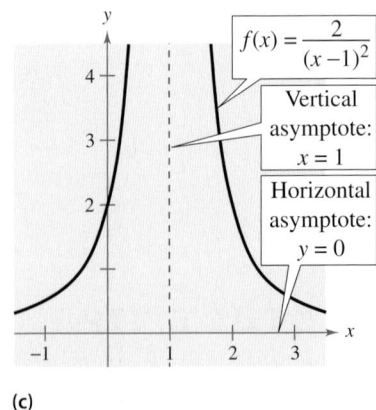

(c)

FIGURE **2.37**

The graphs of $f(x) = 1/x$ in Figure 2.36 and $f(x) = (2x + 1)/(x + 1)$ in Figure 2.37(a) are **hyperbolas.** You will study hyperbolas in Section 10.4.

Additional Example

Identify all horizontal and vertical asymptotes of the graph of

$$f(x) = \frac{x}{x^2 - 9}.$$

Solution

The function has a horizontal asymptote at $y = 0$ because the degree of the numerator is less than the degree of the denominator. The function has two vertical asymptotes at $x = 3$ and $x = -3$, the zeros of the denominator.

Asymptotes of a Rational Function

Let f be the rational function given by

$$f(x) = \frac{N(x)}{D(x)} = \frac{a_n x^n + a_{n-1} x^{n-1} + \cdots + a_1 x + a_0}{b_m x^m + b_{m-1} x^{m-1} + \cdots + b_1 x + b_0}$$

where $N(x)$ and $D(x)$ have no common factors.

1. The graph of f has *vertical* asymptotes at the zeros of $D(x)$.

2. The graph of f has one or no *horizontal* asymptote determined by comparing the degrees of $N(x)$ and $D(x)$.

    a. If $n < m$, the graph of f has the line $y = 0$ (the x-axis) as a horizontal asymptote.

    b. If $n = m$, the graph of f has the line $y = a_n / b_m$ as a horizontal asymptote.

    c. If $n > m$, the graph of f has no horizontal asymptote.

Example 2 ▶ **Finding Horizontal and Vertical Asymptotes**

Find all horizontal and vertical asymptotes of the graph of each rational function.

a. $f(x) = \dfrac{2x}{3x^2 + 1}$ **b.** $f(x) = \dfrac{2x^2}{x^2 - 1}$

Solution

a. For this rational function, the degree of the numerator is *less than* the degree of the denominator, so the graph has the line $y = 0$ as a horizontal asymptote. To find any vertical asymptotes, set the denominator equal to zero and solve the resulting equation for x.

$$3x^2 + 1 = 0 \qquad \text{Set denominator equal to zero.}$$

Because this equation has no real solutions, you can conclude that the graph has no vertical asymptote. The graph of the function is shown in Figure 2.38.

b. For this rational function, the degree of the numerator is *equal to* the degree of the denominator. The leading coefficient of the numerator is 2 and the leading coefficient of the denominator is 1, so the graph has the line $y = 2$ as a horizontal asymptote. To find any vertical asymptotes, set the denominator equal to zero and solve the resulting equation for x.

$$x^2 - 1 = 0 \qquad \text{Set denominator equal to zero.}$$
$$(x + 1)(x - 1) = 0 \qquad \text{Factor}$$
$$x + 1 = 0 \implies x = -1 \qquad \text{Set 1st factor equal to 0.}$$
$$x - 1 = 0 \implies x = 1 \qquad \text{Set 2nd factor equal to 0.}$$

This equation has two real solutions, $x = -1$ and $x = 1$. So, the graph has the lines $x = -1$ and $x = 1$ as vertical asymptotes. The graph of the function is shown in Figure 2.39.

FIGURE **2.38**

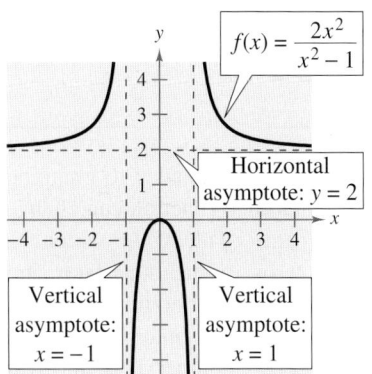

FIGURE **2.39**

Analyzing Graphs of Rational Functions

Guidelines for Analyzing Graphs of Rational Functions

Let $f(x) = N(x)/D(x)$, where $N(x)$ and $D(x)$ are polynomials with no common factors.

1. Find and plot the *y*-intercept (if any) by evaluating $f(0)$.

2. Find the zeros of the numerator (if any) by solving the equation $N(x) = 0$. Then plot the corresponding *x*-intercepts.

3. Find the zeros of the denominator (if any) by solving the equation $D(x) = 0$. Then sketch the corresponding vertical asymptotes.

4. Find and sketch the horizontal asymptote (if any) by using the rule for finding the horizontal asymptote of a rational function.

5. Test for symmetry.

6. Plot at least one point *between* and one point *beyond* each *x*-intercept and vertical asymptote.

7. Use smooth curves to complete the graph between and beyond the vertical asymptotes.

Technology

Some graphing utilities have difficulty graphing rational functions that have vertical asymptotes. Often, the utility will connect parts of the graph that are not supposed to be connected. For instance, the screen below on the left shows the graph of $f(x) = 1/(x - 2)$.

Notice that the graph should consist of two *separated* portions—one to the left of $x = 2$ and the other to the right

of $x = 2$. To eliminate this problem, you can try changing the *mode* of the graphing utility to *dot mode*. The problem with this is that the graph is then represented as a collection of dots (as shown in the screen below on the right) rather than as a smooth curve.

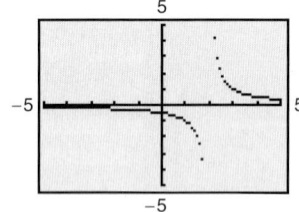

The concept of *test intervals* from Section 2.2 can be extended to graphing of rational functions. To do this, use the fact that a rational function can change signs only at its zeros and its undefined values (the *x*-values for which its denominator is zero). Between two consecutive zeros of the numerator and the denominator, a rational function must be entirely positive or entirely negative. This means that when the zeros of the numerator and the denominator of a rational function are put in order, they divide the real number line into test intervals in which the function has no sign changes. A representative *x*-value is chosen to determine if the value of the rational function is positive (the graph lies above the *x*-axis) or negative (the graph lies below the *x*-axis).

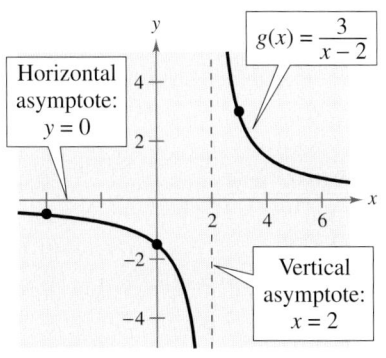

FIGURE 2.40

STUDY TIP

You can use transformations to help you sketch graphs of rational functions. For instance, the graph of g in Example 3 is a vertical stretch and a right shift of the graph of $f(x) = 1/x$ because

$$g(x) = \frac{3}{x - 2}$$

$$= 3\left(\frac{1}{x - 2}\right)$$

$$= 3f(x - 2).$$

Example 3 ▶ **Sketching the Graph of a Rational Function**

Sketch the graph of $g(x) = \dfrac{3}{x - 2}$ and state its domain.

Solution

y-Intercept:	$\left(0, -\frac{3}{2}\right)$, because $g(0) = -\frac{3}{2}$
x-Intercept:	None, because $3 \neq 0$
Vertical asymptote:	$x = 2$, zero of denominator
Horizontal asymptote:	$y = 0$, because degree of $N(x) <$ degree of $D(x)$
Additional points:	

Test Interval	Representative x-value	Value of g	Sign	Point on Graph
$(-\infty, 2)$	-4	$g(-4) = -0.5$	Negative	$(-4, -0.5)$
$(2, \infty)$	3	$g(3) = 3$	Positive	$(3, 3)$

By plotting the intercepts, asymptotes, and a few additional points, you can obtain the graph shown in Figure 2.40. The domain of g is all real numbers except $x = 2$.

Example 4 ▶ **Sketching the Graph of a Rational Function**

Sketch the graph of

$$f(x) = \frac{2x - 1}{x}$$

and state its domain.

Solution

y-Intercept:	None, because $x = 0$ is not in the domain
x-Intercept:	$\left(\frac{1}{2}, 0\right)$, from $2x - 1 = 0$
Vertical asymptote:	$x = 0$, zero of denominator
Horizontal asymptote:	$y = 2$, because degree of $N(x) =$ degree of $D(x)$
Additional points:	

Test Interval	Representative x-value	Value of f	Sign	Point on Graph
$(-\infty, 0)$	-1	$f(-1) = 3$	Positive	$(-1, 3)$
$\left(0, \frac{1}{2}\right)$	$\frac{1}{4}$	$f\left(\frac{1}{4}\right) = -2$	Negative	$\left(\frac{1}{4}, -2\right)$
$\left(\frac{1}{2}, \infty\right)$	4	$f(4) = 1.75$	Positive	$(4, 1.75)$

By plotting the intercepts, asymptotes, and a few additional points, you can obtain the graph shown in Figure 2.41. The domain of f is all real numbers except $x = 0$.

FIGURE 2.41

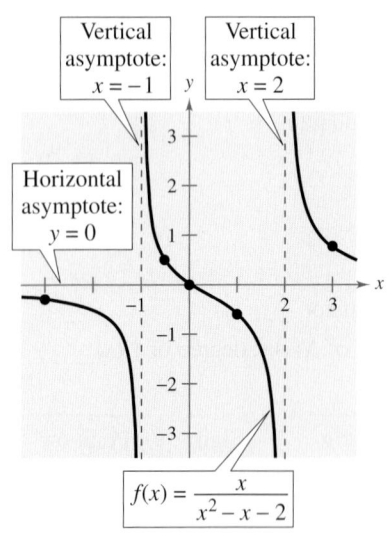

$$f(x) = \frac{x}{x^2 - x - 2}$$

FIGURE 2.42

STUDY TIP

If you are unsure of the shape of a portion of the graph of a rational function, plot some additional points.

A computer animation of this example appears in the Interactive CD-ROM and Internet versions of this text.

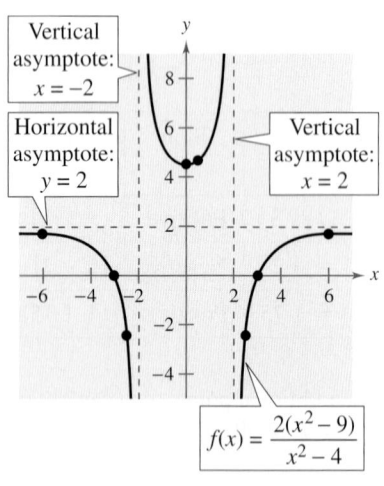

$$f(x) = \frac{2(x^2 - 9)}{x^2 - 4}$$

FIGURE 2.43

Example 5 ▶ **Sketching the Graph of a Rational Function**

Sketch the graph of $f(x) = x/(x^2 - x - 2)$.

Solution

Factoring the denominator, you have $f(x) = \dfrac{x}{(x + 1)(x - 2)}$.

y-Intercept: $(0, 0)$, because $f(0) = 0$ *x-Intercept:* $(0, 0)$

Vertical asymptotes: $x = -1$, $x = 2$, zeros of denominator

Horizontal asymptote: $y = 0$, because degree of $N(x) <$ degree of $D(x)$

Additional points:

Test Interval	Representative x-value	Value of f	Sign	Point on Graph
$(-\infty, -1)$	-3	$f(-3) = -0.3$	Negative	$(-3, -0.3)$
$(-1, 0)$	-0.5	$f(-0.5) = 0.4$	Positive	$(-0.5, 0.4)$
$(0, 2)$	1	$f(1) = -0.5$	Negative	$(1, -0.5)$
$(2, \infty)$	3	$f(3) = 0.75$	Positive	$(3, 0.75)$

The graph is shown in Figure 2.42.

Example 6 ▶ **Sketching the Graph of a Rational Function**

Sketch the graph of $f(x) = 2(x^2 - 9)/(x^2 - 4)$.

Solution

Factoring the numerator and denominator, you have $f(x) = \dfrac{2(x - 3)(x + 3)}{(x - 2)(x + 2)}$.

y-Intercept: $\left(0, \frac{9}{2}\right)$, because $f(0) = \frac{9}{2}$

x-Intercepts: $(-3, 0)$ and $(3, 0)$

Vertical asymptotes: $x = -2$, $x = 2$, zeros of denominator

Horizontal asymptote: $y = 2$, because degree of $N(x) =$ degree of $D(x)$

Symmetry: With respect to y-axis, because $f(-x) = f(x)$

Additional points:

Test Interval	Representative x-value	Value of f	Sign	Point on Graph
$(-\infty, -3)$	-6	$f(-6) = 1.69$	Positive	$(-6, 1.69)$
$(-3, -2)$	-2.5	$f(-2.5) = -2.44$	Negative	$(-2.5, -2.44)$
$(-2, 2)$	0.5	$f(0.5) = 4.67$	Positive	$(0.5, 4.67)$
$(2, 3)$	2.5	$f(2.5) = -2.44$	Negative	$(2.5, -2.44)$
$(3, \infty)$	6	$f(6) = 1.69$	Positive	$(6, 1.69)$

The graph is shown in Figure 2.43.

Slant Asymptotes

Consider a rational function whose denominator is of degree one or greater. If the degree of the numerator is exactly *one more* than the degree of the denominator, the graph of the function has a **slant** (or **oblique**) **asymptote.** For example, the graph of

$$f(x) = \frac{x^2 - x}{x + 1}$$

has a slant asymptote, as shown in Figure 2.44. To find the equation of a slant asymptote, use long division. For instance, by dividing $x + 1$ into $x^2 - x$, you obtain

$$f(x) = \frac{x^2 - x}{x + 1} = \underbrace{x - 2}_{\text{Slant asymptote}} + \frac{2}{x + 1}.$$

$$\text{Slant asymptote}$$
$$(y = x - 2)$$

As x increases or decreases without bound, the remainder term $2/(x + 1)$ approaches 0, so the graph of f approaches the line $y = x - 2$, as shown in Figure 2.44.

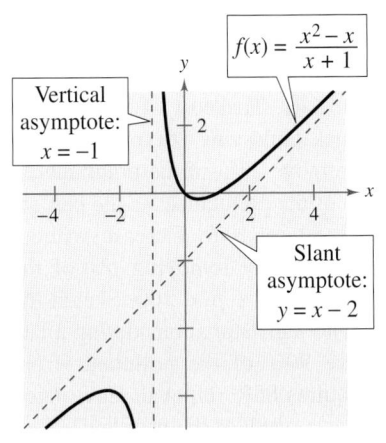

Vertical asymptote: $x = -1$

$f(x) = \dfrac{x^2 - x}{x + 1}$

Slant asymptote: $y = x - 2$

FIGURE 2.44

| Example 7 ▶ | **A Rational Function with a Slant Asymptote** |

Sketch the graph of $f(x) = \dfrac{x^2 - x - 2}{x - 1}$.

Solution

Factoring the numerator as $(x - 2)(x + 1)$ allows you to recognize the x-intercepts. Using long division

$$f(x) = \frac{x^2 - x - 2}{x - 1} = x - \frac{2}{x - 1}$$

allows you to recognize that the line $y = x$ is a slant asymptote of the graph.

y-Intercept: $(0, 2)$, because $f(0) = 2$

x-Intercepts: $(-1, 0)$ and $(2, 0)$

Vertical asymptote: $x = 1$, zero of denominator

Slant asymptote: $y = x$

Additional points:

Test Interval	Representative x-value	Value of f	Sign	Point on Graph
$(-\infty, -1)$	-2	$f(-2) = -1.33$	Negative	$(-2, -1.33)$
$(-1, 1)$	0.5	$f(0.5) = 4.5$	Positive	$(0.5, 4.5)$
$(1, 2)$	1.5	$f(1.5) = -2.5$	Negative	$(1.5, -2.5)$
$(2, \infty)$	3	$f(3) = 2$	Positive	$(3, 2)$

The graph is shown in Figure 2.45.

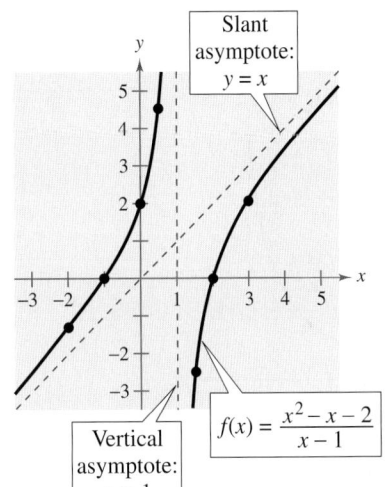

Slant asymptote: $y = x$

$f(x) = \dfrac{x^2 - x - 2}{x - 1}$

Vertical asymptote: $x = 1$

FIGURE 2.45

Applications

There are many examples of asymptotic behavior in real life. For instance, Example 8 shows how a vertical asymptote can be used to analyze the cost of removing pollutants from smokestack emissions.

Example 8 ▶ **Cost-Benefit Model**

A utility company burns coal to generate electricity. The cost of removing a certain *percent* of the pollutants from smokestack emissions is typically not a linear function. That is, if it costs C dollars to remove 25% of the pollutants, it would cost more than $2C$ dollars to remove 50% of the pollutants. As the percent of removed pollutants approaches 100%, the cost tends to increase without bound, becoming prohibitive. The cost C (in dollars) of removing $p\%$ of the smokestack pollutants is $C = 80,000p/(100 - p)$ for $0 \le p < 100$. Sketch the graph of this function. You are a member of a state legislature considering a law that would require utility companies to remove 90% of the pollutants from their smokestack emissions. The current law requires 85% removal. How much additional cost would the utility company incur as a result of the new law?

Solution

The graph of this function is shown in Figure 2.46. Note that the graph has a vertical asymptote at $p = 100$. Because the current law requires 85% removal, the current cost to the utility company is

$$C = \frac{80,000(85)}{100 - 85} \approx \$453,333. \qquad \text{Evaluate } C \text{ at } p = 85.$$

If the new law increases the percent removal to 90%, the cost to the utility company will be

$$C = \frac{80,000(90)}{100 - 90} = \$720,000. \qquad \text{Evaluate } C \text{ at } p = 90.$$

So, the new law would require the utility company to spend an additional

$$720,000 - 453,333 = \$266,667. \qquad \begin{array}{l}\text{Subtract 85\% removal cost}\\\text{from 90\% removal cost.}\end{array}$$

FIGURE **2.46**

Activities

1. Sketch a graph of
$$f(x) = \frac{3x + 4}{x^2 + x - 6}.$$

Answer:

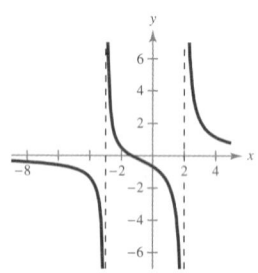

2. Find the slant asymptote.
$$g(x) = \frac{4x^2 - 2x + 1}{x - 1}$$
Answer: $y = 4x + 2$

3. Write a rational function with vertical asymptote $x = 4$, slant asymptote $y = x + 4$, and zero $x = 3$.

Answer: $f(x) = \dfrac{x^2 - 9}{x - 4}$

Ultraviolet Radiation

$$T = \frac{0.37s + 23.8}{s}$$

Exposure time (in hours)

Sunsor Scale reading

FIGURE 2.47

Example 9 ▶ **Ultraviolet Radiation**

For a person with sensitive skin, the amount of time T (in hours) the person can be exposed to the sun with minimal burning can be modeled by

$$T = \frac{0.37s + 23.8}{s}, \qquad 0 < s \le 120$$

where s is the Sunsor Scale reading. The Sunsor Scale is based on the level of intensity of UVB rays. (Source: Sunsor, Inc.)

a. Find the amount of time a person with sensitive skin can be exposed to the sun with minimal burning for $s = 10$, $s = 25$, and $s = 100$.

b. What is the horizontal asymptote of this function, and what does it represent?

Solution

a. When $s = 10$, $T = \dfrac{0.37(10) + 23.8}{10}$

$$= 2.75 \text{ hours.}$$

When $s = 25$, $T = \dfrac{0.37(25) + 23.8}{25}$

$$\approx 1.32 \text{ hours.}$$

When $s = 100$, $T = \dfrac{0.37(100) + 23.8}{100}$

$$\approx 0.61 \text{ hour.}$$

b. As shown in Figure 2.47, the horizontal asymptote is the line $T = 0.37$. This line represents the shortest possible exposure time with minimal burning.

Writing ABOUT MATHEMATICS

Common Factors in the Numerator and Denominator When sketching the graph of a rational function, be sure that the rational function has no factor that is common to its numerator and denominator. To see why, consider the function

$$f(x) = \frac{2x^2 + x - 1}{x + 1}$$

$$= \frac{(x + 1)(2x - 1)}{x + 1}$$

which has a common factor of $x + 1$ in the numerator and denominator. Sketch the graph of this function. Does it have a vertical asymptote at $x = -1$?

Decide whether each function below has a vertical asymptote. Write a short paragraph to explain your reasoning. Include a graph of each function in your explanation.

a. $f(x) = \dfrac{x^2 - 4}{x + 2}$ **b.** $f(x) = \dfrac{x^2 - 4}{x}$ **c.** $f(x) = \dfrac{x^2 - 4}{2 - x}$

2.6 **Exercises**

In Exercises 1–4, (a) complete each table, (b) determine the vertical and horizontal asymptotes of the function, and (c) find the domain of the function.

x	$f(x)$
0.5	
0.9	
0.99	
0.999	

x	$f(x)$
1.5	
1.1	
1.01	
1.001	

x	$f(x)$
5	
10	
100	
1000	

1. $f(x) = \dfrac{1}{x - 1}$

2. $f(x) = \dfrac{5x}{x - 1}$

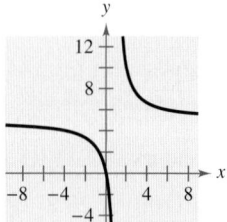

3. $f(x) = \dfrac{3x^2}{x^2 - 1}$

4. $f(x) = \dfrac{4x}{x^2 - 1}$

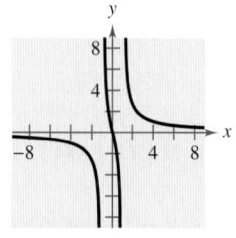

In Exercises 5–12, find the domain of the function and identify any horizontal and vertical asymptotes.

5. $f(x) = \dfrac{1}{x^2}$

6. $f(x) = \dfrac{4}{(x - 2)^3}$

7. $f(x) = \dfrac{2 + x}{2 - x}$

8. $f(x) = \dfrac{1 - 5x}{1 + 2x}$

9. $f(x) = \dfrac{x^3}{x^2 - 1}$

10. $f(x) = \dfrac{2x^2}{x + 1}$

11. $f(x) = \dfrac{3x^2 + 1}{x^2 + x + 9}$

12. $f(x) = \dfrac{3x^2 + x - 5}{x^2 + 1}$

In Exercises 13–16, match the rational function with its graph. [The graphs are labeled (a), (b), (c), and (d).]

(a)

(b)

(c)

(d)
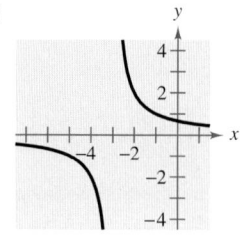

13. $f(x) = \dfrac{2}{x + 3}$

14. $f(x) = \dfrac{1}{x - 5}$

15. $f(x) = \dfrac{x - 1}{x - 4}$

16. $f(x) = -\dfrac{x + 2}{x + 4}$

In Exercises 17–20, find the zeros (if any) of the rational function.

17. $g(x) = \dfrac{x^2 - 1}{x + 1}$

18. $h(x) = 2 + \dfrac{5}{x^2 + 2}$

19. $f(x) = 1 - \dfrac{3}{x - 3}$

20. $g(x) = \dfrac{x^3 - 8}{x^2 + 1}$

In Exercises 21–40, (a) identify all intercepts, (b) find any vertical and horizontal asymptotes, (c) check for symmetry, and (d) plot additional solution points as needed and sketch the graph of the rational function.

21. $f(x) = \dfrac{1}{x + 2}$

22. $f(x) = \dfrac{1}{x - 3}$

23. $h(x) = \dfrac{-1}{x + 2}$

24. $g(x) = \dfrac{1}{3 - x}$

25. $C(x) = \dfrac{5 + 2x}{1 + x}$

26. $P(x) = \dfrac{1 - 3x}{1 - x}$

27. $g(x) = \dfrac{1}{x + 2} + 2$

28. $f(x) = 2 - \dfrac{3}{x^2}$

29. $f(x) = \dfrac{x^2}{x^2 + 9}$

30. $f(t) = \dfrac{1 - 2t}{t}$

31. $h(x) = \dfrac{x^2}{x^2 - 9}$

32. $g(x) = \dfrac{x}{x^2 - 9}$

33. $g(s) = \dfrac{s}{s^2 + 1}$

34. $f(x) = -\dfrac{1}{(x - 2)^2}$

35. $g(x) = \dfrac{4(x + 1)}{x(x - 4)}$

36. $h(x) = \dfrac{2}{x^2(x - 2)}$

37. $f(x) = \dfrac{3x}{x^2 - x - 2}$

38. $f(x) = \dfrac{2x}{x^2 + x - 2}$

39. $f(x) = \dfrac{2x^2 - 5x - 3}{x^3 - 2x^2 - x + 2}$

40. $f(x) = \dfrac{x^2 - x - 2}{x^3 - 2x^2 - 5x + 6}$

Analytical, Numerical, and Graphical Analysis In Exercises 41–44, do the following.

(a) Determine the domains of *f* and *g*.

(b) Simplify *f* and find any vertical asymptotes of *f*.

(c) Compare the functions by completing the table.

 (d) Use a graphing utility to graph *f* and *g* in the same viewing window.

 (e) Explain why the graphing utility may not show the difference in the domains of *f* and *g*.

41. $f(x) = \dfrac{x^2 - 1}{x + 1}, \qquad g(x) = x - 1$

x	-3	-2	-1.5	-1	-0.5	0	1
$f(x)$							
$g(x)$							

42. $f(x) = \dfrac{x^2(x - 2)}{x^2 - 2x}, \qquad g(x) = x$

x	-1	0	1	1.5	2	2.5	3
$f(x)$							
$g(x)$							

43. $f(x) = \dfrac{x - 2}{x^2 - 2x}, \qquad g(x) = \dfrac{1}{x}$

x	-0.5	0	0.5	1	1.5	2	3
$f(x)$							
$g(x)$							

44. $f(x) = \dfrac{2x - 6}{x^2 - 7x + 12}, \qquad g(x) = \dfrac{2}{x - 4}$

x	0	1	2	3	4	5	6
$f(x)$							
$g(x)$							

In Exercises 45–50, state the domain of the function and identify any vertical and slant asymptotes.

45. $h(x) = \dfrac{x^2 - 4}{x}$

46. $g(x) = \dfrac{x^2 + 5}{x}$

47. $f(t) = -\dfrac{t^2 + 1}{t + 5}$

48. $f(x) = \dfrac{x^2}{3x + 1}$

49. $f(x) = \dfrac{x^3 - 1}{x^2 - x}$

50. $f(x) = \dfrac{x^4 + x}{x^3}$

In Exercises 51–58, (a) identify all intercepts, (b) find any vertical and slant asymptotes, (c) check for symmetry, and (d) plot additional solution points as needed and sketch the graph of the rational function.

51. $f(x) = \dfrac{2x^2 + 1}{x}$

52. $f(x) = \dfrac{1 - x^2}{x}$

53. $g(x) = \dfrac{x^2 + 1}{x}$

54. $h(x) = \dfrac{x^2}{x - 1}$

55. $f(x) = \dfrac{x^3}{x^2 - 1}$

56. $g(x) = \dfrac{x^3}{2x^2 - 8}$

57. $f(x) = \dfrac{x^2 - x + 1}{x - 1}$

58. $f(x) = \dfrac{2x^2 - 5x + 5}{x - 2}$

In Exercises 59–62, use a graphing utility to graph the rational function. Give the domain of the function and identify any asymptotes. Then zoom out sufficiently far so that the graph appears as a line. Identify the line.

59. $f(x) = \dfrac{x^2 + 5x + 8}{x + 3}$

60. $f(x) = \dfrac{2x^2 + x}{x + 1}$

61. $g(x) = \dfrac{1 + 3x^2 - x^3}{x^2}$

62. $h(x) = \dfrac{12 - 2x - x^2}{2(4 + x)}$

Graphical Reasoning In Exercises 63–66, (a) use the graph to determine any *x*-intercepts of the rational function and (b) set *y* = 0 and solve the resulting equation to confirm your result in part (a).

63. $y = \dfrac{x + 1}{x - 3}$

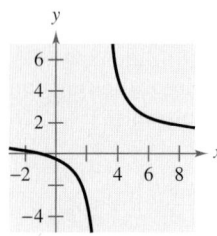

64. $y = \dfrac{2x}{x - 3}$

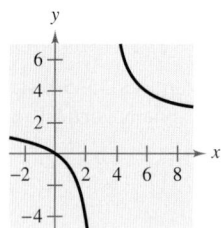

65. $y = \dfrac{1}{x} - x$

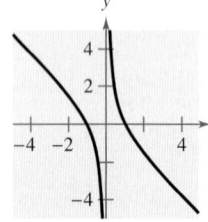

66. $y = x - 3 + \dfrac{2}{x}$

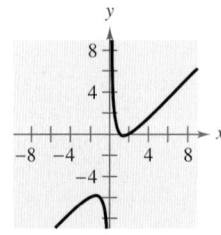

67. *Pollution* The cost *C* (in millions of dollars) of removing *p*% of the industrial and municipal pollutants discharged into a river is

$$C = \frac{255p}{100 - p}, \qquad 0 \le p < 100.$$

(a) Find the cost of removing 10% of the pollutants.

(b) Find the cost of removing 40% of the pollutants.

(c) Find the cost of removing 75% of the pollutants.

(d) According to this model, would it be possible to remove 100% of the pollutants? Explain.

68. *Recycling* In a pilot project, a rural township is given recycling bins for separating and storing recyclable products. The cost *C* (in dollars) for supplying bins to *p*% of the population is

$$C = \frac{25{,}000p}{100 - p}, \qquad 0 \le p < 100.$$

(a) Find the cost of supplying bins to 15% of the population.

(b) Find the cost of supplying bins to 50% of the population.

(c) Find the cost of supplying bins to 90% of the population.

(d) According to this model, would it be possible to supply bins to 100% of the residents? Explain.

69. *Population Growth* The game commission introduces 100 deer into newly acquired state game lands (see figure). The population *N* of the herd is modeled by

$$N = \frac{20(5 + 3t)}{1 + 0.04t}, \qquad t \ge 0$$

where *t* is the time in years (see figure).

(a) Find the population when *t* = 5, *t* = 10, and *t* = 25.

(b) What is the limiting size of the herd as time increases?

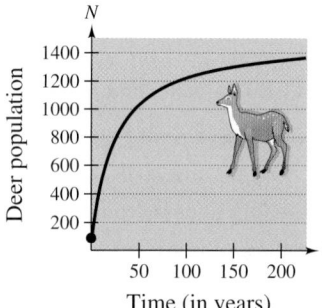

Time (in years)

70. *Concentration of a Mixture* A 1000-liter tank contains 50 liters of a 25% brine solution. You add *x* liters of a 75% brine solution to the tank.

(a) Show that the concentration *C*, the proportion of brine to total solution, in the final mixture is

$$C = \frac{3x + 50}{4(x + 50)}.$$

(b) Determine the domain of the function based on the physical constraints of the problem.

(c) Sketch a graph of the concentration function.

(d) As the tank is filled, what happens to the rate at which the concentration of brine is increasing? What percent does the concentration of brine appear to approach?

71. *Geometry* A rectangular region of length *x* and width *y* has an area of 500 square meters.

(a) Write the width *y* as a function of *x*.

(b) Determine the domain of the function based on the physical constraints of the problem.

(c) Sketch a graph of the function and determine the width of the rectangle when *x* = 30 meters.

72. *Minimum Area*   A rectangular page is designed to contain 64 square inches of print. The margins at the top and bottom of the page are each 1 inch deep. The margins on each side are $1\frac{1}{2}$ inches wide. What should the dimensions of the page be so that the least amount of paper is used?

73. *Medicine*   The concentration C of a chemical in the bloodstream t hours after injection into muscle tissue is

$$C = \frac{3t^2 + t}{t^3 + 50}, \qquad t > 0.$$

(a) Determine the horizontal asymptote of the function and interpret its meaning in the context of the problem.

 (b) Use a graphing utility to graph the function and approximate the time when the bloodstream concentration is greatest.

▶ Model It

74. *Average Speed*   A driver averaged 50 miles per hour on the round trip between Akron, Ohio and Columbus, Ohio, 100 miles away. The average speeds for going and returning were x and y miles per hour, respectively.

(a) Show that $y = \dfrac{25x}{x - 25}$.

 (c) Use a graphing utility to graph the function.

(b) Determine the vertical and horizontal asymptotes of the function.

(d) Complete the table.

x	30	35	40	45	50	55	60
y							

(e) Are the results in the table unexpected? Explain.

(f) Is it possible to average 20 miles per hour in one direction and still average 50 miles per hour on the round trip? Explain.

Synthesis

True or False?   **In Exercises 75 and 76, determine whether the statement is true or false. Justify your answer.**

75. A polynomial can have infinitely many vertical asymptotes.

76. The graph of a rational function can never cross one of its asymptotes.

Think About It   **In Exercises 77 and 78, write a rational function f that has the specified characteristics. (There are many correct answers.)**

77. Vertical asymptote: none

Horizontal asymptote: $y = 2$

78. Vertical asymptotes: $x = 0, x = \frac{5}{2}$

Horizontal asymptote: $y = -3$

79. *Think About It*   Give an example of a rational function whose domain is the set of all real numbers. Give an example of a rational function whose domain is the set of all real numbers except $x = 20$.

80. *Writing*   Describe what is meant by an asymptote of a graph.

81. *Think About It*   Write a rational function satisfying the following criteria.

Vertical asymptote: $x = 2$

Slant asymptote: $y = x + 1$

Zero of the function: $x = -2$

82. *Think About It*   Write a rational function satisfying the following criteria.

Vertical asymptote: $x = -1$

Slant asymptote: $y = x + 2$

Zero of the function: $x = 3$

Think About It   **In Exercises 83 and 84, use a graphing utility to graph the function. Explain why there is no vertical asymptote when a superficial examination of the function may indicate that there should be one.**

83. $h(x) = \dfrac{6 - 2x}{3 - x}$ **84.** $g(x) = \dfrac{x^2 + x - 2}{x - 1}$

Review

In Exercises 85–88, completely factor the expression.

85. $x^2 - 15x + 56$ **86.** $3x^2 + 23x - 36$

87. $x^3 - 5x^2 + 4x - 20$ **88.** $x^3 + 6x^2 - 2x - 12$

In Exercises 89–92, solve the inequality and show the solution on the real number line.

89. $10 - 3x \le 0$ **90.** $5 - 2x > 5(x + 1)$

91. $|4(x - 2)| < 20$ **92.** $\frac{1}{2}|2x + 3| \ge 5$

2.7 Partial Fractions

▶ **What you should learn**

- How to recognize partial fraction decompositions of rational expressions
- How to find partial fraction decompositions of rational expressions

▶ **Why you should learn it**

Partial fractions can help you analyze the behavior of a rational function. For instance, in Exercise 57 on page 185, you can analyze the exhaust temperatures of a diesel engine using partial fractions.

Introduction

In this section, you will learn to write a rational expression as the sum of two or more simpler rational expressions. For example, the rational expression

$$\frac{x+7}{x^2-x-6}$$

can be written as the sum of two fractions with first-degree denominators. That is,

Partial fraction decomposition

of $\dfrac{x+7}{x^2-x-6}$

$$\underbrace{\frac{x+7}{x^2-x-6}}_{} = \underbrace{\frac{2}{x-3}}_{\substack{\text{Partial}\\\text{fraction}}} + \underbrace{\frac{-1}{x+2}}_{\substack{\text{Partial}\\\text{fraction}}}.$$

Each fraction on the right side of the equation is a **partial fraction,** and together they make up the **partial fraction decomposition** of the left side.

Decomposition of $N(x)/D(x)$ into Partial Fractions

1. *Divide if improper:* If $N(x)/D(x)$ is an improper fraction [degree of $N(x) \geq$ degree of $D(x)$], divide the denominator into the numerator to obtain

$$\frac{N(x)}{D(x)} = (\text{polynomial}) \ + \frac{N_1(x)}{D(x)}$$

and apply Steps 2, 3, and 4 below to the proper rational expression $N_1(x)/D(x)$. Note that $N_1(x)$ is the remainder from the division of $N(x)$ by $D(x)$.

2. *Factor the denominator:* Completely factor the denominator into factors of the form

$$(px + q)^m \quad \text{and} \quad (ax^2 + bx + c)^n$$

where $(ax^2 + bx + c)$ is irreducible.

3. *Linear factors:* For *each* factor of the form $(px + q)^m$, the partial fraction decomposition must include the following sum of m fractions.

$$\frac{A_1}{(px + q)} + \frac{A_2}{(px + q)^2} + \cdots + \frac{A_m}{(px + q)^m}$$

4. *Quadratic factors:* For *each* factor of the form $(ax^2 + bx + c)^n$, the partial fraction decomposition must include the following sum of n fractions.

$$\frac{B_1x + C_1}{ax^2 + bx + c} + \frac{B_2x + C_2}{(ax^2 + bx + c)^2} + \cdots + \frac{B_nx + C_n}{(ax^2 + bx + c)^n}$$

STUDY TIP

Section A.4, shows you how to combine expressions such as

$$\frac{1}{x-2} + \frac{-1}{x+3} = \frac{5}{(x-2)(x+3)}.$$

The method of partial fractions shows you how to reverse this process.

$$\frac{5}{(x-2)(x+3)} = \frac{?}{x-2} + \frac{?}{x+3}$$

Partial Fraction Decomposition

Algebraic techniques for determining the constants in the numerators of partial fractions are demonstrated in the examples that follow. Note that the techniques vary slightly, depending on the type of factors of the denominator: linear or quadratic, distinct or repeated.

Example 1 ▶ Distinct Linear Factors

Write the partial fraction decomposition of $\dfrac{x + 7}{x^2 - x - 6}$.

Solution

The expression is not improper, so factor the denominator. Because $x^2 - x - 6 = (x - 3)(x + 2)$, you should include one partial fraction with a constant numerator for each linear factor of the denominator. Write the form of the decomposition as follows.

$$\frac{x + 7}{x^2 - x - 6} = \frac{A}{x - 3} + \frac{B}{x + 2} \qquad \text{Write form of decomposition.}$$

Multiplying each side of this equation by the least common denominator, $(x - 3)(x + 2)$, leads to the **basic equation**

$$x + 7 = A(x + 2) + B(x - 3). \qquad \text{Basic equation}$$

Because this equation is true for all x, you can substitute any *convenient* values of x that will help determine the constants A and B. Values of x that are especially convenient are ones that make the factors $(x + 2)$ and $(x - 3)$ equal to zero. For instance, let $x = -2$. Then

$$-2 + 7 = A(-2 + 2) + B(-2 - 3) \qquad \text{Substitute } -2 \text{ for } x.$$
$$5 = A(0) + B(-5)$$
$$5 = -5B$$
$$-1 = B.$$

To solve for A, let $x = 3$ and obtain

$$3 + 7 = A(3 + 2) + B(3 - 3) \qquad \text{Substitute 3 for } x.$$
$$10 = A(5) + B(0)$$
$$10 = 5A$$
$$2 = A.$$

So, the decomposition is

$$\frac{x + 7}{x^2 - x - 6} = \frac{2}{x - 3} + \frac{-1}{x + 2}$$

as indicated at the beginning of this section. Check this result by combining the two partial fractions on the right side of the equation, or by using your graphing utility.

Technology

You can use a graphing utility to check *graphically* the decomposition found in Example 1. To do this, graph

$$y_1 = \frac{x + 7}{x^2 - x - 6}$$

and

$$y_2 = \frac{2}{x - 3} + \frac{-1}{x + 2}$$

in the same viewing window. The graphs should be identical, as shown below.

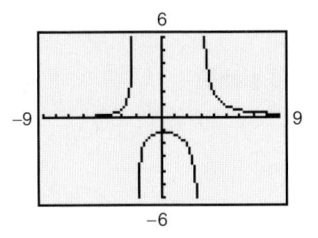

The next example shows how to find the partial fraction decomposition of a rational expression whose denominator has a repeated linear factor.

Example 2 ▶ **Repeated Linear Factors**

Write the partial fraction decomposition of $\dfrac{x^4 + 2x^3 + 6x^2 + 20x + 6}{x^3 + 2x^2 + x}$.

Solution

This rational expression is improper, so you should begin by dividing the numerator by the denominator to obtain

$$x + \frac{5x^2 + 20x + 6}{x^3 + 2x^2 + x}.$$

Have students check some of their answers to Exercises 15–52 on page 184 or the answers to some of the examples by combining the partial fractions.

Because the denominator of the remainder factors as

$$x^3 + 2x^2 + x = x(x^2 + 2x + 1) = x(x + 1)^2$$

you should include one partial fraction with a constant numerator for each power of x and $(x + 1)$ and write the form of the decomposition as follows.

$$\frac{5x^2 + 20x + 6}{x(x + 1)^2} = \frac{A}{x} + \frac{B}{x + 1} + \frac{C}{(x + 1)^2}$$

Multiplying by the LCD, $x(x + 1)^2$, leads to the basic equation

$$5x^2 + 20x + 6 = A(x + 1)^2 + Bx(x + 1) + Cx. \qquad \text{Basic equation}$$

Letting $x = -1$ eliminates the A- and B-terms and yields

$$5(-1)^2 + 20(-1) + 6 = A(-1 + 1)^2 + B(-1)(-1 + 1) + C(-1)$$

$$5 - 20 + 6 = 0 + 0 - C$$

$$C = 9.$$

Letting $x = 0$ eliminates the B- and C-terms and yields

$$5(0)^2 + 20(0) + 6 = A(0 + 1)^2 + B(0)(0 + 1) + C(0)$$

$$6 = A(1) + 0 + 0$$

$$6 = A.$$

At this point, you have exhausted the most convenient choices for x, so to find the value of B, use *any other value* for x along with the known values of A and C. So, using $x = 1$, $A = 6$, and $C = 9$,

$$5(1)^2 + 20(1) + 6 = 6(1 + 1)^2 + B(1)(1 + 1) + 9(1)$$

$$31 = 6(4) + 2B + 9$$

$$-2 = 2B$$

$$-1 = B.$$

Therefore, the partial fraction decomposition is

$$\frac{x^4 + 2x^3 + 6x^2 + 20x + 6}{x^3 + 2x^2 + x} = x + \frac{6}{x} + \frac{-1}{x + 1} + \frac{9}{(x + 1)^2}.$$

The procedure used to solve for the constants in Examples 1 and 2 works well when the factors of the denominator are linear. However, when the denominator contains irreducible quadratic factors, you should use a different procedure, which involves writing the right side of the basic equation in polynomial form and *equating the coefficients* of like terms.

Example 3 ▶ **Distinct Linear and Quadratic Factors**

Write the partial fraction decomposition of

$$\frac{3x^2 + 4x + 4}{x^3 + 4x}.$$

Solution

This expression is not improper, so factor the denominator. Because the denominator factors as

$$x^3 + 4x = x(x^2 + 4)$$

you should include one partial fraction with a constant numerator and one partial fraction with a linear numerator and write the form of the decomposition as follows.

$$\frac{3x^2 + 4x + 4}{x^3 + 4x} = \frac{A}{x} + \frac{Bx + C}{x^2 + 4}$$

Multiplying by the LCD, $x(x^2 + 4)$, yields the basic equation

$$3x^2 + 4x + 4 = A(x^2 + 4) + (Bx + C)x. \qquad \text{Basic equation}$$

Expanding this basic equation and collecting like terms produces

$$3x^2 + 4x + 4 = Ax^2 + 4A + Bx^2 + Cx$$

$$= (A + B)x^2 + Cx + 4A. \qquad \text{Polynomial form}$$

Finally, because two polynomials are equal if and only if the coefficients of like terms are equal,

$$3x^2 + 4x + 4 = (A + B)x^2 + Cx + 4A \qquad \text{Equate coefficients of like terms.}$$

you obtain the equations

$$3 = A + B, \qquad 4 = C, \qquad \text{and} \qquad 4 = 4A.$$

So, $A = 1$ and $C = 4$. Moreover, substituting $A = 1$ in the equation $3 = A + B$ yields

$$3 = 1 + B$$

$$2 = B.$$

Therefore, the partial fraction decomposition is

$$\frac{3x^2 + 4x + 4}{x^3 + 4x} = \frac{1}{x} + \frac{2x + 4}{x^2 + 4}.$$

Historical Note

John Bernoulli (1667–1748), a Swiss mathematician, introduced the method of partial fractions and was instrumental in the early development of calculus. Bernoulli was a professor at the University of Basel and taught many outstanding students, the most famous of whom was Leonhard Euler.

The Granger Collection

The next example shows how to find the partial fraction decomposition of a rational function whose denominator has a *repeated* quadratic factor.

Example 4 ▶ **Repeated Quadratic Factors**

Write the partial fraction decomposition of

$$\frac{8x^3 + 13x}{(x^2+2)^2}.$$

Solution

You need to include one partial fraction with a linear numerator for each power of $(x^2 + 2)$.

$$\frac{8x^3 + 13x}{(x^2+2)^2} = \frac{Ax + B}{x^2+2} + \frac{Cx + D}{(x^2+2)^2}$$

Multiplying by the LCD, $(x^2+2)^2$, yields the basic equation

$$8x^3 + 13x = (Ax + B)(x^2+2) + Cx + D \qquad \text{Basic equation}$$

$$= Ax^3 + 2Ax + Bx^2 + 2B + Cx + D$$

$$= Ax^3 + Bx^2 + (2A + C)x + (2B + D). \qquad \text{Polynomial form}$$

Equating coefficients of like terms

$$8x^3 + 0x^2 + 13x + 0 = Ax^3 + Bx^2 + (2A + C)x + (2B + D)$$

produces

$$8 = A, \; 0 = B, \; 13 = 2A + C, \text{ and } 0 = 2B + D. \qquad \text{Equate coefficients.}$$

Finally, use the values $A = 8$ and $B = 0$ to obtain the following.

$$13 = 2A + C$$

$$= 2(8) + C$$

$$-3 = C$$

$$0 = 2B + D$$

$$= 2(0) + D$$

$$0 = D$$

Therefore,

$$\frac{8x^3 + 13x}{(x^2+2)^2} = \frac{8x}{x^2+2} + \frac{-3x}{(x^2+2)^2}.$$

By equating coefficients of like terms in Examples 3 and 4, you obtained several equations involving A, B, C, and D, which were solved by *substitution*. In a later chapter you will study a more general method for solving such *systems of equations*.

Guidelines for Solving the Basic Equation

Linear Factors

1. Substitute the *zeros* of the distinct linear factors into the basic equation.

2. For repeated linear factors, use the coefficients determined in step 1 above to rewrite the basic equation. Then substitute *other* convenient values of x and solve for the remaining coefficients.

Quadratic Factors

1. Expand the basic equation.

2. Collect terms according to powers of x.

3. Equate the coefficients of like terms to obtain equations involving A, B, C, and so on.

4. Use substitution to solve for $A, B, C, \dots$

Activities

1. Write the partial fraction decomposition of
$$\frac{5x - 10}{(x + 2)(2x - 1)}.$$
Answer: $\dfrac{4}{x + 2} - \dfrac{3}{2x - 1}$

2. Write the partial fraction decomposition of
$$\frac{4x^3 + 9x^2 - 2x + 6}{x(x + 2)}.$$
Answer: $4x + 1 + \dfrac{3}{x} - \dfrac{7}{x + 2}$

Keep in mind that for *improper* rational expressions such as

$$\frac{N(x)}{D(x)} = \frac{2x^3 + x^2 - 7x + 7}{x^2 + x - 2}$$

you must first divide before applying partial fraction decomposition.

Writing ABOUT MATHEMATICS

Error Analysis Suppose you are tutoring a student in algebra. In trying to find a partial fraction decomposition, your student writes the following.

$$\frac{x^2 + 1}{x(x - 1)} = \frac{A}{x} + \frac{B}{x - 1}$$

$$\frac{x^2 + 1}{x(x - 1)} = \frac{A(x - 1)}{x(x - 1)} + \frac{Bx}{x(x - 1)}$$

$$x^2 + 1 = A(x - 1) + Bx \qquad \text{Basic equation}$$

By substituting $x = 0$ and $x = 1$ into the basic equation, your student concludes that $A = -1$ and $B = 2$. However, in checking this solution, your student obtains the following.

$$\frac{-1}{x} + \frac{2}{x - 1} = \frac{(-1)(x - 1) + 2(x)}{x(x - 1)}$$

$$= \frac{x + 1}{x(x - 1)}$$

$$\neq \frac{x^2 + 1}{x(x - 1)}$$

What has gone wrong?

2.7 Exercises

In Exercises 1–4, match the rational expression with the form of its decomposition. [The decompositions are labeled (a), (b), (c), and (d).]

(a) $\dfrac{A}{x} + \dfrac{B}{x+2} + \dfrac{C}{x-2}$

(b) $\dfrac{A}{x} + \dfrac{B}{x-4}$

(c) $\dfrac{A}{x} + \dfrac{B}{x^2} + \dfrac{C}{x-4}$

(d) $\dfrac{A}{x} + \dfrac{Bx+C}{x^2+4}$

1. $\dfrac{3x-1}{x(x-4)}$

2. $\dfrac{3x-1}{x^2(x-4)}$

3. $\dfrac{3x-1}{x(x^2+4)}$

4. $\dfrac{3x-1}{x(x^2-4)}$

In Exercises 5–14, write the form of the partial fraction decomposition of the rational expression. Do not solve for the constants.

5. $\dfrac{7}{x^2-14x}$

6. $\dfrac{x-2}{x^2+4x+3}$

7. $\dfrac{12}{x^3-10x^2}$

8. $\dfrac{x^2-3x+2}{4x^3+11x^2}$

9. $\dfrac{4x^2+3}{(x-5)^3}$

10. $\dfrac{6x+5}{(x+2)^4}$

11. $\dfrac{2x-3}{x^3+10x}$

12. $\dfrac{x-6}{2x^3+8x}$

13. $\dfrac{x-1}{x(x^2+1)^2}$

14. $\dfrac{x+4}{x^2(3x-1)^2}$

In Exercises 15–38, write the partial fraction decomposition of the rational expression. Check your result algebraically.

15. $\dfrac{1}{x^2-1}$

16. $\dfrac{1}{4x^2-9}$

17. $\dfrac{1}{x^2+x}$

18. $\dfrac{3}{x^2-3x}$

19. $\dfrac{1}{2x^2+x}$

20. $\dfrac{5}{x^2+x-6}$

21. $\dfrac{3}{x^2+x-2}$

22. $\dfrac{x+1}{x^2+4x+3}$

23. $\dfrac{x^2+12x+12}{x^3-4x}$

24. $\dfrac{x+2}{x(x-4)}$

25. $\dfrac{4x^2+2x-1}{x^2(x+1)}$

26. $\dfrac{2x-3}{(x-1)^2}$

27. $\dfrac{3x}{(x-3)^2}$

28. $\dfrac{6x^2+1}{x^2(x-1)^2}$

29. $\dfrac{x^2-1}{x(x^2+1)}$

30. $\dfrac{x}{(x-1)(x^2+x+1)}$

31. $\dfrac{x}{x^3-x^2-2x+2}$

32. $\dfrac{x+6}{x^3-3x^2-4x+12}$

33. $\dfrac{x^2}{x^4-2x^2-8}$

34. $\dfrac{2x^2+x+8}{(x^2+4)^2}$

35. $\dfrac{x}{16x^4-1}$

36. $\dfrac{x+1}{x^3+x}$

37. $\dfrac{x^2+5}{(x+1)(x^2-2x+3)}$

38. $\dfrac{x^2-4x+7}{(x+1)(x^2-2x+3)}$

In Exercises 39–44, write the partial fraction decomposition of the improper rational expression.

39. $\dfrac{x^2-x}{x^2+x+1}$

40. $\dfrac{x^2-4x}{x^2+x+6}$

41. $\dfrac{2x^3-x^2+x+5}{x^2+3x+2}$

42. $\dfrac{x^3+2x^2-x+1}{x^2+3x-4}$

43. $\dfrac{x^4}{(x-1)^3}$

44. $\dfrac{16x^4}{(2x-1)^3}$

In Exercises 45–52, write the partial fraction decomposition of the rational expression. Use a graphing utility to check your result graphically.

45. $\dfrac{5-x}{2x^2+x-1}$

46. $\dfrac{3x^2-7x-2}{x^3-x}$

47. $\dfrac{x-1}{x^3+x^2}$

48. $\dfrac{4x^2-1}{2x(x+1)^2}$

49. $\dfrac{x^2+x+2}{(x^2+2)^2}$

50. $\dfrac{x^3}{(x+2)^2(x-2)^2}$

51. $\dfrac{2x^3-4x^2-15x+5}{x^2-2x-8}$

52. $\dfrac{x^3-x+3}{x^2+x-2}$

Graphical Analysis In Exercises 53–56, write the partial fraction decomposition of the rational function. Identify the graph of the rational function and the graph of each term of its decomposition. State any relationship between the vertical asymptotes of the rational function and the vertical asymptotes of the terms of the decomposition. To print an enlarged copy of the graph, go to the website *www.mathgraphs.com*.

53. $y = \dfrac{x - 12}{x(x - 4)}$

54. $y = \dfrac{2(x + 1)^2}{x(x^2 + 1)}$

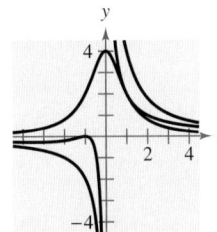

55. $y = \dfrac{2(4x - 3)}{x^2 - 9}$

56. $y = \dfrac{2(4x^2 - 15x + 39)}{x^2(x^2 - 10x + 26)}$

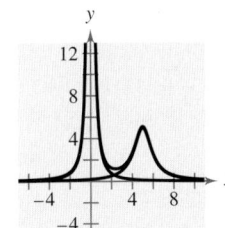

▶ Model It

57. *Thermodynamics* The magnitude of the range R of exhaust temperatures (in degrees Fahrenheit) in an experimental diesel engine is approximated by

$$R = \frac{2000(4 - 3x)}{(11 - 7x)(7 - 4x)}, \qquad 0 < x \le 1$$

where x is the relative load (in foot-pounds).

(a) Write the partial fraction decomposition of the equation.

(b) The decomposition in part (a) is the difference of two fractions. The absolute values of the terms give the expected maximum and minimum temperatures of the exhaust gases for different loads.

Ymax $= |$1st term$|$ Ymin $= |$2nd term$|$

Write the equations for Ymax and Ymin.

▶ Model It *(continued)*

 (c) Use a graphing utility to graph each equation from part (b) in the same viewing window.

(d) Determine the expected maximum and minimum temperatures for a relative load of 0.5.

Synthesis

58. *Writing* Describe two ways of solving for the constants in a partial fraction decomposition.

True or False? In Exercises 59 and 60, determine whether the statement is true or false. Justify your answer.

59. For the rational expression

$$\frac{x}{(x + 10)(x - 10)^2}$$

the partial fraction decomposition is of the form

$$\frac{A}{x + 10} + \frac{B}{(x - 10)^2}.$$

60. When writing the partial fraction decomposition of the expression

$$\frac{x^3 + x - 2}{x^2 - 5x + 14}$$

the first step is to factor the denominator.

In Exercises 61–64, write the partial fraction decomposition of the rational expression. Check your result algebraically. Then assign a value to the constant a to check the result graphically.

61. $\dfrac{1}{a^2 - x^2}$

62. $\dfrac{1}{x(x + a)}$

63. $\dfrac{1}{y(a - y)}$

64. $\dfrac{1}{(x + 1)(a - x)}$

Review

In Exercises 65–68, sketch the graph of the function.

65. $f(x) = x^2 - 9x + 18$

66. $f(x) = 2x^2 - 9x - 5$

67. $f(x) = -x^2(x - 3)$

68. $f(x) = \frac{1}{2}x^3 - 1$

In Exercises 69 and 70, sketch the graph of the rational function.

69. $f(x) = \dfrac{x^2 + x - 6}{x + 5}$

70. $f(x) = \dfrac{3x - 1}{x^2 + 4x - 12}$

Chapter Summary

▶ *What* did you learn?

Section 2.1 Review Exercises
☐ How to analyze graphs of quadratic functions 1–6
☐ How to write quadratic functions in standard form and sketch their graphs 7–18
☐ How to use quadratic functions to model and solve real-life problems 19–22

Section 2.2
☐ How to use transformations to sketch graphs of polynomial functions 23–28
☐ How to use the Leading Coefficient Test to determine the end behavior of graphs of polynomial functions 29–32
☐ How to use zeros of polynomial functions as sketching aids 33–42
☐ How to use the Intermediate Value Theorem to help locate zeros of polynomial functions 43–46

Section 2.3
☐ How to use long division to divide polynomials by other polynomials 47–52
☐ How to use synthetic division to divide polynomials by binomials 53–60
☐ How to use the Remainder Theorem and the Factor Theorem 61–64

Section 2.4
☐ How to use the imaginary unit i to write complex numbers 65–68
☐ How to add, subtract, and multiply complex numbers 69–74
☐ How to use complex conjugates to write the quotient of two complex numbers 75–78
☐ How to find complex solutions of quadratic equations 79–82

Section 2.5
☐ How to use the Fundamental Theorem of Algebra to determine the number of zeros of polynomial functions 83–88
☐ How to find rational zeros of polynomial functions 89–96
☐ How to find conjugate pairs of complex zeros 97, 98
☐ How to use factoring, Descartes' Rule of Signs, and the Upper and Lower Bound Rules to find zeros of polynomial functions 99–110

Section 2.6
☐ How to find the domains of rational functions 111–114
☐ How to find the horizontal and vertical asymptotes of graphs of rational functions 115–118
☐ How to analyze and sketch graphs of rational functions 119–130
☐ How to sketch graphs of rational functions that have slant asymptotes 131–134
☐ How to use rational functions to model and solve real-life problems 135–138

Section 2.7
☐ How to recognize and find partial fraction decompositions of rational expressions 139–150

Review Exercises

2.1 In Exercises 1–4, find the quadratic function that has the indicated vertex and whose graph passes through the given point.

1.

2.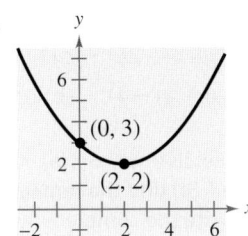

3. Vertex: $(1, -4)$; Point: $(2, -3)$

4. Vertex: $(2, 3)$; Point: $(-1, 6)$

In Exercises 5 and 6, graph each function. Compare the graph of each function with the graph of $y = x^2$.

5. (a) $f(x) = 2x^2$ (b) $g(x) = -2x^2$
   (c) $h(x) = x^2 + 2$ (d) $k(x) = (x + 2)^2$

6. (a) $f(x) = x^2 - 4$ (b) $g(x) = 4 - x^2$
   (c) $h(x) = (x - 3)^2$ (d) $k(x) = \frac{1}{2}x^2 - 1$

In Exercises 7–18, write the quadratic function in standard form and sketch its graph. Identify the vertex and x-intercepts.

7. $g(x) = x^2 - 2x$ **8.** $f(x) = 6x - x^2$

9. $f(x) = x^2 + 8x + 10$ **10.** $h(x) = 3 + 4x - x^2$

11. $f(t) = -2t^2 + 4t + 1$ **12.** $f(x) = x^2 - 8x + 12$

13. $h(x) = 4x^2 + 4x + 13$ **14.** $f(x) = x^2 - 6x + 1$

15. $h(x) = x^2 + 5x - 4$ **16.** $f(x) = 4x^2 + 4x + 5$

17. $f(x) = \frac{1}{3}(x^2 + 5x - 4)$

18. $f(x) = \frac{1}{2}(6x^2 - 24x + 22)$

19. *Geometry* The perimeter of a rectangle is 200 meters.

(a) Draw a rectangle that gives a visual representation of the problem. Label the length and width in terms of x and y, respectively.

(b) Write y as a function of x. Use the result to write the area as a function of x.

(c) Of all possible rectangles with perimeters of 200 meters, find the dimensions of the one with the maximum area.

20. *Maximum Profit* A real estate office handles 50 apartment units. When the rent is $540 per month, all units are occupied. However, for each $30 increase in rent, one unit becomes vacant. Each occupied unit requires an average of $18 per month for service and repairs. What rent should be charged to obtain the maximum profit?

21. *Minimum Cost* A soft drink manufacturer has daily production costs of

$$C = 70{,}000 - 120x + 0.055x^2$$

where C is the total cost (in dollars) and x is the number of units produced. How many units should be produced each day to yield a minimum cost?

22. *Sociology* The average age of the groom at a first marriage for a given age of the bride can be approximated by the model $y = -0.107x^2 + 5.68x - 48.5$, $20 \le x \le 25$, where y is the age of the groom and x is the age of the bride. For what age of the bride is the average age of the groom 26? (Source: U.S. Census Bureau)

2.2 In Exercises 23–28, sketch the graphs of $y = x^n$ and the transformation.

23. $y = x^3$, $f(x) = -(x - 4)^3$

24. $y = x^3$, $f(x) = -4x^3$

25. $y = x^4$, $f(x) = 2 - x^4$

26. $y = x^4$, $f(x) = 2(x - 2)^4$

27. $y = x^5$, $f(x) = (x - 3)^5$

28. $y = x^5$, $f(x) = \frac{1}{2}x^5 + 3$

In Exercises 29–32, determine the right-hand and left-hand behavior of the graph of the polynomial function.

29. $f(x) = -x^2 + 6x + 9$ **30.** $f(x) = \frac{1}{2}x^3 + 2x$

31. $g(x) = \frac{3}{4}(x^4 + 3x^2 + 2)$

32. $h(x) = -x^5 - 7x^2 + 10x$

In Exercises 33–38, find all the real zeros of the function. Determine the multiplicity of each zero.

33. $f(x) = 2x^2 + 11x - 21$ **34.** $f(x) = x(x + 3)^2$

35. $f(t) = t^3 - 3t$ **36.** $f(x) = x^3 - 8x^2$

37. $f(x) = -12x^3 + 20x^2$ **38.** $g(x) = x^4 - x^3 - 2x^2$

In Exercises 39–42, sketch the graph of the function by (a) applying the Leading Coefficient Test, (b) finding the zeros of the polynomial, (c) plotting sufficient solution points, and (d) drawing a continuous curve though the points.

39. $f(x) = -x^3 + x^2 - 2$ **40.** $g(x) = 2x^3 + 4x^2$

41. $f(x) = x(x^3 + x^2 - 5x + 3)$

42. $h(x) = 3x^2 - x^4$

In Exercises 43–46, use the Intermediate Value Theorem and the *table* feature of a graphing utility to find intervals one unit in length in which the polynomial function is guaranteed to have a zero. Adjust the table to approximate the zeros of the function. Use the *zero* or *root* feature of a graphing utility to verify your results.

43. $f(x) = 3x^3 - x^2 + 3$

44. $f(x) = 0.25x^3 - 3.65x + 6.12$

45. $f(x) = x^4 - 5x - 1$

46. $f(x) = 7x^4 + 3x^3 - 8x^2 + 2$

2.3 In Exercises 47–52, use long division to divide.

47. $\dfrac{24x^2 - x - 8}{3x - 2}$ **48.** $\dfrac{4x + 7}{3x - 2}$

49. $\dfrac{5x^3 - 13x^2 - x + 2}{x^2 - 3x + 1}$ **50.** $\dfrac{3x^4}{x^2 - 1}$

51. $\dfrac{x^4 - 3x^3 + 4x^2 - 6x + 3}{x^2 + 2}$

52. $\dfrac{6x^4 + 10x^3 + 13x^2 - 5x + 2}{2x^2 - 1}$

In Exercises 53–56, use synthetic division to divide.

53. $\dfrac{6x^4 - 4x^3 - 27x^2 + 18x}{x - 2}$

54. $\dfrac{0.1x^3 + 0.3x^2 - 0.5}{x - 5}$

55. $\dfrac{2x^3 - 19x^2 + 38x + 24}{x - 4}$

56. $\dfrac{3x^3 + 20x^2 + 29x - 12}{x + 3}$

In Exercises 57 and 58, use synthetic division to determine whether the given values of x are zeros of the function.

57. $f(x) = 20x^4 + 9x^3 - 14x^2 - 3x$

(a) $x = -1$ (b) $x = \frac{3}{4}$ (c) $x = 0$ (d) $x = 1$

58. $f(x) = 3x^3 - 8x^2 - 20x + 16$

(a) $x = 4$ (b) $x = -4$ (c) $x = \frac{2}{3}$ (d) $x = -1$

In Exercises 59 and 60, use synthetic division to find the specified value of the function.

59. $f(x) = x^4 + 10x^3 - 24x^2 + 20x + 44$

(a) $f(-3)$ (b) $f(-1)$

60. $g(t) = 2t^5 - 5t^4 - 8t + 20$

(a) $g(-4)$ (b) $g(\sqrt{2})$

In Exercises 61–64, (a) verify the given factor(s) of the function f, (b) find the remaining factors of f, (c) use your results to write the complete factorization of f, (d) list all real zeros of f, and (e) confirm your results by using a graphing utility to graph the function.

Function	*Factor(s)*
61. $f(x) = x^3 + 4x^2 - 25x - 28$	$(x - 4)$
62. $f(x) = 2x^3 + 11x^2 - 21x - 90$	$(x + 6)$
63. $f(x) = x^4 - 4x^3 - 7x^2 + 22x + 24$	$(x + 2)(x - 3)$
64. $f(x) = x^4 - 11x^3 + 41x^2 - 61x + 30$	$(x - 2)(x - 5)$

2.4 In Exercises 65–68, write the complex number in standard form.

65. $6 + \sqrt{-4}$ **66.** $3 - \sqrt{-25}$

67. $i^2 + 3i$ **68.** $-5i + i^2$

In Exercises 69–74, perform the operation and write the result in standard form.

69. $(7 + 5i) + (-4 + 2i)$

70. $\left(\dfrac{\sqrt{2}}{2} - \dfrac{\sqrt{2}}{2}i\right) - \left(\dfrac{\sqrt{2}}{2} + \dfrac{\sqrt{2}}{2}i\right)$

71. $5i(13 - 8i)$ **72.** $(1 + 6i)(5 - 2i)$

73. $(10 - 8i)(2 - 3i)$ **74.** $i(6 + i)(3 - 2i)$

In Exercises 75 and 76, write the quotient in standard form.

75. $\dfrac{6 + i}{4 - i}$ **76.** $\dfrac{3 + 2i}{5 + i}$

In Exercises 77 and 78, perform the operation and write the result in standard form.

77. $\dfrac{4}{2 - 3i} + \dfrac{2}{1 + i}$ **78.** $\dfrac{1}{2 + i} - \dfrac{5}{1 + 4i}$

In Exercises 79–82, find all solutions of the equation.

79. $3x^2 + 1 = 0$

80. $2 + 8x^2 = 0$

81. $x^2 - 2x + 10 = 0$

82. $6x^2 + 3x + 27 = 0$

2.5 In Exercises 83–88, find all the zeros of the function.

83. $f(x) = 3x(x - 2)^2$

84. $f(x) = (x - 4)(x + 9)^2$

85. $f(x) = x^2 - 9x + 8$

86. $f(x) = x^3 + 6x$

87. $f(x) = (x + 4)(x - 6)(x - 2i)(x + 2i)$

88. $f(x) = (x - 8)(x - 5)^2(x - 3 + i)(x - 3 - i)$

In Exercises 89 and 90, use the Rational Zero Test to list all possible rational zeros of f.

89. $f(x) = -4x^3 + 8x^2 - 3x + 15$

90. $f(x) = 3x^4 + 4x^3 - 5x^2 - 8$

In Exercises 91–96, find all the real zeros of the function.

91. $f(x) = x^3 - 2x^2 - 21x - 18$

92. $f(x) = 3x^3 - 20x^2 + 7x + 30$

93. $f(x) = x^3 - 10x^2 + 17x - 8$

94. $f(x) = x^3 + 9x^2 + 24x + 20$

95. $f(x) = x^4 + x^3 - 11x^2 + x - 12$

96. $f(x) = 25x^4 + 25x^3 - 154x^2 - 4x + 24$

In Exercises 97 and 98, find a polynomial with real coefficients that has the given zeros.

97. $\frac{2}{3}, 4, \sqrt{3}i$

98. $2, -3, 1 - 2i$

In Exercises 99–102, use the given zero to find all the zeros of the function.

Function	*Zero*
99. $f(x) = x^3 - 12x^2 + x - 12$	i
100. $h(x) = -x^3 + 2x^2 - 16x + 32$	$-4i$
101. $g(x) = 2x^4 - 3x^3 - 13x^2 + 37x - 15$	$2 + i$
102. $f(x) = 4x^4 - 11x^3 + 14x^2 - 6x$	$1 - i$

In Exercises 103–106, find all the zeros of the function and write the polynomial as a product of linear factors.

103. $f(x) = x^3 + 4x^2 - 5x$

104. $g(x) = x^3 - 7x^2 + 36$

105. $g(x) = x^4 + 4x^3 - 3x^2 + 40x + 208$

106. $f(x) = x^4 + 8x^3 + 8x^2 - 72x - 153$

In Exercises 107 and 108, use Descartes's Rule of Signs to determine the possible numbers of positive and negative zeros of the function.

107. $g(x) = 5x^3 + 3x^2 - 6x + 9$

108. $h(x) = -2x^5 + 4x^3 - 2x^2 + 5$

In Exercises 109 and 110, use synthetic division to verify the upper and lower bounds of the real zeros of f.

109. $f(x) = 4x^3 - 3x^2 + 4x - 3$

(a) Upper: $x = 1$ (b) Lower: $x = -\frac{1}{4}$

110. $f(x) = 2x^3 - 5x^2 - 14x + 8$

(a) Upper: $x = 8$ (b) Lower: $x = -4$

2.6 In Exercises 111–114, find the domain of the rational function.

111. $f(x) = \dfrac{5x}{x + 12}$

112. $f(x) = \dfrac{3x^2}{1 + 3x}$

113. $f(x) = \dfrac{8}{x^2 - 10x + 24}$

114. $f(x) = \dfrac{x^2 + x - 2}{x^2 + 4}$

In Exercises 115–118, identify any horizontal or vertical asymptotes.

115. $f(x) = \dfrac{4}{x + 3}$

116. $f(x) = \dfrac{2x^2 + 5x - 3}{x^2 + 2}$

117. $g(x) = \dfrac{x^2}{x^2 - 4}$

118. $g(x) = \dfrac{1}{(x - 3)^2}$

In Exercises 119–130, identify intercepts, check for symmetry, identify any vertical or horizontal asymptotes, and sketch the graph of the rational function.

119. $f(x) = \dfrac{-5}{x^2}$

120. $f(x) = \dfrac{4}{x}$

121. $g(x) = \dfrac{2 + x}{1 - x}$

122. $h(x) = \dfrac{x - 3}{x - 2}$

123. $p(x) = \dfrac{x^2}{x^2 + 1}$

124. $f(x) = \dfrac{2x}{x^2 + 4}$

125. $f(x) = \dfrac{x}{x^2 + 1}$

126. $h(x) = \dfrac{4}{(x - 1)^2}$

127. $f(x) = \dfrac{-6x^2}{x^2 + 1}$

128. $y = \dfrac{2x^2}{x^2 - 4}$

129. $y = \dfrac{x}{x^2 - 1}$

130. $g(x) = \dfrac{-2}{(x + 3)^2}$

In Exercises 131–134, state the domain of the function and identify any vertical and slant asymptotes. Then sketch the graph of the rational function.

131. $f(x) = \dfrac{2x^3}{x^2 + 1}$

132. $f(x) = \dfrac{x^2 + 1}{x + 1}$

133. $f(x) = \dfrac{x^2 + 3x - 10}{x + 2}$

134. $f(x) = \dfrac{x^3}{x^2 - 4}$

135. *Average Cost* A business has a cost C of $C = 0.5x + 500$ for producing x units. The average cost per unit is

$$\overline{C} = \frac{C}{x} = \frac{0.5x + 500}{x}, \qquad x > 0.$$

Determine the average cost per unit as x increases without bound. (Find the horizontal asymptote.)

136. *Seizure of Illegal Drugs* The cost C (in millions of dollars) for the federal government to seize $p\%$ of an illegal drug as it enters the country is

$$C = \frac{528p}{100 - p}, \qquad 0 \le p < 100.$$

(a) Find the cost of seizing 25% of the drug.

(b) Find the cost of seizing 50% of the drug.

(c) Find the cost of seizing 75% of the drug.

(d) According to this model, would it be possible to seize 100% of the drug?

137. *Minimum Area* A page that is x inches wide and y inches high contains 30 square inches of print. The top and bottom margins are 2 inches deep, and the margins on each side are 2 inches wide.

(a) Draw a diagram that gives a visual representation of the problem.

(b) Show that the total area A on the page is

$$A = \frac{2x(2x + 7)}{x - 4}.$$

(c) Determine the domain of the function based on the physical constraints of the problem.

(d) Use a graphing utility to graph the area function and approximate the page size for which the least amount of paper will be used.

138. *Photosynthesis* The amount y of CO_2 uptake in milligrams per square decimeter per hour at optimal temperatures and with the natural supply of CO_2 is approximated by the model

$$y = \frac{18.47x - 2.96}{0.23x + 1}, \qquad x > 0$$

where x is the light intensity (in watts per square meter.) Use a graphing utility to graph the function and determine the limiting amount of CO_2 uptake.

2.7 In Exercises 139–142, write the form of the partial fraction decomposition for the rational expression. Do not solve for the constants.

139. $\dfrac{3}{x^2 + 20x}$

140. $\dfrac{x - 8}{x^2 - 3x - 28}$

141. $\dfrac{3x - 4}{x^3 - 5x^2}$

142. $\dfrac{x - 2}{x(x^2 + 2)^2}$

In Exercises 143–150, write the partial fraction decomposition for the rational expression.

143. $\dfrac{4 - x}{x^2 + 6x + 8}$

144. $\dfrac{-x}{x^2 + 3x + 2}$

145. $\dfrac{x^2}{x^2 + 2x - 15}$

146. $\dfrac{9}{x^2 - 9}$

147. $\dfrac{x^2 + 2x}{x^3 - x^2 + x - 1}$

148. $\dfrac{4x - 2}{3(x - 1)^2}$

149. $\dfrac{3x^3 + 4x}{(x^2 + 1)^2}$

150. $\dfrac{4x^2}{(x - 1)(x^2 + 1)}$

Synthesis

True or False? In Exercises 151 and 152, determine whether the statement is true or false. Justify your answer.

151. A fourth-degree polynomial can have -5, $-8i$, $4i$, and 5 as its zeros.

152. The domain of a rational function can never be the set of all real numbers.

153. Write quadratic equations that have (a) two distinct real solutions, (b) two complex solutions, and (c) no real solution.

154. Given the function $f(x) = a(x - h)^2 + k$, state the values of a, h, and k that yield a reflection in the x-axis with either a shrink or a stretch of the graph of the function $f(x) = x^2$.

155. What is the degree of a function that has exactly two real zeros and two complex zeros?

156. Because $i^2 = -1$, is the square of any complex number a real number? Explain.

Chapter Test

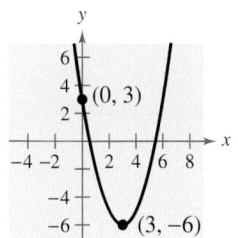

$(0, 3)$

$(3, -6)$

The *Interactive* CD-ROM and *Internet* versions of this text offer Chapter Pre-Tests and Chapter Post-Tests, both of which have randomly generated exercises with diagnostic capabilities.

Take this test as you would take a test in class. When you are finished, check your work against the answers given in the back of the book.

1. Describe how the graph of g differs from the graph of $f(x) = x^2$.

    (a) $g(x) = 2 - x^2$

    (b) $g(x) = \left(x - \frac{3}{2}\right)^2$

2. Find an equation of the parabola shown in the figure at the left.

3. The path of a ball is given by $y = -\frac{1}{20}x^2 + 3x + 5$, where y is the height (in feet) of the ball and x is the horizontal distance (in feet) from where the ball was thrown. Find (a) the maximum height of the ball and (b) the distance the ball travels.

4. Determine the right-hand and left-hand behavior of the graph of the function $h(t) = -\frac{3}{4}t^5 + 2t^2$. Then sketch its graph.

5. Divide by long division: $3x^3 + 4x - 1 \div x^2 + 1$.

6. Use synthetic division to show that $x = \sqrt{3}$ is a zero of the function $f(x) = 4x^3 - x^2 - 12x + 3$. Use the result to factor the polynomial function completely and list all the real zeros of the function.

7. Perform the operation and write the result in standard form.

    (a) $10i - \left(3 + \sqrt{-25}\right)$

    (b) $\left(2 + \sqrt{3}i\right)\left(2 - \sqrt{3}i\right)$

8. Write the quotient in standard form: $\dfrac{5}{2 + i}$.

In Exercises 9 and 10, find all the real zeros of the function.

9. $g(t) = 2t^4 - 3t^3 + 16t - 24$ 10. $h(x) = 3x^5 + 2x^4 - 3x - 2$

11. Find all zeros of $f(x) = x^4 - x^3 + 2x^2 - 4x - 8$ given that $f(2i) = 0$.

In Exercises 12 and 13, find a polynomial function with integer coefficients that has the given zeros.

12. $0, 3, 3 + i, 3 - i$ 13. $1 + \sqrt{3}i, 1 - \sqrt{3}i, 2, 2$

In Exercises 14–16, sketch the graph of the rational function by hand. Be sure to identify all intercepts and asymptotes.

14. $f(x) = \dfrac{3 - x^2}{3 + x^2}$ 15. $f(x) = \dfrac{x + 1}{x^2 + x - 12}$ 16. $g(x) = \dfrac{x^2 + 2}{x - 1}$

In Exercises 17–20, write the partial fraction decomposition for the rational expression.

17. $\dfrac{2x + 5}{x^2 - x - 2}$ 18. $\dfrac{3x^2 - 2x + 4}{x^2(2 - x)}$ 19. $\dfrac{x^2 + 5}{x^3 - x}$ 20. $\dfrac{x^2 - 4}{x^3 + 2x}$

Proofs in Mathematics

These two pages contain proofs of four important theorems and polynomial functions. The first two theorems are from Section 2.3, and the second two theorems are from Section 2.5.

The Remainder Theorem   *(p. 138)*

If a polynomial $f(x)$ is divided by $x - k$, the remainder is

$$r = f(k).$$

Proof

From the Division Algorithm, you have

$$f(x) = (x - k)q(x) + r(x)$$

and because either $r(x) = 0$ or the degree of $r(x)$ is less than the degree of $x - k$, you know that $r(x)$ must be a constant. That is, $r(x) = r$. Now, by evaluating $f(x)$ at $x = k$, you have

$$f(k) = (k - k)q(k) + r$$

$$= (0)q(k) + r = r.$$

To be successful in algebra, it is important that you understand the connection among *factors* of a polynomial, *zeros* of a polynomial function, and *solutions* or *roots* of a polynomial equation. The Factor Theorem is the basis for this connection.

The Factor Theorem   *(p. 138)*

A polynomial $f(x)$ has a factor $(x - k)$ if and only if $f(k) = 0$.

Proof

Using the Division Algorithm with the factor $(x - k)$, you have

$$f(x) = (x - k)q(x) + r(x).$$

By the Remainder Theorem, $r(x) = r = f(k)$, and you have

$$f(x) = (x - k)q(x) + f(k)$$

where $q(x)$ is a polynomial of lesser degree than $f(x)$. If $f(k) = 0$, then

$$f(x) = (x - k)q(x)$$

and you see that $(x - k)$ is a factor of $f(x)$. Conversely, if $(x - k)$ is a factor of $f(x)$, division of $f(x)$ by $(x - k)$ yields a remainder of 0. So, by the Remainder Theorem, you have $f(k) = 0$.

The Fundamental Theorem of Algebra

The Linear Factorization Theorem is closely related to the Fundamental Theorem of Algebra. The Fundamental Theorem of Algebra has a long and interesting history. In the early work with polynomial equations, The Fundamental Theorem of Algebra was thought to have been not true, because imaginary solutions were not considered. In fact, in the very early work by mathematicians such as Abu al-Khwarizmi (c. 800 A.D.), negative solutions were also not considered.

Once imaginary numbers were accepted, several mathematicians attempted to give a general proof of the Fundamental Theorem of Algebra. These included Gottfried von Leibniz (1702), Jean D`Alembert (1740), Leonhard Euler (1749), Joseph-Louis Lagrange (1772), and Pierre Simon Laplace (1795). The mathematician usually credited with the first correct proof of the Fundamental Theorem of Algebra is Carl Friedrich Gauss, who published the proof in his doctoral thesis in 1799.

Linear Factorization Theorem   *(p. 150)*

If $f(x)$ is a polynomial of degree n, where $n > 0$, then f has precisely n linear factors

$$f(x) = a_n(x - c_1)(x - c_2) \cdots (x - c_n)$$

where $c_1, c_2, \ldots, c_n$ are complex numbers.

Proof

Using the Fundamental Theorem of Algebra, you know that f must have at least one zero, c_1. Consequently, $(x - c_1)$ is a factor of $f(x)$, and you have

$$f(x) = (x - c_1)f_1(x).$$

If the degree of $f_1(x)$ is greater than zero, you again apply the Fundamental Theorem to conclude that f_1 must have a zero c_2, which implies that

$$f(x) = (x - c_1)(x - c_2)f_2(x).$$

It is clear that the degree of $f_1(x)$ is $n - 1$, that the degree of $f_2(x)$ is $n - 2$, and that you can repeatedly apply the Fundamental Theorem n times until you obtain

$$f(x) = a_n(x - c_1)(x - c_2) \cdots (x - c_n)$$

where a_n is the leading coefficient of the polynomial $f(x)$.

Factors of a Polynomial   *(p. 154)*

Every polynomial of degree $n > 0$ with real coefficients can be written as the product of linear and quadratic factors with real coefficients, where the quadratic factors have no real zeros.

Proof

To begin, you use the Linear Factorization Theorem to conclude that $f(x)$ can be *completely* factored in the form

$$f(x) = d(x - c_1)(x - c_2)(x - c_3) \cdots (x - c_n).$$

If each c_i is real, there is nothing more to prove. If any c_i is complex ($c_i = a + bi$, $b \neq 0$), then, because the coefficients of $f(x)$ are real, you know that the conjugate $c_j = a - bi$ is also a zero. By multiplying the corresponding factors, you obtain

$$(x - c_i)(x - c_j) = [x - (a + bi)][x - (a - bi)]$$
$$= x^2 - 2ax + (a^2 + b^2)$$

where each coefficient is real.

1. Use the form $f(x) = (x - k)q(x) + r$ to create a cubic function that (a) passes through the point $(2, 5)$ and rises to the right and (b) passes through the point $(-3, 1)$ and falls to the right. (There are many correct answers.)

2. In 2000 B.C. the Babylonians solved polynomial equations by referring to tables of values. One such table gave the values of $y^3 + y^2$. To be able to use this table, the Babylonians sometimes had to manipulate the equation as shown below.

$$ax^3 + bx^2 = c \qquad \text{Original equation}$$

$$\frac{a^3 x^3}{b^3} + \frac{a^2 x^2}{b^2} = \frac{a^2 c}{b^3} \qquad \text{Multiply each side by } \frac{a^2}{b^3}.$$

$$\left(\frac{ax}{b}\right)^3 + \left(\frac{ax}{b}\right)^2 = \frac{a^2 c}{b^3} \qquad \text{Rewrite.}$$

Then they would find $(a^2 c)/b^3$ in the $y^3 + y^2$ column of the table. Because they knew that the corresponding y-value was equal to $(ax)/b$, they could conclude that $x = (by)/a$.

(a) Calculate $y^3 + y^2$ for $y = 1, 2, 3, \ldots, 10$. Record the values in a table.

Use the table from part (a) and the method from above to solve each equation.

(b) $x^3 + x^2 = 252$ (c) $x^3 + 2x^2 = 288$

(d) $3x^3 + x^2 = 90$ (e) $2x^3 + 5x^2 = 2500$

(f) $7x^3 + 6x^2 = 1728$ (g) $10x^3 + 3x^2 = 297$

Using the methods from this chapter, verify your solution to each euqation.

3. Show that if

$$f(x) = ax^3 + bx^2 + cx + d$$

then $f(k) = r$ where

$$r = ak^3 + bk^2 + ck + d$$

using long division. In other words, verify the Remainder Theorem for a third-degree polynomial function.

4. At a glassware factory, molten cobalt glass is poured into molds to make paperweights. Each mold is a rectangular prism whose height is 3 inches greater than the length of each side of the square base. A machine pours 20 cubic inches of liquid glass into each mold. What are dimensions of the mold?

5. The parabola shown in the figure has an equation of the form $y = ax^2 + bx + c$. Find the equation for this parabola by the following methods. (a) Find the equation analytically. (b) Use the *regression* feature of a graphing utility to find the equation.

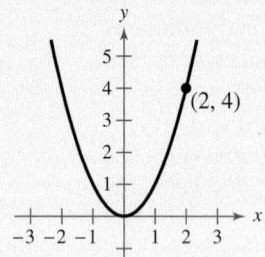
6. One of the fundamental themes of calculus is to find the slope of the tangent line to a curve at a point. To see how this can be done, consider the point $(2, 4)$ on the graph of the quadratic function $f(x) = x^2$.

(a) Find the slope of the line joining $(2, 4)$ and $(3, 9)$. Is the slope of the tangent line at $(2, 4)$ greater than or less than the slope of the line through $(2, 4)$ and $(3, 9)$?

(b) Find the slope of the line joining $(2, 4)$ and $(1, 1)$. Is the slope of the tangent line at $(2, 4)$ greater than or less than the slope of the line through $(2, 4)$ and $(1, 1)$?

(c) Find the slope of the line joining $(2, 4)$ and $(2.1, 4.41)$. Is the slope of the tangent line at $(2, 4)$ greater than or less than the slope of the line through $(2, 4)$ and $(2.1, 4.41)$?

(d) Find the slope of the line joining $(2, 4)$ and $(2 + h, f(2 + h))$ in terms of h $(h \neq 0)$.

(e) Evaluate the slope formula from part (d) for $h = -1, 1$, and 0.1. Compare these values with those in parts (a) to (c).

(f) What can you conclude the slope of the tangent line at $(2, 4)$ to be? Explain your answer.

7. Find a formula for the polynomial division: $\dfrac{x^n - 1}{x - 1}$.

8. A wire 100 centimeters in length is cut into two pieces. One piece is bent to form a square and the other to form a circle. Let x equal the length of the wire used to form the square.

(a) Write the function that represents the area of the two figures.

(b) Determine the domain of the function.

(c) Find the value(s) of x that yield a maximum and minimum area.

(d) Explain your reasoning.

9. Match the graph of the rational function

$$f(x) = \frac{ax + b}{cx + d}$$

with the given conditions.

(a)

(b)

(c)

(d)

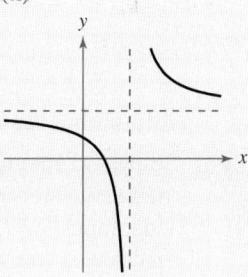

(i) $a > 0$	(ii) $a > 0$	(iii) $a < 0$	(iv) $a > 0$
$b < 0$	$b > 0$	$b > 0$	$b < 0$
$c > 0$	$c < 0$	$c > 0$	$c > 0$
$d < 0$	$d < 0$	$d < 0$	$d > 0$

10. Consider the function

$$f(x) = \frac{2x^2 + x - 1}{x + 1}.$$

(a) Use a graphing utility to graph the function. Does the graph have a vertical asymptote at $x = -1$?

(b) Complete the table. What value is f approaching as x approaches -1 from the left and from the right?

x	-1.1	-1.01	-1.001	-1
$f(x)$				

x	-0.999	-0.99	-0.9
$f(x)$			

(c) Use the *zoom* and *trace* features to determine the value of the graph near $x = -1$.

(d) Use the following viewing window to adjust your graph in part (a).

    Xmin: -9.4 Xmax: 9.4   Xscl: 1

    Ymin: -6.2 Ymax: 6.2   Yscl: 1

    What happens at the point $(-1, 3)$?

(e) Rewrite the function in simplified form. Evaluate the simplified function for $x = -1$.

(f) Sketch the graph of $g(x) = \dfrac{2x^2 - 5x - 12}{x - 4}$.

11. Consider the function

$$f(x) = \frac{ax}{(x - b)^2}.$$

(a) Determine the effect on the graph of f if $b \neq 0$ and a is varied. Consider cases in which a is positive and a is negative.

(b) Determine the effect on the graph of f if $a \neq 0$ and b is varied.

How to study Chapter 3

▶ **What you should learn**

In this chapter you will learn the following skills and concepts:

- How to recognize and evaluate exponential and logarithmic functions
- How to graph exponential and logarithmic functions
- How to use the change-of-base formula to rewrite and evaluate logarithmic expressions
- How to use properties of logarithms to evaluate, rewrite, expand, or condense logarithmic expressions
- How to solve exponential and logarithmic equations
- How to use exponential growth models, exponential decay models, Gaussian models, logistic growth models, and logarithmic models to solve real-life problems

▶ **Important Vocabulary**

As you encounter each new vocabulary term in this chapter, add the term and its definition to your notebook glossary.

Algebraic functions (p. 198)
Transcendental functions (p. 198)
Exponential function *f* with base *a* (p. 198)
Natural base *e* (p. 202)
Natural exponential function (p. 202)
Continuous compounding (p. 203)
Logarithmic function with base *a* (p. 209)
Common logarithmic function (p. 210)
Natural logarithmic function (p. 213)

Exponential growth model (p. 236)
Exponential decay model (p. 236)
Gaussian model (p. 236)
Logistic growth model (p. 236)
Logarithmic models (p. 236)
Bell-shaped curve (p. 240)
Logistic curve (p. 241)
Sigmoidal curve (p. 241)

Study Tools

Learning objectives in each section
Chapter Summary (p. 249)
Review Exercises (pp. 250–253)
Chapter Test (p. 254)
Cumulative Test for Chapters 1–3
   (pp. 255, 256)

Additional Resources

Study and Solutions Guide
Interactive Precalculus
Videotapes/DVD for Chapter 3
Precalculus Website
Student Success Organizer

Bill Ross/Corbis

3

Exponential and Logarithmic Functions

3.1   Exponential Functions and Their Graphs

▶ **What you should learn**

- How to recognize and evaluate exponential functions with base a
- How to graph exponential functions
- How to recognize and evaluate exponential functions with base e
- How to use exponential functions to model and solve real-life applications

▶ **Why you should learn it**

Exponential functions can be used to model and solve real-life problems. For instance, in Exercise 59 on page 207, an exponential function is used to model the amount of defoliation caused by the gypsy moth.

Exponential Functions

So far, this book has dealt only with **algebraic functions,** which include polynomial functions and rational functions. In this chapter you will study two types of nonalgebraic functions—*exponential* functions and *logarithmic* functions. These functions are examples of **transcendental functions.**

Definition of Exponential Function

The **exponential function** f with base a is denoted by

$$f(x) = a^x$$

where $a > 0$, $a \neq 1$, and x is any real number.

The base $a = 1$ is excluded because it yields $f(x) = 1^x = 1$. This is a constant function, not an exponential function.

You already know how to evaluate a^x for integer and rational values of x. For example, you know that $4^3 = 64$ and $4^{1/2} = 2$. However, to evaluate 4^x for any real number x, you need to interpret forms with *irrational* exponents. For the purposes of this book, it is sufficient to think of

$$a^{\sqrt{2}} \quad \text{(where } \sqrt{2} \approx 1.41421356)$$

as the number that has the successively closer approximations

$$a^{1.4},\ a^{1.41},\ a^{1.414},\ a^{1.4142},\ a^{1.41421},\ \ldots\ .$$

Example 1 shows how to use a calculator to evaluate exponential expressions.

Example 1 ▶ **Evaluating Exponential Functions**

Use a calculator to evaluate each function at the indicated value of x.

Function	Value
a. $f(x) = 2^x$	$x = -3.1$
b. $f(x) = 2^{-x}$	$x = \pi$
c. $f(x) = 12^x$	$x = \frac{5}{7}$
d. $f(x) = 0.6^x$	$x = \frac{3}{2}$

Solution

Function Value	Graphing Calculator Keystrokes	Display
a. $f(-3.1) = 2^{-3.1}$	2 [^] [(−)] 3.1 [ENTER]	0.1166291
b. $f(\pi) = 2^{-\pi}$	2 [^] [(−)] π [ENTER]	0.1133147
c. $f\left(\frac{5}{7}\right) = 12^{5/7}$	12 [^] [(] 5 [÷] 7 [)] [ENTER]	5.8998877
d. $f\left(\frac{3}{2}\right) = (0.6)^{3/2}$	.6 [^] [(] 3 [÷] 2 [)] [ENTER]	0.4647580

Graphs of Exponential Functions

The graphs of all exponential functions have similar characteristics, as shown in Examples 2, 3, and 4.

Example 2 ▶ Graphs of $y = a^x$

In the same coordinate plane, sketch the graph of each function.

a. $f(x) = 2^x$ **b.** $g(x) = 4^x$

Solution

The table below lists some values for each function, and Figure 3.1 shows the graphs of these two functions. Note that both graphs are increasing. Moreover, the graph of $g(x) = 4^x$ is increasing more rapidly than the graph of $f(x) = 2^x$.

x	2^x	4^x
-2	$\frac{1}{4}$	$\frac{1}{16}$
-1	$\frac{1}{2}$	$\frac{1}{4}$
0	1	1
1	2	4
2	4	16
3	8	64

FIGURE **3.1**

Example 3 ▶ Graphs of $y = a^{-x}$

In the same coordinate plane, sketch the graph of each function.

a. $F(x) = 2^{-x}$ **b.** $G(x) = 4^{-x}$

Solution

The table below lists some values for each function, and Figure 3.2 shows the graphs of the two functions. Note that both graphs are decreasing. Moreover, the graph of $G(x) = 4^{-x}$ is decreasing more rapidly than the graph of $F(x) = 2^{-x}$.

x	-3	-2	-1	0	1	2
2^{-x}	8	4	2	1	$\frac{1}{2}$	$\frac{1}{4}$
4^{-x}	64	16	4	1	$\frac{1}{4}$	$\frac{1}{16}$

In Example 3, note that the functions $F(x) = 2^{-x}$ and $G(x) = 4^{-x}$ can be rewritten with positive exponents.

$$F(x) = 2^{-x} = \left(\frac{1}{2}\right)^x \quad \text{and} \quad G(x) = 4^{-x} = \left(\frac{1}{4}\right)^x$$

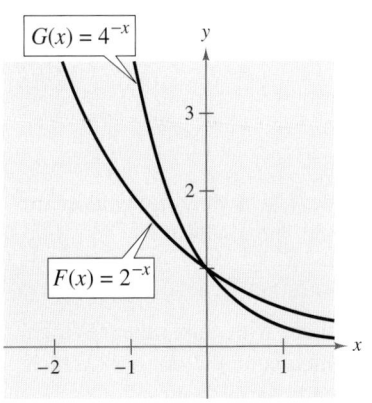

FIGURE **3.2**

STUDY TIP

The table in Example 2 was evaluated by hand. You could, of course, use a graphing utility to construct tables with even more values.

The icon www identifies examples and concepts related to features of the Learning Tools CD-ROM and the *Interactive* and *Internet* versions of this text. For more details see the chart on pages *xxi-xxv*.

Comparing the functions in Examples 2 and 3, observe that

$$F(x) = 2^{-x} = f(-x) \qquad \text{and} \qquad G(x) = 4^{-x} = g(-x).$$

Consequently, the graph of F is a reflection (in the y-axis) of the graph of f. The graphs of G and g have the same relationship. The graphs in Figures 3.1 and 3.2 are typical of the exponential functions $y = a^x$ and $y = a^{-x}$. They have one y-intercept and one horizontal asymptote (the x-axis), and they are continuous. The basic characteristics of these exponential functions are summarized in Figures 3.3 and 3.4.

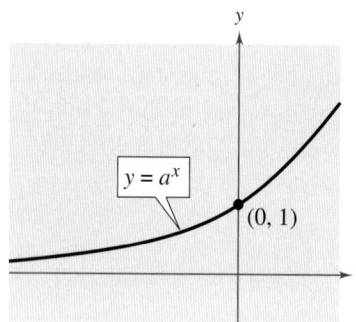

FIGURE 3.3

Graph of $y = a^x, a > 1$

- Domain: $(-\infty, \infty)$
- Range: $(0, \infty)$
- Intercept: $(0, 1)$
- Increasing
- x-Axis is a horizontal asymptote $(a^x \to 0 \text{ as } x \to -\infty)$
- Continuous

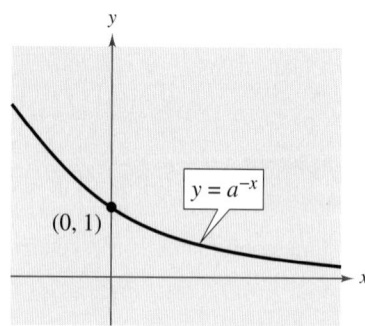

FIGURE 3.4

Graph of $y = a^{-x}, a > 1$

- Domain: $(-\infty, \infty)$
- Range: $(0, \infty)$
- Intercept: $(0, 1)$
- Decreasing
- x-Axis is a horizontal asymptote $(a^{-x} \to 0 \text{ as } x \to \infty)$
- Continuous

Exploration

Use a graphing utility to graph

$$y = a^x$$

for $a = 3, 5,$ and 7 in the same viewing window. (Use a viewing window in which $-2 \le x \le 1$ and $0 \le y \le 2$.) For instance, the graph of

$$y = 3^x$$

is shown in Figure 3.5. How do the graphs compare with each other? Which graph is on the top in the interval $(-\infty, 0)$? Which is on the bottom? Which graph is on the top in the interval $(0, \infty)$? Which is on the bottom?

Repeat this experiment with the graphs of $y = b^x$ for $b = \frac{1}{3}, \frac{1}{5},$ and $\frac{1}{7}$. (Use a viewing window in which $-1 \le x \le 2$ and $0 \le y \le 2$.) What can you conclude about the shape of the graph of $y = b^x$ and the value of b?

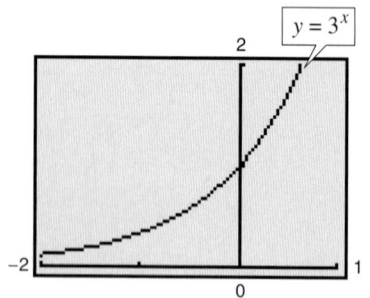

FIGURE 3.5

In the following example, notice how the graph of $y = a^x$ can be used to sketch the graphs of functions of the form $f(x) = b \pm a^{x+c}$.

Example 4 ▶ **Transformations of Graphs of Exponential Functions**

Each of the following graphs is a transformation of the graph of $f(x) = 3^x$.

a. Because $g(x) = 3^{x+1} = f(x + 1)$, the graph of g can be obtained by shifting the graph of f one unit to the *left*, as shown in Figure 3.6.

b. Because $h(x) = 3^x - 2 = f(x) - 2$, the graph of h can be obtained by shifting the graph of f *downward* two units, as shown in Figure 3.7.

c. Because $k(x) = -3^x = -f(x)$, the graph of k can be obtained by *reflecting* the graph of f in the x-axis, as shown in Figure 3.8.

d. Because $j(x) = 3^{-x} = f(-x)$, the graph of j can be obtained by *reflecting* the graph of f in the y-axis, as shown in Figure 3.9.

The *Interactive* CD-ROM and *Internet* versions of this text offer a Quiz for every section of the text.

FIGURE **3.6** *Horizontal shift*

FIGURE **3.7** *Vertical shift*

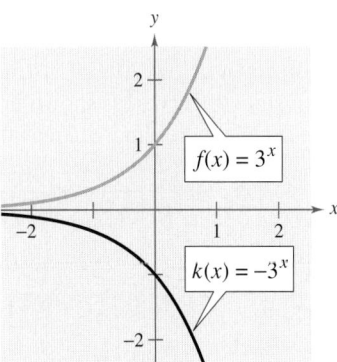

FIGURE **3.8** *Reflection in x-axis*

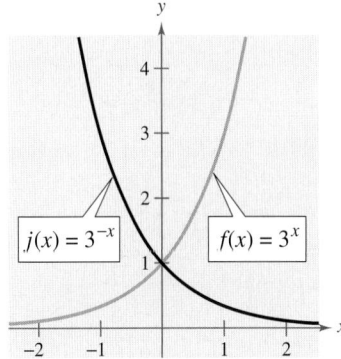

FIGURE **3.9** *Reflection in y-axis*

Notice that the transformations in Figures 3.6, 3.8, and 3.9 keep the x-axis as a horizontal asymptote, but the transformation in Figure 3.7 yields a new horizontal asymptote of $y = -2$. Also, be sure to note how the y-intercept is affected by each transformation.

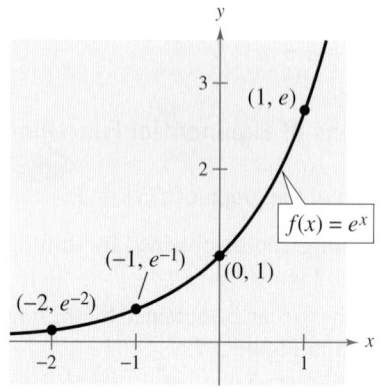

FIGURE **3.10**

The Natural Base e

In many applications, the most convenient choice for a base is the irrational number

$$e \approx 2.718281828 \ldots .$$

This number is called the **natural base.** The function $f(x) = e^x$ is called the **natural exponential function.** Its graph is shown in Figure 3.10. Be sure you see that for the exponential function $f(x) = e^x$, e is the constant $2.718281828 \ldots$, whereas x is the variable.

Example 5 ▶   **Evaluating the Natural Exponential Function**

Use a calculator to evaluate the function $f(x) = e^x$ at each indicated value of x.
a. $x = -2$ **b.** $x = -1$ **c.** $x = 0.25$ **d.** $x = -0.3$

Solution

	Function Value	Graphing Calculator Keystrokes	Display
a.	$f(-2) = e^{-2}$	[eˣ] [(−)] 2 [ENTER]	0.1353353
b.	$f(-1) = e^{-1}$	[eˣ] [(−)] 1 [ENTER]	0.3678794
c.	$f(0.25) = e^{0.25}$	[eˣ] 0.25 [ENTER]	1.2840254
d.	$f(-0.3) = e^{-0.3}$	[eˣ] [(−)] 0.3 [ENTER]	0.7408182

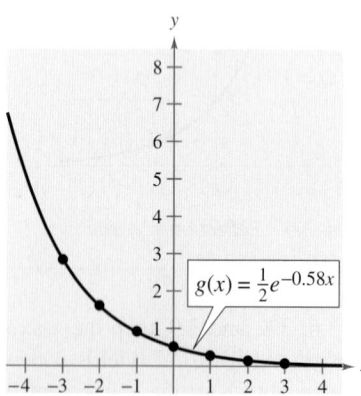

FIGURE **3.11**

Example 6 ▶   **Graphing Natural Exponential Functions**

Sketch the graph of each natural exponential function.

a. $f(x) = 2e^{0.24x}$ **b.** $g(x) = \frac{1}{2}e^{-0.58x}$

Solution

To sketch these two graphs, you can use a graphing utility to construct a table of values, as shown below. After constructing the table, plot the points and connect them with smooth curves, as shown in Figures 3.11 and 3.12. Note that the graph in Figure 3.11 is increasing whereas the graph in Figure 3.12 is decreasing.

FIGURE **3.12**

x	$f(x)$	$g(x)$
-3	0.974	2.849
-2	1.238	1.595
-1	1.573	0.893
0	2.000	0.500
1	2.542	0.280
2	3.232	0.157
3	4.109	0.088

Activities

1. Sketch the graphs of the functions $f(x) = e^x$ and $g(x) = 1 + e^x$ on the same coordinate system.

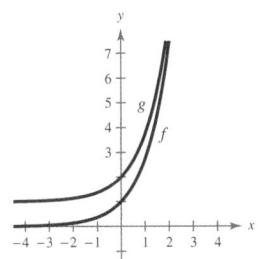

2. Determine the balance A at the end of 20 years if $1500 is invested at 6.5% interest and the interest is compounded (a) quarterly and (b) continuously.

   Answer: (a) $5446.73 (b) $5503.95

3. Determine the amount of money that should be invested at 9% interest, compounded monthly, to produce a final balance of $30,000 in 15 years.

   Answer: $7816.48

Applications

One of the most familiar examples of exponential growth is that of an investment earning *continuously compounded interest*. Using exponential functions, you can now *develop* that formula and show how it leads to continuous compounding.

Suppose a principal P is invested at an annual interest rate r, compounded once a year. If the interest is added to the principal at the end of the year, the new balance P_1 is

$$P_1 = P + Pr$$
$$= P(1 + r).$$

This pattern of multiplying the previous principal by $1 + r$ is then repeated each successive year, as shown below.

Year	Balance After Each Compounding
0	$P = P$
1	$P_1 = P(1 + r)$
2	$P_2 = P_1(1 + r) = P(1 + r)(1 + r) = P(1 + r)^2$
3	$P_3 = P_2(1 + r) = P(1 + r)^2(1 + r) = P(1 + r)^3$
⋮	
t	$P_t = P(1 + r)^t$

To accommodate more frequent (quarterly, monthly, or daily) compounding of interest, let n be the number of compoundings per year and let t be the number of years. Then the rate per compounding is r/n and the account balance after t years is

$$A = P\left(1 + \frac{r}{n}\right)^{nt}. \qquad \text{Amount (balance) with } n \text{ compoundings per year}$$

If you let the number of compoundings n increase without bound, the process approaches what is called **continuous compounding.** In the formula for n compoundings per year, let $m = n/r$. This produces

$$A = P\left(1 + \frac{r}{n}\right)^{nt} \qquad \text{Amount with } n \text{ compoundings per year}$$

$$= P\left(1 + \frac{r}{mr}\right)^{mrt} \qquad \text{Substitute } mr \text{ for } n.$$

$$= P\left(1 + \frac{1}{m}\right)^{mrt} \qquad \text{Simplify.}$$

$$= P\left[\left(1 + \frac{1}{m}\right)^m\right]^{rt}. \qquad \text{Property of exponents}$$

As m increases without bound, it can be shown that $\left[1 + (1/m)\right]^m$ approaches e. (Try the values $m = 10$, $10{,}000$, and $10{,}000{,}000$.) From this, you can conclude that the formula for continuous compounding is

$$A = Pe^{rt}. \qquad \text{Substitute } e \text{ for } (1 + 1/m)^m.$$

Formulas for Compound Interest

After t years, the balance A in an account with principal P and annual interest rate r (in decimal form) is given by the following formulas.

1. For n compoundings per year: $A = P\left(1 + \dfrac{r}{n}\right)^{nt}$

2. For continuous compounding: $A = Pe^{rt}$

Example 7 ▶ **Compound Interest**

A total of $12,000 is invested at an annual interest rate of 9%. Find the balance after 5 years if it is compounded

a. quarterly.

b. monthly.

c. continuously.

Solution

a. For quarterly compoundings, you have $n = 4$. So, in 5 years at 9%, the balance is

$$A = P\left(1 + \frac{r}{n}\right)^{nt}$$ Formula for compound interest

$$= 12{,}000\left(1 + \frac{0.09}{4}\right)^{4(5)}$$ Substitute for P, r, n, and t.

$$\approx \$18{,}726.11.$$ Use a calculator.

b. For monthly compoundings, you have $n = 12$. So, in 5 years at 9%, the balance is

$$A = P\left(1 + \frac{r}{n}\right)^{nt}$$ Formula for compound interest

$$= 12{,}000\left(1 + \frac{0.09}{12}\right)^{12(5)}$$ Substitute for P, r, n, and t.

$$\approx \$18{,}788.17.$$ Use a calculator.

c. For continuous compounding, the balance is

$$A = Pe^{rt}$$ Formula for continuous compounding

$$= 12{,}000e^{0.09(5)}$$ Substitute for P, r, and t.

$$\approx \$18{,}819.75.$$ Use a calculator.

In Example 7, note that continuous compounding yields more than quarterly or monthly compounding. This is typical of the two types of compounding. That is, for a given principal, interest rate, and time, continuous compounding will always yield a larger balance than compounding n times a year.

Example 8 ▶ **Radioactive Decay**

In 1986, a nuclear reactor accident occurred in Chernobyl in what was then the Soviet Union. The explosion spread highly toxic radioactive chemicals, such as plutonium, over hundreds of square miles, and the government evacuated the city and the surrounding area. To see why the city is now uninhabited, consider the model

$$P = 10\left(\frac{1}{2}\right)^{t/24,360}$$

which represents the amount of plutonium P that remains (from an initial amount of 10 pounds) after t years. Sketch the graph of this function over the interval from $t = 0$ to $t = 100,000$, where $t = 0$ represents 1986. How much of the 10 pounds will remain in the year 2005? How much of the 10 pounds will remain after 100,000 years?

Solution

The graph of this function is shown in Figure 3.13. Note from this graph that plutonium has a *half-life* of about 24,360 years. That is, after 24,360 years, *half* of the original amount will remain. After another 24,360 years, one-quarter of the original amount will remain, and so on. In the year 2005 ($t = 19$), there will still be

$$P = 10\left(\frac{1}{2}\right)^{19/24,360} \approx 10\left(\frac{1}{2}\right)^{0.0007800} \approx 9.995 \text{ pounds}$$

of plutonium remaining. After 100,000 years, there will still be

$$P = 10\left(\frac{1}{2}\right)^{100,000/24,360} \approx 10\left(\frac{1}{2}\right)^{4.105} \approx 0.581 \text{ pound}$$

of plutonium remaining.

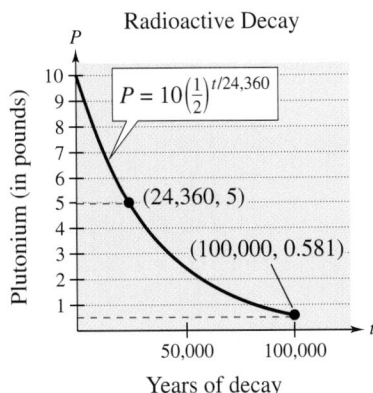

Radioactive Decay

$P = 10\left(\frac{1}{2}\right)^{t/24,360}$

(24,360, 5)

(100,000, 0.581)

Plutonium (in pounds)

Years of decay

FIGURE **3.13**

One way your students might approach this problem is to create a table, covering x-values from -2 through 3, for each of the functions and compare this table with the given tables. If this method is used, you might consider dividing your class into groups of three or six and having the groups assign one or two functions to each member. They should then pool their results and work cooperatively to determine that each function has a y-intercept of $(0, 8)$.

Another approach is a graphical one: the groups can create scatter plots of the data shown in the table and compare them with sketches of the graphs of the given functions. Consider assigning students to groups of four and giving the responsibility for sketching three graphs to each group member.

Writing **ABOUT MATHEMATICS**

Identifying Exponential Functions Which of the following functions generated the two tables below? Discuss how you were able to decide. What do these functions have in common? Are any of them the same? If so, explain why.

a. $f_1(x) = 2^{(x+3)}$ **b.** $f_2(x) = 8\left(\frac{1}{2}\right)^x$ **c.** $f_3(x) = \left(\frac{1}{2}\right)^{(x-3)}$

d. $f_4(x) = \left(\frac{1}{2}\right)^x + 7$ **e.** $f_5(x) = 7 + 2^x$ **f.** $f_6(x) = (8)2^x$

x	-1	0	1	2	3
$g(x)$	7.5	8	9	11	15

x	-2	-1	0	1	2
$h(x)$	32	16	8	4	2

Create two different exponential functions of the forms $y = a(b)^x$ and $y = c^x + d$ with y-intercepts of $(0, -3)$.

3.1 Exercises

The *Interactive* CD-ROM and *Internet* versions of this text contain step-by-step solutions to all odd-numbered exercises. They also provide Tutorial Exercises for additional help.

In Exercises 1–6, evaluate the function at the indicated value of *x*. Round your result to three decimal places.

Function	Value
1. $f(x) = 3.4^x$	$x = 5.6$
2. $f(x) = 2.3^x$	$x = \frac{3}{2}$
3. $f(x) = 5^x$	$x = -\pi$
4. $g(x) = 5000(2^x)$	$x = -1.5$
5. $h(x) = e^{-x}$	$x = \frac{3}{4}$
6. $f(x) = e^x$	$x = 3.2$

In Exercises 7–10, match the exponential function with its graph. [The graphs are labeled (a), (b), (c), and (d).]

(a)

(b)

(c)

(d)
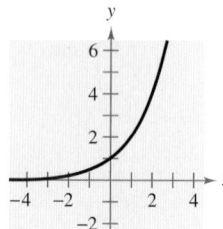

7. $f(x) = 2^x$ **8.** $f(x) = 2^x + 1$

9. $f(x) = 2^{-x}$ **10.** $f(x) = 2^{x-2}$

In Exercises 11–18, use the graph of *f* to describe the transformation that yields the graph of *g*.

11. $f(x) = 3^x$, $g(x) = 3^{x-4}$

12. $f(x) = 4^x$, $g(x) = 4^x + 1$

13. $f(x) = -2^x$, $g(x) = 5 - 2^x$

14. $f(x) = 10^x$, $g(x) = 10^{-x+3}$

15. $f(x) = \left(\frac{3}{5}\right)^x$, $g(x) = -\left(\frac{3}{5}\right)^{x+4}$

16. $f(x) = \left(\frac{7}{2}\right)^x$, $g(x) = -\left(\frac{7}{2}\right)^{-x+6}$

17. $f(x) = 0.3^x$, $g(x) = -0.3^x + 5$

18. $f(x) = 3.6^x$, $g(x) = -3.6^{-x} + 8$

In Exercises 19–32, use a graphing utility to construct a table of values for the function. Then sketch the graph of the function.

19. $f(x) = \left(\frac{1}{2}\right)^x$ **20.** $f(x) = \left(\frac{1}{2}\right)^{-x}$

21. $f(x) = 6^{-x}$ **22.** $f(x) = 6^x$

23. $f(x) = 2^{x-1}$ **24.** $f(x) = 3^{x+2}$

25. $f(x) = e^x$ **26.** $f(x) = e^{-x}$

27. $f(x) = 3e^{x+4}$ **28.** $f(x) = 2e^{-0.5x}$

29. $f(x) = 2e^{x-2} + 4$ **30.** $f(x) = 2 + e^{x-5}$

31. $f(x) = 4^{x-3} + 3$ **32.** $f(x) = -4^{x-3} - 3$

 In Exercises 33–42, use a graphing utility to graph the exponential function.

33. $y = 2^{-x^2}$ **34.** $y = 3^{-|x|}$

35. $y = 3^{x-2} + 1$ **36.** $y = 4^{x+1} - 2$

37. $y = 1.08^{-5x}$ **38.** $y = 1.08^{5x}$

39. $s(t) = 2e^{0.12t}$ **40.** $s(t) = 3e^{-0.2t}$

41. $g(x) = 1 + e^{-x}$ **42.** $h(x) = e^{x-2}$

Compound Interest In Exercises 43–46, complete the table to determine the balance *A* for *P* dollars invested at rate *r* for *t* years and compounded *n* times per year.

n	1	2	4	12	365	Continuous
A						

43. $P = \$2500$, $r = 8\%$, $t = 10$ years

44. $P = \$1000$, $r = 6\%$, $t = 10$ years

45. $P = \$2500$, $r = 8\%$, $t = 20$ years

46. $P = \$1000$, $r = 6\%$, $t = 40$ years

Compound Interest In Exercises 47–50, complete the table to determine the balance *A* for \$12,000 invested at rate *r* for *t* years, compounded continuously.

t	10	20	30	40	50
A					

47. $r = 8\%$ **48.** $r = 6\%$

49. $r = 6.5\%$ **50.** $r = 7.5\%$

51. Trust Fund On the day of a child's birth, a deposit of $25,000 is made in a trust fund that pays 8.75% interest, compounded continuously. Determine the balance in this account on the child's 25th birthday.

52. Trust Fund A deposit of $5000 is made in a trust fund that pays 7.5% interest, compounded continuously. It is specified that the balance will be given to the college from which the donor graduated after the money has earned interest for 50 years. How much will the college receive?

53. Inflation If the annual rate of inflation averages 4% over the next 10 years, the approximate cost C of goods or services during any year in that decade will be modeled by $C(t) = P(1.04)^t$, where t is the time in years and P is the present cost. The price of an oil change for your car is presently $23.95. Estimate the price 10 years from now.

54. Demand The demand equation for a product is

$$p = 5000\left(1 - \frac{4}{4 + e^{-0.002x}}\right).$$

 (a) Use a graphing utility to graph the demand function for $x > 0$ and $p > 0$.

(b) Find the price p for a demand of $x = 500$ units.

 (c) Use the graph in part (a) to approximate the greatest price that will still yield a demand of at least 600 units.

55. Population Growth A certain type of bacterium increases according to the model $P(t) = 100e^{0.2197t}$, where t is the time in hours. Find (a) $P(0)$, (b) $P(5)$, and (c) $P(10)$.

56. Population Growth The population of a town increases according to the model $P(t) = 2500e^{0.0293t}$, where t is the time in years, with $t = 0$ corresponding to 2000. Use the model to estimate the population in (a) 2010 and (b) 2020.

57. Radioactive Decay Let Q represent a mass of radioactive radium (^{226}Ra) (in grams), whose half-life is 1620 years. The quantity of radium present after t years is

$$Q = 25\left(\frac{1}{2}\right)^{t/1620}.$$

(a) Determine the initial quantity (when $t = 0$).

(b) Determine the quantity present after 1000 years.

 (c) Use a graphing utility to graph the function over the interval $t = 0$ to $t = 5000$.

58. Radioactive Decay Let Q represent a mass of carbon 14 (^{14}C) (in grams), whose half-life is 5730 years. The quantity of carbon 14 present after t years is

$$Q = 10\left(\frac{1}{2}\right)^{t/5730}.$$

(a) Determine the initial quantity (when $t = 0$).

(b) Determine the quantity present after 2000 years.

(c) Sketch the graph of this function over the interval $t = 0$ to $t = 10,000$.

▶ Model It

59. Data Analysis To estimate the amount of defoliation caused by the gypsy moth during a given year, a forester counts the number x of egg masses on $\frac{1}{40}$ of an acre (circle of radius 18.6 feet) in the fall. The percent of defoliation y the next spring is shown in the table. (Source: USDA, Forest Service)

Egg masses, x	Percent of defoliation, y
0	12
25	44
50	81
75	96
100	99

A model for the data is

$$y = \frac{100}{1 + 7e^{-0.069x}}.$$

(a) Use a graphing utility to create a scatter plot of the data and graph the model in the same viewing window.

(b) Create a table that compares the model with the sample data.

(c) Estimate the percent of defoliation if 36 egg masses are counted on $\frac{1}{40}$ acre.

(d) You observe that $\frac{2}{3}$ of a forest is defoliated the following spring. Use the graph in part (a) to estimate the number of egg masses per $\frac{1}{40}$ acre.

60. *Data Analysis*   A meteorologist measures the atmospheric pressure P (in pascals) at altitude h (in kilometers). The data is shown in the table.

Altitude, h	Pressure, P
0	101,293
5	54,735
10	23,294
15	12,157
20	5,069

A model for the data is given by

$P = 102,303e^{-0.137h}$.

(a) Sketch a scatter plot of the data and graph the model on the same set of axes.

(b) Estimate the atmospheric pressure at a height of 8 kilometers.

Synthesis

True or False?   In Exercises 61 and 62, determine whether the statement is true or false. Justify your answer.

61. The line $y = -2$ is an asymptote for the graph of $f(x) = 10^x - 2$.

62. $e = \dfrac{271,801}{99,990}$.

Think About It   In Exercises 63–66, use properties of exponents to determine which functions (if any) are the same.

63. $f(x) = 3^{x-2}$
$g(x) = 3^x - 9$
$h(x) = \frac{1}{9}(3^x)$

64. $f(x) = 4^x + 12$
$g(x) = 2^{2x+6}$
$h(x) = 64(4^x)$

65. $f(x) = 16(4^{-x})$
$g(x) = \left(\frac{1}{4}\right)^{x-2}$
$h(x) = 16(2^{-2x})$

66. $f(x) = 5^{-x} + 3$
$g(x) = 5^{3-x}$
$h(x) = -5^{x-3}$

67. Graph the functions $y = 3^x$ and $y = 4^x$ and use the graphs to solve the inequalities.

(a) $4^x < 3^x$ (b) $4^x > 3^x$

68. Graph the functions $y = \left(\frac{1}{2}\right)^x$ and $y = \left(\frac{1}{4}\right)^x$ and use the graphs to solve the inequalities.

(a) $\left(\frac{1}{4}\right)^x < \left(\frac{1}{2}\right)^x$ (b) $\left(\frac{1}{4}\right)^x > \left(\frac{1}{2}\right)^x$

69. Use a graphing utility to graph each function. Use the graph to find any asymptotes of the function.

(a) $f(x) = \dfrac{8}{1 + e^{-0.5x}}$ (b) $g(x) = \dfrac{8}{1 + e^{-0.5/x}}$

70. Use a graphing utility to graph each function. Use the graph to find where the function is increasing and decreasing, and approximate any relative maximum or minimum values.

(a) $f(x) = x^2e^{-x}$ (b) $g(x) = x2^{3-x}$

71. *Graphical Analysis*   Use a graphing utility to graph

$$f(x) = \left(1 + \frac{0.5}{x}\right)^x \quad \text{and} \quad g(x) = e^{0.5}$$

in the same viewing window. What is the relationship between f and g as x increases and decreases without bound?

72. *Conjecture*   Use the result of Exercise 71 to make a conjecture about the value of $[1 + (r/x)]^x$ as x increases without bound. Create a table that illustrates your conjecture for $r = 1$.

73. *Think About It*   Which functions are exponential?

(a) $3x$ (b) $3x^2$
(c) 3^x (d) 2^{-x}

74. *Writing*   Explain why $2^{\sqrt{2}}$ is greater than 2, but less than 4.

Review

In Exercises 75–78, solve for y.

75. $2x - 7y + 14 = 0$ **76.** $x^2 + 3y = 4$

77. $x^2 + y^2 = 25$ **78.** $x - |y| = 2$

In Exercises 79–82, sketch the graph of the rational function.

79. $f(x) = \dfrac{2}{9 + x}$ **80.** $f(x) = \dfrac{4x - 3}{x}$

81. $f(x) = \dfrac{6}{x^2 + 5x - 24}$ **82.** $f(x) = \dfrac{x^2 - 7x + 12}{x + 2}$

▶ **What you should learn**

- How to recognize and evaluate logarithmic functions with base a
- How to graph logarithmic functions
- How to recognize and evaluate natural logarithmic functions
- How to use logarithmic functions to model and solve real-life applications

▶ **Why you should learn it**

You can use logarithmic functions to model and solve real-life problems. For instance, in Exercise 57 on page 217, you can use a logarithmic function to approximate the length of a home mortgage.

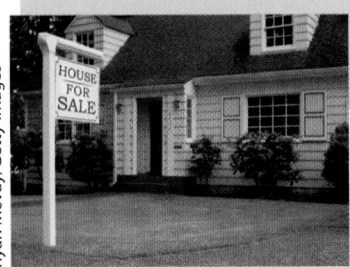

Ryan McVay/Getty Images

Logarithmic Functions

In Section 1.8, you studied the concept of an inverse function. There, you learned that if a function is one-to-one—that is, if the function has the property that no horizontal line intersects the graph of the function more than once—the function must have an inverse function. By looking back at the graphs of the exponential functions introduced in Section 3.1, you will see that every function of the form

$$f(x) = a^x$$

passes the Horizontal Line Test and therefore must have an inverse function. This inverse function is called the **logarithmic function with base a.**

Definition of Logarithmic Function with Base a

For $x > 0$ and $0 < a \neq 1$,

$$y = \log_a x \text{ if and only if } x = a^y.$$

The function given by

$$f(x) = \log_a x$$

is called the **logarithmic function with base a.**

The equations

$$y = \log_a x \qquad \text{and} \qquad x = a^y$$

are equivalent. The first equation is in logarithmic form and the second is in exponential form.

When evaluating logarithms, remember that *a logarithm is an exponent.* This means that $\log_a x$ is the exponent to which a must be raised to obtain x. For instance, $\log_2 8 = 3$ because 2 must be raised to the third power to get 8.

Example 1 ▶ Evaluating Logarithms

Use the definition of logarithmic function to evaluate each logarithm at the indicated value of x.

a. $f(x) = \log_2 x, \quad x = 32$ **b.** $f(x) = \log_3 x, \quad x = 1$

c. $f(x) = \log_4 x, \quad x = 2$ **d.** $f(x) = \log_{10} x, \quad x = \frac{1}{100}$

Solution

a. $f(32) = \log_2 32 = 5$ because $2^5 = 32$.

b. $f(1) = \log_3 1 = 0$ because $3^0 = 1$.

c. $f(2) = \log_4 2 = \frac{1}{2}$ because $4^{1/2} = \sqrt{4} = 2$.

d. $f\left(\frac{1}{100}\right) = \log_{10} \frac{1}{100} = -2$ because $10^{-2} = \frac{1}{10^2} = \frac{1}{100}$.

STUDY TIP

Remember that a logarithm is an exponent. So, to evaluate the logarithmic expression $\log_a x$, you need to ask the question, "To what power must a be raised to obtain x?"

◀ **E x p l o r a t i o n** ▶

Complete the table for
$f(x) = 10^x$.

x	-2	-1	0	1	2
$f(x)$					

Complete the table for
$f(x) = \log_{10} x$.

x	$\frac{1}{100}$	$\frac{1}{10}$	1	10	100
$f(x)$					

Compare the two tables. What is the relationship between
$f(x) = 10^x$ and $f(x) = \log_{10} x$?

The logarithmic function with base 10 is called the **common logarithmic function.** On most calculators, this function is denoted by $\boxed{\text{LOG}}$. Example 2 shows how to use a calculator to evaluate common logarithmic functions. You will learn how to use a calculator to calculate logarithms to any base in the next section.

Example 2 ▶ **Evaluating Common Logarithms on a Calculator**

Use a calculator to evaluate the function $f(x) = \log_{10} x$ at each value of x.

a. $x = 10$ **b.** $x = \frac{1}{3}$

c. $x = 2.5$ **d.** $x = -2$

Solution

Function Value	Graphing Calculator Keystrokes	Display
a. $f(10) = \log_{10} 10$	$\boxed{\text{LOG}}$ 10 $\boxed{\text{ENTER}}$	1
b. $f(\frac{1}{3}) = \log_{10}\frac{1}{3}$	$\boxed{\text{LOG}}$ $\boxed{(}$ 1 $\boxed{\div}$ 3 $\boxed{)}$ $\boxed{\text{ENTER}}$	-0.4771213
c. $f(2.5) = \log_{10} 2.5$	$\boxed{\text{LOG}}$ 2.5 $\boxed{\text{ENTER}}$	0.3979400
d. $f(-2) = \log_{10}(-2)$	$\boxed{\text{LOG}}$ $\boxed{(-)}$ 2 $\boxed{\text{ENTER}}$	ERROR

Note that the calculator displays an error message (or a complex number) when you try to evaluate $\log_{10}(-2)$. The reason for this is that there is no real number power to which 10 can be raised to obtain -2.

The following properties follow directly from the definition of the logarithmic function with base a.

The logarithmic function can be one of the most difficult concepts for students to understand. Remind students that a logarithm is an exponent. Converting back and forth from logarithmic form to exponential form supports this concept.

Properties of Logarithms

1. $\log_a 1 = 0$ because $a^0 = 1$.

2. $\log_a a = 1$ because $a^1 = a$.

3. $\log_a a^x = x$ and $a^{\log_a x} = x$ Inverse Properties

4. If $\log_a x = \log_a y$, then $x = y$.   One-to-One Property

---

Example 3 ▶ **Using Properties of Logarithms**

a. Solve for x: $\log_2 x = \log_2 3$ **b.** Solve for x: $\log_4 4 = x$

c. Simplify: $\log_5 5^x$ **d.** Simplify: $6^{\log_6 20}$

Solution

a. Using the One-to-One Property (Property 4), you can conclude that $x = 3$.

b. Using Property 2, you can conclude that $x = 1$.

c. Using the Inverse Property (Property 3), it follows that $\log_5 5^x = x$.

d. Using the Inverse Property (Property 3), it follows that $6^{\log_6 20} = 20$.

Graphs of Logarithmic Functions

To sketch the graph of $y = \log_a x$, you can use the fact that the graphs of inverse functions are reflections of each other in the line $y = x$.

Example 4 ▶ **Graphs of Exponential and Logarithmic Functions**

In the same coordinate plane, sketch the graph of each function.

a. $f(x) = 2^x$ **b.** $g(x) = \log_2 x$

Solution

a. For $f(x) = 2^x$, construct a table of values.

x	$f(x) = 2^x$
-2	$\frac{1}{4}$
-1	$\frac{1}{2}$
0	1
1	2
2	4
3	8

By plotting these points and connecting them with a smooth curve, you obtain the graph shown in Figure 3.14.

b. Because $g(x) = \log_2 x$ is the inverse of $f(x) = 2^x$, the graph of g is obtained by plotting the points $(f(x), x)$ and connecting them with a smooth curve. The graph of g is a reflection of the graph of f in the line $y = x$, as shown in Figure 3.14.

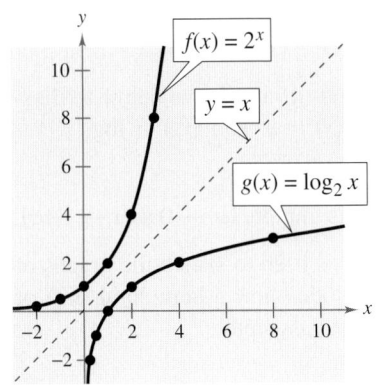

FIGURE **3.14**

Example 5 ▶ **Sketching the Graph of a Logarithmic Function**

Sketch the graph of the common logarithmic function $f(x) = \log_{10} x$. Identify the x-intercept and the vertical asymptote.

Solution

Begin by constructing a table of values. Note that some of the values can be obtained without a calculator by using the Inverse Property of Logarithms. Others require a calculator. Next, plot the points and connect them with a smooth curve, as shown in Figure 3.15. The x-intercept of the graph is $(1, 0)$ and the vertical asymptote is $x = 0$ (y-axis).

	Without calculator				With calculator		
x	$\frac{1}{100}$	$\frac{1}{10}$	1	10	2	5	8
$\log_{10} x$	-2	-1	0	1	0.301	0.699	0.903

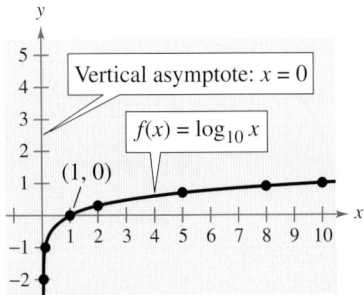

FIGURE **3.15**

The nature of the graph in Figure 3.15 is typical of functions of the form $f(x) = \log_a x, a > 1$. They have one x-intercept and one vertical asymptote. Notice how slowly the graph rises for $x > 1$. The basic characteristics of logarithmic graphs are summarized in Figure 3.16.

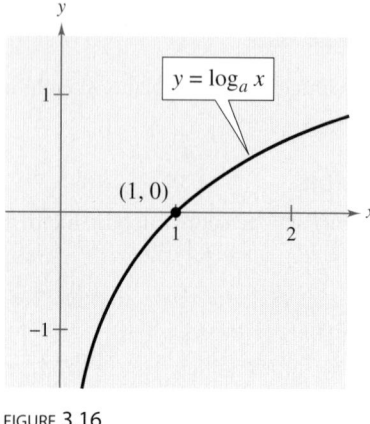

FIGURE 3.16

Graph of $y = \log_a x, a > 1$

- Domain: $(0, \infty)$
- Range: $(-\infty, \infty)$
- x-Intercept: $(1, 0)$
- Increasing
- One-to-one, therefore has an inverse function
- y-Axis is a vertical asymptote $(\log_a x \to -\infty$ as $x \to 0^+)$.
- Continuous
- Reflection of graph of $y = a^x$ about the line $y = x$

The basic characteristics of the graph of $f(x) = a^x$ are shown below to illustrate the inverse relation between the functions $f(x) = a^x$ and $g(x) = \log_a x$.

- Domain: $(-\infty, \infty)$ • Range: $(0, \infty)$
- y-Intercept: $(0,1)$ • x-Axis is a horizontal asymptote $(a^x \to 0$ as $x \to -\infty)$.

In the next example, the graph of $y = \log_a x$ is used to sketch the graphs of functions of the form $f(x) = b \pm \log_a(x + c)$. Notice how a horizontal shift of the graph results in a horizontal shift of the vertical asymptote.

STUDY TIP

You can use your understanding of transformations to identify vertical asymptotes of logarithmic functions. For instance, in Example 6(a) the graph of $g(x) = f(x - 1)$ shifts the graph of $f(x)$ one unit to the right. So the vertical asymptote of $g(x)$ is $x = 1$, one unit to the right of the asymptote of the graph of $f(x)$.

Example 6 ▶ Shifting Graphs of Logarithmic Functions

The graph of each of the functions is similar to the graph of $f(x) = \log_{10} x$.

a. Because $g(x) = \log_{10}(x - 1) = f(x - 1)$, the graph of g can be obtained by shifting the graph of f one unit to the right, as shown in Figure 3.17.

b. Because $h(x) = 2 + \log_{10} x = 2 + f(x)$, the graph of h can be obtained by shifting the graph of f two units upward, as shown in Figure 3.18.

FIGURE 3.17

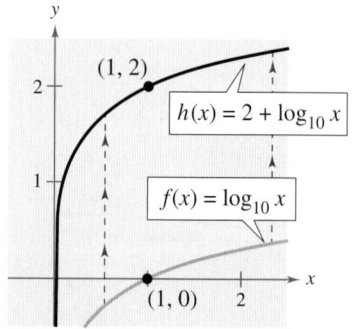

FIGURE 3.18

The Natural Logarithmic Function

By looking back at the graph of the natural exponential function introduced in Section 3.1, you will see that $f(x) = e^x$ is one-to-one and so has an inverse function. This inverse function is called the **natural logarithmic function** and is denoted by the special symbol $\ln x$, read as "the natural log of x" or "el en of x."

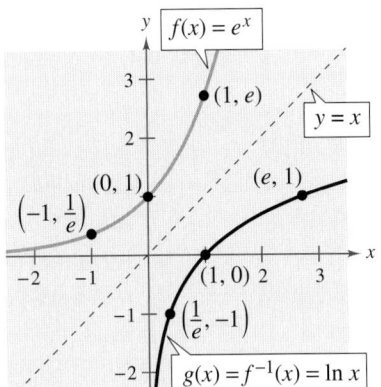

Reflection of graph of $f(x) = e^x$ about the line $y = x$

FIGURE 3.19

The Natural Logarithmic Function

The function defined by

$$f(x) = \log_e x = \ln x, \quad x > 0$$

is called the **natural logarithmic function.**

The definition above implies that the natural logarithmic function and the natural exponential function are inverse functions of each other. So, every logarithmic equation can be written in an equivalent exponential form and every exponential equation can be written in logarithmic form. That is, $y = \ln x$ and $x = e^y$ are equivalent equations.

Because the functions $f(x) = e^x$ and $g(x) = \ln x$ are inverse functions of each other, their graphs are reflections of each other in the line $y = x$. This reflective property is illustrated in Figure 3.19.

The four properties of logarithms listed on page 210 are also valid for natural logarithms.

STUDY TIP

Notice that as with every other logarithmic function, the domain of the natural logarithmic function is the set of *positive real numbers*—be sure you see that $\ln x$ is not defined for zero or for negative numbers.

Properties of Natural Logarithms

1. $\ln 1 = 0$ because $e^0 = 1$.

2. $\ln e = 1$ because $e^1 = e$.

3. $\ln e^x = x$ and $e^{\ln x} = x$ Inverse Properties

4. If $\ln x = \ln y$, then $x = y$.   One-to-One Property

Example 7 ▶ Using Properties of Natural Logarithms

Use the properties of natural logarithms to simplify each expression.

a. $\ln \dfrac{1}{e}$ **b.** $e^{\ln 5}$ **c.** $\dfrac{\ln 1}{3}$ **d.** $2 \ln e$

Solution

a. $\ln \dfrac{1}{e} = \ln e^{-1} = -1$ Inverse Property

b. $e^{\ln 5} = 5$ Inverse Property

c. $\dfrac{\ln 1}{3} = \dfrac{0}{3} = 0$ Property 1

d. $2 \ln e = 2(1) = 2$ Property 2

On most calculators, the natural logarithm is denoted by $\boxed{\text{LN}}$, as illustrated in Example 8.

Example 8 ▶ **Evaluating the Natural Logarithmic Function**

Use a calculator to evaluate the function $f(x) = \ln x$ for each value of x.

a. $x = 2$ **b.** $x = 0.3$ **c.** $x = -1$ **d.** $x = 1 + \sqrt{2}$

Solution

Function Value	Graphing Calculator Keystrokes	Display
a. $f(2) = \ln 2$	$\boxed{\text{LN}}$ 2 $\boxed{\text{ENTER}}$	0.6931472
b. $f(0.3) = \ln 0.3$	$\boxed{\text{LN}}$ .3 $\boxed{\text{ENTER}}$	−1.2039728
c. $f(-1) = \ln(-1)$	$\boxed{\text{LN}}$ $\boxed{\text{(−)}}$ 1 $\boxed{\text{ENTER}}$	ERROR
d. $f(1 + \sqrt{2}) = \ln(1 + \sqrt{2})$	$\boxed{\text{LN}}$ $\boxed{\text{(}}$ 1 $\boxed{\text{+}}$ $\boxed{\sqrt{\ }}$ 2 $\boxed{\text{)}}$ $\boxed{\text{ENTER}}$	0.8813736

In Example 8, be sure you see that $\ln(-1)$ gives an error message on most calculators. This occurs because the domain of $\ln x$ is the set of positive real numbers (see Figure 3.19). So, $\ln(-1)$ is undefined.

Example 9 ▶ **Finding the Domains of Logarithmic Functions**

Find the domain of each function.

a. $f(x) = \ln(x - 2)$

b. $g(x) = \ln(2 - x)$

c. $h(x) = \ln x^2$

Solution

a. Because $\ln(x - 2)$ is defined only if $x - 2 > 0$, it follows that the domain of f is $(2, \infty)$. The graph of f is shown in Figure 3.20.

b. Because $\ln(2 - x)$ is defined only if $2 - x > 0$, it follows that the domain of g is $(-\infty, 2)$. The graph of g is shown in Figure 3.21.

c. Because $\ln x^2$ is defined only if $x^2 > 0$, it follows that the domain of h is all real numbers except $x = 0$. The graph of h is shown in Figure 3.22.

FIGURE 3.20

FIGURE 3.21

FIGURE 3.22

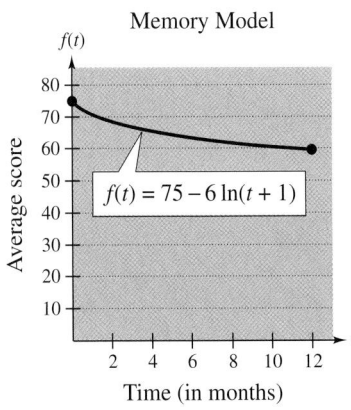

Memory Model

$f(t) = 75 - 6\ln(t + 1)$

FIGURE **3.23**

Application

Example 10 ▶ **Human Memory Model**

Students participating in a psychology experiment attended several lectures on a subject and were given an exam. Every month for a year after the exam, the students were retested to see how much of the material they remembered. The average scores for the group are given by the *human memory model*

$$f(t) = 75 - 6\ln(t + 1), \quad 0 \le t \le 12$$

where t is the time in months. The graph of f is shown in Figure 3.23.

a. What was the average score on the original ($t = 0$) exam?

b. What was the average score at the end of $t = 2$ months?

c. What was the average score at the end of $t = 6$ months?

Solution

a. The original average score was

$$f(0) = 75 - 6\ln(0 + 1) \qquad \text{Substitute 0 for } t.$$
$$= 75 - 6\ln 1 \qquad \text{Simplify.}$$
$$= 75 - 6(0) \qquad \text{Property of natural logarithms}$$
$$= 75. \qquad \text{Solution}$$

b. After 2 months, the average score was

$$f(2) = 75 - 6\ln(2 + 1) \qquad \text{Substitute 2 for } t.$$
$$= 75 - 6\ln 3 \qquad \text{Simplify.}$$
$$\approx 75 - 6(1.0986) \qquad \text{Use a calculator.}$$
$$\approx 68.4. \qquad \text{Solution}$$

c. After 6 months, the average score was

$$f(6) = 75 - 6\ln(6 + 1) \qquad \text{Substitute 6 for } t.$$
$$= 75 - 6\ln 7 \qquad \text{Simplify.}$$
$$\approx 75 - 6(1.9459) \qquad \text{Use a calculator.}$$
$$\approx 63.3. \qquad \text{Solution}$$

Alternative Writing About Mathematics

Use a graphing utility to graph $f(x) = \ln x$. How will the graphs of $h(x) = \ln x + 5$, $j(x) = \ln(x - 3)$, and $l(x) = \ln x - 4$ differ from the graph of f?

How will the basic graph of f be affected when a constant c is introduced: $g(x) = c\ln x$? Use a graphing utility to graph g with several different positive values of c, and summarize the effect of c.

Writing **ABOUT MATHEMATICS**

Analyzing a Human Memory Model Use a graphing utility to determine the time in months when the average score in Example 10 was 60. Explain your method of solving the problem. Describe another way that you can use a graphing utility to determine the answer.

3.2 Exercises

In Exercises 1–8, write the logarithmic equation in exponential form. For example, the exponential form of $\log_5 25 = 2$ is $5^2 = 25$.

1. $\log_4 64 = 3$ **2.** $\log_3 81 = 4$

3. $\log_7 \frac{1}{49} = -2$ **4.** $\log_{10} \frac{1}{1000} = -3$

5. $\log_{32} 4 = \frac{2}{5}$ **6.** $\log_{16} 8 = \frac{3}{4}$

7. $\ln \frac{1}{2} = -0.693\ldots$ **8.** $\ln 4 = 1.386\ldots$

In Exercises 9–18, write the exponential equation in logarithmic form. For example, the logarithmic form of $2^3 = 8$ is $\log_2 8 = 3$.

9. $5^3 = 125$ **10.** $8^2 = 64$

11. $81^{1/4} = 3$ **12.** $9^{3/2} = 27$

13. $6^{-2} = \frac{1}{36}$ **14.** $10^{-3} = 0.001$

15. $e^3 = 20.0855\ldots$ **16.** $e^{1/2} = 1.6487\ldots$

17. $e^x = 4$ **18.** $u^v = w$

In Exercises 19–26, evaluate the function at the indicated value of x without using a calculator.

Function	Value
19. $f(x) = \log_2 x$	$x = 16$
20. $f(x) = \log_{16} x$	$x = 4$
21. $f(x) = \log_7 x$	$x = 1$
22. $f(x) = \log_{10} x$	$x = 10$
23. $g(x) = \ln x$	$x = e^3$
24. $g(x) = \ln x$	$x = e^{-2}$
25. $g(x) = \log_a x$	$x = a^2$
26. $g(x) = \log_b x$	$x = b^{-3}$

 In Exercises 27–32, use a calculator to evaluate the function at the indicated value of x. Round your result to three decimal places.

Function	Value
27. $f(x) = \log_{10} x$	$x = \frac{4}{5}$
28. $f(x) = \log_{10} x$	$x = 12.5$
29. $f(x) = \ln x$	$x = 18.42$
30. $f(x) = 3 \ln x$	$x = 0.32$
31. $g(x) = 2 \ln x$	$x = 0.75$
32. $g(x) = -\ln x$	$x = \frac{1}{2}$

In Exercises 33–38, use the graph of $y = \log_3 x$ to match the given function with its graph. [The graphs are labeled (a), (b), (c), (d), (e), and (f).]

(a)   (b)

(c)   (d)

(e)   (f)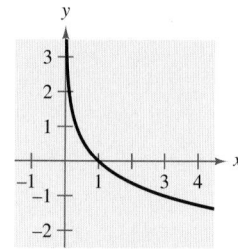

33. $f(x) = \log_3 x + 2$ **34.** $f(x) = -\log_3 x$

35. $f(x) = -\log_3(x + 2)$ **36.** $f(x) = \log_3(x - 1)$

37. $f(x) = \log_3(1 - x)$ **38.** $f(x) = -\log_3(-x)$

In Exercises 39–50, find the domain, x-intercept, and vertical asymptote of the logarithmic function and sketch its graph.

39. $f(x) = \log_4 x$ **40.** $g(x) = \log_6 x$

41. $y = -\log_3 x + 2$ **42.** $h(x) = \log_4(x - 3)$

43. $f(x) = -\log_6(x + 2)$ **44.** $y = \log_5(x - 1) + 4$

45. $y = \log_{10}\left(\frac{x}{5}\right)$ **46.** $y = \log_{10}(-x)$

47. $f(x) = \ln(x - 2)$ **48.** $h(x) = \ln(x + 1)$

49. $g(x) = \ln(-x)$ **50.** $f(x) = \ln(3 - x)$

In Exercises 51–56, use a graphing utility to graph the function. Be sure to use an appropriate viewing window.

51. $f(x) = \log_{10}(x + 1)$ **52.** $f(x) = \log_{10}(x - 1)$

53. $f(x) = \ln(x - 1)$ **54.** $f(x) = \ln(x + 2)$

55. $f(x) = \ln x + 2$ **56.** $f(x) = 3 \ln x - 1$

▶ Model It

57. *Monthly Payment* The model

$$t = 12.542 \ln\left(\frac{x}{x - 1000}\right), \qquad x > 1000$$

approximates the length of a home mortgage of $150,000 at 8% in terms of the monthly payment. In the model, t is the length of the mortgage in years and x is the monthly payment in dollars (see figure).

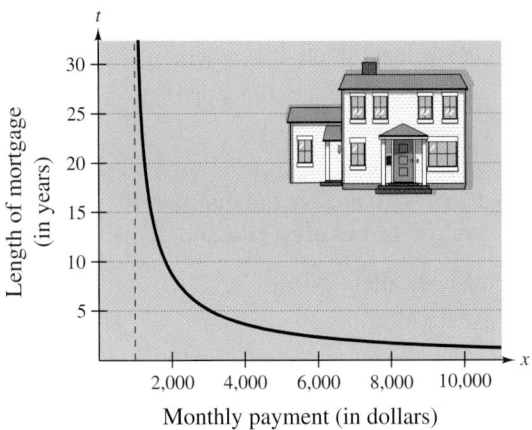

(a) Use the model to approximate the length of a $150,000 mortgage at 8% when the monthly payment is $1100.65 and when the monthly payment is $1254.68.

(b) Approximate the total amount paid over the term of the mortgage with a monthly payment of $1100.65 and with a monthly payment of $1254.68.

(c) Approximate the total interest charge for a monthly payment of $1100.65 and for a monthly payment of $1254.68.

(d) What is the vertical asymptote for the model? Interpret its meaning in the context of the problem.

58. *Compound Interest* A principal P, invested at $9\frac{1}{2}\%$ and compounded continuously, increases to an amount K times the original principal after t years, where t is given by

$$t = \frac{\ln K}{0.095}.$$

(a) Complete the table and interpret your results.

K	1	2	4	6	8	10	12
t							

(b) Sketch a graph of the function.

59. *Population* The time t in years for the world population to double if it is increasing at a continuous rate of r is given by

$$t = \frac{\ln 2}{r}.$$

(a) Complete the table.

r	0.005	0.01	0.015	0.02	0.025	0.03
t						

(b) Sketch a graph of the function.

(c) Use a reference source to decide which value of r best approximates the actual rate of growth for the world population.

60. *Sound Intensity* The relationship between the number of decibels β and the intensity of a sound I in watts per square meter is

$$\beta = 10 \log_{10}\left(\frac{I}{10^{-12}}\right).$$

(a) Determine the number of decibels of a sound with an intensity of 1 watt per square meter.

(b) Determine the number of decibels of a sound with an intensity of 10^{-2} watt per square meter.

(c) The intensity of the sound in part (a) is 100 times as great as that in part (b). Is the number of decibels 100 times as great? Explain.

61. Human Memory Model   Students in a mathematics class were given an exam and then retested monthly with an equivalent exam. The average scores for the class are given by the human memory model

$$f(t) = 80 - 17 \log_{10}(t + 1), \qquad 0 \le t \le 12$$

where t is the time in months.

(a) Use a graphing utility to graph the model over the specified domain.

(b) What was the average score on the original exam $(t = 0)$?

(c) What was the average score after 4 months?

(d) What was the average score after 10 months?

62. (a) Complete the table for the function

$$f(x) = \frac{\ln x}{x}.$$

x	1	5	10	10^2	10^4	10^6
$f(x)$						

(b) Use the table in part (a) to determine what value $f(x)$ approaches as x increases without bound.

(c) Use a graphing utility to confirm the result of part (b).

Synthesis

True or False?   In Exercises 63 and 64, determine whether the statement is true or false. Justify your answer.

63. You can determine the graph of $f(x) = \log_6 x$ by graphing $g(x) = 6^x$ and reflecting it about the x-axis.

64. The graph of $f(x) = \log_3 x$ contains the point $(27, 3)$.

In Exercises 65–68, describe the relationship between the graphs of f and g. What is the relationship between the functions f and g?

65. $f(x) = 3^x$
$g(x) = \log_3 x$

66. $f(x) = 5^x$
$g(x) = \log_5 x$

67. $f(x) = e^x$
$g(x) = \ln x$

68. $f(x) = 10^x$
$g(x) = \log_{10} x$

69. Graphical Analysis   Use a graphing utility to graph f and g in the same viewing window and determine which is increasing at the greater rate as x approaches $+\infty$. What can you conclude about the rate of growth of the natural logarithmic function?

(a) $f(x) = \ln x, \qquad g(x) = \sqrt{x}$

(b) $f(x) = \ln x, \qquad g(x) = \sqrt[4]{x}$

70. Think About It   The table of values was obtained by evaluating a function. Determine which of the statements may be true and which must be false.

x	y
1	0
2	1
8	3

(a) y is an exponential function of x.

(b) y is a logarithmic function of x.

(c) x is an exponential function of y.

(d) y is a linear function of x.

In Exercises 71–73, answer the question for the function $f(x) = \log_{10} x$. Do not use a calculator.

71. What is the domain of f?

72. What is f^{-1}?

73. If x is a real number between 1000 and 10,000, in which interval will $f(x)$ be found?

74. Writing   Explain why $\log_a x$ is defined only for $0 < a < 1$ and $a > 1$.

In Exercises 75 and 76, (a) use a graphing utility to graph the function, (b) use the graph to determine the intervals in which the function is increasing and decreasing, and (c) approximate any relative maximum or minimum values of the function.

75. $f(x) = |\ln x|$ **76.** $h(x) = \ln(x^2 + 1)$

Review

In Exercises 77 and 78, translate the statement into an algebraic expression.

77. The total cost for auto repairs if the cost of parts was $83.95 and there were t hours of labor at $37.50 per hour

78. The area of a rectangle if the length is 10 units more than the width w

3.3 Properties of Logarithms

▶ What you should learn

- How to use the change-of-base formula to rewrite and evaluate logarithmic expressions
- How to use properties of logarithms to evaluate or rewrite logarithmic expressions
- How to use properties of logarithms to expand or condense logarithmic expressions
- How to use logarithmic functions to model and solve real-life applications

▶ Why you should learn it

Logarithmic functions are often used to model scientific observations. For instance, in Exercise 81 on page 224, a logarithmic function is used to model human memory.

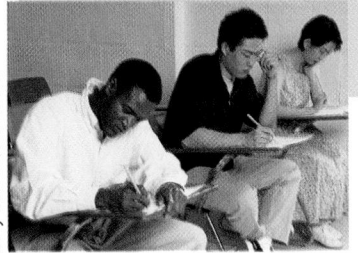

Gary Conner/PhotoEdit

Change of Base

Most calculators have only two types of log keys, one for common logarithms (base 10) and one for natural logarithms (base e). Although common logs and natural logs are the most frequently used, you may occasionally need to evaluate logarithms to other bases. To do this, you can use the following **change-of-base formula**.

> ### Change-of-Base Formula
>
> Let a, b, and x be positive real numbers such that $a \neq 1$ and $b \neq 1$. Then $\log_a x$ can be converted to a different base as follows.
>
> | *Base b* | *Base 10* | *Base e* |
> |---|---|---|
> | $\log_a x = \dfrac{\log_b x}{\log_b a}$ | $\log_a x = \dfrac{\log_{10} x}{\log_{10} a}$ | $\log_a x = \dfrac{\ln x}{\ln a}$ |

One way to look at the change-of-base formula is that logarithms to base a are simply *constant multiples* of logarithms to base b. The constant multiplier is $1/(\log_b a)$.

Example 1 ▶ **Changing Bases Using Common Logarithms**

a. $\log_4 30 = \dfrac{\log_{10} 30}{\log_{10} 4}$ $\log_a x = \dfrac{\log_{10} x}{\log_{10} a}$

$\approx \dfrac{1.47712}{0.60206}$ Use a calculator.

≈ 2.4534 Simplify.

b. $\log_2 14 = \dfrac{\log_{10} 14}{\log_{10} 2} \approx \dfrac{1.14613}{0.30103} \approx 3.8074$

Example 2 ▶ **Changing Bases Using Natural Logarithms**

a. $\log_4 30 = \dfrac{\ln 30}{\ln 4}$ $\log_a x = \dfrac{\ln x}{\ln a}$

$\approx \dfrac{3.40120}{1.38629}$ Use a calculator.

≈ 2.4535 Simplify.

b. $\log_2 14 = \dfrac{\ln 14}{\ln 2} \approx \dfrac{2.63906}{0.69315} \approx 3.8073$

Encourage your students to know these properties well. They will be used for solving logarithmic and exponential equations, as well as in calculus.

Properties of Logarithms

You know from the preceding section that the logarithmic function with base a is the *inverse function* of the exponential function with base a. So, it makes sense that the properties of exponents should have corresponding properties involving logarithms. For instance, the exponential property $a^0 = 1$ has the corresponding logarithmic property $\log_a 1 = 0$.

STUDY TIP

There is no general property that can be used to rewrite $\log_a(u \pm v)$. Specifically, $\log_a(x + y)$ is not equal to $\log_a x + \log_a y$.

Properties of Logarithms

Let a be a positive number such that $a \neq 1$, and let n be a real number. If u and v are positive real numbers, the following properties are true.

Logarithm with Base a	*Natural Logarithm*
1. $\log_a(uv) = \log_a u + \log_a v$	**1.** $\ln(uv) = \ln u + \ln v$
2. $\log_a \dfrac{u}{v} = \log_a u - \log_a v$	**2.** $\ln \dfrac{u}{v} = \ln u - \ln v$
3. $\log_a u^n = n \log_a u$	**3.** $\ln u^n = n \ln u$

Remind your students to note the domain when applying properties of logarithms to a logarithmic function. For example, the domain of $f(x) = \ln x^2$ is all real $x \neq 0$, whereas the domain of $g(x) = 2 \ln x$ is all real $x > 0$.

For a proof of the properties listed above, see Proofs in Mathematics on page 257.

Example 3 ▶ **Using Properties of Logarithms**

Write each logarithm in terms of $\ln 2$ and $\ln 3$.

a. $\ln 6$ **b.** $\ln \dfrac{2}{27}$

Solution

a. $\ln 6 = \ln(2 \cdot 3)$ Rewrite 6 as $2 \cdot 3$.

$\qquad = \ln 2 + \ln 3$ Property 1

b. $\ln \dfrac{2}{27} = \ln 2 - \ln 27$ Property 2

$\qquad\quad = \ln 2 - \ln 3^3$ Rewrite 27 as 3^3.

$\qquad\quad = \ln 2 - 3 \ln 3$ Property 3

The Granger Collection

Historical Note
John Napier, a Scottish mathematician, developed logarithms as a way to simplify some of the tedious calculations of his day. Beginning in 1594, Napier worked about 20 years on the invention of logarithms. Napier was only partially successful in his quest to simplify tedious calculations. Nonetheless, the development of logarithms was a step forward and received immediate recognition.

Example 4 ▶ **Using Properties of Logarithms**

Use the properties of logarithms to verify that $-\log_{10} \frac{1}{100} = \log_{10} 100$.

Solution

$-\log_{10} \frac{1}{100} = -\log_{10}(100^{-1})$ Rewrite $\frac{1}{100}$ as 100^{-1}.

$\qquad\qquad = -(-1)\log_{10} 100$ Property 3

$\qquad\qquad = \log_{10} 100$ Simplify.

Try checking this result on your calculator.

Rewriting Logarithmic Expressions

The properties of logarithms are useful for rewriting logarithmic expressions in forms that simplify the operations of algebra. This is true because these properties convert complicated products, quotients, and exponential forms into simpler sums, differences, and products, respectively.

A common error made in expanding logarithmic expressions is to rewrite log ax^n as n log ax instead of as log $a + n$ log x.

Example 5 ▶ Expanding Logarithmic Expressions

Expand each logarithmic expression.

a. $\log_4 5x^3y$ **b.** $\ln \dfrac{\sqrt{3x-5}}{7}$

Solution

a. $\log_4 5x^3y = \log_4 5 + \log_4 x^3 + \log_4 y$ Property 1

$\qquad\qquad = \log_4 5 + 3 \log_4 x + \log_4 y$ Property 3

b. $\ln \dfrac{\sqrt{3x-5}}{7} = \ln \dfrac{(3x-5)^{1/2}}{7}$ Rewrite using rational exponent.

$\qquad\qquad = \ln(3x-5)^{1/2} - \ln 7$ Property 2

$\qquad\qquad = \dfrac{1}{2}\ln(3x-5) - \ln 7$ Property 3

In Example 5, the properties of logarithms were used to *expand* logarithmic expressions. In Example 6, this procedure is reversed and the properties of logarithms are used to *condense* logarithmic expressions.

A common error made in condensing logarithmic expressions is to rewrite

log x − log y as $\dfrac{\log x}{\log y}$ instead of as log $\dfrac{x}{y}$.

Example 6 ▶ Condensing Logarithmic Expressions

Condense each logarithmic expression.

a. $\frac{1}{2} \log_{10} x + 3 \log_{10}(x+1)$ **b.** $2 \ln(x+2) - \ln x$
c. $\frac{1}{3}[\log_2 x + \log_2(x+1)]$

Solution

a. $\frac{1}{2}\log_{10} x + 3 \log_{10}(x+1) = \log_{10} x^{1/2} + \log_{10}(x+1)^3$ Property 3

$\qquad\qquad\qquad = \log_{10}\left[\sqrt{x}(x+1)^3\right]$ Property 1

b. $2 \ln(x+2) - \ln x = \ln(x+2)^2 - \ln x$ Property 3

$\qquad\qquad\qquad = \ln \dfrac{(x+2)^2}{x}$ Property 2

c. $\frac{1}{3}[\log_2 x + \log_2(x+1)] = \frac{1}{3}\{\log_2[x(x+1)]\}$ Property 1

$\qquad\qquad\qquad = \log_2[x(x+1)]^{1/3}$ Property 3

$\qquad\qquad\qquad = \log_2 \sqrt[3]{x(x+1)}$ Rewrite with a radical.

◀ Exploration ▶

Use a graphing utility to graph the functions

$y_1 = \ln x - \ln(x-3)$

and

$y_2 = \ln \dfrac{x}{x-3}$

in the same viewing window. Does the graphing utility show the functions with the same domain? If so, should it? Explain your reasoning.

Application

One method of determining how the x- and y-values for a set of nonlinear data are related begins by taking the natural log of each of the x- and y-values. If the points are graphed and fall on a straight line, then you can determine that the x- and y-values are related by the equation

$$\ln y = m \ln x$$

where m is the slope of the straight line.

Example 7 ▶ **Finding a Mathematical Model**

The table shows the mean distance x and the period (the time it takes a planet to orbit the sun) y for each of the six planets that are closest to the sun. In the table, the mean distance is given in terms of astronomical units (where Earth's mean distance is defined as 1.0), and the period is given in terms of years. Find an equation that relates y and x.

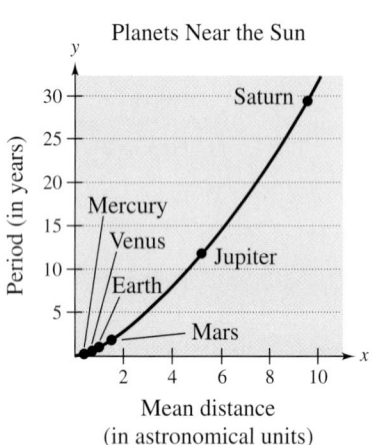

Planets Near the Sun

FIGURE 3.24

Planet	Mean distance, x	Period, y
Mercury	0.387	0.241
Venus	0.723	0.615
Earth	1.000	1.000
Mars	1.524	1.881
Jupiter	5.203	11.862
Saturn	9.555	29.458

Solution

The points in the table are plotted in Figure 3.24. From this figure it is not clear how to find an equation that relates y and x. To solve this problem, take the natural log of each of the x- and y-values in the table. This produces the following results.

Planet	$\ln x$	$\ln y$
Mercury	-0.949	-1.423
Venus	-0.324	-0.486
Earth	0.000	0.000
Mars	0.421	0.632
Jupiter	1.649	2.473
Saturn	2.257	3.383

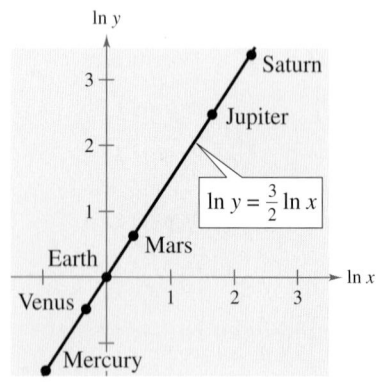

FIGURE 3.25

Now, by plotting the points in the second table, you can see that all six of the points appear to lie in a line (see Figure 3.25). You can use a graphical approach or the algebraic approach discussed in Section 1.9 to find that the slope of this line is $\frac{3}{2}$. You can therefore conclude that $\ln y = \frac{3}{2} \ln x$.

3.3 **Exercises**

In Exercises 1–8, rewrite the logarithm as a ratio of (a) common logarithms and (b) natural logarithms.

1. $\log_5 x$
2. $\log_3 x$
3. $\log_{1/5} x$
4. $\log_{1/3} x$
5. $\log_x \frac{3}{10}$
6. $\log_x \frac{3}{4}$
7. $\log_{2.6} x$
8. $\log_{7.1} x$

In Exercises 9–16, evaluate the logarithm using the change-of-base formula. Round your result to three decimal places.

9. $\log_3 7$
10. $\log_7 4$
11. $\log_{1/2} 4$
12. $\log_{1/4} 5$
13. $\log_9 0.4$
14. $\log_{20} 0.125$
15. $\log_{15} 1250$
16. $\log_3 0.015$

In Exercises 17–38, use the properties of logarithms to expand the expression as a sum, difference, and/or constant multiple of logarithms. (Assume all variables are positive.)

17. $\log_4 5x$
18. $\log_3 10z$
19. $\log_8 x^4$
20. $\log_{10} \frac{y}{2}$
21. $\log_5 \frac{5}{x}$
22. $\log_6 \frac{1}{z^3}$
23. $\ln \sqrt{z}$
24. $\ln \sqrt[3]{t}$
25. $\ln xyz^2$
26. $\log_{10} 4x^2 y$
27. $\ln z(z-1)^2, \; z > 1$
28. $\ln \left(\frac{x^2-1}{x^3} \right), \; x > 1$
29. $\log_2 \frac{\sqrt{a-1}}{9}, \; a > 1$
30. $\ln \frac{6}{\sqrt{x^2+1}}$
31. $\ln \sqrt[3]{\frac{x}{y}}$
32. $\ln \sqrt{\frac{x^2}{y^3}}$
33. $\ln \frac{x^4 \sqrt{y}}{z^5}$
34. $\log_2 \frac{\sqrt{x} \, y^4}{z^4}$
35. $\log_5 \frac{x^2}{y^2 z^3}$
36. $\log_{10} \frac{xy^4}{z^5}$
37. $\ln \sqrt[4]{x^3(x^2+3)}$
38. $\ln \sqrt{x^2(x+2)}$

In Exercises 39–56, condense the expression to the logarithm of a single quantity.

39. $\ln x + \ln 3$
40. $\ln y + \ln t$
41. $\log_4 z - \log_4 y$
42. $\log_5 8 - \log_5 t$
43. $2 \log_2(x+4)$
44. $\frac{2}{3} \log_7(z-2)$
45. $\frac{1}{4} \log_3 5x$
46. $-4 \log_6 2x$
47. $\ln x - 3 \ln(x+1)$
48. $2 \ln 8 + 5 \ln(z-4)$
49. $\log_{10} x - 2 \log_{10} y + 3 \log_{10} z$
50. $3 \log_3 x + 4 \log_3 y - 4 \log_3 z$
51. $\ln x - 4[\ln(x+2) + \ln(x-2)]$
52. $4[\ln z + \ln(z+5)] - 2 \ln(z-5)$
53. $\frac{1}{3}[2 \ln(x+3) + \ln x - \ln(x^2-1)]$
54. $2[3 \ln x - \ln(x+1) - \ln(x-1)]$
55. $\frac{1}{3}[\log_8 y + 2 \log_8(y+4)] - \log_8(y-1)$
56. $\frac{1}{2}[\log_4(x+1) + 2 \log_4(x-1)] + 6 \log_4 x$

In Exercises 57 and 58, compare the logarithmic quantities. If two are equal, explain why.

57. $\dfrac{\log_2 32}{\log_2 4}, \quad \log_2 \dfrac{32}{4}, \quad \log_2 32 - \log_2 4$

58. $\log_7 \sqrt{70}, \quad \log_7 35, \quad \frac{1}{2} + \log_7 \sqrt{10}$

In Exercises 59–74, find the exact value of the logarithm without using a calculator. (If this is not possible, state the reason.)

59. $\log_3 9$
60. $\log_5 \frac{1}{125}$
61. $\log_2 \sqrt[4]{8}$
62. $\log_6 \sqrt[3]{6}$
63. $\log_4 16^{1.2}$
64. $\log_3 81^{-0.2}$
65. $\log_3(-9)$
66. $\log_2(-16)$
67. $\ln e^{4.5}$
68. $3 \ln e^4$
69. $\ln \dfrac{1}{\sqrt{e}}$
70. $\ln \sqrt[4]{e^3}$
71. $\ln e^2 + \ln e^5$
72. $2 \ln e^6 - \ln e^5$
73. $\log_5 75 - \log_5 3$
74. $\log_4 2 + \log_4 32$

In Exercises 75–80, use the properties of logarithms to rewrite and simplify the logarithmic expression.

75. $\log_4 8$

76. $\log_2(4^2 \cdot 3^4)$

77. $\log_5 \frac{1}{250}$

78. $\log_{10} \frac{9}{300}$

79. $\ln(5e^6)$

80. $\ln \frac{6}{e^2}$

▶ Model It

81. *Human Memory Model* Students participating in a psychology experiment attended several lectures and were given an exam. Every month for a year after the exam, the students were retested to see how much of the material they remembered. The average scores for the group can be modeled by the human memory model

$$f(t) = 90 - 15 \log_{10}(t + 1), \qquad 0 \le t \le 12$$

where t is the time in months.

(a) What was the average score on the original exam ($t = 0$)?

(b) What was the average score after 6 months?

(c) What was the average score after 12 months?

(d) When will the average score decrease to 75?

(e) Use the properties of logarithms to write the function in another form.

(f) Sketch the graph of the function over the specified domain.

82. *Sound Intensity* The relationship between the number of decibels β and the intensity of a sound I in watts per square meter is

$$\beta = 10 \log_{10}\left(\frac{I}{10^{-12}}\right).$$

Use the properties of logarithms to write the formula in simpler form, and determine the number of decibels of a sound with an intensity of 10^{-6} watt per square meter.

Synthesis

True or False? In Exercises 83–88, determine whether the statement is true or false given that $f(x) = \ln x$. Justify your answer.

83. $f(0) = 0$

84. $f(ax) = f(a) + f(x), \qquad a > 0, x > 0$

85. $f(x - 2) = f(x) - f(2), \qquad x > 2$

86. $\sqrt{f(x)} = \frac{1}{2}f(x)$

87. If $f(u) = 2f(v)$, then $v = u^2$.

88. If $f(x) < 0$, then $0 < x < 1$.

89. *Proof* Prove that $\log_b \frac{u}{v} = \log_b u - \log_b v$.

90. *Proof* Prove that $\log_b u^n = n \log_b u$.

In Exercises 91–96, use the change-of-base formula to rewrite the logarithm as a ratio of logarithms. Then use a graphing utility to graph both functions in the same viewing window to verify that the functions are equivalent.

91. $f(x) = \log_2 x$

92. $f(x) = \log_4 x$

93. $f(x) = \log_{1/2} x$

94. $f(x) = \log_{1/4} x$

95. $f(x) = \log_{11.8} x$

96. $f(x) = \log_{12.4} x$

97. *Think About It* Consider the functions below.

$$f(x) = \ln \frac{x}{2}, \quad g(x) = \frac{\ln x}{\ln 2}, \quad h(x) = \ln x - \ln 2$$

Which two functions should have identical graphs? Verify your answer by sketching the graphs of all three functions on the same set of coordinate axes.

98. *Exploration* For how many integers between 1 and 20 can the natural logarithms be approximated given that $\ln 2 \approx 0.6931$, $\ln 3 \approx 1.0986$, and $\ln 5 \approx 1.6094$? Approximate these logarithms (do not use a calculator).

Review

In Exercises 99–102, simplify the expression.

99. $\frac{24xy^{-2}}{16x^{-3}y}$

100. $\left(\frac{2x^2}{3y}\right)^{-3}$

101. $(18x^3y^4)^{-3}(18x^3y^4)^3$

102. $xy(x^{-1} + y^{-1})^{-1}$

In Exercises 103–106, solve the equation.

103. $3x^2 + 2x - 1 = 0$

104. $4x^2 - 5x + 1 = 0$

105. $\frac{2}{3x + 1} = \frac{x}{4}$

106. $\frac{5}{x - 1} = \frac{2x}{3}$

3.4 Exponential and Logarithmic Equations

▶ **What you should learn**

- How to solve simple exponential and logarithmic equations
- How to solve more complicated exponential equations
- How to solve more complicated logarithmic equations
- How to use exponential and logarithmic equations to model and solve real-life applications

▶ **Why you should learn it**

Applications of exponential and logarithmic equations are found in consumer safety testing. For instance, in Exercise 119, on page 234, a logarithmic function is used to model crumple zones for automobile crash tests.

Introduction

So far in this chapter, you have studied the definitions, graphs, and properties of exponential and logarithmic functions. In this section, you will study procedures for *solving equations* involving these exponential and logarithmic functions.

There are two basic strategies for solving exponential or logarithmic equations. The first is based on the One-to-One Properties and the second is based on the Inverse Properties. For $a > 0$ and $a \neq 1$, the following properties are true for all x and y for which $\log_a x$ and $\log_a y$ are defined.

One-to-One Properties

$a^x = a^y$ if and only if $x = y$.

$\log_a x = \log_a y$ if and only if $x = y$.

Inverse Properties

$a^{\log_a x} = x$

$\log_a a^x = x$

| Example 1 ▶ | Solving Simple Equations | |

	Original Equation	*Rewritten Equation*	*Solution*	*Property*
a.	$2^x = 32$	$2^x = 2^5$	$x = 5$	One-to-One
b.	$\ln x - \ln 3 = 0$	$\ln x = \ln 3$	$x = 3$	One-to-One
c.	$\left(\frac{1}{3}\right)^x = 9$	$3^{-x} = 3^2$	$x = -2$	One-to-One
d.	$e^x = 7$	$\ln e^x = \ln 7$	$x = \ln 7$	Inverse
e.	$\ln x = -3$	$e^{\ln x} = e^{-3}$	$x = e^{-3}$	Inverse
f.	$\log_{10} x = -1$	$10^{\log_{10} x} = 10^{-1}$	$x = 10^{-1} = \frac{1}{10}$	Inverse

The strategies used in Example 1 are summarized as follows.

Strategies for Solving Exponential and Logarithmic Equations

1. Rewrite the original equation in a form that allows the use of the One-to-One Properties of exponential or logarithmic functions.

2. Rewrite an *exponential* equation in logarithmic form and apply the Inverse Property of logarithmic functions.

3. Rewrite a *logarithmic* equation in exponential form and apply the Inverse Property of exponential functions.

Solving Exponential Equations

Example 2 ▶ Solving Exponential Equations

Solve each equation and approximate the result to three decimal places.

a. $4^x = 72$ **b.** $3(2^x) = 42$

Solution

a.

$4^x = 72$	Write original equation.
$\log_4 4^x = \log_4 72$	Take logarithm (base 4) of each side.
$x = \log_4 72$	Inverse Property
$x = \dfrac{\ln 72}{\ln 4}$	Change-of-base formula
$x \approx 3.085$	Use a calculator.

The solution is $x = \log_4 72 \approx 3.085$. Check this in the original equation.

b.

$3(2^x) = 42$	Write original equation.
$2^x = 14$	Divide each side by 3.
$\log_2 2^x = \log_2 14$	Take log (base 2) of each side.
$x = \log_2 14$	Inverse Property
$x = \dfrac{\ln 14}{\ln 2}$	Change-of-base formula
$x \approx 3.807$	Use a calculator.

The solution is $x = \log_2 14 \approx 3.807$. Check this in the original equation.

In Example 2(a), the exact solution is $x = \log_4 72$ and the approximate solution is $x \approx 3.085$. An exact answer is preferred when the solution is an intermediate step in a larger problem. For a final answer, an approximate solution is easier to comprehend.

Example 3 ▶ Solving an Exponential Equation

Solve $e^x + 5 = 60$ and approximate the result to three decimal places.

Solution

$e^x + 5 = 60$	Write original equation.
$e^x = 55$	Subtract 5 from each side.
$\ln e^x = \ln 55$	Take natural log of each side.
$x = \ln 55$	Inverse Property
$x \approx 4.007$	Use a calculator.

The solution is $x = \ln 55 \approx 4.007$. Check this in the original equation.

Technology

When solving an exponential or logarithmic equation, remember that you can check your solution graphically by "graphing the left and right sides separately" and using the *intersect* feature of your graphing utility to determine the point of intersection. For instance, to check the solution of the equation in Example 2(a), you can graph

$$y_1 = 4^x \quad \text{and} \quad y_2 = 72$$

in the same viewing window, as shown below. Using the *intersect* feature of your graphing utility, you can determine that the graphs intersect when $x \approx 3.085$, which confirms the solution found in Example 2(a).

Additional Example

$2^x = 10$

$\ln 2^x = \ln 10$

$x \ln 2 = \ln 10$

$x = \dfrac{\ln 10}{\ln 2} \approx 3.322$

Note: Using the change-of-base formula or the definition of a logarithmic function, you could write this solution as $x = \log_2 10$.

STUDY TIP

Remember that to evaluate a logarithm such as $\log_3 7.5$, you need to use the change-of-base formula.

$$\log_3 7.5 = \frac{\ln 7.5}{\ln 3} \approx 1.834$$

To ensure that students first solve for the unknown variable algebraically and then use their calculators, you can require both exact algebraic solutions and approximate numerical answers.

| Example 4 ▶ | **Solving an Exponential Equation** | www ▶ |

Solve $2(3^{2t-5}) - 4 = 11$ and approximate the result to three decimal places.

Solution

$2(3^{2t-5}) - 4 = 11$	Write original equation.
$2(3^{2t-5}) = 15$	Add 4 to each side.
$3^{2t-5} = \dfrac{15}{2}$	Divide each side by 2.
$\log_3 3^{2t-5} = \log_3 \dfrac{15}{2}$	Take log (base 3) of each side.
$2t - 5 = \log_3 \dfrac{15}{2}$	Inverse Property
$2t = 5 + \log_3 7.5$	Add 5 to each side.
$t = \dfrac{5}{2} + \dfrac{1}{2}\log_3 7.5$	Divide each side by 2.
$t \approx 3.417$	Use a calculator.

The solution is $t = \frac{5}{2} + \frac{1}{2}\log_3 7.5 \approx 3.417$. Check this in the original equation.

When an equation involves two or more exponential expressions, you can still use a procedure similar to that demonstrated in Examples 2, 3, and 4. However, the algebra is a bit more complicated.

| Example 5 ▶ | **Solving an Exponential Equation of Quadratic Type** |

www ▶

Solve $e^{2x} - 3e^x + 2 = 0$.

Solution

$e^{2x} - 3e^x + 2 = 0$	Write original equation.
$(e^x)^2 - 3e^x + 2 = 0$	Write in quadratic form.
$(e^x - 2)(e^x - 1) = 0$	Factor.
$e^x - 2 = 0$	Set 1st factor equal to 0.
$x = \ln 2$	Solution
$e^x - 1 = 0$	Set 2nd factor equal to 0.
$x = 0$	Solution

The solutions are $x = \ln 2$ and $x = 0$. Check these in the original equation.

In Example 5, use a graphing utility to graph $y = e^{2x} - 3e^x + 2$. The graph should have two x-intercepts: one at $x = \ln 2 \approx 0.693$ and one at $x = 0$.

Solving Logarithmic Equations

To solve a logarithmic equation such as

$$\ln x = 3 \qquad \text{Logarithmic form}$$

write the equation in exponential form as follows.

$$e^{\ln x} = e^3 \qquad \text{Exponentiate each side.}$$

$$x = e^3 \qquad \text{Exponential form}$$

This procedure is called *exponentiating* each side of an equation.

Example 6 ▶ Solving a Logarithmic Equation

a. Solve $\ln x = 2$.

b. Solve $\log_3(5x - 1) = \log_3(x + 7)$.

Solution

a.
$$\ln x = 2 \qquad \text{Write original equation.}$$

$$e^{\ln x} = e^2 \qquad \text{Exponentiate each side.}$$

$$x = e^2 \qquad \text{Inverse Property}$$

The solution is $x = e^2$. Check this in the original equation.

b.
$$\log_3(5x - 1) = \log_3(x + 7) \qquad \text{Write original equation.}$$

$$5x - 1 = x + 7 \qquad \text{One-to-One Property}$$

$$4x = 8 \qquad \text{Add } -x \text{ and 1 to each side.}$$

$$x = 2 \qquad \text{Divide each side by 4.}$$

The solution is $x = 2$. Check this in the original equation.

Example 7 ▶ Solving a Logarithmic Equation

Solve $5 + 2 \ln x = 4$ and approximate the result to three decimal places.

Solution

$$5 + 2 \ln x = 4 \qquad \text{Write original equation.}$$

$$2 \ln x = -1 \qquad \text{Subtract 5 from each side.}$$

$$\ln x = -\frac{1}{2} \qquad \text{Divide each side by 2.}$$

$$e^{\ln x} = e^{-1/2} \qquad \text{Exponentiate each side.}$$

$$x = e^{-1/2} \qquad \text{Inverse Property}$$

$$x \approx 0.607 \qquad \text{Use a calculator.}$$

The solution is $x = e^{-1/2} \approx 0.607$. Check this in the original equation.

Activities

1. Solve for x: $7^x = 3$.

   Answer: $x = \dfrac{\ln 3}{\ln 7} \approx 0.5646$

2. Solve for x:
   $\log_{10}(x + 4) + \log_{10}(x + 1) = 1$.
   Answer: $x = 1$ ($x = -6$ is not in the domain.)

Example 8 ▶ Solving a Logarithmic Equation

Solve $2 \log_5 3x = 4$.

Solution

$2 \log_5 3x = 4$	Write original equation.
$\log_5 3x = 2$	Divide each side by 2.
$5^{\log_5 3x} = 5^2$	Exponentiate each side (base 5).
$3x = 25$	Inverse Property
$x = \dfrac{25}{3}$	Divide each side by 3.

The solution is $x = \frac{25}{3}$. Check this in the original equation.

Because the domain of a logarithmic function generally does not include all real numbers, you should be sure to check for extraneous solutions of logarithmic equations.

Example 9 ▶ Checking for Extraneous Solutions

Solve $\log_{10} 5x + \log_{10}(x - 1) = 2$.

Solution

$\log_{10} 5x + \log_{10}(x - 1) = 2$	Write original equation.
$\log_{10}[5x(x - 1)] = 2$	Product Property of Logarithms
$10^{\log_{10}(5x^2 - 5x)} = 10^2$	Exponentiate each side (base 10).
$5x^2 - 5x = 100$	Inverse Property
$x^2 - x - 20 = 0$	Write in general form.
$(x - 5)(x + 4) = 0$	Factor.
$x - 5 = 0$	Set 1st factor equal to 0.
$x = 5$	Solution
$x + 4 = 0$	Set 2nd factor equal to 0.
$x = -4$	Solution

The solutions appear to be $x = 5$ and $x = -4$. However, when you check these in the original equation, you can see that $x = 5$ is the only solution.

In Example 9, the domain of $\log_{10} 5x$ is $x > 0$ and the domain of $\log_{10}(x - 1)$ is $x > 1$, so the domain of the original equation is $x > 1$. Because the domain is all real numbers greater than 1, the solution $x = -4$ is extraneous.

STUDY TIP

Notice in Example 9 that the logarithmic part of the equation is condensed into a single logarithm before exponentiating each side of the equation.

Technology

You can use a graphing utility to verify that the equation in Example 9 has $x = 5$ as its only solution. Graph

$$y_1 = \log_{10} 5x + \log_{10}(x - 1)$$

and

$$y_2 = 2$$

in the same viewing window. From the graph shown below, it appears that the graphs of the two equations intersect at one point. Use the *intersect* feature or the *zoom* and *trace* features to determine that $x = 5$ is an approximate solution. You can verify this algebraically by substituting $x = 5$ into the original equation.

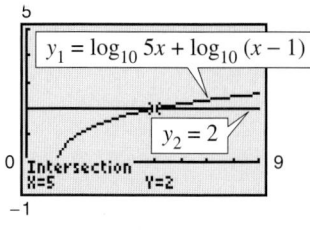

Applications

Activity

Determine the amount of time it would take $1000 to double in an account that pays 6.75% interest, compounded continuously. How does this compare to Example 10?

Answer: ≈ 10.27 years; it takes the same amount of time.

Example 10 ▶ **Doubling an Investment**

You have deposited $500 in an account that pays 6.75% interest, compounded continuously. How long will it take your money to double?

Solution

Using the formula for continuous compounding, you can find that the balance in the account is

$$A = Pe^{rt}$$

$$A = 500e^{0.0675t}.$$

To find the time required for the balance to double, let $A = 1000$ and solve the resulting equation for t.

$500e^{0.0675t} = 1000$	Let $A = 1000$.
$e^{0.0675t} = 2$	Divide each side by 500.
$\ln e^{0.0675t} = \ln 2$	Take natural log of each side.
$0.0675t = \ln 2$	Inverse Property
$t = \dfrac{\ln 2}{0.0675}$	Divide each side by 0.0675.
$t \approx 10.27$	Use a calculator.

The balance in the account will double after approximately 10.27 years. This result is demonstrated graphically in Figure 3.26.

◀ **Exploration** ▶

The *effective yield* of a savings plan is the percent increase in the balance after 1 year. Find the effective yield for each savings plan when $1000 is deposited in a savings account.

a. 7% annual interest rate, compounded annually

b. 7% annual interest rate, compounded continuously

c. 7% annual interest rate, compounded quarterly

d. 7.25% annual interest rate, compounded quarterly

Which savings plan has the greatest effective yield? Which savings plan will have the highest balance after 5 years?

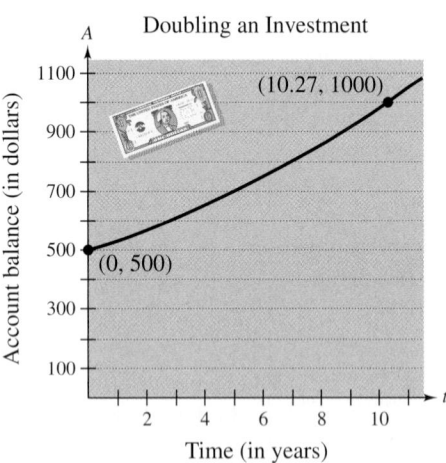

FIGURE **3.26**

In Example 10, an approximate answer of 10.27 years is given. Within the context of the problem, the exact solution, $(\ln 2)/0.0675$ years, does not make sense as an answer.

Average Salary for
Secondary Teachers

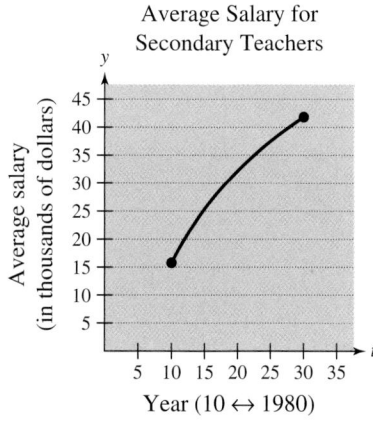

FIGURE **3.27**

Example 11 ▶ **Average Salary for Secondary Teachers**

For selected years from 1980 to 2000, the average salary for secondary teachers y (in thousands of dollars) for the year t can be modeled by the equation

$$y = -38.8 + 23.7 \ln t, \qquad 10 \le t \le 30$$

where $t = 10$ represents 1980 (see Figure 3.27). During which year did the average salary for secondary teachers reach 2.5 times its 1980 level of $16.5 thousand? (Source: National Education Association)

Solution

$-38.8 + 23.7 \ln t = y$	Write original equation.
$-38.8 + 23.7 \ln t = 41.25$	Let $y = (2.5)(16.5) = 41.25$.
$23.7 \ln t = 80.05$	Add 38.8 to each side.
$\ln t \approx 3.378$	Divide each side by 23.7.
$e^{\ln t} \approx e^{3.378}$	Exponentiate each side.
$t \approx e^{3.378}$	Inverse Property
$t \approx 29$	Use a calculator.

The solution is $t \approx 29$ years. Because $t = 10$ represents 1980, it follows that the average salary for secondary teachers reached 2.5 times its 1980 level in 1999.

Writing ABOUT MATHEMATICS

Year, x	Rate, y
5	10.75
8	12.00
11	13.95
15	15.00
19	15.75
21	16.00

Comparing Mathematical Models The table shows the U.S. Postal Service rates y for sending an express mail package for selected years from 1985 through 2001, where $x = 5$ represents 1985. (Source: U.S. Postal Service)

a. Create a scatter plot of the data. Find a linear model for the data, and add its graph to your scatter plot. According to this model, when will the rate for sending an express mail package reach $17.50?

b. Create a new table showing values for $\ln x$ and $\ln y$ and create a scatter plot of this transformed data. Use the method illustrated in Example 7 in Section 3.3 to find a model for the transformed data, and add its graph to your scatter plot. According to this model, when will the rate for sending an express mail package reach $17.50?

c. Solve the model in part (b) for y, and add its graph to your scatter plot in part (a). Which model better fits the original data? Which model will better predict future shipments? Explain.

3.4 Exercises

In Exercises 1–6, determine whether each x-value is a solution (or an approximate solution) of the equation.

1. $4^{2x-7} = 64$

  (a) $x = 5$

  (b) $x = 2$

2. $2^{3x+1} = 32$

  (a) $x = -1$

  (b) $x = 2$

3. $3e^{x+2} = 75$

  (a) $x = -2 + e^{25}$

  (b) $x = -2 + \ln 25$

  (c) $x \approx 1.219$

4. $5^{2x+3} = 812$

  (a) $x = -\frac{3}{2} + \log_5 \sqrt{812}$

  (b) $x \approx 0.581$

  (c) $x = -1.5 + \dfrac{\ln 812}{\ln 5}$

5. $\log_4(3x) = 3$

  (a) $x \approx 20.356$

  (b) $x = -4$

  (c) $x = \frac{64}{3}$

6. $\ln(x - 1) = 3.8$

  (a) $x = 1 + e^{3.8}$

  (b) $x \approx 45.701$

  (c) $x = 1 + \ln 3.8$

In Exercises 7–26, solve for x.

7. $4^x = 16$

8. $3^x = 243$

9. $5^x = 625$

10. $3^x = 729$

11. $7^x = \frac{1}{49}$

12. $8^x = 4$

13. $\left(\frac{1}{2}\right)^x = 32$

14. $\left(\frac{1}{4}\right)^x = 64$

15. $\left(\frac{3}{4}\right)^x = \frac{27}{64}$

16. $\left(\frac{2}{3}\right)^x = \frac{4}{9}$

17. $\ln x - \ln 2 = 0$

18. $\ln x - \ln 5 = 0$

19. $e^x = 2$

20. $e^x = 4$

21. $\ln x = -1$

22. $\ln x = -7$

23. $\log_4 x = 3$

24. $\log_5 x = -3$

25. $\log_{10} x = -1$

26. $\log_{10} x - 2 = 0$

In Exercises 27–30, approximate the point of intersection of the graphs of f and g. Then solve the equation $f(x) = g(x)$ algebraically.

27. $f(x) = 2^x$

  $g(x) = 8$

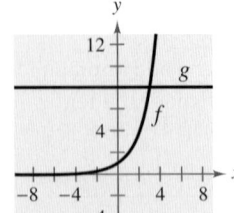

28. $f(x) = 27^x$

  $g(x) = 9$

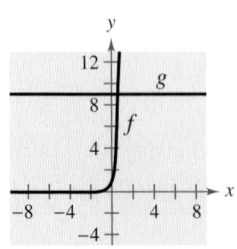

29. $f(x) = \log_3 x$

  $g(x) = 2$

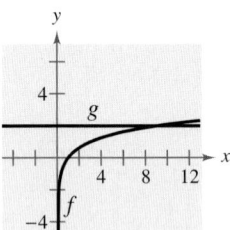

30. $f(x) = \ln(x - 4)$

  $g(x) = 0$

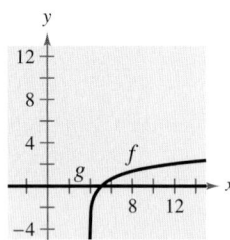

In Exercises 31–68, solve the exponential equation algebraically. Approximate the result to three decimal places.

31. $4(3^x) = 20$

32. $2(5^x) = 32$

33. $2e^x = 10$

34. $4e^x = 91$

35. $e^x - 9 = 19$

36. $6^x + 10 = 47$

37. $3^{2x} = 80$

38. $6^{5x} = 3000$

39. $5^{-t/2} = 0.20$

40. $4^{-3t} = 0.10$

41. $3^{x-1} = 27$

42. $2^{x-3} = 32$

43. $2^{3-x} = 565$

44. $8^{-2-x} = 431$

45. $8(10^{3x}) = 12$

46. $5(10^{x-6}) = 7$

47. $3(5^{x-1}) = 21$

48. $8(3^{6-x}) = 40$

49. $e^{3x} = 12$

50. $e^{2x} = 50$

51. $500e^{-x} = 300$

52. $1000e^{-4x} = 75$

53. $7 - 2e^x = 5$

54. $-14 + 3e^x = 11$

55. $6(2^{3x-1}) - 7 = 9$

56. $8(4^{6-2x}) + 13 = 41$

57. $e^{2x} - 4e^x - 5 = 0$

58. $e^{2x} - 5e^x + 6 = 0$

59. $e^{2x} - 3e^x - 4 = 0$

60. $e^{2x} + 9e^x + 36 = 0$

61. $\dfrac{500}{100 - e^{x/2}} = 20$

62. $\dfrac{400}{1 + e^{-x}} = 350$

63. $\dfrac{3000}{2 + e^{2x}} = 2$

64. $\dfrac{119}{e^{6x} - 14} = 7$

65. $\left(1 + \dfrac{0.065}{365}\right)^{365t} = 4$

66. $\left(4 - \dfrac{2.471}{40}\right)^{9t} = 21$

67. $\left(1 + \dfrac{0.10}{12}\right)^{12t} = 2$

68. $\left(16 - \dfrac{0.878}{26}\right)^{3t} = 30$

In Exercises 69–76, use a graphing utility to solve the equation. Approximate the result to three decimal places. Verify your result algebraically.

69. $6e^{1-x} = 25$

70. $-4e^{-x-1} + 15 = 0$

71. $3e^{3x/2} = 962$

72. $8e^{-2x/3} = 11$

73. $e^{0.09t} = 3$

74. $-e^{1.8x} + 7 = 0$

75. $e^{0.125t} - 8 = 0$

76. $e^{2.724x} = 29$

In Exercises 77–104, solve the logarithmic equation algebraically. Approximate the result to three decimal places.

77. $\ln x = -3$

78. $\ln x = 2$

79. $\ln 2x = 2.4$

80. $\ln 4x = 1$

81. $\log_{10} x = 6$

82. $\log_{10} 3z = 2$

83. $6 \log_3(0.5x) = 11$

84. $5 \log_{10}(x - 2) = 11$

85. $3 \ln 5x = 10$

86. $2 \ln x = 7$

87. $\ln \sqrt{x + 2} = 1$

88. $\ln \sqrt{x - 8} = 5$

89. $7 + 3 \ln x = 5$

90. $2 - 6 \ln x = 10$

91. $\ln x - \ln(x + 1) = 2$

92. $\ln x + \ln(x + 1) = 1$

93. $\ln x + \ln(x - 2) = 1$

94. $\ln x + \ln(x + 3) = 1$

95. $\ln(x + 5) = \ln(x - 1) - \ln(x + 1)$

96. $\ln(x + 1) - \ln(x - 2) = \ln x$

97. $\log_2(2x - 3) = \log_2(x + 4)$

98. $\log_{10}(x - 6) = \log_{10}(2x + 1)$

99. $\log_{10}(x + 4) - \log_{10} x = \log_{10}(x + 2)$

100. $\log_2 x + \log_2(x + 2) = \log_2(x + 6)$

101. $\log_4 x - \log_4(x - 1) = \frac{1}{2}$

102. $\log_3 x + \log_3(x - 8) = 2$

103. $\log_{10} 8x - \log_{10}(1 + \sqrt{x}) = 2$

104. $\log_{10} 4x - \log_{10}(12 + \sqrt{x}) = 2$

 In Exercises 105–108, use a graphing utility to solve the equation. Approximate the result to three decimal places. Verify your result algebraically.

105. $7 = 2^x$

106. $500 = 1500e^{-x/2}$

107. $3 - \ln x = 0$

108. $10 - 4 \ln(x - 2) = 0$

Compound Interest In Exercises 109 and 110, find the time required for a $1000 investment to double at interest rate r, compounded continuously.

109. $r = 0.085$

110. $r = 0.12$

Compound Interest In Exercises 111 and 112, find the time required for a $1000 investment to triple at interest rate r, compounded continuously.

111. $r = 0.085$

112. $r = 0.12$

113. *Demand* The demand equation for a microwave oven is

$$p = 500 - 0.5(e^{0.004x}).$$

Find the demand x for a price of (a) $p = \$350$ and (b) $p = \$300$.

114. *Demand* The demand equation for a hand-held electronic organizer is

$$p = 5000 \left(1 - \frac{4}{4 + e^{-0.002x}}\right).$$

Find the demand x for a price of (a) $p = \$600$ and (b) $p = \$400$.

115. *Forest Yield* The yield V (in millions of cubic feet per acre) for a forest at age t years is

$$V = 6.7e^{-48.1/t}.$$

 (a) Use a graphing utility to graph the function.

(b) Determine the horizontal asymptote of the function. Interpret its meaning in the context of the problem.

(c) Find the time necessary to obtain a yield of 1.3 million cubic feet.

116. *Trees per Acre* The number of trees per acre N of a species is approximated by the model

$$N = 68(10^{-0.04x}), \qquad 5 \le x \le 40$$

where x is the average diameter of the trees 3 feet above the ground. Use the model to approximate the average diameter of the trees in a test plot when $N = 21$.

117. *Average Heights* The percent of American males between the ages of 18 and 24 who are no more than x inches tall is

$$m(x) = \frac{100}{1 + e^{-0.6114(x-69.71)}}$$

and the percent of American females between the ages of 18 and 24 who are no more than x inches tall is

$$f(x) = \frac{100}{1 + e^{-0.66607(x-64.51)}}$$

where m and f are the percents and x is the height in inches. (Source: U.S. National Center for Health Statistics)

(a) Use the graph to determine any horizontal asymptotes of the functions. Interpret the meaning in the context of the problem.

(b) What is the average height of each sex?

Height (in inches)

118. *Learning Curve* In a group project in learning theory, a mathematical model for the proportion P of correct responses after n trials was found to be

$$P = \frac{0.83}{1 + e^{-0.2n}}.$$

(a) Use a graphing utility to graph the function.

(b) Use the graph to determine any horizontal asymptotes of the function. Interpret the meaning of the upper asymptote in the context of this problem.

(c) After how many trials will 60% of the responses be correct?

▶ Model It

119. *Automobiles* Automobiles are designed with crumple zones that help protect their occupants in crashes. The crumple zones allow the occupants to move short distances when the automobiles come to abrupt stops. The greater the distance moved, the fewer g's the crash victims experience. (One g is equal to the acceleration due to gravity. For very short periods of time, humans have withstood as much as 40 g's.) In crash tests with vehicles moving at 90 kilometers per hour, analysts measured the numbers of g's experienced during deceleration by crash dummies that were permitted to move x meters during impact. The data is shown in the table.

x	g's
0.2	158
0.4	80
0.6	53
0.8	40
1.0	32

A model for this data is

$$y = -3.00 + 11.88 \ln x + \frac{36.94}{x}$$

where y is the number of g's.

(a) Complete the table using the model.

x	0.2	0.4	0.6	0.8	1.0
y					

(b) Use a graphing utility to graph the data points and the model in the same viewing window. How do they compare?

(c) Use the model to estimate the distance traveled during impact if the passenger deceleration must not exceed 30 g's.

(d) Do you think it is practical to lower the number of g's experienced during impact to fewer than 23? Explain your reasoning.

120. *Data Analysis* An object at a temperature of 160°C was removed from a furnace and placed in a room at 20°C. The temperature T of the object was measured each hour h and recorded in the table. A model for this data is $T = 20[1 + 7(2^{-h})]$. The graph of this model is shown in the figure.

Hour, h	Temperature, T
0	160°
1	90°
2	56°
3	38°
4	29°
5	24°

(a) Use the graph to identify the horizontal asymptote of the model and interpret the asymptote in the context of the problem.

(b) Use the model to approximate the time when the temperature of the object was 100°C.

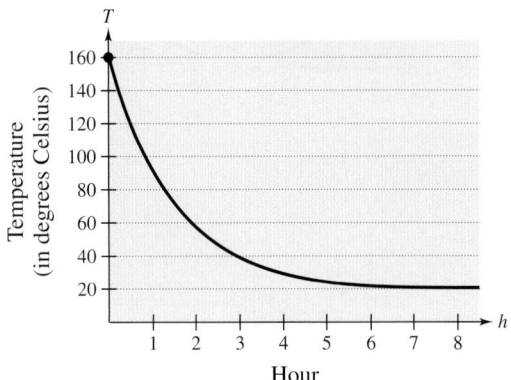

Synthesis

True or False? In Exercises 121–124, rewrite each verbal statement as an equation. Then decide whether the statement is true or false. Justify your answer.

121. The logarithm of the product of two numbers is equal to the sum of the logarithms of the numbers.

122. The logarithm of the sum of two numbers is equal to the product of the logarithms of the numbers.

123. The logarithm of the difference of two numbers is equal to the difference of the logarithms of the numbers.

124. The logarithm of the quotient of two numbers is equal to the difference of the logarithms of the numbers.

125. *Think About It* Is it possible for a logarithmic equation to have more than one extraneous solution? Explain.

126. *Finance* You are investing P dollars at an annual interest rate of r, compounded continuously, for t years. Which of the following would result in the highest value of the investment? Explain your reasoning.

(a) Double the amount you invest.

(b) Double your interest rate.

(c) Double the number of years.

127. *Think About It* Are the times required for the investments in Exercises 109 and 110 to quadruple twice as long as the times for them to double? Give a reason for your answer and verify your answer algebraically.

128. *Writing* Write two or three sentences stating the general guidelines that you follow when solving (a) exponential equations and (b) logarithmic equations.

Review

In Exercises 129–132, simplify the expression.

129. $\sqrt{48x^2y^5}$

130. $\sqrt{32} - 2\sqrt{25}$

131. $\sqrt[3]{25} \cdot \sqrt[3]{15}$

132. $\dfrac{3}{\sqrt{10} - 2}$

In Exercises 133–136, find a mathematical model for the verbal statement.

133. M varies directly as the cube of p.

134. t varies inversely as the cube of s.

135. d varies jointly as a and b.

136. x is inversely proportional to $b - 3$.

In Exercises 137–140, evaluate the logarithm using the change-of-base formula. Approximate your result to three decimal places.

137. $\log_6 9$

138. $\log_3 4$

139. $\log_{3/4} 5$

140. $\log_8 22$

3.5   Exponential and Logarithmic Models

▶ **What you should learn**

- How to recognize the five most common types of models involving exponential and logarithmic functions
- How to use exponential growth and decay functions to model and solve real-life problems
- How to use Gaussian functions to model and solve real-life problems
- How to use logistic growth functions to model and solve real-life problems
- How to use logarithmic functions to model and solve real-life problems

▶ **Why you should learn it**

Exponential growth and decay models are often used to model the population of a country. For instance, in Exercise 36 on page 244, you will use exponential growth and decay models to compare the populations of several countries.

Introduction

The five most common types of mathematical models involving exponential functions and logarithmic functions are as follows.

1. **Exponential growth model:** $y = ae^{bx}, \quad b > 0$
2. **Exponential decay model:** $y = ae^{-bx}, \quad b > 0$
3. **Gaussian model:** $y = ae^{-(x-b)^2/c}$
4. **Logistic growth model:** $y = \dfrac{a}{1 + be^{-rx}}$
5. **Logarithmic models:** $y = a + b \ln x, \quad y = a + b \log_{10} x$

The graphs of the basic forms of these functions are shown in Figure 3.28.

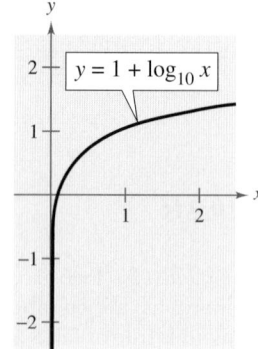

FIGURE 3.28

You can often gain quite a bit of insight into a situation modeled by an exponential or logarithmic function by identifying and interpreting the function's asymptotes. Use the graphs in Figure 3.28 to identify the asymptotes of each function.

This section shows students real-world applications for logarithmic and exponential functions.

Exponential Growth and Decay

Example 1 ► Population Increase

Estimates of the world population (in millions) from 1995 through 2003 are shown in the table. The scatter plot of the data is shown in Figure 3.29. (Source: U.S. Census Bureau)

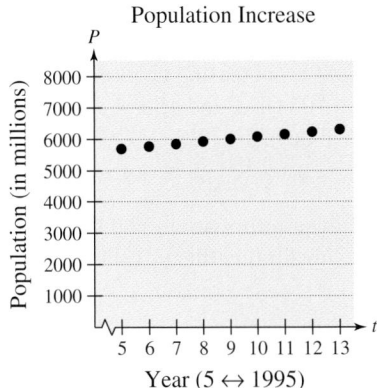

Population Increase

FIGURE 3.29

Year	Population
1995	5691
1996	5769
1997	5847
1998	5925
1999	6003

Year	Population
2000	6080
2001	6157
2002	6234
2003	6311

An exponential growth model that approximates this data is

$$P = 5340e^{0.012922t}, \quad 5 \le t \le 13$$

where P is the population (in millions) and $t = 5$ represents 1995. Compare the values given by the model with the estimates given by the U.S. Census Bureau. According to this model, when will the world population reach 6.8 billion?

Solution

The following table compares the two sets of population figures. The graph of the model is shown in Figure 3.30.

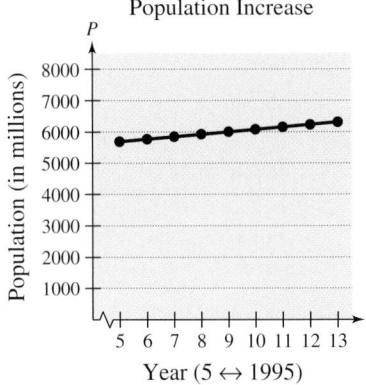

Population Increase

FIGURE 3.30

Year	1995	1996	1997	1998	1999	2000	2001	2002	2003
Population	5691	5769	5847	5925	6003	6080	6157	6234	6311
Model	5696	5771	5846	5922	5999	6077	6156	6236	6317

To find when the world population will reach 6.8 billion, let $P = 6800$ in the model and solve for t.

$5340e^{0.012922t} = P$	Write original model.
$5340e^{0.012922t} = 6800$	Let $P = 6800$.
$e^{0.012922t} \approx 1.27341$	Divide each side by 5340.
$\ln e^{0.012922t} \approx \ln 1.27341$	Take natural log of each side.
$0.012922t \approx 0.241698$	Inverse Property
$t \approx 18.7$	Divide each side by 0.012922.

According to the model, the world population will reach 6.8 billion in 2008.

Technology

Some graphing utilities have curve-fitting capabilities that can be used to find models that represent data. If you have such a graphing utility, try using it to find a model for the data given in Example 1. How does your model compare with the model given in Example 1?

Additional Example

Radioactive iodine is a by-product of some types of nuclear reactors. Its half-life is 60 days. That is, after 60 days, a given amount of radioactive iodine will have decayed to half the original amount. Suppose a contained nuclear accident occurs and gives off an initial amount C of radioactive iodine.

a. Write an equation for the amount of radioactive iodine present at any time t following the accident.

b. How long will it take for the radioactive iodine to decay to a level of 20% of the original amount?

Solution

a. Knowing that half the original amount remains after 60 days, you can use the exponential decay model $y = ae^{-bt}$ to obtain

$$\frac{1}{2}C = Ce^{-b(60)}$$

$$\frac{1}{2} = e^{-60b}$$

$$-\ln 2 = -60b$$

$$b = \frac{\ln 2}{60} \approx 0.0116.$$

So, $y = Ce^{-0.0116t}$.

b. The time required for the radioactive iodine to decay to 20% of the original amount is

$$Ce^{-0.0116t} = (0.2)C$$

$$e^{-0.0116t} = 0.2$$

$$-0.0116t = \ln 0.2$$

$$t = \frac{\ln 0.2}{-0.0116} \approx 139 \text{ days.}$$

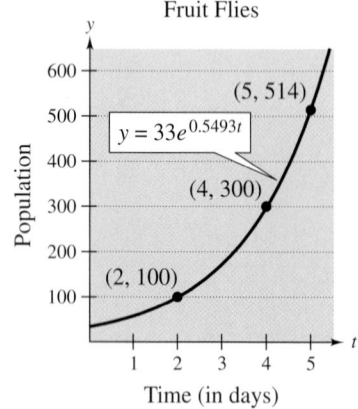

Fruit Flies

$y = 33e^{0.5493t}$

(5, 514)

(4, 300)

(2, 100)

Population

Time (in days)

FIGURE **3.31**

In Example 1, you were given the exponential growth model. But suppose this model were not given; how could you find such a model? One technique for doing this is demonstrated in Example 2.

Example 2 ▶ **Modeling Population Growth**

In a research experiment, a population of fruit flies is increasing according to the law of exponential growth. After 2 days there are 100 flies, and after 4 days there are 300 flies. How many flies will there be after 5 days?

Solution

Let y be the number of flies at time t. From the given information, you know that $y = 100$ when $t = 2$ and $y = 300$ when $t = 4$. Substituting this information into the model $y = ae^{bt}$ produces

$$100 = ae^{2b} \quad \text{and} \quad 300 = ae^{4b}.$$

To solve for b, solve for a in the first equation.

$$100 = ae^{2b} \quad \Longrightarrow \quad a = \frac{100}{e^{2b}} \qquad \text{Solve for } a \text{ in the first equation.}$$

Then substitute the result into the second equation.

$300 = ae^{4b}$	Write second equation.
$300 = \left(\dfrac{100}{e^{2b}}\right)e^{4b}$	Substitute $100/e^{2b}$ for a.
$\dfrac{300}{100} = e^{2b}$	Divide each side by 100.
$\ln 3 = 2b$	Take natural log of each side.
$\dfrac{1}{2}\ln 3 = b$	Solve for b.

Using $b = \frac{1}{2}\ln 3$ and the equation you found for a, you can determine that

$a = \dfrac{100}{e^{2[(1/2)\ln 3]}}$	Substitute $(1/2)\ln 3$ for b.
$= \dfrac{100}{e^{\ln 3}}$	Simplify.
$= \dfrac{100}{3}$	Inverse Property
$\approx 33.$	Simplify.

So, with $a \approx 33$ and $b = \frac{1}{2}\ln 3 \approx 0.5493$, the exponential growth model is

$$y = 33e^{0.5493t}$$

as shown in Figure 3.31. This implies that, after 5 days, the population will be

$$y = 33e^{0.5493(5)} \approx 514 \text{ flies.}$$

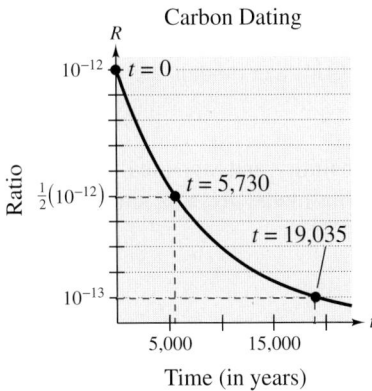

FIGURE 3.32

In living organic material, the ratio of the number of radioactive carbon isotopes (carbon 14) to the number of nonradioactive carbon isotopes (carbon 12) is about 1 to 10^{12}. When organic material dies, its carbon 12 content remains fixed, whereas its radioactive carbon 14 begins to decay with a half-life of 5730 years. To estimate the age of dead organic material, scientists use the following formula, which denotes the ratio of carbon 14 to carbon 12 present at any time t (in years).

$$R = \frac{1}{10^{12}}e^{-t/8267} \qquad \text{Carbon dating model}$$

The graph of R is shown in Figure 3.32. Note that R decreases as t increases.

Example 3 ▶ **Carbon Dating**

The ratio of carbon 14 to carbon 12 in a newly discovered fossil is

$$R = \frac{1}{10^{13}}.$$

Estimate the age of the fossil.

Solution

In the carbon dating model, substitute the given value of R to obtain the following.

$$\frac{1}{10^{12}}e^{-t/8267} = R \qquad \text{Write original model.}$$

$$\frac{e^{-t/8267}}{10^{12}} = \frac{1}{10^{13}} \qquad \text{Let } R = \frac{1}{10^{13}}.$$

$$e^{-t/8267} = \frac{1}{10} \qquad \text{Multiply each side by } 10^{12}.$$

$$\ln e^{-t/8267} = \ln\frac{1}{10} \qquad \text{Take natural log of each side.}$$

$$-\frac{t}{8267} \approx -2.3026 \qquad \text{Inverse Property}$$

$$t \approx 19{,}036 \qquad \text{Multiply each side by } -8267.$$

So, to the nearest thousand years, you can estimate the age of the fossil to be 19,000 years.

The carbon dating model in Example 3 assumed that the carbon 14/carbon 12 ratio was one part in 10,000,000,000,000. Suppose an error in measurement occurred and the actual ratio was only one part in 8,000,000,000,000. The fossil age corresponding to the actual ratio would then be approximately 17,000 years. Try checking this result.

Gaussian Models

As mentioned at the beginning of this section, Gaussian models are of the form

$$y = ae^{-(x-b)^2/c}.$$

This type of model is commonly used in probability and statistics to represent populations that are **normally distributed.** One model for this situation takes the form

$$y = \frac{1}{\sigma\sqrt{2\pi}}e^{-x^2/(2\sigma^2)}$$

where σ is the standard deviation (σ is the lowercase Greek letter sigma). The graph of a Gaussian model is called a **bell-shaped curve.**

The average value for a population can be found from the bell-shaped curve by observing where the maximum y-value of the function occurs. The x-value corresponding to the maximum y-value of the function represents the average value of the independent variable—in this case, x.

Example 4 ▶ **SAT Scores**

In 2001, the Scholastic Aptitude Test (SAT) math scores for college-bound seniors roughly followed a normal distribution

$$y = 0.0035e^{-(x-514)^2/25{,}538}, \quad 200 \le x \le 800$$

where x is the SAT score for mathematics. Sketch the graph of this function. From the graph, estimate the average SAT score.   (Source: College Board)

Solution

The graph of the function is shown in Figure 3.33. From the graph, you can see that the average mathematics score for college-bound seniors in 2001 was 514.

FIGURE **3.33**

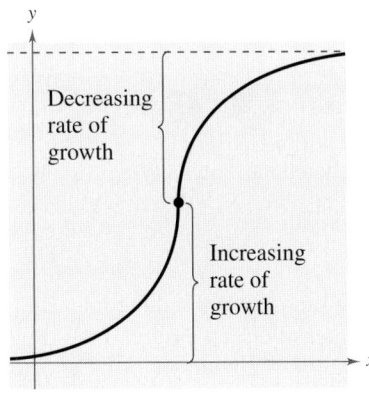

FIGURE **3.34**

Logistic Growth Models

Some populations initially have rapid growth, followed by a declining rate of growth, as indicated by the graph in Figure 3.34. One model for describing this type of growth pattern is the **logistic curve** given by the function

$$y = \frac{a}{1 + be^{-rx}}$$

where y is the population size and x is the time. An example is a bacteria culture that is initially allowed to grow under ideal conditions, and then under less favorable conditions that inhibit growth. A logistic growth curve is also called a **sigmoidal curve.**

Example 5 ▶ **Spread of a Virus**

On a college campus of 5000 students, one student returns from vacation with a contagious and long-lasting flu virus. The spread of the virus is modeled by

$$y = \frac{5000}{1 + 4999e^{-0.8t}}, \quad t \geq 0$$

where y is the total number of students infected after t days. The college will cancel classes when 40% or more of the students are infected.

a. How many students are infected after 5 days?

b. After how many days will the college cancel classes?

Solution

a. After 5 days, the number of students infected is

$$y = \frac{5000}{1 + 4999e^{-0.8(5)}} = \frac{5000}{1 + 4999e^{-4}} \approx 54.$$

b. Classes are canceled when the number infected is $(0.40)(5000) = 2000$.

$$2000 = \frac{5000}{1 + 4999e^{-0.8t}}$$

$$1 + 4999e^{-0.8t} = 2.5$$

$$e^{-0.8t} = \frac{1.5}{4999}$$

$$\ln e^{-0.8t} = \ln \frac{1.5}{4999}$$

$$-0.8t = \ln \frac{1.5}{4999}$$

$$t = -\frac{1}{0.8} \ln \frac{1.5}{4999}$$

$$t \approx 10.1$$

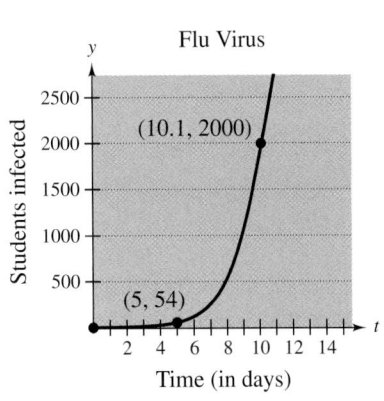

Flu Virus

(10.1, 2000)

(5, 54)

Time (in days)

FIGURE **3.35**

So, after 10 days, at least 40% of the students will be infected, and classes will be canceled. The graph of the function is shown in Figure 3.35.

On January 13, 2001 an earthquake of magnitude 7.7 in El Salvador caused 185 landslides and killed over 800 people.

Logarithmic Models

Example 6 ▶ **Magnitude of Earthquakes**

On the Richter scale, the magnitude R of an earthquake of intensity I is

$$R = \log_{10} \frac{I}{I_0}$$

where $I_0 = 1$ is the minimum intensity used for comparison. Find the intensities per unit of area for the following earthquakes. (Intensity is a measure of the wave energy of an earthquake.)

a. Tokyo and Yokohama, Japan in 1923: $R = 8.3$.

b. El Salvador in 2001: $R = 7.7$.

Solution

a. Because $I_0 = 1$ and $R = 8.3$, you have

$$8.3 = \log_{10} \frac{I}{1} \qquad \text{Substitute 1 for } I_0 \text{ and 8.3 for } R.$$

$$10^{8.3} = 10^{\log_{10} I} \qquad \text{Exponentiate each side.}$$

$$I = 10^{8.3} \approx 199{,}526{,}000. \qquad \text{Inverse property of exponents and logs}$$

b. For $R = 7.7$, you have

$$7.7 = \log_{10} \frac{I}{1} \qquad \text{Substitute 1 for } I_0 \text{ and 7.7 for } R.$$

$$10^{7.7} = 10^{\log_{10} I} \qquad \text{Exponentiate each side.}$$

$$I = 10^{7.7} \approx 50{,}119{,}000. \qquad \text{Inverse property of exponents and logs}$$

Note that an increase of 0.6 unit on the Richter scale (from 7.7 to 8.3) represents an increase in intensity by a factor of

$$\frac{199{,}526{,}000}{50{,}119{,}000} \approx 4.$$

In other words, the earthquake in 1923 had an intensity about 4 times greater than that of the 2001 earthquake.

t	Year	Population
1	1910	91.97
2	1920	105.71
3	1930	122.78
4	1940	131.67
5	1950	151.33
6	1960	179.32
7	1970	203.30
8	1980	226.54
9	1990	248.72
10	2000	281.42

Writing ABOUT MATHEMATICS

Comparing Population Models The population (in millions) of the United States from 1910 to 2000 is shown in the table at the left. (Source: U.S. Census Bureau) Least squares regression analysis gives the best quadratic model for this data as $P = 1.0317t^2 + 9.668t + 81.38$ and the best exponential model for this data as $P = 82.367e^{0.125t}$. Which model better fits the data? Describe the method you used to reach your conclusion.

3.5 Exercises

In Exercises 1–6, match the function with its graph. [The graphs are labeled (a), (b), (c), (d), (e), and (f).]

(a)

(b)

(c)

(d)

(e)

(f)
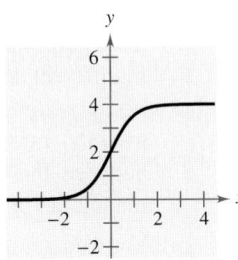

1. $y = 2e^{x/4}$

2. $y = 6e^{-x/4}$

3. $y = 6 + \log_{10}(x + 2)$

4. $y = 3e^{-(x-2)^2/5}$

5. $y = \ln(x + 1)$

6. $y = \dfrac{4}{1 + e^{-2x}}$

Compound Interest In Exercises 7–14, complete the table for a savings account in which interest is compounded continuously.

Initial Investment	Annual % Rate	Time to Double	Amount After 10 Years
7. $1000	12%		
8. $20,000	$10\frac{1}{2}\%$		
9. $750		$7\frac{3}{4}$ yr	
10. $10,000		12 yr	
11. $500			$1505.00
12. $600			$19,205.00
13.	4.5%		$10,000.00
14.	8%		$20,000.00

Compound Interest In Exercises 15 and 16, determine the principal P that must be invested at rate r, compounded monthly, so that $500,000 will be available for retirement in t years.

15. $r = 7\frac{1}{2}\%$, $t = 20$

16. $r = 12\%$, $t = 40$

Compound Interest In Exercises 17 and 18, determine the time necessary for $1000 to double if it is invested at interest rate r compounded (a) annually, (b) monthly, (c) daily, and (d) continuously.

17. $r = 11\%$

18. $r = 10\frac{1}{2}\%$

19. *Compound Interest* Complete the table for the time t necessary for P dollars to triple if interest is compounded continuously at rate r.

r	2%	4%	6%	8%	10%	12%
t						

 20. *Modeling Data* Draw a scatter plot of the data in Exercise 19. Use the *regression* feature of a graphing utility to find a model for the data.

21. *Compound Interest* Complete the table for the time t necessary for P dollars to triple if interest is compounded annually at rate r.

r	2%	4%	6%	8%	10%	12%
t						

22. *Modeling Data* Draw a scatter plot of the data in Exercise 21. Use the *regression* feature of a graphing utility to find a model for the data.

23. *Comparing Models* If $1 is invested in an account over a 10-year period, the amount in the account, where t represents the time in years, is

$$A = 1 + 0.075[\![t]\!] \quad \text{or} \quad A = e^{0.07t}$$

depending on whether the account pays simple interest at $7\frac{1}{2}\%$ or continuous compound interest at 7%. Graph each function on the same set of axes. Which grows at the faster rate? (Remember that $[\![t]\!]$ is the greatest integer function discussed in Section 1.5.)

24. *Comparing Models*   If \$1 is invested in an account over a 10-year period, the amount in the account, where t represents the time in years, is

$$A = 1 + 0.06[\![t]\!] \quad \text{or} \quad A = \left(1 + \frac{0.055}{365}\right)^{[\![365t]\!]}$$

depending on whether the account pays simple interest at 6% or compound interest at $5\frac{1}{2}\%$ compounded daily. Use a graphing utility to graph each function in the same viewing window. Which grows at the faster rate?

Radioactive Decay In Exercises 25–30, complete the table for the radioactive isotope.

Isotope	Half-life (years)	Initial Quantity	Amount After 1000 Years
25. ^{226}Ra	1620	10 g	
26. ^{226}Ra	1620		1.5 g
27. ^{14}C	5730		2 g
28. ^{14}C	5730	3 g	
29. ^{239}Pu	24,360		2.1 g
30. ^{239}Pu	24,360		0.4 g

In Exercises 31–34, find the exponential model $y = ae^{bx}$ that fits the points in the graph or table.

31.

32.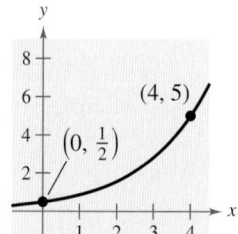

33.

x	0	4
y	5	1

34.

x	0	3
y	1	$\frac{1}{4}$

35. *Population*   The population P of Texas (in thousands) from 1991 through 2000 can be modeled by

$$P = 16{,}968e^{0.019t}$$

where $t = 1$ represents the year 1991. According to this model, when will the population reach 22 million?   (Source: U.S. Census Bureau)

▶ **Model It**

36. *Population*   The table shows the populations (in millions) of five countries in 2000 and the projected populations (in millions) for the year 2010.   (Source: U.S. Census Bureau)

Country	2000	2010
Canada	31.3	34.3
China	1261.8	1359.1
Italy	57.6	57.4
United Kingdom	59.5	60.6
United States	275.6	300.1

(a) Find the exponential growth or decay model $y = ae^{bt}$ or $y = ae^{-bt}$ for the population in each country by letting $t = 0$ correspond to 2000. Use the model to predict the population of each country in 2030.

(b) You can see that the populations of the United States and the United Kingdom are growing at different rates. What constant in the equation $y = ae^{bt}$ is determined by these different growth rates? Discuss the relationship between the different growth rates and the magnitude of the constant.

(c) You can see that the population of China is increasing while the population of Italy is decreasing. What constant in the equation $y = ae^{bt}$ reflects this difference? Explain.

37. *Population*   The population P of Charlotte, North Carolina (in thousands) is

$$P = 548e^{kt}$$

where $t = 0$ represents the year 2000. In 1970, the population was 241,000. Find the value of k, and use this result to predict the population in the year 2010. (Source: U.S. Census Bureau)

38. *Population*   The population P of Lincoln, Nebraska (in thousands) is

$$P = 224e^{kt}$$

where $t = 0$ represents the year 2000. In 1980, the population was 172,000. Find the value of k, and use this result to predict the population in the year 2020. (Source: U.S. Census Bureau)

39. Bacteria Growth The number N of bacteria in a culture is modeled by

$$N = 100e^{kt}$$

where t is the time in hours. If $N = 300$ when $t = 5$, estimate the time required for the population to double in size.

40. Bacteria Growth The number N of bacteria in a culture is modeled by $N = 250e^{kt}$, where t is the time in hours. If $N = 280$ when $t = 10$, estimate the time required for the population to double in size.

41. Radioactive Decay The half-life of radioactive radium (^{226}Ra) is 1620 years. What percent of a present amount of radioactive radium will remain after 100 years?

42. Radioactive Decay Carbon 14 dating assumes that the carbon dioxide on Earth today has the same radioactive content as it did centuries ago. If this is true, the amount of ^{14}C absorbed by a tree that grew several centuries ago should be the same as the amount of ^{14}C absorbed by a tree growing today. A piece of ancient charcoal contains only 15% as much radioactive carbon as a piece of modern charcoal. How long ago was the tree burned to make the ancient charcoal if the half-life of ^{14}C is 5730 years?

43. Depreciation A car that cost $22,000 new has a book value of $13,000 after 2 years.

(a) Find the straight-line model $V = mt + b$.

(b) Find the exponential model $V = ae^{kt}$.

 (c) Use a graphing utility to graph the two models in the same viewing window. Which model depreciates faster in the first 2 years?

(d) Find the book values of the car after 1 year and after 3 years using each model.

(e) Interpret the slope of the straight-line model.

44. Depreciation A computer that costs $2000 new has a book value of $500 after 2 years.

(a) Find the straight-line model $V = mt + b$.

(b) Find the exponential model $V = ae^{kt}$.

 (c) Use a graphing utility to graph the two models in the same viewing window. Which model depreciates faster in the first 2 years?

(d) Find the book values of the computer after 1 year and after 3 years using each model.

(e) Interpret the slope of the straight-line model.

45. Sales The sales S (in thousands of units) of a new CD burner after it has been on the market t years are modeled by $S(t) = 100(1 - e^{kt})$. Fifteen thousand units of the new product were sold the first year.

(a) Complete the model by solving for k.

(b) Sketch the graph of the model.

(c) Use the model to estimate the number of units sold after 5 years.

46. Sales After discontinuing all advertising for a tool kit in 1998, the manufacturer noted that sales began to drop according to the model

$$S = \frac{500,000}{1 + 0.6e^{kt}}$$

where S represents the number of units sold and $t = 0$ represents 1998. In 2000, the company sold 300,000 units.

(a) Complete the model by solving for k.

(b) Estimate sales in 2005.

47. Sales The sales S (in thousands of units) of a cleaning solution after x hundred dollars is spent on advertising are modeled by $S = 10(1 - e^{kx})$. When $500 is spent on advertising, 2500 units are sold.

(a) Complete the model by solving for k.

(b) Estimate the number of units that will be sold if advertising expenditures are raised to $700.

48. Profit Because of a slump in the economy, a department store finds that its annual profits have dropped from $742,000 in 2000 to $632,000 in 2002. The profit follows an exponential pattern of decline. What is the expected profit for 2005? (Let $t = 0$ represent 2000.)

49. Learning Curve The management at a plastics factory has found that the maximum number of units a worker can produce in a day is 30. The learning curve for the number N of units produced per day after a new employee has worked t days is

$$N = 30(1 - e^{kt}).$$

After 20 days on the job, a new employee produces 19 units.

(a) Find the learning curve for this employee (first, find the value of k).

(b) How many days should pass before this employee is producing 25 units per day?

50. *Population Growth*   A conservation organization releases 100 animals of an endangered species into a game preserve. The organization believes that the preserve has a carrying capacity of 1000 animals and that the growth of the herd will be modeled by the logistic curve

$$p(t) = \frac{1000}{1 + 9e^{-0.1656t}}$$

where t is measured in months (see figure).

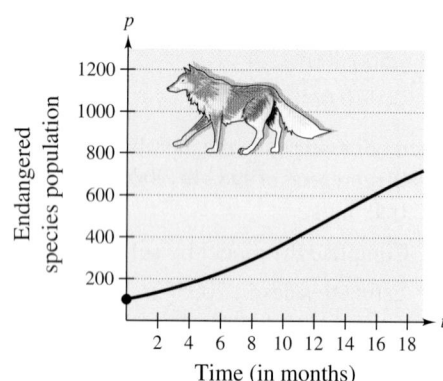

Time (in months)

(a) Estimate the population after 5 months.

(b) After how many months will the population be 500?

 (c) Use a graphing utility to graph the function. Use the graph to determine the horizontal asymptotes, and interpret the meaning of the larger p-value in the context of the problem.

Geology   In Exercises 51 and 52, use the Richter scale for measuring the magnitudes of earthquakes.

51. Find the magnitude R of an earthquake of intensity I (let $I_0 = 1$).

(a) $I = 80,500,000$

(b) $I = 48,275,000$

(c) $I = 251,200$

52. Find the intensity I of an earthquake measuring R on the Richter scale (let $I_0 = 1$).

(a) Chile in 1906, $R = 8.2$

(b) Los Angeles in 1971, $R = 6.7$

(c) India in 2001, $R = 7.7$

Intensity of Sound   In Exercises 53–56, use the following information for determining sound intensity. The level of sound β, in decibels, with an intensity of I is

$$\beta = 10 \log_{10} \frac{I}{I_0}$$

where I_0 is an intensity of 10^{-12} watt per square meter, corresponding roughly to the faintest sound that can be heard by the human ear. In Exercises 53 and 54, find the level of sound, β.

53. (a) $I = 10^{-10}$ watt per m² (faint whisper)

(b) $I = 10^{-5}$ watt per m² (busy street corner)

(c) $I = 10^{-2.5}$ watt per m² (air hammer)

(d) $I = 10^0$ watt per m² (threshold of pain)

54. (a) $I = 10^{-9}$ watt per m² (whisper)

(b) $I = 10^{-3.5}$ watt per m² (jet 4 miles from takeoff)

(c) $I = 10^{-3}$ watt per m² (diesel truck at 25 feet)

(d) $I = 10^{-0.5}$ watt per m² (auto horn at 3 feet)

55. Due to the installation of noise suppression materials, the noise level in an auditorium was reduced from 93 to 80 decibels. Find the percent decrease in the intensity level of the noise as a result of the installation of these materials.

56. Due to the installation of a muffler, the noise level of an engine was reduced from 88 to 72 decibels. Find the percent decrease in the intensity level of the noise as a result of the installation of the muffler.

pH Levels   In Exercises 57–62, use the acidity model given by $pH = -\log_{10} [H^+]$, where acidity (pH) is a measure of the hydrogen ion concentration $[H^+]$ (measured in moles of hydrogen per liter) of a solution.

57. Find the pH if $[H^+] = 2.3 \times 10^{-5}$.

58. Find the pH if $[H^+] = 11.3 \times 10^{-6}$.

59. Compute $[H^+]$ for a solution in which pH $= 5.8$.

60. Compute $[H^+]$ for a solution in which pH $= 3.2$.

61. A fruit has a pH of 2.5 and an antacid tablet has a pH of 9.5. The hydrogen ion concentration of the fruit is how many times the concentration of the tablet?

62. The pH of a solution is decreased by one unit. The hydrogen ion concentration is increased by what factor?

63. Forensics   At 8:30 A.M., a coroner was called to the home of a person who had died during the night. In order to estimate the time of death, the coroner took the person's temperature twice. At 9:00 A.M. the temperature was 85.7°F, and at 11:00 A.M. the temperature was 82.8°F. From these two temperatures, the coroner was able to determine that the time elapsed since death and the body temperature were related by the formula

$$t = -10 \ln \frac{T - 70}{98.6 - 70}$$

where t is the time in hours elapsed since the person died and T is the temperature (in degrees Fahrenheit) of the person's body. Assume that the person had a normal body temperature of 98.6°F at death, and that the room temperature was a constant 70°F. (This formula is derived from a general cooling principle called Newton's Law of Cooling.) Use the formula to estimate the time of death of the person.

 64. Home Mortgage   A $120,000 home mortgage for 35 years at $7\frac{1}{2}\%$ has a monthly payment of $809.39. Part of the monthly payment goes for the interest charge on the unpaid balance, and the remainder of the payment is used to reduce the principal. The amount that goes toward the interest is

$$u = M - \left(M - \frac{Pr}{12}\right)\left(1 + \frac{r}{12}\right)^{12t}$$

and the amount that goes toward the reduction of the principal is

$$v = \left(M - \frac{Pr}{12}\right)\left(1 + \frac{r}{12}\right)^{12t}.$$

In these formulas, P is the size of the mortgage, r is the interest rate, M is the monthly payment, and t is the time in years.

(a) Use a graphing utility to graph each function in the same viewing window. (The viewing window should show all 35 years of mortgage payments.)

(b) In the early years of the mortgage, the larger part of the monthly payment goes for what purpose? Approximate the time when the monthly payment is evenly divided between interest and principal reduction.

(c) Repeat parts (a) and (b) for a repayment period of 20 years ($M = \$966.71$). What can you conclude?

 65. Home Mortgage   The total interest u paid on a home mortgage of P dollars at interest rate r for t years is

$$u = P\left[\frac{rt}{1 - \left(\dfrac{1}{1 + r/12}\right)^{12t}} - 1\right].$$

Consider a $120,000 home mortgage at $7\frac{1}{2}\%$.

(a) Use a graphing utility to graph the total interest function.

(b) Approximate the length of the mortgage for which the total interest paid is the same as the size of the mortgage. Is it possible that some people are paying twice as much in interest charges as the size of the mortgage?

66. Data Analysis   The table shows the time t (in seconds) required to attain a speed of s miles per hour from a standing start for a car.

Speed, s	Time, t
30	3.4
40	5.0
50	7.0
60	9.3
70	12.0
80	15.8
90	20.0

Two models for this data are as follows.

$$t_1 = 40.757 + 0.556s - 15.817 \ln s$$

$$t_2 = 1.2259 + 0.0023s^2$$

(a) Use a graphing utility to fit a linear model t_3 and an exponential model t_4 to the data.

(b) Use a graphing utility to graph the data points and each model in the same viewing window.

(c) Create a table comparing the data with estimates obtained from each model.

(d) Use the results of part (c) to find the sum of the absolute values of the differences between the data and estimated values given by each model. Based on the four sums, which model do you think better fits the data? Explain.

Synthesis

True or False? **In Exercises 67–70, determine whether the statement is true or false. Justify your answer.**

67. The domain of a logistic growth function cannot be the set of real numbers.

68. A logistic growth function will always have an *x*-intercept.

69. The graph of

$$f(x) = \frac{4}{1 + 6e^{-2x}} + 5$$

is the graph of

$$g(x) = \frac{4}{1 + 6e^{-2x}}$$

shifted to the right five units.

70. The graph of a Gaussian model will never have an *x*-intercept.

71. Identify each model as linear, logarithmic, exponential, logistic, or none of the above. Explain your reasoning.

(a)

(b)

(c)

(d)

(e)

(f)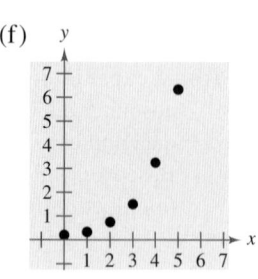

72. ***Writing*** Use your school's library, the Internet, or some other reference source to write a paper describing John Napier's work with logarithms.

Review

In Exercises 73–76, determine the right-hand and left-hand behavior of the polynomial function.

73. $f(x) = 2x^3 - 3x^2 + x - 1$

74. $f(x) = 5 - x^2 - 4x^4$

75. $g(x) = -1.6x^5 + 4x^2 - 2$

76. $g(x) = 7x^6 + 9.1x^5 - 3.2x^4 + 25x^3$

In Exercises 77–80, divide using synthetic division.

77. $\dfrac{4x^3 + 4x^2 - 39x + 36}{x + 4}$

78. $\dfrac{8x^3 - 36x^2 + 54x - 27}{x - \frac{3}{2}}$

79. $(2x^3 - 8x^2 + 3x - 9) \div (x - 4)$

80. $(x^4 - 3x + 1) \div (x + 5)$

In Exercises 81–90, sketch the graph of the equation.

81. $y = 10 - 3x$

82. $y = -4x - 1$

83. $y = -2x^2 - 3$

84. $y = 2x^2 - 7x - 30$

85. $3x^2 - 4y = 0$

86. $-x^2 - 8y = 0$

87. $y = \dfrac{4}{1 - 3x}$

88. $y = \dfrac{x^2}{-x - 2}$

89. $x^2 + (y - 8)^2 = 25$

90. $(x - 4)^2 + (y + 7) = 4$

In Exercises 91–94, graph the exponential function.

91. $f(x) = 2^{x-1} + 5$

92. $f(x) = -2^{-x-1} - 1$

93. $f(x) = 3^x - 4$

94. $f(x) = -3^x + 4$

Chapter Summary

▶ *What* did you learn?

Section 3.1	Review Exercises
☐ How to recognize and evaluate exponential functions with base *a*	1–10
☐ How to graph exponential functions	11–22, 27–30
☐ How to recognize and evaluate exponential functions with base *e*	23–26
☐ How to use exponential functions to model and solve real-life applications	31–36

Section 3.2	
☐ How to recognize and evaluate logarithmic functions with base *a*	37–42
☐ How to graph logarithmic functions	43–48, 55–58
☐ How to recognize and evaluate natural logarithmic functions	49–54
☐ How to use logarithmic functions to model and solve real-life applications	59, 60

Section 3.3	
☐ How to rewrite logarithmic functions with a different base	61–64
☐ How to use properties of logarithms to evaluate or rewrite and expand or condense logarithmic expressions	65–80
☐ How to use logarithmic functions to model and solve real-life applications	81, 82

Section 3.4	
☐ How to solve simple exponential and logarithmic equations	83–92
☐ How to solve more complicated exponential equations	93–106
☐ How to solve more complicated logarithmic equations	107–122
☐ How to use exponential and logarithmic equations to model and solve real-life applications	123, 124

Section 3.5	
☐ How to recognize the five most common types of models involving exponential and logarithmic functions	125–130
☐ How to use exponential growth and decay functions to model and solve real-life problems	131–136
☐ How to use Gaussian functions to model and solve real-life problems	137
☐ How to use logistic growth functions to model and solve real-life problems	138
☐ How to use logarithmic functions to model and solve real-life problems	139, 140

Review Exercises

 3.1 In Exercises 1–6, evaluate the expression. Approximate your result to three decimal places.

1. $(6.1)^{2.4}$

2. $-14(5^{-0.8})$

3. $2^{-0.5\pi}$

4. $\sqrt[5]{1278}$

5. $60^{\sqrt{3}}$

6. $7^{-\sqrt{11}}$

In Exercises 7–10, match the function with its graph. [The graphs are labeled (a), (b), (c), and (d).]

(a)

(b)

(c)

(d)

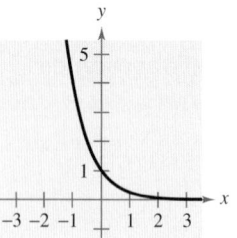

7. $f(x) = 4^x$

8. $f(x) = 4^{-x}$

9. $f(x) = -4^x$

10. $f(x) = 4^x + 1$

In Exercises 11–14, use the graph of f to describe the transformation that yields the graph of g.

11. $f(x) = 5^x, \quad g(x) = 5^{x-1}$

12. $f(x) = 4^x, \quad g(x) = 4^x - 3$

13. $f(x) = \left(\frac{1}{2}\right)^x, \quad g(x) = -\left(\frac{1}{2}\right)^{x+2}$

14. $f(x) = \left(\frac{2}{3}\right)^x, \quad g(x) = 8 - \left(\frac{2}{3}\right)^x$

 In Exercises 15–22, use a graphing utility to construct a table of values. Then sketch the graph of the function.

15. $f(x) = 4^{-x} + 4$

16. $f(x) = -4^x - 3$

17. $f(x) = -2.65^{x+1}$

18. $f(x) = 2.65^{x-1}$

19. $f(x) = 5^{x-2} + 4$

20. $f(x) = 2^{x-6} - 5$

21. $f(x) = \left(\frac{1}{2}\right)^{-x} + 3$

22. $f(x) = \left(\frac{1}{8}\right)^{x+2} - 5$

In Exercises 23–26, evaluate the function $f(x) = e^x$ for the indicated value of x. Approximate your result to three decimal places.

23. $x = 8$

24. $x = \dfrac{5}{8}$

25. $x = -1.7$

26. $x = 0.278$

In Exercises 27–30, use a graphing utility to construct a table of values. Then sketch the graph of the function.

27. $h(x) = e^{-x/2}$

28. $h(x) = 2 - e^{-x/2}$

29. $f(x) = e^{x+2}$

30. $s(t) = 4e^{-2/t}, \quad t > 0$

Compound Interest In Exercises 31 and 32, complete the table to determine the balance A for P dollars invested at rate r for t years and compounded n times per year.

n	1	2	4	12	365	Continuous
A						

31. $P = \$3500, \ r = 6.5\%, \ t = 10$ years

32. $P = \$2000, \ r = 5\%, \ t = 30$ years

33. ***Waiting Times*** The average time between incoming calls at a switchboard is 3 minutes. The probability F of waiting less than t minutes until the next incoming call is approximated by the model $F(t) = 1 - e^{-t/3}$. A call has just come in. Find the probability that the next call will be within

(a) $\frac{1}{2}$ minute.   (b) 2 minutes.   (c) 5 minutes.

34. ***Depreciation*** After t years, the value V of a car that cost \$14,000 is $V(t) = 14,000\left(\frac{3}{4}\right)^t$.

 (a) Use a graphing utility to graph the function.

(b) Find the value of the car 2 years after it was purchased.

(c) According to the model, when does the car depreciate most rapidly? Is this realistic? Explain.

35. ***Trust Fund*** On the day a person was born, a deposit of \$50,000 was made in a trust fund that pays 8.75% interest, compounded continuously.

(a) Find the balance on the person's 35th birthday.

(b) How much longer would the person have to wait to get twice as much?

36. Radioactive Decay Let Q represent a mass of plutonium 241 (^{241}Pu) (in grams), whose half-life is 13 years. The quantity of plutonium 241 present after t years is

$$Q = 100\left(\frac{1}{2}\right)^{t/13}.$$

(a) Determine the initial quantity (when $t = 0$).

(b) Determine the quantity present after 10 years.

(c) Sketch the graph of this function over the interval $t = 0$ to $t = 100$.

3.2 In Exercises 37 and 38, write the exponential equation in logarithmic form.

37. $4^3 = 64$

38. $25^{3/2} = 125$

In Exercises 39–42, evaluate the function at the indicated value of x without using a calculator.

Function	Value
39. $f(x) = \log_{10} x$	$x = 1000$
40. $g(x) = \log_9 x$	$x = 3$
41. $g(x) = \log_2 x$	$x = \frac{1}{8}$
42. $f(x) = \log_4 x$	$x = \frac{1}{4}$

In Exercises 43–48, find the domain, x-intercept, and vertical asymptote of the logarithmic function and sketch its graph.

43. $g(x) = \log_7 x$

44. $g(x) = \log_5 x$

45. $f(x) = \log_{10}\left(\frac{x}{3}\right)$

46. $f(x) = 6 + \log_{10} x$

47. $f(x) = 4 - \log_{10}(x + 5)$

48. $f(x) = \log_{10}(x - 3) + 1$

In Exercises 49–54, use your calculator to evaluate the function $f(x) = \ln x$ for the indicated value of x. Approximate your result to three decimal places if necessary.

49. $x = 22.6$

50. $x = 0.98$

51. $x = e^{-12}$

52. $x = e^7$

53. $x = \sqrt{7} + 5$

54. $x = \frac{\sqrt{3}}{8}$

In Exercises 55–58, find the domain, x-intercept, and vertical asymptote of the logarithmic function and sketch its graph.

55. $f(x) = \ln x + 3$

56. $f(x) = \ln(x - 3)$

57. $h(x) = \ln(x^2)$

58. $f(x) = \frac{1}{4}\ln x$

59. Antler Spread The antler spread a (in inches) and shoulder height h (in inches) of an adult male American elk are related by the model

$$h = 116\log_{10}(a + 40) - 176.$$

Approximate the shoulder height of a male American elk with an antler spread of 55 inches.

60. Snow Removal The number of miles s of roads cleared of snow is approximated by the model

$$s = 25 - \frac{13\ln(h/12)}{\ln 3}, \quad 2 \le h \le 15$$

where h is the depth of the snow in inches. Use this model to find s when $h = 10$ inches.

3.3 In Exercises 61–64, evaluate the logarithm using the change-of-base formula. Do each problem twice, once with common logarithms and once with natural logarithms. Approximate the results to three decimal places.

61. $\log_4 9$

62. $\log_{12} 200$

63. $\log_{1/2} 5$

64. $\log_3 0.28$

In Exercises 65–72, use the properties of logarithms to expand the expression as a sum, difference, and/or multiple of logarithms.

65. $\log_5 5x^2$

66. $\log_{10} 7x^4$

67. $\log_3 \frac{6}{\sqrt[3]{x}}$

68. $\log_7 \frac{\sqrt{x}}{4}$

69. $\ln x^2 y^2 z$

70. $\ln 3xy^2$

71. $\ln\left(\frac{x+3}{xy}\right)$

72. $\ln\left(\frac{y-1}{4}\right)^2, \quad y > 1$

In Exercises 73–80, condense the expression to the logarithm of a single quantity.

73. $\log_2 5 + \log_2 x$

74. $\log_6 y - 2\log_6 z$

75. $\ln x - \frac{1}{4}\ln y$

76. $3\ln x + 2\ln(x + 1)$

77. $\frac{1}{3}\log_8(x + 4) + 7\log_8 y$

78. $-2\log_{10} x - 5\log_{10}(x + 6)$

79. $\frac{1}{2}\ln(2x - 1) - 2\ln(x + 1)$

80. $5\ln(x - 2) - \ln(x + 2) - 3\ln x$

81. ***Climb Rate*** The time t (in minutes) for a small plane to climb to an altitude of h feet is modeled by

$$t = 50 \log_{10} \frac{18,000}{18,000 - h}$$

where 18,000 feet is the plane's absolute ceiling.

(a) Determine the domain of the function appropriate for the context of the problem.

 (b) Use a graphing utility to graph the time function and identify any asymptotes.

(c) As the plane approaches its absolute ceiling, what can be said about the time required to increase its altitude further?

(d) Find the time for the plane to climb to an altitude of 4000 feet.

82. ***Human Memory Model*** Students in a sociology class were given an exam and then were retested monthly with an equivalent exam. The average score for the class was given by the human memory model

$$f(t) = 85 - 14 \log_{10}(t + 1), \quad 0 \le t \le 4$$

where t is the time in months. How did the average score change over the four-month period?

3.4 In Exercises 83–92, solve for x.

83. $8^x = 512$ **84.** $3^x = 729$

85. $6^x = \frac{1}{216}$ **86.** $5^x = \frac{1}{25}$

87. $e^x = 3$ **88.** $e^x = 6$

89. $\log_4 x = 2$ **90.** $\log_6 x = -1$

91. $\ln x = 4$ **92.** $\ln x = -3$

In Exercises 93–102, solve the exponential equation. Approximate your result to three decimal places.

93. $e^x = 12$ **94.** $e^{3x} = 25$

95. $3e^{-5x} = 132$ **96.** $14e^{3x+2} = 560$

97. $2^x + 13 = 35$ **98.** $6^x - 28 = -8$

99. $-4(5^x) = -68$ **100.** $2(12^x) = 190$

101. $e^{2x} - 7e^x + 10 = 0$ **102.** $e^{2x} - 6e^x + 8 = 0$

 In Exercises 103–106, use a graphing utility to graph and solve the equation. Approximate the result to two decimal places.

103. $2^{0.6x} - 3x = 0$ **104.** $4^{-0.2x} + x = 0$

105. $25e^{-0.3x} = 12$ **106.** $4e^{1.2x} = 9$

In Exercises 107–118, solve the logarithmic equation. Approximate the result to three decimal places.

107. $\ln 3x = 8.2$ **108.** $\ln 5x = 7.2$

109. $2 \ln 4x = 15$ **110.** $4 \ln 3x = 15$

111. $\ln x - \ln 3 = 2$ **112.** $\ln \sqrt{x + 8} = 3$

113. $\ln \sqrt{x + 1} = 2$ **114.** $\ln x - \ln 5 = 4$

115. $\log_{10}(x - 1) = \log_{10}(x - 2) - \log_{10}(x + 2)$

116. $\log_{10}(x + 2) - \log_{10} x = \log_{10}(x + 5)$

117. $\log_{10}(1 - x) = -1$

118. $\log_{10}(-x - 4) = 2$

 In Exercises 119–122, use a graphing utility to graph and solve the equation. Approximate the result to two decimal places.

119. $2 \ln(x + 3) + 3x = 8$

120. $6 \log_{10}(x^2 + 1) - x = 0$

121. $4 \ln(x + 5) - x = 10$

122. $x - 2 \log_{10}(x + 4) = 0$

123. ***Compound Interest*** \$7550 is deposited in an account that pays 7.25% interest, compounded continuously. How long will it take the money to triple?

124. ***Demand*** The demand equation for a 32-inch television is modeled by $p = 500 - 0.5e^{0.004x}$. Find the demand x for a price of (a) $p = \$450$ and (b) $p = \$400$.

3.5 In Exercises 125–130, match the function with its graph. [The graphs are labeled (a), (b), (c), (d), (e), and (f).]

(a)

(b)

(c)

(d)

(e)

(f)

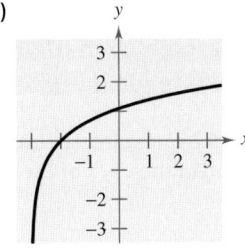

125. $y = 3e^{-2x/3}$

126. $y = 4e^{2x/3}$

127. $y = \ln(x + 3)$

128. $y = 7 - \log_{10}(x + 3)$

129. $y = 2e^{-(x+4)^2/3}$

130. $y = \dfrac{6}{1 + 2e^{-2x}}$

131. ***Population*** The population P of Phoenix, Arizona (in thousands) from 1970 through 2000 can be modeled by $P = 590e^{0.027t}$, where t represents the year, with $t = 0$ corresponding to 1970. According to this model, when will the population reach 1.5 million? (Source: U.S. Census Bureau)

132. ***Radioactive Decay*** The half-life of radioactive uranium II (^{234}U) is 250,000 years. What percent of a present amount of radioactive uranium II will remain after 5000 years?

133. ***Compound Interest*** A deposit of $10,000 is made in a savings account for which the interest is compounded continuously. The balance will double in 5 years.

(a) What is the annual interest rate for this account?

(b) Find the balance after 1 year.

134. ***Bacteria Growth*** The number N of bacteria in a culture is given by the model $N = 200e^{kt}$, where t is the time in hours. If $N = 350$ when $t = 5$, estimate the time required for the population to triple in size.

In Exercises 135 and 136, find the exponential function $y = ae^{bx}$ that passes through the points.

135. $(0, 2), (4, 3)$

136. $\left(0, \frac{1}{2}\right), (5, 5)$

 137. ***Test Scores*** The test scores for a biology test follow a normal distribution modeled by

$y = 0.0499e^{-(x-71)^2/128}$, $40 \le x \le 100$

where x is the test score.

(a) Use a graphing utility to graph the equation.

(b) From the graph, estimate the average test score.

138. ***Typing Speed*** In a typing class, the average number of words per minute typed after t weeks of lessons was found to be

$$N = \frac{157}{1 + 5.4e^{-0.12t}}.$$

Find the time necessary to type (a) 50 words per minute and (b) 75 words per minute.

139. ***Sound Intensity*** The relationship between the number of decibels β and the intensity of a sound I in watts per square centimeter is

$$\beta = 10 \log_{10}\left(\frac{I}{10^{-16}}\right).$$

Determine the intensity of a sound in watts per square centimeter if the decibel level is 125.

140. ***Geology*** On the Richter scale, the magnitude R of an earthquake of intensity I is

$$R = \log_{10}\frac{I}{I_0}$$

where $I_0 = 1$ is the minimum intensity used for comparison. Find the intensity per unit of area for each value of R.

(a) $R = 8.4$ (b) $R = 6.85$ (c) $R = 9.1$

Synthesis

True or False? **In Exercises 141 and 142, determine whether the equation or statement is true or false. Justify your answer.**

141. $\log_b b^{2x} = 2x$

142. $\ln(x + y) = \ln x + \ln y$

143. The graphs of $y = e^{kt}$ are shown for $k = a, b, c,$ and d. Use the graphs to order $a, b, c,$ and d. Which of the four values are negative? Which are positive?

(a)

(b)

(c)

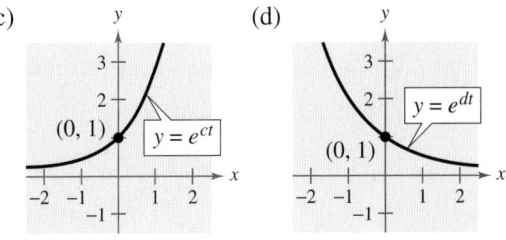

(d)

Chapter Test

Take this test as you would take a test in class. When you are finished, check your work against the answers given in the back of the book.

In Exercises 1–4, evaluate the expression. Approximate your result to three decimal places.

1. $12.4^{2.79}$ **2.** $4^{3\pi/2}$ **3.** $e^{-7/10}$ **4.** $e^{3.1}$

In Exercises 5–7, construct a table of values. Then sketch the graph of the function.

5. $f(x) = 10^{-x}$ **6.** $f(x) = -6^{x-2}$ **7.** $f(x) = 1 - e^{2x}$

8. Evaluate (a) $\log_7 7^{-0.89}$ and (b) $4.6 \ln e^2$.

In Exercises 9–11, construct a table of values. Then sketch the graph of the function. Identify any asymptotes.

9. $f(x) = -\log_{10} x - 6$ **10.** $f(x) = \ln(x - 4)$ **11.** $f(x) = 1 + \ln(x + 6)$

In Exercises 12–14, evaluate the expression. Approximate your result to three decimal places.

12. $\log_7 44$ **13.** $\log_{2/5} 0.9$ **14.** $\log_{24} 68$

In Exercises 15 and 16, use the properties of logarithms to expand the expression as a sum, difference, and/or multiple of logarithms.

15. $\log_2 3a^4$ **16.** $\ln \dfrac{5\sqrt{x}}{6}$

In Exercises 17 and 18, condense the expression to the logarithm of a single quantity.

17. $\log_3 13 + \log_3 y$ **18.** $4 \ln x - 4 \ln y$

In Exercises 19 and 20, solve the equation algebraically. Approximate your result to three decimal places.

19. $\dfrac{1025}{8 + e^{4x}} = 5$ **20.** $\log_{10} x - \log_{10}(8 - 5x) = 2$

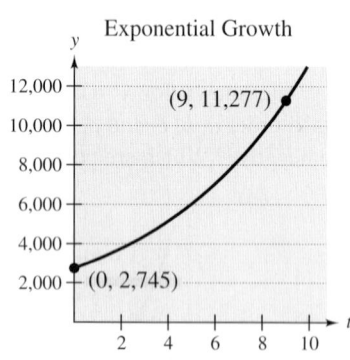

Exponential Growth

(9, 11,277)

(0, 2,745)

FIGURE FOR 21

21. Find an exponential growth model for the graph shown in the figure.

22. The half-life of radioactive actinium (^{227}Ac) is 22 years. What percent of a present amount of radioactive actinium will remain after 19 years?

23. A model that can be used for predicting the height H (in centimeters) of a child based on his or her age is $H = 70.228 + 5.104x + 9.222 \ln x$, $\frac{1}{4} \le x \le 6$, where x is the age of the child in years.   (Source: Snapshots of Applications in Mathematics)

(a) Construct a table of values. Then sketch the graph of the model.

(b) Use the graph from part (a) to estimate the height of a four-year-old child. Then calculate the actual height using the model.

Cumulative Test for Chapters 1–3

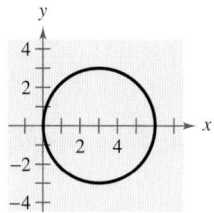

FIGURE FOR 5

Take this test to review the material from earlier chapters. When you are finished, check your work against the answers given in the back of the book.

In Exercises 1–3, use intercepts and symmetry to sketch the graph of the equation.

1. $y = \sqrt{x - 5}$

2. $y = |x - 5|$

3. $y = x^3 - 4$

4. Find an equation for the line passing through $\left(-\frac{1}{2}, 1\right)$ and $(3, 8)$.

5. Explain why the graph at the left does not represent y as a function of x.

6. Evaluate (if possible) the function $f(x) = \dfrac{x}{x - 2}$ for each value.

(a) $f(6)$ (b) $f(2)$ (c) $f(s + 2)$

7. Describe how the graph of each function would differ from the graph of $y = \sqrt[3]{x}$. (*Note:* It is not necessary to sketch the graphs.)

(a) $r(x) = \frac{1}{2}\sqrt[3]{x}$ (b) $h(x) = \sqrt[3]{x} + 2$ (c) $g(x) = \sqrt[3]{x + 2}$

In Exercises 8 and 9, find (a) $(f + g)(x)$, (b) $(f - g)(x)$, (c) $(fg)(x)$, and (d) $(f/g)(x)$. What is the domain of f/g?

8. $f(x) = x - 3$, $g(x) = 4x + 1$

9. $f(x) = \sqrt{x - 1}$, $g(x) = x^2 + 1$

In Exercises 10 and 11, find (a) $f \circ g$ and (b) $g \circ f$.

10. $f(x) = 2x^2$, $g(x) = \sqrt{x + 6}$

11. $f(x) = x - 2$, $g(x) = |x|$

12. Determine whether $h(x) = \sqrt{5x - 3}$ has an inverse function. If so, find it.

13. The power P produced by a wind turbine is proportional to the cube of the wind speed S. A wind speed of 27 miles per hour produces a power output of 750 kilowatts. Find the output for a wind speed of 40 miles per hour.

14. Find the quadratic function $y = a(x - h)^2 + k$ whose graph has a vertex at $(-8, 5)$ and passes through the point $(-4, -7)$.

In Exercises 15–17, sketch the graph of the function without the aid of a graphing utility.

15. $h(x) = -(x^2 + 4x)$ **16.** $f(t) = \frac{1}{4}t(t - 2)^2$ **17.** $g(s) = s^2 + 4s + 10$

In Exercises 18–20, find all the zeros of the function and write the function as a product of linear factors.

18. $f(x) = x^3 + 2x^2 + 4x + 8$ **19.** $f(x) = 6x^3 - 43x^2 + 37x + 140$

20. $f(x) = 2x^4 - 11x^3 + 30x^2 - 62x - 40$

21. Divide $6x^3 - 4x^2$ by $2x^2 + 1$.

22. Use synthetic division to divide $2x^4 + 3x^3 - 6x + 5$ by $x + 2$.

23. Use the Intermediate Value Theorem and a graphing utility to find intervals one unit in length in which the function $g(x) = x^3 + 3x^2 - 6$ is guaranteed to have a zero. Approximate the real zeros of the function.

24. Find a polynomial with integer coefficients that has -5, -2, and $2 + \sqrt{3}i$ as its zeros.

In Exercises 25–27, sketch the graph of the rational function by hand. Be sure to identify all intercepts and asymptotes.

25. $f(x) = \dfrac{2x}{x - 3}$

26. $f(x) = \dfrac{2x}{x^2 - 9}$

27. $g(x) = \dfrac{x^3 - 6x}{x^2 - 2x + 3}$

In Exercises 28 and 29, write the partial fraction decomposition of the rational expression. Check your result algebraically.

28. $\dfrac{8}{x^2 - 4x - 21}$

29. $\dfrac{5x}{(x - 4)^2}$

 In Exercises 30 and 31, use the graph of f to describe the transformation that yields the graph of g. Use a graphing utility to graph both equations in the same viewing window.

30. $f(x) = \left(\frac{2}{5}\right)^x, \quad g(x) = -\left(\frac{2}{5}\right)^{-x+3}$

31. $f(x) = 2.2^x, \quad g(x) = -2.2^x + 4$

In Exercises 32–35, use a calculator to evaluate each expression. Approximate your result to three decimal places.

32. $\log_{10} 98$

33. $\log_{10}\left(\frac{6}{7}\right)$

34. $\ln \sqrt{31}$

35. $\ln\left(\sqrt{40} - 5\right)$

In Exercises 36–38, evaluate the logarithm using the change-of-base formula. Approximate your answer to three decimal places.

36. $\log_7 1.8$

37. $\log_3 0.149$

38. $\log_{1/2} 17$

39. Use the logarithmic properties to expand $\ln\left(\dfrac{x^2 - 16}{x^4}\right)$, where $x > 4$.

40. Write $2 \ln x - \frac{1}{2} \ln(x + 5)$ as a logarithm of a single quantity.

In Exercises 41 and 42, solve the equation.

41. $6e^{2x} = 72$

42. $\log_2 x + \log_2 5 = 6$

43. The numbers D of new car dealerships in the United States from 1994 through 2000 are shown in the table. (Source: National Automobile Dealers Association)

Year, t	Dealerships, D
1994	22,850
1995	22,800
1996	22,750
1997	22,700
1998	22,600
1999	22,400
2000	22,250

(a) Use a graphing utility to create a scatter plot of the data.

(b) A model for this data is given by $D = -16.07t^2 + 126.8t + 22,586$, where t represents the year, with $t = 4$ corresponding to 1994. Use a graphing utility to graph the model in the same viewing window as the scatter plot.

(c) Do you think this model could be used to predict the numbers of new car dealerships in the future? Explain.

44. The number N of bacteria in a culture is given by the model $N = 175e^{kt}$, where t is the time in hours. If $N = 420$ when $t = 8$, estimate the time required for the population to double in size.

Proofs in Mathematics

Each of the following three properties of logarithms can be proved by using properties of exponential functions.

Slide Rules

The slide rule was invented by William Oughtred (1574–1660) in 1625. The slide rule is a computational device with a sliding portion and a fixed portion. A slide rule enables you to perform multiplication by using Property 1 of the Properties of Logarithms. There are other slide rules that allow for the calculation of roots and trigonometric functions. Slide rules were used by mathematicians and engineers until the invention of the handheld calculator in 1972.

Properties of Logarithms (p. 220)

Let a be a positive number such that $a \neq 1$, and let n be a real number. If u and v are positive real numbers, the following properties are true.

Logarithm with Base a	*Natural Logarithm*
1. $\log_a(uv) = \log_a u + \log_a v$	**1.** $\ln(uv) = \ln u + \ln v$
2. $\log_a \dfrac{u}{v} = \log_a u - \log_a v$	**2.** $\ln \dfrac{u}{v} = \ln u - \ln v$
3. $\log_a u^n = n \log_a u$	**3.** $\ln u^n = n \ln u$

Proof

Let

$$x = \log_a u \quad \text{and} \quad y = \log_a v.$$

The corresponding exponential forms of these two equations are

$$a^x = u \quad \text{and} \quad a^y = v.$$

To prove Property 1, multiply u and v to obtain

$$uv = a^x a^y = a^{x+y}.$$

The corresponding logarithmic form of $uv = a^{x+y}$ is $\log_a(uv) = x + y$. So,

$$\log_a(uv) = \log_a u + \log_a v.$$

To prove Property 2, divide u by v to obtain

$$\frac{u}{v} = \frac{a^x}{a^y} = a^{x-y}.$$

The corresponding logarithmic form of $u/v = a^{x-y}$ is $\log_a(u/v) = x - y$. So,

$$\log_a(u/v) = \log_a u - \log_a v.$$

To prove Property 3, substitute a^x for u in the expression $\log_a u^n$, as follows.

$$\log_a u^n = \log_a(a^x)^n \qquad \text{Substitute } a^x \text{ for } u.$$
$$= \log_a a^{nx} \qquad \text{Property of exponents}$$
$$= nx \qquad \text{Inverse Property of Logarithms}$$
$$= n \log_a u \qquad \text{Substitute } \log_a u \text{ for } x.$$

So, $\log_a u^n = n \log_a u.$

1. Graph the exponential function $y = a^x$ for $a = 0.5$, 1.2, and 2.0. Which of these curves intersects the line $y = x$? Determine all positive numbers a for which the curve $y = a^x$ intersects the line $y = x$.

2. Use a graphing utility to graph $y_1 = e^x$ and each of the functions $y_2 = x^2$, $y_3 = x^3$, $y_4 = \sqrt{x}$, and $y_5 = |x|$. Which function increases at the fastest rate as x approaches $+\infty$?

3. Use the result of Exercise 2 to make a conjecture about the rate of growth of $y_1 = e^x$ and $y = x^n$, where n is a natural number and x approaches $+\infty$.

4. Use the results of Exercises 2 and 3 to describe what is implied when it is stated that a quantity is growing exponentially.

5. Given the exponential function

   $$f(x) = a^x$$

   show that

   (a) $f(u + v) = f(u) \cdot f(v)$.

   (b) $f(2x) = [f(x)]^2$.

6. Given that

   $$f(x) = \frac{e^x + e^{-x}}{2} \text{ and } g(x) = \frac{e^x - e^{-x}}{2}$$

   show that

   $$[f(x)]^2 - [g(x)]^2 = 1.$$

7. Use a graphing utility to compare the graph of the function $y = e^x$ with the graph of each given function. [$n!$ (read "n factorial") is defined as $n! = 1 \cdot 2 \cdot 3 \cdots (n - 1) \cdot n$.]

   (a) $y_1 = 1 + \dfrac{x}{1!}$

   (b) $y_2 = 1 + \dfrac{x}{1!} + \dfrac{x^2}{2!}$

   (c) $y_3 = 1 + \dfrac{x}{1!} + \dfrac{x^2}{2!} + \dfrac{x^3}{3!}$

8. Identify the pattern of successive polynomials given in Exercise 7. Extend the pattern one more term and compare the graph of the resulting polynomial function with the graph of $y = e^x$. What do you think this pattern implies?

9. Graph the function

   $$f(x) = e^x - e^{-x}.$$

   From the graph, the function appears to be one-to-one. Assuming that the function has an inverse function, find $f^{-1}(x)$.

10. Find a pattern for $f^{-1}(x)$ if

    $$f(x) = \frac{a^x + 1}{a^x - 1}$$

    where $a > 0$, $a \neq 1$.

11. By observation, identify the equation that corresponds to the graph. Explain your reasoning.

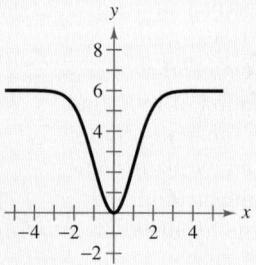

   (a) $y = 6e^{-x^2/2}$

   (b) $y = \dfrac{6}{1 + e^{-x/2}}$

   (c) $y = 6(1 - e^{-x^2/2})$

12. There are two options for investing $500. The first earns 7% compounded annually and the second earns 7% simple interest. The figure shows the growth of each investment over a 30-year period.

    (a) Identify which graph represents each type of investment. Explain your reasoning.

    (b) Verify your answer in part (a) by finding the equations that model the investment growth and graphing the models.

13. Two different samples of radioactive isotopes are decaying. The isotopes have initial amounts of c_1 and c_2, as well as half-lives of k_1 and k_2, respectively. Find the time required for the samples to decay to equal amounts.

14. A lab culture initially contains 500 bacteria. Two hours later, the number of bacteria has decreased to 200. Find the exponential decay model of the form

$$B = B_0 a^{kt}$$

that can be used to approximate the number of bacteria after t hours.

 15. The table shows the colonial population estimates of the American colonies from 1700 to 1780. (Source: U.S. Census Bureau)

Year	Population
1700	250,900
1710	331,700
1720	466,200
1730	629,400
1740	905,600
1750	1,170,800
1760	1,593,600
1770	2,148,100
1780	2,780,400

In each of the following, let y represent the population in the year t, with $t = 0$ corresponding to 1700.

(a) Use the *regression* feature of a graphing utility to find an exponential model for the data.

(b) Use the *regression* feature of the graphing utility to find a quadratic model for the data.

(c) Use the graphing utility to plot the data and the models from parts (a) and (b) in the same viewing window.

(d) Which model is a better fit for the data? Would you use this model to predict the population of the United States in 2010? Explain your reasoning.

16. Show that $\dfrac{\log_a x}{\log_{a/b} x} = 1 + \log_a \dfrac{1}{b}$.

17. Solve $(\ln x)^2 = \ln x^2$.

 18. Use a graphing utility to compare the graph of the function $y = \ln x$ with the graph of each given function.

(a) $y_1 = x - 1$

(b) $y_2 = (x - 1) - \frac{1}{2}(x - 1)^2$

(c) $y_3 = (x - 1) - \frac{1}{2}(x - 1)^2 + \frac{1}{3}(x - 1)^3$

19. Identify the pattern of successive polynomials given in Exercise 18. Extend the pattern one more term and compare the graph of the resulting polynomial function with the graph of $y = \ln x$. What do you think the pattern implies?

20. Using

$$y = ab^x \text{ and } y = ax^b$$

take the natural logarithm of each side of each equation. What are the slope and y-intercept of the line relating x and $\ln y$ for $y = ab^x$? What are the slope and y-intercept of the line relating $\ln x$ and $\ln y$ for $y = ax^b$?

In Exercises 21 and 22, use the model

$$y = 80.4 - 11 \ln x, \quad 100 \le x \le 1500$$

which approximates the minimum required ventilation rate in terms of the air space per child in a public school classroom. In the model, x is the air space per child in cubic feet and y is the ventilation rate in cubic feet per minute.

 21. Use a graphing utility to graph the function and approximate the required ventilation rate if there is 300 cubic feet of air space per child.

22. A classroom is designed for 30 students. The air conditioning system in the room has the capacity of moving 450 cubic feet of air per minute.

(a) Determine the ventilation rate per child, assuming that the room is filled to capacity.

(b) Estimate the air space required per child.

(c) Determine the minimum number of square feet of floor space required for the room if the ceiling height is 30 feet.

How to study Chapter 4

▶ **What you should learn**

In this chapter you will learn the following skills and concepts:

- How to describe an angle and convert between radian and degree measure
- How to identify a unit circle and its relationship to real numbers
- How to evaluate trigonometric functions of any angle
- How to use the fundamental trigonometric identities
- How to sketch the graphs of trigonometric functions and translations of graphs of sine and cosine functions
- How to evaluate the inverse trigonometric functions
- How to evaluate the compositions of trigonometric functions and inverse trigonometric functions

▶ **Important Vocabulary**

As you encounter each new vocabulary term in this chapter, add the term and its definition to your notebook glossary.

Trigonometry (p. 262)
Angle (p. 262)
Initial side (of an angle) (p. 262)
Terminal side (of an angle) (p. 262)
Vertex (of an angle) (p. 262)
Standard position (p. 262)
Coterminal angles (p. 262)
Central angle (p. 263)
Radian (p. 263)
Acute angles (p. 263)
Obtuse angles (p. 263)
Complementary angles (p. 265)
Supplementary angles (p. 265)
Degree (p. 265)
Linear speed (p. 267)
Angular speed (p. 267)
Unit circle (p. 273)

Sine (pp. 274, 280)
Cosecant (pp. 274, 280)
Cosine (pp. 274, 280)
Secant (pp. 274, 280)
Tangent (pp. 274, 280)
Cotangent (pp. 274, 280)
Period (pp. 276, 303)
Angle of elevation (p. 285)
Angle of depression (p. 285)
Reference angles (p. 293)
Amplitude (p. 302)
Phase shift (p. 304)
Damping factor (p. 316)
Inverse sine function (p. 322)
Inverse cosine function (p. 324)
Inverse tangent function (p. 324)

Study Tools

Learning objectives in each section
Chapter Summary (p. 343)
Review Exercises (pp. 344–347)
Chapter Test (p. 348)

Additional Resources

Study and Solutions Guide
Interactive Precalculus
Videotapes/DVD for Chapter 4
Precalculus Website
Student Success Organizer

Raymond Forbes/SuperStock

4

Trigonometry

4.1   Radian and Degree Measure

▶ **What you should learn**

- How to describe angles
- How to use radian measure
- How to use degree measure
- How to use angles to model and solve real-life problems

▶ **Why you should learn it**

You can use angles to model and solve real-life problems. For instance, in Exercise 101 on page 272, you are asked to use angles to find the speed of a bicycle.

Angles

As derived from the Greek language, the word **trigonometry** means "measurement of triangles." Initially, trigonometry dealt with relationships among the sides and angles of triangles and was used in the development of astronomy, navigation, and surveying. With the development of calculus and the physical sciences in the 17th century, a different perspective arose—one that viewed the classic trigonometric relationships as *functions* with the set of real numbers as their domains. Consequently, the applications of trigonometry expanded to include a vast number of physical phenomena involving rotations and vibrations. These phenomena include sound waves, light rays, planetary orbits, vibrating strings, pendulums, and orbits of atomic particles.

The approach in this text incorporates *both* perspectives, starting with angles and their measure.

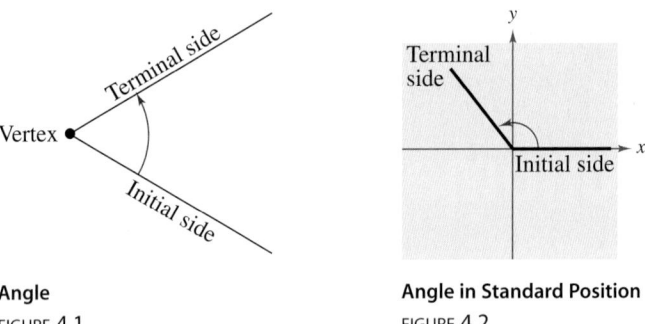

Angle

FIGURE 4.1

Angle in Standard Position

FIGURE 4.2

An **angle** is determined by rotating a ray (half-line) about its endpoint. The starting position of the ray is the **initial side** of the angle, and the position after rotation is the **terminal side,** as shown in Figure 4.1. The endpoint of the ray is the **vertex** of the angle. This perception of an angle fits a coordinate system in which the origin is the vertex and the initial side coincides with the positive *x*-axis. Such an angle is in **standard position,** as shown in Figure 4.2. **Positive angles** are generated by counterclockwise rotation, and **negative angles** by clockwise rotation, as shown in Figure 4.3. Angles are labeled with Greek letters α (alpha), β (beta), and θ (theta), as well as uppercase letters A, B, and C. In Figure 4.4, note that angles α and β have the same initial and terminal sides. Such angles are **coterminal.**

FIGURE 4.3

FIGURE 4.4

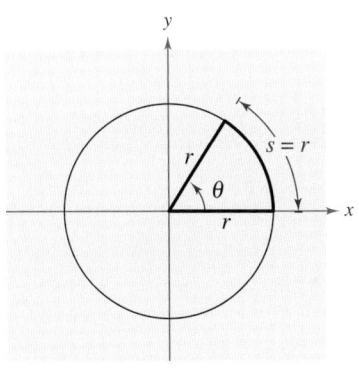

Arc length = *radius when* θ = 1 *radian*
FIGURE 4.5

Radian Measure

The **measure of an angle** is determined by the amount of rotation from the initial side to the terminal side. One way to measure angles is in *radians*. This type of measure is especially useful in calculus. To define a radian, you can use a **central angle** of a circle, one whose vertex is the center of the circle, as shown in Figure 4.5.

Definition of Radian

One **radian** is the measure of a central angle θ that intercepts an arc s equal in length to the radius r of the circle. See Figure 4.5.

Because the circumference of a circle is $2\pi r$ units, it follows that a central angle of one full revolution (counterclockwise) corresponds to an arc length of

$$s = 2\pi r.$$

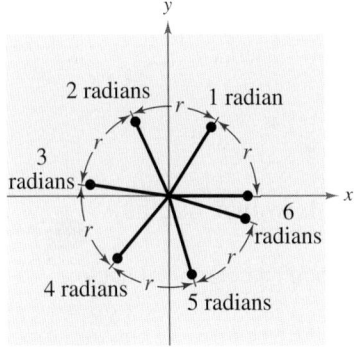

FIGURE 4.6

Moreover, because $2\pi \approx 6.28$, there are just over six radius lengths in a full circle, as shown in Figure 4.6. In general, the radian measure of a central angle θ is obtained by dividing the arc length s by r. That is, $s/r = \theta$, where θ *is measured in radians*. Because the units of measure for s and r are the same, this ratio has no units—it is simply a real number.

Because the radian measure of an angle of one full revolution is 2π, you can obtain the following.

$$\frac{1}{2} \text{ revolution} = \frac{2\pi}{2} = \pi \text{ radians}$$

$$\frac{1}{4} \text{ revolution} = \frac{2\pi}{4} = \frac{\pi}{2} \text{ radians}$$

$$\frac{1}{6} \text{ revolution} = \frac{2\pi}{6} = \frac{\pi}{3} \text{ radians}$$

These and other common angles are shown in Figure 4.7.

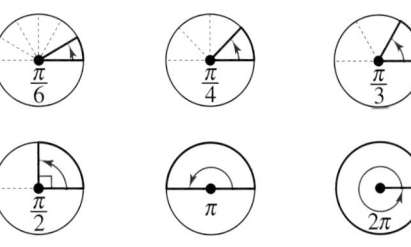

FIGURE 4.7

Recall that the four quadrants in a coordinate system are numbered I, II, III, and IV. Figure 4.8 on page 264 shows which angles between 0 and 2π lie in each of the four quadrants. Note that angles between 0 and $\pi/2$ are **acute** angles and angles between $\pi/2$ and π are **obtuse** angles.

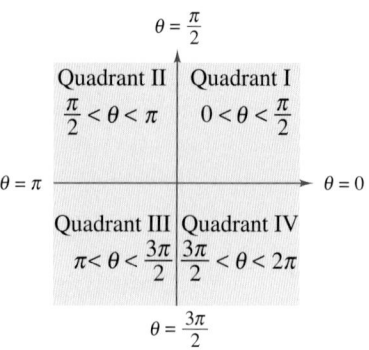

FIGURE 4.8

Two angles are coterminal if they have the same initial and terminal sides. For instance, the angles 0 and 2π are coterminal, as are the angles $\pi/6$ and $13\pi/6$. You can find an angle that is coterminal to a given angle θ by adding or subtracting 2π (one revolution), as demonstrated in Example 1. A given angle θ has infinitely many coterminal angles. For instance, $\theta = \pi/6$ is coterminal with

$$\frac{\pi}{6} + 2n\pi$$

where n is an integer.

Example 1 ▶ **Sketching and Finding Coterminal Angles**

a. For the positive angle $13\pi/6$, subtract 2π to obtain a coterminal angle

$$\frac{13\pi}{6} - 2\pi = \frac{\pi}{6}.$$ See Figure 4.9.

b. For the positive angle $3\pi/4$, subtract 2π to obtain a coterminal angle

$$\frac{3\pi}{4} - 2\pi = -\frac{5\pi}{4}.$$ See Figure 4.10.

c. For the negative angle $-2\pi/3$, add 2π to obtain a coterminal angle

$$-\frac{2\pi}{3} + 2\pi = \frac{4\pi}{3}.$$ See Figure 4.11.

Remind your students to work in radians.

FIGURE 4.9

FIGURE 4.10

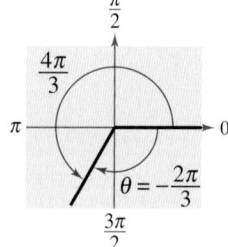

FIGURE 4.11

The icon identifies examples and concepts related to features of the Learning Tools CD-ROM and the *Interactive* and *Internet* versions of this text. For more details see the chart on pages *xxi-xxv*.

You might point out that complementary and supplementary angles do not necessarily share a common side. For example, the acute angles of a right triangle are complementary because the sum of their measures is $\pi/2$.

Two positive angles α and β are **complementary** (complements of each other) if their sum is $\pi/2$. Two positive angles are **supplementary** (supplements of each other) if their sum is π. See Figure 4.12.

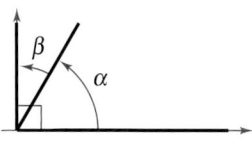

Complementary Angles
FIGURE 4.12

Supplementary Angles

The *Interactive* CD-ROM and *Internet* versions of this text offer a Try It for each example in the text.

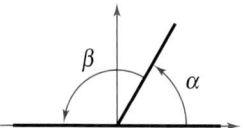

Example 2 ▶ **Complementary and Supplementary Angles**

If possible, find the complement and the supplement of (a) $2\pi/5$ and (b) $4\pi/5$.

Solution

a. The complement of $2\pi/5$ is

$$\frac{\pi}{2} - \frac{2\pi}{5} = \frac{5\pi}{10} - \frac{4\pi}{10} = \frac{\pi}{10}.$$

The supplement of $2\pi/5$ is

$$\pi - \frac{2\pi}{5} = \frac{5\pi}{5} - \frac{2\pi}{5} = \frac{3\pi}{5}.$$

b. Because $4\pi/5$ is greater than $\pi/2$, it has no complement. (Remember to use only positive angles for complements.) The supplement is

$$\pi - \frac{4\pi}{5} = \frac{5\pi}{5} - \frac{4\pi}{5} = \frac{\pi}{5}.$$

Degree Measure

A second way to measure angles is in terms of **degrees,** denoted by the symbol °. A measure of one degree (1°) is equivalent to a rotation of $\frac{1}{360}$ of a complete revolution about the vertex. To measure angles, it is convenient to mark degrees on the circumference of a circle, as shown in Figure 4.13. So, a full revolution (counterclockwise) corresponds to 360°, a half revolution to 180°, a quarter revolution to 90°, and so on.

Because 2π radians corresponds to one complete revolution, degrees and radians are related by the equations

$$360° = 2\pi \text{ rad} \qquad \text{and} \qquad 180° = \pi \text{ rad}.$$

From the latter equation, you obtain

$$1° = \frac{\pi}{180} \text{ rad} \qquad \text{and} \qquad 1 \text{ rad} = \left(\frac{180°}{\pi}\right)$$

which lead to the conversion rules at the top of the next page.

FIGURE 4.13

Converting from degrees to radians and vice versa should help your students become familiar with radian measure.

Conversions Between Degrees and Radians

1. To convert degrees to radians, multiply degrees by $\dfrac{\pi \text{ rad}}{180°}$.

2. To convert radians to degrees, multiply radians by $\dfrac{180°}{\pi \text{ rad}}$.

To apply these two conversion rules, use the basic relationship $\pi \text{ rad} = 180°$. (See Figure 4.14.)

The *Interactive* CD-ROM and *Internet* versions of this text offer a Quiz for every section of the text.

  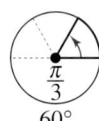

$\dfrac{\pi}{6}$ $\dfrac{\pi}{4}$ $\dfrac{\pi}{3}$
30° 45° 60°

  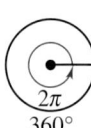

$\dfrac{\pi}{2}$ π 2π
90° 180° 360°

FIGURE **4.14**

When no units of angle measure are specified, *radian measure is implied*. For instance, if you write $\theta = \pi$ or $\theta = 2$, you should mean $\theta = \pi$ radians or $\theta = 2$ radians.

Technology

With calculators it is convenient to use *decimal* degrees to denote fractional parts of degrees. Historically, however, fractional parts of degrees were expressed in *minutes* and *seconds*, using the prime (′) and double prime (″) notations, respectively. That is,

$1' = $ one minute $= \frac{1}{60}(1°)$

$1'' = $ one second $= \frac{1}{3600}(1°)$

Consequently, an angle of 64 degrees, 32 minutes, and 47 seconds is represented by $\theta = 64°\ 32'\ 47''$.

Many calculators have special keys for converting an angle in degrees, minutes, and seconds (D° M′ S″) into decimal degree form, and vice versa.

Example 3 ▶ Converting from Degrees to Radians

a. $135° = (135 \text{ deg})\left(\dfrac{\pi \text{ rad}}{180 \text{ deg}}\right) = \dfrac{3\pi}{4}$ radians   Multiply by $\pi/180$.

b. $540° = (540 \text{ deg})\left(\dfrac{\pi \text{ rad}}{180 \text{ deg}}\right) = 3\pi$ radians   Multiply by $\pi/180$.

c. $-270° = (-270 \text{ deg})\left(\dfrac{\pi \text{ rad}}{180 \text{ deg}}\right) = -\dfrac{3\pi}{2}$ radians   Multiply by $\pi/180$.

Example 4 ▶ Converting from Radians to Degrees

a. $-\dfrac{\pi}{2} \text{ rad} = \left(-\dfrac{\pi}{2} \text{ rad}\right)\left(\dfrac{180 \text{ deg}}{\pi \text{ rad}}\right) = -90°$ Multiply by $180/\pi$.

b. $\dfrac{9\pi}{2} \text{ rad} = \left(\dfrac{9\pi}{2} \text{ rad}\right)\left(\dfrac{180 \text{ deg}}{\pi \text{ rad}}\right) = 810°$ Multiply by $180/\pi$.

c. $2 \text{ rad} = (2 \text{ rad})\left(\dfrac{180 \text{ deg}}{\pi \text{ rad}}\right) = \dfrac{360°}{\pi} \approx 114.59°$ Multiply by $180/\pi$.

If you have a calculator with a "radian-to-degree" conversion key, try using it to verify the result shown in part (c) of Example 4.

Applications

The *radian measure* formula, $\theta = s/r$, can be used to measure arc length along a circle. Specifically, for a circle of radius r, a central angle θ intercepts an arc of length s given by

$$s = r\theta \qquad \text{Length of circular arc}$$

where θ is measured in radians.

> **Example 5** ▶ Finding Arc Length

A circle has a radius of 4 inches. Find the length of the arc intercepted by a central angle of 240°, as shown in Figure 4.15.

Solution

To use the formula $s = r\theta$, first convert 240° to radian measure.

$$240° = (240 \text{ deg})\left(\frac{\pi \text{ rad}}{180 \text{ deg}}\right) \qquad \text{Convert from degrees to radians.}$$

$$= \frac{4\pi}{3} \text{ radians} \qquad \text{Simplify.}$$

Then, using a radius of $r = 4$ inches, you can find the arc length to be

$$s = r\theta \qquad \text{Length of circular arc}$$

$$= 4\left(\frac{4\pi}{3}\right) \qquad \text{Substitute for } r \text{ and } \theta.$$

$$= \frac{16\pi}{3} \approx 16.76 \text{ inches.} \qquad \text{Simplify.}$$

Note that the units for $r\theta$ are determined by the units for r because θ is given in radian measure and so has no units.

The formula for the length of a circular arc can be used to analyze the motion of a particle moving at a *constant speed* along a circular path.

FIGURE **4.15**

Because radian measure is so often used, you may want to encourage your students to be as familiar with the radian measure of angles as they are with degree measure. Measuring arc length along a circle is one of many applications in which radian measure is used.

STUDY TIP

Linear speed measures how fast the particle moves, and angular speed measures how fast the angle changes.

Linear and Angular Speed

Consider a particle moving at a constant speed along a circular arc of radius r. If s is the length of the arc traveled in time t, then the **linear speed** of the particle is

$$\text{Linear speed} = \frac{\text{arc length}}{\text{time}} = \frac{s}{t}.$$

Moreover, if θ is the angle (in radian measure) corresponding to the arc length s, then the **angular speed** of the particle is

$$\text{Angular speed} = \frac{\text{central angle}}{\text{time}} = \frac{\theta}{t}.$$

FIGURE **4.16**

Example 6 ▶ Finding Linear Speed

The second hand of a clock is 10.2 centimeters long, as shown in Figure 4.16. Find the linear speed of the tip of this second hand as it passes around the clock face.

Solution

In one revolution, the arc length traveled is

$$s = 2\pi r$$

$$= 2\pi(10.2) \qquad \text{Substitute for } r.$$

$$= 20.4\pi \text{ centimeters.}$$

The time required for the second hand to travel this distance is

$$t = 1 \text{ minute} = 60 \text{ seconds.}$$

So, the linear speed of the tip of the second hand is

$$\text{Linear speed} = \frac{s}{t}$$

$$= \frac{20.4\pi \text{ centimeters}}{60 \text{ seconds}}$$

$$\approx 1.068 \text{ centimeters per second.}$$

Example 7 ▶ Finding Angular and Linear Speed

A lawn roller with a 10-inch radius (see Figure 4.17) makes 1.2 revolutions per second.

a. Find the angular speed of the roller in radians per second.

b. Find the speed of the tractor that is pulling the roller.

Solution

a. Because each revolution generates 2π radians, it follows that the roller turns $(1.2)(2\pi) = 2.4\pi$ radians per second. In other words, the angular speed is

$$\text{Angular speed} = \frac{\theta}{t}$$

$$= \frac{2.4\pi \text{ radians}}{1 \text{ second}} = 2.4\pi \text{ radians per second.}$$

b. The linear speed (speed of the tractor) is

$$\text{Linear speed} = \frac{s}{t}$$

$$= \frac{r\theta}{t}$$

$$= \frac{10(2.4\pi) \text{ inches}}{1 \text{ second}} \approx 75.4 \text{ inches per second.}$$

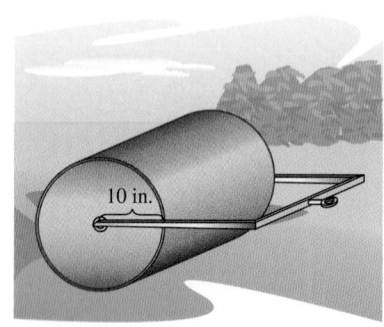

FIGURE **4.17**

Activities

1. Find the supplement of the angle $\theta = \frac{5\pi}{7}$.

   Answer: $\frac{2\pi}{7}$

2. Convert $60°$ from degrees to radians.

   Answer: $\frac{\pi}{3}$

3. On a circle with a radius of 9 inches, find the length of the arc intercepted by a central angle of $140°$.

   Answer: $7\pi \approx 22$ inches

4.1 Exercises

The *Interactive* CD-ROM and *Internet* versions of this text contain step-by-step solutions to all odd-numbered exercises. They also provide Tutorial Exercises for additional help.

In Exercises 1–6, estimate the angle to the nearest one-half radian.

1.   **2.**

3.   **4.**

5.   **6.**

In Exercises 7–12, determine the quadrant in which each angle lies. (The angle measure is given in radians.)

7. (a) $\dfrac{\pi}{5}$ (b) $\dfrac{7\pi}{5}$ **8.** (a) $\dfrac{11\pi}{8}$ (b) $\dfrac{9\pi}{8}$

9. (a) $-\dfrac{\pi}{12}$ (b) -2 **10.** (a) -1 (b) $-\dfrac{11\pi}{9}$

11. (a) 3.5 (b) 2.25 **12.** (a) 6.02 (b) -4.25

In Exercises 13–16, sketch each angle in standard position.

13. (a) $\dfrac{5\pi}{4}$ (b) $-\dfrac{2\pi}{3}$ **14.** (a) $-\dfrac{7\pi}{4}$ (b) $\dfrac{5\pi}{2}$

15. (a) $\dfrac{11\pi}{6}$ (b) -3 **16.** (a) 4 (b) 7π

In Exercises 17–20, determine two coterminal angles (one positive and one negative) for each angle. Give your answers in radians.

17. (a)   (b)

18. (a)   (b)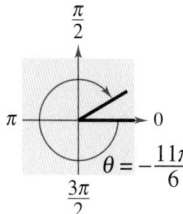

19. (a) $\theta = \dfrac{2\pi}{3}$ (b) $\theta = \dfrac{\pi}{12}$

20. (a) $\theta = -\dfrac{9\pi}{4}$ (b) $\theta = -\dfrac{2\pi}{15}$

In Exercises 21–24, find (if possible) the complement and supplement of each angle.

21. (a) $\dfrac{\pi}{3}$ (b) $\dfrac{3\pi}{4}$ **22.** (a) $\dfrac{\pi}{12}$ (b) $\dfrac{11\pi}{12}$

23. (a) 1 (b) 2 **24.** (a) 3 (b) 1.5

In Exercises 25–28, write each angle in radian measure as a multiple of π. (Do not use a calculator.)

25. (a) $30°$ (b) $150°$

26. (a) $315°$ (b) $120°$

27. (a) $-20°$ (b) $-240°$

28. (a) $-270°$ (b) $144°$

In Exercises 29–36, convert the measure from degrees to radians. Round to three decimal places.

29. $115°$ **30.** $87.4°$

31. $-216.35°$ **32.** $-48.27°$

33. $532°$ **34.** $345°$

35. $-0.83°$ **36.** $0.54°$

In Exercises 37–40, write each angle in degree measure. (Do not use a calculator.)

37. (a) $\dfrac{3\pi}{2}$ (b) $\dfrac{7\pi}{6}$

38. (a) $-\dfrac{7\pi}{12}$ (b) $\dfrac{\pi}{9}$

39. (a) $\dfrac{7\pi}{3}$ (b) $-\dfrac{11\pi}{30}$

40. (a) $\dfrac{11\pi}{6}$ (b) $\dfrac{34\pi}{15}$

In Exercises 41–48, convert the measure from radians to degrees. Round to three decimal places.

41. $\dfrac{\pi}{7}$ **42.** $\dfrac{5\pi}{11}$

43. $\dfrac{15\pi}{8}$ **44.** $\dfrac{13\pi}{2}$

45. -4.2π **46.** 4.8π

47. -2 **48.** -0.57

In Exercises 49–54, estimate the number of degrees in the angle.

49.   **50.**

51.   **52.**

53.   **54.**

In Exercises 55–58, determine the quadrant in which each angle lies.

55. (a) $130°$ (b) $285°$

56. (a) $8.3°$ (b) $257°\,30'$

57. (a) $-132°\,50'$ (b) $-336°$

58. (a) $-260°$ (b) $-3.4°$

In Exercises 59–62, sketch each angle in standard position.

59. (a) $30°$ (b) $150°$

60. (a) $-270°$ (b) $-120°$

61. (a) $405°$ (b) $480°$

62. (a) $-750°$ (b) $-600°$

In Exercises 63–66, determine two coterminal angles (one positive and one negative) for each angle. Give your answers in degrees.

63. (a)   (b) 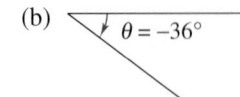 $\theta = -36°$

$\theta = 45°$

64. (a) $\theta = 120°$ (b) $\theta = -420°$

65. (a) $\theta = 240°$ (b) $\theta = -180°$

66. (a) $\theta = -420°$ (b) $\theta = 230°$

In Exercises 67–70, find (if possible) the complement and supplement of each angle.

67. (a) $18°$ (b) $115°$

68. (a) $3°$ (b) $64°$

69. (a) $79°$ (b) $150°$

70. (a) $130°$ (b) $170°$

In Exercises 71–74, convert each angle measure to decimal degree form.

71. (a) $54°\,45'$ (b) $-128°\,30'$

72. (a) $245°\,10'$ (b) $2°\,12'$

73. (a) $85°\,18'\,30''$ (b) $330°\,25''$

74. (a) $-135°\,36''$ (b) $-408°\,16'\,20''$

In Exercises 75–78, convert each angle measure to D° M′ S″ form.

75. (a) $240.6°$ (b) $-145.8°$

76. (a) $-345.12°$ (b) $0.45°$

77. (a) $2.5°$ (b) $-3.58°$

78. (a) $-0.355°$ (b) $0.7865°$

In Exercises 79–82, find the angle in radians.

79.   **80.**

81.

82.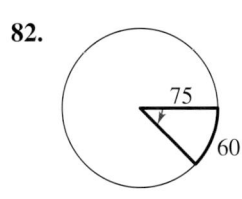

In Exercises 83–86, find the radian measure of the central angle of a circle of radius *r* that intercepts an arc of length *s*.

	Radius r	Arc Length s
83.	27 inches	6 inches
84.	14 feet	8 feet
85.	14.5 centimeters	25 centimeters
86.	80 kilometers	160 kilometers

In Exercises 87–90, find the length of the arc on a circle of radius *r* intercepted by a central angle θ.

	Radius r	Central Angle θ
87.	15 inches	180°
88.	9 feet	60°
89.	3 meters	1 radian
90.	20 centimeters	$\pi/4$ radian

Distance Between Cities **In Exercises 91–94, find the distance between the cities. Assume that Earth is a sphere of radius 4000 miles and that the cities are on the same longitude (one city is due north of the other).**

	City	Latitude
91.	Dallas, Texas	32° 47′ 9″ N
	Omaha, Nebraska	41° 15′ 42″ N
92.	San Francisco, California	37° 46′ 39″ N
	Seattle, Washington	47° 36′ 32″ N
93.	Miami, Florida	25° 46′ 37″ N
	Erie, Pennsylvania	42° 7′ 15″ N
94.	Johannesburg, South Africa	26° 10′ S
	Jerusalem, Israel	31° 47′ N

95. ***Difference in Latitudes*** Assuming that Earth is a sphere of radius 6378 kilometers, what is the difference in the latitudes of Syracuse, New York, and Annapolis, Maryland, where Syracuse is 450 kilometers due north of Annapolis?

96. ***Difference in Latitudes*** Assuming that Earth is a sphere of radius 6378 kilometers, what is the difference in the latitudes of Lynchburg, Virginia and Myrtle Beach, South Carolina, where Lynchburg is 400 kilometers due north of Myrtle Beach?

97. ***Instrumentation*** The pointer on a voltmeter is 6 centimeters in length (see figure). Find the angle through which the pointer rotates when it moves 2.5 centimeters on the scale.

FIGURE FOR 97   FIGURE FOR 98

98. ***Electric Hoist*** An electric hoist is being used to lift a beam (see figure). The diameter of the drum on the hoist is 10 inches, and the beam must be raised 2 feet. Find the number of degrees through which the drum must rotate.

99. ***Angular Speed*** A car is moving at a rate of 65 miles per hour, and the diameter of its wheels is 2.5 feet.
 (a) Find the number of revolutions per minute the wheels are rotating.
 (b) Find the angular speed of the wheels in radians per minute.

100. ***Angular Speed*** A two-inch-diameter pulley on an electric motor that runs at 1700 revolutions per minute is connected by a belt to a four-inch-diameter pulley on a saw arbor.
 (a) Find the angular speed (in radians per minute) of each pulley.
 (b) Find the revolutions per minute of the saw.

▶ Model It

101. *Speed of a Bicycle* The radii of the pedal sprocket, the wheel sprocket, and the wheel of the bicycle in the figure are 4 inches, 2 inches, and 14 inches, respectively. The cyclist is pedaling at a rate of 1 revolution per second.

(a) Find the speed of the bicycle in feet per second and miles per hour.

(b) Use your result from part (a) to write a function for the distance d (in miles) a cyclist travels in terms of the number n of revolutions of the pedal sprocket.

(c) Write a function for the distance d (in miles) a cyclist travels in terms of the time t (in seconds). Compare this function with the function from part (b).

(d) Classify the types of functions you found in parts (b) and (c). Explain your reasoning.

14 in.

4 in.

2 in.

102. *Floppy Disk* The radius of the magnetic disk in a 3.5-inch diskette is 1.68 inches. Find the linear speed of a point on the circumference of the disk if it is rotating at a speed of 360 revolutions per minute.

Synthesis

True or False? In Exercises 103–105, determine whether the statement is true or false. Justify your answer.

103. A measurement of 4 radians corresponds to two complete revolutions from the initial side to the terminal side of an angle.

104. The difference between the measures of two coterminal angles is always a multiple of $360°$ if expressed in degrees and is always a multiple of 2π radians if expressed in radians.

105. An angle that measures $-1260°$ lies in Quadrant III.

106. *Writing* In your own words, explain the meanings of (a) an angle in standard position, (b) a negative angle, (c) coterminal angles, and (d) an obtuse angle.

107. A fan motor turns at a given angular speed. How does the speed of the tips of the blades change if a fan of greater diameter is installed on the motor? Explain.

108. *Think About It* Is a degree or a radian the larger unit of measure? Explain.

109. *Writing* If the radius of a circle is increasing and the magnitude of a central angle is held constant, how is the length of the intercepted arc changing? Explain your reasoning.

110. *Proof* Prove that the area of a circular sector of radius r with central angle θ is $A = \frac{1}{2}\theta r^2$, where θ is measured in radians.

Review

In Exercises 111–114, sketch the graphs of $y = x^5$ and the specified transformation.

111. $f(x) = (x - 2)^5$ **112.** $f(x) = x^5 - 4$

113. $f(x) = 2 - x^5$ **114.** $f(x) = -(x + 3)^5$

In Exercises 115–118, graph the exponential function.

115. $f(x) = 6^x$ **116.** $f(x) = 6^x - 2$

117. $f(x) = 6^{-x}$ **118.** $f(x) = 6^{x+1}$

In Exercises 119–124, graph the logarithmic function.

119. $f(x) = \log_4 x$ **120.** $f(x) = \log_4 x + 5$

121. $f(x) = -\log_4 x$ **122.** $f(x) = \log_4(x + 5)$

123. $f(x) = \log_4(-x)$ **124.** $f(x) = -\log_4(x + 5)$

In Exercises 125–132, simplify the radical expression.

125. $\dfrac{4}{4\sqrt{2}}$ **126.** $\dfrac{2}{\sqrt{3}}$

127. $\dfrac{2\sqrt{3}}{\sqrt{6}}$ **128.** $\dfrac{5\sqrt{5}}{2\sqrt{10}}$

129. $\sqrt{2^2 + 6^2}$ **130.** $\sqrt{18^2 + 12^2}$

131. $\sqrt{18^2 - 6^2}$ **132.** $\sqrt{17^2 - 9^2}$

Trigonometric Functions: The Unit Circle

Richard Megna/Fundamental Photographs

Try demonstrating the wrapping function by using a spool and thread. Demonstrate the real number t as the length of the thread. Then wrap the thread around the spool to show the correspondence between t and the point (x, y) on the circle. For example, if $t = \pi/2$, the point on the unit circle to which it corresponds is $(0, 1)$.

The Unit Circle

The two historical perspectives of trigonometry incorporate different methods for introducing the trigonometric functions. Our first introduction to these functions is based on the unit circle.

Consider the **unit circle** given by

$$x^2 + y^2 = 1 \qquad \text{Unit circle}$$

as shown in Figure 4.18.

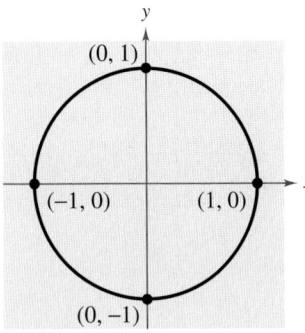

FIGURE **4.18**

Imagine that the real number line is wrapped around this circle, with positive numbers corresponding to a counterclockwise wrapping and negative numbers corresponding to a clockwise wrapping, as shown in Figure 4.19.

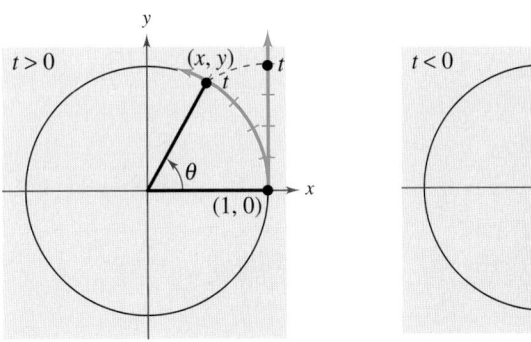

FIGURE **4.19**

As the real number line is wrapped around the unit circle, each real number t corresponds to a point (x, y) on the circle. For example, the real number 0 corresponds to the point $(1, 0)$. Moreover, because the unit circle has a circumference of 2π, the real number 2π also corresponds to the point $(1, 0)$.

In general, each real number t also corresponds to a central angle θ (in standard position) whose radian measure is t. With this interpretation of t, the arc length formula $s = r\theta$ (with $r = 1$) indicates that the real number t is the length of the arc intercepted by the angle θ, given in radians.

The Trigonometric Functions

From the preceding discussion, it follows that the coordinates x and y are two functions of the real variable t. You can use these coordinates to define the six trigonometric functions of t.

sine	cosecant
cosine	secant
tangent	cotangent

These six functions are normally abbreviated sin, csc, cos, sec, tan, and cot, respectively.

Definitions of Trigonometric Functions

Let t be a real number and let (x, y) be the point on the unit circle corresponding to t.

$$\sin t = y \qquad\qquad \csc t = \frac{1}{y}, \qquad y \neq 0$$

$$\cos t = x \qquad\qquad \sec t = \frac{1}{x}, \qquad x \neq 0$$

$$\tan t = \frac{y}{x}, \qquad x \neq 0 \qquad\qquad \cot t = \frac{x}{y}, \qquad y \neq 0$$

Note that the functions in the second column are the *reciprocals* of the corresponding functions in the first column.

In the definitions of the trigonometric functions, note that the tangent and secant are not defined when $x = 0$. For instance, because $t = \pi/2$ corresponds to $(x, y) = (0, 1)$, it follows that $\tan(\pi/2)$ and $\sec(\pi/2)$ are *undefined*. Similarly, the cotangent and cosecant are not defined when $y = 0$. For instance, because $t = 0$ corresponds to $(x, y) = (1, 0)$, cot 0 and csc 0 are *undefined*.

In Figure 4.20, the unit circle has been divided into eight equal arcs, corresponding to t-values of

$$0, \frac{\pi}{4}, \frac{\pi}{2}, \frac{3\pi}{4}, \pi, \frac{5\pi}{4}, \frac{3\pi}{2}, \frac{7\pi}{4}, \text{ and } 2\pi.$$

Similarly, in Figure 4.21, the unit circle has been divided into 12 equal arcs, corresponding to t-values of

$$0, \frac{\pi}{6}, \frac{\pi}{3}, \frac{\pi}{2}, \frac{2\pi}{3}, \frac{5\pi}{6}, \pi, \frac{7\pi}{6}, \frac{4\pi}{3}, \frac{3\pi}{2}, \frac{5\pi}{3}, \frac{11\pi}{6}, \text{ and } 2\pi.$$

Using the (x, y) coordinates in Figures 4.20 and 4.21, you can easily evaluate the trigonometric functions for common t-values. This procedure is demonstrated in Examples 1 and 2.

FIGURE **4.20**

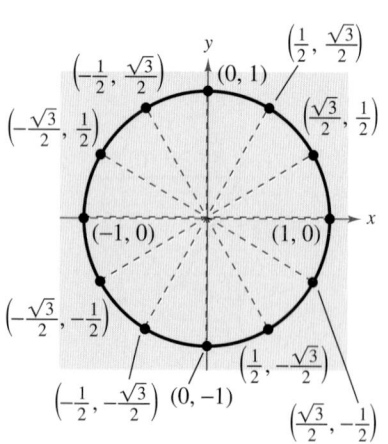

FIGURE **4.21**

Example 1 ▶ **Evaluating Trigonometric Functions**

Evaluate the six trigonometric functions at each real number.

a. $t = \dfrac{\pi}{6}$ **b.** $t = \dfrac{5\pi}{4}$ **c.** $t = 0$ **d.** $t = \pi$

Solution

For each t-value, begin by finding the corresponding point (x, y) on the unit circle. Then use the definitions of trigonometric functions listed on page 274.

a. $t = \pi/6$ corresponds to the point $(x, y) = \left(\sqrt{3}/2,\ 1/2\right)$.

$$\sin \frac{\pi}{6} = y = \frac{1}{2} \qquad\qquad \csc \frac{\pi}{6} = \frac{1}{y} = \frac{1}{1/2} = 2$$

$$\cos \frac{\pi}{6} = x = \frac{\sqrt{3}}{2} \qquad\qquad \sec \frac{\pi}{6} = \frac{1}{x} = \frac{2}{\sqrt{3}} = \frac{2\sqrt{3}}{3}$$

$$\tan \frac{\pi}{6} = \frac{y}{x} = \frac{1/2}{\sqrt{3}/2} = \frac{1}{\sqrt{3}} \qquad\qquad \cot \frac{\pi}{6} = \frac{x}{y} = \frac{\sqrt{3}/2}{1/2} = \sqrt{3}$$

b. $t = 5\pi/4$ corresponds to the point $(x, y) = \left(-\sqrt{2}/2,\ -\sqrt{2}/2\right)$.

$$\sin \frac{5\pi}{4} = y = -\frac{\sqrt{2}}{2} \qquad\qquad \csc \frac{5\pi}{4} = \frac{1}{y} = -\frac{2}{\sqrt{2}} = -\sqrt{2}$$

$$\cos \frac{5\pi}{4} = x = -\frac{\sqrt{2}}{2} \qquad\qquad \sec \frac{5\pi}{4} = \frac{1}{x} = -\frac{2}{\sqrt{2}} = -\sqrt{2}$$

$$\tan \frac{5\pi}{4} = \frac{y}{x} = \frac{-\sqrt{2}/2}{-\sqrt{2}/2} = 1 \qquad\qquad \cot \frac{5\pi}{4} = \frac{x}{y} = \frac{-\sqrt{2}/2}{-\sqrt{2}/2} = 1$$

c. $t = 0$ corresponds to the point $(x, y) = (1, 0)$.

$$\sin 0 = y = 0 \qquad\qquad \csc 0 = \frac{1}{y} \text{ is undefined.}$$

$$\cos 0 = x = 1 \qquad\qquad \sec 0 = \frac{1}{x} = \frac{1}{1} = 1$$

$$\tan 0 = \frac{y}{x} = \frac{0}{1} = 0 \qquad\qquad \cot 0 = \frac{x}{y} \text{ is undefined.}$$

d. $t = \pi$ corresponds to the point $(x, y) = (-1, 0)$.

$$\sin \pi = y = 0 \qquad\qquad \csc \pi = \frac{1}{y} \text{ is undefined.}$$

$$\cos \pi = x = -1 \qquad\qquad \sec \pi = \frac{1}{x} = \frac{1}{-1} = -1$$

$$\tan \pi = \frac{y}{x} = \frac{0}{-1} = 0 \qquad\qquad \cot \pi = \frac{x}{y} \text{ is undefined.}$$

Additional Example

Evaluate the six trigonometric functions at $t = \dfrac{5\pi}{2}$.

Solution

Moving counterclockwise around the unit circle one and a quarter revolutions, you find that $t = 5\pi/2$ corresponds to the point $(x, y) = (0, 1)$.

$\sin \dfrac{5\pi}{2} = y = 1 \qquad \csc \dfrac{5\pi}{2} = \dfrac{1}{y} = 1$

$\cos \dfrac{5\pi}{2} = x = 0$

$\sec \dfrac{5\pi}{2} = \dfrac{1}{x}$ is undefined.

$\tan \dfrac{5\pi}{2} = \dfrac{y}{x}$ is undefined.

$\cot \dfrac{5\pi}{2} = \dfrac{x}{y} = 0$

With your graphing utility in *radian* and *parametric* modes, enter the equations

X1T = cos T   and   Y1T = sin T

and use the following settings.

Tmin = 0, Tmax = 6.3,
Tstep = 0.1
Xmin = -1.5, Xmax = 1.5,
Xscl = 1
Ymin = -1, Ymax = 1,
Yscl = 1

1. Graph the entered equations and describe the graph.

2. Use the *trace* feature to move the cursor around the graph. What do the *t*-values represent? What do the *x*- and *y*-values represent?

3. What are the least and greatest values of *x* and *y*?

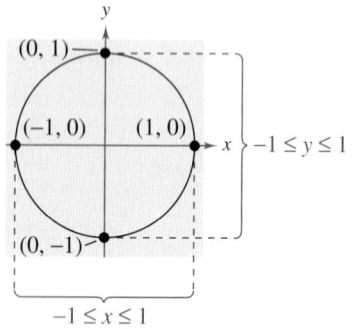

FIGURE 4.22

Example 2 ▶ Evaluating Trigonometric Functions

Evaluate the six trigonometric functions at $t = -\dfrac{\pi}{3}$.

Solution

Moving *clockwise* around the unit circle, it follows that $t = -\pi/3$ corresponds to the point $(x, y) = \left(1/2, -\sqrt{3}/2\right)$.

$$\sin\left(-\frac{\pi}{3}\right) = -\frac{\sqrt{3}}{2} \qquad\qquad \csc\left(-\frac{\pi}{3}\right) = -\frac{2}{\sqrt{3}} = -\frac{2\sqrt{3}}{3}$$

$$\cos\left(-\frac{\pi}{3}\right) = \frac{1}{2} \qquad\qquad \sec\left(-\frac{\pi}{3}\right) = 2$$

$$\tan\left(-\frac{\pi}{3}\right) = \frac{-\sqrt{3}/2}{1/2} = -\sqrt{3} \qquad \cot\left(-\frac{\pi}{3}\right) = \frac{1/2}{-\sqrt{3}/2} = -\frac{1}{\sqrt{3}} = -\frac{\sqrt{3}}{3}$$

Domain and Period of Sine and Cosine

The *domain* of the sine and cosine functions is the set of all real numbers. To determine the *range* of these two functions, consider the unit circle shown in Figure 4.22. Because $r = 1$, it follows that $\sin t = y$ and $\cos t = x$. Moreover, because (x, y) is on the unit circle, you know that $-1 \le y \le 1$ and $-1 \le x \le 1$. So, the values of sine and cosine also range between -1 and 1.

$$-1 \le\ y\ \le 1 \qquad\qquad -1 \le\ x\ \le 1$$
$$\text{and}$$
$$-1 \le \sin t \le 1 \qquad\qquad -1 \le \cos t \le 1$$

Adding 2π to each value of t in the interval $[0, 2\pi]$ completes a second revolution around the unit circle, as shown in Figure 4.23. The values of $\sin(t + 2\pi)$ and $\cos(t + 2\pi)$ correspond to those of $\sin t$ and $\cos t$. Similar results can be obtained for repeated revolutions (positive or negative) on the unit circle. This leads to the general result

$$\sin(t + 2\pi n) = \sin t$$

and

$$\cos(t + 2\pi n) = \cos t$$

for any integer n and real number t. Functions that behave in such a repetitive (or cyclic) manner are called **periodic.**

Definition of Periodic Function

A function f is **periodic** if there exists a positive real number c such that

$$f(t + c) = f(t)$$

for all t in the domain of f. The smallest number c for which f is periodic is called the **period** of f.

$t = \frac{\pi}{2}, \frac{\pi}{2} + 2\pi, \frac{\pi}{2} + 4\pi, \dots$

$t = \frac{3\pi}{4}, \frac{3\pi}{4} + 2\pi, \dots$ $t = \frac{\pi}{4}, \frac{\pi}{4} + 2\pi, \dots$

$t = \pi, 3\pi, \dots$

$t = 0, 2\pi, \dots$

$t = \frac{5\pi}{4}, \frac{5\pi}{4} + 2\pi, \dots$

$t = \frac{7\pi}{4}, \frac{7\pi}{4} + 2\pi, \frac{7\pi}{4} + 4\pi, \dots$

$t = \frac{3\pi}{2}, \frac{3\pi}{2} + 2\pi, \frac{3\pi}{2} + 4\pi, \dots$

FIGURE 4.23

Example 3 ▶ Using the Period to Evaluate the Sine and Cosine

a. Because $\dfrac{13\pi}{6} = 2\pi + \dfrac{\pi}{6}$, you have

$$\sin\frac{13\pi}{6} = \sin\left(2\pi + \frac{\pi}{6}\right) = \sin\frac{\pi}{6} = \frac{1}{2}.$$

b. Because $-\dfrac{7\pi}{2} = -4\pi + \dfrac{\pi}{2}$, you have

$$\cos\left(-\frac{7\pi}{2}\right) = \cos\left(-4\pi + \frac{\pi}{2}\right) = \cos\frac{\pi}{2} = 0.$$

Recall from Section 1.4 that a function f is *even* if $f(-t) = f(t)$, and is *odd* if $f(-t) = -f(t)$.

Even and Odd Trigonometric Functions

The cosine and secant functions are *even*.

$$\cos(-t) = \cos t \qquad \sec(-t) = \sec t$$

The sine, cosecant, tangent, and cotangent functions are *odd*.

$$\sin(-t) = -\sin t \qquad \csc(-t) = -\csc t$$

$$\tan(-t) = -\tan t \qquad \cot(-t) = -\cot t$$

Evaluating Trigonometric Functions with a Calculator

When evaluating a trigonometric function with a calculator, you need to set the calculator to the desired *mode* of measurement (degrees or radians).

Most calculators do not have keys for the cosecant, secant, and cotangent functions. To evaluate these functions, you can use the $\boxed{x^{-1}}$ key with their respective reciprocal functions sine, cosine, and tangent. For example, to evaluate $\csc(\pi/8)$, use the fact that

$$\csc\frac{\pi}{8} = \frac{1}{\sin(\pi/8)}$$

and enter the following keystroke sequence in radian mode.

$\boxed{(}\ \boxed{\text{SIN}}\ \boxed{(}\ \boxed{\pi}\ \boxed{\div}\ \boxed{8}\ \boxed{)}\ \boxed{)}\ \boxed{x^{-1}}\ \boxed{\text{ENTER}}$ Display 2.6131259

Example 4 ▶ Using a Calculator

Function	Mode	Calculator Keystrokes	Display
a. $\sin 2\pi/3$	Radian	$\boxed{\text{SIN}}\ \boxed{(}\ 2\ \boxed{\pi}\ \boxed{\div}\ 3\ \boxed{)}\ \boxed{\text{ENTER}}$	0.8660254
b. $\cot 1.5$	Radian	$\boxed{(}\ \boxed{\text{TAN}}\ 1.5\ \boxed{)}\ \boxed{x^{-1}}\ \boxed{\text{ENTER}}$	0.0709148

4.2 Exercises

In Exercises 1–4, determine the exact values of the six trigonometric functions of the angle θ.

1.

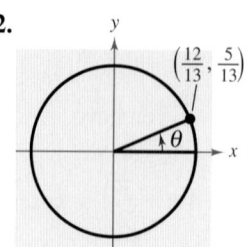

$\left(-\frac{8}{17}, \frac{15}{17}\right)$

2.

$\left(\frac{12}{13}, \frac{5}{13}\right)$

3.

$\left(\frac{12}{13}, -\frac{5}{13}\right)$

4.

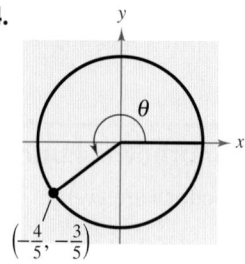

$\left(-\frac{4}{5}, -\frac{3}{5}\right)$

In Exercises 5–12, find the point (x, y) on the unit circle that corresponds to the real number t.

5. $t = \dfrac{\pi}{4}$

6. $t = \dfrac{\pi}{3}$

7. $t = \dfrac{7\pi}{6}$

8. $t = \dfrac{5\pi}{4}$

9. $t = \dfrac{4\pi}{3}$

10. $t = \dfrac{5\pi}{3}$

11. $t = \dfrac{3\pi}{2}$

12. $t = \pi$

In Exercises 13–22, evaluate (if possible) the sine, cosine, and tangent of the real number.

13. $t = \dfrac{\pi}{4}$

14. $t = \dfrac{\pi}{3}$

15. $t = -\dfrac{\pi}{6}$

16. $t = -\dfrac{\pi}{4}$

17. $t = -\dfrac{7\pi}{4}$

18. $t = -\dfrac{4\pi}{3}$

19. $t = \dfrac{11\pi}{6}$

20. $t = \dfrac{5\pi}{3}$

21. $t = -\dfrac{3\pi}{2}$

22. $t = -2\pi$

In Exercises 23–28, evaluate (if possible) the six trigonometric functions of the real number.

23. $t = \dfrac{3\pi}{4}$

24. $t = \dfrac{5\pi}{6}$

25. $t = -\dfrac{\pi}{2}$

26. $t = \dfrac{3\pi}{2}$

27. $t = \dfrac{4\pi}{3}$

28. $t = \dfrac{7\pi}{4}$

In Exercises 29–36, evaluate the trigonometric function using its period as an aid.

29. $\sin 5\pi$

30. $\cos 5\pi$

31. $\cos \dfrac{8\pi}{3}$

32. $\sin \dfrac{9\pi}{4}$

33. $\cos\left(-\dfrac{15\pi}{2}\right)$

34. $\sin \dfrac{19\pi}{6}$

35. $\sin\left(-\dfrac{9\pi}{4}\right)$

36. $\cos\left(-\dfrac{8\pi}{3}\right)$

In Exercises 37–42, use the value of the trigonometric function to evaluate the indicated functions.

37. $\sin t = \frac{1}{3}$
 (a) $\sin(-t)$
 (b) $\csc(-t)$

38. $\sin(-t) = \frac{3}{8}$
 (a) $\sin t$
 (b) $\csc t$

39. $\cos(-t) = -\frac{1}{5}$
 (a) $\cos t$
 (b) $\sec(-t)$

40. $\cos t = -\frac{3}{4}$
 (a) $\cos(-t)$
 (b) $\sec(-t)$

41. $\sin t = \frac{4}{5}$
 (a) $\sin(\pi - t)$
 (b) $\sin(t + \pi)$

42. $\cos t = \frac{4}{5}$
 (a) $\cos(\pi - t)$
 (b) $\cos(t + \pi)$

In Exercises 43–52, use a calculator to evaluate the expression. Round to four decimal places.

43. $\sin \dfrac{\pi}{4}$

44. $\tan \dfrac{\pi}{3}$

45. $\csc 1.3$

46. $\cot 1$

47. $\cos(-1.7)$

48. $\cos(-2.5)$

49. $\csc 0.8$

50. $\sec 1.8$

51. $\sec 22.8$

52. $\sin(-0.9)$

Estimation In Exercises 53 and 54, use the figure and a straightedge to approximate the value of each trigonometric function. To print an enlarged copy of the graph, go to the website *www.mathgraphs.com*.

53. (a) $\sin 5$ (b) $\cos 2$ **54.** (a) $\sin 0.75$ (b) $\cos 2.5$

Estimation In Exercises 55 and 56, use the figure and a straightedge to approximate the solution of each equation, where $0 \le t < 2\pi$. To print an enlarged copy of the graph, go to the website *www.mathgraphs.com*.

55. (a) $\sin t = 0.25$ (b) $\cos t = -0.25$
56. (a) $\sin t = -0.75$ (b) $\cos t = 0.75$

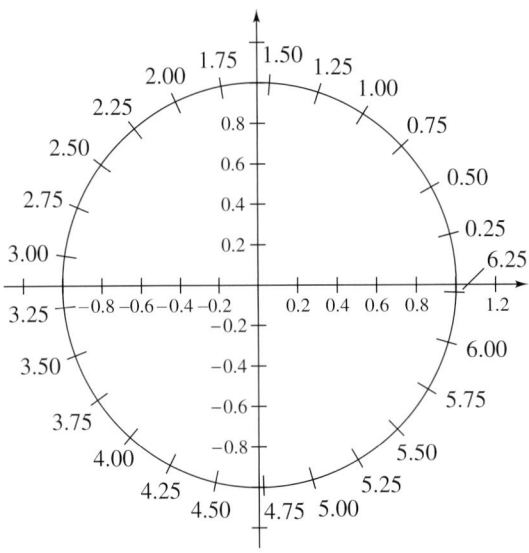

FIGURE FOR 53–56

▶ **Model It**

57. *Harmonic Motion* The displacement from equilibrium of an oscillating weight suspended by a spring and subject to the damping effect of friction is

$$y(t) = \frac{1}{4}e^{-t}\cos 6t$$

where y is the displacement in feet and t is the time in seconds.

(a) Complete the table.

t	0	$\frac{1}{4}$	$\frac{1}{2}$	$\frac{3}{4}$	1
y					

▶ **Model It** *(continued)*

(b) Use the *table* feature of a graphing utility to approximate the time when the weight reaches equilibrium.

(c) What appears to happen to the displacement as t increases?

---

58. *Harmonic Motion* The displacement from equilibrium of an oscillating weight suspended by a spring is $y(t) = \frac{1}{4}\cos 6t$, where y is the displacement in feet and t is the time in seconds. Find the displacement when (a) $t = 0$, (b) $t = \frac{1}{4}$, and (c) $t = \frac{1}{2}$.

Synthesis

True or False? In Exercises 59 and 60, determine whether the statement is true or false. Justify your answer.

59. Because $\sin(-t) = -\sin t$, it can be said that the sine of a negative angle is a negative number.

60. $\tan a = \tan(a - 6\pi)$

61. *Exploration* Let (x_1, y_1) and (x_2, y_2) be points on the unit circle corresponding to $t = t_1$ and $t = \pi - t_1$, respectively.

(a) Identify the symmetry of the points (x_1, y_1) and (x_2, y_2).

(b) Make a conjecture about any relationship between $\sin t_1$ and $\sin(\pi - t_1)$.

(c) Make a conjecture about any relationship between $\cos t_1$ and $\cos(\pi - t_1)$.

62. Use the unit circle to verify that the cosine and secant functions are even and that the sine, cosecant, tangent, and cotangent functions are odd.

63. Verify that $\sin(t_1 + t_2) \ne \sin t_1 + \sin t_2$ by approximating $\sin 0.25$, $\sin 0.75$, and $\sin 1$.

64. *Think About It* Because $f(t) = \sin t$ is an odd function and $g(t) = \cos t$ is an even function, what can be said about the function $h(t) = f(t)g(t)$?

Review

In Exercises 65–68, find the inverse function of the one-to-one function f.

65. $f(x) = \frac{1}{2}(3x - 2)$ **66.** $f(x) = \frac{1}{4}x^3 + 1$

67. $f(x) = \sqrt{x^2 - 4}$, $x \ge 2$ **68.** $f(x) = \dfrac{x + 2}{x - 4}$

4.3   Right Triangle Trigonometry

▶ **What you should learn**

- How to evaluate trigonometric functions of acute angles
- How to use the fundamental trigonometric identities
- How to use a calculator to evaluate trigonometric functions
- How to use trigonometric functions to model and solve real-life problems

▶ **Why you should learn it**

Trigonometric functions are often used to analyze real-life situations. For instance, in Exercise 63 on page 289, you are asked to use trigonometric functions to find the height of a helium-filled balloon.

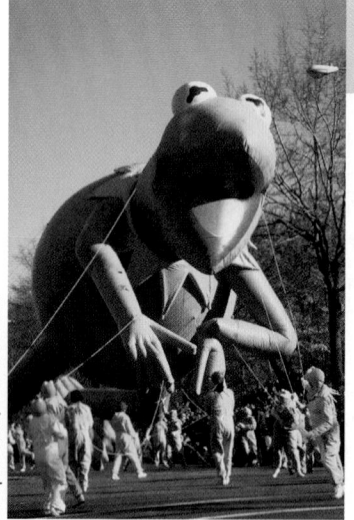

Joseph Sohm; Chromo Sohm

The Six Trigonometric Functions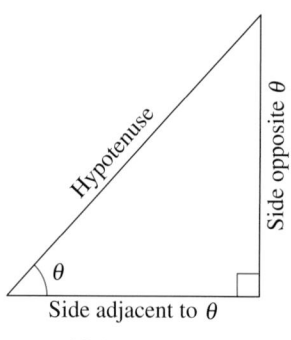

Our second look at the trigonometric functions is from a *right triangle* perspective. Consider a right triangle, with one acute angle labeled θ, as shown in Figure 4.24. Relative to the angle θ, the three sides of the triangle are the **hypotenuse,** the **opposite side** (the side opposite the angle θ), and the **adjacent side** (the side adjacent to the angle θ).

FIGURE 4.24

Using the lengths of these three sides, you can form six ratios that define the six trigonometric functions of the acute angle θ.

sine   cosecant   cosine   secant   tangent   cotangent

In the following definition, it is important to see that $0° < \theta < 90°$ and that for such angles the value of each trigonometric function is *positive*.

Right Triangle Definitions of Trigonometric Functions

Let θ be an *acute* angle of a right triangle. The six trigonometric functions of the angle θ are defined as follows. (Note that the functions in the second row are the *reciprocals* of the corresponding functions in the first row.)

$$\sin \theta = \frac{\text{opp}}{\text{hyp}} \qquad \cos \theta = \frac{\text{adj}}{\text{hyp}} \qquad \tan \theta = \frac{\text{opp}}{\text{adj}}$$

$$\csc \theta = \frac{\text{hyp}}{\text{opp}} \qquad \sec \theta = \frac{\text{hyp}}{\text{adj}} \qquad \cot \theta = \frac{\text{adj}}{\text{opp}}$$

The abbreviations opp, adj, and hyp represent the lengths of the three sides of a right triangle.

opp = the length of the side *opposite* θ

adj = the length of the side *adjacent to* θ

hyp = the length of the *hypotenuse*

You may wish to review the Pythagorean Theorem before presenting the examples in this section.

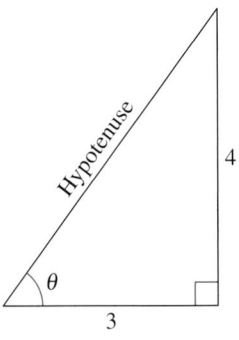

FIGURE **4.25**

Historical Note
Georg Joachim Rhaeticus (1514–1576) was the leading Teutonic mathematical astronomer of the 16th century. He was the first to define the trigonometric functions as ratios of the sides of a right triangle.

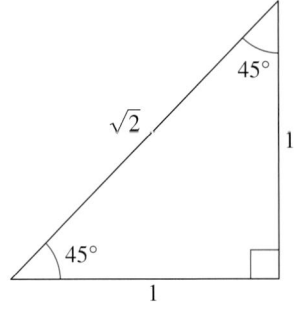

FIGURE **4.26**

Example 1 ▶ Evaluating Trigonometric Functions

Use the triangle in Figure 4.25 to find the values of the six trigonometric functions of θ.

Solution

By the Pythagorean Theorem, $(hyp)^2 = (opp)^2 + (adj)^2$, it follows that

$$hyp = \sqrt{4^2 + 3^2}$$
$$= \sqrt{25}$$
$$= 5.$$

So, the six trigonometric functions of θ are

$$\sin \theta = \frac{opp}{hyp} = \frac{4}{5} \qquad \csc \theta = \frac{hyp}{opp} = \frac{5}{4}$$

$$\cos \theta = \frac{adj}{hyp} = \frac{3}{5} \qquad \sec \theta = \frac{hyp}{adj} = \frac{5}{3}$$

$$\tan \theta = \frac{opp}{adj} = \frac{4}{3} \qquad \cot \theta = \frac{adj}{opp} = \frac{3}{4}.$$

In Example 1, you were given the lengths of two sides of the right triangle, but not the angle θ. Often, you will be asked to find the trigonometric functions of a *given* acute angle θ. To do this, construct a right triangle having θ as one of its angles.

Example 2 ▶ Evaluating Trigonometric Functions of 45°

Find the values of sin 45°, cos 45°, and tan 45°.

Solution

Construct a right triangle having 45° as one of its acute angles, as shown in Figure 4.26. Choose the length of the adjacent side to be 1. From geometry, you know that the other acute angle is also 45°. So, the triangle is isosceles and the length of the opposite side is also 1. Using the Pythagorean Theorem, you find the length of the hypotenuse to be $\sqrt{2}$.

$$\sin 45° = \frac{opp}{hyp} = \frac{1}{\sqrt{2}} = \frac{\sqrt{2}}{2}$$

$$\cos 45° = \frac{adj}{hyp} = \frac{1}{\sqrt{2}} = \frac{\sqrt{2}}{2}$$

$$\tan 45° = \frac{opp}{adj} = \frac{1}{1} = 1$$

Example 3 ▶ Evaluating Trigonometric Functions of 30° and 60°

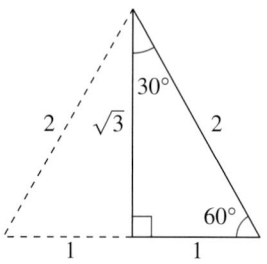

Use the equilateral triangle shown in Figure 4.27 to find the values of sin 60°, cos 60°, sin 30°, and cos 30°.

FIGURE **4.27**

Consider having your students construct the triangle in Figure 4.27 with angles in the corresponding radian measures, then find the six trigonometric functions for each of the acute angles.

Solution

Use the Pythagorean Theorem and the equilateral triangle in Figure 4.27 to verify the lengths of the sides shown in Figure 4.27. For $\theta = 60°$, you have adj = 1, opp = $\sqrt{3}$, and hyp = 2. So,

$$\sin 60° = \frac{\text{opp}}{\text{hyp}} = \frac{\sqrt{3}}{2} \quad \text{and} \quad \cos 60° = \frac{\text{adj}}{\text{hyp}} = \frac{1}{2}.$$

For $\theta = 30°$, adj = $\sqrt{3}$, opp = 1, and hyp = 2. So,

$$\sin 30° = \frac{\text{opp}}{\text{hyp}} = \frac{1}{2} \quad \text{and} \quad \cos 30° = \frac{\text{adj}}{\text{hyp}} = \frac{\sqrt{3}}{2}.$$

STUDY TIP

Because the angles 30°, 45°, and 60° ($\pi/6$, $\pi/4$, and $\pi/3$) occur frequently in trigonometry, you should learn to construct the triangles shown in Figures 4.26 and 4.27.

The triangles in Figures 4.25, 4.26, and 4.27 are useful problem-solving aids. Encourage your students to draw diagrams when they solve problems similar to Examples 1, 2, and 3.

Sines, Cosines, and Tangents of Special Angles

$$\sin 30° = \sin \frac{\pi}{6} = \frac{1}{2} \qquad \cos 30° = \cos \frac{\pi}{6} = \frac{\sqrt{3}}{2} \qquad \tan 30° = \tan \frac{\pi}{6} = \frac{\sqrt{3}}{3}$$

$$\sin 45° = \sin \frac{\pi}{4} = \frac{\sqrt{2}}{2} \qquad \cos 45° = \cos \frac{\pi}{4} = \frac{\sqrt{2}}{2} \qquad \tan 45° = \tan \frac{\pi}{4} = 1$$

$$\sin 60° = \sin \frac{\pi}{3} = \frac{\sqrt{3}}{2} \qquad \cos 60° = \cos \frac{\pi}{3} = \frac{1}{2} \qquad \tan 60° = \tan \frac{\pi}{3} = \sqrt{3}$$

In the box, note that $\sin 30° = \frac{1}{2} = \cos 60°$. This occurs because 30° and 60° are complementary angles. In general, it can be shown from the right triangle definitions that *cofunctions of complementary angles are equal*. That is, if θ is an acute angle, the following relationships are true.

$$\sin(90° - \theta) = \cos \theta \qquad \cos(90° - \theta) = \sin \theta$$

$$\tan(90° - \theta) = \cot \theta \qquad \cot(90° - \theta) = \tan \theta$$

$$\sec(90° - \theta) = \csc \theta \qquad \csc(90° - \theta) = \sec \theta$$

Trigonometric Identities

In trigonometry, a great deal of time is spent studying relationships between trigonometric functions (identities).

These identities will be used many times in trigonometry and later in calculus. Encourage your students to learn them well.

Fundamental Trigonometric Identities

Reciprocal Identities

$$\sin \theta = \frac{1}{\csc \theta} \qquad \cos \theta = \frac{1}{\sec \theta} \qquad \tan \theta = \frac{1}{\cot \theta}$$

$$\csc \theta = \frac{1}{\sin \theta} \qquad \sec \theta = \frac{1}{\cos \theta} \qquad \cot \theta = \frac{1}{\tan \theta}$$

Quotient Identities

$$\tan \theta = \frac{\sin \theta}{\cos \theta} \qquad \cot \theta = \frac{\cos \theta}{\sin \theta}$$

Pythagorean Identities

$$\sin^2 \theta + \cos^2 \theta = 1 \qquad 1 + \tan^2 \theta = \sec^2 \theta$$

$$1 + \cot^2 \theta = \csc^2 \theta$$

Note that $\sin^2 \theta$ represents $(\sin \theta)^2$, $\cos^2 \theta$ represents $(\cos \theta)^2$, and so on.

Example 4 ▶ Applying Trigonometric Identities

Let θ be an acute angle such that $\sin \theta = 0.6$. Find the values of (a) $\cos \theta$ and (b) $\tan \theta$ using trigonometric identities.

Solution

a. To find the value of $\cos \theta$, use the Pythagorean identity

$$\sin^2 \theta + \cos^2 \theta = 1.$$

So, you have

$$(0.6)^2 + \cos^2 \theta = 1 \qquad \text{Substitute 0.6 for } \sin \theta.$$

$$\cos^2 \theta = 1 - (0.6)^2 = 0.64 \qquad \text{Subtract } (0.6)^2 \text{ from each side.}$$

$$\cos \theta = \sqrt{0.64} = 0.8. \qquad \text{Extract the positive square root.}$$

b. Now, knowing the sine and cosine of θ, you can find the tangent of θ to be

$$\tan \theta = \frac{\sin \theta}{\cos \theta}$$

$$= \frac{0.6}{0.8}$$

$$= 0.75.$$

Use the definitions of $\cos \theta$ and $\tan \theta$, and the triangle shown in Figure 4.28, to check these results.

FIGURE **4.28**

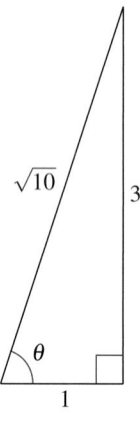

FIGURE 4.29

One of the most common errors students make when they evaluate trigonometric functions with a calculator is not having their calculators set to the correct mode (radian vs. degree).

Example 5 ▶ **Applying Trigonometric Identities**

Let θ be an acute angle such that tan $\theta = 3$. Find the value of each trigonometric function using trigonometric identities.

a. cot θ

b. sec θ

Solution

a. $\cot \theta = \dfrac{1}{\tan \theta} = \dfrac{1}{3}$ Reciprocal identity

b. $\sec^2 \theta = 1 + \tan^2 \theta$ Pythagorean identity

$\sec^2 \theta = 1 + 3^2$

$\sec^2 \theta = 10$

$\sec \theta = \sqrt{10}$

Use the definitions of cot θ and sec θ, and the triangle shown in Figure 4.29, to check these results.

Evaluating Trigonometric Functions with a Calculator

To use a calculator to evaluate trigonometric functions of angles measured in degrees, first set the calculator to *degree* mode and then proceed as demonstrated in Section 4.2. For instance, you can find values of cos 28° and sec 28° as follows.

Function	Calculator Keystrokes	Display
cos 28°	[COS] 28 [ENTER]	0.8829476
sec 28°	([COS] 28) [x^{-1}] [ENTER]	1.1325701

Throughout this text, angles are assumed to be measured in radians unless noted otherwise. For example, sin 1 means the sine of 1 radian and sin 1° means the sine of 1 degree.

Example 6 ▶ **Using a Calculator**

Use a calculator to evaluate sec(5° 40′ 12″).

Solution

Begin by converting to decimal form.

$$5° \, 40' \, 12'' = 5° + \left(\frac{40}{60}\right)^{\circ} + \left(\frac{12}{3600}\right)^{\circ} = 5.67°$$

Then, use a calculator to evaluate sec 5.67°.

$$\sec(5° \, 40' \, 12'') = \sec 5.67° = \frac{1}{\cos 5.67°} \approx 1.00492$$

FIGURE **4.30**

FIGURE **4.31**

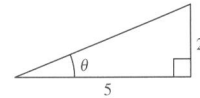
Applications Involving Right Triangles

Many applications of trigonometry involve a process called **solving right triangles.** In this type of application, you are usually given one side of a right triangle and one of the acute angles and asked to find one of the other sides, or you are given two sides and asked to find one of the acute angles.

Example 7 ▶ Using Trigonometry to Solve a Right Triangle

A surveyor is standing 115 feet from the base of the Washington Monument, as shown in Figure 4.30. The surveyor measures the angle of elevation to the top of the monument as 78.3°. How tall is the Washington Monument?

Solution

From Figure 4.30, you can see that

$$\tan 78.3° = \frac{\text{opp}}{\text{adj}} = \frac{y}{x}$$

where $x = 115$ and y is the height of the monument. So, the height of the Washington Monument is

$$y = x \tan 78.3° \approx 115(4.82882) \approx 555 \text{ feet.}$$

The term **angle of elevation** represents the angle from the horizontal upward to an object. For objects that lie below the horizontal, it is common to use the term **angle of depression,** as shown in Figure 4.31.

Example 8 ▶ Using Trigonometry to Solve a Right Triangle

You are 200 yards from a river. Rather than walking directly to the river, you walk 400 yards along a straight path to the river's edge. Find the acute angle θ between this path and the river's edge, as illustrated in Figure 4.32.

FIGURE **4.32**

Solution

From Figure 4.32, you can see that the sine of the angle θ is

$$\sin \theta = \frac{\text{opp}}{\text{hyp}} = \frac{200}{400} = \frac{1}{2}.$$

So, $\theta = 30°$.

By now you are able to recognize that the acute angle that satisfies the equation $\sin\theta = \frac{1}{2}$ is $\theta = 30°$. Suppose, however, that you were given the equation $\sin\theta = 0.6$ and were asked to find the acute angle θ. Because

$$\sin 30° = \frac{1}{2}$$

$$= 0.5000$$

and

$$\sin 45° = \frac{1}{\sqrt{2}}$$

$$\approx 0.7071$$

you might guess that θ lies somewhere between $30°$ and $45°$. A more precise value of θ can be found using the *inverse sine* key on a calculator. To do this, you can use the following keystroke sequence in *degree* mode.

[sin⁻¹] .6 [ENTER]   Display 36.8699

So, you can conclude that if $\sin\theta = 0.6$ and $0° < \theta < 90°$, then $\theta \approx 36.87°$.

Example 9 ▶ **Solving a Right Triangle**

Specifications for a loading dock ramp require a rise of 1 foot for each 3 feet of horizontal length. In Figure 4.33, find the lengths of sides b and c and find the measure of θ.

Solution

From the given specifications, you can write

$$\frac{\text{rise}}{\text{run}} = \frac{1}{3} = \frac{4\text{ ft}}{b\text{ ft}}$$

which implies that $b = 12$ feet. Using the Pythagorean Theorem, you can write

$c^2 = a^2 + b^2$	Pythagorean Theorem
$c^2 = 4^2 + 12^2$	Substitute for a and b.
$c^2 = 160$	Simplify.
$c = 4\sqrt{10}.$	Extract positive square root.

So, $c = 4\sqrt{10} \approx 12.65$ feet. To solve for θ, you can write

$$\tan\theta = \frac{4}{12}$$

$$= \frac{1}{3}.$$

Then, using the calculator keystrokes in *degree* mode

[tan⁻¹] [(] 1 [÷] 3 [)] [ENTER]

you obtain $\theta \approx 18.43°$.

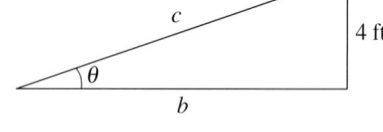

c

4 ft

θ

b

FIGURE **4.33**

4.3 Exercises

In Exercises 1–4, find the exact values of the six trigonometric functions of the angle θ shown in the figure. (Use the Pythagorean Theorem to find the third side of the triangle.)

1.

2.

3.

4.

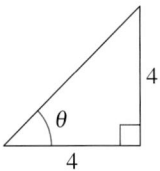

In Exercises 5–8, find the exact values of the six trigonometric functions of the angle θ for each of the two triangles. Explain why the function values are the same.

5.

6.

7.

8.

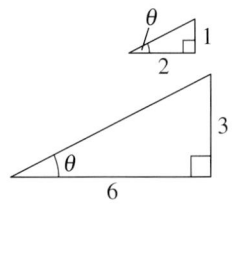

In Exercises 9–16, sketch a right triangle corresponding to the trigonometric function of the acute angle θ. Use the Pythagorean Theorem to determine the third side and then find the other five trigonometric functions of θ.

9. $\sin \theta = \frac{3}{4}$

10. $\cos \theta = \frac{5}{7}$

11. $\sec \theta = 2$

12. $\cot \theta = 5$

13. $\tan \theta = 3$

14. $\sec \theta = 6$

15. $\cot \theta = \frac{3}{2}$

16. $\csc \theta = \frac{17}{4}$

In Exercises 17–22, use the given function value(s), and trigonometric identities (including the cofunction identities), to find the indicated trigonometric functions.

17. $\sin 60° = \dfrac{\sqrt{3}}{2}, \quad \cos 60° = \dfrac{1}{2}$

  (a) $\tan 60°$ (b) $\sin 30°$

  (c) $\cos 30°$ (d) $\cot 60°$

18. $\sin 30° = \dfrac{1}{2}, \quad \tan 30° = \dfrac{\sqrt{3}}{3}$

  (a) $\csc 30°$ (b) $\cot 60°$

  (c) $\cos 30°$ (d) $\cot 30°$

19. $\csc \theta = \dfrac{\sqrt{13}}{2}, \quad \sec \theta = \dfrac{\sqrt{13}}{3}$

  (a) $\sin \theta$ (b) $\cos \theta$

  (c) $\tan \theta$ (d) $\sec(90° - \theta)$

20. $\sec \theta = 5, \quad \tan \theta = 2\sqrt{6}$

  (a) $\cos \theta$ (b) $\cot \theta$

  (c) $\cot(90° - \theta)$ (d) $\sin \theta$

21. $\cos \alpha = \frac{1}{3}$

  (a) $\sec \alpha$ (b) $\sin \alpha$

  (c) $\cot \alpha$ (d) $\sin(90° - \alpha)$

22. $\tan \beta = 5$

  (a) $\cot \beta$ (b) $\cos \beta$

  (c) $\tan(90° - \beta)$ (d) $\csc \beta$

In Exercises 23–26, evaluate the trigonometric function by memory or by constructing an appropriate triangle for the given special angle.

23. (a) $\cos 60°$ (b) $\csc 30°$ (c) $\tan 60°$

24. (a) $\cot 45°$ (b) $\cos 45°$ (c) $\csc 45°$

25. (a) $\sin 45°$ (b) $\cos 30°$ (c) $\tan 30°$

26. (a) $\sin 60°$ (b) $\tan 45°$ (c) $\sec 30°$

In Exercises 27–36, use a calculator to evaluate each function. Round your answers to four decimal places. (Be sure the calculator is in the correct angle mode.)

27. (a) $\sin 10°$ (b) $\cos 80°$

28. (a) $\tan 23.5°$ (b) $\cot 66.5°$

29. (a) $\sin 16.35°$ (b) $\csc 16.35°$

30. (a) $\cos 16° \, 18'$ (b) $\sin 73° \, 56'$

31. (a) $\sec 42° \, 12'$ (b) $\csc 48° \, 7'$

32. (a) $\cos 4° \, 50' \, 15''$ (b) $\sec 4° \, 50' \, 15''$

33. (a) $\cot 11° \, 15'$ (b) $\tan 11° \, 15'$

34. (a) $\sec 56° \, 8' \, 10''$ (b) $\cos 56° \, 8' \, 10''$

35. (a) $\csc 32° \, 40' \, 3''$ (b) $\tan 44° \, 28' \, 16''$

36. (a) $\sec\left(\frac{9}{5} \cdot 20 + 32\right)°$ (b) $\cot\left(\frac{9}{5} \cdot 30 + 32\right)°$

In Exercises 37–42, find the values of θ in degrees ($0° < \theta < 90°$) and radians ($0 < \theta < \pi/2$) without the aid of a calculator.

37. (a) $\sin \theta = \dfrac{1}{2}$ (b) $\csc \theta = 2$

38. (a) $\cos \theta = \dfrac{\sqrt{2}}{2}$ (b) $\tan \theta = 1$

39. (a) $\sec \theta = 2$ (b) $\cot \theta = 1$

40. (a) $\tan \theta = \sqrt{3}$ (b) $\cos \theta = \dfrac{1}{2}$

41. (a) $\csc \theta = \dfrac{2\sqrt{3}}{3}$ (b) $\sin \theta = \dfrac{\sqrt{2}}{2}$

42. (a) $\cot \theta = \dfrac{\sqrt{3}}{3}$ (b) $\sec \theta = \sqrt{2}$

In Exercises 43–46, find the values of θ in degrees ($0° < \theta < 90°$) and radians ($0 < \theta < \pi/2$) by using a calculator.

43. (a) $\sin \theta = 0.0145$ (b) $\sin \theta = 0.4565$

44. (a) $\cos \theta = 0.9848$ (b) $\cos \theta = 0.8746$

45. (a) $\tan \theta = 0.0125$ (b) $\tan \theta = 2.3545$

46. (a) $\sin \theta = 0.3746$ (b) $\cos \theta = 0.3746$

In Exercises 47–56, use trigonometric identities to transform the left side of the equation into the right side.

47. $\tan \theta \cot \theta = 1$

48. $\cos \theta \sec \theta = 1$

49. $\tan \alpha \cos \alpha = \sin \alpha$

50. $\cot \alpha \sin \alpha = \cos \alpha$

51. $(1 + \cos \theta)(1 - \cos \theta) = \sin^2 \theta$

52. $(1 + \sin \theta)(1 - \sin \theta) = \cos^2 \theta$

53. $(\sec \theta + \tan \theta)(\sec \theta - \tan \theta) = 1$

54. $\sin^2 \theta - \cos^2 \theta = 2 \sin^2 \theta - 1$

55. $\dfrac{\sin \theta}{\cos \theta} + \dfrac{\cos \theta}{\sin \theta} = \csc \theta \sec \theta$

56. $\dfrac{\tan \beta + \cot \beta}{\tan \beta} = \csc^2 \beta$

In Exercises 57–60, solve for x, y, or r, as indicated.

57. Solve for x.

58. Solve for y.

59. Solve for x.

60. Solve for r.

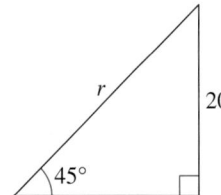

61. *Height* A six-foot person walks from the base of a broadcasting tower directly toward the tip of the shadow cast by the tower. When the person is 132 feet from the tower and 3 feet from the tip of the shadow, the person's shadow starts to appear beyond the tower's shadow.

(a) Draw a right triangle that gives a visual representation of the problem. Show the known quantities of the triangle and use a variable to indicate the height of the tower.

(b) Use a trigonometric function to write an equation involving the unknown quantity.

(c) What is the height of the tower?

62. *Height* A six-foot person standing 20 feet from a streetlight casts a 10-foot shadow (see figure). What is the height of the streetlight?

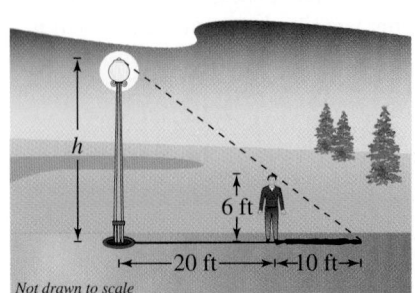

Not drawn to scale

▶ **Model It**

63. *Height* A 20-meter line is used to tether a helium-filled balloon. Because of a breeze, the line makes an angle of approximately 85° with the ground.

   (a) Draw a right triangle that gives a visual representation of the problem. Show the known quantities of the triangle and use a variable to indicate the height of the balloon.

   (b) Use a trigonometric function to write an equation involving the unknown quantity.

   (c) What is the height of the balloon?

   (d) The breeze becomes stronger and the angle the balloon makes with the ground decreases. How does this affect the triangle you drew in part (a)?

   (e) Complete the table, which shows the height (in meters) of the balloon for decreasing angle measures θ.

Angle, θ	80°	70°	60°	50°
Height				

Angle, θ	40°	30°	20°	10°
Height				

   (f) As the angle the balloon makes with the ground approaches 0°, how does this affect the height of the balloon? Draw a right triangle to explain your reasoning.

64. *Angle of Elevation* A ramp 20 feet in length rises to a loading platform that is $3\frac{1}{3}$ feet off the ground.

   (a) Draw a right triangle that gives a visual representation of the problem. Show the known quantities of the triangle and use a variable to indicate the angle of elevation of the ramp.

   (b) Use a trigonometric function to write an equation involving the unknown quantity.

   (c) What is the angle of elevation of the ramp?

65. *Width of a River* A biologist wants to know the width w of a river in order to set instruments for studying the pollutants in the water. From point A, the biologist walks downstream 100 feet and sights to point C (see figure). From this sighting, it is determined that $\theta = 54°$. How wide is the river?

66. *Height of a Mountain* In traveling across flat land, you notice a mountain directly in front of you. Its angle of elevation (to the peak) is 3.5°. After you drive 13 miles closer to the mountain, the angle of elevation is 9°. Approximate the height of the mountain.

67. *Machine Shop Calculations* A steel plate has the form of one-fourth of a circle with a radius of 60 centimeters. Two two-centimeter holes are to be drilled in the plate positioned as shown in the figure. Find the coordinates of the center of each hole.

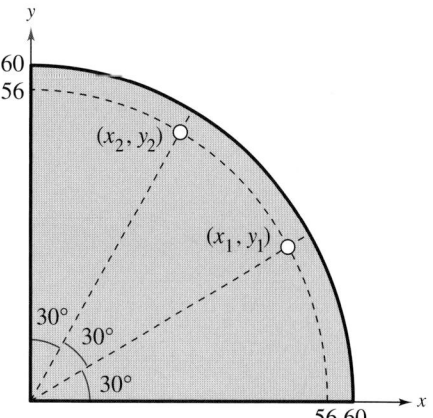

68. *Machine Shop Calculations* A tapered shaft has a diameter of 5 centimeters at the small end and is 15 centimeters long (see figure). The taper is 3°. Find the diameter d of the large end of the shaft.

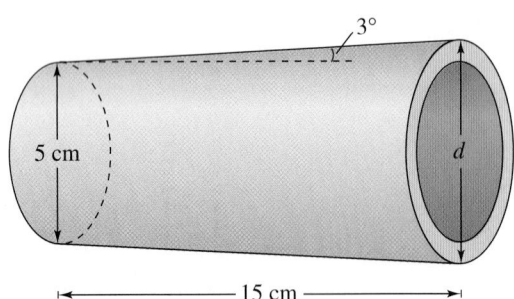

69. *Geometry* Use a compass to sketch a quarter of a circle of radius 10 centimeters. Using a protractor, construct an angle of 20° in standard position (see figure). Drop a perpendicular line from the point of intersection of the terminal side of the angle and the arc of the circle. By actual measurement, calculate the coordinates (x, y) of the point of intersection and use these measurements to approximate the six trigonometric functions of a 20° angle.

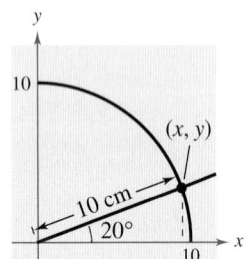

70. *Geometry* Repeat Exercise 69 using a 75° angle.

Synthesis

True or False? In Exercises 71–76, determine whether the statement is true or false. Justify your answer.

71. $\sin 60° \csc 60° = 1$

72. $\sec 30° = \csc 60°$

73. $\sin 45° + \cos 45° = 1$

74. $\cot^2 10° - \csc^2 10° = -1$

75. $\dfrac{\sin 60°}{\sin 30°} = \sin 2°$

76. $\tan[(5°)^2] = \tan^2(5°)$

77. *Writing* In right triangle trigonometry, explain why $\sin 30° = \frac{1}{2}$ regardless of the size of the triangle.

78. *Think About It* You are given only the value $\tan \theta$. Is it possible to find the value of $\sec \theta$ without finding the measure of θ? Explain.

79. *Exploration*

(a) Complete the table.

θ	0.1	0.2	0.3	0.4	0.5
$\sin \theta$					

(b) As θ approaches 0, how do θ and $\sin \theta$ compare? Explain.

80. *Exploration*

(a) Complete the table.

θ	0°	18°	36°	54°	72°	90°
$\sin \theta$						
$\cos \theta$						

(b) Discuss the behavior of the sine function for θ in the range from 0° to 90°.

(c) Discuss the behavior of the cosine function for θ in the range from 0° to 90°.

(d) Use the definitions of the sine and cosine functions to explain the results of parts (b) and (c).

Review

In Exercises 81–84, perform the operations and simplify.

81. $\dfrac{x^2 - 6x}{x^2 + 4x - 12} \cdot \dfrac{x^2 + 12x + 36}{x^2 - 36}$

82. $\dfrac{2t^2 + 5t - 12}{9 - 4t^2} \div \dfrac{t^2 - 16}{4t^2 + 12t + 9}$

83. $\dfrac{3}{x + 2} - \dfrac{2}{x - 2} + \dfrac{x}{x^2 + 4x + 4}$

84. $\dfrac{\left(\dfrac{3}{x} - \dfrac{1}{4}\right)}{\left(\dfrac{12}{x} - 1\right)}$

In Exercises 85 and 86, solve for x.

85. $\dfrac{2}{x + 3} + \dfrac{4}{x - 2} = \dfrac{12}{x^2 + x - 6}$

86. $\dfrac{3x + 2}{x^2 + x - 2} = \dfrac{4}{x + 2} - \dfrac{2}{1 - x}$

Trigonometric Functions of Any Angle

▶ **What you should learn**

- How to evaluate trigonometric functions of any angle
- How to use reference angles to evaluate trigonometric functions
- How to evaluate trigonometric functions of real numbers

▶ **Why you should learn it**

You can use trigonometric functions to model and solve real-life problems. For instance, in Exercise 91 on page 298, you are asked to use trigonometric functions to model the monthly normal temperatures in New York City and Fairbanks, Alaska.

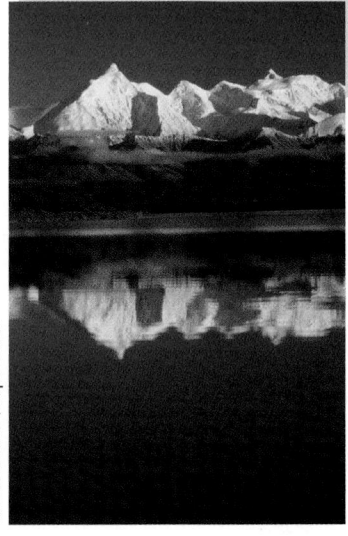

Introduction

In Section 4.3, the definitions of trigonometric functions were restricted to acute angles. In this section, the definitions are extended to cover *any* angle. If θ is an *acute* angle, these definitions coincide with those given in the preceding section.

Definitions of Trigonometric Functions of Any Angle

Let θ be an angle in standard position with (x, y) a point on the terminal side of θ and $r = \sqrt{x^2 + y^2} \neq 0$.

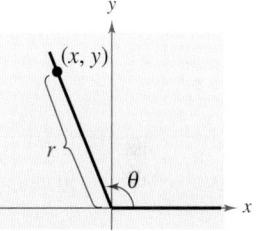

$$\sin \theta = \frac{y}{r} \qquad \cos \theta = \frac{x}{r}$$

$$\tan \theta = \frac{y}{x}, \quad x \neq 0 \qquad \cot \theta = \frac{x}{y}, \quad y \neq 0$$

$$\sec \theta = \frac{r}{x}, \quad x \neq 0 \qquad \csc \theta = \frac{r}{y}, \quad y \neq 0$$

Because $r = \sqrt{x^2 + y^2}$ *cannot* be zero, it follows that the sine and cosine functions are defined for any real value of θ. However, if $x = 0$, the tangent and secant of θ are undefined. For example, the tangent of $90°$ is undefined. Similarly, if $y = 0$, the cotangent and cosecant of θ are undefined.

Example 1 ▶ Evaluating Trigonometric Functions

Let $(-3, 4)$ be a point on the terminal side of θ. Find the sine, cosine, and tangent of θ.

Solution

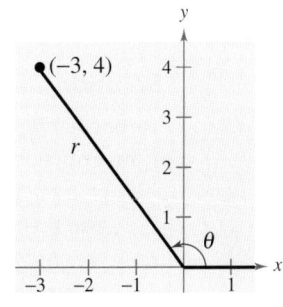

FIGURE **4.34**

Referring to Figure 4.34, you can see that $x = -3$, $y = 4$, and

$$r = \sqrt{x^2 + y^2} = \sqrt{(-3)^2 + 4^2} = \sqrt{25} = 5.$$

So, you have the following.

$$\sin \theta = y/r = 4/5, \qquad \cos \theta = x/r = -3/5, \qquad \tan \theta = y/x = -4/3$$

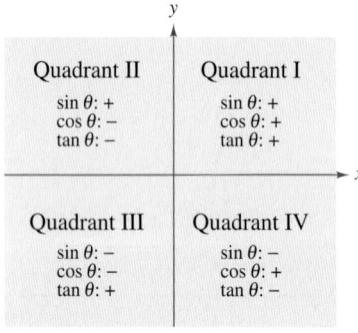

FIGURE **4.35**

The *signs* of the trigonometric functions in the four quadrants can be determined easily from the definitions of the functions. For instance, because $\cos \theta = x/r$, it follows that $\cos \theta$ is positive wherever $x > 0$, which is in Quadrants I and IV. (Remember, r is always positive.) In a similar manner, you can verify the results shown in Figure 4.35.

Example 2 ▶ Evaluating Trigonometric Functions

Given $\tan \theta = -\frac{5}{4}$ and $\cos \theta > 0$, find $\sin \theta$ and $\sec \theta$.

Solution

Note that θ lies in Quadrant IV because that is the only quadrant in which the tangent is negative and the cosine is positive. Moreover, using

$$\tan \theta = \frac{y}{x}$$

$$= -\frac{5}{4}$$

and the fact that y is negative in Quadrant IV, you can let $y = -5$ and $x = 4$. So, $r = \sqrt{16 + 25} = \sqrt{41}$ and you have

$$\sin \theta = \frac{y}{r} = \frac{-5}{\sqrt{41}}$$

$$\approx -0.7809$$

$$\sec \theta = \frac{r}{x} = \frac{\sqrt{41}}{4}$$

$$\approx 1.6008.$$

Example 3 ▶ Trigonometric Functions of Quadrant Angles

Evaluate the sine function at the four quadrant angles 0, $\dfrac{\pi}{2}$, π, and $\dfrac{3\pi}{2}$.

Solution

To begin, choose a point on the terminal side of each angle, as shown in Figure 4.36. For each of the four points, $r = 1$, and you have

$$\sin 0 = \frac{y}{r} = \frac{0}{1} = 0 \qquad (x, y) = (1, 0)$$

$$\sin \frac{\pi}{2} = \frac{y}{r} = \frac{1}{1} = 1 \qquad (x, y) = (0, 1)$$

$$\sin \pi = \frac{y}{r} = \frac{0}{1} = 0 \qquad (x, y) = (-1, 0)$$

$$\sin \frac{3\pi}{2} = \frac{y}{r} = \frac{-1}{1} = -1. \qquad (x, y) = (0, -1)$$

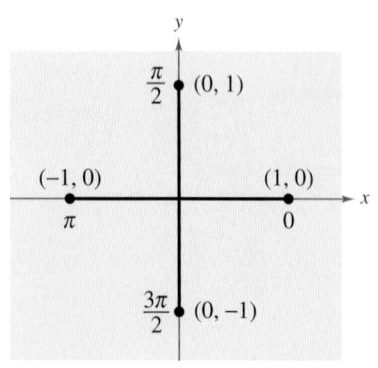

FIGURE **4.36**

Sketching several angles with their reference angles helps reinforce the fact that the reference angle is the acute angle formed with the horizontal.

Reference Angles

The values of the trigonometric functions of angles greater than 90° (or less than 0°) can be determined from their values at corresponding acute angles called **reference angles.**

> ## Definition of Reference Angle
>
> Let θ be an angle in standard position. Its **reference angle** is the acute angle θ' formed by the terminal side of θ and the horizontal axis.

Figure 4.37 shows the reference angles for θ in Quadrants II, III, and IV.

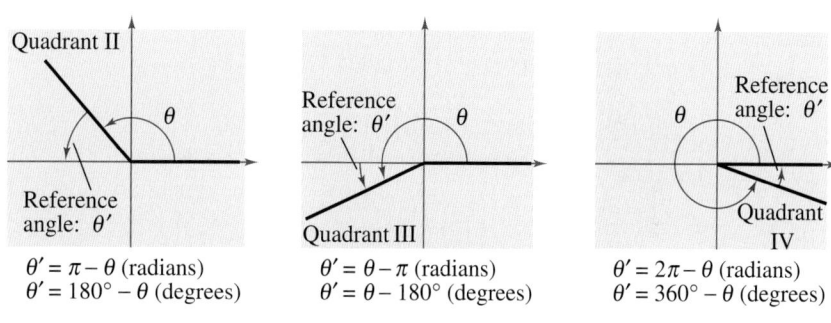

$\theta' = \pi - \theta$ (radians)
$\theta' = 180° - \theta$ (degrees)

$\theta' = \theta - \pi$ (radians)
$\theta' = \theta - 180°$ (degrees)

$\theta' = 2\pi - \theta$ (radians)
$\theta' = 360° - \theta$ (degrees)

FIGURE **4.37**

Example 4 ▶ **Finding Reference Angles**

Find the reference angle θ'.

a. $\theta = 300°$ **b.** $\theta = 2.3$ **c.** $\theta = -135°$

Solution

a. Because 300° lies in Quadrant IV, the angle it makes with the x-axis is

$$\theta' = 360° - 300°$$
$$= 60°. \qquad \text{Degrees}$$

Figure 4.38 shows the angle $\theta = 300°$ and its reference angle $\theta' = 60°$.

b. Because 2.3 lies between $\pi/2 \approx 1.5708$ and $\pi \approx 3.1416$, it follows that it is in Quadrant II and its reference angle is

$$\theta' = \pi - 2.3$$
$$\approx 0.8416. \qquad \text{Radians}$$

Figure 4.39 shows the angle $\theta = 2.3$ and its reference angle $\theta' = \pi - 2.3$.

c. First, determine that $-135°$ is coterminal with 225°, which lies in Quadrant III. So, the reference angle is

$$\theta' = 225° - 180°$$
$$= 45°. \qquad \text{Degrees}$$

Figure 4.40 shows the angle $\theta = -135°$ and its reference angle $\theta' = 45°$.

FIGURE **4.38**

FIGURE **4.39**

FIGURE **4.40**

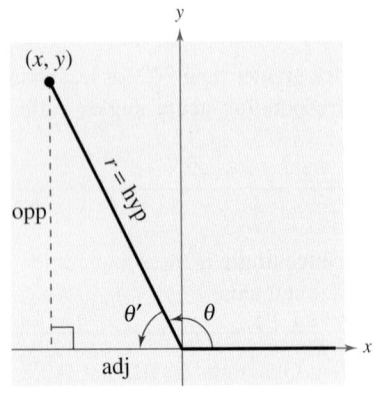

opp = $|y|$, adj = $|x|$

FIGURE 4.41

Trigonometric Functions of Real Numbers

To see how a reference angle is used to evaluate a trigonometric function, consider the point (x, y) on the terminal side of θ, as shown in Figure 4.41. By definition, you know that

$$\sin \theta = \frac{y}{r} \quad \text{and} \quad \tan \theta = \frac{y}{x}.$$

For the right triangle with acute angle θ' and sides of lengths $|x|$ and $|y|$, you have

$$\sin \theta' = \frac{\text{opp}}{\text{hyp}} = \frac{|y|}{r}$$

and

$$\tan \theta' = \frac{\text{opp}}{\text{adj}} = \frac{|y|}{|x|}.$$

So, it follows that $\sin \theta$ and $\sin \theta'$ are equal, *except possibly in sign*. The same is true for $\tan \theta$ and $\tan \theta'$ *and* for the other four trigonometric functions. In all cases, the sign of the function value can be determined by the quadrant in which θ lies.

Evaluating Trigonometric Functions of Any Angle

To find the value of a trigonometric function of any angle θ,

1. determine the function value for the associated reference angle θ';

2. depending on the quadrant in which θ lies, affix the appropriate sign to the function value.

By using reference angles and the special angles discussed in the preceding section, you can greatly extend the scope of *exact* trigonometric values. For instance, knowing the function values of 30° means that you know the function values of all angles for which 30° is a reference angle. For convenience, the table below shows the exact values of the trigonometric functions of special angles and quadrant angles.

STUDY TIP

Learning the table of values at the right is worth the effort. Doing so will increase both your efficiency and your confidence. Here is a pattern for the sine function that may help you remember the values.

θ	0°	30°	45°	60°	90°
$\sin \theta$	$\frac{\sqrt{0}}{2}$	$\frac{\sqrt{1}}{2}$	$\frac{\sqrt{2}}{2}$	$\frac{\sqrt{3}}{2}$	$\frac{\sqrt{4}}{2}$

Reverse the order to get cosine values of the same angles.

Trigonometric Values of Common Angles

θ (degrees)	0°	30°	45°	60°	90°	180°	270°
θ (radians)	0	$\frac{\pi}{6}$	$\frac{\pi}{4}$	$\frac{\pi}{3}$	$\frac{\pi}{2}$	π	$\frac{3\pi}{2}$
$\sin \theta$	0	$\frac{1}{2}$	$\frac{\sqrt{2}}{2}$	$\frac{\sqrt{3}}{2}$	1	0	-1
$\cos \theta$	1	$\frac{\sqrt{3}}{2}$	$\frac{\sqrt{2}}{2}$	$\frac{1}{2}$	0	-1	0
$\tan \theta$	0	$\frac{\sqrt{3}}{3}$	1	$\sqrt{3}$	Undef.	0	Undef.

Example 5 ▶ **Trigonometric Functions of Nonacute Angles**

Evaluate each trigonometric function.

a. $\cos \dfrac{4\pi}{3}$ **b.** $\tan(-210°)$ **c.** $\csc \dfrac{11\pi}{4}$

Solution

a. Because $\theta = 4\pi/3$ lies in Quadrant III, the reference angle is $\theta' = (4\pi/3) - \pi = \pi/3$, as shown in Figure 4.42. Moreover, the cosine is negative in Quadrant III, so

$$\cos \frac{4\pi}{3} = (-) \cos \frac{\pi}{3}$$

$$= -\frac{1}{2}.$$

Emphasize the importance of reference angles in evaluating trigonometric functions of angles greater than 90°.

b. Because $-210° + 360° = 150°$, it follows that $-210°$ is coterminal with the second-quadrant angle $150°$. So, the reference angle is $\theta' = 180° - 150° = 30°$, as shown in Figure 4.43. Finally, because the tangent is negative in Quadrant II, you have

$$\tan(-210°) = (-) \tan 30°$$

$$= -\frac{\sqrt{3}}{3}.$$

c. Because $(11\pi/4) - 2\pi = 3\pi/4$, it follows that $11\pi/4$ is coterminal with the second-quadrant angle $3\pi/4$. So, the reference angle is $\theta' = \pi - (3\pi/4) = \pi/4$, as shown in Figure 4.44. Because the cosecant is positive in Quadrant II, you have

$$\csc \frac{11\pi}{4} = (+) \csc \frac{\pi}{4}$$

$$= \frac{1}{\sin(\pi/4)}$$

$$= \sqrt{2}.$$

FIGURE **4.42**

FIGURE **4.43**

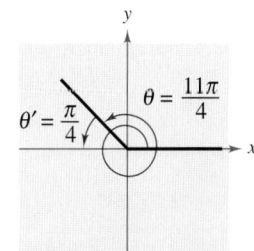

FIGURE **4.44**

Example 6 ▶ Using Trigonometric Identities

Let θ be an angle in Quadrant II such that $\sin \theta = \frac{1}{3}$. Find (a) $\cos \theta$ and (b) $\tan \theta$ by using trigonometric identities.

Solution

a. Using the Pythagorean identity $\sin^2 \theta + \cos^2 \theta = 1$, you obtain

$$\left(\frac{1}{3}\right)^2 + \cos^2 \theta = 1 \qquad \text{Substitute } \tfrac{1}{3} \text{ for } \sin \theta.$$

$$\cos^2 \theta = 1 - \frac{1}{9} = \frac{8}{9}.$$

Because $\cos \theta < 0$ in Quadrant II, you can use the negative root to obtain

$$\cos \theta = -\frac{\sqrt{8}}{\sqrt{9}}$$

$$= -\frac{2\sqrt{2}}{3}.$$

b. Using the trigonometric identity $\tan \theta = \sin \theta / \cos \theta$, you obtain

$$\tan \theta = \frac{1/3}{-2\sqrt{2}/3} \qquad \text{Substitute for } \sin \theta \text{ and } \cos \theta.$$

$$= -\frac{1}{2\sqrt{2}}$$

$$= -\frac{\sqrt{2}}{4}.$$

Students often have difficulty determining angles, especially when the functions given are csc, sec, and/or cot. Have your students rewrite the expression in terms of sin, cos, or tan, whichever is applicable, before evaluating.

Example 7 ▶ Using a Calculator

a. Use a calculator to evaluate $\cot 410°$ and $\sin(-7)$.

b. Use a calculator to solve $\tan \theta = 4.812$, $0 \le \theta < 2\pi$.

Solution

Function	Mode	Calculator Keystrokes	Display
a. $\cot 410°$	Degree	(TAN 410) x^{-1} ENTER	0.8390996
$\sin(-7)$	Radian	SIN ((−) 7) ENTER	−0.6569866

b. To solve the equation $\tan \theta = 4.812$, you can use the inverse tangent key, as follows.

Equation	Mode	Calculator Keystrokes	Display
$\tan \theta = 4.812$	Radian	TAN⁻¹ 4.812 ENTER	1.365898912

The angle $\theta \approx 1.3659$ lies in Quadrant I. A second value of θ lies in Quadrant III (tangent is positive) and is

$$\theta = \pi + 1.3659 \approx 4.5075.$$

Additional Examples

a. Solve the equation
   $\cot \theta = -4.3315, 0° \le \theta < 360°$.

b. Solve the equation $\csc \theta = 1.1034$,
   $0 \le \theta < 2\pi$.

c. Solve the equation
   $\sec \theta = -1.3054, 0 \le \theta < 2\pi$.

Solutions

a. $\tan \theta = \dfrac{1}{\cot \theta} = -0.230866905$;

   $\theta \approx 167°, 347°$

b. $\sin \theta = \dfrac{1}{\csc \theta} = 0.906289650$;

   $\theta \approx 1.13, 2.01$

c. $\cos \theta = \dfrac{1}{\sec \theta} = -0.766048721$;

   $\theta \approx 2.44, 3.84$

4.4 Exercises

In Exercises 1–4, determine the exact values of the six trigonometric functions of the angle θ.

1. (a) (b)

2. (a) (b)

3. (a) (b)

4. (a) (b)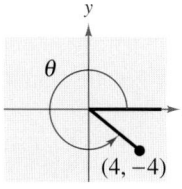

In Exercises 5–10, the point is on the terminal side of an angle in standard position. Determine the exact values of the six trigonometric functions of the angle.

5. $(7, 24)$

6. $(8, 15)$

7. $(-4, 10)$

8. $(-5, -2)$

9. $(-3.5, 6.8)$

10. $\left(3\frac{1}{2}, -7\frac{3}{4}\right)$

In Exercises 11–14, state the quadrant in which θ lies.

11. $\sin \theta < 0$ and $\cos \theta < 0$

12. $\sin \theta > 0$ and $\cos \theta > 0$

13. $\sin \theta > 0$ and $\tan \theta < 0$

14. $\sec \theta > 0$ and $\cot \theta < 0$

In Exercises 15–24, find the values of the six trigonometric functions of θ.

Function Value	Constraint
15. $\sin \theta = \frac{3}{5}$	θ lies in Quadrant II.
16. $\cos \theta = -\frac{4}{5}$	θ lies in Quadrant III.
17. $\tan \theta = -\frac{15}{8}$	$\sin \theta < 0$
18. $\cos \theta = \frac{8}{17}$	$\tan \theta < 0$
19. $\cot \theta = -3$	$\cos \theta > 0$
20. $\csc \theta = 4$	$\cot \theta < 0$
21. $\sec \theta = -2$	$\sin \theta > 0$
22. $\sin \theta = 0$	$\sec \theta = -1$
23. $\cot \theta$ is undefined.	$\pi/2 \leq \theta \leq 3\pi/2$
24. $\tan \theta$ is undefined.	$\pi \leq \theta \leq 2\pi$

In Exercises 25–28, the terminal side of θ lies on the given line in the specified quadrant. Find the values of the six trigonometric functions of θ by finding a point on the line.

Line	Quadrant
25. $y = -x$	II
26. $y = \frac{1}{3}x$	III
27. $2x - y = 0$	III
28. $4x + 3y = 0$	IV

In Exercises 29–36, evaluate the trigonometric function of the quadrant angle.

29. $\cos \pi$

30. $\cos \dfrac{3\pi}{2}$

31. $\sec \dfrac{3\pi}{2}$

32. $\sec \pi$

33. $\tan \dfrac{\pi}{2}$

34. $\tan \pi$

35. $\csc \pi$

36. $\cot \dfrac{\pi}{2}$

In Exercises 37–44, find the reference angle θ', and sketch θ and θ' in standard position.

37. $\theta = 203°$

38. $\theta = 309°$

39. $\theta = -245°$

40. $\theta = -145°$

41. $\theta = \dfrac{2\pi}{3}$

42. $\theta = \dfrac{7\pi}{4}$

43. $\theta = 3.5$

44. $\theta = \dfrac{11\pi}{3}$

In Exercises 45–58, evaluate the sine, cosine, and tangent of the angle without using a calculator.

45. $225°$

46. $300°$

47. $750°$

48. $-405°$

49. $-150°$

50. $-840°$

51. $\dfrac{4\pi}{3}$

52. $\dfrac{\pi}{4}$

53. $-\dfrac{\pi}{6}$

54. $-\dfrac{\pi}{2}$

55. $\dfrac{11\pi}{4}$

56. $\dfrac{10\pi}{3}$

57. $-\dfrac{3\pi}{2}$

58. $-\dfrac{25\pi}{4}$

In Exercises 59–68, use a calculator to evaluate the trigonometric function. Round your answer to four decimal places. (Be sure the calculator is set in the correct angle mode.)

59. $\sin 10°$

60. $\sec 225°$

61. $\cos(-110°)$

62. $\csc(-330°)$

63. $\tan 4.5$

64. $\cot 1.35$

65. $\tan \dfrac{\pi}{9}$

66. $\tan\left(-\dfrac{\pi}{9}\right)$

67. $\sin(-0.65)$

68. $\sin 0.65$

In Exercises 69–74, find two solutions of the equation. Give your answers in degrees ($0° \le \theta < 360°$) and radians ($0 \le \theta < 2\pi$). Do not use a calculator.

69. (a) $\sin \theta = \frac{1}{2}$ (b) $\sin \theta = -\frac{1}{2}$

70. (a) $\cos \theta = \dfrac{\sqrt{2}}{2}$ (b) $\cos \theta = -\dfrac{\sqrt{2}}{2}$

71. (a) $\csc \theta = \dfrac{2\sqrt{3}}{3}$ (b) $\cot \theta = -1$

72. (a) $\sec \theta = 2$ (b) $\sec \theta = -2$

73. (a) $\tan \theta = 1$ (b) $\cot \theta = -\sqrt{3}$

74. (a) $\sin \theta = \dfrac{\sqrt{3}}{2}$ (b) $\sin \theta = -\dfrac{\sqrt{3}}{2}$

In Exercises 75–78, use a calculator to approximate two values of θ ($0° \le \theta < 360°$) that satisfy the equation. Round the values to two decimal places.

75. $\sin \theta = 0.8191$

76. $\cos \theta = 0.8746$

77. $\cos \theta = -0.4367$

78. $\sin \theta = -0.6514$

In Exercises 79–84, use a calculator to approximate two values of θ ($0 \le \theta < 2\pi$) that satisfy the equation. Round the values to three decimal places.

79. $\cos \theta = 0.9848$

80. $\sin \theta = 0.0175$

81. $\tan \theta = 1.192$

82. $\cot \theta = 5.671$

83. $\sec \theta = -2.6667$

84. $\cos \theta = -0.3214$

In Exercises 85–90, find the indicated trigonometric value in the specified quadrant.

	Function	Quadrant	Trigonometric Value
85.	$\sin \theta = -\frac{3}{5}$	IV	$\cos \theta$
86.	$\cot \theta = -3$	II	$\sin \theta$
87.	$\tan \theta = \frac{3}{2}$	III	$\sec \theta$
88.	$\csc \theta = -2$	IV	$\cot \theta$
89.	$\cos \theta = \frac{5}{8}$	I	$\sec \theta$
90.	$\sec \theta = -\frac{9}{4}$	III	$\tan \theta$

▶ Model It

91. ***Data Analysis***   The table shows the monthly normal temperatures (in degrees Fahrenheit) for selected months for New York City *(N)* and Fairbanks, Alaska *(F)*. (Source: National Climatic Data Center)

Month	N	F
January	32	−10
April	53	31
July	77	63
October	58	25
December	37	−7

(a) Use the *regression* feature of a graphing utility to find a model of the form

$$y = a \sin (bt + c) + d$$

for each city. Let t represent the month, with $t = 1$ corresponding to January.

(b) Use the models from part (a) to find the monthly normal temperatures for the two cities in February, March, May, June, August, September, and November.

(c) Compare the models for the two cities.

92. *Sales* A company that produces snowboards, which are seasonal products, forecasts monthly sales over the next 2 years to be

$$S = 23.1 + 0.442t + 4.3 \cos \frac{\pi t}{6}$$

where S is measured in thousands of units and t is the time in months, with $t = 1$ representing January 2003. Predict sales for each of the following months.

(a) February 2003   (b) February 2004

(c) June 2003   (d) June 2004

93. *Harmonic Motion* The displacement from equilibrium of an oscillating weight suspended by a spring is

$$y(t) = 2 \cos 6t$$

where y is the displacement in centimeters and t is the time in seconds. Find the displacement when (a) $t = 0$, (b) $t = \frac{1}{4}$, and (c) $t = \frac{1}{2}$.

94. *Harmonic Motion* The displacement from equilibrium of an oscillating weight suspended by a spring and subject to the damping effect of friction is

$$y(t) = 2e^{-t} \cos 6t$$

where y is the displacement in centimeters and t is the time in seconds. Find the displacement when (a) $t = 0$, (b) $t = \frac{1}{4}$, and (c) $t = \frac{1}{2}$.

95. *Electric Circuits* The current I (in amperes) when 100 volts is applied to a circuit is

$$I = 5e^{-2t} \sin t$$

where t is the time in seconds after the voltage is applied. Approximate the current $t = 0.7$ second after the voltage is applied.

96. *Distance* An airplane, flying at an altitude of 6 miles, is on a flight path that passes directly over an observer (see figure). If θ is the angle of elevation from the observer to the plane, find the distance d from the observer to the plane when (a) $\theta = 30°$, (b) $\theta = 90°$, and (c) $\theta = 120°$.

6 mi

Not drawn to scale

Synthesis

True or False? **In Exercises 97 and 98, determine whether the statement is true or false. Justify your answer.**

97. In each of the four quadrants, the signs of the secant function and sine function will be the same.

98. To find the reference angle for an angle θ (given in degrees), find the integer n such that $0 \le 360°n - \theta \le 360°$. The difference $360°n - \theta$ is the reference angle.

99. *Writing* Consider an angle in standard position with $r = 12$ centimeters, as shown in the figure. Write a short paragraph describing the changes in the magnitudes of x, y, $\sin \theta$, $\cos \theta$, and $\tan \theta$ as θ increases continuously from $0°$ to $90°$.

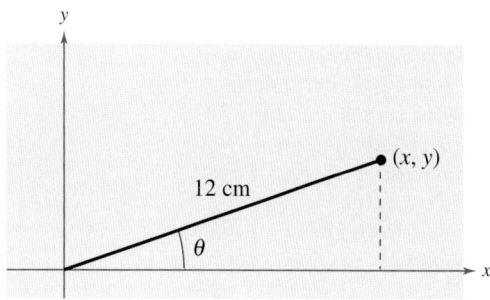

100. *Writing* Explain how reference angles are used to find the trigonometric functions of obtuse angles.

Review

In Exercises 101–110, graph the function. Identify the intercepts, asymptotes, and domain of the function.

101. $y = x^2 + 3x - 4$

102. $y = 2x^2 - 5x$

103. $f(x) = x^3 + 8$

104. $g(x) = x^4 + 2x^2 - 3$

105. $f(x) = \dfrac{x - 7}{x^2 + 4x + 4}$

106. $h(x) = \dfrac{x^2 - 1}{x + 5}$

107. $y = 2^{x-1}$

108. $y = 3^{x+1} + 2$

109. $y = \ln x^4$

110. $y = \log_{10}(x + 2)$

| 4.5 | **Graphs of Sine and Cosine Functions** |

▶ **What you should learn**

- How to sketch the graphs of basic sine and cosine functions
- How to use amplitude and period to help sketch the graphs of sine and cosine functions
- How to sketch translations of the graphs of sine and cosine functions
- How to use sine and cosine functions to model real-life data

▶ **Why you should learn it**

Sine and cosine functions are often used in scientific calculations. For instance, in Exercise 74 on page 309, you can use a trigonometric function to model the percent of the moon's face that is illuminated for any given day in 2005.

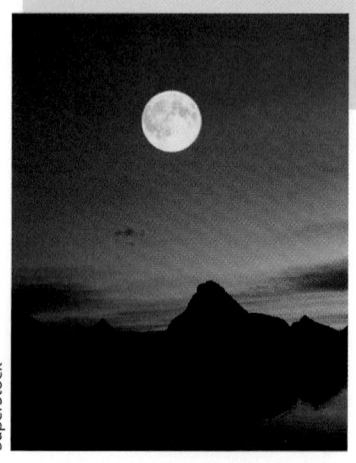

SuperStock

Basic Sine and Cosine Curves

In this section you will study techniques for sketching the graphs of the sine and cosine functions. The graph of the sine function is a **sine curve.** In Figure 4.45, the black portion of the graph represents one period of the function and is called **one cycle** of the sine curve. The gray portion of the graph indicates that the basic sine wave repeats indefinitely in the positive and negative directions. The graph of the cosine function is shown in Figure 4.46.

Recall from Section 4.2 that the domain of the sine and cosine functions is the set of all real numbers. Moreover, the range of each function is the interval $[-1, 1]$, and each function has a period of 2π. Do you see how this information is consistent with the basic graphs shown in Figures 4.45 and 4.46?

FIGURE 4.45

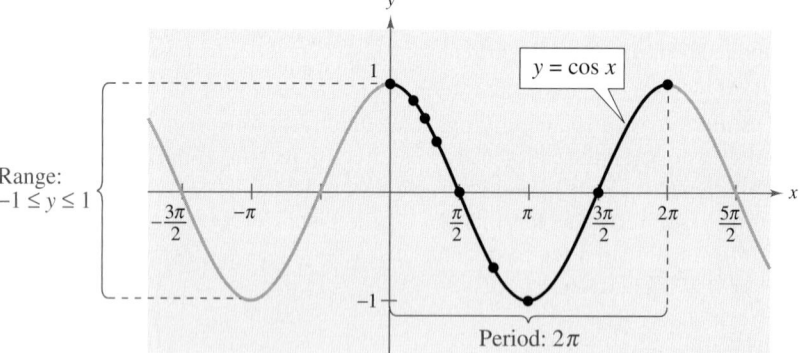

FIGURE 4.46

Note in Figures 4.45 and 4.46 that the sine curve is symmetric with respect to the *origin*, whereas the cosine curve is symmetric with respect to the *y-axis*. These properties of symmetry occur because the sine function is odd and the cosine function is even.

To sketch the graphs of the basic sine and cosine functions by hand, it helps to note five **key points** in one period of each graph: the *intercepts*, *maximum points*, and *minimum points* (see Figure 4.47).

 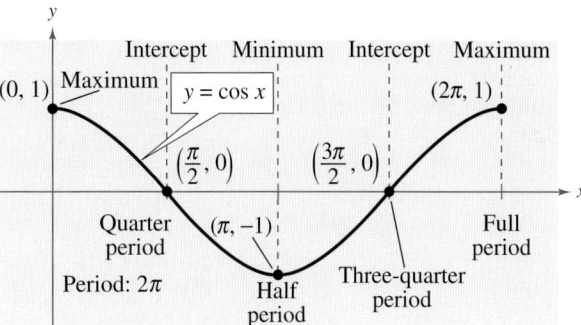

FIGURE **4.47**

Example 1 ▶ Using Key Points to Sketch a Sine Curve

Sketch the graph of $y = 2 \sin x$ on the interval $[-\pi, 4\pi]$.

Solution

Note that

$$y = 2 \sin x = 2(\sin x)$$

indicates that the y-values for the key points will have twice the magnitude of those on the graph of $y = \sin x$. Divide the period 2π into four equal parts to get the key points for $y = 2 \sin x$.

Intercept	*Maximum*	*Intercept*	*Minimum*	*Intercept*
$(0, 0)$,	$\left(\dfrac{\pi}{2}, 2\right)$,	$(\pi, 0)$,	$\left(\dfrac{3\pi}{2}, -2\right)$, and	$(2\pi, 0)$

By connecting these key points with a smooth curve and extending the curve in both directions over the interval $[-\pi, 4\pi]$, you obtain the graph shown in Figure 4.48.

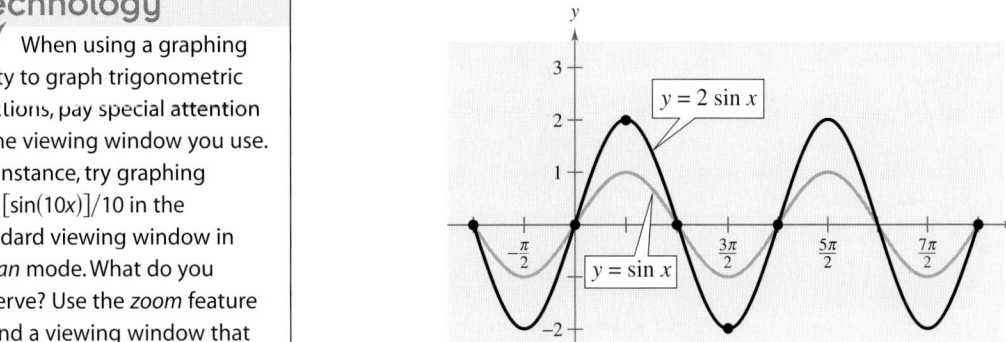

FIGURE **4.48**

Technology

When using a graphing utility to graph trigonometric functions, pay special attention to the viewing window you use. For instance, try graphing $y = [\sin(10x)]/10$ in the standard viewing window in *radian* mode. What do you observe? Use the *zoom* feature to find a viewing window that displays a good view of the graph.

Amplitude and Period

In the remainder of this section you will study the graphic effect of each of the constants a, b, c, and d in equations of the forms

$$y = d + a \sin(bx - c)$$

and

$$y = d + a \cos(bx - c).$$

A quick review of the transformations you studied in Section 1.6 should help in this investigation.

The constant factor a in $y = a \sin x$ acts as a *scaling factor*—a *vertical stretch* or *vertical shrink* of the basic sine curve. If $|a| > 1$, the basic sine curve is stretched, and if $|a| < 1$, the basic sine curve is shrunk. The result is that the graph of $y = a \sin x$ ranges between $-a$ and a instead of between -1 and 1. The absolute value of a is the **amplitude** of the function $y = a \sin x$. The range of the function $y = a \sin x$ for $a > 0$ is $-a \le y \le a$.

Definition of Amplitude of Sine and Cosine Curves

The **amplitude** of $y = a \sin x$ and $y = a \cos x$ represents half the distance between the maximum and minimum values of the function and is given by

$$\text{Amplitude} = |a|.$$

Example 2 ▶ Scaling: Vertical Shrinking and Stretching

On the same coordinate axes, sketch the graph of each function.

a. $y = \dfrac{1}{2} \cos x$

b. $y = 3 \cos x$

Solution

a. Because the amplitude of $y = \frac{1}{2} \cos x$ is $\frac{1}{2}$, the maximum value is $\frac{1}{2}$ and the minimum value is $-\frac{1}{2}$. Divide one cycle, $0 \le x \le 2\pi$, into four equal parts to get the key points

Maximum	Intercept	Minimum	Intercept		Maximum
$\left(0, \dfrac{1}{2}\right),$	$\left(\dfrac{\pi}{2}, 0\right),$	$\left(\pi, -\dfrac{1}{2}\right),$	$\left(\dfrac{3\pi}{2}, 0\right),$	and	$\left(2\pi, \dfrac{1}{2}\right).$

b. A similar analysis shows that the amplitude of $y = 3 \cos x$ is 3, and the key points are

Maximum	Intercept	Minimum	Intercept		Maximum
$(0, 3),$	$\left(\dfrac{\pi}{2}, 0\right),$	$(\pi, -3),$	$\left(\dfrac{3\pi}{2}, 0\right),$	and	$(2\pi, 3).$

The graphs of these two functions are shown in Figure 4.49.

FIGURE 4.49

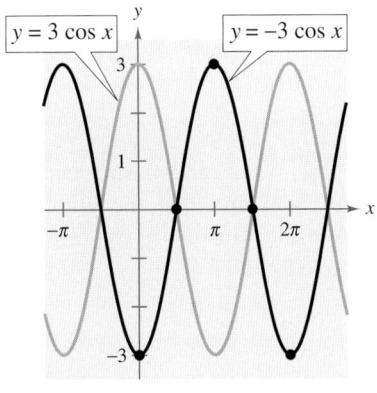

FIGURE 4.50

You know from Section 1.6 that the graph of $y = -f(x)$ is a **reflection** in the x-axis of the graph of $y = f(x)$. For instance, the graph of

$$y = -3 \cos x$$

is a reflection of the graph of

$$y = 3 \cos x$$

as shown in Figure 4.50.

Because $y = a \sin x$ completes one cycle from $x = 0$ to $x = 2\pi$, it follows that $y = a \sin bx$ completes one cycle from $x = 0$ to $x = 2\pi/b$.

Period of Sine and Cosine Functions

Let b be a positive real number. The **period** of $y = a \sin bx$ and $y = a \cos bx$ is $2\pi/b$.

Note that if $0 < b < 1$, the period of $y = a \sin bx$ is greater than 2π and represents a *horizontal stretching* of the graph of $y = a \sin x$. Similarly, if $b > 1$, the period of $y = a \sin bx$ is less than 2π and represents a *horizontal shrinking* of the graph of $y = a \sin x$. If b is negative, the identities $\sin(-x) = -\sin x$ and $\cos(-x) = \cos x$ are used to rewrite the function.

◀ Exploration ▶

Sketch the graph of $y = \cos bx$ for $b = \frac{1}{2}$, 2, and 3. How does the value of b affect the graph? How many complete cycles occur between 0 and 2π for each value of b?

Example 3 ▶ Scaling: Horizontal Stretching

Sketch the graph of $y = \sin \dfrac{x}{2}$.

Solution

The amplitude is 1. Moreover, because $b = \frac{1}{2}$, the period is

$$\frac{2\pi}{b} = \frac{2\pi}{\frac{1}{2}} = 4\pi. \qquad \text{Substitute for } b.$$

Now, divide the period-interval $[0, 4\pi]$ into four equal parts with the values π, 2π, and 3π to obtain the key points on the graph.

Intercept	Maximum	Intercept	Minimum		Intercept
$(0, 0)$,	$(\pi, 1)$,	$(2\pi, 0)$,	$(3\pi, -1)$,	and	$(4\pi, 0)$

The graph is shown in Figure 4.51.

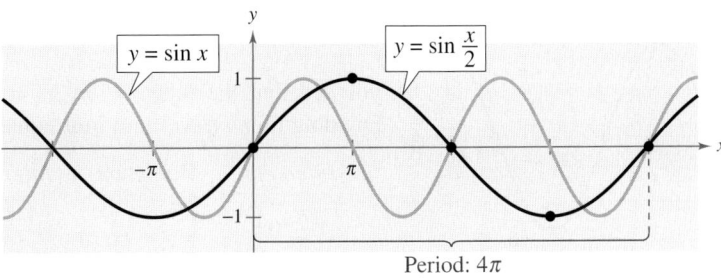

FIGURE 4.51

STUDY TIP

In general, to divide a period-interval into four equal parts, successively add "period/4," starting with the left endpoint of the interval. For instance, for the period-interval $[-\pi/6, \pi/2]$ of length $2\pi/3$, you would successively add

$$\frac{2\pi/3}{4} = \frac{\pi}{6}$$

to get $-\pi/6, 0, \pi/6, \pi/3,$ and $\pi/2$.

Translations of Sine and Cosine Curves

The constant c in the general equations

$$y = a \sin(bx - c) \qquad \text{and} \qquad y = a \cos(bx - c)$$

creates a *horizontal translation* (shift) of the basic sine and cosine curves. Comparing $y = a \sin bx$ with $y = a \sin(bx - c)$, you find that the graph of $y = a \sin(bx - c)$ completes one cycle from $bx - c = 0$ to $bx - c = 2\pi$. By solving for x, you can find the interval for one cycle to be

Left endpoint Right endpoint

$$\overbrace{\frac{c}{b}} \le x \le \overbrace{\frac{c}{b} + \frac{2\pi}{b}}.$$

Period

This implies that the period of $y = a \sin(bx - c)$ is $2\pi/b$, and the graph of $y = a \sin bx$ is shifted by an amount c/b. The number c/b is the **phase shift.**

Graphs of Sine and Cosine Functions

The graphs of $y = a \sin(bx - c)$ and $y = a \cos(bx - c)$ have the following characteristics. (Assume $b > 0$.)

$$\text{Amplitude} = |a| \qquad \text{Period} = \frac{2\pi}{b}$$

The left and right endpoints of a one-cycle interval can be determined by solving the equations $bx - c = 0$ and $bx - c = 2\pi$.

Exploration

Sketch the graph of

$$y = \sin(x - c)$$

where $c = -\pi/4, 0,$ and $\pi/4$. How does the value of c affect the graph?

Example 4 ▶ **Horizontal Translation**

Sketch the graph of $y = \frac{1}{2}\sin(x - \pi/3)$.

Solution

The amplitude is $\frac{1}{2}$ and the period is 2π. By solving the equations

$$x - \frac{\pi}{3} = 0 \quad \Longrightarrow \quad x = \frac{\pi}{3}$$

and

$$x - \frac{\pi}{3} = 2\pi \quad \Longrightarrow \quad x = \frac{7\pi}{3}$$

you see that the interval $[\pi/3, 7\pi/3]$ corresponds to one cycle of the graph. Dividing this interval into four equal parts produces the key points

Intercept	*Maximum*	*Intercept*	*Minimum*		*Intercept*
$\left(\dfrac{\pi}{3}, 0\right)$,	$\left(\dfrac{5\pi}{6}, \dfrac{1}{2}\right)$,	$\left(\dfrac{4\pi}{3}, 0\right)$,	$\left(\dfrac{11\pi}{6}, -\dfrac{1}{2}\right)$,	and	$\left(\dfrac{7\pi}{3}, 0\right)$.

The graph is shown in Figure 4.52.

Period: 2π

FIGURE 4.52

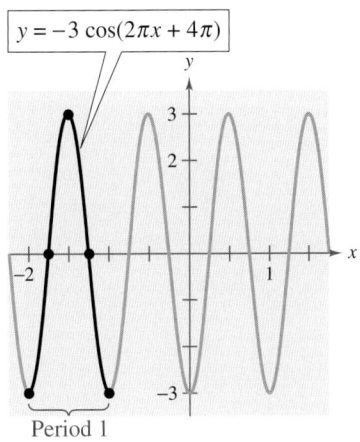

$y = -3 \cos(2\pi x + 4\pi)$

Period 1

FIGURE 4.53

Activities

1. Describe the relationship between the graphs of $f(x) = \sin x$ and $g(x) = 3 \sin(2x + 1)$.

   Answer: The amplitude of the basic sine curve is 1, whereas the amplitude of $g(x)$ is 3. The period of the basic sine curve is 2π, whereas the period of $g(x)$ is π. Lastly, the graph of $g(x)$ has a phase shift $\frac{1}{2}$ unit to the left of the graph of $f(x) = \sin x$.

2. Determine the amplitude and period.

   $y = \frac{1}{2} \cos(\pi x - 1)$

   Answer: Amplitude, $\frac{1}{2}$; period, 2

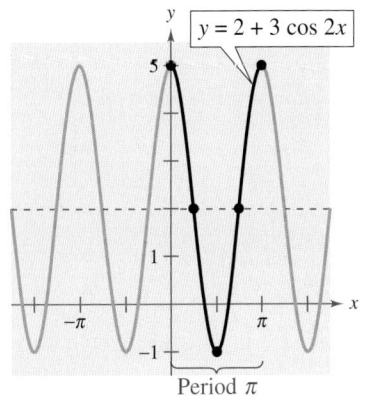

$y = 2 + 3 \cos 2x$

Period π

FIGURE 4.54

Example 5 ▶ **Horizontal Translation**

Sketch the graph of

$$y = -3 \cos(2\pi x + 4\pi).$$

Solution

The amplitude is 3 and the period is $2\pi/2\pi = 1$. By solving the equations

$$2\pi x + 4\pi = 0$$
$$2\pi x = -4\pi$$
$$x = -2$$

and

$$2\pi x + 4\pi = 2\pi$$
$$2\pi x = -2\pi$$
$$x = -1$$

you see that the interval $[-2, -1]$ corresponds to one cycle of the graph. Dividing this interval into four equal parts produces the key points

| *Minimum* | *Intercept* | *Maximum* | *Intercept* | *Minimum* |

$(-2, -3), \quad \left(-\frac{7}{4}, 0\right), \quad \left(-\frac{3}{2}, 3\right), \quad \left(-\frac{5}{4}, 0\right), \quad$ and $\quad (-1, -3).$

The graph is shown in Figure 4.53.

The final type of transformation is the *vertical translation* caused by the constant d in the equations

$$y = d + a \sin(bx - c)$$

and

$$y = d + a \cos(bx - c).$$

The shift is d units upward for $d > 0$ and downward for $d < 0$. In other words, the graph oscillates about the horizontal line $y = d$ instead of the x-axis.

Example 6 ▶ **Vertical Translation**

Sketch the graph of

$$y = 2 + 3 \cos 2x.$$

Solution

The amplitude is 3 and the period is π. The key points over the interval $[0, \pi]$ are

$(0, 5), \quad \left(\frac{\pi}{4}, 2\right), \quad \left(\frac{\pi}{2}, -1\right), \quad \left(\frac{3\pi}{4}, 2\right), \quad$ and $\quad (\pi, 5).$

The graph is shown in Figure 4.54.

Mathematical Modeling

Sine and cosine functions can be used to model many real-life situations, including electric currents, musical tones, radio waves, tides, and weather patterns.

Example 7 ▶ Finding a Trigonometric Model

Throughout the day, the depth of water at the end of a dock in Bar Harbor, Maine, varies with the tides. The table shows the depths (in feet) at various times during the morning. (Source: Nautical Software, Inc.)

Time, t	Depth, y
Midnight	3.4
2 A.M.	8.7
4 A.M.	11.3
6 A.M.	9.1
8 A.M.	3.8
10 A.M.	0.1
Noon	1.2

a. Use a trigonometric function to model this data.

b. Find the depths at 9 A.M. and 3 P.M.

c. A boat needs at least 10 feet of water to moor at the dock. During what times in the afternoon can it safely dock?

Solution

a. Begin by graphing the data, as shown in Figure 4.55. You can use either a sine or cosine model. Suppose you use a cosine model of the form

$$y = a \cos(bt - c) + d.$$

The amplitude is given by

$$a = \frac{1}{2}[(\text{high}) - (\text{low})] = \frac{1}{2}(11.3 - 0.1) = 5.6.$$

The period is

$$p = 2[(\text{low time}) - (\text{high time})] = 2(10 - 4) = 12$$

which implies that

$$b = \frac{2\pi}{p} \approx 0.524.$$

Because high tide occurs 4 hours after midnight, you can conclude that $c/b = 4$, so $c \approx 2.094$. Moreover, because the average depth is $\frac{1}{2}(11.3 + 0.1) = 5.7$, it follows that $d = 5.7$. So, you can model the depth with the function

$$y = 5.6 \cos(0.524t - 2.094) + 5.7.$$

b. The depths at 9 A.M. and 3 P.M. are as follows.

$$y = 5.6 \cos(0.524 \cdot 9 - 2.094) + 5.7$$
$$\approx 0.84 \text{ foot} \qquad\qquad 9 \text{ A.M.}$$
$$y = 5.6 \cos(0.524 \cdot 15 - 2.094) + 5.7$$
$$\approx 10.57 \text{ feet} \qquad\qquad 3 \text{ P.M.}$$

c. To find out when the depth y is at least 10 feet, you can graph the model with the line $y = 10$, as shown in Figure 4.56. From the graph, it follows that the depth is at least 10 feet between 2:42 P.M. ($t \approx 14.7$) and 5:18 P.M. ($t \approx 17.3$).

Changing Tides

FIGURE 4.55

(14.7, 10) (17.3, 10)

FIGURE 4.56

4.5 **Exercises**

In Exercises 1–14, find the period and amplitude.

1. $y = 3 \sin 2x$

2. $y = 2 \cos 3x$

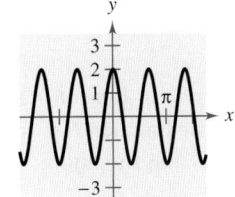

3. $y = \dfrac{5}{2} \cos \dfrac{x}{2}$

4. $y = -3 \sin \dfrac{x}{3}$

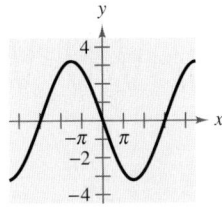

5. $y = \dfrac{1}{2} \sin \dfrac{\pi x}{3}$

6. $y = \dfrac{3}{2} \cos \dfrac{\pi x}{2}$

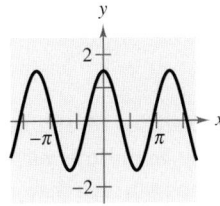

7. $y = -2 \sin x$

8. $y = -\cos \dfrac{2x}{3}$

9. $y = 3 \sin 10x$

10. $y = \dfrac{1}{3} \sin 8x$

11. $y = \dfrac{1}{2} \cos \dfrac{2x}{3}$

12. $y = \dfrac{5}{2} \cos \dfrac{x}{4}$

13. $y = \dfrac{1}{4} \sin 2\pi x$

14. $y = \dfrac{2}{3} \cos \dfrac{\pi x}{10}$

In Exercises 15–22, describe the relationship between the graphs of f and g. Consider amplitude, period, and shifts.

15. $f(x) = \sin x$
$g(x) = \sin(x - \pi)$

16. $f(x) = \cos x$
$g(x) = \cos(x + \pi)$

17. $f(x) = \cos 2x$
$g(x) = -\cos 2x$

18. $f(x) = \sin 3x$
$g(x) = \sin(-3x)$

19. $f(x) = \cos x$
$g(x) = \cos 2x$

20. $f(x) = \sin x$
$g(x) = \sin 3x$

21. $f(x) = \sin 2x$
$g(x) = 3 + \sin 2x$

22. $f(x) = \cos 4x$
$g(x) = -2 + \cos 4x$

In Exercises 23–26, describe the relationship between the graphs of f and g. Consider amplitude, period, and shifts.

23.

24.

25.

26.

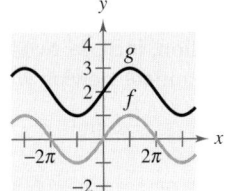

In Exercises 27–34, graph f and g on the same set of coordinate axes. (Include two full periods.)

27. $f(x) = -2 \sin x$
$g(x) = 4 \sin x$

28. $f(x) = \sin x$
$g(x) = \sin \dfrac{x}{3}$

29. $f(x) = \cos x$
$g(x) = 1 + \cos x$

30. $f(x) = 2 \cos 2x$
$g(x) = -\cos 4x$

31. $f(x) = -\dfrac{1}{2} \sin \dfrac{x}{2}$
$g(x) = 3 - \dfrac{1}{2} \sin \dfrac{x}{2}$

32. $f(x) = 4 \sin \pi x$
$g(x) = 4 \sin \pi x - 3$

33. $f(x) = 2 \cos x$
$g(x) = 2 \cos(x + \pi)$

34. $f(x) = -\cos x$
$g(x) = -\cos(x - \pi)$

In Exercises 35–52, sketch the graph of the function. (Include two full periods.)

35. $y = -2 \sin 6x$

36. $y = -3 \cos 4x$

37. $y = \cos 2\pi x$

38. $y = \sin \dfrac{\pi x}{4}$

39. $y = -\sin \dfrac{2\pi x}{3}$

40. $y = -10 \cos \dfrac{\pi x}{6}$

41. $y = \sin\left(x - \dfrac{\pi}{4}\right)$

42. $y = \sin(x - \pi)$

43. $y = 3 \cos(x + \pi)$

44. $y = 4 \cos\left(x + \dfrac{\pi}{4}\right)$

45. $y = 2 - \sin \dfrac{2\pi x}{3}$

46. $y = -3 + 5 \cos \dfrac{\pi t}{12}$

47. $y = 2 + \frac{1}{10} \cos 60\pi x$

48. $y = 2 \cos x - 3$

49. $y = 3 \cos(x + \pi) - 3$

50. $y = 4 \cos\left(x + \dfrac{\pi}{4}\right) + 4$

51. $y = \dfrac{2}{3} \cos\left(\dfrac{x}{2} - \dfrac{\pi}{4}\right)$

52. $y = -3 \cos(6x + \pi)$

 In Exercises 53–58, use a graphing utility to graph the function. Include two full periods. Be sure to choose an appropriate viewing window.

53. $y = -2 \sin(4x + \pi)$

54. $y = -4 \sin\left(\dfrac{2}{3}x - \dfrac{\pi}{3}\right)$

55. $y = \cos\left(2\pi x - \dfrac{\pi}{2}\right) + 1$

56. $y = 3 \cos\left(\dfrac{\pi x}{2} + \dfrac{\pi}{2}\right) - 2$

57. $y = -0.1 \sin\left(\dfrac{\pi x}{10} + \pi\right)$

58. $y = \frac{1}{100} \sin 120\pi t$

Graphical Reasoning In Exercises 59–62, find *a* and *d* for the function $f(x) = a \cos x + d$ such that the graph of *f* matches the figure.

59.

60.

61.

62.

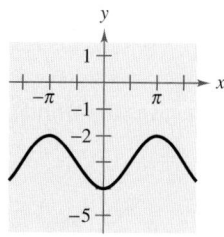

Graphical Reasoning In Exercises 63–66, find *a*, *b*, and *c* for the function $f(x) = a \sin(bx - c)$ such that the graph of *f* matches the figure.

63.

64.

65.

66.

 In Exercises 67 and 68, use a graphing utility to graph y_1 and y_2 in the interval $[-2\pi, 2\pi]$. Use the graphs to find real numbers *x* such that $y_1 = y_2$.

67. $y_1 = \sin x$

$y_2 = -\dfrac{1}{2}$

68. $y_1 = \cos x$

$y_2 = -1$

69. *Respiratory Cycle* For a person at rest, the velocity *v* (in liters per second) of air flow during a respiratory cycle (the time from the beginning of one breath to the beginning of the next) is

$$v = 0.85 \sin \dfrac{\pi t}{3}$$

where *t* is the time in seconds. (Inhalation occurs when $v > 0$, and exhalation occurs when $v < 0$.)

(a) Find the time for one full respiratory cycle.

(b) Find the number of cycles per minute.

(c) Sketch the graph of the velocity function.

70. *Respiratory Cycle*   After exercising for a few minutes, a person has a respiratory cycle for which the velocity of air flow is approximated by

$$v = 1.75 \sin \frac{\pi t}{2}$$

where t is the time in seconds. (Inhalation occurs when $v > 0$, and exhalation occurs when $v < 0$.)

(a) Find the time for one full respiratory cycle.

(b) Find the number of cycles per minute.

(c) Sketch the graph of the velocity function.

71. *Piano Tuning*   When tuning a piano, a technician strikes a tuning fork for the A above middle C and sets up a wave motion that can be approximated by $y = 0.001 \sin 880\pi t$, where t is the time in seconds.

(a) What is the period of the function?

(b) The frequency f is given by $f = 1/p$. What is the frequency of the note?

72. *Health*   The function

$$P = 100 - 20 \cos \frac{5\pi t}{3}$$

approximates the blood pressure P in millimeters of mercury at time t in seconds for a person at rest.

(a) Find the period of the function.

(b) Find the number of heartbeats per minute.

73. *Data Analysis*   The table shows the maximum daily high temperatures for Tallahassee T and Chicago C (in degrees Fahrenheit) for month t, with $t = 1$ corresponding to January. (Source: Southeast Regional Climate Center and National Climatic Data Center)

Month, t	Tallahassee, T	Chicago, C
1	63.9	29.0
2	67.1	33.5
3	73.1	45.8
4	79.9	58.6
5	86.5	70.1
6	90.5	79.6
7	91.3	83.7
8	91.0	81.8
9	88.1	74.8
10	80.8	63.3
11	72.2	48.4
12	65.5	34.0

(a) A model for the temperature in Tallahassee is

$$T(t) = 77.60 + 13.70 \cos\left(\frac{\pi t}{6} - 3.67\right).$$

Find a trigonometric model for Chicago.

(b) Use a graphing utility to graph the data points and the model for the temperatures in Tallahassee. How well does the model fit the data?

(c) Use a graphing utility to graph the data points and the model for the temperatures in Chicago. How well does the model fit the data?

(d) Use the models to estimate the average maximum temperature in each city. Which term of the models did you use? Explain.

(e) What is the period of each model? Are the periods what you expected? Explain.

(f) Which city has the greater variability in temperature throughout the year? Which factor of the models determines this variability? Explain.

▶ Model It

74. *Data Analysis*   The percent y of the moon's face that is illuminated on day x of the year 2005, where $x = 70$ represents March 11, is shown in the table. (Source: U.S. Naval Observatory)

x	y
76	0.5
84	1.0
91	0.5
98	0.0
106	0.5
114	1.0

(a) Create a scatter plot of the data.

(b) Find a trigonometric model that fits the data.

(c) Add the graph of your model in part (b) to the scatter plot. How well does the model fit the data?

(d) What is the period of the model?

(e) Estimate the moon's percent illumination for May 8, 2005.

75. *Fuel Consumption*   The daily consumption C (in gallons) of diesel fuel on a farm is modeled by

$$C = 30.3 + 21.6 \sin\left(\frac{2\pi t}{365} + 10.9\right)$$

where t is the time in days, with $t = 1$ corresponding to January 1.

(a) What is the period of the model? Is it what you expected? Explain.

(b) What is the average daily fuel consumption? Which term of the model did you use? Explain.

(c) Use a graphing utility to graph the model. Use the graph to approximate the time of the year when consumption exceeds 40 gallons per day.

Synthesis

True or False?   **In Exercises 76–78, determine whether the statement is true or false. Justify your answer.**

76. The graph of the function $f(x) = \sin(x + 2\pi)$ translates the graph of $f(x) = \sin x$ exactly one period to the right so that the two graphs look identical.

77. The function $y = \frac{1}{2}\cos 2x$ has an amplitude that is twice that of the function $y = \cos x$.

78. The graph of $y = -\cos x$ is a reflection of the graph of $y = \sin(x + \pi/2)$ in the x-axis.

Conjecture   **In Exercises 79 and 80, graph f and g on the same set of coordinate axes. Include two full periods. Make a conjecture about the functions.**

79. $f(x) = \sin x, \quad g(x) = \cos\left(x - \frac{\pi}{2}\right)$

80. $f(x) = \sin x, \quad g(x) = -\cos\left(x + \frac{\pi}{2}\right)$

81. *Writing*   Use a graphing utility to graph the function $y = a \sin x$ for $a = \frac{1}{2}$, $a = \frac{3}{2}$, and $a = -3$. Write a paragraph describing the changes in the graph corresponding to the specified changes in a.

82. *Writing*   Use a graphing utility to graph the function $y = d + \sin x$ for $d = 2$, $d = 3.5$, and $d = -2$. Write a paragraph describing the changes in the graph corresponding to the specified changes in d.

83. *Writing*   Use a graphing utility to graph the function $y = \sin bx$ for $b = \frac{1}{2}$, $b = \frac{3}{2}$, and $b = 4$. Write a paragraph describing the changes in the graph corresponding to the specified changes in b.

84. *Writing*   Use a graphing utility to graph the function $y = \sin(x - c)$ for $c = 1$, $c = 3$, and $c = -2$. Write a paragraph describing the changes in the graph corresponding to the specified changes in c.

85. *Exploration*   Using calculus, it can be shown that the sine and cosine functions can be approximated by the polynomials

$$\sin x \approx x - \frac{x^3}{3!} + \frac{x^5}{5!} \text{ and } \cos x \approx 1 - \frac{x^2}{2!} + \frac{x^4}{4!}$$

where x is in radians.

(a) Use a graphing utility to graph the sine function and its polynomial approximation in the same viewing window. How do the graphs compare?

(b) Use a graphing utility to graph the cosine function and its polynomial approximation in the same viewing window. How do the graphs compare?

(c) Study the patterns in the polynomial approximations of the sine and cosine functions and guess the next term in each. Then repeat parts (a) and (b). How did the accuracy of the approximations change when additional terms were added?

86. *Exploration*   Use the polynomial approximations for the sine and cosine functions from Exercise 85 to approximate the following functional values. Compare the results with those given by a calculator. Is the error in the approximation the same in each case? Explain.

(a) $\sin \frac{1}{2}$ (b) $\sin 1$ (c) $\sin \frac{\pi}{6}$

(d) $\cos(-0.5)$ (e) $\cos 1$ (f) $\cos \frac{\pi}{4}$

Review

In Exercises 87–90, use the properties of logarithms to write the expression as a sum, difference, and/or constant multiple of a logarithm.

87. $\log_{10} \sqrt{x - 2}$ **88.** $\log_2[x^2(x - 3)]$

89. $\ln \dfrac{t^3}{t - 1}$ **90.** $\ln \sqrt{\dfrac{z}{z^2 + 1}}$

In Exercises 91–94, write the expression as the logarithm of a single quantity.

91. $\frac{1}{2}(\log_{10} x + \log_{10} y)$ **92.** $2 \log_2 x + \log_2(xy)$

93. $\ln 3x - 4 \ln y$

94. $\frac{1}{2}(\ln 2x - 2 \ln x) + 3 \ln x$

4.6 Graphs of Other Trigonometric Functions

▶ What you should learn

- How to sketch the graphs of tangent functions
- How to sketch the graphs of cotangent functions
- How to sketch the graphs of secant and cosecant functions
- How to sketch the graphs of damped trigonometric functions

▶ Why you should learn it

Trigonometric functions can be used to model biological patterns. For instance, in Exercise 75 on page 320, trigonometric functions can be used to model predator-prey cycles.

Tom Brakefield/Corbis

Graph of the Tangent Function

Recall that the tangent function is odd. That is, $\tan(-x) = -\tan x$. Consequently, the graph of $y = \tan x$ is symmetric with respect to the origin. You also know from the identity $\tan x = \sin x / \cos x$ that the tangent is undefined for values at which $\cos x = 0$. Two such values are $x = \pm \pi/2 \approx \pm 1.5708$.

x	$-\dfrac{\pi}{2}$	-1.57	-1.5	$-\dfrac{\pi}{4}$	0	$\dfrac{\pi}{4}$	1.5	1.57	$\dfrac{\pi}{2}$
$\tan x$	Undef.	-1255.8	-14.1	-1	0	1	14.1	1255.8	Undef.

As indicated in the table, $\tan x$ increases without bound as x approaches $\pi/2$ from the left, and decreases without bound as x approaches $-\pi/2$ from the right. So, the graph of $y = \tan x$ has *vertical asymptotes* at $x = \pi/2$ and $x = -\pi/2$, as shown in Figure 4.57. Moreover, because the period of the tangent function is π, vertical asymptotes also occur when $x = \pi/2 + n\pi$, where n is an integer. The domain of the tangent function is the set of all real numbers other than $x = \pi/2 + n\pi$, and the range is the set of all real numbers.

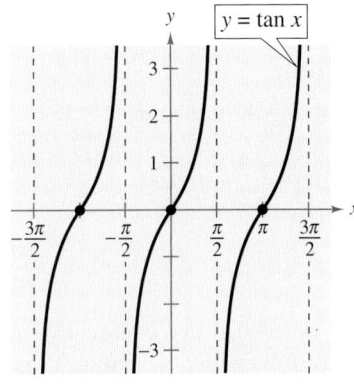

PERIOD: π
DOMAIN: ALL $x \neq \frac{\pi}{2} + n\pi$
RANGE: $(-\infty, \infty)$
VERTICAL ASYMPTOTES: $x = \frac{\pi}{2} + n\pi$

FIGURE 4.57

Sketching the graph of $y = a\tan(bx - c)$ is similar to sketching the graph of $y = a\sin(bx - c)$ in that you locate key points that identify the intercepts and asymptotes. Two consecutive asymptotes can be found by solving the equations

$$bx - c = -\frac{\pi}{2} \quad \text{and} \quad bx - c = \frac{\pi}{2}.$$

The midpoint between two consecutive asymptotes is an x-intercept of the graph. The period of the function $y = a\tan(bx - c)$ is the distance between two consecutive asymptotes. The amplitude of a tangent function is not defined. After plotting the asymptotes and the x-intercept, plot a few additional points between the two asymptotes and sketch one cycle. Finally, sketch one or two additional cycles to the left and right.

Consider reviewing period, range, and domain for all six trigonometric functions, especially emphasizing the difference between the periods of the tangent and cotangent functions.

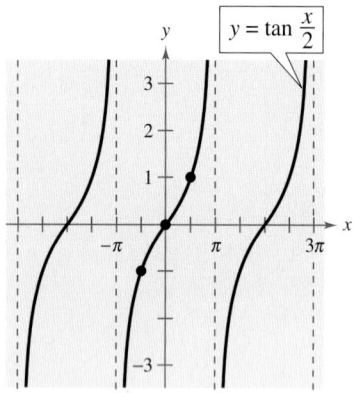

FIGURE 4.58

Example 1 ▶   **Sketching the Graph of a Tangent Function**

Sketch the graph of $y = \tan \dfrac{x}{2}$.

Solution

By solving the equations

$$\frac{x}{2} = -\frac{\pi}{2} \quad \text{and} \quad \frac{x}{2} = \frac{\pi}{2}$$

$$x = -\pi \qquad\qquad x = \pi$$

you can see that two consecutive asymptotes occur at $x = -\pi$ and $x = \pi$. Between these two asymptotes, plot a few points, including the x-intercept, as shown in the table. Three cycles of the graph are shown in Figure 4.58.

x	$-\dfrac{\pi}{2}$	0	$\dfrac{\pi}{2}$
$\tan \dfrac{x}{2}$	-1	0	1

Example 2 ▶   **Sketching the Graph of a Tangent Function**

Sketch the graph of $y = -3 \tan 2x$.

Solution

By solving the equations

$$2x = -\frac{\pi}{2} \quad \text{and} \quad 2x = \frac{\pi}{2}$$

$$x = -\frac{\pi}{4} \qquad\qquad x = \frac{\pi}{4}$$

you can see that two consecutive asymptotes occur at $x = -\pi/4$ and $x = \pi/4$. Between these two asymptotes, plot a few points, including the x-intercept, as shown in the table. Three cycles of the graph are shown in Figure 4.59.

x	$-\dfrac{\pi}{8}$	0	$\dfrac{\pi}{8}$
$-3 \tan 2x$	3	0	-3

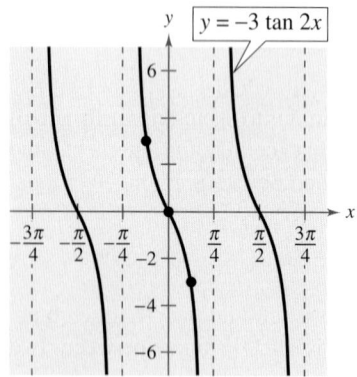

FIGURE 4.59

    By comparing the graphs in Examples 1 and 2, you can see that the graph of $y = a \tan(bx - c)$ increases between consecutive vertical asymptotes when $a > 0$, and decreases between consecutive vertical asymptotes when $a < 0$. In other words, the graph for $a < 0$ is a reflection in the x-axis of the graph for $a > 0$.

Graph of the Cotangent Function

The graph of the cotangent function is similar to the graph of the tangent function. It also has a period of π. However, from the identity

$$y = \cot x = \frac{\cos x}{\sin x}$$

you can see that the cotangent function has vertical asymptotes when $\sin x$ is zero, which occurs at $x = n\pi$, where n is an integer. The graph of the cotangent function is shown in Figure 4.60.

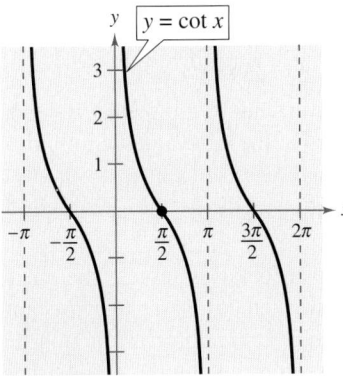

PERIOD: π
DOMAIN: ALL $x \neq n\pi$
RANGE: $(-\infty, \infty)$
VERTICAL ASYMPTOTES: $x = n\pi$

FIGURE 4.60

Example 3 ▶ **Sketching the Graph of a Cotangent Function**

Sketch the graph of $y = 2 \cot \dfrac{x}{3}$.

Solution

To locate two consecutive vertical asymptotes of the graph, solve the equations $x/3 = 0$ and $x/3 = \pi$, as follows.

$$\frac{x}{3} = 0 \qquad \text{and} \qquad \frac{x}{3} = \pi$$

$$x = 0 \qquad\qquad\qquad x = 3\pi$$

Then, between these two asymptotes, plot a few points, including the x-intercept, as shown in the table. Three cycles of the graph are shown in Figure 4.61. (Note that the period is 3π, the distance between consecutive asymptotes.)

x	$\dfrac{3\pi}{4}$	$\dfrac{3\pi}{2}$	$\dfrac{9\pi}{4}$
$2 \cot \dfrac{x}{3}$	2	0	-2

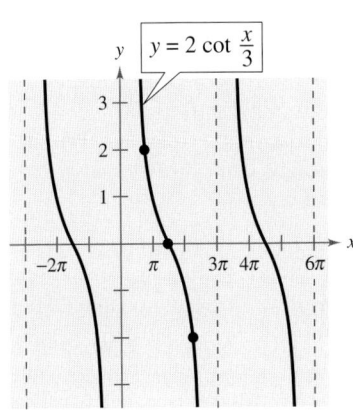

FIGURE 4.61

Graphs of the Reciprocal Functions

Using a graphing utility to graph cosecant and secant functions can help reinforce the need to use the reciprocal functions.

The graphs of the two remaining trigonometric functions can be obtained from the graphs of the sine and cosine functions using the reciprocal identities

$$\csc x = \frac{1}{\sin x} \quad \text{and} \quad \sec x = \frac{1}{\cos x}.$$

For instance, at a given value of x, the y-coordinate of $\sec x$ is the reciprocal of the y-coordinate of $\cos x$. Of course, when $\cos x = 0$, the reciprocal does not exist. Near such values of x, the behavior of the secant function is similar to that of the tangent function. In other words, the graphs of

$$\tan x = \frac{\sin x}{\cos x} \quad \text{and} \quad \sec x = \frac{1}{\cos x}$$

have vertical asymptotes at $x = \pi/2 + n\pi$, where n is an integer, and the cosine is zero at these x-values. Similarly,

$$\cot x = \frac{\cos x}{\sin x} \quad \text{and} \quad \csc x = \frac{1}{\sin x}$$

have vertical asymptotes where $\sin x = 0$—that is, at $x = n\pi$.

To sketch the graph of a secant or cosecant function, you should first make a sketch of its reciprocal function. For instance, to sketch the graph of $y = \csc x$, first sketch the graph of $y = \sin x$. Then take reciprocals of the y-coordinates to obtain points on the graph of $y = \csc x$. This procedure is used to obtain the graphs shown in Figure 4.62.

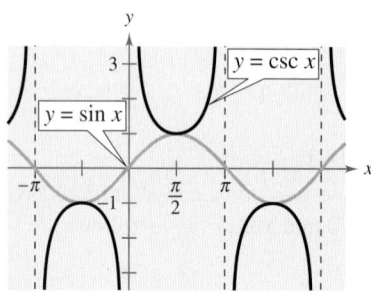

PERIOD: 2π
DOMAIN: ALL $x \neq n\pi$
RANGE: $(-\infty, -1]$ AND $[1, \infty)$
VERTICAL ASYMPTOTES: $x = n\pi$
SYMMETRY: ORIGIN

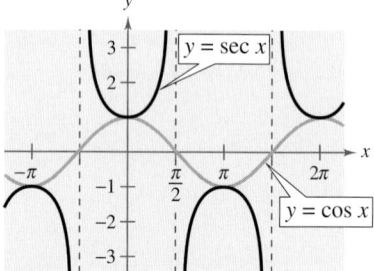

PERIOD: 2π
DOMAIN: ALL $x \neq \frac{\pi}{2} + n\pi$
RANGE: $(-\infty, -1]$ AND $[1, \infty)$
VERTICAL ASYMPTOTES: $x = \frac{\pi}{2} + n\pi$
SYMMETRY: y-AXIS

FIGURE 4.62

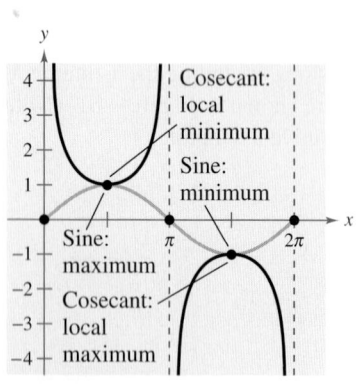

FIGURE 4.63

In comparing the graphs of the cosecant and secant functions with those of the sine and cosine functions, note that the "hills" and "valleys" are interchanged. For example, a hill (or maximum point) on the sine curve corresponds to a valley (a local minimum) on the cosecant curve, and a valley (or minimum point) on the sine curve corresponds to a hill (a local maximum) on the cosecant curve, as shown in Figure 4.63. Additionally, x-intercepts of the sine and cosine functions become vertical asymptotes of the cosecant and secant functions (see Figure 4.63).

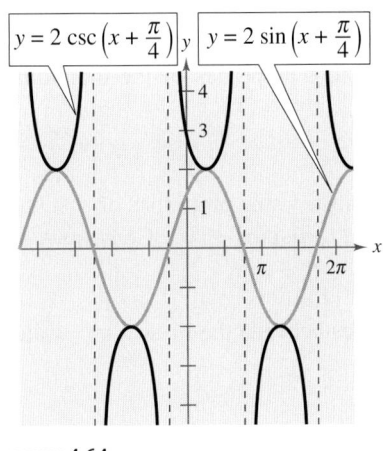

FIGURE **4.64**

Example 4 ▶ **Sketching the Graph of a Cosecant Function**

Sketch the graph of $y = 2 \csc\left(x + \dfrac{\pi}{4}\right)$.

Solution

Begin by sketching the graph of

$$y = 2 \sin\left(x + \frac{\pi}{4}\right).$$

For this function, the amplitude is 2 and the period is 2π. By solving the equations

$$x + \frac{\pi}{4} = 0 \qquad \text{and} \qquad x + \frac{\pi}{4} = 2\pi$$

$$x = -\frac{\pi}{4} \qquad\qquad\qquad x = \frac{7\pi}{4}$$

you can see that one cycle of the sine function corresponds to the interval from $x = -\pi/4$ to $x = 7\pi/4$. The graph of this sine function is represented by the gray curve in Figure 4.64. Because the sine function is zero at the midpoint and endpoints of this interval, the corresponding cosecant function

$$y = 2 \csc\left(x + \frac{\pi}{4}\right)$$

$$= 2\left(\frac{1}{\sin[x + (\pi/4)]}\right)$$

has vertical asymptotes at $x = -\pi/4$, $x = 3\pi/4$, $x = 7\pi/4$, etc. The graph of the cosecant function is represented by the black curve in Figure 4.64.

Example 5 ▶ **Sketching the Graph of a Secant Function**

Sketch the graph of $y = \sec 2x$.

Solution

Begin by sketching the graph of $y = \cos 2x$, as indicated by the gray curve in Figure 4.65. Then, form the graph of $y = \sec 2x$ as the black curve in the figure. Note that the x-intercepts of $y = \cos 2x$

$$\left(-\frac{\pi}{4}, 0\right), \qquad \left(\frac{\pi}{4}, 0\right), \qquad \left(\frac{3\pi}{4}, 0\right), \dots$$

correspond to the vertical asymptotes

$$x = -\frac{\pi}{4}, \qquad x = \frac{\pi}{4}, \qquad x = \frac{3\pi}{4}, \dots$$

of the graph of $y = \sec 2x$. Moreover, notice that the period of $y = \cos 2x$ and $y = \sec 2x$ is π.

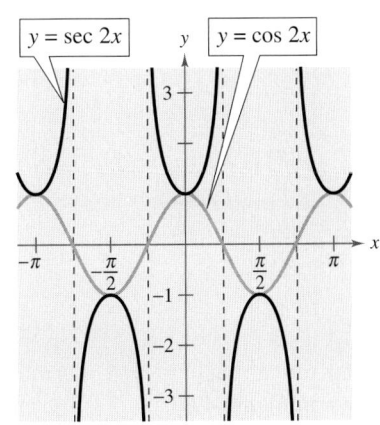

FIGURE **4.65**

Damped Trigonometric Graphs

A *product* of two functions can be graphed using properties of the individual functions. For instance, consider the function

$$f(x) = x \sin x$$

as the product of the functions $y = x$ and $y = \sin x$. Using properties of absolute value and the fact that $|\sin x| \leq 1$, you have $0 \leq |x||\sin x| \leq |x|$. Consequently,

$$-|x| \leq x \sin x \leq |x|$$

which means that the graph of $f(x) = x \sin x$ lies between the lines $y = -x$ and $y = x$. Furthermore, because

$$f(x) = x \sin x = \pm x \quad \text{at} \quad x = \frac{\pi}{2} + n\pi$$

and

$$f(x) = x \sin x = 0 \quad \text{at} \quad x = n\pi$$

the graph of f touches the line $y = -x$ or the line $y = x$ at $x = \pi/2 + n\pi$ and has x-intercepts at $x = n\pi$. A sketch of f is shown in Figure 4.66. In the function $f(x) = x \sin x$, the factor x is called the **damping factor.**

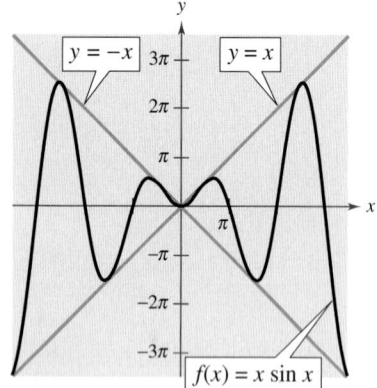

FIGURE 4.66

Example 6 ▶ **Damped Sine Wave**

Sketch the graph of

$$f(x) = e^{-x} \sin 3x.$$

Solution

Consider $f(x)$ as the product of the two functions

$$y = e^{-x} \quad \text{and} \quad y = \sin 3x$$

each of which has the set of real numbers as its domain. For any real number x, you know that $e^{-x} \geq 0$ and $|\sin 3x| \leq 1$. So, $e^{-x}|\sin 3x| \leq e^{-x}$, which means that

$$-e^{-x} \leq e^{-x} \sin 3x \leq e^{-x}.$$

Furthermore, because

$$f(x) = e^{-x} \sin 3x = \pm e^{-x} \quad \text{at} \quad x = \frac{\pi}{6} + \frac{n\pi}{3}$$

and

$$f(x) = e^{-x} \sin 3x = 0 \quad \text{at} \quad x = \frac{n\pi}{3}$$

the graph of f touches the curves $y = -e^{-x}$ and $y = e^{-x}$ at $x = \pi/6 + n\pi/3$ and has intercepts at $x = n\pi/3$. A sketch is shown in Figure 4.67.

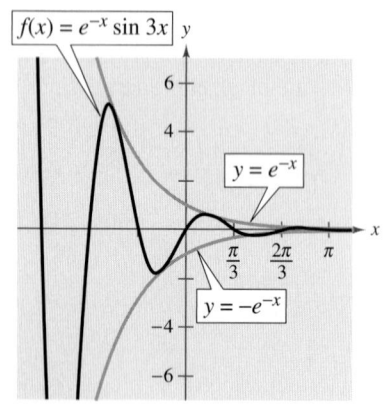

FIGURE 4.67

Figure 4.68 summarizes the six basic trigonometric functions.

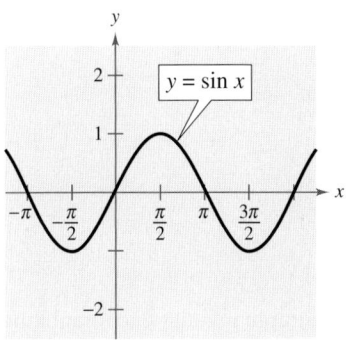

DOMAIN: ALL REALS
RANGE: $[-1, 1]$
PERIOD: 2π

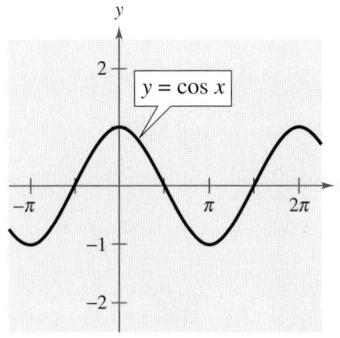

DOMAIN: ALL REALS
RANGE: $[-1, 1]$
PERIOD: 2π

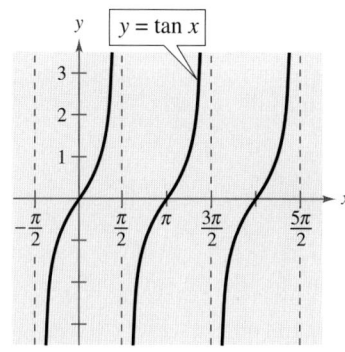

DOMAIN: ALL $x \neq \frac{\pi}{2} + n\pi$
RANGE: $(-\infty, \infty)$
PERIOD: π

DOMAIN: ALL $x \neq n\pi$
RANGE: $(-\infty, -1]$ AND $[1, \infty)$
PERIOD: 2π

FIGURE 4.68

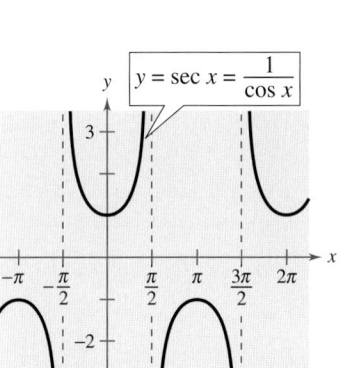

DOMAIN: ALL $x \neq \frac{\pi}{2} + n\pi$
RANGE: $(-\infty, -1]$ AND $[1, \infty)$
PERIOD: 2π

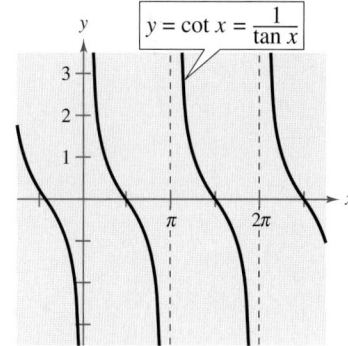

DOMAIN: ALL $x \neq n\pi$
RANGE: $(-\infty, \infty)$
PERIOD: π

Writing **ABOUT MATHEMATICS**

Combining Trigonometric Functions Recall from Section 1.7 that functions can be combined arithmetically. This also applies to trigonometric functions. For each of the functions

$$h(x) = x + \sin x \quad \text{and} \quad h(x) = \cos x - \sin 3x$$

(a) identify two simpler functions f and g that comprise the combination, (b) use a table to show how to obtain the numerical values of $h(x)$ from the numerical values of $f(x)$ and $g(x)$, and (c) use graphs of f and g to show how h may be formed.

Can you find functions

$$f(x) = d + a \sin(bx + c) \quad \text{and} \quad g(x) = d + a \cos(bx + c)$$

such that $f(x) + g(x) = 0$ for all x?

4.6 Exercises

In Exercises 1–6, match the function with its graph. State the period of the function. [The graphs are labeled (a), (b), (c), (d), (e), and (f).]

(a)

(b)

(c)

(d)

(e)

(f)

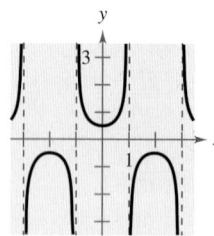

1. $y = \sec 2x$

2. $y = \tan \dfrac{x}{2}$

3. $y = \dfrac{1}{2} \cot \pi x$

4. $y = -\csc x$

5. $y = \dfrac{1}{2} \sec \dfrac{\pi x}{2}$

6. $y = -2 \sec \dfrac{\pi x}{2}$

In Exercises 7–28, sketch the graph of the function. Include two full periods.

7. $y = \frac{1}{3} \tan x$

8. $y = \frac{1}{4} \tan x$

9. $y = \tan 3x$

10. $y = -3 \tan \pi x$

11. $y = -\frac{1}{2} \sec x$

12. $y = \frac{1}{4} \sec x$

13. $y = \csc \pi x$

14. $y = 3 \csc 4x$

15. $y = \sec \pi x - 1$

16. $y = -2 \sec 4x + 2$

17. $y = \csc \dfrac{x}{2}$

18. $y = \csc \dfrac{x}{3}$

19. $y = \cot \dfrac{x}{2}$

20. $y = 3 \cot \dfrac{\pi x}{2}$

21. $y = \frac{1}{2} \sec 2x$

22. $y = -\frac{1}{2} \tan x$

23. $y = \tan \dfrac{\pi x}{4}$

24. $y = \tan(x + \pi)$

25. $y = \csc(\pi - x)$

26. $y = \sec(\pi - x)$

27. $y = \dfrac{1}{4} \csc\left(x + \dfrac{\pi}{4}\right)$

28. $y = 2 \cot\left(x + \dfrac{\pi}{2}\right)$

In Exercises 29–38, use a graphing utility to graph the function. Include two full periods.

29. $y = \tan \dfrac{x}{3}$

30. $y = -\tan 2x$

31. $y = -2 \sec 4x$

32. $y = \sec \pi x$

33. $y = \tan\left(x - \dfrac{\pi}{4}\right)$

34. $y = \dfrac{1}{4} \cot\left(x - \dfrac{\pi}{2}\right)$

35. $y = -\csc(4x - \pi)$

36. $y = 2 \sec(2x - \pi)$

37. $y = 0.1 \tan\left(\dfrac{\pi x}{4} + \dfrac{\pi}{4}\right)$

38. $y = \dfrac{1}{3} \sec\left(\dfrac{\pi x}{2} + \dfrac{\pi}{2}\right)$

In Exercises 39–46, use a graph to solve the equation on the interval $[-2\pi, 2\pi]$.

39. $\tan x = 1$

40. $\tan x = \sqrt{3}$

41. $\cot x = -\dfrac{\sqrt{3}}{3}$

42. $\cot x = 1$

43. $\sec x = -2$

44. $\sec x = 2$

45. $\csc x = \sqrt{2}$

46. $\csc x = -\dfrac{2\sqrt{3}}{3}$

In Exercises 47 and 48, use the graph of the function to determine whether the function is even, odd, or neither.

47. $f(x) = \sec x$

48. $f(x) = \tan x$

49. *Graphical Reasoning* Consider the functions

$$f(x) = 2 \sin x \quad \text{and} \quad g(x) = \dfrac{1}{2} \csc x$$

on the interval $(0, \pi)$.

(a) Graph f and g in the same coordinate plane.

(b) Approximate the interval in which $f > g$.

(c) Describe the behavior of each of the functions as x approaches π. How is the behavior of g related to the behavior of f as x approaches π?

50. *Graphical Reasoning* Consider the functions

$$f(x) = \tan \frac{\pi x}{2} \quad \text{and} \quad g(x) = \frac{1}{2} \sec \frac{\pi x}{2}$$

on the interval $(-1, 1)$.

(a) Use a graphing utility to graph f and g in the same viewing window.

(b) Approximate the interval in which $f < g$.

(c) Approximate the interval in which $2f < 2g$. How does the result compare with that of part (b)? Explain.

 Conjecture In Exercises 59–62, graph the functions f and g. Use the graphs to make a conjecture about the relationship between the functions.

59. $f(x) = \sin x + \cos\left(x + \dfrac{\pi}{2}\right), \quad g(x) = 0$

60. $f(x) = \sin x - \cos\left(x + \dfrac{\pi}{2}\right), \quad g(x) = 2 \sin x$

61. $f(x) = \sin^2 x, \quad g(x) = \frac{1}{2}(1 - \cos 2x)$

62. $f(x) = \cos^2 \dfrac{\pi x}{2}, \quad g(x) = \dfrac{1}{2}(1 + \cos \pi x)$

 In Exercises 51–54, use a graphing utility to graph the two equations in the same viewing window. Determine analytically whether the expressions are equivalent.

51. $y_1 = \sin x \csc x, \quad y_2 = 1$

52. $y_1 = \sin x \sec x, \quad y_2 = \tan x$

53. $y_1 = \dfrac{\cos x}{\sin x}, \quad y_2 = \cot x$

54. $y_1 = \sec^2 x - 1, \quad y_2 = \tan^2 x$

In Exercises 63–66, use a graphing utility to graph the function and the damping factor of the function in the same viewing window. Describe the behavior of the function as x increases without bound.

63. $f(x) = 2^{-x/4} \cos \pi x$ **64.** $f(x) = e^{-x} \cos x$

65. $g(x) = e^{-x^2/2} \sin x$ **66.** $h(x) = 2^{-x^2/4} \sin x$

In Exercises 55–58, match the function with its graph. Describe the behavior of the function as x approaches zero. [The graphs are labeled (a), (b), (c), and (d).]

(a)

(b)

(c)

(d)
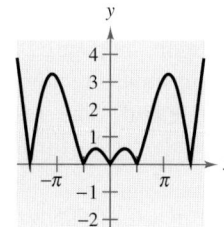

55. $f(x) = |x \cos x|$

56. $f(x) = x \sin x$

57. $g(x) = |x| \sin x$

58. $g(x) = |x| \cos x$

Exploration In Exercises 67–72, use a graphing utility to graph the function. Describe the behavior of the function as x approaches zero.

67. $y = \dfrac{6}{x} + \cos x, \quad x > 0$

68. $y = \dfrac{4}{x} + \sin 2x, \quad x > 0$

69. $g(x) = \dfrac{\sin x}{x}$ **70.** $f(x) = \dfrac{1 - \cos x}{x}$

71. $f(x) = \sin \dfrac{1}{x}$ **72.** $h(x) = x \sin \dfrac{1}{x}$

73. *Distance* A plane flying at an altitude of 7 miles above a radar antenna will pass directly over the radar antenna (see figure). Let d be the ground distance from the antenna to the point directly under the plane and let x be the angle of elevation to the plane from the antenna. (d is positive as the plane approaches the antenna.) Write d as a function of x and graph the function over the interval $0 < x < \pi$.

74. *Television Coverage* A television camera is on a reviewing platform 27 meters from the street on which a parade will be passing from left to right (see figure). Express the distance d from the camera to a particular unit in the parade as a function of the angle x, and graph the function over the interval $-\pi/2 < x < \pi/2$. (Consider x as negative when a unit in the parade approaches from the left.)

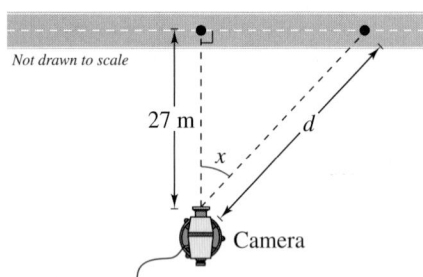

Not drawn to scale

27 m

x

d

Camera

▶ **Model It**

75. *Predator-Prey Model* The population of coyotes (a predator) at time t (in months) in a region is estimated to be

$$C = 5000 + 2000 \sin \frac{\pi t}{12}$$

and the population of rabbits (its prey) is estimated to be

$$R = 25{,}000 + 15{,}000 \cos \frac{\pi t}{12}.$$

(a) Use a graphing utility to graph both models in the same viewing window. Use the window setting $0 \le t \le 100$.

(b) Use the graphs of the models in part (a) to explain the oscillations in the size of each population.

(c) The cycles of each population follow a periodic pattern. Find the period of each model and describe several factors that could be contributing to the cyclical patterns.

76. *Sales* The projected monthly sales S (in thousands of units) of lawn mowers (a seasonal product) are modeled by $S = 74 + 3t - 40 \cos(\pi t/6)$, where t is the time in months, with $t = 1$ corresponding to January. Graph the sales function over 1 year.

77. *Meterology* The normal monthly high temperatures in degrees Fahrenheit for Erie, Pennsylvania are approximated by

$$H(t) = 54.33 - 20.38 \cos \frac{\pi t}{6} - 15.69 \sin \frac{\pi t}{6}$$

and the normal monthly low temperatures are approximated by

$$L(t) = 39.36 - 15.70 \cos \frac{\pi t}{6} - 14.16 \sin \frac{\pi t}{6}$$

where t is the time in months, with $t = 1$ corresponding to January (see figure). (Source: National Oceanic and Atmospheric Administration)

(a) What is the period of each function?

(b) During what part of the year is the difference between the normal high and low temperatures greatest? When is it smallest?

(c) The sun is northernmost in the sky around June 21, but the graph shows the warmest temperatures at a later date. Approximate the lag time of the temperatures relative to the position of the sun.

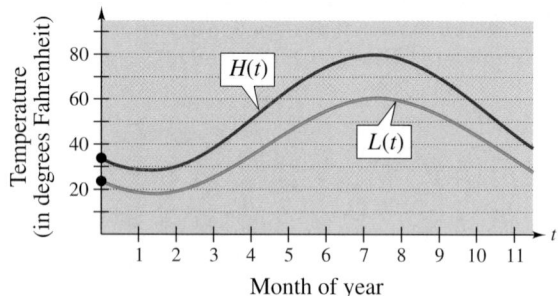

78. *Harmonic Motion* An object weighing W pounds is suspended from the ceiling by a steel spring (see figure on page 321). The weight is pulled downward (positive direction) from its equilibrium position and released. The resulting motion of the weight is described by the function

$$y = \frac{1}{2} e^{-t/4} \cos 4t, \qquad t > 0$$

where y is the distance in feet and t is the time in seconds.

 (a) Use a graphing utility to graph the function.

(b) Describe the behavior of the displacement function for increasing values of time t.

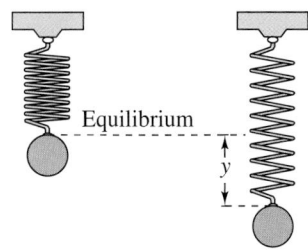

FIGURE FOR 78

Synthesis

True or False? **In Exercises 79 and 80, determine whether the statement is true or false. Justify your answer.**

79. The graph of $y = \csc x$ can be obtained on a calculator by graphing the reciprocal of $y = \sin x$.

80. The graph of $y = \sec x$ can be obtained on a calculator by graphing a translation of the reciprocal of $y = \sin x$.

81. *Writing* Describe the behavior of $f(x) = \tan x$ as x approaches $\pi/2$ from the left and from the right.

82. *Writing* Describe the behavior of $f(x) = \csc x$ as x approaches π from the left and from the right.

83. *Exploration* Consider the function

$$f(x) = x - \cos x.$$

 (a) Use a graphing utility to graph the function and verify that there exists a zero between 0 and 1. Use the graph to approximate the zero.

(b) Starting with $x_0 = 1$, generate a sequence $x_1, x_2, x_3, \ldots$ where $x_n = \cos(x_{n-1})$. For example,

$$x_0 = 1$$
$$x_1 = \cos(x_0)$$
$$x_2 = \cos(x_1)$$
$$x_3 = \cos(x_2)$$
$$\vdots$$

What value does the sequence approach?

84. *Approximation* Using calculus, it can be shown that the tangent function can be approximated by the polynomial

$$\tan x \approx x + \frac{2x^3}{3!} + \frac{16x^5}{5!}$$

where x is in radians. Use a graphing utility to graph the tangent function and its polynomial approximation in the same viewing window. How do the graphs compare?

85. *Approximation* Using calculus, it can be shown that the secant function can be approximated by the polynomial

$$\sec x \approx 1 + \frac{x^2}{2!} + \frac{5x^4}{4!}$$

where x is in radians. Use a graphing utility to graph the secant function and its polynomial approximation in the same viewing window. How do the graphs compare?

86. *Pattern Recognition*

 (a) Use a graphing utility to graph each function.

$$y_1 = \frac{4}{\pi}\left(\sin \pi x + \frac{1}{3}\sin 3\pi x\right)$$

$$y_2 = \frac{4}{\pi}\left(\sin \pi x + \frac{1}{3}\sin 3\pi x + \frac{1}{5}\sin 5\pi x\right)$$

 (b) Identify the pattern started in part (a) and find a function y_3 that continues the pattern one more term. Use a graphing utility to graph y_3.

(c) The graphs in parts (a) and (b) approximate the periodic function in the figure. Find a function y_4 that is a better approximation.

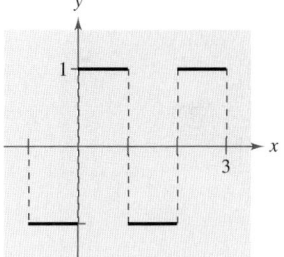

Review

In Exercises 87–90, solve the exponential equation. Round your answer to three decimal places.

87. $e^{2x} = 54$

88. $8^{3x} = 98$

89. $\dfrac{300}{1 + e^{-x}} = 100$

90. $\left(1 + \dfrac{0.15}{365}\right)^{365t} = 5$

In Exercises 91–96, solve the logarithmic equation. Round your answer to three decimal places.

91. $\ln(3x - 2) = 73$

92. $\ln(14 - 2x) = 68$

93. $\ln(x^2 + 1) = 3.2$

94. $\ln \sqrt{x + 4} = 5$

95. $\log_8 x + \log_8(x - 1) = \frac{1}{3}$

96. $\log_6 x + \log_6(x^2 - 1) = \log_6 64x$

4.7 Inverse Trigonometric Functions

▶ **What you should learn**

- How to evaluate the inverse sine function
- How to evaluate the other inverse trigonometric functions
- How to evaluate the compositions of trigonometric functions

▶ **Why you should learn it**

You can use inverse trigonometric functions to model and solve real-life problems. For instance, in Exercise 93 on page 330, an inverse trigonometric function can be used to model the angle subtended by a camera lens x feet from a painting.

John Foxx/Imagestate

Inverse Sine Function

Recall from Section 1.8 that, for a function to have an inverse function, it must be one-to-one—that is, it must pass the Horizontal Line Test. From Figure 4.69 you can see that $y = \sin x$ does not pass the test because different values of x yield the same y-value.

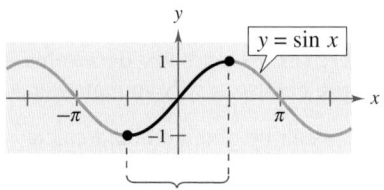

Sin x has an inverse function
on this interval.

FIGURE **4.69**

However, if you restrict the domain to the interval $-\pi/2 \le x \le \pi/2$ (corresponding to the black portion of the graph in Figure 4.69), the following properties hold.

1. On the interval $[-\pi/2, \pi/2]$, the function $y = \sin x$ is increasing.
2. On the interval $[-\pi/2, \pi/2]$, $y = \sin x$ takes on its full range of values, $-1 \le \sin x \le 1$.
3. On the interval $[-\pi/2, \pi/2]$, $y = \sin x$ is one-to-one.

So, on the restricted domain $-\pi/2 \le x \le \pi/2$, $y = \sin x$ has a unique inverse function called the **inverse sine function.** It is denoted by

$$y = \arcsin x \qquad \text{or} \qquad y = \sin^{-1} x.$$

The notation $\sin^{-1} x$ is consistent with the inverse function notation $f^{-1}(x)$. The arcsin x notation (read as "the arcsine of x") comes from the association of a central angle with its subtended *arc length* on a unit circle. So, arcsin x means the angle (or arc) whose sine is x. Both notations, arcsin x and $\sin^{-1} x$, are commonly used in mathematics, so remember that $\sin^{-1} x$ denotes the *inverse* sine function rather than $1/\sin x$. The values of arcsin x lie in the interval $-\pi/2 \le \arcsin x \le \pi/2$. The graph of $y = \arcsin x$ is shown in Figure 4.70 on page 323.

STUDY TIP

When evaluating the inverse sine function, it helps to remember the phrase "the arcsine of x is the angle (or number) whose sine is x."

Definition of Inverse Sine Function

The **inverse sine function** is defined by

$$y = \arcsin x \qquad \text{if and only if} \qquad \sin y = x$$

where $-1 \le x \le 1$ and $-\pi/2 \le y \le \pi/2$. The domain of $y = \arcsin x$ is $[-1, 1]$, and the range is $[-\pi/2, \pi/2]$.

STUDY TIP

As with the trigonometric functions, much of the work with the inverse trigonometric functions can be done by *exact* calculations rather than by calculator approximations. Exact calculations help to increase your understanding of the inverse functions by relating them to the right triangle definitions of the trigonometric functions.

Example 1 ▶ Evaluating the Inverse Sine Function

If possible, find the exact value.

a. $\arcsin\left(-\dfrac{1}{2}\right)$

b. $\sin^{-1}\dfrac{\sqrt{3}}{2}$

c. $\sin^{-1}2$

Solution

a. Because $\sin\left(-\dfrac{\pi}{6}\right) = -\dfrac{1}{2}$ for $-\dfrac{\pi}{2} \le y \le \dfrac{\pi}{2}$, it follows that

$$\arcsin\left(-\dfrac{1}{2}\right) = -\dfrac{\pi}{6}. \qquad \text{Angle whose sine is } -\tfrac{1}{2}$$

b. Because $\sin(\pi/3) = \sqrt{3}/2$ for $-\pi/2 \le y \le \pi/2$, it follows that

$$\sin^{-1}\dfrac{\sqrt{3}}{2} = \dfrac{\pi}{3}. \qquad \text{Angle whose sine is } \sqrt{3}/2$$

c. It is not possible to evaluate $y = \sin^{-1}x$ when $x = 2$ because there is no angle whose sine is 2. Remember that the domain of the inverse sine function is $[-1, 1]$.

You may need to remind your students that the values of the inverse sine function are always in radians.

You may wish to illustrate the reflections of $y = \sin x$ and $y = \arcsin x$ about the line $y = x$. Consider using a graphing utility to do this.

Example 2 ▶ Graphing the Arcsine Function

Sketch a graph of

$$y = \arcsin x.$$

Solution

By definition, the equations $y = \arcsin x$ and $\sin y = x$ are equivalent for $-\pi/2 \le y \le \pi/2$. So, their graphs are the same. From the interval $[-\pi/2, \pi/2]$, you can assign values to y in the second equation to make a table of values. Then plot the points and draw a smooth curve through the points.

y	$-\dfrac{\pi}{2}$	$-\dfrac{\pi}{4}$	$-\dfrac{\pi}{6}$	0	$\dfrac{\pi}{6}$	$\dfrac{\pi}{4}$	$\dfrac{\pi}{2}$
$x = \sin y$	-1	$-\dfrac{\sqrt{2}}{2}$	$-\dfrac{1}{2}$	0	$\dfrac{1}{2}$	$\dfrac{\sqrt{2}}{2}$	1

The resulting graph for $y = \arcsin x$ is shown in Figure 4.70. Note that it is the reflection (in the line $y = x$) of the black portion of the graph in Figure 4.69. Be sure you see that Figure 4.70 shows the *entire* graph of the inverse sine function. Remember that the range of $y = \arcsin x$ is the closed interval $[-\pi/2, \pi/2]$.

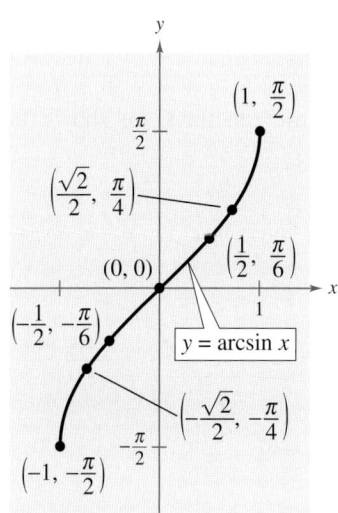

FIGURE 4.70

Other Inverse Trigonometric Functions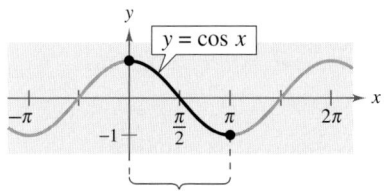

The cosine function is decreasing and one-to-one on the interval $0 \leq x \leq \pi$, as shown in Figure 4.71.

FIGURE **4.71**

Consequently, on this interval the cosine function has an inverse function—the **inverse cosine function**—denoted by

$$y = \arccos x \qquad \text{or} \qquad y = \cos^{-1} x.$$

Similarly, you can define an **inverse tangent function** by restricting the domain of $y = \tan x$ to the interval $(-\pi/2, \pi/2)$. The following list summarizes the definitions of the three most common inverse trigonometric functions. The remaining three are defined in Exercises 100–102.

You may need to point out to your students that the range for each of these functions is different. Students should know these ranges well to ensure that their answers are within the correct range.

Definitions of the Inverse Trigonometric Functions

Function	Domain	Range
$y = \arcsin x$ if and only if $\sin y = x$	$-1 \leq x \leq 1$	$-\dfrac{\pi}{2} \leq y \leq \dfrac{\pi}{2}$
$y = \arccos x$ if and only if $\cos y = x$	$-1 \leq x \leq 1$	$0 \leq y \leq \pi$
$y = \arctan x$ if and only if $\tan y = x$	$-\infty < x < \infty$	$-\dfrac{\pi}{2} < y < \dfrac{\pi}{2}$

The graphs of these three inverse trigonometric functions are shown in Figure 4.72.

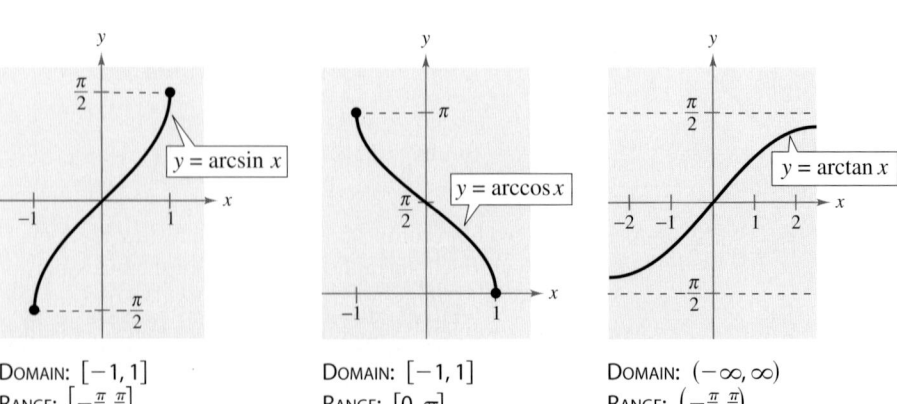

DOMAIN: $[-1, 1]$
RANGE: $\left[-\dfrac{\pi}{2}, \dfrac{\pi}{2}\right]$

DOMAIN: $[-1, 1]$
RANGE: $[0, \pi]$

DOMAIN: $(-\infty, \infty)$
RANGE: $\left(-\dfrac{\pi}{2}, \dfrac{\pi}{2}\right)$

FIGURE **4.72**

Example 3 ▶ Evaluating Inverse Trigonometric Functions

Find the exact value.

a. $\arccos \dfrac{\sqrt{2}}{2}$ **b.** $\cos^{-1}(-1)$

c. $\arctan 0$ **d.** $\tan^{-1}(-1)$

Solution

a. Because $\cos(\pi/4) = \sqrt{2}/2$, and $\pi/4$ lies in $[0, \pi]$, it follows that

$$\arccos \frac{\sqrt{2}}{2} = \frac{\pi}{4}. \qquad \text{Angle whose cosine is } \sqrt{2}/2$$

b. Because $\cos \pi = -1$, and π lies in $[0, \pi]$, it follows that

$$\cos^{-1}(-1) = \pi. \qquad \text{Angle whose cosine is } -1$$

c. Because $\tan 0 = 0$, and 0 lies in $(-\pi/2, \pi/2)$, it follows that

$$\arctan 0 = 0. \qquad \text{Angle whose tangent is } 0$$

d. Because $\tan(-\pi/4) = -1$, and $-\pi/4$ lies in $(-\pi/2, \pi/2)$, it follows that

$$\tan^{-1}(-1) = -\frac{\pi}{4}. \qquad \text{Angle whose tangent is } -1$$

Example 4 ▶ Calculators and Inverse Trigonometric Functions

Use a calculator to approximate the value (if possible).

a. $\arctan(-8.45)$

b. $\sin^{-1} 0.2447$

c. $\arccos 2$

Solution

Function	*Mode*	*Calculator Keystrokes*
a. $\arctan(-8.45)$	Radian	[TAN⁻¹] [(] [(−)] 8.45 [)] [ENTER]

From the display, it follows that $\arctan(-8.45) \approx -1.453001$.

b. $\sin^{-1} 0.2447$	Radian	[SIN⁻¹] 0.2447 [ENTER]

From the display, it follows that $\arcsin 0.2447 \approx 0.2472103$.

c. $\arccos 2$	Radian	[COS⁻¹] 2 [ENTER]

In real number mode, the calculator should display an *error message* because the domain of the inverse cosine function is $[-1, 1]$.

STUDY TIP

It is important to remember that the domain of the inverse sine function and the inverse cosine function is $[-1, 1]$, as indicated in Example 4(c).

In Example 4, if you had set the calculator to degree mode, the displays would have been in degrees rather than radians. This convention is peculiar to calculators. By definition, the values of inverse trigonometric functions are *always in radians.*

Compositions of Functions

Recall from Section 1.8 that for all x in the domains of f and f^{-1}, inverse functions have the properties

$$f(f^{-1}(x)) = x \qquad \text{and} \qquad f^{-1}(f(x)) = x.$$

Inverse Properties of Trigonometric Functions

If $-1 \leq x \leq 1$ and $-\pi/2 \leq y \leq \pi/2$, then

$$\sin(\arcsin x) = x \qquad \text{and} \qquad \arcsin(\sin y) = y.$$

If $-1 \leq x \leq 1$ and $0 \leq y \leq \pi$, then

$$\cos(\arccos x) = x \qquad \text{and} \qquad \arccos(\cos y) = y.$$

If x is a real number and $-\pi/2 < y < \pi/2$, then

$$\tan(\arctan x) = x \qquad \text{and} \qquad \arctan(\tan y) = y.$$

Keep in mind that these inverse properties do not apply for arbitrary values of x and y. For instance,

$$\arcsin\left(\sin\frac{3\pi}{2}\right) = \arcsin(-1) = -\frac{\pi}{2} \neq \frac{3\pi}{2}.$$

In other words, the property

$$\arcsin(\sin y) = y$$

is not valid for values of y outside the interval $\left[-\pi/2, \pi/2\right]$.

Example 5 ▶ **Using Inverse Properties**

If possible, find the exact value.

a. $\tan[\arctan(-5)]$ **b.** $\arcsin\left(\sin\dfrac{5\pi}{3}\right)$ **c.** $\cos(\cos^{-1}\pi)$

Solution

a. Because -5 lies in the domain of the arctan function, the inverse property applies, and you have

$$\tan[\arctan(-5)] = -5.$$

b. In this case, $5\pi/3$ does not lie within the range of the arcsine function, $-\pi/2 \leq y \leq \pi/2$. However, $5\pi/3$ is coterminal with

$$\frac{5\pi}{3} - 2\pi = -\frac{\pi}{3}$$

which does lie in the range of the arcsine function, and you have

$$\arcsin\left(\sin\frac{5\pi}{3}\right) = \arcsin\left[\sin\left(-\frac{\pi}{3}\right)\right] = -\frac{\pi}{3}.$$

c. The expression $\cos(\cos^{-1}\pi)$ is not defined because $\cos^{-1}\pi$ is not defined. Remember that the domain of the inverse cosine function is $[-1, 1]$.

Example 6 shows how to use right triangles to find exact values of compositions of inverse functions. Then, Example 7 shows how to use triangles to convert a trigonometric expression into an algebraic expression. This conversion technique is used frequently in calculus.

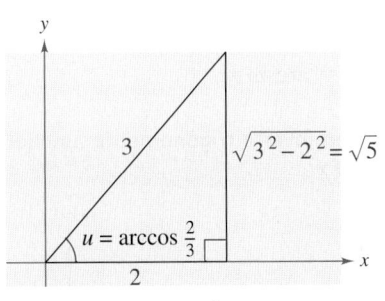

3 $\sqrt{3^2-2^2}=\sqrt{5}$

$u = \arccos \frac{2}{3}$

2

Angle whose cosine is $\frac{2}{3}$

FIGURE **4.73**

Example 6 ▶ **Evaluating Compositions of Functions**

Find the exact value.

a. $\tan\left(\arccos \frac{2}{3}\right)$ **b.** $\cos\left[\arcsin\left(-\frac{3}{5}\right)\right]$

Solution

a. If you let $u = \arccos \frac{2}{3}$, then $\cos u = \frac{2}{3}$. Because $\cos u$ is positive, u is a *first*-quadrant angle. You can sketch and label angle u as shown in Figure 4.73. Consequently,

$$\tan\left(\arccos \frac{2}{3}\right) = \tan u = \frac{\text{opp}}{\text{adj}} = \frac{\sqrt{5}}{2}.$$

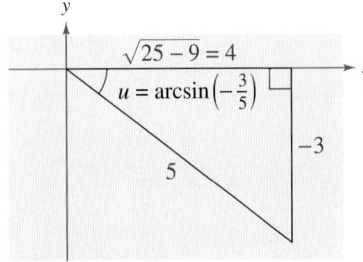

$\sqrt{25-9}=4$

$u = \arcsin\left(-\frac{3}{5}\right)$

-3

5

Angle whose sine is $-\frac{3}{5}$

FIGURE **4.74**

b. If you let $u = \arcsin\left(-\frac{3}{5}\right)$, then $\sin u = -\frac{3}{5}$. Because $\sin u$ is negative, u is a *fourth*-quadrant angle. You can sketch and label angle u as shown in Figure 4.74. Consequently,

$$\cos\left[\arcsin\left(-\frac{3}{5}\right)\right] = \cos u = \frac{\text{adj}}{\text{hyp}} = \frac{4}{5}.$$

Example 7 ▶ **Some Problems from Calculus**

Write each of the following as an algebraic expression in x.

a. $\sin(\arccos 3x), \quad 0 \le x \le \frac{1}{3}$ **b.** $\cot(\arccos 3x), \quad 0 \le x < \frac{1}{3}$

Solution

If you let $u = \arccos 3x$, then $\cos u = 3x$. Because

$$\cos u = \frac{\text{adj}}{\text{hyp}} = \frac{3x}{1}$$

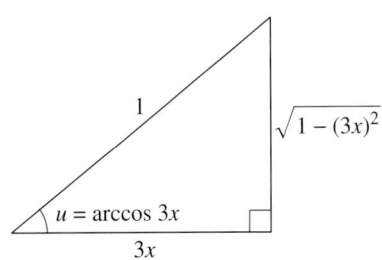

1

$\sqrt{1-(3x)^2}$

$u = \arccos 3x$

$3x$

Angle whose cosine is $3x$

FIGURE **4.75**

you can sketch a right triangle with acute angle u, as shown in Figure 4.75. From this triangle, you can easily convert each expression to algebraic form.

a. $\sin(\arccos 3x) = \sin u = \dfrac{\text{opp}}{\text{hyp}} = \sqrt{1-9x^2}, \quad 0 \le x \le \dfrac{1}{3}$

b. $\cot(\arccos 3x) = \cot u = \dfrac{\text{adj}}{\text{opp}} = \dfrac{3x}{\sqrt{1-9x^2}}, \quad 0 \le x < \dfrac{1}{3}$

You may want to review with students how to rationalize the denominator of a fractional expression.

In Example 7, similar arguments can be made for x-values lying in the interval $\left[-\frac{1}{3}, 0\right]$.

4.7 Exercises

In Exercises 1–16, evaluate the expression without the aid of a calculator.

1. $\arcsin \frac{1}{2}$
2. $\arcsin 0$
3. $\arccos \frac{1}{2}$
4. $\arccos 0$
5. $\arctan \frac{\sqrt{3}}{3}$
6. $\arctan(-1)$
7. $\cos^{-1}\left(-\frac{\sqrt{3}}{2}\right)$
8. $\sin^{-1}\left(-\frac{\sqrt{2}}{2}\right)$
9. $\arctan\left(-\sqrt{3}\right)$
10. $\arctan \sqrt{3}$
11. $\arccos\left(-\frac{1}{2}\right)$
12. $\arcsin \frac{\sqrt{2}}{2}$
13. $\sin^{-1}\frac{\sqrt{3}}{2}$
14. $\tan^{-1}\left(-\frac{\sqrt{3}}{3}\right)$
15. $\tan^{-1} 0$
16. $\cos^{-1} 1$

In Exercises 17–32, use a calculator to approximate the expression. Round your result to two decimal places.

17. $\arccos 0.28$
18. $\arcsin 0.45$
19. $\arcsin(-0.75)$
20. $\arccos(-0.7)$
21. $\arctan(-3)$
22. $\arctan 15$
23. $\sin^{-1} 0.31$
24. $\cos^{-1} 0.26$
25. $\arccos(-0.41)$
26. $\arcsin(-0.125)$
27. $\arctan 0.92$
28. $\arctan 2.8$
29. $\arcsin \frac{3}{4}$
30. $\arccos\left(-\frac{1}{3}\right)$
31. $\tan^{-1}\frac{7}{2}$
32. $\tan^{-1}\left(-\frac{95}{7}\right)$

In Exercises 33 and 34, determine the missing coordinates of the points on the graph of the function.

33.

34.

 In Exercises 35 and 36, use a graphing utility to graph f, g, and y = x in the same viewing window to verify geometrically that g is the inverse function of f. (Be sure to restrict the domain of f properly.)

35. $f(x) = \tan x, \quad g(x) = \arctan x$

36. $f(x) = \sin x, \quad g(x) = \arcsin x$

In Exercises 37–42, use an inverse trigonometric function to write θ as a function of x.

37.
38.
39.
40.
41.
42.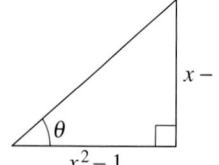

In Exercises 43–48, use the properties of inverse trigonometric functions to evaluate the expression.

43. $\sin(\arcsin 0.3)$
44. $\tan(\arctan 25)$
45. $\cos[\arccos(-0.1)]$
46. $\sin[\arcsin(-0.2)]$
47. $\arcsin(\sin 3\pi)$
48. $\arccos\left(\cos \frac{7\pi}{2}\right)$

In Exercises 49–58, find the exact value of the expression. (Hint: Make a sketch of a right triangle.)

49. $\sin\left(\arctan \frac{3}{4}\right)$
50. $\sec\left(\arcsin \frac{4}{5}\right)$
51. $\cos(\tan^{-1} 2)$
52. $\sin\left(\cos^{-1}\frac{\sqrt{5}}{5}\right)$
53. $\cos\left(\arcsin \frac{5}{13}\right)$
54. $\csc\left[\arctan\left(-\frac{5}{12}\right)\right]$
55. $\sec\left[\arctan\left(-\frac{3}{5}\right)\right]$
56. $\tan\left[\arcsin\left(-\frac{3}{4}\right)\right]$
57. $\sin\left[\arccos\left(-\frac{2}{3}\right)\right]$
58. $\cot\left(\arctan \frac{5}{8}\right)$

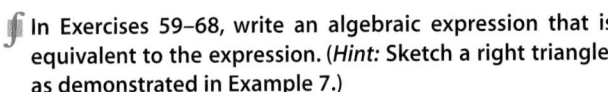

In Exercises 59–68, write an algebraic expression that is equivalent to the expression. (*Hint:* Sketch a right triangle, as demonstrated in Example 7.)

59. $\cot(\arctan x)$

60. $\sin(\arctan x)$

61. $\cos(\arcsin 2x)$

62. $\sec(\arctan 3x)$

63. $\sin(\arccos x)$

64. $\sec[\arcsin(x - 1)]$

65. $\tan\left(\arccos \dfrac{x}{3}\right)$

66. $\cot\left(\arctan \dfrac{1}{x}\right)$

67. $\csc\left(\arctan \dfrac{x}{\sqrt{2}}\right)$

68. $\cos\left(\arcsin \dfrac{x - h}{r}\right)$

In Exercises 69 and 70, use a graphing utility to graph f and g in the same viewing window to verify that the two functions are equal. Explain why they are equal. Identify any asymptotes of the graphs.

69. $f(x) = \sin(\arctan 2x)$, $\quad g(x) = \dfrac{2x}{\sqrt{1 + 4x^2}}$

70. $f(x) = \tan\left(\arccos \dfrac{x}{2}\right)$, $\quad g(x) = \dfrac{\sqrt{4 - x^2}}{x}$

In Exercises 71–74, fill in the blank.

71. $\arctan \dfrac{9}{x} = \arcsin(\quad)$, $\quad x \neq 0$

72. $\arcsin \dfrac{\sqrt{36 - x^2}}{6} = \arccos(\quad)$, $\quad 0 \le x \le 6$

73. $\arccos \dfrac{3}{\sqrt{x^2 - 2x + 10}} = \arcsin(\quad)$

74. $\arccos \dfrac{x - 2}{2} = \arctan(\quad)$, $\quad |x - 2| \le 2$

In Exercises 75–82, sketch a graph of the function.

75. $y = 2 \arccos x$

76. $y = \arcsin \dfrac{x}{2}$

77. $f(x) = \arcsin(x - 1)$

78. $g(t) = \arccos(t + 2)$

79. $f(x) = \arctan 2x$

80. $f(x) = \dfrac{\pi}{2} + \arctan x$

81. $h(v) = \tan(\arccos v)$

82. $f(x) = \arccos \dfrac{x}{4}$

In Exercises 83–88, use a graphing utility to graph the function.

83. $f(x) = 2 \arccos(2x)$

84. $f(x) = \pi \arcsin(4x)$

85. $f(x) = \arctan(2x - 3)$

86. $f(x) = -3 + \arctan(\pi x)$

87. $f(x) = \pi - \sin^{-1}\left(\dfrac{2}{3}\right)$

88. $f(x) = \dfrac{\pi}{2} + \cos^{-1}\left(\dfrac{1}{\pi}\right)$

In Exercises 89 and 90, write the function in terms of the sine function by using the identity

$$A \cos \omega t + B \sin \omega t = \sqrt{A^2 + B^2}\, \sin\left(\omega t + \arctan \dfrac{A}{B}\right).$$

Use a graphing utility to graph both forms of the function. What does the graph imply?

89. $f(t) = 3 \cos 2t + 3 \sin 2t$

90. $f(t) = 4 \cos \pi t + 3 \sin \pi t$

91. *Docking a Boat*   A boat is pulled in by means of a winch located on a dock 5 feet above the deck of the boat (see figure). Let θ be the angle of elevation from the boat to the winch and let s be the length of the rope from the winch to the boat.

(a) Write θ as a function of s.

(b) Find θ when $s = 40$ feet and $s = 20$ feet.

92. *Photography*   A television camera at ground level is filming the lift-off of a space shuttle at a point 750 meters from the launch pad (see figure). Let θ be the angle of elevation to the shuttle and let s be the height of the shuttle.

(a) Write θ as a function of s.

(b) Find θ when $s = 300$ meters and $s = 1200$ meters.

▶ **Model It**

93. *Photography* A photographer is taking a picture of a three-foot-tall painting hung in an art gallery. The camera lens is 1 foot below the lower edge of the painting (see figure). The angle β subtended by the camera lens x feet from the painting is

$$\beta = \arctan \frac{3x}{x^2 + 4}, \qquad x > 0.$$

(a) Use a graphing utility to graph β as a function of x.

(b) Move the cursor along the graph to approximate the distance from the picture when β is maximum.

(c) Identify the asymptote of the graph and discuss its meaning in the context of the problem.

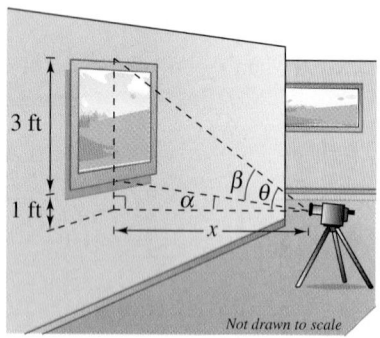

Not drawn to scale

94. *Granular Angle of Repose* Different types of granular substances naturally settle at different angles when stored in cone-shaped piles. This angle θ is called the *angle of repose* (see figure). When rock salt is stored in a cone-shaped pile 11 feet high, the diameter of the pile's base is about 34 feet. (Source: Bulk-Store Structures, Inc.)

(a) Find the angle of repose for rock salt.

(b) How tall is a pile of rock salt that has a base diameter of 40 feet?

95. *Granular Angle of Repose* When whole corn is stored in a cone-shaped pile 20 feet high, the diameter of the pile's base is about 82 feet.

(a) Find the angle of repose for whole corn.

(b) How tall is a pile of corn that has a base diameter of 100 feet?

96. *Angle of Elevation* An airplane flies at an altitude of 6 miles toward a point directly over an observer. Consider θ and x as shown in the figure.

(a) Write θ as a function of x.

(b) Find θ when $x = 7$ miles and $x = 1$ mile.

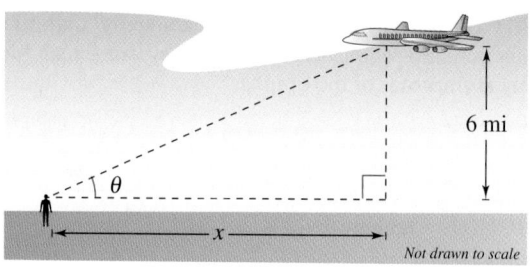

Not drawn to scale

97. *Security Patrol* A security car with its spotlight on is parked 20 meters from a warehouse. Consider θ and x as shown in the figure.

(a) Write θ as a function of x.

(b) Find θ when $x = 5$ meters and $x = 12$ meters.

Not drawn to scale

Synthesis

True or False? In Exercises 98 and 99, determine whether the statement is true or false. Justify your answer.

98. $\sin \dfrac{5\pi}{6} = \dfrac{1}{2}$ ⟹ $\arcsin \dfrac{1}{2} = \dfrac{5\pi}{6}$

99. $\tan \dfrac{5\pi}{4} = 1$ ⟹ $\arctan 1 = \dfrac{5\pi}{4}$

100. Define the inverse cotangent function by restricting the domain of the cotangent function to the interval $(0, \pi)$, and sketch its graph.

101. Define the inverse secant function by restricting the domain of the secant function to the intervals $[0, \pi/2)$ and $(\pi/2, \pi]$, and sketch its graph.

102. Define the inverse cosecant function by restricting the domain of the cosecant function to the intervals $[-\pi/2, 0)$ and $(0, \pi/2]$, and sketch its graph.

103. Use the results of Exercises 100–102 to evaluate each expression without using a calculator.

(a) $\operatorname{arcsec} \sqrt{2}$ (b) $\operatorname{arcsec} 1$

(c) $\operatorname{arccot}\left(-\sqrt{3}\right)$ (d) $\operatorname{arccsc} 2$

104. **Area** In calculus, it is shown that the area of the region bounded by the graphs of $y = 0$, $y = 1/(x^2 + 1)$, $x = a$, and $x = b$ is given by

Area $= \arctan b - \arctan a$

(see figure). Find the area for the following values of a and b.

(a) $a = 0, b = 1$ (b) $a = -1, b = 1$

(c) $a = 0, b = 3$ (d) $a = -1, b = 3$

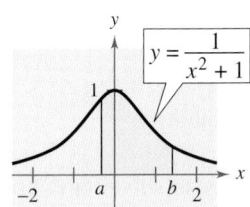

105. **Think About It** Use a graphing utility to graph the functions

$f(x) = \sqrt{x}$ and $g(x) = 6 \arctan x$.

For $x > 0$, it appears that $g > f$. Explain why you know that there exists a positive real number a such that $g < f$ for $x > a$. Approximate the number a.

106. **Think About It** Consider the functions

$f(x) = \sin x$ and $f^{-1}(x) = \arcsin x$.

(a) Use a graphing utility to graph the composite functions $f \circ f^{-1}$ and $f^{-1} \circ f$.

(b) Explain why the graphs in part (a) are not the graph of the line $y = x$. Why do the graphs of $f \circ f^{-1}$ and $f^{-1} \circ f$ differ?

Proof In Exercises 107–112, prove the identity.

107. $\arcsin(-x) = -\arcsin x$

108. $\arctan(-x) = -\arctan x$

109. $\arccos(-x) = \pi - \arccos x$

110. $\arctan x + \arctan \dfrac{1}{x} = \dfrac{\pi}{2}, \quad x > 0$

111. $\arcsin x + \arccos x = \dfrac{\pi}{2}$

112. $\arcsin x = \arctan \dfrac{x}{\sqrt{1 - x^2}}$

Review

In Exercises 113–116, sketch a right triangle corresponding to the trigonometric function of the acute angle θ. Use the Pythagorean Theorem to determine the third side.

113. $\sin \theta = \frac{3}{4}$

114. $\tan \theta = 2$

115. $\cos \theta = \frac{5}{6}$

116. $\sec \theta = 3$

In Exercises 117–120, evaluate the expression. Round your result to three decimal places.

117. $(8.2)^{3.4}$

118. $10(14)^{-2}$

119. $(1.1)^{50}$

120. $16^{-2\pi}$

121. **Partnership Costs** A group of people agree to share equally in the cost of a $250,000 endowment to a college. If they could find two more people to join the group, each person's share of the cost would decrease by $6250. How many people are presently in the group?

122. **Speed** A boat travels at a speed of 18 miles per hour in still water. It travels 35 miles upstream and then returns to the starting point in a total of 4 hours. Find the speed of the current.

4.8 Applications and Models

▶ **What you should learn**

- How to solve real-life problems involving right triangles
- How to solve real-life problems involving directional bearings
- How to solve real-life problems involving harmonic motion

▶ **Why you should learn it**

Trigonometric functions frequently model real-life problems involving cyclical patterns in business. For instance, in Exercise 63 on page 342, you can find a trigonometric model for the sales of an outerwear manufacturer.

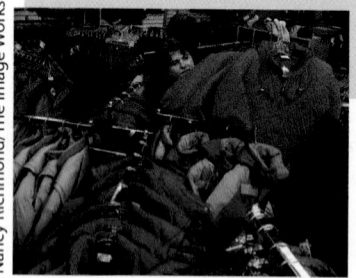

Applications Involving Right Triangles

In this section the three angles of a right triangle are denoted by the letters A, B, and C (where C is the right angle), and the lengths of the sides opposite these angles by the letters a, b, and c (where c is the hypotenuse).

Example 1 ▶ Solving a Right Triangle

Solve the right triangle shown in Figure 4.76 for all unknown sides and angles.

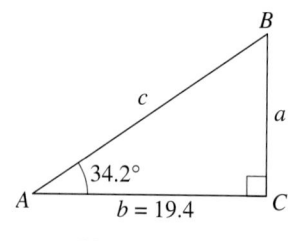

FIGURE **4.76**

Solution

Because $C = 90°$, it follows that $A + B = 90°$ and $B = 90° - 34.2° = 55.8°$. To solve for a, use the fact that

$$\tan A = \frac{\text{opp}}{\text{adj}} = \frac{a}{b} \quad \Longrightarrow \quad a = b \tan A.$$

So, $a = 19.4 \tan 34.2° \approx 13.18$. Similarly, to solve for c, use the fact that

$$\cos A = \frac{\text{adj}}{\text{hyp}} = \frac{b}{c} \quad \Longrightarrow \quad c = \frac{b}{\cos A}.$$

So, $c = \dfrac{19.4}{\cos 34.2°} \approx 23.46$.

Example 2 ▶ Finding a Side of a Right Triangle

A safety regulation states that the maximum angle of elevation for a rescue ladder is 72°. A fire department's longest ladder is 110 feet. What is the maximum safe rescue height?

Solution

A sketch is shown in Figure 4.77. From the equation $\sin A = a/c$, it follows that

$$a = c \sin A = 110 \sin 72° \approx 104.6.$$

So, the maximum safe rescue height is about 104.6 feet above the height of the fire truck.

FIGURE **4.77**

Example 3 ▶ Finding a Side of a Right Triangle

At a point 200 feet from the base of a building, the angle of elevation to the *bottom* of a smokestack is 35°, whereas the angle of elevation to the *top* is 53°, as shown in Figure 4.78. Find the height s of the smokestack alone.

Solution

Note from Figure 4.78 that this problem involves two right triangles. For the smaller right triangle, use the fact that

$$\tan 35° = \frac{a}{200}$$

to conclude that the height of the building is

$$a = 200 \tan 35°.$$

For the larger right triangle, use the equation

$$\tan 53° = \frac{a + s}{200}$$

to conclude that $a + s = 200 \tan 53°$. So, the height of the smokestack is

$$s = 200 \tan 53° - a$$

$$= 200 \tan 53° - 200 \tan 35°$$

$$\approx 125.4 \text{ feet.}$$

FIGURE **4.78**

Example 4 ▶ Finding an Acute Angle of a Right Triangle

A swimming pool is 20 meters long and 12 meters wide. The bottom of the pool is slanted so that the water depth is 1.3 meters at the shallow end and 4 meters at the deep end, as shown in Figure 4.79. Find the angle of depression of the bottom of the pool.

Solution

Using the tangent function, you can see that

$$\tan A = \frac{\text{opp}}{\text{adj}}$$

$$= \frac{2.7}{20}$$

$$= 0.135.$$

So, the angle of depression is

$$A = \arctan 0.135$$

$$\approx 0.13419 \text{ radian}$$

$$\approx 7.69°.$$

FIGURE **4.79**

Trigonometry and Bearings

In surveying and navigation, directions are generally given in terms of **bearings.** A bearing measures the acute angle that a path or line of sight makes with a fixed north-south line, as shown in Figure 4.80. For instance, the bearing S 35° E in Figure 4.80 means 35 degrees east of south.

FIGURE 4.80

Example 5 ▶ **Finding Directions in Terms of Bearings**

A ship leaves port at noon and heads due west at 20 knots, or 20 nautical miles (nm) per hour. At 2 P.M. the ship changes course to N 54° W, as shown in Figure 4.81. Find the ship's bearing and distance from the port of departure at 3 P.M.

FIGURE 4.81

Solution

For triangle BCD, you have $B = 90° - 54° = 36°$. The two sides of this triangle can be determined to be

$$b = 20 \sin 36° \quad \text{and} \quad d = 20 \cos 36°.$$

For triangle ACD, you can find angle A as follows.

$$\tan A = \frac{b}{d + 40} = \frac{20 \sin 36°}{20 \cos 36° + 40} \approx 0.2092494$$

$$A \approx \arctan 0.2092494 \approx 0.2062732 \text{ radian} \approx 11.82°$$

The angle with the north-south line is $90° - 11.82° = 78.18°$. So, the bearing of the ship is N 78.18° W. Finally, from triangle ACD, you have $\sin A = b/c$, which yields

$$c = \frac{b}{\sin A} = \frac{20 \sin 36°}{\sin 11.82°}$$

$$\approx 57.4 \text{ nautical miles.} \qquad \text{Distance from port}$$

STUDY TIP

In *air navigation*, bearings are measured in degrees *clockwise* from north. Examples of air navigation bearings are shown below.

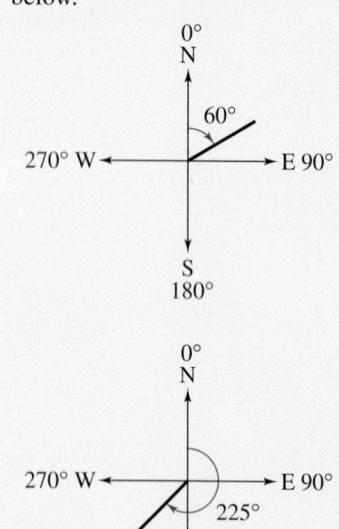

Harmonic Motion

The periodic nature of the trigonometric functions is useful for describing the motion of a point on an object that vibrates, oscillates, rotates, or is moved by wave motion.

For example, consider a ball that is bobbing up and down on the end of a spring, as shown in Figure 4.82. Suppose that 10 centimeters is the maximum distance the ball moves vertically upward or downward from its equilibrium (at rest) position. Suppose further that the time it takes for the ball to move from its maximum displacement above zero to its maximum displacement below zero and back again is $t = 4$ seconds. Assuming the ideal conditions of perfect elasticity and no friction or air resistance, the ball would continue to move up and down in a uniform and regular manner.

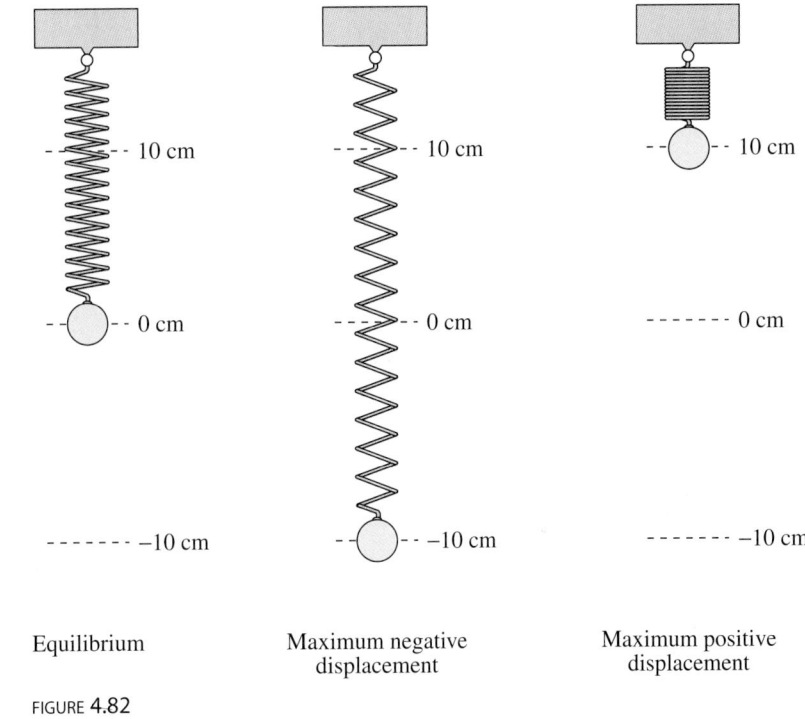

| Equilibrium | Maximum negative displacement | Maximum positive displacement |

FIGURE **4.82**

From this spring you can conclude that the period (time for one complete cycle) of the motion is

Period = 4 seconds

and that its amplitude (maximum displacement from equilibrium) is

Amplitude = 10 centimeters.

Motion of this nature can be described by a sine or cosine function, and is called **simple harmonic motion.**

> ### Definition of Simple Harmonic Motion
>
> A point that moves on a coordinate line is said to be in **simple harmonic motion** if its distance d from the origin at time t is given by either
>
> $$d = a \sin \omega t \quad \text{or} \quad d = a \cos \omega t$$
>
> where a and ω are real numbers such that $\omega > 0$. The motion has amplitude $|a|$, period $2\pi/\omega$, and frequency $\omega/(2\pi)$.

Example 6 ▶ Simple Harmonic Motion

Write the equation for the simple harmonic motion of the ball described in Figure 4.82, where the period is 4 seconds. What is the frequency of this harmonic motion?

Solution

Because the spring is at equilibrium $(d = 0)$ when $t = 0$, you use the equation

$$d = a \sin \omega t.$$

Moreover, because the maximum displacement from zero is 10 and the period is 4, you have

$$\text{Amplitude} = |a| = 10$$

$$\text{Period} = \frac{2\pi}{\omega} = 4 \quad \Longrightarrow \quad \omega = \frac{\pi}{2}.$$

Consequently, the equation of motion is

$$d = 10 \sin \frac{\pi}{2} t.$$

Note that the choice of $a = 10$ or $a = -10$ depends on whether the ball initially moves up or down. The frequency is

$$\text{Frequency} = \frac{\omega}{2\pi}$$

$$= \frac{\pi/2}{2\pi}$$

$$= \frac{1}{4} \text{ cycle per second.}$$

FIGURE **4.83**

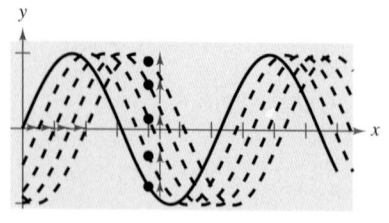

FIGURE **4.84**

One illustration of the relationship between sine waves and harmonic motion can be seen in the wave motion resulting when a stone is dropped into a calm pool of water. The waves move outward in roughly the shape of sine (or cosine) waves, as shown in Figure 4.83. As an example, suppose you are fishing and your fishing bob is attached so that it does not move horizontally. As the waves move outward from the dropped stone, your fishing bob will move up and down in simple harmonic motion, as shown in Figure 4.84.

Example 7 ▶ Simple Harmonic Motion

Given the equation for simple harmonic motion

$$d = 6 \cos \frac{3\pi}{4}t$$

find (a) the maximum displacement, (b) the frequency, (c) the value of d when $t = 4$, and (d) the least positive value of t for which $d = 0$.

Solution

The given equation has the form $d = a \cos \omega t$, with $a = 6$ and $\omega = 3\pi/4$.

a. The maximum displacement (from the point of equilibrium) is given by the amplitude. So, the maximum displacement is 6.

b. Frequency $= \dfrac{\omega}{2\pi}$

$\qquad\qquad = \dfrac{3\pi/4}{2\pi} = \dfrac{3}{8}$ cycle per unit of time

c. $d = 6 \cos\left[\dfrac{3\pi}{4}(4)\right]$

$\qquad = 6 \cos 3\pi$

$\qquad = 6(-1)$

$\qquad = -6$

d. To find the least positive value of t for which $d = 0$, solve the equation

$$d = 6 \cos \frac{3\pi}{4}t = 0$$

to obtain

$$\frac{3\pi}{4}t = \frac{\pi}{2}, \frac{3\pi}{2}, \frac{5\pi}{2}, \ldots \quad \Longrightarrow \quad t = \frac{2}{3}, 2, \frac{10}{3}, \ldots .$$

So, the least positive value of t is $t = \frac{2}{3}$.

(a)

(b)

FIGURE 4.85

Writing ABOUT MATHEMATICS

Radio Waves   Many different physical phenomena can be characterized by wave motion. These phenomena include electromagnetic waves such as radio waves, television waves, and microwaves. Radio waves transmit sound in two different ways. For an AM station, the *amplitude* of the wave is modified to carry sound. The letters AM stand for "amplitude modulation." An FM radio signal has its *frequency* modified in order to carry sound, hence the term "frequency modulation." The FM radio signal is preferred by listeners because of its low-noise and wide-bandwidth qualities. Of the two graphs in Figure 4.85, one shows an AM wave and the other shows an FM wave. Which is which? Explain your reasoning.

4.8 Exercises

In Exercises 1–10, solve the right triangle shown in the figure. Round your answer to two decimal places.

1. $A = 20°$, $b = 10$
2. $B = 54°$, $c = 15$
3. $B = 71°$, $b = 24$
4. $A = 8.4°$, $a = 40.5$
5. $a = 6$, $b = 10$
6. $a = 25$, $c = 35$
7. $b = 16$, $c = 52$
8. $b = 1.32$, $c = 9.45$
9. $A = 12°15'$, $c = 430.5$
10. $B = 65°12'$, $a = 14.2$

FIGURE FOR 1–10

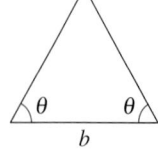

FIGURE FOR 11–14

In Exercises 11–14, find the altitude of the isosceles triangle shown in the figure. Round your answer to two decimal places.

11. $\theta = 52°$, $b = 4$ inches
12. $\theta = 18°$, $b = 10$ meters
13. $\theta = 41°$, $b = 46$ inches
14. $\theta = 27°$, $b = 11$ feet

15. **Length** The sun is 25° above the horizon. Find the length of a shadow cast by a silo that is 50 feet tall (see figure).

16. **Length** The sun is 20° above the horizon. Find the length of a shadow cast by a building that is 600 feet tall.

17. **Height** A ladder 20 feet long leans against the side of a house. Find the height h from the top of the ladder to the ground if the angle of elevation of the ladder is 80°.

18. **Height** The length of a shadow of a tree is 125 feet when the angle of elevation of the sun is 33°. Approximate the height h of the tree.

19. **Height** From a point 50 feet in front of a church, the angles of elevation to the base of the steeple and the top of the steeple are 35° and 47° 40′, respectively.

    (a) Draw right triangles that represent the problem. Label the known and unknown quantities.

    (b) Use a trigonometric function to write an equation involving the unknown height of the steeple.

    (c) Find the height of the steeple.

20. **Height** You are standing 100 feet from the base of a platform from which people are bungee jumping. The angle of elevation from your position to the top of the platform from which they jump is 51°. From what height are the people jumping?

21. **Depth** The sonar of a navy cruiser detects a submarine that is 4000 feet from the cruiser. The angle between the water line and the submarine is 34° (see figure). How deep is the submarine?

Not drawn to scale

22. **Angle of Elevation** An amateur radio operator erects a 75-foot vertical tower for an antenna. Find the angle of elevation to the top of the tower at a point on level ground 50 feet from its base.

23. **Angle of Elevation** The height of an outdoor basketball backboard is $12\frac{1}{2}$ feet, and the backboard casts a shadow $17\frac{1}{3}$ feet long.

    (a) Draw a right triangle that represents the problem. Label the known and unknown quantities.

    (b) Use a trigonometric function to write an equation involving the unknown angle of elevation of the sun.

    (c) Find the angle of elevation of the sun.

24. *Angle of Depression* A Global Positioning System satellite orbits 12,500 miles above Earth's surface. Find the angle of depression from the satellite to the horizon. Assume the radius of Earth is 4000 miles.

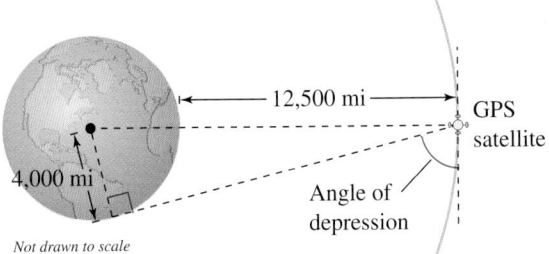

Not drawn to scale

25. *Angle of Depression* A cellular telephone tower that is 150 feet tall is placed on top of a mountain that is 1200 feet above sea level. What is the angle of depression from the top of the tower to a cell phone user who is 5 horizontal miles away and 400 feet above sea level?

26. *Airplane Ascent* During takeoff, an airplane's angle of climb is 18° and its speed is 275 feet per second.

(a) Find the plane's altitude after 1 minute.

(b) How long will it take the plane to climb to an altitude of 10,000 feet?

27. *Mountain Descent* A sign on a roadway at the top of a mountain indicates that for the next 4 miles the grade is 10.5° (see figure). Find the change in elevation for a car descending the mountain.

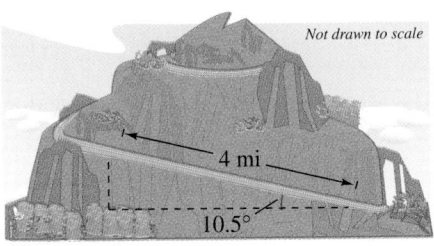

Not drawn to scale

28. *Mountain Descent* A roadway sign at the top of a mountain indicates that for the next 4 miles the grade is 12%. Find the angle of the grade and the change in elevation for a car descending the mountain.

29. *Navigation* An airplane flying at 600 miles per hour has a bearing of 52°. After flying for 1.5 hours, how far north and how far east will the plane have traveled from its point of departure?

30. *Surveying* A surveyor wishes to find the distance across a swamp (see figure). The bearing from A to B is N 32° W. The surveyor walks 50 meters from A, and at the point C the bearing to B is N 68° W. Find (a) the bearing from A to C and (b) the distance from A to B.

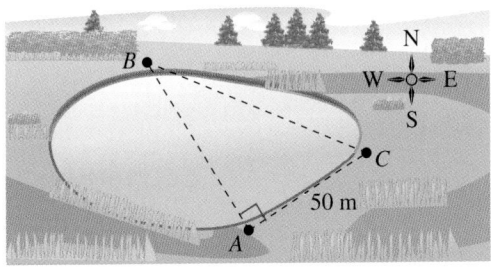

31. *Location of a Fire* Two fire towers are 30 kilometers apart, where tower A is due west of tower B. A fire is spotted from the towers, and the bearings from A and B are E 14° N and W 34° N, respectively (see figure). Find the distance d of the fire from the line segment AB.

Not drawn to scale

32. *Navigation* A ship is 45 miles east and 30 miles south of port. The captain wants to sail directly to port. What bearing should be taken?

33. *Distance* An observer in a lighthouse 350 feet above sea level observes two ships directly offshore. The angles of depression to the ships are 4° and 6.5° (see figure). How far apart are the ships?

Not drawn to scale

34. *Distance* A passenger in an airplane at an altitude of 10 kilometers sees two towns directly to the east of the plane. The angles of depression to the towns are 28° and 55° (see figure). How far apart are the towns?

Not drawn to scale

35. *Altitude* A plane is observed approaching your home and you assume that its speed is 550 miles per hour. The angle of elevation of the plane is 16° at one time and 57° one minute later. Approximate the altitude of the plane.

36. *Height* While traveling across flat land, you notice a mountain directly in front of you. The angle of elevation to the peak is 2.5°. After you drive 17 miles closer to the mountain, the angle of elevation is 9°. Approximate the height of the mountain.

Geometry In Exercises 37 and 38, find the angle α between two nonvertical lines L_1 and L_2. The angle α satisfies the equation

$$\tan \alpha = \left| \frac{m_2 - m_1}{1 + m_2 m_1} \right|$$

where m_1 and m_2 are the slopes of L_1 and L_2, respectively. (Assume that $m_1 m_2 \neq -1$.)

37. L_1: $3x - 2y = 5$ **38.** L_1: $2x - y = 8$
      L_2: $x + y = 1$ L_2: $x - 5y = -4$

39. *Geometry* Determine the angle between the diagonal of a cube and the diagonal of its base, as shown in the figure.

FIGURE FOR 39

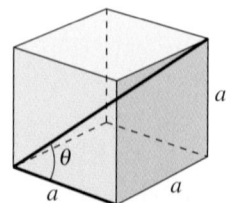

FIGURE FOR 40

40. *Geometry* Determine the angle between the diagonal of a cube and its edge, as shown in the figure.

41. *Geometry* Find the length of the sides of a regular pentagon inscribed in a circle of radius 25 inches.

42. *Geometry* Find the length of the sides of a regular hexagon inscribed in a circle of radius 25 inches.

43. *Hardware* Express the distance y across the flat sides of a hexagonal nut as a function of r, as shown in the figure.

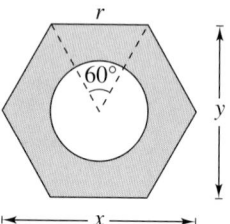

44. *Bolt Holes* The figure shows a circular piece of sheet metal that has a diameter of 40 centimeters and contains 12 equally spaced bolt holes. Determine the straight-line distance between the centers of consecutive bolt holes.

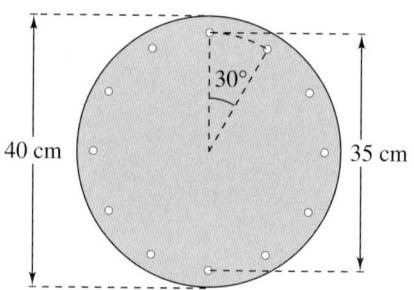

Trusses In Exercises 45 and 46, find all the unknown lengths of the members of the truss.

45.

46.

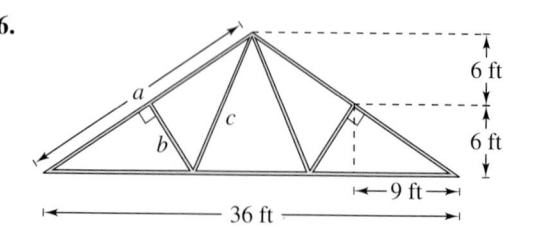

Harmonic Motion In Exercises 47–50, for the simple harmonic motion described by the trigonometric function, find (a) the maximum displacement, (b) the frequency, and (c) the least positive value of t for which $d = 0$.

47. $d = 4 \cos 8\pi t$

48. $d = \frac{1}{2} \cos 20\pi t$

49. $d = \frac{1}{16} \sin 120\pi t$

50. $d = \frac{1}{64} \sin 792\pi t$

Harmonic Motion In Exercises 51–54, find a model for simple harmonic motion satisfying the specified conditions.

	Displacement ($t = 0$)	Amplitude	Period
51.	0	4 centimeters	2 seconds
52.	0	3 meters	6 seconds
53.	3 inches	3 inches	1.5 seconds
54.	2 feet	2 feet	10 seconds

55. *Tuning Fork* A point on the end of a tuning fork moves in simple harmonic motion described by $d = a \sin \omega t$. Find ω given that the tuning fork for middle C has a frequency of 264 vibrations per second.

56. *Wave Motion* A buoy oscillates in simple harmonic motion as waves go past. It is noted that the buoy moves a total of 3.5 feet from its low point to its high point (see figure), and that it returns to its high point every 10 seconds. Write an equation that describes the motion of the buoy if its high point is at $t = 0$.

57. *Oscillation of a Spring* A ball that is bobbing up and down on the end of a spring has a maximum displacement of 3 inches. Its motion (in ideal conditions) is modeled by $y = \frac{1}{4} \cos 16t$ ($t > 0$), where y is in feet and t is in seconds.

(a) Graph the function.

(b) What is the period of the oscillations?

(c) Determine the first time the weight passes the point of equilibrium ($y = 0$).

Synthesis

True or False? In Exercises 58 and 59, determine whether the statement is true or false. Justify your answer.

58. The Leaning Tower of Pisa is not vertical, but if you know the exact angle of elevation θ to the 191-foot tower when you stand near it, then you can determine the exact distance to the tower d by using the formula

$$\tan \theta = \frac{191}{d}.$$

59. For the harmonic motion of a ball bobbing up and down on the end of a spring, one period can be described as the length of one coil of the spring.

60. *Numerical and Graphical Analysis* A two-meter-high fence is 3 meters from the side of a grain storage bin. A grain elevator must reach from ground level outside the fence to the storage bin (see figure). The objective is to determine the shortest elevator that meets the constraints.

(a) Complete four rows of the table.

θ	L_1	L_2	$L_1 + L_2$
0.1	$\dfrac{2}{\sin 0.1}$	$\dfrac{3}{\cos 0.1}$	23.0
0.2	$\dfrac{2}{\sin 0.2}$	$\dfrac{3}{\cos 0.2}$	13.1

(b) Use a graphing utility to generate additional rows of the table. Use the table to estimate the minimum length of the elevator.

(c) Write the length $L_1 + L_2$ as a function of θ.

(d) Use a graphing utility to graph the function. Use the graph to estimate the minimum length. How does your estimate compare with that of part (b)?

61. *Numerical and Graphical Analysis* The cross section of an irrigation canal is an isosceles trapezoid of which three of the sides are 8 feet long (see figure). The objective is to find the angle θ that maximizes the area of the cross section. [*Hint:* The area of a trapezoid is $(h/2)(b_1 + b_2)$.]

(a) Complete seven rows of the table.

Base 1	Base 2	Altitude	Area
8	$8 + 16 \cos 10°$	$8 \sin 10°$	22.1
8	$8 + 16 \cos 20°$	$8 \sin 20°$	42.5

(b) Use a graphing utility to generate additional rows of the table. Use the table to estimate the maximum cross-sectional area.

(c) Write the area A as a function of θ.

(d) Use a graphing utility to graph the function. Use the graph to estimate the maximum cross-sectional area. How does your estimate compare with that of part (b)?

8 ft   8 ft

θ θ

◄——— 8 ft ———►

62. *Data Analysis* The times S of sunset (Greenwich Mean Time) at 40° north latitude on the 15th of each month are: 1(16:59), 2(17:35), 3(18:06), 4(18:38), 5(19:08), 6(19:30), 7(19:28), 8(18:57), 9(18:09), 10(17:21), 11(16:44), 12(16:36). The month is represented by t, with $t = 1$ corresponding to January. A model (in which minutes have been converted to the decimal parts of an hour) for this data is

$$S(t) = 18.09 + 1.41 \sin\left(\frac{\pi t}{6} + 4.60\right).$$

 (a) Use a graphing utility to graph the data points and the model in the same viewing window.

(b) What is the period of the model? Is it what you expected? Explain.

(c) What is the amplitude of the model? What does it represent in the model? Explain.

▶ **Model It**

63. *Data Analysis* The table shows the average sales S (in millions of dollars) of an outerwear manufacturer for each month t, where $t = 1$ represents January.

Time, t	Sales, S
1	13.46
2	11.15
3	8.00
4	4.85
5	2.54
6	1.70
7	2.54
8	4.85
9	8.00
10	11.15
11	13.46
12	14.3

(a) Create a scatter plot of the data.

(b) Find a trigonometric model that fits the data. Graph the model on your scatter plot. How well does the model fit the data?

(c) What is the period of the model? Do you think it is reasonable given the context? Explain your reasoning.

(d) Interpret the meaning of the model's amplitude in the context of the problem.

---

64. *Writing* Is it true that N 24° E means 24 degrees north of east? Explain.

Review

In Exercises 65–72, sketch a graph of the equation.

65. $3x - 2y = 4$ **66.** $5y - 3x = 12$

67. $(y - 2)^2 = 8(x + 2)$ **68.** $(x + 3)^2 = 5y - 8$

69. $\dfrac{x^2}{4} + y^2 = 1$ **70.** $2x^2 + y^2 - 4 = 0$

71. $\dfrac{x^2}{4} + \dfrac{y^2}{4} = 1$ **72.** $(x - 2)^2 + y^2 = 25$

Chapter Summary

▶ *What* did you learn?

Section 4.1	Review Exercises
☐ How to describe angles	1–4
☐ How to use radian and degree measure	5–20
☐ How to use angles to model and solve real-life problems	21, 22

Section 4.2
☐ How to identify a unit circle and its relationship to real numbers — 23–26
☐ How to evaluate trigonometric functions using the unit circle — 27–30
☐ How to use the domain and period to evaluate sine and cosine functions — 31–34
☐ How to use a calculator to evaluate trigonometric functions — 35–38

Section 4.3
☐ How to evaluate trigonometric functions of acute angles — 39–42
☐ How to use the fundamental trigonometric identities — 43–46
☐ How to use a calculator to evaluate trigonometric functions — 47–52
☐ How to use trigonometric functions to model and solve real-life problems — 53, 54

Section 4.4
☐ How to evaluate trigonometric functions of any angle — 55–68
☐ How to use reference angles to evaluate trigonometric functions — 69–76
☐ How to evaluate trigonometric functions of real numbers — 77–82

Section 4.5
☐ How to use amplitude and period to sketch the graphs of sine and cosine functions — 83–86
☐ How to sketch translations of graphs of sine and cosine functions — 87–90
☐ How to use sine and cosine functions to model real-life data — 91, 92

Section 4.6
☐ How to sketch the graphs of tangent and cotangent functions — 93–96
☐ How to sketch the graphs of secant and cosecant functions — 97–100
☐ How to sketch the graphs of damped trigonometric functions — 101, 102

Section 4.7
☐ How to evaluate the inverse sine function — 103–108
☐ How to evaluate the other inverse trigonometric functions — 109–120
☐ How to evaluate the compositions of trigonometric functions — 121–128

Section 4.8
☐ How to solve real-life problems involving right triangles — 129, 130
☐ How to solve real-life problems involving directional bearings — 131
☐ How to solve real-life problems involving harmonic motion — 132

Review Exercises

4.1 In Exercises 1–4, estimate the angle to the nearest one-half radian.

1.

2.

3.

4.

In Exercises 5–12, sketch the angle in standard position. List one positive and one negative coterminal angle.

5. $\dfrac{11\pi}{4}$

6. $\dfrac{2\pi}{9}$

7. $-\dfrac{4\pi}{3}$

8. $-\dfrac{23\pi}{3}$

9. $70°$

10. $280°$

11. $-110°$

12. $-405°$

In Exercises 13–16, convert the measure from radians to degrees. Round your answer to two decimal places.

13. $\dfrac{5\pi}{7}$

14. $-\dfrac{11\pi}{6}$

15. -3.5

16. 5.7

In Exercises 17–20, convert the measure from degrees to radians. Round your answer to four decimal places.

17. $480°$

18. $-127.5°$

19. $-33°\,45'$

20. $196°\,77'$

21. *Phonograph* Compact discs have all but replaced phonograph records. Phonograph records are vinyl discs that rotate on a turntable. A typical record album is 12 inches in diameter and plays at $33\frac{1}{3}$ revolutions per minute.

 (a) What is the angular speed of a record album?

 (b) What is the linear speed of the outer edge of a record album?

22. *Bicycle* At what speed is a bicyclist traveling when his 27-inch-diameter tires are rotating at an angular speed of 5π radians per second?

4.2 In Exercises 23–26, find the point (x, y) on the unit circle that corresponds to the real number t.

23. $t = \dfrac{2\pi}{3}$

24. $t = \dfrac{3\pi}{4}$

25. $t = \dfrac{5\pi}{6}$

26. $t = -\dfrac{4\pi}{3}$

In Exercises 27–30, evaluate (if possible) the six trigonometric functions of the real number.

27. $t = \dfrac{7\pi}{6}$

28. $t = \dfrac{\pi}{4}$

29. $t = -\dfrac{2\pi}{3}$

30. $t = 2\pi$

In Exercises 31–34, evaluate the trigonometric function using its period as an aid.

31. $\sin \dfrac{11\pi}{4}$

32. $\cos 4\pi$

33. $\sin\left(-\dfrac{17\pi}{6}\right)$

34. $\cos\left(-\dfrac{13\pi}{3}\right)$

In Exercises 35–38, use a calculator to evaluate the trigonometric function. Round your answer to two decimal places.

35. $\tan 33$

36. $\csc 10.5$

37. $\sec \dfrac{12\pi}{5}$

38. $\sin\left(-\dfrac{\pi}{9}\right)$

4.3 In Exercises 39–42, find the exact values of the six trigonometric functions of the angle θ shown in the figure.

39.

40.

41.   **42.**

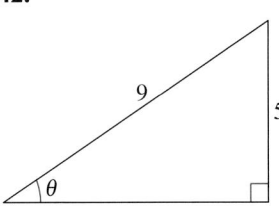

In Exercises 43–46, use the given function value and trigonometric identities (including the cofunction identities) to find the indicated trigonometric functions.

43. $\sin \theta = \frac{1}{3}$

   (a) $\csc \theta$ (b) $\cos \theta$

   (c) $\sec \theta$ (d) $\tan \theta$

44. $\tan \theta = 4$

   (a) $\cot \theta$ (b) $\sec \theta$

   (c) $\cos \theta$ (d) $\csc \theta$

45. $\csc \theta = 4$

   (a) $\sin \theta$ (b) $\cos \theta$

   (c) $\sec \theta$ (d) $\tan \theta$

46. $\csc \theta = 5$

   (a) $\sin \theta$ (b) $\cot \theta$

   (c) $\tan \theta$ (d) $\sec(90° - \theta)$

In Exercises 47–52, use a calculator to evaluate the trigonometric function. Round your answer to two decimal places.

47. $\tan 33°$ **48.** $\csc 11°$

49. $\sin 34.2°$ **50.** $\sec 79.3°$

51. $\cot 15° \, 14'$ **52.** $\cos 78° \, 11' 58''$

53. *Railroad Grade*   A train travels 3.5 kilometers on a straight track with a grade of $1° \, 10'$ (see figure). What is the vertical rise of the train in that distance?

54. *Guy Wire*   A guy wire runs from the ground to the top of a 25-foot telephone pole. The angle formed between the wire and the ground is 52°. How far from the base of the pole is the wire attached to the ground?

4.4 In Exercises 55–62, find the exact values of the six trigonometric functions of the angle θ (in standard position) whose terminal side passes through the point.

55. $(12, 16)$ **56.** $(3, -4)$

57. $\left(\frac{2}{3}, \frac{5}{2}\right)$ **58.** $\left(-\frac{10}{3}, -\frac{2}{3}\right)$

59. $(-0.5, 4.5)$ **60.** $(0.3, 0.4)$

61. $(x, 4x), \; x > 0$ **62.** $(-2x, -3x), \; x > 0$

In Exercises 63–68, find the remaining five trigonometric functions of θ satisfying the condition.

	Function Value	*Constraint*
63.	$\sec \theta = \frac{6}{5}$	$\tan \theta < 0$
64.	$\csc \theta = \frac{3}{2}$	$\cos \theta < 0$
65.	$\sin \theta = \frac{3}{8}$	$\cos \theta < 0$
66.	$\tan \theta = \frac{5}{4}$	$\cos \theta < 0$
67.	$\cos \theta = -\frac{2}{5}$	$\sin \theta > 0$
68.	$\sin \theta = -\frac{2}{4}$	$\cos \theta > 0$

In Exercises 69–76, evaluate the sine, cosine, and tangent of the angle without using a calculator.

69. $\dfrac{\pi}{3}$ **70.** $\dfrac{\pi}{4}$

71. $-\dfrac{7\pi}{3}$ **72.** $-\dfrac{5\pi}{4}$

73. $495°$ **74.** $-150°$

75. $-240°$ **76.** $315°$

In Exercises 77–82, use a calculator to evaluate the trigonometric function of the real number. Round your answer to two decimal places.

77. $\sin 4$ **78.** $\tan 3$

79. $\sin(-3.2)$ **80.** $\cot(-4.8)$

81. $\sec 12\pi/5$ **82.** $\tan(-25\pi/7)$

4.5 In Exercises 83–90, sketch a graph of the function. Include two full periods.

83. $y = \sin x$ **84.** $y = \cos x$

85. $f(x) = 5 \sin \dfrac{2x}{5}$ **86.** $f(x) = 8 \cos\left(-\dfrac{x}{4}\right)$

87. $y = 2 + \sin x$ **88.** $y = -4 - \cos \pi x$

89. $g(t) = \frac{5}{2} \sin(t - \pi)$ **90.** $g(t) = 3 \cos(t + \pi)$

91. *Sound Waves* Sound waves can be modeled by sine functions of the form $y = a \sin bx$, where x is measured in seconds.

(a) Write an equation of a sound wave whose amplitude is 2 and whose period is $\frac{1}{264}$ second.

(b) What is the frequency of the sound wave described in part (a)?

92. *Sound Waves* Use the cosine function $y = a \cos bx$ to model the sound wave described in Exercise 91.

4.6 In Exercises 93–102, sketch a graph of the function. Include two full periods.

93. $f(x) = \tan x$

94. $f(t) = \tan\left(t - \frac{\pi}{4}\right)$

95. $f(x) = \cot x$

96. $g(t) = 2 \cot 2t$

97. $f(x) = \sec x$

98. $h(t) = \sec\left(t - \frac{\pi}{4}\right)$

99. $f(x) = \csc x$

100. $f(t) = 3 \csc\left(2t + \frac{\pi}{4}\right)$

101. $f(x) = x \cos x$

102. $g(x) = x^4 \cos x$

4.7 In Exercises 103–108, evaluate the expression. If necessary, round your answer to two decimal places.

103. $\arcsin\left(-\frac{1}{2}\right)$

104. $\arcsin(-1)$

105. $\arcsin 0.4$

106. $\arcsin 0.213$

107. $\sin^{-1}(-0.44)$

108. $\sin^{-1} 0.89$

In Exercises 109–112, evaluate the expression without the aid of a calculator.

109. $\arccos \dfrac{\sqrt{3}}{2}$

110. $\arccos \dfrac{\sqrt{2}}{2}$

111. $\cos^{-1}(-1)$

112. $\cos^{-1} \dfrac{\sqrt{3}}{2}$

In Exercises 113–120, use a calculator to approximate the value of the expression. Round your answer to two decimal places.

113. $\arccos 0.324$

114. $\arccos(-0.888)$

115. $\arctan 0.123$

116. $\arctan 2.34$

117. $\arctan 5.783$

118. $\arctan 99.1$

119. $\tan^{-1}(-1.5)$

120. $\tan^{-1} 8.2$

In Exercises 121–128, find the exact value of the expression.

121. $\sin(\arcsin 0.72)$

122. $\cos(\arccos 0.25)$

123. $\arctan(\tan \pi)$

124. $\arccos[\cos(-5\pi)]$

125. $\cos\left(\arctan \frac{3}{4}\right)$

126. $\tan\left(\arccos \frac{3}{5}\right)$

127. $\sec\left(\arctan \frac{12}{5}\right)$

128. $\cot\left[\arcsin\left(-\frac{12}{13}\right)\right]$

129. *Angle of Elevation* The height of a radio transmission tower is 70 meters, and it casts a shadow of length 30 meters (see figure). Find the angle of elevation of the sun.

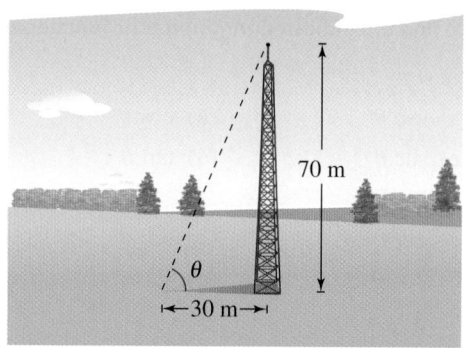

130. *Height* Your football has landed at the edge of the roof of your school building. When you are 25 feet from the base of the building, the angle of elevation to your football is 21°. How high off the ground is your football?

131. *Distance* From city A to city B, a plane flies 650 miles at a bearing of 48°. From city B to city C, the plane flies 810 miles at a bearing of 115°. Find the distance from A to C and the bearing from A to C.

132. *Wave Motion* Your fishing bobber oscillates in simple harmonic motion from the waves in the lake where you fish. Your bobber moves a total of 1.5 inches from its high point to its low point and returns to its high point every 3 seconds. Write an equation modeling the motion of your bobber if it is at its high point at time $t = 0$.

Synthesis

True or False? In Exercises 133–136, determine whether the statement is true or false. Justify your answer.

133. The tangent function is often useful for modeling simple harmonic motion.

134. The inverse sine function $y = \arcsin x$ cannot be defined as a function over any interval that is greater than the interval defined as $-\pi/2 \le y \le \pi/2$.

135. $y = \sin \theta$ is not a function because $\sin 30° = \sin 150°$.

136. Because $\tan 3\pi/4 = -1$, $\arctan(-1) = 3\pi/4$.

In Exercises 137–140, match the function $y = a \sin bx$ with its graph. Base your selection solely on your interpretation of the constants a and b. Explain your reasoning. [The graphs are labeled (a), (b), (c), and (d).]

(a)

(b)

(c)

(d)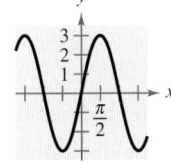

137. $y = 3 \sin x$

138. $y = -3 \sin x$

139. $y = 2 \sin \pi x$

140. $y = 2 \sin \dfrac{x}{2}$

141. *Writing* Describe the behavior of $f(\theta) = \sec \theta$ at the zeros of $g(\theta) = \cos \theta$. Explain your reasoning.

142. *Conjecture*

 (a) Use a graphing utility to complete the table.

θ	0.1	0.4	0.7	1.0	1.3
$\tan\left(\theta - \dfrac{\pi}{2}\right)$					
$-\cot \theta$					

(b) Make a conjecture about the relationship between $\tan\left(\theta - \dfrac{\pi}{2}\right)$ and $-\cot \theta$.

143. *Writing* When graphing the sine and cosine functions, determining the amplitude is part of the analysis. Explain why this is not true for the other four trigonometric functions.

144. *Oscillation of a Spring* A weight is suspended from a ceiling by a steel spring. The weight is lifted (positive direction) from the equilibrium position and released. The resulting motion of the weight is modeled by

$$y = Ae^{-kt} \cos bt = \frac{1}{5}e^{-t/10} \cos 6t$$

where y is the distance in feet from equilibrium and t is the time in seconds. The graph of the function is shown in the figure. For each of the following, describe the change in the system without graphing the resulting function.

(a) A is changed from $\frac{1}{5}$ to $\frac{1}{3}$.

(b) k is changed from $\frac{1}{10}$ to $\frac{1}{3}$.

(c) b is changed from 6 to 9.

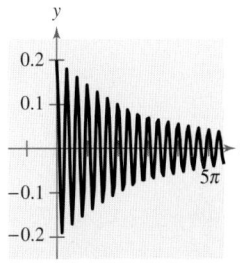

FIGURE FOR **144**

145. *Graphical Reasoning* The formulas for the area of a circular sector and arc length are $A = \frac{1}{2}r^2 \theta$ and $s = 2\theta$, respectively. (r is the radius and θ is the angle measured in radians.)

(a) If $\theta = 0.8$, write the area and arc length as functions of r. What is the domain of each function? Use a graphing utility to graph the functions. Use the graphs to determine which function changes more rapidly as r increases. Explain.

(b) If $r = 10$ centimeters, express the area and arc length of the functions of θ. What is the domain of each function? Use a graphing utility to graph and identify the functions.

146. *Writing* Describe a real-life application that can be represented by a simple harmonic motion model and is different from any that you've seen in this chapter. Explain which function you would use to model your application, and why. Explain how you would determine the amplitude, period, and frequency of the model for your application.

Chapter Test

Take this test as you would take a test in class. When you are finished, check your work against the answers given in the back of the book.

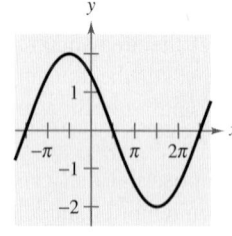

(-2, 6)

θ

FIGURE FOR **3**

1. Consider an angle that measures $5\pi/4$ radians.
   (a) Sketch the angle in standard position.
   (b) Determine two coterminal angles (one positive and one negative).
   (c) Convert the angle to degree measure.

2. A truck is moving at a rate of 90 kilometers per hour, and the diameter of its wheels is 1 meter. Find the angular speed of the wheels in radians per minute.

3. Find the exact values of the six trigonometric functions of the angle θ shown in the figure.

4. Given that $\tan \theta = \frac{3}{2}$, find the other five trigonometric functions of θ.

5. Determine the reference angle θ' of the angle $\theta = 290°$ and sketch θ and θ' in standard position.

6. Determine the quadrant in which θ lies if $\sec \theta < 0$ and $\tan \theta > 0$.

7. Find two values of θ in degrees ($0 \le \theta < 360°$) if $\cos \theta = -\sqrt{3}/2$. (Do not use a calculator.)

8. Use a calculator to approximate two values of θ in radians ($0 \le \theta < 2\pi$) if $\csc \theta = 1.030$. Round the result to two decimal places.

The *Interactive* CD-ROM and *Internet* versions of this text offer Chapter Pre-Tests and Chapter Post-Tests, both of which have randomly generated exercises with diagnostic capabilities.

In Exercises 9 and 10, find the remaining five trigonometric functions of θ satisfying the condition.

9. $\cos \theta = \frac{3}{5}$, $\tan \theta < 0$ 10. $\sec \theta = -\frac{17}{8}$, $\sin \theta > 0$

In Exercises 11 and 12, graph the function through two full periods without the aid of a graphing utility.

11. $g(x) = -2 \sin\left(x - \dfrac{\pi}{4}\right)$ 12. $f(\alpha) = \dfrac{1}{2} \tan 2\alpha$

In Exercises 13 and 14, use a graphing utility to graph the function. If the function is periodic, find its period.

13. $y = \sin 2\pi x + 2 \cos \pi x$ 14. $y = 6e^{-0.12t} \cos(0.25t)$, $0 \le t \le 32$

FIGURE FOR **15**

15. Find a, b, and c for the function $f(x) = a \sin(bx + c)$ such that the graph of f matches the figure.

16. Find the exact value of $\tan\left(\arccos \frac{2}{3}\right)$ without the aid of a calculator.

17. Graph the function $f(x) = 2 \arcsin\left(\frac{1}{2}x\right)$.

18. A plane is 80 miles south and 95 miles east of Cleveland Hopkins International Airport. What bearing should be taken to fly directly to the airport?

19. Write the equation for the simple harmonic motion of a ball on a spring that starts at its lowest point of 6 inches below equilibrium, bounces to its maximum height of 6 inches above equilibrium, and returns to its lowest point in a total of 2 seconds.

Proofs in Mathematics

The Pythagorean Theorem

The Pythagorean Theorem is one of the most famous theorems in mathematics. More than 100 different proofs now exist. James A. Garfield, the twentieth president of the United States, developed a proof of the Pythagorean Theorem in 1876. His proof, shown below, involved the fact that a trapezoid can be formed from two congruent right triangles and an isosceles right triangle.

The Pythagorean Theorem

In a right triangle, the sum of the squares of the lengths of the legs is equal to the square of the length of the hypotenuse, where a and b are the legs and c is the hypotenuse.

$$a^2 + b^2 = c^2$$

Proof

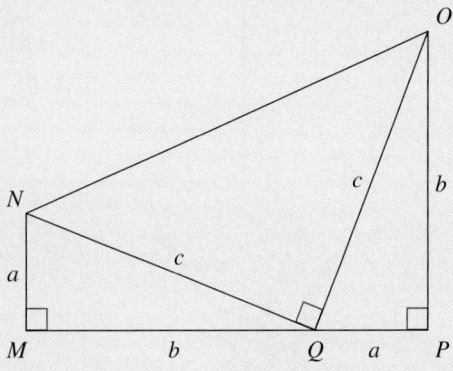

$$\text{Area of trapezoid } MNOP = \text{Area of } \triangle MNQ + \text{Area of } \triangle PQO + \text{Area of } \triangle NOQ$$

$$\frac{1}{2}(a + b)(a + b) = \frac{1}{2}ab + \frac{1}{2}ab + \frac{1}{2}c^2$$

$$\frac{1}{2}(a + b)(a + b) = ab + \frac{1}{2}c^2$$

$$(a + b)(a + b) = 2ab + c^2$$

$$a^2 + 2ab + b^2 = 2ab + c^2$$

$$a^2 + b^2 = c^2$$

1. The restaurant at the top of the Space Needle in Seattle, Washington is circular and has a radius of 47.25 feet. The dining part of the restaurant revolves, making about one complete revolution every 48 minutes. A dinner party was seated at the edge of the revolving restaurant at 6:45 P.M. and was finished at 8:57 P.M.

   (a) Find the angle through which the dinner party rotated.

   (b) Find the distance the party traveled during dinner.

2. A bicycle's gear ratio is the number of times the freewheel turns for every one turn of the chainwheel (see figure). The table shows the numbers of teeth in the freewheel and chainwheel for the first five gears of an 18-speed touring bicycle. The chainwheel completes one rotation for each gear. Find the angle through which the freewheel turns for each gear. Give your answers in both degrees and radians.

Gear number	Number of teeth in freewheel	Number of teeth in chainwheel
1	32	24
2	26	24
3	22	24
4	32	40
5	19	24

Freewheel

Chainwheel

3. A surveyor in a helicopter is trying to determine the width of an island, as shown in the figure.

   (a) What is the shortest distance d the helicopter would have to travel to land on the island?

   (b) What is the horizontal distance x that the helicopter would have to travel before it would be directly over the nearer end of the island?

   (c) Find the width w of the island. Explain how you obtained your answer.

3000 ft

d

x

w

Not drawn to scale

FIGURE FOR 3

4. Use the figure below.

   (a) Explain why $\triangle ABC$, $\triangle ADE$, and $\triangle AFG$ are similar triangles.

   (b) What does similarity imply about the ratios

   $$\frac{BC}{AB}, \frac{DE}{AD}, \text{ and } \frac{FG}{AF}?$$

   (c) Does the value of $\sin A$ depend on which triangle from part (a) is used to calculate it? Would the value of $\sin A$ change if it were found using a different right triangle that was similar to the three given triangles?

   (d) Do your conclusions from part (c) apply to the other five trigonometric functions? Explain.

5. Use a graphing utility to graph h, and use the graph to decide whether h is even, odd, or neither.

   (a) $h(x) = \cos^2 x$ (b) $h(x) = \sin^2 x$

6. If f is an even function and g is an odd function, use the results of Exercise 5 to make a conjecture about h where

   (a) $h(x) = [f(x)]^2$ (b) $h(x) = [g(x)]^2$.

7. The model for the height h of a Ferris wheel car is

   $$h = 50 + 50 \sin 8\pi t$$

   where t is the time in minutes. (The Ferris wheel has a radius of 50 feet.) This model yields a height of 50 feet when $t = 0$. Alter the model so that the height of the car is 1 foot when $t = 0$.

8. A popular theory that attempts to explain the ups and downs of everyday life states that each of us has three cycles, called biorhythms, which begin at birth. These three cycles can be modeled by sine waves.

Physical (23 days): $\quad P = \sin \dfrac{2\pi t}{23}, \quad t \geq 0$

Emotional (28 days): $\quad E = \sin \dfrac{2\pi t}{28}, \quad t \geq 0$

Intellectual (33 days): $\quad I = \sin \dfrac{2\pi t}{33}, \quad t \geq 0$

where t is the number of days since birth. Consider a person who was born on July 20, 1984.

 (a) Use a graphing utility to graph the three models in the same viewing window for $7300 \leq t \leq 7380$

(b) Describe the person's biorhythms during the month of September 2004.

(c) Calculate the person's three energy levels on September 22, 2004.

9. (a) Use a graphing utility to graph the functions

$$f(x) = 2 \cos 2x + 3 \sin 3x$$

and

$$g(x) = 2 \cos 2x + 3 \sin 4x.$$

(b) Use the graphs from part (a) to find the period of each function.

(c) If α and β are positive integers, is the function

$$h(x) = A \cos \alpha x + B \sin \beta x$$

periodic? Explain your reasoning.

10. Two trigonometric functions f and g have periods of 2, and their graphs intersect at $x = 5.35$.

(a) Give one smaller and one larger positive value of x at which the functions have the same value.

(b) Determine one negative value of x at which the graphs intersect.

(c) Is it true that $f(13.35) = g(-4.65)$? Explain your reasoning.

11. The function f is periodic, with period c. So, $f(t + c) = f(t)$. Are the following equal? Explain.

(a) $f(t - 2c) = f(t)$ (b) $f\left(t + \frac{1}{2}c\right) = f\left(\frac{1}{2}t\right)$

(c) $f\left(\frac{1}{2}(t + c)\right) = f\left(\frac{1}{2}t\right)$

12. If you stand in shallow water and look at an object below the surface of the water, the object will look farther away from you than it really is. This is because when light rays pass between air and water, the water refracts, or bends, the light rays. The index of refraction for water is 1.333. This is the ratio of the sine of θ_1 and the sine of θ_2 (see figure).

(a) You are standing in water that is 2 feet deep and are looking at a rock at angle $\theta_1 = 60°$ (measured from a line perpendicular to the surface of the water). Find θ_2.

(b) Find the distances x and y.

(c) Find the distance d between where the rock is and where it appears to be.

(d) What happens to d as you move closer to the rock? Explain your reasoning.

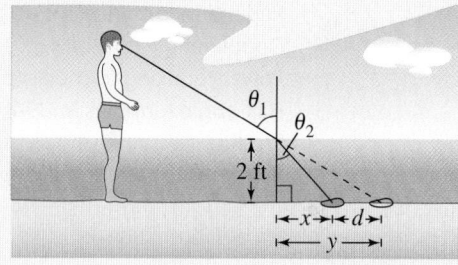

13. In calculus it can be shown that the arctangent function can be approximated by the polynomial

$$\arctan x \approx x - \dfrac{x^3}{3} + \dfrac{x^5}{5} - \dfrac{x^7}{7}$$

where x is in radians.

(a) Use a graphing utility to graph the arctangent function and its polynomial approximation in the same viewing window. How do the graphs compare?

(b) Study the pattern in the polynomial approximation of the arctangent function and guess the next term. Then repeat part (a). How does the accuracy of the approximation change when additional terms are added?

How to study Chapter 5

▶ **What you should learn**

In this chapter you will learn the following skills and concepts:

- How to use fundamental trigonometric identities to evaluate trigonometric functions and simplify trigonometric expressions

- How to verify trigonometric identities

- How to use standard algebraic techniques and inverse trigonometric functions to solve trigonometric equations

- How to use sum and difference formulas, multiple-angle formulas, power-reducing formulas, half-angle formulas, and product-to-sum formulas to rewrite and evaluate trigonometric functions

▶ **Important Vocabulary**

As you encounter each new vocabulary term in this chapter, add the term and its definition to your notebook glossary.

Sum and difference formulas
  (p. 380)
Reduction formulas (p. 382)
Double-angle formulas (p. 387)
Power-reducing formulas (p. 389)
Half-angle formulas (p. 390)
Product-to-sum formulas (p. 391)
Sum-to-product formulas (p. 392)

Study Tools

Learning objectives in each section
Chapter Summary (p. 398)
Review Exercises (pp. 399–401)
Chapter Test (p. 402)

Additional Resources

Study and Solutions Guide
Interactive Precalculus
Videotapes/DVD for Chapter 5
Precalculus Website
Student Success Organizer

Mike Powell/Allsport

5

Analytic Trigonometry

5.1   Using Fundamental Identities

▶ **What you should learn**

- How to recognize and write the fundamental trigonometric identities
- How to use the fundamental trigonometric identities to evaluate trigonometric functions, simplify trigonometric expressions, and rewrite trigonometric expressions

▶ **Why you should learn it**

Fundamental trigonometric identities can be used to simplify trigonometric expressions. For instance, in Exercise 99 on page 361, you can use trigonometric identities to simplify an expression for the coefficient of friction.

Introduction

In Chapter 4, you studied the basic definitions, properties, graphs, and applications of the individual trigonometric functions. In this chapter, you will learn how to use the fundamental identities to do the following.

1. Evaluate trigonometric functions.

2. Simplify trigonometric expressions.

3. Develop additional trigonometric identities.

4. Solve trigonometric equations.

Fundamental Trigonometric Identities

Reciprocal Identities

$$\sin u = \frac{1}{\csc u} \qquad \cos u = \frac{1}{\sec u} \qquad \tan u = \frac{1}{\cot u}$$

$$\csc u = \frac{1}{\sin u} \qquad \sec u = \frac{1}{\cos u} \qquad \cot u = \frac{1}{\tan u}$$

Quotient Identities

$$\tan u = \frac{\sin u}{\cos u} \qquad \cot u = \frac{\cos u}{\sin u}$$

Pythagorean Identities

$$\sin^2 u + \cos^2 u = 1 \qquad 1 + \tan^2 u = \sec^2 u \qquad 1 + \cot^2 u = \csc^2 u$$

Cofunction Identities

$$\sin\left(\frac{\pi}{2} - u\right) = \cos u \qquad \cos\left(\frac{\pi}{2} - u\right) = \sin u$$

$$\tan\left(\frac{\pi}{2} - u\right) = \cot u \qquad \cot\left(\frac{\pi}{2} - u\right) = \tan u$$

$$\sec\left(\frac{\pi}{2} - u\right) = \csc u \qquad \csc\left(\frac{\pi}{2} - u\right) = \sec u$$

Even/Odd Identities

$$\sin(-u) = -\sin u \qquad \cos(-u) = \cos u \qquad \tan(-u) = -\tan u$$

$$\csc(-u) = -\csc u \qquad \sec(-u) = \sec u \qquad \cot(-u) = -\cot u$$

Pythagorean identities are sometimes used in radical form such as

$$\sin u = \pm\sqrt{1 - \cos^2 u}$$

or

$$\tan u = \pm\sqrt{\sec^2 u - 1}$$

where the sign depends on the choice of u.

Using the Fundamental Identities

One common use of trigonometric identities is to use given values of trigonometric functions to evaluate other trigonometric functions.

Technology

You can use a graphing utility to check the result of Example 2. To do this, graph

$$y_1 = \sin x \cos^2 x - \sin x$$

and

$$y_2 = -\sin^3 x$$

in the same viewing window, as shown below. Because Example 2 shows the equivalence algebraically and the two graphs appear to coincide, you can conclude that the expressions are equivalent.

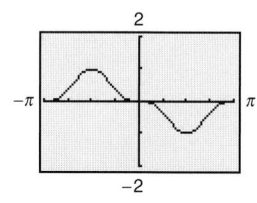

Remind students that they must use an algebraic approach to prove that two expressions are equivalent. A graphical approach can only confirm that the simplification found using algebraic techniques is correct.

Example 1 ▶ Using Identities to Evaluate a Function

Use the values $\sec u = -\frac{3}{2}$ and $\tan u > 0$ to find the values of all six trigonometric functions.

Solution

Using a reciprocal identity, you have

$$\cos u = \frac{1}{\sec u} = \frac{1}{-3/2} = -\frac{2}{3}.$$

Using a Pythagorean identity, you have

$$\sin^2 u = 1 - \cos^2 u$$
$$= 1 - \left(-\frac{2}{3}\right)^2$$
$$= 1 - \frac{4}{9} = \frac{5}{9}.$$

Because $\sec u < 0$ and $\tan u > 0$, it follows that u lies in Quadrant III. Moreover, because $\sin u$ is negative when u is in Quadrant III, you can choose the negative root and obtain $\sin u = -\sqrt{5}/3$. Now, knowing the values of the sine and cosine, you can find the values of all six trigonometric functions.

$$\sin u = -\frac{\sqrt{5}}{3} \qquad\qquad \csc u = \frac{1}{\sin u} = -\frac{3}{\sqrt{5}}$$

$$\cos u = -\frac{2}{3} \qquad\qquad \sec u = \frac{1}{\cos u} = -\frac{3}{2}$$

$$\tan u = \frac{\sin u}{\cos u} = \frac{-\sqrt{5}/3}{-2/3} = \frac{\sqrt{5}}{2} \qquad\qquad \cot u = \frac{1}{\tan u} = \frac{2}{\sqrt{5}}$$

Example 2 ▶ Simplifying a Trigonometric Expression

Simplify $\sin x \cos^2 x - \sin x$.

Solution

Factor the expression and then use a fundamental identity.

$$\sin x \cos^2 x - \sin x = \sin x(\cos^2 x - 1) \qquad \text{Monomial factor}$$
$$= -\sin x(1 - \cos^2 x) \qquad \text{Factor out } -1.$$
$$= -\sin x(\sin^2 x) \qquad \text{Pythagorean identity}$$
$$= -\sin^3 x \qquad \text{Multiply.}$$

The icon identifies examples and concepts related to features of the Learning Tools CD-ROM and the *Interactive* and *Internet* versions of this text. For more details see the chart on pages *xxi-xxv*.

| Example 3 ▶ | **Factoring Trigonometric Expressions** | |

Factor each expression.

a. $\sec^2 \theta - 1$

b. $4 \tan^2 \theta + \tan \theta - 3$

Solution

a. Here you have the difference of two squares, which factors as

$$\sec^2 \theta - 1 = (\sec \theta - 1)(\sec \theta + 1).$$

b. This expression has the polynomial form $ax^2 + bx + c$, and it factors as

$$4 \tan^2 \theta + \tan \theta - 3 = (4 \tan \theta - 3)(\tan \theta + 1).$$

On occasion, factoring or simplifying can best be done by first rewriting the expression in terms of just *one* trigonometric function or in terms of *sine and cosine only*. These strategies are illustrated in Examples 4 and 5, respectively.

| Example 4 ▶ | **Factoring a Trigonometric Expression** | |

Factor $\csc^2 x - \cot x - 3$.

Solution

You can use the identity $\csc^2 x = 1 + \cot^2 x$ to rewrite the expression in terms of the cotangent.

$$\csc^2 x - \cot x - 3 = (1 + \cot^2 x) - \cot x - 3 \qquad \text{Pythagorean identity}$$

$$= \cot^2 x - \cot x - 2 \qquad \text{Combine like terms.}$$

$$= (\cot x - 2)(\cot x + 1) \qquad \text{Factor.}$$

| Example 5 ▶ | **Simplifying a Trigonometric Expression** | |

Simplify $\sin t + \cot t \cos t$.

Solution

Begin by rewriting $\cot t$ in terms of sine and cosine.

$$\sin t + \cot t \cos t = \sin t + \left(\frac{\cos t}{\sin t} \right) \cos t \qquad \text{Quotient identity}$$

$$= \frac{\sin^2 t + \cos^2 t}{\sin t} \qquad \text{Add fractions.}$$

$$= \frac{1}{\sin t} \qquad \text{Pythagorean identity}$$

$$= \csc t \qquad \text{Reciprocal identity}$$

Example 6 ▶   **Adding Trigonometric Expressions**

Perform the addition and simplify.

$$\frac{\sin \theta}{1 + \cos \theta} + \frac{\cos \theta}{\sin \theta}$$

Solution

$$\frac{\sin \theta}{1 + \cos \theta} + \frac{\cos \theta}{\sin \theta} = \frac{(\sin \theta)(\sin \theta) + (\cos \theta)(1 + \cos \theta)}{(1 + \cos \theta)(\sin \theta)}$$

$$= \frac{\sin^2 \theta + \cos^2 \theta + \cos \theta}{(1 + \cos \theta)(\sin \theta)} \qquad \text{Multiply.}$$

$$= \frac{1 + \cos \theta}{(1 + \cos \theta)(\sin \theta)} \qquad \text{Pythagorean identity}$$

$$= \frac{1}{\sin \theta} \qquad \text{Divide out common factor.}$$

$$= \csc \theta \qquad \text{Reciprocal identity}$$

The *Interactive* CD-ROM and *Internet* versions of this text offer a Quiz for every section of the text.

The last two examples in this section involve techniques for rewriting expressions in forms that are used in calculus.

Example 7 ▶   **Rewriting a Trigonometric Expression**

Rewrite $\dfrac{1}{1 + \sin x}$ so that it is *not* in fractional form.

Solution

From the Pythagorean identity $\cos^2 x = 1 - \sin^2 x = (1 - \sin x)(1 + \sin x)$, you can see that by multiplying both the numerator and the denominator by $(1 - \sin x)$ you produce a monomial denominator.

$$\frac{1}{1 + \sin x} = \frac{1}{1 + \sin x} \cdot \frac{1 - \sin x}{1 - \sin x} \qquad \begin{array}{l}\text{Multiply numerator and}\\\text{denominator by } (1 - \sin x).\end{array}$$

$$= \frac{1 - \sin x}{1 - \sin^2 x} \qquad \text{Multiply.}$$

$$= \frac{1 - \sin x}{\cos^2 x} \qquad \text{Pythagorean identity}$$

$$= \frac{1}{\cos^2 x} - \frac{\sin x}{\cos^2 x} \qquad \text{Separate fractions.}$$

$$= \frac{1}{\cos^2 x} - \frac{\sin x}{\cos x} \cdot \frac{1}{\cos x} \qquad \text{Product of fractions}$$

$$= \sec^2 x - \tan x \sec x \qquad \text{Identities}$$

Example 8 ▶ Trigonometric Substitution

Use the substitution $x = 2\tan\theta$, $0 < \theta < \pi/2$, to express

$$\sqrt{4 + x^2}$$

as a trigonometric function of θ.

Solution

Begin by letting $x = 2\tan\theta$. Then, you can obtain

$$\sqrt{4 + x^2} = \sqrt{4 + (2\tan\theta)^2} \qquad \text{Substitute } 2\tan\theta \text{ for } x.$$
$$= \sqrt{4 + 4\tan^2\theta} \qquad \text{Rule of exponents}$$
$$= \sqrt{4(1 + \tan^2\theta)} \qquad \text{Factor.}$$
$$= \sqrt{4\sec^2\theta} \qquad \text{Pythagorean identity}$$
$$= 2\sec\theta. \qquad \sec\theta > 0 \text{ for } 0 < \theta < \pi/2$$

Figure 5.1 shows the right triangle illustration of the trigonometric substitution in Example 8. You can use this triangle to check the solution of Example 8. For $0 < \theta < \pi/2$, you have

$$\text{opp} = x, \quad \text{adj} = 2, \quad \text{and} \quad \text{hyp} = \sqrt{4 + x^2}.$$

With these expressions, you can write the following.

$$\sec\theta = \frac{\text{hyp}}{\text{adj}}$$
$$\sec\theta = \frac{\sqrt{4 + x^2}}{2}$$
$$2\sec\theta = \sqrt{4 + x^2}$$

So, the solution checks.

Activities

1. Simplify, using the fundamental trigonometric identities.

$$\frac{\cot^2\theta}{\csc^2\theta}$$

Answer: $\cos^2\theta$

2. Use the trigonometric substitution $x = 3\cos\theta$ to rewrite the expression $\sqrt{9 - x^2}$ as a trigonometric function of θ, where

$$0 < \theta < \frac{\pi}{2}.$$

Answer: $3\sin\theta$

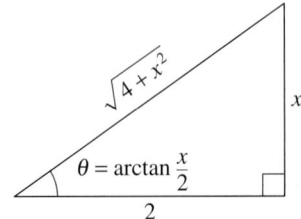

Angle whose tangent is $\frac{x}{2}$.

FIGURE **5.1**

5.1 Exercises

The *Interactive* CD-ROM and *Internet* versions of this text contain step-by-step solutions to all odd-numbered exercises. They also provide Tutorial Exercises for additional help.

In Exercises 1–14, use the given values to evaluate (if possible) the remaining trigonometric functions.

1. $\sin x = \dfrac{\sqrt{3}}{2}, \quad \cos x = -\dfrac{1}{2}$

2. $\tan x = \dfrac{\sqrt{3}}{3}, \quad \cos x = -\dfrac{\sqrt{3}}{2}$

3. $\sec \theta = \sqrt{2}, \quad \sin \theta = -\dfrac{\sqrt{2}}{2}$

4. $\csc \theta = \dfrac{5}{3}, \quad \tan \theta = \dfrac{3}{4}$

5. $\tan x = \dfrac{5}{12}, \quad \sec x = -\dfrac{13}{12}$

6. $\cot \phi = -3, \quad \sin \phi = \dfrac{\sqrt{10}}{10}$

7. $\sec \phi = \dfrac{3}{2}, \quad \csc \phi = -\dfrac{3\sqrt{5}}{5}$

8. $\cos\left(\dfrac{\pi}{2} - x\right) = \dfrac{3}{5}, \quad \cos x = \dfrac{4}{5}$

9. $\sin(-x) = -\dfrac{1}{3}, \quad \tan x = -\dfrac{\sqrt{2}}{4}$

10. $\sec x = 4, \quad \sin x > 0$

11. $\tan \theta = 2, \quad \sin \theta < 0$

12. $\csc \theta = -5, \quad \cos \theta < 0$

13. $\sin \theta = -1, \quad \cot \theta = 0$

14. $\tan \theta$ is undefined, $\quad \sin \theta > 0$

In Exercises 15–20, match the trigonometric expression with one of the following.

(a) sec x   (b) − 1   (c) cot x

(d) 1   (e) − tan x   (f) sin x

15. $\sec x \cos x$

16. $\tan x \csc x$

17. $\cot^2 x - \csc^2 x$

18. $(1 - \cos^2 x)(\csc x)$

19. $\dfrac{\sin(-x)}{\cos(-x)}$

20. $\dfrac{\sin[(\pi/2) - x]}{\cos[(\pi/2) - x]}$

In Exercises 21–26, match the trigonometric expression with one of the following.

(a) csc x   (b) tan x   (c) sin² x

(d) sin x tan x   (e) sec² x   (f) sec² x + tan² x

21. $\sin x \sec x$

22. $\cos^2 x (\sec^2 x - 1)$

23. $\sec^4 x - \tan^4 x$

24. $\cot x \sec x$

25. $\dfrac{\sec^2 x - 1}{\sin^2 x}$

26. $\dfrac{\cos^2[(\pi/2) - x]}{\cos x}$

In Exercises 27–44, use the fundamental identities to simplify the expression. There is more than one correct form of each answer.

27. $\cot \theta \sec \theta$

28. $\cos \beta \tan \beta$

29. $\sin \phi (\csc \phi - \sin \phi)$

30. $\sec^2 x (1 - \sin^2 x)$

31. $\dfrac{\cot x}{\csc x}$

32. $\dfrac{\csc \theta}{\sec \theta}$

33. $\dfrac{1 - \sin^2 x}{\csc^2 x - 1}$

34. $\dfrac{1}{\tan^2 x + 1}$

35. $\sec \alpha \cdot \dfrac{\sin \alpha}{\tan \alpha}$

36. $\dfrac{\tan^2 \theta}{\sec^2 \theta}$

37. $\cos\left(\dfrac{\pi}{2} - x\right)\sec x$

38. $\cot\left(\dfrac{\pi}{2} - x\right)\cos x$

39. $\dfrac{\cos^2 y}{1 - \sin y}$

40. $\cos t (1 + \tan^2 t)$

41. $\sin \beta \tan \beta + \cos \beta$

42. $\csc \phi \tan \phi + \sec \phi$

43. $\cot u \sin u + \tan u \cos u$

44. $\sin \theta \sec \theta + \cos \theta \csc \theta$

In Exercises 45–56, factor the expression and use the fundamental identities to simplify. There is more than one correct form of each answer.

45. $\tan^2 x - \tan^2 x \sin^2 x$

46. $\sin^2 x \csc^2 x - \sin^2 x$

47. $\sin^2 x \sec^2 x - \sin^2 x$

48. $\cos^2 x + \cos^2 x \tan^2 x$

49. $\dfrac{\sec^2 x - 1}{\sec x - 1}$

50. $\dfrac{\cos^2 x - 4}{\cos x - 2}$

51. $\tan^4 x + 2 \tan^2 x + 1$

52. $1 - 2 \cos^2 x + \cos^4 x$

53. $\sin^4 x - \cos^4 x$

54. $\sec^4 x - \tan^4 x$

55. $\csc^3 x - \csc^2 x - \csc x + 1$

56. $\sec^3 x - \sec^2 x - \sec x + 1$

In Exercises 57–60, perform the multiplication and use the fundamental identities to simplify. There is more than one correct form of each answer.

57. $(\sin x + \cos x)^2$

58. $(\cot x + \csc x)(\cot x - \csc x)$

59. $(2 \csc x + 2)(2 \csc x - 2)$

60. $(3 - 3 \sin x)(3 + 3 \sin x)$

In Exercises 61–64, perform the addition or subtraction and use the fundamental identities to simplify. There is more than one correct form of each answer.

61. $\dfrac{1}{1 + \cos x} + \dfrac{1}{1 - \cos x}$

62. $\dfrac{1}{\sec x + 1} - \dfrac{1}{\sec x - 1}$

63. $\dfrac{\cos x}{1 + \sin x} + \dfrac{1 + \sin x}{\cos x}$

64. $\tan x - \dfrac{\sec^2 x}{\tan x}$

In Exercises 65–68, rewrite the expression so that it is not in fractional form. There is more than one correct form of each answer.

65. $\dfrac{\sin^2 y}{1 - \cos y}$

66. $\dfrac{5}{\tan x + \sec x}$

67. $\dfrac{3}{\sec x - \tan x}$

68. $\dfrac{\tan^2 x}{\csc x + 1}$

 Numerical and Graphical Analysis   In Exercises 69–72, use a graphing utility to complete the table and graph the functions. Make a conjecture about y_1 and y_2.

x	0.2	0.4	0.6	0.8	1.0	1.2	1.4
y_1							
y_2							

69. $y_1 = \cos\left(\dfrac{\pi}{2} - x\right), \quad y_2 = \sin x$

70. $y_1 = \sec x - \cos x, \quad y_2 = \sin x \tan x$

71. $y_1 = \dfrac{\cos x}{1 - \sin x}, \quad y_2 = \dfrac{1 + \sin x}{\cos x}$

72. $y_1 = \sec^4 x - \sec^2 x, \quad y_2 = \tan^2 x + \tan^4 x$

 In Exercises 73–76, use a graphing utility to determine which of the six trigonometric functions is equal to the expression. Verify your answer algebraically.

73. $\cos x \cot x + \sin x$

74. $\sec x \csc x - \tan x$

75. $\dfrac{1}{\sin x}\left(\dfrac{1}{\cos x} - \cos x\right)$

76. $\dfrac{1}{2}\left(\dfrac{1 + \sin \theta}{\cos \theta} + \dfrac{\cos \theta}{1 + \sin \theta}\right)$

In Exercises 77–82, use the trigonometric substitution to write the algebraic expression as a trigonometric function of θ, where $0 < \theta < \pi/2$.

77. $\sqrt{9 - x^2}, \quad x = 3 \cos \theta$

78. $\sqrt{64 - 16x^2}, \quad x = 2 \cos \theta$

79. $\sqrt{x^2 - 9}, \quad x = 3 \sec \theta$

80. $\sqrt{x^2 - 4}, \quad x = 2 \sec \theta$

81. $\sqrt{x^2 + 25}, \quad x = 5 \tan \theta$

82. $\sqrt{x^2 + 100}, \quad x = 10 \tan \theta$

In Exercises 83–86, use the trigonometric substitution to write the algebraic equation as a trigonometric function of θ, where $-\pi/2 < \theta < \pi/2$. Then find $\sin \theta$ and $\cos \theta$.

83. $3 = \sqrt{9 - x^2}, \quad x = 3 \sin \theta$

84. $3 = \sqrt{36 - x^2}, \quad x = 6 \sin \theta$

85. $2\sqrt{2} = \sqrt{16 - 4x^2}, \quad x = 2 \cos \theta$

86. $-5\sqrt{3} = \sqrt{100 - x^2}, \quad x = 10 \cos \theta$

In Exercises 87–90, use a graphing utility to solve the equation for θ, where $0 \le \theta < 2\pi$.

87. $\sin \theta = \sqrt{1 - \cos^2 \theta}$

88. $\cos \theta = -\sqrt{1 - \sin^2 \theta}$

89. $\sec \theta = \sqrt{1 + \tan^2 \theta}$

90. $\csc \theta = \sqrt{1 + \cot^2 \theta}$

In Exercises 91–94, rewrite the expression as a single logarithm and simplify the result.

91. $\ln|\cos x| - \ln|\sin x|$

92. $\ln|\sec x| + \ln|\sin x|$

93. $\ln|\cot t| + \ln(1 + \tan^2 t)$

94. $\ln(\cos^2 t) + \ln(1 + \tan^2 t)$

In Exercises 95–98, use a calculator to demonstrate the identity for each value of θ.

95. $\csc^2 \theta - \cot^2 \theta = 1$

(a) $\theta = 132°$,   (b) $\theta = \dfrac{2\pi}{7}$

96. $\tan^2 \theta + 1 = \sec^2 \theta$

(a) $\theta = 346°$,   (b) $\theta = 3.1$

97. $\cos\left(\dfrac{\pi}{2} - \theta\right) = \sin \theta$

(a) $\theta = 80°$,   (b) $\theta = 0.8$

98. $\sin(-\theta) = -\sin \theta$

(a) $\theta = 250°$,   (b) $\theta = \frac{1}{2}$

99. *Friction*   The forces acting on an object weighing W units on an inclined plane positioned at an angle of θ with the horizontal (see figure) are modeled by

$$\mu W \cos \theta = W \sin \theta$$

where μ is the coefficient of friction. Solve the equation for μ and simplify the result.

100. *Rate of Change*   The rate of change of the function

$$f(x) = -\csc x - \sin x$$

is given by the expression

$\csc x \cot x - \cos x.$

Show that this expression can also be written as $\cos x \cot^2 x.$

Synthesis

True or False?   **In Exercises 101 and 102, determine whether the statement is true or false. Justify your answer.**

101. The even and odd trigonometric identities are helpful for determining whether the value of a trigonometric function is positive or negative.

102. A cofunction identity can be used to transform a tangent function so that it can be represented by a cosecant function.

Calculus   **In Exercises 103–106, fill in the blanks.** (*Note: The notation $x \to c^+$ indicates that x approaches c from the right and $x \to c^-$ indicates that x approaches c from the left.*)

103. As $x \to \dfrac{\pi^-}{2}$, $\sin x \to$ [ ] and $\csc x \to$ [ ] .

104. As $x \to 0^+$, $\cos x \to$ [ ] and $\sec x \to$ [ ] .

105. As $x \to \dfrac{\pi^-}{2}$, $\tan x \to$ [ ] and $\cot x \to$ [ ] .

106. As $x \to \pi^+$, $\sin x \to$ [ ] and $\csc x \to$ [ ] .

In Exercises 107–112, determine whether or not the equation is an identity, and give a reason for your answer.

107. $\cos \theta = \sqrt{1 - \sin^2 \theta}$

108. $\cot \theta = \sqrt{\csc^2 \theta + 1}$

109. $\dfrac{(\sin k\theta)}{(\cos k\theta)} = \tan \theta,$ k is a constant.

110. $\dfrac{1}{(5 \cos \theta)} = 5 \sec \theta$

111. $\sin \theta \csc \theta = 1$ **112.** $\sin \theta \csc \theta = 1$

113. Use the definitions of sine and cosine to derive the Pythagorean identity $\sin^2 \theta + \cos^2 \theta = 1$.

114. *Writing*   Use the Pythagorean identity

$$\sin^2 \theta + \cos^2 \theta = 1$$

to derive the other Pythagorean identities, $1 + \tan^2 \theta = \sec^2 \theta$ and $1 + \cot^2 \theta = \csc^2 \theta$. Discuss how to remember these identities and other fundamental identities.

Review

In Exercises 115 and 116, perform the operation and simplify.

115. $\left(\sqrt{x} + 5\right)\left(\sqrt{x} - 5\right)$ **116.** $\left(2\sqrt{z} + 3\right)^2$

In Exercises 117–120, perform the addition or subtraction and simplify.

117. $\dfrac{1}{x + 5} + \dfrac{x}{x - 8}$ **118.** $\dfrac{6x}{x - 4} - \dfrac{3}{4 - x}$

119. $\dfrac{2x}{x^2 - 4} - \dfrac{7}{x + 4}$ **120.** $\dfrac{x}{x^2 - 25} + \dfrac{x^2}{x - 5}$

5.2 Verifying Trigonometric Identities

▶ **What you should learn**

- How to plan a strategy for verifying trigonometric identities
- How to verify trigonometric identities

▶ **Why you should learn it**

You can use trigonometric identities to rewrite trigonometric equations that model real-life situations. For instance, in Exercise 58 on page 368, you can use trigonometric identities to simplify the equation that models the length of a shadow cast by a gnomon.

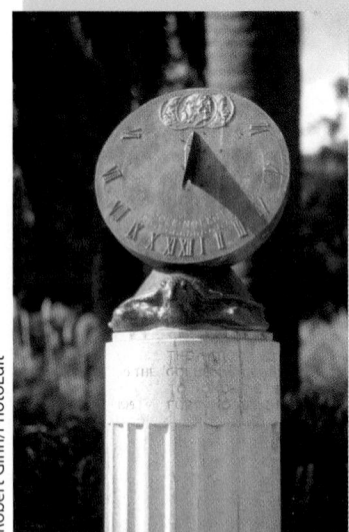

You may want to review the distinctions among expressions, equations, and identities. Have your students look at some algebraic identities and conditional equations before starting this section. It is important for them to understand what it means to verify an identity and not try to solve it as an equation.

Introduction

In this section, you will study techniques for verifying trigonometric identities. In the next section, you will study techniques for solving trigonometric equations. The key to verifying identities *and* solving equations is the ability to use the fundamental identities and the rules of algebra to rewrite trigonometric expressions.

Remember that a *conditional equation* is an equation that is true for only some of the values in its domain. For example, the conditional equation

$$\sin x = 0 \qquad\qquad \text{Conditional equation}$$

is true only for $x = n\pi$, where n is an integer. When you find these values, you are *solving* the equation.

On the other hand, an equation that is true for all real values in the domain of the variable is an *identity*. For example, the familiar equation

$$\sin^2 x = 1 - \cos^2 x \qquad\qquad \text{Identity}$$

is true for all real numbers x. So, it is an identity.

Although there are similarities, verifying that a trigonometric equation is an identity is quite different from solving an equation. There is no well-defined set of rules to follow in verifying trigonometric identities, and the process is best learned by practice.

For instance, to verify that the trigonometric equation $\tan \theta \cos \theta = \sin \theta$ is an identity, begin by working with the more complicated, left side of the equation.

$$\tan \theta \cos \theta = \left(\frac{\sin \theta}{\cos \theta}\right) \cos \theta \qquad\qquad \text{Rewrite } \tan \theta \text{ as } \frac{\sin \theta}{\cos \theta}.$$

$$= \left(\frac{\sin \theta}{\cos \theta}\right) \cos \theta \qquad\qquad \text{Divide out } \cos \theta.$$

$$= \sin \theta \qquad\qquad \text{Simplify.}$$

The result shows that the left side of the equation is equal to the right side. So, the identity has been verified.

Guidelines for Verifying Trigonometric Identities

1. Work with one side of the equation at a time. It is often better to work with the more complicated side first.

2. Look for opportunities to factor an expression, add fractions, square a binomial, or create a monomial denominator.

3. Look for opportunities to use the fundamental identities. Note which functions are in the final expression you want. Sines and cosines pair up well, as do secants and tangents, and cosecants and cotangents.

4. If the preceding guidelines do not help, try converting all terms to sines and cosines.

5. Always try *something*. Even paths that lead to dead ends provide insights.

Verifying Trigonometric Identities

Example 1 ▶ **Verifying a Trigonometric Identity**

Verify the identity $\dfrac{\sec^2 \theta - 1}{\sec^2 \theta} = \sin^2 \theta$.

Solution

Because the left side is more complicated, start with it.

$$\dfrac{\sec^2 \theta - 1}{\sec^2 \theta} = \dfrac{(\tan^2 \theta + 1) - 1}{\sec^2 \theta} \qquad \text{Pythagorean identity}$$

$$= \dfrac{\tan^2 \theta}{\sec^2 \theta} \qquad \text{Simplify.}$$

$$= \tan^2 \theta (\cos^2 \theta) \qquad \text{Reciprocal identity}$$

$$= \dfrac{\sin^2 \theta}{(\cos^2 \theta)} (\cos^2 \theta) \qquad \text{Quotient identity}$$

$$= \sin^2 \theta \qquad \text{Simplify.}$$

Here is another way to verify the identity in Example 1.

$$\dfrac{\sec^2 \theta - 1}{\sec^2 \theta} = \dfrac{\sec^2 \theta}{\sec^2 \theta} - \dfrac{1}{\sec^2 \theta} \qquad \text{Rewrite as the difference of fractions.}$$

$$= 1 - \cos^2 \theta \qquad \text{Reciprocal identity}$$

$$= \sin^2 \theta \qquad \text{Pythagorean identity}$$

As you can see, there can be more than one way to verify an identity. Your method may differ from that used by your instructor or fellow students. Here is a good chance to be creative and establish your own style, but try to be as efficient as possible.

Example 2 ▶ **Combining Fractions Before Using Identities**

Verify the identity $\dfrac{1}{1 - \sin \alpha} + \dfrac{1}{1 + \sin \alpha} = 2 \sec^2 \alpha$.

Solution

$$\dfrac{1}{1 - \sin \alpha} + \dfrac{1}{1 + \sin \alpha} = \dfrac{1 + \sin \alpha + 1 - \sin \alpha}{(1 - \sin \alpha)(1 + \sin \alpha)} \qquad \text{Add fractions.}$$

$$= \dfrac{2}{1 - \sin^2 \alpha} \qquad \text{Simplify.}$$

$$= \dfrac{2}{\cos^2 \alpha} \qquad \text{Pythagorean identity}$$

$$= 2 \sec^2 \alpha \qquad \text{Reciprocal identity}$$

Example 3 ▶   **Verifying a Trigonometric Identity**

Verify the identity

$$(\tan^2 x + 1)(\cos^2 x - 1) = -\tan^2 x.$$

Solution

By applying identities before multiplying, you obtain the following.

$$(\tan^2 x + 1)(\cos^2 x - 1) = (\sec^2 x)(-\sin^2 x) \qquad \text{Pythagorean identities}$$

$$= -\frac{\sin^2 x}{\cos^2 x} \qquad \text{Reciprocal identity}$$

$$= -\left(\frac{\sin x}{\cos x}\right)^2 \qquad \text{Rule of exponents}$$

$$= -\tan^2 x \qquad \text{Quotient identity}$$

Example 4 ▶   **Converting to Sines and Cosines**

Verify the identity

$$\tan x + \cot x = \sec x \csc x.$$

Solution

In this case there appear to be no fractions to add, no products to find, and no opportunities to use the Pythagorean identities. So, try converting the left side into sines and cosines to see what happens.

$$\tan x + \cot x = \frac{\sin x}{\cos x} + \frac{\cos x}{\sin x} \qquad \text{Quotient identities}$$

$$= \frac{\sin^2 x + \cos^2 x}{\cos x \sin x} \qquad \text{Add fractions.}$$

$$= \frac{1}{\cos x \sin x} \qquad \text{Pythagorean identity}$$

$$= \frac{1}{\cos x} \cdot \frac{1}{\sin x} \qquad \text{Product of fractions}$$

$$= \sec x \csc x \qquad \text{Reciprocal identities}$$

STUDY TIP

As shown at the right, $\csc^2 x(1 + \cos x)$ is considered a simplified form of $1/(1 - \cos x)$ because the expression does not contain any fractions.

Recall from algebra that *rationalizing the denominator* using conjugates is, on occasion, a powerful simplification technique. A related form of this technique works for simplifying trigonometric expressions as well. For instance, to simplify $1/(1 - \cos x)$, multiply the numerator and the denominator by $1 + \cos x$.

$$\frac{1}{1 - \cos x} = \frac{1}{1 - \cos x}\left(\frac{1 + \cos x}{1 + \cos x}\right) = \frac{1 + \cos x}{1 - \cos^2 x} = \frac{1 + \cos x}{\sin^2 x}$$

$$= \csc^2 x(1 + \cos x)$$

This technique is demonstrated in the next example.

Example 5 ▶ Verifying Trigonometric Identities

Verify the identity $\sec y + \tan y = \dfrac{\cos y}{1 - \sin y}$.

Solution

Begin with the *right* side. Note that you can create a monomial denominator by multiplying the numerator and denominator by $1 + \sin y$.

$$\frac{\cos y}{1 - \sin y} = \frac{\cos y}{1 - \sin y}\left(\frac{1 + \sin y}{1 + \sin y}\right) \qquad \text{Multiply numerator and denominator by } 1 + \sin y.$$

$$= \frac{\cos y + \cos y \sin y}{1 - \sin^2 y} \qquad \text{Multiply.}$$

$$= \frac{\cos y + \cos y \sin y}{\cos^2 y} \qquad \text{Pythagorean identity}$$

$$= \frac{\cos y}{\cos^2 y} + \frac{\cos y \sin y}{\cos^2 y} \qquad \text{Separate fractions.}$$

$$= \frac{1}{\cos y} + \frac{\sin y}{\cos y} \qquad \text{Simplify.}$$

$$= \sec y + \tan y \qquad \text{Identities}$$

In Examples 1 through 5, you have been verifying trigonometric identities by working with one side of the equation and converting to the form given on the other side. On occasion, it is practical to work with each side *separately*, to obtain one common form equivalent to both sides. This is illustrated in Example 6.

Example 6 ▶ Working with Each Side Separately

Verify the identity $\dfrac{\cot^2 \theta}{1 + \csc \theta} = \dfrac{1 - \sin \theta}{\sin \theta}$.

Solution

Working with the left side, you have

$$\frac{\cot^2 \theta}{1 + \csc \theta} = \frac{\csc^2 \theta - 1}{1 + \csc \theta} \qquad \text{Pythagorean identity}$$

$$= \frac{(\csc \theta - 1)(\csc \theta + 1)}{1 + \csc \theta} \qquad \text{Factor.}$$

$$= \csc \theta - 1. \qquad \text{Simplify.}$$

Now, simplifying the right side, you have

$$\frac{1 - \sin \theta}{\sin \theta} = \frac{1}{\sin \theta} - \frac{\sin \theta}{\sin \theta} \qquad \text{Separate fractions.}$$

$$= \csc \theta - 1. \qquad \text{Reciprocal identity}$$

The identity is verified because both sides are equal to $\csc \theta - 1$.

STUDY TIP

The technique of cross multiplication is not used in verifying trigonometric identities, because you do not know that the expressions are equal. Cross multiplication is used in solving an equation, when you know that the left side equals the right side.

In Example 7, powers of trigonometric functions are rewritten as more complicated sums of products of trigonometric functions. This is a common procedure used in calculus.

Example 7 ▶ **Three Examples from Calculus**

Verify each identity.

a. $\tan^4 x = \tan^2 x \sec^2 x - \tan^2 x$

b. $\sin^3 x \cos^4 x = (\cos^4 x - \cos^6 x) \sin x$

c. $\csc^4 x \cot x = \csc^2 x (\cot x + \cot^3 x)$

Solution

a. $\tan^4 x = (\tan^2 x)(\tan^2 x)$ Separate factors.

$\qquad\qquad = \tan^2 x(\sec^2 x - 1)$ Pythagorean identity

$\qquad\qquad = \tan^2 x \sec^2 x - \tan^2 x$ Multiply.

b. $\sin^3 x \cos^4 x = \sin^2 x \cos^4 x \sin x$ Separate factors.

$\qquad\qquad\quad = (1 - \cos^2 x)\cos^4 x \sin x$ Pythagorean identity

$\qquad\qquad\quad = (\cos^4 x - \cos^6 x) \sin x$ Multiply.

c. $\csc^4 x \cot x = \csc^2 x \csc^2 x \cot.x$ Separate factors.

$\qquad\qquad\quad = \csc^2 x(1 + \cot^2 x) \cot x$ Pythagorean identity

$\qquad\qquad\quad = \csc^2 x(\cot x + \cot^3 x)$ Multiply.

Writing ABOUT MATHEMATICS

Alternative Writing About Mathematics

a. Ask students to assemble a list of techniques and strategies for rewriting trigonometric expressions such as those demonstrated in the examples of this section.

b. Ask students to work in pairs. Each student should create an identity equation from the fundamental trigonometric identities. Partners then trade and verify one another's identities. Then have students write a brief explanation of the techniques they used to create the identities.

Error Analysis   You are tutoring a student in trigonometry. One of the homework problems your student encounters asks whether the following statement is an identity.

$$\tan^2 x \sin^2 x \stackrel{?}{=} \frac{5}{6}\tan^2 x$$

Your student does not attempt to verify the equivalence algebraically, but mistakenly uses only a graphical approach. Using range settings of

Xmin $= -3\pi$	Ymin $= -20$
Xmax $= 3\pi$	Ymax $= 20$
Xscl $= \pi/2$	Yscl $= 1$

your student graphs both sides of the expression on a graphing utility and concludes that the statement is an identity.

What is wrong with your student's reasoning? Explain. Discuss the limitations of verifying identities graphically.

5.2 Exercises

In Exercises 1–40, verify the identity.

1. $\sin t \csc t = 1$

2. $\sec y \cos y = 1$

3. $(1 + \sin \alpha)(1 - \sin \alpha) = \cos^2 \alpha$

4. $\cot^2 y(\sec^2 y - 1) = 1$

5. $\cos^2 \beta - \sin^2 \beta = 1 - 2 \sin^2 \beta$

6. $\cos^2 \beta - \sin^2 \beta = 2 \cos^2 \beta - 1$

7. $\tan^2 \theta + 4 = \sec^2 \theta + 3$

8. $2 - \sec^2 z = 1 - \tan^2 z$

9. $\sin^2 \alpha - \sin^4 \alpha = \cos^2 \alpha - \cos^4 \alpha$

10. $\cos x + \sin x \tan x = \sec x$

11. $\dfrac{\csc^2 \theta}{\cot \theta} = \csc \theta \sec \theta$

12. $\dfrac{\cot^3 t}{\csc t} = \cos t(\csc^2 t - 1)$

13. $\dfrac{\cot^2 t}{\csc t} = \csc t - \sin t$

14. $\dfrac{1}{\tan \beta} + \tan \beta = \dfrac{\sec^2 \beta}{\tan \beta}$

15. $\sin^{1/2} x \cos x - \sin^{5/2} x \cos x = \cos^3 x \sqrt{\sin x}$

16. $\sec^6 x(\sec x \tan x) - \sec^4 x(\sec x \tan x) = \sec^5 x \tan^3 x$

17. $\dfrac{1}{\sec x \tan x} = \csc x - \sin x$

18. $\dfrac{\sec \theta - 1}{1 - \cos \theta} = \sec \theta$

19. $\cot \alpha + \tan \alpha = \csc \alpha \sec \alpha$

20. $\sec x - \cos x = \sin x \tan x$

21. $\dfrac{1}{\tan x} + \dfrac{1}{\cot x} = \tan x + \cot x$

22. $\dfrac{1}{\sin x} - \dfrac{1}{\csc x} = \csc x - \sin x$

23. $\dfrac{\cos \theta \cot \theta}{1 - \sin \theta} - 1 = \csc \theta$

24. $\dfrac{1 + \sin \theta}{\cos \theta} + \dfrac{\cos \theta}{1 + \sin \theta} = 2 \sec \theta$

25. $\dfrac{1}{\sin x + 1} + \dfrac{1}{\csc x + 1} = 1$

26. $\cos x - \dfrac{\cos x}{1 - \tan x} = \dfrac{\sin x \cos x}{\sin x - \cos x}$

27. $\tan\left(\dfrac{\pi}{2} - \theta\right) \tan \theta = 1$

28. $\dfrac{\cos[(\pi/2) - x]}{\sin[(\pi/2) - x]} = \tan x$

29. $\dfrac{\csc(-x)}{\sec(-x)} = -\cot x$

30. $(1 + \sin y)[1 + \sin(-y)] = \cos^2 y$

31. $\dfrac{\sin x \cos y + \cos x \sin y}{\cos x \cos y - \sin x \sin y} = \dfrac{\tan x + \tan y}{1 - \tan x \tan y}$

32. $\dfrac{\tan x + \tan y}{1 - \tan x \tan y} = \dfrac{\cot x + \cot y}{\cot x \cot y - 1}$

33. $\dfrac{\tan x + \cot y}{\tan x \cot y} = \tan y + \cot x$

34. $\dfrac{\cos x - \cos y}{\sin x + \sin y} + \dfrac{\sin x - \sin y}{\cos x + \cos y} = 0$

35. $\sqrt{\dfrac{1 + \sin \theta}{1 - \sin \theta}} = \dfrac{1 + \sin \theta}{|\cos \theta|}$

36. $\sqrt{\dfrac{1 - \cos \theta}{1 + \cos \theta}} = \dfrac{1 - \cos \theta}{|\sin \theta|}$

37. $\cos^2 \beta + \cos^2\left(\dfrac{\pi}{2} - \beta\right) = 1$

38. $\sec^2 y - \cot^2\left(\dfrac{\pi}{2} - y\right) = 1$

39. $\sin t \csc\left(\dfrac{\pi}{2} - t\right) = \tan t$

40. $\sec^2\left(\dfrac{\pi}{2} - x\right) - 1 = \cot^2 x$

In Exercises 41–52, use a graphing utility to determine whether the equation is an identity. If it is, confirm it algebraically.

41. $2 \sec^2 x - 2 \sec^2 x \sin^2 x - \sin^2 x - \cos^2 x = 1$

42. $\csc x(\csc x - \sin x) + \dfrac{\sin x - \cos x}{\sin x} + \cot x = \csc^2 x$

43. $2 + \cos^2 x - 3 \cos^4 x = \sin^2 x(3 + 2 \cos^2 x)$

44. $\tan^4 x + \tan^2 x - 3 = \sec^2 x(4 \tan^2 x - 3)$

45. $\csc^4 x - 2 \csc^2 x + 1 = \cot^4 x$

46. $(\sin^4 \beta - 2 \sin^2 \beta + 1) \cos \beta = \cos^5 \beta$

47. $\sec^4 \theta - \tan^4 \theta = 1 + 2 \tan^2 \theta$

48. $\csc^4 \theta - \cot^4 \theta = 2 \csc^2 \theta - 1$

49. $\dfrac{\cos x}{1 - \sin x} = \dfrac{1 - \sin x}{\cos x}$

50. $\dfrac{\cot \alpha}{\csc \alpha + 1} = \dfrac{\csc \alpha + 1}{\cot \alpha}$

51. $\dfrac{\tan^3 \alpha - 1}{\tan \alpha - 1} = \tan^2 \alpha + \tan \alpha + 1$

52. $\dfrac{\sin^3 \beta + \cos^3 \beta}{\sin \beta + \cos \beta} = 1 - \sin \beta \cos \beta$

In Exercises 53–56, use the cofunction identities to evaluate the expression without the aid of a calculator.

53. $\sin^2 25° + \sin^2 65°$

54. $\cos^2 55° + \cos^2 35°$

55. $\cos^2 20° + \cos^2 52° + \cos^2 38° + \cos^2 70°$

56. $\sin^2 12° + \sin^2 40° + \sin^2 50° + \sin^2 78°$

57. *Rate of Change*   The rate of change of the function

$$f(x) = \sin x + \csc x$$

with respect to change in the variable x is given by the expression $\cos x - \csc x \cot x$. Show that the expression for the rate of change can also be $-\cos x \cot^2 x$.

▶ **Model It**

58. *Shadow Length*   The length s of a shadow cast by a vertical gnomon (a device used to tell time) of height h when the angle of the sun above the horizon is θ (see figure) can be modeled by the equation

$$s = \frac{h \sin(90° - \theta)}{\sin \theta}.$$

(a) Verify that the equation above is equal to $h \cot \theta$.

 (b) Use a graphing utility to complete the table. Let $h = 5$ feet.

θ	10°	20°	30°	40°	50°
s					

θ	60°	70°	80°	90°
s				

▶ **Model It** *(continued)*

(c) Use your table from part (b) to determine the angles of the sun for which the length of the shadow is the greatest and the least.

(d) Based on your results from part (c), what time of day do you think it is when the angle of the sun above the horizon is 90°?

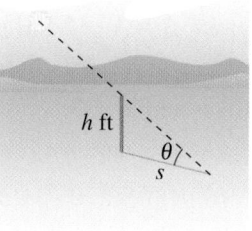

Synthesis

True or False?   In Exercises 59 and 60, determine whether the statement is true or false. Justify your answer.

59. The equation

$$\sin^2 \theta + \cos^2 \theta = 1 + \tan^2 \theta$$

is an identity, because $\sin^2(0) + \cos^2(0) = 1$ and $1 + \tan^2(0) = 1$.

60. The equation $1 + \tan^2 \theta = 1 + \cot^2 \theta$ is *not* an identity, because it is true that $1 + \tan^2(\pi/6) = 1\frac{1}{3}$, and $1 + \cot^2(\pi/6) = 4$.

Think About It   In Exercises 61 and 62, explain why the equation is *not* an identity and find one value of the variable for which the equation is not true.

61. $\sin \theta = \sqrt{1 - \cos^2 \theta}$ **62.** $\tan \theta = \sqrt{\sec^2 \theta - 1}$

Review

In Exercises 63–66, perform the operation and simplify.

63. $(2 + 3i) - \sqrt{-26}$

64. $(2 - 5i)^2$

65. $\sqrt{-16}\left(1 + \sqrt{-4}\right)$

66. $(3 + 2i)^3$

In Exercises 67–70, use the Quadratic Formula to solve the quadratic equation.

67. $x^2 - 6x + 12 = 0$

68. $x^2 + 5x + 7 = 0$

69. $3x^2 + 6x + 12 = 0$

70. $8x^2 - 4x + 3 = 0$

5.3 Solving Trigonometric Equations

▸ **What you should learn**

• How to use standard algebraic techniques to solve trigonometric equations

• How to solve trigonometric equations of quadratic type

• How to solve trigonometric equations involving multiple angles

• How to use inverse trigonometric functions to solve trigonometric equations

▸ **Why you should learn it**

You can use trigonometric equations to solve a variety of real-life problems. For instance, in Exercise 75 on page 379, you can solve a trigonometric equation to help answer questions about the unemployment rate in the United States.

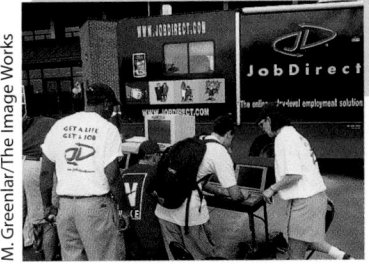

M. Greenlar/The Image Works

Introduction

To solve a trigonometric equation, use standard algebraic techniques such as collecting like terms and factoring. Your preliminary goal in solving a trigonometric equation is to isolate the trigonometric function involved in the equation. For example, to solve the equation $2 \sin x = 1$, divide each side by 2 to obtain

$$\sin x = \frac{1}{2}.$$

To solve for x, note in Figure 5.2 that the equation $\sin x = \frac{1}{2}$ has solutions $x = \pi/6$ and $x = 5\pi/6$ in the interval $[0, 2\pi)$. Moreover, because $\sin x$ has a period of 2π, there are infinitely many other solutions, which can be written as

$$x = \frac{\pi}{6} + 2n\pi \qquad \text{and} \qquad x = \frac{5\pi}{6} + 2n\pi \qquad \text{\small General solution}$$

where n is an integer, as shown in Figure 5.2.

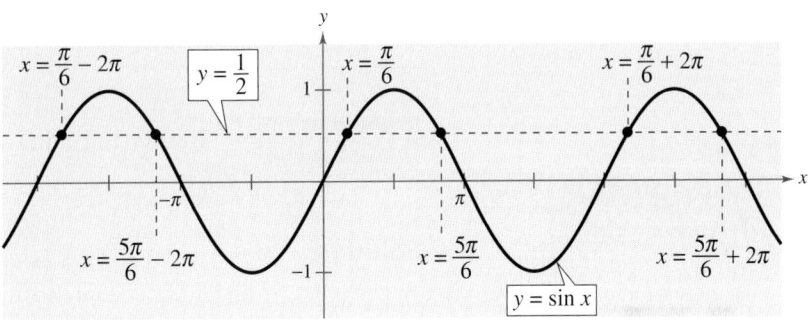

FIGURE 5.2

Another way to show that the equation $\sin x = \frac{1}{2}$ has infinitely many solutions is indicated in Figure 5.3. Any angles that are coterminal with $\pi/6$ or $5\pi/6$ will also be solutions of the equation.

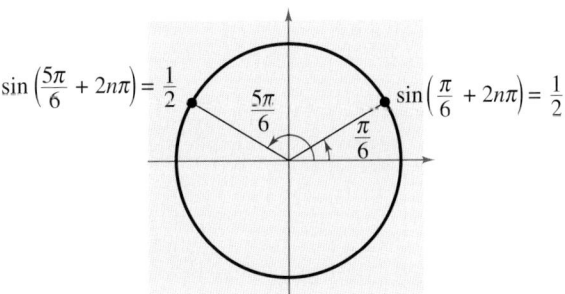

FIGURE 5.3

Encourage your students to give exact answers (rather than decimal approximations using a calculator) when solving these trigonometric equations.

Example 1 ▶ **Collecting Like Terms**

Solve $\sin x + \sqrt{2} = -\sin x$.

Solution

Begin by rewriting the equation so that $\sin x$ is isolated on one side of the equation.

$$\sin x + \sqrt{2} = -\sin x \qquad \text{Write original equation.}$$

$$\sin x + \sin x + \sqrt{2} = 0 \qquad \text{Add } \sin x \text{ to each side.}$$

$$\sin x + \sin x = -\sqrt{2} \qquad \text{Subtract } \sqrt{2} \text{ from each side.}$$

$$2 \sin x = -\sqrt{2} \qquad \text{Combine like terms.}$$

$$\sin x = -\frac{\sqrt{2}}{2} \qquad \text{Divide each side by 2.}$$

Because $\sin x$ has a period of 2π, first find all solutions in the interval $[0, 2\pi)$. These solutions are $x = 5\pi/4$ and $x = 7\pi/4$. Finally, add $2n\pi$ to each of these solutions to get the general form

$$x = \frac{5\pi}{4} + 2n\pi \qquad \text{and} \qquad x = \frac{7\pi}{4} + 2n\pi \qquad \text{General solution}$$

where n is an integer.

Example 2 ▶ **Extracting Square Roots**

Solve $3 \tan^2 x - 1 = 0$.

Solution

Begin by rewriting the equation so that $\tan x$ is isolated on one side of the equation.

$$3 \tan^2 x - 1 = 0 \qquad \text{Write original equation.}$$

$$3 \tan^2 x = 1 \qquad \text{Add 1 to each side.}$$

$$\tan^2 x = \frac{1}{3} \qquad \text{Divide each side by 3.}$$

$$\tan x = \pm \frac{1}{\sqrt{3}} \qquad \text{Extract square roots.}$$

Because $\tan x$ has a period of π, first find all solutions in the interval $[0, \pi)$. These solutions are $x = \pi/6$ and $x = 5\pi/6$. Finally, add $n\pi$ to each of these solutions to get the general form

$$x = \frac{\pi}{6} + n\pi \qquad \text{and} \qquad x = \frac{5\pi}{6} + n\pi \qquad \text{General solution}$$

where n is an integer.

Technology

The solutions in Examples 1 and 2 are obtained analytically. You can use a graphing utility to confirm the solutions graphically. For instance, to confirm the solutions found in Example 2, graph

$$y = 3 \tan^2 x - 1$$

as shown below. Then use the *zero* or *root* feature or the *zoom* and *trace* features to approximate the x-intercepts.

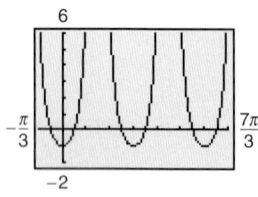

The equations in Examples 1 and 2 involved only one trigonometric function. When two or more functions occur in the same equation, collect all terms on one side and try to separate the functions by factoring or by using appropriate identities. This may produce factors that yield no solutions, as illustrated in Example 3.

Example 3 ▶ **Factoring**

Solve $\cot x \cos^2 x = 2 \cot x$.

Solution

Begin by rewriting the equation so that all terms are collected on one side of the equation.

$$\cot x \cos^2 x = 2 \cot x \qquad \text{Write original equation.}$$

$$\cot x \cos^2 x - 2 \cot x = 0 \qquad \text{Subtract } 2 \cot x \text{ from each side.}$$

$$\cot x (\cos^2 x - 2) = 0 \qquad \text{Factor.}$$

By setting each of these factors equal to zero, you obtain

$$\cot x = 0 \qquad \text{and} \qquad \cos^2 x - 2 = 0$$

$$x = \frac{\pi}{2} \qquad\qquad \cos^2 x = 2$$

$$\cos x = \pm \sqrt{2}.$$

The equation $\cot x = 0$ has the solution $x = \pi/2$. No solution is obtained for $\cos x = \pm \sqrt{2}$ because $\pm \sqrt{2}$ are outside the range of the cosine function. Because $\cot x$ has a period of π, the general form of the solution is obtained by adding multiples of π to $x = \pi/2$, to get

$$x = \frac{\pi}{2} + n\pi \qquad \text{General solution}$$

where n is an integer. You can confirm this graphically by sketching the graph of $y = \cot x \cos^2 x - 2 \cot x$, as shown in Figure 5.4.

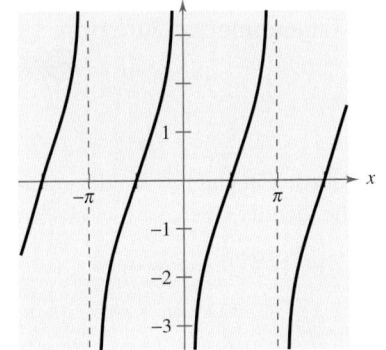

FIGURE 5.4

In Example 3, do not make the mistake of dividing each side of the equation by $\cot x$. If you do this, you lose the solutions. Can you see why?

Equations of Quadratic Type

Many trigonometric equations are of quadratic type. Here are a couple of examples.

Quadratic in sin x	*Quadratic in sec x*
$2 \sin^2 x - \sin x - 1 = 0$	$\sec^2 x - 3 \sec x - 2 = 0$
$2(\sin x)^2 - \sin x - 1 = 0$	$(\sec x)^2 - 3(\sec x) - 2 = 0$

To solve equations of this type, factor the quadratic or, if this is not possible, use the Quadratic Formula.

Example 4 ▶ **Factoring an Equation of Quadratic Type**

Find all solutions of $2 \sin^2 x - \sin x - 1 = 0$ in the interval $[0, 2\pi)$.

Solution

Begin by treating the equation as a quadratic in $\sin x$ and factoring.

$$(2 \sin x + 1)(\sin x - 1) = 0 \qquad \text{Factor.}$$

Setting each factor equal to zero, you can find the solutions in the interval $[0, 2\pi)$.

$$2 \sin x + 1 = 0 \qquad \text{and} \qquad \sin x - 1 = 0$$

$$\sin x = -\frac{1}{2} \qquad\qquad\qquad \sin x = 1$$

$$x = \frac{7\pi}{6}, \frac{11\pi}{6} \qquad\qquad\qquad x = \frac{\pi}{2}$$

When working with an equation of quadratic type, be sure that the equation involves a *single* trigonometric function, as shown in the next example.

Example 5 ▶ **Rewriting with a Single Trigonometric Function**

Solve $2 \sin^2 x + 3 \cos x - 3 = 0$.

Solution

The algebraic model can be difficult for students to visualize. Encourage them to write or visualize the algebraic model, rewrite the corresponding trigonometric equation in terms of a single trigonometric function, and then solve for x. (See Exercises 43 and 44.)

This equation contains both sine and cosine functions. You can rewrite the equation so that it has only cosine functions by using the identity $\sin^2 x = 1 - \cos^2 x$.

$$2 \sin^2 x + 3 \cos x - 3 = 0 \qquad \text{Write original equation.}$$

$$2(1 - \cos^2 x) + 3 \cos x - 3 = 0 \qquad \text{Pythagorean identity}$$

$$2 \cos^2 x - 3 \cos x + 1 = 0 \qquad \text{Multiply each side by } -1.$$

$$(2 \cos x - 1)(\cos x - 1) = 0 \qquad \text{Factor.}$$

By setting each factor equal to zero, you can find the solutions in the interval $[0, 2\pi)$.

$$2 \cos x - 1 = 0 \qquad \text{and} \qquad \cos x - 1 = 0$$

$$\cos x = \frac{1}{2} \qquad\qquad\qquad \cos x = 1$$

$$\qquad\qquad\qquad\qquad\qquad x = 0$$

$$x = \frac{\pi}{3}, \frac{5\pi}{3}$$

Because $\cos x$ has a period of 2π, the general form of the solution is obtained by adding multiples of 2π to get

$$x = 2n\pi, \quad x = \frac{\pi}{3} + 2n\pi, \quad x = \frac{5\pi}{3} + 2n\pi \qquad \text{General solution}$$

where n is an integer.

Sometimes you must square each side of an equation to obtain a quadratic, as demonstrated in the next example. Because this procedure can introduce extraneous solutions, you should check any solutions in the original equation to see whether they are valid or extraneous.

Example 6 ▶ Squaring and Converting to Quadratic Type

Find all solutions of $\cos x + 1 = \sin x$ in the interval $[0, 2\pi)$.

Solution

It is not clear how to rewrite this equation in terms of a single trigonometric function. See what happens when you square each side of the equation.

$$\cos x + 1 = \sin x \qquad \text{Write original equation.}$$

$$\cos^2 x + 2\cos x + 1 = \sin^2 x \qquad \text{Square each side.}$$

$$\cos^2 x + 2\cos x + 1 = 1 - \cos^2 x \qquad \text{Pythagorean identity}$$

$$\cos^2 x + \cos^2 x + 2\cos x + 1 - 1 = 0 \qquad \text{Rewrite equation.}$$

$$2\cos^2 x + 2\cos x = 0 \qquad \text{Combine like terms.}$$

$$2\cos x(\cos x + 1) = 0 \qquad \text{Factor.}$$

Setting each factor equal to zero produces

$$2\cos x = 0 \qquad \text{and} \qquad \cos x + 1 = 0$$

$$\cos x = 0 \qquad\qquad\qquad \cos x = -1$$

$$x = \frac{\pi}{2}, \frac{3\pi}{2} \qquad\qquad\qquad x = \pi.$$

Because you squared the original equation, check for extraneous solutions.

Check for $x = \pi/2$

$$\cos \frac{\pi}{2} + 1 \overset{?}{=} \sin \frac{\pi}{2} \qquad \text{Substitute } \pi/2 \text{ for } x.$$

$$0 + 1 = 1 \qquad \text{Solution checks. } \checkmark$$

Check for $x = 3\pi/2$

$$\cos \frac{3\pi}{2} + 1 \overset{?}{=} \sin \frac{3\pi}{2} \qquad \text{Substitute } 3\pi/2 \text{ for } x.$$

$$0 + 1 \neq -1 \qquad \text{Solution does not check.}$$

Check for $x = \pi$

$$\cos \pi + 1 \overset{?}{=} \sin \pi \qquad \text{Substitute } \pi \text{ for } x.$$

$$-1 + 1 = 0 \qquad \text{Solution checks. } \checkmark$$

Of the three possible solutions, $x = 3\pi/2$ is extraneous. So, in the interval $[0, 2\pi)$, the only two solutions are $x = \pi/2$ and $x = \pi$.

STUDY TIP

You square each side of the equation in Example 6 because the squares of the sine and cosine functions are related by a Pythagorean identity. The same is true for the squares of the secant and tangent functions and the cosecant and cotangent functions.

◀ **Exploration** ▶

Use a graphing utility to confirm the solutions found in Example 6 in two different ways. Do both methods produce the same x-values? Which method do you prefer? Why?

1. Graph both sides of the equation and find the x-coordinates of the points at which the graphs intersect.

   Left side: $y = \cos x + 1$

   Right side: $y = \sin x$

2. Graph the equation

   $y = \cos x + 1 - \sin x$

   and find the x-intercepts of the graph.

Functions Involving Multiple Angles

The next two examples involve trigonometric functions of multiple angles of the forms sin ku and cos ku. To solve equations of these forms, first solve the equation for ku, then divide your result by k.

Example 7 ▶ **Functions of Multiple Angles**

Find all solutions of $2 \cos 3t - 1 = 0$.

Solution

$2 \cos 3t - 1 = 0$	Write original equation.
$2 \cos 3t = 1$	Add 1 to each side.
$\cos 3t = \dfrac{1}{2}$	Divide each side by 2.

In the interval $[0, 2\pi)$, you know that $3t = \pi/3$ and $3t = 5\pi/3$ are the only solutions, so, in general, you have

$$3t = \frac{\pi}{3} + 2n\pi \quad \text{and} \quad 3t = \frac{5\pi}{3} + 2n\pi.$$

Dividing these results by 3, you obtain the general solution

$$t = \frac{\pi}{9} + \frac{2n\pi}{3} \quad \text{and} \quad t = \frac{5\pi}{9} + \frac{2n\pi}{3} \qquad \text{General solution}$$

where n is an integer.

Example 8 ▶ **Functions of Multiple Angles**

Find all solutions of $3 \tan(x/2) + 3 = 0$.

Solution

$3 \tan \dfrac{x}{2} + 3 = 0$	Write original equation.
$3 \tan \dfrac{x}{2} = -3$	Subtract 3 from each side.
$\tan \dfrac{x}{2} = -1$	Divide each side by 3.

In the interval $[0, \pi)$, you know that $x/2 = 3\pi/4$ is the only solution, so, in general, you have

$$\frac{x}{2} = \frac{3\pi}{4} + n\pi.$$

Multiplying this result by 2, you obtain the general solution

$$x = \frac{3\pi}{2} + 2n\pi \qquad \text{General solution}$$

where n is an integer.

Using Inverse Functions

In the next example, you will see how inverse trigonometric functions can be used to solve an equation.

Example 9 ▶ Using Inverse Functions

Find all solutions of $\sec^2 x - 2 \tan x = 4$.

Solution

$\sec^2 x - 2 \tan x = 4$	Write original equation.
$1 + \tan^2 x - 2 \tan x - 4 = 0$	Pythagorean identity
$\tan^2 x - 2 \tan x - 3 = 0$	Combine like terms.
$(\tan x - 3)(\tan x + 1) = 0$	Factor.

Setting each factor equal to zero, you obtain two solutions in the interval $(-\pi/2, \pi/2)$. [Recall that the range of the inverse tangent function is $(-\pi/2, \pi/2)$.]

$$\tan x - 3 = 0 \qquad \text{and} \qquad \tan x + 1 = 0$$

$$\tan x = 3 \qquad\qquad\qquad \tan x = -1$$

$$x = \arctan 3 \qquad\qquad\qquad x = -\frac{\pi}{4}$$

Finally, because $\tan x$ has a period of π, you obtain the general solution by adding multiples of π

$$x = \arctan 3 + n\pi \qquad \text{and} \qquad x = -\frac{\pi}{4} + n\pi \qquad \text{General solution}$$

where n is an integer. You can use a calculator to approximate the value of $\arctan 3$.

Activities

1. Find all solutions of the equation without using a calculator.
   $\tan^2 x = 1$
   Answer: $x = \dfrac{\pi}{4} + n\pi, \dfrac{3\pi}{4} + n\pi$

2. Solve for x, $0 \le x < 2\pi$, without using a calculator.
   $\sin^2 3x - 2 \sin 3x + 1 = 0$
   Answer: $x = \dfrac{\pi}{6}, \dfrac{5\pi}{6}, \dfrac{3\pi}{2}$

3. Solve for x, $0 \le x < 2\pi$.
   $6 \cos^2 x - \cos x - 2 = 0$
   Answer: $x = 0.841, \dfrac{2\pi}{3}, \dfrac{4\pi}{3}, 5.442$

Writing ABOUT MATHEMATICS

Equations with No Solutions   One of the following equations has solutions and the other two do not. Which two equations do not have solutions?

a. $\sin^2 x - 5 \sin x + 6 = 0$

b. $\sin^2 x - 4 \sin x + 6 = 0$

c. $\sin^2 x - 5 \sin x - 6 = 0$

Find conditions involving the constants b and c that will guarantee that the equation

$$\sin^2 x + b \sin x + c = 0$$

has at least one solution on some interval of length 2π.

5.3 Exercises

In Exercises 1–6, verify that the x-values are solutions of the equation.

1. $2 \cos x - 1 = 0$

   (a) $x = \dfrac{\pi}{3}$ (b) $x = \dfrac{5\pi}{3}$

2. $\sec x - 2 = 0$

   (a) $x = \dfrac{\pi}{3}$ (b) $x = \dfrac{5\pi}{3}$

3. $3 \tan^2 2x - 1 = 0$

   (a) $x = \dfrac{\pi}{12}$ (b) $x = \dfrac{5\pi}{12}$

4. $2 \cos^2 4x - 1 = 0$

   (a) $x = \dfrac{\pi}{16}$ (b) $x = \dfrac{3\pi}{16}$

5. $2 \sin^2 x - \sin x - 1 = 0$

   (a) $x = \dfrac{\pi}{2}$ (b) $x = \dfrac{7\pi}{6}$

6. $\csc^4 x - 4 \csc^2 x = 0$

   (a) $x = \dfrac{\pi}{6}$ (b) $x = \dfrac{5\pi}{6}$

In Exercises 7–20, solve the equation.

7. $2 \cos x + 1 = 0$ **8.** $2 \sin x + 1 = 0$

9. $\sqrt{3} \csc x - 2 = 0$ **10.** $\tan x + \sqrt{3} = 0$

11. $3 \sec^2 x - 4 = 0$ **12.** $3 \cot^2 x - 1 = 0$

13. $\sin x(\sin x + 1) = 0$

14. $(3 \tan^2 x - 1)(\tan^2 x - 3) = 0$

15. $4 \cos^2 x - 1 = 0$ **16.** $\sin^2 x = 3 \cos^2 x$

17. $2 \sin^2 2x = 1$ **18.** $\tan^2 3x = 3$

19. $\tan 3x(\tan x - 1) = 0$

20. $\cos 2x(2 \cos x + 1) = 0$

In Exercises 21–32, find all solutions of the equation in the interval [0, 2π).

21. $\cos^3 x = \cos x$ **22.** $\sec^2 x - 1 = 0$

23. $3 \tan^3 x = \tan x$ **24.** $2 \sin^2 x = 2 + \cos x$

25. $\sec^2 x - \sec x = 2$ **26.** $\sec x \csc x = 2 \csc x$

27. $2 \sin x + \csc x = 0$ **28.** $\sec x + \tan x = 1$

29. $2 \cos^2 x + \cos x - 1 = 0$

30. $2 \sin^2 x + 3 \sin x + 1 = 0$

31. $2 \sec^2 x + \tan^2 x - 3 = 0$

32. $\cos x + \sin x \tan x = 2$

In Exercises 33–38, find all solutions of the equation.

33. $\cos 2x = \dfrac{1}{2}$ **34.** $\sin 2x = -\dfrac{\sqrt{3}}{2}$

35. $\tan 3x = 1$ **36.** $\sec 4x = 2$

37. $\cos \dfrac{x}{2} = \dfrac{\sqrt{2}}{2}$ **38.** $\sin \dfrac{x}{2} = -\dfrac{\sqrt{3}}{2}$

In Exercises 39–42, find the x-intercepts of the graph.

39. $y = \sin \dfrac{\pi x}{2} + 1$ **40.** $y = \sin \pi x + \cos \pi x$

 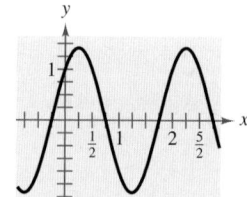

41. $y = \tan^2\left(\dfrac{\pi x}{6}\right) - 3$ **42.** $y = \sec^4\left(\dfrac{\pi x}{8}\right) - 4$

 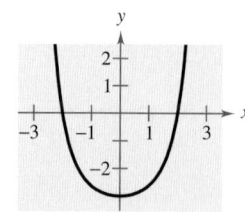

In Exercises 43 and 44, solve both equations. How do the solutions of the algebraic equation compare with the solutions of the trigonometric equation?

43. $6y^2 - 13y + 6 = 0$

    $6 \cos^2 x - 13 \cos x + 6 = 0$

44. $y^2 + y - 20 = 0$

    $\sin^2 x + \sin x - 20 = 0$

In Exercises 45–54, use a graphing utility to approximate the solutions of the equation in the interval [0, 2π).

45. $2 \sin x + \cos x = 0$

46. $4 \sin^3 x + 2 \sin^2 x - 2 \sin x - 1 = 0$

47. $\dfrac{1 + \sin x}{\cos x} + \dfrac{\cos x}{1 + \sin x} = 4$

48. $\dfrac{\cos x \cot x}{1 - \sin x} = 3$

49. $x \tan x - 1 = 0$

50. $x \cos x - 1 = 0$

51. $\sec^2 x + 0.5 \tan x - 1 = 0$

52. $\csc^2 x + 0.5 \cot x - 5 = 0$

53. $2 \tan^2 x + 7 \tan x - 15 = 0$

54. $6 \sin^2 x - 7 \sin x + 2 = 0$

 In Exercises 55–58, use the Quadratic Formula to solve the equation in the interval $[0, 2\pi)$. Then use a graphing utility to approximate the angle x.

55. $12 \sin^2 x - 13 \sin x + 3 = 0$

56. $3 \tan^2 x + 4 \tan x - 4 = 0$

57. $\tan^2 x + 3 \tan x + 1 = 0$

58. $4 \cos^2 x - 4 \cos x - 1 = 0$

In Exercises 59–62, use inverse functions where needed to find all solutions of the equation in the interval $[0, 2\pi)$.

59. $\tan^2 x - 6 \tan x + 5 = 0$

60. $\sec^2 x + \tan x - 3 = 0$

61. $2 \cos^2 x - 5 \cos x + 2 = 0$

62. $2 \sin^2 x - 7 \sin x + 3 = 0$

 In Exercises 63 and 64, (a) use a graphing utility to graph the function and approximate the maximum and minimum points on the graph in the interval $[0, 2\pi)$, and (b) solve the trigonometric equation and demonstrate that its solutions are the x-coordinates of the maximum and minimum points of f. (Calculus is required to find the trigonometric equation.)

Function	Trigonometric Equation
63. $f(x) = \sin x + \cos x$	$\cos x - \sin x = 0$
64. $f(x) = 2 \sin x + \cos 2x$	$2 \cos x - 4 \sin x \cos x = 0$

Fixed Point **In Exercises 65 and 66, find the smallest positive fixed point of the function f. [A fixed point of a function f is a real number c such that $f(c) = c$.]**

65. $f(x) = \tan \dfrac{\pi x}{4}$

66. $f(x) = \cos x$

67. *Graphical Reasoning* Consider the function

$$f(x) = \cos \frac{1}{x}$$

and its graph shown in the figure.

(a) What is the domain of the function?

(b) Identify any symmetry or asymptotes of the graph.

(c) Describe the behavior of the function as $x \to 0$.

(d) How many solutions does the equation

$$\cos \frac{1}{x} = 0$$

have in the interval $[-1, 1]$?

(e) Does the equation $\cos(1/x) = 0$ have a greatest solution? If so, approximate the solution. If not, explain why.

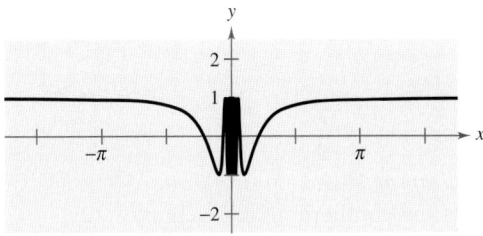

FIGURE FOR 67

68. *Graphical Reasoning* Consider the function

$$f(x) = \frac{\sin x}{x}$$

and its graph shown in the figure.

(a) What is the domain of the function?

(b) Identify any symmetry or asymptotes of the graph.

(c) Describe the behavior of the function as $x \to 0$.

(d) How many solutions does the equation

$$\frac{\sin x}{x} = 0$$

have in the interval $[-8, 8]$? Find the solutions.

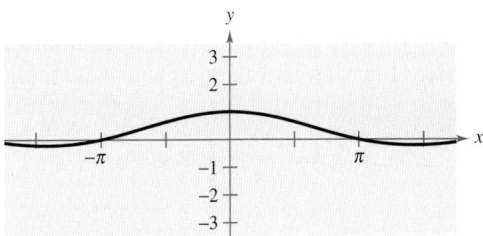

69. Harmonic Motion A weight is oscillating on the end of a spring (see figure). The position of the weight relative to the point of equilibrium is

$$y = \frac{1}{12}(\cos 8t - 3\sin 8t)$$

where y is the displacement in meters and t is the time in seconds. Find the times when the weight is at the point of equilibrium ($y = 0$) for $0 \le t \le 1$.

70. Damped Harmonic Motion The displacement from equilibrium of a weight oscillating on the end of a spring is

$$y = 1.56e^{-0.22t}\cos 4.9t$$

where y is the displacement in feet and t is the time in seconds. Use a graphing utility to graph the displacement function for $0 \le t \le 10$. Find the time beyond which the displacement does not exceed 1 foot from equilibrium.

71. Sales The monthly sales (in thousands of units) of a seasonal product are approximated by

$$S = 74.50 + 43.75 \sin\frac{\pi t}{6}$$

where t is the time in months, with $t = 1$ corresponding to January. Determine the months when sales exceed 100,000 units.

72. Projectile Motion A batted baseball leaves the bat at an angle of θ with the horizontal and an initial velocity of $v_0 = 100$ feet per second. The ball is caught by an outfielder 300 feet from home plate (see figure). Find θ if the range r of a projectile is

$$r = \frac{1}{32}v_0^2 \sin 2\theta.$$

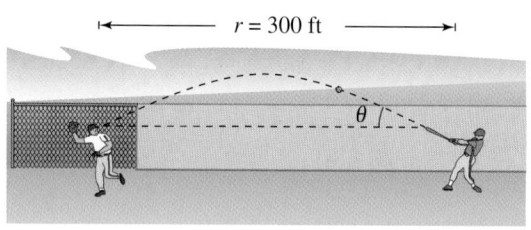

Not drawn to scale

FIGURE FOR **72**

73. Projectile Motion A sharpshooter intends to hit a target at a distance of 1000 yards with a gun that has a muzzle velocity of 1200 feet per second (see figure). Neglecting air resistance, determine the gun's minimum angle of elevation θ if the range r is

$$r = \frac{1}{32}v_0^2 \sin 2\theta.$$

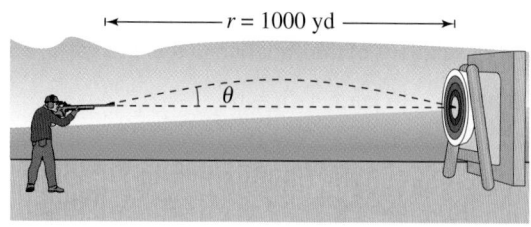

Not drawn to scale

74. Geometry The area of a rectangle (see figure) inscribed in one arc of the graph of $y = \cos x$ is

$$A = 2x \cos x, \qquad 0 < x < \frac{\pi}{2}.$$

 (a) Use a graphing utility to graph the area function, and approximate the area of the largest inscribed rectangle.

(b) Determine the values of x for which $A \ge 1$.

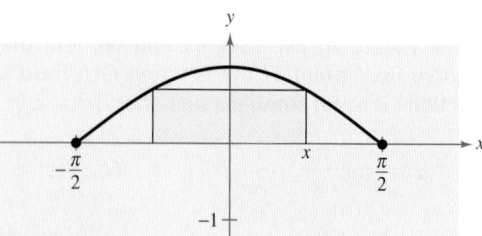

▶ Model It

75. *Data Analysis*   The table shows the unemployment rate r for the years 1990 through 2001 in the United States. The time t is measured in years, with $t = 0$ corresponding to 1990. (Source: U.S. Bureau of Labor Statistics)

Time, t	Rate, r	Time, t	Rate, r
0	5.6	6	5.4
1	6.8	7	4.9
2	7.5	8	4.5
3	6.9	9	4.2
4	6.1	10	4.0
5	5.6	11	4.8

(a) Create a scatter plot of the data.

(b) Which of the following models best represents the data? Explain your reasoning.

   (1) $r = 1.39 \sin(0.48t + 0.42) + 5.51$

   (2) $r = 1.39 \sin(0.48t - 0.01) + 5.51$

   (3) $r = \sin(0.10t + 5.61) + 4.80$

   (4) $r = 896 \sin(0.57t - 2.05) + 6.48$

(c) What term in the model gives the average unemployment rate? What is the rate?

(d) Economists study the lengths of business cycles such as unemployment rates. Based on this short span of time, use the model to give the length of this cycle.

(e) Use the model to estimate the next time the unemployment rate will be 6.5% or more.

76. *Quadratic Approximation*   Consider the function

$f(x) = 3 \sin(0.6x - 2)$.

(a) Approximate the zero of the function in the interval $[0, 6]$.

(b) A quadratic approximation agreeing with f at $x = 5$ is $g(x) = -0.45x^2 + 5.52x - 13.70$. Use a graphing utility to graph f and g in the same viewing window. Describe the result.

(c) Use the Quadratic Formula to find the zeros of g. Compare the zero in the interval $[0, 6]$ with the result of part (a).

Synthesis

True or False?   In Exercises 77 and 78, determine whether the statement is true or false. Justify your answer.

77. The equation $2 \sin 4t - 1 = 0$ has four times the number of solutions in the interval $[0, 2\pi)$ as the equation $2 \sin t - 1 = 0$.

78. If you correctly solve a trigonometric equation down to the statement $\sin x = 3.4$, then you can finish solving the equation by using an inverse function.

In Exercises 79 and 80, use the graph to approximate the number of points of intersection of the graphs of y_1 and y_2.

79. $y_1 = 2 \sin x$

$y_2 = 3x + 1$

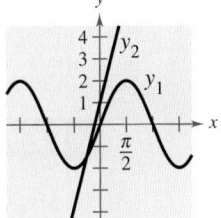

80. $y_1 = 2 \sin x$

$y_2 = \frac{1}{2}x + 1$

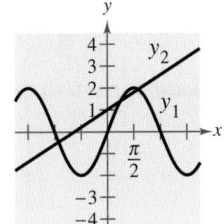

Review

In Exercises 81 and 82, solve triangle ABC by finding all missing angle measures and side lengths.

81.

82.

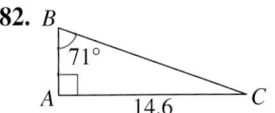

In Exercises 83–86, use reference angles to find the sine, cosine, and tangent of an angle with the given measure.

83. $390°$

84. $570°$

85. $-1845°$

86. $-1410°$

87. *Angle of Depression*   Find the angle of depression from the top of a lighthouse 250 feet above water level to the water line of a ship 2 miles offshore.

88. *Height*   From a point 100 feet in front of the public library, the angles of elevation to the base of the flagpole and the top of the pole are $28°$ and $39° \, 45'$, respectively. The flagpole is mounted on the front of the library's roof. Find the height of the flagpole.

5.4 Sum and Difference Formulas

► **What you should learn**

• How to use sum and difference formulas to evaluate trigonometric functions, verify identities, and solve trigonometric equations

► **Why you should learn it**

You can use identities to rewrite trigonometric expressions. For instance, in Exercise 75 on page 385, you can use an identity to rewrite a trigonometric expression in a form that helps you analyze a harmonic motion equation.

Richard Megna/Fundamental Photographs

Using Sum and Difference Formulas

In this and the following section, you will study the uses of several trigonometric identities and formulas.

Sum and Difference Formulas

$$\sin(u + v) = \sin u \cos v + \cos u \sin v$$

$$\sin(u - v) = \sin u \cos v - \cos u \sin v$$

$$\cos(u + v) = \cos u \cos v - \sin u \sin v$$

$$\cos(u - v) = \cos u \cos v + \sin u \sin v$$

$$\tan(u + v) = \frac{\tan u + \tan v}{1 - \tan u \tan v}$$

$$\tan(u - v) = \frac{\tan u - \tan v}{1 + \tan u \tan v}$$

For a proof of the sum and difference formulas, see Proofs in Mathematics on page 403.

> **Exploration**
>
> Use a graphing utility to graph $y_1 = \cos(x + 2)$ and $y_2 = \cos x + \cos 2$ in the same viewing window. What can you conclude about the graphs? Is it true that $\cos(x + 2) = \cos x + \cos 2$?
>   Use a graphing utility to graph $y_1 = \sin(x + 4)$ and $y_2 = \sin x + \sin 4$ in the same viewing window. What can you conclude about the graphs? Is it true that $\sin(x + 4) = \sin x + \sin 4$?

Examples 1 and 2 show how **sum and difference formulas** can be used to find exact values of trigonometric functions involving sums or differences of special angles.

Example 1 ► **Evaluating a Trigonometric Function**

Find the exact value of $\cos 75°$.

Solution

To find the *exact* value of $\cos 75°$, use the fact that $75° = 30° + 45°$. Consequently, the formula for $\cos(u + v)$ yields

$$\cos 75° = \cos(30° + 45°)$$

$$= \cos 30° \cos 45° - \sin 30° \sin 45°$$

$$= \frac{\sqrt{3}}{2}\left(\frac{\sqrt{2}}{2}\right) - \frac{1}{2}\left(\frac{\sqrt{2}}{2}\right) = \frac{\sqrt{6} - \sqrt{2}}{4}.$$

Try checking this result on your calculator. You will find that $\cos 75° \approx 0.259$.

Historical Note
Hipparchus, considered the most eminent of Greek astronomers, was born about 160 B.C. in Nicaea. He was credited with the invention of trigonometry. He also derived the sum and difference formulas for $\sin(A \pm B)$ and $\cos(A \pm B)$.

Example 2 ▶ **Evaluating a Trigonometric Expression**

Find the exact value of $\sin \dfrac{\pi}{12}$.

Solution

Using the fact that

$$\frac{\pi}{12} = \frac{\pi}{3} - \frac{\pi}{4}$$

together with the formula for $\sin(u - v)$, you obtain

$$\sin \frac{\pi}{12} = \sin\left(\frac{\pi}{3} - \frac{\pi}{4}\right)$$

$$= \sin \frac{\pi}{3} \cos \frac{\pi}{4} - \cos \frac{\pi}{3} \sin \frac{\pi}{4}$$

$$= \frac{\sqrt{3}}{2}\left(\frac{\sqrt{2}}{2}\right) - \frac{1}{2}\left(\frac{\sqrt{2}}{2}\right)$$

$$= \frac{\sqrt{6} - \sqrt{2}}{4}.$$

Example 3 ▶ **Evaluating a Trigonometric Expression**

Find the exact value of $\sin 42° \cos 12° - \cos 42° \sin 12°$.

Solution

Recognizing that this expression fits the formula for $\sin(u - v)$, you can write

$$\sin 42° \cos 12° - \cos 42° \sin 12° = \sin(42° - 12°)$$

$$= \sin 30°$$

$$= \frac{1}{2}.$$

Example 4 ▶ **An Application of a Sum Formula**

Write $\cos(\arctan 1 + \arccos x)$ as an algebraic expression.

Solution

This expression fits the formula for $\cos(u + v)$. Angles $u = \arctan 1$ and $v = \arccos x$ are shown in Figure 5.5. So

$$\cos(u + v) = \cos(\arctan 1)\cos(\arccos x) - \sin(\arctan 1)\sin(\arccos x)$$

$$= \frac{1}{\sqrt{2}} \cdot x - \frac{1}{\sqrt{2}} \cdot \sqrt{1 - x^2}$$

$$= \frac{x - \sqrt{1 - x^2}}{\sqrt{2}}.$$

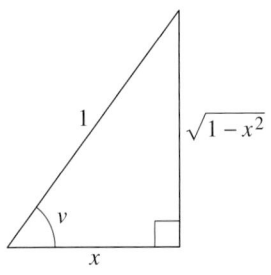

FIGURE 5.5

Example 5 shows how to use a difference formula to prove the cofunction identity

$$\cos\left(\frac{\pi}{2} - x\right) = \sin x.$$

Example 5 ▶ **Proving a Cofunction Identity**

Prove the cofunction identity $\cos\left(\frac{\pi}{2} - x\right) = \sin x.$

Solution

Using the formula for $\cos(u - v)$, you have

$$\cos\left(\frac{\pi}{2} - x\right) = \cos\frac{\pi}{2}\cos x + \sin\frac{\pi}{2}\sin x$$

$$= (0)(\cos x) + (1)(\sin x) = \sin x.$$

Sum and difference formulas can be used to derive **reduction formulas** involving expressions such as

$$\sin\left(\theta + \frac{n\pi}{2}\right) \quad \text{and} \quad \cos\left(\theta + \frac{n\pi}{2}\right), \quad \text{where } n \text{ is an integer.}$$

Example 6 ▶ **Deriving Reduction Formulas**

Simplify each expression.

a. $\cos\left(\theta - \frac{3\pi}{2}\right)$ **b.** $\tan(\theta + 3\pi)$

Solution

a. Using the formula for $\cos(u - v)$, you have

$$\cos\left(\theta - \frac{3\pi}{2}\right) = \cos\theta\cos\frac{3\pi}{2} + \sin\theta\sin\frac{3\pi}{2}$$

$$= (\cos\theta)(0) + (\sin\theta)(-1)$$

$$= -\sin\theta.$$

b. Using the formula for $\tan(u + v)$, you have

$$\tan(\theta + 3\pi) = \frac{\tan\theta + \tan 3\pi}{1 - \tan\theta\tan 3\pi}$$

$$= \frac{\tan\theta + 0}{1 - (\tan\theta)(0)}$$

$$= \tan\theta.$$

The next example was taken from calculus. It is used to derive the derivative of the sine function.

Activities

1. Use the sum and difference formulas to find the exact value of $\cos 50°$.

    Answer: $\dfrac{\sqrt{6} + \sqrt{2}}{4}$

2. Rewrite the expression using the sum and difference formulas.

    $\dfrac{\tan 40° + \tan 10°}{1 - \tan 40° \tan 10°}$

    Answer: $\tan(40° + 10°) = \tan 50°$

3. Verify the identity

    $\sin\left(\dfrac{\pi}{2} - \theta\right) = \cos\theta.$

    Answer:

    $\sin\left(\dfrac{\pi}{2} - \theta\right) = \sin\dfrac{\pi}{2}\cos\theta - \cos\dfrac{\pi}{2}\sin\theta$

    $= (1)\cos\theta - (0)\sin\theta$

    $= \cos\theta$

Example 7 ▶ An Application from Calculus

Verify that

$$\frac{\sin(x + h) - \sin x}{h} = (\cos x)\left(\frac{\sin h}{h}\right) - (\sin x)\left(\frac{1 - \cos h}{h}\right)$$

where $h \neq 0$.

Solution
Using the formula for $\sin(u + v)$, you have

$$\frac{\sin(x + h) - \sin x}{h} = \frac{\sin x \cos h + \cos x \sin h - \sin x}{h}$$

$$= \frac{\cos x \sin h - \sin x(1 - \cos h)}{h}$$

$$= (\cos x)\left(\frac{\sin h}{h}\right) - (\sin x)\left(\frac{1 - \cos h}{h}\right).$$

Example 8 ▶ Solving a Trigonometric Equation

Find all solutions of

$$\sin\left(x + \frac{\pi}{4}\right) + \sin\left(x - \frac{\pi}{4}\right) = -1$$

in the interval $[0, 2\pi)$.

Solution
Using sum and difference formulas, rewrite the equation as

$$\sin x \cos \frac{\pi}{4} + \cos x \sin \frac{\pi}{4} + \sin x \cos \frac{\pi}{4} - \cos x \sin \frac{\pi}{4} = -1$$

$$2 \sin x \cos \frac{\pi}{4} = -1$$

$$2(\sin x)\left(\frac{\sqrt{2}}{2}\right) = -1$$

$$\sin x = -\frac{1}{\sqrt{2}}$$

$$\sin x = -\frac{\sqrt{2}}{2}.$$

So, the only solutions in the interval $[0, 2\pi)$ are

$$x = \frac{5\pi}{4} \quad \text{and} \quad x = \frac{7\pi}{4}.$$

These solutions are checked graphically in Figure 5.6.

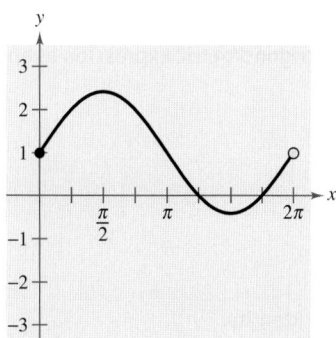

FIGURE 5.6

5.4 Exercises

In Exercises 1–6, find the exact value of each expression.

1. (a) $\cos\left(\dfrac{\pi}{4} + \dfrac{\pi}{3}\right)$ (b) $\cos\dfrac{\pi}{4} + \cos\dfrac{\pi}{3}$

2. (a) $\sin\left(\dfrac{3\pi}{4} + \dfrac{5\pi}{6}\right)$ (b) $\sin\dfrac{3\pi}{4} + \sin\dfrac{5\pi}{6}$

3. (a) $\sin\left(\dfrac{7\pi}{6} - \dfrac{\pi}{3}\right)$ (b) $\sin\dfrac{7\pi}{6} - \sin\dfrac{\pi}{3}$

4. (a) $\cos\left(\dfrac{2\pi}{3} - \dfrac{\pi}{6}\right)$ (b) $\cos\dfrac{2\pi}{3} + \cos\dfrac{\pi}{6}$

5. (a) $\cos(120° + 45°)$ (b) $\cos 120° + \cos 45°$

6. (a) $\sin(135° - 30°)$ (b) $\sin 135° - \cos 30°$

In Exercises 7–14, find the exact values of the sine, cosine, and tangent of the angle.

7. $105° = 60° + 45°$ **8.** $165° = 135° + 30°$

9. $195° = 225° - 30°$ **10.** $255° = 300° - 45°$

11. $\dfrac{11\pi}{12} = \dfrac{3\pi}{4} + \dfrac{\pi}{6}$ **12.** $\dfrac{7\pi}{12} = \dfrac{\pi}{3} + \dfrac{\pi}{4}$

13. $\dfrac{17\pi}{12} = \dfrac{9\pi}{4} - \dfrac{5\pi}{6}$ **14.** $-\dfrac{\pi}{12} = \dfrac{\pi}{6} - \dfrac{\pi}{4}$

In Exercises 15–22, find the exact values of the sine, cosine, and tangent of the angle.

15. $285°$ **16.** $-105°$

17. $-165°$ **18.** $15°$

19. $\dfrac{13\pi}{12}$ **20.** $-\dfrac{7\pi}{12}$

21. $-\dfrac{13\pi}{12}$ **22.** $\dfrac{5\pi}{12}$

In Exercises 23–30, write the expression as the sine, cosine, or tangent of an angle.

23. $\cos 25° \cos 15° - \sin 25° \sin 15°$

24. $\sin 140° \cos 50° + \cos 140° \sin 50°$

25. $\dfrac{\tan 325° - \tan 86°}{1 + \tan 325° \tan 86°}$ **26.** $\dfrac{\tan 140° - \tan 60°}{1 + \tan 140° \tan 60°}$

27. $\sin 3 \cos 1.2 - \cos 3 \sin 1.2$

28. $\cos\dfrac{\pi}{7} \cos\dfrac{\pi}{5} - \sin\dfrac{\pi}{7} \sin\dfrac{\pi}{5}$

29. $\dfrac{\tan 2x + \tan x}{1 - \tan 2x \tan x}$

30. $\cos 3x \cos 2y + \sin 3x \sin 2y$

In Exercises 31–36, find the exact value of the expression.

31. $\sin 330° \cos 30° - \cos 330° \sin 30°$

32. $\cos 15° \cos 60° + \sin 15° \sin 60°$

33. $\sin\dfrac{\pi}{12} \cos\dfrac{\pi}{4} + \cos\dfrac{\pi}{12} \sin\dfrac{\pi}{4}$

34. $\cos\dfrac{\pi}{16} \cos\dfrac{3\pi}{16} - \sin\dfrac{\pi}{16} \sin\dfrac{3\pi}{16}$

35. $\dfrac{\tan 25° + \tan 110°}{1 - \tan 25° \tan 110°}$

36. $\dfrac{\tan(5\pi/4) - \tan(\pi/12)}{1 + \tan(5\pi/4) \tan(\pi/12)}$

In Exercises 37–44, find the exact value of the trigonometric function given that $\sin u = \frac{5}{13}$ and $\cos v = -\frac{3}{5}$. (Both u and v are in Quadrant II.)

37. $\sin(u + v)$ **38.** $\cos(u - v)$

39. $\cos(u + v)$ **40.** $\sin(v - u)$

41. $\tan(u + v)$ **42.** $\csc(u - v)$

43. $\sec(v - u)$ **44.** $\cot(u + v)$

In Exercises 45–50, find the exact value of the trigonometric function given that $\sin u = -\frac{7}{25}$ and $\cos v = -\frac{4}{5}$. (Both u and v are in Quadrant III.)

45. $\cos(u + v)$ **46.** $\sin(u + v)$

47. $\tan(u - v)$ **48.** $\cot(v - u)$

49. $\sec(u + v)$ **50.** $\cos(u - v)$

In Exercises 51–54, write the trigonometric expression as an algebraic expression.

51. $\sin(\arcsin x + \arccos x)$

52. $\sin(\arctan 2x - \arccos x)$

53. $\cos(\arccos x + \arcsin x)$

54. $\cos(\arccos x - \arctan x)$

In Exercises 55–64, verify the identity.

55. $\sin(3\pi - x) = \sin x$ **56.** $\sin\left(\dfrac{\pi}{2} + x\right) = \cos x$

57. $\sin\left(\dfrac{\pi}{6} + x\right) = \dfrac{1}{2}(\cos x + \sqrt{3}\sin x)$

58. $\cos\left(\dfrac{5\pi}{4} - x\right) = -\dfrac{\sqrt{2}}{2}(\cos x + \sin x)$

59. $\cos(\pi - \theta) + \sin\left(\dfrac{\pi}{2} + \theta\right) = 0$

60. $\tan\left(\dfrac{\pi}{4} - \theta\right) = \dfrac{1 - \tan\theta}{1 + \tan\theta}$

61. $\cos(x + y)\cos(x - y) = \cos^2 x - \sin^2 y$

62. $\sin(x + y)\sin(x - y) = \sin^2 x - \sin^2 y$

63. $\sin(x + y) + \sin(x - y) = 2\sin x\cos y$

64. $\cos(x + y) + \cos(x - y) = 2\cos x\cos y$

In Exercises 65–68, simplify the expression algebraically and use a graphing utility to confirm your answer graphically.

65. $\cos\left(\dfrac{3\pi}{2} - x\right)$ **66.** $\cos(\pi + x)$

67. $\sin\left(\dfrac{3\pi}{2} + \theta\right)$ **68.** $\tan(\pi + \theta)$

In Exercises 69–72, find all solutions of the equation in the interval $[0, 2\pi)$.

69. $\sin\left(x + \dfrac{\pi}{3}\right) + \sin\left(x - \dfrac{\pi}{3}\right) = 1$

70. $\sin\left(x + \dfrac{\pi}{6}\right) - \sin\left(x - \dfrac{\pi}{6}\right) = \dfrac{1}{2}$

71. $\cos\left(x + \dfrac{\pi}{4}\right) - \cos\left(x - \dfrac{\pi}{4}\right) = 1$

72. $\tan(x + \pi) + 2\sin(x + \pi) = 0$

 In Exercises 73 and 74, use a graphing utility to approximate the solutions in the interval $[0, 2\pi)$.

73. $\cos\left(x + \dfrac{\pi}{4}\right) + \cos\left(x - \dfrac{\pi}{4}\right) = 1$

74. $\tan(x + \pi) - \cos\left(x + \dfrac{\pi}{2}\right) = 0$

▶ **Model It**

75. ***Harmonic Motion*** A weight is attached to a spring suspended vertically from a ceiling. When a driving force is applied to the system, the weight moves vertically from its equilibrium position, and this motion is modeled by

---

▶ **Model It** *(continued)*

$$y = \dfrac{1}{3}\sin 2t + \dfrac{1}{4}\cos 2t$$

where y is the distance from equilibrium measured in feet and t is the time in seconds.

(a) Use the identity

$$a\sin B\theta + b\cos B\theta = \sqrt{a^2 + b^2}\,\sin(B\theta + C)$$

where $C = \arctan(b/a)$, $a > 0$, to write the model in the form

$$y = \sqrt{a^2 + b^2}\,\sin(Bt + C).$$

(b) Find the amplitude of the oscillations of the weight.

(c) Find the frequency of the oscillations of the weight.

---

76. ***Standing Waves*** The equation of a standing wave is obtained by adding the displacements of two waves traveling in opposite directions (see figure). Assume that each of the waves has amplitude A, period T, and wavelength λ. If the models for these waves are

$$y_1 = A\cos 2\pi\left(\dfrac{t}{T} - \dfrac{x}{\lambda}\right) \quad \text{and}$$

$$y_2 = A\cos 2\pi\left(\dfrac{t}{T} + \dfrac{x}{\lambda}\right)$$

show that

$$y_1 + y_2 = 2A\cos\dfrac{2\pi t}{T}\cos\dfrac{2\pi x}{\lambda}.$$

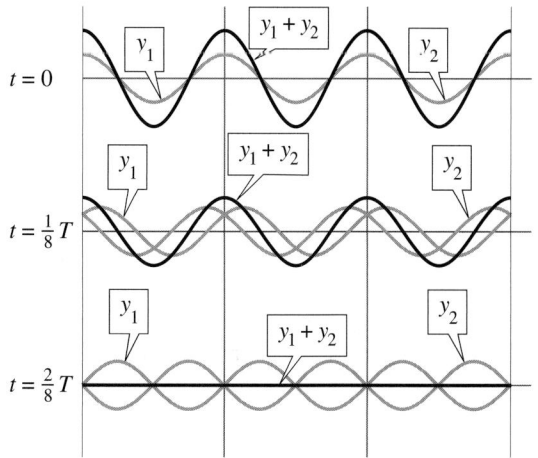

Synthesis

True or False? In Exercises 77–80, determine whether the statement is true or false. Justify your answer.

77. $\sin(u \pm v) = \sin u \pm \sin v$

78. $\cos(u \pm v) = \cos u \pm \cos v$

79. $\cos\left(x - \dfrac{\pi}{2}\right) = -\sin x$

80. $\sin\left(x - \dfrac{\pi}{2}\right) = -\cos x$

In Exercises 81–84, verify the identity.

81. $\cos(n\pi + \theta) = (-1)^n \cos \theta, \quad n$ is an integer

82. $\sin(n\pi + \theta) = (-1)^n \sin \theta, \quad n$ is an integer

83. $a \sin B\theta + b \cos B\theta = \sqrt{a^2 + b^2} \sin(B\theta + C)$, where $C = \arctan(b/a)$ and $a > 0$

84. $a \sin B\theta + b \cos B\theta = \sqrt{a^2 + b^2} \cos(B\theta - C)$, where $C = \arctan(a/b)$ and $b > 0$

In Exercises 85–88, use the formulas given in Exercises 83 and 84 to write the trigonometric expression in the following forms.

(a) $\sqrt{a^2 + b^2} \sin(B\theta + C)$

(b) $\sqrt{a^2 + b^2} \cos(B\theta - C)$

85. $\sin \theta + \cos \theta$

86. $3 \sin 2\theta + 4 \cos 2\theta$

87. $12 \sin 3\theta + 5 \cos 3\theta$

88. $\sin 2\theta - \cos 2\theta$

In Exercises 89 and 90, use the formulas given in Exercises 83 and 84 to write the trigonometric expression in the form $a \sin B\theta + b \cos B\theta$.

89. $2 \sin\left(\theta + \dfrac{\pi}{2}\right)$

90. $5 \cos\left(\theta + \dfrac{3\pi}{4}\right)$

In Exercises 91 and 92, use the figure, which shows two lines whose equations are

$$y_1 = m_1 x + b_1 \quad \text{and} \quad y_2 = m_2 x + b_2.$$

Assume that both lines have positive slopes. Derive a formula for the angle between the two lines. Then use your formula to find the angle between the given pair of lines.

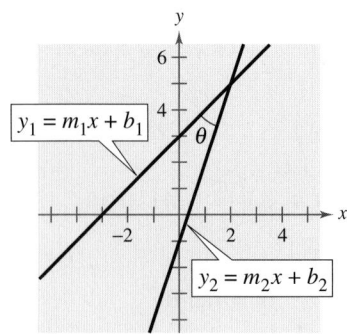

91. $y = x$ and $y = \sqrt{3}x$

92. $y = x$ and $y = \dfrac{1}{\sqrt{3}}x$

93. ***Conjecture*** Consider the function

$$f(\theta) = \sin^2\left(\theta + \dfrac{\pi}{4}\right) + \sin^2\left(\theta - \dfrac{\pi}{4}\right).$$

Use a graphing utility to graph the function and use the graph to create an identity. Prove your conjecture.

94. ***Conjecture*** Three squares of side s are placed side by side (see figure). Make a conjecture about the relationship between the sum $u + v$ and w. Prove your conjecture by using the identity for the tangent of the sum of two angles.

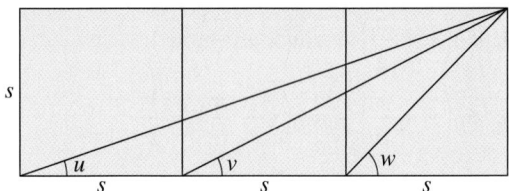

95. ***Proof*** Write a proof for the formula for $\sin(u + v)$.

96. ***Proof*** Write a proof for the formula for $\sin(u - v)$.

Review

In Exercises 97–100, find the inverse function of f. Verify that $f(f^{-1}(x)) = x$ and $f^{-1}(f(x)) = x$.

97. $f(x) = 5(x - 3)$

98. $f(x) = \dfrac{7 - x}{8}$

99. $f(x) = x^2 - 8$

100. $f(x) = \sqrt{x - 16}$

In Exercises 101–104, apply the inverse properties of $\ln x$ and e^x to simplify the expression.

101. $\log_3 3^{4x-3}$

102. $\log_8 8^{3x^2}$

103. $e^{\ln(6x-3)}$

104. $12x + e^{\ln x(x-2)}$

5.5 Multiple-Angle and Product-to-Sum Formulas

▶ **What you should learn**

• How to use multiple-angle formulas to rewrite and evaluate trigonometric functions
• How to use power-reducing formulas to rewrite and evaluate trigonometric functions
• How to use half-angle formulas to rewrite and evaluate trigonometric functions
• How to use product-to-sum and sum-to-product formulas to rewrite and evaluate trigonometric functions

▶ **Why you should learn it**

You can use a variety of trigonometric formulas to rewrite trigonometric functions in more convenient forms. For instance, in Exercise 121 on page 396, you can use a half-angle formula to determine the apex angle of a sound wave cone from the speed of an airplane.

NASA-Liaison Agency

Consider having your students prove the double-angle formulas. Double-angle formulas are often used in calculus.

Multiple-Angle Formulas

In this section you will study four other categories of trigonometric identities.

1. The first category involves *functions of multiple angles* such as $\sin ku$ and $\cos ku$.
2. The second category involves *squares of trigonometric functions* such as $\sin^2 u$.
3. The third category involves *functions of half-angles* such as $\sin(u/2)$.
4. The fourth category involves *products of trigonometric functions* such as $\sin u \cos v$.

You should learn the **double-angle formulas** because they are used most often. For proofs of the formulas, see Proofs in Mathematics on page 404.

Double-Angle Formulas

$$\sin 2u = 2 \sin u \cos u \qquad\qquad \cos 2u = \cos^2 u - \sin^2 u$$

$$\tan 2u = \frac{2 \tan u}{1 - \tan^2 u} \qquad\qquad\qquad = 2\cos^2 u - 1$$

$$\qquad\qquad\qquad\qquad\qquad = 1 - 2\sin^2 u$$

Example 1 ▶ **Solving a Multiple-Angle Equation**

Find all solutions of $2 \cos x + \sin 2x = 0$.

Solution

Begin by rewriting the equation so that it involves functions of x (rather than $2x$). Then factor and solve as usual.

$2 \cos x + \sin 2x = 0$	Write original equation.
$2 \cos x + 2 \sin x \cos x = 0$	Double-angle formula
$2 \cos x(1 + \sin x) = 0$	Factor.
$2 \cos x = 0 \quad$ and $\quad 1 + \sin x = 0$	Set factors equal to zero.
$x = \dfrac{\pi}{2}, \dfrac{3\pi}{2} \qquad\qquad x = \dfrac{3\pi}{2}$	Solutions in $[0, 2\pi)$

So, the general solution is

$$x = \frac{\pi}{2} + 2n\pi \qquad \text{and} \qquad x = \frac{3\pi}{2} + 2n\pi$$

where n is an integer. Try verifying these solutions graphically.

| Example 2 ▶ | Using Double-Angle Formulas to Analyze Graphs |

Use a double-angle formula to rewrite the equation

$$y = 4 \cos^2 x - 2.$$

Then sketch the graph of the equation over the interval $[0, 2\pi]$.

Solution

Using a double-angle formula, you can rewrite the original function as

$$y = 4 \cos^2 x - 2$$

$$= 2(2 \cos^2 x - 1)$$

$$= 2 \cos 2x.$$

Using the techniques discussed in Section 4.5, you can recognize that the graph of this function has an amplitude of 2 and a period of π. The key points in the interval $[0, \pi]$ are as follows.

Maximum	Intercept	Minimum	Intercept	Maximum
$(0, 2)$	$\left(\dfrac{\pi}{4}, 0\right)$	$\left(\dfrac{\pi}{2}, -2\right)$	$\left(\dfrac{3\pi}{4}, 0\right)$	$(\pi, 2)$

Two cycles of the graph are shown in Figure 5.7.

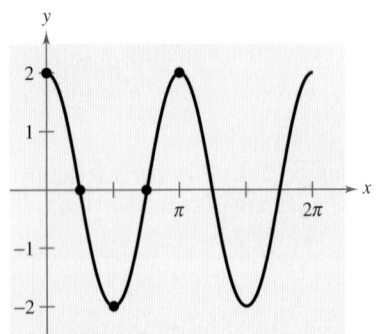

FIGURE **5.7**

| Example 3 ▶ | Evaluating Functions Involving Double Angles |

Use the following to find $\sin 2\theta$, $\cos 2\theta$, and $\tan 2\theta$.

$$\cos \theta = \frac{5}{13}, \qquad \frac{3\pi}{2} < \theta < 2\pi$$

Solution

From Figure 5.8, you can see that $\sin \theta = y/r = -12/13$. Consequently, using each of the double-angle formulas, you can write

$$\sin 2\theta = 2 \sin \theta \cos \theta = 2\left(-\frac{12}{13}\right)\left(\frac{5}{13}\right) = -\frac{120}{169}$$

$$\cos 2\theta = 2 \cos^2 \theta - 1 = 2\left(\frac{25}{169}\right) - 1 = -\frac{119}{169}$$

$$\tan 2\theta = \frac{\sin 2\theta}{\cos 2\theta} = \frac{120}{119}.$$

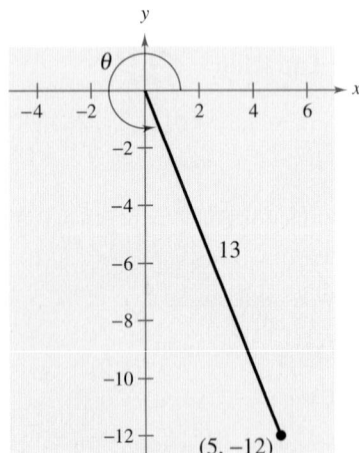

FIGURE **5.8**

The double-angle formulas are not restricted to angles 2θ and θ. Other *double* combinations, such as 4θ and 2θ or 6θ and 3θ, are also valid. Here are two examples.

$$\sin 4\theta = 2 \sin 2\theta \cos 2\theta \qquad \text{and} \qquad \cos 6\theta = \cos^2 3\theta - \sin^2 3\theta$$

By using double-angle formulas together with the sum formulas given in the preceding section, you can form other multiple-angle formulas.

Example 4 ▶ **Deriving a Triple-Angle Formula**

$$\sin 3x = \sin(2x + x)$$

$$= \sin 2x \cos x + \cos 2x \sin x$$

$$= 2 \sin x \cos x \cos x + (1 - 2 \sin^2 x)\sin x$$

$$= 2 \sin x \cos^2 x + \sin x - 2 \sin^3 x$$

$$= 2 \sin x(1 - \sin^2 x) + \sin x - 2 \sin^3 x$$

$$= 2 \sin x - 2 \sin^3 x + \sin x - 2 \sin^3 x$$

$$= 3 \sin x - 4 \sin^3 x$$

Power-Reducing Formulas

The double-angle formulas can be used to obtain the following **power-reducing formulas.** Example 5 shows a typical power reduction that is used in calculus.

Power-reducing formulas are often used in calculus.

Power-Reducing Formulas

$$\sin^2 u = \frac{1 - \cos 2u}{2} \qquad \cos^2 u = \frac{1 + \cos 2u}{2} \qquad \tan^2 u = \frac{1 - \cos 2u}{1 + \cos 2u}$$

For a proof of the power-reducing formulas, see Proofs in Mathematics on page 404.

Example 5 ▶ **Reducing a Power**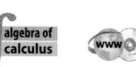

Rewrite $\sin^4 x$ as a sum of first powers of the cosines of multiple angles.

Solution

Note the repeated use of power-reducing formulas.

$$\sin^4 x = (\sin^2 x)^2 \qquad\qquad \text{Rewrite.}$$

$$= \left(\frac{1 - \cos 2x}{2}\right)^2 \qquad\qquad \text{Power-reducing formula}$$

$$= \frac{1}{4}(1 - 2 \cos 2x + \cos^2 2x) \qquad\qquad \text{Expand.}$$

$$= \frac{1}{4}\left(1 - 2 \cos 2x + \frac{1 + \cos 4x}{2}\right) \qquad\qquad \text{Power-reducing formula}$$

$$= \frac{1}{4} - \frac{1}{2} \cos 2x + \frac{1}{8} + \frac{1}{8} \cos 4x \qquad\qquad \text{Distributive Property}$$

$$= \frac{1}{8}(3 - 4 \cos 2x + \cos 4x) \qquad\qquad \text{Factor out common factor.}$$

Half-Angle Formulas

You can derive some useful alternative forms of the power-reducing formulas by replacing u with $u/2$. The results are called **half-angle formulas.**

Half-Angle Formulas

$$\sin \frac{u}{2} = \pm \sqrt{\frac{1 - \cos u}{2}}$$

$$\cos \frac{u}{2} = \pm \sqrt{\frac{1 + \cos u}{2}}$$

$$\tan \frac{u}{2} = \frac{1 - \cos u}{\sin u} = \frac{\sin u}{1 + \cos u}$$

The signs of $\sin \dfrac{u}{2}$ and $\cos \dfrac{u}{2}$ depend on the quadrant in which $\dfrac{u}{2}$ lies.

Example 6 ▶ **Using a Half-Angle Formula**

Find the exact value of $\sin 105°$.

Solution

Begin by noting that $105°$ is half of $210°$. Then, using the half-angle formula for $\sin(u/2)$ and the fact that $105°$ lies in Quadrant II, you have

$$\sin 105° = \sqrt{\frac{1 - \cos 210°}{2}}$$

$$= \sqrt{\frac{1 - (-\cos 30°)}{2}}$$

$$= \sqrt{\frac{1 + (\sqrt{3}/2)}{2}}$$

$$= \frac{\sqrt{2 + \sqrt{3}}}{2}.$$

The positive square root is chosen because $\sin \theta$ is positive in Quadrant II.

Use your calculator to verify the result obtained in Example 6. That is, evaluate $\sin 105°$ and $\left(\sqrt{2 + \sqrt{3}}\right)/2$.

$$\sin 105° \approx 0.9659258$$

$$\frac{\sqrt{2 + \sqrt{3}}}{2} \approx 0.9659258$$

You can see that both values are approximately 0.9659258.

Example 7 ▶ Solving a Trigonometric Equation

Find all solutions of

$$2 - \sin^2 x = 2 \cos^2 \frac{x}{2}$$

in the interval $[0, 2\pi)$.

Solution

STUDY TIP

A common error is to write

$$2 \cos^2 \frac{x}{2}$$

as $\cos^2 x$, rather than to use the correct identity

$$2 \cos^2 \frac{x}{2} = 2\left(\frac{1 + \cos x}{2}\right).$$

$2 - \sin^2 x = 2 \cos^2 \dfrac{x}{2}$	Write original equation.
$2 - \sin^2 x = 2\left(\pm\sqrt{\dfrac{1 + \cos x}{2}}\right)^2$	Half-angle formula
$2 - \sin^2 x = 2\left(\dfrac{1 + \cos x}{2}\right)$	Simplify.
$2 - \sin^2 x = 1 + \cos x$	Simplify.
$2 - (1 - \cos^2 x) = 1 + \cos x$	Pythagorean identity
$\cos^2 x - \cos x = 0$	Simplify.
$\cos x(\cos x - 1) = 0$	Factor.

By setting the factors $\cos x$ and $\cos x - 1$ equal to zero, you find that the solutions in the interval $[0, 2\pi)$ are

$$x = \frac{\pi}{2}, \quad x = \frac{3\pi}{2}, \quad \text{and} \quad x = 0.$$

Product-to-Sum Formulas

Each of the following **product-to-sum formulas** is easily verified using the sum and difference formulas discussed in the preceding section.

Product-to-Sum Formulas

$$\sin u \sin v = \frac{1}{2}[\cos(u - v) - \cos(u + v)]$$

$$\cos u \cos v = \frac{1}{2}[\cos(u - v) + \cos(u + v)]$$

$$\sin u \cos v = \frac{1}{2}[\sin(u + v) + \sin(u - v)]$$

$$\cos u \sin v = \frac{1}{2}[\sin(u + v) - \sin(u - v)]$$

Example 8 ▶ **Writing Products as Sums**

Rewrite the product $\cos 5x \sin 4x$ as a sum or difference.

Solution

Using the appropriate product-to-sum formula, you obtain

$$\cos 5x \sin 4x = \frac{1}{2}[\sin(5x + 4x) - \sin(5x - 4x)]$$

$$= \frac{1}{2}\sin 9x - \frac{1}{2}\sin x.$$

Occasionally, it is useful to reverse the procedure and write a sum of trigonometric functions as a product. This can be accomplished with the following **sum-to-product formulas.**

Sum-to-Product Formulas

$$\sin x + \sin y = 2 \sin\left(\frac{x + y}{2}\right)\cos\left(\frac{x - y}{2}\right)$$

$$\sin x - \sin y = 2 \cos\left(\frac{x + y}{2}\right)\sin\left(\frac{x - y}{2}\right)$$

$$\cos x + \cos y = 2 \cos\left(\frac{x + y}{2}\right)\cos\left(\frac{x - y}{2}\right)$$

$$\cos x - \cos y = -2 \sin\left(\frac{x + y}{2}\right)\sin\left(\frac{x - y}{2}\right)$$

For a proof of the sum-to-product formulas, see Proofs in Mathematics on page 405.

Example 9 ▶ **Using a Sum-to-Product Formula**

Find the exact value of $\cos 195° + \cos 105°$.

Solution

Using the appropriate sum-to-product formula, you obtain

$$\cos 195° + \cos 105° = 2 \cos\left(\frac{195° + 105°}{2}\right)\cos\left(\frac{195° - 105°}{2}\right)$$

$$= 2 \cos 150° \cos 45°$$

$$= 2\left(-\frac{\sqrt{3}}{2}\right)\left(\frac{\sqrt{2}}{2}\right)$$

$$= -\frac{\sqrt{6}}{2}.$$

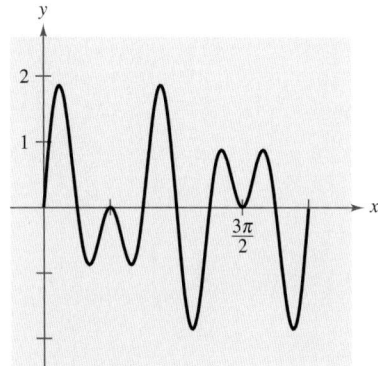

FIGURE 5.9

Example 10 ▶ Solving a Trigonometric Equation

Find all solutions of $\sin 5x + \sin 3x = 0$.

Solution

$$\sin 5x + \sin 3x = 0 \qquad \text{Write original equation.}$$

$$2 \sin\left(\frac{5x + 3x}{2}\right) \cos\left(\frac{5x - 3x}{2}\right) = 0 \qquad \text{Sum-to-product formula}$$

$$2 \sin 4x \cos x = 0 \qquad \text{Simplify.}$$

By setting the factor $2 \sin 4x$ equal to zero, you can find that the solutions in the interval $[0, 2\pi)$ are

$$x = 0, \frac{\pi}{4}, \frac{\pi}{2}, \frac{3\pi}{4}, \pi, \frac{5\pi}{4}, \frac{3\pi}{2}, \frac{7\pi}{4}.$$

The equation $\cos x = 0$ yields no additional solutions, and you can conclude that the solutions are of the form

$$x = \frac{n\pi}{4}$$

where n is an integer. These solutions are verified graphically in Figure 5.9.

Example 11 ▶ Verifying a Trigonometric Identity

Verify the identity

$$\frac{\sin t + \sin 3t}{\cos t + \cos 3t} = \tan 2t.$$

Solution

Using appropriate sum-to-product formulas, you have

$$\frac{\sin t + \sin 3t}{\cos t + \cos 3t} = \frac{2 \sin 2t \cos(-t)}{2 \cos 2t \cos(-t)}$$

$$= \frac{\sin 2t}{\cos 2t}$$

$$= \tan 2t.$$

Writing ABOUT MATHEMATICS

Deriving an Area Formula Describe how you can use a double-angle formula or a half-angle formula to derive a formula for the area of an isosceles triangle. Use a labeled sketch to illustrate your derivation. Then write two examples that show how your formula can be used.

5.5 Exercises

In Exercises 1–8, use the figure to find the exact value of the trigonometric function.

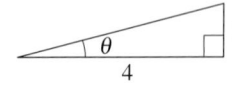

1. $\sin \theta$ **2.** $\tan \theta$

3. $\cos 2\theta$ **4.** $\sin 2\theta$

5. $\tan 2\theta$ **6.** $\sec 2\theta$

7. $\csc 2\theta$ **8.** $\cot 2\theta$

In Exercises 9–18, find the exact solutions of the equation in the interval $[0, 2\pi)$.

9. $\sin 2x - \sin x = 0$ **10.** $\sin 2x + \cos x = 0$

11. $4 \sin x \cos x = 1$ **12.** $\sin 2x \sin x = \cos x$

13. $\cos 2x - \cos x = 0$ **14.** $\cos 2x + \sin x = 0$

15. $\tan 2x - \cot x = 0$ **16.** $\tan 2x - 2 \cos x = 0$

17. $\sin 4x = -2 \sin 2x$ **18.** $(\sin 2x + \cos 2x)^2 = 1$

In Exercises 19–22, use a double-angle formula to rewrite the expression.

19. $6 \sin x \cos x$

20. $6 \cos^2 x - 3$

21. $4 - 8 \sin^2 x$

22. $(\cos x + \sin x)(\cos x - \sin x)$

In Exercises 23–28, find the exact values of sin 2u, cos 2u, and tan 2u using the double-angle formulas.

23. $\sin u = -\dfrac{4}{5}, \quad \pi < u < \dfrac{3\pi}{2}$

24. $\cos u = -\dfrac{2}{3}, \quad \dfrac{\pi}{2} < u < \pi$

25. $\tan u = \dfrac{3}{4}, \quad 0 < u < \dfrac{\pi}{2}$

26. $\cot u = -4, \quad \dfrac{3\pi}{2} < u < 2\pi$

27. $\sec u = -\dfrac{5}{2}, \quad \dfrac{\pi}{2} < u < \pi$

28. $\csc u = 3, \quad \dfrac{\pi}{2} < u < \pi$

In Exercises 29–34, use the power-reducing formulas to rewrite the expression in terms of the first power of the cosine.

29. $\cos^4 x$ **30.** $\sin^8 x$

31. $\sin^2 x \cos^2 x$ **32.** $\sin^4 x \cos^4 x$

33. $\sin^2 x \cos^4 x$ **34.** $\sin^4 x \cos^2 x$

In Exercises 35–40, use the figure to find the exact value of the trigonometric function.

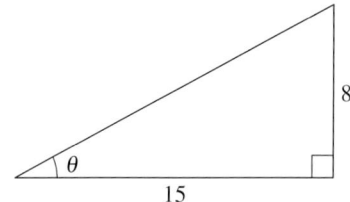

35. $\cos \dfrac{\theta}{2}$ **36.** $\sin \dfrac{\theta}{2}$

37. $\tan \dfrac{\theta}{2}$ **38.** $\sec \dfrac{\theta}{2}$

39. $\csc \dfrac{\theta}{2}$ **40.** $\cot \dfrac{\theta}{2}$

In Exercises 41–48, use the half-angle formulas to determine the exact values of the sine, cosine, and tangent of the angle.

41. $75°$ **42.** $165°$

43. $112° \, 30'$ **44.** $67° \, 30'$

45. $\dfrac{\pi}{8}$ **46.** $\dfrac{\pi}{12}$

47. $\dfrac{3\pi}{8}$ **48.** $\dfrac{7\pi}{12}$

In Exercises 49–54, find the exact values of sin(u/2), cos(u/2), and tan(u/2) using the half-angle formulas.

49. $\sin u = \dfrac{5}{13}, \quad \dfrac{\pi}{2} < u < \pi$

50. $\cos u = \dfrac{3}{5}, \quad 0 < u < \dfrac{\pi}{2}$

51. $\tan u = -\dfrac{5}{8}, \quad \dfrac{3\pi}{2} < u < 2\pi$

52. $\cot u = 3, \quad \pi < u < \dfrac{3\pi}{2}$

53. $\csc u = -\dfrac{5}{3}, \quad \pi < u < \dfrac{3\pi}{2}$

54. $\sec u = -\dfrac{7}{2}, \quad \dfrac{\pi}{2} < u < \pi$

In Exercises 55–58, use the half-angle formulas to simplify the expression.

55. $\sqrt{\dfrac{1 - \cos 6x}{2}}$

56. $\sqrt{\dfrac{1 + \cos 4x}{2}}$

57. $-\sqrt{\dfrac{1 - \cos 8x}{1 + \cos 8x}}$

58. $-\sqrt{\dfrac{1 - \cos(x - 1)}{2}}$

 In Exercises 59–62, find all solutions in the interval $[0, 2\pi)$. Use a graphing utility to graph the function and verify the solutions.

59. $\sin \dfrac{x}{2} + \cos x = 0$

60. $\sin \dfrac{x}{2} + \cos x - 1 = 0$

61. $\cos \dfrac{x}{2} - \sin x = 0$

62. $\tan \dfrac{x}{2} - \sin x = 0$

In Exercises 63–74, use the product-to-sum formulas to write the product as a sum or difference.

63. $6 \sin \dfrac{\pi}{4} \cos \dfrac{\pi}{4}$

64. $4 \cos \dfrac{\pi}{3} \sin \dfrac{5\pi}{6}$

65. $\cos 4\theta \sin 6\theta$

66. $3 \sin 2\alpha \sin 3\alpha$

67. $5 \cos(-5\beta) \cos 3\beta$

68. $\cos 2\theta \cos 4\theta$

69. $\sin(x + y) \sin(x - y)$

70. $\sin(x + y) \cos(x - y)$

71. $\cos(\theta - \pi) \sin(\theta + \pi)$

72. $\sin(\theta + \pi) \sin(\theta - \pi)$

73. $10 \cos 75° \cos 15°$

74. $6 \sin 45° \cos 15°$

In Exercises 75–86, use the sum-to-product formulas to write the sum or difference as a product.

75. $\sin 60° + \sin 30°$

76. $\cos 120° + \cos 30°$

77. $\cos \dfrac{3\pi}{4} - \cos \dfrac{\pi}{4}$

78. $\sin \dfrac{5\pi}{4} - \sin \dfrac{3\pi}{4}$

79. $\sin 5\theta - \sin 3\theta$

80. $\sin 3\theta + \sin \theta$

81. $\cos 6x + \cos 2x$

82. $\sin x + \sin 5x$

83. $\sin(\alpha + \beta) - \sin(\alpha - \beta)$

84. $\cos(\phi + 2\pi) + \cos \phi$

85. $\cos\left(\theta + \dfrac{\pi}{2}\right) - \cos\left(\theta - \dfrac{\pi}{2}\right)$

86. $\sin\left(x + \dfrac{\pi}{2}\right) + \sin\left(x - \dfrac{\pi}{2}\right)$

 In Exercises 87–90, find all solutions in the interval $[0, 2\pi)$. Use a graphing utility to graph the function and verify the solutions.

87. $\sin 6x + \sin 2x = 0$

88. $\cos 2x - \cos 6x = 0$

89. $\dfrac{\cos 2x}{\sin 3x - \sin x} - 1 = 0$

90. $\sin^2 3x - \sin^2 x = 0$

In Exercises 91–94, use the figure and trigonometric identities to find the exact value of the trigonometric function in two ways.

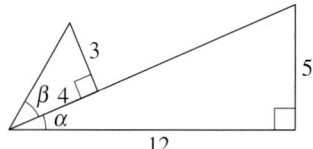

91. $\sin^2 \alpha$

92. $\cos^2 \alpha$

93. $\sin \alpha \cos \beta$

94. $\cos \alpha \sin \beta$

In Exercises 95–110, verify the identity.

95. $\csc 2\theta = \dfrac{\csc \theta}{2 \cos \theta}$

96. $\sec 2\theta = \dfrac{\sec^2 \theta}{2 - \sec^2 \theta}$

97. $\cos^2 2\alpha - \sin^2 2\alpha = \cos 4\alpha$

98. $\cos^4 x - \sin^4 x = \cos 2x$

99. $(\sin x + \cos x)^2 = 1 + \sin 2x$

100. $\sin \dfrac{\alpha}{3} \cos \dfrac{\alpha}{3} = \dfrac{1}{2} \sin \dfrac{2\alpha}{3}$

101. $1 + \cos 10y = 2 \cos^2 5y$

102. $\dfrac{\cos 3\beta}{\cos \beta} = 1 - 4\sin^2 \beta$

103. $\sec \dfrac{u}{2} = \pm \sqrt{\dfrac{2 \tan u}{\tan u + \sin u}}$

104. $\tan \dfrac{u}{2} = \csc u - \cot u$

105. $\dfrac{\sin x \pm \sin y}{\cos x + \cos y} = \tan \dfrac{x \pm y}{2}$

106. $\dfrac{\sin x + \sin y}{\cos x - \cos y} = -\cot \dfrac{x - y}{2}$

107. $\dfrac{\cos 4x + \cos 2x}{\sin 4x + \sin 2x} = \cot 3x$

108. $\dfrac{\cos t + \cos 3t}{\sin 3t - \sin t} = \cot t$

109. $\sin\left(\dfrac{\pi}{6} + x\right) + \sin\left(\dfrac{\pi}{6} - x\right) = \cos x$

110. $\cos\left(\dfrac{\pi}{3} + x\right) + \cos\left(\dfrac{\pi}{3} - x\right) = \cos x$

 In Exercises 111–114, use a graphing utility to verify the identity. Confirm that it is an identity algebraically.

111. $\cos 3\beta = \cos^3 \beta - 3\sin^2 \beta \cos \beta$

112. $\sin 4\beta = 4\sin \beta \cos \beta (1 - 2\sin^2 \beta)$

113. $(\cos 4x - \cos 2x)/(2\sin 3x) = -\sin x$

114. $(\cos 3x - \cos x)/(\sin 3x - \sin x) = -\tan 2x$

In Exercises 115 and 116, graph the function by hand in the interval $[0, 2\pi)$ by using the power-reducing formulas.

115. $f(x) = \sin^2 x$

116. $f(x) = \cos^2 x$

In Exercises 117 and 118, write the trigonometric expression as an algebraic expression.

117. $\sin(2 \arcsin x)$

118. $\cos(2 \arccos x)$

119. *Geometry*   The length of each of the two equal sides of an isosceles triangle is 10 meters (see figure). The angle between the two sides is θ.

  (a) Write the area of the triangle as a function of $\theta/2$.

  (b) Write the area of the triangle as a function of θ. Determine the value of θ such that the area is a maximum.

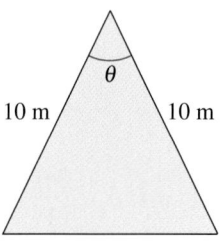

FIGURE FOR 119

120. *Projectile Motion*   The range of a projectile fired at an angle θ with the horizontal and with an initial velocity of v_0 feet per second is

$$r = \frac{1}{32} v_0^2 \sin 2\theta$$

where r is measured in feet. Determine the expression for the range in terms of θ.

▶ **Model It**

121. *Mach Number*   The mach number M of an airplane is the ratio of its speed to the speed of sound. When an airplane travels faster than the speed of sound, the sound waves form a cone behind the airplane. The mach number is related to the apex angle θ of the cone by

$$\sin \frac{\theta}{2} = \frac{1}{M}.$$

  (a) Find the angle θ that corresponds to a mach number of 1.

  (b) Find the angle θ that corresponds to a mach number of 4.5.

  (c) The speed of sound is about 760 miles per hour. Determine the speed of an object with the mach numbers from parts (a) and (b).

  (d) Rewrite the equation in terms of θ.

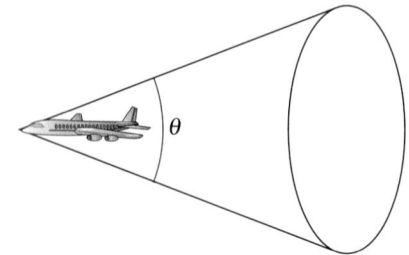

122. *Railroad Track* When two railroad tracks merge, the overlapping portions of the tracks are in the shapes of circular arcs (see figure). The radius of each arc r (in feet) and the angle θ are related by

$$\frac{x}{2} = 2r \sin^2 \frac{\theta}{2}.$$

Write a formula for x in terms of $\cos \theta$.

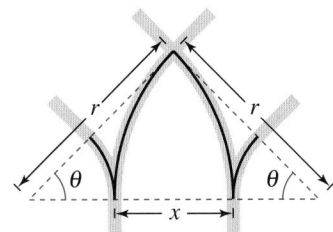

Synthesis

True or False? **In Exercises 123 and 124, determine whether the statement is true or false. Justify your answer.**

123. Because the sine function is an odd function, for a negative number u, $\sin 2u = -2 \sin u \cos u$.

124. $\sin \dfrac{u}{2} = -\sqrt{\dfrac{1 - \cos u}{2}}$ when u is in the second quadrant.

 In Exercises 125 and 126, (a) use a graphing utility to graph the function and approximate the maximum and minimum points on the graph in the interval $[0, 2\pi)$ and (b) solve the trigonometric equation and verify that its solutions are the x-coordinates of the maximum and minimum points of f. (Calculus is required to find the trigonometric equation.)

Function	*Trigonometric Equation*
125. $f(x) = 4 \sin \dfrac{x}{2} + \cos x$	$2 \cos \dfrac{x}{2} - \sin x = 0$
126. $f(x) = \cos 2x - 2 \sin x$	$-2 \cos x(2 \sin x + 1) = 0$

127. *Exploration* Consider the function

$$f(x) = \sin^4 x + \cos^4 x.$$

(a) Use the power-reducing formulas to write the function in terms of cosine to the first power.

 (b) Determine another way of rewriting the function. Use a graphing utility to rule out incorrectly rewritten functions.

 (c) Add a trigonometric term to the function so that it becomes a perfect square trinomial. Rewrite the function as a perfect square trinomial minus the term that you added. Use a graphing utility to rule out incorrectly rewritten functions.

 (d) Rewrite the result of part (c) in terms of the sine of a double angle. Use a graphing utility to rule out incorrectly rewritten functions.

(e) When you rewrite a trigonometric expression, the result may not be the same as a friend's. Does this mean that one of you is wrong? Explain.

128. *Conjecture* Consider the function

$$f(x) = 2 \sin x \left(2 \cos^2 \frac{x}{2} - 1\right).$$

 (a) Use a graphing utility to graph the function.

(b) Make a conjecture about the function that is an identity with f.

(c) Verify your conjecture analytically.

Review

129. *Profit* The total profit for a car manufacturer in October was 16% higher than it was in September. The total profit for the 2 months was $507,600. Find the profit for each month.

130. *Mixture Problem* A 55-gallon barrel contains a mixture with a concentration of 30%. How much of this mixture must be withdrawn and replaced by 100% concentrate to bring the mixture up to 50% concentration?

131. *Distance* A baseball diamond has the shape of a square in which the distance between each of the consecutive bases is 90 feet. Approximate the distance from home plate to second base.

Chapter Summary

▶ *What* did you learn?

Review Exercises

5.1 In Exercises 1–6, name the trigonometric function that is equivalent to the expression.

1. $\dfrac{1}{\cos x}$

2. $\dfrac{1}{\sin x}$

3. $\dfrac{1}{\sec x}$

4. $\dfrac{1}{\tan x}$

5. $\dfrac{\cos x}{\sin x}$

6. $\sqrt{1 + \tan^2 x}$

In Exercises 7–10, use the given values and trigonometric identities to evaluate (if possible) the other trigonometric functions of the angle.

7. $\sin x = \frac{3}{5}$, $\cos x = \frac{4}{5}$

8. $\tan \theta = \dfrac{2}{3}$, $\sec \theta = \dfrac{\sqrt{13}}{3}$

9. $\sin\left(\dfrac{\pi}{2} - x\right) = \dfrac{\sqrt{2}}{2}$, $\sin x = -\dfrac{\sqrt{2}}{2}$

10. $\csc\left(\dfrac{\pi}{2} - \theta\right) = 9$, $\sin \theta = \dfrac{4\sqrt{5}}{9}$

In Exercises 11–22, use the fundamental trigonometric identities to simplify the trigonometric expression.

11. $\dfrac{1}{\cot^2 x + 1}$

12. $\dfrac{\tan \theta}{1 - \cos^2 \theta}$

13. $\tan^2 x(\csc^2 x - 1)$

14. $\cot^2 x(\sin^2 x)$

15. $\dfrac{\sin\left(\dfrac{\pi}{2} - \theta\right)}{\sin \theta}$

16. $\dfrac{\cot\left(\dfrac{\pi}{2} - u\right)}{\cos u}$

17. $\cos^2 x + \cos^2 x \cot^2 x$

18. $\tan^2 \theta \csc^2 \theta - \tan^2 \theta$

19. $(\tan x + 1)^2 \cos x$

20. $(\sec x - \tan x)^2$

21. $\dfrac{1}{\csc \theta + 1} - \dfrac{1}{\csc \theta - 1}$

22. $\dfrac{\cos^2 x}{1 - \sin x}$

23. **Rate of Change** The rate of change of the function $f(x) = \csc x - \cot x$ is the expression $\csc^2 x - \csc x \cot x$. Show that this expression can also be written as

$$\dfrac{(1 - \cos x)}{\sin^2 x}.$$

24. **Rate of Change** The rate of change of the function $f(x) = 2\sqrt{\sin x}$ is the expression $\sin^{-1/2} x \cos x$. Show that this expression can also be written as $\cot x \sqrt{\sin x}$.

5.2 In Exercises 25–32, verify the identity.

25. $\cos x(\tan^2 x + 1) = \sec x$

26. $\sec^2 x \cot x - \cot x = \tan x$

27. $\cos\left(x + \dfrac{\pi}{2}\right) = -\sin x$

28. $\cot\left(\dfrac{\pi}{2} - x\right) = \tan x$

29. $\dfrac{1}{\tan \theta \csc \theta} = \cos \theta$

30. $\dfrac{1}{\tan x \csc x \sin x} = \cot x$

31. $\sin^5 x \cos^2 x = (\cos^2 x - 2\cos^4 x + \cos^6 x)\sin x$

32. $\cos^3 x \sin^2 x = (\sin^2 x - \sin^4 x)\cos x$

5.3 In Exercises 33–38, solve the equation.

33. $\sin x = \sqrt{3} - \sin x$

34. $4\cos \theta = 1 + 2\cos \theta$

35. $3\sqrt{3}\tan u = 3$

36. $\frac{1}{2}\sec x - 1 = 0$

37. $3\csc^2 x = 4$

38. $4\tan^2 u - 1 = \tan^2 u$

In Exercises 39–46, find all solutions of the equation in the interval $[0, 2\pi)$.

39. $2\cos^2 x - \cos x = 1$

40. $2\sin^2 x - 3\sin x = -1$

41. $\cos^2 x + \sin x = 1$

42. $\sin^2 x + 2\cos x = 2$

43. $2\sin 2x - \sqrt{2} = 0$

44. $\sqrt{3}\tan 3x = 0$

45. $\cos 4x(\cos x - 1) = 0$

46. $3\csc^2 5x = -4$

In Exercises 47–50, use inverse functions where needed to find all solutions of the equation in the interval $[0, 2\pi)$.

47. $\sin^2 x - 2\sin x = 0$

48. $2\cos^2 x + 3\cos x = 0$

49. $\tan^2 \theta + \tan \theta - 12 = 0$

50. $\sec^2 x + 6\tan x + 4 = 0$

5.4 In Exercises 51–54, find the exact values of the sine, cosine, and tangent of the angle by using a sum or difference formula.

51. $285° = 315° - 30°$

52. $345° = 300° + 45°$

53. $\dfrac{25\pi}{12} = \dfrac{11\pi}{6} + \dfrac{\pi}{4}$

54. $\dfrac{19\pi}{12} = \dfrac{11\pi}{6} - \dfrac{\pi}{4}$

In Exercises 55–58, write the expression as the sine, cosine, or tangent of an angle.

55. $\sin 60° \cos 45° - \cos 60° \sin 45°$

56. $\cos 45° \cos 120° - \sin 45° \sin 120°$

57. $\dfrac{\tan 25° + \tan 10°}{1 - \tan 25° \tan 10°}$

58. $\dfrac{\tan 68° - \tan 115°}{1 + \tan 68° \tan 115°}$

In Exercises 59–64, find the exact value of the trigonometric function given that $\sin u = \frac{3}{4}$, $\cos v = -\frac{5}{13}$, and u and v are in Quadrant II.

59. $\sin(u + v)$

60. $\tan(u + v)$

61. $\cos(u - v)$

62. $\sin(u - v)$

63. $\cos(u + v)$

64. $\tan(u - v)$

In Exercises 65–68, find all solutions of the equation in the interval $[0, 2\pi)$.

65. $\sin\left(x + \dfrac{\pi}{4}\right) - \sin\left(x - \dfrac{\pi}{4}\right) = 1$

66. $\cos\left(x + \dfrac{\pi}{6}\right) - \cos\left(x - \dfrac{\pi}{6}\right) = 1$

67. $\sin\left(x + \dfrac{\pi}{2}\right) - \sin\left(x - \dfrac{\pi}{2}\right) = \sqrt{3}$

68. $\cos\left(x + \dfrac{3\pi}{4}\right) - \cos\left(x - \dfrac{3\pi}{4}\right) = 0$

5.5 In Exercises 69 and 70, use double-angle formulas to verify the identity algebraically and use a graphing utility to confirm it graphically.

69. $\sin 4x = 8 \cos^3 x \sin x - 4 \cos x \sin x$

70. $\tan^2 x = \dfrac{1 - \cos 2x}{1 + \cos 2x}$

In Exercises 71 and 72, find the exact values of $\sin 2u$, $\cos 2u$, and $\tan 2u$ using the double-angle formulas.

71. $\sin u = -\dfrac{4}{5}, \quad \pi < u < \dfrac{3\pi}{2}$

72. $\cos u = -\dfrac{2}{\sqrt{5}}, \quad \dfrac{\pi}{2} < u < \pi$

73. *Projectile Motion* A baseball leaves the hand of the person at first base at an angle of θ with the horizontal and at an initial velocity of $v_0 = 80$ feet per second. The ball is caught by the person at second base 100 feet away. Find θ if the range r of a projectile is

$$r = \dfrac{1}{32} v_0^2 \sin 2\theta.$$

74. *Projectile Motion* Use the equation in Exercise 73 to find θ when a golf ball is hit at an initial velocity of 50 feet per second and lands 77 feet away.

In Exercises 75–78, use the power-reducing formulas to rewrite the expression in terms of the first power of the cosine.

75. $\tan^2 2x$

76. $\cos^2 3x$

77. $\sin^2 x \tan^2 x$

78. $\cos^2 x \tan^2 x$

In Exercises 79–82, use the half-angle formulas to determine the exact values of the sine, cosine, and tangent of the angle.

79. $-75°$

80. $15°$

81. $\dfrac{19\pi}{12}$

82. $-\dfrac{17\pi}{12}$

In Exercises 83 and 84, use the half-angle formulas to simplify the expression.

83. $-\sqrt{\dfrac{1 + \cos 10x}{2}}$

84. $\dfrac{\sin 6x}{1 + \cos 6x}$

85. Find the exact values of $\sin (u/2)$, $\cos (u/2)$, and $\tan (u/2)$ for $\sin u = \frac{3}{5}$, $0 < u < \frac{\pi}{2}$.

86. *Geometry* A trough for feeding cattle is 4 meters long and its cross sections are isosceles triangles with the two equal sides being $\frac{1}{2}$ meter (see figure on page 401). The angle between the two sides is θ.

(a) Write the trough's volume as a function of $\dfrac{\theta}{2}$.

(b) Write the volume of the trough as a function of θ and determine the value of θ such that the volume is maximum.

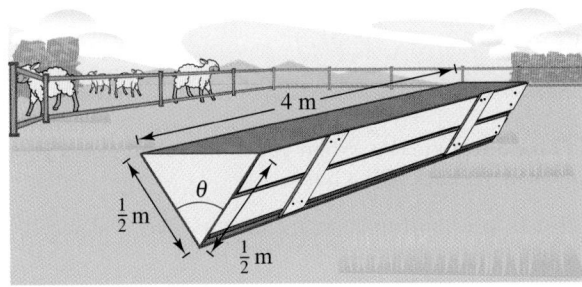

FIGURE FOR 86

In Exercises 87–90, use the product-to-sum formulas to write the product as a sum or difference.

87. $\cos\dfrac{\pi}{6}\sin\dfrac{\pi}{6}$

88. $6\sin 15°\sin 45°$

89. $\cos 5\theta\cos 3\theta$

90. $4\sin 3\alpha\cos 2\alpha$

In Exercises 91–94, use the sum-to-product formulas to write the sum or difference as a product.

91. $\sin 60° + \sin 90°$

92. $\cos 3\theta + \cos 2\theta$

93. $\cos\left(x+\dfrac{\pi}{6}\right) - \cos\left(x-\dfrac{\pi}{6}\right)$

94. $\sin\left(x+\dfrac{\pi}{4}\right) - \sin\left(x-\dfrac{\pi}{4}\right)$

95. **Harmonic Motion**   A weight is attached to a spring suspended vertically from a ceiling. When a driving force is applied to the system, the weight moves vertically from its equilibrium position, and this motion is described by the model

$$y = 1.5\sin 8t - 0.5\cos 8t$$

where y is the distance from equilibrium measured in feet and t is the time in seconds.

(a) Write the model in the form

$$y = \sqrt{a^2+b^2}\,\sin(Bt+C).$$

(b) Find the amplitude of the oscillations of the weight.

(c) Find the frequency of the oscillations of the weight.

Synthesis

True or False?   **In Exercises 96–99, determine whether the statement is true or false. Justify your answer.**

96. If $\dfrac{\pi}{2} < \theta < \pi$, then $\cos\dfrac{\theta}{2} < 0$.

97. $\sin(x+y) = \sin x + \sin y$

98. $4\sin(-x)\cos(-x) = -2\sin 2x$

99. $4\sin 45°\cos 15° = 1 + \sqrt{3}$

100. List the reciprocal identities, quotient identities, and Pythagorean identities from memory.

101. *Think About It*   If a trigonometric equation has an infinite number of solutions, is it true that the equation is an identity? Explain.

102. *Think About It*   Explain why you know from observation that the equation $a\sin x - b = 0$ has no solution if $|a| < |b|$.

In Exercises 103 and 104, use the graphs of y_1 and y_2 to determine how to change one function to form the identity $y_1 = y_2$.

103. $y_1 = \sec^2\left(\dfrac{\pi}{2}-x\right)$

$y_2 = \cot^2 x$

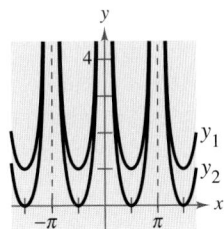

104. $y_1 = \dfrac{\cos 3x}{\cos x}$

$y_2 = (2\sin x)^2$

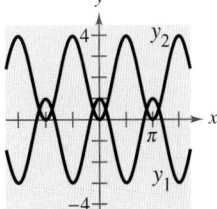

In Exercises 105 and 106, use the *zero* or *root* feature of a graphing utility to approximate the zeros of the function.

105. $y = \sqrt{x+3} + 4\cos x$

106. $y = 2 - \dfrac{1}{2}x^2 + 3\sin\dfrac{\pi x}{2}$

Chapter Test

Take this test as you would take a test in class. When you are finished, check your work against the answers given in the back of the book.

1. If $\tan \theta = \frac{3}{2}$ and $\cos \theta < 0$, use the fundamental identities to evaluate the other five trigonometric functions of θ.

2. Use the fundamental identities to simplify $\csc^2 \beta (1 - \cos^2 \beta)$.

3. Factor and simplify $\dfrac{\sec^4 x - \tan^4 x}{\sec^2 x + \tan^2 x}$.   4. Add and simplify $\dfrac{\cos \theta}{\sin \theta} + \dfrac{\sin \theta}{\cos \theta}$.

5. Determine the values of θ, $0 \leq \theta < 2\pi$, for which $\tan \theta = -\sqrt{\sec^2 \theta - 1}$ is true.

 6. Use a graphing utility to graph the functions $y_1 = \cos x + \sin x \tan x$ and $y_2 = \sec x$. Make a conjecture about y_1 and y_2. Verify the result analytically.

In Exercises 7–12, verify the identity.

7. $\sin \theta \sec \theta = \tan \theta$ 8. $\sec^2 x \tan^2 x + \sec^2 x = \sec^4 x$

9. $\dfrac{\csc \alpha + \sec \alpha}{\sin \alpha + \cos \alpha} = \cot \alpha + \tan \alpha$ 10. $\cos\left(x + \dfrac{\pi}{2}\right) = -\sin x$

11. $\sin(n\pi + \theta) = (-1)^n \sin \theta$, n is an integer.

12. $(\sin x + \cos x)^2 = 1 + \sin 2x$

13. Rewrite $\sin^4 x \tan^2 x$ in terms of the first power of the cosine.

14. Use a half-angle formula to simplify the expression $\dfrac{\sin 4\theta}{1 + \cos 4\theta}$.

15. Write $4 \cos 2\theta \sin 4\theta$ as a sum or difference.

16. Write $\sin 3\theta - \sin 4\theta$ as a product.

In Exercises 17–20, find all solutions of the equation in the interval $[0, 2\pi)$.

17. $\tan^2 x + \tan x = 0$ 18. $\sin 2\alpha - \cos \alpha = 0$

19. $4 \cos^2 x - 3 = 0$ 20. $\csc^2 x - \csc x - 2 = 0$

 21. Use a graphing utility to approximate the solutions of the equation $3 \cos x - x = 0$ accurate to three decimal places.

22. Find the exact value of $\cos 105°$ using the fact that $105° = 135° - 30°$.

23. Use the figure to find the exact values of $\sin 2u$ and $\tan 2u$.

FIGURE FOR 23

 24. Cheyenne, Wyoming has a latitude of 41°N. At this latitude, the position of the sun at sunrise can be modeled by

$$D = 31 \sin\left(\frac{2\pi}{365}t - 1.4\right)$$

where t is the time (in days) and $t = 1$ represents January 1. In this model, D represents the number of degrees north or south of due east that the sun rises. Use a graphing utility to determine the days on which the sun is more than 20° north of due east at sunrise.

Proofs in Mathematics

Sum and Difference Formulas   *(p. 380)*

$$\sin(u + v) = \sin u \cos v + \cos u \sin v$$

$$\sin(u - v) = \sin u \cos v - \cos u \sin v$$

$$\cos(u + v) = \cos u \cos v - \sin u \sin v$$

$$\cos(u - v) = \cos u \cos v + \sin u \sin v$$

$$\tan(u + v) = \frac{\tan u + \tan v}{1 - \tan u \tan v}$$

$$\tan(u - v) = \frac{\tan u - \tan v}{1 + \tan u \tan v}$$

Proof

You can use the figures at the left for the proofs of the formulas for $\cos(u \pm v)$. In the top figure, let A be the point $(1, 0)$ and then use u and v to locate the points $B = (x_1, y_1)$, $C = (x_2, y_2)$, and $D = (x_3, y_3)$ on the unit circle. So, $x_i^2 + y_i^2 = 1$ for $i = 1, 2,$ and 3. For convenience, assume that $0 < v < u < 2\pi$. In the bottom figure, note that arcs AC and BD have the same length. So, line segments AC and BD are also equal in length, which implies that

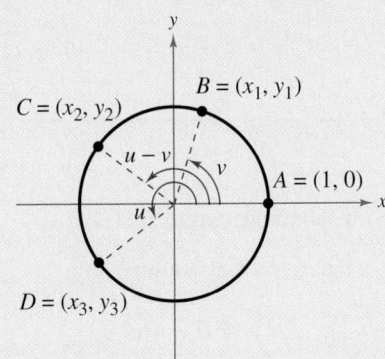

$$\sqrt{(x_2 - 1)^2 + (y_2 - 0)^2} = \sqrt{(x_3 - x_1)^2 + (y_3 - y_1)^2}$$

$$x_2^2 - 2x_2 + 1 + y_2^2 = x_3^2 - 2x_1x_3 + x_1^2 + y_3^2 - 2y_1y_3 + y_1^2$$

$$(x_2^2 + y_2^2) + 1 - 2x_2 = (x_3^2 + y_3^2) + (x_1^2 + y_1^2) - 2x_1x_3 - 2y_1y_3$$

$$1 + 1 - 2x_2 = 1 + 1 - 2x_1x_3 - 2y_1y_3$$

$$x_2 = x_3x_1 + y_3y_1.$$

Finally, by substituting the values $x_2 = \cos(u - v)$, $x_3 = \cos u$, $x_1 = \cos v$, $y_3 = \sin u$, and $y_1 = \sin v$, you obtain $\cos(u - v) = \cos u \cos v + \sin u \sin v$. The formula for $\cos(u + v)$ can be established by considering $u + v = u - (-v)$ and using the formula just derived to obtain

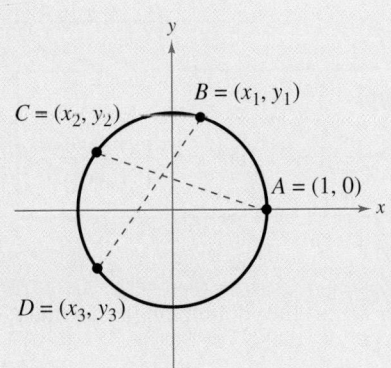

$$\cos(u + v) = \cos[u - (-v)] = \cos u \cos(-v) + \sin u \sin(-v)$$

$$= \cos u \cos v - \sin u \sin v.$$

You can use the sum and difference formulas for sine and cosine to prove the formulas for $\tan(u \pm v)$.

$$\tan(u \pm v) = \frac{\sin(u \pm v)}{\cos(u \pm v)}$$ Quotient identity

$$= \frac{\sin u \cos v \pm \cos u \sin v}{\cos u \cos v \mp \sin u \sin v}$$ Sum and difference formulas

$$= \frac{\dfrac{\sin u \cos v \pm \cos u \sin v}{\cos u \cos v}}{\dfrac{\cos u \cos v \mp \sin u \sin v}{\cos u \cos v}}$$ Divide numerator and denominator by $\cos u \cos v$.

$$= \frac{\dfrac{\sin u \cos v}{\cos u \cos v} \pm \dfrac{\cos u \sin v}{\cos u \cos v}}{\dfrac{\cos u \cos v}{\cos u \cos v} \mp \dfrac{\sin u \sin v}{\cos u \cos v}} \qquad \text{Separate fractions.}$$

$$= \frac{\dfrac{\sin u}{\cos u} \pm \dfrac{\sin v}{\cos v}}{1 \mp \dfrac{\sin u}{\cos u} \cdot \dfrac{\sin v}{\cos v}} \qquad \text{Product of fractions.}$$

$$= \frac{\tan u \pm \tan v}{1 \mp \tan u \tan v} \qquad \text{Quotient identity}$$

Trigonometry and Astronomy

Trigonometry was used by early astronomers to calculate measurements in the universe. Trigonometry was used to calculate the circumference of Earth and the distance from Earth to the moon. Another major accomplishment in astronomy using trigonometry was computing distances to stars.

Double-Angle Formulas *(p. 387)*

$$\sin 2u = 2 \sin u \cos u \qquad\qquad \cos 2u = \cos^2 u - \sin^2 u$$

$$\tan 2u = \frac{2 \tan u}{1 - \tan^2 u} \qquad\qquad\quad = 2 \cos^2 u - 1 = 1 - 2 \sin^2 u$$

Proof

To prove all three formulas, let $v = u$ in the corresponding sum formulas.

$$\sin 2u = \sin(u + u) = \sin u \cos u + \cos u \sin u = 2 \sin u \cos u$$

$$\cos 2u = \cos(u + u) = \cos u \cos u - \sin u \sin u = \cos^2 u - \sin^2 u$$

$$\tan 2u = \tan(u + u) = \frac{\tan u + \tan u}{1 - \tan u \tan u} = \frac{2 \tan u}{1 - \tan^2 u}$$

Power-Reducing Formulas *(p. 389)*

$$\sin^2 u = \frac{1 - \cos 2u}{2} \qquad \cos^2 u = \frac{1 + \cos 2u}{2} \qquad \tan^2 u = \frac{1 - \cos 2u}{1 + \cos 2u}$$

Proof

To prove the first formula, solve for $\sin^2 u$ in the double-angle formula $\cos 2u = 1 - 2 \sin^2 u$, as follows.

$$\cos 2u = 1 - 2 \sin^2 u \qquad \text{Write double-angle formula.}$$

$$2 \sin^2 u = 1 - \cos 2u \qquad \text{Subtract } \cos 2u \text{ from and add } 2 \sin^2 u \text{ to each side.}$$

$$\sin^2 u = \frac{1 - \cos 2u}{2} \qquad \text{Divide each side by 2.}$$

In a similar way you can prove the second formula, by solving for $\cos^2 u$ in the double-angle formula

$$\cos 2u = 2 \cos^2 u - 1.$$

To prove the third formula, use a quotient identity, as follows.

$$\tan^2 u = \frac{\sin^2 u}{\cos^2 u}$$

$$= \frac{\dfrac{1 - \cos 2u}{2}}{\dfrac{1 + \cos 2u}{2}}$$

$$= \frac{1 - \cos 2u}{1 + \cos 2u}$$

Sum-to-Product Formulas *(p. 392)*

$$\sin x + \sin y = 2 \sin\left(\frac{x + y}{2}\right) \cos\left(\frac{x - y}{2}\right)$$

$$\sin x - \sin y = 2 \cos\left(\frac{x + y}{2}\right) \sin\left(\frac{x - y}{2}\right)$$

$$\cos x + \cos y = 2 \cos\left(\frac{x + y}{2}\right) \cos\left(\frac{x - y}{2}\right)$$

$$\cos x - \cos y = -2 \sin\left(\frac{x + y}{2}\right) \sin\left(\frac{x - y}{2}\right)$$

Proof

To prove the first formula, let $x = u + v$ and $y = u - v$. Then substitute $u = (x + y)/2$ and $v = (x - y)/2$ in the product-to-sum formula.

$$\sin u \cos v = \frac{1}{2}[\sin(u + v) + \sin(u - v)]$$

$$\sin\left(\frac{x + y}{2}\right) \cos\left(\frac{x - y}{2}\right) = \frac{1}{2}(\sin x + \sin y)$$

$$2 \sin\left(\frac{x + y}{2}\right) \cos\left(\frac{x - y}{2}\right) = \sin x + \sin y$$

The other sum-to-product formulas can be proved in a similar manner.

1. (a) Write each of the other trigonometric functions of θ in terms of $\sin \theta$.

   (b) Write each of the other trigonometric functions of θ in terms of $\cos \theta$.

2. Verify that for all integers n,

$$\cos\left[\frac{(2n + 1)\pi}{2}\right] = 0.$$

3. Verify that for all integers n,

$$\sin\left[\frac{(12n + 1)\pi}{6}\right] = \frac{1}{2}.$$

 4. A particular sound wave is modeled by

$$p(t) = \frac{1}{4\pi}\left(p_1(t) + 30p_2(t) + p_3(t) + p_5(t) + 30p_6(t)\right)$$

where $p_n(t) = \frac{1}{n}\sin(524n\pi t)$, and t is the time in seconds.

   (a) Find the sine components $p_n(t)$ and use a graphing utility to graph each component. Then verify the graph of p that is shown.

   (b) Find the period of each sine component of p. Is p periodic? If so, what is its period?

   (c) Use the *zero* or *root* feature or the *zoom* and *trace* features of a graphing utility to find the t-intercepts of the graph of p over one cycle.

   (d) Use the *maximum* and *minimum* features of a graphing utility to approximate the absolute maximum and absolute minimum values of p over one cycle.

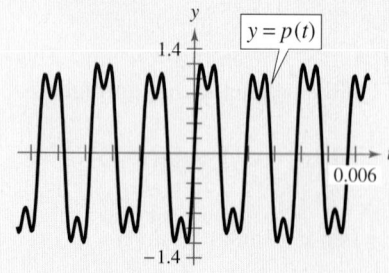

5. The path traveled by an object (neglecting air resistance) that is projected at an initial height of h_0 feet, an initial velocity of v feet per second, and an initial angle θ is given by

$$y = -\frac{16}{v^2 \cos^2 \theta}x^2 + (\tan \theta)x + h_0$$

where x and y are measured in feet. Find a formula for the maximum height of an object projected from ground level at velocity v and angle θ. To do this, find half of the horizontal distance

$$\frac{1}{32} v^2 \sin2\theta$$

and then substitute it for x in the general model for the path of a projectile (where $h_0 = 0$).

6. Verify the following identity used in calculus.

$$\frac{\cos(x + h) - \cos x}{h} = \cos x\left(\frac{\cos h - 1}{h}\right) - \sin x\left(\frac{\sin h}{h}\right)$$

7. Use the figure to derive the formulas for

$$\sin\frac{\theta}{2}, \cos\frac{\theta}{2}, \text{ and } \tan\frac{\theta}{2}$$

when θ is an acute angle.

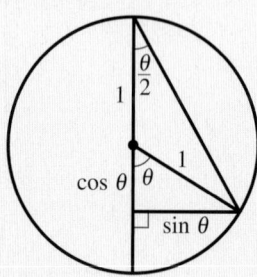

8. The force F (in pounds) on a person's back when he or she bends over at an angle θ is modeled by

$$F = \frac{0.6W \sin(\theta + 90°)}{\sin 12°}$$

where W is the person's weight (in pounds).

   (a) Simplify the model.

 (b) Use a graphing utility to graph the model, where $W = 185$ and $0° < \theta < 90°$.

   (c) At what angle is the force a maximum? At what angle is the force a minimum?

9. The number of hours of daylight that occur at any location on Earth depends on the time of year and the latitude of the location. The following equations model the number of hours of daylight in Seward, Alaska (60° latitude) and New Orleans, Louisiana (30° latitude).

$$D = 12.2 - 6.4 \cos\left[\frac{\pi(t + 0.2)}{182.6}\right] \qquad \text{Seward}$$

$$D = 12.2 - 1.9 \cos\left[\frac{\pi(t + 0.2)}{182.6}\right] \qquad \text{New Orleans}$$

In these models, D represents the number of hours of daylight and t represents the day, with $t = 0$ corresponding to January 1.

(a) Use a graphing utility to graph both models in the same viewing window. Use a viewing window of $0 \le t \le 365$.

(b) Find the days of the year on which both cities receive the same amount of daylight. What are these days called?

(c) Which city has the greater variation in the number of daylight hours? Which constant in each model would you use to determine the difference between the greatest and least numbers of hours of daylight?

(d) Determine the period of each model.

10. The tide, or depth of the ocean near the shore, changes throughout the day. The water depth d (in feet) of a bay can be modeled by

$$d = 35 - 28 \cos\frac{\pi}{6.2} t$$

where t is the time in hours, with $t = 0$ corresponding to 12:00 A.M.

(a) Algebraically find the times at which the high and low tides occur.

(b) Algebraically find the time(s) at which the water depth is 3.5 feet.

(c) Use a graphing utility to verify your results from parts (a) and (b).

11. Find the solution of each inequality in the interval $[0, 2\pi]$.

(a) $\sin x \ge 0.5$ (b) $\cos x \le -0.5$

(c) $\tan x < \sin x$ (d) $\cos x \ge \sin x$

12. The index of refraction n of a transparent material is the ratio of the speed of light in a vacuum to the speed of light in the material. Some common materials and their indices are air (1.00), water (1.33), and glass (1.50). Triangular prisms are often used to measure the index of refraction based on the formula

$$n = \frac{\sin\left(\dfrac{\theta}{2} + \dfrac{\alpha}{2}\right)}{\sin\dfrac{\theta}{2}}.$$

For the prism shown in the figure, $\alpha = 60°$.

(a) Write the index of refraction as a function of $\cot(\theta/2)$.

(b) Find θ for a prism made of glass.

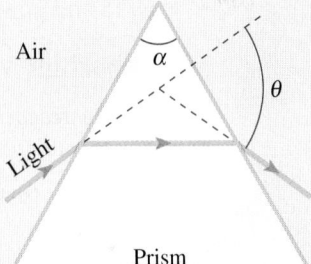

13. (a) Write a sum formula for $\sin(u + v + w)$.

(b) Write a sum formula for $\tan(u + v + w)$.

14. (a) Derive a formula for $\cos 3\theta$.

(b) Derive a formula for $\cos 4\theta$.

15. The heights h (in inches) of pistons 1 and 2 in an automobile engine can be modeled by

$$h_1 = 3.75 \sin 733t + 7.5$$

and

$$h_2 = 3.75 \sin 733\left(t + \frac{4\pi}{3}\right) + 7.5$$

where t is measured in seconds.

(a) Use a graphing utility to graph the heights of these two pistons in the same viewing window for $0 \le t \le 1$.

(b) How often are the pistons at the same height?

407

How to study Chapter 6

▶ **What you should learn**

In this chapter you will learn the following skills and concepts:

- How to use the Law of Sines and the Law of Cosines to solve oblique triangles
- How to find the areas of oblique triangles
- How to write the component forms of vectors and perform basic vector operations
- How to find the direction angles of vectors and the angle between two vectors
- How to multiply and divide complex numbers written in trigonometric form
- How to find powers and *n*th roots of complex numbers

▶ **Important Vocabulary**

As you encounter each new vocabulary term in this chapter, add the term and its definition to your notebook glossary.

Oblique triangle (p. 410)
Law of Sines (p. 410)
Law of Cosines (p. 419)
Directed line segment (p. 427)
Initial point (p. 427)
Terminal point (p. 427)
Magnitude of directed line segment (p. 427)
Vector **v** in the plane (p. 427)
Standard position (p. 428)
Component form of a vector **v** (p. 428)
Zero vector (p. 428)
Magnitude of **v** (p. 428)
Unit vector (p. 428)
Parallelogram law (p. 429)
Resultant (p. 429)

Standard unit vectors (p. 430)
Linear combination of vectors (p. 432)
Direction angle (p. 433)
Dot product (p. 440)
Angle between two nonzero vectors (p. 441)
Orthogonal vectors (p. 442)
Work (p. 446)
Complex plane (p. 449)
Real axis (p. 449)
Imaginary axis (p. 449)
Absolute value of a complex number (p. 449)
Trigonometric form of a complex number (p. 450)
*n*th root of a complex number (p. 454)
*n*th roots of unity (p. 456)

Study Tools

Learning objectives in each section
Chapter Summary (p. 460)
Review Exercises (pp. 461–464)
Chapter Test (p. 465)
Cumulative Test for Chapters 4–6 (pp. 466, 467)

Additional Resources

Study and Solutions Guide
Interactive Precalculus
Videotapes/DVD for Chapter 6
Precalculus Website
Student Success Organizer

Michael Rutherford/SuperStock

6

Additional Topics in Trigonometry

6.1   Law of Sines

▶ **What you should learn**

• How to use the Law of Sines to solve oblique triangles (AAS or ASA)
• How to use the Law of Sines to solve oblique triangles (SSA)
• How to find the areas of oblique triangles
• How to use the Law of Sines to model and solve real-life problems

▶ **Why you should learn it**

You can use the Law of Sines to solve real-life problems involving oblique triangles. For instance, in Exercise 44 on page 418, you will use the Law of Sines to determine the length of the shadow of the Leaning Tower of Pisa.

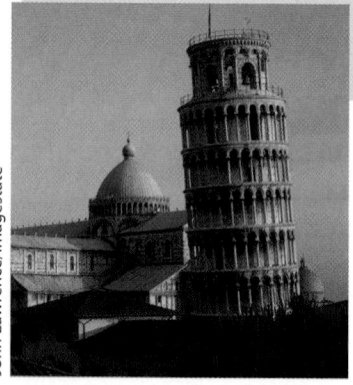

John Lawrence/Imagestate

You may want to illustrate each of the four cases (AAS or ASA, SSA, SSS, SAS) as a quick geometry review for your students.

Introduction

In Chapter 4, you studied techniques for solving right triangles. In this section and the next, you will solve **oblique triangles**—triangles that have no right angles. As standard notation, the angles of a triangle are labeled A, B, and C, and their opposite sides are labeled a, b, and c, as shown in Figure 6.1.

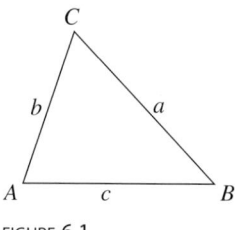

FIGURE **6.1**

To solve an oblique triangle, you need to know the measure of at least one side and any two other parts of the triangle—either two sides, two angles, or one angle and one side. This breaks down into the following four cases.

1. Two angles and any side (AAS or ASA)
2. Two sides and an angle opposite one of them (SSA)
3. Three sides (SSS)
4. Two sides and their included angle (SAS)

The first two cases can be solved using the **Law of Sines,** whereas the last two cases require the Law of Cosines (see Section 6.2).

Law of Sines

If ABC is a triangle with sides a, b, and c, then

$$\frac{a}{\sin A} = \frac{b}{\sin B} = \frac{c}{\sin C}.$$

A is acute. A is obtuse.

The Law of Sines can also be written in the reciprocal form

$$\frac{\sin A}{a} = \frac{\sin B}{b} = \frac{\sin C}{c}.$$

For a proof of the Law of Sines, see Proofs in Mathematics on page 468.

FIGURE **6.2**

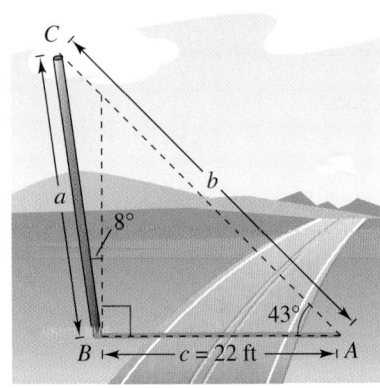

FIGURE **6.3**

Example 1 ▶ **Given Two Angles and One Side—AAS**

For the triangle in Figure 6.2, $C = 102.3°$, $B = 28.7°$, and $b = 27.4$ feet. Find the remaining angle and sides.

Solution

The third angle of the triangle is

$$A = 180° - B - C$$
$$= 180° - 28.7° - 102.3°$$
$$= 49.0°.$$

By the Law of Sines, you have

$$\frac{a}{\sin A} = \frac{b}{\sin B} = \frac{c}{\sin C}.$$

Using $b = 27.4$ produces

$$a = \frac{b}{\sin B}(\sin A) = \frac{27.4}{\sin 28.7°}(\sin 49.0°) \approx 43.06 \text{ feet}$$

and

$$c = \frac{b}{\sin B}(\sin C) = \frac{27.4}{\sin 28.7°}(\sin 102.3°) \approx 55.75 \text{ feet}.$$

Example 2 ▶ **Given Two Angles and One Side—ASA**

A pole tilts *toward* the sun at an 8° angle from the vertical, and it casts a 22-foot shadow. The angle of elevation from the tip of the shadow to the top of the pole is 43°. How tall is the pole?

Solution

From Figure 6.3, note that $A = 43°$ and $B = 90° + 8° = 98°$. So, the third angle is

$$C = 180° - A - B$$
$$= 180° - 43° - 98°$$
$$= 39°.$$

By the Law of Sines, you have

$$\frac{a}{\sin A} = \frac{c}{\sin C}.$$

Because $c = 22$ feet, the length of the pole is

$$a = \frac{c}{\sin C}(\sin A) = \frac{22}{\sin 39°}(\sin 43°) \approx 23.84 \text{ feet}.$$

For practice, try reworking Example 2 for a pole that tilts *away from* the sun under the same conditions.

The icon www⊙ identifies examples and concepts related to features of the Learning Tools CD-ROM and the *Interactive* and *Internet* versions of this text. For more details see the chart on pages *xxi-xxv*.

The Ambiguous Case (SSA)

In Examples 1 and 2 you saw that two angles and one side determine a unique triangle. However, if two sides and one opposite angle are given, three possible situations can occur: (1) no such triangle exists, (2) one such triangle exists, or (3) two distinct triangles may satisfy the conditions.

The Ambiguous Case (SSA)

Consider a triangle in which you are given a, b, and A. $(h = b \sin A)$

	A is acute.	A is acute.	A is acute.	A is acute.	A is obtuse.	A is obtuse.
Sketch					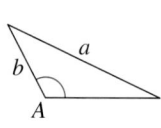	
Necessary condition	$a < h$	$a = h$	$a > b$	$h < a < b$	$a \le b$	$a > b$
Triangles possible	None	One	One	Two	None	One

Example 3 ▶ Single-Solution Case—SSA

For the triangle in Figure 6.4, $a = 22$ inches, $b = 12$ inches, and $A = 42°$. Find the remaining side and angles.

Solution

By the Law of Sines, you have

$$\frac{\sin B}{b} = \frac{\sin A}{a} \qquad \text{Reciprocal form}$$

$$\sin B = b\left(\frac{\sin A}{a}\right) \qquad \text{Multiply each side by } b.$$

$$\sin B = 12\left(\frac{\sin 42°}{22}\right) \qquad \text{Substitute for } A, a, \text{ and } b.$$

$$B \approx 21.41°. \qquad B \text{ is acute.}$$

Now, you can determine that

$$C \approx 180° - 42° - 21.41° = 116.59°.$$

Then, the remaining side is

$$\frac{c}{\sin C} = \frac{a}{\sin A}$$

$$c = \frac{a}{\sin A}(\sin C) = \frac{22}{\sin 42°}(\sin 116.59°) \approx 29.40 \text{ inches.}$$

b = 12 in.

a = 22 in.

42°

A   *c*   *B*

One solution: $a > b$

FIGURE **6.4**

The *Interactive* CD-ROM and *Internet* versions of this text offer a Try It for each example in the text.

Encourage your students to sketch the triangle, keeping in mind that the longest side lies opposite the largest angle of the triangle. For practice, suggest that students also find h.

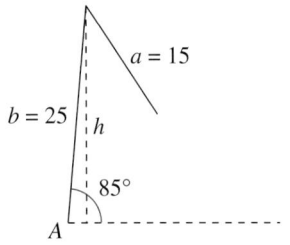

No solution: $a < h$

FIGURE **6.5**

Example 4 ▶ No-Solution Case—SSA

Show that there is no triangle for which $a = 15$, $b = 25$, and $A = 85°$.

Solution

Begin by making the sketch shown in Figure 6.5. From this figure it appears that no triangle is formed. You can verify this using the Law of Sines.

$$\frac{\sin B}{b} = \frac{\sin A}{a}$$ Reciprocal form

$$\sin B = b\left(\frac{\sin A}{a}\right)$$ Multiply each side by b.

$$\sin B = 25\left(\frac{\sin 85°}{15}\right) \approx 1.660 > 1$$

This contradicts the fact that $|\sin B| \leq 1$. So, no triangle can be formed having sides $a = 15$ and $b = 25$ and an angle of $A = 85°$.

Example 5 ▶ Two-Solution Case—SSA

Find two triangles for which $a = 12$ meters, $b = 31$ meters, and $A = 20.5°$.

Solution

By the Law of Sines, you have

$$\frac{\sin B}{b} = \frac{\sin A}{a}$$ Reciprocal form

$$\sin B = b\left(\frac{\sin A}{a}\right) = 31\left(\frac{\sin 20.5°}{12}\right) \approx 0.9047.$$

There are two angles $B_1 \approx 64.8°$ and $B_2 \approx 180° - 64.8° \approx 115.2°$ between $0°$ and $180°$ whose sine is 0.9047. For $B_1 \approx 64.8°$, you obtain

$$C \approx 180° - 20.5° - 64.8° = 94.7°$$

$$c = \frac{a}{\sin A}(\sin C) = \frac{12}{\sin 20.5°}(\sin 94.7°) \approx 34.15 \text{ meters.}$$

For $B_2 \approx 115.2°$, you obtain

$$C \approx 180° - 20.5° - 115.2° = 44.3°$$

$$c = \frac{a}{\sin A}(\sin C) = \frac{12}{\sin 20.5°}(\sin 44.3°) \approx 23.93 \text{ meters.}$$

The resulting triangles are shown in Figure 6.6.

FIGURE **6.6**

Area of an Oblique Triangle

The procedure used to prove the Law of Sines leads to a simple formula for the area of an oblique triangle. Referring to Figure 6.7, note that each triangle has a height of $h = b \sin A$. Consequently, the area of each triangle is

$$\text{Area} = \frac{1}{2}(\text{base})(\text{height}) = \frac{1}{2}(c)(b \sin A) = \frac{1}{2}bc \sin A.$$

By similar arguments, you can develop the formulas

$$\text{Area} = \frac{1}{2}ab \sin C = \frac{1}{2}ac \sin B.$$

  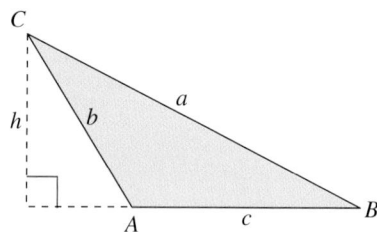

A is acute   *A is obtuse*

FIGURE **6.7**

Activities

1. Use the given information to find (if possible) the remaining side and angles of the oblique triangle. If two solutions exist, find both.

    $A = 58°, \ a = 20, \ c = 10$

    Answer: $B = 97°, \ C = 25°,$
    $\qquad\quad b = 23.4$

2. Use the given information to find (if possible) the remaining side and angles of the oblique triangle. If two solutions exist, find both.

    $B = 78°, \ b = 207, \ c = 210$

    Answer: Two solutions
    $A = 19.1°, \ a = 69.2, \ C = 82.9°$
    $A = 4.9°, \ a = 18.1, \ C = 97.1°$

3. Find the area of the triangle with $B = 120°, \ a = 32, \ c = 50.$

    Answer: Area = 692.8 square units

Area of an Oblique Triangle

The area of any triangle is one-half the product of the lengths of two sides times the sine of their included angle. That is,

$$\text{Area} = \frac{1}{2}bc \sin A = \frac{1}{2}ab \sin C = \frac{1}{2}ac \sin B.$$

Note that if angle A is 90°, the formula gives the area for a right triangle:

$$\text{Area} = \frac{1}{2}bc(\sin 90°) = \frac{1}{2}bc = \frac{1}{2}(\text{base})(\text{height}). \qquad \text{\scriptsize sin 90° = 1}$$

Similar results are obtained for angles C and B equal to 90°.

Example 6 ▶ **Finding the Area of a Triangular Lot**

Find the area of a triangular lot having two sides of lengths 90 meters and 52 meters and an included angle of 102°.

Solution

Consider $a = 90$ meters, $b = 52$ meters, and angle $C = 102°$, as shown in Figure 6.8. Then, the area of the triangle is

$$\text{Area} = \frac{1}{2}ab \sin C = \frac{1}{2}(90)(52)(\sin 102°) \approx 2289 \text{ square meters.}$$

FIGURE **6.8**

FIGURE **6.9**

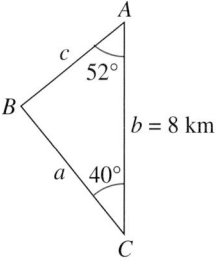

FIGURE **6.10**

Application

Example 7 ▶ An Application of the Law of Sines

The course for a boat race starts at point A and proceeds in the direction S 52° W to point B, then in the direction S 40° E to point C, and finally back to A, as shown in Figure 6.9. Point C lies 8 kilometers directly south of point A. Approximate the total distance of the race course.

Solution

Because lines BD and AC are parallel, it follows that $\angle BCA \cong \angle DBC$. Consequently, triangle ABC has the measures shown in Figure 6.10. For angle B, you have $B = 180° - 52° - 40° = 88°$. Using the Law of Sines

$$\frac{a}{\sin 52°} = \frac{b}{\sin 88°} = \frac{c}{\sin 40°}$$

you can let $b = 8$ and obtain

$$a = \frac{8}{\sin 88°}(\sin 52°) \approx 6.308$$

and

$$c = \frac{8}{\sin 88°}(\sin 40°) \approx 5.145.$$

The total length of the course is approximately

$$\text{Length} \approx 8 + 6.308 + 5.145$$

$$= 19.453 \text{ kilometers.}$$

Alternative Writing About Mathematics: Error Analysis

You are a math instructor, and one of your students hands in the following solution. Discuss what is wrong with your student's solution. How could you help the student avoid making a similar mistake in the future? Use a diagram to illustrate your explanation.

Find side c in a triangle that has $a = 5.8$, $b = 7$, and $C = 82°$.

Student's Solution

Because this is an SSA situation, I can use the Law of Sines.

$$\frac{5.8}{7} = \frac{c}{\sin 82°}$$

$$(\sin 82°)\frac{5.8}{7} = 0.821$$

Writing ABOUT MATHEMATICS

Using the Law of Sines In this section, you have been using the Law of Sines to solve *oblique* triangles. Can the Law of Sines also be used to solve a right triangle? If so, write a short paragraph explaining how to use the Law of Sines to solve each triangle. Is there an easier way to solve these triangles?

a. (AAS)

b. (ASA)

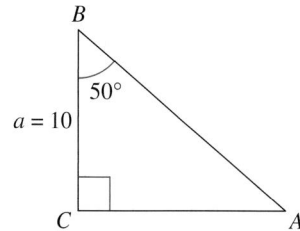

6.1 Exercises

The *Interactive* CD-ROM and *Internet* versions of this text contain step-by-step solutions to all odd-numbered exercises. They also provide Tutorial Exercises for additional help.

In Exercises 1–18, use the information to solve the triangle.

1.

2.

3.

4.

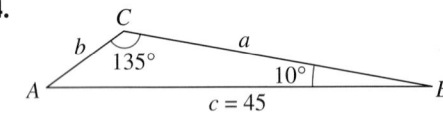

5. $A = 36°$, $a = 8$, $b = 5$

6. $A = 60°$, $a = 9$, $c = 10$

7. $A = 102.4°$, $C = 16.7°$, $a = 21.6$

8. $A = 24.3°$, $C = 54.6°$, $c = 2.68$

9. $A = 83° \, 20'$, $C = 54.6°$, $c = 18.1$

10. $A = 5° \, 40'$, $B = 8° \, 15'$, $b = 4.8$

11. $B = 15° \, 30'$, $a = 4.5$, $b = 6.8$

12. $B = 2° \, 45'$, $b = 6.2$, $c = 5.8$

13. $C = 145°$, $b = 4$, $c = 14$

14. $A = 100°$, $a = 125$, $c = 10$

15. $A = 110° \, 15'$, $a = 48$, $b = 16$

16. $C = 85° \, 20'$, $a = 35$, $c = 50$

17. $A = 55°$, $B = 42°$, $c = \frac{3}{4}$

18. $B = 28°$, $C = 104°$, $a = 3\frac{5}{8}$

In Exercises 19–24, use the information to solve (if possible) the triangle. If two solutions exist, find both.

19. $A = 58°$, $a = 4.5$, $b = 12.8$

20. $A = 58°$, $a = 11.4$, $b = 12.8$

21. $A = 76°$, $a = 18$, $b = 20$

22. $A = 76°$, $a = 34$, $b = 21$

23. $A = 110°$, $a = 125$, $b = 200$

24. $A = 110°$, $a = 125$, $b = 100$

In Exercises 25–28, find a value for b such that the triangle has (a) one solution, (b) two solutions, and (c) no solution.

25. $A = 36°$, $a = 5$ **26.** $A = 60°$, $a = 10$

27. $A = 10°$, $a = 10.8$ **28.** $A = 88°$, $a = 315.6$

In Exercises 29–34, find the area of the triangle having the indicated sides and angle.

29. $C = 120°$, $a = 4$, $b = 6$

30. $B = 130°$, $a = 62$, $c = 20$

31. $A = 43° \, 45'$, $b = 57$, $c = 85$

32. $A = 5° \, 15'$, $b = 4.5$, $c = 22$

33. $B = 72° \, 30'$, $a = 105$, $c = 64$

34. $C = 84° \, 30'$, $a = 16$, $b = 20$

35. *Height* Because of prevailing winds, a tree grew so that it was leaning $4°$ from the vertical. At a point 35 meters from the tree, the angle of elevation to the top of the tree is $23°$ (see figure). Find the height h of the tree.

36. *Height* A flagpole at a right angle to the horizontal is located on a slope that makes an angle of $12°$ with the horizontal. The flagpole's shadow is 16 meters long and points directly up the slope. The angle of elevation from the tip of the shadow to the sun is $20°$.

(a) Draw a triangle that represents the problem. Show the known quantities on the triangle and use a variable to indicate the height of the flagpole.

(b) Write an equation involving the unknown quantity.

(c) Find the height of the flagpole.

37. *Angle of Elevation* A 10-meter telephone pole casts a 17-meter shadow directly down a slope when the angle of elevation of the sun is 42° (see figure). Find θ, the angle of elevation of the ground.

38. *Flight Path* A plane flies 500 kilometers with a bearing of 316° from Naples to Elgin (see figure). The plane then flies 720 kilometers from Elgin to Canton. Find the bearing of the flight from Elgin to Canton.

Not drawn to scale

39. *Bridge Design* A bridge is to be built across a small lake from a gazebo to a dock (see figure). The bearing from the gazebo to the dock is S 41° W. From a tree 100 meters from the gazebo, the bearings to the gazebo and the dock are S 74° E and S 28° E, respectively. Find the distance from the gazebo to the dock.

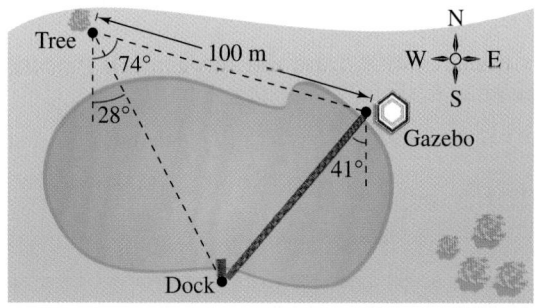

40. *Railroad Track Design* The circular arc of a railroad curve has a chord of length 3000 feet and a central angle of 40°.

(a) Draw a figure that visually represents the problem. Show the known quantities on the figure and use variables *r* and *s* to represent the radius of the arc and the length of the arc, respectively.

(b) Find the radius *r* of the circular arc.

(c) Find the length *s* of the circular arc.

41. *Glide Path* A pilot has just started on the glide path for landing at an airport where the length of the runway is 9000 feet. The angles of depression from the plane to the ends of the runway are 17.5° and 18.8°.

(a) Draw a figure that visually represents the problem.

(b) Find the air distance the plane must travel until touching down on the near end of the runway.

(c) Find the ground distance the plane must travel until touching down.

(d) Find the altitude of the plane when the pilot begins the descent.

42. *Locating a Fire* The bearing from the Pine Knob fire tower to the Colt Station fire tower is N 65° E, and the two towers are 30 kilometers apart. A fire spotted by rangers in each tower has a bearing of N 80° E from Pine Knob and S 70° E from Colt Station. Find the distance of the fire from each tower.

Not drawn to scale

43. *Distance* A boat is sailing due east parallel to the shoreline at a speed of 10 miles per hour. At a given time, the bearing to the lighthouse is S 70° E, and 15 minutes later the bearing is S 63° E (see figure). The lighthouse is located at the shoreline. What is the distance from the boat to the shoreline?

▶ **Model It**

44. **Shadow Length** The Leaning Tower of Pisa in Italy is characterized by its tilt. The tower leans because it was built on a layer of unstable soil—clay, sand, and water. The tower is approximately 58.36 meters tall from its foundation (see figure). The top of the tower leans about 5.45 meters off center.

(a) Find the angle of lean α of the tower.

(b) Write β as a function of d and θ, where θ is the angle of elevation to the sun.

(c) Use the Law of Sines to write an equation for the length d of the shadow cast by the tower.

(d) Use a graphing utility to complete the table.

θ	10°	20°	30°	40°	50°	60°
d						

5.45 m

β

α 58.36 m

θ

d *Not drawn to scale*

(a) Write α as a function of β.

(b) Use a graphing utility to graph the function. Determine its domain and range.

(c) Use the result of part (a) to write c as a function of β.

(d) Use a graphing utility to graph the function in part (c). Determine its domain and range.

(e) Complete the table. What can you infer?

β	0.4	0.8	1.2	1.6	2.0	2.4	2.8
α							
c							

48. **Graphical Analysis**

(a) Write the area A of the shaded region in the figure as a function of θ.

(b) Use a graphing utility to graph the area function.

(c) Determine the domain of the area function. Explain how the area of the region and the domain of the function would change if the eight-centimeter line segment were decreased in length.

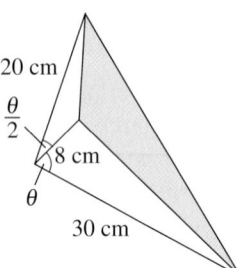

20 cm

$\dfrac{\theta}{2}$

8 cm

θ

30 cm

Synthesis

True or False? In Exercises 45 and 46, determine whether the statement is true or false. Justify your answer.

45. If a triangle contains an obtuse angle, then it must be oblique.

46. Two angles and one side of a triangle do not necessarily determine a unique triangle.

47. **Graphical and Numerical Analysis** In the figure, α and β are positive angles.

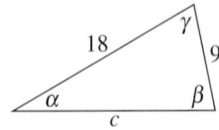

18

γ

9

α

β

c

Review

In Exercises 49–52, use the fundamental trigonometric identities to simplify the expression.

49. $\sin x \cot x$

50. $\tan x \cos x \sec x$

51. $1 - \sin^2\left(\dfrac{\pi}{2} - x\right)$

52. $1 + \cot^2\left(\dfrac{\pi}{2} - x\right)$

In Exercises 53 and 54, write the product as a sum or difference.

53. $6 \sin 8\theta \cos 3\theta$

54. $2 \cos 5\theta \sin 2\theta$

6.2 Law of Cosines

▶ **What you should learn**

• How to use the Law of Cosines to solve oblique triangles (SSS or SAS)

• How to use the Law of Cosines to model and solve real-life problems

• How to use Heron's Area Formula to find the area of a triangle

▶ **Why you should learn it**

You can use the Law of Cosines to solve real-life problems involving oblique triangles. For instance, in Exercise 44 on page 425, you will use the Law of Cosines to determine the maximum distance a piston moves in one cycle.

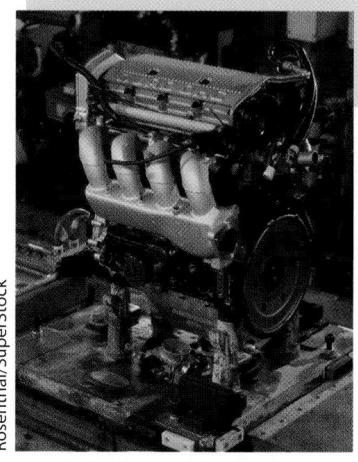

Rosenthal/SuperStock

Introduction

Two cases remain in the list of conditions needed to solve an oblique triangle—SSS and SAS. If you are given three sides (SSS), or two sides and their included angle (SAS), none of the ratios in the Law of Sines would be complete. In such cases, you can use the **Law of Cosines.**

Law of Cosines

Standard Form	*Alternative Form*
$a^2 = b^2 + c^2 - 2bc \cos A$	$\cos A = \dfrac{b^2 + c^2 - a^2}{2bc}$
$b^2 = a^2 + c^2 - 2ac \cos B$	$\cos B = \dfrac{a^2 + c^2 - b^2}{2ac}$
$c^2 = a^2 + b^2 - 2ab \cos C$	$\cos C = \dfrac{a^2 + b^2 - c^2}{2ab}$

For a proof of the Law of Cosines, see Proofs in Mathematics on page 469.

Example 1 ▶ **Three Sides of a Triangle—SSS**

Find the three angles of the triangle in Figure 6.11.

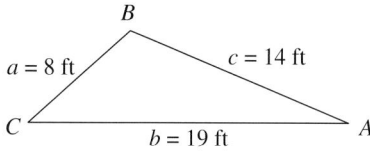

FIGURE **6.11**

Solution

It is a good idea first to find the angle opposite the longest side—side b in this case (see Figure 6.11). Using the Law of Cosines, you find that

$$\cos B = \frac{a^2 + c^2 - b^2}{2ac} = \frac{8^2 + 14^2 - 19^2}{2(8)(14)} \approx -0.45089.$$

Because $\cos B$ is negative, you know that B is an *obtuse* angle given by $B \approx 116.80°$. At this point, it is simpler to use the Law of Sines to determine A.

$$\sin A = a\left(\frac{\sin B}{b}\right) \approx 8\left(\frac{\sin 116.80°}{19}\right) \approx 0.37583$$

Because B is obtuse, you know that A must be acute, because a triangle can have, at most, one obtuse angle. So, $A \approx 22.08°$ and $C \approx 180° - 22.08° - 116.80° = 41.12°$.

◀ E x p l o r a t i o n ▶

What familiar formula do you obtain when you use the third form of the Law of Cosines

$$c^2 = a^2 + b^2 - 2ab \cos C$$

and you let $C = 90°$? What is the relationship between the Law of Cosines and this formula?

Do you see why it was wise to find the largest angle *first* in Example 1? Knowing the cosine of an angle, you can determine whether the angle is acute or obtuse. That is,

$\cos \theta > 0$ for $0° < \theta < 90°$ Acute

$\cos \theta < 0$ for $90° < \theta < 180°$.   Obtuse

So, in Example 1, once you found that angle B was obtuse, you knew that angles A and C were both acute. If the largest angle is acute, the remaining two angles are acute also.

Example 2 ▶   Two Sides and the Included Angle—SAS

Find the remaining angles and side of the triangle in Figure 6.12.

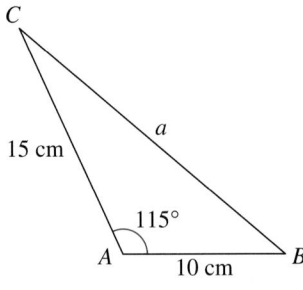

FIGURE **6.12**

Solution

Use the Law of Cosines to find the unknown side a in the figure.

$$a^2 = b^2 + c^2 - 2bc \cos A$$

$$a^2 = 15^2 + 10^2 - 2(15)(10) \cos 115°$$

$$a^2 \approx 451.79$$

$$a \approx 21.26$$

Because $a \approx 21.26$ centimeters, you now know the ratio $\sin A / a$ and you can use the Law of Sines

$$\frac{\sin B}{b} = \frac{\sin A}{a}$$

to solve for B.

$$\sin B = b\left(\frac{\sin A}{a}\right)$$

$$= 15\left(\frac{\sin 115°}{21.26}\right)$$

$$\approx 0.63945$$

So, $B = \arcsin 0.63945 \approx 39.75°$ and $C \approx 180° - 115° - 39.75° = 25.25°$.

Applications

FIGURE **6.13**

Example 3 ▶ An Application of the Law of Cosines

The pitcher's mound on a women's softball field is 43 feet from home plate and the distance between the bases is 60 feet, as shown in Figure 6.13. (The pitcher's mound is not halfway between home plate and second base.) How far is the pitcher's mound from first base?

Solution

In triangle *HPF*, $H = 45°$ (line *HP* bisects the right angle at *H*), $f = 43$, and $p = 60$. Using the Law of Cosines for this SAS case, you have

$$h^2 = f^2 + p^2 - 2fp \cos H$$

$$= 43^2 + 60^2 - 2(43)(60) \cos 45°$$

$$\approx 1800.3$$

So, the approximate distance from the pitcher's mound to first base is

$$h \approx \sqrt{1800.3} \approx 42.43 \text{ feet.}$$

Example 4 ▶ An Application of the Law of Cosines

A ship travels 60 miles due east, then adjusts its course northward, as shown in Figure 6.14. After traveling 80 miles in that direction, the ship is 139 miles from its point of departure. Describe the bearing from point *B* to point *C*.

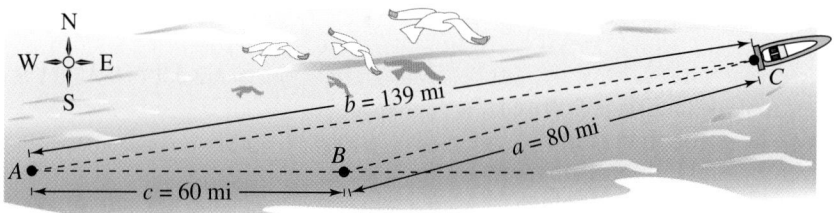

FIGURE **6.14**

Solution

You have $a = 80$, $b = 139$, and $c = 60$; so, using the alternative form of the Law of Cosines, you have

$$\cos B = \frac{a^2 + c^2 - b^2}{2ac}$$

$$= \frac{80^2 + 60^2 - 139^2}{2(80)(60)}$$

$$\approx -0.97094.$$

So, $B \approx \arccos(-0.97094) \approx 166.15°$, and thus, the bearing measured from due north from point *B* to point *C* is $166.15° - 90° = 76.15°$, or N 76.15° E.

Heron's Area Formula

The Law of Cosines can be used to establish the following formula for the area of a triangle. This formula is credited to the Greek mathematician Heron (c. 100 B.C.).

Heron's Area Formula

Given any triangle with sides of lengths a, b, and c, the area of the triangle is

$$\text{Area} = \sqrt{s(s-a)(s-b)(s-c)}$$

where $s = (a+b+c)/2$.

For a proof of Heron's Area Formula, see Proofs in Mathematics on page 470.

Example 5 ▶ **Using Heron's Area Formula**

Find the area of a triangle having sides of lengths $a = 43$ meters, $b = 53$ meters, and $c = 72$ meters.

Solution

Because $s = (a+b+c)/2 = 168/2 = 84$, Heron's Area Formula yields

$$\text{Area} = \sqrt{s(s-a)(s-b)(s-c)}$$
$$= \sqrt{84(41)(31)(12)} \approx 1131.89 \text{ square meters.}$$

Historical Note
Heron of Alexandria (c. 100 B.C.) was a Greek geometer and inventor. His works describe how to find the areas of triangles, quadrilaterals, regular polygons having 3 to 12 sides, and circles as well as the surface areas and volumes of three-dimensional objects.

Writing About Mathematics Suggestion:
You may want to ask students to draw the diagram of a triangle (labeling whatever sides and/or angles are necessary) that is well-suited to each area formula. Then ask students to exchange triangles with a partner to find the area of each.

Writing **ABOUT MATHEMATICS**

The Area of a Triangle You have now studied three different formulas for the area of a triangle. Use the most appropriate formula to find the area of each triangle below. Show your work and give your reasons for choosing each formula.

Standard Formula   Area $= \frac{1}{2}bh$
Oblique Triangle   Area $= \frac{1}{2}bc \sin A = \frac{1}{2}ab \sin C = \frac{1}{2}ac \sin B$
Heron's Area Formula   Area $= \sqrt{s(s-a)(s-b)(s-c)}$

a.
b.
c.
d.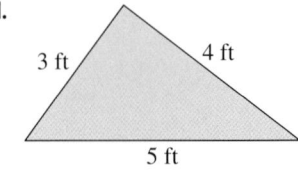

6.2 Exercises

In Exercises 1–16, use the Law of Cosines to solve the triangle.

1.

2.

3.

4.
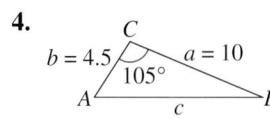

5. $a = 11$, $b = 14$, $c = 20$

6. $a = 55$, $b = 25$, $c = 72$

7. $a = 75.4$, $b = 52$, $c = 52$

8. $a = 1.42$, $b = 0.75$, $c = 1.25$

9. $A = 135°$, $b = 4$, $c = 9$

10. $A = 55°$, $b = 3$, $c = 10$

11. $B = 10° 35'$, $a = 40$, $c = 30$

12. $B = 75° 20'$, $a = 6.2$, $c = 9.5$

13. $B = 125° 40'$, $a = 32$, $c = 32$

14. $C = 15° 15'$, $a = 6.25$, $b = 2.15$

15. $C = 43°$, $a = \frac{4}{9}$, $b = \frac{7}{9}$

16. $C = 103°$, $a = \frac{3}{8}$, $b = \frac{3}{4}$

In Exercises 17–22, complete the table by solving the parallelogram shown in the figure. (The lengths of the diagonals are given by c and d.)

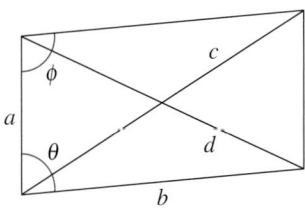

	a	b	c	d	θ	ϕ
17.	5	8			45°	
18.	25	35				120°
19.	10	14	20			
20.	40	60		80		
21.	15		25	20		
22.		25	50	35		

In Exercises 23–28, use Heron's Area Formula to find the area of the triangle.

23. $a = 5$, $b = 7$, $c = 10$

24. $a = 12$, $b = 15$, $c = 9$

25. $a = 2.5$, $b = 10.2$, $c = 9$

26. $a = 75.4$, $b = 52$, $c = 52$

27. $a = 12.32$, $b = 8.46$, $c = 15.05$

28. $a = 3.05$, $b = 0.75$, $c = 2.45$

29. *Navigation* A boat race runs along a triangular course marked by buoys A, B, and C. The race starts with the boats headed west for 3700 meters. The other two sides of the course lie to the north of the first side, and their lengths are 1700 meters and 3000 meters. Draw a figure that gives a visual representation of the problem, and find the bearings for the last two legs of the race.

30. *Navigation* A plane flies 810 miles from Niagara to Cuyahoga with a bearing of 75°. Then it flies 648 miles from Cuyahoga to Rosemount with a bearing of 32°. Draw a figure that visually represents the problem, and find the straight-line distance and bearing from Niagara to Rosemount.

31. *Surveying* To approximate the length of a marsh, a surveyor walks 250 meters from point A to point B, then turns 75° and walks 220 meters to point C (see figure). Approximate the length AC of the marsh.

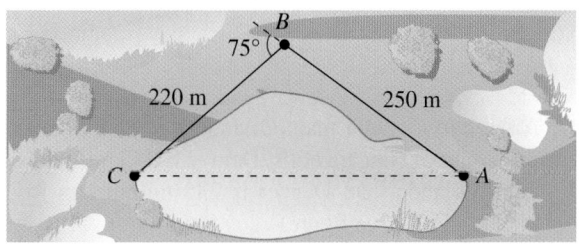

32. *Surveying* A triangular parcel of land has 115 meters of frontage, and the other boundaries have lengths of 76 meters and 92 meters. What angles does the frontage make with the two other boundaries?

33. *Surveying* A triangular parcel of ground has sides of lengths 725 feet, 650 feet, and 575 feet. Find the measure of the largest angle.

34. *Streetlight Design* Determine the angle θ in the design of the streetlight shown in the figure.

35. *Distance* Two ships leave a port at 9 A.M. One travels at a bearing of N 53° W at 12 miles per hour, and the other travels at a bearing of S 67° W at 16 miles per hour. Approximate how far apart they are at noon that day.

36. *Length* A 100-foot vertical tower is to be erected on the side of a hill that makes a 6° angle with the horizontal (see figure). Find the length of each of the two guy wires that will be anchored 75 feet uphill and downhill from the base of the tower.

37. *Navigation* On a map, Orlando is 178 millimeters due south of Niagara Falls, Denver is 273 millimeters from Orlando, and Denver is 235 millimeters from Niagara Falls (see figure).

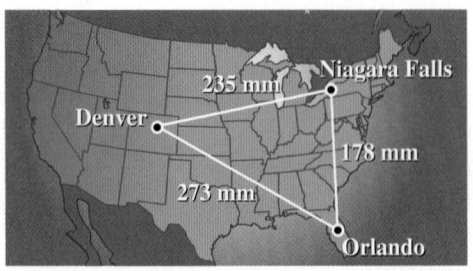

(a) Find the bearing of Denver from Orlando.

(b) Find the bearing of Denver from Niagara Falls.

38. *Navigation* On a map, Minneapolis is 165 millimeters due west of Albany, Phoenix is 216 millimeters from Minneapolis, and Phoenix is 368 millimeters from Albany (see figure).

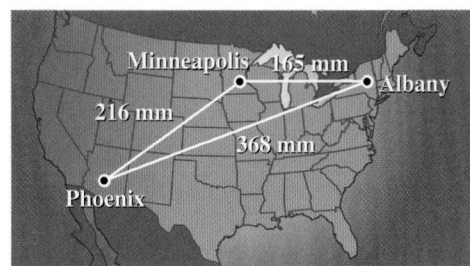

(a) Find the bearing of Minneapolis from Phoenix.

(b) Find the bearing of Albany from Phoenix.

39. *Baseball* On a baseball diamond with 90-foot sides, the pitcher's mound is 60.5 feet from home plate. How far is it from the pitcher's mound to third base?

40. *Baseball* The baseball player in center field is playing approximately 330 feet from the television camera that is behind home plate. A batter hits a fly ball that goes to the wall 420 feet from the camera (see figure). The camera turns 8° to follow the play. Approximately how far does the center fielder have to run to make the catch?

41. *Aircraft Tracking* To determine the distance between two aircraft, a tracking station continuously determines the distance to each aircraft and the angle A between them (see figure). Determine the distance a between the planes when $A = 42°$, $b = 35$ miles, and $c = 20$ miles.

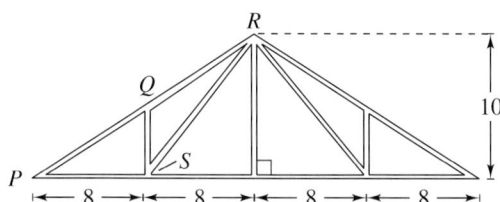

FIGURE FOR 41

42. *Aircraft Tracking*   Use the figure for Exercise 41 to determine the distance *a* between the planes when $A = 11°$, $b = 20$ miles, and $c = 20$ miles.

43. *Trusses* Q is the midpoint of the line segment $\overline{PR}$ in the truss rafter shown in the figure. What are the lengths of the line segments $\overline{PQ}$, $\overline{QS}$, and $\overline{RS}$?

▶ Model It

44. *Engine Design*   An engine has a seven-inch connecting rod fastened to a crank (see figure).

(a) Use the Law of Cosines to write an equation giving the relationship between x and θ.

(b) Write x as a function of θ. (Select the sign that yields positive values of x.)

(c) Use a graphing utility to graph the function in part (b).

(d) Use the graph in part (c) to determine the maximum distance the piston moves in one cycle.

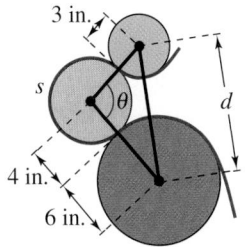

---

45. *Paper Manufacturing*   In a process with continuous paper, the paper passes across three rollers of radii 3 inches, 4 inches, and 6 inches (see figure). The centers of the three-inch and six-inch rollers are *d* inches apart, and the length of the arc in contact with the paper on the four-inch roller is *s* inches. Complete the table.

d (inches)	9	10	12	13	14	15	16
θ (degrees)							
s (inches)							

FIGURE FOR 45

46. *Awning Design*   A retractable awning above a patio door lowers at an angle of 50° from the exterior wall at a height of 10 feet above the ground (see figure). No direct sunlight is to enter the door when the angle of elevation of the sun is greater than 70°. What is the length x of the awning?

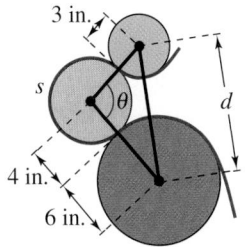

47. *Geometry*   The lengths of the sides of a triangular parcel of land are approximately 200 feet, 500 feet, and 600 feet. Approximate the area of the parcel.

48. *Geometry*   A parking lot has the shape of a parallelogram (see figure). The lengths of two adjacent sides are 70 meters and 100 meters. The angle between the two sides is 70°. What is the area of the parking lot?

Synthesis

True or False? **In Exercises 49–51, determine whether the statement is true or false. Justify your answer.**

49. In Heron's Area Formula

$$\text{Area} = \sqrt{s(s-a)(s-b)(s-c)}$$

s is the average of the lengths of the three sides of the triangle.

50. In addition to SSS and SAS, the Law of Cosines can be used to solve triangles with SSA conditions.

51. A triangle with side lengths of 10 centimeters, 16 centimeters, and 5 centimeters can be solved using the Law of Cosines.

52. ***Circumscribed and Inscribed Circles*** Let R and r be the radii of the circumscribed and inscribed circles of a triangle ABC, respectively (see figure), and let

$$s = \frac{a+b+c}{2}.$$

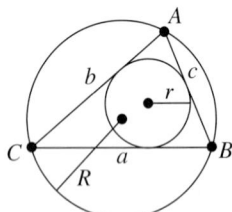

(a) Prove that $2R = \dfrac{a}{\sin A} = \dfrac{b}{\sin B} = \dfrac{c}{\sin C}$.

(b) Prove that $r = \sqrt{\dfrac{(s-a)(s-b)(s-c)}{s}}$.

Circumscribed and Inscribed Circles **In Exercises 53 and 54, use the results of Exercise 52.**

53. Given a triangle with

$a = 25$, $b = 55$, and $c = 72$

find the areas of (a) the triangle, (b) the circumscribed circle, and (c) the inscribed circle.

54. Find the length of the largest circular running track that can be built on a triangular piece of property with sides of lengths 200 feet, 250 feet, and 325 feet.

55. ***Proof*** Use the Law of Cosines to prove that

$$\frac{1}{2}bc(1+\cos A) = \frac{a+b+c}{2}\cdot\frac{-a+b+c}{2}.$$

56. ***Proof*** Use the Law of Cosines to prove that

$$\frac{1}{2}bc(1-\cos A) = \frac{a-b+c}{2}\cdot\frac{a+b-c}{2}.$$

Review

In Exercises 57–62, evaluate the expression without the aid of a calculator.

57. $\arcsin(-1)$

58. $\arccos 0$

59. $\arctan \sqrt{3}$

60. $\arctan -\sqrt{3}$

61. $\arcsin\left(-\dfrac{\sqrt{3}}{2}\right)$

62. $\arccos\left(-\dfrac{\sqrt{3}}{2}\right)$

In Exercises 63–66, write an algebraic expression that is equivalent to the given expression.

63. $\sec(\arcsin 2x)$

64. $\tan(\arccos 3x)$

65. $\cot[\arctan(x-2)]$

66. $\cos\left(\arcsin \dfrac{x-1}{2}\right)$

In Exercises 67–70, use trigonometric substitution to write the algebraic equation as a trigonometric function of θ, where $-\pi/2 < \theta < \pi/2$. Then find $\sec \theta$ and $\csc \theta$.

67. $5 = \sqrt{25-x^2}$, $\quad x = 5\sin\theta$

68. $-\sqrt{2} = \sqrt{4-x^2}$, $\quad x = 2\cos\theta$

69. $-\sqrt{3} = \sqrt{x^2-9}$, $\quad x = 3\sec\theta$

70. $12 = \sqrt{36+x^2}$, $\quad x = 6\tan\theta$

In Exercises 71 and 72, write the sum or difference as a product.

71. $\cos\dfrac{5\pi}{6} - \cos\dfrac{\pi}{3}$

72. $\sin\left(x-\dfrac{\pi}{2}\right) - \sin\left(x+\dfrac{\pi}{2}\right)$

6.3 | Vectors in the Plane

Bill Bachman/Photo Researchers, Inc.

Introduction

Quantities such as force and velocity involve both *magnitude* and *direction* and cannot be completely characterized by a single real number. To represent such a quantity, you can use a **directed line segment,** as shown in Figure 6.15. The directed line segment $\overrightarrow{PQ}$ has **initial point** P and **terminal point** Q. Its **magnitude** (or length) is denoted by $\|PQ\|$ and can be found using the Distance Formula.

Terminal point ● Q

$\overrightarrow{PQ}$

P ● Initial point

FIGURE 6.15   FIGURE 6.16

Two directed line segments that have the same magnitude and direction are equivalent. For example, the directed line segments in Figure 6.16 are all equivalent. The set of all directed line segments that are equivalent to the directed line segment $\overrightarrow{PQ}$ is a **vector v in the plane,** written $\mathbf{v} = \overrightarrow{PQ}$. Vectors are denoted by lowercase, boldface letters such as $\mathbf{u}$, $\mathbf{v}$, and $\mathbf{w}$.

Example 1 ▶ **Vector Representation by Directed Line Segments**

Let $\mathbf{u}$ be represented by the directed line segment from $P = (0, 0)$ to $Q = (3, 2)$, and let $\mathbf{v}$ be represented by the directed line segment from $R = (1, 2)$ to $S = (4, 4)$, as shown in Figure 6.17. Show that $\mathbf{u} = \mathbf{v}$.

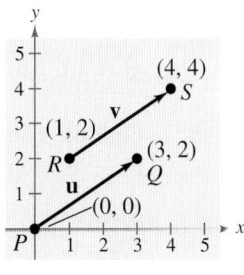

FIGURE 6.17

Solution

From the Distance Formula, it follows that $\overrightarrow{PQ}$ and $\overrightarrow{RS}$ have the *same magnitude*.

$$\|\overrightarrow{PQ}\| = \sqrt{(3 - 0)^2 + (2 - 0)^2} = \sqrt{13}$$

$$\|\overrightarrow{RS}\| = \sqrt{(4 - 1)^2 + (4 - 2)^2} = \sqrt{13}$$

Moreover, both line segments have the *same direction* because they are both directed toward the upper right on lines having a slope of $\frac{2}{3}$. So, $\overrightarrow{PQ}$ and $\overrightarrow{RS}$ have the same magnitude and direction, and it follows that $\mathbf{u} = \mathbf{v}$.

Component Form of a Vector

The directed line segment whose initial point is the origin is often the most convenient representative of a set of equivalent directed line segments. This representative of the vector **v** is in **standard position.**

A vector whose initial point is at the origin $(0, 0)$ can be uniquely represented by the coordinates of its terminal point (v_1, v_2). This is the **component form of a vector v,** written

$$\mathbf{v} = \langle v_1, v_2 \rangle.$$

The coordinates v_1 and v_2 are the *components* of **v.** If both the initial point and the terminal point lie at the origin, **v** is the **zero vector** and is denoted by $\mathbf{0} = \langle 0, 0 \rangle$.

Help students see that $\mathbf{v} = \langle 1, 3 \rangle$ can be thought of as a vector with initial point $(0, 0)$ and terminal point $(1, 3)$, as well as a vector with initial point $(0, -1)$ and terminal point $(1, 2)$, and so on.

Component Form of a Vector

The component form of the vector with initial point $P = (p_1, p_2)$ and terminal point $Q = (q_1, q_2)$ is

$$\overrightarrow{PQ} = \langle q_1 - p_1, q_2 - p_2 \rangle = \langle v_1, v_2 \rangle = \mathbf{v}.$$

The **magnitude** (or length) of **v** is

$$\|\mathbf{v}\| = \sqrt{(q_1 - p_1)^2 + (q_2 - p_2)^2} = \sqrt{v_1^2 + v_2^2}.$$

If $\|\mathbf{v}\| = 1$, **v** is a **unit vector.** Moreover, $\|\mathbf{v}\| = 0$ if and only if **v** is the zero vector **0**.

Two vectors $\mathbf{u} = \langle u_1, u_2 \rangle$ and $\mathbf{v} = \langle v_1, v_2 \rangle$ are *equal* if and only if $u_1 = v_1$ and $u_2 = v_2$. For instance, in Example 1, the vector **u** from $P = (0, 0)$ to $Q = (3, 2)$ is

$$\mathbf{u} = \overrightarrow{PQ} = \langle 3 - 0, 2 - 0 \rangle = \langle 3, 2 \rangle$$

and the vector **v** from $R = (1, 2)$ to $S = (4, 4)$ is

$$\mathbf{v} = \overrightarrow{RS} = \langle 4 - 1, 4 - 2 \rangle = \langle 3, 2 \rangle.$$

Example 2 ▶ Finding the Component Form of a Vector

Find the component form and magnitude of the vector **v** that has initial point $(4, -7)$ and terminal point $(-1, 5)$.

Solution

Let $P = (4, -7) = (p_1, p_2)$ and let $Q = (-1, 5) = (q_1, q_2)$, as shown in Figure 6.18. Then, the components of $\mathbf{v} = \langle v_1, v_2 \rangle$ are

$$v_1 = q_1 - p_1 = -1 - 4 = -5$$
$$v_2 = q_2 - p_2 = 5 - (-7) = 12.$$

So, $\mathbf{v} = \langle -5, 12 \rangle$ and the magnitude of **v** is

$$\|\mathbf{v}\| = \sqrt{(-5)^2 + 12^2}$$
$$= \sqrt{169} = 13.$$

FIGURE **6.18**

FIGURE 6.19

Vector Operations

The two basic vector operations are **scalar multiplication** and **vector addition.** In operations with vectors, numbers are usually referred to as **scalars.** In this text, scalars will always be real numbers. Geometrically, the product of a vector **v** and a scalar k is the vector that is $|k|$ times as long as **v**. If k is positive, k**v** has the same direction as **v**, and if k is negative, k**v** has the direction opposite that of **v**, as shown in Figure 6.19.

To add two vectors geometrically, position them (without changing length or direction) so that the initial point of one coincides with the terminal point of the other. The sum **u** + **v** is formed by joining the initial point of the second vector **v** with the terminal point of the first vector **u**, as shown in Figure 6.20. This technique is called the **parallelogram law** for vector addition because the vector **u** + **v**, often called the **resultant** of vector addition, is the diagonal of a parallelogram having **u** and **v** as its adjacent sides.

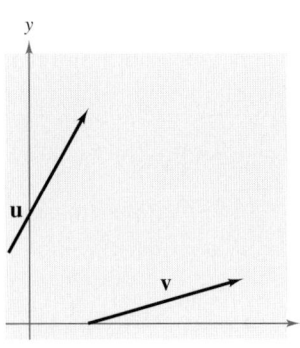

FIGURE 6.20

The graphical representation of the difference of two vectors may not be obvious to your students. You may want to go over this carefully.

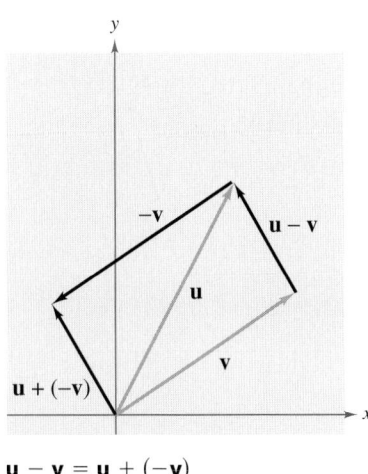

u − **v** = **u** + (−**v**)

FIGURE 6.21

Definitions of Vector Addition and Scalar Multiplication

Let $\mathbf{u} = \langle u_1, u_2 \rangle$ and $\mathbf{v} = \langle v_1, v_2 \rangle$ be vectors and let k be a scalar (a real number). Then the *sum* of **u** and **v** is the vector

$$\mathbf{u} + \mathbf{v} = \langle u_1 + v_1, u_2 + v_2 \rangle \qquad \text{Sum}$$

and the *scalar multiple* of k times **u** is the vector

$$k\mathbf{u} = k\langle u_1, u_2 \rangle = \langle ku_1, ku_2 \rangle. \qquad \text{Scalar multiple}$$

The *negative* of $\mathbf{v} = \langle v_1, v_2 \rangle$ is

$$-\mathbf{v} = (-1)\mathbf{v}$$

$$= \langle -v_1, -v_2 \rangle \qquad \text{Negative}$$

and the *difference* of **u** and **v** is

$$\mathbf{u} - \mathbf{v} = \mathbf{u} + (-\mathbf{v}) \qquad \text{Add } (-\mathbf{v}). \text{ See Figure 8.21.}$$

$$= \langle u_1 - v_1, u_2 - v_2 \rangle. \qquad \text{Difference}$$

To represent **u** − **v** geometrically, you can use directed line segments with the *same* initial point. The difference **u** − **v** is the vector from the terminal point of **v** to the terminal point of **u**, which is equal to **u** + (−**v**), as shown in Figure 6.21.

The component definitions of vector addition and scalar multiplication are illustrated in Example 3. In this example, notice that each of the vector operations can be interpreted geometrically.

Example 3 ▶ **Vector Operations**

Let $\mathbf{v} = \langle -2, 5 \rangle$ and $\mathbf{w} = \langle 3, 4 \rangle$, and find each of the following vectors.

a. $2\mathbf{v}$ **b.** $\mathbf{w} - \mathbf{v}$ **c.** $\mathbf{v} + 2\mathbf{w}$

Solution

a. Because $\mathbf{v} = \langle -2, 5 \rangle$, you have

$$2\mathbf{v} = 2\langle -2, 5 \rangle$$
$$= \langle 2(-2), 2(5) \rangle$$
$$= \langle -4, 10 \rangle.$$

A sketch of $2\mathbf{v}$ is shown in Figure 6.22.

b. The difference of $\mathbf{w}$ and $\mathbf{v}$ is

$$\mathbf{w} - \mathbf{v} = \langle 3 - (-2), 4 - 5 \rangle$$
$$= \langle 5, -1 \rangle.$$

A sketch of $\mathbf{w} - \mathbf{v}$ is shown in Figure 6.23.

c. The sum of $\mathbf{v}$ and $2\mathbf{w}$ is

$$\mathbf{v} + 2\mathbf{w} = \langle -2, 5 \rangle + 2\langle 3, 4 \rangle$$
$$= \langle -2, 5 \rangle + \langle 2(3), 2(4) \rangle$$
$$= \langle -2, 5 \rangle + \langle 6, 8 \rangle$$
$$= \langle -2 + 6, 5 + 8 \rangle$$
$$= \langle 4, 13 \rangle.$$

A sketch of $\mathbf{v} + 2\mathbf{w}$ is shown in Figure 6.24.

FIGURE 6.22

FIGURE 6.23

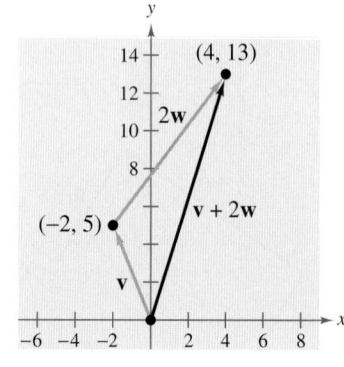

FIGURE 6.24

Vector addition and scalar multiplication share many of the properties of ordinary arithmetic.

Properties of Vector Addition and Scalar Multiplication

Let **u**, **v**, and **w** be vectors and let c and d be scalars. Then the following properties are true.

1. $\mathbf{u} + \mathbf{v} = \mathbf{v} + \mathbf{u}$

2. $(\mathbf{u} + \mathbf{v}) + \mathbf{w} = \mathbf{u} + (\mathbf{v} + \mathbf{w})$

3. $\mathbf{u} + \mathbf{0} = \mathbf{u}$

4. $\mathbf{u} + (-\mathbf{u}) = \mathbf{0}$

5. $c(d\mathbf{u}) = (cd)\mathbf{u}$

6. $(c + d)\mathbf{u} = c\mathbf{u} + d\mathbf{u}$

7. $c(\mathbf{u} + \mathbf{v}) = c\mathbf{u} + c\mathbf{v}$

8. $1(\mathbf{u}) = \mathbf{u}, 0(\mathbf{u}) = \mathbf{0}$

9. $\|c\mathbf{v}\| = |c|\,\|\mathbf{v}\|$

Property 9 can be stated as follows: the magnitude of the vector $c\mathbf{v}$ is the absolute value of c times the magnitude of **v**.

Unit Vectors

In many applications of vectors, it is useful to find a unit vector that has the same direction as a given nonzero vector **v**. To do this, you can divide **v** by its magnitude to obtain

$$\mathbf{u} = \text{unit vector} = \frac{\mathbf{v}}{\|\mathbf{v}\|} = \left(\frac{1}{\|\mathbf{v}\|}\right)\mathbf{v}. \qquad \text{Unit vector in direction of } \mathbf{v}$$

Note that **u** is a scalar multiple of **v**. The vector **u** has magnitude of 1 and the same direction as **v**. The vector **u** is called a **unit vector in the direction of v**.

Example 4 ▶ **Finding a Unit Vector**

Find a unit vector in the direction of $\mathbf{v} = \langle -2, 5 \rangle$ and verify that the result has a magnitude of 1.

Solution

The unit vector in the direction of **v** is

$$\frac{\mathbf{v}}{\|\mathbf{v}\|} = \frac{\langle -2, 5 \rangle}{\sqrt{(-2)^2 + (5)^2}}$$

$$= \frac{1}{\sqrt{29}}\langle -2, 5 \rangle$$

$$= \left\langle \frac{-2}{\sqrt{29}}, \frac{5}{\sqrt{29}} \right\rangle.$$

This vector has a magnitude of 1 because

$$\sqrt{\left(\frac{-2}{\sqrt{29}}\right)^2 + \left(\frac{5}{\sqrt{29}}\right)^2} = \sqrt{\frac{4}{29} + \frac{25}{29}} = \sqrt{\frac{29}{29}} = 1.$$

Historical Note
William Rowan Hamilton (1805–1865), an Irish mathematician, did some of the earliest work with vectors. Hamilton spent many years developing a system of vector-like quantities called quaternions. Although Hamilton was convinced of the benefits of quaternions, the operations he defined did not produce good models for physical phenomena. It wasn't until the latter half of the nineteenth century that the Scottish physicist James Maxwell (1831–1879) restructured Hamilton's quaternions in a form useful for representing physical quantities such as force, velocity, and acceleration.

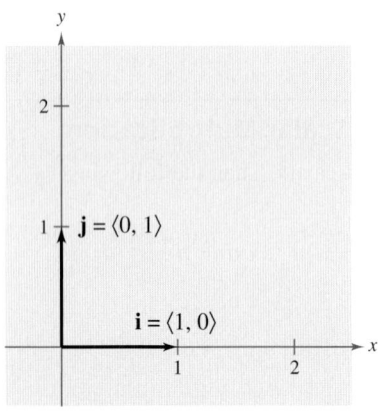

FIGURE 6.25

The unit vectors $\langle 1, 0 \rangle$ and $\langle 0, 1 \rangle$ are called the **standard unit vectors** and are denoted by

$$\mathbf{i} = \langle 1, 0 \rangle \qquad \text{and} \qquad \mathbf{j} = \langle 0, 1 \rangle$$

as shown in Figure 6.25. (Note that the lowercase letter $\mathbf{i}$ is written in boldface to distinguish it from the imaginary number $i = \sqrt{-1}$.) These vectors can be used to represent any vector $\mathbf{v} = \langle v_1, v_2 \rangle$, as follows.

$$\mathbf{v} = \langle v_1, v_2 \rangle$$
$$= v_1 \langle 1, 0 \rangle + v_2 \langle 0, 1 \rangle$$
$$= v_1 \mathbf{i} + v_2 \mathbf{j}$$

The scalars v_1 and v_2 are called the **horizontal** and **vertical components of v,** respectively. The vector sum

$$v_1 \mathbf{i} + v_2 \mathbf{j}$$

is called a **linear combination** of the vectors $\mathbf{i}$ and $\mathbf{j}$. Any vector in the plane can be expressed as a linear combination of the standard unit vectors $\mathbf{i}$ and $\mathbf{j}$.

Example 5 ▶ Writing a Linear Combination of Unit Vectors

Let $\mathbf{u}$ be the vector with initial point $(2, -5)$ and terminal point $(-1, 3)$. Write $\mathbf{u}$ as a linear combination of the standard unit vectors $\mathbf{i}$ and $\mathbf{j}$.

Solution

Begin by writing the component form of the vector $\mathbf{u}$.

$$\mathbf{u} = \langle -1 - 2, 3 + 5 \rangle$$
$$= \langle -3, 8 \rangle$$
$$= -3\mathbf{i} + 8\mathbf{j}$$

This result is shown graphically in Figure 6.26.

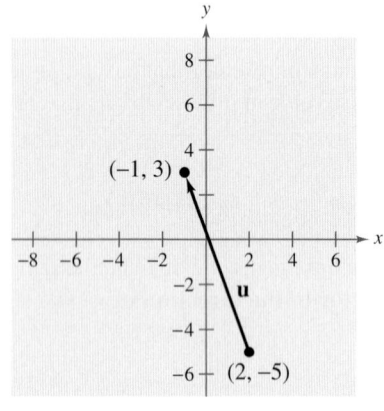

FIGURE 6.26

Example 6 ▶ Vector Operations

Let $\mathbf{u} = -3\mathbf{i} + 8\mathbf{j}$ and let $\mathbf{v} = 2\mathbf{i} - \mathbf{j}$. Find $2\mathbf{u} - 3\mathbf{v}$.

Solution

You could solve this problem by converting $\mathbf{u}$ and $\mathbf{v}$ to component form. This, however, is not necessary. It is just as easy to perform the operations in unit vector form.

$$2\mathbf{u} - 3\mathbf{v} = 2(-3\mathbf{i} + 8\mathbf{j}) - 3(2\mathbf{i} - \mathbf{j})$$
$$= -6\mathbf{i} + 16\mathbf{j} - 6\mathbf{i} + 3\mathbf{j}$$
$$= -12\mathbf{i} + 19\mathbf{j}$$

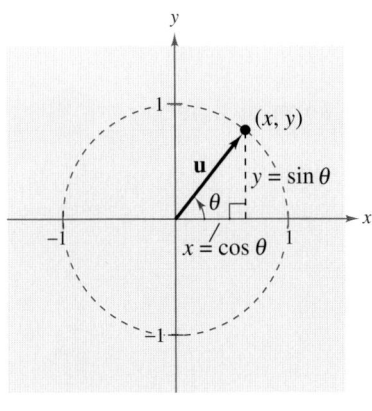

FIGURE 6.27 $\|\mathbf{u}\| = 1$

Direction Angles

If $\mathbf{u}$ is a *unit vector* such that θ is the angle (measured counterclockwise) from the positive x-axis to $\mathbf{u}$, the terminal point of $\mathbf{u}$ lies on the unit circle and you have

$$\mathbf{u} = \langle x, y \rangle = \langle \cos \theta, \sin \theta \rangle = (\cos \theta)\mathbf{i} + (\sin \theta)\mathbf{j}$$

as shown in Figure 6.27. The angle θ is the **direction angle** of the vector $\mathbf{u}$.

Suppose that $\mathbf{u}$ is a unit vector with direction angle θ. If $\mathbf{v}$ is any vector that makes an angle θ with the positive x-axis, it has the same direction as $\mathbf{u}$ and you can write

$$\mathbf{v} = \|\mathbf{v}\| \langle \cos \theta, \sin \theta \rangle$$
$$= \|\mathbf{v}\| (\cos \theta)\mathbf{i} + \|\mathbf{v}\| (\sin \theta)\mathbf{j}.$$

Because $\mathbf{v} = a\mathbf{i} + b\mathbf{j} = \|\mathbf{v}\| (\cos \theta)\mathbf{i} + \|\mathbf{v}\| (\sin \theta)\mathbf{j}$, it follows that the direction angle θ for $\mathbf{v}$ is determined from

$$\tan \theta = \frac{\sin \theta}{\cos \theta} \qquad \text{Quotient identity}$$

$$= \frac{\|\mathbf{v}\| \sin \theta}{\|\mathbf{v}\| \cos \theta} \qquad \text{Multiply numerator and denominator by } \|\mathbf{v}\|.$$

$$= \frac{b}{a}. \qquad \text{Simplify.}$$

Example 7 ▶ **Finding Direction Angles of Vectors**

Find the direction angle of each vector.

a. $\mathbf{u} = 3\mathbf{i} + 3\mathbf{j}$

b. $\mathbf{v} = 3\mathbf{i} - 4\mathbf{j}$

Solution

a. The direction angle is

$$\tan \theta = \frac{b}{a} = \frac{3}{3} = 1.$$

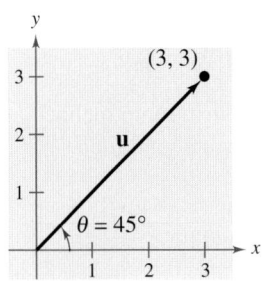

FIGURE 6.28

So, $\theta = 45°$, as shown in Figure 6.28.

b. The direction angle is

$$\tan \theta = \frac{b}{a} = \frac{-4}{3}.$$

Moreover, because $\mathbf{v} = 3\mathbf{i} - 4\mathbf{j}$ lies in Quadrant IV, θ lies in Quadrant IV and its reference angle is

$$\theta = \left| \arctan\left(-\frac{4}{3} \right) \right| \approx \left| -53.13° \right| = 53.13°.$$

So, it follows that $\theta \approx 360° - 53.13° = 306.87°$, as shown in Figure 6.29.

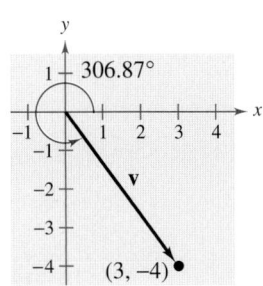

FIGURE 6.29

Applications of Vectors

FIGURE 6.30

Example 8 ▶   Finding the Component Form of a Vector

Find the component form of the vector that represents the velocity of an airplane descending at a speed of 100 miles per hour at an angle 30° below the horizontal, as shown in Figure 6.30.

Solution

The velocity vector **v** has a magnitude of 100 and a direction angle of $\theta = 210°$.

$$\mathbf{v} = \|\mathbf{v}\| (\cos \theta)\mathbf{i} + \|\mathbf{v}\| (\sin \theta)\mathbf{j}$$

$$= 100(\cos 210°)\mathbf{i} + 100(\sin 210°)\mathbf{j}$$

$$= 100\left(\frac{-\sqrt{3}}{2}\right)\mathbf{i} + 100\left(\frac{-1}{2}\right)\mathbf{j}$$

$$= -50\sqrt{3}\,\mathbf{i} - 50\mathbf{j}$$

$$= \langle -50\sqrt{3},\, -50 \rangle$$

You can check that **v** has a magnitude of 100, as follows.

$$\|\mathbf{v}\| = \sqrt{\left(-50\sqrt{3}\right)^2 + (50)^2}$$

$$= \sqrt{7500 + 2500}$$

$$= \sqrt{10{,}000}$$

$$= 100$$

Example 9 ▶   Using Vectors to Determine Weight

A force of 600 pounds is required to pull a boat and trailer up a ramp inclined at 15° from the horizontal. Find the combined weight of the boat and trailer.

Solution

Based on Figure 6.31, you can make the following observations.

$\|\overrightarrow{BA}\|$ = force of gravity = combined weight of boat and trailer

$\|\overrightarrow{BC}\|$ = force against ramp

$\|\overrightarrow{AC}\|$ = force required to move boat up ramp = 600 pounds

By construction, triangles BWD and ABC are similar. So, angle ABC is 15°. So in triangle ABC you have

$$\sin 15° = \frac{\|\overrightarrow{AC}\|}{\|\overrightarrow{BA}\|} = \frac{600}{\|\overrightarrow{BA}\|}$$

$$\|BA\| = \frac{600}{\sin 15°} \approx 2318.$$

Consequently, the combined weight is approximately 2318 pounds. (In Figure 6.31, note that $\overrightarrow{AC}$ is parallel to the ramp.)

FIGURE 6.31

Example 10 ▶ Using Vectors to Find Speed and Direction

An airplane is traveling at a speed of 500 miles per hour on a bearing of 330° at a fixed altitude with a negligible wind velocity as shown in Figure 6.32(a). As the airplane reaches a certain point, it encounters a wind with a velocity of 70 miles per hour in the direction N 45° E, as shown in Figure 6.32(b). What are the resultant speed and direction of the airplane?

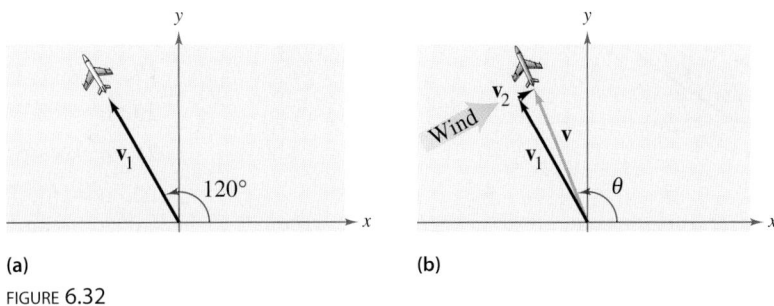

(a)   (b)

FIGURE 6.32

Solution

Using Figure 6.32, the velocity of the airplane (alone) is

$$\mathbf{v}_1 = 500\langle \cos 120°, \sin 120° \rangle$$
$$= \langle -250, 250\sqrt{3} \rangle$$

and the velocity of the wind is

$$\mathbf{v}_2 = 70\langle \cos 45°, \sin 45° \rangle$$
$$= \langle 35\sqrt{2}, 35\sqrt{2} \rangle.$$

So, the velocity of the airplane (in the wind) is

$$\mathbf{v} = \mathbf{v}_1 + \mathbf{v}_2$$
$$= \langle -250 + 35\sqrt{2}, 250\sqrt{3} + 35\sqrt{2} \rangle$$
$$\approx \langle -200.5, 482.5 \rangle$$

and the resultant speed of the airplane is

$$\|\mathbf{v}\| = \sqrt{(-200.5)^2 + (482.5)^2}$$
$$\approx 522.5 \text{ miles per hour.}$$

Finally, if θ is the direction angle of the flight path, you have

$$\tan \theta = \frac{482.5}{-200.5}$$
$$\approx -2.4065$$

which implies that

$$\theta \approx 180° + \arctan(-2.4065) \approx 180° - 67.4° = 112.6°.$$

So, the true direction of the airplane is 337.4°.

Activities

1. Find the component form and the magnitude of the vector with initial point $(-3, 2)$ and terminal point $(1, 4)$.

   Answer: $\langle 4, 2 \rangle; 2\sqrt{5}$

2. Vector **v** has direction angle $\theta = 30°$ and magnitude 6. Find **v**.

   Answer: $\mathbf{v} = \langle 3\sqrt{3}, 3 \rangle$

3. $\mathbf{v} = 7\mathbf{i} - 2\mathbf{j}, \mathbf{w} = -2\mathbf{i} + \mathbf{j}$. Find $2\mathbf{v} + \mathbf{w}$.

   Answer: $12\mathbf{i} - 3\mathbf{j}$

6.3 **Exercises**

In Exercises 1–12, find the component form and the magnitude of the vector **v**.

1.

2.

3.

4.

5.

6.
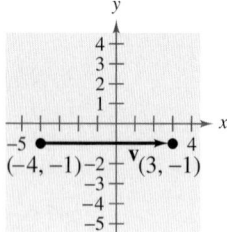

Initial Point	Terminal Point
7. $(-1, 5)$	$(15, 12)$
8. $(1, 11)$	$(9, 3)$
9. $(-3, -5)$	$(5, 1)$
10. $(-3, 11)$	$(9, 40)$
11. $(1, 3)$	$(-8, -9)$
12. $(-2, 7)$	$(5, -17)$

In Exercises 13–18, use the figure to sketch a graph of the specified vector. To print an enlarged copy of the graph, go to the website, *www.mathgraphs.com.*

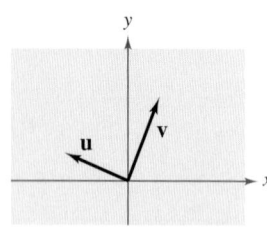

13. $-\mathbf{v}$

14. $5\mathbf{v}$

15. $\mathbf{u} + \mathbf{v}$

16. $\mathbf{u} - \mathbf{v}$

17. $\mathbf{u} + 2\mathbf{v}$

18. $\mathbf{v} - \frac{1}{2}\mathbf{u}$

In Exercises 19–26, find (a) $\mathbf{u} + \mathbf{v}$, (b) $\mathbf{u} - \mathbf{v}$, and (c) $2\mathbf{u} - 3\mathbf{v}$. Then sketch the resultant vector.

19. $\mathbf{u} = \langle 2, 1 \rangle, \quad \mathbf{v} = \langle 1, 3 \rangle$

20. $\mathbf{u} = \langle 2, 3 \rangle, \quad \mathbf{v} = \langle 4, 0 \rangle$

21. $\mathbf{u} = \langle -5, 3 \rangle, \quad \mathbf{v} = \langle 0, 0 \rangle$

22. $\mathbf{u} = \langle 0, 0 \rangle, \quad \mathbf{v} = \langle 2, 1 \rangle$

23. $\mathbf{u} = \mathbf{i} + \mathbf{j}, \quad \mathbf{v} = 2\mathbf{i} - 3\mathbf{j}$

24. $\mathbf{u} = -2\mathbf{i} + \mathbf{j}, \quad \mathbf{v} = -\mathbf{i} + 2\mathbf{j}$

25. $\mathbf{u} = 2\mathbf{i}, \quad \mathbf{v} = \mathbf{j}$

26. $\mathbf{u} = 3\mathbf{j}, \quad \mathbf{v} = 2\mathbf{i}$

In Exercises 27–36, find a unit vector in the direction of the given vector.

27. $\mathbf{u} = \langle 3, 0 \rangle$

28. $\mathbf{u} = \langle 0, -2 \rangle$

29. $\mathbf{v} = \langle -2, 2 \rangle$

30. $\mathbf{v} = \langle 5, -12 \rangle$

31. $\mathbf{v} = 6\mathbf{i} - 2\mathbf{j}$

32. $\mathbf{v} = \mathbf{i} + \mathbf{j}$

33. $\mathbf{w} = 4\mathbf{j}$

34. $\mathbf{w} = -6\mathbf{i}$

35. $\mathbf{w} = \mathbf{i} - 2\mathbf{j}$

36. $\mathbf{w} = 7\mathbf{j} - 3\mathbf{i}$

In Exercises 37–40, find the vector **v** with the given magnitude and the same direction as **u**.

Magnitude	Direction
37. $\|\mathbf{v}\| = 5$	$\mathbf{u} = \langle 3, 3 \rangle$
38. $\|\mathbf{v}\| = 6$	$\mathbf{u} = \langle -3, 3 \rangle$
39. $\|\mathbf{v}\| = 9$	$\mathbf{u} = \langle 2, 5 \rangle$
40. $\|\mathbf{v}\| = 10$	$\mathbf{u} = \langle -10, 0 \rangle$

In Exercises 41–46, find the component form of **v** and sketch the specified vector operations geometrically, where $\mathbf{u} = 2\mathbf{i} - \mathbf{j}$ and $\mathbf{w} = \mathbf{i} + 2\mathbf{j}$.

41. $\mathbf{v} = \frac{3}{2}\mathbf{u}$

42. $\mathbf{v} = \frac{3}{4}\mathbf{w}$

43. $\mathbf{v} = \mathbf{u} + 2\mathbf{w}$

44. $\mathbf{v} = -\mathbf{u} + \mathbf{w}$

45. $\mathbf{v} = \frac{1}{2}(3\mathbf{u} + \mathbf{w})$

46. $\mathbf{v} = \mathbf{u} - 2\mathbf{w}$

In Exercises 47–50, find the magnitude and direction angle of the vector **v**.

47. $\mathbf{v} = 3(\cos 60°\mathbf{i} + \sin 60°\mathbf{j})$

48. $\mathbf{v} = 8(\cos 135°\mathbf{i} + \sin 135°\mathbf{j})$

49. $\mathbf{v} = 6\mathbf{i} - 6\mathbf{j}$ 50. $\mathbf{v} = -5\mathbf{i} + 4\mathbf{j}$

In Exercises 51–58, find the component form of v given its magnitude and the angle it makes with the positive x-axis. Sketch v.

Magnitude	Angle
51. $\|\mathbf{v}\| = 3$	$\theta = 0°$
52. $\|\mathbf{v}\| = 1$	$\theta = 45°$
53. $\|\mathbf{v}\| = \frac{7}{2}$	$\theta = 150°$
54. $\|\mathbf{v}\| = \frac{5}{2}$	$\theta = 45°$
55. $\|\mathbf{v}\| = 3\sqrt{2}$	$\theta = 150°$
56. $\|\mathbf{v}\| = 4\sqrt{3}$	$\theta = 90°$
57. $\|\mathbf{v}\| = 2$	$\mathbf{v}$ in the direction $\mathbf{i} + 3\mathbf{j}$
58. $\|\mathbf{v}\| = 3$	$\mathbf{v}$ in the direction $3\mathbf{i} + 4\mathbf{j}$

In Exercises 59–62, find the component form of the sum of u and v with direction angles $\theta_{\mathbf{u}}$ and $\theta_{\mathbf{v}}$.

Magnitude	Angle
59. $\|\mathbf{u}\| = 5$	$\theta_{\mathbf{u}} = 0°$
$\|\mathbf{v}\| = 5$	$\theta_{\mathbf{v}} = 90°$
60. $\|\mathbf{u}\| = 4$	$\theta_{\mathbf{u}} = 60°$
$\|\mathbf{v}\| = 4$	$\theta_{\mathbf{v}} = 90°$
61. $\|\mathbf{u}\| = 20$	$\theta_{\mathbf{u}} = 45°$
$\|\mathbf{v}\| = 50$	$\theta_{\mathbf{v}} = 180°$
62. $\|\mathbf{u}\| = 50$	$\theta_{\mathbf{u}} = 30°$
$\|\mathbf{v}\| = 30$	$\theta_{\mathbf{v}} = 110°$

In Exercises 63–66, use the Law of Cosines to find the angle α between the vectors. (Assume $0° \le \alpha \le 180°$.)

63. $\mathbf{v} = \mathbf{i} + \mathbf{j}$, $\mathbf{w} = 2\mathbf{i} - 2\mathbf{j}$

64. $\mathbf{v} = 3\mathbf{i} - 2\mathbf{j}$, $\mathbf{w} = 2\mathbf{i} + 2\mathbf{j}$

65. $\mathbf{v} = \mathbf{i} + \mathbf{j}$, $\mathbf{w} = 3\mathbf{i} - \mathbf{j}$

66. $\mathbf{v} = \mathbf{i} + 2\mathbf{j}$, $\mathbf{w} = 2\mathbf{i} - \mathbf{j}$

Resultant Force **In Exercises 67 and 68, find the angle between the forces given the magnitude of their resultant. (*Hint:* Write force 1 as a vector in the direction of the positive x-axis and force 2 as a vector at an angle θ with the positive x-axis.)**

Force 1	Force 2	Resultant Force
67. 45 pounds	60 pounds	90 pounds
68. 3000 pounds	1000 pounds	3750 pounds

69. ***Resultant Force*** Forces with magnitudes of 125 newtons and 300 newtons act on a hook (see figure). The angle between the two forces is 45°. Find the direction and magnitude of the resultant of these forces.

70. ***Resultant Force*** Forces with magnitudes of 2000 newtons and 900 newtons act on a machine part at angles of 30° and −45°, respectively, with the x-axis (see figure). Find the direction and magnitude of the resultant of these forces.

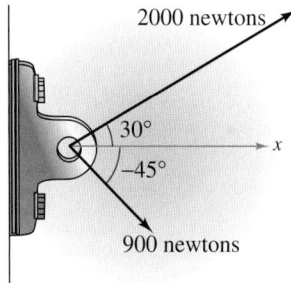

71. ***Resultant Force*** Three forces with magnitudes of 75 pounds, 100 pounds, and 125 pounds act on an object at angles of 30°, 45°, and 120°, respectively, with the positive x-axis. Find the direction and magnitude of the resultant of these forces.

72. ***Resultant Force*** Three forces with magnitudes of 70 pounds, 40 pounds, and 60 pounds act on an object at angles of −30°, 45°, and 135°, respectively, with the positive x-axis. Find the direction and magnitude of the resultant of these forces.

73. *Velocity* A ball is thrown with an initial velocity of 70 feet per second, at an angle of 35° with the horizontal (see figure). Find the vertical and horizontal components of the velocity.

74. *Velocity* A gun with a muzzle velocity of 1200 feet per second is fired at an angle of 6° with the horizontal. Find the vertical and horizontal components of the velocity.

Cable Tension In Exercises 75 and 76, use the figure to determine the tension in each cable supporting the load.

75.

76.
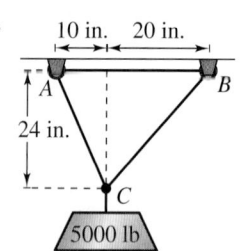

77. *Tow Line Tension* A loaded barge is being towed by two tugboats, and the magnitude of the resultant is 6000 pounds directed along the axis of the barge (see figure). Find the tension in the tow lines if they each make an 18° angle with the axis of the barge.

78. *Rope Tension* To carry a 100-pound cylindrical weight, two people lift on the ends of short ropes that are tied to an eyelet on the top center of the cylinder. Each rope makes a 20° angle with the vertical. Draw a figure that gives a visual representation of the problem, and find the tension in the ropes.

79. *Navigation* An airplane is flying in the direction of 148°, with an airspeed of 875 kilometers per hour. Because of the wind, its groundspeed and direction are 800 kilometers per hour and 140°, respectively (see figure). Find the direction and speed of the wind.

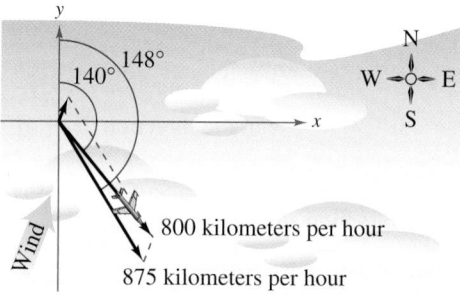

▶ **Model It**

80. *Navigation* A commercial jet is flying from Miami to Seattle. The jet's velocity with respect to the air is 580 miles per hour, and its bearing is 332°. The wind, at the altitude of the plane, is blowing from the southwest with a velocity of 60 miles per hour.

(a) Draw a figure that gives a visual representation of the problem.

(b) Write the velocity of the wind as a vector in component form.

(c) Write the velocity of the jet relative to the air in component form.

(d) What is the speed of the jet with respect to the ground?

(e) What is the true direction of the jet?

81. *Work* A heavy implement is pulled 30 feet across a floor, using a force of 100 pounds. The force is 50° above the horizontal (see figure). Find the work done. (Use the formula for work, $W = FD$, where F is the component of the force in the direction of motion and D is the distance.)

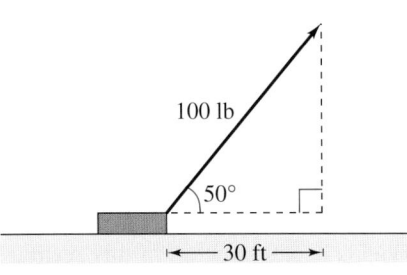

FIGURE FOR 81

82. Rope Tension A tetherball weighing 1 pound is pulled outward from the pole by a horizontal force **u** until the rope makes a 45° angle with the pole (see figure). Determine the resulting tension in the rope and the magnitude of **u**.

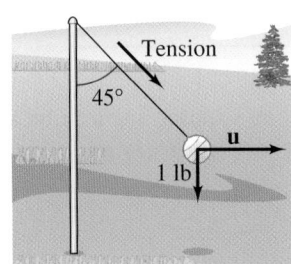

Synthesis

True or False? In Exercises 83 and 84, decide whether the statement is true or false. Justify your answer.

83. If **u** and **v** have the same magnitude and direction, then **u** = **v**.

84. If **u** = a**i** + b**j** is a unit vector, then $a^2 + b^2 = 1$.

85. *Think About It* Consider two forces of equal magnitude acting on a point.

(a) If the magnitude of the resultant is the sum of the magnitudes of the two forces, make a conjecture about the angle between the forces.

(b) If the resultant of the forces is **0**, make a conjecture about the angle between the forces.

(c) Can the magnitude of the resultant be greater than the sum of the magnitudes of the two forces? Explain.

86. *Graphical Reasoning* Consider two forces

$$\mathbf{F}_1 = \langle 10, 0 \rangle \text{ and } \mathbf{F}_2 = 5\langle \cos \theta, \sin \theta \rangle.$$

(a) Find $\|\mathbf{F}_1 + \mathbf{F}_2\|$ as a function of θ.

 (b) Use a graphing utility to graph the function in part (a) for $0 \le \theta < 2\pi$.

 (c) Use the graph in part (b) to determine the range of the function. What is its maximum, and for what value of θ does it occur? What is its minimum, and for what value of θ does it occur?

(d) Explain why the magnitude of the resultant is never 0.

87. *Proof* Prove that $(\cos \theta)\mathbf{i} + (\sin \theta)\mathbf{j}$ is a unit vector for any value of θ.

88. *Technology* Write a program for your graphing utility that graphs two vectors and their difference given the vectors in component form.

In Exercises 89 and 90, use the program in Exercise 88 to find the difference of the vectors shown in the figure.

89.

90.

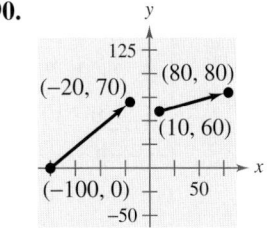

Review

In Exercises 91–94, use the specified trigonometric substitution to write the algebraic expression as a trigonometric function of θ, where $0 < \theta < \pi/2$.

91. $\sqrt{x^2 - 64}$, $x = 8 \sec \theta$

92. $\sqrt{64 - x^2}$, $x = 8 \sin \theta$

93. $\sqrt{x^2 + 36}$, $x = 6 \tan \theta$

94. $\sqrt{(x^2 - 25)^3}$, $x = 5 \sec \theta$

In Exercises 95–98, solve the equation.

95. $\cos x(\cos x + 1) = 0$

96. $\sin x(2 \sin x + \sqrt{2}) = 0$

97. $3 \sec x \sin x - 2\sqrt{3} \sin x = 0$

98. $\cos x \csc x + \cos x\sqrt{2} = 0$

6.4 Vectors and Dot Products

▶ **What you should learn**

- How to find the dot product of two vectors and use the Properties of the Dot Product
- How to find the angle between two vectors and determine whether two vectors are orthogonal
- How to write a vector as the sum of two vector components
- How to use vectors to find the work done by a force

▶ **Why you should learn it**

You can use the dot product of two vectors to solve real-life problems involving two vector quantities. For instance, in Exercise 48 on page 448, you will use the dot product to find the force necessary to keep a truck from rolling down a hill.

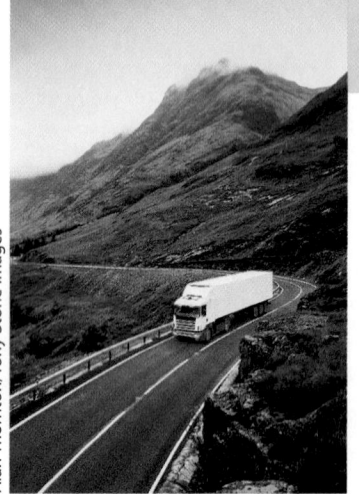

The Dot Product of Two Vectors

So far you have studied two vector operations—vector addition and multiplication by a scalar—each of which yields another vector. In this section you will study a third vector operation, the **dot product.** This product yields a scalar, rather than a vector.

Definition of Dot Product

The **dot product** of $\mathbf{u} = \langle u_1, u_2 \rangle$ and $\mathbf{v} = \langle v_1, v_2 \rangle$ is

$$\mathbf{u} \cdot \mathbf{v} = u_1 v_1 + u_2 v_2.$$

Properties of the Dot Product

Let $\mathbf{u}$, $\mathbf{v}$, and $\mathbf{w}$ be vectors in the plane or in space and let c be a scalar.

1. $\mathbf{u} \cdot \mathbf{v} = \mathbf{v} \cdot \mathbf{u}$

2. $\mathbf{0} \cdot \mathbf{v} = 0$

3. $\mathbf{u} \cdot (\mathbf{v} + \mathbf{w}) = \mathbf{u} \cdot \mathbf{v} + \mathbf{u} \cdot \mathbf{w}$

4. $\mathbf{v} \cdot \mathbf{v} = \|\mathbf{v}\|^2$

5. $c(\mathbf{u} \cdot \mathbf{v}) = c\mathbf{u} \cdot \mathbf{v} = \mathbf{u} \cdot c\mathbf{v}$

For proofs of the Properties of the Dot Product, see Proofs in Mathematics on page 471.

Example 1 ▶ **Finding Dot Products**

Find each dot product.

a. $\langle 4, 5 \rangle \cdot \langle 2, 3 \rangle$ **b.** $\langle 2, -1 \rangle \cdot \langle 1, 2 \rangle$ **c.** $\langle 0, 3 \rangle \cdot \langle 4, -2 \rangle$

Solution

a. $\langle 4, 5 \rangle \cdot \langle 2, 3 \rangle = 4(2) + 5(3)$

$$= 8 + 15$$

$$= 23$$

b. $\langle 2, -1 \rangle \cdot \langle 1, 2 \rangle = 2(1) + (-1)(2) = 2 - 2 = 0$

c. $\langle 0, 3 \rangle \cdot \langle 4, -2 \rangle = 0(4) + 3(-2) = 0 - 6 = -6$

In Example 1, be sure you see that the dot product of two vectors is a scalar (a real number), not a vector. Moreover, notice that the dot product can be positive, zero, or negative.

Example 2 ▸ **Using Properties of Dot Products**

Let $\mathbf{u} = \langle -1, 3 \rangle$, $\mathbf{v} = \langle 2, -4 \rangle$, and $\mathbf{w} = \langle 1, -2 \rangle$. Find each dot product.

a. $(\mathbf{u} \cdot \mathbf{v})\mathbf{w}$ **b.** $\mathbf{u} \cdot 2\mathbf{v}$

Solution

Begin by finding the dot product of $\mathbf{u}$ and $\mathbf{v}$.

$$\mathbf{u} \cdot \mathbf{v} = \langle -1, 3 \rangle \cdot \langle 2, -4 \rangle$$
$$= (-1)(2) + 3(-4)$$
$$= -14$$

a. $(\mathbf{u} \cdot \mathbf{v})\mathbf{w} = -14\langle 1, -2 \rangle$
$$= \langle -14, 28 \rangle$$

b. $\mathbf{u} \cdot 2\mathbf{v} = 2(\mathbf{u} \cdot \mathbf{v})$
$$= 2(-14)$$
$$= -28$$

Notice that the first product is a vector, whereas the second is a scalar. Can you see why?

Example 3 ▸ **Dot Product and Magnitude**

The dot product of $\mathbf{u}$ with itself is 5. What is the magnitude of $\mathbf{u}$?

Solution

Because $\|\mathbf{u}\|^2 = \mathbf{u} \cdot \mathbf{u}$ and $\mathbf{u} \cdot \mathbf{u} = 5$, it follows that

$$\|\mathbf{u}\| = \sqrt{\mathbf{u} \cdot \mathbf{u}}$$
$$= \sqrt{5}.$$

The Angle Between Two Vectors

The **angle between two nonzero vectors** is the angle θ, $0 \le \theta \le \pi$, between their respective standard position vectors, as shown in Figure 6.33 on page 442. This angle can be found using the dot product. (Note that the angle between the zero vector and another vector is not defined.)

Angle Between Two Vectors

If θ is the angle between two nonzero vectors $\mathbf{u}$ and $\mathbf{v}$, then

$$\cos \theta = \frac{\mathbf{u} \cdot \mathbf{v}}{\|\mathbf{u}\| \, \|\mathbf{v}\|}.$$

For a proof of the angle between two vectors, see Proofs in Mathematics on page 471.

| Example 4 ▶ | Finding the Angle Between Two Vectors | |

Find the angle between $\mathbf{u} = \langle 4, 3 \rangle$ and $\mathbf{v} = \langle 3, 5 \rangle$.

Solution

$$\cos \theta = \frac{\mathbf{u} \cdot \mathbf{v}}{\|\mathbf{u}\| \, \|\mathbf{v}\|}$$

$$= \frac{\langle 4, 3 \rangle \cdot \langle 3, 5 \rangle}{\|\langle 4, 3 \rangle\| \, \|\langle 3, 5 \rangle\|}$$

$$= \frac{27}{5\sqrt{34}}$$

This implies that the angle between the two vectors is

$$\theta = \arccos \frac{27}{5\sqrt{34}} \approx 22.2°$$

as shown in Figure 6.33.

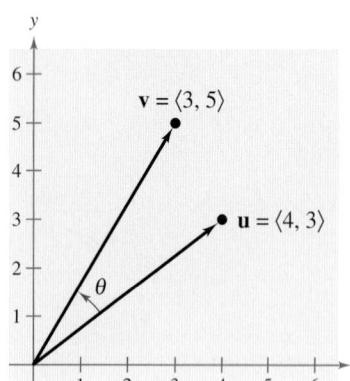

FIGURE 6.33

Rewriting the expression for the angle between two vectors in the form

$$\mathbf{u} \cdot \mathbf{v} = \|\mathbf{u}\| \, \|\mathbf{v}\| \cos \theta \qquad \text{Alternative form of dot product}$$

produces an alternative way to calculate the dot product. From this form, you can see that because $\|\mathbf{u}\|$ and $\|\mathbf{v}\|$ are always positive, $\mathbf{u} \cdot \mathbf{v}$ and $\cos \theta$ will always have the same sign. Figure 6.34 shows the five possible orientations of two vectors.

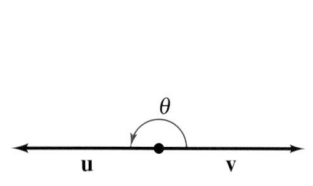

$\theta = \pi$
$\cos \theta = -1$
Opposite Direction
FIGURE 6.34

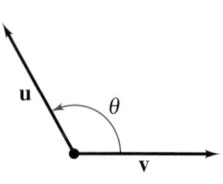

$\frac{\pi}{2} < \theta < \pi$
$-1 < \cos \theta < 0$
Obtuse Angle

$\theta = \frac{\pi}{2}$
$\cos \theta = 0$
90° Angle

$0 < \theta < \frac{\pi}{2}$
$0 < \cos \theta < 1$
Acute Angle

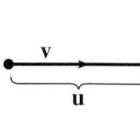

$\theta = 0$
$\cos \theta = 1$
Same Direction

Definition of Orthogonal Vectors

The vectors $\mathbf{u}$ and $\mathbf{v}$ are **orthogonal** if $\mathbf{u} \cdot \mathbf{v} = 0$.

The terms "orthogonal" and "perpendicular" mean essentially the same thing—meeting at right angles. Even though the angle between the zero vector and another vector is not defined, it is convenient to extend the definition of orthogonality to include the zero vector. In other words, the zero vector is orthogonal to every vector $\mathbf{u}$, because $\mathbf{0} \cdot \mathbf{u} = 0$.

Example 5 ▶ **Determining Orthogonal Vectors**

Are the vectors $\mathbf{u} = \langle 2, -3 \rangle$ and $\mathbf{v} = \langle 6, 4 \rangle$ orthogonal?

Solution

Begin by finding the dot product of the two vectors.

$$\mathbf{u} \cdot \mathbf{v} = \langle 2, -3 \rangle \cdot \langle 6, 4 \rangle = 2(6) + (-3)(4) = 0$$

Because the dot product is 0, the two vectors are orthogonal (see Figure 6.35).

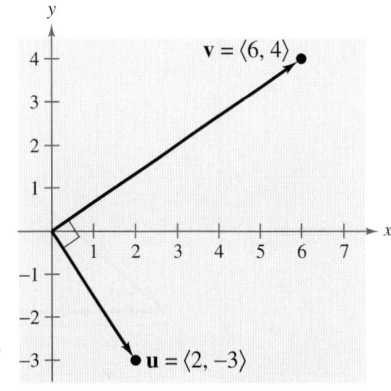

FIGURE 6.35

Finding Vector Components

You have already seen applications in which two vectors are added to produce a resultant vector. Many applications in physics and engineering pose the reverse problem—decomposing a given vector into the sum of two **vector components.**

Consider a boat on an inclined ramp, as shown in Figure 6.36. The force $\mathbf{F}$ due to gravity pulls the boat *down* the ramp and *against* the ramp. These two orthogonal forces, $\mathbf{w}_1$ and $\mathbf{w}_2$, are vector components of $\mathbf{F}$. That is,

$$\mathbf{F} = \mathbf{w}_1 + \mathbf{w}_2. \qquad \text{Vector components of } \mathbf{F}$$

The negative of component $\mathbf{w}_1$ represents the force needed to keep the boat from rolling down the ramp, whereas $\mathbf{w}_2$ represents the force that the tires must withstand against the ramp. A procedure for finding $\mathbf{w}_1$ and $\mathbf{w}_2$ is shown on the following page.

FIGURE 6.36

Definition of Vector Components

Let $\mathbf{u}$ and $\mathbf{v}$ be nonzero vectors such that

$$\mathbf{u} = \mathbf{w}_1 + \mathbf{w}_2$$

where $\mathbf{w}_1$ and $\mathbf{w}_2$ are orthogonal and $\mathbf{w}_1$ is parallel to (or a scalar multiple of) $\mathbf{v}$, as shown in Figure 6.37. The vectors $\mathbf{w}_1$ and $\mathbf{w}_2$ are called vector components of $\mathbf{u}$. The vector $\mathbf{w}_1$ is the **projection** of $\mathbf{u}$ onto $\mathbf{v}$ and is denoted by

$$\mathbf{w}_1 = \text{proj}_{\mathbf{v}}\mathbf{u}.$$

The vector $\mathbf{w}_2$ is given by $\mathbf{w}_2 = \mathbf{u} - \mathbf{w}_1$.

 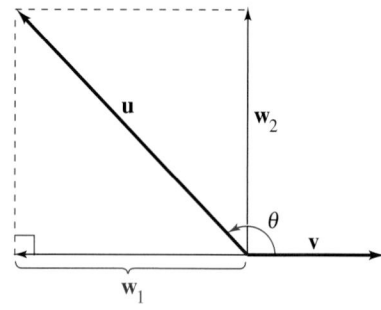

θ *is acute.* θ *is obtuse.*

FIGURE 6.37

From the definition of vector components, you can see that it is easy to find the component $\mathbf{w}_2$ once you have found the projection of $\mathbf{u}$ onto $\mathbf{v}$. To find the projection, you can use the dot product, as follows.

$$\mathbf{u} = \mathbf{w}_1 + \mathbf{w}_2 = c\mathbf{v} + \mathbf{w}_2 \qquad \text{$\mathbf{w}_1$ is a scalar multiple of $\mathbf{v}$.}$$
$$\mathbf{u} \cdot \mathbf{v} = (c\mathbf{v} + \mathbf{w}_2) \cdot \mathbf{v} \qquad \text{Take dot product of each side with $\mathbf{v}$.}$$
$$= c\mathbf{v} \cdot \mathbf{v} + \mathbf{w}_2 \cdot \mathbf{v}$$
$$= c\|\mathbf{v}\|^2 + 0 \qquad \text{$\mathbf{w}_2$ and $\mathbf{v}$ are orthogonal.}$$

So,

$$c = \frac{\mathbf{u} \cdot \mathbf{v}}{\|\mathbf{v}\|^2}$$

and

$$\mathbf{w}_1 = \text{proj}_{\mathbf{v}}\,\mathbf{u} = c\mathbf{v} = \frac{\mathbf{u} \cdot \mathbf{v}}{\|\mathbf{v}\|^2}\,\mathbf{v}.$$

Projection of u onto v

Let $\mathbf{u}$ and $\mathbf{v}$ be nonzero vectors. The projection of $\mathbf{u}$ onto $\mathbf{v}$ is

$$\text{proj}_{\mathbf{v}}\mathbf{u} = \left(\frac{\mathbf{u} \cdot \mathbf{v}}{\|\mathbf{v}\|^2}\right)\mathbf{v}.$$

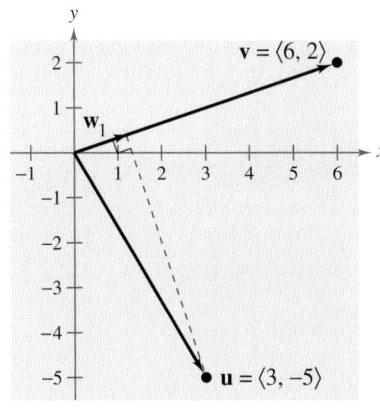

FIGURE **6.38**

Example 6 ▶ Decomposing a Vector into Components

Find the projection of $\mathbf{u} = \langle 3, -5 \rangle$ onto $\mathbf{v} = \langle 6, 2 \rangle$. Then write $\mathbf{u}$ as the sum of two orthogonal vectors, one of which is $\text{proj}_\mathbf{v}\mathbf{u}$.

Solution

The projection of $\mathbf{u}$ onto $\mathbf{v}$ is

$$\mathbf{w}_1 = \text{proj}_\mathbf{v}\mathbf{u} = \left(\frac{\mathbf{u} \cdot \mathbf{v}}{\|\mathbf{v}\|^2}\right)\mathbf{v} = \left(\frac{8}{40}\right)\langle 6, 2 \rangle = \left\langle \frac{6}{5}, \frac{2}{5} \right\rangle$$

as shown in Figure 6.38. The other component, $\mathbf{w}_2$, is

$$\mathbf{w}_2 = \mathbf{u} - \mathbf{w}_1 = \langle 3, -5 \rangle - \left\langle \frac{6}{5}, \frac{2}{5} \right\rangle = \left\langle \frac{9}{5}, -\frac{27}{5} \right\rangle.$$

So,

$$\mathbf{u} = \mathbf{w}_1 + \mathbf{w}_2 = \left\langle \frac{6}{5}, \frac{2}{5} \right\rangle + \left\langle \frac{9}{5}, -\frac{27}{5} \right\rangle = \langle 3, -5 \rangle.$$

Example 7 ▶ Finding a Force

A 200-pound cart sits on a ramp inclined at 30°, as shown in Figure 6.39. What force is required to keep the cart from rolling down the ramp?

Solution

Because the force due to gravity is vertical and downward, you can represent the gravitational force by the vector

$$\mathbf{F} = -200\mathbf{j}. \qquad \text{Force due to gravity}$$

To find the force required to keep the cart from rolling down the ramp, project $\mathbf{F}$ onto a unit vector $\mathbf{v}$ in the direction of the ramp, as follows.

$$\mathbf{v} = (\cos 30°)\mathbf{i} + (\sin 30°)\mathbf{j} = \frac{\sqrt{3}}{2}\mathbf{i} + \frac{1}{2}\mathbf{j} \qquad \text{Unit vector along ramp}$$

Therefore, the projection of $\mathbf{F}$ onto $\mathbf{v}$ is

$$\mathbf{w}_1 = \text{proj}_\mathbf{v}\mathbf{F}$$

$$= \left(\frac{\mathbf{F} \cdot \mathbf{v}}{\|\mathbf{v}\|^2}\right)\mathbf{v}$$

$$= (\mathbf{F} \cdot \mathbf{v})\mathbf{v}$$

$$= (-200)\left(\frac{1}{2}\right)\mathbf{v}$$

$$= -100\left(\frac{\sqrt{3}}{2}\mathbf{i} + \frac{1}{2}\mathbf{j}\right).$$

The magnitude of this force is 100, and so a force of 100 pounds is required to keep the cart from rolling down the ramp.

FIGURE **6.39**

Work

The work W done by a *constant* force $\mathbf{F}$ acting along the line of motion of an object is

$$W = (\text{magnitude of force})(\text{distance}) = \|\mathbf{F}\|\,\|\overrightarrow{PQ}\|$$

as shown in Figure 6.40. If the constant force $\mathbf{F}$ is not directed along the line of motion, as shown in Figure 6.41, the work W done by the force is

$$
\begin{aligned}
W &= \|\operatorname{proj}_{\overrightarrow{PQ}}\mathbf{F}\|\,\|\overrightarrow{PQ}\| \\
&= (\cos\theta)\|\mathbf{F}\|\,\|\overrightarrow{PQ}\| && \|\operatorname{proj}_{\overrightarrow{PQ}}\mathbf{F}\| = (\cos\theta)\|\mathbf{F}\| \\
&= \mathbf{F}\cdot\overrightarrow{PQ}. && \cos\theta(\mathbf{F}\cdot\overrightarrow{PQ})/(\|\mathbf{F}\|\,\|\overrightarrow{PQ}\|)
\end{aligned}
$$

Force acts along the line of motion.
FIGURE **6.40**

Force acts at angle θ with the line of motion.
FIGURE **6.41**

This notion of work is summarized in the following definition.

Definition of Work

The **work** W done by a constant force $\mathbf{F}$ as its point of application moves along the vector $\overrightarrow{PQ}$ is given by either of the following.

1. $W = \|\operatorname{proj}_{\overrightarrow{PQ}}\mathbf{F}\|\,\|\overrightarrow{PQ}\|$ Projection form

2. $W = \mathbf{F}\cdot\overrightarrow{PQ}$ Dot product form

Example 8 ▶ **Finding Work**

To close a sliding door, a person pulls on a rope with a constant force of 50 pounds at a constant angle of 60°, as shown in Figure 6.42. Find the work done in moving the door 12 feet to its closed position.

Solution

Using a projection, you can calculate the work as follows.

$$
\begin{aligned}
W &= \|\operatorname{proj}_{\overrightarrow{PQ}}\mathbf{F}\|\,\|\overrightarrow{PQ}\| && \text{Projection form for work}\\
&= (\cos 60°)\|\mathbf{F}\|\,\|\overrightarrow{PQ}\| \\
&= \frac{1}{2}(50)(12) = 300 \text{ foot-pounds}
\end{aligned}
$$

So, the work done is 300 foot-pounds. You can verify this result by finding the vectors $\mathbf{F}$ and $\overrightarrow{PQ}$ and calculating their dot product.

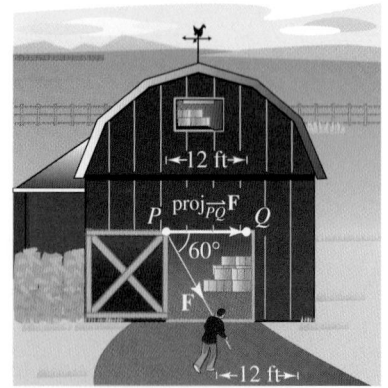

FIGURE **6.42**

6.4 Exercises

In Exercises 1–4, find the dot product of **u** and **v**.

1. $\mathbf{u} = \langle 6, 1 \rangle$
$\mathbf{v} = \langle -2, 3 \rangle$

2. $\mathbf{u} = \langle 5, 12 \rangle$
$\mathbf{v} = \langle -3, 2 \rangle$

3. $\mathbf{u} = 4\mathbf{i} - 2\mathbf{j}$
$\mathbf{v} = \mathbf{i} - \mathbf{j}$

4. $\mathbf{u} = 3\mathbf{i} + 4\mathbf{j}$
$\mathbf{v} = 7\mathbf{i} - 2\mathbf{j}$

In Exercises 5–8, use the vectors $\mathbf{u} = \langle 2, 2 \rangle$ and $\mathbf{v} = \langle -3, 4 \rangle$ to find the indicated quantity. State whether the result is a vector or a scalar.

5. $\mathbf{u} \cdot \mathbf{u}$

6. $\|\mathbf{v}\| + 3$

7. $(\mathbf{u} \cdot \mathbf{v})\mathbf{v}$

8. $3\mathbf{u} \cdot \mathbf{v}$

In Exercises 9–14, use the dot product to find the magnitude of **u**.

9. $\mathbf{u} = \langle -5, 12 \rangle$

10. $\mathbf{u} = \langle 2, -4 \rangle$

11. $\mathbf{u} = 20\mathbf{i} + 25\mathbf{j}$

12. $\mathbf{u} = 12\mathbf{i} - 16\mathbf{j}$

13. $\mathbf{u} = 6\mathbf{j}$

14. $\mathbf{u} = -21\mathbf{i}$

In Exercises 15–24, find the angle θ between the vectors.

15. $\mathbf{u} = \langle 1, 0 \rangle$
$\mathbf{v} = \langle 0, -2 \rangle$

16. $\mathbf{u} = \langle 3, 2 \rangle$
$\mathbf{v} = \langle 4, 0 \rangle$

17. $\mathbf{u} = 3\mathbf{i} + 4\mathbf{j}$
$\mathbf{v} = -2\mathbf{j}$

18. $\mathbf{u} = 2\mathbf{i} - 3\mathbf{j}$
$\mathbf{v} = \mathbf{i} - 2\mathbf{j}$

19. $\mathbf{u} = 2\mathbf{i} - \mathbf{j}$
$\mathbf{v} = 6\mathbf{i} + 4\mathbf{j}$

20. $\mathbf{u} = -6\mathbf{i} - 3\mathbf{j}$
$\mathbf{v} = -8\mathbf{i} + 4\mathbf{j}$

21. $\mathbf{u} = 5\mathbf{i} + 5\mathbf{j}$
$\mathbf{v} = -6\mathbf{i} + 6\mathbf{j}$

22. $\mathbf{u} = 2\mathbf{i} - 3\mathbf{j}$
$\mathbf{v} = 4\mathbf{i} + 3\mathbf{j}$

23. $\mathbf{u} = \cos\left(\frac{\pi}{3}\right)\mathbf{i} + \sin\left(\frac{\pi}{3}\right)\mathbf{j}$
$\mathbf{v} = \cos\left(\frac{3\pi}{4}\right)\mathbf{i} + \sin\left(\frac{3\pi}{4}\right)\mathbf{j}$

24. $\mathbf{u} = \cos\left(\frac{\pi}{4}\right)\mathbf{i} + \sin\left(\frac{\pi}{4}\right)\mathbf{j}$
$\mathbf{v} = \cos\left(\frac{\pi}{2}\right)\mathbf{i} + \sin\left(\frac{\pi}{2}\right)\mathbf{j}$

In Exercises 25–28, use vectors to find the interior angles of the triangle with the given vertices.

25. $(1, 2), (3, 4), (2, 5)$

26. $(-3, -4), (1, 7), (8, 2)$

27. $(-3, 0), (2, 2), (0, 6)$

28. $(-3, 5), (-1, 9), (7, 9)$

In Exercises 29 and 30, find $\mathbf{u} \cdot \mathbf{v}$, where θ is the angle between **u** and **v**.

29. $\|\mathbf{u}\| = 4, \|\mathbf{v}\| = 10, \theta = \frac{2\pi}{3}$

30. $\|\mathbf{u}\| = 100, \|\mathbf{v}\| = 250, \theta = \frac{\pi}{6}$

In Exercises 31–36, determine whether **u** and **v** are orthogonal, parallel, or neither.

31. $\mathbf{u} = \langle -12, 30 \rangle$
$\mathbf{v} = \langle \frac{1}{2}, -\frac{5}{4} \rangle$

32. $\mathbf{u} = \langle 3, 15 \rangle$
$\mathbf{v} = \langle -1, 5 \rangle$

33. $\mathbf{u} = \frac{1}{4}(3\mathbf{i} - \mathbf{j})$
$\mathbf{v} = 5\mathbf{i} + 6\mathbf{j}$

34. $\mathbf{u} = \mathbf{i}$
$\mathbf{v} = -2\mathbf{i} + 2\mathbf{j}$

35. $\mathbf{u} = 2\mathbf{i} - 2\mathbf{j}$
$\mathbf{v} = -\mathbf{i} - \mathbf{j}$

36. $\mathbf{u} = \langle \cos\theta, \sin\theta \rangle$
$\mathbf{v} = \langle \sin\theta, -\cos\theta \rangle$

In Exercises 37–40, find the projection of **u** onto **v** and the vector component of **u** orthogonal to **v**.

37. $\mathbf{u} = \langle 2, 2 \rangle$
$\mathbf{v} = \langle 6, 1 \rangle$

38. $\mathbf{u} = \langle 4, 2 \rangle$
$\mathbf{v} = \langle 1, -2 \rangle$

39. $\mathbf{u} = \langle 0, 3 \rangle$
$\mathbf{v} = \langle 2, 15 \rangle$

40. $\mathbf{u} = \langle -3, -2 \rangle$
$\mathbf{v} = \langle -4, -1 \rangle$

In Exercises 41–44, find two vectors in opposite directions that are orthogonal to the vector **u**. (The answers are not unique.)

41. $\mathbf{u} = \langle 3, 5 \rangle$

42. $\mathbf{u} = \langle -8, 3 \rangle$

43. $\mathbf{u} = \frac{1}{2}\mathbf{i} - \frac{2}{3}\mathbf{j}$

44. $\mathbf{u} = -\frac{5}{2}\mathbf{i} - 3\mathbf{j}$

Work In Exercises 45 and 46, find the work done in moving a particle from P to Q if the magnitude and direction of the force are given by **v**.

45. $P = (0, 0), \quad Q = (4, 7), \quad \mathbf{v} = \langle 1, 4 \rangle$

46. $P = (1, 3), \quad Q = (-3, 5), \quad \mathbf{v} = -2\mathbf{i} + 3\mathbf{j}$

47. *Revenue* The vector $\mathbf{u} = \langle 1650, 3200 \rangle$ gives the numbers of units of two types of baking pans produced by a company. The vector $\mathbf{v} = \langle 15.25, 10.50 \rangle$ gives the price (in dollars) of each pan, respectively.

(a) Find the dot product $\mathbf{u} \cdot \mathbf{v}$ and explain what information it gives.

(b) Identify the vector operation used to increase the prices by 5%.

▶ Model It

48. Braking Load A truck with a gross weight of 30,000 pounds is parked on a slope of $d°$ (see figure). Assume that the only force to overcome is the force of gravity.

(a) Find the force required to keep the truck from rolling down the hill in terms of the slope d.

(b) Use a graphing utility to complete the table.

d	0°	1°	2°	3°	4°	5°
Force						

d	6°	7°	8°	9°	10°
Force					

(c) Find the force perpendicular to the hill when $d = 5°$.

Weight = 30,000 lb

49. Work A 25-kilogram (245-newton) bag of sugar is lifted 3 meters. Determine the work done.

50. Work Determine the work done by a crane lifting a 2400-pound car 5 feet.

51. Work A force of 45 pounds in the direction of 30° above the horizontal is required to slide a table across a floor (see figure). The table is dragged 20 feet. Determine the work done.

45 lb

30°

20 ft

52. Work A tractor pulls a log 800 meters, and the tension in the cable connecting the tractor and log is approximately 1600 kilograms (15,691 newtons). The direction of the force is 35° above the horizontal. Approximate the work done.

Synthesis

True or False? In Exercises 53 and 54, determine whether the statement is true or false. Justify your answer.

53. The work W done by a constant force $\mathbf{F}$ acting along the line of motion of an object is represented by a vector.

54. A sliding door moves along the line of vector $\overrightarrow{PQ}$. If a force is applied to the door along a vector that is orthogonal to $\overrightarrow{PQ}$, then no work is done.

55. Think About It What is known about θ, the angle between two nonzero vectors $\mathbf{u}$ and $\mathbf{v}$, under each condition?

(a) $\mathbf{u} \cdot \mathbf{v} = 0$ (b) $\mathbf{u} \cdot \mathbf{v} > 0$ (c) $\mathbf{u} \cdot \mathbf{v} < 0$

56. Think About It What can be said about the vectors $\mathbf{u}$ and $\mathbf{v}$ under each condition?

(a) The projection of $\mathbf{u}$ onto $\mathbf{v}$ equals $\mathbf{u}$.

(b) The projection of $\mathbf{u}$ onto $\mathbf{v}$ equals $\mathbf{0}$.

57. Proof Use vectors to prove that the diagonals of a rhombus are perpendicular.

58. Proof Prove the following.

$$\|\mathbf{u} - \mathbf{v}\|^2 = \|\mathbf{u}\|^2 + \|\mathbf{v}\|^2 - 2\mathbf{u} \cdot \mathbf{v}$$

Review

In Exercises 59–62, perform the operation and write the result in standard form.

59. $\sqrt{42} \cdot \sqrt{24}$ **60.** $\sqrt{18} \cdot \sqrt{112}$

61. $\sqrt{-3} \cdot \sqrt{-8}$ **62.** $\sqrt{-12} \cdot \sqrt{-96}$

In Exercises 63–66, find the exact solutions of the equation in the interval $[0, 2\pi)$.

63. $\sin 2x - \sqrt{3} \sin x = 0$ **64.** $\sin 2x + \sqrt{2} \cos x = 0$

65. $2 \tan x = \tan 2x$ **66.** $\cos 2x - 3 \sin x = 2$

In Exercises 67–70, find the exact value of the trigonometric function given that $\sin u = -\frac{12}{13}$ and $\cos v = \frac{24}{25}$. (Both u and v are in Quadrant IV.)

67. $\sin(u - v)$ **68.** $\sin(u + v)$

69. $\cos(v - u)$ **70.** $\tan(u - v)$

6.5 Trigonometric Form of a Complex Number

▶ **What you should learn**

- How to plot complex numbers in the complex plane
- How to write the trigonometric forms of complex numbers
- How to multiply and divide complex numbers written in trigonometric form
- How to use DeMoivre's Theorem to find powers of complex numbers
- How to find *n*th roots of complex numbers

▶ **Why you should learn it**

You can use the trigonometric form of a complex number to perform operations with complex numbers. For instance, in Exercises 107–114 on page 459, you will use the trigonometric forms of complex numbers to help you solve polynomial equations.

The Complex Plane

Just as real numbers can be represented by points on the real number line, you can represent a complex number

$$z = a + bi$$

as the point (a, b) in a coordinate plane (the **complex plane**). The horizontal axis is called the **real axis** and the vertical axis is called the **imaginary axis,** as shown in Figure 6.43.

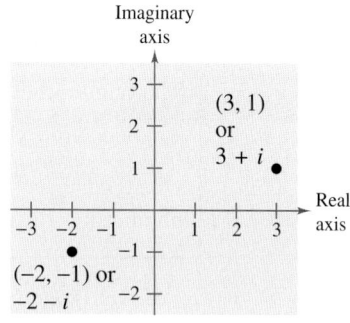

FIGURE **6.43**

The **absolute value** of the complex number $a + bi$ is defined as the distance between the origin $(0, 0)$ and the point (a, b).

Definition of the Absolute Value of a Complex Number

The **absolute value** of the complex number $z = a + bi$ is

$$|a + bi| = \sqrt{a^2 + b^2}.$$

If the complex number $a + bi$ is a real number (that is, if $b = 0$), then this definition agrees with that given for the absolute value of a real number

$$|a + 0i| = \sqrt{a^2 + 0^2} = |a|.$$

Example 1 ▶ Finding the Absolute Value of a Complex Number

Plot $z = -2 + 5i$ and find its absolute value.

Solution

The number is plotted in Figure 6.44. It has an absolute value of

$$|z| = \sqrt{(-2)^2 + 5^2}$$
$$= \sqrt{29}.$$

FIGURE **6.44**

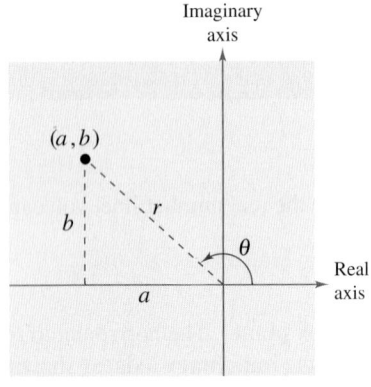

FIGURE **6.45**

Trigonometric Form of a Complex Number

In Section 2.4 you learned how to add, subtract, multiply, and divide complex numbers. To work effectively with *powers* and *roots* of complex numbers, it is helpful to write complex numbers in trigonometric form. In Figure 6.45, consider the nonzero complex number $a + bi$. By letting θ be the angle from the positive real axis (measured counterclockwise) to the line segment connecting the origin and the point (a, b), you can write

$$a = r \cos \theta \quad \text{and} \quad b = r \sin \theta$$

where $r = \sqrt{a^2 + b^2}$. Consequently, you have

$$a + bi = (r \cos \theta) + (r \sin \theta)i$$

from which you can obtain the **trigonometric form of a complex number.**

Trigonometric Form of a Complex Number

The **trigonometric form** of the complex number $z = a + bi$ is

$$z = r(\cos \theta + i \sin \theta)$$

where $a = r \cos \theta$, $b = r \sin \theta$, $r = \sqrt{a^2 + b^2}$, and $\tan \theta = b/a$. The number r is the **modulus** of z, and θ is called an **argument** of z.

The trigonometric form of a complex number is also called the *polar form*. Because there are infinitely many choices for θ, the trigonometric form of a complex number is not unique. Normally, θ is restricted to the interval $0 \le \theta < 2\pi$, although on occasion it is convenient to use $\theta < 0$.

Example 2 ▶ **Writing a Complex Number in Trigonometric Form**

Write the complex number $z = -2 - 2\sqrt{3}i$ in trigonometric form.

Solution

The absolute value of z is

$$r = \left| -2 - 2\sqrt{3}i \right| = \sqrt{(-2)^2 + \left(-2\sqrt{3}\right)^2} = \sqrt{16} = 4$$

and the angle θ is

$$\tan \theta = \frac{b}{a} = \frac{-2\sqrt{3}}{-2} = \sqrt{3}.$$

Because $\tan(\pi/3) = \sqrt{3}$ and $z = -2 - 2\sqrt{3}i$ lies in Quadrant III, you choose θ to be $\theta = \pi + \pi/3 = 4\pi/3$. So, the trigonometric form is

$$z = r(\cos \theta + i \sin \theta)$$
$$= 4\left(\cos \frac{4\pi}{3} + i \sin \frac{4\pi}{3}\right).$$

See Figure 6.46.

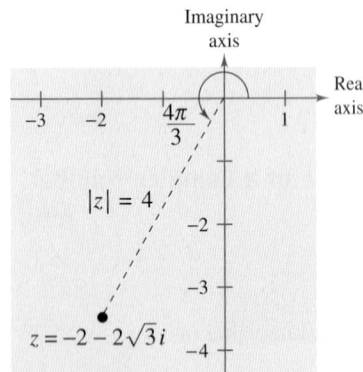

FIGURE **6.46**

Example 3 ▶ Writing a Complex Number in Standard Form

Write the complex number in standard form $a + bi$.

$$z = \sqrt{8}\left[\cos\left(-\frac{\pi}{3}\right) + i\sin\left(-\frac{\pi}{3}\right)\right]$$

Solution

Because $\cos(-\pi/3) = \frac{1}{2}$ and $\sin(-\pi/3) = -\sqrt{3}/2$, you can write

$$z = \sqrt{8}\left[\cos\left(-\frac{\pi}{3}\right) + i\sin\left(-\frac{\pi}{3}\right)\right]$$

$$= 2\sqrt{2}\left(\frac{1}{2} - \frac{\sqrt{3}}{2}i\right)$$

$$= \sqrt{2} - \sqrt{6}i.$$

Technology

A graphing utility can be used to convert a complex number in trigonometric (or polar) form to rectangular form, and vice versa. For specific keystrokes, see the user's manual for your graphing utility.

Multiplication and Division of Complex Numbers

The trigonometric form adapts nicely to multiplication and division of complex numbers. Suppose you are given two complex numbers

$$z_1 = r_1(\cos\theta_1 + i\sin\theta_1) \qquad \text{and} \qquad z_2 = r_2(\cos\theta_2 + i\sin\theta_2).$$

The product of z_1 and z_2 is

$$z_1 z_2 = r_1 r_2(\cos\theta_1 + i\sin\theta_1)(\cos\theta_2 + i\sin\theta_2)$$

$$= r_1 r_2[(\cos\theta_1\cos\theta_2 - \sin\theta_1\sin\theta_2) + i(\sin\theta_1\cos\theta_2 + \cos\theta_1\sin\theta_2)].$$

Using the sum and difference formulas for cosine and sine, you can rewrite this equation as

$$z_1 z_2 = r_1 r_2[\cos(\theta_1 + \theta_2) + i\sin(\theta_1 + \theta_2)].$$

This establishes the first part of the following rule. The second part is left to you (see Exercise 119).

Product and Quotient of Two Complex Numbers

Let $z_1 = r_1(\cos\theta_1 + i\sin\theta_1)$ and $z_2 = r_2(\cos\theta_2 + i\sin\theta_2)$ be complex numbers.

$$z_1 z_2 = r_1 r_2[\cos(\theta_1 + \theta_2) + i\sin(\theta_1 + \theta_2)] \qquad \text{Product}$$

$$\frac{z_1}{z_2} = \frac{r_1}{r_2}[\cos(\theta_1 - \theta_2) + i\sin(\theta_1 - \theta_2)], \quad z_2 \neq 0 \qquad \text{Quotient}$$

Note that this rule says that to *multiply* two complex numbers you multiply moduli and add arguments, whereas to *divide* two complex numbers you divide moduli and subtract arguments.

Example 4 ▶   **Multiplying Complex Numbers**

Find the product of the complex numbers.

$$z_1 = 2\left(\cos\frac{2\pi}{3} + i\sin\frac{2\pi}{3}\right) \qquad z_2 = 8\left(\cos\frac{11\pi}{6} + i\sin\frac{11\pi}{6}\right)$$

Solution

$$z_1z_2 = 2\left(\cos\frac{2\pi}{3} + i\sin\frac{2\pi}{3}\right) \times 8\left(\cos\frac{11\pi}{6} + i\sin\frac{11\pi}{6}\right)$$

$$= 16\left[\cos\left(\frac{2\pi}{3} + \frac{11\pi}{6}\right) + i\sin\left(\frac{2\pi}{3} + \frac{11\pi}{6}\right)\right]$$

$$= 16\left(\cos\frac{5\pi}{2} + i\sin\frac{5\pi}{2}\right)$$

$$= 16\left(\cos\frac{\pi}{2} + i\sin\frac{\pi}{2}\right)$$

$$= 16[0 + i(1)]$$

$$= 16i$$

You can check this result by first converting the complex numbers to the standard forms $z_1 = -1 + \sqrt{3}i$ and $z_2 = 4\sqrt{3} - 4i$ and then multiplying algebraically, as in Section 2.4.

$$z_1z_2 = \left(-1 + \sqrt{3}i\right)\left(4\sqrt{3} - 4i\right)$$

$$= -4\sqrt{3} + 4i + 12i + 4\sqrt{3}$$

$$= 16i$$

Example 5 ▶   **Dividing Complex Numbers**

Find the quotient, z_1/z_2, of the complex numbers.

$$z_1 = 24(\cos 300° + i\sin 300°) \qquad z_2 = 8(\cos 75° + i\sin 75°)$$

Solution

$$\frac{z_1}{z_2} = \frac{24(\cos 300° + i\sin 300°)}{8(\cos 75° + i\sin 75°)}$$

$$= \frac{24}{8}\left[\cos(300° - 75°) + i\sin(300° - 75°)\right]$$

$$= 3(\cos 225° + i\sin 225°)$$

$$= 3\left[\left(-\frac{\sqrt{2}}{2}\right) + i\left(-\frac{\sqrt{2}}{2}\right)\right]$$

$$= -\frac{3\sqrt{2}}{2} - \frac{3\sqrt{2}}{2}i$$

Powers of Complex Numbers

The trigonometric form of a complex number is used to raise a complex number to a power. To accomplish this, consider repeated use of the multiplication rule.

$$z = r(\cos \theta + i \sin \theta)$$

$$z^2 = r(\cos \theta + i \sin \theta)r(\cos \theta + i \sin \theta) = r^2(\cos 2\theta + i \sin 2\theta)$$

$$z^3 = r^2(\cos 2\theta + i \sin 2\theta)r(\cos \theta + i \sin \theta) = r^3(\cos 3\theta + i \sin 3\theta)$$

$$z^4 = r^4(\cos 4\theta + i \sin 4\theta)$$

$$z^5 = r^5(\cos 5\theta + i \sin 5\theta)$$

$$\vdots$$

This pattern leads to the following important theorem, which is named after the French mathematician Abraham DeMoivre (1667–1754).

DeMoivre's Theorem

If $z = r(\cos \theta + i \sin \theta)$ is a complex number and n is a positive integer, then

$$z^n = [r(\cos \theta + i \sin \theta)]^n$$

$$= r^n(\cos n\theta + i \sin n\theta).$$

 Example 6 ▶ **Finding Powers of a Complex Number**

Use DeMoivre's Theorem to find $\left(-1 + \sqrt{3}\,i\right)^{12}$.

Solution

First convert the complex number to trigonometric form using

$$r = \sqrt{(-1)^2 + \left(\sqrt{3}\right)^2} = 2 \quad \text{and} \quad \theta = \arctan \frac{\sqrt{3}}{-1} = \frac{2\pi}{3}.$$

So, the trigonometric form is

$$z = -1 + \sqrt{3}\,i = 2\left(\cos \frac{2\pi}{3} + i \sin \frac{2\pi}{3}\right).$$

Then, by DeMoivre's Theorem, you have

$$(-1 + \sqrt{3}\,i)^{12} = \left[2\left(\cos \frac{2\pi}{3} + i \sin \frac{2\pi}{3}\right)\right]^{12}$$

$$= 2^{12}\left[\cos(12) \frac{2\pi}{3} + i \sin(12) \frac{2\pi}{3}\right]$$

$$= 4096(\cos 8\pi + i \sin 8\pi)$$

$$= 4096(1 + 0)$$

$$= 4096.$$

Historical Note

Abraham DeMoivre (1667–1754) is remembered for his work in probability theory and DeMoivre's Theorem. His book *The Doctrine of Chances* (published in 1718) includes the theory of recurring series and the theory of partial fractions.

Roots of Complex Numbers

Recall that a consequence of the Fundamental Theorem of Algebra is that a polynomial equation of degree n has n solutions in the complex number system. So, the equation $x^6 = 1$ has six solutions, and in this particular case you can find the six solutions by factoring and using the Quadratic Formula.

$$x^6 - 1 = (x^3 - 1)(x^3 + 1)$$
$$= (x - 1)(x^2 + x + 1)(x + 1)(x^2 - x + 1) = 0$$

Consequently, the solutions are

$$x = \pm 1, \qquad x = \frac{-1 \pm \sqrt{3}\,i}{2}, \qquad \text{and} \qquad x = \frac{1 \pm \sqrt{3}\,i}{2}.$$

Each of these numbers is a sixth root of 1. In general, the **nth root** of a complex number is defined as follows.

Definition of nth Root of a Complex Number

The complex number $u = a + bi$ is an **nth root** of the complex number z if

$$z = u^n = (a + bi)^n.$$

To find a formula for an nth root of a complex number, let u be an nth root of z, where

$$u = s(\cos \beta + i \sin \beta)$$

and

$$z = r(\cos \theta + i \sin \theta).$$

By DeMoivre's Theorem and the fact that $u^n = z$, you have

$$s^n(\cos n\beta + i \sin n\beta) = r(\cos \theta + i \sin \theta).$$

Taking the absolute value of each side of this equation, it follows that $s^n = r$. Substituting back into the previous equation and dividing by r, you get

$$\cos n\beta + i \sin n\beta = \cos \theta + i \sin \theta.$$

So, it follows that

$$\cos n\beta = \cos \theta \qquad \text{and} \qquad \sin n\beta = \sin \theta.$$

Because both sine and cosine have a period of 2π, these last two equations have solutions if and only if the angles differ by a multiple of 2π. Consequently, there must exist an integer k such that

$$n\beta = \theta + 2\pi k$$
$$\beta = \frac{\theta + 2\pi k}{n}.$$

By substituting this value of β into the trigonometric form of u, you get the result stated on the following page.

nth Roots of a Complex Number

For a positive integer n, the complex number $z = r(\cos \theta + i \sin \theta)$ has exactly n distinct nth roots given by

$$\sqrt[n]{r}\left(\cos \frac{\theta + 2\pi k}{n} + i \sin \frac{\theta + 2\pi k}{n}\right)$$

where $k = 0, 1, 2, \ldots, n - 1$.

When k exceeds $n - 1$, the roots begin to repeat. For instance, if $k = n$, the angle

$$\frac{\theta + 2\pi n}{n} = \frac{\theta}{n} + 2\pi$$

is coterminal with θ/n, which is also obtained when $k = 0$.

The formula for the nth roots of a complex number z has a nice geometrical interpretation, as shown in Figure 6.47. Note that because the nth roots of z all have the same magnitude $\sqrt[n]{r}$, they all lie on a circle of radius $\sqrt[n]{r}$ with center at the origin. Furthermore, because successive nth roots have arguments that differ by $2\pi/n$, the n roots are equally spaced around the circle.

You have already found the sixth roots of 1 by factoring and by using the Quadratic Formula. Example 7 shows how you can solve the same problem with the formula for nth roots.

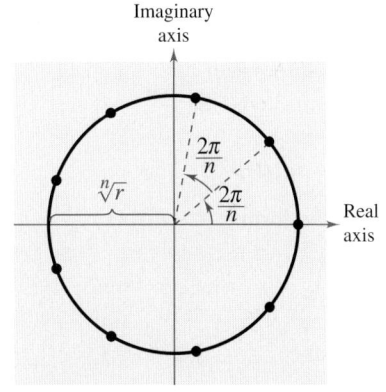

FIGURE 6.47

Example 7 ▶ Finding the nth Roots of a Real Number

Find all the sixth roots of 1.

Solution

First write 1 in the trigonometric form $1 = 1(\cos 0 + i \sin 0)$. Then, by the nth root formula, with $n = 6$ and $r = 1$, the roots have the form

$$\sqrt[6]{1}\left(\cos \frac{0 + 2\pi k}{6} + i \sin \frac{0 + 2\pi k}{6}\right)$$

or simply $\cos(\pi k/3) + i \sin(\pi k/3)$. So, for $k = 0, 1, 2, 3, 4,$ and 5, the sixth roots are as follows. (See Figure 6.48.)

$$\cos 0 + i \sin 0 = 1$$

$$\cos \frac{\pi}{3} + i \sin \frac{\pi}{3} = \frac{1}{2} + \frac{\sqrt{3}}{2}i \qquad \text{Increment by } \frac{2\pi}{n} = \frac{2\pi}{6} = \frac{\pi}{3}$$

$$\cos \frac{2\pi}{3} + i \sin \frac{2\pi}{3} = -\frac{1}{2} + \frac{\sqrt{3}}{2}i$$

$$\cos \pi + i \sin \pi = -1$$

$$\cos \frac{4\pi}{3} + i \sin \frac{4\pi}{3} = -\frac{1}{2} - \frac{\sqrt{3}}{2}i$$

$$\cos \frac{5\pi}{3} + i \sin \frac{5\pi}{3} = \frac{1}{2} - \frac{\sqrt{3}}{2}i$$

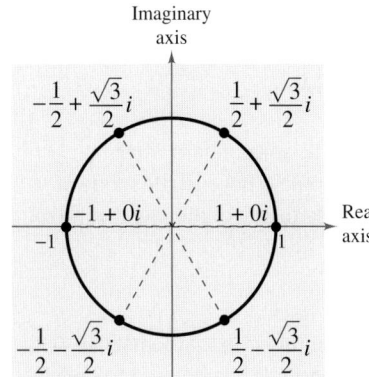

FIGURE 6.48

In Figure 6.48, notice that the roots obtained in Example 7 all have a magnitude of 1 and are equally spaced around the unit circle. Also notice that the complex roots occur in conjugate pairs, as discussed in Section 2.5. The n distinct nth roots of 1 are called the **nth roots of unity.**

Example 8 ▶ Finding the nth Roots of a Complex Number

Find the three cube roots of

$$z = -2 + 2i.$$

Solution

Because z lies in Quadrant II, the trigonometric form for z is

$$z = -2 + 2i$$

$$= \sqrt{8}\,(\cos 135° + i \sin 135°). \qquad \theta = \arctan(2/-2) = 135°$$

By the formula for nth roots, the cube roots have the form

$$\sqrt[6]{8}\left(\cos \frac{135° + 360°k}{3} + i \sin \frac{135° + 360°k}{3}\right).$$

Finally, for $k = 0$, 1, and 2, you obtain the roots

$$\sqrt[6]{8}\left(\cos \frac{135° + 360°(0)}{3} + i \sin \frac{135° + 360°(0)}{3}\right) = \sqrt{2}(\cos 45° + i \sin 45°)$$

$$= 1 + i$$

$$\sqrt[6]{8}\left(\cos \frac{135° + 360°(1)}{3} + i \sin \frac{135° + 360°(1)}{3}\right) = \sqrt{2}(\cos 165° + i \sin 165°)$$

$$\approx -1.3660 + 0.3660i$$

$$\sqrt[6]{8}\left(\cos \frac{135° + 360°(2)}{3} + i \sin \frac{135° + 360°(2)}{3}\right) = \sqrt{2}(\cos 285° + i \sin 285°)$$

$$\approx 0.3660 - 1.3660i.$$

Activities

1. Use DeMoivre's Theorem to find $\left(-2 - 2\sqrt{3}\,i\right)^3$.

   Answer: $64(\cos 4\pi + i \sin 4\pi) = 64$

2. Find the cube roots of

$$8\left(-\frac{1}{2} + \frac{\sqrt{3}}{2}i\right) =$$

$$8\left(\cos \frac{2\pi}{3} + i \sin \frac{2\pi}{3}\right).$$

   Answer: $2\left(\cos \frac{2\pi}{9} + i \sin \frac{2\pi}{9}\right)$

   $2\left(\cos \frac{8\pi}{9} + i \sin \frac{8\pi}{9}\right)$

   $2\left(\cos \frac{14\pi}{9} + i \sin \frac{14\pi}{9}\right)$

3. Find all of the solutions of the equation $x^4 + 1 = 0$.

   Answer:

   $\cos \frac{\pi}{4} + i \sin \frac{\pi}{4} = \frac{\sqrt{2}}{2} + \frac{\sqrt{2}}{2}i$

   $\cos \frac{3\pi}{4} + i \sin \frac{3\pi}{4} = -\frac{\sqrt{2}}{2} + \frac{\sqrt{2}}{2}i$

   $\cos \frac{5\pi}{4} + i \sin \frac{5\pi}{4} = -\frac{\sqrt{2}}{2} - \frac{\sqrt{2}}{2}i$

   $\cos \frac{7\pi}{4} + i \sin \frac{7\pi}{4} = \frac{\sqrt{2}}{2} - \frac{\sqrt{2}}{2}i$

Writing **ABOUT MATHEMATICS**

A Famous Mathematical Formula The famous formula

$$e^{a+bi} = e^a(\cos b + i \sin b)$$

is called Euler's Formula, after the German mathematician Leonhard Euler (1707–1783). Although the interpretation of this formula is beyond the scope of this text, we decided to include it because it gives rise to one of the most wonderful equations in mathematics.

$$e^{\pi i} + 1 = 0$$

This elegant equation relates the five most famous numbers in mathematics—0, 1, π, e, and i—in a single equation. Show how Euler's Formula can be used to derive this equation.

6.5 Exercises

In Exercises 1–6, plot the complex number and find its absolute value.

1. $-7i$

2. -7

3. $-4 + 4i$

4. $5 - 12i$

5. $6 - 7i$

6. $-8 + 3i$

In Exercises 7–10, write the complex number in trigonometric form.

7.

8.

9.

10.

In Exercises 11–26, represent the complex number graphically, and find the trigonometric form of the number.

11. $3 - 3i$

12. $2 + 2i$

13. $\sqrt{3} + i$

14. $4 - 4\sqrt{3}i$

15. $-2(1 + \sqrt{3}i)$

16. $\frac{5}{2}(\sqrt{3} - i)$

17. $-5i$

18. $4i$

19. $-7 + 4i$

20. $3 - i$

21. 7

22. 4

23. $3 + \sqrt{3}i$

24. $2\sqrt{2} - i$

25. $-3 - i$

26. $1 + 3i$

In Exercises 27–34, use a graphing utility to represent the complex number in trigonometric form.

27. $5 + 2i$

28. $8 + 3i$

29. $-3 + i$

30. $-5 - i$

31. $3\sqrt{2} - 7i$

32. $4\sqrt{5} - 4i$

33. $-8 - 5\sqrt{3}i$

34. $-9 - 2\sqrt{10}i$

In Exercises 35–44, represent the complex number graphically, and find the standard form of the number.

35. $3(\cos 120° + i \sin 120°)$

36. $5(\cos 135° + i \sin 135°)$

37. $\frac{3}{2}(\cos 300° + i \sin 300°)$

38. $\frac{1}{4}(\cos 225° + i \sin 225°)$

39. $3.75\left(\cos \dfrac{3\pi}{4} + i \sin \dfrac{3\pi}{4}\right)$

40. $6\left(\cos \dfrac{5\pi}{12} + i \sin \dfrac{5\pi}{12}\right)$

41. $8\left(\cos \dfrac{\pi}{2} + i \sin \dfrac{\pi}{2}\right)$

42. $7(\cos 0 + i \sin 0)$

43. $3[\cos(18° \, 45') + i \sin(18° \, 45')]$

44. $6[\cos(230° \, 30') + i \sin(230° \, 30')]$

In Exercises 45–48, use a graphing utility to represent the complex number in standard form.

45. $5\left(\cos \dfrac{\pi}{9} + i \sin \dfrac{\pi}{9}\right)$

46. $10\left(\cos \dfrac{2\pi}{5} + i \sin \dfrac{2\pi}{5}\right)$

47. $3(\cos 165.5° + i \sin 165.5°)$

48. $9(\cos 58° + i \sin 58°)$

In Exercises 49–60, perform the operation and leave the result in trigonometric form.

49. $\left[2\left(\cos \dfrac{\pi}{4} + i \sin \dfrac{\pi}{4}\right)\right]\left[6\left(\cos \dfrac{\pi}{12} + i \sin \dfrac{\pi}{12}\right)\right]$

50. $\left[\dfrac{3}{4}\left(\cos \dfrac{\pi}{3} + i \sin \dfrac{\pi}{3}\right)\right]\left[4\left(\cos \dfrac{3\pi}{4} + i \sin \dfrac{3\pi}{4}\right)\right]$

51. $\left[\dfrac{5}{3}(\cos 140° + i \sin 140°)\right]\left[\dfrac{2}{3}(\cos 60° + i \sin 60°)\right]$

52. $[0.5(\cos 100° + i \sin 100°)] \times$
$[0.8(\cos 300° + i \sin 300°)]$

53. $[0.45(\cos 310° + i \sin 310°)] \times$
$[0.60(\cos 200° + i \sin 200°)]$

54. $(\cos 5° + i \sin 5°)(\cos 20° + i \sin 20°)$

55. $\dfrac{\cos 50° + i \sin 50°}{\cos 20° + i \sin 20°}$

56. $\dfrac{2(\cos 120° + i \sin 120°)}{4(\cos 40° + i \sin 40°)}$

57. $\dfrac{\cos(5\pi/3) + i \sin(5\pi/3)}{\cos \pi + i \sin \pi}$

58. $\dfrac{5(\cos 4.3 + i \sin 4.3)}{4(\cos 2.1 + i \sin 2.1)}$

59. $\dfrac{12(\cos 52° + i \sin 52°)}{3(\cos 110° + i \sin 110°)}$

60. $\dfrac{6(\cos 40° + i \sin 40°)}{7(\cos 100° + i \sin 100°)}$

In Exercises 61–68, (a) give the trigonometric forms of the complex numbers, (b) perform the indicated operation using the trigonometric forms, and (c) perform the indicated operation using the standard forms, and check your result with that of part (b).

61. $(2 + 2i)(1 - i)$

62. $\left(\sqrt{3} + i\right)(1 + i)$

63. $-2i(1 + i)$

64. $4\left(1 - \sqrt{3}i\right)$

65. $\dfrac{3 + 4i}{1 - \sqrt{3}i}$

66. $\dfrac{1 + \sqrt{3}i}{6 - 3i}$

67. $\dfrac{5}{2 + 3i}$

68. $\dfrac{4i}{-4 + 2i}$

In Exercises 69–72, sketch the graphs of all complex numbers *z* satisfying the given condition.

69. $|z| = 2$

70. $|z| = 3$

71. $\theta = \dfrac{\pi}{6}$

72. $\theta = \dfrac{5\pi}{4}$

In Exercises 73–90, use DeMoivre's Theorem to find the indicated power of the complex number. Write the result in standard form.

73. $(1 + i)^5$

74. $(2 + 2i)^6$

75. $(-1 + i)^{10}$

76. $(3 - 2i)^8$

77. $2\left(\sqrt{3} + i\right)^7$

78. $4\left(1 - \sqrt{3}i\right)^3$

79. $[5(\cos 20° + i \sin 20°)]^3$

80. $[3(\cos 150° + i \sin 150°)]^4$

81. $\left(\cos \dfrac{\pi}{4} + i \sin \dfrac{\pi}{4}\right)^{12}$

82. $\left[2\left(\cos \dfrac{\pi}{2} + i \sin \dfrac{\pi}{2}\right)\right]^8$

83. $[5(\cos 3.2 + i \sin 3.2)]^4$

84. $(\cos 0 + i \sin 0)^{20}$

85. $(3 - 2i)^5$

86. $\left(\sqrt{5} - 4i\right)^3$

87. $[3(\cos 15° + i \sin 15°)]^4$

88. $[2(\cos 10° + i \sin 10°)]^8$

89. $\left[2\left(\cos \dfrac{\pi}{10} + i \sin \dfrac{\pi}{10}\right)\right]^5$

90. $\left[2\left(\cos \dfrac{\pi}{8} + i \sin \dfrac{\pi}{8}\right)\right]^6$

In Exercises 91–106, (a) use the formula on page 455 to find the indicated roots of the complex number, (b) represent each of the roots graphically, and (c) express each of the roots in standard form.

91. Square roots of $5(\cos 120° + i \sin 120°)$

92. Square roots of $16(\cos 60° + i \sin 60°)$

93. Cube roots of $8\left(\cos \dfrac{2\pi}{3} + i \sin \dfrac{2\pi}{3}\right)$

94. Fifth roots of $32\left(\cos \dfrac{5\pi}{6} + i \sin \dfrac{5\pi}{6}\right)$

95. Square roots of $-25i$

96. Fourth roots of $625i$

97. Cube roots of $-\frac{125}{2}\left(1 + \sqrt{3}i\right)$

98. Cube roots of $-4\sqrt{2}(1 - i)$

99. Fourth roots of 16

100. Fourth roots of i

101. Fifth roots of 1

102. Cube roots of 1000

103. Cube roots of -125

104. Fourth roots of -4

105. Fifth roots of $128(-1 + i)$

106. Sixth roots of $64i$

In Exercises 107–114, use the formula on page 455 to find all the solutions of the equation and represent the solutions graphically.

107. $x^4 + i = 0$ **108.** $x^3 + 1 = 0$

109. $x^5 + 243 = 0$ **110.** $x^3 - 27 = 0$

111. $x^4 + 16i = 0$ **112.** $x^6 + 64i = 0$

113. $x^3 - (1 - i) = 0$ **114.** $x^4 + (1 + i) = 0$

Synthesis

True or False? In Exercises 115–118, determine whether the statement is true or false. Justify your answer.

115. Although the square of the complex number bi is given by $(bi)^2 = -b^2$, the absolute value of the complex number $z = a + bi$ is defined as

$$|a + bi| = \sqrt{a^2 + b^2}.$$

116. Geometrically, the nth roots of any complex number z are all equally spaced around the unit circle centered at the origin.

117. The product of two complex numbers

$$z_1 = r_1(\cos \theta_1 + i \sin \theta_1)$$

and

$$z_2 = r_2(\cos \theta_2 + i \sin \theta_2)$$

is zero only when $r_1 = 0$ and/or $r_2 = 0$.

118. By DeMoivre's Theorem,

$$\left(4 + \sqrt{6}\,i\right)^8 = \cos(32) + i \sin\left(8\sqrt{6}\right).$$

119. Given two complex numbers $z_1 = r_1(\cos \theta_1 + i \sin \theta_1)$ and $z_2 = r_2(\cos \theta_2 + i \sin \theta_2)$, $z_2 \neq 0$, show that

$$\frac{z_1}{z_2} = \frac{r_1}{r_2}\left[\cos(\theta_1 - \theta_2) + i \sin(\theta_1 - \theta_2)\right].$$

120. Show that $\bar{z} = r[\cos(-\theta) + i \sin(-\theta)]$ is the complex conjugate of $z = r(\cos \theta + i \sin \theta)$.

121. Use the trigonometric forms of z and $\bar{z}$ in Exercise 120 to find (a) $z\bar{z}$ and (b) $z/\bar{z}$, $\bar{z} \neq 0$.

122. Show that the negative of $z = r(\cos \theta + i \sin \theta)$ is $-z = r[\cos(\theta + \pi) + i \sin(\theta + \pi)]$.

123. Show that $-\frac{1}{2}\left(1 + \sqrt{3}\,i\right)$ is a sixth root of 1.

124. Show that $2^{-1/4}(1 - i)$ is a fourth root of -2.

Graphical Reasoning In Exercises 125 and 126, use the graph of the roots of a complex number.

(a) Write each of the roots in trigonometric form.

(b) Identify the complex number whose roots are given.

 (c) Use a graphing utility to verify the results of part (b).

125.

126.

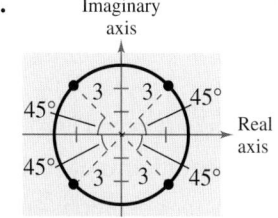

Review

In Exercises 127–132, solve the right triangle shown in the figure. Approximate the result to two decimal places.

127. $A = 22°$, $a = 8$

128. $B = 66°$, $a = 33.5$

129. $A = 30°$, $b = 112.6$

130. $B = 6°$, $b = 211.2$

131. $A = 42° \, 15'$, $c = 11.2$

132. $B = 81° \, 30'$, $c = 6.8$

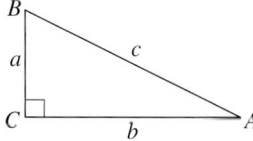

Harmonic Motion In Exercises 133–136, for the simple harmonic motion described by the trigonometric function, find the maximum displacement and the lowest possible value of t for which $d = 0$.

133. $d = 16 \cos \dfrac{\pi}{4} t$ **134.** $d = \dfrac{1}{8} \cos 12\pi t$

135. $d = \dfrac{1}{16} \sin \dfrac{5}{4} \pi t$ **136.** $d = \dfrac{1}{12} \sin 60\pi t$

Chapter Summary

▶ *What* did you learn?

Review Exercises

6.1 In Exercises 1–12, use the Law of Sines to solve (if possible) the triangle. If two solutions exist, list both. Round your answers to two decimal places.

1.

2.

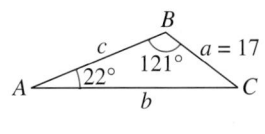

3. $B = 72°$, $C = 82°$, $b = 54$

4. $B = 10°$, $C = 20°$, $c = 33$

5. $A = 16°$, $B = 98°$, $c = 8.4$

6. $A = 95°$, $B = 45°$, $c = 104.8$

7. $A = 24°$, $C = 48°$, $b = 27.5$

8. $B = 64°$, $C = 36°$, $a = 367$

9. $B = 150°$, $b = 30$, $c = 10$

10. $B = 150°$, $a = 10$, $b = 3$

11. $A = 75°$, $a = 51.2$, $b = 33.7$

12. $B = 25°$, $a = 6.2$, $b = 4$

In Exercises 13–16, use the information to find the area of the triangle.

13. $A = 27°$, $b = 5$, $c = 7$

14. $B = 80°$, $a = 4$, $c = 8$

15. $C = 123°$, $a = 16$, $b = 5$

16. $A = 11°$, $b = 22$, $c = 21$

17. *Height* From a certain distance, the angle of elevation to the top of a building is 17°. At a point 50 meters closer to the building, the angle of elevation is 31°. Approximate the height of the building.

18. *Geometry* Find the length of the side w of the parallelogram.

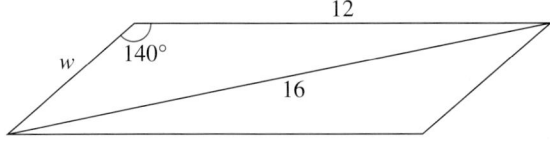

19. *Height* A tree stands on a hillside of slope 28°(from the horizontal). From a point 75 feet down the hill, the angle of elevation to the top of the tree is 45° (see figure). What is the height of the tree?

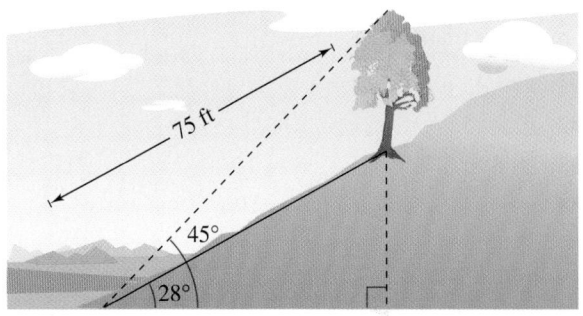

20. *River Width* A surveyor finds that a tree on the opposite bank of a river flowing due east has a bearing of N 22° 30′ E from a certain point and a bearing of N 15° W from a point 400 feet downstream. What is the width of the river?

6.2 In Exercises 21–28, use the Law of Cosines to solve the triangle. Round your answers to two decimal places.

21. $a = 5$, $b = 8$, $c = 10$

22. $a = 80$, $b = 60$, $c = 100$

23. $a = 2.5$, $b = 5.0$, $c = 4.5$

24. $a = 16.4$, $b = 8.8$, $c = 12.2$

25. $B = 110°$, $a = 4$, $c = 4$

26. $B = 150°$, $a = 10$, $c = 20$

27. $C = 43°$, $a = 22.5$, $b = 31.4$

28. $A = 62°$, $b = 11.34$, $c = 19.52$

29. *Surveying* To approximate the length of a marsh, a surveyor walks 425 meters from point A to point B. Then the surveyor turns 65° and walks 300 meters to point C (see figure). Approximate the length AC of the marsh.

30. *Navigation* Two planes leave Raleigh-Durham Airport at approximately the same time. One is flying 425 miles per hour at a bearing of 355°, and the other is flying 530 miles per hour at a bearing of 67°. Draw a figure that gives a visual representation of the problem and determine the distance between the planes after they have flown for 2 hours.

In Exercises 31–34, use Heron's Area Formula to find the area of the triangle.

31. $a = 4$, $b = 5$, $c = 7$

32. $a = 15$, $b = 8$, $c = 10$

33. $a = 12.3$, $b = 15.8$, $c = 3.7$

34. $a = 38.1$, $b = 26.7$, $c = 19.4$

6.3 **In Exercises 35–38, graph the vector with the specified initial point and terminal point.**

Initial Point	*Terminal Point*
35. $(0, 0)$	$(8, 7)$
36. $(3, 4)$	$(-5, -7)$
37. $(-3, 9)$	$(8, -4)$
38. $(-6, -8)$	$(8, 3)$

In Exercises 39–44, find the component form of the vector v satisfying the conditions.

39.

40.

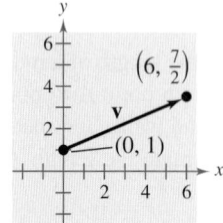

41. Initial point: $(0, 10)$; Terminal point: $(7, 3)$

42. Initial point: $(1, 5)$; Terminal point: $(15, 9)$

43. $\|\mathbf{v}\| = 8$, $\theta = 120°$

44. $\|\mathbf{v}\| = \frac{1}{2}$, $\theta = 225°$

In Exercises 45–48, find the component form of the vector given that $\mathbf{u} = 6\mathbf{i} - 5\mathbf{j}$ and $\mathbf{v} = 10\mathbf{i} + 3\mathbf{j}$. Then sketch your result.

45. $2\mathbf{u} + \mathbf{v}$ **46.** $4\mathbf{u} - 5\mathbf{v}$

47. $3\mathbf{v}$ **48.** $\frac{1}{2}\mathbf{v}$

In Exercises 49–52, write vector u as a linear combination of the standard unit vectors i and j.

49. $\mathbf{u} = \langle -3, 4 \rangle$ **50.** $\mathbf{u} = \langle -6, -8 \rangle$

51. **u** has initial point $(3, 4)$ and terminal point $(9, 8)$.

52. **u** has initial point $(-2, 7)$ and terminal point $(5, -9)$.

In Exercises 53 and 54, write the vector v in the form $\|\mathbf{v}\|(\cos\theta\,\mathbf{i} + \sin\theta\,\mathbf{j})$.

53. $\mathbf{v} = -10\mathbf{i} + 10\mathbf{j}$ **54.** $\mathbf{v} = 4\mathbf{i} - \mathbf{j}$

In Exercises 55–60, find the magnitude and the direction angle of the vector v.

55. $\mathbf{v} = 7(\cos 60°\mathbf{i} + \sin 60°\mathbf{j})$

56. $\mathbf{v} = 3(\cos 150°\mathbf{i} + \sin 150°\mathbf{j})$

57. $\mathbf{v} = 5\mathbf{i} + 4\mathbf{j}$ **58.** $\mathbf{v} = -4\mathbf{i} + 7\mathbf{j}$

59. $\mathbf{v} = -3\mathbf{i} - 3\mathbf{j}$ **60.** $\mathbf{v} = 8\mathbf{i} - \mathbf{j}$

61. *Resultant Force* Forces of 85 pounds and 50 pounds act on a single point. The angle between the forces is 15°. Describe the resultant force.

62. *Rope Tension* A 180-pound weight is supported by two ropes, as shown in the figure. Find the tension exerted on each rope.

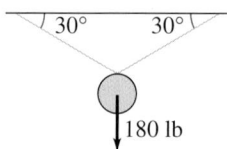

63. *Navigation* An airplane has an airspeed of 430 miles per hour at a bearing of 135°. The wind velocity is 35 miles per hour in the direction of N 30° E. What are the groundspeed and the direction of the plane?

64. *Navigation* An airplane has an airspeed of 724 kilometers per hour at a bearing of 30°. The wind velocity is 32 kilometers per hour from the west. What are the groundspeed and the direction of the plane?

6.4 In Exercises 65–68, find the dot product of **u** and **v**.

65. $\mathbf{u} = \langle 6, 7 \rangle$
$\mathbf{v} = \langle -3, 9 \rangle$

66. $\mathbf{u} = \langle -7, 12 \rangle$
$\mathbf{v} = \langle -4, -14 \rangle$

67. $\mathbf{u} = 3\mathbf{i} + 7\mathbf{j}$
$\mathbf{v} = 11\mathbf{i} - 5\mathbf{j}$

68. $\mathbf{u} = -7\mathbf{i} + 2\mathbf{j}$
$\mathbf{v} = 16\mathbf{i} - 12\mathbf{j}$

In Exercises 69–72, use the vectors $\mathbf{u} = \langle -3, 4 \rangle$ and $\mathbf{v} = \langle 2, 1 \rangle$ to find the quantity. State whether the result is a vector or a scalar.

69. $2\mathbf{u} \cdot \mathbf{u}$

70. $\|\mathbf{v}\|^2$

71. $\mathbf{u}(\mathbf{u} \cdot \mathbf{v})$

72. $3\mathbf{u} \cdot \mathbf{v}$

In Exercises 73–76, find the angle between **u** and **v**.

73. $\mathbf{u} = \cos\dfrac{7\pi}{4}\mathbf{i} + \sin\dfrac{7\pi}{4}\mathbf{j}$
$\mathbf{v} = \cos\dfrac{5\pi}{6}\mathbf{i} + \sin\dfrac{5\pi}{6}\mathbf{j}$

74. $\mathbf{u} = \cos 45°\mathbf{i} + \sin 45°\mathbf{j}$
$\mathbf{v} = \cos 300°\mathbf{i} + \sin 300°\mathbf{j}$

75. $\mathbf{u} = \langle 2\sqrt{2}, -4 \rangle$, $\mathbf{v} = \langle -\sqrt{2}, 1 \rangle$

76. $\mathbf{u} = \langle 3, \sqrt{3} \rangle$, $\mathbf{v} = \langle 4, 3\sqrt{3} \rangle$

In Exercises 77–80, determine whether **u** and **v** are orthogonal, parallel, or neither.

77. $\mathbf{u} = \langle -3, 8 \rangle$
$\mathbf{v} = \langle 8, 3 \rangle$

78. $\mathbf{u} = \langle \frac{1}{4}, -\frac{1}{2} \rangle$
$\mathbf{v} = \langle -2, 4 \rangle$

79. $\mathbf{u} = -\mathbf{i}$
$\mathbf{v} = \mathbf{i} + 2\mathbf{j}$

80. $\mathbf{u} = -2\mathbf{i} + \mathbf{j}$
$\mathbf{v} = 3\mathbf{i} + 6\mathbf{j}$

In Exercises 81–84, find proj$_\mathbf{v}\mathbf{u}$ and the vector component of **u** orthogonal to **v**.

81. $\mathbf{u} = \langle -4, 3 \rangle$, $\mathbf{v} = \langle -8, -2 \rangle$

82. $\mathbf{u} = \langle 5, 6 \rangle$, $\mathbf{v} = \langle 10, 0 \rangle$

83. $\mathbf{u} = \langle 2, 7 \rangle$, $\mathbf{v} = \langle 1, -1 \rangle$

84. $\mathbf{u} = \langle -3, 5 \rangle$, $\mathbf{v} = \langle -5, 2 \rangle$

Work In Exercises 85 and 86, find the work done in moving a particle from P to Q if the magnitude and direction of the force are given by **v**.

85. $P = (5, 3)$, $Q = (8, 9)$, $\mathbf{v} = \langle 2, 7 \rangle$

86. $P = (-2, -9)$, $Q = (-12, 8)$, $\mathbf{v} = 3\mathbf{i} - 6\mathbf{j}$

6.5 In Exercises 87–90, plot the complex number and find its absolute value.

87. $7i$

88. $-6i$

89. $5 + 3i$

90. $-10 - 4i$

In Exercises 91–94, write the trigonometric form of the complex number.

91. $5 - 5i$

92. $5 + 12i$

93. $-3\sqrt{3} + 3i$

94. -7

In Exercises 95 and 96, (a) write the two complex numbers in trigonometric form, and (b) use the trigonometric form to find $z_1 z_2$ and z_1/z_2.

95. $z_1 = 2\sqrt{3} - 2i$, $z_2 = -10i$

96. $z_1 = -3(1 + i)$, $z_2 = 2(\sqrt{3} + i)$

In Exercises 97–100, use DeMoivre's Theorem to find the indicated power of the complex number. Write the result in standard form.

97. $\left[5\left(\cos\dfrac{\pi}{12} + i\sin\dfrac{\pi}{12} \right) \right]^4$

98. $\left[2\left(\cos\dfrac{4\pi}{15} + i\sin\dfrac{4\pi}{15} \right) \right]^5$

99. $(2 + 3i)^6$

100. $(1 - i)^8$

Graphical Reasoning In Exercises 101 and 102, use the graph of the roots of a complex number.

(a) Write each of the roots in trigonometric form.

(b) Identify the complex number whose roots are given.

(c) Use a graphing utility to verify the results of part (b).

101.

102.

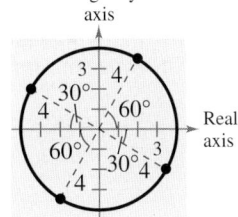

In Exercises 103 and 104, use the formula on page 455 to find the roots of the complex number.

103. Sixth roots of $-729i$

104. Fourth roots of 256

In Exercises 105–108, find all solutions of the equation and represent the solutions graphically.

105. $x^4 + 81 = 0$

106. $x^5 - 32 = 0$

107. $x^3 + 8i = 0$

108. $(x^3 - 1)(x^2 + 1) = 0$

Synthesis

True or False?   In Exercises 109–113, determine whether the statement is true or false. Justify your answer.

109. The Law of Sines is true if one of the angles in the triangle is a right angle.

110. When the Law of Sines is used, the solution is always unique.

111. If **u** is a unit vector in the direction of **v**, then $\mathbf{v} = \|\mathbf{v}\|\,\mathbf{u}$.

112. If $\mathbf{v} = a\mathbf{i} + b\mathbf{j} = \mathbf{0}$, then $a = -b$.

113. $x = \sqrt{3} + i$ is a solution of the equation $x^2 - 8i = 0$.

114. State the Law of Sines from memory.

115. State the Law of Cosines from memory.

116. What characterizes a vector in the plane?

117. Which vectors in the figure appear to be equivalent?

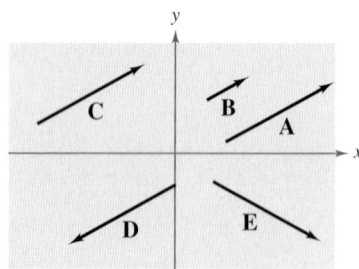

118. The vectors **u** and **v** have the same magnitudes in the two figures. In which figure will the magnitude of the sum be greater? Give a reason for your answer.

(a)

(b)

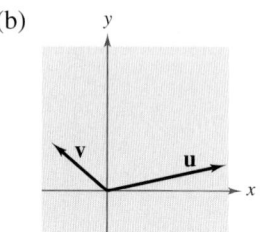

119. Give a geometric description of the scalar multiple $k\mathbf{u}$ of the vector **u**, for $k > 0$ and for $k < 0$.

120. Give a geometric description of the sum of the vectors **u** and **v**.

121. The figure shows z_1 and z_2. Describe $z_1 z_2$ and z_1/z_2.

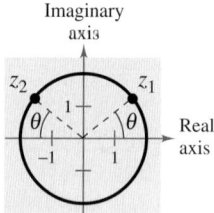

122. One of the fourth roots of a complex number z is shown in the figure.

(a) How many roots are not shown?

(b) Describe the other roots.

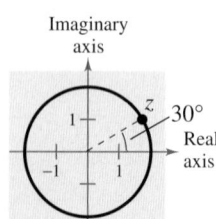

Chapter Test

The *Interactive* CD-ROM and *Internet* versions of this text offer Chapter Pre-Tests and Chapter Post-Tests, both of which have randomly generated exercises with diagnostic capabilities.

Take this test as you would take a test in class. When you are finished, check your work against the answers given in the back of the book.

In Exercises 1–6, use the information to solve the triangle. If two solutions exist, find both.

1. $A = 24°$, $B = 68°$, $a = 12.2$ **2.** $B = 104°$, $C = 33°$, $a = 18.1$

3. $A = 24°$, $a = 11.2$, $b = 13.4$ **4.** $a = 4.0$, $b = 7.3$, $c = 12.4$

5. $B = 100°$, $a = 15$, $b = 23$ **6.** $C = 123°$, $a = 41$, $b = 57$

7. A triangular parcel of land has borders of lengths 60 meters, 70 meters, and 82 meters. Find the area of the parcel of land.

8. An airplane flies 370 miles from point A to point B with a bearing of 24°. It then flies 240 miles from point B to point C with a bearing of 37° (see figure). Find the distance and bearing from point A to point C.

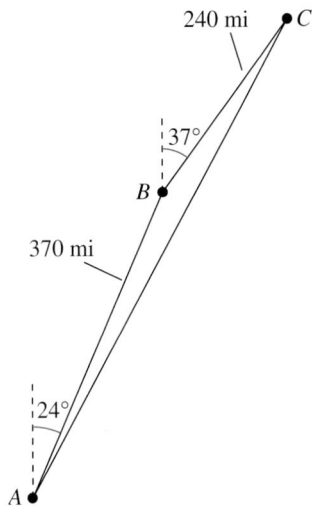

240 mi C

37°

B

370 mi

24°

A

FIGURE FOR 8

In Exercises 9 and 10, find the component form of the vector v with the given components.

9. Initial point of **v**: $(-3, 7)$; Terminal point of **v**: $(11, -16)$

10. Magnitude of **v**: $\|\mathbf{v}\| = 12$; Direction of **v**: $\mathbf{u} = \langle 3, -5 \rangle$

In Exercises 11–13, u = $\langle 3, 5 \rangle$ and v = $\langle -7, 1 \rangle$. Find the resultant vector and sketch its graph.

11. $\mathbf{u} + \mathbf{v}$ **12.** $\mathbf{u} - \mathbf{v}$ **13.** $5\mathbf{u} - 3\mathbf{v}$

14. Find a unit vector in the direction of $\mathbf{u} = \langle 4, -3 \rangle$.

15. Forces with magnitudes of 250 pounds and 130 pounds act on an object at angles of 45° and $-60°$, respectively, with the x-axis. Find the direction and magnitude of the resultant of these forces.

16. Find the angle between the vectors $\mathbf{u} = \langle -1, 5 \rangle$ and $\mathbf{v} = \langle 3, -2 \rangle$.

17. Are the vectors $\mathbf{u} = \langle 6, 10 \rangle$ and $\mathbf{v} = \langle 2, 3 \rangle$ orthogonal?

18. Find the projection of $\mathbf{u} = \langle 6, 7 \rangle$ onto $\mathbf{v} = \langle -5, -1 \rangle$ and the vector component of $\mathbf{u}$ orthogonal to $\mathbf{v}$.

19. Write the complex number $z = 5 - 5i$ in trigonometric form.

20. Write the complex number $z = 6(\cos 120° + i \sin 120°)$ in standard form.

In Exercises 21 and 22, use DeMoivre's Theorem to find the indicated power of the complex number.

21. $\left[3\left(\cos \dfrac{7\pi}{6} + i \sin \dfrac{7\pi}{6} \right) \right]^8$ **22.** $(3 - 3i)^6$

23. Find the fourth roots of $256(1 + \sqrt{3}\,i)$.

24. Find all solutions of the equation $x^3 - 27i = 0$ and represent the solutions graphically.

Cumulative Test for Chapters 4–6

Take this test to review the material from earlier chapters. When you are finished, check your work against the answers given in the back of the book.

1. Consider the angle $\theta = -120°$.
   (a) Sketch the angle in standard position.
   (b) Determine a coterminal angle in the interval $[0°, 360°)$.
   (c) Convert the angle to radian measure.
   (d) Find the reference angle θ'.
   (e) Find the exact values of the six trigonometric functions of θ.

2. Convert the angle of measure 2.35 radians to degrees. Round the answer to one decimal place.

3. Find $\cos \theta$ if $\tan \theta = -\frac{4}{3}$ and $\sin \theta < 0$.

In Exercises 4 and 5, find the period and amplitude, and sketch the graph of the trigonometric function.

4. $f(x) = 3 - 2 \sin \pi x$

5. $g(x) = \frac{1}{2} \tan\left(x - \frac{\pi}{2}\right)$

6. Find a, b, and c such that the graph of the function $h(x) = a \cos(bx + c)$ matches the graph in the figure.

7. Sketch the graph of the function $f(x) = \frac{1}{2}x \sin x$ over the interval $-3\pi \le x \le 3\pi$.

In Exercises 8 and 9, find the exact value of the expression without the aid of a calculator.

8. $\tan(\arctan 6.7)$

9. $\tan\left(\arcsin \frac{3}{5}\right)$

10. Write an algebraic expression equivalent to $\sin(\arccos 2x)$.

11. Use the fundamental identities to simplify: $\cos\left(\frac{\pi}{2} - x\right) \csc x$.

12. Subtract and simplify: $\dfrac{\sin \theta - 1}{\cos \theta} - \dfrac{\cos \theta}{\sin \theta - 1}$.

In Exercises 13–15, prove the identity.

13. $\cot^2 \alpha(\sec^2 \alpha - 1) = 1$

14. $\sin(x + y) \sin(x - y) = \sin^2 x - \sin^2 y$

15. $\sin^2 x \cos^2 x = \frac{1}{8}(1 - \cos 4x)$

In Exercises 16 and 17, find all solutions of the equation in the interval $[0, 2\pi)$.

16. $2 \cos^2 \beta - \cos \beta = 0$

17. $3 \tan \theta - \cot \theta = 0$

18. Use the Quadratic Formula to solve the equation in the interval $[0, 2\pi)$:
$\sin^2 x + 2 \sin x + 1 = 0$.

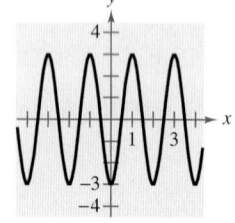

FIGURE FOR 6

19. Given that $\sin u = \frac{12}{13}$, $\cos v = \frac{3}{5}$, and angles u and v are both in Quadrant I, find $\tan(u - v)$.

20. If $\tan \theta = \frac{1}{2}$, find the exact value of $\tan(2\theta)$.

21. If $\tan \theta = \frac{4}{3}$, find the exact value of $\sin \dfrac{\theta}{2}$.

22. Write the product $5 \sin \dfrac{3\pi}{4} \cdot \cos \dfrac{7\pi}{4}$ as a sum or difference.

In Exercises 23–26, use the information to solve the triangle shown in the figure.

23. $A = 30°$, $a = 9$, $b = 8$

24. $A = 30°$, $b = 8$, $c = 10$

25. $A = 30°$, $C = 90°$, $b = 10$

26. $a = 4$, $b = 8$, $c = 9$

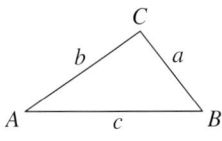

FIGURE FOR **23–26**

27. Two sides of a triangle have lengths 7 inches and 12 inches. Their included angle measures 60°. Find the area of the triangle.

28. Find the area of a triangle with sides of lengths 11 inches, 16 inches, and 17 inches.

29. Write vector $\mathbf{u} = \langle 3, 5 \rangle$ as a linear combination of the standard unit vectors $\mathbf{i}$ and $\mathbf{j}$.

30. Find $\mathbf{u} \cdot \mathbf{v}$ for $\mathbf{u} = 3\mathbf{i} + 4\mathbf{j}$ and $\mathbf{v} = \mathbf{i} - 2\mathbf{j}$.

31. Find the projection of $\mathbf{u} = \langle 8, -2 \rangle$ onto $\mathbf{v} = \langle 1, 5 \rangle$ and the vector component of $\mathbf{u}$ orthogonal to $\mathbf{v}$.

32. Find the trigonometric form of the complex number $-2 + 2i$.

33. Find the product of $[4(\cos 30° + i \sin 30°)][6(\cos 120° + i \sin 120°)]$. Write the answer in standard form.

34. Find the three cube roots of 1.

35. Write all the solutions of the equation $x^4 - 256i = 0$.

36. From a point 200 feet from a flagpole, the angles of elevation to the bottom and top of the flag are $16° \, 45'$ and $18°$, respectively. Approximate the height of the flag to the nearest foot.

37. A compact disc can have an angular speed up to 3142 radians per minute. At this angular speed, how many revolutions per minute would the CD make? How long would it take the CD to make 10,000 revolutions?

38. To determine the angle of elevation of a star in the sky, you get the star in your line of vision with the backboard of a basketball hoop that is 5 feet higher than your eyes (see figure). Your horizontal distance from the backboard is 12 feet. What is the angle of elevation of the star?

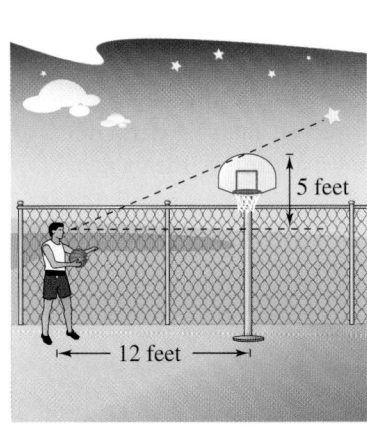

FIGURE FOR **38**

39. Write a model for a particle in simple harmonic motion with a displacement of 4 inches and a period of 8 seconds.

40. An airplane's velocity with respect to the air is 500 kilometers per hour, with a bearing of 30°. The wind at the altitude of the plane has a velocity of 50 kilometers per hour with a bearing of N 60° E. What is the true direction of the plane, and what is its speed relative to the ground?

Proofs in Mathematics

Law of Tangents

Besides the Law of Sines and the Law of Cosines in trigonometry there is also a Law of Tangents developed by Francois Viète (1540–1603). The Law of Tangents follows from the Law of Sines and the sum-to-product formulas for sine and is defined as follows.

$$\frac{a+b}{a-b} = \frac{\tan(A+B)/2}{\tan(A-B)/2}$$

The Law of Tangents can be used to solve a triangle when two sides and the included angle are given (SAS). Before calculators were invented, the Law of Tangents was used to solve the SAS case instead of the Law of Cosines, because computation with a table of tangent values was easier.

A is acute

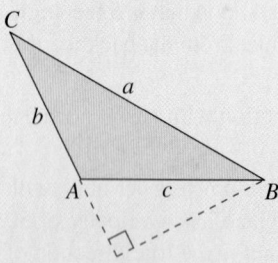

A is obtuse

Law of Sines   *(p. 410)*

If ABC is a triangle with sides a, b, and c, then

$$\frac{a}{\sin A} = \frac{b}{\sin B} = \frac{c}{\sin C}.$$

  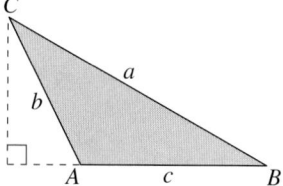

Proof

Let h be the altitude of either triangle found in the figure above. Then you have

$$\sin A = \frac{h}{b} \qquad \text{or} \qquad h = b \sin A$$

$$\sin B = \frac{h}{a} \qquad \text{or} \qquad h = a \sin B.$$

Equating these two values of h, you have

$$a \sin B = b \sin A \qquad \text{or} \qquad \frac{a}{\sin A} = \frac{b}{\sin B}.$$

Note that $\sin A \neq 0$ and $\sin B \neq 0$ because no angle of a triangle can have a measure of $0°$ or $180°$. In a similar manner, construct an altitude from vertex B to side AC (extended in the obtuse triangle), as shown at the left. Then you have

$$\sin A = \frac{h}{c} \qquad \text{or} \qquad h = c \sin A$$

$$\sin C = \frac{h}{a} \qquad \text{or} \qquad h = a \sin C.$$

Equating these two values of h, you have

$$a \sin C = c \sin A \qquad \text{or} \qquad \frac{a}{\sin A} = \frac{c}{\sin C}.$$

By the Transitive Property of Equality you know that

$$\frac{a}{\sin A} = \frac{b}{\sin B} = \frac{c}{\sin C}.$$

So, the Law of Sines is established.

Law of Cosines   *(p. 419)*

Standard Form	*Alternative Form*

$$a^2 = b^2 + c^2 - 2bc \cos A$$

$$\cos A = \frac{b^2 + c^2 - a^2}{2bc}$$

$$b^2 = a^2 + c^2 - 2ac \cos B$$

$$\cos B = \frac{a^2 + c^2 - b^2}{2ac}$$

$$c^2 = a^2 + b^2 - 2ab \cos C$$

$$\cos C = \frac{a^2 + b^2 - c^2}{2ab}$$

Proof

To prove the first formula, consider the top triangle at the left, which has three acute angles. Note that vertex B has coordinates $(c, 0)$. Furthermore, C has coordinates (x, y), where $x = b \cos A$ and $y = b \sin A$. Because a is the distance from vertex C to vertex B, it follows that

$a = \sqrt{(x - c)^2 + (y - 0)^2}$	Distance Formula
$a^2 = (x - c)^2 + (y - 0)^2$	Square each side.
$a^2 = (b \cos A - c)^2 + (b \sin A)^2$	Substitute for x and y.
$a^2 = b^2 \cos^2 A - 2bc \cos A + c^2 + b^2 \sin^2 A$	Expand.
$a^2 = b^2(\sin^2 A + \cos^2 A) + c^2 - 2ab \cos A$	Factor out b^2.
$a^2 = b^2 + c^2 - 2bc \cos A.$	$\sin^2 A + \cos^2 A = 1$

To prove the second formula, consider the bottom triangle at the left, which also has three acute angles. Note that vertex A has coordinates $(c, 0)$. Furthermore, C has coordinates (x, y), where $x = a \cos B$ and $y = a \sin B$. Because b is the distance from vertex C to vertex A, it follows that

$b = \sqrt{(x - c)^2 + (y - 0)^2}$	Distance Formula
$b^2 = (x - c)^2 + (y - 0)^2$	Square each side.
$b^2 = (a \cos B - c)^2 + (a \sin B)^2$	Substitute for x and y.
$b^2 = a^2 \cos^2 B - 2ac \cos B + c^2 + a^2 + \sin^2 B$	Expand.
$b^2 = a^2(\sin^2 B + \cos^2 B) + c^2 - 2ac \cos B$	Factor out a^2.
$b^2 = a^2 + c^2 - 2ac \cos B.$	$\sin^2 B + \cos^2 B = 1$

Try using a similar argument to establish the third formula.

> **Heron's Area Formula**   *(p. 422)*
>
> Given any triangle with sides of lengths a, b, and c, the area of the triangle is
>
> $$\text{Area} = \sqrt{s(s-a)(s-b)(s-c)}$$
>
> where $s = \dfrac{(a+b+c)}{2}$.

Proof

From Section 6.1, you know that

$$\text{Area} = \frac{1}{2}bc\sin A \qquad\qquad \text{Formula for the area of an oblique triangle.}$$

$$= \frac{1}{4}b^2c^2\sin^2 A \qquad\qquad \text{Square the right side.}$$

$$= \sqrt{\frac{1}{4}b^2c^2\sin^2 A} \qquad\qquad \text{Take the square root of the right side.}$$

$$= \sqrt{\frac{1}{4}b^2c^2(1-\cos^2 A)} \qquad\qquad \text{Pythagorean Identity}$$

$$= \sqrt{\left[\frac{1}{2}bc(1+\cos A)\right]\left[\frac{1}{2}bc(1-\cos A)\right]}. \qquad \text{Factor.}$$

Using the Law of Cosines, you can show that

$$\frac{1}{2}bc(1+\cos A) = \frac{a+b+c}{2}\cdot\frac{-a+b+c}{2}$$

and

$$\frac{1}{2}bc(1-\cos A) = \frac{a-b+c}{2}\cdot\frac{a+b-c}{2}.$$

Letting $s = (a+b+c)/2$, these two equations can be rewritten as

$$\frac{1}{2}bc(1+\cos A) = s(s-a)$$

and

$$\frac{1}{2}bc(1-\cos A) = (s-b)(s-c).$$

By substituting into the last formula for area, you can conclude that

$$\text{Area} = \sqrt{s(s-a)(s-b)(s-c)}.$$

Properties of the Dot Product *(p. 440)*

Let **u**, **v**, and **w** be vectors in the place or in space and let c be a scalar.

1. $\mathbf{u} \cdot \mathbf{v} = \mathbf{v} \cdot \mathbf{u}$
2. $\mathbf{0} \cdot \mathbf{v} = 0$
3. $\mathbf{u} \cdot (\mathbf{v} + \mathbf{w}) = \mathbf{u} \cdot \mathbf{v} + \mathbf{u} \cdot \mathbf{w}$
4. $\mathbf{v} \cdot \mathbf{v} = \|\mathbf{v}\|^2$
5. $c(\mathbf{u} \cdot \mathbf{v}) = c\mathbf{u} \cdot \mathbf{v} = \mathbf{u} \cdot c\mathbf{v}$

Proof

Let $\mathbf{u} = \langle u_1, u_2 \rangle$, $\mathbf{v} = \langle v_1, v_2 \rangle$, $\mathbf{w} = \langle w_1, w_2 \rangle$, $\mathbf{0} = \langle 0, 0 \rangle$, and let c be a scalar.

1. $\mathbf{u} \cdot \mathbf{v} = u_1 v_1 + u_2 v_2 = v_1 u_1 + v_2 u_2 = \mathbf{v} \cdot \mathbf{u}$
2. $\mathbf{0} \cdot \mathbf{v} = 0 \cdot v_1 + 0 \cdot v_2 = 0$
3. $\mathbf{u} \cdot (\mathbf{v} + \mathbf{w}) = \mathbf{u} \cdot \langle v_1 + w_1, v_2 + w_2 \rangle$
   $= u_1(v_1 + w_1) + u_2(v_2 + w_2)$
   $= u_1 v_1 + u_1 w_1 + u_2 v_2 + u_2 w_2$
   $= (u_1 v_1 + u_2 v_2) + (u_1 w_1 + u_2 w_2) = \mathbf{u} \cdot \mathbf{v} + \mathbf{u} \cdot \mathbf{w}$
4. $\mathbf{v} \cdot \mathbf{v} = v_1^2 + v_2^2 = \left(\sqrt{v_1^2 + v_2^2} \right)^2 = \|\mathbf{v}\|^2$
5. $c(\mathbf{u} \cdot \mathbf{v}) = c(\langle u_1, u_2 \rangle \cdot \langle v_1, v_2 \rangle)$
   $= c(u_1 v_1 + u_2 v_2) = (cu_1)v_1 + (cu_2)v_2$
   $= \langle cu_1, cu_2 \rangle \cdot \langle v_1, v_2 \rangle = c\mathbf{u} \cdot \mathbf{v}$

Angle Between Two Vectors *(p. 441)*

If θ is the angle between two nonzero vectors $\mathbf{u}$ and $\mathbf{v}$, then $\cos \theta = \dfrac{\mathbf{u} \cdot \mathbf{v}}{\|\mathbf{u}\| \, \|\mathbf{v}\|}$.

Proof

Consider the triangle determined by vectors **u**, **v**, and **v** − **u**, as shown in the figure. By the Law of Cosines, you can write

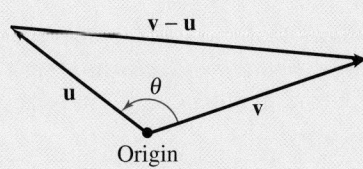

$$\|\mathbf{v} - \mathbf{u}\|^2 = \|\mathbf{u}\|^2 + \|\mathbf{v}\|^2 - 2\|\mathbf{u}\| \, \|\mathbf{v}\|\cos \theta$$

$$(\mathbf{v} - \mathbf{u}) \cdot (\mathbf{v} - \mathbf{u}) = \|\mathbf{u}\|^2 + \|\mathbf{v}\|^2 - 2\|\mathbf{u}\| \, \|\mathbf{v}\| \cos \theta$$

$$(\mathbf{v} - \mathbf{u}) \cdot \mathbf{v} - (\mathbf{v} - \mathbf{u}) \cdot \mathbf{u} = \|\mathbf{u}\|^2 + \|\mathbf{v}\|^2 - 2\|\mathbf{u}\| \, \|\mathbf{v}\| \cos \theta$$

$$\mathbf{v} \cdot \mathbf{v} - \mathbf{u} \cdot \mathbf{v} - \mathbf{v} \cdot \mathbf{u} + \mathbf{u} \cdot \mathbf{u} = \|\mathbf{u}\|^2 + \|\mathbf{v}\|^2 - 2\|\mathbf{u}\| \, \|\mathbf{v}\| \cos \theta$$

$$\|\mathbf{v}\|^2 - 2\mathbf{u} \cdot \mathbf{v} + \|\mathbf{u}\|^2 = \|\mathbf{u}\|^2 + \|\mathbf{v}\|^2 - 2\|\mathbf{u}\| \, \|\mathbf{v}\| \cos \theta$$

$$\cos \theta = \frac{\mathbf{u} \cdot \mathbf{v}}{\|\mathbf{u}\| \, \|\mathbf{v}\|}.$$

1. In the figure, a beam of light is directed at the blue mirror, reflected to the red mirror, and then reflected back to the blue mirror. Find the distance PT that the light travels from the red mirror back to the blue mirror.

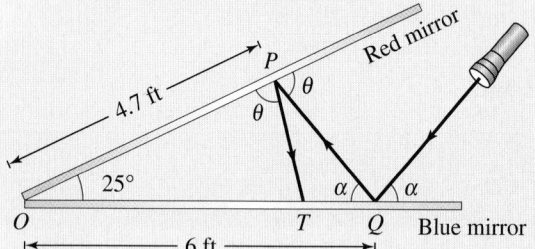

2. A triathlete sets a course to swim S 25° E from a point on shore to a buoy $\frac{3}{4}$ mile away. After swimming 300 yards through a strong current, the triathlete is off course at a bearing of S 35° E. Find the bearing and distance the triathlete needs to swim to correct her course.

3. A hiking party is lost in a national park. Two ranger stations have received an emergency SOS signal from the party. Station B is 75 miles due east of station A. The bearing from station A to the signal is S 60° E and the bearing from station B to the signal is S 75° W.

   (a) Find the distance from each station to the SOS signal.

   (b) A rescue party is in the park 20 miles from station A at a bearing of S 80° E. Find the distance and the bearing the rescue party must travel to reach the lost hiking party.

4. You are seeding a triangular courtyard. One side of the courtyard is 52 feet long and the other side is 46 feet long. The angle opposite the 52-foot side is 65°.

   (a) Draw a diagram that gives a visual representation of the problem.

   (b) How long is the third side of the courtyard?

   (c) One bag of grass covers an area of 50 square feet. How many bags of grass will you need to cover the courtyard?

5. For each pair of vectors, find the following.

   (i) $\|\mathbf{u}\|$ (ii) $\|\mathbf{v}\|$ (iii) $\|\mathbf{u} + \mathbf{v}\|$

   (iv) $\left\|\dfrac{\mathbf{u}}{\|\mathbf{u}\|}\right\|$ (v) $\left\|\dfrac{\mathbf{v}}{\|\mathbf{v}\|}\right\|$ (vi) $\left\|\dfrac{\mathbf{u} + \mathbf{v}}{\|\mathbf{u} + \mathbf{v}\|}\right\|$

   (a) $\mathbf{u} = \langle 1, -1 \rangle$
       $\mathbf{v} = \langle -1, 2 \rangle$

   (b) $\mathbf{u} = \langle 0, 1 \rangle$
       $\mathbf{v} = \langle 3, -3 \rangle$

   (c) $\mathbf{u} = \left\langle 1, \frac{1}{2} \right\rangle$
       $\mathbf{v} = \langle 2, 3 \rangle$

   (d) $\mathbf{u} = \langle 2, -4 \rangle$
       $\mathbf{v} = \langle 5, 5 \rangle$

6. A skydiver is falling at a constant downward velocity of 120 miles per hour. In the figure, vector $\mathbf{u}$ represents the skydiver's velocity. A steady breeze pushes the skydiver to the east at 40 miles per hour. Vector $\mathbf{v}$ represents the wind velocity.

   (a) Write the vectors $\mathbf{u}$ and $\mathbf{v}$ in component form.

   (b) Let $\mathbf{s} = \mathbf{u} + \mathbf{v}$. Use the figure to sketch $\mathbf{s}$. To print an enlarged copy of the graph, go to the website, *www.mathgraphs.com.*

   (c) Find the magnitude of $\mathbf{s}$. What information does the magnitude give you about the skydiver's fall?

   (d) If there were no wind, the skydiver would fall in a path perpendicular to Earth. At what angle to the ground is the path of the skydiver when the skydiver is affected by the 40 mile per hour wind from due west?

   (e) The skydiver is blown to the west at 30 miles per hour. Draw a new figure that gives a visual representation of the problem and find the skydiver's new velocity.

FIGURE FOR 6

7. Write the vector **w** in terms of **u** and **v**, given that the terminal point of **w** bisects the line segment.

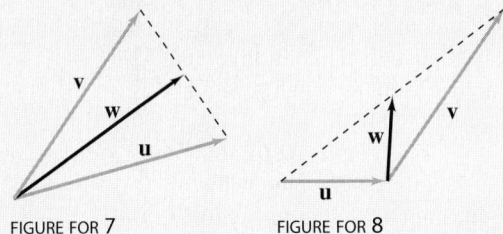

FIGURE FOR 7   FIGURE FOR 8

8. Prove that if **u** is orthogonal to **v** and **w**, then **u** is orthogonal to

$$c\mathbf{v} + d\mathbf{w}$$

for any scalars c and d.

9. Two forces of the same magnitude $\mathbf{F}_1$ and $\mathbf{F}_2$ act at angles θ_1 and θ_2, respectively. Use a diagram to compare the work done by $\mathbf{F}_1$ with the work done by $\mathbf{F}_2$ in moving along the vector PQ if

(a) $\theta_1 = -\theta_2$

(b) $\theta_1 = 60°$ and $\theta_2 = 30°$.

10. Four basic forces are in action during flight: weight, lift, thrust, and drag. To fly through the air, an object must overcome its own *weight*. To do this, it must create an upward force called *lift*. To generate lift, a forward motion called *thrust* is needed. The thrust must be great enough to overcome air resistance, which is called *drag*.

For a commercial jet aircraft, a quick climb is important to maximize efficiency, because the performance of an aircraft at high altitudes is enhanced. In addition, it is necessary to clear obstacles such as buildings and mountains and reduce noise in residential areas. In the diagram, the angle θ is called the climb angle. The velocity of the plane can be represented by a vector **v** with a vertical component $\|\mathbf{v}\| \sin \theta$ (called climb speed) and a horizontal component $\|\mathbf{v}\| \cos \theta$, where $\|\mathbf{v}\|$ is the speed of the plane. When taking off, a pilot must decide how much of the thrust to apply to each component. The more the thrust is applied to the horizontal component, the faster the airplane will gain speed. The more the thrust is applied to the vertical component, the quicker the airplane will climb.

(a) Complete the table for an airplane that has a speed of $\|\mathbf{v}\| = 100$ miles per hour.

θ	0.5°	1.0°	1.5°	2.0°	2.5°	3.0°
$\|\mathbf{v}\| \sin \theta$						
$\|\mathbf{v}\| \cos \theta$						

(b) Does an airplane's speed equal the sum of the vertical and horizontal components of its velocity? If not, how could you find the speed of an airplane whose velocity components were known?

(c) Use the result of part (b) to find the speed of an airplane with the given velocity components.

(i) $\|\mathbf{v}\| \sin \theta = 5.235$ miles per hour

$\|\mathbf{v}\| \cos \theta = 149.909$ miles per hour

(ii) $\|\mathbf{v}\| \sin \theta = 10.463$ miles per hour

$\|\mathbf{v}\| \cos \theta = 149.634$ miles per hour

473

How to study Chapter 7

▶ **What you should learn**

In this chapter you will learn the following skills and concepts:

- How to solve systems of equations by substitution, by elimination, by Gaussian elimination, and by graphing

- How to recognize linear systems in row-echelon form and to use back-substitution to solve the systems

- How to solve nonsquare systems of equations

- How to sketch the graphs of inequalities in two variables and to solve systems of inequalities

- How to solve linear programming problems

- How to use systems of equations and inequalities to model and solve real-life problems

▶ **Important Vocabulary**

As you encounter each new vocabulary term in this chapter, add the term and its definition to your notebook glossary.

System of equations (p. 476)
Solution of a system of equations (p. 476)
Solving a system of equations
  (p. 476)
Method of substitution (p. 476)
Graphical method (p. 480)
Points of intersection (p. 480)
Break-even point (p. 481)
Method of elimination (p. 487)
Equivalent systems (p. 488)
Consistent system (p. 490)
Inconsistent system (p. 490)
Row-echelon form (p. 499)
Ordered triple (p. 499)
Row operations (p. 500)

Gaussian elimination (p. 500)
Nonsquare system of equations
  (p. 504)
Position equation (p. 505)
Solution of an inequality (p. 512)
Graph of an inequality (p. 512)
Linear inequalities (p. 513)
Solution of a system of inequalities (p. 514)
Consumer surplus (p. 517)
Producer surplus (p. 517)
Optimization (p. 523)
Linear programming (p. 523)
Objective function (p. 523)
Constraints (p. 523)
Feasible solutions (p. 523)

Study Tools

Learning objectives in each section
Chapter Summary (p. 533)
Review Exercises (pp. 534–537)
Chapter Test (p. 538)

Additional Resources

Study and Solutions Guide
Interactive Precalculus
Videotapes/DVD for Chapter 7
Precalculus Website
Student Success Organizer

Anthony Boccaccio/Getty Images

7

Systems of Equations and Inequalities

7.1   Solving Systems of Equations

▶ **What you should learn**

- How to use the method of substitution to solve systems of equations in two variables
- How to use a graphical approach to solve systems of equations in two variables
- How to use systems of equations to model and solve real-life problems

▶ **Why you should learn it**

Graphs of systems of equations help you solve real-life problems. For instance, in Exercise 75 on page 485, you can use the graph of a system of equations to approximate the points of intersection of two equations that model the number of visits to hospital emergency departments.

The Method of Substitution

Up to this point in the book, most problems have involved either a function of one variable or a single equation in two variables. However, many problems in science, business, and engineering involve two or more equations in two or more variables. To solve such problems, you need to find solutions of a **system of equations.** Here is an example of a system of two equations in two unknowns.

$$\begin{cases} 2x + y = 5 & \text{Equation 1} \\ 3x - 2y = 4 & \text{Equation 2} \end{cases}$$

A **solution** of this system is an ordered pair that satisfies each equation in the system. Finding the set of all solutions is called **solving the system of equations.** For instance, the ordered pair $(2, 1)$ is a solution of this system. To check this, you can substitute 2 for x and 1 for y in *each* equation.

Check (2, 1) in Equation 1 and Equation 2:

$$2x + y = 5 \qquad \text{Write Equation 1.}$$
$$2(2) + 1 \overset{?}{=} 5 \qquad \text{Substitute 2 for } x \text{ and 1 for } y.$$
$$4 + 1 = 5 \qquad \text{Solution checks in Equation 1. } \checkmark$$

$$3x - 2y = 4 \qquad \text{Write Equation 2.}$$
$$3(2) - 2(1) \overset{?}{=} 4 \qquad \text{Substitute 2 for } x \text{ and 1 for } y.$$
$$6 - 2 = 4 \qquad \text{Solution checks in Equation 2. } \checkmark$$

In this chapter you will study four ways to solve equations, beginning with the **method of substitution.**

Method	Section	Type of System
1. Substitution	7.1	Linear or nonlinear, two variables
2. Graphical method	7.1	Linear or nonlinear, two variables
3. Elimination	7.2	Linear, two variables
4. Gaussian elimination	7.3	Linear, three or more variables

Method of Substitution

1. *Solve* one of the equations for one variable in terms of the other.

2. *Substitute* the expression found in Step 1 into the other equation to obtain an equation in one variable.

3. *Solve* the equation obtained in Step 2.

4. *Back-substitute* the value obtained in Step 3 into the expression obtained in Step 1 to find the value of the other variable.

5. *Check* that the solution satisfies *each* of the original equations.

Example 1 ▶ Solving a System of Equations by Substitution

Solve the system of equations.

$$\begin{cases} x + y = 4 & \text{Equation 1} \\ x - y = 2 & \text{Equation 2} \end{cases}$$

Solution

Begin by solving for y in Equation 1.

$$y = 4 - x \qquad \text{Solve for } y \text{ in Equation 1.}$$

Next, substitute this expression for y into Equation 2 and solve the resulting single-variable equation for x.

$$x - y = 2 \qquad \text{Write Equation 2.}$$
$$x - (4 - x) = 2 \qquad \text{Substitute } 4 - x \text{ for } y.$$
$$x - 4 + x = 2 \qquad \text{Distributive Property}$$
$$2x = 6 \qquad \text{Combine like terms.}$$
$$x = 3 \qquad \text{Divide each side by 2.}$$

Finally, you can solve for y by *back-substituting* $x = 3$ into the equation $y = 4 - x$, to obtain

$$y = 4 - x \qquad \text{Write revised Equation 1.}$$
$$y = 4 - 3 \qquad \text{Substitute 3 for } x.$$
$$y = 1. \qquad \text{Solve for } y.$$

The solution is the ordered pair $(3, 1)$. You can check this solution as follows.

Check

Substitute $(3, 1)$ into Equation 1:

$$x + y = 4 \qquad \text{Write Equation 1.}$$
$$3 + 1 \overset{?}{=} 4 \qquad \text{Substitute for } x \text{ and } y.$$
$$4 = 4 \qquad \text{Solution checks in Equation 1.} ✓$$

Substitute $(3, 1)$ into Equation 2:

$$x - y = 2 \qquad \text{Write Equation 2.}$$
$$3 - 1 \overset{?}{=} 2 \qquad \text{Substitute for } x \text{ and } y.$$
$$2 = 2 \qquad \text{Solution checks in Equation 2.} ✓$$

Because $(3, 1)$ satisfies both equations in the system, it is a solution of the system of equations.

The term *back-substitution* implies that you work *backwards*. First you solve for one of the variables, and then you substitute that value *back* into one of the equations in the system to find the value of the other variable.

The icon identifies examples and concepts related to features of the Learning Tools CD-ROM and the *Interactive* and *Internet* versions of this text. For more details see the chart on pages *xxi-xxv*.

| Example 2 ▶ | Solving a System by Substitution | |

A total of $12,000 is invested in two funds paying 9% and 11% simple interest. The yearly interest is $1180. How much is invested at each rate?

Solution

Verbal Model:

$$\boxed{\begin{array}{c}9\% \\ \text{fund}\end{array}} + \boxed{\begin{array}{c}11\% \\ \text{fund}\end{array}} = \boxed{\begin{array}{c}\text{Total} \\ \text{investment}\end{array}}$$

$$\boxed{\begin{array}{c}9\% \\ \text{interest}\end{array}} + \boxed{\begin{array}{c}11\% \\ \text{interest}\end{array}} = \boxed{\begin{array}{c}\text{Total} \\ \text{interest}\end{array}}$$

> You may want to compare and contrast solving a problem using a system of two equations with solving a problem using one equation.

Labels:

Amount in 9% fund $= x$	(dollars)
Interest for 9% fund $= 0.09x$	(dollars)
Amount in 11% fund $= y$	(dollars)
Interest for 11% fund $= 0.11y$	(dollars)
Total investment $= \$12,000$	(dollars)
Total interest $= \$1,180$	(dollars)

System:

$$\begin{cases} x + y = 12,000 & \text{Equation 1} \\ 0.09x + 0.11y = 1,180 & \text{Equation 2} \end{cases}$$

To begin, it is convenient to multiply each side of Equation 2 by 100. This eliminates the need to work with decimals.

$$100(0.09x + 0.11y) = 100(1180) \qquad \text{Multiply each side by 100.}$$
$$9x + 11y = 118,000 \qquad \text{Revised Equation 2}$$

To solve this system, you can solve for x in Equation 1.

$$x = 12,000 - y \qquad \text{Revised Equation 1}$$

Technology

One way to check the answers you obtain in this section is to use a graphing utility. For instance, enter the two equations in Example 2

$$y_1 = 12,000 - x$$

$$y_2 = \frac{1180 - 0.09x}{0.11}$$

and find an appropriate viewing window that shows where the two lines intersect. Then use the *intersect* feature or the *zoom* and *trace* features to find the point of intersection. Does this point agree with the solution obtained at the right?

Then, substitute this expression for x into revised Equation 2 and solve the resulting equation for y.

$$9x + 11y = 118,000 \qquad \text{Write revised Equation 2.}$$
$$9(12,000 - y) + 11y = 118,000 \qquad \text{Substitute } 12,000 - y \text{ for } x.$$
$$108,000 - 9y + 11y = 118,000 \qquad \text{Distributive Property}$$
$$2y = 10,000 \qquad \text{Combine like terms.}$$
$$y = 5,000 \qquad \text{Divide each side by 2.}$$

Next, back-substitute the value $y = 5000$ to solve for x.

$$x = 12,000 - y \qquad \text{Write revised Equation 1.}$$
$$x = 12,000 - 5000 \qquad \text{Substitute 5000 for } y.$$
$$x = 7000 \qquad \text{Simplify.}$$

The solution is (7000, 5000). So, $7000 is invested at 9% and $5000 is invested at 11%. Check this in the original problem.

The *Interactive* CD-ROM and *Internet* versions of this text offer a Try It for each example in the text.

The equations in Examples 1 and 2 are linear. Substitution can also be used to solve systems in which one or both of the equations are nonlinear.

Example 3 ► Substitution: Two-Solution Case

Solve the system of equations.

$$\begin{cases} x^2 + 4x - y = 7 & \text{Equation 1} \\ 2x - y = -1 & \text{Equation 2} \end{cases}$$

Solution

Begin by solving for y in Equation 2 to obtain $y = 2x + 1$. Next, substitute this expression for y into Equation 1 and solve for x.

$x^2 + 4x - y = 7$	Write Equation 1.
$x^2 + 4x - (2x + 1) = 7$	Substitute $2x + 1$ for y.
$x^2 + 2x - 1 = 7$	Simplify.
$x^2 + 2x - 8 = 0$	General form
$(x + 4)(x - 2) = 0$	Factor.
$x = -4, 2$	Solve for x.

Back-substituting these values of x to solve for the corresponding values of y produces the solutions $(-4, -7)$ and $(2, 5)$. Check these in the original system.

Example 4 ► Substitution: No-Real-Solution Case

Solve the system of equations.

$$\begin{cases} -x + y = 4 & \text{Equation 1} \\ x^2 + y = 3 & \text{Equation 2} \end{cases}$$

Solution

Begin by solving for y in Equation 1 to obtain $y = x + 4$. Next, substitute this expression for y into Equation 2 and solve for x.

$x^2 + y = 3$	Write Equation 2.
$x^2 + (x + 4) = 3$	Substitute $x + 4$ for y.
$x^2 + x + 1 = 0$	Simplify.
$x = \dfrac{-1 \pm \sqrt{1^2 - 4(1)(1)}}{2}$	Use the Quadratic Formula.
$x = \dfrac{-1 \pm \sqrt{-3}}{2}$	Simplify.

Because the discriminant is negative, the equation $x^2 + x + 1 = 0$ has no (real) solution. So, this system has no (real) solution.

◄ **Exploration** ►

Use a graphing utility to graph the two equations in Example 3

$$y_1 = x^2 + 4x - 7$$

$$y_2 = 2x + 1$$

in the same viewing window. How many solutions do you think this system has? Repeat this experiment for the equations in Example 4. How many solutions does this system have? Explain your reasoning.

Point out that it is not practical to solve Equation 2 for x (instead of for y) in Example 3.

The *Interactive* CD-ROM and *Internet* versions of this text offer a Quiz for every section of the text.

Graphical Approach to Finding Solutions

From Examples 2, 3, and 4, you can see that a system of two equations in two unknowns can have exactly one solution, more than one solution, or no solution. By using a **graphical method,** you can gain insight about the number of solutions and the location(s) of the solution(s) of a system of equations by graphing each of the equations in the same coordinate plane. The solutions of the system correspond to the **points of intersection** of the graphs. For instance, the two equations in Figure 7.1 graph as two lines with a *single point* of intersection; the two equations in Figure 7.2 graph as a parabola and a line with *two points* of intersection; and the two equations in Figure 7.3 graph as a line and a parabola that have *no points* of intersection.

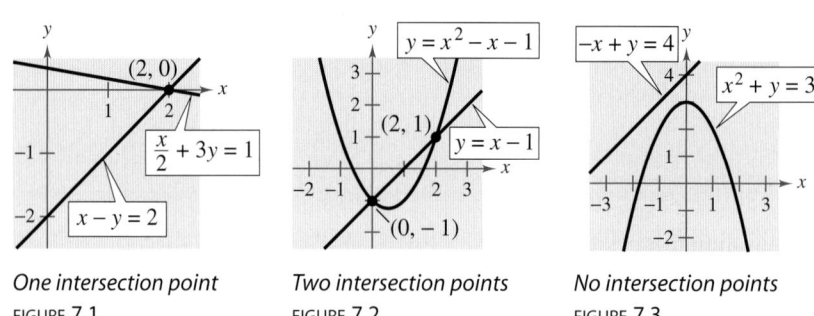

One intersection point	*Two intersection points*	*No intersection points*
FIGURE 7.1	FIGURE 7.2	FIGURE 7.3

Example 5 ▶ **Solving a System of Equations Graphically**

Solve the system of equations.

$$\begin{cases} y = \ln x & \text{Equation 1} \\ x + y = 1 & \text{Equation 2} \end{cases}$$

Solution

Sketch the graphs of the two equations, as shown in Figure 7.4. From the graphs, it is clear that there is only one point of intersection and that $(1, 0)$ is the solution point. You can confirm this by substituting 1 for x and 0 for y in *both* equations.

Check $(1, 0)$ in Equation 1:

$y = \ln x$	Write Equation 1.
$0 = \ln 1$	Equation 1 checks. ✓

Check $(1, 0)$ in Equation 2:

$x + y = 1$	Write Equation 2.
$1 + 0 = 1$	Equation 2 checks. ✓

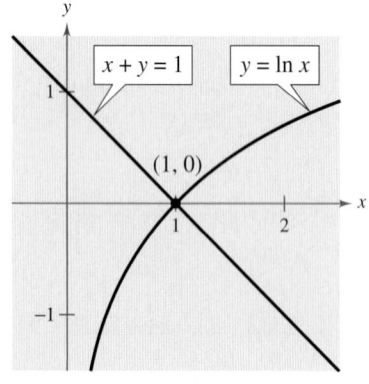

FIGURE 7.4

Example 5 shows the value of a graphical approach to solving systems of equations in two variables. Notice what would happen if you tried only the substitution method in Example 5. You would obtain the equation $x + \ln x = 1$. It would be difficult to solve this equation for x using standard algebraic techniques.

Applications

The total cost C of producing x units of a product typically has two components—the initial cost and the cost per unit. When enough units have been sold so that the total revenue R equals the total cost C, the sales are said to have reached the **break-even point.** You will find that the break-even point corresponds to the point of intersection of the cost and revenue curves.

Example 6 ▶ Break-Even Analysis

A small business invests \$10,000 in equipment to produce a product. Each unit of the product costs \$0.65 to produce and is sold for \$1.20. How many items must be sold before the business breaks even?

Solution

The total cost of producing x units is

$$\frac{\text{Total}}{\text{cost}} = \frac{\text{Cost per}}{\text{unit}} \cdot \frac{\text{Number}}{\text{of units}} + \frac{\text{Initial}}{\text{cost}}$$

$$C = 0.65x + 10,000. \qquad \text{Equation 1}$$

The revenue obtained by selling x units is

$$\frac{\text{Total}}{\text{revenue}} = \frac{\text{Price per}}{\text{unit}} \cdot \frac{\text{Number}}{\text{of units}}$$

$$R = 1.20x. \qquad \text{Equation 2}$$

Because the break-even point occurs when $R = C$, you have $C = 1.20x$, and the system of equations to solve is

$$\begin{cases} C = 0.65x + 10,000 \\ C = 1.20x \end{cases}.$$

Now you can solve by substitution.

$1.20x = 0.65x + 10,000$	Substitute $1.20x$ for C in Equation 1.
$0.55x = 10,000$	Subtract $0.65x$ from each side.
$x \approx 18,182$ units	Divide each side by 0.55.

Note in Figure 7.5 that revenue less than the break-even point corresponds to an overall loss, whereas revenue greater than the break-even point corresponds to a profit.

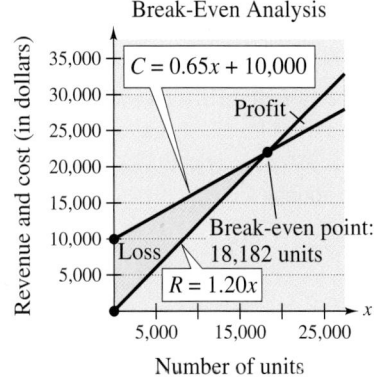

Break-Even Analysis

FIGURE **7.5**

Another way to view the solution in Example 6 is to consider the profit function

$$P = R - C.$$

The break-even point occurs when the profit is 0, which is the same as saying that $R = C$.

Example 7 ▶ **State Population**

From 1990 to 2000, the population of Tennessee was increasing at a faster rate than the population of Missouri. Models that approximate the two populations P (in thousands) are

$$\begin{cases} P = 4866 + 74.5t & \text{Tennessee} \\ P = 5109 + 43.5t & \text{Missouri} \end{cases}$$

where $t = 0$ represents 1990 (see Figure 7.6). According to these two models, when would you expect the population of Tennessee to have exceeded the population of Missouri?   (Source: U.S. Census Bureau)

Solution

Because the first equation has already been solved for P in terms of t, substitute this value into the second equation and solve for t, as follows.

$4866 + 74.5t = 5109 + 43.5t$	Substitute for P in Equation 2.
$74.5t - 43.5t = 5109 - 4866$	Subtract $43.5t$ and 4866 from each side.
$31t = 243$	Combine like terms.
$t \approx 7.84$	Divide each side by 31.

So, from the given models, you would expect that the population of Tennessee exceeded the population of Missouri after $t \approx 7.84$ years, which was sometime during 1997.

State Population

FIGURE 7.6

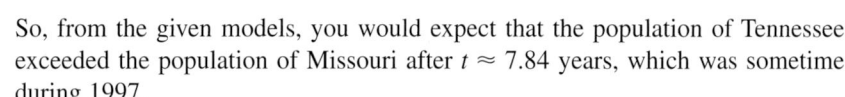

Interpreting Points of Intersection You plan to rent a 14-foot truck for a two-day local move. At truck rental agency A, you can rent a truck for $29.95 per day plus $0.49 per mile. At agency B, you can rent a truck for $50 per day plus $0.25 per mile. The total cost y (in dollars) for the truck from agency A is

$$y = (\$29.95 \text{ per day})(2 \text{ days}) + 0.49x$$
$$= 59.90 + 0.49x$$

where x is the total number of miles the truck is driven.

a. Write a total cost equation in terms of x and y for the total cost of the truck from agency B.

b. Use a graphing utility to graph the two equations in the same viewing window and find the point of intersection. Interpret the meaning of the point of intersection in the context of the problem.

c. Which agency should you choose if you plan to travel a total of 100 miles during the two-day move? Why?

d. How does the situation change if you plan to drive 200 miles during the two-day move?

Writing About Mathematics
Suggestion:

Consider asking your students to make up their own problems that involve a choice of solution methods. Students can then trade their problems with other members of their class. Make sure that students are able to interpret attributes such as slopes and points of intersection.

7.1 Exercises

The *Interactive* CD-ROM and *Internet* versions of this text contain step-by-step solutions to all odd-numbered exercises. They also provide Tutorial Exercises for additional help.

Exercises containing systems with no solutions: 23, 24, 39, 40, 52, 55, 56

In Exercises 1–4, determine which ordered pairs are solutions of the system of equations.

1. $\begin{cases} 4x - y = 1 \\ 6x + y = -6 \end{cases}$ (a) $(0, -3)$ (b) $(-1, -4)$
(c) $\left(-\frac{3}{2}, -2\right)$ (d) $\left(-\frac{1}{2}, -3\right)$

2. $\begin{cases} 4x^2 + y = 3 \\ -x - y = 11 \end{cases}$ (a) $(2, -13)$ (b) $(2, -9)$
(c) $\left(-\frac{3}{2}, -\frac{31}{3}\right)$ (d) $\left(-\frac{7}{4}, -\frac{37}{4}\right)$

3. $\begin{cases} y = -2e^x \\ 3x - y = 2 \end{cases}$ (a) $(-2, 0)$ (b) $(0, -2)$
(c) $(0, -3)$ (d) $(-1, 2)$

4. $\begin{cases} -\log x + 3 = y \\ \frac{1}{9}x + y = \frac{28}{9} \end{cases}$ (a) $\left(9, \frac{37}{9}\right)$ (b) $(10, 2)$
(c) $(1, 3)$ (d) $(2, 4)$

In Exercises 5–14, solve the system by the method of substitution. Check your solution graphically.

5. $\begin{cases} 2x + y = 6 \\ -x + y = 0 \end{cases}$ **6.** $\begin{cases} x - y = -4 \\ x + 2y = 5 \end{cases}$

     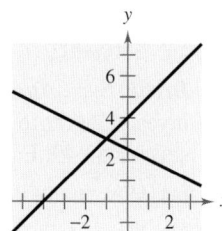

7. $\begin{cases} x - y = -4 \\ x^2 - y = -2 \end{cases}$ **8.** $\begin{cases} 3x + y = 2 \\ x^3 - 2 + y = 0 \end{cases}$

     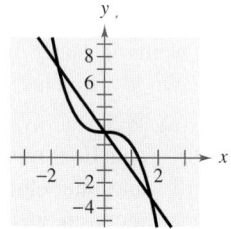

9. $\begin{cases} -2x + y = -5 \\ x^2 + y^2 = 25 \end{cases}$ **10.** $\begin{cases} x + y = 0 \\ x^3 - 5x - y = 0 \end{cases}$

     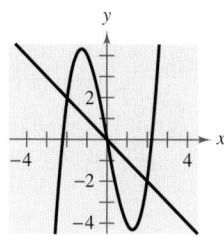

11. $\begin{cases} x^2 + y = 0 \\ x^2 - 4x - y = 0 \end{cases}$ **12.** $\begin{cases} y = -2x^2 + 2 \\ y = 2(x^4 - 2x^2 + 1) \end{cases}$

     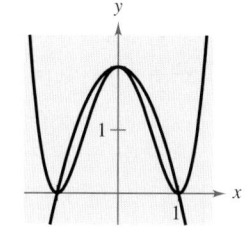

13. $\begin{cases} y = x^3 - 3x^2 + 1 \\ y = x^2 - 3x + 1 \end{cases}$ **14.** $\begin{cases} y = x^3 - 3x^2 + 4 \\ y = -2x + 4 \end{cases}$

     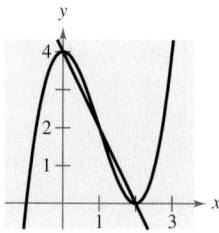

In Exercises 15–28, solve the system by the method of substitution.

15. $\begin{cases} x - y = 0 \\ 5x - 3y = 10 \end{cases}$ **16.** $\begin{cases} x + 2y = 1 \\ 5x - 4y = -23 \end{cases}$

17. $\begin{cases} 2x - y + 2 = 0 \\ 4x + y - 5 = 0 \end{cases}$ **18.** $\begin{cases} 6x - 3y - 4 = 0 \\ x + 2y - 4 = 0 \end{cases}$

19. $\begin{cases} 1.5x + 0.8y = 2.3 \\ 0.3x - 0.2y = 0.1 \end{cases}$

20. $\begin{cases} 0.5x + 3.2y = 9.0 \\ 0.2x - 1.6y = -3.6 \end{cases}$

21. $\begin{cases} \frac{1}{5}x + \frac{1}{2}y = 8 \\ x + y = 20 \end{cases}$ **22.** $\begin{cases} \frac{1}{2}x + \frac{3}{4}y = 10 \\ \frac{3}{4}x - y = 4 \end{cases}$

23. $\begin{cases} 6x + 5y = -3 \\ -x - \frac{5}{6}y = -7 \end{cases}$ **24.** $\begin{cases} -\frac{2}{3}x + y = 2 \\ 2x - 3y = 6 \end{cases}$

25. $\begin{cases} x^2 - y = 0 \\ 2x + y = 0 \end{cases}$ **26.** $\begin{cases} x - 2y = 0 \\ 3x - y^2 = 0 \end{cases}$

27. $\begin{cases} x^3 - y = 0 \\ x - y = 0 \end{cases}$ **28.** $\begin{cases} y = -x \\ y = x^3 + 3x^2 + 2x \end{cases}$

In Exercises 29–42, solve the system graphically.

29. $\begin{cases} -x + 2y = 2 \\ 3x + y = 15 \end{cases}$

30. $\begin{cases} x + y = 0 \\ 3x - 2y = 10 \end{cases}$

31. $\begin{cases} x - 3y = -2 \\ 5x + 3y = 17 \end{cases}$

32. $\begin{cases} -x + 2y = 1 \\ x - y = 2 \end{cases}$

33. $\begin{cases} x + y = 4 \\ x^2 + y^2 - 4x = 0 \end{cases}$

34. $\begin{cases} -x + y = 3 \\ x^2 - 6x - 27 + y^2 = 0 \end{cases}$

35. $\begin{cases} x - y + 3 = 0 \\ x^2 - 4x + 7 = y \end{cases}$

36. $\begin{cases} y^2 - 4x + 11 = 0 \\ -\frac{1}{2}x + y = -\frac{1}{2} \end{cases}$

37. $\begin{cases} 7x + 8y = 24 \\ x - 8y = 8 \end{cases}$

38. $\begin{cases} x - y = 0 \\ 5x - 2y = 6 \end{cases}$

39. $\begin{cases} 3x - 2y = 0 \\ x^2 - y^2 = 4 \end{cases}$

40. $\begin{cases} 2x - y + 3 = 0 \\ x^2 + y^2 - 4x = 0 \end{cases}$

41. $\begin{cases} x^2 + y^2 = 25 \\ 3x^2 - 16y = 0 \end{cases}$

42. $\begin{cases} x^2 + y^2 = 25 \\ (x - 8)^2 + y^2 = 41 \end{cases}$

 In Exercises 43–50, use a graphing utility to solve the system of equations. Find the solution accurate to two decimal places.

43. $\begin{cases} y = e^x \\ x - y + 1 = 0 \end{cases}$

44. $\begin{cases} y = -4e^{-x} \\ y + 3x + 8 = 0 \end{cases}$

45. $\begin{cases} x + 2y = 8 \\ y = \log_2 x \end{cases}$

46. $\begin{cases} y = -2 + \ln(x - 1) \\ 3y + 2x = 9 \end{cases}$

47. $\begin{cases} y = \sqrt{x} \\ y = x \end{cases}$

48. $\begin{cases} x - y = 3 \\ x - y^2 = 1 \end{cases}$

49. $\begin{cases} x^2 + y^2 = 169 \\ x^2 - 8y = 104 \end{cases}$

50. $\begin{cases} x^2 + y^2 = 4 \\ 2x^2 - y = 2 \end{cases}$

In Exercises 51–62, solve the system graphically or algebraically. Explain your choice of method.

51. $\begin{cases} y = 2x \\ y = x^2 + 1 \end{cases}$

52. $\begin{cases} x + y = 4 \\ x^2 + y = 2 \end{cases}$

53. $\begin{cases} 3x - 7y + 6 = 0 \\ x^2 - y^2 = 4 \end{cases}$

54. $\begin{cases} x^2 + y^2 = 25 \\ 2x + y = 10 \end{cases}$

55. $\begin{cases} x - 2y = 4 \\ x^2 - y = 0 \end{cases}$

56. $\begin{cases} y = (x + 1)^3 \\ y = \sqrt{x - 1} \end{cases}$

57. $\begin{cases} y - e^{-x} = 1 \\ y - \ln x = 3 \end{cases}$

58. $\begin{cases} x^2 + y = 4 \\ e^x - y = 0 \end{cases}$

59. $\begin{cases} y = x^4 - 2x^2 + 1 \\ y = 1 - x^2 \end{cases}$

60. $\begin{cases} y = x^3 - 2x^2 + x - 1 \\ y = -x^2 + 3x - 1 \end{cases}$

61. $\begin{cases} xy - 1 = 0 \\ 2x - 4y + 7 = 0 \end{cases}$

62. $\begin{cases} x - 2y = 1 \\ y = \sqrt{x - 1} \end{cases}$

Break-Even Analysis **In Exercises 63–66, find the sales necessary to break even ($R = C$) for the cost C of producing x units and the revenue R obtained by selling x units. (Round to the nearest whole unit.)**

63. $C = 8650x + 250,000, \quad R = 9950x$

64. $C = 2.65x + 350,000, \quad R = 4.15x$

65. $C = 5.5\sqrt{x} + 10,000, \quad R = 3.29x$

66. $C = 7.8\sqrt{x} + 18,500, \quad R = 12.84x$

67. ***Break-Even Analysis*** A small software company invests $16,000 to produce a software package that will sell for $55.95. Each unit can be produced for $35.45.

(a) How many units must be sold to break even?

(b) How many units must be sold to make a profit of $60,000?

68. ***Break-Even Analysis*** A small fast-food restaurant invests $5000 to produce a new food item that will sell for $3.49. Each item can be produced for $2.16.

(a) How many items must be sold to break even?

(b) How many items must be sold to make a profit of $8500?

69. ***Investment Portfolio*** A total of $25,000 is invested in two funds paying 6% and 8.5% simple interest. The 6% investment has a lower risk. The investor wants a yearly interest income of $2000 from the two investments.

(a) Write a system of equations in which one equation represents the total amount invested and the other equation represents the $2000 required in interest. Let x and y represent the amounts invested at 6% and 8.5%, respectively.

(b) Use a graphing utility to graph the two equations in the same viewing window. As the amount invested at 6% increases, how does the amount invested at 8.5% change? How does the amount of interest income change? Explain.

(c) What amount should be invested at 6% to meet the requirement of $2000 per year in interest?

70. *Investment Portfolio*   A total of $20,000 is invested in two funds paying 6.5% and 8.5% simple interest. The 6.5% investment has a lower risk. The investor wants a yearly interest check of $1600 from the two investments.

(a) Write a system of equations in which one equation represents the total amount invested and the other equation represents the $1600 required in interest. Let x and y represent the amounts invested at 6.5% and 8.5%, respectively.

(b) Use a graphing utility to graph the two equations in the same viewing window. As the amount invested at 6.5% increases, how does the amount invested at 8.5% change? How does the amount of interest change? Explain.

(c) What amount should be invested at 6.5% to meet the requirement of $1600 per year in interest?

71. *Choice of Two Jobs*   You are offered two jobs selling dental supplies. One company offers a straight commission of 6% of sales. The other company offers a salary of $350 per week plus 3% of sales. How much would you have to sell in a week in order to make the straight commission offer better?

72. *Choice of Two Jobs*   You are offered two different jobs selling college textbooks. One company offers an annual salary of $25,000 plus a year-end bonus of 2% of your total sales. The other company offers an annual salary of $20,000 plus a year-end bonus of 3% of your total sales. Determine the annual sales required to make the second offer better.

73. *Log Volume*   You are offered two different rules for estimating the number of board feet in a 16-foot log. (A board foot is a unit of measure for lumber equal to a board 1 foot square and 1 inch thick.) The first rule is the *Doyle Log Rule* and is modeled by

$$V_1 = (D - 4)^2, \qquad 5 \le D \le 40$$

and the other is the *Scribner Log Rule* and is modeled by

$$V_2 = 0.79D^2 - 2D - 4, \qquad 5 \le D \le 40$$

where D is the diameter (in inches) of the log and V is its volume in board feet.

(a) Use a graphing utility to graph the two log rules in the same viewing window.

(b) For what diameter do the two scales agree?

(c) You are selling large logs by the board foot. Which scale would you use?

74. *Supply and Demand*   The supply and demand curves for a business dealing with wheat are

Supply: $p = 1.45 + 0.00014x^2$

Demand: $p = (2.388 - 0.007x)^2$

where p is the price in dollars per bushel and x is the quantity in bushels per day. Use a graphing utility to graph the supply and demand equations and find the market equilibrium. (The market equilibrium is the point of intersection of the graphs for $x > 0$.)

▶ Model It

75. *Data Analysis*   The table shows the numbers y (in thousands) of visits to hospital emergency departments in the United States for the years 1996 to 1999. (Source: U.S. National Center for Health Statistics)

Year, t	Number of visits, y
1996	90,347
1997	94,936
1998	100,384
1999	102,765

(a) Use the *regression* feature of a graphing utility to find a linear model f and a quadratic model g for the data. Let t represent the year, with $t = 6$ corresponding to 1996.

(b) Use a graphing utility to graph the data and the two models in the same viewing window.

(c) Use your graph from part (b) to approximate the points of intersection of the graphs of the models.

(d) Approximate the points of intersection of the graphs of the models algebraically. Compare this result with the one obtained in part (c).

(e) Use the models to estimate the number of visits to hospital emergency departments in 2005.

(f) Which model do you think gives the more accurate estimate? Explain.

76. *Data Analysis* The table shows the average hourly earnings y of production workers in manufacturing industries in the United States for the years 1993 to 2000. (Source: U.S. Bureau of Labor Statistics)

Year, t	Average hourly earnings, y
1993	$11.74
1994	$12.07
1995	$12.37
1996	$12.77
1997	$13.17
1998	$13.49
1999	$13.91
2000	$14.38

A linear model that represents the data is given by

$$f(t) = 0.374t + 10.55.$$

A quadratic model that represents the data is given by

$$g(t) = 0.0092t^2 + 0.255t + 10.89.$$

For both models, t represents the year, with $t = 3$ corresponding to 1993.

(a) Use a graphing utility to graph the data and the two models in the same viewing window.

(b) Approximate the points of intersection of the graphs of the models.

Geometry **In Exercises 77–80, find the dimensions of the rectangle meeting the specified conditions.**

77. The perimeter is 30 meters and the length is 3 meters greater than the width.

78. The perimeter is 280 centimeters and the width is 20 centimeters less than the length.

79. The perimeter is 42 inches and the width is three-fourths the length.

80. The perimeter is 210 feet and the length is $1\frac{1}{2}$ times the width.

81. *Geometry* What are the dimensions of a rectangular tract of land if its perimeter is 40 kilometers and its area is 96 square kilometers?

82. *Geometry* What are the dimensions of an isosceles right triangle with a 2-inch hypotenuse and an area of 1 square inch?

Synthesis

True or False? **In Exercises 83 and 84, determine whether the statement is true or false. Justify your answer.**

83. In order to solve a system of equations by substitution, you must always solve for y in one of the two equations and then back-substitute.

84. If a system consists of a parabola and a circle, then the system can have at most two solutions.

85. *Writing* List and explain the steps used to solve a system of equations by substitution.

86. *Think About It* When solving a system of equations by substitution, how do you recognize that the system has no solution?

87. *Exploration* Find an equation of a line whose graph intersects the graph of the parabola $y = x^2$ at (a) two points, (b) one point, and (c) no points. (There is more than one correct answer.)

 88. *Conjecture* Consider the system of equations

$$\begin{cases} y = b^x \\ y = x^b. \end{cases}$$

(a) Use a graphing utility to graph the system for $b = 1, 2, 3,$ and 4.

(b) For a fixed even value of $b > 1$, make a conjecture about the number of points of intersection of the graphs in part (a).

Review

In Exercises 89–94, find the general form of the equation of the line through the two points.

89. $(-2, 7), (5, 5)$ **90.** $(3.5, 4), (10, 6)$

91. $(6, 3), (10, 3)$ **92.** $(4, -2), (4, 5)$

93. $\left(\frac{3}{5}, 0\right), (4, 6)$ **94.** $\left(-\frac{7}{3}, 8\right), \left(\frac{5}{2}, \frac{1}{2}\right)$

In Exercises 95–98, find the domain of the function and identify any horizontal or vertical asymptotes.

95. $f(x) = \dfrac{5}{x - 6}$ **96.** $f(x) = \dfrac{2x - 7}{3x + 2}$

97. $f(x) = \dfrac{x^2 + 2}{x^2 - 16}$ **98.** $f(x) = 3 - \dfrac{2}{x^2}$

7.2 Two-Variable Linear Systems

▶ **What you should learn**

- How to use the method of elimination to solve systems of linear equations in two variables
- How to interpret graphically the numbers of solutions of systems of linear equations in two variables
- How to use systems of equations in two variables to model and solve real-life problems

▶ **Why you should learn it**

You can use systems of equations in two variables to model and solve real-life problems. For instance, in Exercise 61 on page 497, you will solve a system of equations to find a linear model that represents the average room rate for a hotel room in the United States.

The Method of Elimination

In Section 7.1, you studied two methods for solving a system of equations: substitution and graphing. Now you will study the **method of elimination.** The key step in this method is to obtain, for one of the variables, coefficients that differ only in sign so that *adding* the equations eliminates the variable.

$$\begin{array}{ll} 3x + 5y = 7 & \text{Equation 1} \\ \underline{-3x - 2y = -1} & \text{Equation 2} \\ 3y = 6 & \text{Add equations.} \end{array}$$

Note that by adding the two equations, you eliminate the x-terms and obtain a single equation in y. Solving this equation for y produces $y = 2$, which you can then back-substitute into one of the original equations to solve for x.

Example 1 ▶ **Solving a System of Equations by Elimination**

Solve the system of linear equations.

$$\begin{cases} 3x + 2y = 4 & \text{Equation 1} \\ 5x - 2y = 8 & \text{Equation 2} \end{cases}$$

Solution

Because the coefficients of y differ only in sign, you can eliminate the y-terms by adding the two equations.

$$\begin{array}{ll} 3x + 2y = 4 & \text{Write Equation 1.} \\ \underline{5x - 2y = 8} & \text{Write Equation 2.} \\ 8x = 12 & \text{Add equations.} \end{array}$$

So, $x = \frac{3}{2}$. By back-substituting this value into Equation 1, you can solve for y.

$$\begin{array}{ll} 3x + 2y = 4 & \text{Write Equation 1.} \\ 3\left(\dfrac{3}{2}\right) + 2y = 4 & \text{Substitute } \frac{3}{2} \text{ for } x. \\ \dfrac{9}{2} + 2y = 4 & \text{Simplify.} \\ y = -\dfrac{1}{4} & \text{Solve for } y. \end{array}$$

The solution is $\left(\frac{3}{2}, -\frac{1}{4}\right)$. Check this in the original system.

Try using the method of substitution to solve the system given in Example 1. Which method do you think is easier? Many people find that the method of elimination is more efficient.

To be efficient, students should know and understand both the substitution method and the elimination method. You may wish to point out the differences between the two methods and the advantages of one over the other.

STUDY TIP

To obtain coefficients (for one of the variables) that differ only in sign, you often need to multiply one or both of the equations by suitably chosen constants.

Remind your students to multiply the constant as well. A common error is to forget to multiply the constant terms. For instance, in Example 2, students may rewrite Equation 2 as $9x + 3y = -5$ rather than as $9x + 3y = -15$.

Example 2 ▶	Solving a System of Equations by Elimination

Solve the system of linear equations.

$$\begin{cases} 2x - 3y = -7 & \text{Equation 1} \\ 3x + y = -5 & \text{Equation 2} \end{cases}$$

Solution

For this system, you can obtain coefficients that differ only in sign by multiplying Equation 2 by 3.

$2x - 3y = -7$ ⟹	$2x - 3y = -7$	Write Equation 1.
$3x + y = -5$ ⟹	$9x + 3y = -15$	Multiply Equation 2 by 3.
	$11x \quad\quad = -22$	Add equations.

So, you can see that $x = -2$. By back-substituting this value of x into Equation 1, you can solve for y.

$2x - 3y = -7$	Write Equation 1.
$2(-2) - 3y = -7$	Substitute –2 for x.
$-3y = -3$	Combine like terms.
$y = 1$	Solve for y.

The solution is $(-2, 1)$. Check this in the original system, as follows.

Check

$2x - 3y = -7$	Write original Equation 1.
$2(-2) - 3(1) \overset{?}{=} -7$	Substitute into Equation 1.
$-4 - 3 = -7$	Equation 1 checks. ✓
$3x + y = -5$	Write original Equation 2.
$3(-2) + 1 \overset{?}{=} -5$	Substitute into Equation 2.
$-6 + 1 = -5$	Equation 2 checks. ✓

In Example 2, the two systems of linear equations

$$\begin{cases} 2x - 3y = -7 \\ 3x + y = -5 \end{cases}$$

and

$$\begin{cases} 2x - 3y = -7 \\ 9x + 3y = -15 \end{cases}$$

are called **equivalent systems** because they have precisely the same solution set. The operations that can be performed on a system of linear equations to produce an equivalent system are (1) interchanging any two equations, (2) multiplying an equation by a nonzero constant, and (3) adding a multiple of one equation to any other equation in the system.

STUDY TIP

Keep in mind that the terminology and methods discussed in this section and the following section apply only to systems of *linear* equations.

Method of Elimination

1. *Obtain coefficients* for x (or y) that differ only in sign by multiplying all terms of one or both equations by suitably chosen constants.

2. *Add* the equations to eliminate one variable, and solve the resulting equation.

3. *Back-substitute* the value obtained in Step 2 into either of the original equations and solve for the other variable.

4. *Check* your solution in both of the original equations.

◀ **Exploration** ▶

Rewrite each system of equations in slope-intercept form and sketch the graph of each system. What is the relationship between the slopes of the two lines and the number of points of intersection?

a. $\begin{cases} 5x - y = -1 \\ -x + y = -5 \end{cases}$

b. $\begin{cases} 4x - 3y = 1 \\ -8x + 6y = -2 \end{cases}$

c. $\begin{cases} x + 2y = 3 \\ x + 2y = -8 \end{cases}$

Consider having your students solve Example 3 by eliminating the *x*-terms instead of the *y*-terms to reinforce the fact that either variable can be eliminated first.

Example 3 ▶ Solving a System of Equations by Elimination

Solve the system of linear equations.

$$\begin{cases} 5x + 3y = 9 & \text{Equation 1} \\ 2x - 4y = 14 & \text{Equation 2} \end{cases}$$

Solution

You can obtain coefficients that differ only in sign by multiplying Equation 1 by 4 and multiplying Equation 2 by 3.

$$5x + 3y = 9 \quad\Longrightarrow\quad 20x + 12y = 36 \qquad \text{Multiply Equation 1 by 4.}$$

$$\underline{2x - 4y = 14} \quad\Longrightarrow\quad \underline{6x - 12y = 42} \qquad \text{Multiply Equation 2 by 3.}$$

$$26x \qquad\quad = 78 \qquad \text{Add equations.}$$

From this equation, you can see that $x = 3$. By back-substituting this value of x into Equation 2, you can solve for y.

$$\begin{aligned} 2x - 4y &= 14 & \text{Write Equation 2.} \\ 2(3) - 4y &= 14 & \text{Substitute 3 for } x. \\ -4y &= 8 & \text{Collect like terms.} \\ y &= -2 & \text{Solve for y.} \end{aligned}$$

The solution is $(3, -2)$. Check this in the original system.

Technology

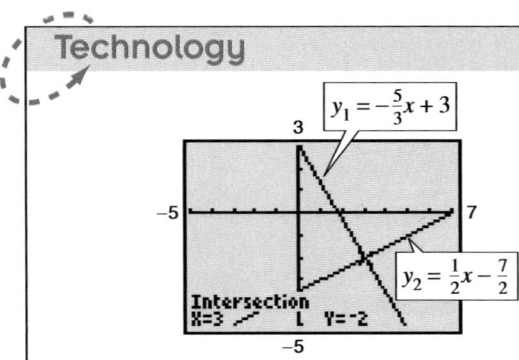

Remember that you can check the solution of a system of equations graphically. For instance, to check the solution found in Example 3, solve each equation for y. Then use a graphing utility to graph $y_1 = -\frac{5}{3}x + 3$ and $y_2 = \frac{1}{2}x - \frac{7}{2}$ in the same viewing window, as shown in the figure at the left. Use the *intersect* feature or the *zoom* and *trace* features to approximate the point of intersection of the graphs. From the graph, the point of intersection is $(3, -2)$.

Graphical Interpretation of Solutions

It is possible for a *general* system of equations to have exactly one solution, two or more solutions, or no solution. If a system of *linear* equations has two different solutions, it must have an *infinite* number of solutions. To see why this is true, consider the following graphical interpretations of a system of two linear equations in two variables.

Graphical Interpretations of Solutions

For a system of two linear equations in two variables, the number of solutions is one of the following.

Number of Solutions	*Graphical Interpretation*	*Slopes of Lines*
1. Exactly one solution	The two lines intersect at one point.	The slopes of the two lines are not equal.
2. Infinitely many solutions	The two lines are coincident (identical).	The slopes of the two lines are equal.
3. No solution	The two lines are parallel.	The slopes of the two lines are equal.

A system of linear equations is **consistent** if it has at least one solution. It is **inconsistent** if it has no solution.

> **Example 4** ▶ **Recognizing Graphs of Linear Systems**

Match the system of linear equations with its graph in Figure 7.7. State whether the system is consistent or inconsistent and describe the number of solutions.

a. $\begin{cases} 2x - 3y = 3 \\ -4x + 6y = 6 \end{cases}$ **b.** $\begin{cases} 2x - 3y = 3 \\ x + 2y = 5 \end{cases}$ **c.** $\begin{cases} 2x - 3y = 3 \\ -4x + 6y = -6 \end{cases}$

i.   **ii.**   **iii.**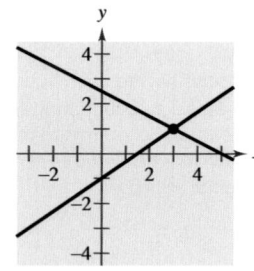

FIGURE 7.7

Solution

a. The graph of system (a) is a pair of parallel lines (ii). The lines have no point of intersection, so the system has no solution. The system is inconsistent.

b. The graph of system (b) is a pair of intersecting lines (iii). The lines have one point of intersection, so the system has exactly one solution. The system is consistent.

c. The graph of system (c) is a pair of lines that coincide (i). The lines have infinitely many points of intersection, so the system has infinitely many solutions. The system is consistent.

STUDY TIP

A comparison of the slopes of two lines gives useful information about the number of solutions of the corresponding system of equations. To solve a system of equations graphically, it helps to begin by writing the equations in slope-intercept form. Try doing this for the systems in Example 4.

In Examples 5 and 6, note how you can use the method of elimination to determine that a system of linear equations has no solution or infinitely many solutions.

Example 5 ▶ No-Solution Case: Method of Elimination

Solve the system of linear equations.

$$\begin{cases} x - 2y = 3 & \text{Equation 1} \\ -2x + 4y = 1 & \text{Equation 2} \end{cases}$$

Solution

To obtain coefficients that differ only in sign, multiply Equation 1 by 2.

$x - 2y = 3$ ⟹	$2x - 4y = 6$	Multiply Equation 1 by 2.
$-2x + 4y = 1$ ⟹	$-2x + 4y = 1$	Write Equation 2.
	$0 = 7$	False statement

Because there are no values of x and y for which $0 = 7$, you can conclude that the system is inconsistent and has no solution. The lines corresponding to the two equations in this system are shown in Figure 7.8. Note that the two lines are parallel and therefore have no point of intersection.

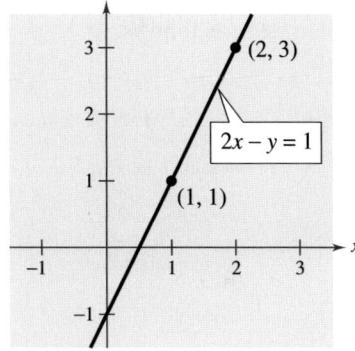

FIGURE 7.8

In Example 5, note that the occurrence of a false statement, such as $0 = 7$, indicates that the system has no solution. In the next example, note that the occurrence of a statement that is true for all values of the variables, such as $0 = 0$, indicates that the system has infinitely many solutions.

Example 6 ▶ Many-Solution Case: Method of Elimination

Solve the system of linear equations.

$$\begin{cases} 2x - y = 1 & \text{Equation 1} \\ 4x - 2y = 2 & \text{Equation 2} \end{cases}$$

Solution

To obtain coefficients that differ only in sign, multiply Equation 2 by $-\frac{1}{2}$.

$2x \quad y = 1$ ⟹	$2x - y = \quad 1$	Write Equation 1.
$4x - 2y = 2$ ⟹	$-2x + y = -1$	Multiply Equation 2 by $-\frac{1}{2}$.
	$0 = \quad 0$	Add equations.

Because the two equations turn out to be equivalent (have the same solution set), you can conclude that the system has infinitely many solutions. The solution set consists of all points (x, y) lying on the line $2x - y = 1$, as shown in Figure 7.9. Letting $x = a$, where a is any real number, you can see that the solutions to the system are $(a, 2a - 1)$.

FIGURE 7.9

Example 7 illustrates a strategy for solving a system of linear equations that has decimal coefficients.

Example 7 ▶ A Linear System Having Decimal Coefficients

Solve the system of linear equations.

$$\begin{cases} 0.02x - 0.05y = -0.38 & \text{Equation 1} \\ 0.03x + 0.04y = 1.04 & \text{Equation 2} \end{cases}$$

Solution

Because the coefficients in this system have two decimal places, you can begin by multiplying each equation by 100. (This produces a system in which the coefficients are all integers.)

$$\begin{cases} 2x - 5y = -38 & \text{Revised Equation 1} \\ 3x + 4y = 104 & \text{Revised Equation 2} \end{cases}$$

Now, to obtain coefficients that differ only in sign, multiply Equation 1 by 3 and multiply Equation 2 by -2.

$$2x - 5y = -38 \implies 6x - 15y = -114 \quad \text{Multiply Equation 1 by 3.}$$

$$3x + 4y = 104 \implies \underline{-6x - 8y = -208} \quad \text{Multiply Equation 2 by } -2.$$

$$-23y = -322 \quad \text{Add equations.}$$

So, you can conclude that

$$y = \frac{-322}{-23}$$

$$= 14.$$

Back-substituting this value into Equation 2 produces the following.

$3x + 4y = 104$	Write revised Equation 2.
$3x + 4(14) = 104$	Substitute 14 for y.
$3x = 48$	Combine like terms.
$x = 16$	Solve for x.

The solution is $(16, 14)$. Check this in the original system, as follows.

Check

$0.02x - 0.05y = -0.38$	Write original Equation 1.
$0.02(16) - 0.05(14) \stackrel{?}{=} -0.38$	Substitute into Equation 1.
$0.32 - 0.70 = -0.38$	Equation 1 checks. ✓
$0.03x + 0.04y = 1.04$	Write original Equation 2.
$0.03(16) + 0.04(14) \stackrel{?}{=} 1.04$	Substitute into Equation 2.
$0.48 + 0.56 = 1.04$	Equation 2 checks. ✓

Activities

1. Solve the system by the elimination method.

$$\begin{cases} 3x - 2y = 7 \\ 8x + 4y = 0 \end{cases}$$

Answer: $(1, -2)$

2. How many milliliters of a 30% acid solution and a 55% acid solution must be mixed to obtain 100 milliliters of a 50% acid solution?
Answer: 20 milliliters of the 30% acid solution and 80 milliliters of the 55% acid solution

3. Find the equilibrium point if the demand equation is $p = 110 - 5x$ and the supply equation is $p = 60 + 20x$.
Answer: $x = 2, p = \$100.00$.

Applications

At this point, you may be asking the question "How can I tell which application problems can be solved using a system of linear equations?" The answer comes from the following considerations.

1. Does the problem involve more than one unknown quantity?

2. Are there two (or more) equations or conditions to be satisfied?

If one or both of these situations occur, the appropriate mathematical model for the problem may be a system of linear equations. Example 8 shows how to construct such a model.

Example 8 ▶ An Application of a Linear System

An airplane flying into a headwind travels the 2000-mile flying distance between Chicopee, Massachusetts and Salt Lake City, Utah in 4 hours and 24 minutes. On the return flight, the same distance is traveled in 4 hours. Find the airspeed of the plane and the speed of the wind, assuming that both remain constant.

Solution

The two unknown quantities are the speeds of the wind and the plane. If r_1 is the speed of the plane and r_2 is the speed of the wind, then

$$r_1 - r_2 = \text{speed of the plane against the wind}$$

$$r_1 + r_2 = \text{speed of the plane with the wind}$$

as shown in Figure 7.10. Using the formula distance = (rate)(time) for these two speeds, you obtain the following equations.

$$2000 = (r_1 - r_2)\left(4 + \frac{24}{60}\right)$$

$$2000 = (r_1 + r_2)(4)$$

These two equations simplify as follows.

$$\begin{cases} 5000 = 11r_1 - 11r_2 & \text{Equation 1} \\ 500 = r_1 + r_2 & \text{Equation 2} \end{cases}$$

To solve this system by elimination, multiply Equation 2 by 11.

$$5000 = 11r_1 - 11r_2 \quad\Longrightarrow\quad 5000 = 11r_1 - 11r_2 \quad \text{Write Equation 1.}$$

$$500 = r_1 + r_2 \quad\Longrightarrow\quad \underline{5500 = 11r_1 + 11r_2} \quad \text{Multiply Equation 2 by 11.}$$

$$10{,}500 = 22r_1 \quad \text{Add equations.}$$

So,

$$r_1 = \frac{10{,}500}{22} = \frac{5250}{11} \approx 477.27 \text{ miles per hour} \qquad \text{Speed of plane}$$

$$r_2 = 500 - \frac{5250}{11} = \frac{250}{11} \approx 22.73 \text{ miles per hour.} \qquad \text{Speed of wind}$$

Check this solution in the original statement of the problem.

Original flight

Return flight

FIGURE **7.10**

In a free market, the demands for many products are related to the prices of the products. As the prices decrease, the demands by consumers increase and the amounts that producers are able or willing to supply decrease.

Example 9 ▶   **Finding the Equilibrium Point**

The demand and supply functions for a new type of calculator are

$$\begin{cases} p = 150 - 0.00001x & \text{Demand equation} \\ p = 60 + 0.00002x & \text{Supply equation} \end{cases}$$

where p is the price in dollars and x represents the number of units. Find the equilibrium point for this market. The equilibrium point is the price p and number of units x that satisfy both the demand and supply equations.

Solution

Begin by substituting the value of p given in the supply equation into the demand equation.

$$p = 150 - 0.00001x \qquad \text{Write demand equation.}$$

$$60 + 0.00002x = 150 - 0.00001x \qquad \text{Substitute } 60 + 0.00002x \text{ for } p.$$

$$0.00003x = 90 \qquad \text{Combine like terms.}$$

$$x = 3{,}000{,}000 \qquad \text{Solve for } x.$$

So, the equilibrium point occurs when the demand and supply are each 3 million units. (See Figure 7.11.) The price that corresponds to this x-value is obtained by back-substituting $x = 3{,}000{,}000$ into either of the original equations. For instance, back-substituting into the demand equation produces

$$p = 150 - 0.00001(3{,}000{,}000)$$

$$= 150 - 30$$

$$= \$120.$$

The solution is $(3{,}000{,}000, \ 120)$. You can check this as follows.

Check

Substitute $(3{,}000{,}000, \ 120)$ into the demand equation.

$$p = 150 - 0.00001x \qquad \text{Write demand equation.}$$

$$120 \stackrel{?}{=} 150 - 0.00001(3{,}000{,}000) \qquad \text{Substitute 120 for } p \text{ and 3,000,000 for } x.$$

$$120 = 120 \qquad \text{Solution checks in demand equation.} \checkmark$$

Substitute $(3{,}000{,}000, \ 120)$ into the supply equation.

$$p = 60 + 0.00002x \qquad \text{Write supply equation.}$$

$$120 \stackrel{?}{=} 60 + 0.00002(3{,}000{,}000) \qquad \text{Substitute 120 for } p \text{ and 3,000,000 for } x.$$

$$120 = 120 \qquad \text{Solution checks in supply equation.} \checkmark$$

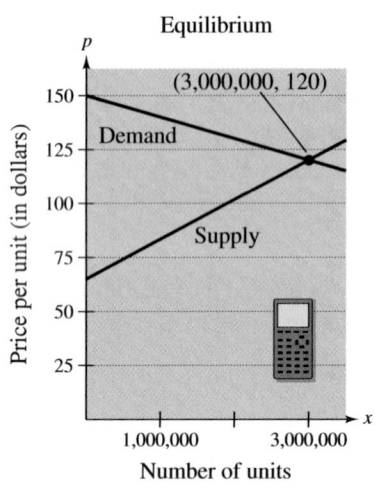

FIGURE 7.11

You may want to point out that if two equations are each written such that one variable is represented in terms of the other variable, substitution is usually more efficient.

7.2 Exercises

Exercises containing systems with no solutions: 5, 6, 19, 20
Exercises containing systems with infinitely many solutions: 7, 8, 22, 23, 24

In Exercises 1–10, solve by elimination. Label each line with its equation. To print an enlarged copy of the graph, go to the website *www.mathgraphs.com*.

1. $\begin{cases} 2x + y = 5 \\ x - y = 1 \end{cases}$ **2.** $\begin{cases} x + 3y = 1 \\ -x + 2y = 4 \end{cases}$

     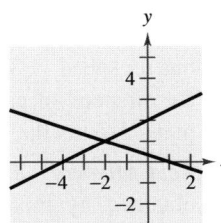

3. $\begin{cases} x + y = 0 \\ 3x + 2y = 1 \end{cases}$ **4.** $\begin{cases} 2x - y = 3 \\ 4x + 3y = 21 \end{cases}$

     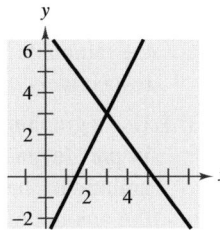

5. $\begin{cases} x - y = 2 \\ -2x + 2y = 5 \end{cases}$ **6.** $\begin{cases} 3x + 2y = 3 \\ 6x + 4y = 14 \end{cases}$

     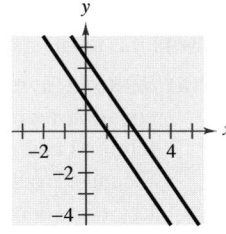

7. $\begin{cases} 3x - 2y = 5 \\ -6x + 4y = -10 \end{cases}$ **8.** $\begin{cases} 9x - 3y = -15 \\ -3x + y = 5 \end{cases}$

     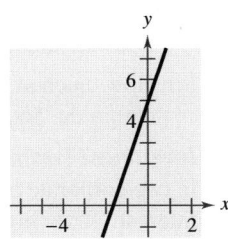

9. $\begin{cases} 9x + 3y = 1 \\ 3x - 6y = 5 \end{cases}$ **10.** $\begin{cases} 5x + 3y = -18 \\ 2x - 6y = 1 \end{cases}$

     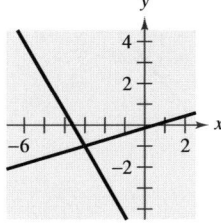

In Exercises 11–30, solve the system by elimination and check any solutions algebraically.

11. $\begin{cases} x + 2y = 4 \\ x - 2y = 1 \end{cases}$ **12.** $\begin{cases} 3x - 5y = 2 \\ 2x + 5y = 13 \end{cases}$

13. $\begin{cases} 2x + 3y = 18 \\ 5x - y = 11 \end{cases}$ **14.** $\begin{cases} x + 7y = 12 \\ 3x - 5y = 10 \end{cases}$

15. $\begin{cases} 3x + 2y = 10 \\ 2x + 5y = 3 \end{cases}$ **16.** $\begin{cases} 2r + 4s = 5 \\ 16r + 50s = 55 \end{cases}$

17. $\begin{cases} 5u + 6v = 24 \\ 3u + 5v = 18 \end{cases}$ **18.** $\begin{cases} 3x + 11y = 4 \\ -2x - 5y = 9 \end{cases}$

19. $\begin{cases} 1.8x + 1.2y = 4 \\ 9x + 6y = 3 \end{cases}$ **20.** $\begin{cases} 3.1x - 2.9y = -10.2 \\ 15.5x - 14.5y = 21 \end{cases}$

21. $\begin{cases} \dfrac{x}{4} + \dfrac{y}{6} = 1 \\ x - y = 3 \end{cases}$ **22.** $\begin{cases} \dfrac{2}{3}x + \dfrac{1}{6}y = \dfrac{2}{3} \\ 4x + y = 4 \end{cases}$

23. $\begin{cases} 2.5x - 3y = 1.5 \\ 2x - 2.4y = 1.2 \end{cases}$ **24.** $\begin{cases} 6.3x + 7.2y = 5.4 \\ 5.6x + 6.4y = 4.8 \end{cases}$

25. $\begin{cases} 0.05x - 0.03y = 0.21 \\ 0.07x + 0.02y = 0.16 \end{cases}$

26. $\begin{cases} 0.2x - 0.5y = -27.8 \\ 0.3x + 0.4y = 68.7 \end{cases}$

27. $\begin{cases} 4b + 3m = 3 \\ 3b + 11m = 13 \end{cases}$ **28.** $\begin{cases} 2x + 5y = 8 \\ 5x + 8y = 10 \end{cases}$

29. $\begin{cases} \dfrac{x+3}{4} + \dfrac{y-1}{3} = 1 \\ 2x - y = 12 \end{cases}$

30. $\begin{cases} \dfrac{x-1}{2} + \dfrac{y+2}{3} = 4 \\ x - 2y = 5 \end{cases}$

In Exercises 31–34, match the system of linear equations with its graph. [The graphs are labeled (a), (b), (c) and (d).]

(a)

(b)

(c)

(d)
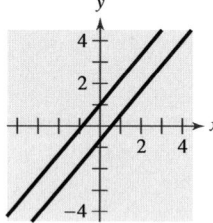

31. $\begin{cases} 2x - 5y = 0 \\ x - y = 3 \end{cases}$ **32.** $\begin{cases} -7x + 6y = -4 \\ 14x - 12y = 8 \end{cases}$

33. $\begin{cases} 2x - 5y = 0 \\ 2x - 3y = -4 \end{cases}$ **34.** $\begin{cases} 7x - 6y = -6 \\ -7x + 6y = -4 \end{cases}$

In Exercises 35–42, use any method to solve the system.

35. $\begin{cases} 3x - 5y = 7 \\ 2x + y = 9 \end{cases}$ **36.** $\begin{cases} -x + 3y = 17 \\ 4x + 3y = 7 \end{cases}$

37. $\begin{cases} y = 2x - 5 \\ y = 5x - 11 \end{cases}$ **38.** $\begin{cases} 7x + 3y = 16 \\ y = x + 2 \end{cases}$

39. $\begin{cases} x - 5y = 21 \\ 6x + 5y = 21 \end{cases}$ **40.** $\begin{cases} y = -3x - 8 \\ y = 15 - 2x \end{cases}$

41. $\begin{cases} -2x + 8y = 19 \\ y = x - 3 \end{cases}$ **42.** $\begin{cases} 4x - 3y = 6 \\ -5x + 7y = -1 \end{cases}$

Supply and Demand **In Exercises 43–46, find the equilibrium point of the demand and supply equations.**

	Demand	*Supply*
43.	$p = 50 - 0.5x$	$p = 0.125x$
44.	$p = 100 - 0.05x$	$p = 25 + 0.1x$
45.	$p = 140 - 0.00002x$	$p = 80 + 0.00001x$
46.	$p = 400 - 0.0002x$	$p = 225 + 0.0005x$

47. *Airplane Speed*   An airplane flying into a headwind travels the 1800-mile flying distance between Pittsburgh, Pennsylvania and Phoenix, Arizona in 3 hours and 36 minutes. On the return flight, the distance is traveled in 3 hours. Find the airspeed of the plane and the speed of the wind, assuming that both remain constant.

48. *Airplane Speed*   Two planes start from Los Angeles International Airport and fly in opposite directions. The second plane starts $\frac{1}{2}$ hour after the first plane, but its speed is 80 kilometers per hour faster. Find the airspeed of each plane if 2 hours after the first plane departs the planes are 3200 kilometers apart.

49. *Acid Mixture*   Ten liters of a 30% acid solution is obtained by mixing a 20% solution with a 50% solution.

(a) Write a system of equations in which one equation represents the amount of final mixture required and the other represents the percent of acid in the final mixture. Let x and y represent the amounts of the 20% and 50% solutions, respectively.

 (b) Use a graphing utility to graph the two equations in part (a) in the same viewing window. As the amount of the 20% solution increases, how does the amount of the 50% solution change?

(c) How much of each solution is required to obtain the specified concentration of the final mixture?

50. *Fuel Mixture*   Five hundred gallons of 89 octane gasoline is obtained by mixing 87 octane gasoline with 92 octane gasoline.

(a) Write a system of equations in which one equation represents the amount of final mixture required and the other represents the amounts of 87 and 92 octane gasolines in the final mixture. Let x and y represent the numbers of gallons of 87 octane and 92 octane gasolines, respectively.

 (b) Use a graphing utility to graph the two equations in part (a) in the same viewing window. As the amount of 87 octane gasoline increases, how does the amount of 92 octane gasoline change?

(c) How much of each type of gasoline is required to obtain the 500 gallons of 89 octane gasoline?

51. *Investment Portfolio*   A total of $12,000 is invested in two corporate bonds that pay 7.5% and 9% simple interest. The investor wants an annual interest income of $990 from the investments. What amount should be invested in the 7.5% bond?

52. *Investment Portfolio* A total of \$32,000 is invested in two municipal bonds that pay 5.75% and 6.25% simple interest. The investor wants an annual interest income of \$1900 from the investments. What amount should be invested in the 5.75% bond?

53. *Ticket Sales* At a local high school city championship basketball game, 1435 tickets were sold. A student admission ticket cost \$1.50 and an adult admission ticket cost \$5.00. The total ticket receipts for the basketball game were \$3552.50. How many of each type of ticket were sold?

54. *Consumer Awareness* A department store held a sale to sell all of the 214 winter jackets that remained after the season ended. Until noon, each jacket in the store was priced at \$31.95. At noon, the price of the jackets was further reduced to \$18.95. After the last jacket was sold, total receipts for the clearance sale were \$5108.30. How many jackets were sold before noon and how many were sold after noon?

 Fitting a Line to Data **In Exercises 55–60, find the least squares regression line** $y = ax + b$ **for the points**

$$(x_1, y_1), (x_2, y_2), \ldots, (x_n, y_n)$$

by solving the system for a **and** b.

$$nb + \left(\sum_{i=1}^{n} x_i\right)a = \sum_{i=1}^{n} y_i$$

$$\left(\sum_{i=1}^{n} x_i\right)b + \left(\sum_{i=1}^{n} x_i^2\right)a = \sum_{i=1}^{n} x_i y_i$$

Then use the graphing utility to confirm the result. (If you are unfamiliar with summation notation, look at the discussion in Section 9.1 or in Appendix B at the website for this text at *college.hmco.com*.**)**

55. $\begin{cases} 5b + 10a = 20.2 \\ 10b + 30a = 50.1 \end{cases}$ **56.** $\begin{cases} 5b + 10a = 11.7 \\ 10b + 30a = 25.6 \end{cases}$

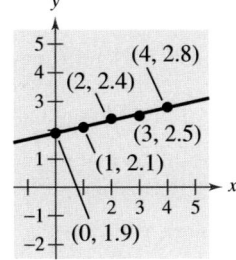

57. $\begin{cases} 7b + 21a = 35.1 \\ 21b + 91a = 114.2 \end{cases}$ **58.** $\begin{cases} 6b + 15a = 23.6 \\ 15b + 55a = 48.8 \end{cases}$

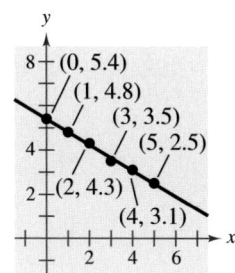

59. $(0, 4), (1, 3), (1, 1), (2, 0)$

60. $(1, 0), (2, 0), (3, 0), (3, 1), (4, 1), (4, 2), (5, 2), (6, 2)$

▶ Model It

61. *Data Analysis* The table shows the average room rates y for a hotel room in the United States for the years 1995 through 1999. (Source: American Hotel & Motel Association)

Year, t	Average room rate, y
1995	\$66.65
1996	\$70.93
1997	\$75.31
1998	\$78.62
1999	\$81.33

(a) Use the technique demonstrated in Exercises 55–60 to find the least squares regression line $y = at + b$. Let t represent the year, with $t = 5$ corresponding to 1995.

 (b) Use the *regression* feature of a graphing utility to find a linear model for the data. How does this model compare with the model obtained in part (a)?

(c) Use the linear model to create a table of estimated values of y. Compare the estimated values with the actual data.

(d) Use the linear model to predict the average room rate in 2005.

(e) Use the linear model to predict when the average room rate will be \$100.00.

62. *Data Analysis* A farmer used four test plots to determine the relationship between wheat yield in bushels per acre and the amount of fertilizer in hundreds of pounds per acre. The results are shown in the table.

Fertilizer, x	Yield, y
1.0	32
1.5	41
2.0	48
2.5	53

(a) Use the technique demonstrated in Exercises 55–60 to find the least squares regression line $y = ax + b$.

(b) Use the linear model to predict the yield for a fertilizer application of 160 pounds per acre.

Synthesis

True or False? In Exercises 63 and 64, determine whether the statement is true or false. Justify your answer.

63. If two lines do not have exactly one point of intersection, then they must be parallel.

64. Solving a system of equations graphically will always give an exact solution.

Think About It In Exercises 65 and 66, the graphs of the two equations appear to be parallel. Yet, when the system is solved algebraically, you find that the system does have a solution. Find the solution and explain why it does not appear on the portion of the graph that is shown.

65. $\begin{cases} 100y - x = 200 \\ 99y - x = -198 \end{cases}$ **66.** $\begin{cases} 21x - 20y = 0 \\ 13x - 12y = 120 \end{cases}$

   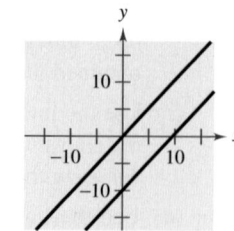

67. *Writing* Briefly explain whether or not it is possible for a consistent system of linear equations to have exactly two solutions.

68. *Think About It* Give examples of (a) a system of linear equations that has no solution and (b) a system that has an infinite number of solutions.

In Exercises 69 and 70, find the value of k such that the system of linear equations is inconsistent.

69. $\begin{cases} 4x - 8y = -3 \\ 2x + ky = 16 \end{cases}$ **70.** $\begin{cases} 15x + 3y = 6 \\ -10x + ky = 9 \end{cases}$

Review

In Exercises 71–78, solve the inequality and graph the solution on the real number line.

71. $-11 - 6x \geq 33$

72. $2(x - 3) > -5x + 1$

73. $8x - 15 \leq -4(2x - 1)$

74. $-6 \leq 3x - 10 < 6$

75. $|x - 8| < 10$

76. $|x + 10| \geq -3$

77. $2x^2 + 3x - 35 < 0$

78. $3x^2 + 12x > 0$

In Exercises 79 and 80, write the partial fraction decomposition for the rational expression.

79. $\dfrac{x - 1}{x^2 + 11x + 30}$ **80.** $\dfrac{3}{x(x^2 - 1)}$

In Exercises 81–84, write the expression as the logarithm of a single quantity.

81. $\ln x + \ln 6$

82. $\ln x - 5 \ln(x + 3)$

83. $\log_9 12 - \log_9 x$

84. $\frac{1}{4} \log_6 3x$

In Exercises 85 and 86, solve the system by the method of substitution.

85. $\begin{cases} 2x - y = 4 \\ -4x + 2y = -12 \end{cases}$

86. $\begin{cases} 30x - 40y - 33 = 0 \\ 10x + 20y - 21 = 0 \end{cases}$

7.3 Multivariable Linear Systems

▶ **What you should learn**

- How to use back-substitution to solve linear systems in row-echelon form
- How to use Gaussian elimination to solve systems of linear equations
- How to solve nonsquare systems of linear equations
- How to use systems of linear equations in three or more variables to model and solve application problems

▶ **Why you should learn it**

Systems of linear equations in three or more variables can be used to model and solve real-life problems. For instance, in Exercise 71 on page 510, a system of linear equations can be used to analyze the reproduction rates of deer in a wildlife preserve.

Jeanne Drake/Tony Stone Images

Row-Echelon Form and Back-Substitution

The method of elimination can be applied to a system of linear equations in more than two variables. In fact, this method easily adapts to computer use for solving linear systems with dozens of variables.

When elimination is used to solve a system of linear equations, the goal is to rewrite the system in a form to which back-substitution can be applied. To see how this works, consider the following two systems of linear equations.

System of Three Linear Equations in Three Variables: (See Example 3.)

$$\begin{cases} x - 2y + 3z = 9 \\ -x + 3y = -4 \\ 2x - 5y + 5z = 17 \end{cases}$$

Equivalent System in Row-Echelon Form: (See Example 1.)

$$\begin{cases} x - 2y + 3z = 9 \\ y + 3z = 5 \\ z = 2 \end{cases}$$

The second system is said to be in **row-echelon form,** which means that it has a "stair-step" pattern with leading coefficients of 1. After comparing the two systems, it should be clear that it is easier to solve the system in row-echelon form, using back-substitution.

Example 1 ▶ **Using Back-Substitution in Row-Echelon Form**

Solve the system of linear equations.

$$\begin{cases} x - 2y + 3z = 9 & \text{Equation 1} \\ y + 3z = 5 & \text{Equation 2} \\ z = 2 & \text{Equation 3} \end{cases}$$

Solution

From Equation 3, you know the value of z. To solve for y, substitute $z = 2$ into Equation 2 to obtain

$$y + 3(2) = 5 \qquad \text{Substitute 2 for } z.$$
$$y = -1. \qquad \text{Solve for } y.$$

Finally, substitute $y = -1$ and $z = 2$ into Equation 1 to obtain

$$x - 2(-1) + 3(2) = 9 \qquad \text{Substitute } -1 \text{ for } y \text{ and 2 for } z.$$
$$x = 1. \qquad \text{Solve for } x.$$

The solution is $x = 1$, $y = -1$, and $z = 2$, which can be written as the **ordered triple** $(1, -1, 2)$. Check this in the original system of equations.

Historical Note

One of the most influential Chinese mathematics books was the *Chui-chang suan-shu* or *Nine Chapters on the Mathematical Art* (written in approximately 250 B.C.). Chapter Eight of the *Nine Chapters* contained solutions of systems of linear equations using positive and negative numbers. One such system was as follows.

$$\begin{cases} 3x + 2y + z = 39 \\ 2x + 3y + z = 34 \\ x + 2y + 3z = 26 \end{cases}$$

This system was solved using column operations on a matrix. Matrices (plural for matrix) will be discussed in the next chapter.

STUDY TIP

As demonstrated in the first step in the solution of Example 2, interchanging rows is an easy way of obtaining a leading coefficient of 1.

Gaussian Elimination

Two systems of equations are *equivalent* if they have the same solution set. To solve a system that is not in row-echelon form, first convert it to an *equivalent* system that is in row-echelon form by using the following operations.

Operations That Produce Equivalent Systems

Each of the following **row operations** on a system of linear equations produces an *equivalent* system of linear equations.

1. Interchange two equations.

2. Multiply one of the equations by a nonzero constant.

3. Add a multiple of one of the equations to another equation to replace the latter equation.

To see how this is done, take another look at the method of elimination, as applied to a system of two linear equations.

Example 2 ▶ **Using Gaussian Elimination to Solve a System**

Solve the system of linear equations.

$$\begin{cases} 3x - 2y = -1 \\ x - y = 0 \end{cases}$$

Solution

There are two strategies that seem reasonable: eliminate the variable x or eliminate the variable y. The following steps show how to use the first strategy.

$$\begin{cases} x - y = 0 \\ 3x - 2y = -1 \end{cases}$$ Interchange two equations in the system.

$$-3x + 3y = 0$$ Multiply the first equation by -3.

$$\begin{aligned} -3x + 3y &= 0 \\ \underline{3x - 2y} &= \underline{-1} \\ y &= -1 \end{aligned}$$ Add the multiple of the first equation to the second equation to obtain a new equation.

$$\begin{cases} x - y = 0 \\ y = -1 \end{cases}$$ New system in row-echelon form

Now, using back-substitution, you can determine that the solution is $y = -1$ and $x = -1$, which can be written as the ordered pair $(-1, -1)$. Check this solution in the original system of equations.

As shown in Example 2, rewriting a system of linear equations in row-echelon form usually involves a chain of equivalent systems, each of which is obtained by using one of the three basic row operations listed above. This process is called **Gaussian elimination,** after the German mathematician Carl Friedrich Gauss (1777–1855).

Example 3 ▶ **Using Gaussian Elimination to Solve a System**

Solve the system of linear equations.

$$\begin{cases} x - 2y + 3z = 9 & \text{Equation 1} \\ -x + 3y \quad\quad = -4 & \text{Equation 2} \\ 2x - 5y + 5z = 17 & \text{Equation 3} \end{cases}$$

Solution

Because the leading coefficient of the first equation is 1, you can begin by saving the x at the upper left and eliminating the other x-terms from the first column.

$$\begin{array}{ll} x - 2y + 3z = 9 & \text{Write Equation 1.} \\ \underline{-x + 3y \quad\quad = -4} & \text{Write Equation 2.} \\ y + 3z = 5 & \text{Add Equation 1 to Equation 2.} \end{array}$$

$$\begin{cases} x - 2y + 3z = 9 \\ \quad\quad y + 3z = 5 \\ 2x - 5y + 5z = 17 \end{cases}$$

> Adding the first equation to the second equation produces a new second equation.

$$\begin{array}{ll} -2x + 4y - 6z = -18 & \text{Multiply Equation 1 by } -2. \\ \underline{2x - 5y + 5z = \quad 17} & \text{Write Equation 3.} \\ -y - z = -1 & \text{Add revised Equation 1 to Equation 3.} \end{array}$$

$$\begin{cases} x - 2y + 3z = 9 \\ \quad\quad y + 3z = 5 \\ \quad\quad -y - z = -1 \end{cases}$$

> Adding -2 times the first equation to the third equation produces a new third equation.

Now that all but the first x have been eliminated from the first column, go to work on the second column. (You need to eliminate y from the third equation.)

$$\begin{cases} x - 2y + 3z = 9 \\ \quad\quad y + 3z = 5 \\ \quad\quad\quad 2z = 4 \end{cases}$$

> Adding the second equation to the third equation produces a new third equation.

Finally, you need a coefficient of 1 for z in the third equation.

$$\begin{cases} x - 2y + 3z = 9 \\ \quad\quad y + 3z = 5 \\ \quad\quad\quad z = 2 \end{cases}$$

> Multiplying the third equation by $\frac{1}{2}$ produces a new third equation.

This is the same system that was solved in Example 1, and, as in that example, you can conclude that the solution is

$$x = 1, \quad y = -1, \quad \text{and} \quad z = 2.$$

In Example 3, you can check the solution by substituting $x = 1$, $y = -1$, and $z = 2$ into each original equation, as follows.

Equation 1: $1 - 2(-1) + 3(2) = 9$ ✓

Equation 2: $-1 + 3(-1) \quad\quad = -4$ ✓

Equation 3: $2(1) - 5(-1) + 5(2) = 17$ ✓

The next example involves an inconsistent system—one that has no solution. The key to recognizing an inconsistent system is that at some stage in the elimination process you obtain a false statement such as $0 = -2$.

Example 4 ▶ **An Inconsistent System**

Solve the system of linear equations.

$$\begin{cases} x - 3y + z = 1 & \text{Equation 1} \\ 2x - y - 2z = 2 & \text{Equation 2} \\ x + 2y - 3z = -1 & \text{Equation 3} \end{cases}$$

Solution

$$\begin{cases} x - 3y + z = 1 \\ 5y - 4z = 0 \\ x + 2y - 3z = -1 \end{cases}$$

Adding -2 times the first equation to the second equation produces a new second equation.

$$\begin{cases} x - 3y + z = 1 \\ 5y - 4z = 0 \\ 5y - 4z = -2 \end{cases}$$

Adding -1 times the first equation to the third equation produces a new third equation.

$$\begin{cases} x - 3y + z = 1 \\ 5y - 4z = 0 \\ 0 = -2 \end{cases}$$

Adding -1 times the second equation to the third equation produces a new third equation.

Because the third "equation" is impossible, you can conclude that this system is inconsistent and so has no solution. Moreover, because this system is equivalent to the original system, you can conclude that the original system also has no solution.

As with a system of linear equations in two variables, the solution(s) of a system of linear equations in more than two variables must fall into one of three categories.

The Number of Solutions of a Linear System

For a system of linear equations, exactly one of the following is true.

1. There is exactly one solution.

2. There are infinitely many solutions.

3. There is no solution.

In Section 7.2, you learned that a system of two linear equations in two variables can be represented graphically as a pair of lines that are intersecting, coincident, or parallel. A system of three linear equations in three variables has a similar graphical representation—it can be represented as three planes in space that intersect in one point (exactly one solution) [see Figure 7.12], intersect in a line or a plane (infinitely many solutions) [see Figures 7.13 and 7.14], or have no points common to all three planes (no solution) [see Figures 7.15 and 7.16].

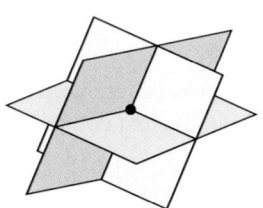

FIGURE 7.12   *Solution: one point*

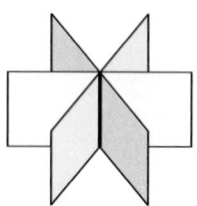

FIGURE 7.13   *Solution: one line*

FIGURE 7.14   *Solution: one plane*

FIGURE 7.15   *Solution: none*

FIGURE 7.16   *Solution: none*

Example 5 ▶ A System with Infinitely Many Solutions

Solve the system of linear equations.

$$\begin{cases} x + y - 3z = -1 & \text{Equation 1} \\ y - z = 0 & \text{Equation 2} \\ -x + 2y = 1 & \text{Equation 3} \end{cases}$$

Solution

$$\begin{cases} x + y - 3z = -1 \\ y - z = 0 \\ 3y - 3z = 0 \end{cases}$$

Adding the first equation to the third equation produces a new third equation.

$$\begin{cases} x + y - 3z = -1 \\ y - z = 0 \\ 0 = 0 \end{cases}$$

Adding -3 times the second equation to the third equation produces a new third equation.

This means that Equation 3 depends on Equations 1 and 2 in the sense that it gives us no additional information about the variables. So, the original system is equivalent to the system

$$\begin{cases} x + y - 3z = -1 \\ y - z = 0. \end{cases}$$

In this last equation, solve for y in terms of z to obtain $y = z$. Back-substituting for y in the previous equation produces $x = 2z - 1$. Finally, letting $z = a$, where a is a real number, you can see that the solutions to the given system are all of the form

$$x = 2a - 1, \qquad y = a, \qquad \text{and} \qquad z = a.$$

So, every ordered triple of the form

$$(2a - 1, a, a), \qquad a \text{ is a real number}$$

is a solution of the system.

In Example 5, there are other ways to write the same infinite set of solutions. For instance, letting $x = b$, the solutions could have been written as

$$\left(b, \tfrac{1}{2}(b + 1), \tfrac{1}{2}(b + 1)\right), \qquad b \text{ is a real number.}$$

To convince yourself that this description produces the same set of solutions, consider the following.

Substitution	*Solution*	
$a = 0$	$(2(0) - 1, 0, 0) = (-1, 0, 0)$	Same solution
$b = -1$	$\left(-1, \tfrac{1}{2}(-1 + 1), \tfrac{1}{2}(-1 + 1)\right) = (-1, 0, 0)$	
$a = 1$	$(2(1) - 1, 1, 1) = (1, 1, 1)$	Same solution
$b = 1$	$\left(1, \tfrac{1}{2}(1 + 1), \tfrac{1}{2}(1 + 1)\right) = (1, 1, 1)$	
$a = 2$	$(2(2) - 1, 2, 2) = (3, 2, 2)$	Same solution
$b = 3$	$\left(3, \tfrac{1}{2}(3 + 1), \tfrac{1}{2}(3 + 1)\right) = (3, 2, 2)$	

Look closely at the original equations in Example 5 and remind students how to recognize equivalent equations (see Section 7.2 for information on equivalent systems). Because Equations 2 and 3 are equivalent, there are infinitely many solutions because there are really only two equations and three unknowns.

STUDY TIP

In Example 5, x and y are solved in terms of the third variable z. To write a solution to the system that does not use any of the three variables of the system, let a represent any real number and let $z = a$. Then solve for x and y. The solution can then be written in terms of a, which is not one of the variables of the system.

STUDY TIP

When comparing descriptions of an infinite solution set, keep in mind that there is more than one way to describe the set.

Nonsquare Systems

So far, each system of linear equations you have looked at has been *square*, which means that the number of equations is equal to the number of variables. In a **nonsquare** system, the number of equations differs from the number of variables. A system of linear equations cannot have a unique solution unless there are at least as many equations as there are variables in the system.

Example 6 ▶ **A System with Fewer Equations than Variables**

Solve the system of linear equations.

$$\begin{cases} x - 2y + z = 2 & \text{Equation 1} \\ 2x - y - z = 1 & \text{Equation 2} \end{cases}$$

Solution

Begin by rewriting the system in row-echelon form.

$$\begin{cases} x - 2y + z = 2 \\ \phantom{x - {}} 3y - 3z = -3 \end{cases}$$

> Adding -2 times the first equation to the second equation produces a new second equation.

$$\begin{cases} x - 2y + z = 2 \\ \phantom{x - 2{}} y - z = -1 \end{cases}$$

> Multiplying the second equation by $\frac{1}{3}$ produces a new second equation.

Solve for y in terms of z, to obtain

$$y = z - 1.$$

By back-substituting into Equation 1, you can solve for x, as follows.

$x - 2y + z = 2$	Write Equation 1.
$x - 2(z - 1) + z = 2$	Substitute for y in Equation 1.
$x - 2z + 2 + z = 2$	Distributive Property
$x = z$	Solve for x.

Finally, by letting $z = a$, where a is a real number, you have the solution

$$x = a, \qquad y = a - 1, \qquad \text{and} \qquad z = a.$$

So, every ordered triple of the form

$$(a, a - 1, a), \qquad a \text{ is a real number}$$

is a solution of the system. Because there were originally three variables and only two equations, the system cannot have a unique solution.

In Example 6, try choosing some values of a to obtain different solutions of the system, such as $(1, 0, 1)$, $(2, 1, 2)$, and $(3, 2, 3)$. Then check each of the solutions in the original system.

Activities

Solve the systems of equations.

1. $\begin{cases} x - y + z = 4 \\ x + 3y - 2z = -3 \\ 3x + 2y + 2z = 6 \end{cases}$
   Answer: $(2, -1, 1)$

2. $\begin{cases} x - 2y - z = -5 \\ 2x + y + z = 5 \end{cases}$
   Answer: $(a, 3a, 5 - 5a)$

3. $\begin{cases} x - 2y + z = 4 \\ 3x - 6y + 3z = 7 \\ 2x + y + 4z = 2 \end{cases}$
   Answer: No solution

s

FIGURE 7.17

Applications

Example 7 ▶ Vertical Motion

The height at time t of an object that is moving in a (vertical) line with constant acceleration a is given by the **position equation**

$$s = \tfrac{1}{2}at^2 + v_0 t + s_0.$$

The height s is measured in feet, the acceleration a is measured in feet per second squared, t is measured in seconds, v_0 is the initial velocity (at $t = 0$), and s_0 is the initial height. Find the values of a, v_0, and s_0 if $s = 52$ at $t = 1$, $s = 52$ at $t = 2$, and $s = 20$ at $t = 3$. (See Figure 7.17.)

Solution

By substituting the three values of t and s into the position equation, you can obtain three linear equations in a, v_0, and s_0.

When $t = 1$: $\tfrac{1}{2}a(1)^2 + v_0(1) + s_0 = 52$ ⟹ $a + 2v_0 + 2s_0 = 104$

When $t = 2$: $\tfrac{1}{2}a(2)^2 + v_0(2) + s_0 = 52$ ⟹ $2a + 2v_0 + s_0 = 52$

When $t = 3$: $\tfrac{1}{2}a(3)^2 + v_0(3) + s_0 = 20$ ⟹ $9a + 6v_0 + 2s_0 = 40$

Solving this system yields $a = -32$, $v_0 = 48$, and $s_0 = 20$. This solution results in a position equation of $s = -16t^2 + 48t + 20$ and implies that the object was thrown upward at a velocity of 48 feet per second from a height of 20 feet.

Example 8 ▶ Partial Fractions

Write the partial fraction decomposition of $\dfrac{3x + 4}{x^3 - 2x - 4}$.

Solution

Because $x^3 - 2x - 4 = (x - 2)(x^2 + 2x + 2)$, you can write

$$\frac{3x + 4}{x^3 - 2x - 4} = \frac{A}{x - 2} + \frac{Bx + C}{x^2 + 2x + 2}$$

$$3x + 4 = A(x^2 + 2x + 2) + (Bx + C)(x - 2)$$

$$3x + 4 = (A + B)x^2 + (2A - 2B + C)x + (2A - 2C).$$

By equating coefficients of like powers on each side of the expanded equation, you obtain the following system in A, B, and C.

$$\begin{cases} A + B = 0 \\ 2A - 2B + C = 3 \\ 2A - 2C = 4 \end{cases}$$

You can solve this system to find that $A = 1$, $B = -1$, and $C = -1$. So, the partial fraction decomposition is

$$\frac{3x + 4}{x^3 - 2x - 4} = \frac{1}{x - 2} + \frac{-x - 1}{x^2 + 2x + 2} = \frac{1}{x - 2} - \frac{x + 1}{x^2 + 2x + 2}.$$

Example 9 ▶ Data Analysis: Curve-Fitting

Find a quadratic equation,

$$y = ax^2 + bx + c$$

whose graph passes through the points $(-1, 3)$, $(1, 1)$, and $(2, 6)$.

Solution

Because the graph of $y = ax^2 + bx + c$ passes through the points $(-1, 3)$, $(1, 1)$, and $(2, 6)$, you can write the following.

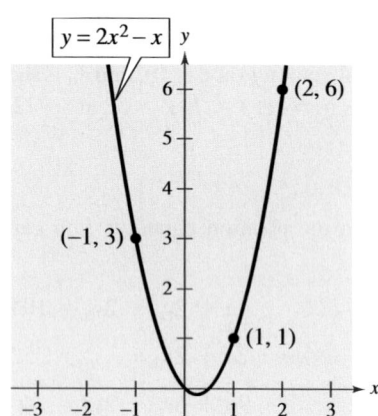

$y = 2x^2 - x$

(2, 6)

(−1, 3)

(1, 1)

FIGURE 7.18

When $x = -1, y = 3$: $a(-1)^2 + b(-1) + c = 3$

When $x = 1, y = 1$: $a(1)^2 + b(1) + c = 1$

When $x = 2, y = 6$: $a(2)^2 + b(2) + c = 6$

This produces the following system of linear equations.

$$\begin{cases} a - b + c = 3 & \text{Equation 1} \\ a + b + c = 1 & \text{Equation 2} \\ 4a + 2b + c = 6 & \text{Equation 3} \end{cases}$$

The solution of this system is $a = 2$, $b = -1$, and $c = 0$. So, the equation of the parabola is $y = 2x^2 - x$, as shown in Figure 7.18.

Example 10 ▶ Investment Analysis

An inheritance of $12,000 was invested among three funds: a money-market fund that paid 5% annually, municipal bonds that paid 6% annually, and mutual funds that paid 12% annually. The amount invested in mutual funds was $4000 more than the amount invested in municipal bonds. The total interest earned during the first year was $1120. How much was invested in each type of fund?

Solution

Let x, y, and z represent the amounts invested in the money-market fund, municipal bonds, and mutual funds, respectively. From the given information, you can write the following equations.

$$\begin{cases} x + y + z = 12{,}000 & \text{Equation 1} \\ z = y + 4000 & \text{Equation 2} \\ 0.05x + 0.06y + 0.12z = 1120 & \text{Equation 3} \end{cases}$$

Rewriting this system in standard form without decimals produces the following.

$$\begin{cases} x + y + z = 12{,}000 & \text{Equation 1} \\ -y + z = 4{,}000 & \text{Equation 2} \\ 5x + 6y + 12z = 112{,}000 & \text{Equation 3} \end{cases}$$

Using Gaussian elimination to solve this system yields $x = 2000$, $y = 3000$, and $z = 7000$. So, $2000 was invested in the money-market fund, $3000 was invested in municipal bonds, and $7000 was invested in mutual funds.

7.3 Exercises

Exercises containing systems with no solutions: 19, 20, 33
Exercises containing systems with infinitely many solutions: 23–30, 37, 38

In Exercises 1–4, determine which ordered triples are solutions of the system of equations.

1. $\begin{cases} 3x - y + z = 1 \\ 2x \quad\;\; - 3z = -14 \\ \quad\;\; 5y + 2z = 8 \end{cases}$

(a) $(2, 0, -3)$ (b) $(-2, 0, 8)$
(c) $(0, -1, 3)$ (d) $(-1, 0, 4)$

2. $\begin{cases} 3x + 4y - z = 17 \\ 5x - y + 2z = -2 \\ 2x - 3y + 7z = -21 \end{cases}$

(a) $(3, -1, 2)$ (b) $(1, 3, -2)$
(c) $(4, 1, -3)$ (d) $(1, -2, 2)$

3. $\begin{cases} 4x + y - z = 0 \\ -8x - 6y + z = -\frac{7}{4} \\ 3x - y \quad\;\; = -\frac{9}{4} \end{cases}$

(a) $\left(\frac{1}{2}, -\frac{3}{4}, -\frac{7}{4}\right)$ (b) $\left(-\frac{3}{2}, \frac{5}{4}, -\frac{5}{4}\right)$
(c) $\left(-\frac{1}{2}, \frac{3}{4}, -\frac{5}{4}\right)$ (d) $\left(-\frac{1}{2}, \frac{1}{6}, -\frac{3}{4}\right)$

4. $\begin{cases} -4x - y - 8z = -6 \\ \quad\;\; y + z = 0 \\ 4x - 7y \quad\;\; = 6 \end{cases}$

(a) $(-2, -2, 2)$ (b) $\left(-\frac{33}{2}, -10, 10\right)$
(c) $\left(\frac{1}{8}, -\frac{1}{2}, \frac{1}{2}\right)$ (d) $\left(-\frac{11}{2}, -4, 4\right)$

In Exercises 5–10, use back-substitution to solve the system of linear equations.

5. $\begin{cases} 2x - y + 5z = 24 \\ \quad\;\; y + 2z = 6 \\ \quad\;\; z - 4 \end{cases}$

6. $\begin{cases} 4x - 3y - 2z = 21 \\ \quad\;\; 6y - 5z = -8 \\ \quad\;\; z - -2 \end{cases}$

7. $\begin{cases} 2x + y - 3z = 10 \\ \quad\;\; y + z = 12 \\ \quad\;\; z = 2 \end{cases}$

8. $\begin{cases} x - y + 2z = 22 \\ \quad\;\; 3y - 8z = -9 \\ \quad\;\; z = -3 \end{cases}$

9. $\begin{cases} 4x - 2y + z = 8 \\ \quad\;\; -y + z = 4 \\ \quad\;\; z = 2 \end{cases}$

10. $\begin{cases} 5x \quad\;\; - 8z = 22 \\ \quad\;\; 3y - 5z = 10 \\ \quad\;\; z = -4 \end{cases}$

In Exercises 11 and 12, perform the row operation and write the equivalent system.

11. Add Equation 1 to Equation 2.

$\begin{cases} x - 2y + 3z = 5 & \text{Equation 1} \\ -x + 3y - 5z = 4 & \text{Equation 2} \\ 2x \quad\;\; - 3z = 0 & \text{Equation 3} \end{cases}$

What did this operation accomplish?

12. Add -2 times Equation 1 to Equation 3.

$\begin{cases} x - 2y + 3z = 5 & \text{Equation 1} \\ -x + 3y - 5z = 4 & \text{Equation 2} \\ 2x \quad\;\; - 3z = 0 & \text{Equation 3} \end{cases}$

What did this operation accomplish?

In Exercises 13–38, solve the system of linear equations and check any solution algebraically.

13. $\begin{cases} x + y + z = 6 \\ 2x - y + z = 3 \\ 3x \quad\;\; - z = 0 \end{cases}$

14. $\begin{cases} x + y + z = 3 \\ x - 2y + 4z = 5 \\ \quad\;\; 3y + 4z = 5 \end{cases}$

15. $\begin{cases} 2x \quad\;\; + 2z = 2 \\ 5x + 3y \quad\;\; = 4 \\ \quad\;\; 3y - 4z = 4 \end{cases}$

16. $\begin{cases} 2x + 4y + z = 1 \\ x - 2y - 3z = 2 \\ x + y - z = -1 \end{cases}$

17. $\begin{cases} 6y + 4z = -12 \\ 3x + 3y \quad\;\; = 9 \\ 2x \quad\;\; - 3z = 10 \end{cases}$

18. $\begin{cases} 2x + 4y - z = 7 \\ 2x - 4y + 2z = -6 \\ x + 4y + z = 0 \end{cases}$

19. $\begin{cases} 2x + y - z = 7 \\ x - 2y + 2z = -9 \\ 3x - y + z = 5 \end{cases}$

20. $\begin{cases} 5x - 3y + 2z = 3 \\ 2x + 4y - z = 7 \\ x - 11y + 4z = 3 \end{cases}$

21. $\begin{cases} 3x - 5y + 5z = 1 \\ 5x - 2y + 3z = 0 \\ 7x - y + 3z = 0 \end{cases}$

22. $\begin{cases} 2x + y + 3z = 1 \\ 2x + 6y + 8z = 3 \\ 6x + 8y + 18z = 5 \end{cases}$

23. $\begin{cases} x + 2y - 7z = -4 \\ 2x + y + z = 13 \\ 3x + 9y - 36z = -33 \end{cases}$

24. $\begin{cases} 2x + y - 3z = 4 \\ 4x \quad\;\; + 2z = 10 \\ -2x + 3y - 13z = -8 \end{cases}$

25. $\begin{cases} 3x - 3y + 6z = 6 \\ x + 2y - z = 5 \\ 5x - 8y + 13z = 7 \end{cases}$

26. $\begin{cases} x \quad\;\; + 2z = 5 \\ 3x - y - z = 1 \\ 6x - y + 5z = 16 \end{cases}$

27. $\begin{cases} x - 2y + 5z = 2 \\ 4x \qquad - z = 0 \end{cases}$ **28.** $\begin{cases} x - 3y + 2z = 18 \\ 5x - 13y + 12z = 80 \end{cases}$

29. $\begin{cases} 2x - 3y + z = -2 \\ -4x + 9y \quad = 7 \end{cases}$

30. $\begin{cases} 2x + 3y + 3z = 7 \\ 4x + 18y + 15z = 44 \end{cases}$

31. $\begin{cases} x \qquad\qquad + 3w = 4 \\ 2y - z - w = 0 \\ 3y \qquad - 2w = 1 \\ 2x - y + 4z \qquad = 5 \end{cases}$

32. $\begin{cases} x + y + z + w = 6 \\ 2x + 3y \qquad - w = 0 \\ -3x + 4y + z + 2w = 4 \\ x + 2y - z + w = 0 \end{cases}$

33. $\begin{cases} x \qquad + 4z = 1 \\ x + y + 10z = 10 \\ 2x - y + 2z = -5 \end{cases}$

34. $\begin{cases} 2x - 2y - 6z = -4 \\ -3x + 2y + 6z = 1 \\ x - y - 5z = -3 \end{cases}$

35. $\begin{cases} 2x + 3y \quad = 0 \\ 4x + 3y - z = 0 \\ 8x + 3y + 3z = 0 \end{cases}$ **36.** $\begin{cases} 4x + 3y + 17z = 0 \\ 5x + 4y + 22z = 0 \\ 4x + 2y + 19z = 0 \end{cases}$

37. $\begin{cases} 12x + 5y + z = 0 \\ 23x + 4y - z = 0 \end{cases}$ **38.** $\begin{cases} 2x - y - z = 0 \\ -2x + 6y + 4z = 2 \end{cases}$

In Exercises 39–42, find the equation of the parabola

$y = ax^2 + bx + c$

that passes through the points. To verify your result, use a graphing utility to plot the points and graph the parabola.

39. $(0, 0), (2, -2), (4, 0)$ **40.** $(0, 3), (1, 4), (2, 3)$

41. $(2, 0), (3, -1), (4, 0)$ **42.** $(1, 3), (2, 2), (3, -3)$

In Exercises 43–46, find the equation of the circle

$x^2 + y^2 + Dx + Ey + F = 0$

that passes through the points. To verify your result, use a graphing utility to plot the points and graph the circle.

43. $(0, 0), (2, 2), (4, 0)$ **44.** $(0, 0), (0, 6), (3, 3)$

45. $(-3, -1), (2, 4), (-6, 8)$

46. $(0, 0), (0, -2), (3, 0)$

Vertical Motion   **In Exercises 47–50, an object moving vertically is at the given heights at the specified times. Find the position equation** $s = \frac{1}{2}at^2 + v_0t + s_0$ **for the object.**

47. At $t = 1$ second, $s = 128$ feet

  At $t = 2$ seconds, $s = 80$ feet

  At $t = 3$ seconds, $s = 0$ feet

48. At $t = 1$ second, $s = 48$ feet

  At $t = 2$ seconds, $s = 64$ feet

  At $t = 3$ seconds, $s = 48$ feet

49. At $t = 1$ second, $s = 452$ feet

  At $t = 2$ seconds, $s = 372$ feet

  At $t = 3$ seconds, $s = 260$ feet

50. At $t = 1$ second, $s = 132$ feet

  At $t = 2$ seconds, $s = 100$ feet

  At $t = 3$ seconds, $s = 36$ feet

51. *Sports*   The University of Michigan and the University of Tennessee scored a total of 62 points during the 2002 Florida Citrus Bowl. The points came from a total of 18 different scoring plays, which were a combination of touchdowns, extra-point kicks, and field goals, worth 6, 1, and 3 points, respectively. The same number of extra points and touchdowns were scored. How many touchdowns, extra-point kicks, and field goals were scored? (Source: National Collegiate Athletic Association)

52. *Sports*   During the second game of the 2002 Western Conference finals, the Los Angeles Lakers scored a total of 90 points, resulting from a combination of three-point baskets, two-point baskets, and one-point free-throws. There were 11 times as many two-point baskets as three-point baskets and five times as many free-throws as three-point baskets. What combination of scoring accounted for the Lakers' 90 points? (Source: National Basketball Association)

53. *Finance*   A small corporation borrowed $775,000 to expand its clothing line. Some of the money was borrowed at 8%, some at 9%, and some at 10%. How much was borrowed at each rate if the annual interest owed was $67,500 and the amount borrowed at 8% was four times the amount borrowed at 10%?

54. *Finance*   A small corporation borrowed $800,000 to expand its line of toys. Some of the money was borrowed at 8%, some at 9%, and some at 10%. How much was borrowed at each rate if the annual interest owed was $67,000 and the amount borrowed at 8% was five times the amount borrowed at 10%?

Investment Portfolio In Exercises 55 and 56, consider an investor with a portfolio totaling $500,000 that is invested in certificates of deposit, municipal bonds, blue-chip stocks, and growth or speculative stocks. How much is invested in each type of investment?

55. The certificates of deposit pay 10% annually, and the municipal bonds pay 8% annually. Over a five-year period, the investor expects the blue-chip stocks to return 12% annually and the growth stocks to return 13% annually. The investor wants a combined annual return of 10% and also wants to have only one-fourth of the portfolio invested in stocks.

56. The certificates of deposit pay 9% annually, and the municipal bonds pay 5% annually. Over a five-year period, the investor expects the blue-chip stocks to return 12% annually and the growth stocks to return 14% annually. The investor wants a combined annual return of 10% and also wants to have only one-fourth of the portfolio invested in stocks.

57. *Truck Scheduling* A small company that manufactures two models of exercise machines has an order for 15 units of the standard model and 16 units of the deluxe model. The company has trucks of three different sizes that can haul the products, as shown in the table.

Truck	Standard	Deluxe
Large	6	3
Medium	4	4
Small	0	3

How many trucks of each size are needed to deliver the order? Give two possible solutions.

58. *Agriculture* A mixture of 12 liters of chemical A, 16 liters of chemical B, and 26 liters of chemical C is required to kill a destructive crop insect. Commercial spray X contains 1, 2, and 2 parts, respectively, of these chemicals. Commercial spray Y contains only chemical C. Commercial spray Z contains only chemicals A and B in equal amounts. How much of each type of commercial spray is needed to get the desired mixture?

59. *Acid Mixture* A chemist needs 10 liters of a 25% acid solution. The solution is to be mixed from three solutions whose concentrations are 10%, 20%, and 50%. How many liters of each solution should the chemist use so that as little as possible of the 50% solution is used?

60. *Electrical Network* Applying Kirchhoff's Laws to the electrical network in the figure, the currents I_1, I_2, and I_3 are the solution of the system

$$\begin{cases} I_1 - I_2 + I_3 = 0 \\ 3I_1 + 2I_2 \qquad = 7 \\ \qquad 2I_2 + 4I_3 = 8. \end{cases}$$

Find the currents.

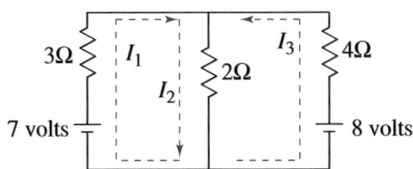

61. *Pulley System* A system of pulleys is loaded with 128-pound and 32-pound weights (see figure). The tensions t_1 and t_2 in the ropes and the acceleration a of the 32-pound weight are found by solving the system of equations

$$\begin{cases} t_1 - 2t_2 \qquad = 0 \\ t_1 \qquad - 2a = 128 \\ \qquad t_2 + a = 32 \end{cases}$$

where t_1 and t_2 are measured in pounds and a is measured in feet per second squared. Solve this system.

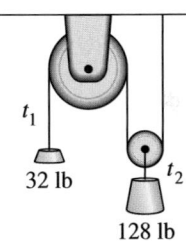

32 lb   128 lb

62. *Pulley System* The 32-pound weight in the pulley system in Exercise 61 is replaced by a 64-pound weight. The new pulley system will be modeled by the following system of equations.

$$\begin{cases} t_1 - 2t_2 \qquad = 0 \\ t_1 \qquad - 2a = 128 \\ \qquad t_2 + 2a = 64 \end{cases}$$

Solve this system and use your answer for the acceleration to describe what (if anything) is happening in the pulley system.

Partial Fraction Decomposition In Exercises 63–66, write the partial fraction decomposition of the rational expression.

63. $\dfrac{1}{x^3 - x} = \dfrac{A}{x} + \dfrac{B}{x - 1} + \dfrac{C}{x + 1}$

64. $\dfrac{3}{x^2 + x - 2} = \dfrac{A}{x - 1} + \dfrac{B}{x + 2}$

65. $\dfrac{x^2 - 3x - 3}{x(x - 2)(x + 3)} = \dfrac{A}{x} + \dfrac{B}{x - 2} + \dfrac{C}{x + 3}$

66. $\dfrac{12}{x(x - 2)(x + 3)} = \dfrac{A}{x} + \dfrac{B}{x - 2} + \dfrac{C}{x + 3}$

Fitting a Parabola In Exercises 67–70, find the least squares regression parabola $y = ax^2 + bx + c$ for the points $(x_1, y_1), (x_2, y_2), \ldots, (x_n, y_n)$ by solving the following system of linear equations for a, b, and c. Then use the *regression* feature of a graphing utility to confirm the result. (If you are unfamiliar with summation notation, look at the discussion in Section 9.1 or in Appendix B at the website for this text at *college.hmco.com*.)

$$nc + \left(\sum_{i=1}^{n} x_i \right) b + \left(\sum_{i=1}^{n} x_i^2 \right) a = \sum_{i=1}^{n} y_i$$

$$\left(\sum_{i=1}^{n} x_i \right) c + \left(\sum_{i=1}^{n} x_i^2 \right) b + \left(\sum_{i=1}^{n} x_i^3 \right) a = \sum_{i=1}^{n} x_i y_i$$

$$\left(\sum_{i=1}^{n} x_i^2 \right) c + \left(\sum_{i=1}^{n} x_i^3 \right) b + \left(\sum_{i=1}^{n} x_i^4 \right) a = \sum_{i=1}^{n} x_i^2 y_i$$

67.

68.

69.

70.

▶ **Model It**

71. Data Analysis A wildlife management team studied the reproduction rates of deer in three tracts of a wildlife preserve. Each tract contained 5 acres. In each tract, the number of females, and the percent of females that had offspring the following year, were recorded. The results are shown in the table.

Number, x	Percent, y
100	75
120	68
140	55

(a) Use the technique demonstrated in Exercises 67–70 to find a least squares regression parabola that models the data.

(b) Use a graphing utility to graph the parabola and the data in the same viewing window.

(c) Use the model to create a table of estimated values of y. Compare the estimated values with the actual data.

(d) Use the model to estimate the percent of females that had offspring when there were 170 females.

(e) Use the model to estimate the number of females when 40% of the females had offspring.

72. Data Analysis In testing a new automobile braking system, the speed in miles per hour and the stopping distance in feet were recorded in the table.

Speed, x	Stopping distance, y
30	55
40	105
50	188

(a) Use the technique demonstrated in Exercises 67–70 to find a least squares regression parabola that models the data.

(b) Graph the parabola and the data on the same set of axes.

(c) Use the model to estimate the stopping distance when the speed is 70 miles per hour.

𝒻 *Advanced Applications* In Exercises 73–76, find *x*, *y*, and *λ* satisfying the system. These systems arise in certain optimization problems in calculus, and *λ* is called a Lagrange multiplier.

73. $\begin{cases} y + \lambda = 0 \\ x + \lambda = 0 \\ x + y - 10 = 0 \end{cases}$

74. $\begin{cases} 2x + \lambda = 0 \\ 2y + \lambda = 0 \\ x + y - 4 = 0 \end{cases}$

75. $\begin{cases} 2x - 2x\lambda = 0 \\ -2y + \lambda = 0 \\ y - x^2 = 0 \end{cases}$

76. $\begin{cases} 2 + 2y + 2\lambda = 0 \\ 2x + 1 + \lambda = 0 \\ 2x + y - 100 = 0 \end{cases}$

Synthesis

True or False? In Exercises 77 and 78, determine whether the statement is true or false. Justify your answer.

77. The system

$\begin{cases} x + 3y - 6z = -16 \\ 2y - z = -1 \\ z = 3 \end{cases}$

is in row-echelon form.

78. If a system of three linear equations is inconsistent, then its graph has no points common to all three equations.

79. *Think About It* Are the following two systems of equations equivalent? Give reasons for your answer.

$\begin{cases} x + 3y - z = 6 \\ 2x - y + 2z = 1 \\ 3x + 2y - z = 2 \end{cases}$ $\begin{cases} x + 3y - z = 6 \\ -7y + 4z = 1 \\ -7y - 4z = -16 \end{cases}$

80. *Writing* When using Gaussian elimination to solve a system of linear equations, explain how you can recognize that the system has no solution. Give an example that illustrates your answer.

In Exercises 81–84, find two systems of linear equations that have the ordered triple as a solution. (The answers are not unique.)

81. $(4, -1, 2)$

82. $(-5, -2, 1)$

83. $\left(3, -\frac{1}{2}, \frac{7}{4}\right)$

84. $\left(-\frac{3}{2}, 4, -7\right)$

Review

In Exercises 85–88, solve the percent problem.

85. What is $7\frac{1}{2}\%$ of 85?

86. 225 is what percent of 150?

87. 0.5% of what number is 400?

88. 48% of what number is 132?

In Exercises 89–94, perform the operation and write the result in standard form.

89. $(7 - i) + (4 + 2i)$

90. $(-6 + 3i) - (1 + 6i)$

91. $(4 - i)(5 + 2i)$

92. $(1 + 2i)(3 - 4i)$

93. $\dfrac{i}{1 + i} + \dfrac{6}{1 - i}$

94. $\dfrac{i}{4 + i} - \dfrac{2i}{8 - 3i}$

In Exercises 95–98, (a) determine the real zeros of *f* and (b) sketch the graph of *f*.

95. $f(x) = x^3 + x^2 - 12x$

96. $f(x) = -8x^4 + 32x^2$

97. $f(x) = 2x^3 + 5x^2 - 21x - 36$

98. $f(x) = 6x^3 - 29x^2 - 6x + 5$

In Exercises 99–102, use a graphing utility to construct a table of values for the equation. Then sketch the graph of the equation by hand.

99. $y = 4^{x-4} - 5$

100. $y = \left(\frac{5}{2}\right)^{-x+1} - 4$

101. $y = 1.9^{-0.8x} + 3$

102. $y = 3.5^{-x+2} + 6$

In Exercises 103 and 104, solve the system by elimination.

103. $\begin{cases} 2x + y = 120 \\ x + 2y = 120 \end{cases}$

104. $\begin{cases} 6x - 5y = 3 \\ 10x - 12y = 5 \end{cases}$

7.4 Systems of Inequalities

▶ **What you should learn**

- How to sketch the graphs of inequalities in two variables
- How to solve systems of inequalities
- How to use systems of inequalities in two variables to model and solve real-life problems

▶ **Why you should learn it**

You can use systems of inequalities in two variables to model and solve real-life problems. For instance, in Exercise 73 on page 521, you will use a system of inequalities to analyze the number of electric-powered vehicles in the United States.

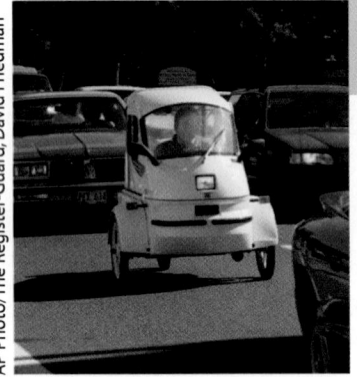

The Graph of an Inequality

The statements $3x - 2y < 6$ and $2x^2 + 3y^2 \geq 6$ are inequalities in two variables. An ordered pair (a, b) is a **solution of an inequality** in x and y if the inequality is true when a and b are substituted for x and y, respectively. The **graph of an inequality** is the collection of all solutions of the inequality. To sketch the graph of an inequality, begin by sketching the graph of the *corresponding equation*. The graph of the equation will normally separate the plane into two or more regions. In each such region, one of the following must be true.

1. *All* points in the region are solutions of the inequality.
2. *No* point in the region is a solution of the inequality.

So, you can determine whether the points in an entire region satisfy the inequality by simply testing *one* point in the region.

> **Sketching the Graph of an Inequality in Two Variables**
>
> 1. Replace the inequality sign by an equal sign, and sketch the graph of the resulting equation. (Use a dashed line for $<$ or $>$ and a solid line for $\leq$ or $\geq$.)
>
> 2. Test one point in each of the regions formed by the graph in Step 1. If the point satisfies the inequality, shade the entire region to denote that every point in the region satisfies the inequality.

Example 1 ▶ Sketching the Graph of an Inequality

To sketch the graph of $y \geq x^2 - 1$, begin by graphing the corresponding *equation* $y = x^2 - 1$, which is a parabola, as shown in Figure 7.19. By testing a point *above* the parabola $(0, 0)$ and a point *below* the parabola $(0, -2)$, you can see that the points that satisfy the inequality are those lying above (or on) the parabola.

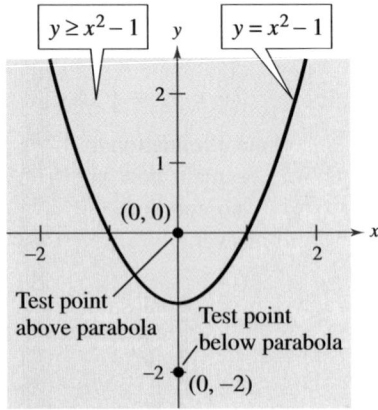

FIGURE **7.19**

The inequality in Example 1 is a nonlinear inequality in two variables. Most of the following examples involve **linear inequalities** such as $ax + by < c$ (a and b are not both zero). The graph of a linear inequality is a half-plane lying on one side of the line $ax + by = c$.

Example 2 ▶ **Sketching the Graph of a Linear Inequality**

Sketch the graph of each linear inequality.

a. $x > -2$ **b.** $y \leq 3$

Solution

a. The graph of the corresponding equation $x = -2$ is a vertical line. The points that satisfy the inequality $x > -2$ are those lying to the right of this line, as shown in Figure 7.20.

b. The graph of the corresponding equation $y = 3$ is a horizontal line. The points that satisfy the inequality $y \leq 3$ are those lying below (or on) this line, as shown in Figure 7.21.

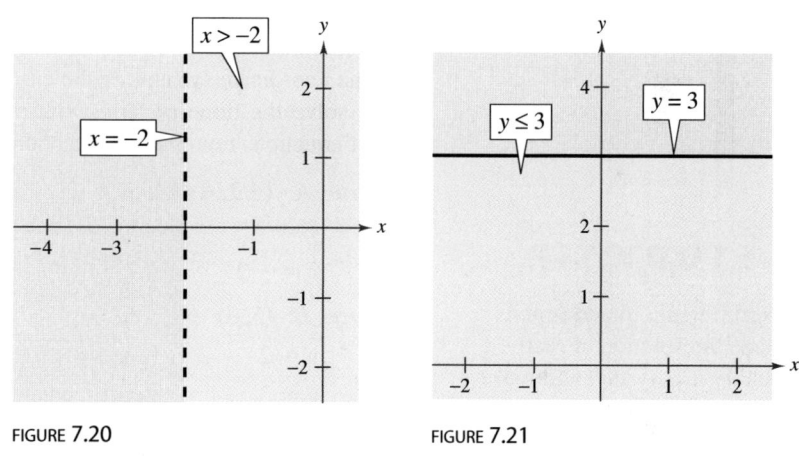

FIGURE 7.20   FIGURE 7.21

Technology

A graphing utility can be used to graph an inequality or a system of inequalities. Consult the user's guide for your graphing utility for the required keystrokes. The graph of the inequality in Example 3 is shown below.

Example 3 ▶ **Sketching the Graph of a Linear Inequality**

Sketch the graph of $x - y < 2$.

Solution

The graph of the corresponding equation $x - y = 2$ is a line, as shown in Figure 7.22. Because the origin $(0, 0)$ satisfies the inequality, the graph consists of the half-plane lying above the line. (Try checking a point below the line. Regardless of which point you choose, you will see that it does not satisfy the inequality.)

To graph a linear inequality, it can help to write the inequality in slope-intercept form. For instance, by writing $x - y < 2$ in the form

$$y > x - 2$$

you can see that the solution points lie *above* the line $x - y = 2$ (or $y = x - 2$), as shown in Figure 7.22.

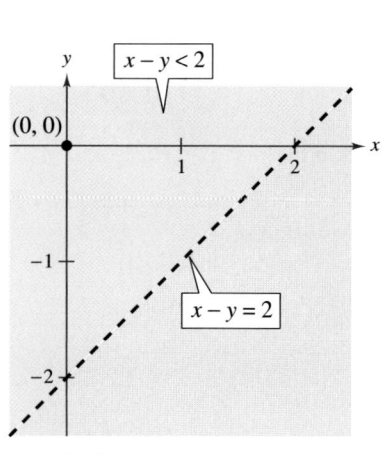

FIGURE 7.22

Systems of Inequalities

Many practical problems in business, science, and engineering involve systems of linear inequalities. A **solution** of a system of inequalities in x and y is a point (x, y) that satisfies each inequality in the system.

To sketch the graph of a system of inequalities in two variables, first sketch the graph of each individual inequality (on the same coordinate system) and then find the region that is *common* to every graph in the system. For systems of *linear* inequalities, it is helpful to find the vertices of the solution region.

Example 4 ▶ Solving a System of Inequalities

Sketch the graph (and label the vertices) of the solution set of the system.

$$\begin{cases} x - y < 2 & \text{Inequality 1} \\ \quad\; x > -2 & \text{Inequality 2} \\ \quad\; y \leq 3 & \text{Inequality 3} \end{cases}$$

Solution

The graphs of these inequalities are shown in Figures 7.20 to 7.22. The triangular region common to all three graphs can be found by superimposing the graphs on the same coordinate system, as shown in Figure 7.23. To find the vertices of the region, solve the three systems of corresponding equations obtained by taking *pairs* of equations representing the boundaries of the individual regions.

Vertex A: $(-2, -4)$

$$\begin{cases} x - y = \;\; 2 & \text{Boundary of Inequality 1} \\ \quad\quad x = -2 & \text{Boundary of Inequality 2} \end{cases}$$

Vertex B: $(5, 3)$

$$\begin{cases} x - y = 2 & \text{Boundary of Inequality 1} \\ \quad\quad y = 3 & \text{Boundary of Inequality 3} \end{cases}$$

Vertex C: $(-2, 3)$

$$\begin{cases} x = -2 & \text{Boundary of Inequality 2} \\ y = \;\; 3 & \text{Boundary of Inequality 3} \end{cases}$$

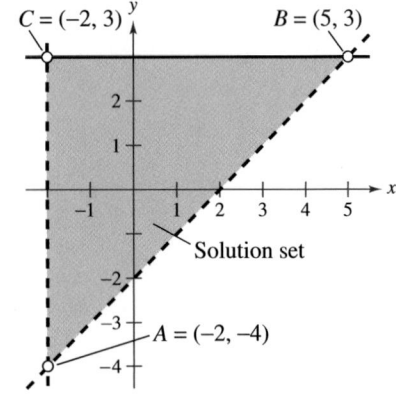

FIGURE **7.23**

For the triangular region shown in Figure 7.23, each point of intersection of a pair of boundary lines corresponds to a vertex. With more complicated regions, two border lines can sometimes intersect at a point that is not a vertex of the region, as shown in Figure 7.24. To keep track of which points of intersection are actually vertices of the region, you should sketch the region and refer to your sketch as you find each point of intersection.

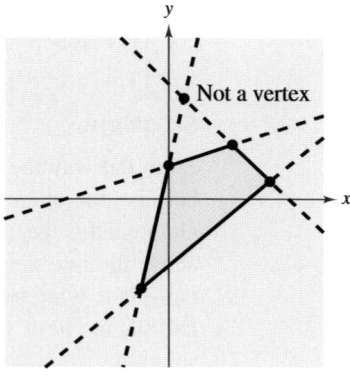

FIGURE **7.24**

Example 5 ▶ **Solving a System of Inequalities**

Sketch the region containing all points that satisfy the system of inequalities.

$$\begin{cases} x^2 - y \le 1 & \text{Inequality 1} \\ -x + y \le 1 & \text{Inequality 2} \end{cases}$$

Solution

As shown in Figure 7.25, the points that satisfy the inequality

$$x^2 - y \le 1 \qquad \text{Inequality 1}$$

are the points lying above (or on) the parabola given by

$$y = x^2 - 1. \qquad \text{Parabola}$$

The points satisfying the inequality

$$-x + y \le 1 \qquad \text{Inequality 2}$$

are the points lying below (or on) the line given by

$$y = x + 1. \qquad \text{Line}$$

To find the points of intersection of the parabola and the line, solve the system of corresponding equations.

$$\begin{cases} x^2 - y = 1 \\ -x + y = 1 \end{cases}$$

Using the method of substitution, you can find the solutions to be $(-1, 0)$ and $(2, 3)$, as shown in Figure 7.25.

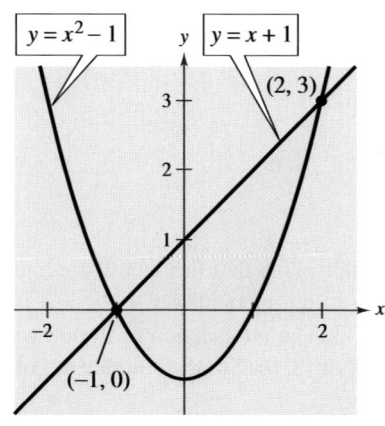

FIGURE **7.25**

When solving a system of inequalities, you should be aware that the system might have no solution *or* it might be represented by an unbounded region in the plane. These two possibilities are shown in Examples 6 and 7.

Example 6 ▶ **A System with No Solution**

Sketch the solution set of the system of inequalities.

$$\begin{cases} x + y > 3 & \text{Inequality 1} \\ x + y < -1 & \text{Inequality 2} \end{cases}$$

Solution

From the way the system is written, it is clear that the system has no solution, because the quantity $(x + y)$ cannot be both less than -1 and greater than 3. Graphically, the inequality $x + y > 3$ is represented by the half-plane lying above the line $x + y = 3$, and the inequality $x + y < -1$ is represented by the half-plane lying below the line $x + y = -1$, as shown in Figure 7.26. These two half-planes have no points in common. So, the system of inequalities has no solution.

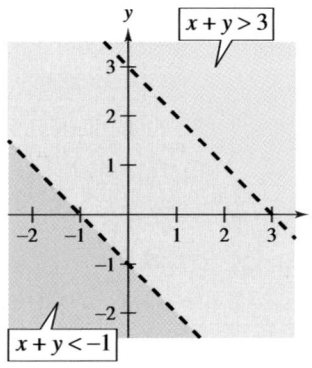

FIGURE 7.26

Example 7 ▶ **An Unbounded Solution Set**

Sketch the solution set of the system of inequalities.

$$\begin{cases} x + y < 3 & \text{Inequality 1} \\ x + 2y > 3 & \text{Inequality 2} \end{cases}$$

Solution

The graph of the inequality $x + y < 3$ is the half-plane that lies below the line $x + y = 3$, as shown in Figure 7.27. The graph of the inequality $x + 2y > 3$ is the half-plane that lies above the line $x + 2y = 3$. The intersection of these two half-planes is an *infinite wedge* that has a vertex at $(3, 0)$. So, the solution set of the system of inequalities is unbounded.

FIGURE 7.27

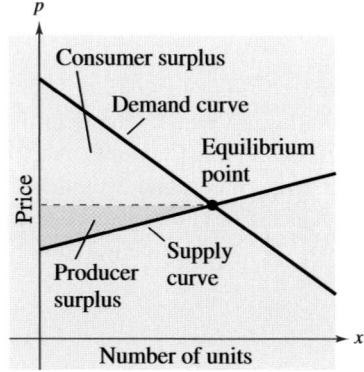

FIGURE **7.28**

Applications

Example 9 in Section 7.2 discussed the *equilibrium point* for a system of demand and supply functions. The next example discusses two related concepts that economists call **consumer surplus** and **producer surplus.** As shown in Figure 7.28, the consumer surplus is defined as the area of the region that lies *below* the demand curve, *above* the horizontal line passing through the equilibrium point, and to the right of the *p*-axis. Similarly, the producer surplus is defined as the area of the region that lies *above* the supply curve, *below* the horizontal line passing through the equilibrium point, and to the right of the *p*-axis. The consumer surplus is a measure of the amount that consumers would have been willing to pay *above what they actually paid*, whereas the producer surplus is a measure of the amount that producers would have been willing to receive *below what they actually received*.

Example 8 ▶ Consumer Surplus and Producer Surplus

The demand and supply functions for a new type of calculator are given by

$$\begin{cases} p = 150 - 0.00001x & \text{Demand equation} \\ p = 60 + 0.00002x & \text{Supply equation} \end{cases}$$

where p is the price in dollars and x represents the number of units. Find the consumer surplus and producer surplus for these two equations.

Solution

Begin by finding the equilibrium point (when supply and demand are equal) by solving the equation

$$60 + 0.00002x = 150 - 0.00001x.$$

In Example 9 in Section 7.2, you saw that the solution is $x = 3{,}000{,}000$ units, which corresponds to an equilibrium price of $p = \$120$. So, the consumer surplus and producer surplus are the areas of the following triangular regions.

Consumer Surplus	*Producer Surplus*
$\begin{cases} p \le 150 - 0.00001x \\ p \ge 120 \\ x \ge 0 \end{cases}$	$\begin{cases} p \ge 60 + 0.00002x \\ p \le 120 \\ x \ge 0 \end{cases}$

In Figure 7.29, you can see that the consumer and producer surpluses are defined as the areas of the shaded triangles.

$$\text{Consumer surplus} = \frac{1}{2}(\text{base})(\text{height})$$

$$= \frac{1}{2}(3{,}000{,}000)(30) = \$45{,}000{,}000$$

$$\text{Producer surplus} = \frac{1}{2}(\text{base})(\text{height})$$

$$= \frac{1}{2}(3{,}000{,}000)(60) = \$90{,}000{,}000$$

FIGURE **7.29**

Example 9 ▶ **Nutrition**

The minimum daily requirements from the liquid portion of a diet are 300 calories, 36 units of vitamin A, and 90 units of vitamin C. A cup of dietary drink X provides 60 calories, 12 units of vitamin A, and 10 units of vitamin C. A cup of dietary drink Y provides 60 calories, 6 units of vitamin A, and 30 units of vitamin C. Set up a system of linear inequalities that describes how many cups of each drink should be consumed each day to meet the minimum daily requirements for calories and vitamins.

Solution

Begin by letting x and y represent the following.

x = number of cups of dietary drink X

y = number of cups of dietary drink Y

To meet the minimum daily requirements, the following inequalities must be satisfied.

$$\begin{cases} 60x + 60y \geq 300 & \text{Calories} \\ 12x + 6y \geq 36 & \text{Vitamin A} \\ 10x + 30y \geq 90 & \text{Vitamin C} \\ x \geq 0 \\ y \geq 0 \end{cases}$$

The last two inequalities are included because x and y cannot be negative. The graph of this system of inequalities is shown in Figure 7.30. (More is said about this application in Example 6 in Section 7.5.)

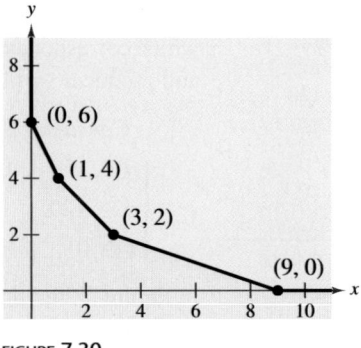

FIGURE 7.30

If you use graphing utilities in your course, you may want your students to work together on the following activity. Consider grouping students with the same model of graphing calculator together so that they can help one another with this activity.

Activity

Using the user's guide for your graphing utility, find how to graph a system of inequalities. Then use the graphing utility to graph each system.

$$\begin{cases} y \leq 4 - x^2 \\ y \geq 2x - 3 \end{cases} \qquad \begin{cases} y \leq 4 - x^2 \\ y \geq x^2 - 4 \end{cases}$$

Writing ABOUT MATHEMATICS

Creating a System of Inequalities Plot the points $(0, 0)$, $(4, 0)$, $(3, 2)$, and $(0, 2)$ in a coordinate plane. Draw the quadrilateral that has these four points as its vertices. Write a system of linear inequalities that has the quadrilateral as its solution. Explain how you found the system of inequalities.

7.4 **Exercises**

Exercise containing system with no solution: 39

In Exercises 1–12, sketch the graph of the inequality.

1. $x \geq 2$ **2.** $x \leq 4$

3. $y \geq -1$ **4.** $y \leq 3$

5. $y < 2 - x$ **6.** $y > 2x - 4$

7. $2y - x \geq 4$ **8.** $5x + 3y \geq -15$

9. $(x + 1)^2 + (y - 2)^2 < 9$

10. $y^2 - x < 0$

11. $y \leq \dfrac{1}{1 + x^2}$ **12.** $y > \dfrac{-15}{x^2 + x + 4}$

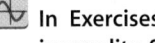 In Exercises 13–24, use a graphing utility to graph the inequality. Shade the region representing the solution.

13. $y < \ln x$ **14.** $y \geq 6 - \ln(x + 5)$

15. $y < 3^{-x-4}$ **16.** $y \leq 2^{2x-0.5} - 7$

17. $y \geq \frac{2}{3}x - 1$ **18.** $y \leq 6 - \frac{3}{2}x$

19. $y < -3.8x + 1.1$ **20.** $y \geq -20.74 + 2.66x$

21. $x^2 + 5y - 10 \leq 0$ **22.** $2x^2 - y - 3 > 0$

23. $\frac{5}{2}y - 3x^2 - 6 \geq 0$ **24.** $-\frac{1}{10}x^2 - \frac{3}{8}y < -\frac{1}{4}$

In Exercises 25–28, write an inequality for the shaded region shown in the figure.

25.

26.

27.

28.
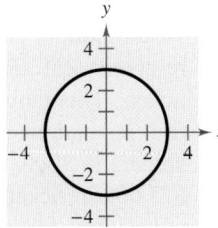

In Exercises 29–32, determine which ordered pairs are solutions of the system of linear inequalities.

29. $\begin{cases} x \geq -4 \\ y > -3 \\ y \leq -8x - 3 \end{cases}$ (a) $(0, 0)$ (b) $(-1, -3)$

                  (c) $(-4, 0)$ (d) $(-3, 11)$

30. $\begin{cases} -2x + 5y \geq 3 \\ y < 4 \\ -4x + 2y < 7 \end{cases}$

(a) $(0, 2)$ (b) $(-6, 4)$

(c) $(-8, -2)$ (d) $(-3, 2)$

31. $\begin{cases} 3x + y > 1 \\ -y - \frac{1}{2}x^2 \leq -4 \\ -15x + 4y > 0 \end{cases}$

(a) $(0, 10)$ (b) $(0, -1)$

(c) $(2, 9)$ (d) $(-1, 6)$

32. $\begin{cases} x^2 + y^2 \geq 36 \\ -3x + y \leq 10 \\ \frac{2}{3}x - y \geq 5 \end{cases}$

(a) $(-1, 7)$ (b) $(-5, 1)$

(c) $(6, 0)$ (d) $(4, -8)$

In Exercises 33–46, sketch the graph and label the vertices of the solution of the system of inequalities.

33. $\begin{cases} x + y \leq 1 \\ -x + y \leq 1 \\ y \geq 0 \end{cases}$ **34.** $\begin{cases} 3x + 2y < 6 \\ x > 0 \\ y > 0 \end{cases}$

35. $\begin{cases} x^2 + y \leq 5 \\ x \geq -1 \\ y \geq 0 \end{cases}$ **36.** $\begin{cases} 2x^2 + y \geq 2 \\ x \leq 2 \\ y \leq 1 \end{cases}$

37. $\begin{cases} -3x + 2y < 6 \\ x - 4y > -2 \\ 2x + y < 3 \end{cases}$ **38.** $\begin{cases} x - 7y > -36 \\ 5x + 2y > 5 \\ 6x - 5y > 6 \end{cases}$

39. $\begin{cases} 2x + y > 2 \\ 6x + 3y < 2 \end{cases}$ **40.** $\begin{cases} x - 2y < -6 \\ 5x - 3y > -9 \end{cases}$

41. $\begin{cases} x > y^2 \\ x < y + 2 \end{cases}$ **42.** $\begin{cases} x - y^2 > 0 \\ x - y > 2 \end{cases}$

43. $\begin{cases} x^2 + y^2 \leq 9 \\ x^2 + y^2 \geq 1 \end{cases}$ **44.** $\begin{cases} x^2 + y^2 \leq 25 \\ 4x - 3y \leq 0 \end{cases}$

45. $\begin{cases} 3x + 4 \geq y^2 \\ x - y < 0 \end{cases}$ **46.** $\begin{cases} x < 2y - y^2 \\ 0 < x + y \end{cases}$

In Exercises 47–52, use a graphing utility to graph the inequalities. Shade the region representing the solution of the system.

47. $\begin{cases} y \le \sqrt{3x} + 1 \\ y \ge x^2 + 1 \end{cases}$ **48.** $\begin{cases} y < -x^2 + 2x + 3 \\ y > x^2 - 4x + 3 \end{cases}$

49. $\begin{cases} y < x^3 - 2x + 1 \\ y > -2x \\ x \le 1 \end{cases}$ **50.** $\begin{cases} y \ge x^4 - 2x^2 + 1 \\ y \le 1 - x^2 \end{cases}$

51. $\begin{cases} x^2 y \ge 1 \\ 0 < x \le 4 \\ y \le 4 \end{cases}$

52. $\begin{cases} y \le e^{-x^2/2} \\ y \ge 0 \\ -2 \le x \le 2 \end{cases}$

In Exercises 53–62, derive a set of inequalities to describe the region.

53.

54.

55.

56.

57.

58.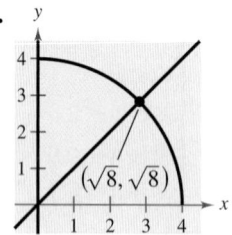

$(\sqrt{8}, \sqrt{8})$

59. Rectangle: Vertices at $(2, 1)$, $(5, 1)$, $(5, 7)$, $(2, 7)$

60. Parallelogram: Vertices at $(0, 0)$, $(4, 0)$, $(1, 4)$, $(5, 4)$

61. Triangle: Vertices at $(0, 0)$, $(5, 0)$, $(2, 3)$

62. Triangle: Vertices at $(-1, 0)$, $(1, 0)$, $(0, 1)$

Supply and Demand In Exercises 63–66, find the consumer surplus and producer surplus for the demand and supply equations.

	Demand	*Supply*
63.	$p = 50 - 0.5x$	$p = 0.125x$
64.	$p = 100 - 0.05x$	$p = 25 + 0.1x$
65.	$p = 140 - 0.00002x$	$p = 80 + 0.00001x$
66.	$p = 400 - 0.0002x$	$p = 225 + 0.0005x$

67. *Production* A furniture company can sell all the tables and chairs it produces. Each table requires 1 hour in the assembly center and $1\frac{1}{3}$ hours in the finishing center. Each chair requires $1\frac{1}{2}$ hours in the assembly center and $1\frac{1}{2}$ hours in the finishing center. The company's assembly center is available 12 hours per day, and its finishing center is available 15 hours per day. Find and graph a system of inequalities describing all possible production levels.

68. *Inventory* A store sells two models of computers. Because of the demand, the store stocks at least twice as many units of model A as of model B. The costs to the store for the two models are \$800 and \$1200, respectively. The management does not want more than \$20,000 in computer inventory at any one time, and it wants at least four model A computers and two model B computers in inventory at all times. Find and graph a system of inequalities describing all possible inventory levels.

69. *Investment Analysis* A person plans to invest up to \$20,000 in two different interest-bearing accounts. Each account is to contain at least \$5000. Moreover, the amount in one account should be at least twice the amount in the other account. Find and graph a system of inequalities to describe the various amounts that can be deposited in each account.

70. *Ticket Sales* For a concert event, there are \$30 reserved seat tickets and \$20 general admission tickets. There are 2000 reserved seats available, and fire regulations limit the number of paid ticket holders to 3000. The promoter must take in at least \$75,000 in ticket sales. Find and graph a system of inequalities describing the different numbers of tickets that can be sold.

71. *Shipping*   A warehouse supervisor is told to ship at least 50 packages of gravel that weigh 55 pounds each and at least 40 bags of stone that weigh 70 pounds each. The maximum weight capacity in the truck he is loading is 7500 pounds. Find and graph a system of inequalities describing the numbers of bags of stone and gravel that he can send.

72. *Nutrition*   A dietitian is asked to design a special dietary supplement using two different foods. Each ounce of food X contains 20 units of calcium, 15 units of iron, and 10 units of vitamin B. Each ounce of food Y contains 10 units of calcium, 10 units of iron, and 20 units of vitamin B. The minimum daily requirements of the diet are 300 units of calcium, 150 units of iron, and 200 units of vitamin B. Find and graph a system of inequalities describing the different amounts of food X and food Y that can be used.

▶ Model It

73. *Data Analysis*   The table shows the numbers y of electric-powered vehicles in the United States for the years 1996 through 2000.   (Source: U.S. Energy Information Administration)

Year, t	Number of vehicles, y
1996	3280
1997	4040
1998	5243
1999	6417
2000	7590

(a) Use the *regression* feature of a graphing utility to find a linear model for the data. Let t represent the year, with $t = 6$ corresponding to 1996.

(b) The total number of electric-powered vehicles in the United States during this five-year period can be approximated by finding the area of the trapezoid bounded by the linear model you found in part (a) and the lines $y = 0$, $t = 5.5$, and $t = 10.5$. Use a graphing utility to graph this region.

(c) Use the formula for the area of a trapezoid to approximate the total number of electric-powered vehicles.

---

74. *Physical Fitness Facility*   An indoor running track is to be constructed with a space for body-building equipment inside the track (see figure). The track must be at least 125 meters long, and the body-building space must have an area of at least 500 square meters.

(a) Find a system of inequalities describing the requirements of the facility.

(b) Graph the system from part (a).

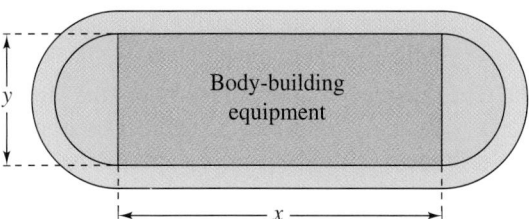

Synthesis

True or False?   **In Exercises 75 and 76, determine whether the statement is true or false. Justify your answer.**

75. The area of the figure defined by the system

$$\begin{cases} x \geq -3 \\ x \leq 6 \\ y \leq 5 \\ y \geq -6 \end{cases}$$

is 99 square units.

76. The graph below shows the solution of the system

$$\begin{cases} y \leq 6 \\ -4x - 9y > 6. \\ 3x + y^2 \geq 2 \end{cases}$$

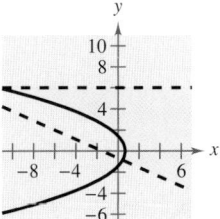

77. *Writing*   Explain the difference between the graphs of the inequality $x \leq 4$ on the real number line and on the rectangular coordinate system.

78. *Think About It*   After graphing the boundary of an inequality in x and y, how do you decide on which side of the boundary the solution set of the inequality lies?

79. *Graphical Reasoning* Two concentric circles have radii x and y, where $y > x$. The area between the circles must be at least 10 square units.

(a) Find a system of inequalities describing the constraints on the circles.

 (b) Use a graphing utility to graph the system of inequalities in part (a). Graph the line $y = x$ in the same viewing window.

(c) Identify the graph of the line in relation to the boundary of the inequality. Explain its meaning in the context of the problem.

80. The graph of the solution of the inequality $x + 2y < 6$ is shown in the figure. Describe how the solution set would change for each of the following.

(a) $x + 2y \le 6$ (b) $x + 2y > 6$

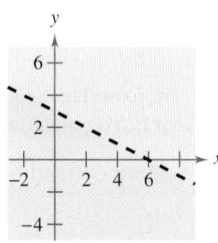

In Exercises 81–84, match the system of inequalities with the graph of its solution. [The graphs are labeled (a), (b), (c), and (d).]

(a)

(b)

(c)

(d)

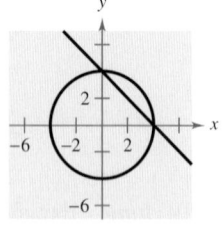

81. $\begin{cases} x^2 + y^2 \le 16 \\ x + y \ge 4 \end{cases}$ **82.** $\begin{cases} x^2 + y^2 \le 16 \\ x + y \le 4 \end{cases}$

83. $\begin{cases} x^2 + y^2 \ge 16 \\ x + y \ge 4 \end{cases}$ **84.** $\begin{cases} x^2 + y^2 \ge 16 \\ x + y \le 4 \end{cases}$

Review

In Exercises 85–90, find the equation of the line passing through the two points.

85. $(-2, 6), (4, -4)$ **86.** $(-8, 0), (3, -1)$

87. $\left(\frac{3}{4}, -2\right), \left(-\frac{7}{2}, 5\right)$ **88.** $\left(-\frac{1}{2}, 0\right), \left(\frac{11}{2}, 12\right)$

89. $(3.4, -5.2), (-2.6, 0.8)$

90. $(-4.1, -3.8), (2.9, 8.2)$

91. *Data Analysis* The table shows the amount y (in trillions of dollars) of personal expenditures for medical care in the United States for the years 1994 through 1999. (Source: U.S. Bureau of Economic Analysis)

Year, t	Expenditures, y
1994	833.7
1995	888.6
1996	912.8
1997	977.6
1998	1040.9
1999	1102.6

(a) Use the *regression* feature of a graphing utility to find a linear model and a quadratic model for the data. Let t represent the year, with $t = 4$ corresponding to 1994.

(b) Use a graphing utility to plot the data and the models in the same viewing window.

(c) How closely do the models represent the data?

92. *Compound Interest* Determine the amount after 5 years if $4000 is invested in an account earning 6% interest compounded monthly.

In Exercises 93–96, evaluate the function at the indicated value of x. Round your result to three decimal places.

Function	Value
93. $f(x) = 2.7^x$	$x = 3.99$
94. $f(x) = 1.5^{-x}$	$x = 3\pi$
95. $f(x) = e^x$	$x = -\frac{11}{4}$
96. $f(x) = e^{-x}$	$x = \sqrt{13}$

7.5 Linear Programming

▶ **What you should learn**

- How to solve linear programming problems
- How to use linear programming to model and solve real-life problems

▶ **Why you should learn it**

Linear programming is often useful in making real-life economic decisions. For example, Exercise 35 on page 530 shows how a merchant can use linear programming to analyze the profitability of two models of compact disc players.

Linear Programming: A Graphical Approach

Many applications in business and economics involve a process called **optimization,** in which you are asked to find the minimum or maximum of a quantity. In this section you will study an optimization strategy called **linear programming.**

A two-dimensional linear programming problem consists of a linear **objective function** and a system of linear inequalities called **constraints.** The objective function gives the quantity that is to be maximized (or minimized), and the constraints determine the set of **feasible solutions.** For example, suppose you are asked to maximize the value of

$$z = ax + by \qquad \text{Objective function}$$

subject to a set of constraints that determines the shaded region in Figure 7.31.

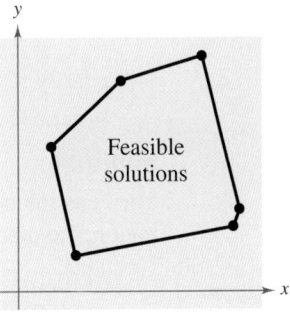

FIGURE 7.31

Because every point in the shaded region satisfies each constraint, it is not clear how you should find the point that yields a maximum value of z. Fortunately, it can be shown that if there is an optimal solution, it must occur at one of the vertices. This means that *you can find the maximum value of z by testing z at each of the vertices.*

Optimal Solution of a Linear Programming Problem

If a linear programming problem has a solution, it must occur at a vertex of the set of feasible solutions. If there is more than one solution, at least one of them must occur at such a vertex. In either case, the value of the objective function is unique.

Some guidelines for solving a linear programming problem in two variables are listed at the top of the next page.

It is important that students immediately become familiar with the terminology of this section. Emphasize that linear programming is powerful in that it identifies quickly those few points out of many that can be easily tested to find the point that gives the maximum or minimum value.

Solving a Linear Programming Problem

1. Sketch the region corresponding to the system of constraints. (The points inside or on the boundary of the region are *feasible solutions*.)

2. Find the vertices of the region.

3. Test the objective function at each of the vertices and select the values of the variables that optimize the objective function. For a bounded region, both a minimum and a maximum value will exist. (For an unbounded region, *if* an optimal solution exists, it will occur at a vertex.)

Example 1 ▶ Solving a Linear Programming Problem

Find the maximum value of

$$z = 3x + 2y \qquad \text{Objective function}$$

subject to the following constraints.

$$\left. \begin{array}{r} x \geq 0 \\ y \geq 0 \\ x + 2y \leq 4 \\ x - y \leq 1 \end{array} \right\} \qquad \text{Constraints}$$

Solution

The constraints form the region shown in Figure 7.32. At the four vertices of this region, the objective function has the following values.

At $(0, 0)$: $z = 3(0) + 2(0) = 0$
At $(1, 0)$: $z = 3(1) + 2(0) = 3$
At $(2, 1)$: $z = 3(2) + 2(1) = 8$ Maximum value of z
At $(0, 2)$: $z = 3(0) + 2(2) = 4$

So, the maximum value of z is 8, and this occurs when $x = 2$ and $y = 1$.

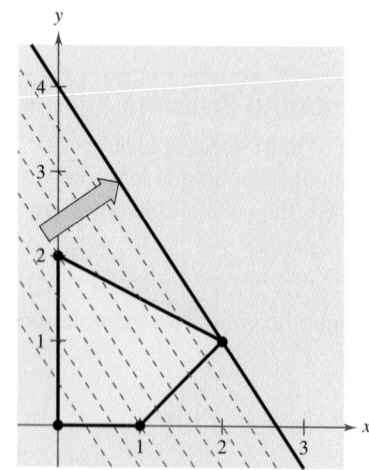

FIGURE **7.32**

In Example 1, try testing some of the *interior* points in the region. You will see that the corresponding values of z are less than 8. Here are some examples.

At $(1, 1)$: $z = 3(1) + 2(1) = 5$ At $\left(\frac{1}{2}, \frac{3}{2}\right)$: $z = 3\left(\frac{1}{2}\right) + 2\left(\frac{3}{2}\right) = \frac{9}{2}$

To see why the maximum value of the objective function in Example 1 must occur at a vertex, consider writing the objective function in slope-intercept form

$$y = -\frac{3}{2}x + \frac{z}{2} \qquad \text{Family of lines}$$

where $z/2$ is the y-intercept of the objective function. This equation represents a family of lines, each of slope $-\frac{3}{2}$. Of these infinitely many lines, you want the one that has the largest z-value while still intersecting the region determined by the constraints. In other words, of all the lines whose slope is $-\frac{3}{2}$, you want the one that has the largest y-intercept *and* intersects the given region, as shown in Figure 7.33. From the graph you can see that such a line will pass through one (or more) of the vertices of the region.

FIGURE **7.33**

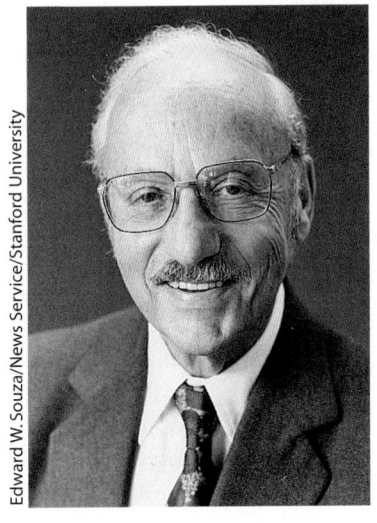

FIGURE 7.34

The next example shows that the same basic procedure can be used to solve a problem in which the objective function is to be *minimized*.

Example 2 ▶ Minimizing an Objective Function

Find the minimum value of

$$z = 5x + 7y \qquad \text{Objective function}$$

where $x \geq 0$ and $y \geq 0$, subject to the following constraints.

$$\left.\begin{array}{r} 2x + 3y \geq 6 \\ 3x - y \leq 15 \\ -x + y \leq 4 \\ 2x + 5y \leq 27 \end{array}\right\} \qquad \text{Constraints}$$

Solution

The region bounded by the constraints is shown in Figure 7.34. By testing the objective function at each vertex, you obtain the following.

At $(0, 2)$: $z = 5(0) + 7(2) = 14$ Minimum value of z

At $(0, 4)$: $z = 5(0) + 7(4) = 28$

At $(1, 5)$: $z = 5(1) + 7(5) = 40$

At $(6, 3)$: $z = 5(6) + 7(3) = 51$

At $(5, 0)$: $z = 5(5) + 7(0) = 25$

At $(3, 0)$: $z = 5(3) + 7(0) = 15$

So, the minimum value of z is 14, and this occurs when $x = 0$ and $y = 2$.

Example 3 ▶ Maximizing an Objective Function

Find the maximum value of

$$z = 5x + 7y \qquad \text{Objective function}$$

where $x \geq 0$ and $y \geq 0$, subject to the following constraints.

$$\left.\begin{array}{r} 2x + 3y \geq 6 \\ 3x - y \leq 15 \\ -x + y \leq 4 \\ 2x + 5y \leq 27 \end{array}\right\} \qquad \text{Constraints}$$

Solution

This linear programming problem is identical to that given in Example 2 above, *except* that the objective function is maximized instead of minimized. Using the values of z at the vertices shown above, you can conclude that the maximum value of

$$z = 5(6) + 7(3) = 51$$

occurs when $x = 6$ and $y = 3$.

Historical Note
George Dantzig (1914–) was the first to propose the simplex method, or linear programming, in 1947. This technique defined the steps needed to find the optimal solution to a complex multivariable problem.

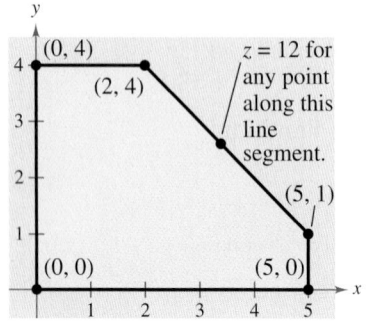

FIGURE **7.35**

It is possible for the maximum (or minimum) value in a linear programming problem to occur at *two* different vertices. For instance, at the vertices of the region shown in Figure 7.35, the objective function

$$z = 2x + 2y \qquad \text{Objective function}$$

has the following values.

At $(0, 0)$: $z = 2(0) + 2(0) = 0$
At $(0, 4)$: $z = 2(0) + 2(4) = 8$
At $(2, 4)$: $z = 2(2) + 2(4) = 12$ Maximum value of z
At $(5, 1)$: $z = 2(5) + 2(1) = 12$ Maximum value of z
At $(5, 0)$: $z = 2(5) + 2(0) = 10$

In this case, you can conclude that the objective function has a maximum value not only at the vertices $(2, 4)$ and $(5, 1)$; it also has a maximum value (of 12) at *any point on the line segment connecting these two vertices*. Note that the objective function in slope-intercept form $y = -x + \frac{1}{2}z$ has the same slope as the line through the vertices $(2, 4)$ and $(5, 1)$.

Some linear programming problems have no optimal solutions. This can occur if the region determined by the constraints is *unbounded*. Example 4 illustrates such a problem.

Example 4 ▶   An Unbounded Region

Find the maximum value of

$$z = 4x + 2y \qquad \text{Objective function}$$

where $x \geq 0$ and $y \geq 0$, subject to the following constraints.

$$\left.\begin{array}{r} x + 2y \geq 4 \\ 3x + y \geq 7 \\ -x + 2y \leq 7 \end{array}\right\} \qquad \text{Constraints}$$

Solution

The region determined by the constraints is shown in Figure 7.36. For this unbounded region, there is no maximum value of z. To see this, note that the point $(x, 0)$ lies in the region for all values of $x \geq 4$. Substituting this point into the objective function, you get

$$z = 4(x) + 2(0) = 4x.$$

By choosing x to be large, you can obtain values of z that are as large as you want. So, there is no maximum value of z.

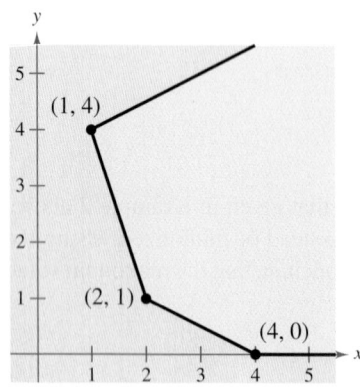

FIGURE **7.36**

Although the objective function in Example 4 has no maximum, there *is* a minimum value of z.

At $(1, 4)$: $z = 4(1) + 2(4) = 12$
At $(2, 1)$: $z = 4(2) + 2(1) = 10$ Minimum value of z
At $(4, 0)$: $z = 4(4) + 2(0) = 16$

So, the minimum value of z is 10, and this occurs when $x = 2$ and $y = 1$.

1. Sketch the region determined by the constraints $x \geq 0$, $y \geq 0$, and $3x + 2y < 6$, and then find the minimum and maximum values of the objective function $z = 4x + 5y$ and where they occur, subject to the constraints.

Answer: Minimum: 0 at (0, 0); Maximum: 15 at (0, 3)

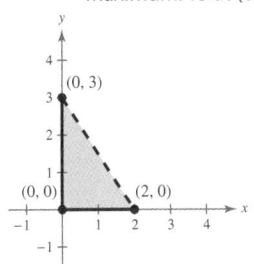

2. Find the maximum value of the objective function $z = 6x + 5y$, and where it occurs, subject to the constraints $3x + 2y \leq 16$, $x + 4y \leq 22$, $x \geq 0$, and $y \geq 0$.

Answer: Maximum: 37 at (2, 5)

3. Find the maximum value, and where it occurs, of $z = 2x + 5y$ where $x \geq 0$ and $y \geq 0$ subject to the constraints $x + 2y \geq 8$, $3x + y \geq 14$, and $-x + y \leq 10$.

Answer: There is no maximum value of z.

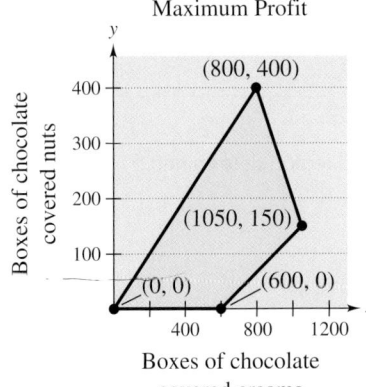

Maximum Profit

FIGURE 7.37

Applications

Example 5 shows how linear programming can be used to find the maximum profit in a business application.

Example 5 ► **Maximum Profit**

A candy manufacturer wants to maximize the profit for two types of boxed chocolates. A box of chocolate covered creams yields a profit of $1.50 per box, and a box of chocolate covered nuts yields a profit of $2.00 per box. Market tests and available resources have indicated the following constraints.

1. The combined production level should not exceed 1200 boxes per month.

2. The demand for a box of chocolate covered nuts is no more than half the demand for a box of chocolate covered creams.

3. The production level of a box of chocolate covered creams should be less than or equal to 600 boxes plus three times the production level of a box of chocolate covered nuts.

Solution

Let x be the number of boxes of chocolate covered creams and let y be the number of boxes of chocolate covered nuts. So, the objective function (for the combined profit) is given by

$$P = 1.5x + 2y. \qquad \text{Objective function}$$

The three constraints translate into the following linear inequalities.

1. $x + y \leq 1200$ ⟹ $x + y \leq 1200$

2. $y \leq \frac{1}{2}x$ ⟹ $-x + 2y \leq 0$

3. $x \leq 600 + 3y$ ⟹ $x - 3y \leq 600$

Because neither x nor y can be negative, you also have the two additional constraints of $x \geq 0$ and $y \geq 0$. Figure 7.37 shows the region determined by the constraints. To find the maximum profit, test the values of P at the vertices of the region.

$$
\begin{aligned}
\text{At } (0, 0): \quad & P = 1.5(0) + 2(0) = 0 \\
\text{At } (800, 400): \quad & P = 1.5(800) + 2(400) = 2000 \qquad \text{Maximum profit} \\
\text{At } (1050, 150): \quad & P = 1.5(1050) + 2(150) = 1875 \\
\text{At } (600, 0): \quad & P = 1.5(600) + 2(0) = 900
\end{aligned}
$$

So, the maximum profit is $2000, and it occurs when the monthly production consists of 800 boxes of chocolate covered creams and 400 boxes of chocolate covered nuts.

In Example 5, the manufacturer improved the production of chocolate covered creams so that it yielded a profit of $2.50 per unit. The maximum profit can then be found using the objective function $P = 2.5x + 2y$. By testing the values of P at the vertices of the region, you find the maximum profit is $2925 and that it now occurs when $x = 1050$ and $y = 150$.

Example 6 ▶ Minimum Cost

The minimum daily requirements from the liquid portion of a diet are 300 calories, 36 units of vitamin A, and 90 units of vitamin C. A cup of dietary drink X costs $0.12 and provides 60 calories, 12 units of vitamin A, and 10 units of vitamin C. A cup of dietary drink Y costs $0.15 and provides 60 calories, 6 units of vitamin A, and 30 units of vitamin C. How many cups of each drink should be consumed each day to minimize the cost and still meet the daily requirements?

Solution

As in Example 9 on page 518, let x be the number of cups of dietary drink X and let y be the number of cups of dietary drink Y.

$$\left.\begin{array}{lr} \text{For calories:} & 60x + 60y \geq 300 \\ \text{For vitamin A:} & 12x + 6y \geq 36 \\ \text{For vitamin C:} & 10x + 30y \geq 90 \\ x \geq 0 \\ y \geq 0 \end{array}\right\} \quad \text{Constraints}$$

The cost C is given by $C = 0.12x + 0.15y$.   Objective function

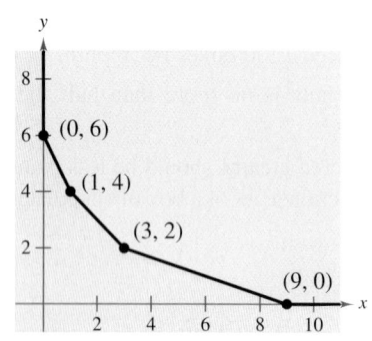

FIGURE **7.38**

The graph of the region corresponding to the constraints is shown in Figure 7.38. To determine the minimum cost, test C at each vertex of the region.

At $(0, 6)$: $C = 0.12(0) + 0.15(6) = 0.90$

At $(1, 4)$: $C = 0.12(1) + 0.15(4) = 0.72$

At $(3, 2)$: $C = 0.12(3) + 0.15(2) = 0.66$ Minimum value of C

At $(9, 0)$: $C = 0.12(9) + 0.15(0) = 1.08$

So, the minimum cost is $0.66 per day, and this occurs when three cups of drink X and two cups of drink Y are consumed each day.

Writing **ABOUT MATHEMATICS**

Creating a Linear Programming Problem Sketch the region determined by the following constraints.

$$\left.\begin{array}{r} x + 2y \leq 8 \\ x + y \leq 5 \\ x \geq 0 \\ y \geq 0 \end{array}\right\} \quad \text{Constraints}$$

Find, if possible, an objective function of the form $z = ax + by$ that has a maximum at the indicated vertex of the region.

a. $(0, 4)$ **b.** $(2, 3)$

c. $(5, 0)$ **d.** $(0, 0)$

Explain how you found each objective function.

Alternative Writing About Mathematics

Explain what difficulties you might encounter with each set of linear programming constraints.

a. $\left.\begin{array}{r} x - y < 0 \\ 3x + y > 9 \\ -4x + y > -2 \end{array}\right\}$ Constraints

b. $\left.\begin{array}{r} 2x + y > 11 \\ x - y > 0 \\ x < 4 \\ y < 0 \end{array}\right\}$ Constraints

7.5 Exercises

Exercise with no feasible solutions: 46
Exercises with unbounded regions: 17, 19, 44

In Exercises 1–12, find the minimum and maximum values of the objective function and where they occur, subject to the indicated constraints. (For each exercise, the graph of the region determined by the constraints is provided.)

1. Objective function:
$z = 4x + 3y$
Constraints:
$x \geq 0$
$y \geq 0$
$x + y \leq 5$

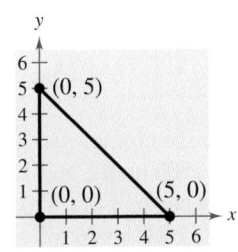

2. Objective function:
$z = 2x + 8y$
Constraints:
$x \geq 0$
$y \geq 0$
$2x + y \leq 4$

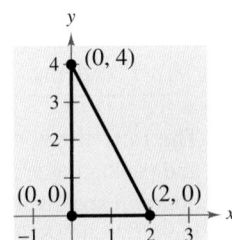

3. Objective function:
$z = 3x + 8y$
Constraints:
(See Exercise 1.)

4. Objective function:
$z = 7x + 3y$
Constraints:
(See Exercise 2.)

5. Objective function:
$z = 3x + 2y$
Constraints:
$x \geq 0$
$y \geq 0$
$x + 3y \leq 15$
$4x + y \leq 16$

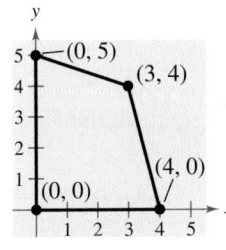

6. Objective function:
$z = 4x + 5y$
Constraints:
$x \geq 0$
$2x + 3y \geq 6$
$3x - y \leq 9$
$x + 4y \leq 16$

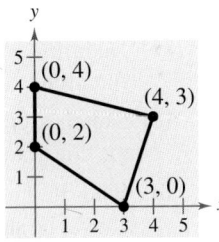

7. Objective function:
$z = 5x + 0.5y$
Constraints:
(See Exercise 5.)

8. Objective function:
$z = 2x + y$
Constraints:
(See Exercise 6.)

9. Objective function:
$z = 10x + 7y$
Constraints:
$0 \leq x \leq 60$
$0 \leq y \leq 45$
$5x + 6y \leq 420$

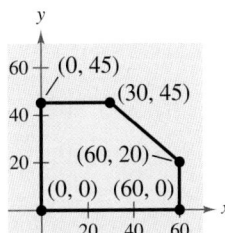

10. Objective function:
$z = 25x + 35y$
Constraints:
$x \geq 0$
$y \geq 0$
$8x + 9y \leq 7200$
$8x + 9y \geq 3600$

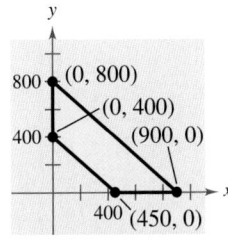

11. Objective function:
$z = 25x + 30y$
Constraints:
(See Exercise 9.)

12. Objective function:
$z = 15x + 20y$
Constraints:
(See Exercise 10.)

In Exercises 13–20, sketch the region determined by the constraints. Then find the minimum and maximum values of the objective function and where they occur, subject to the indicated constraints.

13. Objective function:
$z = 6x + 10y$
Constraints:
$x \geq 0$
$y \geq 0$
$2x + 5y \leq 10$

14. Objective function:
$z = 7x + 8y$
Constraints:
$x \geq 0$
$y \geq 0$
$x + \frac{1}{2}y \leq 4$

15. Objective function:
$z = 9x + 24y$
Constraints:
(See Exercise 13.)

16. Objective function:
$z = 7x + 2y$
Constraints:
(See Exercise 14.)

17. Objective function:
$z = 4x + 5y$
Constraints:
$x \geq 0$
$y \geq 0$
$x + y \geq 8$
$3x + 5y \geq 30$

18. Objective function:
$z = 4x + 5y$
Constraints:
$x \geq 0$
$y \geq 0$
$2x + 2y \leq 10$
$x + 2y \leq 6$

19. Objective function:

$z = 2x + 7y$

Constraints:
(See Exercise 17.)

20. Objective function:

$z = 2x - y$

Constraints:
(See Exercise 18.)

🔖 **In Exercises 21–24, use a graphing utility to graph the region determined by the constraints. Then find the minimum and maximum values of the objective function and where they occur, subject to the constraints.**

21. Objective function:

$z = 4x + y$

Constraints:

$$x \geq 0$$
$$y \geq 0$$
$$x + 2y \leq 40$$
$$2x + 3y \geq 72$$

22. Objective function:

$z = x$

Constraints:

$$x \geq 0$$
$$y \geq 0$$
$$2x + 3y \leq 60$$
$$2x + y \leq 28$$
$$4x + y \leq 48$$

23. Objective function:

$z = x + 4y$

Constraints:
(See Exercise 21.)

24. Objective function:

$z = y$

Constraints:
(See Exercise 22.)

In Exercises 25–28, find the maximum value of the objective function and where it occurs, subject to the constraints $x \geq 0$, $y \geq 0$, $3x + y \leq 15$, and $4x + 3y \leq 30$.

25. $z = 2x + y$ **26.** $z = 5x + y$

27. $z = x + y$ **28.** $z = 3x + y$

In Exercises 29–32, find the maximum value of the objective function and where it occurs, subject to the constraints $x \geq 0$, $y \geq 0$, $x + 4y \leq 20$, $x + y \leq 18$, and $2x + 2y \leq 21$.

29. $z = x + 5y$ **30.** $z = 2x + 4y$

31. $z = 4x + 5y$ **32.** $z = 4x + y$

33. *Maximum Profit* A manufacturer produces two models of bicycles. The times (in hours) required for assembling, painting, and packaging each model are shown in the table.

Process	Hours, model A	Hours, model B
Assembling	2	2.5
Painting	4	1
Packaging	1	0.75

The total times available for assembling, painting, and packaging are 4000 hours, 4800 hours, and 1500 hours, respectively. The profits per unit are $45 for model A and $50 for model B. How many of each type should be produced to maximize profit? What is the maximum profit?

34. *Maximum Profit* A manufacturer produces two models of bicycles. The times (in hours) required for assembling, painting, and packaging each model are shown in the table.

Process	Hours, model A	Hours, model B
Assembling	2.5	3
Painting	2	1
Packaging	0.75	1.25

The total times available for assembling, painting, and packaging are 4000 hours, 2500 hours, and 1500 hours, respectively. The profits per unit are $50 for model A and $52 for model B. How many of each type should be produced to maximize profit? What is the maximum profit?

▶ **Model It**

35. *Maximum Profit* A merchant plans to sell two models of compact disc players at costs of $150 and $200. The $150 model yields a profit of $25 per unit and the $200 model yields a profit of $40 per unit. The merchant estimates that the total monthly demand will not exceed 250 units. The merchant does not want to invest more than $40,000 in inventory for these products.

(a) Write an objective function that models the profit for the compact disc players.

(b) Determine the constraints for the objective function.

(c) Sketch a graph of the region determined by the constraints from part (b).

(d) Find the number of units of each model that should be stocked in order to maximize profit.

(e) What is the maximum profit?

36. Maximum Profit A fruit grower has 150 acres of land available to raise two crops, A and B. It takes 1 day to trim an acre of crop A and 2 days to trim an acre of crop B, and there are 240 days per year available for trimming. It takes 0.3 day to pick an acre of crop A and 0.1 day to pick an acre of crop B, and there are 30 days available for picking. The profit is $140 per acre for crop A and $235 per acre for crop B. Find the number of acres of each fruit that should be planted to maximize profit. What is the maximum profit?

37. Minimum Cost A farming cooperative mixes two brands of cattle feed. Brand X costs $25 per bag and contains two units of nutritional element A, two units of element B, and two units of element C. Brand Y costs $20 per bag and contains one unit of nutritional element A, nine units of element B, and three units of element C. The minimum requirements of nutrients A, B, and C are 12 units, 36 units, and 24 units, respectively. Find the number of bags of each brand that should be mixed to produce a mixture having a minimum cost. What is the minimum cost?

38. Minimum Cost Two gasolines, type A and type B, have octane ratings of 87 and 93, respectively. Type A costs $1.13 per gallon and type B costs $1.28 per gallon. Determine the blend of minimum cost with an octane rating of at least 89. What is the minimum cost? Is the cost cheaper than the advertised cost of $1.20 per gallon for gasoline with an octane rating of 89? (*Hint:* Let x be the fraction of each gallon that is type A and let y be the fraction that is type B.)

39. Maximum Revenue An accounting firm has 800 hours of staff time and 96 hours of reviewing time available each week. The firm charges $2000 for an audit and $300 for a tax return. Each audit requires 100 hours of staff time and 8 hours of review time. Each tax return requires 12.5 hours of staff time and 2 hours of review time. What numbers of audits and tax returns will yield the maximum revenue? What is the maximum revenue?

40. Maximum Revenue The accounting firm in Exercise 39 lowers its charge for an audit to $1000. What numbers of audits and tax returns will yield the maximum revenue? What is the maximum revenue?

41. Investment Portfolio An investor has up to $250,000 to invest in two types of investments. Type A pays 8% annually and type B pays 10% annually. To have a well-balanced portfolio, the investor imposes the following conditions. At least one-fourth of the total portfolio is to be allocated to type A investments and at least one-fourth of the portfolio is to be allocated to type B investments. How much should be allocated to each type of investment to obtain a maximum return?

42. Investment Portfolio An investor has up to $450,000 to invest in two types of investments. Type A pays 6% annually and type B pays 10% annually. To have a well-balanced portfolio, the investor imposes the following conditions. At least one-half of the total portfolio is to be allocated to type A investments and at least one-fourth of the portfolio is to be allocated to type B investments. How much should be allocated to each type of investment to obtain a maximum return?

In Exercises 43–48, the linear programming problem has an unusual characteristic. Sketch a graph of the solution region for the problem and describe the unusual characteristic. Find the maximum value of the objective function and where it occurs.

43. Objective function:
$z = 2.5x + y$
Constraints:
$x \geq 0$
$y \geq 0$
$3x + 5y \leq 15$
$5x + 2y \leq 10$

44. Objective function:
$z = x + y$
Constraints:
$x \geq 0$
$y \geq 0$
$-x + y \leq 1$
$-x + 2y \leq 4$

45. Objective function:
$z = -x + 2y$
Constraints:
$x \geq 0$
$y \geq 0$
$x \leq 10$
$x + y \leq 7$

46. Objective function:
$z = x + y$
Constraints:
$x \geq 0$
$y \geq 0$
$-x + y \leq 0$
$-3x + y \geq 3$

47. Objective function:
$z = 3x + 4y$
Constraints:
$x \geq 0$
$y \geq 0$
$x + y \leq 1$
$2x + y \leq 4$

48. Objective function:
$z = x + 2y$
Constraints:
$x \geq 0$
$y \geq 0$
$x + 2y \leq 4$
$2x + y \leq 4$

Synthesis

True or False? In Exercises 49 and 50, determine whether the statement is true or false. Justify your answer.

49. If an objective function has a maximum value at the vertices $(4, 7)$ and $(8, 3)$, you can conclude that it also has a maximum value at the points $(4.5, 6.5)$ and $(7.8, 3.2)$.

50. When solving a linear programming problem, if the objective function has a maximum value at more than one vertex, you can assume that there are an infinite number of points that will produce the maximum value.

In Exercises 51 and 52, determine values of t such that the objective function has maximum values at the indicated vertices.

51. Objective function:

$z = 3x + ty$

Constraints:

$$x \geq 0$$
$$y \geq 0$$
$$x + 3y \leq 15$$
$$4x + y \leq 16$$

(a) $(0, 5)$

(b) $(3, 4)$

52. Objective function:

$z = 3x + ty$

Constraints:

$$x \geq 0$$
$$y \geq 0$$
$$x + 2y \leq 4$$
$$x - y \leq 1$$

(a) $(2, 1)$

(b) $(0, 2)$

Think About It In Exercises 53–56, find an objective function that has a maximum or minimum value at the indicated vertex of the constraint region shown below. (There are many correct answers.)

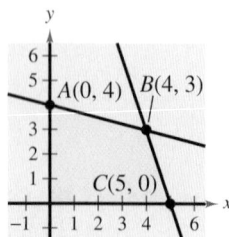

53. The maximum occurs at vertex A.

54. The maximum occurs at vertex B.

55. The maximum occurs at vertex C.

56. The minimum occurs at vertex C.

Review

In Exercises 57–60, simplify the compound fraction.

57. $\dfrac{\left(\dfrac{9}{x}\right)}{\left(\dfrac{6}{x} + 2\right)}$

58. $\dfrac{\left(1 + \dfrac{2}{x}\right)}{\left(x - \dfrac{4}{x}\right)}$

59. $\dfrac{\left(\dfrac{4}{x^2 - 9} + \dfrac{2}{x - 2}\right)}{\left(\dfrac{1}{x + 3} + \dfrac{1}{x - 3}\right)}$

60. $\dfrac{\left(\dfrac{1}{x + 1} + \dfrac{1}{2}\right)}{\left(\dfrac{3}{2x^2 + 4x + 2}\right)}$

In Exercises 61–66, solve the equation algebraically. Round the result to three decimal places.

61. $e^{2x} + 2e^x - 15 = 0$

62. $e^{2x} - 10e^x + 24 = 0$

63. $8(62 - e^{x/4}) = 192$

64. $\dfrac{150}{e^{-x} - 4} = 75$

65. $7 \ln 3x = 12$

66. $\ln(x + 9)^2 = 2$

In Exercises 67 and 68, solve the system of linear equations and check any solution algebraically.

67. $\begin{cases} -x - 2y + 3z = -23 \\ 2x + 6y - z = 17 \\ 5y + z = 8 \end{cases}$

68. $\begin{cases} 7x - 3y + 5z = -28 \\ 4x + 4z = -16 \\ 7x + 2y - z = 0 \end{cases}$

Chapter Summary

▶ *What* did you learn?

Exercise containing system with no solution: 22; Exercises containing systems with infinitely many solutions: 21, 33, 35, 36; Exercises with unbounded regions: 66, 67, 70

Review Exercises

7.1 In Exercises 1–4, solve the system by the method of substitution.

1. $\begin{cases} x^2 - y^2 = 9 \\ x - y = 1 \end{cases}$

2. $\begin{cases} x^2 + y^2 = 169 \\ 3x + 2y = 39 \end{cases}$

3. $\begin{cases} y = 2x^2 \\ y = x^4 - 2x^2 \end{cases}$

4. $\begin{cases} x = y + 3 \\ x = y^2 + 1 \end{cases}$

In Exercises 5–8, solve the system graphically.

5. $\begin{cases} 2x - y = 10 \\ x + 5y = -6 \end{cases}$

6. $\begin{cases} y^2 - 2y + x = 0 \\ x + y = 0 \end{cases}$

7. $\begin{cases} y = 2x^2 - 4x + 1 \\ y = x^2 - 4x + 3 \end{cases}$

8. $\begin{cases} y = 2(6 - x) \\ y = 2^{x-2} \end{cases}$

In Exercises 9 and 10, use a graphing utility to solve the system of equations. Find the solution accurate to two decimal places.

9. $\begin{cases} y = -2e^{-x} \\ 2e^x + y = 0 \end{cases}$

10. $\begin{cases} y = \ln(x - 1) - 3 \\ y = 4 - \frac{1}{2}x \end{cases}$

11. **Break-Even Analysis** You set up a business and make an initial investment of $50,000. The unit cost of the product is $2.15 and the selling price is $6.95. How many units must you sell to break even?

12. **Choice of Two Jobs** You are offered two sales jobs. One company offers an annual salary of $22,500 plus a year-end bonus of 1.5% of your total sales. The other company offers an annual salary of $20,000 plus a year-end bonus of 2% of your total sales. What amount of sales will make the second offer better? Explain.

13. **Geometry** The perimeter of a rectangle is 480 meters and its length is 150% of its width. Find the dimensions of the rectangle.

14. **Geometry** The perimeter of a rectangle is 68 feet and its width is $\frac{8}{9}$ times its length. Find the dimensions of the rectangle.

7.2 In Exercises 15–22, solve the system by elimination.

15. $\begin{cases} 2x - y = 2 \\ 6x + 8y = 39 \end{cases}$

16. $\begin{cases} 40x + 30y = 24 \\ 20x - 50y = -14 \end{cases}$

17. $\begin{cases} 0.2x + 0.3y = 0.14 \\ 0.4x + 0.5y = 0.20 \end{cases}$

18. $\begin{cases} 12x + 42y = -17 \\ 30x - 18y = 19 \end{cases}$

19. $\begin{cases} 3x - 2y = 0 \\ 3x + 2(y + 5) = 10 \end{cases}$

20. $\begin{cases} 7x + 12y = 63 \\ 2x + 3(y + 2) = 21 \end{cases}$

21. $\begin{cases} 1.25x - 2y = 3.5 \\ 5x - 8y = 14 \end{cases}$

22. $\begin{cases} 1.5x + 2.5y = 8.5 \\ 6x + 10y = 24 \end{cases}$

In Exercises 23–26, match the system of linear equations with its graph. [The graphs are labeled (a), (b), (c), and (d).]

(a)

(b)

(c)

(d)
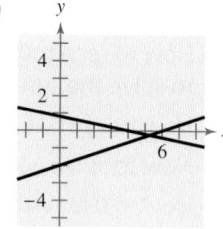

23. $\begin{cases} x + 5y = 4 \\ x - 3y = 6 \end{cases}$

24. $\begin{cases} -3x + y = -7 \\ 9x - 3y = 21 \end{cases}$

25. $\begin{cases} 3x - y = 7 \\ -6x + 2y = 8 \end{cases}$

26. $\begin{cases} 2x - y = -3 \\ x + 5y = 4 \end{cases}$

Supply and Demand In Exercises 27 and 28, find the equilibrium point.

Demand Function	Supply Function
27. $p = 37 - 0.0002x$	$p = 22 + 0.00001x$
28. $p = 120 - 0.0001x$	$p = 45 + 0.0002x$

7.3 In Exercises 29 and 30, use back-substitution to solve the system.

29. $\begin{cases} x - 4y + 3z = 3 \\ -y + z = -1 \\ z = -5 \end{cases}$

30. $\begin{cases} x - 7y + 8z = 85 \\ y - 9z = -35 \\ z = 3 \end{cases}$

In Exercises 31–34, use Gaussian elimination to solve the system of equations.

31.
$$\begin{cases} x + 2y + 6z = 4 \\ -3x + 2y - z = -4 \\ 4x \quad\quad + 2z = 16 \end{cases}$$

32.
$$\begin{cases} x + 3y - z = 13 \\ 2x \quad\quad - 5z = 23 \\ 4x - y - 2z = 14 \end{cases}$$

33.
$$\begin{cases} x - 2y + z = -6 \\ 2x - 3y \quad = -7 \\ -x + 3y - 3z = 11 \end{cases}$$

34.
$$\begin{cases} 2x \quad\quad + 6z = -9 \\ 3x - 2y + 11z = -16 \\ 3x - y + 7z = -11 \end{cases}$$

In Exercises 35 and 36, solve the nonsquare system of equations.

35.
$$\begin{cases} 5x - 12y + 7z = 16 \\ 3x - 7y + 4z = 9 \end{cases}$$

36.
$$\begin{cases} 2x + 5y - 19z = 34 \\ 3x + 8y - 31z = 54 \end{cases}$$

In Exercises 37 and 38, find the equation of the parabola $y = ax^2 + bx + c$ that passes through the points. Use a graphing utility to verify your result.

37.

38.
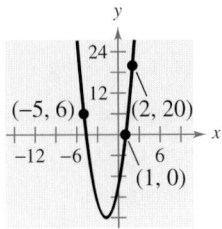

In Exercises 39 and 40, find the equation of the circle $x^2 + y^2 + Dx + Ey + F = 0$ that passes through the points. Use a graphing utility to verify your result.

39.

40.
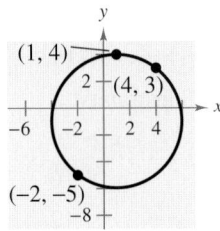

In Exercises 41–44, write the partial fraction decomposition of the rational expression.

41. $\dfrac{4 - x}{x^2 + 6x + 8} = \dfrac{A}{x + 4} + \dfrac{B}{x + 2}$

42. $\dfrac{9}{x^2 - 9} = \dfrac{A}{x + 3} + \dfrac{B}{x - 3}$

43. $\dfrac{x}{x^2 + 3x + 2} = \dfrac{A}{x + 1} + \dfrac{B}{x + 2}$

44. $\dfrac{x^2}{x^2 + 2x - 15} = \dfrac{A}{x + 5} + \dfrac{B}{x - 3}$

45. *Data Analysis* The table shows the numbers y (in thousands) of DVD players sold in the United States for the years 1998 through 2000. (Source: Electronics Industries Association)

Year, x	DVD players sold, y
1998	1079
1999	4072
2000	8258

(a) Use the technique demonstrated in Exercises 67–70 in Section 7.3 to find a least squares regression parabola that models the data. Let x represent the year, with $x = 8$ corresponding to 1998.

(b) Use a graphing utility to graph the parabola and the data in the same viewing window. How well does the model fit the data?

(c) Use the model to estimate the number of DVD players sold in 2005. Does your answer seem reasonable?

46. *Agriculture* A mixture of 6 gallons of chemical A, 8 gallons of chemical B, and 13 gallons of chemical C is required to kill a destructive crop insect. Commercial spray X contains 1, 2, and 2 parts, respectively, of these chemicals. Commercial spray Y contains only chemical C. Commercial spray Z contains chemicals A, B, and C in equal amounts. How much of each type of commercial spray is needed to get the desired mixture?

47. *Investment Analysis* An inheritance of $40,000 was divided among three investments yielding $3500 in interest per year. The interest rates for the three investments were 7%, 9%, and 11%. Find the amount placed in each investment if the second and third were $3000 and $5000 less than the first, respectively.

48. *Vertical Motion* An object moving vertically is at the given heights at the specified times. Find the position equation $s = \frac{1}{2}at^2 + v_0t + s_0$ for the object.

(a) At $t = 1$ second, $s = 134$ feet

   At $t = 2$ seconds, $s = 86$ feet

   At $t = 3$ seconds, $s = 6$ feet

(b) At $t = 1$ second, $s = 184$ feet

   At $t = 2$ seconds, $s = 116$ feet

   At $t = 3$ seconds, $s = 16$ feet

7.4 In Exercises 49–52, sketch the graph of the inequality.

49. $y \le 5 - \frac{1}{2}x$

50. $3y - x \ge 7$

51. $y - 4x^2 > -1$

52. $y \le \dfrac{3}{x^2 + 2}$

In Exercises 53–60, sketch a graph and label the vertices of the solution set of the system of inequalities.

53.
$\begin{cases} x + 2y \le 160 \\ 3x + \ y \le 180 \\ \quad\ x \ge \ \ 0 \\ \quad\ y \ge \ \ 0 \end{cases}$

54.
$\begin{cases} 2x + 3y \le 24 \\ 2x + \ y \le 16 \\ \quad\ x \ge \ 0 \\ \quad\ y \ge \ 0 \end{cases}$

55.
$\begin{cases} 3x + 2y \ge 24 \\ \ x + 2y \ge 12 \\ 2 \le x \le 15 \\ \quad\ y \le 15 \end{cases}$

56.
$\begin{cases} 2x + \ y \ge 16 \\ \ x + 3y \ge 18 \\ 0 \le x \le 25 \\ 0 \le y \le 25 \end{cases}$

57.
$\begin{cases} y < x + 1 \\ y > x^2 - 1 \end{cases}$

58.
$\begin{cases} y \le 6 - 2x - x^2 \\ y \ge x + 6 \end{cases}$

59.
$\begin{cases} 2x - 3y \ge 0 \\ 2x - \ y \le 8 \\ \quad\ y \ge 0 \end{cases}$

60.
$\begin{cases} x^2 + y^2 \le 9 \\ (x - 3)^2 + y^2 \le 9 \end{cases}$

In Exercises 61 and 62, determine a system of inequalities that models the description. Use a graphing utility to graph and shade the solution of the system.

61. *Fruit Distribution* A Pennsylvania fruit grower has 1500 bushels of apples that are to be divided between markets in Harrisburg and Philadelphia. These two markets need at least 400 bushels and 600 bushels, respectively.

62. *Inventory Costs* A warehouse operator has 24,000 square feet of floor space in which to store two products. Each unit of product I requires 20 square feet of floor space and costs $12 per day to store. Each unit of product II requires 30 square feet of

floor space and costs $8 per day to store. The total storage cost per day cannot exceed $12,400.

Supply and Demand In Exercises 63 and 64, find the consumer surplus and producer surplus for the demand and supply equations. Sketch the graph of the equations and shade the regions representing the consumer surplus and producer surplus.

	Demand	*Supply*
63.	$p = 160 - 0.0001x$	$p = 70 + 0.0002x$
64.	$p = 130 - 0.0002x$	$p = 30 + 0.0003x$

7.5 In Exercises 65–70, sketch the region determined by the constraints. Then find the minimum and maximum values of the objective function and where they occur, subject to the indicated restraints.

65. Objective function:

$z = 3x + 4y$

Constraints:

$x \ge \ 0$

$y \ge \ 0$

$2x + 5y \le 50$

$4x + \ y \le 28$

66. Objective function:

$z = 10x + 7y$

Constraints:

$x \ge \ \ 0$

$y \ge \ \ 0$

$2x + y \ge 100$

$x + y \ge \ 75$

67. Objective function:

$z = 1.75x + 2.25y$

Constraints:

$x \ge \ 0$

$y \ge \ 0$

$2x + \ y \ge 25$

$3x + 2y \ge 45$

68. Objective function:

$z = 50x + 70y$

Constraints:

$x \ge \ \ \ 0$

$y \ge \ \ \ 0$

$x + 2y \le 1500$

$5x + 2y \le 3500$

69. Objective function:

$z = 5x + 11y$

Constraints:

$x \ge \ 0$

$y \ge \ 0$

$x + 3y \le 12$

$3x + 2y \le 15$

70. Objective function:

$z = -2x + y$

Constraints:

$x \ge \ 0$

$y \ge \ 0$

$x + \ y \ge \ 7$

$5x + 2y \ge 20$

71. Maximum Revenue A student is working part time as a hairdresser to pay college expenses. The student may work no more than 24 hours per week. Haircuts cost $25 and require an average of 20 minutes, and permanents cost $70 and require an average of 1 hour and 10 minutes. What combination of haircuts and/or permanents will yield a maximum revenue? What is the maximum revenue?

72. Maximum Profit A shoe manufacturer produces a walking shoe and a running shoe yielding profits of $18 and $24, respectively. Each shoe must go through three processes, for which the required times per unit are shown in the table.

	Process I	Process II	Process III
Hours for Walking Shoe	4	1	1
Hours for Running Shoe	2	2	1
Hours Available per Day	24	9	8

Find the daily production level for each shoe to maximize the profit. What is the maximum profit?

73. Minimum Cost A pet supply company mixes two brands of dry dog food. Brand X costs $15 per bag and contains eight units of nutritional element A, one unit of nutritional element B, and two units of nutritional element C. Brand Y costs $30 per bag and contains two units of nutritional element A, one unit of nutritional element B, and seven units of nutritional element C. Each bag of mixed dog food must contain at least 16 units, 5 units, and 20 units of nutritional elements A, B, and C, respectively. Find the numbers of bags of brands X and Y that should be mixed to produce a mixture meeting the minimum nutritional requirements and having a minimum cost. What is the minimum cost?

74. Minimum Cost Two gasolines, type A and type B, have octane ratings of 87 and 92, respectively. Type A costs $1.25 per gallon and type B costs $1.55 per gallon. Determine the blend of minimum cost with an octane rating of at least 89. What is the minimum cost? (*Hint:* Let x be the fraction of each gallon that is type A and let y be the fraction that is type B.)

Synthesis

True or False? In Exercises 75 and 76, determine whether the statement is true or false. Justify your answer.

75. The system
$$\begin{cases} y \le 5 \\ y \ge -2 \\ y \ge \frac{7}{2}x - 9 \\ y \ge -\frac{7}{2}x + 26 \end{cases}$$
represents the region covered by an isosceles trapezoid.

76. It is possible for an objective function of a linear programming problem to have exactly 10 maximum value points.

In Exercises 77–80, find a system of linear equations having the ordered pair as a solution. (There is more than one correct answer.)

77. $(-6, 8)$
78. $(5, -4)$
79. $\left(\frac{4}{3}, 3\right)$
80. $\left(-1, \frac{9}{4}\right)$

In Exercises 81–84, find a system of linear equations having the ordered triple as a solution. (There is more than one correct answer.)

81. $(4, -1, 3)$
82. $(-3, 5, 6)$
83. $\left(5, \frac{3}{2}, 2\right)$
84. $\left(\frac{3}{4}, -2, 8\right)$

85. Writing Explain what is meant by an inconsistent system of linear equations.

86. How can you tell graphically that a system of linear equations in two variables has no solution? Give an example.

87. Writing Write a brief paragraph describing any advantages of substitution over the graphical method of solving a system of equations.

Chapter Test

The *Interactive* CD-ROM and *Internet* versions of this text offer Chapter Pre-Tests and Chapter Post-Tests, both of which have randomly generated exercises with diagnostic capabilities.

Take this test as you would take a test in class. When you are finished, check your work against the answers given in the back of the book.

In Exercises 1–3, solve the system by the method of substitution.

1. $\begin{cases} x - y = -7 \\ 4x + 5y = 8 \end{cases}$ **2.** $\begin{cases} y = x - 1 \\ y = (x - 1)^3 \end{cases}$ **3.** $\begin{cases} 2x - y^2 = 0 \\ x - y = 4 \end{cases}$

In Exercises 4–6, solve the system graphically.

4. $\begin{cases} 2x - 3y = 0 \\ 2x + 3y = 12 \end{cases}$ **5.** $\begin{cases} y = 9 - x^2 \\ y = x + 3 \end{cases}$ **6.** $\begin{cases} y - \ln x = 12 \\ 7x - 2y + 11 = -6 \end{cases}$

In Exercises 7–10, solve the linear system by elimination.

7. $\begin{cases} 2x + 3y = 17 \\ 5x - 4y = -15 \end{cases}$

8. $\begin{cases} 2.5x - y = 6 \\ 3x + 4y = 2 \end{cases}$

9. $\begin{cases} x - 2y + 3z = 11 \\ 2x \quad\;\; - z = 3 \\ \quad\; 3y + z = -8 \end{cases}$

10. $\begin{cases} 3x + 2y + z = 17 \\ -x + y + z = 4 \\ x - y - z = 3 \end{cases}$

In Exercises 11–13, sketch the graph and label the vertices of the solution of the system of inequalities.

11. $\begin{cases} 2x + y \le 4 \\ 2x - y \ge 0 \\ x \ge 0 \end{cases}$ **12.** $\begin{cases} y < -x^2 + x + 4 \\ y > 4x \end{cases}$ **13.** $\begin{cases} x^2 + y^2 \le 16 \\ x \ge 1 \\ y \ge -3 \end{cases}$

14. Find the maximum value of the objective function $z = 20x + 12y$ and where it occurs, subject to the following constraints.

$$\left. \begin{array}{r} x \ge 0 \\ y \ge 0 \\ x + 4y \le 32 \\ 3x + 2y \le 36 \end{array} \right\} \quad \text{Constraints}$$

15. A total of $50,000 is invested in two funds paying 8% and 8.5% simple interest. The yearly interest is $4150. How much is invested at each rate?

16. Find the equation of the parabola $y = ax^2 + bx + c$ passing through the points $(0, 6)$, $(-2, 2)$, and $\left(3, \frac{9}{2}\right)$.

	Model I	Model II
Assembling	0.5	0.75
Staining	2.0	1.5
Packaging	0.5	0.5

17. A manufacturer produces two types of television stands. The amounts of time for assembling, staining, and packaging the two models are shown in the table at the left. The total amounts of time available for assembling, staining, and packaging are 4000, 8950, and 2650 hours, respectively. The profits per unit are $30 (model I) and $40 (model II). How many of each model should be produced to maximize the profit? What is the maximum profit?

Proofs in Mathematics

An **indirect proof** can be useful in proving statements of the form "p implies q." Recall that the conditional statement $p \rightarrow q$ is false only when p is true and q is false. To prove a conditional statement indirectly, assume that p is true and q is false. If this assumption leads to an impossibility, then you have proved that the conditional statement is true. An indirect proof is also called a **proof by contradiction.**

You can use an indirect proof to prove the conditional statement, "If a is a positive integer and a^2 is divisible by 2, then a is divisible by 2," as follows. Assume that p, "a is a positive integer and a^2 is divisible by 2," is true and q, "a is divisible by 2," is false. This means that a is not divisible by 2. If so, a is odd and can be written as $a = 2n + 1$, where n is an integer.

$$a = 2n + 1 \qquad \text{Definition of an odd integer}$$

$$a^2 = 4n^2 + 4n + 1 \qquad \text{Square each side.}$$

$$a^2 = 2(2n^2 + 2n) + 1 \qquad \text{Distributive Property}$$

So, by the definition of an odd integer, a^2 is odd. This contradicts the assumption, and you can conclude that a is divisible by 2.

Example ▶ Using an Indirect Proof

Use an indirect proof to prove that $\sqrt{2}$ is an irrational number.

Solution

Begin by assuming that $\sqrt{2}$ is *not* an irrational number. Then $\sqrt{2}$ can be written as the quotient of two integers a and $b (b \neq 0)$ that have no common factors.

$$\sqrt{2} = \frac{a}{b} \qquad \text{Assume that } \sqrt{2} \text{ is a rational number.}$$

$$2 = \frac{a^2}{b^2} \qquad \text{Square each side.}$$

$$2b^2 = a^2 \qquad \text{Multiply each side by } b^2.$$

This implies that 2 is a factor of a^2. So, 2 is also a factor of a, and a can be written as $2c$, where c is an integer.

$$2b^2 = (2c)^2 \qquad \text{Substitute } 2c \text{ for } a.$$

$$2b^2 = 4c^2 \qquad \text{Simplify.}$$

$$b^2 = 2c^2 \qquad \text{Divide each side by 2.}$$

This implies that 2 is a factor of b^2 and also a factor of b. So, 2 is a factor of both a and b. This contradicts the assumption that a and b have no common factors. So, you can conclude that $\sqrt{2}$ is an irrational number.

1. A theorem from geometry states that if a triangle is inscribed in a circle such that one side of the triangle is a diameter of the circle, then the triangle is a right triangle. Show that this theorem is true for the circle

$$x^2 + y^2 = 100$$

and the triangle formed by the lines

$y = 0$, $y = \frac{1}{2}x + 5$, and $y = -2x + 20$.

2. Find k_1 and k_2 such that the system of equations has an infinite number of solutions.

$$\begin{cases} 3x - 5y = 8 \\ 2x + k_1 y = k_2 \end{cases}$$

3. Consider the following system of linear equations in x and y.

$$\begin{cases} ax + by = e \\ cx + dy = f \end{cases}$$

Under what conditions will the system have exactly one solution?

4. Graph the lines determined by each system of linear equations. Then use Gaussian elimination to solve each system. At each step of the elimination process, graph the corresponding lines. What do you observe?

(a) $\begin{cases} x - 4y = -3 \\ 5x - 6y = 13 \end{cases}$ (b) $\begin{cases} 2x - 3y = 7 \\ -4x + 6y = -14 \end{cases}$

5. A system of two equations in two unknowns is solved and has a finite number of solutions. Determine the maximum number of solutions of the system satisfying each condition.

(a) Both equations are linear.

(b) One equation is linear and the other is quadratic.

(c) Both equations are quadratic.

6. In the 2000 presidential election, approximately 104.779 million voters divided their votes among four presidential candidates. George W. Bush received 537,000 votes less than Al Gore. Ralph Nader and Pat Buchanan together received 3.18% of the votes. Write and solve a system of equations to find the total number of votes cast for each candidate. Let B represent the total votes cast for Bush, G the total votes cast for Gore, and T the total votes cast for Nader and Buchanan together. (Source: Congressional Quarterly)

7. The Vietnam Veterans Memorial (or "The Wall") in Washington, D.C. was designed by Maya Ying Lin when she was a student at Yale University. This monument has two vertical, triangular sections of black granite with a common side (see figure). The top of each section is level with the ground. The bottoms of the two sections can be approximately modeled by the equations $2x + 50y = -505$ and $2x - 50y = 505$ when the x-axis is superimposed on the top of the wall. Each unit in the coordinate system represents 1 foot. How deep is the memorial at the point where the two sections meet? How long is each section?

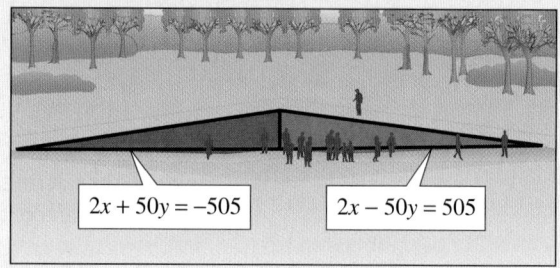

$2x + 50y = -505$ $2x - 50y = 505$

8. Weights of atoms and molecules are measured in atomic mass units (u). A molecule of C_2H_6 (ethane) is made up of two carbon atoms and six hydrogen atoms and weighs 30.07 u. A molecule of C_3H_8 (propane) is made up of three carbon atoms and eight hydrogen atoms and weighs 44.097 u. Find the weights of a carbon atom and a hydrogen atom.

9. To connect a VCR to a television set, a cable with special connectors is required at both ends. You buy a six-foot cable for $15.50 and a three-foot cable for $10.25. Assuming that the cost of a cable is the sum of the cost of the two connectors and the cost of the cable itself, what is the cost of a four-foot cable? Explain your reasoning.

10. A hotel 35 miles from the airport runs a shuttle service to and from the airport. The 9:00 A.M. bus leaves for the airport traveling at 30 miles per hour. The 9:15 A.M. bus leaves for the airport traveling at 40 miles per hour. Write a system of linear equations that represents distance as a function of time for each bus. Graph and solve the system. How far from the airport will the 9:15 A.M. bus catch up to the 9:00 A.M. bus?

11. Solve each system of equations by letting $X = 1/x$, $Y = 1/y$, and $Z = 1/z$.

(a) $\begin{cases} \dfrac{12}{x} - \dfrac{12}{y} = 7 \\ \dfrac{3}{x} + \dfrac{4}{y} = 0 \end{cases}$

(b) $\begin{cases} \dfrac{2}{x} + \dfrac{1}{y} - \dfrac{3}{z} = 4 \\ \dfrac{4}{x} + \dfrac{2}{z} = 10 \\ -\dfrac{2}{x} + \dfrac{3}{y} - \dfrac{13}{z} = -8 \end{cases}$

12. What values should be given to a, b, and c so that the linear system shown has $(-1, 2, -3)$ as its only solution?

$$\begin{cases} x + 2y - 3z = a \\ -x - y + z = b \\ 2x + 3y - 2z = c \end{cases}$$

13. The following system has one solution: $x = 1$, $y = -1$, and $z = 2$.

$$\begin{cases} 4x - 2y + 5z = 16 & \text{Equation 1} \\ x + y = 0 & \text{Equation 2} \\ -x - 3y + 2z = 6 & \text{Equation 3} \end{cases}$$

Solve the system given by (a) Equation 1 and Equation 2, (b) Equation 1 and Equation 3, and (c) Equation 2 and Equation 3. (d) How many solutions does each of these systems have?

14. Each day, an average adult moose can process about 32 kilograms of terrestrial vegetation (twigs and leaves) and aquatic vegetation. From this food, it needs to obtain about 1.9 grams of sodium and 11,000 calories of energy. Aquatic vegetation has about 0.15 gram of sodium per kilogram and about 193 calories of energy per kilogram, whereas terrestrial vegetation has minimal sodium and about four times more energy than aquatic vegetation. Write and graph a system of inequalities that describes the amounts t and a of terrestrial and aquatic vegetation, respectively, for the daily diet of an average adult moose. (Source: *Biology by Numbers*)

15. For a healthy person who is 4 feet 10 inches tall, the recommended minimum weight is about 91 pounds and increases by about 3.7 pounds for each additional inch of height. The recommended maximum weight is about 119 pounds and increases by about 4.9 pounds for each additional inch of height. (Source: Dietary Guidelines Advisory Committee)

(a) Let x be the number of inches by which a person's height exceeds 4 feet 10 inches and let y be the person's weight in pounds. Write a system of inequalities that describes the possible values of x and y for a healthy person.

(b) Use a graphing utility to graph the system of inequalities from part (a).

(c) What is the recommended weight range for someone 6 feet tall?

16. The cholesterol in human blood is necessary, but too much cholesterol can lead to health problems. A blood cholesterol test gives three readings: LDL "bad" cholesterol, HDL "good" cholesterol, and total cholesterol (LDL + HDL). It is recommended that your LDL cholesterol level be less than 130 milligrams per deciliter, your HDL cholesterol level be at least 35 milligrams per deciliter, and your total cholesterol level be no more than 200 milligrams per deciliter. (Source: WebMD, Inc.)

(a) Write a system of linear inequalities for the recommended cholesterol levels. Let x represent HDL cholesterol and let y represent LDL cholesterol.

(b) Graph the system of inequalities from part (a). Label any vertices of the solution region.

(c) Are the following cholesterol levels within recommendations? Explain your reasoning.

LDL: 120 milligrams per deciliter
HDL: 90 milligrams per deciliter
Total: 210 milligrams per deciliter

(d) Give an example of cholesterol levels in which the LDL cholesterol level is too high but the HDL and total cholesterol levels are acceptable.

(e) Another recommendation is that the ratio of total cholesterol to HDL cholesterol be less than 4. Find a point in your solution region from part (b) that meets this recommendation, and show that it does.

How to study Chapter 8

▶ **What you should learn**

In this chapter you will learn the following skills and concepts:

- How to use matrices, Gaussian elimination, and Gauss-Jordan elimination to solve systems of linear equations
- How to add and subtract matrices, multiply matrices by scalars, and multiply two matrices
- How to find the inverses of matrices and use inverse matrices to solve systems of linear equations
- How to find minors, cofactors, and determinants of square matrices
- How to use Cramer's Rule to solve systems of linear equations
- How to use determinants and matrices to model and solve problems

▶ **Important Vocabulary**

As you encounter each new vocabulary term in this chapter, add the term and its definition to your notebook glossary.

Matrix (p. 544)
Entry of a matrix (p. 544)
Order of a matrix (p. 544)
Square matrix (p. 544)
Main diagonal (p. 544)
Row matrix (p. 544)
Column matrix (p. 544)
Augmented matrix (p. 545)
Coefficient matrix (p. 545)
Elementary row operations (p. 546)
Row-equivalent matrices (p. 546)
Row-echelon form (p. 548)

Reduced row-echelon form (p. 548)
Gauss-Jordan elimination (p. 551)
Scalars (p. 560)
Scalar multiple (p. 560)
Zero matrix (p. 563)
Matrix multiplication (p. 564)
Identity matrix of order n (p. 566)
Inverse of a matrix (p. 573)
Determinant (pp. 577, 582)
Minors (p. 584)
Cofactors (p. 584)
Cramer's Rule (p. 590)

Study Tools

Learning objectives in each section
Chapter Summary (p. 602)
Review Exercises (pp. 603–607)
Chapter Test (p. 608)

Additional Resources

Study and Solutions Guide
Interactive Precalculus
Videotapes/DVD for Chapter 8
Precalculus Website
Student Success Organizer

Layne Kennedy/Corbis

Matrices and Determinants

8

8.1 Matrices and Systems of Equations

▶ **What you should learn**

- How to write a matrix and identify its order
- How to perform elementary row operations on matrices
- How to use matrices and Gaussian elimination to solve systems of linear equations
- How to use matrices and Gauss-Jordan elimination to solve systems of linear equations

▶ **Why you should learn it**

You can use matrices to solve systems of linear equations in two or more variables. For instance, in Exercise 90 on page 557, you will use a matrix to find a model for the retail sales for drug stores in the United States.

Larry Mulvehill/The Image Works

Matrices

In this section you will study a streamlined technique for solving systems of linear equations. This technique involves the use of a rectangular array of real numbers called a **matrix.** The plural of matrix is *matrices*.

Definition of Matrix

If m and n are positive integers, an $m \times n$ (read "m by n") matrix is a rectangular array

$$
\begin{array}{c}
\text{Row 1} \\
\text{Row 2} \\
\text{Row 3} \\
\vdots \\
\text{Row } m
\end{array}
\begin{bmatrix}
a_{11} & a_{12} & a_{13} & \cdots & a_{1n} \\
a_{21} & a_{22} & a_{23} & \cdots & a_{2n} \\
a_{31} & a_{32} & a_{33} & \cdots & a_{3n} \\
\vdots & \vdots & \vdots & & \vdots \\
a_{m1} & a_{m2} & a_{m3} & \cdots & a_{mn}
\end{bmatrix}
$$

Column 1 Column 2 Column 3 $\cdots$ Column n

in which each **entry,** a_{ij}, of the matrix is a number. An $m \times n$ matrix has m rows and n columns.

The entry in the ith row and jth column is denoted by the *double subscript* notation a_{ij}. For instance, a_{23} refers to the entry in the second row, third column. A matrix having m rows and n columns is said to be of **order** $m \times n$. If $m = n$, the matrix is **square** of order n. For a square matrix, the entries $a_{11}, a_{22}, a_{33}, \ldots$ are the **main diagonal** entries.

Example 1 ▶ Order of Matrices

Determine the order of each matrix.

a. $\begin{bmatrix} 2 \end{bmatrix}$ 　　　　**b.** $\begin{bmatrix} 1 & -3 & 0 & \frac{1}{2} \end{bmatrix}$

c. $\begin{bmatrix} 0 & 0 \\ 0 & 0 \end{bmatrix}$ 　　**d.** $\begin{bmatrix} 5 & 0 \\ 2 & -2 \\ -7 & 4 \end{bmatrix}$

Solution

a. This matrix has *one* row and *one* column. The order of the matrix is 1×1.

b. This matrix has *one* row and *four* columns. The order of the matrix is 1×4.

c. This matrix has *two* rows and *two* columns. The order of the matrix is 2×2.

d. This matrix has *three* rows and *two* columns. The order of the matrix is 3×2.

A matrix that has only one row is called a **row matrix,** and a matrix that has only one column is called a **column matrix.**

The icon identifies examples and concepts related to features of the Learning Tools CD-ROM and the *Interactive* and *Internet* versions of this text. For more details see the chart on pages *xxi-xxv*.

A matrix derived from a system of linear equations (each written in standard form with the constant term on the right) is the **augmented matrix** of the system. Moreover, the matrix derived from the coefficients of the system (but not including the constant terms) is the **coefficient matrix** of the system.

$$\text{System} \quad \begin{cases} x - 4y + 3z = 5 \\ -x + 3y - z = -3 \\ 2x \quad\quad - 4z = 6 \end{cases}$$

$$\text{Augmented Matrix} \quad \begin{bmatrix} 1 & -4 & 3 & \vdots & 5 \\ -1 & 3 & -1 & \vdots & -3 \\ 2 & 0 & -4 & \vdots & 6 \end{bmatrix}$$

$$\text{Coefficient Matrix} \quad \begin{bmatrix} 1 & -4 & 3 \\ -1 & 3 & -1 \\ 2 & 0 & -4 \end{bmatrix}$$

Note the use of 0 for the missing y-variable in the third equation, and also note the fourth column of constant terms in the augmented matrix.

When forming either the coefficient matrix or the augmented matrix of a system, you should begin by vertically aligning the variables in the equations and using zeros for the missing variables.

Example 2 ▶ Writing an Augmented Matrix

Write the augmented matrix for the system of linear equations.

$$\begin{cases} x + 3y - w = 9 \\ -y + 4z + 2w = -2 \\ x - 5z - 6w = 0 \\ 2x + 4y - 3z = 4 \end{cases}$$

What is the order of the augmented matrix?

Solution

Begin by rewriting the linear system and aligning the variables.

$$\begin{cases} x + 3y \quad\quad - w = 9 \\ -y + 4z + 2w = -2 \\ x \quad\quad - 5z - 6w = 0 \\ 2x + 4y - 3z \quad\quad = 4 \end{cases}$$

Next, use the coefficients as the matrix entries. Include zeros for the missing coefficients.

$$\begin{matrix} R_1 \\ R_2 \\ R_3 \\ R_4 \end{matrix} \begin{bmatrix} 1 & 3 & 0 & -1 & \vdots & 9 \\ 0 & -1 & 4 & 2 & \vdots & -2 \\ 1 & 0 & -5 & -6 & \vdots & 0 \\ 2 & 4 & -3 & 0 & \vdots & 4 \end{bmatrix}$$

The augmented matrix has four rows and five columns, so it is a 4×5 matrix. The notation R_n is used to designate each row in the matrix. For example, Row 1 is represented by R_1.

Elementary Row Operations

In Section 7.3, you studied three operations that can be used on a system of linear equations to produce an equivalent system.

1. Interchange two equations.

2. Multiply an equation by a nonzero constant.

3. Add a multiple of an equation to another equation.

In matrix terminology, these three operations correspond to **elementary row operations.** An elementary row operation on an augmented matrix of a given system of linear equations produces a new augmented matrix corresponding to a new (but equivalent) system of linear equations. Two matrices are **row-equivalent** if one can be obtained from the other by a sequence of elementary row operations.

Elementary Row Operations

1. Interchange two rows.

2. Multiply a row by a nonzero constant.

3. Add a multiple of a row to another row.

Students should recognize that the elementary row operations are essentially the same as the operations that led to equivalent systems of equations in Chapter 7.

Although elementary row operations are simple to perform, they involve a lot of arithmetic. Because it is easy to make a mistake, you should get in the habit of noting the elementary row operations performed in each step so that you can go back and check your work.

Example 3 ▶ **Elementary Row Operations**

a. Interchange the first and second rows.

Original Matrix

$$\begin{bmatrix} 0 & 1 & 3 & 4 \\ -1 & 2 & 0 & 3 \\ 2 & -3 & 4 & 1 \end{bmatrix}$$

New Row-Equivalent Matrix

$$\begin{matrix} R_2 \\ R_1 \end{matrix} \begin{bmatrix} -1 & 2 & 0 & 3 \\ 0 & 1 & 3 & 4 \\ 2 & -3 & 4 & 1 \end{bmatrix}$$

b. Multiply the first row by $\frac{1}{2}$.

Original Matrix

$$\begin{bmatrix} 2 & -4 & 6 & -2 \\ 1 & 3 & -3 & 0 \\ 5 & -2 & 1 & 2 \end{bmatrix}$$

New Row-Equivalent Matrix

$$\frac{1}{2}R_1 \rightarrow \begin{bmatrix} 1 & -2 & 3 & -1 \\ 1 & 3 & -3 & 0 \\ 5 & -2 & 1 & 2 \end{bmatrix}$$

c. Add -2 times the first row to the third row.

Original Matrix

$$\begin{bmatrix} 1 & 2 & -4 & 3 \\ 0 & 3 & -2 & -1 \\ 2 & 1 & 5 & -2 \end{bmatrix}$$

New Row-Equivalent Matrix

$$\begin{bmatrix} 1 & 2 & -4 & 3 \\ 0 & 3 & -2 & -1 \\ 0 & -3 & 13 & -8 \end{bmatrix}$$

$-2R_1 + R_3 \rightarrow$

Note that the elementary row operation is written beside the row that is *changed*.

> **Technology**
>
> Most graphing utilities can perform elementary row operations on matrices. Consult the user's guide for your graphing utility for the required keystrokes.
>
> After performing a row operation, the new row-equivalent matrix that is displayed on your graphing utility is stored in the *answer* variable. You should use the *answer* variable and not the original matrix for subsequent row operations.

In Example 3 in Section 7.3, you used Gaussian elimination with back-substitution to solve a system of linear equations. The next example demonstrates the matrix version of Gaussian elimination. The two methods are essentially the same. The basic difference is that with matrices you do not need to keep writing the variables.

Example 4 ▶ Comparing Linear Systems and Matrix Operations

Arithmetic errors are often made when elementary row operations are performed. Have students note the operation performed in each step so that they can go back and check their work.

Linear System

$$\begin{cases} x - 2y + 3z = 9 \\ -x + 3y = -4 \\ 2x - 5y + 5z = 17 \end{cases}$$

Associated Augmented Matrix

$$\begin{bmatrix} 1 & -2 & 3 & \vdots & 9 \\ -1 & 3 & 0 & \vdots & -4 \\ 2 & -5 & 5 & \vdots & 17 \end{bmatrix}$$

Add the first equation to the second equation.

$$\begin{cases} x - 2y + 3z = 9 \\ y + 3z = 5 \\ 2x - 5y + 5z = 17 \end{cases}$$

Add the first row to the second row.

$$R_1 + R_2 \rightarrow \begin{bmatrix} 1 & -2 & 3 & \vdots & 9 \\ 0 & 1 & 3 & \vdots & 5 \\ 2 & -5 & 5 & \vdots & 17 \end{bmatrix}$$

Add -2 times the first equation to the third equation.

$$\begin{cases} x - 2y + 3z = 9 \\ y + 3z = 5 \\ -y - z = -1 \end{cases}$$

Add -2 times the first row to the third row.

$$-2R_1 + R_3 \rightarrow \begin{bmatrix} 1 & -2 & 3 & \vdots & 9 \\ 0 & 1 & 3 & \vdots & 5 \\ 0 & -1 & -1 & \vdots & -1 \end{bmatrix}$$

Add the second equation to the third equation.

$$\begin{cases} x - 2y + 3z = 9 \\ y + 3z = 5 \\ 2z = 4 \end{cases}$$

Add the second row to the third row.

$$R_2 + R_3 \rightarrow \begin{bmatrix} 1 & -2 & 3 & \vdots & 9 \\ 0 & 1 & 3 & \vdots & 5 \\ 0 & 0 & 2 & \vdots & 4 \end{bmatrix}$$

Multiply the third equation by $\frac{1}{2}$.

$$\begin{cases} x - 2y + 3z = 9 \\ y + 3z = 5 \\ z = 2 \end{cases}$$

Multiply the third row by $\frac{1}{2}$.

$$\tfrac{1}{2}R_3 \rightarrow \begin{bmatrix} 1 & -2 & 3 & \vdots & 9 \\ 0 & 1 & 3 & \vdots & 5 \\ 0 & 0 & 1 & \vdots & 2 \end{bmatrix}$$

At this point, you can use back-substitution to find x and y.

$$y + 3(2) = 5 \qquad \text{Substitute 2 for } z.$$

$$y = -1 \qquad \text{Solve for } y.$$

$$x - 2(-1) + 3(2) = 9 \qquad \text{Substitute } -1 \text{ for } y \text{ and 2 for } z.$$

$$x = 1 \qquad \text{Solve for } x.$$

The solution is $x = 1$, $y = -1$, and $z = 2$.

Remember that you can check a solution by substituting the values of x, y, and z into each equation in the original system.

The last matrix in Example 4 is said to be in **row-echelon form.** The term *echelon* refers to the stair-step pattern formed by the nonzero elements of the matrix. To be in this form, a matrix must have the following properties.

Row-Echelon Form and Reduced Row-Echelon Form

A matrix in **row-echelon form** has the following properties.

1. All rows consisting entirely of zeros occur at the bottom of the matrix.

2. For each row that does not consist entirely of zeros, the first nonzero entry is 1 (called a leading 1).

3. For two successive (nonzero) rows, the leading 1 in the higher row is farther to the left than the leading 1 in the lower row.

A matrix in *row-echelon form* is in **reduced row-echelon form** if every column that has a leading 1 has zeros in every position above and below its leading 1.

Example 5 ▶   **Row-Echelon Form**

The following matrices are in row-echelon form.

a.
$$\begin{bmatrix} 1 & 2 & -1 & 4 \\ 0 & 1 & 0 & 3 \\ 0 & 0 & 1 & -2 \end{bmatrix}$$
b.
$$\begin{bmatrix} 0 & 1 & 0 & 5 \\ 0 & 0 & 1 & 3 \\ 0 & 0 & 0 & 0 \end{bmatrix}$$

c.
$$\begin{bmatrix} 1 & -5 & 2 & -1 & 3 \\ 0 & 0 & 1 & 3 & -2 \\ 0 & 0 & 0 & 1 & 4 \\ 0 & 0 & 0 & 0 & 1 \end{bmatrix}$$
d.
$$\begin{bmatrix} 1 & 0 & 0 & -1 \\ 0 & 1 & 0 & 2 \\ 0 & 0 & 1 & 3 \\ 0 & 0 & 0 & 0 \end{bmatrix}$$

The matrices in (b) and (d) also happen to be in *reduced* row-echelon form. The following matrices are not in row-echelon form.

e.
$$\begin{bmatrix} 1 & 2 & -3 & 4 \\ 0 & 2 & 1 & -1 \\ 0 & 0 & 1 & -3 \end{bmatrix}$$
f.
$$\begin{bmatrix} 1 & 2 & -1 & 2 \\ 0 & 0 & 0 & 0 \\ 0 & 1 & 2 & -4 \end{bmatrix}$$

For the matrix in (e), the first nonzero row entry in Row 2 is not 1. For the matrix in (f), the row that consists entirely of zeros is not at the bottom of the matrix.

Every matrix is row-equivalent to a matrix in row-echelon form. For instance, in Example 5, you can change the matrix in part (e) to row-echelon form by multiplying its second row by $\frac{1}{2}$.

$$\frac{1}{2}R_2 \rightarrow \begin{bmatrix} 1 & 2 & -3 & 4 \\ 0 & 1 & \frac{1}{2} & -\frac{1}{2} \\ 0 & 0 & 1 & -3 \end{bmatrix}$$

What elementary row operation could you perform on the matrix in part (f) so that it would be in row-echelon form?

Gaussian Elimination with Back-Substitution

Gaussian elimination with back-substitution works well for solving systems of linear equations by hand or with a computer. For this algorithm, the order in which the elementary row operations are performed is important. You should operate from left to right by columns, using elementary row operations to obtain zeros in all entries directly below the leading 1's.

Example 6 ▶ **Gaussian Elimination with Back-Substitution**

Solve the system $\begin{cases} y + z - 2w = -3 \\ x + 2y - z = 2 \\ 2x + 4y + z - 3w = -2 \\ x - 4y - 7z - w = -19 \end{cases}$.

Solution

$$\begin{bmatrix} 0 & 1 & 1 & -2 & \vdots & -3 \\ 1 & 2 & -1 & 0 & \vdots & 2 \\ 2 & 4 & 1 & -3 & \vdots & -2 \\ 1 & -4 & -7 & -1 & \vdots & -19 \end{bmatrix}$$ Write augmented matrix.

$\begin{matrix} R_2 \\ R_1 \end{matrix}$ $\begin{bmatrix} 1 & 2 & -1 & 0 & \vdots & 2 \\ 0 & 1 & 1 & -2 & \vdots & -3 \\ 2 & 4 & 1 & -3 & \vdots & -2 \\ 1 & -4 & -7 & -1 & \vdots & -19 \end{bmatrix}$ Interchange R_1 and R_2 so first column has leading 1 in upper left corner.

$\begin{matrix} \\ \\ -2R_1 + R_3 \rightarrow \\ -R_1 + R_4 \rightarrow \end{matrix}$ $\begin{bmatrix} 1 & 2 & -1 & 0 & \vdots & 2 \\ 0 & 1 & 1 & -2 & \vdots & -3 \\ 0 & 0 & 3 & -3 & \vdots & -6 \\ 0 & -6 & -6 & -1 & \vdots & -21 \end{bmatrix}$ Perform operations on R_3 and R_4 so first column has zeros below its leading 1.

$\begin{matrix} \\ \\ \\ 6R_2 + R_4 \rightarrow \end{matrix}$ $\begin{bmatrix} 1 & 2 & -1 & 0 & \vdots & 2 \\ 0 & 1 & 1 & -2 & \vdots & -3 \\ 0 & 0 & 3 & -3 & \vdots & -6 \\ 0 & 0 & 0 & -13 & \vdots & -39 \end{bmatrix}$ Perform operations on R_4 so second column has zeros below its leading 1.

$\begin{matrix} \\ \\ \frac{1}{3}R_3 \rightarrow \\ -\frac{1}{13}R_4 \rightarrow \end{matrix}$ $\begin{bmatrix} 1 & 2 & -1 & 0 & \vdots & 2 \\ 0 & 1 & 1 & -2 & \vdots & -3 \\ 0 & 0 & 1 & -1 & \vdots & -2 \\ 0 & 0 & 0 & 1 & \vdots & 3 \end{bmatrix}$ Perform operations on R_3 and R_4 so third and fourth columns have leading 1's.

The matrix is now in row-echelon form, and the corresponding system is

$$\begin{cases} x + 2y - z = 2 \\ y + z - 2w = -3 \\ z - w = -2 \\ w = 3. \end{cases}$$

Using back-substitution, the solution is $x = -1$, $y = 2$, $z = 1$, and $w = 3$.

The procedure for using Gaussian elimination with back-substitution is summarized below.

Gaussian Elimination with Back-Substitution

1. Write the augmented matrix of the system of linear equations.

2. Use elementary row operations to rewrite the augmented matrix in row-echelon form.

3. Write the system of linear equations corresponding to the matrix in row-echelon form, and use back-substitution to find the solution.

When solving a system of linear equations, remember that it is possible for the system to have no solution. If, in the elimination process, you obtain a row with zeros except for the last entry, it is unnecessary to continue the elimination process. You can simply conclude that the system has no solution, or is *inconsistent*.

Example 7 ▶ A System with No Solution

Solve the system $\begin{cases} x - y + 2z = 4 \\ x \quad\;\; + z = 6 \\ 2x - 3y + 5z = 4 \\ 3x + 2y - z = 1 \end{cases}$.

Solution

$$\begin{bmatrix} 1 & -1 & 2 & \vdots & 4 \\ 1 & 0 & 1 & \vdots & 6 \\ 2 & -3 & 5 & \vdots & 4 \\ 3 & 2 & -1 & \vdots & 1 \end{bmatrix}$$

Write augmented matrix.

$$\begin{matrix} \\ -R_1 + R_2 \rightarrow \\ -2R_1 + R_3 \rightarrow \\ -3R_1 + R_4 \rightarrow \end{matrix} \begin{bmatrix} 1 & -1 & 2 & \vdots & 4 \\ 0 & 1 & -1 & \vdots & 2 \\ 0 & -1 & 1 & \vdots & -4 \\ 0 & 5 & -7 & \vdots & -11 \end{bmatrix}$$

Perform row operations.

$$\begin{matrix} \\ \\ R_2 + R_3 \rightarrow \\ \\ \end{matrix} \begin{bmatrix} 1 & -1 & 2 & \vdots & 4 \\ 0 & 1 & -1 & \vdots & 2 \\ 0 & 0 & 0 & \vdots & -2 \\ 0 & 5 & -7 & \vdots & -11 \end{bmatrix}$$

Perform row operations.

Note that the third row of this matrix consists of zeros except for the last entry. This means that the original system of linear equations is inconsistent. You can see why this is true by converting back to a system of linear equations.

$$\begin{cases} x - y + 2z = 4 \\ \quad\;\; y - z = 2 \\ \qquad\quad 0 = -2 \\ \quad\;\; 5y - 7z = -11 \end{cases}$$

Because the third equation is not possible, the system has no solution.

Reinforce the importance of recognizing systems with no solutions or systems with infinitely many solutions from row-echelon matrices.

Gauss-Jordan Elimination

With Gaussian elimination, elementary row operations are applied to a matrix to obtain a (row-equivalent) row-echelon form of the matrix. A second method of elimination, called **Gauss-Jordan elimination,** after Carl Friedrich Gauss and Wilhelm Jordan (1842–1899), continues the reduction process until a *reduced* row-echelon form is obtained. This procedure is demonstrated in Example 8.

Example 8 ▶ Gauss-Jordan Elimination

Use Gauss-Jordan elimination to solve the system $\begin{cases} x - 2y + 3z = 9 \\ -x + 3y = -4. \\ 2x - 5y + 5z = 17 \end{cases}$

Solution

In Example 4, Gaussian elimination was used to obtain the row-echelon form of the linear system above.

$$\begin{bmatrix} 1 & -2 & 3 & \vdots & 9 \\ 0 & 1 & 3 & \vdots & 5 \\ 0 & 0 & 1 & \vdots & 2 \end{bmatrix}$$

Now, apply elementary row operations until you obtain zeros above each of the leading 1's, as follows.

$$2R_2 + R_1 \rightarrow \begin{bmatrix} 1 & 0 & 9 & \vdots & 19 \\ 0 & 1 & 3 & \vdots & 5 \\ 0 & 0 & 1 & \vdots & 2 \end{bmatrix}$$

Perform operations on R_1 so second column has a zero above its leading 1.

$$\begin{matrix} -9R_3 + R_1 \rightarrow \\ -3R_3 + R_2 \rightarrow \end{matrix} \begin{bmatrix} 1 & 0 & 0 & \vdots & 1 \\ 0 & 1 & 0 & \vdots & -1 \\ 0 & 0 & 1 & \vdots & 2 \end{bmatrix}$$

Perform operations on R_1 and R_2 so third column has zeros above its leading 1.

The matrix is now in reduced row-echelon form. Converting back to a system of linear equations, you have

$$\begin{cases} x = 1 \\ y = -1. \\ z = 2 \end{cases}$$

Now you can simply read the solution.

The elimination procedures described in this section sometimes result in fractional coefficients. For instance, in the elimination procedure for the system

$$\begin{cases} 2x - 5y + 5z = 17 \\ 3x - 2y + 3z = 11 \\ -3x + 3y = -6 \end{cases}$$

you may be inclined to multiply the first row by $\frac{1}{2}$ to produce a leading 1, which will result in working with fractional coefficients. You can sometimes avoid fractions by judiciously choosing the order in which you apply elementary row operations.

STUDY TIP

The advantage of using Gauss-Jordan elimination to solve a system of linear equations is that the solution of the system is easily found without using back-substitution, as illustrated in Example 8.

Group Activity Suggestion:
Because it can be difficult for students to find their own errors when applying Gauss-Jordan elimination to matrices, you might consider making up several more examples of common errors to give them additional practice.

| Example 9 ▶ | A System with an Infinite Number of Solutions |

Solve the system.

$$\begin{cases} 2x + 4y - 2z = 0 \\ 3x + 5y = 1 \end{cases}$$

Solution

$$\begin{bmatrix} 2 & 4 & -2 & \vdots & 0 \\ 3 & 5 & 0 & \vdots & 1 \end{bmatrix}$$

$$\tfrac{1}{2}R_1 \rightarrow \begin{bmatrix} 1 & 2 & -1 & \vdots & 0 \\ 3 & 5 & 0 & \vdots & 1 \end{bmatrix}$$

$$-3R_1 + R_2 \rightarrow \begin{bmatrix} 1 & 2 & -1 & \vdots & 0 \\ 0 & -1 & 3 & \vdots & 1 \end{bmatrix}$$

$$-R_2 \rightarrow \begin{bmatrix} 1 & 2 & -1 & \vdots & 0 \\ 0 & 1 & -3 & \vdots & -1 \end{bmatrix}$$

$$-2R_2 + R_1 \rightarrow \begin{bmatrix} 1 & 0 & 5 & \vdots & 2 \\ 0 & 1 & -3 & \vdots & -1 \end{bmatrix}$$

The corresponding system of equations is

$$\begin{cases} x + 5z = 2 \\ y - 3z = -1 \end{cases}$$

Solving for x and y in terms of z, you have

$$x = -5z + 2$$

and

$$y = 3z - 1.$$

To write a solution to the system that does not use any of the three variables of the system, let a represent any real number and let

$$z = a.$$

Now substitute a for z in the equations for x and y.

$$x = -5z + 2 = -5a + 2$$

$$y = 3z - 1 = 3a - 1$$

So, the solution set has the form

$$(-5a + 2, 3a - 1, a)$$

where a is any real number. Try substituting values for a to obtain a few solutions. Then check each solution in the original equation.

STUDY TIP

In Example 9, x and y are solved for in terms of the third variable z. To write a solution to the system that does not use any of the three variables of the system, let a represent any real number and let $z = a$. Then solve for x and y. The solution can then be written in terms of a, which is not one of the variables of the system.

It is worth noting that the row-echelon form of a matrix is not unique. That is, two different sequences of elementary row operations may yield different row-echelon forms. This is demonstrated in Example 10.

Example 10 ▶ **Comparing Row-Echelon Forms**

Compare the following row-echelon form with the one found in Example 4. Is it the same? Does it yield the same solution?

$$\begin{cases} x - 2y + 3z = 9 \\ -x + 3y = -4 \\ 2x - 5y + 5z = 17 \end{cases}$$

$$\begin{bmatrix} 1 & -2 & 3 & \vdots & 9 \\ -1 & 3 & 0 & \vdots & -4 \\ 2 & -5 & 5 & \vdots & 17 \end{bmatrix}$$

$$\begin{matrix} R_2 \\ R_1 \end{matrix} \begin{bmatrix} -1 & 3 & 0 & \vdots & -4 \\ 1 & -2 & 3 & \vdots & 9 \\ 2 & -5 & 5 & \vdots & 17 \end{bmatrix}$$

$$-R_1 \to \begin{bmatrix} 1 & -3 & 0 & \vdots & 4 \\ 1 & -2 & 3 & \vdots & 9 \\ 2 & -5 & 5 & \vdots & 17 \end{bmatrix}$$

$$\begin{matrix} -R_1 + R_2 \to \\ -2R_1 + R_3 \to \end{matrix} \begin{bmatrix} 1 & -3 & 0 & \vdots & 4 \\ 0 & 1 & 3 & \vdots & 5 \\ 0 & 1 & 5 & \vdots & 9 \end{bmatrix}$$

$$-R_2 + R_3 \to \begin{bmatrix} 1 & -3 & 0 & \vdots & 4 \\ 0 & 1 & 3 & \vdots & 5 \\ 0 & 0 & 2 & \vdots & 4 \end{bmatrix}$$

$$\tfrac{1}{2}R_3 \to \begin{bmatrix} 1 & -3 & 0 & \vdots & 4 \\ 0 & 1 & 3 & \vdots & 5 \\ 0 & 0 & 1 & \vdots & 2 \end{bmatrix}$$

Solution

This row-echelon form is different from that obtained in Example 4. The corresponding system of linear equations for this row-echelon matrix is

$$\begin{cases} x - 3y = 4 \\ y + 3z = 5. \\ z = 2 \end{cases}$$

Using back-substitution on this system, you obtain the solution

$$x = 1, y = -1, \text{ and } z = 2$$

which is the same solution that was obtained in Example 4.

You have seen that the row-echelon form of a given matrix *is not* unique; however, the *reduced* row-echelon form of a given matrix *is* unique. Try applying Gauss-Jordan elimination to the row-echelon matrix in Example 10 to see that you obtain the same reduced row-echelon form as in Example 8.

Activities

1. Set up the augmented matrix needed to solve the system.

$$\begin{cases} 2x + 5y - z + w = 13 \\ x - 4y + 3w = 7 \\ 5x + w = 13 \\ x + 2y + 3z = 1 \end{cases}$$

Answer:

$$\begin{bmatrix} 2 & 5 & -1 & 1 & \vdots & 13 \\ 1 & -4 & 0 & 3 & \vdots & 7 \\ 5 & 0 & 0 & 1 & \vdots & 13 \\ 1 & 2 & 3 & 0 & \vdots & 1 \end{bmatrix}$$

2. Use Gauss-Jordan elimination to solve the system.

$$\begin{cases} x + 2y + z = -4 \\ 2x - y + z = -4 \\ x + 3y - z = -7 \end{cases}$$

Answer: $(-3, -1, 1)$

8.1 Exercises

The *Interactive* CD-ROM and *Internet* versions of this text contain step-by-step solutions to all odd-numbered exercises. They also provide Tutorial Exercises for additional help.

Exercises containing systems with no solutions: 57, 69, 70
Exercises containing systems with infinitely many solutions: 58, 65, 66, 67, 68, 71, 72, 75, 76

In Exercises 1–6, determine the order of the matrix.

1. $\begin{bmatrix} 7 & 0 \end{bmatrix}$

2. $\begin{bmatrix} 5 & -3 & 8 & 7 \end{bmatrix}$

3. $\begin{bmatrix} 2 \\ 36 \\ 3 \end{bmatrix}$

4. $\begin{bmatrix} -3 & 7 & 15 & 0 \\ 0 & 0 & 3 & 3 \\ 1 & 1 & 6 & 7 \end{bmatrix}$

5. $\begin{bmatrix} 33 & 45 \\ -9 & 20 \end{bmatrix}$

6. $\begin{bmatrix} -7 & 6 & 4 \\ 0 & -5 & 1 \end{bmatrix}$

In Exercises 7–12, write the augmented matrix for the system of linear equations.

7. $\begin{cases} 4x - 3y = -5 \\ -x + 3y = 12 \end{cases}$

8. $\begin{cases} 7x + 4y = 22 \\ 5x - 9y = 15 \end{cases}$

9. $\begin{cases} x + 10y - 2z = 2 \\ 5x - 3y + 4z = 0 \\ 2x + y = 6 \end{cases}$

10. $\begin{cases} -x - 8y + 5z = 8 \\ -7x - 15z = -38 \\ 3x - y + 8z = 20 \end{cases}$

11. $\begin{cases} 7x - 5y + z = 13 \\ 19x - 8z = 10 \end{cases}$

12. $\begin{cases} 9x + 2y - 3z = 20 \\ -25y + 11z = -5 \end{cases}$

In Exercises 13–18, write the system of linear equations represented by the augmented matrix. (Use variables x, y, z, and w.)

13. $\left[\begin{array}{cc:c} 1 & 2 & 7 \\ 2 & -3 & 4 \end{array}\right]$

14. $\left[\begin{array}{cc:c} 7 & -5 & 0 \\ 8 & 3 & -2 \end{array}\right]$

15. $\left[\begin{array}{ccc:c} 2 & 0 & 5 & -12 \\ 0 & 1 & -2 & 7 \\ 6 & 3 & 0 & 2 \end{array}\right]$

16. $\left[\begin{array}{ccc:c} 4 & -5 & -1 & 18 \\ -11 & 0 & 6 & 25 \\ 3 & 8 & 0 & -29 \end{array}\right]$

17. $\left[\begin{array}{cccc:c} 9 & 12 & 3 & 0 & 0 \\ -2 & 18 & 5 & 2 & 10 \\ 1 & 7 & -8 & 0 & -4 \\ 3 & 0 & 2 & 0 & -10 \end{array}\right]$

18. $\left[\begin{array}{cccc:c} 6 & 2 & -1 & -5 & -25 \\ -1 & 0 & 7 & 3 & 7 \\ 4 & -1 & -10 & 6 & 23 \\ 0 & 8 & 1 & -11 & -21 \end{array}\right]$

In Exercises 19–22, fill in the blank(s) using elementary row operations to form a row-equivalent matrix.

19. $\begin{bmatrix} 1 & 4 & 3 \\ 2 & 10 & 5 \end{bmatrix}$ $\begin{bmatrix} 1 & 4 & 3 \\ 0 & \blacksquare & -1 \end{bmatrix}$

20. $\begin{bmatrix} 3 & 6 & 8 \\ 4 & -3 & 6 \end{bmatrix}$ $\begin{bmatrix} 1 & \blacksquare & \frac{8}{3} \\ 4 & -3 & 6 \end{bmatrix}$

21. $\begin{bmatrix} 1 & 1 & 4 & -1 \\ 3 & 8 & 10 & 3 \\ -2 & 1 & 12 & 6 \end{bmatrix}$

22. $\begin{bmatrix} 2 & 4 & 8 & 3 \\ 1 & -1 & -3 & 2 \\ 2 & 6 & 4 & 9 \end{bmatrix}$

$\begin{bmatrix} 1 & 1 & 4 & -1 \\ 0 & 5 & \blacksquare & \blacksquare \\ 0 & 3 & \blacksquare & \blacksquare \end{bmatrix}$

$\begin{bmatrix} 1 & \blacksquare & \blacksquare & \blacksquare \\ 1 & -1 & -3 & 2 \\ 2 & 6 & 4 & 9 \end{bmatrix}$

$\begin{bmatrix} 1 & 1 & 4 & -1 \\ 0 & 1 & -\frac{2}{5} & \frac{6}{5} \\ 0 & 3 & \blacksquare & \blacksquare \end{bmatrix}$

$\begin{bmatrix} 1 & 2 & 4 & \frac{3}{2} \\ 0 & \blacksquare & -7 & \frac{1}{2} \\ 0 & 2 & \blacksquare & \blacksquare \end{bmatrix}$

In Exercises 23–26, identify the elementary row operation(s) being performed to obtain the new row-equivalent matrix.

Original Matrix   *New Row-Equivalent Matrix*

23. $\begin{bmatrix} -2 & 5 & 1 \\ 3 & -1 & -8 \end{bmatrix}$ $\begin{bmatrix} 13 & 0 & -39 \\ 3 & -1 & -8 \end{bmatrix}$

Original Matrix   *New Row-Equivalent Matrix*

24. $\begin{bmatrix} 3 & -1 & -4 \\ -4 & 3 & 7 \end{bmatrix}$ $\begin{bmatrix} 3 & -1 & -4 \\ 5 & 0 & -5 \end{bmatrix}$

Original Matrix   *New Row-Equivalent Matrix*

25. $\begin{bmatrix} 0 & -1 & -5 & 5 \\ -1 & 3 & -7 & 6 \\ 4 & -5 & 1 & 3 \end{bmatrix}$ $\begin{bmatrix} -1 & 3 & -7 & 6 \\ 0 & -1 & -5 & 5 \\ 0 & 7 & -27 & 27 \end{bmatrix}$

Original Matrix   *New Row-Equivalent Matrix*

26. $\begin{bmatrix} -1 & -2 & 3 & -2 \\ 2 & -5 & 1 & -7 \\ 5 & 4 & -7 & 6 \end{bmatrix}$ $\begin{bmatrix} -1 & -2 & 3 & -2 \\ 0 & -9 & 7 & -11 \\ 0 & -6 & 8 & -4 \end{bmatrix}$

In Exercises 27–30, determine whether the matrix is in row-echelon form. If it is, determine if it is also in reduced row-echelon form.

27. $\begin{bmatrix} 1 & 0 & 0 & 0 \\ 0 & 1 & 1 & 5 \\ 0 & 0 & 0 & 0 \end{bmatrix}$

28. $\begin{bmatrix} 1 & 3 & 0 & 0 \\ 0 & 0 & 1 & 8 \\ 0 & 0 & 0 & 0 \end{bmatrix}$

29. $\begin{bmatrix} 2 & 0 & 4 & 0 \\ 0 & -1 & 3 & 6 \\ 0 & 0 & 1 & 5 \end{bmatrix}$

30. $\begin{bmatrix} 1 & 0 & 2 & 1 \\ 0 & 1 & -3 & 10 \\ 0 & 0 & 1 & 0 \end{bmatrix}$

31. Perform the sequence of row operations on the matrix. What did the operations accomplish?

$$\begin{bmatrix} 1 & 2 & 3 \\ 2 & -1 & -4 \\ 3 & 1 & -1 \end{bmatrix}$$

(a) Add -2 times R_1 to R_2.

(b) Add -3 times R_1 to R_3.

(c) Add -1 times R_2 to R_3.

(d) Multiply R_2 by $-\frac{1}{5}$.

(e) Add -2 times R_2 to R_1.

32. Perform the sequence of row operations on the matrix. What did the operations accomplish?

$$\begin{bmatrix} 7 & 1 \\ 0 & 2 \\ -3 & 4 \\ 4 & 1 \end{bmatrix}$$

(a) Add R_3 to R_4.

(b) Interchange R_1 and R_4.

(c) Add 3 times R_1 to R_3.

(d) Add -7 times R_1 to R_4.

(e) Multiply R_2 by $\frac{1}{2}$.

(f) Add the appropriate multiples of R_2 to R_1, R_3, and R_4.

In Exercises 33–36, write the matrix in row-echelon form. Remember that the row-echelon form of a matrix is not unique.

33. $\begin{bmatrix} 1 & 1 & 0 & 5 \\ -2 & -1 & 2 & -10 \\ 3 & 6 & 7 & 14 \end{bmatrix}$

34. $\begin{bmatrix} 1 & 2 & -1 & 3 \\ 3 & 7 & -5 & 14 \\ -2 & -1 & -3 & 8 \end{bmatrix}$

35. $\begin{bmatrix} 1 & -1 & -1 & 1 \\ 5 & -4 & 1 & 8 \\ -6 & 8 & 18 & 0 \end{bmatrix}$

36. $\begin{bmatrix} 1 & -3 & 0 & -7 \\ -3 & 10 & 1 & 23 \\ 4 & -10 & 2 & -24 \end{bmatrix}$

In Exercises 37–42, use the matrix capabilities of a graphing utility to write the matrix in *reduced* row-echelon form.

37. $\begin{bmatrix} 3 & 3 & 3 \\ -1 & 0 & -4 \\ 2 & 4 & -2 \end{bmatrix}$

38. $\begin{bmatrix} 1 & 3 & 2 \\ 5 & 15 & 9 \\ 2 & 6 & 10 \end{bmatrix}$

39. $\begin{bmatrix} 1 & 2 & 3 & -5 \\ 1 & 2 & 4 & -9 \\ -2 & -4 & -4 & 3 \\ 4 & 8 & 11 & -14 \end{bmatrix}$

40. $\begin{bmatrix} -2 & 3 & -1 & -2 \\ 4 & -2 & 5 & 8 \\ 1 & 5 & -2 & 0 \\ 3 & 8 & -10 & -30 \end{bmatrix}$

41. $\begin{bmatrix} -3 & 5 & 1 & 12 \\ 1 & -1 & 1 & 4 \end{bmatrix}$

42. $\begin{bmatrix} 5 & 1 & 2 & 4 \\ -1 & 5 & 10 & -32 \end{bmatrix}$

In Exercises 43–46, write the system of linear equations represented by the augmented matrix. Then use back-substitution to solve. (Use variables x, y, and z.)

43. $\begin{bmatrix} 1 & -2 & \vdots & 4 \\ 0 & 1 & \vdots & -3 \end{bmatrix}$

44. $\begin{bmatrix} 1 & 5 & \vdots & 0 \\ 0 & 1 & \vdots & -1 \end{bmatrix}$

45. $\begin{bmatrix} 1 & -1 & 2 & \vdots & 4 \\ 0 & 1 & -1 & \vdots & 2 \\ 0 & 0 & 1 & \vdots & -2 \end{bmatrix}$

46. $\begin{bmatrix} 1 & 2 & -2 & \vdots & -1 \\ 0 & 1 & 1 & \vdots & 9 \\ 0 & 0 & 1 & \vdots & -3 \end{bmatrix}$

In Exercises 47–50, an augmented matrix that represents a system of linear equations (in variables x, y, and z) has been reduced using Gauss-Jordan elimination. Write the solution represented by the augmented matrix.

47. $\begin{bmatrix} 1 & 0 & \vdots & 3 \\ 0 & 1 & \vdots & -4 \end{bmatrix}$

48. $\begin{bmatrix} 1 & 0 & \vdots & -6 \\ 0 & 1 & \vdots & 10 \end{bmatrix}$

49. $\begin{bmatrix} 1 & 0 & 0 & \vdots & -4 \\ 0 & 1 & 0 & \vdots & -10 \\ 0 & 0 & 1 & \vdots & 4 \end{bmatrix}$

50. $\begin{bmatrix} 1 & 0 & 0 & \vdots & 5 \\ 0 & 1 & 0 & \vdots & -3 \\ 0 & 0 & 1 & \vdots & 0 \end{bmatrix}$

In Exercises 51–70, use matrices to solve the system of equations (if possible). Use Gaussian elimination with back-substitution or Gauss-Jordan elimination.

51. $\begin{cases} x + 2y = 7 \\ 2x + y = 8 \end{cases}$

52. $\begin{cases} 2x + 6y = 16 \\ 2x + 3y = 7 \end{cases}$

53. $\begin{cases} 3x - 2y = -27 \\ x + 3y = 13 \end{cases}$

54. $\begin{cases} -x + y = 4 \\ 2x - 4y = -34 \end{cases}$

55. $\begin{cases} -2x + 6y = -22 \\ x + 2y = -9 \end{cases}$

56. $\begin{cases} 5x - 5y = -5 \\ -2x - 3y = 7 \end{cases}$

57. $\begin{cases} -x + 2y = 1.5 \\ 2x - 4y = 3 \end{cases}$

58. $\begin{cases} x - 3y = 5 \\ -2x + 6y = -10 \end{cases}$

59. $\begin{cases} x - 3z = -2 \\ 3x + y - 2z = 5 \\ 2x + 2y + z = 4 \end{cases}$

60. $\begin{cases} 2x - y + 3z = 24 \\ 2y - z = 14 \\ 7x - 5y = 6 \end{cases}$

61. $\begin{cases} -x + y - z = -14 \\ 2x - y + z = 21 \\ 3x + 2y + z = 19 \end{cases}$

62. $\begin{cases} 2x + 2y - z = 2 \\ x - 3y + z = -28 \\ -x + y = 14 \end{cases}$

63. $\begin{cases} x + 2y - 3z = -28 \\ 4y + 2z = 0 \\ -x + y - z = -5 \end{cases}$

64. $\begin{cases} 3x - 2y + z = 15 \\ -x + y + 2z = -10 \\ x - y - 4z = 14 \end{cases}$

65. $\begin{cases} x + y - 5z = 3 \\ x - 2z = 1 \\ 2x - y - z = 0 \end{cases}$

66. $\begin{cases} 2x + 3z = 3 \\ 4x - 3y + 7z = 5 \\ 8x - 9y + 15z = 9 \end{cases}$

67. $\begin{cases} x + 2y + z + 2w = 8 \\ 3x + 7y + 6z + 9w = 26 \end{cases}$

68. $\begin{cases} 4x + 12y - 7z - 20w = 22 \\ 3x + 9y - 5z - 28w = 30 \end{cases}$

69. $\begin{cases} -x + y = -22 \\ 3x + 4y = 4 \\ 4x - 8y = 32 \end{cases}$

70. $\begin{cases} x + 2y = 0 \\ x + y = 6 \\ 3x - 2y = 8 \end{cases}$

⚡ **In Exercises 71–76, use the matrix capabilities of a graphing utility to reduce the augmented matrix corresponding to the system of equations, and solve the system.**

71. $\begin{cases} 3x + 3y + 12z = 6 \\ x + y + 4z = 2 \\ 2x + 5y + 20z = 10 \\ -x + 2y + 8z = 4 \end{cases}$

72. $\begin{cases} 2x + 10y + 2z = 6 \\ x + 5y + 2z = 6 \\ x + 5y + z = 3 \\ -3x - 15y - 3z = -9 \end{cases}$

73. $\begin{cases} 2x + y - z + 2w = -6 \\ 3x + 4y + w = 1 \\ x + 5y + 2z + 6w = -3 \\ 5x + 2y - z - w = 3 \end{cases}$

74. $\begin{cases} x + 2y + 2z + 4w = 11 \\ 3x + 6y + 5z + 12w = 30 \\ x + 3y - 3z + 2w = -5 \\ 6x - y - z + w = -9 \end{cases}$

75. $\begin{cases} x + y + z + w = 0 \\ 2x + 3y + z - 2w = 0 \\ 3x + 5y + z = 0 \end{cases}$

76. $\begin{cases} x + 2y + z + 3w = 0 \\ x - y + w = 0 \\ y - z + 2w = 0 \end{cases}$

In Exercises 77–80, determine whether the two systems of linear equations yield the same solutions. If so, find the solutions using matrices.

77. (a) $\begin{cases} x - 2y + z = -6 \\ y - 5z = 16 \\ z = -3 \end{cases}$ (b) $\begin{cases} x + y - 2z = 6 \\ y + 3z = -8 \\ z = -3 \end{cases}$

78. (a) $\begin{cases} x - 3y + 4z = -11 \\ y - z = -4 \\ z = 2 \end{cases}$

(b) $\begin{cases} x + 4y = -11 \\ y + 3z = 4 \\ z = 2 \end{cases}$

79. (a) $\begin{cases} x - 4y + 5z = 27 \\ y - 7z = -54 \\ z = 8 \end{cases}$ (b) $\begin{cases} x - 6y + z = 15 \\ y + 5z = 42 \\ z = 8 \end{cases}$

80. (a) $\begin{cases} x + 3y - z = 19 \\ y + 6z = -18 \\ z = -4 \end{cases}$

(b) $\begin{cases} x - y + 3z = -15 \\ y - 2z = 14 \\ z = -4 \end{cases}$

81. Use the system $\begin{cases} x + 3y + z = 3 \\ x + 5y + 5z = 1 \\ 2x + 6y + 3z = 8 \end{cases}$ to write two different matrices in row-echelon form that yield the same solutions.

82. *Electrical Network* The currents in an electrical network are given by the solution of the system

$$\begin{cases} I_1 - I_2 + I_3 = 0 \\ 3I_1 + 4I_2 = 18 \\ I_2 + 3I_3 = 6 \end{cases}$$

where $I_1, I_2,$ and I_3 are measured in amperes. Solve the system of equations using matrices.

83. *Partial Fractions* Use a system of equations to write the partial fraction decomposition of the rational expression. Solve the system using matrices.

$$\frac{4x^2}{(x+1)^2(x-1)} = \frac{A}{x-1} + \frac{B}{x+1} + \frac{C}{(x+1)^2}$$

84. *Partial Fractions* Use a system of equations to write the partial fraction decomposition of the rational expression. Solve the system using matrices.

$$\frac{8x^2}{(x-1)^2(x+1)} = \frac{A}{x+1} + \frac{B}{x-1} + \frac{C}{(x-1)^2}$$

85. *Finance* A small shoe corporation borrowed $1,500,000 to expand its line of shoes. Some of the money was borrowed at 7%, some at 8%, and some at 10%. Use a system of equations to determine how much was borrowed at each rate if the annual interest was $130,500 and the amount borrowed at 10% was 4 times the amount borrowed at 7%. Solve the system using matrices.

86. *Finance* A small software corporation borrowed $500,000 to expand its software line. Some of the money was borrowed at 9%, some at 10%, and some at 12%. Use a system of equations to determine how much was borrowed at each rate if the annual interest was $52,000 and the amount borrowed at 10% was $2\frac{1}{2}$ times the amount borrowed at 9%. Solve the system using matrices.

In Exercises 87 and 88, use a system of equations to find the specified equation that passes through the points. Solve the system using matrices. Use a graphing utility to verify your results.

87. Parabola:
$y = ax^2 + bx + c$

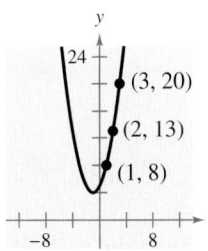

88. Parabola:
$y = ax^2 + bx + c$

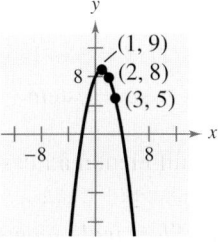

89. *Mathematical Modeling* A videotape of the path of a ball thrown by a baseball player was analyzed with a grid covering the TV screen. The tape was paused three times, and the position of the ball was measured each time. The coordinates obtained are shown in the table. (x and y are measured in feet.)

Horizontal distance, x	Height, y
0	5.0
15	9.6
30	12.4

(a) Use a system of equations to find the equation of the parabola $y = ax^2 + bx + c$ that passes through the three points. Solve the system using matrices.

(b) Use a graphing utility to graph the parabola.

(c) Graphically approximate the maximum height of the ball and the point at which the ball struck the ground.

(d) Analytically find the maximum height of the ball and the point at which the ball struck the ground.

(e) Compare your results from parts (c) and (d).

▶ **Model It**

90. *Data Analysis* The table shows the retail sales y (in billions of dollars) for drug stores in the United States for the years 1998 through 2000. (Source: U.S. Department of Commerce and National Association of Chain Drug Stores Economics Department)

Year, t	Retail sales, y
1998	106.7
1999	122.6
2000	134.4

(a) Use a system of equations to find the equation of the parabola $y = at^2 + bt + c$ that passes through the points. Let $t = 8$ represent 1998. Solve the system using matrices.

(b) Use a graphing utility to graph the parabola.

(c) Use the equation in part (a) to estimate the retail sales in 2001. How does this value compare with the actual 2001 sales of $147.4 billion?

(d) Use the equation in part (a) to estimate y in the year 2004. Is the estimate reasonable? Explain.

Network Analysis   **In Exercises 91 and 92, answer the questions about the specified network. (In a network it is assumed that the total flow into each junction is equal to the total flow out of each junction.)**

91. Water flowing through a network of pipes (in thousands of cubic meters per hour) is shown in the figure.

   (a) Solve this system using matrices for the water flow represented by x_i, $i = 1, 2, \ldots, 7$.

   (b) Find the network flow pattern when $x_6 = x_7 = 0$.

   (c) Find the network flow pattern when $x_5 = 1000$ and $x_6 = 0$.

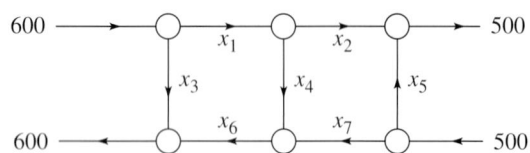

92. The flow of traffic (in vehicles per hour) through a network of streets is shown in the figure.

   (a) Solve this system using matrices for the traffic flow represented by x_i, $i = 1, 2, \ldots, 5$.

   (b) Find the traffic flow when $x_2 = 200$ and $x_3 = 50$.

   (c) Find the traffic flow when $x_2 = 150$ and $x_3 = 0$.

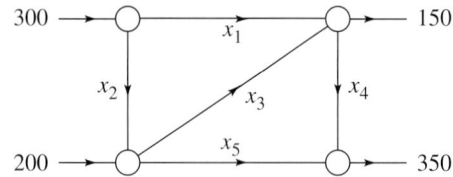

Synthesis

True or False?   **In Exercises 93–95, determine whether the statement is true or false. Justify your answer.**

93. $\begin{bmatrix} 5 & 0 & -2 & 7 \\ -1 & 3 & -6 & 0 \end{bmatrix}$ is a 4×2 matrix.

94. The matrix $\begin{bmatrix} 0 & 0 & 0 & 0 \\ 0 & 0 & 1 & -4 \\ 0 & 1 & 0 & 2 \\ 1 & 0 & 0 & 5 \end{bmatrix}$ is in reduced row-echelon form.

95. Gaussian elimination reduces a matrix until a reduced row-echelon form is obtained.

96. *Think About It*   The augmented matrix represents a system of linear equations (in variables x, y, and z) that has been reduced using Gauss-Jordan elimination. Write a system of equations with nonzero coefficients that is represented by the reduced matrix. (The answer is not unique.)

$$\begin{bmatrix} 1 & 0 & 3 & \vdots & -2 \\ 0 & 1 & 4 & \vdots & 1 \\ 0 & 0 & 0 & \vdots & 0 \end{bmatrix}$$

97. *Think About It*

   (a) Describe the row-echelon form of an augmented matrix that corresponds to a system of linear equations that is inconsistent.

   (b) Describe the row-echelon form of an augmented matrix that corresponds to a system of linear equations that has an infinite number of solutions.

98. Describe the three elementary row operations that can be performed on an augmented matrix.

99. What is the relationship between the three elementary row operations performed on an augmented matrix and the operations that lead to equivalent systems of equations?

100. *Writing*   In your own words, describe the difference between a matrix in row-echelon form and a matrix in reduced row-echelon form.

Review

In Exercises 101–104, sketch the graph of the function. Do not use a graphing utility.

101. $f(x) = 2^{x-1}$

102 $g(x) = 3^{-x+2}$

103. $h(x) = \ln(x - 1)$

104. $f(x) = 3 + \ln x$

8.2 Operations with Matrices

▶ **What you should learn**

- How to decide whether two matrices are equal
- How to add and subtract matrices and multiply matrices by real numbers
- How to multiply two matrices
- How to use matrix operations to model and solve real-life problems

▶ **Why you should learn it**

Matrix operations can be used to model and solve real-life problems. For instance, in Exercise 61 on page 571, matrix multiplication is used to analyze the profit a fruit farmer makes on two fruit crops.

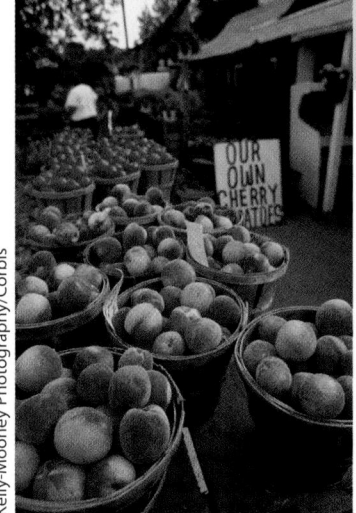

Equality of Matrices

In Section 8.1, you used matrices to solve systems of linear equations. Matrices, however, can do much more than this. There is a rich mathematical theory of matrices, and its applications are numerous. This section and the next two introduce some fundamentals of matrix theory. It is standard mathematical convention to represent matrices in any of the following three ways.

1. A matrix can be denoted by an uppercase letter such as A, B, or C.
2. A matrix can be denoted by a representative element enclosed in brackets, such as $[a_{ij}]$, $[b_{ij}]$, or $[c_{ij}]$.
3. A matrix can be denoted by a rectangular array of numbers such as

$$A = [a_{ij}] = \begin{bmatrix} a_{11} & a_{12} & a_{13} & \cdots & a_{1n} \\ a_{21} & a_{22} & a_{23} & \cdots & a_{2n} \\ a_{31} & a_{32} & a_{33} & \cdots & a_{3n} \\ \vdots & \vdots & \vdots & & \vdots \\ a_{m1} & a_{m2} & a_{m3} & \cdots & a_{mn} \end{bmatrix}.$$

Two matrices $A = [a_{ij}]$ and $B = [b_{ij}]$ are equal if they have the same order $(m \times n)$ and $a_{ij} = b_{ij}$ for $1 \leq i \leq m$ and $1 \leq j \leq n$. In other words, two matrices are equal if their corresponding entries are equal.

Example 1 ▶ **Equality of Matrices**

Solve for a_{11}, a_{12}, a_{21}, and a_{22} in the following matrix equation.

$$\begin{bmatrix} a_{11} & a_{12} \\ a_{21} & a_{22} \end{bmatrix} = \begin{bmatrix} 2 & -1 \\ -3 & 0 \end{bmatrix}$$

Solution

Because two matrices are equal only if their corresponding entries are equal, you can conclude that

$$a_{11} = 2, \quad a_{12} = -1, \quad a_{21} = -3, \quad \text{and} \quad a_{22} = 0.$$

Be sure you see that for two matrices to be equal, they must have the same order *and* their corresponding entries must be equal. For instance,

$$\begin{bmatrix} 2 & -1 \\ \sqrt{4} & \frac{1}{2} \end{bmatrix} = \begin{bmatrix} 2 & -1 \\ 2 & 0.5 \end{bmatrix}$$

but

$$\begin{bmatrix} 2 & -1 \\ 3 & 4 \\ 0 & 0 \end{bmatrix} \neq \begin{bmatrix} 2 & -1 \\ 3 & 4 \end{bmatrix}.$$

Historical Note

Arthur Cayley (1821–1895), a British mathematician, invented matrices around 1858. Cayley was a Cambridge University graduate and a lawyer by profession. His groundbreaking work on matrices was begun as he studied the theory of transformations. Cayley also was instrumental in the development of determinants. Cayley and two American mathematicians, Benjamin Peirce (1809–1880) and his son Charles S. Peirce (1839–1914), are credited with developing "matrix algebra."

Matrix Addition and Scalar Multiplication

In this section, three basic matrix operations will be covered. The first two are matrix addition and scalar multiplication. With matrix addition, you can add two matrices (of the same order) by adding their corresponding entries.

Definition of Matrix Addition

If $A = [a_{ij}]$ and $B = [b_{ij}]$ are matrices of order $m \times n$, their sum is the $m \times n$ matrix given by

$$A + B = [a_{ij} + b_{ij}].$$

The sum of two matrices of different orders is undefined.

Example 2 ▶ **Addition of Matrices**

a. $\begin{bmatrix} -1 & 2 \\ 0 & 1 \end{bmatrix} + \begin{bmatrix} 1 & 3 \\ -1 & 2 \end{bmatrix} = \begin{bmatrix} -1+1 & 2+3 \\ 0-1 & 1+2 \end{bmatrix}$

$$= \begin{bmatrix} 0 & 5 \\ -1 & 3 \end{bmatrix}$$

b. $\begin{bmatrix} 0 & 1 & -2 \\ 1 & 2 & 3 \end{bmatrix} + \begin{bmatrix} 0 & 0 & 0 \\ 0 & 0 & 0 \end{bmatrix} = \begin{bmatrix} 0 & 1 & -2 \\ 1 & 2 & 3 \end{bmatrix}$

c. $\begin{bmatrix} 1 \\ -3 \\ -2 \end{bmatrix} + \begin{bmatrix} -1 \\ 3 \\ 2 \end{bmatrix} = \begin{bmatrix} 0 \\ 0 \\ 0 \end{bmatrix}$

d. The sum of

$$A = \begin{bmatrix} 2 & 1 & 0 \\ 4 & 0 & -1 \\ 3 & -2 & 2 \end{bmatrix} \quad \text{and}$$

$$B = \begin{bmatrix} 0 & 1 \\ -1 & 3 \\ 2 & 4 \end{bmatrix}$$

is undefined because A and B have different orders.

In operations with matrices, numbers are usually referred to as **scalars.** In this text, scalars will always be real numbers. You can multiply a matrix A by a scalar c by multiplying each entry in A by c.

Definition of Scalar Multiplication

If $A = [a_{ij}]$ is an $m \times n$ matrix and c is a scalar, the **scalar multiple** of A by c is the $m \times n$ matrix given by

$$cA = [ca_{ij}].$$

The symbol $-A$ represents the negation of A, or the scalar product $(-1)A$. Moreover, if A and B are of the same order, then $A - B$ represents the sum of A and $(-1)B$. That is,

$$A - B = A + (-1)B.$$ Subtraction of matrices

Example 3 ▶ **Scalar Multiplication and Matrix Subtraction**

For the following matrices, find (a) $3A$, (b) $-B$, and (c) $3A - B$.

$$A = \begin{bmatrix} 2 & 2 & 4 \\ -3 & 0 & -1 \\ 2 & 1 & 2 \end{bmatrix} \quad \text{and} \quad B = \begin{bmatrix} 2 & 0 & 0 \\ 1 & -4 & 3 \\ -1 & 3 & 2 \end{bmatrix}$$

Solution

a. $3A = 3\begin{bmatrix} 2 & 2 & 4 \\ -3 & 0 & -1 \\ 2 & 1 & 2 \end{bmatrix}$ Scalar multiplication

$$= \begin{bmatrix} 3(2) & 3(2) & 3(4) \\ 3(-3) & 3(0) & 3(-1) \\ 3(2) & 3(1) & 3(2) \end{bmatrix}$$ Multiply each entry by 3.

$$= \begin{bmatrix} 6 & 6 & 12 \\ -9 & 0 & -3 \\ 6 & 3 & 6 \end{bmatrix}$$ Simplify.

b. $-B = (-1)\begin{bmatrix} 2 & 0 & 0 \\ 1 & -4 & 3 \\ -1 & 3 & 2 \end{bmatrix}$ Definition of negation

$$= \begin{bmatrix} -2 & 0 & 0 \\ -1 & 4 & -3 \\ 1 & -3 & -2 \end{bmatrix}$$ Multiply each entry by -1.

c. $3A - B = \begin{bmatrix} 6 & 6 & 12 \\ -9 & 0 & -3 \\ 6 & 3 & 6 \end{bmatrix} - \begin{bmatrix} 2 & 0 & 0 \\ 1 & -4 & 3 \\ -1 & 3 & 2 \end{bmatrix}$ Matrix subtraction

$$= \begin{bmatrix} 4 & 6 & 12 \\ -10 & 4 & -6 \\ 7 & 0 & 4 \end{bmatrix}$$ Subtract corresponding entries.

STUDY TIP

The order of operations for matrix expressions is similar to that for real numbers. In particular, you perform scalar multiplication before matrix addition and subtraction, as shown in Example 3(c).

It is often convenient to rewrite the scalar multiple cA by factoring c out of every entry in the matrix. For instance, in the following example, the scalar $\frac{1}{2}$ has been factored out of the matrix.

$$\begin{bmatrix} \frac{1}{2} & -\frac{3}{2} \\ \frac{5}{2} & \frac{1}{2} \end{bmatrix} = \begin{bmatrix} \frac{1}{2}(1) & \frac{1}{2}(-3) \\ \frac{1}{2}(5) & \frac{1}{2}(1) \end{bmatrix}$$

$$= \frac{1}{2}\begin{bmatrix} 1 & -3 \\ 5 & 1 \end{bmatrix}$$

The properties of matrix addition and scalar multiplication are similar to those of addition and multiplication of real numbers.

Properties of Matrix Addition and Scalar Multiplication

Let A, B, and C be $m \times n$ matrices and let c and d be scalars.

1. $A + B = B + A$	Commutative Property of Matrix Addition
2. $A + (B + C) = (A + B) + C$	Associative Property of Matrix Addition
3. $(cd)A = c(dA)$	Associative Property of Scalar Multiplication
4. $1A = A$	Scalar Identity Property
5. $c(A + B) = cA + cB$	Distributive Property
6. $(c + d)A = cA + dA$	Distributive Property

Note that the Associative Property of Matrix Addition allows you to write expressions such as $A + B + C$ without ambiguity because the same sum occurs no matter how the matrices are grouped. In other words, you obtain the same sum whether you group $A + B + C$ as $(A + B) + C$ or as $A + (B + C)$. This same reasoning applies to sums of four or more matrices.

Example 4 ▶ Addition of More than Two Matrices

By adding corresponding entries, you obtain the following sum of four matrices.

$$\begin{bmatrix} 1 \\ 2 \\ -3 \end{bmatrix} + \begin{bmatrix} -1 \\ -1 \\ 2 \end{bmatrix} + \begin{bmatrix} 0 \\ 1 \\ 4 \end{bmatrix} + \begin{bmatrix} 2 \\ -3 \\ -2 \end{bmatrix} = \begin{bmatrix} 2 \\ -1 \\ 1 \end{bmatrix}$$

Example 5 ▶ Using the Distributive Property

$$3\left(\begin{bmatrix} -2 & 0 \\ 4 & 1 \end{bmatrix} + \begin{bmatrix} 4 & -2 \\ 3 & 7 \end{bmatrix} \right) = 3\begin{bmatrix} -2 & 0 \\ 4 & 1 \end{bmatrix} + 3\begin{bmatrix} 4 & -2 \\ 3 & 7 \end{bmatrix}$$

$$= \begin{bmatrix} -6 & 0 \\ 12 & 3 \end{bmatrix} + \begin{bmatrix} 12 & -6 \\ 9 & 21 \end{bmatrix}$$

$$= \begin{bmatrix} 6 & -6 \\ 21 & 24 \end{bmatrix}$$

Technology

Most graphing utilities can add and subtract matrices and multiply matrices by scalars. Try using a graphing utility to find the sum of the matrices

$$A = \begin{bmatrix} 2 & -3 \\ -1 & 0 \end{bmatrix}$$

and

$$B = \begin{bmatrix} -1 & 4 \\ 2 & -5 \end{bmatrix}.$$

In Example 5, you could add the two matrices first and then multiply the matrix by 3, as follows.

$$3\left(\begin{bmatrix} -2 & 0 \\ 4 & 1 \end{bmatrix} + \begin{bmatrix} 4 & -2 \\ 3 & 7 \end{bmatrix} \right) = 3\begin{bmatrix} 2 & -2 \\ 7 & 8 \end{bmatrix}$$

$$= \begin{bmatrix} 6 & -6 \\ 21 & 24 \end{bmatrix}$$

Note that the result is the same.

One important property of addition of real numbers is that the number 0 is the additive identity. That is, $c + 0 = c$ for any real number c. For matrices, a similar property holds. That is, if A is an $m \times n$ matrix and O is the $m \times n$ **zero matrix** consisting entirely of zeros, then $A + O = A$.

In other words, O is the **additive identity** for the set of all $m \times n$ matrices. For example, the following matrices are the additive identities for the set of all 2×3 and 2×2 matrices.

$$O = \begin{bmatrix} 0 & 0 & 0 \\ 0 & 0 & 0 \end{bmatrix} \quad \text{and} \quad O = \begin{bmatrix} 0 & 0 \\ 0 & 0 \end{bmatrix}$$

2 × 3 zero matrix   2 × 2 zero matrix

The algebra of real numbers and the algebra of matrices have many similarities. For example, compare the following solutions.

Real Numbers *(Solve for x.)*	*$m \times n$ Matrices* *(Solve for X.)*
$x + a = b$	$X + A = B$
$x + a + (-a) = b + (-a)$	$X + A + (-A) = B + (-A)$
$x + 0 = b - a$	$X + O = B - A$
$x = b - a$	$X = B - A$

The algebra of real numbers and the algebra of matrices also have important differences, which will be discussed later.

Example 6 ▶ Solving a Matrix Equation

Solve for X in the equation $3X + A = B$, where

$$A = \begin{bmatrix} 1 & -2 \\ 0 & 3 \end{bmatrix} \quad \text{and} \quad B = \begin{bmatrix} -3 & 4 \\ 2 & 1 \end{bmatrix}.$$

Solution

Begin by solving the equation for X to obtain

$$3X = B - A$$

$$X = \frac{1}{3}(B - A).$$

Now, using the matrices A and B, you have

$$X = \frac{1}{3}\left(\begin{bmatrix} -3 & 4 \\ 2 & 1 \end{bmatrix} - \begin{bmatrix} 1 & -2 \\ 0 & 3 \end{bmatrix} \right) \qquad \text{Substitute the matrices.}$$

$$= \frac{1}{3}\begin{bmatrix} -4 & 6 \\ 2 & -2 \end{bmatrix} \qquad \text{Subtract matrix } A \text{ from matrix } B.$$

$$= \begin{bmatrix} -\frac{4}{3} & 2 \\ \frac{2}{3} & -\frac{2}{3} \end{bmatrix}. \qquad \text{Multiply the matrix by } \frac{1}{3}.$$

Matrix Multiplication

The third basic matrix operation is **matrix multiplication.** At first glance, the definition may seem unusual. You will see later, however, that this definition of the product of two matrices has many practical applications.

Definition of Matrix Multiplication

If $A = [a_{ij}]$ is an $m \times n$ matrix and $B = [b_{ij}]$ is an $n \times p$ matrix, the product AB is an $m \times p$ matrix

$$AB = [c_{ij}]$$

where $c_{ij} = a_{i1}b_{1j} + a_{i2}b_{2j} + a_{i3}b_{3j} + \cdots + a_{in}b_{nj}.$

The definition of matrix multiplication indicates a *row-by-column* multiplication, where the entry in the ith row and jth column of the product AB is obtained by multiplying the entries in the ith row of A by the corresponding entries in the jth column of B and then adding the results. The general pattern for matrix multiplication is as follows.

$$
\begin{bmatrix}
a_{11} & a_{12} & a_{13} & \cdots & a_{1n} \\
a_{21} & a_{22} & a_{23} & \cdots & a_{2n} \\
a_{31} & a_{32} & a_{33} & \cdots & a_{3n} \\
\vdots & \vdots & \vdots & & \vdots \\
a_{i1} & a_{i2} & a_{i3} & \cdots & a_{in} \\
\vdots & \vdots & \vdots & & \vdots \\
a_{m1} & a_{m2} & a_{m3} & \cdots & a_{mn}
\end{bmatrix}
\begin{bmatrix}
b_{11} & b_{12} & \cdots & b_{1j} & \cdots & b_{1p} \\
b_{21} & b_{22} & \cdots & b_{2j} & \cdots & b_{2p} \\
b_{31} & b_{32} & \cdots & b_{3j} & \cdots & b_{3p} \\
\vdots & \vdots & & \vdots & & \vdots \\
b_{n1} & b_{n2} & \cdots & b_{nj} & \cdots & b_{np}
\end{bmatrix}
=
\begin{bmatrix}
c_{11} & c_{12} & \cdots & c_{1j} & \cdots & c_{1p} \\
c_{21} & c_{22} & \cdots & c_{2j} & \cdots & c_{2p} \\
\vdots & \vdots & & \vdots & & \vdots \\
c_{i1} & c_{i2} & \cdots & c_{ij} & \cdots & c_{ip} \\
\vdots & \vdots & & \vdots & & \vdots \\
c_{m1} & c_{m2} & \cdots & c_{mj} & \cdots & c_{mp}
\end{bmatrix}
$$

$$a_{i1}b_{1j} + a_{i2}b_{2j} + a_{i3}b_{3j} + \cdots + a_{in}b_{nj} = c_{ij}$$

Example 7 ▶ **Finding the Product of Two Matrices**

First, note that the product AB is defined because the number of columns of A is equal to the number of rows of B. Moreover, the product AB has order 3×2. To find the entries of the product, multiply each row of A by each column of B, as follows.

$$AB = \begin{bmatrix} -1 & 3 \\ 4 & -2 \\ 5 & 0 \end{bmatrix} \begin{bmatrix} -3 & 2 \\ -4 & 1 \end{bmatrix}$$

$$= \begin{bmatrix} (-1)(-3) + (3)(-4) & (-1)(2) + (3)(1) \\ (4)(-3) + (-2)(-4) & (4)(2) + (-2)(1) \\ (5)(-3) + (0)(-4) & (5)(2) + (0)(1) \end{bmatrix}$$

$$= \begin{bmatrix} -9 & 1 \\ -4 & 6 \\ -15 & 10 \end{bmatrix}$$

This pattern for the order of the product of matrix multiplication is an effective memory device. You may want to demonstrate this pattern on several multiplication examples.

Be sure you understand that for the product of two matrices to be defined, the number of *columns* of the first matrix must equal the number of *rows* of the second matrix. That is, the middle two indices must be the same. The outside two indices give the order of the product, as shown below.

$$
\underset{m \times n}{A} \quad \times \quad \underset{n \times p}{B} \quad = \quad \underset{m \times p}{AB}
$$

Equal

Order of AB

Example 8 ▶ Finding the Product of Two Matrices

Find the product AB where

$$
A = \begin{bmatrix} 1 & 0 & 3 \\ 2 & -1 & -2 \end{bmatrix} \quad \text{and} \quad B = \begin{bmatrix} -2 & 4 \\ 1 & 0 \\ -1 & 1 \end{bmatrix}.
$$

Solution

Note that the order of A is 2×3 and the order of B is 3×2. So, the product AB has order 2×2.

$$
AB = \begin{bmatrix} 1 & 0 & 3 \\ 2 & -1 & -2 \end{bmatrix} \begin{bmatrix} -2 & 4 \\ 1 & 0 \\ -1 & 1 \end{bmatrix}
$$

$$
= \begin{bmatrix} 1(-2) + 0(1) + 3(-1) & 1(4) + 0(0) + 3(1) \\ 2(-2) + (-1)(1) + (-2)(-1) & 2(4) + (-1)(0) + (-2)(1) \end{bmatrix}
$$

$$
= \begin{bmatrix} -5 & 7 \\ -3 & 6 \end{bmatrix}
$$

Example 9 ▶ Patterns in Matrix Multiplication

◀ Exploration ▶

Use a graphing utility to multiply the matrices

$$
A = \begin{bmatrix} 1 & 2 \\ 3 & 4 \end{bmatrix} \quad \text{and}
$$

$$
B = \begin{bmatrix} 0 & 1 \\ 2 & 3 \end{bmatrix}.
$$

Do you obtain the same result for the product AB as for the product BA? What does this tell you about matrix multiplication and commutativity?

a. $\begin{bmatrix} 3 & 4 \\ -2 & 5 \end{bmatrix} \begin{bmatrix} 1 & 0 \\ 0 & 1 \end{bmatrix} = \begin{bmatrix} 3 & 4 \\ -2 & 5 \end{bmatrix}$

$\quad 2 \times 2 \qquad 2 \times 2 \qquad\quad 2 \times 2$

b. $\begin{bmatrix} 6 & 2 & 0 \\ 3 & -1 & 2 \\ 1 & 4 & 6 \end{bmatrix} \begin{bmatrix} 1 \\ 2 \\ -3 \end{bmatrix} = \begin{bmatrix} 10 \\ -5 \\ -9 \end{bmatrix}$

$\quad\ \ 3 \times 3 \qquad\quad 3 \times 1 \quad\ 3 \times 1$

c. The product AB for the following matrices is not defined.

$$
A = \begin{bmatrix} -2 & 1 \\ 1 & -3 \\ 1 & 4 \end{bmatrix} \quad \text{and} \quad B = \begin{bmatrix} -2 & 3 & 1 & 4 \\ 0 & 1 & -1 & 2 \\ 2 & -1 & 0 & 1 \end{bmatrix}
$$

$\qquad\qquad 3 \times 2 \qquad\qquad\qquad\qquad 3 \times 4$

Example 10 ▶ Patterns in Matrix Multiplication

a. $\begin{bmatrix} 1 & -2 & -3 \end{bmatrix} \begin{bmatrix} 2 \\ -1 \\ 1 \end{bmatrix} = \begin{bmatrix} 1 \end{bmatrix}$ **b.** $\begin{bmatrix} 2 \\ -1 \\ 1 \end{bmatrix} \begin{bmatrix} 1 & -2 & -3 \end{bmatrix} = \begin{bmatrix} 2 & -4 & -6 \\ -1 & 2 & 3 \\ 1 & -2 & -3 \end{bmatrix}$

$\quad\quad 1 \times 3 \quad\quad 3 \times 1 \quad 1 \times 1 \quad\quad 3 \times 1 \quad\quad 1 \times 3 \quad\quad\quad\quad 3 \times 3$

In Example 10, note that the two products are different. Even if AB and BA are defined, matrix multiplication is not, in general, commutative. That is, for most matrices, $AB \neq BA$.

Properties of Matrix Multiplication

Let A, B, and C be matrices and let c be a scalar.

1. $A(BC) = (AB)C$ Associative Property of Multiplication

2. $A(B + C) = AB + AC$ Distributive Property

3. $(A + B)C = AC + BC$ Distributive Property

4. $c(AB) = (cA)B = A(cB)$ Associative Property of Scalar Multiplication

---

Definition of Identity Matrix

The $n \times n$ matrix that consists of 1's on its main diagonal and 0's elsewhere is called the **identity matrix of order n** and is denoted by

$$I_n = \begin{bmatrix} 1 & 0 & 0 & \dots & 0 \\ 0 & 1 & 0 & \dots & 0 \\ 0 & 0 & 1 & \dots & 0 \\ \vdots & \vdots & \vdots & & \vdots \\ 0 & 0 & 0 & \dots & 1 \end{bmatrix}.$$ Identity matrix

Note that an identity matrix must be *square*. When the order is understood to be n, you can denote I_n simply by I.

If A is an $n \times n$ matrix, the identity matrix has the property that $AI_n = A$ and $I_nA = A$. For example,

$$\begin{bmatrix} 3 & -2 & 5 \\ 1 & 0 & 4 \\ -1 & 2 & -3 \end{bmatrix} \begin{bmatrix} 1 & 0 & 0 \\ 0 & 1 & 0 \\ 0 & 0 & 1 \end{bmatrix} = \begin{bmatrix} 3 & -2 & 5 \\ 1 & 0 & 4 \\ -1 & 2 & -3 \end{bmatrix}$$

and

$$\begin{bmatrix} 1 & 0 & 0 \\ 0 & 1 & 0 \\ 0 & 0 & 1 \end{bmatrix} \begin{bmatrix} 3 & -2 & 5 \\ 1 & 0 & 4 \\ -1 & 2 & -3 \end{bmatrix} = \begin{bmatrix} 3 & -2 & 5 \\ 1 & 0 & 4 \\ -1 & 2 & -3 \end{bmatrix}.$$

Applications

Matrix multiplication can be used to represent a system of linear equations. Note how the system

$$\begin{cases} a_{11}x_1 + a_{12}x_2 + a_{13}x_3 = b_1 \\ a_{21}x_1 + a_{22}x_2 + a_{23}x_3 = b_2 \\ a_{31}x_1 + a_{32}x_2 + a_{33}x_3 = b_3 \end{cases}$$

can be written as the matrix equation $AX = B$, where A is the *coefficient matrix* of the system, and X and B are column matrices.

$$\begin{bmatrix} a_{11} & a_{12} & a_{13} \\ a_{21} & a_{22} & a_{23} \\ a_{31} & a_{32} & a_{33} \end{bmatrix} \begin{bmatrix} x_1 \\ x_2 \\ x_3 \end{bmatrix} = \begin{bmatrix} b_1 \\ b_2 \\ b_3 \end{bmatrix}$$

$$A \qquad \times \quad X \; = \; B$$

Example 11 ▶ **Solving a System of Linear Equations**

Consider the following system of linear equations.

$$\begin{cases} x_1 - 2x_2 + x_3 = -4 \\ x_2 + 2x_3 = 4 \\ 2x_1 + 3x_2 - 2x_3 = 2 \end{cases}$$

a. Write this system as a matrix equation, $AX = B$.

b. Use Gauss-Jordan elimination on the augmented matrix $[A \vdots B]$ to solve for the matrix X.

Solution

a. In matrix form, $AX = B$, the system can be written as follows.

$$\begin{bmatrix} 1 & -2 & 1 \\ 0 & 1 & 2 \\ 2 & 3 & -2 \end{bmatrix} \begin{bmatrix} x_1 \\ x_2 \\ x_3 \end{bmatrix} = \begin{bmatrix} -4 \\ 4 \\ 2 \end{bmatrix}$$

b. The augmented matrix is formed by adjoining matrix B to matrix A.

$$[A \vdots B] = \begin{bmatrix} 1 & -2 & 1 & \vdots & -4 \\ 0 & 1 & 2 & \vdots & 4 \\ 2 & 3 & -2 & \vdots & 2 \end{bmatrix}$$

Using Gauss-Jordan elimination, you can rewrite this equation as

$$[I \vdots X] = \begin{bmatrix} 1 & 0 & 0 & \vdots & -1 \\ 0 & 1 & 0 & \vdots & 2 \\ 0 & 0 & 1 & \vdots & 1 \end{bmatrix}.$$

So, the solution of the system of linear equations is $x_1 = -1$, $x_2 = 2$, and $x_3 = 1$, and the solution of the matrix equation is

$$X = \begin{bmatrix} x_1 \\ x_2 \\ x_3 \end{bmatrix} = \begin{bmatrix} -1 \\ 2 \\ 1 \end{bmatrix}.$$

You may also wish to discuss some of the application problems in the exercise set. (See, for example, Exercises 59–66 on pages 571 and 572.)

Example 12 ▶ Softball Team Expenses

Two softball teams submit equipment lists to their sponsors.

	Women's Team	Men's Team
Bats	12	15
Balls	45	38
Gloves	15	17

Each bat costs $80, each ball costs $6, and each glove costs $60. Use matrices to find the total cost of equipment for each team.

Solution

The equipment lists E and the costs per item C can be written in matrix form as

$$E = \begin{bmatrix} 12 & 15 \\ 45 & 38 \\ 15 & 17 \end{bmatrix}$$

and

$$C = \begin{bmatrix} 80 & 6 & 60 \end{bmatrix}.$$

The total cost of equipment for each team is given by the product

$$CE = \begin{bmatrix} 80 & 6 & 60 \end{bmatrix} \begin{bmatrix} 12 & 15 \\ 45 & 38 \\ 15 & 17 \end{bmatrix}$$

$$= \begin{bmatrix} 80(12) + 6(45) + 60(15) & 80(15) + 6(38) + 60(17) \end{bmatrix}$$

$$= \begin{bmatrix} 2130 & 2448 \end{bmatrix}.$$

So, the total cost of equipment for the women's team is $2130 and the total cost of equipment for the men's team is $2448.

Group Activity

Discuss the requirements for the order of the dimensions m and n for the multiplication of two $m \times n$ matrices. Determine which of the following matrix multiplications AB is (are) defined. For each case in which AB is defined, what is the order of the resulting matrix?

a. A is of order 1×3
   B is of order 2×1

b. A is of order 2×3
   B is of order 2×3

c. A is of order 3×4
   B is of order 4×2

d. A is of order 3×1
   B is of order 3×3

Discuss why matrix multiplication is not, in general, commutative. Work together to find an example of two 2×2 matrices such that $AB \neq BA$. Find an example of two 2×2 matrices such that $AB = BA$.

Writing ABOUT MATHEMATICS

Problem Posing Write a matrix multiplication application problem that uses the matrix

$$A = \begin{bmatrix} 20 & 42 & 33 \\ 17 & 30 & 50 \end{bmatrix}.$$

Exchange problems with another student in your class. Form the matrices that represent the problem, and solve the problem. Interpret your solution in the context of the problem. Check with the creator of the problem to see if you are correct. Discuss other ways to represent and/or approach the problem.

8.2 Exercises

Exercises where the operation is not possible: 11a,11b, 11d, 12a, 12b, 12d, 27, 28, 38, 39, 45c, 46c, 69, 70, 71, 74

In Exercises 1–4, find x and y.

1. $\begin{bmatrix} x & -2 \\ 7 & y \end{bmatrix} = \begin{bmatrix} -4 & -2 \\ 7 & 22 \end{bmatrix}$

2. $\begin{bmatrix} -5 & x \\ y & 8 \end{bmatrix} = \begin{bmatrix} -5 & 13 \\ 12 & 8 \end{bmatrix}$

3. $\begin{bmatrix} 16 & 4 & 5 & 4 \\ -3 & 13 & 15 & 6 \\ 0 & 2 & 4 & 0 \end{bmatrix} = \begin{bmatrix} 16 & 4 & 2x+1 & 4 \\ -3 & 13 & & 15 & 3x \\ 0 & 2 & 3y-5 & 0 \end{bmatrix}$

4. $\begin{bmatrix} x+2 & 8 & -3 \\ 1 & 2y & 2x \\ 7 & -2 & y+2 \end{bmatrix} = \begin{bmatrix} 2x+6 & 8 & -3 \\ 1 & 18 & -8 \\ 7 & -2 & 11 \end{bmatrix}$

In Exercises 5–12, if possible, find (a) $A + B$, (b) $A - B$, (c) $3A$, and (d) $3A - 2B$.

5. $A = \begin{bmatrix} 1 & -1 \\ 2 & -1 \end{bmatrix}$, $B = \begin{bmatrix} 2 & -1 \\ -1 & 8 \end{bmatrix}$

6. $A = \begin{bmatrix} 1 & 2 \\ 2 & 1 \end{bmatrix}$, $B = \begin{bmatrix} -3 & -2 \\ 4 & 2 \end{bmatrix}$

7. $A = \begin{bmatrix} 6 & -1 \\ 2 & 4 \\ -3 & 5 \end{bmatrix}$, $B = \begin{bmatrix} 1 & 4 \\ -1 & 5 \\ 1 & 10 \end{bmatrix}$

8. $A = \begin{bmatrix} 2 & 1 & 1 \\ -1 & -1 & 4 \end{bmatrix}$, $B = \begin{bmatrix} 2 & -3 & 4 \\ -3 & 1 & -2 \end{bmatrix}$

9. $A = \begin{bmatrix} 2 & 2 & -1 & 0 & 1 \\ 1 & 1 & -2 & 0 & -1 \end{bmatrix}$,

$B = \begin{bmatrix} 1 & 1 & -1 & 1 & 0 \\ -3 & 4 & 9 & -6 & -7 \end{bmatrix}$

10. $A = \begin{bmatrix} -1 & 4 & 0 \\ 3 & -2 & 2 \\ 5 & 4 & -1 \\ 0 & 8 & -6 \\ -4 & -1 & 0 \end{bmatrix}$, $B = \begin{bmatrix} -3 & 5 & 1 \\ 2 & -4 & -7 \\ 10 & -9 & -1 \\ 3 & 2 & -4 \\ 0 & 1 & -2 \end{bmatrix}$

11. $A = \begin{bmatrix} 6 & 0 & 3 \\ -1 & -4 & 0 \end{bmatrix}$, $B = \begin{bmatrix} 8 & -1 \\ 4 & -3 \end{bmatrix}$

12. $A = \begin{bmatrix} 3 \\ 2 \\ -1 \end{bmatrix}$, $B = \begin{bmatrix} -4 & 6 & 2 \end{bmatrix}$

In Exercises 13–18, evaluate the expression.

13. $\begin{bmatrix} -5 & 0 \\ 3 & -6 \end{bmatrix} + \begin{bmatrix} 7 & 1 \\ -2 & -1 \end{bmatrix} + \begin{bmatrix} -10 & -8 \\ 14 & 6 \end{bmatrix}$

14. $\begin{bmatrix} 6 & 8 \\ -1 & 0 \end{bmatrix} + \begin{bmatrix} 0 & 5 \\ -3 & -1 \end{bmatrix} + \begin{bmatrix} -11 & -7 \\ 2 & -1 \end{bmatrix}$

15. $4\left(\begin{bmatrix} -4 & 0 & 1 \\ 0 & 2 & 3 \end{bmatrix} - \begin{bmatrix} 2 & 1 & -2 \\ 3 & -6 & 0 \end{bmatrix} \right)$

16. $\frac{1}{2}\left(\begin{bmatrix} 5 & -2 & 4 & 0 \end{bmatrix} + \begin{bmatrix} 14 & 6 & -18 & 9 \end{bmatrix} \right)$

17. $-3\left(\begin{bmatrix} 0 & -3 \\ 7 & 2 \end{bmatrix} + \begin{bmatrix} -6 & 3 \\ 8 & 1 \end{bmatrix} \right) - 2\begin{bmatrix} 4 & -4 \\ 7 & -9 \end{bmatrix}$

18. $-1\begin{bmatrix} 4 & 11 \\ -2 & -1 \\ 9 & 3 \end{bmatrix} + \frac{1}{6}\left(\begin{bmatrix} -5 & -1 \\ 3 & 4 \\ 0 & 13 \end{bmatrix} + \begin{bmatrix} 7 & 5 \\ -9 & -1 \\ 6 & -1 \end{bmatrix} \right)$

In Exercises 19–22, use the matrix capabilities of a graphing utility to evaluate each expression. Round your results to three decimal places, if necessary.

19. $\frac{3}{7}\begin{bmatrix} 2 & 5 \\ -1 & -4 \end{bmatrix} + 6\begin{bmatrix} -3 & 0 \\ 2 & 2 \end{bmatrix}$

20. $55\left(\begin{bmatrix} 14 & -11 \\ -22 & 19 \end{bmatrix} + \begin{bmatrix} -22 & 20 \\ 13 & 6 \end{bmatrix} \right)$

21. $-\begin{bmatrix} 3.211 & 6.829 \\ -1.004 & 4.914 \\ 0.055 & -3.889 \end{bmatrix} - \begin{bmatrix} -1.630 & -3.090 \\ 5.256 & 8.335 \\ -9.768 & 4.251 \end{bmatrix}$

22. $-12\left(\begin{bmatrix} 6 & 20 \\ 1 & -9 \\ -2 & 5 \end{bmatrix} + \begin{bmatrix} 14 & -15 \\ -8 & -6 \\ 7 & 0 \end{bmatrix} + \begin{bmatrix} -31 & -19 \\ 16 & 10 \\ 24 & -10 \end{bmatrix} \right)$

In Exercises 23–26, solve for X when

$$A = \begin{bmatrix} -2 & -1 \\ 1 & 0 \\ 3 & -4 \end{bmatrix} \quad \text{and} \quad B = \begin{bmatrix} 0 & 3 \\ 2 & 0 \\ -4 & -1 \end{bmatrix}.$$

23. $X = 3A - 2B$ **24.** $2X = 2A - B$

25. $2X + 3A = B$ **26.** $2A + 4B = -2X$

In Exercises 27–34, find AB, if possible.

27. $A = \begin{bmatrix} 2 & 1 \\ -3 & 4 \\ 1 & 6 \end{bmatrix}$, $B = \begin{bmatrix} 0 & -1 & 0 \\ 4 & 0 & 2 \\ 8 & -1 & 7 \end{bmatrix}$

28. $A = \begin{bmatrix} 1 & 0 & 3 & -2 \\ 6 & 13 & 8 & -17 \end{bmatrix}$, $B = \begin{bmatrix} 1 & 6 \\ 4 & 2 \end{bmatrix}$

29. $A = \begin{bmatrix} 0 & -1 & 0 \\ 4 & 0 & 2 \\ 8 & -1 & 7 \end{bmatrix}$, $B = \begin{bmatrix} 2 & 1 \\ -3 & 4 \\ 1 & 6 \end{bmatrix}$

30. $A = \begin{bmatrix} -1 & 3 \\ 4 & -5 \\ 0 & 2 \end{bmatrix}$, $B = \begin{bmatrix} 1 & 2 \\ 0 & 7 \end{bmatrix}$

31. $A = \begin{bmatrix} 1 & 0 & 0 \\ 0 & 4 & 0 \\ 0 & 0 & -2 \end{bmatrix}$, $B = \begin{bmatrix} 3 & 0 & 0 \\ 0 & -1 & 0 \\ 0 & 0 & 5 \end{bmatrix}$

32. $A = \begin{bmatrix} 5 & 0 & 0 \\ 0 & -8 & 0 \\ 0 & 0 & 7 \end{bmatrix}$, $B = \begin{bmatrix} \frac{1}{5} & 0 & 0 \\ 0 & -\frac{1}{8} & 0 \\ 0 & 0 & \frac{1}{2} \end{bmatrix}$

33. $A = \begin{bmatrix} 0 & 0 & 5 \\ 0 & 0 & -3 \\ 0 & 0 & 4 \end{bmatrix}$, $B = \begin{bmatrix} 6 & -11 & 4 \\ 8 & 16 & 4 \\ 0 & 0 & 0 \end{bmatrix}$

34. $A = \begin{bmatrix} 10 \\ 12 \end{bmatrix}$, $B = \begin{bmatrix} 6 & -2 & 1 & 6 \end{bmatrix}$

📈 In Exercises 35–40, use the matrix capabilities of a graphing utility to find AB.

35. $A = \begin{bmatrix} 5 & 6 & -3 \\ -2 & 5 & 1 \\ 10 & -5 & 5 \end{bmatrix}$, $B = \begin{bmatrix} 1 & -1 & 2 \\ 8 & 1 & 4 \\ 4 & -2 & 9 \end{bmatrix}$

36. $A = \begin{bmatrix} 11 & -12 & 4 \\ 14 & 10 & 12 \\ 6 & -2 & 9 \end{bmatrix}$, $B = \begin{bmatrix} 12 & 10 \\ -5 & 12 \\ 15 & 16 \end{bmatrix}$

37. $A = \begin{bmatrix} -3 & 8 & -6 & 8 \\ -12 & 15 & 9 & 6 \\ 5 & -1 & 1 & 5 \end{bmatrix}$, $B = \begin{bmatrix} 3 & 1 & 6 \\ 24 & 15 & 14 \\ 16 & 10 & 21 \\ 8 & -4 & 10 \end{bmatrix}$

38. $A = \begin{bmatrix} -2 & 4 & 8 \\ 21 & 5 & 6 \\ 13 & 2 & 6 \end{bmatrix}$, $B = \begin{bmatrix} 2 & 0 \\ -7 & 15 \\ 32 & 14 \\ 0.5 & 1.6 \end{bmatrix}$

39. $A = \begin{bmatrix} 9 & 10 & -38 & 18 \\ 100 & -50 & 250 & 75 \end{bmatrix}$,

$B = \begin{bmatrix} 52 & -85 & 27 & 45 \\ 40 & -35 & 60 & 82 \end{bmatrix}$

40. $A = \begin{bmatrix} 15 & -18 \\ -4 & 12 \\ -8 & 22 \end{bmatrix}$, $B = \begin{bmatrix} -7 & 22 & 1 \\ 8 & 16 & 24 \end{bmatrix}$

In Exercises 41–46, find (a) AB, (b) BA, and, if possible, (c) A^2. (*Note:* $A^2 = AA$.)

41. $A = \begin{bmatrix} 1 & 2 \\ 4 & 2 \end{bmatrix}$, $B = \begin{bmatrix} 2 & -1 \\ -1 & 8 \end{bmatrix}$

42. $A = \begin{bmatrix} 2 & -1 \\ 1 & 4 \end{bmatrix}$, $B = \begin{bmatrix} 0 & 0 \\ 3 & -3 \end{bmatrix}$

43. $A = \begin{bmatrix} 3 & -1 \\ 1 & 3 \end{bmatrix}$, $B = \begin{bmatrix} 1 & -3 \\ 3 & 1 \end{bmatrix}$

44. $A = \begin{bmatrix} 1 & -1 \\ 1 & 1 \end{bmatrix}$, $B = \begin{bmatrix} 1 & 3 \\ -3 & 1 \end{bmatrix}$

45. $A = \begin{bmatrix} 7 \\ 8 \\ -1 \end{bmatrix}$, $B = \begin{bmatrix} 1 & 1 & 2 \end{bmatrix}$

46. $A = \begin{bmatrix} 3 & 2 & 1 \end{bmatrix}$, $B = \begin{bmatrix} 2 \\ 3 \\ 0 \end{bmatrix}$

In Exercises 47–50, evaluate the expression. Use the matrix capabilities of a graphing utility to verify your answer.

47. $\begin{bmatrix} 3 & 1 \\ 0 & -2 \end{bmatrix} \begin{bmatrix} 1 & 0 \\ -2 & 2 \end{bmatrix} \begin{bmatrix} 1 & 0 \\ 2 & 4 \end{bmatrix}$

48. $-3\left(\begin{bmatrix} 6 & 5 & -1 \\ 1 & -2 & 0 \end{bmatrix} \begin{bmatrix} 0 & 3 \\ -1 & -3 \\ 4 & 1 \end{bmatrix} \right)$

49. $\begin{bmatrix} 0 & 2 & -2 \\ 4 & 1 & 2 \end{bmatrix} \left(\begin{bmatrix} 4 & 0 \\ 0 & -1 \\ -1 & 2 \end{bmatrix} + \begin{bmatrix} -2 & 3 \\ -3 & 5 \\ 0 & -3 \end{bmatrix} \right)$

50. $\begin{bmatrix} 3 \\ -1 \\ 5 \\ 7 \end{bmatrix} ([5 \quad -6] + [7 \quad -1] + [-8 \quad 9])$

In Exercises 51–58, (a) write each system of linear equations as a matrix equation, $AX = B$, and (b) use Gauss-Jordan elimination on the augmented matrix $[A \vdots B]$ to solve for the matrix X.

51. $\begin{cases} -x_1 + x_2 = 4 \\ -2x_1 + x_2 = 0 \end{cases}$

52. $\begin{cases} 2x_1 + 3x_2 = 5 \\ x_1 + 4x_2 = 10 \end{cases}$

53. $\begin{cases} -2x_1 - 3x_2 = -4 \\ 6x_1 + x_2 = -36 \end{cases}$

54. $\begin{cases} -4x_1 + 9x_2 = -13 \\ x_1 - 3x_2 = 12 \end{cases}$

55. $\begin{cases} x_1 - 2x_2 + 3x_3 = 9 \\ -x_1 + 3x_2 - x_3 = -6 \\ 2x_1 - 5x_2 + 5x_3 = 17 \end{cases}$

56. $\begin{cases} x_1 + x_2 - 3x_3 = 9 \\ -x_1 + 2x_2 = 6 \\ x_1 - x_2 + x_3 = -5 \end{cases}$

57. $\begin{cases} x_1 - 5x_2 + 2x_3 = -20 \\ -3x_1 + x_2 - x_3 = 8 \\ -2x_2 + 5x_3 = -16 \end{cases}$

58. $\begin{cases} x_1 - x_2 + 4x_3 = 17 \\ x_1 + 3x_2 = -11 \\ -6x_2 + 5x_3 = 40 \end{cases}$

59. *Manufacturing* A corporation has three factories, each of which manufactures acoustic guitars and electric guitars. The number of units of guitars produced at factory j in one day is represented by a_{ij} in the matrix

$$A = \begin{bmatrix} 70 & 50 & 25 \\ 35 & 100 & 70 \end{bmatrix}.$$

Find the production levels if production is increased by 20%.

60. *Manufacturing* A corporation has four factories, each of which manufactures sport utility vehicles and pickup trucks. The number of units of vehicle i produced at factory j in one day is represented by a_{ij} in the matrix

$$A = \begin{bmatrix} 100 & 90 & 70 & 30 \\ 40 & 20 & 60 & 60 \end{bmatrix}.$$

Find the production levels if production is increased by 10%.

▶ Model It

61. *Agriculture* A fruit grower raises two crops, apples and peaches. Each of these crops is sent to three different outlets for sale. These outlets are The Farmer's Market, The Fruit Stand, and The Fruit Farm. The numbers of bushels of apples sent to the three outlets are 125, 100, and 75, respectively. The numbers of bushels of peaches sent to the three outlets are 100, 175, and 125, respectively. The profit per bushel for apples is $3.50 and the profit per bushel for peaches is $6.00.

(a) Write a matrix A that represents the number of bushels of each crop i that are shipped to each outlet j. State what each entry a_{ij} of the matrix represents.

(b) Write a matrix B that represents the profit per bushel of each fruit. State what each entry b_{ij} of the matrix represents.

(c) Find the product BA and state what each entry of the matrix represents.

---

62. *Revenue* A manufacturer of electronics produces three models of portable CD players, which are shipped to two warehouses. The number of units of model i that are shipped to warehouse j is represented by a_{ij} in the matrix

$$A = \begin{bmatrix} 5,000 & 4,000 \\ 6,000 & 10,000 \\ 8,000 & 5,000 \end{bmatrix}.$$

The price per unit is represented by the matrix

$$B = [\$39.50 \quad \$44.50 \quad \$56.50].$$

Compute BA and interpret the result.

63. *Inventory* A company sells five models of computers through three retail outlets. The inventories are represented by S.

Model

$$S = \begin{matrix} & \begin{matrix} A & B & C & D & E \end{matrix} & \\ & \begin{bmatrix} 3 & 2 & 2 & 3 & 0 \\ 0 & 2 & 3 & 4 & 3 \\ 4 & 2 & 1 & 3 & 2 \end{bmatrix} & \begin{matrix} 1 \\ 2 \\ 3 \end{matrix} \end{matrix} \quad \text{Outlet}$$

The wholesale and retail prices are represented by T.

Price

$$T = \begin{matrix} & \begin{matrix} \text{Wholesale} & \text{Retail} \end{matrix} & \\ & \begin{bmatrix} \$840 & \$1100 \\ \$1200 & \$1350 \\ \$1450 & \$1650 \\ \$2650 & \$3000 \\ \$3050 & \$3200 \end{bmatrix} & \begin{matrix} A \\ B \\ C \\ D \\ E \end{matrix} \end{matrix} \quad \text{Model}$$

Compute ST and interpret the result.

64. *Voting Preferences* The matrix

From

$$P = \begin{matrix} & \begin{matrix} R & D & I \end{matrix} & \\ & \begin{bmatrix} 0.6 & 0.1 & 0.1 \\ 0.2 & 0.7 & 0.1 \\ 0.2 & 0.2 & 0.8 \end{bmatrix} & \begin{matrix} R \\ D \\ I \end{matrix} \end{matrix} \quad \text{To}$$

is called a *stochastic matrix*. Each entry $p_{ij} (i \neq j)$ represents the proportion of the voting population that changes from party i to party j, and p_{ii} represents the proportion that remains loyal to the party from one election to the next. Compute and interpret P^2.

65. Voting Preferences Use a graphing utility to find P^3, P^4, P^5, P^6, P^7, and P^8 for the matrix given in Exercise 64. Can you detect a pattern as P is raised to higher powers?

66. Labor/Wage Requirements A company that manufactures boats has the following labor-hour and wage requirements.

Labor per boat

Department

$$S = \begin{bmatrix} 1.0\text{ hr} & 0.5\text{ hr} & 0.2\text{ hr} \\ 1.6\text{ hr} & 1.0\text{ hr} & 0.2\text{ hr} \\ 2.5\text{ hr} & 2.0\text{ hr} & 1.4\text{ hr} \end{bmatrix} \begin{matrix} \text{Small} \\ \text{Medium} \\ \text{Large} \end{matrix}$$

Cutting Assembly Packaging / Boat size

Wages per hour

Plant

$$T = \begin{bmatrix} \$12 & \$10 \\ \$9 & \$8 \\ \$8 & \$7 \end{bmatrix} \begin{matrix} \text{Cutting} \\ \text{Assembly} \\ \text{Packaging} \end{matrix}$$

A B / Department

Compute ST and interpret the result.

Synthesis

True or False? In Exercises 67 and 68, determine whether the statement is true or false. Justify your answer.

67. Two matrices can be added only if they have the same order.

68. $\begin{bmatrix} -6 & -2 \\ 2 & -6 \end{bmatrix}\begin{bmatrix} 4 & 0 \\ 0 & -1 \end{bmatrix} = \begin{bmatrix} 4 & 0 \\ 0 & -1 \end{bmatrix}\begin{bmatrix} -6 & -2 \\ 2 & -6 \end{bmatrix}$

Think About It In Exercises 69–76, let matrices A, B, C, and D be of orders 2×3, 2×3, 3×2, and 2×2, respectively. Determine whether the matrices are of proper order to perform the operation(s). If so, give the order of the answer.

69. $A + 2C$

70. $B - 3C$

71. AB

72. BC

73. $BC - D$

74. $CB - D$

75. $D(A - 3B)$

76. $(BC - D)A$

77. Think About It If a, b, and c are real numbers such that $c \neq 0$ and $ac = bc$, then $a = b$. However, if A, B, and C are nonzero matrices such that $AC = BC$, then A is not necessarily equal to B. Illustrate this using the following matrices.

$$A = \begin{bmatrix} 0 & 1 \\ 0 & 1 \end{bmatrix}, \quad B = \begin{bmatrix} 1 & 0 \\ 1 & 0 \end{bmatrix}, \quad C = \begin{bmatrix} 2 & 3 \\ 2 & 3 \end{bmatrix}$$

78. Think About It If a and b are real numbers such that $ab = 0$, then $a = 0$ or $b = 0$. However, if A and B are matrices such that $AB = O$, it is not necessarily true that $A = O$ or $B = O$. Illustrate this using the following matrices.

$$A = \begin{bmatrix} 3 & 3 \\ 4 & 4 \end{bmatrix}, \quad B = \begin{bmatrix} 1 & -1 \\ -1 & 1 \end{bmatrix}$$

79. Exploration Let A and B be unequal diagonal matrices of the same order. (A diagonal matrix is a square matrix in which each entry not on the main diagonal is zero.) Determine the products AB for several pairs of such matrices. Make a conjecture about a quick rule for such products.

80. Exploration Let $i = \sqrt{-1}$ and let

$$A = \begin{bmatrix} i & 0 \\ 0 & i \end{bmatrix} \quad \text{and} \quad B = \begin{bmatrix} 0 & -i \\ i & 0 \end{bmatrix}.$$

(a) Find A^2, A^3, and A^4. Identify any similarities with i^2, i^3, and i^4.

(b) Find and identify B^2.

Review

In Exercises 81–86, solve the equation.

81. $3x^2 + 20x - 32 = 0$

82. $8x^2 - 10x - 3 = 0$

83. $4x^3 + 10x^2 - 3x = 0$

84. $3x^3 + 22x^2 - 45x = 0$

85. $3x^3 - 12x^2 + 5x - 20 = 0$

86. $2x^3 - 5x^2 - 12x + 30 = 0$

In Exercises 87–90, solve the system of linear equations both graphically and algebraically.

87. $\begin{cases} -x + 4y = -9 \\ 5x - 8y = 39 \end{cases}$

88. $\begin{cases} 8x - 3y = -17 \\ -6x + 7y = 27 \end{cases}$

89. $\begin{cases} -x + 2y = -5 \\ -3x - y = -8 \end{cases}$

90. $\begin{cases} 6x - 13y = 11 \\ 9x + 5y = 41 \end{cases}$

▶ **What you should learn**

- How to verify that two matrices are inverses of each other
- How to use Gauss-Jordan elimination to find the inverses of matrices
- How to use a formula to find the inverses of 2×2 matrices
- How to use inverse matrices to solve systems of linear equations

▶ **Why you should learn it**

You can use inverse matrices to model and solve real-life problems. For instance, in Exercise 72 on page 581, an inverse matrix is used to find a linear model for the number of vehicle registrations in the United States.

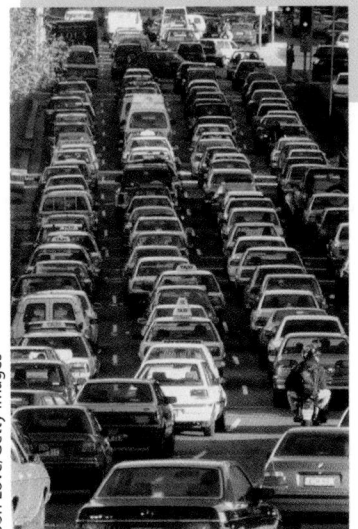

Jon Love/Getty Images

The Inverse of a Matrix

This section further develops the algebra of matrices. To begin, consider the real number equation $ax = b$. To solve this equation for x, multiply each side of the equation by a^{-1} (provided that $a \neq 0$).

$$ax = b$$
$$(a^{-1}a)x = a^{-1}b$$
$$(1)x = a^{-1}b$$
$$x = a^{-1}b$$

The number a^{-1} is called the *multiplicative inverse of a* because $a^{-1}a = 1$. The definition of the multiplicative **inverse of a matrix** is similar.

Definition of the Inverse of a Square Matrix

Let A be an $n \times n$ matrix and let I_n be the $n \times n$ identity matrix. If there exists matrix A^{-1} such that

$$AA^{-1} = I_n = A^{-1}A$$

then A^{-1} is called the **inverse** of A. The symbol A^{-1} is read "A inverse."

Example 1 ▶ The Inverse of a Matrix

Show that B is the inverse of A, where

$$A = \begin{bmatrix} -1 & 2 \\ -1 & 1 \end{bmatrix}$$

and

$$B = \begin{bmatrix} 1 & -2 \\ 1 & -1 \end{bmatrix}.$$

Solution

To show that B is the inverse of A, show that $AB = I = BA$, as follows.

$$AB = \begin{bmatrix} -1 & 2 \\ -1 & 1 \end{bmatrix}\begin{bmatrix} 1 & -2 \\ 1 & -1 \end{bmatrix} = \begin{bmatrix} -1+2 & 2-2 \\ -1+1 & 2-1 \end{bmatrix} = \begin{bmatrix} 1 & 0 \\ 0 & 1 \end{bmatrix}$$

$$BA = \begin{bmatrix} 1 & -2 \\ 1 & -1 \end{bmatrix}\begin{bmatrix} -1 & 2 \\ -1 & 1 \end{bmatrix} = \begin{bmatrix} -1+2 & 2-2 \\ -1+1 & 2-1 \end{bmatrix} = \begin{bmatrix} 1 & 0 \\ 0 & 1 \end{bmatrix}$$

Recall that it is not always true that $AB = BA$, even if both products are defined. However, if A and B are both square matrices and $AB = I_n$, it can be shown that $BA = I_n$. So, in Example 1, you need only to check that $AB = I_2$.

Finding Inverse Matrices

If a matrix A has an inverse, A is called **invertible** (or **nonsingular**); otherwise, A is called **singular.** A nonsquare matrix cannot have an inverse. To see this, note that if A is of order $m \times n$ and B is of order $n \times m$ (where $m \neq n$), the products AB and BA are of different orders and so cannot be equal to each other. Not all square matrices have inverses (see the matrix at the bottom of page 576). If, however, a matrix does have an inverse, that inverse is unique. Example 2 shows how to use a system of equations to find the inverse of a matrix.

Example 2 ▶ **Finding the Inverse of a Matrix**

Find the inverse of

$$A = \begin{bmatrix} 1 & 4 \\ -1 & -3 \end{bmatrix}.$$

Solution

To find the inverse of A, try to solve the matrix equation $AX = I$ for X.

$$\underset{A}{\begin{bmatrix} 1 & 4 \\ -1 & -3 \end{bmatrix}} \underset{X}{\begin{bmatrix} x_{11} & x_{12} \\ x_{21} & x_{22} \end{bmatrix}} = \underset{I}{\begin{bmatrix} 1 & 0 \\ 0 & 1 \end{bmatrix}}$$

$$\begin{bmatrix} x_{11} + 4x_{21} & x_{12} + 4x_{22} \\ -x_{11} - 3x_{21} & -x_{12} - 3x_{22} \end{bmatrix} = \begin{bmatrix} 1 & 0 \\ 0 & 1 \end{bmatrix}$$

Equating corresponding entries, you obtain two systems of linear equations.

$$\begin{cases} x_{11} + 4x_{21} = 1 \\ -x_{11} - 3x_{21} = 0 \end{cases}$$ Linear system with two variables, x_{11} and x_{21}.

$$\begin{cases} x_{12} + 4x_{22} = 0 \\ -x_{12} - 3x_{22} = 1 \end{cases}$$ Linear system with two variables, x_{12} and x_{22}.

From the first system you can determine that $x_{11} = -3$ and $x_{21} = 1$, and from the second system you can determine that $x_{12} = -4$ and $x_{22} = 1$. Therefore, the inverse of A is

$$X = A^{-1}$$

$$= \begin{bmatrix} -3 & -4 \\ 1 & 1 \end{bmatrix}.$$

You can use matrix multiplication to check this result.

Check

$$AA^{-1} = \begin{bmatrix} 1 & 4 \\ -1 & -3 \end{bmatrix} \begin{bmatrix} -3 & -4 \\ 1 & 1 \end{bmatrix} = \begin{bmatrix} 1 & 0 \\ 0 & 1 \end{bmatrix} \checkmark$$

$$A^{-1}A = \begin{bmatrix} -3 & -4 \\ 1 & 1 \end{bmatrix} \begin{bmatrix} 1 & 4 \\ -1 & -3 \end{bmatrix} = \begin{bmatrix} 1 & 0 \\ 0 & 1 \end{bmatrix} \checkmark$$

In Example 2, note that the two systems of linear equations have the *same coefficient matrix A*. Rather than solve the two systems represented by

$$\begin{bmatrix} 1 & 4 & \vdots & 1 \\ -1 & -3 & \vdots & 0 \end{bmatrix}$$

and

$$\begin{bmatrix} 1 & 4 & \vdots & 0 \\ -1 & -3 & \vdots & 1 \end{bmatrix}$$

separately, you can solve them *simultaneously* by *adjoining* the identity matrix to the coefficient matrix to obtain

$$\begin{matrix} A & & & I \\ \end{matrix}$$
$$\begin{bmatrix} 1 & 4 & \vdots & 1 & 0 \\ -1 & -3 & \vdots & 0 & 1 \end{bmatrix}.$$

This "doubly augmented" matrix can be represented as $[A \;\vdots\; I]$. By applying Gauss-Jordan elimination to this matrix, you can solve *both* systems with a single elimination process.

$$\begin{bmatrix} 1 & 4 & \vdots & 1 & 0 \\ -1 & -3 & \vdots & 0 & 1 \end{bmatrix}$$

$$R_1 + R_2 \rightarrow \begin{bmatrix} 1 & 4 & \vdots & 1 & 0 \\ 0 & 1 & \vdots & 1 & 1 \end{bmatrix}$$

$$-4R_2 + R_1 \rightarrow \begin{bmatrix} 1 & 0 & \vdots & -3 & -4 \\ 0 & 1 & \vdots & 1 & 1 \end{bmatrix}$$

So, from the "doubly augmented" matrix $[A \;\vdots\; I]$, you obtained the matrix $[I \;\vdots\; A^{-1}]$.

$$\begin{matrix} A & & & I \\ \end{matrix} \qquad \begin{matrix} I & & & A^{-1} \\ \end{matrix}$$
$$\begin{bmatrix} 1 & 4 & \vdots & 1 & 0 \\ -1 & -3 & \vdots & 0 & 1 \end{bmatrix} \implies \begin{bmatrix} 1 & 0 & \vdots & -3 & -4 \\ 0 & 1 & \vdots & 1 & 1 \end{bmatrix}$$

This procedure (or algorithm) works for an arbitrary square matrix that has an inverse.

Technology

You can find the inverse of a matrix with a graphing utility. Enter the matrix in the graphing utility, press the inverse key $\boxed{x^{-1}}$, and press $\boxed{\text{ENTER}}$. The inverse of the matrix will be displayed on the screen.

Finding an Inverse Matrix

Let A be a square matrix of order n.

1. Write the $n \times 2n$ matrix that consists of the given matrix A on the left and the $n \times n$ identity matrix I on the right to obtain $[A \;\vdots\; I]$.

2. If possible, row reduce A to I using elementary row operations on the *entire* matrix $[A \;\vdots\; I]$. The result will be the matrix $[I \;\vdots\; A^{-1}]$. If this is not possible, A is not invertible.

3. Check your work by multiplying to see that $AA^{-1} = I = A^{-1}A$.

Example 3 ▶   Finding the Inverse of a Matrix

Find the inverse of

$$A = \begin{bmatrix} 1 & -1 & 0 \\ 1 & 0 & -1 \\ 6 & -2 & -3 \end{bmatrix}.$$

Solution

Begin by adjoining the identity matrix to A to form the matrix

$$[A \;\vdots\; I] = \begin{bmatrix} 1 & -1 & 0 & \vdots & 1 & 0 & 0 \\ 1 & 0 & -1 & \vdots & 0 & 1 & 0 \\ 6 & -2 & -3 & \vdots & 0 & 0 & 1 \end{bmatrix}.$$

Use elementary row operations to obtain the form $[I \;\vdots\; A^{-1}]$, as follows.

$$\begin{matrix} \\ -R_1 + R_2 \to \\ -6R_1 + R_3 \to \end{matrix} \begin{bmatrix} 1 & -1 & 0 & \vdots & 1 & 0 & 0 \\ 0 & 1 & -1 & \vdots & -1 & 1 & 0 \\ 0 & 4 & -3 & \vdots & -6 & 0 & 1 \end{bmatrix}$$

$$\begin{matrix} R_2 + R_1 \to \\ \\ -4R_2 + R_3 \to \end{matrix} \begin{bmatrix} 1 & 0 & -1 & \vdots & 0 & 1 & 0 \\ 0 & 1 & -1 & \vdots & -1 & 1 & 0 \\ 0 & 0 & 1 & \vdots & -2 & -4 & 1 \end{bmatrix}$$

$$\begin{matrix} R_3 + R_1 \to \\ R_3 + R_2 \to \\ \\ \end{matrix} \begin{bmatrix} 1 & 0 & 0 & \vdots & -2 & -3 & 1 \\ 0 & 1 & 0 & \vdots & -3 & -3 & 1 \\ 0 & 0 & 1 & \vdots & -2 & -4 & 1 \end{bmatrix} = [I \;\vdots\; A^{-1}]$$

So, the matrix A is invertible and its inverse is

$$A^{-1} = \begin{bmatrix} -2 & -3 & 1 \\ -3 & -3 & 1 \\ -2 & -4 & 1 \end{bmatrix}.$$

Confirm this result by multiplying A and A^{-1} to obtain I, as follows.

Check

$$AA^{-1} = \begin{bmatrix} 1 & -1 & 0 \\ 1 & 0 & -1 \\ 6 & -2 & -3 \end{bmatrix} \begin{bmatrix} -2 & -3 & 1 \\ -3 & -3 & 1 \\ -2 & -4 & 1 \end{bmatrix} = \begin{bmatrix} 1 & 0 & 0 \\ 0 & 1 & 0 \\ 0 & 0 & 1 \end{bmatrix} = I$$

The process shown in Example 3 applies to any $n \times n$ matrix A. If A has an inverse, this process will find it. On the other hand, if A does not have an inverse (if A is *singular*), the process will tell you so. That is, matrix A will not reduce to the identity matrix. For instance, the following matrix has no inverse.

$$A = \begin{bmatrix} 1 & 2 & 0 \\ 3 & -1 & 2 \\ -2 & 3 & -2 \end{bmatrix}$$

Explain how the elimination process shows that this matrix is singular.

You may want to show what happens when A^{-1} does not exist. For example,

$$A = \begin{bmatrix} 3 & 6 \\ 1 & 2 \end{bmatrix} \text{ or}$$

$$B = \begin{bmatrix} 3 & 2 & 1 \\ 1 & 0 & -1 \\ 0 & 1 & 2 \end{bmatrix}.$$

The Inverse of a 2 × 2 Matrix

Using Gauss-Jordan elimination to find the inverse of a matrix works well (even as a computer technique) for matrices of order 3×3 or greater. For 2×2 matrices, however, many people prefer to use a formula for the inverse rather than Gauss-Jordan elimination. This simple formula, which works *only* for 2×2 matrices, is explained as follows. If A is a 2×2 matrix given by

$$A = \begin{bmatrix} a & b \\ c & d \end{bmatrix}$$

then A is invertible if and only if $ad - bc \neq 0$. Moreover, if $ad - bc \neq 0$, the inverse is given by

$$A^{-1} = \frac{1}{ad - bc} \begin{bmatrix} d & -b \\ -c & a \end{bmatrix}.$$ Formula for inverse of matrix A

The denominator $ad - bc$ is called the **determinant** of the 2×2 matrix A. You will study determinants in the next section.

Example 4 ▶   Finding the Inverse of a 2 × 2 Matrix

If possible, find the inverse of each matrix.

a. $A = \begin{bmatrix} 3 & -1 \\ -2 & 2 \end{bmatrix}$

b. $B = \begin{bmatrix} 3 & -1 \\ -6 & 2 \end{bmatrix}$

Solution

a. For the matrix A, apply the formula for the inverse of a 2×2 matrix to obtain

$$ad - bc = (3)(2) - (-1)(-2)$$
$$= 4.$$

Because this quantity is not zero, the inverse is formed by interchanging the entries on the main diagonal, changing the signs of the other two entries, and multiplying by the scalar $\frac{1}{4}$, as follows.

$$A^{-1} = \frac{1}{4} \begin{bmatrix} 2 & 1 \\ 2 & 3 \end{bmatrix}$$ Substitute for a, b, c, d, and the determinant.

$$= \begin{bmatrix} \frac{1}{2} & \frac{1}{4} \\ \frac{1}{2} & \frac{3}{4} \end{bmatrix}$$ Multiply by the scalar $\frac{1}{4}$.

b. For the matrix B, you have

$$ad - bc = (3)(2) - (-1)(-6)$$
$$= 0$$

which means that B is not invertible.

Systems of Linear Equations

You know that a system of linear equations can have exactly one solution, infinitely many solutions, or no solution. If the coefficient matrix A of a *square* system (a system that has the same number of equations as variables) is invertible, the system has a unique solution, which is defined as follows.

A System of Equations with a Unique Solution

If A is an invertible matrix, the system of linear equations represented by $AX = B$ has a unique solution given by

$$X = A^{-1}B.$$

Example 5 ▶   **Solving a System Using an Inverse**

You are going to invest \$10,000 in AAA-rated bonds, AA-rated bonds, and B-rated bonds and want an annual return of \$730. The average yields are 6% on AAA bonds, 7.5% on AA bonds, and 9.5% on B bonds. You will invest twice as much in AAA bonds as in B bonds. Your investment can be represented as

$$\begin{cases} x + y + z = 10{,}000 \\ 0.06x + 0.075y + 0.095z = 730 \\ x \quad\quad - 2z = 0 \end{cases}$$

where x, y, and z represent the amounts invested in AAA, AA, and B bonds, respectively. Use an inverse matrix to solve the system.

Solution

Begin by writing the system in the matrix form $AX = B$.

$$\begin{bmatrix} 1 & 1 & 1 \\ 0.06 & 0.075 & 0.095 \\ 1 & 0 & -2 \end{bmatrix} \begin{bmatrix} x \\ y \\ z \end{bmatrix} = \begin{bmatrix} 10{,}000 \\ 730 \\ 0 \end{bmatrix}$$

Then, use Gauss-Jordan elimination to find A^{-1}.

$$A^{-1} = \begin{bmatrix} 15 & -200 & -2 \\ -21.5 & 300 & 3.5 \\ 7.5 & -100 & -1.5 \end{bmatrix}$$

Finally, multiply B by A^{-1} on the left to obtain the solution.

$$X = A^{-1}B$$

$$= \begin{bmatrix} 15 & -200 & -2 \\ -21.5 & 300 & 3.5 \\ 7.5 & -100 & -1.5 \end{bmatrix} \begin{bmatrix} 10{,}000 \\ 730 \\ 0 \end{bmatrix} = \begin{bmatrix} 4000 \\ 4000 \\ 2000 \end{bmatrix}$$

The solution to the system is $x = 4000$, $y = 4000$, and $z = 2000$. So, you will invest \$4000 in AAA bonds, \$4000 in AA bonds, and \$2000 in B bonds.

8.3 Exercises

Exercises in which the inverse matrix does not exist: 17, 19, 20, 24, 32, 35, 41
Exercise containing system with no solution: 55
Exercises containing systems with infinitely many solutions: 61, 62

In Exercises 1–10, show that B is the inverse of A.

1. $A = \begin{bmatrix} 2 & 1 \\ 5 & 3 \end{bmatrix}$, $B = \begin{bmatrix} 3 & -1 \\ -5 & 2 \end{bmatrix}$

2. $A = \begin{bmatrix} 1 & -1 \\ -1 & 2 \end{bmatrix}$, $B = \begin{bmatrix} 2 & 1 \\ 1 & 1 \end{bmatrix}$

3. $A = \begin{bmatrix} 1 & 2 \\ 3 & 4 \end{bmatrix}$, $B = \begin{bmatrix} -2 & 1 \\ \frac{3}{2} & -\frac{1}{2} \end{bmatrix}$

4. $A = \begin{bmatrix} 1 & -1 \\ 2 & 3 \end{bmatrix}$, $B = \begin{bmatrix} \frac{3}{5} & \frac{1}{5} \\ -\frac{2}{5} & \frac{1}{5} \end{bmatrix}$

5. $A = \begin{bmatrix} 2 & -17 & 11 \\ -1 & 11 & -7 \\ 0 & 3 & -2 \end{bmatrix}$, $B = \begin{bmatrix} 1 & 1 & 2 \\ 2 & 4 & -3 \\ 3 & 6 & -5 \end{bmatrix}$

6. $A = \begin{bmatrix} -4 & 1 & 5 \\ -1 & 2 & 4 \\ 0 & -1 & -1 \end{bmatrix}$, $B = \begin{bmatrix} -\frac{1}{2} & 1 & \frac{3}{2} \\ \frac{1}{4} & -1 & -\frac{11}{4} \\ -\frac{1}{4} & 1 & \frac{7}{4} \end{bmatrix}$

7. $A = \begin{bmatrix} 2 & 0 & 1 & 1 \\ 3 & 0 & 0 & 1 \\ -1 & 1 & -2 & 1 \\ 4 & -1 & 1 & 0 \end{bmatrix}$,

$B = \begin{bmatrix} -1 & 2 & -1 & -1 \\ -4 & 9 & -5 & -6 \\ 0 & 1 & -1 & -1 \\ 3 & -5 & 3 & 3 \end{bmatrix}$

8. $A = \begin{bmatrix} -2 & 0 & 1 & 0 \\ 1 & -1 & -3 & 0 \\ -2 & -1 & 0 & -2 \\ 0 & 1 & 3 & -1 \end{bmatrix}$,

$B = \begin{bmatrix} -3 & -3 & 1 & -2 \\ 12 & 14 & -5 & 10 \\ -5 & -6 & 2 & -4 \\ -3 & -4 & 1 & -3 \end{bmatrix}$

9. $A = \begin{bmatrix} -2 & 2 & 3 \\ 1 & -1 & 0 \\ 0 & 1 & 4 \end{bmatrix}$, $B = \dfrac{1}{3}\begin{bmatrix} -4 & -5 & 3 \\ -4 & -8 & 3 \\ 1 & 2 & 0 \end{bmatrix}$

10. $A = \begin{bmatrix} -1 & 1 & 0 & -1 \\ 1 & -1 & 1 & 0 \\ -1 & 1 & 2 & 0 \\ 0 & -1 & 1 & 1 \end{bmatrix}$,

$B = \dfrac{1}{3}\begin{bmatrix} -3 & 1 & 1 & -3 \\ -3 & -1 & 2 & -3 \\ 0 & 1 & 1 & 0 \\ -3 & -2 & 1 & 0 \end{bmatrix}$

In Exercises 11–26, find the inverse of the matrix (if it exists).

11. $\begin{bmatrix} 2 & 0 \\ 0 & 3 \end{bmatrix}$

12. $\begin{bmatrix} 1 & 2 \\ 3 & 7 \end{bmatrix}$

13. $\begin{bmatrix} 1 & -2 \\ 2 & -3 \end{bmatrix}$

14. $\begin{bmatrix} -7 & 33 \\ 4 & -19 \end{bmatrix}$

15. $\begin{bmatrix} -1 & 1 \\ -2 & 1 \end{bmatrix}$

16. $\begin{bmatrix} 11 & 1 \\ -1 & 0 \end{bmatrix}$

17. $\begin{bmatrix} 2 & 4 \\ 4 & 8 \end{bmatrix}$

18. $\begin{bmatrix} 2 & 3 \\ 1 & 4 \end{bmatrix}$

19. $\begin{bmatrix} 2 & 7 & 1 \\ -3 & -9 & 2 \end{bmatrix}$

20. $\begin{bmatrix} -2 & 5 \\ 6 & -15 \\ 0 & 1 \end{bmatrix}$

21. $\begin{bmatrix} 1 & 1 & 1 \\ 3 & 5 & 4 \\ 3 & 6 & 5 \end{bmatrix}$

22. $\begin{bmatrix} 1 & 2 & 2 \\ 3 & 7 & 9 \\ -1 & -4 & -7 \end{bmatrix}$

23. $\begin{bmatrix} 1 & 0 & 0 \\ 3 & 4 & 0 \\ 2 & 5 & 5 \end{bmatrix}$

24. $\begin{bmatrix} 1 & 0 & 0 \\ 3 & 0 & 0 \\ 2 & 5 & 5 \end{bmatrix}$

25. $\begin{bmatrix} -8 & 0 & 0 & 0 \\ 0 & 1 & 0 & 0 \\ 0 & 0 & 4 & 0 \\ 0 & 0 & 0 & -5 \end{bmatrix}$

26. $\begin{bmatrix} 1 & 3 & -2 & 0 \\ 0 & 2 & 4 & 6 \\ 0 & 0 & -2 & 1 \\ 0 & 0 & 0 & 5 \end{bmatrix}$

 In Exercises 27–38, use the matrix capabilities of a graphing utility to find the inverse of the matrix (if it exists).

27. $\begin{bmatrix} 1 & 2 & -1 \\ 3 & 7 & -10 \\ -5 & -7 & -15 \end{bmatrix}$

28. $\begin{bmatrix} 10 & 5 & -7 \\ -5 & 1 & 4 \\ 3 & 2 & -2 \end{bmatrix}$

29. $\begin{bmatrix} 1 & 1 & 2 \\ 3 & 1 & 0 \\ -2 & 0 & 3 \end{bmatrix}$

30. $\begin{bmatrix} 3 & 2 & 2 \\ 2 & 2 & 2 \\ -4 & 4 & 3 \end{bmatrix}$

31. $\begin{bmatrix} -\frac{1}{2} & \frac{3}{4} & \frac{1}{4} \\ 1 & 0 & -\frac{3}{2} \\ 0 & -1 & \frac{1}{2} \end{bmatrix}$

32. $\begin{bmatrix} -\frac{5}{6} & \frac{1}{3} & \frac{11}{6} \\ 0 & \frac{2}{3} & 2 \\ 1 & -\frac{1}{2} & -\frac{5}{2} \end{bmatrix}$

33. $\begin{bmatrix} 0.1 & 0.2 & 0.3 \\ -0.3 & 0.2 & 0.2 \\ 0.5 & 0.4 & 0.4 \end{bmatrix}$

34. $\begin{bmatrix} 0.6 & 0 & -0.3 \\ 0.7 & -1 & 0.2 \\ 1 & 0 & -0.9 \end{bmatrix}$

35. $\begin{bmatrix} 1 & 0 & 3 & 0 \\ 0 & 2 & 0 & 4 \\ 1 & 0 & 3 & 0 \\ 0 & 2 & 0 & 4 \end{bmatrix}$

36. $\begin{bmatrix} 4 & 8 & -7 & 14 \\ 2 & 5 & -4 & 6 \\ 0 & 2 & 1 & -7 \\ 3 & 6 & -5 & 10 \end{bmatrix}$

37. $\begin{bmatrix} -1 & 0 & 1 & 0 \\ 0 & 2 & 0 & -1 \\ 2 & 0 & -1 & 0 \\ 0 & -1 & 0 & 1 \end{bmatrix}$ **38.** $\begin{bmatrix} 1 & -2 & -1 & -2 \\ 3 & -5 & -2 & -3 \\ 2 & -5 & -2 & -5 \\ -1 & 4 & 4 & 11 \end{bmatrix}$

In Exercises 39–44, use the formula on page 577 to find the inverse of the matrix.

39. $\begin{bmatrix} 5 & -2 \\ 2 & 3 \end{bmatrix}$ **40.** $\begin{bmatrix} 7 & 12 \\ -8 & -5 \end{bmatrix}$

41. $\begin{bmatrix} -4 & -6 \\ 2 & 3 \end{bmatrix}$ **42.** $\begin{bmatrix} -12 & 3 \\ 5 & -2 \end{bmatrix}$

43. $\begin{bmatrix} \frac{7}{2} & -\frac{3}{4} \\ \frac{1}{5} & \frac{4}{5} \end{bmatrix}$ **44.** $\begin{bmatrix} -\frac{1}{4} & \frac{9}{4} \\ \frac{5}{3} & \frac{8}{9} \end{bmatrix}$

In Exercises 45–48, use the inverse matrix found in Exercise 13 to solve the system of linear equations.

45. $\begin{cases} x - 2y = 5 \\ 2x - 3y = 10 \end{cases}$ **46.** $\begin{cases} x - 2y = 0 \\ 2x - 3y = 3 \end{cases}$

47. $\begin{cases} x - 2y = 4 \\ 2x - 3y = 2 \end{cases}$ **48.** $\begin{cases} x - 2y = 1 \\ 2x - 3y = -2 \end{cases}$

In Exercises 49 and 50, use the inverse matrix found in Exercise 21 to solve the system of linear equations.

49. $\begin{cases} x + y + z = 0 \\ 3x + 5y + 4z = 5 \\ 3x + 6y + 5z = 2 \end{cases}$ **50.** $\begin{cases} x + y + z = -1 \\ 3x + 5y + 4z = 2 \\ 3x + 6y + 5z = 0 \end{cases}$

In Exercises 51 and 52, use the inverse matrix found in Exercise 38 to solve the system of linear equations.

51. $\begin{cases} x_1 - 2x_2 - x_3 - 2x_4 = 0 \\ 3x_1 - 5x_2 - 2x_3 - 3x_4 = 1 \\ 2x_1 - 5x_2 - 2x_3 - 5x_4 = -1 \\ -x_1 + 4x_2 + 4x_3 + 11x_4 = 2 \end{cases}$

52. $\begin{cases} x_1 - 2x_2 - x_3 - 2x_4 = 1 \\ 3x_1 - 5x_2 - 2x_3 - 3x_4 = -2 \\ 2x_1 - 5x_2 - 2x_3 - 5x_4 = 0 \\ -x_1 + 4x_2 + 4x_3 + 11x_4 = -3 \end{cases}$

In Exercises 53–60, use an inverse matrix to solve (if possible) the system of linear equations.

53. $\begin{cases} 3x + 4y = -2 \\ 5x + 3y = 4 \end{cases}$ **54.** $\begin{cases} 18x + 12y = 13 \\ 30x + 24y = 23 \end{cases}$

55. $\begin{cases} -0.4x + 0.8y = 1.6 \\ 2x - 4y = 5 \end{cases}$ **56.** $\begin{cases} 0.2x - 0.6y = 2.4 \\ -x + 1.4y = -8.8 \end{cases}$

57. $\begin{cases} -\frac{1}{4}x + \frac{3}{8}y = -2 \\ \frac{3}{2}x + \frac{3}{4}y = -12 \end{cases}$ **58.** $\begin{cases} \frac{5}{6}x - y = -20 \\ \frac{4}{3}x - \frac{7}{2}y = -51 \end{cases}$

59. $\begin{cases} 4x - y + z = -5 \\ 2x + 2y + 3z = 10 \\ 5x - 2y + 6z = 1 \end{cases}$ **60.** $\begin{cases} 4x - 2y + 3z = -2 \\ 2x + 2y + 5z = 16 \\ 8x - 5y - 2z = 4 \end{cases}$

 In Exercises 61–66, use the matrix capabilities of a graphing utility to solve (if possible) the system of linear equations.

61. $\begin{cases} 5x - 3y + 2z = 2 \\ 2x + 2y - 3z = 3 \\ x - 7y + 8z = -4 \end{cases}$ **62.** $\begin{cases} 2x + 3y + 5z = 4 \\ 3x + 5y + 9z = 7 \\ 5x + 9y + 17z = 13 \end{cases}$

63. $\begin{cases} 3x - 2y + z = -29 \\ -4x + y - 3z = 37 \\ x - 5y + z = -24 \end{cases}$

64. $\begin{cases} -8x + 7y - 10z = -151 \\ 12x + 3y - 5z = 86 \\ 15x - 9y + 2z = 187 \end{cases}$

65. $\begin{cases} 7x - 3y + 2w = 41 \\ -2x + y - w = -13 \\ 4x + z - 2w = 12 \\ -x + y - w = -8 \end{cases}$

66. $\begin{cases} 2x + 5y + w = 11 \\ x + 4y + 2z - 2w = -7 \\ 2x - 2y + 5z + w = 3 \\ x - 3w = -1 \end{cases}$

Investment Portfolio In Exercises 67–70, consider a person who invests in AAA-rated bonds, A-rated bonds, and B-rated bonds. The average yields are 6.5% on AAA bonds, 7% on A bonds, and 9% on B bonds. The person invests twice as much in B bonds as in A bonds. Let x, y, and z represent the amounts invested in AAA, A, and B bonds, respectively.

$$\begin{cases} x + y + z = \text{(total investment)} \\ 0.065x + 0.07y + 0.09z = \text{(annual return)} \\ 2y - z = 0 \end{cases}$$

Use the inverse of the coefficient matrix of this system to find the amount invested in each type of bond.

	Total Investment	Annual Return
67.	$10,000	$705
68.	$10,000	$760
69.	$12,000	$835
70.	$500,000	$38,000

71. *Circuit Analysis* Consider the circuit in the figure. The currents I_1, I_2, and I_3, in amperes, are the solution of the system of linear equations

$$\begin{cases} 2I_1 \quad\;\; + 4I_3 = E_1 \\ \qquad I_2 + 4I_3 = E_2 \\ I_1 + I_2 - \;\; I_3 = 0 \end{cases}$$

where E_1 and E_2 are voltages. Use the inverse of the coefficient matrix of this system to find the unknown currents for the voltages.

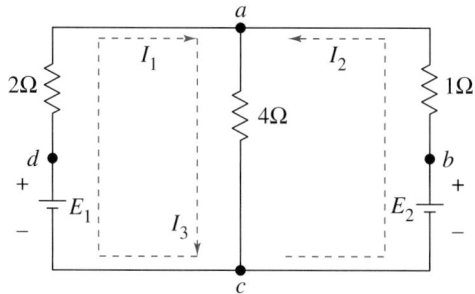

(a) $E_1 = 14$ volts, $E_2 = 28$ volts

(b) $E_1 = 24$ volts, $E_2 = 23$ volts

▶ **Model It**

72. *Data Analysis* The table shows the numbers y (in millions) of motor vehicle registrations in the United States for the years 1997 through 1999. (Source: U.S. Federal Highway Administration)

Year, t	Registrations, y
1997	207.8
1998	211.6
1999	216.3

(a) Use the technique demonstrated in Exercises 55–60 in Section 7.2 to create a system of linear equations for the data. Let t represent the year, with $t = 7$ corresponding to 1997.

(b) Use the matrix capabilities of a graphing utility to find an inverse matrix to solve the system from part (a) and find the least squares regression line $y = at + b$.

(c) Use the result of part (b) to estimate the number of motor vehicle registrations in 2000.

▶ **Model It** *(continued)*

(d) The actual number of motor vehicle registrations in 2000 was 221.5 million. How does this value compare with your estimate from part (c)?

(e) Use the result of part (b) to estimate when the number of vehicle registrations will reach 240 million.

Synthesis

True or False? In Exercises 73 and 74, determine whether the statement is true or false. Justify your answer.

73. Multiplication of an invertible matrix and its inverse is commutative.

74. If you multiply two square matrices and obtain the identity matrix, you can assume that the matrices are inverses of one another.

75. If A is a 2×2 matrix $A = \begin{bmatrix} a & b \\ c & d \end{bmatrix}$, then A is invertible if and only if $ad - bc \neq 0$. If $ad - bc \neq 0$, verify that the inverse is

$$A^{-1} = \frac{1}{ad - bc} \begin{bmatrix} d & -b \\ -c & a \end{bmatrix}.$$

76. *Exploration* Consider matrices of the form

$$A = \begin{bmatrix} a_{11} & 0 & 0 & 0 & \cdots & 0 \\ 0 & a_{22} & 0 & 0 & \cdots & 0 \\ 0 & 0 & a_{33} & 0 & \cdots & 0 \\ \vdots & \vdots & \vdots & \vdots & \cdots & \vdots \\ 0 & 0 & 0 & 0 & \cdots & a_{nn} \end{bmatrix}.$$

(a) Write a 2×2 matrix and a 3×3 matrix in the form of A. Find the inverse of each.

(b) Use the result of part (a) to make a conjecture about the inverses of matrices in the form of A.

Review

In Exercises 77 and 78, solve the inequality and sketch the solution on the real number line.

77. $|x + 7| \geq 2$

78. $|2x - 1| < 3$

In Exercises 79–82, solve the equation.

79. $3^{x/2} = 315$

80. $2000e^{-x/5} = 400$

81. $\log_2 x - 2 = 4.5$

82. $\ln x + \ln(x - 1) = 0$

8.4 The Determinant of a Square Matrix

▶ **What you should learn**

- How to find the determinants of 2×2 matrices
- How to find minors and cofactors of square matrices
- How to find the determinants of square matrices

▶ **Why you should learn it**

Determinants are often used in other branches of mathematics. For instance, Exercises 79–84 on page 589 show some types of determinants that are useful when changes in variables are made in calculus.

The Determinant of a 2 × 2 Matrix

Every *square* matrix can be associated with a real number called its **determinant.** Determinants have many uses, and several will be discussed in this and the next section. Historically, the use of determinants arose from special number patterns that occur when systems of linear equations are solved. For instance, the system

$$\begin{cases} a_1 x + b_1 y = c_1 \\ a_2 x + b_2 y = c_2 \end{cases}$$

has a solution

$$x = \frac{c_1 b_2 - c_2 b_1}{a_1 b_2 - a_2 b_1} \quad \text{and} \quad y = \frac{a_1 c_2 - a_2 c_1}{a_1 b_2 - a_2 b_1}$$

provided that $a_1 b_2 - a_2 b_1 \neq 0$. Note that the denominators of the two fractions are the same. This denominator is called the *determinant* of the coefficient matrix of the system.

Coefficient Matrix   *Determinant*

$$A = \begin{bmatrix} a_1 & b_1 \\ a_2 & b_2 \end{bmatrix} \qquad \det(A) = a_1 b_2 - a_2 b_1$$

The determinant of the matrix A can also be denoted by vertical bars on both sides of the matrix, as indicated in the following definition.

Definition of the Determinant of a 2 × 2 Matrix

The **determinant** of the matrix

$$A = \begin{bmatrix} a_1 & b_1 \\ a_2 & b_2 \end{bmatrix}$$

is given by

$$\det(A) = |A| = \begin{vmatrix} a_1 & b_1 \\ a_2 & b_2 \end{vmatrix} = a_1 b_2 - a_2 b_1.$$

In this book, $\det(A)$ and $|A|$ are used interchangeably to represent the determinant of A. Although vertical bars are also used to denote the absolute value of a real number, the context will show which use is intended.

A convenient method for remembering the formula for the determinant of a 2×2 matrix is shown in the following diagram.

$$\det(A) = \begin{vmatrix} a_1 & b_1 \\ a_2 & b_2 \end{vmatrix} = a_1 b_2 - a_2 b_1$$

Note that the determinant is the difference of the products of the two diagonals of the matrix.

Point out to your students that a matrix is an array of numbers, but a determinant is a single numerical value.

Example 1 ▶ **The Determinant of a 2 × 2 Matrix**

Find the determinant of each matrix.

a. $A = \begin{bmatrix} 2 & -3 \\ 1 & 2 \end{bmatrix}$

b. $B = \begin{bmatrix} 2 & 1 \\ 4 & 2 \end{bmatrix}$

c. $C = \begin{bmatrix} 0 & \frac{3}{2} \\ 2 & 4 \end{bmatrix}$

Solution

a. $\det(A) = \begin{vmatrix} 2 & -3 \\ 1 & 2 \end{vmatrix}$

$= 2(2) - 1(-3)$

$= 4 + 3 = 7$

b. $\det(B) = \begin{vmatrix} 2 & 1 \\ 4 & 2 \end{vmatrix}$

$= 2(2) - 4(1)$

$= 4 - 4 = 0$

c. $\det(C) = \begin{vmatrix} 0 & \frac{3}{2} \\ 2 & 4 \end{vmatrix}$

$= 0(4) - 2\left(\frac{3}{2}\right)$

$= 0 - 3 = -3$

◀ **Exploration** ▶

Use a graphing utility to find the determinant of the following matrix.

$$A = \begin{bmatrix} 1 & 2 \\ -1 & 0 \\ 3 & -2 \end{bmatrix}$$

What message appears on the screen? Why does the graphing utility display this message?

Notice in Example 1 that the determinant of a matrix can be positive, zero, or negative.

The determinant of a matrix of order 1×1 is defined simply as the entry of the matrix. For instance, if $A = \begin{bmatrix} -2 \end{bmatrix}$, then $\det(A) = -2$.

Technology

Most graphing utilities can evaluate the determinant of a matrix. For instance, you can evaluate the determinant of

$$A = \begin{bmatrix} 2 & -3 \\ 1 & 2 \end{bmatrix}$$

by entering the matrix as $[A]$ and then choosing the *determinant* feature. The result should be 7, as in Example 1(a). Try evaluating the determinants of other matrices.

Minors and Cofactors

To define the determinant of a square matrix of order 3×3 or higher, it is convenient to introduce the concepts of **minors** and **cofactors.**

Sign Pattern for Cofactors

$$\begin{bmatrix} + & - & + \\ - & + & - \\ + & - & + \end{bmatrix}$$

3×3 matrix

$$\begin{bmatrix} + & - & + & - \\ - & + & - & + \\ + & - & + & - \\ - & + & - & + \end{bmatrix}$$

4×4 matrix

$$\begin{bmatrix} + & - & + & - & + & \cdots \\ - & + & - & + & - & \cdots \\ + & - & + & - & + & \cdots \\ - & + & - & + & - & \cdots \\ + & - & + & - & + & \cdots \\ \vdots & \vdots & \vdots & \vdots & \vdots & \end{bmatrix}$$

$n \times n$ matrix

Minors and Cofactors of a Square Matrix

If A is a square matrix, the **minor** M_{ij} of the entry a_{ij} is the determinant of the matrix obtained by deleting the ith row and jth column of A. The **cofactor** C_{ij} of the entry a_{ij} is

$$C_{ij} = (-1)^{i+j} M_{ij}.$$

In the sign pattern for cofactors at the left, notice that *odd* positions (where $i + j$ is odd) have negative signs and *even* positions (where $i + j$ is even) have positive signs.

Example 2 ▶ **Finding the Minors and Cofactors of a Matrix**

Find all the minors and cofactors of

$$A = \begin{bmatrix} 0 & 2 & 1 \\ 3 & -1 & 2 \\ 4 & 0 & 1 \end{bmatrix}.$$

Solution

To find the minor M_{11}, delete the first row and first column of A and evaluate the determinant of the resulting matrix.

$$\begin{bmatrix} 0 & 2 & 1 \\ 3 & -1 & 2 \\ 4 & 0 & 1 \end{bmatrix}, \quad M_{11} = \begin{vmatrix} -1 & 2 \\ 0 & 1 \end{vmatrix} = -1(1) - 0(2) = -1$$

Similarly, to find M_{12}, delete the first row and second column.

$$\begin{bmatrix} 0 & 2 & 1 \\ 3 & -1 & 2 \\ 4 & 0 & 1 \end{bmatrix}, \quad M_{12} = \begin{vmatrix} 3 & 2 \\ 4 & 1 \end{vmatrix} = 3(1) - 4(2) = -5$$

Continuing this pattern, you obtain the minors.

$$
\begin{array}{lll}
M_{11} = -1 & M_{12} = -5 & M_{13} = 4 \\
M_{21} = 2 & M_{22} = -4 & M_{23} = -8 \\
M_{31} = 5 & M_{32} = -3 & M_{33} = -6
\end{array}
$$

Now, to find the cofactors, combine the checkerboard pattern of signs for a 3×3 matrix (at left above) with these minors.

$$
\begin{array}{lll}
C_{11} = -1 & C_{12} = 5 & C_{13} = 4 \\
C_{21} = -2 & C_{22} = -4 & C_{23} = 8 \\
C_{31} = 5 & C_{32} = 3 & C_{33} = -6
\end{array}
$$

The Determinant of a Square Matrix

The definition below is called *inductive* because it uses determinants of matrices of order $n - 1$ to define determinants of matrices of order n.

Determinant of a Square Matrix

If A is a square matrix (of order 2×2 or greater), the determinant of A is the sum of the entries in any row (or column) of A multiplied by their respective cofactors. For instance, expanding along the first row yields

$$|A| = a_{11}C_{11} + a_{12}C_{12} + \cdots + a_{1n}C_{1n}.$$

Applying this definition to find a determinant is called expanding by *cofactors*.

Try checking that for a 2×2 matrix

$$A = \begin{bmatrix} a_1 & b_1 \\ a_2 & b_2 \end{bmatrix}$$

this definition of the determinant yields $|A| = a_1 b_2 - a_2 b_1$, as previously defined.

You may need to remind your students to use the appropriate signs when expanding a determinant by cofactors. (Refer them to the Sign Pattern for Cofactors chart on page 584.)

Example 3 ▶ **The Determinant of a Matrix of Order 3 × 3**

Find the determinant of

$$A = \begin{bmatrix} 0 & 2 & 1 \\ 3 & -1 & 2 \\ 4 & 0 & 1 \end{bmatrix}.$$

Solution

Note that this is the same matrix that was in Example 2. There you found the cofactors of the entries in the first row to be

$$C_{11} = -1, \quad C_{12} = 5, \quad \text{and} \quad C_{13} = 4.$$

So, by the definition of a determinant, you have

$$\begin{aligned} |A| &= a_{11}C_{11} + a_{12}C_{12} + a_{13}C_{13} && \text{First-row expansion} \\ &= 0(-1) + 2(5) + 1(4) \\ &= 14. \end{aligned}$$

You might want to consider showing students the following alternative method that can be used to evaluate the determinant of a 3×3 matrix A. (Note that this method works only for 3×3 matrices.) Copy the first and second columns of A to form fourth and fifth columns. The determinant of A is obtained by adding the products of the three "downward diagonals" and subtracting the products of the three "upward diagonals" as shown below.

Subtract these products.

$$\begin{matrix} a_{11} & a_{12} & a_{13} & a_{11} & a_{12} \\ a_{21} & a_{22} & a_{23} & a_{21} & a_{22} \\ a_{31} & a_{32} & a_{33} & a_{31} & a_{32} \end{matrix}$$

Add these products.

That is,

$$\begin{aligned} |A| = {} & a_{11}a_{22}a_{33} + a_{12}a_{23}a_{31} + \\ & a_{13}a_{21}a_{32} - a_{31}a_{22}a_{13} - \\ & a_{32}a_{23}a_{11} - a_{33}a_{21}a_{12}. \end{aligned}$$

Try using this method to find $|A|$ in Example 3.

In Example 3, the determinant was found by expanding by the cofactors in the first row. You could have used any row or column. For instance, you could have expanded along the second row to obtain

$$\begin{aligned} |A| &= a_{21}C_{21} + a_{22}C_{22} + a_{23}C_{23} && \text{Second-row expansion} \\ &= 3(-2) + (-1)(-4) + 2(8) \\ &= 14. \end{aligned}$$

When expanding by cofactors, you do not need to find cofactors of zero entries, because zero times its cofactor is zero.

$$a_{ij}C_{ij} = (0)C_{ij} = 0$$

So, the row (or column) containing the most zeros is usually the best choice for expansion by cofactors. This is demonstrated in the next example.

Example 4 ▶ The Determinant of a Matrix of Order 4 × 4

Find the determinant of

$$A = \begin{bmatrix} 1 & -2 & 3 & 0 \\ -1 & 1 & 0 & 2 \\ 0 & 2 & 0 & 3 \\ 3 & 4 & 0 & 2 \end{bmatrix}.$$

Solution

After inspecting this matrix, you can see that three of the entries in the third column are zeros. So, you can eliminate some of the work in the expansion by using the third column.

$$|A| = 3(C_{13}) + 0(C_{23}) + 0(C_{33}) + 0(C_{43})$$

Because C_{23}, C_{33}, and C_{43} have zero coefficients, you need only find the cofactor C_{13}. To do this, delete the first row and third column of A and evaluate the determinant of the resulting matrix.

$$C_{13} = (-1)^{1+3} \begin{vmatrix} -1 & 1 & 2 \\ 0 & 2 & 3 \\ 3 & 4 & 2 \end{vmatrix} \qquad \text{Delete 1st row and 3rd column.}$$

$$= \begin{vmatrix} -1 & 1 & 2 \\ 0 & 2 & 3 \\ 3 & 4 & 2 \end{vmatrix} \qquad \text{Simplify.}$$

Expanding by cofactors in the second row yields

$$C_{13} = 0(-1)^3 \begin{vmatrix} 1 & 2 \\ 4 & 2 \end{vmatrix} + 2(-1)^4 \begin{vmatrix} -1 & 2 \\ 3 & 2 \end{vmatrix} + 3(-1)^5 \begin{vmatrix} -1 & 1 \\ 3 & 4 \end{vmatrix}$$

$$= 0 + 2(1)(-8) + 3(-1)(-7)$$

$$= 5.$$

So, you obtain

$$|A| = 3C_{13}$$

$$= 3(5)$$

$$= 15.$$

Try using a graphing utility to confirm the result of Example 4.

Students may have difficulty choosing the best row or column about which to expand a determinant using cofactors. You might consider using the following matrices as exercises to give students practice in choosing the row or column that yields the most efficient expansion.

$$A = \begin{bmatrix} 0 & -1 & 3 \\ 4 & 0 & 3 \\ 2 & 0 & -3 \end{bmatrix}$$

$$B = \begin{bmatrix} -1 & 3 & 0 & 1 \\ 2 & 0 & 4 & -3 \\ -2 & 1 & 7 & 0 \\ 3 & 2 & 0 & 5 \end{bmatrix}$$

$$C = \begin{bmatrix} -6 & 0 & 1 & 3 & -2 \\ 2 & -1 & 4 & 0 & -3 \\ 7 & 0 & -1 & 0 & 0 \\ 1 & -3 & 0 & 2 & 2 \\ 0 & 4 & 1 & 3 & 2 \end{bmatrix}$$

8.4 Exercises

In Exercises 1–16, find the determinant of the matrix.

1. $[5]$

2. $[-8]$

3. $\begin{bmatrix} 2 & 1 \\ 3 & 4 \end{bmatrix}$

4. $\begin{bmatrix} -3 & 1 \\ 5 & 2 \end{bmatrix}$

5. $\begin{bmatrix} 5 & 2 \\ -6 & 3 \end{bmatrix}$

6. $\begin{bmatrix} 2 & -2 \\ 4 & 3 \end{bmatrix}$

7. $\begin{bmatrix} -7 & 0 \\ 3 & 0 \end{bmatrix}$

8. $\begin{bmatrix} 4 & -3 \\ 0 & 0 \end{bmatrix}$

9. $\begin{bmatrix} 2 & 6 \\ 0 & 3 \end{bmatrix}$

10. $\begin{bmatrix} 2 & -3 \\ -6 & 9 \end{bmatrix}$

11. $\begin{bmatrix} -3 & -2 \\ -6 & -1 \end{bmatrix}$

12. $\begin{bmatrix} 4 & 7 \\ -2 & 5 \end{bmatrix}$

13. $\begin{bmatrix} 9 & 0 \\ 7 & 8 \end{bmatrix}$

14. $\begin{bmatrix} 0 & 6 \\ -3 & 2 \end{bmatrix}$

15. $\begin{bmatrix} -\frac{1}{2} & \frac{1}{3} \\ -6 & \frac{1}{3} \end{bmatrix}$

16. $\begin{bmatrix} \frac{2}{3} & \frac{4}{3} \\ -1 & -\frac{1}{3} \end{bmatrix}$

In Exercises 17–22, use the matrix capabilities of a graphing utility to find the determinant of the matrix.

17. $\begin{bmatrix} 0.3 & 0.2 & 0.2 \\ 0.2 & 0.2 & 0.2 \\ -0.4 & 0.4 & 0.3 \end{bmatrix}$

18. $\begin{bmatrix} 0.1 & 0.2 & 0.3 \\ -0.3 & 0.2 & 0.2 \\ 0.5 & 0.4 & 0.4 \end{bmatrix}$

19. $\begin{bmatrix} 0.9 & 0.7 & 0 \\ -0.1 & 0.3 & 1.3 \\ -2.2 & 4.2 & 6.1 \end{bmatrix}$

20. $\begin{bmatrix} 0.1 & 0.1 & -4.3 \\ 7.5 & 6.2 & 0.7 \\ 0.3 & 0.6 & -1.2 \end{bmatrix}$

21. $\begin{bmatrix} 1 & 4 & -2 \\ 3 & 6 & -6 \\ -2 & 1 & 4 \end{bmatrix}$

22. $\begin{bmatrix} 2 & 3 & 1 \\ 0 & 5 & -2 \\ 0 & 0 & -2 \end{bmatrix}$

In Exercises 23–30, find all (a) minors and (b) cofactors of the matrix.

23. $\begin{bmatrix} 3 & 4 \\ 2 & -5 \end{bmatrix}$

24. $\begin{bmatrix} 11 & 0 \\ -3 & 2 \end{bmatrix}$

25. $\begin{bmatrix} 3 & 1 \\ -2 & -4 \end{bmatrix}$

26. $\begin{bmatrix} -6 & 5 \\ 7 & -2 \end{bmatrix}$

27. $\begin{bmatrix} 4 & 0 & 2 \\ -3 & 2 & 1 \\ 1 & -1 & 1 \end{bmatrix}$

28. $\begin{bmatrix} 1 & -1 & 0 \\ 3 & 2 & 5 \\ 4 & -6 & 4 \end{bmatrix}$

29. $\begin{bmatrix} 3 & -2 & 8 \\ 3 & 2 & -6 \\ -1 & 3 & 6 \end{bmatrix}$

30. $\begin{bmatrix} -2 & 9 & 4 \\ 7 & -6 & 0 \\ 6 & 7 & -6 \end{bmatrix}$

In Exercises 31–36, find the determinant of the matrix by the method of expansion by cofactors. Expand using the indicated row or column.

31. $\begin{bmatrix} -3 & 2 & 1 \\ 4 & 5 & 6 \\ 2 & -3 & 1 \end{bmatrix}$
    (a) Row 1
    (b) Column 2

32. $\begin{bmatrix} -3 & 4 & 2 \\ 6 & 3 & 1 \\ 4 & -7 & -8 \end{bmatrix}$
    (a) Row 2
    (b) Column 3

33. $\begin{bmatrix} 5 & 0 & -3 \\ 0 & 12 & 4 \\ 1 & 6 & 3 \end{bmatrix}$
    (a) Row 2
    (b) Column 2

34. $\begin{bmatrix} 10 & -5 & 5 \\ 30 & 0 & 10 \\ 0 & 10 & 1 \end{bmatrix}$
    (a) Row 3
    (b) Column 1

35. $\begin{bmatrix} 6 & 0 & -3 & 5 \\ 4 & 13 & 6 & -8 \\ -1 & 0 & 7 & 4 \\ 8 & 6 & 0 & 2 \end{bmatrix}$
    (a) Row 2
    (b) Column 2

36. $\begin{bmatrix} 10 & 8 & 3 & -7 \\ 4 & 0 & 5 & -6 \\ 0 & 3 & 2 & 7 \\ 1 & 0 & -3 & 2 \end{bmatrix}$
    (a) Row 3
    (b) Column 1

In Exercises 37–52, find the determinant of the matrix. Expand by cofactors on the row or column that appears to make the computations easiest.

37. $\begin{bmatrix} 2 & -1 & 0 \\ 4 & 2 & 1 \\ 4 & 2 & 1 \end{bmatrix}$

38. $\begin{bmatrix} -2 & 2 & 3 \\ 1 & -1 & 0 \\ 0 & 1 & 4 \end{bmatrix}$

39. $\begin{bmatrix} 6 & 3 & -7 \\ 0 & 0 & 0 \\ 4 & -6 & 3 \end{bmatrix}$

40. $\begin{bmatrix} 1 & 1 & 2 \\ 3 & 1 & 0 \\ -2 & 0 & 3 \end{bmatrix}$

41. $\begin{bmatrix} -1 & 2 & -5 \\ 0 & 3 & 4 \\ 0 & 0 & 3 \end{bmatrix}$

42. $\begin{bmatrix} 1 & 0 & 0 \\ -4 & -1 & 0 \\ 5 & 1 & 5 \end{bmatrix}$

43. $\begin{bmatrix} 1 & 4 & -2 \\ 3 & 2 & 0 \\ -1 & 4 & 3 \end{bmatrix}$

44. $\begin{bmatrix} 2 & -1 & 3 \\ 1 & 4 & 4 \\ 1 & 0 & 2 \end{bmatrix}$

45. $\begin{bmatrix} 2 & 4 & 6 \\ 0 & 3 & 1 \\ 0 & 0 & -5 \end{bmatrix}$

46. $\begin{bmatrix} -3 & 0 & 0 \\ 7 & 11 & 0 \\ 1 & 2 & 2 \end{bmatrix}$

47. $\begin{vmatrix} 2 & 6 & 6 & 2 \\ 2 & 7 & 3 & 6 \\ 1 & 5 & 0 & 1 \\ 3 & 7 & 0 & 7 \end{vmatrix}$ **48.** $\begin{vmatrix} 3 & 6 & -5 & 4 \\ -2 & 0 & 6 & 0 \\ 1 & 1 & 2 & 2 \\ 0 & 3 & -1 & -1 \end{vmatrix}$

49. $\begin{vmatrix} 5 & 3 & 0 & 6 \\ 4 & 6 & 4 & 12 \\ 0 & 2 & -3 & 4 \\ 0 & 1 & -2 & 2 \end{vmatrix}$ **50.** $\begin{vmatrix} 1 & 4 & 3 & 2 \\ -5 & 6 & 2 & 1 \\ 0 & 0 & 0 & 0 \\ 3 & -2 & 1 & 5 \end{vmatrix}$

51. $\begin{vmatrix} 3 & 2 & 4 & -1 & 5 \\ -2 & 0 & 1 & 3 & 2 \\ 1 & 0 & 0 & 4 & 0 \\ 6 & 0 & 2 & -1 & 0 \\ 3 & 0 & 5 & 1 & 0 \end{vmatrix}$

52. $\begin{vmatrix} 5 & 2 & 0 & 0 & -2 \\ 0 & 1 & 4 & 3 & 2 \\ 0 & 0 & 2 & 6 & 3 \\ 0 & 0 & 3 & 4 & 1 \\ 0 & 0 & 0 & 0 & 2 \end{vmatrix}$

In Exercises 53–60, use the matrix capabilities of a graphing utility to evaluate the determinant.

53. $\begin{vmatrix} 3 & 8 & -7 \\ 0 & -5 & 4 \\ 8 & 1 & 6 \end{vmatrix}$ **54.** $\begin{vmatrix} 5 & -8 & 0 \\ 9 & 7 & 4 \\ -8 & 7 & 1 \end{vmatrix}$

55. $\begin{vmatrix} 7 & 0 & -14 \\ -2 & 5 & 4 \\ -6 & 2 & 12 \end{vmatrix}$ **56.** $\begin{vmatrix} 3 & 0 & 0 \\ -2 & 5 & 0 \\ 12 & 5 & 7 \end{vmatrix}$

57. $\begin{vmatrix} 1 & -1 & 8 & 4 \\ 2 & 6 & 0 & -4 \\ 2 & 0 & 2 & 6 \\ 0 & 2 & 8 & 0 \end{vmatrix}$ **58.** $\begin{vmatrix} 0 & -3 & 8 & 2 \\ 8 & 1 & -1 & 6 \\ -4 & 6 & 0 & 9 \\ -7 & 0 & 0 & 14 \end{vmatrix}$

59. $\begin{vmatrix} 3 & -2 & 4 & 3 & 1 \\ -1 & 0 & 2 & 1 & 0 \\ 5 & -1 & 0 & 3 & 2 \\ 4 & 7 & -8 & 0 & 0 \\ 1 & 2 & 3 & 0 & 2 \end{vmatrix}$

60. $\begin{vmatrix} -2 & 0 & 0 & 0 & 0 \\ 0 & 3 & 0 & 0 & 0 \\ 0 & 0 & -1 & 0 & 0 \\ 0 & 0 & 0 & 2 & 0 \\ 0 & 0 & 0 & 0 & -4 \end{vmatrix}$

In Exercises 61–68, find (a) $|A|$, (b) $|B|$, (c) AB, and (d) $|AB|$.

61. $A = \begin{bmatrix} -1 & 0 \\ 0 & 3 \end{bmatrix}$, $B = \begin{bmatrix} 2 & 0 \\ 0 & -1 \end{bmatrix}$

62. $A = \begin{bmatrix} -2 & 1 \\ 4 & -2 \end{bmatrix}$, $B = \begin{bmatrix} 1 & 2 \\ 0 & -1 \end{bmatrix}$

63. $A = \begin{bmatrix} 4 & 0 \\ 3 & -2 \end{bmatrix}$, $B = \begin{bmatrix} -1 & 1 \\ -2 & 2 \end{bmatrix}$

64. $A = \begin{bmatrix} 5 & 4 \\ 3 & -1 \end{bmatrix}$, $B = \begin{bmatrix} 0 & 6 \\ 1 & -2 \end{bmatrix}$

65. $A = \begin{bmatrix} 0 & 1 & 2 \\ -3 & -2 & 1 \\ 0 & 4 & 1 \end{bmatrix}$, $B = \begin{bmatrix} 3 & -2 & 0 \\ 1 & -1 & 2 \\ 3 & 1 & 1 \end{bmatrix}$

66. $A = \begin{bmatrix} 3 & 2 & 0 \\ -1 & -3 & 4 \\ -2 & 0 & 1 \end{bmatrix}$, $B = \begin{bmatrix} -3 & 0 & 1 \\ 0 & 2 & -1 \\ -2 & -1 & 1 \end{bmatrix}$

67. $A = \begin{bmatrix} -1 & 2 & 1 \\ 1 & 0 & 1 \\ 0 & 1 & 0 \end{bmatrix}$, $B = \begin{bmatrix} -1 & 0 & 0 \\ 0 & 2 & 0 \\ 0 & 0 & 3 \end{bmatrix}$

68. $A = \begin{bmatrix} 2 & 0 & 1 \\ 1 & -1 & 2 \\ 3 & 1 & 0 \end{bmatrix}$, $B = \begin{bmatrix} 2 & -1 & 4 \\ 0 & 1 & 3 \\ 3 & -2 & 1 \end{bmatrix}$

In Exercises 69–74, evaluate the determinant(s) to verify the equation.

69. $\begin{vmatrix} w & x \\ y & z \end{vmatrix} = -\begin{vmatrix} y & z \\ w & x \end{vmatrix}$

70. $\begin{vmatrix} w & cx \\ y & cz \end{vmatrix} = c\begin{vmatrix} w & x \\ y & z \end{vmatrix}$

71. $\begin{vmatrix} w & x \\ y & z \end{vmatrix} = \begin{vmatrix} w & x + cw \\ y & z + cy \end{vmatrix}$

72. $\begin{vmatrix} w & x \\ cw & cx \end{vmatrix} = 0$

73. $\begin{vmatrix} 1 & x & x^2 \\ 1 & y & y^2 \\ 1 & z & z^2 \end{vmatrix} = (y - x)(z - x)(z - y)$

74. $\begin{vmatrix} a + b & a & a \\ a & a + b & a \\ a & a & a + b \end{vmatrix} = b^2(3a + b)$

In Exercises 75–78, solve for x.

75. $\begin{vmatrix} x - 1 & 2 \\ 3 & x - 2 \end{vmatrix} = 0$

76. $\begin{vmatrix} x - 2 & -1 \\ -3 & x \end{vmatrix} = 0$

77. $\begin{vmatrix} x + 3 & 2 \\ 1 & x + 2 \end{vmatrix} = 0$

78. $\begin{vmatrix} x + 4 & -2 \\ 7 & x - 5 \end{vmatrix} = 0$

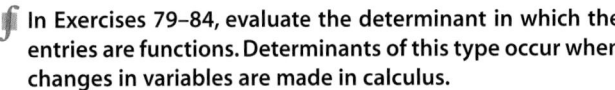 In Exercises 79–84, evaluate the determinant in which the entries are functions. Determinants of this type occur when changes in variables are made in calculus.

79. $\begin{vmatrix} 4u & -1 \\ -1 & 2v \end{vmatrix}$

80. $\begin{vmatrix} 3x^2 & -3y^2 \\ 1 & 1 \end{vmatrix}$

81. $\begin{vmatrix} e^{2x} & e^{3x} \\ 2e^{2x} & 3e^{3x} \end{vmatrix}$

82. $\begin{vmatrix} e^{-x} & xe^{-x} \\ -e^{-x} & (1-x)e^{-x} \end{vmatrix}$

83. $\begin{vmatrix} x & \ln x \\ 1 & 1/x \end{vmatrix}$

84. $\begin{vmatrix} x & x\ln x \\ 1 & 1 + \ln x \end{vmatrix}$

Synthesis

True or False? In Exercises 85 and 86, determine whether the statement is true or false. Justify your answer.

85. If a square matrix has an entire row of zeros, the determinant will always be zero.

86. If two columns of a square matrix are the same, the determinant of the matrix will be zero.

87. *Exploration* Find square matrices A and B to demonstrate that

$$|A + B| \neq |A| + |B|.$$

88. *Exploration* Consider square matrices in which the entries are consecutive integers. An example of such a matrix is

$$\begin{bmatrix} 4 & 5 & 6 \\ 7 & 8 & 9 \\ 10 & 11 & 12 \end{bmatrix}.$$

(a) Use a graphing utility to evaluate the determinants of four matrices of this type. Make a conjecture based on the results.

(b) Verify your conjecture.

89. *Writing* Write a brief paragraph explaining the difference between a square matrix and its determinant.

90. *Think About It* If A is a matrix of order 3×3 such that $|A| = 5$, is it possible to find $|2A|$? Explain.

Properties of Determinants In Exercises 91 and 92, a property of determinants is given. State how the property has been applied to the given determinants and use a graphing utility to verify the results.

91. If A and B are square matrices and B is obtained from A by interchanging two rows of A or interchanging two columns of A, then $|B| = -|A|$.

(a) $\begin{vmatrix} 1 & 3 & 4 \\ -7 & 2 & -5 \\ 6 & 1 & 2 \end{vmatrix} = -\begin{vmatrix} 1 & 4 & 3 \\ -7 & -5 & 2 \\ 6 & 2 & 1 \end{vmatrix}$

(b) $\begin{vmatrix} 1 & 3 & 4 \\ -2 & 2 & 0 \\ 1 & 6 & 2 \end{vmatrix} = -\begin{vmatrix} 1 & 6 & 2 \\ -2 & 2 & 0 \\ 1 & 3 & 4 \end{vmatrix}$

92. If A and B are square matrices and B is obtained from A by adding a multiple of a row of A to another row of A or by adding a multiple of a column of A to another column of A, then $|B| = |A|$.

(a) $\begin{vmatrix} 1 & -3 \\ 5 & 2 \end{vmatrix} = \begin{vmatrix} 1 & -3 \\ 0 & 17 \end{vmatrix}$

(b) $\begin{vmatrix} 5 & 4 & 2 \\ 2 & -3 & 4 \\ 7 & 6 & 3 \end{vmatrix} = \begin{vmatrix} 1 & 10 & -6 \\ 2 & -3 & 4 \\ 7 & 6 & 3 \end{vmatrix}$

Review

In Exercises 93–98, find the domain of the function.

93. $f(x) = x^3 - 2x$

94. $g(x) = \sqrt[3]{x}$

95. $h(x) = \sqrt{16 - x^2}$

96. $A(x) = \dfrac{3}{36 - x^2}$

97. $g(t) = \ln(t - 1)$

98. $f(s) = 625e^{-0.5s}$

In Exercises 99 and 100, sketch the graph of the system of inequalities.

99. $\begin{cases} x + y \leq 8 \\ x \geq -3 \\ 2x - y < 5 \end{cases}$

100. $\begin{cases} -x - y > 4 \\ y \leq 1 \\ 7x + 4y \leq -10 \end{cases}$

In Exercises 101–104, find the inverse of the matrix (if it exists).

101. $\begin{bmatrix} -4 & 1 \\ 8 & -1 \end{bmatrix}$

102. $\begin{bmatrix} -5 & -8 \\ 3 & 6 \end{bmatrix}$

103. $\begin{bmatrix} -7 & 2 & 9 \\ 2 & -4 & -6 \\ 3 & 5 & 2 \end{bmatrix}$

104. $\begin{bmatrix} -6 & 2 & 0 \\ 1 & 3 & -2 \\ -2 & 0 & 1 \end{bmatrix}$

8.5 Applications of Matrices and Determinants

▶ **What you should learn**

- How to use Cramer's Rule to solve systems of linear equations
- How to use determinants to find the areas of triangles
- How to use a determinant to test for collinear points and find an equation of a line passing through two points
- How to use matrices to code and decode messages

▶ **Why you should learn it**

You can use Cramer's Rule to solve real-life problems. For instance, in Exercise 56 on page 601, Cramer's Rule is used to find a quadratic model for the number of U.S. Supreme Court cases waiting to be tried.

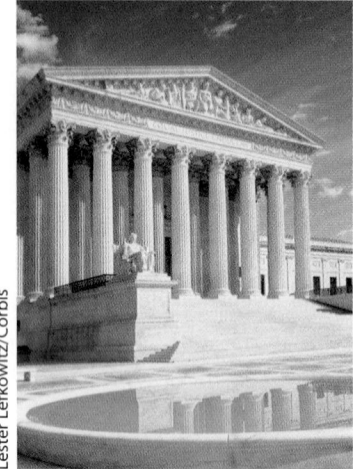

Lester Lefkowitz/Corbis

Cramer's Rule

So far, you have studied three methods for solving a system of linear equations: substitution, elimination with equations, and elimination with matrices. In this section, you will study one more method, **Cramer's Rule,** named after Gabriel Cramer (1704–1752). This rule uses determinants to write the solution of a system of linear equations. To see how Cramer's Rule works, take another look at the solution described at the beginning of Section 8.4. There, it was pointed out that the system

$$\begin{cases} a_1x + b_1y = c_1 \\ a_2x + b_2y = c_2 \end{cases}$$

has a solution

$$x = \frac{c_1b_2 - c_2b_1}{a_1b_2 - a_2b_1}$$

and

$$y = \frac{a_1c_2 - a_2c_1}{a_1b_2 - a_2b_1}$$

provided that $a_1b_2 - a_2b_1 \neq 0$. Each numerator and denominator in this solution can be expressed as a determinant, as follows.

$$x = \frac{c_1b_2 - c_2b_1}{a_1b_2 - a_2b_1} = \frac{\begin{vmatrix} c_1 & b_1 \\ c_2 & b_2 \end{vmatrix}}{\begin{vmatrix} a_1 & b_1 \\ a_2 & b_2 \end{vmatrix}}$$

$$y = \frac{a_1c_2 - a_2c_1}{a_1b_2 - a_2b_1} = \frac{\begin{vmatrix} a_1 & c_1 \\ a_2 & c_2 \end{vmatrix}}{\begin{vmatrix} a_1 & b_1 \\ a_2 & b_2 \end{vmatrix}}$$

Relative to the original system, the denominator for x and y is simply the determinant of the *coefficient* matrix of the system. This determinant is denoted by D. The numerators for x and y are denoted by D_x and D_y, respectively. They are formed by using the column of constants as replacements for the coefficients of x and y, as follows.

Coefficient Matrix	D	D_x	D_y
$\begin{bmatrix} a_1 & b_1 \\ a_2 & b_2 \end{bmatrix}$	$\begin{vmatrix} a_1 & b_1 \\ a_2 & b_2 \end{vmatrix}$	$\begin{vmatrix} c_1 & b_1 \\ c_2 & b_2 \end{vmatrix}$	$\begin{vmatrix} a_1 & c_1 \\ a_2 & c_2 \end{vmatrix}$

Example 1 ▶ **Using Cramer's Rule for a 2 × 2 System**

Use Cramer's Rule to solve the system of linear equations.

$$\begin{cases} 4x - 2y = 10 \\ 3x - 5y = 11 \end{cases}$$

Solution

To begin, find the determinant of the coefficient matrix.

$$D = \begin{vmatrix} 4 & -2 \\ 3 & -5 \end{vmatrix} = -20 - (-6) = -14$$

Because this determinant is not zero, you can apply Cramer's Rule to find the solution, as follows.

$$x = \frac{D_x}{D} = \frac{\begin{vmatrix} 10 & -2 \\ 11 & -5 \end{vmatrix}}{-14} \qquad y = \frac{D_y}{D} = \frac{\begin{vmatrix} 4 & 10 \\ 3 & 11 \end{vmatrix}}{-14}$$

$$= \frac{-50 - (-22)}{-14} \qquad\qquad = \frac{44 - 30}{-14}$$

$$= \frac{-28}{-14} \qquad\qquad\qquad = \frac{14}{-14}$$

$$= 2 \qquad\qquad\qquad\qquad = -1$$

So, the solution is $x = 2$ and $y = -1$. Check this in the original system.

Cramer's Rule generalizes easily to systems of n equations in n variables. The value of each variable is given as the quotient of two determinants. The denominator is the determinant of the coefficient matrix, and the numerator is the determinant of the matrix formed by replacing the column corresponding to the variable (being solved for) with the column representing the constants. For instance, the solution for x_3 in the system

$$\begin{cases} a_{11}x_1 + a_{12}x_2 + a_{13}x_3 = b_1 \\ a_{21}x_1 + a_{22}x_2 + a_{23}x_3 = b_2 \\ a_{31}x_1 + a_{32}x_2 + a_{33}x_3 = b_3 \end{cases}$$

is given by

$$x_3 = \frac{|A_3|}{|A|} = \frac{\begin{vmatrix} a_{11} & a_{12} & b_1 \\ a_{21} & a_{22} & b_2 \\ a_{31} & a_{32} & b_3 \end{vmatrix}}{\begin{vmatrix} a_{11} & a_{12} & a_{13} \\ a_{21} & a_{22} & a_{23} \\ a_{31} & a_{32} & a_{33} \end{vmatrix}}.$$

Cramer's Rule

If a system of n linear equations in n variables has a coefficient matrix A with a nonzero determinant $|A|$, the solution of the system is

$$x_1 = \frac{|A_1|}{|A|}, \quad x_2 = \frac{|A_2|}{|A|}, \quad \dots \quad , \quad x_n = \frac{|A_n|}{|A|}$$

where the ith column of A_i is the column of constants in the system of equations. If the determinant of the coefficient matrix is zero, the system has either no solution or infinitely many solutions.

Example 2 ▶ **Using Cramer's Rule for a 3 × 3 System**

Use Cramer's Rule to solve the system of linear equations.

$$\begin{cases} -x + 2y - 3z = 1 \\ 2x \qquad + z = 0 \\ 3x - 4y + 4z = 2 \end{cases}$$

Solution

The coefficient matrix

$$\begin{bmatrix} -1 & 2 & -3 \\ 2 & 0 & 1 \\ 3 & -4 & 4 \end{bmatrix}$$

can be expanded along the second row, as follows.

$$D = 2(-1)^3 \begin{vmatrix} 2 & -3 \\ -4 & 4 \end{vmatrix} + 0(-1)^4 \begin{vmatrix} -1 & -3 \\ 3 & 4 \end{vmatrix} + 1(-1)^5 \begin{vmatrix} -1 & 2 \\ 3 & -4 \end{vmatrix}$$

$$= -2(-4) + 0 - 1(-2) = 10$$

Because this determinant is not zero, you can apply Cramer's Rule to find the solution, as follows.

$$x = \frac{D_x}{D} = \frac{\begin{vmatrix} 1 & 2 & -3 \\ 0 & 0 & 1 \\ 2 & -4 & 4 \end{vmatrix}}{10} = \frac{8}{10} = \frac{4}{5}$$

$$y = \frac{D_y}{D} = \frac{\begin{vmatrix} -1 & 1 & -3 \\ 2 & 0 & 1 \\ 3 & 2 & 4 \end{vmatrix}}{10} = \frac{-15}{10} = -\frac{3}{2}$$

$$z = \frac{D_z}{D} = \frac{\begin{vmatrix} -1 & 2 & 1 \\ 2 & 0 & 0 \\ 3 & -4 & 2 \end{vmatrix}}{10} = \frac{-16}{10} = -\frac{8}{5}$$

The solution is $\left(\frac{4}{5}, -\frac{3}{2}, -\frac{8}{5}\right)$. Check this in the original system.

Area of a Triangle

Another application of matrices and determinants is finding the area of a triangle whose vertices are given as points in a coordinate plane.

> ### Area of a Triangle
>
> The area of a triangle with vertices (x_1, y_1), (x_2, y_2), and (x_3, y_3) is
>
> $$\text{Area} = \pm \frac{1}{2} \begin{vmatrix} x_1 & y_1 & 1 \\ x_2 & y_2 & 1 \\ x_3 & y_3 & 1 \end{vmatrix}$$
>
> where the symbol $\pm$ indicates that the appropriate sign should be chosen to yield a positive area.

Example 3 ▶ Finding the Area of a Triangle

Find the area of a triangle whose vertices are $(1, 0)$, $(2, 2)$, and $(4, 3)$, as shown in Figure 8.1.

Solution

Let $(x_1, y_1) = (1, 0)$, $(x_2, y_2) = (2, 2)$, and $(x_3, y_3) = (4, 3)$. Then, to find the area of the triangle, evaluate the determinant.

$$\begin{vmatrix} x_1 & y_1 & 1 \\ x_2 & y_2 & 1 \\ x_3 & y_3 & 1 \end{vmatrix} = \begin{vmatrix} 1 & 0 & 1 \\ 2 & 2 & 1 \\ 4 & 3 & 1 \end{vmatrix}$$

$$= 1(-1)^2 \begin{vmatrix} 2 & 1 \\ 3 & 1 \end{vmatrix} + 0(-1)^3 \begin{vmatrix} 2 & 1 \\ 4 & 1 \end{vmatrix} + 1(-1)^4 \begin{vmatrix} 2 & 2 \\ 4 & 3 \end{vmatrix}$$

$$= 1(-1) + 0 + 1(-2) = -3.$$

Using this value, you can conclude that the area of the triangle is

$$\text{Area} = -\frac{1}{2} \begin{vmatrix} 1 & 0 & 1 \\ 2 & 2 & 1 \\ 4 & 3 & 1 \end{vmatrix} \qquad \text{Choose } (-) \text{ so that the area is positive.}$$

$$= -\frac{1}{2}(-3)$$

$$= \frac{3}{2} \text{ square units.}$$

Try using determinants to find the area of a triangle with vertices $(3, -1)$, $(7, -1)$, and $(7, 5)$. Confirm your answer by plotting the points in a coordinate plane and using the formula

$$\text{Area} = \frac{1}{2}(\text{base})(\text{height}).$$

FIGURE **8.1**

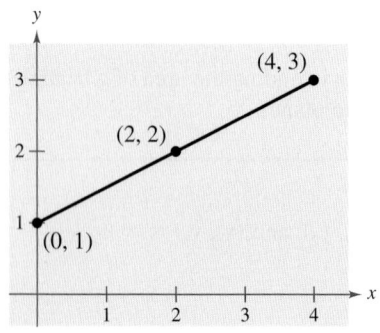

FIGURE **8.2**

Lines in a Plane

What if the three points in Example 3 had been on the same line? What would have happened had the area formula been applied to three such points? The answer is that the determinant would have been zero. Consider, for instance, the three collinear points $(0, 1)$, $(2, 2)$, and $(4, 3)$, as shown in Figure 8.2. The area of the "triangle" that has these three points as vertices is

$$\frac{1}{2}\begin{vmatrix} 0 & 1 & 1 \\ 2 & 2 & 1 \\ 4 & 3 & 1 \end{vmatrix} = \frac{1}{2}\left[0(-1)^2\begin{vmatrix} 2 & 1 \\ 3 & 1 \end{vmatrix} + 1(-1)^3\begin{vmatrix} 2 & 1 \\ 4 & 1 \end{vmatrix} + 1(-1)^4\begin{vmatrix} 2 & 2 \\ 4 & 3 \end{vmatrix}\right]$$

$$= \frac{1}{2}[0 - 1(-2) + 1(-2)]$$

$$= 0.$$

The result is generalized as follows.

Test for Collinear Points

Three points (x_1, y_1), (x_2, y_2), and (x_3, y_3) are collinear (lie on the same line) if and only if

$$\begin{vmatrix} x_1 & y_1 & 1 \\ x_2 & y_2 & 1 \\ x_3 & y_3 & 1 \end{vmatrix} = 0.$$

Example 4 ▶ Testing for Collinear Points

Determine whether the points $(-2, -2)$, $(1, 1)$, and $(7, 5)$ lie on the same line. (See Figure 8.3.)

Solution

Letting $(x_1, y_1) = (-2, -2)$, $(x_2, y_2) = (1, 1)$, and $(x_3, y_3) = (7, 5)$, you have

$$\begin{vmatrix} x_1 & y_1 & 1 \\ x_2 & y_2 & 1 \\ x_3 & y_3 & 1 \end{vmatrix} = \begin{vmatrix} -2 & -2 & 1 \\ 1 & 1 & 1 \\ 7 & 5 & 1 \end{vmatrix}$$

$$= -2(-1)^2\begin{vmatrix} 1 & 1 \\ 5 & 1 \end{vmatrix} + (-2)(-1)^3\begin{vmatrix} 1 & 1 \\ 7 & 1 \end{vmatrix} + 1(-1)^4\begin{vmatrix} 1 & 1 \\ 7 & 5 \end{vmatrix}$$

$$= -2(-4) + (2)(-6) + 1(-2)$$

$$= -6.$$

Because the value of this determinant is *not* zero, you can conclude that the three points do not lie on the same line.

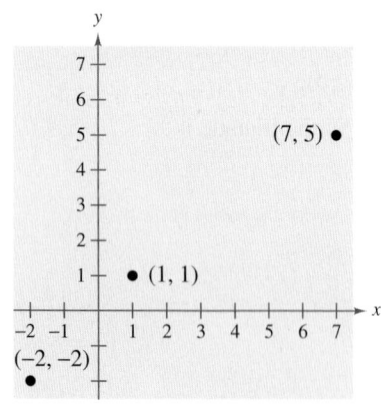

FIGURE **8.3**

The test for collinear points can be adapted to another use. That is, if you are given two points on a rectangular coordinate system, you can find an equation of the line passing through the two points, as follows.

Two-Point Form of the Equation of a Line

An equation of the line passing through the distinct points (x_1, y_1) and (x_2, y_2) is given by

$$\begin{vmatrix} x & y & 1 \\ x_1 & y_1 & 1 \\ x_2 & y_2 & 1 \end{vmatrix} = 0.$$

Example 5 ▶ Finding an Equation of a Line

Find an equation of the line passing through the two points $(2, 4)$ and $(-1, 3)$, as shown in Figure 8.4.

Solution

Applying the determinant formula for the equation of a line produces

$$\begin{vmatrix} x & y & 1 \\ 2 & 4 & 1 \\ -1 & 3 & 1 \end{vmatrix} = 0.$$

To evaluate this determinant, you can expand by cofactors along the first row to obtain the following.

$$x(-1)^2 \begin{vmatrix} 4 & 1 \\ 3 & 1 \end{vmatrix} + y(-1)^3 \begin{vmatrix} 2 & 1 \\ -1 & 1 \end{vmatrix} + 1(-1)^4 \begin{vmatrix} 2 & 4 \\ -1 & 3 \end{vmatrix} = 0$$

$$x(1)(1) + y(-1)(3) + (1)(1)(10) = 0$$

$$x - 3y + 10 = 0$$

So, an equation of the line is

$$x - 3y + 10 = 0.$$

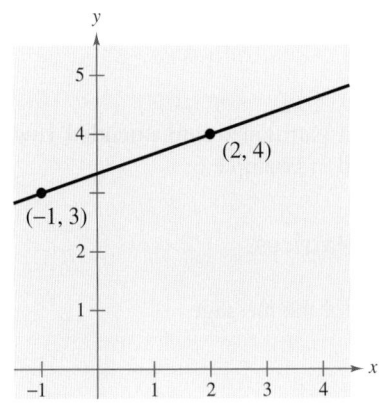

FIGURE 8.4

Note that this method of finding the equation of a line works for all lines, including horizontal and vertical lines. For instance, the equation of the vertical line through $(2, 0)$ and $(2, 2)$ is

$$\begin{vmatrix} x & y & 1 \\ 2 & 0 & 1 \\ 2 & 2 & 1 \end{vmatrix} = 0$$

$$4 - 2x = 0$$

$$x = 2.$$

Cryptography

A **cryptogram** is a message written according to a secret code. (The Greek word *kryptos* means "hidden.") Matrix multiplication can be used to encode and decode messages. To begin, you need to assign a number to each letter in the alphabet (with 0 assigned to a blank space), as follows.

0 = _	9 = I	18 = R
1 = A	10 = J	19 = S
2 = B	11 = K	20 = T
3 = C	12 = L	21 = U
4 = D	13 = M	22 = V
5 = E	14 = N	23 = W
6 = F	15 = O	24 = X
7 = G	16 = P	25 = Y
8 = H	17 = Q	26 = Z

Then the message is converted to numbers and partitioned into **uncoded row matrices,** each having n entries, as demonstrated in Example 6.

Example 6 ▶   Forming Uncoded Row Matrices

Write the uncoded row matrices of order 1×3 for the message

    MEET ME MONDAY.

Solution

Partitioning the message (including blank spaces, but ignoring punctuation) into groups of three produces the following uncoded row matrices.

$$[13 \quad 5 \quad 5] \quad [20 \quad 0 \quad 13] \quad [5 \quad 0 \quad 13] \quad [15 \quad 14 \quad 4] \quad [1 \quad 25 \quad 0]$$
$$\text{M} \quad \text{E} \quad \text{E} \quad \text{T} \quad\quad \text{M} \quad \text{E} \quad\quad \text{M} \quad \text{O} \quad \text{N} \quad \text{D} \quad \text{A} \quad \text{Y}$$

Note that a blank space is used to fill out the last uncoded row matrix.

Activities

1. Solve for z using Cramer's Rule.
$$\begin{cases} x - 2y - z = 4 \\ 4x + y + z = 7 \\ x + 3y - 4z = -1 \end{cases}$$
Answer: $z = 0$

2. Use a determinant to find the area of the triangle with vertices $(1, -3)$, $(2, 3)$, and $(3, 1)$.
Answer: 4 square units

3. Use a determinant to find an equation of the line through the points $(-1, 2)$ and $(3, 4)$.
Answer: $-x + 2y - 5 = 0$

To encode a message, choose an $n \times n$ invertible matrix such as

$$A = \begin{bmatrix} 1 & -2 & 2 \\ -1 & 1 & 3 \\ 1 & -1 & -4 \end{bmatrix}$$

and multiply the uncoded row matrices by A (on the right) to obtain **coded row matrices.** Here is an example.

Uncoded Matrix   *Encoding Matrix A*   *Coded Matrix*

$$[13 \quad 5 \quad 5] \begin{bmatrix} 1 & -2 & 2 \\ -1 & 1 & 3 \\ 1 & -1 & -4 \end{bmatrix} = [13 \quad -26 \quad 21]$$

Example 7 ▶   **Encoding a Message**

Use the following invertible matrix to encode the message MEET ME MONDAY.

$$A = \begin{bmatrix} 1 & -2 & 2 \\ -1 & 1 & 3 \\ 1 & -1 & -4 \end{bmatrix}$$

Solution

The coded row matrices are obtained by multiplying each of the uncoded row matrices found in Example 6 by the matrix A, as follows.

Uncoded Matrix   Encoding Matrix A   Coded Matrix

$$\begin{bmatrix} 13 & 5 & 5 \end{bmatrix} \begin{bmatrix} 1 & -2 & 2 \\ -1 & 1 & 3 \\ 1 & -1 & -4 \end{bmatrix} = \begin{bmatrix} 13 & -26 & 21 \end{bmatrix}$$

$$\begin{bmatrix} 20 & 0 & 13 \end{bmatrix} \begin{bmatrix} 1 & -2 & 2 \\ -1 & 1 & 3 \\ 1 & -1 & -4 \end{bmatrix} = \begin{bmatrix} 33 & -53 & -12 \end{bmatrix}$$

$$\begin{bmatrix} 5 & 0 & 13 \end{bmatrix} \begin{bmatrix} 1 & -2 & 2 \\ -1 & 1 & 3 \\ 1 & -1 & -4 \end{bmatrix} = \begin{bmatrix} 18 & -23 & -42 \end{bmatrix}$$

$$\begin{bmatrix} 15 & 14 & 4 \end{bmatrix} \begin{bmatrix} 1 & -2 & 2 \\ -1 & 1 & 3 \\ 1 & -1 & -4 \end{bmatrix} = \begin{bmatrix} 5 & -20 & 56 \end{bmatrix}$$

$$\begin{bmatrix} 1 & 25 & 0 \end{bmatrix} \begin{bmatrix} 1 & -2 & 2 \\ -1 & 1 & 3 \\ 1 & -1 & -4 \end{bmatrix} = \begin{bmatrix} -24 & 23 & 77 \end{bmatrix}$$

So, the sequence of coded row matrices is

$$\begin{bmatrix} 13 & -26 & 21 \end{bmatrix} \begin{bmatrix} 33 & -53 & -12 \end{bmatrix} \begin{bmatrix} 18 & -23 & -42 \end{bmatrix} \begin{bmatrix} 5 & -20 & 56 \end{bmatrix} \begin{bmatrix} -24 & 23 & 77 \end{bmatrix}.$$

Finally, removing the matrix notation produces the following cryptogram.

$$13 \ -26 \ 21 \ 33 \ -53 \ -12 \ 18 \ -23 \ -42 \ 5 \ -20 \ 56 \ -24 \ 23 \ 77$$

For those who do not know the encoding matrix A, decoding the cryptogram found in Example 7 is difficult. But for an authorized receiver who knows the encoding matrix A, decoding is simple. The receiver need only multiply the coded row matrices by A^{-1} (on the right) to retrieve the uncoded row matrices. Here is an example.

$$\underbrace{\begin{bmatrix} 13 & -26 & 21 \end{bmatrix}}_{\text{Coded}} A^{-1} = \underbrace{\begin{bmatrix} 13 & 5 & 5 \end{bmatrix}}_{\text{Uncoded}}$$

Group Activity Suggestion:

Ask each group to work together to decide on their code's number scheme for assigning numbers to letters, to select a message to encode (some of the group members could work on the number scheme while the others are deciding on a message), and to find their invertible encoding matrix A. (A few group members could be asked to make up a matrix, and the rest of the group could determine if it is invertible. You might also use this as an opportunity to discuss the creation of invertible matrices; suggest starting with the identity matrix and applying a series of elementary row operations.) Students can work together to partition their message into uncoded row matrices; each student can then be responsible for encoding several of the row matrices, and then the group can reassemble the coded message from each member's work. To decode the message they receive, the group can partition the message into coded row matrices, with each member being responsible for decoding several of these matrices, and then reassemble the message from each member's work. Alternatively, to save time, you might supply the entire class with a given number-to-letter code and an invertible matrix A. The groups must then only select a message to encode, divide up the message to encode with A, trade messages with another group, find A^{-1}, and decode the message they received.

Example 8 ▶ Decoding a Message

Use the inverse of the matrix

$$A = \begin{bmatrix} 1 & -2 & 2 \\ -1 & 1 & 3 \\ 1 & -1 & -4 \end{bmatrix}$$

to decode the cryptogram

13 −26 21 33 −53 −12 18 −23 −42 5 −20 56 −24 23 77.

Solution

First find A^{-1} by using the techniques demonstrated in Section 8.3. A^{-1} is the decoding matrix. Then partition the message into groups of three to form the coded row matrices. Finally, multiply each coded row matrix by A^{-1} (on the right).

Coded Matrix   Decoding Matrix A^{-1} Decoded Matrix

$$\begin{bmatrix} 13 & -26 & 21 \end{bmatrix} \begin{bmatrix} -1 & -10 & -8 \\ -1 & -6 & -5 \\ 0 & -1 & -1 \end{bmatrix} = \begin{bmatrix} 13 & 5 & 5 \end{bmatrix}$$

$$\begin{bmatrix} 33 & -53 & -12 \end{bmatrix} \begin{bmatrix} -1 & -10 & -8 \\ -1 & -6 & -5 \\ 0 & -1 & -1 \end{bmatrix} = \begin{bmatrix} 20 & 0 & 13 \end{bmatrix}$$

$$\begin{bmatrix} 18 & -23 & -42 \end{bmatrix} \begin{bmatrix} -1 & -10 & -8 \\ -1 & -6 & -5 \\ 0 & -1 & -1 \end{bmatrix} = \begin{bmatrix} 5 & 0 & 13 \end{bmatrix}$$

$$\begin{bmatrix} 5 & -20 & 56 \end{bmatrix} \begin{bmatrix} -1 & -10 & -8 \\ -1 & -6 & -5 \\ 0 & -1 & -1 \end{bmatrix} = \begin{bmatrix} 15 & 14 & 4 \end{bmatrix}$$

$$\begin{bmatrix} -24 & 23 & 77 \end{bmatrix} \begin{bmatrix} -1 & -10 & -8 \\ -1 & -6 & -5 \\ 0 & -1 & -1 \end{bmatrix} = \begin{bmatrix} 1 & 25 & 0 \end{bmatrix}$$

So, the message is as follows.

$$\begin{bmatrix} 13 & 5 & 5 \end{bmatrix} \begin{bmatrix} 20 & 0 & 13 \end{bmatrix} \begin{bmatrix} 5 & 0 & 13 \end{bmatrix} \begin{bmatrix} 15 & 14 & 4 \end{bmatrix} \begin{bmatrix} 1 & 25 & 0 \end{bmatrix}$$

M E E   T   M E   M O N D A Y

Writing ABOUT MATHEMATICS

Cryptography Use your school's library, the Internet, or some other reference source to research information about another type of cryptography. Write a short paragraph describing how mathematics is used to code and decode messages.

8.5 Exercises

In Exercise 12, Cramer's Rule does not apply.
In Exercises 30, 31, and 34, the points are not collinear.

In Exercises 1–8, use Cramer's Rule to solve (if possible) the system of equations.

1. $\begin{cases} 3x + 4y = -2 \\ 5x + 3y = 4 \end{cases}$ **2.** $\begin{cases} -4x - 7y = 47 \\ -x + 6y = -27 \end{cases}$

3. $\begin{cases} -0.4x + 0.8y = 1.6 \\ 0.2x + 0.3y = 2.2 \end{cases}$

4. $\begin{cases} 2.4x - 1.3y = 14.63 \\ -4.6x + 0.5y = -11.51 \end{cases}$

5. $\begin{cases} 4x - y + z = -5 \\ 2x + 2y + 3z = 10 \\ 5x - 2y + 6z = 1 \end{cases}$ **6.** $\begin{cases} 4x - 2y + 3z = -2 \\ 2x + 2y + 5z = 16 \\ 8x - 5y - 2z = 4 \end{cases}$

7. $\begin{cases} x + 2y + 3z = -3 \\ -2x + y - z = 6 \\ 3x - 3y + 2z = -11 \end{cases}$ **8.** $\begin{cases} 5x - 4y + z = -14 \\ -x + 2y - 2z = 10 \\ 3x + y + z = 1 \end{cases}$

In Exercises 9–12, use a graphing utility and Cramer's Rule to solve (if possible) the system of equations.

9. $\begin{cases} 3x + 3y + 5z = 1 \\ 3x + 5y + 9z = 2 \\ 5x + 9y + 17z = 4 \end{cases}$ **10.** $\begin{cases} x + 2y - z = -7 \\ 2x - 2y - 2z = -8 \\ -x + 3y + 4z = 8 \end{cases}$

11. $\begin{cases} 2x + y + 2z = 6 \\ -x + 2y - 3z = 0 \\ 3x + 2y - z = 6 \end{cases}$ **12.** $\begin{cases} 2x + 3y + 5z = 4 \\ 3x + 5y + 9z = 7 \\ 5x + 9y + 17z = 13 \end{cases}$

In Exercises 13–22, use a determinant and the given vertices of a triangle to find the area of the triangle.

13.

14.

15.

16.

17.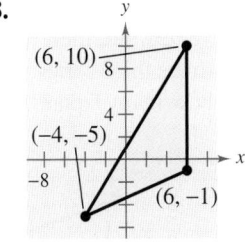

18.

19. $(-2, 4), (2, 3), (-1, 5)$

20. $(0, -2), (-1, 4), (3, 5)$

21. $(-3, 5), (2, 6), (3, -5)$

22. $(-2, 4), (1, 5), (3, -2)$

In Exercises 23 and 24, find a value of x such that the triangle with the given vertices has an area of 4 square units.

23. $(-5, 1), (0, 2), (-2, x)$

24. $(-4, 2), (-3, 5), (-1, x)$

In Exercises 25 and 26, find a value of x such that the triangle with the given vertices has an area of 6 square units.

25. $(-2, -3), (1, -1), (-8, x)$

26. $(1, 0), (5, -3), (-3, x)$

27. *Area of a Region* A large region of forest has been infested with gypsy moths. The region is roughly triangular, as shown in the figure. From the northernmost vertex A of the region, the distances to the other vertices are 25 miles south and 10 miles east (for vertex B), and 20 miles south and 28 miles east (for vertex C). Use a graphing utility to approximate the number of square miles in this region.

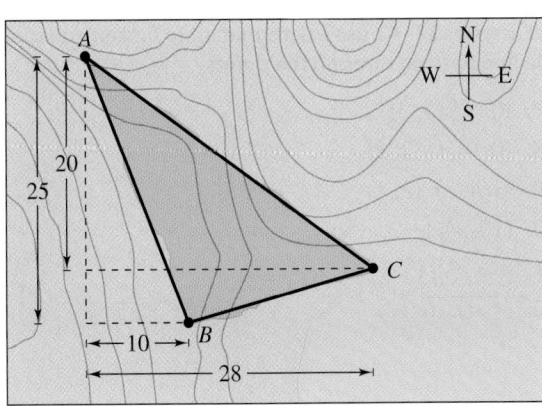

28. *Area of a Region*   You own a triangular tract of land, as shown in the figure. To estimate the number of square feet in the tract, you start at one vertex, walk 65 feet east and 50 feet north to the second vertex, and then walk 85 feet west and 30 feet north to the third vertex. Use a graphing utility to determine how many square feet there are in the tract of land.

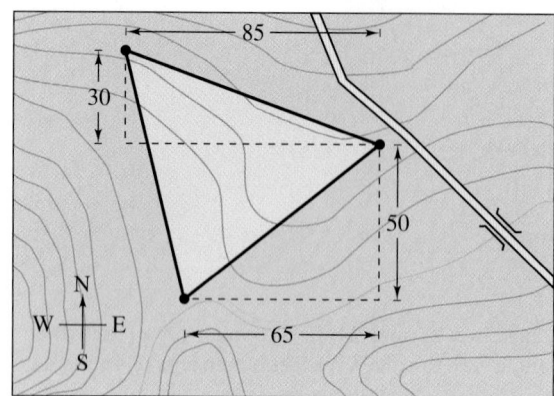

In Exercises 29–34, use a determinant to determine whether the points are collinear.

29. $(3, -1), (0, -3), (12, 5)$
30. $(-3, -5), (6, 1), (10, 2)$
31. $\left(2, -\frac{1}{2}\right), (-4, 4), (6, -3)$
32. $(0, 1), (4, -2), \left(-2, \frac{5}{2}\right)$
33. $(0, 2), (1, 2.4), (-1, 1.6)$
34. $(2, 3), (3, 3.5), (-1, 2)$

In Exercises 35 and 36, find x such that the points are collinear.

35. $(2, -5), (4, x), (5, -2)$
36. $(-6, 2), (-5, x), (-3, 5)$

In Exercises 37–42, use a determinant to find an equation of the line passing through the points.

37. $(0, 0), (5, 3)$
38. $(0, 0), (-2, 2)$
39. $(-4, 3), (2, 1)$
40. $(10, 7), (-2, -7)$
41. $\left(-\frac{1}{2}, 3\right), \left(\frac{5}{2}, 1\right)$
42. $\left(\frac{2}{3}, 4\right), (6, 12)$

In Exercises 43 and 44, find the uncoded 1×3 row matrices for the message. Then encode the message using the encoding matrix.

Message   *Encoding Matrix*

43. TROUBLE IN RIVER CITY $\begin{bmatrix} 1 & -1 & 0 \\ 1 & 0 & -1 \\ -6 & 2 & 3 \end{bmatrix}$

44. PLEASE SEND MONEY $\begin{bmatrix} 4 & 2 & 1 \\ -3 & -3 & -1 \\ 3 & 2 & 1 \end{bmatrix}$

In Exercises 45–48, write a cryptogram for the message using the matrix A.

$$A = \begin{bmatrix} 1 & 2 & 2 \\ 3 & 7 & 9 \\ -1 & -4 & -7 \end{bmatrix}.$$

45. CALL AT NOON
46. ICEBERG DEAD AHEAD
47. HAPPY BIRTHDAY
48. OPERATION OVERLOAD

In Exercises 49–52, use A^{-1} to decode the cryptogram.

49. $A = \begin{bmatrix} 1 & 2 \\ 3 & 5 \end{bmatrix}$

11 21 64 112 25 50 29 53 23 46
40 75 55 92

50. $A = \begin{bmatrix} -5 & 2 \\ -7 & 3 \end{bmatrix}$

-136 58 -173 72 -120 51 -95 38
-178 73 -70 28 -242 101 -115 47
-90 36 -115 49 -199 82

51. $A = \begin{bmatrix} 1 & -1 & 0 \\ 1 & 0 & -1 \\ -6 & 2 & 3 \end{bmatrix}$

9 -1 -9 38 -19 -19 28 -9 -19
-80 25 41 -64 21 31 9 -5 -4

52. $A = \begin{bmatrix} 3 & -4 & 2 \\ 0 & 2 & 1 \\ 4 & -5 & 3 \end{bmatrix}$

112 -140 83 19 -25 13 72 -76 61
95 -118 71 20 21 38 35 -23 36 42
-48 32

In Exercises 53 and 54, decode the cryptogram by using the inverse of the matrix *A*.

$$A = \begin{bmatrix} 1 & 2 & 2 \\ 3 & 7 & 9 \\ -1 & -4 & -7 \end{bmatrix}$$

53. 20 17 -15 -12 -56 -104 1 -25 -65
62 143 181

54. 13 -9 -59 61 112 106 -17 -73 -131
11 24 29 65 144 172

55. The following cryptogram was encoded with a 2×2 matrix.

8 21 -15 -10 -13 -13 5 10 5 25 5
19 -1 6 20 40 -18 -18 1 16

The last word of the message is _RON. What is the message?

▶ Model It

56. *Data Analysis*   The table shows the numbers *y* of U.S. Supreme Court cases waiting to be tried for the years 1997 through 1999. (Source: Office of the Clerk, Supreme Court of the United States)

Year, *t*	Number of cases, *y*
1997	7692
1998	8083
1999	8445

(a) Use the technique demonstrated in Exercises 67–70 in Section 7.3 to create a system of linear equations for the data. Let *t* represent the year, with $t = 7$ corresponding to 1997.

(b) Use Cramer's Rule to solve the system from part (a) and find the least squares regression parabola $y = at^2 + bt + c$.

(c) Use a graphing utility to graph the parabola from part (b).

(d) Use the graph from part (c) to estimate when the number of U.S. Supreme Court cases waiting to be tried will reach 9800.

Synthesis

True or False?   In Exercises 57–59, determine whether the statement is true or false. Justify your answer.

57. In Cramer's Rule, the numerator is the determinant of the coefficient matrix.

58. You cannot use Cramer's Rule when solving a system of linear equations if the determinant of the coefficient matrix is zero.

59. In a system of linear equations, if the determinant of the coefficient matrix is zero, the system has no solution.

60. *Writing*   At this point in the book, you have learned several methods for solving systems of linear equations. Briefly describe which method(s) you find easiest to use and which method(s) you find most difficult to use.

Review

In Exercises 61–64, use any method to solve the system of equations.

61. $\begin{cases} -x - 7y = -22 \\ 5x + y = -26 \end{cases}$ **62.** $\begin{cases} 3x + 8y = 11 \\ -2x + 12y = -16 \end{cases}$

63. $\begin{cases} -x - 3y + 5z = -14 \\ 4x + 2y - z = -1 \\ 5x - 3y + 2z = -11 \end{cases}$

64. $\begin{cases} 5x - y - z = 7 \\ -2x + 3y + z = -5 \\ 4x + 10y - 5z = -37 \end{cases}$

In Exercises 65 and 66, sketch the constraint region. Then find the minimum and maximum values of the objective function and where they occur, subject to the constraints.

65. Objective function:
$z = 6x + 4y$
Constraints:
$x \geq 0$
$y \geq 0$
$x + 6y \leq 30$
$6x + y \leq 40$

66. Objective function:
$z = 6x + 7y$
Constraints:
$x \geq 0$
$y \geq 0$
$4x + 3y \geq 24$
$x + 3y \geq 15$

Chapter Summary

▶ *What* did you learn?

Exercises containing systems with no solutions: 22, 24, 30
Exercise containing system with infinitely many solutions: 21

▶ Review Exercises **603**

Review Exercises

8.1 **In Exercises 1–4, determine the order of the matrix.**

1. $\begin{bmatrix} -4 \\ 0 \\ 5 \end{bmatrix}$

2. $\begin{bmatrix} 3 & -1 & 0 & 6 \\ -2 & 7 & 1 & 4 \end{bmatrix}$

3. $[3]$

4. $\begin{bmatrix} 6 & 2 & -5 & 8 & 0 \end{bmatrix}$

In Exercises 5 and 6, form the augmented matrix for the system of linear equations.

5. $\begin{cases} 3x - 10y = 15 \\ 5x + 4y = 22 \end{cases}$

6. $\begin{cases} 8x - 7y + 4z = 12 \\ 3x - 5y + 2z = 20 \\ 5x + 3y - 3z = 26 \end{cases}$

In Exercises 7 and 8, write the system of linear equations represented by the augmented matrix. (Use variables x, y, z, and w.)

7. $\begin{bmatrix} 5 & 1 & 7 & \vdots & -9 \\ 4 & 2 & 0 & \vdots & 10 \\ 9 & 4 & 2 & \vdots & 3 \end{bmatrix}$

8. $\begin{bmatrix} 13 & 16 & 7 & 3 & \vdots & 2 \\ 1 & 21 & 8 & 5 & \vdots & 12 \\ 4 & 10 & -4 & 3 & \vdots & -1 \end{bmatrix}$

In Exercises 9 and 10, write the matrix in row-echelon form. Remember that the row-echelon form of a matrix is not unique.

9. $\begin{bmatrix} 0 & 1 & 1 \\ 1 & 2 & 3 \\ 2 & 2 & 2 \end{bmatrix}$

10. $\begin{bmatrix} 4 & 8 & 16 \\ 3 & -1 & 2 \\ -2 & 10 & 12 \end{bmatrix}$

In Exercises 11–14, write the system of linear equations represented by the augmented matrix. Then use back-substitution to solve. (Use variables x, y, and z.)

11. $\begin{bmatrix} 1 & 2 & 3 & \vdots & 9 \\ 0 & 1 & -2 & \vdots & 2 \\ 0 & 0 & 1 & \vdots & 0 \end{bmatrix}$

12. $\begin{bmatrix} 1 & 3 & -9 & \vdots & 4 \\ 0 & 1 & -1 & \vdots & 10 \\ 0 & 0 & 1 & \vdots & -2 \end{bmatrix}$

13. $\begin{bmatrix} 1 & -5 & 4 & \vdots & 1 \\ 0 & 1 & 2 & \vdots & 3 \\ 0 & 0 & 1 & \vdots & 4 \end{bmatrix}$

14. $\begin{bmatrix} 1 & -8 & 0 & \vdots & -2 \\ 0 & 1 & -1 & \vdots & -7 \\ 0 & 0 & 1 & \vdots & 1 \end{bmatrix}$

In Exercises 15–24, use matrices to solve the system of equations (if possible). Use Gaussian elimination with back-substitution.

15. $\begin{cases} 5x + 4y = 2 \\ -x + y = -22 \end{cases}$

16. $\begin{cases} 2x - 5y = 2 \\ 3x - 7y = 1 \end{cases}$

17. $\begin{cases} 0.3x - 0.1y = -0.13 \\ 0.2x - 0.3y = -0.25 \end{cases}$

18. $\begin{cases} 0.2x - 0.1y = 0.07 \\ 0.4x - 0.5y = -0.01 \end{cases}$

19. $\begin{cases} 2x + 3y + z = 10 \\ 2x - 3y - 3z = 22 \\ 4x - 2y + 3z = -2 \end{cases}$

20. $\begin{cases} 2x + 3y + 3z = 3 \\ 6x + 6y + 12z = 13 \\ 12x + 9y - z = 2 \end{cases}$

21. $\begin{cases} 2x + y + 2z = 4 \\ 2x + 2y = 5 \\ 2x - y + 6z = 2 \end{cases}$

22. $\begin{cases} x + 2y + 6z = 1 \\ 2x + 5y + 15z = 4 \\ 3x + y + 3z = -6 \end{cases}$

23. $\begin{cases} 2x + y + z = 6 \\ -2y + 3z - w = 9 \\ 3x + 3y - 2z - 2w = -11 \\ x + z + 3w = 14 \end{cases}$

24. $\begin{cases} x + 2y + w = 3 \\ -3y + 3z = 0 \\ 4x + 4y + z + 2w = 0 \\ 2x + z = 3 \end{cases}$

In Exercises 25–28, use matrices to solve the system of equations. Use Gauss-Jordan elimination.

25. $\begin{cases} -x + y + 2z - 1 \\ 2x + 3y + z = -2 \\ 5x + 4y + 2z = 4 \end{cases}$

26. $\begin{cases} 4x + 4y + 4z = 5 \\ 4x - 2y - 8z = 1 \\ 5x + 3y + 8z = 6 \end{cases}$

27. $\begin{cases} 2x - y + 9z = -8 \\ -x - 3y + 4z = -15 \\ 5x + 2y - z = 17 \end{cases}$

28. $\begin{cases} -3x + y + 7z = -20 \\ 5x - 2y - z = 34 \\ -x + y + 4z = -8 \end{cases}$

In Exercises 29 and 30, use the matrix capabilities of a graphing utility to reduce the augmented matrix corresponding to the system of equations, and solve the system.

29. $\begin{cases} 3x - y + 5z - 2w = -44 \\ x + 6y + 4z - w = 1 \\ 5x - y + z + 3w = -15 \\ 4y - z - 8w = 58 \end{cases}$

30. $\begin{cases} 4x + 12y + 2z = 20 \\ x + 6y + 4z = 12 \\ x + 6y + z = 8 \\ -2x - 10y - 2z = -10 \end{cases}$

8.2 In Exercises 31–34, find x and y.

31. $\begin{bmatrix} -1 & x \\ y & 9 \end{bmatrix} = \begin{bmatrix} -1 & 12 \\ -7 & 9 \end{bmatrix}$

32. $\begin{bmatrix} -1 & 0 \\ x & 5 \\ -4 & y \end{bmatrix} = \begin{bmatrix} -1 & 0 \\ 8 & 5 \\ -4 & 0 \end{bmatrix}$

33. $\begin{bmatrix} x+3 & -4 & 4y \\ 0 & -3 & 2 \\ -2 & y+5 & 6x \end{bmatrix} = \begin{bmatrix} 5x-1 & -4 & 44 \\ 0 & -3 & 2 \\ -2 & 16 & 6 \end{bmatrix}$

34. $\begin{bmatrix} -9 & 4 & 2 & -5 \\ 0 & -3 & 7 & -4 \\ 6 & -1 & 1 & 0 \end{bmatrix} = \begin{bmatrix} -9 & 4 & x-10 & -5 \\ 0 & -3 & 7 & 2y \\ \frac{1}{2}x & -1 & 1 & 0 \end{bmatrix}$

In Exercises 35–38, if possible, find (a) $A + B$, (b) $A - B$, (c) $4A$, and (d) $A + 3B$.

35. $A = \begin{bmatrix} 2 & -2 \\ 3 & 5 \end{bmatrix}$, $B = \begin{bmatrix} -3 & 10 \\ 12 & 8 \end{bmatrix}$

36. $A = \begin{bmatrix} 5 & 4 \\ -7 & 2 \\ 11 & 2 \end{bmatrix}$, $B = \begin{bmatrix} 4 & 12 \\ 20 & 40 \\ 15 & 30 \end{bmatrix}$

37. $A = \begin{bmatrix} 5 & 4 \\ -7 & 2 \\ 11 & 2 \end{bmatrix}$, $B = \begin{bmatrix} 0 & 3 \\ 4 & 12 \\ 20 & 40 \end{bmatrix}$

38. $A = \begin{bmatrix} 6 & -5 & 7 \end{bmatrix}$, $B = \begin{bmatrix} -1 \\ 4 \\ 8 \end{bmatrix}$

In Exercises 39–42, perform the matrix operations. If it is not possible, explain why.

39. $\begin{bmatrix} 7 & 3 \\ -1 & 5 \end{bmatrix} + \begin{bmatrix} 10 & -20 \\ 14 & -3 \end{bmatrix}$

40. $\begin{bmatrix} -11 & 16 & 19 \\ -7 & -2 & 1 \end{bmatrix} - \begin{bmatrix} 6 & 0 \\ 8 & -4 \\ -2 & 10 \end{bmatrix}$

41. $-2\begin{bmatrix} 1 & 2 \\ 5 & -4 \\ 6 & 0 \end{bmatrix} + 8\begin{bmatrix} 7 & 1 \\ 1 & 2 \\ 1 & 4 \end{bmatrix}$

42. $-\begin{bmatrix} 8 & -1 & 8 \\ -2 & 4 & 12 \\ 0 & -6 & 0 \end{bmatrix} - 5\begin{bmatrix} -2 & 0 & -4 \\ 3 & -1 & 1 \\ 6 & 12 & -8 \end{bmatrix}$

In Exercises 43 and 44, use a graphing utility to perform the matrix operations.

43. $3\begin{bmatrix} 8 & -2 & 5 \\ 1 & 3 & -1 \end{bmatrix} + 6\begin{bmatrix} 4 & -2 & -3 \\ 2 & 7 & 6 \end{bmatrix}$

44. $-5\begin{bmatrix} 2 & 0 \\ 7 & -2 \\ 8 & 2 \end{bmatrix} + 4\begin{bmatrix} 4 & -2 \\ 6 & 11 \\ -1 & 3 \end{bmatrix}$

In Exercises 45–48, solve for X when

$$A = \begin{bmatrix} -4 & 0 \\ 1 & -5 \\ -3 & 2 \end{bmatrix} \quad \text{and} \quad B = \begin{bmatrix} 1 & 2 \\ -2 & 1 \\ 4 & 4 \end{bmatrix}.$$

45. $X = 3A - 2B$

46. $6X = 4A + 3B$

47. $3X + 2A = B$

48. $2A - 5B = 3X$

In Exercises 49–52, find AB, if possible.

49. $A = \begin{bmatrix} 2 & -2 \\ 3 & 5 \end{bmatrix}$, $B = \begin{bmatrix} -3 & 10 \\ 12 & 8 \end{bmatrix}$

50. $A = \begin{bmatrix} 5 & 4 \\ -7 & 2 \\ 11 & 2 \end{bmatrix}$, $B = \begin{bmatrix} 4 & 12 \\ 20 & 40 \\ 15 & 30 \end{bmatrix}$

51. $A = \begin{bmatrix} 5 & 4 \\ -7 & 2 \\ 11 & 2 \end{bmatrix}$, $B = \begin{bmatrix} 4 & 12 \\ 20 & 40 \end{bmatrix}$

52. $A = \begin{bmatrix} 6 & -5 & 7 \end{bmatrix}$, $B = \begin{bmatrix} -1 \\ 4 \\ 8 \end{bmatrix}$

In Exercises 53–60, perform the matrix operations. If it is not possible, explain why.

53. $\begin{bmatrix} 1 & 2 \\ 5 & -4 \\ 6 & 0 \end{bmatrix} \begin{bmatrix} 6 & -2 & 8 \\ 4 & 0 & 0 \end{bmatrix}$

54. $\begin{bmatrix} 1 & 5 & 6 \\ 2 & -4 & 0 \end{bmatrix} \begin{bmatrix} 6 & -2 & 8 \\ 4 & 0 & 0 \end{bmatrix}$

55. $\begin{bmatrix} 1 & 5 & 6 \\ 2 & -4 & 0 \end{bmatrix} \begin{bmatrix} 6 & 4 \\ -2 & 0 \\ 8 & 0 \end{bmatrix}$

56. $\begin{bmatrix} 1 & 3 & 2 \\ 0 & 2 & -4 \\ 0 & 0 & 3 \end{bmatrix} \begin{bmatrix} 4 & -3 & 2 \\ 0 & 3 & -1 \\ 0 & 0 & 2 \end{bmatrix}$

57. $\begin{bmatrix} 4 \\ 6 \end{bmatrix} \begin{bmatrix} 6 & -2 \end{bmatrix}$

58. $\begin{bmatrix} 4 & -2 & 6 \end{bmatrix} \begin{bmatrix} -2 & 1 \\ 0 & -3 \\ 2 & 0 \end{bmatrix}$

59. $\begin{bmatrix} 2 & 1 \\ 6 & 0 \end{bmatrix} \left(\begin{bmatrix} 4 & 2 \\ -3 & 1 \end{bmatrix} + \begin{bmatrix} -2 & 4 \\ 0 & 4 \end{bmatrix} \right)$

60. $-3 \begin{bmatrix} 1 & -1 \\ 4 & 2 \end{bmatrix} \left(\begin{bmatrix} 0 & 3 \\ 1 & 2 \end{bmatrix} \begin{bmatrix} 1 & 0 \\ 5 & -3 \end{bmatrix} \right)$

In Exercises 61 and 62, use a graphing utility to perform the matrix operations.

61. $\begin{bmatrix} 4 & 1 \\ 11 & -7 \\ 12 & 3 \end{bmatrix} \begin{bmatrix} 3 & -5 & 6 \\ 2 & -2 & -2 \end{bmatrix}$

62. $\begin{bmatrix} -2 & 3 & 10 \\ 4 & -2 & 2 \end{bmatrix} \begin{bmatrix} 1 & 1 \\ -5 & 2 \\ 3 & 2 \end{bmatrix}$

63. **Manufacturing** A corporation has four factories, each of which manufactures three types of cordless power tools. The number of units of cordless power tools produced at factory j in one day is represented by a_{ij} in the matrix

$$A = \begin{bmatrix} 80 & 70 & 90 & 40 \\ 50 & 30 & 80 & 20 \\ 90 & 60 & 100 & 50 \end{bmatrix}.$$

Find the production levels if production is increased by 20%.

64. **Manufacturing** A manufacturing company produces three kinds of computer games that are shipped to two warehouses. The number of units of game i that are shipped to warehouse j is represented by a_{ij} in the matrix

$$A = \begin{bmatrix} 8200 & 7400 \\ 6500 & 9800 \\ 5400 & 4800 \end{bmatrix}.$$

The price per unit is represented by the matrix

$$B = [\$10.25 \quad \$14.50 \quad \$17.75].$$

Compute BA and interpret the result.

8.3 **In Exercises 65–68, show that B is the inverse of A.**

65. $A = \begin{bmatrix} -4 & -1 \\ 7 & 2 \end{bmatrix}, \quad B = \begin{bmatrix} -2 & -1 \\ 7 & 4 \end{bmatrix}$

66. $A = \begin{bmatrix} 5 & -1 \\ 11 & -2 \end{bmatrix}, \quad B = \begin{bmatrix} -2 & 1 \\ -11 & 5 \end{bmatrix}$

67. $A = \begin{bmatrix} 1 & 1 & 0 \\ 1 & 0 & 1 \\ 6 & 2 & 3 \end{bmatrix}, \quad B = \begin{bmatrix} -2 & -3 & 1 \\ 3 & 3 & -1 \\ 2 & 4 & -1 \end{bmatrix}$

68. $A = \begin{bmatrix} 1 & -1 & 0 \\ -1 & 0 & -1 \\ 8 & -4 & 2 \end{bmatrix}, \quad B = \begin{bmatrix} -2 & 1 & \frac{1}{2} \\ -3 & 1 & \frac{1}{2} \\ 2 & -2 & -\frac{1}{2} \end{bmatrix}$

In Exercises 69–72, find the inverse of the matrix (if it exists).

69. $\begin{bmatrix} -6 & 5 \\ -5 & 4 \end{bmatrix}$

70. $\begin{bmatrix} -3 & -5 \\ 2 & 3 \end{bmatrix}$

71. $\begin{bmatrix} -1 & -2 & -2 \\ 3 & 7 & 9 \\ 1 & 4 & 7 \end{bmatrix}$

72. $\begin{bmatrix} 0 & -2 & 1 \\ -5 & -2 & -3 \\ 7 & 3 & 4 \end{bmatrix}$

In Exercises 73–76, use a graphing utility to find the inverse of the matrix (if it exists).

73. $\begin{bmatrix} 2 & 0 & 3 \\ -1 & 1 & 1 \\ 2 & -2 & 1 \end{bmatrix}$

74. $\begin{bmatrix} 1 & 4 & 6 \\ 2 & -3 & 1 \\ -1 & 18 & 16 \end{bmatrix}$

75. $\begin{bmatrix} 1 & 3 & 1 & 6 \\ 4 & 4 & 2 & 6 \\ 3 & 4 & 1 & 2 \\ -1 & 2 & -1 & -2 \end{bmatrix}$

76. $\begin{bmatrix} 8 & 0 & 2 & 8 \\ 4 & -2 & 0 & -2 \\ 1 & 2 & 1 & 4 \\ -1 & 4 & 1 & 1 \end{bmatrix}$

In Exercises 77–80, let

$$A = \begin{bmatrix} a & b \\ c & d \end{bmatrix}.$$

Find the inverse of the matrix above

$$A^{-1} = \frac{1}{ad - bc}\begin{bmatrix} d & -b \\ -c & a \end{bmatrix}$$

(if it exists).

77. $\begin{bmatrix} -7 & 2 \\ -8 & 2 \end{bmatrix}$ **78.** $\begin{bmatrix} 10 & 4 \\ 7 & 3 \end{bmatrix}$

79. $\begin{bmatrix} -\frac{1}{2} & 20 \\ \frac{3}{10} & -6 \end{bmatrix}$ **80.** $\begin{bmatrix} -\frac{3}{4} & \frac{5}{2} \\ -\frac{4}{5} & -\frac{8}{3} \end{bmatrix}$

In Exercises 81–88, use an inverse matrix to solve (if possible) the system of linear equations.

81. $\begin{cases} -x + 4y = 8 \\ 2x - 7y = -5 \end{cases}$ **82.** $\begin{cases} 5x - y = 13 \\ -9x + 2y = -24 \end{cases}$

83. $\begin{cases} -3x + 10y = 8 \\ 5x - 17y = -13 \end{cases}$ **84.** $\begin{cases} 4x - 2y = -10 \\ -19x + 9y = 47 \end{cases}$

85. $\begin{cases} 3x + 2y - z = 6 \\ x - y + 2z = -1 \\ 5x + y + z = 7 \end{cases}$

86. $\begin{cases} -x + 4y - 2z = 12 \\ 2x - 9y + 5z = -25 \\ -x + 5y - 4z = 10 \end{cases}$

87. $\begin{cases} -2x + y + 2z = -13 \\ -x - 4y + z = -11 \\ -y - z = 0 \end{cases}$

88. $\begin{cases} 3x - y + 5z = -14 \\ -x + y + 6z = 8 \\ -8x + 4y - z = 44 \end{cases}$

In Exercises 89–92, use a graphing utility to solve (if possible) the system of linear equations using the inverse of the coefficient matrix.

89. $\begin{cases} x + 2y = -1 \\ 3x + 4y = -5 \end{cases}$ **90.** $\begin{cases} x + 3y = 23 \\ -6x + 2y = -18 \end{cases}$

91. $\begin{cases} -3x - 3y - 4z = 2 \\ y + z = -1 \\ 4x + 3y + 4z = -1 \end{cases}$

92. $\begin{cases} x - 3y - 2z = 8 \\ -2x + 7y + 3z = -19 \\ x - y - 3z = 3 \end{cases}$

8.4 In Exercises 93–96, find the determinant of the matrix.

93. $\begin{bmatrix} 8 & 5 \\ 2 & -4 \end{bmatrix}$ **94.** $\begin{bmatrix} -9 & 11 \\ 7 & -4 \end{bmatrix}$

95. $\begin{bmatrix} 50 & -30 \\ 10 & 5 \end{bmatrix}$ **96.** $\begin{bmatrix} 14 & -24 \\ 12 & -15 \end{bmatrix}$

In Exercises 97–100, find all (a) minors and (b) cofactors of the matrix.

97. $\begin{bmatrix} 2 & -1 \\ 7 & 4 \end{bmatrix}$ **98.** $\begin{bmatrix} 3 & 6 \\ 5 & -4 \end{bmatrix}$

99. $\begin{bmatrix} 3 & 2 & -1 \\ -2 & 5 & 0 \\ 1 & 8 & 6 \end{bmatrix}$ **100.** $\begin{bmatrix} 8 & 3 & 4 \\ 6 & 5 & -9 \\ -4 & 1 & 2 \end{bmatrix}$

In Exercises 101–104, find the determinant of the matrix. Expand by cofactors on the row or column that appears to make the computations easiest.

101. $\begin{bmatrix} -2 & 4 & 1 \\ -6 & 0 & 2 \\ 5 & 3 & 4 \end{bmatrix}$ **102.** $\begin{bmatrix} 4 & 7 & -1 \\ 2 & -3 & 4 \\ -5 & 1 & -1 \end{bmatrix}$

103. $\begin{bmatrix} 3 & 0 & -4 & 0 \\ 0 & 8 & 1 & 2 \\ 6 & 1 & 8 & 2 \\ 0 & 3 & -4 & 1 \end{bmatrix}$

104. $\begin{bmatrix} -5 & 6 & 0 & 0 \\ 0 & 1 & -1 & 2 \\ -3 & 4 & -5 & 1 \\ 1 & 6 & 0 & 3 \end{bmatrix}$

8.5 In Exercises 105–108, use Cramer's Rule to solve (if possible) the system of equations.

105. $\begin{cases} 5x - 2y = 6 \\ -11x + 3y = -23 \end{cases}$

106. $\begin{cases} 3x + 8y = -7 \\ 9x - 5y = 37 \end{cases}$

107. $\begin{cases} -2x + 3y - 5z = -11 \\ 4x - y + z = -3 \\ -x - 4y + 6z = 15 \end{cases}$

108. $\begin{cases} 5x - 2y + z = 15 \\ 3x - 3y - z = -7 \\ 2x - y - 7z = -3 \end{cases}$

In Exercises 109–112, use a determinant and the given vertices of a triangle to find the area of the triangle.

109.

110.

111.

112.

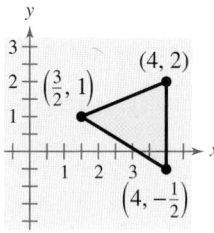

In Exercises 113 and 114, use a determinant to decide whether the points are collinear.

113. $(-1, 7), (3, -9), (-3, 15)$

114. $(0, -5), (-2, -6), (8, -1)$

In Exercises 115–118, use a determinant to find an equation of the line passing through the points.

115. $(-4, 0), (4, 4)$
116. $(2, 5), (6, -1)$

117. $\left(-\frac{5}{2}, 3\right), \left(\frac{7}{2}, 1\right)$
118. $(-0.8, 0.2), (0.7, 3.2)$

In Exercises 119 and 120, find the uncoded 1×3 row matrices for the message. Then encode the message using the encoding matrix.

Message	Encoding Matrix

119. LOOK OUT BELOW
$$\begin{bmatrix} 2 & -2 & 0 \\ 3 & 0 & -3 \\ -6 & 2 & 3 \end{bmatrix}$$

120. RETURN TO BASE
$$\begin{bmatrix} 2 & 1 & 0 \\ -6 & -6 & -2 \\ 3 & 2 & 1 \end{bmatrix}$$

In Exercises 121 and 122, decode the cryptogram by using the inverse of the matrix

$$A = \begin{bmatrix} -5 & 4 & -3 \\ 10 & -7 & 6 \\ 8 & -6 & 5 \end{bmatrix}.$$

121. $-5 \quad 11 \quad -2 \quad 370 \quad -265 \quad 225 \quad -57 \quad 48 \quad -33$
$32 \quad -15 \quad 20 \quad 245 \quad -171 \quad 147$

122. $145 \quad -105 \quad 92 \quad 264 \quad -188 \quad 160 \quad 23 \quad -16 \quad 15$
$129 \quad -84 \quad 78 \quad -9 \quad 8 \quad -5 \quad 159 \quad -118 \quad 100$
$219 \quad -152 \quad 133 \quad 370 \quad -265 \quad 225 \quad -105 \quad 84$
-63

Synthesis

True or False? In Exercises 123 and 124, determine whether the statement is true or false. Justify your answer.

123. It is possible to find the determinant of a 4×5 matrix.

124.
$$\begin{vmatrix} a_{11} & a_{12} & a_{13} \\ a_{21} & a_{22} & a_{23} \\ a_{31} + c_1 & a_{32} + c_2 & a_{33} + c_3 \end{vmatrix} =$$
$$\begin{vmatrix} a_{11} & a_{12} & a_{13} \\ a_{21} & a_{22} & a_{23} \\ a_{31} & a_{32} & a_{33} \end{vmatrix} + \begin{vmatrix} a_{11} & a_{12} & a_{13} \\ a_{21} & a_{22} & a_{23} \\ c_1 & c_2 & c_3 \end{vmatrix}$$

125. Under what conditions does a matrix have an inverse?

126. ***Writing*** What is meant by the cofactor of an entry of a matrix? How are cofactors used to find the determinant of the matrix?

127. Three people were asked to solve a system of equations using an augmented matrix. Each person reduced the matrix to row-echelon form. The reduced matrices were

$$\begin{bmatrix} 1 & 2 & \vdots & 3 \\ 0 & 1 & \vdots & 1 \end{bmatrix},$$
$$\begin{bmatrix} 1 & 0 & \vdots & 1 \\ 0 & 1 & \vdots & 1 \end{bmatrix},$$
and
$$\begin{bmatrix} 1 & 2 & \vdots & 3 \\ 0 & 0 & \vdots & 0 \end{bmatrix}.$$

Can all three be right? Explain.

128. ***Think About It*** Describe the row-echelon form of an augmented matrix that corresponds to a system of linear equations that has a unique solution.

129. Solve the equation

$$\begin{vmatrix} 2 - \lambda & 5 \\ 3 & -8 - \lambda \end{vmatrix} = 0.$$

Chapter Test

The *Interactive* CD-ROM and *Internet* versions of this text offer Chapter Pre-Tests and Chapter Post-Tests, both of which have randomly generated exercises with diagnostic capabilities.

Take this test as you would take a test in class. When you are finished, check your work against the answers given in the back of the book.

In Exercises 1 and 2, write the matrix in reduced row-echelon form.

1. $\begin{bmatrix} 1 & -1 & 5 \\ 6 & 2 & 3 \\ 5 & 3 & -3 \end{bmatrix}$

2. $\begin{bmatrix} 1 & 0 & -1 & 2 \\ -1 & 1 & 1 & -3 \\ 1 & 1 & -1 & 1 \\ 3 & 2 & -3 & 4 \end{bmatrix}$

3. Write the augmented matrix corresponding to the system of equations and solve the system.

$$\begin{cases} 4x + 3y - 2z = 14 \\ -x - y + 2z = -5 \\ 3x + y - 4z = 8 \end{cases}$$

4. Find (a) $A - B$, (b) $3A$, (c) $3A - 2B$, and (d) AB (if possible).

$$A = \begin{bmatrix} 5 & 4 \\ -4 & -4 \end{bmatrix}, \quad B = \begin{bmatrix} 4 & -1 \\ -4 & 0 \end{bmatrix}$$

In Exercises 5 and 6, find the inverse of the matrix (if it exists).

5. $\begin{bmatrix} -6 & 4 \\ 10 & -5 \end{bmatrix}$

6. $\begin{bmatrix} -2 & 4 & -6 \\ 2 & 1 & 0 \\ 4 & -2 & 5 \end{bmatrix}$

7. Use the result of Exercise 5 to solve the system.

$$\begin{cases} -6x + 4y = 10 \\ 10x - 5y = 20 \end{cases}$$

In Exercises 8–10, evaluate the determinant of the matrix.

8. $\begin{bmatrix} -9 & 4 \\ 13 & 16 \end{bmatrix}$

9. $\begin{bmatrix} \frac{5}{2} & \frac{13}{4} \\ -8 & \frac{6}{5} \end{bmatrix}$

10. $\begin{bmatrix} 6 & -7 & 2 \\ 3 & -2 & 0 \\ 1 & 5 & 1 \end{bmatrix}$

In Exercises 11 and 12, use Cramer's Rule to solve (if possible) the system of equations.

11. $\begin{cases} 7x + 6y = 9 \\ -2x - 11y = -49 \end{cases}$

12. $\begin{cases} 6x - y + 2z = -4 \\ -2x + 3y - z = 10 \\ 4x - 4y + z = -18 \end{cases}$

13. Use a determinant to find the area of the triangle in the figure.

14. Find the uncoded 1×3 row matrices for the message KNOCK ON WOOD. Then encode the message using the matrix A at the left.

15. One hundred liters of a 50% solution is obtained by mixing a 60% solution with a 20% solution. How many liters of each solution must be used to obtain the desired mixture?

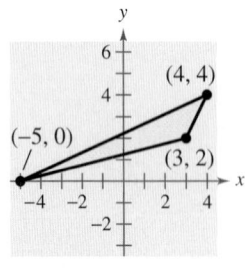

FIGURE FOR 13

$$A = \begin{bmatrix} 1 & -1 & 0 \\ 1 & 0 & -1 \\ 6 & -2 & -3 \end{bmatrix}$$

MATRIX FOR 14

Proofs in Mathematics

Proofs without words are pictures or diagrams that give a visual understanding of why a theorem or statement is true. They can also provide a starting point for writing a formal proof. The following proof shows that a 2×2 determinant is the area of a parallelogram.

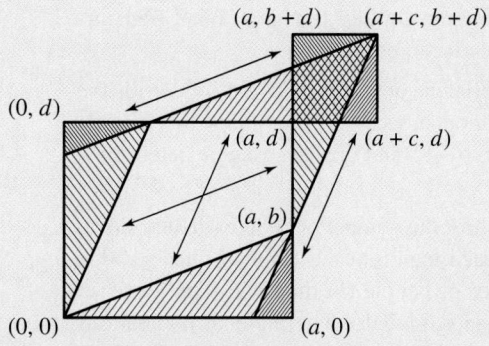

$$\begin{vmatrix} a & b \\ c & d \end{vmatrix} = ad - bc = \|\square\| - \|\square\| = \|\square\|$$

The following is a color-coded version of the proof along with a brief explanation of why this proof works.

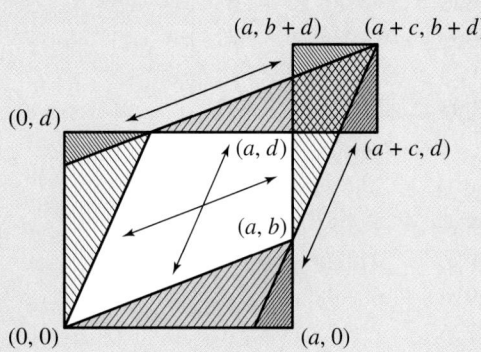

$$\begin{vmatrix} a & b \\ c & d \end{vmatrix} = ad - bc = \|\square\| - \|\square\| = \|\square\|$$

Area of $\square$ = Area of orange $\triangle$ + Area of yellow $\triangle$ + Area of blue $\triangle$ + Area of pink $\triangle$ + Area of white quadrilateral

Area of $\square$ = Area of orange $\triangle$ + Area of pink $\triangle$ + Area of green quadrilateral

Area of $\square$ = Area of white quadrilateral + Area of blue $\triangle$ + Area of yellow $\triangle$ − Area of green quadrilateral
= Area of $\square$ − Area of $\square$

Exercise taken from "Proof Without Words" by Solomon W. Golomb, *Mathematics Magazine*, March 1985. Used by permission of the author.

1. The columns of matrix T show the coordinates of the vertices of a triangle. Matrix A is a transformation matrix.

$$A = \begin{bmatrix} 0 & -1 \\ 1 & 0 \end{bmatrix} \quad T = \begin{bmatrix} 1 & 2 & 3 \\ 1 & 4 & 2 \end{bmatrix}$$

(a) Find AT and AAT. Then sketch the original triangle and the two transformed triangles. What transformation does A represent?

(b) Given the triangle determined by AAT, describe the transformation process that produces the triangle determined by AT and then the triangle determined by T.

2. The matrices show the number of people (in thousands) who lived in each region of the United States in 2000 and the number of people (in thousands) projected to live in each region in 2015. The regional populations are separated into three age categories. (Source: U.S. Census Bureau)

2000

	0–17	18–64	65 +
Northeast	13,049	33,175	7,372
Midwest	16,646	39,386	8,263
South	25,569	62,235	12,437
Mountain	4,935	11,210	2,031
Pacific	12,098	28,036	4,893

2015

	0–17	18–64	65 +
Northeast	12,589	34,081	8,165
Midwest	15,886	41,038	10,101
South	25,916	68,998	17,470
Mountain	5,226	12,626	3,270
Pacific	14,906	33,296	6,565

(a) The total population in 2000 was 281,335,000 and the projected total population in 2015 is 310,133,000. Rewrite the matrices to give the information as percents of the total population.

(b) Write a matrix that gives the projected change in the percent of the population in each region and age group from 2000 to 2015.

(c) Based on the result of part (b), which region(s) and age group(s) are projected to show relative growth from 2000 to 2015?

3. Determine whether the matrix is idempotent. A square matrix is **idempotent** if $A^2 = A$.

(a) $\begin{bmatrix} 1 & 0 \\ 0 & 0 \end{bmatrix}$ (b) $\begin{bmatrix} 0 & 1 \\ 1 & 0 \end{bmatrix}$

(c) $\begin{bmatrix} 2 & 3 \\ -1 & -2 \end{bmatrix}$ (d) $\begin{bmatrix} 2 & 3 \\ 1 & 2 \end{bmatrix}$

4. Let $A = \begin{bmatrix} 1 & 2 \\ -2 & 1 \end{bmatrix}$.

(a) Show that $A^2 - 2A + 5I = 0$, where I is the identity matrix of order 2.

(b) Show that $A^{-1} = \frac{1}{5}(2I - A)$.

(c) Show in general that for any square matrix satisfying

$$A^2 - 2A + 5I = 0$$

the inverse of A is given by

$$A^{-1} = \frac{1}{5}(2I - A).$$

5. Find x such that the matrix is equal to its own inverse.

$$A = \begin{bmatrix} 3 & x \\ -2 & -3 \end{bmatrix}$$

6. Find x such that the matrix is singular.

$$A = \begin{bmatrix} 4 & x \\ -2 & -3 \end{bmatrix}$$

7. Find an example of a singular 2×2 matrix satisfying $A^2 = A$.

8. Verify the following equation.

$$\begin{vmatrix} 1 & 1 & 1 \\ a & b & c \\ a^2 & b^2 & c^2 \end{vmatrix} = (a - b)(b - c)(c - a)$$

9. Verify the following equation.

$$\begin{vmatrix} 1 & 1 & 1 \\ a & b & c \\ a^3 & b^3 & c^3 \end{vmatrix} = (a - b)(b - c)(c - a)(a + b + c)$$

10. Verify the following equation.

$$\begin{vmatrix} x & 0 & c \\ -1 & x & b \\ 0 & -1 & a \end{vmatrix} = ax^2 + bx + c$$

11. Use the equation given in Exercise 10 as a model to find a determinant that is equal to $ax^3 + bx^2 + cx + d$.

12. The atomic masses of three compounds are shown in the table. Use a linear system and Cramer's Rule to find the atomic masses of sulfur (S), nitrogen (N), and fluorine (F).

Compound	Formula	Atomic mass
Tetrasulphur tetranitride	S_4N_4	184
Sulfur hexafluoride	SF_6	146
Dinitrogen tetrafluoride	N_2F_4	104

13. A walkway lighting package includes a transformer, a certain length of wire, and a certain number of lights on the wire. The price of each lighting package depends on the length of wire and the number of lights on the wire. Use the following information to find the cost of a transformer, the cost per foot of wire, and the cost of a light. Assume that the cost of each item is the same in each lighting package.

• A package that contains a transformer, 25 feet of wire, and 5 lights costs $20.

• A package that contains a transformer, 50 feet of wire, and 15 lights costs $35.

• A package that contains a transformer, 100 feet of wire, and 20 lights costs $50.

14. Use the inverse of matrix A to decode the cryptogram.

$$A = \begin{bmatrix} 1 & -2 & 2 \\ 1 & 1 & -3 \\ 1 & -1 & 4 \end{bmatrix}$$

23 13 −34 31 −34 63 25 −17 61
24 14 −37 41 −17 −8 20 −29 40
38 −56 116 13 −11 1 22 −3 −6
41 −53 85 28 −32 16

15. The **transpose** of a matrix, denoted A^T, is formed by writing its columns as rows. Find the transpose of each matrix and verify that $(AB)^T = B^T A^T$.

$$A = \begin{bmatrix} -1 & 1 & -2 \\ 2 & 0 & 1 \end{bmatrix} \quad \text{and} \quad B = \begin{bmatrix} -3 & 0 \\ 1 & 2 \\ 1 & -1 \end{bmatrix}$$

16. A code breaker intercepted the encoded message below.

45 −35 38 −30 18 −18 35 −30 81 −60
42 −28 75 −55 2 −2 22 −21 15
−10

Let

$$A^{-1} = \begin{bmatrix} w & x \\ y & z \end{bmatrix}.$$

(a) You know that $[45 \quad -35]A^{-1} = [10 \quad 15]$ and that $[38 \quad -30]A^{-1} = [8 \quad 14]$, where A^{-1} is the inverse of the encoding matrix A. Write and solve two systems of equations to find w, x, y, and z.

(b) Decode the message.

 17. Let

$$A = \begin{bmatrix} 6 & 4 & 1 \\ 0 & 2 & 3 \\ 1 & 1 & 2 \end{bmatrix}.$$

Use a graphing utility to find A^{-1}. Compare $|A^{-1}|$ with $|A|$. Make a conjecture about the determinant of the inverse of a matrix.

18. Let A be an $n \times n$ matrix each of whose rows adds up to zero. Find $|A|$.

19. Consider matrices of the form

$$A = \begin{bmatrix} 0 & a_{12} & a_{13} & a_{14} & \dots & a_{1n} \\ 0 & 0 & a_{23} & a_{24} & \dots & a_{2n} \\ 0 & 0 & 0 & a_{34} & \dots & a_{3n} \\ \vdots & \vdots & \vdots & \vdots & \dots & \vdots \\ 0 & 0 & 0 & 0 & \dots & a_{(n-1)n} \\ 0 & 0 & 0 & 0 & \dots & 0 \end{bmatrix}$$

(a) Write a 2×2 matrix and a 3×3 matrix in the form of A.

(b) Use a graphing utility to raise each of the matrices to higher powers. Describe the result.

(c) Use the result of part (b) to make a conjecture about powers of A if A is a 4×4 matrix. Use a graphing utility to test your conjecture.

(d) Use the results of parts (b) and (c) to make a conjecture about powers of A if A is an $n \times n$ matrix.

How to study Chapter 9

▶ **What you should learn**

In this chapter you will learn the following skills and concepts:

- How to use sequence, factorial, and summation notation to write the terms and sum of a sequence

- How to recognize, write, and manipulate arithmetic sequences and geometric sequences

- How to use mathematical induction to prove a statement involving a positive integer *n*

- How to use the Binomial Theorem and Pascal's Triangle to calculate binomial coefficients and binomial expansions

- How to solve counting problems using the Fundamental Counting Principle, permutations, and combinations

- How to find the probabilities of events and their complements

▶ **Important Vocabulary**

As you encounter each new vocabulary term in this chapter, add the term and its definition to your notebook glossary.

Infinite sequence (p. 614)
Terms of a sequence (p. 614)
Finite sequence (p. 614)
Factorial (p. 616)
Summation or sigma notation (p. 618)
Finite series (p. 619)
Infinite series (p. 619)
Arithmetic sequence (p. 625)
Common difference (p. 625)
Geometric sequence (p. 634)
Common ratio (p. 634)
Geometric series (p. 638)
Mathematical induction (p. 644)
Binomial coefficients (p. 654)

Binomial Theorem (p. 654)
Fundamental Counting Principle (p. 663)
Permutation (p. 664)
Distinguishable permutations (p. 666)
Combination (p. 667)
Experiment (p. 672)
Outcomes (p. 672)
Sample space (p. 672)
Event (p. 672)
Probability (p. 673)
Mutually exclusive (p. 676)
Independent events (p. 678)
Complement of an event (p. 679)

Study Tools

Learning objectives in each section
Chapter Summary (p. 685)
Review Exercises (pp. 686–689)
Chapter Test (p. 690)
Cumulative Test for Chapters 7–9 (pp. 691, 692)

Additional Resources

Study and Solutions Guide
Interactive Precalculus
Videotapes/DVD for Chapter 9
Precalculus Website
Student Success Organizer

Gavin Hellier/Getty Images

9

Sequences, Series, and Probability

613

9.1   Sequences and Series

▶ **What you should learn**

- How to use sequence notation to write the terms of a sequence
- How to use factorial notation
- How to use summation notation to write sums
- How to find the sum of an infinite series
- How to use sequences and series to model and solve real-life problems

▶ **Why you should learn it**

Sequences and series can be used to model real-life problems. For instance, in Exercise 107 on page 623, sequences are used to model the number of Circuit City Stores from 1991 through 2000.

Bob Daemmrich/The Image Works

Sequences

In mathematics, the word *sequence* is used in much the same way as in ordinary English. Saying that a collection is listed in *sequence* means that it is ordered so that it has a first member, a second member, a third member, and so on.

Mathematically, you can think of a sequence as a *function* whose domain is the set of positive integers.

$$f(1) = a_1, \ f(2) = a_2, \ f(3) = a_3, \ f(4) = a_4, \ldots, f(n) = a_n, \ldots$$

Rather than using function notation, however, sequences are usually written using subscript notation, as indicated in the following definition.

Definition of Sequence

An **infinite sequence** is a function whose domain is the set of positive integers. The function values

$$a_1, a_2, a_3, a_4, \ldots, a_n, \ldots$$

are the **terms** of the sequence. If the domain of the function consists of the first n positive integers only, the sequence is a **finite sequence.**

On occasion it is convenient to begin subscripting a sequence with 0 instead of 1 so that the terms of the sequence become $a_0, a_1, a_2, a_3, \ldots.$

Example 1 ▶   **Finding Terms of a Sequence**

Find the first four terms of the sequences given by

a. $a_n = 3n - 2$ **b.** $a_n = 3 + (-1)^n.$

Solution

a. The first four terms of the sequence given by $a_n = 3n - 2$ are

$$a_1 = 3(1) - 2 = 1 \qquad \text{1st term}$$
$$a_2 = 3(2) - 2 = 4 \qquad \text{2nd term}$$
$$a_3 = 3(3) - 2 = 7 \qquad \text{3rd term}$$
$$a_4 = 3(4) - 2 = 10. \qquad \text{4th term}$$

b. The first four terms of the sequence given by $a_n = 3 + (-1)^n$ are

$$a_1 = 3 + (-1)^1 = 3 - 1 = 2 \qquad \text{1st term}$$
$$a_2 = 3 + (-1)^2 = 3 + 1 = 4 \qquad \text{2nd term}$$
$$a_3 = 3 + (-1)^3 = 3 - 1 = 2 \qquad \text{3rd term}$$
$$a_4 = 3 + (-1)^4 = 3 + 1 = 4. \qquad \text{4th term}$$

Write out the first five terms of the sequence whose nth term is

$$a_n = \frac{(-1)^{n+1}}{2n-1}.$$

Are they the same as the first five terms of the sequence in Example 2? If not, how do they differ?

Additional Example

Write an expression for the apparent nth term a_n of the sequence

$$\frac{2}{1}, \frac{3}{2}, \frac{4}{3}, \frac{5}{4}, \ldots$$

$$\begin{array}{llllll}
n: & 1 & 2 & 3 & 4 & \ldots n \\
\textit{Terms:} & \dfrac{2}{1} & \dfrac{3}{2} & \dfrac{4}{3} & \dfrac{5}{4} & \ldots a_n
\end{array}$$

Apparent pattern: Each term has a numerator that is 1 greater than its denominator, which implies that

$$a_n = \frac{n+1}{n}.$$

Technology

To graph a sequence using a graphing utility, set the mode to *seq* and *dot* and enter the sequence. The graph of the sequence in Example 3(a) is shown below. You can use the *trace* feature to identify its terms.

Example 2 ▶ A Sequence Whose Terms Alternate in Sign

The first five terms of the sequence given by $a_n = \dfrac{(-1)^n}{2n-1}$ are as follows.

$$a_1 = \frac{(-1)^1}{2(1)-1} = \frac{-1}{2-1} = -1 \qquad \text{1st term}$$

$$a_2 = \frac{(-1)^2}{2(2)-1} = \frac{1}{4-1} = \frac{1}{3} \qquad \text{2nd term}$$

$$a_3 = \frac{(-1)^3}{2(3)-1} = \frac{-1}{6-1} = -\frac{1}{5} \qquad \text{3rd term}$$

$$a_4 = \frac{(-1)^4}{2(4)-1} = \frac{1}{8-1} = \frac{1}{7} \qquad \text{4th term}$$

$$a_5 = \frac{(-1)^5}{2(5)-1} = \frac{-1}{10-1} = -\frac{1}{9} \qquad \text{5th term}$$

Simply listing the first few terms is not sufficient to define a unique sequence—the nth term *must be given*. To see this, consider the following sequences, both of which have the same first three terms.

$$\frac{1}{2}, \frac{1}{4}, \frac{1}{8}, \frac{1}{16}, \ldots, \frac{1}{2^n}, \ldots$$

$$\frac{1}{2}, \frac{1}{4}, \frac{1}{8}, \frac{1}{15}, \ldots, \frac{6}{(n+1)(n^2-n+6)}, \ldots$$

Example 3 ▶ Finding the nth Term of a Sequence

Write an expression for the apparent nth term (a_n) of each sequence.

a. $1, 3, 5, 7, \ldots$ **b.** $2, -5, 10, -17, \ldots$

Solution

a.
$$\begin{array}{lllll}
n: & 1 & 2 & 3 & 4 & \ldots n \\
\textit{Terms:} & 1 & 3 & 5 & 7 & \ldots a_n
\end{array}$$

Apparent pattern: Each term is 1 less than twice n, which implies that

$$a_n = 2n - 1.$$

b.
$$\begin{array}{lllll}
n: & 1 & 2 & 3 & 4 & \ldots n \\
\textit{Terms:} & 2 & -5 & 10 & -17 & \ldots a_n
\end{array}$$

Apparent pattern: The terms have alternating signs with those in the even positions being negative. Each term is 1 more than the square of n, which implies that

$$a_n = (-1)^{n+1}(n^2 + 1)$$

The icon identifies examples and concepts related to features of the Learning Tools CD-ROM and the *Interactive* and *Internet* versions of this text. For more details see the chart on pages *xxi-xxv*.

Some sequences are defined **recursively.** To define a sequence recursively, you need to be given one or more of the first few terms. All other terms of the sequence are then defined using previous terms. A well-known example is the Fibonacci sequence shown in Example 4.

Example 4 ► **The Fibonacci Sequence: A Recursive Sequence**

The Fibonacci sequence is defined recursively, as follows.

$$a_0 = 1, \ a_1 = 1, \ a_k = a_{k-2} + a_{k-1}, \text{ where } k \geq 2$$

Write the first six terms of this sequence.

Solution

$$a_0 = 1 \qquad \text{0th term is given.}$$
$$a_1 = 1 \qquad \text{1st term is given.}$$
$$a_2 = a_{2-2} + a_{2-1} = a_0 + a_1 = 1 + 1 = 2 \qquad \text{Use recursion formula.}$$
$$a_3 = a_{3-2} + a_{3-1} = a_1 + a_2 = 1 + 2 = 3 \qquad \text{Use recursion formula.}$$
$$a_4 = a_{4-2} + a_{4-1} = a_2 + a_3 = 2 + 3 = 5 \qquad \text{Use recursion formula.}$$
$$a_5 = a_{5-2} + a_{5-1} = a_3 + a_4 = 3 + 5 = 8 \qquad \text{Use recursion formula.}$$

STUDY TIP

Any variable can be used as a subscript. The most commonly used variable subscripts in sequence and series notation are i, j, k, and n.

The *Interactive* CD-ROM and *Internet* versions of this text offer a Try It for each example in the text.

Factorial Notation

Some very important sequences in mathematics involve terms that are defined with special types of products called **factorials.**

Definition of Factorial

If n is a positive integer, **n factorial** is defined as

$$n! = 1 \cdot 2 \cdot 3 \cdot 4 \cdots (n-1) \cdot n.$$

As a special case, zero factorial is defined as $0! = 1$.

Here are some values of $n!$ for the first several nonnegative integers. Notice that $0!$ is 1 by definition.

$$0! = 1$$
$$1! = 1$$
$$2! = 1 \cdot 2 = 2$$
$$3! = 1 \cdot 2 \cdot 3 = 6$$
$$4! = 1 \cdot 2 \cdot 3 \cdot 4 = 24$$
$$5! = 1 \cdot 2 \cdot 3 \cdot 4 \cdot 5 = 120$$

The value of n does not have to be very large before the value of $n!$ becomes huge. For instance, $10! = 3,628,800$.

Factorials follow the same conventions for order of operations as do exponents. For instance,

$$2n! = 2(n!) = 2(1 \cdot 2 \cdot 3 \cdot 4 \cdots n)$$

whereas $(2n)! = 1 \cdot 2 \cdot 3 \cdot 4 \cdots 2n$.

Example 5 ▶ **Finding Terms of a Sequence Involving Factorials**

List the first five terms of the sequence given by

$$a_n = \frac{2^n}{n!}.$$

Begin with $n = 0$. Then plot the points on a set of coordinate axes.

Solution

$$a_0 = \frac{2^0}{0!} = \frac{1}{1} = 1 \qquad \text{0th term}$$

$$a_1 = \frac{2^1}{1!} = \frac{2}{1} = 2 \qquad \text{1st term}$$

$$a_2 = \frac{2^2}{2!} = \frac{4}{2} = 2 \qquad \text{2nd term}$$

$$a_3 = \frac{2^3}{3!} = \frac{8}{6} = \frac{4}{3} \qquad \text{3rd term}$$

$$a_4 = \frac{2^4}{4!} = \frac{16}{24} = \frac{2}{3} \qquad \text{4th term}$$

FIGURE 9.1

Figure 9.1 shows the first five terms of the sequence.

When working with fractions involving factorials, you will often find that the fractions can be reduced.

Example 6 ▶ **Evaluating Factorial Expressions**

Evaluate each factorial expression.

a. $\dfrac{8!}{2! \cdot 6!}$ **b.** $\dfrac{2! \cdot 6!}{3! \cdot 5!}$ **c.** $\dfrac{n!}{(n - 1)!}$

Solution

a. $\dfrac{8!}{2! \cdot 6!} = \dfrac{1 \cdot 2 \cdot 3 \cdot 4 \cdot 5 \cdot 6 \cdot 7 \cdot 8}{1 \cdot 2 \cdot 1 \cdot 2 \cdot 3 \cdot 4 \cdot 5 \cdot 6} = \dfrac{7 \cdot 8}{2} = 28$

b. $\dfrac{2! \cdot 6!}{3! \cdot 5!} = \dfrac{1 \cdot 2 \cdot 1 \cdot 2 \cdot 3 \cdot 4 \cdot 5 \cdot 6}{1 \cdot 2 \cdot 3 \cdot 1 \cdot 2 \cdot 3 \cdot 4 \cdot 5} = \dfrac{6}{3} = 2$

c. $\dfrac{n!}{(n - 1)!} = \dfrac{1 \cdot 2 \cdot 3 \cdots (n - 1) \cdot n}{1 \cdot 2 \cdot 3 \cdots (n - 1)} = n$

Reading and writing the upper and lower limits of summation correctly will help with problems involving upper and lower limits in calculus.

Summation Notation

There is a convenient notation for the sum of the terms of a finite sequence. It is called **summation notation** or **sigma notation** because it involves the use of the uppercase Greek letter sigma, written as Σ.

Definition of Summation Notation

The sum of the first n terms of a sequence is represented by

$$\sum_{i=1}^{n} a_i = a_1 + a_2 + a_3 + a_4 + \cdots + a_n$$

where i is called the **index of summation**, n is the **upper limit of summation**, and 1 is the **lower limit of summation**.

Example 7 ▶ Summation Notation for Sums

Find each sum.

a. $\displaystyle\sum_{i=1}^{5} 3i$ **b.** $\displaystyle\sum_{k=3}^{6} (1 + k^2)$ **c.** $\displaystyle\sum_{i=0}^{8} \frac{1}{i!}$

Solution

a. $\displaystyle\sum_{i=1}^{5} 3i = 3(1) + 3(2) + 3(3) + 3(4) + 3(5)$

$$= 3(1 + 2 + 3 + 4 + 5)$$
$$= 3(15)$$
$$= 45$$

b. $\displaystyle\sum_{k=3}^{6} (1 + k^2) = (1 + 3^2) + (1 + 4^2) + (1 + 5^2) + (1 + 6^2)$

$$= 10 + 17 + 26 + 37$$
$$= 90$$

c. $\displaystyle\sum_{i=0}^{8} \frac{1}{i!} = \frac{1}{0!} + \frac{1}{1!} + \frac{1}{2!} + \frac{1}{3!} + \frac{1}{4!} + \frac{1}{5!} + \frac{1}{6!} + \frac{1}{7!} + \frac{1}{8!}$

$$= 1 + 1 + \frac{1}{2} + \frac{1}{6} + \frac{1}{24} + \frac{1}{120} + \frac{1}{720} + \frac{1}{5040} + \frac{1}{40,320}$$
$$\approx 2.71828$$

For this summation, note that the sum is very close to the irrational number $e \approx 2.718281828$. It can be shown that as more terms of the sequence whose nth term is $1/n!$ are added, the sum becomes closer and closer to e.

In Example 7, note that the lower limit of a summation does not have to be 1. Also note that the index of summation does not have to be the letter i. For instance, in part (b), the letter k is the index of summation.

STUDY TIP

Variations in the upper and lower limits of summation can produce quite different-looking summation notations for *the same sum*. For example, the following two sums have the same terms.

$$\sum_{i=1}^{3} 3(2^i) = 3(2^1 + 2^2 + 2^3)$$

$$\sum_{i=0}^{2} 3(2^{i+1}) = 3(2^1 + 2^2 + 2^3)$$

Properties of Sums

1. $\displaystyle\sum_{i=1}^{n} c = cn,$ c is a constant. **2.** $\displaystyle\sum_{i=1}^{n} ca_i = c\sum_{i=1}^{n} a_i,$ c is a constant.

3. $\displaystyle\sum_{i=1}^{n} (a_i + b_i) = \sum_{i=1}^{n} a_i + \sum_{i=1}^{n} b_i$ **4.** $\displaystyle\sum_{i=1}^{n} (a_i - b_i) = \sum_{i=1}^{n} a_i - \sum_{i=1}^{n} b_i$

For proofs of these properties, see Proofs in Mathematics on page 693.

Series

Many applications involve the sum of the terms of a finite or infinite sequence. Such a sum is called a **series.**

Definition of Series

Consider the infinite sequence $a_1, a_2, a_3, \ldots, a_i, \ldots$.

1. The sum of the first n terms of the sequence is called a **finite series** or the **nth partial sum** of the sequence and is denoted by

$$a_1 + a_2 + a_3 + \cdots + a_n = \sum_{i=1}^{n} a_i.$$

2. The sum of all terms of the infinite sequence is called an **infinite series** and is denoted by

$$a_1 + a_2 + a_3 + \cdots + a_i + \cdots = \sum_{i=1}^{\infty} a_i.$$

Example 8 ▶ Finding the Sum of a Series

For the series $\displaystyle\sum_{i=1}^{\infty} \frac{3}{10^i}$, find (a) the third partial sum and (b) the sum.

Solution

a. The third partial sum is

$$\sum_{i=1}^{3} \frac{3}{10^i} = \frac{3}{10^1} + \frac{3}{10^2} + \frac{3}{10^3} = 0.3 + 0.03 + 0.003 = 0.333.$$

b. The sum of the series is

$$\sum_{i=1}^{\infty} \frac{3}{10^i} = \frac{3}{10^1} + \frac{3}{10^2} + \frac{3}{10^3} + \frac{3}{10^4} + \frac{3}{10^5} + \cdots$$

$$= 0.3 + 0.03 + 0.003 + 0.0003 + 0.00003 + \cdots$$

$$= 0.33333\ldots = \frac{1}{3}.$$

Application

Sequences have many applications in business and science. One such application is illustrated in Example 9.

| Example 9 ▶ | Population of the United States | |

For the years 1970 to 2000, the resident population of the United States can be approximated by the model

$$a_n = 204.8 + 2.09n + 0.009n^2, \qquad n = 0, 1, \ldots, 30$$

where a_n is the population in millions and n represents the calendar year, with $n = 0$ corresponding to 1970. Find the last five terms of this finite sequence, which represent the U.S. population for the years 1996 to 2000.   (Source: U.S. Census Bureau)

Activities

1. Write the first five terms of the sequence. (Assume that n begins with 1.)

$$a_n = \frac{2n - 1}{2n}$$

Answer: $\dfrac{1}{2}, \dfrac{3}{4}, \dfrac{5}{6}, \dfrac{7}{8}, \dfrac{9}{10}$

2. Write an expression for the apparent nth term of the sequence

$$0, \frac{1}{2}, \frac{2}{6}, \frac{3}{24}, \frac{4}{120}.$$

Answer: $\dfrac{n - 1}{n!}$

3. Find the sum.

$$\sum_{k=1}^{4} (-1)^k 2k$$

Answer: 4

Solution

The last five terms of this finite sequence are as follows.

$a_{26} = 204.8 + 2.09(26) + 0.009(26)^2 \approx 265.2$	1996 population
$a_{27} = 204.8 + 2.09(27) + 0.009(27)^2 \approx 267.8$	1997 population
$a_{28} = 204.8 + 2.09(28) + 0.009(28)^2 \approx 270.4$	1998 population
$a_{29} = 204.8 + 2.09(29) + 0.009(29)^2 \approx 273.0$	1999 population
$a_{30} = 204.8 + 2.09(30) + 0.009(30)^2 \approx 275.6$	2000 population

The bar graph in Figure 9.2 graphically represents the population given by this sequence for the entire 31-year period from 1970 to 2000.

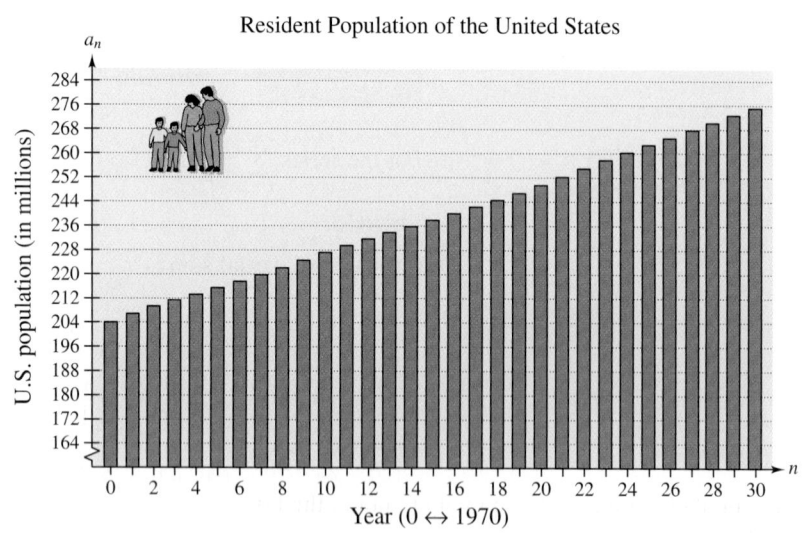

FIGURE 9.2

9.1 Exercises

The *Interactive* CD-ROM and *Internet* versions of this text contain step-by-step solutions to all odd-numbered exercises. They also provide Tutorial Exercises for additional help.

In Exercises 1–24, write the first five terms of the sequence. (Assume that n begins with 1.)

1. $a_n = 3n + 1$ **2.** $a_n = 5n - 3$

3. $a_n = 2^n$ **4.** $a_n = \left(\frac{1}{2}\right)^n$

5. $a_n = (-2)^n$ **6.** $a_n = \left(-\frac{1}{2}\right)^n$

7. $a_n = \dfrac{n+2}{n}$ **8.** $a_n = \dfrac{n}{n+2}$

9. $a_n = \dfrac{6n}{3n^2 - 1}$ **10.** $a_n = \dfrac{3n^2 - n + 4}{2n^2 + 1}$

11. $a_n = \dfrac{1 + (-1)^n}{n}$ **12.** $a_n = 1 + (-1)^n$

13. $a_n = 2 - \dfrac{1}{3^n}$ **14.** $a_n = \dfrac{2^n}{3^n}$

15. $a_n = \dfrac{1}{n^{3/2}}$ **16.** $a_n = \dfrac{10}{n^{2/3}}$

17. $a_n = \dfrac{3^n}{n!}$ **18.** $a_n = \dfrac{n!}{n}$

19. $a_n = \dfrac{(-1)^n}{n^2}$ **20.** $a_n = (-1)^n\left(\dfrac{n}{n+1}\right)$

21. $a_n = \frac{2}{3}$ **22.** $a_n = 0.3$

23. $a_n = n(n-1)(n-2)$ **24.** $a_n = n(n^2 - 6)$

In Exercises 25–30, find the indicated term of the sequence.

25. $a_n = (-1)^n(3n - 2)$

$a_{25} = $ ▨

26. $a_n = (-1)^{n-1}[n(n-1)]$

$a_{16} = $ ▨

27. $a_n = \dfrac{2^n}{n!}$ **28.** $a_n = \dfrac{n!}{2n}$

$a_{10} = $ ▨ $a_8 = $ ▨

29. $a_n = \dfrac{4n}{2n^2 - 3}$ **30.** $a_n = \dfrac{4n^2 - n + 3}{n(n-1)(n+2)}$

$a_{11} = $ ▨ $a_{13} = $ ▨

In Exercises 31–36, use a graphing utility to graph the first 10 terms of the sequence.

31. $a_n = \dfrac{3}{4}n$ **32.** $a_n = 2 - \dfrac{4}{n}$

33. $a_n = 16(-0.5)^{n-1}$ **34.** $a_n = 8(0.75)^{n-1}$

35. $a_n = \dfrac{2n}{n+1}$ **36.** $a_n = \dfrac{n^2}{n^2 + 2}$

In Exercises 37–40, match the sequence with the graph of its first 10 terms. [The graphs are labeled (a), (b), (c), and (d).]

(a)

(b)

(c)

(d)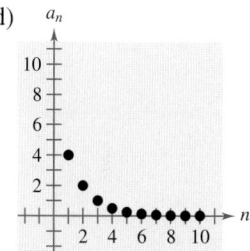

37. $a_n = \dfrac{8}{n+1}$ **38.** $a_n = \dfrac{8n}{n+1}$

39. $a_n = 4(0.5)^{n-1}$ **40.** $a_n = \dfrac{4^n}{n!}$

In Exercises 41–54, write an expression for the *apparent* nth term of the sequence. (Assume that n begins with 1.)

41. $1, 4, 7, 10, 13, \ldots$ **42.** $3, 7, 11, 15, 19, \ldots$

43. $0, 3, 8, 15, 24, \ldots$ **44.** $2, -4, 6, -8, 10, \ldots$

45. $\dfrac{-2}{3}, \dfrac{3}{4}, \dfrac{-4}{5}, \dfrac{5}{6}, \dfrac{-6}{7}, \ldots$

46. $\dfrac{1}{2}, \dfrac{-1}{4}, \dfrac{1}{8}, \dfrac{-1}{16}, \ldots$ **47.** $\dfrac{2}{1}, \dfrac{3}{3}, \dfrac{4}{5}, \dfrac{5}{7}, \dfrac{6}{9}, \ldots$

48. $\dfrac{1}{3}, \dfrac{2}{9}, \dfrac{4}{27}, \dfrac{8}{81}, \ldots$ **49.** $1, \dfrac{1}{4}, \dfrac{1}{9}, \dfrac{1}{16}, \dfrac{1}{25}, \ldots$

50. $1, \dfrac{1}{2}, \dfrac{1}{6}, \dfrac{1}{24}, \dfrac{1}{120}, \ldots$ **51.** $1, -1, 1, -1, 1, \ldots$

52. $1, 2, \dfrac{2^2}{2}, \dfrac{2^3}{6}, \dfrac{2^4}{24}, \dfrac{2^5}{120}, \ldots$

53. $1 + \dfrac{1}{1}, 1 + \dfrac{1}{2}, 1 + \dfrac{1}{3}, 1 + \dfrac{1}{4}, 1 + \dfrac{1}{5}, \ldots$

54. $1 + \dfrac{1}{2}, 1 + \dfrac{3}{4}, 1 + \dfrac{7}{8}, 1 + \dfrac{15}{16}, 1 + \dfrac{31}{32}, \ldots$

In Exercises 55–58, write the first five terms of the sequence defined recursively.

55. $a_1 = 28$, $a_{k+1} = a_k - 4$

56. $a_1 = 15$, $a_{k+1} = a_k + 3$

57. $a_1 = 3$, $a_{k+1} = 2(a_k - 1)$

58. $a_1 = 32$, $a_{k+1} = \frac{1}{2}a_k$

In Exercises 59–62, write the first five terms of the sequence defined recursively. Use the pattern to write the nth term of the sequence as a function of n. (Assume that n begins with 1.)

59. $a_1 = 6$, $a_{k+1} = a_k + 2$

60. $a_1 = 25$, $a_{k+1} = a_k - 5$

61. $a_1 = 81$, $a_{k+1} = \frac{1}{3}a_k$

62. $a_1 = 14$, $a_{k+1} = (-2)a_k$

In Exercises 63–70, simplify the factorial expression.

63. $\dfrac{4!}{6!}$

64. $\dfrac{5!}{8!}$

65. $\dfrac{10!}{8!}$

66. $\dfrac{25!}{23!}$

67. $\dfrac{(n+1)!}{n!}$

68. $\dfrac{(n+2)!}{n!}$

69. $\dfrac{(2n-1)!}{(2n+1)!}$

70. $\dfrac{(3n+1)!}{(3n)!}$

In Exercises 71–82, find the sum.

71. $\displaystyle\sum_{i=1}^{5}(2i+1)$

72. $\displaystyle\sum_{i=1}^{6}(3i-1)$

73. $\displaystyle\sum_{k=1}^{4}10$

74. $\displaystyle\sum_{k=1}^{5}5$

75. $\displaystyle\sum_{i=0}^{4}i^2$

76. $\displaystyle\sum_{i=0}^{5}2i^2$

77. $\displaystyle\sum_{k=0}^{3}\frac{1}{k^2+1}$

78. $\displaystyle\sum_{j=3}^{5}\frac{1}{j^2-3}$

79. $\displaystyle\sum_{k=2}^{5}(k+1)^2(k-3)$

80. $\displaystyle\sum_{i=1}^{4}[(i-1)^2+(i+1)^3]$

81. $\displaystyle\sum_{i=1}^{4}2^i$

82. $\displaystyle\sum_{j=0}^{4}(-2)^j$

In Exercises 83–86, use a calculator to find the sum.

83. $\displaystyle\sum_{j=1}^{6}(24-3j)$

84. $\displaystyle\sum_{j=1}^{10}\frac{3}{j+1}$

85. $\displaystyle\sum_{k=0}^{4}\frac{(-1)^k}{k+1}$

86. $\displaystyle\sum_{k=0}^{4}\frac{(-1)^k}{k!}$

In Exercises 87–96, use sigma notation to write the sum.

87. $\dfrac{1}{3(1)}+\dfrac{1}{3(2)}+\dfrac{1}{3(3)}+\cdots+\dfrac{1}{3(9)}$

88. $\dfrac{5}{1+1}+\dfrac{5}{1+2}+\dfrac{5}{1+3}+\cdots+\dfrac{5}{1+15}$

89. $\left[2\left(\frac{1}{8}\right)+3\right]+\left[2\left(\frac{2}{8}\right)+3\right]+\cdots+\left[2\left(\frac{8}{8}\right)+3\right]$

90. $\left[1-\left(\frac{1}{6}\right)^2\right]+\left[1-\left(\frac{2}{6}\right)^2\right]+\cdots+\left[1-\left(\frac{6}{6}\right)^2\right]$

91. $3-9+27-81+243-729$

92. $1-\frac{1}{2}+\frac{1}{4}-\frac{1}{8}+\cdots-\frac{1}{128}$

93. $\dfrac{1}{1^2}-\dfrac{1}{2^2}+\dfrac{1}{3^2}-\dfrac{1}{4^2}+\cdots-\dfrac{1}{20^2}$

94. $\dfrac{1}{1\cdot 3}+\dfrac{1}{2\cdot 4}+\dfrac{1}{3\cdot 5}+\cdots+\dfrac{1}{10\cdot 12}$

95. $\frac{1}{4}+\frac{3}{8}+\frac{7}{16}+\frac{15}{32}+\frac{31}{64}$

96. $\frac{1}{2}+\frac{2}{4}+\frac{6}{8}+\frac{24}{16}+\frac{120}{32}+\frac{720}{64}$

In Exercises 97–100, find the indicated partial sum of the series.

97. $\displaystyle\sum_{i=1}^{\infty}5\left(\frac{1}{2}\right)^i$,

Fourth partial sum

98. $\displaystyle\sum_{i=1}^{\infty}2\left(\frac{1}{3}\right)^i$,

Fifth partial sum

99. $\displaystyle\sum_{n=1}^{\infty}4\left(-\frac{1}{2}\right)^n$,

Third partial sum

100. $\displaystyle\sum_{n=1}^{\infty}8\left(-\frac{1}{4}\right)^n$,

Fourth partial sum

In Exercises 101–104, find the sum of the infinite series.

101. $\displaystyle\sum_{i=1}^{\infty}6\left(\frac{1}{10}\right)^i$

102. $\displaystyle\sum_{k=1}^{\infty}\left(\frac{1}{10}\right)^k$

103. $\displaystyle\sum_{k=1}^{\infty}7\left(\frac{1}{10}\right)^k$

104. $\displaystyle\sum_{i=1}^{\infty}2\left(\frac{1}{10}\right)^i$

105. *Compound Interest* A deposit of $5000 is made in an account that earns 8% interest compounded quarterly. The balance in the account after n quarters is

$$A_n = 5000\left(1+\frac{0.08}{4}\right)^n, \qquad n = 1, 2, 3, \ldots .$$

(a) Compute the first eight terms of this sequence.

(b) Find the balance in this account after 10 years by computing the 40th term of the sequence.

106. *Compound Interest*   A deposit of $100 is made each month in an account that earns 12% interest compounded monthly. The balance in the account after n months is

$$A_n = 100(101)[(1.01)^n - 1], \quad n = 1, 2, 3, \ldots$$

(a) Compute the first six terms of this sequence.

(b) Find the balance in this account after 5 years by computing the 60th term of the sequence.

(c) Find the balance in this account after 20 years by computing the 240th term of the sequence.

▶ **Model It**

107. *Data Analysis*   The table shows the numbers a_n of Circuit City stores for the years 1991 to 2000.
(Source: Circuit City Stores, Inc.)

Year, n	Number of stores, a_n
1991	228
1992	260
1993	294
1994	352
1995	419
1996	493
1997	556
1998	587
1999	616
2000	629

(a) Use the *regression* feature of a graphing utility to find a linear sequence that models the data. Let n represent the year, with $n = 1$ corresponding to 1991.

(b) Use the *regression* feature of a graphing utility to find a quadratic sequence that models the data.

(c) Evaluate the sequences from parts (a) and (b) for $n = 1, 2, \ldots, 10$. Compare these values with those shown in the table. Which model is a better fit for the data? Explain.

(d) Which model do you think would better predict the number of Circuit City stores in the future? Use the model you chose to predict the number of Circuit City stores in 2005.

---

108. *Medicine*   The numbers a_n (in millions) of AIDS cases reported from 1994 to 1999 can be approximated by the model

$$a_n = 0.3944n^3 - 7.738n^2 + 41.48n + 10.2,$$
$$n = 4, 5, \ldots, 9$$

where n is the year, with $n = 4$ corresponding to 1994. Find the terms of this finite sequence. Use a graphing utility to construct a bar graph that represents the sequence. (Source: U.S. Centers for Disease Control and Prevention)

109. *Federal Debt*   From 1990 to 2000, the federal debt of the United States rose from just over $3 trillion to more than $5 trillion. The federal debt a_n (in billions of dollars) from 1990 to 2000 is approximated by the model

$$a_n = -20.613n^2 + 452.92n + 3183.1,$$
$$n = 0, 1, \ldots, 10$$

where n is the year, with $n = 0$ corresponding to 1990. Find the terms of this finite sequence. Use a graphing utility to construct a bar graph that represents the sequence. (Source: U.S. Office of Management and Budget)

110. *Net Profit*   The net profits a_n (in millions of dollars) of Walgreen for the years 1991 through 2001 are shown in the figure. These profits can be approximated by the model

$$a_n = 5.547n^2 + 184.7, \quad n = 1, 2, \ldots, 11$$

where $n = 1$ represents 1991. Use this model to approximate the total net income from 1991 through 2001. Compare this sum with the result of adding the incomes shown in the figure. (Source: Walgreen Company)

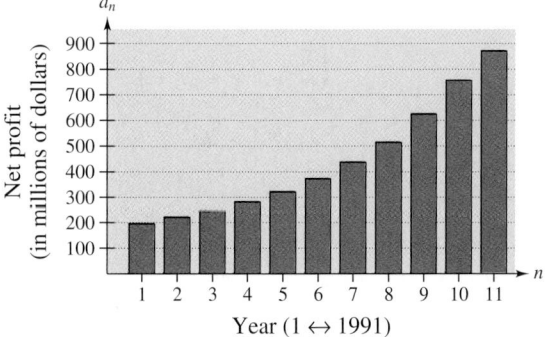

Synthesis

True or False? In Exercises 111 and 112, determine whether the statement is true or false. Justify your answer.

111. $\sum_{i=1}^{4}(i^2 + 2i) = \sum_{i=1}^{4}i^2 + 2\sum_{i=1}^{4}i$

112. $\sum_{j=1}^{4}2^j = \sum_{j=3}^{6}2^{j-2}$

Fibonacci Sequence In Exercises 113 and 114, use the Fibonacci sequence. (See Example 4.)

113. Write the first 12 terms of the Fibonacci sequence a_n and the first 10 terms of the sequence given by

$$b_n = \frac{a_{n+1}}{a_n}, \quad n \geq 1.$$

114. Using the definition for b_n in Exercise 113, show that b_n can be defined recursively by

$$b_n = 1 + \frac{1}{b_{n-1}}.$$

Arithmetic Mean In Exercises 115–118, use the following definition of the arithmetic mean $\bar{x}$ of a set of n measurements $x_1, x_2, x_3, \ldots, x_n$.

$$\bar{x} = \frac{1}{n}\sum_{i=1}^{n}x_i$$

115. Find the arithmetic mean of the six checking account balances $327.15, $785.69, $433.04, $265.38, $604.12, and $590.30. Use the statistical capabilities of a graphing utility to verify your result.

116. Find the arithmetic mean of the following prices per gallon for regular unleaded gasoline at five gasoline stations in a city: $1.279, $1.259, $1.289, $1.329, and $1.349. Use the statistical capabilities of a graphing utility to verify your result.

117. ***Proof*** Prove that

$$\sum_{i=1}^{n}(x_i - \bar{x}) = 0.$$

118. ***Proof*** Prove that

$$\sum_{i=1}^{n}(x_i - \bar{x})^2 = \sum_{i=1}^{n}x_i^2 - \frac{1}{n}\left(\sum_{i=1}^{n}x_i\right)^2.$$

In Exercises 119–122, find the first five terms of the sequence.

119. $a_n = \dfrac{x^n}{n!}$

120. $a_n = \dfrac{(-1)^n x^{2n+1}}{2n+1}$

121. $a_n = \dfrac{(-1)^n x^{2n}}{(2n)!}$

122. $a_n = \dfrac{(-1)^n x^{2n+1}}{(2n+1)!}$

Review

In Exercises 123–126, determine whether the function has an inverse function. If it does, find its inverse function.

123. $f(x) = 4x - 3$

124. $g(x) = \dfrac{3}{x}$

125. $h(x) = \sqrt{5x + 1}$

126. $f(x) = (x - 1)^2$

In Exercises 127–130, find (a) $A - B$, (b) $4B - 3A$, (c) AB, and (d) BA.

127. $A = \begin{bmatrix} 6 & 5 \\ 3 & 4 \end{bmatrix}$, $B = \begin{bmatrix} -2 & 4 \\ 6 & -3 \end{bmatrix}$

128. $A = \begin{bmatrix} 10 & 7 \\ -4 & 6 \end{bmatrix}$, $B = \begin{bmatrix} 0 & -12 \\ 8 & 11 \end{bmatrix}$

129. $A = \begin{bmatrix} -2 & -3 & 6 \\ 4 & 5 & 7 \\ 1 & 7 & 4 \end{bmatrix}$, $B = \begin{bmatrix} 1 & 4 & 2 \\ 0 & 1 & 6 \\ 0 & 3 & 1 \end{bmatrix}$

130. $A = \begin{bmatrix} -1 & 4 & 0 \\ 5 & 1 & 2 \\ 0 & -1 & 3 \end{bmatrix}$, $B = \begin{bmatrix} 0 & 4 & 0 \\ 3 & 1 & -2 \\ -1 & 0 & 2 \end{bmatrix}$

In Exercises 131–134, find the determinant of the matrix.

131. $A = \begin{bmatrix} 3 & 5 \\ -1 & 7 \end{bmatrix}$

132. $A = \begin{bmatrix} -2 & 8 \\ 12 & 15 \end{bmatrix}$

133. $A = \begin{bmatrix} 3 & 4 & 5 \\ 0 & 7 & 3 \\ 4 & 9 & -1 \end{bmatrix}$

134. $A = \begin{bmatrix} 16 & 11 & 10 & 2 \\ 9 & 8 & 3 & 7 \\ -2 & -1 & 12 & 3 \\ -4 & 6 & 2 & 1 \end{bmatrix}$

9.2 Arithmetic Sequences and Partial Sums

▶ **What you should learn**

- How to recognize and write arithmetic sequences
- How to find an *n*th partial sum of an arithmetic sequence
- How to use arithmetic sequences to model and solve real-life problems

▶ **Why you should learn it**

Arithmetic sequences have practical real-life applications. For instance, in Exercise 85 on page 633, an arithmetic sequence is used to model the per capita personal income in the United States from 1990 through 2000.

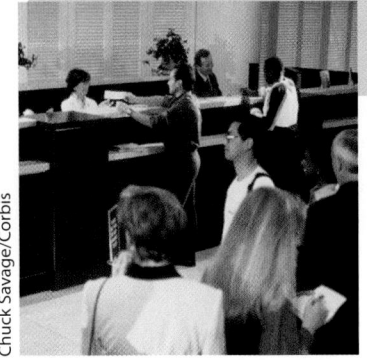

Chuck Savage/Corbis

Arithmetic Sequences

A sequence whose consecutive terms have a common difference is called an **arithmetic sequence.**

Definition of Arithmetic Sequence

A sequence is **arithmetic** if the differences between consecutive terms are the same. So, the sequence

$$a_1, a_2, a_3, a_4, \ldots, a_n, \ldots$$

is arithmetic if there is a number d such that

$$a_2 - a_1 = a_3 - a_2 = a_4 - a_3 = \cdots = d$$

and so on. The number d is the **common difference** of the arithmetic sequence.

Example 1 ▶ **Examples of Arithmetic Sequences**

a. The sequence whose *n*th term is $4n + 3$ is arithmetic. For this sequence, the common difference between consecutive terms is 4.

$$7, 11, 15, 19, \ldots, 4n + 3, \ldots \qquad \text{Begin with } n = 1.$$

$$11 - 7 = 4$$

b. The sequence whose *n*th term is $7 - 5n$ is arithmetic. For this sequence, the common difference between consecutive terms is -5.

$$2, -3, -8, -13, \ldots, 7 - 5n, \ldots \qquad \text{Begin with } n = 1.$$

$$-3 - 2 = -5$$

c. The sequence whose *n*th term is $\frac{1}{4}(n + 3)$ is arithmetic. For this sequence, the common difference between consecutive terms is $\frac{1}{4}$.

$$1, \frac{5}{4}, \frac{3}{2}, \frac{7}{4}, \ldots, \frac{n + 3}{4}, \ldots \qquad \text{Begin with } n = 1.$$

$$\tfrac{5}{4} - 1 = \tfrac{1}{4}$$

The sequence 1, 4, 9, 16, . . . , whose *n*th term is n^2, is *not* arithmetic. The difference between the first two terms is

$$a_2 - a_1 = 4 - 1 = 3$$

but the difference between the second and third terms is

$$a_3 - a_2 = 9 - 4 = 5.$$

In Example 1, notice that each of the arithmetic sequences has an nth term that is of the form $dn + c$, where the common difference of the sequence is d. An arithmetic sequence may be thought of as a linear function whose domain is the set of natural numbers.

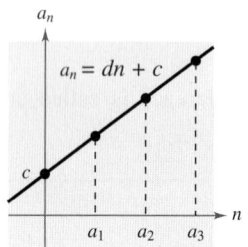

FIGURE **9.3**

> ### The nth Term of an Arithmetic Sequence
>
> The nth term of an arithmetic sequence has the form
>
> $$a_n = dn + c$$
>
> where d is the common difference between consecutive terms of the sequence and $c = a_1 - d$. A graphical representation of this definition is shown in Figure 9.3.

In the figure: $a_n = dn + c$, with axis labels a_n, c, n, and points a_1, a_2, a_3.

As an aid to learning the formula for the nth term of an arithmetic sequence, consider having your students intuitively find the nth term of each of the following sequences.

1. $a, a + 2, a + 4, a + 6, \ldots$

   Answer: $2n + a - 2$

2. $5, 8, 11, 14, 17, \ldots$

   Answer: $3n + 2$

Example 2 ▶ **Finding the nth Term of an Arithmetic Sequence**

Find a formula for the nth term of the arithmetic sequence whose common difference is 3 and whose first term is 2.

Solution

Because the sequence is arithmetic, you know that the formula for the nth term is of the form $a_n = dn + c$. Moreover, because the common difference is $d = 3$, the formula must have the form

$$a_n = 3n + c. \qquad \text{Substitute 3 for } d.$$

Because $a_1 = 2$, it follows that

$$c = a_1 - d$$
$$= 2 - 3 \qquad \text{Substitute 2 for } a_1 \text{ and 3 for } d.$$
$$= -1.$$

So, the formula for the nth term is

$$a_n = 3n - 1.$$

The sequence therefore has the following form.

$$2, 5, 8, 11, 14, \ldots, 3n - 1, \ldots$$

Another way to find a formula for the nth term of the sequence in Example 2 is to begin by writing the terms of the sequence.

a_1	a_2	a_3	a_4	a_5	a_6	a_7	$\cdots$
2	$2 + 3$	$5 + 3$	$8 + 3$	$11 + 3$	$14 + 3$	$17 + 3$	$\cdots$
2	5	8	11	14	17	20	$\cdots$

From these terms, you can reason that the nth term is of the form

$$a_n = dn + c$$
$$= 3n - 1.$$

You can find a_1 in Example 3 by using the alternative form of the nth term of an arithmetic sequence, as follows.

$$a_n = a_1 + (n - 1)d$$

$$a_4 = a_1 + (n - 1)d$$

$$20 = a_1 + (4 - 1)5$$

$$20 = a_1 + 15$$

$$5 = a_1$$

Example 3 ▶ **Writing the Terms of an Arithmetic Sequence**

The fourth term of an arithmetic sequence is 20, and the 13th term is 65. Write the first several terms of this sequence.

Solution

The fourth and 13th terms of the sequence are related by

$$a_{13} = a_4 + 9d.$$

Using $a_4 = 20$ and $a_{13} = 65$, you can conclude that $d = 5$, which implies that the sequence is as follows.

a_1	a_2	a_3	a_4	a_5	a_6	a_7	a_8	a_9	a_{10}	a_{11}	...
5	10	15	20	25	30	35	40	45	50	55	...

If you know the nth term of an arithmetic sequence *and* you know the common difference of the sequence, you can find the $(n + 1)$th term by using the *recursion formula*

$$a_{n+1} = a_n + d. \qquad \text{Recursion formula}$$

With this formula, you can find any term of an arithmetic sequence, *provided* that you know the preceding term. For instance, if you know the first term, you can find the second term. Then, knowing the second term, you can find the third term, and so on.

If you substitute $a_1 - d$ for c in the formula $a_n = dn + c$, the nth term of an arithmetic sequence has the alternative recursion formula

$$a_n = a_1 + (n - 1)d. \qquad \text{Alternative recursion formula}$$

Use this formula to solve Example 4. You should get the same answer.

Example 4 ▶ **Using a Recursion Formula**

Find the ninth term of the arithmetic sequence that begins with 2 and 9.

Solution

For this sequence, the common difference is $d = 9 - 2 = 7$. There are two ways to find the ninth term. One way is simply to write out the first nine terms (by repeatedly adding 7).

$$2, 9, 16, 23, 30, 37, 44, 51, 58$$

Another way to find the ninth term is first to find a formula for the nth term. Because the first term is 2, it follows that

$$c = a_1 - d = 2 - 7 = -5.$$

Therefore, a formula for the nth term is

$$a_n = 7n - 5$$

which implies that the ninth term is

$$a_9 = 7(9) - 5 = 58.$$

The Sum of a Finite Arithmetic Sequence

There is a simple formula for the *sum* of a finite arithmetic sequence.

> **The Sum of a Finite Arithmetic Sequence**
>
> The sum of a finite arithmetic sequence with n terms is
>
> $$S_n = \frac{n}{2}(a_1 + a_n).$$

For a proof of the sum of a finite arithmetic sequence, see Proofs in Mathematics on page 694.

Example 5 ▶ Finding the Sum of a Finite Arithmetic Sequence

Find the sum: $1 + 3 + 5 + 7 + 9 + 11 + 13 + 15 + 17 + 19$.

Solution

To begin, notice that the sequence is arithmetic (with a common difference of 2). Moreover, the sequence has 10 terms. So, the sum of the sequence is

$$S_n = \frac{n}{2}(a_1 + a_n) \qquad \text{Formula for sum of a sequence}$$

$$= \frac{10}{2}(1 + 19) \qquad \text{Substitute 10 for } n, \text{ 1 for } a_1, \text{ 19 for } a_n.$$

$$= 5(20) = 100. \qquad \text{Simplify.}$$

Example 6 ▶ Finding the Sum of a Finite Arithmetic Sequence

Find the sum of the integers (a) from 1 to 100 and (b) from 1 to N.

Solution

The integers from 1 to 100 form an arithmetic sequence that has 100 terms. So, you can use the formula for the sum of an arithmetic sequence, as follows.

a. $S_n = 1 + 2 + 3 + 4 + 5 + 6 + \cdots + 99 + 100$

$$= \frac{n}{2}(a_1 + a_n) \qquad \text{Formula for sum of a sequence}$$

$$= \frac{100}{2}(1 + 100) \qquad \text{Substitute 100 for } n, \text{ 1 for } a_1, \text{ 100 for } a_n.$$

$$= 50(101) = 5050 \qquad \text{Simplify.}$$

b. $S_n = 1 + 2 + 3 + 4 + \cdots + N$

$$= \frac{n}{2}(a_1 + a_n) \qquad \text{Formula for sum of a sequence}$$

$$= \frac{N}{2}(1 + N) \qquad \text{Substitute } N \text{ for } n, \text{ 1 for } a_1, N \text{ for } a_n.$$

The Granger Collection

Historical Note
A teacher of Carl Friedrich Gauss (1777–1855) asked him to add all the integers from 1 to 100. When Gauss returned with the correct answer after only a few moments, the teacher could only look at him in astounded silence. This is what Gauss did:

$$1 + \quad 2 + \quad 3 + \cdots + 100$$
$$100 + \ 99 + \ 98 + \cdots + \quad 1$$
$$\overline{101 + 101 + 101 + \cdots + 101}$$
$$\frac{100 \times 101}{2} = 5050$$

The sum of the first n terms of an infinite sequence is the *nth partial sum*. The nth partial sum can be found by using the formula for the sum of a finite arithmetic sequence.

Example 7 ▶ Finding a Partial Sum of an Arithmetic Sequence

Find the 150th partial sum of the arithmetic sequence

$$5, 16, 27, 38, 49, \ldots .$$

Solution

For this arithmetic sequence, $a_1 = 5$ and $d = 16 - 5 = 11$. So,

$$c = a_1 - d = 5 - 11 = -6$$

and the nth term is $a_n = 11n - 6$. Therefore, $a_{150} = 11(150) - 6 = 1644$, and the sum of the first 150 terms is

$$S_n = \frac{n}{2}(a_1 + a_n) \qquad \text{\textit{n}th partial sum formula}$$

$$= \frac{150}{2}(5 + 1644) \qquad \text{Substitute for } n, a_1, \text{ and } a_{150}.$$

$$= 75(1649) \qquad \text{Simplify.}$$

$$= 123{,}675. \qquad \text{\textit{n}th partial sum}$$

Applications

Example 8 ▶ Seating Capacity

An auditorium has 20 rows of seats. There are 20 seats in the first row, 21 seats in the second row, 22 seats in the third row, and so on. How many seats are there in all 20 rows?

Solution

The numbers of seats in the 20 rows form an arithmetic sequence in which the common difference is $d = 1$. Because

$$c = a_1 - d = 20 - 1 = 19$$

you can determine that the formula for the nth term of the sequence is $a_n = n + 19$. Therefore, the 20th term in the sequence is $a_{20} = 20 + 19 = 39$ (see Figure 9.4), and the total number of seats is

$$S_n = 20 + 21 + 22 + \cdots + 39$$

$$= \frac{n}{2}(a_1 + a_{20}) \qquad \text{\textit{n}th partial sum formula}$$

$$= \frac{20}{2}(20 + 39) \qquad \text{Substitute for } n, a_1, \text{ and } a_{20}.$$

$$= 10(59) = 590. \qquad \text{Simplify.}$$

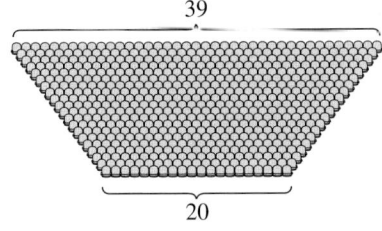

FIGURE **9.4**

Example 9 ▶ **Total Sales**

1. Determine which of the following are arithmetic sequences.
   (a) $3, 5, 7, 9, 11, \ldots$
   (b) $3, 6, 12, 24, 48, \ldots$
   (c) $-3, 6, -9, 12, -15, \ldots$
   (d) $5, 0, -5, -10, -15, \ldots$
   (e) $1, 3, 6, 10, 15, 21, \ldots$
   Answer: (a) and (d)

2. Find the first five terms of the arithmetic sequence with $a_1 = 13$ and $d = -4$.
   Answer: $13, 9, 5, 1, -3$

3. Find the sum.
   $$\sum_{n=1}^{100} (2 + 3n)$$
   Answer: 15,350

A small business sells \$10,000 worth of skin care products during its first year. The owner of the business has set a goal of increasing annual sales by \$7500 each year for 9 years. Assuming that this goal is met, find the total sales during the first 10 years this business is in operation.

Solution

The annual sales form an arithmetic sequence in which $a_1 = 10,000$ and $d = 7500$. So,

$$c = a_1 - d$$
$$= 10,000 - 7500$$
$$= 2500$$

and the nth term of the sequence is

$$a_n = 7500n + 2500.$$

This implies that the 10th term of the sequence is

$$a_{10} = 77,500. \qquad \text{See Figure 9.5.}$$

The sum of the first 10 terms of the sequence is

$$S_n = \frac{n}{2}(a_1 + a_{10}) \qquad \text{nth partial sum formula}$$

$$= \frac{10}{2}(10,000 + 77,500) \qquad \text{Substitute for n, a_1, and a_{10}.}$$

$$= 5(87,500) \qquad \text{Simplify.}$$

$$= 437,500. \qquad \text{Simplify.}$$

So, the total sales for the first 10 years will be \$437,500.

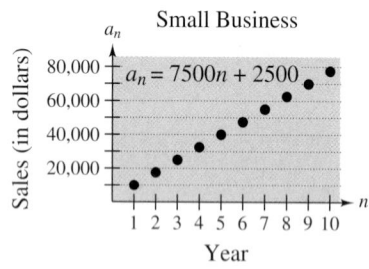

FIGURE 9.5

Writing ABOUT MATHEMATICS

Numerical Relationships Decide whether it is possible to fill in the blanks in each of the sequences such that the resulting sequence is arithmetic. If so, find a recursion formula for the sequence.

a. $-7,$ ___, ___, ___, ___, ___, 11

b. $17,$ ___, ___, ___, ___, ___, ___, ___, 71

c. $2, 6,$ ___, ___, 162

d. $4, 7.5,$ ___, ___, ___, ___, ___, ___, ___, 39

e. $8, 12,$ ___, ___, ___, 60.75

9.2 Exercises

In Exercises 1–10, determine whether the sequence is arithmetic. If it is, find the common difference.

1. 10, 8, 6, 4, 2, . . .

2. 4, 7, 10, 13, 16, . . .

3. 1, 2, 4, 8, 16, . . .

4. 80, 40, 20, 10, 5, . . .

5. $\frac{9}{4}, 2, \frac{7}{4}, \frac{3}{2}, \frac{5}{4}, \ldots$

6. $3, \frac{5}{2}, 2, \frac{3}{2}, 1, \ldots$

7. $\frac{1}{3}, \frac{2}{3}, 1, \frac{4}{3}, \frac{5}{6}, \ldots$

8. 5.3, 5.7, 6.1, 6.5, 6.9, . . .

9. ln 1, ln 2, ln 3, ln 4, ln 5, . . .

10. $1^2, 2^2, 3^2, 4^2, 5^2, \ldots$

In Exercises 11–18, write the first five terms of the sequence. Determine whether the sequence is arithmetic, and if it is, find the common difference. (Assume that n begins with 1.)

11. $a_n = 5 + 3n$

12. $a_n = 100 - 3n$

13. $a_n = 3 - 4(n - 2)$

14. $a_n = 1 + (n - 1)4$

15. $a_n = (-1)^n$

16. $a_n = 2^{n-1}$

17. $a_n = \dfrac{(-1)^n 3}{n}$

18. $a_n = (2^n)n$

In Exercises 19–24, write the first five terms of the arithmetic sequence. Find the common difference and write the nth term of the sequence as a function of n.

19. $a_1 = 15, \quad a_{k+1} = a_k + 4$

20. $a_1 = 6, \quad a_{k+1} = a_k + 5$

21. $a_1 = 200, \quad a_{k+1} = a_k - 10$

22. $a_1 = 72, \quad a_{k+1} = a_k - 6$

23. $a_1 = \frac{5}{8}, \quad a_{k+1} = a_k - \frac{1}{8}$

24. $a_1 = 0.375, \quad a_{k+1} = a_k + 0.25$

In Exercises 25–32, write the first five terms of the arithmetic sequence.

25. $a_1 = 5, d = 6$

26. $a_1 = 5, d = -\frac{3}{4}$

27. $a_1 = -2.6, d = -0.4$

28. $a_1 = 16.5, d = 0.25$

29. $a_1 = 2, a_{12} = 46$

30. $a_4 = 16, a_{10} = 46$

31. $a_8 = 26, a_{12} = 42$

32. $a_3 = 19, a_{15} = -1.7$

In Exercises 33–44, find a formula for a_n for the arithmetic sequence.

33. $a_1 = 1, d = 3$

34. $a_1 = 15, d = 4$

35. $a_1 = 100, d = -8$

36. $a_1 = 0, d = -\frac{2}{3}$

37. $a_1 = x, d = 2x$

38. $a_1 = -y, d = 5y$

39. $4, \frac{3}{2}, -1, -\frac{7}{2}, \ldots$

40. 10, 5, 0, −5, −10, . . .

41. $a_1 = 5, a_4 = 15$

42. $a_1 = -4, a_5 = 16$

43. $a_3 = 94, a_6 = 85$

44. $a_5 = 190, a_{10} = 115$

In Exercises 45–48, match the arithmetic sequence with its graph. [The graphs are labeled (a), (b), (c), and (d).]

(a)

(b)

(c)

(d)
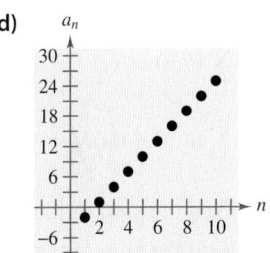

45. $a_n = -\frac{3}{4}n + 8$

46. $a_n = 3n - 5$

47. $a_n = 2 + \frac{3}{4}n$

48. $a_n = 25 - 3n$

 In Exercises 49–52, use a graphing utility to graph the first 10 terms of the sequence.

49. $a_n = 15 - \frac{3}{2}n$

50. $a_n = -5 + 2n$

51. $a_n = 0.2n + 3$

52. $a_n = -0.3n + 8$

In Exercises 53–60, find the indicated nth partial sum of the arithmetic sequence.

53. 8, 20, 32, 44, . . . , $n = 10$

54. 2, 8, 14, 20, . . . , $n = 25$

55. 4.2, 3.7, 3.2, 2.7, . . . , $n = 12$

56. 0.5, 0.9, 1.3, 1.7, . . . , $n = 10$

57. 40, 37, 34, 31, . . . , $n = 10$

58. 75, 70, 65, 60, . . . , $n = 25$

59. $a_1 = 100, a_{25} = 220$, $n = 25$

60. $a_1 = 15, a_{100} = 307$, $n = 100$

In Exercises 61–68, find the partial sum.

61. $\sum_{n=1}^{50} n$

62. $\sum_{n=1}^{100} 2n$

63. $\sum_{n=10}^{100} 6n$

64. $\sum_{n=51}^{100} 7n$

65. $\sum_{n=11}^{30} n - \sum_{n=1}^{10} n$

66. $\sum_{n=51}^{100} n - \sum_{n=1}^{50} n$

67. $\sum_{n=1}^{400} (2n - 1)$

68. $\sum_{n=1}^{250} (1000 - n)$

In Exercises 69–74, use a calculator to find the partial sum.

69. $\sum_{n=1}^{20} (2n + 5)$

70. $\sum_{n=0}^{50} (1000 - 5n)$

71. $\sum_{n=1}^{100} \frac{n + 4}{2}$

72. $\sum_{n=0}^{100} \frac{8 - 3n}{16}$

73. $\sum_{i=1}^{60} \left(250 - \frac{8}{3}i\right)$

74. $\sum_{j=1}^{200} (4.5 + 0.025j)$

75. Find the sum of the first 100 positive odd integers.

76. Find the sum of the integers from -10 to 50.

Job Offer **In Exercises 77 and 78, consider a job offer with the given starting salary and the given annual raise.**

(a) Determine the salary during the sixth year of employment.

(b) Determine the total compensation from the company through six full years of employment.

	Starting Salary	*Annual Raise*
77.	$32,500	$1500
78.	$36,800	$1750

79. *Seating Capacity* Determine the seating capacity of an auditorium with 30 rows of seats if there are 20 seats in the first row, 24 seats in the second row, 28 seats in the third row, and so on.

80. *Seating Capacity* Determine the seating capacity of an auditorium with 36 rows of seats if there are 15 seats in the first row, 18 seats in the second row, 21 seats in the third row, and so on.

81. *Brick Pattern* A brick patio has the approximate shape of a trapezoid (see figure). The patio has 18 rows of bricks. The first row has 14 bricks and the 18th row has 31 bricks. How many bricks are in the patio?

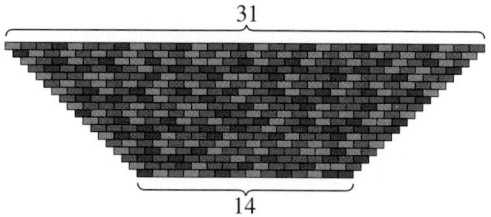

82. *Brick Pattern* A triangular brick wall is made by cutting some bricks in half to use in the first column of every other row. The wall has 28 rows. The top row is one-half brick wide and the bottom row is 14 bricks wide. How many bricks are used in the finished wall?

83. *Falling Object* An object with negligible air resistance is dropped from a plane. During the first second of fall, the object falls 4.9 meters; during the second second, it falls 14.7 meters; during the third second, it falls 24.5 meters; during the fourth second, it falls 34.3 meters. If this arithmetic pattern continues, how many meters will the object fall in 10 seconds?

84. *Falling Object* An object with negligible air resistance is dropped from the top of the Petronas Towers in Malaysia at a height of 1483 feet. During the first second of fall, the object falls 16 feet; during the second second, it falls 48 feet; during the third second, it falls 80 feet; during the fourth second, it falls 112 feet. If this arithmetic pattern continues, how many feet will the object fall in 7 seconds?

▶ Model It

85. *Data Analysis* The table shows the per capita personal income in the United States from 1990 to 2000. (Source: U.S. Department of Commerce, Bureau of Economic Analysis)

Year, n	Per capita personal income, a_n
1990	$19,188
1991	$19,652
1992	$20,576
1993	$21,231
1994	$22,086
1995	$23,562
1996	$24,651
1997	$25,924
1998	$27,203
1999	$28,546
2000	$29,676

(a) Find an arithmetic sequence that models the data. Let a_n represent the per capita personal income and let n represent the year, with $n = 0$ corresponding to 1990.

(b) Use the *regression* feature of a graphing utility to find a linear model for the data. How does this model compare with the arithmetic sequence you found in part (a)?

(c) Use a graphing utility to graph the terms of the finite sequence you found in part (a).

(d) Use the sequence from part (a) to estimate the per capita personal income in 2001 and 2003.

(e) Use your school's library, the Internet, or some other reference source to find the actual per capita personal income in 2001 and 2003, and compare these values with the estimates from part (d).

Synthesis

86. *Writing* Explain how to use the first two terms of an arithmetic sequence to find the nth term.

True or False? In Exercises 87 and 88, determine whether the statement is true or false. Justify your answer.

87. Given an arithmetic sequence for which only the first two terms are known, it is possible to find the nth term.

88. If the only known information about a finite arithmetic sequence is its first term and its last term, then it is possible to find the sum of the sequence.

89. *Exploration*
(a) Graph the first 10 terms of the arithmetic sequence $a_n = 2 + 3n$.
(b) Graph the equation of the line $y = 3x + 2$.
(c) Discuss any differences between the graph of $a_n = 2 + 3n$ and the graph of $y = 3x + 2$.
(d) Compare the slope of the line in part (b) with the common difference of the sequence in part (a). What can you conclude about the slope of a line and the common difference of an arithmetic sequence?

90. *Pattern Recognition*
(a) Compute the following sums of positive odd integers.
$1 + 3 =$
$1 + 3 + 5 =$
$1 + 3 + 5 + 7 =$
$1 + 3 + 5 + 7 + 9 =$
$1 + 3 + 5 + 7 + 9 + 11 =$
(b) Use the sums in part (a) to make a conjecture about the sums of positive odd integers. Check your conjecture for the sum
$1 + 3 + 5 + 7 + 9 + 11 + 13 =$.
(c) Verify your conjecture analytically.

91. *Think About It* The sum of the first 20 terms of an arithmetic sequence with a common difference of 3 is 650. Find the first term.

92. *Think About It* The sum of the first n terms of an arithmetic sequence with first term a_1 and common difference d is S_n. Determine the sum if each term is increased by 5. Explain.

Review

In Exercises 93–96, find the slope and y-intercept (if possible) of the equation of the line. Sketch the line.

93. $2x - 4y = 3$ **94.** $9x + y = -8$
95. $x - 7 = 0$ **96.** $y + 11 = 0$

9.3 Geometric Sequences and Series

▶ **What you should learn**

- How to recognize and write geometric sequences
- How to find the sum of a geometric sequence
- How to find the sum of an infinite geometric series
- How to use geometric sequences to model and solve real-life problems

▶ **Why you should learn it**

Geometric sequences can be used to model and solve real-life problems. For instance, in Exercise 97 on page 641, you will use a geometric sequence to model the population of China.

Geometric Sequences

In Section 9.2, you learned that a sequence whose consecutive terms have a common *difference* is an arithmetic sequence. In this section, you will study another important type of sequence called a **geometric sequence.** Consecutive terms of a geometric sequence have a common *ratio.*

> ### Definition of Geometric Sequence
>
> A sequence is **geometric** if the ratios of consecutive terms are the same. So, the sequence $a_1, a_2, a_3, a_4, \ldots, a_n \ldots$ is geometric if there is a number r such that
>
> $$\frac{a_2}{a_1}, \frac{a_3}{a_2}, \frac{a_4}{a_3} = \ldots = r, \qquad r \neq 0$$
>
> and so on. The number r is the **common ratio** of the sequence.

Example 1 ▶   Examples of Geometric Sequences

a. The sequence whose nth term is 2^n is geometric. For this sequence, the common ratio of consecutive terms is 2.

$$2, 4, 8, 16, \ldots, 2^n, \ldots \qquad \text{Begin with } n = 1.$$

$$\tfrac{4}{2} = 2$$

b. The sequence whose nth term is $4(3^n)$ is geometric. For this sequence, the common ratio of consecutive terms is 3.

$$12, 36, 108, 324, \ldots, 4(3^n), \ldots \qquad \text{Begin with } n = 1.$$

$$\tfrac{36}{12} = 3$$

c. The sequence whose nth term is $\left(-\tfrac{1}{3}\right)^n$ is geometric. For this sequence, the common ratio of consecutive terms is $-\tfrac{1}{3}$.

$$-\frac{1}{3}, \frac{1}{9}, -\frac{1}{27}, \frac{1}{81}, \ldots, \left(-\frac{1}{3}\right)^n, \ldots \qquad \text{Begin with } n = 1.$$

$$\tfrac{1/9}{-1/3} = -\tfrac{1}{3}$$

The sequence $1, 4, 9, 16, \ldots$, whose nth term is n^2, is *not* geometric. The ratio of the second term to the first term is

$$\frac{a_2}{a_1} = \frac{4}{1} = 4$$

but the ratio of the third term to the second term is $\dfrac{a_3}{a_2} = \dfrac{9}{4}$.

In Example 1, notice that each of the geometric sequences has an nth term that is of the form ar^n, where the common ratio of the sequence is r. A geometric sequence may be thought of as an exponential function whose domain is the set of natural numbers.

The nth Term of a Geometric Sequence

The nth term of a geometric sequence has the form

$$a_n = a_1 r^{n-1}$$

where r is the common ratio of consecutive terms of the sequence. So, every geometric sequence can be written in the following form.

$$a_1, \quad a_2, \quad a_3, \quad a_4, \quad a_5, \dots \dots, \quad a_n, \dots \dots$$
$$\downarrow \quad \downarrow \quad \downarrow \quad \downarrow \quad \downarrow \quad\quad\quad \downarrow$$
$$a_1, a_1r, a_1r^2, a_1r^3, a_1r^4, \dots, a_1r^{n-1}, \dots$$

If you know the nth term of a geometric sequence, you can find the $(n+1)$th term by multiplying by r. That is, $a_{n+1} = ra_n$.

Example 2 ▶ **Finding the Terms of a Geometric Sequence**

Write the first five terms of the geometric sequence whose first term is $a_1 = 3$ and whose common ratio is $r = 2$. Then plot the points on a set of coordinate axes.

Solution

Starting with 3, repeatedly multiply by 2 to obtain the following.

$a_1 = 3$	1st term
$a_2 = 3(2^1) = 6$	2nd term
$a_3 = 3(2^2) = 12$	3rd term
$a_4 = 3(2^3) = 24$	4th term
$a_5 = 3(2^4) = 48$	5th term

Figure 9.6 shows the first five terms of this geometric sequence.

Example 3 ▶ **Finding a Term of a Geometric Sequence**

Find the 15th term of the geometric sequence whose first term is 20 and whose common ratio is 1.05.

Solution

$a_{15} = a_1 r^{n-1}$	Formula for geometric sequence
$\quad = 20(1.05)^{15-1}$	Substitute for a_1, r, and n.
$\quad \approx 39.599$	Use a calculator.

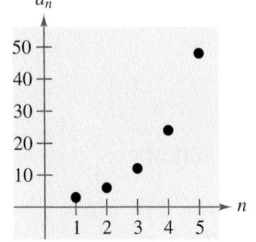

FIGURE **9.6**

| Example 4 ▶ | Finding a Term of a Geometric Sequence | |

Find the 12th term of the geometric sequence

$$5, 15, 45, \ldots.$$

Solution

The common ratio of this sequence is

$$r = \frac{15}{5} = 3.$$

Because the first term is $a_1 = 5$, you can determine the 12th term ($n = 12$) to be

$$a_n = a_1 r^{n-1} \qquad \text{Formula for geometric sequence}$$
$$a_{12} = 5(3)^{12-1} \qquad \text{Substitute for } a_1, r, \text{ and } n.$$
$$= 5(177,147) \qquad \text{Use a calculator.}$$
$$= 885,735. \qquad \text{Simplify.}$$

If you know any two terms of a geometric sequence, you can use that information to find a formula for the nth term of the sequence.

| Example 5 ▶ | Finding a Term of a Geometric Sequence |

The fourth term of a geometric sequence is 125, and the 10th term is 125/64. Find the 14th term. (Assume that the terms of the sequence are positive.)

Solution

The 10th term is related to the fourth term by the equation

$$a_{10} = a_4 r^6. \qquad \text{Multiply 4th term by } r^{10-4}.$$

Because $a_{10} = 125/64$ and $a_4 = 125$, you can solve for r as follows.

$$\frac{125}{64} = 125 r^6 \qquad \text{Substitute } \tfrac{125}{64} \text{ for } a_{10} \text{ and } 125 \text{ for } a_4.$$

$$\frac{1}{64} = r^6 \qquad \text{Divide each side by 125.}$$

$$\frac{1}{2} = r \qquad \text{Take the sixth root of each side.}$$

You can obtain the 14th term by multiplying the 10th term by r^4.

$$a_{14} = a_{10} r^4 \qquad \text{Multiply the 10th term by } r^{14-10}.$$

$$= \frac{125}{64}\left(\frac{1}{2}\right)^4 \qquad \text{Substitute } \tfrac{125}{64} \text{ for } a_{10} \text{ and } \tfrac{1}{2} \text{ for } r.$$

$$= \frac{125}{1024} \qquad \text{Simplify.}$$

STUDY TIP

Remember that r is the common ratio of consecutive terms of a sequence. So in Example 5,

$$a_{10} = a_1 r^9$$
$$= a_1 \cdot r \cdot r \cdot r \cdot r^6$$
$$= a_1 \cdot \frac{a_2}{a_1} \cdot \frac{a_3}{a_2} \cdot \frac{a_4}{a_3} \cdot r^6$$
$$= a_4 r^6.$$

The Sum of a Finite Geometric Sequence

The formula for the sum of a *finite* geometric sequence is as follows.

The Sum of a Finite Geometric Sequence

The sum of the finite geometric sequence

$$a_1, \ a_1r, \ a_1r^2, \ a_1r^3, \ a_1r^4, \ \ldots, a_1r^{n-1}$$

with common ratio $r \neq 1$ is given by

$$S_n = \sum_{i=1}^{n} a_1 \, r^{i-1} = a_1\left(\frac{1 - r^n}{1 - r}\right).$$

For a proof of the sum of a finite geometric sequence, see Proofs in Mathematics on page 694.

Example 6 ▶ Finding the Sum of a Finite Geometric Sequence

Find the sum $\displaystyle\sum_{n=1}^{12} 4(0.3)^n$.

Solution

By writing out a few terms, you have

$$\sum_{n=1}^{12} 4(0.3)^n = 4(0.3)^1 + 4(0.3)^2 + 4(0.3)^3 + \cdots + 4(0.3)^{12}.$$

Now, because $a_1 = 4(0.3)$, $r = 0.3$, and $n = 12$, you can apply the formula for the sum of a finite geometric sequence to obtain

$$S_n = a_1\left(\frac{1 - r^n}{1 - r}\right) \qquad \text{Formula for sum of a sequence}$$

$$= 4(0.3)\left[\frac{1 - (0.3)^{12}}{1 - 0.3}\right] \qquad \text{Substitute for } a_1, r, \text{ and } n.$$

$$\approx 1.714. \qquad \text{Use a calculator.}$$

When using the formula for the sum of a geometric sequence, be careful to check that the index begins at $i = 1$. If the index begins at $i = 0$, you must adjust the formula for the nth partial sum. For instance, if the index in Example 6 had begun with $n = 0$, the sum would have been

$$\sum_{n=0}^{12} 4(0.3)^n = 4(0.3)^0 + \sum_{n=1}^{12} 4(0.3)^n$$

$$= 4 + \sum_{n=1}^{12} 4(0.3)^n$$

$$\approx 4 + 1.714$$

$$= 5.714.$$

Geometric Series

The summation of the terms of an infinite geometric *sequence* is called an **infinite geometric series** or simply a **geometric series.**

    The formula for the sum of a *finite* geometric *sequence* can, depending on the value of r, be extended to produce a formula for the sum of an *infinite* geometric *series.* Specifically, if the common ratio r has the property that $|r| < 1$, it can be shown that r^n becomes arbitrarily close to zero as n increases without bound. Consequently,

$$a_1\left(\frac{1 - r^n}{1 - r}\right) \longrightarrow a_1\left(\frac{1 - 0}{1 - r}\right) \quad \text{as} \quad n \longrightarrow \infty.$$

This result is summarized as follows.

The Sum of an Infinite Geometric Series

If $|r| < 1$, the infinite geometric series

$$a_1 + a_1r + a_1r^2 + a_1r^3 + \cdots + a_1r^{n-1} + \cdots$$

has the sum

$$S = \sum_{i=0}^{\infty} a_1r^i = \frac{a_1}{1 - r}.$$

Note that if $|r| \geq 1$, the series does not have a sum.

Example 7 ▶   **Finding the Sum of an Infinite Geometric Series**

Find each sum.

a. $\displaystyle\sum_{n=1}^{\infty} 4(0.6)^{n-1}$

b. $3 + 0.3 + 0.03 + 0.003 + \cdots$

Solution

a. $\displaystyle\sum_{n=1}^{\infty} 4(0.6)^{n-1} = 4 + 4(0.6) + 4(0.6)^2 + 4(0.6)^3 + \cdots + 4(0.6)^{n-1} + \cdots$

$$= \frac{4}{1 - (0.6)} \qquad\qquad \frac{a_1}{1 - r}$$

$$= 10$$

b. $3 + 0.3 + 0.03 + 0.003 + \cdots = 3 + 3(0.1) + 3(0.1)^2 + 3(0.1)^3 + \cdots$

$$= \frac{3}{1 - (0.1)} \qquad\qquad \frac{a_1}{1 - r}$$

$$= \frac{10}{3}$$

$$\approx 3.33$$

Application

Example 8 ▶ Increasing Annuity

A deposit of $50 is made on the first day of each month in a savings account that pays 6% compounded monthly. What is the balance at the end of 2 years? (This type of savings plan is called an **increasing annuity.**)

Solution

The first deposit will gain interest for 24 months, and its balance will be

$$A_{24} = 50\left(1 + \frac{0.06}{12}\right)^{24}$$

$$= 50(1.005)^{24}.$$

The second deposit will gain interest for 23 months, and its balance will be

$$A_{23} = 50\left(1 + \frac{0.06}{12}\right)^{23}$$

$$= 50(1.005)^{23}.$$

The last deposit will gain interest for only 1 month, and its balance will be

$$A_1 = 50\left(1 + \frac{0.06}{12}\right)^{1}$$

$$= 50(1.005).$$

The total balance in the annuity will be the sum of the balances of the 24 deposits. Using the formula for the sum of a finite geometric sequence, with $A_1 = 50(1.005)$ and $r = 1.005$, you have

$$S_{24} = 50(1.005)\left[\frac{1 - (1.005)^{24}}{1 - 1.005}\right] \qquad \text{Substitute for } A_1, r, \text{ and } n.$$

$$= \$1277.96.$$

Writing ABOUT MATHEMATICS

An Experiment You will need a piece of string or yarn, a pair of scissors, and a tape measure. Measure out any length of string at least 5 feet long. Double over the string and cut it in half. Take one of the resulting halves, double it over, and cut it in half. Continue this process until you are no longer able to cut a length of string in half. How many cuts were you able to make? Construct a sequence of the resulting string lengths after each cut, starting with the original length of the string. Find a formula for the *n*th term of this sequence. How many cuts could you theoretically make? Discuss why you were not able to make that many cuts.

9.3 **Exercises**

In Exercises 1–10, determine whether the sequence is geometric. If it is, find the common ratio.

1. $5, 15, 45, 135, \ldots$

2. $3, 12, 48, 192, \ldots$

3. $3, 12, 21, 30, \ldots$

4. $36, 27, 18, 9, \ldots$

5. $1, -\frac{1}{2}, \frac{1}{4}, -\frac{1}{8}, \ldots$

6. $5, 1, 0.2, 0.04, \ldots$

7. $\frac{1}{8}, \frac{1}{4}, \frac{1}{2}, 1, \ldots$

8. $9, -6, 4, -\frac{8}{3}, \ldots$

9. $1, \frac{1}{2}, \frac{1}{3}, \frac{1}{4}, \ldots$

10. $\frac{1}{5}, \frac{2}{7}, \frac{3}{9}, \frac{4}{11}, \ldots$

In Exercises 11–20, write the first five terms of the geometric sequence.

11. $a_1 = 2, r = 3$

12. $a_1 = 6, r = 2$

13. $a_1 = 1, r = \frac{1}{2}$

14. $a_1 = 1, r = \frac{1}{3}$

15. $a_1 = 5, r = -\frac{1}{10}$

16. $a_1 = 6, r = -\frac{1}{4}$

17. $a_1 = 1, r = e$

18. $a_1 = 3, r = \sqrt{5}$

19. $a_1 = 2, r = \dfrac{x}{4}$

20. $a_1 = 5, r = 2x$

In Exercises 21–26, write the first five terms of the geometric sequence. Determine the common ratio and write the nth term of the sequence as a function of n.

21. $a_1 = 64, \quad a_{k+1} = \frac{1}{2}a_k$

22. $a_1 = 81, \quad a_{k+1} = \frac{1}{3}a_k$

23. $a_1 = 7, \quad a_{k+1} = 2a_k$

24. $a_1 = 5, \quad a_{k+1} = -2a_k$

25. $a_1 = 6, \quad a_{k+1} = -\frac{3}{2}a_k$

26. $a_1 = 48, \quad a_{k+1} = -\frac{1}{2}a_k$

In Exercises 27–38, write an expression for the nth term of the geometric sequence.

27. $a_1 = 4, r = \frac{1}{2}, n = 10$

28. $a_1 = 5, r = \frac{3}{2}, n = 8$

29. $a_1 = 6, r = -\frac{1}{3}, n = 12$

30. $a_1 = 64, r = -\frac{1}{4}, n = 10$

31. $a_1 = 100, r = e^x, n = 9$

32. $a_1 = 1, r = \sqrt{3}, n = 8$

33. $a_1 = 500, r = 1.02, n = 40$

34. $a_1 = 1000, r = 1.005, n = 60$

35. $a_1 = 16, a_4 = \frac{27}{4}, n = 3$

36. $a_2 = 3, a_5 = \frac{3}{64}, n = 1$

37. $a_4 = -18, a_7 = \frac{2}{3}, n = 6$

38. $a_3 = \frac{16}{3}, a_5 = \frac{64}{27}, n = 7$

In Exercises 39–42, match the geometric sequence with its graph. [The graphs are labeled (a), (b), (c), and (d).]

(a)

(b)

(c)

(d)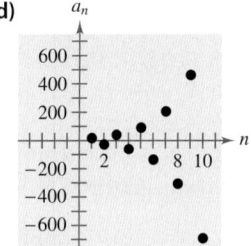

39. $a_n = 18\left(\frac{2}{3}\right)^{n-1}$

40. $a_n = 18\left(-\frac{2}{3}\right)^{n-1}$

41. $a_n = 18\left(\frac{3}{2}\right)^{n-1}$

42. $a_n = 18\left(-\frac{3}{2}\right)^{n-1}$

In Exercises 43–50, use a graphing utility to graph the first 10 terms of the sequence.

43. $a_n = 12(-0.75)^{n-1}$

44. $a_n = 10(1.5)^{n-1}$

45. $a_n = 12(-0.4)^{n-1}$

46. $a_n = 20(-1.25)^{n-1}$

47. $a_n = 2(1.3)^{n-1}$

48. $a_n = 10(1.2)^{n-1}$

49. $a_n = 2(-1.4)^{n-1}$

50. $a_n = 12(-1.2)^{n-1}$

In Exercises 51–70, find the sum of the finite geometric sequence.

51. $\displaystyle\sum_{n=1}^{9} 2^{n-1}$

52. $\displaystyle\sum_{n=1}^{10} \left(\frac{5}{2}\right)^{n-1}$

53. $\displaystyle\sum_{n=1}^{9} (-2)^{n-1}$

54. $\displaystyle\sum_{n=1}^{8} 5\left(-\frac{3}{2}\right)^{n-1}$

55. $\displaystyle\sum_{i=1}^{7} 64\left(-\frac{1}{2}\right)^{i-1}$

56. $\displaystyle\sum_{i=1}^{10} 2\left(\frac{1}{4}\right)^{i-1}$

57. $\displaystyle\sum_{i=1}^{6} 32\left(\frac{1}{4}\right)^{i-1}$

58. $\displaystyle\sum_{i=1}^{12} 16\left(\frac{1}{2}\right)^{i-1}$

59. $\displaystyle\sum_{n=0}^{20} 3\left(\frac{3}{2}\right)^n$

60. $\displaystyle\sum_{n=0}^{40} 5\left(\frac{3}{5}\right)^n$

61. $\displaystyle\sum_{n=0}^{15} 2\left(\frac{4}{3}\right)^n$

62. $\displaystyle\sum_{n=0}^{20} 10\left(\frac{1}{5}\right)^n$

63. $\displaystyle\sum_{n=0}^{5} 300(1.06)^n$

64. $\displaystyle\sum_{n=0}^{6} 500(1.04)^n$

65. $\displaystyle\sum_{n=0}^{40} 2\left(-\frac{1}{4}\right)^n$

66. $\displaystyle\sum_{n=0}^{50} 10\left(\frac{2}{3}\right)^{n-1}$

67. $\displaystyle\sum_{i=1}^{10} 8\left(-\frac{1}{4}\right)^{i-1}$

68. $\displaystyle\sum_{i=0}^{25} 8\left(-\frac{1}{2}\right)^i$

69. $\displaystyle\sum_{i=1}^{10} 5\left(-\frac{1}{3}\right)^{i-1}$

70. $\displaystyle\sum_{i=1}^{100} 15\left(\frac{2}{3}\right)^{i-1}$

In Exercises 71–76, use summation notation to express the sum.

71. $5 + 15 + 45 + \cdots + 3645$

72. $7 + 14 + 28 + \cdots + 896$

73. $2 - \dfrac{1}{2} + \dfrac{1}{8} - \cdots + \dfrac{1}{2048}$

74. $15 - 3 + \dfrac{3}{5} - \cdots - \dfrac{3}{625}$

75. $0.1 + 0.4 + 1.6 + \cdots + 102.4$

76. $32 + 24 + 18 + \cdots + 10.125$

In Exercises 77–90, find the sum of the infinite geometric series.

77. $\displaystyle\sum_{n=0}^{\infty} \left(\frac{1}{2}\right)^n$

78. $\displaystyle\sum_{n=0}^{\infty} 2\left(\frac{2}{3}\right)^n$

79. $\displaystyle\sum_{n=0}^{\infty} \left(-\frac{1}{2}\right)^n$

80. $\displaystyle\sum_{n=0}^{\infty} 2\left(-\frac{2}{3}\right)^n$

81. $\displaystyle\sum_{n=0}^{\infty} 4\left(\frac{1}{4}\right)^n$

82. $\displaystyle\sum_{n=0}^{\infty} \left(\frac{1}{10}\right)^n$

83. $\displaystyle\sum_{n=0}^{\infty} (0.4)^n$

84. $\displaystyle\sum_{n=0}^{\infty} 4(0.2)^n$

85. $\displaystyle\sum_{n=0}^{\infty} -3(0.9)^n$

86. $\displaystyle\sum_{n=0}^{\infty} -10(0.2)^n$

87. $8 + 6 + \dfrac{9}{2} + \dfrac{27}{8} + \cdots$

88. $9 + 6 + 4 + \dfrac{8}{3} + \cdots$

89. $\dfrac{1}{9} - \dfrac{1}{3} + 1 - 3 + \cdots$

90. $-\dfrac{125}{36} + \dfrac{25}{6} - 5 + 6 - \cdots$

In Exercises 91–94, find the rational number representation of the repeating decimal.

91. $0.\overline{36}$

92. $0.\overline{297}$

93. $0.3\overline{18}$

94. $1.3\overline{8}$

Graphical Reasoning In Exercises 95 and 96, use a graphing utility to graph the function. Identify the horizontal asymptote of the graph and determine its relationship to the sum.

95. $f(x) = 6\left[\dfrac{1 - (0.5)^x}{1 - (0.5)}\right]$, $\quad \displaystyle\sum_{n=0}^{\infty} 6\left(\frac{1}{2}\right)^n$

96. $f(x) = 2\left[\dfrac{1 - (0.8)^x}{1 - (0.8)}\right]$, $\quad \displaystyle\sum_{n=0}^{\infty} 2\left(\frac{4}{5}\right)^n$

▶ **Model It**

97. *Data Analysis* The table shows the population of China (in millions) from 1995 through 2001. (Source: U.S. Census Bureau)

Year, n	Population, a_n
1995	1203.1
1996	1210.0
1997	1221.6
1998	1236.9
1999	1246.9
2000	1261.8
2001	1273.1

(a) Use the *regression* feature of a graphing utility to find a geometric (exponential) sequence that models the data. Let a_n represent the population and let n represent the year, with $n = 5$ corresponding to 1995.

(b) Use the sequence from part (a) to describe the rate at which the population of China is growing.

(c) Use the sequence from part (a) to predict the population of China in 2010.

(d) Use the sequence from part (a) to determine when the population of China will reach 1.3 billion.

98. *Compound Interest* A principal of $1000 is invested at 6% interest. Find the amount after 10 years if the interest is compounded (a) annually, (b) semiannually, (c) quarterly, (d) monthly, and (e) daily.

99. *Compound Interest* A principal of $2500 is invested at 8% interest. Find the amount after 20 years if the interest is compounded (a) annually, (b) semiannually, (c) quarterly, (d) monthly, and (e) daily.

100. *Depreciation* A tool and die company buys a machine for $135,000 and it depreciates at a rate of 30% per year. (In other words, at the end of each year the depreciated value is 70% of what it was at the beginning of the year.) Find the depreciated value of the machine after 5 full years.

101. *Annuities* A deposit of $100 is made at the beginning of each month in an account that pays 6%, compounded monthly. The balance A in the account at the end of 5 years is

$$A = 100\left(1 + \frac{0.06}{12}\right)^1 + \cdots + 100\left(1 + \frac{0.06}{12}\right)^{60}.$$

Find A.

102. *Annuities* A deposit of $50 is made at the beginning of each month in an account that pays 8%, compounded monthly. The balance A in the account at the end of 5 years is

$$A = 50\left(1 + \frac{0.08}{12}\right)^1 + \cdots + 50\left(1 + \frac{0.08}{12}\right)^{60}.$$

Find A.

103. *Annuities* A deposit of P dollars is made at the beginning of each month in an account earning an annual interest rate r, compounded monthly. The balance A after t years is

$$A = P\left(1 + \frac{r}{12}\right) + P\left(1 + \frac{r}{12}\right)^2 + \cdots +$$

$$P\left(1 + \frac{r}{12}\right)^{12t}.$$

Show that the balance is

$$A = P\left[\left(1 + \frac{r}{12}\right)^{12t} - 1\right]\left(1 + \frac{12}{r}\right).$$

104. *Annuities* A deposit of P dollars is made at the beginning of each month in an account earning an annual interest rate r, compounded continuously. The balance A after t years is

$$A = Pe^{r/12} + Pe^{2r/12} + \cdots + Pe^{12tr/12}.$$

Show that the balance is

$$A = \frac{Pe^{r/12}(e^{rt} - 1)}{e^{r/12} - 1}.$$

Annuities In Exercises 105–108, consider making monthly deposits of P dollars in a savings account earning an annual interest rate r. Use the results of Exercises 103 and 104 to find the balance A after t years if the interest is compounded (a) monthly and (b) continuously.

105. $P = \$50$, $r = 7\%$, $t = 20$ years

106. $P = \$75$, $r = 9\%$, $t = 25$ years

107. $P = \$100$, $r = 10\%$, $t = 40$ years

108. $P = \$20$, $r = 6\%$, $t = 50$ years

109. *Annuities* Consider an initial deposit of P dollars in an account earning an annual interest rate r, compounded monthly. At the end of each month, a withdrawal of W dollars will occur and the account will be depleted in t years. The amount of the initial deposit required is

$$P = W\left(1 + \frac{r}{12}\right)^{-1} + W\left(1 + \frac{r}{12}\right)^{-2} + \cdots +$$

$$W\left(1 + \frac{r}{12}\right)^{-12t}.$$

Show that the initial deposit is

$$P = W\left(\frac{12}{r}\right)\left[1 - \left(1 + \frac{r}{12}\right)^{-12t}\right].$$

110. *Annuities* Determine the amount required in a retirement account for an individual who retires at age 65 and wants an income of $2000 from the account each month for 20 years. Use the result of Exercise 109 and assume that the account earns 9% compounded monthly.

111. *Geometry* The sides of a square are 16 inches in length. A new square is formed by connecting the midpoints of the sides of the original square, and two of the resulting triangles are shaded (see figure). If this process is repeated five more times, determine the total area of the shaded region.

112. *Sales* The annual sales a_n (in millions of dollars) for Merck & Co., Inc. for 1991 through 2000 can be approximated by the model

$$a_n = 6942.2e^{0.173n}, \qquad n = 1, 2, \ldots, 10$$

where $n = 1$ represents 1991. Use this model and the formula for the sum of a finite geometric sequence to approximate the total sales earned during this 10-year period. (Source: Merck & Co., Inc.)

113. *Salary* An investment firm has a job opening with a salary of $30,000 for the first year. Suppose that during the next 39 years, there is a 5% raise each year. Find the total compensation over the 40-year period.

114. *Distance* A ball is dropped from a height of 16 feet. Each time it drops h feet, it rebounds $0.81h$ feet.

(a) Find the total vertical distance traveled by the ball.

(b) The ball takes the following times for each fall.

$s_1 = -16t^2 + 16,$ $s_1 = 0$ if $t = 1$

$s_2 = -16t^2 + 16(0.81),$ $s_2 = 0$ if $t = 0.9$

$s_3 = -16t^2 + 16(0.81)^2,$ $s_3 = 0$ if $t = (0.9)^2$

$s_4 = -16t^2 + 16(0.81)^3,$ $s_4 = 0$ if $t = (0.9)^3$

$\vdots$ $\vdots$

$s_n = -16t^2 + 16(0.81)^{n-1},$ $s_n = 0$ if $t = (0.9)^{n-1}$

Beginning with s_2, the ball takes the same amount of time to bounce up as it does to fall, and so the total time elapsed before it comes to rest is

$$t = 1 + 2\sum_{n=1}^{\infty}(0.9)^n.$$

Find this total.

Synthesis

True or False? In Exercises 115 and 116, determine whether the statement is true or false. Justify your answer.

115. A sequence is geometric if the ratios of consecutive differences of consecutive terms are the same.

116. You can find the nth term of a geometric sequence by multiplying its common ratio by the first term of the sequence raised to the $(n - 1)$th power.

117. *Writing* Write a brief paragraph explaining why the terms of a geometric sequence decrease in magnitude when $-1 < r < 1$.

118. Find two different geometric series with sums of 4.

Review

In Exercises 119–122, evaluate the function for $f(x) = 3x + 1$ and $g(x) = x^2 - 1$.

119. $g(x + 1)$ **120.** $f(x + 1)$

121. $f(g(x + 1))$ **122.** $g(f(x + 1))$

In Exercises 123–126, completely factor the expression over the rational numbers.

123. $9x^3 - 64x$

124. $x^2 + 4x - 63$

125. $6x^2 - 13x - 5$

126. $16x^2 - 4x^4$

In Exercises 127–132, perform the indicated operation(s) and simplify.

127. $\dfrac{3}{x + 3} \cdot \dfrac{x(x + 3)}{x - 3}$

128. $\dfrac{x - 2}{x + 7} \cdot \dfrac{2x(x + 7)}{6x(x - 2)}$

129. $\dfrac{x}{3} \div \dfrac{3x}{6x + 3}$

130. $\dfrac{x - 5}{x - 3} \div \dfrac{10 - 2x}{2(3 - x)}$

131. $5 + \dfrac{7}{x + 2} + \dfrac{2}{x - 2}$

132. $8 - \dfrac{x - 1}{x + 4} - \dfrac{4}{x - 1} - \dfrac{x + 4}{(x - 1)(x + 4)}$

9.4 Mathematical Induction

▶ **What you should learn**

- How to use mathematical induction to prove a statement
- How to find the sums of powers of integers
- How to recognize patterns and write the nth term of a sequence
- How to find finite differences of a sequence

▶ **Why you should learn it**

Finite differences can be used to determine what type of model can be used to represent a sequence. For instance, in Exercise 59 on page 653, you will use finite differences to find a model that represents the total prize money awarded at professional rodeos.

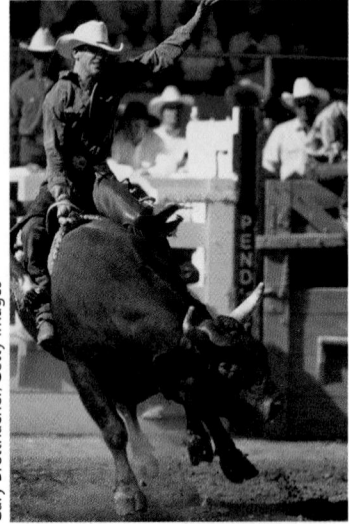

Gary Brettnacher/Getty Images

Introduction

In this section you will study a form of mathematical proof called **mathematical induction.** It is important that you see clearly the logical need for it, so take a closer look at the problem discussed in Example 5 on page 628.

$$S_1 = 1 = 1^2$$
$$S_2 = 1 + 3 = 2^2$$
$$S_3 = 1 + 3 + 5 = 3^2$$
$$S_4 = 1 + 3 + 5 + 7 = 4^2$$
$$S_5 = 1 + 3 + 5 + 7 + 9 = 5^2$$

Judging from the pattern formed by these first five sums, it appears that the sum of the first n odd integers is

$$S_n = 1 + 3 + 5 + 7 + 9 + \cdots + (2n - 1) = n^2.$$

Although this particular formula *is* valid, it is important for you to see that recognizing a pattern and then simply *jumping to the conclusion* that the pattern must be true for all values of n is *not* a logically valid method of proof. There are many examples in which a pattern appears to be developing for small values of n and then at some point the pattern fails. One of the most famous cases of this was the conjecture by the French mathematician Pierre de Fermat (1601–1665), who speculated that all numbers of the form

$$F_n = 2^{2^n} + 1, \quad n = 0, 1, 2, \ldots$$

are prime. For $n = 0$, 1, 2, 3, and 4, the conjecture is true.

$$F_0 = 3$$
$$F_1 = 5$$
$$F_2 = 17$$
$$F_3 = 257$$
$$F_4 = 65,537$$

The size of the next Fermat number ($F_5 = 4{,}294{,}967{,}297$) is so great that it was difficult for Fermat to determine whether it was prime or not. However, another well-known mathematician, Leonhard Euler (1707–1783), later found the factorization

$$F_5 = 4{,}294{,}967{,}297$$
$$= 641(6{,}700{,}417)$$

which proved that F_5 is not prime and therefore Fermat's conjecture was false.

Just because a rule, pattern, or formula seems to work for several values of n, you cannot simply decide that it is valid for all values of n without going through a *legitimate proof.* Mathematical induction is one method of proof.

The Principle of Mathematical Induction

Let P_n be a statement involving the positive integer n. If

1. P_1 is true, and

2. the truth of P_k implies the truth of P_{k+1} for every positive k,

then P_n must be true for all positive integers n.

To apply the Principle of Mathematical Induction, you need to be able to determine the statement P_{k+1} for a given statement P_k.

Example 1 ▶ A Preliminary Example

Find P_{k+1} for each P_k.

a. $P_k : S_k = \dfrac{k^2(k+1)^2}{4}$

b. $P_k : S_k = 1 + 5 + 9 + \cdots + [4(k-1) - 3] + (4k - 3)$

c. $P_k : k + 3 < 5k^2$

d. $P_k : 3^k \geq 2k + 1$

Solution

a. $P_{k+1} : S_{k+1} = \dfrac{(k+1)^2(k+1+1)^2}{4}$ Replace k by $k + 1$.

$\qquad\qquad\quad = \dfrac{(k+1)^2(k+2)^2}{4}$ Simplify.

b. $P_{k+1} : S_{k+1} = 1 + 5 + 9 + \cdots + \{4[(k+1) - 1] - 3\} + [4(k+1) - 3]$

$\qquad\qquad\quad = 1 + 5 + 9 + \cdots + (4k - 3) + (4k + 1)$

c. $P_{k+1} : (k+1) + 3 < 5(k+1)^2$

$\qquad\qquad\quad k + 4 < 5(k^2 + 2k + 1)$

d. $P_{k+1} : 3^{k+1} \geq 2(k+1) + 1$

$\qquad\qquad\quad 3^{k+1} \geq 2k + 3$

FIGURE **9.7**

A well-known illustration used to explain why the Principle of Mathematical Induction works is the unending line of dominoes shown in Figure 9.7. If the line actually contains infinitely many dominoes, it is clear that you could not knock the entire line down by knocking down only *one domino* at a time. However, suppose it were true that each domino would knock down the next one as it fell. Then you could knock them all down simply by pushing the first one and starting a chain reaction. Mathematical induction works in the same way. If the truth of P_k implies the truth of P_{k+1} and if P_1 is true, the chain reaction proceeds as follows: P_1 implies P_2, P_2 implies P_3, P_3 implies P_4, and so on.

When using mathematical induction to prove a *summation* formula (such as the one in Example 2), it is helpful to think of S_{k+1} as

$$S_{k+1} = S_k + a_{k+1}$$

where a_{k+1} is the $(k + 1)$th term of the original sum.

Example 2 ▶   **Using Mathematical Induction**

Use mathematical induction to prove the following formula.

$$S_n = 1 + 3 + 5 + 7 + \cdots + (2n - 1)$$

$$= n^2$$

Solution

Mathematical induction consists of two distinct parts. First, you must show that the formula is true when $n = 1$.

1. When $n = 1$, the formula is valid, because

$$S_1 = 1 = 1^2.$$

The second part of mathematical induction has two steps. The first step is to assume that the formula is valid for *some* integer k. The second step is to use this assumption to prove that the formula is valid for the next integer, $k + 1$.

2. Assuming that the formula

$$S_k = 1 + 3 + 5 + 7 + \cdots + (2k - 1)$$

$$= k^2$$

is true, you must show that the formula $S_{k+1} = (k + 1)^2$ is true.

$$S_{k+1} = 1 + 3 + 5 + 7 + \cdots + (2k - 1) + [2(k + 1) - 1]$$

$$= [1 + 3 + 5 + 7 + \cdots + (2k - 1)] + (2k + 2 - 1)$$

$$= S_k + (2k + 1) \qquad \text{Group terms to form } S_k.$$

$$= k^2 + 2k + 1 \qquad \text{Replace } S_k \text{ by } k^2.$$

$$= (k + 1)^2$$

Combining the results of parts (1) and (2), you can conclude by mathematical induction that the formula is valid for all positive integer values of n.

Your students may benefit from many demonstrations of proof by induction. Consider using proofs of the following.

$3 + 6 + 9 + 12 + \cdots + 3n = \frac{3}{2}n(n + 1)$

$5 + 7 + 9 + 11 + 13 + \cdots +$
$\qquad (3 + 2n) = n(n + 4)$

It occasionally happens that a statement involving natural numbers is not true for the first $k - 1$ positive integers but is true for all values of $n \geq k$. In these instances, you use a slight variation of the Principle of Mathematical Induction in which you verify P_k rather than P_1. This variation is called the *extended principle of mathematical induction*. To see the validity of this, note from Figure 8.7 that all but the first $k - 1$ dominoes can be knocked down by knocking over the kth domino. This suggests that you can prove a statement P_n to be true for $n \geq k$ by showing that P_k is true and that P_k implies P_{k+1}. In Exercises 35–40 of this section, you are asked to apply this extension of mathematical induction.

Example 3 ▶ **Using Mathematical Induction**

Use mathematical induction to prove the formula

$$S_n = 1^2 + 2^2 + 3^2 + 4^2 + \cdots + n^2$$

$$= \frac{n(n + 1)(2n + 1)}{6}.$$

Solution

1. When $n = 1$, the formula is valid, because

$$S_1 = 1^2 = \frac{1(2)(3)}{6}.$$

2. Assuming that

$$S_k = 1^2 + 2^2 + 3^2 + 4^2 + \cdots + k^2$$

$$= \frac{k(k + 1)(2k + 1)}{6}$$

you must show that

$$S_{k+1} = \frac{(k + 1)(k + 1 + 1)[2(k + 1) + 1]}{6}$$

$$= \frac{(k + 1)(k + 2)(2k + 3)}{6}.$$

To do this, write the following.

$$S_{k+1} = S_k + a_{k+1}$$

$$= (1^2 + 2^2 + 3^2 + 4^2 + \cdots + k^2) + (k + 1)^2$$

$$= \frac{k(k + 1)(2k + 1)}{6} + (k + 1)^2 \qquad \text{By assumption}$$

$$= \frac{k(k + 1)(2k + 1) + 6(k + 1)^2}{6}$$

$$= \frac{(k + 1)[k(2k + 1) + 6(k + 1)]}{6}$$

$$= \frac{(k + 1)(2k^2 + 7k + 6)}{6}$$

$$= \frac{(k + 1)(k + 2)(2k + 3)}{6}$$

Combining the results of parts (1) and (2), you can conclude by mathematical induction that the formula is valid for *all* integers $n \geq 1$.

When proving a formula using mathematical induction, the only statement that you *need* to verify is P_1. As a check, however, it is good to try verifying other statements. For instance, in Example 3, try verifying P_2 and P_3.

Sums of Powers of Integers

The formula in Example 3 is one of a collection of useful summation formulas. This and other formulas dealing with the sums of various powers of the first n positive integers are as follows.

Sums of Powers of Integers

1. $1 + 2 + 3 + 4 + \cdots + n = \dfrac{n(n + 1)}{2}$

2. $1^2 + 2^2 + 3^2 + 4^2 + \cdots + n^2 = \dfrac{n(n + 1)(2n + 1)}{6}$

3. $1^3 + 2^3 + 3^3 + 4^3 + \cdots + n^3 = \dfrac{n^2(n + 1)^2}{4}$

4. $1^4 + 2^4 + 3^4 + 4^4 + \cdots + n^4 = \dfrac{n(n + 1)(2n + 1)(3n^2 + 3n - 1)}{30}$

5. $1^5 + 2^5 + 3^5 + 4^5 + \cdots + n^5 = \dfrac{n^2(n + 1)^2(2n^2 + 2n - 1)}{12}$

Example 4 ▶   **Finding a Sum of Powers of Integers**

Find each sum.

a. $\displaystyle\sum_{i=1}^{7} i^3 = 1^3 + 2^3 + 3^3 + 4^3 + 5^3 + 6^3 + 7^3$ **b.** $\displaystyle\sum_{i=1}^{4} (6i - 4i^2)$

Solution

a. Using the formula for the sum of the cubes of the first n positive integers, you obtain

$$\sum_{i=1}^{7} i^3 = 1^3 + 2^3 + 3^3 + 4^3 + 5^3 + 6^3 + 7^3$$

$$= \frac{7^2(7 + 1)^2}{4} = \frac{49(64)}{4} = 784.$$

b. $\displaystyle\sum_{i=1}^{4} (6i - 4i^2) = \sum_{i=1}^{4} 6i - \sum_{i=1}^{4} 4i^2$

$$= 6\sum_{i=1}^{4} i - 4\sum_{i=1}^{4} i^2$$

$$= 6\left[\frac{4(4 + 1)}{2}\right] - 4\left[\frac{4(4 + 1)(8 + 1)}{6}\right]$$

$$= 6(10) - 4(30)$$

$$= 60 - 120 = -60$$

Example 5 ▶ Proving an Inequality by Mathematical Induction

Prove that $n < 2^n$ for all positive integers n.

Solution

1. For $n = 1$ or 2, the statement is true, because

$$1 < 2^1 \quad \text{and} \quad 2 < 2^2.$$

2. Assuming that

$$k < 2^k$$

you need to show that $k + 1 < 2^{k+1}$. For $n = k$, you have

$$2^{k+1} = 2(2^k) > 2(k) = 2k. \qquad \text{By assumption}$$

Because $2k = k + k > k + 1$ for all $k > 1$, it follows that

$$2^{k+1} > 2k > k + 1$$

or

$$k + 1 < 2^{k+1}.$$

So, $n < 2^n$ for all integers $n \geq 1$.

To check a result that you have proved by mathematical induction, it helps to list the statement for several values of n. For instance, in Example 5, you could list

$$1 < 2^1 = 2, \qquad 2 < 2^2 = 4, \qquad 3 < 2^3 = 8,$$
$$4 < 2^4 = 16, \qquad 5 < 2^5 = 32, \qquad 6 < 2^6 = 64.$$

From this list, your intuition confirms that the statement $n < 2^n$ is reasonable.

Pattern Recognition

Although choosing a formula on the basis of a few observations does *not* guarantee the validity of the formula, pattern recognition *is* important. Once you have a pattern or formula that you think works, you can try using mathematical induction to prove your formula.

Finding a Formula for the *n*th Term of a Sequence

To find a formula for the nth term of a sequence, consider these guidelines.

1. Calculate the first several terms of the sequence. It is often a good idea to write the terms in both simplified and factored forms.

2. Try to find a recognizable pattern for the terms and write a formula for the nth term of the sequence. This is your *hypothesis* or *conjecture*. You might try computing one or two more terms in the sequence to test your hypothesis.

3. Use mathematical induction to prove your hypothesis.

Example 6 ▶	Finding a Formula for a Finite Sum

Find a formula for the finite sum and prove its validity.

$$\frac{1}{1 \cdot 2} + \frac{1}{2 \cdot 3} + \frac{1}{3 \cdot 4} + \frac{1}{4 \cdot 5} + \cdots + \frac{1}{n(n + 1)}$$

Solution

Begin by writing out the first few sums.

$$S_1 = \frac{1}{1 \cdot 2} = \frac{1}{2} = \frac{1}{1 + 1}$$

$$S_2 = \frac{1}{1 \cdot 2} + \frac{1}{2 \cdot 3} = \frac{4}{6} = \frac{2}{3} = \frac{2}{2 + 1}$$

$$S_3 = \frac{1}{1 \cdot 2} + \frac{1}{2 \cdot 3} + \frac{1}{3 \cdot 4} = \frac{9}{12} = \frac{3}{4} = \frac{3}{3 + 1}$$

$$S_4 = \frac{1}{1 \cdot 2} + \frac{1}{2 \cdot 3} + \frac{1}{3 \cdot 4} + \frac{1}{4 \cdot 5} = \frac{48}{60} = \frac{4}{5} = \frac{4}{4 + 1}$$

From this sequence, it appears that the formula for the kth sum is

$$S_k = \frac{1}{1 \cdot 2} + \frac{1}{2 \cdot 3} + \frac{1}{3 \cdot 4} + \frac{1}{4 \cdot 5} + \cdots + \frac{1}{k(k + 1)} = \frac{k}{k + 1}.$$

To prove the validity of this hypothesis, use mathematical induction, as follows. Note that you have already verified the formula for $n = 1$, so you can begin by assuming that the formula is valid for $n = k$ and trying to show that it is valid for $n = k + 1$.

$$S_{k+1} = \left[\frac{1}{1 \cdot 2} + \frac{1}{2 \cdot 3} + \frac{1}{3 \cdot 4} + \frac{1}{4 \cdot 5} + \cdots + \frac{1}{k(k + 1)}\right] + \frac{1}{(k + 1)(k + 2)}$$

$$= \frac{k}{k + 1} + \frac{1}{(k + 1)(k + 2)} \qquad \text{By assumption}$$

$$= \frac{k(k + 2) + 1}{(k + 1)(k + 2)}$$

$$= \frac{k^2 + 2k + 1}{(k + 1)(k + 2)}$$

$$= \frac{(k + 1)^2}{(k + 1)(k + 2)}$$

$$= \frac{k + 1}{k + 2}$$

So, the hypothesis is valid.

Finite Differences

The **first differences** of a sequence are found by subtracting consecutive terms. The **second differences** are found by subtracting consecutive first differences. The first and second differences of the sequence $3, 5, 8, 12, 17, 23, \ldots$ are as follows.

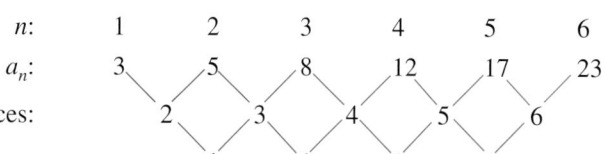

For this sequence, the second differences are all the same. When this happens, the sequence has a perfect *quadratic* model. If the first differences are all the same, the sequence has a *linear* model. That is, it is arithmetic.

Example 7 ▶ **Finding a Quadratic Model**

Find the quadratic model for the sequence

$$3, 5, 8, 12, 17, 23, \ldots .$$

Solution

You know from the second differences shown above that the model is quadratic and has the form

$$a_n = an^2 + bn + c.$$

By substituting 1, 2, and 3 for n, you can obtain a system of three linear equations in three variables.

$a_1 = a(1)^2 + b(1) + c = 3$ Substitute 1 for n.

$a_2 = a(2)^2 + b(2) + c = 5$ Substitute 2 for n.

$a_3 = a(3)^2 + b(3) + c = 8$ Substitute 3 for n.

You now have a system of three equations in a, b, and c.

$$\begin{cases} a + b + c = 3 & \text{Equation 1} \\ 4a + 2b + c = 5 & \text{Equation 2} \\ 9a + 3b + c = 8 & \text{Equation 3} \end{cases}$$

Using the techniques discussed in Chapter 7, you can find the solution to be $a = \frac{1}{2}$, $b = \frac{1}{2}$, and $c = 2$. So, the quadratic model is

$$a_n = \frac{1}{2}n^2 + \frac{1}{2}n + 2.$$

Try checking the values of a_1, a_2, and a_3.

Group Activity

A regular n-sided polygon is a polygon that has n equal sides and n equal angles. For instance, an equilateral triangle is a regular three-sided polygon. Each angle of an equilateral triangle measures 60°, and the sum of all three angles is 180°. Similarly, the sum of the four angles of a four-sided polygon (a square) is 360°.

Polygon	Number of Sides	Sum of Angles
Equilateral triangle	3	180°
Square	4	360°
Regular pentagon	5	540°
Regular hexagon	6	720°

a. The list above shows the sums of the angles of four regular polygons. Use this data to write a conjecture about the sum of the angles of any regular n-sided polygon.

b. Discuss how you could prove that your formula is valid.

9.4 Exercises

In Exercises 1–4, find P_{k+1} for the given P_k.

1. $P_k = \dfrac{5}{k(k+1)}$

2. $P_k = \dfrac{1}{2(k+2)}$

3. $P_k = \dfrac{k^2(k+1)^2}{4}$

4. $P_k = \dfrac{k}{3}(2k+1)$

In Exercises 5–18, use mathematical induction to prove the formula for every positive integer n.

5. $2 + 4 + 6 + 8 + \cdots + 2n = n(n+1)$

6. $3 + 7 + 11 + 15 + \cdots + (4n-1) = n(2n+1)$

7. $2 + 7 + 12 + 17 + \cdots + (5n-3) = \dfrac{n}{2}(5n-1)$

8. $1 + 4 + 7 + 10 + \cdots + (3n-2) = \dfrac{n}{2}(3n-1)$

9. $1 + 2 + 2^2 + 2^3 + \cdots + 2^{n-1} = 2^n - 1$

10. $2(1 + 3 + 3^2 + 3^3 + \cdots + 3^{n-1}) = 3^n - 1$

11. $1 + 2 + 3 + 4 + \cdots + n = \dfrac{n(n+1)}{2}$

12. $1^2 + 2^2 + 3^2 + 4^2 + \cdots + n^2 = \dfrac{n(n+1)(2n+1)}{6}$

13. $1^3 + 2^3 + 3^3 + 4^3 + \cdots + n^3 = \dfrac{n^2(n+1)^2}{4}$

14. $\left(1 + \dfrac{1}{1}\right)\left(1 + \dfrac{1}{2}\right)\left(1 + \dfrac{1}{3}\right) \cdots \left(1 + \dfrac{1}{n}\right) = n + 1$

15. $\displaystyle\sum_{i=1}^{n} i^5 = \dfrac{n^2(n+1)^2(2n^2+2n-1)}{12}$

16. $\displaystyle\sum_{i=1}^{n} i^4 = \dfrac{n(n+1)(2n+1)(3n^2+3n-1)}{30}$

17. $\displaystyle\sum_{i=1}^{n} i(i+1) = \dfrac{n(n+1)(n+2)}{3}$

18. $\displaystyle\sum_{i=1}^{n} \dfrac{1}{(2i-1)(2i+1)} = \dfrac{n}{2n+1}$

In Exercises 19–28, find the sum using the formulas for the sums of powers of integers.

19. $\displaystyle\sum_{n=1}^{15} n$

20. $\displaystyle\sum_{n=1}^{30} n$

21. $\displaystyle\sum_{n=1}^{6} n^2$

22. $\displaystyle\sum_{n=1}^{10} n^3$

23. $\displaystyle\sum_{n=1}^{5} n^4$

24. $\displaystyle\sum_{n=1}^{8} n^5$

25. $\displaystyle\sum_{n=1}^{6} (n^2 - n)$

26. $\displaystyle\sum_{n=1}^{20} (n^3 - n)$

27. $\displaystyle\sum_{i=1}^{6} (6i - 8i^3)$

28. $\displaystyle\sum_{j=1}^{10} \left(3 - \tfrac{1}{2}j + \tfrac{1}{2}j^2\right)$

In Exercises 29–34, find a formula for the sum of the first n terms of the sequence.

29. $1, 5, 9, 13, \ldots$

30. $25, 22, 19, 16, \ldots$

31. $1, \dfrac{9}{10}, \dfrac{81}{100}, \dfrac{729}{1000}, \ldots$

32. $3, -\dfrac{9}{2}, \dfrac{27}{4}, -\dfrac{81}{8}, \ldots$

33. $\dfrac{1}{4}, \dfrac{1}{12}, \dfrac{1}{24}, \dfrac{1}{40}, \ldots, \dfrac{1}{2n(n+1)}, \ldots$

34. $\dfrac{1}{2 \cdot 3}, \dfrac{1}{3 \cdot 4}, \dfrac{1}{4 \cdot 5}, \dfrac{1}{5 \cdot 6}, \ldots,$

$\dfrac{1}{(n+1)(n+2)}, \ldots$

In Exercises 35–40, prove the inequality for the indicated integer values of n.

35. $n! > 2^n, \quad n \ge 4$

36. $\left(\tfrac{4}{3}\right)^n > n, \quad n \ge 7$

37. $\dfrac{1}{\sqrt{1}} + \dfrac{1}{\sqrt{2}} + \dfrac{1}{\sqrt{3}} + \cdots + \dfrac{1}{\sqrt{n}} > \sqrt{n}, \quad n \ge 2$

38. $\left(\dfrac{x}{y}\right)^{n+1} < \left(\dfrac{x}{y}\right)^n, \quad n \ge 1$ and $0 < x < y$

39. $(1 + a)^n \ge na, \quad n \ge 1$ and $a > 0$

40. $2n^2 > (n+1)^2, \quad n \ge 3$

In Exercises 41–48, use mathematical induction to prove the property for all positive integers n.

41. $(ab)^n = a^n b^n$

42. $\left(\dfrac{a}{b}\right)^n = \dfrac{a^n}{b^n}$

43. If $x_1 \ne 0, x_2 \ne 0, \ldots, x_n \ne 0$, then

$(x_1 x_2 x_3 \cdots x_n)^{-1} = x_1^{-1} x_2^{-1} x_3^{-1} \cdots x_n^{-1}.$

44. If $x_1 > 0, x_2 > 0, \ldots, x_n > 0$, then

$\ln(x_1 x_2 \cdots x_n) = \ln x_1 + \ln x_2 + \cdots + \ln x_n.$

45. Generalized Distributive Law:

$x(y_1 + y_2 + \cdots + y_n) = xy_1 + xy_2 + \cdots + xy_n$

46. $(a + bi)^n$ and $(a - bi)^n$ are complex conjugates for all $n \ge 1$.

47. A factor of $(n^3 + 3n^2 + 2n)$ is 3.

48. A factor of $(2^{2n-1} + 3^{2n-1})$ is 5.

In Exercises 49–54, write the first six terms of the sequence. Then calculate the first and second differences of the sequence. Does the sequence have a linear model, a quadratic model, or neither?

49. $a_1 = 0$

$a_n = a_{n-1} + 3$

50. $a_1 = 2$

$a_n = a_{n-1} + 2$

51. $a_1 = 3$

$a_n = a_{n-1} - n$

52. $a_2 = -3$

$a_n = -2a_{n-1}$

53. $a_0 = 2$

$a_n = (a_{n-1})^2$

54. $a_0 = 0$

$a_n = a_{n-1} + n$

In Exercises 55–58, find a quadratic model for the sequence with the indicated terms.

55. $a_0 = 3,\ a_1 = 3,\ a_4 = 15$

56. $a_0 = 7,\ a_1 = 6,\ a_3 = 10$

57. $a_0 = -3,\ a_2 = 1,\ a_4 = 9$

58. $a_0 = 3,\ a_2 = 0,\ a_6 = 36$

▶ Model It

59. *Data Analysis*   The table shows the total prize money awarded (in millions of dollars) at professional rodeos from 1995 through 1999.   (Source: Professional Rodeo Cowboys Association)

Year, n	Prize money, a_n
1995	24.5
1996	26.4
1997	28.0
1998	29.9
1999	31.1

(a) Find the first differences of the data shown in the table.

(b) Use your results from part (a) to determine whether a linear model can be used to approximate the data. If so, find a model. Let a_n represent the total prize money awarded and let n represent the year, with $n = 5$ corresponding to 1995.

(c) Use the model to estimate the total prize money awarded in 2004.

Synthesis

60. *Writing*   In your own words, explain what is meant by a proof by mathematical induction.

True or False?   In Exercises 61–64, determine whether the statement is true or false. Justify your answer.

61. If the statement P_1 is true but the true statement P_6 does *not* imply that the statement P_7 is true, then P_n is not necessarily true for all positive integers n.

62. If the statement P_k is true and P_k implies P_{k+1}, then P_1 is also true.

63. If the second differences of a sequence are all zero, then the sequence is arithmetic.

64. A sequence with n terms has $n - 1$ second differences.

Review

In Exercises 65–68, find the product.

65. $(2x^2 - 1)^2$

66. $(2x - y)^2$

67. $(5 - 4x)^3$

68. $(2x - 4y)^3$

In Exercises 69–72, use synthetic division to divide.

69. $(x^3 + x^2 - 10x + 8) \div (x - 1)$

70. $(x^3 - 4x^2 - 29x - 24) \div (x - 8)$

71. $(4x^3 + 11x^2 - 43x + 10) \div (x + 5)$

72. $(6x^3 - 35x^2 - 8x + 12) \div (x - 6)$

In Exercises 73–76, (a) identify all intercepts, (b) find any vertical and horizontal asymptotes, (c) check for symmetry, and (d) plot additional solution points as needed and sketch the graph of the rational function.

73. $f(x) = \dfrac{x}{x + 3}$

74. $g(x) = \dfrac{x^2}{x^2 - 4}$

75. $h(t) = \dfrac{t - 7}{t}$

76. $f(x) = \dfrac{5 + x}{1 - x}$

9.5 The Binomial Theorem

Rob Gage/Getty Images

Binomial Coefficients

Recall that a *binomial* is a polynomial that has two terms. In this section, you will study a formula that gives a quick method of raising a binomial to a power. To begin, look at the expansion of $(x + y)^n$ for several values of n.

$$(x + y)^0 = 1$$

$$(x + y)^1 = x + y$$

$$(x + y)^2 = x^2 + 2xy + y^2$$

$$(x + y)^3 = x^3 + 3x^2y + 3xy^2 + y^3$$

$$(x + y)^4 = x^4 + 4x^3y + 6x^2y^2 + 4xy^3 + y^4$$

$$(x + y)^5 = x^5 + 5x^4y + 10x^3y^2 + 10x^2y^3 + 5xy^4 + y^5$$

There are several observations you can make about these expansions.

1. In each expansion, there are $n + 1$ terms.
2. In each expansion, x and y have symmetrical roles. The powers of x decrease by 1 in successive terms, whereas the powers of y increase by 1.
3. The sum of the powers of each term is n. For instance, in the expansion of $(x + y)^5$, the sum of the powers of each term is 5.

$$4 + 1 = 5 \quad 3 + 2 = 5$$

$$(x + y)^5 = x^5 + 5x^4y^1 + 10x^3y^2 + 10x^2y^3 + 5x^1y^4 + y^5$$

4. The coefficients increase and then decrease in a symmetric pattern.

The coefficients of a binomial expansion are called **binomial coefficients.** To find them, you can use the **Binomial Theorem.**

The Binomial Theorem

In the expansion of $(x + y)^n$

$$(x + y)^n = x^n + nx^{n-1}y + \cdots + {}_nC_r\, x^{n-r} y^r + \cdots + nxy^{n-1} + y^n$$

the coefficient of $x^{n-r} y^r$ is

$${}_nC_r = \frac{n!}{(n - r)!r!}.$$

The symbol $\binom{n}{r}$ is often used in place of ${}_nC_r$ to denote binomial coefficients.

For a proof of the Binomial Theorem, see Proofs in Mathematics on page 695.

Technology

Most graphing calculators are programmed to evaluate $_nC_r$. Consult your user's manual and then evaluate $_8C_5$. You should get an answer of 56.

Example 1 ▶ Finding Binomial Coefficients

Find each binomial coefficient.

a. $_8C_2$ **b.** $\dbinom{10}{3}$ **c.** $_7C_0$ **d.** $\dbinom{8}{8}$

Solution

a. $_8C_2 = \dfrac{8!}{6! \cdot 2!} = \dfrac{(8 \cdot 7) \cdot 6!}{6! \cdot 2!} = \dfrac{8 \cdot 7}{2 \cdot 1} = 28$

b. $\dbinom{10}{3} = \dfrac{10!}{7! \cdot 3!} = \dfrac{(10 \cdot 9 \cdot 8) \cdot 7!}{7! \cdot 3!} = \dfrac{10 \cdot 9 \cdot 8}{3 \cdot 2 \cdot 1} = 120$

c. $_7C_0 = \dfrac{7!}{7! \cdot 0!} = 1$ **d.** $\dbinom{8}{8} = \dfrac{8!}{0! \cdot 8!} = 1$

When $r \neq 0$ and $r \neq n$, as in parts (a) and (b) above, there is a simple pattern for evaluating binomial coefficients.

$$\overbrace{_8C_2 = \dfrac{8 \cdot 7}{2 \cdot 1}}^{\text{2 factors}} \quad \text{and} \quad \overbrace{\dbinom{10}{3} = \dfrac{10 \cdot 9 \cdot 8}{3 \cdot 2 \cdot 1}}^{\text{3 factors}}$$

2 factors   3 factors

Example 2 ▶ Finding Binomial Coefficients

Find each binomial coefficient.

a. $_7C_3$ **b.** $\dbinom{7}{4}$ **c.** $_{12}C_1$ **d.** $\dbinom{12}{11}$

Solution

a. $_7C_3 = \dfrac{7 \cdot 6 \cdot 5}{3 \cdot 2 \cdot 1} = 35$

b. $\dbinom{7}{4} = \dfrac{7 \cdot 6 \cdot 5 \cdot 4}{4 \cdot 3 \cdot 2 \cdot 1} = 35$

c. $_{12}C_1 = \dfrac{12}{1} = 12$

d. $\dbinom{12}{11} = \dfrac{12!}{1! \cdot 11!} = \dfrac{(12) \cdot 11!}{1! \cdot 11!} = \dfrac{12}{1} = 12$

It is not a coincidence that the results in parts (a) and (b) of Example 2 are the same and that the results in parts (c) and (d) are the same. In general, it is true that

$$_nC_r = {_nC_{n-r}}.$$

This shows the symmetric property of binomial coefficients that was identified earlier.

Pascal's Triangle

There is a convenient way to remember the pattern for binomial coefficients. By arranging the coefficients in a triangular pattern, you obtain **Pascal's Triangle.** This triangle is named after the famous French mathematician Blaise Pascal (1623–1662).

Complete the table and describe the result.

n	r	$_nC_r$	$_nC_{n-r}$
9	5		
7	1		
12	4		
6	0		
10	7		

What characteristic of Pascal's Triangle is illustrated by this table?

```
                    1
                 1     1
              1     2     1
           1     3     3     1
        1     4     6     4     1
     1     5    10    10     5     1              4 + 6 = 10
  1     6    15    20    15     6     1
1     7    21    35    35    21     7     1      1  15 + 6 = 21
```

The first and last numbers in each row of Pascal's Triangle are 1. Every other number in each row is formed by adding the two numbers immediately above the number. Pascal noticed that numbers in this triangle are precisely the same numbers that are the coefficients of binomial expansions, as follows.

$$(x + y)^0 = 1 \qquad \text{0th row}$$

$$(x + y)^1 = 1x + 1y \qquad \text{1st row}$$

$$(x + y)^2 = 1x^2 + 2xy + 1y^2 \qquad \text{2nd row}$$

$$(x + y)^3 = 1x^3 + 3x^2y + 3xy^2 + 1y^3 \qquad \text{3rd row}$$

$$(x + y)^4 = 1x^4 + 4x^3y + 6x^2y^2 + 4xy^3 + 1y^4 \qquad \vdots$$

$$(x + y)^5 = 1x^5 + 5x^4y + 10x^3y^2 + 10x^2y^3 + 5xy^4 + 1y^5$$

$$(x + y)^6 = 1x^6 + 6x^5y + 15x^4y^2 + 20x^3y^3 + 15x^2y^4 + 6xy^5 + 1y^6$$

$$(x + y)^7 = 1x^7 + 7x^6y + 21x^5y^2 + 35x^4y^3 + 35x^3y^4 + 21x^2y^5 + 7xy^6 + 1y^7$$

The top row in Pascal's Triangle is called the *zeroth row* because it corresponds to the binomial expansion $(x + y)^0 = 1$. Similarly, the next row is called the *first row* because it corresponds to the binomial expansion $(x + y)^1 = 1(x) + 1(y)$. In general, the *nth row* in Pascal's Triangle gives the coefficients of $(x + y)^n$.

Example 3 ▶ **Using Pascal's Triangle**

Use the seventh row of Pascal's Triangle to find the binomial coefficients.

$$_8C_0, \,_8C_1, \,_8C_2, \,_8C_3, \,_8C_4, \,_8C_5, \,_8C_6, \,_8C_7, \,_8C_8$$

Solution

```
      1      7      21     35     35     21      7      1
     / \    / \    / \    / \    / \    / \    / \    / \
   1     8     28    56     70    56    28      8      1
   |     |     |     |      |     |     |       |      |
 8C0   8C1   8C2   8C3    8C4   8C5   8C6    8C7    8C8
```

Binomial Expansions

As mentioned at the beginning of this section, when you write out the coefficients for a binomial that is raised to a power, you are **expanding a binomial.** The formulas for binomial coefficients give you an easy way to expand binomials, as demonstrated in the next four examples.

Example 4 ▶ **Expanding a Binomial**

Write the expansion for the expression

$(x + 1)^3$.

Solution

The binomial coefficients from the third row of Pascal's Triangle are

$1, 3, 3, 1$.

So, the expansion is as follows.

$(x + 1)^3 = (1)x^3 + (3)x^2(1) + (3)x(1^2) + (1)(1^3)$

$= x^3 + 3x^2 + 3x + 1$

To expand binomials representing *differences* rather than sums, you alternate signs. Here are two examples.

$(x - 1)^3 = x^3 - 3x^2 + 3x - 1$

$(x - 1)^4 = x^4 - 4x^3 + 6x^2 - 4x + 1$

Example 5 ▶ **Expanding a Binomial**

Write the expansion for each expression.

a. $(2x - 3)^4$ **b.** $(x - 2y)^4$

Solution

a. The binomial coefficients from the fourth row of Pascal's Triangle are

$1, 4, 6, 4, 1$.

So, the expansion is as follows.

$(2x - 3)^4 = (1)(2x)^4 - (4)(2x)^3(3) + (6)(2x)^2(3^2) - (4)(2x)(3^3) + (1)(3^4)$

$= 16x^4 - 96x^3 + 216x^2 - 216x + 81$

b. The binomial coefficients from the fourth row of Pascal's Triangle are

$1, 4, 6, 4, 1$.

So, the expansion is as follows.

$(x - 2y)^4 = (1)x^4 - (4)x^3(2y) + (6)x^2(2y)^2 - (4)x(2y)^3 + (1)(2y)^4$

$= x^4 - 8x^3y + 24x^2y^2 - 32xy^3 + 16y^4$

Historical Note

Precious Mirror "Pascal's" Triangle and forms of the Binomial Theorem were known in Eastern cultures prior to the Western "discovery" of the theorem. A Chinese text entitled *Precious Mirror* contains a triangle of binomial expansions through the eighth power.

Activities

1. Expand and simplify $(x - 3)^4$.

Answer:
$x^4 - 12x^3 + 54x^2 - 108x + 81$

2. Find the fifth term in the expansion of $(2x + 1)^9$.

Answer:
$\dfrac{9 \cdot 8 \cdot 7 \cdot 6 \cdot 5}{5 \cdot 4 \cdot 3 \cdot 2 \cdot 1}(2x)^5(1)^4 = 4032x^5$

3. Evaluate $_8C_3$.

Answer: $\dfrac{8 \cdot 7 \cdot 6}{3 \cdot 2 \cdot 1} = 56$

Group Activity

Add the binomial coefficients in each of the first five rows of Pascal's Triangle. What pattern do you see? Work together to use the pattern to find the sums of the terms in the 10th, 15th, and 20th rows of Pascal's Triangle. Check your answer by actually adding the terms of the 10th, 15th, and 20th rows.

Example 6 ▶   **Expanding a Binomial**

Write the expansion for $(x^2 + 4)^3$.

Solution

Use the third row of Pascal's Triangle, as follows.

$$(x^2 + 4)^3 = (1)(x^2)^3 + (3)(x^2)^2(4) + (3)x^2(4^2) + (1)(4^3)$$
$$= x^6 + 12x^4 + 48x^2 + 64$$

Example 7 ▶   **Finding a Term in a Binomial Expansion**

a. Find the sixth term of $(a + 2b)^8$.

b. Find the coefficient of the term a^6b^5 in the expansion of $(3a - 2b)^{11}$.

Solution

a. For the first term of the binomial expansion, you would use $n = 8$ and $r = 0$ to get ${}_8C_0a^{8-0}(2b)^0$. For the second term of the binomial expansion, you would use $n = 8$ and $r = 1$ to get ${}_8C_1a^{8-1}(2b)^1$. So, for the sixth term of this binomial expansion, use $n = 8$ and $r = 5$ to obtain

$${}_8C_5a^{8-5}(2b)^5 = 56 \cdot a^3 \cdot (2b)^5$$
$$= 56(2^5)a^3b^5$$
$$= 1792a^3b^5.$$

b. From the Binomial Theorem, you can see that the $(r + 1)$th term is ${}_nC_r x^{n-r} y^r$. So in this case, $n = 11$, $r = 5$, $x = 3a$, and $y = -2b$. Substitute these values to obtain

$${}_nC_r x^{n-r} y^r = {}_{11}C_5(3a)^6(-2b)^5$$
$$= (462)(729a^6)(-32b^5)$$
$$= -10,777,536a^6b^5.$$

So, the coefficient is $-10,777,536$.

Writing ABOUT MATHEMATICS

Error Analysis   You are a math instructor and receive the following solutions from one of your students on a quiz. Find the error(s) in each solution. Discuss ways that your student could avoid the error(s) in the future.

a. Find the second term in the expansion of $(2x - 3y)^5$.

$5(2x)^4(3y)^2 = 720x^4y^2$

b. Find the fourth term in the expansion of $(\frac{1}{2}x + 7y)^6$.

${}_6C_4(\frac{1}{2}x)^2(7y)^4 = 9003.75x^2y^4$

9.5 Exercises

In Exercises 1–10, find the binomial coefficient.

1. $_5C_3$

2. $_8C_6$

3. $_{12}C_0$

4. $_{20}C_{20}$

5. $_{20}C_{15}$

6. $_{12}C_5$

7. $\dbinom{10}{4}$

8. $\dbinom{10}{6}$

9. $\dbinom{100}{98}$

10. $\dbinom{100}{2}$

In Exercises 11–14, evaluate using Pascal's Triangle.

11. $\dbinom{8}{5}$

12. $\dbinom{8}{7}$

13. $_7C_4$

14. $_6C_3$

In Exercises 15–34, use the Binomial Theorem to expand and simplify the expression.

15. $(x + 1)^4$

16. $(x + 1)^6$

17. $(a + 6)^4$

18. $(a + 5)^5$

19. $(y - 4)^3$

20. $(y - 2)^5$

21. $(x + y)^5$

22. $(c + d)^3$

23. $(r + 3s)^6$

24. $(x + 2y)^4$

25. $(3a - b)^5$

26. $(2x - y)^5$

27. $(1 - 2x)^3$

28. $(5 - 3y)^3$

29. $(x^2 + 5)^4$

30. $(x^2 + y^2)^6$

31. $\left(\dfrac{1}{x} + y\right)^5$

32. $\left(\dfrac{1}{x} + 2y\right)^6$

33. $2(x - 3)^4 + 5(x - 3)^2$

34. $3(x + 1)^5 - 4(x + 1)^3$

In Exercises 35–38, expand the binomial using Pascal's Triangle to determine the coefficients.

35. $(2t - s)^5$

36. $(3 - 2z)^4$

37. $(x + 2y)^5$

38. $(2v + 3)^6$

In Exercises 39–46, find the specified nth term in the expansion of the binomial.

39. $(x + y)^{10}$, $\quad n = 4$

40. $(x - y)^6$, $\quad n = 7$

41. $(x - 6y)^5$, $\quad n = 3$

42. $(x - 10z)^7$, $\quad n = 4$

43. $(4x + 3y)^9$, $\quad n = 8$

44. $(5a + 6b)^5$, $\quad n = 5$

45. $(10x - 3y)^{12}$, $\quad n = 9$

46. $(7x + 2y)^{15}$, $\quad n = 7$

In Exercises 47–54, find the coefficient a of the term in the expansion of the binomial.

Binomial	Term
47. $(x + 3)^{12}$	ax^5
48. $(x^2 + 3)^{12}$	ax^8
49. $(x - 2y)^{10}$	ax^8y^2
50. $(4x - y)^{10}$	ax^2y^8
51. $(3x - 2y)^9$	ax^4y^5
52. $(2x - 3y)^8$	ax^6y^2
53. $(x^2 + y)^{10}$	ax^8y^6
54. $(z^2 - t)^{10}$	az^4t^8

In Exercises 55–58, use the Binomial Theorem to expand and simplify the expression.

55. $\left(\sqrt{x} + 3\right)^4$

56. $\left(2\sqrt{t} - 1\right)^3$

57. $(x^{2/3} - y^{1/3})^3$

58. $(u^{3/5} + 2)^5$

In Exercises 59–62, expand the expression in the difference quotient and simplify.

$$\dfrac{f(x + h) - f(x)}{h} \qquad \text{Difference quotient}$$

59. $f(x) = x^3$

60. $f(x) = x^4$

61. $f(x) = \sqrt{x}$

62. $f(x) = \dfrac{1}{x}$

In Exercises 63–68, use the Binomial Theorem to expand the complex number. Simplify your result.

63. $(1 + i)^4$

64. $(2 - i)^5$

65. $(2 - 3i)^6$

66. $\left(5 + \sqrt{-9}\right)^3$

67. $\left(-\dfrac{1}{2} + \dfrac{\sqrt{3}}{2}i\right)^3$

68. $\left(5 - \sqrt{3}i\right)^4$

Approximation In Exercises 69–72, use the Binomial Theorem to approximate the quantity accurate to three decimal places. For example, in Exercise 69, use the expansion

$$(1.02)^8 = (1 + 0.02)^8 = 1 + 8(0.02) + 28(0.02)^2 + \cdots.$$

69. $(1.02)^8$

70. $(2.005)^{10}$

71. $(2.99)^{12}$

72. $(1.98)^9$

Graphical Reasoning In Exercises 73 and 74, use a graphing utility to graph f and g in the same viewing window. What is the relationship between the two graphs? Use the Binomial Theorem to write the polynomial function g in standard form.

73. $f(x) = x^3 - 4x, \quad g(x) = f(x + 4)$

74. $f(x) = -x^4 + 4x^2 - 1, \quad g(x) = f(x - 3)$

Probability In Exercises 75–78, consider n independent trials of an experiment in which each trial has two possible outcomes: "success" or "failure." The probability of a success on each trial is p, and the probability of a failure is $q = 1 - p$. In this context, the term $_nC_k\, p^k q^{n-k}$ in the expansion of $(p + q)^n$ gives the probability of k successes in the n trials of the experiment.

75. A fair coin is tossed seven times. To find the probability of obtaining four heads, evaluate the term

$$_7C_4\left(\frac{1}{2}\right)^4\left(\frac{1}{2}\right)^3$$

in the expansion of $\left(\frac{1}{2} + \frac{1}{2}\right)^7$.

76. The probability of a baseball player getting a hit during any given time at bat is $\frac{1}{4}$. To find the probability that the player gets three hits during the next 10 times at bat, evaluate the term

$$_{10}C_3\left(\frac{1}{4}\right)^3\left(\frac{3}{4}\right)^7$$

in the expansion of $\left(\frac{1}{4} + \frac{3}{4}\right)^{10}$.

77. The probability of a sales representative making a sale with any one customer is $\frac{1}{3}$. The sales representative makes eight contacts a day. To find the probability of making four sales, evaluate the term

$$_8C_4\left(\frac{1}{3}\right)^4\left(\frac{2}{3}\right)^4$$

in the expansion of $\left(\frac{1}{3} + \frac{2}{3}\right)^8$.

78. To find the probability that the sales representative in Exercise 77 makes four sales if the probability of a sale with any one customer is $\frac{1}{2}$, evaluate the term

$$_8C_4\left(\frac{1}{2}\right)^4\left(\frac{1}{2}\right)^4$$

in the expansion of $\left(\frac{1}{2} + \frac{1}{2}\right)^8$.

▶ **Model It**

79. *Data Analysis* The table shows the per capita consumption of bottled water $f(t)$ (in gallons) in the United States from 1985 through 1999. (Source: U.S. Department of Agriculture)

Year, t	Consumption, $f(t)$
1985	4.5
1986	5.0
1987	5.7
1988	6.5
1989	7.3
1990	8.0
1991	8.0
1992	8.2
1993	9.4
1994	10.7
1995	11.6
1996	12.5
1997	13.1
1998	16.0
1999	18.1

(a) Use the *regression* feature of a graphing utility to find a cubic model for the data. Let t represent the year, with $t = 5$ corresponding to 1985.

(b) Use a graphing utility to plot the data and the model in the same viewing window.

(c) You want to adjust the model so that $t = 0$ corresponds to 1990 rather than 1980. To do this, you shift the graph of f 10 units *to the left* to obtain $g(t) = f(t + 10)$. Write $g(t)$ in standard form.

(d) Use a graphing utility to graph g in the same viewing window as f.

(e) Use both models to estimate the per capita consumption of bottled water in 2004. Do you obtain the same answer?

(f) Describe the overall trend in the data. What factors do you think may have contributed to the increase in the per capita consumption of bottled water?

80. *Life Insurance* The average amount of life insurance per household $f(t)$ (in thousands of dollars) from 1980 through 1999 can be approximated by

$$f(t) = 0.020t^2 + 5.16t + 41.2, \quad 0 \le t \le 19$$

where $t = 0$ represents 1980 (see figure). (Source: American Council of Life Insurance)

Year (0 ↔ 1980)

You want to adjust this model so that $t = 0$ corresponds to 1990 rather than 1980. To do this, you shift the graph of f 10 units *to the left* and obtain $g(t) = f(t + 10)$.

(a) Write $g(t)$ in standard form.

(b) Use a graphing utility to graph f and g in the same viewing window.

Synthesis

True or False? **In Exercises 81–83, determine whether the statement is true or false. Justify your answer.**

81. The Binomial Theorem could be used to produce each row of Pascal's Triangle.

82. A binomial that represents a difference cannot always be accurately expanded using the Binomial Theorem.

83. The x^{10}-term and the x^{14}-term of the expansion of $(x^2 + 3)^{12}$ have identical coefficients.

84. *Writing* In your own words, explain how to form the rows of Pascal's Triangle.

85. Form rows 8–10 of Pascal's Triangle.

86. *Think About It* How many terms are in the expansion of $(x + y)^n$?

87. *Think About It* How do the expansions of $(x + y)^n$ and $(x - y)^n$ differ?

88. *Graphical Reasoning* Which two functions have identical graphs, and why? Use a graphing utility to graph the functions in the given order and in the same viewing window. Compare the graphs.

(a) $f(x) = (1 - x)^3$ (b) $g(x) = 1 - x^3$

(c) $h(x) = 1 + 3x + 3x^2 + x^3$

(d) $k(x) = 1 - 3x + 3x^2 - x^3$

(e) $p(x) = 1 + 3x - 3x^2 + x^3$

Proof **In Exercises 89–92, prove the property for all integers r and n where $0 \le r \le n$.**

89. ${}_nC_r = {}_nC_{n-r}$

90. ${}_nC_0 - {}_nC_1 + {}_nC_2 - \cdots \pm {}_nC_n = 0$

91. ${}_{n+1}C_r = {}_nC_r + {}_nC_{r-1}$

92. The sum of the numbers in the nth row of Pascal's Triangle is 2^n.

Review

In Exercises 93–96, the graph of $y = g(x)$ is shown. Graph f and use the graph to write an equation for the graph of g.

93. $f(x) = x^2$

94. $f(x) = x^2$

95. $f(x) = \sqrt{x}$

96. $f(x) = \sqrt{x}$

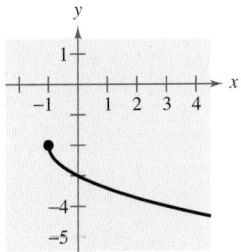

In Exercises 97 and 98, find the inverse of the matrix.

97. $\begin{bmatrix} -6 & 5 \\ -5 & 4 \end{bmatrix}$

98. $\begin{bmatrix} 1.2 & -2.3 \\ -2 & 4 \end{bmatrix}$

9.6 Counting Principles

▶ What you should learn

- How to solve simple counting problems
- How to use the Fundamental Counting Principle to solve counting problems
- How to use permutations to solve counting problems
- How to use combinations to solve counting problems

▶ Why you should learn it

You can use counting principles to solve counting problems that occur in real life. For instance, in Exercise 67 on page 671, you are asked to use counting principles to determine the number of possible ways of selecting the winning numbers in the Powerball lottery.

Simple Counting Problems

This section and Section 9.7 present a brief introduction to some of the basic counting principles and their application to probability. In Section 9.7 you will see that much of probability has to do with counting the number of ways an event can occur. The following two examples describe simple counting problems.

Example 1 ▶ Selecting Pairs of Numbers at Random

Eight pieces of paper are numbered from 1 to 8 and placed in a box. One piece of paper is drawn from the box, its number is written down, and the piece of paper is *replaced in the box*. Then, a second piece of paper is drawn from the box, and its number is written down. Finally, the two numbers are added together. How many different ways can a sum of 12 be obtained?

Solution

To solve this problem, count the different ways that a sum of 12 can be obtained using two numbers from 1 to 8.

First number	4	5	6	7	8
Second number	8	7	6	5	4

From this list, you can see that a sum of 12 can occur in five different ways.

Example 2 ▶ Selecting Pairs of Numbers at Random

Eight pieces of paper are numbered from 1 to 8 and placed in a box. Two pieces of paper are drawn from the box *at the same time*, and the numbers on the pieces of paper are written down and totaled. How many different ways can a sum of 12 be obtained?

Solution

To solve this problem, count the different ways that a sum of 12 can be obtained *using two different numbers* from 1 to 8.

First number	4	5	7	8
Second number	8	7	5	4

So, a sum of 12 can be obtained in four different ways.

The difference between the counting problems in Examples 1 and 2 can be expressed by saying that the random selection in Example 1 occurs **with replacement,** whereas the random selection in Example 2 occurs **without replacement,** which eliminates the possibility of choosing two 6's.

You may want to consider opening class by asking students if they can predict which offers more choices for license plates: (a) a plate with three different letters of the alphabet in any order or (b) a plate with four different nonzero digits in any order. You may want to end class by verifying the answers: (a) offers $26 \cdot 25 \cdot 24 = 15{,}600$ choices and (b) offers $9 \cdot 8 \cdot 7 \cdot 6 = 3024$ choices.

The Fundamental Counting Principle

Examples 1 and 2 describe simple counting problems in which you can *list* each possible way that an event can occur. When it is possible, this is always the best way to solve a counting problem. However, some events can occur in so many different ways that it is not feasible to write out the entire list. In such cases, you must rely on formulas and counting principles. The most important of these is the **Fundamental Counting Principle.**

Fundamental Counting Principle

Let E_1 and E_2 be two events. The first event E_1 can occur in m_1 different ways. After E_1 has occurred, E_2 can occur in m_2 different ways. The number of ways that the two events can occur is $m_1 \cdot m_2$.

The Fundamental Counting Principle can be extended to three or more events. For instance, the number of ways that three events E_1, E_2, and E_3 can occur is $m_1 \cdot m_2 \cdot m_3$.

 Using the Fundamental Counting Principle

How many different pairs of letters from the English alphabet are possible?

Solution

There are two events in this situation. The first event is the choice of the first letter, and the second event is the choice of the second letter. Because the English alphabet contains 26 letters, it follows that the number of two-letter pairs is $26 \cdot 26 = 676$.

 Using the Fundamental Counting Principle

Telephone numbers in the United States currently have 10 digits. The first three are the *area code* and the next seven are the *local telephone number*. How many different telephone numbers are possible within each area code? (Note that at this time, a local telephone number cannot begin with 0 or 1.)

Solution

Because the first digit cannot be 0 or 1, there are only eight choices for the first digit. For each of the other six digits, there are 10 choices.

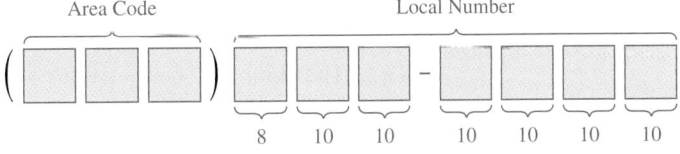

So, the number of local telephone numbers that are possible *within* each area code is $8 \cdot 10 \cdot 10 \cdot 10 \cdot 10 \cdot 10 \cdot 10 = 8{,}000{,}000$.

Permutations

One important application of the Fundamental Counting Principle is in determining the number of ways that n elements can be arranged (in order). An ordering of n elements is called a **permutation** of the elements.

Definition of Permutation

A **permutation** of n different elements is an ordering of the elements such that one element is first, one is second, one is third, and so on.

Example 5 ▶ **Finding the Number of Permutations of n Elements**

How many permutations are possible for the letters A, B, C, D, E, and F?

Solution

Consider the following reasoning.

First position: Any of the *six* letters

Second position: Any of the remaining *five* letters

Third position: Any of the remaining *four* letters

Fourth position: Any of the remaining *three* letters

Fifth position: Any of the remaining *two* letters

Sixth position: The *one* remaining letter

So, the numbers of choices for the six positions are as follows.

Permutations of six letters

6	5	4	3	2	1

The total number of permutations of the six letters is

$$6! = 6 \cdot 5 \cdot 4 \cdot 3 \cdot 2 \cdot 1$$

$$= 720.$$

Number of Permutations of n Elements

The number of permutations of n elements is

$$n \cdot (n - 1) \cdots 4 \cdot 3 \cdot 2 \cdot 1 = n!.$$

In other words, there are $n!$ different ways that n elements can be ordered.

Additional Example

How many permutations are possible for the numbers 0, 1, 2, and 3?

Solution

$4! = 24$

Eleven thoroughbred racehorses hold the title of Triple Crown winner for winning the Kentucky Derby, the Preakness, and the Belmont Stakes in the same year. Forty-six horses have won two out of the three races.

It is useful, on occasion, to order a *subset* of a collection of elements rather than the entire collection. For example, you might want to choose and order *r* elements out of a collection of *n* elements. Such an ordering is called a **permutation of *n* elements taken *r* at a time.**

Example 6 ▶ **Counting Horse Race Finishes**

Eight horses are running in a race. In how many different ways can these horses come in first, second, and third? (Assume that there are no ties.)

Solution

Here are the different possibilities.

Win (first position): *Eight* choices

Place (second position): *Seven* choices

Show (third position): *Six* choices

Using the Fundamental Counting Principle, multiply these three numbers together to obtain the following.

Different orders of horses

So, there are 8 · 7 · 6 = 336 different orders.

Technology

Most graphing calculators are programmed to evaluate $_nP_r$. Consult your user's manual and then evaluate $_8P_5$. You should get an answer of 6720.

Permutations of *n* Elements Taken *r* at a Time

The number of permutations of *n* elements taken *r* at a time is

$$_nP_r = \frac{n!}{(n-r)!}$$

$$= n(n-1)(n-2)\cdots(n-r+1).$$

Using this formula, you can rework Example 6 to find that the number of permutations of eight horses taken three at a time is

$$_8P_3 = \frac{8!}{(8-3)!}$$

$$= \frac{8!}{5!}$$

$$= \frac{8 \cdot 7 \cdot 6 \cdot 5!}{5!}$$

$$= 336$$

which is the same answer obtained in the example.

Remember that for permutations, order is important. So, if you are looking at the possible permutations of the letters A, B, C, and D taken three at a time, the permutations (A, B, D) and (B, A, D) are counted as different because the *order* of the elements is different.

Suppose, however, that you are asked to find the possible permutations of the letters A, A, B, and C. The total number of permutations of the four letters would be $_4P_4 = 4!$. However, not all of these arrangements would be *distinguishable* because there are two A's in the list. To find the number of distinguishable permutations, you can use the following formula.

Distinguishable Permutations

Suppose a set of n objects has n_1 of one kind of object, n_2 of a second kind, n_3 of a third kind, and so on, with

$$n = n_1 + n_2 + n_3 + \cdots + n_k .$$

Then the number of **distinguishable permutations** of the n objects is

$$\frac{n!}{n_1! \cdot n_2! \cdot n_3! \cdots \cdot n_k!}.$$

Example 7 ▶   Distinguishable Permutations

In how many distinguishable ways can the letters in BANANA be written?

Solution

This word has six letters, of which three are A's, two are N's, and one is a B. So, the number of distinguishable ways the letters can be written is

$$\frac{n!}{n_1! \cdot n_2! \cdot n_3!} = \frac{6!}{3! \cdot 2! \cdot 1!}$$

$$= \frac{6 \cdot 5 \cdot 4 \cdot 3!}{3! \cdot 2!}$$

$$= 60.$$

The 60 different distinguishable permutations are as follows.

Additional Example

In how many different ways can the letters in INDIANA be written?

Solution

630

AAABNN	AAANBN	AAANNB	AABANN	AABNAN	AABNNA
AANABN	AANANB	AANBAN	AANBNA	AANNAB	AANNBA
ABAANN	ABANAN	ABANNA	ABNAAN	ABNANA	ABNNAA
ANAABN	ANAANB	ANABAN	ANABNA	ANANAB	ANANBA
ANBAAN	ANBANA	ANBNAA	ANNAAB	ANNABA	ANNBAA
BAAANN	BAANAN	BAANNA	BANAAN	BANANA	BANNAA
BNAAAN	BNAANA	BNANAA	BNNAAA	NAAABN	NAAANB
NAABAN	NAABNA	NAANAB	NAANBA	NABAAN	NABANA
NABNAA	NANAAB	NANABA	NANBAA	NBAAAN	NBAANA
NBANAA	NBNAAA	NNAAAB	NNAABA	NNABAA	NNBAAA

Combinations

When you count the number of possible permutations of a set of elements, *order* is important. As a final topic in this section, you will look at a method of selecting subsets of a larger set in which order is *not* important. Such subsets are called **combinations of *n* elements taken *r* at a time.** For instance, the combinations

$$\{A, B, C\} \quad \text{and} \quad \{B, A, C\}$$

are equivalent because both sets contain the same three elements, and the order in which the elements are listed is not important. So, you would count only one of the two sets. A common example of how a combination occurs is a card game in which the player is free to reorder the cards after they have been dealt.

Careful attention to detail and numerous examples will help students understand when to count different orders and when not to. You may want to discuss the misnaming of the "combination lock" according to the definitions presented in this section.

Example 8 ▶ **Combinations of *n* Elements Taken *r* at a Time**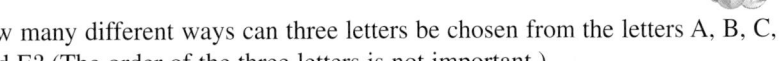

In how many different ways can three letters be chosen from the letters A, B, C, D, and E? (The order of the three letters is not important.)

Solution

The following subsets represent the different combinations of three letters that can be chosen from the five letters.

$\{A, B, C\}$	$\{A, B, D\}$
$\{A, B, E\}$	$\{A, C, D\}$
$\{A, C, E\}$	$\{A, D, E\}$
$\{B, C, D\}$	$\{B, C, E\}$
$\{B, D, E\}$	$\{C, D, E\}$

From this list, you can conclude that there are 10 different ways that three letters can be chosen from five letters.

STUDY TIP

When solving problems involving counting principles, you need to be able to distinguish among the various counting principles in order to determine which is necessary to solve the problem correctly. To do this, ask yourself the following questions.

1. Is the order of the elements important? *Permutation*

2. Are the chosen elements a subset of a larger set in which order is not important? *Combination*

3. Does the problem involve two or more separate events? *Fundamental Counting Principle*

> **Combinations of *n* Elements Taken *r* at a Time**
>
> The number of combinations of *n* elements taken *r* at a time is
>
> $$_nC_r = \frac{n!}{(n-r)!r!}.$$

Note that the formula for $_nC_r$ is the same one given for binomial coefficients. To see how this formula is used, solve the counting problem in Example 8. In that problem, you are asked to find the number of combinations of five elements taken three at a time. So, $n = 5$, $r = 3$, and the number of combinations is

$$_5C_3 = \frac{5!}{2!3!} = \frac{5 \cdot \overset{2}{\cancel{4}} \cdot \cancel{3!}}{2 \cdot 1 \cdot \cancel{3!}} = 10$$

which is the same answer obtained in the example.

Example 9 ▶   **Counting Card Hands**

A standard poker hand consists of five cards dealt from a deck of 52. How many different poker hands are possible? (After the cards are dealt, the player may reorder them, and so order is not important.)

Solution

You can find the number of different poker hands by using the formula for the number of combinations of 52 elements taken five at a time, as follows.

$$_{52}C_5 = \frac{52!}{(52 - 5)!5!}$$

$$= \frac{52!}{47!5!}$$

$$= \frac{52 \cdot 51 \cdot 50 \cdot 49 \cdot 48 \cdot 47!}{5 \cdot 4 \cdot 3 \cdot 2 \cdot 1 \cdot 47!}$$

$$= 2{,}598{,}960$$

Example 10 ▶   **The Number of Subsets of a Set**

Find the total number of subsets of a set that has 10 elements.

Solution

Begin by considering the number of subsets with 0 elements, the number with 1 element, the number with 2 elements, and so on.

Number of subsets	=	Subsets with 0 elements	+	Subsets with 1 element	+	Subsets with 2 elements	+ · · · +	Subsets with 10 elements

$$= \binom{10}{0} + \binom{10}{1} + \binom{10}{2} + \cdots + \binom{10}{10}$$

By comparing this expression with the binomial expansion of $(1 + 1)^{10}$, you see that they are the same.

$$(1 + 1)^{10} = \binom{10}{0}1^{10}1^0 + \binom{10}{1}1^91^1 + \binom{10}{2}1^81^2 + \cdots + \binom{10}{10}1^01^{10}$$

$$= \binom{10}{0} + \binom{10}{1} + \binom{10}{2} + \cdots + \binom{10}{10}$$

This implies that the total number of subsets of a set of 10 elements is

$$(1 + 1)^{10} = 2^{10}$$

$$= 1024.$$

The result of Example 10 can be generalized to conclude that the total number of subsets of a set of n elements is 2^n.

9.6 Exercises

Random Selection In Exercises 1–8, determine the number of ways a computer can randomly generate one or more such integers from 1 through 12.

1. An odd integer

2. An even integer

3. A prime integer

4. An integer that is greater than 9

5. An integer that is divisible by 4

6. An integer that is divisible by 3

7. Two integers whose sum is 8

8. Two *distinct* integers whose sum is 8

9. ***Entertainment Systems*** A customer can choose one of three amplifiers, one of two compact disc players, and one of five speaker models for an entertainment system. Determine the number of possible system configurations.

10. ***Computer Systems*** A customer in a computer store can choose one of four monitors, one of three keyboards, and one of five computers. If all the choices are compatible, determine the number of possible system configurations.

11. ***Job Applicants*** A college needs two additional faculty members: a chemist and a statistician. In how many ways can these positions be filled if there are five applicants for the chemistry position and three applicants for the statistics position?

12. ***Course Schedule*** A college student is preparing a course schedule for the next semester. The student may select one of two mathematics courses, one of three science courses, and one of five courses from the social sciences and humanities. How many schedules are possible?

13. ***True-False Exam*** In how many ways can a six-question true-false exam be answered? (Assume that no questions are omitted.)

14. ***True-False Exam*** In how many ways can a 12-question true-false exam be answered? (Assume that no questions are omitted.)

15. ***Toboggan Ride*** Three people are lining up for a ride on a toboggan, but only two of the three are willing to take the first position. With that constraint, in how many ways can the three people be seated on the toboggan?

16. ***Aircraft Boarding*** Eight people are boarding an aircraft. Two have tickets for first class and board before those in the economy class. In how many ways can the eight people board the aircraft?

17. ***License Plate Numbers*** In the state of Pennsylvania, each automobile license plate number consists of three letters followed by a four-digit number. How many distinct license plate numbers can be formed?

18. ***License Plate Numbers*** In a certain state, each automobile license plate number consists of two letters followed by a four-digit number. To avoid confusion between "O" and "zero" and between "I" and "one," the letters "O" and "I" are not used. How many distinct license plate numbers can be formed?

19. ***Three-Digit Numbers*** How many three-digit numbers can be formed under each condition?

    (a) The leading digit cannot be zero.

    (b) The leading digit cannot be zero and no repetition of digits is allowed.

    (c) The leading digit cannot be zero and the number must be a multiple of 5.

    (d) The number is at least 400.

20. ***Four-Digit Numbers*** How many four-digit numbers can be formed under each condition?

    (a) The leading digit cannot be zero.

    (b) The leading digit cannot be zero and no repetition of digits is allowed.

    (c) The leading digit cannot be zero and the number must be less than 5000.

    (d) The leading digit cannot be zero and the number must be even.

21. ***Combination Lock*** A combination lock will open when the right choice of three numbers (from 1 to 40, inclusive) is selected. How many different lock combinations are possible?

22. ***Combination Lock*** A combination lock will open when the right choice of three numbers (from 1 to 50, inclusive) is selected. How many different lock combinations are possible?

23. Concert Seats Four couples have reserved seats in a row for a concert. In how many different ways can they be seated if

(a) there are no seating restrictions?

(b) the two members of each couple wish to sit together?

24. Single File In how many orders can four girls and four boys walk through a doorway single file if

(a) there are no restrictions?

(b) the girls walk through before the boys?

In Exercises 25–30, evaluate $_nP_r$.

25. $_4P_4$

26. $_5P_5$

27. $_8P_3$

28. $_{20}P_2$

29. $_5P_4$

30. $_7P_4$

In Exercises 31 and 32, solve for n.

31. $14 \cdot {}_nP_3 = {}_{n+2}P_4$

32. $_nP_5 = 18 \cdot {}_{n-2}P_4$

In Exercises 33–38, evaluate using a calculator.

33. $_{20}P_5$

34. $_{100}P_5$

35. $_{100}P_3$

36. $_{10}P_8$

37. $_{20}C_5$

38. $_{10}C_7$

In Exercises 39–42, find the number of distinguishable permutations of the group of letters.

39. A, A, G, E, E, E, M

40. B, B, B, T, T, T, T, T

41. A, L, G, E, B, R, A

42. M, I, S, S, I, S, S, I, P, P, I

43. Write all permutations of the letters A, B, C, and D.

44. Write all permutations of the letters A, B, C, and D if the letters B and C must remain between the letters A and D.

45. Write all possible selections of two letters that can be formed from the letters A, B, C, D, E, and F. (The order of the two letters is not important.)

46. Write all possible selections of three letters that can be formed from the letters A, B, C, D, E, and F. (The order of the three letters is not important.)

47. Posing for a Photograph In how many ways can five children line up in a row?

48. Riding in a Car In how many ways can six people sit in a six-passenger car?

49. Choosing Officers From a pool of 12 candidates, the offices of president, vice-president, secretary, and treasurer will be filled. In how many different ways can the offices be filled?

50. Assembly Line Production There are four processes involved in assembling a product, and these processes can be performed in any order. The management wants to test each order to determine which is the least time-consuming. How many different orders will have to be tested?

51. Forming an Experimental Group In order to conduct an experiment, five students are randomly selected from a class of 20. How many different groups of five students are possible?

52. Test Questions You can answer any 10 questions from a total of 12 questions on an exam. In how many different ways can you select the questions?

53. Lottery Choices There are 35 numbers in the Massachusetts Mass Cash game. In how many ways can a player select five of the numbers?

54. Lottery Choices There are 40 numbers in the Louisiana Lotto game. In how many ways can a player select six of the numbers?

55. Number of Subsets How many subsets of four elements can be formed from a set of 100 elements?

56. Number of Subsets How many subsets of five elements can be formed from a set of 80 elements?

57. Geometry Three points that are not on a line determine three lines. How many lines are determined by seven points, no three of which are on a line?

58. Defective Units A shipment of 10 microwave ovens contains three defective units. In how many ways can a vending company purchase four of these units and receive (a) all good units, (b) two good units, and (c) at least two good units?

59. Job Applicants A toy manufacturer interviews eight people for four openings in the research and development department of the company. Three of the eight people are women. If all eight are qualified, in how many ways can the employer fill the four positions if (a) the selection is random and (b) exactly two selections are women?

60. Poker Hand You are dealt five cards from an ordinary deck of 52 playing cards. In how many ways can you get a full house? (A full house consists of three of one kind and two of another. For example, A-A-A-5-5 and K-K-K-10-10 are full houses.)

61. *Forming a Committee* Four people are to be selected at random from a group of four couples. In how many ways can this be done under the following conditions?

(a) There are no restrictions.

(b) The group must have at least one couple.

(c) Each couple must be represented in the group.

62. *Interpersonal Relationships* The complexity of the interpersonal relationships increases dramatically as the size of a group increases. Determine the number of different two-person relationships in a group of people of size (a) 3, (b) 8, (c) 12, and (d) 20.

Geometry In Exercises 63–66, find the number of diagonals of the polygon. (A line segment connecting any two nonadjacent vertices is called a diagonal of the polygon.)

63. Pentagon

64. Hexagon

65. Octagon

66. Decagon (10 sides)

▶ Model It

67. *Lottery* Powerball is a lottery game that is operated by the Multi-State Lottery Association and its 24 current state members. The game is played by drawing five white balls out of a drum of 53 white balls (numbered 1–53) and one red powerball out of a drum of 42 red balls (numbered 1–42). The jackpot is won by matching all five white balls in any order and the red powerball.

(a) Find the possible number of winning Powerball numbers.

(b) Find the possible number of winning Powerball numbers if the jackpot is won by matching all five white balls in order and the red power ball.

(c) Compare the results of part (a) with a state lottery in which a jackpot is won by matching six balls from a drum of 53 balls.

Synthesis

True or False? In Exercises 68–70, determine whether the statement is true or false. Justify your answer.

68. The number of letter pairs that can be formed from any of the first 13 letters in the alphabet (A–M) is an example of a permutation.

69. The number of permutations of n elements can be determined by using the Fundamental Counting Principle.

70. The value of $_nP_r$ is always greater than the value of $_nC_r$.

71. What is the relationship between $_nC_r$ and $_nC_{n-r}$?

72. Without calculating the numbers, determine which of the following is greater. Explain.

(a) The combinations of 10 elements taken six at a time

(b) The permutations of 10 elements taken six at a time

Proof In Exercises 73–76, prove the identity.

73. $_nP_{n-1} = {_nP_n}$

74. $_nC_n = {_nC_0}$

75. $_nC_{n-1} = {_nC_1}$

76. $_nC_r = \dfrac{_nP_r}{r!}$

 77. *Think About It* Can your calculator evaluate $_{100}P_{80}$? If not, explain why.

78. *Writing* Explain in words the meaning of $_nP_r$.

Review

In Exercises 79–82, evaluate the function at the specified values of the independent variable.

79. $f(x) = 3x^2 + 8$

(a) $f(3)$ (b) $f(0)$ (c) $f(-5)$

80. $g(x) = \sqrt{x-3} + 2$

(a) $g(3)$ (b) $g(7)$ (c) $g(x+3)$

81. $f(x) = -|x-5| + 6$

(a) $f(-5)$ (b) $f(-1)$ (c) $f(11)$

82. $f(x) = \begin{cases} x^2 - 2x + 5, & x \le -4 \\ -x^2 - 2, & x > -4 \end{cases}$

(a) $f(-4)$ (b) $f(-1)$ (c) $f(-20)$

In Exercises 83–86, solve the equation. Round your answer to two decimal places, if necessary.

83. $\sqrt{x-3} = x - 6$

84. $\dfrac{4}{t} + \dfrac{3}{2t} = 1$

85. $\log_2(x-3) = 5$

86. $e^{x/3} = 16$

In Exercises 87–90, use the Binomial Theorem to expand and simplify the expression.

87. $(x+1)^5$

88. $(y-2)^6$

89. $(x^2 + 2y)^5$

90. $(x^2 - y^2)^4$

9.7 Probability

▶ **What you should learn**

• How to find the probabilities of events
• How to find the probabilities of mutually exclusive events
• How to find the probabilities of independent events
• How to find the probability of the complement of an event

▶ **Why you should learn it**

You can use probability to solve a variety of problems that occur in real life. For instance, in Exercise 35 on page 681, you are asked to use probability to help analyze the voting-age population distribution in the United States.

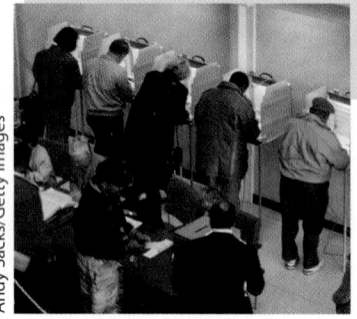

Andy Sacks/Getty Images

The Probability of an Event

Any happening for which the result is uncertain is called an **experiment.** The possible results of the experiment are **outcomes,** the set of all possible outcomes of the experiment is the **sample space** of the experiment, and any subcollection of a sample space is an **event.**

For instance, when a six-sided die is tossed, the sample space can be represented by the numbers 1 through 6. For this experiment, each of the outcomes is *equally likely.*

To describe sample spaces in such a way that each outcome is equally likely, you must sometimes distinguish between or among various outcomes in ways that appear artificial. Example 1 illustrates such a situation.

Example 1 ▶	Finding the Sample Space	

Find the sample space for each of the following.

a. One coin is tossed.

b. Two coins are tossed.

c. Three coins are tossed.

Solution

a. Because the coin will land either heads up (denoted by H) or tails up (denoted by T), the sample space is

$$S = \{H, T\}.$$

b. Because either coin can land heads up or tails up, the possible outcomes are as follows.

HH = heads up on both coins

HT = heads up on first coin and tails up on second coin

TH = tails up on first coin and heads up on second coin

TT = tails up on both coins

So, the sample space is

$$S = \{HH, HT, TH, TT\}.$$

Note that this list distinguishes between the two cases HT and TH, even though these two outcomes appear to be similar.

c. Following the notation of part (b), the sample space is

$$S = \{HHH, HHT, HTH, HTT, THH, THT, TTH, TTT\}.$$

Note that this list distinguishes among the cases HHT, HTH, and THH, and among the cases HTT, THT, and TTH.

Example 5 ▶   The Probability of Winning a Lottery

In the Arizona state lottery, a player chooses six different numbers from 1 to 41. If these six numbers match the six numbers drawn by the lottery commission, the player wins (or shares) the top prize. What is the probability of winning?

Solution

To find the number of elements in the sample space, use the formula for the number of combinations of 41 elements taken six at a time.

$$n(S) = {}_{41}C_6$$

$$= \frac{41 \cdot 40 \cdot 39 \cdot 38 \cdot 37 \cdot 36}{6 \cdot 5 \cdot 4 \cdot 3 \cdot 2 \cdot 1}$$

$$= 4{,}496{,}388$$

If a person buys only one ticket, the probability of winning is

$$P(E) = \frac{n(E)}{n(S)}$$

$$= \frac{1}{4{,}496{,}388}.$$

Example 6 ▶   Random Selection

The numbers of colleges and universities in various regions of the United States in 2001 are shown in Figure 9.10. One institution is selected at random. What is the probability that the institution is in one of the three southern regions?   (Source: U.S. National Center for Education Statistics)

Solution

From the figure, the total number of colleges and universities is 4178. Because there are $687 + 274 + 383 = 1344$ colleges and universities in the three southern regions, the probability that the institution is in one of these regions is

$$P(E) = \frac{n(E)}{n(S)} = \frac{1344}{4178} \approx 0.322.$$

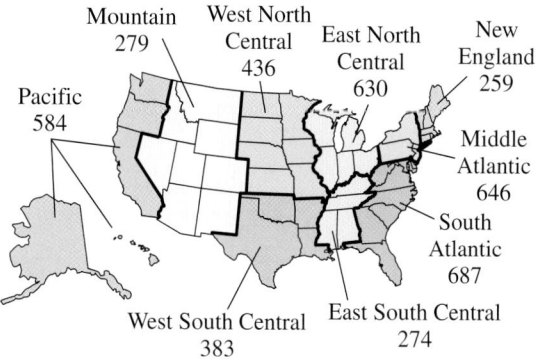

FIGURE **9.10**

Mutually Exclusive Events

Two events A and B (from the same sample space) are **mutually exclusive** if A and B have no outcomes in common. In the terminology of sets, the intersection of A and B is the empty set, which is expressed as

$$P(A \cap B) = 0.$$

For instance, if two dice are tossed, the event A of rolling a total of 6 and the event B of rolling a total of 9 are mutually exclusive. To find the probability that one or the other of two mutually exclusive events will occur, you can *add* their individual probabilities.

Probability of the Union of Two Events

If A and B are events in the same sample space, the probability of A or B occurring is given by

$$P(A \cup B) = P(A) + P(B) - P(A \cap B).$$

If A and B are mutually exclusive, then

$$P(A \cup B) = P(A) + P(B).$$

Example 7 ▶   The Probability of a Union of Events

One card is selected from a standard deck of 52 playing cards. What is the probability that the card is either a heart or a face card?

Solution

Because the deck has 13 hearts, the probability of selecting a heart (event A) is

$$P(A) = \frac{13}{52}.$$

Similarly, because the deck has 12 face cards, the probability of selecting a face card (event B) is

$$P(B) = \frac{12}{52}.$$

Because three of the cards are hearts *and* face cards (see Figure 9.11), it follows that

$$P(A \cap B) = \frac{3}{52}.$$

Finally, applying the formula for the probability of the union of two events, you can conclude that the probability of selecting a heart or a face card is

$$P(A \cup B) = P(A) + P(B) - P(A \cap B)$$

$$= \frac{13}{52} + \frac{12}{52} - \frac{3}{52} = \frac{22}{52} \approx 0.423.$$

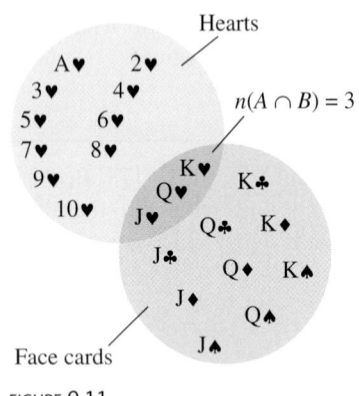

Hearts

$n(A \cap B) = 3$

Face cards

FIGURE 9.11

Example 8 ▶ **Probability of Mutually Exclusive Events**

The personnel department of a company has compiled data on the numbers of employees who have been with the company for various periods of time. The results are shown in the table.

Years of service	Number of Employees
0–4	157
5–9	89
10–14	74
15–19	63
20–24	42
25–29	38
30–34	37
35–39	21
40–44	8

If an employee is chosen at random, what is the probability that the employee has 9 or fewer years of service?

Solution

To begin, add the number of employees and find that the total is 529. Next, let event A represent choosing an employee with 0 to 4 years of service and let event B represent choosing an employee with 5 to 9 years of service. Then

$$P(A) = \frac{157}{529}$$

and

$$P(B) = \frac{89}{529}.$$

Because A and B have no outcomes in common, you can conclude that these two events are mutually exclusive and that

$$P(A \cup B) = P(A) + P(B)$$

$$= \frac{157}{529} + \frac{89}{529}$$

$$= \frac{246}{529}$$

$$\approx 0.465.$$

So, the probability of choosing an employee who has 9 or fewer years of service is about 0.465.

Additional Examples

a. If an employee from Example 8 is chosen at random, what is the probability that the employee has 30 or more years of service?

b. If an employee from Example 8 is chosen at random, what is the probability that the employee has either less than 15 years or more than 34 years of service?

Solutions

a. ≈ 0.125

b. ≈ 0.660

Independent Events

Two events are **independent** if the occurrence of one has no effect on the occurrence of the other. For instance, rolling a total of 12 with two six-sided dice has no effect on the outcome of future rolls of the dice. To find the probability that two independent events will occur, *multiply* the probabilities of each.

Probability of Independent Events

If A and B are independent events, the probability that both A and B will occur is

$$P(A \text{ and } B) = P(A) \cdot P(B).$$

Example 9 ▶   **Probability of Independent Events**

A random number generator on a computer selects three integers from 1 to 20. What is the probability that all three numbers are less than or equal to 5?

Solution

The probability of selecting a number from 1 to 5 is

$$P(A) = \frac{5}{20}$$

$$= \frac{1}{4}.$$

So, the probability that all three numbers are less than or equal to 5 is

$$P(A) \cdot P(A) \cdot P(A) = \left(\frac{1}{4}\right)\left(\frac{1}{4}\right)\left(\frac{1}{4}\right)$$

$$= \frac{1}{64}.$$

Example 10 ▶   **Probability of Independent Events**

In 2000, approximately 65% of the population of the United States was 25 years old or older. In a survey, 10 people were chosen at random from the population. What is the probability that all 10 were 25 years old or older? (Source: U.S. Census Bureau)

Solution

Let A represent choosing a person who was 25 years old or older. Because the probability of choosing a person who was 25 years old or older was 0.65, you can conclude that the probability that all 10 people were 25 years old or older is

$$[P(A)]^{10} = (0.65)^{10}$$

$$\approx 0.0135.$$

You are in a class with 22 other people. What is the probability that at least two out of the 23 people will have a birthday on the same day of the year?

The complement of the probability that at least two people have the same birthday is the probability that all 23 birthdays are different. So, first find the probability that all 23 people have different birthdays and then find the complement.

Now, determine the probability that in a room with 50 people at least two people have the same birthday.

The Complement of an Event

The **complement of an event** A is the collection of all outcomes in the sample space that are *not* in A. The complement of event A is denoted by A'. Because $P(A \text{ or } A') = 1$ and because A and A' are mutually exclusive, it follows that $P(A) + P(A') = 1$. So, the probability of A' is

$$P(A') = 1 - P(A).$$

For instance, if the probability of *winning* a certain game is

$$P(A) = \frac{1}{4}$$

the probability of *losing* the game is

$$P(A') = 1 - \frac{1}{4}$$

$$= \frac{3}{4}.$$

Probability of a Complement

Let A be an event and let A' be its complement. If the probability of A is $P(A)$, the probability of the complement is

$$P(A') = 1 - P(A).$$

Example 11 ▶ **Finding the Probability of a Complement**

A manufacturer has determined that a machine averages one faulty unit for every 1000 it produces. What is the probability that an order of 200 units will have one or more faulty units?

Solution

To solve this problem as stated, you would need to find the probabilities of having exactly one faulty unit, exactly two faulty units, exactly three faulty units, and so on. However, using complements, you can simply find the probability that all units are perfect and then subtract this value from 1. Because the probability that any given unit is perfect is 999/1000, the probability that all 200 units are perfect is

$$P(A) = \left(\frac{999}{1000}\right)^{200}$$

$$\approx 0.8186.$$

So, the probability that at least one unit is faulty is

$$P(A') = 1 - P(A)$$

$$\approx 0.1814.$$

9.7 Exercises

In Exercises 1–6, determine the sample space for the experiment.

1. A coin and a six-sided die are tossed.

2. A six-sided die is tossed twice and the sum of the points is recorded.

3. A taste tester has to rank three varieties of yogurt, A, B, and C, according to preference.

4. Two marbles are selected from a sack containing two red marbles, two blue marbles, and one black marble. The color of each marble is recorded.

5. Two county supervisors are selected from five supervisors, A, B, C, D, and E, to study a recycling plan.

6. A sales representative makes presentations of a product in three homes per day. In each home, there may be a sale (denote by S) or there may be no sale (denote by F).

Heads or Tails In Exercises 7–10, find the probability for the experiment of tossing a coin three times. Use the sample space $S = \{HHH, HHT, HTH, HTT, THH, THT, TTH, TTT\}$.

7. The probability of getting exactly one tail

8. The probability of getting a head on the first toss

9. The probability of getting at least one head

10. The probability of getting at least two heads

Drawing a Card In Exercises 11–14, find the probability for the experiment of selecting one card from a standard deck of 52 playing cards.

11. The card is a face card.

12. The card is not a face card.

13. The card is a red face card.

14. The card is a 6 or less.

Tossing a Die In Exercises 15–20, find the probability for the experiment of tossing a six-sided die twice.

15. The sum is 4.

16. The sum is at least 7.

17. The sum is less than 11.

18. The sum is 2, 3, or 12.

19. The sum is odd and no more than 7.

20. The sum is odd or prime.

Drawing Marbles In Exercises 21–24, find the probability for the experiment of drawing two marbles (without replacement) from a bag containing one green, two yellow, and three red marbles.

21. Both marbles are red.

22. Both marbles are yellow.

23. Neither marble is yellow.

24. The marbles are of different colors.

In Exercises 25–28, you are given the probability that an event *will* happen. Find the probability that the event *will not* happen.

25. $p = 0.7$ 26. $p = 0.36$

27. $p = \dfrac{1}{3}$ 28. $p = \dfrac{5}{6}$

In Exercises 29–32, you are given the probability that an event *will not* happen. Find the probability that the event *will* happen.

29. $p = 0.15$ 30. $p = 0.84$

31. $p = \dfrac{13}{20}$ 32. $p = \dfrac{87}{100}$

33. *Data Analysis* A study of the effectiveness of a flu vaccine was conducted with a sample of 500 people. Some in the study were given no vaccine, some were given one injection, and others were given two injections. The results of the study are listed in the table.

	No vaccine	One injection	Two injections	Total
Flu	7	2	13	22
No flu	149	52	277	478
Total	156	54	290	500

A person is selected at random from the sample. Find the specified probability.

(a) The person had two injections.

(b) The person did not get the flu.

(c) The person got the flu and had one injection.

34. *Data Analysis*   One hundred college students were interviewed to determine their political party affiliations and whether they favored a balanced-budget amendment to the Constitution. The results of the study are listed in the table, where *D* represents Democrat and *R* represents Republican.

	Favor	Not Favor	Unsure	Total
D	23	25	7	55
R	32	9	4	45
Total	55	34	11	100

A person is selected at random from the sample. Find the probability that the described person is selected.

(a) A person who doesn't favor the amendment

(b) A Republican

(c) A Democrat who favors the amendment

> ▶ **Model It**

35. *Graphical Reasoning*   In 2000, the voting-age population of the United States was approximately 203 million. The figure shows the regions in which these people lived.   (Source: U.S. Census Bureau)

Voting-Age Population

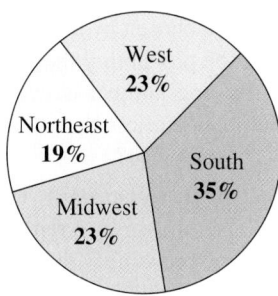

(a) Estimate the voting-age population of the Northeast.

(b) A person is selected at random from the voting-age population. What is the probability that the person lives in the West?

(c) A person is selected at random from the voting-age population. What is the probability that the person lives in the Midwest or the South?

36. *Graphical Reasoning*   In 2000, there were approximately 131.4 million employees in nonfarm establishments in the United States. The figure shows the types of occupations of these employees.   (Source: U.S. Bureau of Labor Statistics)

Employees

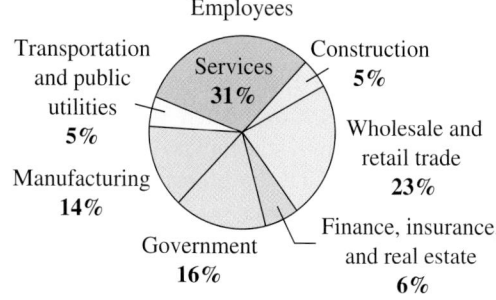

(a) Estimate the number of employees in the manufacturing industry.

(b) What is the probability that a person selected at random from the population of employees in nonfarm establishments works in construction?

(c) What is the probability that a person selected at random from the population of employees in nonfarm establishments works in the service industry or works for the government?

37. *Alumni Association*   A college sends a survey to selected members of the class of 2002. Of the 1254 people who graduated that year, 672 are women, of whom 124 went on to graduate school. Of the 582 male graduates, 198 went on to graduate school. An alumnus member is selected at random. What is the probability that the person is (a) female, (b) male, and (c) female and did not attend graduate school?

38. *Education*   In a high school graduating class of 72 students, 28 are on the honor roll. Of these, 18 are going on to college, and of the other 44 students, 12 are going on to college. A student is selected at random from the class. What is the probability that the person chosen is (a) going to college, (b) not going to college, and (c) on the honor roll, but not going to college?

39. *Winning an Election*   Taylor, Moore, and Jenkins are candidates for public office. It is estimated that Moore and Jenkins have about the same probability of winning, and Taylor is believed to be twice as likely to win as either of the others. Find the probability of each candidate winning the election.

40. *Winning an Election* Three people have been nominated for president of a class. From a poll, it is estimated that the first has a 37% chance of winning and the second has a 44% chance of winning. What is the probability that the third candidate will win?

In Exercises 41–52, the sample spaces are large and you should use the counting principles discussed in Section 9.6.

41. *Preparing for a Test* A class is given a list of 20 study problems, from which 10 will be part of an upcoming exam. A student knows how to solve 15 of the problems. Find the probability that the student will be able to answer (a) all 10 questions on the exam, (b) exactly eight questions on the exam, and (c) at least nine questions on the exam.

42. *Preparing for a Test* A class is given a list of eight study problems, from which five will be part of an upcoming exam. A student knows how to solve six of the problems. Find the probability that the student will be able to answer (a) all five questions on the exam, (b) exactly four questions on the exam, and (c) at least four questions on the exam.

43. *Letter Mix-Up* Four letters and envelopes are addressed to four different people. The letters are randomly inserted into the envelopes. What is the probability that (a) exactly one will be inserted in the correct envelope and (b) at least one will be inserted in the correct envelope?

44. *Payroll Mix-Up* Five paychecks and envelopes are addressed to five different people. The paychecks are randomly inserted into the envelopes. What is the probability that (a) exactly one will be inserted in the correct envelope and (b) at least one will be inserted in the correct envelope?

45. *Game Show* On a game show, you are given five digits to arrange in the proper order to form the price of a car. If you are correct, you win the car. What is the probability of winning, given the following conditions?

(a) You guess the position of each digit.

(b) You know the first digit and guess the positions of the others.

46. *Game Show* On a game show, you are given five digits in the price of a car. The first digit is 1, and you are given the other four digits to arrange in the correct order to win the car. What is your probability of winning given the following conditions?

(a) You guess the position of each digit.

(b) You know the second digit but guess the others.

47. *Drawing Cards from a Deck* Two cards are selected at random from an ordinary deck of 52 playing cards. Find the probability that two aces are selected, given the following conditions.

(a) The cards are drawn in sequence, with the first card being replaced and the deck reshuffled prior to the second drawing.

(b) The two cards are drawn consecutively, without replacement.

48. *Poker Hand* Five cards are drawn from an ordinary deck of 52 playing cards. What is the probability that the hand drawn is a full house? (A full house is a hand that consists of two of one kind and three of another kind.)

49. *Defective Units* A shipment of 12 microwave ovens contains three defective units. A vending company has ordered four of these units, and because each is identically packaged, the selection will be random. What is the probability that (a) all four units are good, (b) exactly two units are good, and (c) at least two units are good?

50. *Defective Units* A shipment of 20 compact disc players contains four defective units. A retail outlet has ordered five of these units. What is the probability that (a) all five units are good, (b) exactly four units are good, and (c) at least one unit is defective?

51. *Random Number Generator* Two integers from 1 through 30 are chosen by a random number generator. What is the probability that (a) the numbers are both even, (b) one number is even and one is odd, (c) both numbers are less than 10, and (d) the same number is chosen twice?

52. *Random Number Generator* Two integers from 1 through 40 are chosen by a random number generator. What is the probability that (a) the numbers are both even, (b) one number is even and one is odd, (c) both numbers are less than 30, and (d) the same number is chosen twice?

53. *Backup System* A space vehicle has an independent backup system for one of its communication networks. The probability that either system will function satisfactorily during a flight is 0.985. What is the probability that during a given flight (a) both systems function satisfactorily, (b) at least one system functions satisfactorily, and (c) both systems fail?

54. *Backup Vehicle* A fire company keeps two rescue vehicles. Because of the demand on the vehicles and the chance of mechanical failure, the probability that a specific vehicle is available when needed is 90%. The availability of one vehicle is *independent* of the availability of the other. Find the probability that (a) both vehicles are available at a given time, (b) neither vehicle is available at a given time, and (c) at least one vehicle is available at a given time.

55. *Making a Sale* A sales representative makes a sale on approximately one-fourth of all calls. On a given day, the representative contacts five potential clients. What is the probability that a sale will be made with (a) each of the five contacts, (b) none of the contacts, and (c) at least one contact?

56. *A Boy or a Girl?* Assume that the probability of the birth of a child of a particular sex is 50%. In a family with four children, what is the probability that (a) all the children are boys, (b) all the children are the same sex, and (c) there is at least one boy?

57. *Flexible Work Hours* In a survey, people were asked if they would prefer to work flexible hours— even if it meant slower career advancement—so they could spend more time with their families. The results of the survey are shown in the figure. Three people from the survey were chosen at random. What is the probability that all three people would prefer flexible work hours?

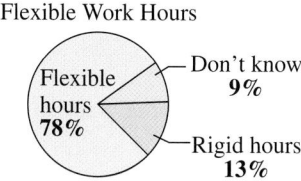

Flexible Work Hours

Flexible hours **78%**

Don't know **9%**

Rigid hours **13%**

58. *Consumer Awareness* Suppose that the methods used by shoppers to pay for merchandise are as shown in the circle graph. Two shoppers are chosen at random. What is the probability that both shoppers paid for their purchases only in cash?

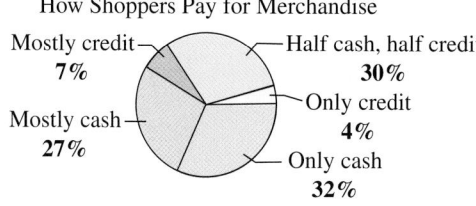

How Shoppers Pay for Merchandise

Mostly credit **7%**

Mostly cash **27%**

Half cash, half credit **30%**

Only credit **4%**

Only cash **32%**

59. *Geometry* You and a friend agree to meet at your favorite fast-food restaurant between 5:00 and 6:00 P.M. The one who arrives first will wait 15 minutes for the other, and then will leave (see figure). What is the probability that the two of you will actually meet, assuming that your arrival times are random within the hour?

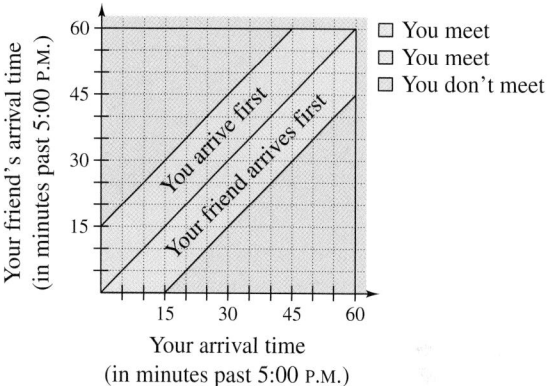

☐ You meet
☐ You meet
☐ You don't meet

You arrive first

Your friend arrives first

Your friend's arrival time (in minutes past 5:00 P.M.)

Your arrival time (in minutes past 5:00 P.M.)

60. *Estimating* π A coin of diameter d is dropped onto a paper that contains a grid of squares d units on a side (see figure).

(a) Find the probability that the coin covers a vertex of one of the squares on the grid.

(b) Perform the experiment 100 times and use the results to approximate π.

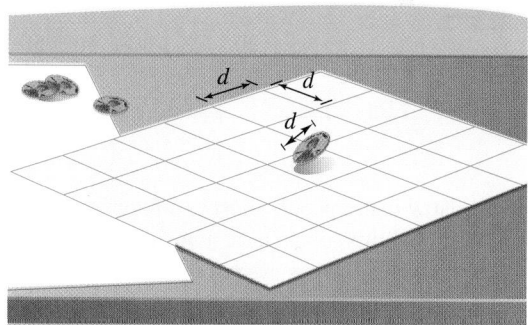

Synthesis

True or False? **In Exercises 61 and 62, determine whether the statement is true or false. Justify your answer.**

61. If A and B are independent events with nonzero probabilities, then A can occur when B occurs.

62. Rolling a number less than 3 on a normal six-sided die has a probability of $\frac{1}{3}$. The complement of this event is to roll a number greater than 3, and its probability is $\frac{1}{2}$.

63. *Pattern Recognition and Exploration*   Consider a group of n people.

(a) Explain why the following pattern gives the probabilities that the n people have distinct birthdays.

$$n = 2: \quad \frac{365}{365} \cdot \frac{364}{365} = \frac{365 \cdot 364}{365^2}$$

$$n = 3: \quad \frac{365}{365} \cdot \frac{364}{365} \cdot \frac{363}{365} = \frac{365 \cdot 364 \cdot 363}{365^3}$$

(b) Use the pattern in part (a) to write an expression for the probability that $n = 4$ people have distinct birthdays.

(c) Let P_n be the probability that the n people have distinct birthdays. Verify that this probability can be obtained recursively by

$$P_1 = 1 \text{ and } P_n = \frac{365 - (n - 1)}{365} P_{n-1}.$$

(d) Explain why $Q_n = 1 - P_n$ gives the probability that at least two people in a group of n people have the same birthday.

(e) Use the results of parts (c) and (d) to complete the table.

n	10	15	20	23	30	40	50
P_n							
Q_n							

(f) How many people must be in a group so that the probability of at least two of them having the same birthday is greater than $\frac{1}{2}$? Explain.

64. *Think About It*   A weather forecast indicates that the probability of rain is 40%. What does this mean?

Review

In Exercises 65–68, find all real solutions of the polynomial equation.

65. $6x^2 + 8 = 0$

66. $4x^2 + 6x - 12 = 0$

67. $x^3 - x^2 - 3x = 0$

68. $x^5 + x^3 - 2x = 0$

In Exercises 69–74, find all real solutions of the rational equation.

69. $\dfrac{12}{x} = -3$

70. $\dfrac{32}{x} = 2x$

71. $\dfrac{2}{x - 5} = 4$

72. $\dfrac{3}{2x + 3} - 4 = \dfrac{-1}{2x + 3}$

73. $\dfrac{3}{x - 2} + \dfrac{x}{x + 2} = 1$

74. $\dfrac{2}{x} - \dfrac{5}{x - 2} = \dfrac{-13}{x^2 - 2x}$

In Exercises 75–80, find all real solutions of the exponential equation.

75. $e^x = 27$ **76.** $e^x + 7 = 35$

77. $e^{2x} - 4e^x + 3 = 0$ **78.** $e^{2x} - 7e^x + 12 = 0$

79. $200e^{-x} = 75$ **80.** $800e^{-x} = 250$

In Exercises 81–84, find all real solutions of the logarithmic equation.

81. $\ln x = 8$ **82.** $3 - 4 \ln x = 6$

83. $4 \ln 6x = 16$ **84.** $5 \ln 2x - 4 = 11$

In Exercises 85–88, sketch the graph of the solution of the system of inequalities.

85. $\begin{cases} y \geq -3 \\ x \geq -1 \\ -x - y \geq -8 \end{cases}$ **86.** $\begin{cases} x \leq 3 \\ y \leq 6 \\ 5x + 2y \geq 10 \end{cases}$

87. $\begin{cases} x^2 + y \geq -2 \\ y \geq x - 4 \end{cases}$ **88.** $\begin{cases} x^2 + y^2 \leq 4 \\ x + y \geq -2 \end{cases}$

In Exercises 89–92, evaluate $_nC_r$.

89. $_6C_2$ **90.** $_9C_5$

91. $_{11}C_8$ **92.** $_{16}C_3$

Chapter Summary

▶ *What* did you learn?

Section 9.1	Review Exercises
☐ How to use sequence notation to write the terms of a sequence	1–8
☐ How to use factorial notation	9–12
☐ How to use summation notation to write sums	13–18
☐ How to find the sum of an infinite series	19–24
☐ How to use sequences and series to model and solve real-life problems	25, 26

Section 9.2	
☐ How to recognize and write arithmetic sequences	27–40
☐ How to find an nth partial sum of an arithmetic sequence	41–46
☐ How to use arithmetic sequences to model and solve real-life problems	47, 48

Section 9.3	
☐ How to recognize and write geometric sequences	49–60
☐ How to find the sum of a geometric sequence	61–70
☐ How to find the sum of an infinite geometric series	71–76
☐ How to use geometric sequences to model and solve real-life problems	77, 78

Section 9.4	
☐ How to use mathematical induction to prove a statement	79–82
☐ How to find the sums of powers of integers	83–86
☐ How to recognize patterns and write the nth term of a sequence	87–90
☐ How to find finite differences of a sequence	91–94

Section 9.5	
☐ How to use the Binomial Theorem to calculate binomial coefficients	95–98
☐ How to use Pascal's Triangle to calculate binomial coefficients	99–102
☐ How to use binomial coefficients to write binomial expansions	103–108

Section 9.6	
☐ How to solve simple counting problems	109, 110
☐ How to use the Fundamental Counting Principle to solve counting problems	111, 112
☐ How to use permutations to solve counting problems	113, 114
☐ How to use combinations to solve counting problems	115, 116

Section 9.7	
☐ How to find the probabilities of events	117, 118
☐ How to find the probabilities of mutually exclusive events	119, 120
☐ How to find the probabilities of independent events	121, 122
☐ How to find the probability of the complement of an event	123, 124

Review Exercises

9.1 In Exercises 1–4, write the first five terms of the sequence. (Assume that n begins with 1.)

1. $a_n = 2 + \dfrac{6}{n}$

2. $a_n = \dfrac{(-1)^n 5n}{2n - 1}$

3. $a_n = \dfrac{72}{n!}$

4. $a_n = n(n - 1)$

In Exercises 5–8, write an expression for the *apparent* nth term of the sequence. (Assume that n begins with 1.)

5. $-2, 2, -2, 2, -2, \ldots$

6. $-1, 2, 7, 14, 23, \ldots$

7. $4, 2, \frac{4}{3}, 1, \frac{4}{5}, \ldots$

8. $1, -\frac{1}{2}, \frac{1}{3}, -\frac{1}{4}, \frac{1}{5}, \ldots$

In Exercises 9–12, evaluate the factorial expression.

9. $5!$

10. $3! \cdot 2!$

11. $\dfrac{3! \cdot 5!}{6!}$

12. $\dfrac{7! \cdot 6!}{6! \cdot 8!}$

In Exercises 13–18, find the sum.

13. $\displaystyle\sum_{i=1}^{6} 5$

14. $\displaystyle\sum_{k=2}^{5} 4k$

15. $\displaystyle\sum_{j=1}^{4} \dfrac{6}{j^2}$

16. $\displaystyle\sum_{i=1}^{8} \dfrac{i}{i + 1}$

17. $\displaystyle\sum_{k=1}^{10} 2k^3$

18. $\displaystyle\sum_{j=0}^{4} (j^2 + 1)$

In Exercises 19 and 20, use sigma notation to write the sum.

19. $\dfrac{1}{2(1)} + \dfrac{1}{2(2)} + \dfrac{1}{2(3)} + \cdots + \dfrac{1}{2(20)}$

20. $\dfrac{1}{2} + \dfrac{2}{3} + \dfrac{3}{4} + \cdots + \dfrac{9}{10}$

In Exercises 21–24, find the sum of the infinite series.

21. $\displaystyle\sum_{i=1}^{\infty} \dfrac{5}{10^i}$

22. $\displaystyle\sum_{i=1}^{\infty} \dfrac{3}{10^i}$

23. $\displaystyle\sum_{k=1}^{\infty} \dfrac{2}{100^k}$

24. $\displaystyle\sum_{k=2}^{\infty} \dfrac{9}{10^k}$

25. *Job Offer* The starting salary for an accountant is $34,000 with a guaranteed salary increase of $2250 per year. Determine (a) the salary during the fifth year and (b) the total compensation through 5 full years of employment.

26. *Baling Hay* In the first two trips baling hay around a large field, a farmer obtains 123 bales and 112 bales, respectively. Because each round gets shorter, the farmer estimates that the same pattern will continue. Estimate the total number of bales made if there are another six trips around the field.

9.2 In Exercises 27–30, determine whether the sequence is arithmetic. If it is, find the common difference.

27. $5, 3, 1, -1, -3, \ldots$

28. $0, 1, 3, 6, 10, \ldots$

29. $\frac{1}{2}, 1, \frac{3}{2}, 2, \frac{5}{2}, \ldots$

30. $\frac{9}{9}, \frac{8}{9}, \frac{7}{9}, \frac{6}{9}, \frac{5}{9}, \ldots$

In Exercises 31–34, write the first five terms of the arithmetic sequence.

31. $a_1 = 4, d = 3$

32. $a_1 = 6, d = -2$

33. $a_1 = 25, a_{k+1} = a_k + 3$

34. $a_1 = 4.2, a_{k+1} = a_k + 0.4$

In Exercises 35–40, find a formula for a_n for the arithmetic sequence.

35. $a_1 = 7, d = 12$

36. $a_1 = 25, d = -3$

37. $a_1 = y, d = 3y$

38. $a_1 = -2x, d = x$

39. $a_2 = 93, a_6 = 65$

40. $a_7 = 8, a_{13} = 6$

In Exercises 41–44, find the partial sum.

41. $\displaystyle\sum_{j=1}^{10} (2j - 3)$

42. $\displaystyle\sum_{j=1}^{8} (20 - 3j)$

43. $\displaystyle\sum_{k=1}^{11} \left(\tfrac{2}{3}k + 4\right)$

44. $\displaystyle\sum_{k=1}^{25} \left(\dfrac{3k + 1}{4}\right)$

45. Find the sum of the first 100 positive multiples of 5.

46. Find the sum of the integers from 20 to 80 (inclusive).

47. *Running* The first time you run a five-mile distance course, it takes you 49 minutes. You run the same course 30 seconds faster each week. How fast can you run the five-mile course after 12 weeks?

48. *Running* On the first day of a new training schedule, you run 2 miles. You increase your distance by one-half mile every day. How many total miles will you run in 14 days?

`9.3` In Exercises 49–52, determine whether the sequence is geometric. If it is, find the common ratio.

49. 5, 10, 20, 40, . . .

50. 54, -18, 6, -2, . . .

51. $\frac{1}{3}, -\frac{2}{3}, \frac{4}{3}, -\frac{8}{3}, \ldots$

52. $\frac{1}{4}, \frac{2}{5}, \frac{3}{6}, \frac{4}{7}, \ldots$

In Exercises 53–56, write the first five terms of the geometric sequence.

53. $a_1 = 4$, $r = -\frac{1}{4}$

54. $a_1 = 2$, $r = 2$

55. $a_1 = 9$, $a_3 = 4$

56. $a_1 = 2$, $a_3 = 12$

In Exercises 57–60, write an expression for the nth term of the geometric sequence and find the sum of the first 20 terms of the sequence.

57. $a_1 = 16, a_2 = -8$

58. $a_3 = 6, a_4 = 1$

59. $a_1 = 100, r = 1.05$

60. $a_1 = 5, r = 0.2$

In Exercises 61–66, find the sum.

61. $\sum_{i=1}^{7} 2^{i-1}$

62. $\sum_{i=1}^{5} 3^{i-1}$

63. $\sum_{i=1}^{4} \left(\frac{1}{2}\right)^{i}$

64. $\sum_{i=1}^{6} \left(\frac{1}{3}\right)^{i-1}$

65. $\sum_{i=1}^{5} (2)^{i-1}$

66. $\sum_{i=1}^{4} 6(3)^{i}$

In Exercises 67–70, use a graphing utility to find the sum.

67. $\sum_{i=1}^{10} 10\left(\frac{3}{5}\right)^{i-1}$

68. $\sum_{i=1}^{15} 20(0.2)^{i-1}$

69. $\sum_{i=1}^{25} 100(1.06)^{i-1}$

70. $\sum_{i=1}^{20} 8\left(\frac{6}{5}\right)^{i-1}$

In Exercises 71–76, find the sum of the infinite geometric series.

71. $\sum_{i=1}^{\infty} \left(\frac{7}{8}\right)^{i-1}$

72. $\sum_{i=1}^{\infty} \left(\frac{1}{3}\right)^{i-1}$

73. $\sum_{i=1}^{\infty} (0.1)^{i-1}$

74. $\sum_{i=1}^{\infty} (0.5)^{i-1}$

75. $\sum_{k=1}^{\infty} 4\left(\frac{2}{3}\right)^{k-1}$

76. $\sum_{k=1}^{\infty} 1.3\left(\frac{1}{10}\right)^{k-1}$

77. *Depreciation* A paper manufacturer buys a machine for \$120,000. During the next 5 years, it will depreciate at a rate of 30% per year. (That is, at the end of each year the depreciated value will be 70% of what it was at the beginning of the year.)

(a) Find the formula for the nth term of a geometric sequence that gives the value of the machine t full years after it was purchased.

(b) Find the depreciated value of the machine at the end of 5 full years.

78. *Total Compensation* A computer programming position pays a salary of \$32,000 the first year. During the next 39 years, there is a 5.5% raise each year. What would be the total amount earned over the 40-year period?

`9.4` In Exercises 79–82, use mathematical induction to prove the formula for every positive integer n.

79. $3 + 5 + 7 + \cdots + (2n + 1) = n(n + 2)$

80. $1 + \frac{3}{2} + 2 + \frac{5}{2} + \cdots + \frac{1}{2}(n + 1) = \frac{n}{4}(n + 3)$

81. $\sum_{i=0}^{n-1} ar^{i} = \frac{a(1 - r^{n})}{1 - r}$

82. $\sum_{k=0}^{n-1} (a + kd) = \frac{n}{2}[2a + (n - 1)d]$

In Exercises 83–86, find the sum using the formulas for the sums of powers of integers.

83. $\sum_{n=1}^{30} n$

84. $\sum_{n=1}^{10} n^{2}$

85. $\sum_{n=1}^{7} (n^{4} - n)$

86. $\sum_{n=1}^{6} (n^{5} - n^{2})$

In Exercises 87–90, find a formula for the sum of the first n terms of the sequence.

87. 9, 13, 17, 21, . . .

88. 68, 60, 52, 44, . . .

89. $1, \frac{3}{5}, \frac{9}{25}, \frac{27}{125}, \ldots$

90. $12, -1, \frac{1}{12}, -\frac{1}{144}, \ldots$

In Exercises 91–94, find the first five terms of the sequence. Then calculate the first and second differences of the sequence. Does the sequence have a linear model, a quadratic model, or neither?

91. $a_1 = 5$
    $a_n = a_{n-1} + 5$

92. $a_1 = -3$
    $a_n = a_{n-1} - 2n$

93. $a_1 = 16$
    $a_n = a_{n-1} - 1$

94. $a_0 = 0$
    $a_n = n - a_{n-1}$?

9.5   In Exercises 95–98, use the Binomial Theorem to calculate the binomial coefficient.

95. $_6C_4$

96. $_{10}C_7$

97. $_8C_5$

98. $_{12}C_3$

In Exercises 99–102, use Pascal's Triangle to calculate the binomial coefficient.

99. $\binom{7}{3}$

100. $\binom{9}{4}$

101. $\binom{8}{6}$

102. $\binom{5}{3}$

In Exercises 103–108, use the Binomial Theorem to expand the binomial. Simplify your answer. (Remember that $i = \sqrt{-1}$.)

103. $\left(\dfrac{x}{2} + y\right)^4$

104. $\left(\dfrac{2}{x} - 3x\right)^6$

105. $(a - 3b)^5$

106. $(3x + y^2)^7$

107. $(5 + 2i)^4$

108. $(4 - 5i)^3$

9.6 **109.** *Dice*   In how many different ways can a pair of dice be rolled to obtain a total of 10?

110. *Numbers in a Hat*   Slips of paper numbered 1 through 14 are placed in a hat. In how many ways can you draw two numbers with replacement that total 12?

111. *Telephone Numbers*   The same three-digit prefix is used for all of the telephone numbers in a small town. How many different telephone numbers are possible by changing only the last four digits?

112. *Telephone Numbers*   A telephone number in another town can use any one of five different three-digit prefixes. How many different telephone numbers are possible in this town?

113. *Bike Race*   There are 10 bicyclists entered in a race. In how many different orders could these 10 bicyclists finish?

114. *Bike Race*   There are 10 bicyclists entered in a race. In how many different ways could the top three places be decided?

115. *Apparel*   You have eight different suits to choose from to take on a trip. How many combinations of three suits could you take?

116. *Apparel*   You have 20 different neckties in your wardrobe. How many combinations of three ties could you choose?

9.7 **117.** *Apparel*   A man has five pairs of socks, of which no two pairs are the same color. He randomly selects two socks from a drawer. What is the probability that he gets a matched pair?

118. *Bookshelf Order*   A child returns a five-volume set of books to a bookshelf. The child is not able to read, and so cannot distinguish one volume from another. What is the probability that the books are shelved in the correct order?

119. *Students by Class*   At a particular high school, the numbers of students in the four classes are broken down by percents, as shown in the table.

Class	Percent
Freshman	31
Sophomores	26
Juniors	25
Seniors	18

A single student is picked randomly by lottery for a cash scholarship. What is the probability that the scholarship winner is

(a) a junior or senior?

(b) a freshman, sophomore, or junior?

120. *Data Analysis*   A sample of college students, faculty, and administration were asked whether they favored a proposed increase in the annual activity fee to enhance student life on campus. The results of the study are listed in the table.

	Students	Faculty	Admin.	Total
Favor	237	37	18	292
Oppose	163	38	7	208
Total	400	75	25	500

A person is selected at random from the sample. Find the specified probability.

(a) The person is not in favor of the proposal.

(b) The person is a student.

(c) The person is a faculty member and is in favor of the proposal.

121. *Tossing a Die*   A six-sided die is rolled three times. What is the probability of a 6 on each roll?

122. Tossing a Die A six-sided die is rolled six times. What is the probability that each side appears exactly once?

123. Drawing a Card You randomly select a card from a 52-card deck. What is the probability that the card is *not* a club?

124. Tossing a Coin Find the probability of obtaining at least one tail when a coin is tossed five times.

Synthesis

True or False? In Exercises 125–128, determine whether the statement is true or false. Justify your answer.

125. $\dfrac{(n+2)!}{n!} = (n+2)(n+1)$

126. $\displaystyle\sum_{i=1}^{5}(i^3 + 2i) = \sum_{i=1}^{5}i^3 + \sum_{i=1}^{5}2i$

127. $\displaystyle\sum_{k=1}^{8}3k = 3\sum_{k=1}^{8}k$

128. $\displaystyle\sum_{j=1}^{6}2^j = \sum_{j=3}^{8}2^{j-2}$

129. Think About It An infinite sequence is a function. What is the domain of the function?

130. Think About It How do the two sequences differ?

(a) $a_n = \dfrac{(-1)^n}{n}$

(b) $a_n = \dfrac{(-1)^{n+1}}{n}$

131. Writing In your own words, explain what makes a sequence (a) arithmetic and (b) geometric.

132. Graphical Reasoning The graphs of two sequences are shown below. Identify each sequence as arithmetic or geometric. Explain your reasoning.

(a)

(b)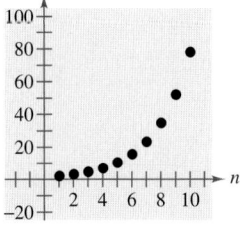

133. Writing Explain what a recursion formula is.

134. Writing Explain why the terms of a geometric sequence decrease when $0 < r < 1$.

Graphical Reasoning In Exercises 135–138, match the sequence or sum of a sequence with its graph without doing any calculations. Explain your reasoning. [The graphs are labeled (a), (b), (c), and (d).]

(a)

(b)

(c)

(d)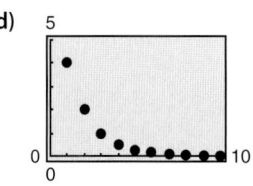

135. $a_n = 4\left(\frac{1}{2}\right)^{n-1}$

136. $a_n = 4\left(-\frac{1}{2}\right)^{n-1}$

137. $a_n = \displaystyle\sum_{k=1}^{n}4\left(\frac{1}{2}\right)^{k-1}$

138. $a_n = \displaystyle\sum_{k=1}^{n}4\left(-\frac{1}{2}\right)^{k-1}$

139. Consider an idealized population with the characteristic that each member of the population produces one offspring at the end of every time period. If each member has a life span of three time periods and the population begins with 10 newborn members, then the following table shows the population during the first five time periods.

		Time Period				
Age Bracket		1	2	3	4	5
0–1		10	10	20	40	70
1–2			10	10	20	40
2–3				10	10	20
Total		10	20	40	70	130

The sequence for the total population has the property that

$$S_n = S_{n-1} + S_{n-2} + S_{n-3}, \quad n > 3.$$

Find the total population during the next five time periods.

140. The probability of an event must be a real number in what interval? Is the interval open or closed?

Chapter Test

Take this test as you would take a test in class. When you are finished, check your work against the answers given in the back of the book.

1. Write the first five terms of the sequence $a_n = \dfrac{(-1)^n}{3n+2}$.

2. Write an expression for the nth term of the sequence.

   $$\frac{3}{1!}, \frac{4}{2!}, \frac{5}{3!}, \frac{6}{4!}, \frac{7}{5!}, \cdots$$

3. Find the next three terms of the series. Then find the fifth partial sum of the series.

   $$6 + 17 + 28 + 39 + \cdots$$

4. The fifth term of an arithmetic series is 5.4, and the 12th term is 11.0. Find the nth term.

5. Write the first five terms of the sequence $a_n = 5(2)^{n-1}$. (Assume that n begins with 1.)

6. Find the sum of the finite series $\displaystyle\sum_{i=1}^{50} (2i^2 + 5)$.

7. Find the sum of the infinite series $\displaystyle\sum_{i=1}^{\infty} 4\left(\tfrac{1}{2}\right)^i$.

8. Use mathematical induction to prove the formula.

   $$5 + 10 + 15 + \cdots + 5n = \frac{5n(n+1)}{2}$$

9. Use the Binomial Theorem to expand the expression $(x + 2y)^4$.

10. To dress for a party, you can choose from six different pairs of slacks, 10 different shirts, and three different pairs of shoes. How many possible outfit combinations do you have?

In Exercises 11 and 12, evaluate each expression.

11. (a) $_9P_2$ (b) $_{70}P_3$ 12. (a) $_{11}C_4$ (b) $_{66}C_4$

13. Eight people are going for a ride in a boat that seats eight people. The owner of the boat will drive, and only three of the remaining people are willing to ride in the two bow seats. How many seating arrangements are possible?

14. You attend a karaoke night and hope to hear your favorite song. The karaoke song book has 300 different songs. Assuming that the singers are equally likely to pick any song and no song is repeated, what is the probability that your favorite song is one of the 20 that you hear?

15. You are with seven of your friends at a party. Names of all of the 60 guests are placed in a hat and drawn randomly to award eight door prizes. Each guest is limited to one prize. What is the probability that you and your friends win all eight of the prizes?

16. The weather report calls for a 75% chance of rain. According to this report, what is the probability that it will not rain?

Cumulative Test for Chapters 7–9

Take this test to review the material from earlier chapters. When you are finished, check your work against the answers given in the back of the book.

In Exercises 1–4, solve the system by the specified method.

1. Substitution

$$\begin{cases} y = 3 - x^2 \\ 2(y - 2) = x - 1 \end{cases}$$

2. Elimination

$$\begin{cases} x + 3y = -1 \\ 2x + 4y = 0 \end{cases}$$

3. Elimination

$$\begin{cases} -2x + 4y - z = 3 \\ x - 2y + 2z = -6 \\ x - 3y - z = 1 \end{cases}$$

4. Gauss-Jordan Elimination

$$\begin{cases} x + 3y - 2z = -7 \\ -2x + y - z = -5 \\ 4x + y + z = 3 \end{cases}$$

In Exercises 5 and 6, sketch the graph of the solution set of the system of inequalities.

5. $\begin{cases} 2x + y \geq -3 \\ x - 3y \leq 2 \end{cases}$

6. $\begin{cases} x - y > 6 \\ 5x + 2y < 10 \end{cases}$

7. Sketch a graph of the solution of the constraints and maximize the objective function $z = 3x + 2y$ subject to the constraints.

$$\begin{aligned} x + 4y &\leq 20 \\ 2x + y &\leq 12 \\ x &\geq 0 \\ y &\geq 0 \end{aligned}$$

8. A custom-blend bird seed is to be mixed from seed mixtures costing $0.75 per pound and $1.25 per pound. How many pounds of each seed mixture are used to make 200 pounds of custom-blend bird seed costing $0.95 per pound?

9. Find the equation of the parabola $y = ax^2 + bx + c$ passing through the points $(0, 4)$, $(3, 1)$, and $(6, 4)$.

$$\begin{cases} -x + 2y - z = 9 \\ 2x - y + 2z = -9 \\ 3x + 3y - 4z = 7 \end{cases}$$

SYSTEM FOR 10 AND 11

In Exercises 10 and 11, use the system of equations at the left.

10. Write the augmented matrix corresponding to the system of equations.

11. Solve the system using the matrix and Gauss-Jordan elimination.

In Exercises 12–15, use the following matrices.

$$A = \begin{bmatrix} 4 & 0 \\ -1 & 2 \end{bmatrix}, \quad B = \begin{bmatrix} -1 & 3 \\ 1 & 0 \end{bmatrix}$$

$$\begin{bmatrix} 8 & 0 & -5 \\ 1 & 3 & -1 \\ -2 & 6 & 4 \end{bmatrix}$$

MATRIX FOR 16

12. Find $A - B$.

13. Find $-2B$.

14. Find $A - 2B$.

15. Find AB, if possible.

16. Find the determinant of the matrix at the left.

17. Find the inverse (if it exists): 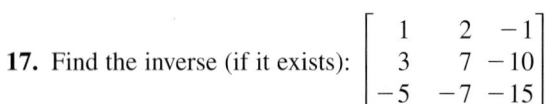 $\begin{bmatrix} 1 & 2 & -1 \\ 3 & 7 & -10 \\ -5 & -7 & -15 \end{bmatrix}$.

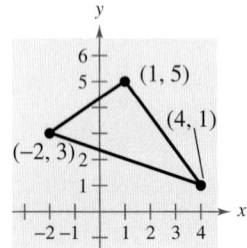

	Gym shoes	Jogging shoes	Walking shoes
14–17	0.13	0.14	0.03
Age group 18–24	0.06	0.11	0.04
25–34	0.10	0.17	0.09

MATRIX FOR 18

18. The percents (by age group) of the total amounts spent on three types of footwear in 1999 are shown in the matrix. The total amounts (in millions) spent by each age group on the three types of footwear were $554.93 (14–17 age group), $405.34 (18–24 age group), and $727.85 (25–34 age group). How many dollars worth of gym shoes, jogging shoes, and walking shoes were sold in 1999?   (Source: National Sporting Goods Association)

In Exercises 19 and 20, use Cramer's Rule to solve the system of equations.

19. $\begin{cases} 8x - 3y = -52 \\ 3x + 5y = 5 \end{cases}$

20. $\begin{cases} 5x + 4y + 3z = 7 \\ -3x - 8y + 7z = -9 \\ 7x - 5y - 6z = -53 \end{cases}$

21. Find the area of the triangle in the figure.

FIGURE FOR 21

22. Write the first five terms of the sequence $a_n = \dfrac{(-1)^{n+1}}{2n+3}$ (assume that n begins with 1).

23. Write an expression for the nth term of the sequence.

$$\frac{2!}{4}, \frac{3!}{5}, \frac{4!}{6}, \frac{5!}{7}, \frac{6!}{8}, \cdots$$

24. Sum the first 20 terms of the arithmetic sequence 8, 12, 16, 20, ...

25. The sixth term of an arithmetic sequence is 20.6, and the ninth term is 30.2.
    (a) Find the 20th term.
    (b) Find the nth term

26. Write the first five terms of the sequence $a_n = 3(2)^{n-1}$ (assume that n begins with 1).

27. Find the sum: $\displaystyle\sum_{i=0}^{\infty} 1.3\left(\frac{1}{10}\right)^{i-1}$.

28. Use mathematical induction to prove the formula

$$3 + 7 + 11 + 15 + \cdots + (4n - 1) = n(2n + 1).$$

29. Use the Binomial Theorem to expand and simplify $(z - 3)^4$.

In Exercises 30–33, evaluate the expression.

30. $_7P_3$ 31. $_{25}P_2$ 32. $\dbinom{8}{4}$ 33. $_{10}C_3$

34. A personnel manager at a department store has 10 applicants to fill three different sales positions. In how many ways can this be done, assuming that all the applicants are qualified for any of the three positions?

35. On a game show, the digits 3, 4, and 5 must be arranged in the proper order to form the price of an appliance. If the digits are arranged correctly, the contestant wins the appliance. What is the probability of winning if the contestant knows that the price is at least $400?

Proofs in Mathematics

Properties of Sums *(p. 619)*

1. $\displaystyle\sum_{i=1}^{n} c = nc,$ c is a constant.   2. $\displaystyle\sum_{i=1}^{n} ca_i = c\sum_{i=1}^{n} a_i,$ c is a constant.

3. $\displaystyle\sum_{i=1}^{n} (a_i + b_i) = \sum_{i=1}^{n} a_i + \sum_{i=1}^{n} b_i$

4. $\displaystyle\sum_{i=1}^{n} (a_i - b_i) = \sum_{i=1}^{n} a_i - \sum_{i=1}^{n} b_i$

Infinite Series

The study of infinite series was considered a novelty in the fourteenth century. Logician Richard Suiseth, whose nickname was Calculator, solved this problem.

If throughout the first half of a given time interval a variation continues at a certain intensity; throughout the next quarter of the interval at double the intensity; throughout the following eighth at triple the intensity and so ad infinitum; The average intensity for the whole interval will be the intensity of the variation during the second subinterval (or double the intensity).

This is the same as saying that the sum of the infinite series

$$\frac{1}{2} + \frac{2}{4} + \frac{3}{8} + \cdots + \frac{n}{2^n} + \cdots$$

is 2.

Proof

Each of these properties follows directly from the properties of real numbers.

1. $\displaystyle\sum_{i=1}^{n} c = c + c + c + \cdots + c = nc$ n terms

The Distributive Property is used in the proof of Property 2.

2. $\displaystyle\sum_{i=1}^{n} ca_i = ca_1 + ca_2 + ca_3 + \cdots + ca_n$

$$= c(a_1 + a_2 + a_3 + \cdots + a_n) = c\sum_{i=1}^{n} a_i$$

The proof of Property 3 uses the Commutative and Associative Properties of Addition.

3.
$$\sum_{i=1}^{n} (a_i + b_i) = (a_1 + b_1) + (a_2 + b_2) + (a_3 + b_3) + \cdots + (a_n + b_n)$$
$$= (a_1 + a_2 + a_3 + \cdots + a_n) + (b_1 + b_2 + b_3 + \cdots + b_n)$$
$$= \sum_{i=1}^{n} a_i + \sum_{i=1}^{n} b_i$$

The proof of Property 4 uses the Commutative and Associative Properties of Addition and the Distributive Property.

4.
$$\sum_{i=1}^{n} (a_i - b_i) = (a_1 - b_1) + (a_2 - b_2) + (a_3 - b_3) + \cdots + (a_n - b_n)$$
$$= (a_1 + a_2 + a_3 + \cdots + a_n) + (-b_1 - b_2 - b_3 - \cdots - b_n)$$
$$= (a_1 + a_2 + a_3 + \cdots + a_n) - (b_1 + b_2 + b_3 + \cdots + b_n)$$
$$= \sum_{i=1}^{n} a_i - \sum_{i=1}^{n} b_i$$

The Sum of a Finite Arithmetic Sequence *(p. 628)*

The sum of a finite arithmetic sequence with n terms is

$$S_n = \frac{n}{2}(a_1 + a_n).$$

Proof

Begin by generating the terms of the arithmetic sequence in two ways. In the first way, repeatedly add d to the first term to obtain

$$S_n = a_1 + a_2 + a_3 + \cdots + a_{n-2} + a_{n-1} + a_n$$
$$= a_1 + [a_1 + d] + [a_1 + 2d] + \cdots + [a_1 + (n-1)d].$$

In the second way, repeatedly subtract d from the nth term to obtain

$$S_n = a_n + a_{n-1} + a_{n-2} + \cdots + a_3 + a_2 + a_1$$
$$= a_n + [a_n - d] + [a_n - 2d] + \cdots + [a_n - (n-1)d].$$

If you add these two versions of S_n, the multiples of d subtract out and you obtain

$$2S_n = (a_1 + a_n) + (a_1 + a_n) + (a_1 + a_n) + \cdots + (a_1 + a_n) \quad n \text{ terms}$$
$$2S_n = n(a_1 + a_n)$$
$$S_n = \frac{n}{2}(a_1 + a_n).$$

The Sum of a Finite Geometric Sequence *(p. 637)*

The sum of the finite geometric sequence

$$a_1, \ a_1r, \ a_1r^2, \ a_1r^3, \ a_1r^4, \ \ldots, a_1r^{n-1}$$

with common ratio $r \neq 1$ is given by $S_n = \displaystyle\sum_{i=1}^{n} a_1 r^{i-1} = a_1\left(\frac{1-r^n}{1-r}\right).$

Proof

$$S_n = a_1 + a_1r + a_1r^2 + \cdots + a_1r^{n-2} + a_1r^{n-1}$$
$$rS_n = a_1r + a_1r^2 + a_1r^3 + \cdots + a_1r^{n-1} + a_1r^n \qquad \text{Multiply by } r.$$

Subtracting the second equation from the first yields

$$S_n - rS_n = a_1 - a_1r^n.$$

So, $S_n(1 - r) = a_1(1 - r^n)$, and, because $r \neq 1$, you have $S_n = a_1\left(\dfrac{1-r^n}{1-r}\right).$

The Binomial Theorem *(p. 654)*

In the expansion of $(x + y)^n$

$$(x + y)^n = x^n + nx^{n-1}y + \cdots + {}_nC_r\,x^{n-r}y^r + \cdots + nxy^{n-1} + y^n$$

the coefficient of $x^{n-r}y^r$ is

$${}_nC_r = \frac{n!}{(n-r)!\,r!}.$$

Proof

The Binomial Theorem can be proved quite nicely using mathematical induction. The steps are straightforward but look a little messy, so only an outline of the proof is presented.

1. If $n = 1$, you have $(x + y)^1 = x^1 + y^1 = {}_1C_0 x + {}_1C_1 y$, and the formula is valid.

2. Assuming that the formula is true for $n = k$, the coefficient of $x^{k-r}y^r$ is

$${}_kC_r = \frac{k!}{(k-r)!\,r!} = \frac{k(k-1)(k-2)\cdots(k-r+1)}{r!}.$$

To show that the formula is true for $n = k + 1$, look at the coefficient of $x^{k+1-r}y^r$ in the expansion of

$$(x + y)^{k+1} = (x + y)^k(x + y).$$

From the right-hand side, you can determine that the term involving $x^{k+1-r}y^r$ is the sum of two products.

$$\left({}_kC_r x^{k-r}y^r\right)(x) + \left({}_kC_{r-1}x^{k+1-r}y^{r-1}\right)(y)$$

$$= \left[\frac{k!}{(k-r)!\,r!} + \frac{k!}{(k+1-r)!(r-1)!}\right]x^{k+1-r}y^r$$

$$= \left[\frac{(k+1-r)k!}{(k+1-r)!\,r!} + \frac{k!r}{(k+1-r)!\,r!}\right]x^{k+1-r}y^r$$

$$= \left[\frac{k!(k+1-r+r)}{(k+1-r)!\,r!}\right]x^{k+1-r}y^r$$

$$= \left[\frac{(k+1)!}{(k+1-r)!\,r!}\right]x^{k+1-r}y^r$$

$$= {}_{k+1}C_r x^{k+1-r}y^r$$

So, by mathematical induction, the Binomial Theorem is valid for all positive integers n.

1. Let $x_0 = 1$ and consider the sequence x_n given by

$$x_n = \frac{1}{2}x_{n-1} + \frac{1}{x_{n-1}}, \quad n = 1, 2, \ldots$$

Use a graphing utility to compute the first 10 terms of the sequence and make a conjecture about the value of x_n as n approaches infinity.

2. Consider the sequence

$$a_n = \frac{n+1}{n^2+1}.$$

 (a) Use a graphing utility to graph the first 10 terms of the sequence.

(b) Use the graph from part (a) to estimate the value of a_n as n approaches infinity.

(c) Complete the table.

n	1	10	100	1000	10,000
a_n					

(d) Use the table from part (c) to determine (if possible) the value of a_n as n approaches infinity.

3. Consider the sequence

$$a_n = 3 + (-1)^n.$$

 (a) Use a graphing utility to graph the first 10 terms of the sequence.

(b) Use the graph from part (a) to describe the behavior of the graph of the sequence.

(c) Complete the table.

n	1	10	101	1000	10,001
a_n					

(d) Use the table from part (c) to determine (if possible) the value of a_n as n approaches infinity.

4. The following operations are performed on each term of an arithmetic sequence. Determine if the resulting sequence is arithmetic, and if so, state the common difference.

(a) A constant C is added to each term.

(b) Each term is multiplied by a nonzero constant C.

(c) Each term is squared.

5. The following sequence of perfect squares is not arithmetic.

1, 4, 9, 16, 25, 36, 49, 64, 81, . . .

However, you can form a related sequence that is arithmetic by finding the differences of consecutive terms.

(a) Write the first eight terms of the related arithmetic sequence described above. What is the nth term of this sequence?

(b) Describe how you can find an arithmetic sequence that is related to the following sequence of perfect cubes.

1, 8, 27, 64, 125, 216, 343, 512, 729, . . .

(c) Write the first seven terms of the related sequence in part (b) and find the nth term of the sequence.

(d) Describe how you can find the arithmetic sequence that is related to the following sequence of perfect fourth powers.

1, 16, 81, 256, 625, 1296, 2401, 4096, 6561, . . .

(e) Write the first six terms of the related sequence in part (d) and find the nth term of the sequence.

6. Can the Greek hero Achilles, running at 20 feet per second, ever catch a tortoise, starting 20 feet ahead of Achilles and running at 10 feet per second? The Greek mathematician Zeno said no. When Achilles runs 20 feet, the tortoise will be 10 feet ahead. Then, when Achilles runs 10 feet, the tortoise will be 5 feet ahead. Achilles will keep cutting the distance in half but will never catch the tortoise. The table shows Zeno's reasoning. From the table you can see that both the distances and the times required to achieve them form infinite geometric series. Using the table, show that both series have finite sums. What do these sums represent?

Distance (in feet)	Time (in seconds)
20	1
10	0.5
5	0.25
2.5	0.125
1.25	0.0625
0.625	0.03125

7. Recall that a *fractal* is a geometric figure that consists of a pattern that is repeated infinitely on a smaller and smaller scale. A well-known fractal is called the *Sierpinski Triangle*. In the first stage, the midpoints of the three sides are used to create the vertices of a new triangle, which is then removed, leaving three triangles. The first three stages are shown below. Note that each remaining triangle is similar to the original triangle. Assume that the length of each side of the original triangle is one unit. Write a formula that describes the side length of the triangles that will be generated in the nth stage. Write a formula for the area of the triangles that will be generated in the nth stage.

8. You can define a sequence using a piecewise formula. The following is an example of a piecewise-defined sequence.

$$a_1 = 7, \quad a_n = \begin{cases} \dfrac{a_{n-1}}{2}, & \text{if } a_{n-1} \text{ is even} \\ 3a_{n-1} + 1, & \text{if } a_{n-1} \text{ is odd} \end{cases}$$

(a) Write the first 10 terms of the sequence.

(b) Choose three different values for a_1 (other than $a_1 = 7$). For each value of a_1, find the first 10 terms of the sequence. What conclusions can you make about the behavior of this sequence?

9. The numbers 1, 5, 12, 22, 35, 51, . . . are called pentagonal numbers because they represent the numbers of dots used to make pentagons, as shown below. Use mathematical induction to prove that the nth pentagonal number P_n is given by

$$P_n = \frac{n(3n - 1)}{2}.$$

  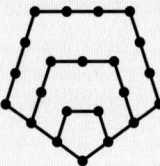

10. What conclusion can be drawn from the information about the sequence of statements P_n?

(a) P_3 is true and P_k implies P_{k+1}.

(b) $P_1, P_2, P_3, \ldots, P_{50}$ are all true.

(c) $P_1, P_2,$ and P_3 are all true, but the truth of P_k does not imply that P_{k+1} is true.

(d) P_2 is true and P_{2k} implies P_{2k+2}.

11. Let $f_1, f_2, \ldots, f_n, \ldots$ be the Fibonacci sequence.

(a) Use mathematical induction to prove that $f_1 + f_2 + \cdots + f_n = f_{n+2} - 1$.

(b) Find the sum of the first 20 terms of the Fibonacci sequence.

12. The odds in favor of an event occurring are the ratio of the probability that the event will occur to the probability that the event will not occur. The reciprocal of this ratio represents the odds against the event occurring.

(a) Six marbles in a bag are red. The odds against choosing a red marble are "4 to 1." How many marbles are in the bag?

(b) A bag contains three blue marbles and seven yellow marbles. What are the odds in favor of choosing a blue marble? What are the odds against choosing a blue marble?

(c) Write a formula for converting the odds in favor of an event to the probability of the event.

(d) Write a formula for converting the probability of an event to the odds in favor of the event.

13. You are taking a test that contains only multiple choice questions. You are on the last question and you know that the answer is not B or D, but you are not sure about answers A, C, and E. What is the probability that you will get the right answer if you take a guess?

14. A dart is thrown at the circular target shown. The dart is equally likely to hit any point inside the target. What is the probability that it hits the region outside the triangle?

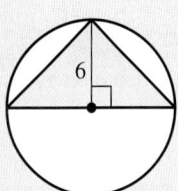

How to study Chapter 10

▶ **What you should learn**

In this chapter you will learn the following skills and concepts:

- How to find the inclination of a line, the angle between two lines, and the distance between a point and a line
- How to write the standard form of the equation of a parabola, an ellipse, and a hyperbola
- How to eliminate the *xy*-term in the equation of a conic and use the discriminant to identify a conic
- How to rewrite a set of parametric equations as a rectangular equation and find a set of parametric equations for a graph
- How to write equations in polar form and graph polar equations

▶ **Important Vocabulary**

As you encounter each new vocabulary term in this chapter, add the term and its definition to your notebook glossary.

Inclination (p. 700)
Angle between two lines (p. 701)
Conic section or conic (pp. 707, 764)
Parabola (pp. 708, 764)
Directrix (p. 708)
Focus or foci (pp. 708, 716)
Focal chord (p. 710)
Latus rectum (p. 710)
Tangent (p. 710)
Ellipse (pp. 716, 764)
Vertices (pp. 716, 725)
Major axis (p. 716)
Minor axis (p. 716)
Center (pp. 716, 725)
Eccentricity (pp. 720, 729, 764)

Hyperbola (pp. 725, 764)
Branches (p. 725)
Transverse axis (p. 725)
Asymptotes (p. 727)
Conjugate axis (p. 727)
Invariant under rotation (p. 738)
Discriminant (p. 738)
Parameter (p. 742)
Parametric equations (p. 742)
Plane curve (p. 742)
Orientation (p. 743)
Polar coordinate system (p. 750)
Pole or origin (p. 750)
Polar axis (p. 750)
Polar coordinates (p. 750)

Study Tools

Learning objectives in each section
Chapter Summary (p. 771)
Review Exercises (pp. 772–775)
Chapter Test (p. 776)

Additional Resources

Study and Solutions Guide
Interactive Precalculus
Videotapes/DVD for Chapter 10
Precalculus Website
Student Success Organizer

www.PerfectPhoto.CA/© Rob vonNostrand

10

Topics in Analytic Geometry

10.1   Lines

▶ **What you should learn**

- How to find the inclination of a line
- How to find the angle between two lines
- How to find the distance between a point and a line

▶ **Why you should learn it**

The inclination of a line can be used to measure heights indirectly. For instance, in Exercise 56 on page 706, the inclination of a line can be used to determine the change in elevation from the top of the Johnstown Inclined Plane.

AP/Wide World Photos

Inclination of a Line

In Section 1.2, you learned that the graph of the linear equation

$$y = mx + b$$

is a nonvertical line with slope m and y-intercept $(0, b)$. There, the slope of a line was described as the rate of change in y with respect to x. In this section, you will look at the slope of a line in terms of the angle of inclination of the line.

Every nonhorizontal line must intersect the x-axis. The angle formed by such an intersection determines the **inclination** of the line, as specified in the following definition.

Definition of Inclination

The **inclination** of a nonhorizontal line is the positive angle θ (less than π) measured counterclockwise from the x-axis to the line. (See Figure 10.1.)

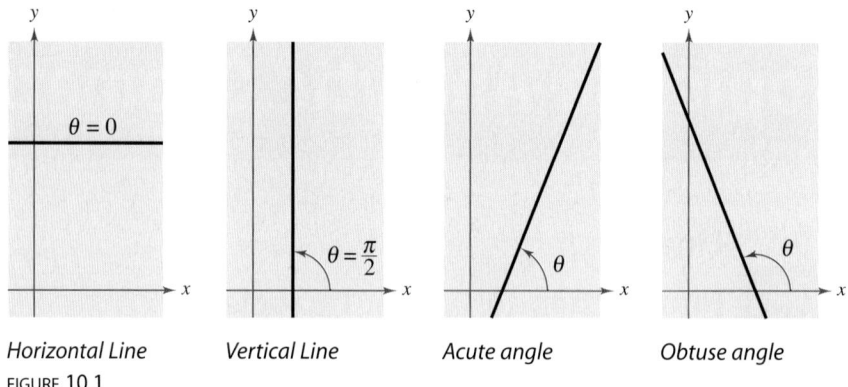

| Horizontal Line | Vertical Line | Acute angle | Obtuse angle |

FIGURE 10.1

The inclination of a line is related to its slope in the following manner.

Inclination and Slope

If a nonvertical line has inclination θ and slope m, then

$$m = \tan \theta.$$

For a proof of the relation between inclination and slope, see Proofs in Mathematics on page 777.

The icon identifies examples and concepts related to features of the Learning Tools CD-ROM and the *Interactive* and *Internet* versions of this text. For more details see the chart on pages *xxi-xxv*.

Example 1 ▶ Finding the Inclination of a Line

Find the inclination of the line $2x + 3y = 6$.

Solution

The slope of this line is $m = -\frac{2}{3}$. So, its inclination is determined from the equation

$$\tan \theta = -\frac{2}{3}.$$

From Figure 10.2, it follows that $\frac{\pi}{2} < \theta < \pi$. This means that

$$\theta = \pi + \arctan\left(-\frac{2}{3}\right)$$

$$\approx \pi + (-0.588)$$

$$= \pi - 0.588$$

$$\approx 2.554.$$

The angle of inclination is about 2.554 radians or about 146.3°.

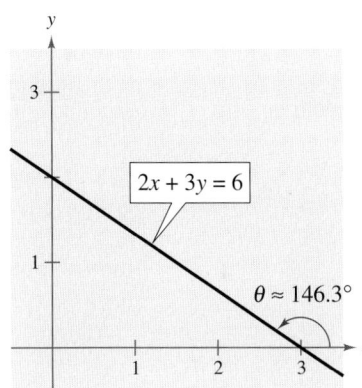

FIGURE **10.2**

The *Interactive* CD-ROM and *Internet* versions of this text offer a Try It for each example in the text.

The Angle Between Two Lines

Two distinct lines in a plane are either parallel or intersecting. If they intersect and are nonperpendicular, their intersection forms two pairs of opposite angles. One pair is acute and the other pair is obtuse. The smaller of these angles is called the **angle between the two lines.** As shown in Figure 10.3, you can use the inclinations of the two lines to find the angle between the two lines. Specifically, if two lines have inclinations θ_1 and θ_2, the angle between the two lines is

$$\theta = \theta_2 - \theta_1$$

where $\theta_1 < \theta_2$. You can use the formula for the tangent of the difference of two angles

$$\tan \theta = \tan(\theta_2 - \theta_1)$$

$$= \frac{\tan \theta_2 - \tan \theta_1}{1 + \tan \theta_1 \tan \theta_2}$$

to obtain the formula for the angle between two lines.

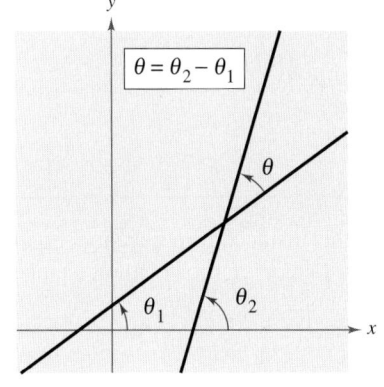

FIGURE **10.3**

Angle Between Two Lines

If two nonperpendicular lines have slopes m_1 and m_2, the angle between the two lines is

$$\tan \theta = \left| \frac{m_2 - m_1}{1 + m_1 m_2} \right|.$$

Example 2 ▶ **Finding the Angle Between Two Lines**

Find the angle between the two lines.

$$\text{Line 1: } 2x - y - 4 = 0 \qquad \text{Line 2: } 3x + 4y - 12 = 0$$

Solution

The two lines have slopes of $m_1 = 2$ and $m_2 = -\frac{3}{4}$, respectively. So, the tangent of the angle between the two lines is

$$\tan \theta = \left| \frac{m_2 - m_1}{1 + m_1 m_2} \right| = \left| \frac{(-3/4) - 2}{1 + (2)(-3/4)} \right| = \left| \frac{-11/4}{-2/4} \right| = \frac{11}{2}.$$

Finally, you can conclude that the angle is

$$\theta = \arctan \frac{11}{2} \approx 1.391 \text{ radians} \approx 79.70°$$

as shown in Figure 10.4.

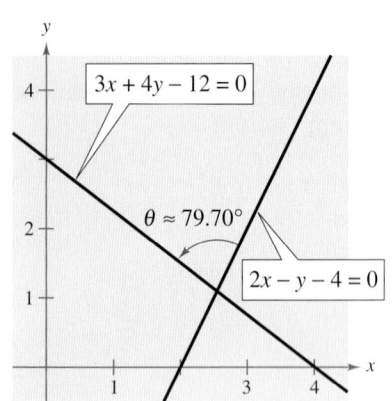

FIGURE 10.4

The Distance Between a Point and a Line

Finding the distance between a line and a point not on the line is an application of perpendicular lines. This distance is defined as the length of the perpendicular line segment joining the point to the line, as shown in Figure 10.5.

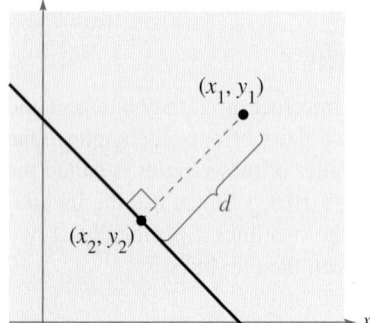

FIGURE 10.5

Distance Between a Point and a Line

The distance between the point (x_1, y_1) and the line $Ax + By + C = 0$ is

$$d = \frac{|Ax_1 + By_1 + C|}{\sqrt{A^2 + B^2}}.$$

Remember that the values of A, B, and C in this distance formula correspond to the general equation of a line, $Ax + By + C = 0$. For a proof of the distance between a point and a line, see Proofs in Mathematics on page 777.

Example 3 ▶ **Finding the Distance Between a Point and a Line**

Find the distance between the point $(4, 1)$ and the line $y = 2x + 1$.

Solution

The general form of the equation is

$$-2x + y - 1 = 0.$$

So, the distance between the point and the line is

$$d = \frac{|-2(4) + 1(1) - 1|}{\sqrt{(-2)^2 + 1^2}} = \frac{8}{\sqrt{5}} \approx 3.58 \text{ units.}$$

The line and the point are shown in Figure 10.6.

FIGURE 10.6

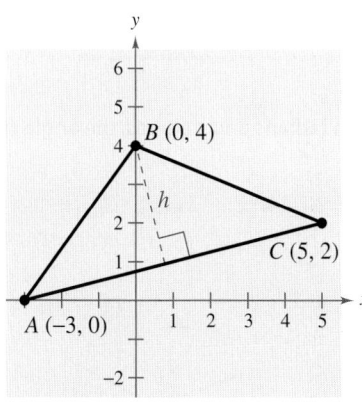

FIGURE **10.7**

Activities

1. Find the inclination of the line
   $5x - 4y = 20$.
   Answer: $\theta = 0.896$ radian or $51.34°$
2. Find the angle θ between the lines
   $x + 2y = 5$ and $3x - y = 6$.
   Answer: $\theta = 1.429$ radians or $81.87°$
3. Find the distance between the point
   $(3, -1)$ and the line
   $4x - 3y - 12 = 0$.
   Answer: $d = \frac{3}{5}$ unit

The *Interactive* CD-ROM and *Internet* versions of this text offer a Quiz for every section of the text.

Example 4 ▶ An Application of Two Distance Formulas

Figure 10.7 shows a triangle with vertices $A(-3, 0)$, $B(0, 4)$, and $C(5, 2)$.

a. Find the altitude from vertex B to side AC.

b. Find the area of the triangle.

Solution

a. To find the altitude, use the formula for the distance between line AC and the point $(0, 4)$. The equation of line AC is obtained as follows.

$$\text{Slope: } m = \frac{2 - 0}{5 + 3} = \frac{2}{8} = \frac{1}{4}$$

$$\text{Equation: } \quad y - 0 = \frac{1}{4}(x + 3) \qquad \text{Point-slope form}$$

$$4y = x + 3 \qquad \text{Multiply each side by 4.}$$

$$x - 4y + 3 = 0 \qquad \text{General form}$$

So, the distance between this line and the point $(0, 4)$ is

$$\text{Altitude} = h = \frac{|1(0) + (-4)(4) + 3|}{\sqrt{1^2 + (-4)^2}} = \frac{13}{\sqrt{17}} \text{ units.}$$

b. Using the formula for the distance between two points, you can find the length of the base AC to be

$$b = \sqrt{(5 + 3)^2 + (2 - 0)^2} \qquad \text{Distance Formula}$$

$$= \sqrt{8^2 + 2^2} \qquad \text{Simplify.}$$

$$= \sqrt{68} \qquad \text{Simplify.}$$

$$= 2\sqrt{17} \text{ units.} \qquad \text{Simplify.}$$

Finally, the area of the triangle in Figure 10.7 is

$$A = \frac{1}{2}bh \qquad \text{Formula for the area of a triangle}$$

$$= \frac{1}{2}\left(2\sqrt{17}\right)\left(\frac{13}{\sqrt{17}}\right) \qquad \text{Substitute for } b \text{ and } h.$$

$$= 13 \text{ square units.} \qquad \text{Simplify.}$$

Group Activity: Graphing Utility

Put your students in groups of two. Ask each group to write a graphing calculator program that finds the angle between two lines based on user input. Ask each group to demonstrate the program on an example or exercise in this section.

Writing ABOUT MATHEMATICS

Inclination and the Angle Between Two Lines Discuss why the inclination of a line can be an angle that is larger than $\pi/2$, but the angle between two lines cannot be larger than $\pi/2$. Decide whether the following statement is true or false: "The inclination of a line is the angle between the line and the x-axis." Explain.

10.1 Exercises

The *Interactive* CD-ROM and *Internet* versions of this text contain step-by-step solutions to all odd-numbered exercises. They also provide Tutorial Exercises for additional help.

In Exercises 1–8, find the slope of the line with inclination θ.

1.

2.

3.

4.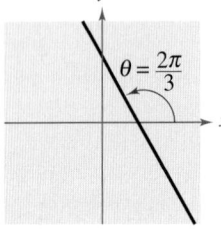

5. $\theta = \dfrac{\pi}{3}$ radians

6. $\theta = \dfrac{5\pi}{6}$ radians

7. $\theta = 1.27$ radians

8. $\theta = 2.88$ radians

In Exercises 9–14, find, in radians and degrees, the inclination θ of the line with a slope of m.

9. $m = -1$

10. $m = -2$

11. $m = 1$

12. $m = 2$

13. $m = \frac{3}{4}$

14. $m = -\frac{5}{2}$

In Exercises 15–18, find, in radians and degrees, the inclination θ of the line passing through the points.

15. $(6, 1), (10, 8)$

16. $(12, 8), (-4, -3)$

17. $(-2, 20), (10, 0)$

18. $(0, 100), (50, 0)$

In Exercises 19–22, find, in radians and degrees, the inclination θ of the line.

19. $6x - 2y + 8 = 0$

20. $4x + 5y - 9 = 0$

21. $5x + 3y = 0$

22. $x - y - 10 = 0$

In Exercises 23–32, find, in radians and degrees, the angle θ between the lines.

23. $3x + y = 3$
    $x - y = 2$

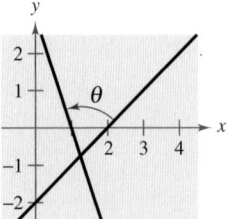

24. $x + 3y = 2$
    $x - 2y = -3$

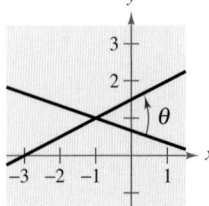

25. $x - y = 0$
    $3x - 2y = -1$

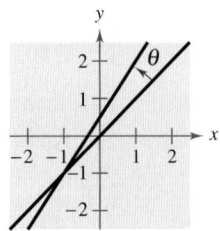

26. $2x - y = 2$
    $4x + 3y = 24$

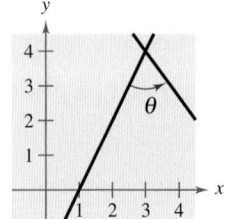

27. $x - 2y = 7$
    $6x + 2y = 5$

28. $5x + 2y = 16$
    $3x - 5y = -1$

29. $x + 2y = 8$
    $x - 2y = 2$

30. $3x - 5y = 3$
    $3x + 5y = 12$

31. $0.05x - 0.03y = 0.21$
    $0.07x + 0.02y = 0.16$

32. $0.02x - 0.05y = -0.19$
    $0.03x + 0.04y = 0.52$

Angle Measurement In Exercises 33–36, find the slope of each side of the triangle and use the slopes to find the measures of the interior angles.

33.

34.

35.

36.

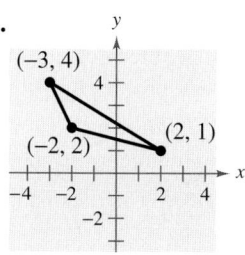

In Exercises 37–44, find the distance between the point and the line.

Point	Line
37. $(0, 0)$	$4x + 3y = 0$
38. $(0, 0)$	$2x - y = 4$
39. $(2, 3)$	$4x + 3y = 10$
40. $(-2, 1)$	$x - y = 2$
41. $(6, 2)$	$x + 1 = 0$
42. $(10, 8)$	$y - 4 = 0$
43. $(0, 8)$	$6x - y = 0$
44. $(4, 2)$	$x - y = 20$

Area **In Exercises 45–48, (a) find the altitude from vertex B of the triangle to side AC, and (b) find the area of the triangle.**

45. $A = (0, 0),\ B = (1, 4),\ C = (4, 0)$

46. $A = (0, 0),\ B = (4, 5),\ C = (5, -2)$

47. $A = \left(-\frac{1}{2}, \frac{1}{2}\right),\ B = (2, 3),\ C = \left(\frac{5}{2}, 0\right)$

48. $A = (-4, -5),\ B = (3, 10),\ C = (6, 12)$

In Exercises 49 and 50, find the distance between the parallel lines.

49. $x + y = 1$
$\ x + y = 5$

50. $3x - 4y = 1$
$\ 3x - 4y = 10$

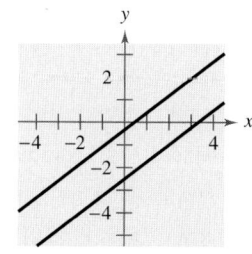

51. *Grade of a Road* A straight road rises with an inclination of 0.10 radian from the horizontal (see figure). Find the slope of the road and the change in elevation over a two-mile stretch of the road.

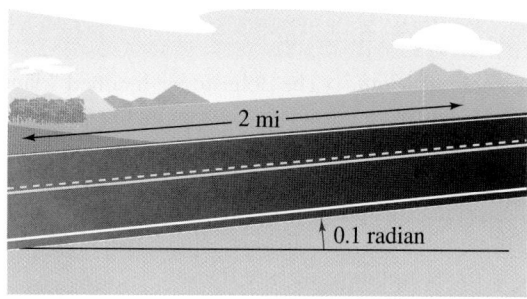

FIGURE FOR 51

52. *Grade of a Road* A straight road rises with an inclination of 0.20 radian from the horizontal. Find the slope of the road and the change in elevation over a one-mile stretch of the road.

53. *Conveyor Design* A moving conveyor is built so that it rises 1 meter for each 3 meters of horizontal travel.

(a) Find the inclination of the conveyor.

(b) The conveyor runs between two floors in a factory. The distance between the floors is 5 meters. Find the length of the conveyor.

54. *Pitch of a Roof* A roof has a rise of 3 feet for every horizontal change of 5 feet (see figure). Find the inclination of the roof.

55. *Truss* Find the angles α and β shown in the drawing of the roof truss.

▶ Model It

56. *Inclined Plane*   The Johnstown Inclined Plane in Johnstown, Pennsylvania is an inclined railway that was designed to carry people to the hilltop community of Westmont. It also proved useful in carrying people and vehicles to safety during severe floods. The railway is 896.5 feet long with a 70.9% uphill grade (see figure).

(a) Find the inclination θ of the railway.

(b) Find the change in elevation from the top of the railway.

(c) Using the origin as the base of the inclined plane, find the equation of the line that models the railway track.

(d) Sketch a graph of the equation you found in part (c).

896.5 ft

θ

Not drawn to scale

Synthesis

True or False?   In Exercises 57 and 58, determine whether the statement is true or false. Justify your answer.

57. A line that has an inclination greater than $\pi/2$ radians has a negative slope.

58. To find the angle between two lines whose angles of inclination θ_1 and θ_2 are known, substitute θ_1 and θ_2 for m_1 and m_2, respectively, in the formula for the angle between two lines.

59. *Exploration*   Consider a line with slope m and y-intercept $(0, 4)$.

(a) Write the distance d between the origin and the line as a function of m.

(b) Graph the function in part (a).

(c) Find the slope that yields the maximum distance between the origin and the line.

(d) Find the asymptote of the graph in part (b) and interpret its meaning in the context of the problem.

60. *Exploration*   Consider a line with slope m and y-intercept $(0, 4)$.

(a) Write the distance d between the point $(3, 1)$ and the line as a function of m.

(b) Graph the function in part (a).

(c) Find the slope that yields the maximum distance between the point and the line.

(d) Is it possible for the distance to be 0? If so, what is the slope of the line that yields a distance of 0?

(e) Find the asymptote of the graph in part (b) and interpret its meaning in the context of the problem.

Review

In Exercises 61–66, find all x-intercepts and y-intercepts of the graph of the quadratic function.

61. $f(x) = (x - 7)^2$

62. $f(x) = (x + 9)^2$

63. $f(x) = (x - 5)^2 - 5$

64. $f(x) = (x + 11)^2 + 12$

65. $f(x) = x^2 - 7x - 1$

66. $f(x) = x^2 + 9x - 22$

In Exercises 67–72, write the quadratic function in standard form by completing the square. Identify the vertex of the function.

67. $f(x) = 3x^2 + 2x - 16$

68. $f(x) = 2x^2 - x - 21$

69. $f(x) = 5x^2 + 34x - 7$

70. $f(x) = -x^2 - 8x - 15$

71. $f(x) = 6x^2 - x - 12$

72. $f(x) = -8x^2 - 34x - 21$

In Exercises 73–76, graph the quadratic function.

73. $f(x) = (x - 4)^2 + 3$

74. $f(x) = 6 - (x + 1)^2$

75. $g(x) = 2x^2 - 3x + 1$

76. $g(x) = -x^2 + 6x - 8$

10.2 Introduction to Conics: Parabolas

► **What you should learn**

- How to recognize a conic as the intersection of a plane and a double-napped cone
- How to write the standard form of the equation of a parabola
- How to use the reflective property of parabolas to solve real-life problems

► **Why you should learn it**

Parabolas can be used to model and solve many types of real-life problems. For instance, in Exercise 62 on page 713, a parabola is used to model the cables of the Golden Gate Bridge.

Cosmo Condina/Getty Images

Conics

Conic sections were discovered during the classical Greek period, 600 to 300 B.C. The early Greeks were concerned largely with the geometric properties of conics. It was not until the 17th century that the broad applicability of conics became apparent and played a prominent role in the early development of calculus.

Each **conic section** (or simply **conic**) is the intersection of a plane and a double-napped cone. Notice in Figure 10.8 that in the formation of the four basic conics, the intersecting plane does not pass through the vertex of the cone. When the plane does pass through the vertex, the resulting figure is a **degenerate conic,** as shown in Figure 10.9.

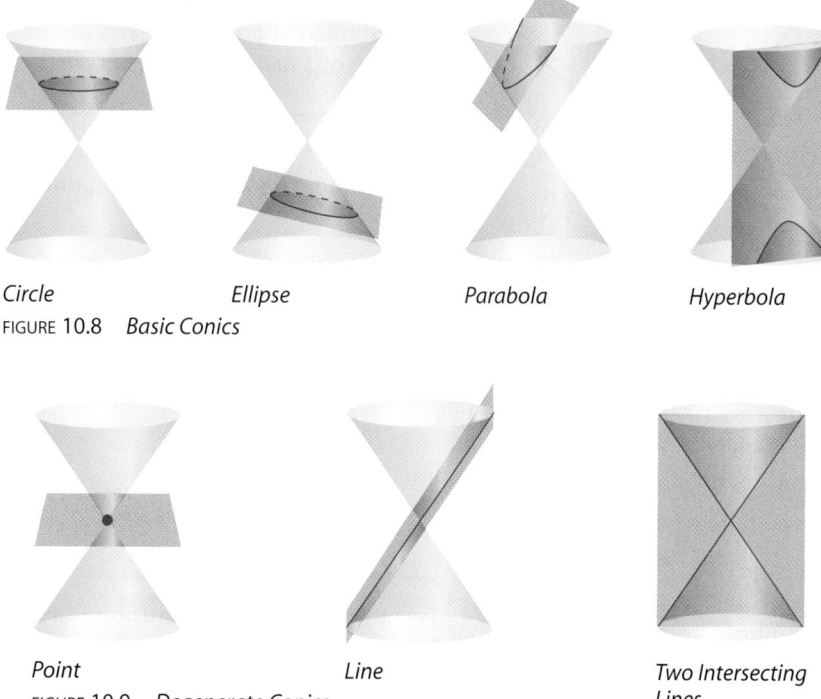

Circle   Ellipse   Parabola   Hyperbola

FIGURE 10.8 *Basic Conics*

Point   Line   Two Intersecting Lines

FIGURE 10.9 *Degenerate Conics*

There are several ways to approach the study of conics. You could begin by defining conics in terms of the intersections of planes and cones, as the Greeks did, or you could define them algebraically, in terms of the general second-degree equation

$$Ax^2 + Bxy + Cy^2 + Dx + Ey + F = 0.$$

However, you will study a third approach, in which each of the conics is defined as a **locus** (collection) of points satisfying a geometric property. For example, a circle is defined as the collection of all points (x, y) that are equidistant from a fixed point (h, k). This leads to the standard equation of a circle

$$(x - h)^2 + (y - k)^2 = r^2. \qquad \text{Equation of circle}$$

This study of conics is from a locus-of-points approach, which leads to the development of the standard equation for each conic. Your students should know the standard equations of all conics well. Make sure they understand the relationship of h and k to the horizontal and vertical shifts.

Parabolas

In Section 2.1, you learned that the graph of the quadratic function

$$f(x) = ax^2 + bx + c$$

is a parabola that opens upward or downward. The following definition of a parabola is more general in the sense that it is independent of the orientation of the parabola.

Definition of Parabola

A **parabola** is the set of all points (x, y) in a plane that are equidistant from a fixed line (**directrix**) and a fixed point (**focus**) not on the line.

The midpoint between the focus and the directrix is called the **vertex,** and the line passing through the focus and the vertex is called the **axis** of the parabola. Note in Figure 10.10 that a parabola is symmetric with respect to its axis. Using the definition of a parabola, you can derive the following **standard form** of the equation of a parabola whose directrix is parallel to the x-axis or to the y-axis.

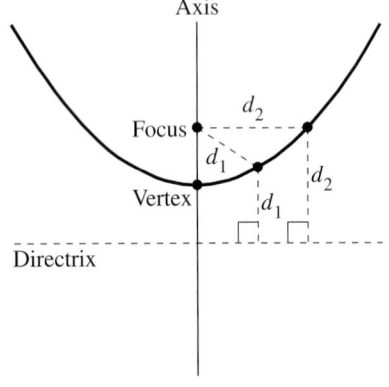

FIGURE 10.10   *Parabola*

Standard Equation of a Parabola

The **standard form of the equation of a parabola** with vertex at (h, k) is as follows.

$$(x - h)^2 = 4p(y - k), \ p \neq 0 \qquad \text{Vertical axis, directrix: } y = k - p$$

$$(y - k)^2 = 4p(x - h), \ p \neq 0 \qquad \text{Horizontal axis, directrix: } x = h - p$$

The focus lies on the axis p units (*directed distance*) from the vertex. If the vertex is at the origin $(0, 0)$, the equation takes one of the following forms.

$$x^2 = 4py \qquad \text{Vertical axis}$$

$$y^2 = 4px \qquad \text{Horizontal axis}$$

See Figure 10.11.

For a proof of the standard form of the equation of a parabola, see Proofs in Mathematics on page 778.

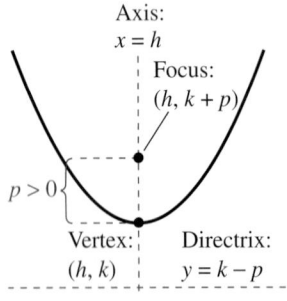

(a) $(x - h)^2 = 4p(y - k)$
    Vertical axis: $p > 0$

(b) $(x - h)^2 = 4p(y - k)$
    Vertical axis: $p < 0$

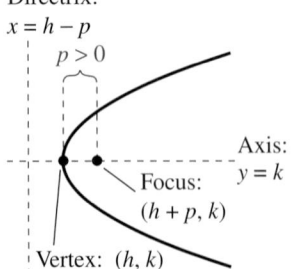

(c) $(y - k)^2 = 4p(x - h)$
    Horizontal axis: $p > 0$

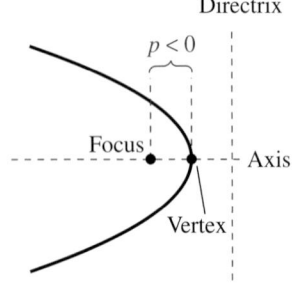

(d) $(y - k)^2 = 4p(x - h)$
    Horizontal axis: $p < 0$

FIGURE **10.11**

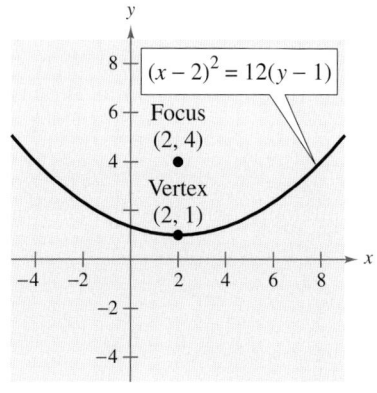

FIGURE 10.12

STUDY TIP

You may want to review the technique of completing the square found in Appendix A.5, which will be used to rewrite each of the conics in standard form.

Example 1 ▶ Finding the Standard Equation of a Parabola

Find the standard form of the equation of the parabola with vertex $(2, 1)$ and focus $(2, 4)$.

Solution

Because the axis of the parabola is vertical, consider the equation

$$(x - h)^2 = 4p(y - k)$$

where $h = 2$, $k = 1$, and $p = 4 - 1 = 3$. So, the standard form is

$$(x - 2)^2 = 12(y - 1).$$

You can obtain the more common quadratic form as follows.

$$x^2 - 4x + 4 = 12y - 12 \qquad \text{Multiply.}$$

$$x^2 - 4x + 16 = 12y \qquad \text{Add 12 to each side.}$$

$$\frac{1}{12}(x^2 - 4x + 16) = y \qquad \text{Divide each side by 12.}$$

The graph of this parabola is shown in Figure 10.12.

Example 2 ▶ Finding the Focus of a Parabola

Find the focus of the parabola

$$y = -\frac{1}{2}x^2 - x + \frac{1}{2}.$$

Solution

To find the focus, convert to standard form by completing the square.

$$y = -\frac{1}{2}x^2 - x + \frac{1}{2} \qquad \text{Write original equation.}$$

$$-2y = x^2 + 2x - 1 \qquad \text{Multiply each side by –2.}$$

$$1 - 2y = x^2 + 2x \qquad \text{Add 1 to each side.}$$

$$1 + 1 - 2y = x^2 + 2x + 1 \qquad \text{Complete the square.}$$

$$2 - 2y = x^2 + 2x + 1 \qquad \text{Combine like terms.}$$

$$-2(y - 1) = (x + 1)^2 \qquad \text{Standard form}$$

Comparing this equation with

$$(x - h)^2 = 4p(y - k)$$

you can conclude that $h = -1$, $k = 1$, and $p = -\frac{1}{2}$. Because p is negative, the parabola opens downward, as shown in Figure 10.13. So, the focus of the parabola is

$$(h, k + p) = \left(-1, \frac{1}{2}\right). \qquad \text{Focus}$$

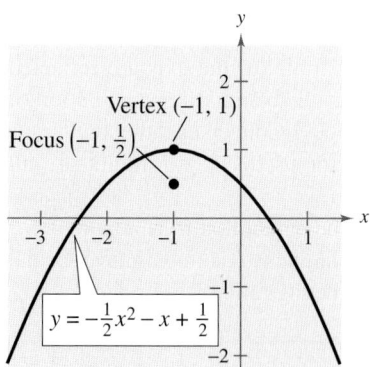

FIGURE 10.13

Example 3 ▶ Vertex at the Origin

Find the standard equation of the parabola with vertex at the origin and focus $(2, 0)$.

Solution

The axis of the parabola is horizontal, passing through $(0, 0)$ and $(2, 0)$, as shown in Figure 10.14.

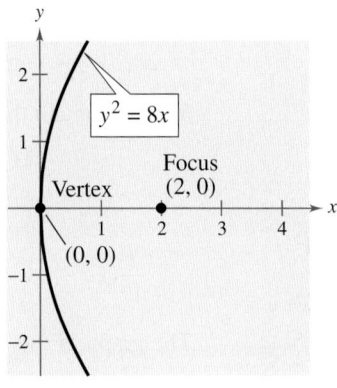

$$y^2 = 8x$$

Focus $(2, 0)$

Vertex $(0, 0)$

FIGURE **10.14**

So, the standard form is $y^2 = 4px$, where $h = 0$, $k = 0$, and $p = 2$. So, the equation is $y^2 = 8x$.

Application

A line segment that passes through the focus of a parabola and has endpoints on the parabola is called a **focal chord.** The specific focal chord perpendicular to the axis of the parabola is called the **latus rectum.**

Parabolas occur in a wide variety of applications. For instance, a parabolic reflector can be formed by revolving a parabola around its axis. The resulting surface has the property that all incoming rays parallel to the axis are reflected through the focus of the parabola. This is the principle behind the construction of the parabolic mirrors used in reflecting telescopes. Conversely, the light rays emanating from the focus of a parabolic reflector used in a flashlight are all parallel to one another, as shown in Figure 10.15.

A line is **tangent** to a parabola at a point on the parabola if the line intersects, but does not cross, the parabola at the point. Tangent lines to parabolas have special properties related to the use of parabolas in constructing reflective surfaces.

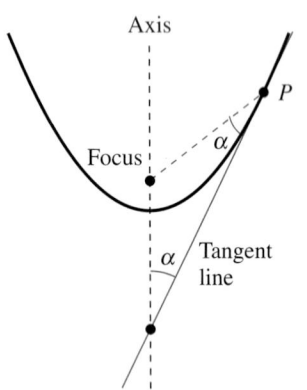

Light source at focus

Focus   Axis

Parabolic reflector: Light is reflected in parallel rays.

FIGURE **10.15**

Axis

P

α

Focus

α Tangent line

FIGURE **10.16**

Reflective Property of a Parabola

The tangent line to a parabola at a point P makes equal angles with the following two lines (see Figure 10.16).

1. The line passing through P and the focus

2. The axis of the parabola

Your students may question why $d_1 = \frac{1}{4} - b$ rather than $b - \frac{1}{4}$. You may need to explain that the distance must be positive, so the order of subtraction is important.

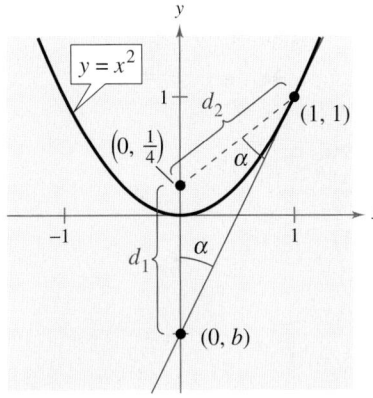

FIGURE 10.17

Activities

1. Find the vertex, focus, and directrix of the parabola $x^2 - 6x - 4y + 5 = 0$.
   Answer: Vertex $(3, -1)$; Focus $(3, 0)$; Directrix $y = -2$

2. Find an equation of the parabola with vertex $(4, 0)$ and directrix $x = 5$.
   Answer: $y^2 + 4x - 16 = 0$

3. Find an equation of the tangent line to the parabola $y = 2x^2$ at the point $(1, 2)$.
   Answer: $y = 4x - 2$

Example 4 ▶ **Finding the Tangent Line at a Point on a Parabola**

Find the equation of the tangent line to the parabola given by $y = x^2$ at the point $(1, 1)$.

Solution

For this parabola, $p = \frac{1}{4}$ and the focus is $\left(0, \frac{1}{4}\right)$, as shown in Figure 10.17. You can find the y-intercept $(0, b)$ of the tangent line by equating the lengths of the two sides of the isosceles triangle shown in Figure 10.17:

$$d_1 = \frac{1}{4} - b$$

and

$$d_2 = \sqrt{(1 - 0)^2 + [1 - (1/4)]^2} = \frac{5}{4}.$$

Setting $d_1 = d_2$ produces

$$\frac{1}{4} - b = \frac{5}{4}$$

$$b = -1.$$

So, the slope of the tangent line is

$$m = \frac{1 - (-1)}{1 - 0} = 2$$

and the equation of the tangent line in slope-intercept form is

$$y = 2x - 1.$$

Writing ABOUT MATHEMATICS

Television Antenna Dishes Cross sections of television antenna dishes are parabolic in shape. Write a paragraph explaining why these dishes are parabolic.

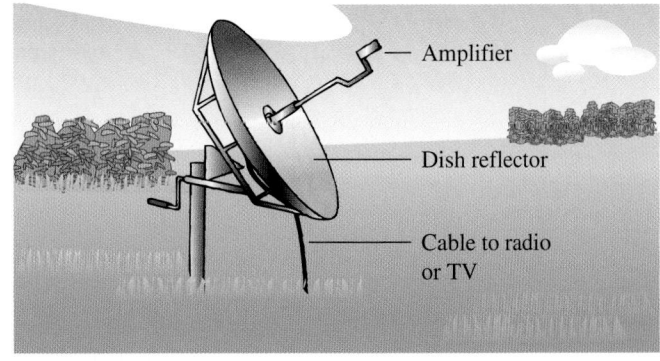

10.2 Exercises

In Exercises 1–4, describe in words how a plane could intersect with the double-napped cone shown to form the conic section.

1. Circle
2. Ellipse
3. Parabola
4. Hyperbola

In Exercises 5–10, match the equation with its graph. [The graphs are labeled (a), (b), (c), (d), (e), and (f).]

(a)

(b)

(c)

(d)

(e)

(f)
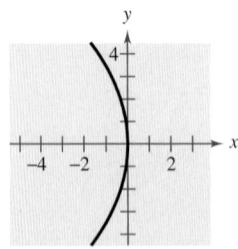

5. $y^2 = -4x$
6. $x^2 = 2y$
7. $x^2 = -8y$
8. $y^2 = -12x$
9. $(y - 1)^2 = 4(x - 3)$
10. $(x + 3)^2 = -2(y - 1)$

In Exercises 11–24, find the vertex, focus, and directrix of the parabola and sketch its graph.

11. $y = \frac{1}{2}x^2$
12. $y = -2x^2$
13. $y^2 = -6x$
14. $y^2 = 3x$
15. $x^2 + 6y = 0$
16. $x + y^2 = 0$
17. $(x - 1)^2 + 8(y + 2) = 0$
18. $(x + 5) + (y - 1)^2 = 0$
19. $\left(x + \frac{3}{2}\right)^2 = 4(y - 2)$
20. $\left(x + \frac{1}{2}\right)^2 = 4(y - 1)$
21. $y = \frac{1}{4}(x^2 - 2x + 5)$
22. $x = \frac{1}{4}(y^2 + 2y + 33)$
23. $y^2 + 6y + 8x + 25 = 0$
24. $y^2 - 4y - 4x = 0$

 In Exercises 25–28, find the vertex, focus, and directrix of the parabola. Use a graphing utility to graph the parabola.

25. $x^2 + 4x + 6y - 2 = 0$
26. $x^2 - 2x + 8y + 9 = 0$
27. $y^2 + x + y = 0$
28. $y^2 - 4x - 4 = 0$

 In Exercises 29 and 30, the equations of a parabola and a tangent line to the parabola are given. Use a graphing utility to graph both equations in the same viewing window. Determine the coordinates of the point of tangency.

	Parabola	*Tangent Line*
29.	$y^2 - 8x = 0$	$x - y + 2 = 0$
30.	$x^2 + 12y = 0$	$x + y - 3 = 0$

In Exercises 31–42, find the standard form of the equation of the parabola with its vertex at the origin.

31.

32.
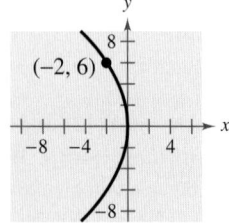

33. Focus: $\left(0, -\frac{3}{2}\right)$
34. Focus: $(2, 0)$
35. Focus: $(-2, 0)$
36. Focus: $(0, -2)$
37. Directrix: $y = -1$
38. Directrix: $y = 3$

39. Directrix: $x = 2$ **40.** Directrix: $x = -3$

41. Horizontal axis and passes through the point $(4, 6)$

42. Vertical axis and passes through the point $(-3, -3)$

In Exercises 43–52, find the standard form of the equation of the parabola.

43.

44.

45.

46.
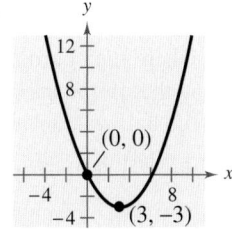

47. Vertex: $(5, 2)$; Focus: $(3, 2)$

48. Vertex: $(-1, 2)$; Focus: $(-1, 0)$

49. Vertex: $(0, 4)$; Directrix: $y = 2$

50. Vertex: $(-2, 1)$; Directrix: $x = 1$

51. Focus: $(2, 2)$; Directrix: $x = -2$

52. Focus: $(0, 0)$; Directrix: $y = 8$

In Exercises 53 and 54, change the equation of the parabola so that its graph matches the description.

53. $(y - 3)^2 = 6(x + 1)$; upper half of parabola

54. $(y + 1)^2 = 2(x - 4)$; lower half of parabola

In Exercises 55–58, find an equation of the tangent line to the parabola at the given point, and find the x-intercept of the line.

55. $x^2 = 2y$, $(4, 8)$ **56.** $x^2 = 2y$, $\left(-3, \frac{9}{2}\right)$

57. $y = -2x^2$, $(-1, -2)$ **58.** $y = -2x^2$, $(2, -8)$

 59. *Revenue*   The revenue R generated by the sale of x units of a patio furniture set is $(x - 106)^2 = -\frac{4}{5}(R - 14{,}045)$. Use a graphing utility to graph the function and approximate the number of sales that will maximize revenue.

 60. *Revenue*   The revenue R generated by the sale of x units of a digital camera is

$$(x - 135)^2 = -\frac{5}{7}(R - 25{,}515).$$

Use a graphing utility to graph the function and approximate the number of sales that will maximize revenue.

61. *Satellite Antenna*   The receiver in a parabolic television dish antenna is 4.5 feet from the vertex and is located at the focus (see figure). Find an equation of a cross section of the reflector. (Assume that the dish is directed upward and the vertex is at the origin.)

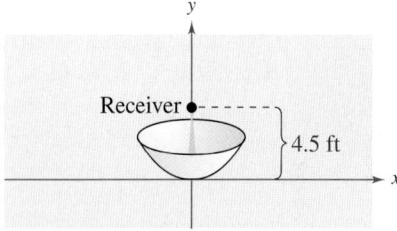

▶ Model It

62. *Suspension Bridge*   Each cable of the Golden Gate Bridge is suspended (in the shape of a parabola) between two towers that are 1280 meters apart. The top of each tower is 152 meters above the roadway. The cables touch the roadway midway between the towers.

(a) Draw a sketch of the bridge. Locate the origin of a rectangular coordinate system at the center of the roadway. Label the coordinates of the known points.

(b) Write an equation that models the cables.

(c) Complete the table by finding the height y of the suspension cables over the roadway at a distance of x meters from the center of the bridge.

Distance, x	Height, y
0	
250	
400	
500	
1000	

63. *Road Design* Roads are often designed with parabolic surfaces to allow rain to drain off. A particular road that is 32 feet wide is 0.4 foot higher in the center than it is on the sides (see figure).

(a) Find an equation of the parabola that models the road surface. (Assume that the origin is at the center of the road.)

(b) How far from the center of the road is the road surface 0.1 foot lower than in the middle?

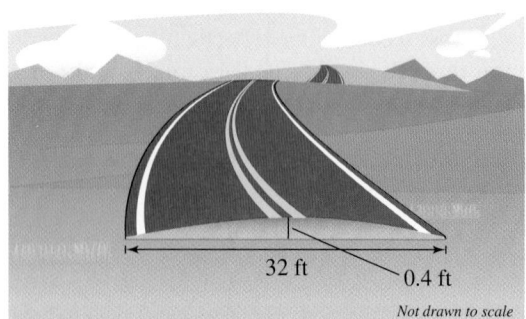

Cross section of road surface

64. *Highway Design* Highway engineers design a parabolic curve for an entrance ramp from a straight street to an interstate highway (see figure). Find an equation of the parabola.

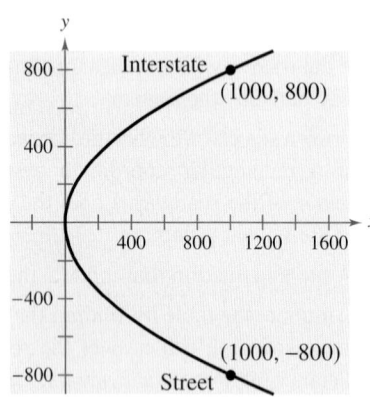

65. *Satellite Orbit* An Earth satellite in a 100-mile-high circular orbit around Earth has a velocity of approximately 17,500 miles per hour. If this velocity is multiplied by $\sqrt{2}$, the satellite will have the minimum velocity necessary to escape Earth's gravity and it will follow a parabolic path with the center of Earth as the focus (see figure).

(a) Find the escape velocity of the satellite.

(b) Find an equation of the parabolic path of the satellite (assume that the radius of Earth is 4000 miles).

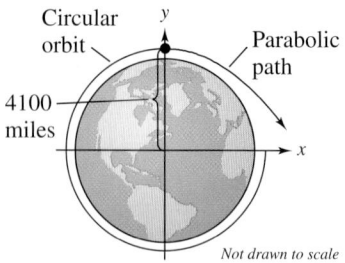

FIGURE FOR 65

66. *Path of a Softball* The path of a softball is modeled by

$$-12.5(y - 7.125) = (x - 6.25)^2$$

where the coordinates x and y are measured in feet, with $x = 0$ corresponding to the position from which the ball was thrown.

(a) Use a graphing utility to graph the trajectory of the softball.

(b) Use the *trace* feature of the graphing utility to approximate the highest point and the range of the trajectory.

Projectile Motion In Exercises 67 and 68, consider the path of a projectile projected horizontally with a velocity of v feet per second at a height of s feet, where the model for the path is

$$x^2 = -\frac{v^2}{16}(y - s).$$

In this model, air resistance is disregarded and y is the height (in feet) of the projectile and x is the horizontal distance (in feet) the projectile travels.

67. A ball is thrown from the top of a 75-foot tower with a velocity of 32 feet per second.

(a) Find the equation of the parabolic path.

(b) How far does the ball travel horizontally before striking the ground?

68. A bomber flying due east at 550 miles per hour at an altitude of 42,000 feet releases a bomb. Determine the distance the bomb travels horizontally before striking the ground.

Synthesis

True or False? **In Exercises 69 and 70, determine whether the statement is true or false. Justify your answer.**

69. It is possible for a parabola to intersect its directrix.

70. If the vertex and focus of a parabola are on a horizontal line, then the directrix of the parabola is vertical.

71. *Exploration*   Consider the parabola $x^2 = 4py$.

 (a) Use a graphing utility to graph the parabola for $p = 1$, $p = 2$, $p = 3$, and $p = 4$. Describe the effect on the graph when p increases.

(b) Locate the focus for each parabola in part (a).

(c) For each parabola in part (a), find the length of the chord passing through the focus and parallel to the directrix (see figure). How can the length of this chord be determined directly from the standard form of the equation of the parabola?

(d) Explain how the result of part (c) can be used as a sketching aid when graphing parabolas.

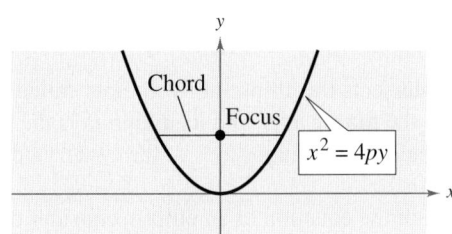

72. *Geometry*   The area of the shaded region in the figure is

$$A = \frac{8}{3}p^{1/2}b^{3/2}.$$

(a) Find the area when $p = 2$ and $b = 4$.

(b) Give a geometric explanation of why the area approaches 0 as p approaches 0.

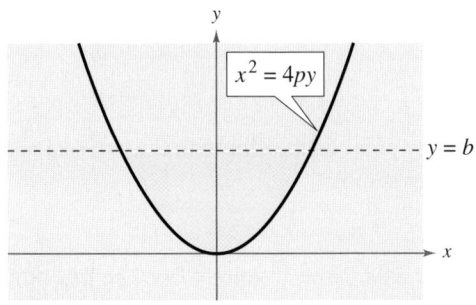

73. *Exploration*   Let (x_1, y_1) be the coordinates of a point on the parabola $x^2 = 4py$. The equation of the line tangent to the parabola at the point is

$$y - y_1 = \frac{x_1}{2p}(x - x_1).$$

What is the slope of the tangent line?

74. *Writing*   In your own words, state the reflective property of a parabola.

Review

In Exercises 75–78, list the possible rational zeros given by the Rational Zero Test.

75. $f(x) = x^3 - 2x^2 + 2x - 4$

76. $f(x) = 2x^3 + 4x^2 - 3x + 10$

77. $f(x) = 2x^5 + x^2 + 16$

78. $f(x) = 3x^3 - 12x + 22$

79. Find a polynomial with integer coefficients that has the zeros 3, $2 + i$, and $2 - i$.

80. Find all the zeros of

$$f(x) = 2x^3 - 3x^2 + 50x - 75$$

if one of the zeros is $x = \frac{3}{2}$.

81. Find all the zeros of the function

$$g(x) = 6x^4 + 7x^3 - 29x^2 - 28x + 20$$

if two of the zeros are $x = \pm 2$.

 82. Use a graphing utility to graph the function

$$h(x) = 2x^4 + x^3 - 19x^2 - 9x + 9.$$

Use the graph to approximate the zeros of h.

In Exercises 83–90, use the information to solve the triangle.

83. $A = 35°$, $a = 10$, $b = 7$

84. $B = 54°$, $b = 18$, $c = 11$

85. $A = 40°$, $B = 51°$, $c = 3$

86. $B = 26°$, $C = 104°$, $a = 19$

87. $a = 7$, $b = 10$, $c = 16$

88. $a = 58$, $b = 28$, $c = 75$

89. $A = 65°$, $b = 5$, $c = 12$

90. $B = 71°$, $a = 21$, $c = 29$

10.3 Ellipses

▶ **What you should learn**

- How to write the standard form of the equation of an ellipse
- How to use properties of ellipses to model and solve real-life problems
- How to find the eccentricity of an ellipse

▶ **Why you should learn it**

Ellipses can be used to model and solve many types of real-life problems. For instance, in Exercise 52 on page 723, an ellipse is used to model the orbit of Halley's comet.

Introduction

The second type of conic is called an **ellipse,** and is defined as follows.

Definition of Ellipse

An **ellipse** is the set of all points (x, y) in a plane, the sum of whose distances from two distinct fixed points **(foci)** is constant. See Figure 10.18.

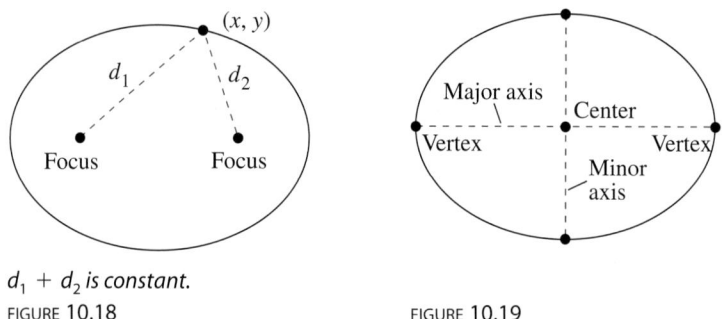

$d_1 + d_2$ is constant.

FIGURE 10.18

FIGURE 10.19

The line through the foci intersects the ellipse at two points called **vertices.** The chord joining the vertices is the **major axis,** and its midpoint is the **center** of the ellipse. The chord perpendicular to the major axis at the center is the **minor axis** of the ellipse. See Figure 10.19.

To derive the standard form of the equation of an ellipse, consider the ellipse in Figure 10.20 with the following points: center, (h, k); vertices, $(h \pm a, k)$; foci, $(h \pm c, k)$. Note that the center is the midpoint of the segment joining the foci.

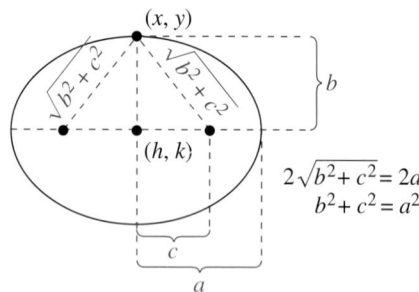

$$2\sqrt{b^2 + c^2} = 2a$$
$$b^2 + c^2 = a^2$$

FIGURE 10.20

The sum of the distances from any point on the ellipse to the two foci is constant. Using a vertex point, this constant sum is

$$(a + c) + (a - c) = 2a \qquad \text{Length of major axis}$$

or simply the length of the major axis. Now, if you let (x, y) be *any* point on the ellipse, the sum of the distances between (x, y) and the two foci must also be $2a$.

Harvard College Observatory/SPL/Photo Researchers, Inc.

That is,

$$\sqrt{[x - (h - c)]^2 + (y - k)^2} + \sqrt{[x - (h + c)]^2 + (y - k)^2} = 2a.$$

Finally, in Figure 10.20, you can see that $b^2 = a^2 - c^2$, which implies that the equation of the ellipse is

$$b^2(x - h)^2 + a^2(y - k)^2 = a^2 b^2$$

$$\frac{(x - h)^2}{a^2} + \frac{(y - k)^2}{b^2} = 1.$$

You would obtain a similar equation in the derivation by starting with a vertical major axis. Both results are summarized as follows.

Standard Equation of an Ellipse

The standard form of the equation of an ellipse, with center (h, k) and major and minor axes of lengths $2a$ and $2b$, respectively, where $0 < b < a$, is

$$\frac{(x - h)^2}{a^2} + \frac{(y - k)^2}{b^2} = 1 \qquad \text{Major axis is horizontal.}$$

$$\frac{(x - h)^2}{b^2} + \frac{(y - k)^2}{a^2} = 1. \qquad \text{Major axis is vertical.}$$

The foci lie on the major axis, c units from the center, with $c^2 = a^2 - b^2$. If the center is at the origin $(0, 0)$, the equation takes one of the following forms.

$$\frac{x^2}{a^2} + \frac{y^2}{b^2} = 1 \quad \text{Major axis is horizontal.} \qquad \frac{x^2}{b^2} + \frac{y^2}{a^2} = 1 \quad \text{Major axis is vertical.}$$

Figure 10.21 shows both the horizontal and vertical orientations for an ellipse.

Major axis is horizontal.

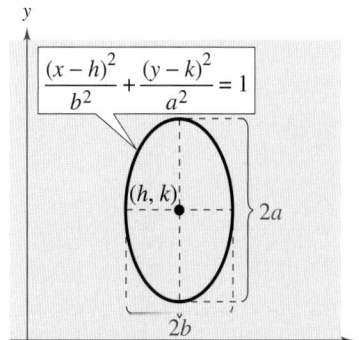

Major axis is vertical.

FIGURE **10.21**

You can visualize the definition of an ellipse by imagining two thumbtacks placed at the foci, as shown in Figure 10.22. If the ends of a fixed length of string are fastened to the thumbtacks and the string is drawn taut with a pencil, the path traced by the pencil will be an ellipse.

FIGURE **10.22**

Example 1 ▶ Finding the Standard Equation of an Ellipse

Find the standard form of the equation of the ellipse having foci at $(0, 1)$ and $(4, 1)$ and a major axis of length 6.

Solution

Because the foci occur at $(0, 1)$ and $(4, 1)$, the center of the ellipse is $(2, 1)$ and the distance from the center to one of the foci is $c = 2$. Because $2a = 6$, you know that $a = 3$. Now, from $c^2 = a^2 - b^2$, you have

$$b = \sqrt{a^2 - c^2} = \sqrt{3^2 - 2^2} = \sqrt{5}.$$

Because the major axis is horizontal, the standard equation is

$$\frac{(x - 2)^2}{3^2} + \frac{(y - 1)^2}{(\sqrt{5})^2} = 1.$$

This equation simplifies to

$$\frac{(x - 2)^2}{9} + \frac{(y - 1)^2}{5} = 1.$$

See Figure 10.23.

$$\frac{(x - 2)^2}{9} + \frac{(y - 1)^2}{5} = 1$$

$b = \sqrt{5}$

$(0, 1)$ $(2, 1)$ $(4, 1)$

$a = 3$

FIGURE **10.23**

In Example 1, note the use of the equation $c^2 = a^2 - b^2$. Do not confuse this equation with the Pythagorean Theorem—there is a difference in sign.

Example 2 ▶ Writing an Equation in Standard Form

Sketch the graph of the ellipse $x^2 + 4y^2 + 6x - 8y + 9 = 0$.

Solution

Begin by writing the original equation in standard form. In the fourth step, note that 9 and 4 are added to *both* sides of the equation when completing the squares.

$$x^2 + 4y^2 + 6x - 8y + 9 = 0 \qquad \text{Write original equation.}$$

$$\left(x^2 + 6x + \boxed{}\right) + \left(4y^2 - 8y + \boxed{}\right) = -9 \qquad \text{Group terms.}$$

$$\left(x^2 + 6x + \boxed{}\right) + 4\left(y^2 - 2y + \boxed{}\right) = -9 \qquad \text{Factor 4 out of } y\text{-terms.}$$

$$(x^2 + 6x + 9) + 4(y^2 - 2y + 1) = -9 + 9 + 4(1)$$

$$(x + 3)^2 + 4(y - 1)^2 = 4 \qquad \text{Write in completed square form.}$$

$$\frac{(x + 3)^2}{4} + \frac{(y - 1)^2}{1} = 1 \qquad \text{Divide each side by 4.}$$

$$\frac{(x + 3)^2}{2^2} + \frac{(y - 1)^2}{1^2} = 1 \qquad \text{Write in standard form.}$$

From this standard form, it follows that the center is $(h, k) = (-3, 1)$. Because the denominator of the x-term is $a^2 = 2^2$, the endpoints of the major axis lie two units to the right and left of the center. Similarly, because the denominator of the y-term is $b^2 = 1^2$, the endpoints of the minor axis lie one unit up and down from the center. The ellipse is shown in Figure 10.24.

Remind your students that completing the square must be performed twice to write the equation of the ellipse in standard form in Example 2.

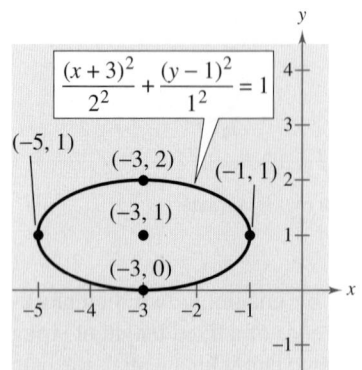

$$\frac{(x + 3)^2}{2^2} + \frac{(y - 1)^2}{1^2} = 1$$

$(-5, 1)$

$(-3, 2)$

$(-1, 1)$

$(-3, 1)$

$(-3, 0)$

FIGURE **10.24**

Example 3 ▶ Analyzing an Ellipse

Find the center, vertices, and foci of the ellipse $4x^2 + y^2 - 8x + 4y - 8 = 0$.

Solution

By completing the square, you can write the original equation in standard form.

$$4x^2 + y^2 - 8x + 4y - 8 = 0$$

$$\left(4x^2 - 8x + \quad\right) + \left(y^2 + 4y + \quad\right) = 8$$

$$4\left(x^2 - 2x + \quad\right) + \left(y^2 + 4y + \quad\right) = 8$$

$$4(x^2 - 2x + 1) + (y^2 + 4y + 4) = 8 + 4(1) + 4$$

$$4(x - 1)^2 + (y + 2)^2 = 16$$

$$\frac{(x - 1)^2}{4} + \frac{(y + 2)^2}{16} = 1$$

$$\frac{(x - 1)^2}{2^2} + \frac{(y + 2)^2}{4^2} = 1$$

The major axis is vertical, where $h = 1$, $k = -2$, $a = 4$, $b = 2$, and

$$c = \sqrt{a^2 - b^2} = \sqrt{16 - 4} = \sqrt{12} = 2\sqrt{3}.$$

So, you have the following.

Center: $(1, -2)$ Vertices: $(1, -6)$ Foci: $\left(1, -2 - 2\sqrt{3}\right)$
$(1, 2)$ $\left(1, -2 + 2\sqrt{3}\right)$

The graph of the ellipse is shown in Figure 10.25.

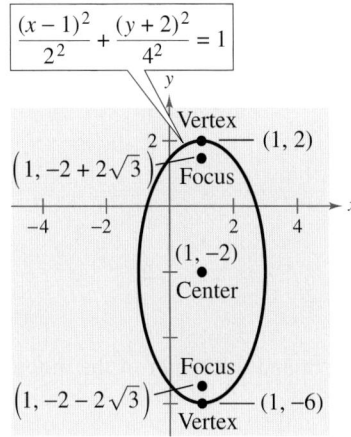

$$\frac{(x - 1)^2}{2^2} + \frac{(y + 2)^2}{4^2} = 1$$

FIGURE **10.25**

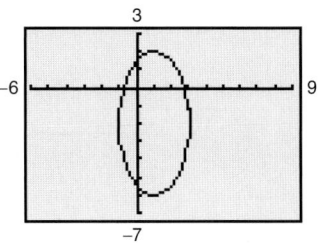

Technology

You can use a graphing utility to graph an ellipse by graphing the upper and lower portions in the same viewing window. For instance, to graph the ellipse in Example 3, first solve for y to get

$$y_1 = -2 + 4\sqrt{1 - \frac{(x - 1)^2}{4}} \quad \text{and} \quad y_2 = -2 - 4\sqrt{1 - \frac{(x - 1)^2}{4}}.$$

Use a viewing window in which $-6 \leq x \leq 9$ and $-7 \leq y \leq 3$. You should obtain the graph shown below.

Application

Ellipses have many practical and aesthetic uses. For instance, machine gears, supporting arches, and acoustic designs often involve elliptical shapes. The orbits of satellites and planets are also ellipses. Example 4 investigates the elliptical orbit of the moon about Earth.

Example 4 ▶ An Application Involving an Elliptical Orbit

The moon travels about Earth in an elliptical orbit with Earth at one focus, as shown in Figure 10.26. The major and minor axes of the orbit have lengths of 768,806 kilometers and 767,746 kilometers, respectively. Find the greatest and smallest distances (the *apogee* and *perigee*) from Earth's center to the moon's center.

Solution

Because $2a = 768,806$ and $2b = 767,746$, you have

$$a = 384,403 \text{ and } b = 383,873$$

which implies that

$$c = \sqrt{a^2 - b^2}$$
$$= \sqrt{384,403^2 - 383,873^2}$$
$$\approx 20,179.$$

So, the greatest distance between the center of Earth and the center of the moon is

$$a + c \approx 404,582 \text{ kilometers}$$

and the smallest distance is

$$a - c \approx 364,224 \text{ kilometers}.$$

767,746 km

768,806 km

Earth

Moon

Perigee   Apogee

FIGURE **10.26**

Eccentricity

One of the reasons it was difficult for early astronomers to detect that the orbits of the planets are ellipses is that the foci of the planetary orbits are relatively close to their centers, and so the orbits are nearly circular. To measure the ovalness of an ellipse, you can use the concept of **eccentricity.**

Ask students to make a conjecture about the eccentricity of a circle before going further.

Definition of Eccentricity

The **eccentricity** e of an ellipse is given by the ratio

$$e = \frac{c}{a}.$$

Note that $0 < e < 1$ for *every* ellipse.

Activities

1. Find the center, foci, vertices, and eccentricity of the ellipse

$$\frac{(x-2)^2}{25} + \frac{(y+1)^2}{9} = 1.$$

Answer: Center $(2, -1)$;
Foci $(-2, -1)$, $(6, -1)$;
Vertices $(-3, -1)$, $(7, -1)$; $e = \frac{4}{5}$

2. Rewrite the equation of the ellipse in standard form:

$$9x^2 + 5y^2 + 36x - 30y + 36 = 0.$$

Answer: $\dfrac{(x+2)^2}{5} + \dfrac{(y-3)^2}{9} = 1$

To see how this ratio is used to describe the shape of an ellipse, note that because the foci of an ellipse are located along the major axis between the vertices and the center, it follows that

$$0 < c < a.$$

For an ellipse that is nearly circular, the foci are close to the center and the ratio c/a is small, as shown in Figure 10.27. On the other hand, for an elongated ellipse, the foci are close to the vertices, and the ratio c/a is close to 1, as shown in Figure 10.28.

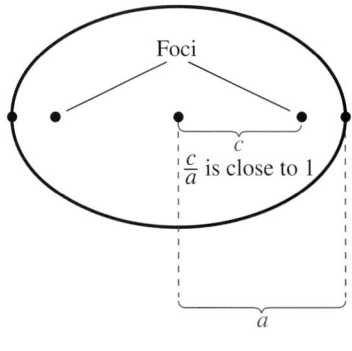

FIGURE 10.27   FIGURE 10.28

The orbit of the moon has an eccentricity of $e \approx 0.0525$, and the eccentricities of the nine planetary orbits are as follows.

Mercury:	$e \approx 0.2056$	Saturn:	$e \approx 0.0543$
Venus:	$e \approx 0.0068$	Uranus:	$e \approx 0.0460$
Earth:	$e \approx 0.0167$	Neptune:	$e \approx 0.0082$
Mars:	$e \approx 0.0934$	Pluto:	$e \approx 0.2481$
Jupiter:	$e \approx 0.0484$		

NASA

The time it takes Saturn to orbit the sun is equal to 29.5 Earth years.

 ABOUT MATHEMATICS

Ellipses and Circles

a. Show that the equation of an ellipse can be written as

$$\frac{(x-h)^2}{a^2} + \frac{(y-k)^2}{a^2(1-e^2)} = 1.$$

b. For the equation in part (a), let $a = 4$, $h = 1$, and $k = 2$, and use a graphing utility to graph the ellipse for $e = 0.95$, $e = 0.75$, $e = 0.5$, $e = 0.25$, and $e = 0.1$. Discuss the changes in the shape of the ellipse as e approaches 0.

c. Make a conjecture about the shape of the graph in part (b) when $e = 0$. What is the equation of this ellipse? What is another name for an ellipse with an eccentricity of 0?

10.3 Exercises

In Exercises 1–6, match the equation with its graph. [The graphs are labeled (a), (b), (c), (d), (e), and (f).]

(a)

(b)

(c)

(d)

(e)

(f)
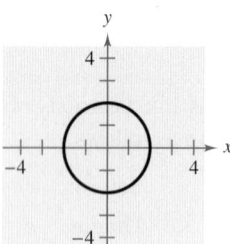

1. $\dfrac{x^2}{4} + \dfrac{y^2}{9} = 1$

2. $\dfrac{x^2}{9} + \dfrac{y^2}{4} = 1$

3. $\dfrac{x^2}{4} + \dfrac{y^2}{25} = 1$

4. $\dfrac{x^2}{4} + \dfrac{y^2}{4} = 1$

5. $\dfrac{(x-2)^2}{16} + (y+1)^2 = 1$

6. $\dfrac{(x+2)^2}{9} + \dfrac{(y+2)^2}{4} = 1$

In Exercises 7–22, find the center, vertices, foci, and eccentricity of the ellipse, and sketch its graph.

7. $\dfrac{x^2}{25} + \dfrac{y^2}{16} = 1$

8. $\dfrac{x^2}{81} + \dfrac{y^2}{144} = 1$

9. $\dfrac{x^2}{5} + \dfrac{y^2}{9} = 1$

10. $\dfrac{x^2}{64} + \dfrac{y^2}{28} = 1$

11. $\dfrac{(x+3)^2}{16} + \dfrac{(y-5)^2}{25} = 1$

12. $\dfrac{(x-4)^2}{12} + \dfrac{(y+3)^2}{16} = 1$

13. $\dfrac{(x+5)^2}{9/4} + (y-1)^2 = 1$

14. $(x+2)^2 + \dfrac{(y+4)^2}{1/4} = 1$

15. $9x^2 + 4y^2 + 36x - 24y + 36 = 0$

16. $9x^2 + 4y^2 - 54x + 40y + 37 = 0$

17. $x^2 + 5y^2 - 8x - 30y - 39 = 0$

18. $3x^2 + y^2 + 18x - 2y - 8 = 0$

19. $6x^2 + 2y^2 + 18x - 10y + 2 = 0$

20. $x^2 + 4y^2 - 6x + 20y - 2 = 0$

21. $16x^2 + 25y^2 - 32x + 50y + 16 = 0$

22. $9x^2 + 25y^2 - 36x - 50y + 60 = 0$

In Exercises 23–26, use a graphing utility to graph the ellipse. Find the center, foci, and vertices. (Recall that it may be necessary to solve the equation for y and obtain two equations.)

23. $5x^2 + 3y^2 = 15$

24. $3x^2 + 4y^2 = 12$

25. $12x^2 + 20y^2 - 12x + 40y - 37 = 0$

26. $36x^2 + 9y^2 + 48x - 36y - 72 = 0$

In Exercises 27–34, find the standard form of the equation of the ellipse with center at the origin.

27.

28.
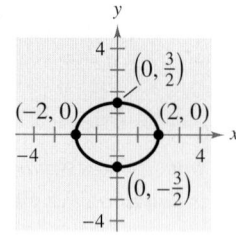

29. Vertices: $(\pm 6, 0)$; Foci: $(\pm 2, 0)$

30. Vertices: $(0, \pm 8)$; Foci: $(0, \pm 4)$

31. Foci: $(\pm 5, 0)$; Major axis of length 12

32. Foci: $(\pm 2, 0)$; Major axis of length 8

33. Vertices: $(0, \pm 5)$; Passes through the point $(4, 2)$

34. Major axis vertical; Passes through the points $(0, 4)$ and $(2, 0)$

In Exercises 35–46, find the standard form of the equation of the ellipse.

35.

36.

37.

38.
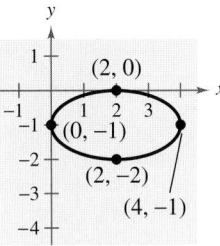

39. Vertices: $(0, 4)$, $(4, 4)$; Minor axis of length 2

40. Foci: $(0, 0)$, $(4, 0)$; Major axis of length 8

41. Foci: $(0, 0)$, $(0, 8)$; Major axis of length 16

42. Center: $(2, -1)$; Vertex: $\left(2, \frac{1}{2}\right)$; Minor axis of length 2

43. Center: $(0, 4)$; $a = 2c$; Vertices: $(-4, 4)$, $(4, 4)$

44. Center: $(3, 2)$; $a = 3c$; Foci: $(1, 2)$, $(5, 2)$

45. Vertices: $(0, 2)$, $(4, 2)$; Endpoints of the minor axis: $(2, 3)$, $(2, 1)$

46. Vertices: $(5, 0)$, $(5, 12)$; Endpoints of the minor axis: $(1, 6)$, $(9, 6)$

47. Find an equation of the ellipse with vertices $(\pm 5, 0)$ and eccentricity $e = \frac{3}{5}$.

48. Find an equation of the ellipse with vertices $(0, \pm 8)$ and eccentricity $e = \frac{1}{2}$.

49. *Architecture* A semielliptical arch over a tunnel for a road through a mountain has a major axis of 80 feet and a height at the center of 30 feet.

(a) Draw a rectangular coordinate system on a sketch of the tunnel with the center of the road entering the tunnel at the origin. Identify the coordinates of the known points.

(b) Find an equation of the semielliptical arch over the tunnel.

(c) Determine the height of the arch 5 feet from each edge of the tunnel.

50. *Architecture* A fireplace arch is to be constructed in the shape of a semiellipse. The opening is to have a height of 2 feet at the center and a width of 6 feet along the base (see figure). The contractor draws the outline of the ellipse using tacks as described at the beginning of this section. Give the required positions of the tacks and the length of the string.

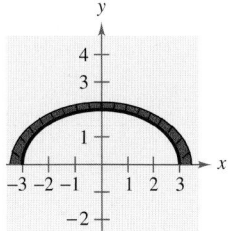

51. *Geometry* The area of the ellipse in the figure is twice the area of the circle. What is the length of the major axis? (*Hint:* The area of an ellipse is $A = \pi ab$.)

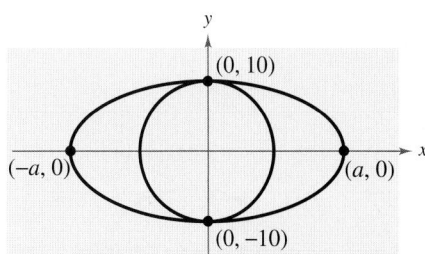

▶ **Model It**

52. *Comet Orbit* Halley's comet has an elliptical orbit, with the sun at one focus. The eccentricity of the orbit is approximately 0.97. The length of the major axis of the orbit is approximately 36.18 astronomical units. (An astronomical unit is about 93 million miles.)

(a) Find an equation of the orbit. Place the center of the orbit at the origin, and place the major axis on the x-axis.

(b) Use a graphing utility to graph the equation of the orbit.

(c) Find the greatest (apogee) and smallest (perigee) distances from the sun's center to the comet's center.

53. Satellite Orbit The first artificial satellite to orbit Earth was Sputnik I (launched by Russia in 1957). Its highest point above Earth's surface was 938 kilometers, and its lowest point was 212 kilometers (see figure). The radius of Earth is 6378 kilometers. Find the eccentricity of the orbit.

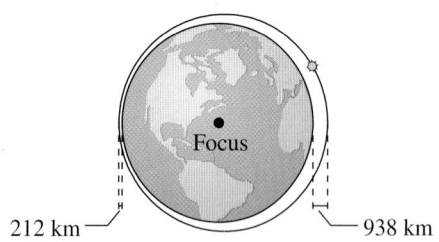

212 km — 938 km

54. Geometry A line segment through a focus of an ellipse with endpoints on the ellipse and perpendicular to the major axis is called a **latus rectum** of the ellipse. Therefore, an ellipse has two latera recta. Knowing the length of the latera recta is helpful in sketching an ellipse because it yields other points on the curve (see figure). Show that the length of each latus rectum is $2b^2/a$.

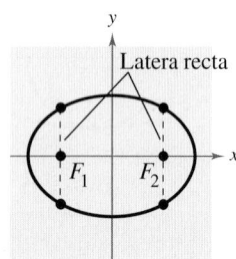

Latera recta

In Exercises 55–58, sketch the graph of the ellipse, using latera recta (see Exercise 54).

55. $\dfrac{x^2}{9} + \dfrac{y^2}{16} = 1$ **56.** $\dfrac{x^2}{4} + \dfrac{y^2}{1} = 1$

57. $5x^2 + 3y^2 = 15$ **58.** $9x^2 + 4y^2 = 36$

Synthesis

True or False? In Exercises 59 and 60, determine whether the statement is true or false. Justify your answer.

59. The graph of $x^2 + 4y^4 - 4 = 0$ is an ellipse.

60. It is easier to distinguish the graph of an ellipse from the graph of a circle if the eccentricity of the ellipse is large (close to 1).

61. Exploration Consider the ellipse

$$\frac{x^2}{a^2} + \frac{y^2}{b^2} = 1, \quad a + b = 20.$$

(a) The area of the ellipse is $A = \pi ab$. Write the area of the ellipse as a function of a.

(b) Find the equation of an ellipse with an area of 264 square centimeters.

(c) Complete the table using your equation from part (a), and make a conjecture about the shape of the ellipse with maximum area.

a	8	9	10	11	12	13
A						

(d) Use a graphing utility to graph the area function and use the graph to make a conjecture about the shape of the ellipse that yields a maximum area.

62. Think About It At the beginning of this section it was noted that an ellipse can be drawn using two thumbtacks, a string of fixed length (greater than the distance between the two tacks), and a pencil. If the ends of the string are fastened at the tacks and the string is drawn taut with a pencil, the path traced by the pencil is an ellipse.

(a) What is the length of the string in terms of a?

(b) Explain why the path is an ellipse.

Review

In Exercises 63–66, determine whether the sequence is arithmetic, geometric, or neither.

63. 80, 40, 20, 10, 5, . . .   **64.** 66, 55, 44, 33, 22, . . .

65. $-\frac{1}{2}, \frac{1}{2}, \frac{3}{2}, \frac{5}{2}, \frac{7}{2}, . . .$ **66.** $\frac{1}{4}, \frac{1}{2}, 1, 2, 4, . . .$

In Exercises 67–70, find a formula for a_n for the arithmetic sequence.

67. $a_1 = 0, \ d = -\frac{1}{4}$ **68.** $a_1 = 13, \ d = 3$

69. $a_3 = 27, \ a_8 = 72$ **70.** $a_1 = 5, \ a_4 = 9.5$

In Exercises 71–74, find the sum.

71. $\displaystyle\sum_{n=0}^{6} (-3)^n$ **72.** $\displaystyle\sum_{n=0}^{6} 3^n$

73. $\displaystyle\sum_{n=0}^{10} 5\left(\frac{4}{3}\right)^n$ **74.** $\displaystyle\sum_{n=1}^{10} 4\left(\frac{3}{4}\right)^{n-1}$

10.4 Hyperbolas

▶ **What you should learn**

- How to write the standard form of the equation of a hyperbola
- How to find the asymptotes of a hyperbola
- How to use properties of hyperbolas to solve real-life problems
- How to classify a conic from its general equation

▶ **Why you should learn it**

Hyperbolas can be used to model and solve many types of real-life problems. For instance, in Exercise 39 on page 733, hyperbolas are used in long-distance radio navigation for aircraft and ships.

Introduction

The third type of conic is called a **hyperbola.** The definition of a hyperbola is similar to that of an ellipse. The difference is that for an ellipse the *sum* of the distances between the foci and a point on the ellipse is fixed, whereas for a hyperbola the *difference* of the distances between the foci and a point on the hyperbola is fixed.

> ### Definition of Hyperbola
> A **hyperbola** is the set of all points (x, y) in a plane, the difference of whose distances from two distinct fixed points (**foci**) is a positive constant. See Figure 10.29.

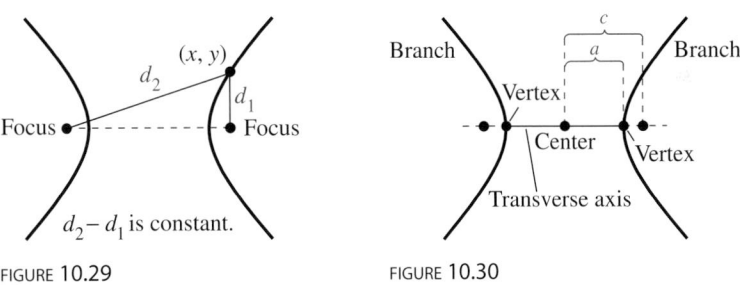

FIGURE **10.29**   FIGURE **10.30**

The graph of a hyperbola has two disconnected **branches.** The line through the two foci intersects the hyperbola at its two **vertices.** The line segment connecting the vertices is the **transverse axis,** and the midpoint of the transverse axis is the **center** of the hyperbola. See Figure 10.30. The development of the standard form of the equation of a hyperbola is similar to that of an ellipse.

> ### Standard Equation of a Hyperbola
> The **standard form of the equation of a hyperbola** with center (h, k) is
>
> $$\frac{(x - h)^2}{a^2} - \frac{(y - k)^2}{b^2} = 1 \qquad \text{Transverse axis is horizontal.}$$
>
> $$\frac{(y - k)^2}{a^2} - \frac{(x - h)^2}{b^2} = 1. \qquad \text{Transverse axis is vertical.}$$
>
> The vertices are a units from the center, and the foci are c units from the center. Moreover, $c^2 = a^2 + b^2$. If the center of the hyperbola is at the origin $(0, 0)$, the equation takes one of the following forms.
>
> $$\frac{x^2}{a^2} - \frac{y^2}{b^2} = 1 \quad \begin{array}{l}\text{Transverse axis}\\ \text{is horizontal.}\end{array} \qquad \frac{y^2}{a^2} - \frac{x^2}{b^2} = 1 \quad \begin{array}{l}\text{Transverse axis}\\ \text{is vertical.}\end{array}$$

Note that a, b, and c are related differently for hyperbolas than for ellipses.

Figure 10.31 shows both the horizontal and vertical orientations for a hyperbola.

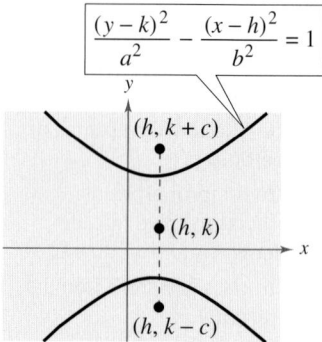

Transverse axis is horizontal.   Transverse axis is vertical.

FIGURE 10.31

Example 1 ▶   **Finding the Standard Equation of a Hyperbola**

Find the standard form of the equation of the hyperbola with foci $(-1, 2)$ and $(5, 2)$ and vertices $(0, 2)$ and $(4, 2)$.

Solution

Because the vertices occur at $(0, 2)$ and $(4, 2)$, the center of the hyperbola occurs at the point $(2, 2)$. Furthermore, $c = 3$ and $a = 2$, and it follows that

$$b = \sqrt{c^2 - a^2} = \sqrt{3^2 - 2^2} = \sqrt{9 - 4} = \sqrt{5}.$$

So, the equation of the hyperbola is

$$\frac{(x - 2)^2}{2^2} - \frac{(y - 2)^2}{\left(\sqrt{5}\right)^2} = 1. \qquad \text{See Figure 10.32.}$$

This equation simplifies to

$$\frac{(x - 2)^2}{4} - \frac{(y - 2)^2}{5} = 1.$$

FIGURE 10.32

Conjugate axis

$(h, k + b)$

Asymptote

(h, k)

$(h, k - b)$

Asymptote

$(h - a, k)$ $(h + a, k)$

FIGURE 10.33

Asymptotes of a Hyperbola

Each hyperbola has two **asymptotes** that intersect at the center of the hyperbola, as shown in Figure 10.33. The asymptotes pass through the vertices of a rectangle of dimensions $2a$ by $2b$, with its center at (h, k). The line segment of length $2b$ joining $(h, k + b)$ and $(h, k - b)$ [or $(h + b, k)$ and $(h - b, k)$] is the **conjugate axis** of the hyperbola.

Asymptotes of a Hyperbola

The equations for the asymptotes of a hyperbola are

$$y = k \pm \frac{b}{a}(x - h) \qquad \text{Transverse axis is horizontal.}$$

$$y = k \pm \frac{a}{b}(x - h). \qquad \text{Transverse axis is vertical.}$$

Example 2 ▶ **Using Asymptotes to Sketch a Hyperbola**

Sketch the hyperbola whose equation is $4x^2 - y^2 = 16$.

Solution

Divide each side of the original equation by 16, and rewrite the equation in standard form.

$$\frac{x^2}{2^2} - \frac{y^2}{4^2} = 1 \qquad \text{Write in standard form.}$$

From this, you can conclude that $a = 2$, $b = 4$, and the transverse axis is horizontal. So, the vertices occur at $(-2, 0)$ and $(2, 0)$, and the ends of the conjugate axis occur at $(0, -4)$ and $(0, 4)$. Using these four points, you are able to sketch the rectangle shown in Figure 10.34. Finally, by drawing the asymptotes through the corners of this rectangle, you can complete the sketch shown in Figure 10.35.

FIGURE 10.34

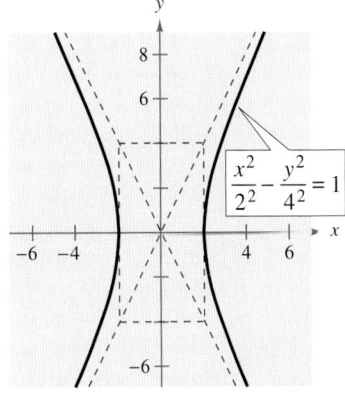

FIGURE 10.35

Example 3 ▶ **Finding the Asymptotes of a Hyperbola**

Sketch the hyperbola given by $4x^2 - 3y^2 + 8x + 16 = 0$ and find the equations of its asymptotes.

Solution

$4x^2 - 3y^2 + 8x + 16 = 0$	Write original equation.
$(4x^2 + 8x) - 3y^2 = -16$	Group terms.
$4(x^2 + 2x) - 3y^2 = -16$	Factor.
$4(x^2 + 2x + 1) - 3y^2 = -16 + 4$	Add 4 to each side.
$4(x + 1)^2 - 3y^2 = -12$	Complete the square.
$-\dfrac{(x + 1)^2}{3} + \dfrac{y^2}{4} = 1$	Divide each side by -12.
$\dfrac{y^2}{2^2} - \dfrac{(x + 1)^2}{\left(\sqrt{3}\right)^2} = 1$	Write in standard form.

From this equation you can conclude that the hyperbola is centered at $(-1, 0)$, has vertices $(-1, 2)$ and $(-1, -2)$, and has a conjugate axis with ends $\left(-1 - \sqrt{3}, 0\right)$ and $\left(-1 + \sqrt{3}, 0\right)$. To sketch the hyperbola, draw a rectangle through these four points. The asymptotes are the lines passing through the corners of the rectangle, as shown in Figure 10.36. Finally, using $a = 2$ and $b = \sqrt{3}$, you can conclude that the equations of the asymptotes are

$$y = \frac{2}{\sqrt{3}}(x + 1) \qquad \text{and} \qquad y = -\frac{2}{\sqrt{3}}(x + 1).$$

The figure at left shows the graph of the hyperbola $4x^2 - 3y^2 + 8x + 16 = 0$ with points $(-1, 2)$, $(-1, 0)$, and $(-1, -2)$.

FIGURE 10.36

Technology

You can use a graphing utility to graph a hyperbola by graphing the upper and lower portions in the same viewing window. For instance, to graph the hyperbola in Example 3, first solve for y to get

$$y_1 = 2\sqrt{1 + \frac{(x + 1)^2}{3}} \qquad \text{and} \qquad y_2 = -2\sqrt{1 + \frac{(x + 1)^2}{3}}.$$

Use a viewing window in which $-9 \leq x \leq 9$ and $-6 \leq y \leq 6$. You should obtain the graph shown below.

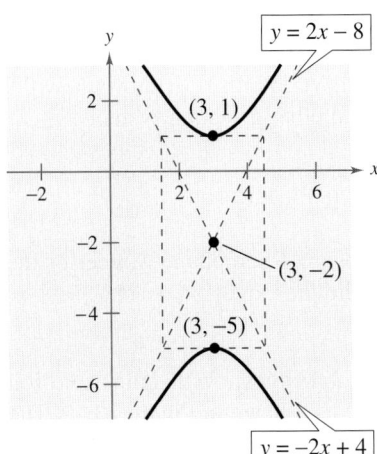

FIGURE **10.37**

Example 4 ▶ **Using Asymptotes to Find the Standard Equation**

Find the standard form of the equation of the hyperbola having vertices $(3, -5)$ and $(3, 1)$ and having asymptotes

$$y = 2x - 8 \qquad \text{and} \qquad y = -2x + 4$$

as shown in Figure 10.37.

Solution

Because the vertices occur at $(3, -5)$ and $(3, 1)$, the center of the hyperbola is $(3, -2)$. Furthermore, the hyperbola has a vertical transverse axis with $a = 3$. From the original equations, you can determine the slopes of the asymptotes to be

$$m_1 = 2 = \frac{a}{b} \qquad \text{and} \qquad m_2 = -2 = -\frac{a}{b}$$

and, because $a = 3$

$$2 = \frac{a}{b} \implies 2 = \frac{3}{b} \implies b = \frac{3}{2}.$$

So, the standard form of the equation is

$$\frac{(y + 2)^2}{3^2} - \frac{(x - 3)^2}{\left(\dfrac{3}{2}\right)^2} = 1.$$

As with ellipses, the **eccentricity** of a hyperbola is

$$e = \frac{c}{a} \qquad \text{Eccentricity}$$

and because $c > a$, it follows that $e > 1$. If the eccentricity is large, the branches of the hyperbola are nearly flat, as shown in Figure 10.38. If the eccentricity is close to 1, the branches of the hyperbola are more pointed, as shown in Figure 10.39.

Additional Example

Find the standard form of the equation of the hyperbola having vertices $(-4, 2)$ and $(1, 2)$ and having foci $(-7, 2)$ and $(4, 2)$.

Answer: $\dfrac{\left(x + \dfrac{3}{2}\right)^2}{\left(\dfrac{5}{2}\right)^2} - \dfrac{(y - 2)^2}{(\sqrt{24})^2} = 1$

FIGURE **10.38**

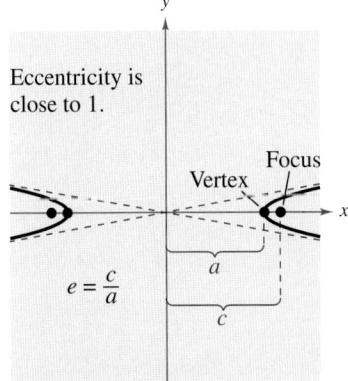

FIGURE **10.39**

Applications

The following application was developed during World War II. It shows how the properties of hyperbolas can be used in radar and other detection systems.

Example 5 ▶ An Application Involving Hyperbolas

Two microphones, 1 mile apart, record an explosion. Microphone A receives the sound 2 seconds before microphone B. Where did the explosion occur?

Solution

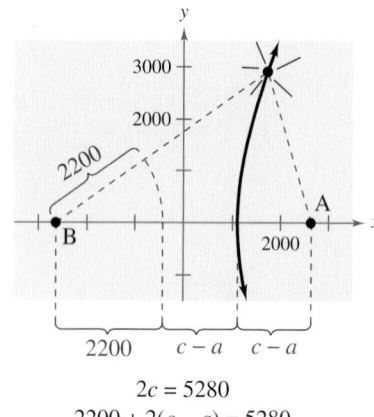

2c = 5280
2200 + 2(c − a) = 5280

FIGURE 10.40

Assuming that sound travels at 1100 feet per second, you know that the explosion took place 2200 feet farther from B than from A, as shown in Figure 10.40. The locus of all points that are 2200 feet closer to A than to B is one branch of the hyperbola

$$\frac{x^2}{a^2} - \frac{y^2}{b^2} = 1$$

where

$$c = \frac{5280}{2} = 2640$$

and

$$a = \frac{2200}{2} = 1100.$$

So, $b^2 = c^2 - a^2 = 2640^2 - 1100^2 = 5,759,600$, and you can conclude that the explosion occurred somewhere on the right branch of the hyperbola

$$\frac{x^2}{1,210,000} - \frac{y^2}{5,759,600} = 1.$$

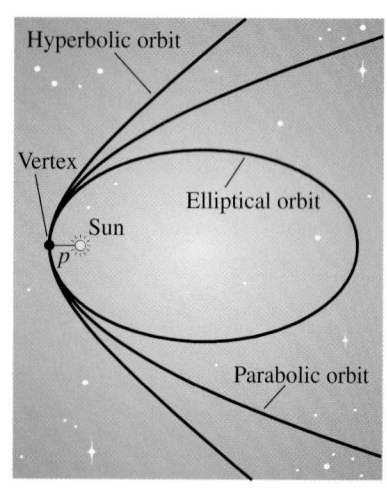

FIGURE 10.41

Another interesting application of conic sections involves the orbits of comets in our solar system. Of the 610 comets identified prior to 1970, 245 have elliptical orbits, 295 have parabolic orbits, and 70 have hyperbolic orbits. The center of the sun is a focus of each of these orbits, and each orbit has a vertex at the point where the comet is closest to the sun, as shown in Figure 10.41. Undoubtedly, there have been many comets with parabolic or hyperbolic orbits that were not identified. We only get to see such comets *once*. Comets with elliptical orbits, such as Halley's comet, are the only ones that remain in our solar system.

If p is the distance between the vertex and the focus in meters, and v is the velocity of the comet at the vertex in meters per second, the type of orbit is determined as follows.

1. Ellipse: $v < \sqrt{2GM/p}$
2. Parabola: $v = \sqrt{2GM/p}$
3. Hyperbola: $v > \sqrt{2GM/p}$

In each of these equations, $M \approx 1.991 \times 10^{30}$ kilograms (the mass of the sun) and $G \approx 6.67 \times 10^{-11}$ cubic meters per kilogram-second squared.

General Equations of Conics

Classifying a Conic from Its General Equation

The graph of $Ax^2 + Cy^2 + Dx + Ey + F = 0$ is one of the following.

1. *Circle:* $\quad A = C$

2. *Parabola:* $\quad AC = 0 \qquad\qquad A = 0$ or $C = 0$, but not both.

3. *Ellipse:* $\quad AC > 0 \qquad\qquad A$ and C have like signs.

4. *Hyperbola:* $AC < 0 \qquad\qquad A$ and C have unlike signs.

The test above is valid if the graph is a conic. The test does not apply to equations such as $x^2 + y^2 = -1$, whose graph is not a conic.

Example 6 ▶ **Classifying Conics from General Equations**

Classify each graph.

a. $4x^2 - 9x + y - 5 = 0$

b. $4x^2 - y^2 + 8x - 6y + 4 = 0$

c. $2x^2 + 4y^2 - 4x + 12y = 0$

d. $2x^2 + 2y^2 - 8x + 12y + 2 = 0$

Solution

a. For the equation $4x^2 - 9x + y - 5 = 0$, you have

$$AC = 4(0) = 0. \qquad \text{Parabola}$$

So, the graph is a parabola.

b. For the equation $4x^2 - y^2 + 8x - 6y + 4 = 0$, you have

$$AC = 4(-1) < 0. \qquad \text{Hyperbola}$$

So, the graph is a hyperbola.

c. For the equation $2x^2 + 4y^2 - 4x + 12y = 0$, you have

$$AC = 2(4) > 0. \qquad \text{Ellipse}$$

So, the graph is an ellipse.

d. For the equation $2x^2 + 2y^2 - 8x + 12y + 2 = 0$, you have

$$A = C = 2. \qquad \text{Circle}$$

So, the graph is a circle.

The Granger Collection

Historical Note

Caroline Herschel (1750–1848) was the first woman to be credited with detecting a new comet. During her long life, this English astronomer discovered a total of eight new comets.

Writing **ABOUT MATHEMATICS**

Sketching Conics Sketch each of the conics described in Example 6. Write a paragraph describing the procedures that allow you to sketch the conics efficiently.

10.4 Exercises

In Exercises 1–4, match the equation with its graph. [The graphs are labeled (a), (b), (c), and (d).]

(a)

(b)

(c)

(d)

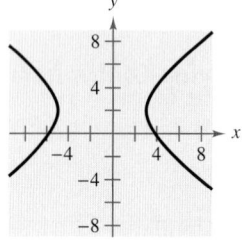

1. $\dfrac{y^2}{9} - \dfrac{x^2}{25} = 1$ **2.** $\dfrac{y^2}{25} - \dfrac{x^2}{9} = 1$

3. $\dfrac{(x-1)^2}{16} - \dfrac{y^2}{4} = 1$ **4.** $\dfrac{(x+1)^2}{16} - \dfrac{(y-2)^2}{9} = 1$

In Exercises 5–16, find the center, vertices, foci, and the equations of the asymptotes of the hyperbola, and sketch its graph.

5. $x^2 - y^2 = 1$ **6.** $\dfrac{x^2}{9} - \dfrac{y^2}{25} = 1$

7. $\dfrac{y^2}{25} - \dfrac{x^2}{81} = 1$ **8.** $\dfrac{x^2}{36} - \dfrac{y^2}{4} = 1$

9. $\dfrac{(x-1)^2}{4} - \dfrac{(y+2)^2}{1} = 1$

10. $\dfrac{(x+3)^2}{144} - \dfrac{(y-2)^2}{25} = 1$

11. $\dfrac{(y+6)^2}{1/9} - \dfrac{(x-2)^2}{1/4} = 1$

12. $\dfrac{(y-1)^2}{1/4} - \dfrac{(x+3)^2}{1/16} = 1$

13. $9x^2 - y^2 - 36x - 6y + 18 = 0$

14. $x^2 - 9y^2 + 36y - 72 = 0$

15. $x^2 - 9y^2 + 2x - 54y - 80 = 0$

16. $16y^2 - x^2 + 2x + 64y + 63 = 0$

In Exercises 17–20, find the center, vertices, foci, and the equations of the asymptotes of the hyperbola. Use a graphing utility to graph the hyperbola and its asymptotes.

17. $2x^2 - 3y^2 = 6$ **18.** $6y^2 - 3x^2 = 18$

19. $9y^2 - x^2 + 2x + 54y + 62 = 0$

20. $9x^2 - y^2 + 54x + 10y + 55 = 0$

In Exercises 21–26, find the standard form of the equation of the hyperbola with center at the origin.

21. Vertices: $(0, \pm 2)$; Foci: $(0, \pm 4)$

22. Vertices: $(\pm 4, 0)$; Foci: $(\pm 6, 0)$

23. Vertices: $(\pm 1, 0)$; Asymptotes: $y = \pm 5x$

24. Vertices: $(0, \pm 3)$; Asymptotes: $y = \pm 3x$

25. Foci: $(0, \pm 8)$; Asymptotes: $y = \pm 4x$

26. Foci: $(\pm 10, 0)$; Asymptotes: $y = \pm \frac{3}{4}x$

In Exercises 27–38, find the standard form of the equation of the hyperbola.

27. Vertices: $(2, 0), (6, 0)$; Foci: $(0, 0), (8, 0)$

28. Vertices: $(2, 3), (2, -3)$; Foci: $(2, 6), (2, -6)$

29. Vertices: $(4, 1), (4, 9)$; Foci: $(4, 0), (4, 10)$

30. Vertices: $(-2, 1), (2, 1)$; Foci: $(-3, 1), (3, 1)$

31. Vertices: $(2, 3), (2, -3)$;
Passes through the point $(0, 5)$

32. Vertices: $(-2, 1), (2, 1)$;
Passes through the point $(5, 4)$

33. Vertices: $(0, 4), (0, 0)$;
Passes through the point $(\sqrt{5}, -1)$

34. Vertices: $(1, 2), (1, -2)$;
Passes through the point $(0, \sqrt{5})$

35. Vertices: $(1, 2), (3, 2)$;
Asymptotes: $y = x$, $y = 4 - x$

36. Vertices: $(3, 0), (3, 6)$;
Asymptotes: $y = 6 - x$, $y = x$

37. Vertices: $(0, 2), (6, 2)$;
Asymptotes: $y = \frac{2}{3}x$, $y = 4 - \frac{2}{3}x$

38. Vertices: $(3, 0), (3, 4)$;
Asymptotes: $y = \frac{2}{3}x$, $y = 4 - \frac{2}{3}x$

▶ Model It

39. **LORAN** Long distance radio navigation for aircraft and ships uses synchronized pulses transmitted by widely separated transmitting stations. These pulses travel at the speed of light (186,000 miles per second). The difference in the times of arrival of these pulses at an aircraft or ship is constant on a hyperbola having the transmitting stations as foci. Assume that two stations, 300 miles apart, are positioned on the rectangular coordinate system at points with coordinates $(-150, 0)$ and $(150, 0)$, and that a ship is traveling on a hyperbolic path with coordinates $(x, 75)$ (see figure).

(a) Find the x-coordinate of the position of the ship if the time difference between the pulses from the transmitting stations is 1000 microseconds (0.001 second).

(b) Determine the distance between the ship and Station 1 when the ship reaches the shore.

(c) The ship wants to enter a bay located between the two stations. The bay is 30 miles from Station 1. What should the time difference between the pulses be?

(d) The ship is 60 miles offshore when the time difference in part (c) is obtained. What is the position of the ship?

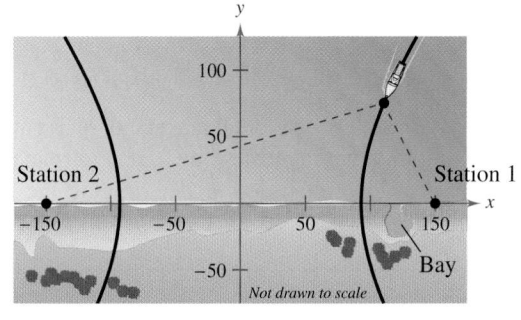

40. **Hyperbolic Mirror** A hyperbolic mirror (used in some telescopes) has the property that a light ray directed at a focus will be reflected to the other focus. The focus of a hyperbolic mirror (see figure) has coordinates $(24, 0)$. Find the vertex of the mirror if the mount at the top edge of the mirror has coordinates $(24, 24)$.

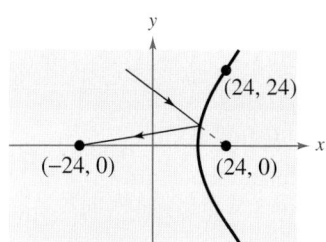

FIGURE FOR **40**

In Exercises 41–48, classify the graph of the equation as a circle, a parabola, an ellipse, or a hyperbola.

41. $x^2 + y^2 - 6x + 4y + 9 = 0$

42. $x^2 + 4y^2 - 6x + 16y + 21 = 0$

43. $4x^2 - y^2 - 4x - 3 = 0$

44. $y^2 - 6y - 4x + 21 = 0$

45. $4x^2 + 3y^2 + 8x - 24y + 51 = 0$

46. $4y^2 - 2x^2 - 4y - 8x - 15 = 0$

47. $25x^2 - 10x - 200y - 119 = 0$

48. $4y^2 + 4x^2 - 24x + 35 = 0$

Synthesis

True or False? In Exercises 49 and 50, determine whether the statement is true or false. Justify your answer.

49. In the standard form of the equation of a hyperbola, the larger the ratio of b to a, the larger the eccentricity of the hyperbola.

50. In the standard form of the equation of a hyperbola, the trivial solution of two intersecting lines occurs when $b = 0$.

51. Consider a hyperbola centered at the origin with a horizontal transverse axis. Use the definition of a hyperbola to derive its standard form.

52. *Writing* Explain how the central rectangle of a hyperbola can be used to sketch its asymptotes.

Review

In Exercises 53–56, factor the polynomial completely.

53. $x^3 - 16x$

54. $x^2 + 14x + 49$

55. $2x^3 - 24x^2 + 72x$

56. $6x^3 - 11x^2 - 10x$

In Exercises 57–60, sketch a graph of the function. Include two full periods.

57. $y = 2 \cos x + 1$

58. $y = \sin \pi x$

59. $y = \tan 2x$

60. $y = -\frac{1}{2} \sec x$

10.5 Rotation of Conics

▶ **What you should learn**

- How to rotate the coordinate axes to eliminate the *xy*-term in the equation of a conic
- How to use the discriminant to classify a conic

▶ **Why you should learn it**

As illustrated in Exercises 7–18 on page 740, rotation of the coordinate axes can help you identify the graph of a general second-degree equation.

Rotation

In the preceding section, you learned that the equation of a conic with axes parallel to one of the coordinate axes has a standard form that can be written in the general form

$$Ax^2 + Cy^2 + Dx + Ey + F = 0. \qquad \text{Horizontal or vertical axis}$$

In this section, you will study the equations of conics whose axes are rotated so that they are not parallel to either the *x*-axis or the *y*-axis. The general equation for such conics contains an *xy*-term.

$$Ax^2 + Bxy + Cy^2 + Dx + Ey + F = 0 \qquad \text{Equation in } xy\text{-plane}$$

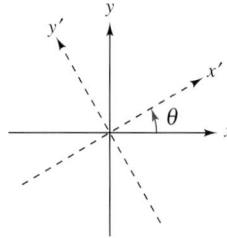

FIGURE 10.42

To eliminate this *xy*-term, you can use a procedure called **rotation of axes.** The objective is to rotate the *x*- and *y*-axes until they are parallel to the axes of the conic. The rotated axes are denoted as the *x′*-axis and the *y′*-axis, as shown in Figure 10.42. After the rotation, the equation of the conic in the new *x′y′*-plane will have the form

$$A'(x')^2 + C'(y')^2 + D'x' + E'y' + F' = 0. \qquad \text{Equation in } x'y'\text{-plane}$$

Because this equation has no *xy*-term, you can obtain a standard form by completing the square. The following theorem identifies how much to rotate the axes to eliminate the *xy*-term and also the equations for determining the new coefficients A', C', D', E', and F'.

Rotation of Axes to Eliminate an *xy*-Term

The general second-degree equation $Ax^2 + Bxy + Cy^2 + Dx + Ey + F = 0$ can be rewritten as

$$A'(x')^2 + C'(y')^2 + D'x' + E'y' + F' = 0$$

by rotating the coordinate axes through an angle θ, where

$$\cot 2\theta = \frac{A - C}{B}.$$

The coefficients of the new equation are obtained by making the substitutions $x = x' \cos \theta - y' \sin \theta$ and $y = x' \sin \theta + y' \cos \theta$.

Remember that the substitutions

$$x = x' \cos \theta - y' \sin \theta$$

and

$$y = x' \sin \theta + y' \cos \theta$$

were developed to eliminate the $x'y'$-term in the rotated system. You can use this as a check on your work. In other words, if your final equation contains an $x'y'$-term, you know that you made a mistake.

Example 1 ▶ **Rotation of Axes for a Hyperbola**

Write the equation $xy - 1 = 0$ in standard form.

Solution

Because $A = 0$, $B = 1$, and $C = 0$, you have

$$\cot 2\theta = \frac{A - C}{B} = 0 \quad \Longrightarrow \quad 2\theta = \frac{\pi}{2} \quad \Longrightarrow \quad \theta = \frac{\pi}{4}$$

which implies that

$$x = x' \cos \frac{\pi}{4} - y' \sin \frac{\pi}{4}$$

$$= x'\left(\frac{1}{\sqrt{2}}\right) - y'\left(\frac{1}{\sqrt{2}}\right)$$

$$= \frac{x' - y'}{\sqrt{2}}$$

and

$$y = x' \sin \frac{\pi}{4} + y' \cos \frac{\pi}{4}$$

$$= x'\left(\frac{1}{\sqrt{2}}\right) + y'\left(\frac{1}{\sqrt{2}}\right)$$

$$= \frac{x' + y'}{\sqrt{2}}.$$

The equation in the $x'y'$-system is obtained by substituting these expressions in the equation $xy - 1 = 0$.

$$\left(\frac{x' - y'}{\sqrt{2}}\right)\left(\frac{x' + y'}{\sqrt{2}}\right) - 1 = 0$$

$$\frac{(x')^2 - (y')^2}{2} - 1 = 0$$

$$\frac{(x')^2}{(\sqrt{2})^2} - \frac{(y')^2}{(\sqrt{2})^2} = 1 \qquad \text{Write in standard form.}$$

In the $x'y'$-system, this is a hyperbola centered at the origin with vertices at $(\pm\sqrt{2}, 0)$, as shown in Figure 10.43. To find the coordinates of the vertices in the xy-system, substitute the coordinates $(\pm\sqrt{2}, 0)$ in the equations

$$x = \frac{x' - y'}{\sqrt{2}} \qquad \text{and} \qquad y = \frac{x' + y'}{\sqrt{2}}.$$

This substitution yields the vertices $(1, 1)$ and $(-1, -1)$ in the xy-system. Note also that the asymptotes of the hyperbola have equations $y' = \pm x'$, which correspond to the original x- and y-axes.

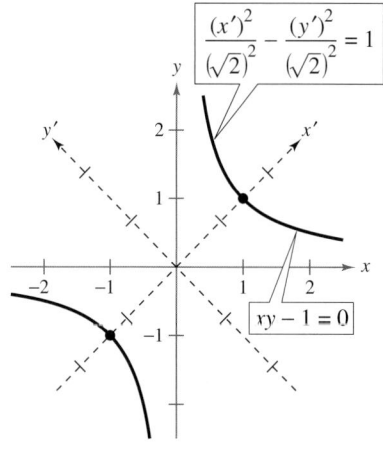

Vertices:
In $x'y'$-system: $(\sqrt{2}, 0), (-\sqrt{2}, 0)$
In xy-system: $(1, 1), (-1, -1)$
FIGURE 10.43

Example 2 ▶   **Rotation of Axes for an Ellipse**

Sketch the graph of $7x^2 - 6\sqrt{3}\,xy + 13y^2 - 16 = 0$.

Solution

Because $A = 7$, $B = -6\sqrt{3}$, and $C = 13$, you have

$$\cot 2\theta = \frac{A - C}{B} = \frac{7 - 13}{-6\sqrt{3}} = \frac{1}{\sqrt{3}}$$

which implies that $\theta = \pi/6$. The equation in the $x'y'$-system is obtained by making the substitutions

$$x = x' \cos \frac{\pi}{6} - y' \sin \frac{\pi}{6}$$

$$= x'\left(\frac{\sqrt{3}}{2}\right) - y'\left(\frac{1}{2}\right)$$

$$= \frac{\sqrt{3}\,x' - y'}{2}$$

and

$$y = x' \sin \frac{\pi}{6} + y' \cos \frac{\pi}{6}$$

$$= x'\left(\frac{1}{2}\right) + y'\left(\frac{\sqrt{3}}{2}\right)$$

$$= \frac{x' + \sqrt{3}\,y'}{2}$$

in the original equation. So, you have

$$7x^2 - 6\sqrt{3}\,xy + 13y^2 - 16 = 0$$

$$7\left(\frac{\sqrt{3}\,x' - y'}{2}\right)^2 - 6\sqrt{3}\left(\frac{\sqrt{3}\,x' - y'}{2}\right)\left(\frac{x' + \sqrt{3}\,y'}{2}\right)$$

$$+ 13\left(\frac{x' + \sqrt{3}\,y'}{2}\right)^2 - 16 = 0$$

which simplifies to

$$4(x')^2 + 16(y')^2 - 16 = 0$$

$$4(x')^2 + 16(y')^2 = 16$$

$$\frac{(x')^2}{4} + \frac{(y')^2}{1} = 1$$

$$\frac{(x')^2}{2^2} + \frac{(y')^2}{1^2} = 1. \qquad \text{Write in standard form.}$$

This is the equation of an ellipse centered at the origin with vertices $(\pm 2, 0)$ in the $x'y'$-system, as shown in Figure 10.44.

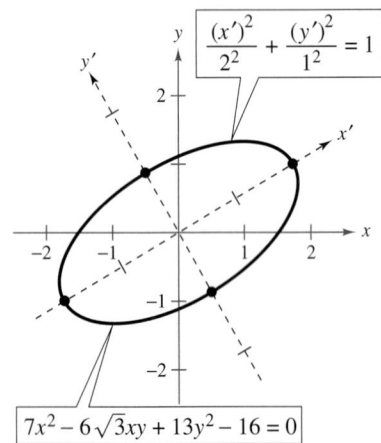

$$\frac{(x')^2}{2^2} + \frac{(y')^2}{1^2} = 1$$

$7x^2 - 6\sqrt{3}xy + 13y^2 - 16 = 0$

Vertices:
In $x'y'$-system: $(\pm 2, 0), (0, \pm 1)$
In xy-system: $\left(\sqrt{3}, 1\right), \left(-\sqrt{3}, -1\right),$
$\left(\dfrac{1}{2}, -\dfrac{\sqrt{3}}{2}\right), \left(-\dfrac{1}{2}, \dfrac{\sqrt{3}}{2}\right)$

FIGURE **10.44**

Example 3 ▶ Rotation of Axes for a Parabola

Sketch the graph of $x^2 - 4xy + 4y^2 + 5\sqrt{5}y + 1 = 0$.

Solution

Because $A = 1$, $B = -4$, and $C = 4$, you have

$$\cot 2\theta = \frac{A - C}{B} = \frac{1 - 4}{-4} = \frac{3}{4}.$$

Using the identity $\cot 2\theta = (\cot^2\theta - 1)/(2\cot\theta)$ produces

$$\cot 2\theta = \frac{\cot^2\theta - 1}{2\cot\theta} = \frac{3}{4}$$

from which you obtain the equation

$$4\cot^2\theta - 4 = 6\cot\theta$$

$$4\cot^2\theta - 6\cot\theta - 4 = 0$$

$$(2\cot\theta - 4)(2\cot\theta + 1) = 0.$$

Considering $0 < \theta < \pi/2$, you have $2\cot\theta = 4$. So,

$$\cot\theta = 2 \quad \Longrightarrow \quad \theta \approx 26.6°.$$

From the triangle in Figure 10.45, you obtain $\sin\theta = 1/\sqrt{5}$ and $\cos\theta = 2/\sqrt{5}$. Consequently, you use the substitutions

$$x = x'\cos\theta - y'\sin\theta$$

$$= x'\left(\frac{2}{\sqrt{5}}\right) - y'\left(\frac{1}{\sqrt{5}}\right) = \frac{2x' - y'}{\sqrt{5}}$$

$$y = x'\sin\theta + y'\cos\theta$$

$$= x'\left(\frac{1}{\sqrt{5}}\right) + y'\left(\frac{2}{\sqrt{5}}\right) = \frac{x' + 2y'}{\sqrt{5}}.$$

Substituting these expressions in the original equation, you have

$$x^2 - 4xy + 4y^2 + 5\sqrt{5}y + 1 = 0$$

$$\left(\frac{2x' - y'}{\sqrt{5}}\right)^2 - 4\left(\frac{2x' - y'}{\sqrt{5}}\right)\left(\frac{x' + 2y'}{\sqrt{5}}\right) + 4\left(\frac{x' + 2y'}{\sqrt{5}}\right)^2 + 5\sqrt{5}\left(\frac{x' + 2y'}{\sqrt{5}}\right) + 1 = 0$$

which simplifies as follows.

$$5(y')^2 + 5x' + 10y' + 1 = 0$$

$$5(y' + 1)^2 = -5x' + 4 \qquad \text{Complete the square.}$$

$$(y' + 1)^2 = (-1)\left(x' - \frac{4}{5}\right) \qquad \text{Write in standard form.}$$

The graph of this equation is a parabola with vertex $\left(\frac{4}{5}, -1\right)$. Its axis is parallel to the x'-axis in the $x'y'$-system, as shown in Figure 10.46.

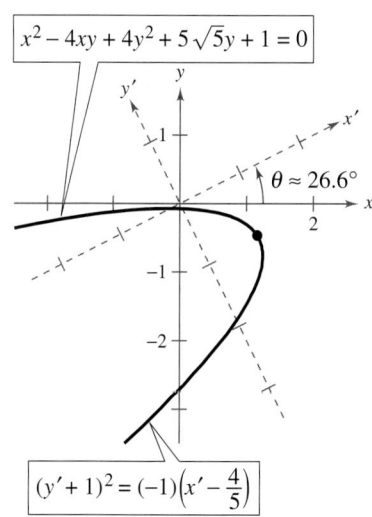

$$\left[(y' + 1)^2 = (-1)\left(x' - \frac{4}{5}\right)\right]$$

Vertex:

In $x'y'$-system: $\left(\frac{4}{5}, -1\right)$

In xy-system: $\left(\frac{13}{5\sqrt{5}}, -\frac{6}{5\sqrt{5}}\right)$

FIGURE **10.46**

FIGURE **10.45**

Invariants Under Rotation

In the rotation of axes theorem listed at the beginning of this section, note that the constant term is the same in both equations, $F' = F$. Such quantities are **invariant under rotation.** The next theorem lists some other rotation invariants.

Rotation Invariants

The rotation of the coordinate axes through an angle θ that transforms the equation $Ax^2 + Bxy + Cy^2 + Dx + Ey + F = 0$ into the form

$$A'(x')^2 + C'(y')^2 + D'x' + E'y' + F' = 0$$

has the following rotation invariants.

1. $F = F'$

2. $A + C = A' + C'$

3. $B^2 - 4AC = (B')^2 - 4A'C'$

You can use the results of this theorem to classify the graph of a second-degree equation *with* an xy-term in much the same way you do for a second-degree equation *without* an xy-term. Note that because $B' = 0$, the invariant $B^2 - 4AC$ reduces to

$$B^2 - 4AC = -4A'C'. \qquad \text{Discriminant}$$

This quantity is called the **discriminant** of the equation

$$Ax^2 + Bxy + Cy^2 + Dx + Ey + F = 0.$$

Now, from the classification procedure given in Section 10.4, you know that the sign of $A'C'$ determines the type of graph for the equation

$$A'(x')^2 + C'(y')^2 + D'x' + E'y' + F' = 0.$$

Consequently, the sign of $B^2 - 4AC$ will determine the type of graph for the original equation, as given in the following classification.

Classification of Conics by the Discriminant

The graph of the equation $Ax^2 + Bxy + Cy^2 + Dx + Ey + F = 0$ is, except in degenerate cases, determined by its discriminant as follows.

1. *Ellipse or circle:* $B^2 - 4AC < 0$

2. *Parabola:* $\quad\quad\quad B^2 - 4AC = 0$

3. *Hyperbola:* $\quad\quad B^2 - 4AC > 0$

For example, in the general equation

$$3x^2 + 7xy + 5y^2 - 6x - 7y + 15 = 0$$

you have $A = 3$, $B = 7$, and $C = 5$. So the discriminant is

$$B^2 - 4AC = 7^2 - 4(3)(5) = 49 - 60 = -11.$$

Because $-11 < 0$, the graph of the equation is an ellipse or a circle.

FIGURE 10.47

FIGURE 10.48

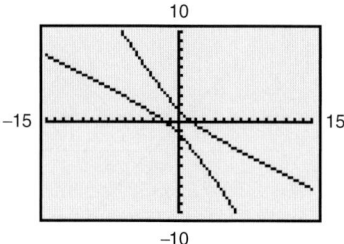

FIGURE 10.49

Activities

1. Use the discriminant to classify each equation.

   a. $x^2 - 4xy + y^2 + 2x - 3y + 1 = 0$

   b. $4x^2 - xy + 4y^2 + 2x - 3y + 1 = 0$

   c. $x^2 - xy + 4y^2 + 2x - 3y + 1 = 0$

   d. $x^2 - 4xy + 4y^2 + 2x - 3y + 1 = 0$

   Answer: (a) Hyperbola, (b) Ellipse or circle, (c) Ellipse or circle, (d) Parabola

2. Find the angle of rotation necessary to eliminate the xy-term in the equation $3x^2 + 2xy - y^2 + x - 1 = 0$.

   Answer: $\theta \approx 13.28°$

3. Rotate the axes to eliminate the xy-term in the equation $x^2 + 2xy + y^2 - \sqrt{2}y = 0$.

   Answer: $2(x')^2 - x' - y' = 0$, $\theta = \dfrac{\pi}{4}$

Example 4 ▶ Rotation and Graphing Utilities

For each of the following, classify the graph, use the Quadratic Formula to solve for y, and then use a graphing utility to graph the equation.

a. $2x^2 - 3xy + 2y^2 - 2x = 0$ **b.** $x^2 - 6xy + 9y^2 - 2y + 1 = 0$

c. $3x^2 + 8xy + 4y^2 - 7 = 0$

Solution

a. Because $B^2 - 4AC = 9 - 16 < 0$, the graph is a circle or an ellipse. Solve for y as follows.

$$2x^2 - 3xy + 2y^2 - 2x = 0 \qquad \text{Write original equation.}$$

$$2y^2 - 3xy + (2x^2 - 2x) = 0 \qquad \text{Quadratic form } ay^2 + by + c = 0$$

$$y = \frac{-(-3x) \pm \sqrt{(-3x)^2 - 4(2)(2x^2 - 2x)}}{2(2)}$$

Graph both of the equations to obtain the ellipse shown in Figure 10.47.

$$y = \frac{3x + \sqrt{9x^2 - 16(x^2 - x)}}{4} \qquad \text{Top half of ellipse}$$

$$y = \frac{3x - \sqrt{9x^2 - 16(x^2 - x)}}{4} \qquad \text{Bottom half of ellipse}$$

b. Because $B^2 - 4AC = 36 - 36 = 0$, the graph is a parabola.

$$x^2 - 6xy + 9y^2 - 2y + 1 = 0 \qquad \text{Write original equation.}$$

$$9y^2 - (6x + 2)y + (x^2 + 1) = 0 \qquad \text{Quadratic form } ay^2 + by + c = 0$$

$$y = \frac{(6x + 2) \pm \sqrt{(6x + 2)^2 - 4(9)(x^2 + 1)}}{18}$$

Graphing the resulting two equations gives the parabola shown in Figure 10.48.

c. Because $B^2 - 4AC = 64 - 48 > 0$, the graph is a hyperbola.

$$3x^2 + 8xy + 4y^2 - 7 = 0 \qquad \text{Write original equation.}$$

$$4y^2 + 8xy + (3x^2 - 7) = 0 \qquad \text{Quadratic form } ay^2 + by + c = 0$$

$$y = \frac{-8x \pm \sqrt{(8x)^2 - 4(4)(3x^2 - 7)}}{8}$$

The graphs of the resulting two equations yield the hyperbola shown in Figure 10.49.

Writing ABOUT MATHEMATICS

Classifying a Graph as a Hyperbola In Section 2.6, it was mentioned that the graph of $f(x) = 1/x$ is a hyperbola. Discuss how you could use the techniques in this section to verify this, and then do so. Compare your statement with that of another student.

10.5 Exercises

In Exercises 1–6, the $x'y'$-coordinate system has been rotated θ degrees from the xy-coordinate system. The coordinates of a point in the xy-coordinate system are given. Find the coordinates of the point in the rotated coordinate system.

1. $\theta = 90°, (0, 3)$ **2.** $\theta = 45°, (3, 3)$

3. $\theta = 30°, (1, 3)$ **4.** $\theta = 60°, (3, 1)$

5. $\theta = 45°, (2, 1)$ **6.** $\theta = 30°, (2, 4)$

In Exercises 7–18, rotate the axes to eliminate the xy-term. Sketch the graph of the resulting equation, showing both sets of axes.

7. $xy + 1 = 0$

8. $xy - 2 = 0$

9. $x^2 - 2xy + y^2 - 1 = 0$

10. $xy + x - 2y + 3 = 0$

11. $xy - 2y - 4x = 0$

12. $2x^2 - 3xy - 2y^2 + 10 = 0$

13. $5x^2 - 6xy + 5y^2 - 12 = 0$

14. $13x^2 + 6\sqrt{3}xy + 7y^2 - 16 = 0$

15. $3x^2 - 2\sqrt{3}xy + y^2 + 2x + 2\sqrt{3}y = 0$

16. $16x^2 - 24xy + 9y^2 - 60x - 80y + 100 = 0$

17. $9x^2 + 24xy + 16y^2 + 90x - 130y = 0$

18. $9x^2 + 24xy + 16y^2 + 80x - 60y = 0$

In Exercises 19–26, use a graphing utility to graph the conic. Determine the angle θ through which the axes are rotated. Explain how you used the graphing utility to obtain the graph.

19. $x^2 + 2xy + y^2 = 20$

20. $x^2 - 4xy + 2y^2 = 6$

21. $17x^2 + 32xy - 7y^2 = 75$

22. $40x^2 + 36xy + 25y^2 = 52$

23. $32x^2 + 48xy + 8y^2 = 50$

24. $24x^2 + 18xy + 12y^2 = 34$

25. $4x^2 - 12xy + 9y^2 + (4\sqrt{13} - 12)x$
$$- (6\sqrt{13} + 8)y = 91$$

26. $6x^2 - 4xy + 8y^2 + (5\sqrt{5} - 10)x$
$$- (7\sqrt{5} + 5)y = 80$$

In Exercises 27–32, match the graph with its equation. [The graphs are labeled (a), (b), (c), (d), (e), and (f).]

(a)

(b)

(c)

(d)

(e)

(f)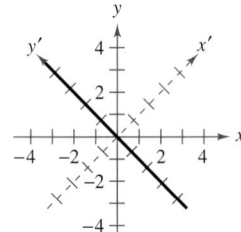

27. $xy + 2 = 0$

28. $x^2 + 2xy + y^2 = 0$

29. $-2x^2 + 3xy + 2y^2 + 3 = 0$

30. $x^2 - xy + 3y^2 - 5 = 0$

31. $3x^2 + 2xy + y^2 - 10 = 0$

32. $x^2 - 4xy + 4y^2 + 10x - 30 = 0$

In Exercises 33–40, use the discriminant to classify the graph. Then use the Quadratic Formula to solve for y and use a graphing utility to graph the equation.

33. $16x^2 - 8xy + y^2 - 10x + 5y = 0$

34. $x^2 - 4xy - 2y^2 - 6 = 0$

35. $12x^2 - 6xy + 7y^2 - 45 = 0$

36. $2x^2 + 4xy + 5y^2 + 3x - 4y - 20 = 0$

37. $x^2 - 6xy - 5y^2 + 4x - 22 = 0$

38. $36x^2 - 60xy + 25y^2 + 9y = 0$

39. $x^2 + 4xy + 4y^2 - 5x - y - 3 = 0$

40. $x^2 + xy + 4y^2 + x + y - 4 = 0$

In Exercises 41–44, sketch (if possible) the graph of the degenerate conic.

41. $y^2 - 9x^2 = 0$

42. $x^2 + y^2 - 2x + 6y + 10 = 0$

43. $x^2 + 2xy + y^2 - 1 = 0$

44. $x^2 - 10xy + y^2 = 0$

In Exercises 45–58, find any points of intersection of the graphs algebraically and then verify using a graphing utility.

45. $-x^2 + y^2 + 4x - 6y + 4 = 0$

$\quad x^2 + y^2 - 4x - 6y + 12 = 0$

46. $-x^2 - y^2 - 8x + 20y - 7 = 0$

$\quad x^2 + 9y^2 + 8x + 4y + 7 = 0$

47. $-4x^2 - y^2 - 16x + 24y - 16 = 0$

$\quad 4x^2 + y^2 + 40x - 24y + 208 = 0$

48. $\quad\ \ x^2 - 4y^2 - 20x - 64y - 172 = 0$

$\quad 16x^2 + 4y^2 - 320x + 64y + 1600 = 0$

49. $x^2 - y^2 - 12x + 16y - 64 = 0$

$\quad x^2 + y^2 - 12x - 16y + 64 = 0$

50. $x^2 + 4y^2 - 2x - 8y + 1 = 0$

$\quad -x^2 + 2x - 4y - 1 = 0$

51. $-16x^2 - y^2 + 24y - 80 = 0$

$\quad 16x^2 + 25y^2 - 400 = 0$

52. $16x^2 - y^2 + 16y - 128 = 0$

$\quad y^2 - 48x - 16y - 32 = 0$

53. $x^2 + y^2 - 4 = 0$

$\quad 3x - y^2 = 0$

54. $4x^2 + 9y^2 - 36y = 0$

$\quad x^2 + 9y - 27 = 0$

55. $x^2 + 2y^2 - 4x + 6y - 5 = 0$

$\quad -x + y - 4 = 0$

56. $x^2 + 2y^2 - 4x + 6y - 5 = 0$

$\quad x^2 - 4x - y + 4 = 0$

57. $xy + x - 2y + 3 = 0$

$\quad x^2 + 4y^2 - 9 = 0$

58. $5x^2 - 2xy + 5y^2 - 12 = 0$

$\quad x + y - 1 = 0$

Synthesis

True or False? **In Exercises 59 and 60, determine whether the statement is true or false. Justify your answer.**

59. The graph of the equation

$$x^2 + xy + ky^2 + 6x + 10 = 0$$

where k is any constant less than $\frac{1}{4}$, is a hyperbola.

60. After a rotation of axes is used to eliminate the xy-term from an equation of the form

$$Ax^2 + Bxy + Cy^2 + Dx + Ey + F = 0$$

the coefficients of the x^2- and y^2-terms remain A and C, respectively.

61. Show that the equation

$$x^2 + y^2 = r^2$$

is invariant under rotation of axes.

62. Find the lengths of the major and minor axes of the ellipse graphed in Exercise 14.

Review

In Exercises 63–68, find the zeros (if any) of the rational function.

63. $f(x) = \dfrac{x^2 - 9}{x + 1}$

64. $f(x) = \dfrac{3}{x^2 + 1}$

65. $f(x) = 4 - \dfrac{8}{x^2 - 2}$

66. $f(x) = \dfrac{x^3 - 27}{x^2 - 1}$

67. $f(x) = \dfrac{x^2 + 4x + 4}{x^2 + 3}$

68. $f(x) = \dfrac{x^2 - 1}{2x^2 + 3x - 2}$

In Exercises 69–76, graph the rational function. Identify all intercepts and asymptotes.

69. $g(x) = \dfrac{2}{2 - x}$

70. $f(x) = \dfrac{2x}{2 - x}$

71. $g(t) = \dfrac{2}{1 + t}$

72. $h(t) = \dfrac{2t}{2 + t}$

73. $g(x) = \dfrac{x^2 - 2x - 3}{x - 2}$

74. $f(x) = \dfrac{x^2}{2 - x}$

75. $h(s) = \dfrac{2}{4 - s^2}$

76. $f(t) = \dfrac{t}{t^2 - t - 6}$

10.6 Parametric Equations

▶ **What you should learn**

• How to evaluate a set of parametric equations for a given value of the parameter
• How to sketch the curve that is represented by a set of parametric equations
• How to rewrite a set of parametric equations as a single rectangular equation
• How to find a set of parametric equations for a graph

▶ **Why you should learn it**

Parametric equations are useful for modeling the path of an object. For instance, in Exercise 59 on page 748, you will use a set of parametric equations to model the path of a baseball.

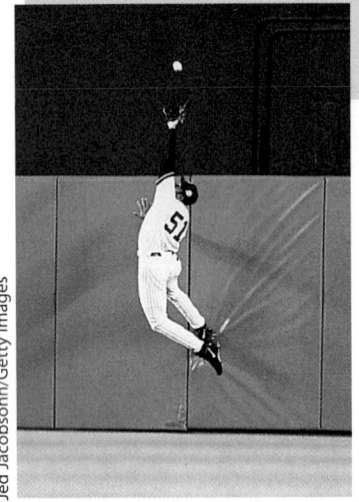

Jed Jacobsohn/Getty Images

Plane Curves

Up to this point you have been representing a graph by a single equation involving the *two* variables x and y. In this section, you will study situations in which it is useful to introduce a *third* variable to represent a curve in the plane.

To see the usefulness of this procedure, consider the path followed by an object that is propelled into the air at an angle of 45°. If the initial velocity of the object is 48 feet per second, it can be shown that the object follows the parabolic path

$$y = -\frac{x^2}{72} + x. \qquad \text{Rectangular equation}$$

However, this equation does not tell the whole story. Although it does tell you *where* the object has been, it doesn't tell you *when* the object was at a given point (x, y) on the path. To determine this time, you can introduce a third variable t, called a **parameter**. It is possible to write both x and y as functions of t to obtain the **parametric equations**

$$x = 24\sqrt{2}\,t \qquad \text{Parametric equation for } x$$

$$y = -16t^2 + 24\sqrt{2}\,t. \qquad \text{Parametric equation for } y$$

From this set of equations you can determine that at time $t = 0$, the object is at the point $(0, 0)$. Similarly, at time $t = 1$, the object is at the point $\left(24\sqrt{2},\ 24\sqrt{2} - 16\right)$, and so on, as shown in Figure 10.50.

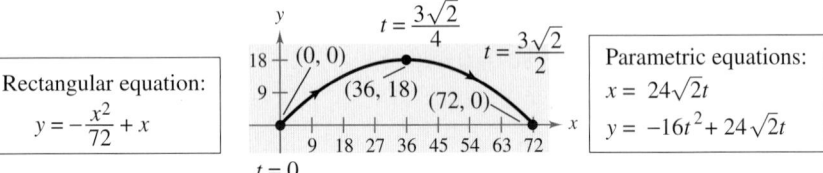

Rectangular equation:
$$y = -\frac{x^2}{72} + x$$

Parametric equations:
$$x = 24\sqrt{2}\,t$$
$$y = -16t^2 + 24\sqrt{2}\,t$$

FIGURE 10.50   *Curvilinear Motion: Two Variables for Position, One Variable for Time*

For this particular motion problem, x and y are continuous functions of t, and the resulting path is a **plane curve.** (For this text, it is sufficient to think of a *continuous function* as one whose graph can be traced without lifting the pencil from the paper.)

Definition of Plane Curve

If f and g are continuous functions of t on an interval I, the set of ordered pairs $(f(t), g(t))$ is a **plane curve** C. The equations

$$x = f(t) \qquad \text{and} \qquad y = g(t)$$

are **parametric equations** for C, and t is the **parameter.**

Sketching a Plane Curve

When sketching a curve represented by a pair of parametric equations, you still plot points in the *xy*-plane. Each set of coordinates (x, y) is determined from a value chosen for the parameter *t*. Plotting the resulting points in the order of *increasing* values of *t* traces the curve in a specific direction. This is called the **orientation** of the curve.

Example 1 ▶ Sketching a Curve

Sketch the curve described by the parametric equations

$$x = t^2 - 4 \quad \text{and} \quad y = \frac{t}{2}, \quad -2 \le t \le 3.$$

Solution

Using values of *t* in the interval, the parametric equations yield the points (x, y) shown in the table.

t	x	y
−2	0	−1
−1	−3	−1/2
0	−4	0
1	−3	1/2
2	0	1
3	5	3/2

By plotting these points in the order of increasing *t*, you obtain the curve *C* shown in Figure 10.51. Note that the arrows on the curve indicate its orientation as *t* increases from −2 to 3.

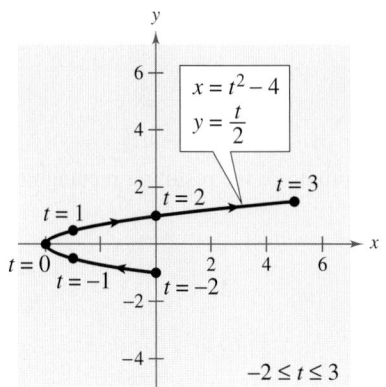

FIGURE 10.51

Note that the graph shown in Figure 10.51 does not define *y* as a function of *x*. This points out one benefit of parametric equations—they can be used to represent graphs that are more general than graphs of functions.

It often happens that two different sets of parametric equations have the same graph. For example, the set of parametric equations

$$x = 4t^2 - 4 \quad \text{and} \quad y = t, \quad -1 \le t \le \frac{3}{2}$$

has the same graph as the set given in Example 1. However, by comparing the values of *t* in Figures 10.51 and 10.52, you see that this second graph is traced out more *rapidly* (considering *t* as time) than the first graph. So, in applications, different parametric representations can be used to represent various *speeds* at which objects travel along a given path.

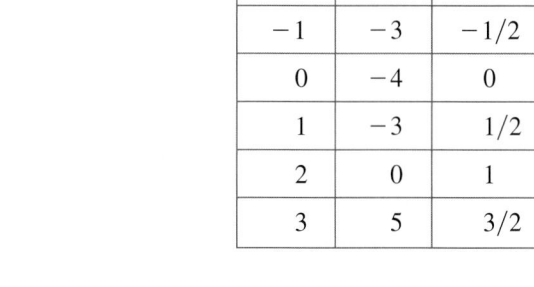

FIGURE 10.52

Eliminating the Parameter

Example 1 uses simple point plotting to sketch the curve. This tedious process can sometimes be simplified by finding a rectangular equation (in x and y) that has the same graph. This process is called **eliminating the parameter.**

Parametric equations	⇨	Solve for t in one equation.	⇨	Substitute in other equation.	⇨	Rectangular equation

$$x = t^2 - 4 \qquad\qquad t = 2y \qquad\qquad x = (2y)^2 - 4 \qquad\qquad x = 4y^2 - 4$$
$$y = t/2$$

Emphasize that converting equations from parametric to rectangular form is primarily an aid in graphing.

Now you can recognize that the equation $x = 4y^2 - 4$ represents a parabola with a horizontal axis and vertex $(-4, 0)$.

When converting equations from parametric to rectangular form, you may need to alter the domain of the rectangular equation so that its graph matches the graph of the parametric equations. Such a situation is demonstrated in Example 2.

Example 2 ▶ **Eliminating the Parameter**

Sketch the curve represented by the equations

$$x = \frac{1}{\sqrt{t + 1}} \qquad \text{and} \qquad y = \frac{t}{t + 1}$$

by eliminating the parameter and adjusting the domain of the resulting rectangular equation.

Solution

Solving for t in the equation for x, you have

$$x = \frac{1}{\sqrt{t + 1}} \qquad \Longrightarrow \qquad x^2 = \frac{1}{t + 1}$$

which implies that

$$t = \frac{1 - x^2}{x^2}.$$

Now, substituting in the equation for y, you obtain

$$y = \frac{t}{t + 1} = \frac{\dfrac{(1 - x^2)}{x^2}}{\left[\dfrac{(1 - x^2)}{x^2}\right] + 1} = \frac{\dfrac{1 - x^2}{x^2}}{\dfrac{1 - x^2}{x^2} + 1} \cdot \frac{x^2}{x^2} = 1 - x^2.$$

The rectangular equation, $y = 1 - x^2$, is defined for all values of x, but from the parametric equation for x you can see that the curve is defined only when $t > -1$. This implies that you should restrict the domain of x to positive values, as shown in Figure 10.53.

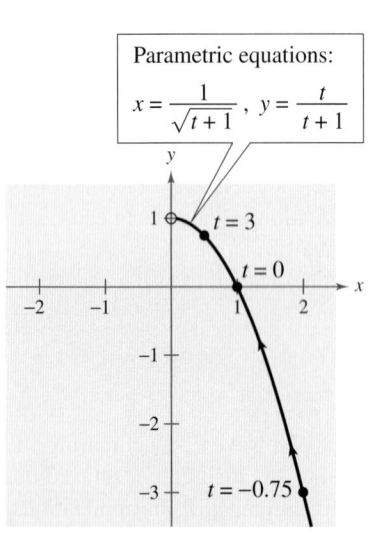

Parametric equations:
$$x = \frac{1}{\sqrt{t + 1}}, \ y = \frac{t}{t + 1}$$

$t = 3$
$t = 0$
$t = -0.75$

FIGURE 10.53

It is not necessary for the parameter in a set of parametric equations to represent time. The next example uses an *angle* as the parameter.

Example 3 ▶ **Eliminating the Parameter**

Sketch the curve represented by

$$x = 3 \cos \theta \quad \text{and} \quad y = 4 \sin \theta, \quad 0 \leq \theta \leq 2\pi$$

by eliminating the parameter.

Solution

Begin by solving for $\cos \theta$ and $\sin \theta$ in the equations.

$$\cos \theta = \frac{x}{3} \quad \text{and} \quad \sin \theta = \frac{y}{4} \qquad \text{Solve for } \cos \theta \text{ and } \sin \theta.$$

Make use of the identity $\sin^2 \theta + \cos^2 \theta = 1$ to form an equation involving only x and y.

$$\cos^2 \theta + \sin^2 \theta = 1 \qquad \text{Trigonometric identity}$$

$$\left(\frac{x}{3}\right)^2 + \left(\frac{y}{4}\right)^2 = 1 \qquad \text{Substitute } \frac{x}{3} \text{ for } \cos \theta \text{ and } \frac{y}{4} \text{ for } \sin \theta.$$

$$\frac{x^2}{9} + \frac{y^2}{16} = 1 \qquad \text{Rectangular equation}$$

From this rectangular equation, you can see that the graph is an ellipse centered at $(0, 0)$, with vertices $(0, 4)$ and $(0, -4)$ and minor axis of length $2b = 6$, as shown in Figure 10.54. Note that the elliptic curve is traced out *counterclockwise* as θ varies from 0 to 2π.

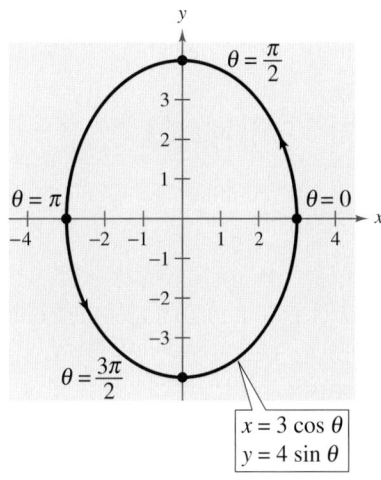

$$x = 3 \cos \theta$$
$$y = 4 \sin \theta$$

FIGURE 10.54

In Examples 2 and 3, it is important to realize that eliminating the parameter is primarily an *aid to curve sketching*. If the parametric equations represent the path of a moving object, the graph alone is not sufficient to describe the object's motion. You still need the parametric equations to tell you the *position*, *direction*, and *speed* at a given time.

Finding Parametric Equations for a Graph

You have been studying techniques for sketching the graph represented by a set of parametric equations. Now consider the reverse problem—that is, how can you find a set of parametric equations for a given graph or a given physical description? From the discussion following Example 1, you know that such a representation is not unique. That is, the equations

$$x = 4t^2 - 4 \quad \text{and} \quad y = t, \quad -1 \leq t \leq \frac{3}{2}$$

produced the same graph as the equations

$$x = t^2 - 4 \quad \text{and} \quad y = \frac{t}{2}, \quad -2 \leq t \leq 3.$$

This is further demonstrated in Example 4.

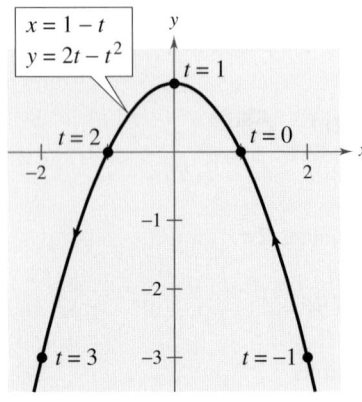

FIGURE 10.55

Example 4 ▶ Finding Parametric Equations for a Graph

Find a set of parametric equations to represent the graph of $y = 1 - x^2$, using the following parameters.

a. $t = x$ **b.** $t = 1 - x$

Solution

a. Letting $t = x$, you obtain the parametric equations

$$x = t \quad \text{and} \quad y = 1 - x^2 = 1 - t^2.$$

b. Letting $t = 1 - x$, you obtain the parametric equations

$$x = 1 - t \quad \text{and} \quad y = 1 - x^2 = 1 - (1 - t)^2 = 2t - t^2.$$

In Figure 10.55, note how the resulting curve is oriented by the increasing values of t. For part (a), the curve would have the opposite orientation.

Example 5 ▶ Parametric Equations for a Cycloid

Point out that a single rectangular equation can have many different parametric representations. To reinforce this, demonstrate along with parts (a) and (b) of Example 4 the parametric equation representations of the graph of $y = 1 - x^2$ using the parameters $t = 2x$ and $t = 2 - 3x$. A graphing utility can be a helpful tool in demonstrating that each of these representations yields the same graph.

Describe the **cycloid** traced out by a point P on the circumference of a circle of radius a as the circle rolls along a straight line in a plane.

Solution

As the parameter, let θ be the measure of the circle's rotation, and let the point $P = (x, y)$ begin at the origin. When $\theta = 0$, P is at the origin; when $\theta = \pi$, P is at a maximum point $(\pi a, 2a)$; and when $\theta = 2\pi$, P is back on the x-axis at $(2\pi a, 0)$. From Figure 10.56, you can see that $\angle APC = 180° - \theta$. So, you have

$$\sin \theta = \sin(180° - \theta) = \sin(\angle APC) = \frac{AC}{a} = \frac{BD}{a}$$

$$\cos \theta = -\cos(180° - \theta) = -\cos(\angle APC) = \frac{AP}{-a}$$

STUDY TIP

In Example 5, $\overparen{PD}$ represents the arc of the circle between points P and D.

which implies that $AP = -a \cos \theta$ and $BD = a \sin \theta$. Because the circle rolls along the x-axis, you know that $OD = \overparen{PD} = a\theta$. Furthermore, because $BA = DC = a$, you have

$$x = OD - BD = a\theta - a \sin \theta \quad \text{and} \quad y = BA + AP = a - a \cos \theta.$$

So, the parametric equations are $x = a(\theta - \sin \theta)$ and $y = a(1 - \cos \theta)$.

Technology

Use a graphing utility in *parametric* mode to obtain a graph similar to Figure 10.56 by graphing the following equations.

$$X_{1T} = T - \sin T$$

$$Y_{1T} = 1 - \cos T$$

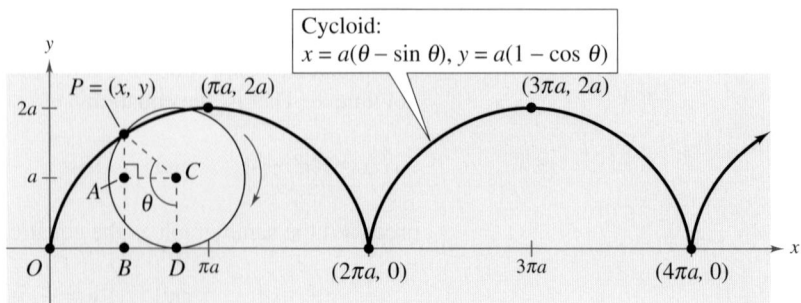

FIGURE 10.56

10.6 Exercises

1. Consider the parametric equations $x = \sqrt{t}$ and $y = 3 - t$.
   (a) Create a table of x- and y-values using $t = 0, 1, 2, 3,$ and 4.
   (b) Plot the points (x, y) generated in part (a), and sketch a graph of the parametric equations.
   (c) Find the rectangular equation by eliminating the parameter. Sketch its graph. How do the graphs differ?

2. Consider the parametric equations $x = 4\cos^2\theta$ and $y = 2\sin\theta$.
   (a) Create a table of x- and y-values using $\theta = -\pi/2, -\pi/4, 0, \pi/4,$ and $\pi/2$.
   (b) Plot the points (x, y) generated in part (a), and sketch a graph of the parametric equations.
   (c) Find the rectangular equation by eliminating the parameter. Sketch its graph. How do the graphs differ?

In Exercises 3–22, sketch the curve represented by the parametric equations (indicate the orientation of the curve) by eliminating the parameter and adjusting the domain of the resulting rectangular equation.

3. $x = 3t - 3$
   $y = 2t + 1$
4. $x = 3 - 2t$
   $y = 2 + 3t$
5. $x = \frac{1}{4}t$
   $y = t^2$
6. $x = t$
   $y = t^3$
7. $x = t + 2$
   $y = t^2$
8. $x = \sqrt{t}$
   $y = 1 - t$
9. $x = t + 1$
   $y = t/(t + 1)$
10. $x = t - 1$
    $y = t/(t - 1)$
11. $x = 2(t + 1)$
    $y = |t - 2|$
12. $x = |t - 1|$
    $y = t + 2$
13. $x = 3\cos\theta$
    $y = 3\sin\theta$
14. $x = 2\cos\theta$
    $y = 3\sin\theta$
15. $x = 4\sin 2\theta$
    $y = 2\cos 2\theta$
16. $x = \cos\theta$
    $y = 2\sin 2\theta$
17. $x = 4 + 2\cos\theta$
    $y = -1 + \sin\theta$
18. $x = 4 + 2\cos\theta$
    $y = 2 + 3\sin\theta$
19. $x = e^{-t}$
    $y = e^{3t}$
20. $x = e^{2t}$
    $y = e^t$

21. $x = t^3$
    $y = 3\ln t$
22. $x = \ln 2t$
    $y = 2t^2$

In Exercises 23 and 24, determine how the plane curves differ from each other.

23. (a) $x = t$
    $y = 2t + 1$
    (b) $x = \cos\theta$
    $y = 2\cos\theta + 1$
    (c) $x = e^{-t}$
    $y = 2e^{-t} + 1$
    (d) $x = e^t$
    $y = 2e^t + 1$

24. (a) $x = t$
    $y = t^2 - 1$
    (b) $x = t^2$
    $y = t^4 - 1$
    (c) $x = \sin t$
    $y = \sin^2 t - 1$
    (d) $x = e^t$
    $y = e^{2t} - 1$

In Exercises 25–28, eliminate the parameter and obtain the standard form of the rectangular equation.

25. Line through (x_1, y_1) and (x_2, y_2):
    $x = x_1 + t(x_2 - x_1), \ y = y_1 + t(y_2 - y_1)$
26. Circle:
    $x = h + r\cos\theta, \ y = k + r\sin\theta$
27. Ellipse:
    $x = h + a\cos\theta, \ y = k + b\sin\theta$
28. Hyperbola:
    $x = h + a\sec\theta, \ y = k + b\tan\theta$

In Exercises 29–36, use the results of Exercises 25–28 to find a set of parametric equations for the line or conic.

29. Line: Passes through $(0, 0)$ and $(6, -3)$
30. Line: Passes through $(2, 3)$ and $(6, -3)$
31. Circle: Center: $(3, 2)$; Radius: 4
32. Circle: Center: $(-3, 2)$; Radius: 5
33. Ellipse: Vertices: $(\pm 4, 0)$; Foci: $(\pm 3, 0)$
34. Ellipse: Vertices: $(4, 7), (4, -3)$;
    Foci: $(4, 5), (4, -1)$
35. Hyperbola: Vertices: $(\pm 4, 0)$; Foci: $(\pm 5, 0)$
36. Hyperbola: Vertices: $(\pm 2, 0)$; Foci: $(\pm 4, 0)$

In Exercises 37–44, find a set of parametric equations for the rectangular equation using (a) $t = x$ and (b) $t = 2 - x$.

37. $y = 3x - 2$

38. $x = 3y - 2$

39. $y = x^2$

40. $y = x^3$

41. $y = x^2 + 1$

42. $y = 2 - x$

43. $y = \dfrac{1}{x}$

44. $y = \dfrac{1}{2x}$

 In Exercises 45–52, use a graphing utility to graph the curve represented by the parametric equations.

45. Cycloid: $x = 4(\theta - \sin \theta),\ y = 4(1 - \cos \theta)$

46. Cycloid: $x = \theta + \sin \theta,\ y = 1 - \cos \theta$

47. Prolate cycloid: $x = \theta - \frac{3}{2}\sin \theta,\ y = 1 - \frac{3}{2}\cos \theta$

48. Prolate cycloid: $x = 2\theta - 4\sin \theta,\ y = 2 - 4\cos \theta$

49. Hypocycloid: $x = 3\cos^3 \theta,\ y = 3\sin^3 \theta$

50. Curtate cycloid: $x = 8\theta - 4\sin \theta,\ y = 8 - 4\cos \theta$

51. Witch of Agnesi: $x = 2\cot \theta,\ y = 2\sin^2 \theta$

52. Folium of Descartes: $x = \dfrac{3t}{1 + t^3},\ y = \dfrac{3t^2}{1 + t^3}$

In Exercises 53–56, match the parametric equations with the correct graph and describe the domain and range. [The graphs are labeled (a), (b), (c), and (d).]

(a)

(b)

(c)

(d)

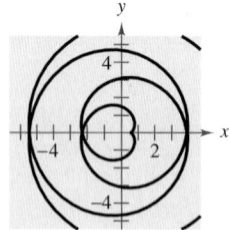

53. Lissajous curve: $x = 2\cos \theta$
$$y = \sin 2\theta$$

54. Evolute of ellipse: $x = 4\cos^3 \theta$
$$y = 6\sin^3 \theta$$

55. Involute of circle: $x = \frac{1}{2}(\cos \theta + \theta \sin \theta)$
$$y = \frac{1}{2}(\sin \theta - \theta \cos \theta)$$

56. Serpentine curve: $x = \frac{1}{2}\cot \theta$
$$y = 4\sin \theta \cos \theta$$

 Projectile Motion   A projectile is launched at a height of h feet above the ground and at an angle θ with the horizontal. The initial velocity is v_0 feet per second and the path of the projectile is modeled by the parametric equations

$$x = (v_0 \cos \theta)t \quad \text{and} \quad y = h + (v_0 \sin \theta)t - 16t^2.$$

In Exercises 57 and 58, use a graphing utility to graph the paths of a projectile launched from ground level at each value of θ and v_0. For each case, use the graph to approximate the maximum height and the range of the projectile.

57. (a) $\theta = 60°,\quad v_0 = 88$ feet per second

(b) $\theta = 60°,\quad v_0 = 132$ feet per second

(c) $\theta = 45°,\quad v_0 = 88$ feet per second

(d) $\theta = 45°,\quad v_0 = 132$ feet per second

58. (a) $\theta = 15°,\quad v_0 = 60$ feet per second

(b) $\theta = 15°,\quad v_0 = 100$ feet per second

(c) $\theta = 30°,\quad v_0 = 60$ feet per second

(d) $\theta = 30°,\quad v_0 = 100$ feet per second

▶ **Model It**

59. *Sports*   The center field fence in Yankee Stadium is 7 feet high and 408 feet from home plate. A baseball is hit 3 feet above the ground. It leaves the bat at an angle of θ degrees with the horizontal at a speed of 100 miles per hour (see figure).

(a) Write a set of parametric equations that model the path of the baseball.

 (b) Use a graphing utility to graph the path of the baseball when $\theta = 15°$. Is the hit a home run?

 (c) Use a graphing utility to graph the path of the baseball when $\theta = 23°$. Is the hit a home run?

(d) Find the minimum angle required for the hit to be a home run.

7 ft

3 ft ---- 408 ft

Not drawn to scale

60. Sports An archer releases an arrow from a bow 5 feet above the ground. The arrow leaves the bow at an angle of 10° with the horizontal and at an initial speed of 240 feet per second.

(a) Write a set of parametric equations that model the path of the arrow.

(b) Assuming the ground is level, find the distance the arrow travels before it hits the ground. (Ignore air resistance.)

(c) Use a graphing utility to graph the path of the arrow and approximate its maximum height.

(d) Find the total time the arrow is in the air.

61. Projectile Motion Eliminate the parameter t from the parametric equations $x = (v_0 \cos \theta)t$ and $y = h + (v_0 \sin \theta)t - 16t^2$ for the motion of a projectile to show that the rectangular equation is

$$y = -\frac{16 \sec^2 \theta}{v_0^2}x^2 + (\tan \theta)x + h.$$

62. Path of a Projectile The path of a projectile is given by the rectangular equation

$$y = 7 + x - 0.02x^2.$$

(a) Use the result of Exercise 61 to find h, v_0, and θ. Find the parametric equations of the path.

(b) Use a graphing utility to graph the rectangular equation for the path of the projectile. Confirm your answer in part (a) by sketching the curve represented by the parametric equations.

(c) Use a graphing utility to approximate the maximum height of the projectile and its range.

63. Curtate Cycloid A wheel of radius a units rolls along a straight line without slipping. The curve traced by a point P that is b units from the center $(b < a)$ is called a **curtate cycloid** (see figure). Use the angle θ shown in the figure to find a set of parametric equations for the curve.

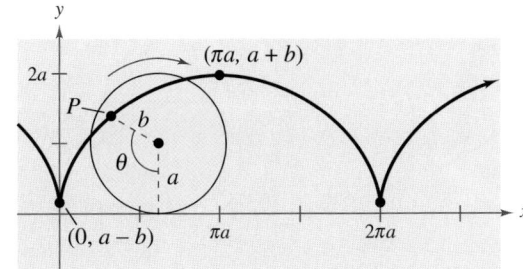

64. Epicycloid A circle of radius one unit rolls around the outside of a circle of radius two units without slipping. The curve traced by a point on the circumference of the smaller circle is called an **epicycloid** (see figure). Use the angle θ shown in the figure to find a set of parametric equations for the curve.

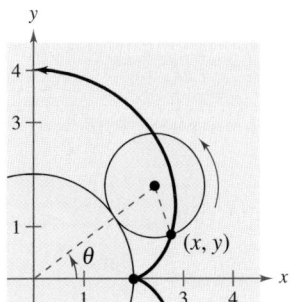

Synthesis

True or False? In Exercises 65 and 66, determine whether the statement is true or false. Justify your answer.

65. The two sets of parametric equations $x = t$, $y = t^2 + 1$ and $x = 3t$, $y = 9t^2 + 1$ have the same rectangular equation.

66. The graph of the parametric equations $x = t^2$ and $y = t^2$ is the line $y = x$.

Review

In Exercises 67–70, solve the system of equations.

67. $\begin{cases} 5x - 7y = 11 \\ -3x + y = -13 \end{cases}$

68. $\begin{cases} 3x + 5y = 9 \\ 4x - 2y = -14 \end{cases}$

69. $\begin{cases} 3a - 2b + c = 8 \\ 2a + b - 3c = -3 \\ a - 3b + 9c = 16 \end{cases}$

70. $\begin{cases} 5u + 7v + 9w = 4 \\ u - 2v - 3w = 7 \\ 8u - 2v + w = 20 \end{cases}$

In Exercises 71–74, find the reference angle θ', and sketch θ and θ' in standard position.

71. $\theta = 105°$

72. $\theta = 230°$

73. $\theta = -\dfrac{2\pi}{3}$

74. $\theta = \dfrac{5\pi}{6}$

In Exercises 75–78, sketch a graph of the function.

75. $y = \arcsin(x + 1)$

76. $y = \arccos(x - 1)$

77. $f(x) = 2 \arctan x$

78. $f(x) = \arctan \dfrac{x}{2}$

10.7 Polar Coordinates

▶ **What you should learn**

- How to plot points on the polar coordinate system
- How to convert points from rectangular to polar form and vice versa
- How to convert equations from rectangular to polar form and vice versa

▶ **Why you should learn it**

Polar coordinates offer a different mathematical perspective on graphing. For instance, in Exercises 1–8 on page 754, you are asked to find multiple representations of polar coordinates.

Introduction

So far, you have been representing graphs of equations as collections of points (x, y) on the rectangular coordinate system, where x and y represent the directed distances from the coordinate axes to the point (x, y). In this section you will study a different system called the **polar coordinate system.**

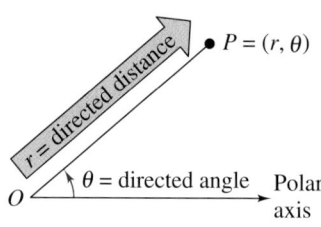

FIGURE 10.57

To form the polar coordinate system in the plane, fix a point O, called the **pole** (or **origin**), and construct from O an initial ray called the **polar axis,** as shown in Figure 10.57. Then each point P in the plane can be assigned **polar coordinates** (r, θ) as follows.

1. $r = $ *directed distance* from O to P
2. $\theta = $ *directed angle*, counterclockwise from polar axis to segment $\overline{OP}$

Example 1 ▶ **Plotting Points on the Polar Coordinate System**

a. The point $(r, \theta) = (2, \pi/3)$ lies two units from the pole on the terminal side of the angle $\theta = \pi/3$, as shown in Figure 10.58.

b. The point $(r, \theta) = (3, -\pi/6)$ lies three units from the pole on the terminal side of the angle $\theta = -\pi/6$, as shown in Figure 10.59.

c. The point $(r, \theta) = (3, 11\pi/6)$ coincides with the point $(3, -\pi/6)$, as shown in Figure 10.60.

FIGURE 10.58

FIGURE 10.59

FIGURE 10.60

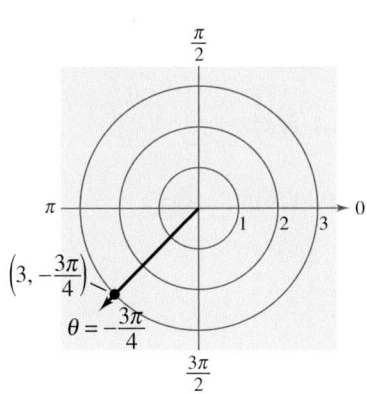

$\left(3, -\frac{3\pi}{4}\right) = \left(3, \frac{5\pi}{4}\right) = \left(-3, -\frac{7\pi}{4}\right) = \left(-3, \frac{\pi}{4}\right) = \dots$

FIGURE **10.61**

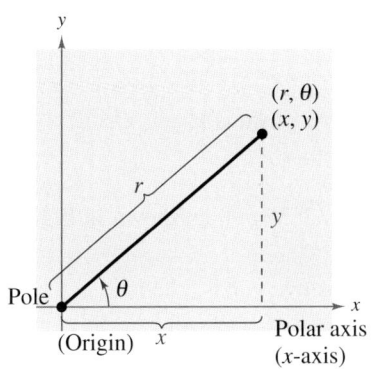

FIGURE **10.62**

In rectangular coordinates, each point (x, y) has a unique representation. This is not true for polar coordinates. For instance, the coordinates (r, θ) and $(r, \theta + 2\pi)$ represent the same point, as illustrated in Example 1. Another way to obtain multiple representations of a point is to use negative values for r. Because r is a *directed distance*, the coordinates (r, θ) and $(-r, \theta + \pi)$ represent the same point. In general, the point (r, θ) can be represented as

$$(r, \theta) = (r, \theta \pm 2n\pi) \quad \text{or} \quad (r, \theta) = (-r, \theta \pm (2n + 1)\pi)$$

where n is any integer. Moreover, the pole is represented by $(0, \theta)$, where θ is any angle.

Example 2 ▶   Multiple Representations of Points

Plot the point $(3, -3\pi/4)$ and find three additional polar representations of this point, using $-2\pi < \theta < 2\pi$.

Solution

The point is shown in Figure 10.61. Three other representations are as follows.

$$\left(3, -\frac{3\pi}{4} + 2\pi\right) = \left(3, \frac{5\pi}{4}\right) \qquad \text{Add } 2\pi \text{ to } \theta.$$

$$\left(-3, -\frac{3\pi}{4} - \pi\right) = \left(-3, -\frac{7\pi}{4}\right) \qquad \text{Replace } r \text{ by } -r; \text{ subtract } \pi \text{ from } \theta.$$

$$\left(-3, -\frac{3\pi}{4} + \pi\right) = \left(-3, \frac{\pi}{4}\right) \qquad \text{Replace } r \text{ by } -r; \text{ add } \pi \text{ to } \theta.$$

Coordinate Conversion

To establish the relationship between polar and rectangular coordinates, let the polar axis coincide with the positive x-axis and the pole with the origin, as shown in Figure 10.62. Because (x, y) lies on a circle of radius r, it follows that $r^2 = x^2 + y^2$. Moreover, for $r > 0$, the definitions of the trigonometric functions imply that

$$\tan \theta = \frac{y}{x}, \qquad \cos \theta = \frac{x}{r}, \qquad \text{and} \qquad \sin \theta = \frac{y}{r}.$$

If $r < 0$, you can show that the same relationships hold.

Coordinate Conversion

The polar coordinates (r, θ) are related to the rectangular coordinates (x, y) as follows.

$$x = r \cos \theta \qquad \text{and} \qquad \tan \theta = \frac{y}{x}$$

$$y = r \sin \theta \qquad \qquad r^2 = x^2 + y^2$$

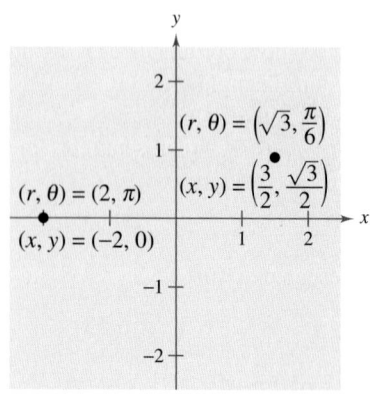

FIGURE **10.63**

Activities

1. Find three additional polar representations of the point $\left(-2, \dfrac{\pi}{3}\right)$.

   Answer: $\left(2, \dfrac{4\pi}{3}\right), \left(2, -\dfrac{2\pi}{3}\right)$, and $\left(-2, -\dfrac{5\pi}{3}\right)$

2. Convert the point $(-4, 2)$ from rectangular to polar form.

   Answer: $(2\sqrt{5}, -0.4636)$ or $(-2\sqrt{5}, 2.6779)$

FIGURE **10.64**

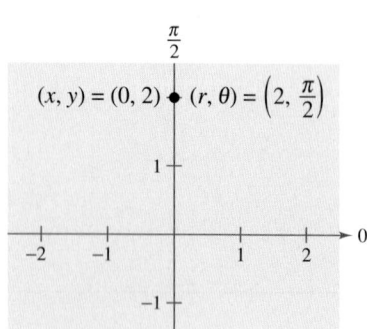

FIGURE **10.65**

Example 3 ▶ **Polar-to-Rectangular Conversion**

Convert the points to rectangular coordinates. (See Figure 10.63.)

a. $(2, \pi)$ **b.** $\left(\sqrt{3}, \pi/6\right)$

Solution

a. For the point $(r, \theta) = (2, \pi)$, you have

$$x = r \cos \theta = 2 \cos \pi = -2$$

and

$$y = r \sin \theta = 2 \sin \pi = 0.$$

The rectangular coordinates are $(x, y) = (-2, 0)$.

b. For the point $(r, \theta) = \left(\sqrt{3}, \pi/6\right)$, you have

$$x = \sqrt{3} \cos \frac{\pi}{6} = \sqrt{3}\left(\frac{\sqrt{3}}{2}\right) = \frac{3}{2}$$

and

$$y = \sqrt{3} \sin \frac{\pi}{6} = \sqrt{3}\left(\frac{1}{2}\right) = \frac{\sqrt{3}}{2}.$$

The rectangular coordinates are $(x, y) = \left(3/2, \sqrt{3}/2\right)$.

Example 4 ▶ **Rectangular-to-Polar Conversion**

Convert the points to polar coordinates.

a. $(-1, 1)$ **b.** $(0, 2)$

Solution

a. For the second-quadrant point $(x, y) = (-1, 1)$, you have

$$\tan \theta = \frac{y}{x}$$

$$\tan \theta = -1$$

$$\theta = \frac{3\pi}{4}.$$

Because θ lies in the same quadrant as (x, y), use positive r.

$$r = \sqrt{x^2 + y^2} = \sqrt{(-1)^2 + (1)^2} = \sqrt{2}$$

So, *one* set of polar coordinates is $(r, \theta) = \left(\sqrt{2}, 3\pi/4\right)$, as shown in Figure 10.64.

b. Because the point $(x, y) = (0, 2)$ lies on the positive y-axis, choose

$$\theta = \frac{\pi}{2} \quad \text{and} \quad r = 2.$$

This implies that *one* set of polar coordinates is $(r, \theta) = (2, \pi/2)$, as shown in Figure 10.65.

Multiple representations of points and equations in the polar system can cause confusion. You may want to discuss several examples.

Activities

1. Convert the polar equation $r = 3 \cos \theta$ to rectangular form.

   Answer: $x^2 + y^2 - 3x = 0$

2. Convert the rectangular equation $x = 4$ to polar form.

   Answer: $r = 4 \sec \theta$

FIGURE **10.66**

FIGURE **10.67**

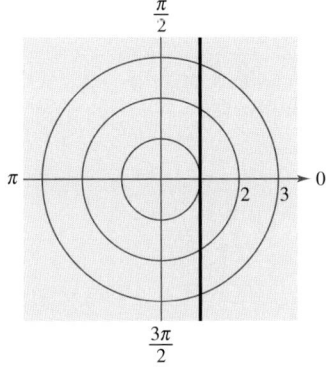

FIGURE **10.68**

Equation Conversion

By comparing Examples 3 and 4, you can see that point conversion from the polar to the rectangular system is straightforward, whereas point conversion from the rectangular to the polar system is more involved. For equations, the opposite is true. To convert a rectangular equation to polar form, you simply replace x by $r \cos \theta$ and y by $r \sin \theta$. For instance, the rectangular equation $y = x^2$ can be written in polar form as follows.

$$y = x^2 \qquad \text{Rectangular equation}$$

$$r \sin \theta = (r \cos \theta)^2 \qquad \text{Polar equation}$$

$$r = \sec \theta \tan \theta \qquad \text{Simplest form}$$

On the other hand, converting a polar equation to rectangular form requires considerable ingenuity.

Example 5 demonstrates several polar-to-rectangular conversions that enable you to sketch the graphs of some polar equations.

Example 5 ▶ **Converting Polar Equations to Rectangular Form**

Describe the graph of each polar equation and find the corresponding rectangular equation.

a. $r = 2$ **b.** $\theta = \dfrac{\pi}{3}$ **c.** $r = \sec \theta$

Solution

a. The graph of the polar equation $r = 2$ consists of all points that are two units from the pole. In other words, this graph is a circle centered at the origin with a radius of 2, as shown in Figure 10.66. You can confirm this by converting to rectangular form, using the relationship $r^2 = x^2 + y^2$.

$$\underbrace{r = 2}_{\text{Polar equation}} \implies r^2 = 2^2 \implies \underbrace{x^2 + y^2 = 2^2}_{\text{Rectangular equation}}$$

b. The graph of the polar equation $\theta = \pi/3$ consists of all points on the line that makes an angle of $\pi/3$ with the positive polar axis, as shown in Figure 10.67. To convert to rectangular form, make use of the relationship $\tan \theta = y/x$.

$$\underbrace{\theta = \dfrac{\pi}{3}}_{\text{Polar equation}} \implies \tan \theta = \sqrt{3} \implies \underbrace{y = \sqrt{3}x}_{\text{Rectangular equation}}$$

c. The graph of the polar equation $r = \sec \theta$ is not evident by simple inspection, so convert to rectangular form by using the relationship $r \cos \theta = x$.

$$\underbrace{r = \sec \theta}_{\text{Polar equation}} \implies r \cos \theta = 1 \implies \underbrace{x = 1}_{\text{Rectangular equation}}$$

Now you see that the graph is a vertical line, as shown in Figure 10.68.

10.7 **Exercises**

In Exercises 1–8, plot the point given in polar coordinates and find two additional polar representations.

1. $\left(4, -\dfrac{\pi}{3}\right)$

2. $\left(-1, -\dfrac{3\pi}{4}\right)$

3. $\left(0, -\dfrac{7\pi}{6}\right)$

4. $\left(16, \dfrac{5\pi}{2}\right)$

5. $\left(\sqrt{2}, 2.36\right)$

6. $(-3, -1.57)$

7. $\left(2\sqrt{2}, 4.71\right)$

8. $(-5, -2.36)$

In Exercises 9–16, a point in polar coordinates is given. Convert the point to rectangular coordinates.

9. $\left(3, \dfrac{\pi}{2}\right)$

10. $\left(3, \dfrac{3\pi}{2}\right)$

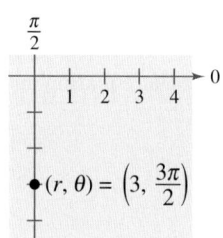

11. $\left(-1, \dfrac{5\pi}{4}\right)$

12. $(0, -\pi)$

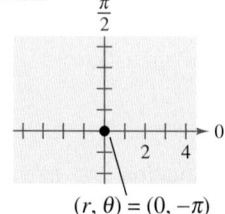

13. $\left(2, \dfrac{3\pi}{4}\right)$

14. $\left(-2, \dfrac{7\pi}{6}\right)$

15. $(-2.5, 1.1)$

16. $(8.25, 3.5)$

In Exercises 17–26, a point in rectangular coordinates is given. Convert the point to polar coordinates.

17. $(1, 1)$

18. $(-3, -3)$

19. $(-6, 0)$

20. $(0, -5)$

21. $(-3, 4)$

22. $(3, -1)$

23. $\left(-\sqrt{3}, -\sqrt{3}\right)$

24. $\left(\sqrt{3}, -1\right)$

25. $(6, 9)$

26. $(5, 12)$

In Exercises 27–32, use a graphing utility to find one set of polar coordinates of the point given in rectangular coordinates.

27. $(3, -2)$

28. $(-5, 2)$

29. $\left(\sqrt{3}, 2\right)$

30. $\left(3\sqrt{2}, 3\sqrt{2}\right)$

31. $\left(\dfrac{5}{2}, \dfrac{4}{3}\right)$

32. $\left(\dfrac{7}{4}, \dfrac{3}{2}\right)$

In Exercises 33–48, convert the rectangular equation to polar form.

33. $x^2 + y^2 = 9$

34. $x^2 + y^2 = 16$

35. $y = 4$

36. $y = x$

37. $x = 10$

38. $x = 4a$

39. $3x - y + 2 = 0$

40. $3x + 5y - 2 = 0$

41. $xy = 16$

42. $2xy = 1$

43. $y^2 - 8x - 16 = 0$

44. $(x^2 + y^2)^2 = 9(x^2 - y^2)$

45. $x^2 + y^2 = a^2$

46. $x^2 + y^2 = 9a^2$

47. $x^2 + y^2 - 2ax = 0$

48. $x^2 + y^2 - 2ay = 0$

In Exercises 49–64, convert the polar equation to rectangular form.

49. $r = 4 \sin \theta$

50. $r = 2 \cos \theta$

51. $\theta = \dfrac{2\pi}{3}$

52. $\theta = \dfrac{5\pi}{3}$

53. $r = 4$

54. $r = 10$

55. $r = 4 \csc \theta$

56. $r = -3 \sec \theta$

57. $r^2 = \cos \theta$

58. $r^2 = \sin 2\theta$

59. $r = 2 \sin 3\theta$

60. $r = 3 \cos 2\theta$

61. $r = \dfrac{2}{1 + \sin \theta}$

62. $r = \dfrac{1}{1 - \cos \theta}$

63. $r = \dfrac{6}{2 - 3 \sin \theta}$

64. $r = \dfrac{6}{2 \cos \theta - 3 \sin \theta}$

In Exercises 65–70, convert the polar equation to rectangular form and sketch its graph.

65. $r = 6$

66. $r = 8$

67. $\theta = \dfrac{\pi}{6}$

68. $\theta = \dfrac{3\pi}{4}$

69. $r = 3 \sec \theta$

70. $r = 2 \csc \theta$

Synthesis

True or False? In Exercises 71 and 72, determine whether the statement is true or false. Justify your answer.

71. If $\theta_1 = \theta_2 + 2\pi n$ for some integer n, then (r, θ_1) and (r, θ_2) represent the same point on the polar coordinate system.

72. If $|r_1| = |r_2|$, then (r_1, θ) and (r_2, θ) represent the same point on the polar coordinate system.

73. Convert the polar equation $r = 2(h \cos \theta + k \sin \theta)$ to rectangular form and verify that it is the equation of a circle. Find the radius and the rectangular coordinates of the center of the circle.

74. Convert the polar equation $r = \cos \theta + 3 \sin \theta$ to rectangular form and identify the graph.

75. *Think About It*

(a) Show that the distance between the points (r_1, θ_1) and (r_2, θ_2) is $\sqrt{r_1^2 + r_2^2 - 2r_1 r_2 \cos(\theta_1 - \theta_2)}$.

(b) Describe the positions of the points relative to each other for $\theta_1 = \theta_2$. Simplify the Distance Formula for this case. Is the simplification what you expected? Explain.

(c) Simplify the Distance Formula for $\theta_1 - \theta_2 = 90°$. Is the simplification what you expected? Explain.

(d) Choose two points on the polar coordinate system and find the distance between them. Then choose different polar representations of the same two points and apply the Distance Formula again. Discuss the result.

76. *Exploration*

(a) Set the window format of your graphing utility on rectangular coordinates and locate the cursor at any position off the coordinate axes. Move the cursor horizontally and observe any changes in the displayed coordinates of the points. Explain the changes. Now repeat the process moving the cursor vertically.

(b) Set the window format of your graphing utility on polar coordinates and locate the cursor at any position off the coordinate axes. Move the cursor horizontally and observe any changes in the displayed coordinates of the points. Explain the changes. Now repeat the process moving the cursor vertically.

(c) Explain why the results of parts (a) and (b) are not the same.

Review

In Exercises 77–80, use the properties of logarithms to expand the expression as a sum, difference, and/or constant multiple of logarithms. (Assume that all variables are positive.)

77. $\log_6 \dfrac{x^2 z}{3y}$

78. $\log_4 \dfrac{\sqrt{2x}}{y}$

79. $\ln x(x + 4)^2$

80. $\ln 5x^2(x^2 + 1)$

In Exercises 81–84, condense the expression to the logarithm of a single quantity.

81. $\log_7 x - \log_7 3y$

82. $\log_5 a + 8 \log_5(x + 1)$

83. $\dfrac{1}{2}\ln x + \ln(x - 2)$

84. $\ln 6 + \ln y - \ln(x - 3)$

In Exercises 85–90, use Cramer's Rule to solve the system of equations.

85. $\begin{cases} 5x - 7y = -11 \\ -3x + y = -3 \end{cases}$

86. $\begin{cases} 3x - 5y = 10 \\ 4x - 2y = -5 \end{cases}$

87. $\begin{cases} 3a - 2b + c = 0 \\ 2a + b - 3c = 0 \\ a - 3b + 9c = 8 \end{cases}$

88. $\begin{cases} 5u + 7v + 9w = 15 \\ u - 2v - 3w = 7 \\ 8u - 2v + w = 0 \end{cases}$

89. $\begin{cases} -x + y + 2z = 1 \\ 2x + 3y + z = -2 \\ 5x + 4y + 2z = 4 \end{cases}$

90. $\begin{cases} 2x_1 + x_2 + 2x_3 = 4 \\ 2x_1 + 2x_2 = 5 \\ 2x_1 - x_2 + 6x_3 = 2 \end{cases}$

In Exercises 91–94, use a determinant to determine whether the points are collinear.

91. $(4, -3), (6, -7), (-2, -1)$

92. $(-2, 4), (0, 1), (4, -5)$

93. $(-6, -4), (-1, -3), (1.5, -2.5)$

94. $(-2.3, 5), (-0.5, 0), (1.5, -3)$

10.8 Graphs of Polar Equations

▶ What you should learn

- How to graph polar equations by point plotting
- How to use symmetry to sketch graphs of polar equations
- How to use zeros and maximum r-values to sketch graphs of polar equations
- How to recognize special polar graphs

▶ Why you should learn it

Equations of several common figures are simpler in polar form than in rectangular form. For instance, Exercise 6 on page 762 shows the graph of a circle and its polar equation.

Introduction

In previous chapters you spent a lot of time learning how to sketch graphs on rectangular coordinate systems. You began with the basic point-plotting method, which was then enhanced by sketching aids such as symmetry, intercepts, asymptotes, periods, and shifts. This section approaches curve sketching on the polar coordinate system similarly, beginning with a demonstration of point plotting.

Example 1 ▶ Graphing a Polar Equation by Point Plotting

Sketch the graph of the polar equation $r = 4 \sin \theta$.

Solution

The sine function is periodic, so you can get a full range of r-values by considering values of θ in the interval $0 \le \theta \le 2\pi$, as shown in the following table.

θ	r
0	0
$\dfrac{\pi}{6}$	2
$\dfrac{\pi}{3}$	$2\sqrt{3}$
$\dfrac{\pi}{2}$	4
$\dfrac{2\pi}{3}$	$2\sqrt{3}$
$\dfrac{5\pi}{6}$	2
π	0
$\dfrac{7\pi}{6}$	-2
$\dfrac{3\pi}{2}$	-4
$\dfrac{11\pi}{6}$	-2
2π	0

Emphasize setting up the table of θ values. Your students will benefit from labeling the points as they plot them.

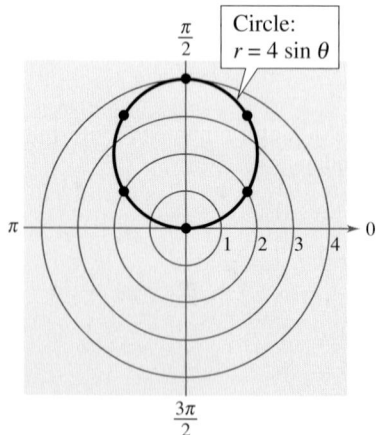

FIGURE 10.69

If you plot these points as shown in Figure 10.69, it appears that the graph is a circle of radius 2 whose center is at the point $(x, y) = (0, 2)$.

Symmetry

In Figure 10.69, note that as θ increases from 0 to 2π the graph is traced out twice. Moreover, note that the graph is *symmetric with respect to the line* $\theta = \pi/2$. Had you known about this symmetry and retracing ahead of time, you could have used fewer points.

Symmetry with respect to the line $\theta = \pi/2$ is one of three important types of symmetry to consider in polar curve sketching. (See Figure 10.70.)

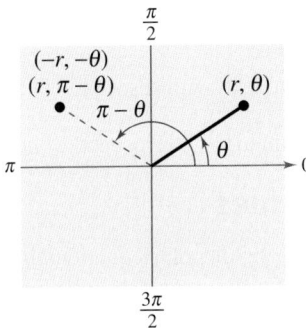
Symmetry with Respect to the Line $\theta = \dfrac{\pi}{2}$

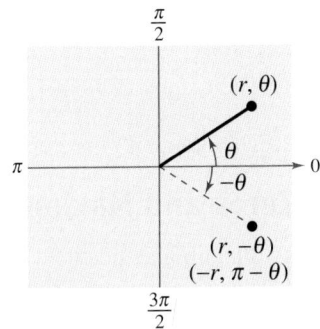
Symmetry with Respect to the Polar Axis

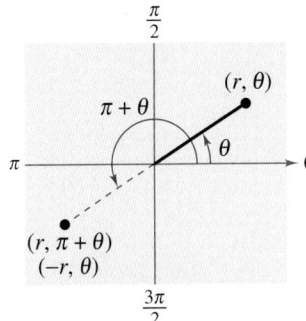
Symmetry with Respect to the Pole

FIGURE 10.70

Point out to your students that these tests are sufficient for showing symmetry; however, they are not necessary. A polar graph can exhibit symmetry even when the tests fail to indicate symmetry.

Tests for Symmetry in Polar Coordinates

The graph of a polar equation is symmetric with respect to the following if the given substitution yields an equivalent equation.

1. *The line $\theta = \pi/2$:*   Replace (r, θ) by $(r, \pi - \theta)$ or $(-r, -\theta)$.

2. *The polar axis:*   Replace (r, θ) by $(r, -\theta)$ or $(-r, \pi - \theta)$.

3. *The pole:*   Replace (r, θ) by $(r, \pi + \theta)$ or $(-r, \theta)$.

Example 2 ▶   **Using Symmetry to Sketch a Polar Graph** www

Use symmetry to sketch the graph of $r = 3 + 2\cos\theta$.

Solution

Replacing (r, θ) by $(r, -\theta)$ produces $r = 3 + 2\cos(-\theta) = 3 + 2\cos\theta$. So, you can conclude that the curve is symmetric with respect to the polar axis. Plotting the points in the table and using polar axis symmetry, you obtain the graph of a **limaçon**, as shown in Figure 10.71.

θ	0	$\dfrac{\pi}{3}$	$\dfrac{\pi}{2}$	$\dfrac{2\pi}{3}$	π
r	5	4	3	2	1

FIGURE 10.71

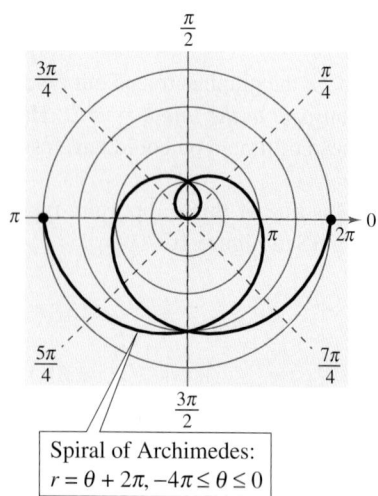

Spiral of Archimedes:
$r = \theta + 2\pi, -4\pi \le \theta \le 0$

FIGURE **10.72**

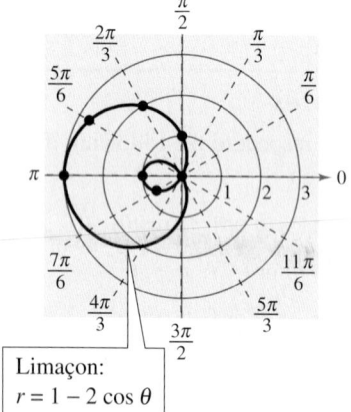

Limaçon:
$r = 1 - 2\cos\theta$

FIGURE **10.73**

The three tests for symmetry in polar coordinates listed on page 757 are sufficient to guarantee symmetry, but they are not necessary. For instance, Figure 10.72 shows the graph of $r = \theta + 2\pi$ to be symmetric with respect to the line $\theta = \pi/2$, and yet the tests on page 757 fail to indicate symmetry.

The equations discussed in Examples 1 and 2 are of the form

$$r = 4\sin\theta = f(\sin\theta) \qquad \text{and} \qquad r = 3 + 2\cos\theta = g(\cos\theta).$$

The graph of the first equation is symmetric with respect to the line $\theta = \pi/2$, and the graph of the second equation is symmetric with respect to the polar axis. This observation can be generalized to yield the following *quick tests for symmetry.*

1. The graph of $r = f(\sin\theta)$ is symmetric with respect to the line $\theta = \dfrac{\pi}{2}$.

2. The graph of $r = g(\cos\theta)$ is symmetric with respect to the polar axis.

Zeros and Maximum *r*-Values

Two additional aids to sketching graphs of polar equations involve knowing the θ-values for which $|r|$ is maximum and knowing the θ-values for which $r = 0$. For instance, in Example 1, the maximum value of $|r|$ for $r = 4\sin\theta$ is $|r| = 4$, and this occurs when $\theta = \pi/2$, as shown in Figure 10.69. Moreover, $r = 0$ when $\theta = 0$.

Example 3 ▶ **Sketching a Polar Graph**

Sketch the graph of

$$r = 1 - 2\cos\theta.$$

Solution

From the equation $r = 1 - 2\cos\theta$, you can obtain the following.

Symmetry: With respect to the polar axis

Maximum value of $|r|$: $r = 3$ when $\theta = \pi$

Zero of r: $r = 0$ when $\theta = \dfrac{\pi}{3}$

The table shows several θ-values in the interval $[0, \pi]$. By plotting the corresponding points, you can sketch the graph shown in Figure 10.73.

θ	0	$\dfrac{\pi}{6}$	$\dfrac{\pi}{3}$	$\dfrac{\pi}{2}$	$\dfrac{2\pi}{3}$	$\dfrac{5\pi}{6}$	π
r	-1	-0.73	0	1	2	2.73	3

Note how the negative r-values determine the *inner loop* of the graph in Figure 10.73. This graph, like the one in Figure 10.71, is a limaçon.

Some curves reach their zeros and maximum r-values at more than one point, as shown in Example 4.

Example 4 ▶ **Sketching a Polar Graph**

Sketch the graph of $r = 2 \cos 3\theta$.

Solution

Symmetry:	With respect to the polar axis
Maximum value of $|r|$:	$|r| = 2$ when $3\theta = 0, \pi, 2\pi, 3\pi$ or $\theta = 0, \pi/3, 2\pi/3, \pi$
Zeros of r:	$r = 0$ when $3\theta = \pi/2, 3\pi/2, 5\pi/2$ or $\theta = \pi/6, \pi/2, 5\pi/6$

θ	0	$\dfrac{\pi}{12}$	$\dfrac{\pi}{6}$	$\dfrac{\pi}{4}$	$\dfrac{\pi}{3}$	$\dfrac{5\pi}{12}$	$\dfrac{\pi}{2}$
r	2	$\sqrt{2}$	0	$-\sqrt{2}$	-2	$-\sqrt{2}$	0

By plotting these points and using the specified symmetry, zeros, and maximum values, you can obtain the graph shown in Figure 10.74. This graph is called a **rose curve,** and each of the loops on the graph is called a *petal* of the rose curve. Note how the entire curve is generated as θ increases from 0 to π.

$0 \le \theta \le \dfrac{\pi}{6}$

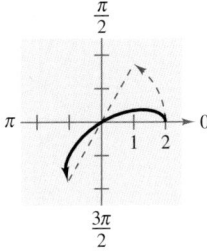
$0 \le \theta \le \dfrac{\pi}{3}$

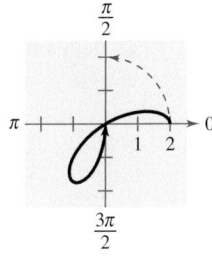
$0 \le \theta \le \dfrac{\pi}{2}$

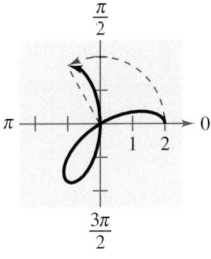
$0 \le \theta \le \dfrac{2\pi}{3}$

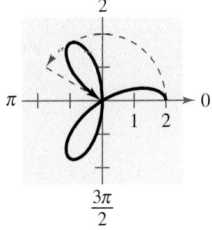
$0 \le \theta \le \dfrac{5\pi}{6}$

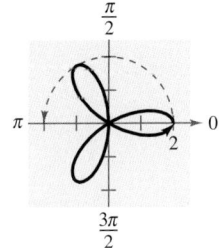
$0 \le \theta \le \pi$

FIGURE 10.74

Technology

Use a graphing utility in *polar* mode to verify the graph of $r = 2 \cos 3\theta$ shown in Figure 10.74.

Special Polar Graphs

Several important types of graphs have equations that are simpler in polar form than in rectangular form. For example, the circle

$$r = 4 \sin \theta$$

in Example 1 has the more complicated rectangular equation

$$x^2 + (y - 2)^2 = 4.$$

Several other types of graphs that have simple polar equations are shown below.

Limaçons

$r = a \pm b \cos \theta$

$r = a \pm b \sin \theta$

$(a > 0, b > 0)$

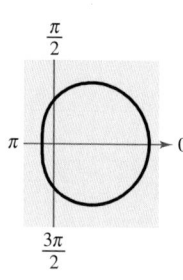

$\dfrac{a}{b} < 1$

Limaçon with inner loop

$\dfrac{a}{b} = 1$

Cardioid (heart-shaped)

$1 < \dfrac{a}{b} < 2$

Dimpled limaçon

$\dfrac{a}{b} \geq 2$

Convex limaçon

Rose Curves

n petals if n is odd,

$2n$ petals if n is even

$(n \geq 2)$

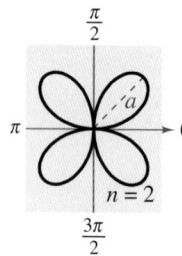

$r = a \cos n\theta$

Rose curve

$r = a \cos n\theta$

Rose curve

$r = a \sin n\theta$

Rose curve

$r = a \sin n\theta$

Rose curve

Circles and Lemniscates

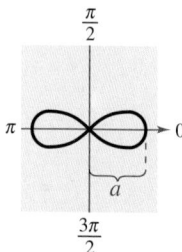

The quick tests for symmetry presented in this section can be especially useful when graphing these special polar graphs.

$r = a \cos \theta$

Circle

$r = a \sin \theta$

Circle

$r^2 = a^2 \sin 2\theta$

Lemniscate

$r^2 = a^2 \cos 2\theta$

Lemniscate

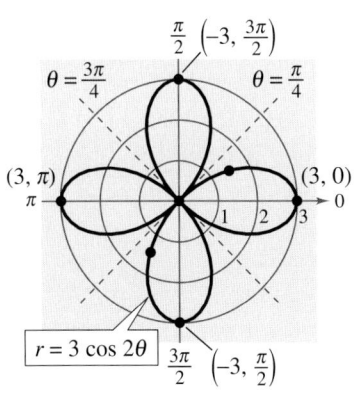

$\frac{\pi}{2}$ $\left(-3, \frac{3\pi}{2}\right)$

$\theta = \frac{3\pi}{4}$ $\theta = \frac{\pi}{4}$

$(3, \pi)$ π $(3, 0)$ 0

$r = 3\cos 2\theta$ $\frac{3\pi}{2}$ $\left(-3, \frac{\pi}{2}\right)$

FIGURE **10.75**

Activities

1. Test $r^2 = 3\sin\theta$ for symmetry.

   Answer: Symmetric with respect to the pole

2. Find the maximum value of $|r|$ and any zeros of r for the polar equation $r = 2 + 2\cos\theta$.

   Answer: Maximum value of $|r| = 4$ when $\theta = 0$, and $r = 0$ when $\theta = \pi$.

3. Identify the shape of the graph of the polar equation $r = 2\sin 3\theta$.

   Answer: Rose curve with 3 petals

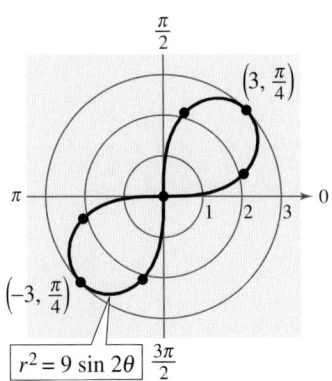

$\frac{\pi}{2}$

$\left(3, \frac{\pi}{4}\right)$

π 0

$\left(-3, \frac{\pi}{4}\right)$

$r^2 = 9\sin 2\theta$ $\frac{3\pi}{2}$

FIGURE **10.76**

Example 5 ▶ **Sketching a Rose Curve**

Sketch the graph of $r = 3\cos 2\theta$.

Solution

Type of curve: Rose curve with $2n = 4$ petals

Symmetry: With respect to polar axis, the line $\theta = \pi/2$, and the pole

Maximum value of $|r|$: $|r| = 3$ when $\theta = 0, \pi/2, \pi, 3\pi/2$

Zeros of r: $r = 0$ when $\theta = \pi/4, 3\pi/4$

Using this information together with the additional points shown in the following table, you obtain the graph shown in Figure 10.75.

θ	0	$\frac{\pi}{6}$	$\frac{\pi}{4}$	$\frac{\pi}{3}$
r	3	$\frac{3}{2}$	0	$-\frac{3}{2}$

Example 6 ▶ **Sketching a Lemniscate**

Sketch the graph of $r^2 = 9\sin 2\theta$.

Solution

Type of curve: Lemniscate

Symmetry: With respect to the pole

Maximum value of $|r|$: $|r| = 3$ when $\theta = \frac{\pi}{4}$

Zeros of r: $r = 0$ when $\theta = 0, \frac{\pi}{2}$

If $\sin 2\theta < 0$, this equation has no solution points. So, you restrict the values of θ to those for which $\sin 2\theta \geq 0$.

$$0 \leq \theta \leq \frac{\pi}{2} \quad \text{or} \quad \pi \leq \theta \leq \frac{3\pi}{2}$$

Moreover, using symmetry, you need to consider only the first of these two intervals. By finding a few additional points (see table below), you can obtain the graph shown in Figure 10.76.

θ	0	$\frac{\pi}{12}$	$\frac{\pi}{4}$	$\frac{5\pi}{12}$	$\frac{\pi}{2}$
$r = \pm 3\sqrt{\sin 2\theta}$	0	$\frac{\pm 3}{\sqrt{2}}$	± 3	$\frac{\pm 3}{\sqrt{2}}$	0

10.8 Exercises

In Exercises 1–6, identify the type of polar graph.

1.

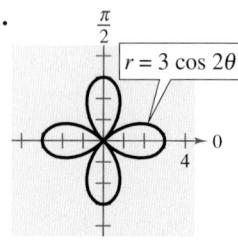

$r = 3 \cos 2\theta$

2.

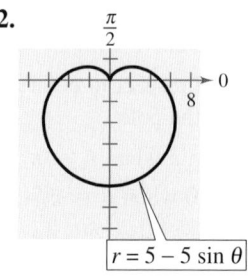

$r = 5 - 5 \sin \theta$

3.

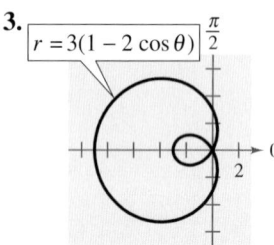

$r = 3(1 - 2 \cos \theta)$

4.

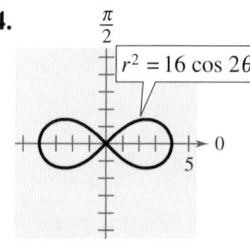

$r^2 = 16 \cos 2\theta$

5.

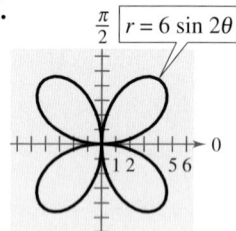

$r = 6 \sin 2\theta$

6.

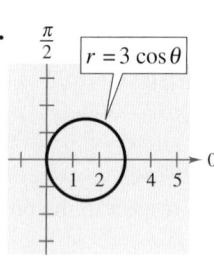

$r = 3 \cos \theta$

In Exercises 7–12, test for symmetry with respect to $\theta = \pi/2$, the polar axis, and the pole.

7. $r = 5 + 4 \cos \theta$

8. $r = 16 \cos 3\theta$

9. $r = \dfrac{2}{1 + \sin \theta}$

10. $r = \dfrac{3}{2 + \cos \theta}$

11. $r^2 = 16 \cos 2\theta$

12. $r^2 = 36 \sin 2\theta$

In Exercises 13–16, find the maximum value of $|r|$ and any zeros of r.

13. $r = 10(1 - \sin \theta)$

14. $r = 6 + 12 \cos \theta$

15. $r = 4 \cos 3\theta$

16. $r = 3 \sin 2\theta$

In Exercises 17–40, sketch the graph of the polar equation.

17. $r = 5$

18. $r = 2$

19. $r = \dfrac{\pi}{6}$

20. $r = -\dfrac{3\pi}{4}$

21. $r = 3 \sin \theta$

22. $r = 4 \cos \theta$

23. $r = 3(1 - \cos \theta)$

24. $r = 4(1 - \sin \theta)$

25. $r = 4(1 + \sin \theta)$

26. $r = 2(1 + \cos \theta)$

27. $r = 3 + 6 \sin \theta$

28. $r = 4 - 3 \sin \theta$

29. $r = 1 - 2 \sin \theta$

30. $r = 1 - 2 \cos \theta$

31. $r = 3 - 4 \cos \theta$

32. $r = 4 + 3 \cos \theta$

33. $r = 5 \sin 2\theta$

34. $r = 3 \cos 2\theta$

35. $r = 2 \sec \theta$

36. $r = 5 \csc \theta$

37. $r = \dfrac{3}{\sin \theta - 2 \cos \theta}$

38. $r = \dfrac{6}{2 \sin \theta - 3 \cos \theta}$

39. $r^2 = 9 \cos 2\theta$

40. $r^2 = 4 \sin \theta$

 In Exercises 41–46, use a graphing utility to graph the polar equation.

41. $r = 8 \cos \theta$

42. $r = \cos 2\theta$

43. $r = 3(2 - \sin \theta)$

44. $r = 2 \cos(3\theta - 2)$

45. $r = 8 \sin \theta \cos^2 \theta$

46. $r = 2 \csc \theta + 5$

 In Exercises 47–52, use a graphing utility to graph the polar equation. Find an interval for θ for which the graph is traced only once.

47. $r = 3 - 4 \cos \theta$

48. $r = 5 + 4 \cos \theta$

49. $r = 2 \cos\left(\dfrac{3\theta}{2}\right)$

50. $r = 3 \sin\left(\dfrac{5\theta}{2}\right)$

51. $r^2 = 9 \sin 2\theta$

52. $r^2 = \dfrac{1}{\theta}$

In Exercises 53–56, use a graphing utility to graph the polar equation and show that the indicated line is an asymptote of the graph.

	Name of Graph	Polar Equation	Asymptote
53.	Conchoid	$r = 2 - \sec \theta$	$x = -1$
54.	Conchoid	$r = 2 + \csc \theta$	$y = 1$
55.	Hyperbolic spiral	$r = \dfrac{3}{\theta}$	$y = 3$
56.	Strophoid	$r = 2 \cos 2\theta \sec \theta$	$x = -2$

Synthesis

True or False? **In Exercises 57 and 58, determine whether the statement is true or false. Justify your answer.**

57. In the polar coordinate system, if a graph that has symmetry with respect to the polar axis were folded on the line $\theta = 0$, the portion of the graph above the polar axis would coincide with the portion of the graph below the polar axis.

58. In the polar coordinate system, if a graph that has symmetry with respect to the pole were folded on the line $\theta = 3\pi/4$, the portion of the graph on one side of the fold would coincide with the portion of the graph on the other side of the fold.

59. ***Exploration*** Sketch the graph of $r = 6 \cos \theta$ over each interval. Describe the part of the graph obtained in each case.

(a) $0 \le \theta \le \dfrac{\pi}{2}$

(b) $\dfrac{\pi}{2} \le \theta \le \pi$

(c) $-\dfrac{\pi}{2} \le \theta \le \dfrac{\pi}{2}$

(d) $\dfrac{\pi}{4} \le \theta \le \dfrac{3\pi}{4}$

 60. ***Graphical Reasoning*** Use a graphing utility to graph the polar equation

$r = 6[1 + \cos(\theta - \phi)]$

for (a) $\phi = 0$, (b) $\phi = \pi/4$, and (c) $\phi = \pi/2$. Use the graphs to describe the effect of the angle ϕ. Write the equation as a function of $\sin \theta$ for part (c).

61. The graph of $r = f(\theta)$ is rotated about the pole through an angle ϕ. Show that the equation of the rotated graph is $r = f(\theta - \phi)$.

62. Consider the graph of $r = f(\sin \theta)$.

(a) Show that if the graph is rotated counterclockwise $\pi/2$ radians about the pole, the equation of the rotated graph is $r = f(-\cos \theta)$.

(b) Show that if the graph is rotated counterclockwise π radians about the pole, the equation of the rotated graph is $r = f(-\sin \theta)$.

(c) Show that if the graph is rotated counterclockwise $3\pi/2$ radians about the pole, the equation of the rotated graph is $r = f(\cos \theta)$.

In Exercises 63–66, use the results of Exercises 61 and 62.

63. Write an equation for the limaçon $r = 2 - \sin \theta$ after it has been rotated by the given amount.

(a) $\dfrac{\pi}{4}$ (b) $\dfrac{\pi}{2}$ (c) π (d) $\dfrac{3\pi}{2}$

64. Write an equation for the rose curve $r = 2 \sin 2\theta$ after it has been rotated by the given amount.

(a) $\dfrac{\pi}{6}$ (b) $\dfrac{\pi}{2}$ (c) $\dfrac{2\pi}{3}$ (d) π

65. Sketch the graph of each equation.

(a) $r = 1 - \sin \theta$ (b) $r = 1 - \sin\left(\theta - \dfrac{\pi}{4}\right)$

66. Sketch the graph of each equation.

(a) $r = 3 \sec \theta$ (b) $r = 3 \sec\left(\theta - \dfrac{\pi}{4}\right)$

(c) $r = 3 \sec\left(\theta + \dfrac{\pi}{3}\right)$ (d) $r = 3 \sec\left(\theta - \dfrac{\pi}{2}\right)$

 67. ***Exploration*** Use a graphing utility to graph and identify $r = 2 + k \sin \theta$ for $k = 0, 1, 2,$ and 3.

 68. ***Exploration*** Consider the equation $r = 3 \sin k\theta$.

(a) Use a graphing utility to graph the equation for $k = 1.5$. Find the interval for θ over which the graph is traced only once.

(b) Use a graphing utility to graph the equation for $k = 2.5$. Find the interval for θ over which the graph is traced only once.

(c) Is it possible to find an interval for θ over which the graph is traced only once for any rational number k? Explain.

Review

In Exercises 69–72, find the zeros (if any) of the rational function.

69. $f(x) = \dfrac{x^2 - 9}{x + 1}$ **70.** $f(x) = 6 + \dfrac{4}{x^2 + 4}$

71. $f(x) = 5 - \dfrac{3}{x - 2}$ **72.** $f(x) = \dfrac{x^3 - 27}{x^2 + 4}$

In Exercises 73 and 74, find the standard form of the equation of the ellipse. Then sketch the ellipse.

73. Vertices: $(-4, 2), (2, 2)$; Minor axis of length 4

74. Foci: $(3, 2), (3, -4)$; Major axis of length 8

10.9 Polar Equations of Conics

▶ **What you should learn**

- How to define conics in terms of eccentricity
- How to write equations of conics in polar form
- How to use equations of conics in polar form to model real-life problems

▶ **Why you should learn it**

The orbits of planets and satellites can be modeled with polar equations. For instance, in Exercise 57 on page 769, a polar equation is used to model the orbit of a satellite.

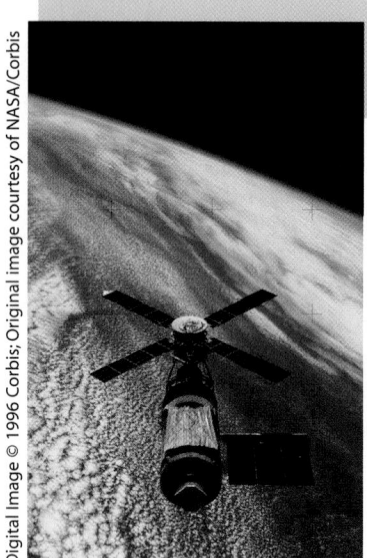

Alternative Definition of Conic

In Sections 10.3 and 10.4, you learned that the rectangular equations of ellipses and hyperbolas take simple forms when the origin lies at their *centers*. As it happens, there are many important applications of conics in which it is more convenient to use one of the *foci* as the origin. In this section you will learn that polar equations of conics take simple forms if one of the foci lies at the pole.

To begin, consider the following alternative definition of conic that uses the concept of eccentricity.

Alternative Definition of Conic

The locus of a point in the plane that moves so that its distance from a fixed point (focus) is in a constant ratio to its distance from a fixed line (directrix) is a **conic.** The constant ratio is the **eccentricity** of the conic and is denoted by e. Moreover, the conic is an **ellipse** if $e < 1$, a **parabola** if $e = 1$, and a **hyperbola** if $e > 1$. (See Figure 10.77.)

In Figure 10.77, note that for each type of conic, the focus is at the pole.

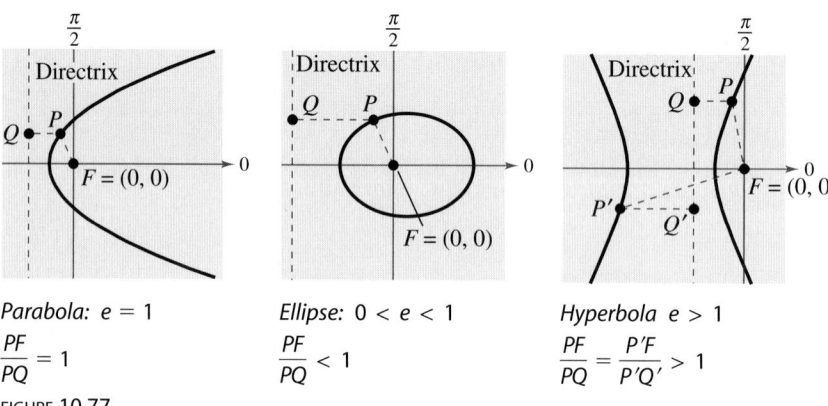

Parabola: $e = 1$
$\dfrac{PF}{PQ} = 1$

Ellipse: $0 < e < 1$
$\dfrac{PF}{PQ} < 1$

Hyperbola $e > 1$
$\dfrac{PF}{PQ} = \dfrac{P'F}{P'Q'} > 1$

FIGURE 10.77

Polar Equations of Conics

The benefit of locating a focus of a conic at the pole is that the equation of the conic takes on a simpler form. For a proof of the polar equations of conics, see Proofs in Mathematics on page 779.

Polar Equations of Conics

The graph of a polar equation of the form

1. $r = \dfrac{ep}{1 \pm e \cos \theta}$ or   **2.** $r = \dfrac{ep}{1 \pm e \sin \theta}$

is a conic, where $e > 0$ is the eccentricity and $|p|$ is the distance between the focus (pole) and the directrix.

The equations

$$r = \frac{ep}{1 \pm e \cos \theta}$$ Vertical directrix

correspond to conics with vertical directrices, and the equations

$$r = \frac{ep}{1 \pm e \sin \theta}$$ Horizontal directrix

correspond to conics with horizontal directrices. Moreover, the converse is also true—that is, any conic with a focus at the pole and having a horizontal or vertical directrix can be represented by one of the given equations.

Example 1 ▶ **Sketching a Conic from Its Polar Equation**

Identify the conic $r = \dfrac{15}{3 - 2 \cos \theta}$ and sketch its graph.

Solution

To identify the type of conic, rewrite the equation as

$$r = \frac{15}{3 - 2 \cos \theta} = \frac{5}{1 - (2/3) \cos \theta}.$$ Divide numerator and denominator by 3.

Because $e = \frac{2}{3} < 1$, you can conclude that the graph is an ellipse. You can sketch the upper half of the ellipse by plotting points from $\theta = 0$ to $\theta = \pi$, as shown in Figure 10.78. Using symmetry with respect to the polar axis, you can sketch the lower half.

Additional Example

Identify the conic and sketch its graph.

$$r = \frac{4}{2 + 2 \sin \theta}$$

Solution

Parabola

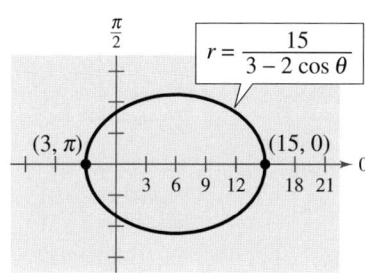

FIGURE 10.78

For the ellipse in Figure 10.78, the major axis is horizontal and the vertices lie at $(15, 0)$ and $(3, \pi)$. So, the length of the *major* axis is $2a = 18$. To find the length of the *minor* axis, you can use the equations $e = c/a$ and $b^2 = a^2 - c^2$ to conclude that

$$b^2 = a^2 - c^2 = a^2 - (ea)^2 = a^2(1 - e^2).$$ Ellipse

Because $e = \frac{2}{3}$, you have $b^2 = 9^2\left[1 - \left(\frac{2}{3}\right)^2\right] = 45$, which implies that $b = \sqrt{45} = 3\sqrt{5}$. So, the length of the minor axis is $2b = 6\sqrt{5}$. A similar analysis for hyperbolas yields

$$b^2 = c^2 - a^2 = (ea)^2 - a^2 = a^2(e^2 - 1).$$ Hyperbola

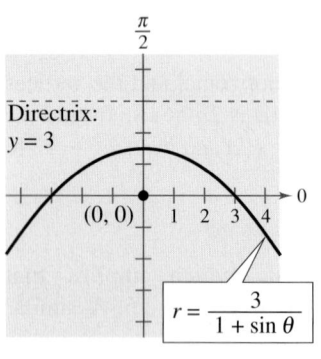

$$r = \frac{32}{3 + 5 \sin \theta}$$

FIGURE 10.79

Example 2 ▶ Sketching a Conic from Its Polar Equation

Identify the conic $r = 32/(3 + 5 \sin \theta)$ and sketch its graph.

Solution

Dividing the numerator and denominator by 3, you have

$$r = \frac{32/3}{1 + (5/3) \sin \theta}.$$

Because $e = \frac{5}{3} > 1$, the graph is a hyperbola. The transverse axis of the hyperbola lies on the line $\theta = \pi/2$, and the vertices occur at $(4, \pi/2)$ and $(-16, 3\pi/2)$. Because the length of the transverse axis is 12, you can see that $a = 6$. To find b, write

$$b^2 = a^2(e^2 - 1) = 6^2 \left[\left(\frac{5}{3} \right)^2 - 1 \right] = 64.$$

So, $b = 8$. Finally, you can use a and b to determine the asymptotes of the hyperbola and obtain the sketch shown in Figure 10.79.

In the next example, you are asked to find a polar equation of a specified conic. To do this, let p be the distance between the pole and the directrix.

1. *Horizontal directrix above the pole:* $r = \dfrac{ep}{1 + e \sin \theta}$

2. *Horizontal directrix below the pole:* $r = \dfrac{ep}{1 - e \sin \theta}$

3. *Vertical directrix to the right of the pole:* $r = \dfrac{ep}{1 + e \cos \theta}$

4. *Vertical directrix to the left of the pole:* $r = \dfrac{ep}{1 - e \cos \theta}$

Technology

Most graphing utilities have a *polar* mode. Try using a graphing utility set in *polar* mode to verify the four orientations shown at the right. Remember that e must be positive, but p can be positive or negative.

Example 3 ▶ Finding the Polar Equation of a Conic

Find the polar equation of the parabola whose focus is the pole and whose directrix is the line $y = 3$.

Solution

From Figure 10.80, you can see that the directrix is horizontal and above the pole, so you can choose an equation of the form

$$r = \frac{ep}{1 + e \sin \theta}.$$

Moreover, because the eccentricity of a parabola is $e = 1$ and the distance between the pole and the directrix is $p = 3$, you have the equation

$$r = \frac{3}{1 + \sin \theta}.$$

Directrix:
$y = 3$

$$r = \frac{3}{1 + \sin \theta}$$

FIGURE 10.80

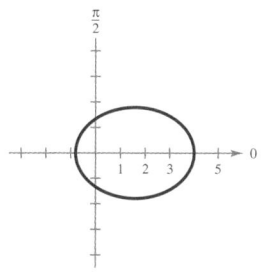

Applications

Kepler's Laws (listed below), named after the German astronomer Johannes Kepler (1571–1630), can be used to describe the orbits of the planets about the sun.

1. Each planet moves in an elliptical orbit with the sun at one focus.

2. A ray from the sun to the planet sweeps out equal areas of the ellipse in equal times.

3. The square of the period (the time it takes for a planet to orbit the sun) is proportional to the cube of the mean distance between the planet and the sun.

Although Kepler simply stated these laws on the basis of observation, they were later validated by Isaac Newton (1642–1727). In fact, Newton was able to show that each law can be deduced from a set of universal laws of motion and gravitation that govern the movement of all heavenly bodies, including comets and satellites. This is illustrated in the next example, which involves the comet named after the English mathematician and physicist Edmund Halley (1656–1742).

If you use Earth as a reference with a period of 1 year and a distance of 1 astronomical unit (an *astronomical unit* is defined as the mean distance between Earth and the sun, or about 93 million miles), the proportionality constant in Kepler's third law is 1. For example, because Mars has a mean distance to the sun of $d = 1.523$ astronomical units, its period P is given by $d^3 = P^2$. So, the period of Mars is $P = 1.88$ years.

Example 4 ▶ **Halley's Comet**

Halley's comet has an elliptical orbit with an eccentricity of $e \approx 0.97$. The length of the major axis of the orbit is approximately 36.18 astronomical units. Find a polar equation for the orbit. How close does Halley's comet come to the sun?

Solution

Using a vertical axis, as shown in Figure 10.81, choose an equation of the form $r = ep/(1 + e \sin\theta)$. Because the vertices of the ellipse occur when $\theta = \pi/2$ and $\theta = 3\pi/2$, you can determine the length of the major axis to be the sum of the r-values of the vertices. That is,

$$2a = \frac{0.97p}{1 + 0.97} + \frac{0.97p}{1 - 0.97} \approx 32.83p \approx 36.18.$$

So, $p \approx 1.102$ and $ep \approx (0.97)(1.102) \approx 1.069$. Using this value of ep in the equation, you have

$$r = \frac{1.069}{1 + 0.97 \sin \theta}$$

where r is measured in astronomical units. To find the closest point to the sun (the focus), substitute $\theta = \pi/2$ in this equation to obtain

$$r = \frac{1.069}{1 + 0.97 \sin(\pi/2)} \approx 0.54 \text{ astronomical unit} \approx 50{,}000{,}000 \text{ miles.}$$

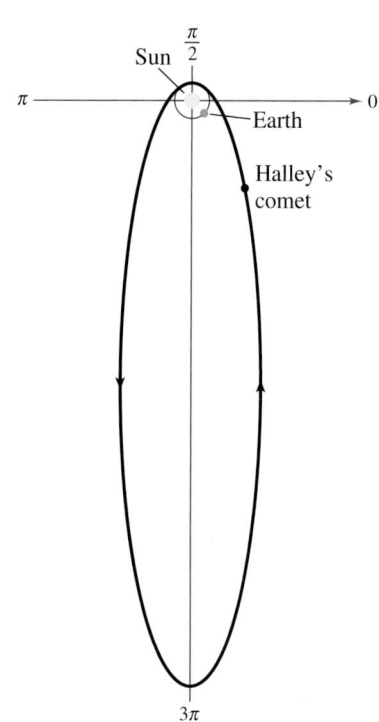

FIGURE **10.81**

10.9 Exercises

In Exercises 1–4, write the polar equation of the conic for $e = 1$, $e = 0.5$, and $e = 1.5$. Identify the conic for each equation. Verify your answers with a graphing utility.

1. $r = \dfrac{4e}{1 + e \cos \theta}$

2. $r = \dfrac{4e}{1 - e \cos \theta}$

3. $r = \dfrac{4e}{1 - e \sin \theta}$

4. $r = \dfrac{4e}{1 + e \sin \theta}$

In Exercises 5–10, match the polar equation with its graph. [The graphs are labeled (a), (b), (c), (d), (e), and (f).]

(a)

(b)

(c)

(d)

(e)

(f)
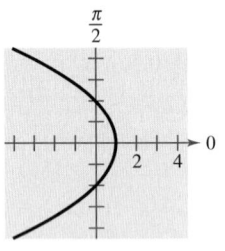

5. $r = \dfrac{2}{1 + \cos \theta}$

6. $r = \dfrac{3}{2 - \cos \theta}$

7. $r = \dfrac{3}{1 + 2 \sin \theta}$

8. $r = \dfrac{2}{1 - \sin \theta}$

9. $r = \dfrac{4}{2 + \cos \theta}$

10. $r = \dfrac{4}{1 - 3 \sin \theta}$

In Exercises 11–24, identify the conic and sketch its graph.

11. $r = \dfrac{2}{1 - \cos \theta}$

12. $r = \dfrac{3}{1 + \sin \theta}$

13. $r = \dfrac{5}{1 + \sin \theta}$

14. $r = \dfrac{6}{1 + \cos \theta}$

15. $r = \dfrac{2}{2 - \cos \theta}$

16. $r = \dfrac{3}{3 + \sin \theta}$

17. $r = \dfrac{6}{2 + \sin \theta}$

18. $r = \dfrac{9}{3 - 2 \cos \theta}$

19. $r = \dfrac{3}{2 + 4 \sin \theta}$

20. $r = \dfrac{5}{-1 + 2 \cos \theta}$

21. $r = \dfrac{3}{2 - 6 \cos \theta}$

22. $r = \dfrac{3}{2 + 6 \sin \theta}$

23. $r = \dfrac{4}{2 - \cos \theta}$

24. $r = \dfrac{2}{2 + 3 \sin \theta}$

 In Exercises 25–28, use a graphing utility to graph the polar equation. Identify the graph.

25. $r = \dfrac{-1}{1 - \sin \theta}$

26. $r = \dfrac{-5}{2 + 4 \sin \theta}$

27. $r = \dfrac{3}{-4 + 2 \cos \theta}$

28. $r = \dfrac{4}{1 - 2 \cos \theta}$

 In Exercises 29–32, use a graphing utility to graph the rotated conic.

29. $r = \dfrac{2}{1 - \cos(\theta - \pi/4)}$ (See Exercise 11.)

30. $r = \dfrac{3}{3 + \sin(\theta - \pi/3)}$ (See Exercise 16.)

31. $r = \dfrac{6}{2 + \sin(\theta + \pi/6)}$ (See Exercise 17.)

32. $r = \dfrac{5}{-1 + 2 \cos(\theta + 2\pi/3)}$ (See Exercise 20.)

In Exercises 33–48, find a polar equation of the conic with its focus at the pole.

Conic	Eccentricity	Directrix
33. Parabola	$e = 1$	$x = -1$
34. Parabola	$e = 1$	$y = -2$
35. Ellipse	$e = \frac{1}{2}$	$y = 1$
36. Ellipse	$e = \frac{3}{4}$	$y = -3$
37. Hyperbola	$e = 2$	$x = 1$
38. Hyperbola	$e = \frac{3}{2}$	$x = -1$

Conic	Vertex or Vertices
39. Parabola	$(1, -\pi/2)$
40. Parabola	$(6, 0)$
41. Parabola	$(5, \pi)$
42. Parabola	$(10, \pi/2)$
43. Ellipse	$(2, 0), (10, \pi)$
44. Ellipse	$(2, \pi/2), (4, 3\pi/2)$
45. Ellipse	$(20, 0), (4, \pi)$
46. Hyperbola	$(2, 0), (8, 0)$
47. Hyperbola	$(1, 3\pi/2), (9, 3\pi/2)$
48. Hyperbola	$(4, \pi/2), (1, \pi/2)$

49. **Planetary Motion** The planets travel in elliptical orbits with the sun at one focus. Assume that the focus is at the pole, the major axis lies on the polar axis, and the length of the major axis is $2a$ (see figure). Show that the polar equation of the orbit is

$$r = \frac{(1 - e^2)a}{1 - e \cos \theta}$$

where e is the eccentricity.

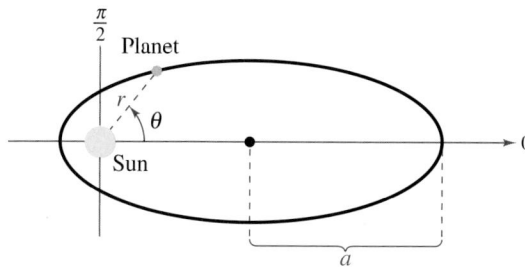

50. **Planetary Motion** Use the result of Exercise 49 to show that the minimum distance (*perihelion distance*) from the sun to the planet is $r = a(1 - e)$ and the maximum distance (*aphelion distance*) is $r = a(1 + e)$.

In Exercises 51–56, use the results of Exercises 49 and 50 to find the polar equation of the planet's orbit and the perihelion and aphelion distances.

51. Earth $a = 92.960 \times 10^6$ miles
               $e = 0.0167$

52. Saturn $a = 1.429 \times 10^9$ kilometers
               $e = 0.0543$

53. Pluto $a = 5.900 \times 10^9$ kilometers
               $e = 0.2481$

54. Mercury $a = 35.98 \times 10^6$ miles
               $e = 0.2056$

55. Mars $a = 141.00 \times 10^6$ miles
               $e = 0.0934$

56. Jupiter $a = 778.40 \times 10^6$ kilometers
               $e = 0.0484$

▶ Model It

57. **Satellite Tracking** A satellite in a 100-mile-high circular orbit around Earth has a velocity of approximately 17,500 miles per hour. If this velocity is multiplied by $\sqrt{2}$, the satellite will have the minimum velocity necessary to escape Earth's gravity and it will follow a parabolic path with the center of Earth as the focus (see figure).

(a) Find a polar equation of the parabolic path of the satellite (assume the radius of Earth is 4000 miles).

(b) Use a graphing utility to graph the equation you found in part (a).

(c) Find the distance between the surface of the Earth and the satellite when $\theta = 30°$.

(d) Find the distance between the surface of Earth and the satellite when $\theta = 60°$.

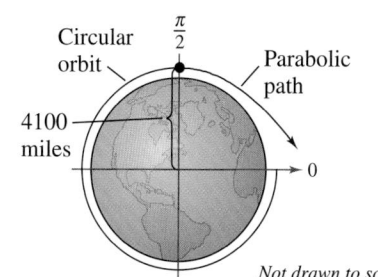

Not drawn to scale

Synthesis

58. *Exploration*   The equation

$$r = \frac{ep}{1 \pm e \sin \theta}$$

is the equation of an ellipse with $e < 1$. What happens to the lengths of both the major axis and the minor axis when the value of e remains fixed and the value of p changes? Use an example to explain your reasoning.

True or False?   In Exercises 59 and 60, determine whether the statement is true or false. Justify your answer.

59. For a given value of $e > 1$ over the interval $\theta = 0$ to $\theta = 2\pi$, the graph of

$$r = \frac{ex}{1 - e \cos \theta}$$

is the same as the graph of

$$r = \frac{e(-x)}{1 + e \cos \theta}.$$

60. The graph of

$$r = \frac{4}{-3 - 3 \sin \theta}$$

has a horizontal directrix above the pole.

61. Show that the polar equation of the ellipse

$$\frac{x^2}{a^2} + \frac{y^2}{b^2} = 1 \quad \text{is} \quad r^2 = \frac{b^2}{1 - e^2 \cos^2 \theta}.$$

62. Show that the polar equation of the hyperbola

$$\frac{x^2}{a^2} - \frac{y^2}{b^2} = 1 \quad \text{is} \quad r^2 = \frac{-b^2}{1 - e^2 \cos^2 \theta}.$$

In Exercises 63–68, use the results of Exercises 61 and 62 to write the polar form of the equation of the conic.

63. $\dfrac{x^2}{169} + \dfrac{y^2}{144} = 1$

64. $\dfrac{x^2}{25} + \dfrac{y^2}{16} = 1$

65. $\dfrac{x^2}{9} - \dfrac{y^2}{16} = 1$

66. $\dfrac{x^2}{36} - \dfrac{y^2}{4} = 1$

67. Hyperbola   One focus: $(5, \pi/2)$
Vertices: $(4, \pi/2), (4, -\pi/2)$

68. Ellipse   One focus: $(4, 0)$
Vertices: $(5, 0), (5, \pi)$

Review

In Exercises 69–74, solve the trigonometric equation.

69. $4\sqrt{3} \tan \theta - 3 = 1$

70. $6 \cos x - 2 = 1$

71. $12 \sin^2 \theta = 9$

72. $9 \csc^2 x - 10 = 2$

73. $2 \cot x = 5 \cos \dfrac{\pi}{2}$

74. $\sqrt{2} \sec \theta = 2 \csc \dfrac{\pi}{4}$

In Exercises 75–78, find the value of the trigonometric function given that u and v are in Quadrant IV and $\sin u = -\frac{3}{5}$ and $\cos v = 1/\sqrt{2}$.

75. $\cos(u + v)$

76. $\sin(u + v)$

77. $\cos(u - v)$

78. $\sin(u - v)$

In Exercises 79 and 80, find the exact values of sin 2u, cos 2u, and tan 2u using the double-angle formulas.

79. $\sin u = \dfrac{4}{5}, \dfrac{\pi}{2} < u < \pi$

80. $\tan u = -\sqrt{3}, \dfrac{3\pi}{2} < u < 2\pi$

In Exercises 81–84, evaluate the expression. Do not use a calculator.

81. $_{12}C_a$

82. $_{18}C_{16}$

83. $_{10}P_3$

84. $_{29}P_2$

Chapter Summary

► *What* did you learn?

Review Exercises

In Exercises 1–4, find, in radians and degrees, the inclination θ of the line with the given characteristics.

1. Passes through the points $(-1, 2)$ and $(2, 5)$
2. Passes through the points $(3, 4)$ and $(-2, 7)$
3. Equation: $y = 2x + 4$
4. Equation: $6x - 7y - 5 = 0$

In Exercises 5–8, find, in radians and degrees, the angle θ between the lines.

5. $\begin{aligned} 4x + y &= 2 \\ -5x + y &= -1 \end{aligned}$

6. $\begin{aligned} -5x + 3y &= 3 \\ -2x + 3y &= 1 \end{aligned}$

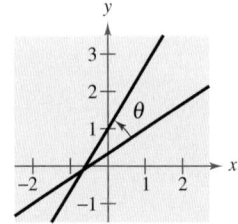

7. $\begin{aligned} 2x - 7y &= 8 \\ 0.4x + y &= 0 \end{aligned}$

8. $\begin{aligned} 0.02x + 0.07y &= 0.18 \\ 0.09x - 0.04y &= 0.17 \end{aligned}$

In Exercises 9 and 10, find the distance between the point and the line.

Point	Line
9. $(1, 2)$	$x - y - 3 = 0$
10. $(0, 4)$	$x + 2y - 2 = 0$

In Exercises 11 and 12, state what type of conic is formed by the intersection of the plane and the double-napped cone.

11.

12.

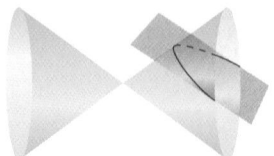

In Exercises 13–16, find the standard form of the equation of the parabola.

13. Vertex: $(4, 2)$
   Focus: $(4, 0)$

14. Vertex: $(2, 0)$
   Focus: $(0, 0)$

15. Vertex: $(0, 2)$
   Directrix: $x = -3$

16. Vertex: $(2, 2)$
   Directrix: $y = 0$

In Exercises 17 and 18, find an equation of a tangent line to the parabola at the given point, and find the x-intercept of the line.

17. $x^2 = -2y, \ (2, -2)$
18. $x^2 = -2y, \ (-4, -8)$

19. **Architecture** A parabolic archway is 12 meters high at the vertex. At a height of 10 meters, the width of the archway is 8 meters (see figure). How wide is the archway at ground level?

FIGURE FOR 19

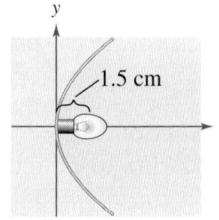

FIGURE FOR 20

20. **Flashlight** The light bulb in a flashlight is at the focus of its parabolic reflector, 1.5 centimeters from the vertex of the reflector (see figure). Write an equation of a cross section of the flashlight's reflector with its focus on the positive x-axis and its vertex at the origin.

In Exercises 21–24, find the standard form of the equation of the ellipse.

21. Vertices: $(-3, 0), (7, 0)$; Foci: $(0, 0), (4, 0)$
22. Vertices: $(2, 0), (2, 4)$; Foci: $(2, 1), (2, 3)$
23. Vertices: $(0, 1), (4, 1)$;
   Endpoints of the minor axis: $(2, 0), (2, 2)$
24. Vertices: $(-4, -1), (-4, 11)$;
   Endpoints of the minor axis: $(-6, 5), (-2, 5)$

25. **Architecture** A semielliptical archway is set on pillars that are 10 feet apart. Its height (atop the pillars) is 4 feet. Where should the foci be placed in order to sketch the semielliptical arch?

26. *Wading Pool* You are building a wading pool that is in the shape of an ellipse. Your plans include an equation for the elliptical shape of the pool measured in feet as

$$\frac{x^2}{324} + \frac{y^2}{196} = 1.$$

Find the longest distance across the pool, the shortest distance, and the distance between the foci.

In Exercises 27–30, find the center, vertices, foci, and eccentricity of the ellipse.

27. $\dfrac{(x + 2)^2}{81} + \dfrac{(y - 1)^2}{100} = 1$

28. $\dfrac{(x - 5)^2}{1} + \dfrac{(y + 3)^2}{36} = 1$

29. $16x^2 + 9y^2 - 32x + 72y + 16 = 0$

30. $4x^2 + 25y^2 + 16x - 150y + 141 = 0$

10.4 In Exercises 31–34, find the standard form of the equation of the hyperbola.

31. Vertices: $(0, \pm 1)$; Foci: $(0, \pm 3)$

32. Vertices: $(2, 2), (-2, 2)$; Foci: $(4, 2), (-4, 2)$

33. Foci: $(0, 0), (8, 0)$; Asymptotes: $y = \pm 2(x - 4)$

34. Foci: $(3, \pm 2)$; Asymptotes: $y = \pm 2(x - 3)$

In Exercises 35–38, find the center, vertices, foci, and the equations of the asymptotes of the hyperbola, and sketch its graph.

35. $\dfrac{(x - 3)^2}{16} - \dfrac{(y + 5)^2}{4} = 1$

36. $\dfrac{(y - 1)^2}{4} - x^2 = 1$

37. $9x^2 - 16y^2 - 18x - 32y - 151 = 0$

38. $-4x^2 + 25y^2 - 8x + 150y + 121 = 0$

39. *LORAN* Radio transmitting station A is located 200 miles east of transmitting station B. A ship is in an area to the north and 40 miles west of station A. Synchronized radio pulses transmitted at 186,000 miles per second by the two stations are received 0.0005 second sooner from station A than from station B. How far north is the ship?

40. *Locating an Explosion* Two of your friends live 4 miles apart and on the same "east-west" street, and you live halfway between them. You are talking on a three-way phone call when you hear an explosion. Six seconds later, your friend to the east hears the explosion, and your friend to the west hears it 8 seconds after you do. Find equations of two hyperbolas that would locate the explosion. (Sound travels at a rate of 1100 feet per second.)

In Exercises 41 and 42, classify the graph of the equation as a circle, a parabola, an ellipse, or a hyperbola.

41. $5x^2 - 2y^2 + 10x - 4y + 17 = 0$

42. $-4y^2 + 5x + 3y + 7 = 0$

10.5 In Exercises 43–46, rotate the axes to eliminate the xy-term. Sketch the graph of the resulting equation, showing both sets of axes.

43. $xy - 4 = 0$

44. $x^2 - 10xy + y^2 + 1 = 0$

45. $5x^2 - 2xy + 5y^2 - 12 = 0$

46. $4x^2 + 8xy + 4y^2 + 7\sqrt{2}x + 9\sqrt{2}y = 0$

 In Exercises 47–50, use the discriminant to classify the graph. Then use the Quadratic Formula to solve for y, and use a graphing utility to graph the equation.

47. $16x^2 - 24xy + 9y^2 - 30x - 40y = 0$

48. $13x^2 - 8xy + 7y^2 - 45 = 0$

49. $x^2 + y^2 + 2xy + 2\sqrt{2}x - 2\sqrt{2}y + 2 = 0$

50. $x^2 - 10xy + y^2 + 1 = 0$

10.6 In Exercises 51–54, evaluate the parametric equations $x = 3 \cos \theta$ and $y = 2 \sin^2 \theta$ for the given value of θ.

51. $\theta = 0$

52. $\theta = \dfrac{\pi}{3}$

53. $\theta = \dfrac{\pi}{6}$

54. $\theta = -\dfrac{\pi}{4}$

In Exercises 55–60, sketch the curve represented by the parametric equations (indicate the orientation of the curve) and, where possible, write the corresponding rectangular equation by eliminating the parameter. Verify your result with a graphing utility.

55. $x = 2t$
       $y = 4t$

56. $x = 1 + 4t$
       $y = 2 - 3t$

57. $x = t^2$

$y = \sqrt{t}$

58. $x = t + 4$

$y = t^2$

59. $x = 6 \cos \theta$

$y = 6 \sin \theta$

60. $x = 3 + 3 \cos \theta$

$y = 2 + 5 \sin \theta$

61. Find a parametric representation of the circle with the center $(5, 4)$ and radius 6.

62. Find a parametric representation of the ellipse with center $(-3, 4)$, major axis horizontal and eight units in length, and minor axis six units in length.

63. Find a parametric representation of the hyperbola with vertices $(0, \pm 4)$ and foci $(0, \pm 5)$.

64. *Involute of a Circle* The *involute* of a circle is described by the endpoint P of a string that is held taut as it is unwound from a spool (see figure). The spool does not rotate. Show that a parametric representation of the involute of a circle is

$x = r(\cos \theta + \theta \sin \theta)$

$y = r(\sin \theta - \theta \cos \theta)$.

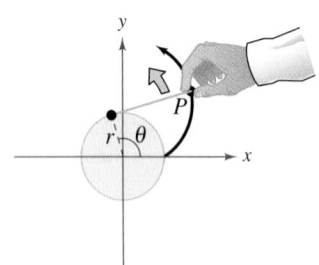

10.7 In Exercises 65–68, plot the point given in polar coordinates and find two additional polar representations.

65. $\left(2, \dfrac{\pi}{4}\right)$

66. $\left(-5, -\dfrac{\pi}{3}\right)$

67. $(-7, 4.19)$

68. $\left(\sqrt{3}, 2.62\right)$

In Exercises 69–72, a point in polar coordinates is given. Convert the point to rectangular coordinates.

69. $\left(-1, \dfrac{\pi}{3}\right)$

70. $\left(2, \dfrac{5\pi}{4}\right)$

71. $\left(3, \dfrac{3\pi}{4}\right)$

72. $\left(0, \dfrac{\pi}{2}\right)$

In Exercises 73–76, a point in rectangular coordinates is given. Convert the point to polar coordinates.

73. $(0, 2)$

74. $\left(-\sqrt{5}, \sqrt{5}\right)$

75. $(4, 6)$

76. $(3, -4)$

In Exercises 77–80, convert the rectangular equation to polar form.

77. $x^2 + y^2 - 6y = 0$

78. $x^2 + y^2 - 4x = 0$

79. $xy = 5$

80. $xy = -2$

In Exercises 81–84, convert the polar equation to rectangular form.

81. $r = 3 \cos \theta$

82. $r = 8 \sin \theta$

83. $r^2 = \sin \theta$

84. $r^2 = \cos 2\theta$

10.8 In Exercises 85–94, determine the symmetry of r, the maximum value of $|r|$, and any zeros of r. Then sketch the graph of the polar equation.

85. $r = 4$

86. $r = 11$

87. $r = 4 \sin 2\theta$

88. $r = \cos 5\theta$

89. $r = -2(1 + \cos \theta)$

90. $r = 3 - 4 \cos \theta$

91. $r = 2 + 6 \sin \theta$

92. $r = 5 - 5 \cos \theta$

93. $r = -3 \cos 2\theta$

94. $r = \cos 2\theta$

In Exercises 95–98, identify the type of polar graph.

95. $r = 3(2 - \cos \theta)$

96. $r = 3(1 - 2 \cos \theta)$

97. $r = 4 \cos 3\theta$

98. $r^2 = 9 \cos 2\theta$

10.9 In Exercises 99–102, identify the conic and sketch its graph.

99. $r = \dfrac{1}{1 + 2 \sin \theta}$

100. $r = \dfrac{2}{1 + \sin \theta}$

101. $r = \dfrac{4}{5 - 3 \cos \theta}$

102. $r = \dfrac{16}{4 + 5 \cos \theta}$

In Exercises 103–106, find a polar equation of the conic with its focus at the pole.

103. Parabola   Vertex: $(2, \pi)$

104. Parabola   Vertex: $(2, \pi/2)$

105. Ellipse   Vertices: $(5, 0), (1, \pi)$

106. Hyperbola   Vertices: $(1, 0), (7, 0)$

107. *Explorer 18* On November 26, 1963, the United States launched Explorer 18. Its low and high points above the surface of Earth were 119 miles and 122,000 miles, respectively (see figure). The center of Earth is at one focus of the orbit. Find the polar equation of the orbit and find the distance between the surface of Earth (assume a radius of 4000 miles) and the satellite when $\theta = \pi/3$ radians.

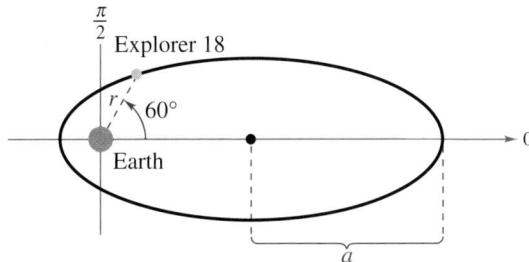

108. *Asteroid* An asteroid takes a parabolic path with Earth as its focus. It is about 6,000,000 miles from Earth at its closest approach. Write the polar equation of the path of the asteroid with its vertex at $\theta = \pi/2$. Find the distance between the asteroid and Earth when $\theta = -\pi/3$.

Synthesis

True or False? In Exercises 109–112, determine whether the statement is true or false. Justify your answer.

109. When $B = 0$ in an equation of the form $Ax^2 + Bxy + Cy^2 + Dx + Ey + F = 0$, the graph of the equation can be a parabola only if $C = 0$ also.

110. The graph of $(x^2/4) - y^4 = 1$ is a hyperbola.

111. Only one set of parametric equations can represent the line $y = 3 - 2x$.

112. There is a unique polar coordinate representation of each point in the plane.

113. Consider an ellipse with the major axis horizontal and 10 units in length. The number b in the standard form of the equation of the ellipse must be less than what real number? Explain the change in the shape of the ellipse as b approaches this number.

114. The graph of the parametric equations $x = 2 \sec t$ and $y = 3 \tan t$ is shown in the figure. Would the graph change for the equations $x = 2 \sec(-t)$ and $y = 3 \tan(-t)$? If so, how would it change?

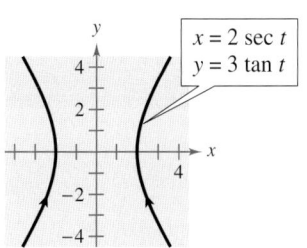

FIGURE FOR **114**

115. A moving object is modeled by the parametric equations $x = 4 \cos t$ and $y = 3 \sin t$, where t is time (see figure). How would the orbit change for the following?

(a) $x = 4 \cos 2t, \quad y = 3 \sin 2t$

(b) $x = 5 \cos t, \quad y = 3 \sin t$

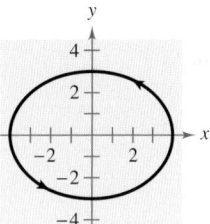

116. Identify the type of symmetry each of the following polar points has with the point in the figure.

(a) $\left(-4, \dfrac{\pi}{6}\right)$

(b) $\left(4, -\dfrac{\pi}{6}\right)$

(c) $\left(-4, -\dfrac{\pi}{6}\right)$

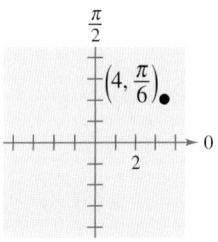

117. What is the relationship between the graphs of the rectangular and polar equations?

(a) $x^2 + y^2 = 25, \quad r = 5$

(b) $x - y = 0, \quad \theta = \dfrac{\pi}{4}$

Chapter Test

Take this test as you would take a test in class. When you are finished, check your work against the answers given in the back of the book.

The *Interactive* CD-ROM and *Internet* versions of this text offer Chapter Pre-Tests and Chapter Post-Tests, both of which have randomly generated exercises with diagnostic capabilities.

1. Find the inclination of the line $2x - 7y + 3 = 0$.

2. Find the angle between the lines $3x + 2y - 4 = 0$ and $4x - y + 6 = 0$.

3. Find the distance between the point $(7, 5)$ and the line $y = 5 - x$.

In Exercises 4–7, classify the conic and write the equation in standard form. Identify the center, vertices, foci, and asymptotes (if any). Then sketch the graph of the conic.

4. $y^2 - 4x + 4 = 0$

5. $x^2 - 4y^2 - 4x = 0$

6. $9x^2 + 16y^2 + 54x - 32y - 47 = 0$

7. $2x^2 + 2y^2 - 8x - 4y + 9 = 0$

8. Find the standard form of the equation of the parabola with vertex $(3, -2)$, with vertical axis, and passing through the point $(0, 4)$.

9. Find the standard form of the equation of the hyperbola with foci $(0, 0)$ and $(0, 4)$ and asymptotes $y = \pm\frac{1}{2}x + 2$.

10. (a) Determine the number of degrees the axis must be rotated to eliminate the xy-term of the conic $x^2 + 6xy + y^2 - 6 = 0$.

    (b) Graph the conic and use a graphing utility to confirm your result.

11. Sketch the curve represented by the parametric equations $x = 2 + 3\cos\theta$ and $y = 2\sin\theta$. Eliminate the parameter and write the corresponding rectangular equation.

12. Find a set of parametric equations of the line passing through the points $(2, -3)$ and $(6, 4)$. (The answer is not unique.)

13. Convert the polar coordinate $(-2, 5\pi/6)$ to rectangular form.

14. Convert the rectangular coordinate $(2, -2)$ to polar form and find two additional representations of this point.

15. Convert the rectangular equation $x^2 + y^2 - 4y = 0$ to polar form.

In Exercises 16–19, sketch the graph of the polar equation. Identify the type of graph.

16. $r = \dfrac{4}{1 + \cos\theta}$

17. $r = \dfrac{4}{2 + \cos\theta}$

18. $r = 2 + 3\sin\theta$

19. $r = 3\sin 2\theta$

20. A straight road rises with an inclination of 0.15 radian from the horizontal. Find the slope of the road and the change in elevation over a one-mile stretch of the road.

21. A baseball is hit 3 feet above the ground toward the left field fence. The fence is 10 feet high and 375 feet from home plate. The path of the baseball can be modeled by the parametric equations $x = (115\cos\theta)t$ and $y = 3 + (115\sin\theta)t - 16t^2$. Does the baseball go over the fence when it is hit at an angle of $\theta = 30°$? Does the baseball go over the fence when $\theta = 35°$?

Proofs in Mathematics

Inclination and Slope (p. 700)

If a nonvertical line has inclination θ and slope m, then $m = \tan \theta$.

Proof

If $m = 0$, the line is horizontal and $\theta = 0$. So, the result is true for horizontal lines because $m = 0 = \tan 0$.

If the line has a positive slope, it will intersect the x-axis. Label this point $(x_1, 0)$, as shown in the figure. If (x_2, y_2) is a second point on the line, the slope is

$$m = \frac{y_2 - 0}{x_2 - x_1} = \frac{y_2}{x_2 - x_1} = \tan \theta.$$

The case in which the line has a negative slope is left for you to prove.

Distance Between a Point and a Line (p. 702)

The distance between the point (x_1, y_1) and the line $Ax + By + C = 0$ is

$$d = \frac{|Ax_1 + By_1 + C|}{\sqrt{A^2 + B^2}}.$$

Proof

For simplicity's sake, assume that the given line is neither horizontal nor vertical (see figure). By writing the equation $Ax + By + C = 0$ in slope-intercept form

$$y = -\frac{A}{B}x - \frac{C}{B}$$

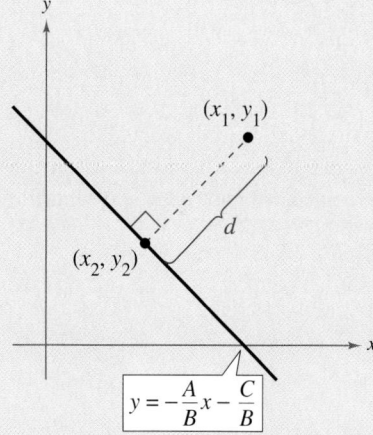

you can see that the line has a slope of $m = -A/B$. So, the slope of the line passing through (x_1, y_1) and perpendicular to the given line is B/A, and its equation is $y - y_1 = (B/A)(x - x_1)$. These two lines intersect at the point (x_2, y_2), where

$$x_2 = \frac{B(Bx_1 - Ay_1) - AC}{A^2 + B^2} \quad \text{and} \quad y_2 = \frac{A(-Bx_1 + Ay_1) - BC}{A^2 + B^2}.$$

Finally, the distance between (x_1, y_1) and (x_2, y_2) is

$$d = \sqrt{(x_2 - x_1)^2 + (y_2 - y_1)^2}$$

$$= \sqrt{\left(\frac{B^2x_1 - ABy_1 - AC}{A^2 + B^2} - x_1\right)^2 + \left(\frac{-ABx_1 + A^2y_1 - BC}{A^2 + B^2} - y_1\right)^2}$$

$$= \sqrt{\frac{A^2(Ax_1 + By_1 + C)^2 + B^2(Ax_1 + By_1 + C)^2}{(A^2 + B^2)^2}}$$

$$= \frac{|Ax_1 + By_1 + C|}{\sqrt{A^2 + B^2}}.$$

Parabolic Paths

There are many natural occurrences of parabolas in real life. For instance, the famous astronomer Galileo discovered in the 17th century that an object that is projected upward and obliquely to the pull of gravity travels in a parabolic path. Examples of this are the center of gravity of a jumping dolphin and the path of water molecules of a drinking fountain

Parabola with vertical axis

Parabola with horizontal axis

Standard Equation of a Parabola   *(p. 708)*

The standard form of the equation of a parabola with vertex at (h, k) is as follows.

$$(x - h)^2 = 4p(y - k), \quad p \neq 0 \qquad \text{Vertical axis, directrix: } y = k - p$$

$$(y - k)^2 = 4p(x - h), \quad p \neq 0 \qquad \text{Horizontal axis, directrix: } x = h - p$$

The focus lies on the axis p units (*directed distance*) from the vertex. If the vertex is at the origin $(0, 0)$, the equation takes one of the following forms.

$$x^2 = 4py \qquad \qquad \text{Vertical axis}$$

$$y^2 = 4py \qquad \qquad \text{Horizontal axis}$$

Proof

For the case in which the directrix is parallel to the x-axis and the focus lies above the vertex, as shown in the top figure, if (x, y) is any point on the parabola, then, by definition, it is equidistant from the focus $(h, k + p)$ and the directrix $y = k - p$. So, you have

$$\sqrt{(x - h)^2 + [y - (k + p)]^2} = y - (k - p)$$

$$(x - h)^2 + [y - (k + p)]^2 = [y - (k - p)]^2$$

$$(x - h)^2 + y^2 - 2y(k + p) + (k + p)^2 = y^2 - 2y(k - p) + (k - p)^2$$

$$(x - h)^2 + y^2 - 2ky - 2py + k^2 + 2pk + p^2 = y^2 - 2ky + 2py + k^2 - 2pk + p^2$$

$$(x - h)^2 - 2py + 2pk = 2py - 2pk$$

$$(x - h)^2 = 4p(y - k).$$

For the case in which the directrix is parallel to the y-axis and the focus lies to the right of the vertex, as shown in the bottom figure, if (x, y) is any point on the parabola, then, by definition, it is equidistant from the focus $(h + p, k)$ and the directrix $x = h - p$. So, you have

$$\sqrt{[x - (h + p)]^2 + (y - k)^2} = x - (h - p)$$

$$[x - (h + p)]^2 + (y - k)^2 = [x - (h - p)]^2$$

$$x^2 - 2x(h + p) + (h + p)^2 + (y - k)^2 = x^2 - 2x(h - p) + (h - p)^2$$

$$x^2 - 2hx - 2px + h^2 + 2ph + p^2 + (y - k)^2 = x^2 - 2hx + 2px + h^2 - 2ph + p^2$$

$$-2px + 2ph + (y - k)^2 = 2px - 2ph$$

$$(y - k)^2 = 4p(x - h).$$

Polar Equations of Conics *(p. 764)*

The graph of a polar equation of the form

1. $r = \dfrac{ep}{1 \pm e \cos \theta}$

or

2. $r = \dfrac{ep}{1 \pm e \sin \theta}$

is a conic, where $e > 0$ is the eccentricity and $|p|$ is the distance between the focus (pole) and the directrix.

Proof

A proof for $r = ep/(1 + e \cos \theta)$ with $p > 0$ is listed here. The proofs of the other cases are similar. In the figure, consider a vertical directrix, p units to the right of the focus $F = (0, 0)$. If $P = (r, \theta)$ is a point on the graph of

$$r = \frac{ep}{1 + e \cos \theta}$$

the distance between P and the directrix is

$$\begin{aligned}
PQ &= |p - x| \\
&= |p - r \cos \theta| \\
&= \left| p - \left(\frac{ep}{1 + e \cos \theta} \right) \cos \theta \right| \\
&= \left| p \left(1 - \frac{e \cos \theta}{1 + e \cos \theta} \right) \right| \\
&= \left| \frac{p}{1 + e \cos \theta} \right| \\
&= \left| \frac{r}{e} \right|.
\end{aligned}$$

Moreover, because the distance between P and the pole is simply $PF = |r|$, the ratio of PF to PQ is

$$\begin{aligned}
\frac{PF}{PQ} &= \frac{|r|}{|r/e|} \\
&= |e| \\
&= e
\end{aligned}$$

and, by definition, the graph of the equation must be a conic.

1. Several mountain climbers are located in a mountain pass between two peaks. The angles of elevation to the two peaks are 0.84 radian and 1.10 radians. A range finder shows that the distances to the peaks are 3250 feet and 6700 feet, respectively (see figure).

   (a) Find the angle between the two lines of sight to the peaks.

   (b) Approximate the amount of vertical climb that is necessary to reach the summit of each peak.

1.10 radians 3250 ft 0.84 radian

2. Statuary Hall is an elliptical room in the United States Capitol in Washington D.C. The room is also called the Whispering Gallery because a person standing at one focus of the room can hear even a whisper spoken by a person standing at the other focus. This occurs because any sound that is emitted from one focus of an ellipse will reflect off the side of the ellipse to the other focus. Statuary Hall is 46 feet wide and 97 feet long.

   (a) Find an equation that models the shape of the room.

   (b) How far apart are the two foci?

   (c) What is the area of the floor of the room? (The area of an ellipse is $A = \pi ab$.)

3. Find the equation(s) of all parabolas that have the x-axis as the axis of symmetry and focus at the origin.

4. Find the area of the square inscribed in the ellipse below.

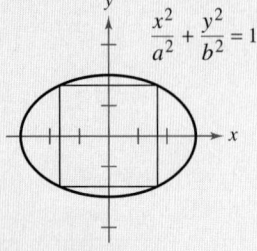

$$\frac{x^2}{a^2} + \frac{y^2}{b^2} = 1$$

5. A tour boat travels between two islands that are 12 miles apart (see figure). For a trip between the islands, there is enough fuel for a 20-mile trip.

   (a) Explain why the region in which the boat can travel is bounded by an ellipse.

   (b) Let $(0, 0)$ represent the center of the ellipse. Find the coordinates of each island.

   (c) The boat travels from one island, straight past the other island to the vertex of the ellipse, and back to the second island. How many miles does the boat travel? Use your answer to find the coordinates of the vertex.

   (d) Use the results from parts (b) and (c) to write an equation for the ellipse that bounds the region in which the boat can travel.

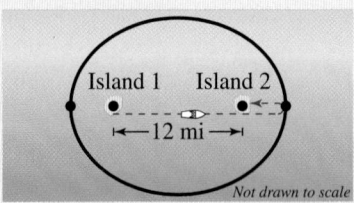

Island 1   Island 2

←—12 mi—→

Not drawn to scale

6. Find an equation of the hyperbola such that for any point on the hyperbola, the difference between its distances from the points $(2, 2)$ and $(10, 2)$ is 6.

7. Prove that the graph of the equation

   $$Ax^2 + Cy^2 + Dx + Ey + F = 0$$

   is one of the following (except in degenerate cases).

Conic	Condition
(a) Circle	$A = C$
(b) Parabola	$A = 0$ or $C = 0$ (but not both)
(c) Ellipse	$AC > 0$
(d) Hyperbola	$AC < 0$

8. The following sets of parametric equations model projectile motion.

$$x = (v_0 \cos \theta)t \qquad x = (v_0 \cos \theta)t$$
$$y = (v_0 \sin \theta)t \qquad y = h + (v_0 \sin \theta)t - 16t^2$$

(a) Under what circumstances would you use each model?

(b) Eliminate the parameter for each set of equations.

(c) In which case is the path of the moving object not affected by a change in the velocity v? Explain.

9. As t increases, the ellipse given by the parametric equations

$$x = \cos t \text{ and } y = 2 \sin t$$

is traced out *counterclockwise*. Find a parametric representation for which the same ellipse is traced out *clockwise*.

 10. A **hypocycloid** has the parametric equations

$$x = (a - b) \cos t + b \cos \left(\frac{a - b}{b} t \right)$$

and

$$y = (a - b) \sin t - b \sin \left(\frac{a - b}{b} t \right).$$

Use a graphing utility to graph the hypocycloid for each value of a and b. Describe each graph.

(a) $a = 2, b = 1$ (b) $a = 3, b = 1$
(c) $a = 4, b = 1$ (d) $a = 10, b = 1$
(e) $a = 3, b = 2$ (f) $a = 4, b = 3$

11. The curve given by the parametric equations

$$x = \frac{1 - t^2}{1 + t^2}$$

and

$$y = \frac{t(1 - t^2)}{1 + t^2}$$

is called a **strophoid**.

(a) Find a rectangular equation of the strophoid.

(b) Find a polar equation of the strophoid.

 (c) Use a graphing utility to graph the strophoid.

12. The rose curves described in this chapter are of the form

$$r = a \cos n\theta \qquad \text{or} \qquad r = a \sin n\theta$$

where n is a positive integer that is greater than or equal to 2. Use a graphing utility to graph $r = a \cos n\theta$ and $r = a \sin n\theta$ for some noninteger values of n. Describe the graphs.

13. What conic section does the polar equation

$$r = a \sin \theta + b \cos \theta$$

represent?

14. The graph of the polar equation

$$r = e^{\cos\theta} - 2 \cos 4\theta + \sin^5 \left(\frac{\theta}{12} \right)$$

is called *the butterfly curve*, as shown in the figure.

(a) The graph below was produced using $0 \le \theta \le 2\pi$. Does this show the entire graph? Explain your reasoning.

(b) Approximate the maximum r-value of the graph. Does this value change if you use $0 \le \theta \le 4\pi$ instead of $0 \le \theta \le 2\pi$? Explain.

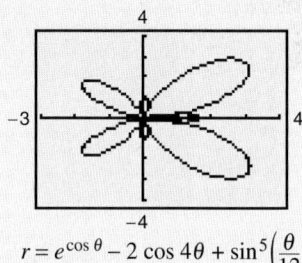

$$r = e^{\cos \theta} - 2 \cos 4\theta + \sin^5 \left(\frac{\theta}{12} \right)$$

15. Use a graphing utility to graph the polar equation

$$r = \cos 5\theta + n \cos \theta$$

for $0 \le \theta \le \pi$ for the integers $n = -5$ to $n = 5$. As you graph these equations, you should see the graph change shape from a heart to a bell. Write a short paragraph explaining what values of n produce the heart portion of the curve and what values of n produce the bell portion.

Appendix A Review of Fundamental Concepts of Algebra

A.1 Real Numbers and Their Properties

▶ **What you should learn**

• How to represent and classify real numbers
• How to order real numbers and use inequalities
• How to find the absolute values of real numbers and find the distance between two real numbers
• How to evaluate algebraic expressions
• How to use the basic rules and properties of algebra

▶ **Why you should learn it**

Real numbers are used to represent many real-life quantities. For example, in Exercise 69 on page A9, you will use real numbers to represent the federal deficit.

Real Numbers

Real numbers are used in everyday life to describe quantities such as age, miles per gallon, container size, and population. Real numbers are represented by symbols such as

$$-5, 9, 0, \frac{4}{3}, 0.666\ldots, 28.21, \sqrt{2}, \pi, \text{ and } \sqrt[3]{-32}.$$

Here are some important subsets of the real numbers.

$$\{1, 2, 3, 4, \ldots\} \quad \text{Set of natural numbers}$$
$$\{0, 1, 2, 3, 4, \ldots\} \quad \text{Set of whole numbers}$$
$$\{\ldots, -3, -2, -1, 0, 1, 2, 3, \ldots\} \quad \text{Set of integers}$$

A real number is **rational** if it can be written as the ratio p/q of two integers, where $q \neq 0$. For instance, the numbers

$$\frac{1}{3} = 0.3333\ldots = 0.\overline{3}, \frac{1}{8} = 0.125, \text{ and } \frac{125}{111} = 1.126126\ldots = 1.\overline{126}$$

are rational. The decimal representation of a rational number either repeats $\left(\text{as in } \frac{173}{55} = 3.1\overline{45}\right)$ or terminates $\left(\text{as in } \frac{1}{2} = 0.5\right)$. A real number that cannot be written as the ratio of two integers is called **irrational.** Irrational numbers have infinite nonrepeating decimal representations. For instance, the numbers

$$\sqrt{2} \approx 1.4142136 \quad \text{and} \quad \pi \approx 3.1415927$$

are irrational. (The symbol $\approx$ means "is approximately equal to.")

Real numbers are represented graphically by a **real number line.** The point 0 on the real number line is the **origin.** Numbers to the right of 0 are positive, and numbers to the left of 0 are negative, as shown in Figure A.1. The term **nonnegative** describes a number that is either positive or zero.

Every point on the real number line corresponds to exactly one real number.

Every real number corresponds to exactly one point on the real number line.

FIGURE A.2   *One-to-One Correspondence*

FIGURE A.1   *The Real Number Line*

As illustrated in Figure A.2, there is a *one-to-one correspondence* between real numbers and points on the real number line.

The icon identifies examples and concepts related to features of the Learning Tools CD-ROM and the *Interactive* and *Internet* versions of this text. For more details see the chart on pages *xxi-xxv.*

Ordering Real Numbers

One important property of real numbers is that they are *ordered*.

Definition of Order on the Real Number Line

If a and b are real numbers, a is less than b if $b - a$ is positive. The **order** of a and b is denoted by the **inequality**

$$a < b.$$

This relationship can also be described by saying that b is *greater than a* and writing $b > a$. The inequality $a \le b$ means that a is *less than or equal to b*, and the inequality $b \ge a$ means that b is *greater than or equal to a*. The symbols $<$, $>$, $\le$, and $\ge$ are *inequality symbols*.

FIGURE A.3   *a < b if and only if a lies to the left of b.*

Geometrically, this definition implies that $a < b$ if and only if a lies to the *left* of b on the real number line, as shown in Figure A.3.

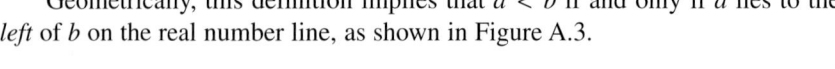   **Example 1** ▶   Interpreting Inequalities

Describe the subset of real numbers represented by each inequality.

a. $x \le 2$ **b.** $-2 \le x < 3$

Solution

FIGURE A.4

a. The inequality $x \le 2$ denotes all real numbers less than or equal to 2, as shown in Figure A.4.

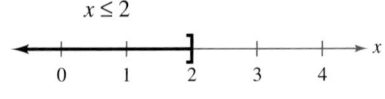

FIGURE A.5

b. The inequality $-2 \le x < 3$ means that $x \ge -2$ and $x < 3$. This "double inequality" denotes all real numbers between -2 and 3, including -2 but not including 3, as shown in Figure A.5.

Inequalities can be used to describe subsets of real numbers called **intervals**. In the bounded intervals below, the real numbers a and b are the **endpoints** of each interval.

Bounded Intervals on the Real Number Line

Notation	Interval Type	Inequality	Graph
$[a, b]$	Closed	$a \le x \le b$	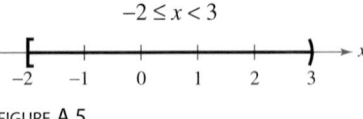
(a, b)	Open	$a < x < b$	
$[a, b)$		$a \le x < b$	
$(a, b]$		$a < x \le b$	

The symbols ∞, **positive infinity,** and −∞, **negative infinity,** do not represent real numbers. They are simply convenient symbols used to describe the unboundedness of an interval such as $(1, \infty)$ or $(-\infty, 3]$.

Unbounded Intervals on the Real Number Line

Notation	Interval Type	Inequality	Graph
$[a, \infty)$		$x \geq a$	
(a, ∞)	Open	$x > a$	
$(-\infty, b]$		$x \leq b$	
$(-\infty, b)$	Open	$x < b$	
$(-\infty, \infty)$	Entire real line	$-\infty < x < \infty$	

Example 2 ▶ **Using Inequalities to Represent Intervals**

Use inequality notation to describe each of the following.

a. c is at most 2.

b. m is at least -3.

c. All x in the interval $(-3, 5]$

Solution

a. The statement "c is at most 2" can be represented by $c \leq 2$.

b. The statement "m is at least -3" can be represented by $m \geq -3$.

c. "All x in the interval $(-3, 5]$" can be represented by $-3 < x \leq 5$.

Example 3 ▶ **Interpreting Intervals**

Give a verbal description of each interval.

a. $(-1, 0)$ **b.** $[2, \infty)$ **c.** $(-\infty, 0)$

Solution

a. This interval consists of all real numbers that are greater than -1 and less than 0.

b. This interval consists of all real numbers that are greater than or equal to 2.

c. This interval consists of all real numbers that are less than zero (the negative real numbers).

The **Law of Trichotomy** states that for any two real numbers a and b, *precisely* one of three relationships is possible:

$$a = b, \quad a < b, \quad \text{or} \quad a > b. \qquad \text{Law of Trichotomy}$$

Absolute Value and Distance

The **absolute value** of a real number is its *magnitude*, or the distance between the origin and the point representing the real number on the real number line.

Definition of Absolute Value

If a is a real number, then the absolute value of a is

$$|a| = \begin{cases} a, & \text{if } a \geq 0 \\ -a, & \text{if } a < 0. \end{cases}$$

Notice in this definition that the absolute value of a real number is never negative. For instance, if $a = -5$, then $|-5| = -(-5) = 5$. The absolute value of a real number is either positive or zero. Moreover, 0 is the only real number whose absolute value is 0. So, $|0| = 0$.

Example 4 ▶   **Evaluating the Absolute Value of a Number**

Evaluate $\dfrac{|x|}{x}$ for (a) $x > 0$ and (b) $x < 0$.

Solution

a. If $x > 0$, then $|x| = x$ and $\dfrac{|x|}{x} = \dfrac{x}{x} = 1$.

b. If $x < 0$, then $|x| = -x$ and $\dfrac{|x|}{x} = \dfrac{-x}{x} = -1$.

Properties of Absolute Values

1. $|a| \geq 0$ **2.** $|-a| = |a|$

3. $|ab| = |a||b|$ **4.** $\left|\dfrac{a}{b}\right| = \dfrac{|a|}{|b|}, \qquad b \neq 0$

Absolute value can be used to define the distance between two points on the real number line. For instance, the distance between -3 and 4 is

$$|-3 - 4| = |-7|$$
$$= 7$$

as shown in Figure A.6.

FIGURE **A.6**   *The distance between* -3 *and 4 is 7.*

Distance Between Two Points on the Real Line

Let a and b be real numbers. The **distance between a and b** is

$$d(a, b) = |b - a| = |a - b|.$$

Algebraic Expressions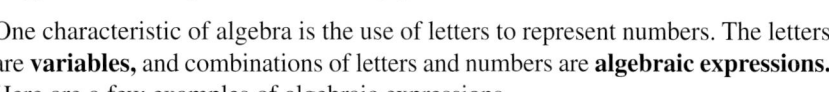

One characteristic of algebra is the use of letters to represent numbers. The letters are **variables,** and combinations of letters and numbers are **algebraic expressions.** Here are a few examples of algebraic expressions.

$$5x, \qquad 2x - 3, \qquad \frac{4}{x^2 + 2}, \qquad 7x + y$$

Definition of an Algebraic Expression

An **algebraic expression** is a collection of letters (**variables**) and real numbers (**constants**) combined using the operations of addition, subtraction, multiplication, division, and exponentiation.

The **terms** of an algebraic expression are those parts that are separated by *addition.* For example,

$$x^2 - 5x + 8 = x^2 + (-5x) + 8$$

has three terms: x^2 and $-5x$ are the **variable terms** and 8 is the **constant term.** The numerical factor of a variable term is the **coefficient** of the variable term. For instance, the coefficient of $-5x$ is -5, and the coefficient of x^2 is 1.

To **evaluate** an algebraic expression, substitute numerical values for each of the variables in the expression. Here are two examples.

Expression	Value of Variable	Substitute	Value of Expression
$-3x + 5$	$x = 3$	$-3(3) + 5$	$-9 + 5 = -4$
$3x^2 + 2x - 1$	$x = -1$	$3(-1)^2 + 2(-1) - 1$	$3 - 2 - 1 = 0$

When an algebraic expression is evaluated, the **Substitution Principle** is used. It states that "If $a = b$, then a can be replaced by b in any expression involving a." In the first evaluation shown above, for instance, 3 is *substituted* for x in the expression $-3x + 5$.

Basic Rules of Algebra

There are four arithmetic operations with real numbers: *addition, multiplication, subtraction,* and *division,* denoted by the symbols $+$, $\times$ or $\cdot$, $-$, and $\div$. Of these, addition and multiplication are the two primary operations. Subtraction and division are the inverse operations of addition and multiplication, respectively.

Subtraction: Add the opposite. *Division:* Multiply by the reciprocal.

$$a - b = a + (-b) \qquad\qquad \text{If } b \neq 0, \text{ then } a/b = a\left(\frac{1}{b}\right) = \frac{a}{b}.$$

In these definitions, $-b$ is the **additive inverse** (or opposite) of b, and $1/b$ is the **multiplicative inverse** (or reciprocal) of b. In the fractional form a/b, a is the **numerator** of the fraction and b is the **denominator.**

Because the properties of real numbers on page A6 are true for variables and algebraic expressions as well as for real numbers, they are often called the **Basic Rules of Algebra.**

STUDY TIP

Try to formulate a verbal description of each property. For instance, the first property states that *the order in which two real numbers are added does not affect their sum.*

Basic Rules of Algebra

Let a, b, and c be real numbers, variables, or algebraic expressions.

Property		Example
Commutative Property of Addition:	$a + b = b + a$	$4x + x^2 = x^2 + 4x$
Commutative Property of Multiplication:	$ab = ba$	$(4 - x)x^2 = x^2(4 - x)$
Associative Property of Addition:	$(a + b) + c = a + (b + c)$	$(x + 5) + x^2 = x + (5 + x^2)$
Associative Property of Multiplication:	$(ab)c = a(bc)$	$(2x \cdot 3y)(8) = (2x)(3y \cdot 8)$
Distributive Properties:	$a(b + c) = ab + ac$	$3x(5 + 2x) = 3x \cdot 5 + 3x \cdot 2x$
	$(a + b)c = ac + bc$	$(y + 8)y = y \cdot y + 8 \cdot y$
Additive Identity Property:	$a + 0 = a$	$5y^2 + 0 = 5y^2$
Multiplicative Identity Property:	$a \cdot 1 = a$	$(4x^2)(1) = 4x^2$
Additive Inverse Property:	$a + (-a) = 0$	$5x^3 + (-5x^3) = 0$
Multiplicative Inverse Property:	$a \cdot \dfrac{1}{a} = 1, \quad a \neq 0$	$(x^2 + 4)\left(\dfrac{1}{x^2 + 4}\right) = 1$

Because subtraction is defined as "adding the opposite," the Distributive Properties are also true for subtraction. So, the first Distributive Property can be applied to an expression of the form $a(b - c)$ as follows.

$$a(b - c) = ab - ac$$

Properties of Negation

Let a and b be real numbers, variables, or algebraic expressions.

	Property	Example
1.	$(-1)a = -a$	$(-1)7 = -7$
2.	$-(-a) = a$	$-(-6) = 6$
3.	$(-a)b = -(ab) = a(-b)$	$(-5)3 = -(5 \cdot 3) = 5(-3)$
4.	$(-a)(-b) = ab$	$(-2)(-x) = 2x$
5.	$-(a + b) = (-a) + (-b)$	$-(x + 8) = (-x) + (-8)$
		$= -x - 8$

STUDY TIP

Be sure you see the difference between the *opposite of a number* and a *negative number*. If a is already negative, then its opposite, $-a$, is positive. For instance, if $a = -5$, then

$$-a = -(-5) = 5.$$

Properties of Equality

Let a, b, and c be real numbers, variables, or algebraic expressions.

1. If $a = b$, then $a + c = b + c$.		Add c to each side.
2. If $a = b$, then $ac = bc$.		Multiply each side by c.
3. If $a + c = b + c$, then $a = b$.		Subtract c from each side.
4. If $ac = bc$ and $c \neq 0$, then $a = b$.		Divide each side by c.

Properties of Zero

Let a and b be real numbers, variables, or algebraic expressions.

1. $a + 0 = a$ and $a - 0 = a$ **2.** $a \cdot 0 = 0$

3. $\dfrac{0}{a} = 0, \qquad a \neq 0$ **4.** $\dfrac{a}{0}$ is undefined.

5. Zero-Factor Property: If $ab = 0$, then $a = 0$ or $b = 0$.

Properties and Operations of Fractions

Let a, b, c, and d be real numbers, variables, or algebraic expressions such that $b \neq 0$ and $d \neq 0$.

1. Equivalent Fractions: $\dfrac{a}{b} = \dfrac{c}{d}$ if and only if $ad = bc$.

2. Rules of Signs: $-\dfrac{a}{b} = \dfrac{-a}{b} = \dfrac{a}{-b}$ and $\dfrac{-a}{-b} = \dfrac{a}{b}$

3. Generate Equivalent Fractions: $\dfrac{a}{b} = \dfrac{ac}{bc}, \qquad c \neq 0$

4. Add or Subtract with Like Denominators: $\dfrac{a}{b} \pm \dfrac{c}{b} = \dfrac{a \pm c}{b}$

5. Add or Subtract with Unlike Denominators: $\dfrac{a}{b} \pm \dfrac{c}{d} = \dfrac{ad \pm bc}{bd}$

6. Multiply Fractions: $\dfrac{a}{b} \cdot \dfrac{c}{d} = \dfrac{ac}{bd}$

7. Divide Fractions: $\dfrac{a}{b} \div \dfrac{c}{d} = \dfrac{a}{b} \cdot \dfrac{d}{c} = \dfrac{ad}{bc}, \qquad c \neq 0$

Example 5 ▶ **Properties and Operations of Fractions**

a. Equivalent fractions: $\dfrac{x}{5} = \dfrac{3 \cdot x}{3 \cdot 5} = \dfrac{3x}{15}$ **b.** Divide fractions: $\dfrac{7}{x} \div \dfrac{3}{2} = \dfrac{7}{x} \cdot \dfrac{2}{3} = \dfrac{14}{3x}$

c. Add fractions with unlike denominators: $\dfrac{x}{3} + \dfrac{2x}{5} = \dfrac{5 \cdot x + 3 \cdot 2x}{3 \cdot 5} = \dfrac{11x}{15}$

If a, b, and c are integers such that $ab = c$, then a and b are **factors** or **divisors** of c. A **prime number** is an integer that has exactly two positive factors:— itself and 1—such as 2, 3, 5, 7, and 11. The numbers 4, 6, 8, 9, and 10 are **composite** because they can be written as the product of two or more prime numbers. The number 1 is neither prime nor composite. The **Fundamental Theorem of Arithmetic** states that every positive integer greater than 1 can be written as the product of prime numbers in precisely one way (disregarding order). For instance, the *prime factorization* of 24 is $24 = 2 \cdot 2 \cdot 2 \cdot 3$.

A.1 Exercises

In Exercises 1–6, determine which numbers are (a) natural numbers, (b) integers, (c) rational numbers, and (d) irrational numbers.

1. $-9, -\frac{7}{2}, 5, \frac{2}{3}, \sqrt{2}, 0, 1, -4, 2, -11$
2. $\sqrt{5}, -7, -\frac{7}{3}, 0, 3.12, \frac{5}{4}, -3, 12, 5$
3. $2.01, 0.666\ldots, -13, 0.010110111\ldots, 1, -6$
4. $2.3030030003\ldots, 0.7575, -4.63, \sqrt{10}, -75, 4$
5. $-\pi, -\frac{1}{3}, \frac{6}{3}, \frac{1}{2}\sqrt{2}, -7.5, -1, 8, -22$
6. $25, -17, -\frac{12}{5}, \sqrt{9}, 3.12, \frac{1}{2}\pi, 7, -11.1, 13$

In Exercises 7–10, use a calculator to find the decimal form of the rational number. If it is a nonterminating decimal, write the repeating pattern.

7. $\frac{5}{8}$
8. $\frac{1}{3}$
9. $\frac{41}{333}$
10. $\frac{6}{11}$

In Exercises 11 and 12, approximate the numbers and place the correct symbol (< or >) between them.

11.

12.

In Exercises 13–18, plot the two real numbers on the real number line. Then place the appropriate inequality symbol (< or >) between them.

13. $-4, -8$
14. $-3.5, 1$
15. $\frac{3}{2}, 7$
16. $1, \frac{16}{3}$
17. $\frac{5}{6}, \frac{2}{3}$
18. $-\frac{8}{7}, -\frac{3}{7}$

In Exercises 19–28, verbally describe the subset of real numbers represented by the inequality. Then sketch the subset on the real number line. State whether the interval is bounded or unbounded.

19. $x \le 5$
20. $x \ge -2$
21. $x < 0$
22. $x > 3$
23. $x \ge 4$
24. $x < 2$
25. $-2 < x < 2$
26. $0 \le x \le 5$
27. $-1 \le x < 0$
28. $0 < x \le 6$

In Exercises 29–36, use inequality notation to describe the set.

29. All x in the interval $(-2, 4]$

30. All y in the interval $[-6, 0)$
31. y is nonnegative.
32. y is no more than 25.
33. t is at least 10 and at most 22.
34. k is less than 5 but no less than -3.
35. The dog's weight W is more than 65 pounds.
36. The annual rate of inflation r is expected to be at least 2.5% but no more than 5%.

In Exercises 37–40, give a verbal description of the interval.

37. $[0, 8)$
38. $[-5, 7]$
39. $(-6, \infty)$
40. $(-\infty, 4]$

In Exercises 41–50, evaluate the expression.

41. $|-10|$
42. $|0|$
43. $|3 - 8|$
44. $|4 - 1|$
45. $|-1| - |-2|$
46. $-3 - |-3|$
47. $\dfrac{-5}{|-5|}$
48. $-3|-3|$
49. $\dfrac{|x + 2|}{x + 2}, \quad x < -2$
50. $\dfrac{|x - 1|}{x - 1}, \quad x > 1$

In Exercises 51–56, place the correct symbol (<, >, or =) between the pair of real numbers.

51. $|-3| \quad\rule{1cm}{0.4pt}\quad -|-3|$
52. $|-4| \quad\rule{1cm}{0.4pt}\quad |4|$
53. $-5 \quad\rule{1cm}{0.4pt}\quad -|5|$
54. $-|-6| \quad\rule{1cm}{0.4pt}\quad |-6|$
55. $-|-2| \quad\rule{1cm}{0.4pt}\quad -|2|$
56. $-(-2) \quad\rule{1cm}{0.4pt}\quad -2$

In Exercises 57–64, find the distance between a and b.

57.

58.

59. $a = 126, b = 75$
60. $a = -126, b = -75$
61. $a = -\frac{5}{2}, b = 0$
62. $a = \frac{1}{4}, b = \frac{11}{4}$
63. $a = \frac{16}{5}, b = \frac{112}{75}$
64. $a = 9.34, b = -5.65$

Budget Variance In Exercises 65–68, the accounting department of a sports drink bottling company is checking to see whether the actual expenses of a department differ from the budgeted expenses by more than $500 or by more than 5%. Fill in the missing parts of the table, and determine whether each actual expense passes the "budget variance test."

	Budgeted Expense, b	Actual Expense, a	$\lvert a - b \rvert$	$0.05b$
65. Wages	$112,700	$113,356		
66. Utilities	$9,400	$9,772		
67. Taxes	$37,640	$37,335		
68. Insurance	$2,575	$2,613		

69. *Federal Deficit* The bar graph shows the federal government receipts (in billions of dollars) for selected years from 1960 through 2000. (Source: U.S. Office of Management and Budget)

(a) Complete the table. (*Hint:* Find |Receipts – Expenditures|.)

Year	Expenditures (in billions)	Surplus or deficit (in billions)
1960	$92.2	
1970	$195.6	
1980	$590.9	
1990	$1253.2	
2000	$1788.8	

(b) Use the table in part (a) to construct a bar graph showing the magnitude of the surplus or deficit for each year.

70. *Veterans* The table shows the number of surviving spouses of deceased veterans of United States wars (as of May 2001). Construct a circle graph showing the percent of surviving spouses for each war as a fraction of the total number of surviving spouses of deceased war veterans. (Source: Department of Veteran Affairs)

War	Number of surviving spouses
Civil War	1
Indian Wars	0
Spanish-American War	386
Mexican Border War	181
World War I	25,573
World War II	272,793
Korean War	63,579
Vietnam War	114,514
Gulf War	6,261

In Exercises 71–78, use absolute value notation to describe the situation.

71. While traveling on the Pennsylvania Turnpike, you pass milepost 57 near Pittsburgh, then milepost 236 near Gettysburg. How far do you travel during that time period?

72. While traveling on the Pennsylvania Turnpike, you pass milepost 326 near Valley Forge, then milepost 351 near Philadelphia. How far do you travel during that time period?

73. The temperature in Bismarck, North Dakota, was 60° at noon, then 23° at midnight. What was the change in temperature over the 12-hour period?

74. The temperature in Chicago, Illinois was 48° last night at midnight, then 82° at noon today. What was the change in temperature over the 12-hour period?

75. The distance between x and 5 is no more than 3.

76. The distance between x and -10 is at least 6.

77. y is at least six units from 0.

78. y is at most two units from a.

In Exercises 79–84, identify the terms. Then identify the coefficients of the variable terms of the expression.

79. $7x + 4$

80. $6x^3 - 5x$

81. $\sqrt{3}x^2 - 8x - 11$

82. $3\sqrt{3}x^2 + 1$

83. $4x^3 + \dfrac{x}{2} - 5$　　　　**84.** $3x^4 - \dfrac{x^2}{4}$

In Exercises 85–90, evaluate the expression for each value of x. (If not possible, state the reason.)

Expression	Values
85. $4x - 6$	(a) $x = -1$　(b) $x = 0$
86. $9 - 7x$	(a) $x = -3$　(b) $x = 3$
87. $x^2 - 3x + 4$	(a) $x = -2$　(b) $x = 2$
88. $-x^2 + 5x - 4$	(a) $x = -1$　(b) $x = 1$
89. $\dfrac{x+1}{x-1}$	(a) $x = 1$　(b) $x = -1$
90. $\dfrac{x}{x+2}$	(a) $x = 2$　(b) $x = -2$

In Exercises 91–100, identify the rule(s) of algebra illustrated by the statement.

91. $x + 9 = 9 + x$　　　**92.** $2\left(\frac{1}{2}\right) = 1$

93. $\dfrac{1}{h+6}(h+6) = 1, \quad h \neq -6$

94. $(x+3) - (x+3) = 0$

95. $2(x+3) = 2x + 6$　　**96.** $(z-2) + 0 = z - 2$

97. $1 \cdot (1 + x) = 1 + x$

98. $x + (y + 10) = (x + y) + 10$

99. $x(3y) = (x \cdot 3)y = (3x)y$

100. $\frac{1}{7}(7 \cdot 12) = \left(\frac{1}{7} \cdot 7\right)12 = 1 \cdot 12 = 12$

In Exercises 101–108, perform the operation(s). (Write fractional answers in simplest form.)

101. $\frac{3}{16} + \frac{5}{16}$　　　　　**102.** $\frac{6}{7} - \frac{4}{7}$

103. $\frac{5}{8} - \frac{5}{12} + \frac{1}{6}$　　　**104.** $\frac{10}{11} + \frac{6}{33} - \frac{13}{66}$

105. $12 \div \frac{1}{4}$　　　　　**106.** $-\left(6 \cdot \frac{4}{8}\right)$

107. $\dfrac{2x}{3} - \dfrac{x}{4}$　　　　**108.** $\dfrac{5x}{6} \cdot \dfrac{2}{9}$

109. (a) Use a calculator to complete the table.

n	1	0.5	0.01	0.0001	0.000001
$5/n$					

　　(b) Use the result from part (a) to make a conjecture about the value of $5/n$ as n approaches 0.

110. (a) Use a calculator to complete the table.

n	1	10	100	10,000	100,000
$5/n$					

　　(b) Use the result from part (a) to make a conjecture about the value of $5/n$ as n increases without bound.

Synthesis

True or False? In Exercises 111 and 112, determine whether the statement is true or false. Justify your answer.

111. If $a < b$, then $\dfrac{1}{a} < \dfrac{1}{b}$, where $a \neq b \neq 0$.

112. Because $\dfrac{a+b}{c} = \dfrac{a}{c} + \dfrac{b}{c}$, then $\dfrac{c}{a+b} = \dfrac{c}{a} + \dfrac{c}{b}$.

113. ***Exploration*** Consider $|u + v|$ and $|u| + |v|$.

　　(a) Are the values of the expressions always equal? If not, under what conditions are they unequal?

　　(b) If the two expressions are not equal for certain values of u and v, is one of the expressions always greater than the other? Explain.

114. ***Think About It*** Is there a difference between saying that a real number is positive and saying that a real number is nonnegative? Explain.

115. ***Think About It*** Because every even number is divisible by 2, is it possible that there exist any even prime numbers? Explain.

116. ***Writing*** Describe the differences among the sets of natural numbers, integers, rational numbers, and irrational numbers.

In Exercises 117 and 118, use the real numbers A, B, and C shown on the number line. Determine the sign of each expression.

117. (a) $-A$　　　　**118.** (a) $-C$

　　(b) $B - A$　　　　　(b) $A - C$

119. ***Writing*** You may hear it said that to take the absolute value of a real number you simply remove any negative sign and make the number positive. Can it ever be true that $|a| = -a$ for a real number a? Explain.

A.2 Exponents and Radicals

▶ **Why you should learn it**

Real numbers and algebraic expressions are often written with exponents and radicals. For instance, in Exercise 113 on page A22, you will use an expression involving rational exponents to find the time required for a funnel to empty for different water heights.

Integer Exponents

Repeated *multiplication* can be written in **exponential form.**

Repeated Multiplication	Exponential Form
$a \cdot a \cdot a \cdot a \cdot a$	a^5
$(-4)(-4)(-4)$	$(-4)^3$
$(2x)(2x)(2x)(2x)$	$(2x)^4$

In general, if a is a real number and n is a positive integer, then

$$a^n = \underbrace{a \cdot a \cdot a \cdots a}_{n \text{ factors}}$$

where n is the **exponent** and a is the **base.** The expression a^n is read "a to the nth **power.**" In Property 3 below, be sure you see how to use a negative exponent.

Properties of Exponents

Let a and b be real numbers, variables, or algebraic expressions, and let m and n be integers. (All denominators and bases are nonzero.)

Property	Example
1. $a^m a^n = a^{m+n}$	$3^2 \cdot 3^4 = 3^{2+4} = 3^6 = 729$
2. $\dfrac{a^m}{a^n} = a^{m-n}$	$\dfrac{x^7}{x^4} = x^{7-4} = x^3$
3. $a^{-n} = \dfrac{1}{a^n} = \left(\dfrac{1}{a}\right)^n$	$y^{-4} = \dfrac{1}{y^4} = \left(\dfrac{1}{y}\right)^4$
4. $a^0 = 1, \quad a \neq 0$	$(x^2 + 1)^0 = 1$
5. $(ab)^m = a^m b^m$	$(5x)^3 = 5^3 x^3 = 125x^3$
6. $(a^m)^n = a^{mn}$	$(y^3)^{-4} = y^{3(-4)} = y^{-12} = \dfrac{1}{y^{12}}$
7. $\left(\dfrac{a}{b}\right)^m = \dfrac{a^m}{b^m}$	$\left(\dfrac{2}{x}\right)^3 = \dfrac{2^3}{x^3} = \dfrac{8}{x^3}$
8. $\lvert a^2 \rvert = \lvert a \rvert^2 = a^2$	$\lvert (-2)^2 \rvert = \lvert -2 \rvert^2 = (2)^2 = 4$

It is important to recognize the difference between expressions such as $(-2)^4$ and -2^4. In $(-2)^4$, the parentheses indicate that the exponent applies to the negative sign as well as to the 2, but in $-2^4 = -(2^4)$, the exponent applies only to the 2. So,

$$(-2)^4 = 16 \quad \text{and} \quad -2^4 = -16.$$

The properties of exponents listed on the preceding page apply to *all* integers m and n, not just to positive integers. For instance, by Property 2, you can write

$$\frac{3^4}{3^{-5}} = 3^{4-(-5)} = 3^{4+5} = 3^9.$$

Example 1 ▶   Using Properties of Exponents

Use the properties of exponents to simplify each expression.

a. $(-3ab^4)(4ab^{-3})$ **b.** $(2xy^2)^3$ **c.** $3a(-4a^2)^0$ **d.** $\left(\frac{5x^3}{y}\right)^2$

Solution

a. $(-3ab^4)(4ab^{-3}) = (-3)(4)(a)(a)(b^4)(b^{-3}) = -12a^2b$

b. $(2xy^2)^3 = 2^3(x)^3(y^2)^3 = 8x^3y^6$

c. $3a(-4a^2)^0 = 3a(1) = 3a, \quad a \neq 0$

d. $\left(\frac{5x^3}{y}\right)^2 = \frac{5^2(x^3)^2}{y^2} = \frac{25x^6}{y^2}$

Example 2 ▶   Rewriting the Positive Exponents

Rewrite each expression with positive exponents.

a. x^{-1} **b.** $\frac{1}{3x^{-2}}$ **c.** $\frac{12a^3b^{-4}}{4a^{-2}b}$ **d.** $\left(\frac{3x^2}{y}\right)^{-2}$

Solution

a. $x^{-1} = \frac{1}{x}$ Property 3

b. $\frac{1}{3x^{-2}} = \frac{1(x^2)}{3} = \frac{x^2}{3}$ The exponent -2 does not apply to 3.

c. $\frac{12a^3b^{-4}}{4a^{-2}b} = \frac{12a^3 \cdot a^2}{4b \cdot b^4}$ Property 3

      $= \frac{3a^5}{b^5}$ Property 1

d. $\left(\frac{3x^2}{y}\right)^{-2} = \frac{3^{-2}(x^2)^{-2}}{y^{-2}}$ Properties 5 and 7

      $= \frac{3^{-2}x^{-4}}{y^{-2}}$ Property 6

      $= \frac{y^2}{3^2x^4}$ Property 3

      $= \frac{y^2}{9x^4}$ Simplify.

Scientific Notation

Exponents provide an efficient way of writing and computing with very large (or very small) numbers. For instance, there are about 359 billion billion gallons of water on Earth—that is, 359 followed by 18 zeros.

$$359,000,000,000,000,000,000$$

It is convenient to write such numbers in **scientific notation.** This notation has the form $c \times 10^n$, where $1 \leq c < 10$ and n is an integer. So, the number of gallons of water on Earth can be written in scientific notation as

$$3.59 \times 100,000,000,000,000,000,000 = 3.59 \times 10^{20}.$$

The *positive* exponent 20 indicates that the number is *large* (10 or more) and that the decimal point has been moved 20 places. A *negative* exponent indicates that the number is *small* (less than 1). For instance, the mass (in grams) of one electron is approximately

$$9.0 \times 10^{-28} = 0.00000000000000000000000000009.$$

28 decimal places

Example 3 ▶ **Scientific Notation**

Write the number in scientific notation.

a. 0.0000782   **b.** 836,100,000

Solution

a. $0.0000782 = 7.82 \times 10^{-5}$

b. $836,100,000 = 8.361 \times 10^{8}$

Example 4 ▶ **Decimal Notation**

Write the number in decimal notation.

a. 9.36×10^{-6} **b.** 1.345×10^{2}

Solution

a. $9.36 \times 10^{-6} = 0.00000936$ **b.** $1.345 \times 10^{2} = 134.5$

Technology

Most calculators automatically switch to scientific notation when they are showing large (or small) numbers that exceed the display range.

To *enter* numbers in scientific notation, your calculator should have an exponential entry key labeled

[EE]   or   [EXP].

Consult the user's guide for your calculator for instructions on keystrokes and how numbers in scientific notation are displayed.

Radicals and Their Properties

A **square root** of a number is one of its two equal factors. For example, 5 is a square root of 25 because 5 is one of the two equal factors of 25. In a similar way, a **cube root** of a number is one of its three equal factors, as in $125 = 5^3$.

Definition of *n*th Root of a Number

Let a and b be real numbers and let $n \geq 2$ be a positive integer. If

$$a = b^n$$

then b is an ***n*th root of *a*.** If $n = 2$, the root is a **square root.** If $n = 3$, the root is a **cube root.**

Some numbers have more than one *n*th root. For example, both 5 and -5 are square roots of 25. The *principal square root* of 25, written as $\sqrt{25}$, is the positive root, 5. The **principal *n*th root** of a number is defined as follows.

Principal *n*th Root of a Number

Let a be a real number that has at least one *n*th root. The **principal *n*th root of *a*** is the *n*th root that has the same sign as a. It is denoted by a **radical symbol**

$$\sqrt[n]{a}. \qquad \text{Principal } n\text{th root}$$

The positive integer n is the **index** of the radical, and the number a is the **radicand.** If $n = 2$, omit the index and write $\sqrt{a}$ rather than $\sqrt[2]{a}$. (The plural of index is *indices*.)

A common misunderstanding is that the square root sign implies both negative and positive roots. This is not correct. The square root sign implies only a positive root. When a negative root is needed, you must use the negative sign with the square root sign.

Incorrect: $\sqrt{4} = \pm 2$ *Correct:* $-\sqrt{4} = -2$ *and* $\sqrt{4} = 2$

Example 5 ▶   Evaluating Expressions Involving Radicals

a. $\sqrt{36} = 6$ because $6^2 = 36$.

b. $-\sqrt{36} = -6$ because $6^2 = 36$.

c. $\sqrt[3]{\dfrac{125}{64}} = \dfrac{5}{4}$ because $\left(\dfrac{5}{4}\right)^3 = \dfrac{5^3}{4^3} = \dfrac{125}{64}$.

d. $\sqrt[5]{-32} = -2$ because $(-2)^5 = -32$.

e. $\sqrt[4]{-81}$ is not a real number because there is no real number that can be raised to the fourth power to produce -81.

Here are some generalizations about the *n*th roots of real numbers.

Generalizations About *n*th Roots of Real Numbers

Real number a	Integer n	Root(s) of a	Example
$a > 0$	$n > 0$, is even.	$\sqrt[n]{a}, -\sqrt[n]{a}$	$\sqrt[4]{81} = 3, -\sqrt[4]{81} = -3$
$a > 0$ or $a < 0$	n is odd.	$\sqrt[n]{a}$	$\sqrt[3]{-8} = -2$
$a < 0$	n is even.	No real roots	$\sqrt{-4}$ is not a real number.
$a = 0$	n is even or odd.	$\sqrt[n]{0} = 0$	$\sqrt[5]{0} = 0$

Integers such as 1, 4, 9, 16, 25, and 36 are called **perfect squares** because they have integer square roots. Similarly, integers such as 1, 8, 27, 64, and 125 are called **perfect cubes** because they have integer cube roots.

Properties of Radicals

Let a and b be real numbers, variables, or algebraic expressions such that the indicated roots are real numbers, and let m and n be positive integers.

Property

1. $\sqrt[n]{a^m} = \left(\sqrt[n]{a}\right)^m$
2. $\sqrt[n]{a} \cdot \sqrt[n]{b} = \sqrt[n]{ab}$
3. $\dfrac{\sqrt[n]{a}}{\sqrt[n]{b}} = \sqrt[n]{\dfrac{a}{b}}, \quad b \neq 0$
4. $\sqrt[m]{\sqrt[n]{a}} = \sqrt[mn]{a}$
5. $\left(\sqrt[n]{a}\right)^n = a$
6. For n even, $\sqrt[n]{a^n} = |a|$.
   For n odd, $\sqrt[n]{a^n} = a$.

Example

$\sqrt[3]{8^2} = \left(\sqrt[3]{8}\right)^2 = (2)^2 = 4$

$\sqrt{5} \cdot \sqrt{7} = \sqrt{5 \cdot 7} = \sqrt{35}$

$\dfrac{\sqrt[4]{27}}{\sqrt[4]{9}} = \sqrt[4]{\dfrac{27}{9}} = \sqrt[4]{3}$

$\sqrt[3]{\sqrt{10}} = \sqrt[6]{10}$

$\left(\sqrt{3}\right)^2 = 3$

$\sqrt{(-12)^2} = |-12| = 12$

$\sqrt[3]{(-12)^3} = -12$

A common special case of Property 6 is $\sqrt{a^2} = |a|$.

Example 6 ▶ Using Properties of Radicals

Use the properties of radicals to simplify each expression.

a. $\sqrt{8} \cdot \sqrt{2}$ **b.** $\left(\sqrt[3]{5}\right)^3$ **c.** $\sqrt[3]{x^3}$ **d.** $\sqrt[6]{y^6}$

Solution

a. $\sqrt{8} \cdot \sqrt{2} = \sqrt{8 \cdot 2} = \sqrt{16} = 4$
b. $\left(\sqrt[3]{5}\right)^3 = 5$
c. $\sqrt[3]{x^3} = x$
d. $\sqrt[6]{y^6} = |y|$

Simplifying Radicals

An expression involving radicals is in **simplest form** when the following conditions are satisfied.

1. All possible factors have been removed from the radical.
2. All fractions have radical-free denominators (accomplished by a process called *rationalizing the denominator*).
3. The index of the radical is reduced.

     To simplify a radical, factor the radicand into factors whose exponents are multiples of the index. The roots of these factors are written outside the radical, and the "leftover" factors make up the new radicand.

STUDY TIP

When you simplify a radical, it is important that both expressions are defined for the same values of the variable. For instance, in Example 7(b), $\sqrt{75x^3}$ and $5x\sqrt{3x}$ are both defined only for nonnegative values of x. Similarly, in Example 7(c), $\sqrt[4]{(5x)^4}$ and $5|x|$ are both defined for all real values of x.

Example 7 ▶   **Simplifying Even Roots**

         Perfect   Leftover
         4th power   factor

a. $\sqrt[4]{48} = \sqrt[4]{16 \cdot 3} = \sqrt[4]{2^4 \cdot 3} = 2\sqrt[4]{3}$

         Perfect   Leftover
         square   factor

b. $\sqrt{75x^3} = \sqrt{25x^2 \cdot 3x}$ Find largest square factor.

        $= \sqrt{(5x)^2 \cdot 3x}$

        $= 5x\sqrt{3x}$ Find root of perfect square.

c. $\sqrt[4]{(5x)^4} = |5x| = 5|x|$

     In Example 7(b), the expression $\sqrt{75x^3}$ makes sense only for nonnegative values of x.

Example 8 ▶   **Simplifying Odd Roots**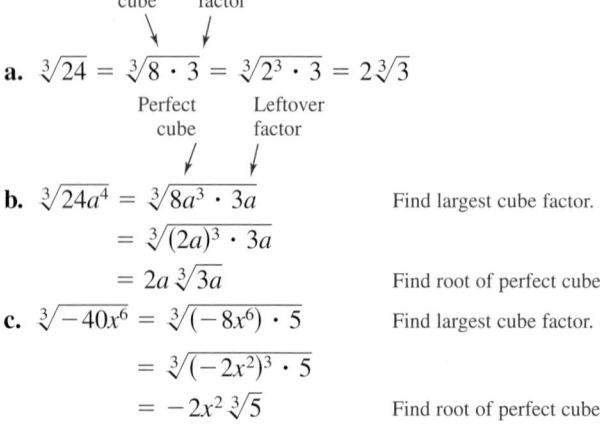

         Perfect   Leftover
         cube   factor

a. $\sqrt[3]{24} = \sqrt[3]{8 \cdot 3} = \sqrt[3]{2^3 \cdot 3} = 2\sqrt[3]{3}$

         Perfect   Leftover
         cube   factor

b. $\sqrt[3]{24a^4} = \sqrt[3]{8a^3 \cdot 3a}$ Find largest cube factor.

        $= \sqrt[3]{(2a)^3 \cdot 3a}$

        $= 2a\sqrt[3]{3a}$ Find root of perfect cube.

c. $\sqrt[3]{-40x^6} = \sqrt[3]{(-8x^6) \cdot 5}$ Find largest cube factor.

        $= \sqrt[3]{(-2x^2)^3 \cdot 5}$

        $= -2x^2\sqrt[3]{5}$ Find root of perfect cube.

Radical expressions can be combined (added or subtracted) if they are **like radicals**—that is, if they have the same index and radicand. For instance, $\sqrt{2}$, $3\sqrt{2}$, and $\frac{1}{2}\sqrt{2}$ are like radicals, but $\sqrt{3}$ and $\sqrt{2}$ are unlike radicals. To determine whether two radicals can be combined, you should first simplify each radical.

Example 9 ▶ **Combining Radicals**

a.
$$2\sqrt{48} - 3\sqrt{27} = 2\sqrt{16 \cdot 3} - 3\sqrt{9 \cdot 3} \qquad \text{Find square factors.}$$
$$= 8\sqrt{3} - 9\sqrt{3} \qquad \text{Find square roots.}$$
$$= (8 - 9)\sqrt{3} \qquad \text{Combine like terms.}$$
$$= -\sqrt{3} \qquad \text{Simplify.}$$

b.
$$\sqrt[3]{16x} - \sqrt[3]{54x^4} = \sqrt[3]{8 \cdot 2x} - \sqrt[3]{27 \cdot x^3 \cdot 2x} \qquad \text{Find cube factors.}$$
$$= 2\sqrt[3]{2x} - 3x\sqrt[3]{2x} \qquad \text{Find cube roots.}$$
$$= (2 - 3x)\sqrt[3]{2x} \qquad \text{Combine like terms.}$$

Rationalizing Denominators and Numerators

To rationalize a denominator or numerator of the form $a - b\sqrt{m}$ or $a + b\sqrt{m}$, multiply both numerator and denominator by a **conjugate**: $a + b\sqrt{m}$ and $a - b\sqrt{m}$ are conjugates of each other. If $a = 0$, then the rationalizing factor for $\sqrt{m}$ is itself, $\sqrt{m}$. For cube roots, choose a rationalizing factor that generates a perfect cube.

Example 10 ▶ **Rationalizing Single-Term Denominators**

Rationalize the denominator of each expression.

a. $\dfrac{5}{2\sqrt{3}}$ **b.** $\dfrac{2}{\sqrt[3]{5}}$

Solution

a.
$$\frac{5}{2\sqrt{3}} = \frac{5}{2\sqrt{3}} \cdot \frac{\sqrt{3}}{\sqrt{3}} \qquad \sqrt{3} \text{ is rationalizing factor.}$$
$$= \frac{5\sqrt{3}}{2(3)}$$
$$= \frac{5\sqrt{3}}{6}$$

b.
$$\frac{2}{\sqrt[3]{5}} = \frac{2}{\sqrt[3]{5}} \cdot \frac{\sqrt[3]{5^2}}{\sqrt[3]{5^2}} \qquad \sqrt[3]{5^2} \text{ is rationalizing factor.}$$
$$= \frac{2\sqrt[3]{5^2}}{\sqrt[3]{5^3}}$$
$$= \frac{2\sqrt[3]{25}}{5}$$

Example 11 ▶ **Rationalizing a Denominator with Two Terms**

$$\frac{2}{3+\sqrt{7}} = \frac{2}{3+\sqrt{7}} \cdot \frac{3-\sqrt{7}}{3-\sqrt{7}}$$
Multiply numerator and denominator by conjugate of denominator.

$$= \frac{2(3-\sqrt{7})}{3(3)+3(-\sqrt{7})+\sqrt{7}(3)-(\sqrt{7})(\sqrt{7})}$$
Use Distributive Property.

$$= \frac{2(3-\sqrt{7})}{(3)^2-(\sqrt{7})^2}$$
Simplify.

$$= \frac{2(3-\sqrt{7})}{9-7}$$
Square terms of denominator.

$$= \frac{2(3-\sqrt{7})}{2} = 3-\sqrt{7}$$
Simplify.

Sometimes it is necessary to rationalize the numerator of an expression. For instance, in Section A.4 you will use the technique shown in the next example to rationalize the numerator of an expression from calculus.

Example 12 ▶ **Rationalizing a Numerator**

$$\frac{\sqrt{5}-\sqrt{7}}{2} = \frac{\sqrt{5}-\sqrt{7}}{2} \cdot \frac{\sqrt{5}+\sqrt{7}}{\sqrt{5}+\sqrt{7}}$$
Multiply numerator and denominator by conjugate of numerator.

$$= \frac{(\sqrt{5})^2-(\sqrt{7})^2}{2(\sqrt{5}+\sqrt{7})}$$
Simplify.

$$= \frac{5-7}{2(\sqrt{5}+\sqrt{7})}$$
Square terms of numerator.

$$= \frac{-2}{2(\sqrt{5}+\sqrt{7})} = \frac{-1}{\sqrt{5}+\sqrt{7}}$$
Simplify.

Rational Exponents

Definition of Rational Exponents

If a is a real number and n is a positive integer such that the principal nth root of a exists, then $a^{1/n}$ is defined as

$$a^{1/n} = \sqrt[n]{a}, \text{ where } 1/n \text{ is the } \textbf{rational exponent} \text{ of } a.$$

Moreover, if m is a positive integer that has no common factor with n, then

$$a^{m/n} = (a^{1/n})^m = (\sqrt[n]{a})^m \quad \text{and} \quad a^{m/n} = (a^m)^{1/n} = \sqrt[n]{a^m}.$$

The symbol ∫ indicates an example or exercise that highlights algebraic techniques specifically used in calculus.

The numerator of a rational exponent denotes the *power* to which the base is raised, and the denominator denotes the *index* or the *root* to be taken.

$$b^{m/n} = \left(\sqrt[n]{b}\right)^m = \sqrt[n]{b^m}$$

(with labels: Power, Index)

When you are working with rational exponents, the properties of integer exponents still apply. For instance,

$$2^{1/2}2^{1/3} = 2^{(1/2)+(1/3)} = 2^{5/6}.$$

Example 13 ▶ **Changing from Radical to Exponential Form**

a. $\sqrt{3} = 3^{1/2}$

b. $\sqrt{(3xy)^5} = \sqrt[2]{(3xy)^5} = (3xy)^{(5/2)}$

c. $2x\sqrt[4]{x^3} = (2x)(x^{3/4}) = 2x^{1+(3/4)} = 2x^{7/4}$

Example 14 ▶ **Changing from Exponential to Radical Form**

a. $(x^2 + y^2)^{3/2} = \left(\sqrt{x^2 + y^2}\right)^3 = \sqrt{(x^2 + y^2)^3}$

b. $2y^{3/4}z^{1/4} = 2(y^3z)^{1/4} = 2\sqrt[4]{y^3z}$

c. $a^{-3/2} = \dfrac{1}{a^{3/2}} = \dfrac{1}{\sqrt{a^3}}$

d. $x^{0.2} = x^{1/5} = \sqrt[5]{x}$

Rational exponents are useful for evaluating roots of numbers on a calculator, for reducing the index of a radical, and for simplifying expressions in calculus.

Example 15 ▶ **Simplifying with Rational Exponents**

a. $(-32)^{-4/5} = \left(\sqrt[5]{-32}\right)^{-4} = (-2)^{-4} = \dfrac{1}{(-2)^4} = \dfrac{1}{16}$

b. $(-5x^{5/3})(3x^{-3/4}) = -15x^{(5/3)-(3/4)} = -15x^{11/12}, \qquad x \neq 0$

c. $\sqrt[9]{a^3} = a^{3/9} = a^{1/3} = \sqrt[3]{a}$ $\qquad$ Reduce index.

d. $\sqrt[3]{\sqrt{125}} = \sqrt[6]{125} = \sqrt[6]{(5)^3} = 5^{3/6} = 5^{1/2} = \sqrt{5}$

e. $(2x - 1)^{4/3}(2x - 1)^{-1/3} = (2x - 1)^{(4/3)-(1/3)}$

$$= 2x - 1, \qquad x \neq \frac{1}{2}$$

f. $\dfrac{x - 1}{(x - 1)^{-1/2}} = \dfrac{x - 1}{(x - 1)^{-1/2}} \cdot \dfrac{(x - 1)^{1/2}}{(x - 1)^{1/2}}$

$$= \dfrac{(x - 1)^{3/2}}{(x - 1)^0}$$

$$= (x - 1)^{3/2}, \qquad x \neq 1$$

A.2 Exercises

In Exercises 1–4, write the expression as a repeated multiplication problem.

1. 8^5

2. $(-2)^7$

3. -0.4^6

4. 11.3^4

In Exercises 5–8, write the expression using exponential notation.

5. $(4.9)(4.9)(4.9)(4.9)(4.9)(4.9)$

6. $\left(2\sqrt{5}\right)\left(2\sqrt{5}\right)\left(2\sqrt{5}\right)\left(2\sqrt{5}\right)$

7. $(-10)(-10)(-10)(-10)(-10)$

8. $-\left(\frac{3}{2} \times \frac{3}{2} \times \frac{3}{2} \times \frac{3}{2}\right)$

In Exercises 9–16, evaluate each expression.

9. (a) $3^2 \cdot 3$ (b) $3 \cdot 3^3$

10. (a) $\dfrac{5^5}{5^2}$ (b) $\dfrac{3^2}{3^4}$

11. (a) $(3^3)^2$ (b) -3^2

12. (a) $(2^3 \cdot 3^2)^2$ (b) $\left(-\frac{3}{5}\right)^3\left(\frac{5}{3}\right)^2$

13. (a) $\dfrac{3 \cdot 4^{-4}}{3^{-4} \cdot 4^{-1}}$ (b) $32(-2)^{-5}$

14. (a) $\dfrac{4 \cdot 3^{-2}}{2^{-2} \cdot 3^{-1}}$ (b) $(-2)^0$

15. (a) $2^{-1} + 3^{-1}$ (b) $(2^{-1})^{-2}$

16. (a) $3^{-1} + 2^{-2}$ (b) $(3^{-2})^2$

In Exercises 17–20, use a calculator to evaluate the expression. (If necessary, round your answer to three decimal places.)

17. $(-4)^3(5^2)$

18. $(8^{-4})(10^3)$

19. $\dfrac{3^6}{7^3}$

20. $\dfrac{4^3}{3^{-4}}$

In Exercises 21–28, evaluate the expression for the given value of x.

Expression	Value
21. $-3x^3$	2
22. $7x^{-2}$	4
23. $6x^0$	10
24. $5(-x)^3$	3
25. $2x^3$	-3
26. $-3x^4$	-2
27. $4x^2$	$-\frac{1}{2}$
28. $5(-x)^3$	$\frac{1}{3}$

In Exercises 29–34, simplify each expression.

29. (a) $(-5z)^3$ (b) $5x^4(x^2)$

30. (a) $(3x)^2$ (b) $(4x^3)^2$

31. (a) $6y^2(2y^4)^2$ (b) $\dfrac{3x^5}{x^3}$

32. (a) $(-z)^3(3z^4)$ (b) $\dfrac{25y^8}{10y^4}$

33. (a) $\dfrac{7x^2}{x^3}$ (b) $\dfrac{12(x+y)^3}{9(x+y)}$

34. (a) $\dfrac{r^4}{r^6}$ (b) $\left(\dfrac{4}{y}\right)^3\left(\dfrac{3}{y}\right)^4$

In Exercises 35–40, rewrite each expression with positive exponents and simplify.

35. (a) $(x+5)^0, \quad x \neq -5$ (b) $(2x^2)^{-2}$

36. (a) $(2x^5)^0, \quad x \neq 0$ (b) $(z+2)^{-3}(z+2)^{-1}$

37. (a) $(-2x^2)^3(4x^3)^{-1}$ (b) $\left(\dfrac{x}{10}\right)^{-1}$

38. (a) $(4y^{-2})(8y^4)$ (b) $\left(\dfrac{x^{-3}y^4}{5}\right)^{-3}$

39. (a) $3^n \cdot 3^{2n}$ (b) $\left(\dfrac{a^{-2}}{b^{-2}}\right)\left(\dfrac{b}{a}\right)^3$

40. (a) $\dfrac{x^2 \cdot x^n}{x^3 \cdot x^n}$ (b) $\left(\dfrac{a^{-3}}{b^{-3}}\right)\left(\dfrac{a}{b}\right)^3$

In Exercises 41–44, write the number in scientific notation.

41. Land area of Earth: 57,300,000 square miles

42. Light year: 9,460,000,000,000 kilometers

43. Relative density of hydrogen: 0.0000899 gram per cubic centimeter

44. One micron (millionth of a meter): 0.00003937 inch

In Exercises 45–48, write the number in decimal notation.

45. Worldwide daily consumption of Coca-Cola: 4.568×10^9 servings (Source: The Coca-Cola Company)

46. Interior temperature of the sun: 1.5×10^7 degrees Celsius

47. Charge of an electron: 1.602×10^{-19} coulomb

48. Width of a human hair: 9.0×10^{-5} meter

In Exercises 49 and 50, evaluate each expression without using a calculator.

49. (a) $\sqrt{25 \times 10^8}$ (b) $\sqrt[3]{8 \times 10^{15}}$

50. (a) $(1.2 \times 10^7)(5 \times 10^{-3})$ (b) $\dfrac{(6.0 \times 10^8)}{(3.0 \times 10^{-3})}$

In Exercises 51–54, use a calculator to evaluate each expression. (Round your answer to three decimal places.)

51. (a) $750\left(1 + \dfrac{0.11}{365}\right)^{800}$

     (b) $\dfrac{67{,}000{,}000 + 93{,}000{,}000}{0.0052}$

52. (a) $(9.3 \times 10^6)^3(6.1 \times 10^{-4})$

     (b) $\dfrac{(2.414 \times 10^4)^6}{(1.68 \times 10^5)^5}$

53. (a) $\sqrt{4.5 \times 10^9}$ (b) $\sqrt[3]{6.3 \times 10^4}$

54. (a) $(2.65 \times 10^{-4})^{1/3}$ (b) $\sqrt{9 \times 10^{-4}}$

In Exercises 55–66, fill in the missing form of the expression.

Radical Form	Rational Exponent Form
55. $\sqrt{9}$	
56. $\sqrt[3]{64}$	
57.	$32^{1/5}$
58.	$-(144^{1/2})$
59.	$196^{1/2}$
60. $\sqrt[3]{614.125}$	
61. $\sqrt[3]{-216}$	
62.	$(-243)^{1/5}$
63.	$27^{2/3}$
64. $\left(\sqrt[4]{81}\right)^3$	
65. $\sqrt[4]{81^3}$	
66.	$16^{5/4}$

In Exercises 67–74, evaluate each expression without using a calculator.

67. (a) $\sqrt{9}$ (b) $\sqrt[3]{8}$

68. (a) $\sqrt{49}$ (b) $\sqrt[3]{\dfrac{27}{8}}$

69. (a) $\left(\sqrt[3]{-125}\right)^3$ (b) $27^{1/3}$

70. (a) $\sqrt[4]{562^4}$ (b) $36^{3/2}$

71. (a) $32^{-3/5}$ (b) $\left(\dfrac{16}{81}\right)^{-3/4}$

72. (a) $100^{-3/2}$ (b) $\left(\dfrac{9}{4}\right)^{-1/2}$

73. (a) $\left(-\dfrac{1}{64}\right)^{-1/3}$ (b) $\left(\dfrac{1}{\sqrt{32}}\right)^{-2/5}$

74. (a) $\left(-\dfrac{125}{27}\right)^{-1/3}$ (b) $-\left(\dfrac{1}{125}\right)^{-4/3}$

In Exercises 75–78, use a calculator to approximate the number. (Round your answer to three decimal places.)

75. (a) $\sqrt{57}$ (b) $\sqrt[5]{-27^3}$

76. (a) $\sqrt[3]{45^2}$ (b) $\sqrt[6]{125}$

77. (a) $(-12.4)^{-1.8}$ (b) $\left(5\sqrt{3}\right)^{-2.5}$

78. (a) $\dfrac{7 - (4.1)^{-3.2}}{2}$ (b) $\left(\dfrac{13}{3}\right)^{-3/2} - \left(-\dfrac{3}{2}\right)^{13/3}$

In Exercises 79–84, simplify by removing all possible factors from each radical.

79. (a) $\sqrt{8}$ (b) $\sqrt[3]{24}$

80. (a) $\sqrt[3]{\dfrac{16}{27}}$ (b) $\sqrt{\dfrac{75}{4}}$

81. (a) $\sqrt{72x^3}$ (b) $\sqrt{\dfrac{18^2}{z^3}}$

82. (a) $\sqrt{54xy^4}$ (b) $\sqrt{\dfrac{32a^4}{b^2}}$

83. (a) $\sqrt[3]{16x^5}$ (b) $\sqrt{75x^2y^{-4}}$

84. (a) $\sqrt[4]{(3x^2)^4}$ (b) $\sqrt[5]{96x^5}$

In Exercises 85–88, perform the operations and simplify.

85. $\dfrac{(2x^2)^{3/2}}{2^{1/2}x^4}$

86. $\dfrac{x^{4/3}y^{2/3}}{(xy)^{1/3}}$

87. $\dfrac{x^{-3} \cdot x^{1/2}}{x^{3/2} \cdot x^{-1}}$

88. $\dfrac{5^{-1/2} \cdot 5x^{5/2}}{(5x)^{3/2}}$

In Exercises 89–92, rationalize the denominator of the expression. Then simplify your answer.

89. $\dfrac{1}{\sqrt{3}}$

90. $\dfrac{5}{\sqrt{10}}$

91. $\dfrac{2}{5 - \sqrt{3}}$

92. $\dfrac{3}{\sqrt{5} + \sqrt{6}}$

In Exercises 93–96, rationalize the numerator of the expression. Then simplify your answer.

93. $\dfrac{\sqrt{8}}{2}$

94. $\dfrac{\sqrt{2}}{3}$

95. $\dfrac{\sqrt{5} + \sqrt{3}}{3}$

96. $\dfrac{\sqrt{7} - 3}{4}$

In Exercises 97 and 98, reduce the index of each radical.

97. (a) $\sqrt[4]{3^2}$ (b) $\sqrt[6]{(x + 1)^4}$

98. (a) $\sqrt[6]{x^3}$ (b) $\sqrt[4]{(3x^2)^4}$

In Exercises 99 and 100, write each expression as a single radical. Then simplify your answer.

99. (a) $\sqrt{\sqrt{32}}$ (b) $\sqrt{\sqrt[4]{2x}}$

100. (a) $\sqrt{\sqrt{243(x + 1)}}$ (b) $\sqrt{\sqrt[3]{10a^7 b}}$

In Exercises 101–106, simplify each expression.

101. (a) $2\sqrt{50} + 12\sqrt{8}$ (b) $10\sqrt{32} - 6\sqrt{18}$

102. (a) $4\sqrt{27} - \sqrt{75}$ (b) $\sqrt[3]{16} + 3\sqrt[3]{54}$

103. (a) $5\sqrt{x} - 3\sqrt{x}$ (b) $-2\sqrt{9y} + 10\sqrt{y}$

104. (a) $8\sqrt{49x} - 14\sqrt{100x}$
  (b) $-3\sqrt{48x^2} + 7\sqrt{75x^2}$

105. (a) $3\sqrt{x + 1} + 10\sqrt{x + 1}$
  (b) $7\sqrt{80x} - 2\sqrt{125x}$

106. (a) $-\sqrt{x^3 - 7} + 5\sqrt{x^3 - 7}$
  (b) $11\sqrt{245x^3} - 9\sqrt{45x^3}$

In Exercises 107–110, complete the statement with $<$, $=$, or $>$.

107. $\sqrt{5} + \sqrt{3}$ ___ $\sqrt{5 + 3}$

108. $\sqrt{\dfrac{3}{11}}$ ___ $\dfrac{\sqrt{3}}{\sqrt{11}}$

109. 5 ___ $\sqrt{3^2 + 2^2}$ **110.** 5 ___ $\sqrt{3^2 + 4^2}$

111. *Period of a Pendulum* The period T (in seconds) of a pendulum is

$$T = 2\pi\sqrt{\dfrac{L}{32}}$$

where L is the length of the pendulum (in feet). Find the period of a pendulum whose length is 2 feet.

The symbol indicates an example or exercise that highlights algebraic techniques specifically used in calculus.

The symbol indicates an exercise or parts of an exercise in which you are instructed to use a graphing utility.

112. *Erosion* A stream of water moving at the rate of v feet per second can carry particles of size $0.03\sqrt{v}$ inches. Find the size of the largest particle that can be carried by a stream flowing at the rate of $\frac{3}{4}$ foot per second.

113. *Mathematical Modeling* A funnel is filled with water to a height of h centimeters. The time t (in seconds) for the funnel to empty is

$$t = 0.03[12^{5/2} - (12 - h)^{5/2}], \quad 0 \le h \le 12.$$

 (a) Use the *table* feature of a graphing utility to find the times required for the funnel to empty for water heights of $h = 0$, $h = 1$, $h = 2, \ldots$ $h = 12$ centimeters.

  (b) Is there a limiting value of time required for the water to empty as the height of the water becomes closer to 12 centimeters? Explain.

114. *Speed of Light* The speed of light is approximately 11,180,000 miles per minute. The distance from the sun to Earth is approximately 93,000,000 miles. Find the time for light to travel from the sun to Earth.

Synthesis

True or False? In Exercises 115 and 116, determine whether the statement is true or false. Justify your answer.

115. $\dfrac{x^{k+1}}{x} = x^k$ **116.** $(a^n)^k = a^{n^k}$

117. Verify that $a^0 = 1$, $a \ne 0$. (*Hint:* Use the property of exponents $a^m / a^n = a^{m-n}$.)

118. Explain why each of the following pairs is not equal.

  (a) $(3x)^{-1} \ne \dfrac{3}{x}$ (b) $y^3 \cdot y^2 \ne y^6$

  (c) $(a^2 b^3)^4 \ne a^6 b^7$ (d) $(a + b)^2 \ne a^2 + b^2$

  (e) $\sqrt{4x^2} \ne 2x$ (f) $\sqrt{2} + \sqrt{3} \ne \sqrt{5}$

119. *Exploration* List all possible digits that occur in the units place of the square of a positive integer. Use that list to determine whether $\sqrt{5233}$ is an integer.

120. *Think About It* Square the real number $2/\sqrt{5}$ and note that the radical is eliminated from the denominator. Is this equivalent to rationalizing the denominator? Why or why not?

A.3 Polynomials and Factoring

▶ **Why you should learn it**

Polynomials can be used to model and solve real-life problems. For instance, in Exercise 178 on page A34, a polynomial is used to model the stopping distance of an automobile.

Polynomials

The most common type of algebraic expression is the **polynomial.** Some examples are

$$2x + 5, \quad 3x^4 - 7x^2 + 2x + 4, \quad \text{and} \quad 5x^2y^2 - xy + 3.$$

The first two are *polynomials in x* and the third is a *polynomial in x and y*. The terms of a polynomial in x have the form ax^k, where a is the **coefficient** and k is the **degree** of the term. For instance, the polynomial

$$2x^3 - 5x^2 + 1 = 2x^3 + (-5)x^2 + (0)x + 1$$

has coefficients $2, -5, 0,$ and 1.

Definition of Polynomial in x

Let $a_0, a_1, a_2, \ldots, a_n$ be real numbers and let n be a nonnegative integer. A polynomial in x is an expression of the form

$$a_n x^n + a_{n-1} x^{n-1} + \cdots + a_1 x + a_0$$

where $a_n \neq 0$. The polynomial is of **degree** n, a_n is the **leading coefficient,** and a_0 is the **constant term.**

Polynomials with one, two, and three terms are called **monomials, binomials,** and **trinomials,** respectively. In **standard form,** a polynomial is written with descending powers of x.

Example 1 ▶ Writing Polynomials in Standard Form

	Polynomial	*Standard Form*	*Degree*
a.	$4x^2 - 5x^7 - 2 + 3x$	$-5x^7 + 4x^2 + 3x - 2$	7
b.	$4 - 9x^2$	$-9x^2 + 4$	2
c.	8	$8 \ (8 = 8x^0)$	0

A polynomial that has all zero coefficients is called the zero polynomial, denoted by 0. No degree is assigned to this particular polynomial. For polynomials in more than one variable, the degree of a *term* is the sum of the exponents of the variables in the term. The degree of the *polynomial* is the degree of the highest-degree term. The leading coefficient of the polynomial is the coefficient of the highest-degree term. Expressions such as the following are not polynomials.

$$x^3 - \sqrt{3x} = x^3 - (3x)^{1/2} \qquad \text{The exponent "1/2" is not an integer.}$$

$$x^2 + 5x^{-1} \qquad \text{The exponent "}-1\text{" is not a nonnegative integer.}$$

Operations with Polynomials

You can add and subtract polynomials in much the same way you add and subtract real numbers. Simply add or subtract the *like terms* (terms having the same variables to the same powers) by adding their coefficients. For instance, $-3xy^2$ and $5xy^2$ are like terms and their sum is

$$-3xy^2 + 5xy^2 = (-3 + 5)xy^2 = 2xy^2.$$

> **STUDY TIP**
>
> A common mistake is to fail to change the sign of each term inside parentheses preceded by a negative sign. For instance, note that
>
> $$-(x^2 - x + 3)$$
> $$= -x^2 + x - 3$$
>
> and
>
> $$-(x^2 - x + 3)$$
> $$\neq -x^2 - x + 3.$$

Example 2 ▶ **Sums and Differences of Polynomials**

Perform the operation on the polynomials.

a. $(5x^3 - 7x^2 - 3) + (x^3 + 2x^2 - x + 8)$

b. $(7x^4 - x^2 - 4x + 2) - (3x^4 - 4x^2 + 3x)$

Solution

a. $(5x^3 - 7x^2 - 3) + (x^3 + 2x^2 - x + 8)$

$\qquad = (5x^3 + x^3) + (2x^2 - 7x^2) - x + (8 - 3)$ Group like terms.

$\qquad = 6x^3 - 5x^2 - x + 5$ Combine like terms.

b. $(7x^4 - x^2 - 4x + 2) - (3x^4 - 4x^2 + 3x)$

$\qquad = 7x^4 - x^2 - 4x + 2 - 3x^4 + 4x^2 - 3x$ Distributive Property

$\qquad = (7x^4 - 3x^4) + (4x^2 - x^2) + (-3x - 4x) + 2$ Group like terms.

$\qquad = 4x^4 + 3x^2 - 7x + 2$ Combine like terms.

To find the **product** of two polynomials, use the left and right Distributive Properties.

Example 3 ▶ **Multiplying Polynomials: The FOIL Method**

Multiply $(3x - 2)$ by $(5x + 7)$.

Solution

$$(3x - 2)(5x + 7) = 3x(5x + 7) - 2(5x + 7)$$
$$= (3x)(5x) + (3x)(7) - (2)(5x) - (2)(7)$$
$$= 15x^2 + 21x - 10x - 14$$

Product of	Product of	Product of	Product of
First terms	Outer terms	Inner terms	Last terms

$$= 15x^2 + 11x - 14$$

Note that in this **FOIL Method** for binomials, the outer (O) and inner (I) terms are like terms and can be combined.

Special Products

Some binomial products have special forms that occur frequently in algebra.

Special Products

Let u and v be real numbers, variables, or algebraic expressions.

Special Product	*Example*

Sum and Difference of Same Terms

$$(u + v)(u - v) = u^2 - v^2 \qquad (x + 4)(x - 4) = x^2 - 4^2$$
$$= x^2 - 16$$

Square of a Binomial

$$(u + v)^2 = u^2 + 2uv + v^2 \qquad (x + 3)^2 = x^2 + 2(x)(3) + 3^2$$
$$= x^2 + 6x + 9$$

$$(u - v)^2 = u^2 - 2uv + v^2 \qquad (3x - 2)^2 = (3x)^2 - 2(3x)(2) + 2^2$$
$$= 9x^2 - 12x + 4$$

Cube of a Binomial

$$(u + v)^3 = u^3 + 3u^2v + 3uv^2 + v^3 \qquad (x + 2)^3 = x^3 + 3x^2(2) + 3x(2^2) + 2^3$$
$$= x^3 + 6x^2 + 12x + 8$$

$$(u - v)^3 = u^3 - 3u^2v + 3uv^2 - v^3 \qquad (x - 1)^3 = x^3 - 3x^2(1) + 3x(1^2) - 1^3$$
$$= x^3 - 3x^2 + 3x - 1$$

Example 4 ▶ **Multiplying Polynomials: Special Products**

Find each product.

a. $(5x + 9)(5x - 9)$ **b.** $(3x + 2)^3$ **c.** $(x + y - 2)(x + y + 2)$

Solution

a. The product of a sum and a difference of the same two terms has no middle term and takes the form $(u + v)(u - v) = u^2 - v^2$.

$$(5x + 9)(5x - 9) - (5x)^2 \quad 9^?$$
$$= 25x^2 - 81$$

b. $(3x + 2)^3 = (3x)^3 + 3(3x)^2(2) + 3(3x)(2)^2 + 2^3$
$$= 27x^3 + 54x^2 + 36x + 8$$

c. By grouping $x + y$ in parentheses, you can write the product of the trinomials as a special product.

$$(x + y - 2)(x + y + 2) = [(x + y) - 2][(x + y) + 2]$$
$$= (x + y)^2 - 2^2$$
$$= x^2 + 2xy + y^2 - 4$$

Factoring

The process of writing a polynomial as a product is called **factoring.** It is an important tool for solving equations and for simplifying rational expressions.

Unless noted otherwise, when you are asked to factor a polynomial, you can assume that you are looking for factors with integer coefficients. If a polynomial cannot be factored using integer coefficients, then it is **prime** or **irreducible over the integers.** For instance, the polynomial $x^2 - 3$ is irreducible over the integers. Over the *real numbers*, this polynomial can be factored as

$$x^2 - 3 = \left(x + \sqrt{3}\right)\left(x - \sqrt{3}\right).$$

A polynomial is **completely factored** when each of its factors is prime. For instance,

$$x^3 - x^2 + 4x - 4 = (x - 1)(x^2 + 4) \qquad \text{Completely factored}$$

is completely factored, but

$$x^3 - x^2 - 4x + 4 = (x - 1)(x^2 - 4) \qquad \text{Not completely factored}$$

is not completely factored. Its complete factorization is

$$x^3 - x^2 - 4x + 4 = (x - 1)(x + 2)(x - 2).$$

The simplest type of factoring involves a polynomial that can be written as the product of a monomial and another polynomial. The technique used here is the Distributive Property, $a(b + c) = ab + ac$, in the *reverse* direction.

$$ab + ac = a(b + c) \qquad \text{a is a common factor.}$$

Removing (factoring out) a common factor is the first step in completely factoring a polynomial.

Example 5 ▶   **Removing Common Factors**

Factor each expression.

a. $6x^3 - 4x$

b. $-4x^2 + 12x - 16$

c. $(x - 2)(2x) + (x - 2)(3)$

Solution

a. $6x^3 - 4x = 2x(3x^2) - 2x(2) \qquad \text{$2x$ is a common factor.}$

$\qquad\qquad\quad = 2x(3x^2 - 2)$

b. $-4x^2 + 12x - 16 = -4(x^2) + (-4)(-3x) + (-4)4 \qquad \text{-4 is a common factor.}$

$\qquad\qquad\qquad\qquad\quad = -4(x^2 - 3x + 4)$

c. $(x - 2)(2x) + (x - 2)(3) = (x - 2)(2x + 3) \qquad \text{$x - 2$ is a common factor.}$

Factoring Special Polynomial Forms

Some polynomials have special forms that you should learn to recognize so that you can factor such polynomials easily.

Factoring Special Polynomial Forms

Factored Form	*Example*

Difference of Two Squares

$$u^2 - v^2 = (u + v)(u - v)$$

$$9x^2 - 4 = (3x)^2 - 2^2 = (3x + 2)(3x - 2)$$

Perfect Square Trinomial

$$u^2 + 2uv + v^2 = (u + v)^2$$

$$x^2 + 6x + 9 = x^2 + 2(x)(3) + 3^2 = (x + 3)^2$$

$$u^2 - 2uv + v^2 = (u - v)^2$$

$$x^2 - 6x + 9 = x^2 - 2(x)(3) + 3^2 = (x - 3)^2$$

Sum or Difference of Two Cubes

$$u^3 + v^3 = (u + v)(u^2 - uv + v^2)$$

$$x^3 + 8 = x^3 + 2^3 = (x + 2)(x^2 - 2x + 4)$$

$$u^3 - v^3 = (u - v)(u^2 + uv + v^2)$$

$$27x^3 - 1 = (3x)^3 - 1^3 = (3x - 1)(9x^2 + 3x + 1)$$

One of the easiest special polynomial forms to factor is the difference of two squares. Think of this form as follows.

$$u^2 - v^2 = (u + v)(u - v)$$

↑   ↑   ↑

Difference   Opposite signs

To recognize perfect square terms, look for coefficients that are squares of integers and variables raised to *even powers*.

STUDY TIP

In Example 6, note that the first step in factoring a polynomial is to check for a common factor. Once the common factor has been removed, it is often possible to recognize patterns that were not immediately obvious.

Example 6 ▶ **Removing a Common Factor First**

Factor $3 - 12x^2$.

Solution

$$3 - 12x^2 = 3(1 - 4x^2) \qquad \text{3 is a common factor.}$$

$$= 3[1^2 - (2x)^2]$$

$$= 3(1 + 2x)(1 - 2x) \qquad \text{Difference of two squares}$$

Example 7 ▶ **Factoring the Difference of Two Squares**

a. $(x + 2)^2 - y^2 = [(x + 2) + y][(x + 2) - y] = (x + 2 + y)(x + 2 - y)$

b. $16x^4 - 81 = (4x^2)^2 - 9^2$

$$= (4x^2 + 9)(4x^2 - 9) \qquad \text{Difference of two squares}$$

$$= (4x^2 + 9)[(2x)^2 - 3^2]$$

$$= (4x^2 + 9)(2x + 3)(2x - 3) \qquad \text{Difference of two squares}$$

A perfect square trinomial is the square of a binomial, and it has the following form.

$$u^2 + 2uv + v^2 = (u + v)^2 \qquad \text{or} \qquad u^2 - 2uv + v^2 = (u - v)^2$$

Like signs   Like signs

Note that the first and last terms are squares and the middle term is twice the product of u and v.

Example 8 ▶   **Factoring Perfect Square Trinomials**

Factor each trinomial.

a. $x^2 - 10x + 25$ **b.** $16x^2 + 8x + 1$

Solution

a. $x^2 - 10x + 25 = x^2 - 2(x)(5) + 5^2$

$$= (x - 5)^2$$

b. $16x^2 + 8x + 1 = (4x)^2 + 2(4x)(1) + 1^2$

$$= (4x + 1)^2$$

The next two formulas show the sums and differences of cubes. Pay special attention to the signs of the terms.

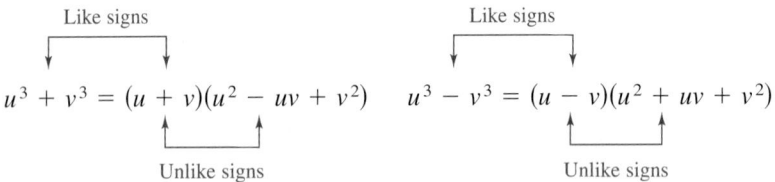

Like signs   Like signs

$$u^3 + v^3 = (u + v)(u^2 - uv + v^2) \qquad u^3 - v^3 = (u - v)(u^2 + uv + v^2)$$

Unlike signs   Unlike signs

Example 9 ▶   **Factoring the Difference of Cubes**

Factor $x^3 - 27$.

Solution

$x^3 - 27 = x^3 - 3^3$	Rewrite 27 as 3^3.
$= (x - 3)(x^2 + 3x + 9)$	Factor.

Example 10 ▶   **Factoring the Sum of Cubes**

a. $y^3 + 8 = y^3 + 2^3$	Rewrite 8 as 2^3.
$= (y + 2)(y^2 - 2y + 4)$	Factor.
b. $3(x^3 + 64) = 3(x^3 + 4^3)$	Rewrite 64 as 4^3.
$= 3(x + 4)(x^2 - 4x + 16)$	Factor.

Trinomials with Binomial Factors

To factor a trinomial of the form $ax^2 + bx + c$, use the following pattern.

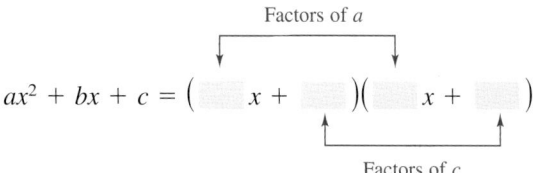

The goal is to find a combination of factors of a and c such that the outer and inner products add up to the middle term bx. For instance, in the trinomial $6x^2 + 17x + 5$, you can write

$$(2x + 5)(3x + 1) = 6x^2 + 2x + 15x + 5$$

$$= 6x^2 + 17x + 5.$$

Note that the outer (O) and inner (I) products add up to $17x$.

Example 11 ▶ **Factoring a Trinomial: Leading Coefficient Is 1**

Factor $x^2 - 7x + 12$.

Solution

The possible factorizations are

$$(x - 2)(x - 6), \quad (x - 1)(x - 12), \quad \text{and} \quad (x - 3)(x - 4).$$

Testing the middle term, you will find the correct factorization to be

$$x^2 - 7x + 12 = (x - 3)(x - 4).$$

Example 12 ▶ **Factoring a Trinomial: Leading Coefficient Is Not 1**

Factor $2x^2 + x - 15$.

Solution

The eight possible factorizations are as follows.

$$(2x - 1)(x + 15) \qquad (2x + 1)(x - 15)$$
$$(2x - 3)(x + 5) \qquad (2x + 3)(x - 5)$$
$$(2x - 5)(x + 3) \qquad (2x + 5)(x - 3)$$
$$(2x - 15)(x + 1) \qquad (2x + 15)(x - 1)$$

Testing the middle term, you will find the correct factorization to be

$$2x^2 + x - 15 = (2x - 5)(x + 3). \qquad \text{O + I} = 6x - 5x = x$$

STUDY TIP

If the original trinomial has no common monomial factor, its binomial factors cannot have common monomial factors. For instance, when factoring $4x^2 - 3x - 10$, you do not have to test factors, such as $(2x - 2)$, that have a common factor of 2.

Factoring by Grouping

Sometimes polynomials with more than three terms can be factored by a method called **factoring by grouping.** It is not always obvious which terms to group, and sometimes several different groupings will work.

Example 13 ▶ Factoring By Grouping

Use factoring by grouping to factor $x^3 - 2x^2 - 3x + 6$.

Solution

$$x^3 - 2x^2 - 3x + 6 = (x^3 - 2x^2) - (3x - 6) \qquad \text{Group terms.}$$
$$= x^2(x - 2) - 3(x - 2) \qquad \text{Factor groups.}$$
$$= (x - 2)(x^2 - 3) \qquad \text{Distributive Property}$$

STUDY TIP

Another way to factor the polynomial in Example 13 is to group the terms as follows.

$$x^3 - 2x^2 - 3x + 6$$
$$= (x^3 - 3x) - (2x^2 - 6)$$
$$= x(x^2 - 3) - 2(x^2 - 3)$$
$$= (x^2 - 3)(x - 2)$$

As you can see, you obtain the same result as in Example 13.

Factoring a trinomial can involve quite a bit of trial and error. Some of this trial and error can be lessened by using factoring by grouping. The key to this method of factoring is knowing how to rewrite the middle term. In general, to factor a trinomial $ax^2 + bx + c$ by grouping, choose factors of the product ac that add up to b and use these factors to rewrite the middle term. This technique is illustrated in Example 14.

Example 14 ▶ Factoring a Trinomial By Grouping

Use factoring by grouping to factor $2x^2 + 5x - 3$.

Solution

In the trinomial $2x^2 + 5x - 3$, $a = 2$ and $c = -3$, which implies that the product ac is -6. Now, -6 factors as $(6)(-1)$ and $6 - 1 = 5 = b$. So, you can rewrite the middle term as $5x = 6x - x$. This produces the following.

$$2x^2 + 5x - 3 = 2x^2 + 6x - x - 3 \qquad \text{Rewrite middle term.}$$
$$= (2x^2 + 6x) - (x + 3) \qquad \text{Group terms.}$$
$$= 2x(x + 3) - (x + 3) \qquad \text{Factor groups.}$$
$$= (x + 3)(2x - 1) \qquad \text{Distributive Property}$$

So, the trinomial factors as $2x^2 + 5x - 3 = (x + 3)(2x - 1)$.

Guidelines for Factoring Polynomials

1. Factor out any common factors using the Distributive Property.

2. Factor according to one of the special polynomial forms.

3. Factor as $ax^2 + bx + c = (mx + r)(nx + s)$.

4. Factor by grouping.

A.3 Exercises

In Exercises 1–6, match the polynomial with its description. [The polynomials are labeled (a), (b), (c), (d), (e), and (f).]

(a) $3x^2$ (b) $1 - 2x^3$

(c) $x^3 + 3x^2 + 3x + 1$ (d) 12

(e) $-3x^5 + 2x^3 + x$ (f) $\frac{2}{3}x^4 + x^2 + 10$

1. A polynomial of degree 0

2. A trinomial of degree 5

3. A binomial with leading coefficient -2

4. A monomial of positive degree

5. A trinomial with leading coefficient $\frac{2}{3}$

6. A third-degree polynomial with leading coefficient 1

In Exercises 7–10, write a polynomial that fits the description. (There are many correct answers.)

7. A third-degree polynomial with leading coefficient -2

8. A fifth-degree polynomial with leading coefficient 6

9. A fourth-degree binomial with a negative leading coefficient

10. A third-degree binomial with an even leading coefficient

In Exercises 11–16, find the degree and leading coefficient of the polynomial.

11. $3 + 2x$ 12. $-3x^4 + 2x^2 - 5$

13. $1 - x + 6x^4 - 4x^5$

14. 3

15. $4x^3y - 3xy^2 + x^2y^3$

16. $-x^5y + 2x^2y^2 + xy^4$

In Exercises 17–22, is the expression a polynomial? If so, write the polynomial in standard form.

17. $2x - 3x^3 + 8$ 18. $2x^3 + x - 3x^{-1}$

19. $\dfrac{3x + 4}{x}$ 20. $\dfrac{x^2 + 2x - 3}{2}$

21. $y^2 - y^4 + y^3$ 22. $\sqrt{y^2 - y^4}$

In Exercises 23–38, perform the operation and write the result in standard form.

23. $(2x^2 + 1) - (x^2 - 2x + 1)$

24. $-(5x^2 - 1) - (-3x^2 + 5)$

25. $(15x^2 - 6) - (-8.3x^3 - 14.7x^2 - 17)$

26. $(15.2x^4 - 18x - 19.1) - (13.9x^4 - 9.6x + 15)$

27. $5z - [3z - (10z + 8)]$

28. $(y^3 + 1) - [(y^2 + 1) + (3y - 7)]$

29. $3x(x^2 - 2x + 1)$

30. $y^2(4y^2 + 2y - 3)$

31. $-5z(3z - 1)$

32. $(-3x)(5x + 2)$

33. $(1 - x^3)(4x)$

34. $-4x(3 - x^3)$

35. $(2.5x^2 + 3)(3x)$

36. $(2 - 3.5y)(2y^3)$

37. $-4x\left(\frac{1}{8}x + 3\right)$

38. $2y\left(4 - \frac{7}{8}y\right)$

In Exercises 39–72, multiply or find the special product.

39. $(x + 3)(x + 4)$ 40. $(x - 5)(x + 10)$

41. $(3x - 5)(2x + 1)$ 42. $(7x - 2)(4x - 3)$

43. $(2x + 3)^2$ 44. $(4x + 5)^2$

45. $(2x - 5y)^2$ 46. $(5 - 8x)^2$

47. $(x + 10)(x - 10)$

48. $(2x + 3)(2x - 3)$

49. $(x + 2y)(x - 2y)$

50. $(2x + 3y)(2x - 3y)$

51. $[(m - 3) + n][(m - 3) - n]$

52. $[(x + y) + 1][(x + y) - 1]$

53. $[(x - 3) + y]^2$ 54. $[(x + 1) - y]^2$

55. $(2r^2 - 5)(2r^2 + 5)$

56. $(3a^3 - 4b^2)(3a^3 + 4b^2)$

57. $(x + 1)^3$ 58. $(x - 2)^3$

59. $(2x - y)^3$ 60. $(4x^3 - 3)^2$

61. $\left(\frac{1}{2}x - 3\right)^2$ 62. $\left(\frac{2}{3}t + 5\right)^2$

63. $\left(\frac{1}{3}x - 2\right)\left(\frac{1}{3}x + 2\right)$ 64. $\left(2x + \frac{1}{5}\right)\left(2x - \frac{1}{5}\right)$

65. $(1.2x + 3)^2$ 66. $(1.5y - 3)^2$

67. $(1.5x - 4)(1.5x + 4)$

68. $(2.5y + 3)(2.5y - 3)$

69. $5x(x + 1) - 3x(x + 1)$

70. $(2x - 1)(x + 3) + 3(x + 3)$

71. $(u + 2)(u - 2)(u^2 + 4)$

72. $(x + y)(x - y)(x^2 + y^2)$

In Exercises 73–76, find the product. The expressions are not polynomials, but the formulas can still be used.

73. $\left(\sqrt{x} + \sqrt{y}\right)\left(\sqrt{x} - \sqrt{y}\right)$

74. $\left(5 + \sqrt{x}\right)\left(5 - \sqrt{x}\right)$

75. $\left(x - \sqrt{5}\right)^2$

76. $\left(x + \sqrt{3}\right)^2$

In Exercises 77–80, determine whether the polynomial is completely factored. If not, give the complete factorization.

77. $x^3 + 2x^2 + x + 2 = (x + 2)(x^2 + 1)$

78. $x^3 + 3x^2 - 9x - 27 = (x + 3)(x^2 - 9)$

79. $x^3 + x^2 - 7x - 7 = (x^2 - 7)(x + 1)$

80. $4x^4 + 12x^3 - x^2 - 3x = (x^2 + 3x)(4x^2 - 1)$

In Exercises 81–88, factor out the common factor.

81. $3x + 6$

82. $5y - 30$

83. $2x^3 - 6x$

84. $4x^3 - 6x^2 + 12x$

85. $x(x - 1) + 6(x - 1)$

86. $3x(x + 2) - 4(x + 2)$

87. $(x + 3)^2 - 4(x + 3)$

88. $(3x - 1)^2 + (3x - 1)$

In Exercises 89–92, find the greatest common factor such that the remaining factors have only integer coefficients.

89. $\frac{1}{2}x^3 + 2x^2 - 5x$

90. $\frac{1}{3}y^4 - 5y^2 + 2y$

91. $\frac{2}{3}x(x - 3) - 4(x - 3)$

92. $\frac{4}{5}y(y + 1) - 2(y + 1)$

In Exercises 93–100, factor the difference of two squares.

93. $16y^2 - 9$

94. $49 - 9y^2$

95. $16x^2 - \frac{1}{9}$

96. $\frac{4}{25}y^2 - 64$

97. $(x - 1)^2 - 4$

98. $25 - (z + 5)^2$

99. $9u^2 - 4v^2$

100. $25x^2 - 16y^2$

In Exercises 101–108, factor the perfect square trinomial.

101. $x^2 - 4x + 4$

102. $x^2 + 10x + 25$

103. $36y^2 - 108y + 81$

104. $9x^2 - 12x + 4$

105. $9u^2 + 24uv + 16v^2$

106. $4x^2 - 4xy + y^2$

107. $x^2 - \frac{4}{3}x + \frac{4}{9}$

108. $z^2 + z + \frac{1}{4}$

In Exercises 109–116, factor the sum or difference of cubes.

109. $x^3 - 8$

110. $x^3 - 27$

111. $y^3 + 64$

112. $z^3 + 125$

113. $8t^3 - 1$

114. $27x^3 + 8$

115. $u^3 + 27v^3$

116. $64x^3 - y^3$

In Exercises 117–128, factor the trinomial.

117. $x^2 + x - 2$

118. $x^2 + 5x + 6$

119. $s^2 - 5s + 6$

120. $t^2 - t - 6$

121. $20 - y - y^2$

122. $24 + 5z - z^2$

123. $3x^2 - 5x + 2$

124. $2x^2 - x - 1$

125. $5x^2 + 26x + 5$

126. $12x^2 + 7x + 1$

127. $-9z^2 + 3z + 2$

128. $-5u^2 - 13u + 6$

In Exercises 129–134, factor by grouping.

129. $x^3 - x^2 + 2x - 2$

130. $x^3 + 5x^2 - 5x - 25$

131. $2x^3 - x^2 - 6x + 3$

132. $6 + 2x - 3x^3 - x^4$

133. $6x^3 - 2x + 3x^2 - 1$

134. $8x^5 - 6x^2 + 12x^3 - 9$

In Exercises 135–138, factor the trinomial by grouping.

135. $3x^2 + 10x + 8$

136. $2x^2 + 9x + 9$

137. $15x^2 - 11x + 2$

138. $12x^2 - 13x + 1$

In Exercises 139–160, completely factor the expression.

139. $6x^2 - 54$

140. $12x^2 - 48$

141. $x^3 - 4x^2$

142. $x^3 - 9x$

143. $2x^2 + 4x - 2x^3$

144. $2y^3 - 7y^2 - 15y$

145. $3x^3 + x^2 + 15x + 5$

146. $13x + 6 + 5x^2$

147. $\frac{1}{81}x^2 + \frac{2}{9}x - 8$

148. $\frac{1}{8}x^2 - \frac{1}{96}x - \frac{1}{16}$

149. $x^4 - 4x^3 + x^2 - 4x$

150. $3u - 2u^2 + 6 - u^3$

151. $(x^2 + 1)^2 - 4x^2$

152. $(x^2 + 8)^2 - 36x^2$

153. $2t^3 - 16$

154. $5x^3 + 40$

155. $4x(2x - 1) + (2x - 1)^2$

156. $5(3 - 4x)^2 - 8(3 - 4x)(5x - 1)$

157. $7(3x + 2)^2(1 - x)^2 + (3x + 2)(1 - x)^3$

158. $7x(2)(x^2 + 1)(2x) - (x^2 + 1)^2(7)$

159. $3(x - 2)^2(x + 1)^4 + (x - 2)^3(4)(x + 1)^3$

160. $5(x^6 + 1)^4(6x^5)(3x + 2)^3 + 3(3x + 2)^2(3)(x^6 + 1)^5$

In Exercises 161–164, find all values of *b* for which the trinomial can be factored.

161. $x^2 + bx - 15$

162. $x^2 + bx + 50$

163. $x^2 + bx - 12$

164. $x^2 + bx + 24$

In Exercises 165–168, find two integer values of *c* such that the trinomial can be factored. (There are many correct answers.)

165. $2x^2 + 5x + c$

166. $3x^2 - 10x + c$

167. $3x^2 - x + c$

168. $2x^2 + 9x + c$

169. *Cost, Revenue, and Profit*   An electronics manufacturer can produce and sell x radios per week. The total cost C (in dollars) for producing x radios is

$$C = 73x + 25{,}000$$

and the total revenue R (in dollars) is

$$R = 95x.$$

Find the profit P obtained by selling 5000 radios per week.

170. *Cost, Revenue, and Profit*   An artist can produce and sell x craft items per month. The total cost C (in dollars) for producing x craft items is

$$C = 460 + 12x$$

and the total revenue R (in dollars) is

$$R = 36x.$$

Find the profit P obtained by selling 42 craft items per month.

171. *Compound Interest*   After 2 years, an investment of $500 compounded annually at an interest rate r will yield an amount of

$$500(1 + r)^2.$$

(a) Write this polynomial in standard form.

(b) Use a calculator to evaluate the polynomial for the values of r in the table.

r	$2\frac{1}{2}\%$	3%	4%	$4\frac{1}{2}\%$	5%
$500(1 + r)^2$					

(c) What conclusion can you make from the table?

172. *Compound Interest*   After 3 years, an investment of $1200 compounded annually at an interest rate r will yield an amount of

$$1200(1 + r)^3.$$

(a) Write this polynomial in standard form.

(b) Use a calculator to evaluate the polynomial for the values of r in the table.

r	2%	3%	$3\frac{1}{2}\%$	4%	$5\frac{1}{2}\%$
$1200(1 + r)^3$					

(c) What conclusion can you make from the table?

173. *Volume of a Box* A take-out fast-food restaurant is constructing an open box by cutting squares from the corners of a piece of cardboard that is 18 centimeters by 26 centimeters (see figure). The edge of each cut-out square is x centimeters. Find the volume when $x = 1$, $x = 2$, and $x = 3$.

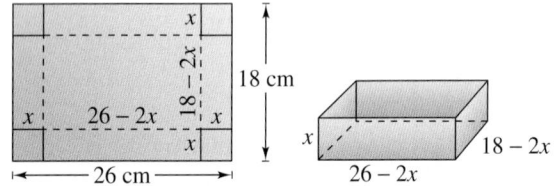

174. *Geometry* Find the area of the shaded region in each figure. Write your result as a polynomial in standard form.

(a)   (b)

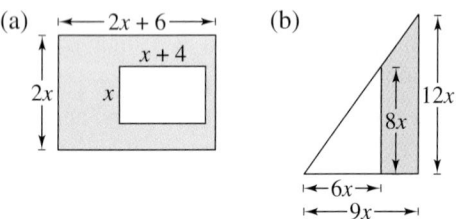

175. *Geometry* Find the area of the shaded region in each figure. Write your result as a polynomial in standard form.

(a)   (b)

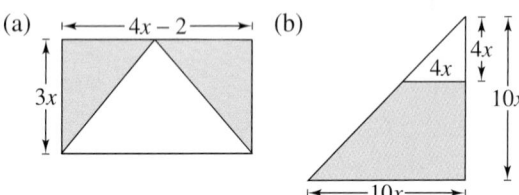

Geometry **In Exercises 176 and 177, find a polynomial that represents the total number of square feet for the floor plan shown in the figure.**

176.

177.

178. *Stopping Distance* The stopping distance of an automobile is the distance traveled during the driver's reaction time plus the distance traveled after the brakes are applied. In an experiment, these distances were measured (in feet) when the automobile was traveling at a speed of x miles per hour on dry, level pavement, as shown in the bar graph. The distance traveled R during the reaction time was

$$R = 1.1x$$

and the braking distance B was

$$B = 0.0475x^2 - 0.001x + 0.23.$$

(a) Determine the polynomial that represents the total stopping distance T.

(b) Use the result of part (a) to estimate the total stopping distance when $x = 30$, $x = 40$, and $x = 55$ miles per hour.

(c) Use the bar graph to make a statement about the total stopping distance required for increasing speeds.

Geometric Modeling   In Exercises 179 and 180, draw a "geometric factoring model" to represent the factorization. For instance, a factoring model for

$$2x^2 + 3x + 1 = (2x + 1)(x + 1)$$

is shown in the figure.

179. $3x^2 + 7x + 2 = (3x + 1)(x + 2)$
180. $2x^2 + 7x + 3 = (2x + 1)(x + 3)$

Geometry   In Exercises 181–184, write an expression in factored form for the area of the shaded portion of the figure.

181.

182.

183.

184.

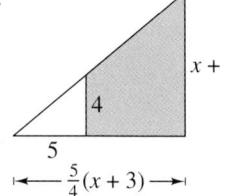

185. *Geometry*   The volume V of concrete used to make the cylindrical concrete storage tank shown in the figure is

$$V = \pi R^2 h - \pi r^2 h.$$

(a) Factor the expression for the volume.

(b) From the result of part (a), show that the volume of concrete is

$$2\pi \ (\text{average radius})(\text{thickness of the tank})h.$$

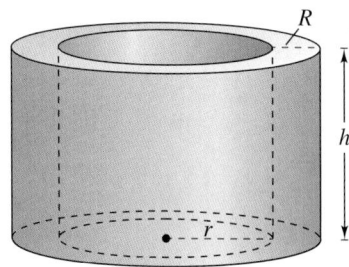

FIGURE FOR 185

186. *Chemistry*   The rate of change of an autocatalytic chemical reaction is $kQx - kx^2$, where Q is the amount of the original substance, x is the amount of substance formed, and k is a constant of proportionality. Factor the expression.

Synthesis

True or False?   In Exercises 187–190, determine whether the statement is true or false. Justify your answer.

187. The product of two binomials is always a second-degree polynomial.

188. The sum of two binomials is always a binomial.

189. The difference of two perfect squares can be factored as the product of conjugate pairs.

190. The sum of two perfect squares can be factored as the binomial sum squared.

191. Find the degree of the product of two polynomials of degrees m and n.

192. Find the degree of the sum of two polynomials of degrees m and n if $m < n$.

193. *Logical Reasoning*   Verify that $(x + y)^2$ is not equal to $x^2 + y^2$ by letting $x = 3$ and $y = 4$ and evaluating both expressions. Are there any values of x or y for which $(x + y)^2 = x^2 + y^2$? Explain.

194. *Pattern Recognition*   Perform each multiplication.

(a) $(x - 1)(x + 1)$

(b) $(x - 1)(x^2 + x + 1)$

(c) $(x - 1)(x^3 + x^2 + x + 1)$

From the pattern formed by these products, can you predict the result of $(x - 1)(x^4 + x^3 + x^2 + x + 1)$?

195. Factor $x^{2n} - y^{2n}$ completely.

196. Factor $x^{3n} + y^{3n}$ completely.

197. Factor $x^{3n} - y^{2n}$ completely.

A.4   Rational Expressions

▶ **What you should learn**

- How to find domains of algebraic expressions
- How to simplify rational expressions
- How to add, subtract, multiply, and divide rational expressions
- How to simplify complex fractions

▶ **Why you should learn it**

Rational expressions can be used to solve real-life problems. For instance, in Exercise 78 on page A45, a rational expression is used to model the cost per ounce of precious metals from 1994 through 1999.

Domain of an Algebraic Expression

The set of real numbers for which an algebraic expression is defined is the **domain** of the expression. Two algebraic expressions are **equivalent** if they have the same domain and yield the same values for all numbers in their domain. For instance, $(x + 1) + (x + 2)$ and $2x + 3$ are equivalent because

$$(x + 1) + (x + 2) = x + 1 + x + 2$$
$$= x + x + 1 + 2$$
$$= 2x + 3.$$

Example 1 ▶   Finding the Domain of an Algebraic Expression

a. The domain of the polynomial

$$2x^3 + 3x + 4$$

is the set of all real numbers. In fact, the domain of any polynomial is the set of all real numbers, unless the domain is specifically restricted.

b. The domain of the radical expression

$$\sqrt{x - 2}$$

is the set of real numbers greater than or equal to 2, because the square root of a negative number is not a real number.

c. The domain of the expression

$$\frac{x + 2}{x - 3}$$

is the set of all real numbers except $x = 3$, which would produce an undefined division by zero.

The quotient of two algebraic expressions is a *fractional expression*. Moreover, the quotient of two *polynomials* such as

$$\frac{1}{x}, \qquad \frac{2x - 1}{x + 1}, \qquad \text{or} \qquad \frac{x^2 - 1}{x^2 + 1}$$

is a **rational expression.** Recall that a fraction is in simplest form if its numerator and denominator have no factors in common aside from ±1. To write a fraction in simplest form, divide out common factors.

$$\frac{a \cdot \cancel{c}}{b \cdot \cancel{c}} = \frac{a}{b}, \quad c \neq 0$$

The key to success in simplifying rational expressions lies in your ability to *factor* polynomials.

Simplifying Rational Expressions

When simplifying rational expressions, be sure to factor each polynomial completely before concluding that the numerator and denominator have no factors in common.

> **Example 2** ▶ Simplifying a Rational Expression
>
> Write $\dfrac{x^2 + 4x - 12}{3x - 6}$ in simplest form.
>
> **Solution**
>
> $$\dfrac{x^2 + 4x - 12}{3x - 6} = \dfrac{(x + 6)(x - 2)}{3(x - 2)}$$ Factor completely.
>
> $$= \dfrac{x + 6}{3}, \qquad x \neq 2$$ Divide out common factors.
>
> Note that the original expression is undefined when $x = 2$ (because division by zero is undefined). To make sure that the simplified expression is *equivalent* to the original expression, you must restrict the domain of the simplified expression by excluding the value $x = 2$.

Sometimes it may be necessary to change the sign of a factor to simplify a rational expression, as shown in Example 3(b).

> **Example 3** ▶ Simplifying Rational Expressions
>
> Write each expression in simplest form.
>
> **a.** $\dfrac{x^3 - 4x}{x^2 + x - 2}$ **b.** $\dfrac{12 + x - x^2}{2x^2 - 9x + 4}$
>
> **Solution**
>
> **a.** $\dfrac{x^3 - 4x}{x^2 + x - 2} = \dfrac{x(x^2 - 4)}{(x + 2)(x - 1)}$
>
> $$= \dfrac{x(x + 2)(x - 2)}{(x + 2)(x - 1)}$$ Factor completely.
>
> $$= \dfrac{x(x - 2)}{(x - 1)}, \qquad x \neq -2$$ Divide out common factors.
>
> **b.** $\dfrac{12 + x - x^2}{2x^2 - 9x + 4} = \dfrac{(4 - x)(3 + x)}{(2x - 1)(x - 4)}$ Factor completely.
>
> $$= \dfrac{-(x - 4)(3 + x)}{(2x - 1)(x - 4)}$$ $(4 - x) = -(x - 4)$
>
> $$= -\dfrac{3 + x}{2x - 1}, \qquad x \neq 4$$ Divide out common factors.

Operations with Rational Expressions

To multiply or divide rational expressions, use the properties of fractions discussed in Section A.1. Recall that to divide fractions, you invert the divisor and multiply.

Example 4 ▶ **Multiplying Rational Expressions**

$$\frac{2x^2 + x - 6}{x^2 + 4x - 5} \cdot \frac{x^3 - 3x^2 + 2x}{4x^2 - 6x} = \frac{(2x - 3)(x + 2)}{(x + 5)(x - 1)} \cdot \frac{x(x - 2)(x - 1)}{2x(2x - 3)}$$

$$= \frac{(x + 2)(x - 2)}{2(x + 5)}, \qquad x \neq 0, x \neq 1, x \neq \tfrac{3}{2}$$

In this text, when performing operations with rational expressions, the convention of listing *by the simplified expression* all values of x that must be specifically excluded from the domain in order to make the domains of the simplified and original expressions agree is followed. In Example 4, for instance, the restrictions $x \neq 0$, $x \neq 1$, and $x \neq \tfrac{3}{2}$ are listed with the simplified expression in order to make the two domains agree. Note that the value $x = -5$ is excluded from both domains, so it is not necessary to list this value.

Example 5 ▶ **Dividing Rational Expressions**

$$\frac{x^3 - 8}{x^2 - 4} \div \frac{x^2 + 2x + 4}{x^3 + 8} = \frac{x^3 - 8}{x^2 - 4} \cdot \frac{x^3 + 8}{x^2 + 2x + 4} \qquad \text{Invert and multiply.}$$

$$= \frac{(x - 2)(x^2 + 2x + 4)}{(x + 2)(x - 2)} \cdot \frac{(x + 2)(x^2 - 2x + 4)}{x^2 + 2x + 4}$$

$$= x^2 - 2x + 4, \qquad x \neq \pm 2 \qquad \begin{array}{l}\text{Divide out} \\ \text{common factors.}\end{array}$$

To add or subtract rational expressions, you can use the LCD (least common denominator) method or the basic definition

$$\frac{a}{b} \pm \frac{c}{d} = \frac{ad \pm bc}{bd}, \qquad b \neq 0, d \neq 0. \qquad \text{Basic definition}$$

This definition provides an efficient way of adding or subtracting *two* fractions that have no common factors in their denominators.

Example 6 ▶ **Subtracting Rational Expressions**

$$\frac{x}{x - 3} - \frac{2}{3x + 4} = \frac{x(3x + 4) - 2(x - 3)}{(x - 3)(3x + 4)} \qquad \text{Basic definition}$$

$$= \frac{3x^2 + 4x - 2x + 6}{(x - 3)(3x + 4)} \qquad \text{Distributive Property}$$

$$= \frac{3x^2 + 2x + 6}{(x - 3)(3x + 4)} \qquad \text{Combine like terms.}$$

For three or more fractions, or for fractions with a repeated factor in the denominators, the LCD method works well. Recall that the least common denominator of several fractions consists of the product of all prime factors in the denominators, with each factor given the highest power of its occurrence in any denominator. Here is a numerical example.

$$\frac{1}{6}+\frac{3}{4}-\frac{2}{3}=\frac{1\cdot 2}{6\cdot 2}+\frac{3\cdot 3}{4\cdot 3}-\frac{2\cdot 4}{3\cdot 4}$$ The LCD is 12.

$$=\frac{2}{12}+\frac{9}{12}-\frac{8}{12}$$

$$=\frac{3}{12}$$

$$=\frac{1}{4}$$

Sometimes the numerator of the answer has a factor in common with the denominator. In such cases the answer should be simplified. For instance, in the example above, $\frac{3}{12}$ was simplified to $\frac{1}{4}$.

Example 7 ▶ Combining Rational Expressions: The LCD Method

Perform the operations and simplify.

$$\frac{3}{x-1}-\frac{2}{x}+\frac{x+3}{x^2-1}$$

Solution

Using the factored denominators $(x-1)$, x, and $(x+1)(x-1)$, you can see that the LCD is $x(x+1)(x-1)$.

$$\frac{3}{x-1}-\frac{2}{x}+\frac{x+3}{(x+1)(x-1)}$$

$$=\frac{3(x)(x+1)}{x(x+1)(x-1)}-\frac{2(x+1)(x-1)}{x(x+1)(x-1)}+\frac{(x+3)(x)}{x(x+1)(x-1)}$$

$$=\frac{3(x)(x+1)-2(x+1)(x-1)+(x+3)(x)}{x(x+1)(x-1)}$$

$$=\frac{3x^2+3x-2x^2+2+x^2+3x}{x(x+1)(x-1)}$$ Distributive Property

$$=\frac{3x^2-2x^2+x^2+3x+3x+2}{x(x+1)(x-1)}$$ Group like terms.

$$=\frac{2x^2+6x+2}{x(x+1)(x-1)}$$ Combine like terms.

$$=\frac{2(x^2+3x+1)}{x(x+1)(x-1)}$$ Factor.

Complex Fractions

Fractional expressions with separate fractions in the numerator, denominator, or both are called **complex fractions.** Here are two examples.

$$\frac{\left(\dfrac{1}{x}\right)}{x^2+1} \quad \text{and} \quad \frac{\left(\dfrac{1}{x}\right)}{\left(\dfrac{1}{x^2+1}\right)}$$

A complex fraction can be simplified by combining the fractions in its numerator into a single fraction and then combining the fractions in its denominator into a single fraction. Then invert the denominator and multiply.

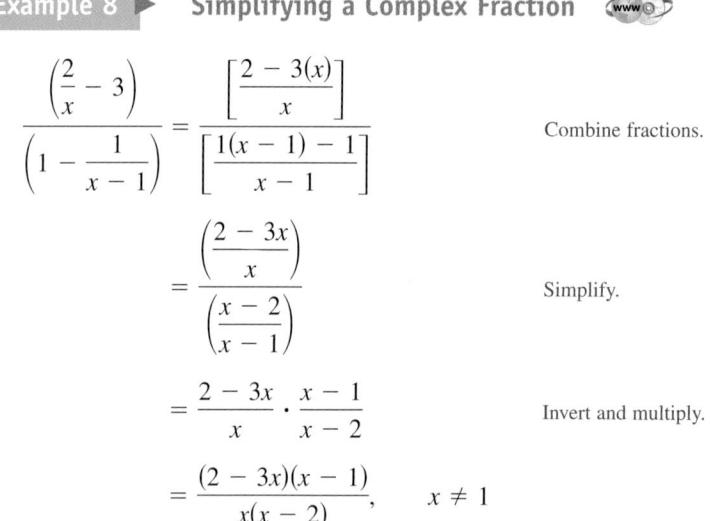

Example 8 ▶ Simplifying a Complex Fraction

$$\frac{\left(\dfrac{2}{x}-3\right)}{\left(1-\dfrac{1}{x-1}\right)} = \frac{\left[\dfrac{2-3(x)}{x}\right]}{\left[\dfrac{1(x-1)-1}{x-1}\right]} \qquad \text{Combine fractions.}$$

$$= \frac{\left(\dfrac{2-3x}{x}\right)}{\left(\dfrac{x-2}{x-1}\right)} \qquad \text{Simplify.}$$

$$= \frac{2-3x}{x} \cdot \frac{x-1}{x-2} \qquad \text{Invert and multiply.}$$

$$= \frac{(2-3x)(x-1)}{x(x-2)}, \qquad x \neq 1$$

Another way to simplify a complex fraction is to multiply its numerator and denominator by the LCD of all fractions in its numerator and denominator. This method is applied to the fraction in Example 8 as follows.

$$\frac{\left(\dfrac{2}{x}-3\right)}{\left(1-\dfrac{1}{x-1}\right)} = \frac{\left(\dfrac{2}{x}-3\right)}{\left(1-\dfrac{1}{x-1}\right)} \cdot \frac{x(x-1)}{x(x-1)} \qquad \text{LCD is } x(x-1).$$

$$= \frac{\left(\dfrac{2-3x}{x}\right) \cdot x(x-1)}{\left(\dfrac{x-2}{x-1}\right) \cdot x(x-1)}$$

$$= \frac{(2-3x)(x-1)}{x(x-2)}, \qquad x \neq 1$$

The next three examples illustrate some methods for simplifying rational expressions involving negative exponents and radicals. These types of expressions occur frequently in calculus.

To simplify an expression with negative exponents, one method is to begin by factoring out the common factor with the smaller exponent. Remember that when factoring, you subtract exponents. For instance, in $3x^{-5/2} + 2x^{-3/2}$ the smaller exponent is $-\frac{5}{2}$ and the common factor is $x^{-5/2}$.

$$3x^{-5/2} + 2x^{-3/2} = x^{-5/2}[3(1) + 2x^{-3/2-(-5/2)}]$$

$$= x^{-5/2}(3 + 2x^1)$$

$$= \frac{3 + 2x}{x^{5/2}}$$

Example 9 ▶ **Simplifying an Expression**

Simplify the following expression containing negative exponents.

$$x(1 - 2x)^{-3/2} + (1 - 2x)^{-1/2}$$

Solution

Begin by factoring out the common factor with the *smaller exponent*.

$$x(1 - 2x)^{-3/2} + (1 - 2x)^{-1/2} = (1 - 2x)^{-3/2}[x + (1 - 2x)^{(-1/2)-(-3/2)}]$$

$$= (1 - 2x)^{-3/2}[x + (1 - 2x)^1]$$

$$= \frac{1 - x}{(1 - 2x)^{3/2}}$$

A second method for simplifying an expression with negative exponents is shown in the next example.

Example 10 ▶ **Simplifying a Complex Fraction**

$$\frac{(4 - x^2)^{1/2} + x^2(4 - x^2)^{-1/2}}{4 - x^2}$$

$$= \frac{(4 - x^2)^{1/2} + x^2(4 - x^2)^{-1/2}}{4 - x^2} \cdot \frac{(4 - x^2)^{1/2}}{(4 - x^2)^{1/2}}$$

$$= \frac{(4 - x^2)^1 + x^2(4 - x^2)^0}{(4 - x^2)^{3/2}}$$

$$= \frac{4 - x^2 + x^2}{(4 - x^2)^{3/2}}$$

$$= \frac{4}{(4 - x^2)^{3/2}}$$

| Example 11 ▶ | Rewriting a Difference Quotient | |

The expression from calculus

$$\frac{\sqrt{x + h} - \sqrt{x}}{h}$$

is an example of a *difference quotient*. Rewrite this expression by rationalizing its numerator.

Solution

$$\frac{\sqrt{x + h} - \sqrt{x}}{h} = \frac{\sqrt{x + h} - \sqrt{x}}{h} \cdot \frac{\sqrt{x + h} + \sqrt{x}}{\sqrt{x + h} + \sqrt{x}}$$

$$= \frac{\left(\sqrt{x + h}\right)^2 - \left(\sqrt{x}\right)^2}{h\left(\sqrt{x + h} + \sqrt{x}\right)}$$

$$= \frac{h}{h\left(\sqrt{x + h} + \sqrt{x}\right)}$$

$$= \frac{1}{\sqrt{x + h} + \sqrt{x}}, \qquad h \neq 0$$

Notice that the original expression is undefined when $h = 0$. So, you must exclude $h = 0$ from the domain of the simplified expression so that the expressions are equivalent.

Difference quotients, such as that in Example 11, occur frequently in calculus. Often, they need to be rewritten in an equivalent form that can be evaluated when $h = 0$. Note that the equivalent form is not simpler than the original form, but it has the advantage that it is defined when $h = 0$.

A.4 Exercises

In Exercises 1–8, find the domain of the expression.

1. $3x^2 - 4x + 7$

2. $2x^2 + 5x - 2$

3. $4x^3 + 3, \quad x \geq 0$

4. $6x^2 - 9, \quad x > 0$

5. $\dfrac{1}{x - 2}$

6. $\dfrac{x + 1}{2x + 1}$

7. $\sqrt{x + 1}$

8. $\sqrt{6 - x}$

In Exercises 9 and 10, find the missing factor in the numerator such that the two fractions are equivalent.

9. $\dfrac{5}{2x} = \dfrac{5(\quad)}{6x^2}$

10. $\dfrac{3}{4} = \dfrac{3(\quad)}{4(x + 1)}$

In Exercises 11–28, write the rational expression in simplest form.

11. $\dfrac{15x^2}{10x}$

12. $\dfrac{18y^2}{60y^5}$

13. $\dfrac{3xy}{xy + x}$

14. $\dfrac{2x^2 y}{xy - y}$

15. $\dfrac{4y - 8y^2}{10y - 5}$

16. $\dfrac{9x^2 + 9x}{2x + 2}$

17. $\dfrac{x - 5}{10 - 2x}$

18. $\dfrac{12 - 4x}{x - 3}$

19. $\dfrac{y^2 - 16}{y + 4}$

20. $\dfrac{x^2 - 25}{5 - x}$

21. $\dfrac{x^3 + 5x^2 + 6x}{x^2 - 4}$

22. $\dfrac{x^2 + 8x - 20}{x^2 + 11x + 10}$

23. $\dfrac{y^2 - 7y + 12}{y^2 + 3y - 18}$

24. $\dfrac{x^2 - 7x + 6}{x^2 + 11x + 10}$

25. $\dfrac{2 - x + 2x^2 - x^3}{x^2 - 4}$

26. $\dfrac{x^2 - 9}{x^3 + x^2 - 9x - 9}$

27. $\dfrac{z^3 - 8}{z^2 + 2z + 4}$

28. $\dfrac{y^3 - 2y^2 - 3y}{y^3 + 1}$

In Exercises 29 and 30, complete the table. What can you conclude?

29.

x	0	1	2	3	4	5	6
$\dfrac{x^2 - 2x - 3}{x - 3}$							
$x + 1$							

30.

x	0	1	2	3	4	5	6
$\dfrac{x - 3}{x^2 - x - 6}$							
$\dfrac{1}{x + 2}$							

31. *Error Analysis* Describe the error.

$$\frac{5x^3}{2x^3 + 4} = \frac{5x^3}{2x^3 + 4} = \frac{5}{2 + 4} = \frac{5}{6}$$

32. *Error Analysis* Describe the error.

$$\frac{x^3 + 25x}{x^2 - 2x - 15} = \frac{x(x^2 + 25)}{(x - 5)(x + 3)}$$

$$= \frac{x(x - 5)(x + 5)}{(x - 5)(x + 3)} = \frac{x(x + 5)}{x + 3}$$

Geometry **In Exercises 33 and 34, find the ratio of the area of the shaded portion of the figure to the total area of the figure.**

33.

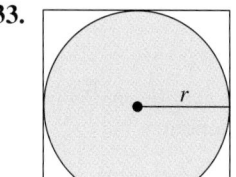

34.

In Exercises 35–42, perform the multiplication or division and simplify.

35. $\dfrac{5}{x - 1} \cdot \dfrac{x - 1}{25(x - 2)}$

36. $\dfrac{x + 13}{x^3(3 - x)} \cdot \dfrac{x(x - 3)}{5}$

37. $\dfrac{r}{r - 1} \cdot \dfrac{r^2 - 1}{r^2}$

38. $\dfrac{4y - 16}{5y + 15} \cdot \dfrac{2y + 6}{4 - y}$

39. $\dfrac{t^2 - t - 6}{t^2 + 6t + 9} \cdot \dfrac{t + 3}{t^2 - 4}$

40. $\dfrac{x^2 + xy - 2y^2}{x^3 + x^2y} \cdot \dfrac{x}{x^2 + 3xy + 2y^2}$

41. $\dfrac{x^2 - 36}{x} \div \dfrac{x^3 - 6x^2}{x^2 + x}$

42. $\dfrac{x^2 - 14x + 49}{x^2 - 49} \div \dfrac{3x - 21}{x + 7}$

In Exercises 43–52, perform the addition or subtraction and simplify.

43. $\dfrac{5}{x - 1} + \dfrac{x}{x - 1}$

44. $\dfrac{2x - 1}{x + 3} + \dfrac{1 - x}{x + 3}$

45. $6 - \dfrac{5}{x + 3}$

46. $\dfrac{3}{x - 1} - 5$

47. $\dfrac{3}{x - 2} + \dfrac{5}{2 - x}$

48. $\dfrac{2x}{x - 5} - \dfrac{5}{5 - x}$

49. $\dfrac{1}{x^2 - x - 2} - \dfrac{x}{x^2 - 5x + 6}$

50. $\dfrac{2}{x^2 - x - 2} + \dfrac{10}{x^2 + 2x - 8}$

51. $-\dfrac{1}{x} + \dfrac{2}{x^2 + 1} + \dfrac{1}{x^3 + x}$

52. $\dfrac{2}{x + 1} + \dfrac{2}{x - 1} + \dfrac{1}{x^2 - 1}$

∫ In Exercises 53–58, factor the expression by removing the common factor with the smaller exponent.

53. $x^5 - 2x^{-2}$

54. $x^5 - 5x^{-3}$

55. $x^2(x^2 + 1)^{-5} - (x^2 + 1)^{-4}$

56. $2x(x - 5)^{-3} - 4x^2(x - 5)^{-4}$

57. $2x^2(x - 1)^{1/2} - 5(x - 1)^{-1/2}$

58. $4x^3(2x - 1)^{3/2} - 2x(2x - 1)^{-1/2}$

Error Analysis In Exercises 59 and 60, describe the error.

59. $\dfrac{x + 4}{x + 2} - \dfrac{3x - 8}{x + 2} = \dfrac{x + 4 - 3x - 8}{x + 2}$

$= \dfrac{-2x - 4}{x + 2}$

$= \dfrac{-2(x + 2)}{x + 2}$

$= -2$

60. $\dfrac{6 - x}{x(x + 2)} + \dfrac{x + 2}{x^2} + \dfrac{8}{x^2(x + 2)}$

$= \dfrac{x(6 - x) + (x + 2)^2 + 8}{x^2(x + 2)}$

$= \dfrac{6x - x^2 + x^2 + 4 + 8}{x^2(x + 2)}$

$= \dfrac{6(x + 2)}{x^2(x + 2)} = \dfrac{6}{x^2}$

In Exercises 61–70, simplify the complex fraction.

61. $\dfrac{\left(\dfrac{x}{2} - 1\right)}{(x - 2)}$

62. $\dfrac{(x - 4)}{\left(\dfrac{x}{4} - \dfrac{4}{x}\right)}$

63. $\dfrac{\left[\dfrac{x^2}{(x + 1)^2}\right]}{\left[\dfrac{x}{(x + 1)^3}\right]}$

64. $\dfrac{\left(\dfrac{x^2 - 1}{x}\right)}{\left[\dfrac{(x - 1)^2}{x}\right]}$

65. $\dfrac{\left[\dfrac{1}{(x + h)^2} - \dfrac{1}{x^2}\right]}{h}$

66. $\dfrac{\left(\dfrac{x + h}{x + h + 1} - \dfrac{x}{x + 1}\right)}{h}$

67. $\dfrac{\left(\sqrt{x} - \dfrac{1}{2\sqrt{x}}\right)}{\sqrt{x}}$

68. $\dfrac{\left(\dfrac{t^2}{\sqrt{t^2 + 1}} - \sqrt{t^2 + 1}\right)}{t^2}$

69. $\dfrac{3x^{1/3} - x^{-2/3}}{3x^{-2/3}}$

70. $\dfrac{-x^3(1 - x^2)^{-1/2} - 2x(1 - x^2)^{1/2}}{x^4}$

∫ In Exercises 71 and 72, rationalize the numerator of the expression.

71. $\dfrac{\sqrt{x + 2} - \sqrt{x}}{2}$

72. $\dfrac{\sqrt{z - 3} - \sqrt{z}}{3}$

Probability In Exercises 73 and 74, consider an experiment in which a marble is tossed into a box whose base is shown in the figure. The probability that the marble will come to rest in the shaded portion of the box is equal to the ratio of the shaded area to the total area of the figure. Find the probability.

73.

74.
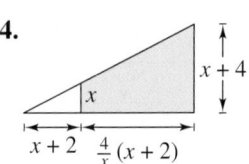

75. *Rate* A photocopier copies at a rate of 16 pages per minute.

(a) Find the time required to copy one page.

(b) Find the time required to copy x pages.

(c) Find the time required to copy 60 pages.

76. *Finance* The formula that approximates the annual interest rate r of a monthly installment loan is given by

$$r = \frac{\left[\dfrac{24(NM - P)}{N}\right]}{\left(P + \dfrac{NM}{12}\right)}$$

where N is the total number of payments, M is the monthly payment, and P is the amount financed.

(a) Approximate the annual interest rate for a four-year car loan of $16,000 that has monthly payments of $400.

(b) Simplify the expression for the annual interest rate r, and then rework part (a).

77. *Refrigeration* When food (at room temperature) is placed in a refrigerator, the time required for the food to cool depends on the amount of food, the air circulation in the refrigerator, the original temperature of the food, and the temperature of the refrigerator. The model that gives the temperature of food that has an original temperature of 75°F and is placed in a 40°F refrigerator is

$$T = 10\left(\frac{4t^2 + 16t + 75}{t^2 + 4t + 10}\right)$$

where T is the temperature (in degrees Fahrenheit) and t is the time (in hours).

(a) Complete the table.

t	0	2	4	6	8	10
T						

t	12	14	16	18	20	22
T						

(b) What value of T does the mathematical model appear to be approaching?

78. *Precious Metals* The costs per fine ounce of gold and per troy ounce of platinum for the years 1994 through 1999 are shown in the table. (Source: U.S. Bureau of Mines, U.S. Geological Survey)

Year, t	Gold	Platinum
1994	$385	$411
1995	$386	$425
1996	$389	$398
1997	$332	$397
1998	$295	$373
1999	$285	$365

Mathematical models for this data are

$$\text{Cost of gold} = \frac{6.79t^2 - 95.6t + 356}{0.0205t^2 - 0.278t + 1}$$

and

$$\text{Cost of platinum} = \frac{-148.2t + 192}{-0.46t + 1}$$

where $t = 4$ corresponds to the year 1994.

(a) Create a table using the models to estimate the costs of the two metals for the given years.

(b) Compare the estimates given by the models with the actual costs.

(c) Determine a model for the ratio of the cost of gold to the cost of platinum.

(d) Use the model from part (c) to find the ratio over the given years. Over this period of time, did the cost of gold increase or decrease relative to the cost of platinum?

Synthesis

True or False? In Exercises 79 and 80, determine whether the statement is true or false. Justify your answer.

79. $\dfrac{x^{2n} - 1^{2n}}{x^n - 1^n} = x^n + 1^n$

80. $\dfrac{x^2 - 3x + 2}{x - 1} = x - 2$ for all values of x.

81. *Think About It* How do you determine whether a rational expression is in simplest form?

A.5 Solving Equations

▶ **What you should learn**

- How to identify different types of equations
- How to solve linear equations in one variable
- How to solve quadratic equations by factoring, extracting square roots, completing the square, and using the Quadratic Formula
- How to solve polynomial equations of degree three or greater
- How to solve equations involving radicals
- How to solve equations involving absolute values

▶ **Why you should learn it**

Linear equations are used in many real-life applications. For example, in Exercises 185 and 186 on page A57, linear equations can be used to model the relationship between the length of a thigh bone and the height of a person, helping researchers learn about ancient cultures.

Equations and Solutions of Equations

An **equation** in x is a statement that two algebraic expressions are equal. For example

$$3x - 5 = 7, \quad x^2 - x - 6 = 0, \quad \text{and} \quad \sqrt{2x} = 4$$

are equations. To **solve** an equation in x means to find all values of x for which the equation is true. Such values are **solutions.** For instance, $x = 4$ is a solution of the equation

$$3x - 5 = 7$$

because $3(4) - 5 = 7$ is a true statement.

The solutions of an equation depend on the kinds of numbers being considered. For instance, in the set of rational numbers, $x^2 = 10$ has no solution because there is no rational number whose square is 10. However, in the set of real numbers, the equation has the two solutions $\sqrt{10}$ and $-\sqrt{10}$.

An equation that is true for *every* real number in the domain of the variable is called an **identity.** For example

$$x^2 - 9 = (x + 3)(x - 3) \qquad \text{Identity}$$

is an identity because it is a true statement for any real value of x, and

$$\frac{x}{3x^2} = \frac{1}{3x} \qquad \text{Identity}$$

where $x \neq 0$, is an identity because it is true for any nonzero real value of x.

An equation that is true for just *some* (or even none) of the real numbers in the domain of the variable is called a **conditional equation.** For example, the equation

$$x^2 - 9 = 0 \qquad \text{Conditional equation}$$

is conditional because $x = 3$ and $x = -3$ are the only values in the domain that satisfy the equation. The equation $2x - 4 = 2x + 1$ is conditional because there are no real values of x for which the equation is true. Learning to solve conditional equations is the primary focus of this section.

Linear Equations in One Variable

Definition of Linear Equation

A **linear equation in one variable** x is an equation that can be written in the standard form

$$ax + b = 0$$

where a and b are real numbers with $a \neq 0$.

A linear equation has exactly one solution. To see this, consider the following steps. (Remember that $a \neq 0$.)

$$ax + b = 0 \qquad \text{Write original equation.}$$

$$ax = -b \qquad \text{Subtract } b \text{ from each side.}$$

$$x = -\frac{b}{a} \qquad \text{Divide each side by } a.$$

To solve a conditional equation in x, isolate x on one side of the equation by a sequence of **equivalent** (and usually simpler) **equations,** each having the same solution(s) as the original equation. The operations that yield equivalent equations come from the Substitution Principle and simplification techniques.

Generating Equivalent Equations

An equation can be transformed into an *equivalent equation* by one or more of the following steps.

	Given Equation	*Equivalent Equation*
1. Remove symbols of grouping, combine like terms, or simplify fractions on one or both sides of the equation.	$2x - x = 4$	$x = 4$
2. Add (or subtract) the same quantity to (from) *each* side of the equation.	$x + 1 = 6$	$x = 5$
3. Multiply (or divide) *each* side of the equation by the same *nonzero* quantity.	$2x = 6$	$x = 3$
4. Interchange the two sides of the equation.	$2 = x$	$x = 2$

Example 1 ▶ Solving a Linear Equation

a. $3x - 6 = 0$ \qquad Original equation

$\qquad 3x = 6$ \qquad Add 6 to each side.

$\qquad\quad x = 2$ \qquad Divide each side by 3.

b. $5x + 4 = 3x - 8$ \qquad Original equation

$\quad 2x + 4 = -8$ \qquad Subtract $3x$ from each side.

$\qquad 2x = -12$ \qquad Subtract 4 from each side.

$\qquad\quad x = -6$ \qquad Divide each side by 2.

To solve an equation involving fractional expressions, find the least common denominator (LCD) of all terms and multiply every term by the LCD.

Example 2 ▶ An Equation Involving Fractional Expressions

Solve $\dfrac{x}{3} + \dfrac{3x}{4} = 2$.

Solution

$$\frac{x}{3} + \frac{3x}{4} = 2 \qquad \text{Write original equation.}$$

$$(12)\frac{x}{3} + (12)\frac{3x}{4} = (12)2 \qquad \text{Multiply each term by the LCD of 12.}$$

$$4x + 9x = 24 \qquad \text{Divide out and multiply.}$$

$$13x = 24 \qquad \text{Combine like terms.}$$

$$x = \frac{24}{13} \qquad \text{Divide each side by 13.}$$

The solution is $x = \frac{24}{13}$. Check this in the original equation.

When multiplying or dividing an equation by a *variable* quantity, it is possible to introduce an extraneous solution. An **extraneous solution** is one that does not satisfy the original equation.

Example 3 ▶ An Equation with an Extraneous Solution

Solve $\dfrac{1}{x-2} = \dfrac{3}{x+2} - \dfrac{6x}{x^2 - 4}$.

Solution

The LCD is $x^2 - 4$, or $(x+2)(x-2)$. Multiply each term by this LCD.

$$\frac{1}{x-2}(x+2)(x-2) = \frac{3}{x+2}(x+2)(x-2) - \frac{6x}{x^2-4}(x+2)(x-2)$$

$$x + 2 = 3(x-2) - 6x, \qquad x \neq \pm 2$$

$$x + 2 = 3x - 6 - 6x$$

$$x + 2 = -3x - 6$$

$$4x = -8$$

$$x = -2$$

In the original equation, $x = -2$ yields a denominator of zero. So, $x = -2$ is an extraneous solution, and the original equation has *no solution*.

Quadratic Equations   www

A **quadratic equation** in x is an equation that can be written in the general form

$$ax^2 + bx + c = 0$$

where a, b, and c are real numbers, with $a \neq 0$. A quadratic equation in x is also known as a **second-degree polynomial equation** in x.

You should be familiar with the following four methods of solving quadratic equations.

Solving a Quadratic Equation

Factoring: If $ab = 0$, then $a = 0$ or $b = 0$.

Example:
$$x^2 - x - 6 = 0$$
$$(x - 3)(x + 2) = 0$$
$$x - 3 = 0 \implies x = 3$$
$$x + 2 = 0 \implies x = -2$$

Square Root Principle: If $u^2 = c$, where $c > 0$, then $u = \pm\sqrt{c}$.

Example:
$$(x + 3)^2 = 16$$
$$x + 3 = \pm 4$$
$$x = -3 \pm 4$$
$$x = 1 \quad \text{or} \quad x = -7$$

Completing the Square: If $x^2 + bx = c$, then

$$x^2 + bx + \left(\frac{b}{2}\right)^2 = c + \left(\frac{b}{2}\right)^2$$

$$\left(x + \frac{b}{2}\right)^2 = c + \frac{b^2}{4}.$$

Example:
$$x^2 + 6x = 5$$
$$x^2 + 6x + 3^2 = 5 + 3^2$$
$$(x + 3)^2 = 14$$
$$x + 3 = \pm\sqrt{14}$$
$$x = -3 \pm \sqrt{14}$$

Quadratic Formula: If $ax^2 + bx + c = 0$, then $x = \dfrac{-b \pm \sqrt{b^2 - 4ac}}{2a}$.

Example:
$$2x^2 + 3x - 1 = 0$$
$$x = \frac{-3 \pm \sqrt{3^2 - 4(2)(-1)}}{2(2)}$$
$$= \frac{-3 \pm \sqrt{17}}{4}$$

STUDY TIP

The Square Root Principle is also referred to as *extracting square roots.*

STUDY TIP

You can solve every quadratic equation by completing the square or using the Quadratic Formula.

> **Example 4** ▶ **Solving a Quadratic Equation by Factoring**

a.

$2x^2 + 9x + 7 = 3$	Original equation
$2x^2 + 9x + 4 = 0$	Write in general form.
$(2x + 1)(x + 4) = 0$	Factor.
$2x + 1 = 0 \implies x = -\dfrac{1}{2}$	Set 1st factor equal to 0.
$x + 4 = 0 \implies x = -4$	Set 2nd factor equal to 0.

The solutions are $x = -\frac{1}{2}$ and $x = -4$. Check these in the original equation.

b.

$6x^2 - 3x = 0$	Original equation
$3x(2x - 1) = 0$	Factor.
$3x = 0 \implies x = 0$	Set 1st factor equal to 0.
$2x - 1 = 0 \implies x = \dfrac{1}{2}$	Set 2nd factor equal to 0.

The solutions are $x = 0$ and $x = \frac{1}{2}$. Check these in the original equation.

Note that the method of solution in Example 4 is based on the Zero-Factor Property from Section A.1. Be sure you see that this property works *only* for equations written in general form (in which the right side of the equation is zero). So, all terms must be collected on one side *before* factoring. For instance, in the equation

$$(x - 5)(x + 2) = 8$$

it is *incorrect* to set each factor equal to 8. Try to solve this equation correctly.

> **Example 5** ▶ **Extracting Square Roots**

Solve each equation by extracting square roots.

a. $4x^2 = 12$ **b.** $(x - 3)^2 = 7$

Solution

a.

$4x^2 = 12$	Write original equation.
$x^2 = 3$	Divide each side by 4.
$x = \pm\sqrt{3}$	Extract square roots.

The solutions are $x = \sqrt{3}$ and $x = -\sqrt{3}$. Check these in the original equation.

b.

$(x - 3)^2 = 7$	Write original equation.
$x - 3 = \pm\sqrt{7}$	Extract square roots.
$x = 3 \pm \sqrt{7}$	Add 3 to each side.

The solutions are $x = 3 \pm \sqrt{7}$. Check these in the original equation.

Example 6 ▶ **The Quadratic Formula: Two Distinct Solutions**

Use the Quadratic Formula to solve

$$x^2 + 3x = 9.$$

Solution

$x^2 + 3x = 9$	Write original equation.
$x^2 + 3x - 9 = 0$	Write in general form.
$x = \dfrac{-b \pm \sqrt{b^2 - 4ac}}{2a}$	Quadratic Formula
$x = \dfrac{-3 \pm \sqrt{(3)^2 - 4(1)(-9)}}{2(1)}$	Substitute $a = 1$, $b = 3$, and $c = -9$.
$x = \dfrac{-3 \pm \sqrt{45}}{2}$	Simplify.
$x = \dfrac{-3 \pm 3\sqrt{5}}{2}$	Simplify.

The equation has two solutions:

$$x = \frac{-3 + 3\sqrt{5}}{2} \quad \text{and} \quad x = \frac{-3 - 3\sqrt{5}}{2}.$$

Check these in the original equation.

Example 7 ▶ **The Quadratic Formula: One Solution**

Use the Quadratic Formula to solve

$$8x^2 - 24x + 18 = 0.$$

Solution

$8x^2 - 24x + 18 = 0$	Write original equation.
$4x^2 - 12x + 9 = 0$	Divide out common factor of 2.
$x = \dfrac{-b \pm \sqrt{b^2 - 4ac}}{2a}$	Quadratic Formula
$x = \dfrac{-(-12) \pm \sqrt{(-12)^2 - 4(4)(9)}}{2(4)}$	Substitute.
$x = \dfrac{12 \pm \sqrt{0}}{8}$	Simplify.
$x = \dfrac{3}{2}$	Simplify.

This quadratic equation has only one solution: $x = \frac{3}{2}$. Check this in the original equation.

Polynomial Equations of Higher Degree

The methods used to solve quadratic equations can sometimes be extended to polynomials of higher degree.

Example 8 ▶ Solving a Polynomial Equation by Factoring

Solve $3x^4 = 48x^2$.

Solution

First write the polynomial equation in general form with zero on one side, factor the other side, and then set each factor equal to zero.

$3x^4 = 48x^2$	Write original equation.
$3x^4 - 48x^2 = 0$	Write in general form.
$3x^2(x^2 - 16) = 0$	Factor out common factor.
$3x^2(x + 4)(x - 4) = 0$	Write in factored form.
$3x^2 = 0 \implies x = 0$	Set 1st factor equal to 0.
$x + 4 = 0 \implies x = -4$	Set 2nd factor equal to 0.
$x - 4 = 0 \implies x = 4$	Set 3rd factor equal to 0.

You can check these solutions by substituting in the original equation, as follows.

Check

$3x^4 = 48x^2$	Write original equation.
$3(0)^4 = 48(0)^2$	0 checks. ✓
$3(-4)^4 = 48(-4)^2$	-4 checks. ✓
$3(4)^4 = 48(4)^2$	4 checks. ✓

So, you can conclude that the solutions are $x = 0$, $x = -4$, and $x = 4$.

Example 9 ▶ Solving a Polynomial Equation by Factoring

Solve $x^3 - 3x^2 - 3x + 9 = 0$.

Solution

$x^3 - 3x^2 - 3x + 9 = 0$	Write original equation.
$x^2(x - 3) - 3(x - 3) = 0$	Factor by grouping.
$(x - 3)(x^2 - 3) = 0$	Distributive Property
$x - 3 = 0 \implies x = 3$	Set 1st factor equal to 0.
$x^2 - 3 = 0 \implies x = \pm\sqrt{3}$	Set 2nd factor equal to 0.

The solutions are $x = 3$, $x = \sqrt{3}$, and $x = -\sqrt{3}$.

Equations Involving Radicals

The steps involved in solving the remaining equations in this section will often introduce *extraneous solutions*. Extraneous solutions occur during operations such as squaring each side of an equation, raising each side of an equation to a rational power, and multiplying each side by a variable quantity. So, when you use any of these operations, checking is crucial.

Example 10 ▶ Solving Equations Involving Radicals

a.
$$\sqrt{2x + 7} - x = 2$$ Original equation

$$\sqrt{2x + 7} = x + 2$$ Isolate radical.

$$2x + 7 = x^2 + 4x + 4$$ Square each side.

$$0 = x^2 + 2x - 3$$ Write in general form.

$$0 = (x + 3)(x - 1)$$ Factor.

$$x + 3 = 0 \implies x = -3$$ Set 1st factor equal to 0.

$$x - 1 = 0 \implies x = 1$$ Set 2nd factor equal to 0.

By checking these values, you can determine that the only solution is $x = 1$.

b.
$$\sqrt{2x - 5} - \sqrt{x - 3} = 1$$ Original equation

$$\sqrt{2x - 5} = \sqrt{x - 3} + 1$$ Isolate $\sqrt{2x - 5}$.

$$2x - 5 = x - 3 + 2\sqrt{x - 3} + 1$$ Square each side.

$$2x - 5 = x - 2 + 2\sqrt{x - 3}$$ Combine like terms.

$$x - 3 = 2\sqrt{x - 3}$$ Isolate $2\sqrt{x - 3}$.

$$x^2 - 6x + 9 = 4(x - 3)$$ Square each side.

$$x^2 - 10x + 21 = 0$$ Write in general form.

$$(x - 3)(x - 7) = 0$$ Factor.

$$x - 3 = 0 \implies x = 3$$ Set 1st factor equal to 0.

$$x - 7 = 0 \implies x = 7$$ Set 2nd factor equal to 0.

The solutions are $x = 3$ and $x = 7$. Check these in the original equation.

Example 11 ▶ Solving an Equation Involving a Rational Exponent

$$(x - 4)^{2/3} = 25$$ Original equation

$$x - 4 = 25^{3/2}$$ Raise each side to the $\frac{3}{2}$ power.

$$x - 4 = 125$$ Simplify.

$$x = 129$$ Add 4 to each side.

The solution is $x = 129$. Check this in the original equation.

Equations with Absolute Values

To solve an equation involving an absolute value, remember that the expression inside the absolute value signs can be positive or negative. This results in *two* separate equations, each of which must be solved. For instance, the equation

$$|x - 2| = 3$$

results in the two equations $x - 2 = 3$ and $-(x - 2) = 3$, which implies that the equation has two solutions: $x = 5$ and $x = -1$.

Example 12 ▶ **Solving an Equation Involving Absolute Value**

Solve $|x^2 - 3x| = -4x + 6$.

Solution

Because the variable expression inside the absolute value signs can be positive or negative, you must solve the following two equations.

First Equation

$x^2 - 3x = -4x + 6$	Use positive expression.
$x^2 + x - 6 = 0$	Write in general form.
$(x + 3)(x - 2) = 0$	Factor.
$x + 3 = 0 \implies x = -3$	Set 1st factor equal to 0.
$x - 2 = 0 \implies x = 2$	Set 2nd factor equal to 0.

Second Equation

$-(x^2 - 3x) = -4x + 6$	Use negative expression.
$x^2 - 7x + 6 = 0$	Write in general form.
$(x - 1)(x - 6) = 0$	Factor.
$x - 1 = 0 \implies x = 1$	Set 1st factor equal to 0.
$x - 6 = 0 \implies x = 6$	Set 2nd factor equal to 0.

Check

$\lvert(-3)^2 - 3(-3)\rvert \overset{?}{=} -4(-3) + 6$	Substitute -3 for x.
$18 = 18$	-3 checks. ✓
$\lvert(2)^2 - 3(2)\rvert \overset{?}{=} -4(2) + 6$	Substitute 2 for x.
$2 \neq -2$	2 does not check.
$\lvert(1)^2 - 3(1)\rvert \overset{?}{=} -4(1) + 6$	Substitute 1 for x.
$2 = 2$	1 checks. ✓
$\lvert(6)^2 - 3(6)\rvert \overset{?}{=} -4(6) + 6$	Substitute 6 for x.
$18 \neq -18$	6 does not check.

The solutions are $x = -3$ and $x = 1$.

A.5 **Exercises**

In Exercises 1–10, determine whether the equation is an identity or a conditional equation.

1. $2(x - 1) = 2x - 2$

2. $3(x + 2) = 5x + 4$

3. $-6(x - 3) + 5 = -2x + 10$

4. $3(x + 2) - 5 = 3x + 1$

5. $4(x + 1) - 2x = 2(x + 2)$

6. $-7(x - 3) + 4x = 3(7 - x)$

7. $x^2 - 8x + 5 = (x - 4)^2 - 11$

8. $x^2 + 2(3x - 2) = x^2 + 6x - 4$

9. $3 + \dfrac{1}{x + 1} = \dfrac{4x}{x + 1}$

10. $\dfrac{5}{x} + \dfrac{3}{x} = 24$

In Exercises 11–26, solve the equation and check your solution.

11. $x + 11 = 15$

12. $7 - x = 19$

13. $7 - 2x = 25$

14. $7x + 2 = 23$

15. $8x - 5 = 3x + 20$

16. $7x + 3 = 3x - 17$

17. $2(x + 5) - 7 = 3(x - 2)$

18. $3(x + 3) = 5(1 - x) - 1$

19. $x - 3(2x + 3) = 8 - 5x$

20. $9x - 10 = 5x + 2(2x - 5)$

21. $\dfrac{5x}{4} + \dfrac{1}{2} = x - \dfrac{1}{2}$

22. $\dfrac{x}{5} - \dfrac{x}{2} = 3 + \dfrac{3x}{10}$

23. $\frac{3}{2}(z + 5) - \frac{1}{4}(z + 24) = 0$

24. $\dfrac{3x}{2} + \dfrac{1}{4}(x - 2) = 10$

25. $0.25x + 0.75(10 - x) = 3$

26. $0.60x + 0.40(100 - x) = 50$

In Exercises 27–48, solve the equation and check your solution. (If not possible, explain why.)

27. $x + 8 = 2(x - 2) - x$

28. $8(x + 2) - 3(2x + 1) = 2(x + 5)$

29. $\dfrac{100 - 4x}{3} = \dfrac{5x + 6}{4} + 6$

30. $\dfrac{17 + y}{y} + \dfrac{32 + y}{y} = 100$

31. $\dfrac{5x - 4}{5x + 4} = \dfrac{2}{3}$

32. $\dfrac{10x + 3}{5x + 6} = \dfrac{1}{2}$

33. $10 - \dfrac{13}{x} = 4 + \dfrac{5}{x}$

34. $\dfrac{15}{x} - 4 = \dfrac{6}{x} + 3$

35. $\dfrac{x}{x + 4} + \dfrac{4}{x + 4} + 2 = 0$

36. $3 = 2 + \dfrac{2}{z + 2}$

37. $\dfrac{1}{x} + \dfrac{2}{x - 5} = 0$

38. $\dfrac{7}{2x + 1} - \dfrac{8x}{2x - 1} = -4$

39. $\dfrac{2}{(x - 4)(x - 2)} = \dfrac{1}{x - 4} + \dfrac{2}{x - 2}$

40. $\dfrac{4}{x - 1} + \dfrac{6}{3x + 1} = \dfrac{15}{3x + 1}$

41. $\dfrac{1}{x - 3} + \dfrac{1}{x + 3} = \dfrac{10}{x^2 - 9}$

42. $\dfrac{1}{x - 2} + \dfrac{3}{x + 3} = \dfrac{4}{x^2 + x - 6}$

43. $\dfrac{3}{x^2 - 3x} + \dfrac{4}{x} = \dfrac{1}{x - 3}$

44. $\dfrac{6}{x} - \dfrac{2}{x + 3} = \dfrac{3(x + 5)}{x^2 + 3x}$

45. $(x + 2)^2 + 5 = (x + 3)^2$

46. $(x + 1)^2 + 2(x - 2) = (x + 1)(x - 2)$

47. $(x + 2)^2 - x^2 = 4(x + 1)$

48. $(2x + 1)^2 = 4(x^2 + x + 1)$

In Exercises 49–54, write the quadratic equation in general form.

49. $2x^2 = 3 - 8x$

50. $x^2 = 16x$

51. $(x - 3)^2 = 3$

52. $13 - 3(x + 7)^2 = 0$

53. $\frac{1}{5}(3x^2 - 10) = 18x$

54. $x(x + 2) = 5x^2 + 1$

In Exercises 55–68, solve the quadratic equation by factoring.

55. $6x^2 + 3x = 0$

56. $9x^2 - 1 = 0$

57. $x^2 - 2x - 8 = 0$

58. $x^2 - 10x + 9 = 0$

59. $x^2 + 10x + 25 = 0$

60. $4x^2 + 12x + 9 = 0$

61. $3 + 5x - 2x^2 = 0$

62. $2x^2 = 19x + 33$

63. $x^2 + 4x = 12$

64. $-x^2 + 8x = 12$

65. $\frac{3}{4}x^2 + 8x + 20 = 0$ **66.** $\frac{1}{8}x^2 - x - 16 = 0$

67. $x^2 + 2ax + a^2 = 0$ **68.** $(x + a)^2 - b^2 = 0$

In Exercises 69–82, solve the equation by extracting square roots. List both the exact solution and the decimal solution rounded to two decimal places.

69. $x^2 = 49$

70. $x^2 = 169$

71. $x^2 = 11$

72. $x^2 = 32$

73. $3x^2 = 81$

74. $9x^2 = 36$

75. $(x - 12)^2 = 16$

76. $(x + 13)^2 = 25$

77. $(x + 2)^2 = 14$

78. $(x - 5)^2 = 30$

79. $(2x - 1)^2 = 18$

80. $(4x + 7)^2 = 44$

81. $(x - 7)^2 = (x + 3)^2$ **82.** $(x + 5)^2 = (x + 4)^2$

In Exercises 83–92, solve the quadratic equation by completing the square.

83. $x^2 - 2x = 0$

84. $x^2 + 4x = 0$

85. $x^2 + 4x - 32 = 0$

86. $x^2 - 2x - 3 = 0$

87. $x^2 + 6x + 2 = 0$

88. $x^2 + 8x + 14 = 0$

89. $9x^2 - 18x = -3$

90. $9x^2 - 12x = 14$

91. $8 + 4x - x^2 = 0$

92. $4x^2 - 4x - 99 = 0$

In Exercises 93–116, use the Quadratic Formula to solve the equation.

93. $2x^2 + x - 1 = 0$

94. $2x^2 - x - 1 = 0$

95. $16x^2 + 8x - 3 = 0$

96. $25x^2 - 20x + 3 = 0$

97. $2 + 2x - x^2 = 0$

98. $x^2 - 10x + 22 = 0$

99. $x^2 + 14x + 44 = 0$

100. $6x = 4 - x^2$

101. $x^2 + 8x - 4 = 0$

102. $4x^2 - 4x - 4 = 0$

103. $12x - 9x^2 = -3$

104. $16x^2 + 22 = 40x$

105. $9x^2 + 24x + 16 = 0$

106. $36x^2 + 24x - 7 = 0$

107. $4x^2 + 4x = 7$

108. $16x^2 - 40x + 5 = 0$

109. $28x - 49x^2 = 4$

110. $3x + x^2 - 1 = 0$

111. $8t = 5 + 2t^2$

112. $25h^2 + 80h + 61 = 0$

113. $(y - 5)^2 = 2y$

114. $(z + 6)^2 = -2z$

115. $\frac{1}{2}x^2 + \frac{3}{8}x = 2$

116. $\left(\frac{5}{7}x - 14\right)^2 = 8x$

In Exercises 117–124, use the Quadratic Formula to solve the equation. (Round your answers to three decimal places.)

117. $5.1x^2 - 1.7x - 3.2 = 0$

118. $2x^2 - 2.50x - 0.42 = 0$

119. $-0.067x^2 - 0.852x + 1.277 = 0$

120. $-0.005x^2 + 0.101x - 0.193 = 0$

121. $422x^2 - 506x - 347 = 0$

122. $1100x^2 + 326x - 715 = 0$

123. $12.67x^2 + 31.55x + 8.09 = 0$

124. $-3.22x^2 - 0.08x + 28.651 = 0$

In Exercises 125–134, solve the equation using any convenient method.

125. $x^2 - 2x - 1 = 0$ **126.** $11x^2 + 33x = 0$

127. $(x + 3)^2 = 81$ **128.** $x^2 - 14x + 49 = 0$

129. $x^2 - x - \frac{11}{4} = 0$ **130.** $x^2 + 3x - \frac{3}{4} = 0$

131. $(x + 1)^2 = x^2$ **132.** $a^2x^2 - b^2 = 0$

133. $3x + 4 = 2x^2 - 7$

134. $4x^2 + 2x + 4 = 2x + 8$

In Exercises 135–152, find all solutions of the equation. Check your solutions in the original equation.

135. $4x^4 - 18x^2 = 0$ **136.** $20x^3 - 125x = 0$

137. $x^4 - 81 = 0$ **138.** $x^6 - 64 = 0$

139. $x^3 + 216 = 0$ **140.** $27x^3 - 512 = 0$

141. $5x^3 + 30x^2 + 45x = 0$

142. $9x^4 - 24x^3 + 16x^2 = 0$

143. $x^3 - 3x^2 - x + 3 = 0$

144. $x^3 + 2x^2 + 3x + 6 = 0$

145. $x^4 - x^3 + x - 1 = 0$

146. $x^4 + 2x^3 - 8x - 16 = 0$

147. $x^4 - 4x^2 + 3 = 0$

148. $x^4 + 5x^2 - 36 = 0$

149. $4x^4 - 65x^2 + 16 = 0$

150. $36t^4 + 29t^2 - 7 = 0$

151. $x^6 + 7x^3 - 8 = 0$

152. $x^6 + 3x^3 + 2 = 0$

In Exercises 153–170, find all solutions of the equation. Check your solutions in the original equation.

153. $\sqrt{2x} - 10 = 0$ **154.** $4\sqrt{x} - 3 = 0$

155. $\sqrt{x - 10} - 4 = 0$ **156.** $\sqrt{5 - x} - 3 = 0$

157. $\sqrt[3]{2x + 5} + 3 = 0$ **158.** $\sqrt[3]{3x + 1} - 5 = 0$

159. $-\sqrt{26 - 11x} + 4 = x$

160. $x + \sqrt{31 - 9x} = 5$

161. $\sqrt{x + 1} = \sqrt{3x + 1}$

162. $\sqrt{x + 5} = \sqrt{x - 5}$

163. $(x - 5)^{3/2} = 8$ **164.** $(x + 3)^{3/2} = 8$

165. $(x + 3)^{2/3} = 8$ **166.** $(x + 2)^{2/3} = 9$

167. $(x^2 - 5)^{3/2} = 27$

168. $(x^2 - x - 22)^{3/2} = 27$

169. $3x(x - 1)^{1/2} + 2(x - 1)^{3/2} = 0$

170. $4x^2(x - 1)^{1/3} + 6x(x - 1)^{4/3} = 0$

In Exercises 171–184, find all solutions of the equation. Check your solutions in the original equation.

171. $\dfrac{20 - x}{x} = x$ **172.** $\dfrac{4}{x} - \dfrac{5}{3} = \dfrac{x}{6}$

173. $\dfrac{1}{x} - \dfrac{1}{x + 1} = 3$ **174.** $\dfrac{x}{x^2 - 4} + \dfrac{1}{x + 2} = 3$

175. $x = \dfrac{3}{x} + \dfrac{1}{2}$ **176.** $4x + 1 = \dfrac{3}{x}$

177. $\dfrac{4}{x + 1} - \dfrac{3}{x + 2} = 1$ **178.** $\dfrac{x + 1}{3} - \dfrac{x + 1}{x + 2} = 0$

179. $|2x - 1| = 5$ **180.** $|3x + 2| = 7$

181. $|x| = x^2 + x - 3$ **182.** $|x^2 + 6x| = 3x + 18$

183. $|x + 1| = x^2 - 5$ **184.** $|x - 10| = x^2 - 10x$

Anthropology In Exercises 185 and 186, use the following information. The relationship between the length of an adult's femur (thigh bone) and the height of the adult can be approximated by the linear equations

$y = 0.432x - 10.44$ Female

$y = 0.449x - 12.15$ Male

where y is the length of the femur in inches and x is the height of the adult in inches (see figure).

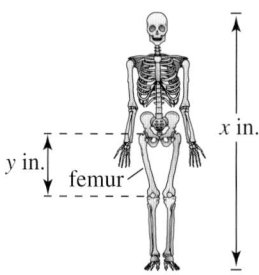

185. An anthropologist discovers a femur belonging to an adult human female. The bone is 16 inches long. Estimate the height of the female.

186. From the foot bones of an adult human male, an anthropologist estimates that the person's height was 69 inches. A few feet away from the site where the foot bones were discovered, the anthropologist discovers a male adult femur that is 19 inches long. Is it likely that the foot bones and the femur came from the same person?

187. *Operating Cost* A delivery company has a fleet of vans. The annual operating cost C per van is

$C = 0.32m + 2500$

where m is the number of miles traveled by a van in a year. What number of miles will yield an annual operating cost of \$10,000?

188. *Flood Control* A river has risen 8 feet above its flood stage. The water begins to recede at a rate of 3 inches per hour. Write a mathematical model that shows the number of feet above flood stage after t hours. If the water continually recedes at this rate, when will the river be 1 foot above its flood stage?

189. *Floor Space* The floor of a one-story building is 14 feet longer than it is wide. The building has 1632 square feet of floor space.

(a) Draw a diagram that gives a visual representation of the floor space. Represent the width as w and show the length in terms of w.

(b) Write a quadratic equation in terms of w.

(c) Find the length and width of the floor of the building.

190. *Packaging* An open box with a square base (see figure) is to be constructed from 84 square inches of material. The height of the box is 2 inches. What are the dimensions of the box? (*Hint:* The surface area is $S = x^2 + 4xh$.)

191. *Geometry* The hypotenuse of an isosceles right triangle is 5 centimeters long. How long are its sides?

192. *Geometry* An equilateral triangle has a height of 10 inches. How long is one of its sides? (*Hint:* Use the height of the triangle to partition the triangle into two congruent right triangles.)

193. *Flying Speed* Two planes leave simultaneously from Chicago's O'Hare Airport, one flying due north and the other due east (see figure). The northbound plane is flying 50 miles per hour faster than the eastbound plane. After 3 hours the planes are 2440 miles apart. Find the speed of each plane.

194. *Airline Passengers* An airline offers daily flights between Chicago and Denver. The total monthly cost C (in millions of dollars) of these flights is

$$C = \sqrt{0.2x + 1}$$

where x is the number of passengers (in thousands). The total cost of the flights for June is 2.5 million dollars. How many passengers flew in June?

195. *Demand* The demand equation for a product is $p = 20 - 0.0002x$, where p is the price per unit and x is the number of units sold. The total revenue for selling x units is

Revenue $= xp = x(20 - 0.0002x)$.

How many units must be sold to produce a revenue of $500,000?

196. *Demand* The demand equation for a video game is modeled by

$$p = 40 - \sqrt{0.01x + 1}$$

where x is the number of units demanded per day and p is the price per unit. Approximate the demand if the price is $37.55.

197. *Saturated Steam* The temperature T (in degrees Fahrenheit) of saturated steam increases as pressure increases. This relationship is approximated by the model

$$T = 75.82 - 2.11x + 43.51\sqrt{x}, \quad 5 \le x \le 40$$

where x is the absolute pressure (in pounds per square inch). Approximate the pressure when the temperature of the steam is 240°F.

198. *Sports* A baseball diamond has the shape of a square where the distance from home plate to second base is approximately $127\frac{1}{2}$ feet. Approximate the distance between the bases.

Synthesis

True or False? In Exercises 199–202, determine whether the statement is true or false. Justify your answer.

199. The equation $x(3 - x) = 10$ is a linear equation.

200. If $(2x - 3)(x + 5) = 8$, then $2x - 3 = 8$ or $x + 5 = 8$.

201. When solving an absolute value equation, you will always have to check more than one solution.

202. An equation can never have more than one extraneous solution.

203. To solve the equation

$$2x^2 + 3x = 15x$$

a student divides each side by x and solves the equation $2x + 3 = 15$. The resulting solution $(x = 6)$ satisfies the original equation. Is there an error? Explain.

204. *Think About It* What is meant by "equivalent equations"? Give an example of two equivalent equations.

205. *Writing* In your own words, describe the steps used to transform an equation into an equivalent equation.

206. Solve $3(x + 4)^2 + (x + 4) - 2 = 0$ in two ways.

(a) Let $u = x + 4$, and solve the resulting equation for u. Then solve the u-solution for x.

(b) Expand and collect like terms in the equation, and solve the resulting equation for x.

(c) Which method is easier? Explain.

207. Solve the equations, given that a and b are not zero.

(a) $ax^2 + bx = 0$ (b) $ax^2 - ax = 0$

208. Write a quadratic equation that has the solutions $x = -2$ and $x = \frac{1}{2}$. (Answers are not unique.)

In Exercises 209 and 210, consider an equation of the form $x + |x - a| = b$, where a and b are constants.

209. Find a and b when the solution to the equation is $x = 9$. (There are many correct answers.)

210. *Writing* Write a short paragraph listing the steps required to solve this equation involving absolute value.

A.6   Solving Inequalities

Introduction

Simple inequalities were reviewed in Section A.1. There, you used the inequality symbols $<$, $\leq$, $>$, and $\geq$ to compare two numbers and to denote subsets of real numbers. For instance, the simple inequality

$$x \geq 3$$

denotes all real numbers x that are greater than or equal to 3.

In this section you will expand your work with inequalities to include more involved statements such as

$$5x - 7 < 3x + 9$$

and

$$-3 \leq 6x - 1 < 3.$$

As with an equation, you **solve an inequality** in the variable x by finding all values of x for which the inequality is true. Such values are **solutions** and are said to **satisfy** the inequality. The set of all real numbers that are solutions of an inequality is the **solution set** of the inequality. For instance, the solution set of

$$x + 1 < 4$$

is all real numbers that are less than 3.

The set of all points on the real number line that represent the solution set is the **graph of the inequality.** Graphs of many types of inequalities consist of intervals on the real number line. See Section A.1 to review the nine basic types of intervals on the real number line. Note that each type of interval can be classified as *bounded* or *unbounded*.

Example 1 ▶   Intervals and Inequalities

Write an inequality to represent each interval, and state whether the interval is bounded or unbounded.

a. $(-3, 5]$

b. $(-3, \infty)$

c. $[0, 2]$

d. $(-\infty, \infty)$

Solution

a. $(-3, 5]$ corresponds to $-3 < x \leq 5$.   Bounded

b. $(-3, \infty)$ corresponds to $-3 < x$.   Unbounded

c. $[0, 2]$ corresponds to $0 \leq x \leq 2$.   Bounded

d. $(-\infty, \infty)$ corresponds to $-\infty < x < \infty$.   Unbounded

---

Properties of Inequalities

The procedures for solving linear inequalities in one variable are much like those for solving linear equations. To isolate the variable, you can make use of the **Properties of Inequalities.** These properties are similar to the properties of equality, but there are two important exceptions. When each side of an inequality is multiplied or divided by a negative number, the direction of the inequality symbol must be reversed. Here is an example.

$$-2 < 5 \qquad \text{Original inequality}$$
$$(-3)(-2) > (-3)(5) \qquad \text{Multiply each side by } -3 \text{ and reverse inequality.}$$
$$6 > -15 \qquad \text{Simplify.}$$

Two inequalities that have the same solution set are **equivalent.** For instance, the inequalities

$$x + 2 < 5$$

and

$$x < 3$$

are equivalent. To obtain the second inequality from the first, you can subtract 2 from each side of the inequality. The following list describes the operations that can be used to create equivalent inequalities.

Properties of Inequalities

Let a, b, c, and d be real numbers.

1. Transitive Property
$$a < b \text{ and } b < c \implies a < c$$

2. Addition of Inequalities
$$a < b \text{ and } c < d \implies a + c < b + d$$

3. Addition of a Constant
$$a < b \implies a + c < b + c$$

4. Multiplication by a Constant
$$\text{For } c > 0, a < b \implies ac < bc$$
$$\text{For } c < 0, a < b \implies ac > bc$$

Each of the properties above is true if the symbol < is replaced by ≤ and the symbol > is replaced by ≥. For instance, another form of the multiplication property would be as follows.

$$\text{For } c > 0, a \le b \implies ac \le bc$$
$$\text{For } c < 0, a \le b \implies ac \ge bc$$

Linear Inequalities

The simplest type of inequality is a **linear inequality** in one variable. For instance, $2x + 3 > 4$ is a linear inequality in x.

In the following examples, pay special attention to the steps in which the inequality symbol is reversed. Remember that when you multiply or divide by a negative number, you must reverse the inequality symbol.

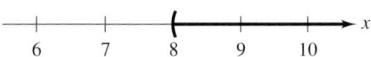 Example 2 ▶ Solving Linear Inequalities

Solve each inequality.

a. $5x - 7 > 3x + 9$

b. $1 - \dfrac{3x}{2} \geq x - 4$

Solution

a.

$5x - 7 > 3x + 9$	Write original inequality.
$2x - 7 > 9$	Subtract $3x$ from each side.
$2x > 16$	Add 7 to each side.
$x > 8$	Divide each side by 2.

The solution set is all real numbers that are greater than 8, which is denoted by $(8, \infty)$. The graph of this solution set is shown in Figure A.7.

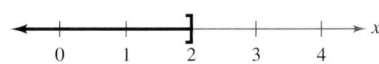

Solution interval: $(8, \infty)$

FIGURE **A.7**

b.

$1 - \dfrac{3x}{2} \geq x - 4$	Write original inequality.
$2 - 3x \geq 2x - 8$	Multiply each side by 2.
$2 - 5x \geq -8$	Subtract $2x$ from each side.
$-5x \geq -10$	Subtract 2 from each side.
$x \leq 2$	Divide each side by -5 and reverse the inequality.

The solution set is all real numbers that are less than or equal to 2, which is denoted by $(-\infty, 2]$. The graph of this solution set is shown in Figure A.8.

Solution interval: $(-\infty, 2]$

FIGURE **A.8**

Sometimes it is possible to write two inequalities as a **double inequality.** For instance, you can write the two inequalities $-4 \leq 5x - 2$ and $5x - 2 < 7$ more simply as

$$-4 \leq 5x - 2 < 7.$$

This form allows you to solve the two inequalities together, as demonstrated in Example 3.

Example 3 ▶ Solving a Double Inequality

To solve a double inequality, you can isolate x as the middle term.

$-3 \leq 6x - 1 < 3$	Write original inequality.
$-3 + 1 \leq 6x - 1 + 1 < 3 + 1$	Add 1 to each part.
$-2 \leq 6x < 4$	Simplify.
$\dfrac{-2}{6} \leq \dfrac{6x}{6} < \dfrac{4}{6}$	Divide each part by 6.
$-\dfrac{1}{3} \leq x < \dfrac{2}{3}$	Simplify.

The solution set is all real numbers that are greater than or equal to $-\frac{1}{3}$ and less than $\frac{2}{3}$, which is denoted by $\left[-\frac{1}{3}, \frac{2}{3}\right)$. The graph of this solution set is shown in Figure A.9.

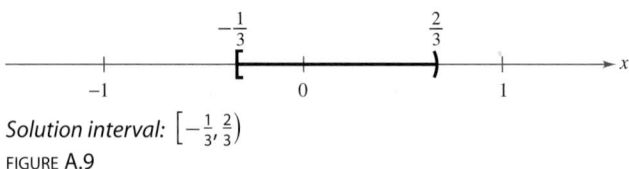

Solution interval: $\left[-\frac{1}{3}, \frac{2}{3}\right)$

FIGURE A.9

The double inequality in Example 3 could have been solved in two parts as follows.

$$-3 \leq 6x - 1 \quad \text{and} \quad 6x - 1 < 3$$
$$-2 \leq 6x \qquad\qquad\qquad 6x < 4$$
$$-\frac{1}{3} \leq x \qquad\qquad\qquad x < \frac{2}{3}$$

The solution set consists of all real numbers that satisfy *both* inequalities. In other words, the solution set is the set of all values of x for which

$$-\frac{1}{3} \leq x < \frac{2}{3}.$$

When combining two inequalities to form a double inequality, be sure that the inequalities satisfy the Transitive Property. For instance, it is *incorrect* to combine the inequalities $3 < x$ and $x \leq -1$ as $3 < x \leq -1$. This "inequality" is wrong because 3 is not less than -1.

Inequalities Involving Absolute Values

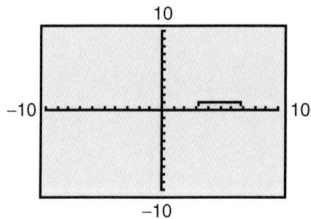
Solving an Absolute Value Inequality

Let x be a variable or an algebraic expression and let a be a real number such that $a \geq 0$.

1. The solutions of $|x| < a$ are all values of x that lie between $-a$ and a.

$$|x| < a \qquad \text{if and only if} \qquad -a < x < a.$$

2. The solutions of $|x| > a$ are all values of x that are less than $-a$ or greater than a.

$$|x| > a \qquad \text{if and only if} \qquad x < -a \quad \text{or} \quad x > a.$$

These rules are also valid if $<$ is replaced by $\leq$ and $>$ is replaced by $\geq$.

Example 4 ▶ Solving an Absolute Value Inequality

Solve each inequality.

a. $|x - 5| < 2$ **b.** $|x + 3| \geq 7$

Solution

a. $|x - 5| < 2$ Write original inequality.

$\qquad -2 < x - 5 < 2$ Write equivalent inequalities.

$\qquad -2 + 5 < x - 5 + 5 < 2 + 5$ Add 5 to each part.

$\qquad\qquad 3 < x < 7$ Simplify.

The solution set is all real numbers that are greater than 3 and less than 7, which is denoted by $(3, 7)$. The graph of this solution set is shown in Figure A.10.

b. $\qquad |x + 3| \geq 7$ Write original inequality.

$\qquad x + 3 \leq -7 \qquad \text{or} \qquad x + 3 \geq 7$ Write equivalent inequalities.

$\qquad x + 3 - 3 \leq -7 - 3 \qquad x + 3 - 3 \geq 7 - 3$ Subtract 3 from each side.

$\qquad\qquad x \leq -10 \qquad\qquad\qquad x \geq 4$ Simplify.

The solution set is all real numbers that are less than or equal to -10 *or* greater than or equal to 4. The interval notation for this solution set is $(-\infty, -10] \cup [4, \infty)$. The symbol $\cup$ is called a *union* symbol and is used to denote the combining of two sets. The graph of this solution set is shown in Figure A.11.

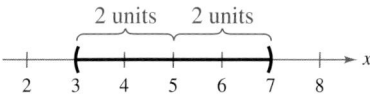

$|x - 5| < 2$: *Solutions lie inside* $(3, 7)$
FIGURE A.10

$|x + 3| \geq 7$: *Solutions lie outside* $(-10, 4)$
FIGURE A.11

Other Types of Inequalities

To solve a polynomial inequality, you can use the fact that a polynomial can change signs only at its zeros (the x-values that make the polynomial equal to zero). Between two consecutive zeros, a polynomial must be entirely positive or entirely negative. This means that when the real zeros of a polynomial are put in order, they divide the real number line into intervals in which the polynomial has no sign changes. These zeros are the **critical numbers** of the inequality, and the resulting intervals are the **test intervals** for the inequality.

Example 5 ▶ Solving a Polynomial Inequality

Solve

$$x^2 - x - 6 < 0.$$

Solution

By factoring the polynomial as

$$x^2 - x - 6 = (x + 2)(x - 3)$$

you can see that the critical numbers are

$$x = -2 \quad \text{and} \quad x = 3.$$

So, the polynomial's test intervals are

$$(-\infty, -2), \quad (-2, 3), \quad \text{and} \quad (3, \infty). \qquad \text{Test intervals}$$

In each test interval, choose a representative x-value and evaluate the polynomial.

Interval	x-Value	Polynomial Value	Conclusion
$(-\infty, -2)$	$x = -3$	$(-3)^2 - (-3) - 6 = 6$	Positive
$(-2, 3)$	$x = 0$	$(0)^2 - (0) - 6 = -6$	Negative
$(3, \infty)$	$x = 4$	$(4)^2 - (4) - 6 = 6$	Positive

From this you can conclude that the inequality is satisfied for all x-values in $(-2, 3)$. This implies that the solution of the inequality $x^2 - x - 6 < 0$ is the interval $(-2, 3)$, as shown in Figure A.12.

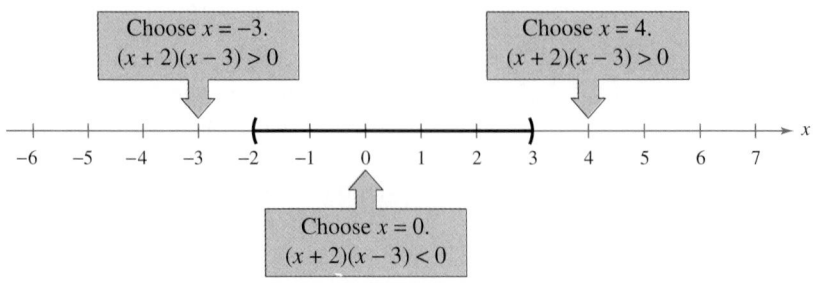

FIGURE **A.12**

STUDY TIP

As with linear inequalities, you can check the reasonableness of a solution by substituting x-values into the original inequality. For instance, to check the solution found in Example 5, try substituting several x-values from the interval $(-2, 3)$ into the inequality

$$x^2 - x - 6 < 0.$$

Regardless of which x-values you choose, the inequality should be satisfied.

The concepts of critical numbers and test intervals can be extended to rational inequalities. To do this, use the fact that the value of a rational expression can change sign only at its zeros (the x-values for which its numerator is zero) and its *undefined values* (the x-values for which its denominator is zero). These two types of numbers make up the *critical numbers* of a rational inequality.

Example 6 ▶ Solving a Rational Inequality

Solve $\dfrac{2x-7}{x-5} \le 3$.

Solution

Begin by writing the rational inequality in general form.

$$\frac{2x-7}{x-5} \le 3 \qquad\qquad \text{Write original inequality.}$$

$$\frac{2x-7}{x-5} - 3 \le 0 \qquad\qquad \text{Write in general form.}$$

$$\frac{2x-7-3x+15}{x-5} \le 0 \qquad\qquad \text{Add fractions.}$$

$$\frac{-x+8}{x-5} \le 0 \qquad\qquad \text{Simplify.}$$

Critical numbers: $\quad x = 5, x = 8 \qquad$ Zeros and undefined values of rational expression

Test intervals: $\qquad (-\infty, 5), (5, 8), (8, \infty)$

Test: $\qquad\qquad$ Is $\dfrac{-x+8}{x-5} \le 0$?

After testing these intervals, as shown in Figure A.13, you can see that the inequality is satisfied on the open intervals $(-\infty, 5)$ and $(8, \infty)$. Moreover, because $(-x+8)/(x-5) = 0$ when $x = 8$, you can conclude that the solution set consists of all real numbers in the intervals $(-\infty, 5) \cup [8, \infty)$. (Be sure to use a closed interval to indicate that x can equal 8.)

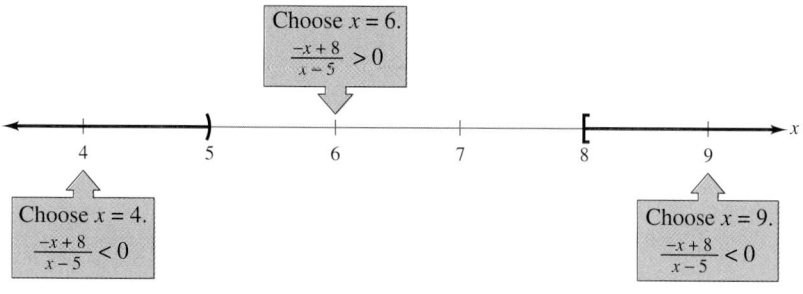

FIGURE A.13

A common application of inequalities is finding the domain of an expression that involves a square root, as shown in Example 7.

Example 7 ▶ **Finding the Domain of an Expression**

Find the domain of

$$\sqrt{64 - 4x^2}.$$

Solution

Remember that the domain of an expression is the set of all x-values for which the expression is defined. Because $\sqrt{64 - 4x^2}$ is defined (has real values) only if $64 - 4x^2$ is nonnegative, the domain is given by $64 - 4x^2 \geq 0$.

$$64 - 4x^2 \geq 0 \qquad \text{Write in general form.}$$
$$16 - x^2 \geq 0 \qquad \text{Divide each side by 4.}$$
$$(4 - x)(4 + x) \geq 0 \qquad \text{Write in factored form.}$$

So, the inequality has two critical numbers: -4 and 4. You can use these two numbers to test the inequality as follows.

Critical numbers: $x = -4, x = 4$

Test intervals: $(-\infty, -4), (-4, 4), (4, \infty)$

Test: Is $(4 - x)(4 + x) \geq 0$?

A test shows that the inequality is satisfied on the *closed interval* $[-4, 4]$. So, the domain of the expression $\sqrt{64 - 4x^2}$ is the interval $[-4, 4]$, as shown in Figure A.14.

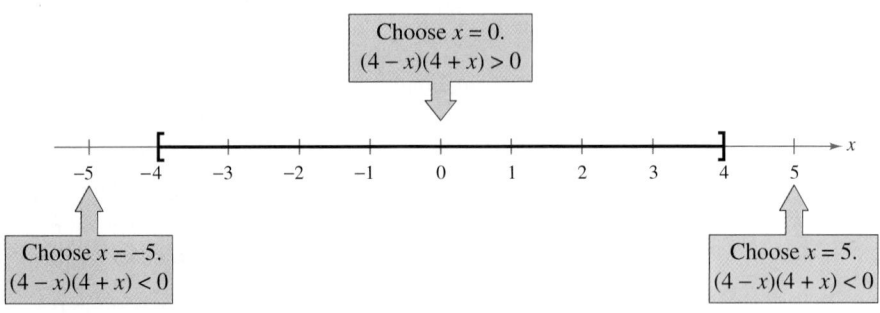

FIGURE A.14

A.6 Exercises

In Exercises 1–6, write an inequality that represents the interval, and state whether the interval is bounded or unbounded.

1. $[-1, 5]$

2. $(2, 10]$

3. $(11, \infty)$

4. $[-5, \infty)$

5. $(-\infty, -2)$

6. $(-\infty, 7]$

In Exercises 7–12, match the inequality with its graph. [The graphs are labeled (a), (b), (c), (d), (e), and (f).]

(a)

(b)

(c)

(d)

(e)

(f)

7. $x < 3$

8. $x \geq 5$

9. $-3 < x \leq 4$

10. $0 \leq x \leq \frac{9}{2}$

11. $|x| < 3$

12. $|x| > 4$

In Exercises 13–18, determine whether each value of x is a solution of the inequality.

Inequality	Values

13. $5x - 12 > 0$ (a) $x = 3$ (b) $x = -3$
    (c) $x = \frac{5}{2}$ (d) $x = \frac{3}{2}$

14. $2x + 1 < -3$ (a) $x = 0$ (b) $x = -\frac{1}{4}$
    (c) $x = -4$ (d) $x = -\frac{3}{2}$

15. $0 < \dfrac{x - 2}{4} < 2$ (a) $x = 4$ (b) $x = 10$
    (c) $x = 0$ (d) $x = \frac{7}{2}$

16. $-1 < \dfrac{3 - x}{2} \leq 1$ (a) $x = 0$ (b) $x = -5$
    (c) $x = 1$ (d) $x = 5$

17. $|x - 10| \geq 3$ (a) $x = 13$ (b) $x = -1$
    (c) $x = 14$ (d) $x = 9$

Inequality	Values

18. $|2x - 3| < 15$ (a) $x = -6$ (b) $x = 0$
    (c) $x = 12$ (d) $x = 7$

In Exercises 19–44, solve the inequality and sketch the solution on the real number line. (Some inequalities have no solution.)

19. $4x < 12$

20. $10x < -40$

21. $-2x > -3$

22. $-6x > 15$

23. $x - 5 \geq 7$

24. $x + 7 \leq 12$

25. $2x + 7 < 3 + 4x$

26. $3x + 1 \geq 2 + x$

27. $2x - 1 \geq 1 - 5x$

28. $6x - 4 \leq 2 + 8x$

29. $4 - 2x < 3(3 - x)$

30. $4(x + 1) < 2x + 3$

31. $\frac{3}{4}x - 6 \leq x - 7$

32. $3 + \frac{2}{7}x > x - 2$

33. $\frac{1}{2}(8x + 1) \geq 3x + \frac{5}{2}$

34. $9x - 1 < \frac{3}{4}(16x - 2)$

35. $3.6x + 11 \geq -3.4$

36. $15.6 - 1.3x < -5.2$

37. $1 < 2x + 3 < 9$

38. $-8 \leq -(3x + 5) < 13$

39. $-4 < \dfrac{2x - 3}{3} < 4$

40. $0 \leq \dfrac{x + 3}{2} < 5$

41. $\frac{3}{4} > x + 1 > \frac{1}{4}$

42. $-1 < 2 - \dfrac{x}{3} < 1$

43. $3.2 \leq 0.4x - 1 \leq 4.4$

44. $4.5 > \dfrac{1.5x + 6}{2} > 10.5$

In Exercises 45–60, solve the inequality and sketch the solution on the real number line. (Some inequalities have no solution.)

45. $|x| < 6$

46. $|x| > 4$

47. $\left|\dfrac{x}{2}\right| > 1$

48. $\left|\dfrac{x}{5}\right| > 3$

49. $|x - 5| < -1$

50. $|x - 5| \geq 0$

51. $|x - 20| \leq 6$

52. $|x - 7| < -5$

53. $|3 - 4x| \geq 9$

54. $|1 - 2x| < 5$

55. $\left|\dfrac{x - 3}{2}\right| \geq 4$

56. $\left|1 - \dfrac{2x}{3}\right| < 1$

57. $|9 - 2x| - 2 < -1$

58. $|x + 14| + 3 > 17$

59. $2|x + 10| \geq 9$

60. $3|4 - 5x| \leq 9$

Graphical Analysis In Exercises 61–68, use a graphing utility to graph the inequality and identify the solution set.

61. $6x > 12$

62. $3x - 1 \le 5$

63. $5 - 2x \ge 1$

64. $3(x + 1) < x + 7$

65. $|x - 8| \le 14$

66. $|2x + 9| > 13$

67. $2|x + 7| \ge 13$

68. $\frac{1}{2}|x + 1| \le 3$

In Exercises 69–74, find the interval(s) on the real number line for which the radicand is nonnegative (greater than or equal to zero).

69. $\sqrt{x - 5}$

70. $\sqrt{x - 10}$

71. $\sqrt{x + 3}$

72. $\sqrt{3 - x}$

73. $\sqrt[4]{7 - 2x}$

74. $\sqrt[4]{6x + 15}$

In Exercises 75–82, use absolute value notation to define the interval (or pair of intervals) on the real number line.

75.

76.

77.

78.

79. All real numbers within 10 units of 12

80. All real numbers at least 5 units from 8

81. All real numbers more than 5 units from -3

82. All real numbers no more than 7 units from -6

In Exercises 83–86, determine whether each value of x is a solution of the inequality.

Inequality   *Values*

83. $x^2 - 3 < 0$ (a) $x = 3$ (b) $x = 0$

               (c) $x = \frac{3}{2}$ (d) $x = -5$

84. $x^2 - x - 12 \ge 0$ (a) $x = 5$ (b) $x = 0$

               (c) $x = -4$ (d) $x = -3$

85. $\frac{x + 2}{x - 4} \ge 3$ (a) $x = 5$ (b) $x = 4$

               (c) $x = -\frac{9}{2}$ (d) $x = \frac{9}{2}$

86. $\frac{3x^2}{x^2 + 4} < 1$ (a) $x = -2$ (b) $x = -1$

               (c) $x = 0$ (d) $x = 3$

In Exercises 87–90, find the critical numbers.

87. $2x^2 - x - 6$

88. $9x^3 - 25x^2$

89. $2 + \frac{3}{x - 5}$

90. $\frac{x}{x + 2} - \frac{2}{x - 1}$

In Exercises 91–106, solve the inequality and graph the solution on the real number line.

91. $x^2 \le 9$

92. $x^2 < 36$

93. $(x + 2)^2 < 25$

94. $(x - 3)^2 \ge 1$

95. $x^2 + 4x + 4 \ge 9$

96. $x^2 - 6x + 9 < 16$

97. $x^2 + x < 6$

98. $x^2 + 2x > 3$

99. $x^2 + 2x - 3 < 0$

100. $x^2 - 4x - 1 > 0$

101. $x^2 + 8x - 5 \ge 0$

102. $-2x^2 + 6x + 15 \le 0$

103. $x^3 - 3x^2 - x + 3 > 0$

104. $x^3 + 2x^2 - 4x - 8 \le 0$

105. $x^3 - 2x^2 - 9x - 2 \ge -20$

106. $2x^3 + 13x^2 - 8x - 46 \ge 6$

In Exercises 107–112, solve the inequality and write the solution set in interval notation.

107. $4x^3 - 6x^2 < 0$

108. $4x^3 - 12x^2 > 0$

109. $x^3 - 4x \ge 0$

110. $2x^3 - x^4 \le 0$

111. $(x - 1)^2(x + 2)^3 \ge 0$

112. $x^4(x - 3) \le 0$

In Exercises 113–126, solve the inequality and graph the solution on the real number line.

113. $\frac{1}{x} - x > 0$

114. $\frac{1}{x} - 4 < 0$

115. $\frac{x + 6}{x + 1} - 2 < 0$

116. $\frac{x + 12}{x + 2} - 3 \ge 0$

117. $\frac{3x - 5}{x - 5} > 4$

118. $\frac{5 + 7x}{1 + 2x} < 4$

119. $\dfrac{4}{x+5} > \dfrac{1}{2x+3}$

120. $\dfrac{5}{x-6} > \dfrac{3}{x+2}$

121. $\dfrac{1}{x-3} \le \dfrac{9}{4x+3}$

122. $\dfrac{1}{x} \ge \dfrac{1}{x+3}$

123. $\dfrac{x^2+2x}{x^2-9} \le 0$

124. $\dfrac{x^2+x-6}{x} \ge 0$

125. $\dfrac{5}{x-1} - \dfrac{2x}{x+1} < 1$

126. $\dfrac{3x}{x-1} \le \dfrac{x}{x+4} + 3$

In Exercises 127–132, find the domain of x in the expression.

127. $\sqrt{4-x^2}$

128. $\sqrt{x^2-4}$

129. $\sqrt{x^2-7x+12}$

130. $\sqrt{144-9x^2}$

131. $\sqrt{\dfrac{x}{x^2-2x-35}}$

132. $\sqrt{\dfrac{x}{x^2-9}}$

In Exercises 133–138, solve the inequality. (Round your answers to two decimal places.)

133. $0.4x^2 + 5.26 < 10.2$

134. $-1.3x^2 + 3.78 > 2.12$

135. $-0.5x^2 + 12.5x + 1.6 > 0$

136. $1.2x^2 + 4.8x + 3.1 < 5.3$

137. $\dfrac{1}{2.3x-5.2} > 3.4$ **138.** $\dfrac{2}{3.1x-3.7} > 5.8$

139. *Car Rental*   You can rent a midsize car from Company A for $250 per week with unlimited mileage. A similar car can be rented from Company B for $150 per week plus 25 cents for each mile driven. How many miles must you drive in a week in order for the rental fee for Company B to be greater than that for Company A?

140. *Copying Costs*   Your department sends its copying to the photocopy center of your company. The center bills your department $0.10 per page. You have investigated the possibility of buying a departmental copier for $3000. With your own copier, the cost per page would be $0.03. The expected life of the copier is 4 years. How many copies must you make in the four-year period to justify buying the copier?

141. *Investment*   In order for an investment of $1000 to grow to more than $1062.50 in 2 years, what must the annual interest rate be? $[A = P(1 + rt)]$

142. *Athletics*   For 60 men enrolled in a weightlifting class, the relationship between body weight x (in pounds) and maximum bench-press weight y (in pounds) can be modeled by the equation $y = 1.266x - 35.766$. Use this model to estimate the range of body weights of the men in this group that can bench press more than 200 pounds.

143. *Height*   The heights h of two-thirds of the members of a population satisfy the inequality

$$\left| \dfrac{h - 68.5}{2.7} \right| \le 1$$

where h is measured in inches. Determine the interval on the real number line in which these heights lie.

144. *Meteorology*   An electronic device is to be operated in an environment with relative humidity h in the interval defined by

$$|h - 50| \le 30.$$

What are the minimum and maximum relative humidities for the operation of this device?

145. *Geometry*   A rectangular playing field with a perimeter of 100 meters is to have an area of at least 500 square meters. Within what bounds must the length of the rectangle lie?

146. *Geometry*   A rectangular parking lot with a perimeter of 440 feet is to have an area of at least 8000 square feet. Within what bounds must the length of the rectangle lie?

147. *Investment* P dollars, invested at interest rate r compounded annually, increases to an amount

$$A = P(1 + r)^2$$

in 2 years. An investment of $1000 is to increase to an amount greater than $1100 in 2 years. The interest rate must be greater than what percent?

148. Cost, Revenue, and Profit The revenue and cost equations for a product are

$$R = x(50 - 0.0002x)$$

and

$$C = 12x + 150,000$$

where R and C are measured in dollars and x represents the number of units sold. How many units must be sold to obtain a profit of at least $1,650,000?

149. Resistors When two resistors of resistance R_1 and R_2 are connected in parallel (see figure), the total resistance R satisfies the equation

$$\frac{1}{R} = \frac{1}{R_1} + \frac{1}{R_2}.$$

Find R_1 for a parallel circuit in which $R_2 = 2$ ohms and R must be at least 1 ohm.

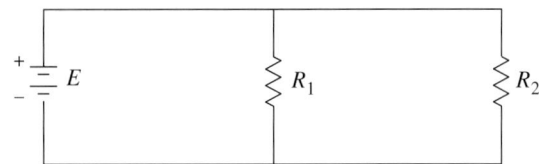

150. Safe Load The maximum safe load uniformly distributed over a one-foot section of a two-inch-wide wooden beam is approximated by the model

$$\text{Load} = 168.5d^2 - 472.1$$

where d is the depth of the beam.

(a) Evaluate the model for $d = 4$, $d = 6$, $d = 8$, $d = 10$, and $d = 12$. Use the results to create a bar graph.

(b) Determine the minimum depth of the beam that will safely support a load of 2000 pounds.

Synthesis

True or False? In Exercises 151–154, determine whether the statement is true or false. Justify your answer.

151. If a, b, and c are real numbers, and $a \le b$, then $ac \le bc$.

152. If $-10 \le x \le 8$, then $-10 \ge -x$ and $-x \ge -8$.

153. The zeros of the polynomial $x^3 - 2x^2 - 11x + 12 \ge 0$ divide the real number line into four test intervals.

154. The solution set of the inequality $\frac{3}{2}x^2 + 3x + 6 \ge 0$ is the set of real numbers.

155. Identify the graph of the inequality $|x - a| \ge 2$.

(a) ├────────┤ x
    $a-2$ a $a+2$

(b) ←─┤   ├──→ x
    $a-2$ a $a+2$

(c) ←─┤   ├──→ x
    $2-a$ 2 $2+a$

(d) ├────────┤ x
    $2-a$ 2 $2+a$

156. Find sets of values for a, b, and c such that $0 \le x \le 10$ is a solution of the inequality $|ax - b| \le c$.

157. Think About It The graph of $|x - 5| < 3$ can be described as all real numbers within 3 units of 5. Give a similar description of $|x - 10| < 8$.

158. Think About It The graph of $|x - 2| > 5$ can be described as all real numbers more than 5 units from 2. Give a similar description of $|x - 8| > 4$.

Exploration In Exercises 159–162, find the interval for b such that the equation has at least one real solution.

159. $x^2 + bx + 4 = 0$

160. $x^2 + bx - 4 = 0$

161. $3x^2 + bx + 10 = 0$

162. $2x^2 + bx + 5 = 0$

163. Conjecture Write a conjecture about the interval for b in Exercises 159–162. Explain your reasoning.

164. Think About It What is the center of the interval for b in Exercises 159–162?

165. Consider the polynomial $(x - a)(x - b)$ and the real number line shown below.

(a) Identify the points on the line at which the polynomial is zero.

(b) In each of the three subintervals of the line, write the sign of each factor and the sign of the product.

(c) For what x-values does the polynomial change signs?

<table>
<tr><td>**A.7**</td><td>**Errors and the Algebra of Calculus**</td></tr>
</table>

▶ **What you should learn**

• How to avoid common algebraic errors

• How to recognize and use algebraic techniques that are common in calculus

▶ **Why you should learn it**

An efficient command of algebra is critical in the study of calculus.

Algebraic Errors to Avoid

This section contains five lists of common algebraic errors: errors involving parentheses, errors involving fractions, errors involving exponents, errors involving radicals, and errors involving dividing out. Many of these errors are made because they seem to be the *easiest* things to do. For instance, the operations of subtraction and division are often believed to be commutative and associative. The following examples illustrate the fact that subtraction and division are neither commutative nor associative.

Not commutative

$$4 - 3 \neq 3 - 4$$

$$15 \div 5 \neq 5 \div 15$$

Not associative

$$8 - (6 - 2) \neq (8 - 6) - 2$$

$$20 \div (4 \div 2) \neq (20 \div 4) \div 2$$

Errors Involving Parentheses

Potential Error	*Correct Form*	*Comment*
	$a - (x - b) = a - x + b$	Change all signs when distributing minus sign.
$(a + b)^2 = a^2 + b^2$	$(a + b)^2 = a^2 + 2ab + b^2$	Remember the middle term when squaring binomials.
$\left(\frac{1}{2}a\right)\left(\frac{1}{2}b\right) = \frac{1}{2}(ab)$	$\left(\frac{1}{2}a\right)\left(\frac{1}{2}b\right) = \frac{1}{4}(ab) = \frac{ab}{4}$	$\frac{1}{2}$ occurs twice as a factor.
$(3x + 6)^2 = 3(x + 2)^2$	$(3x + 6)^2 = [3(x + 2)]^2$ $= 3^2(x + 2)^2$	When factoring, apply exponents to all factors.

Errors Involving Fractions

Potential Error	*Correct Form*	*Comment*
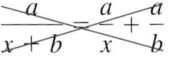	Leave as $\dfrac{a}{x + b}$.	Do not add denominators when adding fractions.
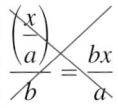	$\dfrac{\left(\dfrac{x}{a}\right)}{b} = \left(\dfrac{x}{a}\right)\left(\dfrac{1}{b}\right) = \dfrac{x}{ab}$	Multiply by the reciprocal when dividing fractions.
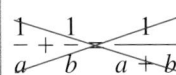	$\dfrac{1}{a} + \dfrac{1}{b} = \dfrac{b + a}{ab}$	Use the property for adding fractions.
	$\dfrac{1}{3x} = \dfrac{1}{3} \cdot \dfrac{1}{x}$	Use the property for multiplying fractions.
	$(1/3)x = \dfrac{1}{3} \cdot x = \dfrac{x}{3}$	Be careful when using a slash to denote division.
	$(1/x) + 2 = \dfrac{1}{x} + 2 = \dfrac{1 + 2x}{x}$	Be careful when using a slash to denote division.

Errors Involving Exponents

Potential Error	Correct Form	Comment
$(x^2)^3 = x^5$	$(x^2)^3 = x^{2\cdot3} = x^6$	Multiply exponents when raising a power to a power.
$x^2 \cdot x^3 = x^6$	$x^2 \cdot x^3 = x^{2+3} = x^5$	Add exponents when multiplying powers with like bases.
$2x^3 = (2x)^3$	$2x^3 = 2(x^3)$	Exponents have priority over coefficients.
$\dfrac{1}{x^2 - x^3} = x^{-2} - x^{-3}$	Leave as $\dfrac{1}{x^2 - x^3}$.	Do not move term-by-term from denominator to numerator.

Errors Involving Radicals

Potential Error	Correct Form	Comment
$\sqrt{5x} = 5\sqrt{x}$	$\sqrt{5x} = \sqrt{5}\sqrt{x}$	Radicals apply to every factor inside the radical.
$\sqrt{x^2 + a^2} = x + a$	Leave as $\sqrt{x^2 + a^2}$.	Do not apply radicals term-by-term.
$\sqrt{-x + a} = -\sqrt{x - a}$	Leave as $\sqrt{-x + a}$.	Do not factor minus signs out of square roots.

Errors Involving Dividing Out

Potential Error	Correct Form	Comment
$\dfrac{a + bx}{a} = 1 + bx$	$\dfrac{a + bx}{a} = \dfrac{a}{a} + \dfrac{bx}{a} = 1 + \dfrac{b}{a}x$	Divide out common factors, not common terms.
$\dfrac{a + ax}{a} = a + x$	$\dfrac{a + ax}{a} = \dfrac{a(1 + x)}{a} = 1 + x$	Factor before dividing out.
$1 + \dfrac{x}{2x} = 1 + \dfrac{1}{x}$	$1 + \dfrac{x}{2x} = 1 + \dfrac{1}{2} = \dfrac{3}{2}$	Divide out common factors.

A good way to avoid errors is to work *slowly, write neatly,* and *talk to yourself.* Each time you write a step, ask yourself why the step is algebraically legitimate. You can justify the step below because *dividing the numerator and denominator by the same nonzero number produces an equivalent fraction.*

$$\frac{2x}{6} = \frac{2 \cdot x}{2 \cdot 3} = \frac{x}{3}$$

Example 1 ▶   **Using the Property for Adding Fractions**

Describe and correct the error. $\dfrac{1}{2x} + \dfrac{1}{3x} = \dfrac{1}{5x}$

Solution

When adding fractions, use the property for adding fractions: $\dfrac{1}{a} + \dfrac{1}{b} = \dfrac{b + a}{ab}$.

$$\frac{1}{2x} + \frac{1}{3x} = \frac{3x + 2x}{6x^2} = \frac{5x}{6x^2} = \frac{5}{6x}$$

Some Algebra of Calculus

In calculus it is often necessary to take a simplified algebraic expression and "unsimplify" it. See the following lists, taken from a standard calculus text.

Unusual Factoring

Expression	Useful Calculus Form	Comment
$\dfrac{5x^4}{8}$	$\dfrac{5}{8}x^4$	Write with fractional coefficient.
$\dfrac{x^2 + 3x}{-6}$	$-\dfrac{1}{6}(x^2 + 3x)$	Write with fractional coefficient.
$2x^2 - x - 3$	$2\left(x^2 - \dfrac{x}{2} - \dfrac{3}{2}\right)$	Factor out the leading coefficient.
$\dfrac{x}{2}(x + 1)^{-1/2} + (x + 1)^{1/2}$	$\dfrac{(x + 1)^{-1/2}}{2}[x + 2(x + 1)]$	Factor out factor with lowest power.

Writing with Negative Exponents

Expression	Useful Calculus Form	Comment
$\dfrac{9}{5x^3}$	$\dfrac{9}{5}x^{-3}$	Move the factor to the numerator and change the sign of the exponent.
$\dfrac{7}{\sqrt{2x - 3}}$	$7(2x - 3)^{-1/2}$	Move the factor to the numerator and change the sign of the exponent.

Writing a Fraction as a Sum

Expression	Useful Calculus Form	Comment
$\dfrac{x + 2x^2 + 1}{\sqrt{x}}$	$x^{1/2} + 2x^{3/2} + x^{-1/2}$	Divide each term by $x^{1/2}$.
$\dfrac{1 + x}{x^2 + 1}$	$\dfrac{1}{x^2 + 1} + \dfrac{x}{x^2 + 1}$	Rewrite the fraction as the sum of fractions.
$\dfrac{2x}{x^2 + 2x + 1}$	$\dfrac{2x + 2 - 2}{x^2 + 2x + 1}$	Add and subtract the same term.
	$= \dfrac{2x + 2}{x^2 + 2x + 1} - \dfrac{2}{(x + 1)^2}$	Rewrite the fraction as the difference of fractions.
$\dfrac{x^2 - 2}{x + 1}$	$x - 1 - \dfrac{1}{x + 1}$	Use long division. (See Section 2.3.)
$\dfrac{x + 7}{x^2 - x - 6}$	$\dfrac{2}{x - 3} - \dfrac{1}{x + 2}$	Use the method of partial fractions. (See Section 2.7.)

Inserting Factors and Terms

Expression	*Useful Calculus Form*	*Comment*
$(2x - 1)^3$	$\dfrac{1}{2}(2x - 1)^3(2)$	Multiply and divide by 2.
$7x^2(4x^3 - 5)^{1/2}$	$\dfrac{7}{12}(4x^3 - 5)^{1/2}(12x^2)$	Multiply and divide by 12.
$\dfrac{4x^2}{9} - 4y^2 = 1$	$\dfrac{x^2}{9/4} - \dfrac{y^2}{1/4} = 1$	Write with fractional denominators.
$\dfrac{x}{x + 1}$	$\dfrac{x + 1 - 1}{x + 1} = 1 - \dfrac{1}{x + 1}$	Add and subtract the same term.

The next five examples demonstrate many of the steps in the preceding lists.

Example 2 ▶   **Factors Involving Negative Exponents**

Factor $x(x + 1)^{-1/2} + (x + 1)^{1/2}$.

Solution

When multiplying factors with like bases, you add exponents. When factoring, you are undoing multiplication, and so you *subtract* exponents.

$$x(x + 1)^{-1/2} + (x + 1)^{1/2} = (x + 1)^{-1/2}[x(x + 1)^0 + (x + 1)^1]$$
$$= (x + 1)^{-1/2}[x + (x + 1)]$$
$$= (x + 1)^{-1/2}(2x + 1)$$

Here is another way to simplify the expression in Example 2.

$$x(x + 1)^{-1/2} + (x + 1)^{1/2} = x(x + 1)^{-1/2} + (x + 1)^{1/2} \cdot \frac{(x + 1)^{1/2}}{(x + 1)^{1/2}}$$
$$= \frac{x(x + 1)^0 + (x + 1)^1}{(x + 1)^{1/2}} = \frac{2x + 1}{\sqrt{x + 1}}$$

Example 3 ▶   **Inserting Factors in an Expression**

Insert the required factor: $\dfrac{x + 2}{(x^2 + 4x - 3)^2} = (\quad)\dfrac{1}{(x^2 + 4x - 3)^2}(2x + 4)$.

Solution

The expression on the right side of the equation is twice the expression on the left side. To make both sides equal, insert a factor of $\frac{1}{2}$.

$$\frac{x + 2}{(x^2 + 4x - 3)^2} = \left(\frac{1}{2}\right)\frac{1}{(x^2 + 4x - 3)^2}(2x + 4)$$
     Right side is multiplied and divided by 2.

Example 4 ▶ Rewriting Fractions

Explain the following.

$$\frac{4x^2}{9} - 4y^2 = \frac{x^2}{9/4} - \frac{y^2}{1/4}$$

Solution

To write the expression on the left side of the equation in the form given on the right side, multiply the numerators and denominators of both terms by $\frac{1}{4}$.

$$\frac{4x^2}{9} - 4y^2 = \frac{4x^2}{9}\left(\frac{1/4}{1/4}\right) - 4y^2\left(\frac{1/4}{1/4}\right)$$

$$= \frac{x^2}{9/4} - \frac{y^2}{1/4}$$

Example 5 ▶ Rewriting with Negative Exponents

Rewrite each expression using negative exponents.

a. $\dfrac{-4x}{(1-2x^2)^2}$ **b.** $\dfrac{2}{5x^3} - \dfrac{1}{\sqrt{x}} + \dfrac{3}{5(4x)^2}$

Solution

a. $\dfrac{-4x}{(1-2x^2)^2} = -4x(1-2x^2)^{-2}$

b. Begin by writing the second term in exponential form.

$$\frac{2}{5x^3} - \frac{1}{\sqrt{x}} + \frac{3}{5(4x)^2} = \frac{2}{5x^3} - \frac{1}{x^{1/2}} + \frac{3}{5(4x)^2}$$

$$= \frac{2}{5}x^{-3} - x^{-1/2} + \frac{3}{5}(4x)^{-2}$$

Example 6 ▶ Writing a Fraction as a Sum of Terms

Rewrite each fraction as the sum of three terms.

a. $\dfrac{x^2 - 4x + 8}{2x}$ **b.** $\dfrac{x + 2x^2 + 1}{\sqrt{x}}$

Solution

a. $\dfrac{x^2 - 4x + 8}{2x} = \dfrac{x^2}{2x} - \dfrac{4x}{2x} + \dfrac{8}{2x}$

$$= \frac{x}{2} - 2 + \frac{4}{x}$$

b. $\dfrac{x + 2x^2 + 1}{\sqrt{x}} = \dfrac{x}{x^{1/2}} + \dfrac{2x^2}{x^{1/2}} + \dfrac{1}{x^{1/2}}$

$$= x^{1/2} + 2x^{3/2} + x^{-1/2}$$

A.7 Exercises

In Exercises 1–18, describe and correct the error.

1. $2x - (3y + 4) = 2x - 3y + 4$
2. $5z + 3(x - 2) = 5z + 3x - 2$
3. $\dfrac{4}{16x - (2x + 1)} = \dfrac{4}{14x + 1}$
4. $\dfrac{1 - x}{(5 - x)(-x)} = \dfrac{x - 1}{x(x - 5)}$
5. $(5z)(6z) = 30z$
6. $x(yz) = (xy)(xz)$
7. $a\left(\dfrac{x}{y}\right) = \dfrac{ax}{ay}$
8. $(4x)^2 = 4x^2$
9. $\sqrt{x + 9} = \sqrt{x} + 3$
10. $\sqrt{25 - x^2} = 5 - x$
11. $\dfrac{2x^2 + 1}{5x} = \dfrac{2x + 1}{5}$
12. $\dfrac{6x + y}{6x - y} = \dfrac{x + y}{x - y}$
13. $\dfrac{1}{a^{-1} + b^{-1}} = \left(\dfrac{1}{a + b}\right)^{-1}$
14. $\dfrac{1}{x + y} = \dfrac{y}{x + 1}$
15. $(x^2 + 5x)^{1/2} = x(x + 5)^{1/2}$
16. $x(2x - 1)^2 = (2x^2 - x)^2$
17. $\dfrac{3}{x} + \dfrac{4}{y} = \dfrac{7}{x + y}$
18. $\dfrac{1}{2y} = (1/2)y$

In Exercises 19–38, insert the required factor in the parentheses.

19. $\dfrac{3x + 2}{5} = \dfrac{1}{5}(\quad)$
20. $\dfrac{7x^2}{10} = \dfrac{7}{10}(\quad)$
21. $\tfrac{2}{3}x^2 + \tfrac{1}{3}x + 5 = \tfrac{1}{3}(\quad)$
22. $\tfrac{3}{4}x + \tfrac{1}{2} = \tfrac{1}{4}(\quad)$
23. $x^2(x^3 - 1)^4 = (\quad)(x^3 - 1)^4(3x^2)$
24. $x(1 - 2x^2)^3 = (\quad)(1 - 2x^2)^3(-4x)$
25. $\dfrac{4x + 6}{(x^2 + 3x + 7)^3} = (\quad)\dfrac{1}{(x^2 + 3x + 7)^3}(2x + 3)$
26. $\dfrac{x + 1}{(x^2 + 2x - 3)^2} = (\quad)\dfrac{1}{(x^2 + 2x - 3)^2}(2x + 2)$
27. $\dfrac{3}{x} + \dfrac{5}{2x^2} - \dfrac{3}{2}x = (\quad)(6x + 5 - 3x^3)$
28. $\dfrac{(x - 1)^2}{169} + (y + 5)^2 = \dfrac{(x - 1)^3}{169(\quad)} + (y + 5)^2$
29. $\dfrac{9x^2}{25} + \dfrac{16y^2}{49} = \dfrac{x^2}{(\quad)} + \dfrac{y^2}{(\quad)}$
30. $\dfrac{3x^2}{4} - \dfrac{9y^2}{16} = \dfrac{x^2}{(\quad)} - \dfrac{y^2}{(\quad)}$
31. $\dfrac{x^2}{1/12} - \dfrac{y^2}{2/3} = \dfrac{12x^2}{(\quad)} - \dfrac{3y^2}{(\quad)}$
32. $\dfrac{x^2}{4/9} + \dfrac{y^2}{7/8} = \dfrac{9x^2}{(\quad)} + \dfrac{8y^2}{(\quad)}$
33. $x^{1/3} - 5x^{4/3} = x^{1/3}(\quad)$
34. $3(2x + 1)x^{1/2} + 4x^{3/2} = x^{1/2}(\quad)$
35. $(1 - 3x)^{4/3} - 4x(1 - 3x)^{1/3} = (1 - 3x)^{1/3}(\quad)$
36. $\dfrac{1}{2\sqrt{x}} + 5x^{3/2} - 10x^{5/2} = \dfrac{1}{2\sqrt{x}}(\quad)$
37. $\dfrac{1}{10}(2x + 1)^{5/2} - \dfrac{1}{6}(2x + 1)^{3/2} = \dfrac{(2x + 1)^{3/2}}{15}(\quad)$
38. $\dfrac{3}{7}(t + 1)^{7/3} - \dfrac{3}{4}(t + 1)^{4/3} = \dfrac{3(t + 1)^{4/3}}{28}(\quad)$

In Exercises 39–44, write the fraction as a sum of two or more terms.

39. $\dfrac{16 - 5x - x^2}{x}$
40. $\dfrac{x^3 - 5x^2 + 4}{x^2}$
41. $\dfrac{4x^3 - 7x^2 + 1}{x^{1/3}}$
42. $\dfrac{2x^5 - 3x^3 + 5x - 1}{x^{3/2}}$
43. $\dfrac{3 - 5x^2 - x^4}{\sqrt{x}}$
44. $\dfrac{x^3 - 5x^4}{3x^2}$

In Exercises 45–56, simplify the expression.

45. $\dfrac{-2(x^2 - 3)^{-3}(2x)(x + 1)^3 - 3(x + 1)^2(x^2 - 3)^{-2}}{[(x + 1)^3]^2}$
46. $\dfrac{x^5(-3)(x^2 + 1)^{-4}(2x) - (x^2 + 1)^{-3}(5)x^4}{(x^5)^2}$
47. $\dfrac{(6x + 1)^3(27x^2 + 2) - (9x^3 + 2x)(3)(6x + 1)^2(6)}{[(6x + 1)^3]^2}$
48. $\dfrac{(4x^2 + 9)^{1/2}(2) - (2x + 3)(\frac{1}{2})(4x^2 + 9)^{-1/2}(8x)}{[(4x^2 + 9)^{1/2}]^2}$
49. $\dfrac{(x + 2)^{3/4}(x + 3)^{-2/3} - (x + 3)^{1/3}(x + 2)^{-1/4}}{[(x + 2)^{3/4}]^2}$
50. $(2x - 1)^{1/2} - (x + 2)(2x - 1)^{-1/2}$
51. $\dfrac{2(3x - 1)^{1/3} - (2x + 1)(\frac{1}{3})(3x - 1)^{-2/3}(3)}{(3x - 1)^{2/3}}$
52. $\dfrac{(x + 1)(\frac{1}{2})(2x - 3x^2)^{-1/2}(2 - 6x) - (2x - 3x^2)^{1/2}}{(x + 1)^2}$
53. $\dfrac{1}{(x^2 + 4)^{1/2}} \cdot \dfrac{1}{2}(x^2 + 4)^{-1/2}(2x)$

54. $\dfrac{1}{x^2 - 6}(2x) + \dfrac{1}{2x + 5}(2)$

55. $(x^2 + 5)^{1/2}\left(\dfrac{3}{2}\right)(3x - 2)^{1/2}(3) +$
$\qquad\qquad (3x - 2)^{3/2}\left(\dfrac{1}{2}\right)(x^2 + 5)^{-1/2}(2x)$

56. $(3x + 2)^{-1/2}(3)(x - 6)^{1/2}(1) +$
$\qquad\qquad (x - 6)^3\left(-\dfrac{1}{2}\right)(3x + 2)^{-3/2}(3)$

57. *Athletics*   A triathlete has set up a course for train-ing as part of her regimen in preparation for an upcoming triathlon. She is dropped off by a boat 2 miles from the nearest point on shore. The finish line is 4 miles down the coast and 2 miles inland (see figure). She can swim at 2 miles per hour and run at 6 miles per hour. The time t (in hours) required for her to reach the finish line can be approximated by the model

$$t = \dfrac{\sqrt{x^2 + 4}}{2} + \dfrac{\sqrt{(4 - x)^2 + 4}}{6}$$

where x is the distance down the coast (in miles) to which she swims and then leaves the water to start her run.

(a) Find the time required for the triathlete to finish when she swims to the points $x = 0.5$, $x = 1.0$, $x = 1.5,\ \ldots,\ x = 3.5$, and $x = 4.0$ miles down the coast.

(b) Use your results from part (a) to determine the distance down the coast that will yield the min-imum amount of time required for the triathlete to reach the finish line.

(c) The expression below was obtained using calculus. It can be used to find the minimum amount of time required for the triathlete to reach the finish line. Simplify the expression.

$$\dfrac{1}{2}x(x^2 + 4)^{-1/2} + \dfrac{1}{6}(x - 4)(x^2 - 8x + 20)^{-1/2}$$

58. (a) Verify that $y_1 = y_2$ analytically.

$$y_1 = x^2\left(\dfrac{1}{3}\right)(x^2 + 1)^{-2/3}(2x) + (x^2 + 1)^{1/3}(2x)$$

$$y_2 = \dfrac{2x(4x^2 + 3)}{3(x^2 + 1)^{2/3}}$$

(b) Complete the table and demonstrate the equality in part (a) numerically.

x	-2	-1	$-\frac{1}{2}$	0	1	2	$\frac{5}{2}$
y_1							
y_2							

Synthesis

True or False?   **In Exercises 59–62, determine whether the statement is true or false. Justify your answer.**

59. $x^{-1} + y^{-2} = \dfrac{y^2 + x}{xy^2}$

60. $\dfrac{1}{x^{-2} + y^{-1}} = x^2 + y$

61. $\dfrac{1}{\sqrt{x} + 4} = \dfrac{\sqrt{x} - 4}{x - 16}$

62. $\dfrac{x^2 - 9}{\sqrt{x} - 3} = \sqrt{x} + 3$

In Exercises 63–66, find and correct any errors.

63. $x^n \cdot x^{3n} = x^{3n^2}$

64. $(x^n)^{2n} + (x^{2n})^n = 2x^{2n^2}$

65. $x^{2n} + y^{2n} = (x^n + y^n)^2$

66. $\dfrac{x^{2n} \cdot x^{3n}}{x^{3n} + x^2} = \dfrac{x^{5n}}{x^{3n} + x^2}$

67. *Think About It*   You are taking a course in calculus, and for one of the homework problems you obtain the following answer.

$$\dfrac{1}{10}(2x - 1)^{5/2} + \dfrac{1}{6}(2x - 1)^{3/2}$$

The answer in the back of the book is

$$\dfrac{1}{15}(2x - 1)^{3/2}(3x + 1).$$

Are these two answers equivalent? If so, show how the second answer can be obtained from the first.

A.8 Graphical Representation of Data

▶ Why you should learn it

The Cartesian plane can be used to represent relationships between two variables. For instance, in Exercise 27 on page A85, a graph represents the minimum wage in the United States from 1950 to 2000.

The Cartesian Plane

Just as you can represent real numbers by points on a real number line, you can represent ordered pairs of real numbers by points in a plane called the **rectangular coordinate system,** or the **Cartesian plane,** named after the French mathematician René Descartes (1596–1650).

The Cartesian plane is formed by using two real number lines intersecting at right angles, as shown in Figure A.15. The horizontal real number line is usually called the **x-axis,** and the vertical real number line is usually called the **y-axis.** The point of intersection of these two axes is the **origin,** and the two axes divide the plane into four parts called **quadrants.**

FIGURE A.15   FIGURE A.16

Each point in the plane corresponds to an **ordered pair** (x, y) of real numbers x and y, called **coordinates** of the point. The **x-coordinate** represents the directed distance from the y-axis to the point, and the **y-coordinate** represents the directed distance from the x-axis to the point, as shown in Figure A.16.

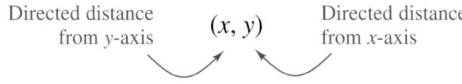

The notation (x, y) denotes both a point in the plane and an open interval on the real number line. The context will tell you which meaning is intended.

Example 1 ▶ Plotting Points in the Cartesian Plane

Plot the points $(-1, 2)$, $(3, 4)$, $(0, 0)$, $(3, 0)$, and $(-2, -3)$.

Solution

To plot the point $(-1, 2)$, imagine a vertical line through -1 on the x-axis and a horizontal line through 2 on the y-axis. The intersection of these two lines is the point $(-1, 2)$. The other four points can be plotted in a similar way, as shown in Figure A.17.

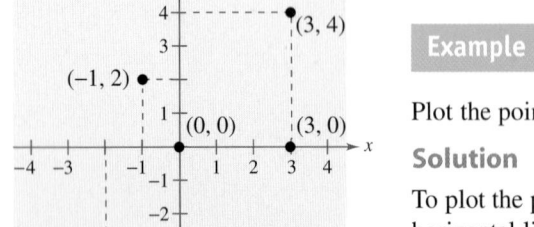

FIGURE A.17

The beauty of a rectangular coordinate system is that it allows you to *see* relationships between two variables. It would be difficult to overestimate the importance of Descartes's introduction of coordinates in the plane. Today, his ideas are in common use in virtually every scientific and business-related field.

Example 2 ▶ **Sketching a Scatter Plot**

From 1990 through 1999, the amount A (in millions of dollars) spent on skiing equipment in the United States is shown in the table, where t represents the year. Sketch a scatter plot of the data.   (Source: National Sporting Goods Association)

Solution

To sketch a *scatter plot* of the data shown in the table, you simply represent each pair of values by an ordered pair (t, A) and plot the resulting points, as shown in Figure A.18. For instance, the first pair of values is represented by the ordered pair $(1990, 475)$. Note that the break in the t-axis indicates that the numbers between 0 and 1990 have been omitted.

Year, t	Amount, A
1990	475
1991	577
1992	521
1993	569
1994	609
1995	562
1996	707
1997	723
1998	718
1999	739

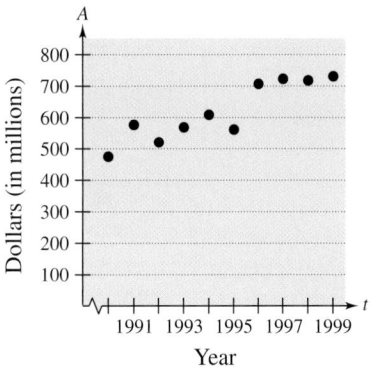

FIGURE A.18

STUDY TIP

In Example 2, you could have let $t = 1$ represent the year 1990. In that case, the horizontal axis would not have been broken, and the tick marks would have been labeled 1 through 10 (instead of 1990 through 1999).

Technology

The scatter plot in Example 2 is only one way to represent the data graphically. Two other techniques are shown at the right. The first is a bar graph and the second is a line graph. All three graphical representations were created with a computer. If you have access to a graphing utility, try using it to represent graphically the data given in Example 2.

Bar Graph

Line Graph

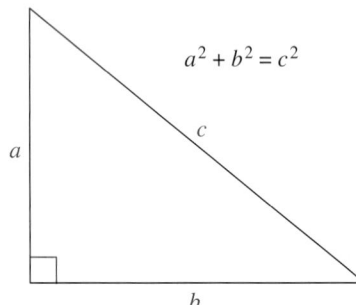

$$a^2 + b^2 = c^2$$

FIGURE **A.19**

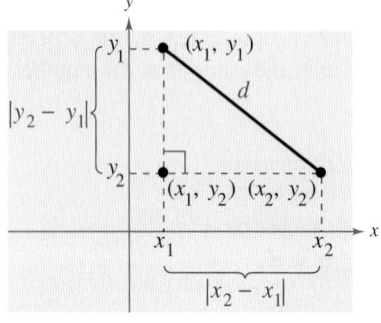

FIGURE **A.20**

The Distance Formula

Recall from the Pythagorean Theorem that, for a right triangle with hypotenuse of length c and sides of lengths a and b, you have

$$a^2 + b^2 = c^2 \qquad \text{Pythagorean Theorem}$$

as shown in Figure A.19. (The converse is also true. That is, if $a^2 + b^2 = c^2$, then the triangle is a right triangle.)

Suppose you want to determine the distance d between two points (x_1, y_1) and (x_2, y_2) in the plane. With these two points, a right triangle can be formed, as shown in Figure A.20. The length of the vertical side of the triangle is $|y_2 - y_1|$, and the length of the horizontal side is $|x_2 - x_1|$. By the Pythagorean Theorem, you can write

$$d^2 = |x_2 - x_1|^2 + |y_2 - y_1|^2$$

$$d = \sqrt{|x_2 - x_1|^2 + |y_2 - y_1|^2}$$

$$d = \sqrt{(x_2 - x_1)^2 + (y_2 - y_1)^2}.$$

This result is the **Distance Formula.**

The Distance Formula

The distance d between the points (x_1, y_1) and (x_2, y_2) in the plane is

$$d = \sqrt{(x_2 - x_1)^2 + (y_2 - y_1)^2}.$$

Example 3 ▶ **Finding a Distance**

Find the distance between the points $(-2, 1)$ and $(3, 4)$.

Solution

Let $(x_1, y_1) = (-2, 1)$ and $(x_2, y_2) = (3, 4)$. Then apply the Distance Formula.

$$d = \sqrt{(x_2 - x_1)^2 + (y_2 - y_1)^2} \qquad \text{Distance Formula}$$

$$= \sqrt{[3 - (-2)]^2 + (4 - 1)^2} \qquad \text{Substitute for } x_1, y_1, x_2, \text{ and } y_2.$$

$$= \sqrt{(5)^2 + (3)^2} \qquad \text{Simplify.}$$

$$= \sqrt{34} \qquad \text{Simplify.}$$

$$\approx 5.83 \qquad \text{Use a calculator.}$$

Note in Figure A.21 that a distance of 5.83 looks about right. You can use the Pythagorean Theorem to check that the distance is correct.

$$d^2 \overset{?}{=} 3^2 + 5^2 \qquad \text{Pythagorean Theorem}$$

$$\left(\sqrt{34}\right)^2 \overset{?}{=} 3^2 + 5^2 \qquad \text{Substitute for } d.$$

$$34 = 34 \qquad \text{Distance checks.} \checkmark$$

FIGURE **A.21**

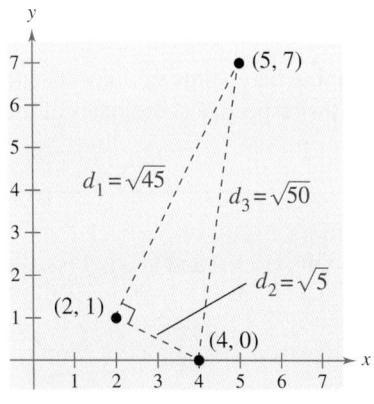

FIGURE A.22

Example 4 ▶ Verifying a Right Triangle

Show that the points $(2, 1)$, $(4, 0)$, and $(5, 7)$ are vertices of a right triangle.

Solution

The three points are plotted in Figure A.22. Using the Distance Formula, you can find the lengths of the three sides as follows.

$$d_1 = \sqrt{(5-2)^2 + (7-1)^2} = \sqrt{9+36} = \sqrt{45}$$
$$d_2 = \sqrt{(4-2)^2 + (0-1)^2} = \sqrt{4+1} = \sqrt{5}$$
$$d_3 = \sqrt{(5-4)^2 + (7-0)^2} = \sqrt{1+49} = \sqrt{50}$$

Because

$$(d_1)^2 + (d_2)^2 = 45 + 5$$
$$= 50$$
$$= (d_3)^2$$

you can conclude that the triangle must be a right triangle.

The figures provided with Examples 3 and 4 were not really essential to the solution. Nevertheless, it is strongly recommended that you develop the habit of including sketches with your solutions—even if they are not required.

Example 5 ▶ Finding the Length of a Pass

During the first quarter of the 2002 Orange Bowl, Brock Berlin, the quarterback for the University of Florida, threw a pass from the 37-yard line, 40 yards from the sideline. The pass was caught by the wide receiver Taylor Jacobs on the 3-yard line, 20 yards from the same sideline, as shown in Figure A.23. How long was the pass?

Solution

You can find the length of the pass by finding the distance between the points $(40, 37)$ and $(20, 3)$.

$$d = \sqrt{(40-20)^2 + (37-3)^2}$$ Distance Formula
$$= \sqrt{400 + 1156}$$ Simplify.
$$= \sqrt{1556}$$ Simplify.
$$\approx 39$$ Use a calculator.

So, the pass was about 39 yards long.

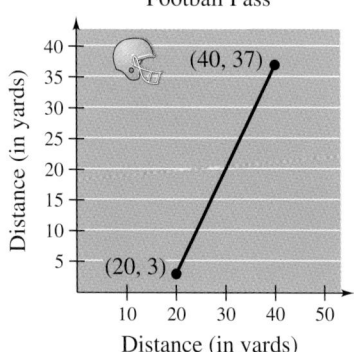

FIGURE A.23

In Example 5, the scale along the goal line does not normally appear on a football field. However, when you use coordinate geometry to solve real-life problems, you are free to place the coordinate system in any way that is convenient for the solution of the problem.

The Midpoint Formula

To find the **midpoint** of the line segment that joins two points in a coordinate plane, you can simply find the average values of the respective coordinates of the two endpoints using the **Midpoint Formula.**

The Midpoint Formula

The midpoint of the line segment joining the points (x_1, y_1) and (x_2, y_2) is given by the Midpoint Formula

$$\text{Midpoint} = \left(\frac{x_1 + x_2}{2}, \frac{y_1 + y_2}{2} \right).$$

Example 6 ▶ Finding a Line Segment's Midpoint

Find the midpoint of the line segment joining the points $(-5, -3)$ and $(9, 3)$, as shown in Figure A.24.

Solution

Let $(x_1, y_1) = (-5, -3)$ and $(x_2, y_2) = (9, 3)$.

$$\text{Midpoint} = \left(\frac{x_1 + x_2}{2}, \frac{y_1 + y_2}{2} \right) \qquad \text{Midpoint Formula}$$

$$= \left(\frac{-5 + 9}{2}, \frac{-3 + 3}{2} \right) \qquad \text{Substitute for } x_1, y_1, x_2, \text{ and } y_2.$$

$$= (2, 0) \qquad \text{Simplify.}$$

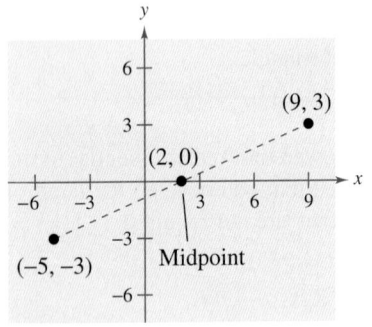

FIGURE **A.24**

Example 7 ▶ Estimating Annual Revenue

The United Parcel Service had annual revenues of $24.8 billion in 1998 and $29.8 billion in 2000. Without knowing any additional information, what would you estimate the 1999 revenue to have been? (Source: United Parcel Service of America Corp.)

Solution

One solution to the problem is to assume that revenue followed a linear pattern. With this assumption, you can estimate the 1999 revenue by finding the midpoint of the line segment connecting the points (1998, 24.8) and (2000, 29.8).

$$\text{Midpoint} = \left(\frac{1998 + 2000}{2}, \frac{24.8 + 29.8}{2} \right)$$

$$= (1999, 27.3)$$

So, you would estimate the 1999 revenue to have been about $27.3 billion, as shown in Figure A.25. (The actual 1999 revenue was $27.1 billion.)

United Parcel Service
Annual Revenue

FIGURE **A.25**

Application

Example 8 ▶ **Translating Points in the Plane**

The triangle in Figure A.26 has vertices at the points $(-1, 2)$, $(1, -4)$, and $(2, 3)$. Shift the triangle three units to the right and two units upward and find the vertices of the shifted triangle, as shown in Figure A.27.

FIGURE A.26

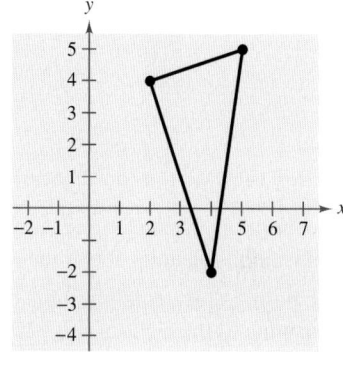

FIGURE A.27

Solution

To shift the vertices three units to the right, add 3 to each of the x-coordinates. To shift the vertices two units upward, add 2 to each of the y-coordinates.

Original Point	Translated Point
$(-1, 2)$	$(-1 + 3, 2 + 2) = (2, 4)$
$(1, -4)$	$(1 + 3, -4 + 2) = (4, -2)$
$(2, 3)$	$(2 + 3, 3 + 2) = (5, 5)$

A.8 Exercises

In Exercises 1 and 2, approximate the coordinates of the points.

1.

2.

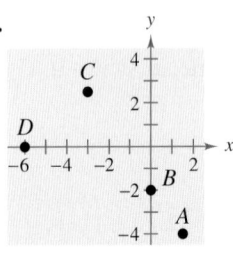

In Exercises 3–6, find the coordinates of the point.

3. The point is located three units to the left of the y-axis and four units above the x-axis.

4. The point is located eight units below the x-axis and four units to the right of the y-axis.

5. The point is located five units below the x-axis and the coordinates of the point are equal.

6. The point is on the x-axis and 12 units to the left of the y-axis.

In Exercises 7–16, determine the quadrant(s) in which (x, y) is located so that the condition(s) is (are) satisfied.

7. $x > 0$ and $y < 0$

8. $x < 0$ and $y < 0$

9. $x = -4$ and $y > 0$

10. $x > 2$ and $y = 3$

11. $y < -5$

12. $x > 4$

13. $(x, -y)$ is in the second quadrant.

14. $(-x, y)$ is in the fourth quadrant.

15. $xy > 0$

16. $xy < 0$

In Exercises 17–20, the polygon is shifted to a new position in the plane. Find the coordinates of the vertices of the polygon in its new position.

17.

18.

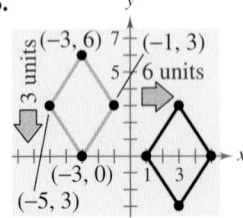

19. Original coordinates of vertices:

$(-7, -2), (-2, 2), (-2, -4), (-7, -4)$

Shift: eight units upward, four units to the right

20. Original coordinates of vertices:

$(5, 8), (3, 6), (7, 6), (5, 2)$

Shift: 6 units downward, 10 units to the left

In Exercises 21 and 22, sketch a scatter plot of the data given in the table.

21. *Meteorology* The table shows the lowest temperature on record y (in degrees Fahrenheit) in Duluth, Minnesota, for each month x, where $x = 1$ represents January. (Source: NOAA)

Month, x	Temperature, y
1	-39
2	-33
3	-29
4	-5
5	17
6	27
7	35
8	32
9	22
10	8
11	-23
12	-34

22. *Number of Stores* The table shows the number y of Wal-Mart stores for each year x from 1993 through 2000. (Source: Wal-Mart Stores, Inc.)

Year, x	Number of stores, y
1993	2440
1994	2759
1995	2943
1996	3054
1997	3406
1998	3599
1999	3985
2000	4190

Retail Price In Exercises 23 and 24, use the graph below, which shows the average retail price of 1 pound of butter from 1993 to 1999. (Source: U.S. Bureau of Labor Statistics)

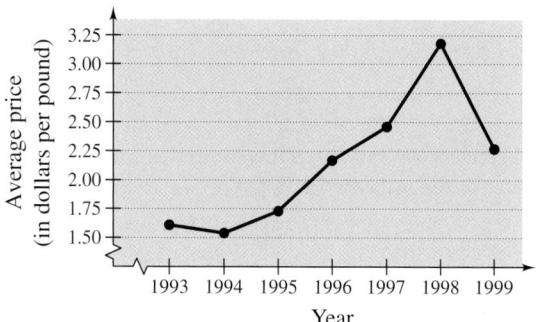

23. Approximate the highest price of a pound of butter shown in the graph. When did this occur?

24. Approximate the percent change in the price of butter from the price in 1994 to the highest price shown in the graph.

Advertising In Exercises 25 and 26, use the graph below, which shows the cost of a 30-second television spot (in thousands of dollars) during the Super Bowl from 1989 to 2001. (Source: USA Today Research)

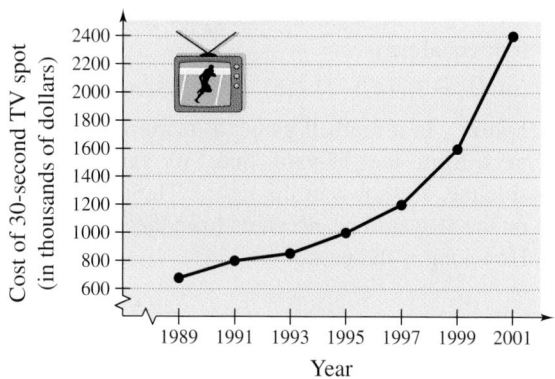

25. Approximate the percent increase in the cost of a 30-second spot from Super Bowl XXIII in 1989 to Super Bowl XXXV in 2001.

26. Estimate the percent increase in the cost of a 30-second spot (a) from Super Bowl XXIII in 1989 to Super Bowl XXVII in 1993 and (b) from Super Bowl XXVII in 1993 to Super Bowl XXXV in 2001.

27. *Labor Force* Use the graph below, which shows the minimum wage in the United States (in dollars) from 1950 to 2000. (Source: U.S. Employment Standards Administration)

(a) Which decade shows the greatest increase in minimum wage?

(b) Approximate the percent increases in the minimum wage from 1990 to 1995 and from 1995 to 2000.

(c) Use the percent increase from 1995 to 2000 to predict the minimum wage in 2005.

(d) Do you believe that your prediction in part (c) is reasonable? Explain.

28. *Data Analysis* Use the table below, which shows the mathematics entrance test scores x and the final examination scores y in an algebra course for a sample of 10 students.

x	22	29	35	40	44
y	53	74	57	66	79

x	48	53	58	65	76
y	90	76	93	83	99

(a) Sketch a scatter plot of the data shown in the table.

(b) Find the entrance exam score of any student with a final exam score in the 80s.

(c) Does a higher entrance exam score imply a higher final exam score? Explain.

In Exercises 29–32, find the distance between the points. (*Note:* In each case, the two points lie on the same horizontal or vertical line.)

29. $(6, -3), (6, 5)$ **30.** $(1, 4), (8, 4)$

31. $(-3, -1), (2, -1)$ **32.** $(-3, -4), (-3, 6)$

In Exercises 33–36, (a) find the length of each side of the right triangle, and (b) show that these lengths satisfy the Pythagorean Theorem.

33.

34.

35.

36.
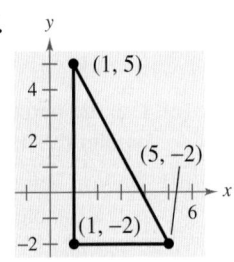

In Exercises 37–46, (a) plot the points, (b) find the distance between the points, and (c) find the midpoint of the line segment joining the points.

37. $(1, 1), (9, 7)$ **38.** $(1, 12), (6, 0)$

39. $(-4, 10), (4, -5)$ **40.** $(-7, -4), (2, 8)$

41. $(-1, 2), (5, 4)$ **42.** $(2, 10), (10, 2)$

43. $\left(\frac{1}{2}, 1\right), \left(-\frac{5}{2}, \frac{4}{3}\right)$ **44.** $\left(-\frac{1}{3}, -\frac{1}{3}\right), \left(-\frac{1}{6}, -\frac{1}{2}\right)$

45. $(6.2, 5.4), (-3.7, 1.8)$

46. $(-16.8, 12.3), (5.6, 4.9)$

Sales **In Exercises 47 and 48, use the Midpoint Formula to estimate the sales of Target Corporation and Kmart Corporation in 1998, given the sales in 1996 and 2000. Assume that the sales followed a linear pattern.**

47. *Target*

Year	Sales (in millions)
1996	$25,371
2000	$36,903

(Source: Target Corporation)

48. *Kmart*

Year	Sales (in millions)
1996	$31,437
2000	$37,028

(Source: Kmart Corporation)

In Exercises 49 and 50, show that the points form the vertices of the indicated polygon.

49. Right triangle: $(4, 0), (2, 1), (-1, -5)$

50. Isosceles triangle: $(1, -3), (3, 2), (-2, 4)$

51. A line segment has (x_1, y_1) as one endpoint and (x_m, y_m) as its midpoint. Find the other endpoint (x_2, y_2) of the line segment in terms of x_1, y_1, x_m, and y_m.

52. Use the result of Exercise 51 to find the coordinates of the endpoint of a line segment if the coordinates of the other endpoint and midpoint are, respectively,

  (a) $(1, -2), (4, -1)$ and (b) $(-5, 11), (2, 4)$.

53. Use the Midpoint Formula three times to find the three points that divide the line segment joining (x_1, y_1) and (x_2, y_2) into four parts.

54. Use the result of Exercise 53 to find the points that divide the line segment joining the given points into four equal parts.

  (a) $(1, -2), (4, -1)$ (b) $(-2, -3), (0, 0)$

55. *Sports* In a football game, a quarterback throws a pass from the 15-yard line, 10 yards from the sideline, as shown in the figure. The pass is caught on the 40-yard line, 45 yards from the same sideline. How long is the pass?

56. *Flying Distance* A jet plane flies from Naples, Italy in a straight line to Rome, Italy, which is 120 kilometers west and 150 kilometers north of Naples. How far does the plane fly?

57. *Make a Conjecture* Plot the points $(2, 1)$, $(-3, 5)$, and $(7, -3)$ on a rectangular coordinate system. Then change the sign of the x-coordinate of each point and plot the three new points on the same rectangular coordinate system. Make a conjecture about the location of a point when each of the following occurs.

(a) The sign of the x-coordinate is changed.

(b) The sign of the y-coordinate is changed.

(c) The signs of both the x- and y-coordinates are changed.

58. *Music* The graph shows the numbers of recording artists who were elected to the Rock and Roll Hall of Fame from 1986 to 2001.

(a) Describe any trends in the data. From these trends, predict the number of artists elected in 2004.

(b) Why do you think the numbers elected in 1986 and 1987 were greater than in other years?

59. *Revenue* Polo Ralph Lauren Corp. had annual revenues of $1713.1 million in 1998 and $2225.8 million in 2000. Use the Midpoint Formula to estimate the revenue in 1999. (Source: Polo Ralph Lauren Corp.)

60. *Revenue* Zale Corp. had annual revenues of $1428.9 million in 1999 and $2068.2 million in 2001. Use the Midpoint Formula to estimate the revenue in 2000. (Source: Zale Corp.)

Synthesis

True or False? **In Exercises 61 and 62, determine whether the statement is true or false. Justify your answer.**

61. In order to divide a line segment into 16 equal parts, you would have to use the Midpoint Formula 16 times.

62. The points $(-8, 4)$, $(2, 11)$, and $(-5, 1)$ represent the vertices of an isosceles triangle.

63. *Think About It* What is the y-coordinate of any point on the x-axis? What is the x-coordinate of any point on the y-axis?

64. *Think About It* When plotting points on the rectangular coordinate system, is it true that the scales on the x- and y-axes must be the same? Explain.

In Exercises 65–68, use the plot of the point (x_0, y_0) in the figure. Match the transformation of the point with the correct plot. [The plots are labeled (a), (b), (c), and (d).]

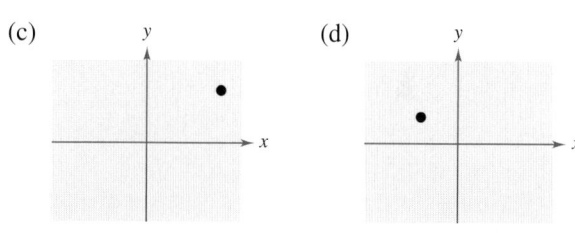

65. $(x_0, -y_0)$

66. $(-2x_0, y_0)$

67. $(x_0, \frac{1}{2}y_0)$

68. $(-x_0, -y_0)$

69. *Proof* Prove that the diagonals of the parallelogram in the figure intersect at their midpoints.

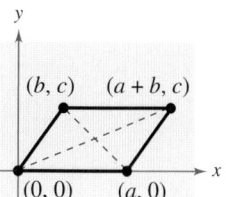

Answers to Odd-Numbered Exercises and Tests

Chapter 1

Section 1.1 *(page 9)*

1. (a) Yes   (b) Yes   **3.** (a) No   (b) Yes

5.

x	-1	0	1	2	$\frac{5}{2}$
y	7	5	3	1	0
(x, y)	$(-1, 7)$	$(0, 5)$	$(1, 3)$	$(2, 1)$	$\left(\frac{5}{2}, 0\right)$

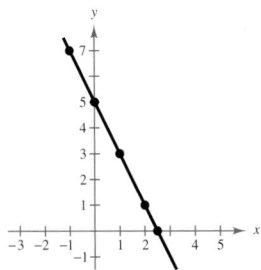

7.

x	-1	0	1	2	3
y	4	0	-2	-2	0
(x, y)	$(-1, 4)$	$(0, 0)$	$(1, -2)$	$(2, -2)$	$(3, 0)$

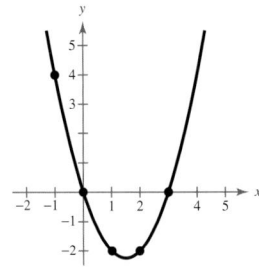

9. x-intercepts: $(\pm 2, 0)$
    y-intercept: $(0, 16)$

11. x-intercept: $\left(\frac{6}{5}, 0\right)$
    y-intercept: $(0, -6)$

13. x-intercept: $(-4, 0)$
    y-intercept: $(0, 2)$

15. x-intercept: $\left(\frac{7}{3}, 0\right)$
    y-intercept: $(0, 7)$

17. x-intercepts: $(0, 0), (2, 0)$
    y-intercept: $(0, 0)$

19. x-intercept: $(6, 0)$
    y-intercepts: $\left(0, \pm\sqrt{6}\right)$

21. y-axis symmetry   **23.** Origin symmetry

25. Origin symmetry   **27.** x-axis symmetry

29.   **31.**

33.   **35.**

37.   **39.**

41.   **43.**

45.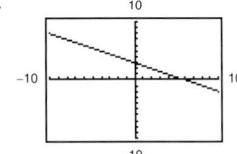

Intercepts: $(6, 0), (0, 3)$

47.

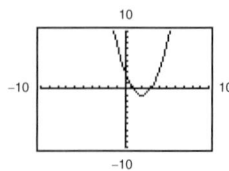

Intercepts: $(3, 0)$, $(1, 0)$, $(0, 3)$

49.

51.

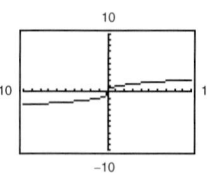

Intercept: $(0, 0)$ Intercept: $(0, 0)$

53.

55.

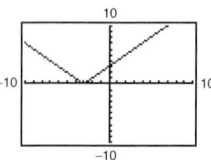

Intercepts: $(0, 0)$, $(-6, 0)$ Intercepts: $(-3, 0)$, $(0, 3)$

57. $x^2 + y^2 = 16$

59. $(x - 2)^2 + (y + 1)^2 = 16$

61. $(x + 1)^2 + (y - 2)^2 = 5$

63. $(x - 3)^2 + (y - 4)^2 = 25$

65. Center: $(0, 0)$; Radius: 5

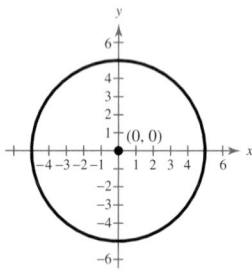

67. Center: $(1, -3)$; Radius: 3

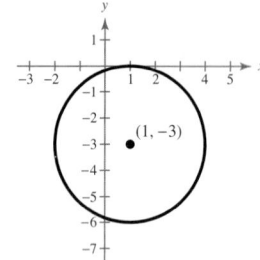

69. Center: $\left(\frac{1}{2}, \frac{1}{2}\right)$; Radius: $\frac{3}{2}$ **71.**

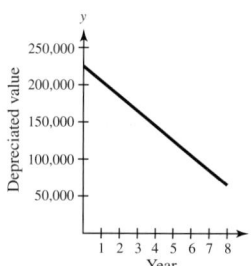

73. (a)   (b) Answers will vary.

(c)

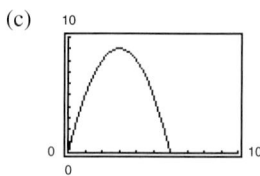

(d) $x = 3$, $w = 3$

75. (a) and (b)

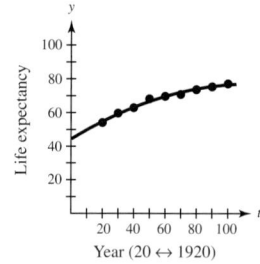

The curve seems to be a good fit for the data.

(c) 2005: 76.8 years; 2010: 77.0 years

(d) No. Because the model is quadratic, life expectancy decreases for $t > 114$ or 2014.

77.

3.9 ohms

79. True. All linear equations of the form $y = mx + b$, which excludes vertical lines, cross the y-axis one time.

81. (a) $a = 1, b = 0$ (b) $a = 0, b = 1$

83. $9x^5$, $4x^3$, -7 **85.** $2\sqrt{2x}$ **87.** $\dfrac{10\sqrt{7x}}{x}$

89. $\sqrt[3]{|t|}$

Section 1.2 *(page 21)*

1. (a) L_2 (b) L_3 (c) L_1

3.

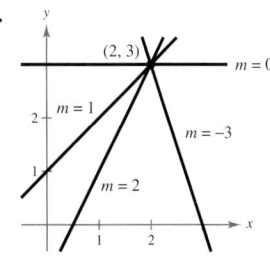

5. $\frac{8}{5}$ **7.** -4

9. $m = 5$; y-intercept: $(0, 3)$ **11.** $m = -\frac{1}{2}$; y-intercept: $(0, 4)$

 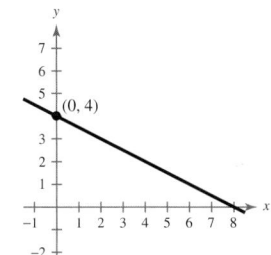

13. m is undefined. There is no y-intercept.

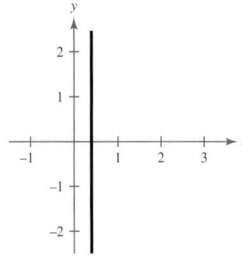

15. $m = -\frac{7}{6}$; y-intercept: $(0, 5)$ **17.** $m = 0$; y-intercept: $(0, 3)$

 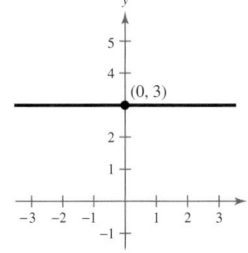

19. m is undefined. There is no y-intercept.

21.

$m = 2$

23.

m is undefined.

25.

$m = -\frac{1}{7}$

27.

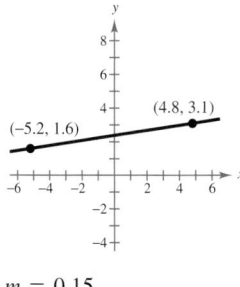

$m = 0.15$

29. Answers will vary. Sample answer:
$(0, 1),\ (3, 1),\ (-1, 1)$

31. Answers will vary. Sample answer:
$(6, -5),\ (7, -4),\ (8, -3)$

33. Answers will vary. Sample answer:
$(-8, 0),\ (-8, 2),\ (-8, 3)$

35. Answers will vary. Sample answer:
$(-4, 6), (-3, 8), (-2, 10)$

37. Answers will vary. Sample answer:
$(9, -1),\ (11, 0),\ (13, 1)$

39. Perpendicular   **41.** Parallel

43. (a) Sales increasing 135 units per year

    (b) No change in sales

    (c) Sales decreasing 40 units per year

45. (a) Greatest increase: 2000-2001
        Smallest increase: 1991-1992

    (b) 0.205

    (c) Each year, the earnings per share increase by $0.205.

47. (a) and (b)

Horizontal measurements

    (c) $y = -\frac{1}{12}x$

(d) For every 12 horizontal measurements, the vertical measurement decreases by 1.

(e) "8.3% grade"

49. $V = 125t + 2165$

51. b; The slope is -20, which represents the decrease in the amount of the loan each week.

52. c; The slope is 2, which represents the hourly wage per unit produced.

53. a; The slope is 0.32, which represents the increase in travel cost for each mile driven.

54. d; The slope is -100, which represents the decrease in the value of the word processor each year.

55. $y = 3x - 2$ **57.** $y = -2x$

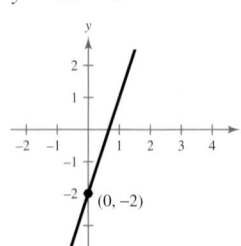

59. $y = -\frac{1}{3}x + \frac{4}{3}$ **61.** $x = 6$

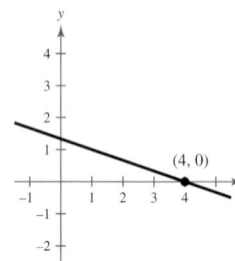

63. $y = \frac{5}{2}$ **65.** $y = 5x + 27.3$

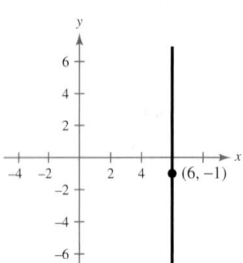

67. $y = -\frac{3}{5}x + 2$ **69.** $x = -8$

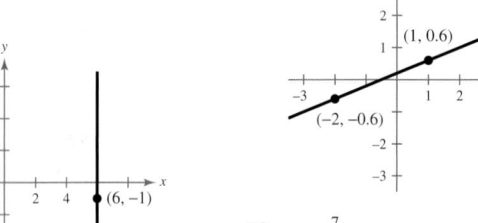

71. $y = -\frac{1}{2}x + \frac{3}{2}$ **73.** $y = -\frac{6}{5}x - \frac{18}{25}$

75. $y = 0.4x + 0.2$ **77.** $y = -1$

79. $x = \frac{7}{3}$

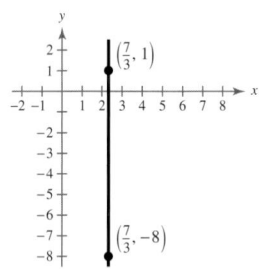

81. $3x + 2y - 6 = 0$ **83.** $12x + 3y + 2 = 0$

85. $x + y - 3 = 0$

87. (a) $y = 2x - 3$ (b) $y = -\frac{1}{2}x + 2$

89. (a) $y = -\frac{3}{4}x + \frac{3}{8}$ (b) $y = \frac{4}{3}x + \frac{127}{72}$

91. (a) $y = 0$ (b) $x = -1$

93. (a) $x = 2$ (b) $y = 5$

95. (a) $y = x + 4.3$ (b) $y = -x + 9.3$

97. Line (b) is perpendicular to line (c).

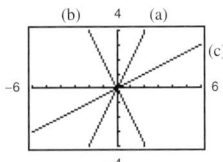

99. Line (a) is parallel to line (b).

Line (c) is perpendicular to line (a) and line (b).

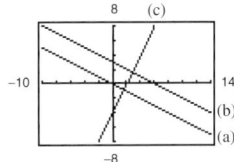

101. $3x - 2y - 1 = 0$ **103.** $80x + 12y + 139 = 0$

105. $y = 0.694t + 0.18$; 2005: \$7.12, 2010: \$10.59

107. \$43,900

109. $V = -175t + 875$ **111.** $S = 0.85L$

113. (a) $C = 16.75t + 36,500$

(b) $R = 27t$

(c) $P = 10.25t - 36,500$

(d) $t \approx 3561$ hours

115. (a)
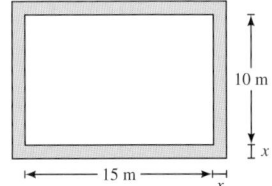

(b) $y = 8x + 50$

(c)
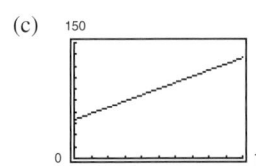

(d) $m = 8$, 8 meters

117. $C = 0.35x + 120$

119. (a) and (b)

Year (0 ↔ 1990)

(c) Answers will vary. Sample answer:
$y = -5.2x + 80.9$

(d) Answers will vary. Sample answer: The initial cost is
\$80.90. Each year, the cellular phone bill decreases an
additional \$5.20.

(e) The model is accurate.

(f) Answers will vary. Sample answer: \$2.90

121. False. The slope with the greatest magnitude corresponds
to the steepest line.

123. Find the distance between each two points and use the
Pythagorean Theorem.

125. No. The slope cannot be determined without knowing the
scale on the y-axis. The slopes could be the same.

127. V-intercept: initial cost; Slope: annual depreciation

129. d   **130.** c   **131.** a   **132.** b

133. -1 **135.** $\frac{7}{2}, 7$ **137.** No solution

Section 1.3 *(page 35)*

1. Yes   **3.** No

5. Yes, each input value has exactly one output value.

7. No, the input values of 7 and 10 each have two different
output values.

9. (a) Function

(b) Not a function, because the element 1 in A corresponds to two elements, -2 and 1, in B.

(c) Function

(d) Not a function, because not every element in A is
matched with an element in B.

11. Each is a function. For each year there corresponds one
and only one circulation.

13. Not a function   **15.** Function   **17.** Function

19. Not a function   **21.** Function

23. (a) -1 (b) -9 (c) $2x - 5$

25. (a) 36π (b) $\frac{9}{2}\pi$ (c) $\frac{32}{3}\pi r^3$

27. (a) 1   (b) 2.5   (c) $3 - 2|x|$

29. (a) $-\frac{1}{9}$ (b) Undefined   (c) $\dfrac{1}{y^2 + 6y}$

31. (a) 1   (b) -1 (c) $\dfrac{|x - 1|}{x - 1}$

33. (a) -1 (b) 2   (c) 6

35. (a) -7 (b) 4   (c) 9

37.

x	-2	-1	0	1	2
$f(x)$	1	-2	-3	-2	1

39.

t	-5	-4	-3	-2	-1
$h(t)$	1	$\frac{1}{2}$	0	$\frac{1}{2}$	1

41.

x	-2	-1	0	1	2
$f(x)$	5	$\frac{9}{2}$	4	1	0

43. 5   **45.** $\frac{4}{3}$ **47.** ±3 **49.** $0, \pm1$

51. $2, -1$ **53.** $3, 0$ **55.** All real numbers

57. All real numbers except $t \neq 0$

59. $y \geq 10$ **61.** $-1 \leq x \leq 1$

63. All real numbers except $x \neq 0, -2$ **65.** $s \geq 1, s \neq 4$

67. $x > 0$

69. $\{(-2, 4), (-1, 1), (0, 0), (1, 1), (2, 4)\}$

71. $\{(-2, 4), (-1, 3), (0, 2), (1, 3), (2, 4)\}$

73. $g(x) = cx^2; c = -2$ **75.** $r(x) = \dfrac{c}{x}; c = 32$

77. $3 + h, h \neq 0$

79. $3x^2 + 3xh + h^2 + 3, h \neq 0$

81. $-\dfrac{x + 3}{9x^2}, x \neq 3$ **83.** $\dfrac{\sqrt{5x} - 5}{x - 5}$ **85.** $A = \dfrac{P^2}{16}$

87. (a) The maximum volume is 1024 cubic centimeters.

(b)

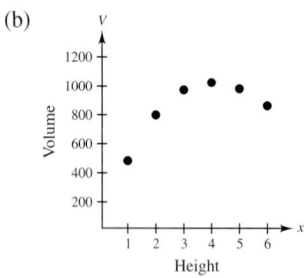

Height

Yes, V is a function of x.

(c) $V = x(24 - 2x)^2, 0 < x < 12$

89. $A = \dfrac{x^2}{2(x - 2)}, x > 2$

91. 1990: \$27,800; 1994: \$33,488;
1996: \$38,440; 1999: \$44,110

93. (a) $C = 12.30x + 98{,}000$

(b) $R = 17.98x$

(c) $P = 5.68x - 98{,}000$

95. (a) $R = \dfrac{240n - n^2}{20}, n \geq 80$

(b)

n	90	100	110	120	130	140	150
$R(n)$	\$675	\$700	\$715	\$720	\$715	\$700	\$675

The revenue is maximum when 120 people take the trip.

97. (a)

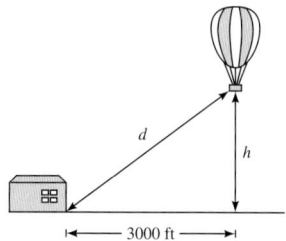

3000 ft

(b) $h = \sqrt{d^2 - 3000^2}, d \geq 3000$

99. (a) The result is 1.8 which is the average increase per year of the number of threatened and endangered fish.

(b) $\begin{cases} 2x + 104 & 6 \leq x \leq 7 \\ 2x + 103 & 8 \leq x \leq 11 \end{cases}$

(c)

x	6	7	8	9	10	11
N	116	118	119	121	123	125

(d) The results are the same.

(e) $y = 1.8x + 105$

The answer in part (b) is more accurate.

101. True. Each x-value corresponds to one y-value.

103. $\frac{15}{8}$ **105.** $-\frac{1}{5}$ **107.** $2x - 3y - 11 = 0$

109. $10x + 9y + 15 = 0$

Section 1.4   *(page 47)*

1. Domain: $(-\infty, -1], [1, \infty)$ **3.** Domain: $[-4, 4]$
Range: $[0, \infty)$ Range: $[0, 4]$

5. (a) 0   (b) -1 (c) 0   (d) -2

7. (a) -3 (b) 0   (c) 1   (d) -3

9. Function   **11.** Not a function   **13.** Function

15. $-\frac{5}{2}, 6$ **17.** 0   **19.** $0, \pm\sqrt{2}$ **21.** $\pm\frac{1}{2}, 6$ **23.** $\frac{1}{2}$

25.

$-\frac{5}{3}$

27.

$-\frac{11}{2}$

29.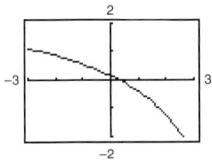

$\frac{1}{3}$

31. Increasing on $(-\infty, \infty)$

33. Increasing on $(-\infty, 0)$ and $(2, \infty)$

Decreasing on $(0, 2)$

35. Increasing on $(-\infty, 0)$ and $(2, \infty)$

Constant on $(0, 2)$

37. Increasing on $(1, \infty)$

Decreasing on $(-\infty, -1)$

Constant on $(-1, 1)$

39. (a)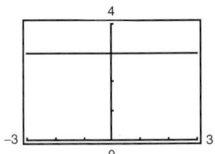

Constant on $(-\infty, \infty)$

(b)

x	-2	-1	0	1	2
$f(x)$	3	3	3	3	3

41. (a)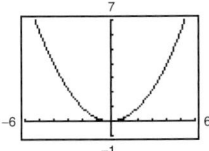

Decreasing on $(-\infty, 0)$; Increasing on $(0, \infty)$

(b)

s	-4	-2	0	2	4
$g(s)$	4	1	0	1	4

43. (a)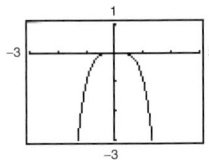

Increasing on $(-\infty, 0)$; Decreasing on $(0, \infty)$

(b)

t	-2	-1	0	1	2
$f(t)$	-16	-1	0	-1	-16

45. (a)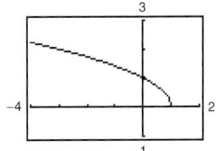

Decreasing on $(-\infty, 1)$

(b)

x	-3	-2	-1	0	1
$f(x)$	2	$\sqrt{3}$	$\sqrt{2}$	1	0

47. (a)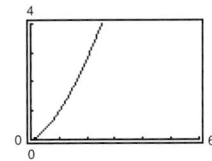

Increasing on $(0, \infty)$

(b)

x	0	1	2	3	4
$f(x)$	0	1	2.8	5.2	8

49.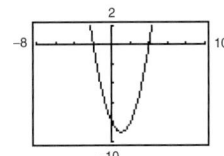

Relative minimum: $(1, -9)$

51.

Relative maximum: $(-1.79, 8.21)$

Relative minimum: $(1.12, -4.06)$

53.

$(-\infty, 4]$

55.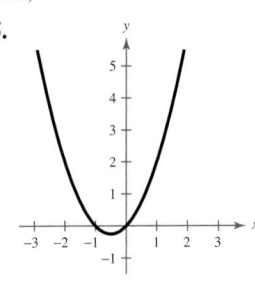

$(-\infty, -1], [0, \infty)$

57.

59.

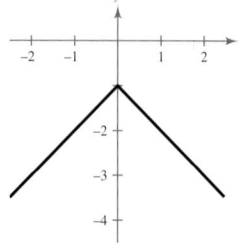

$[1, \infty)$ $f(x) < 0$ for all x

61. Even   **63.** Odd   **65.** Neither even nor odd

67. $h = -x^2 + 4x - 3$ **69.** $h = 2x - x^2$

71. $L = \frac{1}{2}y^2$ **73.** $L = 4 - y^2$

75. (a)

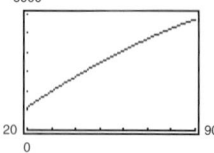

(b) 30 watts

77. (a) ten thousands   (b) ten millions   (c) percent

79. False. The function $f(x) = \sqrt{x^2 + 1}$ has a domain of all real numbers.

81. (a) Even. The graph is a reflection in the x-axis.

(b) Even. The graph is a reflection in the y-axis.

(c) Even. The graph is a vertical translation of f.

(d) Neither. The graph is a horizontal translation of f.

83. (a) $\left(\frac{3}{2}, 4\right)$ (b) $\left(\frac{3}{2}, -4\right)$

85. (a) $(-4, 9)$ (b) $(-4, -9)$

87. (a)

(b)

(c)

(d)

(e)

(f)

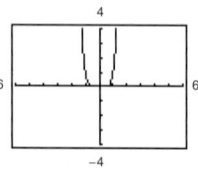

All the graphs pass through the origin. The graphs of the odd powers of x are symmetric with respect to the origin, and the graphs of the even powers are symmetric with respect to the y-axis. As the powers increase, the graphs become flatter in the interval $-1 < x < 1$.

89. 0, 10   **91.** 0, ± 1

93. (a) 37   (b) -28 (c) $5x - 43$

95. (a) -9 (b) $2\sqrt{7} - 9$

(c) The given value is not in the domain of the function.

97. $h + 4$, $h \neq 0$

Section 1.5   *(page 56)*

1. $f(x) = -2x + 6$ **3.** $f(x) = -3x + 11$

    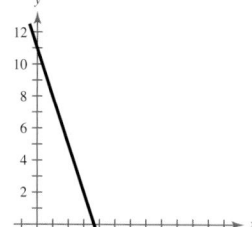

5. $f(x) = -1$ **7.** $f(x) = \frac{6}{7}x - \frac{45}{7}$

9.

11.

13.

15.

17.

19.

21.

23.

25.

27.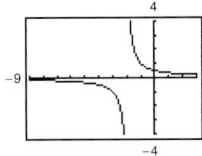

29. (a) 2   (b) 2   (c) -4 (d) 3

31. (a) 1   (b) 3   (c) 7   (d) -19

33. (a) 6   (b) -11 (c) 6   (d) -22

35. (a) -10 (b) -4 (c) -1 (d) 41

37.

39.

41.

43.

45.

47.

49.

51. 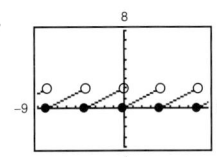   Domain: $(-\infty, \infty)$

Range: $[0, 2)$

Sawtooth pattern

53. $f(x) = |x|$; $g(x) = |x + 2| - 1$

55. $f(x) = x^3$; $g(x) = (x - 1)^3 - 2$

57. $f(x) = 2$; $g(x) = 2$

59. $f(x) = x$; $g(x) = x - 2$

61. $f(x) = x^2$; $g(x) = (x - 3)^2$

63. (a)   (b) \$5.64

65. (a) 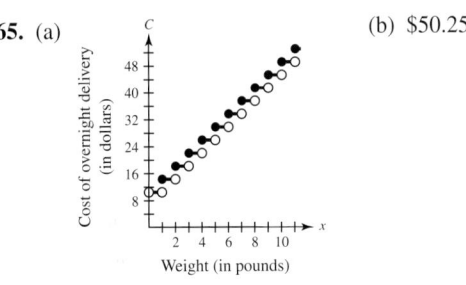   (b) \$50.25

67. (a) $W(30) = 360$; $W(40) = 480$;

$W(45) = 570$; $W(50) = 660$

(b) $W(h) = \begin{cases} 12h, & 0 < h \le 45 \\ 18(h - 45) + 540, & h > 45 \end{cases}$

69.

Interval	Input Pipe	Drainpipe 1	Drainpipe 2
$[0, 5]$	Open	Closed	Closed
$[5, 10]$	Open	Open	Closed
$[10, 20]$	Closed	Closed	Closed
$[20, 30]$	Closed	Closed	Open
$[30, 40]$	Open	Open	Open
$[40, 45]$	Open	Closed	Open
$[45, 50]$	Open	Open	Open
$[50, 60]$	Open	Open	Closed

71. True. The solution sets are the same.

73. $x \le 1$ **75.** Neither

Section 1.6   *(page 64)*

1. (a)

(b)

(c)

3. (a)

(b)

(c)

5. (a)

(b)

(c)

(d)

(e)

(f)

(g)

7. (a)

(b)

(c)

(d)

(e)

(f)

(g)

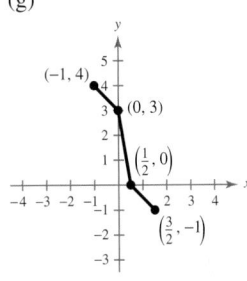

9. (a) $y = x^2 - 1$ (b) $y = 1 - (x + 1)^2$
  (c) $y = -(x - 2)^2 + 6$ (d) $y = (x - 5)^2 - 3$

11. (a) $y = |x| + 5$ (b) $y = -|x + 3|$
  (c) $y = |x - 2| - 4$ (d) $y = -|x - 6| - 1$

13. Horizontal shift of $y = x^3$; $y = (x - 2)^3$

15. Reflection in the x-axis of $y = x^2$; $y = -x^2$

17. Reflection in the x-axis and vertical shift of $y = \sqrt{x}$;
  $y = 1 - \sqrt{x}$

19. Reflection in the x-axis, and vertical shift 12 units upward,
  of $f(x) = x^2$

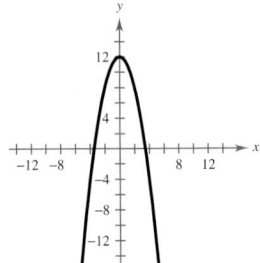

21. Vertical shift seven units upward of $f(x) = x^3$

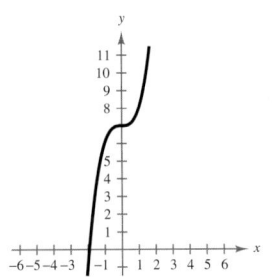

23. Reflection in the x-axis, vertical shift two units upward,
  and horizontal shift five units to the left, of $f(x) = x^2$

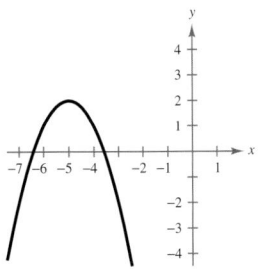

25. Vertical shift two units upward, and horizontal shift one
  unit to the right, of $f(x) = x^3$

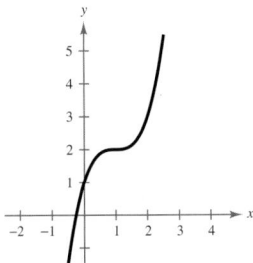

27. Reflection in the x-axis, and vertical shift two units down-
  ward, of $f(x) = |x|$

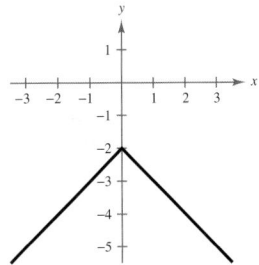

29. Reflection in the x-axis, vertical shift eight units upward,
  and horizontal shift four units to the left, of $f(x) = |x|$

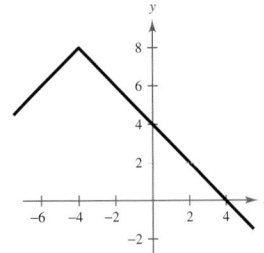

31. Reflection in the *x*-axis, and vertical shift three units upward, of $f(x) = [\![x]\!]$

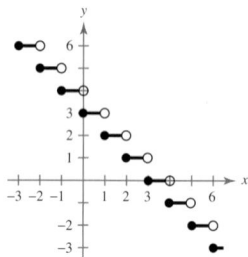

33. Horizontal shift nine units to the right of $f(x) = \sqrt{x}$

35. Reflection in the *y*-axis, vertical shift two units downward, and horizontal shift seven units to the right, of $f(x) = \sqrt{x}$

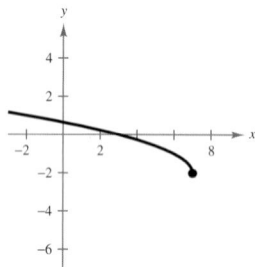

37. Vertical shift four units downward, and horizontal stretch of two, of $f(x) = \sqrt{x}$

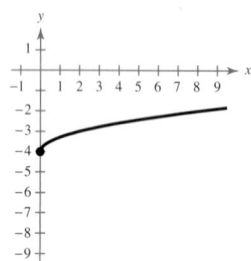

39. $f(x) = (x - 2)^2 - 8$ **41.** $f(x) = (x - 13)^3$

43. $f(x) = -|x| - 10$ **45.** $f(x) = -\sqrt{-x + 6}$

47. (a) $y = -3x^2$ (b) $y = 4x^2 + 3$

49. (a) $y = -\frac{1}{2}|x|$ (b) $y = 3|x| - 3$

51. Vertical stretch of $y = x^3$; $y = 2x^3$

53. Reflection in the *x*-axis and vertical shrink of $y = x^2$; $y = -\frac{1}{2}x^2$

55. Reflection in the *y*-axis and vertical shrink of $y = \sqrt{x}$; $y = \frac{1}{2}\sqrt{-x}$

57. $y = -(x - 2)^3 + 2$ **59.** $y = -\sqrt{x} - 3$

61. (a)

(b)

(c)

(d)

(e)

(f)

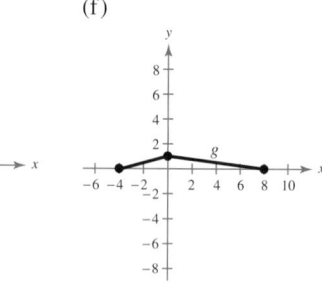

63. (a) Vertical shift of 20.5 units upward and vertical shrink of 0.035

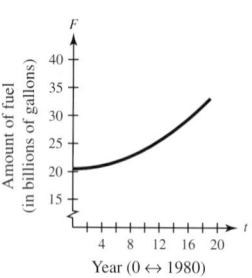

(b) 0.665-billion-gallon increase in fuel usage by trucks each year

(c) $f(t) = 20.5 + 0.035(t + 10)^2$. The graph was shifted 10 units to the left.

(d) 42.375 billion gallons. Yes.

65. True. $|-x| = |x|$

67. (a) $g(t) = \frac{3}{4}f(t)$ (b) $g(t) = f(t) + 10{,}000$

(c) $g(t) = f(t - 2)$

69. $(-2, 0), (-1, 1), (0, 2)$

71. $\dfrac{4}{x(1 - x)}$ **73.** $\dfrac{3x - 2}{x(x - 1)}$ **75.** $\dfrac{(x - 4)\sqrt{x^2 - 4}}{x^2 - 4}$

77. $5(x - 3), \; x \ne -3$

79. (a) 38 (b) $\frac{57}{4}$ (c) $x^2 - 12x + 38$

81. All real numbers $x \ne 11$ **83.** $-9 \le x \le 9$

Section 1.7   *(page 74)*

1. 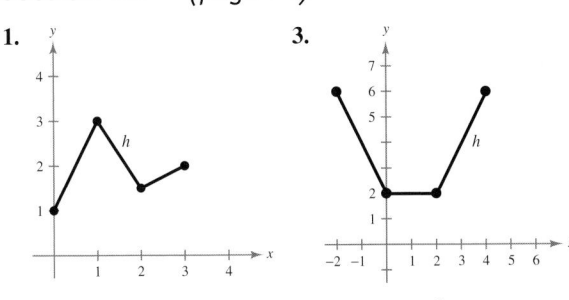 **3.**

5. (a) $2x$ (b) 4 (c) $x^2 - 4$ (d) $\dfrac{x + 2}{x - 2}; \; x \ne 2$

7. (a) $x^2 + 4x - 5$ (b) $x^2 - 4x + 5$

(c) $4x^3 - 5x^2$ (d) $\dfrac{x^2}{4x - 5}; \; x \ne \dfrac{5}{4}$

9. (a) $x^2 + 6 + \sqrt{1 - x}$ (b) $x^2 + 6 - \sqrt{1 - x}$

(c) $(x^2 + 6)\sqrt{1 - x}$ (d) $\dfrac{(x^2 + 6)\sqrt{1 - x}}{1 - x}; \; x < 1$

11. (a) $\dfrac{x + 1}{x^2}$ (b) $\dfrac{x - 1}{x^2}$ (c) $\dfrac{1}{x^3}$ (d) $x; \; x \ne 0$

13. 3 **15.** 5 **17.** $9t^2 - 3t + 5$ **19.** 74

21. 26 **23.** $\frac{3}{5}$

25.   **27.**

29.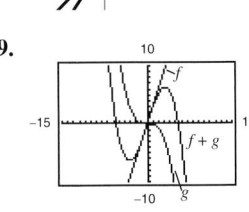

$f(x), g(x)$

31. $T = \frac{3}{4}x + \frac{1}{15}x^2$

33. (a) $y_1 = 1.344t^2 - 9.38t + 163.6$

$y_2 = 17.34t + 238.5$

$y_3 = 3.38t + 28.1$

(b) $y_1 + y_2 + y_3 = 1.344t^2 + 11.34t + 430.2$; the total amount spent on health services and supplies

(c)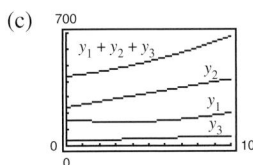

(d) 2003: \$804.76 billion; 2005: \$902.70 billion

35. (a) $(x - 1)^2$ (b) $x^2 - 1$ (c) x^4

37. (a) x (b) x (c) $\sqrt[3]{\sqrt[3]{x - 1} - 1}$

39. (a) $\sqrt{x^2 + 4}$ (b) $x + 4$

Domain of f and $g \circ f$: $x \ge -4$;

Domain of g and $f \circ g$: all real numbers

41. (a) $x + 1$ (b) $\sqrt{x^2 + 1}$

Domain of f and $g \circ f$: all real numbers

Domain of g and $f \circ g$: $x \ge 0$

43. (a) $|x + 6|$ (b) $|x| + 6$

Domain of $f, g, f \circ g,$ and $g \circ f$: all real numbers

45. (a) $\dfrac{1}{x + 3}$ (b) $\dfrac{1}{x} + 3$

Domain of f and $g \circ f$: all real numbers $x \ne 0$

Domain of g: all real numbers

Domain of $f \circ g$: all real numbers $x \ne -3$

47. (a) 3 (b) 0 **49.** (a) 0 (b) 4

51. Answers will vary. Sample answer:
$f(x) = x^2, \; g(x) = 2x + 1$

53. Answers will vary. Sample answer:
$f(x) = \sqrt[3]{x}, \; g(x) = x^2 - 4$

55. Answers will vary. Sample answer:
$f(x) = \dfrac{1}{x}, \; g(x) = x + 2$

57. Answers will vary. Sample answer:

$$f(x) = \frac{x+3}{4+x}, \ g(x) = -x^2$$

59. (a) $r(x) = \dfrac{x}{2}$ (b) $A(r) = \pi r^2$

(c) $(A \circ r)(x) = \pi\left(\dfrac{x}{2}\right)^2$; $(A \circ r)(x)$ represents the area of the circular base of the tank on the square foundation with side length x.

61. False. $(f \circ g)(x) = 6x + 1$ and $(g \circ f)(x) = 6x + 6$

63. $g(f(x))$ represents 3 percent of an amount over \$500,000.

65. Odd   **67.** 3   **69.** $\dfrac{-4}{x(x+h)}$

71. $3x - y - 10 = 0$ **73.** $3x + 2y - 22 = 0$

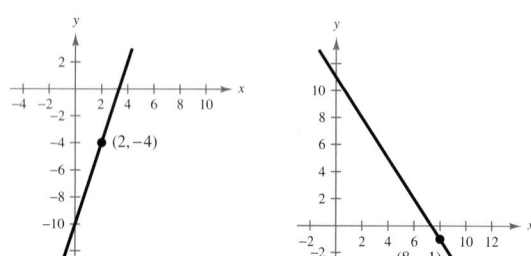

Section 1.8   *(page 83)*

1. c   **2.** b   **3.** a   **4.** d   **5.** $f^{-1}(x) = \frac{1}{6}x$

7. $f^{-1}(x) = x - 9$ **9.** $f^{-1}(x) = \dfrac{x-1}{3}$

11. $f^{-1}(x) = x^3$

13. (a) $f(g(x)) = f\left(\dfrac{x}{2}\right) = 2\left(\dfrac{x}{2}\right) = x$

$g(f(x)) = g(2x) = \dfrac{(2x)}{2} = x$

(b)
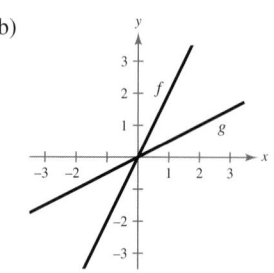

15. (a) $f(g(x)) = f\left(\dfrac{x-1}{7}\right) = 7\left(\dfrac{x-1}{7}\right) + 1 = x$

$g(f(x)) = g(7x+1) = \dfrac{(7x+1)-1}{7} = x$

(b)
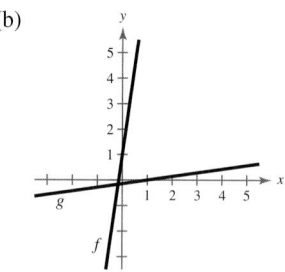

17. (a) $f(g(x)) = f\left(\sqrt[3]{8x}\right) = \dfrac{\left(\sqrt[3]{8x}\right)^3}{8} = x$

$g(f(x)) = g\left(\dfrac{x^3}{8}\right) = \sqrt[3]{8\left(\dfrac{x^3}{8}\right)} = x$

(b)
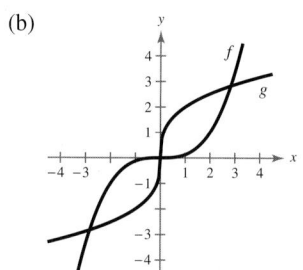

19. (a) $f(g(x)) = f(x^2 + 4), \ x \geq 0$

$= \sqrt{(x^2+4) - 4} = x$

$g(f(x)) = g\left(\sqrt{x-4}\right)$

$= \left(\sqrt{x-4}\right)^2 + 4 = x$

(b)
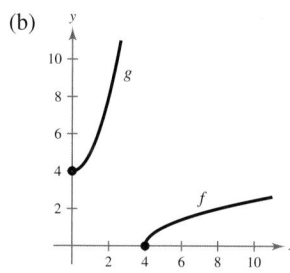

21. (a) $f(g(x)) = f\left(\sqrt{9-x}\right), \ x \leq 9$

$= 9 - \left(\sqrt{9-x}\right)^2 = x$

$g(f(x)) = g(9 - x^2), \ x \geq 0$

$= \sqrt{9 - (9 - x^2)} = x$

(b)
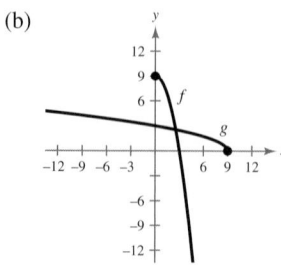

23. (a) $f(g(x)) = f\left(-\dfrac{5x+1}{x-1}\right) = \dfrac{-\left(\dfrac{5x+1}{x-1}\right)-1}{-\left(\dfrac{5x+1}{x-1}\right)+5}$

$= \dfrac{-5x-1-x+1}{-5x-1+5x-5} = x$

$g(f(x)) = g\left(\dfrac{x-1}{x+5}\right) = \dfrac{-5\left(\dfrac{x-1}{x+5}\right)-1}{\dfrac{x-1}{x+5}-1}$

$= \dfrac{-5x+5-x-5}{x-1-x-5} = x$

(b)

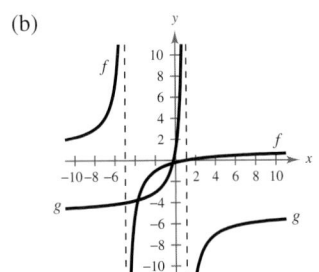

25. No

27.

x	-2	0	2	4	6	8
$f^{-1}(x)$	-2	-1	0	1	2	3

29. Yes   **31.** No

33.

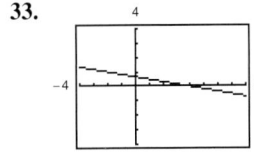

The function has an inverse.

35.

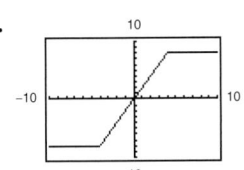

The function does not have an inverse.

37.

The function does not have an inverse.

39. $f^{-1}(x) = \dfrac{x+3}{2}$

41. $f^{-1}(x) = \sqrt[5]{x+2}$

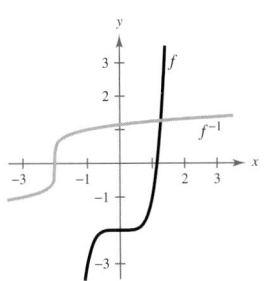

43. $f^{-1}(x) = x^2,\ x \ge 0$

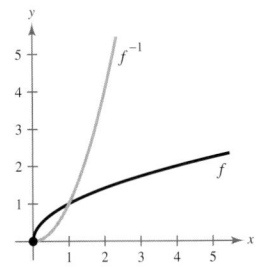

45. $f^{-1}(x) = \sqrt{4-x^2},\ 0 \le x \le 2$

47. $f^{-1}(x) = \dfrac{4}{x}$

49. $f^{-1}(x) = \dfrac{2x+1}{x-1}$

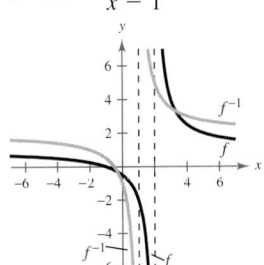

51. $f^{-1}(x) = x^3 + 1$ **53.** $f^{-1}(x) = \dfrac{5x - 4}{6 - 4x}$

 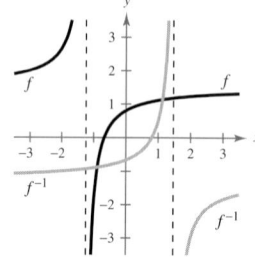

55. No inverse   **57.** $g^{-1}(x) = 8x$ **59.** No inverse

61. $f^{-1}(x) = \sqrt{x} - 3$ **63.** No inverse

65. No inverse   **67.** $f^{-1}(x) = \dfrac{x^2 - 3}{2}, \; x \geq 0$ **69.** 32

71. 600   **73.** $2\sqrt[3]{x + 3}$ **75.** $\dfrac{x + 1}{2}$ **77.** $\dfrac{x + 1}{2}$

79. (a) 9

     (b) f^{-1} yields the year for a given number of households.

     (c) $y = 1266.54x + 92{,}255.54$

     (d) $f^{-1} = \dfrac{x - 92{,}255.54}{1266.54}$ (e) 15

81. (a) Yes

     (b) f^{-1} yields the year for a given number of miles traveled by motor vehicles.

     (c) 8

     (d) No. $f(t)$ would not pass the Horizontal Line Test.

83. (a) $y = \sqrt{\dfrac{x - 245.50}{0.03}}, \; 245.5 < x < 545.5$

     $x = $ degrees Fahrenheit; $y = \%$ load

     (b)   (c) $0 < x < 92.11$

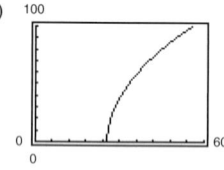

85. False. $f(x) = x^2$ has no inverse.

87.

x	1	3	4	6
y	1	2	6	7

x	1	2	6	7
$f^{-1}(x)$	1	3	4	6

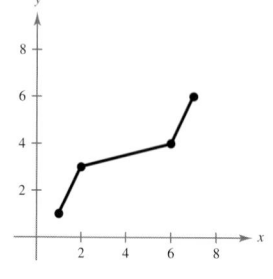

89.

x	-2	-1	3	4
y	6	0	-2	-3

x	-3	-2	0	6
$f^{-1}(x)$	4	3	-1	-2

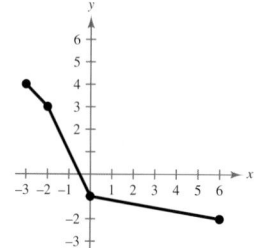

91. $k = \frac{1}{4}$

93. ± 8 **95.** $\frac{3}{2}$ **97.** $3 \pm \sqrt{5}$ **99.** $5, -\frac{10}{3}$

101. 16, 18

Section 1.9   *(page 93)*

1.

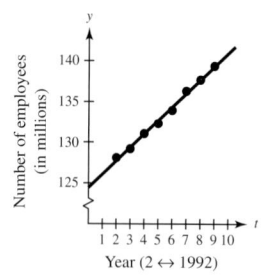

Year (2 $\leftrightarrow$ 1992)

The model is a "good fit" for the actual data.

3. Inversely

5.

x	2	4	6	8	10
$y = kx^2$	4	16	36	64	100

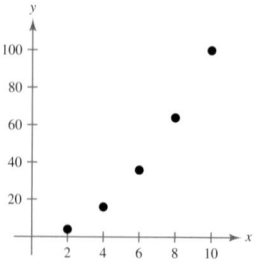

7.

x	2	4	6	8	10
$y = kx^2$	2	8	18	32	50

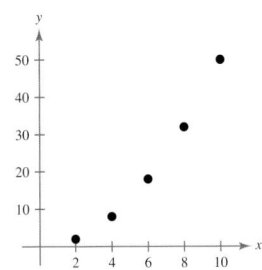

9.

x	2	4	6	8	10
$y = k/x^2$	$\frac{1}{2}$	$\frac{1}{8}$	$\frac{1}{18}$	$\frac{1}{32}$	$\frac{1}{50}$

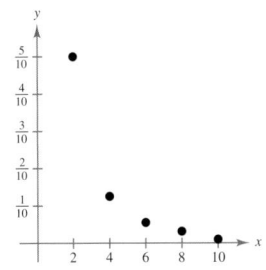

11.

x	2	4	6	8	10
$y = k/x^2$	$\frac{5}{2}$	$\frac{5}{8}$	$\frac{5}{18}$	$\frac{5}{32}$	$\frac{1}{10}$

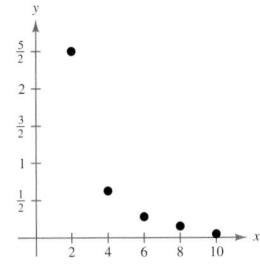

13. $y = \dfrac{5}{x}$ **15.** $y = -\dfrac{7}{10}x$ **17.** $y = \dfrac{12}{5}x$

19. $y = 205x$ **21.** $I = 0.035P$

23. Model: $y = \frac{33}{13}x$; 25.4 centimeters, 50.8 centimeters

25. $y = 0.0368x$; \$7360

27. (a) 0.05 meter   (b) $176\frac{2}{3}$ newtons   **29.** 39.47 pounds

31. $A = kr^2$ **33.** $y = \dfrac{k}{x^2}$ **35.** $F = \dfrac{kg}{r^2}$

37. $P = \dfrac{k}{V}$ **39.** $F = \dfrac{km_1m_2}{r^2}$

41. The area of a triangle is jointly proportional to its base and height.

43. The volume of a sphere varies directly as the cube of its radius.

45. Average speed is directly proportional to the distance and inversely proportional to the time.

47. $A = \pi r^2$ **49.** $y = \dfrac{28}{x}$ **51.** $F = 14rs^3$

53. $z = \dfrac{2x^2}{3y}$ **55.** ≈ 0.61 mile per hour   **57.** 506 feet

59. 400 feet   **61.** The velocity is increased by one-third.

63. (a)

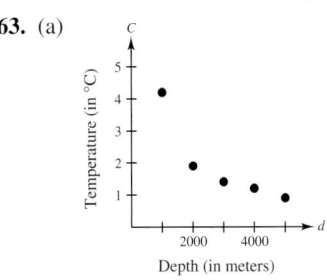

(b) Yes. $k_1 = 4200$, $k_2 = 3800$, $k_3 = 4200$, $k_4 = 4800$, $k_5 = 4500$

(c) $C = \dfrac{4300}{d}$

(d) 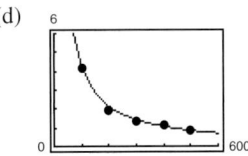   (e) ≈ 1433 meters

65. (a) 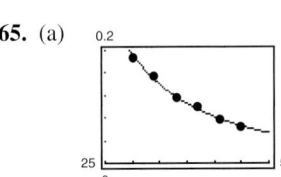   (b) 0.2857 microwatt per square centimeter

67.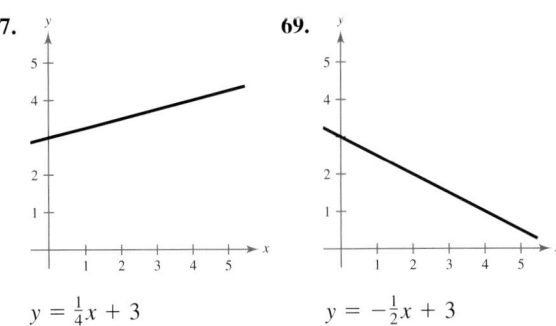

$y = \frac{1}{4}x + 3$ $y = -\frac{1}{2}x + 3$

71. (a) and (b)

$y = t + 128$

(c) $y = 1.08t + 127.7$ (d) The models are similar.

(e) part (b): 232 feet; part (c): 240.02 feet

(f) Analyses will vary.

73. (a) and (c)

(b) $R = 412.9t + 3642$

(d) 2000: \$7771.0 million; 2002: \$8596.8 million

(e) Each year, the annual receipts for motion picture movie theaters increases by \$412.9 million.

75. False. y will increase if k is positive and y will decrease if k is negative.

77. The accuracy is questionable when based on such limited data.

79. $x \le 4, x \ge 6$ **81.** $x > 5$

83. (a) $-\frac{5}{3}$ (b) $-\frac{7}{3}$ (c) 21

Review Exercises   (page 100)

1.

x	-2	-1	0	1	2
y	-11	-8	-5	-2	1

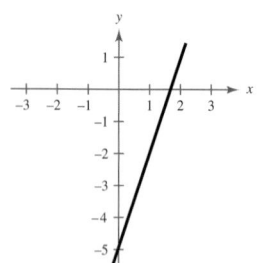

3.

x	-1	0	1	2	3	4
y	4	0	-2	-2	0	4

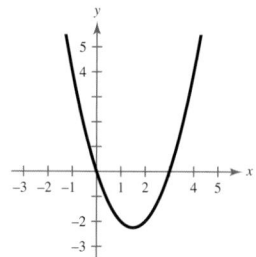

5. x-intercept: $\left(\frac{9}{2}, 0\right)$

y-intercept: $(0, -9)$

7. x-intercept: $(-1, 0)$

y-intercept: $(0, 1)$

9. y-axis symmetry   **11.** No symmetry

    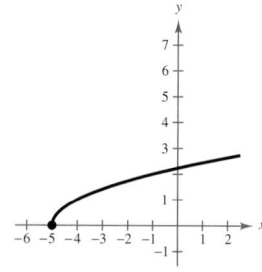

13. Center: $(0, 0)$; Radius: 3   **15.** Center: $(-2, 0)$; Radius: 4

    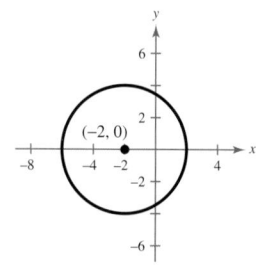

17. $(x - 2)^2 + (y + 3)^2 = 13$

19.

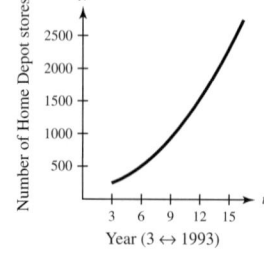

2004

21. $m = 0$; y-intercept: $(0, 6)$ **23.** $m = 3$; y-intercept: $(0, 13)$

25.

$m = -\frac{1}{2}$

27.

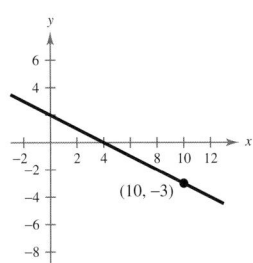

$m = -\frac{5}{11}$

29. $x = 0$ **31.** $4x + 3y - 8 = 0$

33. $3x - 2y - 10 = 0$ **35.** $x + 2y - 4 = 0$

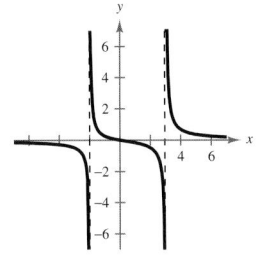

37. (a) $5x - 4y - 23 = 0$ (b) $4x + 5y - 2 = 0$

39. (a) $x = 4$ (b) $y = -1$

41. $V = 850t + 9100,\ 4 \le t \le 9$

43. No   **45.** Yes

47. (a) 5 (b) 17 (c) $t^4 + 1$ (d) $-x^2 - 2x - 2$

49. $-5 \le x \le 5$ **51.** All real numbers $x \ne 3,\ -2$

53. (a) 16 feet per second   (b) 1.5 seconds
     (c) -16 feet per second

55. Function   **57.** Not a function

59. $\frac{7}{3},\ 3$ **61.** $-\frac{3}{8}$

63. Increasing on $(0, \infty)$
     Decreasing on $(-\infty, -1)$
     Constant on $[-1, 0]$

65. Neither even nor odd   **67.** Odd

69. $f(x) = -3x$ **71.**

73.

75.

77.

79.

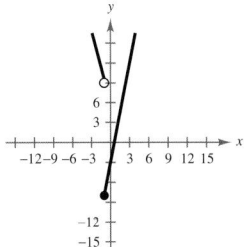

81. $y = (x + 4)^3 + 4$

83. Vertical shift of nine units downward

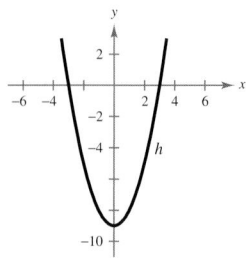

85. Horizontal shift of three units to the left and vertical shift of five units downward

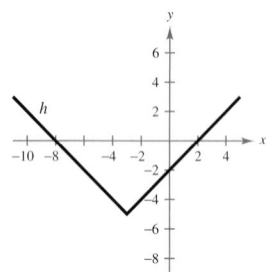

87. Reflection in the x-axis, horizontal shift of one unit to the left, and vertical shift of nine units upward

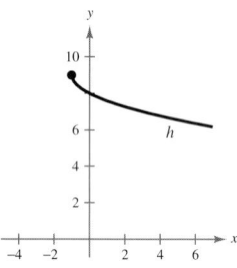

89. Reflection in the x-axis and vertical shift of six units upward

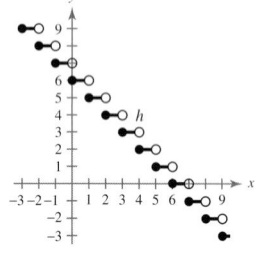

91. (a) $x^2 + 2x + 2$ (b) $x^2 - 2x + 4$

    (c) $2x^3 - x^2 + 6x - 3$ (d) $\dfrac{x^2 + 3}{2x - 1},\ x \neq \dfrac{1}{2}$

93. (a) $x - \dfrac{8}{3}$ (b) $x - 8$

    Domain of $f, g, f \circ g,$ and $g \circ f$: all real numbers

95. $f(x) = x^3, g(x) = 6x - 5$ (Answer is not unique.)

97. $y_1 = 0.207t^2 + 8.65t + 14.2$

    $y_2 = 1.414t^2 - 7.28t + 146.9$

99. $f^{-1}(x) = x + 7$

    $f(f^{-1}(x)) = x + 7 - 7 = x$

    $f^{-1}(f(x)) = x - 7 + 7 = x$

101. The function has an inverse.

103.
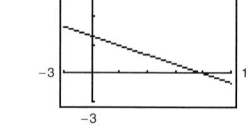
The function has an inverse.

105.
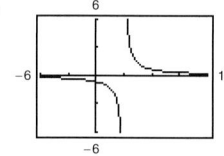
The function has an inverse.

107. (a) $f^{-1}(x) = 2x + 6$

    (b)

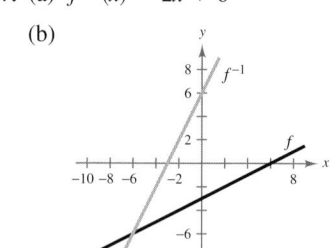

    (c) $f^{-1}(f(x)) = 2\left(\frac{1}{2}x - 3\right) + 6 = x - 6 + 6 = x$

       $f(f^{-1}(x)) = \frac{1}{2}(2x + 6) - 3 = x + 3 - 3 = x$

109. (a) $f^{-1}(x) = x^2 - 1,\ x \geq 0$

    (b)

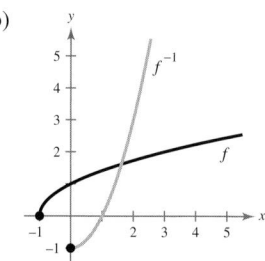

    (c) $f^{-1}(f(x)) = f^{-1}\left(\sqrt{x + 1}\right),\ x \geq -1$

       $= (x + 1) - 1$

       $= x$

      $f(f^{-1}(x)) = f(x^2 - 1),\ x \geq 0$

       $= \sqrt{x^2 - 1 + 1}$

       $= x$

111. $x \geq 4$; $f^{-1}(x) = \sqrt{\dfrac{x}{2}} + 4$

113. (a)

(b) The model is a "good fit" for the actual data.

115. 667 units   **117.** A factor of 4

119. False. The graph is reflected in the x-axis, shifted nine units to the left, and then shifted 13 units downward.

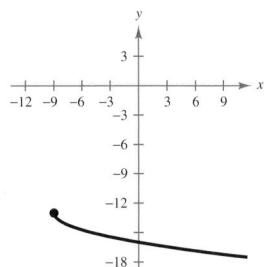

121. The Vertical Line Test is used to determine if the graph of y is a function of x. The Horizontal Line Test is used to determine if a function has an inverse function.

Chapter Test   *(page 104)*

1. No symmetry

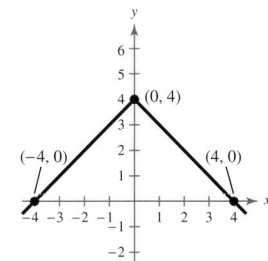

2. y-axis symmetry

3. y-axis symmetry

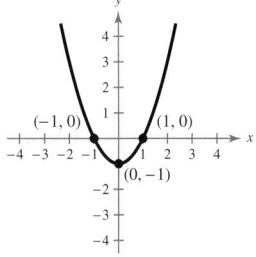

4. $(x - 1)^2 + (y - 3)^2 = 16$

5. $2x + y - 1 = 0$ **6.** $17x + 10y - 59 = 0$

7. (a) $4x - 7y + 44 = 0$ (b) $7x + 4y - 53 = 0$

8. (a) $-\dfrac{1}{8}$ (b) $-\dfrac{1}{28}$ (c) $\dfrac{\sqrt{x}}{x^2 - 18x}$

9. $-10 \leq x \leq 10$

10. (a) $0, \pm 0.4314$

(b)

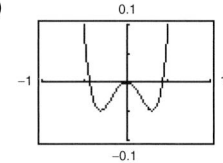

(c) Increasing on $(-0.31, 0)$, $(0.31, \infty)$

Decreasing on $(-\infty, -0.31)$, $(0, 0.31)$

(d) Even

11. (a) $0, 3$

(b)

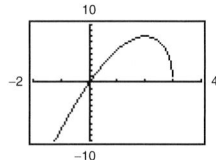

(c) Increasing on $(-\infty, 2)$

Decreasing on $(2, 3)$

(d) Neither even nor odd

12. (a) -5

(b)

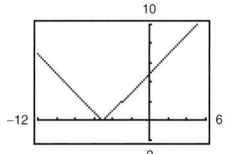

(c) Increasing on $(-5, \infty)$

Decreasing on $(-\infty, -5)$

(d) Neither even nor odd

13.

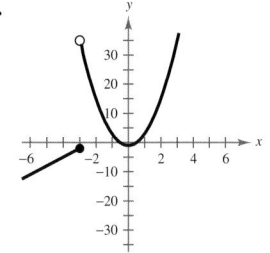

14. Reflection in the x-axis of $y = [\![x]\!]$

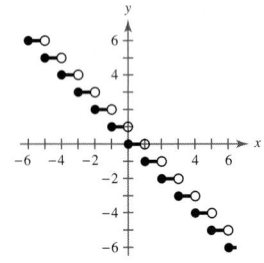

15. Reflection in the x-axis, horizontal shift, and vertical shift of $y = \sqrt{x}$

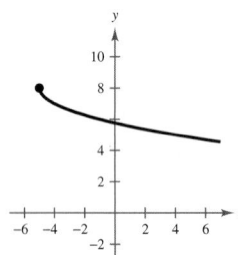

16. (a) $2x^2 - 4x - 2$ (b) $4x^2 + 4x - 12$

(c) $-3x^4 - 12x^3 + 22x^2 + 28x - 35$

(d) $\dfrac{3x^2 - 7}{-x^2 - 4x + 5}, \quad x \neq -5, 1$

(e) $3x^4 + 24x^3 + 18x^2 - 120x + 68$

(f) $-9x^4 + 30x^2 - 16$

17. (a) $\dfrac{1 + 2x^{3/2}}{x}, \quad x > 0$ (b) $\dfrac{1 - 2x^{3/2}}{x}, \quad x > 0$

(c) $\dfrac{2\sqrt{x}}{x}, \quad x > 0$ (d) $\dfrac{1}{2x^{3/2}}, \quad x > 0$

(e) $\dfrac{\sqrt{x}}{2x}, \quad x > 0$ (f) $\dfrac{2\sqrt{x}}{x}, \quad x > 0$

18. $f^{-1}(x) = \sqrt[3]{x - 8}$ **19.** No inverse

20. $f^{-1}(x) = \left(\tfrac{1}{3}x\right)^{2/3}, \; x \geq 0$ **21.** $v = 6\sqrt{s}$

22. $A = \dfrac{25}{6}xy$ **23.** $b = \dfrac{48}{a}$

Problem Solving   *(page 106)*

1. (a) $W_1 = 2000 + 0.07S$ (b) $W_2 = 2300 + 0.05S$

(c)

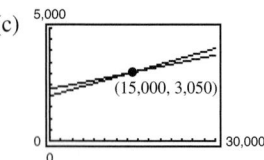

Both jobs pay the same monthly salary if sales equal $15,000.

(d) No. Job 1 would pay $3400 and job 2 would pay $3300.

3. (a) The function will be even.

(b) The function will be odd if the two functions are not equal.

(c) The function will be neither even nor odd.

5. $f(x) = a_{2n}x^{2n} + a_{2n-2}x^{2n-2} + \cdots + a_2x^2 + a_0$

$f(-x) = a_{2n}(-x)^{2n} + a_{2n-2}(-x)^{2n-2}$

$\qquad\qquad + \cdots + a_2(-x)^2 + a_0$

$\qquad = f(x)$

7. (a) $81\tfrac{2}{3}$ hours   (b) $25\tfrac{5}{7}$ miles per hour

(c) $y = \dfrac{-180}{7}x + 3400$

Domain: $0 \leq x \leq \dfrac{1190}{9}$

Range: $0 \leq y \leq 3400$

(d)

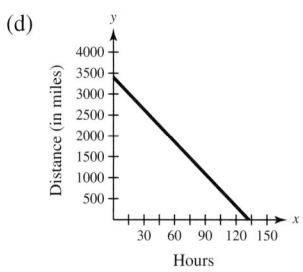

9. (a) $T = \dfrac{1}{2}\sqrt{4 + x^2} + \dfrac{1}{4}\sqrt{x^2 - 6x + 10}$

(b) $0 \leq x \leq 3$

(c)

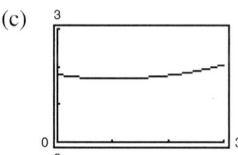

(d) $x = 1$

(e) The distance $x = 1$ yields a time of 1.68 hours.

11. (a) Domain: all real numbers $x \neq 1$

Range: all real numbers

(b) $f(f(x)) = \dfrac{x - 1}{x}$

Domain: all real numbers $x \neq 0, 1$

(c) $f(f(f(x))) = x$

The graph is not a line because there are holes at $x = 0$ and $x = 1$.

13. (a)

(b)

(c)

(d)

(e)

(f)

(g)

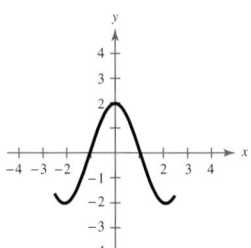

Chapter 2

Section 2.1 *(page 116)*

1. g   **2.** c   **3.** b   **4.** h

5. f   **6.** a   **7.** e   **8.** d

9. (a)

Vertical shrink

(b)

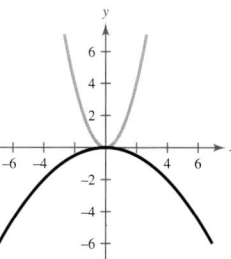

Vertical shrink and
reflection in the x-axis

(c)

Vertical stretch

(d)

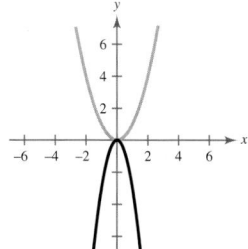

Vertical stretch and
reflection in the x-axis

11. (a)

Horizontal translation

(b)

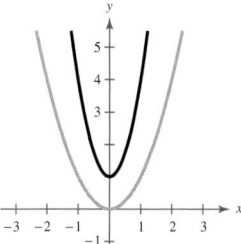

Horizontal shrink and
vertical translation

(c)

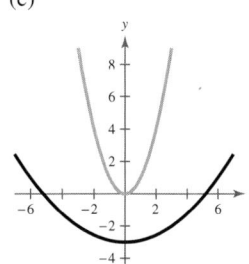

Horizontal stretch and
vertical translation

(d)

Horizontal translation

13.

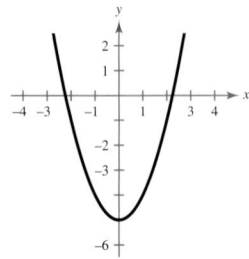

Vertex: $(0, -5)$

x-intercepts: $\left(\pm\sqrt{5}, 0\right)$

15.

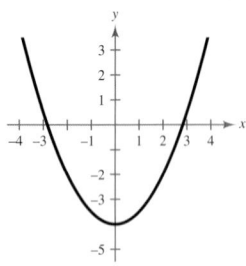

Vertex: $(0, -4)$

x-intercepts: $\left(\pm 2\sqrt{2}, 0\right)$

17.

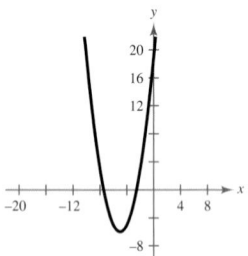

Vertex: $(-5, -6)$

x-intercepts: $\left(-5 \pm \sqrt{6}, 0\right)$

19.

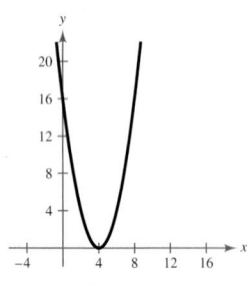

Vertex: $(4, 0)$

x-intercept: $(4, 0)$

21.

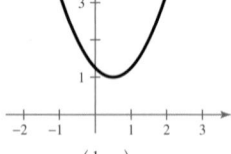

Vertex: $\left(\frac{1}{2}, 1\right)$

No x-intercept

23.

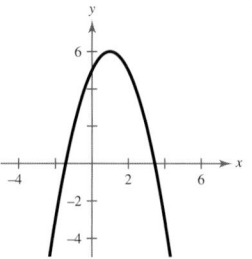

Vertex: $(1, 6)$

x-intercepts: $\left(1 \pm \sqrt{6}, 0\right)$

25.

Vertex: $\left(\frac{1}{2}, 20\right)$

No x-intercept

27.

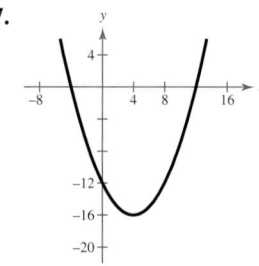

Vertex: $(4, -16)$

x-intercepts: $(-4, 0), (12, 0)$

29.

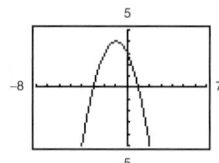

Vertex: $(-1, 4)$

x-intercepts: $(1, 0), (-3, 0)$

31.

Vertex: $(-4, -5)$

x-intercepts: $\left(-4 \pm \sqrt{5}, 0\right)$

33.

Vertex: $(4, -1)$

x-intercepts: $\left(4 \pm \frac{1}{2}\sqrt{2}, 0\right)$

35.

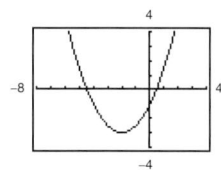

Vertex: $(-2, -3)$

x-intercepts: $\left(-2 \pm \sqrt{6}, 0\right)$

37. $y = (x - 1)^2$ **39.** $y = -(x + 1)^2 + 4$

41. $y = -2(x + 2)^2 + 2$ **43.** $f(x) = (x + 2)^2 + 5$

45. $f(x) = -\frac{1}{2}(x - 3)^2 + 4$ **47.** $f(x) = \frac{3}{4}(x - 5)^2 + 12$

49. $f(x) = -\frac{24}{49}\left(x + \frac{1}{4}\right)^2 + \frac{3}{2}$ **51.** $f(x) = -\frac{16}{3}\left(x + \frac{5}{2}\right)^2$

53. $(\pm 4, 0)$ **55.** $(5, 0), (-1, 0)$

57.   **59.**

$(0, 0), (4, 0)$ $(3, 0), (6, 0)$

61.   **63.**

   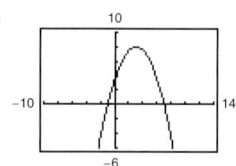

$\left(-\frac{5}{2}, 0\right), (6, 0)$ $(7, 0), (-1, 0)$

65. $f(x) = x^2 - 2x - 3$ **67.** $f(x) = x^2 - 10x$

     $g(x) = -x^2 + 2x + 3$ $g(x) = -x^2 + 10x$

69. $f(x) = 2x^2 + 7x + 3$ **71.** $55, 55$ **73.** $12, 6$

     $g(x) = -2x^2 - 7x - 3$

75. (a) $A = \dfrac{8x(50 - x)}{3}$

(b)

x	5	10	15	20	25	30
A	600	1067	1400	1600	1667	1600

$x = 25$ feet, $y = 33\frac{1}{3}$ feet

(c)

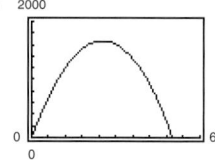

$x = 25$ feet, $y = 33\frac{1}{3}$ feet

(d) $A = -\frac{8}{3}(x - 25)^2 + \frac{5000}{3}$

77. 4500 units   **79.** 20 fixtures   **81.** 350,000 units

83. (a) 4 feet   (b) 16 feet   (c) 25.86 feet

85. (a)

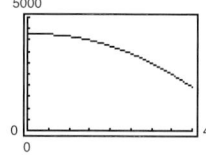   (b) 4265; Yes

(c) 8741 annually; 24 daily

87. (a)

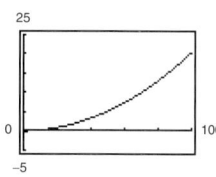   (b) 69.6 miles per hour

89. True. The equation has no real solution, so the graph has no x-intercepts.

91. $f(x) = a\left(x + \dfrac{b}{2a}\right)^2 + \dfrac{4ac - b^2}{4a}$

93. Yes. A graph of a quadratic equation whose vertex is on the x-axis has only one x-intercept.

95. $y = -\frac{1}{3}x + \frac{5}{3}$ **97.** $y = \frac{5}{4}x + 3$ **99.** 27

101. $-\frac{1408}{49}$ **103.** 109

Section 2.2   *(page 130)*

1. c   **2.** g   **3.** h   **4.** f

5. a   **6.** e   **7.** d   **8.** b

9. (a)   (b)

(c)   (d)

11. (a)

(b)

(c)

(d)

(e)

(f)

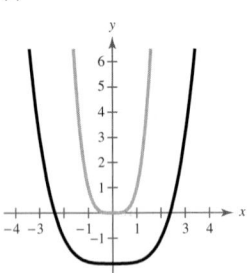

13. Falls to the left, rises to the right

15. Falls to the left, falls to the right

17. Rises to the left, falls to the right

19. Rises to the left, falls to the right

21. Falls to the left, falls to the right

23.

25.

27. ± 5, odd multiplicity   **29.** 3, even multiplicity

31. $-2, 1$, odd multiplicity

33. $0, 2 \pm \sqrt{3}$, odd multiplicity

35. 0, odd multiplicity; 2, even multiplicity

37. 0, odd multiplicity; $\pm\sqrt{3}$, even multiplicity

39. No real zeros   **41.** $\pm 2, -3$, odd multiplicity

43.

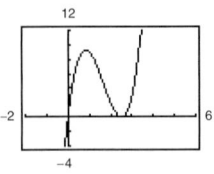

$(0, 0), \left(\frac{5}{2}, 0\right)$

45.

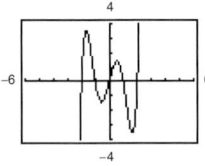

$(0, 0), (\pm 1, 0), (\pm 2, 0)$

47. $f(x) = x^2 - 10x$ **49.** $f(x) = x^2 + 4x - 12$

51. $f(x) = x^3 + 5x^2 + 6x$

53. $f(x) = x^4 - 4x^3 - 9x^2 + 36x$

55. $f(x) = x^2 - 2x - 2$ **57.** $f(x) = x^2 + 4x + 4$

59. $f(x) = x^3 + 2x^2 - 3x$ **61.** $f(x) = x^3 - 3x$

63. $f(x) = x^4 + x^3 - 15x^2 + 23x - 10$

65. $f(x) = x^5 + 16x^4 + 96x^3 + 256x^2 + 256x$

67. (a) Falls to the left, rises to the right

(b) $0, \pm 3$ (c) Answers will vary.

(d)

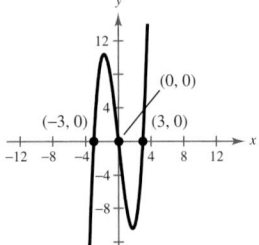

69. (a) Rises to the left, rises to the right

(b) No zeros   (c) Answers will vary.

(d)

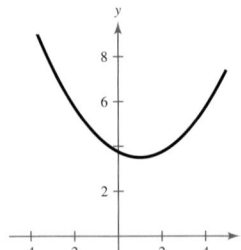

71. (a) Falls to the left, rises to the right

(b) $0, 3$ (c) Answers will vary.

(d)

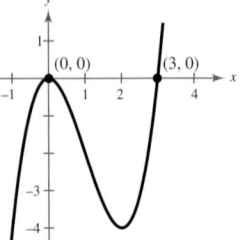

73. (a) Falls to the left, rises to the right

(b) 0, 2, 3   (c) Answers will vary.

(d)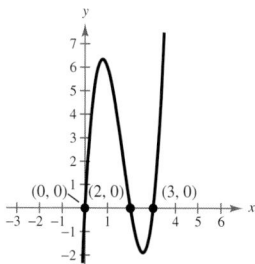

75. (a) Rises to the left, falls to the right

(b) $-5, 0$ (c) Answers will vary.

(d)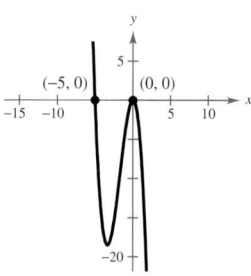

77. (a) Falls to the left, rises to the right

(b) 0, 4   (c) Answers will vary.

(d)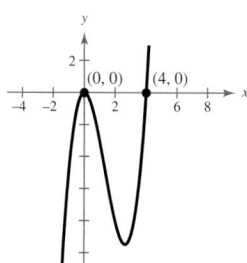

79. (a) Falls to the left, falls to the right

(b) ± 2 (c) Answers will vary.

(d)

81.

Zeros: $0, \pm 2$,
odd multiplicity

83.

Zeros: -1,
even multiplicity;
$3, \frac{9}{2}$, odd multiplicity

85. $[-1, 0], [1, 2], [2, 3]; \approx -0.879, 1.347, 2.532$

87. $[-2, -1], [0, 1]; \approx -1.585, 0.779$

89. (a) $V = l \times w \times h$

$$= (36 - 2x)(36 - 2x)x$$

$$= x(36 - 2x)^2$$

(b) Domain: $0 < x < 18$

(c)

x	1	2	3	4	5	6	7
V	1156	2048	2700	3136	3380	3456	3388

6 inches $\times$ 24 inches $\times$ 24 inches

(d)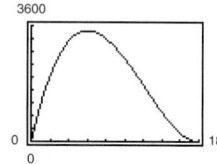

$x = 6$

91. (a)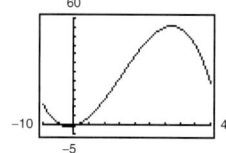

(b) $t \approx 15$

(c) Vertex: $(15.22, 2.54)$

(d) The results are approximately equal.

93. False. A fifth-degree polynomial can have at most four turning points.

95. True. The degree of the function is odd and its leading coefficient is negative, so the graph rises to the left and falls to the right.

97.

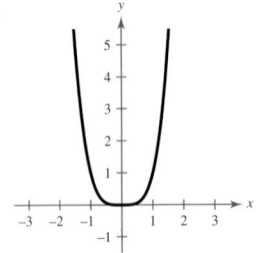

(a) Vertical shift of 2 units; Even

(b) Horizontal shift of 2 units; Neither even nor odd

(c) Reflection in the y-axis; Even

(d) Reflection in the x-axis; Even

(e) Horizontal stretch; Even

(f) Vertical shrink; Even

(g) $g(x) = x^3$; Odd

(h) $g(x) = x^{16}$; Even

99. $-\frac{7}{2}, 4$ **101.** $-\frac{5}{4}, \frac{1}{3}$ **103.** $1 \pm \sqrt{22}$

105. $\dfrac{-5 \pm \sqrt{185}}{4}$ **107.** $(5x - 8)(x + 3)$

109. $x^2(4x + 5)(x - 3)$

111. Horizontal translation four units to the left of $y = x^2$.

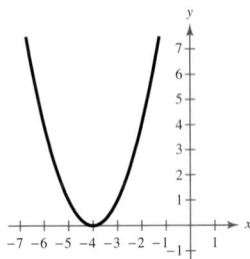

113. Horizontal translation one unit left and vertical translation five units down of $y = \sqrt{x}$

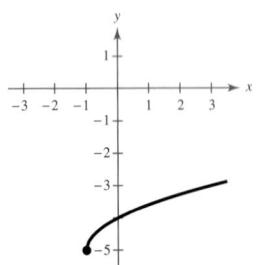

115. Vertical stretch of a factor of 2 and vertical translation nine units up of $y = [\![x]\!]$

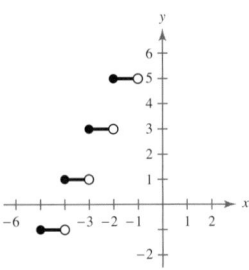

Section 2.3   *(page 140)*

1. Answers will vary.

3.

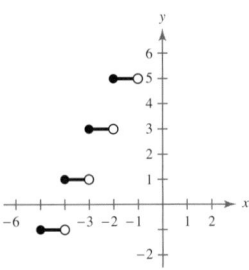

5. $2x + 4$ **7.** $x^2 - 3x + 1$ **9.** $x^3 + 3x^2 - 1$

11. $7 - \dfrac{11}{x + 2}$ **13.** $3x + 5 - \dfrac{2x - 3}{2x^2 + 1}$

15. $x^2 + 2x + 4 + \dfrac{2x - 11}{x^2 - 2x + 3}$

17. $x + 3 + \dfrac{6x^2 - 8x + 3}{(x - 1)^3}$ **19.** $3x^2 - 2x + 5$

21. $4x^2 - 9$ **23.** $-x^2 + 10x - 25$

25. $5x^2 + 14x + 56 + \dfrac{232}{x - 4}$

27. $10x^3 + 10x^2 + 60x + 360 + \dfrac{1360}{x - 6}$

29. $x^2 - 8x + 64$

31. $-3x^3 - 6x^2 - 12x - 24 - \dfrac{48}{x - 2}$

33. $-x^3 - 6x^2 - 36x - 36 - \dfrac{216}{x - 6}$

35. $4x^2 + 14x - 30$

37. $f(x) = (x - 4)(x^2 + 3x - 2) + 3$, $f(4) = 3$

39. $f(x) = \left(x + \frac{2}{3}\right)(15x^3 - 6x + 4) + \frac{34}{3}$,
$f\left(-\frac{2}{3}\right) = \frac{34}{3}$

41. $f(x) = \left(x - \sqrt{2}\right)\left[x^2 + \left(3 + \sqrt{2}\right)x + 3\sqrt{2}\right] - 8$,
$f\left(\sqrt{2}\right) = -8$

43. $f(x) = \left(x - 1 + \sqrt{3}\right)\left[-4x^2 + \left(2 + 4\sqrt{3}\right)x + \left(2 + 2\sqrt{3}\right)\right]$,
$f\left(1 - \sqrt{3}\right) = 0$

45. (a) 1　(b) 4　(c) 4　(d) 1954

47. (a) 97　(b) $-\frac{5}{3}$　(c) 17　(d) -199

49. $(x - 2)(x + 3)(x - 1)$; Zeros: $2, -3, 1$

51. $(2x - 1)(x - 5)(x - 2)$; Zeros: $\frac{1}{2}, 5, 2$

53. $\left(x + \sqrt{3}\right)\left(x - \sqrt{3}\right)(x + 2)$; Zeros: $-\sqrt{3}, \sqrt{3}, -2$

55. $(x - 1)\left(x - 1 - \sqrt{3}\right)\left(x - 1 + \sqrt{3}\right)$;

　　Zeros: $1, \ 1 + \sqrt{3}, \ 1 - \sqrt{3}$

57. (a) Answers will vary.　(b) $2x - 1$

　　(c) $f(x) = (2x - 1)(x + 2)(x - 1)$　(d) $\frac{1}{2}, -2, 1$

　　(e)

59. (a) Answers will vary.　(b) $(x - 1), (x - 2)$

　　(c) $f(x) = (x - 1)(x - 2)(x - 5)(x + 4)$

　　(d) $1, 2, 5, -4$

　　(e)

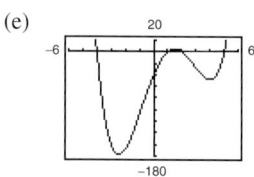

61. (a) Answers will vary.　(b) $x + 7$

　　(c) $f(x) = (x + 7)(2x + 1)(3x - 2)$　(d) $-7, -\frac{1}{2}, \frac{2}{3}$

　　(e)

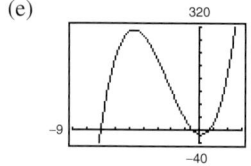

63. (a) Answers will vary.　(b) $\left(x - \sqrt{5}\right)$

　　(c) $f(x) = \left(x - \sqrt{5}\right)\left(x + \sqrt{5}\right)(2x - 1)$　(d) $\pm\sqrt{5}, \frac{1}{2}$

　　(e)

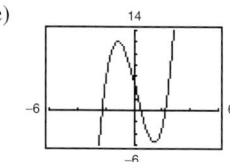

65. (a) Zeros are 2 and $\approx \pm 2.236$.

　　(b) $f(x) = (x - 2)\left(x - \sqrt{5}\right)\left(x + \sqrt{5}\right)$

67. (a) Zeros are $-2, \approx 0.268$, and ≈ 3.732.

　　(b) $h(t) = (t + 2)\left[t - \left(2 + \sqrt{3}\right)\right]\left[t - \left(2 - \sqrt{3}\right)\right]$

69. $2x^2 - x - 1, \ x \neq \frac{3}{2}$　**71.** $x^2 + 2x - 3, \ x \neq -1$

73. $x^2 + 3x, \ x \neq -2, -1$

75. (a) and (b)

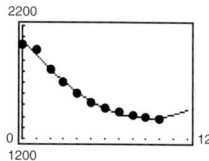

$M = 0.126t^3 + 5.86t^2 - 139.2t + 2070$

(c)

t	0	1	2	3	4	5
M	2070	1937	1816	1709	1615	1536

t	6	7	8	9	10
M	1473	1426	1396	1384	1390

　　(d) 1726 thousand. No, because the model will approach
　　infinity quickly.

77. False. $-\frac{4}{7}$ is a zero of f.

79. True. The degree of the numerator is greater than the
　　degree of the denominator.

81. $x^{2n} + 6x^n + 9$　**83.** The remainder is 0.

85. $c = -210$　**87.** $0; x + 3$ is a factor of f.

89. $\pm\dfrac{5}{3}$　**91.** $-\dfrac{7}{5}, 2$　**93.** $\dfrac{-3 \pm \sqrt{3}}{2}$

95. $f(x) = x^3 - 7x^2 + 12x$

97. $f(x) = x^3 + x^2 - 7x - 3$

Section 2.4　*(page 148)*

1. $a = -10, b = 6$　**3.** $a = 6, b = 5$　**5.** $4 + 3i$

7. $2 - 3\sqrt{3}i$　**9.** $5\sqrt{3}i$　**11.** 8　**13.** $-1 - 6i$

15. $0.3i$　**17.** $11 - i$　**19.** 4　**21.** $3 - 3\sqrt{2}i$

23. $-14 + 20i$　**25.** $\frac{1}{6} + \frac{7}{6}i$　**27.** $-2\sqrt{3}$　**29.** -10

31. $5 + i$　**33.** $12 + 30i$　**35.** 24　**37.** $-9 + 40i$

39. -10　**41.** $6 - 3i, 45$　**43.** $-1 + \sqrt{5}i, 6$

45. $-2\sqrt{5}i, 20$　**47.** $\sqrt{8}, 8$　**49.** $-5i$

51. $\frac{8}{41} + \frac{10}{41}i$　**53.** $\frac{4}{5} + \frac{3}{5}i$　**55.** $-5 - 6i$

57. $-\frac{120}{1681} - \frac{27}{1681}i$　**59.** $-\frac{1}{2} - \frac{5}{2}i$　**61.** $\frac{62}{949} + \frac{297}{949}i$

63. $1 \pm i$　**65.** $-2 \pm \frac{1}{2}i$　**67.** $-\frac{3}{2}, -\frac{5}{2}$

69. $2 \pm \sqrt{2}i$　**71.** $\dfrac{5}{7} \pm \dfrac{5\sqrt{15}}{7}$　**73.** $-1 + 6i$

75. $-5i$　**77.** $-375\sqrt{3}i$　**79.** i

81. (a) 8　(b) 8　(c) 8

83. (a) 1　(b) i　(c) -1　(d) $-i$

85. False. If the complex number is real, the number equals its
　　conjugate.

87. False.

$i^{44} + i^{150} - i^{74} - i^{109} + i^{61} = 1 - 1 + 1 - i + i = 1$

89. Answers will vary. **91.** $-x^2 - 3x + 12$

93. $3x^2 + \frac{23}{2}x - 2$ **95.** -31 **97.** $\frac{27}{2}$

99. $a = \dfrac{\sqrt{3V\pi b}}{2\pi b}$ **101.** 1 liter

Section 2.5 *(page 160)*

1. $0, 6$ **3.** $2, -4$ **5.** $-6, \pm i$ **7.** $\pm 1, \pm 3$

9. $\pm 1, \pm 3, \pm 5, \pm 9, \pm 15, \pm 45, \pm\frac{1}{2}, \pm\frac{3}{2}, \pm\frac{5}{2}, \pm\frac{9}{2}, \pm\frac{15}{2}, \pm\frac{45}{2}$

11. $1, 2, 3$ **13.** $1, -1, 4$ **15.** $-1, -10$

17. $\frac{1}{2}, -1$ **19.** $-2, 3, \pm\frac{2}{3}$ **21.** $-1, 2$ **23.** $-6, \frac{1}{2}, 1$

25. (a) $\pm 1, \pm 2, \pm 4$

(b)

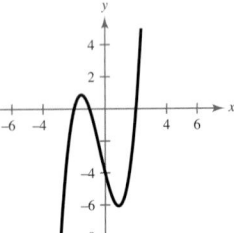

(c) $-2, -1, 2$

27. (a) $\pm 1, \pm 3, \pm\frac{1}{2}, \pm\frac{3}{2}, \pm\frac{1}{4}, \pm\frac{3}{4}$

(b)

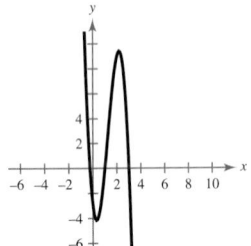

(c) $-\frac{1}{4}, 1, 3$

29. (a) $\pm 1, \pm 2, \pm 4, \pm 8, \pm\frac{1}{2}$

(b)

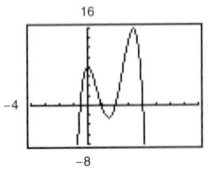

(c) $-\frac{1}{2}, 1, 2, 4$

31. (a) $\pm 1, \pm 3, \pm\frac{1}{2}, \pm\frac{3}{2}, \pm\frac{1}{4}, \pm\frac{3}{4}, \pm\frac{1}{8}, \pm\frac{3}{8}, \pm\frac{1}{16}, \pm\frac{3}{16}, \pm\frac{1}{32}, \pm\frac{3}{32}$

(b)

(c) $1, \frac{3}{4}, -\frac{1}{8}$

33. (a) $\pm 1, \approx\pm 1.414$

(b) $f(x) = (x + 1)(x - 1)\left(x + \sqrt{2}\right)\left(x - \sqrt{2}\right)$

35. (a) $0, 3, 4, \approx\pm 1.414$

(b) $h(x) = x(x - 3)(x - 4)\left(x + \sqrt{2}\right)\left(x - \sqrt{2}\right)$

37. $x^3 - x^2 + 25x - 25$ **39.** $x^3 + 4x^2 - 31x - 174$

41. $3x^4 - 17x^3 + 25x^2 + 23x - 22$

43. (a) $(x^2 + 9)(x^2 - 3)$

(b) $(x^2 + 9)\left(x + \sqrt{3}\right)\left(x - \sqrt{3}\right)$

(c) $(x + 3i)(x - 3i)\left(x + \sqrt{3}\right)\left(x - \sqrt{3}\right)$

45. (a) $(x^2 - 2x - 2)(x^2 - 2x + 3)$

(b) $\left(x - 1 + \sqrt{3}\right)\left(x - 1 - \sqrt{3}\right)(x^2 - 2x + 3)$

(c) $\left(x - 1 + \sqrt{3}\right)\left(x - 1 - \sqrt{3}\right)\left(x - 1 + \sqrt{2}i\right)$
$\left(x - 1 - \sqrt{2}i\right)$

47. $-\frac{3}{2}, \pm 5i$ **49.** $\pm 2i, 1, -\frac{1}{2}$ **51.** $-3 \pm i, \frac{1}{4}$

53. $2, -3 \pm \sqrt{2}i, 1$ **55.** $\pm 5i; (x + 5i)(x - 5i)$

57. $2 \pm \sqrt{3}; \left(x - 2 - \sqrt{3}\right)\left(x - 2 + \sqrt{3}\right)$

59. $\pm 3, \pm 3i; (x + 3)(x - 3)(x + 3i)(x - 3i)$

61. $1 \pm i; (z - 1 + i)(z - 1 - i)$

63. $2, 2 \pm i; (x - 2)(x - 2 + i)(x - 2 - i)$

65. $-2, 1 \pm \sqrt{2}i; (x + 2)\left(x - 1 + \sqrt{2}i\right)\left(x - 1 - \sqrt{2}i\right)$

67. $-\frac{1}{5}, 1 \pm \sqrt{5}i; (5x + 1)\left(x - 1 + \sqrt{5}i\right)\left(x - 1 - \sqrt{5}i\right)$

69. $2, \pm 2i; (x - 2)^2(x + 2i)(x - 2i)$

71. $\pm i, \pm 3i; (x + i)(x - i)(x + 3i)(x - 3i)$

73. $-10, -7 \pm 5i$ **75.** $-\frac{3}{4}, 1 \pm \frac{1}{2}i$ **77.** $-2, -\frac{1}{2}, \pm i$

79. No real zeros **81.** No real zeros

83. One positive zero **85.** One or three positive zeros

87. Answers will vary. **89.** Answers will vary.

91. $1, -\frac{1}{2}$ **93.** $-\frac{3}{4}$ **95.** $\pm 2, \pm\frac{3}{2}$ **97.** $\pm 1, \frac{1}{4}$

99. d **100.** a **101.** b **102.** c

103. (a)

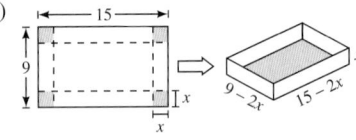

(b) $V = x(9 - 2x)(15 - 2x)$

Domain: $0 < x < \frac{9}{2}$

(c)

1.82 centimeters $\times$ 5.36 centimeters $\times$ 11.36 centimeters

(d) $\frac{1}{2}, \frac{7}{2}, 8$; 8 is not in the domain of V.

105. $x \approx 38.4$, or \$384,000

107. (a) $A = -0.045028t^3 + 0.97071t^2 - 5.8547t + 15.390$

(b)   (c) 1996   (d) 1998

(e) The attendance will increase until 2000. It will then decrease quickly.

109. No. Setting $h = 64$ and solving the resulting equation yields imaginary roots.

111. False. The most complex zeros it can have is two, and the Linear Factorization Theorem guarantees that there are three linear factors, so one zero must be real.

113. r_1, r_2, r_3 **115.** $5 + r_1, 5 + r_2, 5 + r_3$

117. The zeros cannot be determined.

119. (a) $0 < k < 4$ (b) $k = 4$ (c) $k < 0$ (d) $k > 4$

121. $f(x) = -2x^3 + 3x^2 + 11x - 6$

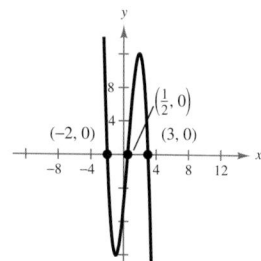

(Equations and graphs will vary.) There are infinitely many possible functions for f.

123. (a) $-2, 1, 4$

(b) The graph touches the x-axis at $x = 1$.

(c) The least possible degree of the function is 4, because there are at least four real zeros (1 is repeated) and a function can have at most the number of real zeros equal to the degree of the function. The degree cannot be odd by the definition of multiplicity.

(d) Positive. From the information in the table, it can be concluded that the graph will eventually rise to the left and rise to the right.

(e) $f(x) = x^4 - 4x^3 - 3x^2 + 14x - 8$

(f)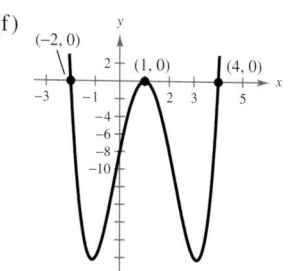

125. (a) $x^2 + b$ (b) $x^2 - 2ax + a^2 + b^2$

127. $-11 + 9i$ **129.** $20 + 40i$

131.   **133.**

135.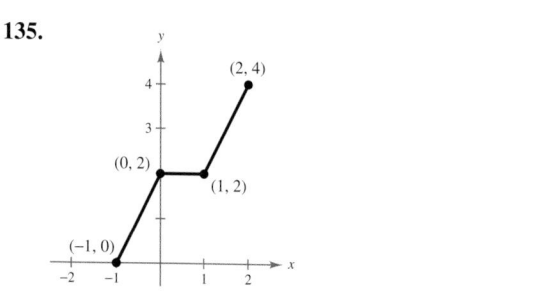

Section 2.6   *(page 174)*

1. (a)

x	$f(x)$	x	$f(x)$	x	$f(x)$
0.5	-2	1.5	2	5	0.25
0.9	-10	1.1	10	10	$0.\overline{1}$
0.99	-100	1.01	100	100	$0.\overline{01}$
0.999	-1000	1.001	1000	1000	$0.\overline{001}$

(b) Vertical asymptote: $x = 1$

Horizontal asymptote: $y = 0$

(c) Domain: all real numbers $x \neq 1$

3. (a)

x	$f(x)$	x	$f(x)$	x	$f(x)$
0.5	-1	1.5	5.4	5	3.125
0.9	-12.79	1.1	17.29	10	$3.\overline{03}$
0.99	-147.8	1.01	152.3	100	$3.\overline{0003}$
0.999	-1498	1.001	1502	1000	3

(b) Vertical asymptotes: $x = \pm 1$
Horizontal asymptote: $y = 3$

(c) Domain: all real numbers $x \neq \pm 1$

5. Domain: all real numbers $x \neq 0$
Vertical asymptote: $x = 0$
Horizontal asymptote: $y = 0$

7. Domain: all real numbers $x \neq 2$
Vertical asymptote: $x = 2$
Horizontal asymptote: $y = -1$

9. Domain: all real numbers $x \neq \pm 1$
Vertical asymptotes: $x = \pm 1$
No horizontal asymptote

11. Domain: all real numbers
Horizontal asymptote: $y = 3$
No vertical asymptote

13. d **14.** a **15.** c **16.** b **17.** 1 **19.** 6

21. (a) y-intercept: $\left(0, \frac{1}{2}\right)$

(b) Vertical asymptote: $x = -2$
Horizontal asymptote: $y = 0$

(c) No axis or origin symmetry

(d)

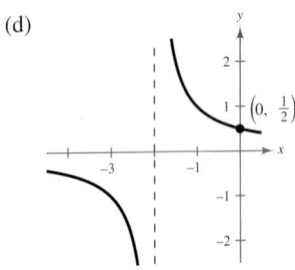

23. (a) y-intercept: $\left(0, -\frac{1}{2}\right)$

(b) Vertical asymptote: $x = -2$
Horizontal asymptote: $y = 0$

(c) No axis or origin symmetry

(d)

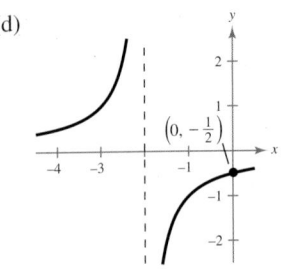

25. (a) x-intercept: $\left(-\frac{5}{2}, 0\right)$
y-intercept: $(0, 5)$

(b) Vertical asymptote: $x = -1$
Horizontal asymptote: $y = 2$

(c) No axis or origin symmetry

(d)

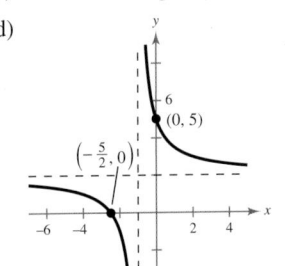

27. (a) x-intercept: $\left(-\frac{5}{2}, 0\right)$
y-intercept: $\left(0, \frac{5}{2}\right)$

(b) Vertical asymptote: $x = -2$
Horizontal asymptote: $y = 2$

(c) No axis or origin symmetry

(d)

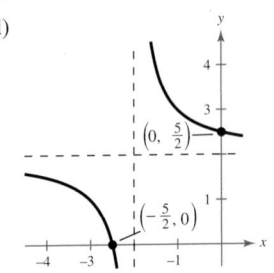

29. (a) Intercept: $(0, 0)$

(b) Horizontal asymptote: $y = 1$

(c) y-axis symmetry

(d)

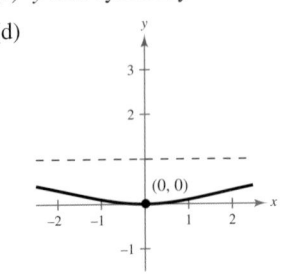

31. (a) Intercept: $(0, 0)$

(b) Vertical asymptotes: $x = 3, x = -3$

Horizontal asymptote: $y = 1$

(c) y-axis symmetry

(d)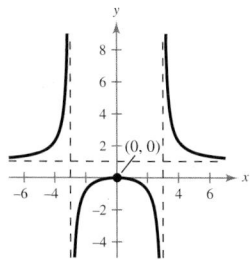

33. (a) Intercept: $(0, 0)$

(b) Horizontal asymptote: $y = 0$

(c) Origin symmetry

(d)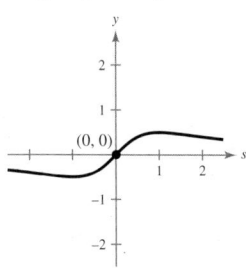

35. (a) x-intercept: $(-1, 0)$

(b) Vertical asymptotes: $x = 0, \ x = 4$

Horizontal asymptote: $y = 0$

(c) No axis or origin symmetry

(d)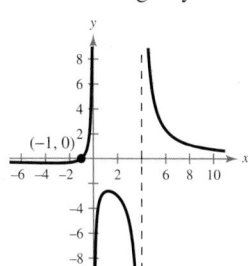

37. (a) Intercept: $(0, 0)$

(b) Vertical asymptotes: $x = -1, \ x = 2$

Horizontal asymptote: $y = 0$

(c) No axis or origin symmetry

(d)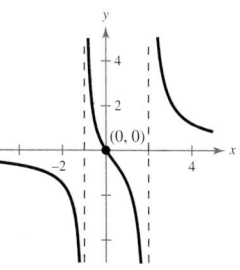

39. (a) x-intercepts: $(3, 0), \left(-\frac{1}{2}, 0\right)$

y-intercept: $\left(0, -\frac{3}{2}\right)$

(b) Vertical asymptotes: $x = 2, x = 1, x = -1$

Horizontal asymptote: $y = 0$

(c) No axis or origin symmetry

(d)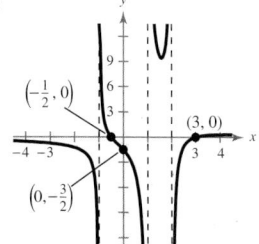

41. (a) Domain of f: all real numbers $x \neq -1$

Domain of g: all real numbers

(b) Vertical asymptote: none

(c)

x	-3	-2	-1.5	-1	-0.5	0	1
$f(x)$	-4	-3	-2.5	Undef.	-1.5	-1	0
$g(x)$	-4	-3	-2.5	-2	-1.5	-1	0

(d)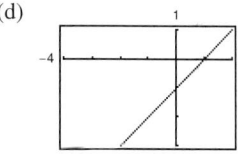

(e) Because there are only a finite number of pixels, the utility may not attempt to evaluate the function where it does not exist.

43. (a) Domain of f: all real numbers $x \neq 0, 2$

Domain of g: all real numbers $x \neq 0$

(b) Vertical asymptote: $x = 0$

(c)

x	-0.5	0	0.5	1	1.5	2	3
$f(x)$	-2	Undef.	2	1	$\frac{2}{3}$	Undef.	$\frac{1}{3}$
$g(x)$	-2	Undef.	2	1	$\frac{2}{3}$	$\frac{1}{2}$	$\frac{1}{3}$

(d)

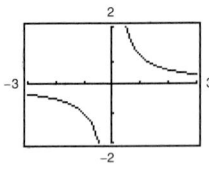

(e) Because there are only a finite number of pixels, the utility may not attempt to evaluate the function where it does not exist.

45. Domain: all real numbers $x \neq 0$

Vertical asymptote: $x = 0$

Slant asymptote: $y = x$

47. Domain: all real numbers $t \neq -5$

Vertical asymptote: $t = -5$

Slant asymptote: $y = -t + 5$

49. Domain: all real numbers $x \neq 0, 1$

Vertical asymptote: $x = 0$

Slant asymptote: $y = x + 1$

51. (a) No intercepts

(b) Vertical asymptote: $x = 0$

Slant asymptote: $y = 2x$

(c) Origin symmetry

(d)

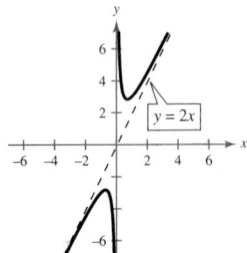

53. (a) No intercepts

(b) Vertical asymptote: $x = 0$

Slant asymptote: $y = x$

(c) Origin symmetry

(d)

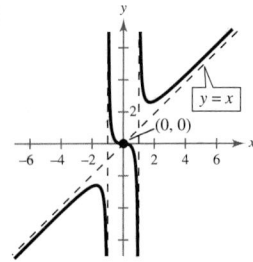

55. (a) Intercept: $(0, 0)$

(b) Vertical asymptotes: $x = \pm 1$

Slant asymptote: $y = x$

(c) Origin symmetry

(d)

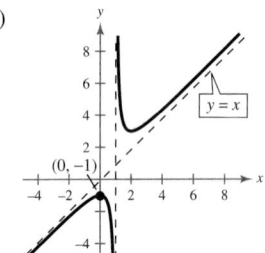

57. (a) y-intercept: $(0, -1)$

(b) Vertical asymptote: $x = 1$

Slant asymptote: $y = x$

(c) No axis or origin symmetry

(d)

59.

Domain: all real numbers $x \neq -3$

Vertical asymptote: $x = -3$

Slant asymptote: $y = x + 2$

$y = x + 2$

61.

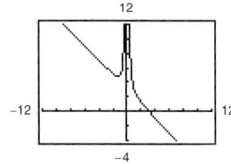

Domain: all real numbers $x \neq 0$

Vertical asymptote: $x = 0$

Slant asymptote: $y = -x + 3$

$y = -x + 3$

63. (a) $(-1, 0)$ (b) -1

65. (a) $(1, 0), (-1, 0)$ (b) ± 1

67. (a) \$28.33 million

   (b) \$170 million

   (c) \$765 million

   (d) No. The function is undefined at $p = 100$.

69. (a) 333 deer, 500 deer, 800 deer   (b) 1500 deer

71. (a) $y = \dfrac{500}{x}$

   (b) $(0, \infty)$

   (c)

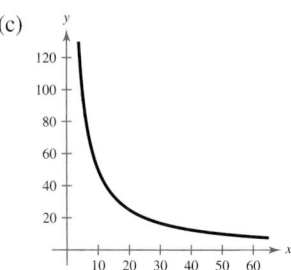

   $16\frac{2}{3}$ meters

73. (a) $C = 0$; The chemical will eventually dissipate.

   (b)

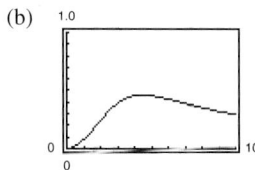

   $t \approx 4.5$ hours

75. False. Polynomials do not have vertical asymptotes.

77. $f(x) = \dfrac{2x^2}{x^2 + 1}$ (Answer is not unique.)

79. $f(x) = \dfrac{1}{x^2 + 2}$, $f(x) = \dfrac{1}{x - 20}$ (Answers are not unique.)

81. $f(x) = \dfrac{x^2 - x - 6}{x - 2}$

83.

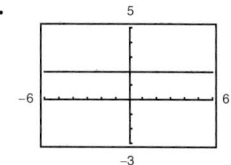

The fraction is not reduced.

85. $(x - 7)(x - 8)$ **87.** $(x - 5)(x + 2i)(x - 2i)$

89. $x \geq \dfrac{10}{3}$ **91.** $-3 < x < 7$

Section 2.7   *(page 184)*

1. b   **2.** c   **3.** d   **4.** a

5. $\dfrac{A}{x} + \dfrac{B}{x - 14}$ **7.** $\dfrac{A}{x} + \dfrac{B}{x^2} + \dfrac{C}{x - 10}$

9. $\dfrac{A}{x - 5} + \dfrac{B}{(x - 5)^2} + \dfrac{C}{(x - 5)^3}$

11. $\dfrac{A}{x} + \dfrac{Bx + C}{x^2 + 10}$ **13.** $\dfrac{A}{x} + \dfrac{Bx + C}{x^2 + 1} + \dfrac{Dx + E}{(x^2 + 1)^2}$

15. $\dfrac{1}{2}\left(\dfrac{1}{x - 1} - \dfrac{1}{x + 1}\right)$

17. $\dfrac{1}{x} - \dfrac{1}{x + 1}$ **19.** $\dfrac{1}{x} - \dfrac{2}{2x + 1}$ **21.** $\dfrac{1}{x - 1} - \dfrac{1}{x + 2}$

23. $-\dfrac{3}{x} - \dfrac{1}{x + 2} + \dfrac{5}{x - 2}$ **25.** $\dfrac{3}{x} - \dfrac{1}{x^2} + \dfrac{1}{x + 1}$

27. $\dfrac{3}{x - 3} + \dfrac{9}{(x - 3)^2}$ **29.** $-\dfrac{1}{x} + \dfrac{2x}{x^2 + 1}$

31. $-\dfrac{1}{x - 1} + \dfrac{x + 2}{x^2 - 2}$

33. $\dfrac{1}{6}\left(\dfrac{2}{x^2 + 2} - \dfrac{1}{x + 2} + \dfrac{1}{x - 2}\right)$

35. $\dfrac{1}{8}\left(\dfrac{1}{2x + 1} + \dfrac{1}{2x - 1} - \dfrac{4x}{4x^2 + 1}\right)$

37. $\dfrac{1}{x + 1} + \dfrac{2}{x^2 - 2x + 3}$ **39.** $1 - \dfrac{2x + 1}{x^2 + x + 1}$

41. $2x - 7 + \dfrac{17}{x + 2} + \dfrac{1}{x + 1}$

43. $x + 3 + \dfrac{6}{x - 1} + \dfrac{4}{(x - 1)^2} + \dfrac{1}{(x - 1)^3}$

45. $\dfrac{3}{2x - 1} - \dfrac{2}{x + 1}$ **47.** $\dfrac{2}{x} - \dfrac{1}{x^2} - \dfrac{2}{x + 1}$

49. $\dfrac{1}{x^2 + 2} + \dfrac{x}{(x^2 + 2)^2}$ **51.** $2x + \dfrac{1}{2}\left(\dfrac{3}{x - 4} - \dfrac{1}{x + 2}\right)$

53. $\dfrac{3}{x} - \dfrac{2}{x-4}$

$y = \dfrac{x-12}{x(x-4)}$ $\qquad y = \dfrac{3}{x}, \ y = -\dfrac{2}{x-4}$

 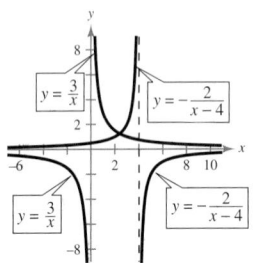

The vertical asymptotes are the same.

55. $\dfrac{3}{x-3} + \dfrac{5}{x+3}$

$y = \dfrac{2(4x-3)}{x^2-9}$ $\qquad y = \dfrac{3}{x-3}, \ y = \dfrac{5}{x+3}$

 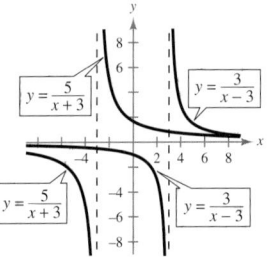

The vertical asymptotes are the same.

57. (a) $\dfrac{2000}{7-4x} - \dfrac{2000}{11-7x}, \quad 0 < x \le 1$

(b) $\text{Ymax} = \left|\dfrac{2000}{7-4x}\right|$

$\text{Ymin} = \left|\dfrac{-2000}{11-7x}\right|$

(c)

(d) Maximum: 400°F

Minimum: 266.7°F

59. False. The partial fraction decomposition is

$\dfrac{A}{x+10} + \dfrac{B}{x-10} + \dfrac{C}{(x-10)^2}.$

61. $\dfrac{1}{2a}\left(\dfrac{1}{a+x} + \dfrac{1}{a-x}\right)$ **63.** $\dfrac{1}{a}\left(\dfrac{1}{y} + \dfrac{1}{a-y}\right)$

65. **67.**

69.

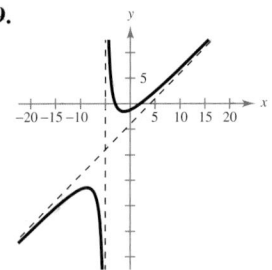

Review Exercises *(page 187)*

1. $f(x) = -\frac{1}{2}(x-4)^2 + 1$ **3.** $f(x) = (x-1)^2 - 4$

5.

(a)

Vertical stretch

(b)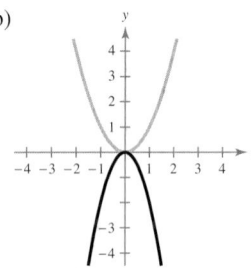

Vertical stretch and reflection in the x-axis

(c)

Vertical translation

(d)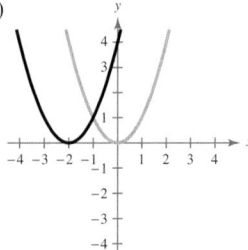

Horizontal translation

7. $g(x) = (x - 1)^2 - 1$

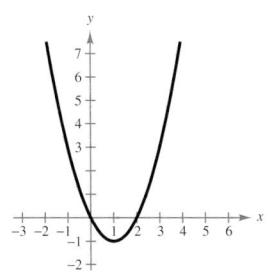

Vertex: $(1, -1)$

x-intercepts: $(0, 0), (2, 0)$

9. $f(x) = (x + 4)^2 - 6$

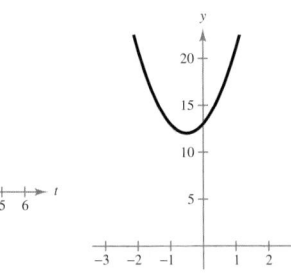

Vertex: $(-4, -6)$

x-intercepts: $\left(-4 \pm \sqrt{6}, 0\right)$

11. $f(t) = -2(t - 1)^2 + 3$

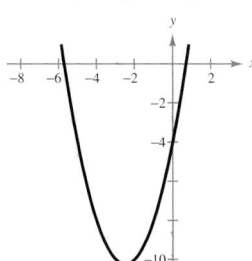

Vertex: $(1, 3)$

t-intercepts: $\left(1 \pm \dfrac{\sqrt{6}}{2}, 0\right)$

13. $h(x) = 4\left(x + \frac{1}{2}\right)^2 + 12$

Vertex: $\left(-\frac{1}{2}, 12\right)$

No x-intercept

15. $h(x) = \left(x + \frac{5}{2}\right)^2 - \frac{41}{4}$

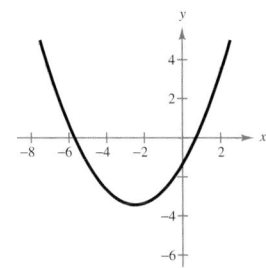

Vertex: $\left(-\frac{5}{2}, -\frac{41}{4}\right)$

x-intercepts: $\left(\dfrac{\pm\sqrt{41} - 5}{2}, 0\right)$

17. $f(x) = \frac{1}{3}\left(x + \frac{5}{2}\right)^2 - \frac{41}{12}$

Vertex: $\left(-\frac{5}{2}, -\frac{41}{12}\right)$

x-intercepts: $\left(\dfrac{\pm\sqrt{41} - 5}{2}, 0\right)$

19. (a)

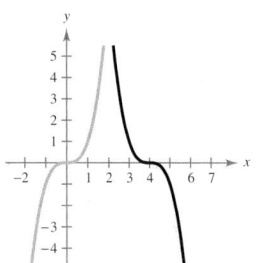

(b) $y = 100 - x$

$A = 100x - x^2$

(c) $x = 50, \ y = 50$

21. 1091 units

23.

25.

27.

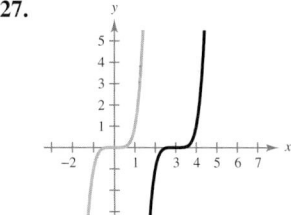

29. Falls to the left, falls to the right

31. Rises to the left, rises to the right

33. $-7, \frac{3}{2}$, odd multiplicity   **35.** $0, \pm\sqrt{3}$, odd multiplicity

37. 0, even multiplicity; $\frac{5}{3}$, odd multiplicity

39. (a) Rises to the left, falls to the right   (b) -1

(c) Answers will vary.

(d)

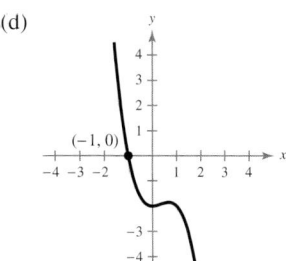

$(-1, 0)$

41. (a) Rises to the right, rises to the left   (b) $-3, 0, 1$

(c) Answers will vary.

(d)

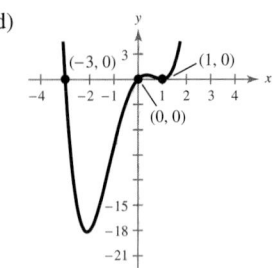

43. $[-1, 0]; \approx -0.900$

45. $[-1, 0], [1, 2]; \approx -0.200, \approx 1.772$

47. $8x + 5 + \dfrac{2}{3x - 2}$ **49.** $5x + 2$

51. $x^2 - 3x + 2 - \dfrac{1}{x^2 + 2}$

53. $6x^3 + 8x^2 - 11x - 4 - \dfrac{8}{x - 2}$ **55.** $2x^2 - 11x - 6$

57. (a) Yes   (b) Yes   (c) Yes   (d) No

59. (a) -421 (b) -9

61. (a) Answers will vary.

(b) $(x + 7), (x + 1)$

(c) $f(x) = (x + 7)(x + 1)(x - 4)$

(d) $-7, -1, 4$

(e)

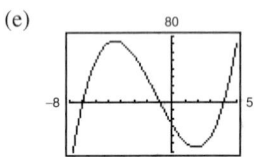

63. (a) Answers will vary.

(b) $(x + 1), (x - 4)$

(c) $f(x) = (x + 1)(x - 4)(x + 2)(x - 3)$

(d) $-2, -1, 3, 4$

(e)

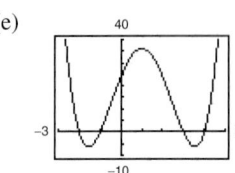

65. $6 + 2i$ **67.** $-1 + 3i$ **69.** $3 + 7i$

71. $40 + 65i$ **73.** $-4 - 46i$ **75.** $\frac{23}{17} + \frac{10}{17}i$

77. $\dfrac{21}{13} - \dfrac{1}{13}i$ **79.** $\pm\dfrac{\sqrt{3}}{3}i$ **81.** $1 \pm 3i$

83. $0, 2$ **85.** $8, 1$ **87.** $-4, 6, \pm 2i$

89. $\pm 1, \pm 3, \pm 5, \pm 15, \pm\frac{1}{2}, \pm\frac{3}{2}, \pm\frac{5}{2}, \pm\frac{15}{2}, \pm\frac{1}{4}, \pm\frac{3}{4}, \pm\frac{5}{4}, \pm\frac{15}{4}$

91. $-1, -3, 6$ **93.** $1, 8$ **95.** $-4, 3$

97. $3x^4 - 14x^3 + 17x^2 - 42x + 24$ **99.** $12, \pm i$

101. $-3, \frac{1}{2}, 2 \pm i$ **103.** $0, 1, -5; f(x) = x(x - 1)(x + 5)$

105. $-4, 2 \pm 3i; g(x) = (x + 4)^2(x - 2 - 3i)(x - 2 + 3i)$

107. Two or no positive real zeros, one negative real zero

109. Answers will vary.

111. Domain: all real numbers $x \neq -12$

113. Domain: all real numbers $x \neq 6, 4$

115. Vertical asymptote: $x = -3$

Horizontal asymptote: $y = 0$

117. Vertical asymptotes: $x = -2, x = 2$

Horizontal asymptote: $y = 1$

119. No intercepts

y-axis symmetry

Vertical asymptote: $x = 0$

Horizontal asymptote: $y = 0$

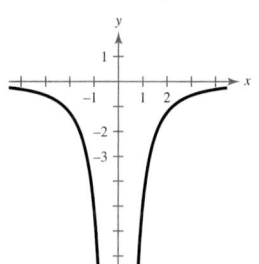

121. x-intercept: $(-2, 0)$

y-intercept: $(0, 2)$

No axis or origin symmetry

Vertical asymptote: $x = 1$

Horizontal asymptote: $y = -1$

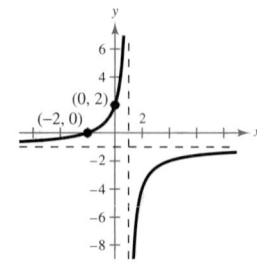

123. Intercept: $(0, 0)$

y-axis symmetry

Horizontal asymptote: $y = 1$

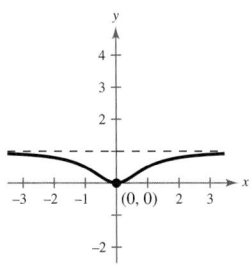

125. Intercept: $(0, 0)$

Origin symmetry

Horizontal asymptote: $y = 0$

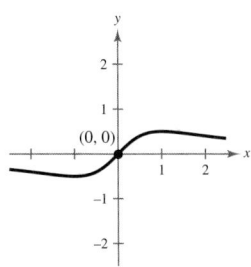

127. Intercept: $(0, 0)$

y-axis symmetry

Horizontal asymptote: $y = -6$

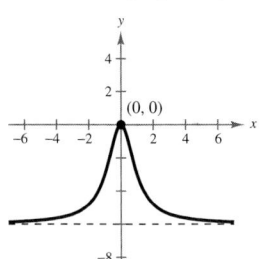

129. Intercept: $(0, 0)$

Origin symmetry

Vertical asymptotes: $x = \pm 1$

Horizontal asymptote: $y = 0$

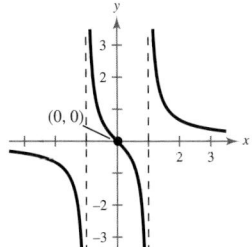

131. Domain: all real numbers

Slant asymptote: $y = 2x$

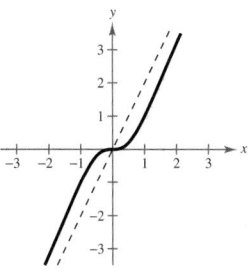

133. Domain: all real numbers $x \neq -2$

Vertical asymptote: $x = -2$

Slant asymptote: $y = x + 1$

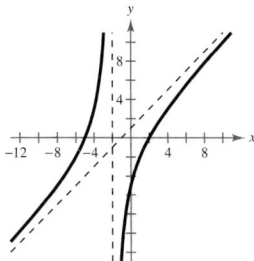

135. As x increases, the cost approaches the horizontal asymptote $\bar{c} = 0.5$. The average cost per unit is \$0.50.

137. (a)

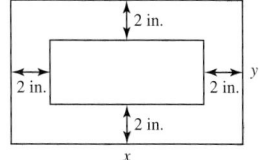

(b) $(x - 4)(y - 4) = 30$

$$y = \frac{4x + 14}{x - 4}$$

$$\text{Area} = x\left(\frac{4x + 14}{x - 4}\right)$$

$$= \frac{2x(2x + 7)}{x - 4}$$

(c) $4 < x < \infty$

(d)

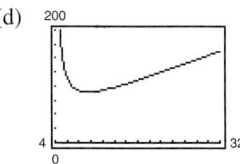

9.48 inches $\times$ 9.48 inches

139. $\dfrac{A}{x} + \dfrac{B}{x + 20}$ **141.** $\dfrac{A}{x} + \dfrac{B}{x^2} + \dfrac{C}{x - 5}$

143. $\dfrac{3}{x+2} - \dfrac{4}{x+4}$ **145.** $1 - \dfrac{25}{8(x+5)} + \dfrac{9}{8(x-3)}$

147. $\dfrac{1}{2}\left(\dfrac{3}{x-1} - \dfrac{x-3}{x^2+1}\right)$ **149.** $\dfrac{3x}{x^2+1} + \dfrac{x}{(x^2+1)^2}$

151. False. A fourth-degree polynomial can have at most four zeros, and complex zeros occur in conjugate pairs.

153. Answers will vary. For example:

(a) $x^2 + 2x - 8 = 0$

(b) $x^2 + x + 5 = 0$

(c) $x^2 + 4 = 0$

155. Fourth degree

Chapter Test   *(page 191)*

1. (a) Reflection in the x-axis followed by a vertical translation of two units upward

(b) Horizontal translation of three half units to the right

2. $y = (x-3)^2 - 6$

3. (a) 50 feet   (b) 61.6 feet

4. Rises to the left, falls to the right

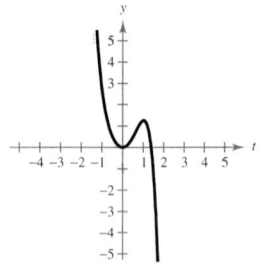

5. $3x + \dfrac{x-1}{x^2+1}$

6. $f(x) = (4x-1)(x-\sqrt{3})(x+\sqrt{3})$;

Real zeros: $\frac{1}{4}, \pm\sqrt{3}$

7. (a) $-3 + 5i$ (b) 7 **8.** $2 - i$

9. $-2, \frac{3}{2}$ **10.** $\pm 1, -\frac{2}{3}$ **11.** $2, -1, \pm 2i$

12. $f(x) = x^4 - 9x^3 + 28x^2 - 30x$

13. $f(x) = x^4 - 6x^3 + 16x^2 - 24x + 16$

14.

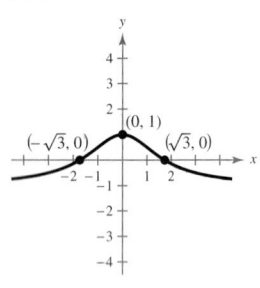

Horizontal asymptote: $y = -1$

15.

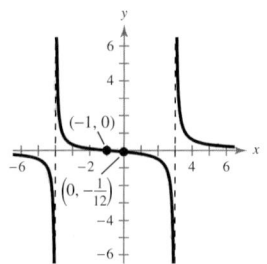

Vertical asymptotes: $x = 3, x = -4$

Horizontal asymptote: $y = 0$

16.

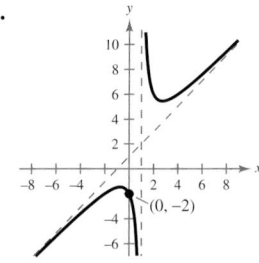

Vertical asymptote: $x = 1$

Slant asymptote: $y = x + 1$

17. $\dfrac{3}{x-2} - \dfrac{1}{x+1}$ **18.** $\dfrac{2}{x^2} - \dfrac{3}{x-2}$

19. $-\dfrac{5}{x} + \dfrac{3}{x-1} + \dfrac{3}{x+1}$ **20.** $-\dfrac{2}{x} + \dfrac{3x}{x^2+2}$

Problem Solving   *(page 194)*

1. (a) $f(x) = (x-2)x^2 + 5 = x^3 - 2x^2 + 5$

(b) $f(x) = -(x+3)x^2 + 1 = -x^3 - 3x^2 + 1$

3. Answers will vary.

5. (a) and (b) $y = -x^2 + 5x - 4$

7. $\dfrac{x^n - 1}{x - 1} = x^{n-1} + x^{n-2} + x^{n-3} + \cdots + 1$

9. (a) iii   (b) ii   (c) iv   (d) i

11. (a) As $|a|$ increases, the graph becomes wider, and as $|a|$ decreases, the graph becomes narrower. For $a < 0$, the graph is reflected in the x-axis.

(b) As $|b|$ increases, the graph becomes wider, and as $|b|$ decreases, the graph becomes narrower. For $b > 0$, the graph is translated to the right. For $b < 0$, the graph is reflected in the x-axis and is translated to the left.

Chapter 3

Section 3.1 *(page 206)*

1. 946.852   **3.** 0.006   **5.** 0.472

7. d   **8.** c   **9.** a   **10.** b

11. Shift the graph of four units to the right.

13. Shift the graph of five units upward.

15. Reflect f in the x-axis and shift four units to the left.

17. Reflect f in the x-axis and shift five units upward.

19.

x	-2	-1	0	1	2
$f(x)$	4	2	1	0.5	0.25

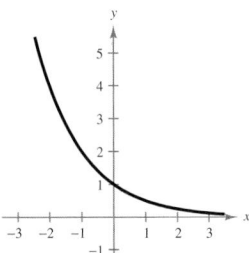

21.

x	-2	-1	0	1	2
$f(x)$	36	6	1	0.167	0.028

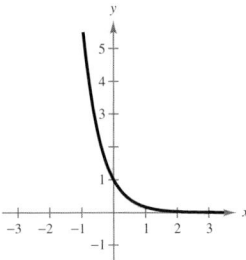

23.

x	-2	-1	0	1	2
$f(x)$	0.125	0.25	0.5	1	2

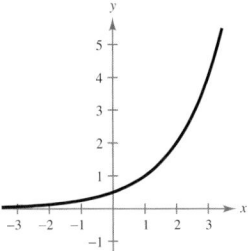

25.

x	-2	-1	0	1	2
$f(x)$	0.135	0.368	1	2.718	7.389

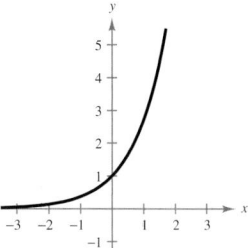

27.

x	-8	-7	-6	-5	-4
$f(x)$	0.055	0.149	0.406	1.104	3

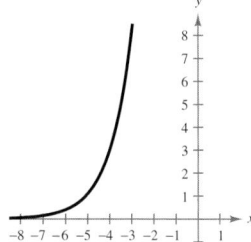

29.

x	-2	-1	0	1	2
$f(x)$	4.037	4.100	4.271	4.736	6

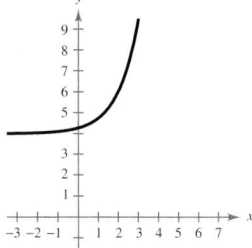

31.

x	-1	0	1	2	3
$f(x)$	3.004	3.016	3.063	3.25	4

33.   **35.**

37.   **39.**

41.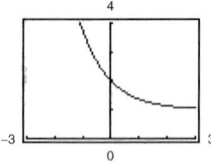

43.

n	1	2	4
A	\$5397.31	\$5477.81	\$5520.10

n	12	365	Continuous
A	\$5549.10	\$5563.36	\$5563.85

45.

n	1	2	4
A	\$11,652.39	\$12,002.55	\$12,188.60

n	12	365	Continuous
A	\$12,317.01	\$12,380.41	\$12,382.58

47.

t	10	20
A	\$26,706.49	\$59,436.39

t	30	40	50
A	\$132,278.12	\$294,390.36	\$655,177.80

49.

t	10	20
A	\$22,986.49	\$44,031.56

t	30	40	50
A	\$84,344.25	\$161,564.86	\$309,484.08

51. \$222,822.57

53. \$35.45   **55.** (a) 100   (b) 300   (c) 900

57. (a) 25 grams   (b) 16.30 grams

(c)

59. (a)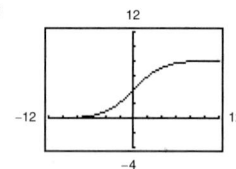

(b)

x	0	25	50	75	100
y	13	45	82	96	99

(c) 63.1%   (d) 38.2

61. True. As $x \to -\infty$, $f(x) \to -2$ but never reaches -2.

63. $f(x) = h(x)$ **65.** $f(x) = g(x) = h(x)$

67. (a) $x < 0$ (b) $x > 0$

69. (a)   Horizontal asymptotes: $y = 0$, $y = 8$

(b) Horizontal asymptote: $y = 4$

Vertical asymptote: $x = 0$

71.

As $x \to \infty$, $f(x) \to g(x)$.

As $x \to -\infty$, $f(x) \to g(x)$.

73. c, d   **75.** $y = \frac{1}{7}(2x + 14)$ **77.** $y = \pm\sqrt{25 - x^2}$

79.

81.

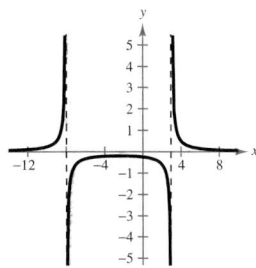

Section 3.2   *(page 216)*

1. $4^3 = 64$ **3.** $7^{-2} = \frac{1}{49}$ **5.** $32^{2/5} = 4$

7. $e^{-0.693\cdots} = \frac{1}{2}$ **9.** $\log_5 125 = 3$ **11.** $\log_{81} 3 = \frac{1}{4}$

13. $\log_6 \frac{1}{36} = -2$ **15.** $\ln 20.0855\ldots = 3$

17. $\ln 4 = x$ **19.** 4   **21.** 0   **23.** 3   **25.** 2

27. -0.097 **29.** 2.913   **31.** -0.575 **33.** c

34. f   **35.** d   **36.** e   **37.** b   **38.** a

39. Domain: $(0, \infty)$

x-intercept: $(1, 0)$

Vertical asymptote: $x = 0$

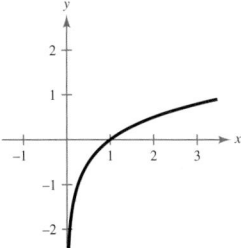

41. Domain: $(0, \infty)$

x-intercept: $(9, 0)$

Vertical asymptote: $x = 0$

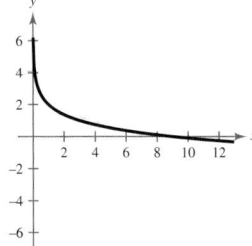

43. Domain: $(-2, \infty)$

x-intercept: $(-1, 0)$

Vertical asymptote: $x = -2$

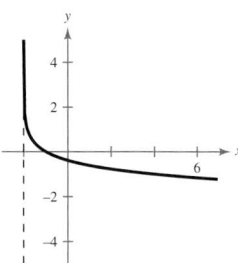

45. Domain: $(0, \infty)$

x-intercept: $(5, 0)$

Vertical asymptote: $x = 0$

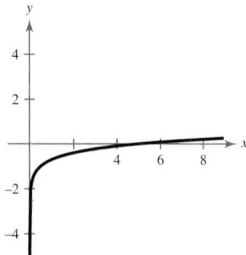

47. Domain: $(2, \infty)$

x-intercept: $(3, 0)$

Vertical asymptote: $x = 2$

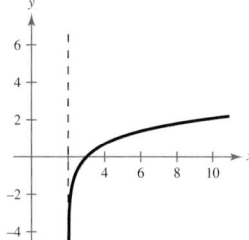

49. Domain: $(-\infty, 0)$

x-intercept: $(-1, 0)$

Vertical asymptote: $x = 0$

51.

53.

55.

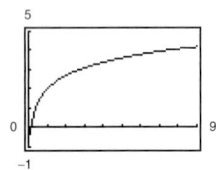

57. (a) 30 years; 20 years   (b) $396,234; $301,123.20

(c) $246,234; $151,123.20

(d) $x = 1000$; The monthly payment must be greater than $1000.

59. (a)

r	0.005	0.01	0.015	0.02	0.025	0.03
t	138.6	69.3	46.2	34.7	27.7	23.1

(b)

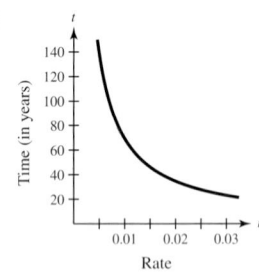

(c) Answers will vary.

61. (a)

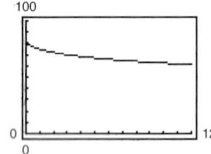

(b) 80   (c) 68.1   (d) 62.3

63. False. Reflecting $g(x)$ about the line $y = x$ will determine the graph of $f(x)$.

65.

$g = f^{-1}$

67.

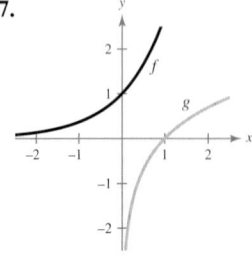

$g = f^{-1}$

69. (a)

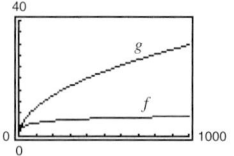

$g(x)$; The natural log function grows at a slower rate than the square root function.

(b)

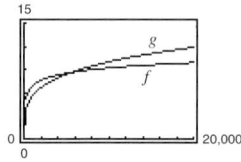

$g(x)$; The natural log function grows at a slower rate than the fourth root function.

71. $(0, \infty)$ **73.** $3 < x < 4$

75. (a)

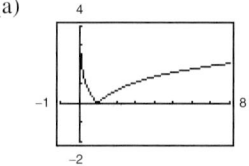

(b) Increasing: $(1, \infty)$

Decreasing: $(0, 1)$

(c) Relative minimum: $(1, 0)$

77. $83.95 + 37.50t$

Section 3.3   *(page 223)*

1. (a) $\dfrac{\log_{10} x}{\log_{10} 5}$ (b) $\dfrac{\ln x}{\ln 5}$ **3.** (a) $\dfrac{\log_{10} x}{\log_{10} \frac{1}{5}}$ (b) $\dfrac{\ln x}{\ln \frac{1}{5}}$

5. (a) $\dfrac{\log_{10} \frac{3}{10}}{\log_{10} x}$ (b) $\dfrac{\ln \frac{3}{10}}{\ln x}$ **7.** (a) $\dfrac{\log_{10} x}{\log_{10} 2.6}$ (b) $\dfrac{\ln x}{\ln 2.6}$

9. 1.771   **11.** -2.000 **13.** -0.417 **15.** 2.633

17. $\log_4 5 + \log_4 x$ **19.** $4 \log_8 x$ **21.** $1 - \log_5 x$

23. $\frac{1}{2} \ln z$ **25.** $\ln x + \ln y + 2 \ln z$

27. $\ln z + 2 \ln(z - 1)$ **29.** $\frac{1}{2} \log_2(a - 1) - \log_2 9$

31. $\frac{1}{3} \ln x - \frac{1}{3} \ln y$ **33.** $4 \ln x + \frac{1}{2} \ln y - 5 \ln z$

35. $2 \log_5 x - 2 \log_5 y - 3 \log_5 z$

37. $\frac{3}{4} \ln x + \frac{1}{4} \ln(x^2 + 3)$ **39.** $\ln 3x$ **41.** $\log_4 \dfrac{z}{y}$

43. $\log_2(x + 4)^2$ **45.** $\log_3 \sqrt[4]{5x}$

47. $\ln \dfrac{x}{(x + 1)^3}$ **49.** $\log_{10} \dfrac{xz^3}{y^2}$ **51.** $\ln \dfrac{x}{(x^2 - 4)^4}$

53. $\ln \sqrt[3]{\dfrac{x(x + 3)^2}{x^2 - 1}}$ **55.** $\log_8 \dfrac{\sqrt[3]{y(y + 4)^2}}{y - 1}$

57. $\log_2 \frac{32}{4} = \log_2 32 - \log_2 4$; Property 2   **59.** 2

61. $\frac{3}{4}$ **63.** 2.4   **65.** -9 is not in the domain of $\log_3 x$.

67. 4.5   **69.** $-\frac{1}{2}$ **71.** 7   **73.** 2

75. $\frac{3}{2}$ **77.** $-3 - \log_5 2$ **79.** $6 + \ln 5$

81. (a) 90   (b) 77   (c) 73   (d) 9 months

(e) $90 - \log_{10}(t + 1)^{15}$

(f)

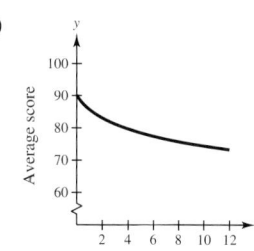

83. False. $\ln 1 = 0$ **85.** False. $\ln(x - 2) \neq \ln x - \ln 2$

87. False. $u = v^2$ **89.** Answers will vary.

91. $f(x) = \dfrac{\log_{10} x}{\log_{10} 2} = \dfrac{\ln x}{\ln 2}$ **93.** $f(x) = \dfrac{\log_{10} x}{\log_{10} \frac{1}{2}} = \dfrac{\ln x}{\ln \frac{1}{2}}$

    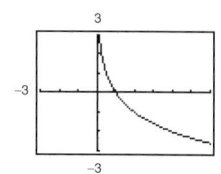

95. $f(x) = \dfrac{\log_{10} x}{\log_{10} 11.8} = \dfrac{\ln x}{\ln 11.8}$

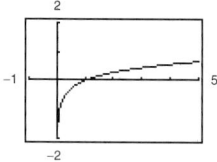

97. $f(x) = h(x)$; Property 2

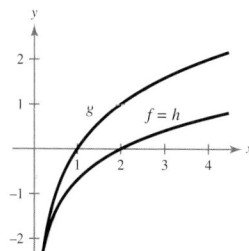

99. $\dfrac{3x^4}{2y^3}$, $x \neq 0$ **101.** $1, x \neq 0, y \neq 0$

103. $-1, \dfrac{1}{3}$ **105.** $\dfrac{-1 \pm \sqrt{97}}{6}$

Section 3.4   *(page 232)*

1. (a) Yes   (b) No

3. (a) No   (b) Yes   (c) Yes, approximate

5. (a) Yes, approximate   (b) No   (c) Yes   **7.** 2

9. 4   **11.** -2 **13.** -5 **15.** 3   **17.** 2

19. $\ln 2 \approx 0.693$ **21.** $e^{-1} \approx 0.368$ **23.** 64

25. $\frac{1}{10}$ **27.** $(3, 8)$ **29.** $(9, 2)$

31. $\dfrac{\ln 5}{\ln 3} \approx 1.465$ **33.** $\ln 5 \approx 1.609$

35. $\ln 28 \approx 3.332$ **37.** $\dfrac{\ln 80}{2 \ln 3} \approx 1.994$ **39.** 2

41. 4   **43.** $3 - \dfrac{\ln 565}{\ln 2} \approx -6.142$

45. $\dfrac{1}{3} \log_{10} \left(\dfrac{3}{2} \right) \approx 0.059$ **47.** $1 + \dfrac{\ln 7}{\ln 5} \approx 2.209$

49. $\dfrac{\ln 12}{3} \approx 0.828$ **51.** $-\ln \dfrac{3}{5} \approx 0.511$ **53.** 0

55. $\dfrac{\ln \frac{8}{3}}{3 \ln 2} + \dfrac{1}{3} \approx 0.805$ **57.** $\ln 5 \approx 1.609$

59. $\ln 4 \approx 1.386$ **61.** $2 \ln 75 \approx 8.635$

63. $\frac{1}{2} \ln 1498 \approx 3.656$ **65.** $\dfrac{\ln 4}{365 \ln \left(1 + \frac{0.065}{365} \right)} \approx 21.330$

67. $\dfrac{\ln 2}{12 \ln \left(1 + \frac{0.10}{12} \right)} \approx 6.960$

69.   **71.**

-0.427 3.847

73.   **75.**

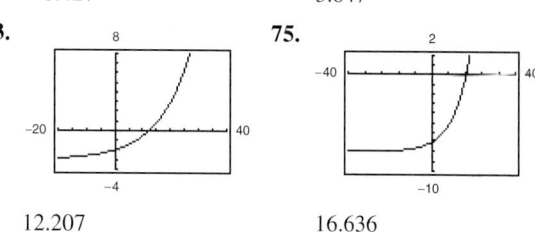

12.207 16.636

77. $e^{-3} \approx 0.050$ **79.** $\dfrac{e^{2.4}}{2} \approx 5.512$ **81.** 1,000,000

83. $2(3^{11/6}) \approx 14.988$ **85.** $\dfrac{e^{10/3}}{5} \approx 5.606$

87. $e^2 - 2 \approx 5.389$ **89.** $e^{-2/3} \approx 0.513$

91. No solution   **93.** $1 + \sqrt{1 + e} \approx 2.928$

95. No solution   **97.** 7   **99.** $\dfrac{-1 + \sqrt{17}}{2} \approx 1.562$

101. 2   **103.** $\dfrac{725 + 125\sqrt{33}}{8} \approx 180.384$

105.

2.807

107.
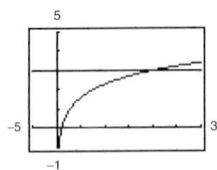
20.086

109. 8.2 years   **111.** 12.9 years

113. (a) 1426 units   (b) 1498 units

115. (a)

(b) $V = 6.7$; the yield will approach 6.7 million cubic feet per acre.

(c) 29.3 years

117. (a) $y = 100$ and $y = 0$; The range falls between 0% and 100%.

(b) Males: 69.71 inches   Females: 64.51 inches

119. (a)

x	0.2	0.4	0.6	0.8	1.0
y	162.6	78.5	52.5	40.5	33.9

(b)
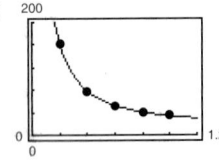

The model appears to fit the data well.

(c) 1.2 meters

(d) No. According to the model, when the number of g's is less than 23, x is between 2.276 meters and 4.404 meters, which isn't realistic in most vehicles.

121. $\log_b uv = \log_b u + \log_b v$

True by Property 1 in Section 3.3.

123. $\log_b(u - v) = \log_b u - \log_b v$

False.

$1.95 \approx \log_{10}(100 - 10) \neq \log_{10} 100 - \log_{10} 10 = 1$

125. Yes. See Exercise 95.

127. Yes. Time to double: $t = \dfrac{\ln 2}{r}$;

Time to quadruple: $t = \dfrac{\ln 4}{r} = 2\left(\dfrac{\ln 2}{r}\right)$

129. $4|x|y^2\sqrt{3y}$ **131.** $5\sqrt[3]{3}$ **133.** $M = kp^3$

135. $d = kab$ **137.** 1.226   **139.** -5.595

Section 3.5   (page 243)

1. c   **2.** e   **3.** b

4. a   **5.** d   **6.** f

Initial Investment	Annual % Rate	Time to Double	Amount After 10 years
7. $1000	12%	5.78 yr	$3320.12
9. $750	8.9438%	7.75 yr	$1834.37
11. $500	11.0%	6.3 yr	$1505.00
13. $6376.28	4.5%	15.4 yr	$10,000.00

15. $112,087.09

17. (a) 6.642 years   (b) 6.330 years

(c) 6.302 years   (d) 6.301 years

19.

r	2%	4%	6%	8%	10%	12%
t	54.93	27.47	18.31	13.73	10.99	9.16

21.

r	2%	4%	6%	8%	10%	12%
t	55.48	28.01	18.85	14.27	11.53	9.69

23.

Continuous compounding

Isotope	Half-life (years)	Initial Quantity	Amount After 1000 Years
25. ^{226}Ra	1620	10 g	6.52 g
27. ^{14}C	5730	2.26 g	2 g
29. ^{239}Pu	24,360	2.16 g	2.1 g

31. $y = e^{0.7675x}$ **33.** $y = 5e^{-0.4024x}$ **35.** 2003

37. $k = 0.0274$; 720,738   **39.** 3.15 hours   **41.** 95.8%

43. (a) $V = -4500t + 22{,}000$ (b) $V = 22{,}000e^{-0.263t}$

(c)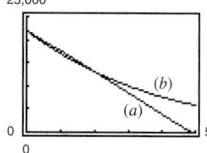

Exponential

(d) 1 year: Straight-line, \$17,500;

Exponential, \$16,912

3 years: Straight-line, \$8500;

Exponential, \$9995

(e) The value decreases \$4500 per year.

45. (a) $S(t) = 100(1 - e^{-0.1625t})$

(b)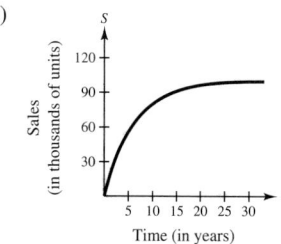

(c) 55,625

47. (a) $S = 10(1 - e^{-0.0575x})$ (b) 3314 units

49. (a) $N = 30(1 - e^{-0.050t})$ (b) 36 days

51. (a) 7.91 (b) 7.68 (c) 5.40

53. (a) 20 decibels (b) 70 decibels

(c) 95 decibels (d) 120 decibels

55. 95% **57.** 4.64 **59.** 1.58×10^{-6} moles per liter

61. 10^7 **63.** 3:00 A.M.

65. (a)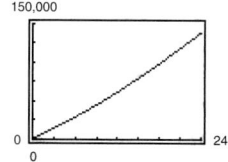

(b) ≈ 21 years; Yes

67. False. The domain can be the set of real numbers for a logistic growth function.

69. False. The graph of $f(x)$ is the graph of $g(x)$ shifted upward five units.

71. (a) Logarithmic (b) Logistic (c) Exponential
(d) Linear (e) None of the above (f) Exponential

73. Rises to the right. **75.** Rises to the left.

Falls to the left. Falls to the right.

77. $4x^2 - 12x + 9$ **79.** $2x^2 + 3 + \dfrac{3}{x - 4}$

81.

83.

85.

87.

89.

91.

93.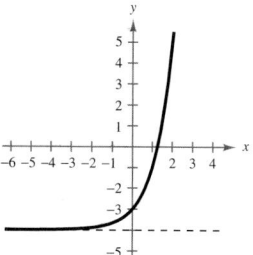

Review Exercises *(page 250)*

1. 76.699 **3.** 0.337 **5.** 1201.845 **7.** c

8. d **9.** a **10.** b

11. Shift the graph of one unit to the right.

13. Reflect f in the x-axis and shift two units to the left.

15.

x	−1	0	1	2	3
f(x)	8	5	4.25	4.063	4.016

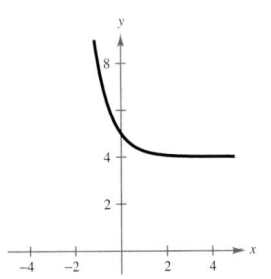

17.

x	−2	−1	0	1	2
f(x)	−0.377	−1	−2.65	−7.023	−18.61

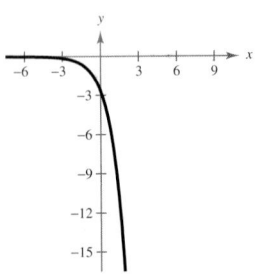

19.

x	−1	0	1	2	3
f(x)	4.008	4.04	4.2	5	9

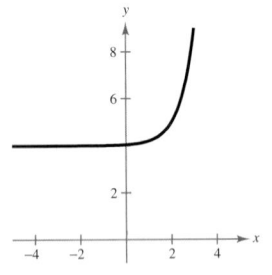

21.

x	−2	−1	0	1	2
f(x)	3.25	3.5	4	5	7

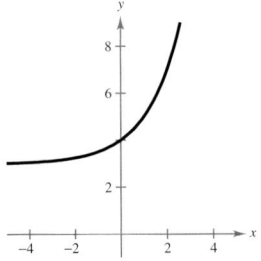

23. 2980.958   **25.** 0.183

27.

x	−2	−1	0	1	2
h(x)	2.72	1.65	1	0.61	0.37

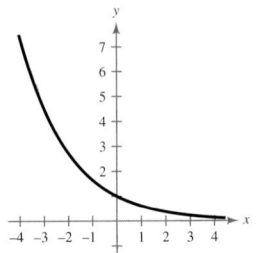

29.

x	−3	−2	−1	0	1
f(x)	0.37	1	2.72	7.39	20.09

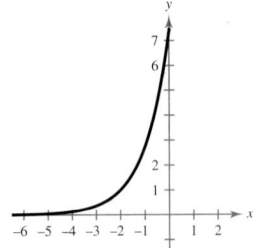

31.

n	1	2	4	12
A	$6569.98	$6635.43	$6669.46	$6692.64

n	365	Continuous
A	$6704.00	$6704.39

33. (a) 0.154   (b) 0.487   (c) 0.811

35. (a) $1,069,047.14   (b) 7.9 years

37. $\log_4 64 = 3$ **39.** 3   **41.** −3

43. Domain: $(0, \infty)$

x-intercept: $(1, 0)$

Vertical asymptote: $x = 0$

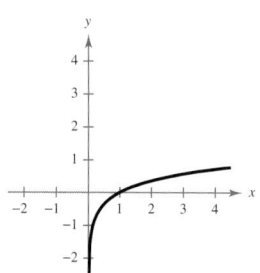

45. Domain: $(0, \infty)$

x-intercept: $(3, 0)$

Vertical asymptote: $x = 0$

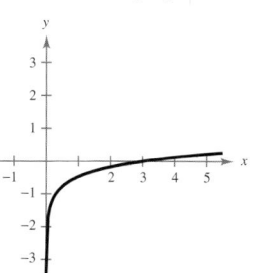

47. Domain: $(-5, \infty)$

x-intercept: $(9995, 0)$

Vertical asymptote: $x = -5$

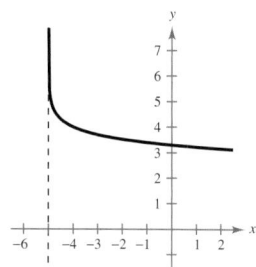

49. 3.118   **51.** -12 **53.** 2.034

55. Domain: $(0, \infty)$

x-intercept: $(e^{-3}, 0)$

Vertical asymptote: $x = 0$

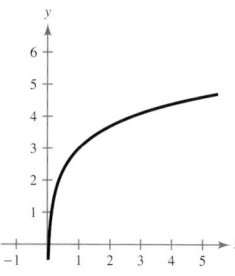

57. Domain: $(-\infty, 0), (0, \infty)$

x-intercept: $(\pm 1, 0)$

Vertical asymptote: $x = 0$

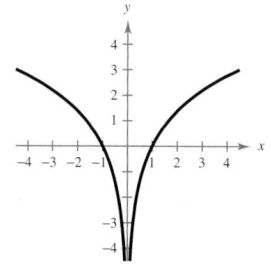

59. 53.4 inches   **61.** 1.585   **63.** -2.322

65. $1 + 2 \log_5 |x|$ **67.** $1 + \log_3 2 - \frac{1}{3} \log_3 x$

69. $2 \ln x + 2 \ln y + \ln z$ **71.** $\ln(x + 3) - \ln x - \ln y$

73. $\log_2 5x$ **75.** $\ln \dfrac{x}{\sqrt[4]{y}}$ **77.** $\log_8 y^7 \sqrt[3]{x + 4}$

79. $\ln \dfrac{\sqrt{|2x - 1|}}{(x + 1)^2}$

81. (a) $0 \le h < 18{,}000$

(b)

Vertical asymptote: $h = 18{,}000$

(c) The plane is climbing at a slower rate, so the time required increases.

(d) 5.46 minutes

83. 3   **85.** -3 **87.** $\ln 3 \approx 1.099$ **89.** 16

91. $e^4 \approx 54.598$

93. $\ln 12 \approx 2.485$ **95.** $-\dfrac{\ln 44}{5} \approx -0.757$

97. $\dfrac{\ln 22}{\ln 2} \approx 4.459$ **99.** $\dfrac{\ln 17}{\ln 5} \approx 1.760$

101. $\ln 2 \approx 0.693$, $\ln 5 \approx 1.609$

103.   **105.**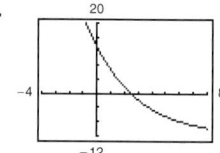

0.39, 7.48   2.45

107. $\frac{1}{3} e^{8.2} \approx 1213.650$ **109.** $\frac{1}{4} e^{7.5} \approx 452.011$

111. $3e^2 \approx 22.167$ **113.** $e^4 - 1 \approx 53.598$

115. No solution   **117.** 0.900

119.   **121.**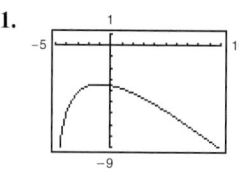

1.64   No solution

123. 15.2 years   **125.** e   **126.** b   **127.** f

128. d   **129.** a   **130.** c   **131.** 2004

133. (a) 13.8629%   (b) \$11,486.98   **135.** $y = 2e^{0.1014x}$

137. (a)   (b) 71

139. $10^{-3.5}$ watt per square centimeter

141. True by the inverse properties

143. $b < d < a < c$

b and d are negative.

a and c are positive.

Chapter Test   *(page 254)*

1. 1123.690   **2.** 687.291   **3.** 0.497   **4.** 22.198

5.

x	-1	$-\frac{1}{2}$	0	$\frac{1}{2}$	1
$f(x)$	10	3.162	1	0.316	0.1

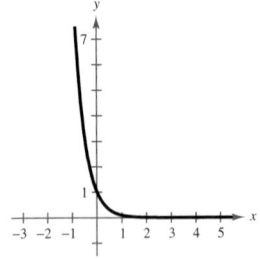

6.

x	-1	0	1	2	3
$f(x)$	-0.005	-0.028	-0.167	-1	-6

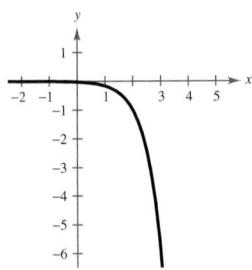

7.

x	-1	$-\frac{1}{2}$	0	$\frac{1}{2}$	1
$f(x)$	0.865	0.632	0	-1.718	-6.389

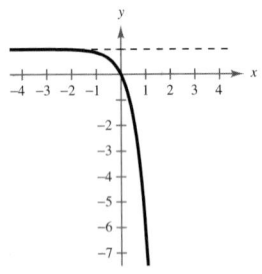

8. (a) -0.89 (b) 9.2

9.

x	$\frac{1}{2}$	1	$\frac{3}{2}$	2	4
$f(x)$	-5.699	-6	-6.176	-6.301	-6.602

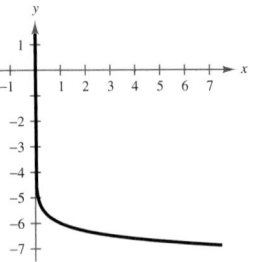

Vertical asymptote: $x = 0$

10.

x	5	7	9	11	13
$f(x)$	0	1.099	1.609	1.946	2.197

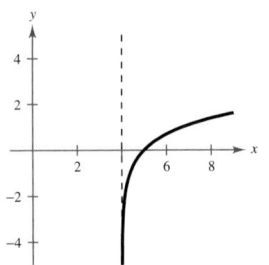

Vertical asymptote: $x = 4$

11.

x	-5	-3	-1	0	1
$f(x)$	1	2.099	2.609	2.792	2.946

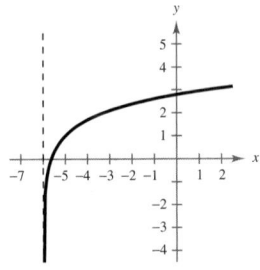

Vertical asymptote: $x = -6$

12. 1.945   **13.** 0.115   **14.** 1.328

15. $\log_2 3 + 4\log_2 |a|$ **16.** $\ln 5 + \frac{1}{2}\ln x - \ln 6$

17. $\log_3 13y$ **18.** $\ln \dfrac{x^4}{y^4}$ **19.** $\dfrac{\ln 197}{4} \approx 1.321$

20. $\frac{800}{501} \approx 1.597$ **21.** $y = 2745e^{0.1570x}$ **22.** 55%

23. (a)

x	$\frac{1}{4}$	1	2	4	5	6
H	58.720	75.332	86.828	103.43	110.59	117.38

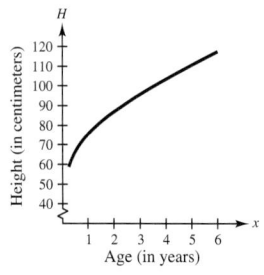

(b) 103 centimeters; 103.43 centimeters

Cumulative Test for Chapters 1–3
(page 255)

1. No axis or origin symmetry

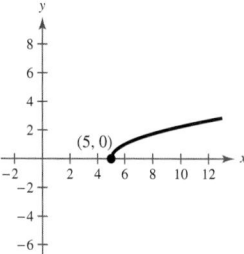

2. No axis or origin symmetry

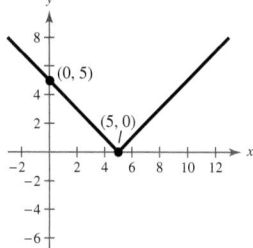

3. No axis or origin symmetry

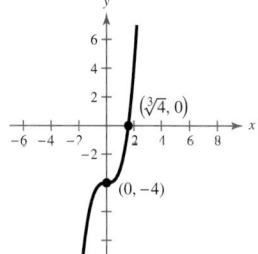

4. $2x - y + 2 = 0$

5. For some values of x there correspond two values of y.

6. (a) $\dfrac{3}{2}$ (b) Division by 0 is undefined.   (c) $\dfrac{s + 2}{s}$

7. (a) Vertical shrink by $\frac{1}{2}$

(b) Vertical shift of two units upward

(c) Horizontal shift of two units to the left

8. (a) $5x - 2$ (b) $-3x - 4$ (c) $4x^2 - 11x - 3$

(d) $\dfrac{x - 3}{4x + 1}$; Domain: all real numbers $x \neq -\dfrac{1}{4}$

9. (a) $\sqrt{x - 1} + x^2 + 1$ (b) $\sqrt{x - 1} - x^2 - 1$

(c) $x^2\sqrt{x - 1} + \sqrt{x - 1}$ (d) $\dfrac{\sqrt{x - 1}}{x^2 + 1}$; Domain: $x \geq 1$

10. (a) $2x + 12$ (b) $\sqrt{2x^2 + 6}$

11. (a) $|x| - 2$ (b) $|x - 2|$

12. $h^{-1}(x) = \frac{1}{5}(x^2 + 3), x \geq 0$ **13.** 2438.65 kilowatts

14. $y = -\frac{3}{4}(x + 8)^2 + 5$

15.   **16.**

17.

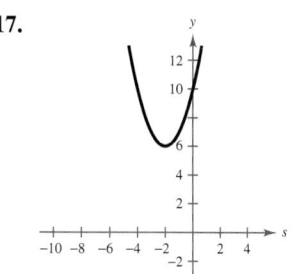

18. Zeros: $-2, \pm 2i$; $f(x) = (x + 2)(x - 2i)(x + 2i)$

19. Zeros: $5, \frac{7}{2}, -\frac{4}{3}$; $f(x) = (x - 5)(2x - 7)(3x + 4)$

20. Zeros: $4, -\frac{1}{2}, 1 \pm 3i$;
$f(x) = (x - 4)(2x + 1)(x - 1 - 3i)(x - 1 + 3i)$

21. $3x - 2 - \dfrac{3x - 2}{2x^2 + 1}$

22. $2x^3 - x^2 + 2x - 10 + \dfrac{25}{x + 2}$

23. $[1, 2] \approx 1.20$ **24.** $x^4 + 3x^3 - 11x^2 + 9x + 70$

25.

Vertical asymptote: $x = 3$

Horizontal asymptote: $y = 2$

26.

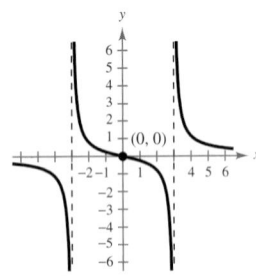

Vertical asymptotes: $x = \pm 3$
Horizontal asymptote: $y = 0$

27.

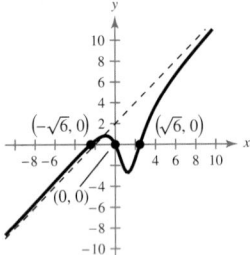

Slant asymptote: $y = x + 2$

28. $\dfrac{1}{5}\left(\dfrac{4}{x - 7} - \dfrac{4}{x + 3}\right)$ **29.** $\dfrac{5}{x - 4} + \dfrac{20}{(x - 4)^2}$

30. Reflect f in the x-axis and y-axis, and shift three units to the right.

31. Reflect f in the x-axis, and shift four units upward.

32. 1.991   **33.** -0.067 **34.** 1.717   **35.** 0.281

36. 0.302   **37.** -1.733 **38.** -4.087

39. $\ln(x + 4) + \ln(x - 4) - 4\ln x$, $x > 4$

40. $\ln\dfrac{x^2}{\sqrt{x + 5}}$, $x > -5$, $x \neq 0$ **41.** $\dfrac{\ln 12}{2} \approx 1.242$

42. $\dfrac{64}{5} = 12.8$

43. (a) and (b)

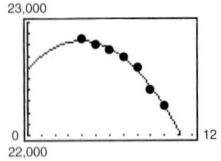

(c) No, because the number of dealerships will eventually become negative.

44. 6.3 hours

Problem Solving   *(page 258)*

1.

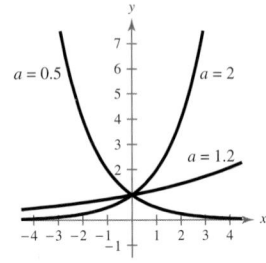

$y = 0.5^x$ and $y = 1.2^x$.

$0 \leq a \leq 1.44$.

3. As $x \to \infty$, the graph of e^x increases at a greater rate than the graph of x^n.

5. Answers will vary.

7. (a)

(b)

(c)

9.

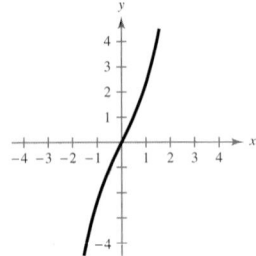

$f^{-1}(x) = \ln\left(\dfrac{x + \sqrt{x^2 + 4}}{2}\right)$

11. c   **13.** $t = \dfrac{\ln c_1 - \ln c_2}{\left(\dfrac{1}{k_2} - \dfrac{1}{k_1}\right)\ln \dfrac{1}{2}}$

15. (a) $y_1 = 252{,}606(1.0310)^t$

(b) $y_2 = 400.88t^2 - 1464.6t + 291{,}782$

(c)

(d) The exponential model is a better fit. No, because the model is rapidly approaching infinity.

17. $1, e^2$

19. $y_4 = (x - 1) - \frac{1}{2}(x - 1)^2 + \frac{1}{3}(x - 1)^3 - \frac{1}{4}(x - 1)^4$

The pattern implies that

$\ln x = (x - 1) - \frac{1}{2}(x - 1)^2 + \frac{1}{3}(x - 1)^3 - \cdots$

21.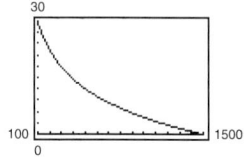

17.7 cubic feet per minute

Chapter 4

Section 4.1 *(page 269)*

1. 2 radians   **3.** -3 radians   **5.** 1 radian

7. (a) Quadrant I   (b) Quadrant III

9. (a) Quadrant IV   (b) Quadrant III

11. (a) Quadrant III   (b) Quadrant II

13. (a)   (b)

15. (a)   (b)

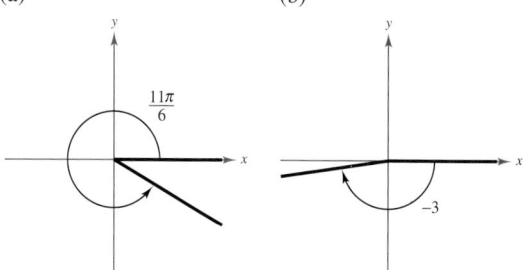

17. (a) $\dfrac{13\pi}{6}, -\dfrac{11\pi}{6}$ (b) $\dfrac{17\pi}{6}, -\dfrac{7\pi}{6}$

19. (a) $\dfrac{8\pi}{3}, -\dfrac{4\pi}{3}$ (b) $\dfrac{25\pi}{12}, -\dfrac{23\pi}{12}$

21. (a) Complement: $\dfrac{\pi}{6}$; Supplement: $\dfrac{2\pi}{3}$

(b) Complement: none; Supplement: $\dfrac{\pi}{4}$

23. (a) Complement: $\dfrac{\pi}{2} - 1 \approx 0.57$;

Supplement: $\pi - 1 \approx 2.14$

(b) Complement: none; Supplement: $\pi - 2 \approx 1.14$

25. (a) $\dfrac{\pi}{6}$ (b) $\dfrac{5\pi}{6}$ **27.** (a) $-\dfrac{\pi}{9}$ (b) $-\dfrac{4\pi}{3}$

29. 2.007   **31.** -3.776 **33.** 9.285   **35.** -0.014

37. (a) $270°$ (b) $210°$ **39.** (a) $420°$ (b) $-66°$

41. $25.714°$ **43.** $337.500°$ **45.** $-756.000°$

47. $-114.592°$ **49.** $210°$ **51.** $-60°$ **53.** $165°$

55. (a) Quadrant II   (b) Quadrant IV

57. (a) Quadrant III   (b) Quadrant I

59. (a)   (b)

61. (a)   (b)

111.

113.

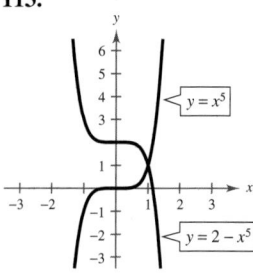

63. (a) $405°, -315°$ (b) $324°, -396°$

65. (a) $600°, -120°$ (b) $180°, -540°$

67. (a) Complement: $72°$; Supplement: $162°$

　　(b) Complement: none; Supplement: $65°$

69. (a) Complement: $11°$; Supplement: $101°$

　　(b) Complement: none; Supplement: $30°$

71. (a) $54.75°$ (b) $-128.5°$

73. (a) $85.308°$ (b) $330.007°$

75. (a) $240°\,36'$ (b) $-145°\,48'$

77. (a) $2°\,30'$ (b) $-3°\,34'\,48''$

79. $\frac{6}{5}$ radians   **81.** $\frac{32}{7}$ radians

83. $\frac{2}{9}$ radian   **85.** $\frac{50}{29}$ radians

87. 15π inches ≈ 47.12 inches   **89.** 3 meters

91. 591.7 miles   **93.** 1141.0 miles

95. 0.071 radian $\approx 4.04°$ **97.** $\frac{5}{12}$ radian

99. (a) 728.3 revolutions per minute

　　(b) 4576 radians per minute

101. (a) $\dfrac{14\pi}{3}$ feet per second; ≈ 10 miles per hour

　　(b) $d = \dfrac{7\pi}{7920}n$ (c) $d = \dfrac{7\pi}{7920}t$

　　(d) The functions are both linear.

103. False. A measurement of 4π radians corresponds to two complete revolutions from the initial to the terminal side of an angle.

105. False. The terminal side of the angle lies on the x-axis.

107. Increases. The linear velocity is proportional to the radius.

109. The arc length increases. If θ is constant, the length of the arc is proportional to the radius $(s = r\theta)$.

115.

117.

119.

121.

123.

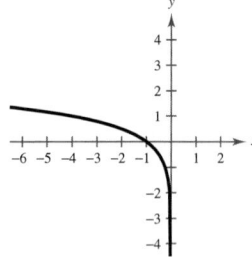

125. $\dfrac{\sqrt{2}}{2}$ **127.** $\sqrt{2}$ **129.** $2\sqrt{10}$ **131.** $12\sqrt{2}$

Section 4.2   *(page 278)*

1. $\sin\theta = \frac{15}{17}$

$\cos\theta = -\frac{8}{17}$

$\tan\theta = -\frac{15}{8}$

$\csc\theta = \frac{17}{15}$

$\sec\theta = -\frac{17}{8}$

$\cot\theta = -\frac{8}{15}$

3. $\sin\theta = -\frac{5}{13}$

$\cos\theta = \frac{12}{13}$

$\tan\theta = -\frac{5}{12}$

$\csc\theta = -\frac{13}{5}$

$\sec\theta = \frac{13}{12}$

$\cot\theta = -\frac{12}{5}$

5. $\left(\dfrac{\sqrt{2}}{2}, \dfrac{\sqrt{2}}{2}\right)$ **7.** $\left(-\dfrac{\sqrt{3}}{2}, -\dfrac{1}{2}\right)$

9. $\left(-\dfrac{1}{2}, -\dfrac{\sqrt{3}}{2}\right)$ **11.** $(0, -1)$

13. $\sin\dfrac{\pi}{4} = \dfrac{\sqrt{2}}{2}$

$\cos\dfrac{\pi}{4} = \dfrac{\sqrt{2}}{2}$

$\tan\dfrac{\pi}{4} = 1$

15. $\sin\left(-\dfrac{\pi}{6}\right) = -\dfrac{1}{2}$

$\cos\left(-\dfrac{\pi}{6}\right) = \dfrac{\sqrt{3}}{2}$

$\tan\left(-\dfrac{\pi}{6}\right) = -\dfrac{\sqrt{3}}{3}$

17. $\sin\left(-\dfrac{7\pi}{4}\right) = \dfrac{\sqrt{2}}{2}$

$\cos\left(-\dfrac{7\pi}{4}\right) = \dfrac{\sqrt{2}}{2}$

$\tan\left(-\dfrac{7\pi}{4}\right) = 1$

19. $\sin\dfrac{11\pi}{6} = -\dfrac{1}{2}$

$\cos\dfrac{11\pi}{6} = \dfrac{\sqrt{3}}{2}$

$\tan\dfrac{11\pi}{6} = -\dfrac{\sqrt{3}}{3}$

21. $\sin\left(-\dfrac{3\pi}{2}\right) = 1$

$\cos\left(-\dfrac{3\pi}{2}\right) = 0$

$\tan\left(-\dfrac{3\pi}{2}\right)$ is undefined.

23. $\sin\dfrac{3\pi}{4} = \dfrac{\sqrt{2}}{2}$ $\csc\dfrac{3\pi}{4} = \sqrt{2}$

$\cos\dfrac{3\pi}{4} = -\dfrac{\sqrt{2}}{2}$ $\sec\dfrac{3\pi}{4} = -\sqrt{2}$

$\tan\dfrac{3\pi}{4} = -1$ $\cot\dfrac{3\pi}{4} = -1$

25. $\sin\left(-\dfrac{\pi}{2}\right) = -1$ $\csc\left(-\dfrac{\pi}{2}\right) = -1$

$\cos\left(-\dfrac{\pi}{2}\right) = 0$ $\sec\left(-\dfrac{\pi}{2}\right)$ is undefined.

$\tan\left(-\dfrac{\pi}{2}\right)$ is undefined. $\cot\left(-\dfrac{\pi}{2}\right) = 0$

27. $\sin\left(\dfrac{4\pi}{3}\right) = -\dfrac{\sqrt{3}}{2}$ $\csc\left(\dfrac{4\pi}{3}\right) = -\dfrac{2\sqrt{3}}{3}$

$\cos\left(\dfrac{4\pi}{3}\right) = -\dfrac{1}{2}$ $\sec\left(\dfrac{4\pi}{3}\right) = -2$

$\tan\left(\dfrac{4\pi}{3}\right) = \sqrt{3}$ $\cot\left(\dfrac{4\pi}{3}\right) = \dfrac{\sqrt{3}}{3}$

29. $\sin 5\pi = \sin \pi = 0$ **31.** $\cos\dfrac{8\pi}{3} = \cos\dfrac{2\pi}{3} = -\dfrac{1}{2}$

33. $\cos\left(-\dfrac{15\pi}{2}\right) = \cos\dfrac{\pi}{2} = 0$

35. $\sin\left(-\dfrac{9\pi}{4}\right) = \sin\dfrac{7\pi}{4} = -\dfrac{\sqrt{2}}{2}$

37. (a) $-\dfrac{1}{3}$ (b) -3 **39.** (a) $-\dfrac{1}{5}$ (b) -5

41. (a) $\dfrac{4}{5}$ (b) $-\dfrac{4}{5}$ **43.** 0.7071 **45.** 1.0378

47. -0.1288 **49.** 1.3940 **51.** -1.4486

53. (a) -1 (b) -0.4

55. (a) 0.25 or 2.89   (b) 1.82 or 4.46

57. (a)

t	0	$\frac{1}{4}$	$\frac{1}{2}$	$\frac{3}{4}$	1
y	0.25	0.0138	−0.1501	−0.0249	0.0883

(b) $t \approx 5.5$ (c) The displacement decreases.

59. False. $\sin(-t) = -\sin t$ means that the function is odd, not that the sine of a negative angle is a negative number.

61. (a) y-axis symmetry   (b) $\sin t_1 = \sin(\pi - t_1)$

(c) $\cos(\pi - t_1) = -\cos t_1$

63. $\sin(0.25) + \sin(0.75) = 0.9290 \neq \sin 1 = 0.8415$

65. $f^{-1}(x) = \dfrac{2}{3}(x + 1)$ **67.** $f^{-1}(x) = \sqrt{x^2 + 4}, \quad x \geq 0$

Section 4.3   *(page 287)*

1. $\sin\theta = \dfrac{3}{5}$ $\csc\theta = \dfrac{5}{3}$

$\cos\theta = \dfrac{4}{5}$ $\sec\theta = \dfrac{5}{4}$

$\tan\theta = \dfrac{3}{4}$ $\cot\theta = \dfrac{4}{3}$

3. $\sin\theta = \dfrac{9}{41}$ $\csc\theta = \dfrac{41}{9}$

$\cos\theta = \dfrac{40}{41}$ $\sec\theta = \dfrac{41}{40}$

$\tan\theta = \dfrac{9}{40}$ $\cot\theta = \dfrac{40}{9}$

5. $\sin\theta = \dfrac{1}{3}$ $\csc\theta = 3$

$\cos\theta = \dfrac{2\sqrt{2}}{3}$ $\sec\theta = \dfrac{3\sqrt{2}}{4}$

$\tan\theta = \dfrac{\sqrt{2}}{4}$ $\cot\theta = 2\sqrt{2}$

The triangles are similar, and corresponding sides are proportional.

7. $\sin\theta = \dfrac{3}{5}$ $\csc\theta = \dfrac{5}{3}$

$\cos\theta = \dfrac{4}{5}$ $\sec\theta = \dfrac{5}{4}$

$\tan\theta = \dfrac{3}{4}$ $\cot\theta = \dfrac{4}{3}$

The triangles are similar, and corresponding sides are proportional.

9.

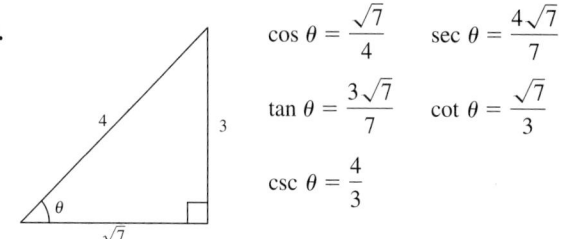

$\cos\theta = \dfrac{\sqrt{7}}{4}$ $\sec\theta = \dfrac{4\sqrt{7}}{7}$

$\tan\theta = \dfrac{3\sqrt{7}}{7}$ $\cot\theta = \dfrac{\sqrt{7}}{3}$

$\csc\theta = \dfrac{4}{3}$

11.

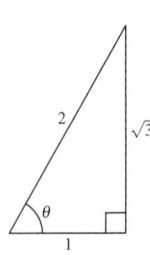

$\sin \theta = \dfrac{\sqrt{3}}{2}$ $\qquad$ $\csc \theta = \dfrac{2\sqrt{3}}{3}$

$\cos \theta = \dfrac{1}{2}$ $\qquad$ $\cot \theta = \dfrac{\sqrt{3}}{3}$

$\tan \theta = \sqrt{3}$

13.

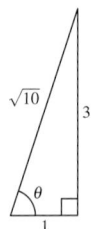

$\sin \theta = \dfrac{3\sqrt{10}}{10}$ $\qquad$ $\sec \theta = \sqrt{10}$

$\cos \theta = \dfrac{\sqrt{10}}{10}$ $\qquad$ $\cot \theta = \dfrac{1}{3}$

$\csc \theta = \dfrac{\sqrt{10}}{3}$

15.

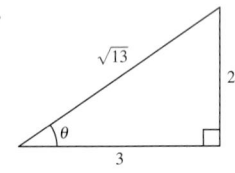

$\sin \theta = \dfrac{2\sqrt{13}}{13}$

$\cos \theta = \dfrac{3\sqrt{13}}{13}$

$\tan \theta = \dfrac{2}{3}$

$\csc \theta = \dfrac{\sqrt{13}}{2}$

$\sec \theta = \dfrac{\sqrt{13}}{3}$

17. (a) $\sqrt{3}$ $\quad$ (b) $\dfrac{1}{2}$ $\quad$ (c) $\dfrac{\sqrt{3}}{2}$ $\quad$ (d) $\dfrac{\sqrt{3}}{3}$

19. (a) $\dfrac{2\sqrt{13}}{13}$ $\quad$ (b) $\dfrac{3\sqrt{13}}{13}$ $\quad$ (c) $\dfrac{2}{3}$ $\quad$ (d) $\dfrac{\sqrt{13}}{2}$

21. (a) 3 $\quad$ (b) $\dfrac{2\sqrt{2}}{3}$ $\quad$ (c) $\dfrac{\sqrt{2}}{4}$ $\quad$ (d) $\dfrac{1}{3}$

23. (a) $\dfrac{1}{2}$ $\quad$ (b) 2 $\quad$ (c) $\sqrt{3}$

25. (a) $\dfrac{\sqrt{2}}{2}$ $\quad$ (b) $\dfrac{\sqrt{3}}{2}$ $\quad$ (c) $\dfrac{\sqrt{3}}{3}$

27. (a) 0.1736 $\quad$ (b) 0.1736

29. (a) 0.2815 $\quad$ (b) 3.5523

31. (a) 1.3499 $\quad$ (b) 1.3432

33. (a) 5.0273 $\quad$ (b) 0.1989

35. (a) 1.8527 $\quad$ (b) 0.9817

37. (a) $30° = \dfrac{\pi}{6}$ $\quad$ (b) $30° = \dfrac{\pi}{6}$

39. (a) $60° = \dfrac{\pi}{3}$ $\quad$ (b) $45° = \dfrac{\pi}{4}$

41. (a) $60° = \dfrac{\pi}{3}$ $\quad$ (b) $45° = \dfrac{\pi}{4}$

43. (a) $0.83° \approx 0.015$ $\quad$ (b) $27° \approx 0.474$

45. (a) $0.72° \approx 0.012$ $\quad$ (b) $67° \approx 1.169$

47–55. Answers will vary. $\qquad$ **57.** $30\sqrt{3}$ $\qquad$ **59.** $\dfrac{32\sqrt{3}}{3}$

61. (a)

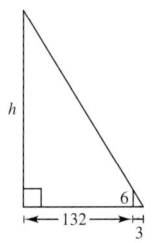

Not drawn to scale

(b) $\cos \theta = \dfrac{6}{3} = \dfrac{h}{135}$

(c) 270 feet

63. (a)

(b) $\sin 85° = \dfrac{h}{20}$ $\quad$ (c) 19.9 meters

(d) The side of the triangle labeled h will become shorter.

(e)

Angle, θ	80°	70°	60°	50°
Height	19.7	18.8	17.3	15.3

Angle, θ	40°	30°	20°	10°
Height	12.9	10.0	6.8	3.5

(f) As $\theta \to 0°$, $h \to 0$.

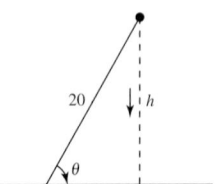

65. 137.6 feet $\qquad$ **67.** $(x_1, y_1) = \left(28\sqrt{3},\ 28\right)$

$(x_2, y_2) = \left(28,\ 28\sqrt{3}\right)$

69. $\sin 20° \approx 0.34$

$\cos 20° \approx 0.94$

$\tan 20° \approx 0.36$

$\csc 20° \approx 2.92$

$\sec 20° \approx 1.06$

$\cot 20° \approx 2.75$

71. True, $\csc x = \dfrac{1}{\sin x}$.   **73.** False, $\dfrac{\sqrt{2}}{2} + \dfrac{\sqrt{2}}{2} \neq 1$.

75. False, $1.7321 \neq 0.0349$.

77. Corresponding sides of similar triangles are proportional.

79. (a)

θ	0.1	0.2	0.3	0.4	0.5
$\sin \theta$	0.0998	0.1987	0.2955	0.3894	0.4794

(b) As θ approaches 0, $\sin \theta$ approaches θ.

81. $\dfrac{x}{x-2}$, $x \neq \pm 6$ **83.** $\dfrac{2(x^2 - 5x - 10)}{(x-2)(x+2)^2}$ **85.** $x = \dfrac{2}{3}$

Section 4.4   (page 297)

1. (a) $\sin \theta = \dfrac{3}{5}$ (b) $\sin \theta = -\dfrac{15}{17}$

$\cos \theta = \dfrac{4}{5}$ $\cos \theta = \dfrac{8}{17}$

$\tan \theta = \dfrac{3}{4}$ $\tan \theta = -\dfrac{15}{8}$

$\csc \theta = \dfrac{5}{3}$ $\csc \theta = -\dfrac{17}{15}$

$\sec \theta = \dfrac{5}{4}$ $\sec \theta = \dfrac{17}{8}$

$\cot \theta = \dfrac{4}{3}$ $\cot \theta = -\dfrac{8}{15}$

3. (a) $\sin \theta = -\dfrac{1}{2}$ (b) $\sin \theta = \dfrac{\sqrt{17}}{17}$

$\cos \theta = -\dfrac{\sqrt{3}}{2}$ $\cos \theta = -\dfrac{4\sqrt{17}}{17}$

$\tan \theta = \dfrac{\sqrt{3}}{3}$ $\tan \theta = -\dfrac{1}{4}$

$\csc \theta = -2$ $\csc \theta = \sqrt{17}$

$\sec \theta = -\dfrac{2\sqrt{3}}{3}$ $\sec \theta = -\dfrac{\sqrt{17}}{4}$

$\cot \theta = \sqrt{3}$ $\cot \theta = -4$

5. $\sin \theta = \dfrac{24}{25}$ $\csc \theta = \dfrac{25}{24}$

$\cos \theta = \dfrac{7}{25}$ $\sec \theta = \dfrac{25}{7}$

$\tan \theta = \dfrac{24}{7}$ $\cot \theta = \dfrac{7}{24}$

7. $\sin \theta = \dfrac{5\sqrt{29}}{29}$ $\csc \theta = \dfrac{\sqrt{29}}{5}$

$\cos \theta = -\dfrac{2\sqrt{29}}{29}$ $\sec \theta = -\dfrac{\sqrt{29}}{2}$

$\tan \theta = -\dfrac{5}{2}$ $\cot \theta = -\dfrac{2}{5}$

9. $\sin \theta = \dfrac{68\sqrt{5849}}{5849} \approx 0.9$ $\csc \theta = \dfrac{\sqrt{5849}}{68} \approx 1.1$

$\cos \theta = -\dfrac{35\sqrt{5849}}{5849} \approx -0.5$ $\sec \theta = -\dfrac{\sqrt{5849}}{35} \approx -2.2$

$\tan \theta = -\dfrac{68}{35} \approx -1.9$ $\cot \theta = -\dfrac{35}{68} \approx -0.5$

11. Quadrant III   **13.** Quadrant II

15. $\sin \theta = \dfrac{3}{5}$ $\csc \theta = \dfrac{5}{3}$

$\cos \theta = -\dfrac{4}{5}$ $\sec \theta = -\dfrac{5}{4}$

$\tan \theta = -\dfrac{3}{4}$ $\cot \theta = -\dfrac{4}{3}$

17. $\sin \theta = -\dfrac{15}{17}$ $\csc \theta = -\dfrac{17}{15}$

$\cos \theta = \dfrac{8}{17}$ $\sec \theta = \dfrac{17}{8}$

$\tan \theta = -\dfrac{15}{8}$ $\cot \theta = -\dfrac{8}{15}$

19. $\sin \theta = -\dfrac{\sqrt{10}}{10}$ $\csc \theta = -\sqrt{10}$

$\cos \theta = \dfrac{3\sqrt{10}}{10}$ $\sec \theta = \dfrac{\sqrt{10}}{3}$

$\tan \theta = -\dfrac{1}{3}$ $\cot \theta = -3$

21. $\sin \theta = \dfrac{\sqrt{3}}{2}$ $\csc \theta = \dfrac{2\sqrt{3}}{3}$

$\cos \theta = -\dfrac{1}{2}$ $\sec \theta = -2$

$\tan \theta = -\sqrt{3}$ $\cot \theta = -\dfrac{\sqrt{3}}{3}$

23. $\sin \theta = 0$ $\csc \theta$ is undefined.

$\cos \theta = -1$ $\sec \theta = -1$

$\tan \theta = 0$ $\cot \theta$ is undefined.

25. $\sin \theta = \dfrac{\sqrt{2}}{2}$ $\csc \theta = \sqrt{2}$

$\cos \theta = -\dfrac{\sqrt{2}}{2}$ $\sec \theta = -\sqrt{2}$

$\tan \theta = -1$ $\cot \theta = -1$

27. $\sin \theta = -\dfrac{2\sqrt{5}}{5}$ $\csc \theta = -\dfrac{\sqrt{5}}{2}$

$\cos \theta = -\dfrac{\sqrt{5}}{5}$ $\sec \theta = -\sqrt{5}$

$\tan \theta = 2$ $\cot \theta = \dfrac{1}{2}$

29. -1 **31.** Undefined

33. Undefined   **35.** Undefined

37. $\theta' = 23°$

39. $\theta' = 65°$

41. $\theta' = \dfrac{\pi}{3}$

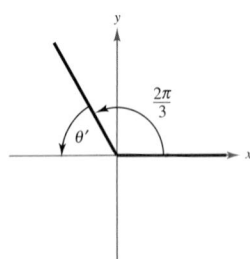

43. $\theta' = 3.5 - \pi$

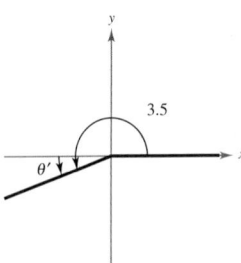

45. $\sin 225° = -\dfrac{\sqrt{2}}{2}$

$\cos 225° = -\dfrac{\sqrt{2}}{2}$

$\tan 225° = 1$

47. $\sin 750° = \dfrac{1}{2}$

$\cos 750° = \dfrac{\sqrt{3}}{2}$

$\tan 750° = \dfrac{\sqrt{3}}{3}$

49. $\sin(-150°) = -\dfrac{1}{2}$

$\cos(-150°) = -\dfrac{\sqrt{3}}{2}$

$\tan(-150°) = \dfrac{\sqrt{3}}{3}$

51. $\sin \dfrac{4\pi}{3} = -\dfrac{\sqrt{3}}{2}$

$\cos \dfrac{4\pi}{3} = -\dfrac{1}{2}$

$\tan \dfrac{4\pi}{3} = \sqrt{3}$

53. $\sin\left(-\dfrac{\pi}{6}\right) = -\dfrac{1}{2}$

$\cos\left(-\dfrac{\pi}{6}\right) = \dfrac{\sqrt{3}}{2}$

$\tan\left(-\dfrac{\pi}{6}\right) = -\dfrac{\sqrt{3}}{3}$

55. $\sin \dfrac{11\pi}{4} = \dfrac{\sqrt{2}}{2}$

$\cos \dfrac{11\pi}{4} = -\dfrac{\sqrt{2}}{2}$

$\tan \dfrac{11\pi}{4} = -1$

57. $\sin\left(-\dfrac{3\pi}{2}\right) = 1$

$\cos\left(-\dfrac{3\pi}{2}\right) = 0$

$\tan\left(-\dfrac{3\pi}{2}\right)$ is undefined.

59. 0.1736 **61.** -0.3420

63. 4.6373 **65.** 0.3640 **67.** -0.6052

69. (a) $30° = \dfrac{\pi}{6},\ 150° = \dfrac{5\pi}{6}$ (b) $210° = \dfrac{7\pi}{6},\ 330° = \dfrac{11\pi}{6}$

71. (a) $60° = \dfrac{\pi}{3},\ 120° = \dfrac{2\pi}{3}$ (b) $135° = \dfrac{3\pi}{4},\ 315° = \dfrac{7\pi}{4}$

73. (a) $45° = \dfrac{\pi}{4},\ 225° = \dfrac{5\pi}{4}$ (b) $150° = \dfrac{5\pi}{6},\ 330° = \dfrac{11\pi}{6}$

75. $54.99°,\ 125.01°$ **77.** $115.89°,\ 244.11°$

79. $0.175,\ 6.109$ **81.** $0.873,\ 4.014$ **83.** $1.955,\ 4.328$

85. $\dfrac{4}{5}$ **87.** $-\dfrac{\sqrt{13}}{2}$ **89.** $\dfrac{8}{5}$

91. (a) $N = 22.66 \sin(0.51t - 2.12) + 54.58$

$F = 37.18 \sin(0.51t - 1.91) + 26.17$

(b) February: $N = 34°,\ F = -3°$

March: $N = 42°,\ F = 12°$

May: $N = 64°,\ F = 48°$

June: $N = 73°,\ F = 60°$

August: $N = 76°,\ F = 57°$

September: $N = 69°,\ F = 43°$

November: $N = 47°,\ F = 6°$

(c) Answers will vary.

93. (a) 2 centimeters   **95.** 0.79 ampere

(b) 0.14 centimeter

(c) -1.98 centimeters

97. False. In each of the four quadrants, the signs of the secant function and cosine function will be the same, because these functions are reciprocals of each other.

99. As θ increases from $0°$ to $90°$, x decreases from 12 cm to 0 cm and y increases from 0 cm to 12 cm. Therefore, $\sin \theta = y/12$ increases from 0 to 1 and $\cos \theta = x/12$ decreases from 1 to 0. Thus, $\tan \theta = y/x$ and increases without bound. When $\theta = 90°$, the tangent is undefined.

101.

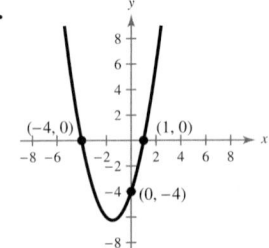

x-intercepts:

$(1, 0),\ (-4, 0)$

y-intercept: $(0, -4)$

Domain: all real numbers

103.

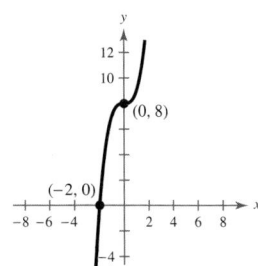

x-intercept: $(-2, 0)$

y-intercept: $(0, 8)$

Domain: all real numbers

105.

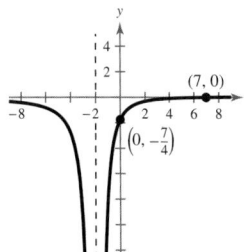

x-intercept: $(7, 0)$

y-intercept: $\left(0, -\frac{7}{4}\right)$

Vertical asymptote:
$x = -2$

Horizontal asymptote:
$y = 0$

Domain: all real numbers,
$\qquad x \neq -2$

107.

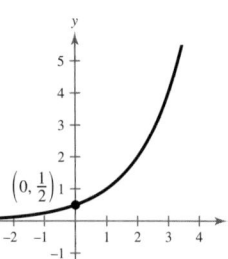

y-intercept: $\left(0, \frac{1}{2}\right)$

Horizontal asymptote:
$y = 0$

Domain: all real numbers

109.

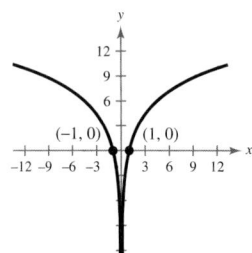

x-intercepts: $(\pm 1, 0)$

Vertical asymptote: $x = 0$

Domain: all real
$\qquad$ numbers, $x \neq 0$

Section 4.5 *(page 307)*

1. Period: π
$\quad$ Amplitude: 3

3. Period: 4π
$\quad$ Amplitude: $\frac{5}{2}$

5. Period: 6
$\quad$ Amplitude: $\frac{1}{2}$

7. Period: 2π
$\quad$ Amplitude: 2

9. Period: $\dfrac{\pi}{5}$
$\quad$ Amplitude: 3

11. Period: 3π
$\quad$ Amplitude: $\frac{1}{2}$

13. Period: 1
$\quad$ Amplitude: $\frac{1}{4}$

15. *g* is a shift of *f* π units to the right.

17. *g* is a reflection of *f* in the *x*-axis.

19. The period of *f* is twice the period of *g*.

21. *g* is a shift of *f* three units upward.

23. The graph of *g* has twice the amplitude of the graph of *f*.

25. The graph of *g* is a horizontal shift of the graph of *f* π units to the right.

27.

29.

31.

33.

35.

37.

39.

41.

43.

45.

47.

49.

51.

53.

55.

57.
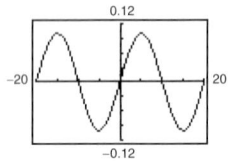

59. $a = 2, d = 1$ **61.** $a = -4, d = 4$

63. $a = -3, b = 2, c = 0$ **65.** $a = 2, b = 1, c = -\dfrac{\pi}{4}$

67.
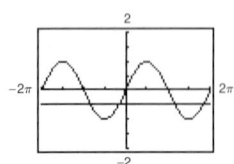

$x = -\dfrac{\pi}{6}, -\dfrac{5\pi}{6}, \dfrac{7\pi}{6}, \dfrac{11\pi}{6}$

69. (a) 6 seconds (b) 10 cycles per minute

(c)
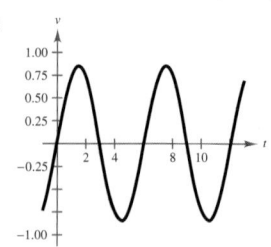

71. (a) $\dfrac{1}{440}$ second (b) 440 cycles per second

73. (a) $C(t) = 56.35 + 27.35 \cos\left(\dfrac{\pi t}{6} - 3.67\right)$

(b)
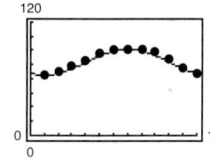

The model is a good fit.

(c)
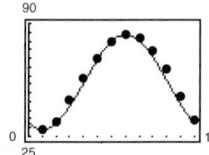

The model is a good fit.

(d) Tallahassee: 77.60°; Chicago: 56.35°

The constant term gives the annual average temperature.

(e) 12. Yes. One full period is 1 year.

(f) Chicago; amplitude: the greater the amplitude, the greater the variability in temperature.

75. (a) 365. Yes. One year is 365 days.

(b) 30.3 gallons; the constant term

(c)
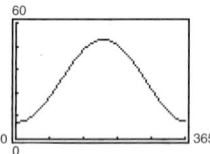

$124 < t < 252$

77. False. The function $y = \frac{1}{2}\cos 2x$ has an amplitude that is one-half that of $y = \cos x$. For $y = a \cos bx$, the amplitude is $|a|$.

79.
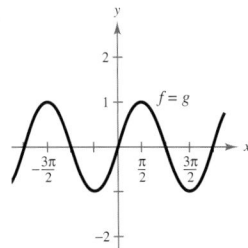

Conjecture:

$$\sin x = \cos\left(x - \frac{\pi}{2}\right)$$

81.

Amplitude changes

83.

Period changes

85. (a)

The graphs appear to coincide from $-\dfrac{\pi}{2}$ to $\dfrac{\pi}{2}$.

(b)

The graphs appear to coincide from $-\dfrac{\pi}{2}$ to $\dfrac{\pi}{2}$.

(c) $-\dfrac{x^7}{7!},\ -\dfrac{x^6}{6!}$

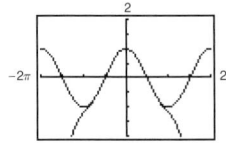

The interval of accuracy increased.

87. $\frac{1}{2}\log_{10}(x-2)$ **89.** $3\ln t - \ln(t-1)$

91. $\log_{10}\sqrt{xy}$ **93.** $\ln\dfrac{3x}{y^4}$

Section 4.6   *(page 318)*

1. e, π **2.** c, 2π **3.** a, 1   **4.** d, 2π

5. f, 4   **6.** b, 4

7.

9.

11.

13.

15.

17.

19.

21.

23.

25.

27.

29.

31.

33.

35.

37.

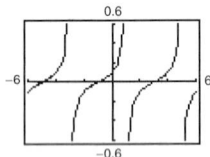

39. $-\dfrac{7\pi}{4}, -\dfrac{3\pi}{4}, \dfrac{\pi}{4}, \dfrac{5\pi}{4}$

41. $-\dfrac{4\pi}{3}, -\dfrac{\pi}{3}, \dfrac{2\pi}{3}, \dfrac{5\pi}{3}$

43. $-\dfrac{4\pi}{3}, -\dfrac{2\pi}{3}, \dfrac{2\pi}{3}, \dfrac{4\pi}{3}$

45. $-\dfrac{7\pi}{4}, -\dfrac{5\pi}{4}, \dfrac{\pi}{4}, \dfrac{3\pi}{4}$

47. Even

49. (a) 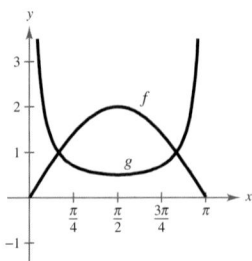 (b) $\dfrac{\pi}{6} < x < \dfrac{5\pi}{6}$

(c) f approaches 0 and g approaches $+\infty$ because the cosecant is the reciprocal of the sine.

51.

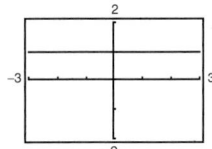

The expressions are equivalent except that when $\sin x = 0$, y_1 is undefined.

53.

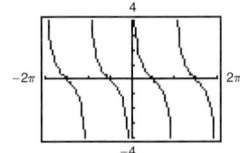

The expressions are equivalent.

55. d, $f \to 0$ as $x \to 0$. **56.** a, $f \to 0$ as $x \to 0$.

57. b, $g \to 0$ as $x \to 0$. **58.** c, $g \to 0$ as $x \to 0$.

59.

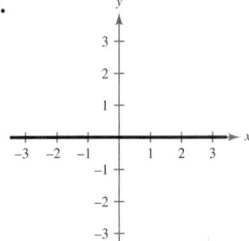

The functions are equal.

61.

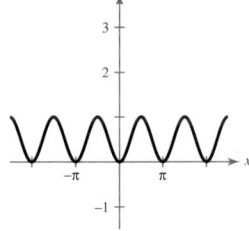

The functions are equal.

63.

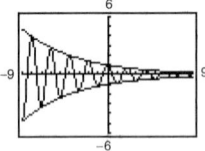

As $x \to \infty$, $f(x) \to 0$.

65.

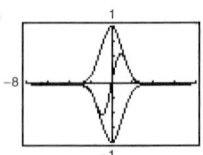

As $x \to \infty$, $g(x) \to 0$.

67.

As $x \to 0$, $y \to \infty$.

69.

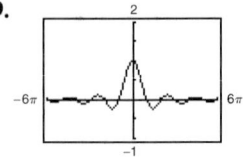

As $x \to 0$, $g(x) \to 1$.

71.

As $x \to 0$, $f(x)$ oscillates between 1 and -1.

73. $d = 7 \cot x$

75. (a)

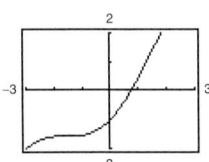

(b) As the predator population increases, the number of prey decreases. When the number of prey is small, the number of predators decreases.

(c) C: 24 months; R: 24 months

77. (a) 12

(b) Summer; Winter

(c) 1 month

79. True. For a given value of x, the y-coordinate of $\csc x$ is the reciprocal of the y-coordinate of $\sin x$.

81. As x approaches $\pi/2$ from the left, f approaches ∞. As x approaches $\pi/2$ from the right, f approaches $-\infty$.

83. (a)

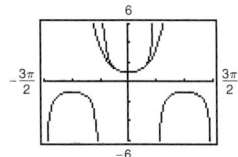

0.7391

(b) 1, 0.5403, 0.8576, 0.6543, 0.7935, 0.7014, 0.7640, 0.7221, 0.7504, 0.7314, . . . ; 0.7391

85.

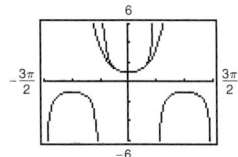

The graphs appear to coincide on the interval $-1.1 \le x \le 1.1$.

87. $\dfrac{\ln 54}{2} \approx 1.994$ **89.** $-\ln 2 \approx -0.693$

91. $\dfrac{2 + e^{73}}{3} \approx 1.684 \times 10^{31}$ **93.** $\pm\sqrt{e^{3.2} - 1} \approx \pm 4.851$

95. 2

Section 4.7   *(page 328)*

1. $\dfrac{\pi}{6}$ **3.** $\dfrac{\pi}{3}$ **5.** $\dfrac{\pi}{6}$ **7.** $\dfrac{5\pi}{6}$ **9.** $-\dfrac{\pi}{3}$ **11.** $\dfrac{2\pi}{3}$

13. $\dfrac{\pi}{3}$ **15.** 0   **17.** 1.29   **19.** -0.85 **21.** -1.25

23. 0.32   **25.** 1.99   **27.** 0.74   **29.** 0.85

31. 1.29   **33.** $-\dfrac{\pi}{3}$, $-\dfrac{\sqrt{3}}{3}$, 1

35.

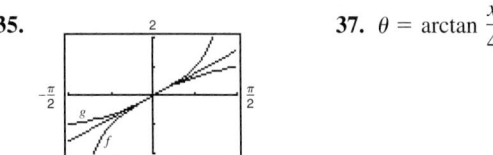

37. $\theta = \arctan \dfrac{x}{4}$

39. $\theta = \arcsin \dfrac{x + 2}{5}$ **41.** $\theta = \arccos \dfrac{x + 3}{2x}$ **43.** 0.3

45. -0.1 **47.** 0   **49.** $\dfrac{3}{5}$ **51.** $\dfrac{\sqrt{5}}{5}$ **53.** $\dfrac{12}{13}$

55. $\dfrac{\sqrt{34}}{5}$ **57.** $\dfrac{\sqrt{5}}{3}$ **59.** $\dfrac{1}{x}$ **61.** $\sqrt{1 - 4x^2}$

63. $\sqrt{1 - x^2}$ **65.** $\dfrac{\sqrt{9 - x^2}}{x}$ **67.** $\dfrac{\sqrt{x^2 + 2}}{x}$

69.

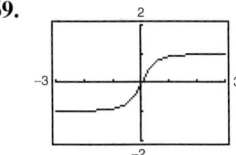

Asymptotes: $y = \pm 1$

71. $\dfrac{9}{\sqrt{x^2 + 81}}$, $x > 0$; $\dfrac{-9}{\sqrt{x^2 + 81}}$, $x < 0$

73. $\dfrac{|x - 1|}{\sqrt{x^2 - 2x + 10}}$

75.

77.

79.

80.

83.

85.

87.

89. $3\sqrt{2}\sin\left(2t + \dfrac{\pi}{4}\right)$

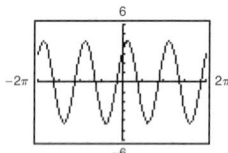

The graph implies that the identity is true.

91. (a) $\theta = \arcsin\dfrac{5}{s}$ (b) $0.13, 0.25$

93. (a)
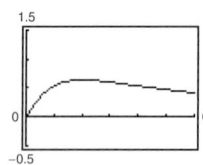

   (b) 2 feet

   (c) $\beta = 0$; As x increases, β approaches 0.

95. (a) $\theta \approx 26.0°$ (b) 24.4 feet

97. (a) $\theta = \arctan\dfrac{x}{20}$ (b) $14.0°, 31.0°$

99. False. $\dfrac{5\pi}{4}$ is not in the range of the arctangent.

101. Domain: $(-\infty, -1] \cup [1, \infty)$

   Range: $[0, \pi/2) \cup (\pi/2, \pi]$

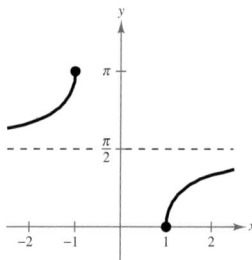

103. (a) $\dfrac{\pi}{4}$ (b) 0   (c) $\dfrac{5\pi}{6}$ (d) $\dfrac{\pi}{6}$

105.
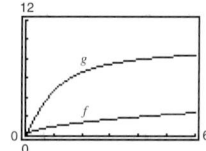

   As x increases to infinity, g approaches 3π, but f has no maximum.

   $a \approx 87.54$

107–111. Answers will vary.

113.

115.
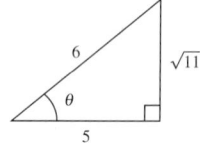

117. 1279.284   **119.** 117.391   **121.** Eight people

Section 4.8   *(page 338)*

1. $a \approx 3.64$

   $c \approx 10.64$

   $B = 70°$

3. $a \approx 8.26$

   $c \approx 25.38$

   $A = 19°$

5. $c \approx 11.66$

   $A \approx 30.96°$

   $B \approx 59.04°$

7. $a \approx 49.48$

   $A \approx 72.08°$

   $B \approx 17.92°$

9. $a \approx 91.34$

   $b \approx 420.70$

   $B = 77°45'$

11. 2.56 inches

13. 19.99 inches   **15.** 107.2 feet   **17.** 19.7 feet

19. (a)

(b) $h = 50(\tan 47° \, 40' - \tan 35°)$ (c) 19.9 feet

21. 2236.8 feet

23. (a)

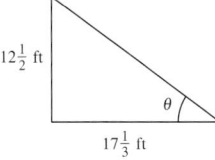

(b) $\tan \theta = \dfrac{12\frac{1}{2}}{17\frac{1}{3}}$

(c) 35.8°

25. 2.06°   **27.** 0.73 mile

29. 554 miles north; 709 miles east   **31.** 5.46 kilometers

33. 1933.3 feet   **35.** ≈ 3.23 miles or $\approx 17{,}054$ feet

37. 78.7°   **39.** 35.3°   **41.** 29.4 inches

43. $y = \sqrt{3}\,r$ **45.** $a \approx 12.2$, $b \approx 7$

47. (a) 4   (b) 4   (c) $\frac{1}{16}$

49. (a) $\frac{1}{16}$ (b) 60   (c) $\frac{1}{120}$ **51.** $d = 4\sin(\pi t)$

53. $d = 3\cos\left(\dfrac{4\pi t}{3}\right)$ **55.** $\omega = 528\pi$

57. (a)

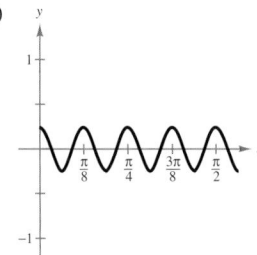

(b) $\dfrac{\pi}{8}$

(c) $\dfrac{\pi}{32}$

59. False. One period is the time for one complete cycle of the motion.

61. (a) and (b)

Base 1	Base 2	Altitude	Area
8	$8 + 16\cos 10°$	$8\sin 10°$	22.1
8	$8 + 16\cos 20°$	$8\sin 20°$	42.5
8	$8 + 16\cos 30°$	$8\sin 30°$	59.7
8	$8 + 16\cos 40°$	$8\sin 40°$	72.7
8	$8 + 16\cos 50°$	$8\sin 50°$	80.5
8	$8 + 16\cos 60°$	$8\sin 60°$	83.1
8	$8 + 16\cos 70°$	$8\sin 70°$	80.7

≈ 83.1 square feet when $\theta = 60°$

(c) $A = 64(1 + \cos\theta)(\sin\theta)$

(d)

≈ 83.1 square feet when $\theta = 60°$

63. (a)

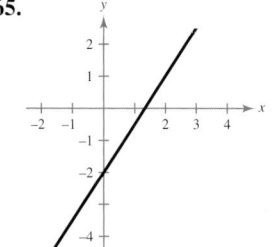

(b) $S = 8 + 6.3\cos\left(\dfrac{\pi}{6}t\right)$ or $S = 8 + 6.3\sin\left(\dfrac{\pi}{6}t + \dfrac{\pi}{2}\right)$

The model is a good fit.

(c) 12. Yes, sales of outerwear are seasonal.

(d) Maximum displacement from average sales of $8 million

65.

67.

69.

71.

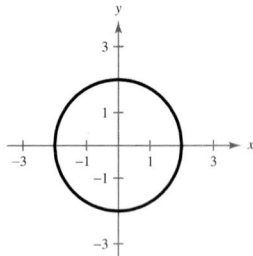

Review Exercises   *(page 344)*

1. 0.5 radian   **3.** 4.5 radians

5.

7.

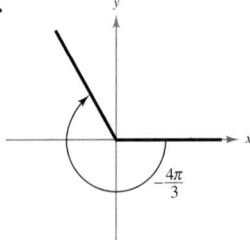

$\dfrac{3\pi}{4}, -\dfrac{5\pi}{4}$ $\dfrac{2\pi}{3}, -\dfrac{10\pi}{3}$

9.

11.

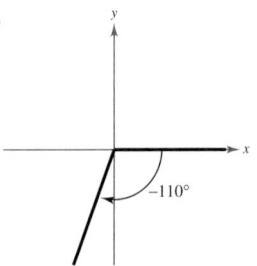

430°, −290°   250°, −470°

13. 128.57°   **15.** −200.54°

17. 8.3776   **19.** −0.5890

21. (a) $66\frac{2}{3}\pi$ radians per minute

    (b) 400π inches per minute

23. $\left(-\dfrac{1}{2}, \dfrac{\sqrt{3}}{2}\right)$ **25.** $\left(-\dfrac{\sqrt{3}}{2}, \dfrac{1}{2}\right)$

27. $\sin\dfrac{7\pi}{6} = -\dfrac{1}{2}$ $\csc\dfrac{7\pi}{6} = -2$

    $\cos\dfrac{7\pi}{6} = -\dfrac{\sqrt{3}}{2}$ $\sec\dfrac{7\pi}{6} = -\dfrac{2\sqrt{3}}{3}$

    $\tan\dfrac{7\pi}{6} = \dfrac{\sqrt{3}}{3}$ $\cot\dfrac{7\pi}{6} = \sqrt{3}$

29. $\sin\left(-\dfrac{2\pi}{3}\right) = -\dfrac{\sqrt{3}}{2}$ $\csc\left(-\dfrac{2\pi}{3}\right) = -\dfrac{2\sqrt{3}}{3}$

    $\cos\left(-\dfrac{2\pi}{3}\right) = -\dfrac{1}{2}$ $\sec\left(-\dfrac{2\pi}{3}\right) = -2$

    $\tan\left(-\dfrac{2\pi}{3}\right) = \sqrt{3}$ $\cot\left(-\dfrac{2\pi}{3}\right) = \dfrac{\sqrt{3}}{3}$

31. $\sin\dfrac{11\pi}{4} = \sin\dfrac{3\pi}{4} = \dfrac{\sqrt{2}}{2}$

33. $\sin\left(-\dfrac{17\pi}{6}\right) = \sin\dfrac{7\pi}{6} = -\dfrac{1}{2}$

35. −75.31   **37.** 3.24

39. $\sin\theta = \dfrac{4\sqrt{41}}{41}$ **41.** $\sin\theta = \dfrac{\sqrt{3}}{2}$

    $\cos\theta = \dfrac{5\sqrt{41}}{41}$ $\cos\theta = \dfrac{1}{2}$

    $\tan\theta = \dfrac{4}{5}$ $\tan\theta = \sqrt{3}$

    $\csc\theta = \dfrac{\sqrt{41}}{4}$ $\csc\theta = \dfrac{2\sqrt{3}}{3}$

    $\sec\theta = \dfrac{\sqrt{41}}{5}$ $\sec\theta = 2$

    $\cot\theta = \dfrac{5}{4}$ $\cot\theta = \dfrac{\sqrt{3}}{3}$

43. (a) 3   (b) $\dfrac{2\sqrt{2}}{3}$ (c) $\dfrac{3\sqrt{2}}{4}$ (d) $\dfrac{\sqrt{2}}{4}$

45. (a) $\dfrac{1}{4}$ (b) $\dfrac{\sqrt{15}}{4}$ (c) $\dfrac{4\sqrt{15}}{15}$ (d) $\dfrac{\sqrt{15}}{15}$

47. 0.65   **49.** 0.56   **51.** 3.67   **53.** 71.3 meters

55. $\sin\theta = \frac{4}{5}$ $\csc\theta = \frac{5}{4}$

    $\cos\theta = \frac{3}{5}$ $\sec\theta = \frac{5}{3}$

    $\tan\theta = \frac{4}{3}$ $\cot\theta = \frac{3}{4}$

57. $\sin\theta = \dfrac{15\sqrt{241}}{241}$ $\csc\theta = \dfrac{\sqrt{241}}{15}$

    $\cos\theta = \dfrac{4\sqrt{241}}{241}$ $\sec\theta = \dfrac{\sqrt{241}}{4}$

    $\tan\theta = \dfrac{15}{4}$ $\cot\theta = \dfrac{4}{15}$

59. $\sin \theta \approx 1$ $\csc \theta \approx 1$

$\cos \theta \approx -0.1$ $\sec \theta \approx -9$

$\tan \theta \approx -9$ $\cot \theta \approx -0.1$

61. $\sin \theta = \dfrac{4\sqrt{17}}{17}$ $\csc \theta = \dfrac{\sqrt{17}}{4}$

$\cos \theta = \dfrac{\sqrt{17}}{17}$ $\sec \theta = \sqrt{17}$

$\tan \theta = 4$ $\cot \theta = \dfrac{1}{4}$

63. $\sin \theta = -\dfrac{\sqrt{11}}{6}$ **65.** $\cos \theta = -\dfrac{\sqrt{55}}{8}$

$\cos \theta = \dfrac{5}{6}$ $\tan \theta = -\dfrac{3\sqrt{55}}{55}$

$\tan \theta = -\dfrac{\sqrt{11}}{5}$ $\csc \theta = \dfrac{8}{3}$

$\csc \theta = -\dfrac{6\sqrt{11}}{11}$ $\sec \theta = -\dfrac{8\sqrt{55}}{55}$

$\cot \theta = -\dfrac{5\sqrt{11}}{11}$ $\cot \theta = -\dfrac{\sqrt{55}}{3}$

67. $\sin \theta = \dfrac{\sqrt{21}}{5}$

$\tan \theta = -\dfrac{\sqrt{21}}{2}$

$\csc \theta = \dfrac{5\sqrt{21}}{21}$

$\sec \theta = -\dfrac{5}{2}$

$\cot \theta = -\dfrac{2\sqrt{21}}{21}$

69. $\sin \dfrac{\pi}{3} = \dfrac{\sqrt{3}}{2};\ \cos \dfrac{\pi}{3} = \dfrac{1}{2};\ \tan \dfrac{\pi}{3} = \sqrt{3}$

71. $\sin \left(-\dfrac{7\pi}{3}\right) = -\dfrac{\sqrt{3}}{2};\ \cos \left(-\dfrac{7\pi}{3}\right) = \dfrac{1}{2};$

$\tan \left(-\dfrac{7\pi}{3}\right) = -\sqrt{3}$

73. $\sin 495° = \dfrac{\sqrt{2}}{2};\ \cos 495° = -\dfrac{\sqrt{2}}{2};\ \tan 495° = -1$

75. $\sin(-240°) = \dfrac{\sqrt{3}}{2};\ \cos(-240°) = -\dfrac{1}{2};$

$\tan(-240°) = -\sqrt{3}$

77. -0.76 **79.** 0.06 **81.** 3.24

83.

85.

87.

89.

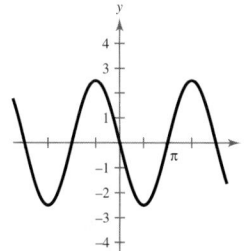

91. (a) $y = 2 \sin 528\pi x$

    (b) 264 cycles per second

93.

95.

97.

99.

101.

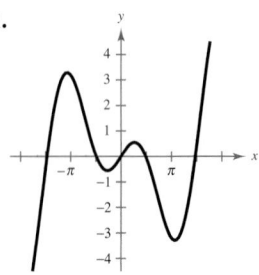

103. $-\dfrac{\pi}{6}$ **105.** 0.41

107. -0.46 **109.** $\dfrac{\pi}{6}$ **111.** π **113.** 1.24

115. 0.12   **117.** 1.40   **119.** -0.98 **121.** 0.72

123. 0   **125.** $\frac{4}{5}$ **127.** $\frac{13}{5}$ **129.** 66.8°

131. 1221 miles, 85.6°

133. False. The sine or cosine function is often useful for modeling simple harmonic motion.

135. False. For each θ there corresponds exactly one value of y.

137. d; The period is 2π and the amplitude is 3.

138. a; The period is 2π and, because $a < 0$, the graph is reflected in the x-axis.

139. b; The period is 2 and the amplitude is 2.

140. c; The period is 4π and the amplitude is 2.

141. The function is undefined because $\sec\theta = 1/\cos\theta$.

143. The ranges of the other four trigonometric functions are $(-\infty, \infty)$ or $(-\infty, -1] \cup [1, \infty)$.

145. (a) $A = 0.4r^2, r > 0$

$s = 0.8r, r > 0$

The area function increases at a greater rate than the arc length.

(b) $A = 50\theta, \theta > 0$

$s = 10\theta, \theta > 0$

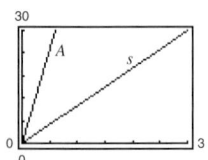

Chapter Test   *(page 348)*

1. (a)

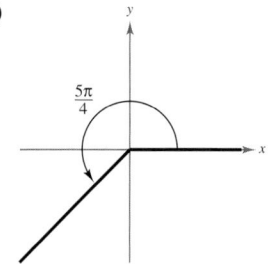

(b) $\dfrac{13\pi}{4}, -\dfrac{3\pi}{4}$

(c) 225°

2. 3000 radians per minute

3. $\sin\theta = \dfrac{3\sqrt{10}}{10}$ $\csc\theta = \dfrac{\sqrt{10}}{3}$

$\cos\theta = -\dfrac{\sqrt{10}}{10}$ $\sec\theta = -\sqrt{10}$

$\tan\theta = -3$ $\cot\theta = -\dfrac{1}{3}$

4. For $0 \le \theta < \dfrac{\pi}{2}$:   For $\pi \le \theta < \dfrac{3\pi}{2}$:

$\sin\theta = \dfrac{3\sqrt{13}}{13}$ $\sin\theta = -\dfrac{3\sqrt{13}}{13}$

$\cos\theta = \dfrac{2\sqrt{13}}{13}$ $\cos\theta = -\dfrac{2\sqrt{13}}{13}$

$\csc\theta = \dfrac{\sqrt{13}}{3}$ $\csc\theta = -\dfrac{\sqrt{13}}{3}$

$\sec\theta = \dfrac{\sqrt{13}}{2}$ $\sec\theta = -\dfrac{\sqrt{13}}{2}$

$\cot\theta = \dfrac{2}{3}$ $\cot\theta = \dfrac{2}{3}$

5. $\theta' = 70°$

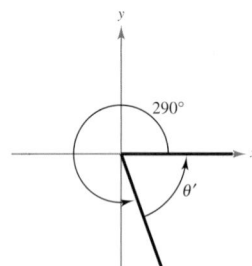

6. Quadrant III   **7.** 150°, 210°   **8.** 1.33, 1.81

9. $\sin\theta = -\frac{4}{5}$ **10.** $\sin\theta = \frac{15}{17}$

$\tan\theta = -\frac{4}{3}$ $\cos\theta = -\frac{8}{17}$

$\csc\theta = -\frac{5}{4}$ $\tan\theta = -\frac{15}{8}$

$\sec\theta = \frac{5}{3}$ $\csc\theta = \frac{17}{15}$

$\cot\theta = -\frac{3}{4}$ $\cot\theta = -\frac{8}{15}$

11.

12.

13.

Period: 2

14.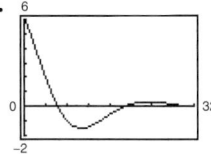

Not periodic

15. $a = -2, b = \dfrac{1}{2}, c = -\dfrac{\pi}{4}$ **16.** $\dfrac{\sqrt{5}}{2}$

17.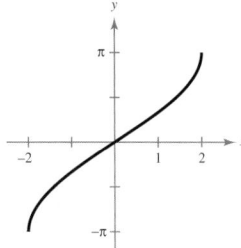

18. $310.1°$ **19.** $d = -6 \cos \pi t$

Problem Solving *(page 350)*

1. (a) $\dfrac{11\pi}{2}$ radians or $990°$ (b) ≈ 816.42 feet

3. (a) 4767 feet (b) 3705 feet

 (c) $\tan 63° = \dfrac{w + 3705}{3000}$,

 $w = 2183$ feet

5. (a)

Even

 (b)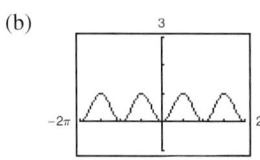

Even

7. $h = 51 - 50 \sin\!\left(8\pi t + \dfrac{\pi}{2}\right)$

9. (a)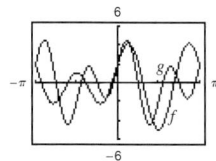

 (b) Period of f: 2π

  Period of g: π

 (c) Yes, because the sine and cosine functions are periodic.

11. (a) Equal; two-period shift

 (b) Not equal; $f\!\left(t + \tfrac{1}{2}c\right)$ is a horizontal translation and $f\!\left(\tfrac{1}{2}t\right)$ is a period change.

 (c) Not equal; For example, $\sin\!\left[\tfrac{1}{2}(\pi + 2\pi)\right] \neq \sin\!\left(\tfrac{1}{2}\pi\right)$.

13. (a)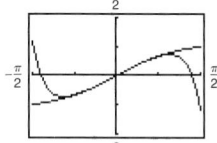

The approximation is accurate over the interval $-1 \leq x \leq 1$.

 (b) $\dfrac{x^9}{9}$

The accuracy improved.

Chapter 5
Section 5.1 *(page 359)*

1. $\tan x = -\sqrt{3}$

 $\csc x = \dfrac{2\sqrt{3}}{3}$

 $\sec x = -2$

 $\cot x = -\dfrac{\sqrt{3}}{3}$

3. $\cos \theta = \dfrac{\sqrt{2}}{2}$

 $\tan \theta = -1$

 $\csc \theta = -\sqrt{2}$

 $\cot \theta = -1$

5. $\sin x = -\dfrac{5}{13}$

$\cos x = -\dfrac{12}{13}$

$\csc x = -\dfrac{13}{5}$

$\cot x = \dfrac{12}{5}$

7. $\sin \phi = -\dfrac{\sqrt{5}}{3}$

$\cos \phi = \dfrac{2}{3}$

$\tan \phi = -\dfrac{\sqrt{5}}{2}$

$\cot \phi = -\dfrac{2\sqrt{5}}{5}$

9. $\sin x = \dfrac{1}{3}$

$\cos x = -\dfrac{2\sqrt{2}}{3}$

$\csc x = 3$

$\sec x = -\dfrac{3\sqrt{2}}{4}$

$\cot x = -2\sqrt{2}$

11. $\sin \theta = -\dfrac{2\sqrt{5}}{5}$

$\cos \theta = -\dfrac{\sqrt{5}}{5}$

$\csc \theta = -\dfrac{\sqrt{5}}{2}$

$\sec \theta = -\sqrt{5}$

$\cot \theta = \dfrac{1}{2}$

13. $\cos \theta = 0$

$\tan \theta$ is undefined.

$\csc \theta = -1$

$\sec \theta$ is undefined.

15. d   **16.** a   **17.** b   **18.** f   **19.** e   **20.** c

21. b   **22.** c   **23.** f   **24.** a   **25.** e   **26.** d

27. $\csc \theta$ **29.** $\cos^2 \phi$ **31.** $\cos x$ **33.** $\sin^2 x$

35. 1   **37.** $\tan x$ **39.** $1 + \sin y$ **41.** $\sec \beta$

43. $\cos u + \sin u$ **45.** $\sin^2 x$ **47.** $\sin^2 x \tan^2 x$

49. $\sec x + 1$ **51.** $\sec^4 x$ **53.** $\sin^2 x - \cos^2 x$

55. $\cot^2 x(\csc x - 1)$ **57.** $1 + 2\sin x \cos x$

59. $4\cot^2 x$ **61.** $2\csc^2 x$ **63.** $2\sec x$

65. $1 + \cos y$ **67.** $3(\sec x + \tan x)$

69.

x	0.2	0.4	0.6	0.8	1.0
y_1	0.1987	0.3894	0.5646	0.7174	0.8415
y_2	0.1987	0.3894	0.5646	0.7174	0.8415

x	1.2	1.4
y_1	0.9320	0.9854
y_2	0.9320	0.9854

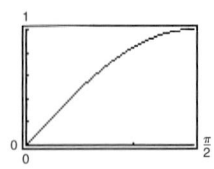

$y_1 = y_2$

71.

x	0.2	0.4	0.6	0.8	1.0
y_1	1.2230	1.5085	1.8958	2.4650	3.4082
y_2	1.2230	1.5085	1.8958	2.4650	3.4082

x	1.2	1.4
y_1	5.3319	11.6814
y_2	5.3319	11.6814

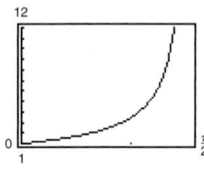

$y_1 = y_2$

73. $\csc x$ **75.** $\tan x$ **77.** $3\sin \theta$ **79.** $3\tan \theta$

81. $5\sec \theta$ **83.** $3\cos \theta = 3$; $\sin \theta = 0$; $\cos \theta = 1$

85. $4\sin \theta = 2\sqrt{2}$; $\sin \theta = \dfrac{\sqrt{2}}{2}$; $\cos \theta = \dfrac{\sqrt{2}}{2}$

87. $0 \le \theta \le \pi$ **89.** $0 \le \theta < \dfrac{\pi}{2}$, $\dfrac{3\pi}{2} < \theta < 2\pi$

91. $\ln|\cot x|$ **93.** $\ln|\csc t \sec t|$

95. (a) $\csc^2 132° - \cot^2 132° \approx 1.8107 - 0.8107 = 1$

(b) $\csc^2 \dfrac{2\pi}{7} - \cot^2 \dfrac{2\pi}{7} \approx 1.6360 - 0.6360 = 1$

97. (a) $\cos(90° - 80°) = \sin 80° \approx 0.9848$

(b) $\cos\left(\dfrac{\pi}{2} - 0.8\right) = \sin 0.8 \approx 0.7174$

99. $\mu = \tan \theta$

101. True. For example, $\sin(-x) = -\sin x$.

103. 1, 1   **105.** $\infty, 0$

107. Not an identity because $\cos \theta = \pm\sqrt{1 - \sin^2 \theta}$

109. Not an identity because $\dfrac{\sin k\theta}{\cos k\theta} = \tan k\theta$

111. Identity because $\sin \theta \cdot \dfrac{1}{\sin \theta} = 1$

113. Answers will vary. For example:

$$\sin^2 \theta + \cos^2 \theta = \dfrac{y^2}{r^2} + \dfrac{x^2}{r^2} = \dfrac{x^2 + y^2}{r^2} = \dfrac{r^2}{r^2} = 1$$

115. $x - 25$

117. $\dfrac{x^2 + 6x - 8}{(x + 5)(x - 8)}$ **119.** $\dfrac{-5x^2 + 8x + 28}{(x^2 - 4)(x + 4)}$

Section 5.2   *(page 367)*

1–39. Answers will vary.

41. Identity   **43.** Not an identity   **45.** Identity

47. Identity   **49.** Not an identity   **51.** Identity

53. 1   **55.** 2   **57.** Answers will vary.

59. False. An identity is an equation that is true for all real values of θ.

61. The equation is not an identity because $\sin \theta = \pm \sqrt{1 - \cos^2 \theta}$.

Possible answer: $\dfrac{7\pi}{4}$

63. $2 + \left(3 - \sqrt{26}\right)i$

65. $-8 + 4i$ **67.** $3 \pm \sqrt{3}\,i$ **69.** $-1 \pm \sqrt{3}\,i$

Section 5.3   *(page 376)*

1–5. Answers will vary.   **7.** $\dfrac{2\pi}{3} + 2n\pi, \dfrac{4\pi}{3} + 2n\pi$

9. $\dfrac{\pi}{3} + 2n\pi, \dfrac{2\pi}{3} + 2n\pi$ **11.** $\dfrac{\pi}{6} + n\pi, \dfrac{5\pi}{6} + n\pi$

13. $n\pi, \dfrac{3\pi}{2} + 2n\pi$ **15.** $\dfrac{\pi}{3} + n\pi, \dfrac{2\pi}{3} + n\pi$

17. $\dfrac{\pi}{8} + \dfrac{n\pi}{2}, \dfrac{3\pi}{8} + \dfrac{n\pi}{2}$ **19.** $\dfrac{n\pi}{3}, \dfrac{\pi}{4} + n\pi$

21. $0, \dfrac{\pi}{2}, \pi, \dfrac{3\pi}{2}$ **23.** $0, \pi, \dfrac{\pi}{6}, \dfrac{5\pi}{6}, \dfrac{7\pi}{6}, \dfrac{11\pi}{6}$

25. $\dfrac{\pi}{3}, \dfrac{5\pi}{3}, \pi$ **27.** No solution   **29.** $\pi, \dfrac{\pi}{3}, \dfrac{5\pi}{3}$

31. $\dfrac{\pi}{6}, \dfrac{5\pi}{6}, \dfrac{7\pi}{6}, \dfrac{11\pi}{6}$ **33.** $\dfrac{\pi}{6} + n\pi, \dfrac{5\pi}{6} + n\pi$

35. $\dfrac{\pi}{12} + \dfrac{n\pi}{3}$ **37.** $\dfrac{\pi}{2} + 4n\pi, \dfrac{7\pi}{2} + 4n\pi$

39. $-1 + 4n$ **41.** $-2 + 6n, 2 + 6n$

43. $\dfrac{2}{3}, \dfrac{3}{2}$; $0.8411 + 2n\pi, 5.4421 + 2n\pi$

45. 2.6779, 5.8195   **47.** 1.0472, 5.2360

49. 0.8603, 3.4256   **51.** 0, 2.6779, 3.1416, 5.8195

53. 0.9828, 1.7682, 4.1244, 4.9098

55. 0.3398, 0.8481, 2.2935, 2.8018

57. 1.9357, 2.7767, 5.0773, 5.9183

59. $\dfrac{\pi}{4}, \dfrac{5\pi}{4}$, arctan 5, arctan $5 + \pi$ **61.** $\dfrac{\pi}{3}, \dfrac{5\pi}{3}$

63. (a)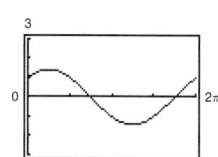

(b) $\dfrac{\pi}{4} \approx 0.7854$;

$\dfrac{5\pi}{4} \approx 3.9270$

Maximum: $(0.7854, 1.4142)$

Minimum: $(3.9270, -1.4142)$

65. 1

67. (a) All real numbers $x \neq 0$

(b) y-axis symmetry; Horizontal asymptote: $y = 1$

(c) Oscillates

(d) Infinitely many solutions

(e) Yes, 0.6366

69. 0.04 second, 0.43 second, 0.83 second

71. February, March, and April   **73.** $1.9°$

75. (a)

Unemployment rate vs. Year (0 ↔ 1990)

(b) (1)

(c) The constant term, 5.51

(d) ≈ 13 years

(e) 2004

77. True. The first equation has a smaller period than the second equation, so it will have more solutions in the interval $[0, 2\pi)$.

79. 1   **81.** $C = 24°$

$a \approx 54.8$

$b \approx 50.1$

83. $\sin 390° = \dfrac{1}{2}$ **85.** $\sin(-1845°) = -\dfrac{\sqrt{2}}{2}$

$\cos 390° = \dfrac{\sqrt{3}}{2}$ $\cos(-1845°) = \dfrac{\sqrt{2}}{2}$

$\tan 390° = \dfrac{\sqrt{3}}{3}$ $\tan(-1845°) = -1$

87. $1.36°$

Section 5.4   *(page 384)*

1. (a) $\dfrac{\sqrt{2} - \sqrt{6}}{4}$ (b) $\dfrac{\sqrt{2} + 1}{2}$

3. (a) $\dfrac{1}{2}$ (b) $\dfrac{-\sqrt{3} - 1}{2}$

5. (a) $\dfrac{-\sqrt{2} - \sqrt{6}}{4}$ (b) $\dfrac{-1 + \sqrt{2}}{2}$

7. $\sin 105° = \dfrac{\sqrt{2}}{4}(\sqrt{3} + 1)$

$\cos 105° = \dfrac{\sqrt{2}}{4}(1 - \sqrt{3})$

$\tan 105° = -2 - \sqrt{3}$

9. $\sin 195° = \dfrac{\sqrt{2}}{4}(1 - \sqrt{3})$

$\cos 195° = -\dfrac{\sqrt{2}}{4}(\sqrt{3} + 1)$

$\tan 195° = 2 - \sqrt{3}$

11. $\sin \dfrac{11\pi}{12} = \dfrac{\sqrt{2}}{4}(\sqrt{3} - 1)$

$\cos \dfrac{11\pi}{12} = -\dfrac{\sqrt{2}}{4}(\sqrt{3} + 1)$

$\tan \dfrac{11\pi}{12} = -2 + \sqrt{3}$

13. $\sin \dfrac{17\pi}{12} = -\dfrac{\sqrt{2}}{4}(\sqrt{3} + 1)$

$\cos \dfrac{17\pi}{12} = \dfrac{\sqrt{2}}{4}(1 - \sqrt{3})$

$\tan \dfrac{17\pi}{12} = 2 + \sqrt{3}$

15. $\sin 285° = -\dfrac{\sqrt{2}}{4}(\sqrt{3} + 1)$

$\cos 285° = \dfrac{\sqrt{2}}{4}(\sqrt{3} - 1)$

$\tan 285° = -(2 + \sqrt{3})$

17. $\sin(-165°) = -\dfrac{\sqrt{2}}{4}(\sqrt{3} - 1)$

$\cos(-165°) = -\dfrac{\sqrt{2}}{4}(1 + \sqrt{3})$

$\tan(-165°) = 2 - \sqrt{3}$

19. $\sin \dfrac{13\pi}{12} = \dfrac{\sqrt{2}}{4}(1 - \sqrt{3})$

$\cos \dfrac{13\pi}{12} = -\dfrac{\sqrt{2}}{4}(1 + \sqrt{3})$

$\tan \dfrac{13\pi}{12} = 2 - \sqrt{3}$

21. $\sin\left(-\dfrac{13\pi}{12}\right) = \dfrac{\sqrt{2}}{4}(\sqrt{3} - 1)$

$\cos\left(-\dfrac{13\pi}{12}\right) = -\dfrac{\sqrt{2}}{4}(\sqrt{3} + 1)$

$\tan\left(-\dfrac{13\pi}{12}\right) = -2 + \sqrt{3}$

23. $\cos 40°$ **25.** $\tan 239°$ **27.** $\sin 1.8$ **29.** $\tan 3x$

31. $-\dfrac{\sqrt{3}}{2}$ **33.** $\dfrac{\sqrt{3}}{2}$ **35.** -1 **37.** $-\dfrac{63}{65}$

39. $\frac{16}{65}$ **41.** $-\frac{63}{16}$ **43.** $\frac{65}{56}$ **45.** $\frac{3}{5}$ **47.** $-\frac{44}{117}$

49. $\frac{5}{3}$ **51.** 1 **53.** 0 **55–63.** Answers will vary.

65. $-\sin x$ **67.** $-\cos \theta$ **69.** $\dfrac{\pi}{2}$ **71.** $\dfrac{5\pi}{4}, \dfrac{7\pi}{4}$

73. $\dfrac{\pi}{4}, \dfrac{7\pi}{4}$ **75.** (a) $y = \dfrac{5}{12} \sin(2t + 0.6435)$

(b) $\dfrac{5}{12}$ feet (c) $\dfrac{1}{\pi}$ cycle per second

77. False. $\sin(u \pm v) = \sin u \cos v \pm \cos u \sin v$

79. False.

$\cos\left(x - \dfrac{\pi}{2}\right) = \cos x \cos \dfrac{\pi}{2} + \sin x \sin \dfrac{\pi}{2} = \sin x$

81. Answers will vary. **83.** Answers will vary.

85. (a) $\sqrt{2} \sin\left(\theta + \dfrac{\pi}{4}\right)$ (b) $\sqrt{2} \cos\left(\theta - \dfrac{\pi}{4}\right)$

87. (a) $13 \sin(3\theta + 0.3948)$ (b) $13 \cos(3\theta - 1.1760)$

89. $2 \cos \theta$ **91.** $15°$

93.

$\sin^2\left(\theta + \dfrac{\pi}{4}\right) + \sin^2\left(\theta - \dfrac{\pi}{4}\right) = 1$

95. Answers will vary. **97.** $f^{-1}(x) = \dfrac{x + 15}{5}$

99. Because f is not one-to-one, f^{-1} does not exist.

101. $4x - 3$ **103.** $6x - 3$

Section 5.5 (page 394)

1. $\dfrac{\sqrt{17}}{17}$ **3.** $\dfrac{15}{17}$ **5.** $\dfrac{8}{15}$ **7.** $\dfrac{17}{8}$

9. $0, \dfrac{\pi}{3}, \pi, \dfrac{5\pi}{3}$ **11.** $\dfrac{\pi}{12}, \dfrac{5\pi}{12}, \dfrac{13\pi}{12}, \dfrac{17\pi}{12}$

13. $0, \dfrac{2\pi}{3}, \dfrac{4\pi}{3}$ **15.** $\dfrac{\pi}{2}, \dfrac{\pi}{6}, \dfrac{5\pi}{6}, \dfrac{7\pi}{6}, \dfrac{3\pi}{2}, \dfrac{11\pi}{6}$

17. $0, \dfrac{\pi}{2}, \pi, \dfrac{3\pi}{2}$ **19.** $3 \sin 2x$ **21.** $4 \cos 2x$

23. $\sin 2u = \dfrac{24}{25}$ **25.** $\sin 2u = \dfrac{24}{25}$

$\cos 2u = -\dfrac{7}{25}$ $\cos 2u = \dfrac{7}{25}$

$\tan 2u = -\dfrac{24}{7}$ $\tan 2u = \dfrac{24}{7}$

27. $\sin 2u = -\dfrac{4\sqrt{21}}{25}$

$\cos 2u = -\dfrac{17}{25}$

$\tan 2u = \dfrac{4\sqrt{21}}{17}$

29. $\dfrac{1}{8}(3 + 4 \cos 2x + \cos 4x)$ **31.** $\dfrac{1}{8}(1 - \cos 4x)$

33. $\dfrac{1}{16}(1 + \cos 2x - \cos 4x - \cos 2x \cos 4x)$

35. $\dfrac{4\sqrt{17}}{17}$ **37.** $\dfrac{1}{4}$ **39.** $\sqrt{17}$

41. $\sin 75° = \dfrac{1}{2}\sqrt{2 + \sqrt{3}}$

$\cos 75° = \dfrac{1}{2}\sqrt{2 - \sqrt{3}}$

$\tan 75° = 2 + \sqrt{3}$

43. $\sin 112° 30' = \dfrac{1}{2}\sqrt{2 + \sqrt{2}}$

$\cos 112° 30' = -\dfrac{1}{2}\sqrt{2 - \sqrt{2}}$

$\tan 112° 30' = -1 - \sqrt{2}$

45. $\sin \dfrac{\pi}{8} = \dfrac{1}{2}\sqrt{2 - \sqrt{2}}$ **47.** $\sin \dfrac{3\pi}{8} = \dfrac{1}{2}\sqrt{2 + \sqrt{2}}$

$\cos \dfrac{\pi}{8} = \dfrac{1}{2}\sqrt{2 + \sqrt{2}}$ $\cos \dfrac{3\pi}{8} = \dfrac{1}{2}\sqrt{2 - \sqrt{2}}$

$\tan \dfrac{\pi}{8} = \sqrt{2} - 1$ $\tan \dfrac{3\pi}{8} = \sqrt{2} + 1$

49. $\sin \dfrac{u}{2} = \dfrac{5\sqrt{26}}{26}$ **51.** $\sin \dfrac{u}{2} = \sqrt{\dfrac{89 - 8\sqrt{89}}{178}}$

$\cos \dfrac{u}{2} = \dfrac{\sqrt{26}}{26}$ $\cos \dfrac{u}{2} = -\sqrt{\dfrac{89 + 8\sqrt{89}}{178}}$

$\tan \dfrac{u}{2} = 5$ $\tan \dfrac{u}{2} = \dfrac{8 - \sqrt{89}}{5}$

53. $\sin \dfrac{u}{2} = \dfrac{3\sqrt{10}}{10}$ **55.** $|\sin 3x|$ **57.** $-|\tan 4x|$

$\cos \dfrac{u}{2} = -\dfrac{\sqrt{10}}{10}$

$\tan \dfrac{u}{2} = -3$

59. π **61.** $\dfrac{\pi}{3}, \pi, \dfrac{5\pi}{3}$

63. $3\left(\sin \dfrac{\pi}{2} + \sin 0\right)$

65. $\dfrac{1}{2}(\sin 10\theta + \sin 2\theta)$ **67.** $\dfrac{5}{2}(\cos 8\beta + \cos 2\beta)$

69. $\dfrac{1}{2}(\cos 2y - \cos 2x)$ **71.** $\dfrac{1}{2}(\sin 2\theta + \sin 2\pi)$

73. $5(\cos 60° + \cos 90°)$ **75.** $2 \sin 45° \cos 15°$

77. $-2 \sin \dfrac{\pi}{2} \sin \dfrac{\pi}{4}$ **79.** $2 \cos 4\theta \sin \theta$

81. $2 \cos 4x \cos 2x$ **83.** $2 \cos \alpha \sin \beta$

85. $-2 \sin \theta \sin \dfrac{\pi}{2}$

87. $0, \dfrac{\pi}{4}, \dfrac{\pi}{2}, \dfrac{3\pi}{4}, \pi, \dfrac{5\pi}{4}, \dfrac{3\pi}{2}, \dfrac{7\pi}{4}$

89. $\dfrac{\pi}{6}, \dfrac{5\pi}{6}$

91. $\dfrac{25}{169}$ **93.** $\dfrac{4}{13}$ **95–109.** Answers will vary.

111.

113.

115.

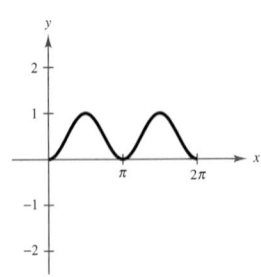

117. $2x\sqrt{1-x^2}$

119. (a) $A = 100 \sin \dfrac{\theta}{2} \cos \dfrac{\theta}{2}$

(b) $A = 50 \sin \theta$

The area is maximum when $\theta = \pi/2$.

121. (a) π

(b) 0.4482

(c) 760 miles per hour; 3420 miles per hour

(d) $\theta = 2 \sin^{-1}\!\left(\dfrac{1}{m}\right)$

123. False. For $u < 0$,

$\sin 2u = -\sin(-2u)$

$\qquad = -2 \sin(-u) \cos(-u)$

$\qquad = -2(-\sin u) \cos u$

$\qquad = 2 \sin u \cos u.$

125. (a)

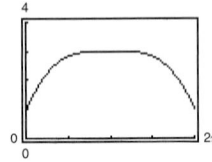

(b) π

Maximum: $(\pi, 3)$

127. (a) $\frac{1}{4}(3 + \cos 4x)$

(b) $2 \cos^4 x - 2 \cos^2 x + 1$

(c) $1 - 2 \sin^2 x \cos^2 x$

(d) $1 - \frac{1}{2} \sin^2 2x$

(e) No. There is often more than one way to rewrite a trigonometric expression.

129. September: $235,000$ October: $272,600$

131. ≈ 127 feet

Review Exercises   *(page 399)*

1. $\sec x$ **3.** $\cos x$ **5.** $\cot x$

7. $\tan x = \dfrac{3}{4}$

$\csc x = \dfrac{5}{3}$

$\sec x = \dfrac{5}{4}$

$\cot x = \dfrac{4}{3}$

9. $\cos x = \dfrac{\sqrt{2}}{2}$

$\tan x = -1$

$\csc x = -\sqrt{2}$

$\sec x = \sqrt{2}$

$\cot x = -1$

11. $\sin^2 x$ **13.** 1 **15.** $\cot \theta$ **17.** $\cot^2 x$

19. $\sec x + 2 \sin x$ **21.** $-2 \tan^2 \theta$

23–31. Answers will vary.

33. $\dfrac{\pi}{3} + 2n\pi, \dfrac{2\pi}{3} + 2n\pi$ **35.** $\dfrac{\pi}{6} + n\pi$

37. $\dfrac{\pi}{3} + n\pi, \dfrac{2\pi}{3} + n\pi$ **39.** $0, \dfrac{2\pi}{3}, \dfrac{4\pi}{3}$

41. $0, \dfrac{\pi}{2}, \pi$ **43.** $\dfrac{\pi}{8}, \dfrac{3\pi}{8}, \dfrac{9\pi}{8}, \dfrac{11\pi}{8}$

45. $0, \dfrac{\pi}{8}, \dfrac{3\pi}{8}, \dfrac{5\pi}{8}, \dfrac{7\pi}{8}, \dfrac{9\pi}{8}, \dfrac{11\pi}{8}, \dfrac{13\pi}{8}, \dfrac{15\pi}{8}$ **47.** $0, \pi$

49. $\arctan(-4) + \pi, \arctan(-4) + 2\pi, \arctan 3,$

$\qquad \pi + \arctan 3$

51. $\sin 285° = -\dfrac{\sqrt{2}}{4}(\sqrt{3} + 1)$

$\cos 285° = \dfrac{\sqrt{2}}{4}(\sqrt{3} - 1)$

$\tan 285° = -2 - \sqrt{3}$

53. $\sin \dfrac{25\pi}{12} = \dfrac{\sqrt{2}}{4}(\sqrt{3} - 1)$

$\cos \dfrac{25\pi}{12} = \dfrac{\sqrt{2}}{4}(\sqrt{3} + 1)$

$\tan \dfrac{25\pi}{12} = 2 - \sqrt{3}$

55. $\sin 15°$ **57.** $\tan 35°$ **59.** $-\frac{3}{52}(5 + 4\sqrt{7})$

61. $\frac{1}{52}(5\sqrt{7} + 36)$ **63.** $\frac{1}{52}(5\sqrt{7} - 36)$

65. $\dfrac{\pi}{4}, \dfrac{7\pi}{4}$ **67.** $\dfrac{\pi}{6}, \dfrac{11\pi}{6}$

69.

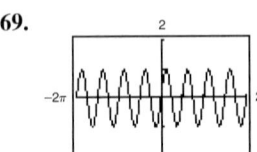

71. $\sin 2u = \frac{24}{25}$

$\cos 2u = -\frac{7}{25}$

$\tan 2u = -\frac{24}{7}$

73. $\theta = 15°$ or $\dfrac{\pi}{12}$ **75.** $\dfrac{1 - \cos 4x}{1 + \cos 4x}$

77. $\dfrac{3 - 4\cos 2x + \cos 4x}{4(1 + \cos 2x)}$

79. $\sin(-75°) = -\dfrac{1}{2}\sqrt{2 + \sqrt{3}}$

$\cos(-75°) = \dfrac{1}{2}\sqrt{2 - \sqrt{3}}$

$\tan(-75°) = -2 - \sqrt{3}$

81. $\sin\dfrac{19\pi}{12} = -\dfrac{1}{2}\sqrt{2 + \sqrt{3}}$ **83.** $-|\cos 5x|$

$\cos\dfrac{19\pi}{12} = \dfrac{1}{2}\sqrt{2 - \sqrt{3}}$

$\tan\dfrac{19\pi}{12} = -2 - \sqrt{3}$

85. $\sin\dfrac{u}{2} = \dfrac{\sqrt{10}}{10}$

$\cos\dfrac{u}{2} = \dfrac{3\sqrt{10}}{10}$

$\tan\dfrac{u}{2} = \dfrac{1}{3}$

87. $\dfrac{1}{2}\sin\dfrac{\pi}{3}$ **89.** $\dfrac{1}{2}(\cos 2\theta + \cos 8\theta)$

91. $2\sin 75°\cos 15°$ **93.** $-2\sin x \sin\dfrac{\pi}{6}$

95. (a) $y = \dfrac{1}{2}\sqrt{10}\sin\left(8t - \arctan\dfrac{1}{3}\right)$

(b) $\dfrac{1}{2}\sqrt{10}$ feet   (c) $\dfrac{4}{\pi}$ cycles per second

97. False. Using the sum and difference formula, $\sin(x + y) = \sin x \cos y + \cos x \sin y$.

99. True by the product-to-sum formula

101. No. For an equation to be an identity, the equation must be true for all real numbers x. $\sin\theta = \dfrac{1}{2}$ has an infinite number of solutions but is not an identity.

103. $y_1 = y_2 + 1$

105. $-1.8431, 2.1758, 3.9903, 8.8935, 9.8820$

Chapter Test   *(page 402)*

1. $\sin\theta = -\dfrac{3\sqrt{13}}{13}$ **2.** 1   **3.** 1   **4.** $\csc\theta\sec\theta$

$\cos\theta = -\dfrac{2\sqrt{13}}{13}$

$\csc\theta = -\dfrac{\sqrt{13}}{3}$

$\sec\theta = -\dfrac{\sqrt{13}}{2}$

$\cot\theta = \dfrac{2}{3}$

5. $\theta = 0, \dfrac{\pi}{2} < \theta \le \pi, \dfrac{3\pi}{2} < \theta < 2\pi$

6.

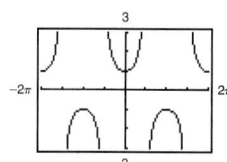

$y_1 = y_2$

7–12. Answers will vary.

13. $\dfrac{1}{16}\left(\dfrac{10 - 15\cos 2x + 6\cos 4x - \cos 6x}{1 + \cos 2x}\right)$ **14.** $\tan 2\theta$

15. $2(\sin 6\theta + \sin 2\theta)$ **16.** $-2\cos\dfrac{7\theta}{2}\sin\dfrac{\theta}{2}$

17. $0, \dfrac{3\pi}{4}, \pi, \dfrac{7\pi}{4}$ **18.** $\dfrac{\pi}{6}, \dfrac{\pi}{2}, \dfrac{5\pi}{6}, \dfrac{3\pi}{2}$

19. $\dfrac{\pi}{6}, \dfrac{5\pi}{6}, \dfrac{7\pi}{6}, \dfrac{11\pi}{6}$ **20.** $\dfrac{\pi}{6}, \dfrac{5\pi}{6}, \dfrac{3\pi}{2}$

21. $-2.938, -2.663, 1.170$

22. $\dfrac{\sqrt{2} - \sqrt{6}}{4}$ **23.** $\sin 2u = \dfrac{4}{5}, \tan 2u = -\dfrac{4}{3}$

24. Day 123 to day 223

Problem Solving   *(page 406)*

1. (a) $\cos\theta = \pm\sqrt{1 - \sin^2\theta}$

$\tan\theta = \pm\dfrac{\sin\theta}{\sqrt{1 - \sin^2\theta}}$

$\cot\theta = \pm\dfrac{\sqrt{1 - \sin^2\theta}}{\sin\theta}$

$\sec\theta = \pm\dfrac{1}{\sqrt{1 - \sin^2\theta}}$

$\csc\theta = \dfrac{1}{\sin\theta}$

(b) $\sin\theta = \pm\sqrt{1 - \cos^2\theta}$

$\tan\theta = \pm\dfrac{\sqrt{1 - \cos^2\theta}}{\cos\theta}$

$\csc\theta = \pm\dfrac{1}{\sqrt{1 - \cos^2\theta}}$

$\sec\theta = \dfrac{1}{\cos\theta}$

$\cot\theta = \pm\dfrac{\cos\theta}{\sqrt{1 - \cos^2\theta}}$

3. Answers will vary.   **5.** $y = \dfrac{1}{64}v^2\sin^2\theta$

7. $\sin \dfrac{\theta}{2} = \sqrt{\dfrac{1 - \cos \theta}{2}}$

$\cos \dfrac{\theta}{2} = \sqrt{\dfrac{1 + \cos \theta}{2}}$

$\tan \dfrac{\theta}{2} = \dfrac{\sin \theta}{1 + \cos \theta}$

9. (a)

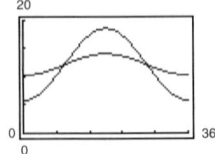

(b) $t = 91, t = 274$; Spring Equinox and Fall Equinox

(c) Seward; The amplitudes: 6.4 and 1.9

(d) 365.2 days

11. (a) $\dfrac{\pi}{6} \le x \le \dfrac{5\pi}{6}$

(b) $\dfrac{2\pi}{3} \le x \le \dfrac{4\pi}{3}$

(c) $\dfrac{\pi}{2} < x < \pi, \dfrac{3\pi}{2} < x < 2\pi$

(d) $0 \le x \le \dfrac{\pi}{4}, \dfrac{5\pi}{4} \le x \le 2\pi$

13. (a) $\sin(u + v + w)$

$= \sin u \cos v \, \cos w - \sin u \sin v \sin w$

$+ \cos u \sin v \cos w + \cos u \cos v \sin w$

(b) $\tan(u + v + w)$

$= \dfrac{\tan u + \tan v + \tan w - \tan u \tan v \tan w}{1 - \tan u \tan v - \tan u \tan w - \tan v \tan w}$

15. (a)

(b) 233.3 times per second

Chapter 6

Section 6.1   *(page 416)*

1. $C = 105°, b \approx 28.28, c \approx 38.64$

3. $C = 120°, b \approx 4.75, c \approx 7.17$

5. $B \approx 21.55°, C \approx 122.45°, c \approx 11.49$

7. $B = 60.9°, b \approx 19.32, c \approx 6.36$

9. $B = 42°4', a \approx 22.05, b \approx 14.88$

11. $A \approx 10°11', C \approx 154°19', c \approx 11.03$

13. $A \approx 25.57°, B \approx 9.43°, a \approx 10.53$

15. $B \approx 18°13', C \approx 51°32', c \approx 40.06$

17. $C = 83°, a \approx 0.62, b \approx 0.51$ **19.** No solution

21. No solution   **23.** No solution

25. (a) $b \le 5, b = \dfrac{5}{\sin 36°}$

(b) $5 < b < \dfrac{5}{\sin 36°}$

(c) $b > \dfrac{5}{\sin 36°}$

27. (a) $b \le 10.8, b = \dfrac{10.8}{\sin 10°}$

(b) $10.8 < b < \dfrac{10.8}{\sin 10°}$

(c) $b > \dfrac{10.8}{\sin 10°}$

29. 10.4   **31.** 1675.2   **33.** 3204.5   **35.** 15.3 meters

37. 16.1°   **39.** 77 meters

41. (a)

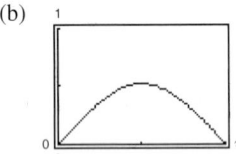

Not drawn to scale

(b) 22.6 miles

(c) 21.4 miles

(d) 7.3 miles

43. 3.2 miles

45. True. If one angle of a triangle is obtuse (greater than 90°), then the other two angles must be acute and therefore less than 90°. The triangle is oblique.

47. (a) $\alpha = \arcsin(0.5 \sin \beta)$

(b)

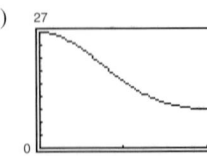

Domain: $0 < \beta < \pi$

Range: $0 < \alpha \le \dfrac{\pi}{6}$

(c) $c = \dfrac{18 \sin[\pi - \beta - \arcsin(0.5 \sin \beta)]}{\sin \beta}$

(d)

Domain: $0 < \beta < \pi$

Range: $9 < c < 27$

(e)

β	0.4	0.8	1.2	1.6
α	0.1960	0.3669	0.4848	0.5234
c	25.95	23.07	19.19	15.33

β	2.0	2.4	2.8
α	0.4720	0.3445	0.1683
c	12.29	10.31	9.27

As β increases from 0 to π, α increases and then decreases, and c decreases from 27 to 9.

49. $\cos x$ **51.** $\sin^2 x$ **53.** $3(\sin 11\theta + \sin 5\theta)$

Section 6.2 *(page 423)*

1. $A \approx 23.07°, B \approx 34.05°, C \approx 122.88°$

3. $B \approx 23.79°, C \approx 126.21°, a \approx 18.59$

5. $A \approx 31.99°, B \approx 42.38°, C \approx 105.63°$

7. $A \approx 92.94°, B \approx 43.53°, C \approx 43.53°$

9. $B \approx 13.45°, C \approx 31.55°, a \approx 12.16$

11. $A \approx 141°45', C \approx 27°40', b \approx 11.87$

13. $A = 27°10', C = 27°10', b \approx 56.94$

15. $A \approx 33.80°, B \approx 103.20°, c \approx 0.54$

	a	b	c	d	θ	ϕ
17.	5	8	12.07	5.69	45°	135°
19.	10	14	20	13.86	68.2°	111.8°
21.	15	16.96	25	20	77.2°	102.8°

23. 16.25 **25.** 10.44 **27.** 52.11

29.

N 37.1° E, S 63.1° E

31. 373.3 meters **33.** 72.3° **35.** 43.3 miles

37. (a) N 58.4° W (b) S 81.5° W **39.** 63.7 feet

41. 24.2 miles **43.** $\overline{PQ} \approx 9.4, \overline{QS} = 5, \overline{RS} \approx 12.8$

45.

d (inches)	9	10	12	13	14
θ (degrees)	60.9°	69.5°	88.0°	98.2°	109.6°
s (inches)	20.88	20.28	18.99	18.28	17.48

d (inches)	15	16
θ (degrees)	122.9°	139.8°
s (inches)	16.55	15.37

47. 46,837.5 square feet

49. False. For s to be the average of the lengths of the three sides of the triangle, s would be equal to $(a + b + c)/3$.

51. False. The three side lengths do not form a triangle.

53. (a) 570.60 (b) 5909.2 (c) 177.09

55. Answers will vary. **57.** $-\dfrac{\pi}{2}$ **59.** $\dfrac{\pi}{3}$

61. $-\dfrac{\pi}{3}$ **63.** $\dfrac{1}{\sqrt{1 - 4x^2}}$ **65.** $\dfrac{1}{x - 2}$

67. $\cos \theta = 1$

$\sec \theta = 1$

$\csc \theta$ is undefined.

69. $\tan \theta = -\dfrac{\sqrt{3}}{3}$

$\sec \theta = \dfrac{2\sqrt{3}}{3}$

$\csc \theta = -2$

71. $-2 \sin \dfrac{7\pi}{12} \sin \dfrac{\pi}{4}$

Section 6.3 *(page 436)*

1. $\mathbf{v} = \langle 3, 2 \rangle; \|\mathbf{v}\| = \sqrt{13}$ **3.** $\mathbf{v} = \langle -3, 2 \rangle; \|\mathbf{v}\| = \sqrt{13}$

5. $\mathbf{v} = \langle 0, 5 \rangle; \|\mathbf{v}\| = 5$ **7.** $\mathbf{v} = \langle 16, 7 \rangle; \|\mathbf{v}\| = \sqrt{305}$

9. $\mathbf{v} = \langle 8, 6 \rangle; \|\mathbf{v}\| = 10$ **11.** $\mathbf{v} = \langle -9, -12 \rangle; \|\mathbf{v}\| = 15$

13.

15.

17.

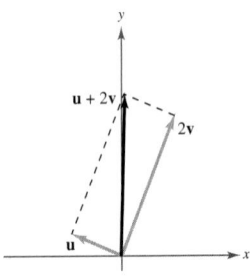

19. (a) $\langle 3, 4 \rangle$

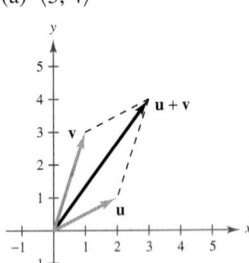

(b) $\langle 1, -2 \rangle$

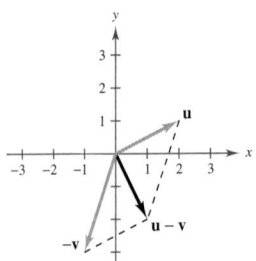

(c) $\langle 1, -7 \rangle$

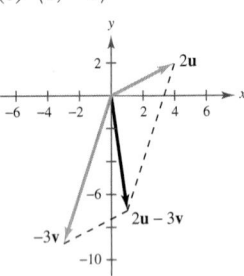

21. (a) $\langle -5, 3 \rangle$ (b) $\langle -5, 3 \rangle$

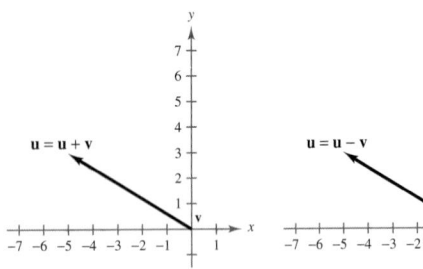

(c) $\langle -10, 6 \rangle$

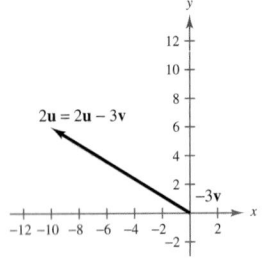

23. (a) $3\mathbf{i} - 2\mathbf{j}$ (b) $-\mathbf{i} + 4\mathbf{j}$

(c) $-4\mathbf{i} + 11\mathbf{j}$

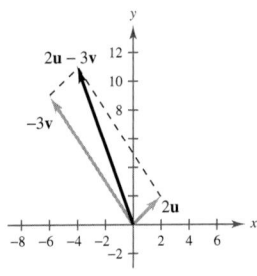

25. (a) $2\mathbf{i} + \mathbf{j}$ (b) $2\mathbf{i} - \mathbf{j}$

(c) $4\mathbf{i} - 3\mathbf{j}$

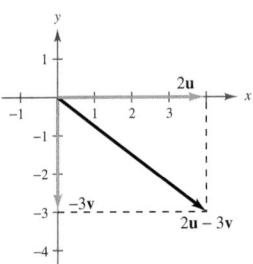

27. $\langle 1, 0 \rangle$ **29.** $\left\langle -\dfrac{\sqrt{2}}{2}, \dfrac{\sqrt{2}}{2} \right\rangle$ **31.** $\dfrac{3\sqrt{10}}{10}\mathbf{i} - \dfrac{\sqrt{10}}{10}\mathbf{j}$

33. $\mathbf{j}$ **35.** $\dfrac{\sqrt{5}}{5}\mathbf{i} - \dfrac{2\sqrt{5}}{5}\mathbf{j}$ **37.** $\left\langle \dfrac{5\sqrt{2}}{2}, \dfrac{5\sqrt{2}}{2} \right\rangle$

39. $\left\langle \dfrac{18\sqrt{29}}{29}, \dfrac{45\sqrt{29}}{2} \right\rangle$

41. $\mathbf{v} = \left\langle 3, -\frac{3}{2} \right\rangle$ **43.** $\mathbf{v} = \langle 4, 3 \rangle$

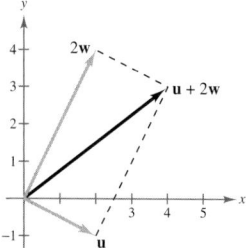

45. $\mathbf{v} = \left\langle \frac{7}{2}, -\frac{1}{2} \right\rangle$

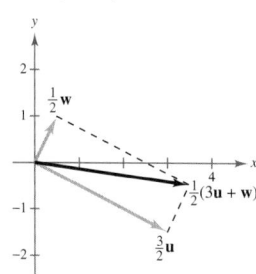

47. $\|\mathbf{v}\| = 3;\ \theta = 60°$ **49.** $\|\mathbf{v}\| = 6\sqrt{2};\ \theta = 315°$

51. $\mathbf{v} = \langle 3, 0 \rangle$ **53.** $\mathbf{v} = \left\langle -\frac{7\sqrt{3}}{4}, \frac{7}{4} \right\rangle$

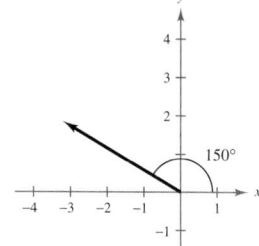

55. $\mathbf{v} = \left\langle -\frac{3\sqrt{6}}{2}, \frac{3\sqrt{2}}{2} \right\rangle$ **57.** $\mathbf{v} = \left\langle \frac{\sqrt{10}}{5}, \frac{3\sqrt{10}}{5} \right\rangle$

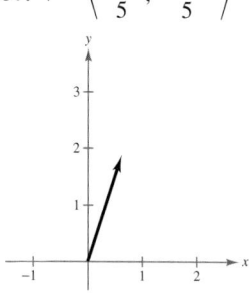

59. $\langle 5, 5 \rangle$ **61.** $\left\langle 10\sqrt{2} - 50, 10\sqrt{2} \right\rangle$ **63.** $90°$

65. $63.4°$ **67.** $62.7°$ **69.** $12.8°;\ 398.32$ newtons

71. $71.3°;\ 228.5$ pounds

73. Vertical component: $70 \sin 35° \approx 40.15$ feet per second

Horizontal component: $70 \cos 35° \approx 57.34$ feet per second

75. $T_{AC} \approx 1758.8$ pounds   **77.** 3154.4 pounds

$T_{BC} \approx 1305.4$ pounds

79. N $21.4°$ E; 138.7 kilometers per hour

81. 1928.4 foot-pounds   **83.** True. See Example 1.

85. (a) $0°$ (b) $180°$

(c) No. The magnitude is at most equal to the sum when the angle between the vectors is $0°$.

87. Answers will vary.   **89.** $\langle 1, 3 \rangle$ or $\langle -1, -3 \rangle$

91. $8 \tan \theta$ **93.** $6 \sec \theta$

95. $\frac{\pi}{2} + n\pi,\ \pi + 2n\pi$ **97.** $n\pi, \frac{\pi}{6} + 2n\pi, \frac{11\pi}{6} + 2n\pi$

Section 6.4   *(page 447)*

1. -9 **3.** 6 **5.** 8; scalar   **7.** $\langle -6, 8 \rangle$; vector

9. 13 **11.** $5\sqrt{41}$ **13.** 6 **15.** $90°$ **17.** $143.13°$

19. $60.26°$ **21.** $90°$ **23.** $\frac{5\pi}{12}$

25. $26.57°, 63.43°, 90°$ **27.** $41.63°, 53.13°, 85.24°$

29. -20 **31.** Parallel   **33.** Neither   **35.** Orthogonal

37. $\frac{1}{37}\langle 84, 14 \rangle, \frac{1}{37}\langle -10, 60 \rangle$ **39.** $\frac{45}{229}\langle 2, 15 \rangle, \frac{6}{229}\langle -15, 2 \rangle$

41. $\langle -5, 3 \rangle, \langle 5, -3 \rangle$ **43.** $\frac{2}{3}\mathbf{i} + \frac{1}{2}\mathbf{j}, -\frac{2}{3}\mathbf{i} - \frac{1}{2}\mathbf{j}$ **45.** 32

47. (a) $\$58,762.50$

This value gives the total revenue that can be earned by selling all of the units.

(b) $1.05\mathbf{v}$

49. 735 newton-meters   **51.** 779.4 foot-pounds

53. False. Work is represented by a scalar.

55. (a) $\theta = \frac{\pi}{2}$ (b) $0 \le \theta < \frac{\pi}{2}$ (c) $\frac{\pi}{2} < \theta \le \pi$

57. Answers will vary.   **59.** $12\sqrt{7}$ **61.** $-2\sqrt{6}$

63. $0, \frac{\pi}{6}, \pi, \frac{11\pi}{6}$ **65.** $0, \pi$ **67.** $-\frac{253}{325}$ **69.** $\frac{204}{325}$

Section 6.5   *(page 457)*

1.

7

3.

$4\sqrt{2}$

5.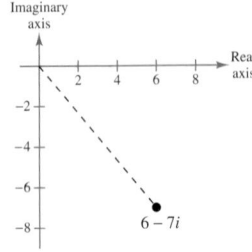

$\sqrt{85}$

7. $3\left(\cos \dfrac{\pi}{2} + i \sin \dfrac{\pi}{2}\right)$ **9.** $\sqrt{10}(\cos 5.96 + i \sin 5.96)$

11.

13.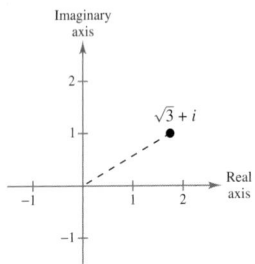

$3\sqrt{2}\left(\cos \dfrac{7\pi}{4} + i \sin \dfrac{7\pi}{4}\right)$ $2\left(\cos \dfrac{\pi}{6} + i \sin \dfrac{\pi}{6}\right)$

15.

17.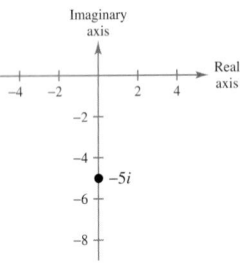

$4\left(\cos \dfrac{4\pi}{3} + i \sin \dfrac{4\pi}{3}\right)$ $5\left(\cos \dfrac{3\pi}{2} + i \sin \dfrac{3\pi}{2}\right)$

19.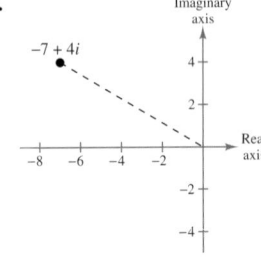

$\sqrt{65}(\cos 2.62 + i \sin 2.62)$

21.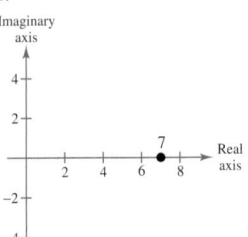

$7(\cos 0 + i \sin 0)$

23.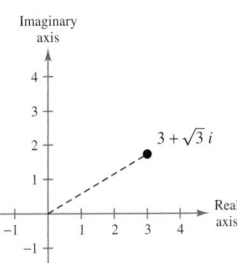

$2\sqrt{3}\left(\cos \dfrac{\pi}{6} + i \sin \dfrac{\pi}{6}\right)$

25.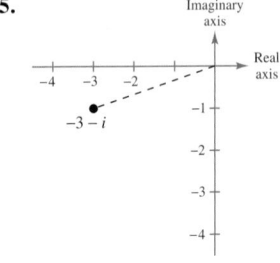

$\sqrt{10}(\cos 3.46 + i \sin 3.46)$

27. $5.39(\cos 0.38 + i \sin 0.38)$

29. $3.16(\cos 2.82 + i \sin 2.82)$

31. $8.19(\cos 5.26 + i \sin 5.26)$

33. $11.79(\cos 3.97 + i \sin 3.97)$

35.

$-\dfrac{3}{2} + \dfrac{3\sqrt{3}}{2}i$

37.

$\dfrac{3}{4} - \dfrac{3\sqrt{3}}{4}i$

39.

$-\dfrac{15\sqrt{2}}{8} + \dfrac{15\sqrt{2}}{8}i$

41.

$8i$

43.

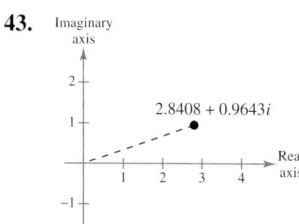

$2.8408 + 0.9643i$

45. $4.6985 + 1.7101i$ **47.** $-2.9044 + 0.7511i$

49. $12\left(\cos\dfrac{\pi}{3} + i\sin\dfrac{\pi}{3}\right)$ **51.** $\dfrac{10}{9}(\cos 200° + i\sin 200°)$

53. $0.27(\cos 150° + i\sin 150°)$ **55.** $\cos 30° + i\sin 30°$

57. $\cos\dfrac{2\pi}{3} + i\sin\dfrac{2\pi}{3}$ **59.** $4(\cos 302° + i\sin 302°)$

61. (a) $\left[2\sqrt{2}\left(\cos\dfrac{\pi}{4} + i\sin\dfrac{\pi}{4}\right)\right]\left[\sqrt{2}\left(\cos\dfrac{7\pi}{4} + i\sin\dfrac{7\pi}{4}\right)\right]$

(b) $4(\cos 0 + i\sin 0) = 4$

(c) 4

63. (a) $2\left(\cos\dfrac{3\pi}{2} + i\sin\dfrac{3\pi}{2}\right)\left[\sqrt{2}\left(\cos\dfrac{\pi}{4} + i\sin\dfrac{\pi}{4}\right)\right]$

(b) $2\sqrt{2}\left(\cos\dfrac{7\pi}{4} + i\sin\dfrac{7\pi}{4}\right) = 2 - 2i$

(c) $-2i - 2i^2 = -2i + 2 = 2 - 2i$

65. (a) $[5(\cos 0.93 + i\sin 0.93)] \div \left[2\left(\cos\dfrac{5\pi}{3} + i\sin\dfrac{5\pi}{3}\right)\right]$

(b) $\dfrac{5}{2}(\cos 1.97 + i\sin 1.97) \approx -0.982 + 2.299i$

(c) $\approx -0.982 + 2.299i$

67. (a) $[5(\cos 0 + i\sin 0)] \div \left[\sqrt{13}(\cos 0.98 + i\sin 0.98)\right]$

(b) $\dfrac{5}{\sqrt{13}}(\cos 5.30 + i\sin 5.30) \approx 0.769 - 1.154i$

(c) $\frac{10}{13} - \frac{15}{13}i \approx 0.769 - 1.154i$

69. **71.**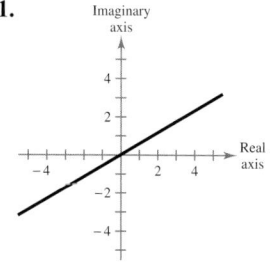

73. $-4 - 4i$ **75.** $-32i$ **77.** $-128\sqrt{3} - 128i$

79. $\dfrac{125}{2} + \dfrac{125\sqrt{3}}{2}i$ **81.** -1

83. $608.0204 + 144.6936i$

85. $-597 - 122i$ **87.** $\dfrac{81}{2} + \dfrac{81\sqrt{3}}{2}i$ **89.** $32i$

91. (a) $\sqrt{5}(\cos 60° + i\sin 60°)$

$\sqrt{5}(\cos 240° + i\sin 240°)$

(b)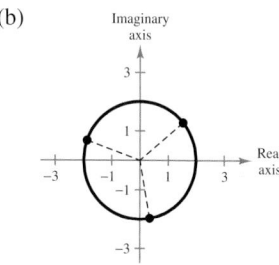

(c) $\dfrac{\sqrt{5}}{2} + \dfrac{\sqrt{15}}{2}i, \ -\dfrac{\sqrt{5}}{2} - \dfrac{\sqrt{15}}{2}i$

93. (a) $2\left(\cos\dfrac{2\pi}{9} + i\sin\dfrac{2\pi}{9}\right)$

$2\left(\cos\dfrac{8\pi}{9} + i\sin\dfrac{8\pi}{9}\right)$

$2\left(\cos\dfrac{14\pi}{9} + i\sin\dfrac{14\pi}{9}\right)$

(b)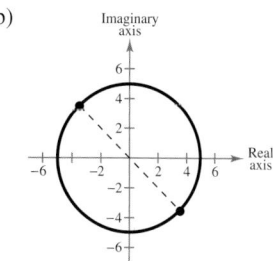

(c) $1.5321 + 1.2856i, \ -1.8794 + 0.6840i,$

$0.3473 - 1.9696i$

95. (a) $5\left(\cos\dfrac{3\pi}{4} + i\sin\dfrac{3\pi}{4}\right)$

$5\left(\cos\dfrac{7\pi}{4} + i\sin\dfrac{7\pi}{4}\right)$

(b)

(c) $-\dfrac{5\sqrt{2}}{2} + \dfrac{5\sqrt{2}}{2}i, \ \dfrac{5\sqrt{2}}{2} - \dfrac{5\sqrt{2}}{2}i$

97. (a) $5\left(\cos\dfrac{4\pi}{9} + i\sin\dfrac{4\pi}{9}\right)$

$5\left(\cos\dfrac{10\pi}{9} + i\sin\dfrac{10\pi}{9}\right)$

$5\left(\cos\dfrac{16\pi}{9} + i\sin\dfrac{16\pi}{9}\right)$

(b)

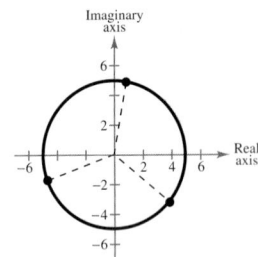

(c) $0.8682 + 4.9240i,\ -4.6985 - 1.7101i,$
$3.8302 - 3.2140i$

99. (a) $2(\cos 0 + i\sin 0)$

$2\left(\cos\dfrac{\pi}{2} + i\sin\dfrac{\pi}{2}\right)$

$2(\cos\pi + i\sin\pi)$

$2\left(\cos\dfrac{3\pi}{2} + i\sin\dfrac{3\pi}{2}\right)$

(b)

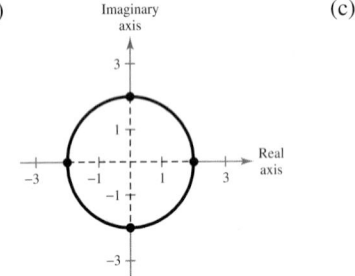

(c) $2, 2i, -2, -2i$

101. (a) $\cos 0 + i\sin 0$

$\cos\dfrac{2\pi}{5} + i\sin\dfrac{2\pi}{5}$

$\cos\dfrac{4\pi}{5} + i\sin\dfrac{4\pi}{5}$

$\cos\dfrac{6\pi}{5} + i\sin\dfrac{6\pi}{5}$

$\cos\dfrac{8\pi}{5} + i\sin\dfrac{8\pi}{5}$

(b)

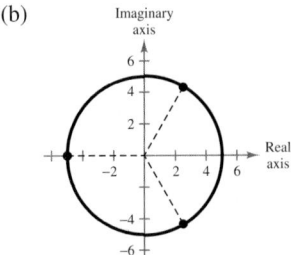

(c) $1, 0.3090 + 0.9511i,\ -0.8090 + 0.5878i,$
$-0.8090 - 0.5878i, 0.3090 - 0.9511i$

103. (a) $5\left(\cos\dfrac{\pi}{3} + i\sin\dfrac{\pi}{3}\right)$

$5(\cos\pi + i\sin\pi)$

$5\left(\cos\dfrac{5\pi}{3} + i\sin\dfrac{5\pi}{3}\right)$

(b)

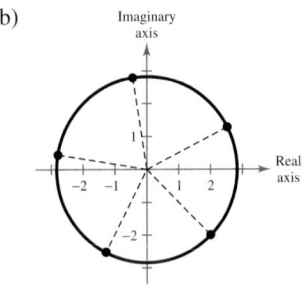

(c) $\dfrac{5}{2} + \dfrac{5\sqrt{3}}{2}i,\ -5,\ \dfrac{5}{2} - \dfrac{5\sqrt{3}}{2}i$

105. (a) $2\sqrt[5]{4\sqrt{2}}\left(\cos\dfrac{3\pi}{20} + i\sin\dfrac{3\pi}{20}\right)$

$2\sqrt[5]{4\sqrt{2}}\left(\cos\dfrac{11\pi}{20} + i\sin\dfrac{11\pi}{20}\right)$

$2\sqrt[5]{4\sqrt{2}}\left(\cos\dfrac{19\pi}{20} + i\sin\dfrac{19\pi}{20}\right)$

$2\sqrt[5]{4\sqrt{2}}\left(\cos\dfrac{27\pi}{20} + i\sin\dfrac{27\pi}{20}\right)$

$2\sqrt[5]{4\sqrt{2}}\left(\cos\dfrac{7\pi}{4} + i\sin\dfrac{7\pi}{4}\right)$

(b)

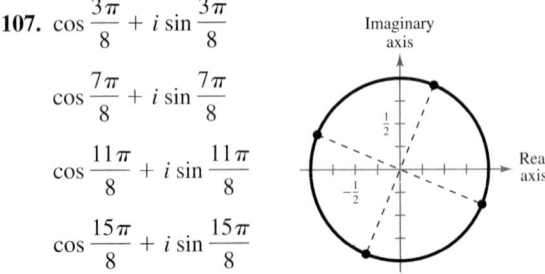

(c) $2.5201 + 1.2841i,\ -0.4425 + 2.7936i,$
$-2.7936 + 0.4425i,\ -1.2841 - 2.5201i,\ 2 - 2i$

107. $\cos\dfrac{3\pi}{8} + i\sin\dfrac{3\pi}{8}$

$\cos\dfrac{7\pi}{8} + i\sin\dfrac{7\pi}{8}$

$\cos\dfrac{11\pi}{8} + i\sin\dfrac{11\pi}{8}$

$\cos\dfrac{15\pi}{8} + i\sin\dfrac{15\pi}{8}$

109. $3\left(\cos\dfrac{\pi}{5} + i\sin\dfrac{\pi}{5}\right)$

$3\left(\cos\dfrac{3\pi}{5} + i\sin\dfrac{3\pi}{5}\right)$

$3(\cos\pi + i\sin\pi)$

$3\left(\cos\dfrac{7\pi}{5} + i\sin\dfrac{7\pi}{5}\right)$

$3\left(\cos\dfrac{9\pi}{5} + i\sin\dfrac{9\pi}{5}\right)$

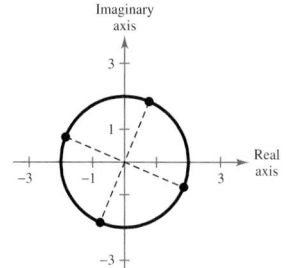

111. $2\left(\cos\dfrac{3\pi}{8} + i\sin\dfrac{3\pi}{8}\right)$

$2\left(\cos\dfrac{7\pi}{8} + i\sin\dfrac{7\pi}{8}\right)$

$2\left(\cos\dfrac{11\pi}{8} + i\sin\dfrac{11\pi}{8}\right)$

$2\left(\cos\dfrac{15\pi}{8} + i\sin\dfrac{15\pi}{8}\right)$

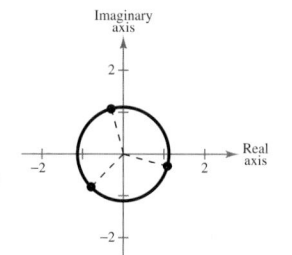

113. $\sqrt[6]{2}\left(\cos\dfrac{7\pi}{12} + i\sin\dfrac{7\pi}{12}\right)$

$\sqrt[6]{2}\left(\cos\dfrac{5\pi}{4} + i\sin\dfrac{5\pi}{4}\right)$

$\sqrt[6]{2}\left(\cos\dfrac{23\pi}{12} + i\sin\dfrac{23\pi}{12}\right)$

115. True, by the definition of the absolute value of a complex number.

117. True. $z_1 z_2 = r_1 r_2[\cos(\theta_1 + \theta_2) + i\sin(\theta_1 + \theta_2)] = 0$ if and only if $r_1 = 0$ and/or $r_2 = 0$.

119. Answers will vary.   **121.** (a) r^2 (b) $\cos 2\theta + i\sin 2\theta$

123. Answers will vary.

125. (a) $2(\cos 30° + i\sin 30°)$ (b) $8i$

$2(\cos 150° + i\sin 150°)$

$2(\cos 270° + i\sin 270°)$

127. $B = 68°, b \approx 19.80, c \approx 21.36$

129. $B = 60°, a \approx 65.01, c \approx 130.02$

131. $B = 47°45', a \approx 7.53, b \approx 8.29$

133. $16; 2$ **135.** $\frac{1}{16}; 0$

Review Exercises   *(page 461)*

1. $C = 74°, b \approx 13.19, c \approx 13.41$

3. $A = 26°, a \approx 24.89, c \approx 56.23$

5. $C = 66°, a \approx 2.53, b \approx 9.11$

7. $B = 108°, a \approx 11.76, c \approx 21.49$

9. $A \approx 20.41°, C \approx 9.59°, a \approx 20.92$

11. $B \approx 39.48°, C \approx 65.52°, c \approx 48.24$

13. 7.9 **15.** 33.5 **17.** 31.1 meters   **19.** 31.01 feet

21. $A \approx 29.69°, B \approx 52.41°, C \approx 97.90°$

23. $A \approx 29.92°, B \approx 86.18°, C \approx 63.90°$

25. $A = 35°, C = 35°, b \approx 6.55$

27. $A \approx 45.76°, B \approx 91.24°, c \approx 21.42$

29. 615.1 meters   **31.** 9.80 **33.** 8.36

35.

37.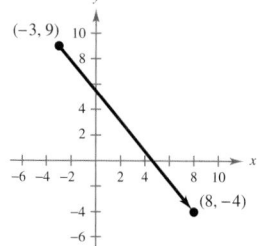

39. $\langle 7, -5\rangle$ **41.** $\langle 7, -7\rangle$ **43.** $\langle -4, 4\sqrt{3}\rangle$

45. $\langle 22, -7\rangle$ **47.** $\langle 30, 9\rangle$

   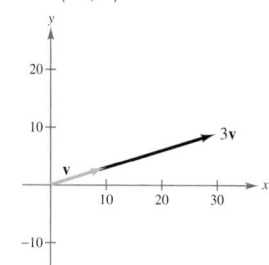

49. $-3i + 4j$ **51.** $6i + 4j$

53. $10\sqrt{2}(\cos 135° \, i + \sin 135° \, j)$ **55.** $\|v\| = 7; \theta = 60°$

57. $\|v\| = \sqrt{41}; \theta = 38.7°$ **59.** $\|v\| = 3\sqrt{2}; \theta = 225°$

61. The resultant force is 133.92 pounds and $5.6°$ from the 85-pound force.

63. 422.30 miles per hour; $130.4°$ **65.** 45 **67.** -2

69. 50; scalar   **71.** $\langle 6, -8\rangle$; vector   **73.** $\dfrac{11\pi}{12}$

75. $160.5°$ **77.** Orthogonal   **79.** Neither

81. $-\frac{13}{17}\langle 4, 1\rangle, \frac{16}{17}\langle -1, 4\rangle$ **83.** $\frac{5}{2}\langle -1, 1\rangle, \frac{9}{2}\langle 1, 1\rangle$ **85.** 48

87.

$7i$

7

89.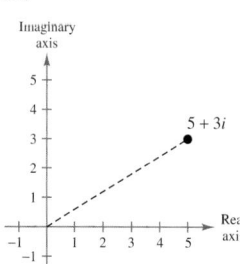

$5 + 3i$

$\sqrt{34}$

91. $5\sqrt{2}\left(\cos\dfrac{7\pi}{4} + i\sin\dfrac{7\pi}{4}\right)$

93. $6\left(\cos\dfrac{5\pi}{6} + i\sin\dfrac{5\pi}{6}\right)$

95. (a) $z_1 = 4\left(\cos\dfrac{11\pi}{6} + i\sin\dfrac{11\pi}{6}\right)$

$z_2 = 10\left(\cos\dfrac{3\pi}{2} + i\sin\dfrac{3\pi}{2}\right)$

(b) $z_1 z_2 = 40\left(\cos\dfrac{10\pi}{3} + i\sin\dfrac{10\pi}{3}\right)$

$\dfrac{z_1}{z_2} = \dfrac{2}{5}\left(\cos\dfrac{\pi}{3} + i\sin\dfrac{\pi}{3}\right)$

97. $\dfrac{625}{2} + \dfrac{625\sqrt{3}}{2}i$ **99.** $2035 - 828i$

101. (a) $4(\cos 60° + i\sin 60°)$ (b) -64

$4(\cos 180° + i\sin 180°)$

$4(\cos 300° + i\sin 300°)$

103. $3\left(\cos\dfrac{\pi}{4} + i\sin\dfrac{\pi}{4}\right)$

$3\left(\cos\dfrac{7\pi}{12} + i\sin\dfrac{7\pi}{12}\right)$

$3\left(\cos\dfrac{11\pi}{12} + i\sin\dfrac{11\pi}{12}\right)$

$3\left(\cos\dfrac{5\pi}{4} + i\sin\dfrac{5\pi}{4}\right)$

$3\left(\cos\dfrac{19\pi}{12} + i\sin\dfrac{19\pi}{12}\right)$

$3\left(\cos\dfrac{23\pi}{12} + i\sin\dfrac{23\pi}{12}\right)$

105. $3\left(\cos\dfrac{\pi}{4} + i\sin\dfrac{\pi}{4}\right) = \dfrac{3\sqrt{2}}{2} + \dfrac{3\sqrt{2}}{2}i$

$3\left(\cos\dfrac{3\pi}{4} + i\sin\dfrac{3\pi}{4}\right) = -\dfrac{3\sqrt{2}}{2} + \dfrac{3\sqrt{2}}{2}i$

$3\left(\cos\dfrac{5\pi}{4} + i\sin\dfrac{5\pi}{4}\right) = -\dfrac{3\sqrt{2}}{2} - \dfrac{3\sqrt{2}}{2}i$

$3\left(\cos\dfrac{7\pi}{4} + i\sin\dfrac{7\pi}{4}\right) = \dfrac{3\sqrt{2}}{2} - \dfrac{3\sqrt{2}}{2}i$

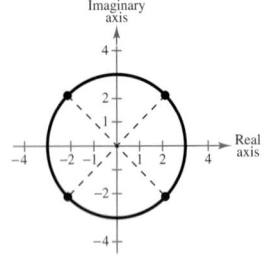

107. $2\left(\cos\dfrac{\pi}{2} + i\sin\dfrac{\pi}{2}\right) = 2i$

$2\left(\cos\dfrac{7\pi}{6} + i\sin\dfrac{7\pi}{6}\right) = -\sqrt{3} - i$

$2\left(\cos\dfrac{11\pi}{6} + i\sin\dfrac{11\pi}{6}\right) = \sqrt{3} - i$

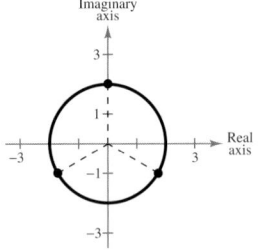

109. True. $\sin 90°$ is defined in the Law of Sines.

111. True. By definition, $\mathbf{u} = \dfrac{\mathbf{v}}{\|\mathbf{v}\|}$, so $\mathbf{v} = \|\mathbf{v}\|\mathbf{u}$

113. False. The solutions to $x^2 - 8i = 0$ are $x = 2 + 2i$ and $-2 - 2i$.

115. $a^2 = b^2 + c^2 - 2bc\cos A,$ **117.** **A** and **C**

$b^2 = a^2 + c^2 - 2ac\cos B,$

$c^2 = a^2 + b^2 - 2ab\cos C$

119. If $k > 0$, the direction is the same and the magnitude is k times as great.

If $k < 0$, the result is a vector in the opposite direction and the magnitude is $|k|$ times as great.

121. $z_1 z_2 = -4;\ \dfrac{z_1}{z_2} = \cos(2\theta - \pi) + i\sin(2\theta - \pi)$

$= -\cos 2\theta - i\sin 2\theta$

Chapter Test   *(page 465)*

1. $C = 88°, b \approx 27.81, c \approx 29.98$

2. $A = 43°, b \approx 25.75, c \approx 14.45$

3. Two solutions:

$B \approx 29.12°, C \approx 126.88°, c \approx 22.03$

$B \approx 150.88°, C \approx 5.12°, c \approx 2.46$

4. No solution   **5.** $A \approx 39.96°, C \approx 40.04°, c \approx 15.02$

6. $A \approx 23.43°, B \approx 33.57°, c \approx 86.46$

7. 2052.5 square meters   **8.** 606.3 miles; 29.1°

9. $\langle 14, -23 \rangle$ **10.** $\left\langle \dfrac{18\sqrt{34}}{17}, -\dfrac{30\sqrt{34}}{17} \right\rangle$

11. $\langle -4, 6 \rangle$

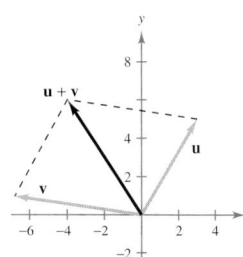

12. $\langle 10, 4 \rangle$

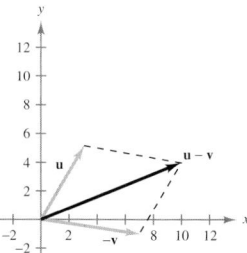

13. $\langle 36, 22 \rangle$

14. $\left\langle \frac{4}{5}, -\frac{3}{5} \right\rangle$

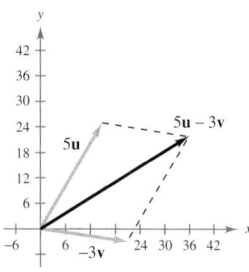

15. $14.9°$; 250.15 pounds **16.** $135°$ **17.** No

18. $\frac{37}{26}\langle 5, 1 \rangle; \frac{29}{26}\langle -1, 5 \rangle$ **19.** $5\sqrt{2}\left(\cos \frac{7\pi}{4} + i \sin \frac{7\pi}{4} \right)$

20. $-3 + 3\sqrt{3}i$ **21.** $-\frac{6561}{2} - \frac{6561\sqrt{3}}{2}i$ **22.** $5832i$

23. $4\sqrt[4]{2}\left(\cos \frac{\pi}{12} + i \sin \frac{\pi}{12} \right)$

$4\sqrt[4]{2}\left(\cos \frac{7\pi}{12} + i \sin \frac{7\pi}{12} \right)$

$4\sqrt[4]{2}\left(\cos \frac{13\pi}{12} + i \sin \frac{13\pi}{12} \right)$

$4\sqrt[4]{2}\left(\cos \frac{19\pi}{12} + i \sin \frac{19\pi}{12} \right)$

24. $3\left(\cos \frac{\pi}{6} + i \sin \frac{\pi}{6} \right)$

$3\left(\cos \frac{5\pi}{6} + i \sin \frac{5\pi}{6} \right)$

$3\left(\cos \frac{3\pi}{2} + i \sin \frac{3\pi}{2} \right)$

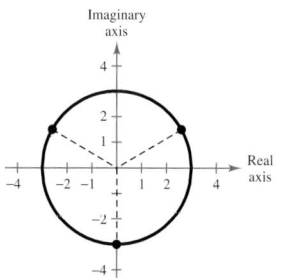

Cumulative Test for Chapters 4–6
(page 466)

1. (a)

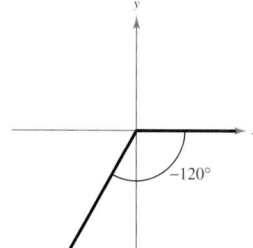

(b) $240°$

(c) $-\frac{2\pi}{3}$

(d) $60°$

(e) $\sin(-120°) = -\frac{\sqrt{3}}{2}$ $\qquad \csc(-120°) = -\frac{2\sqrt{3}}{3}$

$\cos(-120°) = -\frac{1}{2}$ $\qquad \sec(-120°) = -2$

$\tan(-120°) = \sqrt{3}$ $\qquad \cot(-120°) = \frac{\sqrt{3}}{3}$

2. $134.6°$ **3.** $\frac{3}{5}$

4. Period: 2; Amplitude: 2 **5.** Period: π

 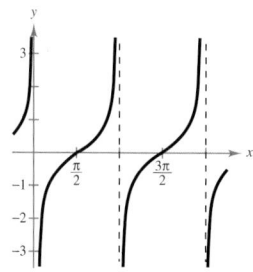

6. $a = -3, b = \pi, c = 0$

7.

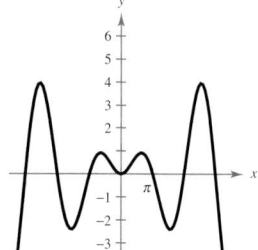

8. 6.7 **9.** $\frac{3}{4}$ **10.** $\sqrt{1 - 4x^2}$ **11.** 1

12. $2 \tan \theta$ **13–15.** Answers will vary.

16. $\frac{\pi}{3}, \frac{\pi}{2}, \frac{3\pi}{2}, \frac{5\pi}{3}$ **17.** $\frac{\pi}{6}, \frac{5\pi}{6}, \frac{7\pi}{6}, \frac{11\pi}{6}$ **18.** $\frac{3\pi}{2}$

19. $\frac{16}{63}$ **20.** $\frac{4}{3}$ **21.** $\frac{\sqrt{5}}{5}, \frac{2\sqrt{5}}{5}$ **22.** $\frac{5}{2}\left(\sin \frac{5\pi}{2} - \sin \pi \right)$

23. $B \approx 26.39°, C \approx 123.61°, c \approx 15.0$

24. $B \approx 52.48°, C \approx 97.52°, a \approx 5.04$

25. $B = 60°, a \approx 5.77, c \approx 11.55$

26. $A = 26.38°, B \approx 62.72°, C \approx 90.90°$

27. 36.4 square inches **28.** 85.2 square inches

29. $3\mathbf{i} + 5\mathbf{j}$ **30.** -5 **31.** $-\frac{1}{13}\langle 1, 5\rangle; \frac{21}{13}\langle 5, -1\rangle$

32. $2\sqrt{2}\left(\cos\dfrac{3\pi}{4} + i\sin\dfrac{3\pi}{4}\right)$ **33.** $-12\sqrt{3} + 12i$

34. $\cos 0 + i\sin 0 = 1$

$\cos\dfrac{2\pi}{3} + i\sin\dfrac{2\pi}{3} = -\dfrac{1}{2} + \dfrac{\sqrt{3}}{2}i$

$\cos\dfrac{4\pi}{3} + i\sin\dfrac{4\pi}{3} = -\dfrac{1}{2} - \dfrac{\sqrt{3}}{2}i$

35. $4\left(\cos\dfrac{\pi}{8} + i\sin\dfrac{\pi}{8}\right)$ **36.** 5 feet

$4\left(\cos\dfrac{5\pi}{8} + i\sin\dfrac{5\pi}{8}\right)$

$4\left(\cos\dfrac{9\pi}{8} + i\sin\dfrac{9\pi}{8}\right)$

$4\left(\cos\dfrac{13\pi}{8} + i\sin\dfrac{13\pi}{8}\right)$

37. ≈ 500 revolutions per minute; ≈ 20 minutes

38. $22.6°$ **39.** $d = 4\cos\dfrac{\pi}{4}t$

40. $32.6°$; 543.9 kilometers per hour

Problem Solving   *(page 472)*

1. 2.01 feet

3. (a) Station A: 27.45 miles; Station B: 53.03 miles
     (b) 11.03 miles; S 21.7° E

5. (a) (i) $\sqrt{2}$ (ii) $\sqrt{5}$ (iii) 1
       (iv) 1   (v) 1   (vi) 1
     (b) (i) 1   (ii) $3\sqrt{2}$ (iii) $\sqrt{13}$
       (iv) 1   (v) 1   (vi) 1
     (c) (i) $\dfrac{\sqrt{5}}{2}$ (ii) $\sqrt{13}$ (iii) $\dfrac{\sqrt{85}}{2}$
       (iv) 1   (v) 1   (vi) 1
     (d) (i) $2\sqrt{5}$ (ii) $5\sqrt{2}$ (iii) $5\sqrt{2}$
       (iv) 1   (v) 1   (vi) 1

7. $\mathbf{w} = \frac{1}{2}(\mathbf{u} + \mathbf{v})$; $\mathbf{w} = \frac{1}{2}(\mathbf{v} - \mathbf{u})$

9. (a)

The amount of work done by $\mathbf{F}_1$ is equal to the amount of work done by $\mathbf{F}_2$.

   (b)
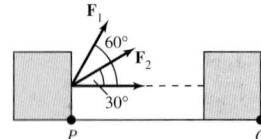

The amount of work done by $\mathbf{F}_2$ is $\sqrt{3}$ times as great as the amount of work done by $\mathbf{F}_1$.

Chapter 7

Section 7.1   *(page 483)*

1. d   **3.** b   **5.** $(2, 2)$ **7.** $(2, 6), (-1, 3)$

9. $(0, -5), (4, 3)$ **11.** $(0, 0), (2, -4)$

13. $(0, 1), (1, -1), (3, 1)$ **15.** $(5, 5)$ **17.** $\left(\frac{1}{2}, 3\right)$

19. $(1, 1)$ **21.** $\left(\frac{20}{3}, \frac{40}{3}\right)$ **23.** No solution

25. $(-2, 4), (0, 0)$ **27.** $(0, 0), (-1, -1), (1, 1)$

29. $(4, 3)$ **31.** $\left(\frac{5}{2}, \frac{3}{2}\right)$ **33.** $(2, 2), (4, 0)$

35. $(1, 4), (4, 7)$ **37.** $\left(4, -\frac{1}{2}\right)$

39. No solution   **41.** $(4, 3), (-4, 3)$

43.

$(0, 1)$

45.

$(4, 2)$

47.

$(0, 0), (1, 1)$

49.
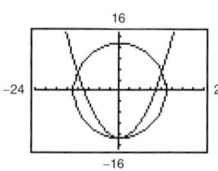
$(0, -13), (\pm 12, 5)$

51. $(1, 2)$ **53.** $(-2, 0), \left(\frac{29}{10}, \frac{21}{10}\right)$ **55.** No solution

57. $(0.287, 1.751)$ **59.** $(-1, 0), (0, 1), (1, 0)$

61. $\left(\frac{1}{2}, 2\right), \left(-4, -\frac{1}{4}\right)$ **63.** 192 units   **65.** 3133 units

67. (a) 781 units   (b) 3708 units

69. (a) $\begin{cases} x + \quad\;\; y = 25{,}000 \\ 0.06x + 0.085y = \;\;2{,}000 \end{cases}$

   (b)
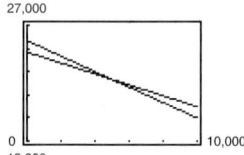

   (c) \$5000

   Decreases; Interest is fixed.

71. More than \$11,666.67

73. (a)

   (b) 24.7 inches

   (c) Doyle Log Rule

75. (a) $f(t) = 4270.2t + 65{,}082$

   $g(t) = -552.00t^2 + 12{,}550.2t + 34{,}722$

(b)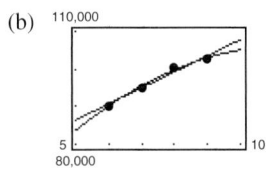

(c) (8.62, 101,882.73), (6.38, 92,334.27)

(d) (8.62, 101,888.70), (6.38, 92,323.45)

(e) $f = 129,135,000$, $g = 98,775,000$

(f) f is more accurate.

77. 6×9 meters   **79.** 9×12 inches

81. 8×12 kilometers

83. False. To solve a system of equations by substitution, you can solve for either variable in one of the two equations and then back-substitute.

85. 1. *Solve* one of the equations for one variable in terms of the other.

2. *Substitute* the expression found in Step 1 into the other equation to obtain an equation in one variable.

3. *Solve* the equation obtained in Step 2.

4. *Back-substitute* the value obtained in Step 3 into the expression obtained in Step 1 to find the value of the other variable.

5. *Check* that the solution satisfies each of the original equations.

87. (a) $y = 2x$ (b) $y = 0$ (c) $y = x - 2$

89. $2x + 7y - 45 = 0$ **91.** $y - 3 = 0$

93. $30x - 17y - 18 = 0$

95. Domain: All real numbers $x \neq 6$

Horizontal asymptote: $y = 0$

Vertical asymptote: $x = 6$

97. Domain: All real numbers $x \neq \pm 4$

Horizontal asymptote: $y = 1$

Vertical asymptotes: $x = \pm 4$

Section 7.2   *(page 495)*

1. $(2, 1)$ **3.** $(1, -1)$

                    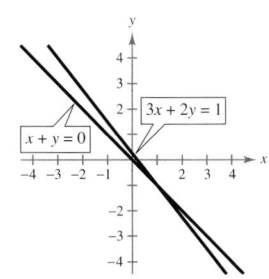

5. No solution

7. $\left(a, \frac{3}{2}a - \frac{5}{2}\right)$

          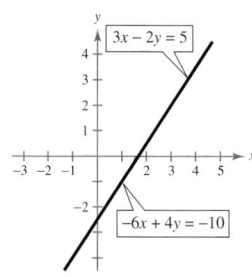

9. $\left(\frac{1}{3}, -\frac{2}{3}\right)$ **11.** $\left(\frac{5}{2}, \frac{3}{4}\right)$

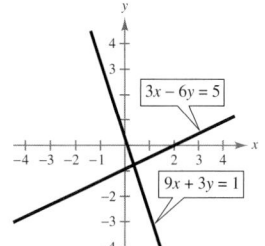

13. $(3, 4)$ **15.** $(4, -1)$

17. $\left(\frac{12}{7}, \frac{18}{7}\right)$ **19.** No solution   **21.** $\left(\frac{18}{5}, \frac{3}{5}\right)$

23. $\left(a, \frac{5}{6}a - \frac{1}{2}\right)$ **25.** $\left(\frac{90}{31}, -\frac{67}{31}\right)$

27. $\left(-\frac{6}{35}, \frac{43}{35}\right)$ **29.** $(5, -2)$

31. b   **32.** a   **33.** c   **34.** d

35. $(4, 1)$ **37.** $(2, -1)$ **39.** $(6, -3)$

41. $\left(\frac{43}{6}, \frac{25}{6}\right)$ **43.** $(80, 10)$ **45.** $(2,000,000, 100)$

47. 550 miles per hour, 50 miles per hour

49. (a) $\begin{cases} x + y = 10 \\ 0.2x + 0.5y = 3 \end{cases}$

(b)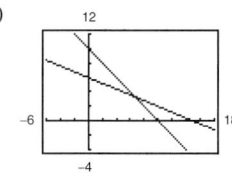

Decreases

(c) 20% solution: $6\frac{2}{3}$ liters

50% solution: $3\frac{1}{3}$ liters

51. \$6000   **53.** 400 adult, 1035 student

55. $y = 0.97x + 2.1$

57. $y = 0.32x + 4.1$

59. $y = -2x + 4$

61. (a) and (b) $y = 3.705t + 48.63$

(c)

Year	1995	1996	1997	1998	1999
y	\$67.16	\$70.86	\$74.57	\$78.27	\$81.98

(d) \$104.21   (e) 2003

63. False. Two lines that coincide have infinitely many points of intersection.

65. (39,600, 398). It is necessary to change the scale on the axes to see the point of intersection.

67. No. Two lines will intersect only once or will coincide, and if they coincide the system will have infinitely many solutions.

69. $k = -4$

71. $x \le -\frac{22}{3}$

73. $x \le \frac{19}{16}$

75. $-2 < x < 18$

77. $-5 < x < \frac{7}{2}$

79. $-\dfrac{6}{x + 5} + \dfrac{7}{x + 6}$ **81.** $\ln 6x$ **83.** $\log_9 \dfrac{12}{x}$

85. No solution

Section 7.3   (page 507)

1. d   **3.** c   **5.** $(1, -2, 4)$ **7.** $(3, 10, 2)$

9. $\left(\frac{1}{2}, -2, 2\right)$

11. $\begin{cases} x - 2y + 3z = 5 \\ \quad\ y - 2z = 9 \\ 2x \qquad\ - 3z = 0 \end{cases}$

First step in putting the system in row-echelon form

13. $(1, 2, 3)$ **15.** $(-4, 8, 5)$ **17.** $(5, -2, 0)$

19. No solution   **21.** $\left(-\frac{1}{2}, 1, \frac{3}{2}\right)$

23. $(-3a + 10, 5a - 7, a)$ **25.** $(-a + 3, a + 1, a)$

27. $(2a, 21a - 1, 8a)$ **29.** $\left(-\frac{3}{2}a + \frac{1}{2}, -\frac{2}{3}a + 1, a\right)$

31. $(1, 1, 1, 1)$ **33.** No solution   **35.** $(0, 0, 0)$

37. $(9a, -35a, 67a)$

39. $y = \frac{1}{2}x^2 - 2x$ **41.** $y = x^2 - 6x + 8$

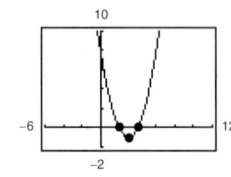

43. $x^2 + y^2 - 4x = 0$ **45.** $x^2 + y^2 + 6x - 8y = 0$

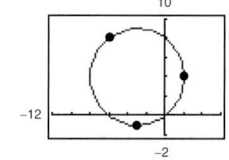

47. $s = -16t^2 + 144$ **49.** $s = -16t^2 - 32t + 500$

51. 8 touchdowns, 8 extra-point kicks, 2 field goals

53. \$300,000 at 8%
\$400,000 at 9%
\$75,000 at 10%

55. $250,000 - \frac{1}{2}s$ in certificates of deposit,
$125,000 + \frac{1}{2}s$ in municipal bonds,
$125,000 - s$ in blue-chip stocks,
s in growth stocks

57. Use four medium trucks or use two large, one medium, and two small trucks. Other answers are possible.

59. No 10% solution, $8\frac{1}{3}$ liters of 20% solution, $1\frac{2}{3}$ liters of 50% solution

61. $t_1 = 96$ pounds
$t_2 = 48$ pounds
$a = -16$ feet per second squared

63. $\dfrac{1}{2}\left(-\dfrac{2}{x} + \dfrac{1}{x - 1} + \dfrac{1}{x + 1}\right)$

65. $\dfrac{1}{2}\left(\dfrac{1}{x} - \dfrac{1}{x - 2} + \dfrac{2}{x + 3}\right)$

67. $y = -\frac{5}{24}x^2 - \frac{3}{10}x + \frac{41}{6}$ **69.** $y = x^2 - x$

71. (a) $y = -0.0075x^2 + 1.3x + 20$

(b)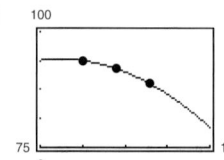

(c)

x	100	120	140
y	75	68	55

The values are the same.

(d) 24.25%   (e) 156 females

73. $x = 5$ **75.** $x = \pm\sqrt{2}/2$ or $x = 0$
$y = 5$ $y = \frac{1}{2}$ $y = 0$
$\lambda = -5$ $\lambda = 1$ $\lambda = 0$

77. False. Equation 2 does not have a leading coefficient of 1.

79. No. Answers will vary.

81. $\begin{cases} 3x + y - z = 9 \\ \quad x + 2y - z = 0 \\ -x + y + 3z = 1 \end{cases}$ $\begin{cases} x + y + z = 5 \\ x \qquad - 2z = 0 \\ \quad\ 2y + z = 0 \end{cases}$

83. $\begin{cases} x + 2y - 4z = -5 \\ -x - 4y + 8z = 13 \\ x + 6y + 4z = 7 \end{cases}$ $\begin{cases} x + 2y + 4z = 9 \\ y + 2z = 3 \\ x - 4z = -4 \end{cases}$

85. 6.375   **87.** 80,000   **89.** $11 + i$

91. $22 + 3i$ **93.** $\frac{7}{2} + \frac{7}{2}i$

95. (a) $-4, 0, 3$ (b)

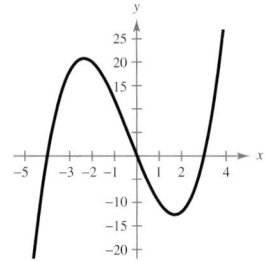

97. (a) $-4, -\frac{3}{2}, 3$

(b)

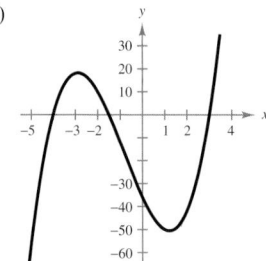

99.

x	-2	0	2	4	5
y	-5	-4.996	-4.938	-4	-1

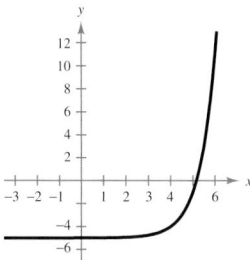

101.

x	-2	-1	0	1	2
y	5.793	4.671	4	3.598	3.358

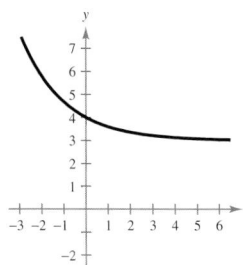

103. $(40, 40)$

Section 7.4   *(page 519)*

1.

3.

5.

7.

9.

11.

13.

15.

17.

19.

21.

23.

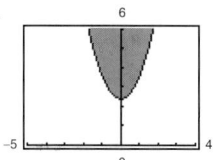

25. $y \leq \frac{1}{2}x + 2$ **27.** $y \geq -\frac{2}{3}x + 2$

29. c and d   **31.** a, c, and d

33.

35.

37.

39. No solution

41.

43.

45.

47.

49.

51.

53. $\begin{cases} y \leq 4 - x \\ x \geq 0 \\ y \geq 0 \end{cases}$ **55.** $\begin{cases} y \geq 4 - x \\ y \geq 2 - \frac{1}{4}x \\ x \geq 0, \ y \geq 0 \end{cases}$

57. $\begin{cases} x^2 + y^2 \leq 16 \\ x \geq 0 \\ y \geq 0 \end{cases}$ **59.** $\begin{cases} 2 \leq x \leq 5 \\ 1 \leq y \leq 7 \end{cases}$ **61.** $\begin{cases} y \leq \frac{3}{2}x \\ y \leq -x + 5 \\ y \geq 0 \end{cases}$

63. Consumer surplus: $1600

Producer surplus: $400

65. Consumer surplus: $40,000,000

Producer surplus: $20,000,000

67. $\begin{cases} x + \frac{3}{2}y \leq 12 \\ \frac{4}{3}x + \frac{3}{2}y \leq 15 \\ x \qquad \geq 0 \\ \qquad y \geq 0 \end{cases}$

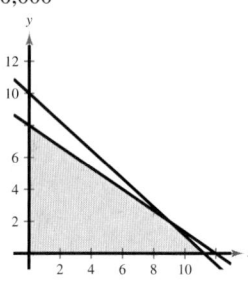

69. $\begin{cases} x + y \leq 20{,}000 \\ \quad y \geq 2x \\ x \quad \geq 5{,}000 \\ \quad y \geq 5{,}000 \end{cases}$

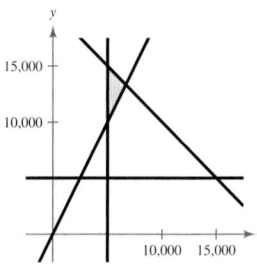

71. $\begin{cases} 55x + 70y \leq 7500 \\ x \qquad \geq 50 \\ \qquad y \geq 40 \end{cases}$

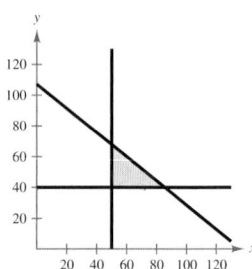

73. (a) $y = 1099.7t - 3484$

(b)

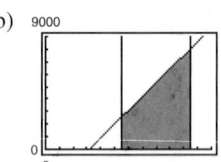

(c) 26,568 electric-powered vehicles

75. True. The figure is a rectangle with a length of 9 units and a width of 11 units.

77. The graph is a half-line on the real number line; on the rectangular coordinate system, the graph is a half-plane.

79. (a) $\begin{cases} \pi y^2 - \pi x^2 \geq 10 \\ \quad\quad y > x \\ \quad\quad x > 0 \end{cases}$

(b)

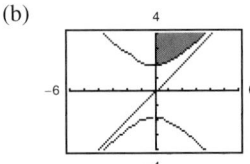

(c) The line is an asymptote to the boundary. The larger the circles, the closer the radii can be and the constraint will still be satisfied.

81. d   **82.** b   **83.** c   **84.** a

85. $5x + 3y - 8 = 0$ **87.** $28x + 17y + 13 = 0$

89. $x + y + 1.8 = 0$

91. (a) $y_1 = 53.32t + 612.8$

$y_2 = 3.400t^2 + 9.12t + 746.5$

(b)

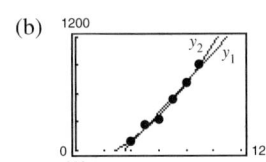

(c) The models are accurate.

93. 52.619   **95.** 0.064

Section 7.5   (page 529)

1. Minimum at $(0, 0)$: 0
Maximum at $(5, 0)$: 20

3. Minimum at $(0, 0)$: 0
Maximum at $(0, 5)$: 40

5. Minimum at $(0, 0)$: 0
Maximum at $(3, 4)$: 17

7. Minimum at $(0, 0)$: 0
Maximum at $(4, 0)$: 20

9. Minimum at $(0, 0)$: 0
Maximum at $(60, 20)$: 740

11. Minimum at $(0, 0)$: 0
Maximum at any point on the line segment connecting $(60, 20)$ and $(30, 45)$: 2100

13.

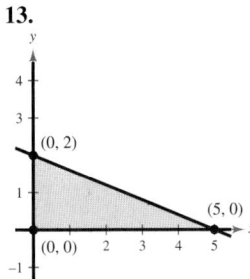

Minimum at $(0, 0)$: 0
Maximum at $(5, 0)$: 30

15.

Minimum at $(0, 0)$: 0
Maximum at $(0, 2)$: 48

17.

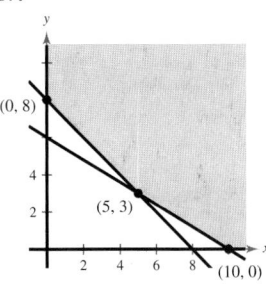

Minimum at $(5, 3)$: 35
No maximum

19.

Minimum at $(10, 0)$: 20
No maximum

21.

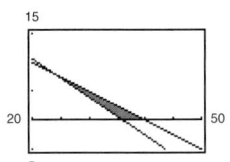

Minimum at $(24, 8)$: 104
Maximum at $(40, 0)$: 160

23.

Minimum at $(36, 0)$: 36
Maximum at $(24, 8)$: 56

25. Maximum at $(3, 6)$: 12   **27.** Maximum at $(0, 10)$: 10

29. Maximum at $(0, 5)$: 25   **31.** Maximum at $\left(\frac{22}{3}, \frac{19}{6}\right)$: $\frac{271}{6}$

33. 750 units of model A
1000 units of model B
Maximum profit: $83,750

35. (a) $P = 25x + 40y$

(b) $150x + 200y \leq 40{,}000$
$x + \quad y \leq 250$
$x \geq 0$
$y \geq 0$

(c)

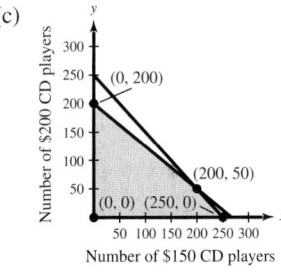

Number of $150 CD players

(d) 0 units of the $150 model
200 units of the $200 model

(e) Maximum profit: $8000

37. Three bags of brand X
Six bags of brand Y
Minimum cost: $195

39. Four audits
32 tax returns
Maximum revenue: $17,600

41. $62,500 to type A
$187,500 to type B

43.

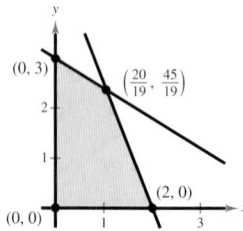

The maximum, 5, occurs at any point on the line segment connecting $(2, 0)$ and $\left(\frac{20}{19}, \frac{45}{19}\right)$.

45.

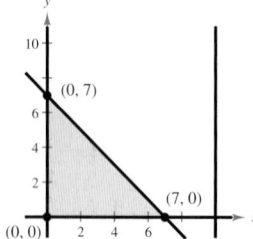

The constraint $x \le 10$ is extraneous. Maximum at $(0, 7)$: 14

47.

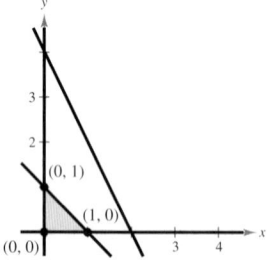

The constraint $2x + y \le 4$ is extraneous. Maximum at $(0, 1)$: 4

49. True. The objective function has a maximum value at any point on the line segment connecting the two vertices.

51. (a) $t \ge 9$ (b) $\frac{3}{4} \le t \le 9$ **53.** $z = x + 5y$

55. $z = 4x + y$

57. $\dfrac{9}{2(x + 3)}$, $x \ne 0$ **59.** $\dfrac{x^2 + 2x - 13}{x(x - 2)}$, $x \ne \pm 3$

61. $\ln 3 \approx 1.099$ **63.** $4 \ln 38 \approx 14.550$

65. $\frac{1}{3}e^{12/7} \approx 1.851$ **67.** $(-4, 3, -7)$

Review Exercises *(page 534)*

1. $(5, 4)$ **3.** $(0, 0), (2, 8), (-2, 8)$ **5.** $(4, -2)$

7. $(1.41, -0.66), (-1.41, 10.66)$

9.

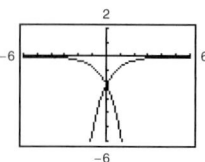

$(0, -2)$

11. 10,417 units **13.** 96×144 meters **15.** $\left(\frac{5}{2}, 3\right)$

17. $(-0.5, 0.8)$ **19.** $(0, 0)$ **21.** $\left(\frac{8}{5}a + \frac{14}{5}, a\right)$

23. d **24.** c **25.** b **26.** a

27. $\left(\dfrac{500,000}{7}, \dfrac{159}{7}\right)$ **29.** $(2, -4, -5)$ **31.** $\left(\frac{24}{5}, \frac{22}{5}, -\frac{8}{5}\right)$

33. $(3a + 4, 2a + 5, a)$ **35.** $(a - 4, a - 3, a)$

37. $y = 2x^2 + x - 5$ **39.** $x^2 + y^2 - 4x + 4y - 1 = 0$

41. $-\dfrac{4}{x + 4} + \dfrac{3}{x + 2}$ **43.** $-\dfrac{1}{x + 1} + \dfrac{2}{x + 2}$

45. (a) $y = 596.50x^2 - 7147.5x + 20,083$

(b)

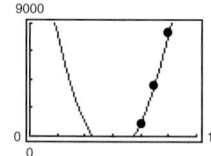

The model is a "good fit" for the data.

(c) 47,083. No.

47. $16,000 at 7%
$13,000 at 9%
$11,000 at 11%

49.

51.

53.

55.

57.

59.

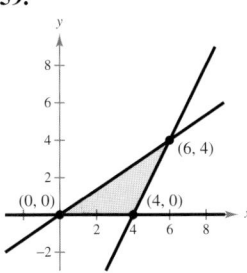

61. $\begin{cases} x + y \leq 1500 \\ x \quad\;\; \geq 400 \\ \quad\;\; y \geq 600 \end{cases}$

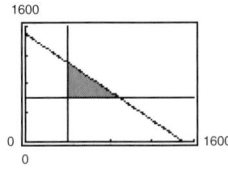

63. Consumer surplus: $4,500,000

Producer surplus: $9,000,000

65.

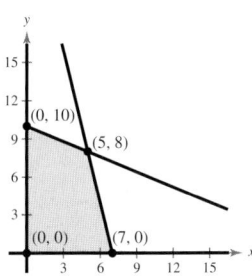

Minimum at $(0, 0)$: 0

Maximum at $(5, 8)$: 47

67.

Minimum at $(15, 0)$: 26.25

No maximum

69.

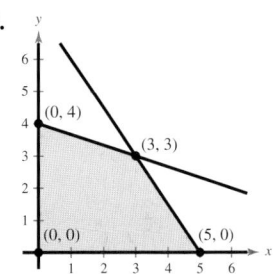

Minimum at $(0, 0)$: 0

Maximum at $(3, 3)$: 48

71. 72 haircuts, 0 permanents; Maximum revenue: $1800

73. Three bags of brand X
Two bags of brand Y
Minimum cost: $105

75. False. To represent a region covered by an isosceles trapezoid, the last two inequality signs should be $\leq$.

77. $\begin{cases} x + y = \quad 2 \\ x - y = -14 \end{cases}$ **79.** $\begin{cases} 3x + \;\; y = 7 \\ -6x + 3y = 1 \end{cases}$

81. $\begin{cases} x + y + z = 6 \\ x + y - z = 0 \\ x - y - z = 2 \end{cases}$ **83.** $\begin{cases} 2x + 2y - 3z = \quad 7 \\ x - 2y + \;\; z = \quad 4 \\ -x + 4y - \;\; z = -1 \end{cases}$

85. An inconsistent system of linear equations has no solution.

87. Answers will vary.

Chapter Test   *(page 538)*

1. $(-3, 4)$ **2.** $(0, -1)$, $(1, 0)$, $(2, 1)$

3. $(8, 4)$, $(2, -2)$

4.

$(3, 2)$

5.

$(-3, 0)$, $(2, 5)$

6.

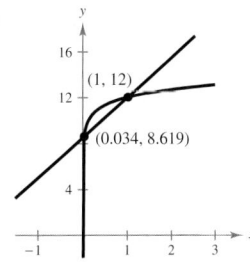

$(1, 12)$, $(0.034, 8.619)$

7. $(1, 5)$ **8.** $(2, -1)$

9. $(2, -3, 1)$ **10.** No solution

11.

12.

13.

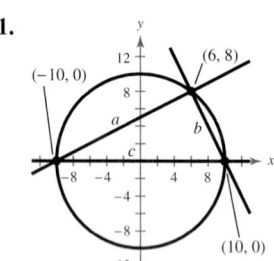

14. Maximum at $(12, 0)$: 240   **15.** 8%: $20,000
8.5%: $30,000

16. $y = -\frac{1}{2}x^2 + x + 6$

17. 0 units of model I
5300 units of model II
Maximum profit: $212,000

Problem Solving   *(page 540)*

1.

$a = 8\sqrt{5}, b = 4\sqrt{5}, c = 20$

$\left(8\sqrt{5}\right)^2 + \left(4\sqrt{5}\right)^2 = 20^2$

Therefore, the triangle is a right triangle.

3. $ad \neq cd$ **5.** (a) One   (b) Two   (c) Four

7. 10.1 feet deep; ≈ 252.7 feet long   **9.** $12.00

11. (a) $(3, -4)$ (b) $\left(\dfrac{2}{-a + 5}, \dfrac{1}{4a - 1}, \dfrac{1}{a}\right)$

13. (a) $(-5a + 16, 5a - 16, 6a)$

(b) $(-11a + 36, 13a - 40, 14a)$

(c) $(-a + 3, a - 3, a)$ (d) Infinitely many

15. (a) $\begin{cases} y \geq 91 + 3.7x \\ y \leq 119 + 4.9x \\ x \geq 0 \\ y \geq 0 \end{cases}$ (b)

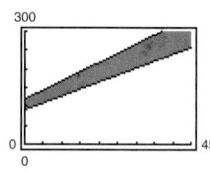

(c) 142.8 pounds $\leq y \leq$ 187.6 pounds

Chapter 8

Section 8.1   *(page 554)*

1. 1×2 **3.** 3×1 **5.** 2×2

7. $\begin{bmatrix} 4 & -3 & \vdots & -5 \\ -1 & 3 & \vdots & 12 \end{bmatrix}$ **9.** $\begin{bmatrix} 1 & 10 & -2 & \vdots & 2 \\ 5 & -3 & 4 & \vdots & 0 \\ 2 & 1 & 0 & \vdots & 6 \end{bmatrix}$

11. $\begin{bmatrix} 7 & -5 & 1 & \vdots & 13 \\ 19 & 0 & -8 & \vdots & 10 \end{bmatrix}$

13. $\begin{cases} x + 2y = 7 \\ 2x - 3y = 4 \end{cases}$ **15.** $\begin{cases} 2x & + 5z = -12 \\ & y - 2z = 7 \\ 6x + 3y & = 2 \end{cases}$

17. $\begin{cases} 9x + 12y + 3z & = 0 \\ -2x + 18y + 5z + 2w = 10 \\ x + 7y - 8z & = -4 \\ 3x & + 2z = -10 \end{cases}$

19. $\begin{bmatrix} 1 & 4 & 3 \\ 0 & 2 & -1 \end{bmatrix}$ **21.** $\begin{bmatrix} 1 & 1 & 4 & -1 \\ 0 & 5 & -2 & 6 \\ 0 & 3 & 20 & 4 \end{bmatrix}$

$\begin{bmatrix} 1 & 1 & 4 & -1 \\ 0 & 1 & -\frac{2}{5} & \frac{6}{5} \\ 0 & 3 & 20 & 4 \end{bmatrix}$

23. Add 5 times Row 2 to Row 1.

25. Interchange Row 1 and Row 2. Add 4 times new Row 1 to Row 3.

27. Reduced row-echelon form

29. Not in row-echelon form

31. (a) $\begin{bmatrix} 1 & 2 & 3 \\ 0 & -5 & -10 \\ 3 & 1 & -1 \end{bmatrix}$ (b) $\begin{bmatrix} 1 & 2 & 3 \\ 0 & -5 & -10 \\ 0 & -5 & -10 \end{bmatrix}$

(c) $\begin{bmatrix} 1 & 2 & 3 \\ 0 & -5 & -10 \\ 0 & 0 & 0 \end{bmatrix}$ (d) $\begin{bmatrix} 1 & 2 & 3 \\ 0 & 1 & 2 \\ 0 & 0 & 0 \end{bmatrix}$

(e) $\begin{bmatrix} 1 & 0 & -1 \\ 0 & 1 & 2 \\ 0 & 0 & 0 \end{bmatrix}$

The matrix is in reduced row-echelon form.

33. $\begin{bmatrix} 1 & 1 & 0 & 5 \\ 0 & 1 & 2 & 0 \\ 0 & 0 & 1 & -1 \end{bmatrix}$ **35.** $\begin{bmatrix} 1 & -1 & -1 & 1 \\ 0 & 1 & 6 & 3 \\ 0 & 0 & 0 & 0 \end{bmatrix}$

37. $\begin{bmatrix} 1 & 0 & 0 \\ 0 & 1 & 0 \\ 0 & 0 & 1 \end{bmatrix}$ **39.** $\begin{bmatrix} 1 & 2 & 0 & 0 \\ 0 & 0 & 1 & 0 \\ 0 & 0 & 0 & 1 \\ 0 & 0 & 0 & 0 \end{bmatrix}$

41. $\begin{bmatrix} 1 & 0 & 3 & 16 \\ 0 & 1 & 2 & 12 \end{bmatrix}$

43. $\begin{cases} x - 2y = 4 \\ \quad\ y = -3 \end{cases}$ **45.** $\begin{cases} x - y + 2z = 4 \\ \quad\ y - z = 2 \\ \quad\quad\ z = -2 \end{cases}$

$(-2, -3)$ $\quad\quad\quad\quad\quad$ $(8, 0, -2)$

47. $(3, -4)$ **49.** $(-4, -10, 4)$ **51.** $(3, 2)$

53. $(-5, 6)$ **55.** $(-1, -4)$ **57.** Inconsistent

59. $(4, -3, 2)$ **61.** $(7, -3, 4)$ **63.** $(-4, -3, 6)$

65. $(2a + 1, 3a + 2, a)$

67. $(4 + 5b + 4a, 2 - 3b - 3a, b, a)$ **69.** Inconsistent

71. $(0, 2 - 4a, a)$ **73.** $(1, 0, 4, -2)$

75. $(-2a, a, a, 0)$ **77.** Yes; $(-1, 1, -3)$ **79.** No

81. $\begin{bmatrix} 1 & 3 & \frac{3}{2} & : & 4 \\ 0 & 1 & \frac{7}{4} & : & -\frac{3}{2} \\ 0 & 0 & 1 & : & 2 \end{bmatrix}$, $\begin{bmatrix} 1 & 3 & 1 & : & 3 \\ 0 & 1 & 2 & : & -1 \\ 0 & 0 & 1 & : & 2 \end{bmatrix}$

83. $\dfrac{4x^2}{(x + 1)^2(x - 1)} = \dfrac{1}{x - 1} + \dfrac{3}{x + 1} - \dfrac{2}{(x + 1)^2}$

85. \$150,000 at 7%

\$750,000 at 8%

\$600,000 at 10%

87. $y = x^2 + 2x + 5$

89. (a) $y = -0.004x^2 + 0.367x + 5$

(b)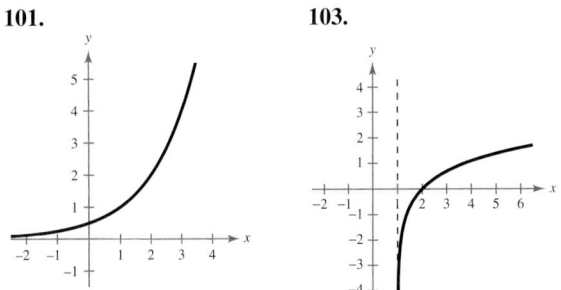

(c) 13 feet, 104 feet

(d) 13.418 feet, 103.793 feet

(e) The results are similar.

91. (a) $x_1 = s$, $x_2 = t$, $x_3 = 600 - s$, $x_4 = s - t$,

$x_5 = 500 - t$, $x_6 = s$, $x_7 = t$

(b) $x_1 = 0$, $x_2 = 0$, $x_3 = 600$, $x_4 = 0$, $x_5 = 500$,

$x_6 = 0$, $x_7 = 0$

(c) $x_1 = 0$, $x_2 = -500$, $x_3 = 600$, $x_4 = 500$,

$x_5 = 1000$, $x_6 = 0$, $x_7 = -500$

93. False. It is a 2×4 matrix.

95. False. Gaussian elimination reduces a matrix until a row-echelon form is obtained; Gauss-Jordan elimination reduces a matrix until a reduced row-echelon form is obtained.

97. (a) There exists a row with all zeros except for the entry in the last column.

(b) There are fewer rows with nonzero entries than there are variables and no rows as in (a).

99. They are the same.

101.

103.

Section 8.2 *(page 569)*

1. $x = -4$, $y = 22$ **3.** $x = 2$, $y = 3$

5. (a) $\begin{bmatrix} 3 & -2 \\ 1 & 7 \end{bmatrix}$ (b) $\begin{bmatrix} -1 & 0 \\ 3 & -9 \end{bmatrix}$ (c) $\begin{bmatrix} 3 & -3 \\ 6 & -3 \end{bmatrix}$

(d) $\begin{bmatrix} -1 & -1 \\ 8 & -19 \end{bmatrix}$

7. (a) $\begin{bmatrix} 7 & 3 \\ 1 & 9 \\ -2 & 15 \end{bmatrix}$ (b) $\begin{bmatrix} 5 & -5 \\ 3 & -1 \\ -4 & -5 \end{bmatrix}$ (c) $\begin{bmatrix} 18 & -3 \\ 6 & 12 \\ -9 & 15 \end{bmatrix}$

(d) $\begin{bmatrix} 16 & -11 \\ 8 & 2 \\ -11 & -5 \end{bmatrix}$

9. (a) $\begin{bmatrix} 3 & 3 & -2 & 1 & 1 \\ -2 & 5 & 7 & -6 & -8 \end{bmatrix}$

(b) $\begin{bmatrix} 1 & 1 & 0 & -1 & 1 \\ 4 & -3 & -11 & 6 & 6 \end{bmatrix}$

(c) $\begin{bmatrix} 6 & 6 & -3 & 0 & 3 \\ 3 & 3 & -6 & 0 & -3 \end{bmatrix}$

(d) $\begin{bmatrix} 4 & 4 & -1 & -2 & 3 \\ 9 & -5 & -24 & 12 & 11 \end{bmatrix}$

11. (a), (b), and (d) not possible

(c) $\begin{bmatrix} 18 & 0 & 9 \\ -3 & -12 & 0 \end{bmatrix}$

13. $\begin{bmatrix} -8 & -7 \\ 15 & -1 \end{bmatrix}$ **15.** $\begin{bmatrix} -24 & -4 & 12 \\ -12 & 32 & 12 \end{bmatrix}$

17. $\begin{bmatrix} 10 & 8 \\ -59 & 9 \end{bmatrix}$ **19.** $\begin{bmatrix} -17.143 & 2.143 \\ 11.571 & 10.286 \end{bmatrix}$

21. $\begin{bmatrix} -1.581 & -3.739 \\ -4.252 & -13.249 \\ 9.713 & -0.362 \end{bmatrix}$

23. $\begin{bmatrix} -6 & -9 \\ -1 & 0 \\ 17 & -10 \end{bmatrix}$ **25.** $\begin{bmatrix} 3 & 3 \\ -\frac{1}{2} & 0 \\ -\frac{13}{2} & \frac{11}{2} \end{bmatrix}$

27. Not possible **29.** $\begin{bmatrix} 3 & -4 \\ 10 & 16 \\ 26 & 46 \end{bmatrix}$ **31.** $\begin{bmatrix} 3 & 0 & 0 \\ 0 & -4 & 0 \\ 0 & 0 & -10 \end{bmatrix}$

33. $\begin{bmatrix} 0 & 0 & 0 \\ 0 & 0 & 0 \\ 0 & 0 & 0 \end{bmatrix}$ **35.** $\begin{bmatrix} 41 & 7 & 7 \\ 42 & 5 & 25 \\ -10 & -25 & 45 \end{bmatrix}$

37. $\begin{bmatrix} 151 & 25 & 48 \\ 516 & 279 & 387 \\ 47 & -20 & 87 \end{bmatrix}$ **39.** Not possible

41. (a) $\begin{bmatrix} 0 & 15 \\ 6 & 12 \end{bmatrix}$ (b) $\begin{bmatrix} -2 & 2 \\ 31 & 14 \end{bmatrix}$ (c) $\begin{bmatrix} 9 & 6 \\ 12 & 12 \end{bmatrix}$

43. (a) $\begin{bmatrix} 0 & -10 \\ 10 & 0 \end{bmatrix}$ (b) $\begin{bmatrix} 0 & -10 \\ 10 & 0 \end{bmatrix}$ (c) $\begin{bmatrix} 8 & -6 \\ 6 & 8 \end{bmatrix}$

45. (a) $\begin{bmatrix} 7 & 7 & 14 \\ 8 & 8 & 16 \\ -1 & -1 & -2 \end{bmatrix}$ (b) $[13]$ (c) Not possible

47. $\begin{bmatrix} 5 & 8 \\ -4 & -16 \end{bmatrix}$ **49.** $\begin{bmatrix} -4 & 10 \\ 3 & 14 \end{bmatrix}$

51. (a) $\begin{bmatrix} -1 & 1 \\ -2 & 1 \end{bmatrix}\begin{bmatrix} x_1 \\ x_2 \end{bmatrix} = \begin{bmatrix} 4 \\ 0 \end{bmatrix}$ (b) $\begin{bmatrix} 4 \\ 8 \end{bmatrix}$

53. (a) $\begin{bmatrix} -2 & -3 \\ 6 & 1 \end{bmatrix}\begin{bmatrix} x_1 \\ x_2 \end{bmatrix} = \begin{bmatrix} -4 \\ -36 \end{bmatrix}$ (b) $\begin{bmatrix} -7 \\ 6 \end{bmatrix}$

55. (a) $\begin{bmatrix} 1 & -2 & 3 \\ -1 & 3 & -1 \\ 2 & -5 & 5 \end{bmatrix}\begin{bmatrix} x_1 \\ x_2 \\ x_3 \end{bmatrix} = \begin{bmatrix} 9 \\ -6 \\ 17 \end{bmatrix}$ (b) $\begin{bmatrix} 1 \\ -1 \\ 2 \end{bmatrix}$

57. (a) $\begin{bmatrix} 1 & -5 & 2 \\ -3 & 1 & -1 \\ 0 & -2 & 5 \end{bmatrix}\begin{bmatrix} x_1 \\ x_2 \\ x_3 \end{bmatrix} = \begin{bmatrix} -20 \\ 8 \\ -16 \end{bmatrix}$ (b) $\begin{bmatrix} -1 \\ 3 \\ -2 \end{bmatrix}$

59. $\begin{bmatrix} 84 & 60 & 30 \\ 42 & 120 & 84 \end{bmatrix}$

61. (a) $A = \begin{bmatrix} 125 & 100 & 75 \\ 100 & 175 & 125 \end{bmatrix}$

The entries represent the numbers of bushels of each crop that are shipped to each outlet.

(b) $B = [\$3.50 \quad \$6.00]$

The entries represent the profits per bushel of each crop.

(c) $BA = [\$1037.50 \quad \$1400 \quad \$1012.50]$

The entries represent the profits from both crops at each of the three outlets.

63. $\begin{bmatrix} \$15,770 & \$18,300 \\ \$26,500 & \$29,250 \\ \$21,260 & \$24,150 \end{bmatrix}$

The entries represent the wholesale and retail values of the inventories at the three outlets.

65. $P^3 = \begin{bmatrix} 0.300 & 0.175 & 0.175 \\ 0.308 & 0.433 & 0.217 \\ 0.392 & 0.392 & 0.608 \end{bmatrix}$

$P^4 = \begin{bmatrix} 0.250 & 0.188 & 0.188 \\ 0.315 & 0.377 & 0.248 \\ 0.435 & 0.435 & 0.565 \end{bmatrix}$

$P^5 = \begin{bmatrix} 0.225 & 0.194 & 0.194 \\ 0.314 & 0.345 & 0.267 \\ 0.461 & 0.461 & 0.539 \end{bmatrix}$

$P^6 = \begin{bmatrix} 0.213 & 0.197 & 0.197 \\ 0.311 & 0.326 & 0.280 \\ 0.477 & 0.477 & 0.523 \end{bmatrix}$

$P^7 = \begin{bmatrix} 0.206 & 0.198 & 0.198 \\ 0.308 & 0.316 & 0.288 \\ 0.486 & 0.486 & 0.514 \end{bmatrix}$

$P^8 = \begin{bmatrix} 0.203 & 0.199 & 0.199 \\ 0.305 & 0.309 & 0.292 \\ 0.492 & 0.492 & 0.508 \end{bmatrix}$

Approaches the matrix

$\begin{bmatrix} 0.2 & 0.2 & 0.2 \\ 0.3 & 0.3 & 0.3 \\ 0.5 & 0.5 & 0.5 \end{bmatrix}$

67. True. The sum of two matrices of different orders is undefined.

69. Not possible **71.** Not possible **73.** 2×2

75. 2×3 **77.** $AC = BC = \begin{bmatrix} 2 & 3 \\ 2 & 3 \end{bmatrix}$

79. AB is a diagonal matrix whose entries are the products of the corresponding entries of A and B.

81. $-8, \dfrac{4}{3}$ **83.** $0, \dfrac{-5 \pm \sqrt{37}}{4}$ **85.** $4, \pm\dfrac{\sqrt{15}}{3}i$

87. $\left(7, -\frac{1}{2}\right)$ **89.** $(3, -1)$

Section 8.3 *(page 579)*

1–9. $AB = I$ and $BA = I$

11. $\begin{bmatrix} \frac{1}{2} & 0 \\ 0 & \frac{1}{3} \end{bmatrix}$ **13.** $\begin{bmatrix} -3 & 2 \\ -2 & 1 \end{bmatrix}$ **15.** $\begin{bmatrix} 1 & -1 \\ 2 & -1 \end{bmatrix}$

17. Does not exist **19.** Does not exist

21. $\begin{bmatrix} 1 & 1 & -1 \\ -3 & 2 & -1 \\ 3 & -3 & 2 \end{bmatrix}$ **23.** $\begin{bmatrix} 1 & 0 & 0 \\ -\frac{3}{4} & \frac{1}{4} & 0 \\ \frac{7}{20} & -\frac{1}{4} & \frac{1}{5} \end{bmatrix}$

25. $\begin{bmatrix} -\frac{1}{8} & 0 & 0 & 0 \\ 0 & 1 & 0 & 0 \\ 0 & 0 & \frac{1}{4} & 0 \\ 0 & 0 & 0 & -\frac{1}{5} \end{bmatrix}$ **27.** $\begin{bmatrix} -175 & 37 & -13 \\ 95 & -20 & 7 \\ 14 & -3 & 1 \end{bmatrix}$

29. $\begin{bmatrix} -1.5 & 1.5 & 1 \\ 4.5 & -3.5 & -3 \\ -1 & 1 & 1 \end{bmatrix}$ **31.** $\begin{bmatrix} -12 & -5 & -9 \\ -4 & -2 & -4 \\ -8 & -4 & -6 \end{bmatrix}$

33. $\begin{bmatrix} 0 & -1.\overline{81} & 0.\overline{90} \\ -10 & 5 & 5 \\ 10 & -2.\overline{72} & -3.\overline{63} \end{bmatrix}$ **35.** Does not exist

37. $\begin{bmatrix} 1 & 0 & 1 & 0 \\ 0 & 1 & 0 & 1 \\ 2 & 0 & 1 & 0 \\ 0 & 1 & 0 & 2 \end{bmatrix}$ **39.** $\begin{bmatrix} \frac{3}{19} & \frac{2}{19} \\ -\frac{2}{19} & \frac{5}{19} \end{bmatrix}$

41. Does not exist **43.** $\begin{bmatrix} \frac{16}{59} & \frac{15}{59} \\ -\frac{4}{59} & \frac{70}{59} \end{bmatrix}$ **45.** $(5, 0)$

47. $(-8, -6)$ **49.** $(3, 8, -11)$ **51.** $(2, 1, 0, 0)$

53. $(2, -2)$ **55.** No solution **57.** $(-4, -8)$

59. $(-1, 3, 2)$ **61.** $\left(\frac{5}{16}a + \frac{13}{16}, \frac{19}{16}a + \frac{11}{16}, a\right)$

63. $(-7, 3, -2)$ **65.** $(5, 0, -2, 3)$

67. $7000 in AAA-rated bonds
$1000 in A-rated bonds
$2000 in B-rated bonds

69. $9000 in AAA-rated bonds
$1000 in A-rated bonds
$2000 in B-rated bonds

71. (a) $I_1 = -3$ amperes (b) $I_1 = 2$ amperes
$I_2 = 8$ amperes $\qquad I_2 = 3$ amperes
$I_3 = 5$ amperes $\qquad I_3 = 5$ amperes

73. True. If B is the inverse of A, then $AB = I = BA$.

75. Answers will vary.

77. $x \geq -5$ or $x \leq -9$

79. $\dfrac{2 \ln 315}{\ln 3} \approx 10.47$ **81.** $2^{6.5} \approx 90.51$

Section 8.4 *(page 587)*

1. 5 **3.** 5 **5.** 27 **7.** 0 **9.** 6 **11.** -9

13. 72 **15.** $\frac{11}{6}$ **17.** -0.002 **19.** -4.842 **21.** 0

23. (a) $M_{11} = -5, M_{12} = 2, M_{21} = 4, M_{22} = 3$

(b) $C_{11} = -5, C_{12} = -2, C_{21} = -4, C_{22} = 3$

25. (a) $M_{11} = -4, M_{12} = -2, M_{21} = 1, M_{22} = 3$

(b) $C_{11} = -4, C_{12} = 2, C_{21} = -1, C_{22} = 3$

27. (a) $M_{11} = 3, M_{12} = -4, M_{13} = 1, M_{21} = 2, M_{22} = 2,$
$M_{23} = -4, M_{31} = -4, M_{32} = 10, M_{33} = 8$

(b) $C_{11} = 3, C_{12} = 4, C_{13} = 1, C_{21} = -2, C_{22} = 2,$
$C_{23} = 4, C_{31} = -4, C_{32} = -10, C_{33} = 8$

29. (a) $M_{11} = 30, M_{12} = 12, M_{13} = 11, M_{21} = -36,$
$M_{22} = 26, M_{23} = 7, M_{31} = -4, M_{32} = -42, M_{33} = 12$

(b) $C_{11} = 30, C_{12} = -12, C_{13} = 11, C_{21} = 36, C_{22} = 26,$
$C_{23} = -7, C_{31} = -4, C_{32} = 42, C_{33} = 12$

31. (a) -75 (b) -75 **33.** (a) 96 (b) 96

35. (a) 170 (b) 170 **37.** 0 **39.** 0 **41.** -9

43. -58 **45.** -30 **47.** -168 **49.** 0 **51.** 412

53. -126 **55.** 0 **57.** -336 **59.** 410

61. (a) -3 (b) -2 (c) $\begin{bmatrix} -2 & 0 \\ 0 & -3 \end{bmatrix}$ (d) 6

63. (a) -8 (b) 0 (c) $\begin{bmatrix} -4 & 4 \\ 1 & -1 \end{bmatrix}$ (d) 0

65. (a) -21 (b) -19 (c) $\begin{bmatrix} 7 & 1 & 4 \\ -8 & 9 & -3 \\ 7 & -3 & 9 \end{bmatrix}$ (d) 399

67. (a) 2 (b) -6 (c) $\begin{bmatrix} 1 & 4 & 3 \\ -1 & 0 & 3 \\ 0 & 2 & 0 \end{bmatrix}$ (d) -12

69–73. Answers will vary. **75.** $-1, 4$ **77.** $-1, -4$

79. $8uv - 1$ **81.** e^{5x} **83.** $1 - \ln x$

85. True. If an entire row is zero, then each cofactor in the expansion is multiplied by zero.

87. Answers will vary.

89. A square matrix is a square array of numbers. The determinant of a square matrix is a real number.

91. (a) Columns 2 and 3 of A were interchanged.
$|A| = -115 = -|B|$

(b) Rows 1 and 3 of A were interchanged.
$|A| = -40 = -|B|$

93. All real numbers **95.** $-4 \leq x \leq 4$

97. All real numbers $t > 1$

99.

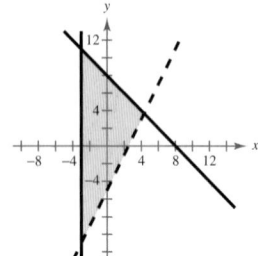

101. $\begin{bmatrix} \frac{1}{4} & \frac{1}{4} \\ 2 & 1 \end{bmatrix}$ **103.** Does not exist

Section 8.5 *(page 599)*

1. $(2, -2)$ **3.** $\left(\frac{32}{7}, \frac{30}{7}\right)$ **5.** $(-1, 3, 2)$

7. $(-2, 1, -1)$ **9.** $\left(0, -\frac{1}{2}, \frac{1}{2}\right)$ **11.** $(1, 2, 1)$ **13.** 7

15. 14   **17.** $\frac{33}{8}$ **19.** $\frac{5}{2}$ **21.** 28   **23.** $\frac{16}{5}$ or 0

25. -3 or -11 **27.** 250 square miles   **29.** Collinear

31. Not collinear   **33.** Collinear   **35.** $x = -3$

37. $3x - 5y = 0$ **39.** $x + 3y - 5 = 0$

41. $2x + 3y - 8 = 0$

43. Uncoded: $[20\ 18\ 15], [21\ 2\ 12], [5\ 0\ 9], [14\ 0\ 18],$
$[9\ 22\ 5], [18\ 0\ 3], [9\ 20\ 25]$

Encoded: $-52\ 10\ 27\ -49\ 3\ 34\ -49\ 13\ 27$
$-94\ 22\ 54\ 1\ 1\ -7\ 0\ -12\ 9$
$-121\ 41\ 55$

45. $-6\ -35\ -69\ 11\ 20\ 17\ 6\ -16\ -58\ 46\ 79\ 67$

47. $-5\ -41\ -87\ 91\ 207\ 257\ 11\ -5\ -41\ 40\ 80$
$84\ 76\ 177\ 227$

49. HAPPY NEW YEAR   **51.** CLASS IS CANCELED

53. SEND PLANES   **55.** MEET ME TONIGHT RON

57. False. The denominator is the determinant of the coefficient matrix.

59. False. If the determinant of the coefficient matrix is zero, the system has either no solution or infinitely many solutions.

61. $(-6, 4)$ **63.** $(-1, 0, -3)$

65.

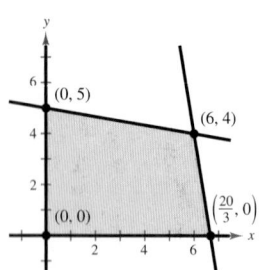

Minimum at $(0, 0)$: 0
Maximum at $(6, 4)$: 52

Review Exercises *(page 603)*

1. 3×1 **3.** 1×1 **5.** $\begin{bmatrix} 3 & -10 & \vdots & 15 \\ 5 & 4 & \vdots & 22 \end{bmatrix}$

7. $\begin{cases} 5x + y + 7z = -9 \\ 4x + 2y = 10 \\ 9x + 4y + 2z = 3 \end{cases}$

9. $\begin{bmatrix} 1 & 2 & 3 \\ 0 & 1 & 1 \\ 0 & 0 & 1 \end{bmatrix}$

11. $\begin{cases} x + 2y + 3z = 9 \\ y - 2z = 2 \\ z = 0 \end{cases}$ **13.** $\begin{cases} x - 5y + 4z = 1 \\ y + 2z = 3 \\ z = 4 \end{cases}$

$(5, 2, 0)$ $(-40, -5, 4)$

15. $(10, -12)$ **17.** $\left(-\frac{1}{5}, \frac{7}{10}\right)$ **19.** $(5, 2, -6)$

21. $\left(-2a + \frac{3}{2}, 2a + 1, a\right)$ **23.** $(1, 0, 4, 3)$

25. $(2, -3, 3)$ **27.** $(2, 3, -1)$ **29.** $(2, 6, -10, -3)$

31. $x = 12, y = -7$ **33.** $x = 1, y = 11$

35. (a) $\begin{bmatrix} -1 & 8 \\ 15 & 13 \end{bmatrix}$ (b) $\begin{bmatrix} 5 & -12 \\ -9 & -3 \end{bmatrix}$

(c) $\begin{bmatrix} 8 & -8 \\ 12 & 20 \end{bmatrix}$ (d) $\begin{bmatrix} -7 & 28 \\ 39 & 29 \end{bmatrix}$

37. (a) $\begin{bmatrix} 5 & 7 \\ -3 & 14 \\ 31 & 42 \end{bmatrix}$ (b) $\begin{bmatrix} 5 & 1 \\ -11 & -10 \\ -9 & -38 \end{bmatrix}$

(c) $\begin{bmatrix} 20 & 16 \\ -28 & 8 \\ 44 & 8 \end{bmatrix}$ (d) $\begin{bmatrix} 5 & 13 \\ 5 & 38 \\ 71 & 122 \end{bmatrix}$

39. $\begin{bmatrix} 17 & -17 \\ 13 & 2 \end{bmatrix}$ **41.** $\begin{bmatrix} 54 & 4 \\ -2 & 24 \\ -4 & 32 \end{bmatrix}$

43. $\begin{bmatrix} 48 & -18 & -3 \\ 15 & 51 & 33 \end{bmatrix}$ **45.** $\begin{bmatrix} -14 & -4 \\ 7 & -17 \\ -17 & -2 \end{bmatrix}$

47. $\begin{bmatrix} 3 & \frac{2}{3} \\ -\frac{4}{3} & \frac{11}{3} \\ \frac{10}{3} & 0 \end{bmatrix}$ **49.** $\begin{bmatrix} -30 & 4 \\ 51 & 70 \end{bmatrix}$ **51.** $\begin{bmatrix} 100 & 220 \\ 12 & -4 \\ 84 & 212 \end{bmatrix}$

53. $\begin{bmatrix} 14 & -2 & 8 \\ 14 & -10 & 40 \\ 36 & -12 & 48 \end{bmatrix}$ **55.** $\begin{bmatrix} 44 & 4 \\ 20 & 8 \end{bmatrix}$

57. $\begin{bmatrix} 24 & -8 \\ 36 & -12 \end{bmatrix}$ **59.** $\begin{bmatrix} 1 & 17 \\ 12 & 36 \end{bmatrix}$

61. $\begin{bmatrix} 14 & -22 & 22 \\ 19 & -41 & 80 \\ 42 & -66 & 66 \end{bmatrix}$ **63.** $\begin{bmatrix} 96 & 84 & 108 & 48 \\ 60 & 36 & 96 & 24 \\ 108 & 72 & 120 & 60 \end{bmatrix}$

65 and 67. $AB = I$ and $BA = I$

69. $\begin{bmatrix} 4 & -5 \\ 5 & -6 \end{bmatrix}$ **71.** $\begin{bmatrix} 13 & 6 & -4 \\ -12 & -5 & 3 \\ 5 & 2 & -1 \end{bmatrix}$

73. $\begin{bmatrix} \frac{1}{2} & -1 & -\frac{1}{2} \\ \frac{1}{2} & -\frac{2}{3} & -\frac{5}{6} \\ 0 & \frac{2}{3} & \frac{1}{3} \end{bmatrix}$ **75.** $\begin{bmatrix} -3 & 6 & -5.5 & 3.5 \\ 1 & -2 & 2 & -1 \\ 7 & -15 & 14.5 & -9.5 \\ -1 & 2.5 & -2.5 & 1.5 \end{bmatrix}$

77. $\begin{bmatrix} 1 & -1 \\ 4 & -\frac{7}{2} \end{bmatrix}$ **79.** $\begin{bmatrix} 2 & \frac{20}{3} \\ \frac{1}{10} & \frac{1}{6} \end{bmatrix}$

81. $(36, 11)$ **83.** $(-6, -1)$ **85.** $(2, -1, -2)$

87. $(6, 1, -1)$ **89.** $(-3, 1)$ **91.** $(1, 1, -2)$

93. -42 **95.** 550

97. (a) $M_{11} = 4, M_{12} = 7, M_{21} = -1, M_{22} = 2$

(b) $C_{11} = 4, C_{12} = -7, C_{21} = 1, C_{22} = 2$

99. (a) $M_{11} = 30, M_{12} = -12, M_{13} = -21,$

$M_{21} = 20, M_{22} = 19, M_{23} = 22, M_{31} = 5,$

$M_{32} = -2, M_{33} = 19$

(b) $C_{11} = 30, C_{12} = 12, C_{13} = -21,$

$C_{21} = -20, C_{22} = 19, C_{23} = -22,$

$C_{31} = 5, C_{32} = 2, C_{33} = 19$

101. 130 **103.** 279 **105.** $(4, 7)$ **107.** $(-1, 4, 5)$

109. 16 **111.** 10 **113.** Collinear

115. $x - 2y + 4 = 0$ **117.** $2x + 6y - 13 = 0$

119. Uncoded: $[12 \quad 15 \quad 15], [11 \quad 0 \quad 15], [21 \quad 20 \quad 0],$

$[2 \quad 5 \quad 12], [15 \quad 23 \quad 0]$

Encoded: $-21 \ 6 \ 0 \ -68 \ 8 \ 45 \ 102 \ -42 \ -60 \ -53$

$20 \ 21 \ 99 \ -30 \ -69$

121. SEE YOU FRIDAY

123. False. The matrix must be square.

125. The matrix must be square and its determinant nonzero.

127. No. The first two matrices describe a system of equations with one solution. The third matrix describes a system with infinitely many solutions.

129. $\lambda = \pm 2\sqrt{10} - 3$

Chapter Test   *(page 608)*

1. $\begin{bmatrix} 1 & 0 & 0 \\ 0 & 1 & 0 \\ 0 & 0 & 1 \end{bmatrix}$ **2.** $\begin{bmatrix} 1 & 0 & -1 & 2 \\ 0 & 1 & 0 & -1 \\ 0 & 0 & 0 & 0 \\ 0 & 0 & 0 & 0 \end{bmatrix}$

3. $\begin{bmatrix} 4 & 3 & -2 & \vdots & 14 \\ -1 & -1 & 2 & \vdots & -5 \\ 3 & 1 & -4 & \vdots & 8 \end{bmatrix}, \left(1, 3, -\frac{1}{2}\right)$

4. (a) $\begin{bmatrix} 1 & 5 \\ 0 & -4 \end{bmatrix}$ (b) $\begin{bmatrix} 15 & 12 \\ -12 & -12 \end{bmatrix}$

(c) $\begin{bmatrix} 7 & 14 \\ -4 & -12 \end{bmatrix}$ (d) $\begin{bmatrix} 4 & -5 \\ 0 & 4 \end{bmatrix}$

5. $\begin{bmatrix} \frac{1}{2} & \frac{2}{5} \\ 1 & \frac{3}{5} \end{bmatrix}$ **6.** $\begin{bmatrix} -\frac{5}{2} & 4 & -3 \\ 5 & -7 & 6 \\ 4 & -6 & 5 \end{bmatrix}$

7. $(13, 22)$ **8.** -196 **9.** 29 **10.** 43

11. $(-3, 5)$ **12.** $(-2, 4, 6)$ **13.** 7

14. Uncoded: $[11 \ 14 \ 15], [3 \ 11 \ 0], [15 \ 14 \ 0], [23 \ 15 \ 15],$

$[4 \ 0 \ 0]$

Encoded: $115 \ -41 \ -59 \ 14 \ -3 \ -11 \ 29 \ -15$

$-14 \ 128 \ -53 \ -60 \ 4 \ -4 \ 0$

15. 75 liters of 60% solution

25 liters of 20% solution

Problem Solving   *(page 610)*

1. (a) $AT = \begin{bmatrix} -1 & -4 & -2 \\ 1 & 2 & 3 \end{bmatrix}$

$AAT = \begin{bmatrix} -1 & -2 & -3 \\ -1 & -4 & -2 \end{bmatrix}$

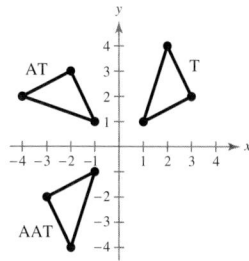

A represents reflections in the origin and in the x-axis.

(b) AAT is rotated clockwise $90°$ to obtain AT. AT is then rotated clockwise $90°$ to obtain T.

3. (a) Yes   (b) No   (c) No   (d) No   **5.** $x = 4$

7. Answers will vary. For example: $A = \begin{bmatrix} 1 & 1 \\ 0 & 0 \end{bmatrix}$

9. Answers will vary.

11. $\begin{vmatrix} x & 0 & 0 & d \\ -1 & x & 0 & c \\ 0 & -1 & x & b \\ 0 & 0 & -1 & a \end{vmatrix}$

13. Transformer: $10.00

Foot of wire: $0.20

Light: $1.00

15. $A^T = \begin{bmatrix} -1 & 2 \\ 1 & 0 \\ -2 & 1 \end{bmatrix}$ $B^T = \begin{bmatrix} -3 & 1 & 1 \\ 0 & 2 & -1 \end{bmatrix}$

$(AB)^T = \begin{bmatrix} 2 & -5 \\ 4 & -1 \end{bmatrix} = B^T A^T$

17. $A^{-1} = \begin{bmatrix} 0.0625 & -0.4375 & 0.625 \\ 0.1875 & 0.6875 & -1.125 \\ -0.125 & -0.125 & 0.75 \end{bmatrix}$

$|A^{-1}| = \dfrac{1}{16}, |A| = 16$

$|A^{-1}| = \dfrac{1}{|A|}$

19. (a) Answers will vary.

(b) Squaring the 2×2 matrix yields the zero matrix. Cubing the 3×3 matrix yields the zero matrix.

(c) A^4 is the zero matrix.

(d) A^n is the zero matrix.

Chapter 9

Section 9.1 *(page 621)*

1. 4, 7, 10, 13, 16   **3.** 2, 4, 8, 16, 32

5. $-2, 4, -8, 16, -32$ **7.** $3, 2, \frac{5}{3}, \frac{3}{2}, \frac{7}{5}$

9. $3, \frac{12}{11}, \frac{9}{13}, \frac{24}{47}, \frac{15}{37}$ **11.** $0, 1, 0, \frac{1}{2}, 0$ **13.** $\frac{5}{3}, \frac{17}{9}, \frac{53}{27}, \frac{161}{81}, \frac{485}{243}$

15. $1, \dfrac{1}{2^{3/2}}, \dfrac{1}{3^{3/2}}, \dfrac{1}{8}, \dfrac{1}{5^{3/2}}$ **17.** $3, \dfrac{9}{2}, \dfrac{9}{2}, \dfrac{27}{8}, \dfrac{81}{40}$

19. $-1, \frac{1}{4}, -\frac{1}{9}, \frac{1}{16}, -\frac{1}{25}$ **21.** $\frac{2}{3}, \frac{2}{3}, \frac{2}{3}, \frac{2}{3}, \frac{2}{3}$

23. 0, 0, 6, 24, 60   **25.** -73

27. 0.000282   **29.** $\frac{44}{239}$

31.

33.

35.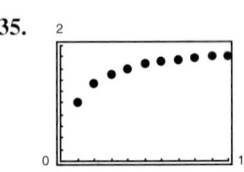

37. c   **38.** b   **39.** d   **40.** a

41. $a_n = 3n - 2$ **43.** $a_n = n^2 - 1$

45. $a_n = \dfrac{(-1)^n(n + 1)}{n + 2}$ **47.** $a_n = \dfrac{n + 1}{2n - 1}$

49. $a_n = \dfrac{1}{n^2}$ **51.** $a_n = (-1)^{n+1}$ **53.** $a_n = 1 + \dfrac{1}{n}$

55. 28, 24, 20, 16, 12   **57.** 3, 4, 6, 10, 18

59. 6, 8, 10, 12, 14   **61.** 81, 27, 9, 3, 1

$a_n = 2n + 4$ $a_n = \dfrac{243}{3^n}$

63. $\dfrac{1}{30}$ **65.** 90   **67.** $n + 1$ **69.** $\dfrac{1}{2n(2n + 1)}$

71. 35   **73.** 40   **75.** 30   **77.** $\frac{9}{5}$ **79.** 88

81. 30   **83.** 81   **85.** $\frac{47}{60}$

87. $\displaystyle\sum_{i=1}^{9} \dfrac{1}{3i}$ **89.** $\displaystyle\sum_{i=1}^{8} \left[2\left(\dfrac{i}{8}\right) + 3\right]$ **91.** $\displaystyle\sum_{i=1}^{6} (-1)^{i+1} 3^i$

93. $\displaystyle\sum_{i=1}^{20} \dfrac{(-1)^{i+1}}{i^2}$ **95.** $\displaystyle\sum_{i=1}^{5} \dfrac{2^i - 1}{2^{i+1}}$ **97.** $\dfrac{75}{16}$ **99.** $-\dfrac{3}{2}$

101. $\frac{2}{3}$ **103.** $\frac{7}{9}$

105. (a) $A_1 = \$5100.00, A_2 = \$5202.00, A_3 = \$5306.04,$
$A_4 = \$5412.16, A_5 = \$5520.40, A_6 = \$5630.81,$
$A_7 = \$5743.43, A_8 = \$5858.30$

(b) $A_{40} = \$11,040.20$

107. (a) $b_n = 50.0n + 168$

(b) $c_n = -1.36n^2 + 65.0n + 138$

(c)

n	1	2	3	4	5
a_n	228	260	294	352	419
b_n	218	268	318	368	418
c_n	202	263	321	376	429

n	6	7	8	9	10
a_n	493	556	587	616	629
b_n	468	518	568	618	668
c_n	479	526	571	613	652

The quadratic model is a better fit.

(d) The quadratic model; 807

109. $a_0 = 3183.1, a_1 = 3615.4, a_2 = 4006.5,$
$a_3 = 4356.3, a_4 = 4665.0, a_5 = 4932.4,$
$a_6 = 5158.6, a_7 = 5343.5, a_8 = 5487.2,$
$a_9 = 5589.7, a_{10} = 5651.0$

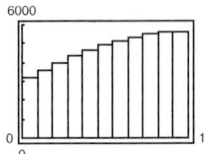

111. True by the Properties of Sums

113. 1, 1, 2, 3, 5, 8, 13, 21, 34, 55, 89, 144

$1, 2, \frac{3}{2}, \frac{5}{3}, \frac{8}{5}, \frac{13}{8}, \frac{21}{13}, \frac{34}{21}, \frac{55}{34}, \frac{89}{55}$

115. $500.95   **117.** Answers will vary.

119. $x, \dfrac{x^2}{2}, \dfrac{x^3}{6}, \dfrac{x^4}{24}, \dfrac{x^5}{120}$

121. $-\dfrac{x^2}{2}, \dfrac{x^4}{24}, -\dfrac{x^6}{720}, \dfrac{x^8}{40{,}320}, -\dfrac{x^{10}}{3{,}628{,}800}$

123. $f^{-1}(x) = \dfrac{x+3}{4}$ **125.** $h^{-1}(x) = \dfrac{x^2-1}{5}, x \ge 0$

127. (a) $\begin{bmatrix} 8 & 1 \\ -3 & 7 \end{bmatrix}$ (b) $\begin{bmatrix} -26 & 1 \\ 15 & -24 \end{bmatrix}$

(c) $\begin{bmatrix} 18 & 9 \\ 18 & 0 \end{bmatrix}$ (d) $\begin{bmatrix} 0 & 6 \\ 27 & 18 \end{bmatrix}$

129. (a) $\begin{bmatrix} -3 & -7 & 4 \\ 4 & 4 & 1 \\ 1 & 4 & 3 \end{bmatrix}$ (b) $\begin{bmatrix} 10 & 25 & -10 \\ -12 & -11 & 3 \\ -3 & -9 & -8 \end{bmatrix}$

(c) $\begin{bmatrix} -2 & 7 & -16 \\ 4 & 42 & 45 \\ 1 & 23 & 48 \end{bmatrix}$ (d) $\begin{bmatrix} 16 & 31 & 42 \\ 10 & 47 & 31 \\ 13 & 22 & 25 \end{bmatrix}$

131. 26   **133.** -194

Section 9.2 *(page 631)*

1. Arithmetic sequence, $d = -2$

3. Not an arithmetic sequence

5. Arithmetic sequence, $d = -\frac{1}{4}$

7. Not an arithmetic sequence

9. Not an arithmetic sequence

11. 8, 11, 14, 17, 20

Arithmetic sequence, $d = 3$

13. 7, 3, -1, -5, -9

Arithmetic sequence, $d = -4$

15. $-1, 1, -1, 1, -1,$

Not an arithmetic sequence

17. $-3, \frac{3}{2}, -1, \frac{3}{4}, -\frac{3}{5}$

Not an arithmetic sequence

19. 15, 19, 23, 27, 31; $d = 4$; $a_n = 4n + 11$

21. 200, 190, 180, 170, 160; $d = -10$; $a_n = -10n + 210$

23. $\frac{5}{8}, \frac{1}{2}, \frac{3}{8}, \frac{1}{4}, \frac{1}{8}$; $d = -\frac{1}{8}$; $a_n = -\frac{1}{8}n + \frac{3}{4}$

25. 5, 11, 17, 23, 29   **27.** $-2.6, -3.0, -3.4, -3.8, -4.2$

29. 2, 6, 10, 14, 18   **31.** $-2, 2, 6, 10, 14$

33. $a_n = 3n - 2$ **35.** $a_n = -8n + 108$

37. $a_n = 2xn - x$ **39.** $a_n = -\frac{5}{2}n + \frac{13}{2}$

41. $a_n = \frac{10}{3}n + \frac{5}{3}$ **43.** $a_n = -3n + 103$

45. b   **46.** d   **47.** c   **48.** a

49. 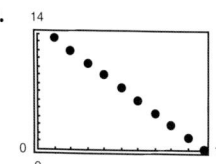   **51.**

53. 620   **55.** 17.4   **57.** 265   **59.** 4000

61. 1275   **63.** 30,030   **65.** 355   **67.** 160,000

69. 520   **71.** 2725   **73.** 10,120   **75.** 10,000

77. (a) $40,000   (b) $217,500

79. 2340 seats   **81.** 405 bricks   **83.** 490 meters

85. (a) $a_n = 1048.8n + 19{,}188$

(b) $y = 1089.5n + 18{,}397$

This model is quite close to the arithmetic sequence.

(c)

(d) 2001: $30,725; 2003: $32,822

(e) Answers will vary.

87. True. Given a_1 and a_2, $d = a_2 - a_1$ and

$a_n = a_1 + (n - 1)d$.

89. (a)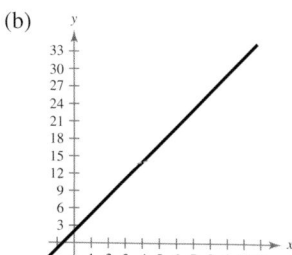

(b)

(c) The graph of $y = 3x + 2$ contains all points on the line. The graph of $a_n = 2 + 3n$ contains only points at the positive integers.

(d) The slope of the line and the common difference of the arithmetic sequence are equal.

91. 4

93. Slope: $\frac{1}{2}$;

y-intercept: $\left(0, -\frac{3}{4}\right)$

95. Slope: undefined;

No y-intercept

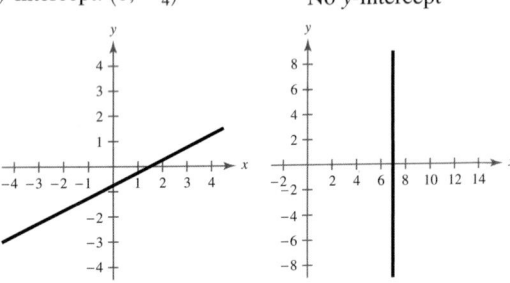

Section 9.3   (page 640)

1. Geometric sequence, $r = 3$

3. Not a geometric sequence

5. Geometric sequence, $r = -\frac{1}{2}$

7. Geometric sequence, $r = 2$

9. Not a geometric sequence

11. 2, 6, 18, 54, 162   **13.** $1, \frac{1}{2}, \frac{1}{4}, \frac{1}{8}, \frac{1}{16}$

15. $5, -\frac{1}{2}, \frac{1}{20}, -\frac{1}{200}, \frac{1}{2000}$ **17.** $1, e, e^2, e^3, e^4$

19. $2, \frac{x}{2}, \frac{x^2}{8}, \frac{x^3}{32}, \frac{x^4}{128}$

21. 64, 32, 16, 8, 4; $r = \frac{1}{2}$; $a_n = 128\left(\frac{1}{2}\right)^n$

23. 7, 14, 28, 56, 112; $r = 2$; $a_n = \frac{7}{2}(2)^n$

25. $6, -9, \frac{27}{2}, -\frac{81}{4}, \frac{243}{8}$; $r = -\frac{3}{2}$; $a_n = -4\left(-\frac{3}{2}\right)^n$

27. $\frac{1}{128}$ **29.** $-\frac{2}{3^{10}}$ **31.** $100e^{8x}$ **33.** 1082.372

35. 9   **37.** -2 **39.** a   **40.** c   **41.** b   **42.** d

43.   **45.**

47.   **49.**

51. 511   **53.** 171   **55.** 43   **57.** $\frac{1365}{32}$

59. 29,921.311   **61.** 592.647   **63.** 2092.596

65. $\frac{8}{5}$ **67.** 6.400   **69.** 3.750

71. $\sum_{n=1}^{7} 5(3)^{n-1}$ **73.** $\sum_{n=1}^{7} 2\left(-\frac{1}{4}\right)^{n-1}$ **75.** $\sum_{n=1}^{6} 0.1(4)^{n-1}$

77. 2   **79.** $\frac{2}{3}$ **81.** $\frac{16}{3}$ **83.** $\frac{5}{3}$ **85.** -30

87. 32   **89.** Undefined   **91.** $\frac{4}{11}$ **93.** $\frac{7}{22}$

95.

Horizontal asymptote: $y = 12$

Corresponds to the sum of the series

97. (a) $a_n = 1142.90(1.01)^n$

(b) The population is growing at a rate of 1% per year.

(c) 1394.6 million

(d) 2003

99. (a) $11,652.39   (b) $12,002.55

(c) $12,188.60   (d) $12,317.01

(e) $12,380.41

101. $7011.89   **103.** Answers will vary.

105. (a) $26,198.27   **107.** (a) $637,678.02

(b) $26,263.88   (b) $645,861.43

109. Answers will vary.   **111.** 126 square inches

113. $3,623,993.23

115. False. A sequence is geometric if the ratios of consecutive terms are the same.

117. The value of a real number between -1 and 1, raised to a power, approaches zero.

119. $x^2 + 2x$ **121.** $3x^2 + 6x + 1$

123. $x(3x + 8)(3x - 8)$ **125.** $(3x + 1)(2x - 5)$

127. $\frac{3x}{x - 3}$, $x \neq -3$ **129.** $\frac{2x + 1}{3}$, $x \neq 0, -\frac{1}{2}$

131. $\frac{5x^2 + 9x - 30}{(x + 2)(x - 2)}$

Section 9.4   (page 652)

1. $\frac{5}{(k + 1)(k + 2)}$ **3.** $\frac{(k + 1)^2(k + 2)^2}{4}$

5–17. Answers will vary.

19. 120   **21.** 91   **23.** 979   **25.** 70   **27.** -3402

29. $S_n = n(2n - 1)$ **31.** $S_n = 10 - 10\left(\frac{9}{10}\right)^n$

33. $S_n = \frac{n}{2(n + 1)}$ **35–47.** Answers will vary.

49. 0, 3, 6, 9, 12, 15

First differences: 3, 3, 3, 3, 3

Second differences: 0, 0, 0, 0

Linear

51. 3, 1, −2, −6, −11, −17

First differences: −2, −3, −4, −5, −6

Second differences: −1, −1, −1, −1

Quadratic

53. 2, 4, 16, 256, 65,536, 4,294,967,296

First differences: 2, 12, 240, 65,280, 4,294,901,760

Second differences: 10, 228, 65,040, 4,294,836,480

Neither

55. $a_n = n^2 − n + 3$ **57.** $a_n = \frac{1}{2}n^2 + n − 3$

59. (a) 1.9, 1.6, 1.9, 1.2

(b) A linear model can be used.

$a_n = 1.67n + 16.3$

(c) \$39.68 million

61. True. P_7 may be false.

63. True. If the second differences are all zero, then the first differences are all the same and the sequence is arithmetic.

65. $4x^4 − 4x^2 + 1$ **67.** $−64x^3 + 240x^2 − 300x + 125$

69. $x^2 + 2x − 8$ **71.** $4x^2 − 9x + 2$

73. (a) Intercept: (0, 0)

(b) Vertical asymptote: $x = −3$

Horizontal asymptote: $y = 1$

(c) No symmetry

(d)

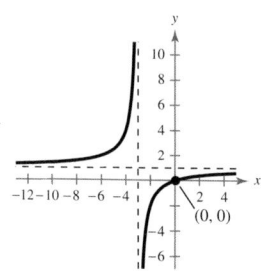

75. (a) t-intercept: (7, 0)

(b) Vertical asymptote: $t = 0$

Horizontal asymptote: $y = 1$

(c) No symmetry

(d)

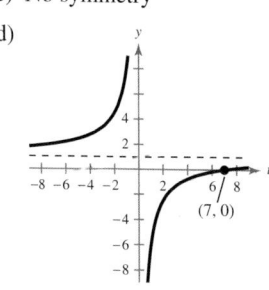

1. 10   **3.** 1   **5.** 15,504   **7.** 210   **9.** 4950

11. 56   **13.** 35   **15.** $x^4 + 4x^3 + 6x^2 + 4x + 1$

17. $a^4 + 24a^3 + 216a^2 + 864a + 1296$

19. $y^3 − 12y^2 + 48y − 64$

21. $x^5 + 5x^4y + 10x^3y^2 + 10x^2y^3 + 5xy^4 + y^5$

23. $r^6 + 18r^5s + 135r^4s^2 + 540r^3s^3 + 1215r^2s^4 + 1458rs^5 + 729s^6$

25. $243a^5 − 405a^4b + 270a^3b^2 − 90a^2b^3 + 15ab^4 − b^5$

27. $1 − 6x + 12x^2 − 8x^3$

29. $x^8 + 20x^6 + 150x^4 + 500x^2 + 625$

31. $\dfrac{1}{x^5} + \dfrac{5y}{x^4} + \dfrac{10y^2}{x^3} + \dfrac{10y^3}{x^2} + \dfrac{5y^4}{x} + y^5$

33. $2x^4 − 24x^3 + 113x^2 − 246x + 207$

35. $32t^5 − 80t^4s + 80t^3s^2 − 40t^2s^3 + 10ts^4 − s^5$

37. $x^5 + 10x^4y + 40x^3y^2 + 80x^2y^3 + 80xy^4 + 32y^5$

39. $120x^7y^3$ **41.** $360x^3y^2$ **43.** $1,259,712x^2y^7$

45. $32,476,950,000x^4y^8$ **47.** $1,732,104$

49. 180   **51.** −326,592   **53.** 210

55. $x^2 + 12x^{3/2} + 54x + 108x^{1/2} + 81$

57. $x^2 − 3x^{4/3}y^{1/3} + 3x^{2/3}y^{2/3} − y$

59. $3x^2 + 3xh + h^2, h \neq 0$

61. $\dfrac{1}{\sqrt{x + h} + \sqrt{x}}, h \neq 0$ **63.** −4   **65.** $2035 + 828i$

67. 1   **69.** 1.172   **71.** 510,568.785

73.

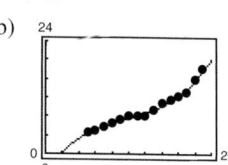

g is shifted four units to the left of f.

$g(x) = x^3 + 12x^2 + 44x + 48$

75. 0.273   **77.** 0.171

79. (a) $f(t) = 0.0071t^3 − 0.209t^2 + 2.55t − 4.1$

(b)

(c) $g(t) = 0.0071t^3 + 0.004t^2 + 0.50t + 7.6$

(d)

(e) 34.9 gallons; Yes

(f) The per capita consumption of bottled water is increasing. Answers will vary.

81. True. The coefficients from the Binomial Theorem can be used to find the numbers in Pascal's Triangle.

83. False. The coefficient of the x^{10}-term is 1,732,104 and the coefficient of the x^{14}-term is 192,456.

85.
$$1 \quad 8 \quad 28 \quad 56 \quad 70 \quad 56 \quad 28 \quad 8 \quad 1$$
$$1 \quad 9 \quad 36 \quad 84 \quad 126 \quad 126 \quad 84 \quad 36 \quad 9 \quad 1$$
$$1 \quad 10 \quad 45 \quad 120 \quad 210 \quad 252 \quad 210 \quad 120 \quad 45 \quad 10 \quad 1$$

87. The signs of the terms in the expansion of $(x - y)^n$ alternate between positive and negative.

89. Answers will vary.   **91.** Answers will vary.

93.   **95.**

                 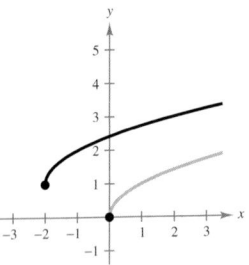

$g(x) = (x - 3)^2$ $g(x) = \sqrt{x + 2} + 1$

97. $\begin{bmatrix} 4 & -5 \\ 5 & -6 \end{bmatrix}$

Section 9.6   *(page 669)*

1. 6   **3.** 5   **5.** 3   **7.** 7   **9.** 30   **11.** 15

13. 64   **15.** 4   **17.** 175,760,000

19. (a) 900   (b) 648   (c) 180   (d) 600   **21.** 64,000

23. (a) 40,320   (b) 384   **25.** 24   **27.** 336

29. 120   **31.** $n = 5$ or $n = 6$ **33.** 1,860,480

35. 970,200   **37.** 15,504   **39.** 420   **41.** 2520

43. ABCD, ABDC, ACBD, ACDB, ADBC, ADCB, BACD, BADC, CABD, CADB, DABC, DACB, BCAD, BDAC, CBAD, CDAB, DBAC, DCAB, BCDA, BDCA, CBDA, CDBA, DBCA, DCBA

45. AB, AC, AD, AE, AF, BC, BD, BE, BF, CD, CE, CF, DE, DF, EF

47. 120   **49.** 11,880   **51.** 15,504   **53.** 324,632

55. 3,921,225   **57.** 21   **59.** (a) 70   (b) 30

61. (a) 70   (b) 54   (c) 16   **63.** 5   **65.** 20

67. (a) 120, 526, 770

(b) 1

(c) There are 22,957,480 possible winning numbers in the state lottery, which is considerably less than the possible number of winning Powerball numbers.

69. True by the definition of the Fundamental Counting Principle.

71. They are equal.

73. Answers will vary.   **75.** Answers will vary.

77. No. For some calculators the number is too great.

79. (a) 35   (b) 8   (c) 83

81. (a) -4 (b) 0   (c) 0   **83.** 8.30   **85.** 35.00

87. $x^5 + 5x^4 + 10x^3 + 10x^2 + 5x + 1$

89. $x^{10} + 10x^8y + 40x^6y^2 + 80x^4y^3 + 80x^2y^4 + 32y^5$

Section 9.7   *(page 680)*

1. $\{(H, 1), (H, 2), (H, 3), (H, 4), (H, 5), (H, 6),$
$(T, 1), (T, 2), (T, 3), (T, 4), (T, 5), (T, 6)\}$

3. $\{ABC, ACB, BAC, BCA, CAB, CBA\}$

5. $\{AB, AC, AD, AE, BC, BD, BE, CD, CE, DE\}$

7. $\frac{3}{8}$ **9.** $\frac{7}{8}$ **11.** $\frac{3}{13}$ **13.** $\frac{3}{26}$ **15.** $\frac{1}{12}$

17. $\frac{11}{12}$ **19.** $\frac{1}{3}$ **21.** $\frac{1}{5}$ **23.** $\frac{2}{5}$ **25.** 0.3

27. $\frac{2}{3}$ **29.** 0.85   **31.** $\frac{7}{20}$

33. (a) 58%   **35.** (a) 38,570,000   **37.** (a) $\frac{112}{209}$

(b) 95.6%   (b) 23%   (b) $\frac{97}{209}$

(c) 0.4%   (c) 58%   (c) $\frac{274}{627}$

39. $P(\{\text{Taylor wins}\}) = \frac{1}{2}$
$P(\{\text{Moore wins}\}) = P(\{\text{Jenkins wins}\}) = \frac{1}{4}$

41. (a) $\frac{21}{1292}$ **43.** (a) $\frac{1}{3}$ **45.** (a) $\frac{1}{120}$

(b) $\frac{225}{646}$ (b) $\frac{5}{8}$ (b) $\frac{1}{24}$

(c) $\frac{49}{323}$

47. (a) $\frac{14}{169}$ **49.** (a) $\frac{14}{55}$ **51.** (a) $\frac{1}{4}$

(b) $\frac{1}{221}$ (b) $\frac{12}{55}$ (b) $\frac{1}{2}$

(c) $\frac{54}{55}$ (c) $\frac{9}{100}$

(d) $\frac{1}{30}$

53. (a) 0.9702   **55.** (a) $\frac{1}{1024}$ **57.** 0.4746   **59.** $\frac{7}{16}$

(b) 0.9998   (b) $\frac{243}{1024}$

(c) 0.0002   (c) $\frac{781}{1024}$

61. True. Two events are independent if the occurrence of one has no effect on the occurrence of the other.

63. (a) As you consider successive people with distinct birthdays, the probabilities must decrease to take into account the birth dates already used. Because the birth dates of people are independent events, multiply the respective probabilities of distinct birthdays.

(b) $\dfrac{365}{365} \cdot \dfrac{364}{365} \cdot \dfrac{363}{365} \cdot \dfrac{362}{365}$ (c) Answers will vary.

(d) Q_n is the probability that the birthdays are *not* distinct, which is equivalent to at least two people having the same birthday.

(e)

n	10	15	20	23	30	40	50
P_n	0.88	0.75	0.59	0.49	0.29	0.11	0.03
Q_n	0.12	0.25	0.41	0.51	0.71	0.89	0.97

(f) 23

65. No real solution   **67.** $0, \dfrac{1 \pm \sqrt{13}}{2}$ **69.** -4

71. $\dfrac{11}{2}$ **73.** -10 **75.** $\ln 27 \approx 3.296$

77. $\ln 1 = 0, \ln 3 \approx 1.099$ **79.** $\ln \dfrac{8}{3} \approx 0.981$

81. $e^8 \approx 2980.958$ **83.** $\dfrac{e^4}{6} \approx 9.100$

85.

87.
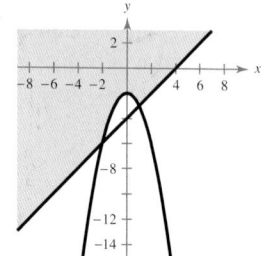
   89. 15   **91.** 165

Review Exercises   *(page 686)*

1. $8, 5, 4, \dfrac{7}{2}, \dfrac{16}{5}$ **3.** $72, 36, 12, 3, \dfrac{3}{5}$ **5.** $a_n = 2(-1)^n$

7. $a_n = \dfrac{4}{n}$ **9.** 120   **11.** 1   **13.** 30   **15.** $\dfrac{205}{24}$

17. 6050   **19.** $\displaystyle\sum_{k=1}^{20} \dfrac{1}{2k}$ **21.** $\dfrac{5}{9}$ **23.** $\dfrac{2}{99}$

25. (a) \$43,000   (b) \$192,500

27. Arithmetic sequence, $d = -2$

29. Arithmetic sequence, $d = \dfrac{1}{2}$

31. $4, 7, 10, 13, 16$ **33.** $25, 28, 31, 34, 37$

35. $a_n = 12n - 5$ **37.** $a_n = 3ny - 2y$

39. $a_n = -7n + 107$ **41.** 80   **43.** 88   **45.** 25,250

47. 43 minutes   **49.** Geometric sequence, $r = 2$

51. Geometric sequence, $r = -2$ **53.** $4, -1, \dfrac{1}{4}, -\dfrac{1}{16}, \dfrac{1}{64}$

55. $9, 6, 4, \dfrac{8}{3}, \dfrac{16}{9}$ or $9, -6, 4, -\dfrac{8}{3}, \dfrac{16}{9}$

57. $a_n = 16\left(-\dfrac{1}{2}\right)^{n-1}, 10.67$

59. $a_n = 100(1.05)^{n-1}, 3306.60$ **61.** 127   **63.** $\dfrac{15}{16}$

65. 31   **67.** 24.85   **69.** 5486.45   **71.** 8   **73.** $\dfrac{10}{9}$

75. 12   **77.** (a) $a_t = 120,000(0.7)^t$ (b) \$20,168.40

79. Answers will vary.   **81.** Answers will vary.   **83.** 465

85. 4648   **87.** $S_n = n(2n + 7)$ **89.** $S_n = \dfrac{5}{2}\left[1 - \left(\dfrac{3}{5}\right)^n\right]$

91. 5, 10, 15, 20, 25

First differences: 5, 5, 5, 5

Second differences: 0, 0, 0

Linear

93. 16, 15, 14, 13, 12

First differences: $-1, -1, -1, -1$

Second differences: 0, 0, 0

Linear

95. 15   **97.** 56   **99.** 35   **101.** 28

103. $\dfrac{x^4}{16} + \dfrac{x^3 y}{2} + \dfrac{3x^2 y^2}{2} + 2xy^3 + y^4$

105. $a^5 - 15a^4 b + 90a^3 b^2 - 270a^2 b^3 + 405ab^4 - 243b^5$

107. $41 + 840i$ **109.** 3   **111.** 10,000

113. 3,628,800   **115.** 56   **117.** $\dfrac{1}{9}$

119. (a) 43%   (b) 82%   **121.** $\dfrac{1}{216}$ **123.** $\dfrac{3}{4}$

125. True. $\dfrac{(n+2)!}{n!} = \dfrac{(n+2)(n+1)n!}{n!} = (n+2)(n+1)$

127. True by Properties of Sums

129. The set of natural numbers

131. (a) Each term is obtained by adding the same constant (common difference) to the preceding term.

(b) Each term is obtained by multiplying the same constant (common ratio) by the preceding term.

133. Each term of the sequence is defined in terms of preceding term.

135. d   **136.** a   **137.** b   **138.** c

139. 240, 440, 810, 1490, 2740

Chapter Test   *(page 690)*

1. $-\dfrac{1}{5}, \dfrac{1}{8}, -\dfrac{1}{11}, \dfrac{1}{14}, -\dfrac{1}{17}$ **2.** $a_n = \dfrac{n+2}{n!}$

3. $50, 61, 72; 140$ **4.** $a_n = 0.8n + 1.4$

5. 5, 10, 20, 40, 80   **6.** 86,100   **7.** 4

8. Answers will vary.

9. $x^4 + 8x^3y + 24x^2y^2 + 32xy^3 + 16y^4$ **10.** 180

11. (a) 72   (b) 328,440   **12.** (a) 330   (b) 720,720

13. 720   **14.** $\frac{1}{15}$ **15.** 3.908×10^{-10} **16.** 25%

Cumulative Test for Chapters 7–9
(page 691)

1. $(1, 2), \left(-\frac{3}{2}, \frac{3}{4}\right)$ **2.** $(2, -1)$

3. $(4, 2, -3)$ **4.** $(1, -2, 1)$

5.

6.

7.

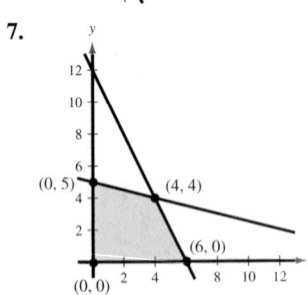

Maximum at $(4, 4)$: $z = 20$

8. $0.75 mixture: 120 pounds;

$1.25 mixture: 80 pounds

9. $y = \frac{1}{3}x^2 - 2x + 4$

10. $\begin{bmatrix} -1 & 2 & -1 & \vdots & 9 \\ 2 & -1 & 2 & \vdots & -9 \\ 3 & 3 & -4 & \vdots & 7 \end{bmatrix}$ **11.** $(-2, 3, -1)$

12. $\begin{bmatrix} 5 & -3 \\ -2 & 2 \end{bmatrix}$ **13.** $\begin{bmatrix} 2 & -6 \\ -2 & 0 \end{bmatrix}$ **14.** $\begin{bmatrix} 6 & -6 \\ -3 & 2 \end{bmatrix}$

15. $\begin{bmatrix} -4 & 12 \\ 3 & -3 \end{bmatrix}$ **16.** 84   **17.** $\begin{bmatrix} -175 & 37 & -13 \\ 95 & -20 & 7 \\ 14 & -3 & 1 \end{bmatrix}$

18. Gym shoes: $1936 million

Jogging shoes: $1502 million

Walking shoes: $3099 million

19. $(-5, 4)$ **20.** $(-3, 4, 2)$ **21.** 9

22. $\frac{1}{5}, -\frac{1}{7}, \frac{1}{9}, -\frac{1}{11}, \frac{1}{13}$ **23.** $a_n = \dfrac{(n + 1)!}{n + 3}$

24. 920   **25.** (a) 65.4   (b) $a_n = 3.2n + 1.4$

26. 3, 6, 12, 24, 48   **27.** $\frac{130}{9}$ **28.** Answers will vary.

29. $z^4 - 12z^3 + 54z^2 - 108z + 81$ **30.** 210   **31.** 600

32. 70   **33.** 120   **34.** 720   **35.** $\frac{1}{4}$

Problem Solving   (page 696)

1. 1, 1.5, 1.41$\overline{6}$, 1.414215686,

1.414213562, 1.414213562, . . .

x_n approaches $\sqrt{2}$.

3. (a)

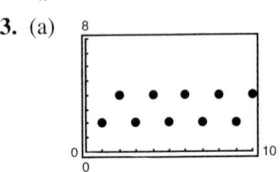

(b) If n is odd, $a_n = 2$, and if n is even, $a_n = 4$.

(c)

n	1	10	101	1000	10,001
a_n	2	4	2	4	2

(d) It is not possible to find the value of a_n as n approaches infinity.

5. (a) 3, 5, 7, 9, 11, 13, 15, 17

$a_n = 2n + 1$

(b) To obtain the arithmetic sequence, find the differences of consecutive terms of the sequence of perfect cubes. Then find the differences of consecutive terms of this sequence.

(c) 12, 18, 24, 30, 36, 42, 48

$a_n = 6n + 6$

(d) To obtain the arithmetic sequence, find the third sequence obtained by taking differences of consecutive terms in consecutive sequences.

(e) 60, 84, 108, 132, 156, 180

$a_n = 24n + 36$

7. $s_n = \left(\frac{1}{2}\right)^{n-1}$

$a_n = \dfrac{\sqrt{3}}{4}s_n^2$

9. Answers will vary.

11. (a) Answers will vary.   (b) 17,710   **13.** $\frac{1}{3}$

Chapter 10

Section 10.1　*(page 704)*

1. $\dfrac{\sqrt{3}}{3}$　**3.** -1　**5.** $\sqrt{3}$　**7.** 3.2236

9. $\dfrac{3\pi}{4}$ radians, 135°　**11.** $\dfrac{\pi}{4}$ radian, 45°

13. 0.6435 radian, 36.9°　**15.** 1.0517 radians, 60.3°

17. 2.1112 radians, 121.0°　**19.** 1.2490 radians, 71.6°

21. 2.1112 radians, 121.0°　**23.** 1.1071 radians, 63.4°

25. 0.1974 radian, 11.3°　**27.** 1.4289 radians, 81.9°

29. 0.9273 radian, 53.1°　**31.** 0.8187 radian, 46.9°

33. (2, 1): 42.3°; (4, 4): 78.7°; (6, 2): 59.0°

35. $(-4, -1)$: 11.9°; (3, 2): 21.8°; (1, 0): 146.3°　**37.** 0

39. $\dfrac{7}{5}$　**41.** 7　**43.** $\dfrac{8\sqrt{37}}{37} \approx 1.3152$

45. (a) 4　(b) 8　**47.** (a) $\dfrac{35\sqrt{37}}{74}$　(b) $\dfrac{35}{8}$

49. $2\sqrt{2}$　**51.** 0.1003, 1054 feet

53. (a) 18.4°　(b) 15.8 meters

55. $\alpha \approx 33.69°$; $\beta \approx 56.31°$

57. True. The inclination of a line is related to its slope by $m = \tan \theta$. If the angle is greater than $\pi/2$ but less than π, then the angle is in the second quadrant, where the tangent function is negative.

59. (a) $d = \dfrac{4}{\sqrt{m^2 + 1}}$

(b)

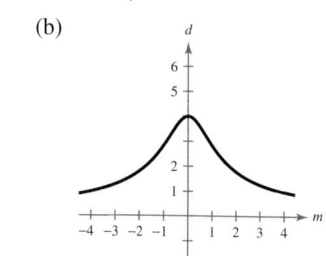

(c) $m = 0$

(d) $d = 0$. As the line approaches the vertical, the distance approaches 0.

61. x-intercept: $(7, 0)$

　y-intercept: $(0, 49)$

63. x-intercepts: $\left(5 \pm \sqrt{5}, 0\right)$

　y-intercept: $(0, 20)$

65. x-intercepts: $\left(\dfrac{7 \pm \sqrt{53}}{2}, 0\right)$

　y-intercept: $(0, -1)$

67. $f(x) = 3\left(x + \tfrac{1}{3}\right)^2 - \tfrac{49}{3}$

　Vertex: $\left(-\tfrac{1}{3}, -\tfrac{49}{3}\right)$

69. $f(x) = 5\left(x + \tfrac{17}{5}\right)^2 - \tfrac{324}{5}$

　Vertex: $\left(-\tfrac{17}{5}, -\tfrac{324}{5}\right)$

71. $f(x) = 6\left(x - \tfrac{1}{12}\right)^2 - \tfrac{289}{24}$

　Vertex: $\left(\tfrac{1}{12}, -\tfrac{289}{24}\right)$

73.

75.

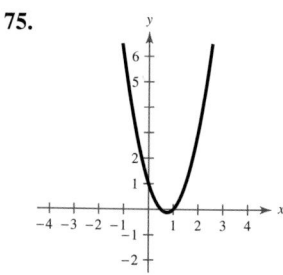

Section 10.2　*(page 712)*

1. A circle is formed when a plane intersects the top or bottom half of a double-napped cone and is perpendicular to the axis of the cone.

3. A parabola is formed when a plane intersects the top or bottom half of a double-napped cone, is parallel to the side of the cone, and does not intersect the vertex.

5. e　**6.** b　**7.** d　**8.** f　**9.** a　**10.** c

11. Vertex: $(0, 0)$

　Focus: $\left(0, \tfrac{1}{2}\right)$

　Directrix: $y = -\tfrac{1}{2}$

13. Vertex: $(0, 0)$

　Focus: $\left(-\tfrac{3}{2}, 0\right)$

　Directrix: $x = \tfrac{3}{2}$

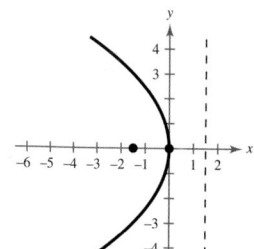

15. Vertex: $(0, 0)$

　Focus: $\left(0, -\tfrac{3}{2}\right)$

　Directrix: $y = \tfrac{3}{2}$

17. Vertex: $(1, -2)$

　Focus: $(1, -4)$

　Directrix: $y = 0$

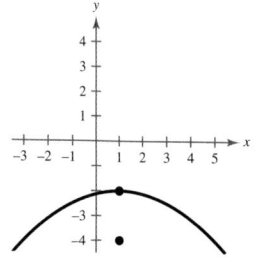

19. Vertex: $\left(-\frac{3}{2}, 2\right)$

Focus: $\left(-\frac{3}{2}, 3\right)$

Directrix: $y = 1$

21. Vertex: $(1, 1)$

Focus: $(1, 2)$

Directrix: $y = 0$

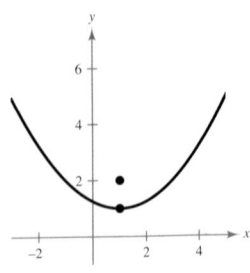

23. Vertex: $(-2, -3)$

Focus: $(-4, -3)$

Directrix: $x = 0$

25. Vertex: $(-2, 1)$

Focus: $\left(-2, -\frac{1}{2}\right)$

Directrix: $y = \frac{5}{2}$

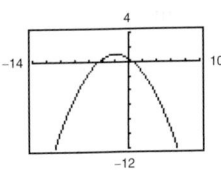

27. Vertex: $\left(\frac{1}{4}, -\frac{1}{2}\right)$

Focus: $\left(0, -\frac{1}{2}\right)$

Directrix: $x = \frac{1}{2}$

29.

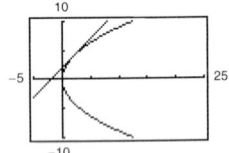

$(2, 4)$

31. $x^2 = \frac{3}{2}y$ **33.** $x^2 = -6y$ **35.** $y^2 = -8x$

37. $x^2 = 4y$ **39.** $y^2 = -8x$ **41.** $y^2 = 9x$

43. $(x - 3)^2 = -(y - 1)$ **45.** $y^2 = 4(x + 4)$

47. $(y - 2)^2 = -8(x - 5)$ **49.** $x^2 = 8(y - 4)$

51. $(y - 2)^2 = 8x$ **53.** $y = \sqrt{6(x + 1)} + 3$

55. $4x - y - 8 = 0$; $(2, 0)$ **57.** $4x - y + 2 = 0$; $\left(-\frac{1}{2}, 0\right)$

59.

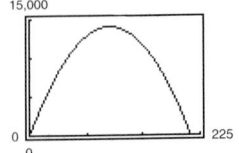

$x = 106$ units

61. $y = \frac{1}{18}x^2$ **63.** (a) $y = -\frac{1}{640}x^2$ (b) 8 feet

65. (a) $17,500\sqrt{2}$ miles per hour

(b) $x^2 = -16,400(y - 4100)$

67. (a) $x^2 = -64(y - 75)$

(b) 69.3 feet

69. False. If the graph crossed the directrix, there would exist points nearer the directrix than the focus.

71. (a)

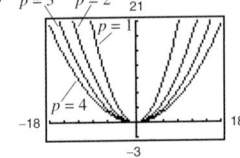

As p increases, the graph becomes wider.

(b) $(0, 1)$, $(0, 2)$, $(0, 3)$, $(0, 4)$

(c) $4, 8, 12, 16$; $4|p|$

(d) Easy way to determine two additional points on the graph

73. $m = \dfrac{x_1}{2p}$ **75.** $\pm 1, \pm 2, \pm 4$

77. $\pm\frac{1}{2}, \pm 1, \pm 2, \pm 4, \pm 8, \pm 16$

79. $y = x^3 - 7x^2 + 17x - 15$ **81.** $\frac{1}{2}, -\frac{5}{3}, \pm 2$

83. $B \approx 23.67°$, $C \approx 121.33°$, $c \approx 14.89$

85. $C = 89°$, $a \approx 1.93$, $b \approx 2.33$

87. $A \approx 16.39°$, $B \approx 23.77°$, $C \approx 139.84°$

89. $B \approx 24.62°$, $C \approx 90.38°$, $a \approx 10.88$

Section 10.3   *(page 722)*

1. b   **2.** c   **3.** d   **4.** f   **5.** a   **6.** e

7. Center: $(0, 0)$

Vertices: $(\pm 5, 0)$

Foci: $(\pm 3, 0)$

Eccentricity: $\frac{3}{5}$

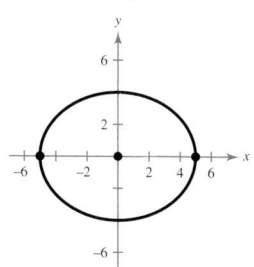

9. Center: $(0, 0)$

Vertices: $(0, \pm 3)$

Foci: $(0, \pm 2)$

Eccentricity: $\frac{2}{3}$

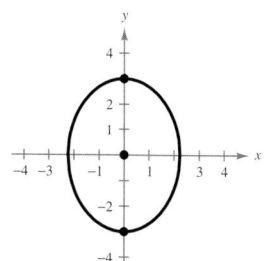

11. Center: $(-3, 5)$

Vertices: $(-3, 10), (-3, 0)$

Foci: $(-3, 8), (-3, 2)$

Eccentricity: $\frac{3}{5}$

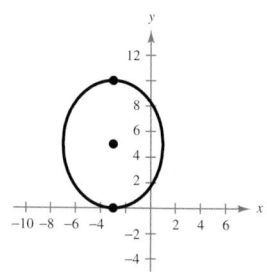

13. Center: $(-5, 1)$

Vertices: $\left(-\frac{7}{2}, 1\right), \left(-\frac{13}{2}, 1\right)$

Foci: $\left(-5 \pm \frac{\sqrt{5}}{2}, 1\right)$

Eccentricity: $\frac{\sqrt{5}}{3}$

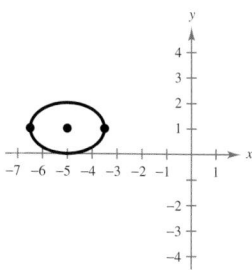

15. Center: $(-2, 3)$

Vertices: $(-2, 6), (-2, 0)$

Foci: $\left(-2, 3 \pm \sqrt{5}\right)$

Eccentricity: $\frac{\sqrt{5}}{3}$

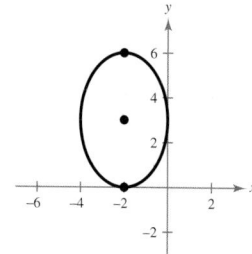

17. Center: $(4, 3)$

Vertices: $(14, 3), (-6, 3)$

Foci: $\left(4 \pm 4\sqrt{5}, 3\right)$

Eccentricity: $\frac{2\sqrt{5}}{5}$

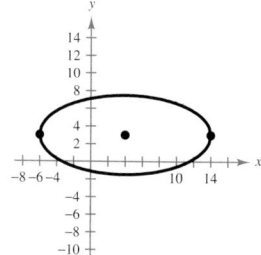

19. Center: $\left(-\frac{3}{2}, \frac{5}{2}\right)$

Vertices: $\left(-\frac{3}{2}, \frac{5}{2} \pm 2\sqrt{3}\right)$

Foci: $\left(-\frac{3}{2}, \frac{5}{2} \pm 2\sqrt{2}\right)$

Eccentricity: $\frac{\sqrt{6}}{3}$

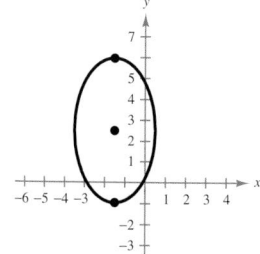

21. Center: $(1, -1)$

Vertices: $\left(\frac{9}{4}, -1\right), \left(-\frac{1}{4}, -1\right)$

Foci: $\left(\frac{7}{4}, -1\right), \left(\frac{1}{4}, -1\right)$

Eccentricity: $\frac{3}{5}$

23.

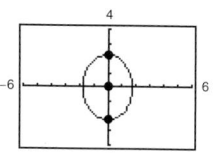

Center: $(0, 0)$

Vertices: $\left(0, \pm \sqrt{5}\right)$

Foci: $\left(0, \pm \sqrt{2}\right)$

25.

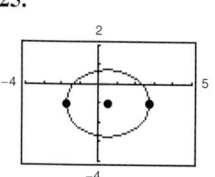

Center: $\left(\frac{1}{2}, -1\right)$

Vertices: $\left(\frac{1}{2} \pm \sqrt{5}, -1\right)$

Foci: $\left(\frac{1}{2} \pm \sqrt{2}, -1\right)$

27. $\dfrac{x^2}{4} + \dfrac{y^2}{16} = 1$ **29.** $\dfrac{x^2}{36} + \dfrac{y^2}{32} = 1$

31. $\dfrac{x^2}{36} + \dfrac{y^2}{11} = 1$ **33.** $\dfrac{21x^2}{400} + \dfrac{y^2}{25} = 1$

35. $\dfrac{(x - 2)^2}{1} + \dfrac{(y - 3)^2}{9} = 1$

37. $\dfrac{(x + 2)^2}{16} + \dfrac{(y - 3)^2}{9} = 1$

39. $\dfrac{(x - 2)^2}{4} + \dfrac{(y - 4)^2}{1} = 1$ **41.** $\dfrac{x^2}{48} + \dfrac{(y - 4)^2}{64} = 1$

43. $\dfrac{x^2}{16} + \dfrac{(y-4)^2}{12} = 1$ **45.** $\dfrac{(x-2)^2}{4} + \dfrac{(y-2)^2}{1} = 1$

47. $\dfrac{x^2}{25} + \dfrac{y^2}{16} = 1$

49. (a)

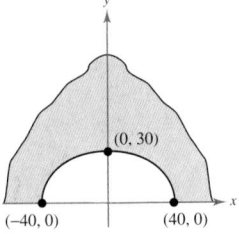

(b) $\dfrac{x^2}{1600} + \dfrac{y^2}{900} = 1$ (c) 14.5 feet

51. 40   **53.** $e \approx 0.052$

55.

57.

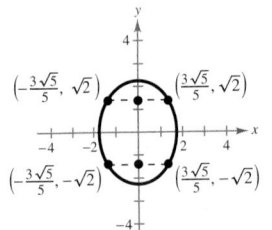

59. False. The equation of an ellipse is second degree in x and y.

61. (a) $A = \pi a(20 - a)$ (b) $\dfrac{x^2}{196} + \dfrac{y^2}{36} = 1$

(c)

a	8	9	10	11	12	13
A	301.6	311.0	314.2	311.0	301.6	285.9

$a = 10$, circle

(d)

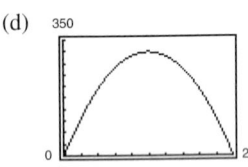

The shape of an ellipse with a maximum area is a circle.

63. Geometric   **65.** Arithmetic   **67.** $a_n = -\frac{1}{4}n + \frac{1}{4}$

69. $a_n = 9n$ **71.** 547   **73.** 340.15

Section 10.4   *(page 732)*

1. b   **2.** c   **3.** a   **4.** d

5. Center: $(0, 0)$
Vertices: $(\pm 1, 0)$
Foci: $\left(\pm\sqrt{2}, 0\right)$
Asymptotes: $y = \pm x$

7. Center: $(0, 0)$
Vertices: $(0, \pm 5)$
Foci: $\left(0, \pm\sqrt{106}\right)$
Asymptotes: $y = \pm\frac{5}{9}x$

 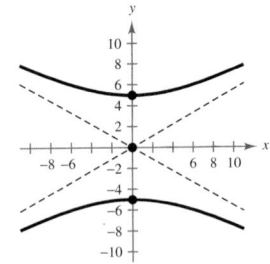

9. Center: $(1, -2)$
Vertices: $(3, -2), (-1, -2)$
Foci: $\left(1 \pm \sqrt{5}, -2\right)$
Asymptotes: $y = -2 \pm \frac{1}{2}(x - 1)$

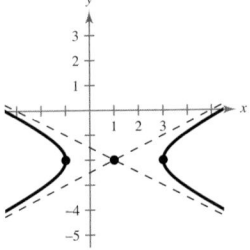

11. Center: $(2, -6)$
Vertices: $\left(2, -\dfrac{17}{3}\right), \left(2, -\dfrac{19}{3}\right)$
Foci: $\left(2, -6 \pm \dfrac{\sqrt{13}}{6}\right)$
Asymptotes: $y = -6 \pm \dfrac{2}{3}(x - 2)$

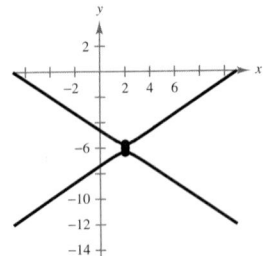

13. Center: $(2, -3)$

Vertices: $(3, -3), (1, -3)$

Foci: $\left(2 \pm \sqrt{10}, -3\right)$

Asymptotes: $y = -3 \pm 3(x - 2)$

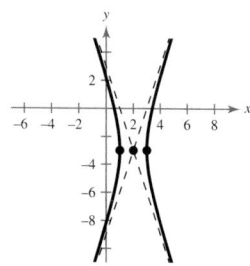

15. The graph of this equation is two lines intersecting at $(-1, -3)$.

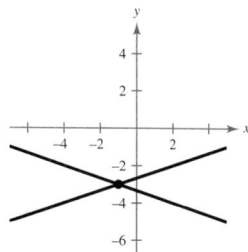

17. Center: $(0, 0)$

Vertices: $\left(\pm\sqrt{3}, 0\right)$

Foci: $\left(\pm\sqrt{5}, 0\right)$

Asymptotes: $y = \pm\dfrac{\sqrt{6}}{3}x$

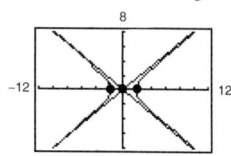

19. Center: $(1, -3)$

Vertices: $\left(1, -3 \pm \sqrt{2}\right)$

Foci: $\left(1, -3 \pm 2\sqrt{5}\right)$

Asymptotes: $y = -3 \pm \frac{1}{3}(x - 1)$

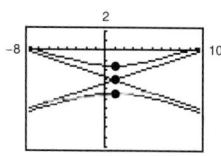

21. $\dfrac{y^2}{4} - \dfrac{x^2}{12} = 1$ **23.** $\dfrac{x^2}{1} - \dfrac{y^2}{25} = 1$

25. $\dfrac{17y^2}{1024} - \dfrac{17x^2}{64} = 1$ **27.** $\dfrac{(x - 4)^2}{4} - \dfrac{y^2}{12} = 1$

29. $\dfrac{(y - 5)^2}{16} - \dfrac{(x - 4)^2}{9} = 1$ **31.** $\dfrac{y^2}{9} - \dfrac{4(x - 2)^2}{9} = 1$

33. $\dfrac{(y - 2)^2}{4} - \dfrac{x^2}{4} = 1$ **35.** $\dfrac{(x - 2)^2}{1} - \dfrac{(y - 2)^2}{1} = 1$

37. $\dfrac{(x - 3)^2}{9} - \dfrac{(y - 2)^2}{4} = 1$

39. (a) $x \approx 110.3$ miles

(b) 57.0 miles

(c) 0.00129 second

(d) The ship is at the position $(144.2, 60)$.

41. Circle   **43.** Hyperbola   **45.** Ellipse

47. Parabola

49. True. For a hyperbola, $c^2 = a^2 + b^2$. The larger the ratio of b to a, the larger the eccentricity of the hyperbola, $e = c/a$.

51. Answers will vary.   **53.** $x(x + 4)(x - 4)$

55. $2x(x - 6)^2$

57. 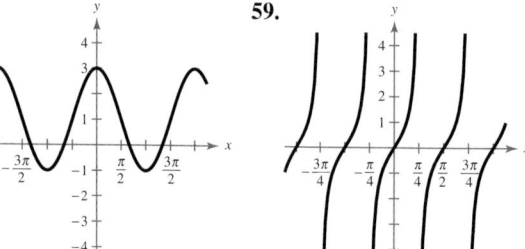   **59.**

Section 10.5   *(page 740)*

1. $(3, 0)$ **3.** $\left(\dfrac{3 + \sqrt{3}}{2}, \dfrac{3\sqrt{3} - 1}{2}\right)$

5. $\left(\dfrac{3\sqrt{2}}{2}, -\dfrac{\sqrt{2}}{2}\right)$

7. $\dfrac{(y')^2}{2} - \dfrac{(x')^2}{2} = 1$ **9.** $y' = \pm\dfrac{\sqrt{2}}{2}$

    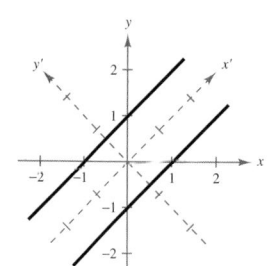

11. $\dfrac{(x' - 3\sqrt{2})^2}{16} - \dfrac{(y' - \sqrt{2})^2}{16} = 1$

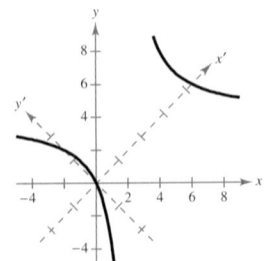

13. $\dfrac{(x')^2}{6} + \dfrac{(y')^2}{\frac{3}{2}} = 1$ **15.** $x' = -(y')^2$

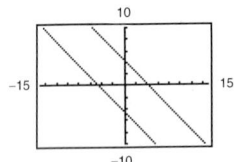

17. $y' = \frac{1}{6}(x')^2 - \frac{1}{3}x'$ **19.**

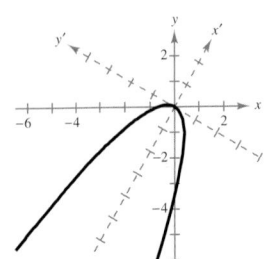

$\theta = 45°$

21.   **23.**

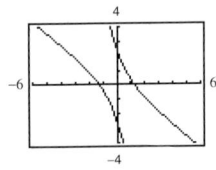

$\theta \approx 26.57°$ $\theta \approx 31.72°$

25.

$\theta \approx 33.69°$

27. e   **28.** f   **29.** b   **30.** a   **31.** d   **32.** c

33. Parabola

$$y = \dfrac{(8x - 5) \pm \sqrt{(8x - 5)^2 - 4(16x^2 - 10x)}}{2}$$

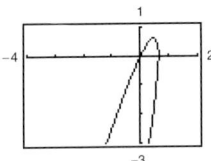

35. Ellipse

$$y = \dfrac{6x \pm \sqrt{36x^2 - 28(12x^2 - 45)}}{14}$$

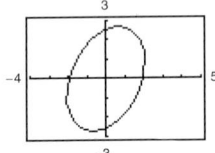

37. Hyperbola

$$y = \dfrac{6x \pm \sqrt{36x^2 + 20(x^2 + 4x - 22)}}{-10}$$

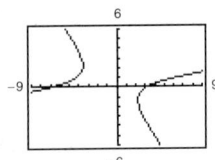

39. Parabola

$$y = \dfrac{-(4x - 1) \pm \sqrt{(4x - 1)^2 - 16(x^2 - 5x - 3)}}{8}$$

41.   **43.**

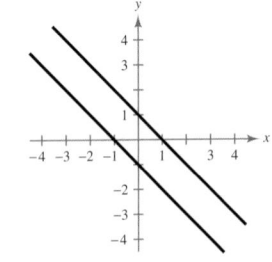

45. $(2, 2), (2, 4)$ **47.** $(-8, 12)$ **49.** $(0, 8), (12, 8)$

51. $(0, 4)$ **53.** $\left(1, \sqrt{3}\right), \left(1, -\sqrt{3}\right)$

55. No solution   **57.** $\left(0, \frac{3}{2}\right), (-3, 0)$

59. True. The graph of the equation can be classified by finding the discriminant. For a graph to be a hyperbola, the discriminant must be greater than zero. If $k \geq \frac{1}{4}$, then the discriminant would be less than or equal to zero.

61. Answers will vary.   **63.** ± 3 **65.** ± 2 **67.** -2

69.

71.

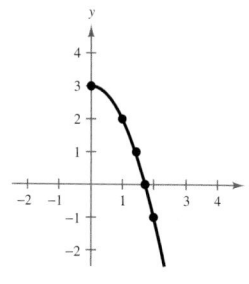

Intercept: $(0, 1)$

Asymptotes: $x = 2, y = 0$

Intercept: $(0, 2)$

Asymptotes: $t = -1, y = 0$

73.

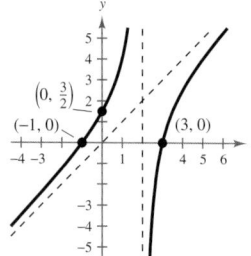

Intercepts: $(-1, 0), (3, 0), \left(0, \frac{3}{2}\right)$

Asymptotes: $x = 2, y = x$

75.

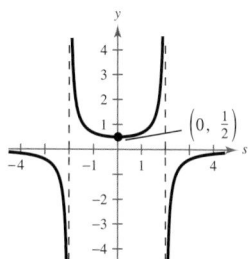

Intercept: $\left(0, \frac{1}{2}\right)$

Asymptotes: $s = \pm 2, y = 0$

Section 10.6   *(page 747)*

1. (a)

t	0	1	2	3	4
x	0	1	$\sqrt{2}$	$\sqrt{3}$	2
y	3	2	1	0	-1

(b)

(c) $y = 3 - x^2$

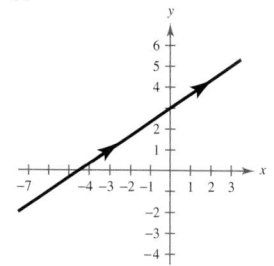

The graph of the rectangular equation shows the entire parabola rather than just the right half.

3.

5.

7.

9.

11.

13.

15.

17.

19.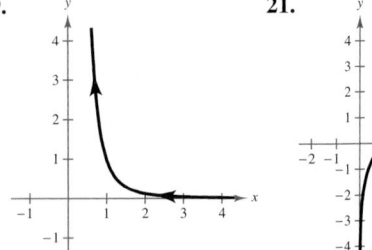

21.

23. Each curve represents a portion of the line $y = 2x + 1$.

	Domain	Orientation
(a)	$(-\infty, \infty)$	Left to right
(b)	$[-1, 1]$	Depends on θ
(c)	$(0, \infty)$	Right to left
(d)	$(0, \infty)$	Left to right

25. $y - y_1 = m(x - x_1)$ **27.** $\dfrac{(x - h)^2}{a^2} + \dfrac{(y - k)^2}{b^2} = 1$

29. $x = 6t$ **31.** $x = 3 + 4 \cos \theta$ **33.** $x = 4 \cos \theta$
$y = -3t$ $y = 2 + 4 \sin \theta$ $y = \sqrt{7} \sin \theta$

35. $x = 4 \sec \theta$ **37.** (a) $x = t, \ y = 3t - 2$
$y = 3 \tan \theta$ (b) $x = -t + 2, \ y = -3t + 4$

39. (a) $x = t, \ y = t^2$
(b) $x = -t + 2, \ y = t^2 - 4t + 4$

41. (a) $x = t, \ y = t^2 + 1$
(b) $x = -t + 2, \ y = t^2 - 4t + 5$

43. (a) $x = t, \ y = \dfrac{1}{t}$
(b) $x = -t + 2, \ y = -\dfrac{1}{t - 2}$

45.

47.

49.

51.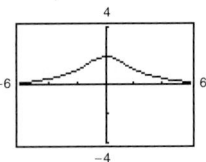

53. b
Domain: $[-2, 2]$
Range: $[-1, 1]$

54. c
Domain: $[-4, 4]$
Range: $[-6, 6]$

55. d
Domain: $(-\infty, \infty)$
Range: $(-\infty, \infty)$

56. a
Domain: $(-\infty, \infty)$
Range: $[-2, 2]$

57. (a)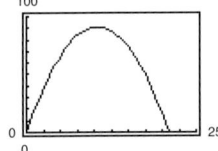

Maximum height: 90.7 feet
Range: 209.6 feet

(b)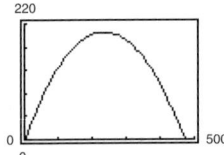

Maximum height: 204.2 feet
Range: 471.6 feet

(c)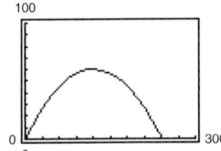

Maximum height: 60.5 feet
Range: 242.0 feet

(d)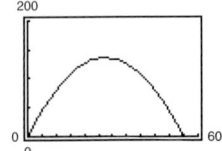

Maximum height: 136.1 feet
Range: 544.5 feet

59. (a) $x = (146.67 \cos \theta)t$

$y = 3 + (146.67 \sin \theta)t - 16t^2$

(b)

No

(c)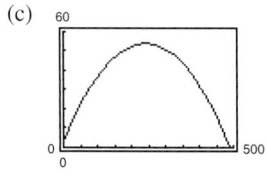

Yes

(d) $19.3°$

61. Answers will vary. **63.** $x = a\theta - b \sin \theta$

$y = a - b \cos \theta$

65. True

$x = t$

$y = t^2 + 1 \Rightarrow y = x^2 + 1$

$x = 3t$

$y = 9t^2 + 1 \Rightarrow y = x^2 + 1$

67. $(5, 2)$ **69.** $(1, -2, 1)$

71. $\theta' = 75°$ **73.** $\theta' = \dfrac{\pi}{3}$

75.   **77.**

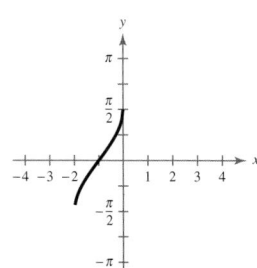

Section 10.7 *(page 754)*

1.   **3.**

$\left(4, \dfrac{5\pi}{3}\right), \left(-4, -\dfrac{4\pi}{3}\right)$ $\left(0, \dfrac{5\pi}{6}\right), \left(0, -\dfrac{13\pi}{6}\right)$

5.   **7.**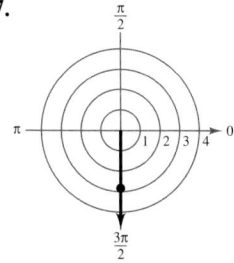

$\left(\sqrt{2}, 8.64\right), \left(-\sqrt{2}, -0.78\right)$ $\left(2\sqrt{2}, 10.99\right), \left(-2\sqrt{2}, 7.85\right)$

9. $(0, 3)$ **11.** $\left(\dfrac{\sqrt{2}}{2}, \dfrac{\sqrt{2}}{2}\right)$ **13.** $\left(-\sqrt{2}, \sqrt{2}\right)$

15. $(-1.1340, -2.2280)$ **17.** $\left(\sqrt{2}, \dfrac{\pi}{4}\right)$ **19.** $(6, \pi)$

21. $(5, 2.2143)$ **23.** $\left(\sqrt{6}, \dfrac{5\pi}{4}\right)$ **25.** $\left(3\sqrt{13}, 0.9828\right)$

27. $\left(\sqrt{13}, 5.6952\right)$ **29.** $\left(\sqrt{7}, 0.8571\right)$

31. $\left(\frac{17}{6}, 0.4900\right)$ **33.** $r = 3$ **35.** $r = 4 \csc \theta$

37. $r = 10 \sec \theta$ **39.** $r = \dfrac{-2}{3 \cos \theta - \sin \theta}$

41. $r^2 = 16 \sec \theta \csc \theta = 32 \csc 2\theta$

43. $r = \dfrac{4}{1 - \cos \theta}$ or $-\dfrac{4}{1 + \cos \theta}$ **45.** $r = a$

47. $r = 2a \cos \theta$ **49.** $x^2 + y^2 - 4y = 0$

51. $\sqrt{3}x + y = 0$ **53.** $x^2 + y^2 = 16$ **55.** $y = 4$

57. $x^2 + y^2 - x^{2/3} = 0$ **59.** $(x^2 + y^2)^2 = 6x^2y - 2y^3$

61. $x^2 + 4y - 4 = 0$ **63.** $4x^2 - 5y^2 - 36y - 36 = 0$

65. $x^2 + y^2 = 36$

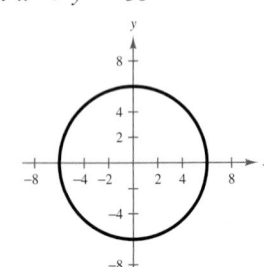

67. $-\sqrt{3}x + 3y = 0$

69. $x - 3 = 0$

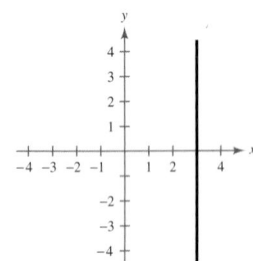

71. True. Because r is a directed distance, the point (r, θ) can be represented as $(r, \theta \pm 2\pi n)$.

73. $(x - h)^2 + (y - k)^2 = h^2 + k^2$

Radius: $\sqrt{h^2 + k^2}$

Center: (h, k)

75. (a) Answers will vary.

(b) (r_1, θ_1), (r_2, θ_2) and the pole are collinear.
$$d = \sqrt{r_1^2 + r_2^2 - 2r_1 r_2} = |r_1 - r_2|$$
This represents the distance between two points on the line $\theta = \theta_1 = \theta_2$.

(c) $d = \sqrt{r_1^2 + r_2^2}$

This is the result of the Pythagorean Theorem.

(d) Answers will vary. For example:

Points: $(3, \pi/6), (4, \pi/3)$

Distance: 2.053

Points: $(-3, 7\pi/6), (-4, 4\pi/3)$

Distance: 2.053

77. $2 \log_6 x + \log_6 z - \log_6 y - \log_6 3$

79. $\ln x + 2 \ln(x + 4)$ **81.** $\log_7 \dfrac{x}{3y}$ **83.** $\ln \sqrt{x(x - 2)}$

85. $(2, 3)$ **87.** $\left(\frac{8}{7}, \frac{88}{35}, \frac{8}{5}\right)$ **89.** $(2, -3, 3)$

91. Not collinear **93.** Collinear

Section 10.8 *(page 762)*

1. Rose curve **3.** Limaçon **5.** Rose curve

7. Polar axis **9.** $\theta = \dfrac{\pi}{2}$ **11.** $\theta = \dfrac{\pi}{2}$, polar axis, pole

13. Maximum: $|r| = 20$ when $\theta = \dfrac{3\pi}{2}$

Zero: $r = 0$ when $\theta = \dfrac{\pi}{2}$

15. Maximum: $|r| = 4$ when $\theta = 0, \dfrac{\pi}{3}, \dfrac{2\pi}{3}$

Zero: $r = 0$ when $\theta = \dfrac{\pi}{6}, \dfrac{\pi}{2}, \dfrac{5\pi}{6}$

17.

19.

21.

23.

25.

27.

29.

31.

33.

35.

37.

39.

41.

43.

45.

47.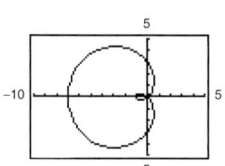

$0 \le \theta < 2\pi$

49.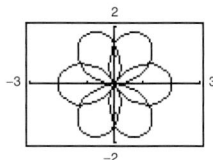

$0 \le \theta < 4\pi$

51.

$0 \le \theta < \pi$

53.

55.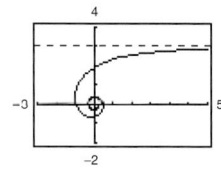

57. True. For a graph to have polar axis symmetry, replace (r, θ) by $(r, -\theta)$ or $(-r, \pi - \theta)$.

59. (a)

(b)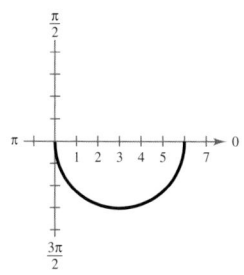

Upper half of circle   Lower half of circle

(c)

(d)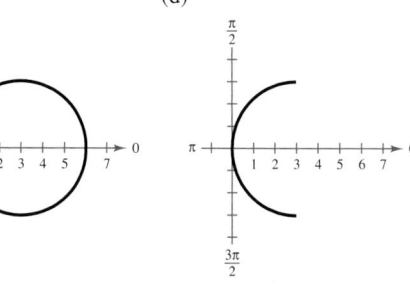

Full circle   Left half of circle

61. Answers will vary.

63. (a) $r = 2 - \sin\left(\theta - \dfrac{\pi}{4}\right)$

(b) $r = 2 + \cos \theta$

(c) $r = 2 + \sin \theta$

(d) $r = 2 - \cos \theta$

65. (a)

(b)

67.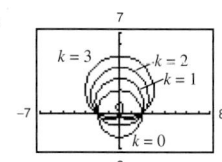

$k = 0$, circle

$k = 1$, limaçon

$k = 2$, cardioid

$k = 3$, limaçon

69. ± 3 **71.** $\dfrac{13}{5}$

73. $\dfrac{(x + 1)^2}{9} + \dfrac{(y - 2)^2}{4} = 1$

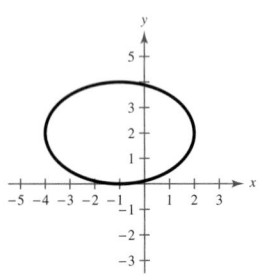

Section 10.9 (page 768)

1. $e = 1$: $r = \dfrac{4}{1 + \cos \theta}$, parabola

$e = 0.5$: $r = \dfrac{2}{1 + 0.5 \cos \theta}$, ellipse

$e = 1.5$: $r = \dfrac{6}{1 + 1.5 \cos \theta}$, hyperbola

3. $e = 1$: $r = \dfrac{4}{1 - \sin \theta}$, parabola

$e = 0.5$: $r = \dfrac{2}{1 - 0.5 \sin \theta}$, ellipse

$e = 1.5$: $r = \dfrac{6}{1 - 1.5 \sin \theta}$, hyperbola

5. f **6.** c **7.** d **8.** e **9.** a **10.** b

11. Parabola **13.** Parabola

15. Ellipse

17. Ellipse

19. Hyperbola

21. Hyperbola

23. Ellipse

25.

Parabola

27.

Ellipse

29.

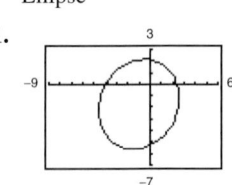

31.

33. $r = \dfrac{1}{1 - \cos \theta}$ **35.** $r = \dfrac{1}{2 + \sin \theta}$

37. $r = \dfrac{2}{1 + 2 \cos \theta}$ **39.** $r = \dfrac{2}{1 - \sin \theta}$

41. $r = \dfrac{10}{1 - \cos \theta}$ **43.** $r = \dfrac{10}{3 + 2 \cos \theta}$

45. $r = \dfrac{20}{3 - 2\cos\theta}$ **47.** $r = \dfrac{9}{4 - 5\sin\theta}$

49. Answers will vary.

51. $r = \dfrac{9.2934 \times 10^7}{1 - 0.0167\cos\theta}$

Perihelion: 9.1408×10^7 miles

Aphelion: 9.4512×10^7 miles

53. $r = \dfrac{5.5368 \times 10^9}{1 - 0.2481\cos\theta}$

Perihelion: 4.4362×10^9 kilometers

Aphelion: 7.3638×10^9 kilometers

55. $r = \dfrac{1.3977 \times 10^8}{1 - 0.0934\cos\theta}$

Perihelion: 1.2783×10^8 miles

Aphelion: 1.5417×10^8 miles

57. (a) $r = \dfrac{8200}{1 + \sin\theta}$

(b)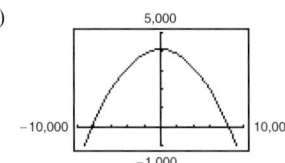

(c) 1467 miles

(d) 394 miles

59. True. The graphs represent the same hyperbola.

61. Answers will vary. **63.** $r^2 = \dfrac{24,336}{169 - 25\cos^2\theta}$

65. $r^2 = \dfrac{144}{25\cos^2\theta - 9}$ **67.** $r^2 = \dfrac{144}{25\cos^2\theta - 16}$

69. $\dfrac{\pi}{6} + n\pi$ **71.** $\dfrac{\pi}{3} + n\pi, \dfrac{2\pi}{3} + n\pi$

73. $\dfrac{\pi}{2} + n\pi$ **75.** $\dfrac{\sqrt{2}}{10}$ **77.** $\dfrac{7\sqrt{2}}{10}$

79. $\sin 2u = -\dfrac{24}{25}$

$\cos 2u = -\dfrac{7}{25}$

$\tan 2u = \dfrac{24}{7}$

81. $\dfrac{12!}{(12 - a)!a!}$ **83.** 720

Review Exercises *(page 772)*

1. $\dfrac{\pi}{4}$ radian, $45°$ **3.** 1.1071 radians, $63.43°$

5. 0.4424 radian, $25.35°$ **7.** 0.6588 radian, $37.75°$

9. $2\sqrt{2}$ **11.** Hyperbola **13.** $(x - 4)^2 = -8(y - 2)$

15. $(y - 2)^2 = 12x$ **17.** $y = -2x + 2; (1, 0)$

19. $8\sqrt{6}$ meters **21.** $\dfrac{(x - 2)^2}{25} + \dfrac{y^2}{21} = 1$

23. $\dfrac{(x - 2)^2}{4} + (y - 1)^2 = 1$

25. The foci occur 3 feet from the center of the arch on a line connecting the tops of the pillars.

27. Center: $(-2, 1)$

Vertices: $(-2, 11), (-2, -9)$

Foci: $\left(-2, 1 \pm \sqrt{19}\right)$

Eccentricity: $\dfrac{\sqrt{19}}{10}$

29. Center: $(1, -4)$

Vertices: $(1, 0), (1, -8)$

Foci: $\left(1, -4 \pm \sqrt{7}\right)$

Eccentricity: $\dfrac{\sqrt{7}}{4}$

31. $y^2 - \dfrac{x^2}{8} = 1$ **33.** $\dfrac{5(x - 4)^2}{16} - \dfrac{5y^2}{64} = 1$

35. Center: $(3, -5)$

Vertices: $(7, -5), (-1, -5)$

Foci: $\left(3 \pm 2\sqrt{5}, -5\right)$

Asymptotes: $y = -5 \pm \frac{1}{2}(x - 3)$

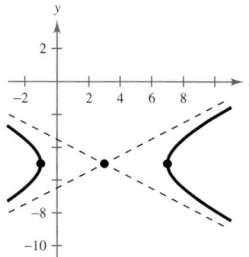

37. Center: $(1, -1)$

Vertices: $(5, -1), (-3, -1)$

Foci: $(6, -1), (-4, -1)$

Asymptotes: $y = -1 \pm \frac{3}{4}(x - 1)$

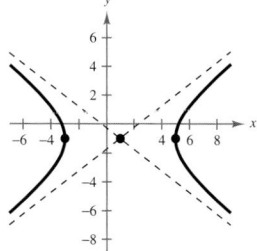

39. 72 miles   **41.** Hyperbola

43. $\dfrac{(x')^2}{8} - \dfrac{(y')^2}{8} = 1$ **45.** $\dfrac{(x')^2}{3} + \dfrac{(y')^2}{2} = 1$

    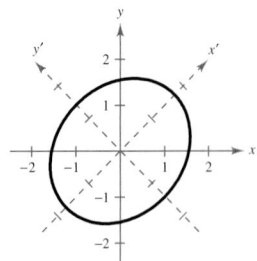

47. Parabola

$$y = \dfrac{24x + 40 \pm \sqrt{(24x + 40)^2 - 36(16x^2 - 30x)}}{18}$$

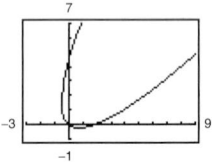

49. Parabola

$$y = \dfrac{-(2x - 2\sqrt{2}) \pm \sqrt{(2x - 2\sqrt{2})^2 - 4(x^2 + 2\sqrt{2}x + 2)}}{2}$$

51. $x = 3,\ y = 0$ **53.** $x = \dfrac{3\sqrt{3}}{2},\ y = \dfrac{1}{2}$

55.   **57.**

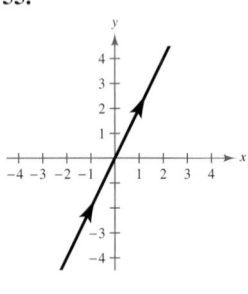

$y = 2x$ $y = \sqrt[4]{x}$

59.

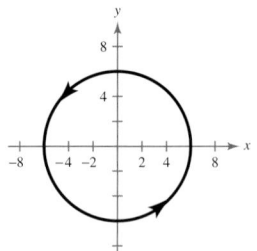

$x^2 + y^2 = 36$

61. $x = 5 + 6\cos\theta$ **63.** $x = 3\tan\theta$
$\quad\ \ y = 4 + 6\sin\theta$ $\quad\ \ y = 4\sec\theta$

65.   **67.**

    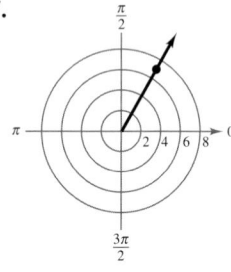

$\left(2, \dfrac{9\pi}{4}\right), \left(-2, \dfrac{5\pi}{4}\right)$ $(7, 1.05), (-7, 10.47)$

69. $\left(-\dfrac{1}{2}, -\dfrac{\sqrt{3}}{2}\right)$ **71.** $\left(-\dfrac{3\sqrt{2}}{2}, \dfrac{3\sqrt{2}}{2}\right)$

73. $\left(2, \dfrac{\pi}{2}\right)$ **75.** $\left(2\sqrt{13}, 0.9828\right)$

77. $r = 6\sin\theta$ **79.** $r^2 = 10\csc 2\theta$
81. $x^2 + y^2 = 3x$ **83.** $x^2 + y^2 = y^{2/3}$

85. Symmetry: $\theta = \dfrac{\pi}{2}$, polar axis, pole

Maximum value of $|r|$: $|r| = 4$ when $\theta = 0, \dfrac{\pi}{2}, \pi, \dfrac{3\pi}{2}$

No zeros of r

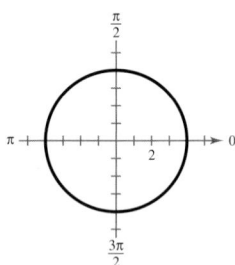

87. Symmetry: $\theta = \dfrac{\pi}{2}$, polar axis and the pole

Maximum value of $|r|$: $|r| = 4$ when $\theta = \dfrac{\pi}{4}, \dfrac{3\pi}{4}, \dfrac{5\pi}{4}, \dfrac{7\pi}{4}$

Zeros of r: $r = 0$ when $\theta = 0, \dfrac{\pi}{2}, \pi, \dfrac{3\pi}{2}$

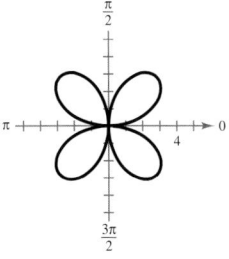

89. Symmetry: polar axis

Maximum value of $|r|$: $|r| = 4$ when $\theta = 0$

Zeros of r: $r = 0$ when $\theta = \pi$

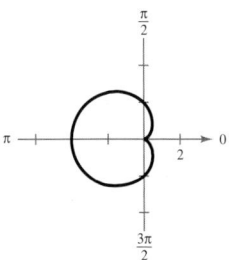

91. Symmetry: $\theta = \dfrac{\pi}{2}$

Maximum value of $|r|$: $|r| = 8$ when $\theta = \dfrac{\pi}{2}$

Zeros of r: $r = 0$ when $\theta = 3.4814, 5.9433$

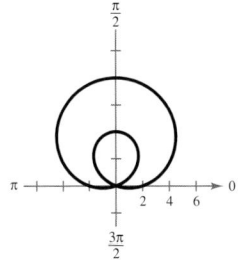

93. Symmetry: $\theta = \dfrac{\pi}{2}$, polar axis and the pole

Maximum value of $|r|$: $|r| = 3$ when $\theta = 0, \dfrac{\pi}{2}, \pi, \dfrac{3\pi}{2}$

Zeros of r: $r = 0$ when $\theta = \dfrac{\pi}{4}, \dfrac{3\pi}{4}, \dfrac{5\pi}{4}, \dfrac{7\pi}{4}$

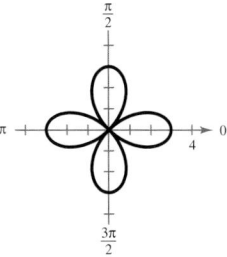

95. Limaçon   **97.** Rose curve

99. Hyperbola   **101.** Ellipse

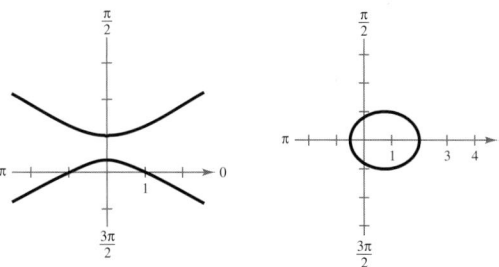

103. $r = \dfrac{4}{1 - \cos\theta}$ **105.** $r = \dfrac{5}{3 - 2\cos\theta}$

107. $r = \dfrac{7977.2}{1 - 0.937\cos\theta}$; 11,008.8 miles

109. False. When classifying an equation of the form $Ax^2 + Bxy + Cy^2 + Dx + Ey + F = 0$, its graph can be determined by its discriminant. For a graph to be a parabola, its discriminant, $B^2 - 4AC$, must equal zero. So, if $B = 0$, then A or C equals 0.

111. False. The following are two sets of parametric equations for the line.

$x = t, \ y = 3 - 2t$

$x = 3t, \ y = 3 - 6t$

113. 5. The ellipse becomes more circular and approaches a circle of radius 5.

115. (a) The speed would double.

(b) The elliptical orbit would be flatter; the length of the major axis would be greater.

117. (a) The graphs are the same.

(b) The graphs are the same.

Chapter Test *(page 776)*

1. 0.2783 radian, 15.9°   **2.** 0.8330 radian, 47.7°

3. $\dfrac{7\sqrt{2}}{2}$

4. Parabola: $y^2 = 4(x - 1)$

Vertex: $(1, 0)$

Focus: $(2, 0)$

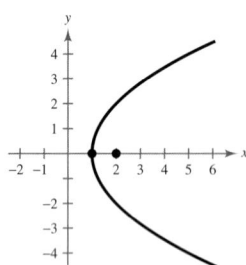

5. Hyperbola: $\dfrac{(x - 2)^2}{4} - y^2 = 1$

Center: $(2, 0)$

Vertices: $(0, 0), (4, 0)$

Foci: $\left(2 \pm \sqrt{5}, 0\right)$

Asymptotes: $y = \pm\frac{1}{2}(x - 2)$

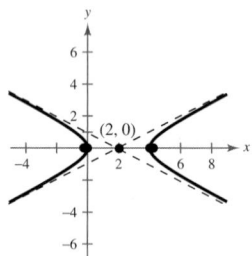

6. Ellipse: $\dfrac{(x + 3)^2}{16} + \dfrac{(y - 1)^2}{9} = 1$

Center: $(-3, 1)$

Vertices: $(1, 1), (-7, 1)$

Foci: $\left(-3 \pm \sqrt{7}, 1\right)$

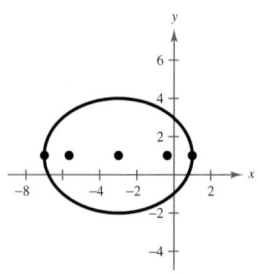

7. Circle: $(x - 2)^2 + (y - 1)^2 = \frac{1}{2}$

Center: $(2, 1)$

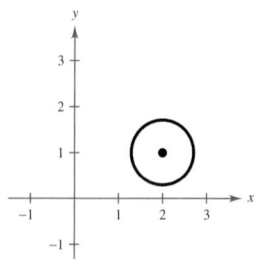

8. $(x - 3)^2 = \dfrac{3}{2}(y + 2)$ **9.** $\dfrac{5(y - 2)^2}{4} - \dfrac{5x^2}{16} = 1$

10. (a) 45°

(b)

11.

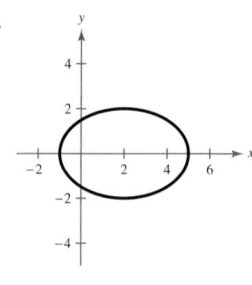

$\dfrac{(x - 2)^2}{9} + \dfrac{y^2}{4} = 1$

12. $x = 6 + 4t$

$y = 4 + 7t$

13. $\left(\sqrt{3}, -1\right)$

14. $\left(2\sqrt{2}, \dfrac{7\pi}{4}\right), \left(-2\sqrt{2}, \dfrac{3\pi}{4}\right), \left(2\sqrt{2}, -\dfrac{\pi}{4}\right)$

15. $r = 4 \sin \theta$

16.

Parabola

17.

Ellipse

18.   **19.**

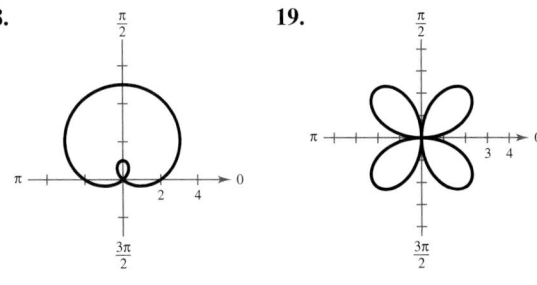

Limaçon   Rose curve

20. Slope: 0.1511; Change in elevation: 789.03 feet

21. No; Yes

Problem Solving   *(page 780)*

1. (a) 1.2016 radians

(b) 2420 feet, 5971 feet

3. $y^2 = 4p(x + p)$

5. (a) The sum of the distances from the two islands the tour boat can travel is constant.

(b) Island 1: $(-6, 0)$;
Island 2: $(6, 0)$

(c) 20 miles; Vertex: $(10, 0)$

(d) $\dfrac{x^2}{100} + \dfrac{y^2}{64} = 1$

7. Answers will vary.

9. Answers will vary. For example:

$x = \cos(-t)$

$y = 2 \sin(-t)$

11. (a) $y^2 = x^2\left(\dfrac{1 - x}{1 + x}\right)$

(b) $\cos 2\theta \sec \theta$

(c)

13. Circle

15.

For $n \ge 1$, a bell is produced.

For $n \le -1$, a heart is produced.

For $n = 0$, a rose curve is produced.

Appendix A
Section A.1   *(page A8)*

1. (a) 5, 1, 2   (b) $-9, 5, 0, 1, -4, 2, -11$

(c) $-9, -\frac{7}{2}, 5, \frac{2}{3}, 0, 1, -4, 2, -11$ (d) $\sqrt{2}$

3. (a) 1   (b) $-13, 1, -6$

(c) $2.01, 0.666 \ldots, -13, 1, -6$ (d) $0.010110111 \ldots$

5. (a) $\frac{6}{3}, 8$ (b) $\frac{6}{3}, -1, 8, -22$

(c) $-\frac{1}{3}, \frac{6}{3}, -7.5, -1, 8, -22$ (d) $-\pi, \frac{1}{2}\sqrt{2}$

7. 0.625   **9.** $0.\overline{123}$ **11.** $-1 < 2.5$

13. $-4 > -8$

15. $\frac{3}{2} < 7$

17. 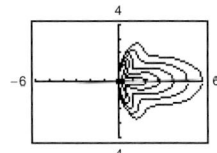 $\frac{5}{6} > \frac{2}{3}$

19. $x \le 5$ denotes the set of all real numbers less than or equal to 5. Unbounded

21. $x < 0$ denotes the set of all negative real numbers. Unbounded

23. $x \ge 4$ denotes the set of all real numbers greater than or equal to 4. Unbounded

25. $-2 < x < 2$ denotes the set of all real numbers greater than -2 and less than 2. Bounded

27. $-1 \le x < 0$ denotes the set of all negative real numbers greater than or equal to -1. Bounded

29. $-2 < x \le 4$ **31.** $y \ge 0$

33. $10 \le t \le 22$ **35.** $W > 65$

37. This interval consists of all real numbers greater than or equal to 0 and less than 8.

39. This interval consists of all real numbers greater than -6.

41. 10   **43.** 5   **45.** -1 **47.** -1 **49.** -1

51. $|-3| > -|-3|$ **53.** $-5 = -|5|$

55. $-|-2| = -|2|$ **57.** 4   **59.** 51   **61.** $\frac{5}{2}$ **63.** $\frac{128}{75}$

65. $|\$113{,}356 - \$112{,}700| = \$656 > \$500$

$0.05(\$112{,}700) = \$5635$

Because the actual expenses differ from the budget by more than $500, there is failure to meet the "budget variance test."

67. $|\$37{,}335 - \$37{,}640| = \$305 < \$500$

$0.05(\$37{,}640) = \$1882$

Because the difference between the actual expenses and the budget is less than $500 and less than 5% of the budgeted amount, there is compliance with the "budget variance test."

69. (a)

Year	Expenditures (in billions)	Surplus or deficit (in billions)
1960	$92.2	$0.3 (s)
1970	$195.6	$2.8 (d)
1980	$590.9	$73.8 (d)
1990	$1253.2	$221.2 (d)
2000	$1788.8	$236.4 (s)

(b)

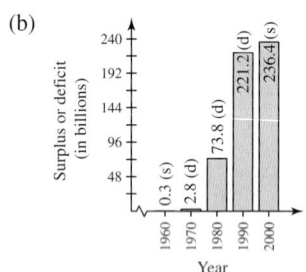

71. $|57 - 236| = 179$ miles   **73.** $|60 - 23| = 37°$

75. $|x - 5| \le 3$ **77.** $|y| \ge 6$

79. $7x$ and 4 are the terms; 7 is the coefficient.

81. $\sqrt{3}x^2$, $-8x$, and -11 are the terms; $\sqrt{3}$ and -8 are the coefficients.

83. $4x^3$, $x/2$, and -5 are the terms; 4 and $\frac{1}{2}$ are the coefficients.

85. (a) -10 (b) -6 **87.** (a) 14   (b) 2

89. (a) Division by 0 is undefined.   (b) 0

91. Commutative Property of Addition

93. Multiplicative Inverse Property

95. Distributive Property

97. Multiplicative Identity Property

99. Associative and Commutative Properties of Multiplication

101. $\frac{1}{2}$ **103.** $\frac{3}{8}$ **105.** 48   **107.** $\frac{5x}{12}$

109. (a)

n	1	0.5	0.01	0.0001	0.000001
$5/n$	5	10	500	50,000	5,000,000

(b) The value of $5/n$ approaches infinity as n approaches 0.

111. False. If $a < b$, then $\frac{1}{a} > \frac{1}{b}$, where $a \ne b \ne 0$.

113. (a) No. If one variable is negative and the other is positive, the expressions are unequal.

(b) $|u + v| \le |u| + |v|$

The expressions are equal when u and v have the same sign. If u and v differ in sign, $|u + v|$ is less than $|u| + |v|$.

115. The only even prime number is 2, because its only factors are itself and 1.

117. (a) Negative   (b) Negative

119. Yes. $|a| = -a$ if $a < 0$.

Section A.2   *(page A20)*

1. $8 \times 8 \times 8 \times 8 \times 8$

3. $-(0.4 \times 0.4 \times 0.4 \times 0.4 \times 0.4 \times 0.4)$ **5.** 4.9^6

7. $(-10)^5$ **9.** (a) 27   (b) 81

11. (a) 729   (b) -9 **13.** (a) $\frac{243}{64}$ (b) -1

15. (a) $\frac{5}{6}$ (b) 4   **17.** -1600 **19.** 2.125

21. -24 **23.** 6   **25.** -54 **27.** 1

29. (a) $-125z^3$ (b) $5x^6$ **31.** (a) $24y^{10}$ (b) $3x^2$

33. (a) $\frac{7}{x}$ (b) $\frac{4}{3}(x + y)^2$ **35.** (a) 1   (b) $\frac{1}{4x^4}$

37. (a) $-2x^3$ (b) $\frac{10}{x}$ **39.** (a) 3^{3n} (b) $\frac{b^5}{a^5}$

41. 5.73×10^7 square miles

43. 8.99×10^{-5} gram per cubic centimeter

45. 4,568,000,000 servings

47. 0.00000000000000000001602 coulomb

49. (a) 50,000   (b) 200,000

51. (a) 954.448   (b) 3.077×10^{10}

53. (a) 67,082.039   (b) 39.791   **55.** $9^{1/2}$

57. $\sqrt[5]{32}$ **59.** $\sqrt{196}$ **61.** $(-216)^{1/3}$

63. $\sqrt[3]{27^2}$ **65.** $81^{3/4}$ **67.** (a) 3   (b) 2

69. (a) -125 (b) 3   **71.** (a) $\frac{1}{8}$ (b) $\frac{27}{8}$

73. (a) -4 (b) 2   **75.** (a) 7.550   (b) -7.225

77. (a) -0.011 (b) 0.005   **79.** (a) $2\sqrt{2}$ (b) $2\sqrt[3]{3}$

81. (a) $6x\sqrt{2x}$ (b) $\frac{18}{z\sqrt{z}}$

83. (a) $2x\sqrt[3]{2x^2}$ (b) $\frac{5|x|\sqrt{3}}{y^2}$ **85.** $\frac{2}{x}$

87. $\frac{1}{x^3}$, $x > 0$ **89.** $\frac{\sqrt{3}}{3}$ **91.** $\frac{5 + \sqrt{3}}{11}$

93. $\dfrac{2}{\sqrt{2}}$ **95.** $\dfrac{2}{3\left(\sqrt{5}-\sqrt{3}\right)}$

97. (a) $\sqrt{3}$ (b) $\sqrt[3]{(x+1)^2}$

99. (a) $2\sqrt[4]{2}$ (b) $\sqrt[8]{2x}$

101. (a) $34\sqrt{2}$ (b) $22\sqrt{2}$ **103.** (a) $2\sqrt{x}$ (b) $4\sqrt{y}$

105. (a) $13\sqrt{x+1}$ (b) $18\sqrt{5x}$

107. $\sqrt{5}+\sqrt{3}>\sqrt{5+3}$

109. $5>\sqrt{3^2+2^2}$ **111.** $\dfrac{\pi}{2}\approx 1.57$ seconds

113. (a)

h	0	1	2	3	4	5	6
t	0	2.93	5.48	7.67	9.53	11.08	12.32

h	7	8	9	10	11	12
t	13.29	14.00	14.50	14.80	14.93	14.96

(b) Yes. $t=8.64\sqrt{3}\approx 14.96$

115. True. When dividing variables, you subtract exponents.

117. $a^0=1,\ a\neq 0$, using the property $\dfrac{a^m}{a^n}=a^{m-n}$: $\dfrac{a^m}{a^m}=a^{m-m}=a^0=1.$

119. When any positive integer is squared, the units digit is 0, 1, 4, 5, 6, or 9. Therefore, $\sqrt{5233}$ is not an integer.

Section A.3   *(page A31)*

1. d   **2.** e   **3.** b   **4.** a   **5.** f   **6.** c

7. $-2x^3+4x^2-3x+20$ (Answers will vary.)

9. $-15x^4+1$ (Answers will vary.)

11. Degree: 1; Leading coefficient: 2

13. Degree: 5; Leading coefficient: -4

15. Degree: 5; Leading coefficient: 1

17. Polynomial: $-3x^3+2x+8$

19. Not a polynomial because of the operation of division

21. Polynomial: $-y^4+y^3+y^2$

23. x^2+2x **25.** $8.3x^3+29.7x^2+11$

27. $12z+8$ **29.** $3x^3-6x^2+3x$ **31.** $-15z^2+5z$

33. $4x^4+4x$ **35.** $7.5x^3+9x$ **37.** $-\frac{1}{2}x^2-12x$

39. $x^2+7x+12$ **41.** $6x^2-7x-5$

43. $4x^2+12x+9$ **45.** $4x^2-20xy+25y^2$

47. x^2-100 **49.** x^2-4y^2 **51.** m^2-n^2-6m+9

53. $x^2+2xy+y^2-6x-6y+9$ **55.** $4r^4-25$

57. x^3+3x^2+3x+1 **59.** $8x^3-12x^2y+6xy^2-y^3$

61. $\frac{1}{4}x^2-3x+9$ **63.** $\frac{1}{9}x^2-4$

65. $1.44x^2+7.2x+9$ **67.** $2.25x^2-16$

69. $2x^2+2x$ **71.** u^4-16 **73.** $x-y$

75. $x^2-2\sqrt{5}x+5$ **77.** Factored   **79.** Factored

81. $3(x+2)$ **83.** $2x(x^2-3)$ **85.** $(x-1)(x+6)$

87. $(x+3)(x-1)$ **89.** $\frac{1}{2}x(x^2+4x-10)$

91. $\frac{2}{3}(x-6)(x-3)$ **93.** $(4y+3)(4y-3)$

95. $\left(4x+\frac{1}{3}\right)\left(4x-\frac{1}{3}\right)$ **97.** $(x+1)(x-3)$

99. $(3u+2v)(3u-2v)$ **101.** $(x-2)^2$

103. $(6y-9)^2$ **105.** $(3u+4v)^2$ **107.** $\left(x-\frac{2}{3}\right)^2$

109. $(x-2)(x^2+2x+4)$ **111.** $(y+4)(y^2-4y+16)$

113. $(2t-1)(4t^2+2t+1)$

115. $(u+3v)(u^2-3uv+9v^2)$

117. $(x+2)(x-1)$ **119.** $(s-3)(s-2)$

121. $-(y+5)(y-4)$ **123.** $(3x-2)(x-1)$

125. $(5x+1)(x+5)$ **127.** $-(3z-2)(3z+1)$

129. $(x-1)(x^2+2)$ **131.** $(2x-1)(x^2-3)$

133. $(3x^2-1)(2x+1)$ **135.** $(x+2)(3x+4)$

137. $(3x-1)(5x-2)$ **139.** $6(x+3)(x-3)$

141. $x^2(x-4)$ **143.** $-2x(x+1)(x-2)$

145. $(3x+1)(x^2+5)$ **147.** $\frac{1}{81}(x+36)(x-18)$

149. $x(x-4)(x^2+1)$ **151.** $(x+1)^2(x-1)^2$

153. $2(t-2)(t^2+2t+4)$ **155.** $(2x-1)(6x-1)$

157. $5(1-x)^2(3x+2)(4x+3)$

159. $(x-2)^2(x+1)^3(7x-5)$

161. $-14,\ 14,\ -2,\ 2$ **163.** $-11,\ 11,\ -4,\ 4,\ -1,\ 1$

165. Two possible answers: 2, -12

167. Two possible answers: $-2,\ -4$ **169.** \$85,000

171. (a) $500r^2+1000r+500$

(b)

r	$2\frac{1}{2}\%$	3%	4%
$500(1+r)^2$	\$525.31	\$530.45	\$540.80

r	$4\frac{1}{2}\%$	5%
$500(1+r)^2$	\$546.01	\$551.25

(c) The amount increases with increasing r.

173. $V=x(26-2x)(18-2x)$
$=4x(x-13)(x-9)$

x (cm)	1	2	3
V (cm³)	384	616	720

175. (a) $6x^2 - 3x$ (b) $42x^2$ **177.** $2x^2 + 46x + 252$

179.

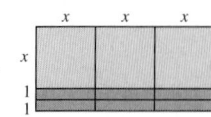

181. $4\pi(r + 1)$ **183.** $4(6 - x)(6 + x)$

185. (a) $V = \pi h(R - r)(R + r)$

(b) $V = 2\pi\left[\left(\dfrac{R + r}{2}\right)(R - r)\right]h$

187. False. $(4x^2 + 1)(3x + 1) = 12x^3 + 4x^2 + 3x + 1$

189. True. $(x^2 - 16) = (x + 4)(x - 4)$ **191.** $m + n$

193. $(3 + 4)^2 = 49 \neq 25 = 3^2 + 4^2$.
If either x or y is zero, then $(x + y)^2 = x^2 + y^2$.

195. $(x^n + y^n)(x^n - y^n)$

197. $x^{3n} - y^{2n}$ is completely factored.

Section A.4 (page A43)

1. All real numbers   **3.** All nonnegative real numbers

5. All real numbers x such that $x \neq 2$

7. All real numbers x such that $x \geq -1$

9. $3x, \ x \neq 0$ **11.** $\dfrac{3x}{2}, \ x \neq 0$ **13.** $\dfrac{3y}{y + 1}, \ x \neq 0$

15. $\dfrac{-4y}{5}, \ y \neq \dfrac{1}{2}$ **17.** $-\dfrac{1}{2}, \ x \neq 5$

19. $y - 4, \ y \neq -4$ **21.** $\dfrac{x(x + 3)}{x - 2}, \ x \neq -2$

23. $\dfrac{y - 4}{y + 6}, \ y \neq 3$ **25.** $\dfrac{-(x^2 + 1)}{(x + 2)}, \ x \neq 2$ **27.** $z - 2$

29.

x	0	1	2	3	4	5	6
$\dfrac{x^2 - 2x - 3}{x - 3}$	1	2	3	Undef.	5	6	7
$x + 1$	1	2	3	4	5	6	7

The expressions are equivalent except at $x = 3$.

31. The expression cannot be simplified.

33. $\dfrac{\pi}{4}, \ r \neq 0$ **35.** $\dfrac{1}{5(x - 2)}, \ x \neq 1$

37. $\dfrac{r + 1}{r}, \ r \neq 1$ **39.** $\dfrac{t - 3}{(t + 3)(t - 2)}, \ t \neq -2$

41. $\dfrac{(x + 6)(x + 1)}{x^2}, \ x \neq 6$ **43.** $\dfrac{x + 5}{x - 1}$ **45.** $\dfrac{6x + 13}{x + 3}$

47. $-\dfrac{2}{x - 2}$ **49.** $-\dfrac{x^2 + 3}{(x + 1)(x - 2)(x - 3)}$

51. $\dfrac{2 - x}{x^2 + 1}, \ x \neq 0$ **53.** $\dfrac{x^7 - 2}{x^2}$ **55.** $\dfrac{-1}{(x^2 + 1)^5}$

57. $\dfrac{2x^3 - 2x^2 - 5}{(x - 1)^{1/2}}$

59. The error was incorrect subtraction in the numerator.

61. $\dfrac{1}{2}, \ x \neq 2$ **63.** $x(x + 1), \ x \neq -1, 0$

65. $-\dfrac{2x + h}{x^2(x + h)^2}, \ h \neq 0$ **67.** $\dfrac{2x - 1}{2x}, \ x > 0$

69. $\dfrac{3x - 1}{3}, \ x \neq 0$ **71.** $\dfrac{1}{\sqrt{x + 2} + \sqrt{x}}$

73. $\dfrac{x}{2(2x + 1)}, \ x \neq 0$

75. (a) $\dfrac{1}{16}$ minute (b) $\dfrac{x}{16}$ minute(s) (c) $\dfrac{60}{16} = \dfrac{15}{4}$ minutes

77. (a)

t	0	2	4	6	8	10
T	75	55.9	48.3	45	43.3	42.3

t	12	14	16	18	20	22
T	41.7	41.3	41.1	40.9	40.7	40.6

(b) The model is approaching a T-value of 40.

79. False. In order for the simplified expression to be equivalent to the original expression, the domain of the simplified expression needs to be restricted. If n is even, $x \neq -1, 1$. If n is odd, $x \neq 1$.

81. Completely factor each polynomial in the numerator and in the denominator. Then conclude that there are no common factors.

Section A.5 (page A55)

1. Identity   **3.** Conditional equation   **5.** Identity

7. Identity   **9.** Conditional equation

11. 4   **13.** -9 **15.** 5   **17.** 9   **19.** No solution

21. -4 **23.** $-\dfrac{6}{5}$ **25.** 9

27. No solution. The x-terms sum to zero

29. 10   **31.** 4   **33.** 3

35. No solution. The variable is divided out.   **37.** $\dfrac{5}{3}$

39. No solution. The solution is extraneous.

41. 5   **43.** No solution. The solution is extraneous.

45. 0   **47.** All real numbers

49. $2x^2 + 8x - 3 = 0$ **51.** $x^2 - 6x + 6 = 0$

53. $3x^2 - 90x - 10 = 0$ **55.** $0, -\dfrac{1}{2}$ **57.** $4, -2$

59. -5 **61.** $3, -\frac{1}{2}$ **63.** $2, -6$ **65.** $-\frac{20}{3}, -4$

67. $-a$ **69.** $\pm 7; \pm 7.00$ **71.** $\pm\sqrt{11}; \pm 3.32$

73. $\pm 3\sqrt{3}; \pm 5.20$ **75.** $8, 16; 8.00, 16.00$

77. $-2 \pm \sqrt{14}; 1.74, -5.74$ **79.** $\dfrac{1 \pm 3\sqrt{2}}{2}; 2.62, -1.62$

81. $2; 2.00$ **83.** $0, 2$ **85.** $4, -8$ **87.** $-3 \pm \sqrt{7}$

89. $1 \pm \dfrac{\sqrt{6}}{3}$ **91.** $2 \pm 2\sqrt{3}$ **93.** $\dfrac{1}{2}, -1$

95. $\frac{1}{4}, -\frac{3}{4}$ **97.** $1 \pm \sqrt{3}$ **99.** $-7 \pm \sqrt{5}$

101. $-4 \pm 2\sqrt{5}$ **103.** $\dfrac{2}{3} \pm \dfrac{\sqrt{7}}{3}$ **105.** $-\dfrac{4}{3}$

107. $-\dfrac{1}{2} \pm \sqrt{2}$ **109.** $\dfrac{2}{7}$ **111.** $2 \pm \dfrac{\sqrt{6}}{2}$

113. $6 \pm \sqrt{11}$ **115.** $-\dfrac{3}{8} \pm \dfrac{\sqrt{265}}{8}$

117. $0.976, -0.643$ **119.** $1.355, -14.071$

121. $1.687, -0.488$ **123.** $-0.290, -2.200$

125. $1 \pm \sqrt{2}$ **127.** $6, -12$ **129.** $\frac{1}{2} \pm \sqrt{3}$

131. $-\dfrac{1}{2}$ **133.** $\dfrac{3}{4} \pm \dfrac{\sqrt{97}}{4}$ **135.** $0, \pm\dfrac{3\sqrt{2}}{2}$

137. $\pm 3, \pm 3i$ **139.** $-6, 3 \pm 3\sqrt{3}i$ **141.** $-3, 0$

143. $3, \pm 1$ **145.** $\pm 1, \dfrac{1}{2} \pm \dfrac{\sqrt{3}}{2}i$ **147.** $\pm\sqrt{3}, \pm 1$

149. $\pm\dfrac{1}{2}, \pm 4$ **151.** $1, -2, 1 \pm \sqrt{3}i, -\dfrac{1}{2} \pm \dfrac{\sqrt{3}i}{2}$

153. 50 **155.** 26 **157.** -16 **159.** $2, -5$

161. 0 **163.** 9 **165.** $-3 \pm 16\sqrt{2}$

167. $\pm\sqrt{14}$ **169.** 1 **171.** $4, -5$ **173.** $\dfrac{-3 \pm \sqrt{21}}{6}$

175. $2, -\frac{3}{2}$ **177.** $-3, 1$ **179.** $3, -2$ **181.** $\sqrt{3}, -3$

183. $3, \dfrac{-1 - \sqrt{17}}{2}$ **185.** 61.2 inches   **187.** $23{,}437.5$ miles

189. (a)   (b) $w(w + 14) = 1632$
(c) $w = 34$ feet
$l = 48$ feet

w ... $w + 14$

191. $\dfrac{5\sqrt{2}}{2} \approx 3.54$ centimeters

193. ≈ 550 miles per hour and 600 miles per hour

195. $50{,}000$ units   **197.** 24.7 pounds per square inch

199. False. $x(3 - x) = 10$
$3x - x^2 = 10$
The equation cannot be written in the form $ax + b = 0$.

201. False. $|x| = 0$ has only one solution to check, 0.

203. Yes. The student should have subtracted $15x$ from both sides to make the right side of the equation equal to zero. Factoring out an x shows that there are two solutions, $x = 0$ and $x = 6$.

205. Remove symbols of grouping, combine like terms, reduce fractions.

Add (or subtract) the same quantity to (from) each side of the equation.

Multiply (or divide) each side of the equation by the same nonzero quantity.

Interchange the two sides of the equation.

207. (a) $x = 0, -\dfrac{b}{a}$ (b) $x = 0, 1$ **209.** $a = 9, b = 9$

Section A.6   (page A67)

1. $-1 \le x \le 5$. Bounded

3. $x > 11$. Unbounded

5. $x < -2$. Unbounded

7. b   **8.** f   **9.** d   **10.** c   **11.** e   **12.** a

13. (a) Yes   (b) No   (c) Yes   (d) No

15. (a) Yes   (b) No   (c) No   (d) Yes

17. (a) Yes   (b) Yes   (c) Yes   (d) No

19. $x < 3$

21. $x < \frac{3}{2}$

23. $x \ge 12$ **25.** $x > 2$

27. $x \ge \frac{2}{7}$

29. $x < 5$

31. $x \ge 4$ **33.** $x \ge 2$

35. $x \geq -4$

37. $-1 < x < 3$

39. $-\frac{9}{2} < x < \frac{15}{2}$

41. $-\frac{3}{4} < x < -\frac{1}{4}$

43. $10.5 \leq x \leq 13.5$

45. $-6 < x < 6$

47. $x < -2, x > 2$

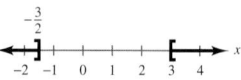

49. No solution

51. $14 \leq x \leq 26$

53. $x \leq -\frac{3}{2}, x \geq 3$

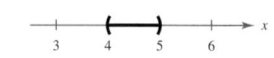

55. $x \leq -5, x \geq 11$

57. $4 < x < 5$

59. $x \leq -\frac{29}{2}, x \geq -\frac{11}{2}$

61.

$x > 2$

63.

$x \leq 2$

65.

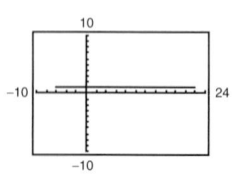

$-6 \leq x \leq 22$

67.

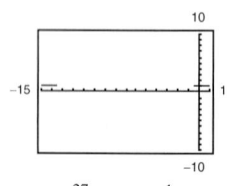

$x \leq -\frac{27}{2}, x \geq -\frac{1}{2}$

69. $[5, \infty)$ **71.** $[-3, \infty)$ **73.** $\left(-\infty, \frac{7}{2}\right]$ **75.** $|x| \leq 3$

77. $|x - 7| \geq 3$ **79.** $|x - 12| < 10$ **81.** $|x + 3| > 5$

83. (a) No   (b) Yes   (c) Yes   (d) No

85. (a) Yes   (b) No   (c) No   (d) Yes

87. $2, -\frac{3}{2}$ **89.** $\frac{7}{2}, 5$

91. $[-3, 3]$

93. $(-7, 3)$

95. $(-\infty, -5], [1, \infty)$

97. $(-3, 2)$

99. $(-3, 1)$

101. $\left(-\infty, -4 - \sqrt{21}\right], \left[-4 + \sqrt{21}, \infty\right)$

103. $(-1, 1), (3, \infty)$ **105.** $[-3, 2], [3, \infty)$

107. $(-\infty, 0), \left(0, \frac{3}{2}\right)$ **109.** $[-2, 0], [2, \infty)$ **111.** $[-2, \infty)$

113. $(-\infty, -1), (0, 1)$

115. $(-\infty, -1), (4, \infty)$

117. $(5, 15)$ **119.** $\left(-5, -\frac{3}{2}\right), (-1, \infty)$

121. $\left(-\frac{3}{4}, 3\right), [6, \infty)$ **123.** $(-3, -2], [0, 3)$

125. $(-\infty, -1), \left(-\frac{2}{3}, 1\right), (3, \infty)$

127. $[-2, 2]$ **129.** $(-\infty, 3], [4, \infty)$

131. $(-5, 0], (7, \infty)$ **133.** $(-3.51, 3.51)$

135. $(-0.13, 25.13)$ **137.** $(2.26, 2.39)$

139. More than 400 miles   **141.** $r > 3.125\%$

143. $65.8 \le h \le 71.2$

145. 13.8 meters $\le L \le$ 36.2 meters   **147.** $r > 4.88\%$

149. $R_1 \ge 2$ ohms   **151.** False. c has to be greater than zero.

153. True. The test intervals are $(-\infty, -3), (-3, 1), (1, 4)$, and $(4, \infty)$.

155. b   **157.** All real numbers within eight units of 10

159. $(-\infty, -4] \cup [4, \infty)$

161. $\left(-\infty, -2\sqrt{30}\,\right] \cup \left[2\sqrt{30}, \infty\right)$

163. If $a > 0$ and $c \le 0$, or $a < 0$ and $c > 0$, b can be any real number. If $a > 0$ and $c > 0$, $b < -2\sqrt{ac}$ or $b > 2\sqrt{ac}$.

165. (a) $x = a, x = b$

(b)

(c) The polynomial changes sign at its zeros.

Section A.7   *(page A76)*

1. Change all signs when distributing the minus sign.
$$2x - (3y + 4) = 2x - 3y - 4$$

3. Change all signs when distributing the minus sign.
$$\frac{4}{16x - (2x + 1)} = \frac{4}{14x - 1}$$

5. z occurs twice as a factor.
$$(5z)(6z) = 30z^2$$

7. The fraction as a whole is multiplied by a, not the numerator and denominator separately.
$$a\left(\frac{x}{y}\right) = \frac{ax}{y}$$

9. $\sqrt{x + 9}$ cannot be simplified.

11. Divide out common factors, not common terms.
$$\frac{2x^2 + 1}{5x} \text{ cannot be simplified.}$$

13. To get rid of negative exponents:
$$\frac{1}{a^{-1} + b^{-1}} = \frac{1}{a^{-1} + b^{-1}} \cdot \frac{ab}{ab} = \frac{ab}{b + a}.$$

15. Factor within grouping symbols before applying exponent to each factor.
$$(x^2 + 5x)^{1/2} = [x(x + 5)]^{1/2} = x^{1/2}(x + 5)^{1/2}$$

17. To add fractions, first find a common denominator.
$$\frac{3}{x} + \frac{4}{y} = \frac{3y + 4x}{xy}$$

19. $3x + 2$ **21.** $2x^2 + x + 15$ **23.** $\frac{1}{3}$ **25.** 2

27. $\frac{1}{2x^2}$ **29.** $\frac{25}{9}, \frac{49}{16}$ **31.** 1, 2   **33.** $1 - 5x$

35. $1 - 7x$ **37.** $3x - 1$ **39.** $\frac{16}{x} - 5 - x$

41. $4x^{8/3} - 7x^{5/3} + \frac{1}{x^{1/3}}$ **43.** $\frac{3}{\sqrt{x}} - 5x^{3/2} - x^{7/2}$

45. $\frac{-7x^2 - 4x + 9}{(x^2 - 3)^3(x + 1)^4}$ **47.** $\frac{27x^2 - 24x + 2}{(6x + 1)^4}$

49. $\frac{-1}{(x + 3)^{2/3}(x + 2)^{7/4}}$ **51.** $\frac{4x - 3}{(3x - 1)^{4/3}}$ **53.** $\frac{x}{x^2 + 4}$

55. $\frac{(3x - 2)^{1/2}(15x^2 - 4x + 45)}{2(x^2 + 5)^{1/2}}$

57. (a)

x	0.5	1.0	1.5	2.0
t	1.70	1.72	1.78	1.89

x	2.5	3.0	3.5	4.0
t	2.02	2.18	2.36	2.57

(b) $x = 0.5$ mile

(c) $\dfrac{3x\sqrt{x^2 - 8x + 20} + (x - 4)\sqrt{x^2 + 4}}{6\sqrt{x^2 + 4}\sqrt{x^2 - 8x + 20}}$

59. True. $x^{-1} + y^{-2} = \dfrac{1}{x} + \dfrac{1}{y^2}$
$$= \frac{y^2 + x}{xy^2}$$

61. True. $\dfrac{1}{\sqrt{x} + 4} = \dfrac{1}{\sqrt{x} + 4} \cdot \dfrac{\sqrt{x} - 4}{\sqrt{x} - 4}$
$$= \frac{\sqrt{x} - 4}{x - 16}$$

63. Add exponents when multiplying powers with like bases.
$$x^n \cdot x^{3n} = x^{4n}$$

65. When a binomial is squared, there is also a middle term.
$$(x^n + y^n)^2 = x^{2n} + 2x^n y^n + y^{2n} \ne x^{2n} + y^{2n}$$

67. The two answers are equivalent and can be obtained by factoring.
$$\tfrac{1}{10}(2x - 1)^{5/2} + \tfrac{1}{6}(2x - 1)^{3/2}$$
$$= \tfrac{1}{60}(2x - 1)^{3/2}[6(2x - 1) + 10]$$
$$= \tfrac{1}{60}(2x - 1)^{3/2}(12x + 4)$$
$$= \tfrac{4}{60}(2x - 1)^{3/2}(3x + 1)$$
$$= \tfrac{1}{15}(2x - 1)^{3/2}(3x + 1)$$

Section A.8 *(page A84)*

1. $A: (2, 6)$, $B: (-6, -2)$, $C: (4, -4)$, $D: (-3, 2)$

3. $(-3, 4)$ **5.** $(-5, -5)$

7. Quadrant IV   **9.** Quadrant II

11. Quadrant III or IV   **13.** Quadrant III

15. Quadrant I or III   **17.** $(0, 1)$, $(4, 2)$, $(1, 4)$

19. $(-3, 6)$, $(2, 10)$, $(2, 4)$, $(-3, 4)$

21.

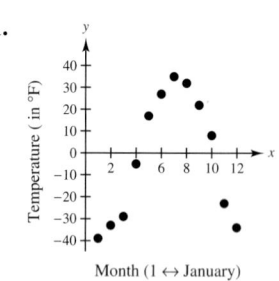

23. $3.20 per pound; 1998   **25.** 242.9%

27. (a) 1990s   (b) 11.8%; 21.2%   (c) $6.24   (d) Yes

29. 8   **31.** 5   **33.** (a) 4, 3, 5   (b) $4^2 + 3^2 = 5^2$

35. (a) 10, 3, $\sqrt{109}$ (b) $10^2 + 3^2 = \left(\sqrt{109}\right)^2$

37. (a)

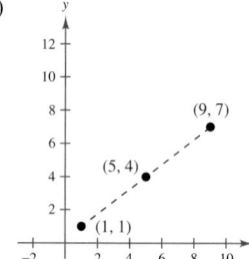

(b) 10

(c) $(5, 4)$

39. (a)

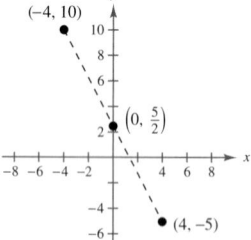

(b) 17

(c) $\left(0, \frac{5}{2}\right)$

41. (a)

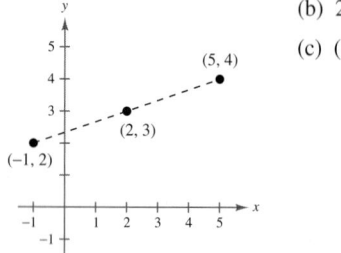

(b) $2\sqrt{10}$

(c) $(2, 3)$

43. (a)

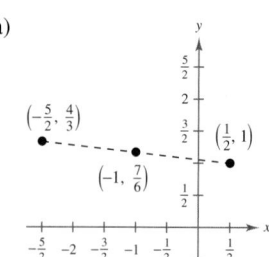

(b) $\dfrac{\sqrt{82}}{3}$

(c) $\left(-1, \frac{7}{6}\right)$

45. (a)

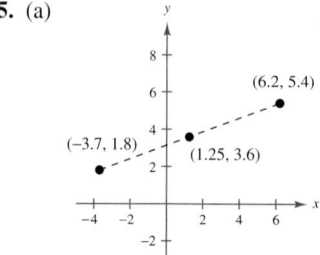

(b) $\sqrt{110.97}$

(c) $(1.25, 3.6)$

47. $31,137 million   **49.** $\left(\sqrt{5}\right)^2 + \left(\sqrt{45}\right)^2 = \left(\sqrt{50}\right)^2$

51. $(2x_m - x_1, 2y_m - y_1)$

53. $\left(\dfrac{3x_1 + x_2}{4}, \dfrac{3y_1 + y_2}{4}\right)$, $\left(\dfrac{x_1 + x_2}{2}, \dfrac{y_1 + y_2}{2}\right)$,

$\left(\dfrac{x_1 + 3x_2}{4}, \dfrac{y_1 + 3y_2}{4}\right)$

55. $5\sqrt{74} \approx 43$ yards

57.

(a) The point is reflected through the *y*-axis.

(b) The point is reflected through the *x*-axis.

(c) The point is reflected through the origin.

59. $1969.45 million

61. False. The Midpoint Formula would be used 15 times.

63. Point on *x*-axis: $y = 0$; Point on *y*-axis: $x = 0$

65. b   **66.** c   **67.** d   **68.** a

69. Use the Midpoint Formula to prove that the diagonals of the parallelogram bisect each other.

$$\left(\frac{b + a}{2}, \frac{c + 0}{2}\right) = \left(\frac{a + b}{2}, \frac{c}{2}\right)$$

$$\left(\frac{a + b + 0}{2}, \frac{c + 0}{2}\right) = \left(\frac{a + b}{2}, \frac{c}{2}\right)$$

Instructor's Answers

Chapter 1

Section 1.1   *(page 9)*

2. (a) Yes   (b) No   **4.** (a) Yes   (b) No

6.

x	-2	0	1	$\frac{4}{3}$	2
y	$-\frac{5}{2}$	-1	$-\frac{1}{4}$	0	$\frac{1}{2}$
(x, y)	$\left(-2, -\frac{5}{2}\right)$	$(0, -1)$	$\left(1, -\frac{1}{4}\right)$	$\left(\frac{4}{3}, 0\right)$	$\left(2, \frac{1}{2}\right)$

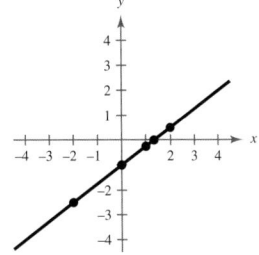

8.

x	-2	-1	0	1	2
y	1	4	5	4	1
(x, y)	$(-2, 1)$	$(-1, 4)$	$(0, 5)$	$(1, 4)$	$(2, 1)$

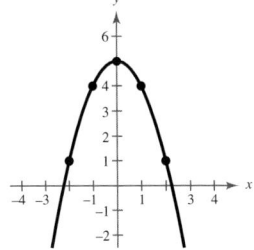

10. x-intercept: $(-3, 0)$
y-intercept: $(0, 9)$

12. x-intercept: $\left(\frac{8}{3}, 0\right)$
y-intercept: $(0, 8)$

14. x-intercept: $\left(\frac{1}{2}, 0\right)$
No y-intercept

16. x-intercept: $(-10, 0)$
y-intercept: $(0, -10)$

18. x-intercepts: $\left(\pm\sqrt{5}, 0\right)$
y-intercept: $(0, -25)$

20. x-intercept: $(-1, 0)$
y-intercepts: $(0, \pm 1)$

22. x-axis symmetry

24. y-axis symmetry

26. y-axis symmetry

28. Origin symmetry

30.

32.

34.

36.

38.

40.

42.

44.

46.

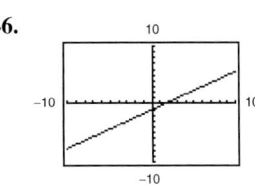

Intercepts: $\left(\frac{3}{2}, 0\right)$, $(0, -1)$

CHAPTER 1

48.

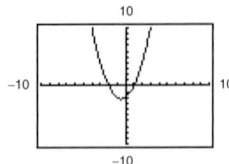

Intercepts: $(-2, 0), (1, 0), (0, -2)$

50.

Intercept: $(0, 4)$

52.

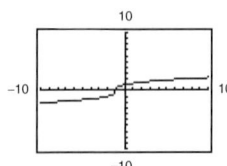

Intercepts: $(-1, 0), (0, 1)$

54.

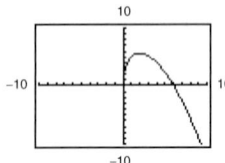

Intercepts: $(0, 0), (6, 0)$

56.

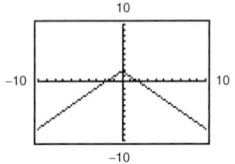

Intercepts: $(\pm 2, 0), (0, 2)$

58. $x^2 + y^2 = 25$ **60.** $(x + 7)^2 + (y + 4)^2 = 49$

62. $(x - 3)^2 + (y + 2)^2 = 25$ **64.** $x^2 + y^2 = 17$

66. Center: $(0, 0)$; Radius: 4

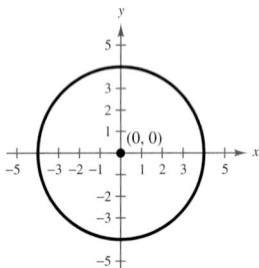

68. Center: $(0, 1)$; Radius: 1

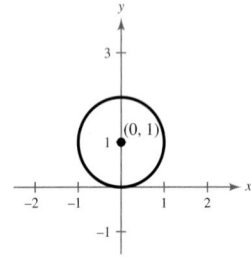

70. Center: $(2, -1)$; Radius: $\sqrt{3}$

72.

74. (a)

(b) Answers will vary.

(c)

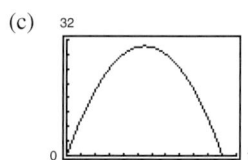

(d) $x = 5.5, w = 5.5$

76.

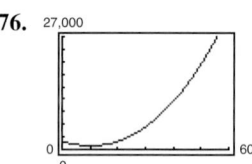

2005: \$26,377.88

78. False. To find y-intercepts, let $x = 0$ and solve the equation for y.

80. The graph does not appear due to the incorrect window settings. Change the viewing window. Examples will vary.

82. Assuming that the graph does not go beyond the vertical limits of the display, you will see the graph for larger values of x.

84. -7^4 **86.** $|x| \sqrt[4]{x}$ **88.** $5(2\sqrt{5} + 3)$ **90.** $\sqrt[6]{y}$

Section 1.2   *(page 21)*

2. (a) L_2 (b) L_1 (c) L_3

4.

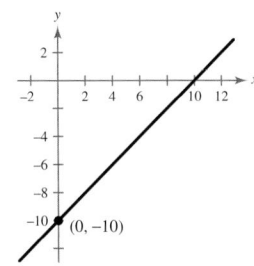

6. $\frac{8}{3}$ **8.** -1

10. $m = 1$; y-intercept: $(0, -10)$

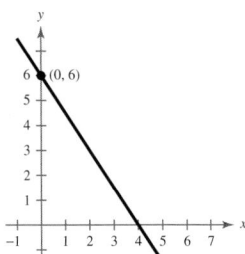

12. $m = -\frac{3}{2}$; y-intercept: $(0, 6)$

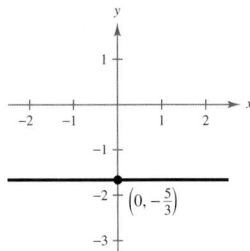

14. $m = 0$; y-intercept: $\left(0, -\frac{5}{3}\right)$

16. $m = -\frac{2}{3}$; y-intercept: $(0, 3)$

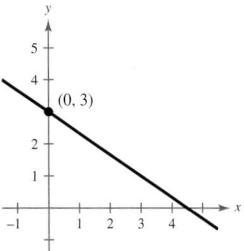

18. $m = 0$; y-intercept: $(0, -4)$

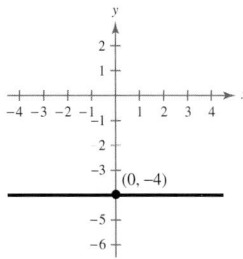

20. m is undefined. There is no y-intercept.

22.

$m = -4$

24.

$m = -\frac{5}{2}$

26.

$m = -\frac{8}{3}$

28.

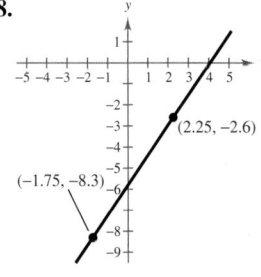

$m = 1.425$

30. Answers will vary. Sample answer:
$(-4, 0), (-4, 3), (-4, 5)$

32. Answers will vary. Sample answer:
$(0, 4), (9, -5), (11, -7)$

34. Answers will vary. Sample answer:
$(-4, -1), (-2, -1), (0, -1)$

36. Answers will vary. Sample answer:
$(-2, -5), (1, -11), (3, -15)$

38. Answers will vary. Sample answer:
$(-3, -5), (1, -7), (5, -9)$

40. Neither parallel nor perpendicular   **42.** Perpendicular

44. (a) Revenues increasing $400 per day.

   (b) Revenues increasing $100 per day.

   (c) No change in revenues.

46. (a) Greatest increase: 1998–1999
      Smallest increase: 1996–1997

   (b) 12.92

   (c) Each year, the net profit increases by $12.92 million.

48. 12 feet   **50.** $V = 4.5t + 142.5$

51. b; The slope is -20, which represents the decrease in the amount of the loan each week.

52. c; The slope is 2, which represents the hourly wage per unit produced.

53. a; The slope is 0.32, which represents the increase in travel cost for each mile driven.

54. d; The slope is -100, which represents the decrease in the value of the word processor each year.

56. $y = -x + 10$ **58.** $y = 4x$

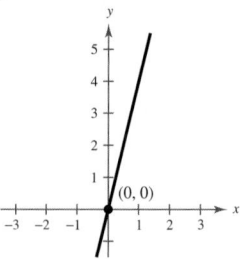

60. $y = \frac{3}{4}x - \frac{7}{2}$ **62.** $x = -10$

64. $y = \frac{3}{2}$

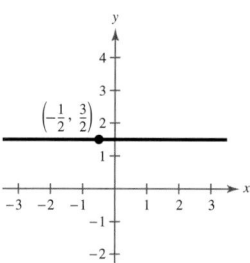

66. $y = -2.5x - 2.75$

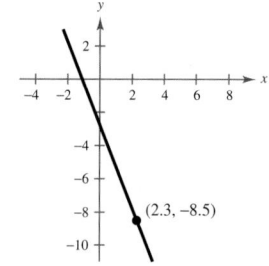

68. $y = \frac{7}{8}x - \frac{1}{2}$

70. $y = 4$

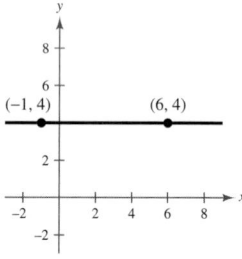

72. $y = -\frac{1}{3}x + \frac{4}{3}$

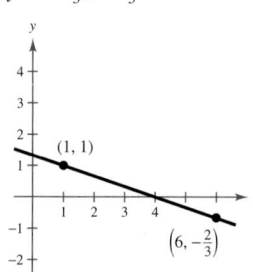

74. $y = -\frac{3}{25}x + \frac{159}{100}$

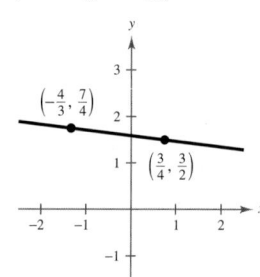

76. $y = 0.3x - 1.8$

78. $y = -2$

80. $x = 1.5$

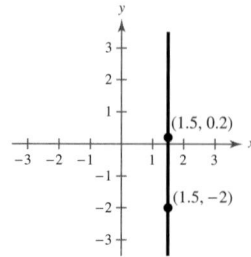

82. $4x - 3y + 12 = 0$ **84.** $3x - y - 2 = 0$

86. $x + y - 1 = 0$

88. (a) $y = -x - 1$ (b) $y = x + 5$

90. (a) $y = -\frac{5}{3}x + \frac{53}{24}$ (b) $y = \frac{3}{5}x + \frac{9}{40}$

92. (a) $y = -2$ (b) $x = 4$

94. (a) $x = -5$ (b) $y = 1$

96. (a) $y = -3x - 13.1$ (b) $y = \frac{1}{3}x - 0.1$

98. Line (a) is parallel to line (c). Line (b) is perpendicular to line (a) and line (c).

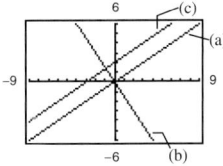

100. Line (a) is parallel to line (b). Line (c) is perpendicular to line (a) and line (b).

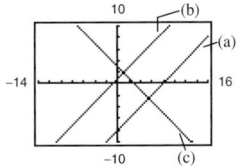

102. $5x + 13y + 2 = 0$ **104.** $128x + 168y + 39 = 0$

106. $y = -31.75t + 3927$; 2005: 3641 stores, 2010: 3483 stores

108. 28,765   **110.** $V = 25,000 - 2300t$

112. $W = 0.75x + 11.50$

114. (a) $x = -\frac{1}{15}p + \frac{266}{3}$ (b) 45   (c) 49

116. $W = 0.07S + 2500$

118. Answers will vary. Sample answer: $y = 199t - 13$

120. (a) and (b)

(c) $y = 4x + 19$ (d) 87

(e) Vertical shift four units upward

122. False. The slope of the first line is $\frac{2}{7}$ and the slope of the second line is $-\frac{11}{7}$.

124. The slope of a vertical line is undefined because division by zero is undefined.

126. The line with a slope of -4 is steeper. The slope with the greatest magnitude corresponds to the steepest line.

128. No. The slopes of two perpendicular lines have opposite signs (assume that neither line is vertical or horizontal).

129. d   **130.** c   **131.** a   **132.** b   **134.** $\frac{5}{2}$

136. $4 \pm \sqrt{13}$ **138.** $\frac{1}{9}, 25$

Section 1.3   (page 35)

2. No   **4.** Yes

6. No, the input values of 0 and 1 each have two different output values.

8. Yes, it does not matter that each input value has the same output value.

10. (a) Not a function, because the element c in A corresponds to two elements, 2 and 3, in B.

(b) Function

(c) Not a function from A to B. (It is instead a function from B to A.)

(d) Function

12. 11 million   **14.** Not a function   **16.** Not a function

18. Not a function   **20.** Function   **22.** Not a function

24. (a) 7   (b) 0   (c) $1 - 3s$

26. (a) 0   (b) -0.75 (c) $x^2 + 2x$

28. (a) 2   (b) 5   (c) $\sqrt{x} + 2$

30. (a) $\frac{11}{4}$ (b) Undefined   (c) $\frac{2x^2 + 3}{x^2}$

32. (a) 6   (b) 6   (c) $x^2 + 4$

34. (a) 6   (b) 3   (c) 10   **36.** (a) 19   (b) 17   (c) 0

38.

x	3	4	5	6	7
$g(x)$	0	1	$\sqrt{2}$	$\sqrt{3}$	2

40.

s	0	1	$\frac{3}{2}$	$\frac{5}{2}$	4
$f(s)$	-1	-1	-1	1	1

42.

x	1	2	3	4	5
$h(x)$	8	5	0	1	2

44. $-\frac{1}{5}$ **46.** $\pm 2\sqrt{3}$ **48.** 3, 5   **50.** 1, ± 2

52. 0, ± 2 **54.** 4   **56.** All real numbers

58. All real numbers $y \neq -5$ **60.** All real numbers

62. $x \leq -3, x \geq 0$ **64.** All real numbers $x \neq 0, 2$

66. $x > -6$ **68.** $x < -3, x > 3$

70. $\{(-2, 1), (-1, -2), (0, -3), (1, -2), (2, 1)\}$

72. $\{(-2, 1), (-1, 0), (0, 1), (1, 2), (2, 3)\}$

74. $f(x) = cx; c = \frac{1}{4}$ **76.** $h(x) = c\sqrt{|x|}; c = 3$

78. $-(5 + h), \ h \neq 0$ **80.** $8x + 4h - 2, h \neq 0$

82. $\dfrac{1}{t - 2}, t \neq 1$ **84.** $\dfrac{x^{2/3} - 4}{x - 8}$ **86.** $A = \dfrac{C^2}{4\pi}$

88. (a) The maximum profit is $3375.

(b)

Yes, P is a function of x.

(c) $P = 45x - 0.15x^2, \ x > 100$

90. $A = 2xy = 2x\sqrt{36 - x^2}, \ 0 < x < 6$

92. (a) $V = x^2y = x^2(108 - 4x)$
$$= 108x^2 - 4x^3, 0 < x < 27$$

(b)

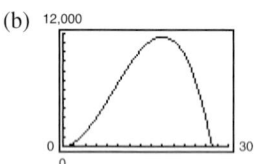

(c) 18 inches $\times$ 18 inches $\times$ 36 inches

94. (a) $C = 6000 + 0.95x$ (b) $\overline{C} = \dfrac{C}{x} = \dfrac{6000}{x} + 0.95$

96. (a)

y	5	10	20
$F(y)$	26,474.08	149,760.00	847,170.49

y	30	40
$F(y)$	2,334,527.36	4,792,320.00

The deeper the water, the greater the force.

(b) 21 feet (c) 21.37 feet

98. Yes, the ball will be at a height of 6 feet.

100. False. The range is $[-1, \infty)$.

102. The domain is the set of inputs of the function, and the range is the set of outputs.

104. 8 **106.** $\frac{2}{3}$ **108.** $x + y - 10 = 0$

110. $10x + 18y - 49 = 0$

Section 1.4 *(page 47)*

2. Domain: $(-\infty, \infty)$ **4.** Domain: $(-\infty, 1), (1, \infty)$
Range: $[0, \infty)$ Range: $-1, 1$

6. (a) 4 (b) 4 (c) 2 (d) 0

8. (a) 0 (b) 1 (c) 2 (d) 3

10. Function **12.** Not a function **14.** Not a function

16. $-8, \frac{2}{3}$ **18.** 2, 7 **20.** $\pm 3, 4$ **22.** $0, \pm\frac{5}{3}$ **24.** $-\frac{2}{3}$

26.

28.

0, 7 26

30.

$\pm\dfrac{3\sqrt{2}}{2}$

32. Increasing on $(2, \infty)$; Decreasing on $(-\infty, 2)$

34. Increasing on $(1, \infty)$; Decreasing on $(-\infty, -1)$

36. Increasing on $(-\infty, -1), (0, \infty)$
Decreasing on $(-1, 0)$

38. Increasing on $(-\infty, -2), (0, \infty)$
Decreasing on $(-2, -1), (-1, 0)$

40. (a)

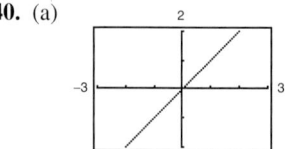

Increasing on $(-\infty, \infty)$

(b)

x	-2	-1	0	1	2
$g(x)$	-2	-1	0	1	2

42. (a)

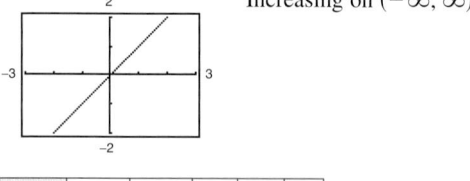

Increasing on $(0, \infty)$;
Decreasing on $(-\infty, 0)$

(b)

x	-2	-1	0	1	2
$h(x)$	0	-3	-4	-3	0

44. (a)

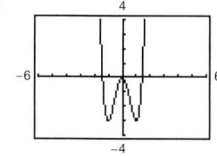

Increasing on $(-1, 0)$, $(1, \infty)$

Decreasing on $(-\infty, -1)$, $(0, 1)$

(b)

x	-2	-1	0	1	2
$f(x)$	24	-3	0	-3	24

46. (a)

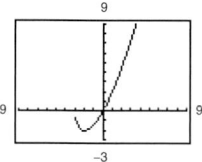

Increasing on $(-2, \infty)$

Decreasing on $(-3, -2)$

(b)

x	-3	-2	-1	0	1
$f(x)$	0	-2	-1.414	0	2

48. (a)

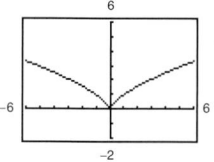

Decreasing on $(-\infty, 0)$; Increasing on $(0, \infty)$

(b)

x	-2	-1	0	1	2
$f(x)$	1.59	1	0	1	1.59

50.

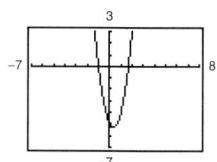

Relative minimum: $\left(\frac{1}{3}, -\frac{16}{3}\right)$

52.

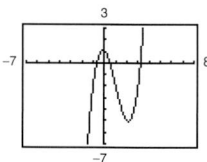

Relative maximum: $(-0.15, 1.08)$

Relative minimum: $(2.15, -5.08)$

54.

$\left[-\frac{1}{2}, \infty\right)$

56.

$(-\infty, 0]$, $[4, \infty)$

58.

$[-2, \infty)$

60.

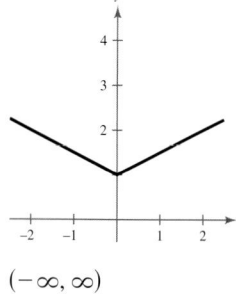

$(-\infty, \infty)$

62. Neither even nor odd   **64.** Odd   **66.** Even

68. $h = 3 - 4x + x^2$ **70.** $h = 2 - \sqrt[3]{x}$

72. $L = 2 - \sqrt[3]{2y}$ **74.** $L = \dfrac{2}{y}$

76. (a) and (e)

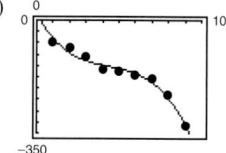

(b) y is a function of x.

(c) $y = -1.3767x^3 + 18.156x^2 - 89.40x + 16.5$

(d) $1 \le x \le 9$

(f) 1996; 1992

78. (a) $A = 64 - 2x^2$, $0 \le x \le 4$

(b)

$32 \le A \le 64$

(c) Square with sides of $4\sqrt{2}$ meters

80. False. An odd function is symmetric with respect to the origin, so its domain must include negative values.

82. Yes. For each value of y there corresponds one and only one value of x.

84. (a) $\left(\frac{5}{3}, -7\right)$ (b) $\left(\frac{5}{3}, 7\right)$

86. (a) $(-5, -1)$ (b) $(-5, 1)$

88. Both graphs will pass through the origin. $y = x^7$ will be symmetric with respect to the origin, and $y = x^8$ will be symmetric with respect to the y-axis.

 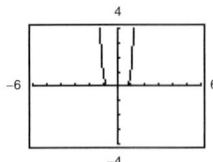

90. $-5, 15$ **92.** $\frac{5}{4}$

94. (a) -24 (b) 144 (c) $x^2 - 18x + 56$

96. (a) -3 (b) $-\frac{87}{16}$ (c) $139 - 2\sqrt{3}$

98. $-6 - h, h \neq 0$

Section 1.5   (page 56)

2. $f(x) = \frac{5}{2}x - \frac{1}{2}$ **4.** $f(x) = 5x - 6$

 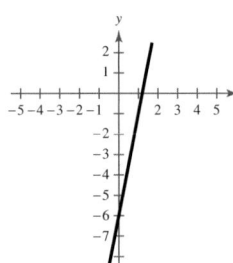

6. $f(x) = -\frac{1}{2}x + 7$ **8.** $f(x) = \frac{3}{4}x - 8$

10.   **12.**

14.   **16.**

18.   **20.**

22.   **24.**

26.   **28.**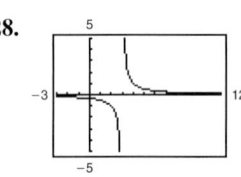

30. (a) -6 (b) 0 (c) 18 (d) 6

32. (a) 7 (b) -1 (c) 31 (d) 11

34. (a) 8 (b) 2 (c) 6 (d) 13

36. (a) -22 (b) -85 (c) 6 (d) -29

38.   **40.**

42.   **44.**

46.   **48.**

50.

52.

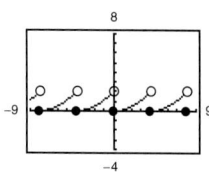

Domain: $(-\infty, \infty)$

Range: $[0, 2)$

Sawtooth pattern

54. $f(x) = \sqrt{x}; g(x) = 1 + \sqrt{x + 2}$

56. $f(x) = \dfrac{1}{x}; g(x) = \dfrac{1}{x} - 2$

58. $f(x) = x^2; g(x) = 1 - (x + 2)^2$

60. $f(x) = [\![x]\!]; g(x) = [\![x - 1]\!]$

62. $f(x) = x^3; g(x) = -x^3$

64. (a) C_2 is the appropriate model, because the cost does not increase until after the next minute of conversation has started.

(b)

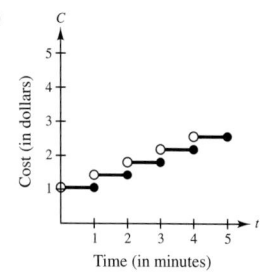

$7.89

66. (a) $C = 9.8 + 2.5[\![x]\!]$

(b)

68. (a) $f(x) = \begin{cases} 0.505x^2 - 1.47x + 6.3, & 1 \le x \le 6 \\ -1.97x + 26.3, & 6 < x \le 12 \end{cases}$

Answers will vary. Sample answer: The domain is determined by inspection of a graph of the data with the two models.

(b)

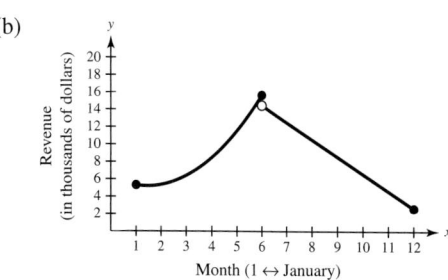

(c) $f(5) = 11.575, f(11) = 4.63$; These values represent the revenue for the months of May and November, respectively.

(d) These values are quite close to the actual data values.

70. False. A piecewise-defined function is a function that is defined by two or more equations over a specified domain. That domain may or may not include x- and y-intercepts.

72. $f(x) = \begin{cases} -\frac{4}{3}x + 6, & 0 \le x \le 3 \\ -\frac{2}{5}x + \frac{16}{5}, & 3 < x \le 8 \end{cases}$

74. $x < \frac{5}{2}$ **76.** Neither

Section 1.6   *(page 64)*

2. (a)

(b)

(c)

CHAPTER 1

4. (a)

(b)

6. (a)

(b)

(c)

(d)

(e)

(f)

(g)

8. (a)

(b)

(c)

(d)

(e)

(f)

(g)

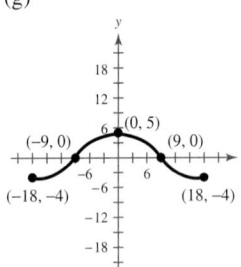

10. (a) $y = 1 - x^3$ (b) $y = (x - 1)^3 + 1$
   (c) $y = -(x + 3)^3 - 1$ (d) $y = (x - 10)^3 - 4$

12. (a) $y = \sqrt{x} - 3$ (b) $y = \sqrt{x + 1} - 7$
   (c) $y = -\sqrt{x - 5} + 5$ (d) $y = -\sqrt{-x + 3} - 4$

14. Vertical shrink of $y = x$; $y = \frac{1}{2}x$

16. Vertical shift of $y = [\![x]\!]$; $y = [\![x]\!] + 4$

18. Horizontal shift of $y = |x|$; $y = |x + 2|$

20. Horizontal shift eight units to the right of $f(x) = x^2$

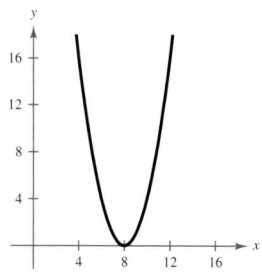

22. Reflection in the x-axis, and vertical shift one unit downward, of $f(x) = x^3$

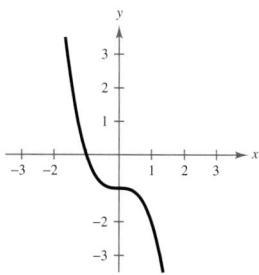

24. Reflection in the x-axis, horizontal shift 10 units to the left, and vertical shift 5 units upward, of $f(x) = x^2$

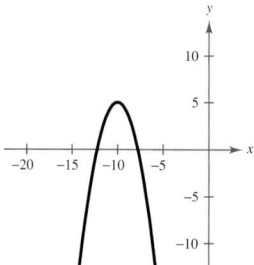

26. Horizontal shift 3 units to the left, and vertical shift 10 units downward, of $f(x) = x^3$

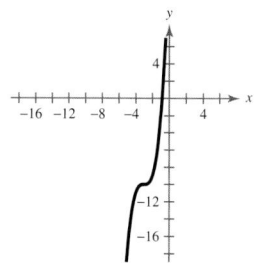

28. Reflection in the x-axis, horizontal shift five units to the left, and vertical shift six units upward, of $f(x) = |x|$

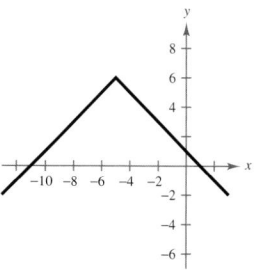

30. Reflection in the y-axis, horizontal shift three units to the right, and vertical shift nine units upward, of $f(x) = |x|$

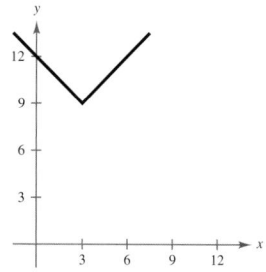

32. Horizontal shift five units to the left, and vertical stretch of two, of $f(x) = [\![x]\!]$

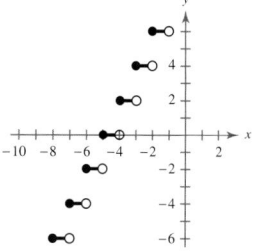

34. Horizontal shift four units to the left, and vertical shift eight units upward, of $f(x) = \sqrt{x}$

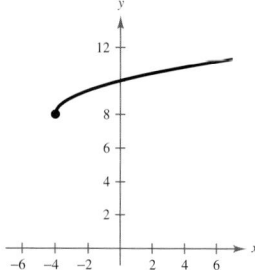

CHAPTER 1

36. Reflection in the x-axis, horizontal shift one unit to the left, and vertical shift of six units downward, of $f(x) = \sqrt{x}$

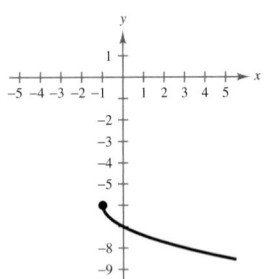

38. Vertical shift one unit upward, and horizontal shrink of $\frac{1}{3}$, of $f(x) = \sqrt{x}$

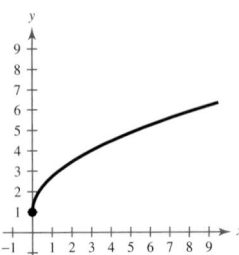

40. $f(x) = -(x+3)^2 + 7$ **42.** $f(x) = (-x-6)^3 - 6$

44. $f(x) = |x+1| - 7$ **46.** $f(x) = -\sqrt{-x} - 9$

48. (a) $y = \frac{1}{4}x^3$ (b) $y = -2x^3$

50. (a) $y = 8\sqrt{x}$ (b) $y = -\frac{1}{4}\sqrt{x}$

52. Vertical stretch of $y = |x|$; $y = 6|x|$

54. Horizontal stretch of $y = [\![x]\!]$; $y = [\![\frac{1}{2}x]\!]$

56. Reflection in the x-axis, vertical shift two units downward, and vertical stretch, of $y = |x|$;
$y = -2|x| - 2$

58. $y = |x+4| - 2$ **60.** $y = (x-2)^2 + 4$

62. (a)   (b)

(c)   (d)

(e)   (f)

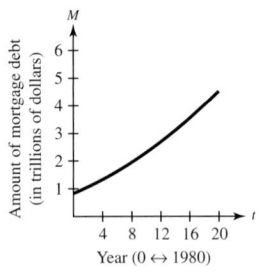

64. (a) Horizontal shift of 14.979 units to the left and vertical shrink of 0.0037

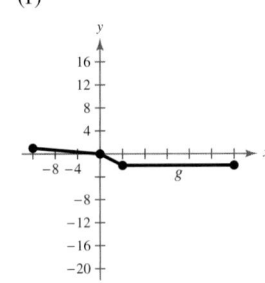

(b) $f(t) = 0.0037(t + 24.979)^2$. The graph was shifted 10 units to the left.

66. False. The point $(-2, -61)$ will lie on the transformation.

68. If you consider the x-axis to be a mirror, the graph of $y = -f(x)$ is the mirror image of the graph of $y = f(x)$.

70. Answers will vary.

72. $\dfrac{-20}{(x+5)(x-5)}$ **74.** $\dfrac{3x-5}{2(x-5)}$

76. $\dfrac{x+1}{x(x+2)}, x \neq 2$ **78.** $\dfrac{x+1}{(x-7)(x+3)}, x \neq 0, -1, -4$

80. (a) -3 (b) 3   (c) $\sqrt{x} - 3$ **82.** $x \geq 3, x \neq 8$

84. All real numbers

Section 1.7   *(page 74)*

2.

4.

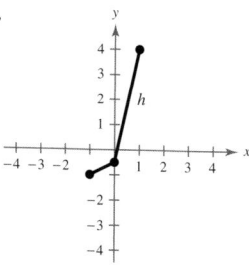

6. (a) $x - 3$ (b) $3x - 7$

(c) $-2x^2 + 9x - 10$ (d) $\dfrac{2x - 5}{2 - x}; x \neq 2$

8. (a) $2x - 1$ (b) $2x - 9$

(c) $8x - 20$ (d) $\frac{1}{2}x - \frac{5}{4}; -\infty < x < \infty$

10. (a) $\sqrt{x^2 - 4} + \dfrac{x^2}{x^2 + 1}$ (b) $\sqrt{x^2 - 4} - \dfrac{x^2}{x^2 + 1}$

(c) $\dfrac{x^2\sqrt{x^2 - 4}}{x^2 + 1}$ (d) $\dfrac{(x^2 + 1)\sqrt{x^2 - 4}}{x^2}; |x| \geq 2$

12. (a) $\dfrac{x^4 + x^3 + x}{x + 1}$ (b) $\dfrac{-x^4 - x^3 + x}{x + 1}$

(c) $\dfrac{x^4}{x + 1}$ (d) $\dfrac{1}{x^2(x + 1)}; x \neq 0, -1$

14. 7   **16.** -1 **18.** $t^2 - 3t - 1$ **20.** -370

22. $-\frac{1}{4}$ **24.** 43

26.

28.

30.

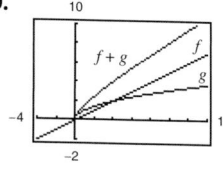

$g(x), f(x)$

32. $R_T = 734 - 7.22t - 0.8t^2$

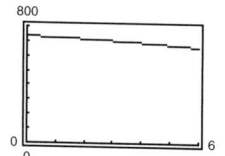

34. (a) For each time t there corresponds one and only one temperature T.

(b) $60°, 72°$

(c) All the temperature changes occur 1 hour later.

(d) The temperature is decreased by 1 degree.

(e) $T(t) = \begin{cases} 60, & 0 \leq t \leq 6 \\ 12t - 12, & 6 < t < 7 \\ 72, & 7 \leq t \leq 20 \\ -12t + 312, & 20 < t < 21 \\ 60, & 21 \leq t \leq 24 \end{cases}$

36. (a) $20 - 3x$ (b) $-3x$ (c) $9x + 20$

38. (a) $\dfrac{1}{x^3}$ (b) $\dfrac{1}{x^3}$ (c) x^9

40. (a) $\sqrt[3]{x^3 - 4}$ (b) $x - 4$

Domain of $f, g, f \circ g,$ and $g \circ f$: all real numbers

42. (a) x^4 (b) x^4

Domain of $f, g, f \circ g,$ and $g \circ f$: all real numbers

44. (a) $\left|-1 - x\right|$ (b) $3 - |x - 4|$

Domain of $f, g, f \circ g,$ and $g \circ f$: all real numbers

46. (a) $\dfrac{3}{x^2 + 2x}$ (b) $\dfrac{x^2 + 2}{x^2 - 1}$

Domain of f and $g \circ f$: all real numbers $x \neq \pm 1$

Domain of g: all real numbers

Domain of $f \circ g$: all real numbers $x \neq 0, -2$

48. (a) -1 (b) 0   **50** (a) 2   (b) 2

52. $f(x) = x^3, g(x) = 1 - x$

54. $f(x) = \sqrt{x}, g(x) = 9 - x$

56. $f(x) = \dfrac{4}{x^2}, g(x) = 5x + 2$

58. $f(x) = \dfrac{27x + 6\sqrt[3]{x}}{10 - 27x}, g(x) = x^3$

60. $(A \circ r)(t) = 0.36\pi t^2$; $(A \circ r)(t)$ represents the area of the circle at time t.

62. True. The range of g must be a subset of the domain of f for $(f \circ g)(x)$ to be defined.

64. Answers will vary.

66. All real numbers $x \neq -\frac{7}{5}$ **68.** $-2x - h$

70.

$$\dfrac{\sqrt{2(x + h) + 1} - \sqrt{2x + 1}}{h} = \dfrac{2}{\sqrt{2(x + h) + 1} + \sqrt{2x + 1}}$$

72. $x + y + 3 = 0$ **74.** $5x - 7y - 35 = 0$

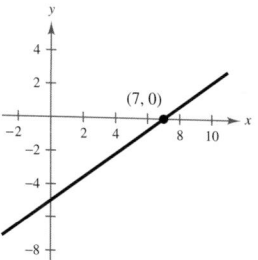

Section 1.8   *(page 83)*

1. c   **2.** b   **3.** a   **4.** d   **6.** $f^{-1}(x) = 3x$

8. $f^{-1}(x) = x + 4$ **10.** $f^{-1}(x) = 5x + 1$

12. $f^{-1}(x) = \sqrt[5]{x}$

14. (a) $f(g(x)) = f(x + 5) = (x + 5) - 5 = x$

$\qquad g(f(x)) = g(x - 5) = (x - 5) + 5 = x$

(b)

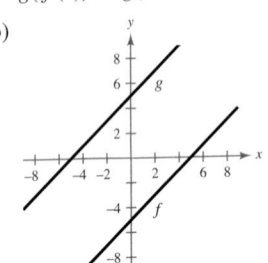

16. (a) $f(g(x)) = f\!\left(\dfrac{3 - x}{4}\right) = 3 - 4\!\left(\dfrac{3 - x}{4}\right) = x$

$\qquad g(f(x)) = g(3 - 4x) = \dfrac{3 - (3 - 4x)}{4} = x$

(b)

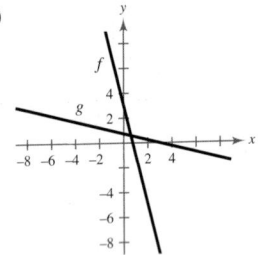

18. (a) $f(g(x)) = f\!\left(\dfrac{1}{x}\right) = \dfrac{1}{1/x} = x$

$\qquad g(f(x)) = g\!\left(\dfrac{1}{x}\right) = \dfrac{1}{1/x} = x$

(b)

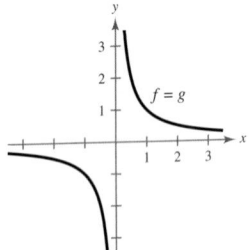

20. (a) $f(g(x)) = f\!\left(\sqrt[3]{1 - x}\,\right)$

$\qquad\qquad = 1 - \left(\sqrt[3]{1 - x}\right)^{3} = x$

$\qquad g(f(x)) = g(1 - x^{3})$

$\qquad\qquad = \sqrt[3]{1 - (1 - x^{3})} = x$

(b)

[figure: graph with f and g]

22. (a) $f(g(x)) = f\!\left(\dfrac{1 - x}{x}\right), \quad 0 < x \le 1$

$\qquad = \dfrac{1}{1 + (1 - x)/x} = \dfrac{x}{x + 1 - x} = x$

$\qquad g(f(x)) = g\!\left(\dfrac{1}{1 + x}\right), \quad x \ge 0$

$\qquad = \dfrac{1 - 1/(1 + x)}{1/(1 + x)} = \dfrac{1 + x - 1}{1} = x$

(b)

[figure: graph with f and g]

24. (a) $f(g(x)) = f\!\left(\dfrac{2x + 3}{x - 1}\right) = \dfrac{\left(\dfrac{2x + 3}{x - 1}\right) + 3}{\left(\dfrac{2x + 3}{x - 1}\right) - 2}$

$\qquad = \dfrac{2x + 3 + 3x - 3}{2x + 3 - 2x + 2} = x$

(b) $g(f(x)) = g\!\left(\dfrac{x + 3}{x - 2}\right) = \dfrac{2\!\left(\dfrac{x + 3}{x - 2}\right) + 3}{\left(\dfrac{x + 3}{x - 2}\right) - 1}$

$\qquad = \dfrac{2x + 6 + 3x - 6}{x + 3 - x + 2} = x$

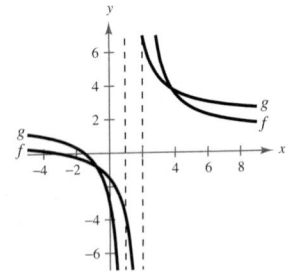

26. Yes

28.

x	-10	-7	-4	-1	2	5
$f^{-1}(x)$	-3	-2	-1	0	1	2

30. No   **32.** Yes

34.

36.

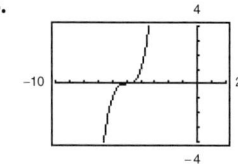

The function does not have an inverse.

The function has an inverse.

38.

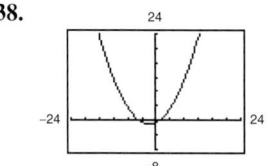

The function does not have an inverse.

40. $f^{-1}(x) = \dfrac{x-1}{3}$ **42.** $f^{-1}(x) = \sqrt[3]{x-1}$

44. $f^{-1}(x) = \sqrt{x}$

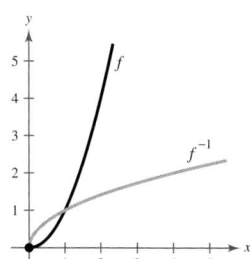

46. $f^{-1}(x) = -\sqrt{x+2}$ **48.** $f^{-1}(x) = -\dfrac{2}{x}$

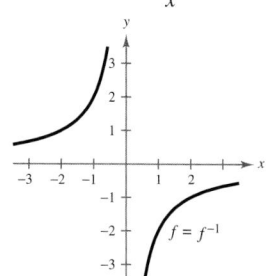

50. $f^{-1}(x) = \dfrac{-2x-3}{x-1}$ **52.** $f^{-1}(x) = x^{5/3}$

54. $f^{-1}(x) = \dfrac{-6x-4}{2x-8}$

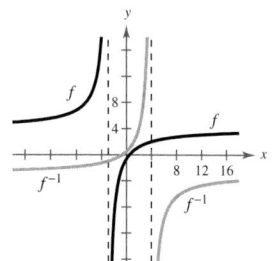

56. No inverse   **58.** $f^{-1}(x) = \dfrac{x-5}{3}$

60. $f^{-1}(x) = \dfrac{5x-4}{3}$ **62.** No inverse

64. No inverse   **66.** $f^{-1}(x) = 2 - x, \ x \geq 0$

68. $f^{-1}(x) = x^2 + 2, \ x \geq 0$ **70.** 0   **72.** $-\sqrt[9]{4}$

74. $2\sqrt[3]{x+3}$ **76.** $\dfrac{x-3}{2}$ **78.** $\dfrac{x-3}{2}$

80. (a) Yes

(b) The inverse, f^{-1}, yields the year for a given per capita consumption of bottled water.

(c) 8

82. (a) $y = \dfrac{x-8}{0.75}$

(b) y = number of units produced; x = hourly wage

(c) 19 units

84. (a) $y = \dfrac{80 - x}{0.35}$

x = total cost; y = number of pounds of the less expensive ground beef

(b) $62.5 \le x \le 80$ (c) 20 pounds

86. True. If $f(x) = x - 6$ and $f^{-1}(x) = x + 6$, then the y-intercept of f is $(0, -6)$ and the x-intercept of f^{-1} is $(-6, 0)$.

88.

x	-2	-1	1	3
y	-5	-2	2	3

x	-5	-2	2	3
$f^{-1}(x)$	-2	-1	1	3

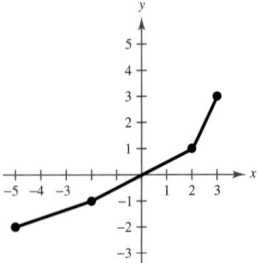

90.

x	-4	-2	0	3
y	3	4	0	-1

The graph of f does not pass the Horizontal Line Test, so $f^{-1}(x)$ does not exist.

92. $k = -\dfrac{1}{2}$ **94.** $5 \pm 2\sqrt{2}$ **96.** $-1, -\dfrac{1}{3}$

98. $-1, 3$ **100.** $\dfrac{11}{8}$

102. $b = \sqrt{10}$ feet, $h = 2\sqrt{10}$ feet

Section 1.9   *(page 93)*

2.

The model is not a "good fit" for the actual data.

4. Directly

6.

x	2	4	6	8	10
$y = kx^2$	8	32	72	128	200

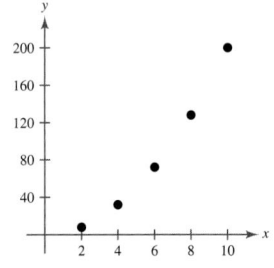

8.

x	2	4	6	8	10
$y = kx^2$	1	4	9	16	25

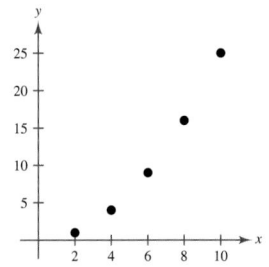

10.

x	2	4	6	8	10
$y = k/x^2$	$\dfrac{5}{4}$	$\dfrac{5}{16}$	$\dfrac{5}{36}$	$\dfrac{5}{64}$	$\dfrac{1}{20}$

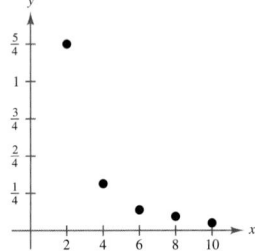

12.

x	2	4	6	8	10
$y = k/x^2$	5	$\dfrac{5}{4}$	$\dfrac{5}{9}$	$\dfrac{5}{16}$	$\dfrac{1}{5}$

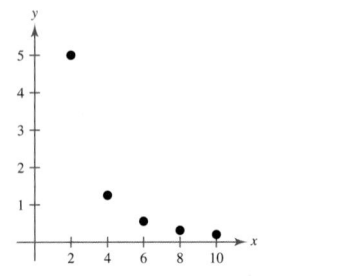

14. $y = \dfrac{2}{5}x$ **16.** $y = \dfrac{120}{x}$ **18.** $y = 7x$

20. $y = \frac{290}{3}x$ **22.** $I = 0.0375P$

24. Model: $y = \frac{53}{14}x$; 18.9 liters, 94.6 liters

26. $y = 0.07x$; \$37.84   **28.** $293\frac{1}{3}$ newtons

30. Combined lifting force $= 2F = 120$ pounds

32. $V = ke^3$ **34.** $h = \dfrac{k}{\sqrt{s}}$ **36.** $z = kx^2y^3$

38. $R = k\left(T - T_e\right)$ **40.** $R = kS(L - S)$

42. The surface area of a sphere varies directly as the square of its radius.

44. The volume of a right circular cylinder is jointly proportional to the product of its height and the square of its radius.

46. ω varies directly as the square root of g and inversely as the square root of W.

48. $y = \dfrac{75}{x}$ **50.** $z = 2xy$ **52.** $P = \dfrac{18x}{y^2}$

54. $v = \dfrac{24pq}{287s^2}$ **56.** $\dfrac{k(2v)^2}{kv^2} = 4$

58. Diameter $= 2r = 0.054$ inch

60. No. The 15-inch pizza is the best buy.

62. (a) The safe load is unchanged.

(b) The safe load is eight times as great.

(c) The safe load is four times as great.

(d) The safe load is one-fourth as great.

64. (a) 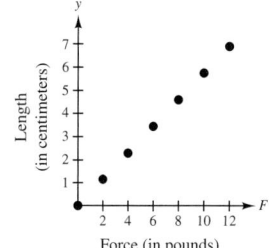   (b) Yes. $k = 0.575$

(c) 15.7 pounds

66. The illumination is reduced to one-fourth of its original value. Explanations will vary.

68. 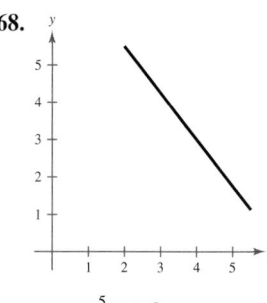   **70.**

$y = -\frac{5}{4}x + 8$ $y = \frac{1}{3}x + 2$

72. (a) and (b)

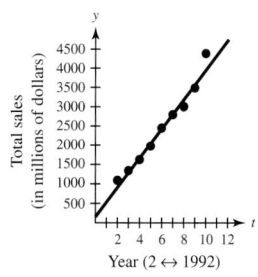

$y = 380t + 140$

(c) $y = 386.47t + 140.8$ (d) The models are similar.

(e) Part (b): \$4700 million; Part (c): \$4778 million

(f) Analyses will vary.

74. (a) $y = -0.43x + 85.4$

(b)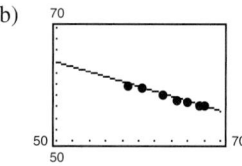

(c) 55.3 million

(d) For every million households with cable television, there is a 0.43 million decrease in the number of daily newspapers in circulation.

76. False. E is jointly proportional to the mass of an object and the square of its velocity.

78. (a) Good approximation   (b) Poor approximation

(c) Poor approximation   (d) Good approximation

80. $-1 < x < 3$ **82.** $x = 0,\ x \geq 8$

84. (a) 6   (b) 9   (c) 383

Review Exercises *(page 100)*

2.

x	-4	-2	0	2	4
y	4	3	2	1	0

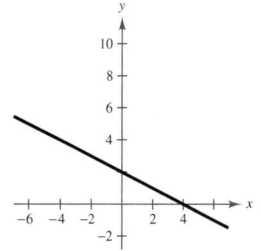

4.

x	-2	-1	0	1	2	3
y	1	-6	-9	-8	-3	6

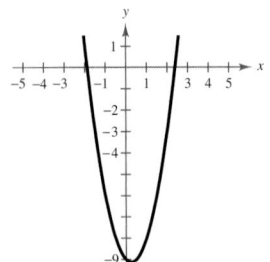

6. x-intercepts:
(0, 0), (8, 0)

y-intercept: (0, 0)

8. x-intercepts:
(0, 0), ($\pm$3, 0)

y-intercept: (0, 0)

10. No symmetry

12. y-axis symmetry

 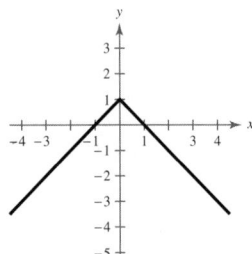

14. Center: (0, 0); Radius: 2

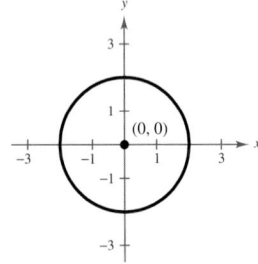

16. Center: (0, 8); Radius: 9

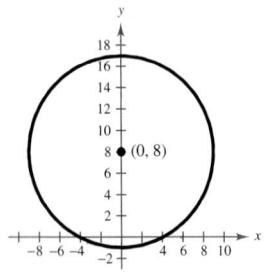

18. $(x - 1)^2 + \left(y + \frac{13}{2}\right)^2 = \frac{85}{4}$

20.

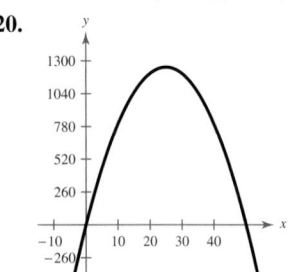

Maximum area: 1250 square feet

Length of sides: 25 feet

22. m is undefined:
No y-intercept

24. $m = -10$:
y-intercept: (0, 9)

26.

$m = -\frac{3}{7}$

28.

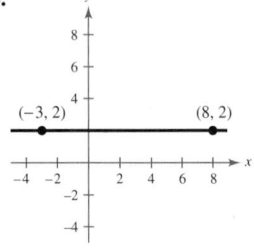

$m = 0$

30. $3x - 2y + 4 = 0$ **32.** $x + 5y - 1 = 0$

34. $y - 6 = 0$ **36.** $x + 8 = 0$

 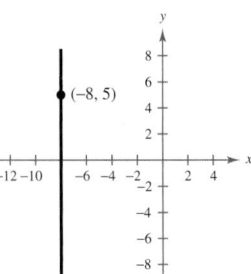

38. (a) $2x + 3y + 7 = 0$ (b) $3x - 2y + 30 = 0$

40. (a) $y = 5$ (b) $x = -2$

42. $V = 5.15t + 52.35, 4 \le t \le 9$

44. Yes   **46.** No

48. (a) -3 (b) -1 (c) 2   (d) 6

50. All real numbers

52. All real numbers

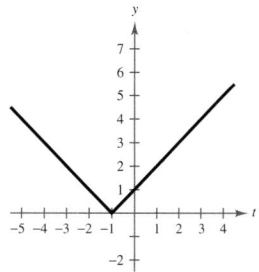

54. (a) $f(x) = 0.4(50 - x) + x = 20 + 0.6x$

(b) Domain: $0 \leq x \leq 50$; Range: $20 \leq y \leq 50$

(c) $8\frac{1}{3}$ liters

56. Function   **58.** Not a function   **60.** $-1, \frac{1}{5}$

62. $1, \pm 5$

64. Increasing on $(-2, 0)$ and $(2, \infty)$

Decreasing on $(-\infty, -2)$ and $(0, 2)$

66. Even   **68.** Even

70. $f(x) = -\frac{3}{4}x - 5$ **72.**

74.   **76.**

78.   **80.**

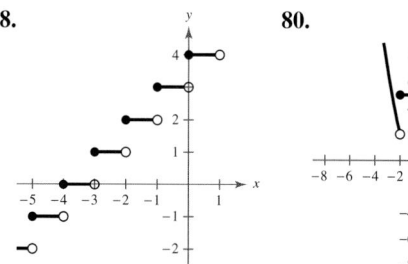

82. $y = -(x + 3)^2$

84. Horizontal shift of seven units to the right

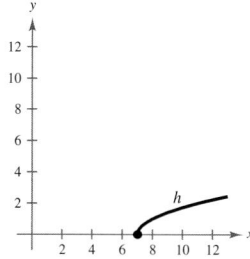

86. Reflection in the x-axis, horizontal shift of three units to the left, and vertical shift of one unit upward

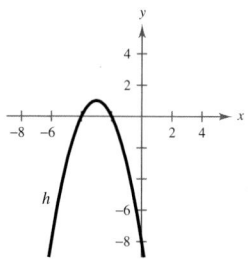

88. Reflection in the x-axis and vertical shrink

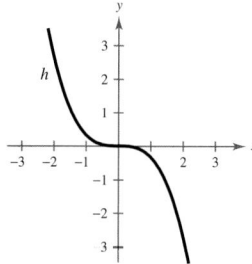

90. Horizontal shift of nine units to the right and vertical stretch

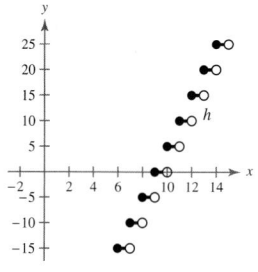

CHAPTER 1

92. (a) $x^2 - 4 + \sqrt{3 - x}$

(b) $x^2 - 4 - \sqrt{3 - x}$

(c) $(x^2 - 4)\sqrt{3 - x}$

(d) $\dfrac{x^2 - 4}{\sqrt{3 - x}}$, $x < 3$

94. (a) $x + 3$

(b) $\sqrt[3]{x^3 + 3}$

Domain of $f, g, f \circ g,$ and $g \circ f$: all real numbers

96. $f(x) = \sqrt[3]{x}, g(x) = x + 2$ (Answer is not unique.)

98.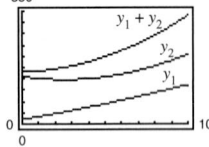

$\$546.4$ billion

100. $f^{-1}(x) = x - 5$

$f(f^{-1}(x)) = x - 5 + 5 = x$

$f^{-1}(f(x)) = x + 5 - 5 = x$

102. The function does not have an inverse.

104.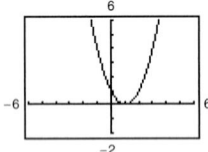

The function does not have an inverse.

106.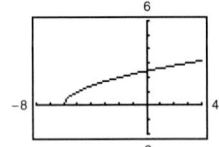

The function has an inverse.

108. (a) $f^{-1}(x) = \dfrac{x + 7}{5}$

(b)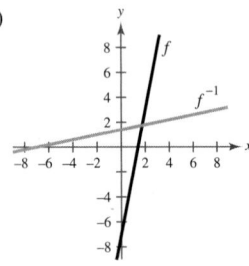

(c) $f^{-1}(f(x)) = f^{-1}(5x - 7)$

$= \dfrac{5x - 7 + 7}{5}$

$= x$

$f(f^{-1}(x)) = f\left(\dfrac{x + 7}{5}\right)$

$= 5\left(\dfrac{x + 7}{5}\right) - 7$

$= x$

110. (a) $f^{-1}(x) = \sqrt[3]{x - 2}$

(b)

(c) $f^{-1}(f(x)) = f^{-1}(x^3 + 2)$

$= \sqrt[3]{x^3 + 2 - 2}$

$= x$

$f(f^{-1}(x)) = f\left(\sqrt[3]{x - 2}\right)$

$= (x - 2) + 2$

$= x$

112. $x \geq 2;\ f^{-1}(x) = x + 2, x \geq 0$

114. Model: $y = \frac{8}{5}x$; 3.2 kilometers, 16.1 kilometers

116. $N = 100$

118. (a) $y = 73.37t + 292.4$

(b) 1392.95 million

(c) Each year, the number of CDs shipped in the United States increases by 73.37 million.

120. True. If $f(x) = x^3$ and $g(x) = \sqrt[3]{x}$, then the domain of g is all real numbers, which is equal to the range of f, and vice versa.

122. The y-intercept is $(0, 0)$.

Problem Solving   (page 106)

2. Mapping numbers onto letters is not a function since each number corresponds to three letters.

Mapping letters onto numbers is a function since every letter is assigned exactly one number.

4. $f(x) = x$ $g(x) = -x$

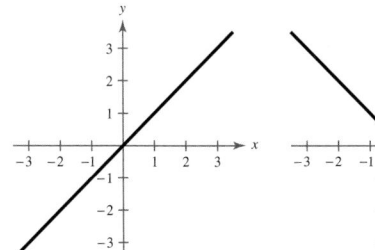

Both graphs are already symmetric with respect to the line $y = x$.

General formula: $y = -x + c, c \geq 0$

6. $(6, 8)$

$$f(x) = \begin{cases} \frac{12}{7}x - \frac{16}{7}, & 2.5 \leq x \leq 6 \\ -\frac{12}{7}x + \frac{128}{7}, & 6 < x \leq 9.5 \end{cases}$$

8. (a) $(f \circ g)(x) = 4x + 24.$ (b) $(f \circ g)^{-1}(x) = \frac{1}{4}x - 6$

(c) $f^{-1}(x) = \frac{1}{4}x; g^{-1}(x) = x - 6$

(d) $(g^{-1} \circ f^{-1})(x) = \frac{1}{4}x - 6$

(e) $(f \circ g)(x) = 8x^3 + 1; (f \circ g)^{-1}(x) = \frac{1}{2}\sqrt[3]{x - 1};$

$\quad f^{-1}(x) = \sqrt[3]{x - 1}; g^{-1}(x) = \frac{1}{2}x;$

$\quad (g^{-1} \circ f^{-1})(x) = \frac{1}{2}\sqrt[3]{x - 1}$

(f) Answers will vary.

(g) $(f \circ g)^{-1}(x) = (g^{-1} \circ f^{-1})(x)$

10. (a)   (b)

(c)   (d)

(e)   (f)

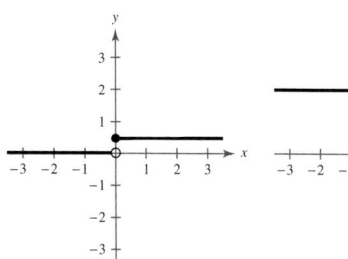

12. Answers will vary. Sample answer:

Let $f(x) = x^2, g(x) = x + 1, h(x) = 2x + 3.$

$(f \circ (g \circ h))(x) = f(g(2x + 3))$

$\qquad\qquad = f(2x + 4)$

$\qquad\qquad = 4x^2 + 16x + 16$

$((f \circ g) \circ h)(x) = f(x + 1) \circ h(x)$

$\qquad\qquad = x^2 + 2x + 1 \circ h(x)$

$\qquad\qquad = 4x^2 + 16x + 16$

14. (a)

x	-4	-2	0	4
$f(f^{-1}(x))$	-4	-2	0	4

(b)

x	-3	-2	0	1
$(f + f^{-1})(x)$	5	1	-3	-5

(c)

x	-3	-2	0	1
$(f \circ f^{-1})(x)$	4	0	2	6

x	-4	-3	0	4
$|f^{-1}(x)|$	2	1	1	3

Chapter 2

Section 2.1   *(page 116)*

1. g   **2.** c   **3.** b   **4.** h

5. f   **6.** a   **7.** e   **8.** d

10. (a)

Vertical translation

(b)

Vertical translation

(c)

Vertical translation

(d)

Vertical translation

12. (a)

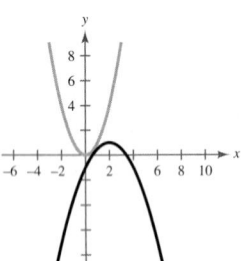

Horizontal translation, vertical shrink, reflection in the x-axis, and vertical translation

(b)

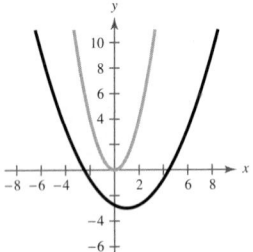

Horizontal translation, vertical shrink, and vertical translation

(c)

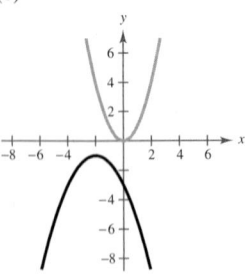

Reflection in the x-axis, vertical shrink, horizontal translation, and vertical translation

(d)

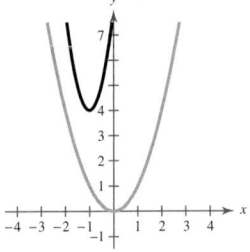

Horizontal translation, vertical stretch, and vertical translation

14.

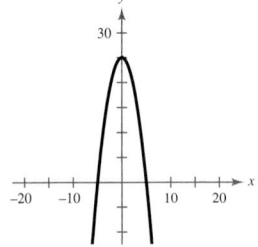

Vertex: $(0, 25)$

x-intercepts: $(\pm 5, 0)$

16.

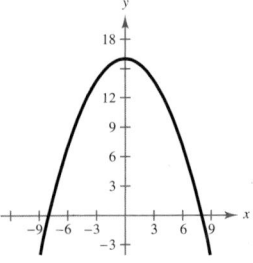

Vertex: $(0, 16)$

x-intercepts: $(\pm 8, 0)$

18.

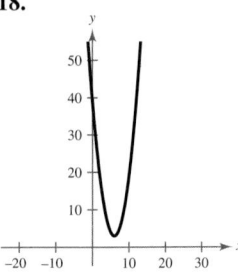

Vertex: $(6, 3)$

No x-intercept

20.

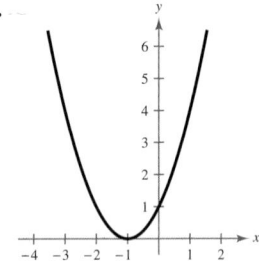

Vertex: $(-1, 0)$

x-intercept: $(-1, 0)$

22.

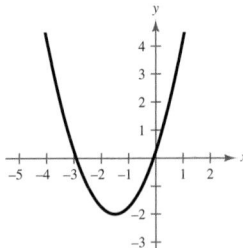

Vertex: $\left(-\frac{3}{2}, -2\right)$

x-intercepts: $\left(-\frac{3}{2} \pm \sqrt{2}, 0\right)$

24.

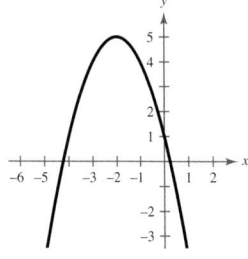

Vertex: $(-2, 5)$

x-intercepts: $(-2 \pm \sqrt{5}, 0)$

26.

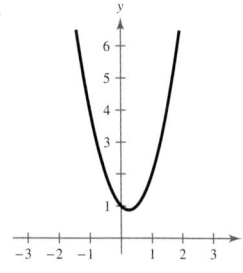

Vertex: $\left(\frac{1}{4}, \frac{7}{8}\right)$

No x-intercept

28.

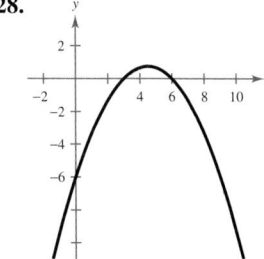

Vertex: $\left(\frac{9}{2}, \frac{3}{4}\right)$

x-intercepts: $(3, 0), (6, 0)$

30.

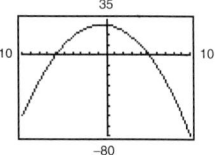

Vertex: $\left(-\frac{1}{2}, \frac{121}{4}\right)$

x-intercepts: $(-6, 0), (5, 0)$

32.

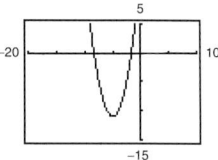

Vertex: $(-5, -11)$

x-intercepts: $\left(-5 \pm \sqrt{11}, 0\right)$

34.

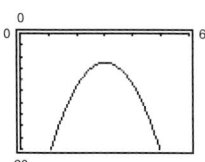

Vertex: $(3, -5)$

No x-intercept

36.

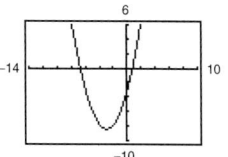

Vertex: $\left(-3, -\frac{42}{5}\right)$

x-intercepts: $\left(-3 \pm \sqrt{14}, 0\right)$

38. $y = -x^2 + 1$ **40.** $y = (x + 2)^2 - 1$

42. $y = 2(x - 2)^2$ **44.** $f(x) = (x - 4)^2 - 1$

46. $f(x) = -\frac{1}{4}(x - 2)^2 + 3$ **48.** $f(x) = 2(x + 2)^2 - 2$

50. $f(x) = \frac{19}{81}\left(x - \frac{5}{2}\right)^2 - \frac{3}{4}$

52. $f(x) = -450(x - 6)^2 + 6$

54. $(3, 0)$ **56.** $(-3, 0), \left(\frac{1}{2}, 0\right)$

58.

60.

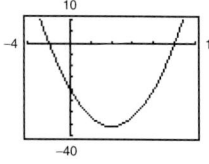

$(0, 0), (5, 0)$ $(-2, 0), (10, 0)$

62.

64.

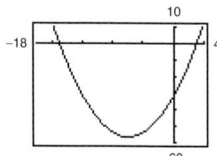

$(-7, 0), \left(\frac{3}{4}, 0\right)$ $(-15, 0), (3, 0)$

66. $f(x) = x^2 - 25$ **68.** $f(x) = x^2 - 12x + 32$

      $g(x) = -x^2 + 25$ $g(x) = -x^2 + 12x - 32$

70. $f(x) = 2x^2 + x - 10$

      $g(x) = -2x^2 - x + 10$

72. $\frac{S}{2}, \frac{S}{2}$ **74.** $21, 7$

76. (a) $r = \frac{1}{2}y; d = y\pi$ (b) $y = \dfrac{200 - 2x}{\pi}$

     (c) $A = x\left(\dfrac{200 - 2x}{\pi}\right)$; $x = 50$ meters, $y = \dfrac{100}{\pi}$ meters

78. $250{,}000$ units   **80.** 1222 units   **82.** \$2000

84. 16 feet

86. (a) and (c)

(b) $y = 5.09x^2 - 61.9x + 930$ (d) 1996 (e) 1147

CHAPTER 2

88. (a) and (c)

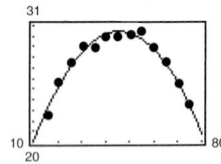

(b) $y = -0.0082x^2 + 0.746x + 13.47$

(d) 45.5 miles per hour

90. True. The vertex of $f(x)$ is $\left(-\frac{5}{4}, \frac{53}{4}\right)$ and the vertex of $g(x)$ is $\left(-\frac{5}{4}, -\frac{71}{4}\right)$.

92. Conditions (a) and (d) are preferable because profits would be increasing.

94. Answers will vary.   **96.** $y = \frac{3}{2}x - \frac{13}{4}$

98. $y = -3x - 20$ **100.** 7   **102.** $-\frac{4}{3}$ **104.** 72

Section 2.2   *(page 130)*

1. c   **2.** g   **3.** h   **4.** f

5. a   **6.** e   **7.** d   **8.** b

10. (a)

(b)

(c)

(d)

12. (a)

(b)

(c)

(d)

(e)

(f)

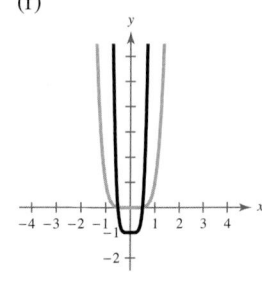

14. Rises to the left, rises to the right

16. Falls to the left, falls to the right

18. Falls to the left, rises to the right

20. Rises to the left, rises to the right

22. Rises to the left, falls to the right

24.

26.

28. ± 7, odd multiplicity   **30.** -5, even multiplicity

32. $\dfrac{-5 \pm \sqrt{37}}{2}$, odd multiplicity

34. $0, 1 \pm \sqrt{2}$, odd multiplicity

36. $5, -4$, odd multiplicity; 0, even multiplicity

38. $0, \pm\sqrt{2}$, odd multiplicity   **40.** $\pm\sqrt{5}$, odd multiplicity

42. $4, \pm 5$, odd multiplicity

44.

46.

$(-2, 0), \left(\frac{1}{2}, 0\right)$ $(0, 0), (\pm 3, 0)$

48. $f(x) = x^2 + 3x$ **50.** $f(x) = x^2 - x - 20$

52. $f(x) = x^3 - 7x^2 + 10x$ **54.** $f(x) = x^5 - 5x^3 + 4x$

56. $f(x) = x^3 - 10x^2 + 27x - 22$

58. $f(x) = x^2 + 12x + 32$

60. $f(x) = x^3 - 9x^2 + 6x + 56$

62. $f(x) = x^3 - 27x^2 + 243x - 729$

64. $f(x) = x^4 - 4x^3 - 23x^2 + 54x + 72$

66. $f(x) = x^5 - 10x^4 + 14x^3 + 88x^2 - 183x + 90$

68. (a) Rises to the left, rises to the right

    (b) $0, \pm 2$ (c) Answers will vary.

    (d)

70. (a) Falls to the left, falls to the right

    (b) $2, 8$ (c) Answers will vary.

    (d)

72. (a) Rises to the left, falls to the right

    (b) 1 (c) Answers will vary.

    (d)

74. (a) Rises to the left, falls to the right

    (b) $-\frac{3}{2}, 0, \frac{5}{2}$ (c) Answers will vary.

    (d)

76. (a) Rises to the left, rises to the right

    (b) $0, \pm 4$ (c) Answers will vary.

    (d)

78. (a) Falls to the left, rises to the right

    (b) $0, 4$ (c) Answers will vary.

    (d)

80. (a) Falls to the left, rises to the right

    (b) $-1, 3$ (c) Answers will vary.

    (d)

82.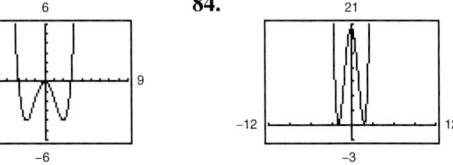

Zeros: $\pm 2\sqrt{2}$, odd multiplicity; 0, even multiplicity

84.

Zeros: $-2, \frac{5}{3}$, even multiplicity

86. $[0, 1], [6, 7], [11, 12]; \approx 0.845, 6.385, 11.588$

88. $[-4, -3], [-1, 0], [0, 1], [3, 4]; \approx \pm 3.113, \pm 0.556$

90. (a) Answers will vary.

(b) Domain: $0 < x < 6$

(c)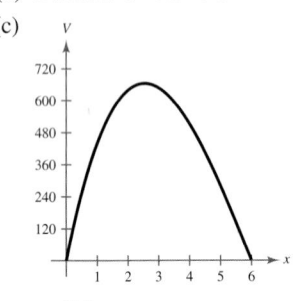

$x \approx 2.6$

92. $x \approx 200$

94. True. $f(x) = (x - 1)^6$ has one repeated solution.

96. (a) Degree: 3; Leading coefficient: positive

(b) Degree: 2; Leading coefficient: positive

(c) Degree: 4; Leading coefficient: positive

(d) Degree: 5; Leading coefficient: positive

98. (a)

y_1 is decreasing. y_2 is increasing.

(b) Either always increasing or always decreasing. The behavior is determined by a.

(c)

Because $H(x)$ is not always increasing or always decreasing, H cannot be written in the form $H(x) = a(x - h)^5 + k$.

100. $-\frac{2}{3}, 8$ **102.** -12 **104.** $4 \pm \sqrt{14}$

106. $\dfrac{-2 \pm \sqrt{31}}{3}$ **108.** $x(6x - 1)(x - 10)$

110. $(y + 6)(y^2 - 6y + 36)$

112. Reflection in the x-axis, and vertical shift of three units up of $y = x^2$

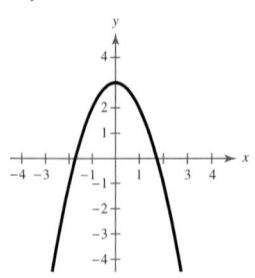

114. Reflection in the x-axis, horizontal translation, and vertical translation of $y = \sqrt{x}$

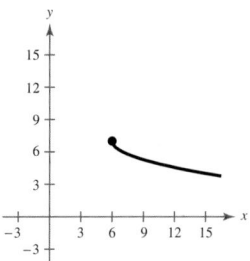

116. Vertical shrink, reflection in the x-axis, horizontal shift of 3 units to the left, vertical shift of 10 units up, and vertical translation of $y = [\![x]\!]$

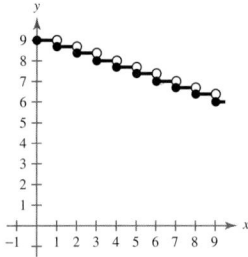

Section 2.3   *(page 140)*

2. Answers will vary.

4.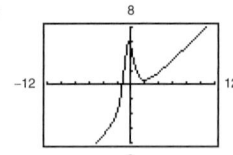

6. $5x + 3$ **8.** $2x^2 - 4x + 3$

10. $x^2 + 7x + 18 + \dfrac{42}{x - 3}$ **12.** $4 - \dfrac{9}{2x + 1}$

14. $x - \dfrac{x + 9}{x^2 + 1}$ **16.** $x^2 + \dfrac{x^2 + 7}{x^3 - 1}$

18. $2x - \dfrac{17x - 5}{x^2 - 2x + 1}$ **20.** $5x^2 + 3x - 2$

22. $9x^2 - 16$ **24.** $3x^2 + 2x + 12$

26. $5x^2 - 10x + 26 - \dfrac{44}{x + 2}$

28. $x^4 - 16x^3 + 48x^2 - 144x + 312 - \dfrac{856}{x + 3}$

30. $x^2 + 9x + 81$

32. $-3x^3 + 6x^2 - 12x + 24 - \dfrac{48}{x + 2}$

34. $-x^2 + 3x - 6 + \dfrac{11}{x + 1}$

36. $3x^2 + \dfrac{1}{2}x + \dfrac{3}{4} + \dfrac{49}{8x - 12}$

38. $f(x) = (x + 2)(x^2 - 7x + 3) + 2, f(-2) = 2$

40. $f(x) = \left(x - \frac{1}{5}\right)(10x^2 - 20x - 7) + \frac{13}{5}, f\left(\frac{1}{5}\right) = \frac{13}{5}$

42. $f(x) = \left(x + \sqrt{5}\right)\left[x^2 + \left(2 - \sqrt{5}\right)x - 2\sqrt{5}\right] + 6,$
$f\left(-\sqrt{5}\right) = 6$

44. $f(x) = \left(x - 2 - \sqrt{2}\right)\left[-3x^2 + \left(2 - 3\sqrt{2}\right)x + 8 - 4\sqrt{2}\right],$
$f\left(2 + \sqrt{2}\right) = 0$

46. (a) 14   (b) 3122   (c) 434   (d) 2

48. (a) -2.5 (b) 20   (c) 65.5   (d) 5668

50. $(x + 4)(x + 2)(x - 6)$; Zeros: $-4, -2, 6$

52. $(3x - 2)(4x - 3)(4x - 1)$; Zeros: $\frac{2}{3}, \frac{3}{4}, \frac{1}{4}$

54. $\left(x - \sqrt{2}\right)\left(x + \sqrt{2}\right)(x + 2)$; Zeros: $\sqrt{2}, -\sqrt{2}, -2$

56. $\left(x - 2 + \sqrt{5}\right)\left(x - 2 - \sqrt{5}\right)(x + 3)$;
Zeros: $2 - \sqrt{5}, 2 + \sqrt{5}, -3$

58. (a) Answers will vary.   (b) $3x - 1$
(c) $f(x) = (3x - 1)(x + 3)(x - 2)$
(d) $\frac{1}{3}, -3, 2$
(e)
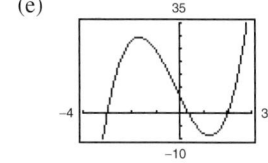

60. (a) Answers will vary.
(b) $(4x + 3), (2x - 1)$
(c) $f(x) = (4x + 3)(2x - 1)(x + 2)(x - 4)$
(d) $-\frac{3}{4}, \frac{1}{2}, -2, 4$
(e)
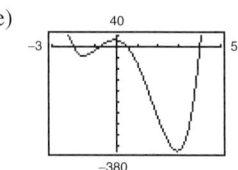

62. (a) Answers will vary.
(b) $x - 3$
(c) $f(x) = (x - 3)(2x + 5)(5x - 3)$
(d) $3, -\frac{5}{2}, \frac{3}{5}$
(e)
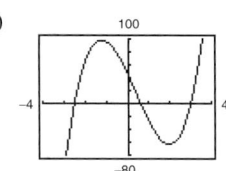

64. (a) Answers will vary.   (b) $x - 4\sqrt{3}$
(c) $f(x) = \left(x - 4\sqrt{3}\right)\left(x + 4\sqrt{3}\right)(x + 3)$
(d) $\pm 4\sqrt{3}, -3$
(e)

66. (a) Zeros are 4 and $\approx \pm 1.414$.
(b) $g(x) = (x - 4)\left(x - \sqrt{2}\right)\left(x + \sqrt{2}\right)$

68. (a) Zeros are 6, ≈ 0.764, and ≈ 5.236.
(b) $f(s) = (s - 6)\left[s - \left(3 + \sqrt{5}\right)\right]\left[s - \left(3 - \sqrt{5}\right)\right]$

70. $x^2 - 7x - 8, \ x \neq -8$ **72.** $2x^2 + 5x + 2, \ x \neq 1$

74. $x^2 + 9x - 1, \ x \neq \pm 2$

76. (a) and (b)
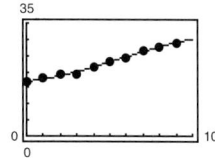

$R = -0.01128t^3 + 0.1913t^2 + 0.527t + 17.03$
(c) \$29.91

78. True.
$f(x) = (2x - 1)(x + 1)(x - 2)(x - 3)(3x + 2)(x + 4)$

80. (a) $f(x) = (x - 2)x^2 + 5 = x^3 - 2x^2 + 5$
(b) $f(x) = -(x + 3)x^2 + 1 = -x^3 - 3x^2 + 1$

82. $x^{2n} - x^n + 3$

84. Multiply the divisor and the quotient to obtain the dividend.

86. $c = 42$

88. Because $f(x)$ is in factored form, it is easier to evaluate directly.

90. $\pm\dfrac{\sqrt{21}}{4}$ **92.** $\dfrac{5}{4}, \dfrac{3}{2}$ **94.** $\dfrac{-3 \pm \sqrt{21}}{2}$

96. $f(x) = x^2 + 5x - 6$

98. $f(x) = x^4 - 3x^3 - 5x^2 + 9x - 2$

Section 2.4   *(page 148)*

2. $a = 13, \ b = 4$ **4.** $a = 0, \ b = -\frac{5}{2}$ **6.** $3 + 4i$

8. $1 + 2\sqrt{2}i$ **10.** $2i$ **12.** 45   **14.** $4 + 2i$

16. $0.02i$ **18.** $8 + 4i$ **20.** $-3 - 11i$ **22.** 4

24. $17 + 18i$ **26.** $-4.2 + 7.5i$ **28.** $-5\sqrt{2}$

30. -75 **32.** $6 - 22i$ **34.** $32 - 72i$

36. $\left(21 + 5\sqrt{2}\right) + \left(7\sqrt{5} - 3\sqrt{10}\right)i$

38. $-5 - 12i$ **40.** $-8i$ **42.** $7 + 12i,\ 193$

44. $-3 - \sqrt{2}\,i,\ 11$ **46.** $-\sqrt{15}\,i,\ 15$

48. $1 + \sqrt{8},\ 9 + 4\sqrt{2}$ **50.** $7i$ **52.** $\frac{5}{2} + \frac{5}{2}i$

54. $4 + i$ **56.** $8 - 4i$ **58.** $\frac{60}{169} - \frac{25}{169}i$ **60.** $\frac{12}{5} + \frac{9}{5}i$

62. $\frac{5}{17} - \frac{20}{17}i$ **64.** $-3 \pm i$ **66.** $\frac{1}{3} \pm 2i$

68. $\frac{1}{8} \pm \frac{\sqrt{11}}{8}i$ **70.** $\frac{3}{7} \pm \frac{\sqrt{34}}{14}i$ **72.** $\frac{1}{3} \pm \frac{\sqrt{23}}{3}i$

74. $-4 + 2i$ **76.** i **78.** -8 **80.** $\frac{1}{8}i$

82. (a) 16   (b) 16   (c) 16   (d) 16

84. (a) $z_1 = 9 + 16i,\ z_2 = 20 - 10i$

    (b) $z = \dfrac{11{,}240}{877} + \dfrac{4630}{877}i$

86. True. $x^4 - x^2 + 14 = 56$

$$\left(-i\sqrt{6}\right)^4 - \left(-i\sqrt{6}\right)^2 + 14 \overset{?}{=} 56$$
$$36 + 6 + 14 \overset{?}{=} 56$$
$$56 = 56$$

88. $\sqrt{-6}\sqrt{-6} = \sqrt{6}\,i\sqrt{6}\,i = 6i^2 = -6$

90. Answers will vary.   **92.** $x^3 + x^2 + 2x - 6$

94. $4x^2 - 20x + 25$ **96.** 14   **98.** $-\frac{4}{3}$

100. $r = \dfrac{\sqrt{\alpha m_1 m_2 F}}{F}$

Section 2.5   *(page 160)*

2. $0, -3, \pm 1$ **4.** $-5, 8$ **6.** $3, 2, \pm 3i$

8. $\pm 1, \pm 2, \pm 4, \pm 8, \pm 16$ **10.** $\pm 1, \pm 2, \pm \frac{1}{2}, \pm \frac{1}{4}$

12. $-2, -1, 3$ **14.** $1, 2, 6$ **16.** 3   **18.** $\frac{1}{3}, 3$

20. $\pm 1, 5, \frac{5}{2}$ **22.** $0, -1, -3, 4$ **24.** $-2, 0, 1$

26. (a) $\pm 1, \pm 2, \pm 4, \pm 8, \pm 16, \pm \frac{1}{3}, \pm \frac{2}{3}, \pm \frac{4}{3}, \pm \frac{8}{3}, \pm \frac{16}{3}$

    (b)

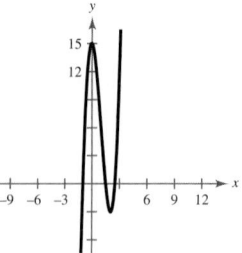

    (c) $\frac{2}{3}, 2, 4$

28. (a) $\pm 1, \pm 3, \pm 5, \pm 15, \pm \frac{1}{2}, \pm \frac{3}{2}, \pm \frac{5}{2}, \pm \frac{15}{2}, \pm \frac{1}{4}, \pm \frac{3}{4}, \pm \frac{5}{4}, \pm \frac{15}{4}$

    (b)

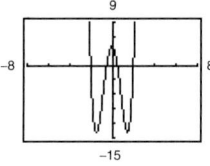

    (c) $-1, \frac{3}{2}, \frac{5}{2}$

30. (a) $\pm 1, \pm 2, \pm 4, \pm \frac{1}{2}, \pm \frac{1}{4}$

    (b)

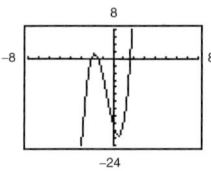

    (c) $\pm 2, \pm \frac{1}{2}$

32. (a) $\pm 1, \pm 2, \pm 3, \pm 6, \pm 9, \pm 18, \pm \frac{1}{2}, \pm \frac{3}{2}, \pm \frac{9}{2}, \pm \frac{1}{4}, \pm \frac{3}{4}, \pm \frac{9}{4}$

    (b)

    (c) $-2, \dfrac{1}{8} \pm \dfrac{\sqrt{145}}{8}$

34. (a) $\pm 2, \approx \pm 1.732$

    (b) $P(t) = (t + 2)(t - 2)\left(t + \sqrt{3}\right)\left(t - \sqrt{3}\right)$

36. (a) $\pm 3, 1.5, 0.333$

    (b) $g(x) = (x + 3)(x - 3)(2x - 3)(3x - 1)$

38. $x^3 - 4x^2 + 9x - 36$ **40.** $x^3 - 10x^2 + 33x - 34$

42. $x^4 + 8x^3 + 9x^2 - 10x + 100$

44. (a) $(x^2 - 6)(x^2 - 2x + 3)$

    (b) $\left(x + \sqrt{6}\right)\left(x - \sqrt{6}\right)(x^2 - 2x + 3)$

    (c) $\left(x + \sqrt{6}\right)\left(x - \sqrt{6}\right)\left(x - 1 - \sqrt{2}\,i\right)\left(x - 1 + \sqrt{2}\,i\right)$

46. (a) $(x^2 + 4)(x^2 - 3x - 5)$

    (b) $(x^2 + 4)\left(x - \dfrac{3 + \sqrt{29}}{2}\right)\left(x - \dfrac{3 - \sqrt{29}}{2}\right)$

    (c) $(x + 2i)(x - 2i)\left(x - \dfrac{3 + \sqrt{29}}{2}\right)\left(x - \dfrac{3 - \sqrt{29}}{2}\right)$

48. $-1, \pm 3i$ **50.** $-3, 5 \pm 2i$ **52.** $-\frac{2}{3}, 1 \pm \sqrt{3}\,i$

54. $-2, -1 \pm 3i$

56. $\dfrac{1 \pm \sqrt{223}\,i}{2}$; $\left(x - \dfrac{1 - \sqrt{223}\,i}{2}\right)\left(x - \dfrac{1 + \sqrt{223}\,i}{2}\right)$

58. $-5 \pm \sqrt{2}$; $(x + 5 + \sqrt{2})(x + 5 - \sqrt{2})$

60. $\pm 5, \pm 5i$; $(y + 5)(y - 5)(y + 5i)(y - 5i)$

62. $1 \pm i, 1$; $(x - 1)(x - 1 + i)(x - 1 - i)$

64. $3 \pm 2i, -4$; $(x + 4)(x - 3 + 2i)(x - 3 - 2i)$

66. $-2 \pm \sqrt{3}\,i, -5$; $(x + 5)(x + 2 + \sqrt{3}\,i)(x + 2 - \sqrt{3}\,i)$

68. $1 \pm \sqrt{3}\,i, -\frac{2}{3}$; $(3x + 2)(x - 1 + \sqrt{3}\,i)(x - 1 - \sqrt{3}\,i)$

70. $-3, \pm i$; $(x + 3)^2(x + i)(x - i)$

72. $\pm 2i, \pm 5i$; $(x + 2i)(x - 2i)(x + 5i)(x - 5i)$

74. $1 \pm 2i, \frac{1}{2}$ **76.** $\frac{1}{3} \pm \frac{2}{3}i, 1$ **78.** $1 \pm \sqrt{3}\,i, 2$

80. Two or no positive zeros

82. Two or no positive zeros

84. One or three positive zeros

86. One or three negative zeros

88. Answers will vary.   **90.** Answers will vary.

92. $-\frac{3}{2}, \frac{1}{3}, \frac{3}{2}$ **94.** $\frac{2}{3}$ **96.** $-3, \frac{1}{2}, 4$

98. $-2, -\frac{1}{3}, \frac{1}{2}$ **99.** d   **100.** a   **101.** b   **102.** c

104. (a) Answers will vary.

(b)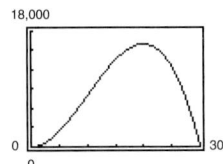

20 inches $\times$ 20 inches $\times$ 40 inches

(c) $15, \dfrac{15 \pm 15\sqrt{5}}{2}$; the value $x = \dfrac{15 - 15\sqrt{5}}{2}$ is physically impossible because x is negative.

106. $x \approx 31.5$ or \$315,000   **108.** $x \approx 40$ or 4000 units

110. No. Setting $p = 9{,}000{,}000$ and solving the resulting equation yields imaginary roots.

112. False. f does not have real coefficients.

114. r_1, r_2, r_3 **116.** $\dfrac{r_1}{2}, \dfrac{r_2}{2}, \dfrac{r_3}{2}$ **118.** $-r_1, -r_2, -r_3$

120. (a) No   (b) No

122. (Answers will vary.)

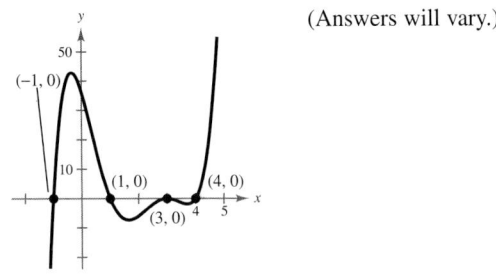

124. (a) $-2, 0, 2$

(b) The graph touches the x-axis at $x = 0$.

(c) The least possible degree of the function is 4, because there are at least four real zeros (0 is repeated) and a function can have at most the number of real zeros equal to the degree of the function. The degree cannot be odd by the definition of multiplicity.

(d) Negative. From the information in the table, it can be concluded that the graph will eventually fall to the left and fall to the right.

(e) $f(x) = -x^4 + 4x^2$

(f)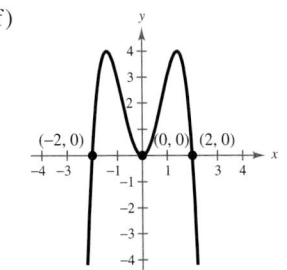

126. (a) Not correct because f has $(0, 0)$ as an intercept.

(b) Not correct because the function must be at least a fourth-degree polynomial.

(c) Correct function

(d) Not correct because k has $(-1, 0)$ as an intercept.

128. $12 + 11i$ **130.** 106

132.   **134.**

136.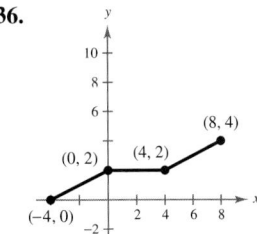

Section 2.6   *(page 174)*

2. (a)

x	$f(x)$	x	$f(x)$	x	$f(x)$
0.5	-5	1.5	15	5	6.25
0.9	-45	1.1	55	10	$5.\overline{55}$
0.99	-495	1.01	505	100	$5.\overline{05}$
0.999	-4995	1.001	5005	1000	$5.\overline{005}$

(b) Vertical asymptote: $x = 1$

Horizontal asymptote: $y = 5$

(c) Domain: all real numbers $x \neq 1$

4. (a)

x	$f(x)$	x	$f(x)$	x	$f(x)$
0.5	$-2.\overline{66}$	1.5	4.8	5	$0.8\overline{33}$
0.9	-18.95	1.1	20.95	10	$0.\overline{40}$
0.99	-199	1.01	201	100	0.04
0.999	-1999	1.001	2001	1000	0.004

(b) Vertical asymptotes: $x = \pm 1$

Horizontal asymptote: $y = 0$

(c) Domain: all real numbers $x \neq \pm 1$

6. Domain: all real numbers $x \neq 2$

Vertical asymptote: $x = 2$

Horizontal asymptote: $y = 0$

8. Domain: all real numbers $x \neq -\frac{1}{2}$

Vertical asymptote: $x = -\frac{1}{2}$

Horizontal asymptote: $y = -\frac{5}{2}$

10. Domain: all real numbers $x \neq -1$

Vertical asymptote: $x = -1$

No horizontal asymptote

12. Domain: all real numbers

Horizontal asymptote: $y = 3$

No vertical asymptote

13. d   **14.** a   **15.** c   **16.** b

18. None   **20.** 2

22. (a) y-intercept: $\left(0, -\frac{1}{3}\right)$

(b) Vertical asymptote: $x = 3$

Horizontal asymptote: $y = 0$

(c) No axis or origin symmetry

(d)

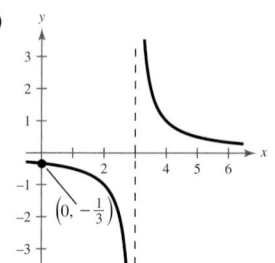

24. (a) y-intercept: $\left(0, \frac{1}{3}\right)$

(b) Vertical asymptote: $x = 3$

Horizontal asymptote: $y = 0$

(c) No axis or origin symmetry

(d)

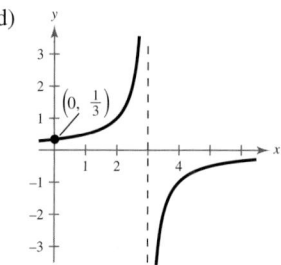

26. (a) x-intercept: $\left(\frac{1}{3}, 0\right)$

y-intercept: $(0, 1)$

(b) Vertical asymptote: $x = 1$

Horizontal asymptote: $y = 3$

(c) No axis or origin symmetry

(d)

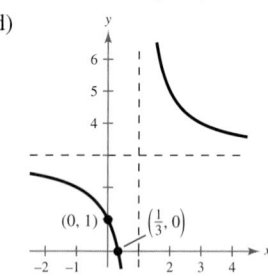

28. (a) x-intercepts: $\left(-\frac{\sqrt{6}}{2}, 0\right), \left(\frac{\sqrt{6}}{2}, 0\right)$

(b) Vertical asymptote: $x = 0$

Horizontal asymptote: $y = 2$

(c) y-axis symmetry

(d)

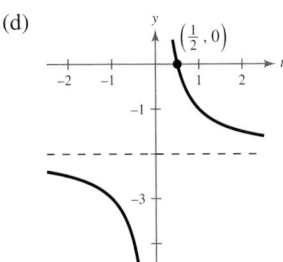

30. (a) t-intercept: $\left(\frac{1}{2}, 0\right)$

   (b) Vertical asymptote: $t = 0$

      Horizontal asymptote: $y = -2$

   (c) No axis or origin symmetry

   (d)

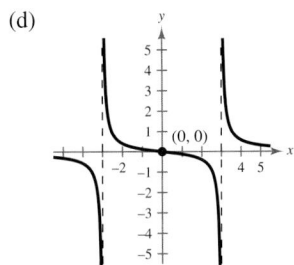

32. (a) Intercept: $(0, 0)$

   (b) Vertical asymptotes: $x = 3, x = -3$

      Horizontal asymptote: $y = 0$

   (c) Origin symmetry

   (d)

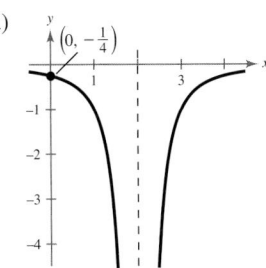

34. (a) y-intercept: $\left(0, -\frac{1}{4}\right)$

   (b) Vertical asymptote: $x = 2$

      Horizontal asymptote: $y = 0$

   (c) No axis or origin symmetry

   (d)

36. (a) No intercepts

   (b) Vertical asymptotes: $x = 0, x = 2$

      Horizontal asymptote: $y = 0$

   (c) No axis or origin symmetry

   (d)

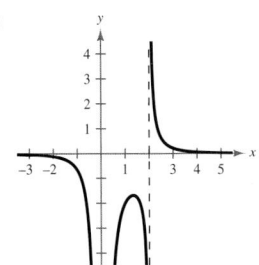

38. (a) Intercept: $(0, 0)$

   (b) Vertical asymptotes: $x = -2, x = 1$

      Horizontal asymptote: $y = 0$

   (c) No axis or origin symmetry

   (d)

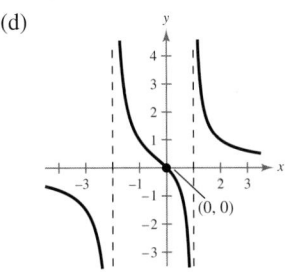

40. (a) x-intercepts: $(-1, 0), (2, 0)$

      y-intercept: $\left(0, -\frac{1}{3}\right)$

   (b) Vertical asymptotes: $x = -2, x = 1, x = 3$

      Horizontal asymptote: $y = 0$

   (c) No axis or origin symmetry

   (d)

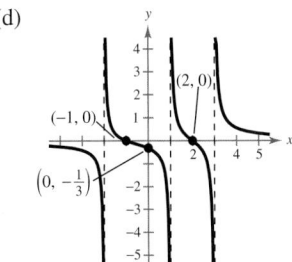

42. (a) Domain of f: all real numbers $x \neq 0, 2$

      Domain of g: all real numbers

   (b) Vertical asymptote: none

   (c)

x	-1	0	1	1.5	2	2.5	3
$f(x)$	-1	Undef.	1	1.5	Undef.	2.5	3
$g(x)$	-1	0	1	1.5	2	2.5	3

(d)

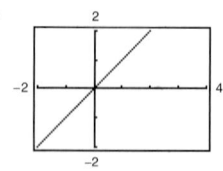

(e) Because there are only a finite number of pixels, the utility may not attempt to evaluate the function where it does not exist.

44. (a) Domain of f: all real numbers $x \neq 3, 4$

Domain of g: all real numbers $x \neq 4$

(b) Vertical asymptote: $x = 4$

(c)

x	0	1	2	3	4	5	6
$f(x)$	$-\frac{1}{2}$	$-\frac{2}{3}$	-1	Undef.	Undef.	2	1
$g(x)$	$-\frac{1}{2}$	$-\frac{2}{3}$	-1	-2	Undef.	2	1

(d)

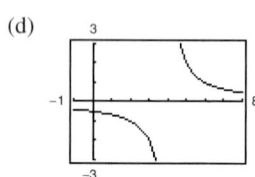

(e) Because there are only a finite number of pixels, the utility may not attempt to evaluate the function where it does not exist.

46. Domain: all real numbers $x \neq 0$

Vertical asymptote: $x = 0$

Slant asymptote: $y = x$

48. Domain: all real numbers $x \neq -\frac{1}{3}$

Vertical asymptote: $x = -\frac{1}{3}$

Slant asymptote: $y = \frac{1}{3}x - \frac{1}{9}$

50. Domain: all real numbers $x \neq 0$

Vertical asymptote: $x = 0$

Slant asymptote: $y = x$

52. (a) x-intercepts: $(-1, 0)$, $(1, 0)$

(b) Vertical asymptote: $x = 0$

Slant asymptote: $y = -x$

(c) Origin symmetry

(d)

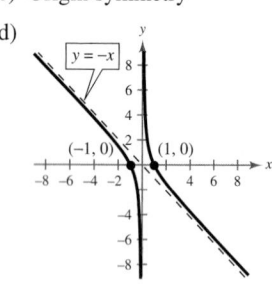

54. (a) Intercept: $(0, 0)$

(b) Vertical asymptote: $x = 1$

Slant asymptote: $y = x + 1$

(c) No axis or origin symmetry

(d)

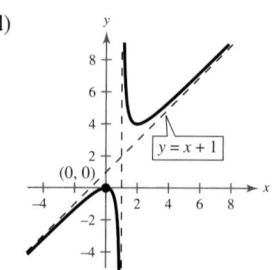

56. (a) Intercept: $(0, 0)$

(b) Vertical asymptotes: $x = \pm 2$

Slant asymptote: $y = \frac{1}{2}x$

(c) Origin symmetry

(d)

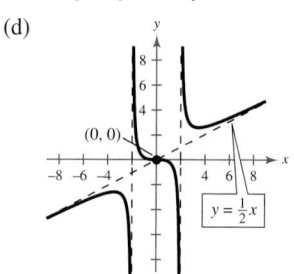

58. (a) y-intercept: $\left(0, -\frac{5}{2}\right)$

(b) Vertical asymptote: $x = 2$

Slant asymptote: $y = 2x - 1$

(c) No axis or origin symmetry

(d)

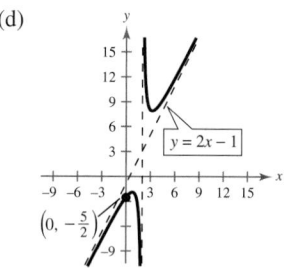

60.

Domain: all real numbers $x \neq -1$

Vertical asymptote: $x = -1$

Slant asymptote: $y = 2x - 1$

$y = 2x - 1$

62.

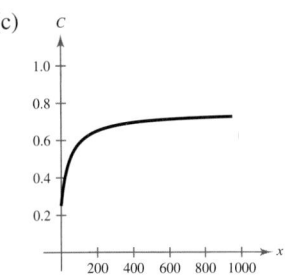

Domain: all real numbers $x \neq -4$

Vertical asymptote: $x = -4$

Slant asymptote: $y = -\frac{1}{2}x + 1$

$y = -\frac{1}{2}x + 1$

64. (a) $(0, 0)$ (b) 0 **66.** (a) $(1, 0), (2, 0)$ (b) $1, 2$

68. (a) \$4411.76

(b) \$25,000

(c) \$225,000

(d) No. The function is undefined at $p = 100$.

70. (a) Answers will vary.   (b) $[0, 950]$

(c)

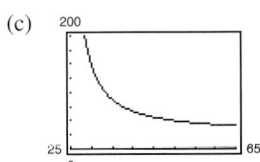

(d) The rate of the increase in concentration decreases; 75%

72. 12.8 inches $\times$ 8.5 inches

74. (a) Answers will vary.

(b) Vertical asymptote: $x = 25$

Horizontal asymptote: $y = 25$

(c)

x	30	35	40	45	50	55	60
y	150	87.5	66.7	56.3	50	45.8	42.9

(e) Yes. You would expect the average speed for the round trip to be the average of the average speeds for the two parts of the trip.

(f) No. At 20 miles per hour you would use more time in one direction than is required for the round trip at an average speed of 50 miles per hour.

76. False. The graph of $f(x) = \dfrac{x}{x^2 + 1}$ crosses $y = 0$, which is a horizontal asymptote.

78. $f(x) = \dfrac{-6x^2 + 1}{x(2x - 5)}$ (Answer is not unique.)

80. An asymptote of a graph is a line to which the graph becomes arbitrarily close as x increases or decreases without bound.

82. $f(x) = \dfrac{x^2 + 3x - 18}{x + 1}$

84.

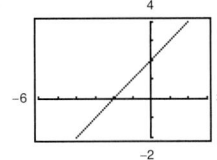

The fraction is not reduced.

86. $(3x - 4)(x + 9)$ **88.** $(x + 6)(x + \sqrt{2})(x - \sqrt{2})$

90. $x < 0$ **92.** $x \leq -\frac{13}{2}, x \geq \frac{7}{2}$

Section 2.7   *(page 184)*

1. b   **2.** c   **3.** d   **4.** a

6. $\dfrac{A}{x + 3} + \dfrac{B}{x + 1}$ **8.** $\dfrac{A}{x} + \dfrac{B}{x^2} + \dfrac{C}{4x + 11}$

10. $\dfrac{A}{x + 2} + \dfrac{B}{(x + 2)^2} + \dfrac{C}{(x + 2)^3} + \dfrac{D}{(x + 2)^4}$

12. $\dfrac{A}{2x} + \dfrac{Bx + C}{x^2 + 4}$ **14.** $\dfrac{A}{x} + \dfrac{B}{x^2} + \dfrac{C}{3x - 1} + \dfrac{D}{(3x - 1)^2}$

16. $\dfrac{1}{6}\left(\dfrac{1}{2x - 3} - \dfrac{1}{2x + 3}\right)$ **18.** $\dfrac{1}{x - 3} - \dfrac{1}{x}$

20. $\dfrac{1}{x - 2} - \dfrac{1}{x + 3}$ **22.** $\dfrac{1}{x + 3}, x \neq -1$

24. $\dfrac{1}{2}\left(\dfrac{3}{x - 4} - \dfrac{1}{x}\right)$ **26.** $\dfrac{2}{x - 1} - \dfrac{1}{(x - 1)^2}$

28. $\dfrac{2}{x} + \dfrac{1}{x^2} - \dfrac{2}{x - 1} + \dfrac{7}{(x - 1)^2}$

30. $\dfrac{1}{3}\left(\dfrac{1}{x - 1} - \dfrac{x - 1}{x^2 + x + 1}\right)$

32. $\dfrac{1}{5}\left(\dfrac{9}{x - 3} + \dfrac{1}{x + 2} - \dfrac{10}{x - 2}\right)$

34. $\dfrac{2}{x^2 + 4} + \dfrac{x}{(x^2 + 4)^2}$ **36.** $\dfrac{1}{x} - \dfrac{x - 1}{x^2 + 1}$

38. $\dfrac{2}{x+1} - \dfrac{x-1}{x^2 - 2x + 3}$

40. $1 - \dfrac{5x+6}{x^2 + x + 6}$

42. $x - 1 + \dfrac{1}{5}\left(\dfrac{27}{x+4} + \dfrac{3}{x-1}\right)$

44. $2x + 3 + \dfrac{6}{2x-1} + \dfrac{4}{(2x-1)^2} + \dfrac{1}{(2x-1)^3}$

46. $\dfrac{2}{x} + \dfrac{4}{x+1} - \dfrac{3}{x-1}$

48. $\dfrac{1}{2}\left[-\dfrac{1}{x} + \dfrac{5}{x+1} - \dfrac{3}{(x+1)^2}\right]$

50. $\dfrac{1}{2}\left[\dfrac{1}{x+2} - \dfrac{1}{(x+2)^2} + \dfrac{1}{x-2} + \dfrac{1}{(x-2)^2}\right]$

52. $x - 1 + \dfrac{1}{x+2} + \dfrac{1}{x-1}$

54. $\dfrac{2}{x} + \dfrac{4}{x^2+1}$

$y = \dfrac{2(x+1)^2}{x(x^2+1)}$ $y = \dfrac{2}{x},\ y = \dfrac{4}{x^2+1}$

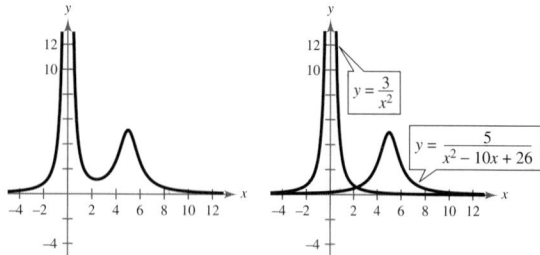

The vertical asymptotes are the same.

56. $\dfrac{3}{x^2} + \dfrac{5}{x^2 - 10x + 26}$

$y = \dfrac{2(4x^2 - 15x + 39)}{x^2(x^2 - 10x + 26)}$ $y = \dfrac{3}{x^2},\ y = \dfrac{5}{x^2 - 10x + 26}$

The vertical asymptotes are the same.

58. Answers will vary. Sample answer: You can substitute any convenient values of x that will help determine constants. You can also find your basic equation, expand it, then equate coefficients of like terms.

60. False. The expression is an improper rational expression, so you must first divide before applying partial fraction decomposition.

62. $\dfrac{1}{a}\left(\dfrac{1}{x} - \dfrac{1}{x+a}\right)$

64. $\dfrac{1}{a+1}\left(\dfrac{1}{x+1} + \dfrac{1}{a-x}\right)$

66.

68.

70.

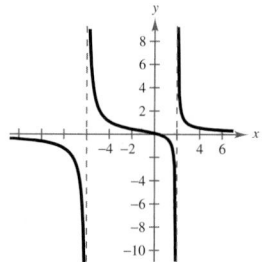

Review Exercises   *(page 187)*

2. $f(x) = \frac{1}{4}(x-2)^2 + 2$

4. $f(x) = \frac{1}{3}(x-2)^2 + 3$

6. (a)

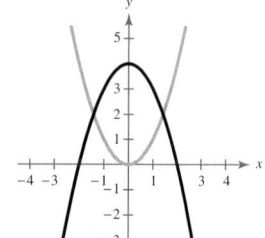

(b)

Vertical translation

Reflection in the x-axis and vertical translation

(c)

(d)

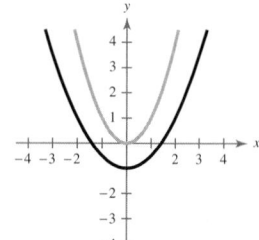

Horizontal translation

Vertical shrink and vertical translation

8. $f(x) = -(x - 3)^2 + 9$

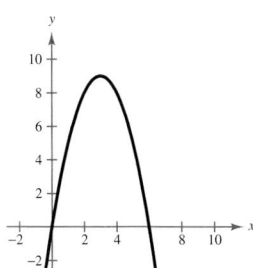

Vertex: $(3, 9)$

x-intercepts: $(0, 0), (6, 0)$

12. $f(x) = (x - 4)^2 - 4$

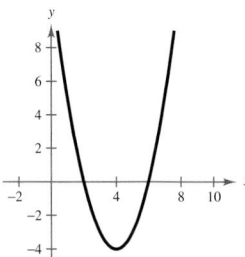

Vertex: $(4, -4)$

x-intercepts: $(2, 0), (6, 0)$

16. $f(x) = 4\left(x + \frac{1}{2}\right)^2 + 4$

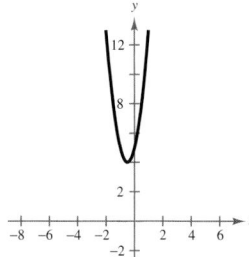

Vertex: $\left(-\frac{1}{2}, 4\right)$

No x-intercept

20. \$1020   **22.** 24 years old

24.

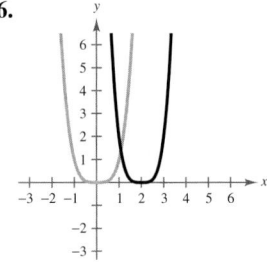

10. $h(x) = -(x - 2)^2 + 7$

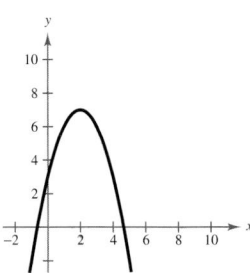

Vertex: $(2, 7)$

x-intercepts: $\left(2 \pm \sqrt{7}, 0\right)$

14. $f(x) = (x - 3)^2 - 8$

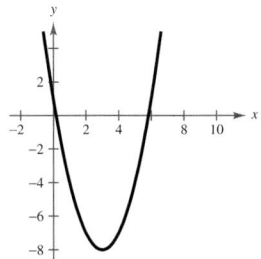

Vertex: $(3, -8)$

x-intercepts: $\left(3 \pm 2\sqrt{2}, 0\right)$

18. $f(x) = 3(x - 2)^2 - 1$

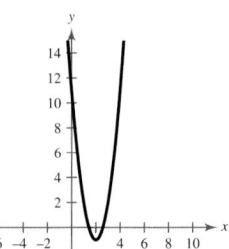

Vertex: $(2, -1)$

x-intercepts: $\left(2 \pm \dfrac{\sqrt{3}}{3}, 0\right)$

26.

28.

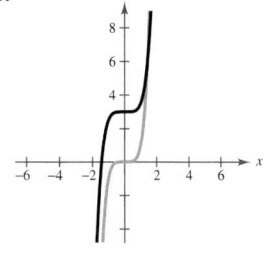

30. Falls to the left, rises to the right

32. Rises to the left, falls to the right

34. 0, odd multiplicity; -3, even multiplicity

36. 8, odd multiplicity; 0, even multiplicity

38. $-1, 2$, odd multiplicity; 0, even multiplicity

40. (a) Rises to the right, falls to the left

(b) $-2, 0$

(c) Answers will vary.

(d)

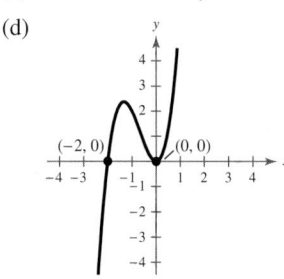

42. (a) Falls to the left, falls to the right

(b) $0, \pm\sqrt{3}$

(c) Answers will vary.

(d)

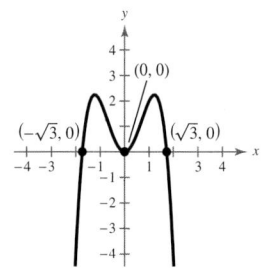

44. $[-5, -4]$; ≈ -4.479

46. $[-2, -1], [-1, 0]$; $\approx -1.211, \approx -0.509$

48. $\dfrac{4}{3} + \dfrac{29}{3(3x - 2)}$ **50.** $3x^2 + 3 + \dfrac{3}{x^2 - 1}$

52. $3x^2 + 5x + 8 + \dfrac{10}{2x^2 - 1}$

54. $0.1x^2 + 0.8x + 4 + \dfrac{19.5}{x - 5}$ **56.** $3x^2 + 11x - 4$

CHAPTER 2

58. (a) Yes   (b) No   (c) Yes   (d) No

60. (a) -3276 (b) 0

62. (a) Answers will vary.   (b) $(2x + 5), (x - 3)$

(c) $f(x) = (2x + 5)(x - 3)(x + 6)$ (d) $-\frac{5}{2}, 3, -6$

(e)

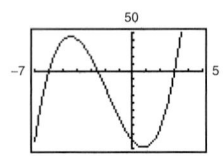

64. (a) Answers will vary.   (b) $(x - 1), (x - 3)$

(c) $f(x) = (x - 1)(x - 3)(x - 2)(x - 5)$ (d) $1, 2, 3, 5$

(e)

66. $3 - 5i$ **68.** $-1 - 5i$ **70.** $-\sqrt{2}\,i$

72. $17 + 28i$ **74.** $9 + 20i$ **76.** $\frac{17}{26} + \frac{7}{26}i$

78. $\frac{9}{85} + \frac{83}{85}i$ **80.** $\pm\frac{1}{2}i$ **82.** $-\frac{1}{4} \pm \frac{\sqrt{71}}{4}i$

84. $-9, 4$ **86.** $0, \pm\sqrt{6}\,i$ **88.** $5, 8, 3 \pm i$

90. $\pm 1, \pm 2, \pm 4, \pm 8, \pm\frac{1}{3}, \pm\frac{2}{3}, \pm\frac{4}{3}, \pm\frac{8}{3}$

92. $-1, \frac{5}{3}, 6$ **94.** $-5, -2$ **96.** $-3, 2, \pm\frac{2}{5}$

98. $x^4 - x^3 - 3x^2 + 17x - 30$

100. $2, \pm 4i$ **102.** $0, \frac{3}{4}, 1 \pm i$

104. $-2, 3, 6; g(x) = (x + 2)(x - 3)(x - 6)$

106. $\pm 3, -4 \pm i;$

$f(x) = (x - 3)(x + 3)(x + 4 - i)(x + 4 + i)$

108. One or three positive zeros, two or no negative zeros

110. Answers will vary.

112. Domain: all real numbers $x \neq -\frac{1}{3}$

114. Domain: all real numbers

116. Horizontal asymptote: $y = 2$

118. Vertical asymptote: $x = 3$

Horizontal asymptote: $y = 0$

120. No intercepts

Origin symmetry

Vertical asymptote: $x = 0$

Horizontal asymptote: $y = 0$

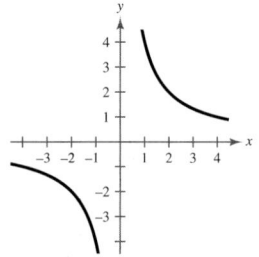

122. x-intercept: $(3, 0)$

y-intercept: $\left(0, \frac{3}{2}\right)$

No axis or origin symmetry

Vertical asymptote: $x = 2$

Horizontal asymptote: $y = 1$

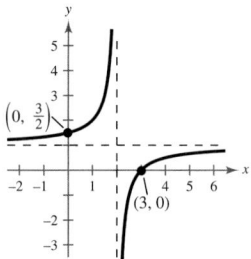

124. Intercept: $(0, 0)$

Origin symmetry

Horizontal asymptote: $y = 0$

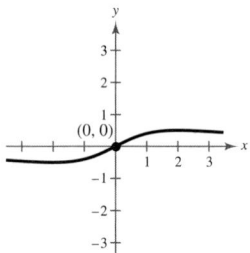

126. y-intercept: $(0, 4)$

No axis or origin symmetry

Vertical asymptote: $x = 1$

Horizontal asymptote: $y = 0$

128. Intercept: $(0, 0)$

y-axis symmetry

Vertical asymptotes: $x = \pm 2$

Horizontal asymptote: $y = 2$

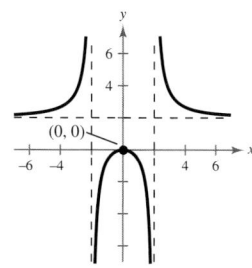

130. y-intercept: $\left(0, -\frac{2}{9}\right)$

No axis or origin symmetry

Vertical asymptote: $x = -3$

Horizontal asymptote: $y = 0$

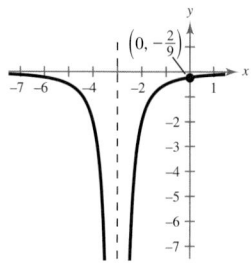

132. Domain: all real numbers $x \neq -1$

Vertical asymptote: $x = -1$

Slant asymptote: $y = x - 1$

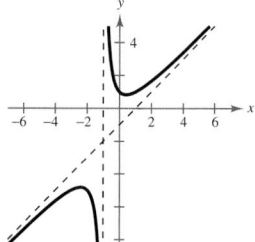

134. Domain: all real numbers $x \neq +2$

Vertical asymptotes: $x = \pm 2$

Slant asymptote: $y = x$

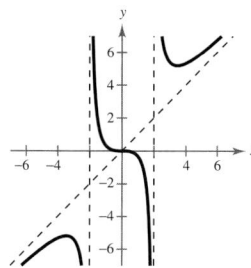

136. (a) $176 million (b) $528 million

(c) $1584 million (d) No

138.

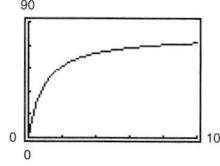

80.3 milligrams per square decimeter per hour

140. $\dfrac{A}{x - 7} + \dfrac{B}{x + 4}$

142. $\dfrac{A}{x} + \dfrac{Bx + C}{x^2 + 2} + \dfrac{Dx + E}{(x^2 + 2)^2}$

144. $\dfrac{1}{x + 1} - \dfrac{2}{x + 2}$

146. $\dfrac{1}{2}\left(\dfrac{3}{x - 3} - \dfrac{3}{x + 3}\right)$

148. $\dfrac{4}{3(x - 1)} + \dfrac{2}{3(x - 1)^2}$

150. $2\left(\dfrac{1}{x - 1} + \dfrac{x + 1}{x^2 + 1}\right)$

152. False. The domain of $f(x) = \dfrac{1}{x^2 + 1}$ is the set of all real numbers.

154. $a < -1$, $h = 0$, and $k = 0$ produce a stretch that is reflected in the x-axis. $-1 < a < 0$, $h = 0$, and $k = 0$ produce a shrink that is reflected in the x-axis.

156. No. The middle term will be an imaginary number, so the answer will be a complex number.

Problem Solving (page 194)

2. (a)

y	1	2	3	4	5
$y^3 + y^2$	2	12	36	80	150

y	6	7	8	9	10
$y^3 + y^2$	252	392	576	810	1100

(b) $x = 6$ (c) $x = 6$

(d) $x = 3$ (e) $x = 10$

(f) $x = 6$ (g) $x = 3$

4. 2 inches $\times$ 2 inches $\times$ 5 inches

6. (a) $m_1 = 5$; less than (b) $m_2 = 3$; greater than

(c) $m_3 = 4.1$; less than (d) $m_h = h + 4$

(e) $m_h = 3, 5, 4.1$. The values are the same.

(f) $m_{\text{tan}} = 4$ since $h = 0$.

8. (a) $A(x) = \dfrac{x^2}{16} + \dfrac{1}{\pi}\left(\dfrac{100 - x}{2}\right)^2$ (b) $0 < x < 100$

(c) Maximum area at $x = 0$; Minimum area at $x = 56$

(d) Answers will vary.

10. (a)

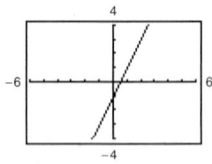

No

(b)

x	-1.1	-1.01	-1.001	-1
$f(x)$	-3.2	-3.02	-3.002	Undef.

x	-0.999	-0.99	-0.9
$f(x)$	-2.998	-2.98	-2.8

-3

(c) -3 (d) There is a hole at $(-1, -3)$.

(e) $f(x) = 2x - 1;\ f(-1) = -3$

(f)

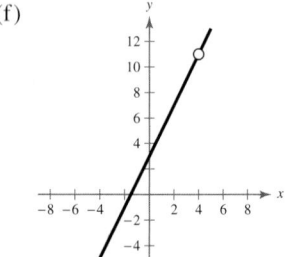

Chapter 3

Section 3.1   *(page 206)*

2. 3.488   **4.** 1767.767

6. 24.533   **7.** d   **8.** c

9. a   **10.** b

12. Shift the graph of f one unit upward.

14. Reflect the graph of f in the y-axis and shift three units to the right.

16. Reflect the graph of f in the x-axis and y-axis and shift six units to the right.

18. Reflect the graph of f in the x-axis and y-axis and shift eight units upward.

20.

x	-2	-1	0	1	2
$f(x)$	0.25	0.5	1	2	4

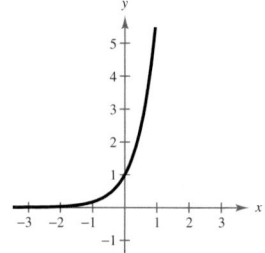

22.

x	-2	-1	0	1	2
$f(x)$	0.028	0.167	1	6	36

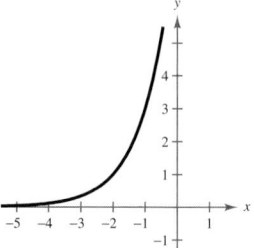

24.

x	-4	-3	-2	-1	0
$f(x)$	0.111	0.333	1	3	9

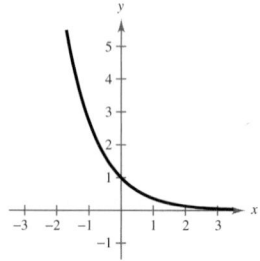

26.

x	-2	-1	0	1	2
$f(x)$	7.389	2.718	1	0.368	0.135

28.

x	-2	-1	0	1	2
$f(x)$	5.437	3.297	2	1.213	0.736

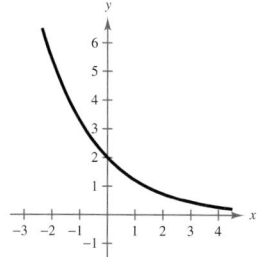

30.

x	0	2	4	5	6
$f(x)$	2.007	2.050	2.368	3	4.718

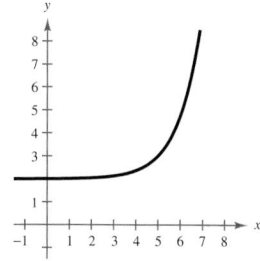

32.

x	-1	0	1	3	4
$f(x)$	-3.004	-3.016	-3.063	-4	-7

34.   **36.**

38.   **40.**

42.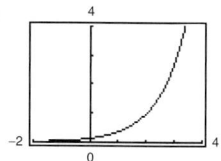

44.

n	1	2	4	12
A	\$1790.85	\$1806.11	\$1814.02	\$1819.40

n	365	Continuous
A	\$1822.03	\$1822.12

46.

n	1	2	4
A	\$10,285.72	\$10,640.89	\$10,828.46

n	12	365	Continuous
A	\$10,957.45	\$11,021.00	\$11,023.18

48.

t	10	20
A	\$21,865.43	\$39,841.40

t	30	40	50
A	\$72,595.77	\$132,278.12	\$241,026.44

50.

t	10	20
A	\$25,404.00	\$53,780.27

t	30	40	50
A	\$113,852.83	\$241,026.44	\$510,252.98

52. \$212,605.41

54. (a)

(b) \$421.12

(c) \$350

56. (a) 3351   (b) 4492

58. (a) 10 grams   (b) 7.85 grams

(c)

60. (a)

(b) 34,190 pascals

62. False. e is an irrational number.

64. $g(x) = h(x)$ **66.** None are equal.

68. (a) $x > 0$ (b) $x < 0$

70. (a)

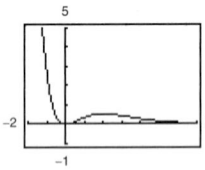

Decreasing: $(-\infty, 0), (2, \infty)$

Increasing: $(0, 2)$

Relative maximum: $(2, 4e^{-2})$

Relative minimum: $(0, 0)$

(b)

Decreasing: $(1.44, \infty)$

Increasing: $(-\infty, 1.44)$

Relative maximum:
    $(1.44, 4.25)$

72. The value of $f(x)$ approaches e^r.

x	1	10	100	200	500
$[1 + (1/x)]^x$	2	2.5937	2.7048	2.7115	2.7156

x	1000	10,000
$[1 + (1/x)]^x$	2.7170	2.718

74. $1 < \sqrt{2} < 2$

    $2^1 < 2^{\sqrt{2}} < 2^2$

76. $y = \frac{1}{3}(4 - x^2)$

78. $y = x - 2$ and $y = -(x - 2), \ x \geq 2$

80.

82.

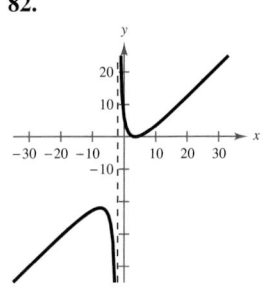

Section 3.2   *(page 216)*

2. $3^4 = 81$ **4.** $10^{-3} = \frac{1}{1000}$ **6.** $16^{3/4} = 8$

8. $e^{1.386\ldots} = 4$ **10.** $\log_8 64 = 2$ **12.** $\log_9 27 = \frac{3}{2}$

14. $\log_{10} 0.001 = -3$ **16.** $\ln 1.6487\ldots = \frac{1}{2}$

18. $\log_u w = v$ **20.** $\frac{1}{2}$ **22.** 1   **24.** -2

26. -3 **28.** 1.097   **30.** -3.418 **32.** 0.693

33. c   **34.** f   **35.** d   **36.** e   **37.** b   **38.** a

40. Domain: $(0, \infty)$

    x-intercept: $(1, 0)$

    Vertical asymptote: $x = 0$

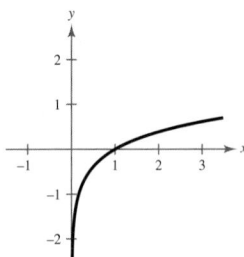

42. Domain: $(3, \infty)$

    x-intercept: $(4, 0)$

    Vertical asymptote: $x = 3$

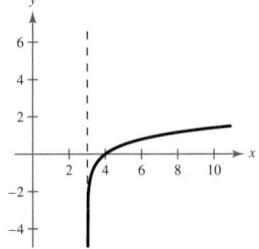

44. Domain: $(1, \infty)$

x-intercept: $\left(\frac{626}{625}, 0\right)$

Vertical asymptote: $x = 1$

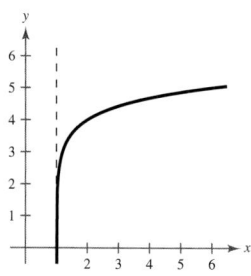

46. Domain: $(-\infty, 0)$

x-intercept: $(-1, 0)$

Vertical asymptote: $x = 0$

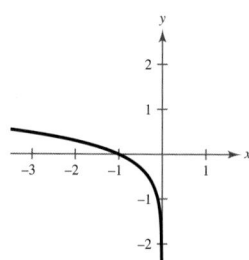

48. Domain: $(-1, \infty)$

x-intercept: $(0, 0)$

Vertical asymptote: $x = -1$

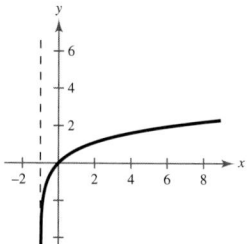

50. Domain: $(-\infty, 3)$

x-intercept: $(2, 0)$

Vertical asymptote: $x = 3$

52.

54.

56.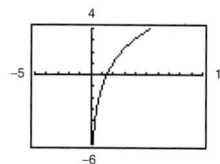

58. (a)

K	1	2	4	6	8	10	12
t	0	7.3	14.6	18.9	21.9	24.2	26.2

The number of years required to multiply the original investment by K increases with K. However, the larger the value of K, the fewer the years required to increase the value of the investment by an additional multiple of the original investment.

(b)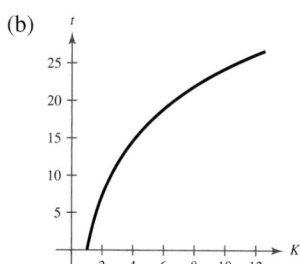

60. (a) 120 decibels

(b) 100 decibels

(c) No, the difference results from the logarithmic relationship between intensity and number of decibels.

62. (a)

x	1	5	10	10^2
$f(x)$	0	0.322	0.230	0.046

x	10^4	10^6
$f(x)$	0.00092	0.0000138

(b) 0

(c)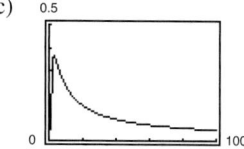

64. True. $\log_3 27 = 3 \Longrightarrow 3^3 = 27$

CHAPTER 3

66.

$g = f^{-1}$

68.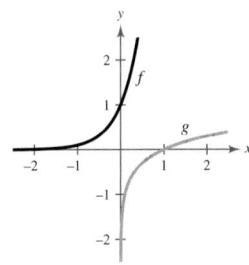

$g = f^{-1}$

70. (a) False   (b) True   (c) True   (d) False

72. $f^{-1}(x) = 10^x$ **74.** Answers will vary.

76. (a)

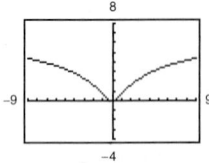

     (b) Increasing: $(0, \infty)$

        Decreasing: $(-\infty, 0)$

     (c) Relative minimum: $(0, 0)$

78. $w^2 + 10w$

Section 3.3   *(page 223)*

2. (a) $\dfrac{\log_{10} x}{\log_{10} 3}$ (b) $\dfrac{\ln x}{\ln 3}$ **4.** (a) $\dfrac{\log_{10} x}{\log_{10} \frac{1}{3}}$ (b) $\dfrac{\ln x}{\ln \frac{1}{3}}$

6. (a) $\dfrac{\log_{10} \frac{3}{4}}{\log_{10} x}$ (b) $\dfrac{\ln \frac{3}{4}}{\ln x}$ **8.** (a) $\dfrac{\log_{10} x}{\log_{10} 7.1}$ (b) $\dfrac{\ln x}{\ln 7.1}$

10. 0.712   **12.** -1.161 **14.** -0.694 **16.** -3.823

18. $\log_3 10 + \log_3 z$ **20.** $\log_{10} y - \log_{10} 2$

22. $-3 \log_6 z$ **24.** $\frac{1}{3} \ln t$

26. $\log_{10} 4 + 2 \log_{10} x + \log_{10} y$

28. $\ln(x + 1) + \ln(x - 1) - 3 \ln x$

30. $\ln 6 - \frac{1}{2} \ln(x^2 + 1)$ **32.** $\frac{1}{2}(2 \ln x - 3 \ln y)$

34. $\frac{1}{2} \log_2 x + 4 \log_2 y - 4 \log_2 z$

36. $\log_{10} x + 4 \log_{10} y - 5 \log_{10} z$

38. $\ln x + \dfrac{1}{2} \ln(x + 2)$ **40.** $\ln yt$ **42.** $\log_5 \dfrac{8}{t}$

44. $\log_7 (z - 2)^{2/3}$ **46.** $\log_6 \dfrac{1}{16x^4}$ **48.** $\ln 64(z - 4)^5$

50. $\log_3 \dfrac{x^3 y^4}{z^4}$ **52.** $\ln \dfrac{z^4(z + 5)^4}{(z - 5)^2}$ **54.** $\ln\left(\dfrac{x^3}{x^2 - 1}\right)^2$

56. $\log_4\left[x^6(x - 1)\sqrt{x + 1}\right]$

58. $\log_7 \sqrt{70} = \frac{1}{2}(\log_7 7 + \log_7 10)$

             $= \frac{1}{2} + \log_7 \sqrt{10}$; Properties 1 and 3

60. -3 **62.** $\frac{1}{3}$ **64.** -0.8

66. -16 is not in the domain of $\log_2 x$.

68. 12   **70.** $\frac{3}{4}$ **72.** 7   **74.** 3   **76.** $4 + 4 \log_2 3$

78. $\log_{10} 3 - 2$ **80.** $\ln 6 - 2$

82. $\beta = 10(\log_{10} I + 12)$; 60 decibels

84. True; Property 1   **86.** False. $f(\sqrt{x}) = \frac{1}{2} f(x)$

88. True   **90.** Answers will vary.

92. $f(x) = \dfrac{\log_{10} x}{\log_{10} 4} = \dfrac{\ln x}{\ln 4}$ **94.** $f(x) = \dfrac{\log_{10} x}{\log_{10} \frac{1}{4}} = \dfrac{\ln x}{\ln \frac{1}{4}}$

 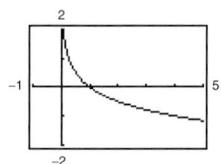

96. $f(x) = \dfrac{\log_{10} x}{\log_{10} 12.4} = \dfrac{\ln x}{\ln 12.4}$

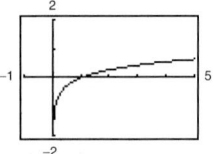

98. $\ln 2 \approx 0.6931$ $\ln 10 \approx 2.3025$

     $\ln 3 \approx 1.0986$ $\ln 12 \approx 2.4848$

     $\ln 4 \approx 1.3862$ $\ln 15 \approx 2.7080$

     $\ln 5 \approx 1.6094$ $\ln 16 \approx 2.7724$

     $\ln 6 \approx 1.7917$ $\ln 18 \approx 2.8903$

     $\ln 8 \approx 2.0793$ $\ln 20 \approx 2.9956$

     $\ln 9 \approx 2.1972$

100. $\dfrac{27y^3}{8x^6}$ **102.** $\dfrac{(xy)^2}{x + y}$ **104.** $1, \dfrac{1}{4}$ **106.** $\dfrac{1 \pm \sqrt{31}}{2}$

Section 3.4   *(page 232)*

2. (a) No   (b) No

4. (a) Yes   (b) Yes, approximate   (c) No

6. (a) Yes   (b) Yes, approximate   (c) No

8. 5   **10.** 6   **12.** $\frac{2}{3}$ **14.** -3

16. 2   **18.** 5   **20.** $\ln 4 \approx 1.386$

22. $e^{-7} \approx 0.000912$ **24.** 0.008   **26.** 100

28. $\left(\dfrac{2}{3}, 9\right)$ **30.** $(5, 0)$ **32.** $\dfrac{\ln 16}{\ln 5} \approx 1.723$

34. $\ln \dfrac{91}{4} \approx 3.125$ **36.** $\dfrac{\ln 37}{\ln 6} \approx 2.015$

38. $\dfrac{\ln 3000}{5 \ln 6} \approx 0.894$ **40.** $-\dfrac{\ln(0.10)}{3 \ln 4} \approx 0.554$ **42.** 8

44. $\dfrac{-\ln 64 - \ln 431}{\ln 8} \approx -4.917$

46. $6 + \log_{10} \dfrac{7}{5} \approx 6.146$ **48.** $6 - \dfrac{\ln 5}{\ln 3} \approx 4.535$

50. $\dfrac{\ln 50}{2} \approx 1.956$ **52.** $-\dfrac{1}{4} \ln \dfrac{3}{40} \approx 0.648$

54. $\ln \dfrac{25}{3} \approx 2.120$ **56.** $3 - \dfrac{\ln \frac{7}{2}}{2 \ln 4} \approx 2.548$

58. $\ln 2 \approx 0.693;\ \ln 3 \approx 1.099$ **60.** No solution

62. $\ln 7 \approx 1.946$ **64.** $\dfrac{\ln 31}{6} \approx 0.572$

66. $\dfrac{\ln 21}{9 \ln 3.938225} \approx 0.247$ **68.** $\dfrac{\ln 30}{3 \ln\left(16 - \frac{0.878}{26}\right)} \approx 0.409$

70.

-2.322

72.

-0.478

74.

1.081

76.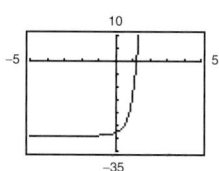

1.236

78. $e^2 \approx 7.389$ **80.** $\dfrac{e}{4} \approx 0.680$ **82.** $\dfrac{100}{3} \approx 33.333$

84. $10^{11/5} + 2 \approx 160.489$ **86.** $e^{7/2} \approx 33.115$

88. $e^{10} + 8 = 22{,}034.466$ **90.** $e^{-4/3} \approx 0.264$

92. $\dfrac{-1 + \sqrt{1 + 4e}}{2} \approx 1.223$ **94.** $\dfrac{-3 + \sqrt{9 + 4e}}{2} \approx 0.729$

96. $\dfrac{3 + \sqrt{13}}{2} \approx 3.303$ **98.** no solution

100. 2   **102.** 9

104. $\dfrac{1225 + 125\sqrt{73}}{2} \approx 1146.500$

106.

2.197

108.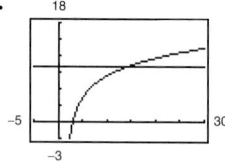

14.182

110. 5.8 years   **112.** 9.2 years

114. (a) 303 units   (b) 528 units

116. 12.76 inches

118. (a)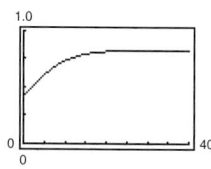

(b) Horizontal asymptotes: $P = 0, P = 0.83$

The proportion of correct responses will approach 0.83 as the number of trials increases.

(c) ≈ 5 trials

120. (a) $T = 20$; Room temperature   (b) ≈ 0.81 hour

122. $\log_b(u + v) = (\log_b u)(\log_b v)$

False.

$2.04 \approx \log_{10}(10 + 100) \neq (\log_{10} 10)(\log_{10} 100) = 2$

124. $\log_b \dfrac{u}{v} = \log_b u - \log_b v$

True by Property 2 in Section 3.3.

126. For $rt < \ln 2$ years, double the amount you invest. For $rt > \ln 2$ years, double your interest rate or double the number of years, because either of these will double the exponent in the exponential function.

128. Answers will vary.

130. $4\sqrt{2} - 10$ **132.** $\dfrac{1}{2}\sqrt{10} + 1$ **134.** $t = \dfrac{k}{s^3}$

136. $x = \dfrac{k}{b - 3}$ **138.** 1.262   **140.** 1.486

Section 3.5   *(page 243)*

1. c   **2.** e   **3.** b   **4.** a   **5.** d   **6.** f

Initial Investment	Annual % Rate	Time to Double	Amount After 10 Years
8. $20,000	10.5%	6.60 yr	$57,153.02
10. $10,000	5.7762%	12 yr	$17,817.97
12. $600	34.66%	2 yr	$19,205.00
14. $8986.58	8%	8.66 yr	$20,000.00

16. $4214.16

18. (a) 6.94 years   (b) 6.63 years

(c) 6.602 years   (d) 6.601 years

CHAPTER 3

20.

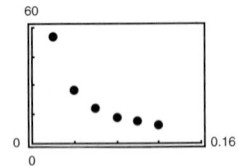

60 · · 0.16 0

Use PwrReg: $t = 1.099r^{-1}$

22.

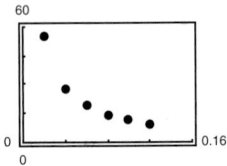

60 · · 0.16 0

Use PwrReg: $t = 1.222r^{-1}$

24.

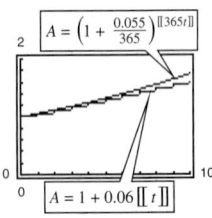

$A = \left(1 + \frac{0.055}{365}\right)^{[\![365t]\!]}$

$A = 1 + 0.06[\![t]\!]$

Daily compounding

Isotope	Half-life (years)	Initial Quantity	Amount After 1000 Years
26. ^{226}Ra	1620	2.30 g	1.5 g
28. ^{14}C	5730	3 g	2.66 g
30. ^{239}Pu	24,360	0.41 g	0.4 g

32. $y = \frac{1}{2}e^{0.5756x}$ **34.** $y = e^{-0.4621x}$

36. (a) Canada: $y = 31.3e^{0.00915t}$; 41.2 million

China: $y = 1261.8e^{0.00743t}$; 1576.9 million

Italy: $y = 57.6e^{-0.0035t}$; 57.0 million

United Kingdom: $y = 59.5e^{0.00183t}$; 62.8 million

United States: $y = 275.6e^{0.00852t}$; 355.8 million

(b) b; The greater the rate of growth, the greater the value of b.

(c) b determines whether the population is increasing ($b > 0$) or decreasing ($b < 0$).

38. $k = 0.0132$; 291,677   **40.** 61.16 hours

42. 15,683 years

44. (a) $V = -750t + 2000$ (b) $V = 2000e^{-0.6931t}$

(c)

2200 (a) (b) 0 5   Exponential

(d) 1 year:
Straight-line, $1250; Exponential, $1000
3 years:
Straight-line, $-$250; Exponential, $250

(e) The value decreases $750 per year.

46. (a) $k \approx 0.053$ (b) 267,450 units

48. $496,880

50. (a) 203 animals

(b) 13 months

(c)

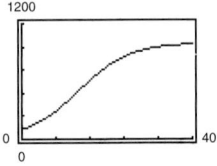

1200 0 40

Horizontal asymptotes: $y = 0$, $y = 1000$. The population size will approach 1000 as time increases.

52. (a) 158,489,319   (b) 5,011,872   (c) 50,118,723

54. (a) 30 decibels   (b) 85 decibels

(c) 90 decibels   (d) 115 decibels

56. 97%   **58.** 4.95

60. $10^{-3.2} \approx 6.3 \times 10^{-4}$ moles per liter   **62.** 10

64. (a)

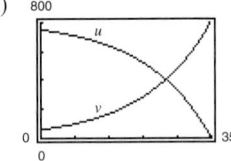

800 u v 0 35

(b) Interest; $t \approx 26$ years

(c)

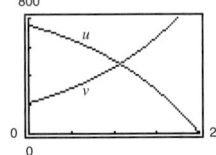

800 u v 0 20

Interest; $t \approx 11$ years; The interest is still the majority of the monthly payment in the early years, but now the principal and interest are nearly equal when $t \approx 11$ years.

66. (a) $t_3 = 0.2729s - 6.0143$

$t_4 = 1.5385e^{0.02913s}$ or $t_4 = 1.5385(1.0296)^s$

(b)

25 t_2 t_4 t_1 t_3 20 100 0

(c)

s	30	40	50	60	70	80	90
t_1	3.6	4.6	6.7	9.4	12.5	15.9	19.6
t_2	3.3	4.9	7.0	9.5	12.5	15.9	19.9
t_3	2.2	4.9	7.6	10.4	13.1	15.8	18.5
t_4	3.7	4.9	6.6	8.9	11.9	15.9	21.2

(d) Model t_1: Sum $= 2.0$

   Model t_2: Sum $= 1.1$

   Model t_3: Sum $= 5.6$

   Model t_4: Sum $= 2.6$

   The quadratic model (model t_2) fits best.

68. False. A logistic growth function never has an x-intercept.

70. True. The graph of a Gaussian model will never have an x-intercept.

72. Answers will vary.

74. Falls to the left.   **76.** Rises to the right.

   Falls to the right.   Rises to the left.

78. $8x^2 - 24x + 18$

80. $x^3 - 5x^2 + 25x - 128 + \dfrac{641}{x + 5}$

82.

84.

86.

88.

90.

92.

94.
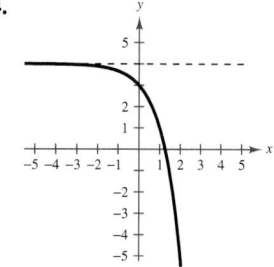

Review Exercises   (page 250)

2. -3.863 **4.** 4.181 **6.** 0.002 **7.** c

8. d   **9.** a   **10.** b

12. Shift the graph of f three units downward.

14. Reflect f in the x-axis and shift f eight units upward.

16.

x	-2	-1	0	1	2
$f(x)$	-3.063	-3.25	-4	-7	-19

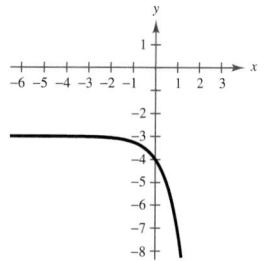

18.

x	-3	-1	0	1	3
$f(x)$	0.020	0.142	0.377	1	7.023

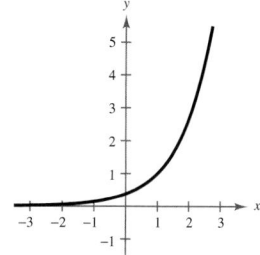

20.

x	0	5	6	7	8	9
$f(x)$	-4.984	-4.5	-4	-3	-1	3

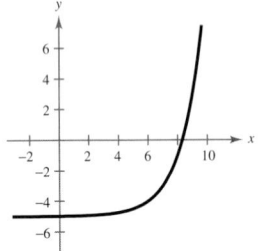

22.

x	-3	-2	-1	0	2
$f(x)$	3	-4	-4.875	-4.984	-5

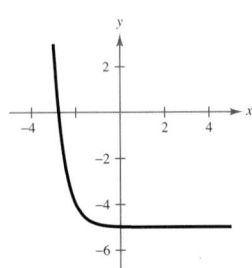

24. 1.868   **26.** 1.320

28.

x	-2	-1	0	1	2
$h(x)$	-0.72	0.35	1	1.39	1.63

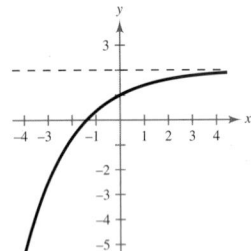

30.

t	$\frac{1}{2}$	1	2	3	4
$s(t)$	0.07	0.54	1.47	2.05	2.43

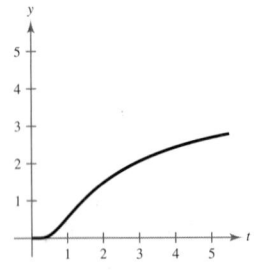

32.

n	1	2	4	12
A	\$8643.88	\$8799.58	\$8880.43	\$8935.49

n	365	Continuous
A	\$8962.46	\$8963.38

34. (a)

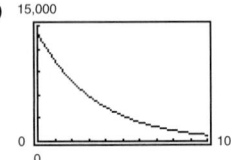

(b) \$7875   (c) At the beginning. Yes

36. (a) 100 grams   (b) 58.7 grams

(c)

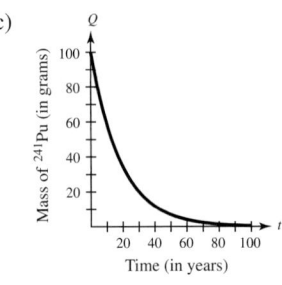

38. $\log_{25} 125 = \frac{3}{2}$ **40.** $\frac{1}{2}$ **42.** -1

44. Domain: $(0, \infty)$

x-intercept: $(1, 0)$

Vertical asymptote: $x = 0$

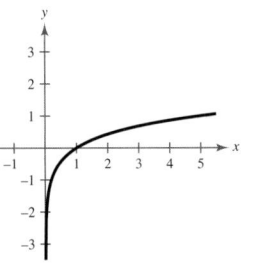

46. Domain: $(0, \infty)$

x-intercept: $(10^{-6}, 0)$

Vertical asymptote: $x = 0$

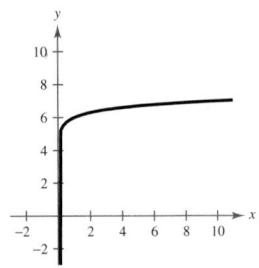

48. Domain: $(3, \infty)$

x-intercept: $(3.1, 0)$

Vertical asymptote: $x = 3$

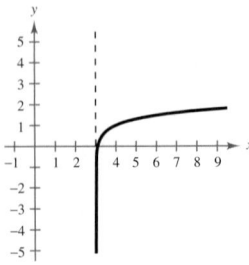

50. -0.020 **52.** 7   **54.** -1.530

56. Domain: $(3, \infty)$ **58.** Domain: $(0, \infty)$

x-intercept: $(4, 0)$ x-intercept: $(1, 0)$

Vertical asymptote: $x = 3$ Vertical asymptote: $x = 0$

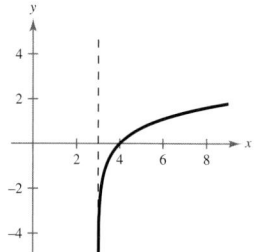

60 27.16 miles   **62.** 2.132   **64.** -1.159

66. $\log_{10} 7 + 4 \log_{10} |x|$ **68.** $\frac{1}{2} \log_7 x - \log_7 4$

70. $\ln 3 + \ln x + 2 \ln y$ **72.** $2 \ln(y - 1) - \ln 16$

74. $\log_6 \dfrac{y}{z^2}$ **76.** $\ln x^3 (x + 1)^2$

78. $\log_{10} \dfrac{1}{x^2(x + 6)^5}$ **80.** $\ln \dfrac{(x - 2)^5}{x^3(x + 2)}$

82. The score decreased 10 points over the four-month period.

84. 6   **86.** -2 **88.** $\ln 6$ **90.** $\frac{1}{6}$ **92.** e^{-3}

94. $\dfrac{\ln 25}{3} \approx 1.073$ **96.** $\frac{1}{3}(\ln 40 - 2) \approx 0.563$

98. $\dfrac{\ln 20}{\ln 6} \approx 1.672$ **100.** $\dfrac{\ln 95}{\ln 12} \approx 1.833$

102. $\ln 2 \approx 0.693$, $\ln 4 \approx 1.386$

104.   **106.**

    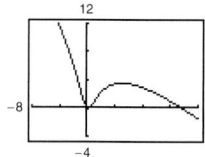

$-1.53, -7.04$ 0.68

108. $\frac{1}{5}e^{7.2} \approx 267.886$ **110.** $\frac{1}{3}e^{15/4} \approx 14.174$

112. $e^6 - 8 \approx 395.429$ **114.** $5e^4 \approx 272.991$

116. $-2 + \sqrt{6} \approx 0.449$ **118.** -104

120.   **122.**

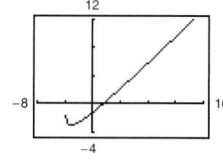

$0, 0.42, 13.63$ $-3.99, 1.48$

124. (a) 1151 units   (b) 1325 units   **125.** e   **126.** b

127. f   **128.** d   **129.** a   **130.** c   **132.** 98.6%

134. 9.8 hours   **136.** $y = \frac{1}{2}e^{0.4605x}$

138. (a) 7.7 weeks   (b) 13.3 weeks

140. (a) 251,188,643   (b) 7,079,458   (c) 1,258,925,412

142. False. $\ln x + \ln y = \ln(xy) \neq \ln(x + y)$

Problem Solving   *(page 258)*

2.

y_1 increases at the fastest rate.

4. Answers will vary.

6. Answers will vary.

8. $y_4 = 1 + \dfrac{x}{1!} + \dfrac{x^2}{2!} + \dfrac{x^3}{3!} + \dfrac{x^4}{4!}$

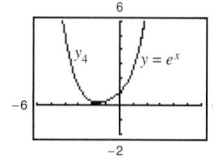

The pattern implies that

$$e^x = 1 + \frac{x}{1!} + \frac{x^2}{2!} + \frac{x^3}{3!} + \cdots$$

10. $f^{-1}(x) = \dfrac{\ln\left(\dfrac{x + 1}{x - 1}\right)}{\ln a}$

12. (a) The upper graph represents the investment compounded annually and the lower graph represents simple interest.

(b) $y_1 = 500(1.07)^t$

$y_2 = 35t + 500$

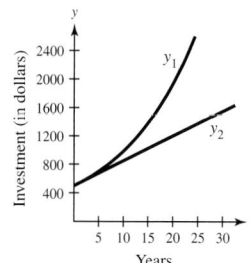

14. $B = 500a^{\left(\frac{\ln 2/5}{\ln a}\right)t}$

16. Answers will vary.

18. (a) (b)

(c)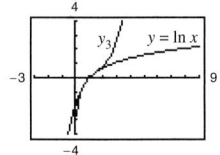

20. Slope $= \ln b$; y-intercept: $(0, \ln a)$

Slope $= b$; y-intercept: $(0, \ln a)$

22. (a) 15 cubic feet per minute

(b) 382.0 cubic feet

(c) 382.0 square feet

Chapter 4

Section 4.1 *(page 269)*

2. 5.5 radians **4.** -4 radians **6.** 6.5 radians

8. (a) Quadrant III (b) Quadrant III

10. (a) Quadrant IV (b) Quadrant II

12. (a) Quadrant IV (b) Quadrant II

14. (a) (b)

16. (a) 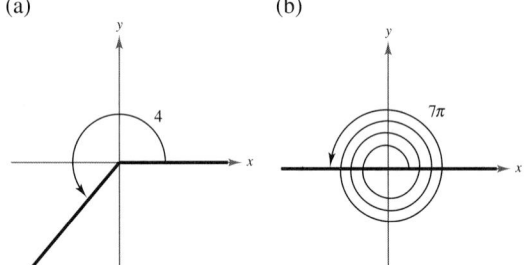 (b)

18. (a) $\dfrac{19\pi}{6}, -\dfrac{5\pi}{6}$ (b) $\dfrac{\pi}{6}, -\dfrac{23\pi}{6}$

20. (a) $\dfrac{7\pi}{4}, -\dfrac{\pi}{4}$ (b) $\dfrac{28\pi}{15}, -\dfrac{32\pi}{15}$

22. (a) Complement: $\dfrac{5\pi}{12}$; Supplement: $\dfrac{11\pi}{12}$

(b) Complement: none; Supplement: $\dfrac{\pi}{12}$

24. (a) Complement: none; Supplement: $\pi - 3 \approx 0.14$

(b) Complement: $\dfrac{\pi}{2} - 1.5 \approx 0.07$;

Supplement: $\pi - 1.5 \approx 1.64$

26. (a) $\dfrac{7\pi}{4}$ (b) $\dfrac{2\pi}{3}$ **28.** (a) $-\dfrac{3\pi}{2}$ (b) $\dfrac{4\pi}{5}$

30. 1.525 **32.** -0.842 **34.** 6.021 **36.** 0.009

38. (a) $-105°$ (b) $20°$ **40.** (a) $330°$ (b) $408°$

42. $81.818°$ **44.** $1170.000°$ **46.** $864.000°$

48. $-32.659°$ **50.** $120°$ **52.** $-330°$ **54.** $10°$

56. (a) Quadrant I (b) Quadrant III

58. (a) Quadrant II (b) Quadrant IV

60. (a) (b)

62. (a) (b)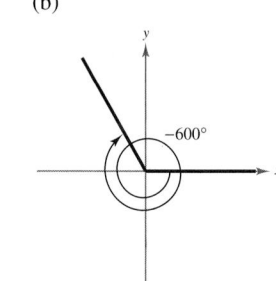

64. (a) $480°, -240°$ (b) $300°, -60°$

66. (a) $300°, -60°$ (b) $590°, -130°$

68. (a) Complement: $87°$; Supplement: $177°$

(b) Complement: $26°$; Supplement: $116°$

70. (a) Complement: none; Supplement: $50°$

(b) Complement: none; Supplement: $10°$

72. (a) $245.167°$ (b) $2.2°$

74. (a) $-135.01°$ (b) $-408.272°$

76. (a) $-345°\,7'12''$ (b) $0°\,27'$

78. (a) $-0°\,21'18''$ (b) $0°\,47'11.4''$

80. $\frac{29}{10}$ radians **82.** $-\frac{4}{5}$ radian

84. $\frac{4}{7}$ radian   **86.** 2 radians   **88.** 3π feet ≈ 9.42 feet

90. 5π centimeters ≈ 15.71 centimeters

92. 686.4 miles   **94.** 4045.7 miles

96. 0.063 radian $\approx 3.59°$ **98.** 275°

100. (a) 3400π radians per minute; 1700π radians per minute

(b) 850 revolutions per minute

102. 20.16π inches per second

104. True. Let α and β represent coterminal angles, and let n represent an integer.

$$\alpha = \beta + n(360°)$$
$$\alpha - \beta = n(360°)$$

106. (a) The vertex is at the origin and the initial side is on the positive x-axis.

(b) Clockwise rotation of the terminal side

(c) Two angles in standard position where the terminal sides coincide

(d) The magnitude of the angle is between 90° and 180°.

108. Radian. 1 radian $\approx 57.3°$ **110.** Answers will vary.

112.

114.

116.

118.

120.

122.

124.

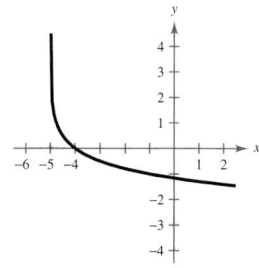

126. $\dfrac{2\sqrt{3}}{3}$ **128.** $\dfrac{5\sqrt{2}}{4}$

130. $6\sqrt{13}$ **132.** $4\sqrt{13}$

Section 4.2   *(page 278)*

2. $\sin\theta = \frac{5}{13}$ $\csc\theta = \frac{13}{5}$

$\cos\theta = \frac{12}{13}$ $\sec\theta = \frac{13}{12}$

$\tan\theta = \frac{5}{12}$ $\cot\theta = \frac{12}{5}$

4. $\sin\theta = -\frac{3}{5}$ $\csc\theta = -\frac{5}{3}$

$\cos\theta = -\frac{4}{5}$ $\sec\theta = -\frac{5}{4}$

$\tan\theta = \frac{3}{4}$ $\cot\theta = \frac{4}{3}$

6. $\left(\dfrac{1}{2}, \dfrac{\sqrt{3}}{2}\right)$ **8.** $\left(-\dfrac{\sqrt{2}}{2}, -\dfrac{\sqrt{2}}{2}\right)$

10. $\left(\dfrac{1}{2}, -\dfrac{\sqrt{3}}{2}\right)$ **12.** $(-1, 0)$

14. $\sin\dfrac{\pi}{3} = \dfrac{\sqrt{3}}{2}$ **16.** $\sin\left(-\dfrac{\pi}{4}\right) = -\dfrac{\sqrt{2}}{2}$

$\cos\dfrac{\pi}{3} = \dfrac{1}{2}$ $\cos\left(-\dfrac{\pi}{4}\right) = \dfrac{\sqrt{2}}{2}$

$\tan\dfrac{\pi}{3} = \sqrt{3}$ $\tan\left(-\dfrac{\pi}{4}\right) = -1$

18. $\sin\left(-\dfrac{4\pi}{3}\right) = \dfrac{\sqrt{3}}{2}$ **20.** $\sin\dfrac{5\pi}{3} = -\dfrac{\sqrt{3}}{2}$

$\cos\left(-\dfrac{4\pi}{3}\right) = -\dfrac{1}{2}$ $\cos\dfrac{5\pi}{3} = \dfrac{1}{2}$

$\tan\left(-\dfrac{4\pi}{3}\right) = -\sqrt{3}$ $\tan\dfrac{5\pi}{3} = -\sqrt{3}$

22. $\sin(-2\pi) = 0$

$\cos(-2\pi) = 1$

$\tan(-2\pi) = 0$

CHAPTER 4

24. $\sin \dfrac{5\pi}{6} = \dfrac{1}{2}$

$\cos \dfrac{5\pi}{6} = -\dfrac{\sqrt{3}}{2}$

$\tan \dfrac{5\pi}{6} = -\dfrac{\sqrt{3}}{3}$

$\csc \dfrac{5\pi}{6} = 2$

$\sec \dfrac{5\pi}{6} = -\dfrac{2\sqrt{3}}{3}$

$\cot \dfrac{5\pi}{6} = -\sqrt{3}$

26. $\sin \dfrac{3\pi}{2} = -1$

$\cos \dfrac{3\pi}{2} = 0$

$\tan \dfrac{3\pi}{2}$ is undefined.

$\csc \dfrac{3\pi}{2} = -1$

$\sec \dfrac{3\pi}{2}$ is undefined.

$\cot \dfrac{3\pi}{2} = 0$

28. $\sin \dfrac{7\pi}{4} = -\dfrac{\sqrt{2}}{2}$

$\cos \dfrac{7\pi}{4} = \dfrac{\sqrt{2}}{2}$

$\tan \dfrac{7\pi}{4} = -1$

$\csc \dfrac{7\pi}{4} = -\sqrt{2}$

$\sec \dfrac{7\pi}{4} = \sqrt{2}$

$\cot \dfrac{7\pi}{4} = -1$

30. $\cos 5\pi = \cos \pi = -1$ **32.** $\sin \dfrac{9\pi}{4} = \sin \dfrac{\pi}{4} = \dfrac{\sqrt{2}}{2}$

34. $\sin \dfrac{19\pi}{6} = \sin \dfrac{7\pi}{6} = -\dfrac{1}{2}$

36. $\cos\left(-\dfrac{8\pi}{3}\right) = \cos \dfrac{4\pi}{3} = -\dfrac{1}{2}$

38. (a) $-\dfrac{3}{8}$ (b) $-\dfrac{8}{3}$ **40.** (a) $-\dfrac{3}{4}$ (b) $-\dfrac{4}{3}$

42. (a) $-\dfrac{4}{5}$ (b) $-\dfrac{4}{5}$ **44.** 1.7321   **46.** 0.6421

48. -0.8011 **50.** -4.4014 **52.** -0.7833

54. (a) 0.7   (b) -0.8

56. (a) 4.0 or 5.4   (b) 0.72 or 5.56

58. (a) 0.25 foot   (b) 0.02 foot   (c) -0.25 foot

60. True. The tangent function has a period of π.

62. Answers will vary.   **64.** Odd

66. $f^{-1}(x) = \sqrt[3]{4(x-1)}$ **68.** $f^{-1}(x) = \dfrac{2(2x+1)}{x-1}$

Section 4.3   (page 287)

2. $\sin \theta = \dfrac{5}{13}$ $\csc \theta = \dfrac{13}{5}$

$\cos \theta = \dfrac{12}{13}$ $\sec \theta = \dfrac{13}{12}$

$\tan \theta = \dfrac{5}{12}$ $\cot \theta = \dfrac{12}{5}$

4. $\sin \theta = \dfrac{\sqrt{2}}{2}$ $\csc \theta = \sqrt{2}$

$\cos \theta = \dfrac{\sqrt{2}}{2}$ $\sec \theta = \sqrt{2}$

$\tan \theta = 1$ $\cot \theta = 1$

6. $\sin \theta = \dfrac{8}{17}$ $\csc \theta = \dfrac{17}{8}$

$\cos \theta = \dfrac{15}{17}$ $\sec \theta = \dfrac{17}{15}$

$\tan \theta = \dfrac{8}{15}$ $\cot \theta = \dfrac{15}{8}$

The triangles are similar, and corresponding sides are proportional.

8. $\sin \theta = \dfrac{\sqrt{5}}{5}$ $\csc \theta = \sqrt{5}$

$\cos \theta = \dfrac{2\sqrt{5}}{5}$ $\sec \theta = \dfrac{\sqrt{5}}{2}$

$\tan \theta = \dfrac{1}{2}$ $\cot \theta = 2$

The triangles are similar, and corresponding sides are proportional.

10.

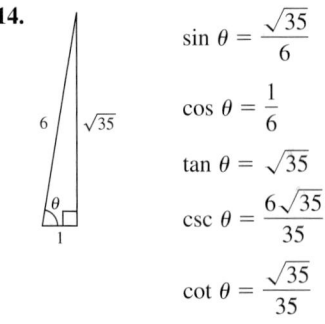

$\sin \theta = \dfrac{2\sqrt{6}}{7}$

$\tan \theta = \dfrac{2\sqrt{6}}{5}$

$\csc \theta = \dfrac{7\sqrt{6}}{12}$

$\sec \theta = \dfrac{7}{5}$

$\cot \theta = \dfrac{5\sqrt{6}}{12}$

12.

$\sin \theta = \dfrac{\sqrt{26}}{26}$ $\csc \theta = \sqrt{26}$

$\cos \theta = \dfrac{5\sqrt{26}}{26}$ $\sec \theta = \dfrac{\sqrt{26}}{5}$

$\tan \theta = \dfrac{1}{5}$

14.

$\sin \theta = \dfrac{\sqrt{35}}{6}$

$\cos \theta = \dfrac{1}{6}$

$\tan \theta = \sqrt{35}$

$\csc \theta = \dfrac{6\sqrt{35}}{35}$

$\cot \theta = \dfrac{\sqrt{35}}{35}$

16.

$$\sin \theta = \frac{4}{17} \qquad\qquad \sec \theta = \frac{17\sqrt{273}}{273}$$

$$\cos \theta = \frac{\sqrt{273}}{17} \qquad\qquad \cot \theta = \frac{\sqrt{273}}{4}$$

$$\tan \theta = \frac{4\sqrt{273}}{273}$$

18. (a) 2 (b) $\dfrac{\sqrt{3}}{3}$ (c) $\dfrac{\sqrt{3}}{2}$ (d) $\sqrt{3}$

20. (a) $\dfrac{1}{5}$ (b) $\dfrac{\sqrt{6}}{12}$ (c) $2\sqrt{6}$ (d) $\dfrac{2\sqrt{6}}{5}$

22. (a) $\dfrac{1}{5}$ (b) $\dfrac{\sqrt{26}}{26}$ (c) $\dfrac{1}{5}$ (d) $\dfrac{\sqrt{26}}{5}$

24. (a) 1 (b) $\dfrac{\sqrt{2}}{2}$ (c) $\sqrt{2}$

26. (a) $\dfrac{\sqrt{3}}{2}$ (b) 1 (c) $\dfrac{2\sqrt{3}}{3}$

28. (a) 0.4348 (b) 0.4348

30. (a) 0.9598 (b) 0.9609

32. (a) 0.9964 (b) 1.0036

34. (a) 1.7946 (b) 0.5572

36. (a) 2.6695 (b) 0.0699

38. (a) $45° = \dfrac{\pi}{4}$ (b) $45° = \dfrac{\pi}{4}$

40. (a) $60° = \dfrac{\pi}{3}$ (b) $60° = \dfrac{\pi}{3}$

42. (a) $60° = \dfrac{\pi}{3}$ (b) $45° = \dfrac{\pi}{4}$

44. (a) $10° \approx 0.175$ (b) $29° \approx 0.506$

46. (a) $22° \approx 0.384$ (b) $68° \approx 1.187$

48–56. Answers will vary.

58. $9\sqrt{3}$ **60.** $20\sqrt{2}$

62. 18 feet

64. (a)

(b) $\sin \theta = \dfrac{3\frac{1}{3}}{20}$ (c) $9.59°$

66. 1.3 miles

68. 6.57 centimeters

70. $\sin 75° \approx 0.97 \qquad \csc 75° \approx 1.04$

$\cos 75° \approx 0.26 \qquad \sec 75° \approx 3.86$

$\tan 75° \approx 3.73 \qquad \cot 75° \approx 0.27$

72. True, $\sec x = \csc(90 - x)$.

74. True, $\cot^2 \theta - \csc^2 \theta = -1$ for all θ.

76. False, $\tan 25° \neq (\tan 5°)(\tan 5°)$.

78. Yes. Tan θ is equal to opp/adj. You can find the value of the hypotenuse by the Pythagorean Theorem, then you can find $\sec \theta$, which is equal to hyp/adj.

80. (a)

θ	0°	18°	36°	54°	72°	90°
$\sin \theta$	0	0.3090	0.5878	0.8090	0.9511	1
$\cos \theta$	0	0.9511	0.8090	0.5878	0.3090	0

(b) Increasing function   (c) Decreasing function

(d) As the angle increases, the length of the side opposite the angle increases relative to the length of the hypotenuse and the length of the side adjacent to the angle decreases relative to the length of the hypotenuse. Thus, the sine increases and the cosine decreases.

82. $\dfrac{2t + 3}{4 - t}$, $t \neq \pm\dfrac{3}{2}$, -4 **84.** $\dfrac{1}{4}$, $x \neq 0, 12$

86. $x = \dfrac{2}{3}$

Section 4.4   *(page 297)*

2. (a) $\sin \theta = -\dfrac{5}{13}$ $\qquad \csc \theta = -\dfrac{13}{5}$

$\cos \theta = -\dfrac{12}{13}$ $\qquad \sec \theta = -\dfrac{13}{12}$

$\tan \theta = \dfrac{5}{12}$ $\qquad \cot \theta = \dfrac{12}{5}$

(b) $\sin \theta = \dfrac{\sqrt{2}}{2}$ $\qquad \csc \theta = \sqrt{2}$

$\cos \theta = -\dfrac{\sqrt{2}}{2}$ $\qquad \sec \theta = -\sqrt{2}$

$\tan \theta = -1$ $\qquad \cot \theta = -1$

4. (a) $\sin \theta = \dfrac{\sqrt{10}}{10}$ $\qquad \csc \theta = \sqrt{10}$

$\cos \theta = \dfrac{3\sqrt{10}}{10}$ $\qquad \sec \theta = \dfrac{\sqrt{10}}{3}$

$\tan \theta = \dfrac{1}{3}$ $\qquad \cot \theta = 3$

(b) $\sin \theta = -\dfrac{\sqrt{2}}{2}$ $\qquad \csc \theta = -\sqrt{2}$

$\cos \theta = \dfrac{\sqrt{2}}{2}$ $\qquad \sec \theta = \sqrt{2}$

$\tan \theta = -1$ $\qquad \cot \theta = -1$

6. $\sin \theta = \frac{15}{17}$ $\csc \theta = \frac{17}{15}$

$\cos \theta = \frac{8}{17}$ $\sec \theta = \frac{17}{8}$

$\tan \theta = \frac{15}{8}$ $\cot \theta = \frac{8}{15}$

8. $\sin \theta = -\dfrac{2\sqrt{29}}{29}$ $\csc \theta = -\dfrac{\sqrt{29}}{2}$

$\cos \theta = -\dfrac{5\sqrt{29}}{29}$ $\sec \theta = -\dfrac{\sqrt{29}}{5}$

$\tan \theta = \dfrac{2}{5}$ $\cot \theta = \dfrac{5}{2}$

10. $\sin \theta = -\dfrac{31\sqrt{1157}}{1157}$ $\csc \theta = -\dfrac{\sqrt{1157}}{31}$

$\cos \theta = \dfrac{14\sqrt{1157}}{1157}$ $\sec \theta = \dfrac{\sqrt{1157}}{14}$

$\tan \theta = -\dfrac{31}{14}$ $\cot \theta = -\dfrac{14}{31}$

12. Quadrant I   **14.** Quadrant IV

16. $\sin \theta = -\frac{3}{5}$ $\csc \theta = -\frac{5}{3}$

$\cos \theta = -\frac{4}{5}$ $\sec \theta = -\frac{5}{4}$

$\tan \theta = \frac{3}{4}$ $\cot \theta = \frac{4}{3}$

18. $\sin \theta = -\frac{15}{17}$ $\csc \theta = -\frac{17}{15}$

$\cos \theta = \frac{8}{17}$ $\sec \theta = \frac{17}{8}$

$\tan \theta = -\frac{15}{8}$ $\cot \theta = -\frac{8}{15}$

20. $\sin \theta = \dfrac{1}{4}$ $\csc \theta = 4$

$\cos \theta = -\dfrac{\sqrt{15}}{4}$ $\sec \theta = -\dfrac{4\sqrt{15}}{15}$

$\tan \theta = -\dfrac{\sqrt{15}}{15}$ $\cot \theta = -\sqrt{15}$

22. $\sin \theta = 0$ $\csc \theta$ is undefined.

$\cos \theta = -1$ $\sec \theta = -1$

$\tan \theta = 0$ $\cot \theta$ is undefined.

24. $\sin \theta = -1$ $\csc \theta = -1$

$\cos \theta = 0$ $\sec \theta$ is undefined.

$\tan \theta$ is undefined. $\cot \theta = 0$

26. $\sin \theta = -\dfrac{\sqrt{10}}{10}$ $\csc \theta = -\sqrt{10}$

$\cos \theta = -\dfrac{3\sqrt{10}}{10}$ $\sec \theta = -\dfrac{\sqrt{10}}{3}$

$\tan \theta = \dfrac{1}{3}$ $\cot \theta = 3$

28. $\sin \theta = -\frac{4}{5}$ $\csc \theta = -\frac{5}{4}$

$\cos \theta = \frac{3}{5}$ $\sec \theta = \frac{5}{3}$

$\tan \theta = -\frac{4}{3}$ $\cot \theta = -\frac{3}{4}$

30. 0   **32.** -1 **34.** 0   **36.** 0

38. $\theta' = 51°$ **40.** $\theta' = 35°$

     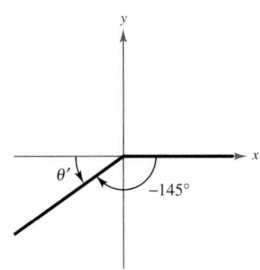

42. $\theta' = \dfrac{\pi}{4}$ **44.** $\theta' = \dfrac{\pi}{3}$

     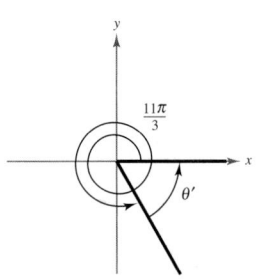

46. $\sin 300° = -\dfrac{\sqrt{3}}{2}$ **48.** $\sin(-405°) = -\dfrac{\sqrt{2}}{2}$

$\cos 300° = \dfrac{1}{2}$ $\cos(-405°) = \dfrac{\sqrt{2}}{2}$

$\tan 300° = -\sqrt{3}$ $\tan(-405°) = -1$

50. $\sin(-840°) = -\dfrac{\sqrt{3}}{2}$

$\cos(-840°) = -\dfrac{1}{2}$

$\tan(-840°) = \sqrt{3}$

52. $\sin \dfrac{\pi}{4} = \dfrac{\sqrt{2}}{2}$ **54.** $\sin\left(-\dfrac{\pi}{2}\right) = -1$

$\cos \dfrac{\pi}{4} = \dfrac{\sqrt{2}}{2}$ $\cos\left(-\dfrac{\pi}{2}\right) = 0$

$\tan \dfrac{\pi}{4} = 1$ $\tan\left(-\dfrac{\pi}{2}\right)$ is undefined.

56. $\sin \dfrac{10\pi}{3} = -\dfrac{\sqrt{3}}{2}$ **58.** $\sin\left(-\dfrac{25\pi}{4}\right) = -\dfrac{\sqrt{2}}{2}$

$\cos \dfrac{10\pi}{3} = -\dfrac{1}{2}$ $\cos\left(-\dfrac{25\pi}{4}\right) = \dfrac{\sqrt{2}}{2}$

$\tan \dfrac{10\pi}{3} = \sqrt{3}$ $\tan\left(-\dfrac{25\pi}{4}\right) = -1$

60. -1.4142 **62.** 2.0000   **64.** 0.2245

66. -0.3640 **68.** 0.6052

70. (a) $45° = \dfrac{\pi}{4}$, $315° = \dfrac{7\pi}{4}$ (b) $135° = \dfrac{3\pi}{4}$, $225° = \dfrac{5\pi}{4}$

72. (a) $60° = \dfrac{\pi}{3}$, $300° = \dfrac{5\pi}{3}$ (b) $120° = \dfrac{2\pi}{3}$, $240° = \dfrac{4\pi}{3}$

74. (a) $60° = \dfrac{\pi}{3}$, $120° = \dfrac{2\pi}{3}$ (b) $240° = \dfrac{4\pi}{3}$, $300° = \dfrac{5\pi}{3}$

76. $29.00°$, $331.00°$ **78.** $220.65°$, $319.35°$

80. 0.018, 3.124 **82.** 0.175, 3.316 **84.** 1.898, 4.385

86. $\dfrac{\sqrt{10}}{10}$ **88.** $-\sqrt{3}$ **90.** $\dfrac{\sqrt{65}}{4}$

92. (a) 26,134 units (b) 31,438 units (c) 21,452 units
(d) 26,756 units

94. (a) 2 centimeters (b) 0.11 centimeter
(c) -1.2 centimeters

96. (a) 12 miles (b) 6 miles (c) 6.9 miles

98. False. For θ in Quadrant II, $\theta' = 180° - \theta$. For θ in Quadrant III, $\theta' = \theta - 180°$. For θ in Quadrant IV, $\theta' = 360° - \theta$.

100. Determine the trigonometric function of the reference angle and prefix the appropriate sign.

102. **104.**

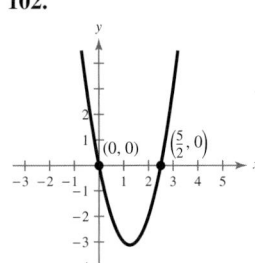

Intercept: $(0, 0)$
x-intercept: $\left(\dfrac{5}{2}, 0\right)$
Domain: all real numbers

x-intercepts: $(1, 0)$, $(-1, 0)$
y-intercept: $(0, -3)$
Domain: all real numbers

106.

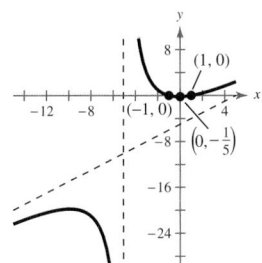

x-intercepts:
$(1, 0)$, $(-1, 0)$
y-intercept: $\left(0, -\dfrac{1}{5}\right)$
Vertical asymptote:
$x = -5$
Slant asymptote:
$y = x - 5$
Domain: all real numbers
$x \neq -5$

108.

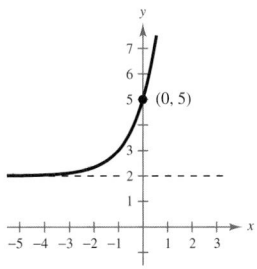

y-intercept: $(0, 5)$
Horizontal asymptote:
$y = 2$
Domain: all real numbers

110.

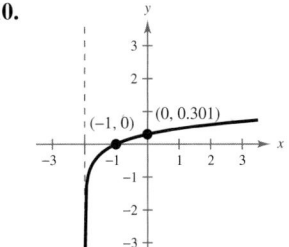

x-intercept: $(-1, 0)$,
y-intercept: $(0, 0.301)$
Vertical asymptote:
$x = -2$
Domain: $x > -2$

Section 4.5 *(page 307)*

2. Period: $\dfrac{2\pi}{3}$ **4.** Period: 6π **6.** Period: 4
Amplitude: 2 Amplitude: 3 Amplitude: $\dfrac{3}{2}$

8. Period: 3π **10.** Period: $\dfrac{\pi}{4}$
Amplitude: 1 Amplitude: $\dfrac{1}{3}$

12. Period: 8π **14.** Period: 20
Amplitude: $\dfrac{5}{2}$ Amplitude: $\dfrac{2}{3}$

16. g is a shift of f π units to the left.

18. g is a reflection of f in the y-axis.

20. The period of g is one-third the period of f.

22. g is a shift of f two units downward.

24. The period of g is $\dfrac{1}{3}$ the period of f.

26. g is a shift of f two units upward.

28. **30.**

32.

34.

52.

36.

38.

54.

56.

58.

40.

42.

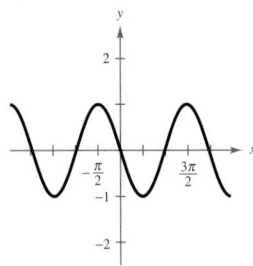

60. $a = 2, d = -1$ **62.** $a = -1, d = -3$

64. $a = 2, b = \dfrac{1}{2}, c = 0$ **66.** $a = 2, b = \dfrac{\pi}{2}, c = -\dfrac{\pi}{2}$

68.

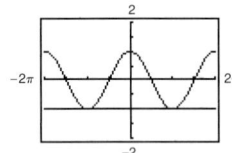

$x = \pi, -\pi$

70. (a) 4 seconds

(b) 15 cycles per minute

(c)

44.

46.

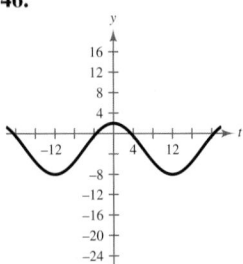

72. (a) $\dfrac{6}{5}$ seconds

(b) 50 heartbeats per minute

48.

50.

74. (a) and (c)

The model is a good fit.

(b) $y = \dfrac{1}{2} + \dfrac{1}{2}\sin\left[\dfrac{\pi}{15}(x - 76)\right]$ (d) 30 days   (e) 0.0

76. False. The graph of $f(x) = \sin(x + 2\pi)$ translates the graph of $f(x) = \sin x$ exactly one period to the left so that the two graphs look identical.

78. True. Because $\cos x = \sin\left(x + \dfrac{\pi}{2}\right)$, $y = -\cos x$ is a reflection in the x-axis of $y = \sin\left(x + \dfrac{\pi}{2}\right)$.

80.

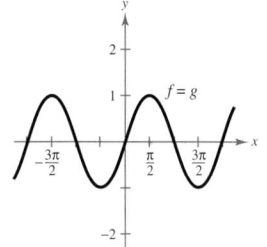

Conjecture:
$$\sin x = -\cos\left(x + \dfrac{\pi}{2}\right)$$

82.

84.

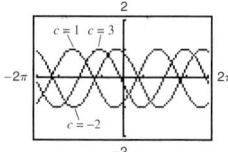

Vertical translations   Horizontal shifts

86. (a) 0.4794, 0.4794   (b) 0.8417, 0.8415   (c) 0.5, 0.5

(d) 0.8776, 0.8776   (e) 0.5417, 0.5403

(f) 0.7074, 0.7071

The error increases as x moves farther away from 0.

88. $2 \log_2 x + \log_2(x - 3)$

90. $\frac{1}{2}\ln z - \frac{1}{2}\ln(z^2 + 1)$ **92.** $\log_2(x^3 y)$

94. $\ln\left(x^3 \sqrt{\dfrac{2x}{x^2}}\right) = \ln\left(x^2\sqrt{2x}\right)$

Section 4.6   *(page 318)*

1. e, π **2.** c, 2π **3.** a, 1

4. d, 2π **5.** f, 4   **6.** b, 4

8.

10.

12.

14.

16.

18.

20.

22.

24.

26.

CHAPTER 4

28.

30.

32.

34.

36.

38.

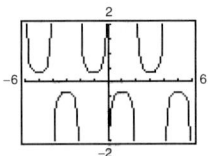

40. $-\dfrac{5\pi}{3}, -\dfrac{2\pi}{3}, \dfrac{\pi}{3}, \dfrac{4\pi}{3}$

42. $-\dfrac{7\pi}{4}, -\dfrac{3\pi}{4}, \dfrac{\pi}{4}, \dfrac{5\pi}{4}$

44. $-\dfrac{5\pi}{3}, -\dfrac{\pi}{3}, \dfrac{\pi}{3}, \dfrac{5\pi}{3}$

46. $-\dfrac{2\pi}{3}, -\dfrac{\pi}{3}, \dfrac{4\pi}{3}, \dfrac{5\pi}{3}$

48. Odd

50. (a)

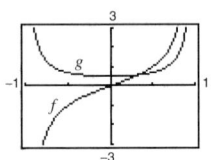

  (b) $\left(-1, \frac{1}{3}\right)$

  (c) $\left(-1, \frac{1}{3}\right)$; The intervals are the same.

52.

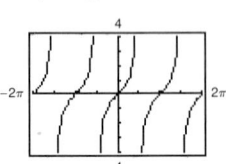

The expressions are equivalent.

54.

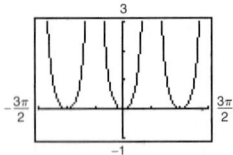

The expressions are equivalent.

55. d, $f \to 0$ as $x \to 0$.   **56.** a, $f \to 0$ as $x \to 0$.

57. b, $g \to 0$ as $x \to 0$.   **58.** c, $g \to 0$ as $x \to 0$.

60.

62.

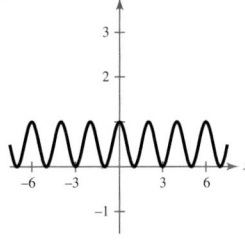

The functions are equal.   The functions are equal.

64.

66.

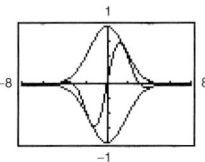

As $x \to \infty, f(x) \to 0$.   As $x \to \infty, h(x) \to 0$.

68.

70.

As $x \to 0, y \to \infty$.   As $x \to 0, f(x) \to 0$.

72.

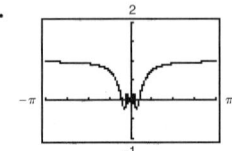

As $x \to 0, h(x)$ oscillates.

74. $d = 27 \sec x$

76.

78. (a)

(b) y approaches 0 as t increases.

80. True. $y = \sec x$ is equal to $y = 1/\cos x$, and if the reciprocal of $y = \sin x$ is translated $\pi/2$ units to the left, then

$$\frac{1}{\sin\left(x + \dfrac{\pi}{2}\right)} = \frac{1}{\cos x} = \sec x.$$

82. As x approaches π from the left, f approaches ∞. As x approaches π from the right, f approaches $-\infty$.

84.

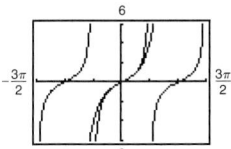

The graphs appear to coincide on the interval $-1.1 \le x \le 1.1$.

86. (a)

 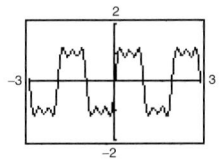

(b) $y_3 = \dfrac{4}{\pi}\left[\sin(\pi x) + \dfrac{1}{3}\sin(3\pi x) + \dfrac{1}{5}\sin(5\pi x)\right.$

$\left. + \dfrac{1}{7}\sin(7\pi x)\right]$

(c) $y_4 = \dfrac{4}{\pi}\left[\sin(\pi x) + \dfrac{1}{3}\sin(3\pi x) + \dfrac{1}{5}\sin(5\pi x)\right.$

$\left. + \dfrac{1}{7}\sin(7\pi x) + \dfrac{1}{9}\sin(9\pi x)\right]$

88. $\dfrac{1}{3}\left(\dfrac{\log_{10} 98}{\log_{10} 8}\right) \approx 0.735$

90. $\dfrac{1}{365}\left(\dfrac{\log_{10} 5}{\log_{10} 1.00041096}\right) \approx 10.732$

92. $\dfrac{14 - e^{68}}{2} \approx -1.702 \times 10^{29}$

94. $e^{10} - 4 \approx 22{,}022.466$ **96.** $\sqrt{65} \approx 8.062$

Section 4.7   *(page 328)*

2. 0   **4.** $\dfrac{\pi}{2}$ **6.** $-\dfrac{\pi}{4}$ **8.** $-\dfrac{\pi}{4}$ **10.** $\dfrac{\pi}{3}$ **12.** $\dfrac{\pi}{4}$

14. $-\dfrac{\pi}{6}$ **16.** 0   **18.** 0.47   **20.** 2.35   **22.** 1.50

24. 1.31   **26.** -0.13 **28.** 1.23   **30.** 1.91

32. -1.50 **34.** $\pi, \dfrac{2\pi}{3}, \dfrac{\sqrt{3}}{2}$

36.

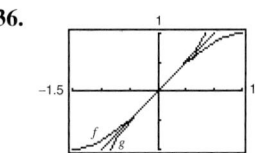

38. $\theta = \arccos\dfrac{4}{x}$

40. $\theta = \arctan\dfrac{x+1}{10}$ **42.** $\theta = \arctan\dfrac{1}{x+1},\ x \ne 1$

44. 25   **46.** -0.2 **48.** $\dfrac{\pi}{2}$ **50.** $\dfrac{5}{3}$ **52.** $\dfrac{2\sqrt{5}}{5}$

54. $-\dfrac{13}{5}$ **56.** $-\dfrac{3\sqrt{7}}{7}$ **58.** $\dfrac{8}{5}$ **60.** $\dfrac{x}{\sqrt{x^2+1}}$

62. $\sqrt{9x^2+1}$ **64.** $\dfrac{1}{\sqrt{2x-x^2}}$ **66.** x

68. $\dfrac{\sqrt{r^2-(x-h)^2}}{r}$

70.

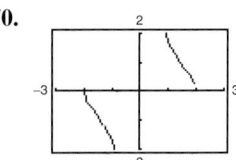

72. $\dfrac{x}{6}$ **74.** $\dfrac{\sqrt{4x-x^2}}{x-2}$

Asymptote: $x = 0$

76.

78.

80.

82.

84.

86.

88.

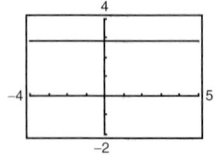

90. $5 \sin\left(\pi t + \arctan \frac{4}{3}\right)$

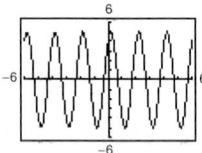

The graph implies that the identity is true.

92. (a) $\theta = \arctan \dfrac{s}{750}$ (b) $21.8°, 58.0°$

94. (a) $\theta = 32.9°$ (b) 12.94 feet

96. (a) $\theta = \arctan \dfrac{6}{x}$ (b) $40.6°, 80.5°$

98. False. $\dfrac{5\pi}{6}$ is not in the range of the arcsine.

100. Domain: $(-\infty, \infty)$

Range: $(0, \pi)$

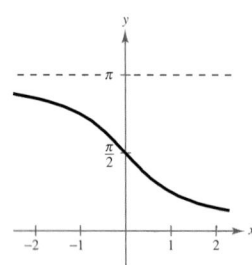

102. Domain: $(-\infty, -1] \cup [1, \infty)$

Range: $[-\pi/2, 0) \cup (0, \pi/2]$

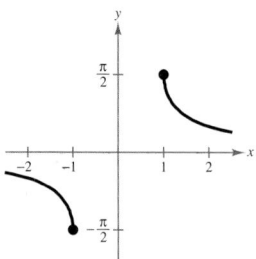

104. (a) $\dfrac{\pi}{4}$ (b) $\dfrac{\pi}{2}$ (c) 1.25 (d) 2.03

106. (a) $f \circ f^{-1}$

$f^{-1} \circ f$

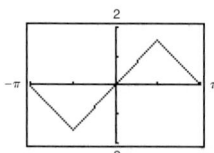

(b) The domains and ranges of the functions are restricted. The graphs of $f \circ f^{-1}$ and $f^{-1} \circ f$ differ because of the domains and ranges of f and f^{-1}.

108–112. Answers will vary.

114.

116.

118. 0.051 **120.** 2.718×10^{-8} **122.** 3 miles per hour

Section 4.8   *(page 338)*

2. $a \approx 8.82$
$b \approx 12.14$
$A = 36°$

4. $b \approx 274.27$
$c \approx 277.24$
$B = 81.6°$

6. $b \approx 24.49$
$A \approx 45.58°$
$B \approx 44.42°$

8. $a \approx 9.36$ **10.** $b \approx 30.73$
      $A \approx 81.97°$ $c \approx 33.85$
      $B \approx 8.03°$ $A = 24°48'$

12. 1.62 meters   **14.** 2.80 feet   **16.** 1648.5 feet

18. 81.2 feet   **20.** 123.5 feet

22. 56.3°   **24.** 75.97°

26. (a) 5099 feet   (b) 117.7 seconds

28. 6.8°; 2516.3 feet

30. (a) N 58° E   (b) 68.82 meters   **32.** N 56.3° W

34. 11.8 kilometers

36. ≈ 1.025 miles or ≈ 5412 feet   **38.** 52.1°   **40.** 54.7°

42. 25 inches   **44.** 9.06 centimeters

46. $a \approx 21.6$ feet, $b \approx 7.2$ feet, $c \approx 13$ feet

48. (a) $\frac{1}{2}$ (b) 10   (c) $\frac{1}{40}$

50. (a) $\frac{1}{64}$ (b) 396   (c) $\frac{1}{792}$ **52.** $d = 3\sin\left(\frac{\pi t}{3}\right)$

54. $d = 2\cos\left(\frac{\pi t}{5}\right)$ **56.** $d = \frac{7}{4}\cos\frac{\pi t}{5}$

58. False. The tower is leaning, so it is not perfectly vertical and does not form a right angle with the ground.

60. (a)

θ	L_1	L_2	$L_1 + L_2$
0.1	$\frac{2}{\sin 0.1}$	$\frac{3}{\cos 0.1}$	23.0
0.2	$\frac{2}{\sin 0.2}$	$\frac{3}{\cos 0.2}$	13.1
0.3	$\frac{2}{\sin 0.3}$	$\frac{3}{\cos 0.3}$	9.9
0.4	$\frac{2}{\sin 0.4}$	$\frac{3}{\cos 0.4}$	8.4

(b)

θ	L_1	L_2	$L_1 + L_2$
0.5	$\frac{2}{\sin 0.5}$	$\frac{3}{\cos 0.5}$	7.6
0.6	$\frac{2}{\sin 0.6}$	$\frac{3}{\cos 0.6}$	7.2
0.7	$\frac{2}{\sin 0.7}$	$\frac{3}{\cos 0.7}$	7.0
0.8	$\frac{2}{\sin 0.8}$	$\frac{3}{\cos 0.8}$	7.1

7.0 (minimum length)

(c) $L = L_1 + L_2 = \frac{2}{\sin\theta} + \frac{3}{\cos\theta}$

(d)   7.0 (minimum length)

62. (a)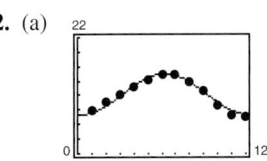

(b) 12. Yes. One period is 1 year.

(c) 1.41. 1.41 represents the maximum change in time from the average time ($d = 18.09$) of sunset.

64. No. N 24° E means 24 degrees east of north.

66.   **68.**

70.   **72.**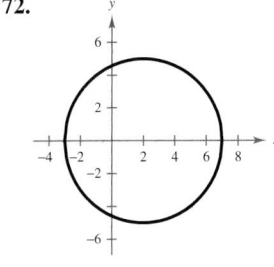

Review Exercises *(page 344)*

2. 2 radians   **4.** -3.5 radians

6.   **8.**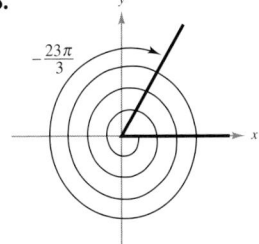

$\frac{20\pi}{9}, -\frac{16\pi}{9}$ $\frac{\pi}{3}, -\frac{17\pi}{3}$

CHAPTER 4

10.

12.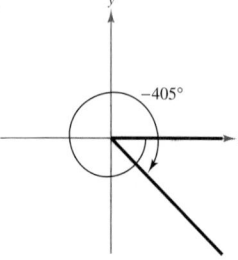

$640°, -80°$

$315°, -45°$

14. $-330.00°$ **16.** $326.59°$ **18.** -2.2253

20. 3.4432 **22.** 212.1 inches per second

24. $\left(-\dfrac{\sqrt{2}}{2}, \dfrac{\sqrt{2}}{2}\right)$ **26.** $\left(-\dfrac{1}{2}, \dfrac{\sqrt{3}}{2}\right)$

28. $\sin \dfrac{\pi}{4} = \dfrac{\sqrt{2}}{2}$ $\csc \dfrac{\pi}{4} = \sqrt{2}$

$\cos \dfrac{\pi}{4} = \dfrac{\sqrt{2}}{2}$ $\sec \dfrac{\pi}{4} = \sqrt{2}$

$\tan \dfrac{\pi}{4} = 1$ $\cot \dfrac{\pi}{4} = 1$

30. $\sin 2\pi = 0$ $\csc 2\pi$ is undefined.

$\cos 2\pi = 1$ $\sec 2\pi = 1$

$\tan 2\pi = 0$ $\csc 2\pi$ is undefined.

32. $\cos 4\pi = \cos 0 = 1$

34. $\cos\left(-\dfrac{13\pi}{3}\right) = \cos \dfrac{5\pi}{3} = \dfrac{1}{2}$ **36.** -1.14 **38.** -0.34

40. $\sin \theta = \dfrac{\sqrt{2}}{2}$ $\csc \theta = \sqrt{2}$

$\cos \theta = \dfrac{\sqrt{2}}{2}$ $\sec \theta = \sqrt{2}$

$\tan \theta = 1$ $\cot \theta = 1$

42. $\sin \theta = \dfrac{5}{9}$ $\csc \theta = \dfrac{9}{5}$

$\cos \theta = \dfrac{2\sqrt{14}}{9}$ $\sec \theta = \dfrac{9\sqrt{14}}{28}$

$\tan \theta = \dfrac{5\sqrt{14}}{28}$ $\cot \theta = \dfrac{2\sqrt{14}}{5}$

44. (a) $\dfrac{1}{4}$ (b) $\sqrt{17}$ (c) $\dfrac{\sqrt{17}}{17}$ (d) $\dfrac{\sqrt{17}}{4}$

46. (a) $\dfrac{1}{5}$ (b) $2\sqrt{6}$ (c) $\dfrac{\sqrt{6}}{12}$ (d) 5 **48.** 5.24

50. 5.39 **52.** 0.20 **54.** 19.5 feet

56. $\sin \theta = -\dfrac{4}{5}$ $\csc \theta = -\dfrac{5}{4}$

$\cos \theta = \dfrac{3}{5}$ $\sec \theta = \dfrac{5}{3}$

$\tan \theta = -\dfrac{4}{3}$ $\cot \theta = -\dfrac{3}{4}$

58. $\sin \theta = -\dfrac{\sqrt{26}}{26}$ $\csc \theta = -\sqrt{26}$

$\cos \theta = -\dfrac{5\sqrt{26}}{26}$ $\sec \theta = -\dfrac{\sqrt{26}}{5}$

$\tan \theta = \dfrac{1}{5}$ $\cot \theta = 5$

60. $\sin \theta = 0.8$ $\csc \theta = 1.25$

$\cos \theta = 0.6$ $\sec \theta \approx 1.67$

$\tan \theta \approx 1.33$ $\cot \theta = 0.75$

62. $\sin \theta = -\dfrac{3\sqrt{13}}{13}$ $\csc \theta = -\dfrac{\sqrt{13}}{3}$

$\cos \theta = -\dfrac{2\sqrt{13}}{13}$ $\sec \theta = -\dfrac{\sqrt{13}}{2}$

$\tan \theta = \dfrac{3}{2}$ $\cot \theta = \dfrac{2}{3}$

64. $\sin \theta = \dfrac{2}{3}$ **66.** $\sin \theta = -\dfrac{5\sqrt{41}}{41}$

$\cos \theta = -\dfrac{\sqrt{5}}{3}$ $\cos \theta = -\dfrac{4\sqrt{41}}{41}$

$\tan \theta = -\dfrac{2\sqrt{5}}{5}$ $\csc \theta = -\dfrac{\sqrt{41}}{5}$

$\sec \theta = -\dfrac{3\sqrt{5}}{5}$ $\sec \theta = -\dfrac{\sqrt{41}}{4}$

$\cot \theta = -\dfrac{\sqrt{5}}{2}$ $\cot \theta = \dfrac{4}{5}$

68. $\cos \theta = \dfrac{\sqrt{3}}{2}$ $\sec \theta = \dfrac{2\sqrt{3}}{3}$

$\tan \theta = -\dfrac{\sqrt{3}}{3}$ $\cot \theta = -\sqrt{3}$

$\csc \theta = -2$

70. $\sin \dfrac{\pi}{4} = \dfrac{\sqrt{2}}{2}$; $\cos \dfrac{\pi}{4} = \dfrac{\sqrt{2}}{2}$; $\tan \dfrac{\pi}{4} = 1$

72. $\sin\left(-\dfrac{5\pi}{4}\right) = \dfrac{\sqrt{2}}{2}$; $\cos\left(-\dfrac{5\pi}{4}\right) = -\dfrac{\sqrt{2}}{2}$;

$\tan\left(-\dfrac{5\pi}{4}\right) = -1$

74. $\sin(-150°) = -\dfrac{1}{2}$; $\cos(-150°) = -\dfrac{\sqrt{3}}{2}$;

$\tan(-150°) = \dfrac{\sqrt{3}}{3}$

76. $\sin 315° = -\dfrac{\sqrt{2}}{2}$; $\cos 315° = \dfrac{\sqrt{2}}{2}$; $\tan 315° = -1$

78. -0.14 **80.** 0.09 **82.** 4.38

84.

86.

88.

90.

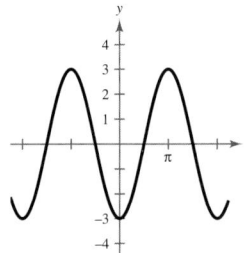

92. $y = 2 \cos 528\pi x$

94.

96.

98.

100.

102.

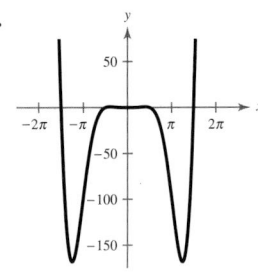

104. $-\dfrac{\pi}{2}$ **106.** 0.21

108. 1.10   **110.** $\dfrac{\pi}{4}$

112. $\dfrac{\pi}{6}$ **114.** 2.66

116. 1.17   **118.** 1.56

120. 1.45   **122.** 0.25

124. π **126.** $\dfrac{4}{3}$

128. $-\dfrac{5}{12}$

130. 9.6 feet   **132.** $d = 0.75 \cos\left(\dfrac{2\pi t}{3}\right)$

134. False. The inverse sine, $y = \arcsin x$, cannot be defined as a function over any interval that is greater than the interval defined as $-\pi/2 \le x \le \pi/2$.

136. False. $3\pi/4$ is not in the range of the arctangent function.

137. d; The period is 2π and the amplitude is 3.

138. a; The period is 2π and, because $a < 0$, the graph is reflected in the x-axis.

139. b; The period is 2 and the amplitude is 2.

140. c; The period is 4π and the amplitude is 2.

142. (a)

θ	0.1	0.4	0.7
$\tan\left(\theta - \dfrac{\pi}{2}\right)$	-9.9666	-2.3652	-1.1872
$-\cot\theta$	-9.9666	-2.3652	-1.1872

θ	1.0	1.3
$\tan\left(\theta - \dfrac{\pi}{2}\right)$	-0.6421	-0.2776
$-\cot\theta$	-0.6421	-0.2776

(b) $\tan\left(\theta - \dfrac{\pi}{2}\right) = -\cot\theta$

144. (a) The displacement is increased.

(b) The friction damps the oscillations more rapidly.

(c) The frequency of the oscillations increases.

146. Answers will vary.

Problem Solving   *(page 350)*

2. Gear 1: $270°, \dfrac{3\pi}{2}$ radians

Gear 2: $\approx 332.3°, \dfrac{24\pi}{13}$ radians

Gear 3: $\approx 392.7°, \dfrac{24\pi}{11}$ radians

Gear 4: $450°, \dfrac{5\pi}{2}$ radians

Gear 5: $\approx 454.7°, \dfrac{48\pi}{19}$ radians

4. (a) Answers will vary.

(b) The ratios are equal.   (c) No; No

(d) Yes, because all six trigonometric functions are ratios of right triangles.

6. (a) $h(x)$ is even.   (b) $h(x)$ is even.

8. (a)

(b)

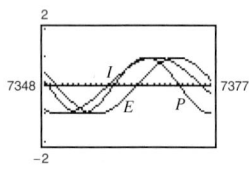

(c) $P(7369) = 0.631$

$E(7369) = 0.901$

$I(7369) = 0.945$

10. (a) 3.35, 7.35

(b) -0.65

(c) Yes. There is a difference of nine periods between the values.

12. (a) $40.5°$

(b) $x \approx 1.71$ feet; $y \approx 3.46$ feet

(c) ≈ 1.75 feet

(d) As you move closer to the rock, d must get smaller and smaller. The angles θ_1 and θ_2 will decrease along with the distance y, so d will decrease

Chapter 5

Section 5.1   *(page 359)*

2. $\sin x = -\dfrac{1}{2}$

$\csc x = -2$

$\sec x = -\dfrac{2\sqrt{3}}{3}$

$\cot x = \sqrt{3}$

4. $\sin \theta = \dfrac{3}{5}$

$\cos \theta = \dfrac{4}{5}$

$\sec \theta = \dfrac{5}{4}$

$\cot \theta = \dfrac{4}{3}$

6. $\cos \phi = -\dfrac{3\sqrt{10}}{10}$

$\tan \phi = -\dfrac{1}{3}$

$\csc \phi = \sqrt{10}$

$\sec \phi = -\dfrac{\sqrt{10}}{3}$

8. $\sin x = \dfrac{3}{5}$

$\tan x = \dfrac{3}{4}$

$\csc x = \dfrac{5}{3}$

$\sec x = \dfrac{5}{4}$

$\cot x = \dfrac{4}{3}$

10. $\sin x = \dfrac{\sqrt{15}}{4}$

$\cos x = \dfrac{1}{4}$

$\tan x = \sqrt{15}$

$\csc x = \dfrac{4\sqrt{15}}{15}$

$\cot x = \dfrac{\sqrt{15}}{15}$

12. $\sin \theta = -\dfrac{1}{5}$

$\cos \theta = -\dfrac{2\sqrt{6}}{5}$

$\tan \theta = \dfrac{\sqrt{6}}{12}$

$\sec \theta = -\dfrac{5\sqrt{6}}{12}$

$\cot \theta = 2\sqrt{6}$

14. $\sin \theta = 1$

$\cos \theta = 0$

$\csc \theta = 1$

$\sec \theta$ is undefined.

$\cot \theta = 0$

15. d   **16.** a   **17.** b   **18.** f   **19.** e   **20.** c

21. b   **22.** c   **23.** f   **24.** a   **25.** e   **26.** d

28. $\sin \beta$ **30.** 1   **32.** $\cot \theta$ **34.** $\cos^2 x$

36. $\sin^2 \theta$ **38.** $\sin x$ **40.** $\sec t$ **42.** $2 \sec \phi$

44. $\csc \theta \sec \theta$ **46.** $\cos^2 x$ **48.** 1   **50.** $\cos x + 2$

52. $\sin^4 x$ **54.** $\sec^2 x + \tan^2 x$ **56.** $\tan^2 x(\sec x - 1)$

58. -1 **60.** $9 \cos^2 x$ **62.** $-2 \cot^2 x$ **64.** $-\cot x$

66. $5(\sec x - \tan x)$ **68.** $\tan^4 x(\csc x - 1)$

70.

x	0.2	0.4	0.6	0.8	1.0
y_1	0.0403	0.1646	0.3863	0.7386	1.3105
y_2	0.0403	0.1646	0.3863	0.7386	1.3105

x	1.2	1.4
y_1	2.3973	5.7135
y_2	2.3973	5.7135

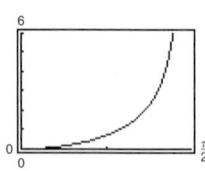

$y_1 = y_2$

72.

x	0.2	0.4	0.6	0.8	1.0
y_1	0.0428	0.2107	0.6871	2.1841	8.3087
y_2	0.0428	0.2107	0.6871	2.1841	8.3087

x	1.2	1.4
y_1	50.3869	1163.6143
y_2	50.3869	1163.6143

$y_1 = y_2$

74. $\cot x$ **76.** $\sec \theta$ **78.** $8 \sin \theta$ **80.** $2 \tan \theta$

82. $10 \sec \theta$ **84.** $6 \cos \theta = 3$; $\sin \theta = \pm\dfrac{\sqrt{3}}{2}$; $\cos \theta = \dfrac{1}{2}$

86. $10 \sin \theta = -5\sqrt{3}$; $\sin \theta = -\dfrac{\sqrt{3}}{2}$; $\cos \theta = \dfrac{1}{2}$

88. $\dfrac{\pi}{2} \le \theta \le \dfrac{3\pi}{2}$ **90.** $0 < \theta < \pi$ **92.** $\ln|\tan x|$

94. 0 **96.** (a) $(\tan 346°)^2 + 1 = (\sec 346°)^2 \approx 1.0622$

(b) $(\tan 3.1)^2 + 1 = (\sec 3.1)^2 \approx 1.0017$

98. (a) $\sin(-250°) = -\sin 250° \approx 0.9397$

(b) $\sin\left(-\tfrac{1}{2}\right) = -\sin\left(\tfrac{1}{2}\right) \approx -0.4794$

100. Answers will vary.

102. False. A cofunction identity can be used to transform a tangent function so that it can be represented by a cotangent function.

104. $1, 1$ **106.** $0, -\infty$

108. Not an identity because $\cot \theta = \pm\sqrt{\csc^2 \theta - 1}$

110. Not an identity because $\dfrac{5}{\cos \theta} \ne \dfrac{1}{5 \cos \theta}$

112. An identity because $\sin \theta(\cos^2 \theta + \sin^2 \theta) = \sin \theta$

114. Answers will vary. For example:

$$\dfrac{\sin^2 \theta + \cos^2 \theta}{\cos^2 \theta} = \dfrac{1}{\cos^2 \theta} \Longrightarrow \tan^2 \theta + 1 = \sec^2 \theta$$

$$\dfrac{\sin^2 \theta + \cos^2 \theta}{\sin^2 \theta} = \dfrac{1}{\sin^2 \theta} \Longrightarrow 1 + \cot^2 \theta = \csc^2 \theta$$

116. $4z + 12\sqrt{z} + 9$

118. $\dfrac{3(2x + 1)}{x - 4}$ **120.** $\dfrac{x(x^2 + 5x + 1)}{x^2 - 25}$

Section 5.2   *(page 367)*

2–40. Answers will vary.

42. Identity   **44.** Not an identity   **46.** Identity

48. Identity   **50.** Not an identity   **52.** Identity

54. 1 **56.** 2

58. (a) Answers will vary.

(b)

θ	10°	20°	30°	40°	50°
s	28.36	13.74	8.66	5.96	4.20

θ	60°	70°	80°	90°
s	2.89	1.82	0.88	0

(c) Greatest: 10°; Least: 90°

(d) Noon

60. True. An identity is an equation that is true for all real values in the domain of the variable.

62. The equation is not an identity because $\tan \theta = \pm\sqrt{\sec^2 \theta - 1}$.

Possible answer: $\dfrac{3\pi}{4}$

64. $-21 - 20i$

66. $-9 + 46i$ **68.** $\dfrac{-5 \pm \sqrt{3}i}{2}$ **70.** $\dfrac{1 \pm \sqrt{5}i}{4}$

Section 5.3   *(page 376)*

2–6. Answers will vary.   **8.** $\dfrac{7\pi}{6} + 2n\pi, \dfrac{11\pi}{6} + 2n\pi$

10. $\dfrac{2\pi}{3} + n\pi$ **12.** $\dfrac{\pi}{3} + n\pi, \dfrac{2\pi}{3} + n\pi$

14. $\dfrac{\pi}{6} + n\pi, \dfrac{5\pi}{6} + n\pi, \dfrac{\pi}{3} + n\pi, \dfrac{2\pi}{3} + n\pi$

16. $\dfrac{\pi}{3} + n\pi, \dfrac{2\pi}{3} + n\pi$ **18.** $\dfrac{\pi}{9} + \dfrac{n\pi}{3}, \dfrac{2\pi}{9} + \dfrac{n\pi}{3}$

20. $\dfrac{\pi}{4} + \dfrac{n\pi}{2}, \dfrac{2\pi}{3} + 2n\pi, \dfrac{4\pi}{3} + 2n\pi$

22. $0, \pi$ **24.** $\dfrac{\pi}{2}, \dfrac{3\pi}{2}, \dfrac{2\pi}{3}, \dfrac{4\pi}{3}$ **26.** $\dfrac{\pi}{3}, \dfrac{5\pi}{3}$ **28.** 0

30. $\dfrac{7\pi}{6}, \dfrac{3\pi}{2}, \dfrac{11\pi}{6}$ **32.** $\dfrac{\pi}{3}, \dfrac{5\pi}{3}$ **34.** $\dfrac{2\pi}{3} + n\pi, \dfrac{5\pi}{6} + n\pi$

36. $\dfrac{\pi}{12} + \dfrac{n\pi}{2}, \dfrac{5\pi}{12} + \dfrac{n\pi}{2}$ **38.** $\dfrac{8\pi}{3} + 4n\pi, \dfrac{10\pi}{3} + 4n\pi$

40. $\dfrac{3}{4} + 4n$ **42.** $-2 + 8n, 2 + 8n$

CHAPTER 5

44. $-5, 4$; No solution

46. 0.7854, 2.3562, 3.6652, 3.9270, 5.4978, 5.7596

48. 0.5236, 2.6180   **50.** 4.9172

52. 0.5153, 2.7259, 3.6569, 5.8675

54. 0.5236, 0.7297, 2.4119, 2.6180

56. 0.5880, 2.0344, 3.7296, 5.1760   **58.** 1.7794, 4.5038

60. $\arctan(-2) + \pi$, $\arctan(-2) + 2\pi$, $\dfrac{\pi}{4}$, $\dfrac{5\pi}{4}$ **62.** $\dfrac{\pi}{6}$, $\dfrac{5\pi}{6}$

64. (a)

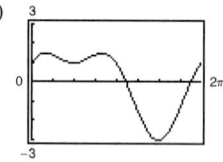

(b) $\dfrac{\pi}{6} \approx 0.5236$

$\dfrac{\pi}{2} \approx 1.5708$

$\dfrac{5\pi}{6} \approx 2.618$

$\dfrac{3\pi}{2} \approx 4.712$

Maximum: $(0.5236, 1.5)$

Maximum: $(2.6180, 1.5)$

Minimum: $(1.5708, 1)$

Minimum: $(4.7124, -3)$

66. 0.739

68. (a) All real numbers $x \neq 0$

(b) y-axis symmetry

(c) y approaches 1.

(d) Four solutions: $\pm\pi$, $\pm 2\pi$

70.

1.96 seconds

72. 36.9°, 53.1°

74. (a)

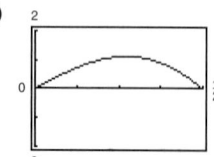

(b) $0.6 < x < 1.1$

$A \approx 1.12$

76. (a) $\dfrac{10}{3}$

(b)

For $3.5 \le x \le 6$, the approximation appears to be good.

(c) 3.46, 8.81

3.46 is close to the zero of f in the interval $[0, 6]$.

78. False. There is no value of x for which $\sin x = 3.4$.

80. 3

82. $C = 19°$

$a \approx 15.4$

$c \approx 5.0$

84. $\sin 570° = -\dfrac{1}{2}$ **86.** $\sin(-1410°) = \dfrac{1}{2}$

$\cos 570° = -\dfrac{\sqrt{3}}{2}$ $\cos(-1410°) = \dfrac{\sqrt{3}}{2}$

$\tan 570° = \dfrac{\sqrt{3}}{3}$ $\tan(-1410°) = \dfrac{\sqrt{3}}{3}$

88. 30 feet

Section 5.4   (page 384)

2. (a) $-\dfrac{\sqrt{6} + \sqrt{2}}{4}$ (b) $\dfrac{\sqrt{2} + 1}{2}$

4. (a) 0   (b) $\dfrac{\sqrt{3} - 1}{2}$

6. (a) $\dfrac{\sqrt{6} + \sqrt{2}}{4}$ (b) $\dfrac{\sqrt{2} - \sqrt{3}}{2}$

8. $\sin 165° = \dfrac{\sqrt{2}}{4}(\sqrt{3} - 1)$

$\cos 165° = -\dfrac{\sqrt{2}}{4}(\sqrt{3} + 1)$

$\tan 165° = -2 + \sqrt{3}$

10. $\sin 255° = -\dfrac{\sqrt{2}}{4}(\sqrt{3} + 1)$

$\cos 255° = \dfrac{\sqrt{2}}{4}(1 - \sqrt{3})$

$\tan 255° = 2 + \sqrt{3}$

12. $\sin \dfrac{7\pi}{12} = \dfrac{\sqrt{2}}{4}(\sqrt{3} + 1)$

$\cos \dfrac{7\pi}{12} = \dfrac{\sqrt{2}}{4}(1 - \sqrt{3})$

$\tan \dfrac{7\pi}{12} = -2 - \sqrt{3}$

14. $\sin\left(-\dfrac{\pi}{12}\right) = \dfrac{\sqrt{2}}{4}(1 - \sqrt{3})$

$\cos\left(-\dfrac{\pi}{12}\right) = \dfrac{\sqrt{2}}{4}(\sqrt{3} + 1)$

$\tan\left(-\dfrac{\pi}{12}\right) = -2 + \sqrt{3}$

16. $\sin(-105°) = -\dfrac{\sqrt{2}}{4}\left(\sqrt{3}+1\right)$

$\cos(-105°) = \dfrac{\sqrt{2}}{4}\left(1-\sqrt{3}\right)$

$\tan(-105°) = 2+\sqrt{3}$

18. $\sin 15° = \dfrac{\sqrt{2}}{4}\left(\sqrt{3}-1\right)$

$\cos 15° = \dfrac{\sqrt{2}}{4}\left(1+\sqrt{3}\right)$

$\tan 15° = 2-\sqrt{3}$

20. $\sin\left(-\dfrac{7\pi}{12}\right) = -\dfrac{\sqrt{2}}{4}\left(\sqrt{3}+1\right)$

$\cos\left(-\dfrac{7\pi}{12}\right) = \dfrac{\sqrt{2}}{4}\left(1-\sqrt{3}\right)$

$\tan\left(-\dfrac{7\pi}{12}\right) = 2+\sqrt{3}$

22. $\sin\dfrac{5\pi}{12} = \dfrac{\sqrt{2}}{4}\left(1+\sqrt{3}\right)$

$\cos\dfrac{5\pi}{12} = \dfrac{\sqrt{2}}{4}\left(\sqrt{3}-1\right)$

$\tan\dfrac{5\pi}{12} = \sqrt{3}+2$

24. $\sin 190°$ **26.** $\tan 80°$ **28.** $\cos\dfrac{12\pi}{35}$

30. $\cos(3x-2y)$ **32.** $\dfrac{\sqrt{2}}{2}$ **34.** $\dfrac{\sqrt{2}}{2}$ **36.** $\dfrac{\sqrt{3}}{3}$

38. $\dfrac{56}{65}$ **40.** $-\dfrac{33}{65}$ **42.** $\dfrac{65}{33}$ **44.** $-\dfrac{16}{63}$ **46.** $\dfrac{4}{5}$

48. $\dfrac{117}{44}$ **50.** $-\dfrac{125}{44}$ **52.** $\dfrac{2x^2-\sqrt{1-x^2}}{\sqrt{4x^2+1}}$

54. $\dfrac{x+x\sqrt{1-x^2}}{\sqrt{x^2+1}}$ **56–64.** Answers will vary.

66. $-\cos x$ **68.** $\tan\theta$ **70.** $\dfrac{\pi}{3}, \dfrac{5\pi}{3}$

72. $0, \dfrac{\pi}{3}, \pi, \dfrac{5\pi}{3}$ **74.** $0, \pi$ **76.** Answers will vary.

78. False. $\cos(u\pm v) = \cos u\cos v \mp \sin u\sin v$

80. True.

$\sin\left(x-\dfrac{\pi}{2}\right) = \sin x\cos\dfrac{\pi}{2} - \cos x\sin\dfrac{\pi}{2} = -\cos x$

82. Answers will vary.   **84.** Answers will vary.

86. (a) $5\sin(2\theta+0.9273)$ (b) $5\cos(2\theta-0.6435)$

88. (a) $\sqrt{2}\sin\left(2\theta-\dfrac{\pi}{4}\right)$ (b) $\sqrt{2}\cos\left(2\theta+\dfrac{\pi}{4}\right)$

90. $-\dfrac{5\sqrt{2}}{2}\sin\theta - \dfrac{5\sqrt{2}}{2}\cos\theta$ **92.** $15°$ **94.** $u+v=w$

96. Answers will vary.   **98.** $f^{-1}(x) = -8x+7$

100. $f^{-1}(x) = x^2+16$ **102.** $3x^2$ **104.** x^2+10x

Section 5.5   *(page 394)*

2. $\dfrac{1}{4}$ **4.** $\dfrac{8}{17}$ **6.** $\dfrac{17}{15}$ **8.** $\dfrac{15}{8}$

10. $\dfrac{\pi}{2}, \dfrac{7\pi}{6}, \dfrac{3\pi}{2}, \dfrac{11\pi}{6}$ **12.** $\dfrac{\pi}{2}, \dfrac{3\pi}{2}, \dfrac{\pi}{4}, \dfrac{3\pi}{4}, \dfrac{5\pi}{4}, \dfrac{7\pi}{4}$

14. $\dfrac{\pi}{2}, \dfrac{7\pi}{6}, \dfrac{11\pi}{6}$ **16.** $\dfrac{\pi}{6}, \dfrac{\pi}{2}, \dfrac{5\pi}{6}, \dfrac{3\pi}{2}$

18. $0, \dfrac{\pi}{4}, \dfrac{\pi}{2}, \dfrac{3\pi}{4}, \pi, \dfrac{5\pi}{4}, \dfrac{3\pi}{2}, \dfrac{7\pi}{4}$

20. $3\cos 2x$ **22.** $\cos 2x$

24. $\sin 2u = -\dfrac{4\sqrt{5}}{9}$ **26.** $\sin 2u = -\dfrac{8}{17}$

$\cos 2u = -\dfrac{1}{9}$ $\cos 2u = \dfrac{15}{17}$

$\tan 2u = 4\sqrt{5}$ $\tan 2u = -\dfrac{8}{15}$

28. $\sin 2u = -\dfrac{4\sqrt{2}}{9}$

$\cos 2u = \dfrac{7}{9}$

$\tan 2u = -\dfrac{4\sqrt{2}}{7}$

30. $\dfrac{1}{128}(35 - 48\cos 2x + 28\cos 4x - 16\cos 2x\cos 4x + \cos 8x)$

32. $\dfrac{1}{128}(3 - 4\cos 4x + \cos 8x)$

34. $\dfrac{1}{16}(1 - \cos 2x - \cos 4x + \cos 2x\cos 4x)$

36. $\dfrac{\sqrt{17}}{17}$ **38.** $\dfrac{\sqrt{17}}{4}$ **40.** 4

42. $\sin 165° = \dfrac{1}{2}\sqrt{2-\sqrt{3}}$

$\cos 165° = -\dfrac{1}{2}\sqrt{2+\sqrt{3}}$

$\tan 165° = \sqrt{3}-2$

44. $\sin 67°\,30' = \dfrac{1}{2}\sqrt{2+\sqrt{2}}$

$\cos 67°\,30' = \dfrac{1}{2}\sqrt{2-\sqrt{2}}$

$\tan 67°\,30' = 1+\sqrt{2}$

46. $\sin\dfrac{\pi}{12} = \dfrac{1}{2}\sqrt{2-\sqrt{3}}$

$\cos\dfrac{\pi}{12} = \dfrac{1}{2}\sqrt{2+\sqrt{3}}$

$\tan\dfrac{\pi}{12} = 2-\sqrt{3}$

CHAPTER 5

48. $\sin \dfrac{7\pi}{12} = \dfrac{1}{2}\sqrt{2+\sqrt{3}}$

$\cos \dfrac{7\pi}{12} = -\dfrac{1}{2}\sqrt{2-\sqrt{3}}$

$\tan \dfrac{7\pi}{12} = -2-\sqrt{3}$

50. $\sin \dfrac{u}{2} = \dfrac{\sqrt{5}}{5}$

$\cos \dfrac{u}{2} = \dfrac{2\sqrt{5}}{5}$

$\tan \dfrac{u}{2} = \dfrac{1}{2}$

52. $\sin \dfrac{u}{2} = \dfrac{1}{2}\sqrt{\dfrac{10+3\sqrt{10}}{5}}$

$\cos \dfrac{u}{2} = -\dfrac{1}{2}\sqrt{\dfrac{10-3\sqrt{10}}{5}}$

$\tan \dfrac{u}{2} = -3-\sqrt{10}$

54. $\sin \dfrac{u}{2} = \dfrac{3\sqrt{14}}{14}$

$\cos \dfrac{u}{2} = \dfrac{\sqrt{70}}{14}$

$\tan \dfrac{u}{2} = \dfrac{3\sqrt{5}}{5}$

56. $|\cos 2x|$ **58.** $-\left|\sin\left(\dfrac{x-1}{2}\right)\right|$

60. $0, \dfrac{\pi}{3}, \dfrac{5\pi}{3}$

62. $0, \dfrac{\pi}{2}, \dfrac{3\pi}{2}$

64. $2\left(\sin \dfrac{7\pi}{6} + \sin \dfrac{\pi}{2}\right)$

66. $\dfrac{3}{2}[\cos(\alpha) - \cos 5\alpha]$ **68.** $\dfrac{1}{2}(\cos 2\theta + \cos 6\theta)$

70. $\dfrac{1}{2}(\sin 2x + \sin 2y)$ **72.** $\dfrac{1}{2}(\cos 2\pi - \cos 2\theta)$

74. $3(\sin 60° + \sin 30°)$ **76.** $2\cos 75° \cos 45°$

78. $2\cos \pi \sin \dfrac{\pi}{4}$ **80.** $2\sin 2\theta \cos \theta$

82. $2\sin 3x \cos 2x$ **84.** $2\cos(\phi + \pi)\cos \pi$

86. $2\sin x \cos \dfrac{\pi}{2}$

88. $0, \dfrac{\pi}{4}, \dfrac{\pi}{2}, \dfrac{3\pi}{4}, \pi, \dfrac{5\pi}{4}, \dfrac{3\pi}{2}, \dfrac{7\pi}{4}$

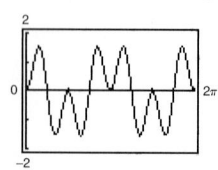

90. $0, \dfrac{\pi}{2}, \pi, \dfrac{3\pi}{2}, \dfrac{\pi}{4}, \dfrac{3\pi}{4}, \dfrac{5\pi}{4}, \dfrac{7\pi}{4}$

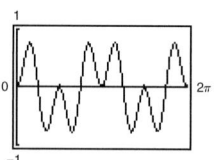

92. $\dfrac{144}{169}$ **94.** $\dfrac{36}{65}$

96–110. Answers will vary.

112.   **114.**

116.

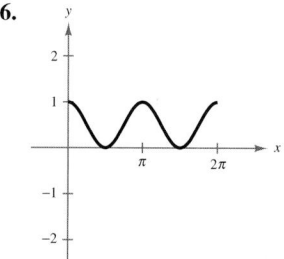

118. $2x^2 - 1$

120. $r = \dfrac{1}{16} v_0{}^2 \sin \theta \cos \theta$ **122.** $x = 2r(1 - \cos \theta)$

124. False. $\sin \dfrac{u}{2} = \sqrt{\dfrac{1-\cos u}{2}}$ when $\dfrac{u}{2}$ is in the second quadrant.

126. (a)

Minima: $\left(\dfrac{\pi}{2}, -3\right)$, $\left(\dfrac{3\pi}{2}, 1\right)$

Maxima: $\left(\dfrac{7\pi}{6}, \dfrac{3}{2}\right)$, $\left(\dfrac{11\pi}{6}, \dfrac{3}{2}\right)$

(b) $\dfrac{\pi}{2}, \dfrac{7\pi}{6}, \dfrac{3\pi}{2}, \dfrac{11\pi}{6}$

128. (a)

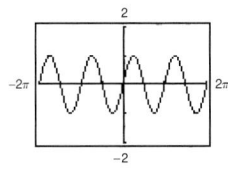

130. ≈ 15.7 gallons

(b) $g(x) = \sin 2x$

(c) Answers will vary.

Review Exercises   *(page 399)*

2. $\csc x$ **4.** $\cot x$ **6.** $|\sec x|$

8. $\sin \theta = \dfrac{2\sqrt{13}}{13}$ **10.** $\cos \theta = \dfrac{1}{9}$

$\cos \theta = \dfrac{3\sqrt{13}}{13}$ $\tan \theta = 4\sqrt{5}$

$\csc \theta = \dfrac{\sqrt{13}}{2}$ $\csc \theta = \dfrac{9\sqrt{5}}{20}$

$\cot \theta = \dfrac{3}{2}$ $\sec \theta = 9$

$\cot \theta = \dfrac{\sqrt{5}}{20}$

12. $\sec \theta \csc \theta$ **14.** $\cos^2 x$ **16.** $\tan u \sec u$ **18.** 1

20. $2 \tan^2 x - 2 \sec x \tan x + 1$ **22.** $1 + \sin x$

24–32. Answers will vary.

34. $\dfrac{\pi}{3} + 2n\pi, \dfrac{5\pi}{3} + 2n\pi$ **36.** $\dfrac{\pi}{3} + 2n\pi, \dfrac{5\pi}{3} + 2n\pi$

38. $\dfrac{\pi}{6} + n\pi, \dfrac{5\pi}{6} + n\pi$ **40.** $\dfrac{\pi}{6}, \dfrac{\pi}{2}, \dfrac{5\pi}{6}$ **42.** 0

44. $0, \dfrac{\pi}{3}, \dfrac{2\pi}{3}, \pi, \dfrac{4\pi}{3}, \dfrac{5\pi}{3}$ **46.** No solution   **48.** $\dfrac{\pi}{2}, \dfrac{3\pi}{2}$

50. $\dfrac{3\pi}{4}, \dfrac{7\pi}{4}, \arctan(-5) + \pi, \arctan(-5) + 2\pi$

52. $\sin 345° = \dfrac{\sqrt{2}}{4}\left(1 - \sqrt{3}\right)$

$\cos 345° = \dfrac{\sqrt{2}}{4}\left(1 + \sqrt{3}\right)$

$\tan 345° = -2 + \sqrt{3}$

54. $\sin \dfrac{19\pi}{12} = -\dfrac{\sqrt{2}}{4}\left(\sqrt{3} + 1\right)$

$\cos \dfrac{19\pi}{12} = \dfrac{\sqrt{2}}{4}\left(\sqrt{3} - 1\right)$

$\tan \dfrac{19\pi}{12} = -2 - \sqrt{3}$

56. $\cos 165°$ **58.** $\tan(-47°)$ **60.** $\dfrac{960 + 507\sqrt{7}}{1121}$

62. $\dfrac{12\sqrt{7} - 15}{52}$ **64.** $\dfrac{-960 + 507\sqrt{7}}{1121}$ **66.** $\dfrac{3\pi}{2}$

68. $0, \pi$

70.

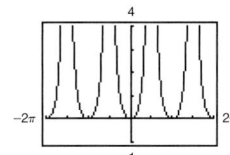

72. $\sin 2u = -\dfrac{4}{5}$

$\cos 2u = \dfrac{3}{5}$

$\tan 2u = -\dfrac{4}{3}$

74. $\theta \approx 40°$ **76.** $\dfrac{1 + \cos 6x}{2}$ **78.** $\dfrac{1 - \cos 2x}{2}$

80. $\sin 15° = \dfrac{1}{2}\sqrt{2 - \sqrt{3}}$

$\cos 15° = \dfrac{1}{2}\sqrt{2 + \sqrt{3}}$

$\tan 15° = 2 - \sqrt{3}$

82. $\sin\left(-\dfrac{17\pi}{12}\right) = \dfrac{1}{2}\sqrt{2 + \sqrt{3}}$

$\cos\left(-\dfrac{17\pi}{12}\right) = -\dfrac{1}{2}\sqrt{2 - \sqrt{3}}$

$\tan\left(-\dfrac{17\pi}{12}\right) = -2 - \sqrt{3}$

84. $\tan 3x$

86. (a) $V = \sin \dfrac{\theta}{2} \cos \dfrac{\theta}{2}$ cubic meters

(b) $V = \dfrac{1}{2} \sin \theta$ cubic meters

Volume is maximum when $\theta = \pi/2$.

88. $3[\cos(-30°) - \cos 60°]$ **90.** $2(\sin 5\alpha + \sin \alpha)$

92. $2 \cos \dfrac{5\theta}{2} \cos \dfrac{\theta}{2}$ **94.** $2 \cos x \sin \dfrac{\pi}{4}$

96. False. If $\dfrac{\pi}{2} < \theta < \pi$, then $\cos \dfrac{\theta}{2} > 0$. The sign of $\cos \dfrac{\theta}{2}$

depends on the quadrant in which $\dfrac{\theta}{2}$ lies.

98. True. $4 \sin(-x) \cos(-x) = 4(-\sin x) \cos x$

$= -4 \sin x \cos x$

$= -2(2 \sin x \cos x)$

$= -2 \sin 2x$

100. Reciprocal identities: $\sin \theta = \dfrac{1}{\csc \theta}, \cos \theta = \dfrac{1}{\sec \theta},$

$\tan \theta = \dfrac{1}{\cot \theta}, \csc \theta = \dfrac{1}{\sin \theta}, \sec \theta = \dfrac{1}{\cos \theta},$

$\cot \theta = \dfrac{1}{\tan \theta}$

Quotient identities: $\tan \theta = \dfrac{\sin \theta}{\cos \theta}, \cot \theta = \dfrac{\cos \theta}{\sin \theta}$

Pythagorean identities: $\sin^2 \theta + \cos^2 \theta = 1,$

$1 + \tan^2 \theta = \sec^2 \theta, 1 + \cot^2 \theta = \csc^2 \theta$

102. $-1 \le \sin x \le 1$ for all x **104.** $y_1 = 1 - y_2$

106. $-3.1395, -2.0000, -0.4378, 2.0000$

Problem Solving *(page 406)*

2. Answers will vary.

4. (a) $p_1(t) = \sin(524\,\pi t)$

$p_2(t) = \frac{1}{2}\sin(1048\,\pi t)$

$p_3(t) = \frac{1}{3}\sin(1572\,\pi t)$

$p_5(t) = \frac{1}{5}\sin(2620\,\pi t)$

$p_6(t) = \frac{1}{6}\sin(3144\,\pi t)$

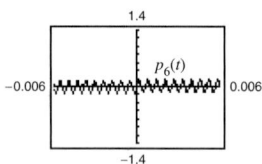

(b) p_1: $\frac{1}{262}$ p_5: $\frac{1}{1310}$

p_2: $\frac{1}{524}$ p_6: $\frac{1}{1572}$

p_3: $\frac{1}{786}$

p is periodic with period $\frac{1}{262}$.

(c) $(0, 0), (0.00096, 0), (0.00191, 0)$
$(0.00285, 0), (0.00382, 0)$

(d) Maximum: $(0.00406, 1.19524)$
Minimum: $(0.00357, -1.19525)$

6. Answers will vary.

8. (a) $F = \dfrac{0.6\,W\cos\theta}{\sin 12°}$

(b)   (c) Maximum: $\theta = 0°$
Minimum: $\theta = 90°$

10. (a) High tides: 6:12 A.M., 6:36 P.M.
Low tides: 12:00 A.M., 12:24 P.M.

(b) The water depth never falls below 7 feet.

(c)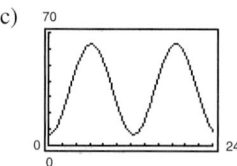

12. (a) $n = \dfrac{1}{2}\left(\cot\dfrac{\theta}{2} + \sqrt{3}\right)$

(b) $\theta \approx 76.5°$

14. (a) $\cos 3\theta = \cos\theta - 4\sin^2\theta\cos\theta$

(b) $\cos 4\theta = \cos^4\theta - 6\sin^2\theta\cos^2\theta + \sin^4\theta$

Chapter 6

Section 6.1 *(page 416)*

2. $A = 35°, a \approx 11.88, b \approx 13.31$

4. $A = 35°, a \approx 36.50, b \approx 11.05$

6. Two solutions:

$B \approx 45.79°, C \approx 74.21°, b \approx 7.45$

$B \approx 14.21°, C \approx 105.79°, b \approx 2.55$

8. $B = 101.1°, a \approx 1.35, b \approx 3.23$

10. $C = 166°5', a \approx 3.30, c \approx 8.05$

12. $A \approx 174°41', C \approx 2°34', a \approx 11.99$

14. $B \approx 75.48°, C \approx 4.52°, b \approx 122.87$

16. $A \approx 44°14', B \approx 50°26', b \approx 38.67$

18. $A = 48°, b \approx 2.29, c \approx 4.73$

20. Two solutions:

$B \approx 72.21°, C \approx 49.79°, c \approx 10.27$

$B \approx 107.79°, C \approx 14.21°, c \approx 3.30$

22. $B \approx 36.82°, C \approx 67.18°, c \approx 32.30$

24. $B \approx 48.74°, C \approx 21.26°, c \approx 48.23$

26. (a) $b \le 10, b = \dfrac{10}{\sin 60°}$ (b) $10 < b < \dfrac{10}{\sin 60°}$

(c) $b > \dfrac{10}{\sin 60°}$

28. (a) $b \le 315.6, b = \dfrac{315.6}{\sin 88°}$ (b) $315.6 < b < \dfrac{315.6}{\sin 88°}$

(c) $b > \dfrac{315.6}{\sin 88°}$

30. 474.9   **32.** 4.5   **34.** 159.3

36. (a)

(b) $\dfrac{16}{\sin 70°} = \dfrac{h}{\sin 32°}$

(c) 9 meters

38. 240°

40. (a)

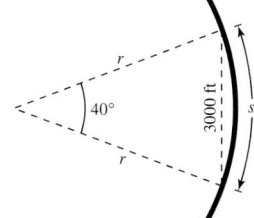

(b) 4385.71 feet

(c) 3061.80 feet

42. From Pine Knob: 42.4 kilometers
From Colt Station: 15.5 kilometers

44. (a) $\alpha \approx 5.36°$ **(b)** $\beta = \sin^{-1}\left(\dfrac{d \sin \theta}{58.36}\right)$

(c) $d = \sin(84.64 - \theta)\left(\dfrac{58.36}{\sin \theta}\right)$

(d)

θ	10°	20°	30°	40°	50°	60°
d	324.1	154.2	95.2	63.8	43.3	28.1

46. False. Two angles and one side determine a unique triangle, while two sides and one opposite angle do not necessarily determine a unique triangle.

48. (a) $A = 20\left(15 \sin \dfrac{3\theta}{2} - 4 \sin \dfrac{\theta}{2} - 6 \sin \theta\right)$

(b)

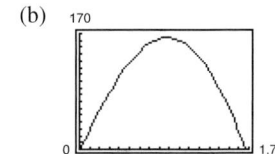

(c) Domain: $0 \le \theta \le 1.6690$

The area would increase and the domain would increase in length.

50. $\tan x$ **52.** $\sec^2 x$ **54.** $\sin 7\theta - \sin 3\theta$

Section 6.2 *(page 423)*

2. $A \approx 61.22°, B \approx 19.19°, C \approx 99.59°$

4. $A \approx 53.73°, B \approx 21.27°, c \approx 11.98$

6. $A \approx 39.35°, B \approx 16.74°, C \approx 123.91°$

8. $A \approx 86.68°, B \approx 31.82°, C \approx 61.50°$

10. $B \approx 16.54°, C \approx 108.46°, a \approx 8.64$

12. $A \approx 37°6', C \approx 67°34', b \approx 9.94$

14. $A \approx 157°2', B \approx 7°43', c \approx 4.21$

16. $A \approx 23.69°, B \approx 53.31°, c \approx 0.91$

	a	b	c	d	θ	ϕ
18.	25	35	52.20	31.22	60°	120°
20.	40	60	63.25	80	104.47°	75.53°
22.	35.18	25	50	35	68.75°	111.25°

24. 54   **26.** 1350.2   **28.** 0.6

30.

1357.8 miles, 56°

32. 41.2°, 52.9°   **34.** 127.2°   **36.** 131.1 feet, 118.6 feet

38. (a) N 59.7° E   **(b)** N 72.8° E   **40.** 103.9 feet

42. 3.8 miles

44. (a) $0 = x^2 - 3x \cos \theta - 46.75$

(b) $x = \frac{1}{2}\left(3 \cos \theta + \sqrt{9 \cos^2 \theta + 187}\right)$

(c)

(d) 8.5 inches

46. 3.95 feet   **48.** 6577.8 square meters

50. False. To solve an SSA triangle, the Law of Sines is needed.

52. Answers will vary.   **54.** 405.3 feet

56. Answers will vary.   **58.** $\dfrac{\pi}{2}$ **60.** $-\dfrac{\pi}{3}$ **62.** $\dfrac{5\pi}{6}$

64. $\dfrac{\sqrt{1 - 9x^2}}{3x}$ **66.** $\dfrac{\sqrt{4 - (x - 1)^2}}{2}$

68. $\sin \theta = -\dfrac{\sqrt{2}}{2}$ **70.** $12 = 6 \sec \theta$

$\sec \theta = \sqrt{2}$ $\sec \theta = 2$

$\csc \theta = -\sqrt{2}$ $\csc \theta = \pm\dfrac{2\sqrt{3}}{3}$

72. $2 \cos x \sin\left(-\dfrac{\pi}{2}\right)$

Section 6.3 *(page 436)*

2. $\mathbf{v} = \langle -4, -2 \rangle; \|\mathbf{v}\| = 2\sqrt{5}$ **4.** $\mathbf{v} = \langle 4, 6 \rangle; \|\mathbf{v}\| = 2\sqrt{13}$

6. $\mathbf{v} = \langle 7, 0 \rangle; \|\mathbf{v}\| = 7$ **8.** $\mathbf{v} = \langle 8, -8 \rangle; \|\mathbf{v}\| = 8\sqrt{2}$

10. $\mathbf{v} = \langle 12, 29 \rangle; \|\mathbf{v}\| = \sqrt{985}$

12. $\mathbf{v} = \langle 7, -24 \rangle; \|\mathbf{v}\| = 25$

CHAPTER 6

14.

16.

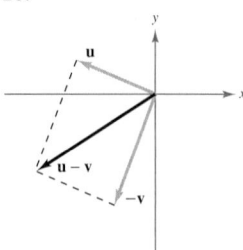

(c) $\langle -6, -3 \rangle$

18.

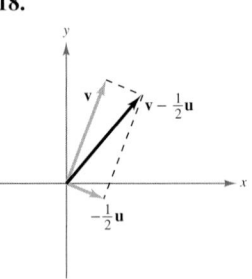

24. (a) $-3\mathbf{i} + 3\mathbf{j}$ (b) $-\mathbf{i} - \mathbf{j}$

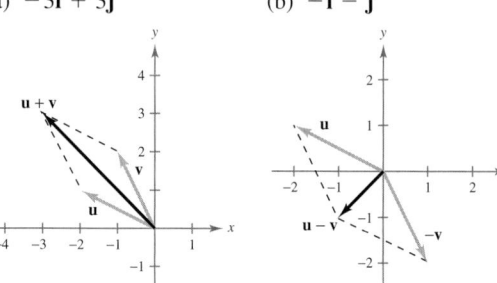

20. (a) $\langle 6, 3 \rangle$ (b) $\langle -2, 3 \rangle$

(c) $-\mathbf{i} - 4\mathbf{j}$

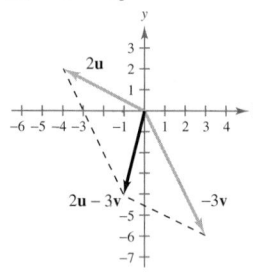

(c) $\langle -8, 6 \rangle$

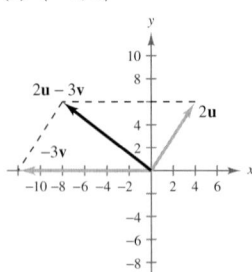

26. (a) $2\mathbf{i} + 3\mathbf{j}$ (b) $-2\mathbf{i} + 3\mathbf{j}$

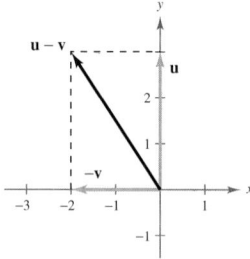

22. (a) $\langle 2, 1 \rangle$ (b) $\langle -2, -1 \rangle$

(c) $-6\mathbf{i} + 6\mathbf{j}$

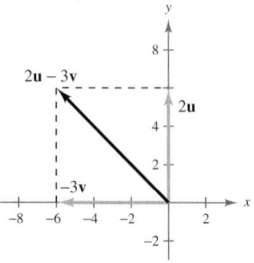

28. $\langle 0, -1 \rangle$ **30.** $\left\langle \dfrac{5}{13}, -\dfrac{12}{13} \right\rangle$ **32.** $\dfrac{\sqrt{2}}{2}\mathbf{i} + \dfrac{\sqrt{2}}{2}\mathbf{j}$

34. $-\mathbf{i}$ **36.** $-\dfrac{3\sqrt{58}}{58}\mathbf{i} + \dfrac{7\sqrt{58}}{58}\mathbf{j}$ **38.** $\langle -3\sqrt{2}, 3\sqrt{2} \rangle$

40. $\langle -10, 0 \rangle$

42. $\mathbf{v} = \langle \tfrac{3}{4}, \tfrac{3}{2} \rangle$ **44.** $\mathbf{v} = \langle -1, 3 \rangle$

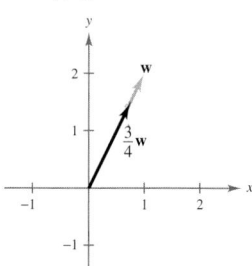

46. $\mathbf{v} = \langle 0, -5 \rangle$

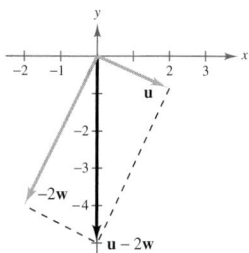

48. $\|\mathbf{v}\| = 8; \theta = 135°$ **50.** $\|\mathbf{v}\| = \sqrt{41}; \theta = 141.3°$

52. $\mathbf{v} = \left\langle \dfrac{\sqrt{2}}{2}, \dfrac{\sqrt{2}}{2} \right\rangle$ **54.** $\mathbf{v} = \left\langle \dfrac{5\sqrt{2}}{4}, \dfrac{5\sqrt{2}}{4} \right\rangle$

    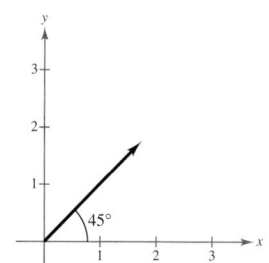

56. $\mathbf{v} = \langle 0, 4\sqrt{3} \rangle$ **58.** $\mathbf{v} = \langle \tfrac{9}{5}, \tfrac{12}{5} \rangle$

    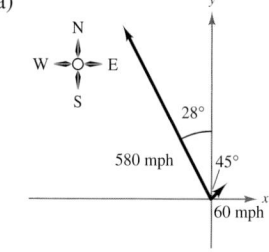

60. $\langle 2, 4 + 2\sqrt{3} \rangle$ **62.** $\langle 33.04, 53.19 \rangle$ **64.** $78.7°$

66. $90°$ **68.** $47.4°$ **70.** $8.7°; 2396.2$ newtons

72. $37.5°; 58.6$ pounds

74. Vertical component: $1200 \sin 6° \approx 125.4$ feet per second

Horizontal component:

$1200 \cos 6° \approx 1193.4$ feet per second

76. $T_{AC} \approx 3611.1$ pounds

$T_{BC} \approx 2169.5$ pounds

78.

53.2 pounds

80. (a)

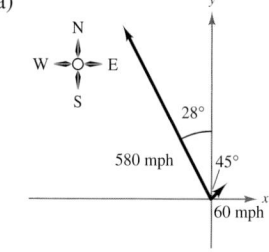

(b) $60 \langle \cos 45°, \sin 45° \rangle$

(c) $580 \langle \cos 118°, \sin 118° \rangle$

(d) 600.3 miles per hour

(e) $337.5°$

82. $\sqrt{2}$ pounds; 1 pound

84. True, by the definition of a unit vector.

86. (a) $5\sqrt{5 + 4 \cos \theta}$

(b)

(c) Range: $[5, 15]$

Maximum is 15 when $\theta = 0$.

Minimum is 5 when $\theta = \pi$.

(d) The magnitudes of $\mathbf{F}_1$ and $\mathbf{F}_2$ are not the same.

88. Answers will vary.   **90.** $\langle 10, 50 \rangle$ or $\langle -10, -50 \rangle$

92. $8 \cos \theta$ **94.** $125 \tan^3 \theta$

96. $n\pi, \dfrac{5\pi}{4} + 2n\pi, \dfrac{7\pi}{4} + 2n\pi$

CHAPTER 6

98. $\dfrac{\pi}{2} + n\pi, \dfrac{5\pi}{4} + 2n\pi, \dfrac{7\pi}{4} + 2n\pi$

Section 6.4   *(page 447)*

2. 9   **4.** 13   **6.** 8; scalar   **8.** 6; scalar   **10.** $2\sqrt{5}$

12. 20   **14.** 21   **16.** 33.69°   **18.** 7.13°

20. 53.13°   **22.** 93.18°   **24.** $\dfrac{\pi}{4}$

26. 41.40°, 64.15°, 74.45°   **28.** 21.80°, 41.63°, 116.57°

30. $12,500\sqrt{3}$ **32.** Neither   **34.** Neither

36. Orthogonal   **38.** $\langle 0, 0 \rangle, \langle 4, 2 \rangle$

40. $\dfrac{14}{17}\langle -4, -1 \rangle, \dfrac{5}{17}\langle 1, -4 \rangle$ **42.** $\langle 3, 8 \rangle, \langle -3, -8 \rangle$

44. $3\mathbf{i} - \dfrac{5}{2}\mathbf{j}, -3\mathbf{i} + \dfrac{5}{2}\mathbf{j}$ **46.** 14

48. (a) Force $= 30{,}000 \sin d$

(b)

d	0°	1°	2°	3°	4°	5°
Force	0	523.6	1047.0	1570.1	2092.7	2614.7

d	6°	7°	8°	9°	10°
Force	3135.9	3656.1	4175.2	4693.0	5209.4

(c) 29,885.8 pounds

50. 12,000 foot-pounds

52. 1,048,514.62 kilogram-meters (10,282,651.78 newton-meters)

54. True. $\cos 90° = 0$

56. (a) **u** and **v** are parallel.   (b) **u** and **v** are orthogonal.

58. Answers will vary.   **60.** $12\sqrt{14}$ **62.** $-24\sqrt{2}$

64. $\dfrac{\pi}{2}, \dfrac{5\pi}{4}, \dfrac{3\pi}{2}, \dfrac{7\pi}{4}$

66. $\dfrac{7\pi}{6}, \dfrac{3\pi}{2}, \dfrac{11\pi}{6}$ **68.** $-\dfrac{323}{325}$ **70.** $-\dfrac{253}{204}$

Section 6.5   *(page 457)*

2.

7

4.

13

6.

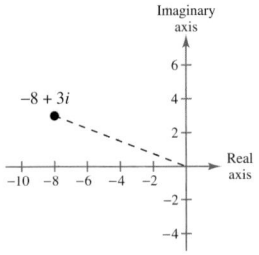

$\sqrt{73}$

8. $2(\cos \pi + i \sin \pi)$ **10.** $2\left(\cos \dfrac{2\pi}{3} + i \sin \dfrac{2\pi}{3}\right)$

12.

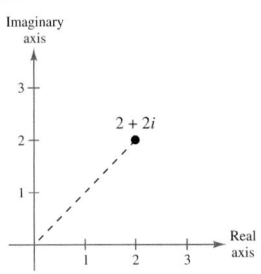

$2\sqrt{2}\left(\cos \dfrac{\pi}{4} + i \sin \dfrac{\pi}{4}\right)$

14.

$8\left(\cos \dfrac{5\pi}{3} + i \sin \dfrac{5\pi}{3}\right)$

16.

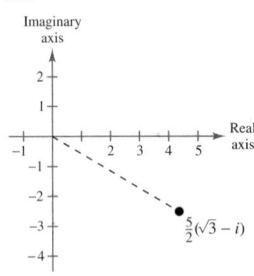

$5\left(\cos \dfrac{11\pi}{6} + i \sin \dfrac{11\pi}{6}\right)$

18.

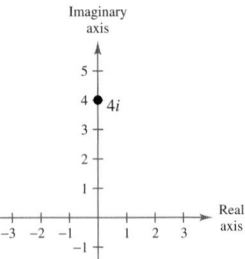

$4\left(\cos \dfrac{\pi}{2} + i \sin \dfrac{\pi}{2}\right)$

20.

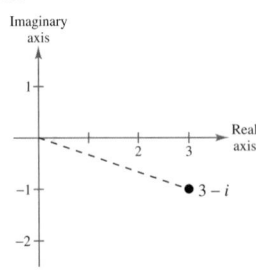

$\sqrt{10}(\cos 5.96 + i \sin 5.96)$

22.

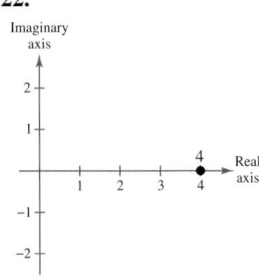

$4(\cos 0 + i \sin 0)$

24.

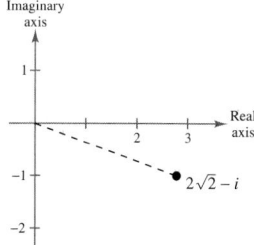

$3(\cos 5.94 + i \sin 5.94)$

26.

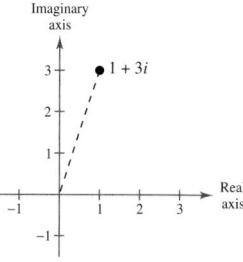

$\sqrt{10}(\cos 1.25 + i \sin 1.25)$

28. $8.54(\cos 0.36 + i \sin 0.36)$

30. $5.10(\cos 3.34 + i \sin 3.34)$

32. $9.80(\cos 5.86 + i \sin 5.86)$

34. $11(\cos 3.75 + i \sin 3.75)$

36.

$-\dfrac{5\sqrt{2}}{2} + \dfrac{5\sqrt{2}}{2}i$

38.

$-\dfrac{\sqrt{2}}{8} - \dfrac{\sqrt{2}}{8}i$

40.

$1.5529 + 5.7956i$

42.

7

44.

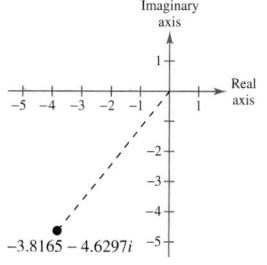

$-3.8165 - 4.6297i$

46. $3.0902 + 9.5106i$

48. $4.7693 + 7.6324i$ **50.** $3\left(\cos\dfrac{13\pi}{12} + i \sin\dfrac{13\pi}{12}\right)$

52. $0.4(\cos 40° + i \sin 40°)$ **54.** $\cos 25° + i \sin 25°$

56. $\frac{1}{2}(\cos 80° + i \sin 80°)$ **58.** $\frac{5}{4}(\cos 2.2 + i \sin 2.2)$

60. $\frac{6}{7}(\cos 300° + i \sin 300°)$

62. (a) $\left[2\left(\cos\dfrac{\pi}{6} + i \sin\dfrac{\pi}{6}\right)\right]\left[\sqrt{2}\left(\cos\dfrac{\pi}{4} + i \sin\dfrac{\pi}{4}\right)\right]$

(b) $2\sqrt{2}\left(\cos\dfrac{5\pi}{12} + i \sin\dfrac{5\pi}{12}\right) \approx 0.732 + 2.732i$

(c) $(\sqrt{3} - 1) + (\sqrt{3} + 1)i \approx 0.732 + 2.732i$

64. (a) $[4(\cos 0 + i \sin 0)]\left[2\left(\cos\dfrac{5\pi}{3} + i \sin\dfrac{5\pi}{3}\right)\right]$

(b) $8\left(\cos\dfrac{5\pi}{3} + i \sin\dfrac{5\pi}{3}\right) = 4 - 4\sqrt{3}i$

(c) $4 - 4\sqrt{3}i$

66. (a) $\left[2\left(\cos\dfrac{\pi}{3} + i \sin\dfrac{\pi}{3}\right)\right] \div$

$[3\sqrt{5}(\cos 5.82) + i \sin 5.82)]$

(b) $\dfrac{2\sqrt{5}}{15}(\cos 1.51 + i \sin 1.51) \approx 0.018 + 0.298i$

(c) $\approx 0.018 + 0.298i$

68. (a) $\left[4\left(\cos\dfrac{\pi}{2} + i \sin\dfrac{\pi}{2}\right)\right] \div [2\sqrt{5}(\cos 2.68 + i \sin 2.68)]$

(b) $\dfrac{2}{\sqrt{5}}(\cos 5.18 + i \sin 5.18) \approx 0.403 - 0.798i$

(c) $\frac{2}{5} - \frac{4}{5}i = 0.400 - 0.800i$

70.

72.

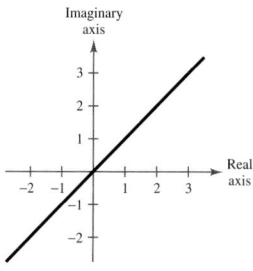

CHAPTER 6

74. $-512i$ **76.** $-239 + 28{,}560i$ **78.** -32

80. $-\dfrac{81}{2} - \dfrac{81\sqrt{3}}{2}i$ **82.** 256 **84.** 1

86. $-43\sqrt{5} + 4i$ **88.** $44.4539 + 252.1108i$

90. $-32\sqrt{2} + 32\sqrt{2}\,i$

92. (a) $4(\cos 30° + i \sin 30°)$

  $4(\cos 210° + i \sin 210°)$

(b)

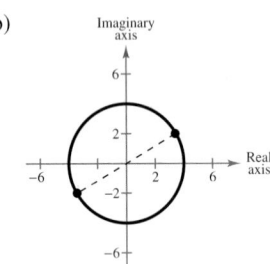

(c) $2\sqrt{3} + 2i,\ -2\sqrt{3} - 2i$

94. (a) $2\left(\cos \dfrac{\pi}{6} + i \sin \dfrac{\pi}{6}\right)$

  $2\left(\cos \dfrac{17\pi}{30} + i \sin \dfrac{17\pi}{30}\right)$

  $2\left(\cos \dfrac{29\pi}{30} + i \sin \dfrac{29\pi}{30}\right)$

  $2\left(\cos \dfrac{41\pi}{30} + i \sin \dfrac{41\pi}{30}\right)$

  $2\left(\cos \dfrac{53\pi}{30} + i \sin \dfrac{53\pi}{30}\right)$

(b)

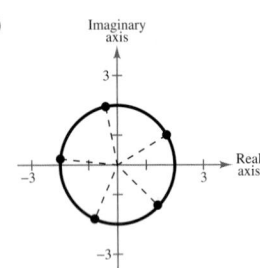

(c) $\sqrt{3} + i,\ -0.4158 + 1.9563i,\ -1.9890 + 0.2091i,$
  $-0.8135 - 1.8271i,\ 1.4863 - 1.3383i$

96. (a) $5\left(\cos \dfrac{\pi}{8} + i \sin \dfrac{\pi}{8}\right)$

  $5\left(\cos \dfrac{5\pi}{8} + i \sin \dfrac{5\pi}{8}\right)$

  $5\left(\cos \dfrac{9\pi}{8} + i \sin \dfrac{9\pi}{8}\right)$

  $5\left(\cos \dfrac{13\pi}{8} + i \sin \dfrac{13\pi}{8}\right)$

(b)

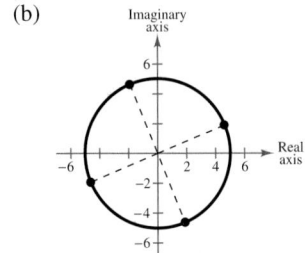

(c) $4.6194 + 1.9134i,\ -1.9134 + 4.6194i,$
  $-4.6194 - 1.9134i,\ 1.9134 - 4.6194i$

98. (a) $2\left(\cos \dfrac{\pi}{4} + i \sin \dfrac{\pi}{4}\right)$

  $2\left(\cos \dfrac{11\pi}{12} + i \sin \dfrac{11\pi}{12}\right)$

  $2\left(\cos \dfrac{19\pi}{12} + i \sin \dfrac{19\pi}{12}\right)$

(b)

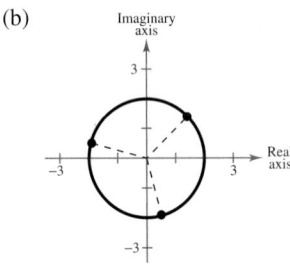

(c) $\sqrt{2} + \sqrt{2}i,\ -1.9319 + 0.5176i,\ 0.5176 - 1.9319i$

100. (a) $\cos \dfrac{\pi}{8} + i \sin \dfrac{\pi}{8}$

  $\cos \dfrac{5\pi}{8} + i \sin \dfrac{5\pi}{8}$

  $\cos \dfrac{9\pi}{8} + i \sin \dfrac{9\pi}{8}$

  $\cos \dfrac{13\pi}{8} + i \sin \dfrac{13\pi}{8}$

(b)

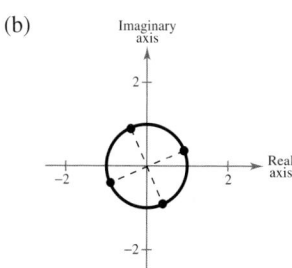

(c) $0.9239 + 0.3827i$, $-0.3827 + 0.9239i$,
    $-0.9239 - 0.3827i$, $0.3827 - 0.9239i$

102. (a) $10(\cos 0 + i \sin 0)$

$10\left(\cos \dfrac{2\pi}{3} + i \sin \dfrac{2\pi}{3}\right)$

$10\left(\cos \dfrac{4\pi}{3} + i \sin \dfrac{4\pi}{3}\right)$

(b)

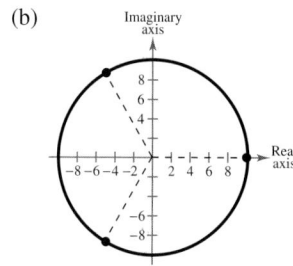

(c) 10, $-5 + 5\sqrt{3}\,i$, $-5 - 5\sqrt{3}\,i$

104. (a) $\sqrt{2}\left(\cos \dfrac{\pi}{4} + i \sin \dfrac{\pi}{4}\right)$

$\sqrt{2}\left(\cos \dfrac{3\pi}{4} + i \sin \dfrac{3\pi}{4}\right)$

$\sqrt{2}\left(\cos \dfrac{5\pi}{4} + i \sin \dfrac{5\pi}{4}\right)$

$\sqrt{2}\left(\cos \dfrac{7\pi}{4} + i \sin \dfrac{7\pi}{4}\right)$

(b)

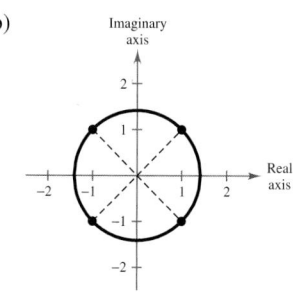

(c) $1 + i$, $-1 + i$, $-1 - i$, $1 - i$

106. (a) $2\left(\cos \dfrac{\pi}{12} + i \sin \dfrac{\pi}{12}\right)$

$2\left(\cos \dfrac{5\pi}{12} + i \sin \dfrac{5\pi}{12}\right)$

$2\left(\cos \dfrac{3\pi}{4} + i \sin \dfrac{3\pi}{4}\right)$

$2\left(\cos \dfrac{13\pi}{12} + i \sin \dfrac{13\pi}{12}\right)$

$2\left(\cos \dfrac{17\pi}{12} + i \sin \dfrac{17\pi}{12}\right)$

$2\left(\cos \dfrac{7\pi}{4} + i \sin \dfrac{7\pi}{4}\right)$

(b)

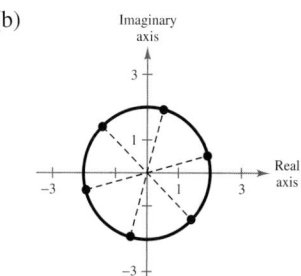

(c) $1.9319 + 0.5176i$, $0.5176 + 1.9319i$,
    $-\sqrt{2} + \sqrt{2}\,i$, $-1.9319 - 0.5176i$,
    $-0.5176 - 1.9319i$, $\sqrt{2} - \sqrt{2}\,i$

108. $\cos \dfrac{\pi}{3} + i \sin \dfrac{\pi}{3}$

$\cos \pi + i \sin \pi$

$\cos \dfrac{5\pi}{3} + i \sin \dfrac{5\pi}{3}$

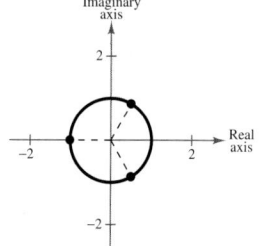

110. $3(\cos 0 + i \sin 0)$

$3\left(\cos \dfrac{2\pi}{3} + i \sin \dfrac{2\pi}{3}\right)$

$3\left(\cos \dfrac{4\pi}{3} + i \sin \dfrac{4\pi}{3}\right)$

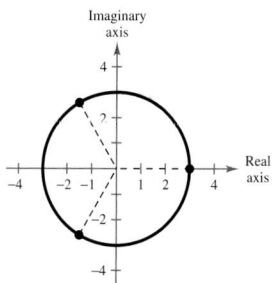

CHAPTER 6

112. $2\left(\cos\dfrac{\pi}{4} + i\sin\dfrac{\pi}{4}\right)$

$2\left(\cos\dfrac{7\pi}{12} + i\sin\dfrac{7\pi}{12}\right)$

$2\left(\cos\dfrac{11\pi}{12} + i\sin\dfrac{11\pi}{12}\right)$

$2\left(\cos\dfrac{5\pi}{4} + i\sin\dfrac{5\pi}{4}\right)$

$2\left(\cos\dfrac{19\pi}{12} + i\sin\dfrac{19\pi}{12}\right)$

$2\left(\cos\dfrac{23\pi}{12} + i\sin\dfrac{23\pi}{12}\right)$

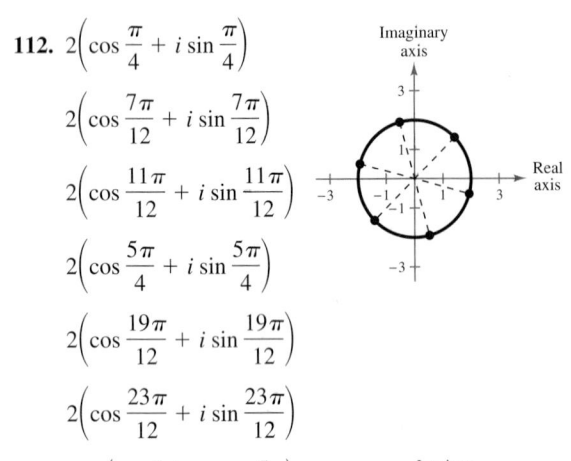

114. $\sqrt[8]{2}\left(\cos\dfrac{5\pi}{16} + i\sin\dfrac{5\pi}{16}\right)$

$\sqrt[8]{2}\left(\cos\dfrac{13\pi}{16} + i\sin\dfrac{13\pi}{16}\right)$

$\sqrt[8]{2}\left(\cos\dfrac{21\pi}{16} + i\sin\dfrac{21\pi}{16}\right)$

$\sqrt[8]{2}\left(\cos\dfrac{29\pi}{16} + i\sin\dfrac{29\pi}{16}\right)$

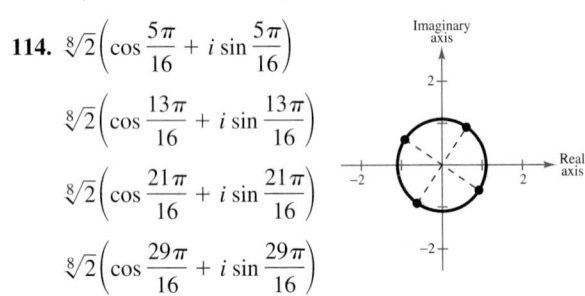

116. False. They are equally spaced along the circle centered at the origin with radius $\sqrt[n]{r}$.

118. False. The complex number needs to be converted to trigonometric form before using DeMoivre's Theorem.
$$\left(4 + \sqrt{6}i\right)^8 = \left[\sqrt{22}(\cos 0.55 + i\sin 0.55)\right]^8$$

120–124. Answers will vary.

126. (a) $3(\cos 45° + i\sin 45°)$

$3(\cos 135° + i\sin 135°)$

$3(\cos 225° + i\sin 225°)$

$3(\cos 315° + i\sin 315°)$

(b) -81

128. $A = 24°, b \approx 75.24, c \approx 82.36$

130. $A = 84°, a \approx 2009.43, c \approx 2020.50$

132. $A = 8°30', a \approx 1.01, b \approx 6.73$

134. $\frac{1}{8}; \frac{1}{24}$ **136.** $\frac{1}{12}; 0$

Review Exercises   *(page 461)*

2. $C = 37°, b \approx 38.90, c \approx 27.31$

4. $A = 150°, a \approx 48.24, b \approx 16.75$

6. $C = 40°, a \approx 162.42, b \approx 115.29$

8. $A = 80°, b \approx 334.95, c \approx 219.04$

10. No solution

12. Two solutions:

$A \approx 40.92°, C \approx 114.08°, c \approx 8.64$

$A \approx 139.08°, C \approx 15.92°, c \approx 2.60$

14. 15.8   **16.** 44.1   **18.** 4.8   **20.** 586.4 feet

22. $A \approx 53.13°, B \approx 36.87°, C = 90°$

24. $A \approx 101.47°, B \approx 31.73°, C \approx 46.80°$

26. $A \approx 9.90°, C \approx 20.10°, b \approx 29.09$

28. $B \approx 35.20°, C \approx 82.80°, a \approx 17.37$

30.

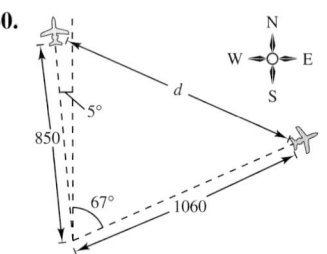

1135.5 miles

32. 36.98   **34.** 242.63

36.

38.

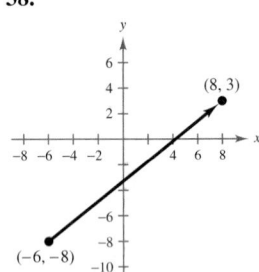

40. $\left\langle 6, \frac{5}{2}\right\rangle$ **42.** $\langle 14, 4\rangle$ **44.** $\left\langle -\dfrac{\sqrt{2}}{4}, -\dfrac{\sqrt{2}}{4}\right\rangle$

46. $\langle -26, -35\rangle$ **48.** $\left\langle 5, \frac{3}{2}\right\rangle$

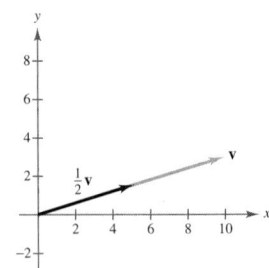

50. $-6\mathbf{i} - 8\mathbf{j}$ **52.** $7\mathbf{i} - 16\mathbf{j}$

54. $\sqrt{17}(\cos 346°\,\mathbf{i} + \sin 346°\,\mathbf{j})$ **56.** $\|\mathbf{v}\| = 3; \theta = 150°$

58. $\|\mathbf{v}\| = \sqrt{65}; \theta = 119.7°$ **60.** $\|\mathbf{v}\| = \sqrt{65}; \theta = 352.9°$

62. 180 pounds each

64. 740.5 kilometers per hour; 32.1°   **66.** -140

68. -136 **70.** 5; scalar **72.** -6; scalar

74. 105° **76.** 22.4° **78.** Parallel **80.** Orthogonal

82. $\langle 5, 0 \rangle, \langle 0, 6 \rangle$ **84.** $\frac{25}{29}\langle -5, 2 \rangle, \frac{19}{29}\langle 2, 5 \rangle$ **86.** -132

88.

6

90.

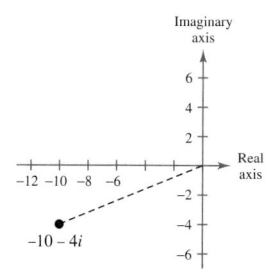

$2\sqrt{29}$

92. $13(\cos 1.176 + i \sin 1.176)$ **94.** $7(\cos \pi + i \sin \pi)$

96. (a) $z_1 = 3\sqrt{2}\left(\cos \frac{5\pi}{4} + i \sin \frac{5\pi}{4}\right)$

$z_2 = 4\left(\cos \frac{\pi}{6} + i \sin \frac{\pi}{6}\right)$

(b) $z_1 z_2 = 12\sqrt{2}\left(\cos \frac{17\pi}{12} + i \sin \frac{17\pi}{12}\right)$

$\frac{z_1}{z_2} = \frac{3\sqrt{2}}{4}\left(\cos \frac{13\pi}{12} + i \sin \frac{13\pi}{12}\right)$

98. $-16 - 16\sqrt{3}i$ **100.** 16

102. (a) $4(\cos 60° + i \sin 60°)$

$4(\cos 150° + i \sin 150°)$

$4(\cos 240° + i \sin 240°)$

$4(\cos 330° + i \sin 330°)$

(b) $-128 - 128\sqrt{3}i$

104. $4(\cos 0 + i \sin 0) = 4$

$4\left(\cos \frac{\pi}{2} + i \sin \frac{\pi}{2}\right) = 4i$

$4(\cos \pi + i \sin \pi) = -4$

$4\left(\cos \frac{3\pi}{2} + i \sin \frac{3\pi}{2}\right) = -4i$

106. $2(\cos 0 + i \sin 0) = 2$

$2\left(\cos \frac{2\pi}{5} + i \sin \frac{2\pi}{5}\right) = 0.6180 + 1.9021i$

$2\left(\cos \frac{4\pi}{5} + i \sin \frac{4\pi}{5}\right) = -1.6180 + 1.1756i$

$2\left(\cos \frac{6\pi}{5} + i \sin \frac{6\pi}{5}\right) = -1.6180 - 1.1756i$

$2\left(\cos \frac{8\pi}{5} + i \sin \frac{8\pi}{5}\right) = 0.6180 - 1.9021i$

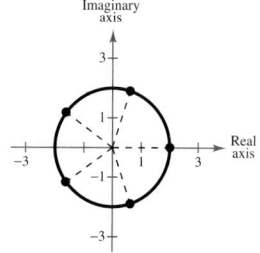

108. $\cos 0 + i \sin 0 = 1$

$\cos \frac{\pi}{2} + i \sin \frac{\pi}{2} = i$

$\cos \frac{2\pi}{3} + i \sin \frac{2\pi}{3} = -\frac{1}{2} + \frac{\sqrt{3}}{2}i$

$\cos \frac{4\pi}{3} + i \sin \frac{4\pi}{3} = -\frac{1}{2} - \frac{\sqrt{3}}{2}i$

$\cos \frac{3\pi}{2} + i \sin \frac{3\pi}{2} = -i$

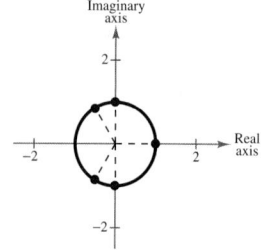

110. False. There may be no solution, one solution, or two solutions.

112. False. If $\mathbf{v} = a\mathbf{i} + b\mathbf{j} = \mathbf{0}$, then $a = b = 0$.

114. $\dfrac{a}{\sin A} = \dfrac{b}{\sin B} = \dfrac{c}{\sin C}$

116. Direction and magnitude

118. a; The angle between the vectors is acute.

120. The diagonal of the parallelogram with $\mathbf{u}$ and $\mathbf{v}$ as its adjacent sides

122. (a) 3

(b) On the circle 120°, 210°, and 300° from the positive x-axis

Problem Solving *(page 472)*

2. S 22.09° E; 1025.88 yards

4. (a)

(b) 50.5 feet

(c) 22 bags

65°

46 ft

52 ft

6. (a) $\mathbf{u} = \langle 0, -120 \rangle$, $\mathbf{v} = \langle 40, 0 \rangle$

(b)

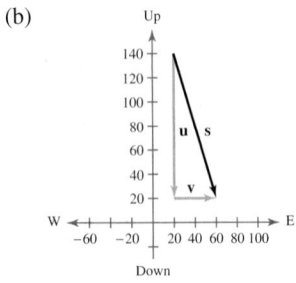

(c) 126.5 miles per hour; The magnitude gives the velocity of the skydiver's fall.

(d) 108.43°

(e)

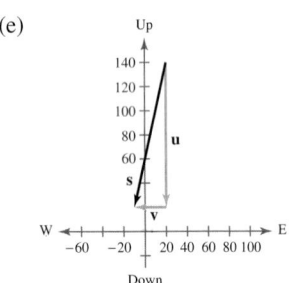

       123.7 miles per hour

8. $\mathbf{u} \cdot \mathbf{v} = 0$ and $\mathbf{u} \cdot \mathbf{w} = 0$

$\mathbf{u} \cdot (c\mathbf{v} + d\mathbf{w})$

$= \mathbf{u} \cdot c\mathbf{v} + \mathbf{u} \cdot d\mathbf{w}$

$= c(\mathbf{u} \cdot \mathbf{v}) + d(\mathbf{u} \cdot \mathbf{w})$

$= 0$

10. (a)

θ	0.5°	1.0°	1.5°
$\|\mathbf{v}\| \sin \theta$	0.873	1.745	2.618
$\|\mathbf{v}\| \cos \theta$	99.996	99.985	99.966

θ	2.0°	2.5°	3.0°
$\|\mathbf{v}\| \sin \theta$	3.490	4.362	5.234
$\|\mathbf{v}\| \cos \theta$	99.939	99.905	99.863

(b) No. Find the square root of the sum of the squares of the vertical and horizontal components.

(c) (i) 150 miles per hour

     (ii) 150 miles per hour

Chapter 7

Section 7.1   *(page 483)*

2. a and d   **4.** b and c   **6.** $(-1, 3)$

8. $\left(-\sqrt{3}, 2 + 3\sqrt{3}\right)$, $(0, 2)$, $\left(\sqrt{3}, 2 - 3\sqrt{3}\right)$

10. $(0, 0), (2, -2), (-2, 2)$ **12.** $(0, 2), (1, 0), (-1, 0)$

14. $(0, 4), (1, 2), (2, 0)$ **16.** $(-3, 2)$ **18.** $\left(\frac{4}{3}, \frac{4}{3}\right)$

20. $\left(2, \frac{5}{2}\right)$ **22.** $\left(\frac{208}{17}, \frac{88}{17}\right)$ **24.** No solution

26. $(0, 0), (12, 6)$ **28.** $(0, 0)$ **30.** $(2, -2)$

32. $(5, 3)$ **34.** $(-3, 0), (3, 6)$ **36.** $(3, 1), (15, 7)$

38. $(2, 2)$ **40.** No solution   **42.** $(3, 4), (3, -4)$

44.   **46.**

   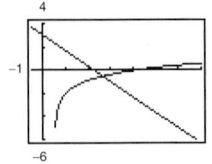

     $(-0.49, -6.53)$ $(5.31, -0.54)$

48.   **50.**

   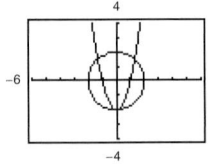

     $(5, 2), (2, -1)$ $(0, -2), (\pm 1.32, 1.50)$

52. No solution   **54.** $(3, 4), (5, 0)$

56. No solution   **58.** $(-1.96, 0.14), (1.06, 2.88)$

60. $(0, -1), (2, 1), (-1, -5)$ **62.** $(1, 0), (5, 2)$

64. 233,333 units   **66.** 1464 units

68. (a) 3759 items   (b) 10,151 items

70. (a) $\begin{cases} x + y = 20{,}000 \\ 0.065x + 0.085y = 1600 \end{cases}$

(b)   (c) \$5000

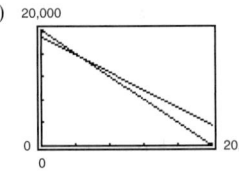

     Decreases; interest is fixed at \$1600.

72. More than \$500,000

74.

     $(99.99, 2.85)$

76. (a)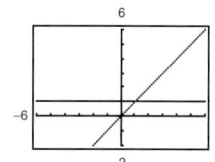

(b) $(4.26, 12.14)$, $(8.67, 13.79)$

80. 42×63 feet   **82.** $\sqrt{2} \times \sqrt{2} \times 2$ inches

84. False. The system can have at most four solutions because a parabola and a circle can intersect at most four times.

86. For a linear system, the result will be a contradictory equation such as $0 = N$, where N is a nonzero real number. For a nonlinear system, there may be an equation with imaginary solutions.

88. (a) $b = 1$ 　　　　　　　　　$b = 2$

$b = 3$ 　　　　　　　　　$b = 4$

　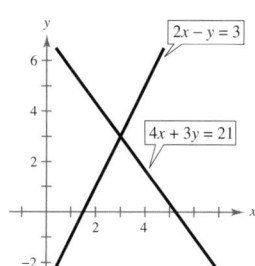

(b) Three points of intersection

90. $4x - 13y + 38 = 0$ **92.** $x - 4 = 0$

94. $45x + 29y - 127 = 0$

96. Domain: All real numbers $x \neq -\frac{2}{3}$

Horizontal asymptote: $y = \frac{2}{3}$

Vertical asymptote: $x = -\frac{2}{3}$

98. Domain: All real numbers $x \neq 0$

Horizontal asymptote: $y = 3$

Vertical asymptote: $x = 0$

Section 7.2   *(page 495)*

2. $(-2, 1)$ 　　　　　　　**4.** $(3, 3)$

　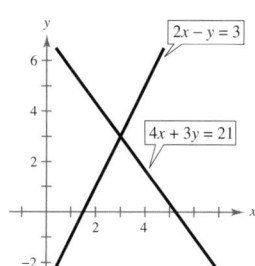

6. No solution   **8.** $(a, 3a + 5)$

　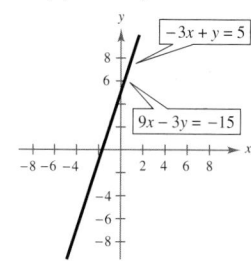

10. $\left(-\frac{35}{12}, -\frac{41}{36}\right)$ **12.** $\left(3, \frac{7}{5}\right)$

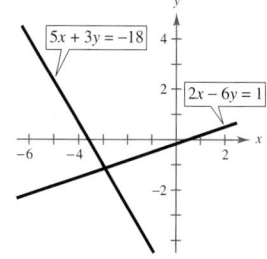

14. $(5, 1)$ **16.** $\left(\frac{5}{6}, \frac{5}{6}\right)$ **18.** $(-17, 5)$ **20.** No solution

22. $(a, 4 - 4a)$ **24.** $(a, -0.875a + 0.75)$

26. $(101, 96)$ **28.** $\left(-\frac{14}{9}, \frac{20}{9}\right)$ **30.** $(7, 1)$

31. b   **32.** a   **33.** c   **34.** d   **36.** $(-2, 5)$

38. $(1, 3)$ **40.** $(-23, 61)$ **42.** $(3, 2)$

44. $(500, 75)$ **46.** $(250,000, 350)$

48. First plane: 880 kilometers per hour
Second plane: 960 kilometers per hour

50. (a) $\begin{cases} x + y = 500 \\ 87x + 92y = 44{,}500 \end{cases}$

(b)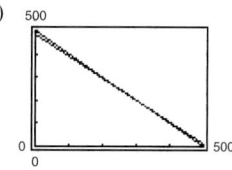

Decreases

(c) 87 octane: 300 gallons; 92 octane: 200 gallons

52. \$20,000

54. Before noon: 81 jackets; After noon: 133 jackets

56. $y = 0.22x + 1.9$ **58.** $y = -0.58x + 5.4$

60. $y = \frac{1}{2}x - \frac{3}{4}$

62. (a) $y = 14x + 19$ (b) 41.4 bushels per acre

64. False. Solving a system of equations algebraically will always give an exact solution.

66. $(300, 315)$. It is necessary to change the scale on the axes to see the point of intersection.

68. (a) $\begin{cases} x + y = 10 \\ x + y = 20 \end{cases}$ (b) $\begin{cases} x + y = 3 \\ 2x + 2y = 6 \end{cases}$ **70.** $k = -2$

72. $x > 1$

74. $\frac{4}{3} \le x < \frac{16}{3}$

76. All real numbers x

78. $x < -4,\ x > 0$

80. $\frac{1}{2}\left(-\frac{6}{x} + \frac{3}{x+1} + \frac{3}{x-1} \right)$ **82.** $\ln \dfrac{x}{(x+3)^5}$

84. $\log_6 \sqrt[4]{3x}$ **86.** $\left(\frac{3}{2}, \frac{3}{10} \right)$

Section 7.3 (page 507)

2. b **4.** a and d **6.** $(2, -3, -2)$

8. $(17, -11, -3)$ **10.** $\left(-2, -\frac{10}{3}, -4 \right)$

12. $\begin{cases} x - 2y + 3z = 5 \\ -x + 3y - 5z = 4 \\ 4y - 9z = -10 \end{cases}$

Eliminated the x-term from the 3rd equation.

14. $\left(\frac{5}{3}, \frac{1}{3}, 1 \right)$ **16.** $(5, -3, 3)$ **18.** $\left(1, \frac{1}{2}, -3 \right)$

20. No solution **22.** $\left(\frac{3}{10}, \frac{2}{5}, 0 \right)$

24. $\left(-\frac{1}{2}a + \frac{5}{2}, 4a - 1, a \right)$ **26.** $(-2a + 5, -7a + 14, a)$

28. $(-5a + 3, -a - 5, a)$ **30.** $\left(-\frac{3}{8}a - \frac{1}{4}, -\frac{3}{4}a + \frac{5}{2}, a \right)$

32. $(1, 0, 3, 2)$ **34.** $\left(3, \frac{7}{2}, \frac{1}{2} \right)$ **36.** $(0, 0, 0)$

38. $\left(\frac{1}{5}a + \frac{1}{5}, -\frac{3}{5}a + \frac{2}{5}, a \right)$

40. $y = -x^2 + 2x + 3$ **42.** $y = -2x^2 + 5x$

44. $x^2 + y^2 - 6y = 0$ **46.** $x^2 + y^2 - 3x + 2y = 0$

48. $s = -16t^2 + 64t$ **50.** $s = -16t^2 + 16t + 132$

52. 3-point baskets: 3 **54.** \$625,000 at 8%
2-point baskets: 33 \$50,000 at 9%
Free-throws: 15 \$125,000 at 10%

56. $406,250 - \frac{1}{2}s$ in certificates of deposit,
$-31,250 + \frac{1}{2}s$ in municipal bonds,
$125,000 - s$ in blue-chip stocks,
s in growth stocks

58. 20 liters of spray X,
18 liters of spray Y,
16 liters of spray Z

60. $I_1 = 1, I_2 = 2, I_3 = 1$

62. $t_1 = 128$ pounds
$t_2 = 64$ pounds
$a = 0$ feet per second squared
The system is stable.

64. $\dfrac{1}{x-1} - \dfrac{1}{x+2}$ **66.** $-\dfrac{2}{x} + \dfrac{6}{5(x-2)} + \dfrac{4}{5(x+3)}$

68. $y = \frac{3}{7}x^2 + \frac{6}{5}x + \frac{26}{35}$ **70.** $y = -\frac{5}{4}x^2 + \frac{9}{20}x + \frac{199}{20}$

72. (a) $y = 0.165x^2 - 6.55x + 103$

(b)

(c) 453 feet

74. $x = 2$ **76.** $x = 25$
$y = 2$ $y = 50$
$\lambda = -4$ $\lambda = -51$

78. True. If a system of three linear equations is inconsistent, then it has no points common to all three equations.

80. There will be a row representing a contradictory equation such as $0 = N$, where N is a nonzero real number.

82. $\begin{cases} x + y + z = -6 \\ -2x - y + 3z = 15 \\ x + 4y - z = -14 \end{cases}$ $\begin{cases} 2x - y - z = -9 \\ -x + 2y + 2z = 3 \\ -3x + y - 2z = 11 \end{cases}$

84. $\begin{cases} 2x - y + 3z = -28 \\ -6x + 4y + z = 18 \\ -4x - 2y - 3z = 19 \end{cases}$ $\begin{cases} 4x + y - 2z = 12 \\ 4y + 2z = 2 \\ -2x + y + z = 0 \end{cases}$

86. 150% **88.** 275 **90.** $-7 - 3i$

92. $11 + 2i$ **94.** $\frac{175}{1241} + \frac{20}{1241}i$

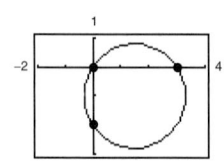

96. (a) $\pm 2, 0$

(b)

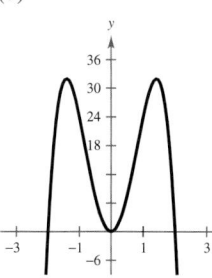

98. (a) $-\frac{1}{2}, \frac{1}{3}, 5$

(b)

100.

x	-2	-1	0	1	2
y	11.625	2.25	-1.5	-3	-3.6

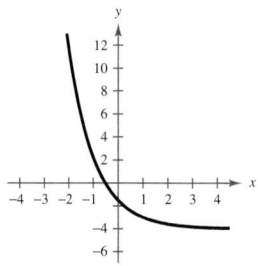

102.

x	$-\frac{1}{2}$	0	$\frac{1}{2}$	1	2
y	28.918	18.25	12.548	9.5	7

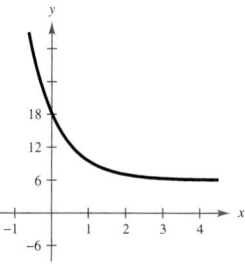

104. $\left(\frac{1}{2}, 0\right)$

Section 7.4 *(page 519)*

2.

4.

6.

8.

10.

12.

14.

16.

18.

20.

22.

24.

26. $y \geq x^2 - 4$ **28.** $x^2 + y^2 \leq 9$ **30.** a   **32.** d

34.

36.

38.

40.

42.

44.

46.

48.

50.

52.

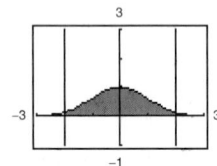

54. $\begin{cases} y < 6 - 2x \\ y \geq x - 3 \\ x \geq 1 \end{cases}$ **56.** $x^2 + y^2 > 4$ **58.** $\begin{cases} x^2 + y^2 \leq 16 \\ x \leq y \\ x \geq 0 \end{cases}$

60. $\begin{cases} 4x - y \geq 0 \\ 4x - y \leq 16 \\ 0 \leq y \leq 4 \end{cases}$ **62.** $\begin{cases} y \leq x + 1 \\ y \leq -x + 1 \\ y \geq 0 \end{cases}$

64. Consumer surplus: \$6250

Producer surplus: \$12,500

66. Consumer surplus: \$6,250,000

Producer surplus: \$15,625,000

68. $\begin{cases} x \qquad\quad \geq 2y \\ 8x + 12y \leq 200 \\ x \qquad\quad \geq 4 \\ \qquad\quad y \geq 2 \end{cases}$

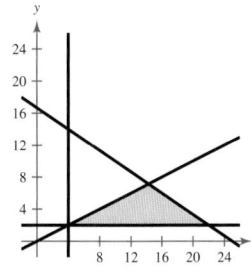

70. $\begin{cases} x + \quad y \leq \;\; 3{,}000 \\ 30x + 20y \geq 75{,}000 \\ x \qquad\quad\; \leq \;\; 2{,}000 \\ x \qquad\qquad \geq \qquad 0 \\ \qquad\quad y \geq \qquad 0 \end{cases}$

72. $\begin{cases} 20x + 10y \geq 300 \\ 15x + 10y \geq 150 \\ 10x + 20y \geq 200 \\ x \qquad\qquad \geq 0 \\ \qquad\quad y \geq 0 \end{cases}$

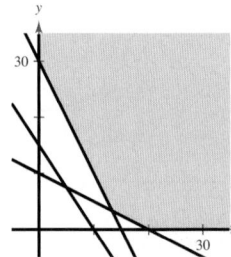

74. (a) $\begin{cases} \qquad xy \geq 500 \\ 2x + \pi y \geq 125 \\ x \qquad\quad \geq \;\; 0 \\ \qquad\quad y \geq \;\; 0 \end{cases}$ (b)

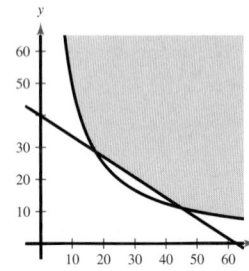

76. False. The graph shows the solution of the system

$$\begin{cases} \qquad y < 6 \\ -4x - 9y < 6. \\ 3x + y^2 \geq 2 \end{cases}$$

78. Test a point on either side.

80. (a) The boundary would be included in the solution.

(b) The solution would be the half-plane on the opposite side of the boundary.

81. d   **82.** b   **83.** c   **84.** a

86. $x + 11y + 8 = 0$ **88.** $2x - y + 1 = 0$

90. $60x - 35y + 113 = 0$ **92.** \$5395.40

94. 0.022   **96.** 0.027

Section 7.5 (page 529)

2. Minimum at $(0, 0)$: 0
Maximum at $(0, 4)$: 32

4. Minimum at $(0, 0)$: 0
Maximum at $(2, 0)$: 14

6. Minimum at $(0, 2)$: 10
Maximum at $(4, 3)$: 31

8. Minimum at $(0, 2)$: 2
Maximum at $(4, 3)$: 11

10. Minimum at $(450, 0)$: $11{,}250$
Maximum at $(0, 800)$: $28{,}000$

12. Minimum at $(450, 0)$: 6750
Maximum at $(0, 800)$: $16{,}000$

14.

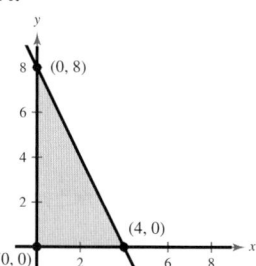

Minimum at $(0, 0)$: 0
Maximum at $(0, 8)$: 64

16.

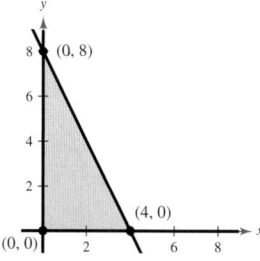

Minimum at $(0, 0)$: 0
Maximum at $(4, 0)$: 28

18.

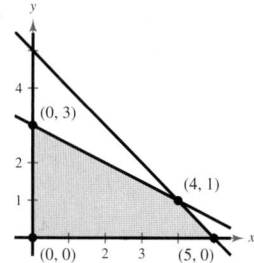

Minimum at $(0, 0)$: 0
Maximum at $(4, 1)$: 21

20.

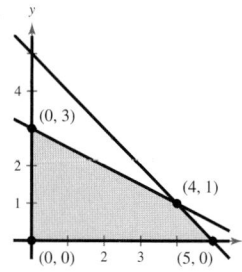

Minimum at $(0, 3)$: -3
Maximum at $(5, 0)$: 10

22.

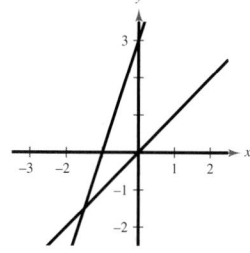

Minimum at any point on the line segment connecting $(0, 0)$ and $(0, 20)$: 0

Maximum at $(12, 0)$: 12

24.

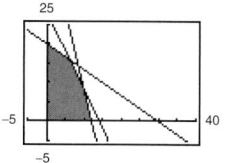

Minimum at any point on the line segment connecting $(0, 0)$ and $(12, 0)$: 0

Maximum at $(0, 20)$: 20

26. Maximum at $(5, 0)$: 25

28. Maximum at any point on the line segment connecting $(3, 6)$ and $(5, 0)$: 15

30. Maximum at $\left(\frac{22}{3}, \frac{19}{6}\right)$: $\frac{82}{3}$

32. Maximum at $\left(\frac{21}{2}, 0\right)$: 42

34. 1000 units of model A
500 units of model B
Maximum profit: $76{,}000

36. 60 acres of crop A
90 acres of crop B
Maximum profit: $29{,}550

38. Type A: $\frac{2}{3}$ gallon
Type B: $\frac{1}{3}$ gallon
Minimum cost: $1.18 per gallon
Yes.

40. No audits
48 tax returns
Maximum revenue: $14{,}400

42. $225{,}000 to type A
$225{,}000 to type B

44.

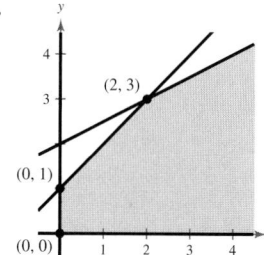

The constraints do not form a closed set of points. Therefore, $z = x + y$ is unbounded.

46.

The feasible set is empty.

48.

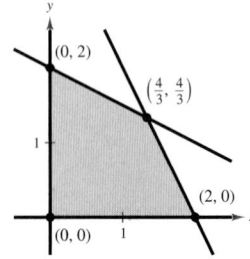

The maximum, 4, occurs at any point on the line segment connecting $(0, 2)$ and $\left(\frac{4}{3}, \frac{4}{3}\right)$.

50. True. If an objective function has a maximum value at more than one vertex, then any point on the line segment connecting the points will produce the maximum value.

52. (a) $-3 < t < 6$ (b) $t > 6$

54. $z = x + y$ **56.** $z = -10x + y$

58. $\dfrac{1}{x - 2}$, $x \neq 0, -2$ **60.** $\dfrac{(x + 1)(x + 3)}{3}$, $x \neq -1$

62. $\ln 4 \approx 1.386$, $\ln 6 \approx 1.792$ **64.** $-\ln 6 \approx -1.792$

66. $e - 9 \approx -6.282$ **68.** $(-1, 2, -3)$

Review Exercises   *(page 534)*

2. $(13, 0)$, $(5, 12)$ **4.** $(5, 2)$, $(2, -1)$

6. $(0, 0)$, $(-3, 3)$ **8.** $(4, 4)$

10.

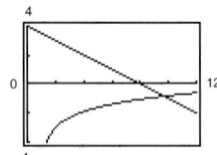

$(9.68, -0.84)$

12. Sales greater than \$500,000   **14.** 16×18 feet

16. $\left(\frac{3}{10}, \frac{2}{5}\right)$ **18.** $\left(\frac{1}{3}, -\frac{1}{2}\right)$ **20.** $(-3, 7)$

22. No solution   **23.** d   **24.** c   **25.** b   **26.** a

28. $(250,000, 95)$ **30.** $(5, -8, 3)$ **32.** $\left(\frac{38}{17}, \frac{40}{17}, -\frac{63}{17}\right)$

34. $\left(-\frac{3}{4}, 0, -\frac{5}{4}\right)$ **36.** $(-3a + 2, 5a + 6, a)$

38. $y = 3x^2 + 11x - 14$

40. $x^2 + y^2 - 2x + 2y - 23 = 0$

42. $\dfrac{1}{2}\left(\dfrac{3}{x - 3} - \dfrac{3}{x + 3}\right)$ **44.** $\dfrac{1}{8}\left(8 + \dfrac{9}{x - 3} - \dfrac{25}{x + 5}\right)$

46. 10 gallons of spray X
5 gallons of spray Y
12 gallons of spray Z

48. (a) $s = -16t^2 + 150$ (b) $s = -16t^2 - 20t + 220$

50.

52.

54.

56.

58.

60.

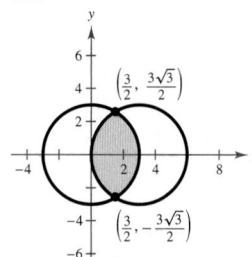

62. $\begin{cases} 20x + 30y \leq 24{,}000 \\ 12x + 8y \leq 12{,}400 \\ \quad x \qquad\quad \geq \quad 0 \\ \quad\qquad y \geq \quad 0 \end{cases}$

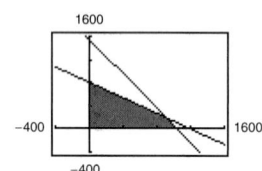

64. Consumer surplus: \$4,000,000
Producer surplus: \$6,000,000

66.

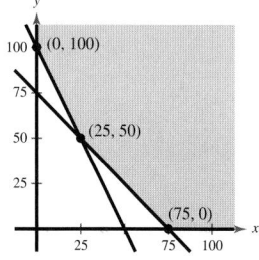

Minimum at (25, 50): 600

No maximum

68.

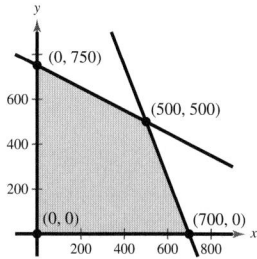

Minimum at (0, 0): 0

Maximum at (500, 500): 60,000

70.

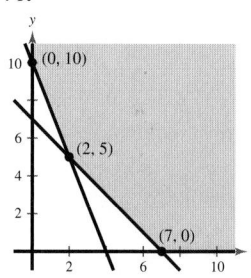

Minimum at (7, 0): −14

No maximum

72. 5 walking shoes
2 running shoes
Maximum profit: $138

74. $\frac{3}{5}$ gallon of type A
$\frac{2}{5}$ gallon of type B
Minimum cost: $1.37

76. False. An objective function can have no maximum value, one point where a maximum value occurs, or an infinite number of points where a maximum value occurs.

78. $\begin{cases} x - y = 9 \\ 3x + y = 11 \end{cases}$
80. $\begin{cases} -x + 4y = 10 \\ 3x - 8y = -21 \end{cases}$

82. $\begin{cases} x - 2y + z = -7 \\ 2x + y - 4z = -25 \\ -x + 3y - z = 12 \end{cases}$
84. $\begin{cases} 4x + y - z = -7 \\ 8x + 3y + 2z = 16 \\ 4x - 2y + 3z = 31 \end{cases}$

86. The lines are distinct and parallel.

$\begin{cases} x + 2y = 3 \\ 2x + 4y = 9 \end{cases}$

Problem Solving *(page 540)*

2. $k_1 = -\frac{10}{3}, k_2 = \frac{16}{3}$

4. (a)

(5, 2)

(b)

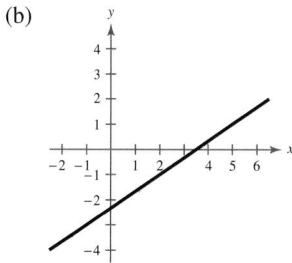

$\left(\frac{3}{2}a + \frac{7}{2}, a\right)$

6. $\begin{cases} B + G + T = 104,779,000 \\ B - G = -537,000 \\ T = 3,331,972 \end{cases}$

Bush: 50,455,014 votes

Gore: 50,992,014 votes

Nader and Buchanan: 3,331,972 votes

8. Carbon: 12.011 u

Hydrogen: 1.008 u

10. $\begin{cases} d_1 = 30t \\ d_2 = 40\left(t - \frac{1}{4}\right) \end{cases}$

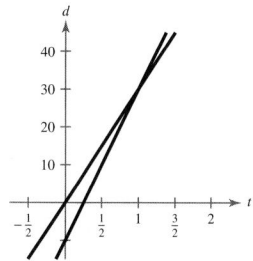

(1, 30)

5 miles from the airport

12. $a = 12, b = -4, c = 10$

14.
$$\begin{cases} a + \quad t \le 32 \\ 0.15a \qquad \ge 1.9 \\ 193a + 772t \ge 11,000 \end{cases}$$

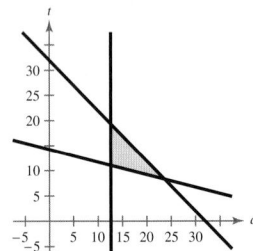

16. (a)
$$\begin{cases} x + y \le 200 \\ x \qquad \ge 35 \\ 0 < y \le 130 \end{cases}$$

(b)

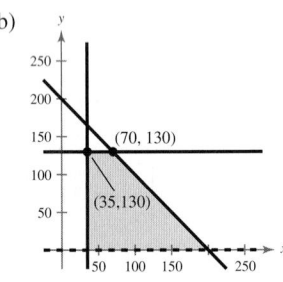

(c) No, because the total cholesterol is greater than 200 milligrams per deciliter.

(d) LDL: 140 milligrams per deciliter

HDL: 50 milligrams per deciliter

Total: 190 milligrams per deciliter

(e) $(50, 120); \frac{170}{50} = 3.4 < 4$

Chapter 8

Section 8.1   *(page 554)*

2. 1×4 **4.** 3×4 **6.** 2×3

8. $\begin{bmatrix} 7 & 4 & \vdots & 22 \\ 5 & -9 & \vdots & 15 \end{bmatrix}$

10. $\begin{bmatrix} -1 & -8 & 5 & \vdots & 8 \\ -7 & 0 & -15 & \vdots & -38 \\ 3 & -1 & 8 & \vdots & 20 \end{bmatrix}$

12. $\begin{bmatrix} 9 & 2 & -3 & \vdots & 20 \\ 0 & -25 & 11 & \vdots & -5 \end{bmatrix}$

14. $\begin{cases} 7x - 5y = 0 \\ 8x + 3y = -2 \end{cases}$ **16.** $\begin{cases} 4x - 5y - z = 18 \\ -11x + 6z = 25 \\ 3x + 8y = -29 \end{cases}$

18. $\begin{cases} 6x + 2y - z - 5w = -25 \\ -x + 7z + 3w = 7 \\ 4x - y - 10z + 6w = 23 \\ 8y + z - 11w = -21 \end{cases}$

20. $\begin{bmatrix} 1 & 2 & \frac{8}{3} \\ 4 & -3 & 6 \end{bmatrix}$

22. $\begin{bmatrix} 1 & 2 & 4 & \frac{3}{2} \\ 1 & -1 & -3 & 2 \\ 2 & 6 & 4 & 9 \end{bmatrix}$ $\begin{bmatrix} 1 & 2 & 4 & \frac{3}{2} \\ 0 & -3 & -7 & \frac{1}{2} \\ 0 & 2 & -4 & 6 \end{bmatrix}$

24. Add 3 times Row 1 to Row 2.

26. Add 2 times Row 1 to Row 2.

Add 5 times Row 1 to Row 3.

28. Reduced row-echelon form

30. Row-echelon form

32. (a) $\begin{bmatrix} 7 & 1 \\ 0 & 2 \\ -3 & 4 \\ 1 & 5 \end{bmatrix}$ (b) $\begin{bmatrix} 1 & 5 \\ 0 & 2 \\ -3 & 4 \\ 7 & 1 \end{bmatrix}$ (c) $\begin{bmatrix} 1 & 5 \\ 0 & 2 \\ 0 & 19 \\ 7 & 1 \end{bmatrix}$

(d) $\begin{bmatrix} 1 & 5 \\ 0 & 2 \\ 0 & 19 \\ 0 & -34 \end{bmatrix}$ (e) $\begin{bmatrix} 1 & 5 \\ 0 & 1 \\ 0 & 19 \\ 0 & -34 \end{bmatrix}$ (f) $\begin{bmatrix} 1 & 0 \\ 0 & 1 \\ 0 & 0 \\ 0 & 0 \end{bmatrix}$

The matrix is in reduced row-echelon form.

34. $\begin{bmatrix} 1 & 2 & -1 & 3 \\ 0 & 1 & -2 & 5 \\ 0 & 0 & 1 & -1 \end{bmatrix}$ **36.** $\begin{bmatrix} 1 & -3 & 0 & -7 \\ 0 & 1 & 1 & 2 \\ 0 & 0 & 0 & 0 \end{bmatrix}$

38. $\begin{bmatrix} 1 & 3 & 0 \\ 0 & 0 & 1 \\ 0 & 0 & 0 \end{bmatrix}$ **40.** $\begin{bmatrix} 1 & 0 & 0 & 0 \\ 0 & 1 & 0 & 0 \\ 0 & 0 & 1 & 0 \\ 0 & 0 & 0 & 1 \end{bmatrix}$

42. $\begin{bmatrix} 1 & 0 & 0 & 2 \\ 0 & 1 & 2 & -6 \end{bmatrix}$

44. $\begin{cases} x + 5y = 0 \\ y = -1 \end{cases}$ **46.** $\begin{cases} x + 2y - 2z = -1 \\ y + z = 9 \\ z = -3 \end{cases}$

$(5, -1)$ $(-31, 12, -3)$

48. $(-6, 10)$ **50.** $(5, -3, 0)$ **52.** $(-1, 3)$

54. $(9, 13)$ **56.** $(-2, -1)$ **58.** $(3a + 5, a)$

60. $(8, 10, 6)$ **62.** $(-6, 8, 2)$ **64.** $(5, -1, -2)$

66. $\left(-\frac{3}{2}a + \frac{3}{2}, \frac{1}{3}a + \frac{1}{3}, a\right)$

68. $(-3b + 96a + 100, b, 52a + 54, a)$

70. Inconsistent   **72.** $(-5a, a, 3)$

74. $(-1, 1, 3, 1)$ **76.** $(-2a, -a, a, a)$

78. No   **80.** No   **82.** $I_1 = 2, I_2 = 3, I_3 = 1$

84. $\dfrac{8x^2}{(x-1)^2(x+1)} = \dfrac{2}{x+1} + \dfrac{6}{x-1} + \dfrac{4}{(x-1)^2}$

86. $100,000 at 9%

$250,000 at 10%

$150,000 at 12%

88. $y = -x^2 + 2x + 8$

90. (a) $y = -2.05t^2 + 50.75t - 168.1$

(b)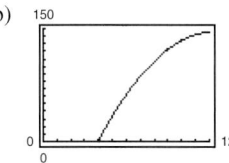

(c) $142.1 billion. This value is fairly close to the actual value.

(d) $140.6 billion. No.

92. (a) $x_1 = 500 - s - t, x_2 = -200 + s + t, x_3 = s,$

$x_4 = 350 - t, x_5 = t$

(b) $x_1 = 100, x_2 = 200, x_3 = 50, x_4 = 0, x_5 = 350$

(c) $x_1 = 150, x_2 = 150, x_3 = 0, x_4 = 0, x_5 = 350$

94. False. A matrix is in reduced row-echelon form if (1) all rows consisting entirely of zeros occur at the bottom of the matrix, (2) for each row that does not consist entirely of zeros, the first nonzero entry is 1, (3) for two successive nonzero rows, the leading 1 in the higher row is farther to the left than the leading 1 in the lower row, and (4) every column that has a leading 1 has zeros in every position above and below its leading 1.

96. Answers will vary. For example:

$$\begin{cases} x + y + 7z = -1 \\ x + 2y + 11z = 0 \\ 2x + y + 10z = -3 \end{cases}$$

98. Interchange two rows.
Multiply a row by a nonzero constant.
Add a multiple of a row to another row.

100. A matrix in reduced row-echelon form has zeros above the leading 1s. A matrix in row-echelon form may have any real numbers above the leading 1s.

102.

104.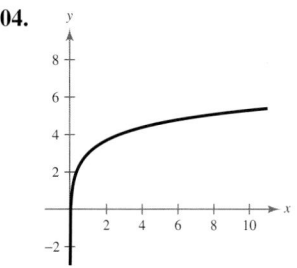

Section 8.2 *(page 569)*

2. $x = 13, \ y = 12$ **4.** $x = -4, \ y = 9$

6. (a) $\begin{bmatrix} -2 & 0 \\ 6 & 3 \end{bmatrix}$ (b) $\begin{bmatrix} 4 & 4 \\ -2 & -1 \end{bmatrix}$

(c) $\begin{bmatrix} 3 & 6 \\ 6 & 3 \end{bmatrix}$ (d) $\begin{bmatrix} 9 & 10 \\ -2 & -1 \end{bmatrix}$

8. (a) $\begin{bmatrix} 4 & -2 & 5 \\ -4 & 0 & 2 \end{bmatrix}$ (b) $\begin{bmatrix} 0 & 4 & -3 \\ 2 & -2 & 6 \end{bmatrix}$

(c) $\begin{bmatrix} 6 & 3 & 3 \\ -3 & -3 & 12 \end{bmatrix}$ (d) $\begin{bmatrix} 2 & 9 & -5 \\ 3 & -5 & 16 \end{bmatrix}$

10. (a) $\begin{bmatrix} -4 & 9 & 1 \\ 5 & -6 & -5 \\ 15 & -5 & -2 \\ 3 & 10 & -10 \\ -4 & 0 & -2 \end{bmatrix}$ (b) $\begin{bmatrix} 2 & -1 & -1 \\ 1 & 2 & 9 \\ -5 & 13 & 0 \\ -3 & 6 & -2 \\ -4 & -2 & 2 \end{bmatrix}$

(c) $\begin{bmatrix} -3 & 12 & 0 \\ 9 & -6 & 6 \\ 15 & 12 & -3 \\ 0 & 24 & -18 \\ -12 & -3 & 0 \end{bmatrix}$ (d) $\begin{bmatrix} 3 & 2 & -2 \\ 5 & 2 & 20 \\ -5 & 30 & -1 \\ -6 & 20 & -10 \\ -12 & -5 & 4 \end{bmatrix}$

12. (a), (b), and (d) not possible

(c) $\begin{bmatrix} 9 \\ 6 \\ -3 \end{bmatrix}$

14. $\begin{bmatrix} -5 & 6 \\ -2 & -2 \end{bmatrix}$ **16.** $\begin{bmatrix} \frac{19}{2} & 2 & -7 & \frac{9}{2} \end{bmatrix}$

18. $\begin{bmatrix} -\frac{11}{3} & -\frac{31}{3} \\ 1 & \frac{3}{2} \\ -8 & -1 \end{bmatrix}$ **20.** $\begin{bmatrix} -440 & 495 \\ -495 & 1375 \end{bmatrix}$

22. $\begin{bmatrix} 132 & 168 \\ -108 & 60 \\ -348 & 60 \end{bmatrix}$ **24.** $\begin{bmatrix} -2 & -\frac{5}{2} \\ 0 & 0 \\ 5 & -\frac{7}{2} \end{bmatrix}$ **26.** $\begin{bmatrix} 2 & -5 \\ -5 & 0 \\ 5 & 6 \end{bmatrix}$

28. Not possible

30. $\begin{bmatrix} -1 & 19 \\ 4 & -27 \\ 0 & 14 \end{bmatrix}$ **32.** $\begin{bmatrix} 1 & 0 & 0 \\ 0 & 1 & 0 \\ 0 & 0 & \frac{7}{2} \end{bmatrix}$

CHAPTER 8

34. $\begin{bmatrix} 60 & -20 & 10 & 60 \\ 72 & -24 & 12 & 72 \end{bmatrix}$

36. $\begin{bmatrix} 252 & 30 \\ 298 & 452 \\ 217 & 180 \end{bmatrix}$ **38.** Not possible

40. $\begin{bmatrix} -249 & 42 & -417 \\ 124 & 104 & 284 \\ 232 & 176 & 520 \end{bmatrix}$

42. (a) $\begin{bmatrix} -3 & 3 \\ 12 & -12 \end{bmatrix}$ (b) $\begin{bmatrix} 0 & 0 \\ 3 & -15 \end{bmatrix}$ (c) $\begin{bmatrix} 3 & -6 \\ 6 & 15 \end{bmatrix}$

44. (a) $\begin{bmatrix} 4 & 2 \\ -2 & 4 \end{bmatrix}$ (b) $\begin{bmatrix} 4 & 2 \\ -2 & 4 \end{bmatrix}$ (c) $\begin{bmatrix} 0 & -2 \\ 2 & 0 \end{bmatrix}$

46. (a) $[12]$ (b) $\begin{bmatrix} 6 & 4 & 2 \\ 9 & 6 & 3 \\ 0 & 0 & 0 \end{bmatrix}$ (c) Not possible

48. $\begin{bmatrix} 27 & -6 \\ -6 & -27 \end{bmatrix}$ **50.** $\begin{bmatrix} 12 & 6 \\ -4 & -2 \\ 20 & 10 \\ 28 & 14 \end{bmatrix}$

52. (a) $\begin{bmatrix} 2 & 3 \\ 1 & 4 \end{bmatrix}\begin{bmatrix} x_1 \\ x_2 \end{bmatrix} = \begin{bmatrix} 5 \\ 10 \end{bmatrix}$ (b) $\begin{bmatrix} -2 \\ 3 \end{bmatrix}$

54. (a) $\begin{bmatrix} -4 & 9 \\ 1 & -3 \end{bmatrix}\begin{bmatrix} x_1 \\ x_2 \end{bmatrix} = \begin{bmatrix} -13 \\ 12 \end{bmatrix}$ (b) $\begin{bmatrix} -23 \\ -\frac{35}{3} \end{bmatrix}$

56. (a) $\begin{bmatrix} 1 & 1 & -3 \\ -1 & 2 & 0 \\ 1 & -1 & 1 \end{bmatrix}\begin{bmatrix} x_1 \\ x_2 \\ x_3 \end{bmatrix} = \begin{bmatrix} 9 \\ 6 \\ -5 \end{bmatrix}$ (b) $\begin{bmatrix} 0 \\ 3 \\ -2 \end{bmatrix}$

58. (a) $\begin{bmatrix} 1 & -1 & 4 \\ 1 & 3 & 0 \\ 0 & -6 & 5 \end{bmatrix}\begin{bmatrix} x_1 \\ x_2 \\ x_3 \end{bmatrix} = \begin{bmatrix} 17 \\ -11 \\ 40 \end{bmatrix}$ (b) $\begin{bmatrix} 4 \\ -5 \\ 2 \end{bmatrix}$

60. $\begin{bmatrix} 110 & 99 & 77 & 33 \\ 44 & 22 & 66 & 66 \end{bmatrix}$

62. $[\$916{,}500 \quad \$885{,}500]$

The entries represent the costs of the three models of the portable CD players at the two warehouses.

64. $\begin{bmatrix} 0.40 & 0.15 & 0.15 \\ 0.28 & 0.53 & 0.17 \\ 0.32 & 0.32 & 0.68 \end{bmatrix}$

P^2 gives the proportions of the voting population that changed parties or remained loyal to their parties from the first election to the third.

66. $\begin{bmatrix} \$18.10 & \$15.40 \\ \$29.80 & \$25.40 \\ \$59.20 & \$50.80 \end{bmatrix}$

The entries represent the labor costs at each plant for each size of boat.

68. False. For most matrices, $AB \neq BA$.

70. Not possible   **72.** 2×2 **74.** Not possible

76. 2×3

78. $AB = \begin{bmatrix} 0 & 0 \\ 0 & 0 \end{bmatrix}$

$AB = O$ and neither A nor B is O.

80. (a) $A^2 = \begin{bmatrix} -1 & 0 \\ 0 & -1 \end{bmatrix}$ and $i^2 = -1$.

$A^3 = \begin{bmatrix} -i & 0 \\ 0 & -i \end{bmatrix}$ and $i^3 = -i$.

$A^4 = \begin{bmatrix} 1 & 0 \\ 0 & 1 \end{bmatrix}$ and $i^4 = 1$.

(b) $B^2 = \begin{bmatrix} 1 & 0 \\ 0 & 1 \end{bmatrix} = I$, the identity matrix.

82. $-\frac{1}{4}, \frac{3}{2}$ **84.** $0, -9, \frac{5}{3}$ **86.** $\frac{5}{2}, \pm\sqrt{6}$

88. $(-1, 3)$ **90.** $(4, 1)$

Section 8.3 (page 579)

2–10. $AB = I$ and $BA = I$

12. $\begin{bmatrix} 7 & -2 \\ -3 & 1 \end{bmatrix}$ **14.** $\begin{bmatrix} -19 & -33 \\ -4 & -7 \end{bmatrix}$

16. $\begin{bmatrix} 0 & -1 \\ 1 & 11 \end{bmatrix}$ **18.** $\begin{bmatrix} \frac{4}{5} & -\frac{3}{5} \\ -\frac{1}{5} & \frac{2}{5} \end{bmatrix}$

20. Does not exist   **22.** $\begin{bmatrix} -13 & 6 & 4 \\ 12 & -5 & -3 \\ -5 & 2 & 1 \end{bmatrix}$

24. Does not exist   **26.** $\begin{bmatrix} 1 & -\frac{3}{2} & -4 & \frac{13}{5} \\ 0 & \frac{1}{2} & 1 & -\frac{4}{5} \\ 0 & 0 & -\frac{1}{2} & \frac{1}{10} \\ 0 & 0 & 0 & \frac{1}{5} \end{bmatrix}$

28. $\begin{bmatrix} -10 & -4 & 27 \\ 2 & 1 & -5 \\ -13 & -5 & 35 \end{bmatrix}$ **30.** $\begin{bmatrix} 1 & -1 & 0 \\ 7 & -8.5 & 1 \\ -8 & 10 & -1 \end{bmatrix}$

32. Does not exist   **34.** $\begin{bmatrix} 3.75 & 0 & -1.25 \\ 3.458\overline{3} & -1 & -1.375 \\ 4.1\overline{6} & 0 & -2.5 \end{bmatrix}$

36. $\begin{bmatrix} 27 & -10 & 4 & -29 \\ -16 & 5 & -2 & 18 \\ -17 & 4 & -2 & 20 \\ -7 & 2 & -1 & 8 \end{bmatrix}$

38. $\begin{bmatrix} -24 & 7 & 1 & -2 \\ -10 & 3 & 0 & -1 \\ -29 & 7 & 3 & -2 \\ 12 & -3 & -1 & 1 \end{bmatrix}$ **40.** $\begin{bmatrix} -\frac{5}{61} & -\frac{12}{61} \\ \frac{8}{61} & \frac{7}{61} \end{bmatrix}$

42. $\begin{bmatrix} -\frac{2}{9} & -\frac{1}{3} \\ -\frac{5}{9} & -\frac{4}{3} \end{bmatrix}$ **44.** $\begin{bmatrix} -\frac{32}{143} & \frac{81}{143} \\ \frac{60}{143} & \frac{9}{143} \end{bmatrix}$

46. $(6, 3)$ **48.** $(-7, -4)$ **50.** $(1, 7, -9)$

52. $(-32, -13, -37, 15)$ **54.** $\left(\frac{1}{2}, \frac{1}{3}\right)$

56. $(6, -2)$ **58.** $(-12, 10)$ **60.** $(5, 8, -2)$

62. $(2a - 1, -3a + 2, a)$ **64.** $(10, -3, 5)$

66. $(6.21, -0.77, -2.67, 2.40)$

68. \$4000 in AAA-rated bonds

$2000 in A-rated bonds

$4000 in B-rated bonds

70. \$200,000 in AAA-rated bonds

$100,000 in A-rated bonds

$200,000 in B-rated bonds

72. (a) $\begin{cases} 3b + 24a = 635.7 \\ 24b + 194a = 5094.1 \end{cases}$

(b) $y = 4.25t + 177.9$ (c) 220.4 million

(d) The value is close to the estimate.   (e) 2004

74. True. If A and B are both square matrices and $AB = I_n$, it can be shown that $BA = I_n$.

76. (a) Answers will vary.

(b) $A^{-1} = \begin{bmatrix} \frac{1}{a_{11}} & 0 & 0 & \cdots & 0 \\ 0 & \frac{1}{a_{22}} & 0 & \cdots & 0 \\ 0 & 0 & \frac{1}{a_{33}} & \cdots & 0 \\ \vdots & \vdots & \vdots & \cdots & \vdots \\ 0 & 0 & 0 & \cdots & \frac{1}{a_{nn}} \end{bmatrix}$

78. $-1 < x < 2$

80. $-5 \ln \frac{1}{5} \approx 8.05$ **82.** $\dfrac{1 + \sqrt{5}}{2} \approx 1.62$

Section 8.4 *(page 587)*

 2. -8 **4.** -11 **6.** 14 **8.** 0 **10.** 0

12. 34 **14.** 18 **16.** $\frac{10}{9}$ **18.** -0.022

20. -11.217 **22.** -20

24. (a) $M_{11} = 2, M_{12} = -3, M_{21} = 0, M_{22} = 11$

(b) $C_{11} = 2, C_{12} = 3, C_{21} = 0, C_{22} = 11$

26. (a) $M_{11} = -2, M_{12} = 7, M_{21} = 5, M_{22} = -6$

(b) $C_{11} = -2, C_{12} = -7, C_{21} = -5, C_{22} = -6$

28. (a) $M_{11} = 38, M_{12} = -8, M_{13} = -26, M_{21} = -4,$

$M_{22} = 4, M_{23} = -2, M_{31} = -5, M_{32} = 5, M_{33} = 5$

(b) $C_{11} = 38, C_{12} = 8, C_{13} = -26, C_{21} = 4,$

$C_{22} = 4, C_{23} = 2, C_{31} = -5, C_{32} = -5, C_{33} = 5$

30. (a) $M_{11} = 36, M_{12} = -42, M_{13} = 85, M_{21} = -82,$

$M_{22} = -12, M_{23} = -68, M_{31} = 24,$

$M_{32} = -28, M_{33} = -51$

(b) $C_{11} = 36, C_{12} = 42, C_{13} = 85, C_{21} = 82,$

$C_{22} = -12, C_{23} = 68, C_{31} = 24, C_{32} = 28,$

$C_{33} = -51$

32. (a) 151   (b) 151   **34.** (a) 650   (b) 650

36. (a) -1167 (b) -1167 **38.** 3

40. -2 **42.** -5 **44.** 2   **46.** -66

48. -108 **50.** 0   **52.** -100 **54.** 223

56. 105   **58.** 7441   **60.** -48

62. (a) 0   **64.** (a) -17

(b) -1 (b) -6

(c) $\begin{bmatrix} -2 & -5 \\ 4 & 10 \end{bmatrix}$ (c) $\begin{bmatrix} 4 & 22 \\ -1 & 20 \end{bmatrix}$

(d) 0   (d) 102

66. (a) -23 **68.** (a) 0

(b) 1   (b) -7

(c) $\begin{bmatrix} -9 & 4 & 1 \\ -5 & -10 & 6 \\ 4 & -1 & -1 \end{bmatrix}$ (c) $\begin{bmatrix} 7 & -4 & 9 \\ 8 & -6 & 3 \\ 6 & -2 & 15 \end{bmatrix}$

(d) -23 (d) 0

70–74. Answers will vary.   **76.** $-1, 3$ **78.** $-2, 3$

80. $3x^2 + 3y^2$ **82.** e^{-2x} **84.** x

86. True. If a square matrix has two columns that are equal, then elementary column operations can be used to create a column with all zeros.

88. (a) For an $n \times n$ matrix $(n > 2)$ with consecutive integer entries, the determinant appears to be 0.

(b) Answers will vary.

90. Yes. $|2A| = 8|A| = 8(5) = 40$

92. (a) Add -5 times Row 1 to Row 2.

$|A| = 17 = |B|$

(b) Add -2 times Row 2 to Row 1.

$|A| = -11 = |B|$

94. All real numbers   **96.** All real numbers $x \neq \pm 6$

98. All real numbers

CHAPTER 8

100.

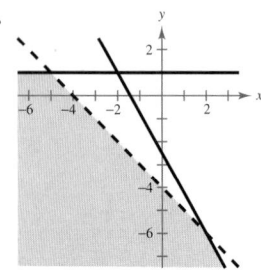

102. $\begin{bmatrix} -1 & -\frac{4}{3} \\ \frac{1}{2} & \frac{5}{6} \end{bmatrix}$ **104.** $\begin{bmatrix} -\frac{1}{4} & \frac{1}{6} & \frac{1}{3} \\ -\frac{1}{4} & \frac{1}{2} & 1 \\ -\frac{1}{2} & \frac{1}{3} & \frac{5}{3} \end{bmatrix}$

Section 8.5   *(page 599)*

2. $(-3, -5)$ **4.** $\left(\frac{8}{5}, -\frac{83}{10}\right)$ **6.** $(5, 8, -2)$

8. $(0, 3, -2)$ **10.** $(-3, -1, 2)$

12. Cramer's Rule does not apply.

14. $\frac{33}{2}$ **16.** $\frac{31}{2}$ **18.** 55 **20.** $\frac{25}{2}$ **22.** $\frac{23}{2}$

24. 19 or 3   **26.** 6 or 0   **28.** 3100 square feet

30. Not collinear   **32.** Collinear   **34.** Not collinear

36. $x = 3$ **38.** $x + y = 0$ **40.** $7x - 6y - 28 = 0$

42. $3x - 2y + 6 = 0$

44. Uncoded: $[16 \quad 12 \quad 5], [1 \quad 19 \quad 5], [0 \quad 19 \quad 5],$
$\qquad\qquad [14 \quad 4 \quad 0], [13 \quad 15 \quad 14], [5 \quad 25 \quad 0]$

      Encoded: $43 \ 6 \ 9 \ -38 \ -45 \ -13$
$\qquad\qquad\qquad -42 \ -47 \ -14 \ 44 \ 16 \ 10 \ 49 \ 9 \ 12$
$\qquad\qquad\qquad -55 \ -65 \ -20$

46. $13 \ 19 \ 10 \ -1 \ -33 \ -77 \ 3 \ -2 \ -14$
$\qquad 4 \ 1 \ -9 \ -5 \ -25 \ -47 \ 4 \ 1 \ -9$

48. $58 \ 122 \ 139 \ 1 \ -37 \ -95 \ 40 \ 67 \ 55 \ 23 \ 17 \ -19 \ 47$
$\qquad 88 \ 88 \ 14 \ 21 \ 11$

50. BRONCOS WIN SUPER BOWL

52. HAVE A GREAT WEEKEND

54. RETURN AT DAWN

56. (a) $\begin{cases} 3c + 24b + 194a = 24{,}220 \\ 24c + 194b + 1584a = 194{,}513 \\ 194c + 1584b + 13{,}058a = 1{,}578{,}265 \end{cases}$

     (b) $y = -14.50t^2 + 608.5t + 4143$

     (c) 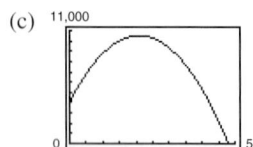   (d) 2004

58. True. If the determinant of the coefficient matrix is zero, then the solution of the system would result in division by zero, which is undefined.

60. Answers will vary.   **62.** $\left(5, -\frac{1}{2}\right)$ **64.** $(2, -2, 5)$

66.

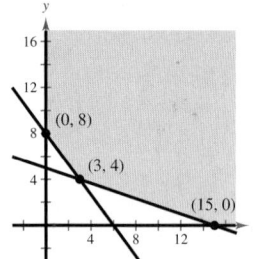

    Minimum at $(3, 4)$: 46

    No maximum

Review Exercises   *(page 603)*

2. 2×4 **4.** 1×5

6. $\begin{bmatrix} 8 & -7 & 4 & \vdots & 12 \\ 3 & -5 & 2 & \vdots & 20 \\ 5 & 3 & -3 & \vdots & 26 \end{bmatrix}$

8. $\begin{cases} 13x + 16y + 7z + 3w = 2 \\ x + 21y + 8z + 5w = 12 \\ 4x + 10y - 4z + 3w = -1 \end{cases}$

10. $\begin{bmatrix} 1 & 2 & 4 \\ 0 & 1 & \frac{10}{7} \\ 0 & 0 & 0 \end{bmatrix}$

12. $\begin{cases} x + 3y - 9z = 4 \\ y - z = 10 \\ z = -2 \end{cases}$ **14.** $\begin{cases} x - 8y = -2 \\ y - z = -7 \\ z = 1 \end{cases}$

    $(-38, 8, -2)$ $(-50, -6, 1)$

16. $(-9, -4)$ **18.** $\left(\frac{3}{5}, \frac{1}{2}\right)$ **20.** $\left(\frac{1}{2}, -\frac{1}{3}, 1\right)$

22. Inconsistent   **24.** Inconsistent   **26.** $\left(\frac{31}{42}, \frac{5}{14}, \frac{13}{84}\right)$

28. $(6, -2, 0)$ **30.** Inconsistent   **32.** $x = 8, y = 0$

34. $x = 12, y = -2$

36. (a) $\begin{bmatrix} 9 & 16 \\ 13 & 42 \\ 26 & 32 \end{bmatrix}$ (b) $\begin{bmatrix} 1 & -8 \\ -27 & -38 \\ -4 & -28 \end{bmatrix}$

    (c) $\begin{bmatrix} 20 & 16 \\ -28 & 8 \\ 44 & 8 \end{bmatrix}$ (d) $\begin{bmatrix} 17 & 40 \\ 53 & 122 \\ 56 & 92 \end{bmatrix}$

38. (a), (b), and (d) not possible

    (c) $[24 \quad -20 \quad 28]$

40. Not possible. The matrices are not of the same order.

42. $\begin{bmatrix} 2 & 1 & 12 \\ -13 & 1 & -17 \\ -30 & -54 & 40 \end{bmatrix}$ **44.** $\begin{bmatrix} 6 & -8 \\ -11 & 54 \\ -44 & 2 \end{bmatrix}$

46. $\begin{bmatrix} -\frac{13}{6} & 1 \\ -\frac{1}{3} & -\frac{17}{6} \\ 0 & \frac{10}{3} \end{bmatrix}$ **48.** $\begin{bmatrix} -\frac{13}{3} & -\frac{10}{3} \\ 4 & -5 \\ -\frac{26}{3} & -\frac{16}{3} \end{bmatrix}$

50. Not possible. The number of columns of A does not equal the number of rows of B.

52. $[30]$

54. Not possible. The number of columns of the first matrix does not equal the number of rows of the second matrix.

56. $\begin{bmatrix} 4 & 6 & 3 \\ 0 & 6 & -10 \\ 0 & 0 & 6 \end{bmatrix}$ **58.** $[4 \quad 10]$

60. $\begin{bmatrix} -12 & 9 \\ -246 & 144 \end{bmatrix}$ **62.** $\begin{bmatrix} 13 & 24 \\ 20 & 4 \end{bmatrix}$

64. $[\$274,150 \quad \$303,150]$

The merchandise shipped to warehouse 1 is worth \$274,150 and the merchandise shipped to warehouse 2 is worth \$303,150.

66 and 68. $AB = I$ and $BA = I$

70. $\begin{bmatrix} 3 & 5 \\ -2 & -3 \end{bmatrix}$ **72.** $\begin{bmatrix} 1 & 11 & 8 \\ -1 & -7 & -5 \\ -1 & -14 & -10 \end{bmatrix}$

74. Does not exist

76. $\begin{bmatrix} -2.5 & 3 & 7 & -2 \\ -4 & 4.5 & 11 & -3 \\ 14.5 & -16 & -40 & 12 \\ -1 & 1 & 3 & -1 \end{bmatrix}$

78. $\begin{bmatrix} \frac{3}{2} & -2 \\ -\frac{7}{2} & 5 \end{bmatrix}$ **80.** $\begin{bmatrix} -\frac{2}{3} & -\frac{5}{8} \\ \frac{1}{5} & -\frac{3}{16} \end{bmatrix}$ **82.** $(2, -3)$

84. $(-2, 1)$ **86.** $(-2, 4, 3)$ **88.** $(-3, 5, 0)$

90. $(5, 6)$ **92.** $(4, -2, 1)$ **94.** -41 **96.** 78

98. (a) $M_{11} = -4, M_{12} = 5, M_{21} = 6, M_{22} = 3$

    (b) $C_{11} = -4, C_{12} = -5, C_{21} = -6, C_{22} = 3$

100. (a) $M_{11} = 19, M_{12} = -24, M_{13} = 26, M_{21} = 2,$

      $M_{22} = 32, M_{23} = 20, M_{31} = -47, M_{32} = -96,$

      $M_{33} = 22$

    (b) $C_{11} = 19, C_{12} = 24, C_{13} = 26, C_{21} = -2,$

      $C_{22} = 32, C_{23} = -20, C_{31} = -47, C_{32} = 96,$

      $C_{33} = 22$

102. -117 **104.** -255 **106.** $(3, -2)$

108. $(6, 8, 1)$ **110.** 24 **112.** $\frac{25}{8}$ **114.** Collinear

116. $3x + 2y - 16 = 0$ **118.** $10x - 5y + 9 = 0$

120. Uncoded: $[18 \ 5 \ 20], [21 \ 18 \ 14], [0 \ 20 \ 15],$

        $[0 \ 2 \ 1], [19 \ 5 \ 0]$

    Encoded: $66 \ 28 \ 10 \ -24 \ -59 \ -22 \ -75 \ -90$

        $-25 \ -9 \ -10 \ -3 \ 8 \ -11 \ -10$

122. MAY THE FORCE BE WITH YOU

124. True. Answers will vary.

126. If A is a square matrix, the cofactor C_{ij} of the entry a_{ij} is $(-1)^{i+j}M_{ij}$, where M_{ij} is the determinant obtained by deleting the ith row and jth column of A. The determinant of A is the sum of the entries of any row or column of A multiplied by their respective cofactors.

128. The part of the matrix corresponding to the coefficients of the system reduces to a matrix in which the number of rows with nonzero entries is the same as the number of variables.

Problem Solving (page 610)

2. (a)

2000

	0–17	18–64	65+
Northeast	4.64	11.79	2.62
Midwest	5.92	14.00	2.94
South	9.09	22.12	4.42
Mountain	1.75	3.98	0.72
Pacific	4.30	9.97	1.74

2015

	0–17	18–64	65+
Northeast	4.06	10.99	2.63
Midwest	5.12	13.23	3.26
South	8.36	22.25	5.63
Mountain	1.69	4.07	1.05
Pacific	4.81	10.74	2.12

(b)

	0–17	18–64	65+
Northeast	-0.58	-0.80	0.01
Midwest	-0.80	-0.77	0.32
South	-0.73	0.13	1.21
Mountain	-0.06	0.09	0.33
Pacific	0.51	0.77	0.38

(c) The Pacific region and the 65+ age group show relative growth.

4. (a) $A^2 - 2A + 5I$

$$= \begin{bmatrix} 1 & 2 \\ -2 & 1 \end{bmatrix}^2 - 2\begin{bmatrix} 1 & 2 \\ -2 & 1 \end{bmatrix} + 5\begin{bmatrix} 1 & 0 \\ 0 & 1 \end{bmatrix}$$

$$= \begin{bmatrix} -3 & 4 \\ -4 & -3 \end{bmatrix} - \begin{bmatrix} 2 & 4 \\ -4 & 2 \end{bmatrix} + \begin{bmatrix} 5 & 0 \\ 0 & 5 \end{bmatrix}$$

$$= \begin{bmatrix} 0 & 0 \\ 0 & 0 \end{bmatrix}$$

(b) $A^{-1} = \frac{1}{5}(2I - A)$

$$\begin{bmatrix} 1 & 2 \\ -2 & 1 \end{bmatrix}^{-1} = \frac{1}{5}\left(2\begin{bmatrix} 1 & 0 \\ 0 & 1 \end{bmatrix} - \begin{bmatrix} 1 & 2 \\ -2 & 1 \end{bmatrix}\right)$$

$$\begin{bmatrix} \frac{1}{5} & -\frac{2}{5} \\ \frac{2}{5} & \frac{1}{5} \end{bmatrix} = \frac{1}{5}\left(\begin{bmatrix} 2 & 0 \\ 0 & 2 \end{bmatrix} - \begin{bmatrix} 1 & 2 \\ -2 & 1 \end{bmatrix}\right)$$

$$\begin{bmatrix} \frac{1}{5} & -\frac{2}{5} \\ \frac{2}{5} & \frac{1}{5} \end{bmatrix} = \frac{1}{5}\begin{bmatrix} 1 & -2 \\ 2 & 1 \end{bmatrix}$$

$$\begin{bmatrix} \frac{1}{5} & -\frac{2}{5} \\ \frac{2}{5} & \frac{1}{5} \end{bmatrix} = \begin{bmatrix} \frac{1}{5} & -\frac{2}{5} \\ \frac{2}{5} & \frac{1}{5} \end{bmatrix}$$

(c) Answers will vary.

6. $x = 6$

8.

$$\begin{vmatrix} 1 & 1 & 1 \\ a & b & c \\ a^2 & b^2 & c^2 \end{vmatrix} = \begin{vmatrix} b & c \\ b^2 & c^2 \end{vmatrix} - \begin{vmatrix} a & c \\ a^2 & c^2 \end{vmatrix} + \begin{vmatrix} a & b \\ a^2 & b^2 \end{vmatrix}$$

$$= bc^2 - b^2c - ac^2 + a^2c + ab^2$$
$$- a^2b$$

$$(a-b)(b-c)(c-a) = -a^2b + a^2c + ab^2 - ac^2$$
$$- b^2c + bc^2$$

10.
$$\begin{vmatrix} x & 0 & c \\ -1 & x & b \\ 0 & -1 & a \end{vmatrix} = x\begin{vmatrix} x & b \\ -1 & a \end{vmatrix} + c\begin{vmatrix} -1 & x \\ 0 & -1 \end{vmatrix}$$

$$= x(ax+b) + c(1)$$
$$= ax^2 + bx + c$$

12. Sulfur: 32 atomic mass units

Nitrogen: 14 atomic mass units

Fluorine: 19 atomic mass units

14. REMEMBER SEPTEMBER THE ELEVENTH

16. (a) $A^{-1} = \begin{bmatrix} 1 & -2 \\ 1 & -3 \end{bmatrix}$

(b) JOHN RETURN TO BASE

18. $|A| = 0$

Chapter 9

Section 9.1 *(page 621)*

2. 2, 7, 12, 17, 22   **4.** $\frac{1}{2}, \frac{1}{4}, \frac{1}{8}, \frac{1}{16}, \frac{1}{32}$

6. $-\frac{1}{2}, \frac{1}{4}, -\frac{1}{8}, \frac{1}{16}, -\frac{1}{32}$ **8.** $\frac{1}{3}, \frac{1}{2}, \frac{3}{5}, \frac{2}{3}, \frac{5}{7}$ **10.** $2, \frac{14}{9}, \frac{28}{19}, \frac{16}{11}, \frac{74}{51}$

12. 0, 2, 0, 2, 0   **14.** $\frac{2}{3}, \frac{4}{9}, \frac{8}{27}, \frac{16}{81}, \frac{32}{243}$

16. $10, \frac{10}{\sqrt[3]{4}}, \frac{10}{\sqrt[3]{9}}, \frac{10}{\sqrt[3]{16}}, \frac{10}{\sqrt[3]{25}}$ **18.** 1, 1, 2, 6, 24

20. $-\frac{1}{2}, \frac{2}{3}, -\frac{3}{4}, \frac{4}{5}, -\frac{5}{6}$ **22.** 0.3, 0.3, 0.3, 0.3, 0.3

24. $-5, -4, 9, 40, 95$ **26.** -240 **28.** 2520   **30.** $\frac{37}{130}$

32.   **34.**

36. 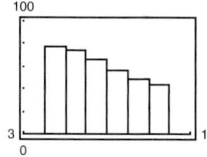   **37.** c   **38.** b

39. d   **40.** a

42. $a_n = 4n - 1$ **44.** $a_n = (-1)^{n+1}(2n)$

46. $a_n = \frac{(-1)^{n+1}}{2^n}$ **48.** $a_n = \frac{2^{n-1}}{3^n}$ **50.** $a_n = \frac{1}{n!}$

52. $a_n = \frac{2^{n-1}}{(n-1)!}$ **54.** $a_n = 1 + \frac{2^n - 1}{2^n}$

56. 15, 18, 21, 24, 27   **58.** 32, 16, 8, 4, 2

60. 25, 20, 15, 10, 5   **62.** $14, -28, 56, -112, 224$

$a_n = 30 - 5n$ $a_n = 14(-2)^{n-1}$

64. $\frac{1}{336}$ **66.** 600   **68.** $(n+2)(n+1)$ **70.** $3n + 1$

72. 57   **74.** 25   **76.** 110   **78.** $\frac{124}{429}$ **80.** 238

82. 11   **84.** 6.06   **86.** $\frac{3}{8}$ **88.** $\sum_{i=1}^{15} \frac{5}{1+i}$

90. $\sum_{i=1}^{6}\left[1 - \left(\frac{i}{6}\right)^2\right]$ **92.** $\sum_{i=0}^{7}\left(-\frac{1}{2}\right)^i$ **94.** $\sum_{i=1}^{10} \frac{1}{i(i+2)}$

96. $\sum_{i=1}^{6} \frac{i!}{2^i}$ **98.** $\frac{242}{243}$ **100.** $-\frac{51}{32}$ **102.** $\frac{1}{9}$ **104.** $\frac{2}{9}$

106. (a) $A_1 = \$101.00, A_2 = \$203.01, A_3 = \$306.04,$
$A_4 = \$410.10, A_5 = \$515.20, A_6 = \$621.35$

(b) $A_{60} = \$8248.64$

(c) $A_{240} = \$99,914.79$

108. $a_4 = 77.6, a_5 = 73.5, a_6 = 65.7,$
$a_7 = 56.7, a_8 = 48.7, a_9 = 44.3$

110. $4838.48 million

112. True. The sums are equal because

$$2^1 + 2^2 + 2^3 + 2^4 = 2^{3-2} + 2^{4-2} + 2^{5-2} + 2^{6-2}.$$

114. Answers will vary.   **116.** $1.301

118. Answers will vary.

120. $-\dfrac{x^3}{3}, \dfrac{x^5}{5}, -\dfrac{x^7}{7}, \dfrac{x^9}{9}, -\dfrac{x^{11}}{11}$

122. $-\dfrac{x^3}{6}, \dfrac{x^5}{120}, -\dfrac{x^7}{5040}, \dfrac{x^9}{362,880}, -\dfrac{x^{11}}{39,916,800}$

124. $g^{-1}(x) = \dfrac{3}{x}$ **126.** No inverse

128. (a) $\begin{bmatrix} 10 & 19 \\ -12 & -5 \end{bmatrix}$ (b) $\begin{bmatrix} -30 & -69 \\ 44 & 26 \end{bmatrix}$

(c) $\begin{bmatrix} 56 & -43 \\ 48 & 114 \end{bmatrix}$ (d) $\begin{bmatrix} 48 & -72 \\ 36 & 122 \end{bmatrix}$

130. (a) $\begin{bmatrix} -1 & 0 & 0 \\ 2 & 0 & 4 \\ 1 & -1 & 1 \end{bmatrix}$ (b) $\begin{bmatrix} 3 & 4 & 0 \\ -3 & 1 & -14 \\ -4 & 3 & -1 \end{bmatrix}$

(c) $\begin{bmatrix} 12 & 0 & -8 \\ 1 & 21 & 2 \\ -6 & -1 & 8 \end{bmatrix}$ (d) $\begin{bmatrix} 20 & 4 & 8 \\ 2 & 15 & -4 \\ 1 & -6 & 6 \end{bmatrix}$

132. -126 **134.** $-11,758$

Section 9.2   *(page 631)*

2. Arithmetic sequence, $d = 3$

4. Not an arithmetic sequence

6. Arithmetic sequence, $d = -\frac{1}{2}$

8. Arithmetic sequence, $d = 0.4$

10. Not an arithmetic sequence

12. 97, 94, 91, 88, 85
Arithmetic sequence, $d = -3$

14. 1, 5, 9, 13, 17
Arithmetic sequence, $d = 4$

16. 1, 2, 4, 8, 16
Not an arithmetic sequence

18. 2, 8, 24, 64, 160
Not an arithmetic sequence

20. 6, 11, 16, 21, 26; $d = 5$; $a_n = 5n + 1$

22. 72, 66, 60, 54, 48; $d = -6$; $a_n = -6n + 78$

24. 0.375, 0.625, 0.875, 1.125, 1.375; $d = 0.25$;
$a_n = 0.25n + 0.125$

26. 5, $\frac{17}{4}, \frac{7}{2}, \frac{11}{4}, 2$ **28.** 16.5, 16.75, 17, 17.25, 17.5

30. 1, 6, 11, 16, 21   **32.** 22.45, 20.725, 19, 17.275, 15.55

34. $a_n = 4n + 11$ **36.** $a_n = -\frac{2}{3}n + \frac{2}{3}$

38. $a_n = 5yn - 6y$ **40.** $a_n = -5n + 15$

42. $a_n = 5n - 9$ **44.** $a_n = -15n + 265$

45. b   **46.** d   **47.** c   **48.** a

50.   **52.**

54. 1850   **56.** 23   **58.** 375   **60.** 16,100

62. 10,100   **64.** 26,425   **66.** 2500   **68.** 218,625

70. 44,625   **72.** -896.375 **74.** 1402.5   **76.** 1220

78. (a) $45,550   (b) $247,050

80. 2430 seats   **82.** 203 bricks   **84.** 784 feet

86. Add the first term to $(n - 1)$ times the common difference.

88. True by the formula for the sum of a finite arithmetic sequence,

$$S_n = \frac{n}{2}(a_1 + a_n)$$

90. (a) 4, 9, 16, 25, 36   (b) n^2; $49 = 7^2$

(c) $\dfrac{n}{2}[1 + (2n - 1)] = n^2$

92. $S_n + 5n$

94. Slope: -9;   **96.** Slope: 0
y-intercept: $(0, -8)$ y-intercept: $(0, -11)$

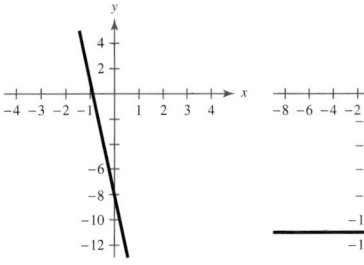

Section 9.3   *(page 640)*

2. Geometric sequence, $r = 4$

4. Not a geometric sequence

6. Geometric sequence, $r = 0.2$

8. Geometric sequence, $r = -\frac{2}{3}$

10. Not a geometric sequence   **12.** 6, 12, 24, 48, 96

14. $1, \frac{1}{3}, \frac{1}{9}, \frac{1}{27}, \frac{1}{81}$ **16.** $6, -\frac{3}{2}, \frac{3}{8}, -\frac{3}{32}, \frac{3}{128}$

18. $3, 3\sqrt{5}, 15, 15\sqrt{5}, 75$ **20.** $5, 10x, 20x^2, 40x^3, 80x^4$

22. 81, 27, 9, 3, 1; $r = \frac{1}{3}$; $a_n = 243\left(\frac{1}{3}\right)^n$

24. $5, -10, 20, -40, 80$; $r = -2$; $a_n = -\frac{5}{2}(-2)^n$

26. $48, -24, 12, -6, 3$; $r = -\frac{1}{2}$; $a_n = -96\left(-\frac{1}{2}\right)^n$

28. $\dfrac{10,935}{128}$ **30.** $-\dfrac{1}{4096}$ **32.** $27\sqrt{3}$

34. 1342.139   **36.** 12   **38.** $\frac{256}{243}$

39. a   **40.** c   **41.** b   **42.** d

44.

46.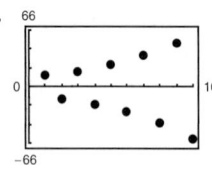

48.

50.

52. 6357.162   **54.** $-\frac{6305}{128}$ **56.** 2.667   **58.** $\frac{4095}{128}$

60. 12.500   **62.** $\frac{25}{2}$ **64.** 3949.147   **66.** 45.000

68. 5.333   **70.** 45   **72.** $\sum_{n=1}^{8} 7(2)^{n-1}$

74. $\sum_{n=1}^{6} 15\left(-\frac{1}{5}\right)^{n-1}$ **76.** $\sum_{n=1}^{5} 32\left(\frac{3}{4}\right)^{n-1}$ **78.** 6

80. $\frac{6}{5}$ **82.** $\frac{10}{9}$ **84.** 5   **86.** $-\frac{25}{2}$ **88.** 27

90. Undefined   **92.** $\frac{11}{37}$ **94.** $\frac{25}{18}$

96.

Horizontal asymptote: $y = 10$

Corresponds to the sum of the series

98. (a) $1790.85   (b) $1806.11   (c) $1814.02

     (d) $1819.40   (e) $1822.03

100. $22,689.45   **102.** $3698.34   **104.** Answers will vary.

106. (a) $84,714.78   (b) $85,196.05

108. (a) $76,122.54   (b) $76,533.16

110. $222,289.91   **112.** $202,794.06 million

114. (a) 152.42 feet   (b) 19 seconds

116. False. $a_n = a_1 r^{n-1}$ **118.** Answers will vary.

120. $3x + 4$ **122.** $9x^2 + 24x + 15$

124. Does not factor   **126.** $4x^2(2 + x)(2 - x)$

128. $\frac{1}{3}, x \neq 2, -7$ **130.** $1, x \neq 3, 5$

132. $\dfrac{7x^2 + 21x - 53}{(x - 1)(x + 4)}$

Section 9.4   *(page 652)*

2. $\dfrac{1}{2(k + 3)}$ **4.** $\dfrac{k + 1}{3}(2k + 3)$

6–18. Answers will vary.   **20.** 465   **22.** 3025

24. 61,776   **26.** 43,890   **28.** 195

30. $S_n = \dfrac{n}{2}(-3n + 53)$ **32.** $S_n = 3\left(-\dfrac{3}{2}\right)^{n-1}$

34. $S_n = \dfrac{n}{2(n + 2)}$ **36–48.** Answers will vary.

50. 2, 4, 6, 8, 10, 12

     First differences: 2, 2, 2, 2, 2

     Second differences: 0, 0, 0, 0

     Linear

52. $\frac{3}{2}, -3, 6, -12, 24, -48$

     First differences: $-\frac{9}{2}, 9, -18, 36, -72$

     Second differences: $\frac{27}{2}, -27, 54, -108$

     Neither

54. 0, 1, 3, 6, 10, 15

     First differences: 1, 2, 3, 4, 5

     Second differences: 1, 1, 1, 1

     Quadratic

56. $a_n = n^2 - 2n + 7$ **58.** $a_n = \frac{7}{4}n^2 - 5n + 3$

60. See page 645.

62. False. P_1 must be proven to be true.

64. False. A sequence with n terms has $n - 2$ second differences.

66. $4x^2 - 4xy + y^2$ **68.** $8x^3 - 48x^2y + 96xy^2 - 64y^3$

70. $x^2 + 4x + 3$ **72.** $6x^2 + x - 2$

74. (a) Intercept: $(0, 0)$

     (b) Vertical asymptotes: $x = 2, x = -2$

         Horizontal asymptote: $y = 1$

     (c) $y = $ axis symmetry

     (d)

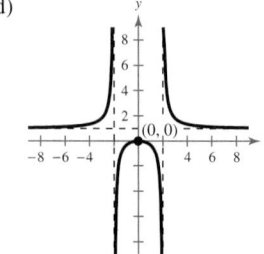

76. (a) x-intercept: $(-5, 0)$

y-intercept: $(0, 5)$

(b) Vertical asymptote: $x = 1$

Horizontal asymptote: $y = -1$

(c) No symmetry

(d)

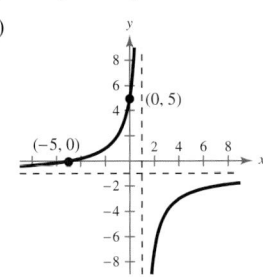

Section 9.5 (page 659)

2. 28   **4.** 1   **6.** 792   **8.** 210

10. 4950   **12.** 8   **14.** 20

16. $x^6 + 6x^5 + 15x^4 + 20x^3 + 15x^2 + 6x + 1$

18. $a^5 + 25a^4 + 250a^3 + 1250a^2 + 3125a + 3125$

20. $y^5 - 10y^4 + 40y^3 - 80y^2 + 80y - 32$

22. $c^3 + 3c^2d + 3cd^2 + d^3$

24. $x^4 + 8x^3y + 24x^2y^2 + 32xy^3 + 16y^4$

26. $32x^5 - 80x^4y + 80x^3y^2 - 40x^2y^3 + 10xy^4 - y^5$

28. $125 - 225y + 135y^2 - 27y^3$

30. $x^{12} + 6x^{10}y^2 + 15x^8y^4 + 20x^6y^6 + 15x^4y^8$

$\quad + 6x^2y^{10} + y^{12}$

32. $\dfrac{1}{x^6} + \dfrac{12y}{x^5} + \dfrac{60y^2}{x^4} + \dfrac{160y^3}{x^3} + \dfrac{240y^4}{x^2} + \dfrac{192y^5}{x} + 64y^6$

34. $3x^5 + 15x^4 + 26x^3 + 18x^2 + 3x - 1$

36. $81 - 216z + 216z^2 - 96z^3 + 16z^4$

38. $64v^6 + 576v^5 + 2160v^4 + 4320v^3 + 4860v^2$

$\quad + 2916v + 729$

40. y^6 **42.** $-35,000x^4z^3$ **44.** $32,400ab^4$

46. $1.293 \times 10^{13}x^9y^6$ **48.** 3,247,695   **50.** 720

52. 16,128   **54.** 45   **56.** $8t^{3/2} - 12t + 6t^{1/2} - 1$

58. $u^3 + 10u^{12/5} + 40u^{9/5} + 80u^{6/5} + 80u^{3/5} + 32$

60. $4x^3 + 6x^2h + 4xh^2 + h^3,\ h \neq 0$

62. $-\dfrac{1}{x(x + h)},\ h \neq 0$

64. $-38 - 41i$ **66.** $-10 + 198i$ **68.** $184 - 440\sqrt{3}i$

70. 1049.890   **72.** 467.721

74.

g is shifted three units to the right of f.

$g(x) = -x^4 + 12x^3 - 50x^2 + 84x - 46$

76. 0.250   **78.** 0.273

80. (a) $g(t) = 0.020t^2 + 5.56t + 94.8$

(b)

82. False. Expanding binomials that represent differences is accurate. The coefficients have alternating signs.

84. The first and last numbers in each row are 1. Every other number in each row is formed by adding the two numbers immediately above the number.

86. $n + 1$ terms

88.

$k(x)$ is the expansion of $f(x)$.

90. Answers will vary.   **92.** Answers will vary.

94.   **96.**

 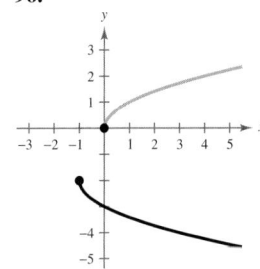

$g(x) = -(x + 2)^2 + 3$ $g(x) = -\sqrt{x + 1} - 2$

98. $\begin{bmatrix} 20 & 11.5 \\ 10 & 6 \end{bmatrix}$

Section 9.6 (page 669)

2. 6   **4.** 3   **6.** 4   **8.** 3   **10.** 60   **12.** 30

14. 4096   **16.** 1440   **18.** 5,760,000

20. (a) 9000   (b) 4536   (c) 4000   (d) 4500

22. 125,000   **24.** (a) 40,320   (b) 576

26. 120   **28.** 380   **30.** 840   **32.** $n = 9$ or $n = 10$

34. 9,034,502,400   **36.** 1,814,400   **38.** 120   **40.** 56

42. 34,650   **44.** ABCD, DBCA, ACBD, DCBA

46. ABC, ABD, ABE, ABF, ACD, ACE, ACF, ADE, ADF, AEF,
BCD, BCE, BCF, BDE, BDF, BEF, CDE, CDF, CEF, DEF

48. 720   **50.** 24   **52.** 66   **54.** 3,838,380

56. 24,040,016   **58.** (a) 35   (b) 63   (c) 203

60. 3744   **62.** (a) 3   (b) 28   (c) 66   (d) 190

64. 9   **66.** 35

68. False. It is an example of a combination.

70. False. $_nP_r > _nC_r$ if $r > 1$ and $_nP_r = _nC_r$ if $r = 0$ or 1.

72. $_{10}P_6 > _{10}C_6$. Changing the order of any of the six elements selected results in a different permutation but the same combination.

74. Answers will vary.   **76.** Answers will vary.

78. The symbol $_nP_r$ denotes the number of ways to choose and order r elements out of a collection of n elements.

80. (a) 2   (b) 4   (c) $\sqrt{x} + 2$

82. (a) 29   (b) -3 (c) 445   **84.** 5.5   **86.** 8.32

88. $y^6 - 12y^5 + 60y^4 - 160y^3 + 240y^2 - 192y + 64$

90. $x^8 - 4x^6y^2 + 6x^4y^4 - 4x^2y^6 + y^8$

Section 9.7   *(page 680)*

2. $\{2, 3, \ldots, 12\}$

4. {(red, red), (red, blue), (red, black),
(blue, blue), (blue, black)}

6. {SSS, SSF, SFS, SFF, FSS, FSF, FFS, FFF}

8. $\frac{1}{2}$ **10.** $\frac{1}{2}$ **12.** $\frac{10}{13}$ **14.** $\frac{6}{13}$ (for A-6)   **16.** $\frac{7}{12}$

18. $\frac{1}{9}$ **20.** $\frac{19}{36}$ **22.** $\frac{1}{15}$ **24.** $\frac{11}{15}$ **26.** 0.64

28. $\frac{1}{6}$ **30.** 0.16   **32.** $\frac{13}{100}$

34. (a) 34%   (b) 45%   (c) 23%

36. (a) 18,396,000   (b) 5%   (c) 47%

38. (a) $\frac{5}{12}$ (b) $\frac{7}{12}$ (c) $\frac{5}{36}$

40. 19%   **42.** (a) $\frac{3}{28}$ (b) $\frac{15}{28}$ (c) $\frac{9}{14}$

44. (a) $\frac{3}{8}$ (b) $\frac{19}{30}$ **46.** (a) $\frac{1}{24}$ (b) $\frac{1}{6}$ **48.** $\frac{6}{4165}$

50. (a) $\frac{91}{323}$ (b) $\frac{455}{969}$ (c) $\frac{232}{323}$

52. (a) $\frac{1}{4}$ (b) $\frac{1}{2}$ (c) $\frac{841}{1600}$ (d) $\frac{1}{40}$

54. (a) 0.81   (b) 0.01   (c) 0.99

56. (a) $\frac{1}{16}$ (b) $\frac{1}{8}$ (c) $\frac{15}{16}$ **58.** 0.1024

60. (a) $\frac{\pi}{4}$ (b) Approximations will vary.

62. False. The complement of the event is to roll a number greater than or equal to 3, and its probability is $\frac{2}{3}$.

64. Meteorological records indicate that over an extended period of time with similar weather conditions it will rain 40% of the time.

66. $\dfrac{-3 \pm \sqrt{57}}{4}$ **68.** $0, \pm 1$ **70.** ± 4 **72.** -1

74. 3   **76.** $\ln 28 \approx 3.332$

78. $\ln 3 \approx 1.099$, $\ln 4 \approx 1.386$ **80.** $\ln 3.2 \approx 1.163$

82. $e^{-3/4} \approx 0.472$ **84.** $\dfrac{e^3}{2} \approx 10.043$

86.   **88.**

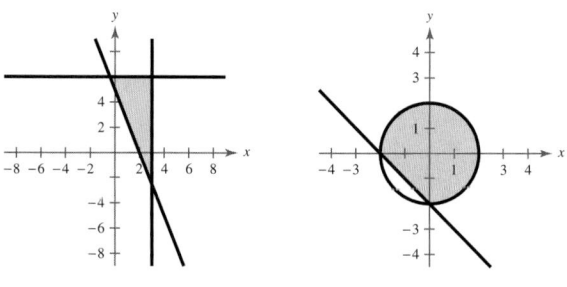

90. 126   **92.** 560

Review Exercises   *(page 686)*

2. $-5, \frac{10}{3}, -3, \frac{20}{7}, -\frac{25}{9}$ **4.** 0, 2, 6, 12, 20

6. $a_n = n^2 - 2$ **8.** $a_n = \dfrac{(-1)^{n+1}}{n}$ **10.** 12   **12.** $\frac{1}{8}$

14. 56   **16.** 6.17   **18.** 35   **20.** $\displaystyle\sum_{k=1}^{9} \dfrac{k}{k+1}$

22. $\frac{1}{3}$ **24.** $\frac{1}{10}$

26. 676 bales   **28.** Not an arithmetic sequence

30. Arithmetic sequence, $d = -\frac{1}{9}$ **32.** 6, 4, 2, 0, -2

34. 4.2, 4.6, 5.0, 5.4, 5.8   **36.** $a_n = -3n + 28$

38. $a_n = nx - 3x$ **40.** $a_n = -\frac{1}{3}n + \frac{31}{3}$ **42.** 52

44. 250   **46.** 3050   **48.** 73.5 miles

50. Geometric sequence, $r = -\frac{1}{3}$

52. Not a geometric sequence   **54.** 2, 4, 8, 16, 32

56. $2, 2\sqrt{6}, 12, 12\sqrt{6}, 72$ or $2, -2\sqrt{6}, 12, -12\sqrt{6}, 72$

58. $a_n = 216\left(\frac{1}{6}\right)^{n-1}$; 259.2   **60.** $a_n = 5(0.2)^{n-1}$; 6.25

62. 121   **64.** $\frac{364}{243}$ **66.** 720   **68.** 25   **70.** 1493.50

72. $\frac{3}{2}$ **74.** 2   **76.** $\frac{13}{9}$ **78.** \$4,371,379.65

80. Answers will vary.   **82.** Answers will vary.

84. 385   **86.** 12,110

88. $S_n = 4n(18 - n)$ **90.** $S_n = \frac{144}{13}\left[1 - \left(-\frac{1}{12}\right)^n\right]$

92. $-3, -7, -13, -21, -31$

First differences: $-4, -6, -8, -10$

Second differences: $-2, -2, -2$

Quadratic

94. $0, 1, 1, 2, 2$

First differences: $1, 0, 1, 0$

Second differences: $-1, 1, -1$

Neither

96. 120   **98.** 220   **100.** 126   **102.** 10

104. $\dfrac{64}{x^6} - \dfrac{576}{x^4} + \dfrac{2160}{x^2} - 4320 + 4860x^2 - 2916x^4 + 729x^6$

106. $2187x^7 + 5103x^6y^2 + 5103x^5y^4 + 2835x^4y^6 + 945x^3y^8$
$+ 189x^2y^{10} + 21xy^{12} + y^{14}$

108. $-236 - 115i$ **110.** 11   **112.** 50,000

114. 720   **116.** 1140   **118.** $\frac{1}{120}$

120. (a) 41.6%   (b) 80%   (c) 7.4%

122. $\frac{5}{324}$ **124.** $\frac{31}{32}$ **126.** True by Properties of Sums

128. True. The sums are equal because
$2^1 + 2^2 + 2^3 + 2^4 + 2^5 + 2^6 =$
$2^{3-2} + 2^{4-2} + 2^{5-2} + 2^{6-2} + 2^{7-2} + 2^{8-2}$.

130. In the sequence in part (a), the odd-numbered terms are negative, whereas in the sequence in part (b), the even-numbered terms are negative.

132. (a) Arithmetic. There is a constant difference between consecutive terms.

(b) Geometric. Each term is a constant multiple of the preceding term. In this case, the common ratio is greater than 1.

134. Increasing powers of real numbers between 0 and 1 approach zero.

135. d   **136.** a   **137.** b   **138.** c

140. $0 \le p \le 1$; Closed interval

Problem Solving   *(page 696)*

2. (a)   (b) 0

(b) 0

(c)

n	1	10	100	1000	10,000
a_n	1	0.1089	0.0101	0.0010	0.0001

(d) 0

4. (a) Arithmetic sequence, difference $= d$

(b) Arithmetic sequence, difference $= dC$

(c) Not an arithmetic sequence

6. $s_d = \dfrac{a_1}{1 - r} = \dfrac{20}{1 - \frac{1}{2}} = 40$

This represents the total distance Achilles ran.

$s_t = \dfrac{a_1}{1 - r} = \dfrac{1}{1 - \frac{1}{2}} = 2$

This represents the total amount of time Achilles ran.

8. (a) 7, 22, 11, 34, 17, 52, 26, 79, 39.5, 119.5

(b) Examples will vary. The differences of consecutive terms of the sequence become greater as n increases.

10. (a) P_n is true for integers $n \ge 3$.

(b) P_n is true for integers $1 \le n \le 50$.

(c) $P_1, P_2,$ and P_3 are true.

(d) P_{2n} is true for any positive integer n.

12. (a) 30 marbles   (b) 3 to 7; 7 to 3

(c) $P(E) = (\text{odds in favor of event } E) \times P(E')$

(d) Odds in favor of event $E = \dfrac{P(E)}{P(E')}$

14. $\dfrac{\pi - 1}{\pi}$

Chapter 10
Section 10.1   *(page 704)*

2. 1   **4.** $-\sqrt{3}$ **6.** $-\dfrac{\sqrt{3}}{3}$ **8.** -0.2677

10. 2.0344 radians, 116.6°   **12.** 1.1071 radians, 63.4°

14. 1.9513 radians, 111.8°   **16.** 0.6023 radian, 34.5°

18. 2.0344 radians, 116.6°   **20.** 2.4669 radians, 141.3°

22. $\dfrac{\pi}{4}$ radian, 45°   **24.** $\dfrac{\pi}{4}$ radian, 45°

26. 1.1071 radians, 63.4°   **28.** 1.4109 radians, 80.8°

30. 1.0808 radians, 61.9°   **32.** 1.0240 radians, 58.7°

34. $(-3, 2)$: 35.8°; $(1, 3)$: 94.4°; $(2, 0)$: 49.8°

36. $(-3, 4)$: 32.5°; $(2, 1)$: 16.9°; $(-2, 2)$: 130.6°

38. $\dfrac{4\sqrt{5}}{5} \approx 1.7889$ **40.** $\dfrac{5\sqrt{2}}{2} \approx 3.5355$ **42.** 4

44. $9\sqrt{2} \approx 12.7279$ **46.** (a) $\dfrac{33\sqrt{29}}{29}$ (b) $\dfrac{31}{2}$

48. (a) $\dfrac{31\sqrt{389}}{389}$ (b) $\dfrac{31}{2}$ **50.** $\dfrac{9}{5}$

52. 0.2027, 1049 feet   **54.** 31.0°

56. (a) 0.6167 radian, 35.3° (b) 518.5 feet

(c) $y = 0.709x$

(d)

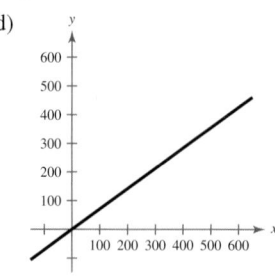

58. False. Substitute $\tan\theta_1$ and $\tan\theta_2$ for m_1 and m_2 in the formula for the angle between two lines.

60. (a) $d = \dfrac{3|m + 1|}{\sqrt{m^2 + 1}}$

(b)

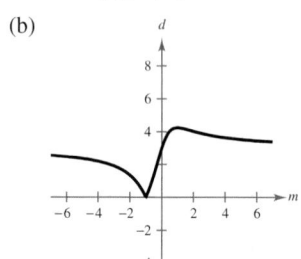

(c) $m = 1$ (d) Yes. $m = -1$

(e) $d = 3$. As the line approaches the vertical, the distance approaches 3.

62. x-intercept: $(-9, 0)$

y-intercept: $(0, 81)$

64. No x-intercepts

y-intercept: $(0, 133)$

66. x-intercepts: $(-11, 0), (2, 0)$

y-intercept: $(0, -22)$

68. $f(x) = 2\left(x - \frac{1}{4}\right)^2 - \frac{169}{8}$

Vertex: $\left(\frac{1}{4}, -\frac{169}{8}\right)$

70. $f(x) = -(x + 4)^2 + 1$

Vertex: $(-4, 1)$

72. $f(x) = -8\left(x + \frac{17}{8}\right)^2 + \frac{121}{8}$

Vertex: $\left(-\frac{17}{8}, \frac{121}{8}\right)$

74.

76.

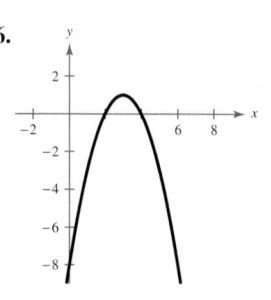

Section 10.2 *(page 712)*

2. An ellipse is formed when a plane intersects only the top or bottom half of a double-napped cone but is not parallel or perpendicular to the axis of the cone, is not parallel to the side of the cone, and does not intersect the vertex.

4. A hyperbola is formed when a plane intersects both halves of a double-napped cone, is parallel to the axis of the cone, and does not intersect the vertex.

5. e **6.** b **7.** d **8.** f **9.** a **10.** c

12. Vertex: $(0, 0)$

Focus: $\left(0, -\frac{1}{8}\right)$

Directrix: $y = \frac{1}{8}$

14. Vertex: $(0, 0)$

Focus: $\left(\frac{3}{4}, 0\right)$

Directrix: $x = -\frac{3}{4}$

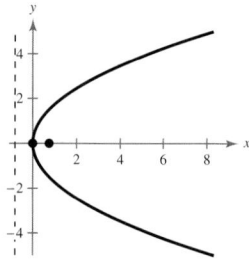

16. Vertex: $(0, 0)$

Focus: $\left(-\frac{1}{4}, 0\right)$

Directrix: $x = \frac{1}{4}$

18. Vertex: $(-5, 1)$

Focus: $\left(-\frac{21}{4}, 1\right)$

Directrix: $x = -\frac{19}{4}$

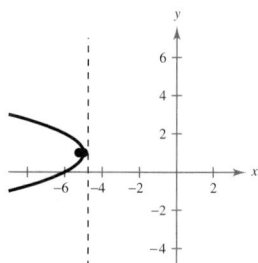

20. Vertex: $\left(-\frac{1}{2}, 1\right)$

Focus: $\left(-\frac{1}{2}, 2\right)$

Directrix: $y = 0$

22. Vertex: $(8, -1)$

Focus: $(9, -1)$

Directrix: $x = 7$

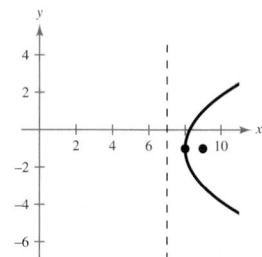

24. Vertex: $(-1, 2)$

Focus: $(0, 2)$

Directrix: $x = -2$

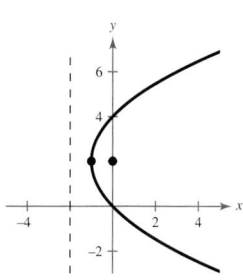

26. Vertex: $(1, -1)$

Focus: $(1, -3)$

Directrix: $y = 1$

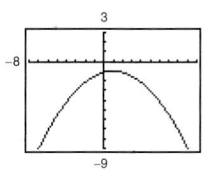

28. Vertex: $(-1, 0)$

Focus: $(0, 0)$

Directrix: $x = -2$

30.

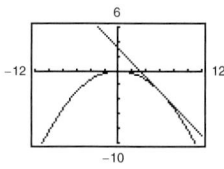

$(6, -3)$

32. $y^2 = -18x$ **34.** $y^2 = 8x$ **36.** $x^2 = -8y$

38. $x^2 = -12y$ **40.** $y^2 = 12x$ **42.** $x^2 = -3y$

44. $(y - 3)^2 = -2(x - 5)$ **46.** $(x - 3)^2 = 3(y + 3)$

48. $(x + 1)^2 = -8(y - 2)$ **50.** $(y - 1)^2 = -12(x + 2)$

52. $x^2 = -16(y - 4)$ **54.** $y = -\sqrt{2(x - 4)} - 1$

56. $6x + 2y + 9 = 0; \left(-\frac{3}{2}, 0\right)$

58. $8x + y - 8 = 0; (1, 0)$

60.

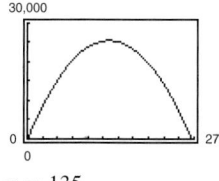

$x = 135$

62. (a)

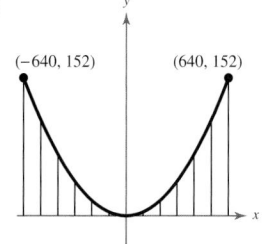

(b) $y = \dfrac{19x^2}{51{,}200}$

(c)

Distance, x	0	250	400	500	1000
Height, y	0	23.19	59.38	92.77	371.09

64. $y^2 = 640x$

66. (a)

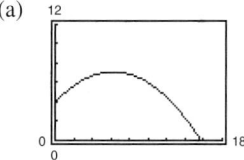

(b) Highest point: $(6.25, 7.125)$

Range: 15.69 feet

68. 41,329.5 feet

70. True. The directrix of a parabola is perpendicular to the axis of the parabola.

72. (a) $\dfrac{64\sqrt{2}}{3} \approx 30.17$

(b) As p approaches zero, the parabola becomes narrower and narrower, thus the area becomes smaller and smaller.

74. Answers will vary.

76. $\pm\frac{1}{2}, \pm1, \pm2, \pm\frac{5}{2}, \pm5, \pm10$

78. $\pm\frac{1}{3}, \pm\frac{2}{3}, \pm1, \pm2, \pm\frac{11}{3}, \pm\frac{22}{3}, \pm11, \pm22$ **80.** $\frac{3}{2}, \pm5i$

82.

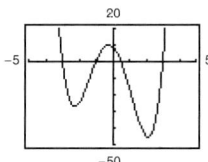

$\frac{1}{2}, -1, \pm3$

84. $A \approx 96.37°, C \approx 29.63°, a \approx 22.11$

86. $A = 50°, b \approx 10.87, c \approx 24.07$

88. $A \approx 43.53°, B \approx 19.42°, C \approx 117.05°$

90. $A \approx 41.85°, C \approx 67.15°, b \approx 29.76$

Section 10.3   *(page 722)*

1. b   **2.** c   **3.** d   **4.** f   **5.** a   **6.** e

8. Center: $(0, 0)$

Vertices: $(0, \pm 12)$

Foci: $\left(0, \pm 3\sqrt{7}\right)$

Eccentricity: $\dfrac{\sqrt{7}}{4}$

10. Center: $(0, 0)$

Vertices: $(\pm 8, 0)$

Foci: $(\pm 6, 0)$

Eccentricity: $\dfrac{3}{4}$

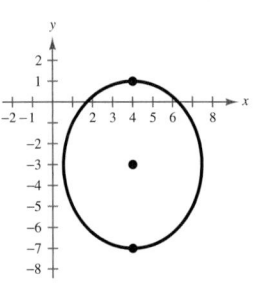

12. Center: $(4, -3)$

Vertices: $(4, 1), (4, -7)$

Foci: $(4, -1), (4, -5)$

Eccentricity: $\frac{1}{2}$

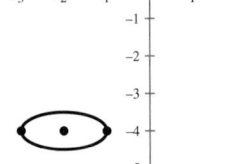

14. Center: $(-2, -4)$

Vertices: $(-3, -4), (-1, -4)$

Foci: $\left(\dfrac{-4 \pm \sqrt{3}}{2}, -4\right)$

Eccentricity: $\dfrac{\sqrt{3}}{2}$

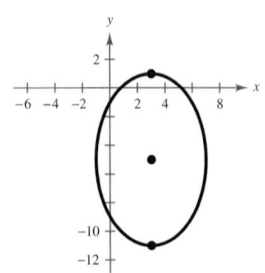

16. Center: $(3, -5)$

Vertices: $(3, 1), (3, -11)$

Foci: $\left(3, -5 \pm 2\sqrt{5}\right)$

Eccentricity: $\dfrac{\sqrt{5}}{3}$

18. Center: $(-3, 1)$

Vertices: $(-3, 7), (-3, -5)$

Foci: $\left(-3, 1 \pm 2\sqrt{6}\right)$

Eccentricity: $\dfrac{\sqrt{6}}{3}$

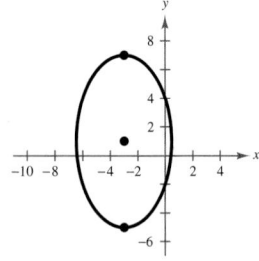

20. Center: $\left(3, -\dfrac{5}{2}\right)$

Vertices: $\left(9, -\dfrac{5}{2}\right), \left(-3, -\dfrac{5}{2}\right)$

Foci: $\left(3 \pm 3\sqrt{3}, -\dfrac{5}{2}\right)$

Eccentricity: $\dfrac{\sqrt{3}}{2}$

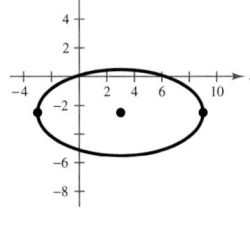

22. Center: $(2, 1)$

Vertices: $\left(\frac{7}{3}, 1\right), \left(\frac{5}{3}, 1\right)$

Foci: $\left(\frac{34}{15}, 1\right), \left(\frac{26}{15}, 1\right)$

Eccentricity: $\frac{4}{5}$

24.

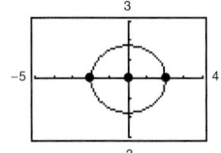

Center: $(0, 0)$

Vertices: $(\pm 2, 0)$

Foci: $(\pm 1, 0)$

26.

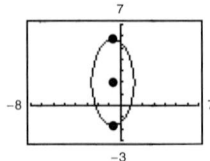

Center: $\left(-\dfrac{2}{3}, 2\right)$

Vertices: $\left(-\dfrac{2}{3}, 2 \pm \dfrac{2\sqrt{31}}{3}\right)$

Foci: $\left(-\dfrac{2}{3}, 2 \pm \dfrac{\sqrt{93}}{3}\right)$

28. $\dfrac{x^2}{4} + \dfrac{4y^2}{9} = 1$ **30.** $\dfrac{x^2}{48} + \dfrac{y^2}{64} = 1$ **32.** $\dfrac{x^2}{16} + \dfrac{y^2}{12} = 1$

34. $\dfrac{x^2}{4} + \dfrac{y^2}{16} = 1$ **36.** $\dfrac{(x-4)^2}{9} + \dfrac{y^2}{16} = 1$

38. $\dfrac{(x-2)^2}{4} + \dfrac{(y+1)^2}{1} = 1$ **40.** $\dfrac{(x-2)^2}{16} + \dfrac{y^2}{12} = 1$

42. $\dfrac{(x-2)^2}{1} + \dfrac{4(y+1)^2}{9} = 1$

44. $\dfrac{(x-3)^2}{36} + \dfrac{(y-2)^2}{32} = 1$

46. $\dfrac{(x-5)^2}{16} + \dfrac{(y-6)^2}{36} = 1$ **48.** $\dfrac{x^2}{48} + \dfrac{y^2}{64} = 1$

50. Positions: $\left(\pm\sqrt{5}, 0\right)$; Length of string: 6 feet

52. (a) $\dfrac{x^2}{327.25} + \dfrac{y^2}{19.34} = 1$

(b)

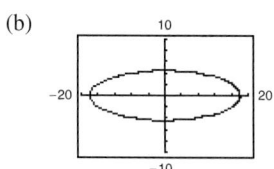

(c) Apogee: 35.64 astronomical units
Perigee: 0.54 astronomical unit

54. Answers will vary.

56.

58.

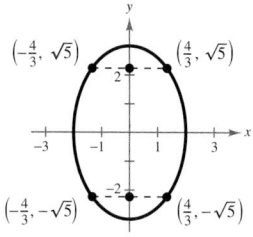

60. True. The ellipse is elongated and the foci are close to the vertices.

62. (a) $2a$

(b) The sum of the distances from the two fixed points is constant.

64. Arithmetic **66.** Geometric **68.** $a_n = 3n + 10$

70. $a_n = 3.5 + 1.5n$ **72.** 1093 **74.** 15.10

Section 10.4 *(page 732)*

1. b **2.** c **3.** a **4.** d

6. Center: $(0, 0)$
Vertices: $(\pm 3, 0)$
Foci: $\left(\pm\sqrt{34}, 0\right)$
Asymptotes: $y = \pm\frac{5}{3}x$

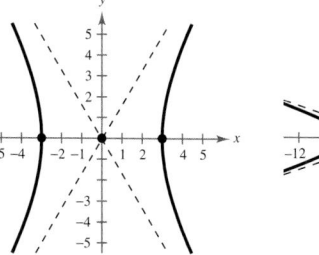

8. Center: $(0, 0)$
Vertices: $(\pm 6, 0)$
Foci: $\left(\pm 2\sqrt{10}, 0\right)$
Asymptotes: $y = \pm\frac{1}{3}x$

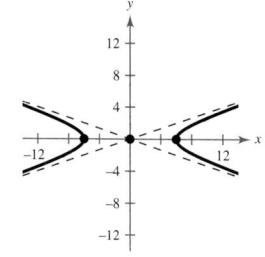

10. Center: $(-3, 2)$
Vertices: $(9, 2), (-15, 2)$
Foci: $(10, 2), (-16, 2)$
Asymptotes:
$y = 2 \pm \frac{5}{12}(x + 3)$

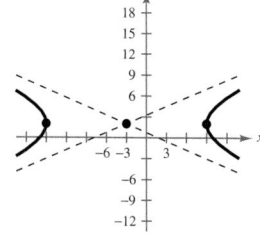

12. Center: $(-3, 1)$
Vertices: $\left(-3, \frac{3}{2}\right), \left(-3, \frac{1}{2}\right)$
Foci: $\left(-3, 1 \pm \frac{\sqrt{5}}{4}\right)$
Asymptotes:
$y = 1 \pm 2(x + 3)$

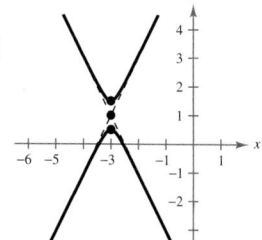

14. Center: $(0, 2)$
Vertices: $(\pm 6, 2)$
Foci: $\left(\pm 2\sqrt{10}, 2\right)$
Asymptotes: $y = 2 \pm \frac{1}{3}x$

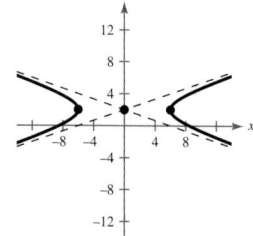

16. The graph of this equation is two lines intersecting at $(1, -2)$.

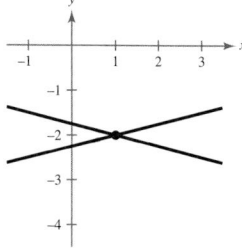

CHAPTER 10

18. Center: $(0, 0)$

Vertices: $(0, \pm\sqrt{3})$

Foci: $(0, \pm 3)$

Asymptotes: $y = \pm\dfrac{\sqrt{2}}{2}x$

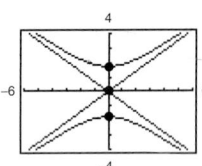

20. Center: $(-3, 5)$

Vertices: $\left(-\dfrac{10}{3}, 5\right), \left(-\dfrac{8}{3}, 5\right)$

Foci: $\left(-3 \pm \dfrac{\sqrt{10}}{3}, 5\right)$

Asymptotes: $y = 5 \pm 3(x + 3)$

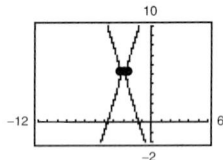

22. $\dfrac{x^2}{16} - \dfrac{y^2}{20} = 1$ **24.** $\dfrac{y^2}{9} - \dfrac{x^2}{1} = 1$

26. $\dfrac{x^2}{64} - \dfrac{y^2}{36} = 1$ **28.** $\dfrac{y^2}{9} - \dfrac{(x-2)^2}{27} = 1$

30. $\dfrac{x^2}{4} - \dfrac{(y-1)^2}{5} = 1$ **32.** $\dfrac{x^2}{4} - \dfrac{7(y-1)^2}{12} = 1$

34. $\dfrac{y^2}{4} - \dfrac{(x-1)^2}{4} = 1$ **36.** $\dfrac{(y-3)^2}{9} - \dfrac{(x-3)^2}{9} = 1$

38. $\dfrac{(y-2)^2}{4} - \dfrac{(x-3)^2}{9} = 1$

40. $\left(12(\sqrt{5} - 1), 0\right) \approx (14.83, 0)$ **42.** Ellipse

44. Parabola   **46.** Hyperbola   **48.** Circle

50. False. For the trivial solution of two intersecting lines to occur, the standard form of the equation of the hyperbola would be equal to zero,

$$\dfrac{(x-h)^2}{a^2} - \dfrac{(y-k)^2}{b^2} = 0 \text{ or } \dfrac{(y-k)^2}{a^2} - \dfrac{(x-h)^2}{b^2} = 0.$$

52. The extended diagonals of the central rectangle are asymptotes of the hyperbola.

54. $(x + 7)^2$ **56.** $x(3x + 2)(2x - 5)$

58.

60.

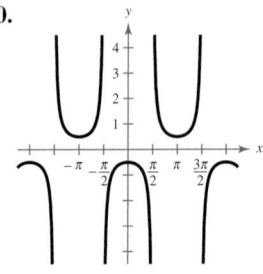

Section 10.5   *(page 740)*

2. $(3\sqrt{2}, 0)$ **4.** $\left(\dfrac{3 + \sqrt{3}}{2}, \dfrac{1 - 3\sqrt{3}}{2}\right)$

6. $\left(\sqrt{3} + 2, 2\sqrt{3} - 1\right)$

8. $\dfrac{(x')^2}{4} - \dfrac{(y')^2}{4} = 1$

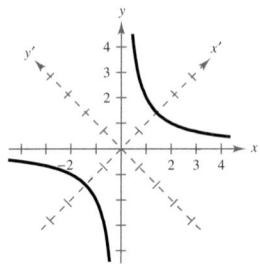

10. $\dfrac{\left[y' + \left(3\sqrt{2}/2\right)\right]^2}{10} - \dfrac{\left[x' - \left(\sqrt{2}/2\right)\right]^2}{10} = 1$

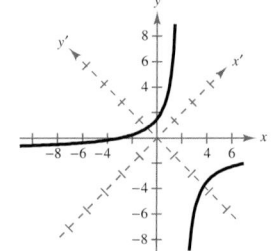

12. $\dfrac{(x')^2}{4} - \dfrac{(y')^2}{4} = 1$ **14.** $\dfrac{(x')^2}{1} + \dfrac{(y')^2}{4} = 1$

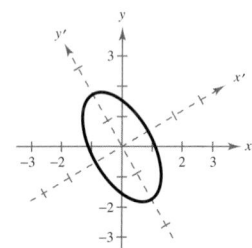

16. $(y')^2 = 4(x' - 1)$ **18.** $y' = \dfrac{1}{4}(x')^2$

20.

$\theta \approx 37.98°$

22.

$\theta \approx 33.69°$

24.

$\theta \approx 28.15°$

26.
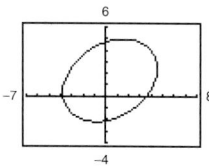

$\theta \approx 31.72°$

27. e **28.** f **29.** b **30.** a **31.** d **32.** c

34. Hyperbola

$$y = \frac{4x \pm \sqrt{16x^2 + 8(x^2 - 6)}}{-4}$$

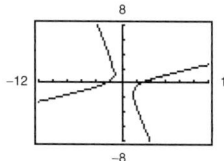

36. Ellipse

$$y = \frac{-(4x - 4) \pm \sqrt{(4x - 4)^2 - 20(2x^2 + 3x - 20)}}{10}$$

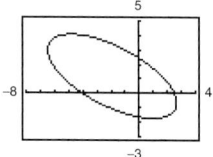

38. Parabola

$$y = \frac{60x - 9 \pm \sqrt{(60x - 9)^2 - 3600x^2}}{50}$$

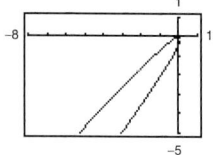

40. Ellipse

$$y = \frac{-(x + 1) \pm \sqrt{(x + 1)^2 - 16(x^2 + x - 4)}}{8}$$

42.
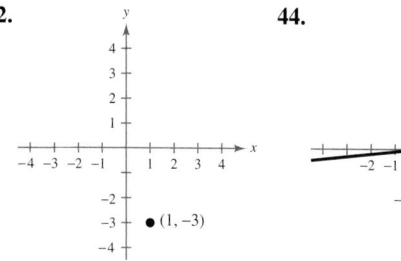

44.

46. $(-7, 0), (-1, 0)$ **48.** $(14, -8), (6, -8)$

50. $(1, 0)$ **52.** $(-2, 8), (5, 8 \pm 4\sqrt{21})$

54. $(\pm 3, 2)$ **56.** $(1, 1), (3, 1)$

58. $(\frac{1}{6}(3 + \sqrt{30}), \frac{1}{6}(3 - \sqrt{30})), (\frac{1}{6}(3 - \sqrt{30}), \frac{1}{6}(3 + \sqrt{30}))$

60. False. The coefficients of the new equation after it has been rotated are obtained by making the substitutions $x = x' \cos \theta - y' \sin \theta$ and $y = x' \sin \theta + y' \cos \theta$.

62. Major axis: 4; Minor axis: 2

64. No zeros **66.** 3 **68.** ± 1

70.
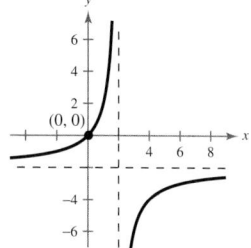

Intercept: $(0, 0)$

Asymptotes: $x = 2, y = -2$

72.
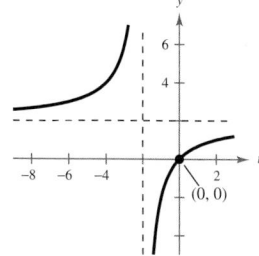

Intercept: $(0, 0)$

Asymptotes: $t = -2, y = 2$

CHAPTER 10

74.

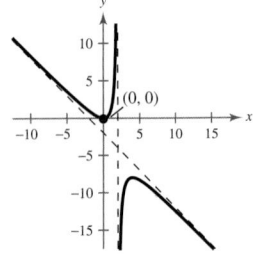

Intercept: $(0, 0)$

Asymptotes: $x = 2, y = -x - 2$

76.

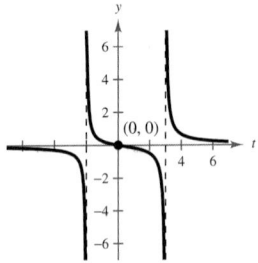

Intercept: $(0, 0)$

Asymptotes: $t = -2, t = 3, y = 0$

Section 10.6   *(page 747)*

2. (a)

θ	$-\dfrac{\pi}{2}$	$-\dfrac{\pi}{4}$	0	$\dfrac{\pi}{4}$	$\dfrac{\pi}{2}$
x	0	2	4	2	0
y	-2	$-\sqrt{2}$	0	$\sqrt{2}$	2

(b)

(c) $x = -y^2 + 4$

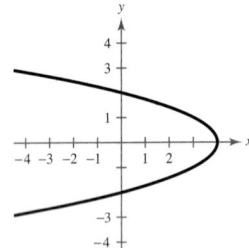

The graph of the rectangular equation continues the graph into the second and third quadrants.

4.

6.

8.

10.

12.

14.

16.

18.

20.

22.

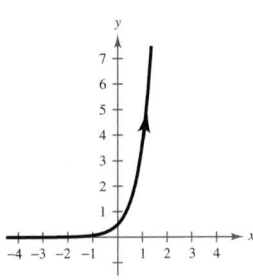

24. Each curve represents a portion of the parabola $y = x^2 - 1$.

	Domain	*Orientation*
(a)	$(-\infty, \infty)$	Left to right
(b)	$[0, \infty)$	Depends on t
(c)	$[-1, 1]$	Depends on t
(d)	$(0, \infty)$	Left to right

26. $(x - h)^2 + (y - k)^2 = r^2$

28. $\dfrac{(x - h)^2}{a^2} - \dfrac{(y - k)^2}{b^2} = 1$

30. $x = 2 + 4t$ **32.** $x = -3 + 5\cos\theta$
    $y = 3 - 6t$ $y = 2 + 5\sin\theta$

34. $x = 4 + 4\cos\theta$ **36.** $x = 2\sec\theta$
    $y = 2 + 5\sin\theta$ $y = 2\sqrt{3}\tan\theta$

38. (a) $x = t, y = \frac{1}{3}(t + 2)$
    (b) $x = -t + 2, y = -\frac{1}{3}(t - 4)$

40. (a) $x = t, y = t^3$
    (b) $x = -t + 2, y = (-t + 2)^3$

42. (a) $x = t, y = 2 - t$
    (b) $x = -t + 2, y = t$

44. (a) $x = t, y = \dfrac{1}{2t}$

    (b) $x = -t + 2, y = \dfrac{1}{-2t + 4}$

46.

48.

50.

52.
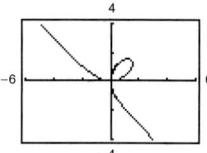

53. b
    Domain: $[-2, 2]$
    Range: $[-1, 1]$

54. c
    Domain: $[-4, 4]$
    Range: $[-6, 6]$

55. d
    Domain: $(-\infty, \infty)$
    Range: $(-\infty, \infty)$

56. a
    Domain: $(-\infty, \infty)$
    Range: $[-2, 2]$

58. (a)
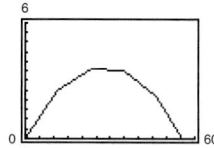

    Maximum height: 3.8 feet
    Range: 56.3 feet

(b)
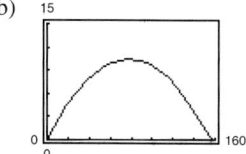

    Maximum height: 10.5 feet
    Range: 156.3 feet

(c)
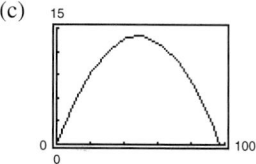

    Maximum height: 14.1 feet
    Range: 97.4 feet

(d)
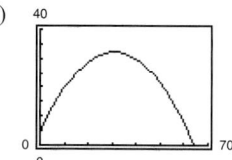

    Maximum height: 39.1 feet
    Range: 270.6 feet

60. (a) $x = (240\cos 10°)t$
    $y = 5 + (240\sin 10°)t - 16t^2$

    (b) 643 feet

    (c)

      32.1 feet

    (d) 2.72 seconds

62. (a) $h = 7, v_0 = 40, \theta = 45°$
    $x = (40\cos 45°)t$
    $y = 7 + (40\sin 45°)t - 16t^2$

    (b)

    (c) Maximum height: 19.5 feet
      Range: 56.2 feet

64. $x = 3 \cos \theta - \cos 3\theta$ **66.** False. $y = x$ for $x \geq 0$
$y = 3 \sin \theta - \sin 3\theta$

68. $(-2, 3)$ **70.** $(3, 1, -2)$

72. $\theta' = 50°$ **74.** $\theta' = \dfrac{\pi}{6}$

76.   **78.**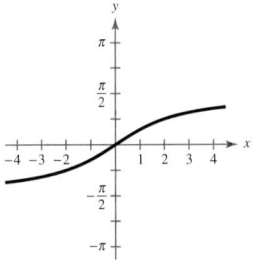

Section 10.7   *(page 754)*

2.   **4.**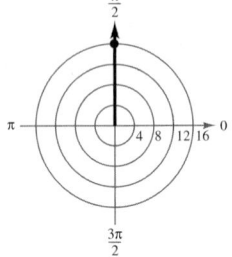

$\left(-1, \dfrac{5\pi}{4}\right), \left(1, \dfrac{\pi}{4}\right)$ $\left(16, \dfrac{\pi}{2}\right), \left(-16, \dfrac{3\pi}{2}\right)$

6.   **8.**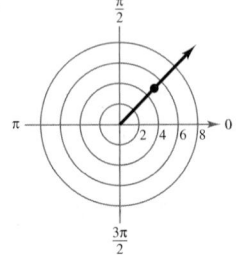

$(-3, 4.7132), (3, 1.5716)$ $(-5, 3.9232), (5, 0.7816)$

10. $(0, -3)$ **12.** $(0, 0)$ **14.** $\left(\sqrt{3}, 1\right)$

16. $(-7.7258, -2.8940)$ **18.** $\left(3\sqrt{2}, \dfrac{5\pi}{4}\right)$

20. $\left(5, \dfrac{3\pi}{2}\right)$ **22.** $\left(\sqrt{10}, 5.9614\right)$ **24.** $\left(2, \dfrac{11\pi}{6}\right)$

26. $(13, 1.1760)$ **28.** $\left(\sqrt{29}, 2.7611\right)$ **30.** $\left(6, \dfrac{\pi}{4}\right)$

32. $(2.3049, 0.7086)$ **34.** $r = 4$ **36.** $\theta = \dfrac{\pi}{4}$

38. $r = 4a \sec \theta$ **40.** $r = \dfrac{2}{3 \cos \theta + 5 \sin \theta}$

42. $r^2 = \frac{1}{2} \sec \theta \csc \theta = \csc 2\theta$

44. $r^2 = 9 \cos 2\theta$ **46.** $r = 3a$ **48.** $r = 2a \sin \theta$

50. $x^2 + y^2 - 2x = 0$ **52.** $\sqrt{3}x + y = 0$

54. $x^2 + y^2 = 100$ **56.** $x = -3$

58. $(x^2 + y^2)^2 = 2xy$ **60.** $(x^2 + y^2)^3 = 9(x^2 - y^2)^2$

62. $y^2 = 2x + 1$ **64.** $2x - 3y = 6$

66. $x^2 + y^2 = 64$ **68.** $x + y = 0$

70. $y - 2 = 0$

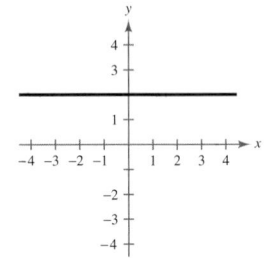

72. False. If $r_1 = -r_2$, then (r_1, θ) and (r_2, θ) are different points.

74. $\left(x - \frac{1}{2}\right)^2 + \left(y - \frac{3}{2}\right)^2 = \frac{5}{2}$; circle

76. (a) Horizontal: x-coordinate changes

Vertical: y-coordinate changes

(b) Horizontal: r and θ both change

Vertical: r and θ both change

(c) Unlike r and θ, x and y measure horizontal and vertical changes, respectively.

78. $\frac{1}{4} + \frac{1}{2} \log_4 x - \log_4 y$ **80.** $\ln 5 + 2 \ln x + \ln(x^2 + 1)$

82. $\log_5 a(x + 1)^8$ **84.** $\ln \dfrac{6y}{x - 3}$ **86.** $\left(-\frac{45}{14}, -\frac{55}{14}\right)$

88. $\left(\frac{295}{89}, \frac{844}{89}, -\frac{672}{89}\right)$ **90.** Cramer's Rule does not apply.

92. Collinear **94.** Not collinear

Section 10.8 *(page 762)*

2. Cardioid **4.** Lemniscate **6.** Circle

8. Polar axis **10.** Polar axis **12.** Pole

14. Maximum: $|r| = 18$ when $\theta = 0$

Zeros: $r = 0$ when $\theta = \frac{2\pi}{3}, \frac{4\pi}{3}$

16. Maximum: $|r| = 3$ when $\theta = \frac{\pi}{4}, \frac{3\pi}{4}, \frac{5\pi}{4}, \frac{7\pi}{4}$

Zeros: $r = 0$ when $\theta = 0, \frac{\pi}{2}, \pi, \frac{3\pi}{2}$

18.   **20.**

22.   **24.**

26.   **28.**

30.   **32.**

34.   **36.**

38.   **40.**

42.   **44.**

46.   **48.**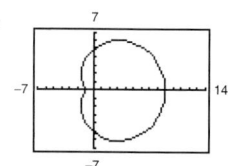

$0 \le \theta < 2\pi$

50.   **52.**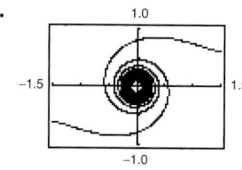

$0 \le \theta < 4\pi$ $0 \le \theta < \infty$

54.   **56.**

58. False. For a graph symmetric with respect to the pole, one portion of the graph coincides with the other portion when rotated π radians about the pole.

60. (a)

(b)

(c)

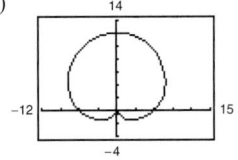

The angle ϕ controls rotation of the axis of symmetry.
$r = 6(1 + \sin \theta)$

62. Answers will vary.

64. (a) $r = 4 \sin\left(\theta - \dfrac{\pi}{6}\right) \cos\left(\theta - \dfrac{\pi}{6}\right)$

(b) $r = -4 \sin \theta \cos \theta$

(c) $r = 4 \sin\left(\theta - \dfrac{2\pi}{3}\right) \cos\left(\theta - \dfrac{2\pi}{3}\right)$

(d) $r = 4 \sin \theta \cos \theta$

66. (a)

(b)

(c)

(d)

68. (a)

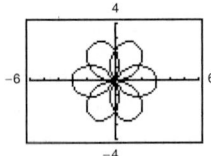

$0 \le \theta < 4\pi$

(b)

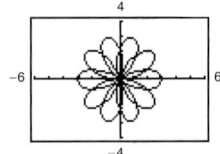

$0 \le \theta < 4\pi$

(c) Yes. Explanations will vary.

70. No zeros   **72.** 3

74. $\dfrac{(x-3)^2}{7} + \dfrac{(y+1)^2}{16} = 1$

Section 10.9   *(page 768)*

2. $e = 1$: $r = \dfrac{4}{1 - \cos \theta}$, parabola

$e = 0.5$: $r = \dfrac{2}{1 - 0.5 \cos \theta}$, ellipse

$e = 1.5$: $r = \dfrac{6}{1 - 1.5 \cos \theta}$, hyperbola

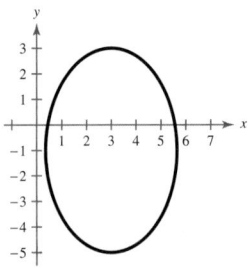

4. $e = 1$: $r = \dfrac{4}{1 + \sin \theta}$, parabola

$e = 0.5$: $r = \dfrac{2}{1 + 0.5 \sin \theta}$, ellipse

$e = 1.5$: $r = \dfrac{6}{1 + 1.5 \sin \theta}$, hyperbola

5. f   **6.** c   **7.** d   **8.** e   **9.** a   **10.** b

12. Parabola

14. Parabola

16. Ellipse

18. Ellipse

20. Hyperbola

22. Hyperbola

24. Hyperbola

26.

Hyperbola

28.

Hyperbola

30.

32.

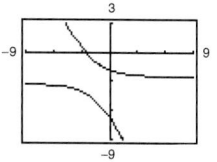

34. $r = \dfrac{2}{1 - \sin \theta}$ **36.** $r = \dfrac{9}{4 - 3 \sin \theta}$

38. $r = \dfrac{3}{2 - 3 \cos \theta}$ **40.** $r = \dfrac{12}{1 + \cos \theta}$

42. $r = \dfrac{20}{1 + \sin \theta}$ **44.** $r = \dfrac{8}{3 + \sin \theta}$

46. $r = \dfrac{16}{3 + 5 \cos \theta}$ **48.** $r = \dfrac{8}{3 + 5 \sin \theta}$

50. Answers will vary.

52. $r = \dfrac{1.4248 \times 10^9}{1 - 0.0543 \cos \theta}$

Perihelion: 1.3514×10^9 kilometers

Aphelion: 1.5066×10^9 kilometers

54. $r = \dfrac{3.4459 \times 10^7}{1 - 0.2056 \cos \theta}$

Perihelion: 2.8583×10^7 miles

Aphelion: 4.3377×10^7 miles

56. $r = \dfrac{7.7658 \times 10^8}{1 - 0.0484 \cos \theta}$

Perihelion: 7.4073×10^8 kilometers

Aphelion: 8.1607×10^8 kilometers

58. If e remains fixed and p changes, then the lengths of both the major axis and the minor axis change. For example, graph

$r = \dfrac{5}{1 - \frac{2}{3} \cos \theta}$, with $e = \frac{2}{3}$ and $p = \frac{15}{2}$, and graph

$r = \dfrac{6}{1 - \frac{2}{3} \cos \theta}$, with $e = \frac{2}{3}$ and $p = 9$, on the same set of coordinate axes.

60. False. The graph has a horizontal directrix below the pole.

62. Answers will vary.   **64.** $r^2 = \dfrac{400}{25 - 9 \cos^2 \theta}$

66. $r^2 = \dfrac{36}{8 \cos^2 \theta - 9}$ **68.** $r^2 = \dfrac{225}{25 - 16 \cos^2 \theta}$

70. $\dfrac{\pi}{3} + 2n\pi, \dfrac{5\pi}{3} + 2n\pi$ **72.** $\dfrac{\pi}{3} + n\pi, \dfrac{2\pi}{3} + n\pi$

74. $\dfrac{\pi}{3} + 2n\pi, \dfrac{5\pi}{3} + 2n\pi$ **76.** $-\dfrac{7\sqrt{2}}{10}$ **78.** $\dfrac{\sqrt{2}}{10}$

CHAPTER 10

80. $\sin 2u = -\dfrac{\sqrt{3}}{2}$ **82.** 153   **84.** 812

$\cos 2u = -\dfrac{1}{2}$

$\tan 2u = \sqrt{3}$

Review Exercises   *(page 772)*

2. 2.6012 radians, 149.04°   **4.** 0.7086 radian, 40.60°

6. 0.4424 radian, 25.35°   **8.** 1.4309 radians, 81.98°

10. $\dfrac{6\sqrt{5}}{5}$ **12.** Parabola   **14.** $y^2 = -8(x - 2)$

16. $(x - 2)^2 = 8(y - 2)$ **18.** $y = 4x + 8; (-2, 0)$

20. $y^2 = 6x$ **22.** $\dfrac{(x - 2)^2}{3} + \dfrac{(y - 2)^2}{4} = 1$

24. $\dfrac{(x + 4)^2}{4} + \dfrac{(y - 5)^2}{36} = 1$

26. Longest distance: 36 feet

   Shortest distance: 28 feet

   Distance between foci: $16\sqrt{2}$ feet

28. Center: $(5, -3)$ **30.** Center: $(-2, 3)$

   Vertices: $(5, 3), (5, -9)$ Vertices: $(3, 3), (-7, 3)$

   Foci: $\left(5, -3 \pm \sqrt{35}\right)$ Foci: $\left(-2 \pm \sqrt{21}, 3\right)$

   Eccentricity: $\dfrac{\sqrt{35}}{6}$ Eccentricity: $\dfrac{\sqrt{21}}{5}$

32. $\dfrac{x^2}{4} - \dfrac{(y - 2)^2}{12} = 1$ **34.** $\dfrac{5y^2}{16} - \dfrac{5(x - 3)^2}{4} = 1$

36. Center: $(0, 1)$

   Vertices: $(0, 3), (0, -1)$

   Foci: $\left(0, 1 \pm \sqrt{5}\right)$

   Asymptotes: $y = 1 \pm 2x$

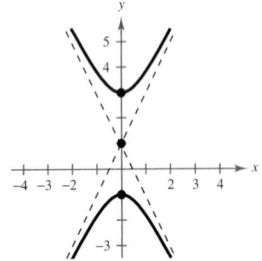

38. Center: $(-1, -3)$

   Vertices: $(-1, -1), (-1, -5)$

   Foci: $\left(-1, -3 \pm \sqrt{29}\right)$

   Asymptotes: $y = -3 \pm \frac{2}{5}(x + 1)$

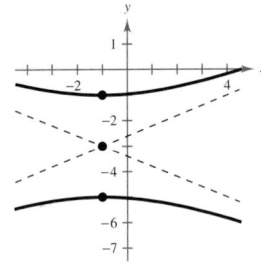

40. $\dfrac{576x^2}{25} - \dfrac{576y^2}{2279} = 1, \dfrac{64(x - 1)^2}{25} - \dfrac{64y^2}{39} = 1$

42. Parabola

44. $\dfrac{(x')^2}{1/4} - \dfrac{(y')^2}{1/6} = 1$ **46.** $y' = -4(x')^2 - 8x'$

   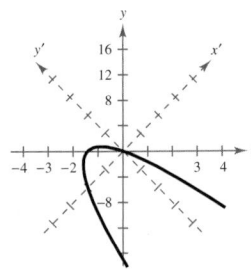

48. Ellipse

   $y = \dfrac{8x \pm \sqrt{64x^2 - 28(13x^2 - 45)}}{14}$

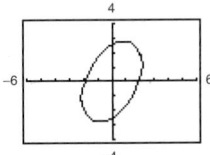

50. Hyperbola

   $y = \dfrac{10x \pm \sqrt{100x^2 - 4(x^2 + 1)}}{2}$

52. $x = \dfrac{3}{2}, y = \dfrac{3}{2}$ **54.** $x = \dfrac{3\sqrt{2}}{2}, y = 1$

56.

58.

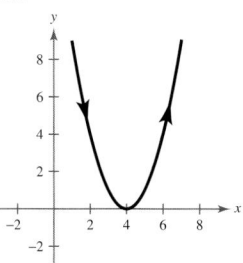

$y = -\frac{3}{4}x + \frac{11}{4}$

$y = (x - 4)^2$

60.

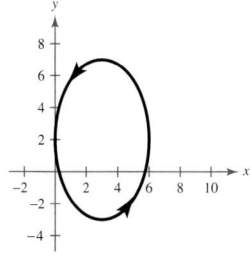

$\dfrac{(x-3)^2}{9} + \dfrac{(y-2)^2}{25} = 1$

62. $x = -3 + 4\cos\theta$

$y = 4 + 3\sin\theta$

64. Answers will vary.

66.

68.

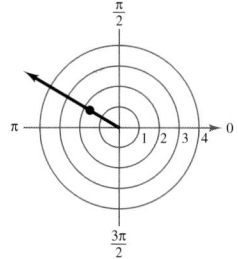

$\left(-5, \dfrac{5\pi}{3}\right), \left(5, \dfrac{2\pi}{3}\right)$ $\left(\sqrt{3}, 8.90\right), \left(-\sqrt{3}, 5.76\right)$

70. $\left(-\sqrt{2}, -\sqrt{2}\right)$ **72.** $(0, 0)$ **74.** $\left(\sqrt{10}, \dfrac{3\pi}{4}\right)$

76. $(5, 5.3559)$ **78.** $r = 4\cos\theta$ **80.** $r^2 = -4\csc 2\theta$

82. $x^2 + y^2 = 8y$ **84.** $(x^2 + y^2)^2 = x^2 - y^2$

86. Symmetry: $\theta = \dfrac{\pi}{2}$, polar axis, pole

Maximum value of $|r|$: $|r| = 11$ when $\theta = 0, \dfrac{\pi}{2}, \pi, \dfrac{3\pi}{2}$

No zeros of r

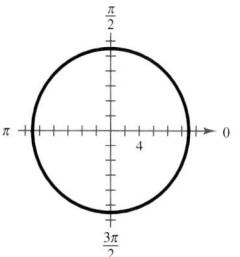

88. Symmetry: polar axis

Maximum value of $|r|$: $|r| = 1$ when $\theta = 0, \dfrac{2\pi}{5}, \dfrac{4\pi}{5}, \dfrac{6\pi}{5}, \dfrac{8\pi}{5}$

Zeros of r: $r = 0$ when $\theta = \dfrac{\pi}{10}, \dfrac{3\pi}{10}, \dfrac{5\pi}{10}, \dfrac{7\pi}{10}, \dfrac{9\pi}{10}$

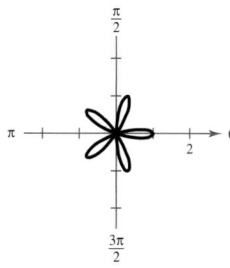

90. Symmetry: polar axis

Maximum value of $|r|$: $|r| = 7$ when $\theta = \pi$

Zeros of r: $r = 0$ when $\theta = \arccos\frac{3}{4}, 2\pi - \arccos\frac{3}{4}$

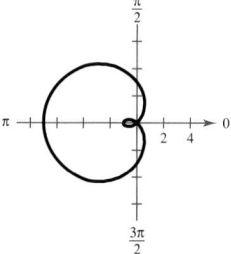

92. Symmetry: polar axis

Maximum value of $|r|$: $|r| = 10$ when $\theta = \pi$

Zero of r: $r = 0$ when $\theta = 0$

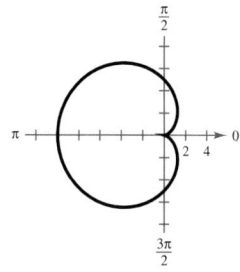

CHAPTER 10

94. Symmetry: $\theta = \dfrac{\pi}{2}$, polar axis

Maximum value of $|r|$: $|r| = 1$ when $\theta = 0, \dfrac{\pi}{2}, \pi, \dfrac{3\pi}{2}$

Zeros of r: $r = 0$ when $\theta = \dfrac{\pi}{4}, \dfrac{3\pi}{4}, \dfrac{5\pi}{4}, \dfrac{7\pi}{4}$

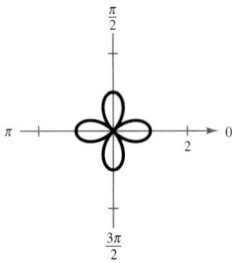

96. Limaçon   **98.** Lemniscate

100. Parabola   **102.** Hyperbola

    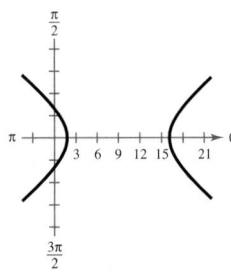

104. $r = \dfrac{4}{1 + \sin \theta}$ **106.** $r = \dfrac{7}{3 + 4 \cos \theta}$

108. $r = \dfrac{12{,}000{,}000}{1 + \sin \theta}$; 89,600,000 miles

110. False. The equation of a hyperbola is a second-degree equation.

112. False. $(2, \pi/4)$, $(-2, 5\pi/4)$, and $(2, 9\pi/4)$ all represent the same point.

114. Yes. The orientation would be reversed.

116. (a) Symmetric to the pole
(b) Symmetric to the polar axis
(c) Symmetric to $\theta = \pi/2$

Problem Solving   (page 780)

2. (a) $\dfrac{x^2}{2352.25} + \dfrac{y^2}{529} = 1$

(b) ≈ 85.4 feet   (c) 1115.5π square feet

4. $A = \dfrac{4\,a^2\,b^2}{a^2 + b^2}$

6. $\dfrac{(x - 6)^2}{9} - \dfrac{(y - 2)^2}{7} = 1$

8. (a) The first set of parametric equations models projectile motion along a straight line. The second set of parametric equations models projectile motion of an object launched at a height of h units above the ground that will eventually fall back to the ground.

(b) $y = (\tan \theta)x$; $y = h + x \tan \theta - \dfrac{16x^2 \sec^2 \theta}{v_0^2}$

(c) In the first case, the path of the moving object is not affected by changing the velocity because eliminating the parameter removes v_0.

10. (a)   (b)

The graph is a line between -2 and 2 on the x-axis.   The graph is a three-sided figure with counter-clockwise orientation.

(c)   (d)

The graph is a four-sided figure with counter-clockwise orientation.   The graph is a 10-sided figure with counter-clockwise orientation.

(e)   (f)

    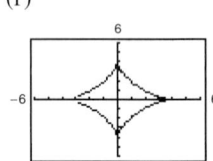

The graph is a three-sided figure with clockwise orientation.   The graph is a four-sided figure with clockwise orientation.

12.

    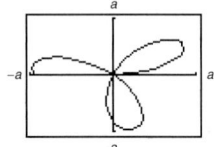

$r = a \cos(3.5\theta)$ $r = a \sin(2.63\theta)$

The graphs are rose curves with partially completed petals.

14. (a) No. Because of the exponential, the graph will continue to trace the butterfly curve at larger values of r.

(b) $r \approx 4.1$. This value will increase if θ is increased.

Explorations

Chapter 1

(page 12)

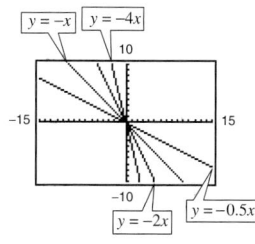

The line $y = 4x$.   The line $y = -4x$.

As $|m|$ increases, the line rises or falls faster.

(page 19)

$$d_1 = \sqrt{1 + m_1^2}, d_2 = \sqrt{1 + m_2^2}; m_1 = -\frac{1}{m_2}$$

(page 46)

Even

Neither

Odd

Even

Neither

Odd

Equations of odd functions contain only odd powers of x. Equations of even functions contain only even powers of x. Odd functions have all variables raised to odd powers and even functions have all variables raised to even powers. A function that has variables raised to even and odd powers is neither odd nor even.

(page 60)

a.

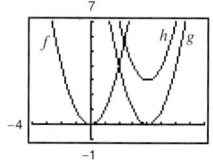

b.

g is a right shift of four units. h is a right shift of four units and an upward shift of three units.

g is a left shift of one unit. h is a left shift of one unit and a downward shift of two units.

c.

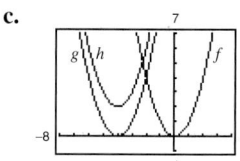

g is a left shift of four units. h is a left shift of four units and an upward shift of two units.

(page 61)

No. $g(x) = -x^4 - 2$. Yes. $h(x) = -(x - 3)^4$.

(page 73)

Option (b), because option (a) takes a 10% discount on a smaller amount. Option (b) represents $f(g(x))$; Option (a) represents $g(f(x))$.

(page 78)

x	-10	0	7	45
$f(f^{-1}(x))$	-10	0	7	45
$f^{-1}(f(x))$	-10	0	7	45

The functions are inverses of each other.

(page 81)

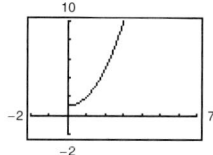

There is an inverse function $f^{-1}(x) = \sqrt{x - 1}$ since the domain of f is equal to the range of f^{-1} and the range of f is equal to the domain of f^{-1}.

Chapter 2

(page 112)

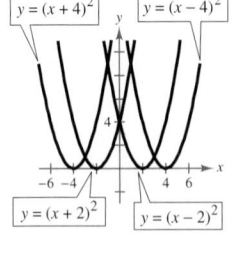

As $|a|$ gets larger, the parabola becomes narrower.

As h gets larger, the parabola shifts to the right.

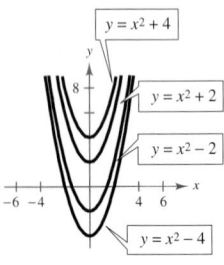

As k gets larger, the parabola shifts upward.

(page 123)

a. Third degree, odd; 1, greater than 0

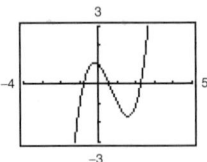

b. Fifth degree, odd; 2, greater than 0

c. Fifth degree, odd; -2, less than 0

d. Third degree, odd; -1, less than 0

e. Second degree, even; 2, greater than 0

f. Fourth degree, even; 1, greater than 0

g. Second degree, even; 1, greater than 0

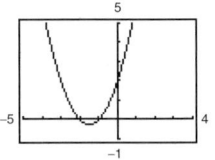

When the degree of the function is odd and the leading coefficient is positive, the graph falls to the left and rises to the right, but if the leading coefficient is negative, the graph falls to the right and rises to the left. When the degree of the function is even and the leading coefficient is positive, the graph rises to the left and right, but if the leading coefficient is negative, the graph falls to the left and right.

(page 145)

$i, -1, -i, 1, i, -1, -i, 1;$

The pattern repeats the first four results. Divide the exponent by 4.

If the remainder is 1, the result is i.

If the remainder is 2, the result is -1.

If the remainder is 3, the result is $-i$.

If the remainder is 0, the result is 1.

Chapter 3

(page 200)

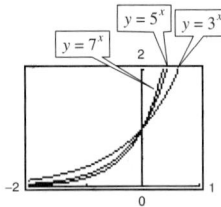

The graphs rise to the right and intersect at $(0, 1)$. $y = 3^x$. $y = 7^x$. $y = 7^x$. $y = 3^x$.

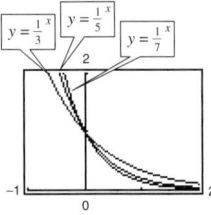

The graphs fall to the right and intersect at $(0, 1)$. $y = \frac{1}{7}^x$. $y = \frac{1}{3}^x$. $y = \frac{1}{3}^x$. $y = \frac{1}{7}^x$. For positive values of x, the greater the value of a, the more steeply the graph rises. The smaller the value of a, the more sharply the graph falls.

(page 203)

$A = \$5466.09$, $A = \$5466.35$, $A = \$5466.36$, $A = \$5466.38$.

No. Explorations will vary.

(page 210)

x	-2	-1	0	1	2
$f(x) = 10^x$	$\frac{1}{100}$	$\frac{1}{10}$	1	10	100

x	$\frac{1}{100}$	$\frac{1}{10}$	1	10	100
$f(x) = \log_{10} x$	-2	-1	0	1	2

The domain of $f(x) = 10^x$ is equal to the range of $f(x) = \log_{10} x$ and vice versa. $f(x) = 10^x$ and $f(x) = \log_{10} x$ are inverses of each other.

(page 221)

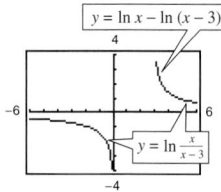

No; the domain of the first graph is $(3, \infty)$ and the domain of the second graph is $(-\infty, 0) \cup (3, \infty)$.

(page 230)

a. 7% **b.** 7.251% **c.** 7.186% **d.** 7.45%

Savings plan (d) will have the greatest effective yield. Savings plan (d) will have the highest balance after 5 years.

Chapter 4

(page 276)

1.

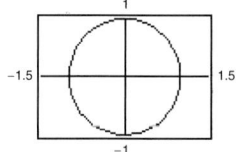

The graph is a circle.

2. The t-values represent the central angle in radians. The x- and y-values represent the location in the coordinate plane.

3. $-1 \le x \le 1$, $-1 \le y \le 1$

(page 303)

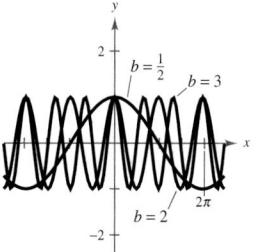

b affects the period of the graph.

$b = \frac{1}{2}$: $\frac{1}{2}$ cycle;

$b = 2$: 2 cycles;

$b = 3$: 3 cycles

(page 304)

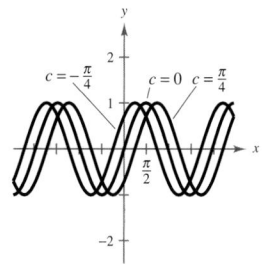

c shifts the graph horizontally.

Chapter 5

(page 373)

Yes. Preferences will vary.

(page 380)

  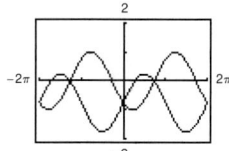

The graphs are different. No, it is not true.

The graphs are different. No, it is not true.

Chapter 6

(page 420)

Pythagorean Theorem.

The Pythagorean Theorem is just a special case of the more general Law of Cosines.

(page 454)

The given equation can be written as

$$x^4 = -16 = 16(\cos \pi + i \sin \pi)$$

which means that you can solve the equation by finding the four fourth roots of -16. Each of these roots has the form

$$\sqrt[4]{16}\left(\cos\frac{\pi + 2\pi k}{4} + i \sin \frac{\pi + 2\pi k}{4}\right).$$

Finally, using $k = 0, 1, 2$, and 3, you obtain the roots

$$2\left(\cos\frac{\pi}{4} + i \sin\frac{\pi}{4}\right) = 2\left(\frac{\sqrt{2}}{2} + \frac{\sqrt{2}}{2}i\right) = \sqrt{2} + \sqrt{2}i$$

$$2\left(\cos\frac{3\pi}{4} + i \sin\frac{3\pi}{4}\right) = 2\left(-\frac{\sqrt{2}}{2} + \frac{\sqrt{2}}{2}i\right) = -\sqrt{2} + \sqrt{2}i$$

$$2\left(\cos\frac{5\pi}{4} + i \sin\frac{5\pi}{4}\right) = 2\left(-\frac{\sqrt{2}}{2} - \frac{\sqrt{2}}{2}i\right) = -\sqrt{2} - \sqrt{2}i$$

$$2\left(\cos\frac{7\pi}{4} + i \sin\frac{7\pi}{4}\right) = 2\left(\frac{\sqrt{2}}{2} - \frac{\sqrt{2}}{2}i\right) = \sqrt{2} - \sqrt{2}i.$$

Chapter 7

(page 477)

No, the coordinates are approximations.

(page 479)

Two solutions   No solution

The number of points of intersection of the graph of a system of equations is the number of solutions the system has.

(page 489)

a.
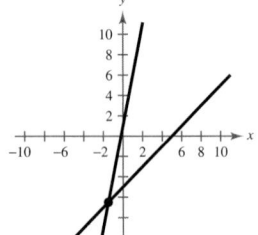

Slopes are not equal. Graphs have one point of intersection.

b.
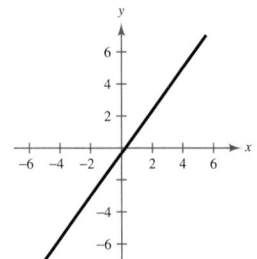

Slopes are equal. Infinitely many points of intersection.

c.
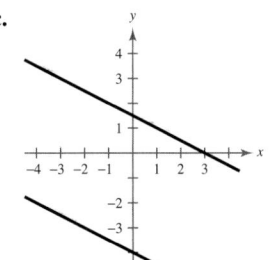

Slopes are equal. Graphs do not intersect.

Chapter 8

(page 565)

No. $AB = \begin{bmatrix} 4 & 7 \\ 8 & 15 \end{bmatrix}$, $BA = \begin{bmatrix} 3 & 4 \\ 11 & 16 \end{bmatrix}$.

Matrix multiplication is not commutative.

(page 577)

An error message appears because

$$1(6) - (-2)(-3) = 0.$$

(page 583)

An error message appears because the matrix is not square.

Chapter 9

(page 615)

$1, -\frac{1}{3}, \frac{1}{5}, -\frac{1}{7}, \frac{1}{9}$. No. The terms have the opposite signs.

(page 638)

As $x \to \infty$, $y \to 2$ for $r = \frac{1}{2}$, $y \to 3$ for $r = \frac{2}{3}$, $y \to 5$ for $r = \frac{4}{5}$.

As $x \to \infty$, $y \to \infty$ for $r = 1.5, 2$, and 3.

(page 656)

n	r	$_nC_r$	$_nC_{n-r}$
9	5	126	126
7	1	7	7
12	4	495	495
6	0	1	1
10	7	120	120

$_nC_r = {_nC_{n-r}}$

This illustrates the symmetry of Pascal's Triangle.

(page 679)

Assuming 365 different birthdays in a year, the probability that at least two out of 23 people will have a birthday on the same day of the year is ≈ 0.51.

The probability that at least two out of 50 people will have a birthday on the same day of the year is ≈ 0.97.

Chapter 10

(page 744)

t should be greater than -1. The upper bound of t varies, but one possibility is $t = 20$.

(page 751)

a. Yes. $\theta \approx 3.927, x \approx -2.121, y \approx -2.121$

b. Yes. Answers and explanations will vary.

Technology

Chapter 1

(page 19)

The lines appear perpendicular with the square setting.

(page 31)

Domain: $[-2, 2]$

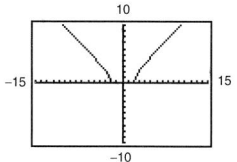

Domain: $(-\infty, -2] \cup [2, \infty)$

Yes, for -2 and 2.

Chapter 2

(page 126)

(a)

Chapter 3

(page 237)

$P = 5340(1.013)^t$. The models are very similar.

Chapter 4

(page 301)

No graph is visible. Try $-\pi \le x \le \pi$ and $-0.5 \le y \le 0.5$ as a viewing window.

Chapter 7

(page 478)

The point of intersection (7000, 5000) agrees with the solution.

(page 480)

a. $(2, 0)$ **b.** $(0, -1), (2, 1)$ **c.** None

Chapter 8

(page 562)

$$A + B = \begin{bmatrix} 1 & 1 \\ 1 & -5 \end{bmatrix}$$

Chapter 10

(page 746)

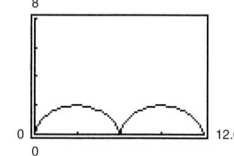

EXPLORATIONS

Writing About Mathematics

Chapter 1

Section 1.3   *(page 34)*

Answers will vary.

Section 1.7   *(page 73)*

a.

x	1	2	3	4	5	6
$g(x)$	0	1	2	0	1	-1

b.

x	1	2	3	4	5	6
$h(x)$	2	1	-3	-1	0	5

Section 1.8   *(page 82)*

a. The function does not have an inverse, because the retail price cannot be determined exactly because the sales tax is rounded.

b. The function does have an inverse because $f(f^{-1}(x)) = x$ and $f^{-1}(f(x)) = x$.

Chapter 2

Section 2.5   *(page 159)*

Answers will vary.

Section 2.6   *(page 173)*

No

a. No

b. Yes

c. No

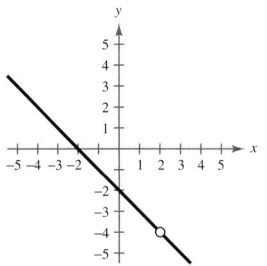

A rational function will not have a vertical asymptote when the function can be factored and reduced so that a variable factor no longer appears in the denominator.

Section 2.7   *(page 183)*

Because $\dfrac{x^2 + 1}{x(x - 1)}$ is an improper fraction, the student should begin by dividing to obtain $\dfrac{x^2 + 1}{x(x - 1)} = 1 + \dfrac{x + 1}{x(x - 1)}$, and decompose $\dfrac{x + 1}{x(x - 1)}$ into its partial fractions by the usual methods.

Chapter 3

Section 3.1   *(page 205)*

$g(x)$ can be generated by f_5.

$h(x)$ can be generated by f_2 or f_3.

All six functions have $(0, 8)$ as their y-intercept.

The functions f_2 and f_3 are the same because

$$f_2(x) = 8\left(\tfrac{1}{2}\right)^x = 2^3(2)^{-x} = 2^{(3-x)} = \left(\tfrac{1}{2}\right)^{-(3-x)}$$

$$= \left(\tfrac{1}{2}\right)^{(x-3)} = f_3(x).$$

The functions f_1 and f_6 are the same because

$$f_1(x) = 2^{(x+3)} = 2^x 2^3 = (8)2^x = f_6(x).$$

Examples of exponential functions with y-intercepts of $(0, -3)$ will vary. Possibilities include $f(x) = -3(2^x)$ and $f(x) = \left(\tfrac{1}{3}\right)^x - 4$.

Section 3.2   *(page 215)*

Approximately 11 months. Explanations will vary.

Section 3.4   (page 231)

a.

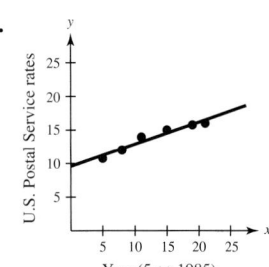

Linear model: $y = 0.329x + 9.58$

2004

b.

ln x	1.6094	2.0794	2.3979	2.7081	2.9444	3.0445
ln y	2.3749	2.4849	2.6355	2.7081	2.7568	2.7726

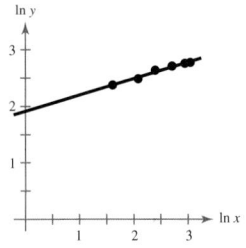

Logarithmic model: $\ln y = 0.28888 \ln x + 1.9103$

2007

c.

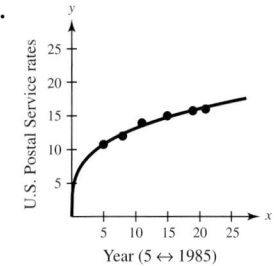

$y = 6.7551x^{0.28888}$ seems to fit the data better and will probably better predict future shipments.

Section 3.5   (page 242)

The quadratic model is better.

Chapter 4

Section 4.6   (page 317)

$h(x) = x + \sin x$

(a) $f(x) = x$ and $g(x) = \sin x$

(b) Tables will vary. One example is:

x	−3	−2	−1
$f(x) = x$	−3	−2	−1
$g(x) = \sin x$	−0.14112	−0.90930	−0.84147
$h(x) = f(x) + g(x)$	−3.14112	−2.90930	−1.84147

x	0	1	2
$f(x) = x$	0	1	2
$g(x) = \sin x$	0	0.84147	0.90930
$h(x) = f(x) + g(x)$	0	1.84147	2.90930

x	3
$f(x) = x$	3
$g(x) = \sin x$	0.14112
$h(x) = f(x) + g(x)$	3.14112

(c) A graph of h can be formed by adding the graphs of f and g point by point.

$h(x) = \cos x - \sin 3x$

(a) $f(x) = \cos x$ and $g(x) = \sin 3x$

(b) Tables will vary. One example is:

x	−3	−2	−1
$f(x) = \cos x$	−0.98999	−0.41615	0.54030
$g(x) = \sin 3x$	−0.41212	0.27942	−0.14112
$h(x) = f(x) - g(x)$	−0.57787	−0.69557	0.68142

x	0	1	2
$f(x) = \cos x$	1	0.54030	−0.41615
$g(x) = \sin 3x$	0	0.14112	−0.27942
$h(x) = f(x) - g(x)$	1	0.39918	−0.13673

x	3
$f(x) = \cos x$	−0.98999
$g(x) = \sin 3x$	0.41212
$h(x) = f(x) - g(x)$	−1.40211

(c) A graph of h can be formed by subtracting the graph of g from the graph of f point by point.

Examples will vary. One example is $f(x) = \sin x$ and

$$g(x) = \cos\left(x + \frac{\pi}{2}\right).$$

Section 4.8   *(page 337)*

(a) Amplitude modulation

(b) Frequency modulation

Explanations will vary.

Chapter 5

Section 5.2   *(page 366)*

This particular set of range settings actually shows the statement's left side and right side as coinciding, when an algebraic verification shows that they are not equal (using a different set of range settings will confirm this). A trigonometric identity should always be verified algebraically first, and then graphically. Showing that the graphs of the left and right sides of a statement appear to coincide is not strong enough proof to conclude that the statement is an identity.

Section 5.3   *(page 375)*

Equations a and b. Either $-2 \le \sqrt{b^2 - 4c} + b \le 2$ or $-2 \le \sqrt{b^2 - 4c} - b \le 2$ must be true.

Section 5.5   *(page 393)*

Let c be the length of the two equal sides of an isosceles triangle, and let θ be the angle between the two equal sides.

$$\text{Area} = \left(\frac{1}{2}\,\text{base}\right)(\text{height})$$

$$= \left(c \sin \frac{\theta}{2}\right)\left(c \cos \frac{\theta}{2}\right)$$

$$= c^2 \sqrt{\frac{1 - \cos \theta}{2}} \sqrt{\frac{1 + \cos \theta}{2}}$$

$$= c^2 \sqrt{\frac{1 - \cos^2\theta}{4}}$$

$$= \frac{1}{2}c^2 \sqrt{\sin^2 \theta}$$

$$= \frac{1}{2}c^2 \sin \theta$$

Examples will vary.

Chapter 6

Section 6.1   *(page 415)*

Yes

(a) $A = 40°$, $a \approx 12.86$, $b \approx 15.32$

(b) $A = 40°$, $b \approx 11.92$, $c \approx 15.56$

It is probably easier to use the right triangle definitions of sine, cosine, and tangent to solve the triangle.

Section 6.2   *(page 422)*

(a) Area $= \frac{1}{2}(2)(4) \sin 50° \approx 3.064$ square feet

(b) Area $= \sqrt{\frac{9}{2}\left(\frac{9}{2} - 2\right)\left(\frac{9}{2} - 3\right)\left(\frac{9}{2} - 4\right)} \approx 2.905$ square feet

(c) Area $= \frac{1}{2}(2)(4) = 4$ square feet

(d) Area $= \sqrt{6(6 - 3)(6 - 4)(6 - 5)} = 6$ square feet

Section 6.5   *(page 456)*

$e^{a+bi} = e^a(\cos b + i \sin b)$

Let $a = 0$ and $b = \pi$.

$$e^{0 + \pi i} = e^0(\cos \pi + i \sin \pi)$$

$$e^{\pi i} = -1$$

$$e^{\pi i} + 1 = 0$$

Chapter 7

Section 7.1   *(page 482)*

a. Agency B cost equation: $y = 100 + 0.25x$

b.

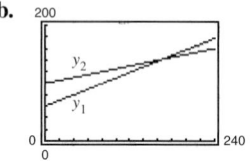

Point of intersection: $(167.08, 141.77)$. This gives the point at which the plans from both agencies cost the same. ($141.77 for 167.08 miles)

c. Agency A. If you plan to drive the truck less than 167 miles, it is less expensive to choose Agency A.

d. Agency B. If you plan to drive more than 167 miles, choose Agency B.

Section 7.4 (page 518)

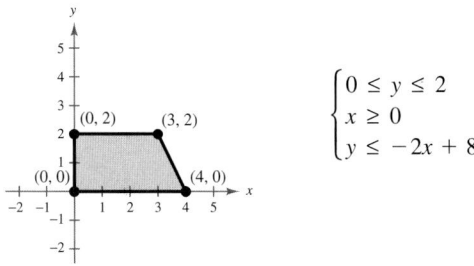

$$\begin{cases} 0 \le y \le 2 \\ x \ge 0 \\ y \le -2x + 8 \end{cases}$$

Section 7.5 (page 528)

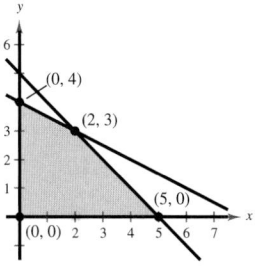

Answers are not unique.

a. $z = -x + y$ **b.** $z = 2x + 3y$

c. $z = x - y$ **d.** $z = -x - y$

Chapter 8

Section 8.2 (page 568)

Problems will vary.

Section 8.5 (page 598)

Answers will vary.

Chapter 9

Section 9.2 (page 630)

a. $-7, -4, -1, 2, 5, 8, 11; a_{n+1} = a_n + 3$

b. $17, 23, 29, 35, 41, 47, 53, 59, 65, 71; a_{n+1} = a_n + 6$

c. Not possible

d. $4, 7.5, 11, 14.5, 18, 21.5, 25, 28.5, 32, 35.5, 39;$ $a_{n+1} = a_n + 3.5$

e. Not possible

Section 9.3 (page 639)

Sequences will vary. One possibility (in inches, when starting with an 8-foot piece of string) is: $96, 48, 24, 12, 6, 3, 1\frac{1}{2}, \frac{3}{4}, \frac{3}{8}, \frac{3}{16}, \frac{3}{32}, \frac{3}{64}$ (and can go no further).

Formula: $a_n = 96\left(\frac{1}{2}\right)^{n-1}$.

You could theoretically make an infinite number of cuts, but realistically the string would become so small that it would be impossible to cut.

Section 9.5 (page 658)

a. Student used the wrong sign and raised $3y$ to the incorrect power in the expansion. Correct solution:
$$-5(2x)^4(3y)^1 = -240x^4y$$

b. Student gave the fifth term instead of the fourth term. Correct solution:
$$_6C_3\left(\frac{1}{2}x\right)^3(7y)^3 = 20\left(\frac{1}{2}x\right)^3(7y)^3$$
$$= 857.5x^3y^3$$

Chapter 10

Section 10.1 (page 703)

The angle of inclination is the positive angle made with the x-axis measured counterclockwise. Therefore, there are two cases: (1) a line with positive slope, implying $\theta < 90°$, and (2) a line with negative slope, implying $90° < \theta < 180°$. The angle between two lines is, by definition, the smaller of the two angles formed by the intersecting lines. The two angles formed are supplementary; therefore, one angle must be acute—i.e., less than $90°$—or, if the lines are perpendicular, both angles equal $90°$.

False. The inclination is the *positive angle measured counterclockwise* from the x-axis, not necessarily the angle between the line and the x-axis.

Section 10.2 (page 711)

When a television signal hits the antenna dish, the parabolic shape of the dish reflects the signal inward to the focus of the parabola. The signal is then transferred to the receiving equipment.

Section 10.3 (page 721)

a. Answers will vary.

b.

As e approaches 0, the shape of the ellipse approaches the shape of a circle.

c. When $e = 0$, the graph of the equation is circular. The equation of the ellipse is

$$\frac{(x - h)^2}{a^2} + \frac{(y - k)^2}{a^2} = 1,$$

otherwise known as the equation of a circle.

Section 10.4   (page 731)

a.

b.

c.

d.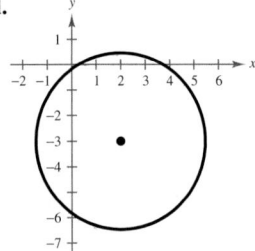

Discussions will vary.

Section 10.5   (page 739)

$f(x) = 1/x$

$y = 1/x$

$xy = 1$

$xy - 1 = 0 \Rightarrow B = 1$ and $F = -1$.

So, $B^2 - 4AC = (1)^2 - 4(0)(0) = 1 > 0$.

Therefore, the graph of $f(x) = 1/x$ is a hyperbola.

Appendix A

Section A.1   (page A8)

2. (a) $12, 5$ (b) $-7, 0, -3, 12, 5$

(c) $-7, -\frac{7}{3}, 0, 3.12, \frac{5}{4}, -3, 12, 5$ (d) $\sqrt{5}$

4. (a) 4 (b) $-75, 4$

(c) $0.7575, -4.63, -75, 4$

(d) $2.3030030003\ldots, \sqrt{10}$

6. (a) $25, \sqrt{9}, 7, 13$ (b) $25, -17, \sqrt{9}, 7, 13$

(c) $25, -17, -\frac{12}{5}, \sqrt{9}, 3.12, 7, -11.1, 13$ (d) $\frac{1}{2}\pi$

8. $0.\overline{3}$ **10.** $0.\overline{54}$ **12.** $-6 < -2.5$

14.

$$-3.5 < 1$$

16.

$$1 < \frac{16}{3}$$

18.

$$-\frac{8}{7} < -\frac{3}{7}$$

20. $x \geq -2$ denotes the set of all real numbers greater than or equal to -2. Unbounded

22. $x > 3$ denotes the set of all real numbers greater than 3. Unbounded

24. $x < 2$ denotes the set of all real numbers less than 2. Unbounded

26. $0 \leq x \leq 5$ denotes the set of all real numbers greater than or equal to zero and less than or equal to 5. Bounded

28. $0 < x \leq 6$ denotes the set of positive real numbers less than or equal to 6. Bounded

30. $-6 \leq y < 0$ **32.** $y \leq 25$

34. $-3 \leq k < 5$ **36.** $2.5\% \leq r \leq 5\%$

38. This interval consists of all real numbers greater than or equal to -5 and less than or equal to 7.

40. This interval consists of all real numbers less than or equal to 4.

42. 0 **44.** 3 **46.** -6 **48.** -9 **50.** 1

52. $|-4| = |4|$ **54.** $-|-6| < |-6|$

56. $-(-2) > -2$ **58.** $\frac{5}{2}$ **60.** 51

62. $\frac{5}{2}$ **64.** 14.99

66. $|\$9772 - \$9400| = \$372 < \$500$

$0.05(\$9400) = \$470$

Because the difference between the actual expenses and the budget is less than \$500 and less than 5% of the budgeted amount, there is compliance with the "budget variance test."

68. $|\$2613 - \$2575| = \$38 < \$500$

$0.05(\$2575) = \$128.75$

Because the difference between the actual expenses and the budget is less than \$500 and less than 5% of the budgeted amount, there is compliance with the "budget variance test."

70.

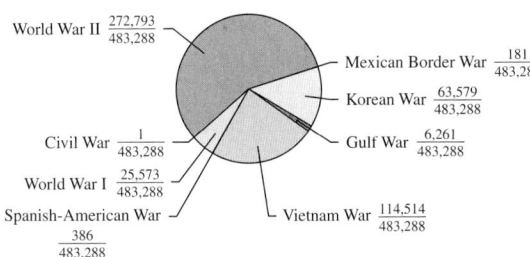

World War II $\frac{272{,}793}{483{,}288}$

Mexican Border War $\frac{181}{483{,}288}$

Korean War $\frac{63{,}579}{483{,}288}$

Civil War $\frac{1}{483{,}288}$

Gulf War $\frac{6{,}261}{483{,}288}$

World War I $\frac{25{,}573}{483{,}288}$

Spanish-American War $\frac{386}{483{,}288}$

Vietnam War $\frac{114{,}514}{483{,}288}$

72. $|326 - 351| = 25$ miles   **74.** $|48 - 82| = 34°$

76. $|x + 10| \geq 6$ **78.** $|y - a| \leq 2$

80. $6x^3$ and $-5x$ are the terms; 6 and -5 are the coefficients.

82. $3\sqrt{3}x^2$ and 1 are the terms; $3\sqrt{3}$ is the coefficient.

84. $3x^4$ and $-x^2/4$ are the terms; 3 and $-\frac{1}{4}$ are the coefficients.

86. (a) 30   (b) -12 **88.** (a) -10 (b) 0

90. (a) $\frac{1}{2}$ (b) Division by 0 is undefined.

92. Multiplicative Inverse Property

94. Additive Inverse Property

96. Additive Identity Property

98. Associative Property of Addition

100. $\frac{1}{7}(7 \cdot 12) = \left(\frac{1}{7} \cdot 7\right)12$ Associative Property of Multiplication

$= 1 \cdot 12$ Multiplicative Inverse Property

$= 12$ Multiplicative Identity Property

102. $\frac{2}{7}$ **104.** $\frac{59}{66}$ **106.** -3 **108.** $\frac{5x}{27}$

110. (a)

n	1	10	100	10,000	100,000
$5/n$	5	0.5	0.05	0.0005	0.00005

(b) The value of $5/n$ approaches 0 as n increases without bound.

112. False. The denominators cannot be added when adding fractions.

114. Yes. y is nonnegative if $y \geq 0$. y is positive if $y > 0$.

116.

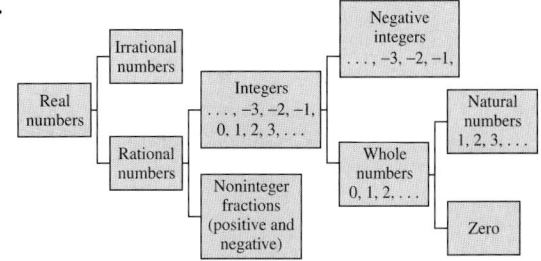

Real numbers

Irrational numbers

Rational numbers

Integers $\dots, -3, -2, -1, 0, 1, 2, 3, \dots$

Noninteger fractions (positive and negative)

Negative integers $\dots, -3, -2, -1,$

Whole numbers $0, 1, 2, \dots$

Natural numbers $1, 2, 3, \dots$

Zero

118. (a) Positive   (b) Positive

Section A.2   *(page A20)*

2. $(-2) \times (-2) \times (-2) \times (-2) \times (-2) \times (-2) \times (-2)$

4. $11.3 \times 11.3 \times 11.3 \times 11.3$ **6.** $\left(2\sqrt{5}\right)^4$

8. $-\left(\frac{3}{2}\right)^4$ **10.** (a) 125   (b) $\frac{1}{9}$

12. (a) 5184   (b) $-\frac{3}{5}$ **14.** (a) $\frac{16}{3}$ (b) 1

16. (a) $\frac{7}{12}$ (b) $\frac{1}{81}$ **18.** 0.244   **20.** 5184

22. $\frac{7}{16}$ **24.** -135 **26.** -48 **28.** $-\frac{5}{27}$

30. (a) $9x^2$ (b) $16x^6$ **32.** (a) $-3z^7$ (b) $\frac{5}{2}y^4$

34. (a) $\frac{1}{r^2}$ (b) $\frac{5184}{y^7}$ **36.** (a) 1   (b) $\frac{1}{(z+2)^4}$

38. (a) $32y^2$ (b) $\frac{125x^9}{y^{12}}$ **40.** (a) $\frac{1}{x}$ (b) 1

42. 9.46×10^{12} kilometers   **44.** 3.937×10^{-5} inch

46. 15,000,000 °C   **48.** 0.00009 meter

50. (a) 60,000   (b) 2.0×10^{11}

52. (a) 4.907×10^{17} (b) 1.479

54. (a) 0.064   (b) 0.030

56. $64^{1/3}$ **58.** $-\sqrt{144}$ **60.** $(614.125)^{1/3}$

62. $\sqrt[5]{-243}$ **64.** $81^{3/4}$ **66.** $\sqrt[4]{16^5}$

68. (a) 7   (b) $\frac{3}{2}$ **70.** (a) 562   (b) 216

72. (a) $\frac{1}{1000}$ (b) $\frac{2}{3}$ **74.** (a) $-\frac{3}{5}$ (b) -625

76. (a) 12.651   (b) 2.236   **78.** (a) 3.495   (b) 5.906

80. (a) $\frac{2\sqrt[3]{2}}{3}$ (b) $\frac{5\sqrt{3}}{2}$

82. (a) $3y^2\sqrt{6x}$ (b) $\frac{4a^2}{|b|}\sqrt{2}$

84. (a) $3x^2$ (b) $2x\sqrt[5]{3}$ **86.** $xy^{1/3}$

88. $\frac{x}{5},\quad x > 0$ **90.** $\frac{\sqrt{10}}{2}$ **92.** $3\left(\sqrt{6} - \sqrt{5}\right)$

94. $\frac{2}{3\sqrt{2}}$ **96.** $-\frac{1}{2\left(\sqrt{7} + 3\right)}$ **98.** (a) $\sqrt{x}$ (b) $3x^2$

100. (a) $3\sqrt[4]{3(x+1)}$ (b) $a\sqrt[6]{10ab}$

102. (a) $7\sqrt{3}$ (b) $11\sqrt[3]{2}$

104. (a) $-84\sqrt{x}$ (b) $23|x|\sqrt{3}$

106. (a) $4\sqrt{x^3-7}$ (b) $50x\sqrt{5x}$

108. $\sqrt{\dfrac{3}{11}} = \dfrac{\sqrt{3}}{\sqrt{11}}$ **110.** $5 = \sqrt{3^2+4^2}$

112. 0.026 inch **114.** 8.32 minutes

116. False. When a power is raised to a power, you multiply the exponents: $(a^n)^k = a^{nk}$.

118. (a) 3 is also raised to the -1 power, so $(3x)^{-1} = \dfrac{1}{3x}$.

(b) When two powers have the same base, the exponents are added: $y^3 \cdot y^2 = y^5$.

(c) When a power is raised to a power, the exponents are multiplied: $(a^2b^3)^4 = a^8b^{12}$.

(d) The square of a binomial contains a cross-product term: $(a+b)^2 = a^2 + 2ab + b^2$.

(e) If $x < 0$, then $\sqrt{4x^2} > 0$ but $2x < 0$: $\sqrt{4x^2} = 2|x|$.

(f) Radicals can only be added together if they have the same radicand and index: $\sqrt{2} + \sqrt{2} = 2\sqrt{2}$.

120. No. Rationalizing the denominator produces a number equivalent to the original fraction; squaring does not.

Section A.3 *(page A31)*

1. d **2.** e **3.** b **4.** a **5.** f **6.** c

8. $6x^5 + 3x + 1$ (Answers will vary.)

10. $20x^3 + 5$ (Answers will vary.)

12. Degree: 4; Leading coefficient: -3

14. Degree: 0; Leading coefficient: 3

16. Degree: 5; Leading coefficient: -1

18. Not a polynomial because of the negative exponent

20. Polynomial: $\frac{1}{2}x^2 + x - \frac{3}{2}$

22. Not a polynomial because of the square root

24. $-2x^2 - 4$ **26.** $1.3x^4 - 8.4x - 34.1$

28. $y^3 - y^2 - 3y + 7$ **30.** $4y^4 + 2y^3 - 3y^2$

32. $-15x^2 - 6x$ **34.** $4x^4 - 12x$ **36.** $-7y^4 + 4y^3$

38. $-\frac{7}{4}y^2 + 8y$ **40.** $x^2 + 5x - 50$

42. $28x^2 - 29x + 6$ **44.** $16x^2 + 40x + 25$

46. $64x^2 - 80x + 25$ **48.** $4x^2 - 9$

50. $4x^2 - 9y^2$ **52.** $x^2 + 2xy + y^2 - 1$

54. $x^2 - 2xy + y^2 + 2x - 2y + 1$

56. $9a^6 - 16b^4$ **58.** $x^3 - 6x^2 + 12x - 8$

60. $16x^6 - 24x^3 + 9$ **62.** $\frac{4}{9}t^2 + \frac{20}{3}t + 25$

64. $4x^2 - \frac{1}{25}$ **66.** $2.25y^2 - 9y + 9$ **68.** $6.25y^2 - 9$

70. $2x^2 + 8x + 6$ **72.** $x^4 - y^4$ **74.** $25 - x$

76. $x^2 + 2x\sqrt{3} + 3$

78. Not factored: $(x+3)^2(x-3)$

80. Not factored: $x(x+3)(2x-1)(2x+1)$

82. $5(y-6)$

84. $2x(2x^2 - 3x + 6)$ **86.** $(x+2)(3x-4)$

88. $3x(3x-1)$ **90.** $\frac{1}{3}y(y^3 - 15y + 6)$

92. $\frac{2}{5}(y+1)(2y-5)$ **94.** $(7+3y)(7-3y)$

96. $\left(\frac{2}{5}y+8\right)\left(\frac{2}{5}y-8\right)$ **98.** $-z(z+10)$

100. $(5x+4y)(5x-4y)$ **102.** $(x+5)^2$

104. $(3x-2)^2$ **106.** $(2x-y)^2$ **108.** $\left(z+\frac{1}{2}\right)^2$

110. $(x-3)(x^2+3x+9)$ **112.** $(z+5)(z^2-5z+25)$

114. $(3x+2)(9x^2-6x+4)$

116. $(4x-y)(16x^2+4xy+y^2)$

118. $(x+2)(x+3)$ **120.** $(t+2)(t-3)$

122. $(8-z)(3+z)$ **124.** $(2x+1)(x-1)$

126. $(3x+1)(4x+1)$ **128.** $(-5u+2)(u+3)$

130. $(x+5)(x^2-5)$ **132.** $(2-x^3)(x+3)$

134. $(4x^3-3)(2x^2+3)$ **136.** $(x+3)(2x+3)$

138. $(x-1)(12x-1)$ **140.** $12(x+2)(x-2)$

142. $x(x+3)(x-3)$ **144.** $y(2y+3)(y-5)$

146. $(5x+3)(x+2)$ **148.** $\frac{1}{96}(4x-3)(3x+2)$

150. $(u+2)(3-u^2)$

152. $(x+2)(x+4)(x-2)(x-4)$

154. $5(x+2)(x^2-2x+4)$ **156.** $(3-4x)(23-60x)$

158. $7(x^2+1)(3x^2-1)$

160. $3(x^6+1)^4(3x+2)^2(33x^6 + 20x^5 + 3)$

162. $-51, 51, -15, 15, -27, 27$

164. $-25, 25, -14, 14, -11, 11, -10, 10$

166. Two possible answers: $3, -8$

168. Two possible answers: $9, 7$

170. $548

172. (a) $1200r^3 + 3600r^2 + 3600r + 1200$

(b)

r	2%	3%	$3\frac{1}{2}$%
$1200(1+r)^3$	$1273.45	$1311.27	$1330.46

r	4%	$5\frac{1}{2}$%
$1200(1+r)^3$	$1349.84	$1409.09

(c) The amount increases with increasing r.

174. (a) $3x^2 + 8x$ (b) $30x^2$

176. $44x + 308$

178. (a) $T = 0.0475x^2 + 1.099x + 0.23$

(b)

x (mi/hr)	30	40	55
T (feet)	75.95	120.19	204.36

(c) The stopping distance increases at an accelerating rate as speed increases.

180.

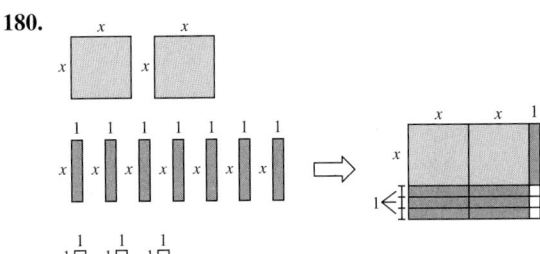

182. $r^2(4 - \pi)$ **184.** $\frac{5}{8}(x + 7)(x - 1)$

186. $kx(Q - x)$

188. False. $(4x + 3) + (-4x + 6)$

$$= 4x + 3 - 4x + 6$$
$$= 3 + 6$$
$$= 9$$

190. False. A perfect square trinomial can be factored as the binomial sum squared.

192. n

194. (a) $x^2 - 1$ (b) $x^3 - 1$ (c) $x^4 - 1$
$(x - 1)(x^4 + x^3 + x^2 + x + 1) = x^5 - 1$

196. $(x^n + y^n)(x^{2n} - x^n y^n + y^{2n})$

Section A.4   *(page A43)*

2. All real numbers   **4.** All positive real numbers

6. All real numbers x such that $x \neq -\frac{1}{2}$

8. All real numbers x such that $x \leq 6$

10. $(x + 1)$, $x \neq -1$ **12.** $\frac{3}{10y^3}$ **14.** $\frac{2x^2}{x - 1}$

16. $\frac{9x}{2}$, $x \neq -1$ **18.** $-4, x \neq 3$

20. $-(x + 5)$, $x \neq 5$ **22.** $\frac{x - 2}{x + 1}$, $x \neq -10$

24. $\frac{(x - 6)(x - 1)}{(x + 10)(x + 1)}$ **26.** $\frac{1}{x + 1}$, $x \neq \pm 3$

28. $\frac{y(y - 3)}{y^2 - y + 1}$, $y \neq -1$

30.

x	0	1	2	3	4	5	6
$\dfrac{x - 3}{x^2 - x - 6}$	$\frac{1}{2}$	$\frac{1}{3}$	$\frac{1}{4}$	Undef.	$\frac{1}{6}$	$\frac{1}{7}$	$\frac{1}{8}$
$\dfrac{1}{x + 2}$	$\frac{1}{2}$	$\frac{1}{3}$	$\frac{1}{4}$	$\frac{1}{5}$	$\frac{1}{6}$	$\frac{1}{7}$	$\frac{1}{8}$

The expressions are equivalent except at $x = 3$.

32. The expression cannot be simplified.

34. $\frac{x + 5}{4(2x + 3)}$, $x \neq -5$ **36.** $-\frac{x + 13}{5x^2}$, $x \neq 3$

38. $-\frac{8}{5}$, $y \neq -3, 4$ **40.** $\frac{x - y}{x(x + y)^2}$, $x \neq -2y$

42. $\frac{1}{3}$, $x \neq \pm 7$ **44.** $\frac{x}{x + 3}$ **46.** $\frac{8 - 5x}{x - 1}$ **48.** $\frac{2x + 5}{x - 5}$

50. $\frac{6(2x + 3)}{(x - 2)(x + 1)(x + 4)}$ **52.** $\frac{4x + 1}{(x - 1)(x + 1)}$

54. $\frac{x^8 - 5}{x^3}$ **56.** $\frac{-2x(x + 5)}{(x - 5)^4}$ **58.** $\frac{4x^3(2x - 1)^2 - 2x}{(2x - 1)^{1/2}}$

60. The error was an incorrect expansion of $(x + 2)^2$ in the numerator.

62. $\frac{4x}{x + 4}$, $x \neq 0, 4$ **64.** $\frac{x + 1}{x - 1}$, $x \neq 0$

66. $\frac{1}{(x + h + 1)(x + 1)}$, $h \neq 0$ **68.** $\frac{-1}{t^2 \sqrt{t^2 + 1}}$

70. $\frac{x^2 - 2}{x^3(1 - x^2)^{1/2}}$ **72.** $\frac{-1}{\sqrt{z - 3} + \sqrt{z}}$ **74.** $\frac{8(x + 2)}{(x + 4)^2}$

76. (a) 9.09%   (b) $\frac{288(MN - P)}{N(MN + 12P)}$; 9.09%

78. (a)

Year	1994	1995	1996	1997	1998	1999
Gold	$381	$390	$383	$334	$293	$288
Platinum	$477	$422	$396	$381	$371	$364

(b) The estimates are fairly close to the actual costs.

(c) Ratio $= \dfrac{-3.123t^3 + 50.77t^2 - 259.4t + 356}{-3.038t^3 + 45.14t^2 - 201.6t + 192}$

(d)

Year	1994	1995	1996	1997	1998	1999
Ratio	0.80	0.92	0.97	0.88	0.79	0.79

Decrease

80. False. The two expressions are equivalent for all values of x such that $x \neq 1$.

Section A.5   *(page A55)*

2. Conditional equation   **4.** Identity

6. Identity   **8.** Identity   **10.** Conditional equation

12. -12 **14.** 3   **16.** -5 **18.** $-\frac{5}{8}$

20. All real numbers   **22.** -5 **24.** 6

26. 50   **28.** No solution. The x-terms sum to zero.

30. $\frac{1}{2}$ **32.** 0   **34.** $\frac{9}{7}$ **36.** 0

38. $\frac{11}{6}$ **40.** $-\frac{13}{3}$ **42.** $\frac{7}{4}$

44. No solution. The solution is extraneous.   **46.** $\frac{1}{5}$

48. No solution. The x-terms sum to zero.

50. $x^2 - 16x = 0$ **52.** $3x^2 + 42x + 134 = 0$

54. $4x^2 - 2x + 1 = 0$ **56.** $-\frac{1}{3}, \frac{1}{3}$ **58.** 9, 1

60. $-\frac{3}{2}$ **62.** $-\frac{3}{2}, 11$ **64.** 2, 6   **66.** $-8, 16$

68. $-a - b, -a + b$ **70.** $\pm 13; \pm 13.00$

72. $\pm 4\sqrt{2}; \pm 5.66$ **74.** $\pm 2; \pm 2.00$

76. $-18, -8; -18.00, -8.00$

78. $5 \pm \sqrt{30}; 10.48, -0.48$

80. $-\frac{7}{4} \pm \frac{\sqrt{11}}{2}; -0.09, -3.41$ **82.** $-\frac{9}{2}; -4.50$

84. $0, -4$ **86.** $3, -1$ **88.** $-4 \pm \sqrt{2}$

90. $\frac{2}{3} \pm \sqrt{2}$ **92.** $\frac{11}{2}, -\frac{9}{2}$ **94.** $1, -\frac{1}{2}$

96. $\frac{3}{5}, \frac{1}{5}$ **98.** $5 \pm \sqrt{3}$ **100.** $-3 \pm \sqrt{13}$

102. $\frac{1}{2} \pm \frac{\sqrt{5}}{2}$ **104.** $\frac{5}{4} \pm \frac{\sqrt{3}}{4}$ **106.** $-\frac{1}{3} \pm \frac{\sqrt{11}}{6}$

108. $\frac{5}{4} \pm \frac{\sqrt{5}}{2}$ **110.** $-\frac{3}{2} \pm \frac{\sqrt{13}}{2}$ **112.** $-\frac{8}{5} \pm \frac{\sqrt{3}}{5}$

114. $-7 \pm \sqrt{13}$ **116.** $\frac{686 \pm 196\sqrt{6}}{25}$

118. $1.400, -0.150$ **120.** $2.137, 18.063$

122. $0.672, -0.968$ **124.** $-2.995, 2.971$

126. $0, -3$ **128.** 7   **130.** $-\frac{3}{2} \pm \sqrt{3}$

132. $-\frac{b}{a}, \frac{b}{a}$ **134.** ± 1 **136.** $0, \pm \frac{5}{2}$

138. $\pm 2, \pm 1 \pm \sqrt{3}i$ **140.** $\frac{8}{3}, -\frac{4}{3} \pm \frac{4\sqrt{3}i}{3}$

142. $0, \frac{4}{3}$ **144.** $-2, \pm\sqrt{3}i$ **146.** $\pm 2, -1 \pm \sqrt{3}i$

148. $\pm 2, \pm 3i$ **150.** $\pm \frac{\sqrt{7}}{6}, \pm i$

152. $-\sqrt[3]{2}, \frac{1 \pm \sqrt{3}i}{2^{2/3}}, -1, \frac{1 \pm \sqrt{3}i}{2}$

154. $\frac{9}{16}$ **156.** -4 **158.** $\frac{124}{3}$ **160.** $3, -2$

162. No solution   **164.** 1

166. $-29, 25$ **168.** $\frac{1 \pm 5\sqrt{5}}{2}$ **170.** $0, 1, \frac{3}{5}$

172. $2, -12$ **174.** $\frac{1 \pm \sqrt{31}}{3}$ **176.** $\frac{3}{4}, -1$ **178.** ± 1

180. $\frac{5}{3}, -3$ **182.** $-6, \pm 3$ **184.** $10, -1$

186. Yes, The estimated height of a male with a 19-inch femur is 69.4 inches.

188. $y = -0.25t + 8$; after about 28 hours

190. 6 inches $\times$ 6 inches $\times$ 2 inches

192. $\frac{20\sqrt{3}}{3} \approx 11.55$ inches

194. 26,250 passengers   **196.** 500 units   **198.** 90 feet

200. False. The product must equal zero for the Zero-Factor Property to be used.

202. False. See Example 12.

204. Equivalent equations have the same solution set, and one is derived from the other by steps for generating equivalent equations.

$2x = 5, \ 2x + 3 = 8$

206. (a) and (b) $x = -5, -\frac{10}{3}$

(c) The method used in part (a) reduces the number of algebraic steps.

208. Answers will vary. Sample answer: $y = 2x^2 + 3x - 2$

210. Isolate the absolute value by subtracting x from both sides of the equation. The expression inside the absolute value signs can be positive or negative, so two separate equations must be solved.

Section A.6   *(page A67)*

2. $2 < x \le 10$. Bounded   **4.** $-5 \le x < \infty$. Unbounded

6. $-\infty < x \le 7$. Unbounded   **7.** b   **8.** f

9. d   **10.** c   **11.** e   **12.** a

14. (a) No   (b) No   (c) Yes   (d) No

16. (a) No   (b) No   (c) Yes   (d) No

18. (a) No   (b) Yes   (c) No   (d) Yes

20. $x < -4$

22. $x < -\frac{5}{2}$

24. $x \leq 5$

26. $x \geq \frac{1}{2}$

28. $x \geq -3$

30. $x < -\frac{1}{2}$

32. $x < 7$

34. $x > \frac{1}{6}$

36. $x > 16$

38. $-6 < x \leq 1$

40. $-3 \leq x < 7$

42. $3 < x < 9$

44. No solution

46. $x < -4, x > 4$

48. $x < -15, \ x > 15$

50. All real numbers x

52. No solution

54. $-2 < x < 3$

56. $0 < x < 3$

58. $x < -28, \ x > 0$

60. $\frac{1}{5} \leq x \leq \frac{7}{5}$

62.

$x \leq 2$

64.

$x < 2$

66.
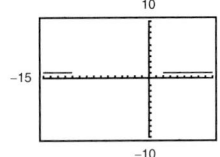

$x < -11, x > 2$

68.
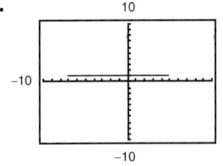

$-7 \leq x \leq 5$

70. $[10, \infty)$ **72.** $(-\infty, 3]$ **74.** $\left[-\frac{5}{2}, \infty\right)$

76. $|x| > 3$ **78.** $|x + 1| \leq 4$ **80.** $|x - 8| \geq 5$

82. $|x + 6| \leq 7$

84. (a) Yes   (b) No   (c) Yes   (d) Yes

86. (a) No   (b) Yes   (c) Yes   (d) No

88. $0, \frac{25}{9}$ **90.** $-2, -1, 1, 4$

92. $(-6, 6)$

94. $(-\infty, 2], [4, \infty)$

96. $(-1, 7)$

98. $(-\infty, -3), (1, \infty)$

100. $\left(-\infty, 2 - \sqrt{5}\right), \left(2 + \sqrt{5}, \infty\right)$

102. $\left(-\infty, \frac{3}{2} - \frac{\sqrt{39}}{2}\right], \left[\frac{3}{2} + \frac{\sqrt{39}}{2}, \infty\right)$

104. $(-\infty, 2]$

106. $\left[-\frac{13}{2}, -2\right], [2, \infty)$

108. $(3, \infty)$ **110.** $(-\infty, 0], [2, \infty)$ **112.** $(-\infty, 3]$

114.

$(-\infty, 0), \left(\frac{1}{4}, \infty\right)$

116. $(-2, 3]$ **118.** $\left(-\infty, -\frac{1}{2}\right), (1, \infty)$

120. $(-14, -2), (6, \infty)$ **122.** $(-\infty, -3), (0, \infty)$

124. $[-3, 0), [2, \infty)$

126. $(-\infty, -4), [-2, 1), [6, \infty)$ **128.** $(-\infty, -2], [2, \infty)$

130. $[-4, 4]$ **132.** $(-3, 0], (3, \infty)$ **134.** $(-1.13, 1.13)$

136. $(-4.42, 0.42)$ **138.** $(1.19, 1.30)$

140. More than 42,857 copies **142.** $x \geq 187$ pounds

144. $20 \leq h \leq 80$ **146.** 45.97 feet $\leq L \leq 174.03$ feet

148. $90{,}000$ units $\leq x \leq 100{,}000$ units

150. (a) $2223.9; 5593.9; 10{,}312; 16{,}378; 23{,}792$

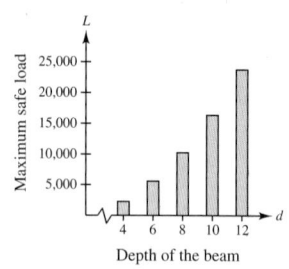

(b) 3.83 inches

152. False. If $-10 \leq x \leq 8$, then $10 \geq -x$ and $-x \geq -8$.

154. True. The y-values are greater than zero for all values of x.

156. One set (the solution is not unique): $a = 1, b = 5, c = 5$

158. All real numbers more than four units from 8

160. $(-\infty, \infty)$ **162.** $\left(-\infty, -2\sqrt{10}\right] \cup \left[2\sqrt{10}, \infty\right)$

164. 0

Section A.7 *(page A76)*

2. The 3 is distributed to both terms.
$$5z + 3(x - 2) = 5z + 3x - 6$$

4. The expression on the right should be negative.
$$\frac{1 - x}{(5 - x)(-x)} = -\frac{x - 1}{x(x - 5)}$$

6. yz is one term, not two. $x(yz) = xyz$

8. The exponent also applies to the coefficient. $(4x)^2 = 16x^2$

10. Do not apply radicals term-by-term.
$$\sqrt{25 - x^2} = \sqrt{(5 + x)(5 - x)}$$

12. $\dfrac{6x + y}{6x - y}$ cannot be simplified.

14. The negative exponent is on a term of the denominator, not a factor.
$$\frac{1}{x + y^{-1}} = \frac{y}{xy + 1}, \ y \neq 0$$

16. Exponents are applied before multiplying.
$$x(2x - 1)^2 = x(4x^2 - 4x + 1) = 4x^3 - 4x^2 + x$$

18. Be careful when using a slash to denote division.
$$(1/2)y = \frac{1}{2} \cdot y = \frac{y}{2}$$

20. x^2 **22.** $3x + 2$ **24.** $-\frac{1}{4}$ **26.** $\frac{1}{2}$ **28.** $x - 1$

30. $\frac{4}{3}, \frac{16}{9}$ **32.** $4, 7$ **34.** $10x + 3$

36. $1 + 10x^2 - 20x^3$ **38.** $4t - 3$ **40.** $x - 5 + \dfrac{4}{x^2}$

42. $2x^{7/2} - 3x^{3/2} + \dfrac{5}{x^{1/2}} - \dfrac{1}{x^{3/2}}$ **44.** $\dfrac{x}{3} - \dfrac{5x^2}{3}$

46. $\dfrac{-11x^2 - 5}{x^6(x^2 + 1)^4}$ **48.** $\dfrac{-6(2x - 3)}{(4x^2 + 9)^{3/2}}$ **50.** $\dfrac{x - 3}{(2x - 1)^{1/2}}$

52. $\dfrac{1 - 4x}{(x + 1)^2(2x - 3x^2)^{1/2}}$ **54.** $\dfrac{2(3x^2 + 5x - 6)}{(x^2 - 6)(2x + 5)}$

56. $\dfrac{3(x - 6)^{1/2}[6x + 4 - (x - 6)^{5/2}]}{2(3x + 2)^{3/2}}$

58. (a) Answers will vary.

(b)

x	-2	-1	$-\frac{1}{2}$	0	1	2	$\frac{5}{2}$
y_1	-8.7	-2.9	-1.1	0	2.9	8.7	12.5
y_2	-8.7	-2.9	-1.1	0	2.9	8.7	12.5

60. False. Cannot move term-by-term from denominator to numerator.

62. False. $x^2 - 9$ does not factor into $\left(\sqrt{x} + 3\right)\left(\sqrt{x} - 3\right)$.

64. There is no error. **66.** There is no error.

Section A.8 *(page A84)*

2. A: $\left(\frac{3}{2}, -4\right)$, B: $(0, -2)$, C: $\left(-3, \frac{5}{2}\right)$, D: $(-6, 0)$

4. $(4, -8)$ **6.** $(-12, 0)$

8. Quadrant III   **10.** Quadrant I

12. Quadrant I or IV   **14.** Quadrant III

16. Quadrant II or IV   **18.** $(3, 3)$, $(1, 0)$, $(3, -3)$, $(5, 0)$

20. $(-5, 2)$, $(-7, 0)$, $(-3, 0)$, $(-5, -4)$

22.

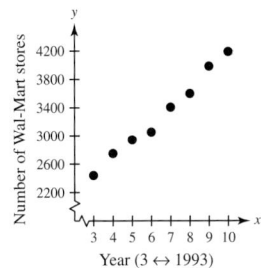

24. 106%

26. (a) 21.4%

(b) 182.4%

28. (a)

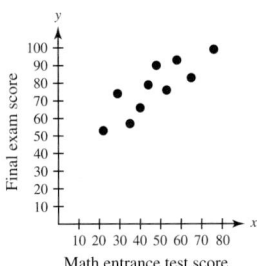

(b) 65

(c) No. There are many variables that will affect the final exam score.

30. 7   **32.** 10   **34.** (a) 5, 12, 13   (b) $5^2 + 12^2 = 13^2$

36. (a) 4, 7, $\sqrt{65}$ (b) $4^2 + 7^2 = \left(\sqrt{65}\right)^2$

38. (a)

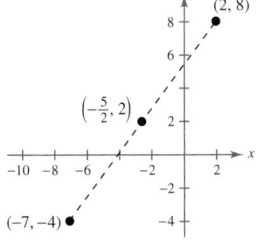

(b) 13

(c) $\left(\frac{7}{2}, 6\right)$

40. (a)

(b) 15

(c) $\left(-\frac{5}{2}, 2\right)$

42. (a)

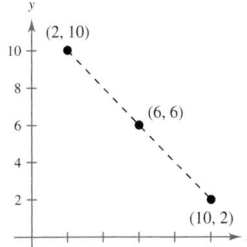

(b) $8\sqrt{2}$

(c) $(6, 6)$

44. (a)

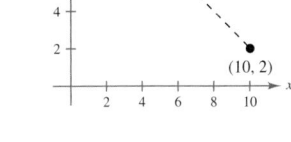

(b) $\dfrac{\sqrt{2}}{6}$

(c) $\left(-\frac{1}{4}, -\frac{5}{12}\right)$

46. (a)

(b) $\sqrt{556.52}$

(c) $(-5.6, 8.6)$

48. $34,232.50 million

50. Distances between the points: $\sqrt{29}$, $\sqrt{58}$, $\sqrt{29}$

52. (a) $(7, 0)$ (b) $(9, -3)$

54. (a) $\left(\frac{7}{4}, -\frac{7}{4}\right)$, $\left(\frac{5}{2}, -\frac{3}{2}\right)$, $\left(\frac{13}{4}, -\frac{5}{4}\right)$

(b) $\left(-\frac{3}{2}, -\frac{9}{4}\right)$, $\left(-1, -\frac{3}{2}\right)$, $\left(-\frac{1}{2}, -\frac{3}{4}\right)$

56. $30\sqrt{41} \approx 192$ kilometers

58. (a) The number of artists elected each year seems to be nearly steady except for the first few years. From six to eight artists will be elected in 2004.

(b) The Rock and Roll Hall of Fame was opened in 1986.

60. $1748.55 million

62. True. Two sides of the triangle have lengths of $\sqrt{149}$, and the third side has a length of $\sqrt{18}$.

64. No. It depends on the magnitudes of the quantities measured.

65. b   **66.** c   **67.** d   **68.** a

Index of Applications

Index

Definition of the Six Trigonometric Functions

Right triangle definitions, where $0 < \theta < \pi/2$.

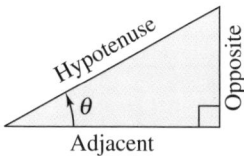

$$\sin \theta = \frac{\text{opp.}}{\text{hyp.}} \qquad \csc \theta = \frac{\text{hyp.}}{\text{opp.}}$$

$$\cos \theta = \frac{\text{adj.}}{\text{hyp.}} \qquad \sec \theta = \frac{\text{hyp.}}{\text{adj.}}$$

$$\tan \theta = \frac{\text{opp.}}{\text{adj.}} \qquad \cot \theta = \frac{\text{adj.}}{\text{opp.}}$$

Circular function definitions, where θ is any angle.

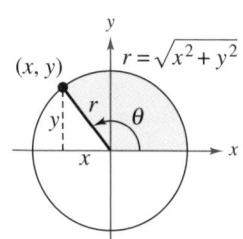

$$\sin \theta = \frac{y}{r} \qquad \csc \theta = \frac{r}{y}$$

$$\cos \theta = \frac{x}{r} \qquad \sec \theta = \frac{r}{x}$$

$$\tan \theta = \frac{y}{x} \qquad \cot \theta = \frac{x}{y}$$

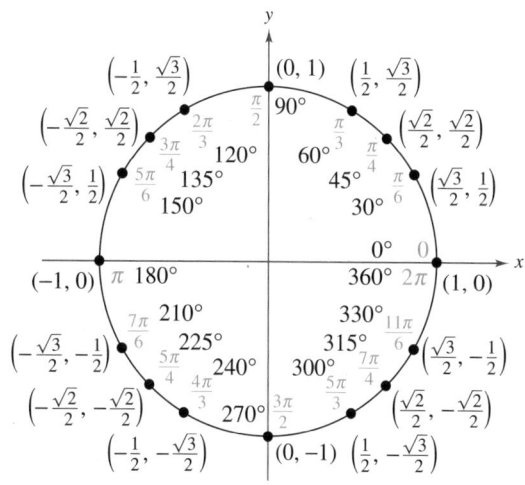

Reciprocal Identities

$$\sin u = \frac{1}{\csc u} \qquad \cos u = \frac{1}{\sec u} \qquad \tan u = \frac{1}{\cot u}$$

$$\csc u = \frac{1}{\sin u} \qquad \sec u = \frac{1}{\cos u} \qquad \cot u = \frac{1}{\tan u}$$

Quotient Identities

$$\tan u = \frac{\sin u}{\cos u} \qquad \cot u = \frac{\cos u}{\sin u}$$

Pythagorean Identities

$$\sin^2 u + \cos^2 u = 1$$

$$1 + \tan^2 u = \sec^2 u \qquad 1 + \cot^2 u = \csc^2 u$$

Cofunction Identities

$$\sin\left(\frac{\pi}{2} - u\right) = \cos u \qquad \cot\left(\frac{\pi}{2} - u\right) = \tan u$$

$$\cos\left(\frac{\pi}{2} - u\right) = \sin u \qquad \sec\left(\frac{\pi}{2} - u\right) = \csc u$$

$$\tan\left(\frac{\pi}{2} - u\right) = \cot u \qquad \csc\left(\frac{\pi}{2} - u\right) = \sec u$$

Even/Odd Identities

$$\sin(-u) = -\sin u \qquad \cot(-u) = -\cot u$$

$$\cos(-u) = \cos u \qquad \sec(-u) = \sec u$$

$$\tan(-u) = -\tan u \qquad \csc(-u) = -\csc u$$

Sum and Difference Formulas

$$\sin(u \pm v) = \sin u \cos v \pm \cos u \sin v$$

$$\cos(u \pm v) = \cos u \cos v \mp \sin u \sin v$$

$$\tan(u \pm v) = \frac{\tan u \pm \tan v}{1 \mp \tan u \tan v}$$

Double-Angle Formulas

$$\sin 2u = 2 \sin u \cos u$$

$$\cos 2u = \cos^2 u - \sin^2 u = 2\cos^2 u - 1 = 1 - 2\sin^2 u$$

$$\tan 2u = \frac{2 \tan u}{1 - \tan^2 u}$$

Power-Reducing Formulas

$$\sin^2 u = \frac{1 - \cos 2u}{2}$$

$$\cos^2 u = \frac{1 + \cos 2u}{2}$$

$$\tan^2 u = \frac{1 - \cos 2u}{1 + \cos 2u}$$

Sum-to-Product Formulas

$$\sin u + \sin v = 2 \sin\left(\frac{u + v}{2}\right)\cos\left(\frac{u - v}{2}\right)$$

$$\sin u - \sin v = 2 \cos\left(\frac{u + v}{2}\right)\sin\left(\frac{u - v}{2}\right)$$

$$\cos u + \cos v = 2 \cos\left(\frac{u + v}{2}\right)\cos\left(\frac{u - v}{2}\right)$$

$$\cos u - \cos v = -2 \sin\left(\frac{u + v}{2}\right)\sin\left(\frac{u - v}{2}\right)$$

Product-to-Sum Formulas

$$\sin u \sin v = \frac{1}{2}[\cos(u - v) - \cos(u + v)]$$

$$\cos u \cos v = \frac{1}{2}[\cos(u - v) + \cos(u + v)]$$

$$\sin u \cos v = \frac{1}{2}[\sin(u + v) + \sin(u - v)]$$

$$\cos u \sin v = \frac{1}{2}[\sin(u + v) - \sin(u - v)]$$

FORMULAS FROM GEOMETRY

Triangle:

$h = a \sin \theta$

$\text{Area} = \dfrac{1}{2}bh$

(Laws of Cosines)

$c^2 = a^2 + b^2 - 2ab \cos \theta$

Right Triangle:

(Pythagorean Theorem)

$c^2 = a^2 + b^2$

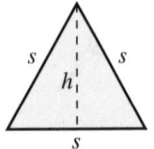

Equilateral Triangle:

$h = \dfrac{\sqrt{3}s}{2}$

$\text{Area} = \dfrac{\sqrt{3}s^2}{4}$

Parallelogram:

$\text{Area} = bh$

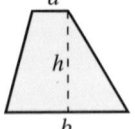

Trapezoid:

$\text{Area} = \dfrac{h}{2}(a + b)$

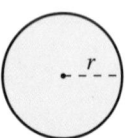

Circle:

$\text{Area} = \pi r^2$

$\text{Circumference} = 2\pi r$

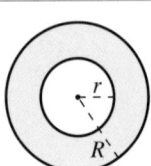

Sector of Circle:

(θ in radians)

$\text{Area} = \dfrac{\theta r^2}{2}$

$s = r\theta$

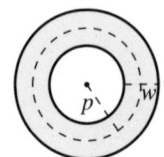

Circular Ring:

(p = average radius,
 w = width of ring)

$\text{Area} = \pi(R^2 - r^2)$
$\quad\quad = 2\pi pw$

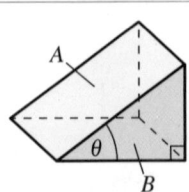

Sector of Circular Ring:

(p = average radius,

  w = width of ring,
  θ in radians)

$\text{Area} = \theta pw$

Ellipse:

$\text{Area} = \pi ab$

$\text{Circumference} \approx 2\pi \sqrt{\dfrac{a^2 + b^2}{2}}$

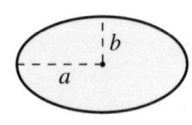

Cone:

(A = area of base)

$\text{Volume} = \dfrac{Ah}{3}$

Right Circular Cone:

$\text{Volume} = \dfrac{\pi r^2 h}{3}$

$\text{Lateral Surface Area} = \pi r \sqrt{r^2 + h^2}$

Frustum of Right Circular Cone:

$\text{Volume} = \dfrac{\pi(r^2 + rR + R^2)h}{3}$

$\text{Lateral Surface Area} = \pi s(R + r)$

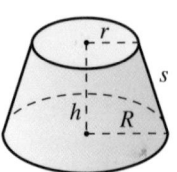

Right Circular Cylinder:

$\text{Volume} = \pi r^2 h$

$\text{Lateral Surface Area} = 2\pi rh$

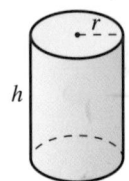

Sphere:

$\text{Volume} = \dfrac{4}{3}\pi r^3$

$\text{Surface Area} = 4\pi r^2$

Wedge:

(A = area of upper face,

  B = area of base)

$A = B \sec \theta$

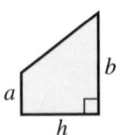